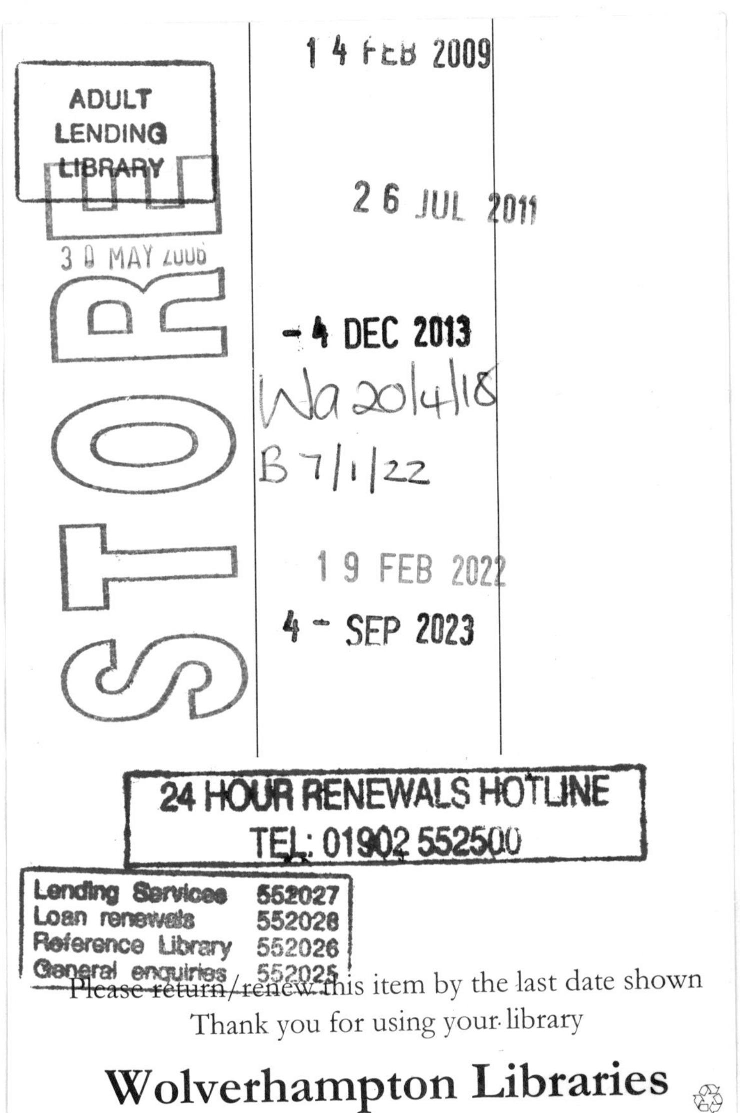
ADULT
LENDING
LIBRARY
STORE
30 MAY 2006
14 FEB 2009
26 JUL 2011
-4 DEC 2013
Wa 20/4/18
B 7/1/22
19 FEB 2022
4 - SEP 2023

ENCYCLOPEDIA OF

OCCULTISM & PARAPSYCHOLOGY

ENCYCLOPEDIA OF OCCULTISM & PARAPSYCHOLOGY

A Compendium of Information on the Occult Sciences, Magic, Demonology, Superstitions, Spiritism, Mysticism, Metaphysics, Psychical Science, and Parapsychology, with Biographical and Bibliographical Notes and Comprehensive Indexes

FOURTH EDITION

In Two Volumes

VOLUME ONE

A-L

Edited by J. Gordon Melton

GALE
an International Thomson Publishing company I(T)P®

J. Gordon Melton, *Editor*

Gale Research staff

Kelle S. Sisung, *Developmental Editor*
Lawrence W. Baker, *Managing Editor*
Allison McNeill, *Contributing Editor*
Jolen Marya Gedridge and Camille Killens, *Associate Editors*
Andrea Kovacs and Jessica Proctor, *Assistant Editors*

Mary Beth Trimper, *Production Director*
Evi Seoud, *Assistant Production Manager*
Shanna Philpott Heilveil, *Production Assistant*

Barbara J. Yarrow, *Graphic Services Manager*
Sherrell Hobbs, *MacIntosh Artist*

Benita L. Spight, *Manager, Data Entry Services*
Gwendolyn S. Tucker, *Data Entry Supervisor*
Johnny R. Carson, Edgar C. Jackson, Constance J. Wells, *Data Entry Associates*

Library of Congress Cataloging in Publication requested.

∞™ This book is printed on acid-free paper that meets the minimum requirements of American National Standard for Information Sciences Permanence Paper for Printed Library Materials, ANSI Z39.48-1984.

ISBN 0-8103-5487-X (Complete set)
ISBN 0-8103-9486-3 (Volume 1)
ISBN 0-8103-9487-1 (Volume 2)
Printed in the United States of America
10 9 8 7 6 5 4 3 2

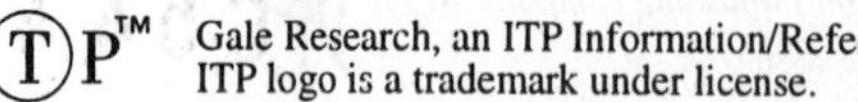

I(T)P™ Gale Research, an ITP Information/Reference Group Company.
ITP logo is a trademark under license.

Contents

Foreword

With this fourth edition of the *Encyclopedia of Occultism & Parapsychology (EOP),* I am relinquishing editorship of a publication with which I have been involved since its inception seventeen years ago. Other matters now claim my attention, and I believe that a new editor can bring a fresh outlook and new insight into the rapidly developing fields of occultism and parapsychology. There could be no better qualified individual to take over this task than Dr. J. Gordon Melton.

Dr. Melton is already famous for his comprehensive publication *The Encyclopedia of American Religions,* a superb reference work that first appeared, coincidentally, in 1978, when the first edition of the present title was published. In addition to editing this research tool, which is especially valuable given the proliferation of controversy surrounding religious and cult movements, Dr. Melton is also an esteemed authority on the whole New Age movement. His research base spans inquiry into alternative healing, altered consciousness, spiritual development, mysticism, cults, and all aspects of the paranormal, including occultism and witchcraft. In addition, Dr. Melton, along with his associates, authored the reference works, *The New Age Encyclopedia* (1990) and the *New Age Almanac* (1991).

Much of the present edition of *EOP* will necessarily contain a considerable body of entries from the period of my own editorship, and, in order to ease the transition to future editions, I have had a hand in updating many of the core entries. I have, as well, contributed a number of new entries. However, with this edition, the reader should note that Dr. Melton embraces the opportunity to shape the publication in new directions, utilizing his own comprehensive research organization.

The *Encyclopedia of Occultism & Parapsychology* has always attempted to enlarge and refine its coverage. Under its new editor it should continue to enhance its reputation as a basic reference work in an important and complex field of human activity.

Leslie A. Shepard
1996

Introduction

This fourth edition of the *Encyclopedia of Occultism & Parapsychology (EOP)* continues the tradition established by its predecessors of providing the most comprehensive coverage of the entire field of occultism and of the scientific evaluation of the occult provided by parapsychology. The first edition, published in 1978, brought together the texts of two of the standard reference works in the field, Lewis Spence's *Encyclopedia of Occultism* (1920) and Nandor Fodor's *Encyclopedia of Psychic Science* (1934). Spence wrote largely out of his involvement with British Spiritualism for which he was somewhat of an apologist, while Fodor was himself a prominent psychical researcher. Editor Leslie Shepard took on the task of updating their observations and supplementing the volume with new entries.

The production of this massively ambitious work was sparked by the heightened wave of interest in psychic phenomena, the occult, witchcraft, and related topics in the 1970s. That interest, which led directly to what was termed the New Age movement in the 1980s, provided a continued wealth of material for parapsychologists to examine, and provoked a popular social reaction among a group of debunkers who organized the Committee for the Scientific Investigation of the Claims of the Paranormal to speak for what they saw as the scientific establishment.

Defining the Terms

The term "occult" remains suspect in many circles. The word derives from the Greek and simply means that which is hidden. However, it eventually came to refer to realities specifically hidden from common sight; the occult realm was invisible to the physical eye but could be seen by an inner "spiritual" vision and/or grasped by a psychic intuition. The occult was the opposite of the "apocalypse," which means that which is revealed. The last book of the Christian Bible is called *The Apocalypse* or *The Revelation* and, subsequently, to many religious people, the term occult came to denote that which is opposite of what God has revealed, hence the realm of Satan and his legions of demons. Some substance for that observation has been provided by individual religious leaders who combine an exploration of occult realms with open opposition to the more traditional religions and religious institutions.

As used in *EOP*, however, occultism more properly refers to (1) that broad area of human experience that goes beyond the five senses (now called extrasensory perception or ESP), (2) the philosophical conclusions drawn from consideration of such experiences, and (3) the social structures created by people who have had extra-sensory experiences, who attempt to produce and cultivate them, and/or who believe in their vital significance for human life. Therefore, occultism (many today, including this editor, prefer the term "paranormal") properly refers to a wide spectrum of experiences from clairvoyance and telepathy to visions and dreams to the sightings of ghosts and the pronouncements of a medium/channel. The paranormal includes the phenomenon known as psychokinesis (commonly referred to as mind over matter)—whether in the dramatic form of levitation or teleportation, or the more commonly experienced miracle of spiritual healing. It certainly includes experiences related to death such as out-of-body travel and death-bed visions.

The occult also includes a host of techniques and practices originally designed and created to contact the extrasensory realm. Most frequently associated with the term occult are the techniques of magic and divination (including astrology, the tarot, and palmistry). In addition, various forms of meditation, yoga, and psychic development should be included, as well as some practices more commonly associated with the religious life such as speaking in tongues, prayer, and mysticism.

By extension, the occult or paranormal can also legitimately include a legion of mysterious phenomena not obviously extra-sensory in nature: anomalous natural occurrences not easily understood and explained by contemporary science. Such phenomena as the Loch Ness monster, unidentified flying objects (UFOs or flying saucers), Bigfoot, and crop circles may eventually be attributed to the realm of ordinary sense perception, but their very elusiveness has led them to be associated with the occult. In addition, some features associated with each are certainly best investigated by a person with parapsychological training. Not only does occult phenomena occur in connection with such anomalous phenomena, many occult teachers regularly speak about their significance as an integral element in their teachings.

The Evolution of Occultism

The present-day view of the occult is highly conditioned by the history of the paranormal in the West in the nineteenth and twentieth centuries. Through the seventeenth century, the great majority believed in the active operation of occult (then termed "supernatural") entities and forces. That belief brought comfort to some; for others, it became a significant source of fear, which led to suffering and even death for many. It allowed some people to rule by their reported ability to manipulate supernatural powers. It made possible the Inquisition and the persecution of thousands of people as "witches" and "Satanists." It allowed unscrupulous religious leaders to deceive people with sham relics and miracles.

By the sixteenth and seventeenth centuries, however, there began a serious critique of the more questionable supernatural phenomena, beginning with relics and extending to the actions of the witchfinders. As Protestantism secularized (denied sacred value to) the world, and then as scientific observation and organization of natural phenomena proceeded, a general spirit of skepticism spread. This skeptical spirit gave birth in the eighteenth century to the first significant movement to challenge the role of the supernatural in human society—Deism.

Deism affirmed the existence of God the Creator, but suggested that God had merely established a system of natural law and left the world he created to run on endlessly by that law. By implication, God was divorced from the world, and supernatural events did not occur; rather the "supernatural" was merely the misobserved "natural." Further, neither angels nor the spirits communicated with humans, and in turn prayer did not reach God's ears. Religious spokespersons responded, of course, and popularized a new definition of "miracle" as God breaking his own natural laws to intervene in the lives of his creatures.

Deist thought was largely confined to a small number of intellectual elites, among them some very powerful and influential people including most of the founding fathers of the United States—Benjamin Franklin, Thomas Jefferson, and George Washington. In the nineteenth century, the skeptical view of the supernatural became the subject of a movement called Freethought, which, while never a belief held by the majority, presented an intellectual and theological challenge that was to be confronted at every level. Theologians regularly began their courses with "proofs" of the existence of God; preachers debated village atheists; evangelists spurred their efforts to reach the godless masses.

In the midst of the debate between traditional religionists and Freethinkers, a few people (who came to be known as Spiritualists) suggested that they had a better approach. Spiritualists proposed that the distinction between this life and the life beyond was a somewhat artificial intellectual construct; everything was part of one larger natural world. To demonstrate and prove scientifically the existence of this larger universe, Spiritualists turned to mediums—people with special access to those realms formerly referred to as supernatural. The early mediums entered a trance state and while in that state brought forth messages containing information that seemingly could not have been known by normal means. They subsequently began to manifest a wide variety of extraordinary phenomena that suggested the existence of unusual forces operating on the physical world, forces unknown or undocumented by the emerging scientific community at the time.

Almost simultaneously with the emergence and spread of Spiritualism, a few intellectuals who retained a tie to traditional religion and were equally compelled by the perspectives of the new science, concluded that scientific observation could be turned to the investigation of this wave of reports of "supernatural" phenomena. Most prevalent were reports of ghosts and hauntings, which sparked the formation of the Ghost Club, founded in England in 1862. Over the next two decades the growth of Spiritualism provided a most fertile field for investigation, and in 1882 a new crop of investigators founded the Society for Psychical Research in London to study both the actual phenomena occurring at Spiritualist seances and incidents of "psychic" phenomena occurring elsewhere (a large part of the founders' energy going into the development of a properly precise and descriptive scientific language to facilitate their investigations).

The period from 1882 to the beginning of World War II can be viewed as the era of a stormy marriage between Spiritualism and psychical research (some would describe it as merely a scandalous illegitimate affair). Spiritualism and the movements it spawned, most notably Theosophy, supplied the phenomena; psychical researchers made the observations, analysis, and reports. With an increasingly sophisticated eye, psychical researchers researched, catalogued, experimented with, and debated the existence of psychical phenomena, with the understanding that psychic events, if verified, had far-reaching implications for our understanding of the world and how it operated.

Psychical researchers amassed a mountain of data and reached a number of conclusions, both positive and negative. On one hand, researchers positively documented a host of basic psychic occurrences (telepathy, clairvoyance, and precognition) and compiled a body of evidence that seemed to support human-spirit contact. At the same time, especially while researching physical mediumship—certainly the most exciting occurrences in all of psychical research—investigators repeatedly discovered that situations involving visible phenomena (materializations, apports, movement of objects) were permeated with fraud. The high incident of deceit and trickery, especially in those cases of mediums previously investigated and pronounced genuine, created a significant problem for all concerned. It challenged the credibility of Spiritualism, and while not suggesting that every medium or member was a fraud, it did insinuate that the movement protected con artists and condoned their work, even in the face of unquestioned evidence of guilt. It also opened psychical researchers who produced any positive evidence to charges that they were either naive, sloppy methodologically, or actually in cahoots with the mediums.

Both Spence's *Encyclopedia of Occultism* and Fodor's *Encyclopedia of Psychic Science* were produced as the interest in physical phenomena was peaking. Spence wrote from a Spiritualist perspective, and was (in 1920) still very hopeful that scientists would find the means of proving the validity of the full range of physical phenomena. He fully accepted the existence of materializations, teleportations, and apports. Fodor's volume, written just a decade and a half later, was produced by a prominent psychical researcher who acknowledged the element of fraud in Spiritualism, but was confident in the larger body of data gathered by his colleagues.

Since Fodor and Spence

Even as Fodor was writing, however, a revolution was starting within the ranks of psychical research. The first shots were fired by J. B. Rhine, a young biologist who suggested an entirely new direction. Psychical research, Rhine noted, had relied mainly upon the studied observation of phenomena in the field and operated by eliminating possible mundane explanations for what was occurring. Investigators visited ghostly haunts, sites of poltergeist occurrences, and Spiritualist seances and then developed detailed reports of what they had seen and heard. After a half century of endeavor, that approach eventually eliminated much fraudulent phenomena, however, psychical researchers had been unsuccessful in convincing their scholarly colleagues not only of the truth of their findings but of the validity of their effort. Psychical research, even though it had attracted some of the most eminent scientists of the era to its ranks, remained science-on-the-fringe. Thus, according to Rhine, the only way to validate future endeavors would be to bring research into the laboratory where scientists create and conduct methodologically sound experiments. Only such experimental data would be compelling to the modern scientifically trained mind.

Rhine's new approach and his early experimental successes provided inspiration for the study of parapsychology superseding the older psychical research. It also provided a means for the positive foundation built by psychical research to expand while the field gracefully distanced itself from the Spiritualist community and the overwhelming evidence of its widespread fraud. Parapsychology by implication called for a reorganization of research around a primary commitment to building a firm body of experimental data on basic psychic experiences. A few psychical researchers wished to continue the more intriguing work of investigating evidence into survival of bodily death and for at least a generation parapsychologists and traditional psychical researchers engaged in intramural warfare. A sort of reconciliation was reached only after parapsychology had proved itself and psychical research's strong identification with the Spiritualist community had been firmly put in the past.

Today, laboratory research dominates the scientific study of the paranormal. Psychics, mediums, and channels are still investigated, but they are now invited into the laboratory for close observation working under an experimental format. Thus, since Spence and Fodor were writing, the whole atmosphere of research on the paranormal, including the language, has changed.

In addition, the place of both Spiritualism and Theosophy in the larger psychical community has radically changed. Both groups had wholeheartedly accepted the new nineteenth-century scientific perspective as their starting point. But science moved on. Quantum mechanics superseded Newtonian physics, and depth psychology, sociology, and cybernetics emerged on the scene. From a position of dominance, Spiritualism and Theosophy have been pushed aside by a host of competing groups who can move more freely in the post-Newtonian environment. In addition, largely as a result of the New Age movement of the 1980s, metaphysical and occult religions enjoy an acceptability in the West unprecedented since the scientific revolution. That acceptability is evident in the amount of favorable comment on television and in print given to psychic and occult phenomena. The absence of Spiritualist mediums and leaders of the Theosophical Society in the New Age movement, which definitely built upon spiritualist and theosophical foundations, was evidence of their inability to articulate their world view in late twentieth-century categories.

The Current Need for a New Edition of *EOP*

In the more than half a century since Spence and Fodor published their volumes, not only has the occult/metaphysical/psychic world changed—a change clearly symbolized in the New Age movement—but the general opinion surrounding Spiritualism, Theosophy, and psychic phenomena has been radically altered by the science of parapsychology. The acceptance of the Parapsychological Association into the American Academy for the Advancement of Science indicated a new tolerance for (if not agreement with) psychical research by the scientific community, while parapsychologists have become methodologically more conservative and less accepting of much of the data from earlier decades.

During the 1970s there was an "occult explosion" in the media while the 1980s saw the emergence of a New Age movement. From a mid 1990s perspective, we can now see, beginning in the late 1960s, almost three decades of a steadily growing interest in psychical phenomena and metaphysical thought. "Fads" can certainly be identified—from exorcism to channeling, from crystals to angels—but what remains constant is that the entire field has become established in mainline society in a way that no one but a psychic could have predicted in the 1950s.

In light of the occult community's evolution and our changing appraisal of the occult in the nineteenth and early twentieth century, it seemed the proper time to plunge into the task of subjecting the *Encyclopedia of Occultism & Parapsychology* to a thorough editing. In particular, entries that came directly from Spence and Fodor cried for revision in light of current research and opinion, although care was taken to retain the core content and at times lengthy discussion of historic cases. Editing has also allowed for the removal of much archaic language. Spence, in particular, writing from a British perspective, had numerous off-the-cuff references to events and people now known only to a few dedicated students of the history of psychical research. As much as possible, additional material has been added to the text to identify such obscure references.

In addition a list of sources for further reading has been added to the majority of entries. Special care was also taken to include recent publications, as well as complete citations of those books mentioned in passing in the body of an entry, especially if quotations from the original source have been included. Many of the items cited are quite rare, but others have been reprinted in recent decades by University, Causeway, and Arno Presses, and are now more generally available.

Finally, more than 300 new entries, concentrating on recent developments in the occult community and parapsychology have been added. Entries cover new occult groups and movements, highlight recent work in parapsychology, and continue to reference events not only in England and North America, but across continental Europe and around the world.

It is important to note that a conscious effort has been made to continue the policy so carefully established by Les Shepard in providing reliable and authoritative information and to treat both the occult and parapsychology in a manner that avoids sensationalism, name-calling, and undue labeling. In that process, it is an unfortunate task to have to cite a number of cases of fraudulent activity, especially by a group of Spiritualist mediums, but in each case, the evidence for such references has also been included.

Format of Entries

The format of this edition follows much the same plan as the third edition. For biographical entries, birth and death dates are given where known. Many of the people covered in this volume were unfortunately not subject to the standard data gathering sources of their era. Individuals often came out of obscurity, briefly participated in a controversial event(s), and then retreated back into obscurity. Therefore, such basic information is often elusive. Every effort has been made to locate that basic data, and numerous new references have been added and others corrected. Where dates are highly debatable the formula "ca." followed by a century or year indicates the period during which the person flourished. A question mark in lieu of a death date indicates that the individual was born pre-1900 and a death date not known.

Cross-references are indicated by bold type within the text or by "See" and "See also" references following an entry.

Indexing

EOP's general index provides readers with access to significant people, movements, cultures, and phenomenon within the world of occultism and parapsychology. With this edition, the topical indexes cover those areas most queried by readers: paranormal phenomena broken down into 52 types including clairvoyance, ESP, and poltergeists; periodicals; and societies and organizations.

Acknowledgments

The *Encyclopedia of Occultism and Parapsychology* could not have been compiled without the combined help of a number of people. Needless to say, it would not be in existence without the original efforts of Lewis Spence and Nandor Fodor, and the tireless work of Les Shepard. Shepard, in the process of turning over editing duties to me, contributed a number of new entries and updated many others.

Special thanks are due to James R. Lewis and Jerome Clark for writing the major entries on astrology and UFOs respectively and for reviewing additional entries that involve their special expertise. I am also grateful to Gordon Stein who pointed out a host of needed corrections and supplied additional information for this new edition and to Tom Csere who, in the final stages of production, acted as fact checker using his personal collection and contacts in the field.

My assuming responsibility for this and future editions has been made possible by the extraordinary collection of occult, parapsychological, and related materials in the Special Collections department of the Davidson Library at the University of California-Santa Barbara. The material was originally compiled by the Institute for the Study of American Religion, which I have headed since its founding in 1969, and was donated to the Davidson Library as the American Religions Collection in 1985. The Institute has continued to support the growth of the collection over the succeeding decade, and is now available as a public collection for the use of scholars and other interested researchers.

Finally, the editor would also like to thank the many individuals and organizations who supplied background materials for creating new entries and assisted in making additions, corrections, and updatings of the existing text.

User Comments Are Welcome

The editor is eager to hear from people who can supply any further corrections, additional information, or suggestions for new entries in future editions. Please address him either c/o Gale Research, 835 Penobscot Bldg., Detroit, MI 48226, or at his office:

Dr. J. Gordon Melton
Institute for the Study of American Religion
Box 90709
Santa Barbara, CA 93190–0709

ENCYCLOPEDIA OF
OCCULTISM & PARAPSYCHOLOGY

A

A∴ A∴

A secret society founded by **Aleister Crowley** (1875–1947) comprised of three orders: the Silver Star, the Rosy Cross, and the Golden Dawn. This society is also described as the **Great White Brotherhood,** although that is a term more properly applied by Theosophists. The initials A∴ A∴ indicate Argenteum Astrum, and the triangle of dots signifies a secret society connected with ancient mysteries.

During his period in the Hermetic Order of the **Golden Dawn** (GD), Crowley believed that he had reached the exalted stage of the Silver Star and was thus a Secret Chief of the Golden Dawn. After 1906 Crowley launched his own order of the Silver Star, or A∴ A∴, using rituals and teachings taken from the Golden Dawn.

In March 1909 he began publishing the magazine the ***Equinox,*** as the official organ of the A∴ A∴, including rituals of the Outer Order of the Society in the second number. This alarmed members of the Golden Dawn, who wished their rituals to remain secret, and **S. L. MacGregor Mathers,** one of the Golden Dawn chiefs, took legal action to restrain Crowley from continuing to publish the rituals. Although a temporary injunction was granted, Mathers did not have funds to contest an appeal setting this aside, and Crowley continued to publish his own version of GD secret rituals.

In addition to the publicity from this legal action, Crowley also gained additional notice through public performance of "the Rites of Eleusis" at Caxton Hall, University of London, in 1910. This ceremony comprised seven invocations of the gods, with dancing by Crowley's disciple **Victor Neuburg,** violin playing by Leila Waddel (named by Crowley as his "Scarlet Woman"), and recital of Crowley's poems. The performances were impressive, if bewildering to ordinary members of the public, who were charged a fee of five guineas a head. Not surprisingly, in the prudish atmosphere of the time, there were sharp criticisms of such a daring presentation.

A hostile review of the Rites appeared in the journal the *Looking Glass,* mocking the lyrics as "gibberish." In a further issue, the *Looking Glass* published sensational allegations about Crowley and his associates **Allan Bennett** and George Cecil Jones. In response, Jones sued the journal in 1911, and Crowley obtained considerable publicity through the court hearing. Although Crowley must have reveled in such public attention, he lost several friends through it, in particular his disciple **J. F. C. Fuller,** who had written the eulogy of Crowley titled *The Star in the West* (1907).

Meanwhile, Crowley had joined another secret order, the **Ordo Templi Orientis** (OTO), which strongly emphasized the power of sex magic. After Crowley departed to the United States toward the end of 1914, the A∴ A∴ ceased working as a group in London.

Sources:

King, Francis. *Ritual Magic in England: 1887 to the Present Day.* London: Neville Spearman, 1970.

Suster, Gerald. *The Legacy of the Beast.* York Beach, Maine: Samuel Weiser, 1989.

Symonds, John. *The Great Beast: The Life and Magick of Aleister Crowley.* London: Macdonald, 1971. Rev. ed.: London, Mayflower, 1973.

Aaron's Rod

A magic wand deriving from the biblical narrative of the rods of Moses and Aaron that were used in the miracles of dividing the waters of the Red Sea and in causing water to gush from a rock in the desert. When Aaron cast his rod before pharaoh and his magicians (Exodus 7), the rod transformed into a serpent, hence the occult use of Aaron's Rod with a motif of a serpent. An old Jewish legend states that Aaron's rod was created on the sixth day of Creation and was retained by Adam after leaving the Garden of Eden, subsequently passing into the hands of a succession of patriarchs. An apocryphal Christian legend states that the rod was cut from the Tree of Knowledge, eventually came into the possession of Judas, and was the beam of the cross on which Christ was crucified.

The hazel wand used by water diviners in **dowsing** echoes the water finding by Aaron's rod in the desert. Some form of wand has always been a symbol of authority. The wand also survives as the magical staff of modern conjuring magicians.

AASC Newsletter See Anthropology of Consciousness

Ab

Semitic magical month. Crossing a river on the twentieth of that month was supposed to bring sickness. Ancient texts state that if a man should eat the flesh of swine on the thirtieth day of Ab, he will be plagued with boils.

Ab is also an ancient Egyptian term for the heart. Since the heart was the seat of the conscience, its preservation was a crucial part of the mummification process.

Abaddon

"The Destroyer," from a Hebrew word meaning "destruction." Chief of the demons of the seventh hierarchy. Abaddon is the name given by St. John in the Apocalypse to the king of the grasshoppers. He is sometimes regarded as the destroying angel or prince of the underworld, also synonymous with Apollyon (Rev. 9:11). (See also **Black Magic**)

Sources:

Barrett, Francis. *The Magus.* London, 1801. Reprint, New Hyde Park, N.Y.: University Books, 1967.

Abadie, Jeannette See Jeannette D'Abadie

Abaris

A Scythian high priest of Apollo and a renowned magician. He chanted the praises of Apollo, his master, so flatteringly that the god gave him a golden arrow on which he could ride through the air like a bird. Therefore, the Greeks called him the Aerobate. Pythagoras, his pupil, stole this arrow from him and thus accomplished many wonderful feats. Abaris foretold the future, pacified storms, banished disease, and lived without eating or drinking. With the bones of Pelops, he made a statue of Minerva, which he sold to the Trojans as a talisman descended from heaven. This was the famous Palladium, which protected and rendered impregnable the town wherein it was lodged.

Abayakoon, Cyrus D. F. (1912- ?)

Astrologer born in Ceylon (now Sri Lanka). He was educated by Buddhist priests who instructed him in the traditional science of astrology. He also became highly skilled in **palmistry** and the curing of disease through Mantra **yoga** (science of sound vibration through sacred utterance). He made a number of accurate predictions of important world events, including the assassination of Gandhi, the fall of Khrushchev, the assassination of Kennedy, and the Watergate scandal.

Sources:

Abayakoon, Cyrus D. F. *Astro-Palmistry: Signs and Seals of the Hand.* New York: ASI, 1975.

———. *Rahu Pimma [and] Yama Kalaya.* Delhi, India, ca. 1957.

Abbott, David P(helps) (1863–1934)

Amateur magician and investigator of Spiritualist mediums. He was born in Falls City, Nebraska, September 22, 1863. His early education consisted of three months a year in a country schoolhouse on Nebraska prairies, and a final nine months in Falls City High School. In later life Abbott followed the trade of a money lender but took a great interest in science and philosophy. He also became an amateur magician, inventing and performing many startling feats of magic. He lived for some years in Omaha, Nebraska.

Abbott published numerous essays and several books on psychical subjects. His book *Behind the Scenes with the Mediums* exposed many techniques of fake mediumship, including **slate writing** and billet tests (see **pellet reading**). In spite of his skepticism regarding the claims of mediumship, however, Abbott did not rule out the possibility of genuine phenomena. In a thoughtful contribution to the second volume of *The Dream Problem* by Ram Narayana (Delhi, 1922), he stated: "I mention these things to show that telepathy is far from established as a fact, yet I must say that I believe it to be possible under certain conditions, but positively it can not be commanded at will in the slightest degree." He then related personal and family experiences of veridical dreaming.

Sources:

Abbott, David P. *Behind the Scenes with the Mediums.* Chicago: Open Court Publishing, 1912.

———. *The History of a Strange Case.* Chicago: Open Court Publishing, 1908.

———. *Spirit Portrait Mystery . . . Its Final Solution.* Chicago: Open Court Publishing, 1913.

Abdelazys

An Arabian astrologer of the tenth century generally known in Europe by his Latin name, Alchabitius. His treatise on **astrology** was highly acclaimed and was translated into Latin and printed in 1473. Other editions have since appeared, the best being that of Venice (1503) entitled *Alchabitius cum commento,* translated by John of Seville.

Aben-Ragel

An Arabian astrologer born at Cordova at the beginning of the fifth century. His book of horoscopes was translated into Latin and published at Venice, 1485, under the title *De Judiciis seu fatis stellarum.* Aben-Ragel's predictions were known for their remarkable accuracy.

Abigor

According to **Johan Weyer,** Abigor is the Grand Duke of Hades. He is shown in the form of a handsome knight bearing a lance, standard, or scepter. He is a demon of the superior order and responds readily to questions concerning war. He can foretell the future and instructs leaders how to make themselves respected by their soldiers. Sixty infernal regions are at his command.

Sources:

Weyer, Johannes. *Witches, Devils, and Doctors in the Renaissance: Johann Weyer, De Praestigiis.* Edited by George Mora. Binghamton, N.Y.: Medieval and Renaissance Texts and Studies, 1991.

Abou-Ryhan

An Arabian astrologer whose real name was Mohammed-ben-Ahmed; he is credited with introducing judicial **astrology.** Many stories told of him in the East show that he possessed an extraordinary power to read the future.

Abracadabra

A magical word said to be formed from the letters of the **abraxas,** written thus:

A
A B
A B R
A B R A
A B R A C
A B R A C A
A B R A C A D
A B R A C A D A
A B R A C A D A B
A B R A C A D A B R
A B R A C A D A B R A

or the reverse way. The pronunciation of this word, according to Julius Africanus, was equally efficacious either way. According to Serenus Sammonicus, it was used as a spell to cure asthma. *Abracalan,* or *aracalan,* another form of the word, is said to have been regarded as the name of a god in Syria and as a magical symbol by the Jews. It seems doubtful whether the abracadabra, or its synonyms, was really the name of a deity.

Sources:

Lévi, Éliphas. *Transcendental Magic.* London: Rider, 1896. Reprint, New York: Samuel Weiser, 1970.

Abraham the Jew (ca. 1362–ca. 1460)

Little biographical information exists concerning this German Jew, who was an alchemist, magician, and philosopher, ca. 1400. What is known is mostly derived from a manuscript in the Archives of the Bibliotheque de l'Arsenal, Paris, an institution rich in occult documents. Written entirely in French, the manuscript purports to be translated from the Hebrew, and the handwriting style indicates that the scribe lived at the beginning of the eighteenth century or possibly somewhat earlier. A distinct illiteracy characterizes the French script, with the punctuation being either inaccurate or conspicuously absent.

Abraham was probably a native of Mayence, and appears to have been born in 1362. His father, Simon, was something of a seer and magician, and the boy took up his occult studies initially under parental guidance, then later under another teacher, Moses, whom Abraham describes as "indeed a good man, but entirely ignorant of The True Mystery, and of The Veritable Magic."

Abraham thereafter decided to continue his education by traveling. With his friend Samuel, a Bohemian by birth, he wandered through Austria and Hungary into Greece, and next into Constantinople (now Istanbul), where he remained two years. Abraham then traveled to Arabia, in those days a renowned center of mystic learning, and afterward to Palestine and Egypt.

In Egypt he became acquainted with Abra-Melin, a famous Egyptian philosopher, who entrusted certain documents to him and confided to him a number of invaluable secrets. Abraham then left Egypt for Europe, where he settled eventually at Würzburg in Germany, became deeply involved in research on **alchemy.** He married a woman who appears to have been his cousin, and had three daughters and two sons, the elder named Joseph and the younger, Lamech.

He instructed both sons in occult affairs, while on each of his three daughters, he settled a dowry of 100,000 golden florins. This considerable sum, together with other vast wealth, Abraham claimed to have earned by traveling as an alchemist. He was well known and was summoned to perform acts of **magic** before many rich and influential people, notably Emperor Sigismund of Germany, the bishop of Würzburg, King Henry VI of England, the duke of Bavaria, and Pope John XXII. No details exist about the rest of Abraham's career, and the date of his death is uncertain, but it is commonly supposed to have occurred about 1460.

The previously mentioned manuscript which yielded this biographical information is entitled *The Book of the Sacred Magic of Abra-Melin, as delivered by Abraham the Jew unto his son Lamech.* This title is rather misleading and not strictly accurate, for Abra-Melin had absolutely no hand in the opening part of the work, which consists of an account of Abraham's own youth and early travels in search of wisdom, along with advice to the young man aspiring to become skilled in occult arts. The second part, on the other hand, is either based on the documents that Abra-Melin handed to Abraham or on the confidences the Egyptian sage disclosed to Abraham. This part of the manuscript deals with the first principles of magic in general, and includes such chapters as "How Many, and what are the Classes of Veritable Magic?" "What we Ought to Take into Consideration before the Undertaking of the Operation," "Concerning the Convocation of the Spirits," and "In what Manner we ought to Carry out the Operations."

The third and last part of the document is mostly derived straight from Abra-Melin, and the author, ignoring theoretical matter as far as possible, gives information about the actual practice of magic. In the first place he tells how "To procure divers Visions," "How one may retain the Familiar Spirits, bound or free, in whatsoever form," and how "To excite Tempests." In other chapters he discusses raising the dead, transforming oneself into "divers shapes and forms," flying in the air, demolishing buildings, discovering thefts, and walking underwater. The author writes about the thaumaturgic healing of leprosy, dropsy, paralysis, and various common ailments such as fever and seasickness. He also offers advice on "How to be beloved by a Woman" and how to command the favor of popes, emperors, and other influential people. He addresses the question of summoning visions in "How to cause Armed Men to Appear," and he tells how to evoke "Comedies, Operas, and all kinds of Music and Dances." Many of these feats are achieved by employing Kabalistic squares of letters. The manuscript details many different signs of this sort.

Abraham's personality and temperament as revealed in this work indicate a man heaping scorn on most other magicians and speaking with great derision of nearly all mystical writings other than his own and those of his hero, Abra-Melin. Abraham fiercely criticizes all those who recant the religion in which they were raised and contends that no one guilty of this will ever attain skill in magic. Nevertheless, throughout the manuscripts, Abraham manifests little selfishness and seems to have worked toward success in his craft with a view to using it for the benefit of mankind in general. His writings also reflect a firm belief in a higher self existing in every man, and a keen desire to develop it. (See also **Nicholas Flamel**)

Sources:

The Book of the Sacred Magic of Abra-Melin the Sage. Translated by S. L. MacGregor-Mathers. Chicago: De Laurence, 1932. Reprint, New York: Causeway Books, 1974.

Abrams, Albert (1863–1924)

A San Francisco physician who devised a system of diagnosis and healing variously termed **radionics,** electronic medicine, or **electronics.** Abrams, who had a distinguished medical background, graduated in medicine at Heidelberg University, Germany, and was professor of pathology at Cooper Medical College, San Francisco, California. Working on cancer patients, he believed that he had discovered that diseased tissue radiated an abnormal wave. His work further led to his invention of the **oscilloclast,** an electrical instrument for generating oscillations involving changes of skin potential, based on an electronic theory of disease. Developments of Abrams's apparatus have since come to be known as **black boxes.** In 1922, just two years before his death, the British Royal Society of Medicine issued a negative report on Abrams, and his work almost died out. It was picked up by **Ruth Drown** during the 1930s.

Sources:

Abrams, Albert. *New Concepts in Diagnosis and Treatment.* San Francisco, Calif.: Physico-Clinical, 1922.

Barr, James. *Abrams' Methods of Diagnosis and Treatment.* London, 1925.

Scott, G. Laughton. *"The Abrams Treatment" in Practice: An Investigation.* London: Bless, 1925.

Stanway, Andrew. *Alternative Medicine.* New York: Penguin, 1982.

Abrams, Stephen Irwin (1938–)

Psychologist who studied extrasensory stimulation of conditioned reflexes in hypnotized subjects. He was born July 15, 1938, in Chicago, Illinois, and studied at the University of Chicago and Oxford University, England. Abrams has served as visiting research fellow at the Parapsychology Laboratory, Duke University, Durham, North Carolina; president of the Parapsychology Laboratory of the University of Chicago (1957–60); and charter associate of the Parapsychological Association. His paper "Extrasensory Behavior" was presented at the Seventh Annual Congress of the Parapsychological Association at Oxford in 1964.

Abraxas (or **Abracax**)

The **Basilidian** sect of Gnostics of the second century claimed Abraxas as their supreme god and said that Jesus Christ was only a phantom sent to Earth by him. They believed that his name contained great mysteries, as it was composed of the seven Greek letters which form the number 365, the number of days in a year. Abraxas, they thought, had under his command 365 gods, to whom they attributed 365 virtues, one for each day. The older mythologists consider Abraxas an Egyptian god, and demonologists describe him as a demon with the head of a king and with serpents forming his feet. Ancient **amulets** depict Abraxas with a whip in his hand, and his name inspired the mystic word **abracadabra.**

Sources:

Drury, Nevill, and Stephen Skinner. *The Search for Abraxas.* London: Spearman, 1972.

Abred

The innermost of three concentric circles representing the totality of being in the cosmology of the **Celts.** Abred represents the stage of struggle and evolution against Cythrawl, the power of evil. (See also **Barddas**)

Absent Healing

Healing at a distance from the subject, sometimes through the subject providing some associational link such as a written request for healing, or in reverse form, by the healer sending a piece of material to be placed on the subject's body where the healing is required, or simply by prayers for the subject's recovery on the part of the healer or a band of healing associates. Many people today, Christian, metaphysical, or modern Spiritualist, hold sessions at which they pray for the recovery of petitioners who write them for help. (See also **Healing by Faith; Psychic Healing**)

Absolute (Theosophy)

Theosophists profess to know nothing further about the Absolute, the **Logos,** the Word of God, than that it exists. The universes with their solar systems are the lowest manifestations of this Being, which humans are capable of perceiving. Human beings themselves are an emanation from the Absolute, with which they will be ultimately reunited.

Abu Yazid al-Bestami (ca. 801–874)

Noted Islamic mystic who founded the ecstatic school of **Sufism.** Born in Bestam in northeastern Persia, he became known as al-Bestami. His claim that the mystic quest could result in complete absorption and identification with divinity is thought to have been an influence of Hindu **Vedanta.** In this respect, his heterodoxy was blasphemous to orthodox Islam.

Beginning with the Sufi concept of approaching divinity as the lover approaches the beloved, al-Bestami claimed that this love was in itself an obstacle. He renounced conventional worship in the mosque, pilgrimage to Mecca, and even the mystical practices of asceticism and meditation. Various miracles were ascribed to al-Bestami.

Sources:

Attar, Farid al-Din. *Muslim Saints and Mystics.* Translated by A. J. Arberry. Chicago: University of Chicago Press, 1966.

Zaehner, R. C. *Hindu and Muslim Mysticism.* London: Athlone Press, 1960.

Abyssum

An herb used in the ceremony of exorcising a haunted house. Abyssum is consecrated by the sign of the cross and hung up at the four corners of the house.

Academia De Estudo Psychicos "Cesare Lombroso"

Cesare Lombroso Academy for Psychical Research, founded in Sao Paolo by José de Freitas Tinoco in September 1919. The academy investigated the mediumship of **Carlos Mirabelli.** In 392 sittings, Mirabelli produced what were considered to be remarkable results as he demonstrated a wide variety of materializations, levitation, psychokinesis, and automatic writing. The academy proclaimed Mirabelli the greatest of all mental and physical mediums, but its 1926 report was called into question by **Theodore Besterman,** who studied Mirabelli for the **American Society for Psychical Research** in 1934. The academy continued to exist into the 1930s.

Sources:

Berger, Arthur S., and Joyce Berger. *The Encyclopedia of Parapsychology and Psychical Research.* New York: Paragon House, 1991.

Academy of Parapsychology and Medicine

An important but short-lived organization founded in California in 1970 with the basic belief that spirit and matter are a unity. The academy held that the true nature of healing must be sought in that unity and the interrelationship of body, mind, and spirit in health and disease. Treatment of disease should be directed at the whole person, and any lasting healing of the physical body should synthesize mental, emotional, and spiritual aspects. This belief restates traditional Hindu Yoga teachings in a Western context.

The academy served its membership by offering symposia, workshops, and publications (including *APM Report,* published quarterly for members). Investigating paranormal and unorthodox healing, the academy presented its research findings to both professional medical and lay communities. It sponsored seven major symposia between 1971 and 1974, primarily in the San Francisco and Los Angeles areas, as well as Chicago, New York, and Philadelphia. Other activities included one-day seminars on **acupuncture** and **biofeedback** and nine two-day acupuncture workshops. In June 1974 the academy presented a symposium on nontraditional approaches to treatment of the developmentally disabled, sponsored jointly with the Division of Retardation of the state of Florida's Department of Health and Rehabilitative Services. The academy laid the groundwork for the formation of the American Holistic Medical Association in 1978. (See also **Healing Center for the Whole Person**)

Sources:

The Dimensions of Healing: A Symposium. Los Altos, Calif.: Academy of Parapsychology and Medicine, 1972.

The Varieties of the Healing Experience. Los Altos, Calif.: Academy of Parapsychology and Medicine, 1971.

Academy of Religion and Psychical Research

Organization founded in 1972 from a proposal developed in 1971 by **J. Gordon Melton,** its first secretary, to operate in those areas where parapsychology and religion intersect. It has served as an academic affiliate of **Spiritual Frontiers Fellowship** (SFF). The academy encourages dialogue, idea exchange, and cooperation between clergy, academics in philosophy and religion, and the researchers and scientists in parapsychology and related fields. It conducts educational programs for scholars, Spiritual Frontiers Fellowship members, and the general public and works closely with related organizations. The academy organized several large conferences soon after its founding beginning with one at Garrett Theological Seminary in 1972, but its activity slowed in the mid-1970s when SFF went through a period of organizational disruption.

Reorganized by the end of the 1970s, the academy now conducts an annual conference, usually in conjunction with the annual meeting of SFF, and occasional seminars. It sponsors an annual competition for the Robert H. Ashby Memorial Award for the best paper on an announced subject. It publishes the *Journal of Religion and Psychical Research* quarterly and *Proceedings* (issued from time to time). The academy may be reached at P.O. Box 614, Bloomfield, CT 06002.

Achad, Frater

The magical name assumed by **Charles Stansfeld Jones** (1886–1950), a British occultist and author who lived in Canada and founded the **Fellowship of Ma-Ion.** He was a follower of magician **Aleister Crowley** who designated him his **magical child.**

Jones is to be distinguished from theosophical writer George Graham Price who channeled two popular texts, *Melchizedek Truth Principles* (1963) and *Ancient Mystical White Brotherhood* (1971), both published under the pseudonym Frater Achad. Little is known of Price's life apart from his channeling the two books.

Sources:

Achad, Frater [George Graham Price]. *Ancient Mystical White Brotherhood.* Lakemont, Ga.: CSA Press, 1971.

———. *Melchizedek Truth Principles.* Phoenix, Ariz.: Lockhart Research Foundation, 1963.

Acheropite

Term used to describe a supernormally produced portrait on cloth. Another term, used for a cloth that bears the miraculous portrait of Jesus, is **veronica,** based on an apocryphal legend of a woman who wiped the face of Jesus during the procession to the Cross. The controversial **Turin Shroud** is one of the more interesting examples of such a cloth.

Achmet See Ahmad ibn Sirin

Aconcio, Jacques See Jacobus Acontius

Acontius, Jacobus (ca. 1500–ca. 1566)

Also known as Jacques Aconcio. Theologian, philosopher, and engineer. Born in Trent, Tyrol, he became curate of that diocese, then became a Calvinist in 1557. Acontius came to England about two years later, where he dedicated his major work, *Stratagemata Satanae* (The Stratagems of Satan), to Queen Elizabeth. The book attributes all doctrines other than the Apostles' Creed to Satan as stratagems to tempt mankind from truth. However, the book was also a strong plea for religious toleration. An English translation was first published in 1648 under the title *Satan's Stratagems; or, The Devil's Cabinet-Council Discovered.*

Active-Agent Telepathy

Term used by parapsychologists for situations in which the agent in telepathic experiments seems to be an active factor in causing mental or behavioral effects in the percipient, or subject, rather than being simply a passive participant whose mental states are recognized by the percipient.

Acupressure

A form of body work which, as the name implies, is based in **acupuncture.** Acupuncturists apply pressure to the designated points on the body with the hand rather than using needles. A popular practice in Japan, it was severely restricted by laws against massage in the nineteenth century. That law was repealed in 1955. As acupressure revived, it found a receptive audience in the West. Acupressure is similar to but distinct from other body techniques like do-in and **shiatsu.** For further information, contact the Acupressure Institute, 1533 Shattuck Ave., Berkeley, CA 94709.

In the 1970s, Michael Reed Gach developed a variation on acupressure that he termed acu-yoga. It combines acupressure with hatha yoga. Individuals are taught to apply pressure on the points while assuming various yoga positions.

Sources:

Cerney, J. V. *Acupressure: Acupuncture without Needles.* West Nyack, N.Y.: Parker Publishing, 1974.

Chan, Pedro. *Finger Acupressure.* New York: Ballantine Books, 1975.

Gach, Michael Reed. *Acu-yoga: Self Help Techniques.* Tokyo: Japan Publications, 1981.

Acupressure News

Quarterly magazine concerned with information on **acupressure.** Includes articles and news items relating to activities, techniques, and attitudes of the medical profession. Address: 2309 Main St., Santa Monica, CA 90405.

Acupressure Workshop

Organization that arranges classes in elementary to advanced study of **acupressure, shiatsu, t'ai chi ch'an,** and **yoga.** Address: 1872 S. Sepulveda Blvd., Los Angeles, CA 90025.

Acupuncture

An ancient Chinese medical system over five thousand years old, recently revived in China and demonstrated to Western doctors. It is based on the belief that subtle energy flows in the body related to the cosmic principles of Yin and Yang. Yin relates to shadow, moon, passivity, softness, femininity; Yang denotes sunlight, activity, masculinity, hardness. The balance of these energies in the human body affects health and disease. Acupuncture therapy alters these energy flows by inserting needles at key points for varying periods of time. Anesthesia for surgical operations can also be effected by acupuncture. Both ancient Chinese and Hindu medical systems are related to a philosophical or mystical view of the universe, and the concept of Yin and Yang and subtle energy flows has much in common with the **kundalini** energy of the Hindu **yoga** system. In hatha yoga, the system of **asanas,** or physical positions, affect the vital energies in the body through muscular tension and relaxation. Comparison may also be made with the theories of **Wilhelm Reich** and his concept of **orgone** energy.

Special developments of acupuncture include **shiatsu** and **acupressure,** a form of acupuncture without needles, and acupuncture charts locating ear and hand points. Dr. Lester Sacks, a Los Angeles doctor, introduced a system of ear acupuncture in which a special "gun" fires a surgical staple into the ear near a particular acupuncture point, to help patients who want to lose weight or stop smoking, drinking, or taking drugs. Whenever the patient feels his craving coming on, he wiggles the staple, and the craving apparently subsides.

A simple device for self-treatment of acupuncture points on the back is the "MA-roller," a specially shaped wooden rod, on which the patient lies. It is marketed by Great Earth Therapeutics, Forest Row, Sussex, England.

Acupuncture came into the West in 1928 when Soulie de Morant, the French consul in China, returned home with the texts he had translated into French and persuaded several doctors to examine the practice. Interest grew steadily throughout Europe and America after World War II. The Acupuncture International Association was founded in 1949 by a group of nonconventional physicians in the United States. J. R. Worsley established the Chinese College of Acupuncture in England in 1960. However, the major opening for acupuncture in the West came in the early 1970s, when the United States reestablished friendly relations with the People's Republic of China. In 1973 the National Institute of Health sponsored an Acupuncture Research Conference, a signal of official approval for the testing of acupuncture's claims. Over the next few years a host of acupuncture texts appeared, acupuncture associations formed, and journals initiated.

The literature of acupuncture is extensive, and there are now several journals devoted to the subject, including *Acupuncture News, American Journal of Acupuncture,* and *Journal of the Acupuncture Association of Great Britain.* The American Association of Acupuncture and Oriental Medicine may be contacted at 1424 16th St. N.W., Washington, DC 20036. There is also an International Veterinary Acupuncture Society at 2140 Conestoga Rd., Chester Springs, PA 19425.

Sources:

Academy of Traditional Chinese Medicine. *An Outline of Chinese Acupuncture.* New York: Pergamon Press, 1975; Peking: Foreign Language Press, 1975.

Austin, Mary. *Acupuncture Therapy.* 2nd ed. New York: ASI Publishers, 1972.

Dubrin, Stanley, and J. Keenan. *Acupuncture and Your Health.* Chatsworth, Calif.: Books for Better Living, 1974.

Hashimoto, M. *Japanese Acupuncture.* New York: Liveright Publishing, 1968; London: Thursons, 1966.

Mann, Felix. *Acupuncture.* New York: Random House, 1963; London: W. Heinemann Medical Books, 1962.

Matsumoto, Teruo. *Acupuncture for Physicians.* Springfield, Ill.: Thomas, 1974.

McGarey, William. *Acupuncture and Body Energies.* Phoenix, Ariz.: Gabriel Press, 1974.

Nanking Army Ear Acupuncture Team. *Ear Acupuncture: A Chinese Medical Report.* Emmaus, Pa.: Rodale Press, 1974.

Nightingale, Michael. *The Healing Power of Acupuncture.* New York: Javalin Books, 1986.

Acuto-manzia

Unusual form of **divination** by pins practiced by Italian psychic Maria Rosa Donati-Evstigneeff. Ten straight pins and three bent pins are used. They are shaken in cupped hands, then dropped onto a surface dusted with powder. This system would seem to involve some psychic faculty, and is related to such forms of divination as **geomancy** and **tea leaves.**

Adalbert (ca. 740 C.E.)

A French pseudo-mystic of the eighth century. He boasted that an angel brought him relics of extraordinary sanctity from all parts of the earth and he claimed to be able to foretell the future, and to read thoughts. "I know what you have done," he would say; "there is no need for confession. Go in peace, your sins are forgiven." Adalbert's so-called "miracles" gained him great popularity, and he gave away many cuttings of his nails and locks of his hair as powerful amulets. He is even said to have set up an altar in his own name.

The small amount of biographical information that exists tells of miraculous powers bestowed by an angel at his birth. Adalbert was accused of showing to his disciples a letter that he declared was brought to him from Jesus Christ and delivered by St. Michael. Adalbert was also accused of composing a mystical prayer invoking uncanonical **angels** believed to be demons.

In 744 C.E. a Church synod denounced him. A year later, after appealing to Pope Zacharius, Adalbert was deprived of priestly office. Later he was condemned to perpetual imprisonment in the monastery of Fulda.

Adam, Book of the Penitence of

A manuscript in the Library of the Arsenal at Paris that deals with kabalistic tradition. It recounts how the first two sons of Adam, Cain and Abel, respectively typifying brute force and intelligence, slew each other, and that Adam's inheritance passed to his third son, Seth. Seth was permitted to advance as far as the gate of the Earthly Paradise without being threatened by the guardian angel with his flaming sword, which is to say that he was an initiate of occult science.

He beheld the Tree of Life and the Tree of Knowledge, which had become grafted upon each other so that they formed one tree. Some commentators believe this to symbolize the harmony of science and religion in the **Kabala.** The guardian angel presented Seth with three seeds from this tree and directed him to place them within the mouth of his father, Adam, when he died. From this planting arose the burning bush, out of which God communicated to Moses his holy name, and from a part of which Moses made his magic wand. This was placed in the Ark of the Covenant and was planted by King David on Mount Zion, where it grew into a triple tree and was later cut down by Solomon to form the pillars Jachin and Boaz, which were placed at the entrance to the Temple.

A third portion was inserted in the threshold of the great gate and acted as a talisman, permitting no unclean thing to enter the sanctuary. However, certain wicked priests removed it, weighted it with stones, and cast it into the Temple reservoir, where it was guarded by an angel, who kept it from the sight of men. During the time of Christ the reservoir was drained and the beam of wood discovered and thrown across the brook Kedron, over which the Savior passed after he was apprehended in the Garden of Olives. It was taken by his executioners and made into the cross.

This legend is markedly similar to those from which the conception of the Holy Grail arose. Man is restored by the wood through the instrumentality of which Adam, the first man, fell. The idea that the Cross was a cutting of the Tree of Knowledge was widespread in the Middle Ages and may be found in the twelfth century *Quete del St. Graal,* ascribed to Walter Map but probably only adapted by him. All the traditions of the Kabala are embodied in the allegory contained in the *Book of the Penitence of Adam,* which supplements and throws considerable light on the entire kabalistic literature.

Adam, L'Abbé

About the time that the **Templars** were being driven from France, the Devil was said to have appeared under various guises to the Abbé Adam, who was journeying with one of the servants from his convent to another part of his abbacy of the Vaux de Cernay. The evil spirit first opposed the progress of the Abbé taking the form of a tree white with frost, which rushed toward him with inconceivable swiftness. The Abbé's horse trembled with fear, as did the servant, but the Abbé himself made the sign of the Cross, and the tree disappeared.

The Abbé concluded that he had seen the Devil and called upon the Virgin to protect him. Nevertheless, the fiend shortly reappeared in the shape of a furious black knight. "Begone," said the Abbé. "Why do you attack me far from my brothers?" The Devil once more left him, but returned in the shape of a tall man with a long, thin neck. To get rid of him, Adam struck him a blow with his fist. The evil spirit shrank and took the stature and countenance of a little cloaked monk, with a glittering weapon under his garb. His little eyes could be seen darting and glancing under his cowl. He tried hard to strike the Abbé with the sword he held, but Adam repulsed the strokes with the sign of the Cross.

The demon became in turn a pig and a long-eared ass. The Abbé, impatient to be on his way, made a circle on the ground with a cross in the center. The fiend was then obliged to withdraw a little distance. He changed his long ears into horns, which did not hinder the Abbé from boldly addressing him. Offended by his plain-speaking, the Devil changed himself into a barrel and rolled into an adjoining field. In a short time he returned in the form of a cart wheel, and, without giving the brother time to put himself on the defensive, rolled heavily over his body, without, however, doing him any injury. After that he left him to pursue his journey in peace. This story is related in *Regne de Philippe le Bel* by Robert Gaguin and in *Histoire de la Magie en France* by Jules Garinet (1818).

Adam Kadmon

A Tree of Life in the **Kabala** in the form of an idealized spiritual being.

Sources:

Halevi, Z'ev ben Shimon. *Adam and the Kabbalistic Tree.* London: Rider, 1974.

Adamantius (ca. fourth century C.E.)

A Jewish doctor, who became a Catholic at Constantinople in the time of Constantine, to whom he dedicated his two volumes on *Physiognomy; or, The Art of Judging People by Their Faces.* This work, full of contradictions and fantasies, was printed in the *Scriptores Physiognomoniae veteres* of Johann G. F. Franz at Attembourg in 1780.

Adams, Evangeline Smith (Mrs. George E. Jordon, Jr.) (1859–1932)

Noted American astrologer. Born February 8, 1859, in Jersey City, New Jersey; daughter of George and Harriette E. (Smith) Adams (of the Adams family of New England); and a descendant of John Quincy Adams, sixth president of the United States. She was educated in Andover, Massachusetts, and Chicago, Illinois, and from childhood she was strongly impressed by the religious and academic atmosphere of Andover, which was then the center of various theological institutions. While still young, Adams had her horoscope read by Dr. J. Herbert Smith, then professor of Materia Medica at Boston University and became profoundly interested in **astrology.** Smith's reading of Adams's horoscope and his personal observation of her character convinced him that she was an ideal personality to help elevate astrology to the dignity of an accepted science. He taught her all he knew, and she supplemented this knowledge by studying Hindu **Vedanta** under **Swami Vivekananda,** pioneer of Hindu philosophy in the United States. After years of study, Adams started practice as a professional astrological consultant in New York.

She became nationally known when she read a chart for the owner of New York's Windsor Hotel on Fifth Avenue predicting a serious disaster that would take place almost immediately. The hotel owner was unaware of any impending problems and took no action, but the next day his hotel was destroyed by fire. The resulting media publicity brought Evangeline Adams immediate fame nationwide. In 1914 she was prosecuted for "fortune-telling" but contested the case in court. She demonstrated her methods of work and made an accurate prediction concerning the judge's son. Judge John H. Freschi acquitted her, stating: "The defendant has raised astrology to the dignity of an exact science."

Adams published various books and pamphlets on astrology, and many famous individuals (including J. Pierpont Morgan, Mary Pickford, singer Enrico Caruso, and King Edward VII of Britain) visited her headquarters at Carnegie Hall. From 1930 onward she broadcast three times weekly, and received thousands of letters requesting astrological readings. As early as 1931, she predicted that the United States would be at war in 1942. In 1932 she was booked for a 21-night lecture tour but canceled it after predicting her own death, which duly occurred. She is generally recognized as the leading astrologer of her time who laid the groundwork for professional astrology in the United States. She died in New York November 10, 1932.

Sources:

Adams, Evangeline. *Astrology: Your Place among the Stars.* New York: Dodd, Mead, 1930.

———. *Astrology: Your Place in the Sun.* New York: Dodd, Mead, 1928.

———. *Astrology for Everyone: What It Is and How It Works.* New York: Dodd, Mead, 1931.

———. *The Bowl of Heaven.* New York: Dodd, Mead, 1926.

Adams, John Q(uincy), III (1938–)

Parapsychologist who experimented with school children and teachers to test clairvoyance and extrasensory effects. He was born March 7, 1938, in Dallas, Texas, and studied at Oberlin College, Ohio (B.A., 1960).

Adamski, George (1891–1965)

First of the 1950s flying saucer **contactees** who claimed direct contact with beings who had traveled to Earth in spaceships from planets in outer space. Adamski was born in Poland on April 17, 1891. He was two years old when his family emigrated to Dunkirk, New York. In 1913 Adamski served with the 13th Cavalry on the Mexican border, received an honorable discharge from the army in 1919, then settled in Laguna Beach, California. He studied occult metaphysics and in 1936 founded the Royal Order of Tibet, through which he offered a course in self-mastery. Although he had no scientific training, he was often referred to as "Professor" by his Royal Order of Tibet mystical philosophy students. In 1940 he moved to the Valley Center with his followers, where they established a farming project. Four years later he moved to the southern slope of Mount Palomar in Southern California. He had no formal connection with the observatory there and worked as a handyman at a hamburger stand.

Soon after the modern flying saucer era began, Adamski emerged in 1947 as a popular lecturer. He claimed to have sighted a UFO in 1946 and in 1949 wrote a novel, *Pioneers in Space,* to promote discussion of the subject by the general public. He also began to show pictures of what he claimed were saucers he had seen near his home near Mount Palomar.

Adamski also coauthored, with **Desmond Leslie,** *Flying Saucers Have Landed* (1953), the book that launched the contactee phenomenon. Adamski claimed that he had been contacted by the Venusian occupant of a flying saucer that landed in the California desert November 20, 1952. Subsequently Adamski claimed to have had contact with spacemen from Mars and Saturn and to have traveled 50,000 miles into space in their craft. After Adamski's revelations, the convention of spaceman contacts, messages from outer space, and warnings about the welfare of the cosmos became firmly established. Adamski expanded upon his revelations in two subsequent volumes: *Inside the Space Ships* (1955) and *Flying Saucers Farewell* (1961).

By the late 1950s Adamski was an international celebrity who lectured to large audiences in North America and Europe. He also had his critics. In 1957 editor James Mosley devoted an issue of *Saucer News* to an exposé of Adamski. In 1962 Adamski's close associate C. A. Honey denounced him after discovering that Adamski had rewritten the original messages from the saucer beings in the Royal Order of Tibet materials. As his following had grown, Adamski had formed his followers into study groups and offered lessons in *cosmic philosophy.* In spite of the critics and defections, he retained a large following at the time of his death on April 23, 1965, from a heart attack, in Washington, D.C. His close associates founded the UFO Education Center in Valley Center, California, and the George Adamski Foundation, in Vista, California, to carry on his legacy.

Sources:

Adamski, George. *Cosmic Philosophy.* Freeman, S.D.: Pine Hill Press, 1961.

———. *Flying Saucer Farewell.* 1961. Reprint, *Behind the Flying Saucer Mystery.* New York: Paperback Library, 1967.

———. *Inside the Space Ships.* 1955. Reprint, *Inside the Flying Saucers.* New York: Paperback Library, 1967.

Barker, Gray. *The Book of Adamski.* Clarksburg, W.V.: Saucerian Publications, 1965.

Leslie, Desmond, and George Adamski. *Flying Saucers Have Landed.* London: Werner Laurie, 1953. Rev. London: Neville Spearman, 1970.

Zinsstag & Timothy Good. *George Adamski: The Untold Story.* Beckenham, U.K.: Ceit Publications, 1983.

Adare, Lord (1841–1926)

Author of a remarkable work, *Experiences in Spiritualism with D. D. Home,* printed privately in 1869 at the request of his father, Earl of Dunraven. To make this book accessible to a large public and in memory of his father to whose title he succeeded, the author agreed in 1924 to a second edition by the **Society for Psychical Research,** omitting the attestation of some of the prominent witnesses of the phenomena. The probable reason for the privacy of the first publication was that the Earl of Dunraven, being a Roman Catholic, wished to avoid the censure of the Church.

The friendship of Lord Adare and **Daniel Douglas Home** dated from 1867. It began at Malvern in Dr. Gully's hydropathic establishment, where Home was a guest and Lord Adare a patient. For the next two years he spent a great deal of time in

Home's company. His friendship for Home (as stated in his preface to the 1924 publication) never diminished or changed thereafter.

The phenomena recorded in the book are of a wide range and embrace almost every spiritualistic manifestation. Only the absence of **apport** phenomena and the penetration of matter through solid matter is conspicuous. Its possibility was stoutly denied by Home. The records fail to meet scientific requirements in many ways. The control was left to the senses, no instruments were introduced, and many points in the narrative were left incomplete.

No attempt was made to appraise the sittings in scientific categories. "Miracle worship" might best describe the attitude of Lord Adare and of his fellow-sitters. On the other hand, while deficient in some ways, these records demonstrate the conscientiousness of those who observed Home. Each wrote letters addressed to the Earl of Dunraven shortly after the séances. Lord Adare, for almost two years, lived most of the time with Home, which bolstered his belief that Home was not perpetrating a large scale deception. The preface states: "We have not, on a single occasion, during the whole series of seances, seen any indication of contrivance on the part of the medium for producing or facilitating the manifestations which have taken place."

ADC Project

Established by Judy and Bill Guggenehim to accumulate first-hand accounts of people who have felt the direct presence of or have actually seen deceased loved ones. They have collected more than two thousand such accounts of "after death contact" (ADC) in their study and welcome any further accounts. Telephone interviews are conducted at the expense of the ADC Project, P.O. Box 536365, Orlando, FL 32853.

Adcock, C(yril) J(ohn) (1904– ?)

Parapsychologist and university lecturer on psychology. Born in England, Adcock studied at the University of New Zealand and the University of London (B.A., M.A., Ph.D.). He lectured at Victoria University, Wellington, New Zealand, and is a member of the Parapsychological Association and American Psychology Association. His work in parapsychology included group testing of ESP and tests of statistical significance of ESP experiments.

Sources:

Pleasants, Helene, ed. *Biographical Dictionary of Parapsychology.* New York: Helix Press, 1964.

Addanc of the Lake

A monster that figures in the **Mabinogion** legend of Peredur. Peredur obtains a magic stone that renders him invisible, and he thus succeeds in slaying this monster, which had daily killed the inhabitants of the palace of the King of Tortures.

Addey, John (1920–)

Theosophist and astrologer, born at Barnsley, Yorkshire, England, on June 15, 1920. Addey earned his master's degree from Saint John's College, Cambridge. He became interested in **astrology** while at Cambridge, and after World War II he joined the Theosophical Society's Astrological Lodge, which brought him into a long-term relationship with **C. E. O. Carter.** In 1948 Carter established the Faculty of Astrological Studies to train astrologers, and Addey became one of its first students, obtaining his diploma in 1951.

Within a few years, however, he found himself doubtful of his art and its scientific underpinnings. He turned to scientific research, his most important focus centering on longevity and people suffering from polio. His observations led him to the development of a "wave" theory of astrology. He subsequently moved to integrate completed and ongoing statistical studies of astrological effects and the insights of Hindu astrology into what he termed *harmonics,* a system of astrology that emphasizes the integral divisions of the horoscope chart. He saw in harmonics a method of bringing a united theoretical base to the many different systems of astrology that were emerging in the postwar world.

In 1958 Addey led in the founding of the Astrological Association, a professional association of astrologers primarily in Great Britain. His underlying agenda was the development of harmonic theory, which he presented in a series of booklets in the 1970s.

Harmonics was initially received with some enthusiasm by Addey's astrological colleagues; however, as astrologers worked with Addey's thought, they found it was too abstract and offered little insight to assist in the essential task of interpreting an astrological chart. As such, Addey's theoretical work was soon forgotten, though his empirical studies remain a major building block of contemporary astrology's attempt to provide astrology with an acceptable scientific base.

In 1970 Addey founded the Urania Trust, which had the exceedingly ambitious goal of reintegrating astrology into astronomy, an objective on which almost no progress has been made. Addey also served a term as editor of the *Astrological Journal.*

Sources:

Addey, John. *Astrology Reborn.* Tempe, Ariz.: American Federation of Astrologers, 1972.

———. *Harmonic Anthology.* Tempe, Ariz.: American Federation of Astrologers, 1976.

———. *Harmonics in Astrology.* Romford: L. N. Fowler, 1976.

———. *Selected Writings.* Tempe, Ariz.: American Federation of Astrologers, 1976.

Lewis, James L. *The Astrology Encyclopedia.* Detroit: Gale Research, 1994.

Additor

A **ouija** board modified by the addition of a little round hollow box with a pointer protruding from it. The hollow box is a miniature cabinet that is believed to accumulate psychic force as it moves under the fingers over a polished board printed with the alphabet.

The term **autoscope** has been given to such devices as the ouija board, **planchette,** and additor, that are believed to facilitate the production of messages from an unknown intelligent source, at times the subconscious mind, at other times from discarnate spirits of the dead. (See also **Automatic Writing**)

Adelphi Organization

The Adelphi Organization dates to 1976 when Richard Kieninger, the founder of the **Stelle Group,** left Stelle, Illinois, and founded a second group near Dallas, Texas. Kieninger's autobiographical volume *The Ultimate Frontier* had provided the main teaching at Stelle, but he was asked to leave the community after his sexual liaisons with several of the married women were discovered. The new organization was modeled on Stelle and had the same goal, which Kieninger had been given by his teacher, of building a new nation that would survive the disasters at the end of the twentieth century.

After Kieninger left Stelle, a significant power struggle developed. His former wife, the president of the corporation, and the entire board of trustees resigned and left the community. Those remaining reestablished relations with Kieninger. Stelle and Adelphi reunited, the headquarters moved to Texas, and Kieninger was named chairman of the board. However, in 1986, Kieninger was again forced out and founded a short-lived group, the Builders of the Nation of God. A short time later Kieninger was accepted back at Adelphi and at that point Adelphi and Stelle went their separate ways.

Adelphi continues with its program of building the new nation that is predicted to arise following an atomic world war in 1999, which purportedly will destroy 90 percent of the population, and the massive disaster in the year 2000, which will see many land masses rearranged. The Adelphi Organization can be reached at 406 Mayfield Ave., Garland, TX 75041.

Sources:

Kieninger, Richard. *The Hidden Christ.* Dallas, Tex.: Paragon Press, 1989.

———. *Observations.* 4 vols. Chicago: Stelle Group, 1971–79.

———. *Spiritual Seekers Guidebook and Hidden Threats to Mental and Spiritual Freedom.* Quinlan, Tex.: Stelle Group, 1986.

Kossy, Donna. *Kooks: A Guide to the Outer Limits of Human Belief.* Portland, Oreg.: Feral House, 1994.

Kueshana, Eklal [Richard Kieninger]. *The Ultimate Frontier.* Chicago: Stelle Group, 1963.

Adelung, Johann Christoph (1732–1806)

German philologist and grammarian. Adelung published a work on the occult entitled *Histoire des folies humaines, on Biographie des plus celebres necromanciens, alchimistes, devins, etc.* (Leipzig, 1785–89). He died at Dresden.

Adepts

According to the **Theosophical Society** and some occultists, adepts are individuals who, after stern self-denial and consistent self-development, have prepared themselves to assist in influencing the advancement of the world. The means by which this is attained are said to be long and arduous, but in the end the successful adept fulfills the purpose for which he was created and transcends other human beings.

The activities of adepts are multifarious, being concerned with the direction and guidance of the activities of other human beings. Theosophists claim that their knowledge, like their powers, far exceeds that of other mortals; they can control forces both in the spiritual and the physical realm and are said to be able to prolong their lives for centuries.

Adepts are also known as the **Great White Brotherhood,** rishis, rahats, or **mahatmas.** Ordinary people who earnestly desire to work for the betterment of the world may become "chelas," or apprentices to adepts, in which case the latter are known as **masters,** but the apprentice must first have practiced self-denial and self-development in order to become sufficiently worthy. The master imparts teaching and wisdom otherwise unattainable (and thus resembles the **guru** in the Hindu tradition) and helps the apprentice by communion and inspiration. **Helena Petrovna Blavatsky** alleged that she was the apprentice of such masters and claimed that they dwelled in the Tibetan Mountains. The term adept was also employed by medieval magicians and alchemists to denote a master of their sciences.

Adhab-Algal

The Islamic purgatory, where the wicked are tormented by the dark angels Munkir and Nekir.

Adjuration

A formula of **exorcism** by which an evil spirit is commanded, in the name of God, to do or say what the exorcist requires of him.

Adler, Margot (1946–)

Margot Adler, author and Wiccan priestess, is the granddaughter of renowned psychotherapist Alfred Adler. She was raised in a nonreligious setting and attended the University of California at Berkeley (B.S., 1968) during its era of political radicalism. Following her graduation she began a career in broadcast journalism at radio station WBAI-FM. In 1978 she accepted her latest position, with National Public Radio.

Living in New York in the early 1970s, she encountered **witchcraft** through a study group founded by the New York Coven of Welsh Traditional Witches. In 1973 she became associated with Gardnerian witchcraft. In 1976 she became the priestess of Iargalon, a Gardnerian coven. During her years as an active priestess, she researched and wrote *Drawing Down the Moon,* a sympathetic history and survey of the modern Wiccan and pagan community. Over the years since, the book, now in its second edition, has introduced many people to witchcraft.

Since 1982 Adler has practiced as a solitary, but remains one of the most visible leaders of the pagan community in North America. In 1988 her handfasting to John Gliedman was the first pagan marriage covered in the *New York Times* society pages.

Sources:

Adler, Margot. *Drawing Down the Moon.* New York: Viking Press, 1979. Rev. ed. Boston, Mass.: Beacon Press, 1986.

Adonai

A Hebrew word signifying "the Lord" and used by Jews when speaking or writing of "YHWH," or Yahweh, the ineffable name of **God.** The Jews entertained the deepest awe for this incommunicable and mysterious name, and this feeling led them to avoid pronouncing it and to substitute the word Adonai for "Jehovah" in their sacred text. The ancients attributed great power to names; to know and pronounce someone's name was to have power over them. Obviously one could not, like the Pagans, suggest that mere creatures had power over God.

This custom in Jewish prayers still prevails, especially among Hasidic Jews, who follow the **Kabala** and believe that the Holy Name of God, associated with miraculous powers, should not be profaned. Yahweh is their invisible protector and king, and no image of him is made. He is worshiped according to his commandments, with an observance of the ritual instituted through Moses. The term "YHWH" means the revealed Absolute Deity, the Manifest, Only, Personal, Holy Creator and Redeemer.

Adoptive Masonry

Masonic societies that adopted women as members. Early in the eighteenth century such societies were established in France, and they spread speedily to other countries. One of the first to "adopt" women was the Mopses. The Felicitaries existed in 1742. The Fendeurs, or Woodcutters, were instituted in 1763 by Bauchaine, Master of a Parisian lodge. It was modeled on the Carbonari, and its popularity led to the establishment of other lodges, notably the Fidelity and the Hatchet.

In 1774 the Grand Orient Lodge of France established a system of three degrees called the Rite of Adoption and elected the duchess of Bourbon as Grand Mistress of France.

The rite has been generally adopted into **Freemasonry,** and various degrees were added from time to time to the number of about twelve in all. Latin and Greek mysteries were added to the rite by the Ladies' Hospitallers of Mount Tabor. The greatest ladies in France joined the French lodges of adoption.

The Rite of Mizraim created lodges for both sexes in 1819, 1821, 1838, and 1853, and the Rite of Memphis in 1839. America founded the Rite of the Eastern Star in five points. In these systems, admission was generally confined to the female relations of Masons. The Order of the Eastern Star and that of Adoptive Masonry were attempted in Scotland but without success.

Adramelech

According to **Johan Weyer,** Adramelech is Chancellor of the infernal regions, Keeper of the Wardrobe of the Demon King, and President of the High Council of the Devils. He was worshiped at Sepharvaim, an Assyrian town, where children were burned on his altar. Rabbis of the period said that he showed himself in the form of a mule or sometimes of a peacock.

Sources:

Weyer, Johannes. *Witches, Devils, and Doctors in the Renaissance: Johann Weyer, De Praestigiis.* Edited by George Mora. Binghamton, N.Y.: Medieval and Renaissance Texts and Studies, 1991.

Advanced Spiritual Church Healing Center

Center founded by British-born psychic **Douglas Johnson.** Holds public meetings and is concerned with psychic and spiritual development. Address: 10945 Camarillo St., North Hollywood, CA 91602.

"AE"

Pen name of **George W. Russell** (1867–1935), Irish poet, painter, mystic, and journalist.

Aerial Phenomena Research Organization (APRO)

Founded in January 1952 in Sturgeon Bay, Wisconsin, "to conduct investigations and research into the phenomenon of unidentified flying objects (**UFOs**) and to find a scientifically acceptable solution to this phenomenon." Led by Jim Lorenzen and his wife, Coral Lorenzen, who authored several popular UFO books, APRO emerged as one of the most outstanding UFO investigation organizations. Through the 1950s the Lorenzens and APRO moved successively to Los Angeles (1954), Alamogordo, New Mexico (1954), and Tucson, Arizona (1960). Beginning as an association of flying saucer clubs that collected accounts of UFOs and commented upon them in the *APRO Bulletin,* APRO grew into a substantial research organization. It was distinguished from the **National Investigations Committee on Aerial Phenomena (NICAP),** the other main UFO research organization of the 1950s, by its coolness to the idea of a government cover-up of UFO data and its interest in sightings of humanoid-like creatures associated with the UFOs.

APRO membership peaked in 1967 with 1,500 members. Then in 1969 it suffered two disasters. First, the University of Colorado report of its study of UFOs, popularly known as the **Condon Report,** struck Ufology (the study of UFOs) a significant blow with the conclusion that nothing was likely to be achieved by further study. As a result, the Air Force dropped its semipublic data collection effort, Project Blue Book. Then APRO suffered a major schism when Walt Andrus, who led a regional office in Illinois, broke away and founded the Midwest UFO Network (now the **Mutual UFO Network**). Membership began a decline from which APRO never recovered. Jim Lorenzen died in 1986, and Coral followed two years later. The board voted to disband the organization shortly thereafter.

Sources:

Clark, Jerome. *The Emergence of a Phenomenon: UFOs from the Beginning through 1959; The UFO Encyclopedia.* Vol. 2. Detroit: Omnigraphics, 1992.

Lorenzen, Coral E. *The Great Flying Saucer Hoax: The UFO Facts and Their Interpretation.* New York: William Frederick Press, 1962. Rev.: *Flying Saucers: The Startling Evidence of Invasion from Outer Space.* New York: New American Library, 1966.

Lorenzen, Coral, and Jim Lorenzen. *Abducted! Confrontations with Beings from Outer Space.* New York: Berkley, 1977.

———. *Encounters with UFO Occupants.* New York: Berkley, 1976.

———. *UFOs: The Whole Story.* New York: New American Library, 1969.

———. *UFOs Over the Americas.* New York: New American Library, 1968.

Aerial Phenomenon Clipping and Information Center

A subscription information service that operated during the 1980s, providing a monthly sampling of reports of unidentified flying objects and related phenomena such as monster or occult occurrences. The reports were compiled from the various wire services, reproduced from original news sources, and sent out from editorial offices in Cleveland, Ohio.

Aeromancy

The art of foretelling future events by the observation of atmospheric phenomena, as, for example, when the death of a great man is presaged by the appearance of a comet. Francois de la Tour Blanche stated that aeromancy is the art of **fortune-telling** by means of specters that are made to appear in the air, or the representation by the aid of demons, of future events, which are projected on the clouds as a film is projected onto a screen. "As for thunder and lightning," he adds, "these are concerned with auguries, and the aspect of the sky and of the planets belong to the science of astrology."

Sources:

Waite, Arthur Edward. *The Occult Sciences.* 1891. Reprint, Secaucus, N.J.: University Books, 1974.

Aetherius Society, The

Founded by **Sir George King,** a British occultist and flying saucer **contactee** from the West country, whose mother had formerly run a healing sanctuary. He was in his apartment one morning in March 1954 when a voice informed him: "Prepare yourself. You are to become the voice of Interplanetary Parliament." It was King's habit to meditate daily, and while so engaged several days later, he was visited by an Indian yoga master who informed him of his mission: the Cosmic Intelligences had selected him as their "primary terrestrial channel." King began to communicate with an entity named Aetherius, a Venusian who was one of the Cosmic Masters of the Interplanetary Parliament located on Saturn. (Jesus Christ is also considered a Parliamentary Master.)

Eventually King went public when he permitted the Master Aetherius to speak through him at a **channeling** held at Caxton Hall in London. He began the magazine *Aetherius Speaks to Earth* (now *Cosmic News*) and in 1956 founded the Aetherius Society. By this time the issue of UFOs had become a matter of public concern, and UFO contactees like King were offering an answer. Before the decade was out, King had attracted a following in the United States, and an American headquarters was established in Los Angeles.

King developed a picture of the cosmos as ruled by an extraterrestrial hierarchy similar to the theosophical spiritual hierarchy. The hierarchy sent spiritual energy to the planet, which could be used to fight the forces of evil, especially those coming from evil extraterrestrials. Spaceships position themselves above the earth at special times of the year, considered the best moments for transmitting the energies from outer space. King authored a series of books spelling out the theology and practices of what emerged as a new occult religion.

King claims that he received a mystical consecration on July 23, 1958, from the Master Jesus for his mission; the Lord Buddha added his consecration on December 5, 1978. In 1980 King was consecrated as an archbishop in an independent Old Catholic lineage. The society has headquarters in London and in Hollywood, California, where it owns a complex of buildings. It may be contacted at 757 Fulham Rd., London SW6 5UU, England, and at 6202 Afton Pl., Hollywood, CA 90028-8298.

Sources:

King, George. *The Nine Freedoms.* Los Angeles: Aetherius Society, 1963.

———. *The Practices of Aetherius.* Hollywood, Calif.: Aetherius Society, 1964.

———. *The Twelve Blessings.* London: Aetherius Press, 1958.

———. *You Are Responsible.* London: Aetherius Press, 1961.

The Story of Aetherius Society. Hollywood, Calif.: Aetherius Society, n.d.

Aetherius Speaks to Earth

Started as a biweekly publication of the **Aetherius Society,** promulgating the teachings of psychic **George King** and providing information on the Society's activities. It was renamed *Aetherius Society Newsletter* and now continues as a monthly periodical under the name *Cosmic Voice.* Address: 6202 Afton Pl., Hollywood, CA 90028.

Aetities (or Aquilaeus)

A precious stone of magical properties, composed of iron oxide with a little silex and alumina, and said to be found in the stomach or neck of the eagle. It is supposed to heal falling sickness and prevent untimely birth. It was worn bound on the arm to prevent abortion and on the thigh to aid parturition.

AFAN See Association for Astrological Networking

Affectability

A term coined by parapsychologist **Charles Stuart** implying susceptibility to feedback in a situation where the subject in an ESP test is told the score on the previous run and asked to estimate the score on the next run. In this context, "affectable" subjects were those who consistently gave estimates that reflected their score on the immediately previous run; "unaffectable subjects" were not so influenced. Stuart also used the term "affectable" for subjects who were markedly extreme in expressing likes or dislikes to various possible interests, while "unaffectable" subjects were relatively indifferent to many of these interests. By measurement on a Stuart Interest Inventory, Stuart claimed that unaffectable subjects appeared to score higher than affectable on ESP perception. However, the term "affectability" can be applied generally to the degree of suggestibility of a subject.

Sources:

Stuart, Charles. "An Analysis to Determine a Test Predictive of Extra-chance Scoring in Card-calling Tests." *Journal of Parapsychology* vol. 5 (1941).

———. "An Interest Inventory Relation to ESP Scores." *Journal of Parapsychology* vol. 10 (1946).

AFRICA

(Note: The north of Africa, including the Sahara and the Sudan, has been Islamic territory for many centuries. For a discussion of Islamic magic and alchemy, see the entry **Arabs.** Instances of Arabic sorcery are also discussed in the **Semites** entry.)

Beliefs and practices thought of as occult in Western society were integral to the traditional tribal religions in the southern two-thirds of Africa, especially those concerning sympathetic **magic,** the cult of the dead, and **witchcraft.** During the history of this region, the basically pantheistic and polytheistic religions have also been cross-fertilized with Islamic and Christian teachings, creating new beliefs and modifying old ones. Today a large but undetermined number of Africans follow traditional beliefs involving deities, ghosts, and spirits as well as an array of special powers in nature presided over by the supreme entity adopted from Christianity and Islam. The latter, somewhat remote from everyday problems, is believed to largely operate on humans through the many other deities.

Southern Africa

Among the Zulu and other Bantu tribes of equatorial and southern Africa, witchcraft or malevolent **sorcery** was traditionally practiced—in secret, for the results of detection were terrible. Tribes instituted a caste of witchfinders assigned the task of tracking down witches.

The nineteenth-century writer Lady Mary Anne Barker observed,

"It is not difficult to understand, bearing in mind the superstition and cruelty which existed in remote parts of England not so very long ago; how powerful such women become among a savage people, or how tempting an opportunity they could furnish of getting rid of an enemy. Of course they are exceptional individuals; more observant, more shrewd, and more dauntless than the average fat, hard-working Kaffir women, besides possessing the contradictory mixture of great physical powers and strong hysterical tendencies. They work themselves up to a pitch of frenzy, and get to believe as firmly in their own supernatural discernment as any individual among the trembling circle of Zulus to whom a touch from the whisk they carry is a sentence of instant death."

The Zulu witchfinders were attended by a circle of girls and women who, like a Greek chorus, clapped their hands and repeated a low chant, the measure and rhythm of which changed at times with a stomp and a swing of the arm. Ceremonial dress was also an important part of the witch doctor's role, for such things appealed directly to the imagination of the crowd and prepared onlookers to be readily swayed by the necromancer's devices. One of the witchfinders, Nozinyanga, was especially impressive. Her fierce face, spotted with gouts of red paint on cheek and brow, was partly overshadowed by a helmetlike plume of the tall feathers of the sakabula bird. In her right hand she carried a light sheaf of *assegais* (spears), and on her left arm was slung a small and pretty shield of dappled oxhide. Her petticoat, made of a couple of large gay handkerchiefs, was worn kiltwise. From neck to waist she was covered with bead-necklaces, goat's-hair fringes, and the scarlet tassels. Her chest rose and fell beneath the baldric of leopard skin, fastened across with huge brazen knobs, while down her back hung a beautifully dried and flattened skin of an enormous boa constrictor.

When the community had resolved that a certain misfortune was caused by witches, the next step was to find and punish them. For this purpose the king summoned a great meeting, his subjects sitting on the ground in a ring or circle for four or five days. The witchfinders took their places in the center, and as they gradually worked themselves up to an ecstatic state, resembling possession, they lightly switched with their quagga-tail one of the trembling spectators, who was immediately dragged away and butchered, along with all of his or her relatives and livestock. Sometimes a whole kraal was exterminated in this way, so reminiscent of European witch-hunts.

Barker also described a sorceress named Nozilwane, whose wistful glance, she noticed, had in it something uncanny and uncomfortable. She was dressed beautifully in lynx skins folded over and over from waist to knee, the upper part of her body covered by strings of wild beasts' teeth and fangs, beads, skeins of gaily colored yarn, strips of snakeskin, and fringes of Angora goat fleece. Lynx tails hung like lappets on each side of her face, which was overshadowed and almost hidden by a profusion of sakabula feathers. "This bird," Barker commented, "has a very beautiful plumage, and is sufficiently rare for the natives to attach a peculiar value and charm to the tail-feathers; they are like those of a young cock, curved and slender, and of a dark chestnut color, with a white eye at the extreme tip of each feather." Among all this thick, floating plumage were interspersed small bladders and skewers or pins wrought out of tusks. Like the other witchfinders, she wore her hair highly greased and twisted up with twine until it ceased to have the appearance of hair and hung around the face like a thick fringe, dyed deep red.

Bent double and with a catlike gait, Nozilwane came forward. Every movement of her undulating body kept time to the beat of the girls' hands and their low crooning chant. Soon she pretended to find the thing she sought, and with a series of wild pirouettes leaped into the air, shaking her spears and brandishing her shield like a bacchante. Nowamso, another of the party, was determined that her companion should not get all the applause, and she too, with a yell and a leap, sprang into the dance to the sound of louder grunts and harder handclaps. Nowamso was anxious to display her back, where a magnificent snakeskin, studded in a regular pattern with brass-headed nails, floated like a stream. She was attired also in a splendid kilt of leopard skins, decorated with red rosettes, and her dress was considered more careful and artistic than any of the others'. Nozilwane, however, had youth and stamina on her side. The others, although they all joined in and hunted out an imaginary enemy, and in turn exulted over his discovery, soon became breathless and spent and were glad when their attendants led them away to be anointed and to drink water.

Central Africa

The magical beliefs of central and eastern Africa were for the most part connected with beliefs and practices concerning the dead and the honoring of images. When the ghost of a dead person was weary of staying in the bush, many believed that the spirit would come for one of the people over whom they exerted the most influence. The spirit would say to that person, "I am tired of dwelling in the bush, please to build for me in the town a little house as close as possible to your own." The spirit would also instruct him to dance and sing, and accordingly he would assemble the women at night to join in dance and song.

Then, the next day, the people would go to the grave of the *obambo,* or ghost, and make a crude image, after which a bamboo bier, on which a body is conveyed to the grave, and some of the dust of the ground were carried into a little hut erected near the house of the visited, and a white cloth was draped over the door. A curious element of the ritual, which seems to show that these people had a legend something like the old Greek myth of Charon and the river Styx, was a song chanted during the ceremony with the following line: "You are well dressed, but you have no canoe to carry you across to the other side."

Possession

In most preindustrial cultures, epileptic diseases were assumed to be the result of demoniac possession. In much of Africa the sufferer was supposed to be possessed by Mbwiri, and the person was relieved only by the intervention of the medicine man (priest) or a spirit or deity. In the middle of the street a hut was built for the sufferer, and there he resided, along with the priest and his disciples, until cured, or maddened. Townspeople held a continuous revel, including what seemed like unending dances to the sound of flute and drum, for ten days to two weeks, engaging in much eating and drinking all at the expense of the patient's relatives.

The patient at some point danced, usually feigning madness, until the epileptic attack came on accompanied by a frenzied stare, convulsed limbs, the gnashing of teeth. The man's actions at this point were not ascribed to himself, but to the demon that had control of him. When a cure, real or pretended, had been effected the patient built a little house for the spirit image, avoided certain kinds of food, and performed certain duties. Sometimes the process terminated in the patient's insanity; some were known to run away to the bush, hide from all human beings, and live on the roots and berries of the forest.

One European writer observed of the tribal medicine man,

"[They] are priest doctors, like those of the ancient Germans. They have a profound knowledge of herbs, and also of human nature, for they always monopolise the real power in the state. But it is very doubtful whether they possess any secrets save that of extracting virtue and poison from plants. During the first trip which I made into the bush I sent for one of these doctors. At that time I was staying among the Shekani, who are celebrated for their fetish [image]. He came attended by half-a-dozen disciples. He was a tall man dressed in white, with a girdle of leopard's skin, from which hung an iron bell, of the same shape as our sheep bells. He had two chalk marks over his eyes. I took some of my own hair, frizzled it with a burning glass, and gave it to him. He popped it with alacrity into his little grass bag; for white man's hair is fetish of the first order. Then I poured out some raspberry vinegar into a glass, drank a little of it first, country fashion, and offered it to him, telling him that it was blood from the brains of great doctors. Upon this he received it with great reverence, and dipping his fingers into it as if it was snap-dragon, sprinkled with it his forehead, both feet between the two first toes, and the ground behind his back. He then handed his glass to a disciple, who emptied it, and smacked his lips afterwards in a very secular manner. I then desired to see a little of his fetish. He drew on the ground with red chalk some hieroglyphics, among which I distinguished the circle, the cross, and the crescent. He said that if I would give him a fine 'dush,' he would tell me about it. But as he would not take anything in reason, and as I knew that he would tell me nothing of very great importance in public, negotiations were suspended."

The claims of the priest to possess supernatural powers were seldom questioned. He was not only a doctor and a priest who intervened with the spirits and deities—two capacities in which his influence was necessarily very powerful—he was also a witchfinder, and this office invested him with a truly formidable authority. When a man of worth died, his death was invariably ascribed to witchcraft, and the aid of the priest was invoked to discover the witch.

When a man was sick a long time, his neighbors called Ngembi, and if she could not make him well, they called the priest. He came at night, in a white dress, with cock's feathers on his head, carrying a bell and a little glass. He called two or three of the victim's relatives together. He did not speak, but always looked in his glass. Then he told them that the sickness was not of Mbwiri, nor of a ghost, nor of God, but that it came from a witch. They would say to him, "What shall we do?" He would then go out and say, "I have told you. I have no more to say." They then gave him a dollar's worth of cloth, and every night they gathered together in the street and cried, "I know that man who bewitched my brother. It is good for you to make him well." Then the witch made him well.

If the man did not recover they called the bush doctor from the Shekani country. At night he went into the street; all the people flocked about him. With a tiger skin in his hand, he walked to and fro, until, singing all the while, he laid the tiger skin at the feet of the witch. At the conclusion of his song the people seized the witch and put him or her in chains, saying, "If you don't restore our brother to health, we will kill you."

Western Occultism in Africa

Today more than 100 million Africans follow a form of Islamic faith, and an almost equal number some form of Christianity. In addition to Roman Catholic and Protestant faiths, there are many variant forms of Christianity, and many Christian groups have become independent of the older missionary churches and reorganized as indigenous religious bodies. The religious picture has been confused in recent years as a result of the unrest attending the throwing off of colonial regimes and the establishment of autonomous governments.

In the midst of these changes, Western occult, metaphysical, and mystical literature has circulated through the continent since the 1920s, especially in South Africa, the central African states, and such West African nations as Ghana and Nigeria. Since World War II there has been a noticeable popular response to such ideas. As early as 1925 the **Rosicrucians** were present in West Africa, and **New Thought** was introduced into Africa in the 1930s when several American teachers toured the country and assisted in the formation of the School of Practical Christianity in 1937 (now known as the School of Truth). Today a broad range of such groups as the Church of Religious Science, the Unity School of Christianity, Swedenborgians, and the **Church Universal and Triumphant** are in existence. In the last two decades, guru-oriented groups such as **ECKANKAR, Subud,** and the Grail

Movement, and some of the new Japanese religions have appeared. Numerous gurus, including Maharishi Mehesh Yogi, Sathya Sai Baba, and Maharaj Ji have a following. The **New Age** movement has been particularly strong in South Africa, mostly among the white population, and has provoked the appearance of a reactionary anti-New Age effort.

Most interesting has been the emergence of new indigenous African metaphysical movements. Typical of these are the Spiritual Fellowship and the Esom Fraternity Company, both operating in Nigeria. The latter, for example, has established a training school specializing in the healing arts and sciences and what is called a "cosmic hospital." The Spiritual Fellowship grew out of the literary efforts of A. Peter Akpan, who has developed an eclectic program of spiritual development aimed at attaining the higher levels of consciousness. Yogi Kane is a Hindu teacher operating in the Senegal, where he teaches what he terms "Egyptian" **yoga.** East and West come together in these new movements in a mutual affirmation of **astrology, divination,** spiritual healing, and an esoteric approach to life. These indigenous have also become an avenue for the advancement of women who often must assume a secondary role in traditional African religions as well as in Christianity and Islam.

Sources:

Gardiner, John. *The New Age Cult in South Africa.* Cape Town: Stuikhof, 1991.

Hackett, Rosalind I. J. "New Age Trends in Nigeria: Ancestral and or Alien Religion?" In *Perspectives on the New Age,* edited by James R. Lewis and J. Gordon Melton. Albany: State University of New York Press, 1992.

———. *Religion in Calabar: The Religious Life and History of a Nigerian Town.* Berlin: Mouton de Gruyter, 1989.

Oosthuizen, Gehardus C. "The 'Newness' of the New Age in South Africa and Reactions to It." In *Perspectives on the New Age,* edited by James R. Lewis and J. Gordon Melton. Albany: State University of New York Press, 1992.

Parrinder, Geoffrey. *African Traditional Religion.* London: Sheldon Press, 1974. Reprint, New York: Harper, 1977.

Wellard, James. *Lost Worlds of Africa.* New York: E. P. Dutton, 1967.

African Architects, Order of

Eighteenth-century Masonic order founded in Prussia in 1767 by Brother Von Kopper and C. F. Koffen, under the auspices of Frederick II. The order was concerned largely with historical research into **freemasonry,** Christianity, **alchemy,** and chivalry and attracted many distinguished European literary figures of the period. A vast building was erected as Grand Chapter, containing an extensive library, museum of natural history, and a chemical laboratory. The Architects published many works of freemasonry and awarded an annual gold medal to the author of the best historical memoir on the subject. Branches of the order were established at Worms, Cologne, and Paris, and it was said to be affiliated with the Society of Alethophilas, or Lovers of Truth, after which it named one of its grades.

There were two temples, comprising the following degrees: (1) Apprentice of Egyptian Secrets, (2) Initiate into Egyptian Secrets, (3) Cosmopolitan, (4) Christian Philosopher, and (5) Alethophilos. Higher Grades: (1) Esquire, (2) Soldier, and (3) Knight, thus supplying Egyptian, Christian, and Templar mysteries to the initiate. In 1806 a pamphlet was published at Berlin entitled *A Discovery Concerning the System of the Order of African Architects.*

Ag

A red flower used by some Hindus to propitiate the deity Sanee (the planet Saturn). It is made into a wreath with jasoon, also a red-colored flower, which is hung round the neck of the god, who is of a congenial nature. This ceremony is performed at night.

Agaberte

Daughter of a certain giant called Vagnoste dwelling in Scandinavia. She was a powerful enchantress and was rarely seen in her true shape. Sometimes she would take the form of an old woman, wrinkled and bent, and hardly able to move about. At one time she would appear weak and ill, and at another tall and strong, so that her head seemed to touch the clouds. She effected these transformations without the smallest effort or trouble. People believed her capable of overthrowing the mountains, tearing up the trees, drying up the rivers with the greatest of ease. They held that nothing less than a legion of demons must be at her command in order for her to accomplish her magic feats. She seems to be like the Scottish Cailleach Bheur, a nature hag.

Agapis

According to ancient tradition, this was a yellow stone said to promote love or charity; it also cured stings and venomous bites when dipped in water and rubbed over the wound.

Agares

According to **Johan Weyer,** Agares is Grand Duke of the eastern region of Hades. He is shown in the form of a benevolent lord mounted on a crocodile and carrying a hawk on his fist. The army he protects in battle is indeed fortunate, for he disperses their enemies and puts new courage into the hearts of the cowards who fly before superior numbers. He distributes place and power, titles and prelacies, teaches all languages, and has other equally remarkable powers. Thirty-one legions are under his command.

Sources:

Weyer, Johannes. *Witches, Devils, and Doctors in the Renaissance: Johann Weyer, De Praestigiis.* Edited by George Mora. Binghamton, N.Y.: Medieval and Renaissance Texts and Studies, 1991.

Agasha Temple of Wisdom

The Agasha Temple of Wisdom is a Spiritualist church that, during its first generation, was built around the mediumship of Rev. Richard Zenor (1911–1978), a channel for the master teacher Agasha. The temple was founded in 1943 and attained some degree of fame after reporter James Crenshaw wrote sympathetically about it in his book *Telephone between Two Worlds.* Toward the end of Zenor's life, an attempt was made to compile the more important discourses of Agasha in several volumes edited by William Eisen. Two years after Zenor's death, Rev. Geary Salvat, also a channel, was chosen to succeed him. Salvat channels the master teacher Ayuibbi Tobabu.

Both Agasha and Ayuibbi Tobabu have articulated what they consider a universal philosophy based on the acceptance of individual responsibility and a spiritual democracy within the larger context of universal laws. Basic laws include the Golden Rule (Do unto others as you would have them do unto you) and the law of compensation (For every action there is an equal and opposite reaction). The temple is headquartered at 460 Western Ave., Los Angeles, CA 90004. It has several centers in the United States and one in Japan.

Sources:

Crenshaw, James. *Telephone between Two Worlds.* Los Angeles: DeVorss, 1950.

Eisen, William. *Agasha, Master of Wisdom.* Marina del Rey, Calif.: DeVorss, 1977.

———. *The English Cabala.* 2 vols. Marina del Rey, Calif.: DeVorss, 1980–82.

Eisen, William, ed. *The Agashan Discourse.* Marina del Rey, Calif.: DeVorss, 1978.

Zenor, Richard. *Maggie Answers You.* San Diego: Philip J. Hastings, 1965.

Agate (or **Achates**)

According to ancient tradition, this precious stone protected against the biting of scorpions or serpents, soothed the mind, drove away contagion, and put a stop to thunder and lightning. It was also said to dispose the wearer to solitude, promote eloquence, and secure the favor of princes. It gave victory over enemies to those who wore it.

Agathion

A **familiar** spirit that was said to appear only at midday. It took the shape of a man or a beast, or even enclosed itself in a talisman, bottle, or magic ring.

Agathodaemon

Benevolent deity in Greek mythology, the "good spirit" of vineyards and cornfields. According to Aristophanes, Agathodaemon was honored by drinking a cup of wine at the end of a meal. He was represented pictorially in the form of a serpent or sometimes as a young man holding a horn of plenty, a bowl, and ears of corn. Winged serpents were also venerated by the ancient Egyptians, Chinese, and other peoples. (See also **Dragon**)

Age of Progress, The

American Spiritualist weekly edited by Stephen Albro, who witnessed and reported on the early demonstrations of the **Davenport Brothers** in the 1850s.

Agent

Term in parapsychology to denote the individual who attempts to communicate information to a percipient, or subject, of **extrasensory** perception.

Agharta (or **Agharti**)

In his book *Agharta* (1951), **Robert Ernst Dickhoff** claimed that Martians colonized Earth 80,000 years ago and built an elaborate system of underground tunnels, starting in Antarctica, with exits in Tibet, Brazil, the United States, and elsewhere. A secret underground port for **UFOs** called Rainbow City was supposed to be still in operation.

This colorful story appears to be related to the Tibetan legend of the subterranean kingdom of Agharti, presided over by "the King of the World." Millions of people are said to live in these underground realms in cities without crime and using a highly developed science. The King of the World understands the people on Earth and influences them secretly. He is to appear before the people of Earth in a final cosmic struggle of good against evil. This legend was recounted in the book *Beasts, Men, and Gods* by Ferdinand Ossendowski. Ossendowski (1876–1945) was a Polish writer who traveled extensively through Central Asia in the 1920s. (See also **Shaver Mystery; Subterranean Cities**)

Sources:

Dickhoff, Robert Ernest. *Agharta.* Mokelumne Hill, Calif.: Health Research, 1964.

Ossendowski, Ferdinand. *Beasts, Men, and Gods.* New York: E. P. Dutton, 1922.

Agla

A word from the **Kabala** formerly used by rabbis for **exorcisms** of the evil spirit. It is made up of the initial letters of the Hebrew words, *Athah gabor leolam, Adonai,* meaning, "Thou art powerful and eternal, Lord." Among superstitious Christians it was also a favorite weapon with which to combat the evil one, as late as the sixteenth century. It is found in many books on magic, notably in the *Enchiridion* ascribed to Pope Leo III.

Aglaophotis

A kind of herb said to grow in the deserts of Arabia and much used by sorcerers for the evocation of demons. Other plants were then employed to retain the evil spirits as long as the sorcerer required them.

Agondonter (Newsletter)

Quarterly publication concerned with the twentieth-century channeled gospel **Urantia,** published by the First Urantia Society of Los Angeles, P.O. Box 563, Los Angeles, CA 90053.

Agpaoa, Tony (1939–1982)

A Filipino Spiritualist healer who claims to perform surgery with his bare hands without anesthetic. Agpaoa passes his hand across the area to be operated, and an incision appears. He operates either with his fingers or a pair of scissors, and the wound appears to suture instantaneously without scar.

As with similar **psychic surgery** in Brazil, such operations are highly controversial. Early reports, such as those by Bernard Jensen, were most positive, but more recent studies have tended to condemn Agapoa and his colleagues as clever conjurers. For example, in his book *Flim-Flam!* **James Randi** points out that when Agpaoa needed to have his own appendix removed, he had the operation at a San Francisco hospital, although there are scores of other psychic surgeons in the Philippines. (See also **José Arigó**)

Sources:

Chesi, Gert. *Faith Healers in the Philippines.* Austria: Perlinger Verlag, 1981.

Jensen, Bernard. *Tony: The Miraculous Spiritual Healer at Work.* Escondido, Calif.: The Author, [1966].

Randi, James. *Flim-Flam!* Buffalo, N.Y.: Prometheus Books, 1982.

Sherman, Harold. *Wonder Healers of the Philippines.* Los Angeles: DeVorss, 1967.

Valentine, Tom. *Psychic Surgery.* Chicago: Henry Regnery, 1973.

Agricola

Name adopted by mineralogist **Georg Bauer** (1490–1555), who had also searched for the **elixir of life** and the secret of the **Philosopher's Stone.**

Agrippa von Nettesheim, Henry Cornelius (1486–1535)

German soldier and physician, and an adept in **alchemy, astrology,** and **magic.** He was born at Cologne September 14, 1486, and educated at the University of Cologne. While still a youth he served under Maximilian I of Germany. In 1509 he lectured at the University of Dole, but a charge of heresy brought against him by a monk named Catilinet compelled him to leave Dole, and he resumed his former occupation of soldier. In the following year he was sent on a diplomatic mission to England, and on his return followed Maximilian to Italy, where he passed seven years, serving various noble patrons.

Thereafter he practiced medicine at Geneva, and was appointed physician to Louise of Savoy, mother of Francis I; but, on being given some task which he found irksome, he left the service of his patroness and denounced her bitterly. He then accepted a post offered him by Margaret, duchess of Savoy, regent of the Netherlands. On her death in 1530, he traveled to France, where he was arrested for some slighting mention of the

Queen-Mother, Louise of Savoy. He was soon released, however, and died at Grenoble in 1535.

Agrippa was a man of great talent and varied attainments. He was acquainted with eight languages and was evidently a talented physician, soldier, and theologian with many noble patrons. Yet, notwithstanding these advantages, he never seemed free from misfortune; persecution and financial difficulties dogged him and in Brussels he suffered imprisonment for debt. He frequently made enemies, and the persecution of the monks with whom he often came into conflict was bitter and increasing.

His principal works were a defense of magic, entitled *De occulta philosophia,* which was not published until 1531, though written some twenty years earlier; and a satirical attack on the scientific pretensions of his day, *De incertitudine et Vanitate Scientiarum et Artium atque Excellentia Verbi Dei Declamatio,* also published at Antwerp in 1531. His other works included a treatise *De Nobilitate et Praecellentia Feminu Sexus,* dedicated to Margaret of Burgundy out of gratitude for her patronage.

His interest in alchemy and magic dated from an early period of his life and gave rise to many tales of his occult powers. It was said that he was always accompanied by a **familiar** in the shape of a large black dog. There is a tradition that on his death he renounced his magical works and addressed his familiar thus: "Begone, wretched animal, the entire cause of my destruction!" The animal fled from the room and plunged into the Saone, where it perished. It was said that at the inns where he stayed, Agrippa paid his bills with money that appeared genuine enough at the time, but which afterward turned to worthless horn or shell, like the fairy money which turned to earth after sunset. He was also said to have summoned the spirit of Cicero (died 43 B.C.E.) to pronounce his oration for Roscius, in the presence of John George, elector of Saxony, the earl of Surrey, Erasmus, and other eminent people. Cicero duly appeared, delivered his famous oration, and left his audience deeply moved. Agrippa was supposed to have a magic glass in which it was possible to see objects distant in time or place.

One other story concerning the magician is worthy of record. About to leave home for a short time, he entrusted his wife with the key of his museum, warning her to permit no one to enter. But a curious boarder in their house begged for the key, till at length the harassed hostess gave it to him. The first thing that caught the student's attention was a book of spells, which he began to read. A knock sounded on the door. The student took no notice, but went on reading, and the knock was repeated. A moment later a demon entered, demanding to know why he had been summoned. The student was too terrified to make reply, and the angry demon seized him by the throat and strangled him. At the same moment Agrippa entered, having returned unexpectedly from his journey. Fearing that he would be charged with the murder of the youth, he persuaded the demon to restore him to life for a little while and walk him up and down the market place. The demon consented; people saw the student apparently alive and in good health, and when the demon allowed the semblance of life to leave the body, they thought the young man had died a natural death. However, an examination clearly showed that he had been strangled. The true state of affairs leaked out, and Agrippa was forced to flee for his life.

These fabrications of the popular imagination were probably encouraged rather than suppressed by Agrippa, who loved to surround his comparatively harmless pursuits of alchemy and astrology with an air of mystery calculated to inspire awe and terror in the minds of the ignorant. It is known that he had correspondents in all parts of the world, and that from their letters he gleaned the knowledge which he was popularly believed to obtain from his familiars.

Sources:

Agrippa, Henry. *Three Books of Occult Philosophy.* London: Chthonois Books, n.d.

Agrippa von Nettesheim, H. C. *Philosophy of Natural Magic.* New Hyde Park, N.Y.: University Books, 1974.

———. *Three Books of Occult Philosophy or Magic.* New York: Samuel Weiser, 1971.

Federmann, Reinhard. *The Royal Art of Alchemy.* New York: Chilton Book, 1969.

Ahazu-Demon

(The Seizer). Little is known of this ancient Semitic demon unless it is the same *ahazie* told of in medical texts, where a man can be stricken by a disease bearing this name.

Ahmad ibn Sirin (ca. ninth century C.E.)

(Also known as Achmet). Arabian seer who wrote a book on dream interpretation, now known only in the Greek and Latin translations, which was published in Paris in 1603 titled *Oneirocritica.*

Ahrimanes

The name given to the chief of the **Cacodaemons,** or fallen angels, by the ancient Persians and Chaldeans. These Cacodaemons were believed to have been expelled from Heaven for their sins; they endeavored to settle down in various parts of the Earth, but were always rejected, and out of revenge they found their pleasure in injuring the inhabitants. Xenocritus thought that penance and self-mortification, though not agreeable to the gods, pacified the malice of the Cacodaemons. Ahrimanes and his followers finally took up their abode in all the space between the Earth and the fixed stars, and there established their domain, which is called Ahriman-abad. As Ahrimanes was the spirit of evil, his counterpart in Persian dualism was Ormuzd, the creative and benevolent being.

Ailuromancy

Divination through superstitions concerning cats. For example, a black cat crossing your path is a bad omen in the United States and Germany, although usually regarded as lucky in Britain. Owning a black cat is also believed to be lucky. A cat washing its face or ears, or climbing up furniture, is said to indicate rain; if the cat washes its face in the parlor, it may indicate visitors. It is a widespread belief that killing or mistreating a cat will bring ill fortune. This may arise from ancient religious beliefs concerning the cat as a sacred animal.

Ainsarii

An Ishmaelite sect of the **Assassins,** who continued to exist after the stronghold of that society was destroyed. They held secret meetings for receptions and possessed signs, words, and a catechism. The Ainsarii are discussed in *The Asian Mystery Illustrated in the Ansaireeh or Nusairis of Syria* by Samuel Lyde, 1860.

Akasha (or Soniferous Ether)

One of the five elementary principles of nature according to Hindu mysticism. Akasha is the first of these principles, and out of it the others are created. These subtle principles, or *tattvas,* are related to the five senses of human beings and to basic elements of matter: earth (*prithivi*), water (*apas*), fire (*tejas*), and air (*vayu*). The all-pervading *akasha* is responsible for vibrations of light and sound.

Sources:

Prasad, Rama. *The Science of Breath and the Philosophy of the Tattvas, Translated from the Sanskrit, with Introductory and Explanatory Essays on Nature's Finer Forces.* London: Theosophical Publishing Society, 1897.

Akashic Records

A theosophical term denoting a kind of central filing system of all events, thoughts, and actions impressed upon an astral plane, which may be consulted in certain conditions of consciousness. Events are believed to make an impression upon the **akasha,** or subtle ether, which may be reanimated by mystics as if they are switching on a celestial television set.

The idea of akashic records was central to the work of seer **Edgar Cayce.** When Cayce went into trance, it was believed that he accessed the records, sometimes referred to as God's Book of Remembrance. The akashic records store the individual's thoughts and information on activities that may be read by certain gifted seers.

Sources:

Neimark, Anne E. *With This Gift: The Story of Edgar Cayce.* New York: William Morrow, 1978.

Puryear, Herbert B. *The Edgar Cayce Primer.* New York: Bantam Books, 1982.

Akathaso

Evil spirits that inhabit trees.

Akhnim

A town of Middle Thebais, which at one time possessed the reputation of being the habitation of the greatest magicians. The French traveler Paul Lucas (1664–1737), in his *Second Voyage,* speaks of the wonderful serpent of Akhnim, which was worshiped by the Muslims as an angel, and which the Christians believed to be the demon **Asmodeus.**

Akiba ben Joseph (ca. 50–132 C.E.)

A Jewish rabbi of the first century, who began as a simple shepherd, then became a learned scholar, spurred by the hope of winning the hand of a young lady he greatly admired. According to Jewish legend, he was taught by the **elemental** spirits, was a wonder worker, and at his peak had as many as 24,000 disciples. He was reputed to be the author of a famous work entitled *Yetzirah* (On the Creation), which is by some ascribed to Abraham, or to Adam. An early Hebrew edition of the *Sepher Yetzirah* was printed at Lemberg in 1680: a Latin version was printed in Paris in 1552.

Rabbi Akiba was a great teacher who developed a rabbinical school at Jaffu, and his Mishnah became the foundation of the religious code. He was involved in the revolt of Bar-Cochba against Hadrian in 132 C.E. and suffered martyrdom by being flayed alive.

Aksakof, Alexander N. (1832–1903)

Imperial councillor to the czar and the pioneer of **Spiritualism** in **Russia,** as well as a **Swedenborg** enthusiast. He was born in Repiofka, Russia, in 1832 and educated for civil duty at the Royal Lyceum, St. Petersburg. He was introduced to modern Spiritualism by **Andrew Jackson Davis**'s *Nature's Divine Revelations* in 1855.

In order to form a correct judgment of both physiological and psychological phenomena, he studied medicine at the University of Moscow for two years. He translated Emanuel Swedenborg's *Heaven and Hell,* Count Szapary's *Magnetic Healing,* and the principal works of **Robert Hare, William Crookes, J. W. Edmonds, Robert Dale Owen** and the Report of the **Dialectical Society.** Because works on Spiritualism in Russian were suppressed by the censor but German publications were tolerated, his literary activity of necessity centered in Germany.

He founded the *Psychische Studien* which, under the new title *Zeitschrift für Parapsychologie,* was instrumental in provoking the first strictly scientific Russian investigation of Spiritualism.

Daniel D. Home, who visited Russia for the first time in 1861, became connected through marriage with Aksakof's family. In 1871 Aksakof introduced Home to Professor Boutlerof and to other professors of the University of St. Petersburg. However, the body of savants was left unconvinced of the reality of his phenomena.

In 1874 the French medium Camille Brédif paid a visit. Professor Wagner attended a seance and was deeply impressed. His article in the *Revue de l'Europe* aroused such a storm that the university felt impelled to delegate an investigating committee and asked Aksakof to make the necessary arrangements for them. Aksakof went to England in 1875 and engaged a nonprofessional medium, using the name of Mrs. Clayer (to whom he was introduced by Crookes) for presentation to the committee. The lady, who is mentioned in Crookes's *Researches,* produced strong physical phenomena in good light. The committee, however, refused to be impressed and Professor Mendeleyeff, its principal member, declared in his report *Materials by Which to Judge Spiritualism* that the medium had an instrument under her skirt and produced table movements and raps by this agency. To this report Aksakof published a caustic reply under the title *A Monument of Scientific Prejudice.*

In 1876 his request for permission to publish in St. Petersburg a monthly *Review of Mediumship* was refused. In 1881 he founded the publication *Rebus,* which was largely subsidized by Aksakof after funds dwindled. It popularized the teachings of Spiritualism.

Aksakof experimented with **Henry Slade** and **Charles Williams** when they visited St. Petersburg, and he made arrangements for Kate Fox-Jencken when the czar desired to consult her for the safe conduct of the coronation ceremonies. **William Eglinton, Elizabeth d'Esperance,** and **Eusapia Palladino** were the next mediums who engaged his attention. His wife was herself mediumistic and helped him in his work. In a *Case of Partial Dematerialisation* (1896), he recorded testimonies of an astounding occurrence with d'Esperance.

His most important book, *Animismus und Spiritismus* (1890), was published in answer to Dr. Edward von Hartmann's *Spiritualism.* **F. W. H. Myers** reviewed it in *Proceedings* of the Society for Psychical Research, where he stated: "I may say at once that on the data as assumed I think that Mr. Aksakof has the better of his opponent." In the book Aksakof says that for the comprehension of mediumistic phenomena we have three hypotheses: 1. Personism (or change of personality) may stand for those unconscious psychical phenomena that are produced within the limits of the medium's own body, those intra-mediumistic phenomena whose distinguishing characteristic is the assumption of a personality changing to that of the medium. 2. Under the name animism we include unconscious psychical phenomena that show themselves outside the limits of the medium's body. Extra-mediumistic operation of objects without contact and finally materialisation. We have here the highest manifestation of the psychic duplication; the elements of personality overstep the limits of the body up to the point of complete externalisation and objectification. 3. Under the name spiritism we include phenomena resembling both personalisation and animism but which we much ascribe to some extra-mediumistic and extra-terrene cause. They differ from the phenomena of personalisation and animism in their intellectual content which affords evidence of an independent personality.

Spiritualism and Science (*Der Spiritualismus und die Wissenschaft*) [1872] was another of Aksakof's important works. His literary output was considerable, and during his lifetime he translated or wrote over 30 books relating to Spiritualism and psychic research. In 1874, he started a German monthly journal *Psychische Studien* (Psychic Studies). One of his last translations was Colonel De Rochas's *Exteriorisation of Motricity.* Under dreadful physical handicaps Aksakof kept on working to the last. His right hand became useless, his eye almost sightless. He died January 17, 1903, after an attack of influenza. Aksakof bequeathed a large sum of money to the British **Society for Psychical Research.** His own work as an experimenter and psychical researcher was well ahead of its time and not properly recognized.

Sources:

Aksakof, A. N. *Animism and Spiritism.* Leipzig: Oswald Mutze, 1980.

Britten, Emma Hardinge. *Nineteenth-Century Miracles.* New York: W. Britten, 1884.

Doyle, Arthur Conan. *The History of Spiritualism.* New York: Charles H. Doran, 1926. Reprint, New York: Arno Press, 1979.

Society for Psychical Research. *Proceedings* Vol. 6: 665.

Al

According to **Éliphas Lévi,** this forms part of the inscription on a **pentacle** that was a frontispiece to the published **Grimoire** of Honorius, an antipope of the thirteenth century. The letters, used to designate a name of God, were reversed on the pentacle, said to be part of a ritual for the evocation of evil spirits.

"AL" was also a word of considerable importance to magician **Aleister Crowley.** It was the name given to the revelation he received in 1904 that became the basis of his new system of thelemic magic, usually called *The Book of the Law* or *Liber AL.* Crowley placed great store in numerology. In his system, AL equated to 31, the number which he felt held the key to unlocking the meaning of *Liber AL.*

Sources:

Crowley, Aleister. *The Law Is for All.* Edited by Israel Regardie. St. Paul, Minn.: Llewellyn Publications, 1975.

Lévi, Éliphas. *The History of Magic.* 1913. Reprint, New York: Samuel Weiser, 1969.

Alain of Lille (ca. 1128–1203)

Also known as Alanus de Insulensis, *Doctor Universalis* (because of his universal knowledge), theologian and poet, presumed author of a treatise on alchemy entitled *Dicta de Lapide Philosophico,* published at Leyden in 1600. Alain de Lille entered the Cistercian order at Clairvaux, taught in Paris, and became bishop of Auxerre. His writings were praised for their clarity of style. However, there is some doubt as to whether he was really the author of the *Dicta,* since it appears to have been written first in German. The work bears the ascription "Alanus Insulensis," but this may have been due to a contemporary practice of ascribing anonymous works to some illustrious individual who had died and was therefore unable to deny authorship. It has been suggested that the real author was Albertus Cranzius, ca. 1430.

Alamut

A mountain in Persia, which became the stronghold of the sect of **Assassins** during the eleventh century C.E.

Sources:

Daraul, Akron. *A History of Secret Societies.* New York: Citadel Press, 1962.

Alary, François

A visionary who had printed at Rouen in 1701, *Prophetie . . . sur la naissance miraculeuse de Louis le Grand* . . . (The Prophecy of Count Bombaste, [Chevalier de la Rose-Croix], nephew of **Paracelsus**), published in 1609 on the birth of Louis the Great.

Alastor

A cruel demon, who, according to **Johan Weyer,** filled the post of chief executioner to the monarch of Hades. The conception of him somewhat resembles that of Nemesis. Zoroaster is said to have called him "The Executioner." Others identify him with the destroying angel. Evil genies were formerly called *alastors.* Plutarch says that Cicero, who bore a grudge against Augustus, conceived the plan of committing suicide on the emperor's hearth, and thus becoming his "alastor."

Sources:

Weyer, Johannes. *Witches, Devils, and Doctors in the Renaissance: Johann Weyer, De Praestigiis.* Edited by George Mora. Binghamton, N.Y.: Medieval and Renaissance Texts and Studies, 1991.

Albertus Magnus (Albert of Cologne) (ca. 1206–1280)

Scholar, philosopher, and scientist traditionally believed to have been an alchemist. No fewer than 21 folio volumes are attributed to him, though it is highly improbable that all of them are really his. In several cases the ascription rests on slender evidence, but those that are incontestably written by him are numerous enough to label him a prolific writer. Tradition holds that he was the inventor of the pistol and the cannon, though the truth of this claim cannot be proven. This does indicate, however, that his scientific skill was recognized by a few of the men of his own time.

Born in Swabia, Germany, he entered the Dominican order in 1223, taught in Paris and Cologne, and became the teacher of Thomas Aquinas. The term *Magnus,* which is usually applied to him, is not the result of his reputation but is the Latin equivalent of his family name, de Groot. As with many other men destined to become famous, he was distinctly stupid as a boy, but from the outset he showed a predilection for religion. One night the Blessed Virgin appeared to him, which caused his intellect to metamorphose, acquiring extraordinary vitality. Albertus therefore decided that he must show his gratitude to the Madonna by entering the priesthood, and eventually he won eminence in the clerical profession. In 1260 he became bishop of Ratisbon. His books include *Summa de Creaturis* and *Summa Theologiae.*

Albertus was repeatedly charged by some of his contemporaries with holding communications with the devil and practicing the craft of magic. He was said to have invited some friends to his house at Cologne, among them William, count of Holland, and when the guests arrived they were amazed to find that, although the season was midwinter and the ground was covered with snow, they were expected to have a meal outside in the garden. Their host urged them to be seated, assuring them that all would be well. Though doubtful, they took their places, and had only begun to eat and drink when their annoyance vanished, for the snow around them melted away and the sun shone brightly.

The alchemist Michael Maier (author of *Museum Chimicum*), declared that Albertus had succeeded in evolving the **philosophers' stone** and passed it to his pupil Thomas Aquinas, who subsequently destroyed it, believing it to be diabolical. The alleged discoverer himself says nothing on this subject, but, in his *De Rebus Metallicis et Mineralibus,* he tells how he had personally tested some gold that had been manufactured by an alchemist, and it resisted many searching fusions. Whether this story is true or not, Albertus was certainly an able scientist, and it is clear that his learning ultimately gained wide recognition, for a collected edition of his vast writings was issued at Leyden as late as 1653.

Albertus died in 1280, was beatified in 1622, and canonized by Pius XI in 1932. There is no firm evidence that Albertus was author of the ever popular occult work ascribed to him under the title *Albertus Magnus . . . Egyptian Secrets; or, White and Black Art for Man and Beast.*

Sources:

Albertus Magnus. *The Book of Secrets of Albertus Magnus: Also, A Book of the Marvels of the World.* Edited by M. R. Best and F. H. Brightman. Oxford: Clarendon Press, 1973.

Federmann, Reinhard. *The Royal Art of Alchemy.* New York: Chilton, 1969.

Kovech, F. J., and R. W. Shahan, eds. *Albert the Great: Commemorative Essays.* Norman Okla.: University of Oklahoma Press, 1980.

Sighart, J. *Albert the Great.* London: Washbourne, 1876.

Albigenses

A sect that originated in the south of France in the twelfth century. They were named for one of their territorial centers, that of Albi, and were a branch of the **Cathari** heresy. It is probable that the heresy came originally from Eastern Europe, since they were often designated "Bulgarians" and undoubtedly kept up relations with such sects as the Bogomils and the Paulicians. It is difficult to form any exact idea about their doctrines, as Albigensian texts are rare and contain little concerning their ethics, but we know that they were strongly opposed to the Roman Catholic Church and protested the corruption of its clergy.

Their opponents claimed that they admitted two fundamental principles, good and bad, saying that God had produced Lucifer from himself; that Lucifer was indeed the son of God who revolted against him; that he had carried with him a rebellious party of angels who were driven from Heaven along with him; that Lucifer in his exile created this world with its inhabitants, where he reigned, and where all was evil. It is alleged that the Albigenses further believed that, for the reestablishment of order, God produced a second son, Jesus Christ. Furthermore the Catholic writers on the Albigenses charged them with believing that the souls of men were demons lodged in mortal bodies in punishment of their crimes.

Following the murder of the legate of Pope Innocent III, who was sent to root out the heresy, a crusade was brought against them, resulting in wholesale massacres. The Inquisition was also set upon them, and they were driven to hide in the forests and among the mountains, where, like the Covenanters of Scotland, they met secretly. The Inquisition so terrorized the district in which they lived that the very name of Albigenses was practically blotted out, and by the year 1330, the records of the Holy Office show no further writs issued against the heretics.

It seems possible that such heresies as the Albigenses and the Cathari, with their belief in Lucifer as lord of the world, may have sometimes merged with the pagan folklore that went to form the **witchcraft** heresy, which was also ruthlessly persecuted by the Inquisition. (See also **Gnostics; Arthur Guirdham**)

Sources:

Holmes, E. G. A. *Albigensian or Catharist Heresy.* London: William & Norgate, 1925.

Lea, Henry C. *A History of the Inquisition of the Middle Ages.* 3 vols. London: Sampson Low, 1888.

Warner, H. J. *The Albigensian Heresy.* 2 vols. London: SPCK, 1922–28.

Albigerius (ca. 400 C.E.)

A Carthaginian soothsayer mentioned by St. Augustine. He would fall into strange ecstasies in which his soul, separated from his body, would travel abroad and find out what was taking place in distant places. He could read people's thoughts and discover anything he wished to learn. These wonders were ascribed to the agency of the Devil. St. Augustine also speaks of a time when the possessed man was ill of a fever. Though not in a trance, he saw the priest who was coming to visit him while he was yet six leagues away, and Albigerius told the company assembled around him the exact moment when the priest would arrive.

Albumazar (or Abu-Maaschar) (805–885 C.E.)

Arabian astrologer of the ninth century. Born in Balkh, he lived in Baghdad and was known principally for his astrological treatise entitled *Thousands of Years,* in which he declares that the world could only have been created when the seven planets were in conjunction in the first degree of Aries, and that the end of the world will take place when these seven planets (the number has now risen to twelve) will be together in the last degree of Pisces. His treatises include *De Magnis Conjunctionibus* (Augsburg, 1489), *Introductorium in Astronomian* (Venice, 1506), and *Flores Astrologici* (Augsburg, 1488). He died at Wasid, Central Asia.

Sources:

McIntosh, Christopher. *The Astrologers and Their Creed: An Historical Outline.* New York: Frederick A. Praeger, 1969.

Alchemy

The art and science by which the chemical philosophers of medieval times attempted to transmute the baser metals into gold and silver. Alchemy is also the name of the Gnostic philosophy that undergirded the alchemical activity, a practical philosophy of spiritual purification. There is considerable disagreement as to which, the scientific or the philosophical, is the dominant aspect and the manner in which the two were integrated (which to some extent varied tremendously from alchemist to alchemist).

There is also considerable divergence of opinion as to the etymology of the word. One highly possible origin is the Arabic *al* (the) and *kimya* (chemistry), which in turn derived from late Greek *chemeia* (chemistry), from *chumeia* (a mingling), or *cheein* (to pour out or mix). The Aryan root is *ghu,* (to pour), whence comes the modern word *gush.* E. A. Wallis Budge, in his *Egyptian Magic,* however, states that it is possible that alchemy may be derived from the Egyptian word *khemeia,* "the preparation of the black ore," or "powder," which was regarded as the active principle in the transmutation of metals. To this name the Arabs affixed the article *al,* resulting in *al-khemeia,* or alchemy.

History of Alchemy

From an early period the Egyptians possessed the reputation of being skillful workers in metals, and, according to Greek writers, they were conversant with their transmutation, employing quicksilver in the process of separating gold and silver from the native matrix. The resulting oxide was supposed to possess marvelous powers, and it was thought that there resided within it the individualities of the various metals—that in it their various substances were incorporated. This black powder was mystically identified with the underworld god Osiris, and consequently was credited with magical properties. Thus there grew up in Egypt the belief that magical powers existed in fluxes and alloys. It is probable such a belief existed throughout Europe in connection with the bronze-working castes of its several races. (See **Shelta Thari**)

It was probably in the Byzantium of the fourth century, however, that alchemical science received embryonic form. There is little doubt that Egyptian tradition, filtering through Alexandrian Hellenic sources, was the foundation upon which the infant science was built, and this is borne out by the circumstance that the art was attributed to **Hermes Trismegistus** and supposed to be contained in its entirety in his works.

The **Arabs,** after their conquest of Egypt in the seventh century, carried on the researches of the Alexandrian school, and through their instrumentality the art was carried to Morocco and in the eighth century to Spain, where it flourished. During the next few centuries Spain served as the repository of alchemical science, and the colleges at Seville, Cordova, and Granada were the centers from which this science radiated throughout Europe. The first practical alchemist was probably the Arabian **Geber,** who flourished in the early to mid-eighth century C.E. His *Summa Perfectionis* implies that alchemical science had already matured in his day, and that he drew his inspiration from a still older unbroken line of **adepts.** He was followed by **Avicenna, Meisner,** and **Rhasis;** in France by **Alain of Lisle, Arnaldus de Villanova,** and **Jean de Meung** the troubadour; in England by **Roger Bacon;** and in Spain by **Raymond Lully.**

Later, in French alchemy, the most illustrious names are those of **Nicolas Flamel** (fourteenth century), and **Bernard Trévisan** (fifteenth century), after which the center of interest changes in the sixteenth century to Germany and in some measure to England, in which countries **Paracelsus, Heinrich Khunrath, Mi-**

chael Maier, Jakob Boehme, Jean Van Helmont, the Brabanter, **George Ripley, Thomas Norton, Thomas Dalton, Jean Martin Charnock,** and **Robert Fludd** kept the alchemical flame burning brightly. In Britain, the great scientist Sir Isaac Newton conducted alchemical research.

It is surprising how little alteration is found throughout the period between the seventh and the seventeenth centuries, the heyday of alchemy, in the theory and practice of the art. The same sentiments and processes put forth by the earliest alchemical authorities are also found expressed by the later experts, and a unanimity regarding the basic canons of the art is expressed by the hermetic students of all periods, thus suggesting the dominance of the philosophical teachings over any "scientific" applications. With the introduction of chemistry as a practical art, alchemical science fell into disuse, already having suffered from the number of charlatans practicing it. Here and there, however, a solitary student of the art lingered, and the subject has to some extent been revived during modern times.

The Theory and Philosophy of Alchemy

The grand objects of the alchemical art were (1) the discovery of a process by which the baser metals might be transmuted into gold and silver; (2) the discovery of an elixir by which life might be prolonged indefinitely; and there is sometimes added (3) the manufacture of an artificial process of human life (see **Homunculus**). Religiously, the transmutation of metals can be thought of as a symbol of the transmutation of the self to a higher consciousness and the discovery of the elixir as an affirmation of eternal life.

The transmutation of metals was to be accomplished by a powder, stone, or elixir often called the **philosophers' stone,** the application of which would effect the transmutation of the baser metals into gold or silver, depending on the length of time of its application. Basing their conclusions on the examination of natural processes and metaphysical speculation concerning the secrets of nature, the alchemists arrived at the axiom that nature was divided into four principal regions: the dry, the moist, the warm, the cold, from which all that exists must be derived. Nature was also divisible into the male and the female. She is the divine breath, the central fire, invisible yet ever active, and is typified by sulphur, which is the mercury of the sages, which slowly fructifies under the genial warmth of nature.

Thus, the alchemist had to be ingenuous, of a truthful disposition, and gifted with patience and prudence, following nature in every alchemical performance. He recalled that like attracts like, and had to know how to obtain the "seed" of metals, which was produced by the four elements through the will of the Supreme Being and the Imagination of Nature. We are told that the original matter of metals was double in its essence, being a dry heat combined with a warm moisture, and that air is water coagulated by fire, capable of producing a universal dissolvent. These terms the neophyte must be cautious of interpreting in their literal sense, for it is likely that alchemists, other than the several frauds, were speaking about the metaphysics of inner spirituality. Great confusion exists in alchemical nomenclature, and the gibberish employed by the scores of charlatans who in later times pretended to a knowledge of alchemical matters did not tend to make things any more clear.

The neophyte alchemist also had to acquire a thorough knowledge of the manner in which metals "grow" in the bowels of the earth. They were said to be engendered by sulphur, which is male, and mercury, which is female, and the crux of alchemy was to obtain their "seed"—a process the alchemistical philosophers did not describe with any degree of clarity. The physical theory of transmutation is based on the composite character of metals, and on the presumed existence of a substance which, applied to matter, exalts and perfects it. This substance, **Eugenius Philalethes** and others called "The Light." The elements of all metals were said to be similar, differing only in purity and proportion. The entire trend of the metallic kingdom was toward the natural manufacture of gold, and the production of the baser metals was only accidental as the result of an unfavorable environment. The philosophers' stone was the combination of the male and female "seeds" that form gold. The composition of these was so veiled by symbolism as to make their precise identification impossible.

Occult scholar **Arthur Edward Waite,** summarized the alchemical process once the secret of the stone was unveiled:

"Given the matter of the stone and also the necessary vessel, the processes which must be then undertaken to accomplish the *magnum opus* are described with moderate perspicuity. There is the calcination or purgation of the stone, in which kind is worked with kind for the space of a philosophical year. There is dissolution which prepares the way for congelation, and which is performed during the black state of the mysterious matter. It is accomplished by water which does not wet the hand. There is the separation of the subtle and the gross, which is to be performed by means of heat. In the conjunction which follows, the elements are duly and scrupulously combined. Putrefaction afterwards takes place, 'Without which pole no seed may multiply.'

"Then, in the subsequent congelation the white colour appears, which is one of the signs of success. It becomes more pronounced in cibation. In sublimation the body is spiritualised, the spirit made corporeal, and again a more glittering whiteness is apparent. Fermentation afterwards fixes together the alchemical earth and water, and causes the mystic medicine to flow like wax. The matter is then augmented with the alchemical spirit of life, and the exaltation of the philosophic earth is accomplished by the natural rectification of its elements. When these processes have been successfully completed, the mystic stone will have passed through three chief stages characterised by different colours, black, white, and red, after which it is capable of infinite multication, and when projected on mercury, it will absolutely transmute it, the resulting gold bearing every test. The base metals made use of must be purified to insure the success of the operation. The process for the manufacture of silver is essentially similar, but the resources of the matter are not carried to so high a degree.

"According to the *Commentary on the Ancient War of the Knights* the transmutations performed by the perfect stone are so absolute that no trace remains of the original metal. It cannot, however, destroy gold, nor exalt it into a more perfect metallic substance; it, therefore, transmutes it into a medicine a thousand times superior to any virtues which can be extracted from it in its vulgar state. This medicine becomes a most potent agent in the exaltation of base metals."

Other modern authorities have denied that the transmutation of metals was the grand object of alchemy, and from reasons highlighted earlier, among others, inferred from the alchemistical writings that the object of the art was the spiritual regeneration of mankind. **Mary Ann Atwood,** author of *A Suggestive Inquiry into the Hermetic Mystery,* and Civil War General Ethan Allen Hitchcock, author of *Remarks upon Alchemy and the Alchemists,* were perhaps the chief protagonists of the belief that, by spiritual processes akin to those of the chemical processes of alchemy, the soul of man may be purified and exalted. Both somewhat overstated their case in their assertion that the alchemical writers did not claim that the transmutation of base metal into gold was their grand object. While the spiritual quest may have been dominant, none of the passages that Atwood and Hitchcock quote was inconsistent with the physical aspect of alchemy. Eugenius Philalethes, for example, in his work *The Marrow of Alchemy,* argues forcefully that the real quest is for gold. It is constantly impressed upon the reader, however, in the perusal of esteemed alchemical works, that only those who are instructed by God can achieve the grand secret. Others, again, state that while a novice might possibly stumble upon it, unless guided by an adept the beginner has small chance of achieving the grand arcanum.

The transcendental view of alchemy, however, rapidly gained ground through the nineteenth century. Among its exponents was A. E. Waite, who argued, "The gold of the philosopher is not a metal, on the other hand, man is a being who possesses within himself the seeds of a perfection which he has never realized, and that he therefore corresponds to those metals which the Hermetic theory supposes to be capable of development. It has been constantly advanced that the conversion of lead into gold was only the assumed object of alchemy, and that it was in reality in search of a process for developing the latent possibilities in the subject man."

At the same time, it must be admitted that the cryptic character of alchemical language was probably occasioned by a fear on the part of the alchemical mystic that he might lay himself open through his magical opinions to the rigors of the law.

Meanwhile, several records of alleged transmutations of base metals into gold have survived. These were reportedly achieved by Nicholas Flamel, Van Helmont, Martini, Richthausen, and Sethon. In nearly every case the transmuting element was said to be a mysterious powder or the "philosophers' stone."

Modern Alchemy

A correspondent writing to the British newspaper *Liverpool Post* in its Saturday, November 28, 1907, edition gave an interesting description of a veritable Egyptian alchemist whom he had encountered in Cairo not long before:

"I was not slow in seizing an opportunity of making the acquaintance of the real alchemist living in Cairo, which the winds of chance had blown in my direction. He received me in his private house in the native quarter, and I was delighted to observe that the appearance of the man was in every way in keeping with my notions of what an alchemist should be. Clad in the flowing robes of a graduate of Al Azhar, his long grey beard giving him a truly venerable aspect, the sage by the eager, far-away expression of his eyes, betrayed the mind of the dreamer, of the man lost to the meaner comforts of the world in his devotion to the secret mysteries of the universe. After the customary salaams, the learned man informed me that he was seeking three things—the philosopher's stone, at whose touch all metal should become gold—the elixir of life, and the universal solvent which would dissolve all substances as water dissolves sugar; the last, he assured me, he had indeed discovered a short time since. I was well aware of the reluctance of the medieval alchemists to divulge their secrets, believing as they did that the possession of them by the vulgar would bring about ruin of states and the fall of divinely constituted princes; and I feared that the reluctance of the modern alchemist to divulge any secrets to a stranger and a foreigner would be no less. However, I drew from my pocket Sir William Crookes's spinthariscope—a small box containing a particle of radium highly magnified—and showed it to the sheikh. When he applied it to his eye and beheld the wonderful phenomenon of this dark speck flashing out its fiery needles on all sides, he was lost in wonder, and when I assured him that it would retain this property for a thousand years, he hailed me as a fellow-worker, and as one who had indeed penetrated into the secrets of the world. His reticence disappeared at once, and he began to tell me the aims and methods of alchemical research, which were indeed the same as those of the ancient alchemists of yore. His universal solvent he would not show me, but assured me of its efficacy. I asked him in what he kept it if it dissolved all things. He replied 'In wax,' this being the one exception. I suspected that he had found some hydrofluoric acid, which dissolves glass, and so has to be kept in wax bottles, but said nothing to dispel his illusion.

"The next day I was granted the unusual privilege of inspecting the sheikh's laboratory, and duly presented myself at the appointed time. My highest expectations were fulfilled; everything was exactly what an alchemist's laboratory should be. Yes, there was the sage, surrounded by his retorts, alembics, crucibles, furnace, and bellows, and, best of all, supported by familiars of gnome-like appearance, squatting on the ground, one blowing the fire (a task to be performed daily for six hours continuously), one pounding substances in a mortar, and another seemingly engaged in doing odd jobs. Involuntarily my eyes sought the **pentacle** inscribed with the mystic word '**Abracadabra**,' but here I was disappointed, for the black arts had no place in this laboratory. One of the familiars had been on a voyage of discovery to London, where he bought a few alchemical materials; another had explored Spain and Morocco, without finding any alchemists, and the third had indeed found alchemists in Algeria, though they had steadily guarded their secrets. After satisfying my curiosity in a general way, I asked the sage to explain the principles of his researches and to tell me on what his theories were based. I was delighted to find that his ideas were precisely those of the medieval alchemists namely, that all metals are debased forms of the original gold, which is the only pure, non-composite metal; all nature strives to return to its original purity, and all metals would return to gold if they could; nature is simple and not complex, and works upon one principle, namely, that of sexual reproduction. It was not easy, as will readily be believed, to follow the mystical explanations of the sheikh. Air was referred to by him as the 'vulture,' fire as the 'scorpion,' water as the 'serpent,' and earth as 'calacant'; and only after considerable cross-questioning and confusion of mind was I able to disentangle his arguments. Finding his notions so entirely medieval, I was anxious to discover whether he was familiar with the phlogistic theory of the seventeenth century. The alchemists of old had noticed that the earthy matter which remains when a metal is calcined is heavier than the metal itself, and they explained this by the hypothesis, that the metal contained a spirit known as 'phlogiston,' which becomes visible when it escapes from the metal or combustible substance in the form of flame; thus the presence of the phlogiston lightened the body just as gas does, and on its being expelled, the body gained weight. I accordingly asked the chemist whether he had found that iron gains weight when it rusts, an experiment he had ample means of making. But no, he had not yet reached the seventeenth century; he had not observed the fact, but was none the less ready with his answer; the rust of iron was an impurity proceeding from within, and which did not affect the weight of the body in that way. He declared that a few days would bring the realisation of his hopes, and that he would shortly send me a sample of the philosopher's stone and of the divine elixir; but although his promise was made some weeks since, I have not yet seen the fateful discoveries."

That alchemy has continued to be studied in relatively modern times there can be no doubt. **Louis Figuier** in his *L'Alchimie et les Alchimistes* (1854), dealing with the subject of modern alchemy, as expressed by the initiates of the first half of the nineteenth century, states that many French alchemists of his time regarded the discoveries of modern science as merely so many evidences of the truth of the doctrines they embraced. Throughout Europe, he said, the positive alchemical doctrine had many adherents at the end of the eighteenth century and the beginning of the nineteenth.

Reportedly, a "vast association of alchemists" called the **Hermetic Society,** founded in Westphalia in 1790, continued to flourish in the year 1819. In 1837 an alchemist of Thuringia presented to the Société Industrielle of Weimar a tincture he averred would effect metallic transmutation. About the same time several French journals announced a public course of lectures on hermetic philosophy by a professor of the University of Munich.

Figuier further stated that many Hanoverian and Bavarian families pursued in common the search for the grand arcanum. Paris, however, was regarded as the alchemistical Mecca. There lived many theoretical alchemists and "empirical adepts." The first pursued the arcanum through the medium of books; the others engaged in practical efforts to effect transmutation.

During the 1840s Figuier frequented the laboratory of a certain Monsieur L., which was the rendezvous of the alchemists of Paris. When Monsieur L's pupils left the laboratory for the day the modern adepts dropped in one by one, and Figuier relates how deeply impressed he was by the appearance and costumes of these strange men. In the daytime he frequently encountered them in the public libraries, buried in the study of gigantic folios, and in the evening they might be seen pacing the solitary bridges with eyes fixed in vague contemplation upon the first pale stars of night. A long cloak usually covered their meager limbs, and their untrimmed beards and matted locks lent them a wild appearance. They walked with a solemn and measured gait, and used the figures of speech employed by the medieval illuminés. Their expression was generally a mixture of the most ardent hope and a fixed despair.

Among the adepts who sought the laboratory of Monsieur L., Figuier noticed especially a young man in whose habits and language he could see nothing in common with those of his strange companions. He confounded the wisdom of the alchemical adept with the tenets of the modern scientist in the most singular fashion, and meeting him one day at the gate of the observatory, M. Figuier renewed the subject of their last discussion, deploring that "a man of his gifts could pursue the semblance of a chimera." Without replying, the young adept led him into the observatory garden and proceeded to reveal to him the mysteries of modern alchemical science.

The young man recognized a limit to the research of the modern alchemists. Gold, he said, according to the ancient authors, has three distinct properties: (1) resolving the baser metals into itself, and interchanging and metamorphosing all metals into one another; (2) curing afflictions and the prolongation of life; and (3) serving as a *spiritus mundi* to bring mankind into rapport with the supermundane spheres. Modern alchemists, he continued, rejected the greater part of these ideas, especially those connected with spiritual contact. The object of modern alchemy might be reduced to the search for a substance having power to transform and transmute all other substances one into another—in short, to discover that medium known to the alchemists of old as the philosophers' stone and now lost to us. In the four principal substances of oxygen, hydrogen, carbon, and azote, we have the *tetractus* of Pythagoras and the *tetragram* of the Chaldeans and Egyptians. All the sixty elements are referable to these original four. The ancient alchemical theory claimed that all the metals are the same in their composition, that all are formed from sulphur and mercury, and that the difference between them is according to the proportion of these substances in their composition. Further, all the products of minerals present in their composition complete identity with those substances most opposed to them. For example, fulminating acid contains precisely the same quantity of carbon, oxygen, and azote as cyanic acid, and "cyanhydric" acid does not differ from formate ammoniac. This new property of matter is known as "isomerism." Figuier's friend then proceeded to quote in support of his thesis the operations and experiments of M. Dumas, a celebrated French savant, as well as those of William Prout and other English chemists of standing.

Passing on to consider the possibility of isomerism in elementary as well as in compound substances, he pointed out to Figuier that if the theory of isomerism can apply to such bodies, the transmutation of metals ceases to be a wild, unpractical dream and becomes a scientific possibility, the transformation being brought about by a molecular rearrangement. Isomerism can be established in the case of compound substances by chemical analysis, showing the identity of their constituent parts. In the case of metals it can be proved by the comparison of the properties of isomeric bodies with the properties of metals, in order to discover whether they have any common characteristics.

M. Dumas, speaking before the British Association, had shown that when three simple bodies displayed great analogies in their properties, such as chlorine, bromide, and iodine, barium, strontium, and calcium, the chemical equivalent of the intermediate body is represented by the arithmetical mean between the equivalents of the other two. Such a statement well showed the isomerism of elementary substances and proved that metals, however dissimilar in outward appearance, were composed of the same matter differently arranged and proportioned. This theory successfully demolished the difficulties in the way of transmutation.

If transmutation is thus theoretically possible, it only remains to show by practical experiment that it is strictly in accordance with chemical laws, and by no means inclines to the supernatural.

At this juncture, the young alchemist proceeded to liken the action of the philosophers' stone on metals to that of a ferment on organic matter. When metals are melted and brought to red heat, a molecular change may be produced analogous to fermentation. Just as sugar, under the influence of a ferment, may be changed into lactic acid without altering its constituents, so metals can alter their character under the influence of the philosophers' stone. The explanation of the latter case is no more difficult than that of the former. The ferment does not take any part in the chemical changes it brings about, and no satisfactory explanation of its effects can be found either in the laws of affinity or in the forces of electricity, light, or heat. As with the ferment, the required quantity of the philosophers' stone is infinitesimal.

The alchemist then averred that medicine, philosophy, every modern science was at one time a source of such errors and extravagances as are associated with medieval alchemy, but they are not therefore neglected and despised. Why, then, should we be blind to the scientific nature of transmutation? One of the foundations of alchemical theories was that minerals grow and develop in the earth, like organic things. It was always the aim of nature to produce gold, the most precious metal, but when circumstances were not favorable the baser metals resulted. The desire of the old alchemists was to surprise nature's secrets, and thus attain the ability to do in a short period what nature takes years to accomplish. Nevertheless, the medieval alchemists appreciated the value of time in their experiments as modern alchemists never do.

Figuier's friend urged him not to condemn these exponents of the hermetic philosophy for their metaphysical tendencies, for, he said, there are facts in our sciences that can only be explained in that light. If, for instance, copper is placed in air or water, there will be no result, but if a touch of some acid is added, it will oxidize. The explanation is that "the acid provokes oxidation of the metal, because it has an affinity for the oxide which tends to form"—a material fact almost metaphysical in its production, and only explicable thereby.

Alchemy in the Twentieth Century

Since the nineteenth-century speculations of Figuier, the modern view of alchemy has primarily regarded it as a mystical approach to chemistry. With the development of subatomic physics and nuclear fission, the transmutation of elements became a reality, culminating in the atomic bomb and atomic power stations, but the vast apparatus and energy needed to transmute elements has increased skepticism that the old alchemists ever succeeded in their dreams.

The alchemical work gave way to ceremonial magic, which today carries most of what is left of the alchemical hermetic tradition. However, there have been a few contemporary figures who followed the alchemical metaphor. Among these was Frater Albertus, who emerged in the 1970s as head of the Paracelsus Research Society in Salt Lake City, Utah. He wrote a number of books about his work, however these only hinted at any alchemical success.

Sources:

Albertus, Frater. *The Alchemist of the Rocky Mountains.* Salt Lake City, Utah: Paracelsus Research Society, 1976.

———. *The Alchemist's Handbook: Manual for Practical Laboratory Alchemy.* Rev. ed. New York: Samuel Weiser, 1974.

Atwood, Mary Anne. *A Suggestive Inquiry Into the Hermetic Mystery.* London, 1850. Rev. ed. Belfast, 1918. Reprint, New York: Julian Press, 1960. Reprint, New York: Arno Press, 1976.

Bacon, Roger. *The Mirror of Alchemy.* London, 1597. Los Angeles: Press of the Pegacycle Lady, 1975.

Barbault, Armand, *Gold of a Thousand Mornings.* London: Neville Spearman, 1975.

Boyle, Robert. *Works.* 5 vols. London, 1744. Rev. ed. 6 vols. London, 1772.
Cummings, Richard. *Alchemists: Fathers of Practical Chemistry.* New York: David O. McKay, 1966.
De Givry, Grillot. *Witchcraft, Magic & Alchemy.* London, 1931. Reprinted as *Illustrated Anthology of Sorcery, Magic & Alchemy.* New York: Causeway, 1973.
De Rola, Stanislaw K. *Alchemy: The Secret Art.* Bounty Books/Crown, 1973. Reprint, London: Thames & Hudson, 1973.
Doberer, Kurt K. *The Goldmakers: Ten Thousand Years of Alchemy.* Westport, Conn.: Greenwood, 1948.
Dobbs, Betty Jo T. *Foundations of Newton's Alchemy; or, The Hunting of the Greene Lyon.* Cambridge, Mass.: Cambridge University Press, 1975.
Eliade, Mircea. *The Forge and the Crucible.* London, 1962.
Federmann, Reinhard. *The Royal Art of Alchemy.* New York: Chilton, 1969.
Ferguson, J. *Bibliotheca Chemica; a Bibliography of Books on Alchemy, Chemistry and Pharmaceutics.* 2 vols. London, 1954.
Figuier, Louis. *L'Alchimie et les Achimistes.* Paris, 1856.
Hitchcock, C. A. *Remarks Upon Alchemy and the Alchemists.* Boston: Crosby, Nichols, 1857. Reprint, New York: Arno Press, 1976.
Journal of the Alchemical Society 3 vols., London, 1913–15.
Jung, C. G. *Psychology and Alchemy.* Volume 12 of the *Collected Works.* Princeton, N.J.: Princeton University Press, 1968.
Laoux, Gaston. *Dictionnaire Hermetique.* Paris, 1695.
Lapidus. *In Pursuit of Gold: Alchemy in Theory and Practice.* London: Neville Spearman, 1976.
Lenglet, Dufresnoy N. *Histoire de la Philosophie Hermetique.* 2 vols. Paris, 1792.
Read, J. *Prelude to Chemistry.* London, 1936. Reprint, Cambridge, Mass.: MIT Press, 1957.
Redgrove, H. Stanley. *Alchemy: Ancient and Modern.* London: Rider, 1922. Reprint, New Hyde Park, N.Y.: University Books, 1969.
———. *Bygone Beliefs.* London, 1920. Reprinted as *Magic & Mysticism: Studies in Bygone Beliefs.* New Hyde Park, N.Y.: University Books, 1971.
Sadoul, Jacques. *Alchemists and Gold.* New York: G. P. Putnam's Sons, 1972. Reprint, London: Neville Spearman, 1972.
Silberer, Herbert. *The Hidden Symbolism of Alchemy and the Occult Arts.* New York: Dover Books, 1971. Reprint, Magnolia, Mass.: Peter Smith, 1972.
Thompson, Charles J. *Alchemy: Source of Chemistry & Medicine.* London, 1897. Reprint, Sentry Press, 1974.
Valentine, Basil. *Triumphal Chariot of Antimony.* London, 1656.
Waite, A. E. *The Alchemical Writings of Edward Kelly.* New York: Samuel Weiser, 1973.
———. *Alchemists Through the Ages.* Blauvelt, N.Y.: Rudolf Steiner Publications, 1970.
———. *Azoth, or the Star in the East.* London, 1893. Reprint, New Hyde Park, N.Y.: University Books, 1973.
———. *The Occult Sciences.* London, 1923. Reprint, New Hyde Park, N.Y.: University Books, 1973.
Waite, A. E., ed. *The Hermetical & Alchemical Writings of Paracelsus.* 2 vols., London, 1894. Reprint, New Hyde Park, N.Y.: University Books, 1967.
———. *The Works of Thomas Vaughan, Mystic and Alchemist.* London, 1919. Reprint, New Hyde Park, N.Y.: University Books, 1968.
Zetznerus, L., ed. *Theatrum Chimicum.* 6 vols. Strasbourg, France, 1659–61.

Alchindus (or Alkindi) (ca. ninth century C.E.)

Arabian doctor and philosopher of the ninth century regarded by some authorities as a magician but by others as merely a superstitious writer. He used charmed words and combinations of figures in order to cure his patients. Demonologists maintained that the devil was responsible for his power, and based their statements on the fact that he had written a work entitled *The Theory of the Magic Arts.* He was probably, however, nothing more formidable than a natural philosopher at a time when all matters of science and philosophy were held in suspicion. Some of his theories were of a magical nature, as when he attempted to explain the phenomena of dreams by saying that they were the work of the **elementals,** who acted their strange fantasies before the mind of the sleeper as actors play in a theater. But on the whole there is little to connect him with the practice of **magic.**

Aldinach

An Egyptian demon, who, according to demonologists, presides over tempests, earthquakes, rainstorms, and hailstorms and sinks ships. When he appears in visible form, he takes the shape of a woman.

Alectorius (or Alectoria)

This stone is about the size of a bean, clear as crystal, sometimes with veins the color of flesh. It is said to be taken from the cock's stomach. According to ancient belief, it renders its owner courageous and invincible, brings him wealth, assuages thirst, and makes the husband love his wife, or, as another author has it, "makes the woman agreeable to her husband." Its most wonderful property is that it helps to regain a lost kingdom and acquire a foreign one.

Alectromancy (or Alectryomancy)

An ancient method of **divination** with a cock. In practicing it, a circle must be made and divided equally into as many parts as there are letters in the alphabet. Then a wheat-corn must be placed on every letter, beginning with A, during which the depositor must repeat a certain verse. This must be done when the sun or moon is in Aries or Leo. A young cock, all white, should then be taken, his claws cut off and the cock forced to swallow them together with a little scroll of parchment made of lambskin upon which has been written certain words. Then the diviner holding the cock should repeat a form of incantation. Next, on placing the cock within the circle, he must repeat two verses of the Psalms, which are exactly in the middle of the 72 verses cited in the entry on **onimancy.**

With the cock inside the circle, it must be observed from which letters he pecks the grains, and upon these letters new grains must be placed. The letters, when written down and put together will reveal the name of the person concerning whom inquiry has been made.

According to legend the magician Iamblicus used this art to discover the person who should succeed Valens Caesar in the empire, but the bird picking up four of the grains, those which lay on the letters "T h e o," left it uncertain whether Theodosius, Theodotus, Theodorus, or Theodectes, was the person designated. Valens, however, learning what had been done, put to death several individuals whose names unhappily began with those letters, and the magician, to avoid the effects of his resentment, took a draught of poison.

A kind of Alectromancy was also sometimes practiced upon the crowing of the cock, and the periods at which it was heard. Ammianus Marcellinus (fourth century C.E.) describes the ritual that accompanied this act rather differently. The sorcerers commenced by placing a basin made of different metals on the ground and drawing around it at equal distances the letters of the alphabet. Then whoever possessed the deepest occult knowledge, advanced, enveloped in a long veil, holding in his hand branches of vervain, and emitting dreadful cries, accompanied by hideous convulsions. He would stop before the magic basin, and become rigid and motionless. He struck on a letter several times with the branch in his hand, and then upon another, until he had selected sufficient letters to form a heroic verse, which was then given out to the assembly.

The details of an operation in Alectromancy are described in the fourth song of the *Caquet Bonbec,* of Jonquieres, a poet of the fourteenth century.

Sources:

Waite, A. E.. *The Occult Sciences.* 1891. Reprint, Secaucus, N.J.: University Books, 1974.

Aleuromancy

An ancient kind of **divination** practiced with flour. Sentences were written on slips of paper, each of which was rolled up in a little ball of flour. These were thoroughly mixed up nine times and divided among the curious who were waiting to learn their fate. Apollo, who was supposed to preside over this form of divination, was surnamed Aleuromantis. The custom lingered in remote districts as late as the nineteenth century.

Sources:

Waite, A. E. *The Occult Sciences.* 1891. Reprint, Secaucus, N.J.: University Books, 1974.

Alexander ab Alexandro (Alexandro Alessandri) (ca. 1461–1523)

A Neapolitan lawyer, who published a dissertation on the marvelous entitled *De Rebus Admirabilibus,* in which he recounts miracles that happened in **Italy,** dreams that were verified, and the circumstances connected with many apparitions and phantoms, which he claims to have witnessed. He followed this dissertation with his celebrated work *Genialium Dierum,* which contains many fantastic accounts.

For instance, one evening he set out to join a party of several friends at a house in Rome said to have been haunted for a long time by specters and demons. In the middle of the night, when all of them were assembled in one room, a frightening specter appeared who called to them in a loud voice and threw about the ornaments in the room. One of the friends approached the specter bearing a light, whereupon it disappeared. Several times afterward the same apparition reentered through the door. Alexander found that the demon had slid underneath the couch he was lying on, and on rising from it, he saw a black arm appear on a table in front of him. By this time several of the company had retired, and the lights were out, but torches were brought in answer to their cries of alarm when the specter opened the door, slid past the advancing domestics, and disappeared.

Alexander of Tralles (ca. sixth century B.C.E.)

A physician born at Tralles in Asia Minor, with a leaning toward medico-magical practice. He prescribed for his patients amulets and charmed words, as, for instance, when he stated in his *Practice of Medicine* that the figure of Hercules strangling the Nemean lion, graven on a stone and set in a ring, was an excellent cure for colic. He also claimed that charms and phylacteries were efficacious remedies for gout and fevers.

Alexander the Paphlagonian (ca. second century C.E.)

The oracle of Abonotica, an obscure Paphlagonian town, who for nearly twenty years held absolute supremacy in the empirical art. Born about the end of the second century, a native of Abonotica, he possessed little in the way of worldly wealth. His sole capital consisted in his good looks, fine presence, exquisite voice, and certain talent for fraud, which he was soon to profit from in an extraordinary manner. His idea was to institute a new oracle, and he chose Chalcedon as a suitable place to begin operations. Finding no great encouragement there, he spread a rumor to the effect that Apollo and his son Aesculapius intended shortly to take up residence at Abonotica. The rumor at length reached the ears of his fellow townsmen, who promptly set to work making a temple for the gods. The way was thus prepared for Alexander, who proceeded to Abonotica, diligently advertising his skill as a prophet, so that on his arrival people from many neighboring towns consulted him, and his fame soon spread as far as Rome. We are told that the Emperor Aurelius himself conferred with Alexander before undertaking an important military enterprise.

Lucian gives a possible explanation of the Paphlagonian prophet's remarkable popularity. Alexander, he says, came in the course of his early travels to Pella in Macedon, where he found a unique breed of serpents, large, beautiful, and so tame and harmless that they were allowed by the inhabitants to enter their houses and play with children. A plan took shape in his brain that would help him attain the fame he craved. Selecting the largest and finest specimen of the Macedonian snakes that he could find, he carried it secretly to his destination. The temple that the credulous natives of Abonotica had raised to Apollo was surrounded by a moat, and Alexander, ever ready to seize an opportunity wherever it presented itself, emptied a goose egg of its contents, placed within the shell a newly hatched serpent, and sunk it in the moat. He then informed the people that Apollo had arrived. Making for the moat with all speed, followed by a curious multitude, he scooped up the egg, and in full view of the people, broke the shell and exposed to their admiring eyes a little, wriggling serpent. When a few days had elapsed, he judged the time ripe for a second demonstration. Gathering together a huge crowd from every part of Paphlagonia, he emerged from the temple with the large Macedonian snake coiled about his neck. The head of the serpent was concealed under the prophet's arm, and an artificial head, somewhat resembling that of a human being, allowed to protrude. The assembly was astonished to find that the tiny serpent of a few days ago had already attained such remarkable proportions and possessed the face of a human being, and they appeared to have little doubt that it was indeed Apollo come to Abonotica.

By means of ingenious mechanical contrivances, the serpent was apparently made to reply to questions put to it. In other cases sealed rolls containing the questions were handed to the oracle and returned with the seals intact and an appropriate answer written inside.

His audacity and ready invention enabled Alexander to impose at will upon the credulous people of his time, and these, combined with a strong and attractive personality, won and preserved for him his remarkable popularity, as they have done for other "prophets" before and since.

Alfarabi (ca. 870–950 C.E.)

An adept of remarkable gifts with an extensive knowledge of all the sciences. Born at Othrar (then called Faral) in Asia Minor, he was named Abou-Nasr-Mohammed-Ibn-Tarkaw, but he was better known as Farabi, or *Alfarabi,* from the town of his birth. Though he was of Turkish extraction, he desired to perfect himself in Arabic, so he went to Baghdad and studied the Greek philosophers under Abou Bachar Maltey. He next stayed for a time in Hanan, where he learned logic from a Christian physician. Having far surpassed his fellow scholars, he left Hanan and drifted at last to Egypt. During his wanderings he came in contact with the learned philosophers of his time, and he wrote books on philosophy, mathematics, astronomy, and other sciences, acquiring proficiency in 70 languages. His treatise on music, proving the connection of sound with atmospheric vibrations and mocking the Pythagorean theory of the music of the spheres, attained some celebrity.

He gained the goodwill and patronage of the sultan of Syria in a somewhat curious fashion. While passing through Syria he visited the court of the sultan, who was at that moment discussing abstruse scientific points with doctors and astrologers. Alfarabi entered in his stained and dusty traveling attire (he had been on a pilgrimage to Mecca), and when the sultan bade him be seated, he, either unaware of or indifferent to the etiquette of court life, sat down boldly on a corner of the royal sofa. The monarch, unused to such informality, spoke in a little-known tongue to a courtier, and asked him to remove the presumptuous philosopher. The latter, however, astonished him by replying in the same language: "Sire, he who acts hastily, in haste repents."

The sultan, interested in his unconventional guest, questioned him and learned of the accomplishments of Alfarabi. The sages who were present were also astounded at his wide learning. When the prince eventually called for some music, Alfarabi accompanied the musicians on a lute with such marvelous skill and grace that the entire company was charmed.

The sultan wished to keep such a valuable philosopher at his court, and some say that Alfarabi accepted his patronage and died peacefully in Syria. Others maintain that he informed the sultan that he would never rest till he had discovered the secret of the **Philosopher's Stone,** which he believed himself on the verge of finding. They say that he set out but was attacked and killed by robbers in the woods of Syria.

Alfridarya

A belief resembling **astrology,** which claims that all the planets in turn influence the life of man, each one governing a certain number of years.

Alis de Tésieux (ca. sixteenth century C.E.)

Spirit of a Spanish nun, as recorded in a book published in Paris in 1528: *La merveilleuse histoire de l'esprit qui, depuis naguère, s'est apparu au monastère des religieuses de Saint Pierre de Lyon, laquelle est pleine de grande admiration, comme on pourra vois par la lecture de ce présent livre, par Adrien de Montalembert, aumonier du roi François Ier.* This work dealt with the appearance in the monastery of the spirit of Alis de Tésieux, a nun who had lived there before the reformation of the monastery in 1513. It seems Alis led a rather worldly life, following pleasure and enjoyment in a manner unbecoming to a nun, finally stealing the ornaments from the altar and selling them. She left the monastery and for a time continued her disgraceful career outside, but before she died she repented of her sins and, through the intercession of the Virgin, received pardon. However, she was refused Christian burial and was interred without the usual prayers and funeral rites.

A number of years later, when the monastery was occupied by other nuns, one of their number, a girl of about eighteen years, was aroused from her sleep by the apparition of Sister Alis. For some time afterward the spirit haunted her wherever she went, continually rapping on the ground near where she stood and even communicating with the other nuns. The spirit who entered the monastery seemed good and devout, but the good sisters, well versed in the wiles of the devil, had their doubts. The bishop of Lyons and the narrator, Adrien de Montalembert, were called in to deal with the evil spirit.

After many prayers and formalities, the spirit of Alis was found to be an innocent one, attended by a guardian angel. She answered a number of questions regarding her present state and her desire for Christian burial, and confirmed the doctrines of the Catholic Church, notably that of purgatory. The remains of Sister Alis were conveyed to consecrated ground, and prayers made for the release of her soul from purgatory, but she continued to follow the young nun for a time, teaching her, on her last visit, five secret prayers composed by St. John the Evangelist.

Alister Hardy Research Centre, The

Originally founded in 1969 as the **Religious Experience Research Unit** at Manchester College, Oxford, England, by Professor Sir **Alister Hardy** after his retirement from the chair of zoology at Oxford University. In 1985, shortly before he died, Sir Alister was named before a group of eminent churchmen and scientists at the Church Centre of the United Nations as the winner of the Templeton Prize, awarded annually for progress in religion.

The purpose of the Alister Hardy Research Centre is "to make a disciplined study of the frequency of report of first hand religious or transcendent experience in contemporary members of human species and to investigate the nature and function of such experiences." The center explores such questions as: How many people in the modern world report religious or transcendent experiences? What do people mean when they say they have had one of these experiences? What sort of things do they describe? How do they interpret them? What effects do they have on their lives? Are the sorts of people who report them more likely to be: Well or poorly educated; impoverished or well provided for; happy or unhappy; mentally unbalanced or stable; socially responsible or self-preoccupied; members of religious institutions or not?

Since its foundation, the center has built up a unique body of research data consisting of more than 5,000 case histories of individuals who have had some form of such experience. Although these case histories have come mainly from Britain, and, to a lesser degree, from other English-speaking countries, many other cultural and religious traditions are represented. The center has also conducted a number of large scale and in-depth surveys of reports of religious experiences in Britain and the United States.

Repeated national polls indicate that between a third and a half of the adult populations in Britain and the United States claim to have been "aware of or influenced by a presence or a power, whether they call it God or not, which is different from their everyday selves." Parallel studies in the United States and Australia (e.g., by the National Opinion Research Center at the University of Chicago, the Survey Research Center of the University of California at Berkeley, and Gallup International) have produced similarly high figures. The center has now completed a number of in-depth studies in Britain, in which random samples of particular social groups (e.g., adult members of the population of an industrial city, a sample of postgraduate students, and a sample of nurses in two large hospitals) have been interviewed personally and at length about their experiences. In all these groups the positive response rate has been over 60 percent.

The center believes that such research is particularly important "in view of the crisis through which Western culture (and hence the world affected by it) is now passing, in part the result of an intellectually restricted perspective which appeared at the time of the European Enlightenment, especially during the eighteenth century." The center claims that modern analyses of the alienation, meaninglessness, and violence increasingly endemic to society have been limited by the proscriptions enforced by this dominant (and materially successful) thought pattern, particularly in failing to comprehend or dismissing the religious or transcendent dimension of human experience.

The address of the British branch is: The Alister Hardy Research Centre, Manchester College, Oxford OX1 3TD, England. The address of the U.S. branch is: The Alister Hardy Research Centre (U.S.S.) Inc., The Gallup Building, 53 Bank St., Princeton, N.J. 08542.

All Hallow's Eve

One of the ancient four great Fire festivals in Britain, supposed to have taken place on November 1, when all fires, save those of the Druids, were extinguished, from whose altars the holy fire had to be purchased by the householders for a certain price. The festival is still known in Ireland as Samhein, or La Samon, i.e., the Feast of the Sun, while in Scotland, it has been given the name of Hallowe'en.

All Hallow's Eve, as observed in the Church of Rome, corresponds with the Feralia of the ancient Romans, when they sacrificed in honor of the dead, offered up prayers for them, and made oblations to them. In ancient times, this festival was celebrated on February 21, but the Roman church transferred it to

November 1. It was originally designed to give rest and peace to the souls of the departed.

In some parts of Scotland, it is still customary for young people to kindle a fire, called a "Hallowe'en bleeze," on the tops of hills. It was customary to surround these bonfires with a circular trench symbolic of the sun.

In Perthshire, the Hallowe'en bleeze is made in the following fashion. Heath, broom, and dressings of flax are tied upon a pole. The torch is lit; a youth takes it and carries it upon his shoulders. When the torch is burned out, a second is tied to the pole and kindled. Several of these blazing torches are often carried through the villages at the same time.

Hallowe'en is believed by the superstitious to be a night on which the invisible world has peculiar power. Further, it is thought that there is no such night in all the year for obtaining insight into the future. His Satanic Majesty is supposed to have great latitude allowed him on this anniversary, in common with witches, who are believed to fly on broomsticks. Others less aerially disposed ride over by-road and heath, seated on the back of cats that have been transformed into coal-black steeds for the journey. The green-robed fairies are also said to hold special festive meetings at their favorite haunts.

There are many folk customs relating to this eve of mystic ceremonies:

The youths, who engage in the ceremony of Pulling the Green Kail, go hand-in-hand, with closed eyes, into a bachelor's or spinster's garden, and pull up the first "kail stalks" that come in their way. Should the stalks prove to be straight in stem, and with a good supply of earth at their roots, the future husbands (or wives) will be young, good looking, and rich in proportion. If the stalks are stunted, crooked, and have little or no earth at their roots, the future spouses will be found lacking in good looks and fortune. The stem's taste (sweet or sour) indicates the temper of the future partner. The stalks are afterward placed above the doors of the respective houses, and the Christian names of those persons who first pass underneath will correspond with those of the future husbands or wives.

Eating the Apple at the Glass: Provide yourself with an apple, and, as the clock strikes twelve, go alone into a room where there is a looking glass. Cut the apple into small pieces, throw one piece over your left shoulder, and advancing to the mirror without looking back, eat the remainder, combing your hair carefully all the time before the glass. It is said that the face of the person you are to marry will be seen peeping over your left shoulder. This Hallowe'en game is supposed to be a relic of that form of divination with mirrors that popes condemned as sorcery.

The Burning Nuts: Take two nuts and place them in the fire, giving one of them your own name; the other that of the object of your affections. Should they burn quietly away, side by side, then the issue of your love affair will be prosperous; but if one starts away from the other, the result will be unfavorable.

Sowing Hemp Seed: Steal forth alone toward midnight and sow a handful of hemp seed, repeating the following rhyme:

"Hemp seed, I sow thee, hemp seed, I sow thee;
And he that is my true love, come behind and harrow me."

Then look over your left shoulder and you will see the person.

Winnowing Corn: This ceremony must also be performed alone. Go to a barn and open both doors, taking them off the hinges if possible. Then take the instrument used in winnowing corn, and go through the motions of letting it down against the wind. Repeat the operation three times, and the figure of your future partner will appear passing in at one door and out at the other. Should those engaging in this ceremony be fated to die young, it is believed that a coffin, followed by mourners, will enter and pursue the too adventurous youth around the barn.

Eating the Bean Stack: Go three times round a bean stack with outstretched arms, as if measuring it, and the third time you will clasp in your arms the shade of your future partner.

Eating the Herring: Just before retiring to rest, eat a raw or roasted salt herring, and in your dreams your future husband (or wife) will come and offer you a drink of water to quench your thirst.

Dipping the Shirt Sleeve: Go alone, or in company with others, to a stream where "three lairds' lands meet," and dip in the left sleeve of a shirt; after this is done not one word must be spoken, otherwise the spell is broken. Then put your sleeve to dry before your bedroom fire. Go to bed, but be careful to remain awake, and you will see the form of your future helpmate enter and turn the sleeve in order that the other side may get dried.

The Three Plates: Place three plates in a row on a table. In one of these put clean water, in another dirty water, and leave the third empty. Blindfold the person wishing to try his or her fortune, and lead him or her up to the table, left hand forward. Should it come in contact with the clean water, then the future spouse will be young, handsome, and a bachelor or maid. The dirty water signifies a widower or a widow, and the empty dish, no spouses. This ceremony is repeated three times, and the plates must be differently arranged after each attempt.

Throwing the Clue: Go alone at night to the nearest lime-kiln and throw in a ball of blue yarn, winding it off on to a fresh ball. As you come near the end, someone will grasp hold of the thread lying in the kiln. You then ask, "Who holds?" and the name of your future partner will be uttered from beneath.

In modern Britain, Halloween customs have merged with the bonfire ceremonies of Guy Fawkes day, on November 5th, when effigies of the conspirator who tried to blow up the Houses of Parliament are burnt all over the country and fireworks set off.

In the United States, Halloween has become one of the most celebrated holidays of the year. It combines a harvest festival with the ancient associations of Halloween with demons and the souls of the dead. Today almost totally secularized, it has become a society-wide costume party. The practice of "Trick or Treat" has lost all conscious associations with the older practice, when fruit or candies were gained from neighbors, a relic of the custom of food offerings for the dead.

Modern Wiccans and Neo-Pagans have revived the eve of November 1 as the pagan New Year, which they term Samhein (pronounced "Sav-en"). It is the beginning of winter, and during the evening hours, the spirits of the departed seek the warmth of the Samhein fire. The day is a time of communing with the dead, but also a time of feasting and drinking in defiance of the approaching days of increasing darkness and cold.

Sources:

Farrar, Janet, and Stewart Farrar. *Eight Sabbats for Witches.* London: Robert Hale, 1981.

Halloween and Other Festivals of Death and Life. Knoxville: University of Tennessee Press, 1994.

Allat (or **Ellat**)

Goddess of the ancient Arabs of pre-Islamic times, associated with the god Dhu-shara, known as Allah (supreme god), worshiped in the form of a rectangular stone, reminiscent of the later Kaaba of Mecca. Allat is mentioned in the Koran as a pagan goddess. She is said to have been joint ruler with Allah and judge of the afterlife.

Allegro, John (Marco) (1923–1988)

British scholar who assisted in the deciphering of the Dead Sea Scrolls, and created a sensation with his book *The Sacred Mushroom and the Cross* (1970), which suggested that the New Testament was written in a secret code for the use of a sect built around the hallucinatory properties of a sacred **mushroom** drug. According to Allegro, Jesus never existed and the crucifixion story was a myth, symbolic of the ecstasy of a drug cult.

In support of this extraordinary theory, Allegro strained philology, comparative linguistics, and semantics in a manner that recalled the eccentricities of John Belleden Ker in the nineteenth century, who wrote several volumes to "prove" that all British proverbs and nursery rhymes were assonantal equivalents of High Dutch invectives against the Roman Catholic Church.

Sources:

Allegro, John. *The Sacred Mushroom and the Cross.* Garden City, N.Y.: Doubleday, 1970.

Allen, James (1864–1912)

British writer of self-improvement books that present a very individual blend of **mysticism** and **New Thought.** Like his contemporary Ralph Waldo Trine in America, Allen helped popularize New Thought in Great Britain with his numerous popular inspirational books. According to his wife, Allen "wrote when he had a message, and it became a message only when he had lived it in his own life and knew that it was good."

Born in Leicester, England, on November 28, 1864, he suffered much ill-health as a child. His father died when he was 14, and he had to earn his living and help support his mother. He worked hard at various jobs and studied poetry, drama, philosophy, and religion in his spare time. At the age of 24, he experienced what he described as "the Cosmic Vision" after reading Sir Edwin Arnold's *Light of Asia* (1879), a famous poem based on the teaching of Buddha. This transient illumination returned in a more permanent form ten years later and led to the writing of his first book, *From Poverty to Power* (1901), which went into seven editions. After the success of this book, Allen found it possible to live by his writings. With his wife, Lily, he moved to Ilfracombe, Devon.

Allen was not ambitious, avoided publicity, and lived simply on a modest income from his writings. He derived inspiration for his books from solitary meditation. He published 19 books and edited two journals: *The Epoch* and *The Light of Reason.* Some of his books were quite short in length but influential in their succinct inspiration. His best-known work, *As a Man Thinketh,* went into six editions and influenced many thousands of readers. It remains a classic of its kind and has been frequently reprinted. Allen died January 24, 1912.

Sources:

Allen, James. *As a Man Thinketh.* 1890. Reprint, Philadelphia: David O. McKay, n.d.

———. *By-Ways of Blessedness.* Libertyville, Ill.: Sheldon University Press, 1909.

———. *From Poverty to Power.* New York: R. F. Fenno, 1907.

———. *The Life Triumphant.* Libertyville, Ill.: Sheldon University Press, 1908.

"Alleyne, John"

Pseudonym of Captain **John Allen Bartlett** (1861–1933), retired British marine officer, who was the psychic medium of part of the **Glastonbury Scripts** in the experiments of **Frederick Bligh Bond** (1864–1945), detailed in Bond's book *Gate of Remembrance* (1918).

Alli Allahis

A continuation of the old sect of the **Magi,** priests of ancient Persia.

Allingham, Cedric

Elusive author of the book *Flying Saucers from Mars* (1954), published a year after the remarkable claims of **George Adamski** in his influential book, written with **Desmond Leslie,** *Flying Saucers Have Landed* (1953).

Cedric Allingham's book claimed that while the author was on a caravan holiday near Lossiemouth, Scotland, in February 1954, he saw a flying saucer and met its Martian pilot. The book included a soft focus photograph of a back view of the alien moving away. Coming so soon after Adamski's book, both books initiated scores of similar "contactee" claims. While flying saucer fans welcomed Allingham's book, skeptics denounced it as a hoax.

The case against the genuineness of the book was strengthened by the fact that attempts to contact the author by other investigators proved fruitless. At the time the book was published in October 1954, Allingham was said to be touring the United States planning to meet Adamski. His publisher then claimed that Allingham was suffering from tuberculosis in a Swiss sanitarium. A few months later, Allingham was said to have died.

Apart from Allingham's publishers, the only other named human contactee was said to have been a fisherman named James Duncan, however Duncan proved just as elusive as Allingham. In 1969 Robert Chapman, a perceptive critic, claimed in his own book *Unidentified Flying Objects* that Allingham never existed and that the story was "probably the biggest **UFO** leg-pull ever perpetrated in Britain." Chapman discovered that Allingham was supposed to have lectured to a flying saucer group in Kent, England, and a photograph purporting to be of Allingham standing by "his 10-inch reflecting telescope" appeared as frontispiece to *Flying Saucers from Mars.*

The hoax was finally resolved in 1986 by journalists Christopher Allan and Steuart Campbell in an article in the journal *Magonia.* Allan and Campbell claimed that Allingham's book was a hoax perpetrated by a British astronomer Patrick Moore, who presents the popular television series "The Sky at Night." Moore had claimed to know Allingham and to have met him at a lecture on UFOs given at a club in Tunbridge Wells, Kent. Allan and Campbell conducted a careful comparison between the Allingham book and the writings of Moore. They found significant similarities of words, phrases, and references, but also some puzzling differences. They concluded that more than one individual was involved in the writing of the book.

Although the publishers refused to disclose the identity or whereabouts of "Allingham," they agreed to forward a letter from Allan and Campbell, asking for details of identity. The letter was returned with the remark on the envelope "not known here for at least twelve years." However, the envelope itself identified the name and address to which the letter had been sent! Allan and Campbell were thus able to contact the individual, Peter Davies, who had been living only nine miles from the home of Patrick Moore in East Grinstead, Sussex. When contacted at a later address, Davies admitted that he had been involved with the book *Flying Saucers from Mars,* that it was written by someone else whom he would not name, but that his task had been to revise the book to conceal the style, and that the frontispiece photograph of "Allingham" was actually of himself in disguise. He also admitted that he had given the lecture to the flying saucer group in Kent, in company with a knowledgeable "assistant" (i.e., Moore) whom he would not name. It also transpired that Davies was an old friend of Patrick Moore.

Allan and Campbell compared the photograph of "Allingham" standing by the side of the 10-inch reflecting telescope with a photograph of the 1½-inch reflector telescope belonging to Patrick Moore, taken in his garden in East Grinstead, Sussex. The telescope and the background of trees, shrub, and a garden seat matched.

The question of Allingham's identity was finally resolved; however, Moore never acknowledged his role in the hoax. Immediately after the 1986 article exposing his initiation of the affair, he tried to refute the idea and threatened to sue any who perpetuated it. He soon lapsed into silence and ufologists discovered that his authorship of the Allingham book was somewhat of an open secret among British scientists. Moore in fact had a long history of poking fun at contactee claims and had written many letters to *Cosmic Voice,* the periodical of the Aetherius Society, which included mention of scientists with names such as L. Puller or Dr. Huizenass.

Sources:

Allen, Christopher, and Steuart Campbell. "Flying Saucer from Moore's?" *Magonia* vol. 23 (July 1986): 15–18.

Allingham, Cedric [Patrick Moore]. *Flying Saucer from Mars.* London: Frederick Muller, 1954.

Chapman, Robert. *Unidentified Flying Objects.* London: Arthur Barker, 1969.

Allison, Lydia W(interhalter) (1880–1959)

Founding member of the **Boston Society for Psychic Research** in 1925, trustee of the **American Society for Psychical Research** (ASPR) (1941–59), chairman of committee on publication (1943–59), and a member of the **Society for Psychical Research,** London, and the International Committee for the Study of Parapsychological Methods.

Allison was born September 14, 1880, in Milwaukee, Wisconsin. She married Edward Wood Allison in 1905. Dealing with his death led her to psychic research in 1920. During the early 1920s she visited the famous medium **Mrs. Osborne Leonard.** Her report on these sittings established her place in the history of psychic research. In 1925, a controversy within the ASPR over the organization's vehement defense of the medium **Mina S. Crandon ("Margery")** led to a schism. Allison, along with Episcopal minister and researcher **Elwood Worcester,** established the Boston Society for Psychic Research. Allison was in charge of the new society's publications. She also assisted in the negotiations that led to the eventual healing of the schism in 1941. She worked with the ASPR's publications committee for the rest of her life.

While her sittings with Leonard are most remembered, along the way Allison also sat with **Minne M. Soule,** and investigated the mediumship of "Margery," **Rudi Schneider,** and **Eileen J. Garrett.** In 1953 she attended the First International Conference of Parapsychological Studies in Utrecht, Holland.

Her careful objective investigations elicited the following tribute from parapsychologist **Gardner Murphy:** "Her combination of unfailing enthusiasm for the highest quality research and solid skepticism regarding unsound methods made her a precious collaborator."

Sources:

Allison, Lydia W. "The American Society for Psychical Research: a Brief History." *SPR Proceedings* vol. 52, no. 1 (1958).

———. *Leonard and Soule Experiments in Psychical Research.* Boston, 1929.

———. "Proxy Sittings with Mrs. Leonard." *SPR Proceedings* vol 42 (1934).

———. "Telepathy or Association." *SPR Proceedings* vol. 35 (1941).

"Obituary and Tributes to Mrs. E. W. Allison." *Journal of the ASPR* vol. 53 (1959): 81.

Pleasants, Helene, ed. *Biographical Dictionary of Parapsychology.* New York: Helix Press, 1964.

Almanach du Diable

A French almanac containing predictions for the years 1737 and 1738 and purported to be published from hell. The book, which was a satire against the Jansenists, was suppressed on account of some over-bold predictions and became very rare. The authorship was ascribed to Quesnel, an ironmonger at Dijon. The Jansenists replied with a pamphlet directed against the Jesuits, which was also suppressed. Entitled *Almanac de Dieu* and dedicated to M. Carré de Montgeron, it was published in 1738 and claimed satirically to be printed in heaven.

Almoganenses

The name given to certain Spanish people who, by the flight and song of **birds,** meetings with wild animals, and various other means, foretold coming events. According to the fifteenth-century humanist Laurentius Valla, "They carefully preserve among themselves books which treat of this science, where they find rules of all sorts of prognostications and predictions. The soothsayers are divided into two classes, one, the masters or principals, the other the disciples and aspirants."

Another kind of knowledge is also attributed to them, that of being able to indicate the way taken by horses and other beasts of burden which are lost, and the road followed by one or more persons. They can specify the kind and shape of the ground, whether the earth is hard or soft, covered with sand or grass, whether it is a broad road, paved or sanded, or narrow, twisting paths, and tell also how many passengers are on the road. They can follow the track of anyone and cause thieves to be apprehended. Those writers who mention the Almoganenses, however, do not specify either the period when they flourished or the country or province they occupied, but it seems possible from their name and other considerations that they were Moorish. (See also **Ornithomancy**)

Almusseri

A nineteenth-century secret society resembling African associations, with secret rites akin to those of the Cabiric and Orphic Mysteries. Their reception took place once a year in a wood, where the candidate pretended to die. The initiates surrounded the neophyte and chanted funeral songs. He was then brought to the temple erected for the purpose and anointed with palm oil. After 40 days of probation, he was said to have obtained a new soul, was greeted with hymns of joy, and conducted home.

Alocer

According to **Johan Weyer,** Alocer is a powerful demon, Grand Duke of Hades. He appears in the shape of a knight mounted on an enormous horse. His face has leonine characteristics; he has a ruddy complexion and burning eyes, and speaks with much gravity. He is said to give family happiness to those whom he takes under his protection and to teach astronomy and liberal arts. Thirty-six legions are controlled by him.

Sources:

Weyer, Johannes. *Witches, Devils, and Doctors in the Renaissance: Johann Weyer, De Praestigiis.* Edited by George Mora. Binghamton, N.Y.: Medieval and Renaissance Texts and Studies, 1991.

Alomancy

Divination by means of salt, of which process little is known. From this ancient practice comes the saying that misfortune is about to fall on the household when the salt cellar is overturned.

Alopecy

A species of charm by the aid of which one can bewitch an enemy whom one wishes to harm.

Alper, Frank (1930–)

Frank Alper, Spiritualist channel and founder of the Arizona Metaphysical Society, was born on January 22, 1930, in Brooklyn, New York. Alper moved to Phoenix in 1970. He founded the society three years later, and in 1979 he aligned the society with the Church of Tzaddi, a Spiritualist denomination headquartered in Boulder, Colorado.

Alper first emerged as a channel in 1975 and has subsequently channeled many volumes of material from "Moses" and "the Christos." However, he is most known for the three volumes he channeled and published in 1982 as *Exploring Atlantis.* According to Alper, one of the masters who periodically spoke through him requested that he channel several sessions on **Atlantis.** The several entities channeled during these sessions claimed to have lived there. According to Alper's volumes, the Atlanteans were extraterrestrials. When their planet became uninhabitable, they used their advanced technology to come to Earth. They settled in

Atlantis, but their island kingdom was destroyed by a natural catastrophe following the tilting of the Earth's axis.

While *Exploring Atlantis* provided some interesting development of thought about the ancient continent, the volumes especially developed a new occult perspective on **crystals.** Alper described Atlantis as a crystal-oriented culture that relied on a power system based on natural symmetrical—flawless—crystals said to concentrate massive amounts of energy. While these crystals could absorb and store electrical energy to be used at a later date, they were most useful in storing universal energy to be used for healing. Crystals of different shapes and colors have different healing uses. During the 1980s crystal power became the subject of numerous books and the starting point of a debate on the power-storing capacity of crystals. Through the early 1990s, the emphasis within the **New Age** community on crystals has considerably waned in the face of a strong critique of Alper's theories.

Sources:

Alper, Frank. *Exploring Atlantis.* 3 vols. Farmington, N.Y.: Coleman Publishing, 1982.

Webster, Sam. "Dr. Frank Alper: Interview with a Metaphysician." *Whole Life Monthly* (March 1987): 20–22.

Alpert, Richard (1931–   )

With Dr. **Timothy Leary,** Alpert became a controversial figure in the psychedelic revolution of the 1960s. Born April 6, 1931, in Boston, he received his Ph.D. in psychology at Stanford University in 1957, then taught at Stanford, University of California at Berkeley, and Harvard University. Leary and Alpert were both dismissed from Harvard for their experiments with psilocybin. They subsequently obtained financing to conduct experiments and to publicize the use of such **drugs** as **LSD** (lysergic acid diethylamide) in producing altered states of consciousness, thus launching the psychedelic revolution.

In propagating the belief that mystical experience could be obtained from a drug, Leary and Alpert were expanding upon suggestions made earlier in **Aldous Huxley**'s book *The Doors of Perception* (1954), which cited the sacramental use of peyote by certain North American Indians. However, the motivations and cultural values of those closely knit groups were left behind in what became a popular movement. The psychedelic revolution contributed to the popularization of mystical experiences in an otherwise materialistic society but at the same time led many into meaningless despair and helped legitimize the widespread use of addictive narcotics drugs, now widely recognized as a major social problem.

In 1967, in a state of spiritual despair, Alpert went to India in search of meaning through mysticism. He studied for a few months under Neem Karoli Baba in the Himalayas, then returned to the United States as "Baba Ram Dass," or "God's servant." Having abandoned psychedelic drugs, he emerged as a disciple of Hindu spirituality and commenced a career of lecturing and writing. In 1969 Ram Dass gave a course on raja **yoga** (**meditation**) at **Esalen Institute,** near San Francisco, California, launching his new role as a transpersonal psychologist speaking on spiritual issues. His first book as Baba Ram Dass, *Be Here Now,* made him a popular figure in what was to become the **New Age movement.** He followed it with a series of books, including *Seed* (1972), *The Only Dance There Is* (1974), and *Grist for the Mill* (1977).

Ram Dass has lectured widely on his present spiritual position and on personality problems of Western life. Royalties from his book *The Only Dance There Is* supported the *Journal of Transpersonal Psychology,* and his activities are conducted under the auspices of the Hanuman Foundation, which distributes his books and lecture tapes. The foundation may be reached at Box 478, Sante Fe, NM 87501. On land near Taos, New Mexico, Baba Ram Dass built the Neem Karoli Baba Hanuman Temple in memory of his guru.

Sources:

Ram Dass, Baba [Richard Alpert]. *Be Here Now.* Christobal, N.Mex.: Lama Foundation, 1972.

———. *Grist for the Mill.* Santa Cruz, Calif.: Unity Press, 1977.

———. *Journey to Awakening.* New York: Bantam Books, 1976.

———. *The Only Dance There Is.* New York: Aronson, 1976.

Alpha Magazine

British journal devoted to parapsychology, earth mysteries, and ancient arts (astrology, dowsing, numerology, psychic healing, and divination). Edited by David Harvey and Roy Stemman, *Alpha* is published by Pendulum Publishing, 20 Regent St., Fleet, Hampshire GU13 9NR, England.

The first issue was dated March–April 1979, but in issue No. 9 (October 1980), the editors stated that the journal was expected to cease publication through lack of financial support. The nine issues maintained a high standard of presentation, including valuable contributions by authoritative writers.

Alpha Wave

A brain wave with a frequency of between 14 and 50 cycles per second, related to relaxation and dream states. Through **biofeedback** machines, subjects can learn to produce alpha waves and induce altered states of consciousness. During the 1970s, many thought alpha waves to be especially associated with **ESP** and worked on producing them as a means of assisting people with psychic development. Today, that enthusiasm has waned.

Sources:

Lawrence, Jodi. *Alpha Brain Waves.* New York: Avon, 1972.

Stern, Jess. *The Power of Alpha Thinking: Miracle of the Mind.* New York: William Morrow, 1976.

Tart, Charles T. *States of Consciousness.* New York: E. P. Dutton, 1975.

Alphitomancy

An ancient method of **divination** used to prove the guilt or innocence of a suspected person with a loaf of barley. When many persons were accused of a crime and it was desired to find the true culprit, a loaf of barley was made and a portion given to each of the suspects. The innocent people suffered no ill-effects, but criminals were said to betray themselves by an attack of indigestion. This practice gave rise to the oath: "If I am deceiving you, may this piece of bread choke me." By means of this method, a lover might know if his mistress were faithful to him, or a wife, her husband.

The procedure was a follows: A quantity of pure barley flour was kneaded with milk and a little salt, without any leaven. It was then rolled up in a greased paper, and cooked among the cinders. It was afterward taken out and rubbed with verbena leaves and given to the person suspected of deceit, who, if the suspicion was justified, would be unable to digest it.

In ancient times, there was said to be a sacred wood at Lavinium, near Rome, where Alphitomancy was practiced in order to test the purity of women. The priests kept a serpent or a dragon in a cavern in the wood. On certain days of the year the young women were sent there, blindfolded, and carrying a cake made of barley flour and honey. Those who were innocent had their cakes eaten by the serpent, while the cakes of the others were refused.

Sources:

Waite, Arthur Edward. *The Occult Sciences.* 1891. Reprint, Secaucus, N.J.: University Books, 1974.

Alpiel

An angel or demon who, according to the Talmud, presides over fruit trees.

Alraun

Images shaped from the roots of mandrake (see **Mandragoras**) or from ash or briony. The term was popular in Germany, where it was also used to indicate a witch or a magician. An alraun had to be treated with great care because of its magical properties. It was wrapped or dressed in a white robe with a golden girdle, bathed every Friday, and kept in a box, otherwise it was believed to shriek for attention. Alrauns were used in magic rituals and were also believed to bring good luck. But possession of them carried the risk of witchcraft prosecution, and in 1630 three women were executed in Hamburg on this charge.

The alraun was difficult to get rid of because there was a superstition that it could only be sold at a higher price than bought, and there are legends that owners who tried to throw an alraun away found it returned to their room.

According to German folklore, an alraun assisted easy childbirth, and water in which it had been infused prevented swellings in animals. Because of the large demand for alrauns, they were often carved from the roots of briony when genuine mandrakes were difficult to find. They were exported from Germany to various countries and sold in England during the reign of Henry VIII.

Sources:

Thompson, C. J. S. *The Mystic Mandrake.* London: Rider, 1934.

Alrunes

Female demons or sorceresses, the mothers of the Huns in ancient Germany. They took all sorts of shapes, but without changing their sex. The name was also given by Germans to little statues of old sorceresses, about a foot high. To these they attributed great virtues, honoring them as fetishes; clothing them richly, housing them comfortably, and serving them with food and drink at every meal. They believed that if these little images were neglected, they would bring misfortunes upon the household.

Alruy (or Alroy), David (twelfth century C.E.)

A Jewish false Messiah, born in Kurdistan ca. 1147. Alruy boasted that he was a descendant of King David. Educated in Baghdad, he received instruction in the magic arts and came to be more proficient than his masters. His false miracles gained so much popularity for him that many Jews believed him to be the Messiah who was to restore their nation to Jerusalem.

According to legends, the king of Persia imprisoned him, but no bolts and bars could hold so formidable a magician. He escaped from his prison and appeared before the eyes of the astonished king, though the courtiers saw nothing. In vain the king called angrily for someone to arrest the imposter. While they groped in search of him, Alruy slipped from the palace with the king in pursuit and all the courtiers running after him. They reached the sea shore, and Alruy turned and showed himself to all the people. Spreading a scarf on the surface of the water, he walked over it lightly, before the boats which were to pursue him were ready. This tale confirmed his reputation as the greatest magician within the memory of man.

It is said that a Turkish prince, a subject of the Persian king, bribed the father-in-law of the sorcerer to kill him, and one night, when Alruy was sleeping peacefully in his bed, a dagger thrust put an end to his existence.

Alruy was the subject of a novel by the politician-author Benjamin Disraeli (1804–1881): *Alroy: A Romance* (1846).

Alternative Medicine Exhibition

Sponsored in Britain July 1985 by the journal *Here's Health* and organized by Swan House Special Events, with exhibitors and workshops in a wide range of subjects, including **acupressure** and **acupuncture,** Alexander Technique, **Aromatherapy, Bach Flower Remedies, biofeedback,** herbalism, homeopathy, **hypnotism,** iridology, **Kirlian** photography, osteopathy, and reflexology. During the year there was significant interest in alternative medicine, with the formation of the Council for Complementary and Alternative Medicine and the Confederation of Healing Organizations. The British Medical Association, with interests vested in orthodox medical practice, undertook a major investigation into alternative medicine, and a pilot project was also undertaken to provide alternative healing on the National Health Service. For information on the exhibition, contact: Swan House Special Events, Thames Meadow, Walton Bridge, Shepperton, Middlesex TW17 8LT, England.

Althotas (ca. eighteenth century C.E.)

The presumed "master" and companion of **Cagliostro.** Considerable doubt has been expressed regarding his existence. The French writer Louis Figuier, author of *L'alchimie et les alchimistes* (Paris, 1854), stated that Althotas was no imaginary character, that the Roman Inquisition collected many proofs of his existence, but none regarding his origin or end. "But," stated Figuier, "he was a magician and doctor as well, possessed divinatory abilities of a high order, was in possession of several Arabic manuscripts, and had great skill in chemistry."

The French writer on occultism **Éliphas Lévi** stated that the name Althotas is composed of the word "thot" with the syllables "al" and "as," which if read cabalistically are *sala,* meaning messenger or envoy; the name as a whole therefore signifies "Thot, the Messenger of the Egyptians."

Althotas has also been identified with Kolmer, the instructor of Adam Weishaupt (a German leader of the **Illuminati**) in **magic,** and at other times with the Comte de **Saint Germain.** The accounts concerning him are certainly conflicting, for whereas Cagliostro stated at his trial in Paris that Althotas had been his lifelong preceptor, another account says that he met him first on the quay at Messina.

Alu-Demon

Ancient Babylonian demon, said to owe his parentage to a human being; he hides himself in caverns and corners and slinks through the streets at night. He also lies in wait for the unwary, and at night enters bed-chambers and terrorizes people, threatening to pounce on them if they shut their eyes.

Amadeus

A visionary who experienced an apocalypse and revelations, in one of which he learned the two psalms composed by Adam, one a mark of joy at the creation of Eve, and the other the dialogue he held with her after they had sinned. Both psalms are printed in the *Codex Pseudepigraphus Veteris Testamenti* of Johann Albert Fabricius, published at Hamburg, 1713–33.

Amadou, Robert (1924–)

French writer and editor in the field of parapsychology. Born February 16, 1924, at Bois-Colombes (Seine), he studied at Sorbonne, University of Paris, where he earned his licencié des lettres and diplôme d'études supérieures de philosophie. From 1952 to 1955 he edited *Revue métapsychique,* and from 1955 to 1959 *La Tour Saint-Jacques.* He was a charter member of the Parapsychological Association and attended the First International Conference of Parapsychological Studies, Utrecht, 1953, the Conference on Philosophy and Parapsychology, Saint Paul de Vence, France, 1954, and the International Symposium on Psychology and Parapsychology, Asnières-sur-Oise, France, 1956. He edited *La Science et le paranormal* (proceedings of the first three International Symposia of Parapsychological Studies), 1955.

Amadou was both ordained as a priest and consecrated as a bishop in the Église Gnostique Universelle, an independent

French gnostic church, in 1944; he took the name Tau Jacques. In 1988 he was elevated as archbishop and assumed the additional role of archbishop of Europe for the Philippine Independent Catholic Church. He contributed numerous articles on parapsychology to various parapsychological journals and several books, including *La Parapsychologie: Essai historique et critique* (1954), *Les Grands Médiums* (1957), and *La Télépathie* (1958).

Sources:

Amadou, Robert. *Les Grands Mediums.* Paris: Editions Denoel, 1957.

———. *La Parapsychologie: Essai historique et critique.* Paris: Editions Denoel, 1954.

Pleasants, Helene, ed. *Biographical Dictionary of Parapsychology.* New York: Helix Press, 1964.

Amaimon (or Amaymon)

One of the four spirits who preside over the four parts of the universe. *Amaimon* is the governor of the eastern part, according to the **grimoire,** or magic manual, of the *Lemegeton of Solomon,* also known as the *Lesser Key* or *Little Key.*

Sources:

The Lesser Key of Solomon. Chicago: De Laurence, Scott, 1916.

Amalgamated Flying Saucer Clubs of America

Founded in 1959 by Gabriel Green (1924–), Amalgamated Flying Saucer Clubs of America (AFSCA) grew out of the Los Angeles Interplanetary Study Groups, which Green had started in 1956. That same year Green also began issuing a magazine, *Thy Kingdom Come.* A photographer, Green became interested in **flying saucers** after his own sighting of a **UFO.** He also claimed to have made telepathic contact with the Space Masters and the **Great White Brotherhood.**

Green intended the AFSCA to create public acceptance of flying saucers, and to further his aims he planned petitions to Congress and held national conventions. At its peak in the early 1960s the AFSCA had 5,000 members in 24 countries. In 1959 *Thy Kingdom Come* was renamed *World Report* (1959–61), then *UFO International* (1962–65). A second periodical, *Flying Saucers International,* began in 1962 and continued until 1969. Green assumed that the flying saucers were manned by friendly extraterrestrials and had a plan for imparting their advanced knowledge to the people of the Earth in order to resolve present world problems. AFSCA was quite active through the 1960s, but after 1969 became a paper organization and for all practical purposes ceased to exist.

Sources:

Biographical Sketch of Gabriel Green. Northridge, Calif.: Amalgamated Flying Saucer Clubs of America, 1974.

Clark, Jerome. *The Emergence of a Phenomenon: UFOs from the Beginning through 1959; The UFO Encyclopedia.* Vol. 2. Detroit: Omnigraphics, 1992.

Green, Gabriel, and Warren Smith. *Let's Face the Facts about Flying Saucers.* New York: Popular Library, 1967.

Amandinus

A variously colored stone, said to enable the wearer of it to solve any question concerning dreams or enigmas.

Amaranth

A flower that is one of the symbols of immortality. It has been said by occult magicians that a crown made with this flower has supernatural properties and will bring fame and favor to those who wear it. It was also regarded in ancient times as a symbol of immortality and was used to decorate images of gods and tombs. In ancient Greece, the flower was sacred to the goddess Artemis of Ephesus, and the name "amaranth" derives from Amarynthos, a hunter of Artemis and king of Euboea.

There are many species of Amaranth, some with poetic folk names such as "prince's feather" and "love-lies-bleeding."

"Amazing Randi, The"

Stage name of professional conjuring magician **James Randi** (or Randall Zwinge), who is the self-appointed arch-enemy of psychics and the paranormal.

Amduscias

Grand Duke of Hades. According to **Johan Weyer,** Amduscias has the form of a unicorn, but when evoked, appears in human shape. He gives concerts, at the command of men, where one hears the sound of all kinds of musical instruments but can see nothing. It is said that the trees themselves bend to his voice. He commands 29 legions.

Sources:

Weyer, Johannes. *Witches, Devils, and Doctors in the Renaissance: Johann Weyer, De Praestigiis.* Edited by George Mora. Binghamton, N.Y.: Medieval and Renaissance Texts and Studies, 1991.

AMERICA, UNITED STATES OF

This entry treats Native American and European American contributions to parapsychology and the occult. See also related items on **Mexico, Central America,** and **South America.** For the history of Spiritualism in America, see the entry on **Spiritualism,** where a summary of the subject will be found.

Native Americans

Among the various native races of the American continent, the supernatural has flourished as universally as in other parts of the world. The oldest writers (of European and Christian background) on Native Americans agreed that they practiced **sorcery** and the magic arts, and were quick to attribute their prowess to Satan. For example, the Rev. Peter Jones, writing as late as the first decade of the nineteenth century, stated: "I have sometimes been inclined to think that if witchcraft still exists in the world, it is to be found among the aborigines of America."

The early French settlers called the Nipissing *Jongleurs* because of the surprising expertness in magic of their medicine men. Some writers observed the use of hypnotic suggestion among the Menominee and Lakota (Sioux) about the middle of the last century, and it is generally admitted that this art, which is known to Americanists as *orenda,* was familiar among most Indian tribes, as James Mooney noted in his *Ghost Dance Religion* (1896). D. G. Brinton, alluding to Indian medicine men and their connection with the occult arts, observed:

"They were also adept in tricks of sleight of hand, and had no mean acquaintance with what is called natural magic. They would allow themselves to be tied hand and foot with knots innumerable, and at a sign would shake them loose as so many wisps of straw; they would spit fire and swallow hot coals, pick glowing stones from the flames, walk with naked feet over live ashes, and plunge their arms to the shoulder in kettles of boiling water with apparent impunity.

"Nor was this all. With a skill not inferior to that of the jugglers of India, they could plunge knives into vital parts, vomit blood, or kill one another out and out to all appearances, and yet in a few minutes be as well as ever; they could set fire to articles of clothing and even houses, and by a touch of their magic restore them instantly as perfect as before. Says Father Bautista: 'They can make a stick look like a serpent, a mat like a centipede, and a piece of stone like a scorpion.' If it were not within our power to see most of these miracles performed any night in our great cities by a well-dressed professional, we should at once deny their possibility. As it is they astonish us but little.

"One of the most peculiar and characteristic exhibitions of their power, was to summon a spirit to answer inquiries concerning the future and the absent. A great similarity marked this proceeding in all northern tribes, from the Eskimos to the Mexicans. A circular or conical lodge of stout poles, four or eight in number, planted firmly in the ground was covered with skins or mats, a small aperture only being left for the seer to enter. Once in, he carefully closed the hole and commenced his incantations. Soon the lodge trembles, the strong poles shake and bend as with the united strength of a dozen men, and strange, unearthly sounds, now far aloft in the air, now deep in the ground, anon approaching near and nearer, reach the ears of the spectators.

"At length the priest announces that the spirit is present, and is prepared to answer questions. An indispensable preliminary to any inquiry is to insert a handful of tobacco, or a string of beads, or some such douceur under the skins, ostensibly for the behalf of the celestial visitor, who would seem not to be above earthly wants and vanities. The replies received, though occasionally singularly clear and correct, are usually of that profoundly ambiguous purport which leaves the anxious inquirer little wiser than he was before.

"For all this, ventriloquism, trickery, and shrewd knavery are sufficient explanations. Nor does it materially interfere with this view, that converted Indians, on whose veracity we can implicitly rely, have repeatedly averred that in performing this rite they themselves did not move the medicine lodge; for nothing is easier than in the state of nervous excitement they were then in to be self-deceived, as the now familiar phenomenon of table-turning illustrates.

"But there is something more than these vulgar arts now and then to be perceived. There are statements supported by unquestionable testimony, which ought not to be passed over in silence, and yet I cannot but approach them with hesitation. They are so revolting to the laws of exact science, so alien, I had almost said, to the experience of our lives. Yet is this true, or are such experiences only ignored and put aside without serious consideration? Are there not in the history of each of us passages which strike our retrospective thought with awe, almost with terror? Are there not in nearly every community individuals who possess a mysterious power, concerning whose origin, mode of action, and limits, we and they are like, in the dark?

"I refer to such organic forces as are popularly summed up under the words clairvoyance, mesmerism, rhabdomancy, animal magnetism, physical spiritualism. Civilized thousands stake their faith and hope here and hereafter, on the truth of these manifestations; rational medicine recognizes their existence, and while she attributes them to morbid and exceptional influences, confesses her want of more exact knowledge, and refrains from barren theorizing. Let us follow her example, and hold it enough to show that such powers, whatever they are, were known to the native priesthood as well as the modern spiritualists and the miracle mongers of the Middle Ages.

"Their highest development is what our ancestors called 'second sight.' That under certain conditions knowledge can pass from one mind to another otherwise than through the ordinary channels of the senses, is shown by the examples of persons *en rapport*. The limit to this we do not know, but it is not unlikely that clairvoyance or second sight is based upon it."

In his autobiography, the celebrated Sac chief, Black Hawk, related that his great grandfather "was inspired by a belief that at the end of four years he should see a white man, who would be to him a father." Under the direction of this vision he travelled eastward to a certain spot, and there, as he was forewarned, met a Frenchman, through whom the nation was brought into alliance with France.

An anecdote related by Captain Jonathan Carver, an English trader, in his little book of travels, describes his travels among the Killistenoes. In 1767 they were in great straits for food, and depending upon the arrival of the traders to rescue them from starvation. They persuaded the chief priest to consult the divinities as to when the relief would arrive. After the usual preliminaries, their magnate announced that the next day, precisely when the sun reached the zenith, a canoe would arrive with further tidings. At the appointed hour, the whole village, together with the incredulous Englishman, was on the beach, and sure enough, at the minute specified, a canoe swung round a distant point of land and brought the expected news.

More spectacular is an account by Col. John Mason Brown published in the *Atlantic Monthly* (July 1866). Some years earlier as the head of a party of voyagers, he set forth in search of a band of Indians somewhere on the vast plains along the tributaries of the Copper-mine and Mackenzie rivers. Danger, disappointment, and the fatigues of the road induced one after another to turn back, until of the original ten only three remained. They were also on the point of giving up the apparently hopeless quest when they were met by some warriors of the very band they were seeking. The leader of these warriors had been sent out by one of their medicine men to find three whites whose horses, arms, attire, and personal appearance he minutely described, which description was repeated to Col. Brown by the warriors before they saw his two companions. Afterward, when the priest, a frank and simple-minded man, was asked to explain this extraordinary occurrence, he could offer no other explanation than that "he saw them coming, and heard them talk on their journey." Many additional tales such as these were recorded by later travelers.

Those nervous conditions associated with the name of **Franz A. Mesmer** were also nothing new to the Native American magical practioners. Rubbing and stroking the sick, and the laying on of hands, were very common parts of their clinical procedures, and at the initiations to their societies they were frequently exhibited. Observers have related that among the Nez Percés of Oregon, the novice was put to sleep by songs, incantations, and "certain passes of the hand," and that with the Dakotas he would be struck lightly on the breast at a preconcerted moment, and instantly "would drop prostrate on his face, his muscles rigid and quivering in every fibre."

White observers also saw magicians working magical tricks, a fact that supported the general distrust of Indians pervading the white culture. In *Bulletin 30* of the Bureau of American Ethnology, Washington Mathews stated:

"Sleight-of-hand was not only much employed in the treatment of disease, but was used on many other occasions. A very common trick among Indian charlatans was to pretend to suck foreign bodies, such as stones, out of the persons of their patients. Records of this are found among many tribes, from the lowest in culture to the highest, even among the Aztecs. Of course, such trickery was not without some therapeutic efficacy, for, like many other proceedings of the shamans, it was designed to cure disease by influence on the imagination. A Hidatsa, residing in Dakota, in 1865, was known by the name of Cherry-in-the-mouth, because he had a trick of producing from his mouth, at any season, what seemed to be fresh wild cherries. He had found some way of preserving cherries, perhaps in whiskey, and it was easy for him to hide them in his mouth before intending to play the trick; but many of the Indians considered it wonderful magic.

"The most astonishing tricks of the Indians were displayed in their fire ceremonies and in handling hot substances, accounts of which performances pertain to various tribes. It is said that Chippewa sorcerers could handle with impunity red-hot stones and burning brands, and could bathe the hands in boiling water or syrup; such magicians were called 'fire-dealers' and 'fire-handlers.' There are authentic accounts from various parts of the world of fire-dancers and fire-walks among barbarous races, and extraordinary fire acts are performed also among widely separated Indian tribes. Among the Arikara of what is now North Dakota, in the autumn of 1865, when a large fire in the center of the medicine lodge had died down until it became a bed of glowing embers, and the light in the lodge was dim, the performers ran with apparently bare feet among the hot coals and threw these around in the lodge with their bare hands, causing the spectators to flee. Among the Navaho, performers, naked except for breechcloth and moccasins, and having their bodies daubed with a white infusorial clay, run at high speed around a fire, holding in their hands great faggots of flaming cedar bark, which they apply to the bare backs of those in front of them and to their own persons. Their wild race around the fire is continued until the faggots are nearly all consumed, but they are never injured by the flame. This immunity may be accounted for by supposing that the cedar bark does not make a very hot fire, and that the clay coating protects the body. Menominee shamans are said to handle fire, as also are the female sorcerers of Honduras.

"Indians know well how to handle venomous serpents with impunity. If they can not avoid being bitten, as they usually can, they seem to be able to avert the fatal consequences of the bite. The wonderful acts performed in the Snake Dance of the Hopi have often been described.

"A trick of Navaho dancers, in the ceremony of the mountain chant, is to pretend to thrust an arrow far down the throat. In this feat an arrow with a telescopic shaft is used; the point is held between the teeth; the hollow part of the handle, covered with plumes, is forced down toward the lips, and thus the arrow appears to be swallowed. There is an account of an arrow of similar construction used early in the eighteenth century by Indians of Canada, who pretended a man was wounded by it and healed instantly. The Navaho also pretend to swallow sticks, which their neighbors of the pueblo of Zuñi actually do in sacred rites, occasionally rupturing the oesophagus in the ordeal of forcing a stick into the stomach. Special societies which practice magic, having for their chief object rainmaking and the cure of disease, exist among the southwestern tribes. Swallowing sticks, arrows, etc., eating and walking on fire, and trampling on cactus, are performed by members of the same fraternity.

"Magicians are usually men; but among the aborigines of the Mosquito Coast in Central America, they are often women who are called *sukias,* and are said to exercise great power. According to Hewitt, Iroquois women are reported traditionally to have been magicians.

"A trick of the juggler among many tribes of the North was to cause himself to be bound hand and foot and then, without visible assistance or effort on his part to release himself from the bonds. Civilized conjurers who perform a similar trick are hidden in a cabinet, and claim supernatural aid; but some Indian jugglers performed this feat under observation. It was common for Indian magicians to pretend they could bring rain, but the trick consisted simply of keeping up ceremonies until rain fell, the last ceremony being the one credited with success. Catlin describes this among the Mandan, in 1832, and the practice is still common among the Pueblo tribes of the arid region. The rain-maker was a special functionary among the Menominee.

"To cause a large plant to grow to maturity in a few moments and out of season is another Indian trick. The Navaho plant the root stalk of a yucca in the ground in the middle of the winter, and apparently cause it to grow, blossom, and bear fruit in a few moments. This is done by the use of artificial flowers and fruit carried under the blankets of the performers; the dimness of the firelight and the motion of the surrounding dancers hide from the spectators the operations of the shaman when he exchanges one artificial object for another. In this way the Hopi grow beans, and the Zuñi corn, the latter using a large cooking pot to cover the growing plant."

European Settlers

The occult history of the European races that occupy the territories now known as the United States of America begins with their initial settlement of North America. The early English, German, and Dutch settlers brought with them an active belief in magic, **witchcraft,** and **sorcery** (malevolent magic). Settlers were aware of a range of magical practices such as image magic, and had a particular fear of curses aimed at them. Should such curses come to pass they would often attribute it to the sorcery of the person pronouncing the course. As early as 1638 in Massachusetts, Jane Hawkins was indicted for practicing witchcraft, though no record of a trial survived. Less than a decade later, however, Alice Young was tried and executed in Connecticut. Hers was the first of a steady stream of trials and a number of executions prior to the famous outbreak at Salem.

The numerous accusations of witchcraft prepared the way for the events at Salem Village (now Danvers), Massachusetts, as did the writings of two leading ministers, Increase Mather (1639–1723) and his son, Cotton Mather (1662–1728). As president of Harvard Increase Mather collected numerous accounts of what today would be called psychic occurrences as evidence of supernatural actions operating in the life of people and published these in *An Essay for the Recording of Illustrious Providences.* Cotton, a brilliant child who entered Harvard at the age of twelve, was only 25 years old when he was placed in charge of North Church, Boston, the largest congregation in the colony. During the early years of his pastorate, he followed his father's interests and collected accounts of some unusual negative experiences of his parishioners which he viewed as the actions of supernatural forces among the people. He argued for the reality of witchcraft, both because the Bible declared it a reality and because he saw instances of it in the deranged behavior of Boston citizens. His conclusions were published in a widely read book published in 1689, *Memorable Provinces Relating to Witchcraft and Possessions.*

The strong belief in the power and presence of negative magic in Salem Village, supported by the writings of the Mathers, emerged in the context of a deep community division between the wealthier landowners and the poorer elements in the village as well as the threat of a war with the natives. For a generation Salem Village had been afflicted by economic tensions and the entire colony faced the threat of open hostilities breaking out as colonists continually expanded into Indian lands.

It began in the depths of winter when the daughters of parish minister the Rev. Samuel Parris began to play games of fortunetelling using the white of an egg as a crystal ball. Panic ensued when one of the girls saw a coffin in the egg. The fearfulness soon found expression in unexplained fits, which disrupted the household and on occasion the church services. A physician suggested witchcraft and while that suggestion was under consideration, a young woman in the village suggested to Tituba and John Indian, a Caribbean Indian couple (not African as is often alleged) who were slaves in the Parris household that they prepare a witch cake (rye meal mixed with the urine of the afflicted girls) to determine if in fact witchcraft was at work. When this plan came to light Tituba and two other women were arrested.

Unfortunately, the girls' fits did not end. They began to name residents of the village who were subsequently arrested. Through the spring months the jails were filled with the accused who could not be tried as the colony was in the midst of a crisis—their charter had expired and had not been renewed. A court was finally and hastily established in June 1692 and the trials began. The first woman tried, Briget Bishop, was sentenced to death. There was little evidence to support the cases against the accused beyond the claims of the girls that spectres of the accused afflicted them and caused their fits. During the trials, when the accused appeared, they would often react as if their mere presence caused them harm. And, as the trials and executions continued and the number of accused grew, the situation in Salem became a matter of colony-wide concern.

Cotton Mather played an active role in the trials. He believed the Devil was at work in Salem, and authored the response of the Boston ministers on the necessity of the trials. However, he warned against a too ready acceptance of spectral evidence. Additionally, he spoke on the occasion of the hanging of former parish minister George Burroughs. When Burroughs flawlessly spoke the Lord's Prayer, which supposedly a witch could not do, Mather rose to quiet the crowd and allowed the execution to continue. However, it was Mather who personally called upon Governor Phelps, who had spent much of the summer away from Boston fighting the Indians, to stop the trials which had reached such large proportions.

In the end, the court sentenced 31 (including 25 women) to death. Nineteen, who pleaded not guilty, were hanged. One Giles Cory refused to plead, thus making use of a legal provision that would prevent his property from being confiscated. One escaped jail and left the colony; two died in jail, and two who were pregnant survived and were freed. Five joined the 55 people who confessed and were later freed.

Reaction to the trials was widespread. Among the most vehement detractors was Thomas Brattle, an educated citizen of Boston, who attacked the proceedings and termed the whole affair utter nonsense. Mather published a reply, defending the court and the idea of witchcraft, *The Wonders of the Invisible World* (1693), but the tide of public opinion was slowly turning against the complex of ideas underlying the trials. Mather continued the debate in his later writings, but his reputation was severely damaged by Robert Calef's attack in *More Wonders of the Invisible World* (1700). Eventually, on January 15, 1697, the jurors who had brought in the guilty verdicts joined in a day of fasting and repentance for the injustices of the trials. In 1702, Samuel Sewell, the judge who presided, publicly confessed his guilt and asked pardon for his role in the proceedings.

Calef's view of Mather and the trial was largely adopted by later generations who came to deny the reality of witchcraft. His reputation was only resurrected when a vigorous reappraisal of witchcraft in seventeenth-century New England occurred by such scholars as Chadwick Hansen, Paul Boyer, Stephen Nissenbaum, and John Putnam Demos.

The whole magical supernatural world present during the Salem trials is also evident in the consideration of **alchemy.** For example, while condemning witchcraft, Cotton Mather praised John Winthrop, Jr., and his son Wait Still Winthrop (1642–1717), both prominent citizens and both also alchemists. While governor of Connecticut, the elder Winthrop conducted alchemical experiments in the governor's mansion. He built one of the largest alchemical libraries in America and on occasion hosted visiting alchemists from Europe. Both the Winthrops joined the debates then going on in medical circles over the introduction of nonorganic substances, i.e., chemical preparations, for the treatment of illnesses.

The Occult in the Nineteenth Century

Post-Revolutionary America is extremely rich in occult history as evidenced in the writings of Spiritualist, magical, and metaphysical teachers such as **Thomas Lake Harris, Andrew Jackson Davis, William Q. Judge, Mary Baker Eddy,** and the people who followed them into Spiritualism, Theosophy, and Christian Science. Hundreds of occult and metaphysical movements have either originated in, or found a home in the United States from the nineteenth century onward.

The **Church of Jesus Christ of Latter-day Saints** (the Mormons) had undoubtedly a semi-occult origin. Its founder, Joseph Smith, Jr. claimed to discover tablets of gold upon which was engraved the new revelation, the *Book of Mormon,* which he translated by a process similar to modern **channeling.** Smith also tied the church loosely to **Freemasonry.**

Theosophy became firmly rooted in America through the efforts of William Q. Judge, and his successor **Katherine B. Tingley,** the founder of the theosophical colony at Point Loma, California. In recent years, however, the American society formerly led by Judge declined and most theosophists now adhere to the **Theosophical Society** headquartered in Adyar, India.

Modern American Occultism and Parapsychology

Throughout the twentieth century, old and new religious movements have appeared, and a few have flourished. Ceremonial magic and Neo-pagan Witchcraft have been imported from England and both have enjoyed their greatest success in the United States. One noteworthy aspect of the American scene has been the association of revivalist evangelism with paranormal **healing,** an association begun in the holiness movement but finding its greatest expression in **Pentecostalism.**

Interestingly enough, Spiritualism (which had grown from the Hydesville rappings association with the **Fox Sisters** in the nineteenth century) took a firmer hold in Great Britain, Europe, and Brazil, than in America. While Spiritualism swept across America, claimed many cultural leaders, and developed into a large organizational structure, it remained a relatively minuscule movement in the midst of a large population. It did become, as in Europe, the subject of a much public scrutiny, but declined in the wake of the discovery of widespread fraud. However, the **National Spiritualist Association of Churches,** founded in 1893, still has more than a hundred affiliated congregations.

The emergence of Spiritualism eventually led in 1885 to the formation of the **American Society for Psychical Research** as a branch of the London-based **Society for Psychical Research.** It investigated the mediumship and the phenomena associated with that movement over the next several generations and included in its leadership a number of outstanding scientists including **William James, Walter Franklin Prince, James H. Hyslop** and **Hereward Carrington.** In 1930, American biologist/psychologist **J. B. Rhine** gave a new direction to the whole of psychical research as director of the Parapsychology Laboratory at Duke University, North Carolina. Whereas psychical research was largely concerned with the phenomena associated with Spiritualist mediums, Rhine and his associates moved research from the séance-room into the laboratory and, under systematic control conditions, began testing the unknown or "extra-sensory" faculties (**ESP** for short) of ordinary individuals.

The new term, **parapsychology,** with its experimental methodology has now largely superseded the earlier approach of psychical research. Organizations also founded in the United States to pursue parapsychological research include the **Psychical Research Foundation** and the **Parapsychology Foundation** in New York, linked with the work and paranormal talents of **Eileen Garrett.** Rhine also led in the foundation of the **Parapsychological Foundation,** now the international professional association of parapsychologists.

At a popular level, belief in **divination,** especially **astrology,** has experienced a steady increase throughout the twentieth century, and is now widespread. More than 20 percent of the population express some acceptance of belief in astrology.

A major occult explosion took place in the 1960s, marked by an increased interest in psychic and occult phenomenon. This phenomenon merged into the New Age movement of the 1970s and 1980s, and earned a new respectability for those involved in the psychic movement, despite the concurrent interest in the more sinister aspects of occultism symbolized by the new Satanism.

The 1960s revival built upon earlier, if less intense, waves of interest, most notably those occurring during the 1920s and 30s. These earlier activities were of specialized coterie interest in line with the more structured society of the period, constituting a kind of occult underground of the kind described in books like *Witchraft: Its Power in the World Today* by **William Seabrook** (1940). The witch craze of the colonial period had long ago died out, although magical practices and beliefs could be found throughout the country's rural areas and in the poorer sections of the urban centers. The last of the witchcraft trials was held in the early eighteenth century, when there were a few cases in Virginia. The twentieth-century revival of witchcraft and Satanism owed more to the freedom of the cities and the new climate of religious and cultural pluralism of the post-World War II era, undoubtedly strengthened by the widespread use of psychedelic drugs.

One of the most widespread popular preoccupations has been the phenomena of flying saucers or unidentified flying objects (**UFOs**), mysterious aerial objects of a disk-like shape. Such sightings had been reported for many centuries, but during the emerging space age of the 1950s, the idea that these UFOs might be spacecraft from other planets captured the popular imagination. In addition, many individuals (who in earlier generations would have become Spiritualist mediums) claimed to have met the occupants of these spacecrafts, taken trips in their crafts, and/or received psychic communications from **space intelligences.** With many thousands of claimed sightings, UFO groups sprang up all over the United States and interest spread to other countries of the world. At its lowest level, the flying saucer phenomenon has become something of a new mythology, comparable with other modern preoccupations such as **near-death experiences.** At a more responsible level, there remains a residuum of inexplicable phenomena that deserves closer investigation.

The emergence of a post-Enlightenment occult belief has been opposed at every level by leaders in the scientific community. The ongoing controversy has most recently led to the formation of the **Committee for the Scientific Investigation of Claims of the Paranormal,** which is devoted to debunking occult and related claims and publishes a journal, *Skeptical Inquirer.*

The United States remains home to a vital popular interest in matters psychical and occult. *Fate,* the oldest of the occult-related periodicals, is but one of hundreds. The occult forms the basis for numerous books, movies, and television shows, and provides the substance for hundreds of religious groups and spiritual organizations, all of which provide the Committee for the Scientific Investigation of the Claims of the Paranormal with an endless agenda.

Sources:

Berger, Arthur S., and Joyce Berger. *The Encyclopedia of Parapsychology and Psychical Research.* New York: Paragon House, 1991.

Boyer, Paul, and Stephen Nissenbaum. *Salem Possessed.* Cambridge, Mass.: Harvard University Press, 1974.

———. *Salem-Village Witchcraft.* Belmont, Calif.: Wadsworth Publishing, 1972.

Brinton, Daniel G. *The Myths of the New World.* Leypoldt and Holt, 1868.

Calef, Robert. *More Wonders of the Invisible World.* London, 1700.

Christopher, Milbourne. *ESP, Seers and Psychics.* New York: Thomas Y. Crowell, 1970.

Clark, Jerome. *The Emergence of a Phenomenon: UFOs from the Beginning through 1959. The UFO Encyclopedia.* Vol. 2. Detroit, Mich.: Omnigraphics, 1992.

Demos, John Putnam. *Entertaining Satan: Witchcraft and the Culture of Early New England.* New York: Oxford University Press, 1982.

Ebon, Martin, ed. *The Signet Handbook of Parapsychology.* New York: New American Library, 1978.

Ellwood, Robert S., Jr. *Religious and Spiritual Groups in Modern America.* Englewood Cliffs, N.J.: Prentice-Hall, 1973.

Freelands, Nat. *The Occult Explosion.* New York: G. P. Putnam's Sons/London: Michael Joseph, 1972.

Fritscher, John. *Popular Witchcraft: Straight from the Witch's Mouth.* Bowling Green, Ohio: Bowling Green University Popular Press, 1972.

Godwin, John. *Occult America.* Garden City, N.Y.: Doubleday, 1972.

Hansen, Chadwick. *Witchcraft at Salem.* New York: George Braziller, 1969. Reprint, New York: New American Library, 1970.

Hohman, Johann George. *Der lange vernorgene Freund.* Reading, Pa., 1819. English edition as *The Long Lost Friend.* Harrisburg, Pa., 1850.

Jack, Alex. *The New Age Dictionary.* Brookline Village, Mass.: Kanthaka Press, 1976.

Jacobs, David M. *The UFO Controversy in America.* Bloomington, Ind.: Indiana University Press, 1975. Reprint, New York: New American Library, 1976.

Khalsa, Parmatma Singh, ed. *Spiritual Community Guide No. 4,* California: Spiritual Community Publications, 1979.

Kittredge, G. L. *Witchcraft in Old and New England.* Cambridge, Mass.: Harvard University Press, 1929.

La Barre, Weston. *Ghost Dance: The Origins of Religion.* Garden City, N.Y.: Doubleday, 1971.

Mather, Cotton. *Wonders of the Invisible World.* Boston, 1693. Reprint, Anherst, Wisc.: Amherst Press, n.d.

Mather, Increase. *Cases of Conscience Concerning Evil Spirits.* Boston, 1693.

Melton, J. Gordon, and Isotta Poggi. *Magic, Witchcraft, and Paganism in America: A Bibliography.* New York: Garland Publishing, 1992.

Mooney, James. "The Ghost-Dance Religion." In *Annual Report of Bureau of American Ethnology.* 14, 2, (1893).

Needleman, Jacob. *The New Religions.* Garden City, N.Y.: Doubleday, 1970.

Rhine, J. B. and Associates. *Parapsychology from Duke to FRNM.* Durham, N.C.: Parapsychology Press, 1965.

Sladek, John. *The New Apocrypha: A Guide to Strange Sciences & Occult Beliefs.* New York: Stein and Day, 1974.

Starkey, Marion L. *The Devil in Massachusetts.* Garden City, N.Y.: Doubleday, 1952. Reprint, New York: Time, 1949.

Upham, Charles W. *Salem Witchcraft with an Account of Salem Village and a History of Opinion on Witchcraft and Kindred Subjects.* 2 Vols. Boston, 1867. Reprint, New York: Ungar, 1959.

White, Rhea A., and Laura A. Dale. *Parapsychology: Sources of Information.* Metheun, N.J.: Scarecrow Press, 1973.

American Academy of Astrologians

An early attempt to bring together the more intellectually and research-oriented astrologers for regular sessions at which serious scientific and philosophical discussions would be held. It was fashioned after some of the early eighteenth-century academies in Europe. The prime mover in the academy's formation was **John Hazelrigg,** a New York astrologer, who with three colleagues called the first meeting, held in New York in 1916. It was limited to 30 members. The membership was self-perpetuating and elected new members to replace any who died or withdrew. Members had to be citizens of the United States. Although most of the members came from the New York City metropolitan area, some came from around the country, such as Inez Perry (Los Angeles), **Llewellyn George** (Los Angeles), and J. U. Giesy (Salt Lake City).

The academy flourished through the 1920s. Hazelrigg, one of the more capable scholars to take up consideration of **astrology,** was inclined toward the occult and for several years issued a yearbook that included some of the more esoteric papers presented by the academy's members.

Sources:

Hartman, William C. *Who's Who in Occultism, New Thought, Psychism, and Spiritualism.* Jamaica, N.Y.: Occult Press, 1927.

Hazelrigg, John. *Astrosophical Principles.* New York: Hermetic Publishing, 1917.

Yearbook of the American Academy of Astrologians. 2 vols. New York: Hermetic Publishing, 1917, 1918.

American Association—Electronic Voice Phenomena

The American Association—Electronic Voice Phenomena was founded in 1972 to collect objective evidence of **survival** after death. It describes itself as "a metaphysical organization interested in spiritual evolvement." Research is primarily centered around what are called **Raudive voices,** voices that seem to appear spontaneously on recording tapes and purport to be the communications of the dead. Such voices, first noticed in the late 1960s, became a well-known phenomenon following the 1971 English publication of Latvian psychologist **Konstantin Raudive**'s book, *Breakthrough,* in which he claimed hundreds of such contacts with the deceased. The association formed in direct response to the popularity of Raudive's findings. The group enjoyed great popularity through the 1980s and by the end of the decade had approximately 200 members. The association supports conferences and publishes a quarterly newsletter. It may be contacted at 726 Dill Rd., Severna Park, MD 21146.

Sources:

Ellis, D. T. *The Mediumship of the Tape Recorder.* Pulborough, U.K.: The Author, 1978.

Raudive, K. *Breakthrough.* New York: Taplinger, 1971.

American Association of Meta-Science

Organization founded in 1977 to study, explore, and observe paranormal phenomena, including **UFOs,** to develop and use instruments to detect and stimulate "subtle, unseen energies," and assist members and others in developing psychic and spiritual abilities. It aims to provide a channel for bringing paranormal discoveries into everyday life. It publishes the quarterly journal *Specula.* Address: P.O. Box 1182, Huntsville, AL 35807.

American Astrological Society

Among the earliest attempts to form a national association of astrologers and astrological organizations, the American Astrological Society was founded on September 22, 1915, with the goal of championing the cause of **astrology** among the public in North America. It had a five-member board. For many years Gustave W. Ekstrome of Minnepolis, Minnesota, was its corresponding secretary. Members came from across the United States and Canada. The society survived into the 1950s.

Sources:

Hartman, William C. *Who's Who in Occultism, New Thought, Psychism, and Spiritualism.* Jamaica, N.Y.: Occult Press, 1927.

American Astrology (Magazine)

Founded in 1923 by Paul G. Clancy, this monthly magazine for general readers is the longest-running astrological periodical in the United States. Each issue includes articles, reflections on world news events, day-by-day guides for signs, and horoscopes of public figures. Address: Starlog, 475 Park Ave., New York, NY 10016.

American Dowser (Magazine)

Quarterly publication for members of the **American Society of Dowsers,** a long-established organization concerned with water witching, discovery of lost articles or persons, and related parapsychological phenomena. Address: The American Society of Dowsers, Danville, VT 05828.

American Federation of Astrologers

Founded in 1938 as a federation of local associations and individuals in 20 countries interested in the advancement of astrology through research and education. The association conducts examinations of individuals interested in **astrology,** maintains a specialized library, publishes educational and research texts as well as the monthly *AFA Bulletin,* and sponsors an annual convention. Address: P.O. Box 22040, Tempe, AZ 85282.

American Folklore Society

Long-established American society, founded in 1888, concerned with the scholarly study, collection, and publication of folklore throughout the world. It holds an annual convention and publishes the quarterly *Journal of American Folklore* and other studies as well as the *American Folklore Newsletter* (six issues per year). Address: American Folklore Society, Maryland State Arts Council, 15 West Mulberry St., Baltimore, MD 21201.

American Healers Association

Founded April 1977 in association with the **Psychical Research Foundation.** The association exists to upgrade the status of healers, educate the public in availability of unconventional healers, provide training courses in healing, investigate and certify reliable healers, and protect legitimate healers from the risk of legal harassment. Address: 2015 Erwin Rd., Durham, NC.

American Institute for Scientific Research

The American Institute for Scientific Research was established in 1904 by **James Hervey Hyslop** (1854–1920), a former professor of logic and ethics at Columbia University. Hyslop was drawn into **psychical research** in the 1880s and within a short time was stripped of his skepticism and came to believe that such research was actually probing the afterlife. Shortly after the turn of the century, his health failed and Hyslop was forced to resign his university appointment. He then turned his attention to psychical research full time and founded the institute as an instrument to raise money for psychical research. He established two branches, one that focused on abnormal psychology and one that centered on psychical research. He received the immediate support of such scientists as psychologist **William James** and physiologist **Charles Richet.**

In 1905, the president of the **American Society for Psychical Research** (ASPR), Richard Hodgson, died, as did his society shortly thereafter. Previously the ASPR had existed as a branch of the British **Society for Psychical Research,** but in 1906 the ASPR was reborn through the psychical research branch of the American Institute for Scientific Research. Soon afterward Hyslop discontinued the institute and it survived as a new, independent ASPR. For the rest of his life Hyslop headed the new organization, through which he was able to pursue his primary interest in mediumship and its possible use for contacting the dead.

Sources:

Berger, Arthur S., and Joyce Berger. *The Encyclopedia of Parapsychology and Psychical Research.* New York: Paragon House, 1991.

Hyslop, James H. *Contact with the Other World.* New York: Century, 1919.

———. *Life after Death: Problems of the Future Life and its Nature.* New York: E. P. Dutton, 1918.

American Museum of Magic

Established in 1977 at 107 E. Michigan, Marshall, Michigan, by Robert Lund, a collector of books, movies, recordings, posters, and apparatus associated with conjuring **magic** and magicians. The collection includes some of the apparatus of the great magician **Harry Houdini.** The museum also issues a periodic newsletter. Postal address: P.O. Box 5, Marshall, MI 49068.

American National Institute for Psychical Research

Publishers of **VISIONS,** monthly magazine of psychic phenomena and related subjects. Address: 30423 Canwood St., No. 125, Agoura Hills, CA 91301.

American Parapsychological Research Foundation

Organization founded in 1971 to encourage interest in the expanding field of parapsychology, to promote an interchange of knowledge between the public and those in the field, to bridge the gap between academic parapsychology and the experimental ESP participation among laymen, and to stimulate interest in scientific research and encourage public involvement in future research. The foundation offers a complete course in parapsychology, including basic theories, principles, and histories of phenomena involving telepathy, clairvoyance, hypnosis, and sensory awareness, and psychometry, psychokinesis, and the human aura. It maintains a consultation and advisory service and awards a certificate after completion of the prescribed course of study in the advancement of psychic research and human understanding. Address: Box 5395, 15446 Sherman Way, Sherman Oaks, CA 91413.

American Psychical Institute and Laboratory

A short-lived parapsychology facility organized in New York in 1920 by **Hereward Carrington** for specialized research. It existed for two years. In 1933 it was reorganized and incorporated at 20 West 58th Street, New York. Carrington became its director, and his wife, Marie Sweet Carrington, became secretary. A long list of scientific men of international repute made up the advisory council. The institute published *Bulletins.*

American Psychical Society

Founded in Boston in 1882. It issued seven quarterly journals, then ceased after two years of existence.

American Society for Psychical Research (ASPR)

Founded in 1885 in Boston, Massachusetts, on the initiative of Prof. **W. F. Barrett.** Its initial officers included president Prof. Simon Newcomb, secretary N. D. C. Hodges, and four vice-presidents, Profs. Stanley Hall, George S. Fullerton, Edward C. Pickering, and Dr. Charles S. Minot. Support was difficult to maintain in the controversial field, even with the strong support of **William James,** and, in 1889, for financial considerations, then-president S. P. Langley affiliated the ASPR to the English **Society for Psychical Research.** The research work of the American Society for Psychical Research was conducted by Dr. **Richard Hodgson** from 1887 until his death in 1905. The society, never strong, was dissolved the following year and continued as a branch of **James Hervey Hyslop**'s **American Institute for Scientific Research.** It was the only active part of Hyslop's institute to develop a program.

When Hyslop died in 1920, the ASPR regained its independent status, and Dr. **Walter Franklin Prince** became the society's director of research and editor of its publications. He carried on a variety of investigations prior to his observations of **Mina S. Crandon,** better known as "Margery." The ASPR board was strongly behind Margery, but Prince believed her to be a **fraud.** When **J. Malcolm Bird,** former assistant editor of the *Scientific American* and author of several items favorable to Margery, was appointed co-research officer with Prince in 1925, Prince was infuriated. He resigned, and with him resigned other disaffected members, including **Gardner Murphy, William McDougall, Elwood Worcester,** and **Lydia Allison,** who together founded the rival **Boston Society for Psychic Research.**

Bird served as research officer for the ASPR, but he suddenly resigned from his position in 1930. Some time later it came to light that he had second thoughts on Margery. He had submitted a confidential report to the board suggesting that Margery had approached him to become a confidant in producing some phenomena for magician **Harry Houdini.** Subsequently, Bird disappeared along with his last manuscript on Margery. Bird was succeeded by **B. K. Thorogood** (1930–39).

Following the merger of the Boston SPR back into the ASPR in 1941, George Hyslop, the son of J. H. Hyslop, became president. Since 1925 he had been a lone voice decrying the slippage of research standards, and he demanded the full exposure of Margery's fraudulent activity. He reestablished the standards demanded during his father's years of leadership, then was succeeded by Gardner Murphy, who served as president of the ASPR for 20 years and was a dominating figure. A distinguished psychologist, Murphy brought new prestige to the organization and recruited talented researchers to carry out its program. During this period, laboratory parapsychology as developed by **J. B. Rhine** at Duke University emerged as the cutting edge of psychic investigations, and the **Parapsychology Association** was established (1957) as the major professional association for scholars engaged in psychic research.

More recently, the ASPR has remained one of the stable organizations in American psychic research and the organizational home of many leading lights in the field, including **Gertrude Schmeidler, Rhea White,** and **Karlis Osis.** Publication of the society's *Journal* and *Proceedings* commenced in 1907 and has continued uninterruptedly to the present.

The nonprofit society located in New York City exists "to advance the understanding of phenomena alleged to be paranormal: telepathy, clairvoyance, precognition, psychokinesis, and related occurrences that are not at present thought to be explicable in terms of physical, psychological and biological theories." In the years since World War II, the society has become concerned with the need to integrate such subjects as paranormal phenomena with a wide range of behavioral and physical sciences, which has demanded major revisions of theoretical constructs.

The ASPR has an active research department and houses a large library for the members use. There are no special requirements for membership, and the society welcomes members of the general public and the professions, as well as active researchers and students. Membership does not imply acceptance of any particular phenomena. Address: 5 West 73rd St., New York, NY 10023.

Sources:

Moore, R. Laurence. *In Search of White Crows.* New York: Oxford University Press, 1977.

Rogo, D. Scott. *Parapsychology: A Century of Inquiry.* New York: Dell, 1975.

American Society of Dowsers

A nonprofit corporation founded in Vermont in 1961 to disseminate knowledge of **dowsing** (water witching, discovery of lost articles or persons, and related parapsychological phenomena), development of its skills, and recognition for its achievements. The society issues the quarterly magazine the *American Dowser.* Address: American Society of Dowsers, Danville, VT 05828. Christopher Bird, a trustee of the society, has written a comprehensive survey of the practice.

Sources:

Bird, Christopher. *The Divining Hand.* New York: E. P. Dutton, 1979.

Stark, Erwin E. *A History of Dowsing and Energy Relationships.* North Hollywood, Calif.: BAC, 1978.

Wyman, Walker D. *Witching for Water, Oil, Pipes, and Precious Minerals.* River Falls: University of Wisconsin Press, 1977.

American Yoga Association

Originally founded in 1971 as the Light of Yoga Society by Alice Christensen, a disciple of Swami Rama of Hardwar, India (1900–1972) (not to be confused with Swami Rama of the **Himalayan International Institute of Yoga Science and Philosophy**). Swami Rama left his home in the 1920s to practice **yoga** and wander through the Himalayas. After three decades as a recluse, he settled in Hardwar as a yoga teacher.

Alice Christensen's yoga practice began with a vision of bright light that she experienced in 1953. She subsequently corresponded for many years with Swami **Sivananda** (1887–1963), founder of the **Divine Life Society** in Rishikesh, India. The year after Swami Sivananda's death, she met her own guru, Swami Rama, and spent a year in India studying with him. After he appointed her his representative in the West, Christensen returned to the U.S. in 1965 to lecture and teach yoga and to gather a group of students.

The Light of Yoga Society transmitted the teachings of Swami Rama, who simplified the complex wisdom of the **Vedanta** and developed it as a practical tool for Western practitioners. The society's program started with **hatha yoga** asanas and **meditation,** both to be practiced daily. Other practices recommended were vegetarianism, the restrained use of sex, the practice of *ahimsa* (nonviolence), and the avoidance of alcohol, tobacco, and drugs. During the life of Swami Rama, he guided eleven centers in India, Australia, and the U.S.

In 1982 the society was renamed the American Yoga Association, and since 1983 directs the headquarter's center in Cleveland Heights, Ohio; a second center in Sarasota, Florida; and two centers in India. Christensen married former student David Rankin and wrote two books with him. The address of the American Yoga Association is: 2134 Lee Rd., Cleveland Heights, OH 44118.

Sources:

Christensen, Alice, and David Rankin. *The Light of Yoga Society Beginner's Manual.* Cleveland Heights, Ohio: Om Ram Productions, 1972. Revised edition as: Christensen, Alice. *The American Yoga Association Beginner's Manual.* New York: Simon & Schuster, 1987.

American Zen College

A **Zen** center derived from the eclectic Chogye Buddhist sect of Korea and the activities of Zen Master Gosung Shin. Shin had been abbot of several large temples in southeastern Korea when he was invited to continue the work begun by Bishop Seo Kyung-Bo, who had previously established the World Zen Center at Spruce Run Mountain, Virginia.

Shin first came to the U.S. in 1970 as a student at Harvard University. In 1971 he moved to Philadelphia and taught religion at Lehigh University. He was offered space for a Zen center at Easton, Pennsylvania, and founded the Hui-Neng Zen Temple. After several years the Temple outgrew its space, and Shin moved to Woodhull, New York, where he established the Kwan Yin Zen Center.

Continued growth led to the closing of the Woodhull center and the creation of two new centers: the Zen Center of Washington (1977), which primarily serves Koreans living in the Washington, D.C. area, and the Seneca Lake Zen Center (1978) at 16815 Germantown Rd., Route 18, Germantown, MD 20767. The name "American Zen College" was adopted as an inclusive designation in the early 1980s. The college publishes the journal *Buddha World.*

Sources:

Shin, Gosung. *Zen Teachings of Emptiness.* Washington, D.C.: American Zen College Press, 1982.

Amethyst

Gemstone believed to have occult properties, described by sixteenth-century writer Camillus Leonardus as "reckoned among the purple and transparent stones, mixed with a violet colour, emitting rosy sparkles." The Indian variety is the most precious. When made into drinking cups or bound on the navel, it was claimed to prevent drunkenness. It was also believed to sharpen the wit, turn away evil thoughts, and give a knowledge of the future in dreams. Drunk in a potion, it was thought to expel poison and render the barren fruitful. In ancient times it was frequently engraved with the head of Bacchus and was a favorite with Roman women.

Amiante

A species of fireproof stone, which **Pliny** and the ancient demonologists recommended as excellent against the charms of magic.

Amityville Horror, The

A well-publicized case of a modern haunting that turned out to be an elaborate hoax. On November 13, 1974, a large colonial house at 112 Ocean Ave., Amityville, Long Island, New York, was the scene of a mass murder. Twenty-four-year old Ronald DeFeo shot his parents, two brothers, and two sisters with a high-powered rifle. At his trial, DeFeo claimed that he had been obsessed by voices who told him to kill, and his attorney entered a plea of insanity. The plea was not accepted, and DeFeo was sentenced to six consecutive life terms.

In view of this horrific tragedy, the spacious Dutch colonial house was offered for sale at a relatively low price, and was purchased by George Lee Lutz of Long Island. He and his wife, Kathleen, and three children moved into their new home on December 18, 1975. They stayed in the house, which had been named "High Hopes" by a previous owner, only 28 days, then fled in terror, claiming they had been plagued by spirits. The hauntings reported were many and varied. Kathy Lutz was levitated one night and her face transformed into the appearance of an aged hag. One of the children talked to the spirit form of an enormous pig named Jodie. There were plagues of flies in the dead of winter, unearthly loud voices, music and footsteps, unpleasant smells, and a green slime that oozed through ceiling, walls, and keyholes. A Catholic priest who attempted to bless the house was commanded by a mysterious voice shouting "Get out!" After the Lutzes left the house, various mediums held seances but became ill afterward.

Mrs. Lutz's story to the press was analyzed on a truth-detecting Psychological Stress Evaluator of a type used in legal proceedings as court evidence. The investigator claimed that the results indicated Mrs. Lutz was telling the truth or what she believed to be the truth. The story of the Amityville hauntings was the subject of a telecast on Channel 5 *Ten O'Clock News* on February 5, 1976, with reporter Steve Bauman. The story was also told at length by author Jay Anson in his book *The Amityville Horror: A True Story* (1977). Anson's book became a best-seller, with paperback editions in the U.S. and Britain, and was turned into a highly successful movie with six sequels.

It now appears that the Lutzes abandoned the house, not because of any hauntings, but because they realized that they had gotten in over their heads financially. They abandoned their furniture when they left because it was so worn it was not worth moving. The idea of the haunting seems to have come from DeFeo's attorney's attempt to have DeFeo's conviction overturned. When insanity proved unacceptable, he tried to blame the murders on the voices.

When Anson began his book on the story, he was not allowed into the house and he never interviewed the Lutzes. He had only several tapes they had made from which to work. He seems to have borrowed heavily from his own screenplay of *The Exorcist* to fill in the gaps and make an entertaining story. Many of the strange events mentioned in the book simply never occurred: there was no levitation, no marching band, no door torn off its hinges, no tracks in the snow (as it had not snowed during the Lutzes' time in the house), no pig's face, etc. In the court hearing in September 1979 on the DeFeo case, the Lutzes admitted under oath that almost everything in the book was fiction. Because of the powerful impact of the movies, few are aware of the fictional nature of the story, which was presented to the public as fact.

The Amityville house was subsequently occupied by new owners, who stated that there were no unusual phenomena whatsoever except extensive harassment from tourists. They sued the Lutzes, the publisher Prentice-Hall, and Jay Anson for $1.1 million damages. (See also **Poltergeist**)

Sources:

Anson, Jay. *The Amityville Horror: A True Story.* Englewood Cliffs, N.J.: Prentice Hall, 1977.

Morris, Robert L. "The Amityville Horror." *The Skeptical Inquirer* Vol. 2, no. 2 (Spring/Summer 1978): 95–102.

Stein, Gordon. *Encyclopedia of Hoaxes.* Detroit: Gale Research, 1993.

Amniomancy

Divination by means of the **caul,** or membrane that sometimes envelopes the head of a child at birth. From an inspection of this caul, wise women predicted the sort of future the baby would have. If it were red, happy days were in store for the child, or if lead-colored, he would have misfortunes.

Sources:

Waite, Arthur Edward. *The Occult Sciences.* 1891. Reprint, Secaucus, N.J.: University Books, 1974.

Amon

According to an ancient **grimoire,** Amon is the great and powerful marquis of the infernal empire. He is represented as a wolf with a serpent's tail, vomiting flame. When he appears in human form, his head resembles that of a large owl with canine teeth. He is the strongest of the princes of the demons, knows the past and the future, and can reconcile friends who have quarreled. He commands 40 legions.

AMORC See Ancient and Mystical Order of the Rosicrucians

Amoymon

According to an ancient **grimoire,** Amoymon is one of the four kings of Hades, of which the eastern part falls to his share. He may be invoked in the morning from nine o'clock till midday and in the evening from three o'clock till six. He has been identified with **Amaimon** (or **Amaymon**). **Asmodeus** is his lieutenant and first prince of his dominions.

Amphiaraus

A famous soothsayer of classical mythology, son of Oicles and Hypermnestra. He hid himself so that he might not have to go to the war of Thebes, because he had foreseen that he should die there. This indeed happened, but he came to life again. A temple was raised to him in Attica, near a sacred fountain by which he had left Hades. He healed the sick by showing them in a dream the remedies they must use. He also founded many oracles. After they sacrificed, those who consulted the oracle slept under a sheep skin and dreamed a dream, which usually found plenty of interpreters after the event. Amphiaraus was an adept in the art of explaining **dreams.** Some prophecies in verse, which are no longer extant, were attributed to him.

Amulets

The charm, amulet, or mascot, derives from **fetishism,** the belief of people that a small object or fetish could contain a spirit. Amulets are said to be of two classes: those which are worn as (1) fetishes, i.e., the dwelling place of spiritual entities who are active on behalf of the wearer; or (2) mascots to ward off bad luck or such influences as the **evil eye.** The amulet, a protective device, is thus distinguished from a **talisman,** a magical charm used to accomplish some end.

There is little doubt that charms were worn by prehistoric peoples, because objects similar in appearance and general description to amulets have been discovered in neolithic tombs. The ancient Egyptians possessed a bewildering variety of amulets, worn by both the living and the dead. Indeed, among the latter, every part of the body had an amulet sacred to itself. These were, as a rule, evolved from various organs of the gods; for example, the eye of Isis, the backbone of Osiris, and so forth. Among savage and semicivilized peoples, the amulet usually took the form of necklaces, bracelets, or anklets, and where belief in **witchcraft** and the evil eye was strong, the faith in these and in charms was always most intense.

Stones, teeth, claws, shells, coral, and symbolic emblems were favored amulets. These item were seen to carry specific characteristics of the animal from which they were taken or to correspond to reality specific to the culture. For example, the desert goat is a sure-footed animal; accordingly, certain Malay tribes carried its tongue as a powerful amulet against falling. Beads resembling teeth were often hung around the necks of Kaffir children in Africa to assist them in teething, and the incisor teeth of the beaver were frequently placed around the necks of Native American girls to promote industriousness.

Certain plants and minerals were believed to indicate by their external character the diseases for which nature intended them as remedies. Thus the euphrasia, or eyebright, was supposed to be good for the eyes because it contains a black pupil-like spot, while the blood-stone was employed for stopping the flow of blood from a wound.

When prehistoric implements, such as arrowheads, were found, they were thought by the peasants of the locality to be of great virtue as amulets. Some light is cast on this custom by the fact that stone arrowheads were in use among medieval British witches. But in most countries they were thought to descend from the sky and were therefore kept to preserve people and cattle from lightning.

Certain roots, which have the shape of snakes, were kept by Malays to protect them against snakebite. This correspondence of root to animal likeness is known as the doctrine of signatures.

The Celts used many kinds of amulets, such as the symbolic wheel of the sun god found frequently in France and Great Britain, pebbles, amulets of the teeth of the wild boar, and pieces of amber. The well-known serpent's egg of the Druids was also probably an amulet of the priests. Indian amulets are numerous, and in Buddhist countries their use was universal, especially where that religion had degenerated. In northern Buddhist countries, it was common to wear an amulet around the neck. These generally represented the leaf of the sacred fig tree and were made in the form of a box that contained a scrap of sacred writing, prayer, or a little picture. Women of position in Tibet wore a chatelaine containing a charm or charms, and the universal amulet of the Tibetan Buddhist priests is the thunderbolt, supposed to have fallen direct from Indra's heaven. This is usually imitated in bronze or other metal and is used for exorcising evil spirits.

Many Muslims wear amulets, and it is said that the prophet Mohammed believed in the evil eye. The Koran is sometimes carried as an amulet, or extracts from it are copied out for that purpose. *Suras* 113 and 114 are directed against **witchcraft.** Other powerful charms for amulets include the names and attributes of gods, the names of the *suras* in the Koran, names of prophets, planets, **angels,** and **magic** squares.

Amulets were also widespread among Jewish people, particularly from the seventeenth to the nineteenth centuries. The phylacteries still worn in certain rituals are believed to be a protection against evil. One, derived from the legend of **Lilith,** bearing the name of three angels, is given to babies to protect them from her. In Jewish folklore, names of God, biblical verses and names of angels were regarded to be powerful amulets. Such amulets have been copied by non-Jewish occultists and used in ritual magic.

With the magical revival of the nineteenth century and the belief in occult powers being directed to various goals by magical practitioners, amulets once again came into widespread use. They were a necessary side effect of the development of talismanic magic, an important part of magical practice featured in the writings of **Francis Barrett** and **Éliphas Lévi.** Today, magicians and Wiccans learn the preparation of amulets as part of their basic magical training.

Sources:

Budge, E. A. W. *Amulets and Talismans.* New Hyde Park, N.Y.: University Books, 1961.

Lippman, Deborah, and Paul Colin. *How to Make Amulets, Charms, and Talismans.* New York: M. Evans, 1974.

Pavitt, William T., and Kate Pavitt. *The Book of Talismans, Amulets, and Zodiacal Gems.* Detroit: Gale Research, 1972.

Amy

According to an ancient **grimoire,** Amy is Grand President of Hades and one of the princes of the infernal monarchy. He appears there enveloped with flame, but on Earth, he is in human form. He teaches the secrets of astrology and liberal arts. He reveals to those who possess his favor the hiding place of treasures guarded by demons. Thirty-six of the infernal legions are under his command. The fallen angels acknowledge his orders, and he hopes that, at the end of 200,000 years, he shall return to heaven to occupy the seventh throne.

Anachitis

A stone used in divination to call up spirits from water; another stone, called synochitis, obliged them to remain while they were interrogated.

Anamelech

An obscure demon, the bearer of ill news. In ancient times he was worshiped at Sepharvaün, a town of the Assyrians. He always revealed himself in the figure of a quail. His name, it is said, signified a "good king," and some authorities declare that this demon was the Moon, as Andramelech is the Sun.

Anancithidus

The sixteenth-century physician Camillus Leonardus described this as "a necromantic stone, whose virtue is to call up evil spirits and ghosts."

Ananda Ashram

Founded to promote the teachings of Dr. Rammurti S. Mishra, the ashram presented **yoga** in a modern context. Mishra was born in India in a Brahmin family and studied traditional yoga teachings along with his professional vocation as endocrinologist, neurosurgeon, and psychiatrist, practicing in India, Canada, and the United States. He is the author of *Fundamentals of Yoga,* a reliable guide to hatha yoga and yoga philosophy, first published in 1959, which has gone through a number of editions. He has also published *The Textbook of Yoga Psychology: A New Translation and Interpretation of Patanjali's Yoga Sutras for Meaningful Application in All Modern Psychologic Disciplines.* Mishra traveled widely, teaching a synthesis of traditional hatha, karma, and raja yoga in terms acceptable to modern sciences. Ananda Ashram is a branch of ICSA (Inter Cosmic Spiritual Association), with branches in various countries. The ashram may be contacted at RD 3, Box 141, Monroe, NY 10950.

Sources:

Mishra, Rammurti. *Dynamics of Yoga-Mudras and Five Successive Suggestions for Meditation.* Pleasant Valley, N.Y.: Kriya Press, 1967.

———. *Fundamentals of Yoga.* New York: Lancer Books, 1969. Reprint, *Yoga Sutras: The Textbook of Yoga Psychology.* New York, 1973.

———. *Isha Upanishad.* Dayton, Ohio: Yoga Society of Dayton, 1962.

———. *Self Analysis and Self Knowledge.* Lakemont, Ga.: CSA Press, 1978.

Ananda Church of God-Realization

An international Hindu group formed by J. Donald Walters (also known as Swami Kriyananda). The church has its base at the Ananda World Brotherhood Village (formerly known as the Ananda Cooperative Village). Ananda is based upon the teachings of **Paramahansa Yogananda,** with whom Walters studied. After Yogananda's death in 1952, Walters served as a minister in the **Self-Realization Fellowship** (SRF), the organization Yogananda had founded, and eventually became SRF's vice president. He left SRF in 1962 and in 1968 founded Ananda Village in the Sierra Mountains in response to Yogananda's admonition to "Cover the earth with world-brotherhood colonies, demonstrating that simplicity of living plus high thinking lead to the greatest happiness."

Kriyananda emerged as a talented leader of a successful cooperative colony, the author of numerous books, musician and composer, and **yoga** teacher. He followed the system of kriya yoga taught by Yogananda, the exact content of which is taught only to initiated disciples.

Branch communities are located along the West Coast of the United States with an additional community in Italy. Approximately 50 centers and meditation groups exist worldwide. Some four hundred people live at the Ananda World Brotherhood Village, and Ananda Church, which was established in 1990, numbers about 1,600 members. Kriyananda has ordained over one hundred ministers. *Clarity Newsletter* and Crystal Clarity Publishers serve the movement. Ananda may be contacted as 14618 Tyler Foote Blvd., Nevada City, CA 95959.

Sources:

Walter, J. Donald [Kriyananda]. *Cities of Light.* Nevada City, Calif.: Crystal Clarity Publishers, 1987.

———. *Cooperative Communities: How to Start Them and Why.* Nevada City, Calif.: Ananda Publications, 1968.

———. *Crises in Modern Thought.* Nevada City, Calif.: Ananda Publications, 1972.

———. *The Path.* Nevada City, Calif.: Ananda Publications, 1977.

Nordquist, Ted A. *Ananda Cooperative Village.* Upsala, Sweden: Borgstroms Tyckeri Ab, 1978.

Ananda Cooperative Village See Ananda Church of God-Realization

Ananda Marga Yoga Society

Controversial Hindu religious group with branches in many Western countries. It was founded in January 1955 in Railway Quarters No. 339, Jamalpur, India, by **Probhat Ranjam Sarkar** (b. 1921), a former railway accounts clerk and journalist known by his religious name, Shrii Shrii Anandamurti. Above and beyond his yoga teachings, Sarkar also taught a political philosophy known as "Prout" (progressive utilization theory), claiming that capitalism makes men slaves and communism makes them beasts; Prout offered a middle way of socialist autocracy. The meditation and yoga materials are generally released under Sarkar's religious name, and his political writings under his birth name. The two movements are officially independent of each other, though informally they are closely associated.

Initiates to Ananda Marga are instructed in the "path of bliss" by a teacher (guru). Included in the instructions are the traditional yogic disciplines of yama and niyama, the do's and don'ts of yoga. The disciple is admonished to abstain from violence, falsehood, theft, incontinence, and acquisitiveness, and to follow a path of purity, contentment, austerities, study, and dedicated activity. They are told to meditate twice daily and work toward bringing all to the path of perfection. Social service is also emphasized.

Both Ananda Marga and the Proutist party developed through the 1960s. In 1967 and 1969 the Proutists ran candidates for office in India. Then in 1971 Sarkar was accused by a former follower of conspiracy to murder, and he was arrested and left in jail awaiting trail. In the meantime, Prime Minister Indira Ghandi proclaimed a national emergency in 1975 and banned Ananda Marga. Members of the organization were involved in several violent incidents, some growing out of their public protests of their leader's imprisonment without a trial. Brought to trial under the emergency, he was not allowed to bring any witnesses in his behalf and was convicted. In 1978 he was retried and found not guilty, and there was general agreement that Sarkar was the victim of political persecution. Since that time the movement has spread worldwide, and the era of social conflict seems to have ended.

Ananda Marga was brought to the United States in September 1969 by Acharya Vimalananda. By 1973 there were more than one hundred centers, three thousand members, and a monthly periodical, *Sadvipra.* Ananda Marga was established in Great Britain under the leadership of an American disciple known as Acharya Bharadwaja. Branches teach meditation and yoga allied with a program of popular social activities such as food cooperatives, prison work, disaster relief, and projects with migrant farm workers. The address of the U.S. headquarters is 97-38 42nd Ave., Corona, NY 11368. There are British centers at 14 Hendrick Ave., London S.W.12 and 8 Ullet Rd., Liverpool 8.

Sources:

Anandamurti, Shrii Shrii. *The Great Universe: Discourses on Society.* Los Altos, Calif.: Ananda Marga Publishers, 1971.

Sarkar, P. R. *Ideas and Ideology.* Calcutta: Acarya Pranavananda Avadhuta, 1978.

The Spiritual Philosophy of Shrii Shrii Anandamurti. Denver, Colo.: Ananda Marga Publications, 1981.

Ananda Metteya

Religious name assumed by occultist **Allan Bennett** (1872–1947) after becoming a Buddhist monk.

Ananda World Brotherhood See Ananda Church of God-Realization

Anandamayi Ma, Sri (1896–1982)

Prominent Indian mystic, revered as a living saint and noted for her spiritual insight and perceptive instructions to devotees. She was born Nirmala Bhattachari on April 30, 1896, of devout Brahmin parents, in Kheora, a small village in the Comilla district of Bangladesh. The name "Nirmala" means "Pure." She began primary school at the age of five and showed unusual facility in learning. However, she preferred devotional songs to books and would often lose consciousness during the singing of hymns or the chanting of names of Hindu deities. At the age of 12, she was married to Ramani Mohan Chakravarty, but her trances continued, and her husband eventually concluded that she was to be his guru rather than a traditional wife. She renamed him "Bholanath," and thereafter their relationship was of guru and disciple rather than wife and husband.

At the age of 18, Nirmala went to the village of Bajitpur in East Bengal. During some five years there she spontaneously assumed yogic postures and recited mantras. For a year and a half she remained silent, then continued the period of silence for another year and a half on returning to her husband's home in 1923. Bholanath had her examined by various holy men and exorcists, but all believed her condition to be a spiritual one.

At the age of 27, Nirmala manifested a profound knowledge of spiritual teachings, although she had no formal training in scriptures, and she was able to fluently discuss spiritual matters with learned professors. One of her followers named Hara Kumar started calling her "Ma" (Mother) and revered her as a saint. In 1924, Jyotish Chandra Roy, a distinguished officer of the Bengal government, renounced his worldly life to become her disciple and attendant. She named him "Bhaiji," and he gave her the name of "Anandamayi" (spiritual bliss).

In 1932, Ma Anandamayi, Bholanath (now known as "Pitaji," or Father), and Bhaiji went to Dehra Dun in the Himalayan foothills and established an ashram there. Subsequently a second ashram (later to become the headquarters) was established at Varanasi (Benares). In time, a number of other ashrams were established throughout India, some with hospitals, high schools, orphanages, and charitable dispensaries. As her fame spread, Anandamayi Ma acquired devotees from Britain, Germany, France, and the U.S.

She has never left India and visits her various ashrams without any special schedule, as the spirit moves her. She has remarkable presence, and many have testified to her spiritual influence on them. She answers questions succinctly, with great spiritual insight. Her disciples in the United States were organized into the Matri Satsang.

Sources:

Anandamayi, Ma Sri. *Matri Vani.* 2 vols. Varnasi, India: Shree Shree Annandamayee Charitable Society, 1977.

———. *Sad Vani.* Calcutta, India: Shree Shree Anandamayi Charitable Society, 1981.

Lipski, Alexander. *Life and Teachings of Sri Anandamayi Ma.* Delhi, India: Motilial Banaridass, 1977.

Anandamurti, Shri

Religious name assumed by **Probhat Ranjan Sarkar** (b. 1921), founder of the controversial international socio-spiritual sect **Ananda Marga.**

Ananisapta

A kabalistic word made up from the initial letters of the prayer *Antidotum Nazareni Auferat Necene Intoxicationis; Sanctificet Alimenta, Poculaque Trinitas Alma.* When written on virgin parchment, it is said to be a powerful **talisman** to protect against disease. (See also **Kabala**)

Anarazel

According to ancient superstition, Anarazel is one of the demons charged with the guardianship of subterranean treasures, which he carries about from one place to another to hide them from men. It is he who, with his companions Gaziel and Fécor, shakes the foundations of houses, raises the tempests, rings the bells at midnight, causes specters to appear, and inspires a thousand terrors.

Anathema

The name was given by the ancients to certain classes of votive offerings, to the nets that the fisherman laid on the altar of the sea nymphs, to the mirror that Laïs consecrated to Venus, and to offerings of vessels, garments, instruments, and various other articles.

The word was also applied to the victim devoted to the infernal gods, and it is this sense that is found among Jews and Christians, referring either to the curse or its object. The man who is anathematized is denied communication with the faithful, and he is delivered to the demon if he dies without absolution. Through the centuries the Church often lavished anathemas upon those considered heretics and enemies, though many such as St. John Chrysostom taught that while it was well to anathematize false doctrine, people who have strayed should be pardoned and prayed for. The use of anathemas has largely dropped out of contemporary Christianity.

Magicians and sorcerers once employed a sort of anathema to discover thieves and witches. Some limpid water was brought, and in it were boiled as many pebbles as there were persons suspected. The pebbles were then buried under the doorstep over which the thief or the sorcerer was to pass, and a plate of tin was attached to it, on which was written the words "Christ is conqueror; Christ is king; Christ is master." Every pebble must bear the name of one of the suspected persons. The stones are removed at sunrise, and the one representing the guilty person is hot and glowing. The seven penitential psalms must then be recited, with the Litanies of the Saints, and the prayers of **exorcism** pronounced against the thief or the sorcerer. His name must be written in a circular figure, and a triangular brass nail driven in above it with a hammer, the handle of which is of cypress wood, while the exorcist declares, "Thou are just, Lord, and just are Thy judgments." At this, the thief would betray himself by a loud cry.

If the anathema has been pronounced by a sorcerer, and one wishes merely to escape the effects of it and cause it to return to him who has cast it, one must take, on Saturday, before sunrise, the branch of a one-year-old hazel tree and recite the following prayer: "I cut thee, branch of this year, in the name of him whom I wish to wound as I wound thee." The branch is then laid on the table and other prayers said, ending with "Holy Trinity, punish him who has done this evil, and take him from among us by Thy great justice, that the sorcerer or sorceress may be anathema, and we safe." Harrison Ainsworth's famous novel, *The Lancashire Witches,* deals with the subject and the Pendleton locality in England.

Ancient and Mystical Order of Seekers

The Ancient and Mystical Order of Seekers was founded in the 1970s by Clifford Bias (d. 1986), the president of the **Universal Spiritualist Association,** as a society for the clergy and the more serious lay students in the association. The order explores the esoteric arts and sciences, those areas generally part of the work of occult orders and magical groups. Bias produced a series of manuals, *The A.M.O.S. Path of Light,* for the order's members. The order may be contacted c/o the Maple Grove Spiritual Retreat, P. O. Box 379, Pendleton, IN 46064-0379.

Sources:

[Bias, Clifford]. *The A.M.O.S. Path of Light.* 19 vols. Anderson, Ind.: Ancient and Mystical Order of Seekers, n.d.

Ancient and Mystical Order of the Rosicrucians (AMORC)

The largest of the several **Rosicrucian** organizations operating in North America and Europe, the Ancient and Mystical Order of the Roase Crucis (AMORC) was founded in 1915 in New York City by **H. Spencer Lewis** (1883–1939). Lewis dates efforts to found the order to 1909 when he met with French Rosicrucians at Toulouse for his original initiation. Upon his return to America, he began holding meetings. AMORC headquarters moved to Florida and then in the early 1920s to San Jose, California, where it is now located. Here Lewis and the order, which were becoming well known due to a publicity campaign, were sued by the older Rosicrucian Fraternity under the leadership of **R. Swinburne Clymer.** AMORC lost the privilege of using the term "Rosicrucian" or "fraternity" as part of its official name.

The AMORC teaches that God created the universe according to a set of immutable laws. Human beings succeed in this life through attaining mastership, the ability to bring into material expression the things which one mentally images. The techniques taught to students are presented through a correspondence course, leading to mastery. As each level is successfully completed, the student is admitted to a higher degree and given a more advanced set of lessons. Members may, but are by no means required to, attend local gatherings of students variously designated as lodges, chapters, or pronaoi, depending upon their strength.

The AMORC sees itself as the continuation of the ancient mystery schools of the Middle East, once headed by Solomon and Amenhotep. According to its own history, the group works in 180-year cycles in which public activity is followed by a period of secrecy and silence. Thus is explained the broken history of the order. A new public cycle began in 1909. Among the famous people claimed as Rosicrucians are Isaac Newton, Rene Descartes, Benjamin Franklin, and Francis Bacon.

H. Spencer Lewis was succeeded by his son, **Ralph M. Lewis** (1904–1987), who headed the order for almost half a century. He was followed by Gary L. Stewart, which proved to be a disastrous choice, as it was discovered that Stewart was quietly moving the order's money into a bank account in the tiny kingdom of Andorra. He was removed from office, and Christian Bernard was selected as the new Grand Imperator.

The AMORC has attained a relatively high profile due to its continuing mass publicity campaign, making it a large international organization with members in 85 countries around the world. In 1990 there were over 250,000 members, 163 chartered groups in the United States, and 44 in Canada. Its Egyptian Museum and headquarters complex located in San Jose is a popular tourist attraction. The order publishes two magazines, *Rosicrucian Digest* and *Rosicrucian Forum,* the latter for members only.

Sources:

Lewis, H. Spencer. *Rosicrucian Manual.* San Jose, Calif.: Rosicrucian Press, 1941.

———. *Rosicrucian Questions and Answers.* San Jose, Calif.: Supreme Grand Lodge of the AMORC, 1969.

Lewis, Ralph M. *Yesterday Has Much to Tell.* San Jose, Calif.: Supreme Grand Lodge of the AMORC, 1973.

"Special Ralph M. Lewis Memorial Issue." *Rosicrucian Digest* (1987).

Ancient Astronaut Society

Founded in 1973 to bring together individuals who desire to determine whether Earth was visited in prehistoric times by extraterrestrial beings and whether advanced civilizations existed on Earth prior to recorded history. Its founder was Gene M. Phillips, who continues to head the organization. The society was established largely out of the popular response to the writings of **Erich von Däniken** who, in his 1969 book, *Chariots of the Gods?,* developed ideas first expressed in the 1950s by writers such as **George Hunt Williamson,** M. K. Jessup, and **Desmond Leslie.** Unlike the earlier texts, however, von Däniken's book became an international best-seller.

The society was inaugurated with a conference in Chicago and has since held annual conferences and conducted expeditions to locations around the world, from Yugoslavia to Brazil, where members can see firsthand the sites discussed in the ancient astronaut literature. The ancient astronaut hypothesis was found unconvincing by ufologists, and was quickly segregated from **UFO** studies. However, von Däniken and Zecharia Sitchin, the most scholarly of the ancient astronaut writers, have continued to reach a substantial audience.

The society's international headquarters is located at 1921 St. Johns Ave., Highland Park, IL 60035. Von Däniken heads a European office in Switzerland. A bimonthly newsletter in English and German, *Ancient Skies,* serves the movement.

Sources:

Sitchin, Zecharia. *The Stairway to Heaven.* New York: Avon, 1980.

———. *The 12th Planet.* New York: Avon, 1976.

Story, Ronald. *The Space Gods Revealed: A Close Look at the Theories of Erich Von Däniken.* New York: Harper & Row, 1976.

Von Däniken, Erich. *Chariots of the Gods?* New York: G. P. Putnam's Sons, 1969.

———. *In Search of Ancient Gods: My Pictorial Evidence for the Impossible.* London: Souvenir, 1974.

Ancient Astronauts (Magazine)

Short-lived bimonthly magazine concerned with the ancient astronaut hypothesis, the possibility that Earth was visited in prehistoric times by extraterrestrial beings, and that advanced civilizations existed on Earth prior to recorded history. The magazine also covered other unexplained events and Fortean phenomena. It was published by Countrywide Publications in New York.

Ancient Mysteries

Secret rituals of pagan religions, known only to select initiates who had qualified for higher spiritual development. Such **mysteries** were kept apart from popular worship, and initiates had to take a binding oath of secrecy, so that even today our knowledge of the mysteries is partly conjectural. Typical mystery cults were those of Eleusis in Greece from about 1500 B.C.E., in turn deriving from the mystery religions of ancient Egypt and the mysteries of Mithras, a Persian deity. Traces of Mithraism existed in Britain. Many secret societies in modern times have claimed that their rituals are a descent of an ancient tradition.

Sources:

Ulansey, David. *The Origins of the Mithraic Mysteries: Cosmology and Salvation in the Ancient World.* New York: Oxford University Press, 1989.

Ancitif

A little-known demon, who, during the **possession** of the nuns of **Louviers** in 1643, was said to have occupied the body of Sister Barbara of St. Michael.

Anderson, Margaret (1920–1986)

Parasychologist fellow and professor of education at the University of Pittsburgh. She became interested in parapsychology in the 1950s when she began working with **Rhea White** on testing ESP in children. They predicted that good relations between teachers and pupils would produce ESP, and bad relations would inhibit it, then conducted tests of clairvoyance and precognition to test their theory.

Anderson moved on and began to create situations that would yield ESP results. Her work led to a series of important papers, and in 1961 she was joint winner (with **R. A. McConnell**) of the McDougall Award for the article "Fantasy Testing for ESP in a Fourth and Fifth Grade Class." She was treasurer of the **Parapsychological Association** in 1961, president in 1962. That year she received her Ph.D. in education and began a career teaching at the University of Pittsburgh. She gradually withdrew from parapsychological circles. She retired from the university in 1985 and died the following year of lung cancer.

Sources:

Anderson, Margaret L. "The Use of Fantasy in Testing for Extrasensory Perception." *Journal* of the ASPR Vol. 60 (1966): 150.

Anderson, Margaret L., and R. A. McConnell. "Fantasy Testing for ESP in a Fourth and Fifth Grade Class." *Journal of Psychology* Vol. 52 (1961): 491.

Berger, Arthur S., and Joyce Berger. *The Encyclopedia of Parapsychology and Psychical Research.* New York: Paragon House, 1991.

Pleasants, Helene, ed. *Biographical Dictionary of Parapsychology.* New York: Helix Press, 1964.

Anderson, Rodger I(van) (1943–)

Writer on parapsychology, with special interest in survival, history of **Spiritualism** and psychic research, and so-called "spirit teachings." He was born in 1943 in Springville, Utah, and educated at the University of Utah (B.S., English, 1971; M.S., philosophy, 1974). Anderson grew up with a strong belief in the occult and the supernatural and was drawn to writings in parapsychology. He became involved in psychic research because of the uncritical acceptance of psychic events he found in many writers. His own interests have centered in the history of Spiritualism, possibilities of demonstrating survival of death, and experimental research. He has authored a number of articles, including philosophical and theological reflections on parapsychological studies, and co-authored two books with **Rhea A. White:** *On Being Psychic: A Reading Guide* (2nd ed., 1989) and *Psychic Experiences: A Bibliography* (1990). In 1983 he won the Robert H. Ashby Memorial Award offered annually by the Academy of Religion and Psychical Research.

Sources:

Anderson, Roger I. "Cahagnet's Contribution to Psychical Research." *Theta* 12, 4 (1983): 74.

———. "Channeling." *Journal of Religion and Psychical Research* Vol. 19 (1988): 5.

———. "Contemporary Survival Research: A Critical Review." *Parapsychology Review* Vol. 12 (1981): 5.

———. "Reincarnation: Can Christianity Accommodate It?" *Journal of Religion and Psychical Research* Vol. 9 (1985): 189.

———. "Swedenborg on the Modus Operandi of Spirit Communication." *Parapsychology Review* Vol. 13 (1982): 6.

Berger, Arthur S., and Joyce Berger. *The Encyclopedia of Parapsychology and Psychical Research.* New York: Paragon House, 1991.

Andrae, Johann Valentin (1586–1654)

Johann Valentin Andrae, the German Lutheran pastor who developed the legend of the **Rosicrucian** occult orders, came from a line of ministers that included a grandfather who had been among Martin Luther's original supporters. Andrae was born August 7, 1586, in Herrenburg, Württemberg. He attended Tübingen University, and after graduation he became chaplain at Stüttgart. In 1607, due to ill health, he returned to Tübingen, where he was introduced to mysticism as a member of the informal circle around Christoph Besold, a local devotee of the occult, especially the **Kabala,** the Jewish mystical system. During his last days in Tübingen he finished and anonymously published the *Fama Fraternitatis,* the first of his Rosicrucian publications. The following year he published the *Confessio,* soon to be followed by the *Chemical Marriage.* By this time he had moved to Vaihingen as the church's deacon.

Andrae's three volumes announced the existence of a secret fraternity founded by Christian Rosencreutz, a high occult initiate. The order had supposedly been founded a century earlier and was only now being made public. The documents further invited inquiries from interested readers but failed to give an address or location for the fraternity. Over the next decades, many would look in vain for the group. In 1619 Andrae published a short work, *The Tower of Babel,* in which he confessed his authorship and told his readers that the Rosicrucian order did not exist. He apparently derived the basic symbolism of the order from Martin Luther's coat of arms, which had a rose and a cross on it. However, by this time the original writings had spread far and wide, and many did not believe Andrae's confession.

Andrae essentially left his Rosicrucian ideas behind and moved to Stüttgart as court prelate to the king of Württemberg. He wrote prolifically (over a hundred books) and became a leader of the Fruit-Bringing Society, one of several German revivalist movements of the seventeenth century. He ended his career at Babenhausen, Bavaria, where he moved in 1650 to become the local abbot. He died on January 27, 1654, at Stüttgart.

Andrae's writings have become the source of intense controversy in the centuries since his death. Some came to believe that he wrote about the society as a hoax, while others just as firmly believed that he was exposing a real organization. Frustrated at their inability to locate the fraternity, people responded to various occultists who came forward as representatives of the Rosicrucians, a practice which has continued into the twentieth century. Rosicrucian orders have been founded in every century, and beginning with the founding of the Rosicrucian Fraternity in the mid-nineteenth century, no fewer than ten currently existing Rosicrucian groups have been founded. In 1968 an English edition of the Rosicrucian works of Andrae, edited by Paul M. Allen, made them generally available to the public again.

Sources:

Allen, Paul M. *A Christian Rosenkreutz Anthology.* Blauvelt, N.Y.: Rudolf Steiner Publications, 1968.

McIntosh, Christopher. *The Rose Cross Unveiled.* Wellingborough, England: Aquarian Press, 1980.

Waite, A. E. *The Brotherhood of the Rosy Cross.* London: Rider, 1924.

Yates, Frances A. *The Rosicrucian Enlightenment.* London: Routledge & Kegan Paul, 1972.

Andrews, Mary (ca. 1871)

One of the earliest mediums for **materialization.** She was a plain, uneducated woman of Moravia, near Auburn, New York. Her seances were held in the house of a farmer named Keeler. In the dark seances, questions were answered by spirit lights, the piano was sounded, water was sprinkled into the faces of the sitters, they were touched by phantom hands, and spirit voices were heard. In the light seances, the second part of the exhibition, the medium sat in a cabinet, and busts, arms, and hands materialized, the lips of phantom faces were seen in motion, and, despite the dim light, many departed relatives were recognized.

T. R. Hazard, Epes Sargent, and Eugene Crowell provided accounts of Andrews's sittings, while John W. Truesdell offered a very critical appraisal of her seances.

Sources:

Crowell, Eugene. *The Identity of Primitive Christianity and Modern Spiritualism.* N.p., 1874.

Hazard, T. R. *Eleven Days in Moravia.* N.p., n.d.

Sargent, Epes. *Proof Palpable of Immortality.* N.p., 1875.

Truesdell, John W. *The Bottom Facts Concerning the Science of Spiritualism.* 1883. Reprint, New York, 1884.

Androdamas

According to ancient belief, the androdamas is a stone resembling the diamond, said to be found in the sands of the Red Sea, in squares or dies. Its name denotes the virtue belonging to it, namely, to restrain anger, mitigate lunacy, and lessen the gravity of the body.

Android

A man made by other means than the natural mode of reproduction. The automaton attributed to **Albertus Magnus,** which St. Thomas destroyed with his stick because its answers to his questions puzzled him, was such an android. Some have attempted to humanize a root called the mandrake, which bears a fantastic resemblance to a human being. In modern times, androids or robots have become commonplace in science fiction stories and films. (See also **Mandragoras**)

Angels

The word "angel" ("angelos" in Greek, "malak" in Hebrew) means a person sent or a messenger. It is a name not of nature but of office, and is applied also to humans in the world who are ambassadors or representatives. In another sense, the word denotes a spiritual being employed in occasional offices; and lastly, men in office as priests or bishops. The "angel of the congregation" among the Jews was the chief of the synagogue. This later usage is also found in Revelation 1 and 2, where the"angel of the church" is regularly addressed. Today, the term is now limited to its principal meaning, and pertains only to the inhabitants of heaven.

Biblical Angels

Mark, the apostle of the Gentiles, speaks of the angels as "ministering spirits, sent forth to minister for them who shall be heirs of salvation," in strict keeping with the import of the term itself. In Mark 1:2, it is applied to John the Baptist: "Behold I send my messenger (i.e., angel) before my face," and the word is the same ("malak") in the corresponding prophecy of Malachi. In Hebrews 12: 22, 24, we read: "Ye have come to an innumerable company of angels, to the spirits of the just," and this idea of their great number is sustained by the words of the Lord, where, for example, he declares that "twelve legions" of them were ready upon his demand. In the Revelation of St. John, a vast idea of their overwhelming number is indicated. Their song of praise is described as "the voice of a great multitude, and as the voice of many waters, and as the voice of mighty thunderings."

The angels form the armies of heaven, and military terms are commonly quoted. It is mentioned in the Bible that the angel host or army will fight God's cosmic battle. For example, an angel destroyed Sennacherib's army encamped around Jerusalem. They appeared to the shepards to announce the birth of Jesus, and Jesus will lead the armies of God in the final conflict at the end of time (Revelation 19:14). The idea of angelic armies would come to the forefront during World War I in the myth of the **Angels of Mons.**

As to the nature of angles, it is essentially the same as that of humans, for not only are understanding and will attributed to them, but they have been mistaken for humans when they appear, and seem capable of disobedience (Hebrews 2:7, 16). The latter possibility is exhibited in its greatest extent by Jude, who speaks of the "angels which kept not their first estate, but left their own habitation," and upon this passage would later lay the foundation of the differences and definitions concerning angels and demons. The former term limited its meaning only to the obedient ministers of the will of the Almighty, and the influence of evil angels is concentrated only on the devil or Satan. These ideas were common to the whole Eastern world, and were probably derived by the Jewish people from the Assyrians. The Pharisees charged Jesus with casting out devils "by Beelzebub the prince of the devils." The idea that evil spirits acted in multitudes under one person appears in Mark 5:9, where, when he is asked his name, the evil spirit answers: "My name is 'Legion' for we are many."

In the Bible two orders are mentioned in scripture, "angels" and "archangels;" but the latter only occurs twice, namely, in Jude, where Michael is called "an archangel," and in I Thessalonians 4:16, where it is written: "the Lord shall descend from heaven with a shout, with the voice of the archangel, and with the trump of God."

Gabriel and Michael are the only angels mentioned by name. The archangel Michael appeared to Daniel and will lead his angelic army against the people of God (Revelation 12:7). The mention of Michael by name occurs five times in scripture, and always in the character of a chief militant. In Daniel, he is the champion of the Jewish church against Persia; in the Revelation, he overcame the dragon; and in Jude he is mentioned in a personal conflict with the devil about the body of Moses. He is called by Gabriel, "Michael, your prince," meaning the prince of the Jewish church. Gabriel first appeared as an angel to give Daniel an interpretation of a dream (Daniel 8:16–27) but earned his lasting fame as the one to announce both the birth of John the Baptist to Zachariah and the coming birth of Jesus to the Virgin Mary (Luke 1:11–38).

Developing Notions about Angels

In the intertestimental period (the centuries just prior to the Christian era) as the Jewish notion of angelic orders developed, Michael and Gabriel were named as two of the seven archangels. The alleged prophecy of Enoch states, "Michael, one of the holy angels who, presiding over human virtue, commands the nations." The same volume notes that Raphael, "presides over the spirits of men." And other angels who will become integral to

Western angelic and magical lore appear: Uriel, who reigns "over clamor and terror"; and Gabriel, who reigns "over Paradise, and over the cherubims."

As the Roman Catholic mass evolved, Michael, now a saint, was invoked as a "most glorious and warlike prince," "the receiver of souls," and "the vanquisher of evil spirits." His symbol is a banner hanging on a cross; he is armed and represents victory, with a dart in one hand and a cross on his forehead. It may be noted that God himself is called the angel of the Covenant, because he embodied in his own person the whole power and representation of the angelic kingdom, as the messenger, not of separate and temporary commands, but of the whole word in its fullness.

Dionysius, or St. Denis, the supposed Areopagite (sixth century C.E.), describes three hierarchies of angels in nine choirs: Seraphim, Cherubim, Thrones, Dominions, Principalities, Powers, Virtues, Angels, and Archangels. These were created by assembling various biblical passages (such as Exodus 25:18–20; Isaiah 6:2–3; Ephesians 3:10) and the book of Enoch. Vartan (or Vertabied), the thirteenth-century Armenian poet and historian, described them under the same terms, but expressly stated: "these orders differ from one another in situation and degree of glory, just as there are different ranks among men, though they are all of one nature."

This description, and all others resembling it (the twelve heavenly worlds of Plato, and the heaven of the Chinese, for example), can be understood as landmarks serving to denote the heights human intelligence has reached at various times in the attempt to represent the eternal and infinite in precise terms. Seventeenth-century mystic **Jakob Boehme** recognized the "whole deep between the stars," as the heaven of one of the three hierarchies, and placed the other two above it; "in the midst of all which," he says, "is the Son of God; no part of either is farther or nearer to him, yet are the three kingdoms circular about him." The visions of **Emanuel Swedenborg** date a century later, and describe his intimacy with the angelic world. The angels described to him in great detail a level of spiritual existence qualitatively different from the visible world of sensation.

Angelic Realms in Jewish Thought

Jewish teachers have developed an elaborate doctrine of a heavenly hierarchy. Some, such as Bechai and Joshua, teach that "every day ministering angels are created out of the river Dinor, or fiery stream, and they sing an anthem and cease to exist; as it is written, they are new every morning." This idea appears to be a misunderstanding of biblical intent—to be "renewed" or "created" in the scriptural sense is to be regenerated. Thus, to be renewed every morning is to be kept in a regenerate state; the fiery stream is the baptism by fire or divine love.

In later doctrine, the angelic hierarchies were understood in correspondence to the ten divine names. Both Christian and astrological elements eventually could be discerned in the presentation that reached its height in the teachings of the **Kabala.**

The following represents the angelic hierarchies answering to the ten divine names:

1. Jehovah, attributed to God the Father, being the pure and simple essence of the divinity, flowing through *Hajoth Hakados* to the angel Metratton and to the ministering spirit, *Reschith Hajalalim,* who guides the *primum mobile,* and bestows the gift of being on all. These names are to be understood as pure essences, or as spheres of angels and blessed spirits, by whose agency the divine providence extends.
2. Jah, attributed to the person of the Messiah or Logos, whose power and influence descends through the angel Masleh into the sphere of the Zodiac. This is the spirit or word that actuated the chaos and ultimately produced the four elements and all creatures, by the agency of a spirit named Raziel, who was the ruler of Adam.
3. Ehjeh, attributed to the Holy Spirit, whose divine light is received by the angel Sabbathi, and communicated from him through the sphere of Saturn. It denotes the beginning of the supernatural generation, and hence of all living souls.

The ancient Jews considered the three superior names to be those above, to be attributed to the divine essence as personal or proper names, while the seven noted below denote the measures (*middoth*) or attributes that are visible in the works of God. But modern Jews, in opposition to the tripersonalists, consider the whole as attributes. The higher three denote the heavens, and the succeeding ones the seven planets or worlds, to each of which a presiding angel is assigned.

4. El, strength, power, and light, through which flows grace, goodness, mercy, piety, and munificence to the angel Zadkiel, and passing through the sphere of Jupiter, fashions the images of all bodies, bestowing clemency, benevolence and justice on all.
5. Elohi, the upholder of the sword and left hand of God. Its influence penetrates the angel Geburah (or Gamaliel) and descends through the sphere of Mars. It imparts fortitude in times of war and affliction.
6. Tsebaoth, the title of God as Lord of hosts. The angel is Raphael, through whom its mighty power passes into the sphere of the sun, giving motion, heat, and brightness to it.
7. Elion, the title of God as the highest. The angel is Michael. The sphere to which he imparts its influence is Mercury, giving benignity, motion, and intelligence, with elegance and consonance of speech.
8. Adonai, master or lord, governing the angel Haniel, and the sphere of Venus.
9. Shaddai. The virtue of this name is conveyed by Cherubim to the angel Gabriel and influences the sphere of the moon. It causes increase and decrease, and rules the jinn and protecting spirits.
10. Elohim, the source of knowledge, understanding, and wisdom, received by the angel Jesodoth, and imparted to the sphere of the Earth.

The division of angels into nine orders or three hierarchies, as derived from Dionysius Areopagus, was made in the Middle Ages, which gave the prevalent division much of its symbolism. With it was held the doctrine of their separate creation; the tradition of the rebellious hierarchy, headed by **Lucifer,** was rendered familiar to society by the epic poetry of John Milton. The medieval development of angelology was passed on to occultists and a description of the angelic orders became integral to **magic** and in the practices of magical rituals.

Angels and Giants

Another leading belief, not so much interwoven with the popular theology, was that of angels' intercourse with women, producing the race of giants. The idea derived from Genesis 4:2, in the adoption of which the Christian fathers followed the opinion of ancient Jewish interpreters, Philo-Judaeus, and Josephus. A particular account of the circumstances is given in the book of Enoch, which makes the angels—Uriel, Gabriel, and Michael—the chief instruments in the subjugation of the adulterers and their formidable offspring. The classic writers have perpetuated similar beliefs of the "hero" race, all of them born either from the love of the gods for women, or of the preference shown for a goddess by some mortal man.

The Persian, Jewish, and Muslim accounts of angels all evince a common origin, and they alike admit a difference of sex. In the latter, the name of Azazil is given to the hierarchy nearest the throne of God, to which the Mohammedan Satan (Eblis or Haris) is supposed to have belonged; also Azreal, the angel of death, and Asrafil (probably the same as Israfil), the angel of the resurrection. The examiners, Moukir and Nakir, are subordinate angels who are armed with whips of iron and fire, and interrogate recently deceased souls as to their lives.

The parallel belief in the Talmud is an account of seven angels who beset the paths of death. The Koran also assigns two angels to every man—one to record his good and the other his evil actions. They are so merciful that if an evil action has been done, it is not recorded until the man has slept, and if at that time he repents, they place on the record that God has pardoned him. The Siamese, besides holding the difference of sex, imagine angels have offspring; but their beliefs concerning the government of the world and the guardianship of the human race are similar to those of other nations.

The Christian fathers, for the most part, believed angels possessed bodies of heavenly substance (Tertullian calls it "angelified flesh"), and, if not, they could assume a corporeal presence at their pleasure. In fact, all the actions recorded of angels in Scripture imply human bodies and attributes.

Some Theosophists regard angels as related to fairy life, part of the "Devic" kingdom (from the Sanskrit term **"deva,"** or "divine being"). Reports of encounters with visitors from **flying saucers** often suggest a secular form of angel life.

Contemporary Interest in Angels

The existence of angels, especially guardian angels, has been a common theme of popular Western lore. It has been the subject of numerous Christian texts and been championed in metaphysical lore by the likes of Flower A. Newhouse, founder of Christward Ministry in Escondido, California. In the late 1980s a significant revival of interest in angels occurred and a number of new books and reprints of old books began to appear. While many of these repeated traditional themes, the majority flowed out of the **New Age** movement and concerned present contact and **channeling** of messages from angelic beings—a source more acceptable and familiar to many with a Christian background than communication with spirits of the deceased.

One interesting variation on the current interest in angels are the writings of artist Leilah Wendell, who has written a series of books concerning her communications with Azrael, the angel of death, and who created a popular museum built around artistic representations of death in New Orleans.

Sources:

Clayton, Rev. George. *Angelology; Agency & Ministry of Holy Angels.* New York, 1851.

Davidson, Gustav. *A Dictionary of Angels: Including the Fallen Angels.* New York: Free Press, 1967.

Duke, H. H. *The Holy Angels: Their Nature & Employments.* London, 1875.

Hodson, Geoffrey. *The Kingdom of Faerie.* London, 1927.

Miller, C. Leslie. *All About Angels: The Other Side of the Spirit World.* Glendale: G/L Regal Books, 1973.

Newhouse, Flower A. *Natives of Eternity.* Vista, Calif.: The Author, 1950.

O'Kennedy, Rev. R. *Book of the Holy Angels.* London, 1887.

Swedenborg, Emanuel. *Earths in Planets & in Starry Heavens: Inhabitants, Spirits & Angels.* London, 1758.

Wendell, Leilah. *The Book of Azrael.* New York: Westgate Press, 1988.

Angel's Hair

A fine, filmy substance observed falling from the sky, sometimes extensively. It has been explained as cobwebs from airborne spiders, but the strands of angel's hair may vary in length from a few inches to over a hundred feet, and often dissolve in contact with the ground. Possibly the earliest account of angel hair occurred in 1741 when it was reported that "flakes or rags about one inch broad and five or six inches long" fell on the towns of Bradly, Selborne, and Alresford in England. In 1881 *Scientific American* carried an account of huge falling spider webs (one as large as 60 feet, over Lake Michigan). Other falls have been reported over the years, and accounts were collected by **Charles Fort,** famous for his assemblage of accounts of anomalous natural events.

In the 1950s angel hair became associated with **UFOs.** A famous case occurred in France in 1952 during which a local high school principal reported seeing a cylindrical-shaped UFO and a circular one. The flying objects left a film behind them, which floated to the earth and fell to the ground covering trees, telephone wires, and roofs of houses. When the material was picked up and rolled into a ball, it turned gelatinous and vanished. Occasional additional accounts have appeared in the literature over the years, though angel hair is by no means a common element of UFO reports. Analysis of angel hair has proved elusive as the material seems to dissolve very quickly. (See also **Devil's Jelly; Falls**)

Sources:

Clark, Jerome. *The Emergence of a Phenomenon: UFOs from the Beginning through 1959.* Detroit: Omnigraphics, 1992.

Corliss, William R., ed. *Handbook of Unusual Natural Phenomena.* Glen Arm, Md.: Sourcebook Project, 1977.

Angels of Mons

A story by British author Arthur Machen, first published in the London *Evening News* for September 14, 1915, on the apparition of phantom English bowmen from the field of Agincourt during the terrible retreat from Mons in World War I. The story quoted the testimony of an officer as follows:

"On the night of the 27th I was riding along the column with two other officers. . . . As we rode along I became conscious of the fact that in the fields on both sides of the road along which we were marching I could see a very large body of horsemen. . . . The other two officers had stopped talking. At last one of them asked me if I saw anything in the fields. I told them what I had seen. The third officer confessed that he, too, had been watching these horsemen for the past twenty minutes. So convinced were we that they were really cavalry, that at the next halt one of the officers took a party of men out to reconnoitre and found no one there. The night then grew darker and we saw no more."

Confirmations poured in. Similar visions of phantom armies were related from different battle fronts. Books were written on the occurrence. Harold Begbie, in *On the Side of the Angels* (1915), quoted testimonies of soldiers. A dying prisoner spoke of the reluctance of the Germans to attack the English lines "because of the thousands of troops behind us." Then Machen confessed that he had invented the whole story. A claim in 1930 added another feature to the story. Friedrich Herzenwirth, a director of the German espionage system, published his memoirs in February 1930 and declared that the Angels of Mons were motion pictures, projected by German flyers on the clouds to make the English troops believe that even God was on the German side. No firm evidence has been produced to support this explanation.

Sources:

Machen, Arthur. *The Angel of Mons: The Bowmen and Other Legends of the War.* New York: G. P. Putnam's Sons, 1915.

Stein, Gordon. *Encyclopedia of Hoaxes.* Detroit: Gale Research, 1993.

Anger, Kenneth (1930–)

Avant-garde filmmaker and writer with a special interest in the occult. Born February 3, 1930, in Santa Monica, California, he was educated at Beverly Hills High School and also attended a school for expressive dancing. At the age of four he played the part of the changeling prince in Max Reinhardt's "A Midsummer Night's Dream" for Warner Brothers. It was the beginning of Anger's fascination with filmmaking.

He grew up in Hollywood and collected a great deal of film memorabilia along with stories and gossip of the film industry, which formed the basis of his book *Hollywood Babylone,* first published in Paris, 1959, and reissued as *Hollywood Babylon* in 1965 and revised in 1975.

On graduation from high school, Anger's grandmother, who had happy memories of Paris, sponsored Anger's visit to Paris, where he met Jean Cocteau. Cocteau was impressed by Anger's first film, "Fireworks," and introduced Anger to writer Anaïs Nin.

In 1955 Anger paid a visit to Cefalù, Sicily, and rediscovered the Abbey of Thelema, the occult community established by **Aleister Crowley** in 1920. Anger uncovered a variety of magical paintings, many with sexual themes, on the abbey walls and doors, hidden by whitewash 37 years earlier by order of the Italian police. Dr. Alfred C. Kinsey, compiler of the famous report *Sexual Behavior in the Human Male* (1948), visited Cefalù, where Anger showed him the unique murals. The story of Anger's discovery was featured in a two-part article in the journal *Picture Post* (November 26–December 3, 1955), illustrated with striking photographs by Fosco Maraini.

Anger did a number of films, among which are those with occult themes, stemming from Anger's fascination with the writings and philosophy of Aleister Crowley. Notable among these are "Thelema Abbey" (1955); "Lord Shiva's Dream" (1954), released as "Inauguration of the Pleasure Dome" (1958); "Scorpio Rising" (1963); "Invocation of My Demon Brother" (1969); and "Lucifer Rising" (1970–80). Anaïs Nin played the part of the goddess Astarte in "Inauguration of the Pleasure Dome," concerned with Crowleyesque rituals. Margorie Cameron, a member of the Ordo Templi Orientis, who was famous for her participation in some magical child rituals with Jack Parsons, also appeared in the movie. Rock singer Mick Jagger provided a soundtrack on Moog synthesizer for "Invocation of My Demon Brother," in which **Anton LaVey** played the part of Satan and hippie musician Bobby Beausoleil played Lucifer. Beausoleil also provided music (performed by the Freedom Orchestra of Tracy Prison) for "Lucifer Rising." Beausoleil, a member of **Charles Manson**'s Family, had by that time been convicted for the 1969 murder of Gary Hinman.

During the preoccupation with occultism of the 1960s, Anger attended some of the Magic Circle discussion group meetings organized by colorful Satanist Anton LaVey in San Francisco. However, Anger has remained something of a loner, following his own individual avant-garde film themes of motorcycle gang mystique, sadomasochistic homosexual encounter, and Crowley's thelemic magick.

Sources:

Robertson, Sandy. *The Aleister Crowley Scrapbook.* York Beach, Maine: Samuel Weiser, 1988.

Anglieri

A Sicilian writer of the seventeenth century, who is known by a work of which he published only two volumes (after promising twenty-four) entitled *Magic Light; or, The Origin, Order, and Government of All Things Celestial, Terrestial, and Infernal, etc.* The antiquary Antonino Mongitore (1663–1743) mentioned it in his *Sicilian Library.*

Angoff, Allan (1910– ?)

Editor and librarian in the field of parapsychology. Angoff was the editor of *Tomorrow* for the Parapsychology Foundation and a frequent contributor to the *Journal of Parapsychology.* He was a major advocate of establishing a central parapsychological library.

Born July 30, 1910, in Boston, Massachusetts, he studied at Boston University and Columbia University. He was a journalist and book critic for *Boston Evening Transcript* (1934–39) and assistant editor of *North American Review* (1940–42). Following the bombing of Pearl Harbor, he joined the U.S. Army and served as a staff sergeant (1942–45). After the war he became an associate editor at Creative Age Press (1945–46). He joined the staff as managing editor of *Tomorrow* magazine in 1946. After five years with the **Parapsychology Foundation,** he moved on successively to be editor-in-chief of Emerson Books, New York (1951–52); editor-in-chief, New York University Press (1953–57); chairman of Evaluation Committee, Adult School of Montcalm, N.J. (1958–59); readers' adviser at Montclair Public Library (1957–60); and since 1960 assistant director of Fair Lawn (N.J.) Public Library. He also served as book review editor of *Tomorrow* (1958–62) and as administrative secretary of the Parapsychology Foundation, New York.

Sources:

Angoff, Allan. *Eileen Garrett and the World Beyond the Senses.* New York: William Morrow, 1974.

Angoff, Allan, ed. *Parapsychology and the Sciences.* New York: Parapsychology Foundation, 1972.

———. *Parapsychology Today: A Geographic View.* New York: Parapsychology Foundation, 1971.

Angoff, Allan, and Diana Barth, eds. *Parapsychology and Anthropology.* New York: Parapsychology Foundation, 1973.

Angoff, Allan, and Betty Shapin, eds. *Proceedings of an International Conference: A Century of Psychical Research.* New York: Parapsychology Foundation, 1971.

Angstadt, L(aura) Jean (1931–)

Parapsychologist who has conducted experiments on teachers and pupils in ESP. She was born April 10, 1931, in Carlisle, Pennsylvania, and studied at Pennsylvania State University (B.S., 1953) and St. John's University, Jamaica, New York (M.S., education, 1961). Angstadt, for a time, was a teacher, then became a guidance counselor to Westbury High School on Long Island, in 1960.

Sources:

Angstadt, L. Jean, and Rhea White. "Student Performance in Two Classroom GESP Experiment with Two Students-Agents Acting Simultaneously." *Journal* of the ASPR 57 (1963): 32.

Angurvadel

The sword, possessing magical properties, which was inherited by Frithjof, the hero of a thirteenth-century Icelandic saga. It had a golden hilt and shone like the Northern Lights. In times of peace, certain characters on its blade were dull and pale, but during a battle they became red.

Anima Mundi

The soul of the world, a pure ethereal spirit that some ancient philosophers said was diffused throughout all nature. Plato is considered to be the originator of this idea, but it is of more ancient origin and prevailed in the systems of certain eastern philosophers. The Stoics believed it to be the only vital force in the universe. Similar concepts have been held by hermetic philosophers like **Paracelsus** and have been incorporated in the philosophy of more modern philosophers like Friedrich Schelling (1775–1854).

Animal Magnetism

Alternative term for **mesmerism.** It appears to have been first used by Michel A. Thouret in his *Recherches et doutes sur le magnétisme animal* (1784) with the intention of disassociating the phenomena from the name of its popularizer **Franz Anton Mesmer** (1733–1815). Thouret reviewed similar phenomena throughout the ages, and the name "animal magnetism" was intended to disassociate it from ferro-magnetism, indicating that the mesmeric or magnetic fluid was associated with unusual phenomena in living organisms.

Animal magnetism became a preferred term for experimenters and writers like **J. P. F. Deleuze** (1753–1835), and

William Gregory (1803–1858), translator of **Baron von Reichenbach**'s works on the "**od,**" or "odic force"(associated with animal magnetism). Animal magnetism embraced such paranormal phenomena as **clairvoyance, transposition of the senses,** and sympathy (rapport between operator and subject). A number of reputable scientists took a serious interest in animal magnetism and conducted numerous experiments, and for many years during the nineteenth century the subject formed a bridge between mesmerism, **Spiritualism,** and **hypnotism.** From time to time various alternative terms were proposed, largely in order to give the subject some scientific dignity. These included "psycodunamy" (Theodore Leger), "electro-psychology," and "electro-biology." Animal magnetism was eventually supplanted by hypnotism, which discarded many of the claimed paranormal aspects of the subject.

Sources:

Binet, Alfred, and Charles Fere. *Animal Magnetism.* London, 1887.

Deleuze, J. P. F. *Practical Instruction in Animal Magnetism.* Providence, R.I.: B. Cranston, 1837. Reprint, New York: Samuel R. Wells, 1879.

DuPoteat, Jules. *Magnetism and Magic.* New York: F. Stokes, n.d.

Gregory, William. *Animal Magnetism or Mesmerism and Its Phenomena.* London, 1909.

Townshend, Chauncy Hare. *Facts in Mesmerism, with Reasons for a Dispassionate Inquiry into It.* London, 1844.

Animals

Animals are believed to exhibit psychic faculties similar to human beings. In her account of a case of haunting in *Proceedings* of the Society for Psychical Research, Vol. 8, R. C. Morton mentions two dogs who saw a ghost. The medium **Mrs. J. H. Conant** believed that her pet dog and cat saw the spirits she described clairvoyantly. The dog barked and snarled; the cat arched its back, spat, and ran to hide. **Sir William Barrett** recorded the case of the Montgomery sisters who saw a ghost floating across the road; their horse stopped and shook with fright. The watchdog of the Rev. Samuel Wesley crouched in terror during the poltergeist manifestations at Epworth Vicarage (see **Epworth Phenomena**). In a poltergeist case on the Baltic Island of Oesel in 1844 a number of horses were frightened by thunderous noises coming from a nearby underground vault. The case is described in **Robert Dale Owen**'s *Footfalls on the Boundary of Another World* (1860).

Ernesto Bozzano collected many cases (published in the *Annals of Psychic Science* in 1905 and in *Animaux et manifestations metapsychiques* in 1926) in which animals as agents induce telepathic hallucinations; in which they act as percipients simultaneously with, or previously to, human beings; in which they see human or animal phantoms, collectively with human beings in which phantom animals are seen in haunted spots or periodically appear as a premonition of death. Out of a total of 69 cases, in 13 the animals were subject to supernormal psychic perceptions in precedence to humans, and in 12 they perceived things that the persons present were unable to see. In more than one-third of the cases, therefore, the animals' perception had precedence to humans. Bozzano pointed out that animals, "besides sharing with man the intermittent exercise of faculties of supernormal psychic perception, show themselves furthermore normally endowed with special psychic faculties unknown to men, such as the so-called instincts of direction and of migration, and the faculty of precognition regarding unforeseen atmospheric disturbances, or the imminence of earthquakes, or volcanic eruptions. Although man is destitute of such superior faculties of instinct, nevertheless these same faculties exist in the unexplored recesses of his subconsciousness." (See also **Earthquake Prediction**)

In the case of avalanches, the presentiments, especially attributed to horses, are still more mysterious. The deathhowl of dogs in anticipation of the death of their master or a member of the household is a well documented phenomenon. Gustave Geley recorded a personal experience of this in *From the Unconscious to the Conscious* (1920).

Supernormal perception may also work in a lower scale of life. Sir William Barrett suggested that the color changes of insect life to suit the environment might be due to causes of stigmata, i.e., suggestion unconsciously derived from the environment.

That there may be latent high faculties in animals which vie with the powers of genius was demonstrated by the famous case of the **Elberfeld Horses,** although many scientists have been skeptical of the evidence. An Italian horse, Tripoli, showed similar talent after a course in mathematics. The dog Rolf, of Mannheim, learned to calculate by attending the lessons given to a child. (See *Proceedings* of the ASPR, Vol. 13 [1919]). Rolf sired Lola who attained considerable fame as narrated in Henry Kindermann's *Lola; or, The Thought and Speech of Animals* (1922). She could calculate, tell the time, and phonetically spell out answers to questions. When she was asked what was the name of the Mannheim dog, she replied "mein fadr" (Mein Vater) i.e., "my father." All present had expected her to answer "Rolf."

Carita Borderieux's *Les Nouveaux Animaux Pensants* (Paris, 1927) tells the story of Zou, the author's calculating dog. In *Proceedings* of the ASPR Vol. 38, **Theodore Besterman** described his personal encounter with Borderieux's dog and claims to have discovered that the dog interpreted unconscious movements of Borderieux's hand. Unconscious movements were also put forward to explain the phenomena of the Elberfeld Horses, but they often gave correct answers to mathematical problems when the answer was not known by the questioner.

Unconscious signals or secret code falls far short as a theory of explanation in the case of Black Bear, the Briarcliff pony, who not only solved mathematical problems and spelled answers by selecting letters from a rack, but, according to narratives in the journal *Psychic Research* (April 1931), exhibited clairvoyant or telepathic powers by correctly describing playing cards which were turned face down. Black Bear either answered correctly or refused to venture an answer at all. He was never at fault and solved his problems with a supreme indifference. Mrs. Fletcher, one of his visitors, whose birthday was to occur shortly—a fact which could not normally have been known to either Black Bear or Mr. Barrett (his trainer)—asked these questions: "Black Bear,—there is an anniversary coming soon. Can you tell me what it is?" The pony spelled out "Birthday." Mrs. Fletcher then said "That is right, now, can you tell me when it will be?" and Black Bear replied "Friday." "What date will it be?" was the next question, and Black Bear at once spelled out "August 3rd."

Regarding the survival of animals, no definite proof is available. **Materialization** seances in which animals are seen do not offer evidence in themselves of survival. It is the continuation of personality and memory of which proof is demanded. Obviously, the barking of dogs is not sufficiently expressive for the purpose. After-death communications, however, do assert that animals also survive. Nevertheless, as an interesting speculation, the **direct voice** communication given to **H. Dennis Bradley** should be registered. According to Bradley, animals such as tigers and snakes, etc., go to an animal kingdom, there to be redrawn upon for physical life on Earth. Animals, such as dogs and cats, that are capable of love and loyalty live with the spirits in their plane. Said **Andrew Lang,** "Knowing cases in which phantasms of dogs have been seen and heard collectively by several persons simultaneously, I tend to agree with the tribes of North-West Central Queensland that dogs, like men, have khoi—have spirits."

In various countries of the world, the special sensory abilities of animals have been used in war and defense situations. Robert Lubow, professor of psychology at Tel Aviv University, Israel, revealed various extraordinary developments in the use of animals in his book *The War Animals* (1977). The Russians trained porpoises and dolphins to recognize different kinds of metal plates in warships in order to lay mines beside enemy ships, rather like the story in the film *Day of the Dolphin.* In Hong Kong, police tested the use of rats to sniff out heroin. In Britain, the Royal Air Force devised a system of coating aircraft flight detectors ("black boxes") with a special substance odorless to human beings but detectable by trained dogs, who can locate the recorders after a crash. During the Vietnam war, Prof. Lubow successfully trained nearly one hundred dogs to find mines and booby-traps. Insects were used at military establishments to detect the presence of intruders. Pigeons were trained for aerial reconnaissance to identify man-made objects from natural features of the landscape; a radio direction finder would be triggered by the pigeon's landing, transmitting the information to a remote patrol. In Israel, dogs have been used successfully to detect letter-bombs in the mail. The scent of the explosive is apparently perceptible to a dog even in a sack of 600 letters. (See also **Anpsi**)

Sources:

Boone, J. Allen. *Kinship with All Life.* New York: Harper & Brothers, 1954.

Bozzano, Ernesto. "Animals and Psychic Perceptions." *Annals of Psychic Science* (August 1905).

Burton, Maurice. *The Sixth Sense of Animals.* New York: Taplinger, 1973; London: Dent, 1973.

Gaddis, Vincent, and Margaret Gaddis. *The Strange World of Animals and Pets.* 1970. Reprint, New York: Pocket Books, 1971.

Kindermann, Henny. *Lola; or, the Thought and Speech of Animals.* New York: E. P. Dutton, 1923.

Lilly, J. *Man and Dolphin.* Graden City, N.Y.: Doubleday, 1961.

Lorenz, Konrad. *King Solomon's Ring.* New York: Time, 1962.

Lubow, Robert. *The War Animals.* Garden City, N.Y.: Doubleday, 1977.

Maeterlinck, Maurice. *The Unknown Guest.* New Hyde Park, N.Y.: University Books, 1975.

Schul, Bill. *The Psychic Power of Animals.* Greenwich, Conn.: Fawcett, 1977.

Selous, Edmund. *Thought-Transference (or What?) in Birds.* London: Constable & Co. Ltd., 1931.

Animism

An obsolete term used by anthropologists and scholars of comparative religions to designate a doctrine of spiritual being, or the concept that a great part, if not the whole, of inanimate nature, as well as of animate beings, is endowed with reason and volition similar to that of man. In the nineteenth century, a popular hypothesis suggested that animism was at the basis of all religious belief, but that idea has fallen by the way.

Sources:

Durkheim, Emile. *The Elementary Forms of the Religious Life.* New York: Collier, 1961.

Ankh

The Egyptian symbol of life, perhaps the life which remains after death. It takes the form of a cross with a loop instead of an upper vertical arm. It is conjectured that it symbolizes the union of the male and female principles, the origins of life, and that like the American cross, it typifies the four winds, the rain-bringers and fertilizers. It is usually carried in the right hand by Egyptian divinities. This symbol of a cross with a handle is also known as *crux ansata.*

Annales des Sciences Psychiques

Monthly magazine founded in 1891 by **Charles Richet** and Dr. X. Dariex, and edited from 1905 by **Count Cesar Baudi De Vesme,** having absorbed his *Revue des etudes psychique.* It ran until 1919, when it was replaced by the *Revue metapsychique,* the official organ of the **Institut Mètapsychique International.** An English edition under the title *Annals of Psychic Science* was published between 1905 and 1910 and was edited by Laura L. Finch.

Annali dello Spiritismo (Annals of Spiritualism)

The first representative spiritualist journal in **Italy.** It was started in Turin in 1863 by Signor Niceforo Filalete (pseudonym of Prof. Vincenzo Scarpa) and ran until 1898.

Anneberg (or Aunabergius)

A demon of the mines, in German folklore. On one occasion he killed with his breath 12 miners who were working in a silver mine. He was sometimes represented as a large goat, sometimes as a horse, with an immense neck and frightful eyes.

Annius de Viterbo (1432–1502)

Preaching friar born at Viterbo who published a collection of manuscripts known as *The Antiquities of Annius,* full of fables and absurdities, and falsely attributed to Berosus, Fabius Victor, Cato, Manettio, and others. He was also responsible for the treatise *The Empire of the Turks* and the book *Future Triumphs of the Christians over the Turks and the Saracens.* These two works are explanations of the Apocalypse. The author claimed that Mahomet was the **antichrist,** and that the end of the world would take place when the Christians overcome the Jews and the Muslims.

Annwyn (or Annwfn)

The Celtic other-world. According to ancient belief, it might be located either on or under the earth or the sea, or might be a group of islands or a revolving castle surrounded by sea, and was variously known as "Land Over Sea," "Land Under Wave," or *Caer Sidi* (revolving castle). It was said to be a land of strange beauty and delight, with a magic caldron having miraculous powers. It is described in such works as the *Book of Taliesin* and the *Mabinogion.* (See also **Hell**)

Sources:

The Mabinogion. London: J. M. Dent, 1949.

Anomalous Thoughts (Newsletter)

Newsletter concerned with unusual and anomalous data. Address: Box 94, Beaumont, TX 77704.

Anomaly

Journal of unusual events of a Fortean kind, such as UFOs, sea monsters, mysterious disappearances, and strange coincidences. Founded in 1969 by researcher **John A. Keel.** Address: P.O. Box 351, Murray Hill Station, New York, NY 10016.

Anomaly Research Bulletin

Bimonthly publication with reports on UFOs, mysterious animals and other Fortean phenomena. Address: 7098 Edinburgh, Lambertville, MI 48144.

Anonymous Adept

Alchemist alluded to in the two-volume work entitled *Mundus subterraneus* (Amsterdam, 1665), published by the learned German Jesuit of the eighteenth century, known to his clerical *confrères* and his flock as Athanasius the Churchman.

This alchemist long endeavored to discover the **philosophers' stone** and met with no success. One day he encountered a venerable individual who said to him: "I see by these glasses and this furnace that you are engaged in search after something very great in chemistry, but, believe me, you will never attain your object by working as you are doing." These words led the alchemist to suspect that his visitor was learned in **alchemy,** so he begged him to display his knowledge. The unknown took a quill and wrote down a formula for making a transmutatory powder, including specific directions for using it.

"Let us proceed together," said the great unknown, and in a little while a fragment of gold was made; however, the wise teacher disappeared immediately afterward. The alchemist now believed himself on the verge of a dazzling fortune, and he immediately tried to manufacture nuggets, but his solo attempts proved futile.

Enraged, he went to the inn where the unknown teacher was staying, but the teacher was gone.

"We see by this true history," remarked Athanasius, "how the devil seeks to deceive men who are led by a lust of riches." He related further that, as a result of this incident, the alchemist destroyed his scientific equipment and renounced alchemy forever.

Anpiel

In ancient Hebrew mysticism, Anpiel is one of the **angels** charged by rabbis with the government of birds, for every known species was put under the protection of one or more angels.

Anpsi

Psi faculty in **animals.** The term "Psi-trailing" is used to indicate a form of Anpsi in which a pet may trace its owner in a distant location it has not previously visited. (See also **Earthquake Prediction; Elberfeld Horses**)

Sources:

Gaddis, Vincent, and Margaret Gaddis. *The Strange World of Animals and Pets.* 1970. Reprint, New York: Pocket Books, 1971.

Kindermann, Henny. *Lola; or, The Thought and Speech of Animals.* New York: E. P. Dutton, 1923.

Maeterlinck, Maurice. *The Unknown Guest.* New Hyde Park, N.Y.: University Books, 1975.

Schul, Bill. *The Psychic Power of Animals.* Greenwich, Conn.: Fawcett, 1977.

Selous, Edmund. *Thought-Transference (or What?) in Birds.* London: Constable & Co. Ltd., 1931.

Anselm de Parma (d. 1440)

An astrologer born in Parma, where he died in 1440. He wrote *Astrological Institutions,* a work that has never been printed. **Johan Weyer** and some other demonologists classed Anselm with sorcerers, because certain charlatans, who healed sores by means of mysterious words, had taken the name of "Anselmites." It has been noted by Naudé, however, that, in fact, sorcerers claimed to have received their gift of healing not from Anselm of Parma, but from St. Anselm of Canterbury.

Sources:

Weyer, Johannes. *Witches, Devils, and Doctors in the Renaissance: Johann Weyer, De Praestigiis.* Edited by George Mora. Binghamton, N.Y.: Medieval and Renaissance Texts and Studies, 1991.

Ansuperomin

A sorcerer of the time of St. Jean de Lus, who, according to information supplied by Pierre Delamere, a councillor of Henry IV, was seen several times at the "sabbath" mounted on a demon in the shape of a goat and playing on the flute for the witches' dance.

Answerer (or Fragarach)

A magical sword belonging to the Irish Sea-God Lir. It was brought from the Celtic otherworld by Lugh, the Irish Sun-God, and was believed that it could pierce any armor.

Anthony, St.

A great demon of enormous stature is said to have approached Anthony one day to offer his services. In response, the saint looked at him sideways and spat in his face. The demon vanished without a word and did not dare to appear on Earth for a long time afterward. In response to this encounter St. Anthony once said: "I fear the demon no more than I fear a fly, and with the sign of the cross I can at once put him to flight."

St. Athanasius, who wrote the biography *St. Anthony,* mingled his hero's adventures with the devil and certain other incidents that contrast strangely. Some philosophers, astonished at the great wisdom of Anthony, asked him in what book he had discovered his doctrine. The saint pointed with one hand to the Earth, and the other to the sky. "There are my books," said he, "I have no others. If men will design to study as I do the marvels of creation, they will find wisdom enough there. Their spirit will soon soar from the creation to the Creator."

Anthropological Research Foundation

The Anthropological Research Foundation was a short-lived channeling group that formed in the early 1970s during the period of discord within **Cosmic Awareness Communications** following the death of William Ralph Duby, the primary channel for the group. The group was organized in San Diego, California, by Jack T. Fletcher and Pat Fletcher and built around the work of a new channel, trance medium Danton Spivey. Spivey claimed to be the continuing voice of "Conscious Awareness," the universal mystical entity who had spoken through Duby.

The organization took its name from its goal of discovering a new culture characterized by wholeness and overcoming the forces that divided humans from each other. They felt that the resources for such wholeness could be found in the ancient cultures of **Atlantis** and **Lemuria.**

The organization announced its existence with a magazine, *Aware,* but it soon faded from the scene and disbanded.

Anthropology of Consciousness

Quarterly publication (formerly the *AASC Newsletter*) of the **Society for the Anthropology of Consciousness** (formerly the Association for the Anthropological Study of Consciousness), covering such topics as multiple personality, shamanism, "past-life regression," psi-related processes, altered states of consciousness, healing, and symbolism of mythology. The association may be reached c/o Dr. Helmut Wautischer, Society for the Anthropology of Consciousness, Box 13758, Berkeley, CA 94712.

Anthropomancy

Ancient practice of **divination** by the entrails of men or women. Herodotus said that Menelaus, detained in Egypt by poor winds, sacrificed two children of the country to discover his destiny by means of anthropomancy. Heliogabalus practiced this means of divination. It is said that in his magical operations, Julian the Apostate caused a large number of children to be killed so that he might consult their entrails. During his last expedition at Carra, in Mesopotamia, he shut himself in the Temple of the Moon. After completing his anthropomancy, he sealed the doors and posted a guard, whose duty it was to see that they were not opened until his return. However, he was killed in battle with the Persians, and those who entered the Temple of Carra, in the reign of Julian's successor, found there a woman hanging by her hair, with her liver torn out. The infamous **Gilles De Laval** may also have practiced this dreadful type of divination.

Sources:

Waite, Arthur Edward. *The Occult Sciences.* 1891. Reprint, Secaucus, N.J.: University Books, 1974.

Anthroposophia Pacifica (Newsletter)

Bimonthly publication concerned with the teachings of **Rudolf Steiner** (1861–1925), including news of Anthroposophical branches. Address: 5906 Pacific Coast Highway No. 12, Redondo Beach, CA 90277.

Anthroposophical Press

Publishers and suppliers of books on the work of **Rudolf Steiner** and anthroposophy, Waldorf education, occult cosmology, self-development, and alternative therapies. The Press issues a comprehensive mail-order catalog. Address: 258 Bell's Pond, Star Route, Hudson, NY 12534.

Anthroposophical Society

Organization founded by **Rudolf Steiner** (1861–1925) to teach an occult philosophy relating man to his natural environment, with special emphasis on the significance of color and rhythm. The name, which derives from the book *Anthroposophia Theomagica* by seventeenth-century mystic **Thomas Vaughan,** implies wisdom relating to man. Anthroposophy covers a wide range of enlightened activity—education, music, painting, eurythmy, biodynamic farming, medicine, and architecture.

There are some 70 anthroposophical schools in various parts of the world, and the society has many branches. Drawing largely upon the work and lectures of the late Rudolf Steiner, the society has established a high standard of enlightened community activity and culture. Its clinics, particularly for retarded children, are conducted with insight and kindness. The **Anthroposophical Press** issues titles by Steiner and other writers in the English language. The society has an impressive international headquarters building named the Goetheanum (acknowledging Steiner's debt to the writings of Goethe) at Dornach, Switzerland.

Sources:

Davey, John, ed. *Work Arising from the Life of Rudolf Steiner.* London: R. Steiner Press, 1975.

Steiner, Rudolf. *Knowledge of the Higher Worlds: How Is It Achieved?.* 1923. Rev. ed., London: R. Steiner Press, 1969.

———. *The Story of My Life.* London: Anthroposophical Publishing, 1928; New York: Anthroposophic Press, 1928.

Anthroposophical Society in America

Organization devoted to the teachings of theosophist and occult mystic **Rudolf Steiner,** whose system of **Anthroposophy** is concerned with "wisdom relating to man." Steiner developed his system of thought to speak directly to issues of education, art, dance and body movement, natural foods, and the religious life. The society promotes Steiner's thinking through a number of local and a variety of specialized organizations such as the School of Eurythmy and the Waldorf Institute (260 Hungry Hollow Rd., Spring Valley, NY), the Bio-Dynamic Association (P.O. Box 550, Kimberton, PA 19442), the Rudolf Steiner Research Foundation (1753 Appleton St., Ste. D, Long Beach, CA 90802), and Weleda USA (841 South Main St., P.O. Box 769, Spring Valley, NY 10977). The Christian Community (309 West 74th St., New York, NY 10023) includes churches that embody Steiner's ideals in Christian expression.

Headquarters of the society are at 21 Madison Ave., New York, NY 10016. It publishes the quarterly *Journal of Anthroposophy* (HCO1, Box 24, Dripping Springs, TX 78620). The numerous books by Steiner are published by the **Anthroposophical Press** (RR4, Box 94A1, Hudson, NY 12534).

Sources:

Directory of Activities and Services. New York: Rudolf Steiner Information Center, n.d.

Richards, M. C. *Toward Wholeness: Rudolf Steiner Education in America.* Middletown, Conn.: Wesleyan University Press, 1980.

Anthroposophical Society in Great Britain

Organization devoted to the teachings of occult mystic **Rudolf Steiner,** whose system of **Anthroposophy** is concerned with a "wisdom relating to man." The London headquarters presents study groups, classes in artistic activities (painting, speech, drama), and performances of eurythmy. The Anthroposophical Society's publications include the *Anthroposophical Quarterly,* the annual magazine the *Golden Blade,* the booklet *Practical Activities Founded on the Work of Rudolf Steiner,* and a catalog of works by Steiner and other writers. Steiner's work ranges across many fields, including education, art therapy, special care and training of retarded children, and agricultural techniques. Address: 35 Park Rd., London NW1 6XT, England. Branches of the Anthroposophical Society and special schools are located in different areas in Britain.

Antichrist

According to early and medieval Christian belief, Antichrist is the universal enemy of human beings who in the latter days will scourge the world for its wickedness. He is only mentioned as a character in the Bible in two brief passages occurring in the First and Second Epistles of John (1 John 2:18, 22, and 4:3; and 2 John 7). However, the "man of Lawlessness" (2 Thessalonians 2:3–12) and the "beast" (Revelation 13) are also commonly thought to represent the Antichrist.

Abbot Bergier described the Antichrist as a tyrant, impious and excessively cruel, the arch enemy of Christ, and the last ruler of the Earth. The persecutions he will inflict on the elect will be the last and most severe ordeal that they will have to endure.

The Antichrist will pose as the Messiah and will perform things wonderful enough to mislead the elect themselves. The thunder will obey him, according to St. John, and Leloyer asserts that the demons below watch over hidden treasures with which he will be able to tempt many. Because of the miracles that he will perform, Boguet calls him the "Ape of God," and it is through this scourge that God will proclaim the final judgment.

Antichrist will have a great number of forerunners and will appear just before the end of the world. St. Jerome claimed that he will be a man fathered by a demon; others said that he will be a demon in the flesh. But, following the thinking of Saints Ireneus, Ambrose, Augustine and almost all of the church fathers, Antichrist will be a man similar to and conceived in the same way as all others, differing from them only in a malice and an impiety more worthy of a demon than of a man. More recently, however, Cardinal Bellarmin asserted that Antichrist will be the son of a demon **incubus** and a sorceress.

He will be a Jew of the tribe of Dan, according to Malvenda, who supported his view with the words the dying Jacob spoke to his sons, "Dan shall be a serpent by the way—an adder in the path": by those of Jeremiah, "The armies of Dan will devour the earth"; and by the seventh chapter of the Apocalypse, where St. John has omitted the tribe of Dan in his enumeration of the other tribes.

Elijah and Enoch will return to convert the Jews and will die by order of Antichrist. Then Christ will descend from the heavens, kill Antichrist with the two-edged sword, which will issue from his mouth, and reign on the earth for a thousand years.

It is claimed by some that the reign of Antichrist will last fifty years; but the opinion of the majority is that his reign will last three and a half years, after which the angels will sound the trumpets of the day of judgment, and Christ will come and judge the world. Boguet declared that the watchword of Antichrist will be "I abjure baptism." Many commentators foresaw the return of Elijah in these words of Malachi "I will send Elijah, the prophet, before the coming of the great and dreadful day of the Lord." But it is not certain that Malachi referred to this ancient prophet, since Christ applied this prediction to John the Baptist when he said, "Elias is come already, and they knew him not"; and when the angel foretold to Zacharias the birth of his son, he said to him: "And he shall go forth before the Lord in the spirit and power of Elias."

The word "Antichrist" probably refers to the persecutors of the Church. Through the centuries, different groups of Christians declared that one or more of their contemporaries was the Antichrist. For example, sixteenth-century Protestants called the pope Antichrist. Even Napoleon was called Antichrist.

The third treatise in the *History véritable et mémorable des trois possédees de Flandre* (1613) by Father Sebastien Michaelis, a Dominican friar, described Antichrist:

"Conceived through the medium of a devil, he will be as malicious as a madman, with such wickedness as was never seen on earth. An inhuman martyr rather than a human one, he will treat Christians as souls are treated in hell. He will have a multitude of synagogue names, and he will be able to fly when he wishes. Beelzebub will be his father, Lucifer his grandfather."

According to Michaelis, exorcised demons revealed that Antichrist was alive in 1613 but had not yet attained his growth. "He was baptized on the Sabbath of the sorcerers, before his mother, a Jewess, called La Belle-Fleur. He was three years old in 1613." **Louis Gaufridi** is said to have baptized him, in a field near Paris. An exorcised sorceress claimed to have held the little Antichrist on her knees. She said that his bearing was proud and that even then he spoke many languages. But he had talons in the place of feet. His father is shown in the figure of a bird, with four feet, a tail, a bull's head much flattened, horns, and black shaggy hair. He will mark his own with a seal representing this in miniature. Michaelis added that things execrable will be around him. He will destroy Rome and the Pope with the help of the Jews. He will resuscitate the dead, and, at the age of 30 will reign with Lucifer, the seven-headed dragon. After a reign of three years, Christ will slay him.

Many such details might be quoted of Antichrist, whose coming has long been threatened but not yet realized (see **End of the World**). A volume by Rusand published many years ago at Lyons, *Les Prècurseurs de l'Antechrist,* stated that the reign of Antichrist, if it has not begun, is drawing near; that the philosophers, encyclopedists, and revolutionaries of the eighteenth century were only demons incarnated to precede and prepare the way for Antichrist. During World War I, there were people who were convinced that Antichrist was none other than the ex-kaiser of Germany.

Another way to recognize Antichrist is by the title "Beast 666," because Revelation describes the beast as a "false prophet." The title "Beast 666" was applied to modern occultist **Aleister Crowley** (1875–1947) by his mother, and he accepted it as a symbol of his break with the severe fundamentalism of his Plymouth Brethren father.

Sources:

Crowley, Aleister. *The Confessions of Aleister Crowley.* Edited by John Symonds and Kenneth Grant. New York: Hill & Wang, 1969.

Kirban, Salem. *666.* Huntingdon Valley, Penn.: Salem Kirban, 1970.

McBirnie, William S. *Anti-Christ.* Dallas, Tex.: International Prison Ministry, 1978.

Antipathy

Early astrologers claimed that the dislike one feels for another person or thing is caused by the stars. Thus, two persons born under the same aspect will be mutually attracted and will love without knowing why. Others born under opposite conjunctions will feel an unreasoning hate for each other.

But what is the explanation for the antipathy people sometimes have for the commonest things? Lamothe-Levayer could not bear to hear the sound of any musical instrument. Caesar could not hear the crowing of a cock without shuddering; Lord Bacon fell into despondency during the eclipse of the moon; Marie de Medicis could not bear to look on a rose, even in a painting, although she loved all other flowers. Cardinal Henry of Cardonne had the same antipathy toward the odor of roses; Marshal d'Albret became ill at dinner when a young wild boar or a suckling pig was served; Henry III of France could not remain in the same room with a cat; Marshal de Schomberg had the same weakness; Ladislas, king of Poland, was much disturbed at the sight of apples; Scaliger trembled at the sight of cress; Erasmus could not taste fish without having the fever; Tycho-Brahe felt his knees give way when he met a hare or a fox; the duke of Epernon fainted at the sight of a leveret; Cardan could not stomach eggs; Ariosto, baths; the son of Croesus, bread; Caesar of Lescalle, the sound of the vielle or violin.

The causes of these antipathies might be found in childhood impressions. A lady who was very fond of pictures and engravings fainted when she found them in a book. She explained her terror thus: When she was a child her father had one day seen her turning over the leaves of the books in his library, in search of pictures. He had roughly taken the book from her hand, telling her in terrible tones that there were devils in these books who would strangle her if she dared touch them. Such threats may have lingering effects that cannot be overcome.

Karl von Reichenbach (1788–1869) investigated human antipathies and their opposite, sympathies, as they relate to colors, metals, magnetic poles, right and left hand polarities, and heat and cold. He distinguished specific antipathies and sympathies that were characteristic of sensitives (mediumistic individuals) and related his findings to **animal magnetism** and **mesmerism.**

Antiphates

A shining black stone, used as an **amulet** in defending oneself against witchcraft.

Antracites (or Antrachas or Anthrax)

A stone, sparkling like fire and girdled with a white vein, supposed by **Albertus Magnus** to be the carbuncle. It was said to cure "imposthumes" (purulent swellings). If smeared with oil it loses its color but sparkles the more for being dipped in water.

Aonbarr

A horse belonging to Manaanan, son of the Irish Sea-God Lir. It was believed to possess magical gifts and could gallop on land or sea.

Apantomancy

Divination by means of any objects that happen to present themselves. To this class belong omens drawn from chance meetings with a hare or an eagle.

Apepi, Book of Overthrowing of

An Egyptian work that forms a considerable portion of the funerary papyrus of Nesi-Amsu. It deals with the diurnal combat between Ra the Sun-God and Apepi the great serpent and personification of spiritual evil. Several chapters (notably 31, 33, and 35–39) are obviously borrowed from the **Book of the Dead,** or Papyrus of Ani. Its 15 chapters contain a great deal of repetition and details concerning various methods for the destruction of Apepi, including many magical directions.

It stipulates that the name of Apepi must be written in green on a papyrus and then burnt. Wax figures of his attendant fiends were to be made, mutilated, and burnt, in the hope that, through the agency of sympathetic magic, their prototypes might be injured or destroyed.

Another portion of the work details the creative process and describes how men and women were formed from the tears of the god Khepera. This portion is known as *The Book of Knowing the Evolutions of Ra.* The work is evidently very ancient, as is shown by the circumstance that many variant readings occur, and only one copy is known. The funeral papyrus in which it is contained was discovered at Thebes in 1860, purchased by the archaeologist A. H. Rhind, and sold to the trustees of the British Museum by David Bremner. The linen on which it is written is of very fine texture, measures 19 feet by 9 inches, and has been translated by Wallis Budge in *Archaeologia* (Vol. 52, Part 2).

Apollonius of Tyana

A Neo-Pythagorean philosopher of Greece who had a great reputation for magical powers. *The Life of Apollonius of Tyana,* written by Philostratus at the urging of Julia, mother of the Emperor Severus, is the only extant source of information concerning the sage, although other biographies, now lost, are known to have existed.

Born at Tyana in Asia Minor, Apollonius was contemporary with Christ. He was educated at Tarsus and at the Temple of Aesculapius in Aegae. At the temple he became an adherent of the sect of Pythagoras, to whose strict discipline he submitted himself throughout his life. In his desire for knowledge he traveled widely in eastern countries, and is said to have performed miracles wherever he went. At Ephesus, for instance, he warned the people of the approach of a terrible plague, but they paid no attention to him until the pestilence was actually in their midst; then they recalled the warning and summoned the potent magician who had uttered it. Apollonius identified a poor, maimed beggar as the cause of the plague and an enemy of the gods, and he advised them to stone the unfortunate wretch to death. The citizens were at first reluctant to comply with the cruel injunction, but something in the expression of the beggar confirmed the prophet's accusation, and the wretch was soon covered with a mound of stones. When the stones were removed, the man had disappeared. In his place was a huge black dog, the cause of the plague that had come upon the Ephesians.

In Rome Apollonius raised from death or apparent death (his biographer does not seem to know which) a young lady of a consular family who had been betrothed and was mourned by the entire city. Yet another story relates how Apollonius saved a friend of his, Menippus of Corinth, from marrying a **vampire.** The youth neglected all the earlier warnings of his counselor, and the preparations for the wedding proceeded. Just as the ceremony was about to begin, Apollonius appeared and caused the wedding feast, the guests, and all the evidences of wealth—which were but illusion—to vanish; then he wrung from the bride the confession that she was a vampire. Many other similar tales are told of the philosopher's clairvoyant and magical powers.

His death is wrapped in mystery, although he is said to have lived to be nearly one hundred years of age. His disciples were quick to say that he had not died at all, but had been caught up to heaven. When he had vanished from the Earth, the inhabitants of his native Tyana built a temple in his honor, and statues were raised to him in various other temples.

The account given by Philostratus was compiled from the memoirs of "Damis the Assyrian," a disciple of Apollonius, but Damis may be a literary fiction. The work seems largely a romance; fictitious stories are often introduced, and the whole account is mystical and symbolical. Nevertheless, it is possible to glimpse the real character of Apollonius beyond the literary artifices of the writer. The purpose of the philosopher of Tyana seems to have been to infuse into paganism practical morality combined with a transcendental doctrine. He himself practiced a very severe asceticism and supplemented his own knowledge by revelations from the gods. Because of his claim to divine enlightenment, some would have refused him a place among the philosophers, but Philostratus holds that this in no way detracts from his philosophic reputation. He points out that Pythagoras, Plato, and Democritus used to visit eastern sages, and they were not charged with dabbling in **magic.** Divine revelations had been given to earlier philosophers; why not also to the Philosopher of Tyana? It may be that Apollonius borrowed considerably from Oriental sources and that his doctrines were more Brahminical than magical.

Sources:

Eells, Charles P. *Life and Times of Apollonius of Tyana, Rendered into English from the Greek of Philostratus the Elder.* Stanford, Calif.: Stanford University Press, 1923.

Mead, G. R. S. *Apollonius of Tyana: The Philosopher-Reformer of the First Century A.D.* 1901. Reprint, New Hyde Park, N.Y.: University Books, 1966.

Philostratus. *The Life of Apollonius of Tyana.* Translated by F. C. Conybeare. London: Macmillan, 1912.

Apollyon

The destroying angel or prince of the underworld (Rev. 9:11), synonymous with **Abaddon.**

Sources:

Barrett, Francis. *The Magus.* 1801. Reprint, New Hyde Park, N.Y.: University Books, 1967.

Apostolic Circle

A sectarian group of early American Spiritualists that claimed to be in communication (through the mediumship of **Mrs. Benedict** of Auburn) with the apostles and prophets of the Bible. The sect also believed in a second advent. James L. Scott, a Seventh Day Baptist minister of Brooklyn, joined the group in 1849. He delivered trance utterances in the name of St. John and edited, jointly with the **Rev. Thomas Lake Harris,** a periodical of the Apostolic Movement: *Disclosures from the Interior and Superior Care for Mortals.*

Not long after, the partnership was dissolved, and in October 1851 the remaining members of the group settled at **Mountain Cove,** Fayette County, Virginia. Scott declared himself medium absolute. Owing to strife and dissension, the settlement was given up in February 1852. Scott went to New York, and as Thomas Lake Harris succeeded in arousing the interest of several wealthy men for the movements, the surrendered property was repurchased. A new era began in which Scott and Harris, the first the mouthpiece of St. John, the second of St. Paul, acted as "the chosen mediums" through which "the Lord would communicate to man on earth."

Their house was called "the House of God," and Mountain Cove was "the Gate of Heaven." They proclaimed themselves to be the two witnesses named in Rev. 10 and claimed to possess the powers spoken of. In one of his prayers Harris said, "Oh Lord, thou knowest we do not wish to destroy man with fire from our mouths!" However, the two "perfect" prophets could not smother the growing discord against their autocratic rule, and soon the whole community dispersed.

Sources:

Cuthbert, Arthur. *The Life Worldwork of Thomas Lake Harris, Written from Direct Personal Knowledge.* Glasgow, Scotland, 1909.

Schneider, Herbert W., and George Lawton. *A Prophet and a Pilgrim.* New York: Columbia University Press, 1942.

Apparitions

An apparition, from Latin *apparere* (to appear), is in its literal sense merely an appearance—a sense perception of any kind, but as used in **psychical research** and **parapsychology** the word denotes an abnormal or paranormal appearance or perception, which cannot be explained by any mundane objective cause. Taken in this sense the word covers all visionary appearances, **hallucinations, clairvoyance,** and similar unusual perceptions. "Apparition" and "ghost" are frequently used as synonymous terms, though the former is, of course, of much wider significance. A **ghost** is a visual apparition of a deceased human being—the term implies that the ghost is the spirit of the person it represents. Apparitions of **animals** and even inanimate objects are also occasionally reported. All apparitions do not take the form of visual images; auditory and tactile false perceptions, although less common, are not unknown. For example, there is record of a house that was "haunted" with the perpetual odor of violets.

Evolution of the Belief in Apparitions

The belief that identifies an apparition with the spirit of the creature it represents—a worldwide belief widely affirmed in all cultures throughout history—has been traced to the ancient doctrine generally called **animism,** which endowed everything in nature, from human beings to the smallest insect, from the heavenly bodies to an insignificant plant or stone, with a separable soul. It is not difficult to understand how the conception of souls may have arisen. Nineteenth-century anthropologist James Frazer, in his classic work, the *Golden Bough,* states,

"As the savage commonly explains the processes of inanimate nature by supposing that they are produced by living beings working in or behind the phenomena, so he explains the phenomena of life itself. If an animal lives and moves, it can only be, he thinks, because there is a little animal inside which moves it. If a man lives and moves, it can only be because he has a little man or animal inside, who moves him. The animal inside the animal, the man inside the man, is the soul. And as the activity of an animal or man is explained by the presence of the soul, so the repose of sleep or death is explained by its absence; sleep or trance being the temporary, death being the permanent absence of the soul."

Sometimes the human soul was represented as a bird—an eagle, a dove, a raven—or as an animal of some sort, just as the soul of a river might be in the form of a horse or a serpent, or the soul of a tree in human shape; but among most peoples the belief was that the soul was an exact reproduction of the body resembling it in every feature, even to details of dress.

When a person saw another in a dream, it was thought either that the soul of the dreamer had visited the person dreamed of, or that the soul of the latter had visited the dreamer. By an easy process of reasoning, this theory was extended to include dreams of animals and inanimate things, which also were endowed with souls.

Telepathy and clairvoyance have been described as appearing in pre-industrial indigenous cultures and have a powerful effect in the development of a belief in apparitions. It is believed that the apparition of a deceased person suggested to some the continuance of the soul's existence beyond the grave; the apparition of a sick person, or one in some other grave crisis could also be regarded as the soul, which at such times was absent from the body.

There is a widely diffused opinion that ghosts are of a filmy, unsubstantial nature, a belief also present in the earliest speculations concerning apparitions. At a very early period (as, for example, in the early chapters of the biblical book of Genesis) we find "spirit" and "breath" identified with each other—an identification continued in the Latin *spiritus* and the Greek *pneuma,* as well as appearing in other languages. It is possible that the breath, which in some climates readily condenses in cold air to a white mist, might be regarded as the stuff that ghosts are made of.

The "misty" nature of the ghost may also have resulted from an early speculation that the shadow is related to soul. Thus "animistic" ideas of the soul offer an explanation of apparitions. Ancient religion also had a belief in a host of spirits that had never taken bodies—true supernatural beings, as distinct from souls, i.e., gods, elementary spirits, and those "evil" spirits to which were attributed disease, disaster, possession, and bewitchment. The ancient deities may have evolved into the **fairies,** elves, brownies, bogies, and goblins of popular folklore, of which many apparitions are recorded.

Primitive Concepts of Apparitions

It is only within the last few generations that scientific investigation of apparitions has begun, growing out of the new post-Enlightenment scientific mythologies, and resulting from the new level of skepticism towards paranormal occurrences that developed in the nineteenth century. There was an almost universal belief in ghosts, a belief which European explorers found among the peoples they encountered as they set out on their empire-building expansions.

One of the most noteworthy features of ghosts in indigenous cultures was the fear and antagonism with which many regarded them. The spirits of the deceased were frequently thought to be unfriendly towards the living, desirous of drawing their souls into the spirit-world. Sometimes, as with the Australian Aborigines, they were represented as malignant demons. Naturally, everything possible was done to keep such ghosts at a distance from the habitations of the living.

Barriers to ghosts were constructed of thorn bushes planted around the beds of surviving relatives. Persons returning from a funeral might pass through a cleft tree, or other narrow aperture, to free themselves from the ghost of the person they just buried. The same reason has been given for the practice, common among Hottentots, Hindus, Native Americans, and many other peoples, of carrying the dead out through a hole in the wall and closing the aperture immediately afterward. The custom of closing the eyes of the dead may have arisen from the fear that the ghost would find its way back again.

To the contrary, the Mayas of the Yucatan (Mexico), used to draw a line with chalk from the tomb to the hearth, so that the soul might return if it desired to do so.

Among many peoples, the names of the departed (in some mysterious manner bound up with the soul, if not identified with it) are not mentioned by the survivors, and any among them possessing the same name change it for another.

Apparitions appeared in many shapes; it might take a human form, or the form of a beast, bird, or fish. Animal ghosts were common among Native Americans in both North and South America. Certain African tribes believed that the souls of evil-doers became jackals (a scavenger animal) on the death of the body. The Tapuya Indians of Brazil thought the souls of the good entered into birds, and this belief was of rather wide diffusion.

When the apparition was in human shape it was generally an exact counterpart of the person it represented, and, like the apparitions reported in more recent times, its dress was that worn by the deceased in its lifetime. It was generally accepted in indigenous cultures that the spirits of the departed mingled with the living, coming and going with no particular object in view or, on occasion, with the special purpose of visiting the scene of his earthly life. It may be that the spirit was demanding its body be buried with the proper ceremonial rites, if this had not been done, for a spirit cannot have any rest until the burial rite has been duly performed.

In China, the most common ghost was that of a person who had been murdered, and sought revenge on his murderer. In Australia, the spirit of one who had been murdered, or had died a violent death, was also considered likely to walk abroad. In many lands, the souls of women who died in childbirth were supposed to become spirits of a particularly malignant type that dwelled in trees and tormented passers-by. The Eastern Europeans believed the neglect of proper burial procedures led the deceased to continued existence as a **vampire.**

Such attention to burial procedures had several very practical benefits. The family in charge of the burial of a deceased relative was provided the opportunity of completing any emotional business they had with the deceased—a process today generally termed grief work. Burial rites of today are designed for the living, not the deceased, and provide a means of affirming life in the community in the face of death.

In many cultures, it is thought that ghosts haunt certain localities. The favorite spot seems to be the burial place, of which there is an almost universal superstitious dread (an emotional reaction to the implied threat of death). However, the Indians of Guyana (South America) believed that every place where anyone had died was haunted. Among the Kaffirs and the Maoris of New Zealand, a hut where a death has occurred was taboo, and was often burned or deserted. Sometimes, even a whole village would be abandoned on account of a death.

In most ancient accounts of apparitions, as well as those from more recent indigenous peoples, ghosts seldom manifest articulate human speech. They chirp like crickets, for instance, among the Algonquin Indians, and their "voices" are only intelligible to the trained ear of the shaman. The ghosts of the Zulus and New Zealander Maoris speak to the magicians in thin, whistling tones. This idea of the semiarticulate nature of ghosts is not confined to anthropological treatises; in his play *Julius Ceasar,* William Shakespeare spoke of "the sheeted dead," who, "did squeak and gibber in the streets of Rome," and the "gibbering" ghost appeared in other connections.

Naturally an articulate apparition would be doubly convincing, since it appealed to two separate senses. Nineteenth-century anthropologist E. B. Tylor argued, "Men who perceive evidently that souls do talk when they present themselves in dream or vision, naturally take for granted at once the objective reality of the ghostly voice, and of the ghostly form from which it proceeds." Spirits that are generally invisible may appear only to selected persons and under certain circumstances. In the Antilles, it was believed that one person traveling alone could see a ghost that would be invisible to a number of people. The various religious functionaries—shamans, medicine men, and magicians—were often able to perceive apparitions that none but they could see. The induction of hallucinations by means of various techniques—fasts, rigid asceticism, solitude, the use of narcotics and intoxicants, dancing, and the performance of elaborate ceremonial rites—was known all over the world. These rituals are still performed today.

Ancient and Modern Ideas Concerning Apparitions

The belief in apparitions was very common in the ancient Middle East. The early Hebrews attributed them to angels, demons, and the souls of the dead, as is shown in the numerous Scriptural instances of apparitions. Dreams (see, for example Genesis 41) were regarded as apparitions if the predictions made in them were fulfilled, or if the dream-figure revealed anything unknown to the dreamer which afterwards proved to be true. That the Hebrews believed in the possibility of the souls of the dead returning is evident from the tale of the witch of Endor (I Samuel 28). In this connection, French biblical scholar **Augustin Calmet** wrote in his classic study, *Dissertations upon the Apparitions of Angels, Demons & Ghosts* (1759), "Whether Samuel was raised up or not, whether his soul, or only a shadow, or even nothing at all appeared to the woman, it is still certain that Saul and his attendants, with the generality of the Hebrews, believed the thing to be possible." Similar beliefs were held by other Mediterranean nations. Among the Greeks and Romans of the classic period apparitions of gods and men seem to have been fairly common. As Calmet further noted,

"The ancient Greeks, who had derived their religion and theology from the Egyptians and Eastern nations, and the Latins, who had borrowed theirs from the Greeks, were all firmly persuaded that the souls of the dead appeared sometimes to the living—that they could be called up by necromancers, that they answered questions, and gave notice of future events; that Apollo gave oracles, and that the priestess, filled with his spirit, and transported with a holy enthusiasm, uttered infallible predictions of things to come. Homer, the most ancient of all the Greek writers, and their greatest divine, relates several apparitions, not only of gods, but of dead men and heroes. In the Odyssey, he introduces Ulysses consulting Teresias, who, having prepared a pit full of blood, in order to call up the Manes, Ulysses draws his sword to hinder them from drinking the blood for which they were very thirsty, till they had answered the questions proposed to them. It was also a prevailing opinion that the souls of men enjoyed no repose, but wandered about near their carcasses as long as they continued unburied. Even after they were buried, it was a custom to offer them something to eat, especially honey, upon the supposition that after having left their graves, they came to feed upon what was brought them. They believed also, that the demons were fond of the smoke of sacrifices, of music, of the blood of victims, and the commerce of women; and that they were confined for a determinate time to certain houses or other places, which they haunted, and in which they appeared.

"They held that souls, when separated from their gross and terrestrial bodies, still retained a finer and more subtle body, of the same form with that which they had quitted; that these bodies were luminous like the stars; and they retained an inclination for the things which they had loved in their life time, and frequently appeared about their graves. When the soul of Patroclus appeared to Achilles, it had his voice, his shape, his eyes, and his dress, but not the same tangible body."

Calmet added of the early Christian church fathers,

"We find that Origen, Tertullian, and St. Irenaus, were clearly of this opinion. Origen, in his second book against Celsus, relates and subscribes to the opinion of Plato, who says, that the shadows and images of the dead, which are seen near sepulchres, are nothing but the soul disengaged from its gross body, but not yet entirely freed from matter; that these souls become in time luminous, transparent, and subtle, or rather are carried in luminous and transparent bodies, as in a vehicle, in which they appeal to the living. . . . Tertullian, in his book concerning the soul, asserts that it is corporeal, and of a certain figure, and appeals to the experience of those who have seen apparitions of departed souls, and to whom they have appeared as corporeal and tangible, though of an aerial colour and consistence. He defines the soul to be a breath from God, immortal, corporeal, and of a certain figure."

It is interesting to note that some of these widely read classic accounts of specters became the model of the melodramatic conceptions of more modern times. The younger Pliny tells of haunted houses whose main features correspond with those of later hauntings—houses haunted by dismal, chained specters, and the ghosts of murdered men who could not rest till their mortal remains had been properly buried.

In the early centuries of Christendom there was no diminution in the number of apparitions witnessed. Visions of saints were frequently seen; their appearances were stimulated by the fasts, rigid austerities, and severe penances practiced by Christian ascetics and penitents. The saints regularly saw visions, and were attended by guardian angels, as well as being harassed by the unwelcome attention of demons, or of their master, the devil.

These beliefs continued into the Middle Ages, when, without decreasing in vigor, they began to assume a more romantic aspect. The witch and **werewolf** superstitions led to many tales of animal apparitions. The **poltergeist** flourished in a congenial atmosphere. Vampires were familiar in Slavonic and African lands, and analogous beings such as the **incubus** and **succubus** were widespread throughout Northern and Western Europe.

In the northern countries, familiar spirits or goblins, similar to the Roman *lares,* or the wicked and mischievous *lemures,* haunted the domestic hearth, and bestowed well-meant, but not always desirable, attentions on the families to which they attached themselves. These beings were accountable for a vast number of apparitions, but the spirits of the dead also walked abroad. Generally they wished to unburden their minds of some weighty secret that hindered them from resting in their graves. The criminal came to confess his guilt, the miser to reveal the spot where he had hidden his gold. The cowled monk walked the dim aisles of a monastery, or haunted the passages of some Rhenish castle until the prayers of the devout won release for his tortured soul.

Tales of apparitions began to emerge in this period. For example, a maiden in white might flit through the corridor of an old mansion, moaning and wringing her hands, enacting in pantomime some long-forgotten tragedy. At the crossroads lingered the ghost of the poor suicide, uncertain which way to take. The old belief in the dread potency of the unburied dead continued to exercise sway. Another story, of German origin, tells of the Bleeding Nun. Many and ghastly had been her crimes during her lifetime, until finally she was murdered by one of her paramours, and her body was left unburied. The castle where she was slain became the scene of her nocturnal wanderings. One traditional story tells of a young woman who wished to elope with her lover and decided to disguise herself as this ghostly specter in order to facilitate their escape. But the unfortunate lover eloped with the veritable Bleeding Nun herself, mistaking her for his mistress!

This, and other traditional tales of apparitions—the Wild Huntsman, the Phantom Coach, and the **Flying Dutchman,** to mention a few of the more widespread and famous—either originated in this period or acquired in it a wildly romantic character which lent itself to treatment by ballad writers. It is in ballad form that many of these stories survived.

Such tales of the apparitions gave way in the eighteenth century to a skepticism among the more educated elements of Western society about the objective nature of apparitions—a skepticism that was destined two centuries later to assume almost universal proportions. Hallucinations, although not yet very well understood, began to be referred to as the "power of imagination." Many apparitions were also attributed to illusion. The belief in apparitions was sustained and given new strength by the clairvoyant powers demonstrated by magnetized subjects and somnambules. **Emanuel Swedenborg,** who had many disciples, did much to encourage the idea that apparitions were both objective and supernatural. To explain the fact that only the seer saw these beings and heard their voices, he argued,

"The speech of an angel or of a spirit with man is heard as sonorously as the speech of one man with another: yet it is not heard by others who stand near, but by the man himself alone. The reason is, the speech of an angel or of a spirit flows in first into the man's thought, and by an internal way into the organ of hearing, and thus actuates it from within, whereas the speech of man flows first into the air, and by an external way into the organ of hearing which it actuates from without. Hence, it is evident, that the speech of an angel and of a spirit with man is heard in man, and, since it equally affects the organ of hearing, that it is equally sonorous."

Ancient and modern ideas on apparitions differed very little in essential particulars, though they were colored by the culture in which they were reported and the time to which they belong. In times past they were thin, gibbering shadows; now they tend to be solid, full-bodied creatures, hardly to be distinguished from real flesh and blood, or again they are rich in romantic accessories; but the laws governing their appearance are the same, and the beliefs concerning them are not greatly different, in whatever culture or time period they may be found.

The belief in apparitions is as old as humanity, but modern culture tends to reduce the phantoms to human shapes. Rare indeed, though not unknown, are accounts like that Plutarch told of Brutus,

"A little before he left Asia he was sitting alone in his tent, by a dim light, and at a late hour. The whole army lay in sleep and silence, while the general, wrapped in meditation, thought he perceived something enter his tent; turning towards the door he saw a horrible and monstrous specter standing silently by his side. 'What art thou,' said he boldly. 'Art thou God or man, and what is thy business with me?' The specter answered, 'I am thy evil genius, Brutus! Thou wilt see me at Philippi.' To which he calmly replied, 'I'll meet thee there.' When the apparition was gone he called his servants, who told him they had neither heard any voice, nor seen any vision."

Types of Apparitions

Psychical research divided apparitions broadly into two classes—induced and spontaneous. To the former class belong hypnotic and post-hypnotic hallucinations and visions induced by the use of narcotics and intoxicants, fasts, ascetic practices, incense, narcotic salves, and various forms of **hypnotism.** The hallucinatory appearances seen in the mediumistic or somnambulistic trance are allied to those of hypnotism, but usually arise spontaneously, and are often associated with clairvoyance.

Crystallomancy or **crystal gazing** is a form of apparition that is believed to be frequently clairvoyant, and in this case the theory of telepathy is especially applicable. Crystal visions fall under the heading of induced apparitions, since gazing in a crystal globe induces in some persons an altered or slight dissociation of consciousness, without which hallucination is impossible.

Another form of clairvoyance is **second sight,** a faculty commonly reported among the Scottish Highlanders. Persons gifted with second sight often see symbolical apparitions; for instance, the vision of a funeral or a coffin when a death is about to occur in the community. Symbolical appearances are indeed a feature of clairvoyance and visions generally. Clairvoyance includes retrocognition and **premonition**—visions of the past and the future respectively—as well as apparitions of contemporary events happening at a distance. Clairvoyant powers are often attributed to the dying. Dreams are, strictly speaking, apparitions, but in ordinary usage the term is applied only to coincidental or genuine dreams, or to those "visions of the night," which are of peculiar vividness.

These subjective apparitions lead quite naturally to a consideration of the question of ghosts. The belief in ghosts has come to us, as has been indicated, from the remotest antiquity, and innumerable theories have been formulated to account for it, from older conceptions of the apparition as an actual soul to modern theories of which the chief are telepathy and spirit materialization. Apparitions of the living also offer a wide field for research, perhaps the most favored hypothesis being that of telepathic hallucination.

Another type of apparition is the **wraith** or **double,** of which the Irish **fetch** is a variant. The wraith is an exact facsimile of a living person, who may himself see it; Goethe, Shelley, and other famous men are said to have seen their own wraiths. The fetch makes its appearance shortly before the death of the person it represents, either to himself or his friends, or both. Another Irish spirit which foretells death is the **banshee,** a being which, according to legend, attaches itself to certain ancient families, and is regularly seen or heard before the death of one of its members.

To the same class of spirits belong the omens of death, in the form of certain animals or birds, which follow some families. The poltergeist, whose playful manifestations must certainly be included among apparitions is suggested as another classification of these as visual, auditory, and tactile, since poltergeist hauntings—or indeed hauntings of any kind—are not confined to apparitions touching any one sense.

Apparitions of the Virgin Mary

One characteristic type of apparition is the appearance of the Virgin Mary, who is usually seen by young girls in Catholic countries. Such appearances involve messages for mankind as a whole, usually admonitions against sin and exhortations to repentance. The apparitions are not sought by the children and youths concerned, and often the messages are well beyond their intellectual capacity. The visions occur in an ecstatic state.

Typical of such apparitions were those at **Lourdes,** in southern France, **Fatima** in Portugal, and **Garabandal** in Spain. Such apparitions have reinforced the faith of thousands of Catholics, though many have pointed out that similar visitations have been recorded widely within non-Catholic Christianity and among most or all of the world's religions and peoples. It is natural that sincere devotees envision a divine figure in the form familiar through the iconography of their own religion. The nineteenth-century Hindu mystic **Sri Ramakrishna** frequently had ecstatic visions of the goddess Kali.

While the unreligious might dismiss such visions as religious hysteria, contemporary psychology has rescued them from the realms of the abnormal and mapped their ecstatic nature along with other transpersonal psychological states, and religious scholars have noted the predominantly meaningful messages they deliver. One might also group such visitations with phenomena like the appearance of fairies, who are said to have a changeable aspect, taking on a form to suit the convention of the percipient. Additionally, in the twentieth century, there have been frequent reports by UFO **contactees** of "shining visitors from outer space" arriving in flying saucers.

Universality of Belief in Apparitions

It is clear that the belief in apparitions, and the varied forms under which this belief exhibits itself in various times and countries, is universal. Both ancient and modern peoples believe in hauntings and the basic principles of the phenomena—the existence of a spiritual world capable of manifesting itself in the sphere of matter, and the survival of the human soul after the dissolution of the body—are the same.

While the beliefs in ancient and medieval times may arouse interest and curiosity for their own sakes, psychical researchers have valued them chiefly as throwing light on modern occurrences and beliefs. The belief in apparitions, for example, has been a root principle of **Spiritualism** and is characteristic of religions that postulate the existence of a human soul. Many individuals who are not Spiritualists in the accepted sense have had experiences that render belief in apparitions inevitable.

Some Typical Examples of Apparitions

The true nature of apparitions is not really known. As Andrew Lang stated: "Only one thing is certain about apparitions, namely this, that they do appear. They really are perceived." How are they seen? When Lord Adare submitted this question to the **control** of the famous medium **D. D. Home,** he received the following answer:

"At times we make passes over the individual to cause him to see us, sometimes we make the actual resemblance of our former clothing, and of what we were, so that we appear exactly as we were known to you on earth; sometimes we project an image that you see, sometimes you see us as we are, with a cloudlike aura of light around us."

The perception is not restricted to the small hours of the night or to times of seclusion. It may occur publicly and at the most unexpected moments, a fact demonstrated by a ghost in evening dress seen one morning in a London street in 1878. As the *Daily Telegraph* reported: "A woman fled in affright, the figure had a most cadaverous look, but the next person the apparition encountered recognized it as that of a friend, a foreigner." Later, this next person, Dr. Armand Leslie, learned the his close friend was found dead in evening clothes in a foreign city at the time his phantasm was seen; but such occurrences are very rare. In the majority of cases there is some mediumistic intervention or some sufficiently potent driving motive to achieve the manifestation to nonsensitive people provided they happen to be in a receptive state.

An instance of the first is Cromwell Varley's oft-quoted testimony before the **London Dialectical Society** in 1869:

"In the Winter of 1864–5 I was busy with the Atlantic cable. I left a gentleman at Birmingham to test the iron wire. He had seen something of Spiritualism but he did not believe in it. He had a brother whom I had never seen in life. One night in my room there were a great number of loud raps. When at length I sat up in bed I saw a man in the air—a spirit—in military dress. I could see the pattern of the paper on the wall through him. Mrs. Varley did not see it. She was in a peculiar state and became entranced. The spirit spoke to me through her. He told me his name and said that he had seen his brother in Birmingham but that what he had to communicate was not understood. He asked me to write a message to his brother, which I did, and received an answer from Birmingham 'Yes, I know my brother has seen you, for he came to me and was able to make known as much.' The spirit informed me that when at school in France he was stabbed. This fact was only known to his eldest surviving brother and his mother. When I narrated this to the survivor he turned very pale and confirmed it."

Why Do They Appear?

Apparitions often occur because they possess an urgent message of extreme danger, worry, illness, or death on the part of the agent. But it is also often a warning of impending danger of death of someone closely connected to the percipient. The mode of delivery in the first group may disclose a confused, perturbed mentality. A phantom form may rush into a room and alarm individuals by its sudden appearance or by its noises. The purpose, nevertheless, is mostly clear and the apparition may come back more than once as if to make sure that the information of the fact of decease was duly understood. Sometimes more is conveyed, especially in cases of accidental or violent death. Successive pictures may arise as if in a vision of the state of the body or of subsequent steps taken in regard to it.

The announcement of death may be quite explicit, as in the case described in the *Proceedings* Society for Psychical Research (vol. 10, pp. 380–82),

"On June 5th, 1887, a Sunday evening, between eleven and twelve at night, being awake, my name was called three times. I answered twice, thinking it was my uncle, 'Come in, Uncle George, I am awake,' but the third time I recognized the voice as that of my mother, who had been dead sixteen years. I said 'Mamma!' She then came round a screen near my bedside with two children in her arms, and placed them in my arms and put the bedclothes over them, and said 'Lucy, promise me to take care of them, for their mother is just dead.' I said 'Yes, Mamma.' She repeated: 'Promise me to take care of them.' I replied 'Yes, I promise you,' and I added: 'Oh, Mamma, stay and speak to me. I am so wretched.' She replied: 'Not yet, my child.' Then she seemed to go round the screen again, and I remained, feeling the children to be still in my arms, and fell asleep. When I awoke, there was nothing. Tuesday morning, June 7th, I received the news of my sister-in-law's death. She had given birth to a child three weeks before which I did not know till after her death."

In a similar case a mother brought the news of the death of her grandson by drowning, the drowned man also appearing to the percipient. In an instance quoted by **Camille Flammarion** in *The Unknown* (1900), the percipient, whose brother was killed in the attack at Sedan, awoke suddenly during the night and saw,

". . . opposite to the window and beside my bed my brother on his knees surrounded by a sort of luminous mist. I tried to speak to him but I could not. I jumped out of bed. I looked out of the window and I saw there was no moonlight. The night was dark and it was raining heavily, great drops pattering on the window panes. My poor Oliver was still there. Then I drew near. I walked right through the apparition. I reached my chamber door, and as I turned the knob to open I looked back once more. The apparition slowly turned its head towards me, and gave me another look full of anguish and love. Then for the first time I observed a wound on his right temple, and from it trickled a little stream of blood. The face was pale as wax, but it was transparent."

A letter later received proved that the dead man had a wound corresponding to that shown by the apparition.

The warning of death is sometimes veiled, an account of which is well illustrated by the instance recorded by the **American Society for Psychical Research** of a salesman, who, in a distant city, had suddenly seen the phantasmal appearance of his sister, full of life and natural, with a bright red scratch on the right side of her face. Perturbed by the vision he immediately broke his journey. At home his mother nearly fainted when he mentioned the scar. She had accidentally scratched her daughter's face after her death and carefully obliterated all its traces with powder. A few weeks later the mother died; but for the vision her son would not have seen her in life again. It is known that Josephine appeared to Napoleon at St. Helena and warned him of his approaching death.

The message left by an apparition is usually brief, as if the power to convey it is limited. The apparition seems to be drawn to the spot by the personality of the percipient. The place may have been totally unknown to him in life. The pictorial and often symbolic nature of the communication has been suggestive of the more subjective explanations of apparitions. In a curious group of cases images are seen instead of the lifelike figure. **Anna Blackwell** testified to such an experience before the London Dialectical Committee in 1870. The face of a beloved relative, like a life-size daguerreotype, appeared on a window pane of the house opposite to her window. It faded away several times, and appeared again. There seemed to be upon the pane a sort of dark iridescence out of which the face evolved, each appearance lasting about eight seconds, and each being darker and fainter than the preceding one. She also quoted the case of a Mrs. M. G. who saw in the tortoiseshell handle of a new parasol the face of Charles Dickens soon after his death. The face was small but with every feature perfectly distinct; and as she gazed upon it in utter amazement, the eyes moved and the mouth smiled.

Such images usually appear on polished surfaces. They may be seen by several people and then disappear after a while. In volume 2 of *Phantasms of the Living* there is a record of an apparition of this kind, of one Capt. Towns, witnessed by eight people. His face was seen on the polished surface of a wardrobe six weeks after his death.

The explorer Ernest Shackleton's experience, recorded in his book *South* (1919), borders on abnormal perception,

"I know that during that long and racking march of thirty-six hours over the unnamed mountains and glaciers of South Georgia it seemed to me often that we were four, not three. I said nothing to my companions on the point, but afterwards Worsley said to me: 'Boss, I had a curious feeling on the march that there was another person with us.'"

Crean confessed to the same idea. Being interviewed by the *Daily Telegraph* (February 1, 1922) on this point, he said: "None of us cares to speak about that. There are some things which can never be spoken of. Almost to hint about them comes perilously near sacrilege. This experience was eminently one of those things."

Apparitions may be accompanied by bright light. A case in the *Proceedings* of the American Society for Psychical Research (vol. 1, p. 405) suggests the objectivity of the occurrence. A physician and his wife, sleeping in separate but adjoining rooms, were awakened by a bright light. The physician saw a figure, and his wife got up and went into her husband's room to see what the light was. By that time the figure had disappeared.

In the Rev. **Charles Tweedale**'s house the disappearance of a phantom on November 14, 1908, was accompanied by a big flash of light and a cloud of smoke that filled the kitchen and the passage. The smoke had no ordinary smell. On another occasion the figure touched and spoke to his wife, then dissolved into a pillar of black vapor.

There are some cases in which the apparition is behind the percipient, yet clearly seen. Again, the phantom may appear quite solid, yet objects may be seen beyond it. Occasionally, it is a reflection only. As reported in *Phantasms of the Living* (vol. 2, p. 35), a Mrs. Searle fainted. Her husband saw her head and face white and bloodless about the same time in a mirror upon a window opposite him.

Meeting Cases

Apparitions seen at deathbeds are in a class of their own. In these so-called "meeting cases," a type of **near-death experience,** it appears as if deceased friends and relatives hasten to the borderland to extend a welcome to the dying.

In *Peak in Darien* (1882), Frances Power Cobbe writes,

"The dying person is lying quietly, when suddenly, in the very act of expiring, he looks up—sometimes starts up in bed—and gazes on what appears to be vacancy, with an expression of astonishment, sometimes developing instantly into joy, and sometimes cut short in the first emotion of solemn wonder and awe. If the dying man were to see some utterly unexpected but instantly recognized vision, causing him great surprise, or rapturous joy, his face could not better reveal the fact. The very instant this phenomenon occurs, death is actually taking place, and the eyes glaze even while they gaze at the unknown sight."

In many cases on record such paranormal perception and death are not simultaneous. "Among all the facts adduced to prove survival these seem to me to be the most disquieting," wrote **Charles Richet,** a psychical researcher who wished to explain all the Spiritistic occurrences by his theory of **cryptesthesia.** Hallucination is effectively barred out by those cases in which others in the room also perceive the phantom forms, but there is sufficient evidence for a genuine phenomenon if the person was not known to be dead to the dying at the moment of perception, or if independent evidence comes forth to prove that the perception was veridical. A striking illustration of the latter instance is the case of Elisa Mannors whose near relatives and friends, concerned in the communications received through Leonora Piper, were known to Richard Hodgson. His account, published in the *Proceedings* of the Society for Psychical Research (vol. 13, p. 378), states:

"The notice of his [F., an uncle of Elisa Mannors] death was in a Boston morning paper, and I happened to see it on my way to the sitting. The first writing of the sitting came from Madame Elisa, without my expecting it. She wrote clearly and strongly, explaining that F. was there with her, but unable to speak directly, that she wished to give me an account of how she had helped F. to reach her. She said that she had been present at his deathbed, and had spoken to him, and she repeated what she had said, an unusual form of expression, and indicated that he had heard and recognized her. This was confirmed in detail in the only way possible at the time, by a very intimate friend of Mme. Elisa and myself, and also of the nearest surviving relative of F. I showed my friend the account of the sitting, and to this friend, a day or two later, the relative, who was present at the deathbed, stated spontaneously that F. when dying said that he saw Madame Elisa who was speaking to him, and he repeated what she was saying. The expression so repeated, which the relative quoted to my friend, was that which I had received from Madame Elisa through Mrs. Piper's trance when the death-bed incident was, of course, entirely unknown to me."

As **Ernesto Bozzano** pointed out, a curious feature of these visions is that the dying only claim to see deceased persons, whereas, if his thoughts alone would be concerned in it, he might be expected to see living persons as frequently as deceased ones. Again, even people who have been skeptical of **survival** all their lives sometimes have given evidence of such visions. The effect on those who witness such rending of the veil is very dramatic. A Dr. Wilson of New York who was present at the death of the well-known American tenor, James Moore, wrote:

"Then something which I shall never forget to my dying day happened, something which is utterly indescribable. While he appeared perfectly rational and as sane as any man I have ever seen, the only way that I can express it is that he was transported into another world, and although I cannot satisfactorily explain the matter to myself, I am fully convinced that he had entered the Golden City—for he said in a stronger voice than he had used since I had attended him: 'There is Mother. Why Mother, have you come here to see me? No, no, I'm coming to see you. Just wait, Mother, I am almost over. I can jump it. Wait, Mother.' On his face there was a look of inexpressible happiness, and the way in which he said the words impressed me as I have never been before, and I am as firmly convinced that he saw and talked with his mother as I am that I am sitting here."

In his *Psychic Facts and Theories* (1893), **Minot J. Savage** quoted the following instance in which the death in question was not known to the dying,

"In a neighbouring city were two little girls, Jennie and Edith, one about eight years of age, and the other but a little older. They were schoolmates and intimate friends. In June, 1889, both were taken ill with diphtheria. At noon on Wednesday Jennie died. Then the parents of Edith, and her physician as well, took particular pains to keep from her the fact that her little playmate was gone. They feared the effect of the knowledge on her own condition. To prove that they succeeded and that she did not know, it may be mentioned that on Saturday, June 8th, at noon, just before she became unconscious of all that was passing about her, she selected two of her photographs to be sent to Jennie, and also told her attendants to bid her goodbye. She died at half-past six o'clock on the evening of Saturday, June 8th. She had roused and bidden her friends goodbye, and was talking of dying and seemed to have no fear. She appeared to see one and another of the friends she knew were dead. So far it was like the common cases.

But now suddenly, and with every appearance of surprise, she turned to her father and exclaimed: 'Why, papa, I am going to take Jennie with me!' Then she added 'Why, papa, why, papa, you did not tell me that Jennie was here.' And immediately she reached out her arms as if in welcome, and said: 'Oh, Jennie, I am so glad you are here. . . .' "

Stainton Moses was quoted by Richet as the source of the following case: Miss H., the daughter of an English clergyman, was tending a dying child. His little brother, aged three to four years, was in a little bed in the same room. As the former was dying, the child woke up, and pointing to the ceiling with every expression of joy, said: "Mother, look at the beautiful ladies round my brother. How lovely they are, they want to take him." The elder child died at that moment.

There is a group of cases in which only some sort of a presence is felt or a cloud of depression experienced, which becomes instantly relieved when the actual news of death arrives. Phenomena of sound are often recorded in place of a visual apparition. Sometimes they attempt to prove identity, imitating the professional work of the departed. They differ from poltergeist phenomena, as the latter do not coincide with death.

If no definite message is conveyed, the apparition may be explained by a spirit's continued interest in earthly occupations. Spiritualists often suggest that some spirits of the deceased apparently cannot adjust immediately to their new surroundings, and they may be seen for a while in favorite haunts or at their usual work, being somehow enabled, when recently freed from the body, to enjoy a fuller perception of earthly scenes than it is afterward possible to retain.

Knowledge and memory are the two main characteristics of after-death apparitions. Local apparitions that are not attached to persons seem to degenerate into mere spectral automations, as witnessed in haunted houses. Somewhat similar, yet belonging to a different class, is illustrated by a case of apparitions *en masse* originally reported by **Eleanor Sidgwick** in the *Proceedings,* of the Society for Psychical Research (vol. 3, p. 76),

"Two ladies, Mrs. F. and her sister, saw in the street during a thick fog numerous human forms passing by. Some were tall persons who seemed to enter the body of one of the two sisters. The servant who was with the two ladies cried out in terror. In this crowd of phantoms there were men, women and dogs. The women wore high bonnets and large shawls of old fashion. Their faces were livid and cadaverous. The whole phantasmal troop accompanied Mrs. F. and her sister about three hundred yards. Sometimes they seemed to be lit up by a kind of yellow light. When Mrs. F., her sister and the servant reached their home, only one single individual of the crowd, taller than the others and hideous in appearance, remained. He then disappeared also."

Prolonged apparitions are very rare, and possibly serve some deeper purpose, as in the case of a sailor who saw his father beside him on the bridge of his ship during a storm for two hours. The message of the apparition is, as a rule, simple and appears to be chosen intelligently in the form that may best suit the percipient's power of understanding. An apparition with empty eye sockets perceived by a sailor's wife, the sound of a terrific storm, or the image of a coffin conveys the intended message nearly as efficiently as the spoken words. The percipient appears to be curiously receptive in such moments and seldom exhibits astonishment at the most unlikely things.

Death-compacts offer another field of study. There are cases on record when the apparition concerned was perceived not after death but before, at the moment of a dangerous accident. In *Phantasms of the Living* there are 12 such cases recorded; the apparitions having appeared within 12 hours of the death. In three cases the agent was still alive. It appears as if such a compact would act effectively both on the subconscious before death and on the spirit after death. How long the efforts as a result of such a compact may continue we cannot tell. It is usually fulfilled shortly after death, but in some cases after years. The living party to the compact may not be sufficiently sensitive to be successfully impressed and others may see a phantom of the departed much sooner than the party in question.

The Genesis of Apparitions

If one accepts a paranormal explanation of apparitions, the primary question then becomes, "Are apparitions objective, produced in space, or are they subjectively seen as the result of a telepathic impact from the agent?" The answer is a qualified one—the subjective nature of the apparition being often unquestionable. The medium **Hélène Smith** wrote to **Theodore Flournoy** in 1926 of an Italian spiritualist from whom she received a letter. She decided to ask him for details of his life. Suddenly, she heard a knock at the door, three sharp and distinct raps. The door opened and she saw a man, holding in each hand a small wickerwork basket, containing grain of different kinds. He made a sign, inviting her attention to the baskets. Two minutes afterwards he disappeared. The door was found shut. After sending off the intended letter, a photograph came, bearing the exact reproduction of the man seen, with the information that the writer was a dealer in corn still living in Genoa.

The objectivity of any apparition might best be decided by the means of the camera. Circumstances, however, are very seldom such that would make possible the acquisition of such evidence. There is, however, a well-authenticated case, furnished by Church of England minister Charles L. Tweedale, the vicar at Weston. He photographed in the breakfast room of the vicarage an old man who was clairvoyantly seen by his wife **Violet Tweedale.** (The photographs obtained by spirit photographers belong to quite a different class, as there is no perceptible apparition during the process.)

Nevertheless, the photograph of the Combermere ghost demands consideration. Lacy C. had rented Combermere Abbey, in Cheshire, Lord Combermere's country house, for the summer. The library in the house was a fine panelled room and the new tenant was anxious to secure a photograph of it. She placed her half-plate camera on its stand in a favorable position—fronting the unoccupied carved oak arm chair on which Lord Combermere always used to sit. On developing the plate by herself, she was amazed to find the figure of a legless old man seated in the carved oak arm chair. The curious coincidence that Lord Combermere was buried a few miles from his country house at the very time the photograph was taken led to the surmise that the ghostly figure resembled the late nobleman. Opinions of the family differed, but on the whole it was considered to be like him, especially in the peculiar attitude that was habitual to him when seated in his chair.

Sir William Barrett, who investigated the case and reported on it in the *Journal* of the Society for Psychical Research (December 1895), was not satisfied. Working on the theory that a manservant may have come in and seated himself in the chair, he took a test photograph and got a picture that was almost a duplicate of the Combermere photograph. With this the matter seemed ended, but, as he told in his book *On the Threshold of the Unseen* (1918), some time later he received a letter from Lord Combermere's daughter-in-law in which she said:

"The face was always too indistinct to be quite convincing to me, though some of his children had no doubt at all of the identity. I may add, none of the menservants in the house in the least resembled the figure and were all young men; whilst the outside men were all attending the funeral, which was taking place at the Church four miles off, at the very time the photograph was being done."

This testimony induced Barrett to change his opinion.

The famous British conjurer **J. N. Maskelyne** in his account of his own experience of drowning (reported in *Phantasms of Living*) spoke about whether an objective apparition is simply an effigy or the actual presence of the person whom it represents. He stated:

"One thing, however, did appear to my mental vision as plainly as though it were actually before my eyes. That was the form of my mother, engaged upon her household duties. Upon returning home, I was utterly astonished to find that she had been as conscious of my danger as I had been, and at the moment when I was so near death."

It seems that when his past life flashed by in the moment of drowning the last thoughts of Maskelyne dwelt on his mother with the effect that he found his mental self gazing at her. Many other apparitions may be simply thought forms, reflections of intense mental anguish experienced in some time past in certain places which are now called haunted or, as **F. W. H. Myers** suggested, they may be visible dreams of the dead.

Edmund Gurney, writing in 1888, believed that there were three conditions that might establish a presumption that an apparition or other immediate manifestation of a dead person is something more than a subjective hallucination. Either (1) more persons than one might be independently affected by the phenomenon; or (2) the phantasm might convey information, afterwards discovered to be true, of something the percipient had never known; or (3) the appearance might be that of a person the percipient himself had never seen, and of whose aspect he was ignorant, and yet his description of it might be sufficiently definite for identification. Gurney also noted that the high number of phantasmal appearances shortly after death is also suggestive, as the calculation of probabilities for telepathic impressions from the living would not result in such a disproportionate number.

Telepathic explanations of apparitions present many difficulties. One has to suppose that a dying man can visualize himself and his condition sufficiently clearly to project a telepathic image as distinctly as perceived. In experimental thought transference it is always the idea on which the agent concentrates that is perceived by the percipients. On the other hand, in some experiments the agent always concentrates on the person to whom he wishes to appear and not on himself. But again in such cases the agent often sees the percipient and brings back an account that can be verified. Such experiences suggest the real presence of the agent and argue against the sufficiency of the telepathic impact theory.

Apparently, this telepathic impulse is first registered on the unconscious part of the mind. If so, the impression may be latent for a time. Strong preoccupation of the conscious mind with the business of life may prevent its emergence. This would explain why the vision of an apparition does not always coincide in time with the actual happening. In *Phantasms of the Living,* such deferred telepathic perceptions are accepted, if they occur within a period of 12 hours. On the other hand, the theory does not bar out the other, that there is an actual presence that does not always find the mind of the percipient sufficiently receptive to take cognition. Reciprocal perceptions are also on record. The telepathic theory has to be twisted and modified to cover the wide range of supernormal perceptions. In case of accidental death, the apparition is sometimes seen at the moment of death, sometimes after it.

Does the mind transform the picture of deadly danger into a picture of death? If this were true, it would suggest that we might come across many cases in which the vision of death was premature as the accident did not prove fatal. We do not see such cases. On the other hand, in cases of suicides the apparition is often found to precede the actual commission of the act. It would seem very credible that brooding over the fatal act and its possible effect on close relations produces a telepathic image.

By all means, the telepathic theory would account for the clothes apparently worn by the ghosts and would eliminate suggestions, like those of d'Assier, of the ghosts of garments. But it meets with difficulties in cases when animals are stricken with terror and register alarm before the man suspects anything unusual.

The greatest stumbling block in the way of the telepathic theory, as an all-inclusive explanation, is presented by those cases in which the apparition is collectively perceived. Gurney attempted to explain these cases by a telepathic transmission that takes place from the percipient's mind to the mind of his neighbors. This theory proved inadequate. There is nothing to prove its possibilities. The hallucinations of the insane or the visions seen in delirium tremens are never communicated to those around them. Why should such a communication take place in cases of apparitions, coinciding with the death of someone distant? What happens when the percipient appears to have traveled to a distant scene and he is actually perceived there?

As early as 1885 Myers began to feel the insufficiency of the telepathic theory. Gurney himself, by the time he died, was convinced of the genuine character of many an apparition. The trance phenomena of medium **Leonora Piper** led Myers to the belief that the evidence for communications from the departed is quite as strong as for telepathic communication between the living. Still there remained a large number of phantasmal manifestations that even communication from the departed could not explain. So Myers proposed a theory of psychical invasion—the creation of a "Phantasmogenetic centre" in the percipient's surroundings by some dissociated elements of the agent's personality, which in some way are potent enough to affect and modify space. He considered it a subliminal operation, resembling the continuous dream life which he supposed to run concurrently with the waking life, not necessarily a profound incident but rather a special idiosyncracy on the part of the agent that tends to make his phantasm easily visible.

From the Greek he coined the word "psychorrhagy" which means "to let the soul break loose." He believed he had discovered a new physiological fact, the psychorrhagic diathesis, essentially a psychical manifestation by some people born with an ability to produce phantasmogenetic effect either on the mind of another person or on a portion of space, in which case several persons may simultaneously discern the phantasm.

This theory enjoyed great support in the early years of psychical research. It was a half-way house between telepathic and Spiritualist explanations of apparitions. The supposition of the double easily explains many an apparition of the living: the "arrival cases" where a man's attention is fixed on his return home, the cases in which there is a strong link of emotion between agent and percipient and the phantom is collectively or repeatedly seen. But there are cases of phantasmal apparitions in which the theory of the double offers no satisfactory explanation. Such was case of Canon Bourne, reported in the *Journal* of the Society for Psychical Research (vol. 6, p. 129), as recounted by Lois Bourne,

"On February 5th, 1887, my father, sister, and I went out hunting. About the middle of the day my sister and I decided to return home with the coachman, while my father went on. Somebody came and spoke to us, and delayed us for a few moments. As we were turning to go home, we distinctly saw my father, waving his hat to us and signing us to follow him. He was on the side of a small hill, and there was a dip between him and us. My sister, the coachman and myself all recognized my father, and also the horse. The horse looked so dirty and shaken that the coachman remarked he thought there had been a nasty accident. As my father waved his hat I clearly saw the Lincoln and Bennett mark inside, though from the distance we were apart it ought to have been utterly impossible for me to have seen it. At the time I mentioned seeing the mark in the hat, though the strangeness of seeing it did not strike me till afterwards.

Fearing an accident, we hurried down the hill. From the nature of the ground we had to lose sight of my father, but it took us very few seconds to reach the place where we had seen him. When we got there, there was no sign of him anywhere, nor could we see anyone in sight at all. We rode about for some time looking for him, but could not see or hear anything of him. We all reached home within a quarter of an hour of each other. My father then told us he had never been in the field, nor near the field, in which we thought we saw him, the whole of that day. He had never waved to us, and had met with no accident. My father was riding the only white horse that was out that day."

Myers believes that Canon Bourne was subliminally dreaming of himself as having had a fall, and as beckoning to his daughters, an incoherent dream but of quite ordinary type. Being born with the psychorrhagic diathesis, a certain psychical element so far detached itself from his organism as to affect a certain portion of space near the daughters of whom he was thinking, to effect it not materially nor even optically, but yet in such a manner that to a certain kind of immaterial and nonoptical sensitivity a phantasm of himself and his horse became discernible.

Myers suggested that hauntings by departed spirits may be similarly explained and that the modification of space into a phantasmogenetic center applies to a phantasmal voice as well.

If this alteration of space is more than a theory it may theoretically happen, so Myers thought, that a bystander may discern the alteration more clearly than the person for whose benefit it was made or that the bystander alone may perceive it. Such seems to be the case of Frances Reddell quoted in *Phantasms of the Living*,

"Helen Alexander (maid to Lady Waldegrave) was lying here very ill with typhoid fever, and was attended by me. I was standing at the table by her bedside, pouring out her medicine, at about 4 o'clock in the morning of the 4th October, 1880. I heard the call bell ring (this had been heard twice before during the night in that same week) and was attracted by the door of the room opening, and by seeing a person entering the room whom I instantly felt to be the mother of the sick woman. She had a brass candlestick in her hand, a red shawl over her shoulder, and a flannel petticoat on which had a hole in the front. I looked at her as much as to say 'I am glad you have come' but the woman looked at me sternly, as much as to say 'Why wasn't I sent for before?' I gave the medicine to Helen Alexander and then turned round to speak to the vision, but no one was there. She had gone. She was a short, dark person, and very stout. At about 6 o'clock that morning Helen Alexander died. Two days after her parents and a sister came to Antony, and arrived between 1 and 2 o'clock in the morning; I and another maid let them in, and it gave me a great turn when I saw the living likeness of the vision I had seen two nights before. I told the sister about the vision, and she said that the description of the dress exactly answered to her mother's, and that they had brass candlesticks at home exactly like the one described. There was not the slightest resemblance between the mother and daughter."

The account was corroborated. Myers believes the vision was meant for the daughter by the mother who, in her anxiety, paid her a psychical visit and affected part of the space with an image corresponding to the conception of her own aspect latent in her mind. A bystander, a susceptible person, happened to see the image while the girl for whom it was meant died without leaving a sign of having perceived it.

A still more curious but, according to Myers, similarly explainable case is the sailor's (*Phantasms of the Living* (vol. 2, p. 144) who, watching by a dying comrade, saw figures around his hammock, apparently representing the dying man's family, in mourning clothes. The family was alarmed by noises, which they took as indication of danger to the dying. According to Myers the wife paid a psychical visit to her husband. The mourning clothes and the figures of the children were symbolical expressions of her thought that her children would be orphans.

Would the alteration of space theory account for changes in physical objects? While Myers is silent on this point, Andrew Lang considers it crucial. For if an apparition can thump, open a door, or pull a curtain, it must be a ghost—real, objective entity, filling space. *Per contra,* "no ghost who does not do this has any strict legal claim to be regarded as other than a telepathic hallucination at best." The statement is rather severe in view of his quotation from Edward Binn's *Anatomy of Sleep* (1842) of the case of the gentlemen who, in a dream, pushed so strongly against a door in a distant house that they could hardly hold it against him.

Apparitions may be produced experimentally by the projection of the double or powerful suggestion. The first attempts in the latter class are recorded from Germany in H. M. Wesermanns' *Der Magnetismus und die allgemeine Weltsprache* (1822). On four occasions he succeeded in inducing four separate acquaintances to dream on matters suggested by himself. On the fifth occasion he produced a collective apparition. The subject and a friend who happened to be in his company saw, in the waking state, the apparition of a woman in accordance with the operator's suggestion.

Theories Concerning Apparitions

Various complex and contradictory theories have already been cited in relation to specific cases of apparitions. From the late-nineteenth century on, apparitions have usually been ascribed to hallucination. Even those who advanced a Spiritualistic view of apparitions frequently inclined to this view, for it was argued that the discarnate intelligence might, by psychical energy alone, produce in the brain of a living person a definite hallucination, corresponding perhaps to the agent's appearance in life. Hallucinations might be either coincidental or noncoincidental. The former, also known as telepathic hallucinations, were those which coincided with a death, or with some other crisis in the life of the person represented by the hallucination.

The nineteenth-century psychical researcher **Frank Podmore** insisted that apparitions resulted from a telepathic impression conveyed from the mind of one living person to that of another, an impression which might be doubly intense in time of stress or exalted emotion, or at the moment of dissolution. Apparitions of the dead could be accounted for by a theory of latent impressions, conveyed to the mind of the percipient during the agent's lifetime, but remaining dormant until some particular train of thought aroused them to activity. This view still finds some support at the present day.

Hallucinations, whether coincidental or otherwise, may and do present themselves to persons who are perfectly sane and normal, but they are also reported by people who are suffering mental disorders, under hypnosis, or in a state of hysteria. Hallucinations are also symptomatic of certain pathological conditions of brain, nerves, and sense-organs. As mentioned earlier, Myers was of the opinion that an apparition represented an actual "psychic invasion," that it was a projection of some of the agent's psychic force. Such a doctrine was, as Myers himself admitted, a reverse animism.

Another theory of apparitions, particularly applicable to haunted houses, was related to **psychometry. Sir Oliver Lodge,** in his *Man and the Universe* (1908) wrote:

"Occasionally a person appears able to respond to stimuli embedded, as it were among psycho-physical surroundings in a manner at present ill understood and almost incredible:—as if strong emotions could be unconsciously recorded in matter, so that the deposit shall thereafter affect a sufficiently sensitive organism, and cause similar emotions to reproduce themselves in its subconsciousness, in a manner analogous to the customary conscious interpretation of photographic or phonographic records, and indeed of pictures or music and artistic embodiment generally."

Take, for example, a haunted house, where one room is the scene of a ghostly representation of some long past tragedy. On a psychometric hypothesis the original tragedy has been literally photographed on its material surroundings, even on the "ether" itself, by reason of the intensity of emotion felt by those who enacted it; and thenceforth in certain persons an hallucinatory effect is experienced corresponding to such impression. It is this theory that accounts for the feeling one has on entering certain rooms, that there is an alien presence therein, though it be invisible and inaudible to mortal sense.

The idea of connecting psychometry with apparitions might seem of considerable interest because of its wide possibilities, but in the end it belongs to the realm of romance rather than science; it is hardly to be considered as a serious theory. Not only is it unsupported by convincing evidence, but it again attempts to explain one unknown by another.

Spiritualistic theories of apparitions also vary, though they agree in referring such appearances to discarnate intelligences, generally to the spirits of the dead. The opinion of some Spiritualist authorities is that the surviving spirit is produced in the mind of the percipient by purely psychic means—an hallucination representing the agent's former bodily appearance.

Others believe that the discarnate spirit can materialize by taking ethereal particles from the external world, and building up a temporary physical organism through which it can communicate with the living. Still others believe that the materialized spirit borrows such temporary physical organism from the medium, and experiments were made which suggested that the medium lost weight during the **materialization.** [The various speculations based on apparitions observed at materialization seances has had to be discharged as the widespread involvement of materialization mediums in fraudulently produced phenomena became widely accepted.]

The ancient belief that the soul itself can become visible is not generally accepted, since it is thought that pure spirit cannot be perceptible to the physical senses. But a compromise has been made in the idea of a "psychic body," midway between soul and body, which theosophists and some spiritualists theorize clothes the soul at the dissolution of the physical body. The psychic body is said to be composed of very fine and subtle material particles, perceptible as a rule, only to the eye of the clairvoyant. It is this astral body, and not the soul, that is seen as an apparition.

Experimental evidence for these and various alternative theories has proven far from conclusive. Since its formation in 1882, the **Society for Psychical Research** and its sister organizations, have collected numerous instances of coincidental hallucinations, many of which were recorded in the monumental work *Phantasms of the Living* (1886) by Edmund Gurney, F. W. H. Myers, and Frank Podmore, from which various cases were cited above. Some 5,705 individuals, chosen at random, had been canvassed for phantasmal visions occurring within the previous 12 years. It concluded: "Between death and apparitions a connection exists not due to chance alone. This we hold a proved fact."

As the scientific world did not consider the evidence of 702 accepted cases sufficient for such a momentous conclusion, an international statistical inquiry named the **Census of Hallucinations** was decided upon in 1889. A sum of 32,000 answers were received, 17,000 in English. The report, published in 1894, fills almost the whole of volume 10 of *Proceedings* of the Society for Psychical Research. Chance coincidence was more powerfully ruled out than before, and the previous conclusion was confirmed. The inquiry of the American Society for Psychical Research and the census of Camille Flammarion in 1899 gave further confirmation.

With the emergence of parapsychology, which has now largely superseded psychical research, and the work of **J. B. Rhine** and associates in ESP (**extrasensory perception**) from 1935 on, experimental researches into paranormal phenomena have placed greater emphasis on telepathy and clairvoyance, and moved away from the study of survival phenomena including apparitions.

Surveys of apparitional or hallucinatory experiences have been carried out in recent decades by parapsychologists, but it is difficult to establish objective criteria for personal anecdotes, and the suspicion must remain that many stories of apparitions may have been consciously or unconsciously invented or embroidered by the percipients. Statistical evaluation of such censuses may establish general patterns of claimed phenomena, but the real meaning of any apparitional experience is primarily for the individual concerned, and even if the individual cannot offer objective evidence of such experience, the subjective aspect can be of great personal importance.

Although spontaneous phenomena like hauntings are not readily amenable to scientific validation, modern parapsychologists have shown some ingenuity in new approaches to such phenomena as apparitions. Besides collecting eyewitness accounts, several researchers have also made a systematic psychological investigation of locations at which apparitions occurred. In one experiment by Michaeleen Maher and **Gertrude Schmeidler,** different psychics have been taken to the location by an individual without knowledge of the claimed phenomena and therefore unable to color any impressions received. The accounts of the different psychics were collated and a total picture of the claimed haunting built up.

Theoretical models for apparitional experience remain somewhat speculative since early investigators like Frank Podmore claimed that apparitions resulted from a telepathic impression conveyed from the mind of one living person to that of another. More recently, British psychical researcher **G. N. M. Tyrrell,** in his monumental survey of *Apparitions,* suggested that the sensory apparatus (like the optic nerve) of the percipient is telepathically affected by other minds. However, from the variety of evidence and discussion, as well as the wide range of types of apparitions, it seems reasonable to believe that we are not dealing with a single phenomenon, and it would be unrealistic to claim one universal explanation that covers the diverse facts and claims.

Sources:

Barrett, William F. *Death Bed Visions.* London, 1926.

Beaumont, John. *An Historical, Physiological & Theological Treatise of Spirits, Apparitions, Witchcraft & Other Magical Practices.* London, 1750.

Bennett, Ernest W. *Apparitions & Haunted Houses: A Survey of Evidence.* London: 1939. Reprint, Ann Arbor, Mich.: Gryphon Books, 1971.

Bozzano, Ernesto. *Phénomènes Psychiques au Moment de la Mort.* Paris, 1923.

Calmet, Dom Augustine. *Dissertations sur les apparitions des anges des démons et des espits, et sur les revenants, et vampires de Hongrie, de Boheme, de Moravie, et de Silésie.* Paris, 1746. Reprinted as *The Phantom World.* 2 vols. London: Richard Bentley, 1850.

Carrington, Hereward. *True Ghost Stories.* London, [1933].

Carrington, Hereward, and Nandor Fodor. *Haunted People: Story of the Poltergeist Down the Centuries.* New York: E. P. Dutton, New American Library, 1951. Reprinted as *The Story of the Poltergeist Down the Centuries.* London: Rider, 1953.

Clarke, Edward H. *Visions: A Study of False Sight.* Boston, 1878.

Cobbe, Frances Power. *The Peak in Darien.* London, 1882.

Crosland, Newton. *Apparitions.* London, 1873.

Crowe, Catherine. *Ghosts and Family Legends.* London, 1859.

———. *The Night Side of Nature.* 1848. Reprint, Philadelphia: R. West, 1978.

[Defoe, Daniel]. *An Essay on the History & Reality of Apparitions.* London, 1727.

Dingwall, Eric J., and Trevor H. Hall. *Four Modern Ghosts.* London, 1958.

Dingwall, Eric J., K. M. Goldney, and Trevor H. Hall. *The Haunting of Borley Rectory.* London: Duckworth, 1955.

Flammarion, Camille. *Death & Its Mystery.* 3 vols. New York: Century, 1921–23.

———. *Haunted Houses.* Paris, 1924. Reprint, New York: Appleton, 1924. Reprint, Detroit: Gale Research, 1971.

Garland, Hamlin. *The Shadow World.* New York, 1908.

Gurney, Edmund, F. W. H. Myers, and Frank Podmore. *Phantasms of the Living.* London: Trubner, 1886. Abridged ed. New Hyde Park, N.Y.: University Books, 1962.

Hamel, Frank. *Human Animals.* London, 1915. Reprint, New Hyde Park, N.Y.: University Books, 1969.

Hibbert, Samuel. *Sketches of the Philosophy of Apparitions.* Edinburgh, 1825.

Lang, Andrew. *Book of Dreams & Ghosts.* London, 1898. Reprint, New York: Causeway, 1974.

MacKenzie, Andrew. *The Unexplained; Some Strange Cases of Psychical Research.* London, 1966. Reprint, New York: Popular Library, 1970.

Maher, Michaeleen, and Gertrude Schmeidler. "Confirmation of a Family's Report of an Apparition." In *Research in Parapsychology 1974.* Edited by J. D. Morris, W. G. Roll, and R. L. Morris. Metuchen, N.J.: Scarecrow Press, 1975.

O'Donnell, Elliott. *Animal Ghosts.* London, 1913.

———. *Byways of Ghostland.* London, 1911.

———. *Confessions of a Ghost Hunter.* London, 1928.

———. *Ghostly Phenomena.* London, n.d.

———. *Ghosts Helpful & Harmful.* London, 1924.

———. *Werewolves.* London, 1912.
Pike, Richard. *Life's Borderland and Beyond.* London, n.d.
Podmore, Frank. *Apparitions & Thought-Transference: An Examination of the Evidence for Telepathy.* New York: G. P. Putnam's Sons, 1894.
———. *Telepathic Hallucinations: The New View of Ghosts.* London, 1909.
Pollock, James S. *Dead and Gone.* London, 1874.
Price, Harry. *The End of Borley Rectory.* London: Harrap, 1946.
———. *The Most Haunted House in England.* London: Longmans, Green, 1940.
Salter, W. H. *Ghosts & Apparitions.* London: G. Bell & Sons, 1938.
Savile, Bourchier W. *Apparitions; A Book of Facts.* London, 1874.
The Secrets of the Invisible World Laid Open, or an Universal History of Apparitions, Sacred & Profane. London, 1770.
Snell, Joy. *The Ministry of Angels.* London, 1918.
Stead, William T. *Real Ghost Stories.* London, 1892. Rev. ed. 1897. Reprinted as *Borderland: A Casebook of True Supernatural Stories.* New Hyde Park, N.Y.: University Books, 1970.
Tregortha, John. *News from the Invisible World.* U.K.: Burslem, 1808.
Tweedale, Violet. *Ghosts I Have Seen.* London, 1920.
Tyrrell, G. N. M. *Apparitions.* London, 1953. Reissued in one volume with Tyrrell's *Science & Psychical Phenomena.* New Hyde Park, N.Y.: University Books, 1961.
Wickwar, J. W. *The Ghost World.* London, n.d.
Wright, Dudley. *Vampires & Vampirism.* London, 1914. Reprinted as *The Book of Vampires.* New York: Causeway, 1973.

Apports

The name given to various objects, such as flowers, jewelry, and even live animals, reportedly materialized in the presence of a medium. During the first hundred years of **Spiritualism,** the production of apports was one of the most prominent and effective features of Spiritualistic seances. Sometimes apports flew through the air and struck the faces of sitters; sometimes they appeared on the table, or in the laps of those present. A favorite form was the scattering of perfume on the company. In the last half century, however, as standards for observing seances improved, and the number of fake mediums exposed increased, the appearances of apports steadily decreased and today can only be found in the small circles of fake mediums that still exist on the fringes of the Spiritualist community.

Systematic experiments conducted in a purely scientific spirit exposed **fraud** in numerous instances where ordinary precautions would not have sufficed for its detection. Frequently it was found that the medium had skillfully concealed the apports in the room or about his or her person. Spiritualists have often argued that even though apports were often produced by obviously unscrupulous means, it does not follow that all **materializations** were performed with fraudulent intent. There are cases where, so far as can be judged, the character of the medium was beyond reproach, as in the case of **Hélène Smith.** The idea has been advanced that any preparations made beforehand, such as the secreting of flowers, must result from a process of activity of the subliminal consciousness. Spiritualists generally believe that apports are actually conveyed to the séance by spirits, or that they are drawn there by magnetic power. Branches of trees, armfuls of fruit and flowers, money, jewels, and live lobsters are among the more extraordinary apports.

Today, however, it is difficult to find anyone making a serious case for the existence of genuine apports. After a century and a half of observation, there is no single case of apports to which one can point as even a highly probable incident of the materialization of an object as a result of a medium's activity.

Were apports genuine, they would constitute one of the most baffling phenomena of Spiritualism. The objects produced in seances differed in size, were both inanimate and living, and appeared none the worse for their strange journey. The phenomenon was first observed by Dr. **G. P. Billot.** In *Recherches psychologique ou correspondence sur le magnetisme vital entre un Solitaire et M. Deleuze* (Paris, 1839) he describes a session on March 5, 1819, with three somnambules and a blind woman. He writes: "Towards the middle of the séance, one of the seeresses exclaimed: 'There is the Dove, it is white as snow, it is flying about the room with something in its beak, it is a piece of paper. Let us pray.' A few moments later she added: 'See, it has let the paper drop at the feet of Madame J.'" Billot saw a paper packet at the spot indicated. He found in it three small pieces of bone glued onto small strips of paper, with the words: "St. Maxime, St. Sabine and Many Martyrs" written beneath the fragments.

With the same blind woman on October 27, 1820, he witnessed flower apports. **J. P. F. Deleuze,** to whom Billot communicated his experience in 1830, answered that he had just received a visit from a distinguished physician who had had similar experiences. His somnambule, however, never professed to have interviews with spirits. Deleuze suggested that the power of **animal magnetism** might better explain the phenomena than the intervention of spirits.

In the history of the curious occurrences in the household of Dr. Larkin of Wrentham, Massachusetts, around his servant girl, Mary Jane, about 1844, it is recorded:

"On one occasion, the whole family being assembled round the couch of the magnetized sleeper and every door being shut, a heavy flat-iron, last seen in the kitchen—quite a distance away—was suddenly placed in their midst, and, at the request of Mrs. Larkin, as suddenly disappeared, and was next found in the kitchen, every door of communication having remained closed."

The apport of a white dove into "The Olive Branch of Peace" circle of Boston was attested, in the early years of American Spiritualism, in an account published in the *New Era* by 11 respectable citizens of Boston. The room was hermetically sealed for 24 hours prior to the promised presentation. In quoting this and similar accounts in her *Modern American Spiritualism* (1870), **Emma Hardinge Britten** remarks on the singular docility of apported birds and says: "Numerous other instances can be cited in which spirits have manifested their power of influencing birds with a degree of readiness and intelligence as unaccountable as it is interesting."

Theories of Explanation

Ever since Britten's report of Larkin's experience, the dove has remained a favorite apport object of the invisible operators. The average apport manifestation, however, is less impressive, though, from the viewpoint of experimental research, the appearance of the smallest object in a closed space to which there is no normal access is of immense import. Unfortunately, observations under strict test conditions are all but nonexistent, and psychical research has classified the phenomenon as among the least attested. Besides the lack of observable data, the chief reason is that the phenomenon itself is exceptional and is considered so contrary to scientific observation to date that even those few great minds who admitted the phenomena of materialization as genuine shied away from apports. It also has to be admitted that the production of tame doves (and other items) from thin air is a common trick of the stage magician.

There are two theories that attempted to bring the phenomena of apports within understanding, on the assumption that genuine cases did occur. One is the fourth dimension, and the other, generally favored by Spiritualists, the disintegration and reintegration of the apported objects. The former was first advocated by German psychical researcher **Johann Zöllner** to explain the phenomenon of interpenetration of matter, which he claimed to observe with **Henry Slade.** It was accepted by **Cesare Lombroso** and **Camille Flammarion** and later endorsed by **W. Whateley Carington** in Britain and **Malcolm Bird** in the United States.

Zöllner's theory implies that there is a higher form of space of which we are not normally cognizant. The objects to be apported are lifted into this dimension, brought to the desired spot and then precipitated into our three-dimensional space, much as we can lift out something which is enclosed in a circle and place it outside. For two-dimensional beings, who experience only length and breadth, and live in a plane, this act of ours would constitute an apport phenomenon.

The other theory has been put forward in séance room communications. According to it, the spirits, by an act of willpower, disintegrate the matter to be transported into its molecular elements without altering its form. In this state the object may pass through the interstices of intervening matter and become reintegrated by a second act of willpower. **René Sudre** believes the medium's mind works upon a molecular scale, so that it can dematerialize and rematerialize objects at ordinary temperatures.

This theory essentially means there is another aggregation of matter. It is proposed that beyond the solid, liquid, and gaseous state is a fourth, fluidic state in which matter becomes invisible and impalpable and possesses, conjointly with an expansion of volume, great molecular malleability. From various observations one would have to suppose the state is one of inertia and that it requires strong thermo-dynamic efforts on the part of the operators to effect the return to the former solid state.

If the disintegration theory is correct, in consonance with the law of the transmutation of energy, a thermic reaction should be expected. Spiritualists have suggested that just such a reaction exists. Stone and metallic apports, especially bigger objects, are often burning or scorching hot on arrival. This sudden increase of heat was noticed by Zöllner in the claimed passage of matter through matter. Other objects were nevertheless found cold. In answer the invisible operators replies that they sometimes prefer to disintegrate a portion of the wood of the door or part of the ceiling to facilitate the entrance of the object in its original state. One would have had to suppose that this is the procedure employed when living things are brought in.

Some spirit operators make no claim for the unobstructed passage of matter through matter. They say a crack in the wall or roof is required for a dematerialized object to pass through to the place where a séance was being held. **Julien Ochorowicz** received this explanation from **Stanislawa Tomczyk.** It is very significant that the apport of a key was described by her as something long and whitish. It did not become a key with its peculiar color and shape until it dropped. She also stated in trance that metals became hot because of the friction of the particles in contracting. Paper, leather, and wood are not sensibly heated because they are not so hard and dense. In darkness an apport can be accomplished without dematerialization if the passage is free. In this case the spirit hand holding it would have to be solidified. In light the object had to be dematerialized.

There is one instance on record which suggests the disintegration and reintegration theory. To quote **Ernesto Bozzano** in *Luce e Ombra* (August–October, 1927):

"In March, 1904, in a sitting in the house of Cavaliere Peretti, in which the medium was an intimate friend of ours, gifted with remarkable physical mediumship, and with whom apports could be obtained at command, I begged the communicating spirit to bring me a small block of pyrites which was lying on my writing table about two kilometres (over a mile) away. The spirit replied (by the mouth of the entranced medium) that the power was almost exhausted, but that all the same he would make the attempt. Soon after the medium sustained the usual spasmodic twitchings which signified the arrival of an apport, but without hearing the fall of any object on the table, or on the floor. We asked for an explanation from the spirit-operator, who informed us that although he had managed to disintegrate a portion of the object desired, and had brought it into the room, there was not enough power for him to be able to re-integrate it. He added 'Light the light.' We did so, and found, to our great surprise, that the table, the clothes, and hair of the sitters, as well as the furniture and carpet of the room, were covered by the thinnest layer of brilliant impalpable pyrites. When I returned home after the sitting I found the little block of pyrites lying on my writing table from which a large fragment, about one third of the whole piece, was missing, this having been scooped out of the block."

Again, as an instance speaking for the fourth dimensional explanation, it is mentioned by Malcolm Bird that "Walter," the control of Margery (**Mina Crandon**), cracked a joke at his expense during the Boston investigation on behalf of the *Scientific American* and promised to get a mate for "Birdie." On November 26, 1923, a live carrier pigeon, showing no resemblance to the pigeons found freely about Boston, appeared in the closed dining room of the house. "Walter," when previously asked where he would deposit the living apport, answered, "I can't say, I have to take a run and leap, and I can't tell where I shall land."

Apports in the Course of Arrival

One might expect that sometimes the circumstances of the arrival of the apport would be noticed. This has indeed happened. A pair of modest earrings, a present from the spirit guide to the **Marquise Carlo Centurione Scotto,** was seen to arrive in the Millesimo seances as described: "We all saw the trumpet (having a phosphorescent band) rise towards the ceiling and turn upside down so as to place the large end uppermost, then we heard something fall heavily into the trumpet, as though the object had dropped from the ceiling."

The arrival of a jar of ointment in full visibility is recorded in **Rev. Charles L. Tweedale**'s *Man's Survival After Death* (1909). He writes:

"Sunday, 13th November, 1910. Mother had sustained a cut on the head, and she, my wife, and I were all in the dining room at 9:20 P.M. We were all close together, mother seated in a chair, self and wife standing. No one else was in the room. My wife was in the act of parting mother's hair with her fingers to examine the cut and I was looking on. At that instant I happened to raise my eyes and I saw something issue from a point close to the ceiling in the corner of the room over the window, and distant from my wife (who had her back to it) three and a quarter yards, and four and a quarter yards from myself, facing it. It shot across the room close to the ceiling and struck the wall over the piano, upon which it then fell, making the strings vibrate, and so on to the floor on which it rolled. I ran and picked it up, and found, to my astonishment, that it was a jar of ointment which mother used specially for cuts and bruises, and which she kept locked up in her wardrobe. The intention was evident, the ointment was for the wound. I saw it come apparently through the wall, near the ceiling, and this with no one within three and a quarter yards of the place. The room is over nine feet high and was brilliantly lighted by a 100 candle-power lamp, and the door and window were shut, the latter fastened, and incapable of being opened from the outside."

Tweedale recorded several other similar observations.

"We were talking about the mysterious disappearance of the keys. Suddenly I saw something bright coming swiftly through the air from the direction of the corner opposite the door and high up towards the ceiling, and so from that part of the room where there is neither door, nor window, nor any opening in the wall. The bright thing rushed through the air and struck my wife on the coil of hair at the back of her head. It came with such a force that it bounced from her head to a distance of nearly three and a half yards from where she stood. My wife uttered a loud cry of alarm, due to the shock and surprise, but owing to the thick mass of hair intervening, she was not hurt in the least. I instantly ran and picked the object up, when, to our amazement, we found it was the bunch of keys missed from my mother's pocket since noon, and of which we had been talking when they were thus projected into the room.

"On another occasion (17th January 1911) a shower of articles came apparently through the ceiling and fell upon the tea-table, in the presence of six witnesses, and in good light. On 11th November 1913, a stick three feet ten inches long came slowly through the solid plaster ceiling in the presence of my daughter Marjorie and the servant in full lamplight, and fell on the table, leaving no trace of its passage; and again, on 29th January 1911, a solid article came apparently through the ceiling in our bedroom, in presence of myself and wife, in broad daylight and slowly descended on to the pillow. All these objects proved to be objective and real when we came to pick them up."

Writing of an earlier occurrence, Tweedale noted,

"At 2 p.m. the door once more opened, and from the top of the door there shot a long stream of white cloudy stuff. This was projected towards mother, who was lying in bed, the distance from the door to her pillow being four and a quarter yards. This extraordinary phenomenon looked like a tube of cloudy material and floated in the air. As it drew near to mother's pillow it slowed down, and when close to her she shrank away from it. At this moment something dropped from the end of the tube, which was close to her, on to the pillow and the tube of cloudy material then floated back to the top of the door and vanished. Thinking that the article which had dropped from it was a ball of wool, mother picked it up, and found to her amazement that it was an egg. She instantly sprang to the door, but found no one upstairs."

Henry Sausse in his book *Des Preuves? En Voila* observed many instances of his medium forming her hand into a cup, in trance and in full light, in the cavity of which a small cloud was seen to form, transforming itself instantly into a small spray of roses, with flowers, buds and leaves complete.

The gradual progress of an apported object was recorded by **Stainton Moses** in his account of August 28, 1872.

"In the dining room there was a little bell. We heard it commence to ring, and could trace it by its sound as it approached the door which separated us from it. What was our astonishment when we found that, in spite of the closed door, the sound drew nearer to us. It was evidently within the room in which we sat, for the bell was carried round the room, ringing loudly the whole time. After completing the circuit of the room, it was brought down, passed under the table, coming up close to my elbow. It was finally placed upon the table."

One must suppose that in this case a hole must have been made through the door to open a free passage to the bell. Naturally, the disintegration could not have occurred in a manner similar to atomic disintegration; otherwise we would have to ask as did **W. W. Smith** a whole series of questions: what becomes of the enormous quantity of energy that must be liberated; how is it prevented from being dissipated; and how is it collected again and recondensed into matter. Spiritualists suggested one way out, to suppose that in some mysterious manner the liberated energy was stored in a reservoir, so to speak, which is not situated in ordinary space at all. Such a conclusion leads back to Zöllner's fourth dimensional theory.

Mediums offered no other explanation of apports, but did complain of the difficulties they had to overcome. "I wanted to bring you a photograph in its frame with the glass but I cannot manage it. I will bring it to you without the glass," opined **"Cristo d'Angelo"** in the séance of July 8, 1928, at Millesimo. On another occasion a large ivy plant, about one meter fifty centimeters in height, was apported in three parts. First came the earth, then the plant with clods sticking to it, and finally the pot. The operators seemingly could not have managed the three things at once. That preparation in advance is often necessary seems to be suggested by similar experiences in **Elizabeth d'Esperance**'s mediumship.

The Wonders of Flower, Fruit and Living Apports

The flower apports of "Yolande," d'Esperance's control, were generally very impressive. On her instructions white sand and plenty of water were always held in readiness in the cabinet. On August 4, 1880, in the presence of William Oxley of Manchester, she directed a Mr. Reimers to pour sand into a water carafe, which he did until it was about half full. Then he was instructed to pour in water. "Yolande" took it, placed it on the floor, covering it lightly with the drapery she took from her shoulders. The circle was directed to sing. While singing they observed the drapery to be rising from the rim of the carafe. "Yolande" several times came out of the cabinet to examine the thing growing under the drapery. Finally she raised the drapery altogether and disclosed a perfect plant, its roots firmly grown and packed in the sand. She presented it to Oxley. Through raps, instructions were given not to discuss the matter but sing something and be quiet. They obeyed. More raps came and told them to examine the plant again. To their great surprise they observed a large circular head of bloom, forming a flower fully five inches in diameter, that had opened while the plant stood on the floor at Oxley's feet. The plant was 22 inches in height, with a thick woody stem that filled the neck of the water carafe. It had 29 leaves, each smooth and glossy. It was impossible to remove the plant from the water bottle, the neck being too small to allow the roots to pass; indeed the comparatively slender stem entirely filled the orifice. The plant was a native of India, an "Ixora Crocata." It had some years of growth. "We could see where other leaves had grown and fallen off, and wound-marks which seemed to have healed and grown over long ago. But there was every evidence to show that the plant had grown in the sand in the bottle as the roots were naturally wound around the inner surface of the glass, all the fibres perfect and unbroken as though they had germinated on the spot and had apparently never been disturbed." The plant was photographed. It lived for three months under the care of Mr. Oxley's gardener and then shrivelled up.

It was a favorite feat of "Yolande" to put a glass of water into the hand of one of her particular friends and tell him to watch it. She would then hold her slender tapered fingers over the glass and while her eyes were closely scrutinizing the water within it a flower would form itself upon it and fill the glass.

Patterns of ferns were often handed to her. She always matched them with others to please the sitters. Roses were frequently produced in the water pitcher she carried on her shoulder. If a special color was required it was obtained. D'Esperance once asked for a black rose. "Yolande" dipped her fingers into the pitcher and instantly brought out a dark object, dripping with moisture. It was a rose of distinctly blue-black color the like of which neither d'Esperance nor any of those assembled had seen.

On June 28, 1890, an overpowering scent was followed by the appearance in a water carafe, which was previously prepared with sand and water, of a golden lily, a foot and a half taller than d'Esperance. From root to point it measured seven feet. It bore eleven large blossoms, and the flowers were perfect, five fully blown. After it was photographed by one Professor Boutleroff, "Yolande" tried to take it back. Her efforts of dematerialization were unsuccessful. "Yolande" was in despair as—according to a message from "Walter," another control—she had gotten the plant on condition of returning it. "Walter" gave instructions to keep the plant in darkness until she could come again and take it. On July 5 the plant vanished as mysteriously as it came. At 9:23 P.M. it stood in the midst of the company, and at 9:30 P.M. it was gone. Not a vestige remained except the photographs and a couple of flowers, which had fallen off. The scent seemed for a moment to fill the room almost overpoweringly, and then it was gone.

Addressing inquiries to "Walter" at the time of the lily's appearance, the sitters were told that the plant was in the room before the sitters came in and "was ready for being put together" at least an hour before they saw it. **Alexander N. Aksakof** also witnessed this apport. On the night of its disappearance a piece of grey cloth was found on its stem. The stem passed through a hole in the center of the cloth. The cloth could not be removed. When, however, "Yolande" instructed Aksakof to remove it, it came off, without a rent, and still showing the round hole through which the stem had passed. She said that she got the piece of cloth from the same country as the flower. On examination the piece of cloth was found to be a scrap of mummy cloth, still aromatic with the perfumes used for embalming. It contained 2,584 meshes to the square inch.

It speaks for the previous preparation of apports that the British medium **Kathleen Barkel** saw in the room of the **British College of Psychic Science** in which **Heinrich Melzer** was to hold an apport séance in 1926, the shadow of a bunch of violets near the electric light bulb. At the séance that evening a quantity of violets did, indeed, appear. However, as Melzer was once detected in fraud, a more practiced explanation would be that the flowers had indeed been prepared and hidden near the light bulb, throwing a shadow.

Another early medium, famous for her flower and fruit apports, was **Agnes Guppy-Volckman.** In her seances the operators honored the requests of the sitters. **Alfred Russel Wallace** wrote that a friend of his asked for a sunflower, and one six feet high fell upon the table, having a large mass of earth around its roots. **Georgina Houghton** testified before the committee of the **London Dialectical Society** in 1869 of a sitting with Guppy-Volckman with 18 ladies and a gentleman present. Everybody could wish for a fruit. The list of the various things brought was a banana, two oranges, a bunch of white grapes, a bunch of black grapes, a cluster of filberts, three walnuts, about a dozen damsons, a slice of candied pineapple, three figs, two apples, an onion, a peach, some almonds, four very large grapes, three dates, a potato, two large pears, a pomegranate, two crystallized greengages, a pile of dried currants, a lemon, and a large bunch of raisins. They were brought in the order they had been wished for.

Signor G. Damiani made the curious observation of Guppy-Volckman's apports before the Dialectical Committee that the ends of the stems of the flowers presented a blackened and burnt appearance. When the reason was asked, the invisible intelligences answered that electricity was the potent "nipper" employed.

In her séance before the Florence Spiritual Society, "a sudden noise was heard as if the chandelier had fallen down; a light was struck, and a thick block of ice, of about a square foot in size, was found upon the table." Henry Wadsworth Longfellow had a sitting with her at Naples. He held both her hands, and while he did so several orange boughs were brought. Longfellow considered this manifestation to be one of the most conclusive he had ever witnessed.

Houghton, in her *Evenings at Home in Spiritual Séance* (1881), described a farewell séance held by Samuel Guppy and his mediumistic wife before their departure from England.

"By and by Mrs. Guppy exclaimed that there were creeping creatures about, and begged to be allowed to light the candle. Upon her request being granted there was a quantity of butterflies travelling about among us and the flowers, some of which were caught and put away in a box; altogether we reckoned that there were about forty of them."

Guppy-Volckman also obtained apports in a lighted room. A tray was placed on her knee, it being touched by the sitter's knee. A large shawl pinned to their necks covered the tray. The objects were then deposited on the tray. It is open to speculation whether the darkness under the tray was necessary for the rematerialization of the object or whether it only served the purpose of excluding the human gaze. Apports were peculiar in this respect. They did not appear before the eye but waited until attention was for a moment diverted, additional reason to suppose their production the result of trickery.

This curious fact was often noticed in the seances of **Charles Bailey,** the well-known Australian apport medium. From a description in *Light* (November 26, 1910), it was noted that "the apports included an Indian blanket containing a human scalp and tomahawk, a block of lead said to be found in Roman strata at Rome and bearing the name of Augustus, a quantity of gravel alleged to have come from Central America and quite unlike anything seen in Australia, two perfect clay tablets covered with cuneiform inscriptions and several thousands of years old, said to have been brought direct from the mounds at Babylon, and finally, a bird's nest containing several eggs and the mother bird undoubtedly alive." He was famous for living apports, jungle sparrows, crabs, turtles. Once an 18-inch-long shark, at another time a 30-inch snake appeared mysteriously in the séance room. The apport of jungle sparrows passed the test of a committee of investigation in Milan. Six years later, however, Bailey got into trouble in Grenoble. The investigators claimed that he smuggled in the birds in his intestinal opening, and they found a local dealer who identified Bailey as the man to whom he sold them.

Discredit was also attached to his archaeological objects when the British Museum found the clay tablets were fake.

Where do apports come from? If one eliminated any consideration of fraud, it would be a difficult question. Flowers were sometimes traced to nearby gardens. During his visit to the British College of Psychic Science in 1926, Heinrich Melzer suddenly fell into a semitrance condition out of doors and in his hands appeared sprays of flowers similar to those in a coster's barow on the other side of the street. Once in a séance with **Mary Baker Thayer, Henry Steel Olcott** received, on a mental request, the leaf of a rare plant which he marked in a garden. The question of source is pertinent as in some cases the apport of precious stones was also recorded. Semiprecious stones of little value often appeared in Bailey's seances. The bringing of pearls as apports is recorded in Georgina Houghton's book. They came in veritable showers in the seances of Stainton Moses. They may not have had any value, but that must have been different with his ruby, sapphire, and emerald apports. Small as they were, great commercial value must have been attached to them. Once he woke up from his sleep and saw a luminous hand near the ceiling, under it a little ball of fire as big as a pea. As he looked, the fingers were unclasped, the hand opened and the little ball of fire fell on his beard. It was a small opalescent stone about the size of a large pea, called sapphirium. Two similar stones were later delivered during a séance, the arrival being preceded by a fit of violent convulsion.

Apports, if real, would therefore raise a moral question. Who do they belong to? On being asked an opinion of fruit and flower apports, "John Watts," **Mrs. Thomas Everitt**'s control, said in a séance on February 28, 1868, recorded in Catherine Berry's *Experiences in Spiritualism* (1876), "I do not approve of bringing them, for they are generally stolen."

In discussing apports, Spiritualists surmised that space appears to be uniformly accessible to the spirit operators. Dr. L. Th. Chazarain, in his pamphlet *Scientific Proofs of the Survival of the Soul* told the story of the placing of two chaplets in the coffin of a child, in the presence of a medium very easily hypnotizable, and of their being returned two days after the burial. He made special marks on the chaplets, did not lose sight of them until the coffin was screwed down, and followed it to the church and to the cemetery. Two days later the mother of the child and Mme. D. suddenly saw something white detach itself from the ceiling and descend slowly, to the ground, in a spiral course. They immediately picked up the little white mass. It was the first chaplet, surrounded with a little wadding which smelled of the corpse, and still having the metallic button (the secret mark) attached. The child's body had been wrapped in wadding. Two days later the second chaplet was returned in the same manner.

Distance, however, appears to be of some consequence. The precipitation of the object was often heralded by a spasmodic seizure of the medium. Sometimes she cried out in agony. Fabian Rossi, in a séance on May 20, 1929, in Genoa, Italy, in which two small stones were apported, complained of great pains after she regained consciousness and said that she had been crushed between two enormous stones. At the time of this statement she did not know the nature of the apported objects. In the case of **Maria Silbert,** a light effect, similar to lightning, accompanied the delivery of the object. The bigger it was the greater the nervous tension. The medium always appeared to suffer more keenly if a greater distance was involved. The objects usually fell with a heavy thud. Breakage, it was noted, seldom occurred.

An alarm clock that was seen to fall at least 16 feet down the well of the stairs on to the flagstones in the hall of Tweedale's house was found to be undamaged and still going. The precipitation is usually effected from the direction of the ceiling. Catherine Berry writes in her *Experiences in Spiritualism*: "I saw coming from the ceiling, at the extreme end of the room, the branch of a tree about three feet in length. At the end was a large branch of white blossoms. I should perhaps say it appeared, in descending, like a flash of lightning."

Objects of unusual dimension and variety were apported at the Millesimo Castle seances with Marquise Centurione Scotto and Fabian Rossi. They were too large to hide about anybody's person, a halberd over six feet long, a plant in its pot over four feet high, large pistols, and swords and dolls of great size. The room was nearly bare of furniture and examined at the beginning of every sitting by Ernesto Bozzano. The story of one of these apport cases is notable. "Cristo d'Angelo," the control, told La Marquise Luisa that a very near relative of hers was destined to die. On her entreaty to tell who it was, "Cristo d'Angelo" replied, "I will bring you his portrait." Soon after the framed photograph of the doomed relative fell at La Marquise Luisa's feet. The last news of the relative had been excellent. Two days later he relapsed, and afterward died as predicted.

It was also observed in the Millesimo seances that the objects that were apported from a neighboring room had sometimes vanished days earlier (suggesting that they had been stolen at an opportune moment). Often they were returned to the room from which they were taken. This return, at least in one case, was only partially successful. A squire appeared and executed a "dance of the lance" in the July 8, 1928, séance in total darkness. Two mailed fists squeezed the hands of some of the sitters. The lance, at the end of the séance, was found in the room, but the mittens of mail were discovered in a distant room beneath the suit of mail, from the sleeves of which they were detached. The detachment of the mittens suggests that the rest of the armor was not apported.

One experiment is on record to test the theory that heavy apports brought about no variation in the weight of the medium. It was done in W. H. Terry's house in Melbourne in 1876 with **Mrs. Paton,** a medium who specialized in apporting her personal property. Sometimes it was a cup of tea she had forgotten to drink before leaving home, once a burning hot flat iron, at another time a glass of wine and a plate of eggs. Her phenomena were mostly recorded between 1872 and 1878.

There could hardly be anything to surpass in wonder the accounts of the apports said to be experienced by General "Lorrison" (Major-General A. W. Drayson) at Portsmouth. The medium was a Mrs. Maggs, the wife of a local editor and a writer herself. In a strictly private circle, apports arrived by the thousand. The household was supplied with eggs straight from Brooklyn from a spirit circle and return gifts were sent through similar means to countries as distant as Spain, Australia, India, and China. It is claimed that once a letter was apported, was read, a corner torn off for identification and then reapported. Ten days later it arrived, addressed to General Drayson. The torn-off piece fitted in and the contents were identical.

In experiments with **Lajos Pap** at the Budapest Metapsychical Museum, Chengery Pap often obtained living insects, frogs, and butterflies. Often they were completely dazed and motionless on arrival but recovered completely after a few minutes. Apports have also frequently been noticed in **poltergeist** cases. In stone throwing the stones may arrive apparently through the window without breaking the glass. In the case reported in the *Journal* of the Society for Psychical Research (vol. 12), stones seemed to pass through the roof of a Mr. Grottendieck's hut in the jungle of Sumatra without making a hole. They were so hot that Grottendieck at first believed them to be meteorites.

Apport Mediums Observed

That the actions of apport mediums require careful attention before the séance is well illustrated. Such was the case of a patient of **Pierre Janet,** a 26-year-old woman called Meb, who had visions of Saint Philomena and claimed to receive apports from her. Philomena was later removed from the Roman Catholic Church's list of saints as a nonexistent person. The apports were pebbles, feathers, flowers, and small pieces of cheap jewelry found lying about on the stairs or in other unlikely spots, or discovered in the patient's bedroom in the morning. On one occasion she found several small objects arranged in the shape of a cross, another time a pair of wings was stretched out on the eiderdown quilt. On one occasion feathers floated down from the ceiling upon the family assembled at their evening meal. In hypnotic sleep, the patient confessed the apports were arranged by herself in a state of somnambulism, that she put a stool on the table, mounted it and fastened small feathers with paste to the ceiling so that the heat of the lamp might bring them fluttering down. In her waking state she had no knowledge of these manipulations. It should be added that Meb was a hysteric.

A number of psychic researchers came to believe in apports. A comprehensive monograph on apports was published by Ernesto Bozzano in *Luce e Ombra* (1930), and subsequently in book form. It deals specifically with apports requested by experimenters, which reduces the possibility of a secret introduction. Of **Eusapia Palladino**'s apports, **Enrico Morselli** said, "This phenomenon was repeated two or three times during our sittings, but I frankly confess I was not convinced by it, which does not imply that under better observation it might not also be real in the case of Paladino, as it seems to have been through the agency of other mediums."

Striking experiments were carried out at the British College of Psychic Science in 1929 with **Thomas Lynn.** He was searched, stripped, and put in a bag. Many small objects, a cheap pearl necklace, a small reel of cotton, a button, a shell and a screw nail were apported and photographed at the moment of their arrival. During the sitting the medium lost 10–12 ounces in weight. The objects appeared to grow out of the body of the medium. The same phenomenon was reported upon by Karl Blacker, of Riga University, with the Medium B. X. (*Zeitschrift für Parapsychologie,* June 1933).

One of the more renowned twentieth-century psychics who produced apports was **Roberto Campagni** in Italy. The Genoanese physicist Alfredo Ferraro stated that he had seen 30 apports materialized by Campagni and had established beyond doubt that no trickery was involved. An interesting aspect is that the apports were often preceded by a blue light emanating from the medium's hands.

In spite of these passing recommendations, by the mid-twentieth century, it became obvious that apports were the product of mediumistic fraud, and consideration of them dropped completely from the literature of psychical research and slowly moved to the edge of Spiritualist claims.

Sources:

D'Esperance, Elizabeth. *Shadow Land or Light from the Outer Side.* London: George Redway, n.d.

Hack, Gwendolyn K. *Modern Psychic Mysteries: Millesimo Castle, Italy.* London: Rider, [1929].

Holms, A. Campbell. *The Facts of Psychic Science and Philosophy Collated and Discussed.* London, 1925. Reprint, New Hyde Park, N.Y.: University Books, 1969.

Richet, Charles. *Thirty Years of Psychical Research: Being a Treatise on Metaphysics.* New York: Macmillan, 1923.

Zöllner, J. C. F. *Transcendental Physics.* London, 1880. Reprint, Boston, Mass.: Colby and Rich, 1881.

APRO See Aerial Phenomena Research Organization

APRO Bulletin

Publication of the **Aerial Phenomena Research Organization,** a long-established body sponsoring conferences on UFOs. The *Bulletin* began a decline in the 1970s due to loss of support by APRO and was discontinued in the 1980s.

Aquarian Age

An age of universal brotherhood and enlightenment that many believe humanity is presently entering. It is often identified with the **New Age.** While astrologers have used it as a technical term for many years, it was popularized by the Broadway musical *Hair* with the song "This Is the Dawning of the Age of Aquarius."

Astrologers believe that the Earth enters a new zodiacal age every 2,160 years, a figure calculated by the changing position of the Sun at the spring equinox each year. Among astrologers and occultists, there is no consensus on the date for the beginning of the Age of Aquarius. According to some calculations, the Aquarian Age began as early as the seventeenth century, while others place it as late as the twenty-first century.

Aquarian Conspiracy, The

Title of a 1980 book by **Marilyn Ferguson.** The title became a catchword to describe a new consciousness revolution involving a leaderless network of many enlightened individuals to bring about radical change in modern culture, based on a greatly enlarged concept of human potential. The book is subtitled *Personal and Social Transformation in the 1980s,* and in her introduction, Ferguson explains her reasons for the choice of the term "conspiracy," which she uses in a positive sense.

In 1975 she founded a twice-monthly newsletter, *Brain/Mind Bulletin,* concerned with research and theory in the fields of learning, health, psychiatry, psychology, states of consciousness, meditation, and related subjects. The newsletter became a focus for other individuals exploring the same territories of experience, and Ferguson began to travel the U.S. to meet such individuals, attend conferences, and deliver lectures. She became aware of a transformative movement involving social change stemming from the personal transformation of individuals in all walks of society, which she discussed in *Brain/Mind Bulletin* (January 1976) (now known as *New Sense*) in her editorial, "The Movement that Has No Name." Ferguson claimed that the conspiracy had infected "medicine, education, social science, hard science, even government with its implications. It is characterized by fluid organizations reluctant to create hierarchical structures, averse to dogma. It operates on the principle that change can only be facilitated, not decreed. It is short on manifestos. It seems to speak to something very old. And perhaps, by integrating magic and science, art and technology, it will succeed where all the king's horses and all the king's men failed."

When writing her book about this new movement, Ferguson felt that the subtle links and mutual recognition among enlightened individuals implied something of an undeclared collusion. She was initially reluctant to use the term "conspiracy" because of its negative connotations until she saw a book of spiritual exercises in which Greek novelist Nikos Kazantzakis said that he wished to signal his comrades "like conspirators" that they might unite for the sake of the earth. The next day she read a report in the *Los Angeles Times* about a speech by Pierre Trudeau, in which he quoted a passage from French Jesuit priest Pierre Teilhard de Chardin urging a "conspiracy of love." As Ferguson points out, the literal meaning of the word "conspiracy" is "to breathe together." Even before her book was published, the use of this term produced friendly correspondence from individuals who signed themselves "co-conspirators."

In the **Aquarian Age** ferment of the 1960s, there was a widespread emphasis on the more sensational aspects of the occult, but as this has subsided, there are signs of a more integrated and mature approach to personal transformation, loosely based on enhanced consciousness on the one hand and holistic approaches to physical health on the other. The term Aquarian Conspiracy has been widely quoted to characterize this widespread transformation.

Sources:

Ferguson, Marilyn. *The Aquarian Conspiracy: Personal and Social Transformation in Our Time.* Los Angeles: J. P. Tarcher/Houghton Mifflin, 1987.

Aquarian Foundation

The Aquarian Foundation is a Spiritualist church built around the mediumship of its founder Rev. Keith Milton Rhinehart. It was founded in 1955 and existed for several decades as a single congregation in Seattle. Rhinehart articulated an eclectic occult perspective that combined elements of **Theosophy** and Eastern religion with more traditional **Spiritualism.** Rhinehart also claimed contact with the ascended masters identified with the **Theosophical Society.** Through the 1960s Rhinehart gained some fame as a "materialization" **medium.** In the 1970s his ideas began to spread across the United States and into Canada. Rhinehart has claimed to possess the stigmata, the extraordinary appearance of the wounds of Christ, which appeared on his body and were seen by many.

The work of the Aquarian Foundation centers upon contact with the ascended masters, who constitute the Great Brotherhood of Cosmic Light (termed by some the **Great White Brotherhood**), the spiritual hierarchy that mediates divine energies to humanity. Many of the sessions during which Rhinehart channeled messages from the masters have been recorded, transcribed, printed, and distributed to the foundations's various centers.

The brotherhood affirms belief in **karma** and **reincarnation,** the evolution of the soul, the law of cause and effect, and the eventual attainment of personal mastery. Among those contacted by Rhinehart are **Saint Germain, Master Morya,** Sanat Kumara, and **Djual Khul** (all prominent figures in Theosophy and the **I Am Movement**). Also included among the masters are the Angel Moroni (the angel who gave the Book of Mormon to Joseph Smith Jr.), Mahatma Ghandi, and flying saucer entities Clarion and Ashtar. The Aquarian Foundation is headquartered at 315 15th Ave. E., Seattle, WA 98112.

Sources:

Rhinehart, Keith Milton. *Soul Mates and Twin Rays.* Seattle, Wash.: Aquarian Foundation, 1972.

Aquarius Rising (Magazine)

Quarterly publication of the Astrology Center of the Northwest. Address: 522 Northeast 165th St., Seattle, WA 98155.

Aquino, Michael A.

Michael A. Aquino, U.S. Army officer and founder of the **Temple of Set,** is a graduate of the University of California, Santa Barbara (B.A., 1968; Ph.D., 1980). In 1968 he joined the army as a specialist in psychological warfare. The next year he joined the **Church of Satan.** His career in the church was put on hold while he served a tour of duty in Vietnam, but shortly after his return to the United States in 1971, he was ordained as a Satanic priest and organized a group (termed a grotto) that met at his home.

Aquino rose to a position of prominence in the Church of Satan, but became dissatisfied with the leadership of church founder **Anton LaVey.** He opposed LaVey's arbitrary leadership and atheistic approach to religion. LaVey actually denied the existence of Satan. In 1972 Aquino resigned and was joined in his revolt by Lilith Sinclair, another prominent leader on the East Coast. In 1975 he sought a new mandate to operate by invoking the devil. Satan responded by appearing as Set, the ancient Egyptian deity, and gave Aquino a document, *The Book of Coming Forth by Night.* He authorized Aquino to found the Temple of Set to supersede the Church of Satan. Aquino created a new religious society built around the worship of Set, of whom Satan is one derivation.

During the 1980s Aquino gained some degree of fame when the media became aware that an army officer led a Satanic group. The temple became the subject of criticism, and Aquino was charged with fabricated tales of Satanic child abuse. Aquino, an officer who has an exemplary record, was investigated and found innocent of any wrongdoing. The molestations he was accused of perpetrating were traced to a fellow officer. Meanwhile, he continues his professional career and his leadership in the temple.

Sources:

Aquino, Michael A. *The Church of Satan.* N.p.: The Author, 1989.

Lyons, Arthur. *Satan Wants You.* New York: Mysterious Press, 1988.

Arabs

The heyday of occultism, especially **astrology** and **alchemy,** occurred among the Arab race at the time when the Moors established their empire in the Spanish peninsula. In the eighth century an Arabian mystic revived the dreams and speculations of the alchemists and discovered some important secrets. **Geber,** who flourished about 720–750, is reputed to have written upwards of five hundred works on the **Philosopher's Stone** and the **elixir of life.** His researches in these occult subjects proved fruitless, but though the secrets of immortal life and boundless wealth eluded him, he discovered silver nitrate, corrosive sublimate, red oxide of mercury, and nitric acid, for he was a brilliant chemist.

His tenets included a belief that a preparation of gold would heal all diseases in animals and plants, as well as in human beings; that the metals were affected with maladies, except the pure, supreme, and precious gold; and that the Philosopher's Stone had often been discovered, but its fortunate discoverers would not reveal the secret to blind, incredulous, and unworthy man.

Geber's *Summa Perfectionis,* a manual for the alchemical student, has been frequently translated. One English version, of which there is a copy in the library of the British Museum, London, was published by an English enthusiast, Richard Russell, at "the Star, in New Market, in Wapping, near the Dock," in 1686. Geber's true name was Abou Moussah Djafar, to which was added Al Sofi, or "The Wise," and he was a native of Houran in Mesopotamia. He was followed by **Avicenna, Averroes,** and others equally gifted and fortunate.

According to Geber and his successors, the metals were not only compound creatures, but they were also all composed of the same two substances. By the nineteenth century, European chemists like William Prout and Humphry Davy were propounding similar ideas. "The improvements," stated Davy, "taking place in the methods of examining bodies, are constantly changing the opinions of chemists with respect to their nature, and there is no reason to suppose that any real indestructible principle has yet been discovered. Matter may ultimately be found to be the same in essence, differing only in the arrangement of its particles; or two or three simple substances may produce all the varieties of compound bodies." The ancient ideas, of Demetrius the Greek physicist and of Geber the Arabian polypharmist are still hovering about the horizon of chemistry. In the twentieth century, successful nuclear fission has validated the transmutation of metals.

The Arabians also taught that the metals are composed of mercury and sulphur in different proportions. They toiled away at making many medicines out of the various mixtures and reactions from the few available chemicals. They believed in transmutation, but they did not strive to effect it. It belonged to their creed rather than to their practice. They were hard-working scientific artisans with their pestles and mortars, their crucibles and furnaces, their alembics and aludels, their vessels for infusion, for decoration, for cohobation, sublimation, fixation, lixiviation, filtration, and coagulation. They believed in transmutation, in the first matter, and in the correspondence of the metals with the planets, to say nothing of potable gold. It is not known where the ancient Arabians derived the sublimer articles of their scientific faith. Perhaps they were the conjectures of their ancestors according to the faith. Perhaps they had them from the Fatimites of Northern Africa, among whose local predecessors it has been seen that it is just possible the doctrine of the four elements and their mutual convertibility may have arisen. Perhaps they drew them from Greece, modifying and adapting them to their own specific forms of matter, mercury, sulphur, and arsenic.

Arabian Astrology

Astrology was also employed by the oracles of Spain. Al-Battani was celebrated for his astronomical science, as were many others; and in geometry, arithmetic, algebraical calculations, and the theory of music, the list of Asiatic and Spanish practitioners is long, but only known by their lives and principal writings. The works of Ptolemy also exercised the ingenuity of the Arabians. But judicial astrology, or the art of foretelling future events from the position and influences of the stars, was a favorite pursuit; and many of their philosophers dedicated all their labors to this futile but lucrative inquiry. They often spoke highly of the iatromathematical discipline, which could control the disorders to which man was subject and regulate the events of life.

The tenets of Islam, which inculcate an unreserved submission to the overruling destinies of heaven, are evidently adverse to the lessons of astrology; but this by no means hindered the practitioners of old Spain and Arabia from attaining a high standard of perfection in the art, which they perhaps first learned from the peoples of Chaldea, the past masters of the ancient world in astronomical science, in **divination,** and the secrets of prophecy. But in Arab Spain, where the tenets of Islam were perhaps more lightly esteemed than in their original home, **magic** unquestionably reached a higher if not more thoughtful standard.

From the Greeks, still in search of science, the Arabs turned their attention to the books of the sages who are esteemed the primitive instructors of mankind, among whom Hermes was deemed the first. They mention the works written by him, or rather by them, as they suppose, like other authors, that there were three of the name. To one the imposing appellation of "Trismegistus" has been given, and the Arabians, presumably from some ancient records, minutely described his character and person. Illustrating their astrological discipline, they also published some writings ascribed to the Persian Zoroaster.

Sources:

Hutin, Serge. *A History of Alchemy.* New York: Walker, 1963. Reprint, New York: Tower Books, n.d.

Jabir ibn Hayyan. *The Works of Geber.* London: Printed for William Cooper, 1686.

Muhammad ibn Umail al-Tamini. *Three Arabic Treatises on Alchemy.* Calcutta: Asiatic Society of Bengal, 1933.

Aradia

The book *Aradia: Gospel of the Witches* by **Charles G. Leland** (1899 and often reprinted) presented traditional witchcraft teachings from **Italy,** which Leland claimed he obtained from a Florentine fortune-teller and hereditary witch in the late nineteenth century. This book is clearly one of the inspirations of the modern witchcraft revival launched by **Gerald B. Gardner,** and it has furnished some materials for the contemporary witches' **Book of Shadows,** the ritual book used by modern witch covens.

Sources:

Leland, Charles Godfrey. *Aradia: Gospel of the Witches.* 1899. Reprint, New York: Hero Press, 1971.

Arael

One of the spirits that the ancient rabbis of the Talmud made princes and governors over the people of the birds.

Arariel

According to the ancient rabbis of the Talmud, Arariel is an angel who takes charge of the waters of the Earth. Fishermen invoked him so that they might catch large fish.

Ararita

According to occultist **Éliphas Lévi,** Ararita is "the *verbum inenarrabile* of the sages of the Alexandrian School," which "Hebrew Kabalists wrote *Javeh* and interpreted by the sound *Ararita,* thus expressing the triplicity of the secondary kabalistic principle, the dualism of the means and the equal unity of the first and final principle, as well as the alliance between the triad and the triad and the tetrad in a word composed of four letters, which form seven by means of a triple and double repetition." (See also **Kabala**)

Sources:

Lévi, Éliphas. *Transcendental Magic.* London: Rider, 1896. Reprint, New York: Samuel Weiser, 1972.

Arbatel

A magical ritual published at Basle in 1575. The text is in Latin and appears to have been influenced by **Paracelsus.** It is of Christian, not Jewish, origin, and although the authorship is unknown, it is probably the work of an Italian. Only one of its nine volumes still exists: dealing with the institutions of **magic,** the work is entitled *Isagoge,* which means "essential or necessary instruction."

The book introduces the ritual of the Olympic spirits who dwell in the air and among the stars and who govern the world. There are, we are told, 196 Olympic provinces in the universe: thus Aratron has 49; Bethor, 42; Phaleg 35; Och, 28; Hagith, 21; Ophiel, 14; and Phul, 7. Each of the Olympic spirits rules alternately for 490 years. They have natural sway over certain departments of the material world, but outside these departments they perform the same operations magically.

Thus Och, the ruler of solar affairs, presides over the preparation of gold naturally in the soil. At the same time, he presides magically over the preparation of that metal by means of **alchemy.** The *Arbatel* states that the sources of occult wisdom are to be found in God, spiritual essences, and corporeal creatures, as well as in nature, but also in the apostate spirits and in the ministers of punishment in Hell and the elementary spirits. The secrets of all magic reside in these, but magicians are born, not made, although they are assisted by contemplation and the love of God.

It is sufficient to describe the powers and offices of one of these spirits. Aratron governs those things that are ascribed astrologically to Saturn. He can convert any living thing into stone, can change coals into treasure, gives familiar spirits to men, and teaches alchemy, magic, medicine, and the secret of invisibility and long life. He should be invoked on a Saturday in the first hour of the day. The *Arbatel* was said to be one of the best authorities on spiritual essences and their powers and degrees.

ARC See Astrological Registration and Communicaton

Arcana Magazine

A journal devoted to cosmology, eschatology, hermetic science and the occult. Published quarterly from Land of Cokaygne, 1 Jesus Terrace, New Square, Cambridge, England.

Arcana Workshops

The Arcana Workshops, one of the more important full moon meditation groups operating in Southern California, grew out of the program of the **Arcane School** and the teachings of **Alice Bailey,** to which it has added insights from the theosophical Agni Yoga Society. The group promotes full moon meditation as a time for transmitting the spiritual energies of the masters to the world. The group also works to unite the efforts of occult groups in Southern California to celebrate the three spring festivals (Easter, Wesak, and Goodwill) originally suggested by Bailey. Arcana Workshops literature refers to them as the festivals of Aries, Taurus, and Gemini.

The Arcana Workshops also offers correspondence courses, publishes a number of pamphlets, and sends out regular mailings to those on their mailing list. The organization may be contacted at Box 605, Manhattan Beach, CA 90266.

Sources:

The Full Moon Story. Beverly Hills, Calif.: Arcana Workshops, 1974.

The Full Moon Workers. Beverly Hills, Calif.: Arcana Workshops, n.d.

What Is Arcana? Beverly Hills, Calif.: Arcana Workshops, n.d.

Arcane

That which is hidden or secret; usually refers to rites associated with the mystery religions or secret societies. (See also **Arcanum, Great**)

Sources:

Yarker, John. *The Arcane Schools.* Belfast, 1909.

Arcane School

The Arcane School, an occult organization founded by Theosophist **Alice A. Bailey** and her husband, Foster Bailey, was designed to bring in the **New Age** by the **Great White Brotherhood,** the spiritual hierarchy of masters who are believed to guide human destiny. As a young woman, Bailey affiliated with the **Theosophical Society,** moved into the Krotona community in Hollywood, California, and became editor of *The Messenger,* the society's journal. She also began to channel material from Djwhal Khul, one of the masters of the theosophical spiritual hierarchy, generally called **"The Tibetan."** Her channeling activity proved unacceptable to the society, and in 1920 she and her husband departed.

They moved to New York where Alice completed the channeling of two books and wrote one herself. They formed the Lucis Trust as a publishing concern and began a magazine, the *Beacon.* The Arcane School was founded in 1923 as an organization for students who responded to the books. Over the next years Bailey dictated a series of books that laid out a program for bringing in the New Age.

Among the several programs nurtured by the school was the New Group of World Servers, founded in 1932. The group sought to unite people of goodwill as harbingers of a coming civilization. Five years later the school launched the Triangles program to bring together groups of three people to work together in spiritual service. The primary task of a triangle is to channel spiritual energy from the hierarchy to the world. To assist the triangles, she released what is possibly her most famous piece of writing, a prayer called "The Great Invocation."

Bailey also began to announce the coming of the New Age and the accompanying appearance of the Christ. This coming of the New Age Savior was also encouraged by the repeating of "The Great Invocation."

Bailey taught that certain moments of the year are especially fruitful times for spiritual work because an abundance of spiritual energy is available. Such a time is the monthly period of the full moon, when members of the school gather on the evening of the full moon to meditate and transmit energy. On three full moon dates the great festivals Easter, Wesak, and Goodwill take place. The festival of Easter does not follow either of the Christian calendars, but is celebrated on the full moon in April as the time of the most active forces for the restoration of the Christ. In May, Wesak is the time when the Buddha's forces are available. In June, at the full moon, the forces of reconstruction are active.

Foster succeeded his wife as head of the school following her death in 1949. Their daughter Mary Bailey succeeded to the leadership after Foster's death in 1977. The school publishes several periodicals, including the *Beacon* and the *World Goodwill Newsletter.* International headquarters are located close to the United Nations building at 113 University Pl., 11th Fl., Box 722, Cooper Sta., New York, NY 10276. There are also European offices in London and Geneva. Several groups such as the **Arcana Workshops,** Meditation Groups, Inc., and the School for Esoteric Studies carry on programs similar to the Arcane School, though they are organizationally separate from it.

Sources:

Bailey, Alice A. *The Unfinished Autobiography.* New York: Lucis Publishing Company, 1951.

Sinclair, John R. *The Alice Bailey Inheritance.* Wellingsborough, England: Turnstone Press, 1984.

Arcanum, Great

The great secret that was supposed to lie behind all alchemical and magical striving. "God and Nature, alike," wrote **Éliphas Lévi,** "have closed the Sanctuary of Transcendent Science . . . so that the revelation of the great magical secret is happily impossible." Elsewhere he states that it makes the magician "master of gold and light."

Sources:

Lévi, Éliphas. *Transcendental Magic.* London: Rider, 1896. Reprint, New York: Samuel Weiser, 1972.

Archaeus Project

A private foundation formed to study techniques for detection and measurement of bioenergetic fields—electric, magnetic, and physical—and their application to diagnosis and treatment of disease. The project issues the bimonthly newsletter *Artifex* and the scholarly journal *Archaeus,* dealing with parapsychological topics and anomalous phenomena. Address: 629 12th Ave. SE, Minneapolis, MN 55414.

Archivo di Documentazione Storica Della Ricerca Psichica

The Archivo di Documentazione Storica Della Ricerca Psichica (the Archives of Historical Documents on Psychical Research) was founded in 1985 in Bologna, Italy, by Gastone de Boni and Ernesto Bozzano. The library and archive of books and materials on **parapsychology, psychical research,** and related topics is the largest such collection in Italy. The archives also published *Luce e Ombra.* The organization may be contacted at Via Orfeo 15, 40124 Bologna, Italy.

Ardat-Lile

Ancient Semitic female spirit or demon who wed human beings and worked great harm in the dwellings of men.

ARE See Association for Research and Enlightenment

ARE Journal

Bimonthly publication founded in 1966 by the **Association for Research and Enlightenment** and concerned with the life and work of **Edgar Cayce** (1877–1945). Articles covered the wide range of subjects mentioned in Cayce's writings. It was superseded in 1984 by *Venture Inward.*

ARGENTINA

Although little has been published abroad on the history of **Spiritualism** and psychical research in Argentina, there has been considerable activity from the late nineteenth century onward. In the early period, Argentine Spiritualism was strongly influenced by the **Spiritism** of French Spiritualist **Allan Kardec.** The journal *Constancia: Revista semanal, Illustrada de Espiritismo, Psicologia, y Socialogia* was founded as early as 1877. Other publications during the 1930s included *La Nota Espiritista* and *Revue Anales.* One early organization Spiritualistic Association Lumen aimed to take the study of Spiritualism in the direction of humanistic science rather than religion.

With the growth of interest in experimental psychology stimulated by such pioneers as Dr. Horacio Rinoldi, scientific techniques began to be applied to the study of the paranormal. The first Institute of Psychology was created in the University of Buenos Aires in November 1931 to investigate general psychology, psychological pathology, psychometry, and psychotechniques. Dr. Enrique Mochet, who headed the Institute, observed activities of various clairvoyants and mediums and included a course on paranormal psychology. Other scientists at the institute included Dr. Fernando Gorriti, Prof. Dr. Gonzalez Bosch, and Prof. José Fernández.

In 1933 Fernández founded the ATMAN Spiritualist Circle and also attended meetings of the Psyke Circle, known for their séances with clairvoyants and mediums. Their successes or failures were assessed statistically, and in 1941 Fernández published the results in the pamphlet *Clairvoyance and Probability.* Although these and other investigations were without rigorous control techniques, they played an important part in the development of parapsychological method in Argentina.

During the wartime period in the early 1940s, parapsychological researches were temporarily suspended, but in 1946 Dr. **Orlando Canavesio** founded the Argentine Medical Association for Parapsychology and launched its journal *Revista Medica de Metapsiquica.* At that time the Argentine government, which considered Spiritualism a "social evil" and attempted to control it sponsored the Institute of Applied Psychopathology. Spiritualists responded by turning increasingly to the research of parapsychologists to validate and support their work.

In 1949 the Argentine Association of Parapsychology brought together scientists and active Spiritualists. The research of Dr. **J. B. Rhine** in the U.S. had become well known to Argentine parapsychologists, and it became possible to develop statistical methods of psi evaluation.

Through the early 1950s Benjamin Odell, Julio C. Di Liscia, and **J. Ricardo Musso** created the Association of Friends of Parapsychology and its official organ, the *Revista Argentina de Parapsicología* in 1955. Musso became president of the Instituto Argentino de Parapsicología in Buenos Aires, which publishes the quarterly journal *Cuadernos de Parapsicología.* The serious study of parapsychology seemed well established.

By 1970 there were over 130 organizations devoted to the study of the paranormal in Argentina and many publications. Then suddenly all of the parapsychology courses at both the Roman Catholic and state universities were canceled, except for the one at the Universidad del Salvador. This action signaled official disapproval of parapsychology, and many of the organizations began to disband. As of the early 1990s, only two research centers remain, both in Buenos Aires. Enrique Novillo Paulí teaches parapsychology at the Universidad del Salvador, and the Institutio Argentino de Parapsycología continues to issue *Cuadernos de Parapsicología.* Address: Calle Ramon Lista 868, 1706, P. F., Sarmiento-Haedo, Buenos Aires, Argentina.

Sources:

Berger, Arthur S., and Joyce Berger. *The Encyclopedia of Parapsychology and Psychical Research.* New York: Paragon House, 1991.

Musso, J. Ricardo. "Parapsychology in Argentina." *Parapsychology Today: A Geographic View.* Edited by Allan Angoff and Betty Shapin. New York: Parapsychology Foundation, 1973.

Argentum, Potabile

A remedy prescribed by ancient alchemists such as **Paracelsus** and composed of sulphur, spirits of wine, and other ingredients.

These practitioners gave the remedy for all types of ailments. Called a sovereign remedy, the name implies "silver," meaning that the preparation reflects the powers of the Moon (associated with silver), just as the Sun implies gold.

Arica

A psychophysical system developed by Oscar Ichazo and named after the town in Chile where Ichazo first trained members. The system includes meditation and exercises connected with vibrations, sounds, and movements to produce a state of enhanced consciousness called "Permanent 24." Arica is a body-mind system adapted from a variety of Eastern and Western mystical teachings of a **Gurdjieff** type. Teaching centers have been established in a number of American cities, with headquarters at the Arica Institute, 150 Fifth Ave., New York, NY 10011.

Sources:

Ichazo, Oscar. *The Human Process for Enlightenment and Freedom.* New York: Arica Institute, 1976.

Interviews with Oscar Ichazo. New York: Arica Institute Press, 1982.

Ariel

One of the two spirits supposed to have attended the seventeenth-century English writer on witchcraft, **John Beaumont.**

Arignote

An early ghost story told by the ancient Greek writer Lucian (second century C.E.). The story relates that at Corinth, in the Cranaüs quarter, there was a certain house that no one would inhabit, because it was haunted by a specter. A man named Arignote, well versed in the lore of Egyptian magical books, shut himself in the house to pass the night and began to read peacefully in the court. Soon the specter made its appearance, and in order to frighten Arignote, it first took the form of a dog, then that of a bull, and finally that of a lion. But Arignote was not at all disturbed. He admonished the specter by a magic spell that he found in his books, and he commanded it to go to a corner of the court, where it disappeared. On the following day the spot to which the specter had retreated was dug up, and a skeleton was found. When it was properly buried, the ghost was not seen again. This anecdote is an adaptation of the adventure of Athenodorus, which Lucian had read in Pliny.

Arigó, José (1918–1971)

Pseudonym of José Pedro de Freitas, a Brazilian psychic healer who performed surgical operations without proper instruments or anesthetics. Arigó, who claimed to be directed by the spirit of "Dr. Adolpho Fritz," performed complex operations at top speed with an unsterilized pocket knife. In 1957 he was sentenced to imprisonment for illegally practicing medicine but was pardoned by the president of Brazil. He was again sentenced in 1964, with an additional charge of practicing "witchcraft" (presumably to account for his uncanny successes), but the case was reviewed the following year and Arigó was released before serving his complete sentence. He was killed in a road accident six years later. (See also **Psychic Surgery**)

Sources:

Fuller, John R. *Arigó: Surgeon of the Rusty Knife.* New York: Thomas Y. Crowell, 1974.

Playfair, Guy Lyon. *The Flying Crow.* London: Souvenir Press, 1975. Reprinted as *The Unknown Power.* New York: Pocket Books, 1976.

Valentine, Tom. *Psychic Surgery.* Chicago: Henry Regnery, 1973.

Arioch

Demon of vengeance, according to some demonologists. Arioch differs from **Alastor** and occupies himself only with vengeance in particular cases where he is employed for that purpose.

Ariolists

Ancient diviners whose special occupation was called *ariolatio* because they accomplished their **divination** by means of altars. They consulted demons on their altars, stated Dangis; they observed whether the altar trembled or performed any marvel and predicted what the Devil inspired them with. François de la Tour Blanche maintained that these people ought to have been put to death as idolators. He based his opinion on Deuteronomy 18 and Revelation 21, which assert that idolators and liars shall be cast into the lake of fire and sulphur, which will be their second death. (See also **Divination**)

Aristaeus (ca. sixth century B.C.E.)

A charlatan who lived in the time of Croesus (sixth century B.C.E.). He claimed that his soul could leave his body whenever he wished and then return to it. Some maintain that it escaped in the sight of his wife and children in the figure of a stag. **Johan Weyer** stated that it took the shape of a crow.

According to Herodotus, in his fourth book, Aristaeus fell dead upon entering a fuller's shop, and the fuller ran to break the news to his parents. When they came to bury him, no corpse could be found. The whole town was astonished. Then some men returning from a voyage assured them that they had met Aristaeus on the way to Crotona and that he appeared to be a species of **vampire.** Herodotus added that Aristaeus reappeared at the end of seven years, composed a poem, and died again.

Leloyer, who regarded Aristaeus as a sorcerer or ecstatic, quoted a certain Apollonius, who said that at the same hour as the vampire disappeared for the second time, he was transported to Sicily, where he became a school master.

Aristaeus is again heard of 340 years later in the town of Metapontus, where he caused certain monuments to be raised that were to be seen in the time of Herodotus. So many wonderful happenings inspired the Sicilians with awe, that they raised a temple to him and worshipped him as a demigod.

Sources:

Herodotus. *The Histories of Herodotus of Halicarnassus.* London: Oxford University Press, 1962.

Weyer, Johannes. *Witches, Devils, and Doctors in the Renaissance: Johann Weyer, De Praestigiis.* Edited by George Mora. Binghamton, N.Y.: Medieval and Renaissance Texts and Studies, 1991.

Arithmancy

Divination by means of numbers (sometimes wrongly called *Arithmomancy*). The ancient Greeks examined the number and value of the letters in the names of two combatants and predicted that he whose name contained the most letters, or letters of the greatest value, would be the victor. Using this science, diviners foretold that Hector would be overcome by Achilles. The Chaldeans, who also practiced it, divided their alphabet into three parts, each composed of seven letters, which they attributed to the seven planets, in order to make predictions from them. The Platonists and the Pythagoreans were also strongly addicted to this method of divination, which is similar to certain aspects of the Jewish **Kabala.**

Sources:

Waite, Arthur Edward. *The Occult Sciences.* 1891. Reprint, Secaucus, N.J.: University Books, 1974.

Armida

The episode of *Armida* in *Jerusalem Delivered* by Torquato Tasso (1554–1595), is founded on a popular tradition related by **Pierre De Lancre.** This skillful enchantress was the daughter of Arbilan, king of Damascus. She was brought up by an uncle, a great magician, who taught his niece to become a powerful sorceress. Nature had so well endowed her that she far surpassed the most beautiful women of the East. Her uncle sent her as a worthy foe against the powerful Christian army that Pope Urban XI had collected under the leadership of Godfrey de Bouillon. And there, De Lancre says, she so charmed the principal leaders of the crusaders with her beautiful eyes that she almost ruined the hopes of the Christians. She kept the valiant knight Renaud for a long time in an enchanted castle, and it was with great difficulty that he was disenchanted.

Sources:

Tasso, Torquato. *Jerusalem Delivered.* Rutherford, N.J.: Fairleigh Dickinson University Press, 1970.

Armomancy

A method of **divination** effected by the inspection of the shoulders. The ancients judged by this means whether a victim was suitable for sacrifice to the gods.

Arnaldus de Villanova (ca. 1235–1311)

Famous early alchemist who was also an astrologer, diplomat, and social reformer. He was regarded as a great authority on **alchemy** and is cited in many histories of the subject. Born in a Catalan family near Valencia, he was educated by Dominicans and studied medicine at Naples. His medical skill brought him a great reputation, and he treated kings, popes, and other famous people, which gave him reason to travel widely in Spain, France, Italy, and North Africa. He studied languages and was fluent in Arabic, Greek, and Latin. He became a favorite physician of James II, king of Aragon, and in 1285 he attended King Peter III of Aragon and was rewarded with the professorial chair of the University of Montpellier and a castle in Tarragona. However, his frank criticisms of the clergy of his time made many enemies in the Church, and in 1299, during a diplomatic mission to Paris on behalf of James II of Aragon, he was arrested by order of the Holy Office and charged with heresy in his book on the Antichrist. After strong protests on his behalf to the King of France and Pope Boniface VIII, he was released in 1301.

He wrote many books on medicine and alchemy, although some works ascribed to him are probably wrongly attributed. During a visit to Naples, he met the famous alchemist **Ramon Lully.** In addition to his writings on alchemy, Arnaldus conducted some practical experiments. He died on a voyage from Sicily to Avignon, where he had been summoned to attend Pope Clement V, who was ill. Arnaldus was buried in Genoa.

His major work on alchemy, *The Treasure of Treasures, Rosary of the Philosophers,* was published in Italian and Latin. There is a lengthy account on Arnaldus in *Histoire littéraire de la France* by J. B. Hauréau, 1881.

Sources:

Waite, Arthur Edward. *Alchemists through the Ages.* Blauvelt, N.Y.: Rudolf Steiner Publications, 1970.

Arnoux, François (ca. 1622)

Canon of Riez, France, who published a popular work on wonders of the other world (*Merveilles de l'autre monde*) in 1622 at Rouen. It was written in a bizarre style and was calculated to disturb feeble imaginations with its tales of visions and apparitions.

Arnuphis (ca. 174 C.E.)

An Egyptian general credited with magical powers. He is said to have saved the army of Marcus Aurelius from defeat by the Quadi (a German tribe) when entangled in a pass which had been closed by the enemy. According to the writer Dio Cassius, the troops of Aurelius were dying of thirst when Arnuphis caused a miraculous storm that confounded the enemy and allowed the Romans to quench their thirst and win the battle. Their triumph was known as "The Miracle of the Thundering Legion," although Christians ascribed the victory to their own prayers rather than to the aid of Mercury and other gods invoked by Arnuphis.

Aromatherapy

Term used for treatment of illness and maintenance of general physical health using essential oils distilled from such plants as camomile, camphor, peppermint, rosemary, lavender, and eucalyptus. Such treatments were known in ancient Egypt, Greece, Rome, and other civilizations, while early Arabian physicians developed the distillation of aromatic oils through experiments in **alchemy.** The term aromatherapy derives from the writings of the French chemist Rene-Maurice Gattefosse, whose book *Aromatherapie* was published in 1928. However, the modern popularity of aromatherapy is generally traced to Marguerite Maury, who developed a new technique for the extraction and use of oils. She published her findings in 1962 and was awarded the Prix international d'esthetique et cosmetologie. Her work was picked up by the **New Age** movement in the 1980s and has become an essential part of the holistic health movement.

Aromatherapy is more than simply a department of **herbalism,** since it postulates subtle energies of aromatic plants related to life force, which can be correlated with ancient Chinese concepts of **Yin and Yang.** (See also **Perfumes**)

Sources:

Stead, Christiane. *The Power of Holistic Aromatherapy.* Poole, England: Javalin Books, 1986.

Thompson, C. J. S. *The Mystery and Lure of Perfume.* London, 1927.

Tisserand, Robert. *Aromatherapy.* 1977. Reprint, London: Mayflower, 1979.

Arphaxat

A Persian sorcerer who was killed by a thunderbolt (according to Abdias of Babylon) as St. Simon and St. Jude were martyred. In the account of the possession of the **nuns of Loudun,** there is also a demon known as Arphaxat, who took possession of the body of Louise de Pinterville.

Arriola, Pepito (ca. 1900)

A Spanish musical prodigy who, in 1900, at the age of three years three months, was introduced by **Charles Richet** to the International Psychical Congress. Arriola had only begun playing the piano a year earlier. With his tiny hands, which appeared to grow while he played, he somehow managed to sound full octaves.

He also composed military and funeral marches, waltzes, minuets, and habaneras and played some 20 difficult pieces from memory. At the time, there was no suggestion of a Spiritualist explanation for this phenomena, but 11 years later the boy exhibited the gift of **automatic writing.** (See also **Rosemary Brown; Music (Paranormal); Jesse Shepard**)

Ars Notoria

Title of a work of magical invocations and prayers attributed to Solomon and therefore related to the celebrated *Key of Solomon the King,* one of the most famous **grimoires,** or book of **ceremonial magic.** *Ars Notoria* is known in the English translation of

Robert Turner (Sloane Manuscript 3648, British Library, London), published by him in 1657.

Artephius (d. ca. 1119)

A well-known exponent of Hermetic philosophy who died in the twelfth century, and is said to have lived more than one thousand years by means of alchemical secrets. François Pic mentions the opinion of certain savants who affirmed that Artephius was identical with **Apollonius of Tyana,** who was born in the first century under that name and who died in the twelfth century under that of Artephius.

Many extravagant and curious works are attributed to Artephius: *De Vita Propaganda* (The Art of Prolonging Life), which he claims, in the preface, to have written at the age of 1,025 years; *The Key to Supreme Wisdom;* and a work on the character of the planets, on the significance of the songs of birds, on things past and future, and on the **philosophers' stone.** Jerome Cardan spoke of these books and believed that they were composed by some practical joker who wished to play on the credulity of the partisans of alchemy.

Some scholars have identified Artephius with the Arabic poet and alchemist Al Toghrai, who died ca. 1119.

Arthur, King

Legendary king of England, son of Uther Pendragon and Igraine. It seems likely that Arthur was a sixth-century leader whose life and deeds became interwoven with romance mythology. The character of King Arthur is strongly identified with occult legends. Not only do we find his court a veritable center of happenings more or less supernatural, but his mysterious origin and the subsequent events of his career contain matter of considerable interest from an occult standpoint.

He is connected with one of the greatest magical names of early times—**Merlin** the Enchanter. It is possible that Merlin was originally a British deity who in later times degenerated from his high position in the popular imagination. There are many accounts concerning him, one of which states that he was the direct offspring of Satan himself, but that a zealous priest succeeded in baptizing him before his infernal parent could carry him off.

From Merlin, Arthur received much good advice, both magical and rational. Merlin was present when the king was gifted with his magic sword, Excalibur, which endowed him with practical invulnerability, and all through his career Merlin was deep in the king's counsels. Merlin's tragic imprisonment by the Lady Viviana, who shut him up eternally in a rock through the agency of one of his own spells, removed him from his sphere of activity at the Arthurian Court, and from that time the shadows were seen to gather swiftly around Arthur's head.

Innumerable are the tales concerning the knights of his court who met with magical adventures, and as the stories grew older in the popular mind, additions to these naturally became the rule. Of note is the offshoot of the Arthurian epic, known as the Holy **Grail,** in which the knights who go in quest of it encounter every description of sorcery for the purpose of retarding their progress.

Arthur's end is as strange as his origin, for he is wafted away by fairy hands, or at least by invisible agency, to the Isle of Avillion, which probably is the same place as the Celtic otherworld across the ocean.

As a legend and a tradition, that of Arthur is undoubtedly the most powerful and persistent in the British imagination. It has employed the pens and enhanced the dreams of many of the giants of English literature from the time of Geoffrey of Monmouth to the present day. Some claim Arthur was buried at Glastonbury, and tourists who visit are shown a tomb site and may purchase the replica of a cross with an inscription concerning Arthur.

Sources:

De Troyes, Chrétien. *Arthurian Romances (Erec and Enide; Cligés; Yvain; Lancelot).* London, 1914.

Lacy, Norris J., ed. *The Arthurian Encyclopedia.* New York: Garland Publishing, 1986.

Reiss, Edmund, Louise Horner Reiss, and Beverly Taylor. *Arthurian Legend and Literature: An Annotated Bibliography.* New York: Garland Publishing, 1984.

Waite, Arthur Edward. *The Holy Grail: The Galahad Quest in the Arthurian Literature.* 1933. Reprint, New York: University Books, 1961.

White, Terence H. *The Once and Future King.* London: Collins, 1958.

Wilhelm, James J., and Laila Zamuelis Gross, eds. *The Romance of Arthur.* New York: Garland Publishing, 1984.

Arthur Findlay College

A residential center in Essex, England, administered by the **Spiritualists' National Union,** where students may attend courses on Spiritualist philosophy, practice, healing, and related subjects. These courses are wide ranging, including acupuncture, radionics, meditation, relaxation, color therapy, and Taoism as well as subjects directly related to **Spiritualism,** such as the practice of mediumship. The college is situated on 15 acres of land in pleasant surroundings and includes the **Britten Memorial Museum,** devoted to exhibits concerned with the history of Spiritualism and psychic phenomena.

The college is named for pioneer Spiritualist **J. Arthur Findlay** (1883–1964), the author of a number of well-known Spiritualist works. Address: Stansted Hall, Stansted, Mountfichet, Essex CM24 8UD, England.

Artifex (Newsletter)

Bimonthly newsletter of the **Archaeus Project** concerned with bioenergetic fields and anomalous phenomena. Address: 629 12 Ave. SE, Minneapolis, MN 55414.

Arundale, George Sydney (1878–1945)

Prominent member of the **Theosophical Society.** Born in Surrey, England, December 1, 1878, he was educated in Italy and Germany before entering St. John's College, Cambridge University, England, from which he graduated M.A., LL.B., D.Lit. He joined the Theosophical Society in 1895 and went to India at the invitation of **Annie Besant.** Arundale served as principal of the Central Hindu College, Benares (1905), examiner to the University of Allahabad and to the government of United Provinces, India, principal of National University of Madras (1917), and minister of education to the government of the Maharaja Holkar (1923). He was also regionary bishop of the **Liberal Catholic Church** in India, deputy chief scout of the Indian Boy Scout Association, and provincial commissioner of the Hindustan Scout Association in Madras Presidency.

In 1917 he was interned with Annie Besant, then president of the Theosophical Society, for principles expressed in membership of the All India Home Rule League. In 1920 he married Rukmini Devi, an Indian girl from a Brahmin family, who was a leading exponent of Hindu classical dancing. She helped to restore respect for Indian dancing as an expression of deep spiritual awareness. Arundale lectured extensively in India, Europe, and Australia and was at one time general secretary of the Theosophical Society in England, Australia, and India. In 1934 he succeeded Besant as president of the Theosophical Society. He also wrote a number of works on Theosophy and edited *The Theosophist, The Theosophical Worker,* and *Conscience* (Madras). His book *Kundalini: An Occult Experience* (1938) has special importance as an early personal description of the arousal of **kundalini** in the body. He died at Adyar, India, August 12, 1945.

Sources:

Arundale, George S. *Fragment of Autobiography.* Adyar, India: Kalaksetra, 1940.

———. *Kundalini: An Occult Experience.* Adyar, India: Theosophical Publishing House, 1938.
———. *Lotus Fire.* Adyar, India: Theosophical Publishing House, 1939.
———. *Thoughts on "At the Feet of the Master."* Adyar, India: Theosophical Publishing House, 1919.
———. *You.* Madras, India: Theosophical Publishing House, 1938. Reprint, Wheaton, Ill.: Theosophical Publishing House, 1973.

As You Like It Library

An unusual organization that maintains a free lending library of books on psychic subjects. Only postage is charged, but a $5 bond is required for borrowers outside the state of Washington. Address: 915 E. Pine St., Room 401, Seattle, WA 98122.

Asal

Known as the King of the Golden Pillars in Irish Celtic mythology. He was the owner of seven swine, which might be killed and eaten every night, yet were found alive every morning.

Asana, Jehangir Jamasji (1890–1954)

Biologist and parapsychologist, a professor of biology at Gujarat College in India, and a correspondent with **J. B. Rhine** and other parapsychologists on the subject of ESP. Born July 21, 1890, at Broach, Bombay State, he was educated at Bombay University (B.A., M.A.) and Cambridge University, England (M.A.). He died December 16, 1954, at Poona, India.

Asanas

The physical positions, or postures, of **hatha yoga.** Many of these are named after living creatures, e.g., cow, peacock, locust, cobra, lion. Early yoga treatises state that there are 8.4 million asanas, of which 84 are the best and 32 the most useful for the health of mankind. Hatha yoga should properly be combined with spiritual development.

Sources:

Hittleman, Richard L. *Richard Hittleman's Yoga for Total Fitness.* New York: Bantam Books, 1983.
Kuvalayananda, Swami. *Popular Yoga Asanas.* Rutland, Vt.: Charles E. Tuttle, 1971.

Asbestos

Asbestos is so called from being inextinguishable even by showers and storms, if once set on fire. The name derives from an ancient Greek term for a fabulous stone. Pagan peoples made use of it for lights in their temples. Plutarch records that the Vestal Virgins used perpetual lamp wicks, while Pausanias mentions a lamp with a wick that was not consumed, being made from a mineral fiber from Cyprus. Asbestos is of woolly texture and is sometimes called the Salamander's Feather. Leonardus stated: "Its fire is nourished by an inseparable unctuous humid flowing from its substance; therefore, being once kindled, it preserves a constant light without feeding it with any moisture."

ASC See Austin Seth Center

Ascent

Journal of spiritual development published by **Yasodhara Ashram,** founded in Canada by **Swami Sivananda Radha,** a disciple of the late Swami Sivananda Saraswati of Rishikesh, Himalayas, India. Address: Yasodhara Ashram, Box 9, Kootenay Bay, British Columbia, Canada V0B 1X0.

Asclepius (or Aesculapius)

In Greek mythology, the son of Apollo and Coronis who was instructed in the arts of healing by the centaur Chiron. Asclepius married Epione, who begat Hygeia (health). So successful was Asclepius in the art of healing that Zeus was fearful that he would make mankind immortal, so he killed him with a thunderbolt. Apollo retaliated by attacking the Cyclopes who had forged the thunderbolt, and Zeus was eventually prevailed upon to admit Asclepius to the ranks of the gods.

The worship of Asclepius centered in Epidaurus, and the cock was offered to him in sacrifice. The serpent and the dog were sacred to him, and his symbol of the serpent coiled about a staff still remains as the sign of medical practice. Asclepius is also featured in the Hermetic literature connected with **Hermes Trismegistus** ("Thrice-greatest Hermes").

Sources:

Edelstein, Emma Jeanette Levy. *Asclepius: a Collection and Interpretation of the Testimonies.* New York: Arno Press, 1975.

Ash Tree

There are many old superstitions of the wonderful influence of the ash tree. The old Christmas log was of ash wood, and its use was helpful to the future prosperity of the family. Venomous animals, it was said, would not take shelter under its branches. A carriage with its axles made of ash wood was believed to go faster than a carriage with its axles made of any other wood, and tools with handles made of this wood were supposed to enable a man to do more work than he could do with tools whose handles were not of ash. Hence the reason that ash wood is generally used for tool handles. It was upon ash branches that witches were enabled to ride through the air, and those who ate the red buds of the tree on St. John's Eve were rendered invulnerable to witches' influence.

In speaking of the ash, reference was often to the mountain ash or rowan tree.

Sources:

Porteous, Alexander. *Forest Folklore, Mythology, and Romance.* London: George Allen & Unwin, 1928.

Ashkir-Jobson Trianion

A guild of psychical researchers formed during the 1930s in Britain to develop apparatus to facilitate communication with spirits of the dead. The name derived from the individuals concerned: George Jobson (an engineer who first introduced the telephone into Britain), A. J. Ashdown, and B. K. Kirkby, and was associated with the mediumship of Mrs. I. E. Singleton (who became warden of the Ashkir-Jobson Trianion Guild).

Jobson, Kirkby, and Ashdown were preoccupied with the question of proving survival after death, and they formed a pact that whoever passed away would attempt to communicate with his comrades through an agreed signal—the initials "B. K. K." In 1930, within three months of the passing of Jobson, the signal was received through a medium not formerly known to the three, and thereafter instructions were communicated for the construction of instruments to facilitate spirit communication. The Ashkir-Jobson Trianion was formed as a nonprofit guild to produce apparatus, which included the **Reflectograph** and **Communigraph.** Another instrument, named the Ashkir-Jobson Vibrator, was designated to produce a continuous musical tone to create a harmonious influence at séances. The vibrator was operated by clockwork, which activated an "A" tuning fork, sending out sonorous but subdued sound vibrations, sustained for up to three hours.

Ashtabula Poltergeist, The

The supposed cause of the extraordinary **poltergeist** disturbances that took place about mid-nineteenth century in the presence of a woman of Ashtabula County, Ohio. First of all, she became a medium on the death of her husband and produced spirit-rappings and other manifestations. Then for a time she studied anatomy in Marlborough, and afterward returned to her home in Austinburg, where an alarming outbreak of weird manifestations occurred. Stair-rods moved after her when she went to her room, light articles flew about the house, and uncanny sounds were heard. At Marlborough, when she resumed her anatomical studies, the disturbances increased in violence, and she and her roommate had a ghastly vision of a corpse they had been dissecting that day. The skeptical Dr. Richmond maintained that these phenomena were the result of "magneto-odylic" emanations from the medium.

Sources:

Podmore, Frank. *Modern Spiritualism.* 2 vols. Rev. ed. as *Mediums of the Nineteenth Century.* New Hyde Park, N.Y.: University Books, 1963.

Asiah

According to the **Kabala,** Asiah is the first of the three classes or natural ranks around the spirits of men, who must advance from the lower to the higher.

Asipu

Priests of ancient Mesopotamia. (See also **Semites**)

Asmodeus

Ancient Persian demon of lust and rage who also appeared in ancient Jewish folklore, where he was believed to cause strife between husband and wife. He is mentioned in the book of Tobit ca. 250 B.C.E., where he attempts to cause trouble between Tobias and his wife, Sarah. Jewish legends claim that Asmodeus was the result of a union between the woman Naamah and a fallen angel. Asmodeus was often represented in magical texts as having three heads—a man, a bull, and a ram, riding a dragon, and carrying a spear. Directions for evoking this demon are contained in the well-known magical textbook *The Magus; or, Celestial Intelligencer* by Francis Barrett (1801).

Sources:

Barrett, Francis. *The Magus.* London, 1801. Reprint, New Hyde Park, N.Y.: University Books, 1967.

Aspidomancy

A little-known form of **divination** practiced in the Indies. According to the seventeenth-century writer Pierre de Lancre, the diviner traces a circle, takes up his position seated on a buckler (shield), and mutters certain conjurations. He becomes entranced and falls into an ecstasy, from which he emerges to answer his client's queries with revelations from the devil.

Asports

The reverse of **apport** phenomena—the disappearance of objects from the séance room through the barriers of intervening matter and their appearance at another spot. It is seldom attempted as an independent demonstration and may more often form part of an apport **materialization,** as in the Millesimo séances with the **Marquis Centurione Scotto** and Mme. Fabian Rossi.

In a sitting on July 8, 1928, the members of the circle were tapped by a little parchment drum and Rossi and Mme. la Marquise Luisa felt their hands squeezed by two iron mittens. At the conclusion of the sittings, these objects were no longer in the room. The drum was found in the large salon where it previously stood, while the mittens were discovered at the foot of the suit of armor from which they had previously been detached.

Sources:

Hack, Gwendolyn K. *Modern Psychic Mysteries: Millesimo Castle, Italy.* London, 1929.

ASPR See American Society for Psychical Research

ASPR Newsletter

The news bulletin of the **American Society for Psychical Research** (5 West 73rd St. New York, NY 10023), which began publication in 1968. It features information on activities of the society and features nontechnical rewrites of articles from the society's *Journal.*

Ass

Many superstitions concern this familiar **animal.** The Egyptians traced his image on the cakes they offered to Typhon, god of evil. The Romans regarded the meeting of an ass as an evil omen, but the animal was honored in Arabia and Judea, and it was in Arabia that the ass of Silenus spoke to his master. Other talking asses were Balaam's ass (Numbers 22), which Mahomet placed in his paradise with Alborack; the ass of Aasis, Queen of Sheba; and the ass on which Jesus Christ rode into Jerusalem.

Some people have found something sacred and mysterious in the innocent beast, and a species of divination employed the head of an ass. At one time a special festival was held for the ass, during which he was led into the church while mass was sung. This reverence in which he was held by Christians was doubtless due to the black cross which he wore on his back, and which, it is said, was given him after the ass of Bethphage carried Christ into Jerusalem. But Pliny, who carefully gathered all that related to the animal, made no mention concerning the color of its coat. It seems likely, therefore, that the ass of today is as he always was.

It was not only the devout who respected the ass, for the wise **Agrippa** offered him an apology in his book, *On the Vanity of the Sciences* (1530). Among the Indians of Madras, the people of the Cavaravadonques, one of the principal castes, claimed to be descended from an ass. These Indians treated the ass as a brother, took his part, and prosecuted those who overburdened or ill-treated him in any way. In rainy weather they would often give him shelter when they denied it to his driver.

One old fable shows the ass in an unfavorable light. Jupiter had just taken possession of Olympus. On his coming, men asked of him an eternal springtime, which he accordingly granted, charging the ass of Silenus to bear the precious treasure to earth. The ass became thirsty and approached a fountain guarded by a snake, who refused to let the ass drink unless he parted with the treasure. The stupid animal thereupon bartered the gift of heaven for a skin of water, and since that time snakes, when they grow old, can change their skin and become young again, for they have the gift of perpetual springtime.

Another fable endows the creature with greater intelligence. In a village a few miles from Cairo, there lived a mountebank who possessed a highly trained ass, so clever that the country people took it to be a demon in disguise. One day the mountebank mentioned in the ass's hearing that the sultan wished to construct a beautiful building and planned to employ all the asses in Cairo to carry the lime, mortar, and stones. The ass immediately lay down and pretended to be dead, and his master begged for money to buy another. When he had collected some, he returned to his old ass. "He is not dead," he said; "he only pretended to die because he knew I had not the wherewithal to buy him food." Still the ass refused to rise, and the mountebank addressed the company, telling them that the sultan had sent out the criers commanding the people to assemble the next day outside Cairo to see the most wonderful sights in the world. He further desired that the most gracious ladies and the most beautiful girls should be mounted on asses. The ass raised himself and pricked up his ears. "The governor of my quarter," added the mountebank, "has begged me to lend my ass for his wife, who is old and toothless, and very ugly." The ass began to limp as though he were old and lame. "Ah, you like beautiful ladies?" said his master. The animal bowed his head. "Oh, well," said the man, "there are many present; show me the most beautiful." The ass obeyed with judgment and discretion.

These marvelous asses, said the demonologists, were, if not demons, at least men metamorphosed, like Apuleius, who was transformed into an ass. Vincent de Beauvais speaks of two women who kept a little inn near Rome and who sold their guests at the market after having changed them into pigs, fowls, or sheep. One of them, he adds, changed a certain comedian into an ass, and as he retained his talents under his new skin, she led him to the fairs on the outskirts of the city, gaining much money thereby. A neighbor bought this wise ass at a good price, and in handing it over the sorcerers felt obliged to warn the purchaser not to let the ass enter water. Its new master attended to the warning for some time, but one day the poor ass managed to get free and jumped into a lake, where it regained its natural shape, to the great surprise of its driver. The matter was brought to the ears of the pope, who had the two witches punished, while the comedian returned to of his profession.

Many stories are told of the ass that carried Jesus Christ into Jerusalem, which is said to have died at Verona, where its remains are still honored. They say the ass is a privileged animal that God formed at the end of the sixth day. Abraham employed it to carry the wood for the sacrifice of Isaac; it also carried the wife and son of Moses in the desert. The rabbis maintained that Balaam's ass was carefully nourished and hidden in a secret place until the coming of the Jewish Messiah.

Assagioli, Roberto (1888–1974)

Psychiatrist, psychotherapist, and parapsychologist. He was born February 27, 1888, in Venice, Italy, and educated at University of Florence (M.D.). As a young psychiatrist he became disenchanted with first Freudian and then Jungian psychoanalysis. Thus he turned his attention to the development of a new psychology he termed psychosynthesis. Psychosynthesis assumes that in addition to the conscious self, or "I", every person also has a pathway to a "Higher Self," which is a reflection of the divine. The purpose of each human life is to participate as fully as possible in self-evolution along that pathway. The system was left open so that both individuals and any psychologists could participate in developing psychosynthesis and incorporate the various occult tools of transformation.

Assagioli founded the Institute of Psychosynthesis in 1926. He met **Alice Bailey** during the early 1930s, and they became friends; their organizations have retained a working association. Psychosynthesis was suppressed during World War II, and Assagioli was arrested. He spent his prison days exploring meditation and altered states of consciousness. After the war he revived his work and promoted the founding of institutes in the United States, Greece, and England.

In 1958 Assagioli became chair of the Psychosynthesis Research Foundation at Greenville, Delaware, and editor of *Psiche-Rivista di Studi Psicologici.* During his mature years, he authored a set of books which became the major statements of psychosynthesis. He died in Capaiona, Italy, on August 23, 1974.

Sources:

Assagioli, Roberto. *The Act of Will.* New York: Viking/Penguin, 1973.

———. *Parapsychological Faculties and Psychological Disturbances.* London: Medical Society for Study of Radiesthesia, 1958.

———. *Psychosynthesis: A Manual of Principles and Techniques.* Rev. ed. New York: Viking/Penguin, 1971.

Assailly, Alain Jean Joseph (1909– ?)

French physician and neuro-endocrinologist who studied psychophysiology of mediumship and hauntings and published articles on these subjects. Born October 17, 1909, at Pontchateau (Loire-Inférieure), France, he became consulting psychiatrist to Bichat Hospital and was awarded the Croix de Guerre in World War II. He contributed the chapter "Modern Man Faced with the Problem of the Supernatural" to the book *Medicine and the Supernatural* (1957).

ASSAP News

Newsletter of the **Association for the Scientific Study of Anomalous Phenomena.** It provides news of individuals and groups concerned with a wide range of anomalous phenomena and was also associated with the ASSAP's quarterly journal *Common Ground* until it ceased publication in 1984. Address: Caroline Wise, 56 Telemann Sq., Kidbrook, London SE3, England.

Assassins

The Assassins, or *Hashishin,* were so called from their use of the drug hashish, distilled from the hemp plant. The Assassins were Ismaelites, an Islamic community that developed out of the Shi'a branch of Islam, which is in the majority in modern Iran (the historic Persia). It was founded in the latter part of the eleventh century by Hassan Sabah in Syria and Persia. Driven from Cairo, Hassan spread a modified form of the Ismaelite doctrine throughout Syria, and in 1090 he became master of the mountain stronghold **Alamut,** in Persia, where he founded a society known as the Assassins, and from which he ostensibly promulgated the principles of the Ismaelites. The difference, however, between the Assassins and other Ismaelites was that they employed secret assassinations against all the enemies of the sect. Their organization was founded upon that of the Western Lodge at Cairo, and at the head of their sect was the Sheik-Al-Gebel, or "Old Man of the Mountain," as the name has been translated by European authors, the more correct translation being "Chief of the Mountain."

The other officers of the society were the grand priors, lesser priors, initiates, associates, and the *fedavi,* or "devoted ones," who were the assassins proper. From these latter young men were chosen the perpetrators of the various deeds of blood for which the Assassins became notorious. They were not initiated into the secret circle of the group, and blind obedience was expected from them. When their services were required they were intoxicated with hashish, taken into the magnificent gardens of the sheik, and surrounded by every pleasure. Told that this was a foretaste of what they might expect in Paradise, they would then proceed to lose their lives in the sheik's service. These young men, for the most part ignorant peasants, consequently displayed a degree of fanaticism that made them fitting instruments of Hassan's policy. But the initiated among the Assassins were convinced of the worthlessness of religion and morality, held no belief, and sneered covertly at the Prophet and his religion.

The early history of the society is one of romantic and absorbing interest. According to one account, Hassan had been a member of a secret Ismaelite society at Cairo, the head of which was the Caliph, "and of which the object was the dissemination of the doctrines of the sect of the Ismaelites."

This society comprised both men and women, who met in separate assemblies, for the common supposition of the insignificance of the latter sex in the east is erroneous. It was presided over by the Chief Missionary (*Dai-al-Doat*) who was always a person of importance in the state, and not infrequently Supreme Judge (*Kadhi-al-Kodhat*). Their assemblies, called Societies of Wisdom (*Mejalis-al-Hiemet*), were held twice a week on Mondays and Wednesdays. All the members appeared clad in white. The president having first waited on the Caliph, and read to him the intended lecture, or, if that could not be done, having got his signature on the back of it, proceeded to the assembly and delivered a written discourse. At the conclusion of it, those present kissed his hand and reverently touched with their forehead the handwriting of the Caliph. In this state the society continued till the reign of that extraordinary madman the Caliph Haken-bi-emr-illah (Judge by the Command of God), who determined to place it on a splendid footing. He erected for it a stately edifice, styled the House of Wisdom (*Dar-al-hiemet*), abundantly furnished with books and mathematical instruments. Its doors were open to all, and paper, pens, and ink were profusely supplied for the use of those who chose to frequent it. Professors of law, mathematics, logic, and medicine were appointed to give instructions; and at the learned disputations which were frequently held in presence of the Caliph, these professors appeared in their state of caftans (*Khalaa*), which, it is said, exactly resembled the robes worn at the English universities. The income assigned to this establishment by the munificence of the Caliph, was 257,000 ducats annually, arising from the tenths paid to the crown.

"The course of instruction in this university proceeded," according to Macrisi, by the following nine degrees. "(1) The object of the first, which was long and tedious, was to infuse doubts and difficulties into the mind of the aspirant, and to lead him to repose a blind confidence in the knowledge and wisdom of his teacher. To this end he was perplexed with captious questions; the absurdities of the literal sense of the Koran and its repugnance to reason, were studiously pointed out, and dark hints were given that beneath this shell lay a kernel sweet to the taste and nutritive to the soul. But all further information was most rigorously withheld till he had consented to bind himself by a most solemn oath to absolute faith and blind obedience to his instructor. (2) When he had taken the oath he was admitted to the second degree, which inculcated the acknowledgement of the imams appointed by God as the sources of all knowledge. (3) The third degree informed him what was the number of these blessed and holy imams; and this was the mystic seven; for, as God had made seven heavens, seven earths, seas, planets, metals, tones, and colors, so seven was the number of these noblest of God's creatures. (4) In the fourth degree the pupil learned that God had sent seven lawgivers into the world, each of whom was commissioned to alter and improve the system of his predecessor; that each of these had seven helpers, who appeared in the interval between him and his successor; these helpers, as they did not appear as public teachers, were called the mute (*samit*), in contradistinction to the speaking lawgivers. The seven lawgivers were Adam, Noah, Abraham, Moses, Jesus, Mohammed, and Ismael, the son of Jaaffer; the seven principal helpers, called Seats (*soos*), were Seth, Shem, Ishmael (the son of Abraham), Aaron, Simon, Ali, and Mohammed, the son of Ismael. It is justly observed that, as this last personage was not more than a century dead, the teacher had it in his power to fix on whom he would as the mute prophet of the present time, and inculcate the belief in, and obedience to, him of all who had not got beyond this degree. (5) The fifth degree taught that each of the seven mute prophets had twelve apostles for the dissemination of his faith. The suitableness of this number was also proved by analogy. There are twelve signs of the Zodiac, twelve months, twelve tribes of Israel, twelve joints in the four fingers of each hand, and so forth. (6) The pupil being led thus far, and having shown no symptoms of restiveness, the precepts of the Koran were once more brought under consideration, and he was told that all the positive portions of religion must be subordinate to philosophy. He was consequently instructed in the systems of Plato and Aristotle during the long space of time; and (7) when esteemed fully qualified, he was admitted to the seventh degree, when instruction was communicated in that mystic Pantheism, which is held and taught by the sect of the Soofees. (8) The positive precepts of religion were again considered, the veil was torn from the eyes of the aspirant, all that had preceded was now declared to have been merely scaffolding to raise the edifice of knowledge, and was to be flung down. Prophets and teachers, heaven and hell, all were nothing; future bliss and misery were idle dreams; all actions were permitted. (9) The ninth degree had only to inculcate that nought was to be believed, everything might be done."

One of Hassan's early intimates was the famous Omar Khayyam, with whom he and another friend contracted a bargain that the most successful of the three would share his good fortune with the others. It is likely that the practical mystic and the astrologer would feel drawn to each other by many common tastes, but whether Omar profited much from the bargain is unknown, so far as Hassan was concerned. The third of the friends, Nizan-al-Melk, achieved an exalted position as vizier to the second of the Seljuk monarchs. Recalling his promise, he offered Omar a government post, but the author of the *Rubaiyat* was too addicted to pleasure to accept active employment. In lieu of the dazzling position offered him, Omar was content with a pension of 1,200 ducats, with which he went into retirement.

Hassan clearly perceived that the plan of the society at Cairo was defective as a means of acquiring temporal power. The Dais might exert themselves and proselytes might be gained, but until possession of some strongholds was obtained and a mode of striking terror into princes devised, nothing effectual could be achieved.

With this object in view he instituted the *Fedavi*, who unhesitatingly obeyed their chief, and, without inquiry or hesitation, plunged their daggers into the bosom of whatever victim was pointed out to them, even though their own lives should be the immediate sacrifice. Their usual garment was (like that of all the sects opposed to the house of Abbas), white; their caps, girdles, or boots were red. Hence they were named the White (*Mubeiyazah*) and the Red (*Muhammere*); but they could with ease assume any guise, even that of the Christian monk, to accomplish their murderous designs.

Hassan was perfectly aware that the compelling power of religion could hold a society together. Whatever, therefore, his private opinions may have been, he resolved to impose on the bulk of his followers the most rigid obedience to the precepts of Islam. He actually put his own son to death for a breach of one of them.

Hassan is said to have rejected two of the degrees of the Ismaelite society at Cairo and to have reduced them to seven, the original number in the plan of Abdallah Maimoon, the first projector of this secret society. Besides these seven degrees, through which the aspirants gradually rose to knowledge, Hassan, in what Hammer terms the breviary of the order, drew up seven regulations or rules for the conduct of the teachers in his society.

(1) The first of these, named Ashinai-Risk (Knowledge of Duty), inculcated the requisite knowledge of human nature for selecting fit persons for admission. To this belong the proverbial expressions said to have been current among the Dais, similar to those used by the ancient Pythagoreans, such as "Sow not on barren ground" (that is, "Waste not your labour on incapable persons), "Speak not in a house where there is a lamp" (that is, "Be silent in the presence of a lawyer"). (2) The second rule was called Teênis (Gaining of Confidence), and taught to win the candidates by flattering their passions and inclinations. (3) The third, of which the name is not given, taught to involve them in doubts and difficulties by pointing out the absurdities of the Quran, and of positive religion. (4) When the aspirant had gone thus far, the solemn oath of silence and obedience, and of communicating his doubts to his teacher alone was to be imposed on the disciple; and then (5) he was to be informed that the doctrines and opinions of the society were those of the greatest men in church and state. (6) The Tessees (Confirmation) directed to put the pupil again through all he had learned, and to confirm him in it. And, (7) finally, the Teêvil (Instruction in Allegory) gave the allegorical mode of interpreting the Quran, and drawing whatever sense might suit their purposes from its pages. Any one who had gone through this course of instruction, and was thus become perfectly imbued with the spirit of the society, was regarded as an accomplished Dai, and employed in

the important office of making proselytes and extending its influence.

The Assassins had absorbed elements of **Sufism,** the Islamic form of mysticism. They viewed God in all and all in God. Such mysticism can produce either deep piety or its opposite. In the eyes of one who thus views God, all the distinctions between vice and virtue become fleeting and uncertain, and crime might gradually lose its atrocity and can be regarded as only a means for the production of a good end. That the Ismaelite Fedavi murdered innocent persons without compunction, when ordered to do so by his superiors, is an undoubted fact, and there is no absurdity in supposing that he and they may have thought that in so doing they were acting rightly and promoting the cause of truth. Of course, the mainstream of Sufism in no wise endorses such criminal interpretations of their beliefs.

The followers of Hassan Sabah were called the Eastern Ismaelites, to distinguish them from those of Africa. They were also named the *Batiniyeh* (Internal or Secret), from the secret meaning which they drew from the text of the Quran, and Moolhad, or Moolahid (Impious), an account of the imputed impiety of their doctrines—names common to them with most of the preceding sects. It is under this last appellation that they were known to Marco Polo, the Venetian traveler. The name, however, by which they are best known in Europe is that of Assassins. This name is very generally derived from that of the founder of their society; but M. De Sacy believed it probable that the Oriental term *Hashishin,* of which the Crusaders made Assassins, comes (as already noted) from Hashish, a preparation of hemp which the Fedavi were in the habit of taking before they engaged in their daring enterprises or to procure delicious visions of the paradise promised to them by the Sheikh-al-Gebel.

It is a curious question how Hassan contrived to infuse into the Fedavi the recklessness of life, joined with the spirit of implicit obedience to the commands of their superiors, which they so invariably displayed. We are told that the system adopted for this purpose was to obtain stout and healthy children from their parents by purchasing or otherwise. They were reared in implicit obedience to the will of the sheik, and, to prepare them for their future office, they were carefully instructed in various languages.

The Assassins soon became a power in Persia and Syria. Their first victim was that very Nizam with whom Hassan and Omar had completed their youthful bargain. His son speedily followed him, as did the sultan of Persia. That monarch's successor made war with them but was so terror-stricken by their murderous tactics that he speedily made peace with them.

Hassan died at an advanced age in 1124, having assassinated both his sons and left as his successor his chief prior, Hia-busurg-Omid, during whose reign the Assassins were far from fortunate. The list of their victims had by this time become a long and illustrious one. The fourth Sheik of the Mountain—another Hassan—made public the secret doctrines of the society, announcing that the religion of Islam was abolished and that the people might give themselves up to feasting and pleasure. He further stated that he was the promised Caliph of God upon earth; but some four years after this announcement he was assassinated and succeeded by his son, Mahomed II, whose rule of 46 years was marked by deeds of revolting cruelty.

Mahomed II had several implacable enemies, including the famous Saladin, and the Syrian branch of the society seceded from his sway and became independent. This was the branch with which the Crusaders came into so much contact and whose emissaries slew Raymond of Tripoli and Conrad of Montferrat. Mahomed's son, Hassan III, restored the old form of doctrine—that is, the people were strictly confined to the practice of Islam, while the initiates were as before, superior and agnostic. His was the only reign in which no assassinations occurred, and he was regarded with friendship by his neighbors.

But after a reign of 12 years, Hassan III was poisoned, and during the minority of his son Mahomed III, assassination was again greatly in vogue. After a reign of 30 years, Mahomed III was slain by his successor, Rukneddin, but vengeance quickly followed, for only a year later the Tartars swept into Persia, took Alamut and other Assassin strongholds, and captured the reigning monarch, who was slain because of his treachery.

Over twelve thousand Assassins were massacred, and their power was completely broken. A similar fate overtook the Syrian branch, which was nearly extirpated by the Egyptian Mamelukes. But in the more isolated valleys of Syria, many of them lingered on. Doctrines similar in character to theirs occasionally surfaced in Northern Syria during the twentieth century.

An account of the manner in which the Assassins aroused in the Fedavis lust of slaughter is given in an Arabic historic romance, *Siret-al-Haken,* or *Memoirs of Hakin:*

"Our narrative now returns to Ismael the chief of the Ismaelites. He took with him his people laden with gold, silver, pearls, and other effects, taken away from the inhabitants of the coasts, and which he had received in the island of Cyprus, and on the part of the King of Egypt, Dhaher, the son of Hakem-biemr-Illah. Having bidden farewell to the Sultan of Egypt at Tripolis, they proceeded to Massyat, when the inhabitants of the castles and fortresses assembled to enjoy themselves, along with the chief Ismael and his people. They put on the rich dresses with which the Sultan had supplied them, and adorned the castle of Massyat with everything that was good and fine. Ismael made his entry into Massyat with the Devoted (*Fedavi*), as no one has ever done at Massyat before him or after him. He stopped there some time to take into his service some more persons whom he might make devoted both in heart and body.

"With this view he had caused to be made a vast garden, into which he had water conducted. In the middle of this garden he built a kiosk raised to the height of four storeys. On each of the four sides were richly ornamented windows joined by four arches, in which were painted stars of gold and silver. He put into it roses, porcelain glasses, and drinking-vessels of gold and silver. He had with him Mamlooks (i.e., slaves), ten males and ten females, who were come with him from the region of the Nile, and who had scarcely attained the age of puberty. He clothed them in silks and in the finest stuffs, and he gave unto them bracelets of gold and of silver. The columns were overlaid with musk, and with amber, and in the four arches of the windows he set four caskets, in which was the purest musk. The columns were polished, and this place was the retreat of the slaves. He divided the garden into four parts. In the first of these were pear-trees, apple-trees, vines, cherries, mulberries, plums, and other kinds of fruit-trees. In the second were oranges, lemons, olives, pomegranates, and other fruits. In the third were cucumbers, melons, leguminous plants, etc. In the fourth were roses, jessamine, tamarinds, narcissi, violets, lilies, anemonies, etc., etc.

"The garden was divided by canals of water, and the kiosk was surrounded with ponds and reservoirs. There were groves in which were seen antelopes, ostriches, asses, and wild cows. Issuing from the ponds, one met ducks, geese, partridges, quails, hares, foxes, and other animals. Around the kiosk the chief Ismael planted walks of tall trees, terminating in the different parts of the garden. He built there a great house, divided into two apartments, the upper and the lower. From the latter covered walks led out into the garden, which was all enclosed with walls, so that no one could see into it, for these walks and buildings were all void of inhabitants. He made a gallery of coolness, which ran from this apartment to the cellar, which was behind. This apartment served as a place of assembly for the men. Having placed himself on a sofa there opposite the door, the chief made his men sit down, and gave them to eat and drink during the whole length of the day until evening. At nightfall he looked around him, and, selecting those whose firmness pleased him, said to them. 'Ho! such-a-one, come and seat thyself near me.' It is thus that Ismael made those whom he had chosen sit near him on the sofa and drink. He then spoke to them of the great and excellent qualities of the imam Ali, of his bravery, his nobleness, and his generosity, until they fell asleep, overcome by the power of the *benjeh* which he had given them, and which never failed to produce its effects in less than a quarter of an hour, so that they fell down as if they were inanimate. As soon as the man had fallen the chief Ismael arose, and, taking him up, brought him into a dormitory, and then, shutting the door, carried him on his shoulders into the gallery of coolness, which was in the garden, and thence into the kiosk, where he committed him to the care of the male and female slaves, directing them to comply with all the desires of the candidate, on whom they flung vinegar till he awoke. When he was come to himself the youths and maidens said to him. 'We are only waiting for thy death, for this place is destined for thee. This is one of the pavilions of Paradise, and we are the houries and the children of Paradise. If thou wert dead thou wouldest be for ever with us, but thou art only dreaming, and wilt soon awake.' Meanwhile, the chief Ismael had returned to the company as soon as he had witnessed the awakening of the candidate, who now perceived nothing but youths and maidens of the greatest beauty, and adorned in the most magnificent manner.

"He looked around the place, inhaled the fragrance of musk and frankincense, and drew near to the garden, where he saw the beasts and the birds, the running water, and the trees. He gazed on the beauty of the kiosk, and the vases of gold and silver, while the youths and maidens kept him in converse. In this way he remained confounded, not knowing whether he was awake or only dreaming. When two hours of the night had gone by, the chief Ismael returned to the dormitory, closed to the door, and thence proceeded to the garden, where his slaves came around him and rose before him. When the candidate perceived him, he said unto him, 'O, chief Ismael, do I dream, or am I awake?' The chief Ismael then made answer to him, 'O, such-a-one beware of relating this vision to any one who is a stranger to this place! Know that the Lord Ali has shown thee the place which is destined for thee in Paradise. Know that at this moment the Lord Ali and I have been sitting together in the regions of the empyrean. So do not hesitate a moment in the service of the imam who has given thee to know his felicity.' Then the chief Ismael ordered supper to be served. It was brought in vessels of gold and silver, and consisted of boiled meats and roast meats, with other dishes. While the candidate ate, he was sprinkled with rose-water; when he called for drink there were brought to him vessels of gold and silver filled with delicious liquors, in which also had been mingled some *benjeh.* When he had fallen asleep, Ismael carried him through the gallery back to the dormitory, and, leaving him there, returned to his company. After a little time he went back, threw vinegar on his face, and then, bringing him out, ordered one of the Mamlooks to shake him. On awaking, and finding himself in the same place among the guests, he said, 'There is no god but God, and Mohammed is the Prophet of God!' The chief Ismael then drew near and caressed him, and he remained, at it were, immersed in intoxication, wholly devoted to the service of the chief, who then said unto him, 'O, such-a-one, know that what thou hast seen was not a dream, but one of the miracles of the imam Ali. Know that he has written thy name among those of his friends. If thou keep the secret thou art certain of thy felicity, but if thou speak of it thou wilt incur the resentment of the imam. If thou die thou art a martyr; but beware of relating this to any person whatever. Thou hast entered by one of the gates to the friendship of the imam, and art become one of his family; but if thou betray the secret, thou wilt become one of his enemies, and be driven from his house.' Thus this man became one of the servants of the chief Ismael, who in this manner surrounded himself with trusty men, until his reputation was established. This is what is related to the chief Ismael and his Devoted."

To these romantic tales of the Paradise of the Old Man of the Mountain we must add another of an even more mystical character, furnished by the learned and venerable Sheik Agd-ur-Rahman (Servant of the Compassionate, or Servant of God) Ben Ebubekr Al-Jeriri of Damascus, which can be found in the twenty-fourth chapter of his work entitled *A Choice Book for Discovering the Secrets of the Art of Imposture.*

Sources:

Burman, Edward. *The Assassins.* Wellingborough, U.K.: Crucible, 1987.

Hackethorn, Charles William. *The Secret Societies of All Ages and Countries.* London: Redway, 1897. Reprint, New Hyde Park, N.Y.: University Books, 1966.

Lewis, Bernard. *The Assassins: A Radical Sect in Islam.* London: Al Saqi, 1985.

MacKenzie, Norman. *Secret Societies.* New York: Collier Books, 1967.

Association for Astrological Networking (AFAN)

AFAN was founded in Chicago in 1982 by members of the **American Federation of Astrology** who were dissatisfied with some of its more conservative policies. The new organization took an aggressive stance toward changing public opinion about **astrology,** seeking to reverse negative rulings concerning astrological practice in the courts and to promote networking among different astrological organizations.

AFAN began by creating an open, democratic organization. In 1984 it moved to Europe and became a catalyst for networking among European astrological organizations. At the 1987 World Astrological Congress in Zurich, delegates created the Astrological Registration and Communication. In 1986 AFAN joined with the **Institute for the Study of American Religion (ISAR)** and the **National Council for Geocosmic Research** in sponsoring the first United Astrology Congress (UAC), which has met at regular intervals since.

On the legal front, AFAN prepared a legal information kit for astrologers, began write-in campaigns to overturn antiastrology ordinances in various cities, worked to defeat an antiastrology statute in Los Angeles County, and backed a case in the California courts guaranteeing astrologers their rights in the state. The long-term strategy is to have the federal courts recognize the legitimacy of astrology.

A media-watch program was instituted to respond to negative coverage of astrology in the United States and Canada. Incorrect statements are refuted and a positive image is projected.

As of the mid-1990s, AFAN had established an international network of astrologers on every continent. It publishes a newsletter, operates a speakers bureau, and manages an education scholarship fund. AFAN's council includes a number of nationally and internationally known astrologers. Address: 8306 Wilshire Blvd., Ste. 537, Beverly Hills, CA 90211.

Association for Research and Enlightenment (ARE)

An organization founded by the late **Edgar Cayce** (1877–1945) in 1931. Cayce, one of the outstanding psychics of the twentieth century, gave readings almost daily during his mature years on subjects ranging from diagnosis of illness to **astrology,** reflections on future earth changes, and the nature of the afterlife. Known as "the sleeping prophet," he gave many thousands of readings to clients who consulted him. He spoke in a rapidly induced trance condition resembling normal sleep, and his statements were taken down by a stenographer.

Cayce moved to Virginia Beach in the 1920s. With the backing of Morton Blumenthal, a wealthy businessman, Cayce hoped to develop a hospital and university. The former opened in 1928 and the latter in 1930, but both failed along with Blumenthal's business enterprises in 1931. With the readings as the basic means of support, Cayce and his close associates founded two organizations: the Association for Research and Enlightenment, (ARE), a public fellowship of Cayce's clients and followers; and the Edgar Cayce Foundation, a private corporation to hold the Cayce papers (especially the transcripts of the readings) and the property.

After Cayce's death in 1945, his son **Hugh Lynn Cayce** became head of the ARE. Personnel began the process of sorting, indexing, and studying the approximately 14,000 transcripts of the Cayce readings. Hugh Lynn began an aggressive program of building the association, but not until the late 1960s, when Jess Stern's biography of Cayce, *The Sleeping Prophet* (1967), became a best-seller, did the ARE begin to grow appreciably. In the wake of *The Sleeping Prophet*'s success, Hugh Lynn contracted with Paperback Library to do a series of books based on the readings. These became highly successful and made the ARE one of the largest and most stable associations in the psychic community.

The ARE sponsors lectures, symposia, psychic research, prayer and meditation workshops, a summer camp, and Search for God study groups. It maintains a therapy department and a 46,000-volume library on metaphysics, psychic phenomena, and related subjects. The Edgar Cayce Foundation has custody of the readings and conducts a continuous program of indexing, extracting, microfilming, and otherwise organizing the material in the data files, which are open to the public in print form and on CD-ROM disc. The ARE has sponsored a host of books and booklets on the Cayce materials, some published by the foundation and some by commercial publishers. Several periodicals are produced, including *Venture Inward* and *Pathways to Health;* its monthly newsletter is the *A.R.E. Community Newsletter* which contains *Extracts from the Edgar Cayce Readings* and *Reflections: A Commentary on the Edgar Cayce Readings.*

The association, which seeks to give physical, mental, and spiritual help through investigation of the Cayce readings, coordinates a medical research program with the ARE Clinic in Phoenix, Arizona. In regard to medical data obtained from the Cayce readings, the ARE recommends that except for noncritical home remedies, all medical information should be used under supervision of a licensed physician.

Currently headed by Edgar Cayce's grandson, **Charles Thomas Cayce,** the ARE may be contacted at Box 595, Virginia Beach, VA 23451.

Sources:

Bolton, Brett, ed. *Edgar Cayce Speaks.* New York: Avon, 1969.

Bro, Harmon Hartzell. *A Seer Out of Season: The Life of Edgar Cayce.* New York: New American Library, 1989.

Cayce, Hugh Lynn, ed. *The Edgar Cayce Reader.* 2 vols. New York: Paperback Library, 1969.

Puryear, Herbert B. *The Edgar Cayce Primer.* New York: Bantam Books, 1982.

Smith, Robert A. *Hugh Lynn Cayce: About My Father's Business.* Norfolk, Va.: Donning, 1988.

Association for the Anthropological Study of Consciousness See **Society for the Anthropology of Consciousness**

Association for the Development of Human Potential

Founded in 1970 with the purpose of promoting scientific investigations into the interrelationship of the physical, mental, emotional, and spiritual aspects of the human being. This research consists of inquiry into those methods of study, practice, and discipline that may be used to broaden and deepen consciousness. The association conducts formal educational programs to disseminate research results, and it publishes books and audiovisual educational materials. It is affiliated with the **Yasodhara Ashram Society.** Address: Box 60, Porthill, ID 83853.

Association for the Scientific Study of Anomalous Phenomena (ASSAP)

British organization founded June 10, 1981, to obtain, store, process, and disseminate information concerning areas of human experience and observed phenomena for which no generally acceptable explanation is as yet forthcoming; to encourage and aid investigation and research into these phenomena by investigative groups; and to provide a multidisciplinary forum for the exchange of views and information concerning these phenomena. "Anomaly" is defined as "irregularity, deviation from the common or natural order, exception condition or circumstance," and anomalous phenomena cover a wide field of the paranormal as well as Fortean phenomena, including altered states of consciousness, apparitions, electronic voice phenomenon, extrasensory perception, falls, firewalking, healing, hypnosis, levitation, ley lines, metal bending, out-of-the-body experiences, poltergeists, telepathy, UFOs, etc.

ASSAP, an integrating body with no corporate views, discourages dogmatism while it adopts a scientific approach at all times. It does not wish to replace existing organizations in the field but rather support and encourage them. It publishes *ASSAP Newsletter.* Its quarterly journal, *Common Ground,* ceased publication in 1984. General Secretary: Hugh Pincott, 30 South Row, London SE3 ORY, England. Membership inquiries: Sue Laws, 1306 Southwood Rd. New Eltham, London SE9 3QN, England.

Association for the Understanding of Man (AUM)

A nonprofit corporation founded in 1971 in Austin, Texas, as a vehicle for the psychic activity of Ray Stanford. Stanford is a trance medium who channels messages from the "Source," believed to be his superconsciousness. Besides its more religious activities, the association carried on a research program in several areas. Project Starlight concerned itself with UFOs; through it the short-lived *Journal of Instrumented UFO Research* was issued. A research division concerned with parapsychology was headed by Ray Stanford's brother, **Rex G. Stanford.** AUM was disbanded in the early 1980s.

Association for Transpersonal Psychology

Organization concerned with the study of transpersonal psychology, defined as "those experiences which seem to be more than just of the self, those perceptions of life and the universe which are basic to sentient beings, those feelings, which express a profound commonality with all that is, and those thoughts and ideas which transcend ego considerations." The association publishes a monthly *Newsletter,* giving news of the association's activities and bibliographies of the subject. Address: P.O. Box 3049, Stanford, CA 94305.

Association Internationale de Recherche Psychotronique (International Association for Psychotronic Research)

Founded in 1973 to study **psychotronics,** the relationship of man to the universe, interaction with other physical bodies and matter, and fields of energy, known or unknown. The association publishes biennial multilingual *Proceedings.* Address: V Chaloupkach 59, Hloubetin, CS–194 01 Prague 9, Czechoslovakia.

Association of Progressive Spiritualists of Great Britain

The first organization representing **Spiritualism** in England, formed in 1865. The first convention was held in Darlington, with the objects of "social communion, interchange of sentiment or opinion to record and catalogue our united experience, and the progress which Spiritualism is making in and around us; to devise means for propagating and diffusing among our fellow men and women the principles and soul saving truths of this Divine philosophy by distribution of the best tracts and books." The third convention in London in 1867 attracted representatives from America, France, and Germany. The association declined after 1868, possibly because it was based on individual membership rather than a firm foundation of local groups, and is no longer in existence.

Association of Sananda and Sanat Kumara

The Association of Sananda and Sanat Kumara was founded in 1965 by Sister Thedra (the religious name of Dorothy Martin), a New Age channel. However, the association was rooted in more than a decade of prior **channeling** activity. In the 1950s Martin had been the leader of an early UFO contactee group that became the subject of a famous sociological study, *When Prophecy Fails* (1956). She was identified as Mrs. Keech in the study.

In *When Prophecy Fails,* the group was described as breaking up, but Martin went on to a lengthy career as a channel and leader within the **contactee** community. In 1954, after the disruption of the group in Illinois, she moved to Peru. She later explained that she had been healed by Sananda (Jesus) and instructed to go to South America. Much of that time was spent at the Brotherhood of the Seven Rays, the community established by fellow contactee George Hunt Williamson. These years were a time of intense growth, and before returning to the United States she began to send out transcripts of the messages she was receiving from the masters.

In 1961 Sister Thedra returned to the United States and settled in Arizona. She established the Association of Sananda and Sanat Kumara in 1965 and a short time later relocated to Mount Shasta, California. The association existed as a far-flung network of people who received the teachings of those who spoke through Sister Thedra. The advanced beings she channeled were seen as both spiritually advanced and coming from outer space.

The association may be reached at Box 35, Mount Shasta, CA 96067. Martin died and no new channel has arisen to take her place.

Sources:

Festinger, Leon, Henry W. Riecken, and Stanley Schachter. *When Prophecy Fails.* New York: Harper & Row, 1956.

Sananda, as recorded by Sister Thedra. *I, the Lord God Says Unto Them.* Mt. Shasta, Calif.: Association of Sananda and Sanat Kumara, [1954].

Thedra. *Excerts of Prophecies from Other Planets Concerning Our Earth.* Mt. Shasta, Calif.: Association of Sananda and Sanat Kumara, [1956].

———. *Mine Intercome Messages from the Realms of Light.* Sedona, Ariz.: Association of Sananda and Sanat Kumara, [1990].

Associazione Italiana Scientifica de Metapsichia

The Associazione Italiana Scientifica di Metaphichica (the Italian Scientific Association of Metaphysics) was established in Milan in 1946 to disseminate information on **parapsychology, psychical research,** and related topics to Italian parapsychological groups and the general public and secondarily to support new research on paranormal phenomena by individuals. It publishes a journal, *Metaphysical,* considered by many as Italy's finest psychical research periodical. The association may be contacted at S. Vittore, 9 Milan, Italy.

Astara

Astara is a hermetic occult fraternity founded in 1951 by Robert and Earlyne Chaney, both former Spiritualists. As a young medium, Robert Chaney had been active in the Spiritualist community in the Midwest in the 1930s and 1940s and was one of the founders of the Spiritualist Episcopal Church in 1941. He became somewhat alienated from Spiritualism after reading theosophical and hermetic literature and accepting some ideas, such as reincarnation, he discovered there. Reincarnation was still a very controversial idea in Spiritualism at the time. Meanwhile, Earlyne Chaney, who had been a clairvoyant since childhood, had held conversations with a spirit being who called himself Kut-Hu-Mi. She later discovered this being described in theosophical literature. Kut-Hu-Mi told Chaney that she had been selected for a special task—teaching the ancient wisdom to the people of the New Age. The Chaneys resigned from their church in Eaton Rapids, Michigan, moved to Los Angeles, and founded Astara.

Astara's teachings are an eclectic body. They draw on Christianity, Spiritualism, **Theosophy, yoga,** and especially on the ancient Egyptian teachings of **Hermes Trismegistus,** who is believed to have organized the original mystery school from which all others ultimately derive. The Chaneys also have made themselves open to new insights from the world's religions and philosophies.

From Hermes, Astara teaches that God is the only uncreated reality and that he has emanated his seven attributes and all that exists. Hermes taught the seven laws beginning with the magical law of correspondence ("As above, so below"). The law concisely states that any part of the world reflects the structure of the whole. Other laws deal with basic observations concerning motion, polarity, cycles, cause and effect, gender, and mind. The acceptance of these laws leads to a number of spiritual practices. Central to Astara is Lama Yoga, a method of mind expansion originally taught to Earlyne Chaney by the masters. The law of vibration has led to the practice of reciting "Om," the Sanskrit word believed to encompass the creative energy of the universe. Along with other yogic and meditative techniques, Astara recommends a natural food diet that leans toward vegetarianism.

Astara is headquartered in a complex in Upland, California, where members congregate and regular Sunday services and a cycle of conferences and retreats are held throughout the year. Most members relate to Astara through a set of correspondence lessons, the *Book of Life.* The *Book of Life* lessons function as a guru to the student and replace any need for a personal teacher. Apart from the lessons, both Chaneys have written a number of books and shorter works. In 1988 there were approximately 18,000 students. Astara may be contacted at 800 W. Arrow Hwy., Box 5003, Upland, CA 91785.

Sources:

Chaney, Earlyne. *Beyond Tomorrow.* Upland, Calif.: Astara, 1985.

———. *Remembering.* Los Angeles: Astara's Library of Mystical Classics, 1974.

Chaney, Earlyne, and William L. Messick. *Kundalini and the Third Eye.* Upland, Calif.: Astara's Library of Mystical Classics, 1980.

Chaney, Robert. *The Inner Way.* Los Angeles: De Vorss, 1962.

———. *Mysticism: The Journey Within.* Upland, Calif.: Astara's Library of Mystical Classics, 1979.

Astolpho

A hero of Italian romance, the son of Otho, king of England. He is the subject of Aristo's *Orlando Furioso.* Astolpho was transformed into a myrtle by Alcina, a sorceress, but later regained his human form through Melissa. He took part in many adventures and cured Orlando of his madness. Astolpho is the allegorical representation of a true man lost through sensuality.

Astragalomancy

A system of **divination** involving casting small bones (each associated with particular interpretations), rather in the manner of throwing dice. Later developments in fact utilized dice in place of bones, the numbers being associated with letters, to form words which had a bearing on the questions put by the diviner. An associated preliminary ritual was sometimes used, involving writing a question on paper and passing it through the smoke of burning juniper wood.

Astral Body

An exact replica of the physical body but composed of finer matter. The term is chiefly employed in **Theosophy,** and those numerous occult systems derived from it, to denote the link between the nervous system and the cosmic reservoir of energy. The astral body corresponds to the **double** of **out-of-the-body** experiences reported in psychic research. The term *double,* however, is less comprehensive and refers only to the living; *astral body* refers specifically to the bodily counterpart of the dead. The **etheric double** or body, in Theosophy, is distinct from the astral, but in Spiritualistic literature they are often interchanged. These concepts derive from traditional Hindu mysticism, though there are also Western precursors.

The astral body is the instrument of passions, emotions, and desires, and, since it interpenetrates and extends beyond the physical body, it is the medium through which these are conveyed to the latter. When it separates from the denser body—during sleep, or by the influence of drugs, or as the result of accidents—it takes with it the capacity for feeling, and only with its return can pain or any other such phenomena be felt. During these periods of separation, the astral body is an exact replica of the physical, and as it is extremely sensitive to thought, the apparitions of dead and dying resemble even to the smallest details the physical bodies which they have lately left.

The **Astral World** is said to be attainable to clairvoyants, and many claim that the appropriate body is therefore visible to them. In accordance with theosophical teaching, thought is not the abstraction it is commonly considered to be, but is built up of definite forms, the shape of which depends on the quality of the thought. It also causes definite vibrations, which are seen as colors. Hence, clairvoyants may tell the state of a man's development from the appearance of his astral body.

For example, some suggest that a nebulous appearance indicates imperfect development, while an ovoid appearance betokens a more perfect development. As the colors are indicative of the kind of thought, the variety of these in the astral body indicates the possessor's character. Inferior thoughts produce loud colors, so that rage, for instance, will be recognized by the red appearance of the astral body. Higher thoughts will be recognizable by the presence of delicate colors; religious thought, for instance, will cause a blue color.

This teaching holds true for the bodies higher than the astral, but the coloration of the astral body is much more familiar to those dwellers in the physical world who can see into the astral plane. Less familiar are the coloration and feelings of the higher bodies, for humans are relatively unacquainted with them.

There is a definite theory underlying the emotional and other functions of the astral body. The astral body is not composed of matter alive with an intelligent life, but it nevertheless possesses a kind of life sufficient to convey an understanding of its own existence and wants. The stage of evolution of this astral life is that of descent, the turning point not having yet been reached. He who possesses the physical body has, on the other hand, commenced to ascend, and there is, therefore, a continual opposition of forces between him and his astral body. Hence, the astral body accentuates in him such grosser, retrograde thoughts as he may nourish, since the direction of these thoughts coincides with its own direction. If, however, he resists the opposition of his astral body, the craving of the latter gradually becomes weaker and weaker, till at last it disappears altogether. The constitution of the astral body is thereby altered, for gross thoughts demand for their medium gross astral matter, while pure thoughts demand fine astral matter. During physical life the various kinds of matter in the astral body are intermingled, but at physical death the elementary life in the matter of the astral body seeks instinctively after self-preservation, and it therefore causes the matter to rearrange itself in a series of seven concentric sheaths, the densest being outside and the finest inside.

Physical vision depends on the eyes, but astral vision depends on the various kinds of astral matter capable of receiving different undulations. To be aware of fine matter, fine matter in the astral body is necessary, and so with the other kinds. Hence, when the rearrangement takes place, vision only of the grossest kinds of matter is possible, since only that kind is represented in the thick outer sheath of the astral body. Under these circumstances, the new inhabitant of the astral sphere sees only the worst of it, and also only the worst of his fellow inhabitants, even though they are not in so low a state as himself.

This state is not eternal, and in accordance with the evolutionary process, according to Theosophists, the gross sheath of astral matter wears slowly away, and the individual remains clothed with the six less gross sheaths. These also, with the passage of time, wear away, being resolved into their compound elements, and at last when the final disintegration of the least gross sheath of all takes place, the individual leaves the Astral World and passes into the Mental. However, this rearrangement of the astral body is not inevitable, and those who have learned and know are able at physical death to prevent it. In such cases the change appears a very small one, and the so-called dead continue to live their lives and do their work much as they did in the physical body. (See also **Avichi**)

Sources:

Mead, George R. S. *The Doctrine of the Subtle Body in Western Tradition.* London: John M. Watkins, 1919. Reprint, Wheaton, Ill.: Theosophical Publishing House, 1967.

Powell, Arthur E. *The Astral Body and Other Astral Phenomena.* London: Theosophical Publishing House, 1927.

Astral Projection

Popular term for the ability to travel outside the physical body during sleep or trance, also known as etheric projection or **out-of-the-body** traveling. Astral projection involves the movement of the consciousness, often pictured as an **astral body** or **double,** some distance away from the physical body. There are numerous reports of this ability in popular psychic literature as well as that of psychic research. For example, the British scientist Dr. **Robert Crookall** collected hundreds of cases from individuals in all walks of life.

Sources:

Crookall, Robert. *The Study and Practice of Astral Projection.* London: Aquarian Press, 1961.

Fox, Oliver [Hugh Callaway]. *Astral Projection.* New Hyde Park, N.Y.: University Books, 1962.

Muldoon, Sylvan, and Hereward Carrington. *The Phenomena of Astral Projection.* London: Rider, 1951.

———. *The Projection of the Astral Body.* London: Rider, 1929.

Rogo, D. Scott. *Leaving the Body.* Englewood Cliffs, N.J.: Prentice-Hall, 1983.

Steiger, Brad. *Astral Projection.* Rockport, Mass.: Para Research, 1982.

Astral World

According to theosophical teaching, the Astral World is the first sphere after bodily death. It is said to be material of a refined texture. There are many speculations concerning this world of existence. **Theosophy** claims definite knowledge of its conditions and its inhabitants and the numerous teachers influenced by Theosophy offer variations on the basic theme. Many descriptive accounts are to be found in spiritualistic after-death communications. All this, however, is inaccessible to experimental research.

In Theosophy, the Kama World is the second lowest of seven worlds, the world of emotions, desires, and passions. Into it man passes at physical death, and there he functions for periods that vary with the state of his development, the primitive savage spending a relatively short time in the Astral World, the civilized man spending relatively longer. The appropriate body is the **astral body,** which although composed of matter as is the physical body, is nevertheless of a texture vastly finer than the latter. Although it is in its aspect of the after-death abode that the Astral

World is of most importance and most interest, it may be said that even during physical life, some clairvoyants and even ordinary people are said to be aware of it. This happens during sleep, or by reason of the action of anesthetics or drugs, or accidents; and the interpenetrating astral body then leaves its denser physical counterpart, taking with it the sense of pleasure and pain, and lives for a short time in its own world. Here again the state of the primitive differs from that of his more advanced fellows. The less advanced body does not travel far from his immediate surroundings, while the more mature one may perform useful, helpful work for the benefit of humanity. Furthermore, note that disembodied people are not the only inhabitants of the Astral World, for very many of its inhabitants are said to be of an altogether nonhuman nature—lower orders of the *devas,* or **angels;** and nature-spirits, or **elementals,** both good and bad, such as **fairies,** which are just beyond the powers of human vision; as well as demons, present to alcoholics in delirium tremens. Following physical death, the Astral World is said to contain both heaven and hell as these are popularly conceived.

The Astral World is comprised of seven divisions which correspond to the seven divisions of matter: the solid, liquid, gaseous, etheric, super-etheric, subatomic, and atomic. These divisions are believed to play a most important part in the immediate destiny of humans: If through ignorance, one has permitted the rearrangement of the matter of the astral body into sheaths, one is cognizant only of part of one's surroundings at a time, and it is not till after experience, much of which may be extremely painful, that one is able to enjoy the bliss that the higher divisions of the Astral World contain.

The lowest of these divisions, the seventh, is the environment of gross and unrestrained passions. Since it and most of the matter in the inhabitants' astral bodies is of the same type, it constitutes a veritable hell and is the only hell which exists. This is **Avichi,** the place of desires that cannot be satisfied because of the absence of the physical body, which was the means of their satisfaction. The tortures of these desires are the analog of the torments of hell-fire in the older Christian orthodoxy. Unlike that orthodoxy, however, Theosophy teaches that the state of torment is not eternal but passes away in time, when the desires—through long gnawing without fulfillment—have at last died. Avichi is more correctly regarded as a purgatorial state.

The ordinary individual, however, does not experience this seventh division of the Astral World, but according to character finds itself in one or other of the three next higher divisions. The sixth division is very little different from physical existence, and the new inhabitant continues in the old surroundings among old friends, who, of course, are unaware of the astral presence. Indeed, the newly disembodied soul often does not realize that it is dead, so far as the physical world is concerned.

The fifth and fourth divisions are in most respects quite similar to this, but their inhabitants become less and less immersed in the activities and interests that previously engrossed them, and each sheath of their astral bodies decays in turn, as did the gross outer sheath of the sensualist's body.

The three higher divisions are still more removed from the ordinary material world, and their inhabitants enjoy a state of bliss of which we can have no conception: worries and cares of earth are altogether absent, the insistence of lower desires has worn out in the lower divisions, and it is now possible to live continually in an environment of the loftiest thoughts and aspirations.

The third division is said to correspond to the **Summerland** of **Spiritualism,** where the inhabitants live in a world of their own creation—the creation of their thoughts. Its cities and all their contents, scenery of life, are all formed by the influence of thought.

The second division is what is properly looked upon as Heaven, and the inhabitants of different races, creeds, and beliefs all find it each according to individual belief. Hence, instead of it being the place taught of by any particular religion, it is the region where every religion finds its own ideal. Christians, Muslims, Hindus, and so on, find it to be just as they conceived it would be. Here, and in the first and highest division, the inhabitants pursue noble aims freed from whatever selfishness was mingled with these aims on earth. The literary man, without thoughts of fame; the artist, the scholar, the preacher, all working without incentive of personal interest, and when their work is pursued long enough, and they are fitted for the change, they leave the Astral World and enter one vastly higher—the Mental.

However, the rearrangement of the matter of the astral body at physical death is said to be the result of ignorance, and those who are sufficiently instructed do not permit this rearrangement to take. They are not, therefore, confined to any one division and do not have to progress from division to division, but they are able to move through any part of the Astral World, laboring always in their various lines of action to assist the great evolutionary scheme. Many such theosophical teachings derive from traditional Hindu mysticism.

Sources:

Besant Annie. *The Ancient Wisdom.* 1897. Reprint, Wheaton, Ill.: Theosophical Press, 1928.

Leadbeater, Charles W. *The Astral Plane.* London: Theosophical Publishing House, 1915.

Mead, George R. S. *The Doctrine of the Subtle Body in Western Tradition.* London: John M. Watkins, 1919. Reprint, Wheaton, Ill.: Theosophical Publishing House, 1967.

Nizida. *The Astral Light.* London: Theosophical Publishing House, 1889. Reprint, Talent, Oreg.: Eastern School Press, 1983.

Astroflash

An IBM computer for use in **astrology,** first set up in Paris in the Pan-Am Building in the Champs Elysées. It was programmed by French astrologer Andre Barbault and was said to cover nearly two billion possible planetary interpretations. Astroflash II, a similar computer, was temporarily installed at Grand Central Station, New York, in June 1969 and offered a 14-page horoscope in two minutes for $5.

Astrologers' Guild of America, Inc.

Organization founded in 1927 for students and other persons interested in **astrology.** The guild seeks to promote astrological research and study and to protect the interests of qualified astrologers. It holds lectures and publishes a quarterly journal, *Astrological Review.* The guild is affiliated with the Congress of Astrological Organizations. Address: Morningstar, Long Pond, PA 18334.

Astrologica (Journal)

South American Spanish-language periodical concerned with the serious study of **astrology.** It is published by the Centro Astrologica de Buenos Aires, Avenida Auintana 142, Buenos Aires, Argentina.

Astrological Association

British professional organization for astrologers. The Astrological Association grew out of the desire of **John Addey** to end the chaos he found in astrological thought and practice in the 1950s. He believed he had found a uniting force in his discovery of harmonic patterns in his astrological research. The organization was founded in 1958, and among those who gave it blessings was **C. E. O. Carter,** the most prominent British astrologer at the time.

Addey found little enthusiasm for his harmonic theories, but the other goals of the association have proved sufficient to maintain it as a vital organization. Addey served as president for more than a decade (1951–63). Address: 396 Caledonian Rd., London, N1 1DN England.

Astrological Houses

Besides the 12 **astrological signs** and the **astrological planets,** the birth chart or horoscope also notes the existence of 12 astrological houses. The 12 houses are determined by drawing certain great circles through the intersection of the horizon and meridian, apportioning the whole globe or sphere into 12 equal parts. In practice, these lines are projected by a very simple method onto a plane. The space in the center of the figure thus delineated may be supposed to represent the situation of the earth.

Each of the 12 divisions or houses rules certain events, in the following order, reckoned from the east:

1. The basic self/physical body
2. Income and possessions
3. Relatives, communication, and short-distance travel
4. Property (house and land), the mother
5. Children, creations, self-expression
6. Health, work, pets
7. Marriage and partnerships
8. Sex, death, inheritance
9. Higher education, in-laws, religion, and long-distance travel
10. Career and public image
11. Friends, ideals, group associations
12. Unconscious mind, institutions, how we limit ourselves

These categories are designed to comprehend all that can possibly befall any individual, and the prognostication is drawn from the configuration of the planets in one or more of these "houses."

First House. The first house, the house of life, includes all that affects one's basic self. The sign ascending will considerably modify the character of the native, so forming an astrological judgment will require combining the indications of the ascending sign and the planet. In what are called horary questions, this house relates to all questions of life, health, and appearance, such as stature, complexion, shape, accidents, and sickness. It shows the events that will occur during journeys and ventures with respect to the life and health of those engaged in them. Regarding questions of a political nature, the first house signifies the people in general, and being of the same nature as Aries, all that is said of that sign may be transferred to this house.

Second House. The second house, which is of the same nature as the sign Taurus, is the house of income and possessions. It signifies advancement in the world with respect to the wealth of the querent. Jupiter, Venus, Mercury, and the Sun in this house indicate good fortune. Saturn, Mars, the Moon, and Uranus are generally unfortunate, though much depends on other factors in the chart. In horary questions the second house signifies the money of the querent or the pecuniary success of any expedition of undertaking. It concerns loans, lawsuits, and everything by which riches may be gained or lost. In political questions it signifies the treasury, public loans, taxes, and subsidies as well as the "death" of national enemies.

Third House. The third house is the house of kindred, particularly of the immediate family in which one was raised. In this house Saturn signifies coldness and distrust; Mars, sudden and hasty quarrels, all unaccountable estrangements; Jupiter, steady relationships; Venus, great love between brothers and sisters and good fortune by their means; the Sun, warm attachment; and the Moon, indifference or fluctuations in relationships. In horary questions the third house signifies the health, fortune, and happiness of the querent's parents, the querent's own patrimony and inheritance, and the ultimate consequences of any undertaking the person may be engaged in. In political questions it denotes the landed interests of a nation; the ancient and chartered rights of all classes, handed down to them from their ancestors; and all public advocates and defenders of those interests and rights.

Fourth House. The fourth house, which is associated with the sign Cancer, is that of the home and relates to one's domicile and other real estate one might own. The fourth house also signifies one's subconscious habit patterns and the nurturing parent (usually the mother). Difficult planets placed in the fourth house show problems with the home or with the nurturing parent. A native whose natal sun is in the fourth house tends to be a home body and likes to spend most of his or her time at home. In a horary chart, the fourth house indicates real estate and the home. In a political chart, the fourth house signifies public lands.

Fifth House. The fifth house, which partakes of the same character as Leo, is the house of children. In birth charts, therefore, it denotes the children of the native, their success, and also the parent's success by means of the children. It also has some reference to women. The health and welfare of children, whether present or absent, are determinable by the planets in this house. It also denotes all questions relative to amusement, on account of the fondness of youth for such pursuits. In political questions the fifth house signifies the rising generation, theaters, exhibitions, public festivals, and national amusements; increase in the population; and music and musical taste, sculpture, painting, and the advancement of the fine arts in general.

Sixth House. The sixth house is that of health, but it also denotes work, particularly service work, pets, and servants. It is usually considered a difficult house because only a few of the planetary configurations that can take place in it are fortunate. It is of the nature of Virgo. When the ruler of the ascendant (rising sign) is placed in the sixth house it denotes a low station in life and, depending on other aspects of the horoscope, may indicate that the native will not rise above menial employment. In horary astrology the sixth house points out servants and cattle, dependents, and small shopkeepers; uncles and aunts on the father's side; and tenants, stewards, shepherds, and farmers. In queries of a political nature, however, this house indicates the underservants of the government; the common seamen in the navy; private soldiers in the army; and the general health of the nation, chiefly regarding contagious and epidemic disorders.

Seventh House. The seventh house, which is of the same nature as Libra, is the house of marriage. Saturn here denotes unhappiness from constitutional causes; Mars, from difference of temper; Uranus, as usual, from some strange and unaccountable dislike. The other planets are mostly causers of good, except for the Moon, which may indicate fluctuating relationships. In horary questions the seventh house denotes love, speculations in business, partners in trade, and litigation. In queries of a political nature it signifies war and the consequences of a treaty; the victorious nation, army, or navy; and outlaws and fugitives, along with the places to which they have retreated.

Eighth House. The eighth house is the house of death. It is of the nature of Scorpio. Saturn in this house may indicate a slow death through a lingering disease, and Uranus a sudden, unexpected death. Jupiter and Venus point out a late and quiet departure. In horary questions it denotes wills, legacies, and all property transferred upon the death of others, as well as one's attitude toward sex. It also denotes the portion or dowry of women, as well as seconds in duels. In political questions the eighth house has a very different significance, namely, the privy council of a king or queen, their friends, and secrets of state. Here again, however, it also relates to death, denoting the rate of mortality among the people.

Ninth House. The ninth house is that of religion, science, and learning. It is related to Sagittarius. Jupiter is the most fortunate planet in it, and if Jupiter is joined by Mercury then the native is promised a character at once learned, estimable, and truly religious. The Sun and Venus are likewise good signs here, but the Moon denotes a changeable mind and frequent alterations in religious principles. Mars portends indifference or even active hostility to religion. In horary questions the ninth house is appropriated to the Church and the clergy and all ecclesiastical matters, dissent, heresy, schism, dreams, and visions. It also denotes voyages and travels to distant lands. In questions of a political nature it represents the religion of the nation as well as all the higher and more solemn courts of law.

Tenth House. The tenth house is considered one of the most important. It is the house of honor, rank, and dignity and is of the nature of Capricorn. In this house the planets are more powerful than in any other, save the first. They point out the employment, success, preferment, and authority of the native. Saturn is here a difficult planet that make's the native's climb to success a long and arduous one. The Moon here shows unusual sensitivity to one's public image, and Uranus shows sudden changes in one's career. Jupiter and the Sun signify advancement by the favor of distinguished men, and Venus by that of distinguished women. In horary questions the tenth house signifies the mother of the querist. In political questions it denotes the sovereign. This is a house in which Mars is not unfortunate if well placed, in which case it denotes warlike achievements and consequent honors.

Eleventh House. The eleventh house is the house of friends and has the nature of Aquarius. In addition to friends it denotes well-wishers, favorites, and flatterers. The Sun is the best planet in this house, and Mars is the worst. In horary questions it signifies the same things as in a birth chart and also denotes the expectations and wishes of the querist. The eleventh house is said to be much influenced by the sign that is in it and to denote legacies if the sign is one of the earth triplicity (Taurus, Virgo, Capricorn) and honor with princes if it is one of the five triplicity (Aries, Leo, Sagittarius). In political questions the eleventh house signifies the allies of the public, the general council of the nation, and newly acquired rights.

The last house, which partakes of the character of Pisces, is the house of the unconscious. It denotes sorrow, anxiety, and all kinds of suffering. Yet here difficult planets are weaker, according to some writers, and good planets stronger than in certain other houses. Very few configurations in the twelfth house are esteemed good for the native, but even unfortunate effects are greatly modified by the planetary influences. In horary questions this house signifies imprisonment, treason, sedition, assassination, and suicide. In political questions it points out deceitful treaties, unsuccessful negotiations, treachery in the offices of state, captivity to princes, and general ill fortune. This house also denotes the criminal code, punishment of culprits, dungeons, and circumstances connected with prison discipline. Venus is the best planet in this house, and Saturn is the worst.

There are numerous astrological house systems, each of which divides up the sky in a slightly different way. All of the commonly used house systems agree that the first house–seventh house axis should be drawn from the eastern horizon to the western horizon. All but one system—the equal house system—use the degree of the zodiac closest to the zenith as the place to begin the tenth house, with the point 180 degrees away (the nadir) designated as the cusp of the fourth house. Hence with the exception of the equal house system, the differences between the most commonly used systems—Placidian, Koch, Campanus—are relatively minor.

Sources:

Holden, Ralph William. *The Elements of House Division.* Essex, U.K.: L. N. Fowler, 1977.

Lewis, James R. *The Astrology Encyclopedia.* Detroit: Gale Research, 1994.

McEvers, Joan. *The Houses: Power Places of the Horoscope.* St. Paul, Minn.: Llwellyn Publications, 1991.

Rudhyar, Dane. *The Astrological Houses: The Spectrum of Individual Experience.* Garden City, N.Y.: Doubleday, 1972.

Astrological Journal

Quarterly publication of the **Astrological Association** of Britain. The journal is published at "Oakfield," Goose Rye Rd., Worplesdon, Surrey, England.

Astrological Lodge of London

The Astrological Lodge of London was established in 1915 as the Astrological Lodge of the Theosophical Society by **Alan Leo** (pen name of William Frederick Allen). Leo had been both an enthusiastic Theosophist and professional astrologer for many years. The lodge continued the thrust of two earlier organizations, the **Astrological Society** (founded in 1895) and the **Society for Astrological Research** (founded in 1903), in both of which Leo had taken a leadership role. Unfortunately, he died in 1917 and the lodge languished for several years. It was revived in the 1920s by **C. E. O. Carter,** who remained its president until 1952. He turned it into the most influential astrological organization in Great Britain. In 1948 Carter led in the founding of the **Faculty of Astrological Studies,** a school sponsored by the lodge. Lodge Address: BM Astrolabe, London WC1N 3XX, England.

Sources:

Naylor, P. I. H. *Astrology: A Fascinating History.* N. Hollywood, Calif.: Wilshire Book Co., 1970.

Astrological Magazine

Long-established English-language magazine published monthly in India since 1895. It includes articles on Indian astrological theory and practice. Address: Raman Publications, Sri Rajeswari 115–1, New Extension, Seshadripuram, Bangalore 560020, India.

Astrological Planets

Traditional **astrology** traced the movement of the planets, the seven wandering celestial bodies, through the heavens and pictured them abstractly in the **horoscope** chart. In the horoscope the planets traversed both **astrological signs** and **astrological houses,** divisions created as a map of meanings in the heavens. Astrologers saw in them the major variables in the astrological chart. The seven traditional planets were the Sun, the Moon, Mercury, Venus, Mars, Jupiter, and Saturn. As other planets were discovered (Uranus, Neptune, and Pluto), they were added to considerations of the horoscope.

Modern astrologers are, of course, fully aware that the Sun and Moon are not planets, but they generally keep the traditional terminology. The Sun is the most important planet in the chart. Individuals are primarily designated by the sign in which the Sun is located in their birth chart. The Moon is second only to the Sun in importance. Whereas the Sun represents the active individual, the Moon, whose light is reflective, designates the more receptive and passive qualities of the person.

Some contemporary astrologers also give consideration to asteroids, particularly to the largest (Ceres, Pallas, Juno, and Vesta, which can be found in the asteroid belt, between the orbits of Mars and Jupiter), as well as to Chiron, a large comet orbiting between Saturn and Uranus.

The practice of astrology is based on the premise that the planets can be related to significant personality traits and correlated with major events on Earth. The traits most often associated with specific planets, beginning with the outermost planet in the solar system, are as follows:

Pluto. The slow-moving outermost planet represents a powerful transforming energy whose effect is relative to its position in the chart. Pluto's qualities are power, elimination, latency, eruption, annihilation, renewal, and regeneration. It is seen as related to subtle underground forces that lie dormant for a time and then suddenly burst forth. The discovery of Pluto came at the same time as the rise of Nazism, the discussions on splitting the atom, and the rise of mass media. Pluto's power is the power of the atom, the power of the masses, and the power of the unconscious.

Neptune. Neptune has come to be associated with those forces that tend to do away with such artificial barriers as time, space, ego, and national borders. It might be seen as the higher, more spiritual, form of Venus. Its qualities include universality, idealism, compassion, spirituality, formlessness, elusiveness, secrecy, mystery, fantasy, and delusion. All states of consciousness that destroy the limitations of normal waking consciousness indicate Neptune's influence.

Uranus. Uranus is by nature extremely cold, dry, and melancholy. Natives with a strong Uranian influence are of small stature, dark or pale complexion, rather light hair, highly nervous temperament, and sedate aspect but have some striking physical feature, light gray eyes, and a delicate constitution. If the planet is well dignified (i.e., there is a high degree of harmony between the planet and the sign it is in), the native is a searcher of science, particularly chemistry, and remarkably attached to the wonderful. The person possesses an extraordinary magnanimity and loftiness of mind, with an uncontrollable and intense desire for pursuits and discoveries of an uncommon nature. If the planet is ill dignified, the native is weak, sickly, and destined to have a short life; is treacherous, given to gross imposture, unfortunate in undertakings, capricious in tastes, and eccentric in his conduct. The effects of Uranus are of a totally unexpected, strange, and unaccountable character. The planet rules over places dedicated to unlawful arts and laboratories. Uranus governs Lapland, Finland, and the Poles.

Saturn. Saturn is by nature cold and dry, a melancholy, earthy, masculine, solitary, and diurnal planet. When Saturn rules the ascendant (rising sign), the native is of average stature and dark or pale complexion, has small black eyes, broad shoulders, and black hair, and is ill shaped about the lower extremities. When Saturn is well dignified, the native is grave and wise, studious and severe, of an active and penetrating mind, reserved and patient, constant in attachment but implacable in resentment, upright and inflexible. If the planet is ill dignified, then the native will be sluggish, covetous, and distrustful; stubborn, malicious, and malcontented.

Jupiter. Jupiter is a diurnal, masculine planet, temperately hot and moist, airy, and sanguine, the lord of the air triplicity. If the planet is well dignified, the native will be of erect carriage and tall stature with a handsome ruddy complexion, high forehead, soft, thick brown hair, handsome shape, and commanding aspect; his voice will be strong, clear, and manly, and his speech grave and sober. If the planet is ill dignified, the native will still be a good-looking person, although of smaller stature and less noble aspect. In the former case, the understanding and character will be of the highest possible description; in the latter case, although the native will be careless and improvident, immoral and irreligious, he or she will never entirely lose the good opinion of friends.

Mars. Mars is a masculine, nocturnal, hot, dry planet, of the fire triplicity. It is the author of strife, and the principle of assertiveness. The native is short but strong, having large bones; ruddy complexion; red or sandy hair and eyebrows; quick, sharp eyes; round, bold face; and fearless aspect. If Mars is well dignified, the native will be courageous and invincible, unsusceptible to fear, careless of death, resolute, and unsubmissive. If the planet is ill dignified, the native will be a trumpeter of his own fame, dishonest, fond of quarrels, and prone to fights. The gallows is said to most often terminate the lives of those born in low circumstances under the influence of Mars. Mars signifies soldiers, surgeons, barbers, and butchers.

Sun. The Sun is a masculine, hot, dry planet with usually favorable influences. The native is very much like one born under Jupiter, but with lighter hair, redder complexion, fatter body, and larger eyes. When the Sun is well dignified, the native is affable, courteous, splendid and sumptuous, proud, liberal, humane, and ambitious. When it is ill dignified, the native is arrogant, mean, loquacious, and sycophantic, resembling the native under Jupiter when ill dignified, but even worse. The Sun indicates that which is most seasonable; professions (kings, lords and all dignified persons, braziers, goldsmiths, and persons employed in mints), and places (kings' courts, palaces, theaters, halls, and places of state).

Moon. The Moon is feminine, nocturnal, cold, moist, and phlegmatic. Its influence in itself is neither fortunate nor unfortunate. The Moon is benevolent or otherwise according to how the other planets conflict or are in harmony with it, and in all circumstances it becomes more powerful than any of them. The native is short and stout with fair, pale complexion, round face, gray eyes, short arms, and thick hands and feet; is very hairy but with light hair; and is phlegmatic. If the Moon is affected by the Sun at the time of birth, the native will have a blemish on or near the eye. When the Moon is well dignified, the native is of soft, engaging manners, imaginative, and a lover of the arts but is also wandering, careless, timorous, and unstable; loves peace; and is averse to activity. When it is ill dignified, the native is of an ill shape, indolent, worthless, and disorderly.

Venus Venus is a feminine planet, temperately cold and moist, the author of mirth and sport. The native is handsome and well formed but not tall, with a clear complexion, bright hazel or black eyes, dark brown or chestnut hair that is thick, soft, and shiny; a soft and sweet voice; and a very prepossessing aspect. If Venus is well dignified, the native is cheerful, friendly, musical, fond of elegant accomplishments, and prone to love but frequently jealous. If it is ill dignified, the native is less handsome in person and in mind, given to every licentiousness and to dishonesty.

Mercury. Mercury is masculine, melancholy, cold, and dry. The native is tall, straight, and thin, with a narrow face and high forehead, long straight nose, black or gray eyes, thin lips and chin, scanty beard, and brown hair; the arms, hands, and fingers are long and slender. If Mercury is in the east at the time of birth, the native is likely to be of a stronger constitution and have sandy hair; if in the west, the native is prone to be sallow, lank, slender, and of a dry habit. When mercury is well dignified, the native has an acute and penetrating mind, a powerful imagination, and a retentive memory; is eloquent; is fond of learning; and is successful in scientific investigation. If engaged in mercantile pursuits, the native is enterprising and skillful. If Mercury is ill dignified, the native is a mean, unprincipled character, a pretender to knowledge, a boastful impostor, and a malicious slanderer.

Asteroids represent highly specific principles and influences, in contrast to the planets, which are associated with a broad range of attributes, personality traits, and principles. The "big four" asteroids are Ceres, Juno, Vesta, and Pallas. Ceres represents the attribute of nurturance, either where and how one is nurtured, or where and how one nurtures others. Juno represents the principle of marriage and indicates traits of one's marriage partner, as well as features of one's marriage(s). Vesta represents the principle of dedicated work. Pallas represents the principle of creative wisdom. Chiron, a large comet in orbit between Saturn and Uranus, has a wide variety of associations but seems to have a particular link with healing and counseling.

Aspects and Relationships

As can be seen from the foregoing descriptions, each planet has picked up a host of associations through the centuries. Each one has also been assigned "rulership" of different astrological signs with which it has a particular affinity. The rulerships are as follows:

Mars and Aries; Venus and Taurus; Mercury and Gemini; Moon and Cancer; Sun and Leo; Mercury and Virgo; Pluto and Scorpio; Jupiter and Sagittarius; Saturn and Capricorn; Uranus and Aquarius; Neptune and Pisces.

Planets "project" certain qualities as they assume geometric relationships to other planets in the birth chart. The major geometric *aspects* of the planets are thus distinguished:

Conjunction. When two planets are in the same degree and minute of a sign, which may be of good or unfortunate import, depending on the nature of the planets and whether their relationship is harmonious or conflicting.

Sextile. When two planets are 60 degrees distant from each other; it is called the aspect of imperfect love or friendship and is generally a favorable omen.

Square. When two planets are 90 degrees distant from each other, making the aspect inharmonious and inclining to conflict and difficulty.

Trine. When the distance is 120 degrees, promising harmonious cooperation and the best blending of energies.

Opposition. When two planets are 180 degrees apart, or exactly opposite each other, which is considered an aspect of tension, implying conflict and difficulties.

Aspects need not be exact, but can be within three to eight degrees of the foregoing geometric relationships, depending on the particular aspect and the planets involved. The closer an aspect is to being exact, the stronger it is.

Sources:

George, Llewellyn. *The New A to Z Horoscope Maker and Delineator.* Rev. ed. St. Paul, Minn.: Llwellyn Publications, 1987.

Lewis, James R. *The Astrology Encyclopedia.* Detroit: Gale Research, 1994.

McEvers, Joan. *Planets: The Astrological Tools.* St. Paul, Minn.: Llwellyn Publications, 1989.

Mayo, Jeff. *The Planets and Human Behavior.* 1972. Reprint, Reno, Nev.: CRCS Publications, 1985.

Astrological Registration and Communication (ARC)

A networking organization for astrologers and astrological organizations worldwide. ARC was created in 1987 by delegates attending the World Astrological Congress meeting in Zurich. ARC is an international computer network with primary stations on every continent. Twenty-one countries were represented at its initiation, and its support has grown steadily year by year. ARC is strongly backed by the **Association for Astrological Networking,** based in North America. Address: PO Box 614, CH-8134 Adliswil, Switzerland.

Astrological Signs

Astrologers divide the heavens into 12 segments tracing the apparent movement of the Sun around the Earth. The measuring of the signs begins with the point where the Sun's apparent path crosses the celestial equator, designated 0° Aries. The 12 signs were named after the stellar constellations that appear in the different segments. The signs are classified according to *quality* and *element.* The three qualities are cardinal (outgoing), fixed (stable), and mutable (variable). The four traditional elements are fire, earth, air, and water, which stand for activity, matter, mind, and feeling, respectively. The three qualities and four elements offer twelve possible combinations, one for each sign. The signs may also be seen as positive or "masculine" (active), in the case of the fire and air signs; or negative or "feminine" (reactive), in the case of the earth and water signs. The signs are also divided into "northern" and "commanding" (the first six), and "southern" and "obeying" (last six).

There are four triplicities among the signs: the earth triplicity, including Taurus, Virgo, and Capricorn; the air triplicity, which includes Gemini, Libra, and Aquarius; the fire triplicity, encompassing Aries, Leo, and Sagittarius; and the water triplicity, containing Cancer, Scorpio, and Pisces. The signs are further divided into diurnal and nocturnal, the diurnal signs being all masculine and the nocturnal feminine. Signs named after quadrupeds are, of course, quadrupedal; those named after human states of endeavor (e.g., water bearer, archer) are called humane. A person born under a fiery, masculine, diurnal sign is hot in temper and bold in character. If it is a quadrupedal sign, the native is somewhat like the animal after which the sign is called. Thus in Taurus, the native is bold and furious; in Leo, fierce and aggressive. Cancer, Scorpio and Pisces are called fruitful or prolific; and Gemini, Leo, and Virgo, barren. Sagittarius, because usually represented as a centaur, is said to produce humane character if located in the first 15 degrees (first half) of the sign, but a savage, brutal, and intractable disposition if found in the last 15 degrees.

Astrologers designate the 12 signs as follows:

Aries, the first sign of the zodiac, is a cardinal fire sign. It is a positive, masculine sign, ruled by the planet Mars. Its symbol is the ram, and its glyph (symbol) is said to represent a ram's horns. It takes its name from the Greek god of war. Aries is associated with the head, and people with an Aries sun sign (the Sun is in the sign Aries in their natal chart) are prone to headaches and injuries to the head and face. The association of the head with Aries is the source of the expression "headstrong," which characterizes people with a strong Aries nature. Aries is dry, vernal and equinoctial (it begins on the vernal equinox), diurnal, movable, commanding, eastern, choleric, and aggressive. The native, that is, the person born under its influence, is tall of stature, of a strong but spare make, long face and neck, thick shoulders, piercing eyes, sandy or red hair, and brown complexion. The native's disposition is warm, hasty, and passionate. The aspects of the planets however, may materially alter these traits. (*Aspects* are the angular relationships between various points in a boroscope; in a natal chart the planets represent the various facets of one's psyche, and aspects between them indicate how these facets conflict or work together.) This sign rules the head and face. As the first sign, the key phrase for Aries is "I am," representing the birth of awareness.

Taurus, the second sign of the zodiac, is a fixed earth sign. It is a negative, feminine sign, ruled by the planet Venus. Its symbol is the bull, and its glyph is said to represent a bull's head and horns. It takes its name from the Greek word for "bull." A sign known for its stubbornness, it is the source of our expressions "bullheaded" and "stubborn as a bull." Taurus is associated with the throat and neck. People with a Taurus sun sign, although they often have beautiful voices, are also prone to sore throats, thyroid irregularities, and other neck problems. Taurus is cold and dry, melancholy, nocturnal, and southern. When influential in a nativity, it usually produces a person with a broad forehead, thick lips, dark curling hair, and melancholy, slow to anger, but when once enraged, violent, furious, and difficult to appease. Places ruled by Taurus are stables, cowhouses, cellars and low rooms, and all places used for or by cattle. The key phrase for Taurus is "I have."

Gemini, the third sign of the zodiac, is a mutable air sign. It is a positive, masculine sign, ruled by the planet Mercury. Its symbol is the twins, and its glyph is said to represent a set of twins. It takes its name from the Latin word for "twins." Gemini is associated with the shoulders, arms, hands, and lungs. The native is tall and straight with long arms and well-formed hands and feet, rather dark complexion, brown hair, and hazel eyes. The native is strong and active in person, sound and acute in judgment, lively, playful, and generally skillful in business. Places ruled by Gemini are hilly and high grounds, the tops of houses, wainscoted rooms, halls and theaters, barns, storehouses, and stairs. The key phrase for Gemini is "I think."

Cancer, the fourth sign of the zodiac, is a cardinal water sign. It is a negative, feminine sign, ruled by the Moon. Its symbol is the crab, and its glyph is said to represent the two claws of a crab. It takes its name from the Latin word for "crab." A moody sign, it is the source of the expression "crabby." Cancer is associated with the breasts and the stomach. It is a cold, moist, nocturnal, and exceedingly fruitful sign, more so than any other. The native is fair and pale, short and small, with the upper part of the body larger in proportion to the lower, a round face, light hair, and blue or gray eyes. The native is phlegmatic and heavy in disposition; weak in constitution, and of a small voice. Places associated with Cancer are the sea and all rivers, swamps, ponds, lakes, wells, ditches, and watery places. The key phrase for Cancer is "I feel."

Leo, the fifth sign of the zodiac, is a fixed fire sign. It is a positive, masculine sign, ruled by the Sun. Its symbol is the lion, and its glyph is said to be a modified version of the initial letter of its Greek name. It takes its name from the Latin word for "lion." Leo is associated with the back and, especially, the heart. The association of Leo with the heart is the astrological basis for the common expression "lion hearted." Leo is hot, dry, commanding, and very barren. When this sign ascends in a nativity, the individual has a tall and powerful frame and is well shaped, with an austere countenance, light, yellowish hair, large piercing eyes, commanding aspect, and ruddy complexion. The character is fierce and aggressive, yet open, generous, and courteous. This sign is more modified by planetary influences than any other. Leo governs woods, forests, deserts and hunting grounds, and fireplaces and furnaces. The key phrase for Leo is "I will."

Virgo, the sixth sign of the zodiac, is a mutable earth sign. It is a negative, feminine sign, ruled by the planet Mercury. Its symbol is a young woman, and its glyph is said to represent a serpent. Virgo takes its name from the Latin word for "virgin." Virgo is associated with the nervous system and, especially, with the bowels. Virgo is cold, dry, barren, and melancholy. The native is handsome and well shaped, slender, of average stature, with a clear, ruddy or brown complexion, dark hair and eyes, a rather round face, and a voice sweet and clear but not strong. The character is amiable and benevolent, witty and studious, but not persevering; and if not opposed by planetary aspects, apt to oratory. Virgo is associated with cornfields and granaries, studies and libraries. The key phrase for Virgo is "I analyze."

Libra, the seventh sign of the zodiac, is a cardinal air sign. It is a positive, masculine sign, ruled by the planet Venus. Its symbol is the scales, which its glyph is said to represent. It takes its name from the Latin word for "pound weight," or "scales." Libra is associated with the lower back, buttocks, and kidneys. Libra is sanguine, hot, moist, and diurnal. The native is tall and well made, very handsome, of a fine, ruddy complexion in youth, which changes to a deep red with advancing years. The native has long, flaxen hair, gray eyes, a courteous disposition, and a just and upright character. The places Libra rules are mountains, sawpits, and newly felled woods. The key phrase for Libra is "I balance."

Scorpio, the eighth sign of the zodiac, is a fixed water sign. It is a negative, feminine sign, ruled by the planet Pluto (in traditional astrology it was ruled by Mars). Its symbology is complex, being the only sign with three symbols—the scorpion, the snake, and the eagle. Its glyph is said to represent a serpent. It takes its name from the Latin word for "scorpion." Scorpio is associated with the sexual organs and the kidneys. Scorpio is a cold, nocturnal sign. The native has a strong, robust, corpulent body, is of average stature, and has a broad visage, dark but not clear complexion, dark gray or light brown eyes, black or very dark brown hair, short, thick legs, and a thick neck. Scorpio governs swampy grounds and stagnant waters, orchards and ruinous houses, especially near water. The key phrase for Scorpio is "I desire."

Sagittarius, the ninth sign of the zodiac, is a mutable fire sign. It is a positive, masculine sign, ruled by the planet Jupiter. Its symbol is the centaur (sometimes, alternately, the archer) and its glyph is an arrow, which refers to the arrow in the bow that the centaur is holding. It takes its name from the Latin word *sagitta,* "arrow." Sagittarius is associated with the hips, the thighs, and the liver. Sagittarius is hot, dry, and diurnal. The native is well formed and of slightly above-average stature, with fine chestnut hair, but inclined to baldness, a visage somewhat long but ruddy and handsome. The body is strong, stout, and hardy. The native is inclined to horsemanship and field sports, careless of danger, generous and intrepid, but hasty and careless. Sagittarius rules the hips and is the cause of gout, rheumatism, and disorders that affect the muscles. Accidents and disorders occasioned by intemperance come under the government of this sign. Sagittarius is associated with stables and parks. The key phrase for Sagittarius is "I see."

Capricorn, the tenth sign of the zodiac, is a cardinal earth sign. It is a negative, feminine sign, ruled by the planet Saturn. Its symbol is a goat with a fishtail, and its glyph is said to reflect this symbol. It takes its name from the Latin *capricornus,* "goat horn." Capricorn is associated with the bones and, especially, with the knees. It is a cold, dry, nocturnal, domestic sign. The native usually is tall, of slender stature and long, thin countenance, with a small beard, dark hair and eyes, long neck, and narrow chest and chin. The native is cheerful and collected, talented and upright. Ruling the knees and hips, Capricorn governs all diseases that afflict them, and also melancholy diseases such as hypochondriasis and hysteria. The places over which it has power are workshops and fallow grounds. The key phrase for Capricorn is "I use."

Aquarius, the eleventh sign of the zodiac, is a fixed air sign. It is a positive, masculine sign, ruled by the planet Uranus (before the outer planets were discovered, it was said to be ruled by Saturn). Its symbol is the water bearer, and its glyph is a pair of wavy lines representing water. Aquarius is associated with the shins, ankles, and the circulatory system. Aquarius is a hot, moist, rational, sanguine sign. The native is a well-made and robust person, of above-average stature, long face, but with a pleasing and delicate countenance, clear, bright complexion, and flaxen hair. The native is fair, open, and honest. Aquarius rules the legs and ankles and causes all diseases that affect them: lameness, swelling, cramping, and gout. It governs mines and quarries, flying machines, roofs of houses, wells, and conduits. The key phrase for Aquarius is "I know."

Pisces, the twelfth sign of the zodiac, is a mutable water sign. It is a negative, feminine sign, ruled by the planet Neptune (in traditional astrology it was ruled by Jupiter). Its symbol is two fish moving in opposite directions, tied together by a rope. Its glyph is said to be a stylized representation of this symbol. It takes its name from the plural of the Latin word for "fish." Pisces is associated with the feet. It is a cold, moist, nocturnal, and extremely fruitful sign, second only to Cancer. The native is short and ill shaped, fleshy, if not corpulent, with thick, round shoulders, light hair and eyes, pale complexion, and a large head and face. The native has a weak and vacillating disposition and is well-meaning but devoid of energy. Pisces rules the feet and causes lameness and every kind of disorder occasioned by watery humors. Pisces governs the same places as Cancer, except for the sea and rivers. The key phrase for Pisces is "I believe."

Interpreting a horoscope begins largely with the astrological signs. A person is usually initially designated by the sign within which the sun was located at the time of his or her birth. The influence of the signs however, is lessened or enhanced by the aspects of the planets within them and by the astrological houses, so these factors also have to be considered in interpreting the horoscope. (See also **Astrological Houses; Astrological Planets**)

Sources:

Cirlot, J. E. *A Dictionary of Symbols.* New York: Dorset Press, 1991.

Evans, Colin. *The New Waite's Compendium of Natal Astrology.* 1917. Revised by Brain E. F. Gardener. York Beach, Maine: Samuel Weiser, 1971.

Green, Landis Knight. *The Astrologer's Manual: Modern Insights into an Ancient Art.* Sebastopol, Calif.: CRCS Publications, 1975.

Hall, Manly P. *Astrological Keywords.* 1958. Reprint, Savage, Md.: Littlefield Adams Quality Paperbacks, 1975.

Lewis, James R. *The Astrology Encyclopedia.* Detroit: Gale Research, 1994.

Astrological Society

An early astrological organization that grew out of the magazine *Modern Astrology,* published in the late nineteenth century in London. The society was organized in 1895 by **Walter Gorn Old. Alan Leo,** a fellow Theosophist, became the first president. The society lasted for approximately eight years but ran into criticism because it was almost exclusively confined to London. In 1903 it was disbanded and the new **Society for Astrological Research,** with a wider national focus, was organized in its stead.

Sources:

Naylor, P. I. H. *Astrology: A Fascinating History.* N. Hollywood, Calif.: Wilshire Book Co. 1970.

Astrology

The art of divining the fate or future of persons from the juxtaposition of the Sun, Moon, and planets. *Judicial astrology* foretells the destinies of individuals and nations, while *Natural astrology* predicts changes of weather and the influence of the stars upon natural things.

The characters used in astrology to denote the 12 signs represent natural objects, but they have also a hieroglyphic or esoteric meaning that has been lost. The figure of Aries represents the head and horns of a ram; that of Taurus, the head and horns of a bull; that of Leo, the head and mane of a lion; that of Gemini, two persons standing together; and so on. The physical or astronomical reasons for the adoption of these figures is explained by the Abbé Pluche in his *Histoire du Ciel* (1739–41), and Charles F. Dupuis, in his *Abrégé de l'Origine de tous les Cultes* (1798), endeavors to establish the principles of an astro-mythology by tracing the progress of the moon through the 12 signs in a series of adventures he compares with the wanderings of Isis.

Nativities

Traditionally, the cases for which astrological predictions have chiefly been sought were nativities, that is, in ascertaining the fate and fortunes of individuals from the positions of the stars at the time of birth, and in questions called *horary,* which comprehend almost every matter that might be the subject of astrological inquiry. Sickness, the success of business undertakings, the outcome of lawsuits, and so on are all objects of horary questions.

A person is said to be born under that planet that ruled the hour of his birth. Thus two hours every day are under the control of Saturn; the first hour after sunrise on Saturday is one of them. Therefore, a person born on Saturday in the first hour after sunrise has Saturn for the lord of his or her ascendant; those born in the next hour, Jupiter; and so on in order. Venus rules the first hour on Friday, Mercury on Wednesday, Jupiter on Thursday, the Sun and Moon on Sunday and Monday, and Mars on Tuesday.

In drawing a nativity or natal chart (horoscope) a figure is divided into 12 portions representing the **astrological houses.** The 12 houses are similar to the 12 **astrological signs,** and the planets, being always in the zodiac, will therefore all fall within these 12 divisions or houses. The line that separates any house from the preceding is called the cusp of the house. The first house is called the ascendant, or the east angle; the fourth, the *imum coeli,* or the north angle; the seventh, the west angle; and the tenth, the *medium coeli,* or the south angle. After this figure is drawn, tables and directions are given for placing the signs, and because one house corresponds to a particular sign, the rest can also be determined. When the signs and planets are all placed in the houses, the astrologer can augur, from their relative position, what influence they will have on the life and fortunes of the native.

History of Astrology in the West

The precise origin of astrology is lost to history, but its practice appears to have developed independently in both China and Mesopotamia, and was quite known early in India. One of the most remarkable astrological treatises of all history is the fabulous **Bhrigu-Samhita** of ancient India, said to contain formulas for ascertaining the names of all individuals, past, present, and future, and their destinies. Unlike popular Western astrology, the key to a *Bhrigu* consultation is not the birth sign and conjunction of planets, but the moment of consultation of the oracle.

Marco Polo found astrology well established in China, although Chinese astrology developed apart from Western history and only recently has been imported into the West. Western astrology seems to have originated in Mesopotamia, and all of the cultures of ancient Iraq and Iran contributed to its creation. Among the earliest records of astrology are the cuneiform tablets from the library of King Ashurbanipal of Assyria (669–626 B.C.E.). Astrologers were making periodic reports to Ashurbanipal on such matters as the possibility of war and the probable size of the harvest. Astrology had been present in the region for at least a millennium but was given a distinctive boost by the Chaldeans who took over the Tigris and Euphrates valleys in 606 B.C.E. The Chaldeans mapped the sky, improved the methods for recording the passing of time, successfully predicted eclipses, and accurately determined the length of the solar year (within 26 minutes).

Thus astrology was well developed in Chaldea when (in the second millennium B.C.E.) the biblical Abraham migrated from Ur of the Chaldees (Gen. 11:31) to Palestine. The conflict between the emerging religions of the Israelites and Babylonian astrology can be seen in Isa. 47:13 and repeatedly in the book of Daniel (e.g. 2:27, 4:7). A primitive astrology had developed among the Greeks, but during the conquests of Alexander in the West beginning in 334 B.C.E, Chaldean astrology flowed into the Mediterranean basin. Alexander's conquests also introduced astrology into India, although the Indians took the Chaldean notions and developed them in a unique direction.

In Egyptian tradition the invention of astrology is attributed to Thoth (called **Hermes Trismegistus** by the Greek), the god of wisdom, learning, and literature. He is the Mercury of the Romans, the eloquent deliverer of the messages of the gods.

In imperial Rome astrology was held in great repute, especially under the reign of Tiberius (14–37 C.E.). Augustus (27 B.C.E.–14 C.E.) had discouraged the practice of astrology by banishing its practitioners from Rome, but his successors recalled them; and although occasional edicts in subsequent reigns restrained and even punished all who divined by the stars, the practices of the astrologers were secretly encouraged and their predictions extensively believed. Domitian (51–96 C.E.), in spite of his hostility toward them, was in fear of their pronouncements. They prophesied the year, the hour, and the manner of his death, and agreed with his father in foretelling that he should perish not by poison, but by the dagger. The early Christians gave some sanction to astrology in the Gospel of Matthew, which opens with the visit of the three magi (Persian astrologers) who, having seen the star in the east, have come to worship Christ.

After the age of the Antonines and the work of the third-century C.E. Roman scholar Censorinus, we hear little of astrology for some generations. In the eighth century the Venerable Bede and his distinguished scholar, Alcuin, are said to have pursued this mystic study. Immediately following, the Arabians revived and encouraged it. Under the patronage of Almaimon, in the year 827, the *Megale Syntaxis* of Ptolemy was translated, under the title *Almagest,* by al-Hazen Ben Yusseph. Albumasar added to this work, and the astral science continued to receive new force from the labors of Alfraganus, Ebennozophim, Alfaragius, and **Geber.**

The conquest of Spain by the Moors carried this knowledge, with all their other treasures of learning, into Spain, and before their cruel expulsion it was naturalized among the Christian savants. Among these Alonzo (or Alfonso) of Castile has immortalized himself by his scientific research, and the Jewish and Christian doctors who arranged the tables named for him were convened from all the accessible parts of civilized Europe. Five years were employed in their discussion, and it has been said that the enormous sum of 400,000 ducats was disbursed in the towers of the Alcazar of Galiana in the adjustment and correction of Ptolemy's calculations. Nor was it only the physical motions of the stars that occupied this grave assembly. The two Kabbalistic volumes, yet existing in cipher, in the royal library of the kings of Spain, and which tradition assigns to Alonzo himself, indicate a more visionary study. In spite of the denunciations against this orthodoxy, which were thundered in his ears on the authority of Tertullian, Basil, and Bonaventure, the fearless monarch gave his sanction to such masters as practiced the art of divination by the stars, and in one part of his code enrolled astrology among the seven liberal sciences.

In Germany many eminent men pursued astrology. A long catalog could be made of those who have considered other sciences with reference to astrology and written on them as such. Faust has, of course, the credit of being an astrologer as well as a wizard, and we find that singular but splendid genius, **Cornelius Agrippa** writing with as much zeal against astrology as on behalf of other occult sciences.

Of the early developments in astrology in England little is known. Bede and Alcuin have been mentioned. Roger Bacon included it among his broad studies. But it is the period of the Stuarts that can be considered the acme of astrology in England. Then **William Lilly** employed the doctrine of the **magical circle,** engaged in the evocation of spirits from the **Ars Notoria** and used the form of prayer prescribed therein to the angel Salmonoeus, and entertained among his familiar acquaintance the guardian spirits of England, Salmael and Malchidael. His ill success with the divining rod induced him to surrender the pursuit of **rhabdomancy.**

The successor of Lilly was Henry Coley, a tailor, who had been his amanuensis and was almost as successful in prophecy as his master.

While astrology flourished in England it was in high repute with its kindred pursuits of **magic, necromancy,** and **alchemy** at the court of France. Catherine de Medicis herself was an adept in the art. At the Revolution, which commenced a new era in France, astrology declined.

Modern Astrology

Astrology has now permeated every activity of modern life, from daily household activities to politics and stock market speculation. Leading names that have emerged in the astrology revival include **Luke D. Broughton, Evangeline Adams, Manly Palmer Hall, Elbert Benjamine Heindel,** and **Llewellyn George.** More recently, figures have included **Sydney Omarr, Jeane Dixon, "Zolar"** (Bruce King), **"Ophiel,"** and **Sybil Leek.** Also still popular in its various editions is the mass circulation almanac of **"Old Moore,"** which first appeared nearly three centuries ago.

The psychologist **C. G. Jung** related astrology to "synchronicity," an acausal connecting principle in nature (as distinct from normal cause and effect), and believed that horoscopes offered useful psychological information on patients. Astrology was widely used during World War II as a psychological weapon by both Germans and British.

The most noticeable aspect of the occult revival of modern times has been the widespread popularity of astrology, particularly among young people. It is estimated that there are more than ten thousand professional astrologers in the United States, with a clientele of more than twenty million people. Most American newspapers run an astrology column. Even the respected *Washington Post* includes a horoscope column.

In 1988 the revelations of former White House Chief of Staff Donald T. Regan (in his book *For the Record*) caused widespread media comment with the claim that Nancy Reagan consulted astrologers on questions relating to presidential schedules of her husband, Ronald Reagan. Joan Quigley was cited as her astrological consultant. Caroline Casey, daughter of a former congressman, was also revealed as a leading astrologer to politicians, high-ranking officials, and Georgetown socialites.

None of this would be surprising to Indian and other Asian celebrities, since the astrologer is still an indispensable figure in Asian society, consulted on marriage dates and partnerships, business enterprises, and affairs of state. But the extent of American involvement with astrology surprised and infuriated many commentators, who condemned "occult superstitions." In May 1988, testifying before the Senate Banking Committee, Donald Regan was asked whether he had ever heard of American stockholders using astrology for guidance. He replied, "Recently a study was made of Wall Street people and stockholders—and 48 percent admitted that they used astrology of one sort or another in the stock market."

One astrologer responded, "What's new? Queen Elizabeth I set her coronation date by her guy, John Dee, and consulted him every day. Kings have always used us—and popes! Some of those guys were do-it-yourselfers, like Fixtus IV and Julius II. Others just kept their astrologers in the closet, like Nancy did."

There has been little new to add to popular belief in astrology in the present revival except its linking with modern technology in the use of an IBM computer for rapid calculation of horoscopes. For some time the giant **Astroflash** computer was a familiar sight to commuters at the Lexington Avenue entrance to Grand Central Station, New York.

In spite of its pseudoscientific basis, deriving from outmoded theories of the planetary system, astrology can point to documented successes, particularly by astrologers who combine their calculations with an intuitive faculty of interpretation. There is also scientific evidence for the influence of lunar and solar rhythms on human activity.

One interesting development in modern astrology has been the research of the French statistician **Michel Gauquelin** and his wife **Francosise Gauquelin,** beginning in 1950. They claimed to find a significant correlation between the position of planets at birth and the chosen professions of a large sample of people from all walks of life. The research of the Gauquelins, whose collaboration lasted until 1980, is so significant that it is the most frequently cited research validating astrology.

Sources:

Collins, Rodney. *The Theory of Celestial Influence.* London: Stuart & Watkins, 1955.

Eisler, Robert. *The Royal Art of Astrology.* London: Herbert Joseph, 1946.

Gauquelin, Michel. *The Cosmic Clocks.* Chicago: Henry Regnery, 1967.

———. *Cosmic Influences on Human Behavior; the Planetary Factors in Personality.* New York: Stein & Day, 1973. Rev. ed. New York: ASI Publishers, 1978.

———. *Dreams and Illusions of Astrology.* Buffalo, N.Y.: Prometheus Books, 1978. Reprint, London: Glover & Blair, 1980.

———. *Scientific Basis of Astrology.* New York: Stein & Day, 1969. Reprinted as *Astrology and Science.* London: P. Davies, 1970.

Hone, Margaret. *Modern Textbook of Astrology.* London: Fowler, 1951.

Howe, Ellic. *Astrology & Psychological Warfare during World War II.* London: Rider, 1972.

Kenton, Warren. *Astrology: The Celestial Mirror.* London: Thames & Hudson, 1974.

Lee, Dal. *Dictionary of Astrology.* New York: Warner, 1968.

Leo, Alan. *Casting the Horoscope.* London: Fowler, 1969.

Lewis, James R. *The Astrology Encyclopedia.* Detroit: Gale Research, 1994.

McIntosh, Christopher. *The Astrologers and their Creed.* London: Praeger, 1969.

Rudhyar, Dane. *From Humanistic to Transpersonal Astrology.* Seed Center, 1975.

Thompson, C. J. S. *The Mystery and Romance of Astrology.* London, 1929. Reprint, Detroit: Singing Tree Press, 1969. Reprint, New York: Causeway, 1973.

Astrology: A Comprehensive Bibliography

A somewhat dated but comprehensive publication issued by **Yes Bookshop** that lists nearly a thousand books on all aspects of **astrology** as practiced in the mid-1970s. It contains sections on cosmobiology, sidereal astrology, Uranian astrology, calendars, ephemerides, and so on. Yes Bookshop is located at 1035 31st Street N.W., Washington, D.C. 20007.

Astrology Guide

Popular magazine stand bimonthly that includes horoscopes of notable personalities, a daily guide for astrological signs, and planetary predictions. It is published by Sterling's Magazines, 355 Lexington Ave., New York, N.Y. 10017.

Astrology Now

Former bimonthly magazine for serious study of **astrology** published in the 1970s and 1980s by Llewellyn Publications in St. Paul, Minnesota.

Astrology Quarterly

Journal of the **Astrological Lodge** of the Theosophical Society of England. It is published from Theosophical headquarters at 6 Queen St., Bloomsbury, London, WCI 3AR.

Astronomical Communications

From time to time, Spiritualist mediums have delivered messages relating to astronomy. In discussing the question whether such communications have led science forward a single step, **Camille Flammarion** returned a negative answer. His conclusion was based on his own automatic scripts which were signed by Galileo and contained nothing new and on the analysis of the writings of Major General A. W. Drayson (1827–1901), professor of military surveying, reconnaissance, and practical astronomy at the Royal Military Academy in Woolwich. Under the title *The Solution of Scientific Problems by Spirits,* Drayson published an article in the journal *Light* (1884) in which he asserted that the spirit of an astronomer, communicating through a medium at his house in 1858, had made known the true orbital movement of the satellites of Uranus.

This planet was discovered by William Herschel in 1781. He observed that its satellites, contrary to all the other satellites of the solar system, traversed their orbits from east to west. The spirit communication said on this point: "The satellites of Uranus do not move in their orbits from East to West: they circle about their planet from West to East, in the same way that the moon moves round the earth. The error comes from the fact that the South Pole of Uranus was turned towards the Earth at the moment of the discovery of this planet."

Flammarion pointed out in *Mysterious Psychic Forces* (1907) that the reasoning of the spirit is false. There is abundant evidence that it was really the North Pole which was at that moment turned toward the Sun and the Earth. Regarding another claim of Drayson that a medium in 1859 disclosed the facts about the two satellites of Mars 18 years before their discovery, Flammarion stated that the claim must remain doubtful as it was not published at the time. Furthermore, after Kepler pointed out the probability of their existence, this subject was discussed several times, notably by Dean Swift and Voltaire. Of Drayson's book *Thirty Thousand Years of the Earth's Past History, Read by Aid of the Discovery of the Second Rotation of the Earth,* which seeks to explain the glacial periods and variations of climate, Flammarion says that it is full of scientific errors unpardonable in a man versed in astronomical studies.

No mention is made by Flammarion of the book *Nature's Divine Revelations* by **Andrew Jackson Davis** which, written in March 1846, speaks of nine planets. Seven planets were known at the time. The existence of an eighth was calculated by Leverrier but was not discovered until September 1846. The statement of the Poughkeepsie seer that its density is four-fifths of water agreed with later findings. The ninth planet, Pluto, was not discovered until 1930. On the other hand, Andrew Jackson Davis only spoke of four planetoids, Ceres, Pallas, Juno, and Vesta, whereas they are now numbered in hundreds.

A further indication that psychic experiences may lead to an advance in science is furnished by the dream of Rev. **Charles Tweedale** of Weston, England, of a comet in the East discoverable before sunrise. He went into the laboratory and found the comet, which was invisible to the naked eye. Shortly afterward he learned that he was preceded in the discovery by Barnard and Hartwig.

Of all the astronomers who devoted time and talent to psychic research, Flammarion's name stands foremost. His interest from 1861 onward was continuous until the time of his death. Many important books testify to his keen judgment and to the importance he attributed to this branch of science.

Another famous astronomer whose name is often mentioned in Spiritualist books was Schiaparelli, director of the Milan observatory, who participated at a number of séances with **Eusapia Palladino** in 1892 at Milan. In a letter to Camille Flammarion he stated:

"If it had been possible entirely to exclude all suspicions of deceit one would have had to recognize in these facts the beginning of a new science pregnant with consequences of the highest importance. I cannot say that I am convinced of the reality of the things which are comprised under the ill-chosen name of Spiritualism. But neither do I believe in our right to deny everything; for in order to have a good basis for denial, it is not sufficient to suspect fraud, it is necessary to prove it. These experiments, which I have found very unsatisfactory, other experimenters of great confidence and of established reputation have been able to make in more favourable circumstances. I have not enough presumption to oppose a dogmatic and unwarranted denial to proofs in which scientists of great critical ability, such as **William Crookes, Alfred Russel Wallace, Charles Richet,** and **Oliver Lodge,** have found a solid basis of fact and one worthy of their examination, to such an extent that they have given it years of study."

Schiaparelli discontinued his investigations because, as he said, "Having passed all my life in the study of nature, which is always sincere in its manifestations and logical in its processes, it is repugnant to me to turn my thoughts to the investigation of a class of truths which it seems as if a malevolent and disloyal power was hiding from us with an obstinacy the motive of which we cannot comprehend."

Flammarion believed the cautious reserves of Schiaparelli were exaggerated. He declared, after reading the records of the Milan sittings, "If fraud has sometimes crept in, still what has been accurately observed remains safe and sound and is an acquisition to science."

A fellow astronomer of Schiaparelli, Prof. Francesco Porro, who attended the same sittings and later a number of others, came to the following conclusion:

"The phenomena are real. They cannot be explained either by fraud or hallucination. From the idea of the unconscious muscular action of the spectators (put forth half a century ago by Faraday) to the projection of protoplasmic activity or to the temporary emanation from the body of the medium imagined by Lodge; from the psychiatric doctrine of Lombroso to the psycho-physiology of Ochorowitz; from the externalisation admitted by Rochas to the eso-psychism of Morselli; from the automatism of Pierre Janet to the duplication of personality of Alfred Binet—there was a perfect flood of explanation, having for their end the elimination of an exterior personality. It is not possible, and never will be, to have a scientific proof of the identity of beings who manifest themselves. It will always be possible to imagine an unknown mechanism by the aid of which elemental substance and power may be drawn from the medium and the sitters and combined in such a way as to produce the indicated effects. It will always be found possible to find in the special aptitudes of the medium, in the thought of the sitters, and even in their attitude of expectant attention, the cause of the human origin of the phenomena. Still I should be inclined to admit it (the spirit hypothesis), if I did not see the possibility that these phenomena might form part of a scheme of things still more vast. In fact, nothing hinders us from believing in the existence of forms of life wholly different from those we know, and of which the life of human beings before birth and after death forms only a special case, just as the organic life of man is a special case of animal life in general."

Other astronomers of renown whose names have gone down in the annals of psychical research are Arago, **Marc Thury, Johann Zöllner,** and Sir William Huggins. Arago made interesting experiments in 1846 with **Angelique Cottin,** "the electric girl"; Thury came to positive conclusions in his investigation of table-turning phenomena and admitted that there may exist in this world other wills than those of man and the animals, wills capable of acting on matter; Zöllner's experiments with Slade are still widely quoted in books on the subject. Crookes was assisted for some time, in his memorable experiments with **D. D. Home,** by Sir William Huggins, ex-president of the Royal Society, well known for his researches in physics and astronomy. (See also **Planetary Travels**)

Astrotalk (Newsletter)

Publication for users of astrological software; features new programs, developments, technologies, compatible hardware, and related news. Address: Matrix Software, 315 Marion Ave., Big Rapids, MI 49307.

Athanor

According to Philostratus in his *Life of Apollonius,* Athanor is an occult hill surrounded by mist except on the southern side, which is clear. It has a well, which is four paces in breadth, from which an azure vapor ascends, which is drawn up by the warm sun. The bottom of the well is covered with red arsenic. Near it is a basin filled with fire from which rises a livid flame, odorless and smokeless, and never higher or lower than the edge of the basin. Also there are two black stone reservoirs, in one of which the wind is kept, and in the other the rain. In extreme drought the rain cistern is opened and clouds escape, which water the whole country.

This description should be interpreted as alchemical symbolism, since the Athanor was also the furnace supplying heat for the alchemical process. The term Athanor is also employed to denote moral and philosophical **alchemy.**

Atkinson, William Walker (1862–1932)

Lawyer William Walker Atkinson was an important early exponent of **New Thought** metaphysics and the **occult,** and, under the name of Swami Ramacharaka, he was a pioneer advocate of Hinduism and **yoga.** Atkinson was born December 5, 1862, in Baltimore, Maryland, and began his legal career after he was admitted to the Pennsylvania bar in 1894. His promising future, however, began to dissolve as he found himself unable to cope with the pressures of the job. Doctors were unable to heal him, but in his search for health, he discovered the mind cure movement and was soon healed.

He moved to Chicago around the turn of the century and there continued his law practice but developed a second career as a metaphysical teacher and writer. His first pamphlet, "The Secret of the I AM," was freely distributed for many years. In 1900 he became the editor of *Suggestion,* a New Thought periodical, and about the same time met publisher and entrepreneur Sydney Flowers. Flowers had created the Psychic Research Company and the New Thought Publishing Company. In 1901 Atkinson became editor of Flowers's monthly *New Thought* magazine. He founded a Psychic Club and the Atkinson School of Mental Science, both of which he headquartered in the same building as Flowers's organizations.

The period of association with Flowers proved fruitful for both men. Through Flowers, Atkinson met publisher Elizabeth Towne, for whom he did a large percentage of his writing over the next decades. The first of his more than 50 books, *Thought-Force: In Business and Everyday Life,* appeared in 1900. It was followed by such prominent New Thought titles as *The Law of New Thought* (1902), *The Inner Consciousness* (1908), *How to Know Human Nature: Its Inner States and Outer Forms* (1913), and *The New Thought: Its History and Principles, or the Message of New Thought* (1915).

Soon after moving to Chicago, Atkinson became deeply involved in Hinduism and saw in yogic philosophy a parallel to his New Thought teachings. In 1903, under the pseudonym Swami Ramacharaka, Atkinson issued his first Hindu text, *Fourteen Lessons in Yoga Philosophy and Oriental Occultism.* It was followed by the *Advanced Course in Yogi Philosophy* (1904), *Hindu Yogi Science of Breath* (1904), *Hatha Yoga* (1905), *Reincarnation and the Law of Karma* (1908), and eight more. As popular as the New Thought books were, those books Atkinson wrote as Swami Ramacharaka have proved more enduring. They have remained in print to the present and have become important texts introducing Westerners to Hindu thought and practice.

Atkinson remained active as a writer and editor into the 1920s. He wrote regularly for *The Nautilus,* Elizabeth Towne's monthly, and issued one set of books he cowrote with Edward E. Beals in the early 1920s. In his later years he retired to California; he died in Los Angeles on November 22, 1932.

Sources:

Atkinson, William Walker. *The Law of New Thought: A Study of Fundamental Principles and Their Application.* Chicago: Psychic Research, 1902.

———. *The New Thought: Its History and Principles; or, the Message of New Thought.* Holyoke, Mass.: Elizabeth Towne, 1915.

———. *Thought Force: In Business and Everyday Life.* 1900. 18th ed. New York: Sydney Flower, 1903.

Swami Ramacharaka [William Walker Atkinson]. *Fourteen Lessons in Yogi Philosophy and Oriental Occultism.* Chicago: Yogi Publication Society, 1903.

———. *Reincarnation and the Law of Karma.* Yogi Publication Society, 1908.

Atlanta Astrologer

Monthly newsletter of the Metropolitan Atlanta Astrological Society; includes news of local membership, psi phenomena, and book reviews. Address: P.O. Box 12075, Atlanta, GA 30305.

Atlanteans, The

Occult society founded in London, England, by a small group guided by the spirit "Helio-Arcanophus," who claimed to have been a high priestess in the lost continent of Atlantis and who spoke through the mediumship of former actress Jacqueline Murray. The Atlanteans seek "to bring Light to this planet by endeavoring to achieve a channel of communication with the gods." Great stress is placed upon the significance of the feminine influence in world affairs, symbolized by the Egyptian goddess Isis. The society publishes the magazine *Atlantean,* a monthly newssheet, and tape recordings of the messages of Helio-Arcanophus. Address: Runnings Park, Croft Bank, West Malvern, Worchester WR14 43P, England.

Sources:

Cosmic Law and the World Today. London: Atlanteans, 1967.

The Mind, Meditation, and Healing. London: Atlanteans, 1972.

Spirit Evolution. London: Atlanteans, 1976.

Atlantis

A mythical island continent said to have existed in the Atlantic Ocean in ancient times. The earliest mention of Atlantis is found in Plato's two dialogues *Timaeus* and *Critias,* from which it emerged as a topic of fascination and speculation over the centuries. It entered occult perspectives through the writings of **Helena Petrovna Blavatsky,** cofounder of the Theosophical Society, in the nineteenth century and has been a topic of popular speculation in the twentieth century. For many, Atlantis has replaced the biblical Garden of Eden as a mythical original home for the human race.

For Plato, Atlantis was a useful myth for conveying several lessons he wanted to make about government and the nature of city-states. In the twentieth century it has been integrated into a myth about overreliance on technology as opposed to personal spiritual and psychic awareness. Plato described Atlantis as a large land located beyond the Straits of Gibraltar. It was a powerful land able to conquer much of the Mediterranean basin, but at the height of its power it was destroyed by geologic forces. Plato supposedly learned of Atlantis as a result of the Athenian lawgiver

Solon, who had brought the story to Greece from Egypt several centuries earlier.

Over time the Atlantis myth grew in proportion, so that by the Middle Ages, Atlantis had been transformed into a massive mid-Atlantic continent. Eventually it became one of the destinations visited by explorers in the European fantastic voyage literature, the most prominent being Captain Nemo in Jules Verne's *Twenty Thousand Leagues Under the Sea* (1870).

Interest in Atlantis was revived in 1882 with the publication of Ignatius Donnelly's *Atlantis, the Antediluvian World.* He argued that Atlantis was the lost origin point of humanity, the place where the race moved out of barbarism to a civilized state. For Donnelly, Atlantis explained many of the prominent similarities between the culture of Egypt and that of Latin America. He believed that the worldwide myth of the flood was really the account of Atlantis's demise.

Blavatsky adopted Donnelly's ideas and integrated Atlantis into the theosophical story of the evolution of the human race. She hypothesized the evolution of humanity through a series of "root races." **Lemuria,** the Pacific equivalent of Atlantis, was the home of the third root race; Atlantis, of the fourth root race. Earth is currently populated by the fifth root race. Blavatsky's ideas were expanded by such Theosophists as **Charles W. Leadbeater,** W. Scott Elliott, and **Rudolf Steiner.**

In the 1920s the subject of Atlantis was taken up by Scottish journalist and anthropologist **Lewis Spence,** who eventually wrote four books on the subject, beginning with *The Problem of Atlantis* (1924). He passed along speculations to psychic **Edgar Cayce** (1877–1945), who frequently spoke of Atlantis, primarily as he described the past lives of his clients. Many were seen as people who had escaped to such places as Egypt or Peru following the destruction of the continent.

Cayce pictured Atlantis as a land of high technological achievement, even by twentieth-century standards. Atlanteans understood universal forces and had learned to fly, had central heating, sonar, and television. Central to Atlantean technologies was a firestone, a large crystal that collected energy from the stars and then gave off energy to power the technology of the land. The misuse of the crystal's power led to the destruction of Atlantis.

The **Association for Research and Enlightenment,** an organization formed to promote and perpetuate Cayce's work, gathered his comments about Atlantis and published them in two books, *Atlantis: Fact or Fiction* (1962) and *Edgar Cayce on Atlantis* (1968), which called attention to a Cayce prediction that a remnant of Atlantis would emerge at the end of the 1960s near the island of Bimini. No such emergence occurred, but a number of Cayce's believers travel to the area in search of underground remnants of the continent.

Amid the numerous speculations about the location of the lost continent, one seems to have emerged as the most likely. In 1969 Greek archaeologist Angelo Galanopoulos released data he had collected on the island of Thera. Galanopoulos had discovered an ancient Minoan city, buried in layers of volcanic ash. It was the center of a once-powerful city-state that was wiped out suddenly by the volcano. With the exception of its location in the Mediterranean rather than outside the Straits of Gibraltar, it fits most precisely the several descriptions of Atlantis reported by Plato.

From Cayce the idea of Atlantis was picked up in the New Age movement. In 1982, Frank Alper, a channel from Arizona, issued an important channeled work, *Exploring Atlantis,* in which he picked up the account in Cayce's writings about the crystal on Atlantis. The three-volume work, which purports a crystal-based culture on the lost continent, became the basis of the faddish use of crystals by New Agers in the 1980s. In particular, Alper describes in some detail the techniques of **crystal healing.**

Sources:

Alper, Frank. *Exploring Atlantis.* 3 vols. Farmingdale, N.Y.: Coleman Publishing, 1982.

Cayce, Edgar. *Atlantis: Fact or Fiction.* Virginia Beach, Va.: ARE Press, 1962.

———. *Edgar Cayce on Atlantis.* New York: Paperback Library, 1968.

Donnelly, Ignatius. *Atlantis: The Antediluvian World.* New York: Harper's, 1882.

Ferro, Robert, and Michael Gromley. *Atlantis: The Autobiography of a Search.* New York: Bell Publishing, 1970.

Galanopoulos, A. G., and E. Bacon. *Atlantis.* London: Nelson, 1969.

Scott-Elliott, W. *The Story of Atlantis.* London: Theosophical Publishing House, 1896.

Spence, Lewis. *Atlantis in America.* London: E. Benn, 1925.

———. *The Problem of Atlantis.* London: Rider, 1924.

Steiner, Rudolf. *Cosmic Memory: Prehistory of Earth and Man.* West Nyack, N.Y.: Paperback Library, 1968.

Atlantis (Magazine)

Monthly publication of the Ancient Mediterranean Research Society; contains articles, book reviews, and news of the society's activities. Address: 1047 Gayley Ave., Suite 201, Los Angeles, CA 90024.

Atlantis Book Shop

One of the two most famous British bookshops specializing in occult literature (the other is **Watkins Book Shop**). Located at 49 Museum St., London W.C.1, near the British Museum, it was started 30 years ago by **Michael Houghton,** poet, writer, publisher, student of the occult, and a friend of **Aleister Crowley.** Houghton wrote under the pen name Michael Juste.

For many years the bookshop was a meeting place for occultists, long before the present occult revival. After the death of Houghton, the shop was taken over by the Collins family, who had hoped to change the character of the stock by specializing in books on science and microscopy, but the association with occultism was too strong to be broken and they were obliged to continue as an occult bookshop. It was run by Geraldine Collins and specialized in witchcraft, mythology, vampires, Atlantis, occultism, and magic rituals. Collins closed the shop in 1989, pending sale as a going concern.

The bookshop opened again in November 1989, acquired by **Psychic News** and moved from its former address of 20 Earlham St., London WC2H 9LW. This resulted in a larger and more varied stock of new and secondhand books on the paranormal, spiritualism, occult studies, and New Age topics. The newspaper *Psychic News* also acquired a new address: 2 Tavistock Chambers, Bloomsbury Way, London WC1A 2SE.

Atmadhyana

In the raja **yoga** philosophy of Sankaracharya, Atmadhyana is the fourteenth of the stages necessary to acquire the knowledge of the unity of the soul with Brahman. It is characterized as the condition of highest joy arising from the belief of the identification of the self (**Atman**) with Brahman.

Sources:

Mishra, Shri Ramamurti. *Self Analysis and Self Knowledge.* Lakemont, Ga.: CSA Press, 1977.

Atman

Usually translated "Soul" but better rendered "Self." In the Hindu religion, Atman means the union of the collective human soul with God (Brahma), eventually merged in the absolute totality of Brahman. It is believed that the soul is neither body nor mind, nor even thought, but that these are merely conditions by which the soul is clouded so that it loses its sense of oneness with God. In the Upanishads it is said, "The Self, smaller than small, greater than great, is hidden in the heart of the creature" and "In the beginning there was Self."

Sources:

Davis, Roy Eugene. *The Path of Soul Liberation.* Lakemont, Ga.: CSA Press, 1975.

Mishra, Shri Ramamurti. *Self Analysis and Self Knowledge.* Lakemont, Ga.: CSA Press, 1977.

Prabhavananda, Swami, with Frederick Manchester. *The Spiritual Heritage of India.* Garden City, N.Y.: Doubleday, 1963.

Atmaniketan Ashram

Founded to propagate the teachings of the Hindu sage **Sri Aurobindo** (1872–1950) as presented by one of his disciples, Sadhu Loncontirth. Atmaniketan maintains a residence center for individuals who desire to dedicate their lives to Aurobindo teachings and arranges classes and seminars for visitors with special emphasis on spiritual expression through painting, music, and dance. The ashram has a research library of Sri Aurobindo's writings and other Hindu spiritual works, and it issues a book catalog. The American headquarters are located at 1291 Weber St., Pomona, CA 91768. The international headquarters is in Europe at Merschstrasse 49, D-4715 Ascheberg 2, Germany.

Atreya, Bhikhan Lal (1897–1967)

Professor of philosophy at Banaras Hindu University, India. Dr. Atreya made a special study of the Yogavasishtha, an important Hindu mystical scripture, and wrote several books about it. He also wrote on parapsychology in the *Journal of the Banaras Hindu University.* He took special interest in **poltergeist** phenomena and **reincarnation** and assisted the researches of Prof. **Ian Stevenson** into certain cases suggestive of reincarnation.

Atwood, Mary Ann (1817–1910)

Author of a remarkable book, *A Suggestive Enquiry into the Hermetic Mystery,* first published in 1850 under her maiden name, M. A. South, putting forward an early statement of the theory that the true goal of **alchemy** was spiritual perfection. Atwood subsequently regretted publication, fearing that she had revealed matters that should remain secret, and she therefore bought up as many copies of the book as possible and destroyed them. However, after her death, a new edition was brought out in 1918, from one of the few surviving copies. The new edition included Atwood memorabilia and an introduction by Walter Leslie Wilmshurst.

Sources:

Atwood, Mary Ann. *A Suggestive Enquiry into the Hermetic Mystery.* 1850. Reprint, New York: Arno Press, 1976.

Atziluth

One of the three worlds of the **Kabala**; the supreme circle; the perfect revelation. According to **Éliphas Lévi,** it is represented in the biblical book of Revelation by the head of the mighty angel with the face of a sun.

Aubert, George (ca. 1920)

Nonprofessional French musical medium who claimed to play the piano under the control of classical composers. His performance was investigated in 1906 by the Institut Général Psychologique in Paris. Various tests were devised to eliminate conscious operation. They asked him to play a Mozart Sonata blindfolded and started two gramophones at the same time, leading the tubes of them into his ears. He did it to perfection. In another experiment Aubert continued playing while he read slowly and attentively a philosophical work that was put before him. The names of the spirit musicians were given as Beethoven, Berlioz, Mendelssohn, Mozart, Chopin, Schumann, Liszt, Wagner, and others. Aubert never studied harmony, technique, or improvisation. However, his improvisations were never reproduced and, all except the records taken at the Institut Général Psychologique, are lost. The story of Aubert's mediumship is told by himself in *La Mediumnité Spirite* (Paris, 1920). Similar musical mediumship has been demonstrated by **Rosemary Brown** and **Jesse F. G. Shepard.**

Aubourg, Michel (1921–)

A professor of anthropology and government official in Haiti. Aubourg was born April 1, 1921, at Les Cayes, Haiti, and studied at the University of Haiti (Bachelier ès lettres, diplôme de la Faculté d'Ethnologie) and at Northwestern University, Evanston, Illinois. He authored several books on Haitian folklore and articles on **divination** in **voudou.**

Sources:

Aubourg, Michel. *Haiti prehistorique.* Port-au-Prince, Haiti: Editiones Panorama, n.d. [1966?].

———. *Le Mouvement folklorique en Haiti.* Port-au-Prince, Haiti: Imprimerie de l'Etat, 1952.

August Order of Light

An Oriental order introduced into England in 1882 by Maurice Vidal Portman. Its object was the development of practical occultism, and it continued at Bradford, Yorkshire, as "The Oriental Order of Light." It had a ritual of three degrees, Novice, Aspirans, Viator. It adopted kabalistic forms and was governed by a Grand Master of the Sacred Crown, or *Kether,* of the **Kabala.**

August Spirits, Shelf of the

In **Japan,** it used to be customary for every house to have a room set apart, called the spirit chamber, in which there was a shelf or shrine with tablets bearing the names of the deceased members of the family, with the sole addition of the word *Mitama* (spirit). This is a species of ancestor worship and is known as "home" worship.

AUM (or OM)

A sacred sound in Hinduism, composed of three syllables—A-U-M—merging into each other. The sound is used to preface and end the reading of sacred scriptures and prayers and is used in most **mantras.** AUM is also the subject of intricate mystical symbolism as a subject for meditation and is said to contain the origin of the alphabet and all sounds. In this respect it parallels the Shemhamforasch of Jewish mysticism and the creation of the universe. The Hindu scripture Mandukya Upanishad is devoted entirely to an exposition of the mysticism of AUM.

Sources:

Prabhavananda, Swami, with Frederick Manchester. *The Spiritual Heritage of India.* Garden City, N.Y.: Doubleday, 1963.

Wood, Thomas E. *The Mandukya Upanishad and the Agama Shastra: An Investigation into the Meaning of the Vedanta.* Honolulu: University of Hawaii Press, 1990.

AUM See Association for the Understanding of Man

AUM Magazine

Monthly magazine presenting the teachings, essays, and poems of Hindu spiritual leader **Sri Chinmoy.** Address: Sri Chinmoy Centers, P.O. Box 32433, Jamaica, NY 11431.

Aura

An emanation said to surround human beings, chiefly encircling the head and supposed to proceed from the nervous system. It is described as a cloud of light suffused with various colors. This is seen clairvoyantly, being imperceptible to the physical sight.

Some authorities trace the existence of the aura in such biblical instances as the bright light shining about Moses, which the children of Israel were unable to look upon when he descended from the mountain bearing the stone tablets engraved with the Ten Commandments (Exod. 34:29–30); in the exceedingly brilliant light that shone about St. Paul's vision at the time of his conversion (Acts 9:3); and in the transfiguration of Jesus Christ, when his raiment shone so brightly that no one on Earth could match it (Matt. 17:1–2). Many of the medieval saints were said to be surrounded with a cloud of light.

It is told that when St. John of the Cross knelt at the altar in prayer, a certain brightness darted from his face. St. Philip Neri was constantly seen enveloped in light, and St. Charles Borromeo was similarly illuminated. This is said to be due to the fact that when a person is engaged in lofty thought and spiritual aspiration, the auric colors become more luminous and translucent and therefore more easily discernible.

In Christian art, around the heads of saints and the sacred characters is portrayed the halo, or nimbus, which is supposed to represent the aura. Medieval saints and mystics distinguished four different types of aura; the Nimbus, the Halo, the Aureola, and the Glory. The first two stream from the head, the aureola from the whole body, the glory is a combination of the two. Theosophists speak of five divisions: the health aura, the vital aura, the karmic aura, the aura of character, and the aura of spiritual nature. Clairvoyants often claim the ability to see the human aura. From its colors they draw inferences as to the emotional state of character. Brilliant red means anger and force; dirty red, passion and sensuality; brown, avarice; rose, affection; yellow, intellectual activity; purple, spirituality; blue, religious devotion; green, deceit and jealousy; a deeper shade of green, sympathy. Polish psychic **Stephan Ossowiecki** occasionally saw a kind of dark aura that always meant the approach of unexpected death. It is also thought that the colors of the body and clothing in medieval paintings and stained glass are intended to represent the auric colors of the person portrayed.

The crowns and distinctive headdresses worn by the kings and priests of antiquity are said to be symbolic of the aura. In many of the sacred books of the East, representations of the great teachers and holy men are given with the light extending around the whole body. Instances of this may be found in the temple caves of India and Ceylon, in the Japanese Buddhistic books, also in Egypt, Greece, Mexico, and Peru.

In occult literature the tradition of the aura is an old one. **Paracelsus** mentioned it in the sixteenth century in the following terms: "The vital force is not enclosed in man, but radiates round him like a luminous sphere, and it may be made to act at a distance. In these semi-natural rays the imagination of man may produce healthy or morbid effects. It may poison the essence of life and cause diseases, or it may purify it after it has been made impure, and restore the health."

Paracelsus said further that "Our thoughts are simply magnetic emanations, which, in escaping from our brains, penetrate into kindred heads and carry thither, with a reflection of our life, the mirage of our secrets."

A theosophical description is as follows:

"The aura is a highly complicated and entangled manifestation, consisting of many influences operating within the same area. Some of the elements composing the aura are projected from the body, others from the astral principles, and others again from the more spiritual principles connected with the "Higher Self," or permanent Ego; and the various auras are not lying one around the other, but are all blended together and occupy the same place. Guided by occult training the clairvoyant faculty may make a complete analysis of the various elements in the aura and can estimate the delicate tints of which it is composed—though all blended together—as if each were seen separately."

Classified more exactly, the divisions of the aura are stated to be (1) the health aura (2) the vital aura, (3) the karmic aura, that of the animal soul in man (4) the aura of character, and (5) the aura of the spiritual nature.

The health aura "is almost colorless, but becomes perceptible by reason of possessing a curious system of radial striation, that is to say, it is composed of an enormous number of straight lines, radiating evenly in all directions from the body." The second, or vital aura, is said to be to a certain extent under the control of the will, when it circulates within the "linga charira" or astral body, of a "delicate rosy tint, which it loses, becoming bluish as it radiates outward." The third aura is "the field of manifestation, or the mirror in which every feeling, every desire is reflected." Of this aura the colors constantly change, as seen by the clairvoyant vision. "An outburst of anger will charge the whole aura with deep red flashes on a dark ground, while sudden terror will, in a moment, change everything to a ghastly grey." The fourth aura is that of the permanent character, and is said to contain the record of the past earth life of the personality. The fifth aura is not often seen even by clairvoyants, but it is described by those who have seen it, only in the cases where the spiritual nature is the most powerful factor, as "outshining all the rest of the auras with startling brilliancy." The auric colors, it is declared, cannot be adequately described in terms of the ordinary colors discernible to the physical vision, being very much brighter and of more varied hues and shades. The symbolic meaning of these is roughly of the following order: rose, pure affection; brilliant red, anger and force; dirty red, passion and sensuality; yellow of the purest lemon color, the highest type of intellectual activity; orange, intellect used for selfish ends as well as pride and ambition; brown, avarice. Green is a color of varied significance; its root meaning is the placing of one's self in the position of another. In its lower aspects it represents deceit and jealousy; higher up in the emotional gamut, it signifies adaptability, and at its very highest, when it takes on the color of foliage, it represents sympathy, the very essence of thinking for other people. In some shades, green stands for the lower intellectual and critical faculties, merging into yellow. Blue indicates religious feeling and devotion, its various shades being said to correspond to different degrees of devotion, rising from fetishism to the loftiest religious idealism. Purple represents psychic faculty, spirituality, regality, spiritual power arising from knowledge, and occult preeminence.

Apart from occult beliefs in the aura, there is also some scientific basis. The most important experimental investigations into the subject were conducted by Dr. **Walter J. Kilner** (1847–1920) of St. Thomas Hospital in London. In the first edition of his book, *The Human Atmosphere* (1911), he describes a dicyanin screen that rendered the aura visible to normal sight. The screen was a solution of coal-tar dye between two hermetically sealed pieces of glass. Looking through it in daylight and then turning the eye to view a naked man in dim light before a dark background, three distinct radiations, all lying in the ultraviolet end of the spectrum, became visible.

The first, dark and colorless, surrounded the body to the depth of a quarter to half an inch. Kilner called this the etheric double. The second, the inner aura, extended three inches beyond. The third, the outer aura, was about a foot in depth.

Kilner tried various experiments. He found that the depth of the aura is influenced by a magnet and that it is sensitive to electric currents, completely vanishing under a negative charge from a Wimshurst machine, then increasing to an additional 50 percent after the charge dissipates. It is also affected by the vapors of various chemicals and loses brilliance in hypnosis. Illness affects both its size and color. Impairment of the mental powers causes a diminution in size and distinctness. Nervous diseases result in highly observable changes.

From all this Kilner concluded that the higher brain centers are intimately concerned in the output of auric force. This suggested an identity with the "nerve-aura" of Dr. **Joseph Rhodes Buchanan,** the first explorer of the mysteries of **psychometry,** which was postulated as early as 1852, and with the "nerve atmosphere" of Dr. Benjamin Richardson.

As death approaches, the aura gradually shrinks. No trace of it is discovered around the corpse. Kilner also claimed the discovery that the aura may be affected by an effort of will, that it may be projected to a longer distance from the body, and change its colors. He said that the auras of different people may show attraction; they may blend and become more intense. From the influence of the state of health on the aura, Kilner drew medical conclusions. Dr. Johnson of Brooklyn followed in his footsteps and based his medical diagnoses on the change in the auric color.

Important as the researches of Kilner were, he was not the first in the field. Baron **Karl von Reichenbach** asserted at an early age that the aura can be plainly seen issuing from the fingertips. Dr. **Hereward Carrington** cited a forgotten book, *Ten Years with Spiritual Mediums* published by Francis Gerry Fairfield in 1874 in America, in which the author anticipated Kilner's conclusions. Claiming that all organic structures have a special form of nerve aura, Fairfield "constantly observed that epileptics, pending the incubation of the fit, appear to be enveloped in a sensitive and highly excited nerve-atmosphere, which . . . heralds the attack; or . . . eventuates in clairvoyance and trance. Though subsensible, observation and experiment seem alike to indicate that the nerve-aura is material—an imponderable nervous ether, possibly related to the odyle. It is thus at once a force and a medium, susceptible of control by the will of the operator, and capable of sensory impression: an atmosphere to take shape of his command, and to dissolve the moment volition ceases, or, when the habit of the medium's will has become fixed in that direction, to come and pass in visible apparitions, without conscious objective impulse on his part."

As the excerpt shows, Fairfield attempted to explain in terms of "nerve-aura" the supernormal manifestations of mediums. To be all-inclusive, he endowed it with a self-directive and self-directing power.

This is essentially the same hypothesis at which **Enrico Morselli, Theodore Flournoy, Gustav Geley,** and Carrington later arrived, relative to the exteriorization of nervous energy in the case of **Eusapia Palladino.** Dr. **Paul Joire**'s experiments in the exteriorization of sensibility also lend support to the theory of the aura, and medical observations occasionally bear it out too.

In the *Annales des sciences psychiques* (July 1905), Dr. Charles Féré of the Asylum Bicêtre quoted two cases of his own experience in which he had seen neuropathic halos. The first was the case of a 28-year-old woman of a neuroarthritic family, subject to various hysterical symptoms:

"It was during an unusually painful attack, accompanied by a sensation of frontal bruising, and by cold in the cyanosic extremities, that I was struck, towards four o'clock in the afternoon (23 February 1883) by the sight of a light possessing a radius of about 20 cm., which encircled her head; the light, which was of an orange colour, diminished in intensity near the periphery. The same phenomenon was manifested around her hands. The skin, which was usually white and matt, had an orange tint of a deeper shade than the halos. The colouring of the skin had preceded, by a few seconds, the lights surrounding the head and hands which had appeared about two hours before my observation. The colouring of the skin and the lights ceased about two hours later at the moment of the habitual vomiting."

The second case was similar to the first, except that, save monthly headaches, nothing indicated nervous trouble.

Dr. O'Donnell of the Chicago Mercy Hospital controlled and confirmed Dr. Kilner's experiments; they were, according to a note by psychic researcher **Harry Price** in *Psychic Research* (June 1930), also revived by Dr. Drysdale Anderson in West Africa. He detected a distinct band "like a wreath of tobacco smoke." This smoky aura appeared to "envelope the body and stream out of the tips of the fingers like white elastic bands."

Modern scientific interest in the aura was stimulated briefly in 1970 by the development of **Kirlian photography,** which many believed made the aura visible. Kirlian photography involved taking a picture of an object placed directly onto an unexposed photonegative by sending an electric current across the film. The object would appear with a discharge of energy coming from it. The corona discharge shown surrounding objects seemed to fluctuate in interesting ways. However, when carefully controlled experiments were done, carefully regulating the pressure between the film and the object photographed, the interesting effects disappeared.

Sources:

Bagnall, Oscar. *The Origin and Properties of the Human Aura.* New Hyde Park, N.Y.: University Books, 1970.

Berger, Ruth. *The Secret Is in the Rainbow: Aura Interrelationships.* Clearwater, Fla.: Beau Geste, 1979.

Cayce, Edgar. *Auras.* Virginia Beach, Va.: ARE Press, 1970.

Johnson, Kendall L. *The Living Aura: Radiation Field Photography and the Kirlian Effect.* New York: Hawthorn Books, 1975.

Kilner, Walter J. *The Human Aura.* 1911. Reprint, New Hyde Park, N.Y.: University Books, 1965.

Krippner, Stanley, and Daniel Rubin. *The Kirlian Aura: Photographing the Galaxies of Life.* Garden City, N.Y.: Anchor Books, 1974.

Ouseley, S. G. J. *The Science of the Auras.* London: L. N. Fowler, 1970.

Roberts, Ursula. *The Mystery of the Human Aura.* London: Spiritualist Association of Great Britain, 1972.

Aurobindo, Sri (1872–1950)

Famous Hindu mystic, philosopher, and poet. Sri Aurobindo Ghosh ("Sri" is an honorific pronounced "Shree") was born Arvinda Ackroyd Ghose in Calcutta, India, on August 15, 1872, and educated in Britain, where he spent nearly 15 years. He studied in London and Cambridge, where he mastered Greek and Latin literature as well as the French, German, and Italian languages. He returned to India and worked as a teacher in Baroda, becoming a scholar in Sanskrit and other Indian languages.

After the partition of Bengal, Aurobindo became a leader of a newly formed National party with the goal of home rule. When violence broke out in Bengal, he was arrested for sedition but was acquitted. He was again arrested and acquitted, but a third prosecution commenced while he was detained in prison. During his imprisonment he underwent profound spiritual experiences, which turned him from politics to mysticism. He developed his own system of synthesized **yoga,** which he called "integral yoga." He retired from public life in 1910 and established an ashram at Pondicherry, where he lived until his death in 1950.

After his death the ashram continued under the guidance of Mira Richards (1878–1973), the wife of a French diplomat who had met Aurobindo in 1914 and embraced his philosophy. Richards became known as "the Mother." The Mother conceived of the idea of Auroville as an ideal international urban center.

Aurobindo taught that the material world should be transformed by making one's own life divine, and claimed that he had realized the "Overmind" in 1926 and was thus able to bring divine consciousness to the task of human evolution. He had retired into seclusion and from that time forward had spoken to his disciples only through the Mother. During his lifetime he wrote 30 volumes relating to the theme of *The Life Divine,* including a 23,000 line poem, *Savitri* dealing with the struggle to unite divine consciousness with historical processes.

With the approval of Indian Prime Minister Indira Gandhi, the ashram at Pondicherry inaugurated many "Sri Aurobindo Action" centers throughout India, and Aurobindo centers were also established in most major European cities and throughout the U.S. For information on Sri Aurobindo publications and organizations, contact the Sri Aurobindo Association, P. O. Box

372, High Falls, NY 12440; or Aurobindo International USA, Box 162489, 3112 O St., Sacramento, CA 95816.

Sources:

Aurobindo, Sri. *Sri Aurobindo Centenary Library.* 50 vols. Pondicherry, India: Sri Aurobindo Library Press, 1970–72.

Donnelly, Morwinna. *Founding the Life Divine.* Lower Lake, Calif.: Dawn Horse Press, 1976.

McDermott, Robert, ed. *The Essential Aurobindo.* New York: Schrocken Books, 1973.

———. *Six Pillars.* Chambersburg, Penn.: Wilson Books, 1974.

Auroville

A utopian project for a religious city in India within five miles of the Bay of Bengal, with a planned population of 50,000. The project was originally the idea of Mira Richards (1878–1973), the leading disciple of **Sri Aurobindo** (1872–1950), known as the Mother, who developed the concept in the 1950s as an extension of Aurobindo's idea. Auroville would be a place where people of good will of all nationalities could live freely as citizens of the world and obey only the truth. The plan was developed over a number of years and was finally inaugurated in 1968, when a group gathered on land adjacent to the Aurobindo Ashram north of Pondicherry, India, to lay the foundation stone. India has recognized Auroville as an international city state.

The plan of the city approximates a giant spiral galaxy. In the center is a giant sphere, the Matrimandir, a giant symbol of the community's aspiration for the divine. Spiraling out from the center are four zones, one each for residences, work, education, and culture and social relations. Citizens are expected to avoid drugs, alcohol, tobacco, and extramarital sex. Crops are grown without chemical fertilizers or insecticides, and automobiles are banned. Auroville is believed by some commentators to be the center for the next worldwide religion, based on Sri Aurobindo's teachings.

Some 500 people, mostly from India, the United States, France, Great Britain, and Holland, settled on the land and began the process of reclaiming the inhospitable site for human habitation. All was well until Richards died in 1973. Without her leadership, the project has suffered numerous internal problems and remains unfinished as of the mid-1990s. Auroville may be contacted in care of Auroville Cooperative, Aspiration, Kottakuppan, Auroville 605104, India.

Sources:

Auroville. Pondicherry, India: Sri Auroville Society, n.d.

Glenn, Jerome Clayton. *Linking the Future: Findhorn, Auroville, Arcosanti.* Cambridge, Mass.: Center on Technology and Society, 1979.

Aurum Solis (Order of the Sacred Word)

Magical society founded in 1897 by occultists Charles Kongold and George Stanton. The society is an initiatory order of the Ogdoatic tradition of the Western Mysteries. This tradition fused pre-Christian mystery teachings of the Eastern Mediterranean with the mystic teachings of the Oriental monasteries of Sinai, Carmel, and St. Sabas. Aurum Solis has had a special interest in alchemical, Gnostic, medieval, and Celtic traditions within a basic framework of kabalistic philosophy, affirmed through special rituals relating to spiritual consciousness.

After World War I, the society's membership became influenced by newer occult trends from such other organizations as the Hermetic Order of the **Golden Dawn,** but authentic kabalistic traditions were strengthened by the work of Rabbi Morris Greenburg, a noted Talmudic scholar. World War II largely suspended the society activities until 1949.

Some years later conflicting trends arose, largely around the issue of magical rituals designed to enhance consciousness and the actual use of occult powers. A schism occurred in 1957, and one group broke away to form the Hermetic Order of the Sacred Word (OSW). The main body of the Aurum Solis reaffirmed the original intent of its rituals so that "the rites and the philosophy of the Order should reflect the joy and freedom of the Spirit which has been so much a part of true Magick in all ages; and that, as in the early days of the Order, the essential standard of judgment on any practice should not simply be that of philosophic and technical correctness, but that of effectiveness."

The breakaway group, the Order of the Sacred Word, emphasized the significance of a mystical word in **Kabala.** For some years this group was enriched by the personality of their warden, Ernest Page, a noted graphologist and astrologer. Page was a kindly and well-loved figure in the bohemian culture of London's Soho, and he spent much time and energy attempting to reconcile the OSW and the Aurum Solis. Although he did not live to see this come about, the desired reunion did occur in 1971.

The Aurum Solis is currently flourishing as a private magical group. Its philosophy has been described in detail by Melita Denning and Osborne Phillips (the pen names of Vivian Barcynski and Leonard R. Barcynski) in their five-volume work, *The Magical Philosophy* (1974–81). Denning and Phillips are Adept Minores of the Aurum Solis. In 1987 Carl Weschcke became the Grand Master of the order.

Sources:

Denning, Melita, and Osborne Phillips. *The Magical Philosophy.* 5 vols. St. Paul, Minn.: Llewellyn Publications, 1974–81.

———. *The Magick of Sex.* St. Paul, Minn.: Llewellyn Publications, 1982.

———. *The Magick of Tarot.* St. Paul, Minn.: Llewellyn Publications, 1983.

Ausar Auset Society

The Ausar Auset Society, a Rosicrucian body especially oriented to meet the needs of African Americans, was founded in the mid-1970s by R. A. Straughn, formerly the head of the Rosicrucian Anthropological League in New York City. Straughn, under his adopted name Ra Un Nefer Amen, has written a number of occult texts on Hermetic and Eastern religions. He has also developed a unique **tarot** card deck.

The program of the society is directed to people of African origin, and its literature regularly integrates more familiar occult themes with material specific to African Americans, emphasizing lessons in African American history and the accomplishments of Africans. Centered in the large African community in the greater New York City area, the society also regularly holds classes in African American communities along the East Coast from Virginia to Connecticut. The society may be contacted at Box 281, Bronx, NY 10462. It publishes a magazine, *Metu Neter.*

Sources:

Ra Un Nefer Amen [R. A. Straughn]. *Black Man's Guide to a Spiritual Union.* Bronx, N.Y.: Oracle of Thoth, 1981.

———. *Meditation Techniques of the Kabalists, Vedantins, and Taoists.* Bronx, N.Y.: Maat Publishing, 1976.

———. *The Oracle of Thoth: The Kabalistical Tarot.* Bronx, N.Y.: Oracle of Thoth, 1977.

———. *The Realization of Neter Nu.* Brooklyn, N.Y.: Maat Publishing, 1975.

Austatikco-Pauligaur

A class of Persian evil spirits. Eight in number, they keep the eight sides of the world. Their names are as follows: (1) Indiren, the king of these genii; (2) Augne-Baugauven, the god of fire; (3) Eemen, king of death and hell; (4) Nerudee, earth in the figure of a giant; (5) Vaivoo, god of the air and winds; (6) Varoonon, god of clouds and rain; (7) Gooberen, god of riches; and (8) Essaunien or Shivven.

Austin Seth Center (ASC)

Organization concerned with the "**Seth**" communications channeled through **Jane Roberts** (1929–1984). It was established in 1979 by Maude Cardwell, Ph.D., to spread the ideas of the Seth Material. In September 1984, the organization became a tax-exempt, nonprofit educational corporation, with the stated purpose "to teach a philosophy that empowers people to change their personal reality with love, fun, and awareness."

The ASC published a quarterly magazine *Reality Change* "for people who want to change their lives"; holds an annual Seth World Conference each June and an annual Intensive Seminar in the Seth Material each winter; and in general networks individuals and groups throughout the world who study the Seth Material. Address: P.O. Box 7786, Austin, TX 78713-7786.

AUSTRALIA

Aboriginal Magic

From birth to death, the Australian aborigine, like most members of tribal societies, was surrounded by magical influences. In many tribes the power to perform **magic,** sympathetic or otherwise, was possessed by only a few people, but among the central tribes it was practiced by both men and women—more often, however, by the former, who conserved the knowledge of certain forms of their own. There was also among them a distinct class of medicine men, whose duty it was to discover whose magic had caused the death of anyone. Among the central tribes, unlike many others, magic was not made a means of profit or emolument. Women were often sternly forbidden to go near the places where the men performed their magical ceremonies. To frighten them away from such spots, the men invented an instrument called a "bull-roarer"—a thin slip of wood swung at the end of a string that makes a screaming, whistling noise, which was believed to be the voice of the Great Spirit. Aborigines also preserved long oval pieces of wood, which they call *churingas.* Since the spirits of their ancestors were thought to reside within, these were kept concealed in the most secret manner.

Sympathetic magic is integral to aboriginal practice. Certain ceremonies are employed to control nature to ensure a plentiful supply of food and water, or to injure an enemy. One of the commonest forms is the use of the pointed stick or bone, which is used in one form or another by all Australian tribes. The former is a small piece of wood, varying in length from three to eighteen inches, resembling a skewer, and tapering to a point. At the handle end it is topped with a knob of resin, to which is attached a strand of human hair. Magical songs are sung over it, to endow it with occult potency. The man who wishes to use it goes into the bush alone, or with a friend, where he will be free from observation, and planting the stick in the ground, mutters over it what he desires to happen to his enemy. It is then left in the ground for a few days. The evil magic is supposed to proceed from the stick to the man, who often succumbs, unless a medicine man chances to discover the implement.

The Australian aborigine has a special dread of magic connected with places at a distance, and any magical apparatus purchased or obtained from faraway tribes is supposed to possess potency of a much greater kind than if it had been made among themselves. Thus certain little stones traded by Northern tribes are supposed to contain a very powerful form of evil magic called *mauia.* These are wrapped up in many folds of bark and string. According to their traditions this type of magic was first introduced by a "batman," who dropped it to Earth, where it made a great explosion at a certain spot where it can still be procured. Sticks procured from a distance, with which the natives chastise their wives, are sufficient by their very sight to make the women obey their husbands.

Much mystery surrounds what are known as "debil-debil" shoes, which consist of a pad of emu feathers, rounded at both ends, in order that no one should be able to trace in which direction the wearer is journeying. These are supposed to be worn by a being called *kurdaitcha,* to whom deaths are attributed. The Australian aborigine believes that death is due to evil magic. A man may become a *kurdaitcha* by submitting to a certain ceremony, in which the little toe of his foot is dislocated. Dressed up and painted grotesquely, he sets out accompanied by a medicine man and wearing the *kurdaitcha* shoes when he desires to slay an enemy. When he spears him, the medicine man closes up the wound, and the victim returns to consciousness oblivious to the fact that he is full of evil magic, but when he later sickens and dies, it is known that he has been attacked by a *kurdaitcha.* Many long and elaborate ceremonies are connected with the *churinga.*

In 1988 the bicentenary celebrations in Australia placed primary emphasis on the achievements of the colonists, against a background of protest from displaced aborigines. Traditional aborigine beliefs and life-styles have suffered severe disruption. Displaced from their own lands, their world of supernatural beliefs shattered by the materialism of white society, many aborigines have succumbed to the alcohol introduced by the settlers, or to suicide. Others endure a miserable poverty-stricken existence, stranded between two contradictory cultures. A few successfully adapted aborigine artists have been acclaimed for their expressive and visionary paintings and poetry.

Spiritualism in Australia

Spiritualism seems to have first become a public issue in Australia in the 1860s when, in Victoria, a gentleman of considerable wealth and learning, writing under the pen name of "Schamlyn," entered into a heated controversy with the editor of the *Collingwood Advertiser* in defense of Spiritualism. Another influential supporter of the Spiritual cause who was an early convert, and for a time became a pillar of strength in its maintenance, was a gentleman connected with the editorial department of the *Melbourne Argus,* one of the leading journals of Victoria, and an organ well calculated to exert a powerful sway over the minds of its readers.

As the tides of public opinion moved on, doctors, lawyers, merchants, and men of eminence began to join the ranks. Tidings of phenomena of the most astounding character poured in from distant towns and districts. Members of the press began to share the general enthusiasm, and although some would not, and others could not, avow their convictions, their private prepossessions induced them to open their columns for debate and correspondence on the subject.

To add to the stimulus imparted, many of the leading colonial journals indulged in tirades of abuse and misrepresentation, which only served to increase the influence without in the least diminishing its force. At length the clergy began to manifest their interest by furious abuse. Denunciation provoked retort; discussion compelled investigation. In Sydney, many converts of rank and influence suddenly appeared. The Hon. John Bowie Wilson, land minister and a champion of temperance, converted to Spiritualism, and his public defense of the cause led many to begin their own investigation. Among many who affiliated with the cause in Sydney were several members of the New South Wales Parliament and Cabinet, the attorney general, and several judges. Possibly most influential of all was William Terry, the editor of the Melbourne *Harbinger of Light.* As American Spiritualist writer Hudson Tuttle notes:

"About 1869 the necessity for a Spiritualistic journal was impressed deeply on the mind of Mr. Terry. He could not cast it off, but pondered over the enterprise. At this time, an exceedingly sensitive patient described a spirit holding a scroll on which was written 'Harbinger of Light' and the motto, 'Dawn approaches, error is passing away; men arising shall hail the day.' This influenced him, and in August 1870, he set to work to prepare the first number, which appeared on the 1st of September of that year.

"There was no organization in Australian Spiritualism, and Mr. Terry saw the advantage and necessity of associative movement. He consulted a few friends, and in November 1870, he organized the first Victorian Association of Spiritualists. A hall was rented, and Sunday services, consisting of essays and reading by members, enlivened by appropriate hymns, were held. In October 1872, impressed with the desirability of forming a Lyceum, he called together a few willing workers, and held the first session on October 20th, 1872. It is, and has been from the first in a flourishing condition, numbering 150 members, with a very handsome and complete outfit, and excellent library. He has remained an officer ever since, and conducted four sessions. He assisted in the establishment of the Spiritualist and Free-thought Association, which succeeded the original one, and was its first president. He has lectured occasionally to appreciative audiences, and his lectures have been widely circulated. His mediumship, which gave such fair promise, both in regard to writing and speaking, became controlled, especially for the relief of the sick. Without the assistance of advertising he had acquired a fine practice. With this he combines a trade in Reform and Spiritualistic publications, as extensive as the colony, and the publication of the *Harbinger of Light,* a Spiritual journal that is an honor to the cause, and well sustains the grand philosophy of immortality. No man is doing more for the cause, or has done more efficient work."

A short but interesting summary of the rise and progress of Spiritualism in Australia is given in the American *Banner of Light* in 1880, in which Terry's pioneering efforts are again lauded.

"*The Harbinger of Light,* published at Melbourne, Australia, furnishes a review of the origin of its publication and the work it has accomplished during the ten years just closed. At its advent in 1870, considerable interest had been awakened in the subject of Spiritualism, by the lectures of Mr. Nayler, in Melbourne, and Mr. Leech, at Castlemaine. The leaders of the church became disturbed, and seeing their gods in danger, sought to stay the progress of what would eventually lessen their influence and possibly their income. But Mr. Nayler spoke and wrote with more vigor; the addresses of Mr. Leech were published from week to week in pamphlet form, and widely distributed. At the same time, Mr. Charles Bright, who had published letters on Spiritualism in the *Argus,* over an assumed name, openly identified himself with the movement, and spoke publicly on the subject. Shortly after, 11 persons met and formed an association, which soon increased to 80 members. A hymn book was compiled, and Sunday services began. As elsewhere, the press ridiculed and the pulpit denounced Spiritualism as a delusion. A number of articles in the *Argus* brought some of the facts prominently before the public, and the growing interest was advanced by a public discussion between Messrs. Tyerman and Blair. In 1872, a Sunday school, on harmonial principles, was established, Mr. W. H. Terry, the proprietor of the *Harbinger,* being its first conductor. Almost simultaneously with this was the visit of Dr. J. M. Peebles, whose public lectures and work in the Lyceum served to consolidate the movement. A controversy in the *Age,* between Rev. Mr. Potter, Mr. Tyerman and Mr. Terry, brought the facts and teachings of Spiritualism into further notice.

"Soon came Dr. Peebles, Thomas Walker, Mrs. Britten and others, who widened the influence of the spiritualistic philosophy, and aided the *Harbinger* in its efforts to establish Spiritualism on a broad rational basis. Mr. W. H. Terry is deserving of all praise for his unselfish and faithful exertions in carrying the *Harbinger* through the years of as hard labor as ever befell any similar enterprise, and we bespeak for him, in his continued efforts to make known the evidences of a future existence, and the illuminating truths of Spiritualism, the hearty co-operation and sympathy of all friends of the cause."

Writing to the *Banner of Light* on the subject of Anglican clergyman J. Tyerman's accession to the Spiritualist ranks, an American correspondent states,

"The Rev. J. Tyerman, of the Church of England, resident in one of the country districts, boldly declared his full reception of Spiritualism as a great fact, and his change of religious faith consequent upon the teachings of spirits. Of course, he was welcomed with open arms by the whole body of Spiritualists in Melbourne, the only city where there was any considerable number enrolled in one association. He soon became the principal lecturer, though not the only one employed by the association, and well has he wielded the sword of the new faith. He is decidedly of the pioneer stamp, a skillful debater, a fluent speaker, ready at any moment to engage with any one, either by word of mouth or as a writer. So widely, indeed, did he make his influence felt, and so individual was it, that a new society grew up around him, called the Free-Thought and Spiritualist Propaganda Society, which remained in existence till Mr. Tyerman removed to Sydney, when it coalesced with the older association, under the combined name of Melbourne Spiritualist and Free-Thought Association."

Another valuable convert to the cause of Spiritualism, at a time when it most needed good service, was Florence Williams, the daughter of the celebrated English novelist G. P. R. James. She officiated for many years at the first Spiritualist meetings convened for Sabbath Day exercises and was an eloquent lecturer.

The visits of several zealous propagandists have been alluded to in previous quotations. Among the first to break ground as a public exponent of Spiritualism was the Rev. **James Martin Peebles,** formerly a minister of Battle Creek, Michigan. Peebles was well known in the United States as a capable writer and lecturer. He visited Australia on two occasions several years apart and in his account, which appeared in the *Banner of Light* some five years after his first visit, he described the changed spirit that marked both the progress of the movement and the alteration in the tone of public opinion.

"Relative to Spiritualism and its divine principles, public sentiment has changed rapidly, and for the better, during the past five years. Upon my late public appearance in Melbourne, the Hon. John McIlwraith, ex-mayor of the city, and commissioner of our Centennial Exhibition, took the chair, introducing me to the audience. On my previous visit some of the Spiritualists seemed a little timid. They preferred being called investigators, remaining a good distance from the front. Then my travelling companion, Dr. Dunn was misrepresented, and meanly vilified in the city journals; while I was hissed in the market, caricatured in *Punch,* burlesqued in a theatre, and published in the daily press as an 'ignorant Yankee,' an 'American trickster,' a 'long-haired apostate,' and 'a most unblushing blasphemer.' But how changed! Recently the secular press treated me fairly. Even the usually abusive *Telegraph* published Mr. Stevenson's article assuring the Rev. Mr. Green that I was willing to meet him at once in a public discussion. The *Melbourne Argus,* one of the best daily papers in the world, the *Australasian,* the *Herald,* and the *Age,* all dealt honorably by me, reporting my lectures, if briefly, with admirable impartiality. The press is a reflector; and those audiences of 2,000 and 2,500 in the great Opera House on each Sunday for several successive months, were not without a most striking moral significance. It seemed to be the general opinion that Spiritualism had never before occupied so prominent yet so favorable a position in the eyes of the public. . . ."

Peebles initially introduced Thomas Walker, a young Englishman, to Australia. Alleging himself to be a "trance speaker" under the control of certain spirits, whom he named, Walker lectured in Sydney, Melbourne, and other places. In March 1878 Walker participated in a debate with a Rev. M. Green, a minister of the Churches of Christ, an American free-church denomination that perpetuated that peculiarly nineteenth-century form of public religious discourse. Green had acquired some reputation in Australia both as a preacher and as one bitterly opposed to Spiritualism, which he constantly ridiculed. The debate, held in the Temperance Hall, Melbourne, attracted large audiences, and was extended for several nights beyond the period originally agreed upon.

Spiritualism was also promoted by the visits of **Emma Hardinge Britten** and medium **Henry Slade.** The *Melbourne Age* of August 20th, 1878, recorded their activities.

"Spiritualism is just now very much to the front in Melbourne. The lectures of Emma Hardinge Britten, delivered to crowded audiences at the Opera House every Sunday evening, have naturally attracted a sort of wondering curiosity to the subject, and the interest has probably been intensified by the strenuous efforts that are being made in some of the orthodox pulpits to prove that the whole thing is an emanation from the devil. The announcement that the famous Dr. Slade had arrived to strengthen the ranks of the Spiritualists, has therefore been made at a very critical juncture, and I should not be surprised to find that the consequence will be to infuse a galvanic activity into the forces on both sides. Though I do not profess to be a Spiritualist, I own to having been infected with the fashionable itch for witnessing 'physical manifestations,' as they are called, and accordingly I have attended several circles with more or less gratification. But Slade is not an ordinary medium even among professionals. The literature of the Spiritualists is full of his extraordinary achievements, attested to all appearance by credible witnesses, who have not been ashamed to append their names to their statements. . . . I see that on one occasion, writing in six different languages was obtained on a single slate, and one day, accompanied by two learned professors, Slade had a sitting with the Grand Duke Constantine, who obtained writing on a new slate held by himself alone. From St. Petersburg, Slade went to Berlin, where he is said to have obtained some marvelous manifestations in the house of Professor **Johann Zöllner,** and where he was visited by the court conjurer to the Emperor, Samuel Bellachini. . . . My object in visiting Slade can be understood when I was introduced to him with my friend, whom I shall call Omega, and who was bent on the same errand. Slade and Mr. Terry constituted the circle of four who sat around the table in the center of the room almost as immediately as we entered it. There was nothing in the room to attract attention. No signs of confederacy, human or mechanical. The hour was eleven in the morning. The window was unshuttered, and the sun was shining brightly. The table at which we sat was a new one, made especially by Wallach Brothers, of Elizabeth Street, of polished cedar, having four slight legs, one flap, and no ledges of any kind underneath. As soon as we examined it Slade took his seat on one side, facing the window, and the rest of us occupied the other three seats. He was particularly anxious that we should see he had nothing about him. It has been said that he wrote on the slate by means of a crumb of pencil stuck in his finger-nails, but his nails were cut to the quick, while his legs and feet were ostentatiously placed away from the table in a side position, exposed to view the whole time. He first produced a slate of the ordinary school size, with a wet sponge, which I used to it. A chip of pencil about the size of a grain of wheat was placed upon it on the table; we joined hands, and immediately taps were heard about the table, and in answer to a question—'Will you write?'—from Slade, three raps were given, and he forthwith took up the slate with the pencil lying on it, and held half of it under the table by his finger and thumb, which clasped the corner of the half that was outside the table, and was therefore easily seen by all present. His left hand remained near the center of the table, resting on those of the two sitters on either side of him. Several convulsive jerks of his arm were now given, then a pause, and immediately the sound of writing was audible to every one, a scratching sound interrupted by the tap of the pencil, which indicated, as we afterwards found, that the t's were being crossed and the i's dotted. The slate was then exposed, and the words written were in answer to the question which had been put by Omega as to whether he had psychic power or not. I pass over the conversation that ensued on the subject, and go on to the next phenomenon. To satisfy myself that the 'trick' was not done by means of sympathetic writing on the slate, I had ten minutes previously purchased a slate from a shop in Bourke Street, containing three leaves, and shutting up book fashion. This I produced, and Slade readily repeated his performance with it. It was necessary to break the pencil down to a mere crumb, in order to insert it between the leaves of the slate. This done, the phenomenon at once recurred with this rather perplexing difference, that the slate, instead of being put half under the table, forced itself by a series of jerks on to my neck, and reposed quietly under my ear, in the eyes of everyone present. The scratching then commenced; I heard the t's crossed and the i's dotted by the moving pencil, and at the usual signal I opened the slate, and found an intelligible reply to the question put. . . . The next manifestation was the levitation of one of the sitters in his chair about a clear foot from the ground, and the levitation of the table about two feet. I ought to have mentioned that during the whole of the *séance* there was a good deal of by-play going on. Everyone felt the touch of hands more or less, and the sitters' chairs were twice wrenched from under them, or nearly so, but the psychic could not possibly have done it. . . .''

Britten includes her own reflections in her *Nineteenth Century Miracles* (1883):

''As personal details are more graphic than the cold narrations of passing events, we deem it expedient in this place to give our readers an inside view of Spiritualism in Australia, by republishing one of the many articles sent by the author to the American Spiritual journals during her sojourn in the colonies. The following excerpt was written as the result of personal experience, and at a time when Spiritualism, in the usual inflated style of journalistic literature was 'in the zenith of its triumphs.' It is addressed to the Editor of the *Banner of Light,* and reads as follows:

'''Spiritualism in these colonies finds little or no public representation outside of Melbourne or Sydney, nevertheless warm friends of the cause are scattered all over the land, and endeavors are being made to enlarge the numerous circles into public meetings, and the fugitive efforts of whole-hearted individuals into associations as powerful as that which exists in Melbourne. At present, the attempt to effect missionary work in any portions of Australia outside Sydney or Melbourne, becomes too great a burden to the luckless individual, who has not only to do the work, but to bear the entire cost of the undertaking, as I have had to do in my visits to various towns in Victoria. Expenses which are cheerfully divided amongst the many in the United States, become all too heavy for endurance when shouldered upon the isolated workers; hence the paucity of public representation, and the impossibility of those who visit the colonies, as I have done, effecting any important pioneer work beyond the two great centers I have named. Mr. Walker at Sydney, and I at Melbourne, have been favored with the largest gatherings ever assembled at colonial Sunday meetings.

'''Having, by desire of my spirit guides, exchanged rostrums, he filling my place at Melbourne, and I his at Sydney, we find simultaneously at the same time, and on the same Sundays, the lessees of the two theaters we occupied raising their rent upon us one hundred and fifty per cent. The freethinkers and Spiritualists had occupied the theatre in Sydney four years at the rate of four pounds per Sunday. For my benefit the landlord raised the rent to ten pounds, whilst the same wonderful spirit of accordance caused the Melbourne manager to increase upon Mr. Walker from eight pounds to a demand of twenty. With our heavy expenses and small admission fees this was tantamount to driving us out altogether. Both of us have succeeded after much difficulty, and fighting Christian warriors with the Christian arms of subtlety and vigilance, in securing other places to lecture in; and despite the fact that the press insult us, the pulpit curse us, and Christians generally devote us to as complete a prophecy of what they would wish us to enjoy everlastingly as their piety can devise, we are each attracting our thousands every Sunday night, and making such unmistakable marks on public opinion as will not easily be effaced again. . . .

'''Dr. Slade's advent in Melbourne since last September has been productive of an immense amount of good. How far his labors here will prove remunerative I am not prepared to say. Frankly speaking, I do not advise Spirit Mediums or speakers to visit these colonies on financial advancement intent. There is an abundant crop of Medium power existing, interest enough in the cause, and many of the kindest hearts and clearest brains in the world to be found here; but the lack of organization, to which I have before alluded, and the imperative necessity for the workers who come here to make their labors remunerative, paralyses all attempts at advancement, except in the sensation line. Still I feel confident that with united action throughout the scattered force of Spiritualistic thought in these colonies, Spiritualism might and would supersede every other phase of religious thought in an incredibly short space of time. I must not omit to mention that the friends in every place I have visited have been more than kind, hospitable and appreciative. The public have defied both press and pulpit in their unstinted support of my lectures. The press have been equally servile, and the Christian world equally stirred, and equally active in desperate attempts to crush out the obvious proofs of immortality Spiritualism brings.

"'In Melbourne, I had to fight my way to comply with an invitation to lecture for the benefit of the City Hospital. I fought and conquered; and the hospital committee revenged itself for a crowded attendance at the Town Hall by taking my money without the grace of thanks, either in public or private, and the simply formal acknowledgement of my services by an official receipt. In Sydney, where I now am, I was equally privileged in lecturing for the benefit of the Temperance Alliance, and equally honored, after an enthusiastic and successful meeting, by the daily press of the city in their utter silence concerning such an important meeting, and their careful record of all sorts of such trash as they disgrace their columns with. So mote it be. The wheel will turn some day!'"

During the years 1881 and 1882 the Australians were favored with visits from three more well-known American Spiritualists. The first of these was **William Denton,** an able and eloquent lecturer on geology, who usually combined his scientific addresses with one or more lectures on Spiritualism. The community also welcomed Ada Foye, a test-writing, **rapping,** and seeing medium, and Mrs. E. L. Watson, a trance-speaker.

All was not an upward path, however, as about this same time the government, through its chief secretary, promulgated an interdict against the proprietor of the Melbourne Opera House, forbidding him to allow Spiritualists to take money at the door for admission to their services, and in effect, forbidding them to hold services there at all. Walker, Peebles, and Britten had occupied the Opera House for months together, and admission fees had been charged regularly at each of their Sunday services, without let or hindrance. As reported in the *Harbinger of Light* of March 1882, Spiritualists organized to fight the new policy.

Psychical Research

Psychical research in Australia can be traced to 1864 when it briefly arose in response to the mediumship of William Archer, a table tilter. It soon died out, however, when it was discovered that Archer was not producing any paranormal phenomena. During Slade's 1878 visit to Sydney, E. Cyril Haviland, latter the author of two pamphlets and other writings on Spiritualism, was initially convinced of the truth of Spiritualism. Haviland, Harold Stephen, and several other gentlemen of literary repute in Sydney combined to form a Psychological Society, the members of which included some leading citizens of the city. However, the society was shortlived. Through the early 1900s, there were sporadic informal attempts to conduct some psychical research, but no sustained interest was generated.

A Society for Psychic Research was organized at Melbourne University in 1948 but soon disbanded. Psychical research was thus still in its infancy in the 1950s when a few courses in parapsychology began to be offered in Australian universities. The first degree in parapsychology was issued in 1960 from the University of Tasmania. Slowly through the 1980s, with the leadership of the likes of Ronald K. H. Rose, **Raynor Johnson, Michael John Scriven, H. H. J. Keil,** and Michael A. Thalbourne, a psychical research community had arisen, in spite of an hostile academic environment.

Currently there is an Australian Institute of Psychic Research (P. O. Box, Lane Cove, NSW 2066) and an Australian Society for Psychical Research, headquartered at Murdoch University in Western Australia. The institute publishes a bulletin, and the society issues *Psi,* a newsletter.

Sources:

Berger, Arthur S., and Joyce Berger. *The Encyclopedia of Parapsychology and Psychical Research.* New York: Paragon House, 1991.

Britten, Emma Hardinge. *Nineteenth Century Miracles.* New York, 1870. Reprint, New Hyde Park, N.Y.: University Books, 1970.

Drury, Nevill, and Gregory Tillett. *Other Temples/Other Gods: The Occult in Australia.* Sydney: Hodder & Stoughton, 1982.

Johnson, Raynor C. *The Imprisoned Splendour.* New York: Harper & Brothers, 1953.

———. *Nurslings of Immortality.* London: Hodder and Stoughton, 1957.

———. *The Spiritual Path.* New York: Harper & Brothers, 1971.

———. *Watcher on the Hills.* New York: Harper & Brothers, 1959.

Rose, Ronald. *Living Magic: The Realities Underlying the Psychical Practices and Beliefs of Australian Aborigines.* New York: Rand McNally, 1956.

Australian Society for Psychical Research

The Australian Society for Psychical Research was founded in the early 1980s by Dr. J. Frodsham, a professor at the School of Communication at Murdoch University, Murdoch, Western Australia. It has functioned as an organization disseminating information on **psychical research, parapsychology,** and related issues in Western Australia. To that end it sponsors seminars and lectures and publishes a newsletter, *Psi.* It may be contacted through Frodsham at Murdoch University, Murdoch, WA 6153, Australia.

Australian UFO Bulletin

Quarterly publication of Victorian UFO Research Society, Box 43, Moorabbin, Victoria, Australia 3189.

AUSTRIA

(For ancient magic among the Teutonic people of Austria, see the entry on the **Teutons;** see also **Hungary**).

Mesmerism

As **Spiritualism** spread across Europe in the 1860s and 1870s, it came also to Austria. The movement was first promulgated by Constantine Delby of Vienna, an adherent of the French **Spiritism** of **Allan Kardec.** Delby founded a Spiritualist society and started a journal. However, the society found little support and was kept alive primarily by Delby's enthusiasm. Spiritualism never obtained much foothold in Vienna. A number of Austrians, such as the mediums **Willi and Rudi Schneider** (from Braunau) attained their fame elsewhere.

It was quite otherwise in Budapest (and at this time Hungary was then part of the larger Austrian Empire). Here a considerable amount of interest was awakened, and many persons of note began to take part in the circles that were being formed there. Among these persons were Anton Prohasker and Dr. Adolf Grunhut. At length a society was formed, and Baron Edmund Vay was elected president. A Mr. Lishner, of Budapest, built a séance room, which the society rented. At that time there were some 110 members, all professing Christians. Vay served as the honorary president, and Grunhut as the active president. The principles of the society, indeed the basis of it, were taken from the *Geist Kraft Stoff* of **Baroness Adelma Vay** and the works of Kardec. It never encouraged paid mediumship. All the officers were voluntary and honorary. It had no physical **medium,** but good trance, writing, and seeing mediums.

Psychical Research

Though Austria has not been a center of parapsychology, there is an Austrian Society for Psychic Research (c/o Prof. Dr. H. Hofman, c/o Technische Hochschule, Gusshausstr. 25,

Vienna). Possibly the best known figure in Austrian parapsychology is Andreas Resch, who edited *Imago Mundi* (former publication of the International Society for Catholic Parapsychologists). Resch has conducted courses in parapsychology at Lateran University in Rome. Resch now edits *Grenzgebiete der Wissenschaft* as the organ of the Institut für Grenzgebiete der Wissenschaft und von Imago Mundi (Resch Verlag, Maximilianstr. 8. Postfach 8 A-6010 Innsbruck).

There is also an International School for Psycho-Physical Training (Bartlemae 17, 9110 Poertschach/ Woerthersee, Kaernten, Austria) and the Arbeitsgemeinschaft für Parapsycholige (Himmelspfortgasse 9/Tür 11, A-1010 Vienna) headed by Gustav Pscholka. Franz Seidl, an electronics engineer from Vienna, has experimented with paranormal taped voices (now generally known as **electronic voice phenomenon**).

Austromancy

A form of **divination** through aerial phenomena, such as thunder and lightning, and a branch of **aeromancy.** Austromancy is concerned with the observance and interpretation of winds, and the significance being attached to their direction and intensity. (See also **Chaomancy**)

Autography

A term sometimes used to denote the Spiritualist phenomenon of **direct writing.**

Automatic Drawing and Painting

The phenomenon of artistic expression without control of the conscious self belongs to the same category as **automatic writing,** but neither necessarily involves the other.

Mrs. William Wilkinson, the wife of one of the pioneer English Spiritualists, could draw, paint, and play music automatically, but she could not produce automatic writing. Her husband developed both gifts. An interpretation of the flowers of joy, love, humility, faith, and the architectural designs emanating from under his wife's hand was forthcoming in his automatic scripts. After many weeks of vain trial, the power of automatic drawing burst forth on William Wilkinson in the following way:

"After waiting less than five minutes it [the pencil] began to move, at first slowly, but presently with increased speed, till in less than a quarter-of-an-hour it moved with such velocity as I had never seen in a hand and arm before, or since. It literally ran away in spiral forms; and I can compare it to nothing else than the fly-wheel of an engine when it was run away. This lasted until a gentleman present touched my arm, when suddenly it fell like an infant's as it goes to sleep, and the pencil dropped out of my hand. I had, however, acquired the power. The consequences of the violent motion of the muscles of the arm were so apparent that I could not for several days lift it without pain."

In most cases visions are being presented to the automatist, and the idea to sketch then comes to him naturally. Georgiana Houghton in *Evenings at Home in Spiritual Séance* (1881) wrote of a Mrs. Puget who saw upon a blank paper "a lovely little face, just like a photograph, which gradually disappeared; then another became visible on another part of the sheet, and they arrested her attention so much that she thought she would like to catch the fleeting image, which she did with a piece of burnt cork, thinking that a piece of pencil would be too trying for her sight." **William Blake** sketched his spiritual visitants as if they were posing. He drew them with the utmost alacrity and composure, looking up from time to time as though he had a real sitter before him. If the vision disappeared, he stopped working until it returned. He wrote: "I am really intoxicated with vision every time I hold a pencil or pen in my hand."

Héléne Smith painted in trance a series of tableaus on biblical subjects in colors. Her fingers moved incoherently over the canvas, executing different details in different parts which later merged into a harmonious whole. She was very slow. The execution of a big picture took more than a year. The vision always returned.

Elizabeth d'Esperance saw a luminous cloud concentrate itself in the darkest corner of the room, become substantial, and form itself into the figure of a child. Nobody else saw the figure, but she could sketch it in the dark, being unconscious of the extraordinary circumstances that she could see the paper and pencil perfectly well. Spirit sketching became a regular phase of her mediumship for a considerable time, but the power waned; the luminosity of the apparitions decreased as soon as she began to study sketching and became more self-conscious of her work.

Dr. **John Ballou Newbrough,** the automatist of *Oahspe,* could paint with both hands at once in total darkness. **Susannah Harris,** being blindfolded on a platform, executed in two hours an oil painting upside-down.

There are various degrees of such automatic activity from inspiration to obsession. The fantastic designs of **Victorien Sardou**—scenes on the Planet Jupiter, the House of Mozart, the House of Zoroaster—were inspired, as he felt it, by Bernard Palissy. In the celebrated Thompson-Gifford case, the impulse amounted to obsession (see **possession and obsession**).

Heinrich Nusslein, a German automatist of the 1920s, developed his powers of painting under the effect of the suggestion of a friend. In approximately two years he painted 2,000 pictures; small pictures took three or four minutes and the largest works took no more than 30 or 40 minutes. Many of them were painted from visions and in complete darkness. Nusslein made portraits of distant sitters by psychometric rapport or by concentrating on a name. His paintings have considerable artistic merit. Augustine Lesage, the French miner painter, produced his first work in 1918 at the age of 35 after attending some séances. In 10 years he produced 57 canvases, the conceptions of which are harmonious and suggest an innate genius for color. He always began at the top of the canvas and worked his way down. Lesage, who believed himself to be the reincarnation of an old Egyptian painter, experienced an inner prompting before he began to paint. In 1926 the Society of French Artists exhibited some of his works.

Marjan Gruzewski, the Polish painting medium, experienced a preponderant subconscious life from early childhood. At school his hand would write something other than what had been dictated; if he tried to write what he was told to do, the pen dropped out of his hand. When he first came into contact with **Spiritualism,** he was discovered to be a medium for telekinesis, ectoplasmic phenomena, and trance mediumship in general. His gifts of automatic painting were discovered at the age of 18 or 19 after the end of the war. In a state of trance and in full daylight, he could produce pictorial representations of anything suggested—scenes from the spirit world, historical events, striking portraits of dead people whom he did not know in life—the compositions were often interwoven with grinning demons and weird faces. In Paris at the Institut Métapsychique, he drew designs and painted portraits in complete darkness, although these were inferior to those produced in light. The quality improved with red light, even if it never reached the table where he was working. Gruzewski also painted portraits under psychometric influence. Before his automatic activity developed, he knew nothing of designing or painting.

Since talented painters, like Ferdinand Desmoulin and Hugo d'Alesi, produced automatic pictures, subconscious activity might well explain the case. But that the explanation is not always satisfactory is well shown by the case of Marguerite Burnat-Provins, a very able author and painter. At the outbreak of World War I, when the church bells tolled out the mobilization order, she was seized by a great emotion, and sudden voices impelled her to write. Later the voice was accompanied by a vision, which she drew with lightninglike quickness. The visions, which represented symbolical character pictures, were sometimes felt subjectively but were often seen objectively in natural colors in space. They developed on some occasions from a cloud-like formation and assumed a great variety of shapes and contents. Over 1,000 pictures were produced by summer 1930, when Dr. **Eugèn Osty** published the result of his study in the *Revue Métapsychique* Burnat-Provins felt anguished if she tried to resist the temptation to draw the visions as soon as they presented themselves, and an exhaustion followed or sometimes preceded the phenomenon. The works produced during these episodes differ entirely in style and character from the painter's ordinary work; most of them resemble caricatures, which she attributed to an extraneous influence.

John Bartlett produced automatic sketches of **Glastonbury Abbey,** bringing out archaeologically verified details with an amazing precision. Bartlett would begin at the left-hand top corner and work downward.

The tremendous speed with which the automatic execution takes place is one of the most puzzling features of this psychic activity. The Seeress of Prevorst (**Frederica Hauffe**) drew complicated geometrical designs. "She threw off the whole drawing," wrote Dr. **Justinus Kerner,** "in an incredibly short time, and employed, in marking the more than a hundred points into which this circle was divided, no compasses or instruments whatever. She made the whole with her hand alone, and failed not in single point. She seemed to work as a spider works its geometric diagrams, without a visible instrument. I recommended her to use a pair of compasses to strike the circles; she tried, and made immediate blunders." **William Howitt,** who had the gift of automatic drawing for five years, wrote on this point: "Having myself, who never received a single lesson in drawing, and never could draw in a normal condition, had a great number of circles struck through my hand under spirit influence, and these filled up with tracing of ever-new invention, without a thought of my own, I at once recognized the truth of Kerner's statement."

F. W. H. Myers observed that independent drawings often exhibit a fusion of arabesque with ideography; that is to say, they partly resemble the forms of ornamentation into which the artistic hand strays when, as it were, dreaming on the paper without definite plan; and partly they afford a parallel to the early attempts at symbolic self-expression of primitives who have not yet learned an alphabet. Like primitive writing, they pass by insensible transitions from direct pictorial symbolism to an abbreviated ideography, mingled in its turn with writing of a fantastic or of an ordinary kind. He often showed to experts strange hieroglyphics obtained automatically, but he found that at the best they appeared to resemble scrawls seen on Chinese plates.

The watercolor pictures of **Catherine Berry,** exhibited in Brighton, England, in 1874, disclosed the vagaries of mind to which Myers alludes. Catherine Berry acknowledged, "By any ordinary observer they would be pronounced as chaotic, but a more minute survey of them reveals a wonderful design in construction and purpose whatever it may be." She was told by her guide that they were illustrative of the origin of species. **Baroness Guldenstubbe** attributed them to the inspiration of a planetary spirit.

Mental patients often exhibit an impulse to decorative and symbolical drawings. Some of their products, like those of Vaslav Nijinsky, are of decided art merit. As a rule, however the automatist is of sound mind. Learning and erudition have nothing to do with the gift. Fabre, a French blacksmith, produced an almost faultless copy of Raphael's *Bataille de Constantin,* the original of which is now in the Vatican. The symbolic ideas often disclosed a high moral purpose: "Never has anything proceeded from these drawings," wrote William Wilkinson in *Spirit Drawings: A Personal Narrative* (1858), "nor from their descriptions, but what has been to us an incentive to a better and holier life." The phenomenon is even recorded in the Bible:

"Then David gave to Solomon his son the pattern of the porch, and of the houses thereof, and of the treasuries thereof, and of the upper chambers thereof, and of the inner parlors thereof, and of the place of the mercy seat and the pattern of all that he had by the Spirit, of the courts of the house of the Lord, and of all the chambers round about it, of the treasuries of the house of God, and of the treasuries of the dedicated things. . . . All this, said David, the Lord made me understand in writing by his hand upon me, even all the works of this pattern" (Chron. 28).

Modern psychic artists include the Brazilian Luiz Gasparetto. Painting in the early 1900s at lightning speed and in semidarkness, the entranced artist produced more than 6,000 paintings, some of them in the unmistakable style of such dead masters as Picasso, Renoir, Toulouse-Lautrec, Gaugin, Modigliani, Van Gogh, Rembrandt, Tissot, Manet, Monet, and Matisse.

Among British psychic artists, radical magician **Austin O. Spare** (1888–1956) portrayed fantastic and demonic spirit forms. In 1927 he exhibited a collection of his "psychic drawings and others of magical and occult manifestations" at St. George's Gallery, London. He also published several books of his powerful drawings.

Another British psychic artist, Coral Polge, sketched people who had passed away and wanted to communicate with members of her audience. At such public demonstrations, Polge often worked in a unique partnership with such clairvoyants as **Doris Collins,** who passed on messages while Polge sketched the communicator.

Some of the most remarkable examples of psychic art have come from the contemporary British medium **Matthew Manning,** who has produced automatic drawings in the style of many great artists.

Sources:

d'Esperance, Elizabeth. *Shadow Land; or, Light from the Other Side.* London, n.d. [1897].

Flournoy, Theodor. *From India to the Planet Mars: A Study of Somnambulism.* New York and London, 1900.

Manning, Matthew. *The Link: The Extraordinary Gifts of a Teenage Psychic.* U.K.: Colin Smythe, 1974. Reprint, New York: Holt, Rinehart, 1975.

Spare, Austin O. *A Book of Automatic Drawing.* London: Catalpa Press, 1972.

Automatic Speaking

The phenomenon of excitation of the vocal chords without the volition of the conscious self. Today this phenomenon is called **channeling.** Speech bursts forth impulsively, whether the **medium** is in trance or a more normal waking state. In the latter case, and in partial trance, the medium may understand the contents of the communication even if it comes in a language unknown to him or her. But the retention of consciousness during automatic speaking is exceptional.

The mediums **Horace Leaf** and Florence Morse were conscious during automatic speech, and this consciousness was also observed by **Eugèn Osty** with Mme. Fraya and M. de Fleurière. The curious case **William James** records in the *Proceedings* of the Society for Psychical Research (vol. 12, pp. 277–98), of the experiences of Mr. "Le Baron" (pseudonym) in 1894 in an American Spiritualist camp meeting, is especially instructive on this score. "Le Baron," who was a journalist, at one of these meetings "felt his head drawn back until he was forced flat on the ground." Then "the force produced a motor disturbance of my head and jaws. My mouth made automatic movements, till in a few seconds I was distinctly conscious of another's voice—unearthly, awful, loud, weird—bursting through the woodland from my own lips, with the despairing words 'Oh, my people.' Mutterings of semipurposive prophecy followed."

James also spoke, as a curious thing, of the generic similarity of trance utterances in different individuals.

"It seems exactly if one author composed more than half of the trance messages, no matter by whom they are uttered. Whether all subconscious selves are peculiarly susceptible to a certain stratum of the Zeitgeist, and get their inspirations from it, I know not."

Spiritualists, of course, reject James's observation and cite as evidence some of the more notable trance utterances and inspirational oratory, such as *The Principles of Nature, Her Divine*

Revelation's and a Voice to Mankind, originally dictated by **Andrew Jackson Davis**) in trance in 1845 and 1846. **Thomas Lake Harris** produced two long poems in a similar manner: *Epic of the Starry Heavens* (1854), a poem containing nearly four thousand lines, and *A Lyric of the Morning Land* (1856), another impressive poetic composition of over five thousand words. Both were dictated in a remarkably short time. **David Duguid's** curious historic romance *Hafed, Prince of Persia* (1876), and its sequel *Hermes, A Disciple of Jesus* (1887), were also taken down from trance dictations.

Interesting Cases of Automatic Speaking

The revelations of **Catherine Emmerich,** the seeress of Westphalia, were taken down and published by Clement Brentano in a work of several volumes. The seeress, who lived at the beginning of the nineteenth century, told the story of the life of Jesus day by day as if she had been an eyewitness of it all. Her account deviated from Roman Catholic teachings at several points, and Roman Catholic apologist **Herbert Thurston** attacked her work by noting the numerous discrepancies in her visions. He put together a formal critical examination and compared her visions with those of other more "orthodox" ecstatics.

Telka, **"Patience Worth"**'s poem of sixty to seventy thousand words in an Anglo-Saxon language, was dictated through **Pearl Curran** as rapidly as it could be written down by a secretary, and the medium was so independent of that which came through her that she was free to smoke a cigarette, to interrupt herself by taking part in the conversation of those present, or go into the next room to answer the telephone. The whole poem, a masterpiece, took a total of 35 hours.

Medium Florence Morse was not only conscious of her inspirational delivery but one of her controls, who had a fund of dry humor, frequently kept her amused by his remarks on some feature of the proceedings, especially when it was a case of answering questions.

Trance singing is a kindred manifestation to automatic speaking. **Jesse Shepard** was the most notable example. In the case of Mrs. A. M. Gage, a New York soprano singer who lost her voice through an attack of hemorrhage of the lungs, it was accompanied by a complete alteration of personality.

One of the most remarkable examples of trance utterance was that of the British medium **Mrs. Louis A. Meurig Morris,** who delivered impressive sermons under the control of the spirit "Power." During these addresses, the medium's soprano voice changed to a ringing masculine baritone and all her mannerisms became masculine.

Psychologists who do not accept the claim of spirit utterance through a medium classify the phenomenon as the creation of a secondary personality, and there are many interesting cases on record of individuals who manifested several quite markedly different personalities. Also related to automatic speaking is the phenomenon of **glossolalia** or "speaking in tongues," as well as **xenoglossis,** the speaking of a language without having studied it.

Sources:

Thurston, Herbert. *Surprising Mystics.* London: Burns & Oates, 1955.

Automatic Writing

Scripts produced without the control of the conscious self. It is the most common form of mediumship, the source of innumerable cases of self-delusion, and at the same time the source of some of the most interesting and intriguing cases of mediumship. Between these two extremes many problems of a complex nature present themselves to **psychical research.** Spiritualists consider automatic writing to be performed "under control"—that is, under the controlling agency of the spirits of the dead—and are therefore not judged to be truly "automatic." Most researchers, however, have ascribed such performances to the subconscious activity of the agent.

Both automatic writing and **automatic speaking** necessarily imply some alternation of the consciousness from the common waking state in the subject, though such alteration need not be pronounced, but may vary from a light state such is common in day-dreaming to a full **trance.** When the phenomena are produced during a state of trance or somnambulism the agent may be entirely unconscious of his or her actions. On the other hand, the automatic writing may be executed while the agent is in a condition varying little from waking and he or she may be quite capable of observing the writing process in a critical spirit.

Between these states of consciousness and complete unconsciousness there are many intermediate stages. The **personality,** as displayed in the writings or utterances, may gain only a partial ascendancy over the primary personality, as may happen in dreams or in the hypnotic trance. As a rule automatic speech and writings display nothing more than a revivifying of faded mental imagery, thoughts and conjectures and impressions that never came to light in the upper consciousness. But at times there appears an extraordinary exaltation of memory, or even of the intellectual facilities.

Cases are on record where lost articles have been recovered by means of automatic writing. Foreign languages that have been forgotten, or with which the subject has small acquaintance, are spoken or written fluently. **Hélène Smith,** the subject of **Theodore Flournoy,** even went so far as to invent a new language, purporting to be that of the Martians, but in reality showing a marked resemblance to French—the mother tongue of the **medium.**

Automatic writing and speaking have been produced in considerable quantities, mainly in connection with Spiritualistic circles, though it existed long before the advent of **Spiritualism** in the speaking in tongues of the early ecstatics. Though the matter and style may on occasion transcend the capabilities of the agent in a normal state, the great body of automatic productions show no erudition or literary excellence beyond the scope of the natural resources of the automatist. The style is generally involved, obscure, inflated, yet possessing a superficial smoothness and a suggestion of flowing periods and musical cadences. The ideas are often shallow and incoherent, and all but lost in a multitude of words.

Among Spiritualists, the best known of automatic writings have been the *Spirit Teachings* (1883) of **Stainton Moses,** and the works of **Andrew Jackson Davis,** which dominated the movement in the nineteenth century. Possibly more important have been the trance utterances of **Leonora Piper,** these last convincing many of the reality of **telepathy.** Much poetry has been produced automatically, notably by the nineteenth century medium **Thomas Lake Harris.** Among famous individuals known to have produced automatic scripts are Goethe, Victor Hugo, and **Victorien Sardou,** among other eminent men of letters.

How is the power of automatic writing acquired? In describing his first experience at a séance of **Frank Herne** and **Charles Williams** in 1872, Stainton Moses wrote in *Spirit Identity* (1879):

"My right arm was seized about the middle of the forearm, and dashed violently up and down with a noise resembling that of a number of paviors at work. It was the most tremendous exhibition of 'unconscious muscular action' I ever saw. In vain I tried to stop it. I distinctly felt the grasps, soft and firm, round my arm, and though perfectly possessed of senses and volition, I was powerless to interfere, although my hand was disabled for some days by the bruising it then got. The object we soon found was to get up the force."

The first experience of **William Howitt** is similarly described by his daughter Anna Mary Watts in *Pioneers of The Spiritual Reformation* (1883):

"My father had not sat many minutes passive, holding a pencil in his hand upon a sheet of paper, ere something resembling an electric shock ran through his arm and hand; whereupon the pencil began to move in circles. The influence becoming stronger and even stronger, moved not alone the hand, but the whole arm in a rotatory motion, until the arm was at length raised, and rapidly—as if it had been the spoke of a wheel propelled by machinery—whirled irresistibly in a wide sweep, and with great speed, for some ten minutes through the air. The effect of this rapid rotation was felt by him in the muscles of the arm for some time afterwards. Then the arm being again at rest the pencil, in the passive fingers, began gently, but clearly and decidedly, to move."

Elizabeth d'Esperance wrote: "I first noticed a tingling, pricking, aching sensation in my arm, as one feels as one strikes one's elbow; then a numb swollen sort of feeling which extended to my finger tips. My hand became quite cold and without sensation, so that I could pinch or nip the flesh without feeling any pain." The insensibility to pain was noticed by **William James,** and psychologist Alfred Binet verified this partial anaesthesia by mechanical means.

In Piper's case the automatic writing began with spasmodic violence, with sweeping the writing materials off the table. She wrote in trance. This returns us to consideration of the phenomenon that automatic writing may be produced either in the waking state or in trance. There are many degrees of the two states and blending is frequent, the important point apparently being to bar the interference of the writer's conscious mind.

In conscious writing it is the writer who moves the pencil; in automatic writing it is the pencil that moves the writer. In the waking state, of course, the writer is fully conscious of the strange thing going on but must remain passive. He or she may watch the flow of sentences, but if the writer is too interested or anxious, the writing becomes disconnected, words are left out, or the meaning becomes unintelligible. It is best for the writer to be occupied with something else, like Moses, who kept on writing consciously with his right hand while his left was in control of his "communicators." All this, however, varies considerably with different mediums. Nearly every automatic writer has conditions of his own. Accordingly, the script, which at first is hardly more than erratic markings on the paper, discloses many curious features. The medium may have an impression of the sense of the communication or may not. The text may be couched in tongues unknown, and the character of the writing may be his own or a strange one. It may be so minute that a strong magnifying glass will be necessary for reading it; it may be mirror writing, if the power is applied from underneath the hand; it may come upside down if the horizontal direction is changed to face a particular sitter; the words may be written in a reverse order, as "latipsoh" for "hospital"; and it may be executed at tremendous speed. The automatic communications alleged to originate from Philip the Evangelist, Cleophas, and **Frederic William Henry Myers,** obtained by **Geraldine Dorothy Cummins,** were sometimes delivered at the extraordinary speed of two thousand words per hour.

Automatic Writing from Living Communicators

A question of paramount importance, especially for Spiritualists, has been the source of the automatic communications. Could they originate from an extraneous mind? This need not necessarily be discarnate. There are cases on record that suggest the contents of the script may emanate from the mind of a *living* individual. **William T. Stead,** who developed the power of automatic writing, often received such curious messages from many of his friends for a period of 15 years. He said that, as a rule, these messages were astonishingly correct and the fact of such communication with the living was as well established for him as the existence of wireless telegraphy. He made it a subject of experimental investigation and found that sometimes the messages so transmitted even came against the direct intention of the agent. He called the phenomenon "automatic telepathy" and asserted that he knew at least ten other automatic writers who received similar messages.

Felicia R. Scatcherd was apparently one of them. She is quoted in **James Coates**'s book *Has W. T. Stead Returned?* (1913) as follows:

"Then came a new phase; I was the recipient of messages from the living—mostly strangers engaged in public affairs, and was startled into a perception of the scientific value of these phenomena. When at a dinner in Paris I met a famous scientist who, in his after-dinner remarks, expressed the identical sentiments I had received as coming from him, many months earlier, in a language with which I was then ill-acquainted. There was no mistake about it. Knowing I should meet him, I had my written record with me, taken down in shorthand and copied in longhand as soon as possible, as was my invariable practice. I disliked receiving information in this way, but could not help it. If I refused these confidences, nothing else came. However, I became more reconciled to it when I found I could often be of service, in one instance preventing suicide, in others forestalling various casualties."

To Stead's direct question: "How is it that a person will tell me things with my hand that he would never tell me with his tongue?", his dead friend Julia replied through automatic writing that the real self will never communicate any intelligence whatever except what it wishes to communicate, but the real self is very different from the physical self, it sits behind the physical senses and the mind, using either as it pleases. "I find," said Stead in a lecture before the **London Spiritualist Alliance** in 1913, "that there are some who will communicate with extraordinary accuracy, so much so that out of a hundred statements there would not be more than one which would be erroneous. I find some who, though they will sign their names correctly, apparently in their own character, make statements that are entirely false." To his question "if the real self does not communicate any intelligence except at its volition, how is it that I can get an answer from my friend without his knowing anything about it?" Julia returned the answer that "the real self does not always take the trouble when he has communicated a thing by the mind through the hand to inform the physical brain that he has done so." In one case the message Stead received from a living friend referred to a calamity that happened three days later.

Stead's theory of automatic telepathy appears to have been borne out in experiments with the planchette, as recorded in *Proceedings* of the Society for Psychical Research (vol. 2, p. 235). A long series of communications between Rev. P. H. Newnham, Vicar of Maker, Devonport, and his wife, indicate that Mrs. Newnham's hand wrote replies to questions of her husband's that she neither heard nor saw.

An even more remarkable illustration is to be found in **Frederick Bligh Bond**'s experiences with S., a woman who figures in the history of the **Glastonbury scripts.** As Bond wrote in *Psychic Research,* April 1929:

"I noticed a very curious thing. The communications which she sent me began more and more to follow the line of my current archaeological enquiry. And after we had met once in the summer of that year, this tendency became increasingly obvious. There was some sort of mental *rapport* of attunement apparently present, and this I attributed to the dominance in both our minds of a very specialized line of interest. On one or two occasions in 1922 this correspondence became more pronounced and the communications took the form of answers to questions which were in my mind, though not consciously formulated. . . . Finally a very strange thing happened. I had a letter from S. in which she sent me a writing she had received automatically in the form of a letter addressed to her by myself and signed with my name, although not in my handwriting. . . . I was and am totally unconscious of having mentally addressed it."

Nevertheless, such communications from the living are comparatively very rare. There is no doubt that, whether the contents disclose a rambling mind or powers of lucid reason, most of the automatic scripts represent a subconscious uprush. Therefore, in judging such scripts the standard of evidence should be very strict. So much more so as automatic writing is known to have been produced by post-hypnotic suggestion.

Automatic Writing Through Hypnotic Suggestion

Edmund Gurney was the first to conduct such experiments. When in trance, his subject was given the suggestion to write "It has begun snowing again" after regaining consciousness. When awakened, the subject wrote with a **planchette,** while his waking self was entirely unaware of what he was doing, "It has begun snowing." Similar experiments were initiated independently by **Pierre Janet** in France.

The primary personality will repudiate the authorship of such scripts and it will also say that they cannot emanate from it because there are things in the automatic writings it never knew. Another curious feature of these experimental scripts is that manufactured personalities, dwelling in separate streams of consciousness according to the depth of hypnotism, will sometimes obstinately cling to their fictitious names and refuse to admit that they are only portions of the automatist himself. In incidents of multiple personality the case is still stronger.

The unexpectedness of an automatically received message is yet no proof for its extraneous origin. As Myers suggested, two separate strata of intelligences may be concerned. Besides, automatic writing is often obtained by the collaboration of two people who touch the planchette simultaneously or one touches the wrist of the other during the process of writing. The source of the messages in such cases may be found in a combined fountain of subconsciousness.

The Identity of Communicators

Eugene Rochas recorded a case where the communicator of the automatic script was found to be a fictional being, a character from a novel. Extreme Spiritualists would attribute such messages to lying spirits, the occultist to thoughtforms, endowed with temporary intelligence. It is very likely, however, that nothing more than a dream of the subconscious had been witnessed in the case. Speculative possibilities are well illustrated by the mediumship of Hélène Smith. If the claim of **reincarnation** and exceptional remembrance of a preincarnate state were to be admitted, both the information contained in the script and the question of the communicators as preincarnate personalities would have to be considered in this light.

The difference in the character of the automatic writing alone does not prove the presence of an outside entity. **Charles Richet** proved in experiments, considered classics, that the new personality he created by hypnotic suggestion completely transformed the handwriting of two hypnotized subjects.

The reproduction of the handwriting of the deceased is a much stronger but, in itself, not yet decisive point. Strict evidentiality requires that this resemblance should not be loosely asserted and that the medium should not have seen the writing of the alleged communicator, as hypnotic experiments reveal uncanny powers of perception and retention on the part of the subconscious mind. In the Blanche Abercromby case of Stainton Moses's mediumship, **F. W. H. Myers** found every requirement satisfactory as both the woman's son and a handwriting expert found the spirit writing identical to that by the woman when living.

The analysis is not an easy task as sometimes the handwriting shows the characteristics of two controls and yet the essential characteristics of the medium may also be discernible.

Even simultaneously obtained messages are not safe from the suspicion that they arise from telepathy. Stead's communicator, "Julia," often wrote through Stead and his secretary, Edith K. Harper, at the same time, but not until the idea was further developed to **cross correspondence:** only by obtaining broken off sentences in each script so that they should complete each other, could these scripts be considered exempt from the influence of living minds.

Psychometry may offer an indirect presumption. If the script emanates from an extraneous intelligence, its psychometric reading should result in the presentation of a character different from the medium's. There is no way of telling, however, to what extent the medium's influence may blend with the script and garble psychometric impressions.

The difficulties, therefore, are very great if we set out to prove that a certain message comes from a discarnate mind. It should not only be clear that the contents of the message were unknown to the medium, but also that they were unascertainable by normal means. And as we do not know the powers of the subconscious to acquire information, those instances in which the information may have been acquired from books should only be provisionally accepted.

Stainton Moses' control "Rector" could read books and proved it in many tests. If a discarnate mind can do so, there is no *à priori* possibility that an *incarnate* mind, freed in trance, may not achieve the same thing.

Another series of difficulties will be encountered if we consider the influence of telepathy. A rigorous inquiry should be held into how far the message could have been influenced by the knowledge contained in a living mind. If every exaggerated scruple is to be satisfied we will have to narrow down considerably the circle of conclusive messages. The revelation of the contents of posthumous sealed letters, of the whereabouts of intentionally hidden objects, or the sudden announcement of death unknown to the sitters may offer a *prima facie* case that the communications come from a discarnate mind.

A good case of the latter kind was quoted by **Alexander N. Aksakof.** A man named Duvanel died by his own hand on January 15, 1887, in a Swiss village where he lived alone. Five hours after his death an automatic message, announcing the decease, was written at Wilna by a Miss Stramm, whom Duvanel wished to marry, but who could have received no news of his tragic end.

Nevertheless the enumeration of the many difficulties in the way of convincing evidence does not mean that the message in question is worthless if it could have been know to the medium. Every case has to be examined as a whole. Sometimes the display of extraordinary erudition or educational training revealed by the scripts is sufficient alone to establish a claim of paranormal origin. The banality of a message is usually taken as a proof of subconscious origin. This attitude is not justified by any means. If you begin to knock on a wall behind which, unseen to you, people are passing, there is no telling who will stop and answer. It may be a fool, a knave, or a man of intelligence and sympathy, bent on helping and teaching. The recipient of the message may have confidence in the good faith of the communicator, but no assurance of good faith alone justifies an unqualified belief in the intrinsic worth of the messages coming through. Good faith and ignorance, and good faith and presumption often go together in this world. There is no reason to rule out their partnership in the beyond.

The question assumes a different aspect after long association between the automatic writer and the communicator. The latter may succeed in convincing the writer of his sincerity, erudition, and high moral purpose. He has his own means of identification. From the sensation produced in the hand the automatist recognizes the presence of the well-known control of the appearance of an intruder.

Occasionally the writing is attributed to preposterous sources. Victor Hugo received automatic messages from the "Shadow of the Tomb" and the "Ass of Balaam." And Jules Bois quoted questions in *Le Mirage Moderne* to which the "Lion of Androcles" gave the answers.

The communicator often avails himself or herself of the services of an amanuensis who appears to have more skill in performing the psychic feat of communication. In the séances of Stainton Moses, "Rector" acted as amanuensis for "Imperator" and many others, producing a large part of the automatic script.

In Leonora Piper's case, the communicators were often unconscious whether their messages were delivered by the spoken word or in automatic writing. The scripts of this famous medium are in a class by themselves. While she was writing, her voice was being used by another communicator. To quote from Dr. **Richard Hodgson**'s report:

"The sense of hearing for the 'hand'-consciousness appears to be in the hand, and the sitter must talk to the hand to be understood. The thoughts that pass through the consciousness controlling the hand tend to be written, and one of the difficulties apparently is to prevent the writing out of thoughts which are not intended for the sitter. Other 'indirect communicators' frequently purport to be present and the 'consciousness of the hand' listens to them with the hand as though they were close by, as it listens to the sitters, presenting the palm of the hand, held in slightly different positions for the purpose by different 'direct communicators' so as to bring usually the region of the junction between the little finger and the palm toward the mouth of the sitter."

In the old days writing was usually mirror writing, which sometimes was obtained in an unusual manner, i.e., Piper wrote a name on paper held to her forehead so that the pencil was turned towards her face.

With the advent of the "Imperator" group of Stainton Moses, "Rector" took over the role of the scribe for all communicators and mirror writing only cropped up occasionally. Sometimes the letters were spelled in an inverted order. The writing appeared to be less of a strain than speaking and these séances lasted for two hours or more.

An extremely interesting intellectual aspect of automatic writing is given from the other side in Geraldine Cummins' *The Road to Immortality* (1932). The spirit of F. W. H. Myers, on the second occasion on which he purported to write through Cummins, wrote:

"The inner mind, is very difficult to deal with from this side. We impress it with our message. We never impress the brain of the medium directly. That is out of the question. But the inner mind receives our message and sends it on to the brain. The brain is a mere mechanism. The inner mind is like soft wax, it receives our thoughts, their whole content, but it must produce the words that clothe it. That is what makes cross-correspondence so very difficult. We may succeed in sending the thought through, but the actual words depend largely on the inner mind's content, on what words will frame the thought. If I am to send half a sentence through one medium and half through another I can only send the same thought with the suggestion that a part of it will come through one medium and a part through another."

The explanation may have been very true in the case of Cummins, yet it need not have general application. She was conscious of the use of her brain by someone else. In the introduction to *The Road to Immortality,* "Myers" observed:

"Soon I am in a condition of half-sleep, a kind of dream-state that yet, in its peculiar way, has more illumination than one's waking state. I have at times distinctly the sensation of a dreamer who has no conscious creative control over the ideas that are being formulated in words. I am a mere listener, and through my stillness and passivity I lend my aid to the stranger who is speaking. It is hard to put such a psychological condition into words. I have the consciousness that my brain is being used by a stranger all the time. It is just as if an endless telegram is being tapped out on it."

Like any other mediumistic faculty, automatic writing may appear at a very early age. Mr. Wason, a well-known Spiritualist from Liverpool, saw the six-month old son of Kate Fox-Jencken, write: "I love this little child. God bless him. Advise his father to go back to London on Monday by all means—Susan." Susan was the name of Mr. Wason's wife. Myers and Hodgson saw a girl of four write the words, "Your Aunt Emma." Celina, a child of three and a half, wrote in the presence of Drs. Dussart and Broquet: "I am glad to manifest through a charming little medium of three and a half who promises well. Promise me not to neglect her."

Glimpses into Automatic Literature

The claims of discarnate authorship present a delicate problem. **Angelo Brofferio** knew a writing medium "to whom Boccaccio, Bruno and Galileo dictated replies that for the elevation of thought were assuredly more worthy of the greatness of that trio than on the level of the medium: I could cite competent testimony to the fact." According to **Cesare Lombroso,** "Dante, or one who stood for him, dictated to Scaramuzza three Cantos in *terza rima.* I read only a few strophes of this but so far as I could judge they were very beautiful."

Many famous writers wrote in a semitrance, having but an imperfect recollection of the work afterwards. Harriet Beecher Stowe, the author of *Uncle Tom's Cabin,* claimed that she did not write it: it was given to her; "it passed before her." In like measure William Blake stated that his poem *Jerusalem* was dictated to him. "The grandest poem that this world contains; I may praise it, since I dare not pretend to be other than the Secretary; the authors are in eternity." Again: "I have written this poem from immediate dictation, twelve or sometimes twenty or thirty lines at a time without premeditation and even against my will."

Parts of the Jewish Bible (the Christian Old Testament) were received through automatic writing, for example 2 Chronicles 21:12 says, "And there came a writing to him from Elijah the prophet saying . . . " In 1833, the book of the German Augustinian nun **Catherine Emmerich,** *The Lowly Life and Bitter Passion of Our Lord Jesus Christ and His Blessed Mother,* was accepted by Catholics as divinely inspired. The remarkable contents of the book came to her in visions and were noted and edited by the poet Clement Brentano.

In America one of the earliest automatically written books was Rev. C. Hammond's *The Pilgrimage of Thomas Payne and Others to the Seventh Circle* (New York, 1852). The book contained 250 octavo pages. It was begun at the end of December 1851 and completed February 1 of the next year. The following year Judge **John W. Edmonds**'s and George T. Dexter's *Spiritualism* was published, which also contains many spirit messages. The same year saw the appearance of John Murray Spear's *Messages from the Spirit Life,* which was followed in 1857 by a large connected work, the *Educator.* A year later, Charles Linton, a bookkeeper of limited education, produced a remarkable book of 100,000 words: *The Healing of the Nation,* which was printed with Wisconsin governor **Nathaniel P. Tallmadge**'s preface. In the following year *Twelve Messages from John Quincey Adams through Joseph D. Stiles* was published.

But all these books pale into insignificance before **Hudson Tuttle**'s *Arcana of Nature* (1862), a volume of broad sweep and scope comparable to the trance writings of Andrew Jackson Davis.

Two late nineteenth-century cases of automatic writing still deserve attention. First, when Victorian novelist **Charles Dickens** died in 1870, he left a novel *The Mystery of Edwin Drood* unfinished. T. P. James, an American mechanic of very slight education, completed it automatically. According to many critics the script is characteristic of Dickens in style and is worthy of his talent. Secondly, a few years later **John Ballou Newbrough** received through the process of automatic typewriting the New Age Bible, *Oahspe* (1882). This volume remains in print, the scripture of several small but persistent religious groups. Less than two decades later, **Aleister Crowley** received a much shorter work through automatic writing, *The Book of the Law,* which has become the scripture for thelemic magicians. In the next decade, James Edward Padgett would begin receiving the writings, four volumes in all, which became the scriptures for the Foundation Church of the Divine Truth.

In France, in the early days of French **Spiritism,** Hermance Dufeaux, a girl of 14, produced two surprising books: a *Life of Jeanne d'Arc,* claimed to be dictated by the maid, and *Confessions of Louis XI.* **Allan Kardec** vouched for the honesty of the girl. On the other hand, the *Divine Revelations of Geneva* in 1854, obtained by a little group of ministers and professors by means of the table-tipping "from Christ and his angels," is, according to Flournoy, insipid and foolish enough to give one nausea.

In England, J. Garth Wilkinson published in 1857 an octavo volume of impressional poetry. The first continued a series of automatically received messages deserving serious attention that were produced by William Stainton Moses between 1870 and 1880. His scripts contained many evidential messages, but their main purpose was the delivery of religious teaching.

The *Scripts of Cleophas, Paul in Athens,* and *The Chronicle of Ephesus,* produced by Cummins under the alleged influence of Philip the Evangelist, and Cleophas, bear signs of close acquaintanceship with the **Apostolic Circle,** an early American Spiritualist group which claimed close contact with Jesus' apostles and other New Testament characters. **Sir Oliver Lodge** claims to have received independent evidence concerning the inspiration of *The Road to Immortality,* Cummins's fourth book, with communications said to be from the spirit of F. W. H. Myers.

The quantity of automatically written books is such that it is difficult to mention more than a few. W. T. Stead's *After Death: Letters From Julia* (1914), was widely read by Spiritualists as was Hester Travers Smith's *Psychic Messages from Oscar Wilde* (1924). *The Glastonbury Scripts* by F. Bligh Bond have an importance of their own because of their role in actually guiding the excavation of the medieval site. Other notable volumes from the early twentieth century would include Elsa Barker's *Letters from a Living Dead Man, War Letters from a Living Dead Man,* and *Last Letters from a Living Dead Man* (the probable communicator being David P. Hutch, a magistrate of Los Angeles), the remarkable books of **"Patience Worth"** produced through **Pearl Curran** of St. Louis, *The Seven Purposes,* by Margaret Cameron (New York, 1918), which unlies the Betty Book literature of Betty and **Stewart Edward White,** the anonymous *Private Dowding* (1917) (by New Age movement precursor W. Tudor Pole), and the curious and interesting automatic scripts of Juliette Hervey of France, which **Eugèn Osty** studied.

Automatic writing has continued as a phenomenon through the twentieth century, though only rarely have it attained any notice, most scripts being privately printed and circulated. Many of the UFO **contactee** writings were so produced. With the emergence of **channeling** and audio recording equipment, automatic speaking (channeling) has become a far more popular endeavor. Among the few products of automatic writing that have attained some notice would be the several writings of New Age author **Ruth Montgomery,** which she received while sitting at her typewriter, such as *Here and Hereafter* (1968), *A World Beyond* (1971), and *Companions Along the Way* (1974).

Sources:

Mühl, Anita M. *Automatic Writing: An Approach to the Unconscious.* New York: Helix Press, 1963.

Thurston, Herbert. *Surprising Mystics.* London: Burns & Oates, 1955.

Automatism

A term indicating organic functions, or inhibitions, not controlled by the conscious self. The word "automatism" is actually a misnomer, as the acts, or inhibitions, are only automatic from the viewpoint of personal consciousness and they may offer the characteristic features of voluntary acts on the part of another consciousness.

F. W. H. Myers divided the phenomena of automatism into two principal classes: motor-automatism (the movement of the limbs, head, or tongue by an inner motor impulse beyond the conscious will) and sensory automatism (externalization of perceptions in inner vision and audition). The first he called "active," the second "passive" automatism, stressing, however, that the impulse from which it originates may be much the same in that one case as in the other. This place of origin is either the subconscious self or a discarnate intelligence. Myers suggested that the excitation of the motor or sensory centers may take place either through the subconscious (subliminal) mind, or the communicating intelligence may find some direct way, for which he proposed the name "telergic."

The phenomena of automatism are often accompanied by organic disturbances, or changes in vasomotor, circulatory, and respiratory systems. The sensory impressions are sometimes accompanied by a feeling of malaise, which is noticeable even in such simple cases as **telepathy.** In the phenomena of dowsing, the disturbance is much keener.

Incapacity for action is an almost rudimentary type of motor-automatism. It may result from a simple subconscious perception or it may be induced by an outside agency to save the subject from grave peril, e.g., from entering a house that is about to collapse or boarding a train that will be derailed. An instructive instance is quoted by **Theodore Flournoy** from his experiments with **Héléne Smith:**

"One day Miss Smith, when desiring to lift down a large and heavy object which lay on a high shelf, was prevented from doing so because her raised arm remained for some seconds as though petrified in the air and incapable of movement. She took this as a warning and gave up the attempt. At a subsequent séance, "Leopold" stated that it was he who thus fixed Helen's arm to prevent her from grasping this object which was much too heavy for her and would have caused her some accident."

This record of spirit cure was published in *Proceedings* of the **Society for Psychical Research** (Vol. 3: 182–87):

"On August 17, 1891, the patient felt for the first time a unique sensation, accompanied by formication and sense of weight in the lower limbs, especially in the feet. This sensation gradually spread over the rest of the body, and when it reached the arms, the hands and forearms began to rotate. These phenomena recurred after dinner every evening, as soon as the patient was quiet in her armchair. . . . The patient placed her two hands on a table. The feeling of "magnetisation" then began in the feet, which began to rotate and the upper parts of the body gradually shared in the same movement. At a certain point, the hands automatically detached themselves from the table by small, gradual shocks, and at the same time the arms assumed a tetanic rigidity somewhat resembling catalepsy.

"One day Mme. X. felt herself lifted from her armchair and compelled to stand upright. Her feet and her whole body then executed a systematic calisthenic exercise, in which all the movements were regulated and made rhythmic with finished art. . . . Mme. X. had never had the smallest notion of chamber gymnastics. . . . These movements would have been very painful and fatiguing had she attempted them of her own will. Yet at the end of each performance she was neither fatigued nor out of breath. . . . . Mme. X is accustomed to arrange her own hair. One morning she said laughingly: 'I wish that a Court hairdresser would do my hair for me: my arms are tired.' At once she felt her hands acting automatically, and with no fatigue for her arms, which seemed to be held up; and the result was a complicated coiffure, which in no way resembled her usual simple mode of arrangement. The oddest of all these automatic phenomena consisted in extremely graceful gestures which Mme. X. was caused to execute with her arms, gestures as though of evocation or adoration of some imaginary divinity, or gestures of benediction . . . . The few persons who witnessed this spectacle are agreed that it was worthy of the powers of the greatest actress. Of such a gift Mme. X. has nothing."

Dr. F. L. H. Willis claimed that he performed a difficult and delicate surgical operation in trance while controlled by "Dr. Mason." At that time Willis had not even started to study medicine.

Myers classified the motor messages in the order of their increasing specialization:

1. Massive motor impulses. Case of the bricklayer (*Phantasms of the Living* Vol. 377), who had a sudden impulse to run home and arrived just in time to save the life of his little boy, who had set himself on fire. Case of Mr. Garrison, who left a religious service in the evening and walked 18 miles under a strong impulse to see his mother, then found her dead (*Journal* of the Society for Psychical Research Vol. 3: 125). Included under this heading the phenomenon of ambulatory automatism: moving about in a secondary state, as a result of an irresistible impulse, and forgetting all about it on return to normal consciousness. It is noticeable in subjects affected with nervous diseases. The mysterious **transportation** of the Italian Pansini children was attributed by some Italian scientists to this cause.
2. Simple subliminal motor impulses that give rise to table tilting and similar phenomena. Georgina Houghton wrote in *Evenings at Home in Spiritual Séance* (1881) that on one occasion, being anxious to find her way to a house which

she had not visited for several years, she entrusted herself to spirit guides and arrived safely.

3. Musical execution, subliminally initiated. **Jesse Shepard,** the famous musical medium, **George Aubert,** and many child prodigies furnish cases of absorbing interest. The heading should be widened to include cases of contagious dancing witnessed in religious revivals, or cases like that of Lina, studied by Col. **Eugene Auguste-A. D. Rochas,** and Madeleine, studied by Emile Magnin, both girls exhibiting remarkable histrionic and dancing talent in trance.
4. **Automatic drawing** and painting.
5. **Automatic writing.**
6. Automatic speech.
7. Telekinetic movements.

J. Maxwell suggested in his *Metapsychical Phenomena* (1905) the following classification:

1. Simple muscular automatism: typtology, alphabetic systems.
2. Graphic muscular automatism: automatic writing, drawing, and painting.
3. Phonetic automatism: trance speaking.
4. Mixed automatism: incarnations.

Sensory automatism embraces the phenomena of **clairvoyance, clairaudience,** and **crystal gazing.** Therefore, according to Myers's scheme, the bulk of the phenomena of psychical research would range under the heading: automatism.

Autoscope

Term used by **Sir William Barrett** in his work *On the Threshold of the Unseen* (1917) to denote any mechanical means whereby communication from the unknown may reach us. The unknown may be an extraneous mind, living or dead, or the subconscious. The **planchette,** the **ouija board,** and the **divining rod** are typical autoscopes.

Sources:

Barrett, William. *On the Threshold of the Unseen.* New York: E. P. Dutton, 1917.

Autoscopy

A term dating from the Mesmeric age and denoting the power of somnambules to see their own organs and give a description of their state. The word was coined by neurologist Charles Féré. He applied it to the vision his patients saw of their **double** in a morbid state. This is external autoscopy, as contrasted by **Baron du Potet** to internal autoscopy: self-diagnosis in a trance. Dr. Sollier wrote a monograph, *Les Phénomènes d'autoscopie* (Paris, 1903), on the subject.

Autosuggestion

System of healing developed by **Emile Coué** (1857–1926), in which some of the remarkable effects of **hypnotism** can be achieved through conscious suggestion employed by the subject. Coué's methods have since become the basis for many popular systems of healing, self-improvement, and mysticism and an integral part of **New Thought** metaphysics.

Avalon (or Avillion)

The enchanted island of Arthurian legend. This terrestrial paradise was known in Welsh mythology as Ynys Avallach (Isle of Apples) or possibly related to the Celtic king of the dead named Avalloc or Afallach. In Geoffrey of Manmouth's twelfth-century chronicle of **King Arthur,** *Historia Regum Britanniae,* it was noted that Arthur's sword was forged in Avalon, and he was returned to Avalon after his last battle so his wounds could heal.

In 1191 the monks at **Glastonbury** announced that it was identical to Avalon and that they had discovered Arthur's burial site. As evidence they produced a cross bearing Arthur's name and the place's name, *Avalonia,* which had been found alongside an exhumed body. Today, replicas of the cross are sold at Glastonbury Abbey.

Sources:

Lacy, Norris J. *The Arthurian Encyclopedia.* New York: Garland Publishing, 1986.

Avalon, Arthur

Pseudonym of Sir John George Woodroffe (1865–1936), a prominent British administrator in India. He was educated at Oxford University and the Inner Temple, London, where he qualified as a barrister. He was advocate, Calcutta High Court, 1890; fellow and Tagore Law Professor, University of Calcutta; standing counsel to the Government of India, 1902–03; Puisne Judge of the High Court of Calcutta, 1904–22; and officiating chief justice of Bengal, November 1915. Upon returning to England, he was reader in Indian Law at Oxford University, 1923–30.

He published scholarly translations of rare Hindu esoteric religious scriptures and became a leading authority on Hindu tantra and **yoga.**

Sources:

Avalon, Arthur. *The Garland of Letters: Varnamala; Studies in the Mantra-Shastra.* Madras, India: Ganesh, 1922.

———. *The Serpent Power.* Madras, India: Ganesh, 1924.

———. *Shakti and Shakta.* 3d ed. Madras, India: Ganesh, 1929.

Avatar

A term used in Hindu religion to indicate the incarnation of a deity. *Avatara* is a Sanskrit word meaning "descent," and the Hindu gods take on animal or human form in different ages for the welfare of the world. In Hindu mythology, the god Brahma (originally known as the creator Prajapati) became successively incarnated as a boar, a tortoise, and a fish, to assist the development of the world in prehistory.

Certain Hindu scriptures ascribe these incarnations to the god Vishnu (the preserver), but since the manifestation of divine power takes many different forms in Hindu mythology, the distinction is academic. Various scriptures ascribe to Vishnu ten major incarnations: (1) *Matsya* (the fish), associated with legends of a great deluge in which Manu, progenitor of the human race, was saved from destruction; (2) *Kurma* (the tortoise), whose back supported great mountains while the gods and demons churned the ocean to retrieve divine objects and entities lost in the deluge; (3) *Vahura* (the boar), who raised up the earth from the seas; (4) *Nara-sinha* (the man-lion), who delivered the world from the tyranny of a demon; (5) *Vamana* (the dwarf), who recovered areas of the universe from demons; (6) *Parasu-rama* (Rama with the axe), who delivered Brahmins from dominion by the warrior caste during the second age of the world; (7) *Rama,* hero of the religious epic *Ramayana,* who opposed the demon Ravana; (8) *Krishna* popular incarnation chronicled in the religious epic *Mahabharata* (especially in the *Bhagavad-Gita* section) and *Srimad Bhagavatam;* (9) *Buddha,* the great religious teacher; and (10) *Kalki,* an incarnation yet to come, who is prophesied to appear on a white horse with a sword blazing like a comet, to destroy the wicked, stabilize creation and restore purity to the world.

In other religious works, as many as 22 incarnations are listed, including various great saints and sages. According to Hindu belief, a perfected human soul has no further karma (action and reaction) and is absorbed into divinity at death, but may elect to be incarnated for the good of the world. The deity Shri Krishna, in the *Bhagavad-Gita* (4:7–8) specifically promises: "Arjuna, whenever there is decline of *dharma* (righteous duty), and unrighteousness is dominant, then I am reborn. For the protection of the virtuous, the destruction of evil-doers, and to reestablish righteousness, I am reborn from age to age." Belief in repeated divine reincarnations of the deities for the good of the world, as distinct from one unique Messianic event, is one of the major theological differences between Hinduism and Western religions such as Judaism and Christianity.

Avenar

A fifteenth-century astrologer who promised the Jews, on the testimony of the planets, that their Messiah should arrive without fail in 1444, or at the latest, in 1464. He gave, for his guarantors, Saturn, Jupiter, "the crab, and the fish." The Jews were said to have kept their windows open to receive the messenger of God who did not arrive.

Averroes (1126–1198)

Name generally used for Abul-Walid Mohammed ibn-Ahmad ibn-Mohammed ibn-Roshd, one of the greatest Arabian philosophers, and a commentator on the works of Aristotle. He was born at Cordova and studied theology, mathematics, medicine, jurisprudence, and philosophy. He traveled widely and died in Morocco.

His writings greatly influenced Christian theologians, especially **Thomas Aquinas,** who obtained copies of his writings as a result of the Crusades. Averroes followed the concept of God as the source of emanation of intelligence and suggested that religious and philosophical truth may be in contradiction.

Avicenna (980–1037)

Named Aben Sina by Hebrew writers, but properly Ebor Sina, or—to give his names in full—Al-Sheikh Al-Rayis Abu Ali Al-Hossein ben Abdallah ben Sina. He was born at Kharmatain, near Bokhara, in the year of the Hegira 370, or 980 C.E., and was educated at Bokhara. He displayed such extraordinary precocity that when he had reached his tenth year, he had completely mastered the Quran and acquired a knowledge of algebra, Muslim theology, and the His ab ul-Hind, or the arithmetic of the Hindus. Under Abdallah Al-Natheli he studied logic, Euclid, and the *Almagest,* and then, as a diversion, devoted himself to the study of medicine.

He was only 21 when he composed his *Kitab al-Majmu* or, *The Book of the Sum Total,* whose mysteries he afterward attempted to clarify in a 20-volume commentary.

Avicenna's reputation for wisdom and erudition was so great that on the death of his father he was promoted by Sultan Magdal Douleth to the high office of grand vizier, which he held with advantage to the state until a political revolution accomplished the downfall of the Samanide dynasty. He then abandoned Bokhara and wandered from place to place, increasing his store of knowledge but yielding himself to a life of sensuality.

About 1012 he retired to Jurjân, where he began his great work on medicine, which is still considered one of the earliest systems of that art with any pretensions to philosophical completeness. It is arranged with singular clearness and presents a very admirable résumé of the doctrines of the ancient Greek physicians. Avicenna subsequently lived at Rai, Karzwîn, and Ispahan, where he became physician to the Persian sovereign. He is said to have been dismissed from this post on account of his debauched living. He then retired to Hamadan, where, worn out with years of sensual indulgence, he died, at the age of 58.

Avicenna wrote nearly 100 works on philosophy, mathematics, and medicine and at least seven treatises on the **philosophers' stone** of **alchemy.** His *Book of the Canon of Medicine* acquired European celebrity and has been translated into Latin several times.

Avichi

A theosophical concept of **hell,** deriving from the Sanskrit word for "isolation." Although it is a place of torment, it differs in great degree from the dominant conception of hell. Its torments are the torments of fleshly cravings, which for want of a physical body cannot be satisfied. People remain after death exactly the same entity as before, and, if in life an individual has been obsessed with strong desires or passions, such obsession still continues, though in the astral plane the satisfaction of these desires or passions is impossible. These torments are of infinite scope, whether it be the confirmed sensualist who suffers them, or more ordinary people who, without being bound to the things of the flesh, have nevertheless allowed the affairs of the world to loom too largely in their lives and are now doomed to regret the small attention they have given to higher matters.

Avichi is a place of regrets for things done and things undone. Its torments are not, however, eternal, and with the passing of time—of which there is no measure in the astral plane—they are gradually discontinued at the cost of terrible suffering.

Avidya

A Hindu religious term also used in **Theosophy** to denote the ignorance of mind which causes those commencing the spiritual pathway to expend vain effort and pursue vain courses. It is the antithesis of *Vidya,* or true knowledge.

Awakener, The (Magazine)

One of several independent journals presenting the teachings of famous mystic **Meher Baba** (1894–1969), regarded by disciples as an **avatar** or descent of divine power. Address: 938 18th St., Hermosa Beach, CA 90254.

Awyntyrs off Arthure at the Tern Wathelyn

An Arthurian poem of the fourteenth or fifteenth century, believed to be of Scottish origin. Among other adventures, the poem relates one which **King Arthur** and his queen, Guinevere, experienced while accompanied by their favorite knight Sir Gawane (or Gawain), hunting in the wilds of Cumberland. Overtaken by darkness which separated them from the rest of the party, the ghost of the queen's mother appeared to them. The apparition told of the torments to which it was being subjected and entreated that prayers be offered up for its release. This the queen and Sir Gawane promised, and on their return to Carlisle millions of masses were ordered to be sung on its behalf.

Sources:

Gates, Robert J. *The Awntyrs off Arthure at the Terne Wathelyne: A Critical Edition.* Philadelphia: University of Pennsylvania Press, 1969.

Hanna, Ralph. *The Awntyrs off Arthure: An Edition Based on Bodleian Library MS. Douce 324.* Manchester, U.K.: Manchester University Press, 1974.

Lacy, Norris J. *The Arthurian Encyclopedia.* New York: Garland Publishing, 1986.

Laing, David. *Select Remains of the Ancient Popular Poetry of Scotland.* Edinburgh: Balfour & Clarke, 1822.

Small, John. *Select Remains of the Ancient Popular and Romance Poetry of Scotland.* London: W. Blackwood & Sons, 1885.

Axinomancy

Divination by means of a hatchet or a woodcutter's axe. Diviners predicted the ruin of Jerusalem with axinomancy (Psalm 74). Francois de la Tour-Blanche, who remarked upon this, does not tell us how the diviners made use of the hatchet, but it may have been related to one of the two methods employed in ancient times and lately practiced in certain northern countries.

The first is as follows: To find a treasure, find a round agate, heat the head of the axe until red hot in the fire, and place it so that its edge stands perpendicularly in the air. Place the agate on the edge. If it remains there, there is no treasure; if it falls, it will roll quickly away. It must, however, be replaced three times, and if it rolls three times toward the same place, there the treasure will be found. If it rolls a different way each time, one must seek about for the treasure.

The second method of divination by the axe is for the purpose of detecting robbers. The hatchet is cast on the ground, head downward, with the handle rising perpendicularly in the air. Those present must dance around it in a ring until the handle of the axe totters and it falls to the ground. The end of the handle indicates the direction in which the thieves must be sought. It is said by some that if this divination is to succeed, the head of the axe must be stuck in a round pot.

Ayperor (or Ipès)

A count of the infernal empire.

Ayton, W(illiam) A(lexander) (1816–1909)

Modern alchemist and member of the famous Hermetic Order of the **Golden Dawn** occult society. He was born April 28, 1816, in London, England, and was educated at Charterhouse School (then in London) and Trinity Hall, Cambridge (matriculating 1837; Latin Prize Essay, 1838–39; B.A., 1841). He was ordained as a deacon in the Church of England in 1841 and became a clergyman two years later. After serving in various country parishes, he was appointed vicar of Chacombe, Northamptonshire, in 1873.

Ayton was a Freemason and Theosophist as well as a member of the **Societas Rosicruciana in Anglia** before becoming one of the early members of the Golden Dawn in July 1888 at the age of 72, together with his wife. He took the magical motto Virtute Orta Occident Rarius (Those that rise by virtue rarely fall), his wife, Anne, took Soror Quam Potero Adjutabo (I will help as much as I can).

Ayton was a good Latin scholar, a firm believer in the **Mahatmas** of **Helena Petrovna Blavatsky,** as well as gnomes and **elementals.** With his wife, he had been a secret practitioner of **alchemy** for many years and claimed to have rediscovered the **elixir of life.** The poet **W. B. Yeats,** also a Golden Dawn member, described Ayton as "the most panic-stricken person" he had known. Presumably as an elderly clergyman, pursuing secret researches in occultism and alchemy, Ayton was fearful of being discovered by his Church superiors. He also had obsessive fears about being under threat of occult attack from Jesuits, whom he designated the "Black Brethren." Yeats apparently regarded Ayton with friendly but amused skepticism. In his book *The Trembling of the Veil* (1922), Yeats wrote:

"This old man took me aside that he might say—'I hope you never invoke spirits—that is a very dangerous thing to do. I am told that even the planetary spirits turn upon us in the end.' I said, 'Have you ever seen an apparition?' 'O, yes, once,' he said. 'I have my alchemical laboratory in a cellar under my house where the Bishop cannot see it. One day I was walking up and down there when I heard another footstep walking up and down beside me. I turned and saw a girl I had been in love with when I was a young man, but she died long ago. She wanted me to kiss her. O no, I would not do that.' 'Why not?' I said. 'O she might have got power over me.' 'Has your alchemical research had any success?' I said. 'Yes, I once made the elixir of life. A French alchemist said it had the right smell and the right colour' (the alchemist may have been **Éliphas Lévi**) 'but the first effect of the elixir is that your nails fall out and your hair falls off. I was afraid that I might have made a mistake and that nothing else might happen, so I put it away on a shelf. I meant to drink it when I was an old man, but when I got it down the other day it had all dried up.'"

Between 1886 and 1905 Ayton conducted an extensive correspondence with fellow Golden Dawn member **F. L. Gardner.** These letters, which contain valuable sidelights on occultism and Golden Dawn personalities, were published by Ellic Howe as *The Alchemist of the Golden Dawn; The Letters of the Revd W. A. Ayton to F. L. Gardner and Others, 1886–1905.*

In 1890 Ayton officiated at the marriage of Moina Bergson to **S. L. MacGregor Mathers,** both of whom played a key part in the history of the Golden Dawn. When **A. E. Waite** reorganized the GD in 1903, Ayton was a senior adept of the Second Order and was coopted as a co-chief. In 1908 Ayton translated Dr. Thomas Smith's *Life of John Dee* (1707) from Latin into English. He also transcribed a number of alchemical texts and Golden Dawn papers.

In his later years, Ayton retired to East Grinstead, Sussex, on a small pension, then to Saffron Walden, Hertfordshire, where he died January 1, 1909, at the age of 92.

Sources:

Howe, Ellic, ed. *The Alchemist of the Golden Dawn: The Letters of the Revd W. A. Ayton to F. L. Gardner and Others, 1886–1905.* Wellingborough, U.K.: Aquarian Press, 1985.

Azael

One of the **angels** who revolted against God. The ancient rabbis stated that he is chained on sharp stones in an obscure part of the desert, awaiting the last judgment.

Azazel

A demon of the second order, guardian of the goat. At the feast of expiation, which the ancient Jews celebrated on the tenth day of the seventh month, two goats were led to the high priest, who drew lots for them, the one for the Lord, the other for Azazel. The one on which the lot of the Lord fell was sacrificed, and his blood served for expiation. The high priest then put his two hands on the head of the other, confessed his sins and those of the people, charged the animal with them, and allowed him to be led into the desert and set free. And the people, having left the care of their iniquities to the goat of Azazel—also known as the scapegoat—return home with clean consciences.

According to Milton, Azazel is the principal standard bearer of the infernal armies. It was also the name of the demon used by Mark the heretic for his magic spells.

Azer

An angel of the elemental fire. According to some accounts, Azer is also the name of the father of Zoroaster, legendary author of the *Zend-Avesta,* the sacred work of the ancient Persians.

Azoth (or Azoch)

Name given by ancient alchemists to Mercury, also known as Astral Quintessence, Flying Salve, Animated Spirit, Ethelia, and Auraric. The term also implied the essential element of the transmutation process.

Sources:

Waite, A. E. *Azoth; or, The Star in the East.* London, 1893. Reprint, New Hyde Park, N.Y.: University Books, 1973.

B

Ba

The Egyptian conception of the soul, which, in the form of a man-headed bird, left the body after death and winged its flight to the gods. It returned at intervals to the mummy for the purpose of comforting it and reassuring it concerning immortality. Sometimes carved on the lid of mummy cases, it might be depicted grasping the **ankh** and the **nif;** occasionally it was represented as flying down the tomb shaft to the deceased or perched on the breast of the mummy. In the *Book of the Dead,* a chapter promises abundance of food to the ba.

The ba, or soul, should not be confused with the **ka,** the human **double.** In **Egypt** the human had both. After death, the ba left the body. The ka remained in the tomb and ventured forth in the likeness of the deceased to haunt family and friends.

Sources:

The Book of the Dead. Translated by E. A. Wallis Budge. New Hyde Park, N.Y.: University Books, 1960.

Baal Shem Tov (1698–1760)

Founder of the Jewish mystical movement called Hasidism that swept through Europe during the eighteenth and nineteenth centuries. Born as Israel, son of Eliezer, he became known as the Baal Shem Tov, "Master of the Good Name," or the Besht. Many legends circulated around the zaddikim, or holy leaders, of Hasidism, who were credited with miracles and spiritual insight.

Sources:

Buber, Martin. *The Legend of the Baal-Shem.* New York: Schocken Books, 1955.

———. *Tales of the Hasidim: The Early Masters.* New York: Schocken Books, 1947.

Hilsenrad, Zalman Aryeh, comp. *The Baal Shem Tov: His Birth and Early Manhood.* Brooklyn, N.Y.: Kehot Publication Society, 1967.

Kaplan, Aryeh. *Chassidic Masters: History, Biography, and Thought.* New York: Maznaim Publishing, 1984.

Baalberith

According to **Johan Weyer,** Baalberith is a demon of the second order, master of the Infernal Alliance. He was said to be secretary and keeper of the archives of hell.

Sources:

Weyer, Johannes. *Witches, Devils, and Doctors in the Renaissance: Johann Weyer, De Praestigiis.* Edited by George Mora. Binghamton, N.Y.: Medieval and Renaissance Texts and Studies, 1991.

Baalzephon

Captain of the guard and sentinels of hell (according to **Johan Weyer**).

Sources:

Weyer, Johannes. *Witches, Devils, and Doctors in the Renaissance: Johann Weyer, De Praestigiis.* Edited by George Mora. Binghamton, N.Y.: Medieval and Renaissance Texts and Studies, 1991.

Baaras

A marvelous plant known to the **Arabs** as the "Golden Plant," which is supposed to grow on Mount Libanus, underneath the road that leads to Damascus. It is said to flower in the month of May, after the melting of the snow. At night it can be seen by torchlight, but through the day it is invisible. It was believed to be of great assistance to alchemists in the transmutation of metals. It is alluded to by the historian Josephus (Lib. 8, Chap. 25.)

Bab

Name given to Mirza Ali Muhammad (1819–1850), who led the movement that was the direct precursor of the **Baha'i Faith.** Baha'u'llah (1817–1892), the founder of the Baha'i Faith, was a member of the babi religion, which was in turn heavily influenced by the traditions of Shia Islam, the form of Islam dominant in Iran (formerly Persia). The Bab, meaning the "Gate" (of revelation), was martyred for his faith.

Sources:

Balyuzi, H. M. *The Bab: The Herald of the Day of Days.* Oxford: G. Ronald, 1973.

Selections from the Writings of the Bab. Comp. Habib Taherzadeh. Haifa, Israel: Bahai World Center, 1976.

Babau

A species of ogre with which the nurses in the central parts of France used to frighten their charges. He was supposed to devour naughty children in salad. The ending "au" suggests a Celtic origin, as for example, "Y Mamau" is Welsh for "fairies."

Babiagora

Certain lakes of a gloomy nature between Hungary and Poland that have figured in various stories of witchcraft. Pools such as these were often used for purposes of **divination,** as by gazing down into clear water the mind is disposed to contemplation, often of a melancholy character. This form of divination is termed **hydromancy** and is similar to **crystal gazing.**

BABYLONIA

Ancient Religion and Magic

Magic was integral to the religion of ancient Babylonia. All the deities (the most prominent ones being Ea, Anu, and Enlil, the elder Bel) retained, even in the last centuries of Babylonian development, traces of their early demonic character. Ea, Anu, and Enlil formed a triad at the dawn of history and appear to have developed from an animistic group of world spirits. Although Ea became specialized as a god of the deep, Anu as a god of the sky, and Enlil as an earth god, each also had titles that emphasized that they had attributes overlapping those of the others. Thus Ea was Enki, earth lord, and as Aa was a lunar deity; he also had solar attributes. In the legend of Etana and the Eagle, his heaven is stated to be in the sky. Anu and Enlil as deities of thunder, rain, and fertility are closely linked to Ea, as Dagan, of the flooding and fertilizing Euphrates.

Each of these deities was accompanied by demonic groups. The spirits of disease were the "beloved sons of Bel"; the fates were the seven daughters of Anu; the seven storm demons, including the dragon and serpent, were of Ea's brood. The following description of Ea's older monstrous form occurs in one of the magical incantations translated by R. C. Thompson:

The head is the head of a serpent,
From his nostrils mucus trickles,
The mouth is beslavered with water;
The ears are those of a basilisk,
His horns are twisted into three curls,
He wears a veil in his head-band,
The body is a sun-fish full of stars,
The base of his feet are claws,
The sole of his foot has no heel;
His name is Sassu-wunnu,
A sea monster, a form of Ea.

Ea was "the great magician of the gods"; his sway over the forces of nature was secured by the performance of magical rites, and his services were obtained by humankind, who performed requisite ceremonies and repeated appropriate spells. Although he might be worshipped and propitiated in his temple at Eridu, he could also be conjured in reed huts. The latter indeed appear to have been the oldest holy places. In the Deluge myth, he makes a revelation in a dream to his human favorite, Pirnapishtim, the Babylonian Noah, of the approaching disaster planned by the gods, by addressing the reed hut in which he slept: "O, reed hut, hear; O, wall, understand." The sleeper received the divine message from the reeds. The reeds were to the Babylonians what rowan branches were to northern Europeans—they protected them against demons. Thus, for example, the dead were buried wrapped in reed mats.

The priesthood included two classes of magicians: the "Ashipu," who were exorcists, and the "Mashmashu," the purifers. The Ashipu priests played a prominent part in ceremonies, which had for their object the magical control of nature; in times of storm, disaster, and eclipse they were especially active. They also took the part of "witch doctors." Victims of disease were supposed to be possessed of devouring demons. In Thompson's translation:

Loudly roaring above, gibbering below,
They are the bitter venom of the gods . . .
Knowing no care, they grind the land like corn;
Knowing no mercy, they rage against mankind,
They spill their blood like rain,
Devouring their flesh and sucking their veins.

It was the business of the Ashipu priests to drive out the demon. Before he could do so he had to identify it. Having done so, he needed next to bring it under his influence. This he accomplished by reciting its history and detailing its characteristics. The secret of the magician's power was his knowledge. To cure toothache, for instance, it was necessary to know the "Legend of the Worm." The worm was **vampire**-like and absorbed the blood of victims, but specialized in gums.

The legend relates that the worm came into existence as follows: Anu created the heavens, the heavens created the earth, the earth created the rivers, and the rivers created the canals, then the canals created marshes, and the marshes created the worm. In due time the worm appeared before Shamash, the sun god, and Ea, god of the deep, weeping and hungry. "What will you give me to eat and drink?" it cried. The gods promised that it would get dried bones and scented wood. Apparently the worm realized that this was the food of death, for it answered: "What are dry bones to me? Set me upon the gums that I may drink the blood of the teeth and take away the strength of the gums." When the worm heard this legend repeated, it came under the magician's power and was dismissed to the marshes, while Ea was invoked to smite it. Different demons were exorcised by different processes. A fever patient might receive the following treatment:

Sprinkle this man with water,
Bring unto him a censer and a torch,
That the plague demon which resteth in the body of the man,
Like water may trickle away.

Demons might also be attacked by a form of image magic. The magician began by fashioning a figure of dough, wax, clay, or pitch. This figure might be placed on a fire, mutilated, or placed in running water to be washed away. As the figure suffered, so did the demon it represented, by the magic of the word of Ea.

In treating the sick, the magician might release a raven at the bedside of the sick person so that it would conjure the demon of fever to take flight likewise. Sacrifices could also be offered, as substitutes for patients, to provide food for the spirit of the disease. A young goat was slain and the priest repeated:

The kid is the substitute for mankind;
He hath given the kid for his life,
He hath given the head of the kid for the head of the man.
A pig might be offered:
Give the pig in his stead
And give the flesh of it for his flesh,
The blood of it for his blood.

The cures were numerous and varied. After the patient recovered, the mashmashu priests purified the house. The ceremony entailed the sprinkling of sacred water, the burning of incense, and the repetition of magical charms. People protected their homes against attack by placing certain plants over the doorways and windows. An ass's halter seems to have been used, as horseshoes have been in Europe to repel witches and evil spirits.

The purification ceremonies suggest the existence of **taboo.** For a period, the sick were "unclean" and had to be isolated. The recently recovered could make their way to the temple, to which was attached a House of Light, where fire ceremonies were performed, and a House of Washing, where patients bathed in sacred water. The priest would anoint the individual with oil to complete the release from uncleanliness. Foods were also tabooed at certain seasons. It was unlawful for a man to eat pork on the thirtieth of Ab (July-August), the twenty-seventh of Tisri, and other dates. Fish, ox flesh, and bread were similarly tabooed on specific dates.

A man's luck depended greatly on his observance of these rules. But although he might observe all ceremonies, he might still meet with ill fortune on unlucky days. On the festival day of Marduk (Merodach) a man must not change his clothes, nor put on white garments, nor offer up sacrifices. Sure disaster would overcome a king if he drove out in a chariot, or a physician if he laid hands on the sick, or a priest who sat in judgment, and so on. On lucky days good fortune was the heritage of everyone. Good fortune meant good health in many cases, and it was sometimes assured by worshiping the dreaded spirit of disease called Ura.

A legend related that this demon once made up his mind to destroy all humankind. His counsellor, Ishun, however, prevailed upon him to change his mind, and he said, "Whoever will laud my name I will bless with plenty. No one will oppose the person who proclaims the glory of my valor. The worshiper who chants the hymn of praise to me will not be afflicted by disease, and he will find favor in the eyes of the King and his nobles."

Ghosts

Among the spirits who were the enemies of mankind the ghosts of the dead were not the least virulent, and especially the ghosts of those who had not been properly buried. These homeless spirits (the grave was the home of the dead) wandered about the streets searching for food and drink, or haunting houses. Not infrequently they did real injury to mankind.

Of horrible aspect, they appeared before children and frightened them to death. They waylaid travelers and mocked those who were in sorrow. The screech-owl was a mother who had died in childbed and wailed her grief nightly in solitary places. Occasionally she appeared in monstrous form and slew wayfarers.

Adam's first wife **Lilith** was a demon who had once been beautiful and was in the habit of deceiving lovers and working ill against them. A hag, Labartu, haunted mountains and marshes and children had to be charmed against her attacks. She also had a human history.

The belief that the spirits of the dead could be conjured from their graves to make revelations was also prevalent in Babylonia. In the Gilgamesh epic, the hero visits the tomb of his old friend and fellow warrior Ea-Bani. The ghost rises like a "weird gust" of wind and answers the various questions addressed to it with great sadness. Babylonian outlook on the future life was tinged by profound gloom and pessimism. It was the fate of even the ghosts of the most fortunate and ceremonially buried dead to exist in darkness and amid dust. The ghost of Ea-Bani said to Gilgamesh: "Were I to inform thee the law of the underworld which I have experienced, Thou wouldst sit down and shed tears all day long." Gilgamesh lamented: "The sorrow of the underworld hath taken hold upon thee."

Priests who performed magical ceremonies had to be clothed in magical garments. They received inspiration from their clothing. Similarly the gods derived power from the skins of animals, with which they were associated from the earliest time. Thus Ea was clad in the skin of the fish—probably the fish totem of the Ea tribe.

The dead were not admitted to the heavens of the gods. When a favored human being, like Utnapishtim, the Babylonian Noah, joined the company of the gods, he was assigned an island paradise where Gilgamesh visited him. There he dwelt with his wife. Gilgamesh was not permitted to land and held converse with his immortal ancestor while sitting in his boat. The deities secured immortality by eating the "food of life" and drinking the "water of life."

Astrology

The ancient Babylonians were credited with some of the first correct astronomical observations, and they were also pioneers of **astrology,** which they attributed to the god Marduk or Bel, said to have created the sun, moon, stars, and five planets. They knew that the length of the solar year was approximately 365.4 days and had divided the period of 24 hours into 12 beru (double hours) in accordance with the divisions of the equator, each of which was divided into 60 minutes, and each minute into 60 seconds. Such data were recorded on clay tablets in the library of the Babylonian king Assurbani-pal, circa 668 B.C.E. Their astrologers attributed human characteristics to planetary influences at birth in much the same way as modern astrologers.

Sources:

Ferry, David. *Gilgamesh: a New Rendering into English Verse.* New York: Farrar, Straus and Giroux, 1992.

Jastrow, Morris. *Aspects of Religious Belief and Practice in Babylonia & Assyria.* New York: G. P. Putnam's Sons, 1911.

Kramer, Samuel N. *From the Tablets of Sumer.* Falcon's Wing, 1956.

———. *Gilgamesh and the Huluppu-tree: A Reconstructed Sumerian Text.* Chicago: University of Chicago Press, 1938.

Lenormant, Francois. *Chaldean Magic: Its Origin & Development.* London: Samuel Bagster, [1877].

Spence, Lewis. *Myths and Legends of Babylonia & Assyria.* London, 1916. Reprint, Detroit: Gale Research, 1975.

Thierens, A. E. *Astrology in Mesopotamian Culture.* Leiden: E. J. Brill, 1935.

Bach, Edward (1886–1936)

British physician who developed an unconventional system of healing. Bach (his name is pronounced "batch") was a graduate of University College Hospital (M.B., B.S., M.R.C.S.). He left his flourishing Harley Street practice in favor of homeopathy, seeking a more natural system of healing than allopathic medicine. He was appointed bacteriologist and pathologist to the London Homeopathic Hospital, but in due course developed his own simple system of healing based on his psychic insight. He concluded that healing should be as simple and natural as the development of plants, which were nourished and given healing properties by earth, air, water, and sun.

Bach believed that he could sense the individual healing properties of flowers by placing his hands over the petals. His remedies were prepared by floating summer flowers in a bowl of clear stream water exposed to sunlight for three hours.

He developed 38 remedies, one for each of the negative states of mind suffered by human beings, which he classified under seven group headings: fear, uncertainty, insufficient interest in present circumstances, loneliness, oversensitivity to influences and ideas, despondency or despair, and overcare for the welfare of others. The Bach remedies can be prescribed for plants, animals, and other living creatures as well as human beings.

In the last years of his life, Bach abandoned his successful medical practice and lived in a cottage on the borders of Buckinghamshire, where he developed and prepared his healing system.

The Bach Centre now carries on the doctors's work at Mount Vernon, Sotwell, Wallingford, Berkshire. Some of Bach's ideas now have greater relevance through modern interest in the interaction between **plants** and human beings. During the last years of his life, he published several short books detailing his research. These and other publications dealing with Bach's works are kept in print by the Bach Centre. In the United States, there is an Edward Bach Healing Society, 644 Merrick Rd., Lynbrook, NY 11563.

As many have observed, the Bach system is a gentle method of healing, and many physicians have reported favorably on it. Much of the efficacy of the Bach remedies seemed to depend upon the fact that they were never mass produced but rather prepared individually with care and love for human beings, a fact that suggests that their value may have rested largely on a placebo effect.

Sources:

Bach, Edward. *Heal Thyself.* London: C. W. Daniel, 1931.

———. *The Twelve Healers and Other Remedies: A Simple Herbal Treatment.* 3d ed. London: C. W. Daniel, 1936.

Bach, Edward, and F. J. Wheeler. *The Bach Flower Remedies.* New Canaan, Conn.: Keats, 1977.

Chancellor, P. *Handbook of the Bach Flower Remedies.* London: C. W. Daniel, 1971.

Weeks, N. *The Medical Discoveries of Edward Bach.* London: C. W. Daniel, 1940.

Wheeler, Francis J. *The Bach Remedies Repertory.* London: C. W. Daniel, 1952.

Bach, Richard (1936–)

Writer on aviation who became famous with his book *Jonathan Livingston Seagull* (Macmillan, 1970; Avon, 1973), written as a result of psychic experience over a period of several years. He was a U.S. Air Force pilot from 1956 to 1959 and a technical writer for Douglas Aircraft and associate editor of *Flying* magazine from 1961 to 1964. Bach was also a director of the Antique Airplane Association and editor of its magazine *Antiquer,* and did some airplane barnstorming in the Midwest. His early books include *Stranger to the Ground* (1963), *Biplane* (1966), and *Nothing by Chance: A Gypsy Pilot's Adventures in Modern America* (1969).

In 1959, while living at Belmont Shore, California, Bach was walking by the waterfront when he heard a disembodied voice say

"Jonathan Livingston Seagull." This was followed by a kind of daydream of a seagull flying alone at sunrise, and a realization of its significance. Bach felt impelled to write this down, using a green ballpoint pen and some old scratch paper (the only writing materials handy), and completed the first part of the story of Jonathan Livingston Seagull up to the point of Jonathan's expulsion from the flock. Not until eight years later in Iowa, 1,500 miles away, did the next section of the book come to Bach in a dream. He immediately typed it out and sent it to a magazine, but it was instantly rejected. Next he sent it to *Private Pilot,* which published it reluctantly at below regular rate, but the reader response was so great that the publisher demanded more seagull stories. Bach sat down at his typewriter and, with virtually no rewriting, knocked out the second and third parts of the J. L. Seagull saga, duly published as magazine stories.

The stories were published in book form through the judgment of Eleanor Friede, then an editor at Macmillan (now president of Eleanor Friede Books), who had an intuition about the book. Within two years the book sold over one million copies, was on best-seller lists for nearly a year, became a Book of the Month Club choice, was condensed by *Reader's Digest* books, and was translated into a dozen languages. It was banned only by the People's Republic of China for no very clear reason, but as composers Beethoven and Mozart also shared this prohibition at that time, Bach thought J. L. Seagull was in very good company.

The widespread success of *Jonathan Livingston Seagull* lies in its simple but inspiring allegory, with spiritual and psychic overtones. It embodies Bach's own philosophy, "Find what it is you want in the world to do, and then do it." Bach does not ascribe his inspired story to any psychic entity, in spite of the strange way it was manifested, but believes that part of his personality on an unconscious level was communicating with his everyday self. However, he has also had several psychic experiences, including **out-of-the-body** travel and healing.

His later books include *A Gift of Wings* (1974); *Illusions: The Adventures of a Reluctant Messiah* (1977); *There's No Such Place as Far Away* (1979).

Sources:

Bach, Richard. *Illusions: The Adventures of a Reluctant Messiah.* New York: Delacorte Press, 1977.

———. *Jonathan Livingston Seagull.* New York: Macmillan, 1970.

———. *One: A Novel.* New York: William Morrow, 1988.

Bach Centre

British center for the preparation and dispensation of the remedies developed by Dr. **Edward Bach** (1886–1936). These were prepared from summer flowers floated on a bowl of clear stream water exposed to sunlight for three hours. Bach developed 38 remedies, one for each of the negative states of mind suffered by human beings, classified under seven group headings: fear, uncertainty, insufficient interest in present circumstances, loneliness, oversensitivity to influences and ideas, despondency or despair, and overcare for the welfare of others.

Bach, who had psychic faculties, believed that his special preparations transferred a subtle force from the flowers to the water. The sunlight released vital astral forces in the flowers, which had a positive effect on human astral forces. Bach spent his last years at a cottage on the borders of Buckinghamshire, England, which has now become the center for his remedies. Address: Bach Centre, Mount Vernon, Sotwell, Wallingford, Berkshire, England.

Books and information relating to the flower remedies of the late Edward Bach are available in the United States from the Dr. Edward Bach Healing Society, 644 Merrick Rd., Lynbrook, NY 11563. The society issues a quarterly newsletter.

Sources:

Bach, Edward, and F. J. Wheeler. *The Bach Flower Remedies.* New Canaan, Conn.: Keats, 1977.

Chancellor, P. *Handbook of the Bach Flower Remedies.* London: C. W. Daniel, 1971.

Weeks, N. *The Medical Discoveries of Edward Bach.* London: C. W. Daniel, 1940.

Bachelor

One of the names given to Satan when he appeared in the guise of a great he-goat for the purpose of sexual intercourse with the witches.

Bacis See Bakis

Back to Godhead (Magazine)

Monthly publication of the **International Society for Krishna Consciousness.** Address: Box 16027, North Hollywood, CA 91615-9900.

Backster, Cleve (b. 1924)

Former interrogator for the CIA who became one of America's leading polygraph (lie detector) specialists. He became director of the Keeler Polygraph Institute in Chicago and later founded the Cleve Backster School of Lie Detection in Manhattan, New York. During the late 1960s, he became famous for his experiments in plant ESP, using polygraph techniques. His experiments tend to support the idea that plants are sensitive to human thoughts. Some of his experiments were sponsored by the Parapsychology Foundation and involved tests to see if plants reacted to the destruction of live cells.

Backster believed **plants** that had become attuned to a particular human being appeared to maintain that link wherever the person went and whatever he did. Backster concluded: "There exists an as yet undefined primary perception in plant life, that animal life termination can serve as a remotely located stimulus to demonstrate this perception capability, and that this perception facility in plants can be shown to function independently of human involvement." Procedures and results were reported in the *International Journal of Parapsychology* in 1968.

The Backster Research Foundation was founded to sponsor Backster's research in plant sensitivity. It was funded by a $10,000 grant from the Mary Reynolds Babcock Foundation of Winston-Salem, North Carolina. William M. Bondurant of the Babcock Foundation stated that Backster's work "indicates there may be a primary form of instantaneous communication among all living things that transcends the physical laws we know now—and that seems to warrant looking into."

While some of Backster's conclusions may seem fantastic, the sensitivity of plant life to environments is indisputable. What is unknown is how much of this sensitivity is related to any paranormal interchange. Much pioneer work in this field was investigated with delicate apparatus by the late **Sir Jagadis Chunder Bose,** an Indian scientist in Calcutta. The careful scientific experiments of Bose were reported in a series of papers and books, notably *Response in the Living and the Non-Living* (1902) and *Plant Autographs and Their Revelations* (1927). Drawing upon the experiments of Bose, later researchers investigated the reactions of plants when stimulated by music and dancing. The work of Cleve Backster, Bose, and others revived the whole question of plant sensitivity. While many were impressed with Backster's data, others were skeptical and suggested alternative explanations for his results while others questioned the methodology.

Sources:

Backster, Cleve. "Evidence of a Primary Perception in Plant Life." *International Journal of Parapsychology* 10 (1968): 329–48.

Galston, Arthur W., and Clifford L. Slayman. "Plant Sensitivity and Sensation." In *Science and the Paranormal: Probing the Evidence of the Supernatural.* Edited by George O. Abell and Barry Singer. New York: Charles Scribner's Sons, 1981.

Tompkins, Peter, and Christopher Bird. *The Secret Life of Plants.* New York: Harper and Row, 1973.

Whitman, John. *The Psychic Power of Plants.* London: New English Library, 1974.

Backward Masking

A technique claimed to be used in some **rock music** (especially heavy metal) in order to convey secret, destructive messages. Some conservative Evangelical Christians have claimed that various words and sentences in rock music songs indicate Satanic messages when played backwards. Reversed rituals are a traditional aspect of black magic spells.

The belief in backward masking rests largely on an understanding of subliminal perception, the ability of the brain to take in and store information quite apart from any conscious realization that the information is being received. While a certain amount of subliminal learning seems possible, the idea of backward masking carries the idea to an extreme by suggesting that the brain can receive a coded message and unscramble it. While many Evangelicals believe that Satanism is a real force among contemporary youth, only a few have paid attention to the highly dubious claims concerning backward masking.

Sources:

Aranza, Jacob. *Backward Masking Unmasked.* Shreveport, Louis.: Huntington House, 1983.

Bacon, Roger (ca. 1220–1292)

Versatile British scientist and philosopher around whom accumulated many legends of occult powers. He was born near Ilchester in Somerset, England. He entered the Order of St. Francis and studied mathematics and medicine in Oxford and Paris. Returning to England, he devoted attention to philosophy and also wrote Latin, Greek, and Hebrew grammars.

Bacon was a pioneer of astronomy and, being acquainted with the properties of lenses, may have foreshadowed the telescope. In the mechanical sciences, Bacon envisioned boats propelled without oars, cars that move without horses, and even machines that fly in the air. In the field of pure chemistry, Bacon's name is associated with the making of gunpowder, for even if the discovery cannot be wholly attributed to him, at least his experiments with niter paved its way.

His study of **alchemy** naturally led him to a belief in the **philosophers' stone,** by which gold might be purified to a degree impossible by any other means, and also to a belief in the elixir of life, which, along similar principles of purification, might fortify the human body against death. Thus man could become practically immortal, and by knowledge of the appropriate herbs or by acquaintance with planetary influences, he could experience the same consummation.

Ahead of his time, Bacon was looked on with considerable suspicion, which eventually led to persecution. The brethren of his order practically cast him out, and he was compelled to retire to Paris and to submit to a régime of repression. A prolific author, he was forbidden to write, and it was not till 1266 that Guy de Foulques, the papal legate in England—later Pope Clement IV—heard of Bacon's fame and invited him to break his enforced silence. Bacon hailed the opportunity and in spite of hardship and poverty, he finished his *Opus Majus, Opus Minus,* and *Opus Tertium.*

Clement seemed to approve of these works, because Bacon was allowed to return to Oxford, where he continued his scientific studies and the composition of scientific works. He attempted a compendium of philosophy which still exists in part, but its subject matter displeased the ruling powers, and Bacon's misfortunes began afresh. His books were burned, and again he was thrown into prison. He remained there for 14 years, during which time he probably continued to write. About 1292 he was given his liberty, however he is believed to have died shortly thereafter.

Of Bacon's works, which were numerous, many still remain in manuscript and about a dozen have been printed at various times. Many are obscure treatises on alchemy, but the works he wrote by invitation of Clement are the most important. The *Opus Majus* is divided into six parts treating of the causes of error, the relation between philosophy and theology, the utility of grammar, mathematical perspective, and experimental science. The *Opus Minus,* of which only part has been preserved, was intended to be a summary of the former work. The *Opus Tertium,* though written after the other two, actually serves as an introduction to them and is in part supplementary to them. These works, large though they be, were intended to be forerunners of an even greater work to examine the principles of all the sciences; however, this latter endeavor was probably little more than begun.

Although much of Bacon's work and many of his beliefs reflect the outlook of his period, in his devotion to the experimental sciences he stood far above his peers. This has led to an accretion of legendary material around Bacon's name, by virtue of which he has been regarded as a great magician. In the sixteenth century, when the study of magic was pursued with increased zeal, Friar Bacon became the subject of a popular book, entitled *The History of Friar Bacon,* and the subject of an often-performed play by Robert Greene, one of the dramatists of the age. The greater part of his history of Friar Bacon is evidently the invention of the writer, who lived in the time of Queen Elizabeth. He adapted some of the older traditions and fleshed out the narrative with fables taken from books of the time, including stories about two other legendary occult conjurers, Friars Bungay and Vandermast. The recital is further enlivened with the pranks of Bacon's servant, Miles.

Sources:

Bacon, Roger. *The Mirror of Alchemy.* Los Angeles: Press of the Pegacycle Lady, 1975.

———. *The Opus Majus of Roger Bacon.* 2 vols. Philadelphia: University of Pennsylvania Press, 1928.

———. *Roger Bacon's Philosophy of Nature: A Critical Edition.* Oxford: Clarendon Press, 1983.

Bridges, John Henry. *The Life and Work of Roger Bacon.* 1914. Reprint, Merrick, N.Y.: Richwood, 1976.

Easton, Stewart C. *Roger Bacon and His Search for a Universal Science.* Westport, Conn.: Greenwood Press, 1970.

Little, A. G. *Roger Bacon Essays.* Oxford: Clarendon Press, 1914.

Bacoti

A common name for the augurs and sorcerers of Tonkin in Indochina. They were often consulted by the friends of deceased persons for the purpose of holding communication with the dead.

Bacstrom, Sigismond (ca. 1750–1805)

Physician who was also an alchemist and a **Rosicrucian.** Believed to be of Scandinavian origin, he spent some time as a ship's surgeon. While visiting the island of Mauritius, he met the mysterious occultist and alchemist Comte Louis de Chazel, who initiated him into a Societas Rosae Crucis. De Chazel owned an extensive library of occult and mystical works and a well-equipped laboratory for astronomical observations and alchemical experiments. He informed Bacstrom that he had succeeded in making the **philosophers' stone** and demonstrated the transmutation of quicksilver into gold. Subsequently Bacstrom lived in London and had discussions with other individuals interested in hermetic subjects. He translated a number of treatises on **alchemy** from German, French, and Latin into English, adding his own commentaries. His manuscript *Essay on Alchemy* was published in a limited edition under the title *Bacstrom's Alchemical Anthology,* edited by J. W. Hamilton-Jones (1960).

Bad

A jinni (or genie) of Persia (modern-day Iran), supposed to have command over the winds and tempests. He presided over the twenty-second day of the month.

Badger

To bury the foot of a badger underneath one's sleeping place is believed by **Voudou** worshipers and some **Gypsies** to excite or awaken love.

Bael

A demon cited in the **Grand Grimoire;** head of the infernal powers. It is with him that **Johan Weyer** commenced his inventory of the famous *Pseudonomarchia Daemonum.* He alluded to Bael as the first monarch of hell and said that his estates are situated on the eastern regions thereof. He had three heads, that of a crab, a cat, and a man. Sixty-six legions obey him.

Sources:

Weyer, Johannes. *Witches, Devils, and Doctors in the Renaissance: Johann Weyer, De Praestigiis.* Edited by George Mora. Binghamton, N.Y.: Medieval and Renaissance Texts and Studies, 1991.

Baggally, William Wortley (d. 1928)

Former member of the Council of the British **Society for Psychical Research.** He cooperated with **Hereward Carrington** and Everard Feilding on investigation of the phenomena of the famous medium **Eusapio Palladino** in Naples during 1908.

Baggally joined the Society for Psychical Research in 1896 because he was interested in establishing experimental proof of survival after death, and he was not satisfied with the standard of evidence among most Spiritualists. His knowledge and proficiency in conjuring magic made him a shrewd and intelligent investigator of psychic phenomena. He experimented with many well-known mediums, including **William Eglinton, Cecil Husk,** Mrs. Corner, **Mary Showers, Etta Wriedt,** and the stage performers **Julius and Mrs. Zancig.** Baggally died March 14, 1928.

Sources:

Baggally, W. W., Everard Fielding, and Hereward Carrington. "Report on a Series of Sittings with Eusapia Palladino." *Proceedings* of the Society for Psychical Research, 23 (1909): 309.

Berger, Arthur S., and Joyce Berger. *Encyclopedia of Parapsychology and Psychical Research.* New York: Paragon House, 1991.

Bagnall, (Reginald) Oscar (Gartside) (b. 1893)

British pioneer of **aura** research. Born March 28, 1893, in Berkshire, England, he was educated at Malvern and Magdalene College, Cambridge, where he read natural sciences (biology, chemistry, and physics) and took his degree in science. After the outbreak of World War I, he left Magdalene to take a commission but was released from active service due to an injury. He returned to Magdalene for advanced studies, working as a schoolmaster and coaching young students for medical examinations.

While a professional biologist, he researched color, as a result of which he became interested in the phenomenon of human radiations. He experimented with dye screens in relation to the mechanics of human vision and in particular the effects of dicyanin, which had been studied by pioneer **Walter J. Kilner,** author of the book *The Human Atmosphere; or, The Aura Made Visible by the Aid of Chemical Screens* (1911).

Bagnall's own valuable book, *The Origin and Properties of the Human Aura* (1937), is also a major study of the subject and validates many of Kilner's findings. Both Kilner and Bagnall brought the phenomena, formerly limited to study by psychics and occultists, onto firmer scientific ground. Since then, modern interest in aura research has been stimulated by the discovery of the **Kirlian aura.**

Sources:

Bagnall, Oscar. *The Origin and Properties of the Human Aura.* 1937. Rev. ed. New Hyde Park, N.Y.: University Books, 1970.

Bagoe

A pythoness (priestess of **Delphi** in ancient Greece) who is believed to have been the Erithryean sibyl. She is said to have been the first woman to have practiced the diviner's art. She practiced in Tuscany and judged all events by the sound of thunder. Some identify Bagoe with **Bigois,** another Tuscan sorcerer.

Bagommedes

A knight mentioned by the poet Gautier in the *Conte du Graal* (a medieval version of the Holy **Grail** legend). It is said that he was fastened to a tree by Kay and left hanging head downward until released by Perceval. On Bagommedes' return to the court, he challenged Kay but was prevented by **King Arthur** from slaying him.

The Baha'i Faith

A world religious body dating from mid-nineteenth century Persia (now Iran). Founded out of Shia Islam, which dominates the religious life of Iran, the Baha'i Faith projected a broad view of the oneness of mankind and coming unity of different religions.

Members of the Baha'i Faith generally look upon three major figures as founding influences on the new religion. Mirza Ali Muhammad (1819–1850), known as the *Bab,* or "Gate," of revelation, founded a movement in Persia in the 1840s based upon the belief that the promised madhi, the successor of Muhammad, was at hand. Most followers believed the Bab to be the madhi. However, he was martyred in 1850.

Two years later, an attempt on the life of the Shah of Persia by a follower of the Bab released further persecutions. Mirza Husayn Ali (1817–1892) was among those imprisoned. During his four months of confinement he came to believe that he was the Holy One predicted by the Bab, though he confided that insight to only a few. He, his family, and many of the Bab's followers were exiled—first to Baghdad, then Adrianople, Constantinople, and eventually in a prison at Acre (now Israel). In 1863, after being moved from Baghdad, he declared his new revelation, and from that time forward people began to recognize him as Bah'u'llah, the Glory of God. Baha'u'llah spent the rest of his life under house arrest in Acre, where he composed the majority of his writings, now considered as scripture by the movement.

Baha'u'llah's son, Abbas Effendi (1844–1921), known as Abdu'l-Baha (or Servant of Baha), is considered the exemplar of the faith. Like his father he was confined at Acre until 1908, when he was released following the Revolution of the Young Turks. He was then able to oversee the worldwide spread of the Baha'i Faith. He was in turn succeeded by his grandson, Shoghi Effendi (1897–1957), considered the guardian of the faith. The writings of the Bab, Baha'u'llah, and Abdu'-Baha are considered scripture by followers of the faith, and those of Shoghi Effendi as infallible commentary.

The teachings of the Faith are universalist, based on the claim that divine revelation is continuous and that the Baha'i Faith is the culmination of the world's major religions. The Baha'i Faith proclaims the unity of God and His Prophets, upholds the principle of an unfettered search after truth, condemns all forms of superstition and prejudice, and teaches that the fundamental purpose of religion is to promote concord and harmony. Religion must go hand-in-hand with science, as it constitutes the sole and ultimate basis of a peaceful, ordered, and progressive society.

Baha'i followers believe in the principle of equal opportunity, rights, and privileges for both sexes; compulsory education; and the abolishment of extremes of poverty and wealth. Work performed in the spirit of service is considered of equal rank to worship. The Faith has become part of the international peace movement and in that regard recommends the adoption of an auxiliary international language, and the formation of the necessary agencies for establishing and safeguarding a permanent and universal peace.

The Baha'i Faith has its international headquarters in Haifa, Israel, and membership now extends to 300 countries and territories, where centers have been established. They remain a minority in contemporary Iran and were among the losers in the revolution that resulted in the departure of the shah in 1979. Many Baha'is were persecuted and executed under the conservative rule of Ayatollah Khomeini. In the United States, the Baha'i National Center is located in Wilmette, Illinois; readings are given from the sacred scriptures in a large and beautiful House of Worship, and the facilities are available for individual worship and meditation. The quarterly journal *World Order* is published by the National Spiritual Assembly of the Baha'is of the U.S. national center at 536 Sheridan Rd., Wilmette, IL 60091. In Britain, the National Spiritual Assembly of the Baha'is of the U.K. is at 27 Rutland Gate, London S.W.7, England.

Sources:

Faizi, Gloria. *The Baha'i Faith: An Introduction.* New Delhi, India: Baha'i Publishing Trust, 1988.

Hatcher, William S., and J. Douglas Martin. *The Baha'i Faith.* San Francisco: Harper & Row, 1984.

Perkins, Mary, and Philip Hainsworth. *The Baha'i Faith.* London: Ward Lock Educational, 1980.

Stockman, Robert H. *The Baha'i Faith in America: Origins, 1892–1900.* Wilmette, Ill.: Baha'i Publishing Trust, 1985.

Bahaman

A jinni (or genie) who, according to Persian tradition, appeased anger; governed oxen, sheep, and all animals of a peaceful disposition.

Bahir

("Brightness"). A mystical Hebrew treatise of the twelfth or thirteenth century, the work of a French rabbi named Isaac ben Abraham of Posquières, commonly called "Isaac the Blind." (See **Kabala**)

Baian (or Baianus)

Son of Simeon, king of the Bulgarians of 970 C.E., and a mighty magician, who was said to transform himself into a wolf whenever he desired. He could also adopt other shapes and render himself invisible. A primary example of what is termed a **werwolf,** he is alluded to by Jean de Nynauld in his book *De la lycanthropie* (Paris, 1615).

Bailey, Alice A(nne) (LaTrobe-Bateman) (1880–1949)

A noted Theosophist who later founded her own **Arcane School** of esoteric teaching. Bailey was born June 16, 1880, in Manchester, England. An unhappy childhood led her to attempt suicide; however, at the age of 15, a mysterious stranger wearing a turban walked into her room, sat beside her, and stated that she should prepare herself for an important mission. For many years she believed her visitor was Jesus Christ, but later she saw a picture on the wall at the **Theosophical Society,** which she knew to be the stranger. It was **Koot Hoomi,** one of the mysterious **mahatmas** claimed to have inspired and communicated with **Helena Petrovna Blavatsky.**

Bailey was raised in the Church of England, and after attending finishing school in London, she worked for the Young Women's Christian Association. She spent some time in India with the YWCA and at a soldier's home there she met Walter Evans. They married in 1907 and moved to Cincinnati, Ohio, where Walter studied for the Episcopal priesthood at Lane Theological Seminary. After graduation, they moved to California, but the marriage was an unhappy one; eventually they divorced. Like **Annie Besant,** who also had an unhappy marriage with an Anglican clergymen, the emotional ordeal of marital breakdown culminated in an interest in Theosophy.

In the case of Alice Bailey, she was introduced to Theosophy by friends in Pacific Grove, California. She was attracted by the Theosophical concepts of a spiritual hierarchy, karma, and **reincarnation.** She joined the society and moved to the headquarters at Krotona in 1917, where she edited the society's periodical, the *Messenger,* and became friendly with Foster Bailey, national secretary of the society.

In November 1919 while walking in the hills, Bailey was contacted by another spiritual master, Djual Khul, who came to be known as "The Tibetan." He requested her to be his amanuensis for a series of books, to be dictated telepathically. The first book, titled *Initiation, Human and Solar* commenced in 1920, and over the next 30 years some 18 other books were produced. She married Foster Bailey in 1920.

The production of the "Tibetan" books and the charge by Alice Bailey that the society was dominated by the Esoteric Section led to disagreements, and both Bailey and her husband left the society. They founded the Lucis Trust to publish the books and the magazine *Beacon.* In 1923 they founded the Arcane School to disseminate spiritual teachings. The school became an international organization, branching into special groups. The New Group of World Servers was dedicated to uniting people of goodwill in the goal of creating a new world civilization. *Triangles* evolved as a spiritual service through groups of three individuals uniting with others.

The books of the Tibetan promoted the ideal of a forthcoming world religion uniting East and West, and the Arcane School developed special prayers and meditations, such as the "Full Moon Meditation" and the "Great Invocation," toward this goal. Another theme arising from the Tibetan writings was the reappearance of the Christ. After the death of Alice Bailey in 1949, the Arcane School split into several groups. Foster Bailey headed the Arcane School and the Lucis Trust until his death in 1977. The work is currently headed by the Baileys' daughter, Mary Bailey.

Sources:

Bailey, Alice A. *The Unfinished Autobiography of Alice A. Bailey.* New York: Lucis Publishing, 1951.

———. *Works.* New York: Lucis Publishing, New York, various dates.

Sinclair, John R. *The Alice Bailey Inheritance.* Wellingborough, England: Turnstone Press, 1984.

Thirty Years' Work. New York: Lucis Publishing, n.d.

Bailey, Charles (1870–1947)

Famous **apport** medium of Melbourne, **Australia,** discussed for years both in Australia and in Europe. Though repeatedly caught in fraud, he was able to continue work with a small group of believers until shortly before his death. Bailey was a bootmaker by trade when he began his mediumship in 1889. For many years he was the private medium of Thomas Welton Stanford, a Melbourne millionaire, who made a collection of Bailey's apports, the first museum of its kind. It is preserved at Stanford University, Palo Alto, California, to which he gave an endowment of $50,000 for psychical research in 1911.

Public attention for Bailey's phenomena was aroused in 1902 by accounts published in the *Harbinger of Light.* In 1904 the records of a long series of experiments appeared in *Rigid Tests of the Occult* by Dr. C. W. McCarthy, one of the leading medical men of Sydney. The conditions of these experiments were severe. The medium was searched, stripped, sometimes dressed in a new suit, tied up in a sealed sack, with openings for the hands to hold the apported object; on special occasions the sitters were also searched and the medium was enclosed in a cage with close mosquito netting. The doors were locked or sealed, no furniture was kept in the room except chairs and a table, the fireplace was blocked, and the only second floor window was papered.

Immediately after Bailey went into trance, the controls took charge of the phenomena. The chief **control** was a "Dr. Whitcombe," sometime physician in Melbourne. Another, "Dr. Robinson," claimed to have been professor of Syro-Chaldaic literature in New York. The apport of old coins and Babylonian clay tablets with cuneiform inscriptions were apparently due to him. A third control was a Hindu named "Abdul." It was he who actually brought the apports. A few minutes were sufficient, and when light was produced, the medium was found to hold a live bird and a nest in each hand. Many of these birds were kept for days in cages. Sometimes they disappeared as mysteriously as they came, and sometimes they died in captivity.

Once a live, shovel-nosed shark, 18 inches long, was brought in. A crab, with dripping seaweed, was similarly apported. Another time a long snake was found coiling around the medium's neck. On being covered with a cloth it disappeared in full light. Undercover apports sometimes appeared in good visibility, or were seen to drop from a height away from the medium. In McCarthy's cap, after being covered by a handkerchief, a turtle was discovered. Another time he found a jewel in his hand under a palm leaf.

The clay tablets and the Egyptian and Indian coins that Bailey apported in abundance were submitted by McCarthy to the Department of Egyptian and Assyrian Antiquities of the British Museum. The tablets were pronounced imitations and the coins genuine but of no rarity or value.

Sir Arthur Conan Doyle related his personal experiences with Bailey in the *History of Spiritualism* (1926), adding that on further inquiry it was found that these forgeries were made by certain Jews in a suburb of Baghdad. He voiced the opinion that a forgery, steeped in recent human magnetism, may be more capable of being handled by the invisible operators than the originals, which have to be searched for in mounds. Bailey produced at least 100 such tablets and told Doyle that they were passed as genuine by the British Museum.

At the sitting in question, besides an Assyrian tablet, Bailey apported a jungle sparrow's nest with an egg in it. The nest was two inches high and showed no sign of any flattening, which ought to have been the case had it been concealed on the medium's person.

On **Marco Falcomer**'s intervention, the Milan Society for Psychical Studies made arrangements with Bailey for a European visit. From February to April 1904, 17 sittings were held in Milan. Bailey was put in a sleeved-sack of thin black satin. The sack was fastened at the neck and wrist with tapes. The tapes were tied and the knots were sealed. His coat and boots were taken off, and the investigators felt over his body, especially in hollow parts where objects could be hidden. Bailey, however, refused to allow himself to be entirely undressed, saying he was afraid of catching cold.

The apports consisted mostly of small articles: two or three live birds; a fish with an acrid, penetrating, saline odor; and a Babylonian tablet enveloped in a hard coating of sand. Some of the birds, nests, and eggs disappeared before the end of the séance. In the dark Bailey demonstrated the rapid growth of a seed in a flower pot and the presence of phosphorescent lights and luminous shapes. The committee's desire to have a specially designated object transported from one room to another was not realized.

The report, signed by Mr. Baccigaluppi, A. Brioschi, Dr. Clericetti, O. Cipriana, Dr. F. Ferrari, A. Marzorati, Odorico, Redealli, and Dr. E. Griffini, stated:

"The Committee . . . whilst it deplores (a) the medium's strange obstinacy in refusing to consent to allow himself to be thoroughly undressed; (b) having been obliged to submit to conditions of total darkness at the critical moment of the apport; (c) having been unable, because of the short time accorded the research and in consequence of the very nature even of the phenomena, to apply any method which might enable the Committee to state, precisely and scientifically, the process and origin of the phenomena in question, is on the other hand obliged to state (i) that during the course of seventeen seances, notwithstanding the search of the medium's person by different individuals and by various methods, nothing has ever been found which might justify the hypothesis of fraud; that even admitting that for some of the phenomena an approximate explanation might be found, as far as others are concerned—e.g., the apport of living birds, the instantaneous disappearance of a small bird, etc.—it does not seem possible to formulate a likely explanation; (ii) that, moreover, the hypothesis of suggestion becomes inadmissible if we take into consideration the number of experimenters, who were constantly being changed and who were differently seated each time, as well as the material traces which were left of the phenomena. Given this, the Committee, whilst making reserves on the archaeological value of certain apports, believes it is able, in principle, to come to a conclusion in favor of the objectivity of the facts, and calls the attention of science to these phenomena which find no sufficient explanation in recognised laws."

From Milan Bailey went on to Rome. After giving two seances to Lady Butt he returned to Australia. Because the Milan findings were criticized in many quarters, plans were set afoot to induce Bailey to make a second European visit. It took some years until the plan materialized.

On the invitation of Col. **Eugene A. D. Rochas** and W. Reichel, Bailey came to Grenoble, where disaster overtook him. In a séance held on February 20, 1910, two small live birds were produced. A local dealer recognized in Bailey the man who bought three similar birds from him two days previously. The investigators claimed that he concealed the birds in his intestinal opening as Bailey did not allow them to make examination there. Matters were made worse by the statement of the Hindu control that the birds came directly from India.

In 1911, under the auspices of Mrs. Foster-Turner, Bailey came to London. In a test séance on July 6 before a committee selected by Dr. Abraham Wallace in which the **Society for Psychical Research** was represented by two well-known members, Bailey was undressed, examined, and shut into a cage. Several controls came, a Hindu took possession, but when addressed in Hindustani by a professor of Oriental languages, he immediately subsided into broken English. Later a bird nest appeared in the medium's hand. The control, however, tore it asunder. Two small eggs were also produced but they were broken by the control when passing them to a member of the committee. After the séance, the committee desired to examine the medium's boots more thoroughly, but he left the house, and as a result an unfavorable verdict was returned. On July 28, at another test sitting, during a period of complete darkness, two small birds appeared between the mosquito netting that enveloped the medium and the cabinet. However, toward the end of the sitting the medium toppled over, and in falling he tore the network, so the verdict was again "not proven" (*Light* September 1911; *Journal* of the Society for Psychical Research Vols. 12 & 15).

Back in Sydney there was another exposure scandal on March 5, 1914. One of the sitters made a grab at a materialized form and caught hold of the drapery. It was wrenched from his hand, and the medium, sick and dazed, was carried to Dr. MacCarthy for medical aid. In the same year Bailey sat for six weeks in Rothesay, Scotland, for a circle selected by **James Coates.** Coates reported in *Light* (August 1, 1914) that Bailey was not only a genuine but a unique medium. They obtained apports: ruby sand and an Indian sparrow's nest containing two eggs. The eggs were in Coates's possession for two weeks, and after being blown, the contents were found fresh. Bailey was also induced to try a trumpet. "The personal indication of the voices was most convincing." Impressions of hands and feet were also obtained on plasticine.

In *Psychic Research* (June 1931), **Harry Price** published extracts from a letter written to him by H. L. Williams, a retired magistrate from the Punjab. According to this, Bailey was still active and produced such objects as "a Saracen helmet of scale armour, each scale (3,000 of them) a silver coin with inscription; 30 to 40 Chinese carved figures in ivory of exquisite workmanship and draped in silk arranged to represent a royal court, a complete mandarin's robe which a friend of Williams saw fall from the ceiling, live birds . . . Babylonian cuneiform tablets . . . punic tablets, faience figures from Egypt, cut and polished stone and coins, coins in gold, silver, and copper with inscriptions in Sanskrit, Persian, and Arabic; plaster casts of hands and feet of adults and children obtained from materialisations, etc. Williams says that half the homes of Sydney are stocked with these apports." Bailey held daily seances and charged a small fee only. It could not possibly cover the cost of fraudulently producing such a wide variety of apports.

Bailey's phenomena confounded many psychic researchers in his own day. Given the more skeptical perspective produced by continuous observation of physical mediums, of which only a few remain, and the revelations of mediums like M. Lamar Keene, it is difficult to see in Bailey anything other than a clever stage magician and in the favorable reports of some observers as the observations of those less competent in detecting fraud. The simple fact remains that no one has been able to produce apports under anything resembling controlled conditions, and their existence is highly doubtful.

However, it seems that Bailey continued to give seances in the late 1930s. According to *Two Worlds* (July 9, 1937), the author and playwright **H. Dennis Bradley** communicated in a circle in Manly, Australia, March 25, 1937, at which Charles Bailey was the medium, and a "fraud-proof" instrument, the "Shastaphone," was used.

Sources:

Berger, Arthur S., and Joyce Berger. *Encyclopedia of Parapsychology and Psychical Research.* New York: Paragon House, 1991.

Doyle, Arthur Conan. *History of Spiritualism.* 2 vols. London: Cassele, 1926.

Irwin, H. J. "Charles Bailey: A Biographical Study of the Australian Apport Medium." *Journal* of the Society for Psychical Research 54 (1987): 97.

Keene, M. Lamar. *The Psychic Mafia.* New York: St. Martin's Press, 1976.

McCarthy, C. W. *Rigid Tests of the Occult.* Melbourne, Australia: Stephens, 1904.

"Mediumship of Mr. C. Bailey." *Journal* of the Society for Psychical Research 12 (1905): 77, 109.

Baker, Douglas M. (1922–)

Poet, scientist, and author of popular books on esoteric and occult subjects. He studied medicine and qualified at Sheffield University, England. Preferring to work in complete freedom, he never registered, despite being fully qualified as a medical practitioner. He prefers to use natural energies and remedies without recourse to drugs.

He is concerned with more than 50 different groups in the United States and Britain and has lectured widely on such subjects as reincarnation, life after death, astral projection, the third eye, powers latent in man, esoteric astrology, etc. He is chancellor and director of studies at Claregate College, England, teaching the subjects on which he lectures.

Bakis (or Bacis)

Derived from a Greek term for "speaker," used as a general term for prophets and oracles in ancient Greece from the eighth to sixth century B.C.E. There were three well-known oracles bearing that name who are mentioned by Suidas, the first a Boeotian, the second an Arcadian, and the third an Athenian. The most famous one was from Boeotia and was supposed to have been inspired by the nymphs of the Corycian caves. His oracular verses were said to have been impressively fulfilled. He is cited by Herodotus and Pausanias.

Balan

According to **Johan Weyer,** a great and terrible demon monarch among the infernal powers. He has three heads, those of a bull, a man, and a ram. Joined to these by the tail is a serpent, the eyes of which burn with fire. Balan rides an enormous bear. He commands 40 of the infernal legions and rules over finesse, ruses, and middle courses.

Sources:

Weyer, Johannes. *Witches, Devils and Doctors in the Renaissance: Johann Weyer, De Praestigiis.* Edited by George Mora. Binghamton, N.Y.: Medieval & Renaissance Texts & Studies, 1991.

Balasius

A precious stone with occult virtues. According to Camillus Leonardus (sixteenth century), it is "of a purple or rosy color, and by some is called the placidus or pleasant. Some think it is the carbuncle diminished in its color and virtue; just as the virtue of the female differs from that of the male. It is often found that the external part of one and the same stone appears a balasius, and the internal a carbuncle, from whence comes the saying that the balasius is the carbuncle's house. The virtue of the balasius is to overcome and repress vain thoughts and luxury; to reconcile quarrels among friends; and it befriends the human body with a good habit of health. Being bruised and drunk with water, it relieves infirmities in the eyes, and gives help in disorders of the liver; and what is still more surprising, if you touch the four corners of a house, garden or vineyard, with the balasius, it will preserve them from lightning, tempest, and worms."

Balcoin, Marie

A sorceress of the Basque-speaking Pays de Labourd who attended an infernal sabbat in the reign of Henry IV of France. The indictment against her alleged that she had eaten the ear of a little child at the sabbatic meeting. For her numerous sorceries she was condemned to be burned.

Balfour, Arthur James (1st Earl of Balfour) (1848–1930)

British prime minister, classical scholar, and one of the most brilliant and eminent students of psychical research. In 1882, through his sister, the wife of **Henry Sidgwick** (first president of the **Society for Psychical Research**), he became interested in psychic phenomena and the question of **survival.** In 1893 he became president of the Society for Psychical Research, serving his term between two periods as vice-president, from 1882 to 1892 and from 1895 to 1930. (His brother, the Rt. Hon. **Gerald W. Balfour,** another keen student of psychical research, was president of the Society for Psychical Research from 1906 to 1907.)

Born July 25, 1848, at Whittinghame, East Lothian, Scotland, Balfour was educated at Eton and Trinity College, Cambridge University (M.A.). He was awarded honorary degrees in law and philosophy by British, American, and Polish universities. From 1874 to 1885, he was a member of the British Parliament, and after holding various official posts, he became prime minister (1902–05), first lord of the admiralty (1915–16), and foreign secretary (1916–19).

In the field of psychical research, he held many sittings with Mrs. Willett (**W. M. S. Coombe-Tennant**). He died March 19,

1930, in Surrey, England. It is reported that as he lay dying, he remarked, "I am longing to get to the other side to see what it's like."

Sources:

Balfour, Arthur James. *Chapters of Autobiography.* London: Cassell, 1930.

———. *The Foundations of Belief.* 8th ed. London: Longmans, Green, 1906.

———. *Science, Religions, and Reality.* London: Sheldon Press, 1925.

———. *Theism and Humanism.* London: Hodder & Stoughton, 1915.

Pleasants, Helene, ed. *Biographical Dictionary of Parapsychology.* New York: Helix Press, 1964.

Prince, Walter Franklin. *Noted Witnesses for Psychical Research.* Boston: Boston Society for Psychical Research, 1928. Reprint, New Hyde Park, N.Y.: University Books, 1963.

Balfour, Gerald William (2nd Earl of Balfour) (1853–1945)

Brother of Arthur J. Balfour, first earl of Balfour. He was a statesman, classical scholar, and student of psychical research. He joined the **Society for Psychical Research** soon after its formation and served as president from 1906 to 1907.

Born April 9, 1853, at Whittinghame, Scotland, Balfour was educated at Eton and Trinity College, Cambridge University (M.A.). In 1887 he married Lady Betty, daughter of the first earl of Lytton. He was elected member of Parliament for Central Leeds from 1885 to 1906 and held various government posts; he was also private secretary to his brother.

Like his brother, he was very active in psychical research and also took an important part in organizing and studying the group of **automatic writings** concerned with "**cross-correspondence**" evidence. He published a number of valuable papers in the *Proceedings* of the Society for Psychical Research, including "The Earl of Dionysius," a study of a cross-correspondence case presenting evidence for **survival.** He died January 14, 1945, at Whittinghame.

Sources:

Balfour, Gerald W. "The Ear of Dionysius: Further Scripts Affording Evidence of Personal Survival." *Proceedings* of the Society for Psychical Research 29, no. 74 (1916–18).

———. "Some Recent Scripts Affording Evidence of Personal Survival." *Proceedings* of the Society for Psychical Research 27, no. 69 (1915).

———. "A Study of the Psychological Aspects of Mrs. Willet's Mediumship." *Proceedings* of the Society for Psychical Research 43, no. 140 (1935).

Ball-of-Light International Data Exchange (BOLIDE)

Project set up to share and disseminate information related to balls of light, with a wide scope of inquiry including ball-lightning, marsh lights, will o' the wisp, and séance room phenomena. The project coordinator is **Hilary Evans,** a British authority on such subjects as **apparitions,** visions, **UFOs,** and alien visitors. BOLIDE plans to circulate data supplied by contributors—articles in scholarly journals, press clippings, private research reports from groups or individuals, or personal speculations and hypothesis. Such data will be sent to subscribers who will pay only the cost of copying and mailing. BOLIDE already has subscribers in France, Spain, Norway, Sweden, Canada, England, and Wales. BOLIDE may be contacted c/o Hilary Evans, 1 Tranquil Vale, London SE3 OBU, England.

Ballard, Edna Ann Wheeler (1886–1971)

Leader of the **I AM Movement** and cofounder of the Saint Germain Foundation. Ballard was born on June 25, 1886, in Burlington, Iowa. She studied harp, and by 1912 she had become a concert harpist, on one occasion playing for the duke of Wales. She married Guy W. Ballard in 1916; they had one son, Donald, born in 1918.

During the 1920s she shared an interest with her husband in the occult and worked for a time in the Philosopher's Nook, a Chicago occult bookstore, and edited the *American Occultists.*

In 1930 Guy Ballard was at Mt. Shasta, California, where he had an encounter with a mysterious being, described as an "ascended master" named Saint Germain. He wrote about his experiences and sent letters to Edna Ballard in Chicago describing them.

After his return to Chicago in 1931 she joined with him in founding the Saint Germain Foundation and the Saint Germain Press, the two main organizational expressions of the I AM Religious Activity, and assumed the role beside him as an "accredited messenger of the ascended masters." Through most of the 1930s she took a secondary role in the organization. Guy Ballard allowed Saint Germain and other masters to speak through him almost daily.

Guy Ballard died in 1939, and Edna and her son, Donald, took control of the movement, but neither operated as a messenger. Shortly after taking control, she, Donald, and a number of the national staff were charged with mail fraud. Acting on accusations of several former adherents, the government contended that the leaders were defrauding people by selling them a religion they knew to be false.

Edna Ballard was convicted, had the ruling overturned, and was then convicted a second time. In 1944 the Supreme Court ruled in one of its most famous decisions (*United States v. Ballard*) that people cannot be made to prove their religious beliefs in a court of law. It took several subsequent court actions over the next decade to completely undo the damage that had been inflicted upon the movement by the original conviction.

During the 1950s, Edna Ballard began to function as a messenger. For the rest of her life she periodically brought new messages from the masters (more than two thousand of whom were recorded). She had a radio show for a while during the 1960s.

After Ballard's death on February 10, 1971, in Chicago, leadership of the Saint Germain Foundation and the Saint Germain Press passed to the board of directors and to several "appointed messengers" who had served as teachers within the movement (though never as direct instruments of the masters, as had the Ballards).

Sources:

Braden, Charles S. *These Also Believe.* New York: Macmillan, 1949.

Ballard, Guy Warren (1878– ?)

Cofounder with his wife **Edna W. Ballard** of the **I AM** Religious Activity and the Saint Germain Foundation. He was born in Newton, Kansas, on July 28, 1878, attended business college, and held several mining jobs prior to his marriage in 1916. He settled in Chicago, but his work carried him across the United States. In 1930 he found himself in northern California, near the small community of Mt. Shasta. While walking on the side of a volcanic mountain, he met, according to his later published account, Ascended Master Saint Germain.

Saint Germain identified himself as a member of the **Great White Brotherhood,** the group of evolved adepts believed to guide the destiny of humankind. He was looking for an appropriate person to whom he could give the message that would usher in a new age on earth. Ballard, his wife, and their son Donald were appointed Messengers of the Masters. The Masters began to speak to and through (in a process very similar to what is today termed channeling) Ballard. The story of his initial encounters and early messages, which provided the basic I AM teachings, were later presented as the first six volumes of I AM books. The first volume, *Unveiled Mysteries,* issued under the pen name Godfre Ray King, appeared in 1934.

Ballard informed his wife of what had happened to him in a set of letters from Mt. Shasta, and upon his return to Chicago, they founded the Saint Germain Foundation and Saint Germain Press. The teachings centered upon the announcement of the existence of and the evocation of the I AM Presence, the spirit of God in each individual. A series of mantric-like prayers called decrees were advocated as the means of such evocation.

The I AM movement was one of the most successful, flamboyant, and controversial of the late 1930s. At its height, however, Ballard unexpectedly died. His death created an immediate problem as some expectation had spread through the movement that he would not die but physically ascend. Several years after his death his wife and son and many of the leaders of the movement were the subject of a landmark judicial process initiated by several ex-members who questioned the sincerity of the movement. The process resulted in a 1944 Supreme Court ruling which suggested that it was not legitimate for government to place a religion, no matter how nonconventional, on trial.

Sources:

King, Godfre Ray [Guy W. Ballard]. *The "I AM" Discourses.* Chicago, Ill.: St. Germain Press, 1935.

———. *The Magic Presence.* Chicago, Ill.: St. Germain Press, 1935.

———. *Unveiled Mysteries.* Chicago, Ill.: St. Germain Press, 1934.

Ballinspittle (Moving Statue)

Ballinspittle is a village in county Cork, Ireland, and the site of a reported paranormal **moving statue** of the Virgin Mary. In the same year, 1985, many statues of the Virgin Mary throughout Ireland were reported to be moving. The first reports began in Asdee, county Kerry, on February 14, when several children claimed to have seen a statue of the Madonna and Child at the parish church of St. Mary open its eyes and move its hands. Other people confirmed that they had seen movements.

In July two teenage girls reported seeing movement in a statue of the Virgin Mary at Ballinspittle, in a grotto some 20 feet up the side of a hill. This was a Marian year shrine, and the statue was illuminated by a halo of 11 electric lights.

Within days of the first reports, thousands of pilgrims visited Ballinspittle every night, some traveling hundreds of miles. At regular intervals prayers were spoken on a public address system and the people joined in. Each night many people claimed that they saw the statue move in some way. The most commonly reported movements included changes of countenance, superimposition of other sacred faces, opening and closing of eyes, movements of the hands, and rocking to and fro.

Ballinspittle and its moving statue rapidly became a media event, reported and discussed in newspapers and on radio and television. Among the many thousands of visitors to the shrine were journalists, camera operators, priests, nuns, doctors, lawyers, engineers, housewives, and ordinary people from all walks of life. Surprisingly, even hardened skeptics reported seeing movement. On one occasion a gang of Hell's Angels motorcyclists stood quietly at the shrine, and although they did not believe that the statue moved, they blessed themselves before putting back their crash helmets and driving off.

Naturally enough the church hierarchy became somewhat concerned. While appreciating the devout atmosphere created by many pilgrims at an open-air shrine, ecclesiastics believed that regular church attendance would be a more practical demonstration of faith. The bishop of Killala stated, "We don't mind people gathering together to pray, but we want them to go into the Church to do it." Moreover many people visited the shrine out of mere curiosity or even skepticism; others criticized what they regarded as mass hysteria. Bishop Michael Murphy of Cork warned that "common sense would demand that we approach the claims made concerning the grotto in Ballinspittle with prudence and caution," but he also relished the fact that "crowds are gathering there in a great spirit of prayer."

Nobody denied that the statue itself was a purely material construction. It was a standard five-foot eight-inch Lourdes model cast in concrete. The statue maker, Maurice O'Donnell, recalled, "Her hands are reinforced with wire, and I remember the day she left the works for Ballinspittle. I was making so many at that time there was no time to dry them out before painting, so lots of statues in the shrines around the country are still unpainted. But that was in the Marian Year, 1954. The bottom has dropped out of the statues market since the Vatican Council."

But in 1985, these statues were reported to be moving in shrines all over the country. Not everyone took the moving statues seriously. With characteristic irreverent wit, Irish comedian Brendan Grace recorded a humorous song titled "Is That You Moving?" A new play was written by Brigid McLoughlin titled "Moving Statues." McLoughlin stated that the play "sends up the rituals and double-standards of Catholicism in Ireland."

Although many people claimed that the statue actually moved physically, it seems clear that the majority of reported movements were imaginary. Some may have been related to what psychologists call "eidetic imagery," in which prolonged staring may combine with imaginary mental imagery to produce an illusion. A team of psychologists from Cork University College established that the phenomena did not register on film or motion sensors. Other observers talked of optical illusions, autosuggestion, or mass hallucination. But to many people, the question of physical or visionary movement seemed irrelevant in the highly spiritually charged atmosphere of the grotto. For them, the real movement was one of the soul. On July 31, a 37-year-old Cork housewife named Frances O'Riordan, who had been completely deaf since age 20, claimed that she had her hearing restored during a visit to the Ballinspittle grotto.

With the sudden influx of thousands of visitors and journalists, telephone kiosks were installed at the grotto, as were two concrete toilets. Special bus services were organized, but there was no commercial exploitation of the grotto. The crowds continued to throng at the shrine for over three months, until on Halloween, October 31, there was a sudden and brutal affront to the respect and devotion of the pilgrims.

Three men drove up in a car. Two of them strode swiftly to the shrine, jumped over the fence, and hacked away at the statue with an axe and a hammer, completely destroying the face and severely damaging the hands. The third man calmly took photographs. The spectators were too stunned and horrified to intervene. Someone said, "You must be from Satan to do such a thing!" The men laughed and said, "Well, you're worse to be adoring false gods." They then drove off in their car. Local people linked the attack to a religious sect that had scattered leaflets at the grotto, stating that people should adore the head of Christ in their local churches. Three men were later arrested and charged with malicious damage to the statue. Meanwhile prayers were said at the grotto, and people claimed to have seen the defaced statue continue to move.

The grotto committee arranged for the statue to be repaired, and since its reinstatement at the grotto, pilgrims have still assembled there.

Meanwhile the three men who had been arrested after the Ballinspittle incident were identified as Robert Draper, Roy Murphy, and Anthony Fowler, members of the Faith Center Movement, a Pentecostal Christian church of American evangelist Dr. Gene Scott of Los Angeles, California. The three men were tried at Portlaoise Circuit Court on Tuesday, March 4, 1986, before a Judge O'Higgins and charged with "causing malicious damage in a place of divine worship." The judge stated that he had to be "particularly zealous in guarding the rights of the three defendants" and dismissed the case on the grounds that the Ballinspittle grotto is not, in fact, a place of divine worship. To the defendants, of course, it was a place of sinful **idolatry.**

Robert Draper, who wielded the axe and hammer at Ballinspittle, emerged from the courtroom triumphantly proclaiming that he was going to demolish other images in wayside shrines. He is since reported to have smashed two more statues, one in Ballyfermot and another in Clondalkin. He appeared with his fellow iconoclasts on the popular "Late Late Show," hosted by Gay Byrne on RTE Television on March 7. Draper arrogantly cited the fourth and fifth commandments of the Old Testament and Exod. 23:24 as giving him divine sanction to smash all religious statues in Ireland, regardless of the rights and views of other people.

As reporter Eoghan Corry stated in an article in the *Sunday Press* (March 9, 1986), "there isn't a safe statue in the country."

Meanwhile from Los Angeles evangelist Scott indignantly disassociated himself from the activities of the Irish statue smashers and described the Robert Draper group as "the most ridiculous association I have ever heard in a lifetime of confronting ridiculous things." In a press statement he specifically said, "I abhor violence in any form. I am in the process of preserving and restoring a 23 million dollar religious shrine in Los Angeles at the present. I am also president of Sunset Mausoleum in Berkeley, California, which has a 16-foot statue of Christ commanding the cathedral chapel, which was made of the marble from the same quarry from which Michelangelo made Moses. I abhor the thought of anyone anywhere in this world defacing any religious object and totally disassociate myself from anyone who claims to perpetrate such activity in my name."

For a fascinating account of the Ballinspittle story and the other moving statues of Ireland, see the book *Seeing is Believing* (1985).

Sources:

Tóibín, Colm, ed. *Seeing is Believing*. Ireland: Pilgrim Press, 1985.

Ballou, Adin (Augustus) (1803–1890)

A Universalist minister, born in Cumberland, Rhode Island, April 23, 1803. In 1842 he formed the **Hopedale Community.** He was one of those whose doctrines prepared the way for Spiritualism in the United States; after the movement had been inaugurated, he became one of its most enthusiastic protagonists. He published a magazine, *The Independent Messenger* (1831–39), and wrote a number of books. Ballou died at Milford, Massachusetts, August 5, 1890.

Sources:

Ballou, Adin. *Autobiography of Adin Ballou, 1803–1890*. Lowell, Mass.: Vox Populi Press, 1896. Reprint, Philadelphia: Porcupine Press, 1975.

———. *Practical Christian Socialism*. New York: Fowler and Wells, 1854. Reprint, New York: AMS Press, 1974.

———. *Primitive Christianity and its Corruptions*. 3 vols. 1870–1900.

Balor

In old Irish mythology, the mighty king of the Formorians, usually called "Balor of the Evil Eye." It was believed that he was able to destroy by means of an angry glance. When his eyelid became heavy with years, it is said that he had it raised by means of ropes and pulleys so that he might continue to make use of his magic gift. He was eventually killed by his grandson, Lugh, the sun god and son of his daughter **Birog,** who crept near him one day when his eyelid had drooped momentarily and slew him with a great stone, sinking it through his eye and brain.

Baltazo

One of the demons supposed to have possessed a young woman of Laon, France, in the year 1566. He went to dine with her husband under the pretext of freeing her from demonic possession, which he did not accomplish. It was observed that at supper he did not drink, which reinforced the belief that demons are averse to water.

Baltus, Jean François (1667–1743)

A learned Jesuit who affirmed that the oracles of the ancients were the work of demons and that they were reduced to silence during the mission of Christ upon the earth. He propounded this view in his reply to Le Bovier de Fontonelle's *L'Histoire des Oracles* under the title *Réponse á L'Historic des Oracles de Mr. de Fontonelle* (1707), translated into English as *An Answer to Mr. de Fontonelle's History of Oracles* (1709).

Bander, Peter (1930–)

British psychologist, lecturer in religious and moral education, director in the publishing house Colin Smythe, Ltd., of Gerrards Cross, Britain, and writer on psychic topics. Bander introduced the English-speaking world to the experiments of Dr. Konstantin Raudive, a Latvian psychologist who pioneered a particular kind of electronic communication with the dead, discovered by **Friedrich Jürgenson** in 1959.

This communication involved paranormal voice recordings obtained on a tape recorder enhanced by a simple diode circuit. Bander translated Raudive's book *Breakthrough* in 1971, after which he appeared on 27 television and radio programs in connection with what came to be called **Raudive voices,** now more popularly known as "electronic voice phenomenon." Besides a number of books not dealing with parapsychology, Bander wrote *The Prophecies of Malachy & Columbkille* (1969), *Eternal Youth & Music* (1970), *Voices from the Tapes* (1973), and *Open to Suggestion* (1974).

Sources:

Bander, Peter. *Voices from the Tapes: Recordings from the Other World*. New York: Drake Publishers, 1973.

Raudive, Konstantin. *Breakthrough*. New York: Taplinger, 1971.

Bangs Sisters, Lizzie and May (early 1900s)

Chicago mediums who specialized in **direct writing** and **direct drawing and painting.** In sealed envelopes that were brought by the sitters and enclosed between two slates, messages in ink were produced in bright daylight. The sitter placed the envelopes between a pair of slates and held them under his or her hand while the medium sat on the opposite side of the table. After waiting from a few minutes to an hour, **raps** signaled that the message was ready.

On behalf of Dr. **I. K. Funk,** who investigated the mediums several times himself and had a high opinion of their powers, **Hereward Carrington** went to Chicago in 1909 and, as narrated in the *Annals of Psychic Science* (July– September 1910), found **fraud.** He addressed a letter in a sealed envelope to "Dearest mother, Jane Thompson" (who never existed) and received a reply addressed to "Dearly loved son Harold," signed by his "devoted mother, Jane Thompson." Admiral W. Usborne Moore, who had many sittings with the Bangs sisters in 1909 and later in 1911, defended the sisters.

In the course of the controversy that ensued Carrington told in a letter to *Light* (May 13, 1911) that **David P. Abbott** had succeeded in duplicating the Bangs sisters' phenomena exactly by trickery. Moore replied that he made a number of tests, that he read carefully an exposé by a Dr. Krebs, that he knew the method employed by Abbott and that it surpassed in skill almost every conjuring trick he had witnessed but that the conditions were as different from those at the séances of the Bangs sisters as a locomotive is different from a teapot. In fact, it was the conjuring performance that finally convinced him that the Bangs sisters must be genuine, he said.

In telling the story of his investigations in *Glimpses of the Next State* (1911) Moore narrates how he took his own slates and inkpot to the sitting. On the advice of **Sir William Crookes** he added lithium citrate to the ink. He obtained a message of eight pages, signed by his spirit guide, "Iola." By later spectrum analysis the presence of lithium was in fact discovered in the ink. This proved to his satisfaction that in some mysterious way his own ink was instrumental in preparing the message in the sealed envelope between his own slates.

Furthermore, he laid his visiting card on top of the slates and tore off one corner for identification. He also wrote a postscript to his questions on a separate piece of paper and placed it alongside the visiting card. The former found its way into the envelope, while the card, in accordance with a message on the outside of the envelope, was discovered in another room in Moore's hat.

The "direct spirit portraits" that the Bangs sisters produced as early as 1894 in color, before the sitters' eyes, and in daylight was an even more mysterious phenomenon. At first a locked box or curtained-off space was used and several sittings were required. Later they were openly precipitated, as if by an airbrush, as quickly as within eight minutes. The arrangement was as follows:

Two identical, paper-mounted canvases in wooden frames were held up, face to face, against the window, the lower edges resting on a table and the sides gripped by each medium with one hand. A short curtain was hung on either side and an opaque blind was drawn over the canvases. With the light streaming from behind, the canvases were translucent.

After a quarter of an hour, the outlines of shadows began to appear and disappear as if the invisible artist were making a preliminary sketch, then the picture began to grow at a feverish rate. When the frames were separated the portrait was found on the paper surface of the canvas next to the sitter. Although the paint was greasy and stuck to the finger on being touched, it left no stain on the paper surface of the other canvas, which closely covered it. The sitters were requested to bring a photograph of their departed friends, but they were not asked to produce it. The portraits were not copies of the concealed photographs, but the facial resemblance was apparently an imitation. Reportedly the tone often grew richer and deeper afterward.

Moore noticed in his experiments that details were added if he did not look, and when once he mentally desired that a gold locket should be enlarged and decorated with a monogram, the thing was done as requested. He often brought his own frames, sealed the window, searched the premises, and closely watched every movement in the room, yet the picture was obtained as before.

The Bangs sisters also produced these phenomena in public halls before great audiences. **Apports** of flowers were a frequent occurrence; objects disappeared incomprehensibly; and chemical effects, like ink changing into dirty water, were witnessed.

An early slate-writing séance with Lizzie Bangs is described by A. B. Richmond in *What I Saw at Cassadaga Lake* (1888):

"Soon I heard a faint noise between the slates. It did not sound like writing, but more like the crawling of an insect imprisoned between them, in a few moments there came three distinct raps. I opened the slates and found two messages written in the Morse alphabet, one of them signed by the one to whom the interrogatory was directed, and who could not in this life read or write telegraphy, the other by a prominent jurist who died a number of years ago."

After a trial of many days Richmond obtained three communications between two screwed-together slates. One was signed by Henry Seybert, and the handwriting was the same as that he had obtained a year before in a séance with **Pierre Keeler.**

The most spectacular direct-writing demonstration by Lizzie Bangs was the direct operation of a typewriter. As described by Quaestor Vitae in *Light* (January 25, 1896), the machine kept on working when held up in the air by four of the men present. The hand alleged to have done the work also materialized.

In his investigation of the sisters' phenomena, Hereward Carrington refers to an exposé regarding the letter writing inside a sealed enveolope (*Journal* of the Society for Psychical Research, vol. 10). The writer claims to have seen the tricks by means of a small hand mirror that he held beneath the table. He found that, under cover of the writing pad placed against the edges of the slate resting on the table, May Bangs, one of the sisters, wedged open the slate by means of a small rubber wedge; the letter, when abstracted, was dropped on to a sort of "gridiron" arrangement that lay on the carpet. It was promptly drawn backward under a slit in the door into the next room, where Lizzie Bangs, the other sister, steamed the envelope. In the meantime the ink in the cup had time to evaporate so that it appeared to have been used.

A number of testimonies vouching for the Bangs sisters are printed in **James Coates**'s *Photographing the Invisible.* But there is no doubt that some of the charges of fraud brought against them in their early career were well borne out. In 1880 and in 1891 they were seized as masquerading materialized spirits under very damaging circumstances, and in 1890 a Colonel Bundy charged them in the *Religio-Philosophical Journal* with fraud in slate writing. Dr. **Richard Hodgson** made a thorough investigation of the respective documents. His findings were against the mediums (*Light,* 1899).

A collection of portraits produced by the Bangs sisters has been preserved in the gallery at the Spiritualist Camp at Chesterfield, Indiana.

Sources:

Abbott, David P. *Behind the Scenes With the Mediums.* LaSalle, Ill.: Open Court Publishing, 1909.

———. *Spirit Portrait Mystery; Its Final Solution.* Chicago, 1913.

[Bangs Sisters]. *The Bangs Sisters' Manifesto to the World.* Chicago, 1909.

Moore, W. Usborne. *Glimpses of the Next State (The Education of an Agnostic).* London: Watts, 1911.

Banner of Light (Periodical)

Spiritualist weekly, "an exponent of the spiritual philosophy of the twentieth century," founded in 1857 and published in Boston and New York. It ceased publication after 1910.

Banshee

An Irish supernatural being of the wraith type. The name derives from the Gaelic *bean si* and implies "female fairy." She is usually the possession of a specific family, to a member or members of which she appears before the death of one of them.

T. F. Thistleton Dyer, writing on the banshee in his book *The Ghost World* (1898), states:

"Unlike, also, many of the legendary beliefs of this kind, the popular accounts illustrative of it are related on the evidence of all sections of the community, many an enlightened and well-informed advocate being enthusiastic in his vindication of its reality. It would seem, however, that no family which is not of an ancient and noble stock is honored with this visit of the Banshee and hence its nonappearance has been regarded as an indication of disqualification in this respect on the part of the person about to die. 'If I am rightly informed,' writes Sir Walter Scott, 'the distinction of a Banshee is only allowed to families of the pure Milesian stock, and is never ascribed to any descendant of the proudest Norman or the boldest Saxon who followed the banner of Strongbow, much less to adventurers of later dates who have obtained settlements in the Green Isle.' Thus, an amusing story is contained in an Irish elegy to the effect that on the death of one of the Knights of Kerry, when the Banshee was heard to lament his decease at Dingle—a seaport town, the property of those knights—all the merchants of this place were thrown into a state of alarm lest the mournful and ominous wailing should be a forewarning of the death of one of them, but, as the poet humorously points out, there was no necessity for them to be anxious on this point. Although, through misfortune, a family may be brought down from high estate to the rank of peasant tenants, the Banshee never leaves nor forgets it till the last member has been gathered to his fathers in the churchyard. The MacCarthys,

O'Flahertys, Magraths, O'Rileys, O'Sullivans, O'Reardons, have their Banshees, though many representatives of these names are in abject poverty.

"'The Banshee,' says D. R. McAnally [in his book *Irish Wonders* (1888)], 'is really a disembodied soul, that of one who in life was strongly attached to the family, or who had good reason to hate all its members. Thus, in different instances, the Banshee's song may be inspired by different motives. When the Banshee loves those she calls, the song is a low, soft chant giving notice, indeed, of the close proximity of the angel of death, but with a tenderness of tone that reassures the one destined to die and comforts the survivors; rather a welcome than a warning, and having in its tones a thrill of exultation, as though the messenger spirit were bringing glad tidings to him summoned to join the waiting throng of his ancest[o]rs.' To a doomed member of the family of the O'Reardons the Banshee generally appears in the form of a beautiful woman, 'and sings a song so sweetly solemn as to reconcile him to his approaching fate.' But if, during his lifetime, the Banshee was an enemy of the family, the cry is the scream of a fiend, howling with demoniac delight over the coming death agony of another of his foes.

"Hence, in Ireland, the hateful 'Banshee' is a source of dread to many a family against which she has an enmity. 'It appears,' adds McAnally, 'that a noble family, whose name is still familiar in Mayo, is attended by a Banshee of this description—the spirit of a young girl deceived, and afterwards murdered by a former head of the family. With her dying breath she cursed her murderer, and promised she would attend him and his forever. After many years the chieftain reformed his ways, and his youthful crime was almost forgotten even by himself, when one night, as he and his family were seated by the fire, the most terrible shrieks were suddenly heard outside the castle walls. All ran out, but saw nothing. During the night the screams continued as though the castle were besieged by demons, and the unhappy man recognised in the cry of the Banshee the voice of the young girl he had murdered. The next night he was assassinated by one of his followers, when again the wild unearthly screams were heard exulting over his fate. Since that night "hateful Banshee" has, it is said, never failed to notify the family, with shrill cries of revengeful gladness, when the time of one of their number has arrived.'

"Among some of the recorded instances of the Banshee's appearance may be mentioned one related by Miss Lefrau, the niece of [Richard] Sheridan, in the memoirs of her grandmother, Mrs. Frances Sheridan. From this account we gather that Miss Elizabeth Sheridan was a firm believer in the Banshee, and firmly maintained that the one attached to the Sheridan family was distinctly heard lamenting beneath the windows of the family residence before the news arrived from France of Mrs. Frances Sheridan's death at Blois. She added that a niece of Miss Sheridan made her very angry by observing that as Mrs. Frances Sheridan was by birth a Chamberlaine, a family of English extraction, she had no right to the guardianship of an Irish fairy, and that therefore the Banshee must have made a mistake. Then there is the well-known case related by Lady Fanshawe who tells us how, when on a visit in Ireland, she was awakened at midnight by a loud scream outside her window. On looking out she saw a young and rather handsome woman, with dishevelled hair, who vanished before her eyes with another shriek. On communicating the circumstance in the morning, her host replied, 'A near relation of mine died last night in the castle, and before such an event happens, the female spectre whom you have seen is always visible.'

"This weird apparition is generally supposed to assume the form of a woman, sometimes young, but more often old. She is usually attired in a loose white drapery, and her long ragged locks hang over her thin shoulders. As night time approaches she occasionally becomes visible, and pours forth her mournful wail—a sound said to resemble the melancholy moaning of the wind. . . . Oftentimes she is not seen but only heard, yet she is supposed to be always clearly discernible to the person upon whom she specially waits. Respecting the history of the Banshee, popular tradition in many instances accounts for its presence as the spirit of some mortal woman whose destinies have become linked by some accident with those of the family she follows. It is related how the Banshee of the family of the O'Briens of Thomond was originally a woman who had been seduced by one of the chiefs of that race—an act of indiscretion which ultimately brought about her death."

The banshee is not confined to Ireland, since she is also the subject of folktales in the highlands of Scotland, where she is known as *bean-nighe,* or "little-washer-by-the-ford." She is said to be seen by the side of a river, washing the blood from the clothes of those who will die. (See also **Fairies**)

Sources:

Lysaght, Patricia. *The Banshee.* Dublin, 1986.

McAnally, D. R. *Irish Wonders.* 1888. Reprint, Detroit: Grand River Books, 1971.

O'Donnell, Elliot. *The Banshee.* London, 1919.

Yeats, W. B. *Fairy and Folk Tales of the Irish Peasantry.* London: Walter Scott, [1888].

Bapak

An Indonesian name for "father," given affectionately to patrons, gurus, and charismatic leaders, especially to **Muhammad Subuh,** founder of the **Subud** movement, a modern mystical school combining Sufi insights with elements of the thought of **Georgei I. Gurdjieff** and **P. D. Ouspensky.**

Baphomet

The goat idol of the **Templars** and the deity of the sorcerers' **Sabbat.** Some authorities hold that the Baphomet was a monstrous head, others that it was a demon in the form of a goat. One account of a veritable Baphometic idol describes it thusly:

"A pantheistic and magical figure of the Absolute. The torch placed between the two horns, represents the equilibrating intelligence of the triad. The goat's head, which is synthetic, and unites some characteristics of the dog, bull, and ass, represents the exclusive responsibility of matter and the expiation of bodily sins in the body. The hands are human, to exhibit the sanctity of labor; they make the sign of esotericism above and below, to impress mystery on initiates, and they point at two lunar crescents, the upper being white and the lower black, to explain the correspondences of good and evil, mercy and justice. The lower part of the body is veiled, portraying the mysteries of universal generation, which is expressed solely by the symbol of the caduceus. The belly of the goat is scaled, and should be colored green, the semicircle above should be blue; the plumage, reaching to the breast, should be of various hues. The goat has female breasts, and thus its only characteristics are those of maternity and toil, otherwise the signs of redemption. On its forehead, between the horns and beneath the torch, is the sign of the microcosm, or the pentagram with one beam in the ascendant, symbol of human intelligence, which, placed thus below the torch, makes the flame of the latter an image of divine revelation. This Pantheos should be seated on a cube, and its footstool should be a single ball, or a ball and a triangular stool."

In *Narratives of Sorcery and Magic* (1851), Thomas Wright states:

"Another charge in the accusation of the Templars seems to have been to a great degree proved by the depositions of witnesses[:] the idol or head which they are said to have worshipped, but the real character or meaning of which we are totally unable to explain. Many Templars confessed to having seen this idol, but as they described it differently, we must suppose that it was not in all cases represented under the same form. Some said it was a frightful head, with long beard and sparkling eyes; others said it was a man's skull; some described it as having three faces; some said it was of wood, and others of metal; one witness described it as a painting (*tabula picta*) representing the image of a man (*imago hominis*) and said that when it was shown to him, he was ordered to 'adore Christ, his creator.' According to some it was a gilt figure, either of wood or metal; while others described it as painted black and white. According to another deposition, the idol had four feet, two before and two behind; the one belonging to the order at Paris, was said to be a silver head, with two faces and a beard. The novices of the order were told always to regard this idol as their saviour. Deodatus Jaffet, a knight from the south of France, who had been received at Pedenat, deposed that the person who in his case performed the ceremonies of reception, showed him a head or idol, which appeared to have three faces, and said, 'You must adore this as your saviour, and the saviour of the order of the Temple' and that he was made to worship the idol, saying, 'Blessed be he who shall save my soul.' Cettus Ragonis, a knight received at Rome in a chamber of the palace of the Lateran, gave a somewhat similar account. Many other witnesses spoke of having seen these heads, which, however, were, perhaps, not shown to everybody, for the greatest number of those who spoke on this subject, said that they had heard speak of the head, but that they had never seen it themselves; and many of them declared their disbelief in its existence. A friar minor deposed in England that an English Templar had assured him that in that country the order had four principal idols, one at London, in the Sacristy of the Temple, another at Bristelham, a third at Brueria (Bruern in Lincolnshire), and a fourth beyond the Humber."

Some occultists have suggested that the Baphomet of the Templars was really the god of the witches deriving from the nature god Pan. During the nineteenth century, the Austrian Orientalist Baron Joseph von Hammer-Pürgstall discovered an inscription on a coffer in Burgundy that he claimed showed that the name Baphomet derived from two Greek words meaning "Baptism of Metis [Wisdom]"; the inscription exalted Metis or Baphomet as the true divinity.

When Karl Kellner and other early twentieth century German occultists founded the secret order **OTO** (Ordo Templi Orientis, or Order of Templars in the East), they adopted an emblem of Baphomet taken from Richard Payne Knight's *A Discourse on the Worship of Priapus* as the seal of the order's grand master. At a later date, when British occultist **Aleister Crowley** became head of the British section, he took the name Baphomet as his motto. He had previously wrestled with the numerological significance of the name.

Sources:

Crowley, Aleister. *The Confessions of Aleister Crowley.* Edited by John Symons and Kenneth Grant. New York: Hill and Wang, 1969.

Lévi, Éliphas. *Transcendental Magic.* London: Rider, 1896. Reprint, New York: Samuel Weiser, 1972.

Partner, Peter. *The Murdered Magicians: The Templars and their Myth.* Oxford: Oxford University Press, 1981. Reprint, N.p.: Crucible, 1987.

Wright, Thomas. *Narratives of Sorcery and Magic.* London: R. Bentley, 1851. Reprint, Detroit: Grand River Books, 1971.

Baptism of the Devil

It was said that at the witches' **Sabbat** children and toads were baptized with certain horrible rites. This was called "the baptism of the devil."

Baptism of the Line

A curious rite performed on persons crossing the equator for the first time. The sailors dressed themselves in quaint costumes. The "father of the line" arrived in a cask, accompanied by a courier, a devil, a hairdresser, and a miller. The unfortunate passenger had his hair curled, was liberally sprinkled with flour, and then had water showered upon him, if he was not dunked. The origin of this custom is not known, nor is it quite clear what part the devil played in it. The custom is reminiscent of the traditional initiatory rites of apprentices in trade guilds such as printing, and it may also be a precursor of **initiations** in college fraternities.

Baquet

A large circular tub that figured prominently in the magnetic treatment that Charles d'Eslon, a friend and follower of **Franz A. Mesmer**'s, prescribed for his patients. The marquis of Puységur tells us in his book *Du Magnétisme Animal* (1807) that some bottles, arranged in a particular manner, were placed in the *baquet* and partly covered with water. The tub was fitted with a lid having several holes through which passed iron rods connecting the patients, who sat around the contrivance. The operator was armed with a shorter iron rod. While the patients waited for a response to the treatment, someone played a pianoforte, a device frequently used at Spiritualist séances. Reactions included violent convulsions, cries, laughter, and vomiting. This state, called the *crisis,* was supposed to hasten the healing process.

A commission appointed in 1784 by the French government to report on **mesmerism** suggested that such practices were exceedingly dangerous and in no way proved the existence of an alleged magnetic fluid.

Sources:

Darnton, Robert. *Mesmerism and the End of the Enlightenment in France.* Cambridge, Mass.: Harvard University Press, 1968.

Harte, Richard. *Hypnotism and the Doctors. I. Mesmer/De Puységur.* London: L. N. Fowler, 1902.

Baraduc, Hyppolite (1850–1902)

Noted nineteenth-century French psychical researcher who made interesting experiments in "thought photography" and in 1895 addressed a communication on the subject to the French Academy of Medicine. By photographic means he also claimed to have proved that something misty and vaporous leaves the human body at the moment of death. His contribution to the study of vital emanation is significant. He constructed an instrument, called Baraduc's **biometer,** that indicated the action of a nervous force and unknown vibrations outside the human body. His experiments are described in his books *The Human Soul* (1913), *Iconographie de la Force Vitale Cosmique Od* (1896), *Méthode de Radiographie Humaine* (1897), *Note Sommaire sur la Décondensation Cérébrale* (1901), *Photographie des Etats Hypervibratoires de la Vitalité Humaine* (1897), *Les Vibrations de la Vitalité Humaine* (1904), and *La Force Vitale, Notre Corps Vital, Fulidique, une Formule Barometrique* (1905). (See also **Sthenometer**)

Sources:

Baraduc, Hyppolite. *The Human Soul.* Paris, 1913.

———. *Les Vibrations de la Vitalité Humaine.* Paris, 1904.

Berger, Arthur S., and Joyce Berger. *The Encyclopedia of Parapsychology and Psychical Research.* New York: Paragon House, 1991.

Barbanell, Maurice (1902–1981)

Veteran British lecturer, journalist, and author in the field of **Spiritualism.** He served as editor of the **Psychic News** and **The Two Worlds** for over three decades. Many in North America first heard of him through his book *This is Spiritualism* (1959), a survey of the phenomena and personalities associated with Spiritualism. Barbanell was noted for his vigorous journalism in support of Spiritualism, and he frequently lectured across both Europe and North America. Born in London, May 3, 1902, he was the son of a barber who also practiced dentistry. Young Barbanell's first job involved sweeping up hair and acting as lather boy.

As a young man Barbanell was an atheist like his father. He became unpaid secretary of a social and literary club in London's East End. One evening, there was a talk by a young man on the subject of Spiritualism. Although antagonistic to the subject, Barbanell said that this was a subject on which only those with personal experience could venture any worthwhile opinions.

When challenged as to whether he was prepared to back this position by undertaking a six-month period of personal investigation of Spiritualism, he said yes. He joined a home circle with the medium Mrs. Blaustein, who was controlled by various entities who spoke through her while she was in a state of trance.

Barbanell was not very impressed by this phenomenon and at one sitting he "fell asleep." When he awoke he learned to his surprise that he had been in a mediumistic trance himself and that an Indian spirit guide had spoken through him.

Barbanell subsequently formed his own home circle at which the Indian guide, "Silver Birch," gave regular teachings through Barbanell's mediumship. Later, the famous journalist and Spiritualist **Hannen Swaffer** became a member of this home circle and an enthusiastic proponent of the teachings of "Silver Birch."

In 1932 Barbanell married Sylvia Abrahams, who had attended the home circle sittings with Mrs. Blaustein. The newspaper *Psychic News* was also founded in 1932, as a result of a message from "Red Cloud," the spirit guide of the medium **Estelle Roberts.** Barbanell edited the newspaper for 14 years, resigning in 1946 when unable to agree with **J. Arthur Findlay** on terms for purchase of *Psychic News.* However, 16 years later, in June 1962, Barbanell was able to resume editorship of the newspaper, which by then was in some difficulty. His tireless and enthusiastic work restored the position of *Psychic News* as the preeminent British Spiritualist publication.

Meanwhile, Barbanell's own role in the "Silver Birch" messages continued to be anonymous. Hannen Swaffer thought the teachings should reach a larger audience, but Barbanell believed that he would be open to criticism if he publicized his own mediumship in *Psychic News.* Eventually it was agreed that the "Silver Birch" teachings should be published, provided that Barbanell's identity continued to be withheld. However, these communications attracted so much attention that after some time Barbanell was obliged to make it known that he was the medium.

During his active life as editor, lecturer, and author in the cause of Spiritualism, Barbanell was a friend of every major British medium. Less than a week after his death at age 79, on July 17, 1981, spirit messages from him were claimed through the mediumship of Gordon Higginson, a close friend.

In addition to Barbanell's vast output for his two periodicals, he wrote books on psychical research and Spiritualism.

Sources:

Barbanell, Maurice. *Across the Gulf.* N.p., 1940.

———. *Where There is a Will.* N.p., 1962.

Barbanell, Sylvia, ed. *Silver Birch Speak* . . . . London: Psychic Book Club, 1949.

McCulloch, Joseph. *The Trumpet Shall Sound.* London, M. Joseph, Ltd., 1944.

Naylor, William, ed. *Silver Birch Anthology.* London: Psychic Book Club, 1955.

Pleasants, Helene, ed. *Biographical Dictionary of Parapsychology.* New York: Helix Press, 1964.

The Wisdom of Silver Birch. London: Psychic Book Club, 1944.

Barbault, André (1921-)

Contemporary French astrologer, born at Champignelled/Yonne, France, on October 1, 1921. Barbault began his study of **astrology** in the mid-1930s and a short time later discovered **Sigmund Freud.** He saw Freudian psychology as an excellent tool for assisting in astrological interpretation. Barbault emerged from the disruptions of World War II as a professional astrologer and a charter member of the Centre International d'Astrologie, founded in 1946. He was vice president of the center for 14 years, during which time he published his first books, *De la Psychanalyses de l'Astrologie* (1961) and *Traité pratique d'Astrologie* (1961), an exposition of his Freudian theories and a basic astrological textbook.

In 1967 Barbault attained a level of international fame by opening Ordinastral-Astroflash, a computerized astrology service capable of turning out hundreds of charts daily for Parisians. It was the first such service in the world and in spite of the criticisms of more traditional colleagues quickly spread internationally. Countering critics of the popularizing effects of the computer, Barbault also founded *l'Astrologie,* an academic journal of astrological studies.

Barbault's psychological approach to astrology has come to characterize French astrology. However, he has spent much of his mature years in the equally fascinating realm of mundane astrology, attempting to correlate astrological facts with historical events. His first such study was published in 1967 as *Les Astres et l'historie.* This led to a system of predicting political events from astrological studies. Barbault has written more than thirty books, but they have yet to be translated into English.

Sources:

Barbault, André. *Les Astres et l'historie.* Paris, J.-J. Pauvert, 1967.

———. *De la Psychanalyses de l'Astrologie.* Paris: Editions du Seuil, 1961.

———. *Traité pratique d'Astrologie.* Paris, 1961.

Brau, Jean-Louis, Helen Weaver, and Allan Edmands, eds. *Larousse Encyclopedia of Astrology.* New York: New American Library, 1982.

Barguest (or **Barghest**)

A goblin or phantom of mischievous character traditionally reported in the north of England and also in Wales. The meaning of the term is disputed, some believing it to be "town ghost" (*burhghest*), others suggesting it derives from the German *berggeist* ("mountain demon"). The goblin often appears in the form of a monstrous dog with huge teeth and claws. Another tradition suggests that the phantom is named from his habit of sitting on bars or gates. A writer in the mid-nineteenth-century *Encyclopaedia Metropolitana* relates a story of a woman he knew who had been brought up in the country. As a child, she had been passing through the fields one morning and saw someone sitting on a stile; as she drew near, however, the figure vanished.

Barkel, Kathleen (ca. 1930)

British trance medium, controlled by "White Hawk," who claimed to be a chief of the Sioux who had lived 800 years earlier. Barkel had psychic gifts as a child, and her mediumship began to develop in 1922. For years she did excellent work at the **British College of Psychic Science,** giving psychic healing sessions in conjunction with her husband and offering voice séances with her daughter. Sitters often received **apports** in the form of beautifully cut stones. "White Hawk" would place Barkel's hand over that of the sitter and the stone would appear to grow in between them.

Sources:

Bradley, H. Dennis. . . . *And After.* London, 1931.

Barker, Elsa (d. 1954)

American novelist and poet, born in Leicester, Vermont. She allegedly produced through **automatic writing** the scripts for *Letters from a Living Dead Man* (1914), *War Letters from the Living Dead Man* (1915), and *Last Letters from a Living Dead Man* (1919). These remarkable communications attracted much attention in England, where they were first published. At the time the scripts were produced, Elsa Barker was new to automatic writing, and was also unaware that the communicator (subsequently identified as David P. Hatch, a Los Angeles lawyer), who signed the communications "X," had passed away. These letters record the impressions of an intelligent traveler in a strange country, his mistakes, prejudices, ideals, and new insights.

Elsa Barker's other publications include *The Son of Mary Bethel* (1909), *The Frozen Grail & Other Poems* (1910), *Stories from the New Testament for Children* (1911), *The Body of Love* (1912), *Fielding*

Sargent (1922), *The Cobra Candlestick* (1928), *The C.I.D. of Dexter Drake* (1929), and *The Redman Cave Murder* (1930).

Barker died August 31, 1954.

Sources:

Barker, Elsa. *War Letters from the Living Dead Man.* London: W. Rider & Son, 1915.

Barker, Gray (1925–1984)

Writer on UFOs who launched the story of **Albert K. Bender** and the **men in black,** who are supposed to have silenced Bender's revelations about **flying saucers.** Barker's book *They Knew Too Much About Flying Saucers* (1956) started other similar conspiracy accusations against mysterious officials or unidentified aliens. A number of **UFO** researchers have since reported sinister telephone warnings, slow knockings at the door, confiscation of documents, and other harassment.

Born May 2, 1925, in Riffle, West Virginia, Barker studied at Glenville State College (B.A., 1947). He was a public school teacher (1948–49), then a sales agent and theater owner. In 1952 he became interested in flying saucers and began writing for *Space Review,* the magazine of Bender's International Flying Saucer Bureau. In the fall of 1953 Bender closed the bureau and Barker began his own magazine, *The Saucerian,* later called *The Saucerian Bulletin* (1953–62). Barker then became obsessed with Bender's claim of having been threatened by three mysterious men in black and eventually wrote his first book about the Bender case, *They Knew Too Much About Flying Saucers* (1956). He also founded Saucerian Press (later the New Age Press), which published its first title, *From Outer Space to You,* by **contactee** Howard Menger in 1959.

Barker emerged in the 1960s as a collector of tales that floated through the flying saucer community, especially stories dealing with claims of actual contact with outer space beings and accounts exhibiting a paranoid element. Barker wrote and edited several books, including the *Bender Mystery Confirmed* (1962), *Gray Barker's Book of Saucers* (1965), *Gray Barker's Book of Adamski* (1967), *The Silver Bridge* (1970), and *Gray Barker at Giant Rock* (1974). Among his last publications were two bibliographical books, his own *A UFO Guide to "Fate" Magazine* (1981) and Bruce Walton's *A Guide to he Inner Earth* (1983). In the 1970s Barker began to issue an irregular publication, *Gray Barker's Newsletter.* He was president of the Saucers and Unexplained Celestial Events Research Society (SAUCERS) and a member of the National UFO Congress, the National Audio-Visual Association, and the Mountaineer Educational Media Association. He died December 6, 1984.

Sources:

Barker, Gray. *The Silver Bridge.* Clarksburg, W.Va.: Saucerian Books, 1970.

———. *They Knew Too Much About Flying Saucers.* New York: University Books, 1956.

Clark, Jerome. *The Emergence of a Phenomenon: UFOs from the Beginning through 1959.* Vol. 2, *The UFO Encyclopedia.* Detroit: Omnigraphics, 1992.

Bar-Lgura

Ancient Semitic demon said to sit on the roofs of houses and leap on the inhabitants. People so afflicted were called *d'baregara.*

Barlow, Fred (d. 1964)

Fred Barlow, photography expert for the **Society for Psychical Research,** became interested in the claims various people made of having taken photographs of spirit entities. He entered his study hopeful that photography might provide evidence of **survival** after death and for a while he emerged as a staunch defender of **spirit photography.** However, by mid-century, especially after his investigations of the work of spirit photographers George Moss and **William Hope,** he reversed his opinion. This change resulted from his own inability to produce any spirit photographs under test conditions (where the possibility of **fraud** was ruled out) and the discovery that every spirit photograph could consistently be traced to some existing photograph of which it was an exact copy. While he never discounted the possibility of genuine spirit photographs, his testimonies became an important force in killing the phenomenon.

Barlow died in 1964, and **Eric J. Dingwall** inherited his collection of photographs. Dingwall deposited them at the British Museum.

Sources:

Barlow, Fred. "Report on an Investigation into Spirit-Photography." *Proceedings* of the Society for Psychical Research 41.

Dingwall, E. J. "The Need for Responsibility in Psychology." In *A Skeptic's Handbook of Parapsychology.* Edited by Paul Kurtz. N.p., 1985.

Barnaud, Nicholas (sixteenth century)

A sixteenth-century physician who claimed to have discovered the **philosophers' stone.** He published many short treatises on the subject of **alchemy,** which are contained in the third volume of the *Theatrum Chimicum* of Zetzner, published at Strasbourg in 1659.

Barqu

According to legend, the demon that holds the secret of the **philosophers' stone.**

Barrett, Sir William Fletcher (1844–1925)

One of the distinguished early psychical researchers, a principal founder in 1882 of the **Society for Psychical Research** in England. Born February 10, 1844, in Jamaica, West Indies, Barrett was educated at Old Trafford Grammar School, Manchester, England. He became a science master, physics lecturer, and, from 1873 to 1910, professor of physics at the Royal College of Science, Dublin, Ireland. In 1916 he married Florence Willey. He was a fellow of the Royal Society, the Philosophical Society, and the Royal Society of Literature and a member of the Institute of Electrical Engineers and the Royal Irish Academy. He was a highly respected scientist, responsible for important developments in the fields of metal alloys and vision.

Studies in **mesmerism** aroused Barrett's curiosity for the physical phenomena of **Spiritualism.** He began his first investigations in 1874. Two years later he submitted a paper, "Some Phenomena Associated with Abnormal Conditions of Mind," to the British Association for the Advancement of Science. The Biological Committee refused it, and the Anthropological subsection only accepted it on the casting vote of the chairman, Dr. **Alfred Russel Wallace.** The paper contained an exposition of the professor's experiments in **telepathy,** the existence of which he considered proved, holding that this method of communication is probably explainable by some form of nervous induction.

Barrett was inclined to attribute the more marvelous physical phenomena of Spiritualism (**levitation,** the **fire ordeal**) to **hallucination.** He declared that he himself had heard psychic raps in broad daylight, out-of-doors under conditions that made trickery impossible.

In January 1882 Barrett called a conference in the offices of the **British National Association of Spiritualists.** At this conference the Society for Psychical Research was born. During a visit to the United States in 1885 he gave the impetus to the foundation of the **American Society for Psychical Research.** His theory of hallucination as the cause of the greater part of physical phenomena was soon abandoned. He found mediums among personal friends who were above suspicion, and he could carry out experiments in daylight.

Every branch of psychical research claimed his attention, but his most important studies were on the **divining rod.** He collaborated with **Theodore Besterman** on a brilliant and comprehensive study of the subject. He did one of the earliest studies of **near-death experiences** and explored the philosophical implications of psychic matters. In his paper "Some Reminiscences of Fifty Years of Psychical Research" (1924), he concludes that there is convincing evidence for (1) the existence of a spiritual world, (2) for **survival** after death, and (3) for occasional communications from those who have died.

Barrett was convinced of the possibility of life of some kind in the "luminiferous ether." "It is in harmony with all we know," he writes in *On the Threshold of the Unseen,* "to entertain a belief in an unseen world, in which myriads of living creatures exist, some with faculties like our own, and others with faculties beneath or transcending our own; and it is possible that the evolutionary development of such a world has run on parallel lines to our own. The rivalry of life, the existence of instinct, intellect, conscience, will, right and wrong are as probable there as here, and, in course of time, consciousness of our human existence may have come to our unseen neighbours, and some means of mental, or even material communications with us may have been found."

Although Barrett is remembered for his work in psychical research, he also did outstanding work as a physicist and in 1899 was elected a fellow of the Royal Society. He died May 26, 1925, in London.

Sources:

Barrett, Sir William F. *Death-Bed Visions.* London: Methuen, 1926. Reprint, Wellingborough, England: Aquarian Press, 1986.

———. *The Divining Rod.* New Hyde Park, N.Y.: University Books, 1968.

———. *On the Threshold of a New World of Thought: An Examination of the Phenomena of Spiritualism and of the Evidence for Survival after Death.* New York: E. P. Dutton, 1918.

———. *On the Threshold of the Unseen.* 1917. Reprint, New York: E. P. Dutton, 1918.

———. *Psychical Research.* New York: H. Holt, [1911].

———. "Some Reminiscences of Fifty Years of Psychical Research," *Proceedings* of the Society for Psychical Research 34 (1924).

Berger, Arthur S., and Joyce Berger. *The Encyclopedia of Parapsychology and Psychical Research.* New York: Paragon House, 1991.

Inglis, Brian. "Sir William Barrett (1844–1925)." *Journal* of the Society for Psychical Research 55 (1988): 16.

"Bartholomew"

"Bartholomew," the entity channeled through Mary-Margaret Moore, has emerged through the several books of his teachings as one of the more popular entities in the **New Age** world. Described as an "energy vortex" or alternatively as "the higher and wiser level of energy," "Bartholomew" made his initial appearance in the mid-1970s. Moore was visiting with her friends John and Louise Aiken. John Aiken hypnotized Moore in an attempt to relieve her back pains, and "Bartholomew" began to speak.

Hesitantly Moore accepted "Bartholomew's" presence and allowed him to speak through her, but she also initially tested him. Noting the possibility that she was simply involved in a massive self-delusion, she monitored the information from "Bartholomew" and gauged it according to its helpful effects. Her acceptance of "Bartholomew" was also helped by consulting the **I Ching,** a Chinese divination method that involves the throwing of sticks that can create one of 64 hexagram patterns. She got the fiftieth, which refers to the "hollow" ruler who is receptive to the wisdom of a sage; and the first, which refers to the creative power of the Deity. She decided that she was the ruler and "Bartholomew" the sage and thus that the channeling was a valid experience.

Equally important, she observed that she and others who began to act out of Bartholomew's wisdom were benefiting from it. For herself, Moore discovered a balance between the use of her rational thinking abilities when appropriate and her intuitive self at other suitable moments. The channeling activity itself seemed to bring a sense of peace, gratitude, and love.

The first volume of selected materials from the channeling sessions with "Bartholomew" was published in 1984 as *I Come as a Brother: A Remembrance of Illusions.* As many people became aware of "Bartholomew," Moore attained some celebrity status within the New Age community. Moore soon produced a second volume, *From the Heart of a Gentle Brother* (1987). "Bartholomew" argues for the importance of relating to a higher reality. He calls upon people to turn within and discover the place of knowingness inside the self, assures people that they are not alone in the universe and that they need to open themselves to the energies that permeate it, allowing those energies to transform the self. Self-love and self-acceptance are additional important components of the transforming personality.

"Bartholomew" also emphasizes a life of harmlessness. The shift of people and of society as a whole to a higher level of consciousness is dependent upon the acceptance of a life of harmlessness and a move away from thoughts, words, and actions that lead to harm of others.

Sources:

Moore, Mary-Margaret. *From the Heart of a Gentle Brother.* Taos, N.Mex.: High Mesa Press, 1987.

———. *I Come as a Brother: A Remembrance of Illusions.* Taos, N.Mex.: High Mesa Publishing, 1984.

Bartlett, John Allen (1861–1933)

Retired English marine officer and songwriter who was the psychic medium of part of the **Glastonbury Scripts,** in which indications were given regarding the site and characteristics of the long-lost Edgar and Loretto Chapels of the Abbey at Glastonbury. Bartlett was a friend of **Frederick Bligh Bond**'s, with whom the experiments were conducted and who excavated the abbey site. In his book *The Gate of Remembrance* (1918), Bond, using the pseudonym "John Alleyne" for his friend Bartlett, describes these experiments and their outcome.

Bond believed that the scripts and also the automatic sketches made by Bartlett gave archaeologically correct information, confirmed by the later excavations. Critics of Bond's book believed that such claims were not justified.

Sources:

Bond, Frederick Bligh. *The Gate of Remembrance.* Oxford: Blackwell, 1918.

Baru

Caste of priests in ancient Mesopotamia. (See **Semites**)

Bashir, Mir (1907–)

Kashmiri palmist noted for his serious study of the subject. During his research on **palmistry** he collaborated with physicians and criminologists, maintaining a library of over fifty thousand handprints. Mir Bashir moved to England in 1948. He wrote *How to Read Hands* (1955).

Basil (Astrologer)

A Florentine astrologer of the fifteenth century.

Basil (Herb)

Aromatic herb of the mint family (genus *Ocimum*) with a pungent clovelike flavor, much used in soups and other recipes. Many traditions and superstitions are connected with basil.

There are two suggested derivations of its popular name. It was once thought to be an antidote for the poison of the fabulous

basilisk or cockatrice. Another tradition cites an early Greek name, *basilikon,* implying that the herb was used in a royal ceremony.

Some traditions believed it sacred, others that it was dedicated to the Devil. Greeks believed it was an emblem of hatred, Italians that it was appropriate to lovers. In both Greece and Rome there were ancient rituals involving cursing when the herb was planted, which were believed to assist growth. In Moldavia it was a folk superstition that a sprig of basil flowers handed by a girl to a wayward lover would ensure the boy's fidelity and love.

Basil is much prized in India, where it is known as *tulsi* (or *tulasi*) and regarded as sacred to the god Vishnu and the goddess Lakshmi. It is grown in pots near Hindu homes and temples. It is used in cooking and is also believed to help secure children.

Basilidians

A Gnostic sect founded by Basilides of Alexandria, who claimed to have received his esoteric doctrines from Glaucias, a disciple of the apostle Peter. Basilides recognized one supreme being named **Abraxas.** The sect posited three grades of existence—material, intellectual, and spiritual—and possessed two allegorical statues, male and female. The doctrine had many points of resemblance to that of the **Ophites** and the Jewish **Kabala.**

Sources:

Legge, Francis. *Forerunners and Rivals of Christianity from 333 B.C. to 330 A.D.* 2 vols. 1915. Reprint, New Hyde Park, N.Y.: University Books, 1964.

Basilisk (or Cockatrice)

A fabulous reptilian monster of ancient and medieval legend believed to be generated from a cock's egg hatched by a serpent or a toad in a dunghill. Accounts of this monster vary, but it was generally said to have either the face of a **cock** or a distorted human face, with the wings and feet of a fowl and the tail of a serpent. It was represented this way in heraldry.

It was reputed to be a deadly creature with a destructive power similar to that of the fabulous Gorgons of Greek legend. A human being could survive its deadly glare only by viewing it in a mirror; however, if anyone saw the basilisk before it saw that person, the creature would die. It was even believed to kill itself if it saw its own image in a mirror. Even its breath was poisonous to plants and animals, as well as to humans, and was believed to have the power to split rocks. It is possible that this fearsome creature really evolved from exaggerated travelers' tales of the horned adder or the hooded cobra, confused with such awesome reptiles as the Gila monster.

Basilisk has also been applied to a group of iguanalike lizards (*Basiliscus*), found on the banks of rivers and streams in Central America and Mexico.

Sources:

Borges, Jorge Luis, with Margarita Guerrero. *The Book of Imaginary Beings.* Translated by Norman Thomas de Giovanni. New York: E. P. Dutton, 1970.

Bassantin (or Bassantoun), James (d. 1568)

Scottish astrologer and mathematician, the son of the laird of Bassandean in the Merse, Berwickshire, Scotland, born in the reign of James IV. After studying mathematics at the University of Glasgow, he traveled for further studies on the Continent. He subsequently went to Paris, where for some years he taught mathematics at the university. He returned to Scotland in 1562.

There was a prevailing belief in judicial **astrology** at that time, particularly in France. On his way home through England, according to Sir James Melville's memoirs, Bassantin met with Sir Robert Melville (brother of Sir James), who was at that time engaged on the part of the unfortunate Mary, Queen of Scots in endeavoring to effect a meeting between her and Elizabeth. Bassantin predicted that all his efforts would be in vain, which proved to be true.

Bassantin was a zealous Protestant. His principal work is a treatise on astronomy, written in French and translated into Latin by John Tornaesius, which was published at Geneva in 1599. He wrote four other treatises on mathematics and horoscopes, but they do not appear to have been published.

Bastian, Harry (nineteenth century)

Nineteenth-century American **materialization** medium whose exposure in Vienna on February 11, 1884, led Archduke John to publish a pamphlet under the title *A Glimpse into Spiritualism.*

Bastian traveled to Vienna at **Baron Hellenbach**'s request expressly for the purpose of sitting for Archduke John and Crown Prince Rudolph. According to the baron, Bastian's powers had waned in 1882 and he had retired from giving séances. Nevertheless, he felt sufficiently confident of himself to honor the baron's request.

In the first séance nothing particular occurred. In the second, a bell that was pushed out of the circle by one of the sitters with his foot flew back ringing within the circle on request. Before the séance, a naval officer had bound Bastian to his chair. A few minutes later he was free, but his hands were tied in such a manner that the cords had to be cut.

At the third séance, after the company retired to an adjacent lighted apartment, phantoms appeared. When the fifth spirit walked in, the door between the dark room and the figure was, by a cord arrangement, suddenly shut by Archduke John. The "spirit" was caught and found to be Bastian without his shoes. The spirit costume, however, disappeared, and no trace of it was found either on Bastian's person or in the **cabinet.** Hellenbach, responding to the archduke's accusation of **fraud** in his *The Logic of Facts,* asserts, "There can scarcely be any doubt that Bastian would have been acquitted through a closer acquaintance with these phenomena."

However, this was not the first occasion on which Bastian was accused of fraud. In August 1874, during a séance with Bastian, a lady caught the medium's hand where a spirit hand should have been (see report in *Medium,* August 14, 1874). At another séance in Arnhem, an electric lamp was suddenly introduced, providing a moment's glimpse of Bastian holding a guitar in his hand over the heads of the sitters (*Medium,* January 15, 1875). On this occasion, the editor of the *Medium* and some other sitters insisted that this could have been a spirit hand in the act of dematerializing and sinking back into the medium's body.

Bat

There is an Oriental belief that the bat is specially adapted to occult uses. In the Tyrol, there is a folklore belief that the man who wears the left eye of a bat may become invisible, and in Hesse, he who wears the heart of a bat tied to his arm with red thread will always be lucky at cards.

"Bataille, Dr."

The alleged author of *Le Diable au XIX. Siècle,* published in Paris in 1892, a book that created a sensation with its revelations of the secret rites and orgies of many diabolic societies. The author claimed personal experience with **devil worship.** This exciting and colorful work of some 800,000 words attracted enormous attention and its stories of worldwide diabolic conspiracies associated with **Freemasonry** were widely discussed. It was first thought to be the work of Dr. Charles Hacks, who contributed a preface entitled "Revelations of an Occultist." Hacks was a real, although shadowy, figure. The book was later revealed to be the work of journalist and editor **Gabriel Jogand-Pagés,** also known as "Leo Taxil," who confessed to fabricating the book as an anti-Freemasonry, anticlerical hoax. (See also **Diana Vaughan**)

Sources:

Bataille, Dr. [Gabriel Jogand-Pagés]. *Le Diable au XIX. Siècle.* Paris, 1892.

Batcheldor, Kenneth J. (1921–1988)

British psychical researcher who specialized in the study of **psychokinesis,** or PK (the ability to move objects by means of mental concentration). He made a great contribution to identifying the conditions under which such phenomena are most likely to occur.

Before his detailed investigations, he had been a principal clinical psychologist for a group of hospitals in Devon, United Kingdom. At a social occasion in 1964, after a guest had told ghost stories, Batcheldor suggested the group "[have] a go at tabletipping just for fun." Although there were no perceptible unusual phenomena, a sitting at a later date was marked by a loud noise. During a subsequent séance in darkness, the table rose from the floor, apparently of its own volition. Batcheldor was sufficiently intrigued to continue experimental sittings in an attempt to explain the phenomenon. In 1976 he took early retirement and spent more time in the systematic study of what has become known as "macro-PK." He was assisted by fellow researcher Coin Brooked-Smith and other friends. He published some valuable papers on the subject, supported by the papers of Coin Brooked-Smith.

Batcheldor was fully aware of the difference between unconscious muscular activity and paranormal movement of a table, and of the part played by belief and a nonskeptical state of mind in facilitating the production of genuine phenomena. He stated:

"There's something about table-tipping that enables a group of ordinary people to succeed in generating PK without even trying, provided they are reasonably open-minded. It is this—in most cases the table will start to move due to unconscious muscular activity. This can give an amazing illusion that the table is moving of its own accord as if animated by some mysterious force. You get the impression you are already succeeding in generating paranormal movements. This has precisely the same impact on you as real success would have—it sweeps your doubts aside and produces total faith."

Such faith, he believed, was an essential factor in producing general PK effects. Other researchers have from time to time also discovered that rigid objectivity and skepticism are barriers to producing PK phenomena. The problems of possible **fraud** and repeatability under controlled conditions remain difficult for researchers.

According to Batcheldor, in a letter to Guy Lyon Playfair in 1966, "It is as if the universe allows **psi** to occur, now and then, quite easily and quickly provided the circumstances are such that it is accidental and not under conscious control. Perhaps if things were otherwise, reality would be too unstable." Playfair took part in a number of Batcheldor's investigations, and in an obituary for his friend (*Journal* of the Society for Psychical Research, vol. 55, July 1988) states, "It could even be argued that PK takes place only under conditions that make its verification impossible. . . . However, some of Ken's evidence is very compelling, especially the videotaped episodes in which the table can be seen moving in ways that do not appear normal. . . ."

Batcheldor died March 6, 1988. His paper "Notes on the Elusiveness Problem in Relation to a Radical View of Paranormality" (compiled, edited, and with a preface by Patrick V. Giesler) was published posthumously in the *Journal* of the American Society for Psychical Research. Batcheldor did much to encourage the production and investigation of PK phenomena among various groups and identified the conditions under which such phenomena could more readily occur.

Sources:

Batcheldor, Kenneth. "Contributions to the Theory of PK Induction from Sitter-Group Work." *Journal* of the American Society for Psychical Research 78 (1984).

———. "Notes on the Elusiveness Problem in Relation to a Radical View of Paranormality." *Journal* of the American Society for Psychical Research 88 (April 1994).

———. "Report on a Case of Table-Levitation and Associated Phenomena." *Journal* of the Society for Psychical Research 43 (1966).

Batcheldor, Kenneth, and D. W. Hunt. "Some Experiments in Psychokinesis." *Journal* of the Society for Psychical Research 43 (1966).

Berger, Arthur S., and Joyce Berger. *The Encyclopedia of Parapsychology and Psychical Research.* New York: Paragon House, 1991.

Brooked-Smith, Coin. "Data-tape Recorded Experimental PK Phenomena." *Journal* of the Society for Psychical Research 47 (1973).

Bathym

According to **Johan Weyer,** Bathym is a duke of the infernal regions, also known as Marthin. He has the appearance of a robust man, but his body ends in a serpent's tail. He rides a steed of livid color and is able to transport men from one place to another with wondrous speed. He is well versed in the virtues of herbs and precious stones. Thirty legions obey his behests.

Sources:

Weyer, Johannes. *Witches, Devils and Doctors in the Renaissance: Johann Weyer, De Praestigiis.* Edited by George Mora. Binghamton, N.Y.: Medieval & Renaissance Texts & Studies, 1991.

Baton, The Devil's

There is preserved in the Market of the Arcane, Tolentino, Mexico, a baton that it is said the Devil used.

Bauer, Eberhard (1944–)

Eberhard Bauer, leading German parapsychologist, is a professor of psychology at the University of Freiburg, Germany. Bauer emerged in the period of recovery of German psychical research after World War II and became the leading German historian of parapsychology. In 1981 he led in the founding of the Wissenschaftliche Gesellschaft zur Förderung der Parapsychologie, the first successful academic parapsychology organization in the post-Nazi era. He also became the managing editor of *Zeitschrift für Parapsychologie und Grenzgebiete der Parapsychologie,* the leading parapsychological journal published in Germany. For Bauer's accomplishments as a historian and as a researcher in psychokinesis (**PK**), the **Society for Psychical Research** in England has made him a corresponding member.

Sources:

Bauer, Eberhard. "Criticism and Controversies in Parapsychology." *European Journal of Parapsychology* 5 (1984): 141.

Bauer, Georg (1490–1555)

German scholar and "father of mineralogy." He Latinized his surname (which means "boor" or "husbandman") to "Agricola" ("farmer"). Bauer was born March 24, 1490, at Glauchau, Saxony. An able and industrious man, he acquired considerable knowledge of the principles of medicine, which led him, as it led many of his contemporaries, to search for the **elixir of life** and the **philosophers' stone.** A treatise on these interesting subjects, which he published at Cologne in 1531, secured him the favor of Duke Maurice of Saxony, who appointed him superintendent of his silver mines at Chemnitz. In this post he obtained a practical acquaintance with the properties of metals, which dissipated his wild notions of their possible transmutation into gold; but if he abandoned one superstition he adopted another, and from the legends of the miners he imbibed a belief in the existence of good and evil spirits in the bowels of the earth, and in the creation of explosive gases and firedamp by the malicious agency of the latter.

Bauer's major work, *De Re metallica,* completed in 1550 and published in 1556, has an illustration showing dowsers at work searching for minerals with a **divining rod.**

He died in Chemnitz on November 21, 1555.

Bave

Daughter of the wizard Calatin in ancient Irish mythology. She figures in the famous Irish legend *The Cattle Raid of Quelgny.* By taking the form of one of Niam's handmaids, she succeeded in enticing Niam away from **Cuchulain** and led her forth to wander in the woods.

Bayemon

Named in the **grimoire** of Honorius as a powerful demon and monarch of the western parts of the infernal regions. To him the following invocation is addressed:

"*O King Bayemon,* most mighty, who reigneth towards the western parts, I call upon thee and invoke thy name in the name of the Divinity. I command thee in the name of the Most High to present thyself before this circle, thee and the other spirits who are thy subjects, in the name of Passiel and Rosus, for the purpose of replying to all that which I demand of thee. If thou dost not come I will torment thee with a sword of heavenly fire. I will augment thy pains and burn thee. Obey, *O King Bayemon.*"

Although ascribed to Pope Honorius III and supported by what is claimed as a papal bull authorizing ordained priests to invoke spirits and control demons, this grimoire is denounced by Roman Catholic writers as a forgery. The grimoire became popular among seventeenth-century **occult** magicians.

Beacon

Journal presenting the teachings of **Alice A. Bailey** (1880–1949), former Theosophist who founded her own **Arcane School.** Address: Lucis Publishing Co., 113 University Pl., 11th Fl., Box 722, Cooper Sta., New York, NY 10017.

Beads of Truth (Magazine)

Quarterly publication presenting the teachings of Eastern mystic Yogi Bhajan and news of the activities of the Healthy, Happy, Holy Organization (3HO), the educational affiliate of the Sikh Dharma. Both the Sikh Dharma and the 3HO may be contacted at 1620 Press Rd., Los Angeles, CA 90035.

"Beale, Dr."

The spirit doctor of Hulham House, near Exmouth, England, working through the medium Miss Rose. "Dr. Beale" is credited with the **healing** of many hopeless cases, as narrated in *One Thing I Know* (1919), *Dr. Beale* (1921), and *The House of Wonder* (1928), by E. M. S. (E. M. Storr), a lady patient, whom he cured.

According to his own claims, "Dr. Beale" had been a physician on Earth. He performed no operations, and his treatment mostly consisted of diet, bath, and massages. Hulham House was acquired in 1921 and was run on humanitarian principles. Patients who were unable to come to the home were often treated at a distance if they sent some articles of apparel to establish the link.

Miss Rose, as a rule, went into trance when "Dr. Beale" possessed her body and made the diagnosis. This was often preceded by another possession when "Madeleine," a spirit nurse, came through and prepared everything for the doctor as Miss Rose herself did not understand nursing. Another worker in "Dr. Beale's" band was "Dr. Nova," who worked through Sister Mercia, a fully trained nurse in a small town in Devon. Miss Rose often visited patients, and this way the healing was superintended by "Dr. Beale."

Bealings Bells

Title of a book by Major Edward Moore, F.R.S., that was published in 1841 on the mysterious bell ringing in his house at Great Bealings, Suffolk, England, which began February 2, 1834, and lasted for 53 days. Every attempt to discover the cause of the mysterious ringing was fruitless, and by no effort could the same clamorous, rapid ringing be normally produced. After three days of the strange experience, Major Moore concluded, "I am thoroughly convinced that the ringing is by no human agency." The psychic researcher **Frank Podmore,** in *Modern Spiritualism* (1902), believed the conviction too hastily formed and pointed out that the Major, the sole witness, did not describe a single occasion on which every member of the household was accounted for when the bell ringing occurred. However, no comment was passed by him on the sequel to Major Moore's story as told in the *Ipswich Journal.* Readers of the paper sent 14 communications of similar happenings in different parts of England, some of them recurring and having an ancestry of 100 years.

In *My Life* (1901), Dr. **Alfred Russel Wallace** quoted the testimony of Professor Anstead: "A neighbour and friend of mine at Great Bealings has had the most wonderful things happen in his house, which no one has ever been able to find a cause for. He has often told me about the bells ringing when no one was in the house. He was a very clever man, and I am sure what he says is true, and many people in the neighbourhood were witnesses t."

Sources:

Podmore, Frank. *Modern Spiritualism.* London: Methuen, 1902. Reprinted as *Mediums of the Nineteenth Century.* New Hyde Park, N.Y.: University Books, 1963.

Beans

The consumption of beans was prohibited by Pythagoras and Plato to those who desired veracious dreams, as they tended to inflate; and for the purpose of truthful dreaming, the animal nature must be made to lie quiet. Cicero, however, laughed at this prohibition, asking if it is the stomach and not the mind with which one dreams.

Sources:

Cunningham, Scott. *Cunningham's Encyclopedia of Magical Herbs.* St. Paul, Minn.: Llewellyn Publications, 1985.

Bearded Demon

The demon who teaches the secret of the **philosophers' stone.** He is not well known. The *démon barbu* is not to be confused with Barbatos, a great and powerful demon said to be a duke in Hades, although not a philosopher; nor with Barbas, who is interested in mechanics. It is said that the bearded demon is so called on account of his remarkable beard.

Beare, Charles Albert (ca. 1931)

Famous British fake medium, who demonstrated claimed clairvoyance and trumpet and psychometry phenomena. In 1920 he joined the Spiritualist organization the Temple of Light and promoted himself as a medium. His "phenomena" were tested by the Temple of Light, which presented Beare with a diploma certifying his mediumistic "gifts" and accrediting him as an authorized medium. Beare claimed to have a spirit guide named "Shauna," supposed to be a Greek who had lived 130 years earlier.

In 1931, however, Beare published a confession in the newspaper *Daily Express* (September 18). He stated: "I have deceived hundreds of people. . . . I have been guilty of **fraud** and deception in spiritualistic practices by pretending that I was controlled by a spirit guide. . . . I am frankly and whole-heartedly sorry that I have allowed myself to deceive people."

On November 4, 1931, Beare gave a talk to members of the **National Laboratory of Psychical Research,** founded by psychical researcher **Harry Price.** Beare demonstrated his mediumistic frauds and stated that he was now absolutely disgusted with himself.

Beattie, John (ca. 1873)

A retired British photographer of Clifton, Bristol, England, with 20 years' experience, who decided to test the claims of **Frederick A. Hudson** in regard to **spirit photography.** In the early stage of the experiments, in which he was assisted by Dr. G. S. Thompson, he registered failure after failure. Sometimes 20 plates were exposed without result, but in 1873 he obtained important results. The medium, a tradesman, described minutely and correctly in advance the appearances that were to be impressed on the plates. He claimed to see them clairvoyantly. The developed pictures tallied with his descriptions. The experiments were reported by Rev. **Stainton Moses** and others in *Human Nature* (vol. 8, 1874).

Beaumont, John (d. 1731)

British geologist, surgeon, and author of *An Historical Physiological and Theological Treatise of Spirits, Apparitions, Witchcrafts, and Other Magical Practises* published in 1705. He is described as "a man of hypochondriacal disposition, with a considerable degree of reading, but with a strong bias to credulity." Laboring under this affliction, he saw hundreds of imaginary men and women about him, though, as he added, he never saw anything in the night, unless by fire or candlelight, or in the moonshine. He said:

"I had two spirits, who constantly attended me, night and day, for above three months together, who called each other by their names; and several spirits would call at my chamber door, and ask whether such spirits lived there, and they would answer they did. As for the other spirits that attended me, I heard none of their names mentioned only I asked one spirit, which came for some nights together, and rung a little bell in my ear, what his name was, who answered *Ariel.* The two spirits that constantly attended myself appeared both in women's habit, they being of brown complexion, about three feet in stature; they had both black loose net-work gowns, tied with a black sash about the middle, and within the net-work appeared a gown of a golden colour, with somewhat of a light striking through it. Their heads were not dressed in top-knots, but they had white linen caps on, with lace on them about three fingers' breadth, and over it they had a black loose net-work hood."

He added: "I would not, for the whole world, undergo what I have undergone, upon spirits coming twice to me; their first coming was most dreadful to me, the thing being then altogether new, and consequently most surprising, though at the first coming they did not appear to me but only called to me at my chamber-windows, rung bells, sung to me, and played on music, etc.; but the last coming also carried terror enough; for when they came, being only five in number, the two women before mentioned, and three men (though afterwards there came hundreds), they told me they would kill me if I told any person in the house of their being there, which put me in some consternation; and I made a servant sit up with me four nights in my chamber, before a fire, it being in the Christmas holidays, telling no person of their being there. One of these spirits, in women's dress, lay down upon the bed by me every night; and told me, if I slept, the spirits would kill me, which kept me waking for three nights. In the meantime, a near relation of mine went (though unknown to me) to a physician of my acquaintance, desiring him to prescribe me somewhat for sleeping, which he did, and a sleeping potion was brought me; but I set it by, being very desirous and inclined to sleep without it. The fourth night I could hardly forbear sleeping; but the spirit, lying on the bed by me, told me again, I should be killed if I slept; whereupon I rose and sat by the fireside, and in a while returned to my bed; and so I did a third time, but was still threatened as before; whereupon I grew impatient, and asked the spirits what they would have? Told them I had done the part of a Christian, in humbling myself to God and feared them not; and rose from my bed, took a cane, and knocked at the ceiling of my chamber, a near relation of mine then lying over me, who presently rose and came down to me about two o'clock in the morning, to whom I said, 'You have seen me disturbed these four days past, and that I have not slept: the occasion of it was, that five spirits, which are not in the room with me, have threatened to kill me if I told any person of their being here, or if I slept; but I am not able to forbear sleeping longer, and acquaint you with it, and now stand in defiance of them'; and thus I exerted myself about them and notwithstanding their continued threats I slept very well the next night, and continued to do so, though they continued with me above three months, day and night."

Beausoleil, Jean du Chatelot, Baron de (ca. 1576–1643)

German mineralogist and alchemist who lived during the first half of the seventeenth century. He traveled over most European countries looking for metals with the aid of a divining ring. In 1626 his instruments were seized under the pretext that they were bewitched, and he was imprisoned in the Bastille, where he died in 1643. In 1617 he published a work entitled *Diorisinus, id est defintis verae philisophice de materia prima lapidis philosophalis.* Beausoleil was the greatest of French metallurgists of his time. (See also **Radiesthesia**)

Bechard

A demon alluded to in the ancient **grimoire, The Key of Solomon,** as having power over the winds and the tempests. He makes hail, thunder, and rain.

Sources:

Mathers, S. L. MacGregor. *The Greater Key of Solomon.* Chicago: de Laurence, 1914.

Becker, Robert O(tto) (1923–)

Orthopedic surgeon and authority on the biological effects of electromagnetism, with special interest in the relationship between bioelectromagnetics and **parapsychology.** He was formerly chief of orthopedic surgery at the Veterans Administration Hospital, Syracuse, New York, and later clinical professor of orthopedic surgery at the State University of New York Upstate Medical Center and the Louisiana Medical Center in Shreveport.

Becker has published over 150 scientific papers relating to growth and healing electrical control mechanisms, and the effects of applied electrical currents and/or magnetic fields on living organisms.

His pioneering research in biological electricity and regeneration contributed to the emerging field of energy medicine, which explores alternative medical treatments such as **acupuncture,** electrotherapy, visualization, and **hypnosis,** all of which appear to use an invisible common source—the body's innate electrical systems. Becker initiated the first official hearings on power transmission line safety (1973–80, New York State Public Service Commission). He also served as an expert witness in congressional hearings before the House Subcommittee on Water and Power Resources.

His publications include *Cross Currents* (1990) and *The Body Electric* (1985). He has contributed chapters to numerous medical and scientific books and is associate editor for vols. 1–3 of *Advances in Parapsychology* (1977, 1978, 1982). Becker delivered the 1990 Gardner Murphy Memorial Lecture for the **American Soci-**

ety for **Psychical Research,** titled "The Relationship between Bioelectromagnetics and Psychic Phenomena."

Sources:

Becker, Robert O. *The Body Electric.* Los Angeles: J. P. Tarcher, 1990. Distributed by St. Martin's Press.

———. *Cross Currents.* New York: Quill, 1985.

Bed (Graham's Magnetic)

A magnetic contrivance, similar to the **baquet,** made use of by James Graham, eighteenth-century physician and magnetist of Edinburgh, Scotland. His entire house, which he dubbed the Temple of Hygeia and opened in 1779, was of great magnificence, especially the room with the magnetic bed. The bed itself rested on six transparent pillars; the mattresses were soaked with oriental perfumes; the bedclothes were of satin in tints of purple and sky blue. A healing stream of magnetism, as well as fragrant and strengthening medicines, were introduced into the sleeping apartment through glass tubes and cylinders. To these attractions were added the soft strains of hidden flutes, harmonicons, and a large organ. Use of this celestial couch was said to sooth shattered nerves and was allowed only to those who sent a written application to its owner and enclosed £50 sterling.

Bees

It was maintained by certain demonologists that if a sorceress ate a queen bee before being captured, she would be able to sustain her trial and tortures without making a confession. In some parts of Brittany it was claimed that these insects were very sensitive to the fortunes and misfortunes of their master, and would not thrive unless he was careful to tie a piece of black cloth to the hive when a death occurred in the family, and a piece of red cloth when there was any occasion of rejoicing.

The Latin grammarian Gaius Julius Solinus (third century C.E.) wrote that there are no bees in Ireland, and even if a little Irish earth be taken to another country and spread about the hives, the bees would abandon the place, so fatal to them is the earth of Ireland. The same story is found in the *Origines* of Isodore. "Must we seek," says Pierre Lebrun, author of *Critical History of Superstitious Practices* (1702), "the source of this calumny of Irish earth? No; for it is sufficient to say that it is a fable, and that many bees are to be found in Ireland."

There are many ancient superstitions about bees. In biblical times they were thought to originate in the bodies of dead cattle, hence the riddle by Samson in Judges 14:8, "Out of the eater came forth meat, and out of the strong came forth sweetness." In fact, the skeletonized rib cage skeleton of dead cattle provided a natural beehive. In Egyptian mythology, bees arose from the tears of the sun god Ra, while a Breton superstition said they came from the tears of Christ on the cross. In Hindu mythology, bees formed the bowstring of Kama, the Indian Cupid.

Popular folklore claimed that bee stings aided arthritis and rheumatism sufferers and recently bee venom has been revived as a possible treatment for multiple sclerosis.

In rural districts all over the world, the old custom of "telling the bees" persisted when there was a death in the family or someone left home. In Ireland, the bees also told secrets or advised on new projects. In ancient European folklore, bees were regarded as messengers to the gods, and the custom of "telling the bees" might have been a remnant of the idea of keeping the gods advised of human affairs.

Believe It

Publication (newsletter) of the Maryland Center for Investigation of Unconventional Phenomena, concerned with UFOs, Bigfoot, monsters, and related phenomena. Address: 131 Clifton Rd., Silver Spring, MD 20904.

Belin, Dom Jean Albert (1610–1677)

A Benedictine born at Besancon, France, in 1610. His principal works, a treaty on talismans and a dissertation upon astral figures, were published at Paris in 1671 and again in 1709. He also published several texts on **alchemy,** *Sympathetic Powder Justified* in 1671 and *Les aventures du Philosophe inconnu, en la recherche et en l'invention de la Pierre philosophale* (Adventures of an unknown philosopher in the search for and the manufacture of the Philosopher's Stone) (Paris, 1664, 1674). This latter work is divided into four books and speaks very clearly of the manner in which the **Philosophers' Stone** is made. However, Belin ascribed the authorship to another hand, and some of the adventures appear symbolical rather than factual.

Belk Psychic Research Foundation

Organization founded by **Henry Belk,** the eldest son of William Henry Belk Sr. of North Carolina (of department store fame), to investigate genuine ESP research. He had the early encouragement of Norman Vincent Peale and Dr. Charles Francis Potter. In cooperation with **Harold Sherman,** Belk was an early investigator of the phenomenon of **psychic surgery** as performed by **Tony Agpaoa** and other Philippine healers. The foundation was headquartered in New York City.

Sources:

Sherman, Harold. *"Wonder" Healers of the Philippines.* London: Psychic Press, 1967.

Belli Paaro

A former secret society of Liberia, Africa, the cult of which consisted in a description of brotherhood with departed spirits. The seventeenth-century author Olfert Dapper, writing of this society, stated: "They have also another custom which they call *Belli Paaro* of which they say it is a death, a new birth and an incorporation in the community of spirits or soul with whom the common folk associate in the bush, and help to eat the offerings prepared for the spirits." This description is far from clear, but apparently those who joined the society wished to be regarded as spiritualized, or as having died and having been brought to life again; and that their society was a confraternity of all those who had passed through this training in common.

Belloc, Jeanne (ca. 1609)

An alleged witch of the Labourd district in the Basque region of France, who in the reign of Henry IV was indicted for sorcery at the age of 84 years. In answer to Pierre De Lancre who interrogated her, she stated that she first attended the sabbatic meetings of Satan in winter 1609, where she was presented to the Devil, who kissed her—a mark of approbation that he bestowed upon the greatest sorcerers only. She described the Sabbat as a masked ball to which some came in their ordinary forms, while others joined the dance in the guise of dogs, cats, donkeys, pigs, and other animals.

However, no reliance can be placed on the confessions of any victims of De Lancre, as he used torture and believed that most of the 30,000 inhabitants of Labourd, including the priests, were infected with **witchcraft.**

Bélmez Faces

Strange pictures that appeared on the stone hearth in the kitchen of Juan Pereira Sanchez in the village of Bélmez de la Moraleda, Spain, during 1971. The Sanchez family was puzzled and frightened when the first face gradually manifested on the hearth, and eventually the son of the family hacked out the face with a pickaxe and filled in the hole with cement and sand. Soon afterward, however, a second face appeared near the site of the first one.

As the news spread, neighbors and later sightseers visited to see this phenomenon. The second face was hacked out and placed on a kitchen wall under glass. On the advice of the village mayor, the hearth was excavated and a shaft over six feet dug out. Bones were discovered, and it was later learned that the house was built on the site of an old cemetery. The second face had an agonized expression and resembled a Byzantine sketch. Other faces continued to appear.

The case was investigated in 1972 by German de Argumosa, who reported on some 18 "Bélmez faces" that had "grown" beyond the cemented hearth on the tiled kitchen floor. Even when the professor covered and sealed the floor with plastic, new faces appeared under the plastic, although the seals were not tampered with. Tape recordings were also made of voices associated with the face phenomena.

Belocolus

A fabulous white stone with a black pupil, said to render its bearer invisible in a field of battle.

Beloff, John (1920–)

Psychologist and parapsychologist; served as president of the **Parapsychological Association** in 1972 and again in 1982; president of the **Society for Psychical Research,** 1974–76; and editor of the society's *Journal.*

He studied philosophy and psychology at the University of London, England; became research assistant at the University of Illinois (1952); lecturer in psychology at Queen's University, Belfast, Ireland (1953); then was appointed senior lecturer in psychology at the University of Edinburgh, Scotland, in 1956. He has had a long career of research and writing in parapsychology. Among his numerous books, *Psychological Sciences* (1974) and *New Directions in Parapsychology* (1975) have been translated into several foreign languages. He was program committee chair for the joint Society for Psychical Research/Parapsychology Association Centenary Conference at Cambridge, England, in 1982.

Sources:

Beloff, John. *Existence of Mind.* New York: Citadel, 1964.

———. *The Importance of Psychical Research.* London: Society for Psychical Research, 1988.

———. *New Direction in Parapsychology.* Metuchen, N.J.: Scarecrow Press, 1975.

———. *Parapsychology: The Way Ahead.* Turnbridge Wells, U.K.: Institute for Cultural Research, 1974.

———. *Psychological Sciences: A Review of Modern Psychology.* New York: Barnes & Noble, 1974.

Belomancy

A method of **divination** by arrows that dates as far back as ancient Chaldea. It existed among the Greeks, and still later among the Arabians, although its use was forbidden by the Quran. One popular method was to throw a certain number of arrows into the air, and the direction in which the arrow inclined as it fell pointed out the course to be taken by the enquirer. Divination by arrows is related to **rhabdomancy.**

Sources:

Waite, Arthur Edward. *The Occult Sciences.* 1891. Reprint, Secaucus, N.J.: University Books, 1974.

Belphegor

The demon of discoveries and ingenious inventions. He was said to appear in the shape of a young woman. The ancient Moabites, who called him Baalphegor, adored him on Mount Phegor. He was believed to bestow riches.

Bender, Albert K.

Organizer of an American **flying saucer** bureau who claimed to have discovered important data on the origin of **UFOs** but is supposed to have been silenced in September 1953 by the visit of three mysterious men dressed in black. Three years later this story was released by publisher/writer Gray Barker in *They Knew Too Much about Flying Saucers.* The book firmly established the MIB (Men in Black) in UFO mythology. In 1962 Bender published his own book, *Flying Saucers and the Three Men,* notwithstanding the alleged sinister silencers, in which the somewhat anticlimactic secret was supposed to be an **Agharta**-type underground UFO base in Antarctica, discovered during an astral projection. Barker, always aware of the public appetite for paranoia, used the Bender story as the basis for writing two further books, *Bender Mystery Confirmed* (1962) and *MIB: The Secret Terror among Us* (1983).

Sources:

Barker, Gray, ed. *Bender Mystery Confirmed.* Clarksburg, W. Va.: Saucerian Books, 1962.

———. *MIB: The Secret Terror Among Us.* Jane Lew, W. Va.: New Age Press, 1983.

———. *They Knew Too Much about Flying Saucers.* Clarksburg, W. Va.: Saucerian Press, 1962. Reprint, New York: Tower, 1967.

Clark, Jerome. *The Emergence of a Phenomenon: UFOs from the Beginning through 1959; The UFO Encyclopedia.* Vol. 2. Detroit: Omnigraphics, 1992.

Bender, Hans (1907–1991)

Professor of psychology, author, noted parapsychologist. He was born February 5, 1907, at Freiburg im Breisgau, Germany. He studied with Pierre Janet in Paris during the 1930s and received his Ph.D. from the Psychological Institute at Bonn University in 1936. He was the only parapsychologist to avoid the general suppression of psychical research during the Nazi era. In 1954 he obtained the Chair for Psychology and Border Areas of Psychology at the University of Freiburg, which became the center from which parapsychology was slowly revived after World War II. He retired from the university in 1975; since then he directed the independent institute known as the **Institute Für Grenzgebiete der Psychologie und Psychohygiene** (Institute for Border Areas of Psychology and Mental Hygiene). From 1957, Bender has been editor of the *Zeitshrift für Parapsychologie und Grenzgebiete der Psychologie* (Journal of Parapsychology and Border Areas of Psychology). He is a member of the Deutsche Gesellschaft für Psychologie and the Parapsychological Association, an honorary member of Società Italiana di Parapsicologia, and a corresponding member of the Society for Psychical Research, London.

A distinguished parapsychologist who has written a number of books and articles on a wide range of subjects including ESP, psychokinesis, mediumship, spontaneous phenomena, and spiritual healing, Bender is best known in the English-speaking world for his work on **poltergeists,** about which he has authored a number of papers. The Institute für Grenzgebiete der Psychologie und Psychohygiene houses a large library relating to border areas of psychology. The library is administered by the University Library of Freiburg, and the address of the Institute is: Eichhalde 12, D-7800 Freiburg im Breisgau, Germany.

Sources:

Bender, Hans. "New Developments in Poltergeist Research." *Proceedings of the Parapsychological Association* 6 (1969): 81.

———. *Unser sechter Sinn.* Stuttgart: Wilhelm Goldman Verlag, 1982.

Bendit, L(aurence) J(ohn) (1898–1974)

Psychiatrist, author, parapsychologist. Born in France May 14, 1898, he was educated at Cambridge University, England, and in 1923 established his psychiatric practice in London. In 1939 he married Phoebe Daphne Payne, with whom he would later write several books. He became interested in psychical research during his college years and joined the Society for Psychical Research, London, in 1937. His doctorate in medicine was the first to be granted for work in **parapsychology** by a British university. His thesis, *Paranormal Cognition,* was published in 1944, followed by *Living Together Again* (1946) and *This World and That* (1948).

Bendit was also a devoted member of the **Theosophical Society** and served as the general secretary of the society in London for three years (1958–61). When his term in office ended, the American section invited him to take up residence at the headquarters in Wheaton, Illinois. In 1962 Bendit headed the research department and produced the small volume, *Key Words in the Wisdom Tradition.* Later that year, he and his wife moved to Ojai, California, and led in the revival of the Krotona Institute of Theosophy's educational program.

Bendit was a prolific author, and he and his wife collaborated on a number of important texts. He specialized in the question of psychic ability in relation to psychological problems.

Sources:

Bendit, Laurence J. *The Mirror of Life and Death.* Adyar, Madras, India: Theosophical Publishing House, 1965.

———. *Self Knowledge: A Yoga for the West.* Wheaton, Ill.: Theosophical Publishing House, 1967.

Bendit, Laurence J., and Phoebe D. Bendit. *Man Incarnate.* 1957. Reprinted as *The Etheric Body of Man.* Wheaton, Ill.: Theosophical Publishing House, 1977.

———. *This Transforming Mind.* Wheaton, Ill.: Theosophical Publishing House, 1970.

Mills, Joy. *One Hundred Years of Theosophy: A History of the Theosophical Society in America.* Wheaton, Ill.: Theosophical Publishing House, 1987.

Bendit, Phoebe Daphne (Payne) (1891– ?)

Psychotherapist, author, and collaborator with her husband, Dr. **L. J. Bendit,** in parapsychological studies. Phoebe Bendit was also clairvoyant and associated with the **British College of Psychic Science** in London. She was sole author of several books and coauthor of other books with her husband. In 1961 she moved with her husband to Wheaton, Illinois, and the following year to Ojai, California, where they revived the work of the Krotona Institute of Theosophy.

Sources:

Bendit, L. J., and Phoebe Bendit. *Living Together Again.* London, Gramol Publications, 1946.

———. *Man Incarnate.* N.p., 1957. Reprinted as *The Etheric Body of Man.* Wheaton, Ill.: Theosophical Publishing House, 1977.

———. *This Transforming Mind.* Wheaton, Ill.: Theosophical Publishing House, 1970.

Bendit, Phoebe. *Man's Latent Powers.* London, Faber and Faber, 1938.

———. *The Psychic Child or Over-sensitive Child.* N.p., 1955.

Bendit, Phoebe, and Laurence J. Bendit. *The Psychic Sense.* London: Faber and Faber, 1943.

———. *This World and That.* London: Faber and Faber, 1950.

Benedict, Mrs. (ca. 1850)

Of Auburn, New York, official medium of the **Apostolic Circle,** the first American psychic after the **Fox sisters.** Her psychic faculties were developed in Katie Fox's circle in Auburn. Her channeling from the biblical apostles and prophets was edited and published by **Thomas Lake Harris.**

Benedict XIV, Pope (1678–1758)

Pope Benedict XIV, born Prospero Lambertini of a noble Italian family, is credited with making the first modern objective "scientific" studies of the paranormal in Italy. Lambertini became one of the best educated people of his day, attaining doctorates in both law and theology. Ordained to the priesthood, he became bishop, cardinal (1728), then archbishop of Bologna (1731). From 1702 to 1722 he served as the "devil's advocate" in a series of cases of people proposed for canonization by the Roman Catholic Church. Among the issues the Church investigated in that process were alleged miraculous occurrences credited to the candidate proposed for sainthood.

Lambertini quickly gained a reputation as one who admitted the possibility of miracles but took a very skeptical view of reports of paranormal phenomena. He refused to regard as a "miracle" any event that could result from natural phenomena. He made independent studies of luminous phenomena, nonconventional healings, and **extrasensory perception** (**ESP**). He came to see ESP as a natural phenomenon neither spiritually nor diabolically based. He capped his career with the publication of a four-volume work, *De Canonization Santorum* (1734–38), which had a marked effect upon the thinking of the Church on miracles in a still very superstitious age.

Lambertini was elected to the papal chair in 1740. He gained a reputation as an educated and witty leader and earned the approbation of Voltaire, who dedicated one of his plays to him.

Sources:

Haynes, R. *Philosopher King: The Humanist Pope Benedict XIV.* London: Weidenfield & Nicolson, 1970.

Benedict IX (ca. 1021–ca. 1054)

During the tenth and eleventh centuries, when the papacy was much abused, the papal crown was more than once offered for sale. Thus the office fell into the hands of a high and ambitious family who held it for a boy of 12—Benedict IX—who became pope from 1033 to 1048. As he grew older the boy lost no opportunity to disgrace his position by his depraved mode of life.

But, according to legends, he excelled in sorcery and various forms of **magic.** One story tells how he made the Roman matrons follow him over hill and dale, through forests and across rivers, by the charm of his magic, as though he were a sort of Pied Piper.

Benedict was finally driven from Rome by the Marquis of Tuscany in July 1048. He died a few years later.

Benemmerinen

According to ancient Hebrew belief, Benemmerinen are witches who haunt women in childbirth for the purpose of stealing newborn infants.

Benjamine, Elbert (1882–1951)

Elbert Benjamine, one of America's leading astrologers in the early twentieth century and the founder of the **Church of Light,** was born December 12, 1882, in Iowa. He began to study the occult as a teenager and in 1900 made contact with the Heremetic Brotherhood of Luxor, a small occult order headquartered in Denver, Colorado. The Hermetic Brotherhood was the outward expression of the Brotherhood of Light, a mystical order of enlightened beings believed by occultists to guide the destiny of humankind. The Brotherhood of Light was believed to have been founded in ancient Egypt and to have continued to the present under the leadership of a group of teachers not presently incarnated on the physical plane. The group is popularly known by many as the **Great White Brotherhood.** The Hermetic Brotherhood of Luxor circulated a series of lessons written by the Hermetic Brotherhood's founder, **Thomas H. Burgoyne.**

In 1907 Benjamine directly contacted what he believed to be the Brotherhood of Light in response to his prayer for direction in his life. The members of the brotherhood assured him that he had an important task ahead of him. Two years later he was called to Denver to become the Hermetic Brotherhood's astrologer, taking over the position formerly held by Minnie Higgins, who had recently died. He declined, but the next year he accepted an assignment to prepare a series of lessons on the 21 branches of occult science. After five years of intense study, he felt ready to write. His work would take some 20 years to complete.

Meanwhile, the Hermetic Brotherhood of Luxor was closed and Benjamine was left as an independent representative of the Brotherhood of Light. In 1915 he moved to Los Angeles and began holding classes. Only a small group gathered during the war years, but in 1918 he opened the brotherhood to the public and began his first public class on Armistice Day. As the lessons were completed, they were mimeographed and used as class texts. Eventually Benjamine would publish them under the pseudonym C. C. Zain, the name he used for all official brotherhood writings.

In the 1920s Benjamine also emerged as a specialist in **astrology,** the area of occult science he enjoyed the most, and he became an important force in rebuilding astrology in the modern world. In the 1940s, having completed his writing task for the brotherhood, he issued a number of important astrological texts, including *How to Use the Modern Ephemerides* (1940), *Stellar Dietetics* (1942), *The Beginner's Horoscope Maker* (1940), and *Astrological Lore of All Ages* (1945).

In 1932 Benjamine incorporated with Church of Light as a new esoteric expression of the Brotherhood of Light. He led the church until his death on November 18, 1951, by which time membership had spread across the United States and into Canada, England, Mexico, Nigeria, and Liberia.

Sources:

Benjamine, Elbert. *Astrological Lore of All Ages.* Chicago: Aries Press, 1945.

———. *Beginner's Horoscope Maker.* Chicago: Aries Press, 1940.

———. *Stellar Dietetics.* Chicago: Aries Press, 1942.

"The Founders of the Church of Light." *Church of Light Quarterly* 45, no. 1 (February 1970): 1–2.

Zain, C. C. [Elbert Benjamine]. *Brotherhood of Light Lessons.* 22 vols. Los Angeles: Church of Light, 1922–32.

Benjees, The

Said to be a former Indian cult that engaged in **devil worship.** It seems likely that this belief was based on a misunderstanding of the symbolism of images of Indian temples.

Bennett, (Charles Henry) Allan (1872–1923)

British occultist, at one time the teacher of **Aleister Crowley,** whom he met when they were both members of the Hermetic Order of the **Golden Dawn.** However, Bennett's inclination was primarily toward **mysticism** rather than the occult. He lived in London in great poverty, racked by illness, but made a profound impression on a small circle of perceptive friends for his dedication to Buddhist principles and ideals. Aleister Crowley claimed that he had once witnessed Bennett levitate while in a state of meditation.

Bennett was born in London on December 8, 1872. Orphaned at an early age, he was adopted by **S. L. M. Mathers,** one of the founders of the Golden Dawn. Bennett was educated at Hollesley College and at Bath, England, and took a special interest in scientific research. As a young man he earned a living in a chemical laboratory. Although originally brought up by his mother as a Roman Catholic, he was introduced to occultism through his foster father, who eventually initiated him into the Golden Dawn, in which he was known as Frater Iehi Aour ("Let there be light"). He displayed a great talent for occultism and also conducted a number of dangerous experiments upon himself with poisonous drugs, investigating the borderline between subconscious and supernormal aspects of the mind. Most of the time he lived simply in a small London apartment, where he first studied Sir Edwin Arnold's *The Light of Asia,* one of the first translations of a Buddhist text readily available to the public. He became increasingly fascinated by Buddhism, and at the age of 28 decided to travel abroad to study Buddhism and to seek relief for his asthma.

He traveled to Ceylon in 1898 and studied Pali at Kamburugamuwa. In Colombo he became a pupil of the yogi Shri Paranananda, who taught him Hatha Yoga asanas and pranayama as well as meditation techniques. Bennett went on to Burma, where he became a Buddhist monk in the monastery of Akyab, taking the name Bhikku Ananda Metteya ("bliss of loving kindness"). The name was appropriate since he was a particularly compassionate individual. He founded the Buddhasasana Samagama, or International Buddhist Society, in 1903. He initially served as its secretary general.

He still suffered considerably with poor health and his doctors recommended he travel to California where the air might be better for his lungs. He came back to England on the first stage of his journey, but the intervention of World War I prevented further financial assistance from the East, and he was obliged to stay in London. Here he was befriended by the playwright Clifford Bax and published the *Buddhist Review,* propagating the cause of Buddhism in England. He never got to California, spent his time in London in great poverty and ill health, and died March 9, 1923.

Sources:

Bennett, Allan. *The Wisdom of the Aryas.* London, 1923.

Crowley, Aleister. *The Confessions of Aleister Crowley.* Edited by John Symonds and Kenneth Grant. New York: Hill and Wang, 1969.

Oliver, Ian P. *Buddhism in Britain.* London: Rider, 1979.

Bennett, Ernest (Nathaniel) (1868–1947)

British politician and writer on psychic phenomena. Born December 8, 1868, at Rede, Suffolk, England, he was educated at Durham School and Hertford College, Oxford, and in 1915 he married Marguerite Kleinwort. Elected to Parliament in 1906, he later served as the parliamentary private secretary (1909) and assistant postmaster-general (1932–35). He was knighted in 1930.

As a member of the **Society for Psychical Research,** London, Bennett was particularly interested in investigating **haunted houses,** about which he wrote one book. He died February 2, 1947.

Sources:

Bennett, Ernest. *Apollonius; or, The Future of Psychical Research.* N.p., 1927.

———. *Apparitions and Haunted Houses.* London: Faber and Faber, 1939.

———. *Christianity and Paganism in the Fourth and Fifth Centuries.* London: Rivingtons, 1900.

———. *The Downfall of the Dervishes.* New York: Negro University Press, 1969.

Bennett, J(ohn) G(odolphin) (1897–1974)

Mathematician, industrial research director, and author of books on **parapsychology** and the paranormal. He was born in London, England, and was educated at Kings College School, London; the Royal Military Academy at Woolwich; the School of Military Engineering at Chatham; and the School of Oriental Studies, London. He had an outstanding career as a scientist, and in his mature years served as chair and director of the Institute for the Comparative Study of History, Philosophy, and the Sciences, (1946–59).

Bennett took a special interest in the work and teachings of **Georgei I. Gurdjieff** and after Gurdjieff's death he helped launch the British section of the **Subud** movement at the headquarters at Coombe Springs, Kingston-on-Thames, England. He wrote a number of books including an autobiography, *Witness* (1962). Although Bennett's major interest was in the philosophy and techniques of Gurdjieff, he also drew upon other techniques of human transformation and self-awareness, the **Shivapuri Baba** (a Nepalese saint), dervish dancing, and Sufism. Bennett was particularly concerned with group dynamics in the fields of communication and education.

In 1962–63, Bennett visited Shivapuri Baba (then 136 years old) in the Himalayas, a trip described in his 1965 book, *Long Pilgrimage.* Both Bennett and his wife, Elisabeth, then entered the Catholic faith (see Bennett's *Spiritual Psychology* [1964]), following contact with the author **Sayed Idries Shah,** to whose movement the institute donated its estate at Coombe Springs. This was subsequently sold. In 1971 another estate was acquired in Sherborne, Gloucestershire, and the **International Academy for Continuous Education** was set up "to achieve, in a short space of time, the effective transmission of a whole corpus of practical techniques for self-development and self-liberation, so that people could learn effectively to direct their own inner work and to adapt to the rapid changes in the inner and outer life of man." This program included a synthesis of such disciplines as **mantra** yoga, Gurdjieff movements, Sufi teachings, prayers, and dervish dances. Eventually the Sufi community **Beshara** took over the academy.

Bennett died in December 1974. His work is carried on in the United States by the **Claymont Society for Continuous Education,** Box 122, Charlestown, WV 25414. In Great Britain his disciples may be contacted at Daglingworth Manor, Daglingworth, Gloucester GL7 7AH, England.

Sources:

Bennett, John. *Creative Thinking.* Sherbourne, U.K.: Coombe Springs Press, 1964.

———. *Enneagram Studies.* York Beach, Maine: Samuel Weiser, 1983.

———. *Gurdjieff: Making a New World.* New York: Harper & Row, 1973.

———. *Is There "Life" on Earth?* Santa Fe, N.Mex.: Bennett Books, 1989.

———. *Long Pilgrimage: Shivapuri Baba.* Clearlake, Calif.: Dawn Horse Press, 1983.

———. *Spiritual Psychology.* Lakemont, Ga.: CSA Press, 1974.

———. *Witness.* New York: Dharma Book Co., 1962.

Bennett, Sidney Kimball (1892–1958?)

Prominent figure in twentieth-century astrology. Bennett was born in Chicago on February 10, 1892. Although biographical facts are scarce, he seems to have started his study of **astrology** around 1915 and to have become a professional in the early 1920s. His first book, *Your Birthday and the Year Ahead,* appeared in 1928.

During the late 1920s, a series of events came to radically alter his view of astrology. He had received complaints from clients that his predictions for them had not worked as expected. He turned away the criticisms as the result of faulty birth data, which led to mistakes in the placement of planets in the horoscope chart. However, privately he had noted that the failed predictions had derived from his use of what astrologers termed *progressions,* an old tool for manipulating the chart. (Progressions are based on the notion that there is a relationship between the first day of a person's life and the first year of that person's life. In like measure there is a relationship between the second day and the second year. Thus by examining on the chart the same number of days after the person's birth as the person's age in years, the astrologer supposedly can make some judgments about the present and the immediate future.)

Then two events, one the death of a client in an accident and the other a failed business trip for which Bennett had had high hopes, led to his discarding progressions altogether. He moved on to develop a system based on the solar return (the sun's return to its position in a birth chart, which occurs every seven years), which he called the "Key Cycle."

Bennett functioned publicly under the pen name Wynn. He began *Wynn's Astrology Magazine* in 1931, and for the next two decades it was one of the most influential in the emerging field. He also contributed a column to the *New York Daily News* and wrote a number of popular books. He retired in the 1950s, and his last days are undocumented. Dal Lee, in *Dictionary of Astrology,* reports a rumor that Bennett ended his own life in Australia in 1958, but that event is unverified.

Sources:

Holden, James H., and Robert A. Hughes. *Astrological Pioneers of America.* Tempe, Ariz.: American Federation of Astrologers, 1988.

Lee, Dal. *Dictionary of Astrology.* New York: Coronet Communications, 1968.

Wynn [Sidney K. Bennett]. *Astrology, Science of Prediction.* Los Angeles: Wynn Publishing, 1945.

———. *Astrology, Your Path to Success.* Philadelphia: David McKay, 1938.

———. *The Key Cycle.* 1931. Reprint, Tempe, Ariz.: American Federation of Astrologers, 1970.

Benson, E(dward) F(rederic) (1867–1940)

British novelist, essayist, and biographer, who published 80 works, including some of the most eerie and horrific short stories on occult themes ever written. "The Room in the Tower" and "Mrs. Amworth" have become classic **vampire** stories.

Born July 24, 1867, at Wellington College (where his father E. W. Benson was headmaster, before becoming archbishop of Canterbury), he was educated at Marlborough, and at King's College, Cambridge University. He worked at Athens for the British Archaeological School, 1892–95, and in Egypt for the Hellenic Society, 1896; he also traveled in Algiers, Egypt, Greece, and Italy. He was elected mayor of Rye, Sussex, 1934–37, living at the famous Lamb House that had been the residence of American novelist Henry James for 18 years. He was an honorary fellow of Magdalene College, Cambridge, and was also made a member of the Order of the British Empire for his services to literature.

His best-known fiction works were the series about social climber "Lucia Pillson," later dramatized on British radio and television. His short stories on horror and fantasy themes showed him to be a master of the macabre. He died February 29, 1940.

An E. F. Benson Society has been organized in Britain, arranging social and literary events relating to Benson and his writings, and publishing the journal *Dodo* (named for one of his early novels) for members. Address: Allan Downend, 88 Tollington Park, London N.4., England.

Sources:

Benson, E. F. *The Horror Horn, and Other Stories.* Edited by Alexis Lykiard. London: Panther, 1974.

———. *More Spook Stories.* London: Hutchinson, 1934.

———. *The Room in the Tower, and Other Stories.* London: Mills & Boon, 1912.

———. *Spook Stories.* London: Hutchinson, 1928.

———. *Visible and Invisible.* London: Hutchinson, 1923.

Bensozia

According to Dom Jacques Martin (1684–1751) in his *Religion de Gaulois* (1727), Bensozia was "chief deviless" of a certain **witchcraft** Sabbat held in France in the twelfth and thirteenth centuries. She was, he says, the Diana of the Ancient Gauls and was also called Nocticula, Herodias, and "The Moon." One finds in the fourteenth-century manuscripts of the church at Couserans that women were said to go on horseback to the nocturnal revelries of Bensozia. All of them were forced to inscribe their names in a sabbatic catalog along with those of the sorcerers proper, and after this ceremony they believed themselves to be fairies. In eighteenth-century Montmorillin in Poitou, in a portion of an ancient temple was discovered a bas-relief with the figure of a naked woman carved upon it, and it is not unlikely, according to J. Collin de Plancy (author of *Dictionnaire Infernal,*

6th ed., 1803), that this figure was the original deity of the Bensozia cult.

Bentley, W(illiam) Perry (1880– ?)

Engineer and parapsychologist born February 22, 1880, at Westerly, Rhode Island. He was educated at Trinity College, Hartford, Connecticut, and Massachusetts Institute of Technology, and became chairman of Uvalde Construction, Dallas, Texas. Bentley was a member of the American Association for Advancement of Science, the **American Society for Psychical Research,** and the **Society for Psychical Research,** London, England. He contributed to a fund for a fellowship in **parapsychology** at Duke University, Durham, North Carolina.

Beowulf

An Anglo-Saxon poem of mythological wonders. The folk tales on which the poem is based may date from the fifth century. The epic itself was composed ca. 700 C.E. Beowulf was most likely regarded as one of the Sons of Light or Men of the Sun whose business it was to fight the powers of darkness until they themselves fell.

The legend recounts the tale of Beowulf fighting the monster Grendel; after losing the fight, the giant escapes only by leaving his arm in Beowulf's grip. But Grendel's mother, a mer-woman (see **mermaids**), revenges him and slays many people. When Beowulf hears of this, he takes up the quarrel. Diving to the bottom of the sea, where her palace lay, he kills her after a fierce fight.

Later on Beowulf is made regent and then king of Gothland, where he reigns about 40 years. He is eventually poisoned by the fangs of a dragon during a mighty struggle and dies from the effects. He is buried on a hill named Hronesnas and is deeply mourned by his people.

There are numerous translations of *Beowulf* (see C. B. Tinker, *The Translations of Beowulf,* 1903), as well as many critical works and study guides. A manuscript *Beowulf* (Cotton Vitellius A. xv) ca. 1000 C.E. is preserved in the British Museum Library in London.

Sources:

Beowulf. Edited by F. Klaeber. Boston, 1950.

Beowulf. Translated by John R. Clarke. Rev. ed. New York: C. L. Wrenn, 1954.

Berande

An alleged sorceress burnt at Maubec, in France, in 1577, at the height of the **witchcraft** hysteria. She was confronted and accused of sorcery, and when she denied it, her accuser exclaimed, "Dost thou not remember how at the last dance at the Croix du Paté, thou didst carry a pot of poison?" Then Berande confessed and was burnt along with her accuser.

Beraud, Marthe

Also known as **Eva C.** She was the medium of **Charles Richet**'s experiments in **materialization** phenomena at the Villa Carmen in Algiers, 1905.

Berendt, H(einz) C(haim) (1911–)

Parapsychologist born in Berlin, Germany, who moved to Jerusalem in the 1930s. A dentist, he practiced as a dental surgeon from 1937 on and became an instructor in radiodontics at Hebrew University in Jerusalem from 1957 to 1960. He published several papers on developmental disturbances and orthodontics.

Berendt became interested in **parapsychology** and, beginning in 1959, was an acting committee member of the Parapsychological Study Group of Israel. He later served as president of the Israel Parapsychology Society in Jerusalem. He conducted research on paranormal **metal bending** and eventually came to believe that it is possible.

Sources:

Berendt, Heinz C. "A New Israeli Metal-Bender (with Film)." In *Research in Parapsychology, 1982.* Edited by William Roll, John Beloff, and Rhea W. White. Metuchen, N.J.: Scarecrow Press, 1983.

———. *Parapsychology: The World beyond Our Five Senses.* N.p., 1966.

Bereschit

Universal Genesis, one of the two parts into which the **Kabala** was divided by the rabbis; also the name of the first book of the Hebrew Bible, meaning "in the beginning."

Berger, Arthur Seymour (1920–)

American attorney who in 1970 became active in the field of **death** education and the investigation and teaching of psychic phenomena. In 1978 he taught courses in death and dying and **parapsychology** for the **Psychical Research Foundation,** and a sponsored program of Duke University at Durham, North Carolina. In 1979 he became coordinator of education and a research associate for the Psychical Research Foundation, then taught parapsychology at the Institute for Retired Professionals at Nova University in Fort Lauderdale, Florida, in 1981. He established a PRF Research Center in Florida and became president of **Survival Research Foundation,** a scientific and educational center investigating the question of survival after death, serving as associate editor of the journal *Theta.*

Berger published many papers and research briefs dealing with the survival question, one of which earned him the Robert H. Ashby Award from the **Academy for Religion and Psychical Research** in 1985. Besides his work on survival, he has written several historical and encyclopedic works on parapsychology.

Sources:

Berger, Arthur S. *Aristocracy of the Dead.* Jefferson, N.C.: McFarland, 1987.

———. *Evidence of Life after Death: A Casebook for the Tough-Minded.* Springfield, Ill.: Charles C. Thomas, 1988.

———. *Lives and Letters in American Parapsychology: A Biographical History, 1850–1987.* Jefferson, N.C.: McFarland, 1988.

Berger, Arthur S., and Joyce Berger. *The Encyclopedia of Parapsychology and Psychical Research.* New York: Paragon House, 1991.

Bergier, Jacques (1912–1978)

Co-author with Louis Pauwels of the sensational best-selling work *Le Matin des magiciens* (France, 1960), translated as *The Dawn of Magic* (London, 1963) and *The Morning of the Magicians* (1971). This book significantly influenced the magical revival in Europe with its observations about the part that black magic played in the career of Hitler and the establishment of Nazi philosophy.

Bergier, born in 1912 in Doessa in a Jewish family, emigrated to France in 1920. In 1931, he and fellow student Alfred Eskenazi established a laboratory in Paris to study chemical and nuclear reactions, propagating the release of nuclear energy from lighter elements. Bergier was arrested and tortured by the Gestapo in 1943. After the war, Bergier founded and edited the magazine *Planeté,* which appeared in various foreign editions as *Planeta* (Spain), *Pianeta* (Italy), *Planeta* (Brazil), and *Planet* (Germany). He also wrote a number of additional books on occult and ancient astronaut themes. Originally published in French, they had a wide appeal in their English editions, with their constant themes of paranoia, conspiracy, and alternative history.

Sources:

Bergier, Jacques. *Extraterrestrial Visitations from Prehistoric Times to the Present.* Chicago: Henry Regnery, 1973. Reprinted as *Myster-*

ies of the Earth: The Hidden World of the Extra-Terrestrials. London: Sidgwick and Jackson, 1974.

———. *Secret Doors of the Earth.* Chicago: Henry Regnery, 1975.

Bergier, Jacques, and INFO editors. *Extraterrestrial Intervention: The Evidence.* Chicago: Henry Regnery, 1974.

Pauwels, Louis, and Jacques Bergier. *The Eternal Man.* London: Souvenir, 1972.

———. *Impossible Possibilities.* New York: Stein and Day, 1971.

———. *Le Matin des magiciens.* Paris: Editions Gallimard, 1960. Translated as *The Dawn of Magic.* London: Anthony Gibbs and Phillips, 1963. Reprinted as *The Morning of the Magicians.* New York: Stein and Day, 1964.

Bergman, Samuel Hugo (1883– ?)

Born December 25, 1883, at Prague, Czechoslovakia, he received his Ph.D. from German University, Prague, 1905. He was librarian of the Jewish National and University Library, Jerusalem, 1920–35, and professor of philosophy, rector, and dean of the humanities faculty at Hebrew University, Israel, beginning 1935. Bergman has written on philosophical subjects, with a special interest in parapsychology in relation to philosophy. He served on the committee of the Parapsychological Study Group, Israel. His writings include *Experimente über Telepathie* (Experiments in Telepathy) (1911). Hebrew University bestowed an honorary Ph.D. on Bergman in 1959.

Bergson, Henri (1859–1941)

Famous French philosopher whose concepts of free will, intuition, and mental life have relevance to psychic research and are frequently cited in that context. Born October 18, 1859, in Paris of Anglo-Jewish parents, he became a naturalized French citizen and studied at the École Normale Supérieure. He taught philosophy at academies in Angers, Clermont, and Paris, then succeeded Emile Ollivier at the Academie Française in 1918 but soon abandoned teaching for international affairs. Heading a mission to the United States After World War I, he served as president of the Committee of Intellectual Cooperation.

His books, which brought him the Nobel Prize in literature in 1928, included *Matiére et mémoire* (1896), *L'évolution créatrice* (1907), *Durée et simultanéité* (1922), *L'énergie spirituelle* (1919), *Les Deux Sources de la morale et de la religion* (1932), and *La Pensée et le mouvant* (1935).

His main concept was of an eternal flux in which everything is moving, changing, and becoming, including all matter in the cosmos. Conscious life itself is not a succession of states but an unceasing becoming. Bergson believed that intuition could apprehend reality independently of the limitations of intellect, and he distinguished between the soul and mental life, the soul being independent of, although influenced by, mental life. He claimed that free will is the very nature of our lives and the expression of individuality, although much of our life is largely automatic, deriving from habits and conventions. Bergson's ideas were quite compatible wiith occult philosophies; his sister, Mina Bergson, married ritual magician **MacGregor Mathers,** who had moved to Paris in 1891. Bergson died January 4, 1941, in Paris.

Sources:

Bergson, Henri. *Creative Evolution.* New York: Modern Library, 1944.

———. *The World of Dreams.* New York: Philosophical Library, 1958.

Kolakowski, Leszek. *Bergson.* Oxford: Oxford University Press, 1989.

Bérigard of Pisa (1578?–1664)

French alchemist born Claude Guillermet de Bérigard (surname is sometimes spelled Beauregard). He was popularly known as Bérigard of Pisa because of his residence in Pisa, Italy. The date of his birth is uncertain—some authorities claim it to be 1578; others believe it is considerably later—but all agree on Moulins being his native town, and that, while a young man, he evinced a keen love for science in its various branches and began to dabble in **alchemy.**

He appears to have studied for a while at the Sorbonne, University of Paris, then was appointed professor of natural philosophy at the University of Pisa until 1640. He held an analogous position at Padua, where he died in 1664. His most important contribution to scientific literature is *Dubitationes in Dialogum Ealilaei pro Terrae immobilitate,* a quarto published at Florence in 1632, but he was also author of *Circulus Pisanus,* issued at Udine in 1643, in which he comments on Aristotle's ideas on physics. Bérigard's writings are now virtually forgotten, but they are valuable as documents illustrating the state of scientific knowledge in the seventeenth century.

Berlitz, Charles (1914–)

Popular writer on the Bermuda Triangle and similar mysteries. Born November 23, 1914, in New York City, Berlitz is the grandson of the founder of the famous Berlitz language schools and is familiar with some 30 languages. He studied at Yale University (B.A. magna cum laude, 1936) and during World War II served in the army, becoming a captain in counterintelligence in Europe and Latin America.

He has written or edited dozens of textbooks, language dictionaries, and tourist phrase books in his capacity as vice-president of the Berlitz Schools of Language. His leisure time allowed him to pursue interests in such areas as the **Bermuda triangle, Atlantis, UFOs,** and **ancient astronauts,** which stemmed from his prior interest in archaeology and scuba diving. His first book in this vein, *The Mystery of Atlantis* (1969), reached a popular audience and was followed by a host of others, including *Mysteries from Forgotten Worlds* (1972), *The Bermuda Triangle* (1974), *Doomsday 1999 A.D.* (1981), and *The Dragon's Triangle* (1989).

In 1979 Berlitz and UFO researcher William L. Moore became unwitting accomplices in spreading the hoax usually referred to as the **Philadelphia Experiment.** The story recounts a reported incident in which the U.S. Navy developed a device that transported a destroyer from Philadelphia to Norfolk, Virginia. In the early 1960s Carlos Alende (real name Carl Allen) claimed to have witnessed the experiment and states that the navy classified it and denied that it ever happened.

Sources:

Berlitz, Charles. *The Bermuda Triangle.* New York: Doubleday, 1974.

———. *The Dragon's Triangle.* New York: Wynwood Press, 1989.

———. *Mysteries from Forgotten Worlds.* Garden City, N.Y.: Doubleday, 1972.

———. *Without a Trace: New Information from the Triangle.* Garden City, N.Y.: Doubleday, 1977.

———. *World of Strange Phenomena.* New York: Wynwood Press, 1988.

Berlitz, Charles, and J. Manson Valentine. *Doomsday 1999 A.D.* Garden City, N.Y. Doubleday, 1981.

Berlitz, Charles, and William L. Moore. *The Roswell Incident.* New York: Grosset & Dunlap, 1980.

Moore, William L., and Charles Berlitz. *The Philadelphia Experiment.* New York: Grosset & Dunlap, 1979.

"Bermechobus"

The supposed writings of St. Methodius of Olympus (martyred 311 C.E.); or the saint of the same name who was patriarch of Constantinople and who died in 846. The real name of the work is *Bea-Methodius,* a contraction for *Beatus Methodivo,* which was misprinted "Bermechobus." The work is of the nature of a prophetic Apocalypse and tells the history and destiny of the world. It was handed down by the Gnostics and printed in the

Mirabilis Liber. There are no grounds, however, to suppose that the writings were the work of either of the saints mentioned.

The book recounts how Seth sought a new country in the east and came to the country of the initiates, and how the children of Cain instituted a system of **black magic** in India. The author identifies the Ishmaelites with those tribes who overthrew the Roman power and tells of a powerful northern people whose reign will be overturned by the **Antichrist.** A universal kingdom will thereafter be founded, governed by a prince of French blood, after which a prolonged period of justice will supervene.

Bermuda Triangle

An area of the Western Atlantic between Bermuda and Florida where ships and planes are said to have vanished without a trace. During the late 1960s, inspired largely by the volume by Vincent Gaddis, *Invisible Horizons: True Mysteries of the Sea* (1965), a popular controversy erupted around claims that since 1945 over 100 ships and planes and more than 1,000 people have disappeared in the Bermuda triangle. The area was also termed "the Hoodoo Sea," "the Devil's Triangle," "Limbo of the Lost," "the Twilight Zone," and "Port of Missing Ships." **Charles Berlitz,** who wrote several books on the triangle, speculated on the possibility of time warps, electromagnetic impulses from vanished civilizations, and extraterrestrial activities in **UFOs.**

The controversy was largely put to rest by **Lawrence David Kusche** in his book *The Bermuda Triangle Mystery—Solved.* Kusche destroyed the mystery in a case-by-case discussion of the alleged disappearances. Many had been solved, but popular writers were unaware of the relevant literature. Others happened outside of the triangle. Many had perfectly normal explanations. Since Kusche's book appeared, discussion of the Bermuda triangle has been confined to the fringe, though a few writers like Berlitz have tried to perpetuate interest.

Among the more interesting theories put forward to solve the alleged mystery was proposed by Russian oceanographer Vladimir Azhazha. In articles published in reputable scientific journals in the U.S.S.R. and the United States, Azhazha suggested that storms in the triangle area generate "infrasound"—low-frequency waves that are inaudible to human beings but that can be magnified by special conditions to become a force powerful enough to destroy ships and planes. Infrasound is a frequency lower than 16 cycles per second. In an interview in Moscow published in the *National Enquirer* (November 15, 1977), Azhazha stated that he believed infrasonic waves in the Devil's Triangle are amplified by such factors as changes in water temperature and a powerful undersea river running in an opposite direction to ocean currents.

Scientists at the Wave Propagation Laboratory of the U.S. National Oceanic and Atmospheric Administration (NOAA) confirm that the power of infrasonic vibrations does increase in a storm and that sound can be carried thousands of miles. A NOAA research oceanographer stated that there are very sharp changes in the temperature of the water in the Devil's Triangle because of the Gulf Stream, and that different temperatures in water could cause differences in the intensity of infrasound, either increasing it or decreasing it.

In the *National Enquirer,* Azhazha stated: "An infrasonic sound wave can travel thousands of miles to find its victim in a calm sea. If the wave is gigantic enough, a crew can perish almost instantly. Death will come from stopping of the heart or destruction of the cardiovascular system." In the resulting panic, a ship's crew might even abandon ship. Azhazha claimed that the hull and masts of the ship would begin to vibrate in tune with the infrasound, cracking the ship and breaking it up.

Azhazha's theory was published in the Soviet magazine *Science and Life,* and a similar theory was also put forward by Soviet science writer I. Boyetin. Tests conducted in France have supported the theory that infrasound can damage ships, and Dr. Freeman Hall, chief of the atmospheric acoustic program at NOAA Wave Propagation Laboratory, Boulder, Colorado, confirmed that severe storms can generate such a phenomenon, and that it can also be dangerous to human beings. The theory has not been tested, however, because the mystery was largely accounted for by other means. (See also **Devil's Jaw,** another area of claimed mysterious disappearances.)

Sources:

Berlitz, Charles F. *The Dragon's Triangle.* New York: Wynwood Press, 1989.

Berlitz, Charles, and J. Manson Valentine. *The Bermuda Triangle.* Garden City, N.Y.: Doubleday, 1974.

The Bermuda Triangle: An Annotated Bibliography. Buffalo, N.Y.: Buffalo and Erie County Public Library Librarians Association and Buffalo and Erie County Library, 1975.

Kusche, Lawrence D. *The Bermuda Triangle—Solved.* New York: Harper & Row, 1975.

Kusche, Lawrence David, and Deborah K. Blouin. *Bermuda Triangle Bibliography.* Tempe, Ariz.: Arizona State University Library, 1974.

Winer, Richard. *The Devil's Triangle.* New York: Bantam Books, 1974.

Bernard, Pierre (Arnold) (1875–1955)

A pioneer teacher of hatha and tantric **yoga** in the United States. He was born in Leon, Iowa, in 1875 as Peter Coons. As a young man, he moved to California and worked at various seasonal jobs like fruit picking and salmon packing. In 1905 he teamed up with Mortimer K. Hargis to found the Bacchante Academy to teach **hypnotism** and "soul charming" (concerned with sex mysteries), but the organization disappeared a year later in the wake of the San Francisco earthquake.

Coons changed his name to Pierre Arnold Bernard after founding his Sanskrit College in New York in 1909. The venture was not altogether successful, and Bernard moved to New Jersey where he married a Miss de Vries, a professional dancer. Together they launched a highly successful "health system of Tantrism," embodying **hatha yoga,** dancing, and psychophysical education.

In 1919 Bernard's organization, the Brae Burn Club, was situated in a mansion and estate at Nyack on the Hudson river. The club was well conducted and supported by wealthy followers and socialites, although the practice of hatha yoga was sufficiently novel at that date to attract criticism and scandal-mongering from outside. However, it was Bernard's policy never to give interviews or contradict false stories. He was something of a showman as well as an occultist, and he delighted in staging bizarre publicity stunts, such as his own specialty dance with a baby elephant.

The tantric side of his activities seemed confined to a sensible scheme of sex education allied with psychophysical health, and he said he wanted "to teach men and women to love, and make women feel like queens." His enlightened work in body-building and character-training attracted the interest of Dr. Charles Francis Potter, a liberal New York City minister and one of the founders of Humanism. Potter said that Bernard had "all the earmarks of genius" and "combined knowledge of age-old Indian methods of curing disease of mind and body with the best of Western methods, plus a refreshing amount of common sense." By all reports, the club members, mostly professional and business men and women from New York, were healthy and happy.

There was an inner circle of the club called "The Secret Order of Tantriks," to which a number of wealthy people belonged. Bernard was their guru, known as "Oom the Omnipotent," and his initiates would chant their version of the Tibetan prayer-wheel mantra—"Oom ma na padma oom." Bernard had a special talent for explaining abstruse Hindu **Vedanta** and yoga teachings in crisp, simple language. Affectionately known as "P.A." to club members, he was no ascetic and was known to enjoy a cigar or a game of billiards.

Many well-known and talented people visited the club or became members, including **Francis Yeats-Brown** and **Sir Paul**

Dukes, both pioneer writers on yoga; composer Cyril Scott; and conductor Leopold Stokowski. There were some later criticisms that Bernard was influenced unfavorably by his own material and business success, but in general he seems to have been a pioneer of hatha yoga and sane occultism in the United States.

During his period at Nyack, Bernard became director and later treasurer of the local chamber of commerce. He owned controlling stock in the bank at Pearl River, served as its president in 1931, and owned $12 million worth of property in Rockland County. He closed his yoga center during World War II and turned over his estate to the Wertheim family, who used it to house refugees from Nazi Gemany.

Bernard died in Nyack on September 28, 1955, in his eightieth year. His nephew **Theos Bernard,** who had been a member of the Nyack Community, wrote an authoritative thesis on hatha yoga while at Columbia University. It was first published in 1944 under the title *Hatha Yoga: The Report of a Personal Experience* and has been frequently reprinted.

Sources:

Bernard, Pierre. *In Re Fifth Veda. International Journal of the Tantrik Order.* New York: Tantrik Order in America, [1909].

Boswell, Charles. "The Great Fume and Fuss over the Omnipotent Oom." *True* (January 1965): 31–33, 86–91.

Bernard, Theos (1908–1947)

Early writer and teacher on **hatha yoga,** who drew from his own experience in undertaking a traditional training course. Little has been recorded about the life of Theos Bernard, a nephew of **Pierre Bernard,** one of the pioneer yoga teachers in the United States, who undoubtably introduced him to the subject.

Bernard was born in Tombstone, Arizona. As a child he had hoped to become an athlete, but he suffered from ill health for many years. While at university, he read books on yoga, and one day was visited by a **guru** from India (possibly **Shri Yogendra**) who taught Bernard a graduated system of hatha yoga **asanas** and hygiene practices, combined with traditional yoga philosophy of duty and self-purification. Bernard was already practicing yoga while still at law school and arranged to travel to India to perfect his studies. In India Bernard undertook traditional training under a guru, after first traveling throughout India to familiarize himself with the people and beliefs of the country. He spent several months visiting colleges, libraries, museums, temples, shrines, and ashrams from Calcutta to Bombay, from Kashmir to Ceylon. In Bombay he met Dr. Kovoor T. Behanan, author of the important study *Yoga: A Scientific Evaluation* (1937), and he visited **Swami Kuvalayananda,** a noted yoga teacher, at his ashram in Lonavala. Bernard studied hatha yoga under various teachers, especially in Bombay, which had become the center from which hatha yoga had been revived in India in the late 1800s.

After he obtained his degree in law (M.A., LL.B.), he studied at Columbia University and earned a doctorate in philosophy. His treatise on hatha yoga was first published in 1944 by Columbia University Press and has since been frequently reprinted. *Hatha yoga* covers all the traditional aspects of hatha yoga and correlates his personal training with the major Indian texts: the *Hatha Yoga Pradipika,* the *Gheranda Samhita,* and the *Yoga Sutras of Patanjali.* Bernard achieved the classic requirement of being able to maintain steadiness in performance of the main asanas for a period of three hours each. He went on to practice the traditional forms of mental concentration and meditation.

In order to further his studies, Bernard traveled through Tibet, and at the holy city of Lhasa he was accepted as an incarnation of the Tibetan saint Padma Sambhava. This enabled him to take part in many special religious ceremonies and to discuss Tibetan teachings with some of the leading lamas at famous Tibetan monasteries. He described his experiences in his book *Land of a Thousand Buddhas* (1939).

Bernard died in 1947 while on a mission to a monastery in western Tibet in search of special manuscripts. While en route in a remote area, rioting broke out among Hindus and Moslems, and after the dissident Hindus killed Moslem men, women, and children, they pursued the Moslems who accompanied Bernard as guides and muleteers. These Moslems fled, leaving Bernard and a Tibetan boy alone on the trail. It is believed that both were shot and their bodies thrown into the river.

Sources:

Bernard, Theos. *Hatha Yoga.* New York: Columbia University Press, 1944.

———. *Heaven Lies Within Us.* New York: Scribner's Sons, Ltd., 1939.

———. *Hindu Philosophy.* New York: Philosophical Library, 1947.

———. *Land of a Thousand Buddhas.* London: Rider, 1952.

———. *Philosophical Foundations of India.* London: Rider, 1945.

———. *A Simplified Grammar of the Literary Tibetan Language.* Santa Barbara, Calif.: Tibetan Text Society, 1946.

Bernstein, Morey (1919–)

Businessman and hypnotist from Pueblo, Colorado, who wrote the best-seller *The Search for Bridey Murphy,* published in 1956. His book opened public discussion of **reincarnation** and uncovered a large popular interest and belief in it that had been growing in the West through the twentieth century. The book claimed that under hypnosis by the author, Colorado housewife "Ruth Simmons" (pseudonym of Virginia Tighe) recalled memories of a previous existence in nineteenth-century Belfast, Ireland.

In a series of hypnotic sessions, Bernstein probed Tighe's early memories back to childhood, then as it seemed, to an earlier life as Bridey Murphy, an Irish girl, for which Tighe was able to provide many details. Bernstein instituted a search in Ireland to validate these details. The *Denver Post* sent a reporter to Ireland, and although the findings were somewhat ambiguous, they were added as a supplement to the paperback edition of Bernstein's book.

The tremendous success of Bernstein's book revived interest in **hypnotism** and stimulated pop songs on the theme of reincarnation. An album of some of Tighe's trance sessions was even released. In the wake of the attention given the book, the *Chicago American* published a series of articles questioning wether Tighe was really Bridey Murphy in a former existence. An astute reporter investigated Tighe's early childhood in Chicago and identified names and places that had been woven into an unconscious fantasy of previous life. Across the street from Tighe's girlhood home lived an Irish family with a Mrs. Corkell, whose maiden name had been Bridie Murphy. The *Chicago American* articles went into syndication by the Hearst press, and they ran in the New York *Journal American* (June 10–18, 1956) and in *Time* (June 18, 1956) and *Life* (June 25, 1956). An amusing and witty exposé of the Bridey Murphy story appeared in *Fads and Fallacies in the Name of Science* by Martin Gardner.

The Bridey Murphy case highlights the remarkable ability of the subconscious mind to create fantasies of other lives and personalities that can be elicited under hypnosis. The same faculty is present in the creative imagination of novelists, although consciously controlled. Since the Bridey Murphy case was published, there have been numerous cases of claimed memories of former existence under hypnosis, but few have found them evidential, given the inherent problem of hypnotists guiding the sessions and making leading suggestions to the subject.

Hypnotism continues to be used in counseling situations, and reports of past life recall have gained a large audience among people who have already accepted reincarnation as a fact.

Sources:

Bernstein, Morey. *The Search for Bridey Murphy.* Garden City, N.Y.: Doubleday, 1956.

"Bridey Murphy—Fact, Fraud, or Fancy?" Special issue of *Tomorrow* 4, no. 4 (summer 1956).

Fiore, Edith. *You Have Been Here Before: A Psychologist Looks at Past Lives.* New York: Coward, McCann & Geoghegan, 1978.

Gardner, Martin. *Fads and Fallacies in the Name of Science.* New York: Dover Publications, 1957.

Berosus (fl. 290 B.C.E.)

Berosus is the Babylonian priest most responsible for spreading Chaldean astrological ideas to **Greece.** Berosus was born and raised in Babylon (present-day Iraq). He was a contemporary of Alexander the Great, who died at Babylon when Berosus was still a child. As an adult he traveled to Greece and settled on the Island of Cos, where he founded a school of **astrology.** Around 280 B.C.E. he wrote a history of his homeland; only fragments of this document remain. His greater influence came from the number of students he trained who went on to teach astrology throughout Greece. The Babylonian astrologers were the first to carefully map the night sky and to calculate the length of the solar years (to within 26 minutes). They greatly improved methods of forecasting eclipses and recording time.

Sources:

Brau, Jean-Louis, Helen Weaver, and Allan Edmands. *Larousse Encyclopedia of Astrology.* New York: New American Library, 1977.

Berridge, Edward (ca. 1843–1923)

British homeopathic physician who played an important role in the Isis-Urania Temple of the occult society known as the Hermetic Order of the **Golden Dawn.** Berridge is believed to have qualified as a medical doctor in London and as a homoeopathist in the United States. He was influenced by the writings of **Thomas Lake Harris** and **Andrew Jackson Davis,** whom he probably encountered during a period in the United States. He returned to England in the 1850s and founded an Adventist organization called the **Brotherhood of the New Life,** devoted to the "reorganization of the industrial world." He was also interested in psychosexual theories and practices in relation to the occult.

Berridge joined the Golden Dawn in May 1889, taking the magical name "Respiro" and the motto "Resurgam" (I shall rise again). He associated with the London members who supported **MacGregor Mathers,** including **Aleister Crowley,** who later ridiculed Berridge with typical malice in his *Confessions* and under the name "Dr. Balloch" in the novel *Moonchild.*

Sources:

Crowley, Aleister. *The Confessions of Aleister Crowley.* New York: Hill and Wang, 1969.

Howe, Ellic. *The Magicians of the Golden Dawn.* London: Routledge and Kegan Paul, 1972.

Berry, Catherine (1813–1891)

Nineteenth-century English medium active in the 1870s. She discovered her gift in 1864 after a sitting with **Mary Marshall.** It was alleged that she could throw sitters to the ground by a wave of her hand. Many well-known mediums of the period came to sit with her to be charged with more power. The early issues of the *Medium* contain many accounts of her seances. In her sole presence, however, psychical phenomena were very few. At the **Spiritual Institution** in London in 1870, she sat publicly with the medium **Frank Herne.** Her book, *Experiences in Spiritualism* (London, 1876), records frequent sittings with **Charles Williams,** Frank Herne, **Agnes Guppy,** and **Mrs. Everitt.**

She developed **automatic drawing, painting,** and healing power. In 1874 she exhibited 500 curious watercolors at Brighton. In 1870 she published some prophecies regarding the Franco-Prussian war by pointing out Bible texts illustrative of passing events.

Sources:

Berry, Catherine. *Experiences in Spiritualism.* London, 1876.

Berry, George (d. 1947)

First president of the British-based organization **International Spiritualists' Federation** (ISF). He was a member of the **Spiritualist's National Union** prior to World War I. In 1916 he joined the council on which he served for many years. He became vice-president in 1919 and afterward served as president (1920–22) and general secretary (1922–32). He also edited the publication *National Spiritualist Monthly* from July 1924 to December 1932.

Berry participated in the inaugural meeting of the International Spiritualists' Federation in 1922 in London and the next year traveled to Liége, Belgium, when a constitution was drawn up. Berry was elected first president and served a six-year term. He was succeeded by **Ernest W. Oaten,** whom he had previously followed in the presidency of the Spiritualist's National Union. In 1936 Berry suffered a stroke, which obliged him to relinquish his ISF duties. He died July 13, 1947.

Beryl

Group of precious stones that includes emerald and aquamarine. Colorless beryl is known as goshenite; rose beryl is called verobyerite or morganite; golden beryl is called heliodor; and there are also pale blue stones (aquamarine) and blue-green stones. Beryl was traditionally recommended for curing throat or liver disorders. It was also said to preserve wedded love and to be a good medium for magical vision. (See also **Crystal Gazing**)

Besant, Annie (1847–1933)

Prominent Theosophist and successor to **Helena Petrovna Blavatsky** as the international leader of the Theosophical movement. Besant was born Annie Wood in London, England, October 1, 1847. She was raised by a widowed mother in a very religious environment and in 1867 married Frank Besant, a Church of England minister. However, when she became increasingly skeptical of Christian teachings and refused to silence her doubts, the marriage ended in separation (1873) and divorce (1878). In 1874 she met atheist and freethinker **Charles Bradlaugh,** leader of the National Secular Society, became friends with him, joined the society, began to write for the *National Reformer,* and was elected vice-president of the society in 1875. Her first public lecture concerned the political rights of women. In 1876 she and Bradlaugh formed a partnership, the Freethought Publishing Company, and Besant became co-editor of the *National Reformer.*

Pursuing her feminist agenda, Besant led in the publication of Charles Knowlton's *The Fruits of Philosophy,* an early text advocating birth control. In 1877 she and Bradlaugh were arrested on charges of publishing obscene literature, and in a sensational trial, which became a forum for both to present their opinions to the public, they were convicted of intending to corrupt morals (the conviction was later overturned on a technicality). The trial established Besant's reputation as one of England's finest orators, an atheist, and advocate for women's rights.

In the 1880s she was drawn into the circle of George Bernard Shaw's associates. Besant became a socialist, which led to her break with Bradlaugh, and in 1887 she resigned as co-editor of the *National Reformer.* She joined Shaw's Fabian Society. Meanwhile, she championed the strike of the underpaid matchgirls in 1888 and became the first woman to be accepted at the University of London.

In 1888 she was given a copy of *The Secret Doctrine* for review. The event proved life-changing. She found the answers that had eluded her in Christianity and in freethought. She soon became a close associate of Blavatsky, joined the editorial staff of the Theosophical Society's magazine, *Lucifer,* and turned her oratorical skills to defend her new mentor and promote Theosophy. In 1890 she made her first trip to the United States to revive the society badly shaken by the scandal that followed when **Richard Hodgson** of the **American Society for Psychical Research** accused Blavatsky of **fraud.**

After Blavatsky's death in 1891, Besant headed the Esoteric Section, the group of Blavatsky's personal occult students. In 1892 Besant published her first theosophical books, *Karma* and *The Seven Principles of Man.* In 1893 she visited India for the first time and made a triumphal American tour climaxing with an appearance at the World's Parliament of Religions. She settled in India at the society's headquarters at Adyar, Madras, where she resided for the rest of her life. She had to head off the challenge to her power from **William Q. Judge,** the third co-founder of the society, who remained in America when Blavatsky and Henry S. Olcott moved to India. Besant kept him marginalized internationally, but her efforts cost the society most of its American members. Succeeding to the presidency of the society following Olcott's death in 1907, she had to devote considerable energies to rebuilding the American work.

In 1908 she became sponsor (with **C. W. Leadbeater**) of **Jiddu Krishnamurti** as the vehicle of the world savior, and to that end in 1909 organized the **Order of the Star of the East.** The order flourished for 20 years, but was dissolved when Krishnamurti abandoned it in 1929.

Besant became deeply involved in Indian life. In 1917 she was elected to the Indian Nationalist Congress, one of the organizations promoting Indian home rule. She also led in the founding of many schools, including some of the first for Indian women.

Besant, who came to the society because of her acceptance of its ideas and worldview, did not manifest or claim any outstanding occult abilities. After Blavatsky's death, Besant had no close associates until she met Leadbeater, who claimed to possess clairvoyant vision capable of seeing the occult worlds, and they developed a close friendship and professional working relationship. She co-authored several books based on his occult experiences and generally promoted him in the society. Besant paid dearly for this friendship, as Leadbeater was homosexual and his attraction to young boys became a second major scandal for the society.

Besant led the society until her death on September 21, 1933. She wrote several hundred books (many are transcripts of her lectures) that cover the scope of theosophical philosophy. She also explored Hinduism and gave the society its current focus on Hindu thought, as opposed to the Buddhism that had attracted many of the first generation leaders.

Sources:

Besant, Annie. *Annie Besant: An Autobiography.* London, 1893.

———. *Autobiographical Sketches.* London: Freethought Publishing, 1885.

———. *My Path to Atheism.* London, 1877.

———. *Why I became a Theosophist.* London: Theosphical Publishing Society, 1891.

Besterman, Theodore. *A Bibliography of Annie Besant.* London: Theosophical Society in England, 1924.

Nethercot, A. H. *The First Five Lives of Annie Besant.* Chicago: University of Chicago Press, 1961.

———. *The Last Four Lives of Annie Besant.* Chicago: University of Chicago, 1963.

Beshara (Community)

A Sufi organization devoted to the study of the writings of Muhyiddin Ibn'Arabi, a twelfth-century mystic born in Andalucia, Spain. The community was founded in 1971 at Swyre Farm, Gloucestershire, England, and has since moved to the center that once housed **John G. Bennett**'s **International Academy for Continuous Education** at Sherborne, also in Gloucestershire. United around the basic questions of identity and purpose in life and accepting the absolute unity of existence, Beshara offers courses on the fundamental principles necessary to complete self-knowledge and awareness of reality. The center at Sherborne also holds an Open Day, as well as a regular "Zikr," or meeting, devoted to discovering divine purpose in life.

Affiliated groups emerged throughout the United Kingdom and were opened in Canada, the Netherlands, and Australia. Beshara came to the United States in 1976 when a center was opened in Berkeley, California. The group's strength remains in the San Francisco Bay Area. The center publishes a *Beshara News Bulletin* and may be contacted at Sherborne Stables, Sherborne, Near Cheltenham, Gloucestershire GL54 3DZ, England.

Sources:

al-Arabi, Ibn. *Sufis of Andalucia.* Berkley: University of California Press, 1971.

Landau, Ron. *The Philosophy of Ibn 'Arabi.* London: Allen and Unwin, 1959.

Besinnet, Ada M. (d. 1936)

American physical medium who produced psychic lights, direct voices known for singing and whistling, and **materializations.** She was married to William Wallace Roche and lived for many years in Toledo, Ohio.

After a formal investigation during 1909–10 in 70 test sittings, **James H. Hyslop** wrote in *Proceedings* of the American Society for Psychical Research (vol. 5, 1911) that the medium produced phenomena herself, but while in a hysterical state of secondary personality and without the slightest degree of moral responsibility in her own person for the **fraud.** After six months of study, the **British College for Psychic Science** in London reached the opposite conclusion in 1921. According to **J. Hewat McKenzie**'s report in *Psychic Science* (April 1922), those actions of the medium which Hyslop attributed to hysteria could be fully accounted for as due to the action of controlling spirits.

Dr. **Hereward Carrington** concluded in *The Story of Psychic Science* (1930), "My own sittings with this medium left me entirely unconvinced of their genuineness." Nevertheless, he admitted that he observed very curious lights at a séance in 1922. On request, the lights hovered for a few moments over exposed photographic plates, and the plates, when developed, showed unusual markings that he failed to obtain by artificial means.

Besinnet had two principal controls, both Indians: "Pansy," a little girl, and "Black Cloud." As a rule Besinnet sat in the dark, unbound; then during the séance, as a feat of her stock performance, her hands and feet were often tied to her chair by invisible hands. The sitters usually did not join hands, but placed them on the table. Her materializations were incomplete. The faces seen had a corpse-like appearance and often resembled her own face. It is said that she disappeared several times from the séance room altogether and was found transported in a deep coma in another room. In *Glimpses of the Next State* (1911), Osborne Moore described several séances with the medium. He found the phenomena supernormal and entirely convincing. Besinnet died in 1936.

Bessemans, Joseph François Antoine Albert (1888– ?)

Belgian physician and public official who became active in many branches of parapsychology beginning in 1913. Bessemans held many academic appointments during his distinguished career. He investigated such phenomena as clairvoyance, psychometry, and ESP, although his conclusions were skeptical.

Besterman, Theodore (Deodatus Nathaniel) (1904–1976)

Librarian, world authority on bibliography, psychical researcher, and member of the **Theosophical Society.** He was born September 18, 1904, in Geneva, Switzerland, and was educated at Lycée de Londres and Oxford University. In addition to his activities in the field of psychic research, he also established a worldwide reputation as a bibliographer. He was a special lecturer at the London School of Librarianship (1931–38), then worked for the Association of Special Libraries and the Department for the Exchange of Information for UNESCO. He devoted two decades of his life to work on Voltaire and was editor of the

Studies on Voltaire and the Eighteenth Century and the *Complete Works of Voltaire.*

Besterman, who became a Theosophist as a young man, soon combined his interests and professional credentials in such texts as *Bibliography of Annie Besant* (1924), *A Dictionary of Theosophy* (1927), *The Mind of Annie Besant* (1928), and a 1930 plea for a better relationship between the **Society for Psychcical Research** (SPR) and the Theosophical Society. Theosophy led Besterman to psychic research. He became librarian of the SPR in 1927 and editor of the society's *Proceedings* and *Journal* in 1929; he also served as investigation officer. Demanding high standards, he was critical of any sloppy work in the field. He openly denounced Albert von Schrenck-Notzing and **Charles Richet,** questioned the legitimacy of **Mina Crandon** ("Margery"), and regularly called attention to the problems inherent in human observation. His criticisms of Italian researcher **Ernesto Bozzano** caused **Sir Arthur Conan Doyle** to resign from the SPR.

His publications in the field of psychic research include *Crystal Gazing* (1924), *In the Way of Heaven* (1926), *Library Catalogue of the Society for Psychical Research* (1927), and *Some Modern Mediums* (1930). With **Sir William Barrett,** he produced *The Divining Rod: An Experimental and Psychological Investigation* (1926). Besterman severed his relationship with the society and with psychic research in 1935 and enjoyed a distinguished career as a bibliographer and editor. A final work of earlier writings was published in 1968 as *Collected Papers on the Paranormal.* He died November 11, 1976.

Sources:

Berger, Arthur S., and Joyce Berger. *The Encyclopedia of Parapsychology and Psychical Research.* New York: Paragon House, 1991.

Besterman, Theodore. *A Bibliography of Annie Besant.* London: Theosophical Society in England, 1924.

———. *Collected Papers on the Paranormal.* New York: Garrett Publicaions, 1968.

———. *Dictionary of Theosophy.* London: Theosophical Publishing House, 1927.

———. *The Mind of Annie Besant.* London: Theosophical Publishing House, 1927.

———. *Mrs. Annie Besant: A Modern Prophet.* London: Kegan Paul, Trench, Trubner, 1934.

Bersterman, Theodore, and Sir William Barrett. *The Divining Rod: An Experimental and Psychological Investigation.* 1926. Reprint. New Hyde Park, N.Y.: University Books, 1968.

"Betty Book, The"

A classical channeled text published in 1937 by **Stewart Edward White** from the statements made by his wife, **Elizabeth "Betty" White,** while in trance. Betty channeled for more than 20 years and White believed these channeled communications embodied valuable philosophical and religious messages for daily life. *The Betty Book* was but the first of a series of books developed from Betty's sittings. The third volume, *Across the Unknown,* (1939) rivals *The Betty Book* in popularity.

Sources:

Melton, J. Gordon. *The Betty Book Literature of Stewart Edward White.* Evanston, Ill.: The Author, 1971.

White, Stewart Edward. *The Betty Book.* New York: E. P. Dutton, 1937.

Beyond (Magazine)

Former British Spiritualistic monthly edited by trance medium **W. H. Evans** and published in London into the early years of the twentieth century.

Beyond Reality (Magazine)

American newsstand magazine published six times per year during the 1970s and 1980s. It carried articles covering the range of psychic and occult topics as well as such diverse subjects as Atlantis, time travel, and UFOs.

Bezoar

A red precious stone that was supposed to possess magical properties and was found in the bodies of certain animals. At one time these stones fetched ten times their weight in gold as a remedy against poison and contagion; and for this purpose they were taken both internally and worn round the neck. There were said to be nine varieties of bezoar that differed greatly in composition but were generally divided into those composed mainly from minerals and those composed of organic matter.

A strange origin was assigned to this stone by some of the early naturalists. It is said that aging Oriental stags fed upon serpents, which renewed their youth. In order to counteract the poison which was absorbed into their system they plunged into a running stream, keeping their heads only above water. This caused a viscous fluid to be distilled from their eyes, which was indurated by the heat of the sun and formed the bezoar.

Bezucha, Vlastimil (1928–)

Czechoslovakian chemist and member of the Czechoslovak Parapsychology Study Group, headed by Dr. **Milan Ryzl.** Bezucha was born January 10, 1928, at Nemyslovice and studied at High Chemical School, College of Chemical Technology, Prague. In 1955 he married Eva Ficková.

Bhagavan Sri Ramana Maharshi Center

American center devoted to the teachings of **Sri Ramana Maharshi** (1879–1950), a highly esteemed Hindu mystic. The center focuses on his method of self-realization and surrender to the Supreme Self through self-enquiry, expressed in the simple formula "Who Am I?" This is not merely a mental enquiry but is an attempt to locate the essential subtle self that is independent of ego and individuality and exists in all stages of consciousness—waking life, dreaming, and deep sleep.

The center maintains an urban ashram, Arunachala Ashram, named after the sacred hill at Tiruvannamalai, South India, where the Sri Ramana Ashram was first established during the sage's lifetime. In addition to the urban ashram, there is also an ashram farm in Nova Scotia for devotees who wish to follow an intensive spiritual schedule. Address: 342 East 6th St., New York, NY 10003.

Bhaktivedanta, Swami Prabhupada (1896–1977)

The religious name of Abhay Charan De, leader of the successful Hare Krishna movement that emerged in North America and Europe in the 1970s and is organizationally embodied in the **International Society for Krishna Consciousness** (ISKCON). Born in Calcutta, India, September 1, 1896, he studied philosophy, economics, and English at the University of Calcutta. As a young man he was a follower of Gandhi and advocated independence for India, and he refused to accept his degree in order to show solidarity with Gandhi. Intensely religious even as a child, he nevertheless followed his father's wishes by marrying and going into business. He was initiated into the Goudiya Vaishnava Society by Vaishnava holy man Shi Srimad Bhaktisiddhanta Saraswati Goswami, and followed the Bhaki ("devotional") worship of Vishnu's incarnation as Krishna, which had been initiated by Chaitanya, a Bengali saint of the sixteenth century. Krishna's life is described in the Hindu scriptural texts Bhagavad-Gita and the Srimad-Bhagavatam.

Prabhupada managed a pharmaceutical business in order to support his family, but his guru, who died in 1936, ordered his disciples to preach the Chaitanya message in the West. The honorific name "Bhaktivedanta" was bestowed upon

Prabhupada by the Gaudiya Vishnava Society. During this period he authored his first books, an *Introduction to the Geetopanishad* and the *Bajgavad-Gita as It Is*, a translation and commentary on the Gita from the Chaitaya perspective. In 1956, when his family duties were accomplished, Prabhupada renounced his secular life, including his family, to devote his whole life to religious teaching. His actions followed the ancient Hindu tradition of renunciation of everyday householder life when one's responsibilities were fully discharged.

At the age of 58 Prabhupada became a swami, and in 1965, shortly before the change in American immigration laws relative to India, he immigrated to America. He preached the worship of Krishna in New York and soon attracted students and dropouts, offering his brand of Vaishnava Hinduism in place of radicalism or drug counterculture. Large contributions were made to ISKCON funds by ex-Beatle George Harrison and B. M. Birla, a wealthy Indian textile magnate.

Swami Bhaktivedanta spent much of his time distributing his translation of the Bhagavad-Gita and completing his translation and commentary on Srimad-Bhagavatam and a variety of other writings. He kept up a voluminous correspondence and taught his devotees the basics of Krishna devotion. Like his devotees, he spent much time chanting the Hare Krishna mantra, and his devotees reported that he sometimes exhibited such emotional transports as weeping and dancing. They regarded him as a transcendental being and gave him the title H.D.G.—His Divine Grace.

Prabhupada saw his movement spread internationally, and he experienced the harsh criticism of the new anticult movement. Swami Bhaktivedanta died of heart failure on November 14, 1977, at the age of 81, at Vrindavana, India, the district in Mathura where Sri Krishna spent his childhood. By the late 1970s ISKCON had some 5,000 American disciples and had gained the support of many Indian Americans, who found it like the worship they had left behind when migrating. The movement was left in the control of initiating gurus and a governing board. It experienced intense attacks by anticult groups and suffered some tumultuous internal conflicts, but ISKCON has emerged in the 1990s as a stable Hindu body that has begun to integrate a second generation in its adult membership.

ISKCON has temples across North America, in most countries of Europe, and in numeorus locations around the world. For information, contact the ISKCON International Ministry of Public Affairs, 1030 Grand Ave., San Diego, CA 92109.

Sources:

Bromley, David G., and Larry D. Shinn, eds. *Krishna Consciousness in the West.* Lewisburg: Bucknell University Press, 1989.

Gelberg, Steven, ed. *Hare Krishna, Hare Krishna.* New York: Grove Press, 1983.

Goswami, Satsvarupa dasa. *Srila Prabhupada-lilamrta.* 6 vols. Los Angeles: Bhaktivedanta Book Trust, 1980–83.

Prabhupada, A. C. Bhaktivedanta Swami. *Bhagavad-Gita as It Is.* New York: Bhativedanta Book Trust, 1972.

———. *KRSHA: The Supreme Personality of Godhead.* 3 vols. New York: Bhaktivedanta Book Trust, 1970.

———. *The Nectar of Devotion.* Los Angeles: Bhaktivedanta Book Trust, 1970.

———. *Teachings of Lord Chaitanya.* Los Angeles: Bhaktivedanta Book Trust, 1974.

Bhaktivedanta Institute of Religion and Culture

An informal and independent association of members of the **International Society for Krishna Consciousness** (ISKCON). Founded in the 1970s by Subananda das (Steven Gelberg), the Bhaktivedanta Insititute concerned itself with intellectual and academic pursuits—particularly in the humanities and social sciences. Members of the institute were concerned with the scholarly study of ISKCON (the "Hare Krishna movement") as well as the application of Vaisnava thought to modern academic disciplines. During its brief existence, the institute issued several issues of the *ISKCON Review,* a biannual interdisciplinary publication intended to stimulate and communicate research and reflection on all aspects of the Hare Krishna movement.

Although sponsored by the ISKCON movement, the institute and its *Review* were independent and autonomous, thus providing a meeting place between ISKCON and informed scholars of religious history, theologians, sociologists, and others.

Bharati, Agehananda (1923–   )

Scholar of Eastern religion and mysticism who was ordained as Acharya in Dashanami Mahavidyalaya, Benares, India, in 1951. Scholars in the West considered him an important interpreter of Hindu tradition, especially **tantra.** He became a professor and chair of the department of anthropology at Syracuse University, New York. He traveled throughout Thailand and Japan as a visiting professor and is the author of a number of scholarly but somewhat skeptical writings about Eastern **mysticism.** In 1974 he contributed an important paper on "Separate Realities: Sense and (Mostly) Nonsense in Parapsychology" to the Rhine-Swanton Interdisciplinary Symposium on Parapsychology and Anthropology.

Sources:

Bharati, Agehananda. *The Light at the Center: Context and Pretext of Modern Mysticism.* Santa Barbara, Calif.: Ross-Erickson, 1976.

———. *The Ochre Robe.* Garden City, N.Y.: Doubleday, 1970.

———. "Separate Realities: Sense and (Mostly) Nonsense in Parapsychology." In *Extrasensory Ecology: Parapsychology and Anthropology.* Edited by Joseph K. Long. Metuchen, N.J.: Scarecrow Press, 1977.

———. *The Tantric Tradition.* London: Rider, 1965.

Bhrigu-Samhita

An ancient Hindu astrological treatise, said to contain details of millions of lives, with horoscopes drawn for the time of consultation. The original Bhrigu was a Vedic sage and is mentioned in the Mahabharata. As the Bhrigus were a sacred race, it is difficult to identify the compiler of the Bhrigu-Samhita, but according to legend he lived 10,000 years ago and had a divine vision of everyone who was to be born in every country of the world. He compiled this information in his great treatise on **astrology,** originally written on palm leaves.

No complete manuscript is known, but large sections are rumored to exist somewhere in India. A printed version is said to comprise some 200 volumes, but most Indian astrologers who use the system work with loose manuscript pages. These are supposed to give the name of the client compiled from Sanskrit syllables approximating names in any language, with details of past, present, and future life, as well as previous incarnations.

In addition to his fee, the astrologer usually proposes the sponsorship of a special religious rite to propitiate the gods for past sins. Indian astrologers reported using the Bhrigu-Samhita include Pandit Devakinandan Shastri of Swarsati Phatak, in the old city of Benares; and Pandit Biswanath Bannerjee of Sadananda Road (near the Ujjala movie house) in Calcutta.

In *Fate* magazine (June 1982), **David Christopher Lane,** a noted scholar of spiritual movements and cults, described a personal consultation with Hindu astrologers in Hoshiarpur, Punjab, India, who were custodians of a set of Bhrigu-Samhita leaves. At the time Lane was researching the Radhasoami movement in India, on which he has become a world-famous authority. On July 22, 1978, Lane was taken by his friend Swami Yogeshwar Ananda Saraswati to a house in a back street of Hoshiarpur, where two astrologers had charge of a large set of Bhrigu-Samhita leaves tied in bundles.

The astrologers first compiled a graph, rather like a Western horoscope, but featuring the date of Lane's arrival at the house. According to Hindu tradition, all consultations with the Bhrigu-

Samhita are preordained, and the moment of arrival is the key to discovery of the correct leaf, which indicates not only the life pattern and destiny of the inquirer, but also his name in a Sanskrit equivalent of the language of the inquirer.

Lane stated that after inspection of various bundles of leaves, taken down from the shelf and examined, the correct leaf was found in about 15 or 20 minutes. Lane was shown the leaf, and the Sanskrit inscriptions were translated: "A young man has come from a far-off land across the sea. His name is David Lane and he has come with a pandit [scholar] and a swami." Lane questioned how his name could be known, and the swami showed him the Sanskrit equivalent of the Bhrigu leaf. The reading continued: "The young man is here to study dharma [religious duty] and meet with holy men and saints." Other personal details were also given, including a sketch of Lane's past and present lives.

He expected to be able to make a copy of the leaf with its reading, but to his surprise he was told that he could keep the original leaf. The astrologer explained: "The *Bhrigu-Samhita* replenishes itself, sometimes with very old leaves and with some less aged. We do nothing; there is no need to. The astral records manifest physically at the appropriate time and place."

It was something of an anticlimax when the last lines of the horoscope stated that in order to expiate a sin in a previous life, Lane was advised to pay 150 rupees (approximately $20). But no pressure whatever was put on Lane to pay this modest sum, and the attitude of the astrologers and Swami Yogeshwar that there had been a divine revelation convinced Lane that this was no vulgar fraud. For such a small sum, the preparation of a fake Bhrigu leaf, and the willingness to allow Lane to take it away with him (and thus verify its antiquity) would have been out of all proportion to the work involved. Moreover, the specific details of the horoscope could not have been known in advance of Lane's visit.

Lane's experience was not unique, since a Canadian named H. G. McKenzie recorded that he used the Bhrigu-Samhita in the early 1970s and also verified its accuracy. He wrote: "I consulted *Bhrigu-Samhita* and found my name mentioned there, besides so many other things about my life that shows that one has no free will. . . . The *Bhrigu-Samhita* states about me that I, Mr. McKenzie from Canada, am here with such and such people. It states some events of my past life and also predicts the future course of my life."

In 1980 Lane met and talked with Anders Johanssen, a professional astrologer from Sweden who was then visiting Los Angeles. Johanssen stated that he had used the Bhrigu-Samhita at least seven times and was convinced that it was an authentic work and the most accurate treatise he had encountered. He believed that the copy in Hoshiarpur was the most complete, although other versions were known in Delhi, Meerut, and Benares.

However, it was not clear what the nature of a Bhrigu consultation was on subsequent visits. If the leaf from the first consultation was freely offered (as in the case of David Lane), were other leaves available for each of the later visits? In Lane's case, his Bhrigu horoscope contained the prediction: "This young man will come again several times." On the first visit, Lane accepted the offered leaf, but left it with Swami Yogeshwar to make an exact English translation, planning to collect the original leaf and translation a few weeks later. However, Lane curtailed his trip due to illness and was later unable to contact the swami. Lane made a second visit to Bhrigu-Samhita at Hoshiarpur three years later, in 1981, in company with Prof. Bhagat Ram Kamal. He gave two days' notice of the intended visit, but no leaf for the visit could be discovered, arguing for the genuineness of the astrologers, since no fee was requested. (See also **Astrology**)

Sources:

Kriyananda, Swami. *The Book of Bhrigu.* San Francisco: Hansa Publications, 1967.

Lane, David Christopher. *Fate* (June 1982).

Pagal Baba. *Temple of the Phallic King: The Mind of India; Yogis, Swamis, Sufis, and Avataras.* New York: Simon & Schuster, 1973.

Bianchi, P. Benigno (ca. 1890)

Professor of psychiatry at Naples, director of the Salerne Insane Asylum, and later minister of education, who investigated the phenomena of medium **Eusapia Palladino.** He was present at the sitting in March 1891 that was also attended by **Cesare Lombroso.**

On Marco Falcomer's invitation, Bianchi attended a séance with Nilda Bonardi and, in a spirit of skepticism, asked if the intelligent force directing the movement of the table could indicate the names of two of his uncles, deceased, and also reveal a family secret. The table immediately gave the name of both and proceeded to disclose the secret with so much exactitude that Bianchi hastily cried "Stop!" Subsequently he wrote in a letter to Falcomer: "The entirety of the facts observed and noted by me in the course of various sittings have profoundly shaken my scepticism; and now I can no longer give myself out to be a sceptic, as, for the time being, numerous facts incline me to believe in **spiritualism.**"

Bible of the Devil

Believed to be a **grimoire** or similar work. **Pierre De Lancre** stated that the Devil informed sorcerers that he possessed a bible consisting of sacred books, having a theology of its own, which was dilated upon by various professors. De Lancre claimed the one great magician, who was brought before the Parliament of Paris, avowed that there dwelt at Toledo 63 masters in the faculty of **magic** who took for their textbook the Devil's Bible.

Bibliomancy

A method of discovering whether or not a person was innocent of sorcery, by weighing him against the great Bible in the church. If the person weighed less than the Bible, he was innocent of practicing **witchcraft.** A more popular system of bibliomancy was to open a Bible at random after asking a question. The passage on which one's finger rested was supposed to have special applicability to the question posed. Other books consulted in this way included Greek epics, classical poetry, or the works of Shakespeare, and the term **rhapsodomancy** also has been used for this practice. Another term for bibliomancy is stichomancy.

Sources:

Waite, Arthur Edward. *The Occult Sciences.* 1891. Reprint. Secaucus, N.J.: University Books, 1974.

Biffant

A little-known demon, chief of a legion who was said to have entered the body of Denise de la Caille and who was obliged to sign with his claws the *proces verbal* of exorcisms.

Bifrons

A demon of monstrous guise who, according to **Johan Weyer,** often took the form of a man well versed in astrology and planetary influences. He excels in geometry, is acquainted with the virtues of herbs, precious stones, and plants, and, it is said, he is able to transport corpses from one place to another. He also lights the strange corpse lights above the tombs of the dead. Twenty-six of the infernal regions obey his commands.

Sources:

Weyer, Johannes. *Witches, Devils, and Doctors in the Renaissance: Johann Weyer, De Praestigiis.* Edited by George Mora. Binghamton, N.Y.: Medieval and Renaissance Texts and Studies, 1991.

Bigfoot Information Center

Organization concerned with information and reported sightings of the mysterious humanoid creature variously known as Bigfoot, Sasquatch, Omah, Yowie, Yeti, and Abominable Snowman. The center was established by Peter Byrne in the 1960s as a central clearing house of information on Bigfoot. The center issues a monthly *Bigfoot News*. Address: P.O. Box 777, Hood River, OR 97031. (See also **Monsters**)

Sources:

Byrne, Peter. *The Search for Big Foot: Monster, Myth, or Man?* New York: Pocket Books, 1976.

Bigois (or Bigotis)

A sorcerer in ancient Tuscany who is said to have composed a learned work on the nature of prognostications, especially those connected with thunder and lightning. The book is thought to be irretrievably lost. Some believed Bigois to be the same as **Bagoe,** a sibyl of Erithryea, but this is merely surmise.

BILK Newsletter

Publication concerned primarily with water monsters (such as the **Loch Ness** monster), but also dealing with other aspects of **cryptozoology,** such as **mermaids** and cephalopods. The title is an acronym formed from Behemoth (fresh-water monster), Isis (mermaids), Leviathan (sea serpents), and Kraken (giant cephalopods). Address: Ulrich Magin, Stuhlbruderhofstrasse. 4, D-6704 Mutterstadt, Germany.

Billot, G. P. (ca. 1840)

French physician who practiced during the age of **animal magnetism** and was acquainted with most of the phenomena of **Spiritualism.** His *Recherches psychologiques sur la cause des phénomènes extraordinaires observés chez les modernes voyans, improprement dits somnambules magnétiques, ou correspondance sur le Magnétisme vital, entre un solitaire et M. Deleuze* (2 vols.) was published in Paris in 1839. It contains an interesting exchange of letters and discussions on the subject of **mesmerism** with **J. P. F. Deleuze.** Whereas Deleuze admitted many supernormal phenomena but remained very cautious as to their public avowal, Billot openly affirmed his belief in the existence of spirits and in communication with the departed.

Bilocation

Simultaneous presence in two different places. The term is often used in histories of saints, but there are also many secular examples. (See **double**)

Binah

In the supreme triangle of the **Kabala,** the three sides are reason, which is named *Kether;* necessity, *Chochmah;* and liberty, *Binah.*

Binski, Sigurd R(obert) (1921–)

German government official and parapsychologist who experimented with **psychokinesis** and with psi capacities in **hypnosis.** Born February 18, 1921, in Berlin, he studied at the University of Bonn (B.A., Ph.D.) and afterward served in the German army, 1939–65. After deportation, he suffered forced labor in the Soviet Union. Binski, a government official in Germany since 1957, has written articles for various journals, including the *Journal of Parapsychology,* and was a charter member of the **Parapsychological Association.**

Biocommunication

Preferred term for **telepathy** by Russian parapsychologists.

Biofeedback

A term covering a range of EEG (electroencephalographic) feedback instruments and techniques, as well as apparatus giving information on other biological functions. Biofeedback instruments can convey to the subject the characteristics of his own brainwaves, skin resistance, or heartbeats so that he can learn to modify these functions consciously. In this way, the subject can enhance his capacity for relaxation or reproduce some of the psycho-physiological control shown by yogis and Zen masters.

Modification of brainwaves by biofeedback machines was first introduced in the United States by Joe Kamiya in the late 1960s; Elmer Green of the Menninger Clinic promoted the practice through the 1970s. It appeared that biofeedback could become a major technique within transpersonal psychology, and that subjects could be trained to control or to generate brain wave activity at will, thus achieving altered states of consciousness leading to the production of various psychic, spiritual, and mystical experiences.

The chief brain waves identified within biofeedback studies are: alpha (related to relaxation and dream states), frequency 8 to 13 cycles per second (cps); beta (mental and visual activity), 14 to 50 cps; theta (dream and sleep states), 4 to 7 cps; and delta (deep sleep states), 0.5 to 3.5 cps.

The simple relationship first thought to exist between brain waves and psychic and spiritual development proved to be much more complicated and ambiguous than originally believed. At present biofeedback has been used mainly in teaching people to alter various body functions to improve their health; it has been particularly effective in cases of migraine headaches.

Sources:

Green, Elmer. "Biofeedback for Mind-Body Self-Regulation: Healing and Creativity." In *The Varieties of Healing Experience: Exploring Psychic Phenomena and Healing.* Los Altos, Calif.: Academy of Parapsychology and Medicine, 1971.

Kamiya, Joe. "Conscious Control of Brain Waves." *Psychology Today* 1, no. 11 (April 1968).

Stearn, Jess. *The Power of Alpha-Thinking: Miracle of the Mind.* New York: William Morrow, 1976. Reprint, New York: New American Library, 1977.

Timmons, Beverly, and Joe Kamiya. "The Psychology and Physiology of Meditation and Related Phenomena." *Journal of Transpersonal Psychology* 1 (1970).

Bioinformation

Preferred term for extrasensory perception by Russian parapsychologists.

Bio-introscopy

Term for eyeless sight or "skin vision" used by parapsychologists in **Russia.** Among the more famous individuals demonstrating this faculty were **Rosa Kuleshova** (1955–78) and Tania Bykovskaia. Kuleshova was only five years old when the first newspaper coverage of her abilities appeared. She was later tested by the Nizhne-Tagil Pedagogical Instituite, which found her abilities unusual but not paranormal. Bykovskaia was tested by a commission from Kuban Medical Institute in Krasnodar, which reported on her ability to distinguish the colors of two balls hidden from sight.

In 1965 at the Scientific Conference of the Ural Division of the Society of Psychologists in Perm, Dr. S. N. Dobronravov of Sverdlovsk stated that some 72 percent of children had skin sight potential, especially between the ages of seven and twelve years. Dr. Abram Novomeisky of the psychology laboratory at the Nizhne-Tagil Institute experimented with Vasily B., a metallurgist who had been totally blind for seven years, and found that Vasily could distinguish colors by touch and at a distance. As with other subjects, the ability diminished in the diminution or absence of light. Experiments suggested that bright electric light enhanced the faculty of eyeless sight. Another frequently reported observation was that different colors had specific sensations that aided identification. For example, red seemed to burn, orange to warm, yellow less so, green was neutral, light blue cooling, navy blue freezing. Other subjects reported that red had a sticky sensation and blue felt smooth. (See also **Dermo-Optical Perception; Eyeless Sight; Jules Romains; Seeing with the Stomach; Transposition of the Senses**)

Sources:

Ostrander, Sheila, and Lynn Schroeder. *Psychic Discoveries behind the Iron Curtain.* 1970. Reprint. New York: Bantam Books, 1971.

Biolater

A small electronic calculator for charting **biorhythm** cycles to predict high, low, and danger points of one's personal biochemistry. It looks very much like a normal pocket-size battery-operated calculator with mathematical functions.

Biological Phenomena

Term used by parapsychologists for psychokinetic influences on living systems, such as accelerating or retarding growth of seeds, plants, or bacteria or apparently revivifying anesthetized mice. **J. B. Rhine** used the term "psychokinesis on living targets," (expressed in the acronym "PK-LT.")

Stimulating the growth of plants is a phenomenon occasionally met with in spiritualist literature. It was claimed that marked mango seeds were made to sprout by **Charles Bailey,** the Australian **apport** medium. An Indian myrtle developed from seed to a height of 16 inches in 20 minutes. A loquat seed similarly grew with accelerated speed. His investigators at Milan, Italy, in 1904 could not detect **fraud** in the performance. However, Bailey was once detected in fraud, which has thrown doubt upon his other phenomena. Moreover, the sudden growth of mango plants is a well-known conjuring trick performed by Hindu jugglers.

In *Angelic Revelations* published anonymously in 1875, William Oxley wrote of a séance with **Elizabeth d'Esperance:** "Yolande brought me a rose with a short stem not more than an inch long which I put into my bosom. Feeling something was transpiring, I drew it out and found there were two roses. I then replaced them and withdrawing them at the conclusion of the meeting, to my astonishment the stem had elongated to seven inches with three full blown roses and a bud upon it with several thorns."

In certain individuals, some vital force seems to destroy bacteria, prevent decomposition, and add vigor to dying flowers. (See also **emanations**)

Biological Review

A short-lived British Spiritualistic monthly that ran for a brief period in winter 1858–59 and was published by **Kenneth R. H. Mackenzie.** The chief contributor was Jacob Dixon.

Biomate

A manual computer used for charting **biorhythm** cycles to predict high, low, and danger points in an individual's biochemistry. (See also **biolater**)

Biometer of Baraduc

An instrument to register vibrations and nervous force of human bodies. It consists of a needle suspended by a fine thread under a glass shade. If the hand is brought near the shade, the needle is deflected. The angle of deflection, according to the inventor, **Hyppolite Baraduc,** depended on various mental, physical, and moral conditions of the experimenter. He believed that the biometer indicated aspects of such conditions.

Similar instruments intended to indicate nervous or psychic force include the **sthenometer** developed by **Paul Joire** and the **De Tromelin cylinder.** These are lightly suspended or balanced indicators that have been tested extensively to preclude the possibility of movement caused by air currents or heat from the hand of the operator. Such movement is believed to be connected with the **dowsing** faculty or with **psychokinesis.**

Bioplasma

A term used by Russian parapsychologists to indicate a theoretical energy field counterpart of the human body, involved in extrasensory perception and psychokinetic phenomena. Such a concept has some affinity with the **astral body** spoken of by Theosophists.

Sources:

Ostrander, Sheila, and Lynn Schroeder. *Psychic Discoveries behind the Iron Curtain.* 1970. Reprint. New York: Bantam Books, 1971.

Biorhythm

Theory of biochemical phasing, which claims that human beings experience three major biological cycles: (1) a 23-day cycle of physical strength, energy, and endurance, (2) a 28-day cycle of emotional sensibility, intuition, and creative ability; and (3) a 33-day cycle of mental activity, reasoning, and ambition. Charts of these cycles indicate periods of maximum or minimum potential in any of the three cycles, as well as critical dates of stress when two or three of the cycles intersect. By studying such advantageous or disadvantageous points of the cycles, it is claimed that an individual can be aware of the best and worst dates to maximize effort for success and confidence and avoid over-stress at dates of minimal confidence and energy. The theory has some attraction as it relates to other natural cycles such as the ebb and flow of the tides and the menstrual cycle in women.

Since body cycles relate to birth dates, the system of biorhythms is analagous with medical **astrology.** During the 1970s the system became a popular fad. Some physicians attempted to use biorhythm diagnostically, and some used biorhythms to predict football games. Billie Jean King is said to have won her famous match against Bobby Riggs when at a "high" in two of her cycles. Practitioners claimed that Judy Garland and Marilyn Monroe committed suicide on their critical days. The Omi Railway in Japan credited biorhythms with their accident-free record of safety. Other Japanese firms and several European airlines tested the use of biorhythms.

The concept of biorhythms was first proposed by William Fliess, a German friend of Sigmund Freud. Fliess proposed two basic cycles, and Austrian engineer Alfed Teltscher added the idea of a third cycle. Herman Swoboda tied the cycles to the birth date. Other writers also explored the idea through the twentieth century, but in the early 1960s the writings of George S. Thommen succeeded in popularizing the idea. Thommen found a leading supporter in Bernard Gittelson. Apparatus designed to simplify charting of biorhythm cycles have been developed and include the **biomate** (a manual computer), and the **biolater** (a small electronic calculator with mathematical functions).

During the 1970s various trials attempted to verify the claims about biorhythm. The most notable were in the field of sports where, it was predicted, outstanding performances would tend to appear on days of biorhythmic highs. In fact, no such patterns emerged. No empirical data exists to support the biorhythm theory.

Sources:

Bainbridge, William S. "Biorhythms: Evaluating a Pseudoscience." *Skeptical Inquirer* (spring/summer 1978): 41–56.

Gittelson, Bernard. *Bio-Rhythms: A Personal Science.* New York: Warner Books, 1977.

Luce, Gay Gaer. *Body Time: Physiological Rhythms and Social Stress.* New York: Pantheon Books, 1971.

———. *Biological Rhythms in Psychiatry and Medicine.* Washington, D.C.: National Institute of Mental Health, 1970. Reprinted as *Biological Rhythms in Human and Animal Physiology.* New York: Dover Books, 1971.

Schadewald, Robert. "Biorhythms: A Critical Look at Critical Days." *Fate* (February 1979): 75–80.

Thommen, George. *Is This Your Day?* New York: Award, 1964.

Wernli, Hans J. *Biorhythm: A Scientific Exploration into the Life Cycles of the Individual.* New York: Crown, 1961.

Biosophical Institute

Founded in the 1940s by Dr. **Frederick Kettner** to promote his system of **biosophy.** He defined biosophy (from the words *bios,* meaning life, and *sophia,* meaning intelligence) as "the science and art of intelligent living based on the awareness and practice of spiritual values, ethical-social principles and character qualities essential to individual freedom and social harmony." In his booklet, *The Need for a Thousand Year Plan* (1948), Kettner acknowledged the part played by the human mind in creating civilization but stated, "Humanity's next problem is to realize the creativity of the heart of man." Through biosophy he hoped to create a world-fellowship of peace-loving men and women who have overcome religious, national, racial, and social prejudices and who would work creatively for the growth of democracy and world peace.

Biosophy groups were founded in various U.S. cities and in South and Central America, Europe, Australia, and India. Kettner counted Albert Einstein, Pierre leComte du Nouy, Havelock Ellis, and Lal Sharma among his supporters. No sign of institute activity has been observed in recent years.

Bird, J(ames) Malcolm (1886– ?)

Author and research officer of the **American Society for Psychical Research** (ASPR) from 1925 to 1931. His first contact with psychic research occurred in 1922. He was then secretary of a committee investigating physical phenomena of **Spiritualism,** which was sponsored by the *Scientific American* on which Bird was an associate editor. The committee administered the $2,000 reward offered by the magazine to anyone who could produce satisfactory paranormal physical phenomena. On **Sir Arthur Conan Doyle**'s recommendation, Bird was sent to Europe to collect observations for a supplement to the report. He sat with **John C. Sloan, Gladys Osborne Leonard, William Hope, Ada Emma Deane, Evan Powell,** and **Maria Vollhardt.** In *My Psychic Adventures* (1924), he concluded that the phenomena were truly objective, that is, they were neither due to hallucination nor collective hypnosis, and that a good degree of probability existed for the genuineness of some of the psychic phenomena he witnessed. In *"Margery," The Medium* (1925) Bird traced the development of **Mina Crandon**'s powers from the incipient stage and gave an account of the investigation of her mediumship to the *Scientific American.*

Though Bird was convinced that Margery's work was genuine, the committee could not reach a verdict. When his articles in the *Scientific American* created undue anticipation for a verdict in Margery's favor, he resigned his position on the committee and soon after severed his connections with the magazine. The American Society for Psychical Research appointed Bird as research officer alongside **Walter F. Prince,** which brought to a head the disagreement within the leadership of the ASPR over Margery. Prince, who believed her a **fraud,** resigned from the ASPR and with others founded the **Boston Society for Psychical Research.**

Bird's continuing fascination with the Margery phenomena, and his public endorsement of it as genuine, led to accusations of investigative incompetence and even to confederacy in fraud. At the time Bird strenuously denied the accusations, but many years later, a confidential report that Bird made to the ASPR trustees came to light. In it Bird claimed that he strongly doubted the paranormal character of much of the phenomena and on one occasion proposed that Margery engaged in fraud, this being the time when **Harry Houdini** was to investigate her mediumship. Apparently Bird's doubts on the phenomena caused consternation in the ASPR, which had been placed in the position of competent investigation and support for the phenomena. Publication of Bird's doubts and criticisms would have had an unfavorable influence on the credibility of the society, particularly in light of the scandal surrounding Bird himself.

In December 1930 Bird resigned from the society, after which a lengthy issue of the ASPR *Proceedings* that Bird had compiled was never published and apparently vanished from the archives. Bird himself disappeared from the scene of psychic research; and there appears to be no record of his subsequent career.

Sources:

Berger, Arthur S., and Joyce Berger. *The Encyclopedia of Parapsychology and Psychical Research.* New York: Paragon House, 1991.

Bird, J. Malcolm. *"Margery," The Medium.* Boston: Small, Maynard, 1925.

———. *My Psychic Adventure.* London: George Allen & Unwin, 1923.

Tiertze, Thomas R. *Margery.* New York: Harper & Row, 1973.

Bird Voices

Paranormal messages supposedly conveyed through the medium of the twittering of budgerigars, as distinct from mere imitation of human voices. (See also **electronic voice phenomenon; Friedrich Jürgenson; Raudive voices**)

Birds

It was a common belief amongst primitive tribes that the souls of the dead were conveyed to the land of the hereafter by birds. Some West African peoples would bind a bird to the body of the deceased and then sacrifice it to carry the man's soul to the afterworld. The Bagos also offered up a bird on the corpse of a deceased person for the same reason. The South Sea Islanders used to bury their dead in coffins shaped like the bird that was to bear away the spirits, while the natives of Borneo represented Tempon Telon's **Ship of the Dead** as having the form of a bird. The Native American tribes of the Northwest had rattles shaped like ravens with a large face painted on the breast. The probable significance is that the raven was to carry the disembodied soul to the region of the sun.

The flight of birds was also studied as part of the methods of **divination** in **ornithomancy.**

Birge, Raymond T(hayer) (1887– ?)

A professor of physics at the University of California, Berkeley, who made a special study of **magic** and superstition. He was born March 13, 1887, in Brooklyn, New York, and studied at the University of Wisconsin and University of California. His retiring vice-presidential address to the American Association for the Advancement of Science in 1958 was *"Science, Pseudo-Science, and Parapsychology."*

Birog

A Druidess in ancient Irish legend. The Fomorian king **Balor** had a beautiful daughter named Ethlinn whom he kept imprisoned because of a Druidic prophecy that he would be slain by his grandson. Balor had stolen a magical cow from three brothers, Kian, Sawan, and Goban.

Through the magical spells of Birog, Kian, disguised as a woman, was able to enter the tower where Ethlinn was imprisoned. He then slept with Ethlinn, who in due course delivered three sons at one birth. Balor commanded them to be drowned, but one of them, named Hugh, survived, and in the course of time fulfilled the Druidic prophecy and slew Balor.

Birraark

Practitioners of **necromancy** in Australia.

Al-Biruni (973–1048)

Al-Biruni, born Abu'l-Rayhan Muhammad ibn Ahmad Al-Biruni, an outstanding eleventh-century astrologer whose writings compiled the astrological teachings of several cultures. Al-Biruni was born in Uzbek, a country until recently a part of the former Soviet Union, located just north of Iran and Afghanistan. He grew up under the multicultural influences of Persia, India, and the Greek empire of Alexander. Here Zoroastrian and Manichean teaching mingled with Hinduism and emerging Islam. In the areas of astronomy, mathematics, and **astrology,** this area of the world, making the transition to Islam, was far ahead of Europe, then only beginning to recover its classical tradition.

As a young man, Al-Biruni began to travel through Persia, Afghanistan, and India and to gather the material for one of his important books, *Chronologies of Ancient Nations,* detailing the histories of the peoples of the area. It was completed near the end of the century. Around 1010 he settled in his native land for a decade until the ruler (who was also his patron) was overthrown and the nobility was exiled. Al-Biruni then lived in India for an extended time and wrote a volume on the people of the Indus Valley as well as his most remembered text, *The Book of Instruction in the Elements of the Art of Astrology,* generally called the *Tafhim.*

The *Tafhim,* designed as an introductory textbook for the young astrologer, addresses all of the subjects an astrologer would be expected to have mastered, including mathematics, geography, history, and astronomy, all of which are treated before any consideration of astrology. Al-Biruni picked up this learning from the foundational Tetrabiblos of Ptolemy, upon which astrology is built, and he compared Persian astrology with its Hindu counterpart.

The *Tafhim* was reproduced and widely circulated in Southern Asia and found its way to Europe, where it was read three centuries later by **Guido Bonati** and influenced his important *Liber Astronomie.* It was translated into English in 1934 by R. Ramsey Wright.

Sources:

Al-Biruni. *The Book of Instruction in the Elements of the Art of Astrology.* Trans. R. Ramsey Wright. London: Luzac, 1934.

———. *The Chronologies of Ancient Nations.* Translated by Edward Sachau. London: W. H. Allen, 1879.

Biscar, Jeanette

An alleged sorceress of the Basque district of Labourd in France, who was said to have been transported to the witches' Sabbat by the Devil in the form of a goat. As punishment she was suspended in midair head downward. She was one of thousands of supposed witches persecuted through the efforts of witch-hunter **Pierre de Lancre** in the early seventeenth century.

Bisclaveret

The name of the **werwolf** in Brittany. It was believed to be a human being transformed by magic into a fearsome man-devouring beast that roamed about the woods, seeking people to kill.

Bisson, Juliette (Madame Alexandre Bisson)

Sculptress and wife of French playwright Alexandre Bisson. The Bissons conducted a series of séances between 1909 and 1913 with the celebrated materialization medium Marthe Beraud (known as **Eva C.**) In May 1909 **Baron von Schrenck-Notzing** joined the circle and began his detailed scientific observations.

Sources:

Schrenck-Notzing, Albert von. *Materialisationspaenomene.* Munich: Ernst Reinhart, 1914. Translated as *Phenomena of Materialisation: A Contribution to the Investigation of Mediumistic Teleplastics.* London, 1923.

Bitru

According to the demonologist **Johan Weyer,** Bitru is a great Prince of Hell, also known as Sytry. He appeared in the form of a leopard with the wings of a **griffin.** But whenever he adopted a human appearance, it was invariably one of great beauty. It is he who awakes lust in the human heart. Seventy legions obey his commands.

Sources:

Weyer, Johannes. *Witches, Devils, and Doctors in the Renaissance: Johann Weyer, De Praestigiis.* Edited by George Mora. Binghamton, N.Y.: Medieval and Renaissance Texts and Studies, 1991.

Bitumen

Bitumen was greatly used in magical practices. Images for the purpose of sympathetic magic were often made of this substance, and it was also used in ceremonies for the cleansing of houses in which any uncleanness had appeared—being spread on the floor like clay.

Bjelfvenstam, Nils Erik (1896– ?)

Swedish educator. He was born January 14, 1896, at Köping, Sweden, and educated at the University of Uppsala. He served as president of the Parapsychology Society, Stockholm, beginning in 1948, and of the Institute of Psychological Research, Uppsala, beginning in 1955. He contributed a section to the book *Abnormal Hypnotic Phenomena: A Survey of Nineteenth-Century Cases* in 1967.

Björkhem, John (1910–1963)

Swedish physician in psychiatry and neurology and a parapsychologist. He was born July 20, 1910, at Blekinge, Sweden, and educated at the University of Uppsala. He tested some 400 subjects for psychometric faculty and wrote and lectured on parapsychology in relation to hypnosis. His book *Det Ockulta Problemet* (1939) was translated into Finnish, Norwegian, Danish, and German. His other books dealing with parapsychology include *Nervstralningens Problem* (The Problem of Nerve Irradiation, 1940) and *De Hypnotiska Hallucinationera* (Hypnotic Hallucination, 1942).

Black Box

A general term for **radionics** devices used to diagnose disease. These devices supposedly tap the unknown forces involved in **radiesthesia** and **dowsing,** where instruments such as water-witching rods or small pendulums test for sensitivity to water, metals, or health conditions. The original "Black Box" was devised by Dr. **Albert Abrams,** an unconventional San Francisco physician in the early twentieth century. It consisted of a box, variously called the ERA or the Oscilloclast, with several variable rheostats and a thin sheet of rubber mounted over a metal plate. A blood sample from the patient would be put into the machine, which was connected with a metal plate placed on the forehead of a healthy person. By tapping on the abdomen of this person, the doctor determined the disease of the patient according to the "areas of dullness" identified by dial readings on the apparatus. This strange procedure brought together various techniques: Auscultation is part of normal medical practice, but the suggestion of a psychic relationship between a patient and his blood sample, plus the indications obtained from stroking the rubber sheet with the fingers, involved the paranormal sensitivities used in water witching with rod or pendulum.

Long after the death of Abrams in 1924, his theories and techniques were developed by Dr. **Ruth Drown** in the United States and **George De la Warr** in Britain. De la Warr devised a black box that produced photographs relating to the individual whose sample was placed in the machine. These photographs were more like thought processes than normal images. De la Warr claimed that they registered a radiation pattern related to the shape and chemical structure of the radiating body, and, given a suitable sample, the camera plate would register not only regional tissue but its pathology.

However, the black box did not operate uniformly, and thus it appears that the individual operators were greatly affecting the results. The inability to standardize results would deny its operation any scientific standing. One woman sued the De la Warr laboratories because she was unable to obtain satisfactory results. The case was dismissed on the grounds that there had been no intent to defraud, although the judge severely criticized the apparatus as bogus. Use of the black box is against the law in the United States. However, in a more sympathetic investigation of the apparatus, Lucian Landau suggested that success depended upon the special sensitivity of the operator. In this respect, the apparatus would be related to the phenomenon of thought photography as attempted by **Ted Serios.** For a negative view of Abrams, see the volume by Gardner.

Sources:

Abrams, Albert. *New Concepts in Diagnosis and Treatment.* Physico-Clinical, 1924.

Barr, Sir James. *Abrams' Methods of Diagnosis and Treatment.* London, 1925.

De la Warr, George, with Langston Day. *New Worlds Beyond the Atom.* London: Vincent Stewart Publishers, 1956.

Firebrace, R. C., and Lucien Landau. "The Delawarr Camera." *Light: A Journal of Psychic Science* 77, no. 3430 (March 1937).

Gardner, Martin. *Fads and Fallacies in the Name of Science.* New York: Dover Publications, 1957.

Radionic Therapy (leaflet). Oxford, England: Delawarr Laboratories, 1953.

Black Hen, Fast of the

In Hungary and adjacent countries it was believed that if a person who had been robbed wished to discover the thief, then the victim must take a black hen and fast strictly for nine Fridays. The thief would then either return the plunder or die. This is called "taking up a black fast" against someone. A great deal of lore concerning black hens may be found in the works of Angelo de Gubernatis.

Black Magic

Black magic as practiced in medieval times may be defined as the use of the supernatural knowledge of magic for evil purposes; the invocation of diabolic and infernal powers to blind them as slaves and emissaries to man's will; in short, a perversion of legitimate mystical science. While black magicians certainly existed, there is every reason to believe that the majority of the reports of the spread of black magic were simply polemics against idealogical and personal enemies. Thus, members of the Hermetic Order of the **Golden Dawn** accused **Aleister Crowley** of practicing black magic while Crowley complained that black magicians had perverted his system.

The existence of the black art and its attendant practices can be traced from the time of the ancient Egyptians and Persians, from the Greeks and Hebrews, to the period when reports of black magic were most numerous, during the Middle Ages, thus forming an unbroken chain. In medieval magic may be found a degraded form of popular pagan rites—the ancient gods had become devils, their mysteries orgies, their worship sorcery.

Some historians have tried to trace the areas in Europe most affected by these devilish practices. Spain is said to have excelled all in infamy, to have plumbed the depths of the abyss. The south of France next became a hotbed of sorcery, branching northward to Paris and the countries and islands beyond, southward to Italy, finally extending into the Tyrol and Germany.

Many diseases, including catalepsy, somnambulism, hysteria, and insanity, were attributed to black magic. It followed that curative medicine was also a branch of magic, not a rational science, the suggested cures being such fantastic treatments as incantations and exorcisms, amulets and talismans of precious stones, medicines rendered powerful by spells and philters and enchanted drinks. The use of herbs and chemicals, which later became the foundation of modern curative science, then had more enchanted and symbolic significance when they were first prescribed by magicians.

Folk history surely exaggerated its intimations that the followers of the black art swarmed everywhere. The fraternity had grades from the pretenders, charlatans, and diviners of the common people to the various secret societies and orders of initiates, among whom were kings, queens, popes, and dignitaries of church and state. In these advanced levels, knowledge and ritual were carefully cherished and preserved in manuscripts, some of which still exist. These ancient **grimoires,** variously termed the Black, the Red, the Great Grimoire, are full of weird rites, formulas, conjurations, and evocations of evil malice and lust in the names of barbaric deities; charms and bewitchments clothed in incomprehensible jargon; and ceremonial processes for the fulfillment of imprecations of misfortune, calamity, sin, and death.

The deity who was worshiped and whose powers were invoked in the practice of black magic had many names: the Source and Creator of Evil, Satanas, Belial, the evil, a debased descendent of the Egyptian Set, the Persian Ahriman, the Python of the Greeks, the Jewish Serpent, **Baphomet** of the Templars, the Goat-deity of the Witches' Sabbat. He was said to have the head and legs of a goat and the breasts of a woman.

His followers called him by the names of forgotten deities as well as the Black One, the Black He-goat, the Black Raven, the Dog, the Wolf and Snake, the Dragon, the Hell-hound, Hell-hand, and Hell-bolt. His transformations were unlimited, as is indicated by many of his names; other favorite and familiar forms were a cat, a mouse, a toad, or worm, or again, the human form, especially a young and handsome man as he would appear on his amorous adventures. The signs by which he might be identified, though not invariably, were the cloven hoof, the goat's beard, cock's feathers, or the ox's tail.

In the Devil are embedded ancient mysteries and their symbols, the detritus of dead faiths and faded civilizations. The Greek Pan with the goat limbs masquerades as the Devil, also the goat as emblematic of fire and symbol of generation, and perhaps traces of the Jewish tradition where two goats were taken, one pure, the other impure, the first offered as sacrifice in expiation of sin, the other, the impure burdened with sins by imprecation and driven into the wilderness, in short, the scapegoat. In the Hebrew **Kabala,** Satan's name is Jehovah reversed. He is not a devil, but the negation of deity.

Beneath the Devil's sway were innumerable hordes and legions of demons and spirits, ready and able to procure and work any and every evil or disaster the mind of man might conceive and desire. In one grimoire, as presented in Francis Barrett's *The Magus,* it tells of nine orders of evil spirits, these being False Gods, Lying Spirits, Vessels of Iniquity, Revenge led by Asmodeus, Deluders by the Serpent, Turbulents by Merigum, Furies by Apollyon, Calumniators by Astaroth, and Tempters by Mammon. These demons again are named separately, the meaning of each name indicating the possessor's capacity, such as destroyer, devastator, tumult, ravage, and so forth.

Each earthly vice and calamity was personified by a demon—Moloch, who devours infants; Nisroch, god of hatred, despair, fatality; Astarte, Lilith, and Astaroth, deities of debauchery and abortion; Adramelek, of murder, and Belial, of red anarchy.

According to the grimoires, the rites and rules are multifarious, each demon demanding special invocation and procedure. The ends that might be obtained by performing the rites are indicated in such chapter headings as these: "to take possession of all kinds of treasure," "to live in opulence," "to ruin possessions," "to demolish buildings and strongholds," "to cause armed men to appear," "to excite every description of hatred, discord, failure, and vengeance," "to excite tempest," "to excite love in a virgin, or in a married person," "to procure adulteries," "to cause enchanted music and lascivious dances to appear," "to learn all secrets from those of Venus to Mars," "to render oneself invisible," "to fly in the air and travel," "to operate underwater for twenty-four hours," "to open every kind of lock without a key, without noise, and thus gain entrance to prison, larder, or charnel-house," "to innoculate the walls of houses with plague and diseases," "to bind **familiar** spirits," "to cause a dead body to revive," "to transform one's self," "to transform men into animals or animals into men."

These rites were classified as **divination,** bewitchments, and **necromancy.** Divination was carried out by magical readings of fire, smoke, water, or blood; by letters of names, numbers, symbols, or arrangements of dots; by lines of hand or fingernails; by birds and their flight or their entrails; by dice, cards, rings, or mirrors. Bewitchments were carried out by means of nails, animals, toads, or waxen figures and mostly to bring about suffering or death. Necromancy was the raising of the dead by evocations and sacrilegious rites, for the customary purposes of evil. These rites might take place around pits filled with blood, in a darkened and suffocating room, in a churchyard, or beneath swinging gibbets, and the number of ghosts so summoned and galvanized into life might be one of legion.

Regardless of desired outcome the procedure usually included profanation of Christian ritual, such as diabolical masses and administration of polluted sacraments to animals and reptiles; bloody sacrifices of animals, often of children; of orgiastic dances, generally of circular formation, such as that of the Witches' Sabbat.

For paraphernalia and accessories the sorcerers scoured the world and the imagination and mind of man and bent all things, beautiful or horrible, to their service. Because different planets were believed to rule over certain objects and states and invocations, such would be of great potency if delivered under the planets' auspices. Mars favored wars and strife, Venus love, Jupiter ambition and intrigue, Saturn malediction and death.

Vestments and symbols proper to the occasion were donned. The furs of the panther, lynx, and cat added their quota of influence to the ceremonies. Colors were also observed and suitable ornaments. For operations of vengeance, the robe had to be the hue of leaping flame, or rust and blood, with belt and bracelets of steel, and crown of rue and wormwood. Blue, green, and rose were the colors for amorous incantations; black for encompassing death, with belt of lead and wreath of cypress, amid loathsome incense of sulphur and assafoetida.

Precious stones and metals also influenced spells. Geometrical figures, stars, pentagrams, columns, and triangles were used; also herbs, such as belladonna and assafoetida; flowers, honeysuckle, being the witches' ladder, the arum, deadly nightshade, and black poppies; distillations and philters composed of the virus of loathsome diseases, venom of reptiles, secretions of animals, and poisonous sap, fungi, and fruits, such as the fatal manchineel, pulverized flint, impure ashes, and human blood. **Amulets** and **talismans** were made of the skins of criminals wrought from the skulls of hanged men, ornaments rifled from corpses and thus of special virtue, or the pared nails of an executed thief.

To make themselves invisible, it is said that sorcerers used an unguent compounded from the incinerated bodies of newborn infants mixed with the blood of nightbirds. For personal preparation, the sorceror fasted for 15 days, then got drunk every five days, after sundown, on wine in which poppies and hemp had been steeped.

For the actual rites the light came from candles made from the fat of corpses and fashioned in the form of a cross; the bowls were made from skulls, those of parricides being of greatest virtue; the fires were fed with cypress branches, with the wood of desecrated crucifixes and bloodstained gibbets; the magic fork was fashioned of hazel or almond, severed at one blow; the ceremonial cloth, was to be woven by a prostitute, and around the mystic circle were the embers of a polluted cross. Another potent instrument of magic was the **mandragora,** unearthed from beneath gallows where corpses were suspended, tied to a dog. The dog was then killed by a mortal blow, after which its soul was to pass into the fantastic root, attracting also that of the hanged man.

Widespread belief in black magic pervaded the Middle Ages. Machinations and counter-machinations engaged church and state, rich and poor, learned and ignorant. In persecutions and prosecutions, the persecutor and judge often met the same fate they dealt to the victim and condemned. In this dreadful phantasmagoria and procession can be found the haughty **Templars,** the blood-stained **Gilles de Laval,** the original of Bluebeard, **Catherine de Medici** the Marshals of France, as well as popes, princes, and priests. Literature divulges traces of black magic in weird legends and monstrous tales, in stories of spells and enchantments. The tale of Dr. Faustus recounts his pact with the Devil, his pleasures and their penalty when he must forfeit his soul to Hell. Traces exist in lewd verses and songs. Infernal influence is seen in pictures, sculptures, and carvings decorating palaces and cathedrals; the Devil's likeness peeps out from carven screen and stall, and his demons appear in gargoyles grinning and leering from niche and corner and clustering beneath the eaves.

The atmosphere of superstition and fevered imagination coexisted with religious dogma and repression. The great **witchcraft** manias flourished from the Middle Ages onward. The thousands of innocent men, women, and children who were brutally tortured and executed have left a deep stain on the Church. (See also **Black Mass; Evocation**)

Sources:

Cavendish, Richard. *The Black Arts.* New York: G. P. Putnam's Sons, 1967.

Black Mass

According to the inquisitors, the Black Mass epitomized the worship of Satan and perverted the most holy mystery of Christian worship—the Christian mass. Evidence of such occurrences was confirmed in the confessions forced from accussed witches and sorcerers, who claimed that the devil had mass said at his Sabbat. Pierre Aupetit, an apostate priest of the village of Fossas, France, was burned for celebrating the mysteries of the Devil's mass. Instead of speaking the holy words of consecration, the frequenters of the Sabbat were alleged to have said: "Beelzebub, Beelzebub, Beelzebub." The devil in the shape of a butterfly flew around those who were celebrating the mass, who then ate a black host, which they were obliged to chew before swallowing.

It is possible that the concept of the Black Mass derived from underground traditions of **Cathar** heretics, who were put down by orthodox Christianity during the fourteenth century. The Cathars believed in two gods, the God of light and the Prince of darkness, the maker of all material things. However, the idea of a Black Mass only became operative in the fifteenth century when the Roman Catholic Church turned on the "witches" as followers of Satan, whom because they believed in the magic of the Christian mass, hence could conceive a vulgar misuse of its powers. Several printed accounts which may have fueled the concept document strange occurrences, including the 1335 story of a shepherd found nude performing a parody of the mass and the 1458 story of a priest who mixed semen with the holy oil used for annointing people.

However, Satanism, as defined by the Church at the end of the fifteenth century, existed solely in the imaginaton of the inquisitors. Its ideas and practices were carried from generation to generation by the writings of Christians involved in the pursuit of witches and the stamping out of its practice. No evidence of anyone actually holding a Black Mass appears until the seventeenth century in France, when police arrested a fortune-teller named Catherine Deshayes, known as "La Voisin." Allegedly committing poisonings and sacrilege, La Voisin was a well-known abortionist, and was suspected of providing infants for ritual sacrifice in a Black Mass conducted by a libertine priest, Abbé Guibourg.

These masses were purportedly celebrated on the body of a naked woman. It was claimed that at the moment of consecration of the host, an infant's throat was cut, the blood was poured into the chalice, and prayers were offered to the demons Asmodeus and Ashtaroth. Other obscene rites were associated with the host.

At the trial of La Voisin, evidence was given that some Black Masses had been held at the request of the royal mistress the Marquise de Montespan, in order to retain the favor of Louis XIV. Other masses were associated with murder and poison plots, and many famous names were involved. Over 300 individuals were arrested, although fewer than half were tried; de Montespan was spared. La Voisin was subjected to brutal torture for three days, but she would not confess to poisoning, and on February 22, 1680, she was burned alive.

The modern Black Mass seems to have appeared as part of the magical revival in late ninteeth-century France. J. K. Huysmans is generally credited with reintroduing Satanism and the Black Mass in his book *La-Bas* (Down There), which includes a detailed description of a Satanic service. More recently the **Church of Satan** in San Francisco has based its much publicized diabolism upon a rejection of the Christian ethics of self-denial and humility. Its founder, **Anton La Vey,** published his own version of a Black Mass. (See also **Black Magic**)

Sources:

Cavendish, Richard. *The Black Arts.* New York: G. P. Putnam's Sons, 1967.

Huysmans, J. K. *Down There (La-Bas): A Study in Satanism.* Translated by Keene Willis. New Hyde Park, N.Y.: University Books, 1958.

La Vey, Anton. *The Compleat Witch; or, What to Do When Virtue Fails.* New York: Dodd, Mead, 1971.

———. *The Satanic Bible.* Seacaucus, N.J.: University Books, 1969.

———. *The Satanic Rituals.* Seacaucus, N.J.: University Books, 1972.

———. *The Satanic Witch.* Los Angeles, Calif.: Feral House, 1989.

Rhodes, H. T. F. *The Satanic Mass.* London, 1954.

"Black Pullet, The"

A French **grimoire** of **black magic** supposedly first printed in 1740, but probably much later. *La Poule Noire* actually bears the imprint of Egypt, "740," and the year 740, but this is manifestly false. It has been reprinted in Paris from time to time in editions for collectors, but without any indication of its true origin. The full title translates as *The Black Pullet; or, the Hen with the Golden Eggs, comprising the Science of Magical Talismans and Rings, the Art of Necromancy and of the Kabalah, for the Conjuration of Aerial and Infernal Spirits, of Sylphs, Undines, and Gnomes, serviceable for the aquisition of the Secret Sciences, for the Discovery of Treasures, for obtaining power to command all beings, and to unmask all Sciences and Bewitchments. The whole following the Doctrines of Socrates, Pythagoras, Zoroaster, Son of the Grand Aromasis, and other philosophers whose works in MS. escaped the conflagration of the Library of Ptolemy. Translated from the Language of the Magi and that of the Hieroglyphs by the Doctors Mizzaboula-Jabamia, Danhuzerus, Nehmahmiah, Judahim, and Eliaeb. Rendered into French by A.J.S.D.R.L.G.F.* It purports to be a narrative of an officer who was employed in Egypt. While in Egypt the narrator fell in with an occult magician to whom he rendered considerable service, and who at his death left him the secret of manufacturing a black pullet that would be skillful in finding gold.

Probably a nineteenth-century concoction, the story seems to be based on the the seventeenth-century volume **Comte de Gabalis** (see **Elementary Spirits**). The whole work, if interesting, is distinctly derivative. It contains many illustrations of **talismans** and magical rings. The procedure for bringing the black pullet into existence describes that a black hen should be set to hatch one of its own eggs, and that during the process a hood should be drawn over its eyes so that it cannot see. It is also to be placed in a box lined with black material. The chick thus hatched will have a particular instinct for detecting the places where gold is hidden.

Sources:

The Black Pullet: Science of Talismanic Magic. New York: Samuel Weiser, 1972.

Blackmore, Susan J. (1951–)

British parapsychologist, best known for her study of **out-of-the-body** experiences (OBEs). She completed a Ph.D. course in **parapsychology** in 1980 at the University of Surrey, England, then worked in the Parapsychological Laboratory at the University of Utrecht, in the Netherlands.

She held the Perrott-Warrick Studentship for four years, researching out-of-the-body and **near-death experiences** at the Brain and Perception Laboratory of Bristol University, England. She proposed a theory of OBEs as a psychological process involving memory and imagination, an altered state of consciousness like dream or drug states, and investigated relationships between OBEs, mental imagery, and other cognitive skills. Blackmore developed her theories in a series of research papers and the book *Beyond the Body: An Investigation of Out-of-the-Body Experiences* (1981).

Her special interest in the OBE phenomenon arises from the fact that she had an OBE years earlier. Lasting about three hours, it appeared to be a classic **astral projection** case, complete with the often-reported "silver cord" linking the astral and physical bodies. At the time, Blackmore was reading physiology and psychology at Oxford University, England. She became convinced that in spite of the vivid feeling of reality that accompanies the experience, there should be an acceptable explanation within terms of normal physiology and psychology, and that such an explanation might also explain other claimed paranormal phenomena such as **ESP, psychokinesis, ghosts, poltergeists,** and near-death experiences. Blackmore conducted many experiments to test a general theory of **psi,** which proposed that psi and memory are aspects of the same process. In the case of OBEs, she suggested that when an individual's cognitive system is disturbed and loses input control, its normal reality construct is replaced with one drawing upon memory. This might explain the intense sensation of reality during an OBE, as well as in vivid dreams.

However, her experimental efforts to replicate or validate psi phenomena were largely negative, and after some ten years of careful research, she became increasingly skeptical about the validity of parapsychology itself. Of course, other researchers have also grappled with the age-old problem of the inability to replicate spontaneous phenomena under scientific conditions, and it may be that the whole question of evidence, particularly in the case of OBEs, lies in qualities of consciousness rather than objective demonstration or repeatable material measurement.

Blackmore has raised important questions for parapsychology, and as a conscientious and thoroughly honest investigator, she has not hesitated to discuss such matters quite openly. Her somewhat rueful article, "The Elusive Open Mind: Ten Years of Negative Research in Parapsychology," was first presented at the 1986 CSICOP (Committee for the Scientific Investigation of Claims of the Paranormal) Conference at the University of Colorado in Boulder, and details basic problems of parapsychology in a frank and stimulating way. She expanded upon the paper in a book, *Adventures of a Parapsychologist* (1986).

Sources:

Berger, Arthur S., and Joyce Berger. *The Encyclopedia of Parapsychology and Psychical Research.* New York: Paragon House, 1991.

Blackmore, Susan J. *Adventures of a Parapsychologist.* Buffalo, N.Y.: Prometheus Books, 1986.

———. *Beyond the Body: An Investigation of Out-of-the-Body Experiences.* London: Heineman, 1981.

———. "The Elusive Open Mind: Ten Years of Negative Research in Parapsychology." *The Skeptical Inquirer* 9, no. 3 (spring 1987).

———. *Parapsychology and Out-of-the-Body Experience.* London: Society for Psychical Research; Hove, England: Transpersonal Books, 1978.

———. "A Psychological Theory of the OBE." In *Research in Parapsychology 1984.* Edited by Rhea A. White and Jerry Solfvin. 1985.

Blackmore, Susan J., and John Harris. "OBEs and Perceptual Distortions in Schizophrenic Patients and Students." In *Research in Parapsychology 1982.* Edited by William G. Roll, John Beloff, and Rhea A. White. 1983.

Blackwell, Anna (ca. 1870)

British author and publicist for **Spiritualism** and **Spiritism,** which is the name generally given to the form of Spiritualism developed in France by **Allan Kardec.** Spiritism differed from Spiritualism by its incorporation of **reincarnation** into its belief system. Blackwell became a follower of Spirtualism in the 1860s, a belief conformed by her own experiences. In 1869 she gave evidence to the Committee of the **London Dialectical Society** and contributed a paper dated July 1870 and published in their *Report on Spiritualism* (London, 1871). She had had some psychic experiences herself, having seen visions and had spirit forms appear on photographs that she had taken. During the 1870s she encountered Kardec's writings and began the process of translating them into English. She emerged as a prominent exponent of his teachings. Her mature thought was presented in her last book, co-authored with G. F. Green, *The Probable Effect of Spiritualism upon the Social, Moral, and Religious Condition of Society* (1876).

Sources:

Kardec, Allan. *Heaven and Hell.* Translated by Anna Blackwell. 1878.

———. *The Mediums' Book.* Translated by Anna Blackwell. 1876. Reprint. New York: Samuel Weiser, 1970.

———. *The Spirits' Book.* Translated by Anna Blackwell. 1875. Reprint. Sao Paulo, Brazil: Lake-Livraria Allan Kardec Editora, 1972.

Blackwood, Algernon (Henry) (1869–1951)

British author famous for his brilliant stories on occult themes. He was born March 14, 1869, in Kent, England. At the age of 17 his interest in the mystical and occult was first aroused after reading a translation of the *Yoga Sutrus* of Patanjali. In 1890 he immigrated to Canada at the age of 20 and had a varied career in Canada and the United States. He worked as a journalist, a dairy farmer, a hotel proprietor, and an actor among other occupations, suffering intense poverty until for a time he became secretary to James Speyer, a millionaire banker.

He returned to Britain in 1899, where he wrote most of his well-known occult stories. "The Willows" (1907) is considered by many as the finest supernatural tale in English. In 1900 he became a member of the famous occult society, the Hermetic Order of the **Golden Dawn.** Blackwood was something of a mystic, particularly responsive to wild natural scenery, and believed that humons possessed latent occult faculties. He died in December 1951 at the age of 82.

Sources:

Blackwood, Algernon. *Best Ghost Stories of Algernon Blackwood.* Edited by E. F. Bleiler. New York: Dover Publications, 1973.

———. *Episodes before Thirty.* New York: E. P. Dutton, 1924.

———. *The Human Chord.* London: Macmillan, 1910.

———. *Tales of the Supernatural.* Woodbridge, England: Boydell Press, 1983.

———. *Tales of Terror and Darkness.* London; New York: Spring Books, 1977. Distributed by Transatlantic Arts.

———. *The Willows, and Other Queer Tales.* 1934.

Sullivan, Jack, ed. *The Penguin Encyclopedia of Horror and the Supernatural.* New York: Viking, 1986.

Blake, Elizabeth (d. 1920)

Unusually powerful direct voice medium of Bradrick, Ohio. The voices were regularly heard in broad daylight. **James H. Hyslop** published a favorable report on her mediumship in the *Proceedings* of the **American Society for Psychical Research** (vol. 7: 570–788).

Two expert conjurers, **David P. Abbott** of the ASPR and E. A. Parsons, investigated Blake in 1906 and became convinced of the identity of the spirit communicators. Blake used a 2-foot long double trumpet; putting the small end to her ear and the larger one at that of the sitter, it appeared as if the voices came from her ear. If she covered the small end with her palm, the result was the same. The voices grew from whispers to such loudness that occasionally they were heard at a distance of 100 feet.

The endorsement by David P. Abbott is of particular importance, since he created a wonderful trick in which voices appeared to come from a teapot when the spout was held to an ear; the teapot also answered questions. With his expert experience of such illusions, Abbott would have been expected to discover any similar tricks by Spiritualist mediums.

Blake, William (1757–1827)

Poet, mystic, painter, and engraver, Blake is one of the most enigmatic yet most significant figures in the history of English literature, and a man who has likewise exerted strong influence on the graphic arts. He was born in London, England, November 28, 1757. Little is known definitely about his family's ancestry, but it seems probable that his parents and other relatives were humble folk.

William Blake manifested his artistic predilections at a very early age, and his father and mother did not discourage him. They offered to place him in the studio of a painter. The young man refused, however, pointing out that the apprenticeship was a costly one and saying that his numerous brothers and sisters should be considered; he held that it was not fair to impoverish his family on his behalf. Then engraving was suggested to him as a profession, because it required less expensive training than painting and was likely to yield a speedier financial return. Accepting this offer, Blake went at the age of 14 to study under James Basire, an engraver not very well known today, but who then enjoyed considerable reputation and was employed officially by the Society of Antiquaries.

Blake worked under Basire for seven years and was engaged mainly in making drawings of Westminster Abbey to illustrate a huge book then in progress, the *Sepulchral Monuments* of Richard Gough. It is said that Blake was chosen by his master to do these drawings not so much because he showed particular aptitude for drafting, but because he was eternally quarreling with his fellow apprentices; the young artist apparently believed he was superior to his *confrères* and made enemies by failing to conceal his belief. While at the Westminster Abbey, Blake asserted that he saw many visions.

In 1778 he entered the then recently founded Royal Academy School, where he studied under George Moser, a chaser and enameller who engraved the first great seal of George III. Yet it was not to Moser that the budding visionary looked for instruction; he was far more occupied with studying prints of the old masters, especially Michelangelo and Raphael. A short time later Blake left the Royal Academy and began to work on his own.

He had to work hard, however, for meanwhile his affections had been engaged by a young woman, Catherine Boucher, and he needed funds for the pair to marry. Blake engraved illustrations for magazines and the like, and his marriage was solemnized in 1782. His wife's name indicates that she was of French origin, but it is not known if she was related to François Boucher or to the fine engraver of the French Empire, Boucher-Desnoyers. The marriage proved a singularly happy one.

Regarding Catherine's appearance there still exists a small pencil-drawing by Blake, commonly supposed to be a portrait of his wife. It shows a slim, graceful woman, just the type of woman predominating in Blake's other pictures, so it may be presumed that she frequently acted as his model.

After his marriage Blake took lodgings on Green Street in Leicester Fields, and he opened a print shop on Broad Street. He made many friends at this period; the most favored among them was Flaxman, the sculptor. Flaxman introduced him to Mr. Matthew, a clergyman of artistic tastes who manifested keen interest in the few poems Blake had already written and generously offered to defray the cost of printing them. The writer accepted the offer and brought out a tiny volume, *Poetical Sketches.*

Thus encouraged, Blake gave up his print-selling business, moved to Poland Street, and soon after published his *Songs of Innocence,* the letterpress enriched by his own designs. In addition, the whole volume was printed by the author himself by a new method of his own invention.

Blake lived on Poland Street for five years, during which time he achieved and issued *The Book of Thel, The Marriage of Heaven and Hell,* and the first book of *The French Revolution.* In 1792 he moved to the Hercules Buildings in Lambeth, where dire poverty forced him to do much of his commercial work, notably a series of illustrations to Young's *Night Thoughts,* yet he also found time for original drawing and writing, including the *Gates of Paradise* and *Songs of Experience.*

Eventually he tired of London, however, and moved to Felpham, near Bognor in Sussex, taking a cottage close to where Aubrey Beardsley would live at a later date. Here Blake composed *Milton, Jerusalem,* and a large part of the *Prophetic Books,* and made a new friend, William Hayley, who repeatedly aided him monetarily. The Sussex scenery—afterward to inspire Whistler and Conder—appealed keenly to Blake, and in one of his lyrics he exclaimed, "Away to sweet Felpham, for Heaven is there," while to Flaxman he wrote: "Felpham is a sweet place for study, because it is more spiritual than London. Heaven opens here on all sides her golden gates; her windows are not obstructed by vapours, voices of celestial inhabitants are more distinctly heard, and their forms more distinctly seen and my cottage is also a shadow of their houses."

Eventually Blake returned to London, taking a house in South Molton Street in 1803. Here again he endured much poverty and was forced into doing illustrations for Virgil and also a series of designs for Blair's *Grave;* but later his financial horizon was brightened by help from John Linnell, the landscape painter. Shortly afterward Blake did some of his finest work, including his *Spiritual Portraits* and his drawings for *The Book of Job,* after which he began illustrating the *Divine Comedy* of Dante.

In 1821 he again changed his home to Fountain Court in Strand and continued to work at the Dante drawings, but only seven of them were ever published, for Blake's health was beginning to fail, his energies were waning, and he died August 12, 1827.

Sixteen years before his death, Blake held a public exhibition of his drawings, engravings, illustrations, and the like, and only one paper saw fit to print a criticism of it—*The Examiner,* edited by Leigh Hunt. It is customary for Blake's idolators today to scorn those who then disdained his work, but Blake's work emerged as somewhat of a novelty, especially the mysticism permeating his pictures, which had virtually no parallel in English painting prior to his advent. Also, Blake was still maturing as a technician and still had many grave limitations which are quite evident when placed beside that of his contemporaries.

If Blake the draftsman and illustrator was a fierce iconoclast who turned his back resolutely on the styles current in his time, most assuredly Blake the poet was sublimely contemptuous of the conventions of Augustanism, and thus he prepared the way for Burns, Wordsworth, and Shelley.

Had Blake written only his *Poetical Sketches,* his *Songs of Innocence* and the subsequent *Songs of Experience,* his contemporaries could never have leveled the charge of madness against him. It was his later writings like *The Book of Thel* and the *Prophetic Books* that branded him, for in these later poems the writer threw simplicity to the winds. Giving literary form to visions, Blake is so purely spiritual and ethereal, so far beyond the realm of normal human speech, that mysticism frequently devolves into crypticism. His rhythm, too, is often so subtle that it hardly seems rhythm at all.

Yet even in his weirdest flights Blake is still the master. And if, as already observed, the coloring in many of his watercolor drawings is thin, the very reverse is true of the poems written toward the close of his life. Their glowing and gorgeous tones have the barbaric pomp of Gautier's finest prose and the glitter and opulence of Berlioz's or Wagner's orchestration.

Sources:

Digby, George. *Symbol and Image in William Blake.* Oxford: Oxford University Press, 1957.

Erdman, David, ed. *The Illuminated Blake.* Garden City, N.Y.: Doubleday, 1974.

Keynes, Geoffrey, ed. *Blake: Complete Writings.* Oxford: Oxford University Press, 1974.

King, James. *William Blake: His Life.* London: Weidenfeld and Nicolson, 1991.

Nesfeld-Cookson, Bernard. *William Blake: Prophet of Universal Brotherhood.* U.K.: Crucible, 1987.

Raine, Kathleen. *From Blake to "A Vision."* Dublin: Dolman Press, 1979.

———. *William Blake.* Westport, Conn.: Praeger, 1971.

Wilke, Joanne. *William Blake's Epic: Imagination Unbound.* London: Croom Helm, 1986.

Wilson, Mona. *The Life of William Blake.* London: Oxford University Press, 1971.

Wolf-Gumpold, Kaethe. *William Blake: Painter, Poet, Visionary: An Attempt at and Introduction to his Life and Work.* London: Rudolf Steiner Press, 1969.

Blanchfleur

Granddaughter of the Duke of Ferrara and heroine of the old romance *Florice and Blanchefleur,* which was popular throughout Europe during the sixteenth century, and is probably of Spanish origin. Blanchfleur and Florice (son of the King of Murcia) loved each other from infancy, and she gave him a magical ring. He was banished for his love, and Blanchfleur was eventually shipped to Alexandria to be sold as a slave. Florice, however, found her there, partly by aid of the mystic ring, and they were happily united. Versions of the Florice or Florio romance seem to have existed in the thirteenth century.

Blatchford, Robert (Peel Glanville) (1851–1943)

Rationalist author, journalist, and socialist who was converted to the cause of **Spiritualism** in later life. Born March 17, 1851, in Maidstone, Kent, England, he was the son of two touring actors and grew up in a working-class background. He was apprenticed to a brushmaker at the age of 14, but six years later ran away, tramped from armouth to London, starved for some weeks, then enlisted in the army, becoming a sergeant.

After leaving the army in 1878, he worked for six years as a clerk and then turned to journalism. From 1885 to 1891 he wrote for the *Sunday Chronicle.* He contributed soldier stories and wrote on the land war in Ireland and the slums of Manchester. His experiences turned him to Socialism, and in 1891 he lost his job over it. With friends he started the *Clarion* as a socialist newspaper. His series of articles, *Merrie England,* were reissued in book form in 1893 and had a tremendous popular sale in a penny edition. The articles lifted the *Clarion* circulation to 60,000 and the book became famous as the first really popular work on socialism, selling over two million copies. It was followed by *Britain for the British* (1902), and *God and my Neighbor* (1903), a criticism of Christianity expressing his agnostic or atheistic convictions. He believed that the quality of individual life was positively determined by environment and training. In 1909 he warned Britain of Germany's determination to provoke war, but this lost him many readers. His book, *The Sorcery Shop,* (1907) expressed utopian views and has been compared to *New from Nowhere* by William Morris.

In 1920 Blatchford began to consider the claims of Spiritualism. He read widely on the subject, and after the death of his wife in 1921, he had sittings with **Gladys Osborne Leonard** and other mediums, through which he obtained definite and convincing evidence of the continued existence and affection of his wife. After several years of careful research, he published *More Things in Heaven and Earth* (1925), in which he argued that the evidence for Spiritualism was incontrovertible and that he was assured of his wife's continued presence and interest.

Because of the enormous popularity of his Socialist and agnostic writings, Blatchford is often quoted as a freethinker without reference to his later views. In 1931 he published his autobiography, *My Eighty Years.* He died at Norsham, Sussex, December 17, 1943.

Blätter Aus Prevorst (Periodical)

"Leaves from Prevorst," a psychic periodical founded by Dr. **Justinus Kerner** in 1831. After publication of 12 volumes, it was superseded in 1839 by *Magikon: Archire für Beobachtunger aus dem Gebiete der Geisterkunde und des magnetischen vad magischa Lebens* (*Magikon; or, Archives for Observations Concerning the Realms of the Spirit World of Magnetic Life*). This publication continued until 1853.

Blavatsky, Helena Petrovna (1831–1891)

One of the most influential occult thinkers of the nineteenth century, Blavatsky left behind conflicting images of adventuress, author, mystic, guru, occultist, and charlatan. Born at Ekaterinoslav, Russia, July 31, 1831, she was the daughter of Col. Peter Hahn, a member of a Mecklenburg family settled in Russia. With the aid of Col. **Henry Olcott** and **William Q. Judge**, she founded the **Theosophical Society** in New York in 1875. In order to gain converts to Theosophy, she felt obliged to appear to perform miracles. This she did with a large measure of success, but her "methods" were on several occasions detected as fraudulent. Nevertheless, her commanding personality secured for her a large following.

An enigmatic personality, she was brought up in an atmosphere saturated with superstition and fantasy. She loved to surround herself with mystery as a child and claimed to her playmates that in the subterranean corridors of their old house at Saratow, where she used to wander about, she was never alone, but had companions and playmates whom she called her "hunchbacks."

She was often discovered in a dark tower underneath the roof, where she put pigeons into a mesmeric sleep by stroking them. She was unruly, and as she grew older she often shocked her relatives by her masculine behavior. Once, riding astride a Cossack horse, she fell from the saddle and her foot became entangled in the stirrup. She claimed that she ought to have been killed outright were it not "for the strange sustaining power she distinctly felt around her, which seemed to hold her up in defiance of gravitation."

According to the records of her sister, Blavatsky showed frequent evidence of somnambulism as a child, speaking aloud and often walking in her sleep. She saw eyes glaring at her from inanimate objects or from phantasmal forms, from which she would run away screaming and frighten the entire household. In later years she claimed to have seen a phantom protector whose imposing appearance had dominated her imagination.

Her powers of make-believe were remarkable. She possessed great natural musical talents, had a fearful temper, a passionate curiosity for the unknown and weird, and an intense craving for independence and action.

At the age of 17, she was married to General Blavatsky, an old man from whom she escaped three months later. She then fled abroad and led a wild, wandering life for ten years all over the world, in search of mysteries. When she returned to Russia she possessed well-developed mediumistic gifts. Raps, whisperings, and other mysterious sounds were heard all over the house, objects moved about in obedience to her will, their weight decreased and increased as she wished, and winds swept through the apartment, extinguishing lamps and candles. She gave exhibitions of clairvoyance, discovered a murderer for the police, and narrowly escaped being charged as an accomplice.

In 1860 she became severely ill. A wound below the heart, which she received from a sword cut in magical practice in the East, opened again, causing her intense agony, convulsions, and trance. After Blavatsky recovered, her spontaneous physical phenomena disappeared, and she claimed that they only occurred after that time in obedience to her will.

She again went abroad, and, disguised as a man, she fought under Garibaldi and was left for dead in the battle of Mentana. She fought back to life, had a miraculous escape at sea on a Greek vessel that was blown up, and, in 1871 in Cairo, she founded the Societé Spirite. It was a dubious venture that soon expired amid cries of **fraud** and embezzlement, reflecting considerably on the reputation of the founder.

Her closer ties with **Spiritualism** dated from her arrival in New York in July 1873. Blavatsky first worked as a dressmaker to obtain a living and, after her acquaintance with Col. Henry Steel Olcott at Chittenden, Vermont, in the house of the **Eddy Brothers,** she took up journalism, writing mostly on Spiritualism for magazines and translating Olcott's articles into Russian. "For over 15 years have I fought my battle for the blessed truth," she wrote in *The Spiritual Scientist,* published in Boston (December 3, 1874); "For the sake of Spiritualism I have left my house; an easy life amongst a civilised society, and have become a wanderer upon the face of this earth."

Her second marital venture, which occurred during this period, ended in failure and escape. The starting point of her real career was the foundation of the Theosophical Society in 1875. It professed to expound the esoteric tradition of Buddhism and aimed at forming a universal brotherhood of man; studying and making known the ancient religions, philosophies, and sciences; investigating the laws of nature; and developing the divine powers latent in man. It was claimed to be directed by secret Mahatmas, or Masters of Wisdom.

Olcott, who was elected president, was a tireless organizer and propagandist. His relationship to Blavatsky was that of pupil to teacher. He did the practical work, and Blavatsky the literary work. Their joint efforts soon put the society on a prosperous footing, and at the end of 1878 a little party of four left, under their leadership, for Bombay. Soon after the theosophical movement gained added impetus from the publicity launched by **A. P. Sinnett,** editor of the *Pioneer,* who had embraced Buddhism in Ceylon.

The publicity had its disadvantages as well. The attention of the **Society for Psychical Research** (SPR) was aroused at reports of the theosophic marvels, and **Richard Hodgson** was sent to Adyar, India, where the central headquarters of the theosophical movement was established, to investigate. The investigation had a disastrous effect for Blavatsky and dealt a nearly fatal blow to Theosophy. Hodgson reported that he found nothing but palpable fraud and extreme credulity on the part of the believers. The Coulombs, a couple who had joined Blavatsky in Bombay in 1880 and were her acquaintances from the time of the Cairo adventure, confessed to having manufactured, in conspiracy with Blavatsky, a large number of the theosophical miracles: they revealed the secret of the sliding panels of the shrine in the Occult Room through which, from Blavatsky's bedroom, the "astral" Mahatma letters were deposited; disclosed impersonation of the Mahatmas by a dummy head and shoulders; declared that the Mahatma letters were written by Blavatsky in a disguised hand and that they were projected through cracks in the ceiling by means of spring contrivances; and they produced the correspondence between them and Blavatsky in proof of their self-confessed complicity. Hodgson's investigations, which lasted for three months, entirely demolished the first private and confidential report of the SPR issued in December 1884, which was theoretically favorable to Blavatsky's claims. Hodgson's conclusions were published in the *Proceedings* of the SPR:

"In the first place a large number of letters produced by M. and Mme. Coulomb, formerly Librarian and Assistant Corresponding Secretary, respectively, of the Theosophical Society were, in the opinion of the best experts in handwriting, written by Madame Blavatsky. These letters, which extended over the years of 1880–1883, inclusive, and some of which were published in the Madras Christian College magazine for September, 1884, prove that Mme. Blavatsky has been engaged in the production of a varied and long-continued series of fraudulent phenomena, in which she has been assisted by the Coulombs. The circumstantial evidence which I was able to obtain concerning the incidents referred to in these letters, corroborates the judgment of the experts in handwriting.

"In the second place, apart altogether from either these letters or the statements of the Coulombs, who themselves allege that they were confederates of Mme. Blavatsky, it appears from my own inquiries concerning the existence and the powers of the supposed Adepts or Mahatmas, and the marvellous phenomena alleged to have occurred in connection with the Theosophical Society,

1. That the primary witnesses to the existence of a Brotherhood with occult powers—viz., Madame Blavatsky, Mr. Damodar K. Mavalankar, Mr. Bhavani Shankar and Mr. Babajee D. Nath—have in other matters deliberately made statements which they must have known to be false, and that, therefore, their assertions cannot establish the existence of the Brotherhood in question.
2. That the comparison of handwriting further tends to show that Koot Hoomi Lal Sing and Mahatma Morya are fictitious personages, and that most of the documents purporting to have emanated from these "personages" and especially from "K.H." (Koot Hoomi Lal Sing) are in the disguised handwriting of Madame Blavatsky herself, who originated the style of the K.H. handwriting; and that some of the K.H. writing is the handiwork of Mr. Damodar in imitation of the writing developed by Madame Blavatsky.
3. That in no single phenomenon which came within the scope of my investigation in India, was the evidence such as would entitle it to be regarded as genuine, the witnesses for the most part being extraordinarily inaccurate in observation or memory, and having neglected to exercise due care for the exclusion of fraud; while in the case of some of the witnesses there has been much conscious exaggeration and culpable mis-statement.
4. That not only was the evidence insufficient to establish the genuineness of the alleged marvels, but that evidence furnished partly by my own inspection, and partly by a large number of witnesses, most of them Theosophists, concerning the structure, position and environment of the Shrine, concerning "Mahatma" communications received independently of the Shrine, and concerning various other incidents, including many of the phenomena mentioned in the Occult World, besides the numerous additional suspicious circumstances which I have noted in the course of dealing in detail with the cases considered, renders the conclusion unavoidable that the phenomena in question were actually due to fraudulent arrangement."

On the basis of Hodgson's findings, the committee of the SPR declared: "For our own part we regard her neither as the mouthpiece of hidden seers nor as a mere vulgar adventuress; we think that she has achieved a title to permanent remembrance as one of the most accomplished and interesting impostors in history."

The publication of the report, which followed the printing of the Coulomb letters in the *Madras Christian Magazine,* created an immense sensation. In response, Olcott, whose honesty was not impugned by the report, banished Blavatsky from Adyar. The proofs of her guilt were overwhelming, for the defense was built up with great difficulties. With the Theosophical Society thus discredited, recovery looked hopeless.

Nevertheless, **Annie Besant,** who would become Blavatsky's successor, and Sinnett valiantly took on the task. Hodgson answered and insisted on his conclusions. In the literature that subsequently grew up on the subject, V. S. Solovyoff claimed in *A Modern Priestess of Isis* (1895) that Blavatsky acknowledged her fraudulent practices to the author. *Blavatsky's Posthumous Memoirs* (1896) was a most curious artifact of the time that was said to have been dictated by Blavatsky's spirit. The text (which furnished strong, internal proofs of its apocryphal character) was obtained in independent typewriting on a Yost machine under the supervision of the spirit of its inventor, Mr. G. W. N. Yost.

Blavatsky nevertheless succeeded in living down every attack during her lifetime, continued her work, gained many new adherents to Theosophy, and published a work, *The Secret Doctrine,* which was claimed to have been written in a supernormal condition. Whatever conclusions are reached about her complex character, it must be admitted that she was an extraordinarily gifted individual and it does seem probable that she indeed possessed psychic powers which, however, fell far short of the miraculous feats she constantly aimed at. Even Solovyoff admits some remarkable experiences, and though he furnished natural explanations for many of them, the assumption that withstands challenge is that she had, as plainly pointed out by Olcott himself, unusual hypnotic powers.

Her famous feats of duplicating letters and other small objects are plainly ascribable to this source when common fraud does not cover the ground. She never troubled about test conditions. Most of her phenomena were produced under circumstances wide open to suspicion and strongly savoring of a conjuring performance; like the finding of an extra cup and saucer at a picnic at Simla in 1880 in the Sinnett garden under the ground at a designated spot; the clairvoyant discovery of the lost brooch of Mrs. Hume in a flower bed; the astral dispatch of marked cigarettes to places she indicated; and the Mahatma scripts imposed over the text of private letters which the post had just delivered.

There is no end of these and similar miracles, and the testimony of the truth is sometimes so surprising that one can conclude that imposture occasionally blended with genuine psychic performance. The general character of Blavatsky's phenomena is of a different order from those of the Spiritualist medium. Her early physical phenomena subsided at a later age, although the power to cause raps remained, and once, in New York, Olcott claimed that he witnessed the materialization of a Mahatma from a mist rising from her shoulders. As a rule the Mahatmas were not supposed to depend upon Blavatsky's organism for appearance, and controlled her body but seldom. *Isis Unveiled* and the *Secret Doctrine* were claimed to have been produced under such control.

Whereas there is a limit to the phenomena of every Spiritualistic medium, Blavatsky apparently knew none. From the materialization of grapes for the thirsty Col. Olcott in New York to the duplication of precious stones in India, or the creation of toys for children out of nothingness, she undertook almost any magical task and successfully performed it, to everyone's amazement.

Sinnett must have genuinely suffered in his admission: "That she sometimes employed the Coulombs, husband and wife, as confederates in trickery is the painful though hardly intelligible state of the facts. Even with me she has done this. For example on my return to India, after having published the *Occult World*—after she knew that I was rooted in a personal conviction not only that she possessed magic powers, but that I was in touch with the Masters and devoted to the theosophical cause, she employed M. Coulomb to drop a letter from the Master intended for me through a crack in the rafters above, trying to make me believe that it had been dropped by the Master himself—materialised then and there after transmission by occult means from Tibet. M. Coulomb told Hodgson that he had been so employed on this occasion, and his statement fits in with the minor circumstances of the incident."

The Hodgson Report left a deep shadow over Blavatsky's final years. Besant's conversion to Theosophy resulted after she had been requested by W. T. Stead to review *The Secret Doctrine* in 1889. Blavatsky suggested that she read the Hodgson Report before forming any firm conclusions, but Besant was not adversely affected and requested to be Blavatsky's pupil. Thereafter Besant provided a secure refuge for the aging Theosophist at her own home in London. In her last years here, Blavatsky became the center of a memorable group of talented individuals. She died peacefully May 5, 1891.

Blavatsky's character was too complex for instant judgments. She manifested elements of philosophical mastery and undoubtedly perpetuated numerous psychic frauds. The Hodgson Report, which cast such a shadow over Blavatsky's later years, is not itself beyond reproach. Hodgson was criticized for jumping to conclusions on inadequate evidence and for unsatisfactory examination of the handwriting evidence (though the main body of the report stands as written). The April 1986 edition of the *Journal* of the Society for Psychical Research published a persuasive contribution by Vernon Harrison, "J'Accuse: An Examination of the Hodgson Report of 1885," a paper later reissued in booklet form by the Theosophical History Centre in London.

It is somewhat easier to assess Blavatsky's long-term effect on Western culture. She exercised an enormous influence over some of the most talented individuals of her time, and they passed along her ideas to a wider culture. Through the Theosophical Society, she stimulated translation of important Hindu scriptures and philosophical works. She encouraged national pride in Indian culture, literature, religion, and aspirations for home rule, and she founded an important archive of Sanskrit manuscripts at Adyar, Madras.

The Theosophical Society she co-founded was a forerunner of the famous secret society the Hermetic Order of the **Golden Dawn** and numeorus other occult groups. The Irish literary renaissance owes much to the Hindu mysticism of **William Butler Yeats** and **George W. Russell,** who were both influenced by the teachings of the Theosophical Society.

Sources:

Barker, A. T. *Collected Writings.* 14 vols. Wheaton, Ill.: Theosophical Publishing House, 1950–87.

Besant, Annie. *H. P. Blavatsky and the Masters of Wisdom.* London, 1907.

Blavatsky, Helena P. *From the Caves and Jungles of Hindustan.* London: Theosophical Publishing Society, 1892.

———. *Isis Unveiled.* 2 vols. New York: J. W. Bouton, 1877.

———. *The Key to Theosophy.* Pasadena, Calif.: Theosophical University Press, 1972.

———. *The Secret Doctrine.* 2 vols. London: Theosophical Publishing House, 1889. Reprint, London: Thesophical Publishing House, 1928.

———. *Theosophical Glossary.* New York: Theosophical Publishing House, 1892.

Butt, G. Baseden. *Life of Madame Blavatsky.* London: Rider, 1926.

Cleather, Alice L. *H. P. Blavatsky: A Great Betrayal.* Calcutta: Thacker, Spink, 1922.

Endersby, Victor. *Hall of Magic Mirrors.* New York: Carlton Press, 1969.

Fuller, Jean Overton. *Blavatsky and Her Teachers: An Investigative Biography.* London: East-West Publications/Theosophical Publishing House, 1988.

Gomes, Michael. *Dawning of the Theosophical Movement.* Wheaton, Ill.: Theosophical Publishing House, 1987.

———. *Theosophy in the Nineteenth Century: An Annotated Bibliography.* New York: Garland Publishing, 1994.

Hodgson, Richard. "Report on Phenomena Connected with Theosophy." *Proceedings* of the Society for Psychical Research 3 (1885).

Kingsland, William. *The Real H. P. Blavatsky.* London: Theosophical Publishing House, 1928.

Lillie, Arthur. *Mme. Blavatsky and Her Theosophy.* London: Swan Sonnonschein, 1895.

Meade, Marion. *Madame Blavatsky: The Woman Behind the Myth.* New York: G. P. Putnam's Sons, 1980.

Olcott, Henry Steel. *Old Diary Leaves.* 4 vols. Reprinted as *Inside the Occult: The True Story of Madame H. P. Blavatsky.* Philadephia: Running Press, 1995.

Ransom, Josephine. *A Short History of the Theosophical Society.* Madras, India: Theosophical Publishing House, 1938.

Sinnett, A. P. *Incidents in the Life of Madame Blavatsky.* London: George Redway, 1886.

Solovyoff, V. S. *A Modern Priestess of Isis.* London: Longmans, Green, 1895.

Wachmeister, Countess Constance. *Reminiscences of H. P. Blavatsky and the Secret Doctrine.* London: Theosophical Publishing Society, 1893.

Waterman, Adlai E. [Walter A. Carrithers] *Obituary: The "Hodgson Report" on Madame Blavatsky, 1885–1960.* Adyar, India: Theosophical Publishing House, 1963.

Williams, Gertrude M. *Priestess of the Occult: Madame Blavatsky.* New York: Alfred A. Knopf, 1946.

Yost, G. W. N. *Blavatsky's Posthumous Memoirs.* Boston: Joseph M. Wade, 1896.

Bleksley, Arthur Edward Herbert (1908–1984)

South African professor of applied mathematics and lecturer on science and parapsychology. Born April 27, 1908, in East Griqualand, South Africa, he had a distinguished academic career, becoming professor of applied mathematics at Zeiss Planetarium, Witwatersrand University, and president of South African Association for the Advancement of Sciences. He also became director of the South African Institute for Parapsychological Research, Johannesburg.

He conducted investigations into ESP, telepathy in the classroom situation, and random-number tables. He published various articles on parapsychology, especially on extrasensory perception during sleep. He has been credited with raising the status of parapsychcology in South Africa, and toward the end of his life he was given the Willliam McDougall Award for Distinguished Work in Parapsychology. In addition to various textbooks, he published *The Secret of the Atom Bomb* (1945) and *Travellers through Space* (1962).

Sources:

Bleksley, A. E. H. "An Experiment of Long-Distance ESP During Sleep." *Journal of Parapsychology* 27 (1963): 1.

Blewett, Duncan Bassett (1920–)

Canadian psychologist who has studied telepathy in relation to drug-induced psychedelic experiences. He was born October 28, 1920, in Edmonton, Alberta, Canada, and studied at the University of British Columbia (B.A., 1947; M.A., 1950) and the

University of London (Ph.D., 1953). Beginning in 1961, he was an associate professor of psychology at the Regina campus of the University of Saskatchewan. At the beginning of interest in psychedelic drugs in the mid-1950s, he conducted research on their power to affect telepathic abilities. He presented the results at the 1958 Conference on Parapsychology and Psychedelics in New York. He also contributed papers to the *Journal of Mental Science.*

Blind

Term used by parapsychologists in experiments where the evaluator of targets and responses to them is without knowledge of information that would reveal the **target.** (See also **Double Blind**)

Blindfolding a Corpse

The Afritans of the Shari River in Central America used to blindfold a corpse before burying it to prevent it from returning to haunt the survivors.

Blind-Matching

A term used by parapsychologists in relation to tests for clairvoyance with ESP cards. The subject holds the pack of **Zener cards** face downward and sorts them into five piles, which are later compared to key cards already hidden in envelopes.

Blockula

Believed to be the assembly place for the witches Sabbat at Mora, Sweden, during the great witchcraft hysteria of 1669–70. It was said to be a large meadow with a house where there was a long table set with "broth with colworts and bacon in it, oatmeal, bread spread with butter, milk and cheese." This fairyland repast sometimes "tasted very well, and sometimes very ill."

Blofeld, John (Eaton Calthorpe) (1913–1987)

Author and translator of books on Eastern religion and **mysticism.** Blofeld was born April 2, 1913, in London, England. During World War II he served as a captain with the British War Office (1940–42), and then as a cultural attache at the British Embassy, Chungking, China (1942–46), but returned to England after the war to complete his college work at Downing College, Cambridge (M.A., 1947) and the School of Oriental Studies, London. In 1947 he married Meifang Chang, a teacher. After completing his studies, he moved to Thailand where he would live for the rest of his life. In 1951 he became a lecturer in English literature at Chulalongkorn University, Bangkok, Thailand, a post he held for a decade. During the 1960s he was the chief of editorial services at the U.N. Economic Commission for Asia and the Far East (UNECAFE), Bangkok, and in 1974 he became a lecturer in English at Kasetsart University, Bangkok.

Blofeld became a Buddhist in the 1930s and joined the Buddhist Society in London. His work in China and Thailand allowed him a great deal of freedom to wander around the Orient staying in Buddhist and Taoist communities. His visits provided him with material for his books and numerous articles (some written under the pseudonym Chu Ch'an). His popular books contributed to the spread of Eastern religion in the West through the 1970s and 1980s.

Sources:

Blofeld, John. *Beyond the Gods.* New York: E. P. Dutton, 1974.

———. *Bodhisattva of Compassion: The Mystical Tradition of KuaYin.* Boulder, Colo.: Shambhala, 1977.

———. *The Jewel in the Lotus: An Outline of Present-Day Buddhism in China.* London: Sidgwick & Jackson, 1948.

———. *Mahayana Buddhism in Southeast Asia.* Singapore: Asia Pacific Press, 1971.

———. *Mantras: Sacred Words of Power.* New York: E. P. Dutton, 1977.

———. *The Secret and Sublime.* New York: E. P. Dutton, 1973.

———. *Tantric Mysticism of Tibet: A Practical Guide.* New York: Dutton, 1970. Reprinted as *The Way of Power.* London: Allen & Unwin, 1970.

———. *The Wheel of Life.* London: Rider, 1959. Rev. ed. Boulder, Colo.: Shambhala, 1972.

Bloxham, Arnall (ca. 1881– ?)

British hypnotherapist who spent over 20 years tape-recording hypnotic sessions with subjects whose memories apparently regressed to former incarnations. Bloxham followed up on his tapes and attempted to uncover corroborating evidence relative to his subject's claims of former earth lives, unlike **Morey Bernstein,** who did little research on the claims of his hypnotized subject Virginia Tighe, whose reveries of a former life as "Bridey Murphy" were the subject of a best-selling book. Bloxham assembled data on some 400 cases of claimed **reincarnation.**

He grew up in Pershore, a small village in Worcestershire, England, and was educated at Worcester Grammar School. During childhood, he had vivid dreams of people and events that suggested past lives, and some of the details of these dreams were later verified in adult life. His interest in **hypnotism** dated from his schooldays, when he discovered his ability for **mesmerism,** as it was then called, and used it to cure a friend's headache. He planned to become a doctor and thought that mesmerism might be a useful asset. However at the age of 18, Bloxham joined the Royal Navy on the outbreak of World War I. After being taken ill with typhoid fever, he was told that he could never work in a hospital, so he became a hypnotherapist and practiced for more than 40 years.

During World War II he again served in the navy, this time as a naval lieutenant, and afterward he settled in Cardiff, South Wales. Here his reputation as a hypnotist gained him a thriving practice. He gave public lectures, appeared on television shows, and cooperated with a dentist to prove that teeth could be extracted under hypnosis instead of anesthetic. Hypnotherapy became increasingly recognized by the British medical profession. In 1972 Bloxham served as president of the British Society of Hypnotherapists.

The activity for which he is best known took place with the assistance of his wife, Dulcie, hypnotizing subjects, regressing their memories to "former existences," and making tape recordings of the sessions. Some of these tapes were played at informal meetings with individuals interested in reincarnation or the law of **karma** (the Eastern philosophy of action and reaction extended over several lives). In 1958 Dulcie published a book titled *Who Was Ann Ockenden?* about one of her husband's subjects, a schoolteacher whose memories under hypnosis regressed to seven different "lives." The regular meetings came to an end soon after the death of Dulcie Bloxham.

The 400 cases that make up the Bloxham Tapes are of ordinary people who lived humdrum lives and whose memories of previous "lives" are equally ordinary, although studded with circumstantial information that seemed as if it could be corroborated. For example, the tapes detailed the account of a Welsh housewife who described the massacre of Jews in twelfth-century York, a press photographer who claimed to have seen the execution of Charles I in Whitehall, London, in 1649, a Welshman who told of life aboard a frigate as a press-ganged seaman in Nelson's Navy. Some of the subjects, like the Welsh housewife, recalled six or seven previous lives.

During the 1970s the vast collection of tape-recorded material was painstakingly investigated by BBC radio and television producer Jeffrey Iverson. With the cooperation of famous television presenter Magnus Magnusson, they presented a television program titled *The Bloxham Tapes,* featuring actual hypnotic sessions with some of Bloxham's subjects and detailing how the evidence of the claimed memories of former lives was corroborated.

Iverson's book *More Lives than One?* (1976) presents the results of his research on the Bloxham Tapes.

A more skeptical view of the Bloxham claims was presented by Ian Wilson in his 1982 text *Reincarnation?* Wilson suggests that some of the claimed former lives of Bloxham subjects were due to **cryptomnesia,** the recasting of subconscious memories from secondary sources into apparently real past life experiences. In the case of "Jane Evans," one of Bloxham's cases, Wilson claims that the source of her apparent recall of a past life in the twelfth century could have been an unconscious reworking of a historical novel since traced by an investigator.

Whether hypnotism can be relied on to create significant proof of reincarnation is itself a controversial contention. Researchers have continually shown problems generated by the hypnotist leading the person in the creation of a fantasy. Individuals in a hypnotized state also show an extraordinary ability to create very convincing stories out of a storehouse of memories in the manner that some artists claim they produced their results and some authors their fictions. Although many authors consciously research and develop plot, characters, and backgrounds, others, such as **Joan Grant,** for example, have found that their stories are "dictated" fluently from the subconscious, as if they were dreams or real memories.

Sources:

Iverson, Jeffrey. *More Lives than One?* London, N.p., 1976.

Wilson, Ian. *Mind Out of Time.* London: Gollancz, 1981.

Blue Star Gazette

Monthly publication of the Palo Alto Society branch of **ECKANKAR,** "the ancient science of soul travel." Address: 880 Emerson St., Palo Alto, CA 94301.

Bo and Peep See Human Individual Metamorphosis

Bodhisattva

A Buddhist term for one who exists in enlightenment of truth and compassion guided by love and wisdom. In Mahayana Buddhism, the bodhisattva is the ideal of progress; in Theravada Buddhism, the bodhisattva is an aspirant for Buddha-hood. In Theosophy the bodhisattva is the director of the spiritual development of each root-race and founder of religions, which he propagates through his messengers.

Sources:

The Bodhisattva Doctrine in Buddhism. Waterloo, Ontario: Canadian Corporation for Studies in Religion, Wilfrid Laurier University Press, 1981.

Candragomin. *Difficult Beginnings: Three Works on the Bodhisattva Path.* Boston, Mass.: Shambhala, 1985.

Dayal, Har. *The Bodhisattva Doctrine in Buddhist Sanskrit Literature.* Delhi, India: Motilal Banarsidass, 1970.

Bodin, Jean (1529–1596)

A jurist and student of demonology who died of the plague in 1596. An Angevin by birth, he studied law, classics, philosophies, and economics in his youth and became professor of Roman law at the University of Toulouse. In 1561 he went to Paris, where he served the king, but lost royal favor on publication of his book *Republique,* which contained concepts of monarchy that were ahead of his time. His most famous work was *De la demonomanie des sorciers* (*Demonomania of witches*), which played a large part in the growth of **witchcraft** persecutions, because it defined witchcraft and laid down methods of interrogation, torture, and execution.

His *Colloquium heptaplomeron de abdites rerum sublimium varcanus,* aroused very unfavorable opinions regarding his religious views. In it Bodin discussed the theological opinions of Jews, Moslems, and deists to the disadvantage of the Christian faith, and although he died a Catholic, he professed in his time the tenets of Protestantism, Judaism, sorcery, atheism, and deism.

The *Demonomanie* was published in Paris in 1580 and again under the title *Flèau des demons et des sorciers* at Wiort in 1616. In his first and second books Bodin demonstrated that spirits have communication with mankind, and he traced the various characteristics and forms that distinguish good spirits from evil. His topics include the methods of diabolic prophecy and communication; evocation of evil existences; of pacts with the devil; of journeys through the air to the sorcerers' Sabbath; of infernal ecstasies; of spells by which one may change himself into a **werwolf,** and of carnal communion with an **incubus** or **succubus.** The third book explains how to prevent the work of sorcerers and obviate their charms and enchantments, and the fourth divulges the manner in which sorcerers may be known. He concluded his study by refuting the work of **Johan Weyer,** or Wierus, who, he asserted, was in error in believing that sorcerers were fools and people of unsound mind. Bodin recommended that Weyer's books should be burned "for the honour of God."

Bodin participated in many witchcraft trials as judge and was responsible for the torture of many suspected witches, including children and invalids. He advised using hot irons to cauterize the flesh so that putrefaction could be cut out. One of his precepts was that presumption and conjecture of witchcraft ranked as proof.

Sources:

Robbins, Rossell Hope. *The Encyclopedia of Witchcraft and Demonology.* New York: Crown Publishers, 1959.

Weyer, Johannes. *Witches, Devils, and Doctors in the Renaissance: Johann Weyer, De Praestigiis.* Edited by George Mora. Binghamton, N.Y.: Medieval and Renaissance Texts and Studies, 1991.

Body, Mind & Spirit Magazine

New title for former *Psychic Guide Magazine,* adopted with the November/December 1987 issue. The title reflected the broad identification of editor Paul Zuromski with the New Age movement. Address: Box 701, Providence, RI 02901.

Boehme, Jakob (1575–1624)

Famous German mystic. His name is sometimes spelled Beem, Behm, Behmon, or Behmont, but the most common form is Boehme, although it is probable that the family name was really Böhme, and Boehme most closely matches the German version.

Born in 1575 at Altsteidenberg in Upper Lusatia, Boehme came from peasant stock, and accordingly his education consisted of brief study at the nearby village school in Seidenberg, and for the greater part of his childhood he tended his father's flocks on Mount Landskrone. Not strong enough physically to make a good shepherd, Boehme left home at the age of 13 to seek his fortune at Görlitz, the nearest town of any size.

To this day, Görlitz is famous for its shoemakers, and it was to a cobbler that the boy went first in search of employment. By 1599 he became a master shoemaker, and soon afterward married Katharina, daughter of Hans Kantzschmann, a butcher. The young couple took a house near the bridge in Neiss Voistadt—their dwelling is still pointed out to tourists—and some years later Boehme improved his business by adding gloves to his stock in trade, a departure which sent him periodically to Prague to acquire consignments.

It is likely that Boehme began to write soon after becoming a master cobbler. About the year 1612 he composed a philosophical treatise, *Aurora, oder die morgenröte in Aufgang.* Though not printed until much later, the manuscript was copied and passed from hand to hand. The writer soon found himself the center of a local circle of thinkers and scholars, many of them people far above him in the social scale. As a result, a charge of heresy was brought against him by the Lutheran church; he was loudly denounced from the pulpit by Gregorius Richter, pastor primarius of Görlitz, and then the town council, fearing to contend with the ecclesiastical authorities, took possession of the original manuscript of Boehme's work and prohibited him from writing.

It seems that he obeyed instructions for a little while, but by 1618 he was busy again, compiling polemical and expository treatises, and in 1622 he wrote short pieces on repentance, resignation, and the like. These last were the only writings published in book form during his lifetime with his consent, but in any event they were not likely to excite clerical hostility. However, Boehme later circulated a less cautious theological work, *Der Weg zu Christa,* which brought a fresh outburst of hatred on the part of the Church. Boehme left town for a period and met with some of his admirers in Dresden. However, while there he was struck down by fever. He was carried with great difficulty to his home at Görlitz, where he died in 1624.

Boehme's literary output falls into three distinct sections. At first he was concerned simply with the study of the deity, and to this period belongs his *Aurora.* Second, he grew interested in the manifestation of the divine in the structure of the world and of man, a predilection which resulted in four great works: *Die Drei Principien Gottlichens Wes Wescus, Vom Dreifachen Leben der Menschen, Von der Menschwerdung Christi,* and *Von der Geburt und Bezlichnung Aller Wescu.* Finally, he devoted himself to advanced theological speculations and researches, the main outcome being his *Von Christi Testamenten* and his *Von der Chadenwahl: Mysterium Magnum.* Other substantive works include his seven *Quellgeister* and his study of the three first properties of eternal nature.

Although not an alchemist himself, Boehme's writings demonstrate that he studied **Paracelsus** closely, and they also reflect the influence of Valentine Weigel and the earliest Protestant mystic, Kaspar Schwenhfeld. Boehme never claims to have conversed with spirits, angels, or saints nor of miracles worked on his behalf, the one exception being a passage where he tells how, when a shepherd boy on the Landskrone, he saw an apparition of a pail of gold. At the same time, he seems to have felt a curious and constant intimacy with the invisible world and he appears to have had a strangely perspicacious vision of the *Urgrund,* or primitive cause.

His wide influence over people inclined to mysticism has been attributed to the clarity with which he sets down his ideas and convictions. Throughout the latter half of the seventeenth century, his works were translated into a number of different languages. They proved an inspiration to William Law, the author of *Christian Perfection* and *A Serious Call to a Devout Life.* Since then various religious bodies that regard Boehme as their high priest have been founded in Great Britain and in Holland, while in America, the sect known as the Philadelphians owe their dominant tenets to him.

Sources:

Boehme, J. *Aurora.* London: John M. Watkins, 1960.

———. *The Confession of Jacob Boehme.* New York: Harper, 1954.

———. *Mysterium Magnum.* London: John M. Watkins, 1965.

———. *The Signature of All Things.* London: James Clarke, 1969.

———. *Six Theosophic Points.* Lansing: University of Michigan Press, 1970.

———. *The Three Principles of the Divine Essence.* Jacksonville, Fla.: Yoga Publication Society, 1909.

———. *The Way to Christ.* New York: Paulist Press, 1978.

Hartmann, Franz. *The Life and Doctrines of Jacob Boehme.* New York: McCoy Publishing, 1929.

Martensen, H. L. *Jacob Boehme.* Rockliff, 1949.

Stoudt, J. J. *Sunrise to Eternity.* Philadelphia: University of Pennsylvania, 1957.

Bogey

An evil spirit. The term may derive from the Slavonic *bog* (god). Other forms of the name of this ancient sprite, specter, or goblin are bug-a-boo, boo (Yorkshire), boggart, bogle (Scotland), boggle, bo-guest, bar-guest, boll, bo-man, and bock. Bullbeggar is probably a form of bu and bogey allied to boll (Northern England), an apparition. (See also **Boh**)

Sources:

Briggs, Katherine. *An Encyclopedia of Fairies: Hobgoblins, Brownies, Bogies, and Other Supernatural Creatures.* New York: Pantheon Books, 1976.

Boggle-Threshold

Term coined by parapsychologist **Renée Haynes** to indicate the level at which the mind "boggles" or is thwarted by the degree of improbability of a phenomenon. It is similar to other measures of the strangeness level of a phenomenon expressed by others.

Boguet, Henri (ca. 1550–1619)

Grand Justice of the district of Saint Claude in Burgundy, France, during the seventeenth-century European **witchcraft** mania. He was the author of a work full of ferocious zeal against sorcerers.

This book, entitled *Discours des sorciers,* was published at the beginning of the seventeenth century and was later burned because of the inhumanities crowding its pages, but it went into 12 editions in two decades. The book is a compilation of procedures for judging sorcerers and their alleged acts, most of which the author himself presided over. They exhibit the most incredible absurdities and criminal credulity.

Its pages contain the proceedings against little Louise Maillat, who at the age of eight was said to be possessed of eight demons; Françoise Secretain, a sorceress who had meetings with said demons and who had the Devil for her lover; and the sorcerers Gros-Jacques and Willirmoz. Claude Gailiard and Roland Duvernois and many others figured in the author's dread judgments.

Boguet detailed the horrible doings of the witches' Sabbat, how the sorcerers caused hail to fall, of which they made a powder to be used as poison, how they used an unguent to carry them to Sabbat, how a sorcerer was able to slay anyone by means of a mere breath, and, when arraigned before a judge, they could not shed tears. He described Devil's mark found on their skins, of how all sorcerers and magicians possess the power to change their forms into those of wolves, and how for these offences they were burned at the stake without sacrament, so that they were destroyed body and soul.

The work ended with instructions to the judges of cases of sorcery, which is often known as the *Code des sorciers.*

Sources:

Boguet, Henri. *Discours des sorciers.* Translated as *Examen of Witches.* New York: Barnes & Noble, 1971.

Boh (or Boo)

A magical word often used to frighten children. *Boe* is a Greek word synonymous with the Latin *Clamor,* signifying the English word "cry," and it is possible that the cry of the ox—"boo"—may have suggested this exclamation, since this sound would quite naturally be very terrifying to a young child. There may be some connection between this monosyllable and the "Boglebo" or "bwgwly" of Welsh people. According to one writer, it was the name of a fierce Gothic general whose name like those of other great conquerors was remembered as a word of terror. (See also **Bogey**)

Bohmius, Jean

Author of a work entitled *Pyschologie,* a treatise on spirits, published at Amsterdam in 1632. Nothing is known of the author.

Boirac, Emile (1851–1917)

Rector of the Dijon Academy and noted French psychical researcher. In the course of his study of human **emanations,** he revived **Franz A. Mesmer**'s theories concerning **animal magnetism,** which he saw as the cause of psychokinesis and other physical phenomena of Spiritualism. His observations on the obscure phenomena of **exteriorization of sensitivity** carried the researches of **Paul Joire** and **Albert de Rochas** a step farther. His major book, *La Psychologie inconnue* (1908), was awarded the Emden Prize by the French Academy of Sciences.

Sources:

Berger, Arthur S., and Joyce Berger. *The Encyclopedia of Parapsychology and Psychical Research.* New York: Paragon House, 1991.

Boirac, Emile. *L'Avenir des sciences psychiques.* Paris, 1917. Translated as *The Psychology of the Future.* London, 1918.

———. *La Psychologie inconnue.* Paris, 1908. Translated as *Psychic Science.* London, 1918. Translated as *Our Hidden Forces.* New York, 1917.

BOLIDE See Ball-of-Light International Data Exchange

Bolton, Gambier (d. 1929)

British author and lecturer on natural history who also investigated various aspects of psychical phenomena. He was educated at Corpus Christi College, Cambridge. He published a large series of animal photographs that he took while traveling in Europe, America, Canada, the Hawaiian Islands, Japan, China, Java, the Malay Peninsula, Burma, India, and South Africa. He accompanied the duke of Newcastle on his world tour 1893–94. Bolton died July 29, 1929.

Sources:

Bolton, Gambier *A Book of Beasts and Birds.* London: G. Newnes, Ltd., 1903.

———. *Ghosts in Solid Form.* London: W. Rider and Son, Ltd., 1919.

Bon, Henri (1885– ?)

French physician and parapsychologist. Born August 1, 1885, at Dijon, France, he studied at the University of Lyons Medical School (M.D., 1912). In 1919 he was founder of the Clinique Médicale of Arguel (Doubs) and served as its director for more than 30 years (1919–52). He is best known outside his native land for his several books, which include *La Mort et ses problèmes* (Death and Its Problems, 1941), *Les Guérisons miraculeuses modernes* (1952; trans. *Modern Miraculous Cures* [1957]) and *Le Miracle devant la science* (Miracle and Science, 1957).

Bonati (or Bonatus), Guido (d. 1300)

Florentine astrologer who flourished in the thirteenth century. He lived in a most original manner and perfected the art of prediction. When the army of Martin IV besieged Forli, a town of the Romagna that was defended by the count of Montferrat, Bonati announced to the count that he would repulse the enemy but would be wounded in the fray. The event transpired as Bonati had predicted, and the count, who had taken with him the necessary materials to staunch his wound in case the prophecy came true, became a devout adherent of **astrology.**

Bonati became a Franciscan toward the close of his life and died in 1300. His works were published by Jacobus Cauterus under the title *Liber Astronomicus* at Augsberg, 1491. Another Florentine astrologer of the same name died 1596.

Bond, Frederick Bligh (1864–1945)

Ecclesiastical architect, archaeologist, and excavator of the lost chapels of **Glastonbury** Abbey. Born June 30, 1864, at Marlborough, Wiltshire, England, he was editor of *Psychic Science* from its inception until 1926, editor of the *Journal* of the **Society for Psychical Research** in 1930, and author of a number of books based on **automatic writing.** Received mostly in conjunction with "John Alleyne" (**John A. Bartlett**) and **Hester Dowden,** involved a form of dual mediumship in which Bond provided the special mental contact.

His vocation and his studies of ancient abbeys apparently predisposed him to receive a range of psychic communications. *The Gospel of Philip the Deacon* was entirely different from the communications habitual in Dowden's mediumship. It is an open question whether *The Scripts of Cleophas,* the first two sections of which came under precisely similar conditions, would have been received by **Geraldine Cummins** without Bond's initial mental impetus. The inspiring influences spoke of themselves as "The Company of Avalon," "The Company of the Watchers," etc. The bulk of the philosophical writings which they inspired was published under the title *The Wisdom of the Watchers* (New York, 1933).

Besides these and his own inspirational writings, Bond conducted experiments in **psychic photography** with **Ada E. Deane** (see **Thoughtforms**) and pursued various other lines of research. He considered the survival of mind, memory, and personality as proved facts. In *The Gate of Remembrance* he proposed that the recall of the olden-time memories were due to a cosmic reservoir of human memory and experience in which the element of personality is preserved and welded into a collective association extending through all times. This, he claimed, would not only perpetuate individual character but actually emphasize the force and clarity of its expression by enriching it with added elements of a sympathetic nature.

Thus individual personality is, in Bond's view, progressively developed and perfected through the multiplying of its sympathetic contacts. He outlined this conception of immortality in a series of articles in 1929 in the *Journal* of the **American Society for Psychical Research.** He pictured the subliminal consciousness as a magnet that is constantly attracting other elements of personality sympathetically linked with the physical being of their host.

Hence we are all alike, sharers in the great life of the subliminal world, and are an integral part of it, the only barriers being our own intellectual and emotional limitations. The communications are based upon sympathetic spiritual association. Where this exists there will always be the probability of a recall of the veridical memories of old and of their right translation into language. But where no such spiritual link is present, there is only the reflection of the personal subconscious mind of the medium, and there will be no sure indication of the entry of a really independent personality. This theory brings the extreme psychological and Spiritualistic views into a well thought-out harmony. Although it has been widely accepted that Bond's claim that psychically acquired information successfully guided the discovery of the lost chapels at Glastonbury, some critics do not accept the case as proved, maintaining that the **Glastonbury Scripts** disclosed nothing that might not have been deduced from existing historical records, as well as containing incorrect statements. This does not necessarily impugn the honesty of Bond.

In November 1927 Bond moved to the United States, where he became educational director of the American Society for Psychical Research at the time of the controversy over the mediumship of "Margery" (**Mina Crandon**). Although at first Bond endorsed her mediumship as genuine, he subsequently expressed grave doubts; in the May 1935 *Proceedings* of the ASPR, he defended the research officer E. E. Dudley, who had been accused of tampering with the famous "Walter" wax thumbprints. In effect, this clearly supported the claim that the prints were fraudulent, and as a result Bond was dismissed. Soon afterward he returned to England, where he retired to North Wales.

Bond is sometimes referred to as "The Rev." This stems from the fact that while in America he was ordained as a priest (1932) and consecrated as a bishop (1933) of the Old Catholic Church in America by Archbishop William Henry Francis Brothers.

Bond died March 8, 1945, in Wales. He left behind an unpublished manuscript comprising claimed communications from Captain Bligh of the H.M.S. *Bounty,* received through an American psychic. Bligh was Bond's great-uncle.

Sources:

Bond, Frederick Bligh. "Athanasia." *Journal* of the American Society for Psychical Research (January–May 1929).

———. *The Company of Avalon.* Oxford: B. H. Blackwell, 1924.

———. *The Gate of Remembrance.* Oxford: B. H. Blackwell, 1918.

Bond, Frederick Bligh, and Thomas Simcox Lea. *Gematria: A Preliminary Investigation of the Cabala.* Wellingborough, England: Thorsons, 1977.

Goodman, Jeffrey. *Psychic Archeology: Time Machine to the Past.* New York: Berkley Publishing, 1977.

Kenawell, William W. *The Quest at Glastonbury.* New York: Helix Press, 1965.

Lambert, G. W. "The Quest at Glastonbury." *Journal* of the Society for Psychical Research 43, no. 748 (June 1966).

Ward, Gary L. *Independent Bishops: An International Directory.* Detroit: Apogee Books, 1990.

Bonewits, P(hilip) E(mmons) I(saac) (1949–)

A Pagan priest who has attained some measure of fame as America's first "academically accredited" practitioner of magic. He holds the first (and only) Bachelor of Arts degree with a major in **magic** from the University of California, Berkeley. Bonewits (pronounced *Bon*-a-wits) was born October 1, 1949, in Michigan, and came to Berkeley from Laguna Beach in 1967. He originally studied psychology, but found this limiting, and succeeded in finding a professor who agreed to sponsor a major in occult science. This degree was granted June 16, 1970, after which Bonewits published a very successful book about his academic sojourn under the title *Real Magic* (1971).

While at Berkeley, Bonewits roomed with Robert Larson, who had previously attended Carleton College. In the 1960s Carleton was the site for the formation of the Reformed Druids of North America. The idea of Druidism appealed to Bonewits, and he and Larson formed a Druid grove in Berkeley. Bonewits was ordained as a Druid priest in 1969.

In 1974 he moved to Minneapolis to become editor of the occult journal *Gnostica* (1974–75). He also established a Druid group in Minneapolis and founded the Aquarian Anti-Defamation League, a short-lived Pagan defense organization. In 1976 Bonewits returned to Berkeley. He finished the compilation of the Druid holy writings, which he published as the *Druid Chronicles (Evolved),* and in 1978 he established the periodical *Druid Chronicles* (later *Pentalpha Journal*).

In the early 1980s Bonewits separated from the Druids and was initiated as a priest in a Gardnerian Pagan group, the New Reformed Orthodox Order of the Golden Dawn (no relation to the Hermetic Order of the Golden Dawn). In 1983 he moved to New York, where he and Shenain Bell founded Ar nDraiocht Fein (Gaelic for "Our Own Druid Faith"). Bonewits was named Archdruid. In 1988 he married Deborah Lipp, a Gardnerian priestess. Together they run a Pagan Way group, and Bonewits remains as head of Ar nDraiocht Fein. A national leader in the Pagan/Wicca community, Bonewits is a major advocate of formal theological training for Pagan leaders.

Sources:

Bonewits, P. E. I. *Authentic Thaumaturgy.* Albany, Calif.: The CHAOSium, 1978.

———. *Druid Chronicles (Evolved).* Berkeley, Calif.: Berkeley Drunemetron Press, 1976.

———. *Real Magic.* Coward, McCann & Geoghegan, 1971. Rev. ed. Berkeley, Calif.: Creative Arts Book Co., 1979.

Boniface VIII (Benedetto Gaetano) (ca. 1228–1303)

Pope who gained an unenviable notoriety in Dante's *Inferno* as "Prince of the new Pharisees" and was regarded by many people as an exponent of **black magic.** A noted jurist, Boniface was born at Anagni in a noble family and was elected pope in 1294. In 1296 he quarreled seriously with Phillippe le Bel, king of France, who wanted to tax the church, and prepared to excommunicate the king. The quarrel arose when Boniface was determined to extend the rule of the papacy throughout the kingdoms of the world and to build up great estates for his family.

In 1303, Phillippe's ministers and agents boldly accused Boniface of heresy and sorcery, and the king called a council at Paris to hear witnesses and pronounce judgment. The pope resisted and refused to acknowledge a council not called by himself. Then the king planned to abduct Boniface and bring him to France. The French attacked the pope in his residence, but could not carry off their escape, and the mistreatment to which Boniface was exposed proved too much for him. He died the same year, in the midst of these vindictive proceedings. His enemies spread abroad a report that in his last moments he had confessed his league with the demon, and that his death was attended with "so much thunder and tempest, with dragons flying in the air and vomiting flames, and such lightning and other prodigies, that the people of Rome believed that the whole city was going to be swallowed up in the abyss."

His successor, Benedict XI, undertook to defend his predecessor's memory, but he died in 1304, the first year of his pontificate (some said he was poisoned), and the holy see remained vacant for 11 months. In mid-June 1305 the archbishop of Bordeaux was elected to the papal chair under the title Clement V. This election was ascribed to the influence of the king, who was said to have stipulated as one condition that Clement should support proceedings against Boniface that would make his memory infamous. However, the prosecution was dropped, and in 1312 Boniface was declared innocent of all offenses with which he had been charged. These had included wild accusations of infidelity, skepticism, and communication with demons. One witness deposed that he had a demon enclosed in a ring which he wore on his finger; one friar (Brother Bernard de Sorano) deposed that when Boniface was a cardinal, he was seen to enter a garden adjacent to the palace of Nicholas III and perform a magical ceremony with a sacrificed cock and a book of spells, conjuring up demons. Such statements must be judged in the light of the king's opposition to Boniface and the superstitions of the time.

Bonnevault, Pierre (ca. seventeenth century)

A self-confessed sorcerer of Poitou in the seventeenth century, the son of **Maturin De Bonnevault.** Bonnevault engaged in **devil worship** and was arrested on his way to the Devil's Sabbat. He stated that the first time he had attended an unholy meeting he had been taken there by his parents and dedicated to the Devil, to whom he had promised to leave his bones after death, but that he had not bargained to leave his immortal soul to his infernal majesty.

Bonnevault admitted that he called Satan "Master," that the Devil had assisted him in various magical acts, and that he had slain various persons through Satanic agency. In the end he was condemned to death. His brother Jean, accused of sorcery at the same time, prayed to the Devil for assistance, and was raised some four or five feet from the ground and dashed back thereon, his skin turning at the same time to a blue-black hue. He confessed that he had met at the Sabbat a young man through whom he had promised one of his fingers to Satan after his death. He also told how he had been transported through the air to the Sabbat, how he had received powders to slay certain people whom he named, and for these crimes he received the punishment of death.

Book of Celestial Chivalry

A work of Spanish origin that appeared in the middle of the sixteenth century. It documents supposed knightly adventures in a semi-romantic, semi-mystical vein.

Book of Shadows

The "bible" of the modern witch coven. It contains basic beliefs, rituals, charms, spells, and incantations. There is no authentic definitive edition, since the form and scope of the book differs from coven to coven. Normal procedure is for a witch to copy the work in her own handwriting and destroy the original, but in many covens, copies are made without destroying the original. However, no copy is intended to be kept by a witch who leaves the coven, and this rule is enforced by various threats and curses.

Although the act of copying the book in manuscript suggests a centuries-old secret tradition, there is little doubt that the material contained in most modern versions of the Book of Shadows derives from sources such as *Aradia; or The Gospel of the Witches* (1899) by **Charles Godfrey Leland,** a compilation of **witchcraft** folklore reportedly collected by Leland from a Florentine fortune-teller and hereditary. It was the first English-language publication of its kind. The average modern Book of Shadows derives from the one constructed in stages by **Gerald B. Gardner** for use in his revived Witchcraft group in Great Britain during the 1940s and 1950s. He borrowed heavily from the writings of **Aleister Crowley,** especially for the third degree. During the 1960s and 1970s various Witches mixed the Gardnerian Book of Shadows with material from modern occult and folklore texts.

The Gardnerian Book of Shadows was actually released in 1964 by a hostile ex-member, and over the years additional variations on the text have been published, as have new Books of Shadows inspired by it. Wide circulation was given to Lady Sheba's *Book of Shadows,* released in 1973.

Sources:

The Book of Shadows and Substance. Owlexandrian Multimedia/Hermetic Educational Institute, n.d.

Budapest, Zsuzsanna Emese. *The Feminist Book of Lights and Shadows.* Venice, Calif.: Luna Publications, 1976.

Rex Nemorensis [Charles Cardell]. *Witch.* London: Privately published, 1964.

Sheba, Lady. *The Book of Shadows.* St. Paul, Minn.: Llewellyn Publications, 1973.

Tarostar. *A Book of Shadows.* New Brunswick, N.J.: Inner Light Publications,1987.

Book of Spirits (or The Spirits' Book)

The English translation of *Le Livre des esprits,* a famous book on Spiritualism by **Allan Kardec** (pseudonym of H. L. D. Rivail, 1804–1869). The original French work was published in 1856. It was translated into English in 1975 by **Anna Blackwell** and frequently reprinted, especially in Brazil, where Kardec has a large following.

Sources:

Kardec, Allan. *The Spirits' Book.* Translated by Anna Blackwell. 1875. Reprint, Sao Paulo, Brazil: Lake-Livraria Allan Kardec Editora, 1972.

Book of the Damned

First of the famous four "Books" of **Charles Fort** (1874–1932) that challenged conventional divisions of thought and science by collating and interpreting phenomena that were usually denied, explained away, or ignored. The "damned" described by Fort as the data that science has excluded, referred to a wide variety of scientific anomalies. *The Book of the Damned* was first published in 1919. It was followed by *New Lands,* 1923; *Lo!* 1931; and *Wild Talents,* 1932. A complete collected edition, *The Books of Charles Fort,* was published in 1941.

Sources:

Fort, Charles. *The Books of Charles Fort.* New York: Henry Holt, 1941.

Book of the Dead

An arbitrary title given to a funerary work from ancient **Egypt** called *pert em hru,* the translation of which is "coming forth by day," or "manifested in the light." Several versions or recensions of this work are known, namely those of Heliopolis, Thebes, and Sais, differing only inasmuch as they were edited by the colleges of priests founded at these centers. Many papyri of the work have been discovered, and passages from it have been inscribed upon the walls of tombs and pyramids and on sarcophagi and mummy-wrappings. One very complete copy is on display at the Egyptian Museum in Turin, Italy.

It is undoubtedly of extremely early date; exactly how early it would be difficult to say, but in the course of centuries it was greatly added to and modified. It contains about 200 chapters, but no complete papyrus has been found. The chapters are quite independent of one another, and were probably all composed at different times. The main subject is the beatification of the dead, who were supposed to recite the chapters in order that they might gain power and enjoy the privileges of the new life.

The work abounds in magical references. The whole trend of the Book of the Dead is thaumaturgic, as its purpose is to guard the dead against the dangers they have to face in reaching the other world. As in most mythologies, the dead Egyptian had to encounter malignant spirits and was threatened by many dangers before reaching his haven of rest.

He also had to undergo judgment by Osiris, and to justify himself before being permitted to enter the realms of bliss. This he imagined he could in great part accomplish by the recitation of various magical formula and spells, which would ward off the evil influences opposed to him. To this end every important Egyptian of means had buried with him a papyrus of the Book of the Dead, containing at least all the chapters necessary for encountering the formidable adversaries at the gates of Amenti, the Egyptian Hades. These chapters would assist him in making replies during his ceremony of justification. First among these spells were the "words of power." The Egyptians believed that to discover the "secret" name of a god was to gain complete ascendancy over him.

Sympathetic magic was in vogue in Egyptian burial practice, which explains the presence, in tombs of people of means, of paintings of tables laden with food and drink, with inscriptions attached conveying the idea of boundless liberality. Inscriptions like the following are extremely common—"To the *ka* [essential double or soul] of so-and-so, 5,000 loaves of bread, 500 geese, and 5,000 jugs of beer." Those dedications cost the generous donors little, as they merely had the objects named painted upon the wall of the tomb, imagining that their **ka** or astral counterpart would be eatable and drinkable by the deceased. This of course is merely an extension of the Neolithic conception that articles buried with a man had their astral counterparts and would be of use to him in another world.

Pictorial representation played a considerable part in the magical ritual of the Book of the Dead. One of the pleasures of the dead was to sail over Heaven in the boat of Ra, and to secure this for the deceased one must paint certain pictures and mutter over them words of power. Regarding this belief, E. A. Wallis Budge states in his book *Egyptian Magic* (1889):

"On a piece of clean papyrus a boat is to be drawn with ink made of green *abut* mixed with *anti* water, and in it are to be figures of Isis, Thoth, Shu, and Khepera, and the deceased; when this had been done the papyrus must be fastened to the breast of the deceased, care being taken that it does not actually touch his body. Then shall his spirit enter into the boat of Ra each day, and the god Thoth shall take heed to him, and he shall sail about with him into any place that he wisheth. Elsewhere it is ordered that the boat of Ra be painted 'in a pure place,' and in the bows is to be painted a figure of the deceased; but Ra was supposed to travel in one boat (called Atet) until noon, and another (called Sektet) until sunset, and provision had to be made for the deceased in both boats. How was this to be done? On one side of the picture of the boat a figure of the morning boat of Ra was to be drawn, and on the other a figure of the afternoon boat; thus the one picture was capable of becoming two boats. And, provided the proper offerings were made for the deceased on the birthday of Osiris, his soul would live for ever, and he would not die a second time. According to the rubric to the chapter in which these directions are given, the text of it is as old, at least, as the time of Hesept, the fifth king of the 1st. dynasty, who reigned about 4350 B.C., and the custom of painting the boat upon papyrus is probably contemporaneous."

The words of power were not to be spoken until after death. They were "a great mystery," but "the eye of no man whatsoever must see it, for it is a thing of abomination for every man to know it. Hide it, therefore, the Book of the Lady of the Hidden Temple is its name." This would seem to refer to some spell uttered by Isis-Hathor that delivered the god Ra or Horus from trouble, or was of benefit to him, thus was concluded to be equally efficacious in the case of the deceased.

Many spells were included in the Book of the Dead for the purpose of preserving the mummy against molding and for assisting the owner of the papyrus to become as a god and to be able to transform himself into any shape he desired. Painted offerings were also provided so the deceased would be able to give gifts to the gods. It is apparent that the Book of the Dead was undoubtedly magical in character, consisting as it did of a series of spells or words of power, which enabled the speaker to have perfect control over all the powers of Amenti.

The only moment in which the dead man is not master of his fate is when his heart is weighed by Thoth before Osiris. If it does not conform to the standard required for justification, he is cast out; except for this, an absolute knowledge of the Book of the Dead safeguarded the deceased in every way from the danger of damnation. A number of the chapters consist of prayers and hymns to the gods, but the directions as to the magical uses of the book are equally numerous; the concept of supplication is mingled with the idea of circumvention by sorcery in the most extraordinary manner.

Book of the Sacred Magic of Abra-Melin

A magic manual by "Abraham the Jew," a magician of the Middle Ages, translated and edited by **S. L. MacGregor Mathers** from a rare manuscript dated 1478 at the Bibliotheque de l'Arsenal, Paris. This translation was first published 1898 and has been frequently reprinted. (See also **Abraham the Jew**)

Sources:

The Book of the Sacred Magic of Abra-Melin the Mage. Translated by S. L. MacGregor-Mathers. 1898. Reprint. Chicago: de Laurence, 1932. Reprint, New York: Causeway Books, 1974.

Book of Thoth

An interpretation of the symbolism of the **tarot** cards written by **Aleister Crowley** toward the end of his life (1875–1974). In 1912 Crowley published "A Description of the Cards of the Tarot" in his biannual journal, *Equinox* (vol. 1, nos. 7–8), about the tarot cards of the Hermetic Order of the **Golden Dawn.** Each member had to make a copy from the original deck, but it was not until **Israel Regardie** published a set of the Golden Dawn tarot cards in the 1980s that the pictures that Crowley was describing became available to the public.

In the 1940s Crowley wrote a commentary on the tarot, which carried the Egyptian symbolism that had come to dominate the thelemic magic system he had developed. He teamed with artist Frieda Harris to create a new deck of tarot cards. The commentary, *The Book of Thoth,* was published in 1944. *The Book of Thoth* was released as Vol. 3, no. 5, of the *Equinox.* It is part of the standard curriculum for members of the **OTO.**

Sources:

Crowley, Aleister. *The Book of Thoth.* New York: Samuel Weiser, 1974.

Book Tests

Experiments in psychic research to exclude the working of **telepathy** in mediumistic communications. In answer to questions or for reasons of personal relevance, the communicator indicates a certain book upon a certain shelf in the home of the sitter and gives the text on a certain page.

In such experiments far more successes were registered than chance would justify. The books selected are usually those of which the communicator was fond in his lifetime, thus offering another suggestion of personal identity. Many excellent cases of book tests are recorded in Lady Glenconner's *The Earthen Vessel* (1921) and in *Some New Evidence for Human Survival* (1922), by the Rev. **Drayton Thomas.** In the preface he wrote to Thomas's book, **Sir William Barrett** reported to have received this communication from the deceased psychical researcher **F. W. H. Myers:**

"There were some books on the right-hand side of a room upstairs in your house in Devonshire Place. On the second shelf, four feet from the ground, in the fourth book counting from the left, at the top of page 78, are some words which you should take as direct answer from him (Myers) to so much of the work you have been doing since he passed over. Asked if the name of the book could be given, the reply was 'No,' but that whilst feeling on the cover of the book he got a sense of 'progression.' Two or three books from this test book are one or two books on matters in which Sir William used to be very interested, but not of late years. It is connected with studies of his youth."

Barrett pointed out that **Gladys Leonard,** the medium who brought in this communication from Myers, never visited his house. He had no idea what books were referred to, but on returning home found that in the exact position indicated, the test book was George Eliot's *Middlemarch.* On the first line at the top of page 78 were the words: "Ay, ay. I remember—you'll see I've remembered 'em all." The quotation was singularly appropriate, because much of Barrett's work since Myers passed over had been concerned with the question of survival after death and whether the memories of friends on earth continued with the discarnate.

But the most remarkable part of the test was yet to be discovered. Unknown to Barrett, the maid, when in dusting the bookshelves, replaced two of Eliot's novels by two volumes of Dr. Tyndall's books, namely, his *Heat and Sound,* which were found exactly in the position indicated. In his youth Barrett was for some years Tyndall's assistant, and these books were written during that time.

By what process does the discarnate intelligence find a relevant passage in closed books? One of the preliminary statements that Thomas received from his father was that he "sensed the appropriate spirit of the passage rather than the letters composing it." After 18 months he appeared to acquire a power of occasionally seeing the words by some sort of clairvoyance. Giving the page number is one of the greatest difficulties. The impression left on Thomas's mind was that when a page had been fixed upon as containing a thought suitable for the test, the operator counted the pages between that and the beginning. He usually started where the flow of thought began and when it ceased and recommenced higher up he concluded that he passed from the bottom of one page to the top of another. This was how they computed the number of pages between the beginning and the passage fixed upon for the test. When verifying, one usually counted from the beginning of the printed matter, disregarding fly-leaves and the printer's numbering.

The experiments were just as successful when a sealed book was used, which was deposited by a friend in Thomas's house;

with an unseen bookshelf; with a parcel in which an antiquarian at random packed in some books and which was unopened; and with books placed in the dark in an iron deed-box.

If these results are to be explained by the medium's supernormal powers, she has to be endowed, as Thomas points out, with such a degree of **clairvoyance** as would permit the making of minute observations in distant places and retaining a memory of things seen there; with ability to extract the general meaning from printed pages in distant houses, despite the fact that the books concerned are not open at the time; with ability to obtain knowledge of happenings in the sitter's home and private life relating both to the present and to the distant past; and with an intelligence which knows how to select from among our host of memories the suitable items for association with the book of passage, or conversely, of finding a suitable passage for the particular memory fished from the depths of our mind. Thomas's own conclusion was that the book tests were obtained by a spirit who gleaned impressions psychometrically and obtained an exact glimpse now and again by clairvoyance.

The underlying idea of book tests goes back to the experiments of **Sir William Crookes.** A lady was writing automatically with the **planchette** and he tried to devise a means for the exclusion of "unconscious cerebration." He asked the invisible intelligence if it could see the contents of the room, and on receiving an affirmative answer, Crookes randomly placed his finger on a copy of the *Times* (of London), which was on a table behind him, without looking at it, and asked the communicator to write down the word covered by his finger. The planchette wrote the word "However." He turned around and saw that this was the word covered by the tip of his finger. This experiment was first published in January 1874 in the *Quarterly Journal of Science.*

The first plain book tests were recorded by **Stainton Moses.** He wrote automatically, under the dictation of "Rector": "Go to the book case and take the last book but one on the second shelf, look at the last paragraph on page 94, and you will find this sentence. . . ." The sentence was found as indicated. The experiment was repeated a number of times.

Of other mediums, **William Eglinton** was particularly successful in direct-writing book tests. Many cases are described in John S. Farmer's *Twixt Two Worlds* (1886). The page and line were selected by tossing coins and reading the last numbers of the dates. In some cases they were still further complicated by prescribing the use of colored chalk in a set order of the words. Book tests combined with incidents of **xenoglossia** are described in Judge Ludwig Dahl's *We Are Here,* published in 1931. The Norwegian judge wrote of the mediumship of his daughter, Ingeborg, and described how her two (deceased) brothers "were represented as going into another room and reading aloud passages from a book still on the shelves, the number of which was selected by one of the sitters—the medium successfully repeating or transmitting what they read in a foreign language and far beyond her comprehension."

Mrs. Henry Sidgwick, in her study of the problem of books tests in *Proceedings* of the **Society for Psychical Research** (April 1921), arrived at the conclusion, "On the whole, I think, the evidence before us does constitute a reasonable *prima facie* case for belief in the perception of external things not known to any one present, but known to someone somewhere."

Sources:

Baird, Alexander T. *One Hundred Cases for Survival after Death.* New York: Bernard Ackerman, 1944.

Besterman, Theodore. *Collected Papers on the Paranormal.* New York: Garrett/Helix, 1968.

Smith, Susy. *The Mediumship of Mrs. Leonard.* New Hyde Park, N.Y.: University Books, 1964.

Thomas, C. Drayton. *Some New Evidence for Human Survival.* London: Collins, 1922.

Booth, Gotthard (1899– ?)

Born May 26, 1899 in Nuremberg, Germany, Booth became a psychiatrist and moved to New York in 1935 to assume duties as a consultant at the General Theological Seminary, New York, and adviser to the Program in Psychiatry and Religion at Union Theological Seminary, New York. In the field of parapsychology he took a special interest in spontaneous psi phenomena occurring in psychotherapy, spiritual healing, and psi phenomena in climbing plants, on which he published numerous articles.

Borak (or **Al Borak**)

The animal brought by the angel Gabriel to convey the prophet Mahommad to the seventh heaven. The name means "the lightning" and Al Borak had the face of a man but the cheeks of a horse; its eyes were like jacinths, but as bright as stars; it had eagle's wings that glistened with radiant light; and it spoke with a human voice. It traveled at each step as far as the keenest sight could see, and it was one of the only ten animals (not of the race of men) received into paradise.

Borderieux, Carita (**Mrs. Pierre Borderieux**) (1874–1953)

Secretary to **Gabriel Delanne,** editor of *La Revue scientifique et morale spiritisme* and founder and editor of the review *Psychica* from 1921 until it ceased in 1940. She organized regular weekly meetings in Paris with speakers on **Spiritualism** and **parapsychology.** Such famous individuals as **Camille Flammarion,** Gabriel Delanne, **Juliette Bisson, Rene Warcollier, Leon Chevreuil, Robert Tocquet,** and **Maurice Maeterlinck** spoke at these meetings. Borderieux had a special interest in clairvoyance and so-called "thinking animals." She published a book on the subject, *Les Nouveaux Animaux pensants* (The New Thinking Animals), and also trained the dog "Zou," which was alleged to answer questions put to it telepathically. Borderieux died February 20, 1953.

Borderland (Magazine)

Quarterly magazine dealing with psychical research and Spiritualism founded by **William T. Stead** and published in Britain from July 1893 until October 1897. Stead was assisted editorially by **Ada Goodrich-Freer.** The title was suggested by the famous Spiritualist **J. J. Morse,** and the magazine's stated aim was "seeking the scientific verification of the life and immortality which were brought to light nineteen hundred years ago."

Borderland Library, The W. T. Stead

Founded by Estelle W. Stead in 1914, for the purpose of continuing the work of **Julia's Bureau,** organized to facilitate psychic communication with the afterlife. The president was Mrs. Bayley Worthington. The Stead Bureau closed in 1936.

Borderland Sciences Research Foundation

Organization founded in 1945 by Meade Layne as Borderland Sciences Research Associates, concerned with the "borderland" region between fantasy and reality, fields of parapsychology, the occult, psychic research, hypnosis, dowsing, radiesthesia, radionics, telepathy, and other phenomena. Layne showed a special concern with **flying saucers.** BSRA published many mimeographed bulletins, including *Flying Roll* and *Round Robin,* and the many flying saucer contactee writings of Riley Hansard Crabb.

Around 1960 the organization evolved into Borderland Sciences Research Foundation, Inc. It explores phenomena that orthodox science cannot or will not investigate, and it offers recognition, understanding, and encouragement to individuals who are having unusual experiences of the borderland type or are conducting research in the occult. The foundation maintains a library on occult science and related fields and publishes the *Journal of Borderland Research*, continuing and extending the subjects formerly covered by BSRA publications. The address of the foundation is: P.O. Box 429, Garberville, CA 95440.

Sources:

Crabb, Riley Hansard. *An Attempt at Cosmic Fellowship*. Vista, Calif.: Borderland Science Research Foundation, 1964.

Layne, Meade. *The Coming of the Guardians*. 5th ed. Vista, Calif.: Borderland Sciences Research Foundation, 1964.

———. *The Ether Ship Mystery*. San Diego, Calif.: Borderland Sciences Research Associates, 1950.

Borderline Magazine

Popular American occult magazine published from 1965 to 1966, edited by Shelly Lowenkopf and astrologer **Sydney Omarr.** Publication ceased after vol. 2, no. 2 (February 1966).

Borderline Science Investigation Group

Formed to investigate folklore, **UFOs,** ghosts, and fairy incidents in the Suffolk area of Britain. Currently publishing the magazine *Lantern*. Address: c/o I. Bunn, 3 Dunwich Way, Oulton Broad, Lowestoft, Suffolk, England.

Borri, Josephe-François (1627–1695)

An alchemical imposter of the seventeenth century who was born at Milan in 1627. In youth his conduct was so wayward that at last he was compelled to seek refuge in a church to escape the vengeance of those he had wronged. There he hid his delinquencies under the cloak of imposture and hypocrisy, and he pretended that God had chosen him to reform mankind and to reestablish God's reign below. He also claimed to be the champion of the papal power against all heretics and Protestants, and he wore a wondrous sword that he alleged had been given to him by Saint Michael.

Borri said that he had seen in heaven a luminous palm branch that was reserved for him. He uttered a number of heretical views, including that the Virgin was divine in nature, that she had conceived through inspiration, and that she was equal to her Son, with whom she was present in the Eucharist, that the Holy Spirit was incarnate in her, and that the second and third Persons of the Trinity were inferior to the Father. All of these views are rejected by the Roman Catholic Church.

According to some writers, Borri later proclaimed himself to be the Holy Spirit incarnate. In any case, he was arrested after the death of Innocent X by order of the Inquisition, and on January 3, 1661, he was condemned to be burned as a heretic. He succeeded in escaping to Germany, where he received money from Queen Christina, to whom he asserted his mastery of **alchemy** and his ability to manufacture the **Philosopher's stone.** He afterward fled to Copenhagen and hoped to sail to Turkey, but he was tracked to a small village nearby and arrested, along with a conspirator.

Borri was sent back to Rome, where he died in prison August 10, 1695. It is claimed that he was the author of *The Key of the Cabinet of the Chevalier Borri*, which bore the imprint of Geneva in 1681, a volume chiefly concerned with elementary spirits. In the nineteenth century, **Abbé de Villars** seems to have drawn upon this book for his work *Le Comte de Gabalis*. However, some commentators suggested that the Borri book is merely a faulty translation and expansion of de Villars's volume, complete with a false publication date to support its claim to priority.

Bors (or Bohors or Boort)

One of **King Arthur**'s knights. He was associated with Sir Galahad and Lancelot in their search for the Holy **Grail.** He is the hero of many magical adventures such as the following. During the quest for the Holy Grail, a damsel offers him her love, which he refuses; then she, with 12 other damsels, threatens to throw herself from a tower. Bors, though of a kindly disposition, thinks they had better lose their souls than his. They fall from the tower, Bors crosses himself, and the whole vanishes, being a deceit of the devil. After the quest is ended, Bors comes to Camelot, where he relates his adventures, which, it is said, were written down and kept in the Abbey of Salisbury.

Bose, Sir Jagadis Chunder (1858–1937)

An Indian scientist who pioneered research into plant physiology. He was born November 30, 1858, in the village of Rarikhal in Vikrampur, East Bengal, India, and educated at Calcutta and in England at Cambridge University. His accomplishments were recognized in his election as president of the Indian Science Congress in 1927 and his being named a member of the International Committee on Intellectual Cooperation of the League of Nations. He also received many honors from scientific communities in Europe.

Bose attempted to demonstrate that the gap between living and nonliving matter was less distinct than normally supposed, and he claimed that even stones had some rate of life related to that of living organisms. In 1901 he demonstrated to the Royal Society in Britain that the responses of metals to poison and other stimuli resembled muscular response in living organisms.

In his delicate experiments with plant physiology, Bose anticipated the work of contemporary experimenters like **Cleve Backster.** As early as 1903 the Royal Society, London, published in their *Philosophical Transactions* Bose's reports of experiments with plants from which he concluded that "all the characteristics of the responses exhibited by the animal tissues, were also found in those of the plant." Bose devised sensitive apparatus to demonstrate plant reactions, many of which resembled nervous responses in animal or human life, and he even measured the electrical forces released in the death-spasms of vegetables. In 1917 Bose was knighted for his many valuable services to science. He died November 23, 1937.

From 1950 on, some of his experiments with plant sensitivity were extended by Dr. T. C. N. Singh of the Department of Botany, Annamalai University, India, who claimed that plants responded measurably to music and to prayer.

Sources:

Bose, J. C. *Growth and Tropic Movements of Plants*. London/New York: Longmans, Green and Co., 1929.

———. *Motor Mechanisms of Plants*. London/New York: Longmans, Green and Co., 1928.

———. *The Nervous Mechanism of Plants*. London/New York: Longmans, Green and Co., 1926.

———. *The Physiology of the Ascent of Sap*. London/New York: Longmans, Green and Co., 1923.

———. *The Physiology of Photosynthesis*. London/New York: Longmans, Green and Co., 1924.

———. *Plant Autographs & Their Revelations*. Washington, 1915.

———. *Plant Response as a Means of Physiological Investigation*. London/New York: Longmans, Green and Co., 1906.

———. *Researches in Irritability of Plants*. London/New York: Longmans Green and Co., 1913.

———. *Response in the Living and Non-Living*. London/New York: Longmans, Green and Co., 1902.

Geddes, Patrick. *The Life and Work of Sir Jagadis C. Bose*. London/New York: Longmans, Green and Co., 1920.

Boston Society For Psychic Research

Founded in May 1925 by **Elwood Worcester, William McDougall, Lydia W. Allison,** and **Walter Franklin Prince.** Worcester, a distinguished Episcopal minister and founder of the healing movement in that church, served as the first president. Prince, having resigned as research officer of the **American Society for Psychical Research,** became the new society's research officer. Allison oversaw the publications program. The occasion for the break was the ASPR's strong advocacy of the mediumship of **Mina S. Crandon** ("Margery"). Under Prince's direction, the Boston Society carried on an active research program, the results of which were published in a set of books and a series of bulletins.

After the death of Walter Franklin Prince in 1934, the Boston SPR began to flounder, and because the issue that brought it into existence had faded in importance, it was formally reunited with the ASPR in 1941.

Sources:

Allison, Lydia W. *Leonard and Soule Experiments in Psychical Research.* Boston: Boston Society for Psychical Research, 1929.

Berger, Arthur S., and Joyce Berger. *The Encyclopedia of Parapsychology and Psychical Research.* New York: Paragon House, 1991.

Prince, Walter F. *The Case of Patience Worth: A Critical Study of Certain Unusual Phenomena.* Boston: Boston Society for Psychical Research, 1927.

———. *Noted Witnesses for Psychic Occurrences.* Boston: Boston Society for Psychical Research, 1928. Reprint, New Hyde Park, N.Y.: University Books, 1963.

Thomas, John F. *Beyond Normal Cognition.* Boston: Boston Society for Psychical Research, 1937.

———. *Case Studies Bearing on Survival.* Boston: Boston Society for Psychical Research, 1929.

Botanomancy

A method of **divination** by means of burning the branches of vervein and brier, upon which were carved the questions of the practitioner. Variant methods involved indications from scattering the leaves of vervein or heather in a high wind. (See also **halomancy**)

Bottazzi, Filippo (ca. 1907)

Professor of physiology and director of the Physiological Institute at the University of Naples and a member of the pioneer Italian psychic research organization, Societa di Studi Psichici, founded in 1901. Bottazzi held sittings with the famous medium **Eusapia Palladino** in 1907. The manifestations, witnessed in the presence of professors De Amicis, Scarpa, and Pansini, were controlled by instruments. Bottazzi became convinced of the reality of the physical phenomena and declared, "The certitude we have acquired is of the same order as that which we attain from the study of chemical, physical or physiological facts." Two years later, he published his findings in *Fenomeni Medianici.*

Bottle Imps

A class of German spirits similar in many ways to **familiars.** The following is a paraphrase of the prescription in an old manuscript in the Bodleian Library, Oxford, England (MS. Ashmole 1406), for the purpose of securing one of these fairies:

"First, take a broad square crystal or Venetian glass, about three inches in breadth and length. Lay it in the blood of a white hen on three Wednesdays or three Fridays. Then take it and wash it with holy water and fumigate it. Then take three hazel sticks a year old; take the bark off them; make them long enough to write on them the name of the fairy or spirit whom you may desire three times on each stick, which must be flat on one side. Bury them under some hill haunted by fairies on the Wednesday before you call her; and on the Friday following dig them out, and call her at eight, or three, or ten o'clock, which are good times for this purpose. In order to do so successfully one must be pure, and face toward the East. When you get her, tie her to the glass."

Bourru

French monkish apparition spoken of in many tales as that of an imaginary phantom which appears to the Parisians, walking the streets in the darkest hours of the night, and glancing in at the windows of timid folk—passing and repassing a number of times. Nurses used to frighten small children with the *Monk Bourru.* The origin of the specter is unknown.

Boursnell, Richard (1832–1909)

British spirit photographer who is supposed to have obtained psychic markings on his plates as early as 1851, but when accused by his partner of spoiling the plates, he stopped taking photographs himself until 40 years later. A repetition of the same annoyance then occurred. **W. T. Stead,** a journalist interested in psychic subjects, claimed that the markings were psychic and prevailed upon Boursnell to sit for spirit photographs. He was strikingly successful, and in 1903 the Spiritualists of London presented him with a signed testimonial and a purse of gold as a mark of their high esteem. A **spirit photography** exhibition of 100 chosen photographs was displayed in the rooms of the Psychological Society at Portman Square. Eighty-nine negatives taken by Boursnell in conjunction with S. W. Woolley between 1897–1907 were preserved at the **British College of Psychic Science.**

Like almost every person engaged in a form of **psychic photography,** Boursnell was accused of **fraud.** William Usborne Moore wrote in *Glimpses of the Next State* (1911) that he provided complete proof of a fraudulent production to the **London Spiritualist Alliance.** Duplicates, triplicates, and quadruplicates of Boursnell's spirit pictures were numerous. A tracing could be made from one form in one photograph to the form in another, and not the slightest difference in detail could be discovered. Nevertheless, Admiral Moore believed that Boursnell had genuine powers and was an excellent clairvoyant, for Boursnell repeatedly described the spirit forms before he made an exposure, and the extra on the plate completely corresponded with his description. However, this is hardly satisfactory as proof, since Boursnell could have been describing extra spirit forms already prepared.

Bowditch, H(enry) P(ickering) (1840–1911)

Physiologist who studied in Europe under Claude Bernard and **Jean Charcot.** He had an outstanding career as a professor of physiology at Harvard University Medical School and served from 1883 to 1893 as the school's dean. He also became a founding member of the **Society for Psychical Research,** London, and a friend of **William James** and **Richard Hodgson.**

Bowditch was born April 4, 1840, in Boston, Massachusetts, and studied at Harvard University (B.A., 1861; M.A., 1866; M.D., 1868). His education was interrupted by the Civil War, during which he rose to the rank of major with the Massachusetts Volunteer Cavalry (1861–65). He contributed many papers to medical and scholarly journals and published *Hints for Teachers of Physiology* (1899; 1904).

Boxhorn, Mark Zuerius (1612–1653)

A celebrated Dutch historian and philologist born at Bergen-op-Zoom. His *Oratio de Somniis* (Treatise on Dreams) (Leyden, 1639) is of great rarity.

Bozzano, Ernesto (1862–1943)

The dean of Italian psychic researchers and Spiritualists during the formative years of psychic research. His attention was first directed to psychic phenomena in 1891 by Prof. Theodore Ribot, who forwarded to him the first number of the *Annales des Sciences Psychique.* He accompanied Profs. **Enrico Morselli** and Porro at many sittings with **Eusapia Palladino** and ended by accepting the spiritualistic hypothesis and by becoming a most prolific writer on psychic subjects. He wrote over two dozen books and contributed, for a period of 30 years, hundreds of articles to the *Luce e Ombra* and the *Revue spirite.* His psychic library at Savona was believed to be unique.

He summarized his belief:

"Whoever, instead of losing himself in idle discussions, undertakes systematic and deep researches in metaphysical phenomena, and who perseveres in them for long years, accumulating immense material in happenings and applying to these the methods of scientific inquiry, must, without fail, end by convincing himself that metaphysical phenomena constitute an admirable assemblage of proofs, all converging as to a centre toward the rigorously scientific demonstration of the existence and of the survival of the Spirit. This is my firm conviction, and I do not doubt that time will show that I am right."

Having accepted the Spiritualist explanation of mediumship, Bozzano was looked upon by his English contemporaries as much too uncritical. In 1930 **Theodore Besterman** wrote a scathing criticism of Bozzano's reports of sittings in his home. (Besterman's article led Spiritualist **Sir Arthur Conan Doyle** to resign from the **Society for Psychical Research.**) In retrospect, however, his methodology of gathering numerous reports of sittings and subjecting them to comparative analysis has been more fully understood and appreciated.

Bozzano's pioneer researches have not been fully recognized outside Europe, because most of his many books have not been translated into English. Among the few available to English-speaking readers are *Animism and Spiritism* (1932), *Polyglot Mediumship* (1932), and *Discarnate Influence in Human Life* (1938). Bozzano also contributed a preface and articles to *Modern Psychic Mysteries* by Gwendolyn K. Hack (1929).

Sources:

Alvarado, C. S. "The Life and Work of an Italian Psychical Researcher; A Review of Ernesto Bozzano: La Vite a l'Opera by Giòvanni Iannuzzo." *Journal* of the American Society for Psychical Research 81 (1987): 37.

Berger, Arthur S., and Joyce Berger. *The Encyclopedia of Parapsychology and Psychical Research.* New York: Paragon House, 1991.

Bozzano, Ernesto. *Polyglot Mediumship.* London: Rider, 1932.

Bracesco, Giovanni (ca. 1550)

A physician, prior, and alchemist of Brescia, Italy, who flourished in the sixteenth century. He gave much study to the Hermetic philosophy, and commented upon the work of the Arab alchemist **Geber.** His publications include *The Tree of Life,* a dissertation upon the uses of the **Philosopher's stone** in medicine, published in Rome in 1542.

Bradlaugh, Charles (1833–1891)

A prominent member of the Committee of the **London Dialectical Society** who was appointed in 1869 to investigate the alleged phenomena of **Spiritualism.** He and Dr. James Edmunds were among those who served on subcommittee No. 5, which held séances with the celebrated medium **Daniel D. Home** at which the phenomena were not all satisfactory. Bradlaugh and Edmunds therefore signed a minority report, containing a careful and critical treatment of the evidence. The *Report on Spiritualism of the Committee of the London Dialectical Society,* first published in London in 1871 and reissued in 1873, is something of a landmark in the development of enlightened interest in Spiritualism and psychical phenomena, and in standards of evidence.

Bradlaugh's association with the investigation of Spiritualist phenomena is noteworthy because of his reputation as a freethinker and atheist. His associate in the cause of **Freethought** and birth control was **Annie Besant,** who later became the president of the **Theosophical Society.**

Born September 26, 1833, Bradlaugh early on became a disciple of Richard Carlile. By 1853 Bradlaugh was a lawyer's clerk and began to lecture and write in the cause of freethought under the name "Iconoclast." From 1860 onward he published the *National Reformer,* which the government prosecuted for alleged sedition and blasphemy. In 1874 Besant became co-editor of the paper. The Bristol publisher of Bradlaugh's *Fruits of Philosophy* (concerned with birth control) was prosecuted in 1876 for indecency, and the pamphlet was suppressed. However, Bradlaugh and Besant boldly republished it in the cause of liberty of thought and were both convicted and sentenced, although the indictment was ultimately quashed on a technicality.

From 1885 onward Besant moved away from Bradlaugh and his ideas into socialism and labor agitation and, as a pupil of **Helena Petrovna Blavatsky,** into Theosophy.

Bradlaugh was elected to Parliament as an advanced radical in 1880 but was unseated after refusing to take the Parliamentary oath. He was successively unseated and reelected, until he eventually took his seat in 1886. Arrogant, dogmatic, but courageous in the cause of freedom of thought and speech, he was a great natural leader in the radical causes of his time. He died January 30, 1891.

Sources:

Autobiography of Mr. Bradlaugh: A Page of His Life. London: Watts, 1873.

Besant, Annie. *Charles Bradlaugh: A Character Sketch.* Adyar, Madras, India: Theosophical Publishing House, 1941.

Bonner, Hypatia Bradlaugh, and J. M. Robertson. *Charles Bradlaugh: His Life and Work.* London, 1898.

Chandrasekhar, Sripati. *"A Dirty Filthy Book."* Berkeley: University of California Press, 1981.

Manvell, Roger. *The Trial of Annie Besant and Charles Bradlaugh.* London: Elek/Pemberton, 1976.

Bradley, Donald A. (1925–1974)

Early scientific researcher in **astrology.** Bradley was born in Nebraska on May 16, 1925. He emerged as a professional astrologer in the years immediately after World War II. He is most noted as an advocate of the fixed, or sidereal, zodiac, which had been championed by Irish astrologer **Cyril Fagan** in a 1950 book, *Zodiacs Old and New.* The argument over the sidereal zodiac was basically about the adjustment of the horoscope chart to reflect the "procession of the equinoxes." The tropical, or moving, zodiac begins each year at the point where the sun is located at the spring equinox. However, that position changes slightly each year. Thus the divisions of the zodiac no longer reflect the actual position of the constellations in the heavens. The sidereal zodiac retains the actual position of the 12 signs.

Had Bradley merely been a champion of Fagan's unfashionable ideas, he would not be remembered today. However, he became the director of the Llewellyn Foundation for Astrological Research and in the later 1940s conducted statistical studies that anticipated the work of Françoise and **Michel Gauquelin.** Most notable was the astrological analysis of 2,492 clergymen. His research was published in a series of publications beginning in 1950.

In his later years Bradley wrote several books under the name Garth Allen. He eventually became the editor of *American Astrology,* a position he held at the time of his death from cancer in Tucson, Arizona, on April 25, 1974.

Sources:

Allen, Garth [Donald Bradley]. *Taking the Kid Gloves Off Astrology.* Tucson, Ariz.: Clancy Publications, 1975.

Bradley, Donald A. *Picking Winners.* St. Paul, Minn.: Llewellyn Publications, 1954.

———. *Profession and Birthdate.* Los Angeles: Llewellyn Publications, 1950.

———. *Stock Market Predictions.* Los Angeles: Llewellyn Foundation for Astrological Research, 1950.

Holden, James H., and Robert A. Hughes. *Astrological Pioneers of America.* Tempe, Ariz.: American Federation of Astrologers, 1988.

Bradley, H(erbert) Dennis (1878–1934)

British author who wrote in support of **Spiritualism** and psychic phenomena. He was also a **direct voice** medium, an ability he claimed he developed after his experiences with the medium **George Valiantine** in America.

The story of his first sittings and Valiantine's first visit to England is told in Bradley's book, *Towards the Stars* (1924). His second volume, *The Wisdom of the Gods* (1925), narrates Valiantine's second visit and gives an account of the author's own séances, at which many prominent people attended. He was approached by the **Society for Psychical Research** (SPR; London) for test sittings, but, on the advice of his controls, he refused. Later Bradley declared open enmity to the SPR, resigned his membership, and in March 1931 issued a pamphlet of indictment.

Bradley was the greatest propagandist and champion of Valiantine's mediumship. He cleared the medium of three exposure charges, only to launch the most serious accusation himself in *And After,* published in October 1931. As a result, R. Sproull took action for libel against the author, obtained a judgment with £500 damages, and the book was withdrawn after July 1932. By now, Bradley's own enthusiasm had considerably abated. In an interview to the London*Daily Express* on October 8, 1931, he declared that the general tendency of Spiritualism in its present public form was toward evil, that as a religion it was a farce, and that, nevertheless, "genuine phenomena do occur and genuine communication with spirit entities is, in certain cases, possible and practicable." Bradley died November 20, 1934.

Bragadini, Mark Antony (d. 1595)

A sixteenth-century alchemist of Venice, who was beheaded in 1595 because he boasted he had made gold from a recipe that he had received from a demon. He was tried at Munich, by order of Duke William II. Two black dogs that accompanied him were also arrested, charged with being **familiars,** and duly tried. They were shot with an arquebuse (portable "hook-gun") in the public square.

Brahan Seer, The

Sixteenth- or seventeenth-century Scottish seer named Coinneach Odhar (Kenneth Mackenzie). Although Coinneach Odhar is still spoken of and believed in as a seer throughout the Highlands of Scotland, and especially in the county of Ross and Cromarty, his reputation is of comparatively recent growth.

The first literary reference to him was made by Hugh Miller in his *Scenes and Legends of the North of Scotland* (1834). About half a century later, a collection of the seer's predictions was published by Alexander Mackenzie of Inverness, the author of several clan histories. Many of these alleged foretellings are of a trivial character. The most important prophecies attributed to Coinneach (Kenneth) are those that refer to the house of Seaforth Mackenzies.

One, which dates to the middle of the seventeenth century, foretold that the last of the Seaforths would be deaf. It was uttered at Brahan Castle, the chief seat of the Seaforths, near Dingwall, after the seer had been condemned to death by Lady Seaforth for some offensive remark. He declared to her ladyship that he would go to heaven, but she would never reach it. As a sign of this he declared that when he was burned, a raven and a dove would hasten toward his ashes. If the dove was the first to arrive it would be proved his hope was well founded.

Notably, the same legend is attached to the memory of **Michael Scott.** According to tradition, Kenneth was burned on Chanonry Point, near Fortrose, although no record survives of this event.

The first authentic evidence regarding the alleged seer was unearthed by William M. Mackenzie, editor of *Barbour's Bruce,* who found among the Scottish parliamentary records of the sixteenth century an order, which was sent to the Ross-shire authorities, to prosecute several wizards, including Coinneach Odhar. This was many years before there was a Seaforth.

It is quite probable that Kenneth was burned, but the legendary cause of the tale must have been a "filling in" of late tradition. Kenneth's memory apparently had attached to it many floating prophecies and sayings, including those attributed to Thomas and Michael Scott. The sayings of "True Thomas" were hawked through the Highlands in Gaelic chapbooks, and so strongly did the bard appeal to the imaginations of the eighteenth-century folk of Inverness, that they associate him with the Fairies and Fingalians (Fians) of the local fairy mound, Tom-na-hurich.

A Gaelic saying runs, "When the horn is blown, True Thomas will come forth." Thomas took the place of Fingal (Finn or Fionn) as chief of the "Seven Sleepers" in Tom-na-hurich, Inverness. At Cromarty, which was once destroyed by the sea, Thomas is alleged to have foretold that it would be thrice destroyed.

Of course, the Rhymer was never in Cromarty and probably knew nothing about it. As he supplanted Fingal and Inverness, so at Cromarty he appears to have supplanted some other legendary individual. The only authentic historical fact that remains is that Coinneach Odhar was a notorious wizard of mature years in the middle of the sixteenth century. Wizards were not necessarily seers. It is significant that no reference is made to Kenneth in the letters received by Pepys from Lord Reay regarding **second sight** in the seventeenth century, or in the account of Dr. Johnson's Highland tour, although the learned doctor investigated the problem sympathetically.

There is little support for the "Brahan Seer" legends, especially when it is found that Kenneth died before the Seaforth branch of the Mackenzies came into existence. Whoever foretold the fall of that house, it was certainly not the "notorious wizard" of the Scottish parliamentary records.

No doubt Kenneth made himself notorious by tyrannizing over a superstitious people in the sixteenth century and was remembered on that account. During his lifetime he must have been credited with many happenings supposed to have been caused by his spells. After his death his reputation for prophecy and piety snowballed through folklore, a not unfamiliar happening in the history of the Scottish Highlands, where Sir William Wallace, St. Patrick, St. Bean, and others were reputed to have been giants who flung glaciated boulders from hilltop to hilltop across wide glens and lochs.

One interesting aspect of the claimed visionary powers of the Brahan Seer is that he was said to use a white or blue stone in which he saw distant or future events, as in **crystal gazing.**

Sources:

MacGregor, Alexander. *Highland Superstitions.* Eneas Mackay, 1901.

———. *The Prophecies of the Brahan Seer.* Inverness, 1896. Reprint, London: Constable, 1977.

Miller, Hugh. *Scenes and Legends in the North of Scotland.* Nimmo, 1834.

Sutherland, Elizabeth. *Ravens and Black Rain.* London: Constable, 1985.

Braid, James (1795?–1860)

Scottish surgeon who originated the word "hypnosis" following his investigations into the phenomena of **mesmerism.** He was born at Rylaw House, in Fifeshire, Scotland, about 1795. He was educated at the University of Edinburgh, apprenticed to a doctor in Leith, then became member of the Royal College of Surgeons, Edinburgh (M.R.C.S.E.). He became surgeon to coal miners in Lanarkshire, then practiced with a doctor in Dumfries. Here Braid assisted a man injured in a stagecoach accident who persuaded him to move to Manchester, where Braid distinguished himself for his medical skill.

In 1841 he attended a lecture on **animal magnetism** given by Charles Lafontaine. Braid began his own experiments becuse he suspected that the subject was illusory or a matter of collusion between operator and subject. He soon believed in the reality of the mesmeric state but concluded that it did not arise from any "magnetic influence" passing from operator to subject. Braid found that an abnormal condition of sleep or suggestibility could be induced by the subject concentrating the gaze on an inanimate object. He designated this condition "neuro-hypnotism," a term later shortened to **hypnotism.** He delivered his paper, "A Practical Essay on the Curative Agency of Neuro-hypnotism," to the British Association at Manchester on July 29, 1842. He used hypnotism to produce anesthesia in some of his surgical patients.

Braid's findings and his writings were translated into French and German. Braid died March 25, 1860, in Manchester.

Sources:

Braid, James. *Observations on J. C. Colquhoun's History of "Magic, Witchcraft, and Animal Magnetism."* Manchester, England: J. T. Parkes, 1852.

———. *Neurypnology: or, The Rationale of Nervous Sleep.* London: J. Churchill, 1843; 1899. New York: Arno Press, 1976.

———. *Observations on the Nature and Treatment of Certain Forms of Paralysis.* London: T. Richards, 1855.

———. *Observations on Trance; or, Human Hibernation.* London: J. Churchill 1850.

———. *The Physiology of Fascination, and the Critics Criticised.* Manchester, England: Grant and Co., 1855.

———. *The Power of the Mind Over the Body.* 1846.

Brain/Mind Bulletin See New Sense

Bram Stoker Club

In 1986 the **Bram Stoker Society** in Dublin, Ireland, reorganized as a club affiliated with the Philosophical Society of Trinity College, Dublin. Since **Bram Stoker,** the author of the novel *Dracula,* was at one time president of the Philosophical Society, the affiliation of the two societies seemed a natural fit.

The inauguration of the club occasioned the opening of the Bram Stoker Archives, which included the Leslie Shepard collection of Bram Stoker first editions, autographed material, related literature, and other memorabilia. Housed in the Graduates Memorial Building at Trinity College, the archives were open to the general public. With the Philosophical Society unable to maintain proper security of the Leslie Shepard collection, the exhibit suffered some disorganization, so Shepard withdrew his materials in 1988, pending availability of a safer permanent venue.

Membership of the Bram Stoker Club, which is open to the general public, involves associate membership of the Philosophical Society. Members receive the club's newsletters and may participate in club activities, including lectures on themes related to Bram Stoker and Irish supernatural literature, the showing of rare Gothic films, and the promoting of public recognition of Bram Stoker and his work.

After the disruption concerning the archives, the Bram Stoker Society reemerged as the parent body of the Bram Stoker Club. The club may be contacted c/o David Lass, Hon. Secretary, Regent House, Trinity College, Dublin 2, Ireland.

Bram Stoker Society, The

An organization to encourage the study, appreciation, and presentation of the work of **Bram Stoker** in his own country, to maintain friendly relations with the **Dracula Society** and similar organizations on matters of common interest, to facilitate research into the Irish associations of the Stoker family, to advise or promote tourist visits to locales associated with Bram Stoker and other Gothic novelists, to campaign for plaques to be placed on Irish sites associated with the Stoker family, to plan social events (such as lectures, film shows, and discussions) connected with Bram Stoker and related Irish authors, and to press for the establishment of a permanent Bram Stoker Museum in Dublin. The society was founded in 1980 by Leslie Shepard, the current chairman. Shepard is the editor of *The Dracula Book of Great Vampire Stories.*

In 1983, through the efforts of the society, the Dublin Tourist Board erected a plaque at No. 30 Kildare Street, Dublin, which was Bram Stoker's first independent address in 1871 after the birthplace at Fairview, Dublin, was sold. The unveiling was performed by Ann Stoker, granddaughter of the novelist; Ivan Stoker-Dixon, Stoker's grandnephew, also attended. In honor of the occasion, the National Library, Kildare Street, Dublin, opened an exhibition of Bram Stoker books and other materials.

The society suspended its independent status in 1986 and reorganized as the **Bram Stoker Club** of the Philosophical Society, Trinity College, Dublin, Ireland. Since Bram Stoker had himself served as president of the Philosophical Society at Trinity College, the affiliation seemed appropriate and was marked by the inauguration of the Bram Stoker Archives at Trinity College. This exhibition in the Graduates Memorial Building displayed the Leslie Shepard collection of Bram Stoker first editions, autographed material, related literature, and other memorabilia and was open to the general public.

It was intended to be a permanent exhibition, but the Philosophical Society was unable to provide proper security, and after the collection suffered some disorganization, it was withdrawn by Leslie Shepard, pending the availability of a safer permanent venue.

The Bram Stoker Society then reemerged as the parent body to the Bram Stoker Club. Since 1991 the society has sponsored the Bram Stoker International Summer School for a weekend each June. The school is held at Clontarf, Dublin, near Stoker's birthplace. The society may be contacted c/o David Lass, Hon. Secretary, Regent House, Trinity College, Dublin 2, Ireland. It publishes a monthly newsletter.

Sources:

Shepard, Les. *The Dracula Book of Great Vampire Stories.* New York: Citadel Press, 1981.

Bray, Charles (1811–1884)

British philosopher and author of *The Philosophy of Necessity* (1841). He also wrote several volumes touching on Spiritualist/occult themes. In *On Force, its Mental and Moral Correlates; and on that which is Supposed to Underlie All Phenomena; with Speculations on Spiritualism, and other Abnormal Conditions of Mind* (1866), Bray postulated that the force which produced the phenomena of Spiritualism is "an emanation from all brains, the medium increasing its density so as to allow others present to come into communion with it; and the intelligence new to every one present is that of some brain in the distance acting through this source upon the mind of the medium, or others of the circle." He also spoke of "a mental or thought atmosphere the result of cerebration, but devoid of consciousness till it becomes reflected in our own organisations." In *The Science of Man* (1868), he dealt with the occult powers of man.

BRAZIL

Brazil has always been a vast melting-pot of various Spiritist and psychic traditions, from the shamanistic magic of the original Tupi Indians, to the mixture of the beliefs of many different African tribes brought to Brazil as slaves by Portuguese settlers, to the French **Spiritism** that developed from circulation of the works of **Allan Kardec** in the nineteenth century.

Through the twentieth century, there have been two main strands of occult religion in Brazil: the magical Afro-Brazilian groups, **Umbanda** and **Macumba,** both analogous to Haitian **voodoo,** and Kardec-style Spiritism. Both have possession by spirits as central to their practice. Brazil is officially a Roman Catholic country, but it is estimated that there are some four million people following these various alternative religions, many regarding themselves also at least as nominal Catholics. The complex interchange of religious and cultural traditions over the centuries makes precise distinctions difficult, since many nominally non-Christian blacks incorporate the figure of Jesus into tribal magic, while many Christians have fused tribal magic with Catholicism.

One of the most striking developments of the last few decades has been the emergence of a form of **psychic surgery** in which it is claimed that psychic healers without medical training perform surgical operations, sometimes with their bare hands, sometimes with such primitive instruments as an old penknife. The wounds, it is claimed, are paranormally closed and healed. Two of the most famous Brazilian psychic surgeons are **Edivaldo Oliveira Silva** and **Jose Arigó,** who performed thousands of operations. Although psychic surgery remains a controversial subject and there have been accusations of **fraud,** there is also strong evidence of genuine operations, endorsed by competent American and European investigators.

Psychic healing has flourished in Brazil, in spite of the fact that both the Roman Catholic Church and the medical society have brought lawsuits for witchcraft or for illegal practice of medicine. Many high officials believe in the efficacy of such healing, a fact illustrated by former Brazilian president Juscelino Kubitschek's bringing his daughter to Arigó for psychic healing. Arigó has also successfully treated statesmen, lawyers, scientists, and doctors from many countries.

In 1939, the São Paulo State Spiritist Federation was founded to provide information and assistance to those in need. It has 200 unpaid volunteers and deals with some 1000 individuals daily. In 1963, Hernani Guimàraes Andrade, a São Paulo engineer and civil servant, founded the Brazilian Institute for Psycho-Biophysical Research. Since then, the institute has collected many case histories, conducted research, and published theoretical papers. Unfortunately most of Andrade's writings have yet to be translated into English. Andrade was joined by Waldo Vieira, who concentrated his study on **out-of-the-body travel.** However, on the whole, parapsychological studies have not prospered in Brazil, in spite of the widespread acceptance of religions that make paranormal claims.

Sources:

Andrade, Hernani Guimàraes. *A material psi.* Matao: Clarim, 1972.

———. *Novos rumos à experimentacao espiritica.* São Paulo: Livraria Batuira, 1960.

———. *Parapsicologia experimental.* São Paulo: Calvario, 1967.

———. *A teorià corpuscular do espirito.* São Paulo: The Author, 1958.

Fuller, John G. *Arigó, Surgeon of the Rusty Knife.* New York: Thomas Y. Crowell, 1972. Reprint, London: Panther, 1975.

Kardec, Allan [H. L. D. Rivail]. *The Book of Spirits.* N.p., 1893.

Langguth, A. J. *Macumba: White & Black Magic in Brazil.* New York: Harper and Row, 1975.

McGregor, Pedro. *Moon and Two Mountains.* London, 1966.

Playfair, Guy Lyon. *The Flying Cow.* London, 1975. Reprinted as *The Unknown Power.* New York: Pocket Books, 1975.

St. Clair, David. *Drum and Candle.* Garden City, N.Y.: Doubleday, 1971.

Breathing

Traditional **yoga** practice is associated with mystical and psychic powers developed through special breathing techniques known as *pranayama.* According to Hindu teaching, there is a subtle vitality known as *prana* in the air that we breath, and management of prana has a special effect on the human organism in energizing the *chakras,* or subtle centers in the body associated with spiritual development and psychic side effects. Pranayama involves special techniques of breathing alternately with right and left nostrils, with a special period of retention. Other exercises involve rapid breathing.

In some instances, **levitation** is said to be achieved by breathing exercises. **Baron Schrenck-Notzing** recorded the case of a young man who thus levitated his own body 27 times. In his book *Mysterious Psychic Forces* (1907), **Camille Flammarion** stated: "The breathing seems to have a very great influence. In the way things take place it seems as if the sitters released by breathing an amount of motor energy comparable to that which they release when rapidly moving their limbs. There is something in this [that is] very curious and difficult to explain."

Hereward Carrington and other psychic researchers have often drawn attention to the so-called "lifting game," in which four persons lift a fifth by their fingertips, each of the four rapidly inhaling and exhaling in unison, then lifting the subject by a fingertip under each arm and leg. Sometimes the subject is seated on a chair to facilitate the positioning of fingertips.

Carrington tried the experiment on the platform of a large self-registering scale, and in *The Story of Psychic Science* (1930) commented:

"On the first lift the recorder stated that the needle on the dial had fallen to 660 lbs. (the combined weight was found previously to be 712 lbs.), a loss of 52 lbs. On the second lift there was an apparent loss of 52 lbs.; on the third lift of 60 lbs.; on the fourth lift of 60 lbs.; and on the fifth lift of 60 lbs. No gain of weight was at any time recorded (owing to the muscular exertion), invariably a loss, which, however, slowly returned to normal as the subject was held for some considerable time in the air. I have no theory to offer as to these observations, which I cannot fully explain."

However, modern commentators suggest that the apparent ease with which the subject is lifted by fingertips is related to the distribution of weight on several points, rather like the principle involved when a fakir lies on a bed of sharp nails without injuring himself. Carrington's method of measuring weight loss was too simple a procedure, ignoring such factors as sudden thrust exerted by the lifters.

The association of pranayama with levitation has been revived more recently by the special "siddhi" program of Maharishi Mahesh Yogi, whose system derives from such standard Hindu texts as the Yoga-Sutras of Patanjali. Bhagwan Shree Rajneesh, another modern Indian religious leader, also prescribed special breathing techniques for his followers, although these did not appear to have similar spectacular psychic results. They were more reminiscent of the techniques of the Western mystic Gurdjieff, whose followers often demonstrated remarkable physical control through special breathing.

Breathing techniques have effects on the human organism and contribute to some yogic feats, and also by the related systems of Japanese **martial arts,** especially kung-fu, where it is claimed that a subtle energy named **ch'i** (analagous to the Hindu prana) is accumulated, amplified, and directed by willpower to specific parts of the body, developing astonishing strength and resilience. This process is normally preceded by a sudden exhalation of breath, sometimes accompanied by a shout or yell. The intake of breath that follows appears to result in hyperventilation of the system, generating vitality that can be directed to hands, feet, or other parts of the body. Practitioners demonstrate the ability to break bricks, tiles, or heavy planks of wood with a bare hand.

It is interesting to note that special techniques of breathing associated with mystical and psychic development are common to many Asian countries, from India, to Tibet, China, and Japan. These all postulate that a subtle principle exists in the air, and a system of management of that principle occurs in the subtle centers of the body. Of course, traditional Indian yoga teachings present psychic feats as merely side effects of spiritual development, to be discarded for the higher goals of **mysticism,** and that advanced pranayama techniques, as well as the special physical positions of **hatha yoga,** should be preceded by strict preliminary practices of *yama* and *niyama* (moral observances and ethical restraints). Pranayama is said to begin spontaneously with the perfection of hatha yoga positions, and proper breathing facilitates the advanced techniques. Also with the development of pranayama, a mystical force known as **kundalini** is aroused and led from the lowest chakras to the highest, culminating in a mystical center in the head, conferring higher consciousness.

Sources:

Bernard, Theos. *Hatha Yoga.* London: Rider, 1950. Reprint, New York: Samuel Weiser, 1970.

Chia, Mantak. *Awaken Healing Energy through the Tao.* New York: Aurora Press, 1983.

Dvivedi, M. N., trans. *The Yoga-Sutras of Patanjali.* London: Theosophical Publishing House, 1890.

Gopi Krishna. *The Secret of Yoga.* New York: Harper & Row, 1972.

Huard, Pierre, and Ming Wong. *Oriental Methods of Mental and Physical Fitness: The Complete Book of Meditation, Kinesitherapy, and Martial Arts in China, India, and Japan.* New York: Funk & Wagnalls, 1971.

Kuvalayananda, Swami. *Pranayama.* Bombay, India: Popular Prakashan, 1931.

Luk, Charles. *The Secrets of Chinese Meditation.* London: Rider, 1964.

———. *Taoist Yoga: Alchemy and Immortality.* London: Rider, 1970.

Prasad, Rama. *The Science of Breath and the Philosophy of the Tattvas, Translated from the Sanskrit, with Introductory and Explanatory Essays on Nature's Finer Forces.* London: Theosophical Publishing House, 1889.

Ramacharaka, Yogi [William W. Atkinson]. *The Hindu-Yogi Sciences of Breath.* Chicago: Yogi Publication Society, 1904.

Van Lysebeth, Andre. *Pranayama.* London: Mandala Books, 1979.

Vishnudevananda, Swami. *The Complete Illustrated Book of Yoga.* New York: Julian Press, 1960. Reprint, New York: Pocket Books, 1971.

Volin, Michael, and Nancy Phelan. *Yoga Breathing.* N.p.: Information Inc., 1966.

Brédif, C. (ca. nineteenth century)

Nineteenth-century French medium who was investigated by the famous astronomer **Camille Flammarion,** who reported that Brédif produced strange apparitions.

Brewster, Sir David (1781–1868)

Famous nineteenth-century scientist whose brief investigation of **Spiritualism** in 1855 led to bitter public acrimony. The medium was **D. D. Home,** to whom Brewster was introduced by Lord Brougham. They attended a séance in Cox's Hotel in Jermyn Street in London's West End, and reportedly both were deeply impressed. Home subsequently wrote to a friend in America, describing the visit and stating that they were unable to account for the phenomena by natural means. The letter, published and commented upon in America, found its way into the London press. Sir David Brewster who, in the meantime, had had another séance at Ealing in the house of Mr. Rymer, a London solicitor, promptly wrote to the *Morning Advertiser,* forcefully disclaiming all belief in Spiritualism and ascribing all the phenomena to imposture. His letter ended: "I saw enough to satisfy myself that they could all be produced by human hands and feet."

A heated newspaper controversy arose. **Edward W. Cox,** sergeant-at-law, who was present at the séance, wrote to the *Morning Advertiser,* to contradict Brewster, and citing Brewster's expression of astonishment: "This upsets the philosophy of fifty years." When Brewster replied that he had not been allowed to look under the table, both Cox and the well-known author T. A. Trollope (brother of novelist Anthony Trollope) also present at the Ealing séance, contradicted him. Yet another statement, one by Benjamin Coleman, quoting Sir David Brewster's admission of the reality of the phenomena in private conversation, was published.

Brewster replied in an angry tone, gave a description of the sitting, and declared: "Rather than believe that spirits made the noise, I will conjecture that the raps were produced by Mr. Home's toes, and rather than believe that spirits raised the table, I will conjecture that it was done by the agency of Mr. Home's feet, which were always below it." He further said that the spirits were powerless above the table but were very active beneath a large round table with copious drapery, beneath which nobody was allowed to look. After describing how a handbell from the neighborhood of Mr. Home's feet came across and placed itself into his and afterward into Lord Brougham's hands, he concluded: "How these things were produced neither Lord Brougham nor I could say, but I conjecture that they may be produced by machinery attached to the lower extremities of Mr. Home."

Throughout this passionate controversy Lord Brougham preserved an inflexible silence. Brewster never appealed to him. D. D. Home, on the other hand, challenged Lord Brougham's testimony. This was half promised but not given. However, a conversation is recorded by Cox in his book *The Mechanism of Man* (1876), in which he claimed that Lord Brougham stated to him: "We were both perfectly satisfied at the time that it was no trick, and that some unknown power was in action." I said "Well, Brewster, what do you think of it?' and he said only 'There are more things in heaven and earth, Horatio, than are dreamt of in our philosophy.'" Lord Brougham also declared that Brewster never told him that he had changed his opinion. The only reason why he himself did not pursue the investigation was that he was then deeply immersed in experiments in optical science and did not have the necessary leisure.

The late earl of Dunraven, in his preface to the original private edition of Lord Adare's records on his experiences with D. D. Home, expressed the belief that Brewster acted out of fear of ridicule. He wrote: "He was present at two séances of Mr. Home's where he stated as is affirmed on the written testimony of persons present, his impression that the phenomena were most striking and startling, and he does not appear then to have expressed any doubt of their genuineness, but he afterwards did so in an offensive manner. I mention this circumstance because I was so struck with what Sir David Brewster—with whom I was well acquainted—had himself told me, that it materially influenced me in determining to examine thoroughly into the reality of the phenomena."

In Home's *Incidents in My Life* (1863), Home wrote that Brewster treated certain of his scientific contemporaries even worse than he treated Home, claiming the credit for other people's inventions. Brewster threatened a libel action but despite Home enlarging the evidence in the second edition of his book, Brewster never carried out his threat.

The final word in this public debate was uttered in 1869 when *The Home Life of Sir David Brewster* was published by his daughter, Mrs. Gordon. A note is printed from the private diary of the scientist, which narrated the phenomena he witnessed in company with Lord Brougham:

"Last of all I went with Lord Brougham to a séance of the new spirit-rapper, Mr. Home, a lad of twenty, the son of a brother of the late Earl Home. He lives in Cox's Hotel, Jermyn Street; and Mr. Cox, who knows Lord Brougham, wished him to have a séance and his Lordship invited me to accompany him in order to assist in finding out the trick. We four sat down at a moderately-sized table, the structure of which we were invited to examine. In a short time the table shuddered, and a tremulous motion ran up all our arms; at our bidding these motions ceased and returned. The most unaccountable rappings were produced in various parts of the table; and the table actually rose from the ground when no hand was upon it. A larger table was produced and exhibited similar movements. A small hand-bell was then laid down with its mouth on the carpet: and, after lying for some time, it actually rang when nothing could have touched it. The bell was then placed on the other side, still upon the carpet, and it came over to me and placed itself in my hand. It did the same to Lord Brougham. These were the principal experiments. We could give no explanation of them and could not conjecture how they could be produced by any kind of mechanism."

The version from Brewster's posthumous book conflicts with his letter to the *Morning Advertiser,* in which Sir David expressly stated that the bell did not ring and that the table "appeared" to rise. A detailed comparison of the two statements reveals many other discrepancies. The *Spectator* stated in its review of Home's book, "The hero of science does not acquit himself as we could wish or expect."

There is no doubt that Brewster came out of the affair badly. He was guilty of misrepresentation when he refused to stand by his original puzzlement at the séance, and thereby was criticized for later contradicting himself. What he actually exclaimed at the time was typical of the last ditch materialist unable to believe his own senses: "Spirit is the last thing I will give in to!"

Briah

In the **Kabala,** Briah is the third of the three stages of spirit progress, the three original ranks or classes. Men are called upon to proceed from the lower to the higher. In the Apocalypse Briah is represented as the feet of "the mighty angel with the face of the sun."

Briccriu

An Ulster chieftain surnamed "of the Poisoned Tongue," mentioned in the myth of Cuchulain, a medieval Irish romance. It is said that on one occasion he asked certain warriors to a feast and raised the question which of them was the greatest. Conall, Laery, and Cuchulain were selected, and a demon called "The Terrible" was requested to decide the point. He suggested that whoever could cut off his (The Terrible's) head today, and allow his own head to be cut off on the following day would be the most courageous, and therefore must deserve the title of champion. Cuchulain succeeded in beheading the devil, who immediately picked up his head and vanished. The next day he reappeared in his usual form in order to cut off Cuchulain's head. On his placing his head on the block, the demon told him to rise, and acknowledged that he was champion of Ireland.

Bridge of Souls

The superstition that the souls of the dead crossed to the other world by means of a bridge is widely disseminated. Rev. S. Baring-Gould stated in *A Book of Folklore* (1913):

"As peoples became more civilised and thought more deeply of the mystery of death, they conceived of a place where the souls lived on, and being puzzled to account for the rainbow, came to the conclusion that it was a bridge by means of which spirits mounted to their abode above the clouds. The Milky Way was called variously the Road of the Gods or the Road of Souls. Among the Norsemen, after Odin had constructed his heavenly palace, aided by the dwarfs, he reared the bridge Bifrost, which men call the rainbow, by which it could be reached. It is of three colours; that in the middle is red, and is of fire, to consume any unworthy souls that would venture up the bridge. In connection with this idea of a bridge uniting heaven and earth, up which souls ascended, arose the custom of persons constructing bridges for the good souls of their kinsfolk. On runic grave-stones in Denmark and Sweden we find such inscriptions as these: 'Nageilfr had this bridge built for Anund, his good son.' 'The mother built the bridge for her only son.' 'Holdfast had the bridge constructed for Hame, his father, who lived in Viby.' 'Holdfast had the road made for Igul and for Ura, his dear wife.' At Sundbystein, in the Uplands, is an inscription showing that three brothers and sisters erected a bridge over a ford for their father.

"The bridge as a means of passage for the soul from this earth to eternity must have been known also to the Ancients for in the cult of Demeter, the goddess of Death, at Eleusis, where her mysteries were gone through, in order to pass at once after death into Elyisium, there was an order of Bridge priestesses; and the goddess bore the name of the Lady of the Bridge. In Rome also the priest was a bridge-builder pontifex, as he undertook the charge of souls. In Austria and parts of Germany it is still supposed that children's souls are led up the rainbow to heaven. Both in England and among the Chinese it is regarded as a sin to point with the finger at the bow. With us no trace of the idea that it is a *Bridge of Souls* remains. Probably this was thought to be a heathen belief and was accordingly forbidden, for children in the North of England to this day when a rainbow appears, make a cross on the ground with a couple of twigs or straws, 'to cross out the bow.' The West Riding recipe for driving away a rainbow is: 'Make a cross of two sticks and lay four pebbles on it, one at each end.'" (See also **Brig of Dread**)

Brig of Dread, The

There is an old belief, alluded to by Sir Walter Scott, that the soul, on leaving the body, has to pass over the *brig of dread,* a bridge as narrow as a thread, crossing a great gulf. If the soul succeeds in passing it he enters heaven; if he falls off, he is lost. (See also **Bridge of Souls**)

Briggs, K(atharine) M(ary) (1898–1980)

British folklorist, critic, novelist, former president of the Folklore Society, London, and expert on folk tales and fairy lore. She is best remembered for her many books on the folklore of the British Isles. Born November 8, 1898, in Hampstead, London, she studied at Lansdowne House, Lady Margaret Hall, Oxford University (M.A., Ph.D.). For fifteen years, she headed an amateur touring company, produced plays in the air force, and wrote and produced plays locally in Perthshire and Oxfordshire. During World War I, she served in the Women's Auxiliary Air Force, then became a free-lance writer. She was a member of the Bibliographical Society, the Historical Association, the American Folklore Society, and the English Folkdance and Song Society. In 1969, she was awarded a D.Litt. by Oxford University.

Her *Dictionary of British Folktales in the English Language* is widely regarded as a monumental scholarly achievement; her various works on fairy lore also established her as a preeminent scholar in this field. However, in spite of her encyclopedic knowledge of fairy lore and her enthusiasm for the subject, she did not believe in the reality of fairy life, stating specifically: "This is not an attempt to prove that fairies are real. . . . I am agnostic on the subject."

Briggs died October 15, 1980, in Kent, England.

Sources:

Briggs, Katherine. *The Anatomy of Puck: An Examination of Fairy Beliefs among Shakespeare's Contemporaries and Successors.* London: Routledge & Paul, 1959.

———. *A Dictionary of British Folktales in the English Language.* 4 vols. Bloomington: Indiana University Press, 1970–71.

———. *An Encyclopedia of Fairies: Hobgoblins, Brownies, Bogies, and Other Supernatural Creatures.* New York: Pantheon Books, 1976.

———. *The Fairies in English Tradition and Literature.* 1967. Reprinted as *The Fairies in Tradition and Literature.* London: Routledge and Kegan Paul, 1967.

———. *Folktales of England.* Chicago: University of Chicago Press, 1965.

———. *The Personnel of Fairyland: A Short Account of the Fairy People of Great Britain for Those Who Tell Stories to Children.* 1953. Reprint. Detroit: Singing Tree Press, 1971.

Brimstone

Pliny (ca. 23–79 C.E.) stated that houses were formerly hallowed against evil spirits by the use of brimstone.

Brisin

An enchantress who figures in the Arthurian romance *Morte d'Arthur.* She played an important part in the annunciation of Galahad and the allurement of Lancelot. (See also **King Arthur**)

British & Irish Skeptic, The (Newsletter)

Newsletter issued by a group associated with CSICOP (the **Committee for Scientific Investigation of Claims of the Paranormal**). It is published bimonthly, and the first issue (January/February 1987) included notes on the **James Randi** exposure of faith healer Peter Popoff, Ireland's claimed phenomena of Marian apparitions at **Knock,** and moving **statues.** The newsletter is edited by Wendy M. Grossman, at One Queens Court, Queens Park, Monkstown, Co. Dublin, Republic of Ireland. The British committee of the Skeptics can be contacted through Michael Hutchinson, 10 Crescent View, Loughton, Essex, IG10 4PZ, England.

British College of Psychic Science

An institution founded in April 1920 in London by **Mr. and Mrs. Hewat McKenzie** to work on lines similar to the **Institut Métapsychique** in Paris. They spared neither time nor expense in their effort to collect evidence for genuine phenomena and to spread the knowledge by means of the college. After Mr. McKenzie's death in 1929, Mrs. McKenzie took charge, but in 1930 she relinquished her post, and **Mrs. Champion de Crespigny** was elected honorary principal.

From 1922 to 1939 the college published *Quarterly Transactions,* subsequently titled *Psychic Science* until 1945, after which it appeared briefly as *Experimental Metaphysics.* In December 1938 the college amalgamated with the **International Institute for Psychical Research,** becoming the Institute for Experimental Metaphysics. During World War II, the society languished and eventually closed in 1947, and its excellent library and records were dispersed or destroyed.

When McKenzie founded the college, the **London Spiritualist Alliance** was already in existence but McKenzie's college had broader aims in providing a center for information, advice, and guidance, where psychic mediums of good reputation could be consulted, and where scientific research into psychic phenomena could take place. After World War II the London Spiritualist Alliance broadened its own aims on similar lines to the college, and in 1955 reorganized under the new name of **College of Psychic Studies.**

British Journal of Psychical Research

Established in 1926 as the official organ of the **National Laboratory of Psychical Research** in London, England, the journal appeared every two months, replaced in the following year by *Proceedings* and later by Bulletins. No longer active.

British National Association of Spiritualists

A society formed in 1873 mainly through the instrumentality of Dawson Rogers to promote the interests of Spiritualism in Great Britain. The British National Association of Spiritualists (BNAS) numbered among its original vice-presidents and members of council the most prominent Spiritualists of the day—Benjamin Coleman, Mrs. Macdougall Gregory, Sir Charles Isham, Mr. Jacken, Dawson Rogers, Morell Theobald, Dr. Wyld, Dr. Stanhope Speer, and many others. Many eminent people of other countries joined the association as corresponding members.

In 1882 BNAS changed its name to the Central Association of Spiritualists. Among its committees was one for systematic research into the phenomena of Spiritualism, in which connection some interesting scientific experiments were made in 1878.

Early in 1882, conferences, which were held at the association's rooms and were presided over by **William Barrett,** resulted in the formation of the **Society for Psychical Research** (SPR). Many members of the SPR were recruited from the council of the BNAS, such as the Rev. **Stainton Moses,** Dr. George Wyld, Dawson Rogers, and Morell Theobald. The BNAS was at first associated with the *Spiritualist,* edited by W. H. Harrison, but in 1879 the reports of its proceedings were transferred to *Spiritual Notes,* a paper which, founded in the previous year, came to an end in 1881, as did the *Spiritualist.* In the latter year Dawson Rogers founded *Light,* with which the society was henceforth associated.

From the beginning, the BNAS held itself apart from religious and philosophical dogmatism and included among its members Spiritualists of all sects and opinions.

In 1884 the association reorganized as the **London Spiritualist Alliance.** The journal *Light* is now published by the **College of Psychic Studies,** London, which developed on similar lines to the former **British College of Psychic Science.**

Sources:

Doyle, Arthur Conan. *The History of Spiritualism.* New York: Charles H. Doran, 1926. Reprint, New York: Arno Press, 1975.

British Society of Dowsers

A long-established society of water-diviners (water-witchers) and people interested in **dowsing** and related skills. The society was formed to encourage the study of all matters connected with the perception of radiation by the human organism with or without an instrument (**divining-rod,** pendulum, etc.), and has issued its *Journal* since 1935, published quarterly from the society's present address: Sycamore Cottage, Tamley Lane, Hastingleigh, Ashford, Kent TN25 5HW, England.

British Spiritual Telegraph

An early Spiritualist newspaper, which was founded as the *Yorkshire Spiritual Telegraph* in April 1855 in Keighley and was renamed the *British Spiritual Telegraph* in 1857. It was first issued weekly, then monthly by W. Horsell until December 1859, when it was superseded by the *Spiritual Magazine,* published in London from 1860 to 1874.

British Spiritualists' Lyceum Union

Founded in Manchester in 1889, bearing the same relation to Spiritualist churches as the Sunday School Unions to the churches of other religious communities. It aimed at the intellectual, moral, and spiritual development of children along the lines of **Andrew Jackson Davis**'s vision of children in the Summerland. The BSLU encountered financial difficulties in 1940, and it eventually merged with the **Spiritualists' National Union** in 1948.

British UFO Research Association (BUFORA)

Originally founded in 1959 as the London UFO Research Organization, which issued a monthly mimeographed magazine *LUFORO Bulletin.* In 1962 LUFORO merged with seven other British UFO groups and incorporated as the British UFO Association, consolidated as BUFORA in 1964. It became legally constituted in 1975 as a nonprofit company, limited by guarantee, with the aims of in-depth research and investigation of UFO phenomena. BUFORA's membership was concentrated in London and the southeast of England, and in the mid-1970s one of the BUFORA investigators in northern England, Jenny Randles, created the Northern UFO Network.

BUFORA issues a bimonthly *BUFORA Bulletin* for members, promotes regular lectures, sponsors conferences, and has produced a detailed Investigator's Manual. It may be contacted c/o Pam Kennedy, 30 Vermont Rd., London SE19 3SR, England.

British UFO Society

Group in Warminster, England, concerned with **UFO**-related events in the Warminster district of England. The society publishes the monthly **Warminster UFO News.** Address: Preston House, Warminster, Wiltshire, England.

British Vampyre Society

A **vampire** interest organization; issues a newsletter. Address: Allen Gittens, 38 Westcroft, Chippenham, Wiltshire, SN14 0LY, England.

Brittain, Annie (ca. 1930)

British trance medium well known during the 1920s. **Sir Arthur Conan Doyle** sent many people to her anonymously and kept records of the reports, which showed a very high average of success. Her psychic gifts were noticed in early childhood, when she is said to have played with spirit children and occasionally fallen into trance.

Sources:

Doyle, Arthur Conan. *The History of Spiritualism.* New York: Charles H. Doran, 1926. Reprint, New York: Arno Press, 1975.

Britten, Emma Hardinge (1823–1899)

Inspirational speaker, medium, and early propagandist for **Spiritualism.** Born in the East End of London, Britten was the daughter of Capt. Floyd, a seafaring man, and she showed gifts as musician, singer, and elocutionist at an early age. At the age of 11 she was earning her living as a musical teacher. Under contract to a theatrical company in 1856, she went to America where, through the mediumship of Ada Hoyt (Mrs. Coan), she converted to Spiritualism, developed her own psychic powers, and sat publicly for the **Society for the Diffusion of Spiritual Knowledge** in New York. Her mediumistic gifts included automatic writing, psychometry, occasional healing, prophecy, and inspirational speaking, which disclosed great erudition. As was common at the time, she spoke extempore on a subject generally chosen by a committee from the audience.

In the early history of spirit return, Britten furnished one of the better attested cases. After the mail steamer *Pacific* sank in the high seas, a member of the crew possessed her body in trance and disclosed the facts of the tragedy. Britten was threatened with prosecution by the owners of the steamer when the story was made public, but it was found to be true.

Britten is best remembered today, not as a medium but as a spokesperson and advocate of Spiritualism, for which she traveled widely across North America and the British Empire. In Manchester, England, she founded and for five years edited *Two Worlds,* long a prominent Spiritualist magazine. Her two chronicles of emergent Spiritualism, *Modern American Spiritualism* (1870) and *Nineteenth-Century Miracles* (1884) became important sources for understanding the origin and spread of the movement worldwide. Among her other writings, *Ghost Land; or, Researches into the Mysteries of Occultism* (1876) and her translation and editing of the anonymous *Art Magic* (1875) were most important. She also for a time edited the American periodical *Western Star* (1872) and the British publication *Unseen Universe* (1892–93). Her early musical talent reemerged in a number of musical compositions and songs written under the name Ernest Reinhold.

Britten was also among the founders of the **Theosophical Society** in New York in 1875, but soon severed her connection with **Helena Petrovna Blavatsky.** Britten's life is told in a biography edited by her sister, Margaret Wilkinson.

She died in England October 2, 1899. The **Britten Memorial Institute and Library** and the **Britten Memorial Museum** were named in her honor.

Sources:

[Britten, Emma Hardinge.] *Art Magic.* Boston, 1875. Reprint, Chicago: Progressive Thinker Publishing House, 1898.

———. *Ghost Land; or, Researches into the Mysteries of Occultism.* Chicago: Progressive Thinker Publishing House, 1897.

———. *Modern American Spiritualism.* New York, 1870. Reprint, New Hyde Park, N.Y.: University Books, 1970.

———. *Nineteenth-Century Miracles.* New York: William Britten, 1884.

Britten Memorial Institute and Library

Originally founded in 1900 at 64A Bridge Street, Manchester, England, as "a school of prophets" for the training of mediums, an idea proposed by nineteenth-century Spiritualist writer **Emma Hardinge Britten.** A trust fund was raised by Mr. A. W. Orr with trustees **E. W. Oaten,** W. A. Herring, and E. A. Keeling. Its library had over 3,000 volumes, many from a collection donated by **Sir Arthur Conan Doyle.** The institute and library are no longer in operation.

Britten Memorial Museum

British museum devoted to exhibits relating to Spiritualism and psychic phenomena. Situated in the grounds of the **Arthur Findlay College,** it is administered by the **Spiritualists' National Union.** The name of the museum derives from the work of pioneer Spiritualist **Emma Hardinge Britten,** who was instrumental in the founding of the Spiritualists' National Federation of Great Britain (later the Spiritualists' National Union).

The museum contains over 1,000 exhibits, including diaries, posters, paintings, books, clothing, regalia, photographs, examples of automatic writing and slate writing, wax hands (formed in **materialization** séances), **apports,** paranormal paintings, and personal effect of famous Spiritualists. The address is Britten Memorial Museum, Britten House, Stansted Hall, Stansted, Mountfitchet, Essex, England.

Bro, Harmon Hartzell (1919–)

Professor of philosophy and religion and specialist in parapsychological aspects of religious life, including meditation, faith-healing, mystical experience, and conversion. He was born December 14, 1919, in Nanking, China. He studied at Williams College and the University of Chicago (B.A.); he pursued graduate education at St. Olaf College, Harvard Divinity School, and the University of Chicago Divinity School (Ph.D.). He was ordained a minister in the Christian Church (Disciples of Christ) in 1943.

Bro served as associate professor of religion and psychology, George Williams College, Chicago, Illinois (1949–55), and held various academic positions and developed experimental programs. He was W. Earl Ledden Associate Professor of Religion and director of Institute for Religious Education at Syracuse University, New York (1956–59) and director of the Institute for Research in Psychology and Religion (1960–65). He has written widely on psychological and pastoral counseling issues.

Bro's friendship with **Edgar Cayce** led to his long relationship with the **Association for Research and Enlightenment** (ARE). His doctoral thesis, *The Charisma of the Seer,* examined the life and work of Cayce. Bro has been a frequent speaker at the ARE and has written a number of books on the Cayce material, including *Edgar Cayce on Dreams* (1968), *Dreams in a Life of Prayer: The Approach of Edgar Cayce* (1970), *Edgar Cayce on Religion and Psychic Experience* (1970), and *A Seer Out of Season: The Life of Edgar Cayce* (1989).

Sources:

Bro, Harmon Hartzell. *Begin a New Life: The Approach of Edgar Cayce.* New York: Harper & Row, 1971.

———. *Dreams in a Life of Prayer: The Approach of Edgar Cayce.* New York: Paperback Library, 1970.

———. *Edgar Cayce on Dreams.* New York: Castle Books, 1968.

———. *Edgar Cayce on Religion and Psychic Experience.* New York: Paperback Library, 1970.

———. *High Play; Turning on without Drugs.* New York: Coward-McCann, 1970.

———. *A Seer Out of Season: The Life of Edgar Cayce.* New York: New American Library, 1989.

Broad, C(harlie) D(unbar) (1889–1971)

Professor of philosophy and president of the **Society for Psychical Research,** London, 1935–36 and 1958–60. Dr. Broad had a distinguished academic career and was a prominent researcher and theorist in the field of parapsychology.

Born December 30, 1887, in Harlesden, Middlesex, England, he was educated at Trinity College, Cambridge University, as a scholar in natural science. His dissertation became the basis of his book *Perception, Physics, and Reality* (1914). He was assistant professor of logic at St. Andrews University, Scotland (1912–20), lecturer at University College, Dundee, Scotland (1914–20), professor of philosophy at Bristol University (1920–23), then began his long tenure at Trinity College, Cambridge (1933–53), where he was eventually named Knightbridge Professor of Moral Philosophy. He wrote numerous books in the philosophy of science and ethics and was noted for his clarity of thought on the many abstruse aspects of philosophy.

Even as a young man Broad was interested in psychic research. He joined the Society for Psychical Research, London, in 1920, where he served as president twice, and trained his analytical mind on this field. His early book, *Mind and Its Place in Nature* (1923) caused a stir in philosophical circles because it included evidence of psychic phenomena that suggested the possibility of human life after death. However, as with his other writings, skeptics of psychic phenomena praised the clarity and accuracy of his reasoning. His more mature *Religion Philosophy, and Psychical Research: Selected Essays* (1953) set forth the idea of "basic limiting principles" which Broad believed formed the framework of modern technological society. Accordingly, any event outside that framework can fittingly be labeled "paranormal."

Broad lived in Cambridge after his retirement and died there on March 11, 1971.

Sources:

Broad, C. D. *Lectures on Psychical Research, Incorporating the Perrott Lectures Given in Cambridge University in 1939 and 1960.* New York: Humanities Press, 1962.

———. *The Mind and Its Place in Nature.* London: Routledge and Kegan Paul, 1925.

———. *Perception, Physics, and Reality: An Inquiry into the Information that Physical Science Can Supply about the Real.* 1914.

———. *Personal Identity and Survival.* London: Society for Psychical Research, 1958.

———. *Religion, Philosophy, and Psychical Research.* London: Routledge and Kegan Paul, 1953.

"In Memoriam: Professor C. D. Broad, 1887–1971." *Journal* of the SPR 46 (1971): 107.

Broceliande

A magic forest in ancient Brittany, identified with the forest of Piampont in modern-day Brittany, which figured in Arthurian legend. It was in this place that Merlin was enchanted by Nimue or Viviana, Lady of the Lake, and imprisoned beneath a huge stone. The name Broceliande is often employed as symbolic of the dim unreality of legendary scenery.

Sources:

Lacy, Norris J. *The Arthurian Encyclopedia.* New York: Garland Publishing, 1986.

Brocken Tryst

A celebrated experiment in magical transformation performed by psychical researcher **Harry Price** in June 1932 in the Hartz Mountains, Germany, during the Goethe centenary. The Brocken is the highest peak of the Hartz range.

Price claimed that a fifteenth-century manuscript of a **magic** ritual for changing a goat into a beautiful youth was delivered mysteriously in his National Laboratory of Psychic Research, London, and he decided to test whether the magic worked. This "Blocksberg Manuscript" detailed a ritual from the High German *Black Book,* a classic manual of **black magic,** and required a magic circle drawn on top of the Brocken on a night of full moon, a fire of pinewood, a goat with a silver cord, and a maiden pure in heart. Price undertook this ritual before scores of pressmen, photographers, and a film cameraman. In fact, the goat was not metamorphosed after all, but Price achieved his objective of securing publicity for paranormal investigation, and magic and psychic phenomena became a talking point in the stifled atmosphere of the 1930s.

Sources:

Price, Harry. *Confessions of a Ghost Hunter.* New York: G. P. Putnam's Sons, 1936. Reprint, New York: Causeway Books, 1974.

Brodie-Innes, J(ohn) W(illiam) (1848–1923)

An Edinburgh lawyer, born in Morayshire, Scotland, who became one of the leading members of the Hermetic Order of the **Golden Dawn**'s Amen-Ra Temple in Scotland. Brodie-Innes was also a member of a bibliophile society, the Sette of Odde Volumes, London, and was its president in 1911. He wrote several novels on witchcraft and magic and is said to have taught **Dion Fortune** (Violet Mary Firth) the secret of developing and directing occult force. He was the model for the "soul-doctor" in Fortune's book *The Secrets of Dr. Tavener* (1926).

Throughout the dissensions of the Golden Dawn, Brodie-Innes remained loyal to **MacGregor Mathers,** and on the death of his chief in 1918, published an affectionate obituary in the *Occult Review* (vol. 29, no. 5 [May 1919]).

Sources:

Brodie-Innes, J.W. *Scottish Witchcraft Trials.* London: Chiswick Press, 1891.

Fortune, Dion. *The Secrets of Dr. Tavener.* London: Noel Douglas, 1926.

Gilbert, R. A., ed. *The Sorcerer and His Apprentice: Unknown Hermetic Writings of S. L. MacGregor Mathers and J. W. Brodie-Innes.* Wellingborough, England: Aquarian Press, 1983.

Richardson, Alan. *Priestess: The Life and Magic of Dion Fortune.* Wellingborough, England: Aquarian Press, 1987.

Brofferio, Angelo (ca. 1890)

Italian scientist who was converted to **Spiritualism** by **Eusapia Palladino**'s mediumship. His first book, *Per lo Spiritismo* (Milan, 1892), endorsed the spirit hypothesis.

Brohou, Jean (ca. seventeenth century)

A physician of Coutarces, France, in the seventeenth century. He was the author of an *Almanack* or *Journal of Astrology,* which contained prognostications for the year 1572 (Rouen, 1571), and a *Description d'une Merveilleuse et Prodiigeuse Comète,* treatise on comets and the events they prognosticate (Paris, 1568).

Brooks, Nona Lovell (1861–1945)

Nona Lovell Brooks, a leader of the Divine Science Church, was born March 22, 1861, in Louisville, Kentucky, and grew up in Charleston, West Virginia, where her family moved to escape the Civil War. She was raised as a Presbyterian in a strongly religious home, and as a child had an intense experience of being engulfed by a supernatural light.

During her teen years, the family moved to Pueblo, Colorado, where Brooks came face to face with **New Thought** metaphysics. She had developed a sore throat that would not clear up. Her sister Althea suggested that she attend some classes being offered by Kate Bingham, an independent teacher of Christian Science. Bingham had been healed while in Chicago under the ministrations of **Emma Curtis Hopkins.** Hopkins's independent brand of Christian Science formed the basis of New Thought.

While sitting in Bingham's class, Brooks was particularly affected by Bingham's discussion of the omnipresence of God. As she came to this fresh understanding of God, she was healed, and that evening, for the first time in many months, she ate a normal meal without pain. The sisters shared the story with their minister, who invited them to speak, but the church elders stepped in. They prevented the talk and fired Brooks from her church school teaching job. She in turn quit the church.

After finishing her schooling in Pueblo, Brooks went east for a year at Wellesley College. After she returned home, she taught school for two years before moving to Denver, where her other sister, Fanny, lived. Fanny was also influenced by Hopkins and Bingham and had been holding metaphysical classes. She also began corresponding with Melinda Cramer, who developed her own variation of Christian Science called Divine Science, and Fanny began to use that name for her work. The two sisters opened the Divine Science College in 1898. Responding to a call from the students that they hold Sunday services, Nona Brooks went to San Francisco to be ordained by Cramer. They held their first service in Denver on January 1, 1899.

Cramer died from injuries received in the April 1906 earthquake in San Francisco. The center of the Divine Science movement shifted to Denver, and Brooks became its key leader for the next four decades. By this time she had started the monthly magazine *Fulfillment.* During the years of World War I, when many metaphysical leaders came together to found the International New Thought Alliance, Brooks helped organize the opposition, primarily among leaders in the western states. However, by 1922 she had worked out her differences with the organization and led the ministers and members of the Divine Science movement into it. She became a prominent leader and popular speaker for the alliance.

The last decades of Brooks's life were ones of triumph. Divine Science grew speedily into an international association of metaphysical churches, and Brooks became a well-recognized religious leader in Denver, overcoming opposition both to her gender and her minority beliefs. In 1926 she was invited to join the local ministerial alliance. She served on a variety of civic boards and agencies, including the Colorado State Prison Board. She tried to retire and for a period in the early 1930s settled in Australia, where she opened several churches, but upon her return to Colorado in 1938 she was immediately asked to resume leadership of the movement. She retired a second time in 1943, two years before her death on March 14, 1945.

Sources:

Braden, Charles. *Spirits in Rebellion.* Dallas, 1963.

Brooks, Louise McNamara. *Early History of Divine Science.* Denver: First Divine Science Church, 1963.

Brooks, Nona L. *Mysteries.* Denver: The Author, 1924.

———. *The Prayer that Never Fails.* Denver: The Author, 1935.

———. *Short Lessons in Divine Science.* Denver: The Author, 1928.

Neale, Hazel. *Powerful Is the Light.* Denver: Divine Science College, 1945.

Broom

In Romania and Tuscany it was a folk belief that a broom laid beneath the pillow would keep witches and evil spirits away. Others suggested that witches and evil spirits could be kept at bay by two crossed brooms in front of a house door or cattle-shed. The British believed that if a girl should stride over a broom handle, she would be a mother before she was a wife. Other superstitions claimed that buying a broom in the month of May would sweep your friends away, hence it was unlucky to make brooms during May. Another popular belief was that a new broom should sweep something into the house before it swept dust out of the house.

Broomstick

Witches were said to ride through the air on switches or broomsticks on their nocturnal journey to the Sabbat. Various other mounts were supposed to be used by witches, including a cleft stick, a staff, a distaff, or even a shovel. These objects were smeared with a special **witchcraft** ointment before the flight. Other witches were believed to make their aerial journeys on such animals as a wolf or a goat. These flights were named **transvection** by demonologists.

Sources:

Robbins, Rossell Hope. *The Encyclopedia of Witchcraft and Demonology.* New York: Crown Publishers, 1959.

Brotherhood of the Ram

The Brotherhood of the Ram was a short-lived Satanic group that operated out of an occult booksotre in the Los Angeles area during the 1960s and 1970s. Members reportedly made a pact with Satan renouncing all other devotions, especially any Christian elements in their past. The pact was then signed in blood. (See **Satanism**)

Brotherhood of the Trowel

A whimsical Masonic society founded in Florence, Italy, in 1512, composed of eminent architects, sculptors, and painters. Its emblems were the trowel, the gavel, and the square, and its patron was St. Andrew. The society may have been an offshoot of an older fraternity of Traveling Masons.

The rites are believed to have been a travesty of genuine Masonry, culminating in a banquet. The society existed until 1737.

Brotherhood of the White Temple

The Brotherhood of the White Temple is a theosophical occult organization founded in 1903 in Denver, Colorado, by **Maurice Doreal** (d. 1963), the religious name of Claude Doggins. A lifelong student of the occult, Doreal claimed to have spent eight years in Tibet during the 1920s. He also claimed to have made contact with the Great White Lodge, the advanced beings who completed their work on earth and who now, as masters, guide the destiny of humankind. Doreal was seen as the agent for the coming Golden Age. Associated with the brotherhood is the **White Temple Church.**

The brotherhood was headquartered in Denver for many years, but immediately after World War II, in the atmosphere of anxiety over a possible atomic war, the brotherhood built a new headquarters complex in Sedalia, Colorado, in a valley surrounded by high mountains. The headquarters were formally moved in 1951. Two years later Doreal predicted the coming biblical Battle of Armageddon for later in the year. It did not occur, but members continued to stockpile food and other resources they might need should war break out.

The brotherhood teaches a system of **Gnosticism** that draws heavily on theosophical and kabalistic writings. The human soul is pictured as a spark of the divine that has devolved into matter. This experience has overwhelmed the soul, which has lost the harmony it had after being created. Teachings emphasize methods of reestablishing harmony and, with the aid of the masters, returning to the divine realms.

New members complete a series of lessons and progress through neophyte and temple grades, which can take four to five years, after which members are invited into the real inner work of the group. Some of the older members reside at the center in Colorado, but the great majority live around the country and stay in contact through correspondence. The organizations publishes a periodical, *Light on the Path,* and a set of booklets written by Doreal called the Little Temple Library. The more than one hundred titles in the library cover a broad range of **occult** topics.

Sources:

Doreal, Maurice. *Maitreya: Lord of the World.* Sedalia, Colo.: Brotherhood of the White Temple, n.d.

———. *Man and the Mystic Universe.* Denver: Brotherhood of the White Temple, n.d.

———. *Personal Experiences among the Masters and Great Adepts in Tibet.* Sedalia, Colo.: Brotherhood of the White Temple, n.d.

———. *Secret Teachings of the Himalayan Gurus.* Denver: Brotherhood of the White Temple, n.d.

Brothers of Purity

An association of Arab philosophers founded at Basra in the tenth century. They had forms of initiation, and they wrote many works that were afterward much studied by the Jews of Spain.

Broughton, Luke Dennis (1828–1898)

Luke Dennis Broughton, the leading astrologer in the United States during the last decades of the nineteenth century, was born April 20, 1828, in Leeds, England, and grew up in an astrologically-oriented family. His grandfather had become a devotee of the stars after reading the *Complete Herbal,* a medical **astrology** text by **Nicolas Culpepper** and one of the few astrological texts to have survived the combined attack of Protestantism and the Enlightenment in the seventeenth and eighteenth centuries. The elder Broughton inspired interest in astrology in his physician son and through him to Luke Broughton and his brothers. Luke Broughton's older brother Mark became the leader of an astrological society in England and then moved to the United States to begin *Broughton's Monthly Horoscope* in 1849.

Luke Broughton began studying astrology during his teen years, and he moved to the United States in the early 1840s to study natural medicine at the Eclectic Medical College in Philadelphia. He began a public career in 1860 when he revived his brother's periodical as *Broughton's Monthly Planet Reader and Astrological Journal* (1860–69). In 1863 he moved his medical office to New York City, his home for the rest of his life. He emphasized astrological medicine and in 1866 began to teach astrology. His initial teaching efforts became the foundation upon which the nation's major astrological center would be built. He developed a distributorship of astrological literature, the great majority of which came from England.

As astrology grew and became the center of renewed controversy, Broughton assumed the dual role of astrology's defender from its enemies and protector from incompetent astrologers. He wrote and at times appeared as a witness in court on astrology's behalf. He also attacked people such as Hiram Butler, Eleanor Kirk, and C. W. Roback, astrologers who, he felt, had insufficient training for their work. At the time of his death in 1898, he left his practice to his daughter, who carried on his work and saw to the publication of his most substantive book, *The Elements of Astrology* (1898).

Sources:

Broughton, Luke D. *The Elements of Astrology.* New York: The Author, 1898.

———. *Planetary Influence.* New York: The Author, 1893.

Brown, John (1826–1883)

The personal servant of **Queen Victoria,** (1819–1901) from December 1865 until his death. A rough-mannered, sometimes inebriated, Highland gillie (attendant on a Scottish chieftain), he exercised an extraordinary fascination for the queen of England during her visits to Balmoral Castle, Scotland, and later at Osborne House, Isle of Wight. Their strange and close association gave rise to many rumors and spiteful gossip.

Brown was born at Crathie, near Balmoral, Aberdeenshire, Scotland, December 8, 1826. He first came to the notice of Queen Victoria during her visits to the Scottish Highlands, when Brown served as her outdoor personal attendant. After the death of her beloved Prince Albert, the widowed queen came to rely heavily on the companionship of Brown, after he had been summoned by her to Osborne House in 1864. He had brought the queen's favorite Highland pony "Lochnagar," and soon afterward, the kilted, red-whiskered Highlander became a privileged associate of the queen, and enjoyed powerful influence. Rumor had it that he was even her secret lover or that he took part in Spiritualist séances with her.

It was an open secret that the queen had a special interest in Spiritualism, particularly after the death of Prince Albert. She certainly held a number of séances and is said to have used the services of medium **Robert James Lees.**

Brown died March 27, 1883, at Windsor Castle and was buried at Crathie cemetery. He was praised by the queen in the Court Circular as her "best and truest friend," and she had a statue erected to him at Balmoral.

Sources:

Underwood, Peter. *Queen Victoria's Other World.* London: Harrap, 1868.

Victoria, Queen. *Leaves from the Journal of Our Life in the Highlands.* Smith, Elder, 1868.

Williams, Henry L. *Life of John Brown. . . . for 30 Years Personal Attendant of . . . The Queen.* London: E. Smith, 1883.

Brown, John Mason (1837–1890)

American lawyer who lived among Indian tribes and studied their beliefs and customs. In 1866 he reported on the gift of prophecy by a medicine man.

Brown, Rosemary

A modern British medium who performs musical compositions on the piano which she claims originate from dead composers. A London housewife with no musical training, Brown performs in the manner of Beethoven, Mozart, Liszt, and other well-known composers. Her psychic performances, which recall those of **Jesse Shepard,** another famous musical medium who died in 1927, have been endorsed by famous concert pianist John Lill, winner of the International Tchaikovsky Competition in Moscow in 1970.

Brown has also drawn watercolors and charcoals and painted oils, which she claims are the original work of dead artists; she has written poems from dead poets, equations purportedly from Einstein, philosophical statements from Bertrand Russell, and psychological observations from C. G. Jung.

In 1973 she started to write a play, *Caesar's Revenge,* which she claimed was dictated to her by the playwright George Bernard Shaw, who died 23 years earlier. Brown stated that she had not previously read any play by Shaw and had only seen a television production of *Pygmalion. Caesar's Revenge* was staged at the Edinburgh Festival in Scotland on Tuesday, August 22, 1978. Patrick Roberts, an English lecturer at University of London and an expert on Shaw commented: "The idea of the play is reminiscent of the hell scene in Shaw's *Man and Superman,* where characters can indulge their fantasies without being interrupted. There is the same light-hearted debate that Shaw enjoyed so much. But the style isn't Shaw's at all. . . . this is colloquial, more in keeping with a play of today." Christopher Gilmore, director of the Mountview Theatre, Hornsey, North London, who staged the two-act play at the Edinburgh Festival, stated: "I'm positive it's Shaw. It rings of him with its length of scenes and satiric remarks couched in sweet language." (See also **Pepito Arriola**)

Sources:

Brown, Rosemary. *Immortals at My Elbow.* London, 1974. Reprinted as *Immortals by My Side.* Chicago: Henry Regnery, 1975.

———. *Unfinished Symphonies: Voices from the Beyond.* London, 1971. Reprint, New York: William Morrow, 1971.

May, Antoinette. *Haunted Ladies.* San Francisco: Chronicle Books, 1975.

Brown, William (1881–1952)

British psychologist, psychiatrist, and psychic researcher. Brown was born December 5, 1881, at Morpeth, England. He studied at Collyer's School in Horsham and at King's College Hospital, London (D.Sc., M.R.C.P., F.R.C.B.). He was consulting psychologist and a reader in psychology at the University of London as well as King's College Hospital. He gave the Terry lectures at Yale University in 1928; in 1936 he became director of the Institute of Experimental Psychology at Oxford University, where he remained until his retirement in 1945. In 1951–52 he was president of the British Psychological Society.

Brown's interest in psychic research began early. He joined the **Society for Psychical Research** and served on its board for 17 years (1923–40). While on the board, he wrote two letters to the *Times* (London) (May 7 & 14, 1932) in which he spoke appreciatively if guardedly of medium **Rudi Schneider**'s powers and declared that they were worthy of the closest scientific investigation. In a lecture delivered during the jubilee celebrations of the Society of Psychical Research, London, he reviewed the evidence collected and examined by the society and declared that it was "sufficient to make survival scientifically extremely probable."

Sources:

Brown, William. *Mind and Personality.* College Park, Md.: McGrath, 1927.

———. *Mind, Medicine, and Metaphysics; The Philosohy of a Physician.* London: Oxford University Press, 1936.

———. *Psychological Methods of Healing; An Introduction to Psychotherapy.* London: University of London Press, Ltd., 1938.

———. *Suggestion and Mental Analysis.* New York: Doran, 1922.

Browne, Sir Thomas (1605–1682)

An English physician whose evidence in a **witchcraft** trial in 1664 is said to have assisted the conviction of two women. The accused were Amy Duny and Rose Cullender, arraigned before Sir Matthew Hale at Bury St. Edmunds. Asked by Hale for his opinion, Browne commented, "That 'the fits were natural, but heightened by the devils co-operating with the malice of the witches, at whose instance he did the villainies," citing similar cases in Denmark.

Besides his famous *Religio Medici* (1642) and *Urn Burial* (1658), Browne was chiefly celebrated by the manner in which he combated fallacies in a work entitled *Pseudoxia Epidemica* (1658), an essay on popular errors in which he examined beliefs accepted in his time as veritable facts, then proved them to be false or doubtful. Although the author frequently replaced one error by another, on the whole his book is accurate, especially considering the date of its composition. The work is divided into seven books, each of which deals with a particular set of errors: those springing from man's love of the marvelous; those arising from popular beliefs concerning plants and metals; absurd beliefs connected with animals; errors relative to man; errors recorded by pictures and cosmographical and historical errors and certain commonly accepted absurdities concerning the wonders of the world. The charges of atheism against him, which arose with the publication of this work, stimulated him to publish his famous *Religio Medici.*

His strangest literary conceit was *The Garden of Cyrus* (1658), an exhaustive survey of the **quincunx** (a special arrangement of five objects).

Browning, Robert (1812–1889)

The famous English poet sat at a séance with the medium **Daniel D. Home,** after which Browning published his satirical poem "Mr. Sludge, the Medium," which was generally thought to refer to Home. It contains these lines:

> Now don't, sir! Don't expose me! Just this once!
> This was the first and only time, I'll swear.
> Look at me—see, I kneel—the only time,
> I swear I ever cheated . . .
> "Well, Sir, since you press—
> (How do you tease the whole thing out of me!)
> Now for it, then! . . .
> I cheated when I could.
> Rapped with my toe-joints, set sham hands at work,
> Wrote down names weak in sympathetic ink,
> Rubbed odic lights with ends of phosphor-match,
> all the rest—"

It was generally supposed that the poet detected Home in fraud, but others suggested that Browning was motivated by spiteful jealousy on account of his wife's (Elizabeth Barrett) interest in **Spiritualism.** Evidence in the book *Elizabeth Barrett Browning: Letters to Her Sister* (London, 1929) suggests that Browning's husband strongly resented her attitude and that Spiritualism was tabooed in their house. Home himself discussed the incident in his book *Incidents in My Life* (1874) and preferred a psychological explanation for the poet's verse.

A wreath of clematis, which the children had gathered in the garden, moved from the table and started to glide toward Elizabeth Browning. Robert Browning, seated at the opposite side, came and stood behind his wife. Then the wreath rose and came to rest on Elizabeth's head. Some of the sitters thought Robert was annoyed at not getting the crown himself, but he voluntarily stated that imposture was out of question. Later he evolved a theory of artificial hands affixed to Home's chair.

In his biography of Browning, G. K. Chesterton ridicules the story and says that Browning "did not dislike Spiritualism but Spiritualists." At any rate, the poem harmed Home's reputation substantially. It was widely quoted in the press, even in America, where Sarah Helen Whitman, the poet to whom some of the finest gems of Edgar Allan Poe's poetry were written, felt prompted to write to a paper and brand it as a "blot on Browning's 'scutcheon."

In spite of Browning's hostility toward Home, tradition has it that Robert Browning was well versed in the Hermetic tradition of occult knowledge and used Hermetic imagery in some of his poems. In *My Browning Family Album* (1979), Vivienne Browning, president of the Browning Society, revealed that her father, Vyvyan Deacon, was a practicing medium and lecturer on the occult and Theosophy and told her that he was carrying on the tradition of his grandfather Reuben Browning, the poet's uncle, who was a Rosicrucian who shared his secret knowledge and training with his nephew Robert.

Sources:

Browning, Robert. *Dramatis Personae.* London: Chapman and Hall, 1864.

Browning, Vivienne. *My Browning Family Album.* London: Springwood Books, 1979.

Porter, Katherine H. *Through a Glass Darkly: Spiritualism in the Browning Circle.* Lawrence, Kans.: University of Kansas Press, 1958.

Bruce, H(enry) Addington (Bayley) (1874–1959)

Canadian author, newspaperman, and lecturer on psychology, education, and sociology. Bruce was born June 27, 1874, in Toronto, Ontario, Canada. He studied at the University of Toronto (B.A., 1859; M.S., 1896) and Harvard University. In 1897 he married Lauretta Augusta Bowers (died, 1941). In the early 1920s, Bruce was a trustee of the **American Society for Psychical Research** (ASPR), but he broke with the ASPR in 1925 and became director of research for the **Boston Society for Psychical Research.** He authored a number of books on psychic subjects and contributed a number of articles to *Tommorrow* magazine. He died February 23, 1959, in Hartford, Connecticut.

Sources:

Bruce, Henry Addington Bayley. *Historic Ghosts and Ghost Hunters.* New York: Moffat, Yard, 1908.

———. *Riddle of Personality.* New York: Moffat, Yard, 1915.

———. *Scientific Mental Healing.* Boston, Little, Brown, 1911.

Bruening, J(oseph) H(erbert) (1929–)

Sociologist at University of Mississippi beginning in 1962 who investigated mediumship and survival. He was born February 10, 1929, in Pittsburgh, Pennsylvania, and studied at the University of Florida (B.S., 1954; M.S., 1956). He joined the Florida Society for Psychical Research, the **Parapsychological Association,** and the **Society for Psychical Research,** London.

Bruers, Antonio (188?–1954)

Italian author, editor, and parapsychologist. Bruers was actively interested in psychical research and parapsychology for many years and was president of the Societa Italiana di Metapsichica. He published books on psychic research and bibliography and was associated with the Istituto di Studi Psichici and edited their publication *Luce e Ombra.* He died November 30, 1954, in Rome, Italy. (See also **Italy**).

Brugmans, Henri J. F. W. (1885–1961)

Professor of psychology at University of Gronigen in the Netherlands and pioneer in performing laboratory experiments on psychic phenomena in his home country. He conducted experiments in telepathy after World War I. In one of his experiments he recorded physiological changes during psi testing. His work laid a foundation for the discipline of parapsychology as developed by **J. B. Rhine.** He attended the First International Congress on Psychical Research in Copenhagen in 1922. He died March 1, 1961.

Sources:

Brugmans, H. J. F. W., G. Heymans, and A. Weinberg. "Some Experiments in Telepathy Performed in the Psychological Institute of the University of Groningen." *Compte-Rendu du Premier Congrés International de Recherches Phychiques.* 1921.

"On the Experiments of Brugmans, Heymans, and Weinberg." *European Journal of Parapsychology* 2 (1978): 247.

Bruillant

One of the characters in the thirteenth-century romance *Grand Saint Graal.* Bruillant discovered the Grail Sword in Solomon's ship, and with it slew Lambor, father of the Fisher-King. For this use of the holy sword, however, the whole of Britain suffered, for no wheat grew, the fruit trees bore no fruit, and there were no fish in the sea. Bruillant himself was punished with death for using the sword.

Bruno, Jean (1909–)

Librarian at the Bibliothèque Nationale in Paris beginning in 1936 who published a number of articles dealing with parapsychology, yoga, and mystical experience. Born July 9, 1909, at La Rochelle, France, he studied at University of Poitiers (Licencié ès lettres, 1933).

Brunton, Paul (1898–1981)

British-born journalist who wrote important books on philosophy and comparative religion. He was educated at Central Foundation School, London, and McKinley-Roosevelt College, Chicago, Illinois. Early in life he became interested in **Spiritualism.** He developed mediumistic powers himself, notably **clairvoyance** and **clairaudience,** and thus verified the existence of psychic faculties from first-hand personal experience. Later he joined the **Theosophical Society,** but left after two years. He contacted various occult groups, comparing their teachings, and became a close friend of Ananda Metteya (**Allan Bennett**), who initiated Brunton into Buddhist meditation.

Brunton assisted Bennett to publish his journal the *Buddhist Review.* According to Brunton, Bennett developed a breath control that enabled him at times to alter the specific gravity of his body, so that while sitting in a yoga posture he could rise a foot or two into the air, and then float gently down to the floor again a short distance from the spot where he first sat. Brunton also stated that around the time of Bennett's death, Bennett had "sacrificed his body in an effort to extricate me from a dangerous position."

Brunton traveled in India and Egypt, and attracted tremendous interest with his famous book, *A Search in Secret India* (1934). This was followed by *A Search in Secret Egypt,* (1935), *A Hermit in the Himalayas* (1937), and *The Quest of the Overself* (1937). Although Brunton was at first concerned primarily with miracle-working holy men, he soon became attracted to the deepest metaphysical aspects of yoga and mysticism and was one of the first Europeans to draw attention to **Sri Ramana Maharshi** of Tiruvannamalai, South India, one of the greatest modern Hindu mystics.

Brunton's books greatly influenced the occult revival and growth of Eastern religion from the 1930s onward, stimulating popular interest in **yoga, meditation,** and the teachings of gurus. In 1956 he retired to Switzerland and devoted himself to meditation. During these years he wrote *The Inner Reality* (1959), *The Hidden Teaching beyond Yoga* (1959), and *The Secret Path* (1959). His thoughts and insights on the spiritual life, which he recorded in a series of notebooks numbering some 7,000 pages, were an exposition of the synthesis of Eastern mysticism and Western rational thought. They were published posthumously as *The Notebooks of Paul Brunton: Perspectives* (1984). Brunton died July 27, 1981, in Vevey, Switzerland.

Buchanan, Joseph Rhodes (1814–1899)

American professor of psychology and medical science. He became dean of the faculty and professor in the Eclectic Medical Institute (which practiced natural medicine) in Covington, Kentucky, and a pioneer researcher in the field of **psychometry.**

The discoverer of "phrenomesmerism," Buchanan published in 1843 a neurological map, a new distribution of the phrenological organs. He anticipated Prof. Ferrier's "center of feeling" by localizing as early as 1838 the "region of sensibility" in which, in a state of high development, he found traces of an unknown psychic faculty for which in 1842 he coined the word "psychometry," the measuring of the soul.

Episcopal Bishop Leonidas Polk (General Polk during the Civil War) told him of his curious sensitivity to atmospheric, electric, and other physical conditions. If he touched brass in the dark, he immediately knew it by its influence and the offensive metallic taste in his mouth. Buchanan began to experiment and soon found out that these sensations were not restricted to the sense of taste alone. Students of a Cincinnati medical school registered distinct impressions from medicines held in their hands. To eliminate thought transference, the substances were wrapped up in paper parcels and mixed.

Slowly the conviction forced itself on Buchanan that **emanations** might be thrown off by all substances, even by the human body, which certain sensitives might feel and interpret in their normal state. He was staggered by the implication of such a possibility and asserted:

"The past is entombed in the present, the world is its own enduring monument; and that which is true of its physical is likewise true of its mental career. The discoveries of Psychometry will enable us to explore the history of man, as those of geology enable us to explore the history of the earth. There are mental fossils for psychologists as well as mineral fossils for the geologists; and I believe that hereafter the psychologist and the geologist will go hand in hand, the one portraying the earth, its animals and its vegetation, while the other portrays the human beings who have roamed over its surface in the shadows, and the darkness of primeval barbarism. Aye, the mental telescope is now discovered which may pierce the depths of the past and bring us in full view of the grand and tragic passages of ancient history."

To the subtle emanation given off by the human body he gave the name "nerve aura." In the *Journal of Man,* which succeeded S. B. Brittan's *Shekinah,* one of the first Spiritualist monthlies, he published a complete exposition of his system of neurology, or anthropology. The paper was mainly devoted to his psychometric experiments, in the course of which he came to believe that an actual clue, something belonging to the person of whom reading is given, is not always necessary and that an index, which leads the mind of the psychometer to the subject, may suffice. He observed:

"Acting upon this view I wrote the name of a friend and placed it in the hands of a good psychometer, who had no difficulty, notwithstanding her doubts of so novel a proceeding, in giving as good a description of the character of Dr. N. as if she had made the description from an autograph. After that experiment I was accustomed to extend my inquiries to ancient and modern historical characters, public men and any person in whose character I was interested, as well as localities I wished to have described."

Buchanan regarded psychometry as a human faculty that did not involve the intervention of spirits. L. A. Coffin, however, in her preface to Buchanan's *Manual of Psychometry* (Boston, 1889) admitted that she was often impressed by spirits. This was not incongruous, as Buchanan himself was an avowed Spiritualist. He published an astounding narrative of his own experiences in the *Light of Truth,* Columbus, Ohio, in 1899.

He stated that from 1849 to 1855 he was the only medical scientist to defend the **Fox Sisters** and repel their assailants. He told his friends that he was "as well acquainted with the spirit world as they were with Europe." This knowledge was derived from instructions given by direct voices through Mrs. Hollis-Billing (**Mary J. Hollis**) and from direct scripts. He was further helped by psychometric explorations that he began in 1879–80 through Cornelia H. Buchanan. "The past was to her as open a book as the present, and during the years in which she portrayed historic characters of whom I knew nothing, I never found her deviating from the truth as far as I could discover."

In the course of these investigations, Buchanan received a direct penciled message signed by "St. John." This was followed by startling communications which, after having been held in reserve for 17 years, were published in 1897 under the title *Primitive Christianity: Containing the Lost Lives of Jesus Christ and the Apostles and the Authentic Gospel of St. John.* Buchanan stated that he tested the St. John script, properly concealed, through three psychometrists: Cornelia H. Buchanan, **Mrs. W. R. Hayden,** and Dr. **James M. Peebles,** and that all three agreed as to its source, giving similar descriptions of a great spirit devoted personally to Jesus Christ. The book was also adorned by an engraving of the spirit form of St. John, which Buchanan received between his own pair of slates held in his hand.

On other occasions but in a similar manner, he claimed to obtain between his slates a portrait of Moses and the Tables of Law, pictures of Aaron, Helen of Troy, and John the Baptist, and communications from Confucius. He asserted that subsequent psychometric reading bore out, in each instance, the genuineness of the manifestation. Buchanan died December 26, 1899, in San Jose, California.

Bucke, R(ichard) M(aurice) (1837–1902)

British-born writer who grew up in Canada and practiced as a psychiatrist. He was born March 18, 1837, in Methwold, Norfolk, England. When only a year old, his father took him to Canada, where he was educated at London Grammar School and studied medicine at McGill University, graduating in 1862. He pursued additional studies in England and France, then he returned to Canada in 1864 to take up medical practice. In 1876 he became medical superintendent of the insane asylum in Hamilton, Ontario, and in 1878 was medical superintendent of the insane asylum in London, Ontario.

He became a great friend of poet Walt Whitman (1819–1892) and was fascinated by the subject of mystical experience. Around 1872 Bucke had what became for him a life-changing mystical experience. He spent the next 30 years seeking out other people who had a similar experience and reflecting upon the significance of such altering of consciousness. The literary result of his study, the book *Cosmic Consciousness* (1901), became a classic work on the subject. He theorized that a higher consciousness was a natural faculty in man at a certain state of development.

He became Whitman's literary executor and helped edit Whitman's complete writings in 1902, then wrote the first major biography of the poet. Bucke died February 19, 1902, in London, Ontario. His *Cosmic Consciousness* gave mystical experience a place in the secular world and provided psychiatry with a means of viewing religious experience in other than pathological terms.

Buckland, Raymond (Brian) (1934–)

Author and Wiccan high priest who, with his wife, Rosemary Buckland, introduced Gardnerian Witchcraft into the United States. Buckland was born August 31, 1934, in London, England, where he attended high school. He served in the Royal Air Force, 1957–59, and earned a Ph.D. in anthropology at King's College, Cambridge.

He came to Witchcraft through his reading of the books of **Margaret Murray** and **Gerald Gardner.** Buckland contacted Gardner and established a relationship with him and his priestess Monique Wilson (Lady Olwen). Shortly before Gardner's death in 1964, Buckland and his wife were initiated by Gardner, and they assumed the religious names Robat and Lady Rowan. After they moved to the United States in 1962, they began the first Gardnerian coven. Whenever Americans contacted Gardner and his followers in England, they were referred to the Bucklands, which established the Gardnerian movement across the United States. They also opened a Witchcraft Museum on Long Island modeled on the museum Gardner had established on the Isle of Man. Buckland also authored a set of books on Wicca, including *Ancient and Modern Witchcraft* (1970) and *Witchcraft from the Inside* (1975).

In the early 1970s Buckland divorced and began to disagree with some of the elements of the Gardnerian tradition. In 1973 he turned the leadership of the Gardnerian movement over to another couple, Lady Theos and Phoenix, and created a new non-secret form of Witchcraft that he called Seax (or Saxon) Wicca. He presented this new Witchcraft in a 1974 book, *The Tree: The Complete Book of Saxon Witchcraft.* That same year he also married Joan Helen Taylor, who became his new high priest.

Buckland then developed a correspondence course in Seax Wicca, which he offered through the 1970s. He also moved to Southern California where his approach to the craft evolved. He continued to write on a wide variety of magical and Witchcraft themes and his latest books include *Practical Color Magick* (1983), *Complete Book of Witchcraft* (1986), and the *Secrets of Gypsy Fortunetelling* (1988), which is of a series of books on gypsy occult practices. As of the mid-1990s, Buckland has written more than 20 books. One, a spoof on the books of **James Churchward,** was called *Mu Revealed* and appeared under the Pseudonym Tony Earll (an anagram for "not really"). Buckland also wrote novels under the pseudonym Jessica Wells.

Sources:

Adler, Margo. *Drawing Down the Moon.* New York: Viking Press, 1979. Rev. ed. Boston: Beacon Press, 1986.

———. *Buckland's Complete Book of Witchcraft.* St. Paul, Minn.: Llewellyn Publications, 1986.

———. *Doors to Other Worlds.* St. Paul, Minn.: Llewellyn Books, 1993.

Guiley, Rosemary E. *Encyclopedia of Witchcraft and Witches.* New York: Facts on File, 1989.

Buckley, James Lord (ca. 1867–1947)

Pioneer British spiritualist and medium. He attracted large audiences in Yorkshire by his remarkable gift of **clairaudience.** He died January 14, 1947.

Budapest, Zsuzsanna E. (1940–)

Founder of the main branch of Dianic (feminist) Wicca and author of a number of books. Budapest was born Zsuzsanna Mokcsay in Budapest, Hungary, but left in the wake Hungarian revolt of 1956. She moved to Austria and them to the United States, where she studied at the University of Chicago. She married and had two children, but the marriage ended in the late-1960s. In 1970 Budapest moved to California and became involved in the women's movement and in Witchcraft. She opened a feminist bookstore and began to develop a form of Wicca that would meld Gardnerian Witchcraft and her growing feminist ideals. In 1976 she published *The Feminist Book of Lights and Shadows,* the basic text of what is known as Dianic Wicca.

Budapest was by this time the priestess of a feminist coven, the Susan B. Anthony Coven, in Venice, California. The coven began a newsletter, *Themis* (now *Thesmorphoria*), and in 1979 she and the coven relocated in the San Francisco Bay Area. Budapest opened the Women's Spirituality Forum, which gave Dianic Wicca a public outreach. Among her many books are *The Holy Book of Women's Mysteries* (1979) and *The Grandmother of Time* (1989).

Sources:

Budapest, Zsuzsanna E. *The Feminist Book of Lights and Shadows.* Venice, Calif.: Luna Publications, 1976.

———. *The Grandmother of Time.* San Francisco: Harper & Row, 1989.

———. *The Holy Book of Women's Mysteries.* Los Angeles: Susan B. Anthony Coven Number One, 1979.

Guiley, Rosemary E. *Encyclopedia of Witchcraft and Witches.* New York: Facts on File, 1989.

Buer

According to **Johan Weyer,** Buer is a demon of the second class who has the form of a star and is gifted with a knowledge of philosophy and of the virtues of medicinal herbs. He gives domestic felicity and health to the sick. He has charge over 15 legions.

Sources:

Weyer, Johannes. *Witches, Devils, and Doctors in the Renaissance: Johann Weyer, De Praestigiis.* Edited by George Mora. Binghamton, N.Y.: Medieval and Renaissance Texts and Studies, 1991.

BUFORA See British UFO Research Association

Buguet, Édouard (ca. 1874)

French spirit photographer who, in an alleged partial trance, produced remarkable likenesses of high artistic quality of deceased relatives of his sitters. Most of these spirit photographs represented well-known people, but comparatively obscure people also reported obtaining surprising evidence of spirit presence. Buguet's reputation rose, and he was acclaimed for the feat of photographing the double of the Rev. **Stainton Moses** in Paris while the medium was sitting in trance in London.

However, his successes in London in 1874 were negated by the huge scandal over **spirit photography** that broke out in Paris in April 1875. Buguet was arrested for **fraud.** After he confessed, he was sentenced to one year of imprisonment and a fine of 500 francs. In his confession he admitted that his spirit photographs were produced by double exposure. First he dressed up his assistant to play the part of the ghost; later he constructed a doll to replace the human assistant for the body of the ghost. The doll and a large stock of heads were seized by the police at Buguet's studio.

A verbatim account of the trial was published in Leymaire's book *Procès des spirites* (Paris, 1875). Leymaire's husband, who was editor of the *Revue Spirite,* admitted having suggested to Buguet to follow in the footsteps of **W. H. Mumler,** and he was also sentenced to one year's imprisonment and a fine of 500 francs. Many witnesses were confronted during the trial with Buguet. Even when Buguet repeated his confession, many protested and refused to doubt the evidence of their senses.

Stainton Moses believed that at least some of Buguet's spirit photographs were genuine and said that the persecution bore traces of clerical origin, that the judge was biased, and that Buguet must have been bribed or terrorized to confess and to manufacture a box full of trick apparatus. In an article in *Human Nature* in May 1875, Moses stated that out of 120 photographs produced by Buguet, evidence of recognition or of the operation being produced under test conditions was available in 40 cases.

William Howitt also spoke of an organized conspiracy of the Jesuits against **Spiritualism.** Lady Caithness was quoted by **Epes Sargent** as declaring that out of 13 spirit photographs obtained by Buguet, "we distinctly recognized the spirit forms of five dear ones whom we had never hoped to see again on earth. We were perfect strangers to the medium, who had never heard of us before. That there may be no doubt about the identity of my late husband, he brings in his hand the family crest and emblem." After his liberation, Buguet himself agreed, retracted his confession, declared that he was tricked into it, and stated that a promise had been held out that in case of confession he would be acquitted.

However, **Camille Flammarion** was convinced that Buguet cheated. In *Mysterious Psychic Forces* (1907), he stated that Buguet, "having allowed me to experiment with him, let me conduct my researches for five weeks before I detected his fraudulent methods and mechanism. While I was pushing my investigation a little farther I saw with my own eyes Buguet's prepared negatives." Buguet was but one prominent example of fraudulent **psychic photography.**

Bull, Titus (1871–1946)

New York physician. He was a member of the American Association for the Advancement of Science and the director of the James H. Hyslop Foundation for the treatment of cases of **obsession** by psychic methods.

Bull was a close friend of the distinguished psychic researcher **James H. Hyslop** (1854–1920). Hyslop had already concluded that some individuals believed to be insane might be victims of spirit obsession. When Hyslop was dying, he requested Bull to carry on investigating this hypothesis. As a responsible physician, Bull first sought conventional explanations and treatment of mental breakdowns, but in certain instances where normal diagnosis and treatment seemed ineffective, he looked for a psychic cause. His procedure in such cases was to bring the patient into contact with a medium who had no prior knowledge of the patient to elicit forgotten memories and sometimes describe obsessing entities.

Helen C. Lambert, secretary to Bull, wrote in *Psychic Science* (July 1927):

"Of patients whom I have seen cured by Dr. Bull's method, three had been in State institutions for the insane, and one of these had to be restrained in a straight jacket. This last is a young girl who is now trying to obtain a position that will enable her to leave the difficult home environment which had much to do with her breakdown. Another is a woman who had been in five different institutions, twice in the Boris Sidis Sanitorium, and was considered incurable when she came to Dr. Bull. Some of the patients are persons who had not reached the point of being put under restraint, and whose condition was only incipient. Certain nervous cases have been persons who were not actually obsessed, but rather overshadowed by entities who pressed too close to them, casting on the patients a reflection of their bodily memories and ills, and causing dissociation."

Mrs. Duke, Dr. Bull's medium through whom he pleaded with the obsessing entities, was a woman of education. At first she was completely conscious of the messages that were given through her, but later speech control developed and proceedings became easier and more efficient. Under the title *Analysis of Unusual Experiences in Healing Relative to Diseased Minds and Results of Materialism Foreshadowed* (1932), Bull published his conclusions after 20 years of research. He ascribed the possibility of obsession to some accidental alteration in the nervous system and fully endorsed the Spiritualistic methods of cure. Somewhat similar work to that of Bull was carried out by Dr. **Carl A. Wickland** in Los Angeles, California.

Sources:

Bull, Titus. "Mental Obsession and the Latent Faculty." *Journal* of the American Society for Psychical Research 32 (1938): 260.

———. "Resistance to Metaphysical Science." *Journal* of the American Society for Psychical Research 17 (1927): 645.

Bune

According to **Johan Weyer,** Bune is a most powerful demon, one of the Grand Dukes of the Infernal Regions. His form is that of a man. He does not speak save by signs only. He removes corpses, haunts cemeteries, and marshals the demons around tombs and the places of the dead. He enriches and renders eloquent those who serve him. Thirty legions of the infernal army obey his call. The demons under his authority are called Bunis and are regarded by the Tartars as exceedingly evil. Their power is great and their number immense. But their sorcerers are ever in communication with these demons by means of whom they carry on their dark practices.

Sources:

Weyer, Johannes. *Witches, Devils, and Doctors in the Renaissance: Johann Weyer, De Praestigiis.* Edited by George Mora. Binghamton, N.Y.: Medieval and Renaissance Texts and Studies, 1991.

Bunyip

Legendary roaring monster of aboriginal peoples of **Australia.** The bunyip is said to live at the bottom of lakes and water holes, into which it drags its victims. The name implies "devil," although bunyips have been given other local names, such as "yaa-loo" and "wowee-wowee."

Some claim that the creature really exists. In 1939, to verify its existence, Gilbert Whitely of the Australian Museum collected reports of a number of sightings. Throughout the nineteenth century, explorers reported seeing and sometimes hearing bunyips, which appeared to be furry, with a dog-like head, long neck, and fins. Whitely concluded, "The bunyip has been thought to have been an extinct marsupial otter-like animal, rumors of whose existence have been handed down in aboriginal legends, the latter corrupted and confused with crocodiles in the north of Australia and seals in the south."

Sources:

Costello, Peter. *In Search of Lake Monsters.* New York: Coward, McCann & Geohegan, 1974. Reprint, London: Panther, 1975.

Bureau for the Investigation of Paranormal Photographs

Organization concerned with research on **psychic photography.** It continues the work first launched by the **Society for the Study of Supernormal Pictures,** which was dissolved in 1923. Its archives contain a wide range of examples, ranging from Mumler's **spirit photography** of the 1860s to photographs of paranormal or psychic phenomena. Address: Cyril Permutt, director, Bureau for the Investigation of Paranormal Photographs, Temple Fortune, London, England.

Burgot, Pierre (d. 1521)

A **werewolf** burned at Besançon, France, in 1521 together with **Michel Verdun.** In his confession, Burgot stated that 19 years earlier he had been collecting his flock of sheep during a great thunderstorm, when he was accosted by three demon horsemen, clad in black. One of these demons asked what troubled him, to which Burgot replied that he was afraid that his sheep might be attacked by wild beasts. The demon told him that if he would serve him as master and renounce God, Our Lady, the company of Heaven, and his baptism, all his sheep would be safe. He would also have money.

Burgot acknowledged the demon. Later, in company with Michel Verdun, he attended a Sabbat of warlocks, where he stripped naked and was anointed with an unguent, after which his limbs became hairy and his feet like those of a beast. Verdun also changed his form, and they both ran like the wind. In the shape of wolves they pursued and attacked children and committed other hideous crimes.

Sources:

Summers, Montague. *The Werewolf.* London, Kegan Paul, Trench, Trübner, 1933. Reprint, New Hyde Park, N.Y.: University Books, 1966.

Burgoyne, Thomas H. (1855–1894)

Thomas H. Burgoyne, an astrologer and founder of the Hermetic Brotherhood of Luxor, was born April 14, 1855, and grew up in his native Scotland. Spontaneously psychic, he claimed that as a child he contacted the Brotherhood of Light, a group of discarnate, advanced beings who attempt to guide the destiny of humankind. At a later date he met a M. Theon, who purported to be an earthly representative of the brotherhood.

Burgoyne moved to the United States around 1880 and soon afterward his writings began to appear in various periodicals. He was brought into contact with Norman Astley of Carmel, California, who also claimed to be in contact with the Brotherhood of Light. Astley suggested that Burgoyne write a set of lessons to introduce the brotherhood's teachings to the public, and Burgoyne accepted Astley's hospitality at Carmel while he worked on the lessons. They were published in 1889 as *The Light of Egypt.* The writing of the lessons occasioned the establishment of the Hermetic Brotherhood of Luxor as an esoteric occult order and outer expression of the Brotherhood of Light. The Hermetic Brotherhood was structured with three leaders, a seer, a scribe/secretary, and an astrologer. Burgoyne became the scribe.

As Burgoyne understood it, the Brotherhood of Light dated to ancient Egypt when an occult order formed in opposition to the dominant religious powers of the day. As the members died, they continued the brotherhood from their new plane of being.

Burgoyne wrote several more books, including *The Language of the Stars* (1892), *Celestial Dynamics* (1896), and a second volume of *The Light of Egypt* (1900). He died in March 1894, still a relatively young man, before the last two were published. Henry and Belle Wagner continued his work. Henry Wagner owned the Astro-Philosophical Publishing House in Denver, Colorado, which published Burgoyne's books. Belle M. Wagner succeeded Burgoyne as scribe of the Hermetic Brotherhood.

Occult historian **Arthur Edward Waite** claimed that Burgoyne was, in fact, a name assumed by Thomas Henry Dalton, who had been imprisoned in Leeds, England, in 1883, on charges of fraud. Waite asserts that it was only after his release that he met a Peter Davidson, the real founder of the Hermetic Brotherhood of Luxor. Dalton fled to the United States to escape the scandal of his arrest and continued the work of the order in California.

Sources:

Burgoyne, Thomas H. *Celestial Dynamics*. Denver: Astro-Philosophical Publishing, 1896.

———. *The Language of the Stars*. Denver: Astro-Philosophical Publishing, 1892.

———. *The Light of Egypt*. 2 vols. Denver: Astro-Philosophical Publishing, 1889, 1900.

Burial with Feet to the East

It was an early custom for Christians to bury their dead with the feet toward the east and the head toward the west. Various reasons were given for this practice, some authorities stating that the corpse was placed thus in preparation for the resurrection, when the dead would rise with their faces toward the east. Others think this mode of burial was practiced in imitation of the posture of prayer.

A possibly related custom is the belief that a body must be carried into a churchyard or cemetery "with the sun," that is, in the direction of sunset, from east to west.

Burland, C(ottie) A(rthur) (1905–1983)

Ethnographer, author, and authority on mythology in relation to the occult. He was born September 17, 1905, in Kensington, London, and studied at Regent Street Polytechnic. Except for his time of service in the Royal Air Force during World War II, he served for 40 years as a civil servant in the Department of Ethnography, British Museum, London (1925–65). He was a fellow of the Royal Anthropological Institute and a member of the Société de Americanistes de Paris, the British Society of Aesthetics, and the Folk-Lore Society (London). In 1965 he received the Imago Mundi Award.

Burland authored numerous books about ancient civilizations and primitive people, notably on the peoples of the ancient Americas—the Mayans, Incas, and Aztecs. His studies in these areas were of special importance, since the Incas had no written language, while the Mayan language was virtually obliterated by the destruction of Aztec manuscripts by early Spanish missionaries.

His studies led him into the study of magical practice among pre-industrial peoples, his 1953 *Magic Books from Mexico* being a first product of this interest. He later produced a series of books on magic in general including *The Magical Arts: A Short History* (1966), *The Arts of the Alchemists* (1967; 1968), *Beyond Science: A Journey into the Supernatural* (1972), *Echoes of Magic: A Study of Seasonal Festivals Through the Ages* (1972), and *Secrets of the Occult* (1972). He was a member of the editorial board of the comprehensive encyclopedia *Man, Myth, and Magic* (1970).

BURMA See MYANMAR

Burns, James (d. 1894)

Pioneer British Spiritualist and publisher, who founded the influential weekly newspaper the *Medium* in 1869, later absorbed with the *Daybreak.* Burns also established the **Progressive Library and Spiritual Institution** in Holborn, London, 1863. With their annual subscription, members were entitled to borrow from the thousands of Spiritualist publications available. The institute was also a center and meeting place for Spiritualists in London and organized programs of séances, developing circles and concerts. Burns was criticized because he opposed such other organizations as the **National Association of Spiritualists.** However, he established a great reputation as a courageous and tireless worker in the cause of **Spiritualism.** He died December 30, 1894.

Burt, Sir Cyril (Lodowic) (1883–1971)

Professor of psychology and psychic researcher. He was born March 3, 1883, in London and studied at Oxford University (M.A., D.Sc.). In 1932 he married Joyce Muriel Wood. Burt was psychologist for the London County Council (1913–32) and professor of education at the University of London (1924–31) prior to assuming his post as professor of psychology at University College, London (1931–50). During his career as a psychologist, he concentrated on the role of heredity in the development of intelligence and the application of psychology to education. He was the author of a number of books, edited the *British Journal of Statistical Psychology,* was president of the Psychological Section of the British Association in 1923, and was president of the British Psychological Society in 1942. He was knighted in 1946.

Burt had a special interest in parapsychology. He assisted the young student Samuel G. Soal, who began his career in parapsychology in Burt's laboratory. Burt carried on studies with mediums and did theoretical work on the nature of survival. He also promoted the need to understand perception in light of our knowledge of parapsychology. Besides a number of papers in parapsychological journals, he authored *Psychology and Psychical Research* (1968).

Burt died October 10, 1971. Since then it has been discovered that he doctored data to support his work on heredity and intelligence and appropriated other people's work as his own. The revelation of fraud and plagiarism has led to much of his early work being set aside.

Sources:

Burt, Cyril. *Psychology and Psychical Research.* London: Society for Psychical Research, 1968.

Hearnshaw, L. S. *Cyril Burt, Psychologist.* London: Hodder and Stoughton, 1979.

Busardier (ca. seventeenth century)

A practitioner of **alchemy** of whom few particulars are recorded. He is said to have lived at Prague with a noble courtier. Falling sick and feeling the approach of death, he sent a letter to his friend Richtausen at Vienna, asking him to come and stay with him during his last moments. Richtausen set out at once but on arriving at Prague found that Busardier was dead.

On inquiring if the **adept** had left anything behind him, the steward of the nobleman with whom he had lived stated that only some powder had been left which the nobleman desired to preserve. Richtausen by some means got possession of the powder and took his departure. On discovering this, the nobleman threatened to hang his steward if he did not recover the powder. The steward, surmising that no one but Richtausen could have taken the powder, armed himself and set out in pursuit.

Overtaking him on the road, he drew a pistol on Richtausen and made him hand over the powder. Richtausen, however, contrived to keep a considerable quantity. Knowing the value of the powder, Richtausen presented himself to Emperor Ferdinand, himself an alchemist, and gave him a quantity of the powder. The emperor, assisted by his mine master Count Russe, succeeded in converting three pounds of mercury into gold by means of one grain of the powder. The emperor is said to have commemorated the event by having a medal struck bearing the effigy of Apollo with the caduceus of Mercury and an appropriate motto.

Richtausen was ennobled under the title of "Baron Chaos." A. E. Waite, in his *Lives of Alchemistical Philosophers* (1888), stated:

"Among many transformations performed by the same powder was one by the Elector of Mayence, in 1651. He made projections with all the precautions possible to a learned and skilful philosopher. The powder enclosed in gum tragacanth to retain it effectually, was put into the wax of a taper, which was lighted, the wax being then placed at the bottom of a cruet. These preparations were undertaken by the Elector himself. He poured four ounces of quicksilver on the wax, and put the whole into a fire covered with charcoal above, below and around. Then they began blowing to the utmost, and in about half an hour on removing the coals, they saw that the melted gold was over red, the proper colour being green. The baron said the matter was yet too high and it was necessary to put some silver into it. The Elector took some coins out of his pocket, put them into the melting pot, combined the liquefied silver with the matter in the cruet, and having poured out the whole when in perfect fusion into a lingot, he found after cooling, that it was very fine gold, but rather hard, which was attributed to the lingot. On again melting, it became exceedingly soft and the Master of the Mint declared to His Highness that it was more than twenty-four carats and that he had never seen so fine a quality of the precious metal."

Sources:

Waite, A. E. *Lives of the Alchemical Philosophers.* London: George Redway, 1888. Reprinted as *Alchemists through the Ages.* Blauvelt, N.Y.: Rudolf Steiner Publications, 1970.

Butcher, Samuel Henry (1850–1910)

Distinguished classical scholar and professor of Greek at University of Edinburgh (1882–1903). He was born April 16, 1850, in Dublin, Ireland, and studied at Marlborough College, and Trinity College, Cambridge (senior classic and chancellors medalist, 1873; M.A. 1876). He was a member of parliament for Cambridge University (1906) and an honorary fellow of University College, Oxford, and Trinity College, Cambridge.

Butcher was not himself involved in psychic research but was a close friend of some of the founders of the **Society for Psychical Research,** London. After his death he was claimed to be a leading "communicator" in a famous **cross correspondence** experiment. He died December 29, 1910.

Butler, Walter (Ernest) (1898– ?)

Author of books on **magic** and other occult subjects. He was born August 23, 1898, in England. In 1924 he married Gladys Irene Newell. After serving in the British Army (1917–29), he worked for many years as an engineer (1929–56). From 1956 to 1963 he was a member of the technical staff in charge of physical chemistry, department workshop, at University of Southampton, England.

He began experimenting with magical studies as a child and studied **yoga** while stationed in India with the British Army. In England, he became associated for a time with occultist **Dion Fortune** and her **Fraternity of the Inner Light.** In 1954 Butler was active in the Southampton Group of the **Churches' Fellowship for Psychical and Spiritual Studies.** His teachings and many books formed the substance of the magical Servants of the Light Association. His *The Magician: His Training and Work* (1959) is a classic text for basic magical training.

Sources:

Butler, Walter E. *Apprenticed to Magic.* 1962. Reprint. Wellingborough, England: Aquarian Press, 1990.

———. *How to Read the Aura, Practice Psychometry, Telepathy, and Clairvoyance.* New York: Warner Destiny Books, 1978.

———. *An Introduction to Telepathy.* 1975.

———. *Magic: Its Ritual, Power, and Purpose.* London: Aquarian Press, 1952.

———. *The Magician: His Training and Work.* London: The Aquarian Press, 1959. Reprint, North Hollywood, Calif.: Wilshire Book, 1959.

Butter, Witches'

According to old superstition, the devil gave to the witches of Sweden cats which were called carriers, because they were sent by their mistresses to steal in the neighborhood. On such occasions, the greedy animals could not resist satisfying their own appetites. Sometimes they ate to repletion and were obliged to disgorge their stolen meal. Their vomit, found in kitchen gardens, was a yellow color, and it was called witches' butter.

C

Caacrinolaas

According to **Johan Weyer,** Caacrinolaas is the Grand President of Hell. He is also known as Caasimolar and Glasya and is represented in the shape of a god with the wings of a griffin. He is supposed to inspire knowledge of the liberal arts and to incite homicides. It is also believed that this fiend is able to render people invisible. He commands 36 legions of devils.

Sources:

Weyer, Johannes. *Witches, Devils and Doctors in the Renaissance: Johann Weyer, De Praestigiis.* Edited by George Mora. Binghamton, N.Y.: Medieval & Renaissance Texts & Studies, 1991.

Cabinet

The curtain-enclosed space in which mediums claim to condense the psychic energy necessary for séance-room manifestations. **Hereward Carrington** suggested an electrical analogy: less expenditure of energy is required to charge a small electric conductor to a given voltage than a large one, so it may be with the cabinet, "which acts as a sort of storage battery, retaining the energy and liberating it in bundles of quanta during the séance."

Nineteenth-century biblical scholar Allen Putnam saw the ark of the covenant as an interesting model by which to understand the Spiritualist cabinet:

"The ark of the covenant was constructed expressly for use as a spirit battery, or an instrument through which to give forth the commands of the Lord. The special care taken to have the ark and all its appurtenances charged with the auras or magnetisms of a selected class of workmen, becomes very interesting in these days when much wonder is expressed at the customary stickling of spirits and mediums for right conditions. Biblical history furnishes precedent for great particularity, when constructing a cabinet for manifestations."

The cabinet is usually of very simple construction. It need not be more than a curtain thrown across a corner of the room. The **Davenport brothers** employed a special one. It had three doors; the middle door had a curtained opening on the top. Through this opening, phantom hands were immediately thrust out after the doors were shut on the mediums tied within to their seats. However, such an elaborate arrangement suggests a conjuror's apparatus, and the phenomenon of the Davenports is considered by many people to have been a stage illusion. It is described in some detail by Houdini in *A Magician among the Spirits.*

By the beginning of the twentieth century, many of the famous mediums, such as **D. D. Home** and **Stainton Moses,** had never used the cabinet. Through the course of the twentieth century it has gone almost entirely out of use; the majority of contemporary psychics and channels have never used the cabinet.

Sources:

Houdini, Harry. *A Magician among the Spirits.* New York: Harper & Brothers, 1924. Reprinted as *Houdini: A Magician among the Spirits.* New York: Arno Press, 1972.

Putnam, Allen. *Bible Marvel Workers.* Boston, 1876.

Cabiri (or Cabeiri)

A group of minor deities of Greek origin. The name appears to be of Semitic origin, signifying the "great gods," and the Cabiri seem to have been connected in some manner with the sea, protecting sailors and vessels. The chief seats of their worship were Lemnos, Samothrace, Thessalia, and Boeotia. They were originally only two in number, the elder identified with Dionysus, and the younger with Hermes, who was also known as Cadmilus.

Their worship was later amalgamated with that of Demeter and Ceres, with the result that two sets of Cabiri came into being—Dionysus and Demeter, and Cadmilus and Ceres. A Greek writer of the second century B.C.E. states that they were four in number—Axisros, Axiokersa, Axiokersos, and Casmilus, corresponding, he states, to Demeter, Persephone, Hades, and Hermes.

The Romans identified the Cabiri with the Penates, the Roman gods of the household. A festival of these deities was held annually in Lemnos and lasted nine days, during which all domestic and other fires were extinguished and sacred fire was brought from Delos. From this fact it has been judged that the Cabiri may have been volcanic demons, although this view has largely been abandoned.

It was in Samothrace that the cult of the Cabiri attained its widest significance, and in that island as early as the fifth century B.C.E., their mysteries, or religious rites, were held with great enthusiasm and attracted almost universal attention. Initiation into this cult was regarded as a safeguard against misfortune of all kinds, and persons of distinction exerted all their influence to become initiates. Interesting details as to the bacchanal cult of the Cabiri were obtained in 1888 by the excavation of their temple near Thebes. Statues of a deity called Cabeiros were found, attended by a boy cupbearer. His attributes appear to be bacchic.

The Cabiri were often mentioned as powerful magicians, and Herodotus and other writers speak of the Cabiri as sons of Vulcan. Cicero, however, regarded them as the children of Proserpine, and Jupiter was often named as their father. Strabo, on the other hand, regarded them as the ministers of Hecate, and Bochart recognized in them the three principal infernal deities, Pluto, Proserpine, and Mercury. Although it is assumed that they were originally of Semitic origin, a temple of Memphis was found consecrated to them in Egypt. It is not unlikely, as Herodotus supposed, that the cult was Pelasgian in origin, as it is known that the Pelasgians occupied the island of Samothrace and established there certain mysteries, which they afterward carried to Athens. There are also traditions that the worship of the Cabiri originally came from the Troad (territory surrounding the ancient city of Troy), a Semitic center. In his book *The Egypt of Herodotus* (1841), John Kenrick brings forward the following conclusions concerning the Cabiri:

"1. The existence of the worship of the Cabiri at Memphis under a pygmy form, and its connection with the worship of Vulcan. The coins of Thessalonica also establish this connection; those which bear the legend 'Kabeiros' having a figure with a hammer in his hand, the pileus and apron of Vulcan, and sometimes an anvil near the feet.

"2. The Cabiri belonged also to the Phoenician theology. The proofs are drawn from the statements of Herodotus. Also the coins of Cossyra, a Phoenician settlement, exhibit a dwarfish figure with the hammer and short apron, and sometimes a radiated head, apparently allusive to the element of fire, like the star of the Dioscuri.

"3. The isle of Lemnos was another remarkable seat of the worship of the Cabiri and of Vulcan, as representing the element of fire. Mystic rites were celebrated here over which they presided, and the coins of the island exhibit the head of Vulcan, or a Cabirus, with the pileus, hammer, and forceps. It was this connection with fire, metallurgy, and the most remarkable product of the act, weapons of war, which caused the Cabiri to be identified with the Cureks of Etolia, the Idaei Dactyli of Crete, the Corybantes of Phrygia, and the Telchines of Rhodes. They were the same probably in Phoenician origin, the same in mystical and orgiastic rites, but different in number, genealogy, and local circumstances, and by the mixture of other mythical traditions, according to the various countries in which their worship prevailed. The fable that one Cabirus had been killed by his brother or brothers was probably a moral mythus representing the result of the invention of armor and analogous to the story of the mutual destruction of the men in brazen armor, who sprang from the dragon's teeth sown by Cadmus and Jason. It is remarkable that the name of the first fratricide signifies a 'lance,' and in Arabic a 'smith.'

"4. The worship of the Cabiri prevailed also in Imbros, near the entrance of the Hellespont, which makes it probable that the great gods in the neighboring island of Samothrace were of the same origin. The Cabiri, Curetes, and Corybantes appear to have represented air as well as fire. This island was inhabited by Pelasgi, who may have derived from the neighboring country of Thrace and Phrygia, and with the old Pelasgic mysteries of Ceres. Hence the various explanations given of the Samothracian deities, and the number of them so differently stated, some making them two, some four, some eight, the latter agreeing with the number of early Egyptian gods mentioned by Herodotus. It is still probable that their original number was two, from their identification with the Dioscuri and Tyndaridae, and from the number of the Pataeci on Phoenician vessels. The addition of Vulcan as their father or brother made them three, and a fourth may have been their mother Cabira.

"5. The Samothracian divinities continued to be held in high veneration in late times, but are commonly spoken of in connection with navigation, as the twin Dioscuri or Tyndaridae; on the other hand the Dioscuri are spoken of as the Curetes or Corybantes. The coins of Tripolis exhibit the spears and star of the Dioscuri, with the legend 'Cabiri.'

"6. The Roman Penates have been identified with the Dioscuri, and Dionysius states that he had seen two figures of ancient workmanship, representing youths armed with spears, which, from an antique inscription on them, he knew to be meant for Penates. So, the 'Lares' of Etruria and Rome.

"7. The worship of the Cabiri furnishes the key to the wanderings of Aeneas, the foundation of Rome, and the War of Troy itself, as well as the Argonautic expedition. Samothrace and the Troad were so closely connected in this worship, that it is difficult to judge in which of the two it originated, and the gods of Lavinium, the supposed colony from Troy, were Samothracian. Also the Palladium, a pygmy image, was connected at once with Aeneas and the Troad, with Rome, Vesta, and the Penates, and the religious belief and traditions of several towns in the south of Italy."

Kenrick also recognizes a mythical personage in Aeneas, whose attributes were derived from those of the Cabiri, and continues with some interesting observations on the Homeric fables. He concludes that the essential part of the War of Troy originated in the desire to connect together and explain the traces of an ancient religion. He also notes one other remarkable circumstance, that the countries in which the Samothracian and Cabiriac worship prevailed were peopled either by the Pelasgi or by the Aeolians, who of all the tribes comprehended under the general name Hellenes, approach the most nearly in antiquity and language to the Pelasgi.

"We seem warranted, then," Kenrick observes, "in two conclusions; first that the Pelasgian tribes in Italy, Greece and Asia were united in times reaching high above the commencement of history, by community of religious ideas and rites, as well as letters, arts, and language. Secondly, large portions of what is called the heroic history of Greece, are nothing else than fictions devised to account for the traces of this affinity, when time and the ascendancy of other nations had destroyed the primitive connection, and rendered the cause of the similarity obscure. The original derivation of the Cabiriac system from Phoenicia and Egypt is a less certain, though still highly probable conclusion."

Kenrick also concluded that "the name Cabiri has been very generally deduced from the Phoenician 'mighty' and this etymology is in accordance with the fact that the gods of Samothrace were called 'Divi potes.'"

Kenrick believed, however, that the Phoenicians used some other name, which the Greeks translated "Kabeiros," and that it denoted the two elements of fire and wind.

In his book *India in Greece* (1856), Edward Pococke claims the Cabiri were the "Khyberi," or people of the "Khyber," or a Buddhist tribe—a totally unlikely origin for them. In the *Generations* of Sanchoniathon, the Cabiri are claimed as Phoenicians, although in a mystical sense. According to the myth, the Wind and the Night gave birth to two moral men, Aeon and Protogonus. The immediate descendants of these two were "Genus" and "Genea," a man and woman. To Genus were born three mortal children, Phôs, Pur, and Phlox, who discovered fire, and these again fathered sons of vast bulk and height, whose names were given to the mountains in which they dwelt, Cassiul, Libanus, Antilibanus, and Brathu. The issue of these giant men by their own mothers were Meinrumus, Hypsuranius, and Usous. Hypsuranius inhabited Tyre; Usous becoming a huntsman, consecrated two pillars to fire and the wind with the blood of the wild beasts that he captured.

Much later, from the race of Hypsuranius issued Agreus and Halieus, inventors, it is said, of the arts of hunting and fishing. From these descended two brothers, one of whom was Chrysor (or Hephaestus), skilled in words, charms, and divinations; he also invented boats and was the first to sail. His brother first built walls with bricks, and their descendants in the second generation seem to have completed the invention of houses by the addition of courts, porticos, and crypts. They are called Aletae and Titans, and in their time began animal husbandry and hunting with dogs. From the Titans descended Amynus, a builder, and Magus, who taught men to construct villages and tend flocks, and of these two were begotten Misor (perhaps Mizraim), whose name signifies Well-freed, and Sydic, whose name denotes the Just; these discovered the use of salt.

From Misor descended Taautus (Thoth, Athothis, or Hermes Trismegistus), who invented letters; and from Sydic descended the Dioscuri, or Cabiri, or Corybantes, or Samothraces. According to Sanchoniathon, first built a complete ship and others descended from them who discovered medicine and charms. All this dates prior to Babylon and the gods of paganism, the elder of whom are next introduced in the *Generations.*

Finally, Sanchoniathon settles Poseidon (Neptune) and the Cabiri at Berytus, but not till circumcision, the sacrifice of human beings, and the portrayal of the gods had been introduced. He describes the Cabiri as husbandmen and fishermen, which leads to the presumption that the people who worshiped those ancient gods were at length called by their name. The method of initiation unto the cult was as follows:

"The candidate for initiation was crowned with a garland of olive, and wore a purple band round his loins. Thus attired, and prepared by secret ceremonies (probably mesmeric), he was seated on a throne brilliantly lighted, and the other initiates then danced round him in hieroglyphic measures. It may be imagined that solemnities of this nature would easily degenerate into orgies of the most immoral tendency, as the ancient faith and reverence for sacred things perished, and such was really the case. Still, the primitive institution was pure in form and beautiful in its mystic signification, which passed from one ritual to another, till its last glimmer expired in the freemasonry of a very recent period. The general idea represented was the passage through death to a higher life, and while the outward senses were held in the thrall of magnetism, it is probable that revelations, good or evil, were made to the high priests of these ceremonies.''

It is extremely difficult to arrive at any conclusion regarding the origin of the Cabiri, but they were probably of Semitic origin, arriving in Greece through Phoenician influence, and that they approximated in character the gods with whom the Greeks identified them is extremely likely.

Sources:

Bryant, Jacob. *A New System; or an Analysis of Ancient Mythology.* 3 vols. 1776. Reprint, New York: Garland, 1979.

Varro, Marcus Terrentius. *De Lingua Latina.* Translated as *On the Latin Language.* Cambridge, Mass.: Harvard University Press, 1958.

Cacodaemons

Ancient deities of inferior rank—one of whom it was believed was attached to each mortal from his birth as a constant companion—capable of giving impulses and acting as a sort of messenger between the gods and men. The cacodaemons were of a hostile nature, as opposed to the **agathodaemons**, who were friendly. It is said that one of the cacodaemons who appeared to Cassius was a man of huge stature and of a black hue. Early astrologers named the twelfth house of the sun Cacodemon, as its influence was regarded as evil.

It is said that the cacodaemons were the rebellious angels who were expelled from heaven for their crimes. They tried in vain to obtain settlement in various parts of the universe, with their final abode believed to be all the space between Earth and the stars. There they abide, hated by all the elements and finding their pleasure in revenge and injury. Their king was called Hades by the Greeks, Typhon by the Egyptians, and Ahrimanes by the Persians and Chaldeans.

Sources:

Kendrick, Tertius T. C. *The Kako-daemon or The Cavern of Anti-Paros.* London, 1825.

Cactomite

A marvelous stone believed by ancient peoples to possess occult properties. Anyone wearing it was supposed to be assured of victory in battle.

Cadoret, Remi Jere (1928–)

Assistant professor, Department of Physiology, University of Manitoba Medical College, Winnipeg, Canada, and member of the **Parapsychological Association** and Canadian Physiological Society. He was born March 28, 1928, in Scranton, Pennsylvania, and educated at Harvard University (B.A., 1949), Yale University (M.D., 1953).

Cadoret conducted tests in ESP, reported in the *Journal of Parapsychology.* In 1977 he was treasurer of the Parapsychological Association, Durham, North Carolina.

Sources:

Berger, Arthur S., and Joyce Berger. *The Encyclopedia of Parapsychology and Psychical Research.* New York: Paragon House, 1991.

Cadoret, Remi J. ''Effect of Novelty in Test Conditions on ESP Performance.'' *Journal of Parapsychology* 16 (1952).

———. ''An Exploratory Experiment: Continuous EEG Recoding During Clairvoyant Card Tests.'' *Journal of Parapsychology* 28 (1964).

Cadoret, Remi J., and J. Fahler. ''ESP Card Tests of College Students With and Without Hypnosis.'' *Journal of Parapsychology* 22 (1958).

Cadoret, Remi J., and J. G. Pratt. ''The Consistent Missing Effect in ESP.'' *Journal of Parapsychology* 14 (1950).

Pleasants, Helene, ed. *Biographical Dictionary of Parapsychology.* New York: Helix Press, 1964.

Caer

The daughter of Ethal Anubal, prince of the **Danaans** of Connaught, mentioned in ancient Irish myths. It was said that she lived alternate years in the form of a maiden and a swan. She was loved by Angus Og, who also found himself transformed into a swan. All who heard the rapturous song of the swan lovers were plunged into a deep sleep, lasting for three days and nights.

Cagliostro (1743–1795)

Considered by some to be one of the greatest occult figures of all time. It was the fashion during the latter half of the nineteenth century to regard Cagliostro as a charlatan and **fraud.** This viewpoint was greatly aided by the savage attack perpetrated on his memory by Thomas Carlyle, who alluded to him as ''the Prince of Quacks.'' Others, such as W. R. H. Trowbridge (1918), have argued that if Cagliostro was not a man of unimpeachable honor, he was by no means the quack and scoundrel so many have made him out to be.

Following is an outline of Cagliostro's life as known before Trowbridge's examination, after which the details of his career are explored in view of what may be termed as Trowbridge's ''discoveries.''

Cagliostro's Mysterious Life

The problem of assembling a biographical sketch of Cagliostro is difficult due to the significant amount of legendary material that surrounds him. It is therefore necessary to apply a critical eye when dealing with the myriad contradictions.

Cagliostro's father, whose name is alleged to have been Peter Balsamo, died young. From infancy, young Joseph Balsamo showed an unconventional individualism, and when placed in a religious seminary at Palermo he more than once ran away from it; usually found in undesirable company. He was sent next to a Benedictine convent, where he was under the care of a father superior. The father superior quickly discovered his natural aptitude, and Balsamo became the assistant of an apothecary attached to the convent, from whom he learned the principles of chemistry and medicine. Even then his desire was more to discover surprising and astonishing chemical combinations than to gain more useful knowledge. Tiring of the life at last, he succeeded in escaping from the convent, and went to Palermo.

In Palermo resided a goldsmith named Marano, a superstitious man who believed devoutly in the efficacy of magic. He became attracted to young Balsamo, who at the age of seventeen posed as being deeply versed in occultism and had been seen evoking spirits. Marano made his acquaintance and confided to him that he had spent a great deal of money upon quack alchemists, but he was convinced that by meeting him he had at last chanced upon a real master of magic. Balsamo willingly ministered to the man's superstitions, and told him as a profound secret that in a nearby field was a buried treasure, which he could locate by the aid of magic ceremonies. But the operation necessitated some expensive preliminaries—at least 60 ounces of gold would be required. To this very considerable sum Marano demurred, and Balsamo coolly asserted that he would enjoy the vast treasure alone. But the credulity of Marano was too strong for his better sense, and at length he agreed to furnish the necessary funds.

At midnight they sought the field where it the supposed treasure was hidden. Balsamo proceeded with his incantations, and Marano, terrified at their dreadful nature, fell to the ground in submission. He was then unmercifully attacked by a number of scoundrels whom Balsamo had collected for that purpose. Palermo rang with the affair, but Balsamo managed to escape to Messina, where he adopted the title "Count Cagliostro."

It was in this town where he first met with the mysterious **Althotas.** He was walking one day in the vicinity of the harbor when he encountered a person of singular dress and countenance. Attracted by his appearance, Cagliostro saluted him, and after some conversation the stranger offered to tell the pseudo count the story of his past and to reveal what was actually passing in his mind at that moment. Cagliostro was interested and made arrangements to visit the stranger.

Cagliostro duly appeared and was led along a narrow passage lit by a single lamp in a niche of the wall. At the end was a spacious apartment illuminated by wax candles and furnished with everything necessary for the practice of alchemy. Althotas expressed himself as a believer in the mutability of physical law (rather than magic), which he regarded as a science having fixed laws discoverable and reducible to reason. He proposed to depart for Egypt and to take Cagliostro with him—a proposal that the latter joyfully accepted. Althotas informed Cagliostro that he possessed no funds but told him that it was an easy matter for him to make sufficient gold to pay the expenses of their voyage.

Accompanied by Cagliostro, Althotas penetrated into Africa and the heart of Egypt, visiting the pyramids, making the acquaintance of the priests of different temples, and receiving from them much knowledge. Following their Egyptian tour, they visited the principal kingdoms of Africa and Asia, and were subsequently located at Rhodes pursuing alchemical operations. At Malta they assisted the grandmaster Pinto, who was infatuated with alchemical experiments, and from that moment Althotas completely disappeared, the memoir of Cagliostro stating that during their residence at Malta he passed away.

On the death of his comrade, Cagliostro traveled to Naples. There he met with a Sicilian prince who conceived a strong predilection for his society and invited him to his castle near Palermo. He had not been long in Palermo when one day he traveled to Messina, where he encountered by chance one of his confederates in the affair of Marano the goldsmith. This man warned him not to enter the town of Palermo, and finally persuaded him to return to Naples to open a gambling house for the fleecing of wealthy foreigners. This scheme the pair carried out, but the Neapolitan authorities regarded them with such grave suspicion that they prudently removed themselves to the papal states. There they parted company, and regarding this time the alleged memoir of Cagliostro is not very clear. Later, in Rome, he established a fraudulent medical practice where he retailed concotions for all the diseases that humans can acquire; a setup that provided considerable wealth and luxury.

It was at this time that he met the young and beautiful Lorenza Feliciani, to whom he proposed marriage; her father, dazzled by Cagliostro's apparent wealth and importance, consented, and the marriage took place with some ceremony. All biographers of Cagliostro agree in stating that Lorenza was a thoroughly good woman, honest, devoted, and modest. The most dreadful accusations have been made concerning the manner in which Cagliostro treated his wife, and it has been alleged that he thoroughly ruined her character and corrupted her mind.

At last Caglistro and Lorenza arrived in Spain by way of Barcelona, where they stayed for six months, proceeding afterward to Madrid and Lisbon. From Lisbon they sailed to England, where Cagliostro lived by duping unwitting foreigners. An English "life of Cagliostro" tells of his adventures in London, how he was robbed of a large sum in plate, jewels, and money, and how he hired apartments in Whitcomb Street, where he spent most of his time in studying chemistry and physics, and giving away money.

In 1772 he returned to France with Lorenza and a certain Duplaisir. At this time it is said that Duplaisir eloped with Lorenza, and when Cagliostro obtained an order for her arrest, she was imprisoned in a penitentiary, where she was detained for several months. At this time Cagliostro had attracted attention in Paris with his alchemical successes. It was the period of mystic enthusiasm in Europe, when princes, bishops, and the nobility generally were keen to probe the secrets of nature, and alchemy.

Cagliostro went too far and eventually his benefactors began to seriously doubt his honesty. He was forced to flee to Brussels, where he made his way to his native town of Palermo. He was immediately arrested by the goldsmith Marano. A certain nobleman, however, interested himself on his behalf, procured his release, and Cagliostro embarked with Lorenza for Malta. From that island they soon retired to Naples, and from there to Marseilles and Barcelona. Their progress was marked by considerable state, and having cheated an alchemist of 100,000 crowns under the pretence of achieving some alchemical secret, they fled to England.

During his second visit to London Cagliostro was initiated into **Freemasonry** and conceived his great idea of employing that system for his own gain. He incessantly visited the various London lodges and ingratiated himself with their principals and officials. At this time he supposedly picked up a manuscript at an obscure London bookstall that is said to have belonged to a certain George Gaston. This document dealt with the mysteries of Egyptian Masonry and abounded in magical and mystical references. It was from this, that Cagliostro allegedly gathered his occult inspirations.

After another tour through Holland, Italy, and Germany, he paid a visit to the **Count de St. Germain.** In his usual eccentric manner, St. Germain arranged their meeting for the hour of two o'clock in the morning, at which time Cagliostro and Lorenza presented themselves before the count's temple of mystery.

The Count de St. Germain sat upon the altar, and at his feet two acolytes swung golden censers. In the book *Lives of the Alchemystical Philosophers,* published anonymously in 1815, this interview is thus detailed:

"The divinity bore upon his breast a diamond pentagram of almost intolerable radiance. A majestic statue, white and diaphanous, upheld on the steps of the altar a vase inscribed, 'Elixir of Immortality,' while a vast mirror was on the wall, and before it a living being, majestic as the statue, walked to and fro. Above the mirror were these singular words—'Store House of Wandering Souls.' The most solemn silence prevailed in this sacred retreat, but at length a voice, which seemed hardly a voice, pronounced these words—'Who are you? Whence come you? What would you?' Then the Count and Countess Cagliostro prostrated themselves, and the former answered after a long pause, 'I come to invoke the God of the faithful, the Son of Nature, the Sire of Truth. I come to demand of him one of the fourteen thousand seven hundred secrets which are treasured in his breast, I come to proclaim myself his slave, his apostle, his martyr.'

"The divinity did not respond, but after a long silence, the same voice asked:—'What does the partner of thy long wanderings intend?'

"'To obey and to serve,' Lorenza answered.

"Simultaneously with her words, profound darkness succeeded the glare of light, uproar followed on tranquillity, terror on trust, and a sharp and menacing voice cried loudly:—'Woe to those who cannot stand the tests.'

"Husband and wife were immediately separated to undergo their respective trials, which they endured with exemplary fortitude and which are detailed in the text of their memoirs. When the romantic mummery was over, the two postulants were led back into the temple with the promise of admission to the divine mysteries. There a man mysteriously draped in a long mantle cried out to them: 'Know ye that the arcanum of our great art is the government of mankind, and that the one means to rule them is never to tell them the truth. Do not foolishly regulate your actions according to the rules of common sense; rather outrage reason and courageously maintain every unbelievable absurdity. Remember that reproduction is the palmary active power in nature, politics and society alike; that it is a mania with mortals to be immortal, to know the future without understanding the present, and to be spiritual while all that surrounds them is material.'

"After this harangue the orator genuflected devoutly before the divinity of the temple and retired. At the same moment a man of gigantic stature led the countess to the feet of the immortal Count de St. Germain who thus spoke:

"'Elected from my tenderest youth to the things of greatness, I employed myself in ascertaining the nature of veritable glory. Politics appeared to me nothing but the science of deception, tactics the art of assassination, philosophy the ambitious imbecility of complete irrationality; physics fine fancies about Nature and the continual mistakes of persons suddenly transplanted, into a country which is utterly unknown to them; theology the science of the misery which results from human pride; history the melancholy spectacle of perpetual perfidy and blundering. Thence I concluded that the statesman was a skillful liar, the hero an illustrious idiot, the philosopher an eccentric creature, the physician a pitiable and blind man, the theologian a fanatical pedagogue, and the historian a word-monger. Then did I hear of the divinity of this temple. I cast my cares upon him, with my incertitudes and aspirations. When he took possession of my soul he caused me to perceive all objects in a new light; I began to read futurity. This universe so limited, so narrow, so desert, was now enlarged. I abode not only with those who are, but with those who were. He united me to the loveliest women of antiquity. I found it eminently delectable to know all without studying anything, to dispose of the treasures of the earth without the solicitations of monarchs, to rule the elements rather than men. Heaven made me liberal; I have sufficient to satisfy my taste; all that surrounds me is rich, loving, predestinated.'

"When the service was finished the costume of ordinary life was resumed. A superb repast terminated the ceremony. During the course of the banquet the two guests were informed that the Elixir of Immortality was merely Tokay coloured green or red according to the necessities of the case. Several essential precepts were enjoined upon them, among others that they must detest, avoid, and calumniate men of understanding, but flatter, foster, and blind fools, that they must spread abroad with much mystery the intelligence that the Court de St. Germain was five hundred years old, and that they must make gold, but dupes before all."

Traveling into Courland (western Latvia), Cagliostro and his wife succeeded in establishing several Masonic lodges according to the rite of what he called Egyptian Freemasonry. Persons of high rank flocked around the couple, and it is even said that he plotted for the sovereignty of the grand duchy. It is also alleged that he collected a very large treasure of presents and money and set out for St. Petersburg, where he established himself as a physician.

A large number of medical cures have been credited to Cagliostro throughout his career, and his methods have been the subject of considerable controversy. But there is little doubt that the basis of them was a species of mesmeric influence. It has been said that he trusted simply to the laying on of hands, that he charged nothing for his services, and that most of his time was occupied in treating the poor.

Returning to Germany, he was received in most of the towns through which he passed as a benefactor of the human race. Some regarded his cures as miracles, others as sorceries, while he himself asserted they were effected by celestial aid.

For three years Cagliostro remained at Strasbourg, honored and praised by all. He formed a strong friendship with the cardinal-archbishop, the Prince de Rohan, who was fired by the idea of achieving alchemical successes. Cagliostro accomplished supposed transmutations under his eyes, and the prince, delighted with the seeming successes, lavished immense sums upon him. He even believed that the elixir of life was known to Cagliostro and built a small house in which he was to undergo a physical regeneration.

When he depleted the prince's finances, Cagliostro went to Lyons, where he occupied himself with the foundation of headquarters for his Egyptian Masonic rite. He then proceeded to Paris, where he assumed the role of master of practical magic and evoked phantoms that he caused to appear at the wish of the inquirer in a vase of clear water or in a mirror. Occult authority **Arthur E. Waite** suggested that in this connection fraud was an impossibility and appears to lean toward the theory that the visions evoked by Cagliostro were such as occur in **crystal gazing** and believed no one was more astonished than the Count himself at the results he obtained. Paris rang with his name and he received the appellation "the Divine Cagliostro."

Introduced to the court of Louis XVI, Cagliostro succeeded in evoking apparitions in mirrors before many spectators—these apparitions included many deceased persons especially selected by those present. His residence was isolated and surrounded by gardens, and there he established a laboratory. His wife affected great privacy and only appeared, in a costume, at certain hours and before a very select company. This heightened the mystery surrounding them, and the elite of Parisian society vied with one another to be present at their magic suppers, at which the evocation of the illustrious dead was the principal amusement. It is even stated that deceased statesmen, authors, and nobles took their seats at Cagliostro's supper table.

Cagliostro's grand objective, however, appeared to have been the spread of his Egyptian Masonic rite. The lodges he founded were androgynal—they admitted both men and women. The ladies were instructed by the master's wife, who figured as the grand mistress of the order, her husband adopting the title of Grand Copt.

There is little doubt that a good deal of money was subscribed by the neophytes of the various lodges. Each woman who joined sacrificed on the altar of mysticism no less than 100 louis, and Cagliostro's immense wealth was established from the numerous gifts that were showered upon him by the powerful and wealthy for the purpose of furthering his Masonic schemes. Although he lived in considerable magnificence, Cagliostro by no means led a life of abandoned luxury, for there is evidence that he gave away vast sums to the poor and needy, attended the sick, and played the part of healer and reformer.

A great deal of mystery surrounded the doings of the Egyptian Masonry in its headquarters in the Faubourg Saint Honoré, and the séances for initiation took place at midnight. The writer Louis Figuier and the Marquis de Luchet gave striking accounts of what occurred during the female initiations. Figuier observed:

"On entering the first apartment the ladies were obliged to disrobe and assume a white garment, with a girdle of various colors. They were divided into six groups, distinguished by the tint of their cinctures. A large veil was also provided, and they were caused to enter a temple lighted from the roof, and furnished with thirty-six arm-chairs covered with black satin. Lorenza clothed in white, was seated on a species of throne, supported by two tall figures, so habited that their sex could not be determined. The light was lowered by degrees till surrounding objects could scarcely be distinguished, when the Grand Mistress commanded the ladies to uncover their left legs as far as the thigh, and raising the right arm to rest it on a neighboring pillar. Two young women then entered sword in hand, and with silk ropes bound all the ladies together by the arms and legs."

"After a period of silence, Lorenza pronounced an oration which preached emancipation of womankind from the bonds imposed on them by the lords of creation.

"These bonds were symbolized by the silken ropes from which the fair initiates were released at the end of the harangue, when they were conducted into separate apartments, each opening onto the garden. There some were pursued by men who persecuted them with solicitations; others encountered admirers who sighed in languishing postures at their feet. More than one discovered the counterpart of her own love, but the oath they had all taken necessitated the most inexorable inhumanity, and all faithfully fulfilled what was required of them. The new spirit infused into the regenerated women triumphed along the whole line of the thirty-six initiates, who with intact and immaculate symbols reentered the temple to receive the congratulations of the sovereign priestess.

"When they had breathed a little after their trials, the vaulted roof opened suddenly, and, on a vast sphere of gold, there descended a man, naked as the unfallen Adam, holding a serpent in his hand, and having a burning star upon his head.

"The Grand Mistress announced that this was the genius of Truth, the immortal, the divine Cagliostro, issued without procreation from the bosom of our father Abraham, and the depositary of all that hath been, is, or shall be known on the universal earth. He was there to initiate them into the secrets of which they had been fraudulently deprived. The Grand Copt thereupon commanded them to dispense with the profanity of clothing, for if they would receive truth they must be as naked as itself. The sovereign priestess setting the example unbound her girdle and permitted her drapery to fall to the ground, and the fair initiates following her example exposed themselves in all the nudity of their charms to the magnetic glances of the celestial genius, who then commenced his revelations.

"He informed his daughters that the much abused magical art was the secret of doing good to humanity. It was the initiation into the mysteries of Nature, and the power to make use of her occult forces. The visions which they had beheld in the Garden where so many had seen and recognised those who were dearest to their hearts, proved the reality of hermetic operations. They had shewn themselves worthy to know the truth; he undertook to instruct them by gradations therein. It was enough at the outset to inform them that the sublime end of that Egyptian Freemasonry which he had brought from the very heart of the Orient was the happiness of mankind. This happiness was illimitable in its nature, including material enjoyments as much as spiritual peace, and the pleasures of the understanding."

At the end of this harangue the Grand Copt once more seated himself upon the sphere of gold and was borne away through the roof.

The Affair of the Diamond Necklace

It was during this period that Cagliostro became implicated in the extraordinary affair of a diamond necklace. He had been on terms of great intimacy with the Cardinal de Rohan. Countess de Lamotte had petitioned that prince for a pension on account of long aristocratic descent. De Rohan greatly desired to become first minister of the throne, but Marie Antoinette, the queen, disliked him and stood in the way of this an honor.

Lamotte soon discovered this and, for purposes of her own, told the cardinal that the queen favored his ambitions. She then either forged, or procured someone else to forge, letters to the cardinal claiming to come from the queen, some of which begged for money for a poor family in which her majesty was interested. Rohan was anxious to please the queen but was already heavily in debt and had also misappropriated the funds of various institutions; he was thus driven into the hands of moneylenders.

The wretched Countess de Lamotte met by chance a poor woman whose resemblance to the queen was exceedingly marked. This person she trained to represent Marie Antoinette, and arranged nightly meetings between her and Rohan, in which the disguised woman made all sorts of promises to the cardinal. Between them the adventuresses mulcted the unfortunate prelate of immense sums of money.

Meanwhile, a certain Bähmer, a jeweler, was very desirous of selling a wonderful diamond necklace in which, for over ten years, he had locked up his whole fortune. Hearing that Mme. de Lamotte had great influence with the queen, he approached her for the purpose of getting her to induce Marie Antoinette to purchase it. She at once corresponded on the matter with de Rohan, who proceeded posthaste to Paris, to be told by Mme. de Lamotte that the queen wished him to be security for the purchase of the necklace, for which she had agreed to pay 1,600,000 livres in four half-yearly installments.

The cardinal was naturally overwhelmed at the suggestion but signed the agreement, and Mme. de Lamotte became the possessor of the necklace. She speedily broke it up, picking the jewels from their setting with an ordinary penknife.

Matters went smoothly enough until the date when the first installment of 400,000 livres became due. De Rohan, never dreaming that the queen would not meet it, could not lay his hands on such a sum; and Bähmer, noting his anxiety, mentioned the matter to one of the queen's ladies-in-waiting, who retorted that he must be mad, as the queen had never purchased the necklace at all. Bähmer went at once to Mme. de Lamotte, who laughed at him, said he was being fooled, insisted it had nothing to do with her, and told him to go to the cardinal. The terrified jeweler did not take her advice, however, but went instead to the king.

The amazed Louis XVI listened to the story quietly enough, then turned to the queen who was present. Marie Antoinette at once broke forth in a tempest of indignation. As a matter of fact, Bähmer had for years pestered her to buy the necklace; but the crowning indignity was that de Rohan, whom she cordially detested, should have been made the medium for such a scandalous disgrace in connection with her name. She at once decreed that the cardinal should be arrested. The king acquiesced in this, and shortly afterward the Countess de Lamotte, Cagliostro and his wife (who were implicated by the countess), and others followed the cardinal to the Bastille.

The trial that followed was one of the most sensational and stirring in the annals of French history. The king was blamed for allowing the affair to become public at all, and there the evidence of such conduct as displayed by aristocrats inflamed public opinion and may have hastened the French Revolution.

Mme. de Lamotte not only charged Cagliostro with the robbery of the necklace, but also invented for him a terrible past, designating him an empiric, alchemist, false prophet, and Jew. This is not the place to deal with the trial at length, but suffice it to say that Cagliostro easily proved his complete innocence. The Parisian public looked to Cagliostro to supply the comedy in this great drama, and assuredly they were not disappointed, for he provided them with what must be described as one of the most romantic, fanciful, and absurd life stories in the history of autobiography.

His Last Years

Although proved innocent, he had offended so many people in high places that he was banished, amid shouts of laughter from everyone in the court. Even the judges were convulsed, but on his return from the courthouse the mob cheered him heartily.

If he had accomplished nothing else, he had at least won the hearts of the populace by his kindness and the many acts of faithful service he had lavished upon them; and it was partly owing to this popularity, and partly to the violent hatred of the court, that he owed the reception accorded him.

He was reunited with his wife and shortly afterward took his departure for London, where he was received with considerable éclat. There he addressed a letter to the people of France, which obtained wide circulation and predicted the French Revolution, the demolishment of the Bastille, and the downfall of the monarchy. Following this, the *Courier de l'Europe*, a French paper published in London, printed a so-called exposure of the real life of Cagliostro from beginning to end. From that moment, his descent was headlong. His reputation had preceded him in Switzerland and Austria, and he could find no rest there.

At last he and Lorenza journeyed to Rome. In the beginning he was well received and was even entertained by several cardinals. He privately studied medicine and lived quietly, but he made the great mistake of attempting to further his Masonic ideas within the bounds of the papal states. Masonry was of course anathema to the Roman church; and upon attempting to found a lodge in the Eternal City itself, he was arrested on September 27, 1789, by order of the Holy Inquisition and imprisoned in the castle of Saint Angelo.

His examination occupied his inquisitors for no less than eighteen months, and he was sentenced to death on April 7, 1791. He was recommended to mercy, however, and the pope commuted his sentence to perpetual imprisonment in the castle of Saint Angelo. On one occasion he made a desperate attempt to escape. Requesting the services of a confessor, he attempted to strangle the brother sent to him, but the burly priest, in whose habit he had intended to disguise himself, proved too strong and quickly overpowered him.

Afterward he was imprisoned in the solitary castle of San Leo near Montefeltro, where he died and was interred in 1795. The manner of his death is unknown.

The Countess Cagliostro's wife was also sentenced by the Inquisition to imprisonment for life. She was confined in the Convent of St. Appolonia, a penitentiary for women in Rome, where it is rumored that she died in 1794.

Cagliostro's manuscript volume entitled "Egyptian Freemasonry" fell with his other papers into the hands of the Inquisition and was solemnly condemned by it as subversive to the interests of Christianity. It was publicly burned; but oddly enough the Inquisition set apart one of its brethren to concoct some kind of life of Cagliostro, which did include particulars concerning his Masonic methods.

Cagliostro as Occult Hero

W. R. H. Trowbridge, one of Cagliostro's biographers, made a convincing case that Cagliostro was not the same as Joseph Balsamo, with whom his detractors have identified him. Balsamo was a Sicilian vagabond adventurer, and the statement that he and Cagliostro were one and the same person originally rests on the word of the editor of the *Courier de l'Europe,* and upon an anonymous letter from Palermo to the chief of the Paris police.

According to Trowbridge, the fact that the names of Cagliostro's wife and the wife of Balsamo were identical amounted to little more than coincidence, as the name Lorenza Feliciani was a very common one in Italy. He also claimed in his biography that the testimony of the handwriting experts as to the remarkable similarity between the writing of Balsamo and Cagliostro was worthless and stated that nobody who had known Balsamo ever saw Cagliostro. He also pointed out that Balsamo, who had been in England in 1771, was "wanted" by the London police. How was it then that six years afterward they did not recognize him in Count Cagliostro, who spent four months in a debtors' prison there, for no fault of his own?

The whole evidence against Cagliostro's character rested with the editor of the *Courier de l'Europe* and his Inquisition biographer, neither of whom could be credited for various reasons. For instance, it must be recollected that the narrative of the Inquisition biographer was supposed to be based upon the confessions of Cagliostro under torture in the castle of Saint Angelo. Neither was the damaging disclosure of the editor of the *Courier de l'Europe* at all topical, as he raked up matter which was at least fourteen years old, and of which he had no personal knowledge.

Trowbridge also claimed that the dossier discovered in the French archives in 1783, which was supposed to embody Madame Cagliostro's confessions when she was imprisoned regarding the career of her husband, was a forgery. He further disposes of the statements that Cagliostro lived on the immoral earnings of his wife.

A born adventurer, Cagliostro was by no means a rogue, as revealed by his beneficence. It is unlikely that the various Masonic lodges that he founded and that were patronized by persons of ample means provided him extensive funds, and it is a known fact that he was subsidized by several extremely wealthy men, who, themselves dissatisfied with the state of affairs in Europe, did not hesitate to place their riches at his disposal for the purpose of undermining the tyrannical powers that then wielded sway.

There is reason to believe that he had at some period of his life acquired a certain working knowledge of practical occultism and that he possessed certain elementary psychic powers of hypnotism and telepathy.

But on the whole, Cagliostro remains a mystery, and in all likelihood the clouds that surround his origin and early years will never be dispersed. Although Cagliostro was by no means an exalted character, he was one of the most picturesque figures in the later history of Europe, and assuredly the aura of mystery that surrounds his origin does not in the least detract from his appeal.

Sources:

Funck-Brentano, Frantz. *Cagliostro and Company.* London, 1900.

Gervaso, Roberto. *Cagliostro: A Biography.* London, 1974.

Trowbridge, W. R. H. *Cagliostro: The Splendour and Misery of a Master of Magic.* London, 1910. Reprinted as *Cagliostro: Savant or Scoundrel?* New York: Gordon Press, 1975. Reprinted as *Cagliostro: Maligned Freemason and Rosicrucian.* Kila, Mont.: Kessiger Publishing, 1992.

Cahagnet, Louis-Alphonse (1805–1885)

A journeyman cabinetmaker who, attracted to the study of somnambulism in 1845, published three years later *Magnétisme: Arcanes de la vie future dévoilé* (English translation: *The Celestial Telegraph,* 1848), the first volume of a remarkable book containing a summary of his experiments with eight somnambulists and spirit communications from 36 entities that claimed to have died over a period dating back two hundred years. The communications give a detailed description of spirit spheres and afterlife.

In January 1849, a second volume of the same book was published. It included the testimonies of the sitters, many of whom were very skeptical and on their guard against deception. In 1860 a third volume appeared.

Adèle Maginot was the medium for these sittings. She furnished striking proof of the personal identity of the communicators. In his book, *Modern Spiritualism* (1902), spiritualist historian Frank Podmore observes, "In the whole literature of Spiritualism I know of no records of the kind which reach a higher evidential standard, nor any in which the writer's good faith and intelligence are alike so conspicuous."

Sources:

Cahagnet, Louis-Alphonse. *Magnétisme arcanes de la vie future dévoilé.* Paris, 1848. Translated as *The Celestial Telegraph.* 2 vols. New York, 1851.

———. *Magnétisme: Encyclopédie magnétique spiritualiste.* N.p., 1861.

———. *Sanctuaire au Spiritualisme.* Paris, 1850. Translated as *The Sanctuary of Spiritualism: A Study of the Human Soul and of Its Relation with the Universe through Somnambulism and Ecstasy.* N.p., 1851.

———. *Thérapeutique du magnétisme et du Somnambulisme appropriée aux maladies les plus communes.* N.p., 1883.

Darnton, Robert. *Mesmerism and the End of the Enlightenment in France.* Cambridge, Mass: Harvard University Press, 1968.

Pleasants, Helene, ed. *Biographical Dictionary of Parapsychology.* New York: Helix Press, 1964.

Podmore, Frank. *Modern Spiritualism.* 2 vols. London, 1902. Reprinted as *Mediums of the Nineteenth Century.* New Hyde Park, N.Y.: University Books, 1963.

Cahiers Astrologiques

French-language bimonthly publication on history of astrology and approaches to different systems. Address: 27 Boulevard de Cressole, 06 Nice, France.

Cahn, Harold A(rchambo) (1922–)

A professor of biology who developed an interest in psychical research. Born July 1, 1922, in Minneapolis, Minnesota, he studied at the University of Minnesota (B.A., zoology, psychology), the University of Wyoming (M.A., zoology, biochemistry), and the University of Iowa (Ph.D., physiology). In 1962 he began teaching at Utica College of Syracuse University. He moved on to Northern Arizona University in 1971.

Cahn gave special attention to parapsychology in relation to problems of psychophysiology. He collaborated in experiments with Dr. **Joseph Rush** on subjects under mescaline narcosis and in experiments investigating sensory deprivation in relation to mental imagery. He reported on preliminary investigations of the Boulder (Colorado) Psychical Research Group at the first conference of the **Parapsychological Association** in 1958 and presented a paper entitled "Image Subsception as a Method of Eliciting Psi" at the fifth conference of the Parapsychological Association in 1962.

In later years, Cahn concerned himself with research in such areas as biosystem characteristics, the abstract structure of biological organization, circadian rhythms, and physiological correlates of claimed paranormal phenomena. Cahn has been a member of the American Association for the Advancement of Science, the **Society for Psychical Research** (London), the Parapsychological Association, and the Society for Psychophysiological Research.

Sources:

Pleasants, Helene, ed. *Biographical Dictionary of Parapsychology.* New York: Helix Press, 1964.

Cailleach (or **Harvest Old Wife**)

In the Highlands of **Scotland,** there was a superstition that whoever was last with his harvesting would be saddled with the Harvest Old Wife to keep until the next year. The first farmer to be finished made a doll of some blades of corn, which was called "the old wife," and sent it to his nearest neighbor. He, in turn, when finished, sent it on to another, and so on until the person last finished had the old wife to keep. Needless to say this fear acted as a spur to the superstitious Highlanders.

Sources:

Thompson, Francis. *The Supernatural Highland.* London: Robert Hale, 1976.

Cain, John (1931–1985)

A British spiritual healer. Born on April 21, 1931 in Eastham, Wirral, England, he manifested healing ability at the age of six, when he used to stroke his mother's forehead to relieve her attacks of migraine. After his twenty-first birthday, he joined the Royal Ordnance Corp of the British army as a physical training instructor; he also acquired a reputation for his skill in massage and manipulation. He left the army in 1952, worked in the shipyard at Birkenhead, then worked at window cleaning, logging, and site demolition.

In 1956 he started his own business as a blacksmith and became financially successful, employing 30 people and driving a Rolls Royce. In the same year, he married. Haunted by the thought that he was born to heal, he lost interest in the business. One morning, his anxieties were dispelled by an ecstatic mood of peace, and he heard the voice of his dead father saying, "Do not worry; born to heal, Dad." In 1972 Cain became a full-time spiritual healer, treating a wide variety of disabilities. These included arthritis, diabetes, paralysis, hardening of the arteries, cervical spondilitis, and malignant growths.

Cain was an unconventional healer. He appeared to put people into an altered state of consciousness during which there seemed to be spontaneous improvement. Sometimes sufferers from muscular problems got up and danced; others performed what appeared to be yoga exercises. Cain believed spirit guides controlled his healing, and these were identified independently by other psychic mediums. Although Cain sometimes physically touched people, a great many of his cures were effected without any direct contact. He occasionally practiced absent healing.

Cain was investigated by parapsychologists and performed healing under laboratory conditions. He was tested by Japanese researchers in Tokyo in 1976, and also by Prof. **John Taylor** in London. In spite of Taylor's skepticism about paranormal phenomena, his findings on Cain's healing powers were positive. Cain also demonstrated successful healing sessions in Canada at Vancouver and Winnipeg.

Cain died on September 28, 1985, only a few days after publisher Peter Bander had approached him to discuss a second edition of the book *Heal, My Son!* He was one of the most celebrated British healers, whose talents were widely endorsed.

Sources:

Green, Peter. *Heal, My Son! The Amazing Story of John Cain.* London: Van Duren, 1977.

Sykes, Pat. *You Don't Know John Cain?* London: Van Duren, 1980.

Caiumarath (or **Kaid-mords**)

According to Persian legend, the first man. He lived 1,000 years and reigned 560. He produced a tree from the fruits of which came the human race. The devil seduced and corrupted the first couple, who after their fall dressed themselves in black garments and sadly awaited the resurrection, for they had introduced sin into the world.

Cala, Carlo (ca. seventeenth century)

A Calabrian nobleman (Duke di Diano and Marquis di Ramonte) who wrote on the occult in the seventeenth century. He published *Memorie historiche dell'apparitione delle cruce prodigiose da Carlo Cala* at Naples in 1661.

Calatin Clan

A poisonous multiform monster of Irish legend. The creature was composed of a father and his 27 sons, any one of whose weapons could, by the merest touch, kill a man within nine days. This monstrosity was sent against **Cuchulain,** who succeeded in catching its 28 spears on his shield. The clan, however, managed to throw him down and grind his face in the gravel. Cuchulain was assisted by the son of an Ulster exile, who cut off the creature's heads while Cuchulain hacked it to pieces.

Calen

Chilean sorcerers. (See also **South America**)

California Directory of Psi Services

Former annual directory of organizations, individuals, shops, and services in the fields of parapsychology, occultism, astrology, witchcraft, psychic science, and New Age spiritual studies. The earliest known edition appeared in 1974 as the *Directory of Psychic Sciences Periodicals.* The later editions had annotated listings of groups and individuals with addresses and telephone numbers to facilitate contact. It was edited by Elizabeth M. Werner, later a member of the editorial board of the comprehensive **Whole Again Resource Guide.**

California Institute of Transpersonal Psychology Newsletter

Quarterly newsletter listing Ph.D. programs, with articles on transpersonal psychology and expanded awareness. Includes news of workshops, conferences, and reviews. Address: P.O. Box 2364, Stanford, CA 94305.

California Parapsychology Foundation

Incorporated in 1957 as an educational and research organization. The foundation maintains a reference and lending library for associates and publishes a newsletter. Address: 3580 Adams Blvd., San Diego, CA 92116.

California Society for Psychical Studies

Meets monthly for lectures on various aspects of psychical studies; issues a newsletter *Iridis.* Address: P.O. Box 844, Berkeley, CA 94704.

Callaway, Hugh G. (1885–1949)

Pioneer British experimenter in the field of **astral projection** or **out-of-the-body traveling,** about which he wrote under the pseudouym Oliver Fox. Born in Southampton, England, November 30, 1885, Callaway studied at the Harley Institute (later renamed Southampton University College), taking a three-year course in science and electrical engineering. In the summer of 1902 he experienced his first astral projection.

Callaway joined a theatrical touring company, but his career as an actor was brief. Afterward he invested in two business ventures, which were both unsuccessful. From 1908 to 1910 the Callaways lived in poverty, but in 1910 Hugh inherited a small legacy. He started writing short stories and poems, with which he had some success. Some had mystical themes based on his own astral experiences.

During the early part of World War I, he worked as a clerk, studying occultism in his spare time. In March 1917 he served in an army labor corps in Germany. After leaving the service in October 1919, he moved to London and continued to publish short stories, many of which have powerful occult themes.

Callaway also contributed articles on his out-of-the-body experiences to the *Occult Review,* edited by the Honorable **Ralph Shirley,** and in 1938 his pioneer work *Astral Projection* was published (under the pseudonym Oliver Fox). He compiled an equally remarkable work in association with "Paul Black" (G. Murray Nash), with whom he established occult rapport in recording *The Golden Book of Azelda.* Only fragments of this large work of automatic writing have so far been published, in pamphlet form. These extracts have a Gnostic character and are said to employ a code of celestial symbolism. Hugh Callaway died April 28, 1949.

Sources:

Fox, Oliver [Hugh Callaway]. *Astral Projection.* London: Rider, 1938. Reprint, New Hyde Park, N.Y.: University Books, 1962.

Muldoon, Sylvan, and Hereward Carrington. *The Projection of the Astral Body.* London: Rider, 1929. Rev. ed. 1958.

Rogo, D. Scott. *Leaving the Body: A Complete Guide to Astral Projection.* Englewood Cliffs, N.J.: Prentice-Hall, 1983.

Calmecacs

Training college of Aztec priests. (See also **Mexico** and **Central America**)

Calmet, Dom Antoine Augustin (1672–1757)

A Benedictine of the congregation of Saint-Vannes and one of the most renowned Bible scholars of his day. Calmet was born February 16, 1672, at Minil-la-Horgne, Lorraine, France. He studied at the Benedictine monastery at Breuil and entered the order in 1688. He was ordained to the priesthood in 1696.

Calmet taught philosophy and theology at the abbey at Moyen-Moutier and during the early years of his career worked on a massive 23-volume commentary of the Bible, which appeared between 1707 and 1716. His biblical writings established him as a leading scholar, and he spent many years trying to popularize the work of biblical exegesis in the Church.

Calmet is most remembered today for his single work, *Dissertations sur les apparitions, des anges, des démons et des esprits, et sur les revenants et vampires de Hongrie, de Boheme, de Moravie et de Silésie* (Paris, 1746 and 1951, the latter being the better edition), a broad survey of supernatural/occult events across Europe. The first volume of this work dealt with spirits and apparitions, but it was the second volume, on revenants and vampires, that stirred up controversy.

Like the work of his Italian colleague Archbishop Gioseppe Davanzati, Calmet's study of vampirism was set off by waves of **vampire** reports form Germany and eastern Europe. Vampirism, for all practical purposes, did not exist in France and was largely unknown to the scholarly community there until the early eighteenth century. Calmet was impressed with the detail and corroborative testimonies of incidents of vampirism coming out of eastern Europe and believed that it was unreasonable to simply dismiss them. As a theologian, he recognized that the existence and actions of such beings could have an important bearing on various theological conclusions concerning the nature of the afterlife. Calmet thought it necessary to establish the veracity of such reports and to understand the phenomena in light of the Church's world view. Calmet finished his work a short time after the Sorbonne roundly condemned the reports and, especially, the desecration of the bodies of people believed to be vampires.

Calmet defined a vampire as a person who had been dead and buried and then returned from the grave to disturb the living by sucking their blood and even causing death. The only remedy for vampirism was to dig up the body of the vampire and either sever its head and drive a stake through the chest or burn the body. Using that definition, Calmet collected as many accounts of vampirism as possible from official reports, newspapers, eyewitness reports, travelogues, and critical pieces from his learned colleagues. The majority of space in his published volume was taken up with the anthology of all his collected data.

Calmet then offered his reflections upon the reports. He condemned the hysteria that followed several of the reported incidents of vampirism and seconded the Sorbonne's condemnation of the mutilation of exhumed bodies. He considered all of the explanations that had been offered to explain the phenomena, from the effects of regional folklore, to normal but little-known body changes after death, to premature burial. He focused a critical eye upon the reports and pointed out problems and internal inconsistencies.

In the end, however, Calmet was unable to reach a conclusion beyond the various natural explanations that had been offered. He left the whole matter open, but seemed to favor the existence of vampires, noting that ". . . it seems impossible not to subscribe to the belief which prevails in these countries that these apparitions do actually come forth from the graves and that they are able to produce the terrible effects which are so widely and so positively attributed to them." He thus set up conditions for the heated debate that was to ensue during the 1850s. Calmet's book became a best-seller. It went through three French printings, in 1746, 1747, and 1748. It appeared in a German edition in 1752 and in an English edition in 1759 (reprinted in 1850 as *The Phantom World*). Calmet was immediately attacked by colleagues for taking the vampire stories seriously. Although he tried to apply such critical methods as he had available to him, he never really questioned the legitimacy of the reports of vampiric manifestations.

As the controversy swelled following publication of his book, coupled by a new outbreak of vampirism reported in Silésia, a skeptical Empress Maria Theresa stepped in. She dispatched her personal physician to investigate. He wrote a report denouncing the incident as supernatural quackery and condemned the mutilation of the bodies. In response, in 1755 and 1756 Maria Theresa issued laws to stop the spread of vampire hysteria, including removing the matter of dealing with such reports from the hands of the clergy and placing it, instead, under civil authority. Maria Theresa's edicts came just before Calmet's death on October 25, 1757.

In the generation after his death, Calmet was treated harshly by French intellectuals, both inside and outside the Church. Later in the century, Diderot condemned him. Possibly the final word on Calmet came from Voltaire, who sarcastically ridiculed him in his *Philosophical Dictionary.* Although Calmet was favorably cited by **Montague Summers,** who used him as a major source for his study of vampires, his importance lay in his reprinting and preserving some of the now obscure texts of the vampire wave of eighteenth-century Europe.

Sources:

Calmet, Dom Augustine. *Dissertations sur les apparitions, des anges, des démons et des esprits, et sur les revenants et vampires de Hongrie, de Boheme, de Moravie et de Silésie.* Rev. ed. Paris, 1751. Reprinted as *The Phantom World.* 2 vols. London: Richard Bentley, 1850.

———. *Treatise on Vampires & Revenants: The Phantom World.* Brighton, Sussex, England: Desert Island Books, 1995.

Digot, A. *Notice biographique et littéraire sur Dom Augustin Calmet.* Nancy, France, 1860.

Frayling, Christopher. *Vampyres: From Lord Byron to Count Dracula.* London: Faber and Faber, 1991.

Summers, Montague. *The Vampire: His Kith and Kin.* London: Routledge, Kegan Paul, Trench, Trubner, 1928. Reprint, New York: University Books, 1960.

Calundronius

A legendary magic stone without form or color said to have the virtues of resisting malign spirits, destroying enchantments, giving an advantage over enemies to the owner, and dissipating despair.

Cambions

According to **Jean Bodin** and **Pierre De Lancre,** the offspring of **incubi** and **succubi.** Some of these demons are said to be more kindly disposed to the human race than others. Luther says in his *Colloquies* that they show no sign of life before seven years of age. He further states that he saw one that cried when he touched it.

In his *Discours des Sorciers* (1608), Henri Boguet quotes a story that a Galician mendicant was in the habit of exciting public pity by carrying about a Cambion. One day a horseman, observing him to be much hampered by the seeming infant in crossing a river, took the "child" before him on his horse. But the "child" was so heavy that the animal sank under the weight. The mendicant later admitted that the child he habitually carried was a little demon he had trained so carefully that no one refused him alms when he carried it.

CAMBODIA See KAMPUCHEA

Cambridge Buddhist Association

Founded to provide instruction in Buddhist meditation in the United States and to make available study materials. The association is nonsectarian and meetings are conducted by priests of different Buddhist sects, in accordance with the wishes of the founder, Shinichi Hisamatsu.

The association has been served by a series of outstanding Buddhist teachers. The first president was Shunryu Suzuki (also of the San Francisco Zen Center). He was succeeded by Rev. Chimyo Horioka of the Shingon sect of Buddhism, who graduated from Koyasan University, Japan, then studied philosophy at the University of Berlin, and science and the history of religion at Hamburg University, becoming instructor of Oriental studies. He immigrated to the United States in 1953 and in 1956 was appointed assistant to the curator of the Asiatic department at the Museum of Fine Arts, Boston.

Horioka was succeeded by Maurine Stuart, a student of the late Soen Naakgawa. Stuart, also a musician, teaches Buddhism at the Philips Exeter Academy in New Hampshire as well. The association provides facilities for **Zen** meditation but is also open to a variety of Buddhist perspectives, and members are active in area interfaith activities. The association is housed in a residential neighborhood at 75 Sparks St., Cambridge, MA 02138.

Sources:

Cambridge Buddhist Association. Cambridge, Mass.: Cambridge Buddhist Association, 1960.

Fujimoto, Rindo. *The Way of Zazen.* Cambridge, Mass.: Cambridge Buddhist Association, 1969.

Renfrew, Sita Paulickpulle. *A Buddhist Guide for Laymen.* Cambridge, Mass.: Cambridge Buddhist Association, 1963.

Cambridge Company, The

Lecture bureau specializing in representation of famous psychics and spiritual teachers for lectures and demonstrations. The company has represented such well-known personalities as Jeane Dixon, Doris Collins, Leslie Flint, and Harold Sherman. Address: 9000 Sunset Blvd., Ste. 319, Beverly Hills, CA 90069.

Camp Meetings

Camp meetings (also known as "assemblies") have occupied an important place in the advancement of **Spiritualism** since 1873, when the first camp meeting was initiated at Lake Pleasant, Massachusetts. These camp meetings were very like the revivalistic camp meetings of the early twentieth century and the successful summer chautauquas at Chautauqua Lake, New York. The meetings lasted throughout the summer season and many of the mediums took up residence on the grounds. Lily Dale in New York and Onset and Lake Pleasant in Massachusetts were the leading camps. Today, a small number of camps, such as Cassadaga (Florida), Chesterfield (Indiana), Silver Belle (Pennsylvania), and Lily Dale, still exist.

Sources:

Karcher, Janet. *The Way to Cassadaga: A Look at Spiritualism, Its Roots, and Beliefs, and Cassadaga, Florida.* Daltona, Fla: J. Hutchinson Productions, 1980.

Campagni, Roberto

Contemporary Italian psychic who reportedly demonstrated abilities of **materialization** and **levitation.** A surveyor by trade, Campagni discovered his psychic gifts at the age of sixteen after the death of his brother Ruggero. An aunt persuaded the family to hold séances, at which Campagni found himself the medium. Campagni continued to sit regularly with a séance group known as Circle 77 in Florence, at which, it has been claimed, **apports** materialized. Psychic researcher Gemma Lasta described how Campagni's hands lit up "like a neon sign" with a glow around his fingers. The medium then passed her what she described as a "cloud of light," a weightless glowing mass from which tiny flames leapt with a slight buzzing noise, after which she found a five-pointed star in embossed silver in her hand. Other witnesses have described a blue light around Campagni's hands when apports are materialized.

Father Eugenio Feriaroti, head of a Roman Catholic order in Genoa, attended one séance, at which he stated that the medium "put a luminous ball of light into my hands." The ball of light then materialized into a small silver angel. Psychic researcher Dr. Luigi Lapi of Florence claims at one séance he saw the medium levitate to the ceiling. Genoanese physicist Alfredo Ferraro states he has seen 30 materialized apports and believes trickery is not involved. Parapsychologist Ugo Dettore, who has also studied Campagni's phenomena, suggests that the blue light from the medium's hands is a form of psychic energy working outside the body.

Campagni himself is a shy individual who refuses to be photographed and has never accepted money for his demonstrations during more than 30 years of part-time psychic activity.

Campbell, Joseph (1904–1987)

A prominent American authority on mythology and leading exponent of the idea of "myth" as an inherent characteristic of humanity. Campbell was born March 26, 1904, in New York City. He studied at Dartmouth College, (1921–22) and Columbia University (A.B., 1925; M.A., 1927). He did additional graduate study at the University of Paris and the University of Munich. He taught for a year at Canterbury School, New Milford, Connecticut, before joining the faculty in the literature department at Sarah Lawrence College, Bronxville, New York (1934–72), where he taught until his retirement.

Campbell began his literary work as editor of the writings of his friend Heinrich Zimmer. His first independent work, *The Hero with a Thousand Faces* (1949), examines a number of "hero" tales from around the world in which Campbell discerns the same basic outline. In the book he offers a thesis that myths provide instruction on how we should live, and says that the common themes of mythology throughout the world show these ideas are inherent in human biology. He also launches his search for what he terms the "monomyth," the single underlying story all the myths tell.

He followed *The Hero with a Thousand Faces* with a four-volume work, *The Masks of God* (1959–68), which traces the development of ancient mythology and argues for the need of a new worldwide mythology adaptable to the emerging worldwide culture.

Campbell's last years were spent writing the proposed six-volume *Historical Atlas of World Mythology,* of which only two volumes were completed. He did complete a series of interviews with Bill Moyers that were broadcast posthumously over the Public Broadcasting Service as "The Power of Myth." The television series brought Campbell's works a measure of acclaim the man himself never enjoyed in life.

Campbell died on October 31, 1987. His library and papers have been deposited at the Pacifica Institute in Santa Barbara, California.

Sources:

Campbell, Joseph. *The Hero With a Thousand Faces.* New York: Pantheon, 1949.

———. *Historical Atlas of World Mythologies.* 2 vols. New York: Harper, 1983–88.

———. *The Masks of God.* 6 vols. New York: Viking, 1959–68.

———. *Myths to Live By.* New York: Viking, 1972.

Camus, Philippe (or Felipe) (ca. fifteenth century)

A Spanish writer of romances who lived in the fifteenth century. To him is attributed a life of **Robert the Devil,** *La Vida de Roberto el Diablo,* later published at Seville in 1629. The legend itself probably dates from the thirteenth century.

Canadian Institute of Psychosynthesis, Inc. See Psychosynthesis Institute

Canadian UFO Report

Former Canadian quarterly publication concerned with UFO activities and related mysteries, published by John Magor of British Columbia. It is now incorporated in *Journal UFO,* published by UP Investigations Research, Inc., Box 455, Streetsville, Mississagua, Ontario, Canada L5M 2B9.

Canavesio, Orlando (1915–1957)

Surgeon and neurologist, born in Buenos Aires, Argentina. In 1946 Canavesio founded the Argentine Medical Association for Parapsychology, the first organization to encourage physicians to explore parapsychology, and commenced publication of the journal *Revista Medica de Metapsiquica.* He utilized the electroencephalograph (EEG) to research the relationship between ESP and brain physiology. In 1948 he was appointed head of the Institute of Applied Psychopathology, which the Argentine government had established to determine whether the Spiritualist movement was injurious to the public welfare. As the leading voice of parapsychology in the country, he was invited to speak at the International Conference on Parapsychology held at Utrecht, the Netherlands, in 1953. He was killed in an automobile accident in 1957.

Sources:

Berger, Arthur S., and Joyce Berger. *The Encyclopedia of Parapsychology and Psychical Research.* New York: Paragon House, 1991.

Candles Burning Blue

There is a superstition that candles and other lights burn blue when spirits are present, because of the sulphurous atmosphere thought to accompany the specters. Some individuals claim to see apparitions and state that there is a change in the temperature and other properties of the ambient air when ghosts appear.

Candomblé Nagó

An Afro-Brazilian religion, one of several derived from the traditional religions of West Africa. *Nagó* refers to the West African Yoruban people, many of whom were taken to Brazil as slaves. Yoruban religion survives primarily among the African people of Brazil.

Candomblé is headed by priests and priestesses who are specialists in contacting the *orixds,* the ancester spirits of the Yoruban people. The *orixds* are usually identified with natural forces such as thunder, water, and the sea, but are also identified with Roman Catholic saints. One of the leading *orixds* is Oxalá, who is often identified with Jesus. Worship, which includes spirit possession, drumming, singing, and dancing, occurs in temples called *terreiros.*

Candomblé is strongest in Bahia, the northeast area of Brazil. In recent decades it has been closely associated with other spirit **possession** groups such as **Umbanda** and **Spiritism.**

Sources:

Bastide, Roger. *The African Religions of Brazil.* Baltimore, Md.: Johns Hopkins Press, 1978.

Hess, David J. *Samba in the Night: Spiritism in Brazil.* New York: Columbia University Press, 1994.

Cannon, Alexander (1896–1963)

British psychiatrist, hypnotist, and author of books on occultism. He was born in Leeds, England, and educated at Leeds, London, Vienna, Hong Kong, and several other universities (eventually receiving both an M.D. and Ph.D.). Later he reinforced his medical qualifications with titles reflecting his training in various Eastern spiritual disciplines, such as "Kushog Yogi of Northern Thibet" and "Master-The-Fifth of the Great White Lodge of the Himalayas." He spent a number of years in Hong Kong, where he was vice president of Hong Kong Medical Society (1929 and 1934), medical officer in charge of prisons, head of the Department of Morbid Anatomy at the University of Hong Kong, and psychiatrist and medical jurist to the High Court of Justice. He also served as His Britannic Majesty's Consul and Port Medical Officer in Canton. He later returned to England, serving as psychiatrist and research scientist at Colney Hatch Mental Hospital. In 1939 he established the Isle of Man Clinic for Nervous Diseases.

During his years in the Orient, Cannon studied occultism and yoga and traveled in India and Tibet. His book *The Invisible Influence* (1933) created something of a sensation with its claim that during his travels he was levitated over a chasm in Tibet, together with his porters and luggage. Because of this claim, the London County Council dismissed him from his position as psychiatrist on the grounds that he was unfit to practice in charge of a mental hospital. However, Cannon was reinstated after bringing action for wrongful dismissal. He subsequently set up private practice in London, as a Harley Street consultant, and he used the services of psychic mediums in diagnosis.

Cannon was regarded as an eccentric in prewar Britain, when occultism was considered highly suspect, and the somewhat wild statements in Cannon's books did not help his reputation. In his book *Sleeping Through Space* (1938) he gives directions for bringing the dead back to life: "[administer] a severe kick with the knee between the shoulder blades" at the same time shouting in [the] left ear "Oye," "Oye," "Oye." He adds: "It is rarely necessary to repeat the operation before life is again resumed, but this can be repeated up to seven times in long-standing cases." Again, in an article, "Some Hypnotic Secrets," published in *The British Journal of Medical Hypnotism* (1949), he states, "If the patient wakes up at all before I have got my hypnotic sleep suggestions home to him, I place both of my thumbs on his carotid arteries vagus nerves and carotic body firmly . . . until he is 'off' again. . . ." It would seem that the unfortunate patient stood a fair chance of being strangled, but doubtless he could be resuscitated by the redoubtable doctor's "Oye, Oye, Oye" technique.

Cannon wrote a number of books on both psychiatry and the occult. He was also an early experimenter in suggestion therapy by means of gramophone recordings. In later life he retired to the Isle of Man, where he died circa 1963.

Sources:

Cannon, Alexander. *Hypnotism, Suggestion & Faith-Healing.* 1932.

———. *The Invisible Influence.* New York: E. P. Dutton, 1934.

———. *The Power of Karma.* N.p., 1936.

———. *Powers That Be.* New York: E. P. Dutton, 1935.

———. *The Science of Hypnotism.* N.p., 1936.

———. *Sleeping Through Space.* N.p., 1938.

———. "Some Hypnotic Secrets." *The British Journal of Medical Hypnotism* 1, 1 (1949).

Canon Episcopi (or Capitulum Episcopi)

An early religious document of unknown origin, erroneously attributed to the Council of Ancyra, which met in 314 C.E. It was first quoted by Regino of Prüm, Abbot of Treves, in 906 C.E. In the twelfth century it was incorporated in the *Corpus Juris Canonici* by Gratian of Bologna and became part of canon law. The importance of this document is that it is an early ecclesiastical statement describing **witchcraft** as the practice of pagan religion and ascribing the acts of witches to dreams and fantasies. The document became important in the rise of the Inquisition, which was limited in its scope to heretics (those Christians who held nonorthodox doctrines) and apostates (those Christians who had rejected the faith). Since witchcraft was related to the practice of another religion, rather than being within the purview of either heretics or apostates, the Inquisition could not touch them.

The Canon Episcopai was overturned by a papal encyclical issued by Pope Innocent VIII in 1484. *Summis desiderantes affectibus* redefined witchcraft as **devil worship,** hence abandoning one's religious fault. The encyclical had the effect of unleashing the Inquisition on people accused of practicing witchcraft.

Sources:

Russell, Jeffrey Burton. *Witchcraft in the Middle Ages.* Ithaca, N.Y.: Cornell University Press, 1972.

Cantilever

A theory of the physical action of **ectoplasm** during the phenomenon of **telekinesis,** or the movement of objects without contact or other physical means. The theory was developed by the psychical investigator Dr. **W. J. Crawford,** who attempted to measure the movement of ectoplasm during his investigations of the **Goligher Circle** in Belfast, Ireland, between 1917 and 1920.

Capnomancy

A form of **divination** in ancient times involving the observation of smoke and consisting of two principal methods. The more important was the smoke of sacrifices, which augured well if it rose lightly from the altar and ascended straight to the clouds, but the contrary if it hung about. Another method was to throw a few jasmine or poppy seeds upon burning coals. There was also a third method involving breathing the smoke of the sacrificial fire.

Sources:

Waite, Arthur Edward. *The Occult Sciences.* 1891. Reprint, Secaucus, N.J.: University Books, 1974.

"Caquet Bombec"

A fourteenth-century song by the poet Jonquieres. It details an operation in **alectromancy,** a form of **divination** using a cock.

Caqueux (or Cacoux)

A former caste of rope makers dwelling in Brittany who in some of the cantons of that country were treated as pariahs, perhaps because the ropes they manufactured were considered the symbols of slavery and death by hanging. They were forbidden to enter the churches and were regarded as sorcerers. They did not hesitate to profit by this evil reputation and dealt in **talismans,** which were supposed to render their wearers invulnerable. They also acted as diviners. They were further credited with the ability to raise and sell winds and tempests like the sorcerers of Finland.

It was believed that the Caqueux were originally of Jewish origin, and they were separated like lepers from other folks. Francois II, duke of Brittany, enacted that they should wear a mark composed of red cloth on a part of their dress where it could be readily seen. (They are mentioned in Jaques de Cambry's 1799 book *Voyage dans le Finistére.*)

Carancini, Francesco (1863– ?)

Italian physical medium. He was widely tested by Baron L. von Erhardt and the Society for Psychical Research of Rome, further studied at Paris by **Cesar Baudi De Vesme,** Lemerle, and M. Mangin, and also investigated at Geneva by Professors Clarapede, **Theodore Flournoy,** and Batelli. He sat in darkness, tightly bound, and produced strong telekinetic phenomena and occasional **materializations,** of which flashlight photographs were taken.

Several times he was accused of cheating, but Baron von Erhardt remarked that the hypothesis of fraud in this case implied that the experimenters were absolute imbeciles. Nevertheless, such charges were made by **W. W. Baggally** (1910) and by others (see *Annales des Sciences Psychiques,* 1913, pp. 243–47).

Sources:

Baggally, W. W. "Some Sittings with Carancini." *Journal* of the Society for Psychical Research 14 (June 1910). Reprinted in Everard Feilding, *Sittings with Eusapio Palladino and Other Studies.* New Hyde Park, N.Y.: University Books, 1963.

Carbuncle

In ancient belief this stone was supposed to give out a natural light without reflection; it was ranked fifth in value after diamonds, emeralds, opals, and pearls. It is among the gems ruled by the sun and is both male and female—the former distinguished by the brightness that appears to burn within it, and the latter by the light it throws off. It takes no color from any other gem applied to it, but imparts its own. The virtue of the carbuncle was said to be its power to drive away poisonous air, repress luxury, and preserve the health of the body. It was also supposed to reconcile differences among friends.

Cardan, Jerome (1501–1576)

Italian mathematician, physician, and astrologer, reputed to be a magician. He was a contemporary of Faustus and **Paracelsus.** He left in his *Memoirs* a frank and detailed analysis of a curiously complicated and abnormal intellect, sensitive, intense, and not altogether free from the taint of insanity. He declared himself subject to strange fits of abstraction and exaltation, the intensity of which became at length so intolerable that he inflicted on himself severe bodily pain as a means of banishing them.

Cardan described three personal peculiarities to which he was prone. The first was the faculty of projecting his spirit outside his body, to the accompaniment of strange physical sensations. The second was the ability to perceive through his senses anything he desired to perceive; as a child, he explains, he saw these images involuntarily and without the power of selection, but when he reached manhood he could control them to suit his choice. The third peculiarity was that before every important event in his life he had a dream that warned him about it. Indeed, he had written a commentary of considerable length on Synesius's treatise on dreams, in which he advanced the theory that any virtuous person can acquire the faculty of interpreting dreams. In fact, he believed anyone can draw up for himself a code of dream interpretations by merely studying carefully his own dreams.

In one instance, at least, Cardan's prediction was not entirely successful. He foretold the date of his own death, and, at age 75, was obliged to abstain from food in order to die at the time he had predicted.

He published books on mathematics, astronomy, astrology, rhetoric, and medicine, including *Ars Magna* (1545), *De Subtilitate Rerum* (1551), and *De Rerum Varietate* (1557).

Sources:

Morley, H. *Jerome Cardan.* London, 1854.

Waters, W. G. *Jerome Cardan.* London, 1898.

Carey, Ken

Ken Carey, a contemporary **New Age** medium and channel, was a postal worker as a young man. Frustrated, he and his family moved to a farm where they lived without most modern conveniences such as electricity, plumbing, radio, television, newspapers, and magazines. Carey apprenticed himself to an Amish farmer. At one point in the later 1970s, lying in bed with a severe cold, he felt a presence and heard a low humming he described as an energy field. Then a voice spoke to him.

During the winter of 1978–79 he channeled for 11 days. The entities that spoke through him sometimes appeared as angels (including the angel **Raphael**) or extraterrestrials. However, during the later sessions, an entity declared, "I am Christ. I am coming this day through the atmosphere of your consciousness. . . . I am the bridegroom, spoken of old. I came to you first through the man named Jesus." The transcripts of these sessions were published as *The Starseed Transmissions* in 1982 and became an early channeled New Age classic. The popular response led to the publication of further volumes based on the channelings.

The entities who spoke through Carey emphasized the central New Age message. They had emerged in order to assist human evolution. It was time to lift the spell of matter and to bring forth a new planetary being. Humankind, Carey argued, is poised on the brink of a momentous transformation: The earth is ripe for harvest. Two resources are available to assist humans in the transformative period: the advanced intelligences, such as those channeling through Carey; and the creative power of thought. As with other New Age channelings, Carey's emphasizes the problems of overreliance on rational thought in problem solving and living with guilt imposed in younger years.

Sources:

Carey, Ken. *Notes to My Children: A Simplified Metaphysics.* Kansas City, Mo.: Uni-Sun, 1984.

———. *Return of the Bird Tribes.* Kansas City, Mo.: Uni-Sun, 1988.

——— [Raphael]. *The Starseed Transmissions: An Extraterrestrial Report.* Kansas City, Mo.: Uni-Sun, 1982.

———. *Terra Christa: The Global Spiritual Awakening.* Kansas City, Mo.: Uni-Sun, 1985.

———. *Vision.* Kansas City, Mo.: Uni-Sun, 1985.

Cargo Cults

Various forms of modern mythologies among the native peoples of Melanesia, arising from folk recollections of the riches brought by white traders, missionaries, or other colonizers. The earliest form of cargo cults appears to have developed in Fiji in the late nineteenth century when prophets would announce the imminent return of ancestors or white men on ships laden with luxuries.

During World War II, another form of cargo cult developed around the Red Cross planes transporting medical supplies to the Pacific Islands; modern leaders erected red crosses in the hope of bringing back supplies. In New Hebrides, there was a group that believed a white man would arrive in a red airplane laden with good things, and sticks were used to mark out a magic airstrip. In the New Hebridean island of Tanna, a strong movement emerged around the mythical messianic figure "John Frum." He appears to favor particular individuals and makes legendary trips to America to visit the president. His "Second Coming" will be manifest to the whole island, and he will bring the good things of the world so long denied to the Tannese.

Cargo cults represent a tragic combination of exploitation by explorers and traders and the culture shock of Christian missionaries displacing native religion.

Sources:

Burridge, Kennelm. *Mambu.* New York: Harper Torchbook, 1978.

Lawrence, Peter. *Road Belong Cargo.* Melbourne, Australia: Melbourne University Press, 1964.

Rice, Edward. *John Frum He Come.* Garden City, N.Y.: Doubleday, 1974.

Worsley, Peter. *The Trumpet Shall Sound.* New York: Schocken Books, 1962.

Carington, W(alter) Whateley (1884–1947)

British psychic researcher who investigated **Mrs. Osborne Leonard** and the Irish medium Kathleen Goligher of the **Goligher Circle.** He was born Walter Whately Smith in London. He studied science at Cambridge University, but had to postpone completion of his degree until after his service in the British army during World War I. In 1933 he adopted his older family name from Brittany, modifying the spelling from Carentan to Carington.

In 1920 he became a member of the council of the **Society for Psychical Research,** London, and worked with **E. J. Dingwall** and others investigating the French medium **Marthe Beraud** (see also **Eva C.**). By the early 1930s he had come to believe that further study of spontaneous cases was a dead end and began to advocate quantitative research. His first important paper was presented in several parts (1934–1937) as "The Quantitative Study of Trance Personalities" and was a watershed paper in **parapsychology.**

As with most parapsychologists, Carington turned his attention to the survival hypothesis. His initial quantitative studies in the 1930s had led him to believe that the mediums' controls were not separate entities but secondary personalities of the medium. He eventually came to postulate the "psyhcon hypothesis" of survival. He believed the mind is a cluster of sense-data and images that together constitute a single system, a system which may survive bodily death and even continue to evolve.

Carington founded and edited the journal *Psychic Research Quarterly* and wrote several books. He turned down an academic post and lived most of his life in poverty in order to devote his time to psychic research. In 1940 he was awarded a Perrott Studentship in Psychical Research and a short time later a Leverhulme Research Grant. He died March 2, 1947, at Sennen, Cornwall, England.

Sources:

Berger, Arthur S., and Joyce Berger. *The Encyclopedia of Parapsychology and Psychical Research.* New York: Paragon House, 1991.

Carington, Walter Whately. *The Death of Materialism.* N.p., 1932.

———. *The Foundations of Spiritualism.* N.p., 1920.

———. *Matter, Mind and Meaning.* Completed by H. H. Price. London: Methuen, 1949.

———. "The Quantitative Study of Trance Personalities." *Proceedings* of the Society for Psychical Research. Part 1, 42 (1934): 173. Part 2, 43 (1935): 319. Part 3, 44 (1937): 189.

———. *Telepathy: An Outline of its Fact, Theory and Implications.* London: Methuen, 1945. Reprint, New York: Gordon Press, 1972.

———. *A Theory of the Mechanism of Survival.* N.p., 1920.

Murphy, Gardner. "W. Wately Carington: In Memoriam." *Journal* of the American Society for Psychical Research 41 (1947): 123.

Pleasants, Helene, ed. *Biographical Dictionary of Parapsychology.* New York: Helix Press, 1964.

Carleson, Rolf Alfred Douglas (1910–)

Accountant and Spiritualist leader in Sweden. He was born January 29, 1910, in Montreal, Canada, but moved to Sweden during his adult life. He held posts as general secretary of the International Spiritualist Federation, editor of *Spiritualisten* (a Swedish psychic magazine), and general manager of Excelsior, a Swedish publishing house specializing in psychic literature.

Carleson was a founder of the Stockholm Spiritualist Society and served as its secretary for twenty years (1937–57). He then became general secretary of the Swedish Spiritualists Union in 1958–59. During this time he was a member of a Swedish psychic circle experimenting with **materialization** and **direct voice** phenomena.

Carleson was also a member of the Society for Parapsychological Research in Stockholm.

Sources:

Pleasants, Helene, ed. *Biographical Dictionary of Parapsychology.* New York: Helix Press, 1964.

Carpocratians

A sect of **Gnostics** founded by Carpocrates of Alexandria. The sect claimed Christ derived the mysteries of his religion from the Temple of Isis in Egypt, where he was said to have studied for six years, and that he taught them to his apostles, who transmitted them to Carpocrates. Members used theurgic incantations and had their own peculiar greetings, signs and words, and symbols and degrees of rank. The Carpocratians believed in metampsychosis and the preexistence of the soul, but rejected the resurrection of the body. They had some beliefs in common with the **Basilideans.** The sect endured until the sixth century.

Sources:

Legge, Francis. *Forerunners and Rivals of Christianity from 330 B.C. to 330 A.D.* 2 vols. 1915. Reprint, New Hyde Park, N.Y.: University Books, 1964.

Carrahdis

A class of aborigine priests in New South Wales, Australia.

Carrel, Alexis (1873–1944)

French surgeon and biologist with a philosophical interest in the unknown possibilities of mankind. Born at Sainte-Foy-les Lyons, France, June 28, 1873, Carrel studied at the Universities of Dijon and Lyons obtaining his M.D. in 1900. In 1904 he went to Canada, hoping to raise cattle, but ended up instead pursuing his surgical skills at the Hull Physiological Laboratory, Chicago.

In 1906 he became a staff member of the Rockefeller Institute for Medical Research, and in 1912 received a Nobel Prize in physiology and medicine for his work on vascular surgery and transplantation of organs. He joined the French army in World War I and with Henry Drysdale Dakin developed the Carrel-Dakin solution for sterilizing infected wounds. His philosophical interests came to the forefront in his first book, *Man the Unknown* (1935), which became a best-seller.

During World War II Carrel lived in France and held an appointment as director of the Foundation for the Study of Human Relations under the Vichy government. After the war he was dismissed as a collaborationist, although it is probable that he was more interested in human biology and physiology than politics. He died in Paris, November 5, 1944. Two of his books, *The Prayer* (1948) and *Voyage to Lourdes* (1950), were published posthumously.

Sources:

Carrel, Alexis. *Man the Unknown.* New York: Harper & Brothers, 1935.

———. *Reflections on Life.* New York: Hawthorn, 1953.

———. *Voyage to Lourdes.* New York: Harper & Brothers, 1950.

Carrington, Hereward (Hubert Lavington) (1880–1958)

Psychical investigator and author of many popular books on psychic subjects. Carrington was born October 17, 1880, in St. Heliers, Jersey, Channel Islands, Britain. He was educated in London and Cranbrook, and immigrated to the United States in 1899. His Ph.D. was obtained later at William Penn College, in Iowa. His interest was in psychical research and he followed an anti-Spiritualist line until the book *Essays in Psychical Research* by "Miss X" (Ada Goodrich Freer) shook his skepticism. In 1900, at age 19, he joined the American branch of the **Society for Psychical Research** and devoted the rest of his life to such studies. He became known for his intellect and knowledge and was a delegate to the First International Psychical Congress in Copenhagen in 1921 and to subsequent congresses in Warsaw (1923), Paris (1927), Athens (1930), and Oslo (1935).

After **Richard Hodgson** (1855–1905) died and the American branch of the Society for Psychical Research was reestablished as the **American Society for Psychical Research** under **James H. Hyslop**'s leadership, Carrington became Hyslop's assistant and worked in that capacity until July 1908. Then, on behalf of the English Society for Psychical Research, and in company with **Everard Feilding** and **W. W. Baggally,** he went to Naples to investigate the phenomena of the medium **Eusapia Palladino.** His experiences, as described in *Eusapia Palladino and Her Phenomena,* moved him even further into the camp of believers. Summarizing his new stance, he stated,

"My own sittings convinced me finally and conclusively that genuine phenomena do occur, and, that being the case, the question of their interpretation naturally looms before me. I think that not only is the Spiritualistic hypothesis justified as a working theory, but it is, in fact, the only one capable of rationally explaining the facts."

This view was shaken after Palladino, on his invitation, visited America in 1909 and was exposed as a **fraud** on two occasions. Carrington stuck by his earlier opinions and did not publish the record of the sittings, which remained in his possession until 1954. In his *Personal Experiences in Spiritualism* (1918), he speculated that the phenomena were specifically of biological origin.

In 1921, with an interested group behind him, Carrington founded the **American Psychical Institute** and Laboratory, which was in active operation for about two years.

In 1924 he sat on a committee of the *Scientific American* investigating the phenomena of **Spiritualism.** He attended many sittings with **Mina Crandon** ("Margery") in Boston and initially considered her mediumship genuine. Then in 1932, following some revelations of probable fraud, his faith was again shaken. He wrote in the *Bulletin* of the **Boston Society for Psychic Research,** "Certainly this throws a cloud over the whole Margery case." Carrington also found fraud in his investigation of **William Cartheuser.**

Carrington believed in the strong pull of the positive evidence for human survival, yet as he grew older, he became far less committed to it. Summarizing his own researches in *The Story of Psychic Science* (1930), he states:

"I may say that I have never, in all that time, witnessed any phenomena which have appeared to me undoubtedly spiritistic in character—though I have, of course, seen many unquestionably supernormal phenomena. At the same time, I realize very fully that other very competent investigators have seen and reported manifestations far more striking than any it has been my good fortune to witness: and these findings have duly impressed me. I, therefore, maintain a perfectly open mind upon this question, while continuing my investigations and shall probably continue in this state of mental equilibrium until some striking and convincing phenomena turn the scales in one direction or in the other."

Those striking and convincing phenomena came Carrington's way with the visit of **Eileen Garrett** at the American Psychical Institute three years later. Having subjected her to psychoanalytic "association tests," combined with an electrical recording apparatus to decide whether the "communicators" were personalities distinct from the medium, he concluded, "I can now say that our experiments seem to have shown the existence of mental entities independent of the control of the medium, and separate and apart from the conscious or subconcious mind of the medium."

Throughout his active life Carrington wrote numerous books, some notable for their sharp perceptions and insightful observations, and others filled with incredible and unfounded opinions. In his later years he moved on to investigate astral projection and wrote a series of classic books with **Sylvan J. Muldoon.** He died December 26, 1958, in Los Angeles.

Sources:

Berger, Arthur S., and Joyce Berger. *The Encyclopedia of Parapsychology and Psychical Research.* New York: Paragon House, 1991.

Carrington, Hereward. *The Case for Psychic Survival.* New York: Citadel Press, 1957.

———. *Loaves and Fishes.* New York: Charles Scribner's Sons, 1935.

———. *Modern Psychic Phenomena.* New York: Dodd, Mead, 1919.

———. *The Physical Phenomena of Spiritualism.* New York: Herbert B. Turner, 1907.

———. *The Problems of Psychic Research.* New York: Dodd, Mead, 1921.

———. *The Story of Psychic Science.* London: Rider, 1930. Reprint, New York: Ives Washburn, 1931.

———. *Your Psychic Powers, and How to Develop Them.* New York: A. L. Burt, 1920.

Carrington, Hereward, and Sylvan J. Muldoon. *The Phenomena of Astral Projection.* London: Rider, 1951.

———. *The Projection of the Astral Body.* 1929. Reprint, New York: Samuel Weiser, 1970.

Pleasants, Helene, ed. *Biographical Dictionary of Parapsychology.* New York: Helix Press, 1964.

Carrithers, Walter Adley, Jr. (1924–)

Writer and commercial artist, member of the **American Society for Psychical Research, Society for Psychical Research,** London, and the **American Federation of Astrologers.** He investigated the question of alleged **fraud** with a view to improving reporting methods. He wrote articles for *Fate* magazine and various theosophical and astrological journals. His essay "Re-Appraising Astrological Concepts, Old and New" won first prize in an international essay contest held by the **American Federation of Astrologers** and was published in its *Bulletin* of March-April 1959.

Over the years Carrithers devoted a significant amount of time to investigating and defending **Helena Petrovna Blavatsky** against the charges of fraud that plagued her during the last years of her life and have haunted the **Theosophical Society** ever since. These efforts led to literary works, the first appearing in response to Gertrude Williams's *Priestess of the Occult,* which had appeared in 1946. In the early 1960s Carrithers focused his attention on the Hodgson Report of 1885, the key document that compiled the greatest amount of evidence against Blavatsky. He wrote a series of articles for the *American Theosophist* in 1961 that were later gathered in booklet form and published by the Theosophical Society. In 1962 he also wrote another article that countered the Hodgson Report, which appeared in the *Journal* of the American Society for Psychical Research. Although he raised a few valid points, on the whole his attempt to refute Hodgson failed to convince many outside the theosophical movement.

Sources:

Carrithers, Walter A., Jr. "Madam Blavatsky: One of the World's Great Jokers." *Journal* of the American Society for Psychical Research 56 (July 1962).

———. *The Truth about Madame Blavatsky: An Open Letter to the Author of the Priestess of the Occult.* Covina, Calif.: Theosophical University Press, 1947.

Waterman, Adlai E. [Walter A. Carrithers, Jr.]. *Obituary: The "Hodgson Report" on Madame Blavatsky.* Adyar, Madras, India: Theosophical Publishing House, 1963.

Carter, Charles Ernest Owen (1887–1968)

Theosophist and astrologer, born in Poole, Dorset, England, in 1887. Carter attended the University of London, became a lawyer (1913), and served in the British army during World War I. As a young man he saw an ad for horoscopes by **Alan Leo** and at age 23 began his study of the subject. In 1917 Leo died, and the **Theosophical Society**'s fledgling Astrological Lodge, of which Leo was the driving force, dwindled. In 1920 Carter picked up Leo's work and turned it once again into a vital force. He was elected president of the lodge and served in that post until his retirement in 1952.

Carter's influence came primarily through his writing. He launched *Uranus,* a periodical of the Astrological Lodge, in 1923, and the quarterly journal *Astrology* in 1926. He edited the magazine *Astrology* for 33 years. His breadth of knowledge of the field was demonstrated in his first book, *The Encyclopedia of Astrology* (1924), and in his textbook, *The Principles of Astrology* (1925), the basic introduction used by a generation of astrologers. It was followed by a host of additional books, including his most popular title, *Astrological Aspects* (1930), which went into ten editions during Carter's lifetime. His last and possibly most original book, *An Introduction to Political Astrology* (1951), stemmed from reflection on events surrounding World War II. His texts were well received on both sides of the Atlantic.

In his mature years Carter led in the founding of the Faculty of Astrological Studies, a facility to train the next generation of astrologers. Among his well-known students was **John Addey,** one of the first to receive the school's diploma in 1951. Carter joined with Addey in forming the Astrological Association, a professional organization for British astrologers. Carter died in London on October 4, 1968.

Sources:

Carter, C. E. O. *Astrological Aspects.* London: L. N. Fowler, 1930.

———. *The Encyclopedia of Astrology.* London: Theosophical Publishing House, 1924.

———. *An Introduction to Political Astrology.* London: L. N. Fowler, 1951.

———. *The Principles of Astrology.* London: Theosophical Publishing House, 1925.

———. *The Zodiac and the Soul.* London: Theosophical Publishing House, 1928.

Holden, James H., and Robert A. Hughes. *Astrological Pioneers of America.* Tempe, Ariz.: American Federation of Astrologers, 1988.

Cartheuser, William (ca. 1930)

American **direct voice** medium. His father was a photo engraver who had lived near Vienna, and his mother was of Hungarian origin. Cartheuser was taken to Europe as a child and lived in Besztercze, Transylvania, until age 16, when the family returned to the United States. During the 1930s, Cartheuser resided at the famous **Lily Dale** Spiritualist Center in New York State.

Malcolm Bird reported in *Psychic Research* (1927, p. 166) on two series of séances that Cartheuser gave in October 1926 to the **American Society for Psychical Research.** He found that one of the voice communicators was actually a living person. Cartheuser's voice mediumship was also investigated by noted researcher Dr. **Nandor Fodor** in 1927 at the house of medium **Arthur Ford** in New York. Fodor noted that although Cartheuser had a harelip, there was no impediment in the voices manifesting during a trumpet séance. Finally, Cartheuser was investigated by **Hereward Carrington,** who concluded that "a high percentage of **fraud** enters into the production of Cartheuser's physical phenomena."

In 1933 nine gramophone recordings of Cartheuser's mediumship were made at the studios of the World Broadcasting Company in New York. The "spirit voices" were so loud that engineers had to ask for them to be lowered. Some voices were recorded by a microphone at ceiling level.

Sources:

Carrington, Hereward. *The Invisible World.* New York: The Beechhurst Press; B. Ackerman Inc., 1946.

Pincock, Mrs. J. O'Hara. *The Traits of Truth.* N.p., 1930.

Cartopedy

Modern term for the ancient Persian science of **divination** through the study of feet, similar to the study of hands in **palmistry.** An official cartopedist was employed by the rulers of ancient Persia and India, to be consulted on such important matters as the choice of a bride. Measurements and footprints were studied intensively, sometimes over a period of weeks, before interpretations were made. The size of the foot, the shape of the heel and toes, and the degree of arch were all considered, as well as the lines or markings on the foot itself. Together they were believed to indicate character, ability, and destiny.

Cartopedy is still practiced in India and Pakistan in conjunction with palmistry. Cartopedists are consulted by parents to assess the characteristics of potential brides or husbands for their children, and some employers engage them in hiring staff. In crime detection the police use the services of *payyindas,* or foot trackers, who can assess the characteristics of a wanted man from his footprints.

Cashen's Gap

An isolated place on the Isle of Man, United Kingdom, known in the Manx dialect as Doarlish Cashen, that was the scene of a celebrated haunting by a talking mongoose named Gef. According to the Irving family, who lived at Cashen's Gap, this creature ate rabbits, spoke in various languages, learned nursery rhymes, and imitated other animals and birds.

The case was investigated personally by **Harry Price** in company with **R. S. Lambert** (then editor of the radio magazine *The Listener*), but the animal refused to manifest until after they had left. The case may have been related to **poltergeist** phenomena, since Voirrey Irving, the 13-year-old daughter in the family, was closely associated with the manifestations of the talking mongoose. Price failed to detect any evidence of **fraud.**

The case was also investigated by Dr. **Nandor Fodor,** then chief research officer of the **International Institute for Psychical Research.** He interviewed several witnesses, some hostile to the phenomenon, but the evidence to support it proved strong. Fodor did not accept a poltergeist explanation and suggested half seriously that Gef may have been a mongoose that had learned to talk.

Many years later, after the whole affair had died down, a strange unidentified animal was killed in the district. Some suggested that it might have been Gef.

Sources:

Price, Harry H., and R. S. Lambert. *The Haunting of Cashen's Gap.* London, 1936.

Cassoli, Piero (1918–)

Physician and psychologist actively concerned with parapsychology. Cassoli was born July 25, 1918, in Bologna, Italy, and educated at the University of Bologna (M.D., 1943). In 1947 he became the secretary of a group of researchers investigating parapsychology. He was one of the founders (1954) and then president (1957–59) of the **Centro Studi Parapsicologia.** He also served as director of the center for many years.

A member of the Italian Society for Parapsychology, Cassoli's interests in parapsychology have been quite varied. He was among the first to promote experimental methods of psychical research in Italy and conducted experiments on **precognition.** He also investigated mediums, uncovering numerous tricks they were creating. As a physician, he also experimented in the use of **hypnosis** for anesthesia as an alternative to drugs.

Cassoli contributed articles on parapsychological subjects to *Minerva Medica* and *Luce e Ombra.* In 1971 he participated in the International Conference on Parapsychology held at St. Paul de Vence, France.

Sources:

Berger, Arthur S., and Joyce Berger. *The Encyclopedia of Parapsychology and Psychical Research.* New York: Paragon House, 1991.

Cassoli, Piero. "Parapsychology in Italy Today." In *Parapsychology Today: A Geographical View.* Edited by Allan Angoff and Betty Shapin. New York: Parapsychology Foundation, 1971.

Castaneda, Carlos (1925–)

An anthropologist and occultist who created a sensation with his best-selling book *The Teachings of Don Juan: A Yaqui Way of Knowledge,* first published in 1968. The volume described his experiences with the mysterious Juan Matus, a Yaqui Indian from Sonora. Don Juan was represented as a sorcerer and metaphysical master of the Mexican border who taught a higher reality involving the visionary potentialities of drugs like mescaline. The books caught the imagination of a generation of spiritual seekers who were using various mind-altering drugs and the attention of social scientists who were opting for new theories about the subjective nature of reality.

Castaneda's background is somewhat obscure. His official biographies say that he was born in Sao Paulo, Brazil, in 1931. However, it is now known that he was born in Cajamarca, Peru, on December 25, 1925. He moved to Lima as a young man and studied at the Colegio Nacienal de Nuestra Senora de Guadalupe and the National Fine Arts School of Peru. He moved to San Francisco in 1951 and later attended Los Angeles City College (1955–59). He became an American citizen in 1959 and that same year enrolled in UCLA. He received his B.A. in anthropology in 1962. He pursued his graduate studies sporadically through the next decade, and he finally completed his Ph.D. in 1973.

In the meantime he published his first three books detailing the material he had learned from Don Juan. His third book,

Journey to Ixtlan, had been presented as his doctoral dissertation. Anthropologists praised Castaneda, and Don Juan became a cult figure, although this elusive sorcerer seems to have manifested only to Castaneda and remained a mystery man.

There is, of course, no proof of the existence of Don Juan outside Castaneda's accounts, and his teachings are often recounted in language that sounds nearer to that of a popular thriller than that of a Yaqui Indian. Typically unconvincing phrases from *Tales of Power* (1975) are: "You're goofing," "You indulge like a son of a bitch," and "You nearly lost your marbles." Alan Brian, a British critic, pointed out in a London *Sunday Times* review (May 11, 1975) that Don Juan appears to be bursting with laughter every few pages.

In the absence of any convincing validation of the actual existence of Don Juan, many readers will prefer to regard him as a product of Castaneda's fertile imagination, a mystification of a similar kind to the **Lopsang Rampa** hoax. For a thoughtful and scholarly analysis of the Castaneda phenomenon, see *Castaneda's Journey; The Power and the Allegory* (1976) by Richard DeMille. DeMille discovered sources, published earlier, for the Don Juan material and views the books as fiction. DeMille's work created a storm within the scholarly community and led to a general discrediting of Castaneda. However, the large public tuned to his psychedelic spiritual vision seemed hardly concerned with the controversy. The reclusive Castaneda continued to publish new books in the Don Juan series through the 1980s.

Sources:

Benitez, Fernando. *In the Magic Land of Peyote.* Austin: University of Texas Press, 1975. Reprint, New York: Warner Books, 1975.

Castaneda, Carlos. *The Eagle's Gift.* New York: Simon & Schuster, 1981.

———. *Journey to Ixtlan: The Lessons of Don Juan.* New York: Simon & Schuster, 1972.

———. *The Power of Silence: Further Lessons of Don Juan.* New York: Simon & Schuster, 1987.

———. *The Second Ring of Power.* New York: Simon & Schuster, 1977.

———. *A Separate Reality: Further Conversations with Don Juan.* New York: Simon & Schuster, 1971.

———. *Tales of Power.* New York: Simon & Schuster, 1974.

———. *The Teachings of Don Juan: A Yaqui Way of Knowledge.* Berkeley: University of California Press, 1968.

DeMille, Richard. *Castaneda's Journey; The Power and the Allegory.* Santa Barbara, Calif.: Capra Press, 1976.

———, ed. *Don Juan Papers: Further Castaneda Controversies.* Santa Barbara, Calif.: Ross-Erickson, 1980. Reprint, Belmont, Calif.: Wadsworth, 1990.

Seeing Casteneda: Reaction to the "Don Juan" Writings of Carlos Castaneda. New York: G. P. Putnam & Sons, 1976.

Silverman, David. *Reading Castaneda: A Prologue to the Social Sciences.* London: Routledge & Kegan Paul, 1975.

Castelvitch, Countess (ca. 1920)

Early twentieth-century private medium of Lisbon, Portugal, whose powers of physical phenomena were carefully observed by Dr. d'Oliveira Feijao, professor of surgery in the Lisbon University and Mme. Madeleine Frondoni-Lacombe. According to Feijao's description:

"Blows were struck, the loudest being on the glass of the bookcase. Articles of furniture sometimes moved. Heavy chairs moved about the room; efforts were made on the locked doors of the bookcase, which were opened; large and heavy books were flung on the floor (our hands being linked all the time); an office bell and a handbell, the half open piano and a guitar in its case all sounded loudly. The table rose as much as 24 inches."

Once a heavy table weighing 160 pounds was raised on two legs when it was barely touched and a smaller table was torn into 200 pieces. Objects were brought into the séance room and out through closed doors and excellent materializations were witnessed, among which there was a unique phantom with a death's-head. This phantom and other claimed materializations were photographed.

The mediumship of the countess was discovered in January 1913. Like **Katie King,** in the celebrated case of **Florence Cook,** her control, who manifested for years, departed after a dramatic farewell on July 14, 1920. The history of the mediumship is well told in Frondoni-Lacombe's *Merveilleux Phenomènes de l'au delà* (Lisbon, 1920).

Sources:

Richet, Charles. *Thirty Years of Psychical Research.* London, 1923.

Castle of the Interior Man, The

The mystical name given to the seven stages of the soul's ascent toward divinity, according to such Christian mystics as St. Teresa of Avila (1515–1582). These seven processes of psychic evolution are as follows: (1) the state of prayer in which one concentrates on God; (2) the state of mental prayer, in which one seeks to discover the mystic significance of all things; (3) the obscure night, believed to be the most difficult, in which self must be utterly renounced; (4) the prayer of quietism, complete surrender to the will of God; (5) the state of union, in which the will of man and the will of God become identified; (6) the state of ecstatic prayer, in which the soul is transported with joy, and love enters into it; (7) the state of ravishment, which is the mystic marriage, the perfect union, and the entrance of God and heaven into the interior man.

Sources:

Ramge, Sebastian. *An Introduction to the Writings of St. Teresa.* Chicago: Henry Regnery, 1963.

Teresa of Avila, St. *The Interior Castle.* Translated by Kieran Kavanaugh and Oyilio Rodriguez. New York: Paulist Press, 1979.

Castruccio, Peter Adelbert (1925–)

Engineer, space technologist, and former director of Westinghouse's Astronautics Institute in Baltimore, Maryland. He was born January 11, 1925, in New York and studied at the University of Genoa, Italy, and Johns Hopkins University, Baltimore. He had a distinguished career in such fields as space communications, space navigation, electrical rocketry, and space technology. Castruccio investigated telepathy and clairvoyance and the possible use of ESP in relation to astronautics.

Catabolignes

Demons who bore men away, killed them, and had the power to break and crush them. The sixteenth-century theologian L. Campester described how these demons treated their agents, the magicians and sorcerers.

Catalepsy

A condition involving the sudden suspension of sensation and volition and the partial suspension of vital functions. The body assumes a rigid appearance, sometimes mistaken for death, and the victim remains unconscious throughout the attack. On occasion, the cataleptic state may be marked by symptoms of intense mental excitement and by apparently volitional speech and action. Sometimes the symptoms are hardly distinguishable from those of hysteria.

The period covered by the attack may vary from a few minutes to several days, although the latter occurs only in exceptional cases. An attack may recur, however, on only trifling provocation in the absence of strong resistance by the victim.

Catalepsy is said to be caused by a pathological condition of the nervous system, generally produced by severe or prolonged mental emotion, and should not be confused with hypnotic trance. The belief that the condition may occur in a perfectly healthy person is probably fallacious. There is speculation that catalepsy, like ecstasy and mediumistic faculties, may at times prove contagious.

Catalepsy is associated with schizophrenia and hysteria, and there is reason to believe that it can be self-induced in certain cases. Eastern *fakirs* have been known to cast themselves into a cataleptic sleep lasting for months, and cases have even been reported where they permitted themselves to be buried, being exhumed when the grass had grown over their graves.

Some forms of trance induced by **hypnotism** appear similar to the cataleptic state.

Sources:

Dendy, W. C. *Philosophy of Mystery*. London, 1841.

Cathari

A medieval Christian gnostic heretical sect that flourished in southern France, especially in the Provençal region. One branch of the sect, originating in the region of Albi, gave rise to the name of followers as **Albigenses.**

As early as the 1100s, a form of dualism that held that Satan was, though a creature of God, an immensely powerful being, appeared in southern France and in the Rhine Valley. Its immediate source may have been beliefs brought back from the Holy Land by crusaders. Within a decade, a more extreme dualism that argued for the existence of Satan prior to the creation of the universe appeared. The dualists in France made common cause with the Bogomil dualists of the southern Balkans and by 1180 had become a significant force in southeastern France and northern Italy. Cathar belief was also strong in Lombardy and the Rhineland. The Roman Catholic Church started a crusade against the Cathars of southern France, centered upon the town of Languedoc. By 1230 the Albigensians were eradicated.

What little we know concerning the Cathar belief and practice derives largely from a Cathar ritual from Provence, recorded in a thirteenth-century manuscript, and from the proceedings of the Roman Catholic inquisitors who ruthlessly persecuted the sect. The group has roots that go back to Manicheanism and origins in the theological problem of the place of good and evil in Christian doctrine. The Cathars believed a dualist concept of two gods or principles. The evil god Satan or Lucifer ruled the material world, which was a purgatorial condition for angels or divine souls imprisoned in flesh after the primal war in heaven. Humans could only recover the divine kingdom through a spiritual rebirth, becoming a vehicle for the Holy Ghost, otherwise death would not bring release. A man who died without such a spiritual rebirth would face **reincarnation** again and again, in human or animal form.

An interesting modern echo of the Cathari and its doctrine of imprisonment in the flesh through various incarnations is found in the strange claim of a modern British physician **Arthur Guirdham** that he has verified information that he and a group of other individuals were reincarnations of Cathars who were brutally persecuted in Languedoc, France, during the twelfth century.

Sources:

Birks, Walter. *The Treasure of Montsagur: A Study of the Cathar Heresy and the Nature of the Cathar Secret.* U.K.: Crucible, 1987.

Guirdham, Arthur. *The Cathars and Reincarnation.* London: Neville Spearman, 1970.

Lea, H. C. *History of the Inquisition in the Middle Ages.* 3 vols. New York: Harper and Bros., 1888.

Russell, Jeffrey Burton. *Witchcraft in the Middle Ages.* Ithaca, N.Y.: Cornell University Press, 1972.

Wakefield, Walter, and Austin P. Evans. *Heresies of the High Middle Ages.* New York, 1969.

Catoptromancy (or Enoptromancy)

A type of **divination** using a mirror, described thus by the second-century Greek traveler Pausanius:

"Before the Temple of Ceres at Patras, there was a fountain, separated from the temple by a wall, and there was an oracle, very truthful, not for all events, but for the sick only. The sick person let down a mirror, suspended by a thread, till its base touched the surface of the water, having first prayed to the goddess and offered incense. Then looking in the mirror, he saw the presage of death or recovery, according as the face appeared fresh and healthy, or of a ghastly aspect."

Another catoptric method was to place the mirror at the back of the head of a boy or girl whose eyes were bandaged. In Thessaly, the response reportedly appeared in characters of blood on the face of the moon, probably represented in the mirror. The Thessalian sorceresses derived their art from the Persians, who always endeavored to plant their religion and mystic rites in the countries they invaded. (See also **crystal gazing**)

Cats, Elfin

These cats were said to be found in the Scottish Highlands and to be of a wild breed as large as dogs, black in color, and with a white spot on the breast. They had arched backs and erect bristles. According to superstition, elfin cats were witches in disguise.

Cattle Mutilations

Since 1973 there have been waves of reports of mysterious attacks on cattle in the midwestern United States. The first of these occurred in Minnesota and Kansas. Some features of these attacks seemed inconsistent with normal explanations of attacks by predatory animals. In many instances the dead cattle appeared to have been mutilated by precise surgery in which certain parts of the body (usually eyes, ears, mouth, rectum, or sex organs) had been removed and the carcass drained of blood. No footprints indicating mutilation by humans were found around the bodies. Authorities in Kansas suggested that "cultists" were probably the perpetrators. Several carcasses were brought in for autopsies, which showed the animals died of blackleg, a cattle disease. By this time, however, the early reports and allegations had circulated around the country.

In 1974 there were reports of cattle mutilations in northeastern Nebraska and eastern South Dakota. Some reports coincided with sightings of UFOs. Along with the absence of footprints or other tracks in the area, there were rumors of large helicopters being used for cattle rustling. Although modern rustlers often use mechanization, it is unlikely that they would leave carcasses behind, and they would have no rationale for mutilating individual cattle.

Some explanations were ingenious but not wholly convincing. The director of men's admissions at the South Dakota State Mental Hospital suggested that the mutilations were the work of a psychotic individual, perhaps a youth from a farm background with hostility toward authority figures. A persuasive suggestion was that the mutilations were the work of Satanist groups, and a few scattered cases of animals who had been drugged were found. However, the cattle mutilations covered a large area and continued undetected for three months, and the possibility of Satanist groups operating from helicopters over such a large area seems unlikely.

The suggestion that the mutilations might have been the work of entities from UFOs is offered by Linda Moulton Howe in her 1980 movie, *Strange Harvest,* and reinforced by additional accounts in her book published in 1989.

More definitive work was begun in 1979 by Kenneth Rommel, who received a grant from the Federal Law Enforcement Assistance Administration to investigate mutilation reports in New Mexico. In 1980, after an extensive investigation of the New Mexico carcasses, and with agreement from sheriffs and pathologists in other states, Rommel announced that he had found no evidence of cattle mutilation apart from normal predator damage. The pattern of disturbance of the carcass was consistent with that of small animals attacking the softest part of the cow, which was largely protected by the extremely strong hide. In 1984 further extensive study of the reports around the nation was made by Daniel Kagan and Ian Summers. Their book, *Mute Evidence* (1984), remains the definitive account of the phenomenon. They examined the origin of cattle mutilation reports and found them based on inept observation and unfounded rumor. Where autopsy reports of "mutilated" cattle were acquired from competent pathologists, they indicated damage by small animals.

In spite of lack of evidence, reports of cattle mutilations and unfounded charges that aliens are attacking hundreds of thousands of the defenseless cows continue to circulate within some of the ufological networks, though most ufologists have dismissed the stories.

The modern-day reports of animal mutilations are not unprecedented. Other stories of attacks on cattle were compiled by the indefatigable chronicler of the bizarre, **Charles Fort,** in his book *Lo!* (1931). Fort recalls that in the winter of 1904–05, during an outbreak of religious revivalism in Wales, there were stories of strange lights in the air and mysterious air vessels, followed by reports of widespread attacks on sheep. In 1910 sheep were killed on a large scale by something that attacked half a dozen each night; rabbits were killed by having their backs broken. Since Fort there have been many similar reports of animal mutilations from various countries. Not all such attacks are mysterious. In October 1980, following reports of a sheep predator active for four years, a Scottish farmer baited a cage and caught a puma. Similarly persistent stalking and killing of sheep by wild dogs is well known to farmers in many countries.

Sources:

Mitchell, John, and Robert J. M. Rickard. *Phenomena: A Book of Wonders.* N.p., 1977.

Rommel, Kenneth M. *Operation Animal Mutilation.* Report of the District Attorney, First Judicial District, State of New Mexico. Sante Fe, N.Mex.: District Attorney, 1980.

Stewart, James R. "Cattle Mutilations: An Episode of Collective Delusion." *The Zetetic* 1, 2 (Spring–Summer 1977): 55–66.

Cauda Pavonis (Newsletter)

Newsletter of the Hermetic Text Society, published twice a year. It includes scholarly material on all aspects of **alchemy** and hermeticism and their influence on literature, philosophy, art, religion, and the history of science and medicine. The approach is interdisciplinary and is not limited to any particular historical period, national emphasis, or methodology. Address: *Cauda Pavonis,* Department of English, Washington State University, Pullman, WA 99164-5020.

Caul

A membrane that sometimes covers the head of a child at birth. It was regarded as a preservative against drowning at sea and was consequently much sought after by seamen. Superstitions concerning the caul are of some antiquity. In ancient Rome, Aelius Lampridius wrote about the life of Antonine Diadumeninus, stating that he was so called from having been brought into the world with a band of membrane round his forehead like a diadem, and that he enjoyed a perpetual state of felicity from this circumstance. Roman midwives offered cauls for sale in the Forum.

Even as late as the 1870s, British newspapers often carried advertisements from would-be purchasers of a caul, offering large sums of money. The caul was also used in a form of divination called **amniomancy.**

In the cultures of northern and eastern Europe, the caul, which marked babies as different, was associated with vampirism. A child born with a caul was thought to become a vampire after death. To prevent such a fate, the caul was removed, dried, ground into fine particles, and fed to the child on its seventh birthday.

CAUS See Citizens Against UFO Secrecy

Causimomancy

Divination by fire. It was supposed to be a good omen when combustible objects cast into the fire did not burn.

Cavanna, Roberto (1927–)

Biochemist, Istituto Superiore di Sanità, Rome, Italy. He was born November 3, 1927, in Rome, and educated at the University of Rome (Ph.D., chemistry, 1949). Cavanna investigated connections between states of consciousness affected by psychopharmacological and psi phenomena and edited several books on consciousness studies.

Sources:

Cavanna, Roberto, ed. *Psi Favorable States of Consciousness.* New York: Parapsychology Foundation, 1970.

Cavanna, Roberto, and Emilio Servadio. *ESP Experiments with LSD 25 and Psilocybin.* New York: Parapsychology Foundation, 1964.

Cavanna, Roberto, and Montague Ullman, eds. *Psi and Altered States of Consciousness.* New York: Parapsychology Foundation, 1968.

Cayce, Charles Thomas Taylor (1942–)

Charles Thomas Taylor Cayce, the president of the **Association for Research and Enlightenment** (ARE) and the grandson of seer **Edgar Cayce,** was born in Virginia Beach, Virginia, on October 7, 1942, the son of **Hugh Lynn Cayce.** The Cayce family had lived at Virginia Beach since 1925. Charles Thomas grew up there and worked in his father's office. He attended Hampden-Sydney College and later did graduate work at the University of California at Berkeley and the University of Maryland, from which he received his Ph.D. in child psychology in 1968. He taught college for several years and worked for the U.S. State Department before returning to Virginia Beach in 1972 and joining the ARE staff as the youth director. As a teenager, Cayce had become alienated from the ARE and had decided to pursue a career elsewhere. However, after delving into his grandfather's work, he found ideas and concepts personally helpful to him. His continued study of the readings made him both open and then supportive of the work.

Four years after Cayce began work at ARE, his father had a heart attack. In the wake of Hugh Lynn's illness, immediate plans for succession were made. With the approval of the board, Charles Thomas was named president of the corporation. In that position, Charles Thomas has emerged as an administrator, rather than a writer or speaker like his father. He has developed a research program testing gifted youth and studying the role of meditation and **dreams** in furthering psychic development.

Sources:

Smith, A. Robert. *Hugh Lynn Cayce: About My Father's Business.* Norfolk, Va.: The Donning Co., 1988.

Zuromski, Paul. "A Conversation with Charles Thomas Cayce." *Psychic Guide* (September–November 1984): 14–19.

Cayce, Edgar (1877–1945)

Outstanding American psychic and founder of the **Association for Research and Enlightenment** (ARE). Cayce was born on March 18, 1877, in Hopkinsville, Kentucky, the son of businessman. He grew up in rural Kentucky and received only a limited formal education. He was a member of the Christian Church

(Disciples of Christ). As an adult he began a career as a photographer.

Cayce's life took a radically different direction in 1898, after he developed a case of laryngitis. He was hypnotized by a friend and while in the trance state prescribed a cure that worked. Neighbors heard of the event and asked Cayce to do similar "readings" for them. In 1909 he did a reading in which he diagnosed and cured a homeopathic physician, Dr. Wesley Ketchum. Ketchum arranged for periodic sittings in which Cayce, who had learned by this time to go into trance without the assistance of a hypnotist, offered his medical advice for the ill. During the next years Cayce gave occasional sittings, but primarily worked in photography.

Then in 1923 Theosophist Arthur Lammers invited Cayce to Dayton, Ohio, to do a set of private readings. These readings were noteworthy because they involved Cayce's initial exploration of individual past lives and because of the imposition upon his readings of Lammers's theosophical opinions, especially concerning reincarnation. These readings encouraged Cayce to become a professional. He soon closed his photography shop and moved to Dayton, and then in 1925 to Virginia Beach, Virginia. Among his early supporters was businessman Morton Blumenthal, who gave financial backing for Cayce Hospital (1928) and a school, Atlantic University (1930). Unfortunately, Blumenthal was financially destroyed by the Great Depression and both enterprises failed.

In 1932 Cayce organized his following as the Association for Research and Enlightenment. With the resources generated by the association, complete records of all the readings for the next 12 years were made. These formed a huge body of material for future consideration, and more than any other characteristic make Cayce's career stand out above that of his contemporaries. Cayce's readings were later indexed, cross-referenced, and used as the basis of numerous books.

Cayce died in 1945, and his son Hugh Lynn Cayce continued the work of the association and promoted the abilities of his father, though he did not claim to possess any special psychic abilities himself. Cayce's work became known by a large audience outside the psychic community in 1967 through a biographical book by Jess Stern, *Edgar Cayce, The Sleeping Prophet.*

Sources:

Bro, Harmon Hartzell. *A Seer Out of Season: The Life of Edgar Cayce.* New York: New American Library, 1989.

Cayce, Edgar. *The Edgar Cayce Reader.* 2 vols. New York: Paperback Library, 1969.

Cayce, Hugh Lynn. *Venture Inward.* New York: Paperback Library, 1966.

Millard, Joseph. *Edgar Cayce.* Greenwich, Conn.: Fawcett, 1967.

Neimark, Anne E. *With This Gift.* New York: William Morrow, 1978.

Puryear, Herbert. *The Edgar Cayce Primer.* New York: Bantam Books, 1982.

———. *A Prophet in His Own Country.* New York: William Morrow, 1974.

Cayce, Hugh Lynn (1907–1982)

Son of psychic **Edgar Cayce** (1877–1945) and president for many years of the **Association for Research and Enlightenment** (ARE). He was born on March 16, 1907, at Bowling Green, Kentucky. He grew up in Kentucky and Alabama, where his father worked as a photographer. His childhood was marked by one event that particularly influenced his life: He burned his eyes severely, and his father went against medical advice and would not allow the doctors to remove one of the eyes. The eye was saved and Hugh Lynn recovered completely.

He moved with his family to Virginia Beach in 1925. After graduating from high school, he entered Norfolk Business College and in 1926 began four years at Washington and Lee University. While there he met Thomas Segrue. Through Segrue, who was enthusiastic about his father's work, Hugh Lynn gained a new appreciation for what had become commonplace in his family. In 1929 the two began a periodical, *The New Tomorrow,* which centered upon Cayce's psychic readings. Later, Segrue would write one of the early biographies of Edgar Cayce, *There is a River* (1942).

After graduating from college, Cayce went to work for the ARE. He helped build the organization through the 1930s, but then went into the army during World War II. Both his parents died while he was in Europe, and when he returned the ARE was failing as a business. He soon set about reviving it and developing a program to replace the readings that were no longer available. His major resource was the library of transcripts of readings that Edgar Cayce gave during the last two decades of his life. Research on these readings began with indexing and cross-referencing them, followed by publication of excerpts from the readings on various topics.

Growth of the ARE was slow until 1966–67 when Cayce and Jess Stern published biographical studies of his father. These books became unexpected successes and led to a series of books on Cayce's teachings that appeared over the next decade, including *The Edgar Cayce Reader* (1969), a two-volume collection of excerpts from his readings compiled by Hugh Lynn. The association experienced rapid growth during that period.

Cayce led the foundation until 1976, when he was forced into semiretirement by a heart attack. His son **Charles Thomas Cayce** succeeded him as president of the ARE, and Hugh Lynn became chairman of the board. During his semiretirement Cayce was able to write several more books. He died July 4, 1982.

Sources:

Cayce, Hugh Lynn. *Earth Changes Update.* Virginia Beach, Va.: ARE Press, 1980.

———. *Faces of Fear.* New York: Berkeley Books, 1980.

———. *The Jesus I Knew.* Virginia Beach, Va.: ARE Press, 1984.

———. *Venture Inward.* New York: Paperback Library, 1966.

Smith, A. Robert. *Hugh Lynn Cayce: About My Father's Business.* Norfolk, Va.: Donning, 1988.

Cazotte, Jacques (1719–1792)

French romance writer and the reputed author of the famous *Prophétie de Cazotte,* concerning the French Revolution. As his sympathies were not with the revolutionary party, his letters were seized, and he and his daughter Elizabeth were thrown into prison. He was later beheaded. He was also the author of the celebrated occult romance *Le Diable Amoureux* (1787).

Sources:

Cazotte, Jacques. *Le Diable.* Paris: B. Grasset, 1921. Translated as *The Devil in Love.* London: Consortium, 1993.

CCCS See Centre for Crop Circle Studies

Celestial Light

According to mystical belief, the sacred light of all the ages, which is "as the lightning which shineth from the west to the east." It is the halo that surrounds certain visions of a mystical nature. The celestial light can only be seen by those who have lived ascetically, when respiration is feeble, and life has almost left the body.

Cellini, Benvenuto (1500–1575)

This celebrated Italian artist and craftsman claimed to have had interesting adventures with demons and practitioners of black magic. The following excerpt from his *Life* gives a vivid account of one such experience:

"It happened, through a variety of odd accidents, that I made acquaintance with a Sicilian priest, who was a man of genius, and well versed in the Latin and Greek authors. Happening one day to have some conversation with him, when the subject turned on the subject of necromancy, I, who had a great desire to know something of the matter, told him, that I had all my life felt a curiosity to be acquainted with the mysteries of this art. The priest made answer, 'That the man must be of a resolute and steady temper who enters upon that study.' I replied, 'That I had fortitude and resolution enough, if I could but find an opportunity.' The priest subjoined, 'If you think you have the heart to venture, I will give you all the satisfaction you can desire.' Thus we agreed to enter upon a plan of necromancy. The priest one evening prepared to satisfy me, and desired me to look out for a companion or two. I invited one Vincenzio Romoli, who was my intimate acquaintance: he brought with him a native of Pistoia, who cultivated the black art himself. We repaired to the Colloseo, and the priest, according to the custom of necromancers, began to draw circles upon the ground with the most impressive ceremonies imaginable: he likewise brought hither assafoetida, several precious perfumes and fire, with some compositions also which diffused noisome odors. As soon as he was in readiness, he made an opening to the circle, and having taken us by the hand, ordered the other necromancer, his partner, to throw the perfumes into the fire at the proper time, intrusting the care of the fire and the perfumes to the rest; and then he began his incantations. This ceremony lasted above an hour and a half, when there appeared several legions of devils insomuch that the amphitheatre was quite filled with them. I was busy about the perfumes, when the priest, perceiving there was a considerable number of infernal spirits, turned to me and said, 'Benvenuto, ask them something.' I answered, 'Let them bring me into the company of my Sicilian mistress, Angelica.' That night we obtained no answer of any sort; but I had received great satisfaction in having my curiosity so far indulged. The necromancer told me, it was requisite we should go a second time, assuring me, that I should be satisfied in whatever I asked; but that I must bring with me a pure immaculate boy.

"I took with me a youth who was in my service, of about twelve years of age, together with the same Vincenzio Romoli, who had been my companion the first time and one Agnolino Gaddi, an intimate acquaintance, whom I likewise prevailed on to assist at the ceremony. When we came to the place appointed, the priest having made his preparations as before, with the same and even more striking ceremonies, placed us within the circle, which he had likewise drawn with a more wonderful art, and in a more solemn manner, than at our former meeting. Thus having committed the care of the perfume and the fire to my friend Vincenzio, who was assisted by Agnolino Gaddi, he put into my hand a pintacula or magical chart, and bid me turn it towards the places that he should direct me; and under the pintacula I held the boy. The necromancer having begun to make his tremendous invocations, called by their names a multitude of demons, who were the leaders of the several legions, and questioned them by the power of the eternal uncreated God, who lives for ever, in the Hebrew language, as likewise in Latin and Greek; insomuch that the amphitheatre was almost in an instant filled with demons more numerous than at the former conjuration. Vincenzio Romoli was busied in making a fire, with the assistance of Agnolino, and burning a great quantity of precious perfumes. I, by the direction of the necromancer, again desired to be in the company of my Angelica. The former thereupon turning to me, said, 'Know, they have declared, that in the space of a month you shall be in her company.'

"He then requested me to stand resolutely by him, because the legions were now above a thousand more in number than he had designed; and, besides these were the most dangerous; so that, after they had answered my question, it behoved him to be civil to them, and dismiss them quietly. At the same time the boy under the pintacula was in a terrible fright, saying, that there were in that place a million of fierce men, who threatened to destroy us; and that, moreover, four armed giants of an enormous stature were endeavoring to break into our circle. During this time, whilst the necromancer, trembling with fear, endeavored by mild and gentle methods to dismiss them in the best way he could, Vincenzio Romoli, who quivered like an aspen leaf, took, care of the perfumes. Though I was as much terrified as any of them, I did my utmost to conceal the terror I felt; so that I greatly contributed to inspire the rest with resolution; but the truth is, I gave myself over for a dead man, seeing the horrid fright the necromancer was in. The boy placed his head between his knees, and said, 'In this posture I will die; for we shall all surely perish.' I told him that all these demons were under us, and what he saw was smoke and shadow; so I bid him hold up his head and take courage. No sooner did he look up, but he cried out, 'The whole amphitheatre is burning, and the fire is just falling upon us;' so covering his eyes with his hands, he again exclaimed that destruction was inevitable, and he desired to see no more. The necromancer entreated me to have a good heart, and take care to burn the proper perfumes; upon which I turned to Romoli, and bid him burn all the most precious perfumes he had. At the same time I cast my eye upon Agnolino Gaddi, who was terrified to such a degree that he could scarce distinguish objects, and seemed to be half-dead. Seeing him in this condition, I said, 'Agnolino, upon these occasions a man should not yield to fear, but should stir about and give his assistance; so come directly and put on some more of these perfumes.' Poor Agnolino, upon attempting to move, was so violently terrified that the effects of his fear overpowered all the perfumes we were burning. The boy, hearing a crepitation, ventured once more to raise his head, when, seeing me laugh, he began to take courage, and said, 'That the devils were flying away with a vengeance.'

"In this condition we stayed till the bell rang for morning prayer. The boy again told us, that there remained but few devils, and these were at a great distance. When the magician had performed the rest of his ceremonies, he stripped off his gown and took up a wallet full of books which he had brought with him. We all went out of the circle together, keeping as close to each other as we possibly could, especially the boy, who had placed himself in the middle, holding the necromancer by the coat, and me by the cloak. As we were going to our houses in the quarter of Banchi, the boy told us that two of the demons whom we had seen at the amphitheatre, went on before us leaping and skipping, sometimes running upon the roofs of the houses, and sometimes upon the ground. The priest declared, that though he had often entered magic circles, nothing so extraordinary had ever happened to him. As we went along, he would fain persuade me to assist with him at consecrating a book, from which, he said, we should derive immense riches: we should then ask the demons to discover to us the various treasures with which the earth abounds, which would raise us to opulence and power; but that those love-affairs were mere follies, from whence no good could be expected. I answered, 'That I would readily have accepted his proposal if I understood Latin': he redoubled his persuasions, assuring me, that the knowledge of the Latin language was by no means material. He added, that he could have Latin scholars enough, if he had thought it worth while to look out for them; but that he could never have met with a partner of resolution and intrepidity equal to mine, and that I should by all means follow his advice. Whilst we were engaged in this conversation, we arrived at our respective homes, and all that night dreamt of nothing but devils."

Sources:

Cellini, Benvenuto. *Autobiography.* New York: Dodd, Mead, 1961.

Pope-Hennessy, John Wyndham. *Cellini.* New York: Abbeville Press, 1985.

Symonds, J. A. *The Life of Benvenuto Cellini.* 2 vols. London, 1888.

Celonitis (or Celontes)

This fabulous stone was said to be found in the tortoise. It was believed to resist fire and to have healing virtues. In addition, when carried under the tongue on the day of the new moon and for the fifteen days following, during the lunar ascension, it inspired its fortunate possessor to foretell future events every day from sunrise to six o'clock.

Celts

The ethnic origins of the Celts are somewhat complex, and often obscured by Celtic-influenced languages. Ancient writers referred to the Celts as tall, fair-haired people with blue or grey eyes, but they are more often considered to be the shorter, dark-complexioned Celtic-speaking peoples of France, Great Britain, and Ireland. In general, the Celts are believed to be a warrior race of the early Iron Age, originating north of the Alps, and spreading through central Europe during the La Tène period (500 B.C.E.–C.E. 1).

The Celts who settled in the British Isles comprised two strains—the Brythons and the Goidels. The former became established in England and Wales, but the Goidels migrated from France to Ireland about the forth century B.C.E. At a later date Goidel contingents from Ireland formed settlements in England, Wales, and Scotland, eventually merging with the Brythons. The Gaelic-speaking Celts dominated in Ireland, Scotland, and the Isle of Man, whereas the Brythonic speakers were more common in Wales.

According to **Lewis Spence,** magic among the Celtic peoples in ancient times was closely identified with Druidism. Celtic origin and its relation to Druidism, however, is a question upon which much discussion has been lavished. Some authorities, including Sir John Rhys, believe it to have been of non-Celtic and even non-Aryan origin; that is, the earliest non-Aryan or so-called Iberian or Megalithic people of Britain introduced the immigrant Celts to the Druidic religion.

The Druids were magi as well as hierophants, in the same sense that the American Indian medicine man was both magus and priest. That is, they were medicine men on a higher scale, possessing a larger share of transcendental knowledge than the shamans of more barbarous races. They may be linked to the shaman and the magus of medieval times. Many of their practices were purely shamanistic, while others were more closely connected with medieval magical rites. The magic of Druidism had many points of comparison with other magic systems and seems to have approximated more closely to the type of black magic that desires power for the sake of power alone rather than any of the more transcendental type. It included the power to render oneself invisible, to change the bodily shape, to produce an enchanted sleep, to induce lunacy, and to cast spells and charms that caused death. Power over the elements was also claimed, as in the case of Broichan, a Caledonian Druid who opposed Saint Columba, as related in St. Adamnan's *Life of St. Columba:*

"Broichan, speaking one day to the holy man, says: 'Tell me, Columba, at what time dost thou propose to sail forth?' 'On the third day,' says the Saint, 'God willing and life remaining, we propose to begin our voyage.' 'Thou wilt not be able to do so,' says Broichan in reply, 'for I can make the wind contrary for thee, and bring dark clouds upon thee.' The Saint says: 'The omnipotence of God rules over all things, in Whose Name all our movements, He Himself governing them, are directed.' What more need be said? On the same day as he had purposed in his heart the Saint came to the long lake of the river Ness, a great crowd following. But the Druids then began to rejoice when they saw a great darkness coming over, and a contrary wind with a tempest. Nor should it be wondered at that these things can be done by the art of demons, God permitting it, so that even winds and waters are roused to fury.

"For it was thus that legions of devils once met the holy Bishop Germanus in mid-ocean, what time he was sailing from the Gallican Gulf (the British Channel) to Britain in the cause of man's salvation, and stirred up dangerous storms and spread darkness over the sky and obscured daylight. All which storms, however, were stilled at the prayer of St. Germanus, and, quicker than said, ceased, and the darkness was swept away.

"Our Columba, therefore, seeing the furious elements stirred up against him, calls upon Christ the Lord, and entering the boat while the sailors are hesitating, he with all the more confidence, orders the sail to be rigged against the wind. Which being done, the whole crowd looking on meanwhile, the boat is borne along against the contrary winds with amazing velocity. And after no great interval, the adverse winds veer round to the advantage of the voyage amid the astonishment of all. And thus, throughout that whole day, the blessed man's boat was driven along by gentle favouring breezes, and reached the desired haven. Let the reader, therefore, consider how great and saintly was that vulnerable man through whom Almighty God manifested His glorious Name by such miraculous powers as have just been described in the presence of a heathen people."

The art of rainmaking, bringing down fire from the sky, and causing mists, snowstorms, and floods was also claimed by the Druids. Many of the spells probably in use among the Druids survived until a comparatively late period—the names of saints being substituted for those of Celtic deities. In pronouncing incantations, the usual method employed was to stand upon one leg and point with the forefinger to the person or object on which the spell was to be laid, at the same time closing an eye, as if to concentrate the force of the entire personality upon that which was to be placed under the spell.

A manuscript preserved in the Monastery of St. Gall, dating from the eighth or ninth century, contains magic formulas for preserving butter and healing certain diseases in the name of the Irish god Diancecht. These bear a close resemblance to Babylonian and Etruscan spells, and this goes to strengthen the hypothesis often put forward that Druidism had an eastern origin. All magic rites were accompanied by spells. Druids often accompanied an army to assist by their magic in confounding the enemy.

The concept of a Druidic priesthood descended down to the beginning of the twentieth century in a more or less debased condition in British Celtic areas; thus the existence of guardians and keepers of wells, said to possess magic properties, and the fact that certain familiar magic spells and formulas are handed down from one generation to another are proof of the survival of Druidic tradition. Females are generally the conservators of these mysteries, and that there were Druid priestesses is fairly certain.

There are also indications that to some extent **witchcraft** in **Scotland** was a survival of Celtic religiomagical practice. **Amulets** were worn extensively by the Celts, the principal forms in use being phallic (to fend against the **evil eye**), coral, the serpent's "egg." The person who passed a number of serpents together forming such an "egg" from their collected spume had to catch it in his cloak before it fell to earth and then flee to avoid the reptiles' vengeance. Totemic amulets were also common.

Sources:

De Jubainville, H. d'Arbois. *Les Droides et les dieux celtiques à forme d'animaux.* Paris, 1906.

Gomme, G. L. *Ethnology in Folklore.* New York: D. Appleton, 1892.

Green, Miranda J. *Dictionary of Celtic Myth and Legend.* London: Thames and Hudson, 1992.

Laing, Lloyd Robert. *Celtic Britain and Ireland, A.D. 200-800: The Myth of the Dark Ages.* Dublin, Ireland: Irish Academic Press, 1990.

Powell, T. G. E. *The Celts.* New York: F. A. Praeger, 1958.

Rhys, John. *Celtic Britain.* London, 1882.

Ross, Anne. *Pagan Celtic Britain.* London: Routledge and Kegan Paul, 1967.

Spence, Lewis. *Magical Arts in Celtic Britain.* London: Rider, n.d.

Squire, Charles. *Mythology of the Ancient Britons.* London, 1905.

Census of Hallucinations

An early survey of public encounters with paranormal **apparitions,** occasioned by the publication of *Phantasms of the Living,* by **Edmund Gurney, F. W. H. Myers,** and **Frank Podmore** (1886), expanded on in 1889 by a committee of the **Society for Psychical**

Research, London. Under **Henry Sidgwick**'s chairmanship the committee consisted of Mrs. Henry Sidgwick, Myers, Podmore, and Alice Johnson. The report of the committee, drawn up by Mrs. Sidgwick, was published in 1894. Seventeen thousand people were canvassed, of which 1,684 answered claiming to have seen apparitions.

Sources:

Berger, Arthur S., and Joyce Berger. *The Encyclopedia of Parapsychology and Psychical Research.* New York: Paragon House, 1991.

Gurney, Edmund, F. W. H. Myers, and Frank Podmore. *Phantasms of the Living.* 2 vols. London: Society for Psychical Research, Trubner & Co., 1886.

"Report of the Census of Hallucinations." *Proceedings* of the Society for Psychical Research 10 (1894): 25.

Center for Archaeoastronomy

Founded in 1978 to investigate mysteries of ancient sites such as **Stonehenge** and the **Nazca** lines in Peru. It is concerned primarily with the science, astronomy, and archaeology of ancient peoples. It grew out of the work of people such as R. J. C. Atkinson, Alexander Thom, Gerald S. Hawkins, and Aubrey Burl on Stonehenge and other megalithic sites in Great Britain. The center publishes a quarterly bulletin, *Archaeoastronomy.* Address: Center for Archaeoastronomy, University of Maryland, College Park, MD 20742.

Sources:

Atkinson, R. C. J. *Stonehenge.* London: Pelican Books, 1960.

Burl, Aubrey. *Prehistoric Astronomy and Ritual.* Aylesbury, Bucks, England: Shire Publications, 1983.

Hawkins, Gerald S. *Stonehenge Decoded.* Garden City, N.Y.: Doubleday, 1965.

Thom, Alexander. *Megalithic Lunar Observatories.* Oxford: Oxford University Press, 1971.

Center for Borderline History

Founded in 1984 by individuals interested in borderline history (defined by the center as "the study of occult forces upon the evolution of the world"). It examines the influences of **occult** forces in past as well as contemporary history, identifies these forces, and defines their objectives. The center disseminates findings in various publications. Address: PO Box 955, Ganges, British Columbia VOS 1EO, Canada.

Center for Frontier Sciences at Temple University

A center designed to encourage greater openness toward novel approaches in science, medicine, and technology. The main focus is on three areas where mounting evidence challenges the contemporary scientific consensus: the mind matter relationship, bioelectromagnetics, and energy medicine. The center is also concerned with the international exchange of information on Eastern and Western science. Some fifty Russian and Eastern European scientists are affiliated with the center, which publishes the magazine *Frontier Perspectives.* Address: Temple University, Ritter Hall 003-00, Room 478, 13th & Montgomery, Philadelphia, PA 19122.

Center for Parapsychological Research

The research division of the former **Association for the Understanding of Man,** which conducted experimental studies of empirical, methodological, and theoretical problems in **parapsychology.** Its research was aimed at providing a scientific understanding of **ESP** and psychokinesis, with special attention to the logical linkage between the hypothesis being tested and the methods used to test them. The center was also active in parapsychological education through sponsorship of lectures, workshops, individual counseling, and dissemination of literature and reading lists concerned with the scientific study of psi events. The director of the center was **Rex G. Stanford,** a parapsychologist and brother of the center's founder, Ray Stanford.

Center for Scientific Anomalies Research (CSAR)

Founded by sociologist Dr. **Marcello Truzzi** in 1981 to bring together scholars and researchers concerned with the responsible, skeptical, and scientific inquiry into claims concerning anomalies—including **UFOs, cryptozoology,** and other similar phenomena originally cataloged by **Charles Fort.** Truzzi had earlier broken with the **Committee for the Scientific Investigation of Claims of the Paranormal** because he had come to reject its hardline debunking stance as opposed to the scientific inquiry he proposed. For a decade he edited the **Zetetic Scholar** (1978–87); CSAR grew out of the response to the journal. CSAR promotes an open and fair-minded inquiry that is also constructively skeptical, although with the discontinuance of the *Zetetic Scholar* its activity level has been greatly reduced. Much emphasis in the 1990s has been focused on the **Institute for Anomalistic Criminology,** one division of CSAR. Address: Center for Scientific Anomalies Research, P.O. Box 1052, Ann Arbor, MI 48106-1052.

Sources:

Clark, Jerome. *Encyclopedia of Strange and Unexplained Phenomena.* Detroit, Mich.: Gale Research, 1993.

"CSAR: Statement of Goals." *Zetetic Scholar* 12/13 (1987): 205–06.

Center for Spiritual Awareness

Organization devoted to the concept that religion is a personal relationship between the individual soul and God, with the goal of becoming dissolved in the mystery of divine essence. The center was founded in 1962 by H. Edwin O'Neal. Later in the decade, Roy Eugene Davis, a disciple of **Paramahansa Yogananda,** associated with the center and merged his organization, New Life Worldwide, with it. Davis succeeded O'Neal as head of CSA in 1977.

Under Davis's leadership, the Center for Spiritual Awareness expanded to become the Church of the Christian Spiritual Alliance (which in spite of its name teaches kriya yoga and Hinduism as originally expounded by Swami Yogananda and the Self-Realization Fellowship). The center is now the teaching department of the Church of the Christian Spiritual Alliance. It publishes *Orion* and **Truth Journal.** Address: Box 7, Lakemont, GA 30552.

Sources:

Davis, Eugene Roy. *An Easy Guide to Meditation.* Lakemont, Ga.: CSA Press, 1978.

———. *God Has Given Us Every Good Thing.* Lakemont, Ga.: CSA Press, 1986.

———. *The Path of Soul Liberation.* Lakemont, Ga.: CSA Press, 1975.

———. *The Teachings of the Masters of Perfection.* Lakemont, Ga.: CSA Press, 1979.

Center for UFO Studies See **J. Allen Hynek Center for UFO Studies**

Central Association of Spiritualists See **British National Association of Spiritualists**

Central Premonitions Registry

Founded by Robert and Nancy Nelson in New York, the Central Premonitions Registry registers and checks **predictions** from any part of the country. The registry invites anyone with claims to **premonition** to send them full details for the special filing system, so that their predictions may be verified. Premonitions are date-stamped and filed under such categories as natural disasters, wars and international relations, aircraft and ship disasters, and prominent personalities—injury or death. All these predictions are monitored and checked. The registry has already verified many remarkably accurate predictions, mostly from ordinary individuals, rather than professional psychics. Robert Nelson first became interested in the paranormal through the telekinetic ability of his identical twin brother, William, to move small objects by mental concentration.

The Central Premonitions Registry is the first private agency in the United States dedicated to the scientific evaluation of precognitive perceptions and their use as an early warning system for assassinations, plane crashes, floods, fires, and other catastrophes. Psychically gifted individuals are encouraged to participate in **dream** and **telepathy** studies at local dream laboratories. The registry also provides lectures to civic groups, schools, and colleges on precognition and related faculties. Address: PO Box 482, Times Square Station, New York, NY 10036.

Central Psi Research Institute

Founded in 1977 with a membership of statisticians, psychologists, physicists, and others interested in paranormal phenomena. The institute is dedicated to furthering the development of **parapsychology** and working to integrate parapsychology into the established academic and scientific arena. Activities include research projects, a midwestern premonitions registry, spontaneous case study files, and a comprehensive education file on parapsychology teachers and courses. The institute offers support services for persons who experience paranormal phenomena daily, conducts in-service educational programs, and arranges classes for educational groups locally. The emphasis is on skepticism and empiricism. The institute publishes a bimonthly newsletter and a journal, *Insight*. Address: 4800 N. Milwaukee Ave., Ste. 210, Chicago, IL 60630.

Centre for Crop Circles Studies (CCCS)

British organization concerned with the phenomenon of **crop circles.** CCCS publishes *The Circular*. Address: 20 Paul St., Frome, Somerset, BA11 1DX, UK.

Centre de Cryptozoologie

Founded by zoologist Bernard Heuvelmans for the study of animals whose existence is conjectural (i.e., on a borderline between fact and myth). Heuvelmans has coined the term **cryptozoology** to characterize the study of such creatures as sea monsters, dragons, hairy dwarfs, and yetis or abominable snowmen.

Heuvelmans was born in Le Havre, France, in 1916, and earned his doctoral degree in zoological sciences at Brussels. His books include *On the Track of Unknown Animals* (1955) and *In the Wake of the Sea-Serpents* (1968), both translated from the French. Several of his later books have not been translated. In 1982 he became one of the founders of the *International Society of Cryptozoology*.

The center has a library of some two thousand volumes and a large collection of magazine articles and illustrations, fully indexed by a card catalog. Address: Verlhiac, St. Chamassy, 24260 Le Bugue, France.

Sources:

Clark, Jerome. *Encyclopedia of Strange and Unexplained Physical Phenomena*. Detroit: Gale Research, 1993.

Heuvelmans, Bernard. "The Birth and Early History of Cryptozoology." *Cryptozoology* 3 (1984): 1–30.

———. *In the Wake of the Sea-Serpents*. New York: Hill and Wang, 1968.

———. *On the Track of Unknown Animals*. New York: Hill and Wang, 1958.

Centre House

A British fellowship founded in 1966 by **New Age** teacher **Christopher Hills** to provide training in **yoga, meditation,** awareness, and sensitivity development. The center consists of a resident community that organizes special courses, lectures, and seminars. An unusual activity is the Inward Bound course, which combines yoga and meditation with mountaineering and is designed to "discover and experience in depth the harmony between individuals and cosmos by development of the relationship between mind, body and Nature."

Hills left the community in the 1970s and went on to found the University of the Trees in Boulder Creek, California. Center Address: 10a, Airlie Gardens, London, W8 7AL, England.

Sources:

Hills, Christopher. *Nuclear Evolution (a Guide to Cosmic Enlightenment)*. London: Centre Community Publications, 1968.

Centro di Ricerca Psichica del Convivio

The Centro di Ricerca Psichica del Convivio (Psychical Research Center of the Convivium) was founded in Rome, Italy. It was one of several such centers that emerged in Italy in the decades after World War II. The center focuses its research on problems of the **survival** of death and conducts public education programs on the subject. It may be contacted c/o Via del Serpenti 100/00184 Rome, Italy.

Centro Italiano de Parapsicologia

The Centro Italiano di Parapsicologia (Italian Center for Parapsychology) was founded in 1960 in Naples, Italy, by Giorgio Di Simone, a French professor who teaches at the University of Naples. The center was opened to investigate life after death, especially through an examination of mediumship. Di Simone has monitored a number of mediumistic sessions at which a series of communications were received from what was termed "Dimension X."

The center is a membership organization and holds monthly meetings for those interested in **parapsychology.** Its several research projects have surveyed people's opinions about and experiences of different kinds of psychic phenomenon. It publishes a journal, *Informazioni Parapsicologia,* and may be reached at Via Belvedere, 87/80127, Naples, Italy.

Centro Studi Parapsicologici

Italian organization founded in 1954 in Bologna for the study of parapsychological phenomena. Its founders had broken their relationship with the Centro Emiliano de Metapsychica (psychical research organization), because they believed it was too dominated by Spiritualists. The leaders, including its director Dr. Piero Cassoli, also wished to emphasize laboratory experiments. It publishes a journal, *Quaderni di Parapsicologia: Giornata Parapsicologica Bolognese*. Address: Via Valeriani, 39, 40134 Bologna, Italy.

Sources:

Berger, Arthur S., and Joyce Berger. *The Encyclopedia of Parapsychology and Psychical Research*. New York: Paragon House, 1991.

Centurione Scotto, Marquis Carlo (ca. 1928)

A famous medium who was a member of the Italian nobility. His family was one of the oldest in Italy, one of the titles of the marquis being Principe del Sacro Romano Impero. He was a member of Parliament for eleven years and undertook research work in the hope of communicating with his deceased son, the

Marquis Vittorio dei Principi Centurione, captain of the Aerial Army, who, while flying over Lake Varese in testing a new machine for the Schneider Cup Race in America was killed on September 21, 1926.

The grief-stricken father was advised to seek comfort in reading **H. Dennis Bradley**'s *Towards the Stars* (1924), which had been translated into Italian. He found hope, and with letters of introduction from **Ernesto Bozzano,** he went to London and participated in séances with the medium **George Valiantine** in Bradley's home. During one séance, he believed that his son spoke to him in a voice that he recognized and gave other evidential information. A trumpet also produced the particular noise of an airplane engine and then the sound of the plane falling. The performance was an imitation of the airplane of Vittorio Centurione, of whose tragic death neither Valiantine nor Bradley knew.

In séances held in New York a similarly noisy manifestation, apparently for identification, was noted in the spring of 1928. After the London séances, Valiantine had presented the marquis with an aluminum trumpet and begged him to sit for **direct voice** mediumship in his own house. Whether this acted as a suggestion to awaken latent faculties or not, the marquis obtained much success from subsequent séances.

However, it was not his dead son who communicated but one named Cristo d'Angelo, who said he had been a Sicilian shepherd. This spirit **control** took charge of the manifestations from the other side. Direct voice was the main feature, but many other supernormal manifestations were also witnessed—**direct writing,** unusual **apports** (for the production of which the presence of another medium, Fabienne Rossi, was involved), a wide range of lesser physical phenomena, **materialization,** and once his own **teleportation** from the locked séance room.

The direct voice usually issued from a corner of the ceiling, but sometimes it came from inside one of the trumpets standing upright. The voices spoke Latin, Spanish, and German, as well five dialects unknown to the medium: Piedmontese, Romagnolo, Neapolitan, Venetian, and Sicilian.

The scientific side of the experiments or the question of propaganda did not interest Centurione Scotto at all. To suggest test conditions was an extremely delicate matter for his chief investigator, Ernesto Bozzano. In the absence of these, strong criticisms of the phenomena were brought forward in **Germany** by **Baron Albert von Schrenck-Notzing** and Rudolf Lambert. In England, for similar reasons, the phenomena were questioned by **Theodore Besterman** of the **Society for Psychical Research** in a manner that the noted champion of **Spiritualism Sir Arthur Conan Doyle** found derogatory to Bozzano's reputation as a competent psychical investigator. As a result Conan Doyle resigned his membership from the society.

Sources:

Huck, Gwendolyn K. *Modern Psychic Mysteries: Millesimo Castle, Italy.* London, 1929.

Cephalomancy

Ancient form of **divination** using the head of a goat or a donkey.

Cepionidus

A stone of many colors, said to reflect the likeness of the beholder.

Ceraunius (or Cerraclus)

A magical stone said to fall from the clouds. It is described as a pyramidical stone and is supposed to preserve from drowning, from injury by lightning, and to give pleasant dreams.

Ceraunoscopy

Ancient system of **divination** practiced by examining the phenomena of the air.

Cerealologist, The

British publication concerned with the phenomenon of **crop circles.** Address: 20 Paul St., Frome, Somerset, BA11 1DX, UK.

Ceremancy

Alternative term for **ceroscopy,** or **divination** through the shapes of molten wax dripped into water. (See also **molybdomancy**)

Ceremonial Magic

Ceremonial magic, also known as ritual magic, is a highly disciplined form of magic in which ceremony and ritual become the central tools used in the magical operation. As described in the older **grimoires,** the books that detail magical operations, ceremonial magic centers upon the art of the invocation (or evocation), and control of spirits. In its more contemporary versions, ceremonial magic concerns the discipline of the self and the art of controlling and directing personal and cosmic power, which may or may not be personified as a demonic or deific form.

In its pre-twentieth-century form, ceremonial magic's rites were religious actions, and the ritual format partook largely of the nature of religious observances. It was not, as generally supposed, a reversed Christianity or Judaism, though it departed radically from orthodox Christianity; nor did it partake of the profanation of religious ritual. It was in effect an attempt to derive power from God for the successful control of evil spirits. Even in the grimoires and keys of **black magic,** the operator was constantly reminded that he or she must meditate continually on the undertaking at hand and center every hope in the infinite goodness of the Great Adonai. The god invoked in black magic was not Satan but the Jehovah of the Jews and the Trinity of the Christians.

The foundation of practical magic was the belief in the power of divine words to compel the obedience of all spirits to those who could pronounce them. Such words and names were supposed to invoke or dismiss the denizens of the spirit world, and they, with suitable prayers, were used in all magical ceremonies. Again it was thought that it was easier to control evil spirits than to enlist the sympathies of angels.

He who would gain such power over demons was exhorted in the magical texts to observe continence and abstinence, to disrobe as seldom and sleep as little as possible during the period of preparation, to meditate continually on the magical work, and center all hopes on God. The fast should be most austere, and human society must be avoided as much as possible. The concluding days of the fast should be additionally strict—sustenance being reduced to bread (then a substantive food) and water. Daily ablutions in water, which had been previously exorcised according to the ritual, were necessary; these cleansings needed to be observed immediately before the ceremony.

Certain periods of the day and night, as found, for instance, in the book known as the **Key of Solomon the King,** were ruled by certain planets. The grimoires agreed that the hours of Saturn, Mars, and Venus were good for communion with spirits—the hour of Saturn for invoking souls in Hell, and the hour of Mars for invoking those who have been slain in battle. In fact these hours and seasons were ruled by the laws of **astrology.** In the preparation of the instruments employed, the ceremonies of purifying and consecrating were carefully observed. A brush, an aspergillum, was used to sprinkle a mixture of mint, marjoram, and rosemary. For fumigation, a chafing dish would be filled with freshly kindled coal and perfumed with aloe-wood or mace, benzoin, or storax. The experiment of holding converse with spirits, i.e., **necromancy,** was often made in the day and hour of Mercury, that is the first or eighth, or the fifteenth or twenty-second.

The *Grand Grimoire* notes that when the night of action has arrived, the operator shall take a rod, a goatskin, a blood-stone, two crowns of vervain, and two candlesticks with candles; also a new steel and two new flints, enough wood to make a fire, half a bottle of brandy, incense and camphor, and four nails from the coffin of a dead child. Either one or three persons must take part in the ceremony—one of whom only must address the spirit.

The Kabalistic circle is formed with strips of kid's skin fastened to the ground by the four nails. With the blood-stone a triangle is traced within the circle, beginning at the eastern point. The letters *a e a j* must be drawn in like manner, as also the name of the Savior between two crosses. The candles and vervain crowns are then set in the left and right sides of the triangle within the circle, and they with the brazier are set alight—the fire being fed with brandy and camphor. A prayer is then repeated. The operator must be careful to have no alloyed metal about him except a gold or silver coin wrapped in paper, which must be cast to the spirit when he appears outside the circle. The spirit is then conjured three times. Should the spirit fail to appear, the two ends of the magic rod must be plunged into the flames of the brazier. This ritual is known as the Rite of Lucifuge and is believed to invoke the demon Lucifuge Rofocale.

Modern Revival

Ceremonial magic declined in the eighteenth century and most of the ritual books became buried in libraries. The surviving knowledge was collected into a single volume by Francis Barrett in *The Magus* (1801). However, in the mid-nineteenth century, a revival of ceremonial magic began with the career and writings of **Éliphas Lévi.** Lévi not only made a new collection of magical knowledge, but, by drawing upon **mesmerism,** reworked it into a system more compatible with the scientific spirit of the age. He integrated divinatory work with the tarot into the new system, thus suppling enough information that readers who chose could begin to practice ceremonial magic once again.

Toward the end of the century, organizations based upon the practice of ceremonial magic began to appear, the most important being the Hermetic Order of the **Golden Dawn** in England. Cofounder **S. L. Mathers** rediscovered many of the older grimoires, which he mined for material to include in the Golden Dawn teachings, and published several of them. His effort was followed by that of **Aleister Crowley,** who developed a more psychologically oriented magical system based upon the exercise of the will (thelema).

Through the twentieth century, ceremonial magic has spread through the West, though it has never been the most popular of activities due to its stringent requirements. Several groups, such as the **Ordo Templi Orientis,** have become international organizations.

Sources:

Howe, Ellic. *The Magicians of the Golden Dawn.* London: Routledge and Kegan Paul, 1972.

King, Francis. *Ritual Magic in England.* London: Neville Spearman, 1970.

Lévi, Éliphas. *Transcendental Magic.* London: G. Redway, 1896. Reprint, New York: Samuel Weiser, 1970.

Melton, J. Gordon, and Isotta Poggi. *Magic, Witchcraft, and Paganism in America: A Bibliography.* New York: Garland Publishing, 1992.

Shah, Idries. *The Secret Lore of Magic.* London, 1957. Reprint, New York: Citadel Press, 1957.

Waite, Arthur E. *The Book of Black Magic and of Pacts.* London: George Redway, 1898. Reprinted as *The Book of Ceremonial Magic.* London: William Rider & Sons, 1911. Reprint, New Hyde Park, N.Y.: University Books, 1961. Reprint, New York: Bell Publishing, 1969.

CERES See Circles Effect Research Unit, The

Ceroscopy

System of **divination** by wax. Fine wax was melted in a brass vessel until it became a liquid of uniform consistency. It was then poured slowly into another vessel filled with cold water in such a way that the wax congealed in tiny disks upon the surface of the water. The magician then interpreted the wax figures.

Sources:

Waite, Arthur Edward. *The Occult Sciences.* N.p., 1891. Reprint, Secaucus, N.J.: University Books, 1974.

Chagrin (or Cagrino)

An evil spirit believed in by European Gypsies. It was said to have the form of a hedgehog, to be yellow in color, and to be about a foot and a half in length. Heinrich von Wlislocki stated: "I am certain, that this creature is none other than the equally demoniac being called Harginn, still believed in by the inhabitants of Northwestern India. Horses were the special prey of the Chagrin, who rode them into a state of exhaustion, like the **Guecubu** of Chile."

When horses appeared to be sick and weary, with tangled manes and bathed in sweat, they were believed to have been attacked by chagrin during the night. When this was observed, they were tethered to a stake that had been rubbed with garlic juice, then a red thread was laid on the ground in the form of a cross, or else some of the hair of the animal was mixed with salt, meal, and the blood of a bat and cooked to bread, with which the hoof of the horse was smeared. The empty vessel containing the mixture was put in the trunk of a high tree while these words were uttered:

Tarry, pipkin, in this tree,
Till such time as full ye be.

Chain, Forming a

In **Spiritualism,** a popular practice entails the joining of hands of sitters around a table, whereby it is believed that a "magnetic" current is established and reinforced. **Baron de Guldenstubbe** gave the following directions for forming a chain: "In order to form a chain, the twelve persons each place their right hand on the table, and their left hand on that of their neighbor, thus making a circle round the table. Observe that the medium or mediums if there be more than one, are entirely isolated from those who form the chain."

Dr. Lapponi, in his *Hypnotism and Spiritism* (1906), gave an alternative account of the proper procedure for the forming a chain.

He [the **medium**] makes those present choose a table, which they may examine as much as they like, and may place in whatever part of the room they choose. He then invites some of the assistants to place their hands on the table in the following manner: The two thumbs of each person are to be touching each other, and each little finger is to be in communication with the little finger of the persons on either side. He himself completes the chain with his two hands.

The concept of forming a continuous circuit for the transmission of psychic force is also related to the procedures of **mesmerism,** in which the hands of all the sitter rest together on the edge of the table. (See also **planetary chains; séance**)

Chair Test

A parapsychology test in which a chair number is chosen randomly from a seating plan for a future meeting at which seats are not reserved or allocated to specific individuals. The person who is being tested attempts to describe the appearance, characteristics, or other details of the individual who will later attend the meeting and occupy the chair. The Dutch sensitive **Gerard Croiset** appears to have had remarkable success with this type of clairvoyant precognition, which also had been earlier demonstrated by the French psychic **Pascal Forthuny.**

Sources:

Pollack, Jack Harrison. *Croiset the Clairvoyant.* Garden City, N.Y.: Doubleday, 1964. Reprint, New York: Bantam Books, 1965.

Chakras

According to Theosophists, the sense organs of the **etheric double** that receive their name from their appearance, which resembles vortices. Altogether there are ten chakras (visible only to clairvoyants) but of these it is advisable to use only seven. They are situated not on the denser physical body, but opposite certain parts of it as follows: (1) the top of the head, (2) between the eyebrows, (3) the throat, (4) the heart, (5) the spleen (where vitality is drawn from the sun), (6) the solar plexus, and (7) the base of the spine. The remaining three chakras are situated in the lower part of the pelvis and normally are not used, but are brought into play only in **black magic.** It is by means of the chakras that the trained occultist can become acquainted with the astral world.

The Theosophical concept of chakras was adapted from the ancient Hindu understanding of **kundalini,** a cosmic energy believed to be latent in the human organism responsible for sexual activity and also conditions of higher consciousness. The Hindu mystics pictured kundalini as a coiled serpent situated at the base of the spine in the subtle body. When aroused by spiritual disciplines, which included breath control and **meditation,** the energy darted up the spine in any of three subtle channels, illuminating the seven major centers or chakras in the body. These centers have been tentatively identified with the major nervous plexi. The seventh chakra, known as the *sahasrara* or "Thousand Petalled Lotus," is located in the area of the crown of the head. Many Indian yogis have described blissful conditions of mystical consciousness resulting from the arousal of kundalini and its successful culmination in the sahasrara. This supreme experience is compared with the sexual embrace of the god Siva and his consort.

Today, the idea of chakras is somewhat universal in occult and **New Age** circles. There is some difference of opinion as to the actual nature of the chakras and the experiences associated with them but some uniformity as to their location. An early identification with the nervous plexi of the body was made by V. G. Rele in his book *The Mysterious Kundalini: The Physical Basis of the "Kundali-Hatha-Yoga" According to our Present Knowledge of Western Anatomy and Physiology* (1939).

For comparative Chinese mysticism and meditation techniques in relation to chakras, see the books of "Charles Luk" (pseudonym of K'uan yü Lu), notably *The Secrets of Chinese Meditation* (London, 1964).

Sources:

Avalon, Arthur. *The Serpent Power.* Madras: Ganesh, 1950. Reprint, New York: Dover Pubications, 1974.

Gopi Krishna. *Kundalini: The Evolutionary Energy in Man.* Boulder, Colo.: Shambhala, 1970.

Judith, Anodea. *Wheels of Life: A User's Guide to the Chakra System.* St. Paul, Minn.: Llewellyn Publications, 1987.

Leadbeater, C. W. *The Chakras.* Wheaton, Ill.: Theosophical Publishing House, 1972.

Rele, V. G. *The Mysterious Kundalini: The Physical Basis of the "Kundali-Hatha-Yoga" According to our Present Knowledge of Western Anatomy and Physiology.* Bombay: Taraporevala, 1939.

Chalcedony

A silica mineral related to quartz. Superstition credits chalcedony with magical and medicinal properties. It is a good specific against fantasy and illusions of evil spirits. It supposedly quickens the power of the body and renders its possessor fortunate in law. To achieve the latter effect, it is to be perforated and suspended by hairs from a donkey. The black variety is believed to prevent hoarseness and clear the voice.

Chamberlain, Houston Stewart (1855–1927)

British-born publicist for neopagan religion in Germany and precursor of Nazi racial theorists. Chamberlain was born at Sothsea, England, on September 9, 1855, the son of an admiral in the British navy. His mother died while he was still an infant, and he was raised by his grandmother and an aunt who lived in Versailles, France. In 1867 he returned to England to attend boarding school. He grew to adulthood with no true sense of his English identity, and in 1870 came under the influence of a German tutor who gave him both a love of Germany and an interest in botany. His father died in 1878, and with the financial independence it gave him he soon married a German woman and settled in Geneva to pursue studies at the university. He quickly finished his basic degree but took many years (because of recurring ill health) to finish his doctorate. During these years he also became an enthusiastic fan of the music of Richard Wagner.

In the 1890s Chamberlain combined his scientific background, which included a critique of Darwinian approaches to evolution, and his increasing mastery of Wagner's ideas into a comprehensive vision: he conceived the idea of producing an epic history of humanity. The result was his most famous and important book, *Foundations of the 19th Century* (1899). Lacking training in history, Chamberlain used artistic license to tell the story of human history in such a way as to substantiate two basic ideas: he argues that humanity is divided into various distinct races, each of which has its own physical structure and mental and moral capacity, and that history is best understood as the struggle between these different races.

Historical epochs were marked by the coming to the fore of a dominant racial type, according to Chamberlain, and modern European civilization was built on the Germanic or Teutonic race. As to the components of modern (i.e., nineteenth century) culture, he hypothesizes six major influences: Hellenic art and philosophy; Roman law and organization; the revelation of Christ; racial chaos in the wake of the fall of the Roman Empire; the negative and destructive influence of the Jews; and the creative and regenerative mission of the Teutonic (or Aryan) race. Chamberlain's anti-Semitism led him to reject the idea of the Jewish-born Messiah of Christianity and to propose an essentially Germanic religion deriving from the symbols of the Aryan race.

The mystical/occult underpinnings of Chamberlain's beliefs had a great influence on Hitler's Nazi faith. He wrote a number of other books, but none were as influential as *Foundations of the 19th Century.* He died at Beyreuth, Germany, on January 9, 1927.

Sources:

Field, Geoffrey G. *Evangelist of Race: The Germanic Vision of Houston Stewart Chamberlain.* New York: Columbia University Press, 1981.

Ravencroft, Trevor. *The Spear of Destiny.* New York: G. P. Putnam's Sons, 1973.

Sklar, Dusty. *Gods and Beasts: The Nazis and the Occult.* New York: Thomas Y. Crowell, 1977.

Williamson, Roger Andrew. "Houston Stewart Chamberlain: A Study of the Man and His Ideas, 1855–1927." Ph.D diss., University of California-Santa Barbara, 1973.

Chambers, Robert (1802–1871)

British writer and publisher who played no public part in **Spiritualism** but whose conversion and anonymous activity, especially his writing, were known to his contemporaries. For example, according to **William Howitt,** he contributed the description of a haunted house at Cheshunt in Mrs. Crowe's *Night-Side of Nature* (2 vols., 1848). It was this house that novelist **Charles Dickens** wanted to investigate. It was partly pulled down and altered at the time; he could not find it. Also, an article in *Chambers' Journal,* May 21, 1853, on the mediumship of **Maria B. Hayden** was understood to have been written by Robert Chambers.

Chambers gave an account of the **séances** of another American visitor, a Mrs. Roberts, concluding that it was difficult to formulate an opinion but that it seemed to him the phenomena appeared to be natural and the medium the victim of self-deception. A few weeks later, however, his opinion underwent a decided change. He obtained movements of the table and answers by it in his own family circle on matters known only to himself. He wrote: "I am satisfied, as before, that the phenomena are natural, but to take them in I think we shall have to widen somewhat our ideas as to the extent and character of what is natural." His 1859 pamphlet *Testimony: Its Posture in the Scientific World* examines the scientific idea of evidence with special relation to psychical phenomena.

Chambers had many experiences with the famous medium **D. D. Home,** and he wrote both the anonymous preface to Home's *Incidents in My Life* and the appendix, "Connection of Mr. Home's Experiences with those of Former Times."

In 1860, in company with **Robert Dale Owen,** he sat with the **Fox sisters** in America. They suspended a dining table from a powerful steelyard balance. Under bright gas light and perfect control the table was made heavier and lighter on request, showing variation of weight between 60 and 164 pounds. He had puzzling experiences with **Charles Foster,** who produced inscriptions on his skin. Chambers sat with a Judge Edmonds's daughter, Laura. In February 1867 he wrote to Dr. **Alfred Russel Wallace,** "I have for many years, known that these phenomena are real, as distinguished from impostures; and it is not of yesterday that I concluded they were calculated to explain much that has been doubtful in the past; and, when fully accepted revolutionise the whole frame of human opinion on many important matters."

Chambers retained his interest in psychic phenomena until his death in 1871. A record of a séance written by him was published by **Violet Tweedale,** his granddaughter, in *Mellow Sheaves.* Extracts from further records as preserved by another granddaughter, Mrs. Edward Fitzgerald, were published by A. W. Trethewy in *Light,* January 6, 1933.

Chambers is best remembered today for his many books (on nonoccult themes), especially the many reference books he wrote, and his collections of Scottish poetry.

Sources:

Chambers, Robert. *Testimony: Its Posture in the Scientific World.* N.p., 1959.

Home, D. D. *Incidents in My Life.* First series. London: Green Longman, Roberts & Green, 1863. Second series. London: Whittingham & Wilkins, 1872.

Chams

A race of Indo-Chinese origin, numbering about 130,000, that settled in Annam, Siam; Cochin, China; and Cambodia. They had some reputation among the surrounding population as sorcerers, probably arising from the mythic influence of a conquered race. Their magicians claimed to be able to slay at a distance and to bring ruin and disease by the aid of magic formulas. Among the Cambodian Chams, sorcerers were detested by the common people, as they were believed to be the source of all the evil that befell them; the majority of them usually ended their days by secret assassinations.

Sorcerers were nearly always women. They entered the sisterhood by means of a secret initiation held in the forest at midnight. The woman who desired to become a sorceress sacrificed a **cock** on a nest of termites. The initiate cut the cock in two from the head to the tail and danced in front of it in the nude until, by force of her incantations, the two halves of the bird approached each other and became once more alive and started crowing again.

Sorceresses were said to be known by the tendency of their complexion to alter its hue and by their swollen and bloodshot eyes. They possessed numerous rites for gaining the favor of evil spirits, in which they implicitly believed. In building a house numerous propitiatory rites had to be observed, accompanied by invocation of the protecting deities. The Chams believed in lucky and unlucky days and were careful not to undertake anything of importance unless favored by benevolent omens.

The Chams also possessed many peculiar superstitions. They would not disturb grain that had been stored during the daytime, as they said it was then asleep; they waited until nightfall before gathering it. They also had many magic agricultural formulas, to ensure that harvests were worthy to be stored. The Brahmanic Chams believed that the souls of good men passed to the sun, those of women to the moon, and those of the coolie class into clouds, but these were only places of temporary stay until such time as all finally come to reside within the center of the earth. The belief in **reincarnation** was also highly popular.

Sources:

Aymonier, Etienne F. *Les Tchames et leur Religions.* Paris, 1891.

Chaton, Aymonier. *Dictionnaire Cam-Française.* Paris, 1906.

———. *Nouvelles recherches sur les chams.* Paris, 1901.

Chang, Garma Chen-Chi (1920–)

An authority on Buddhist philosophy, born in China and educated at Kong-ka Monastery, eastern Tibet. Chang came to the United States after World War II and was a research fellow at the Bollingen Foundation in New York from 1955 onward.

He wrote a number of books, including *The Practice of Zen* (1959), *The Hundred Thousand Songs of Milarepa* (1962), and *The Essential Teachings of the Tibetan Mysticism* (1963). He also wrote an important review of the book *The Third Eye* (1958), by **Lopsang Rampa,** published in *Tomorrow* magazine as part of an exposé of the author. Chang showed that Rampa's knowledge of Buddhism and Tibetan occultism was "inaccurate and superficial" and characterized the book as "interesting and highly imaginative fiction." This review appeared alongside a second article, which noted that "Lopsang Rampa" had been born Cyril Henry Hoskins, son of a British plumber.

Sources:

Chang, Garma Chen-Chi. *Esoteric Teachings of the Tibetan Tantra.* Lausanne, Switzerland: Falcon's Wing Press, 1961.

———. *Teachings of Tibetan Yoga.* New Hyde Park, N.Y.: University Books, 1963.

———. "Tibetan Phantasies." *Tomorrow* 6, 2 (Spring 1958): 13–16.

Chang, Garma Chen-Chi, ed. *The Hundred Thousand Songs of Milarepa.* New Hyde Park, N.Y.: University Books, 1962. Reprint, Boulder, Colo: Shambhala, 1977.

Changelings

A manikin, or elf, secretly substituted for a young child. There are many tales of such occurrences in **Scotland.** The changeling grows up peevish and misshapen, always crying, and gives many proofs of its origin to those versed in such matters. There were many ways of getting rid of him, such as sticking a knife into him, making him sit on a gridiron with a fire below, dropping him into a river, and so on. The changeling sometimes gave himself away by reference to his age. (See also **fairies**)

Sources:

McNeil, F. Marion. *The Silver Bough.* Vol. 1, *Scottish Folklore and Folk-Belief.* Glasgow, Scotland: William Maclellan, 1957.

Channeling

A contemporary term for the earlier Spiritualist idea of mediumship, spirit entities conveying philosophical or spiritual advice or healing through mediums. Mediumship is generally thought of as the special activity of a few people who operate primarily to put people in contact with their dead friends and relatives. Channelers operate primarily to bring philosophical and theological teachings from a disembodied entity. Since the development of modern **Spiritualism,** mediums have also operated as channels and many channels also operate as mediums.

The channeling of philosophical teachings, especially on the nature of continued existence in the afterlife, began with **Andrew Jackson Davis,** who published a number of volumes of channeled material. Numerous platform mediums became known for their spirit discourses, which they would offer in place of lectures or Sunday sermons. Compiled into books, channelled material would often become the basis of new religious groups, one notable example being *Oahspe: The New Age Bible* (1881), channeled by **John Ballou Newbrough** and around which he organized the Faithist religion.

Through the twentieth century other important channeled works such as Levi Dowling's *The Aquarian Gospel of Jesus the Christ* (1907) and James Edward Padgett's *True Gospel Revealed Anew by Jesus* have appeared in profusion. The channeled material of **Grace Cooke** became the basis of the White Eagle Lodge in Great Britain and those of Osker Ernest Bernhardt the basis of the Grail Movement in Austria.

The term "channeling" as presently used seems to have arisen within the **UFO** contactee community, which found its focus around individuals who claimed to regularly channel material telepathically from the space brothers. In the 1950s Charles Boyd Gentzel and Pauline Sharpe began their channeling activity, which still exists as Mark-Age, Inc. Violet Gilbert of the Cosmic Star Temple began her public work in 1960. Even earlier, flying saucer channel **Dorothy Martin,** better known by her spiritual name, Sister Thedra, became the subject of a classic sociological study, *When Prophecy Fails.*

The present popularity of channeling stems mainly from the activities of **Jane Roberts** (1929–1984), the channel for the entity **"Seth"** beginning in 1963. Roberts's first books, *The Seth Material* (1970) and *Seth Speaks* (1972), became best sellers, led to some 20 additional volumes, and gave channeling a popularity it had never previously experienced.

The Seth books expounded a coherent philosophy dealing comprehensively with alterations of consciousness, grades of reality, reincarnation, psychology, and a spiritual universe. Roberts also channeled communications claimed to be from psychologist **William James** and psychotherapist **Carl G. Jung.**

After the death of Jane Roberts in 1984, her husband Robert Butts edited new Seth manuscripts, which were published by Tam Mossman in his journal *Metapsychology; The Journal of Discarnate Intelligence.* Mossman himself also channels an entity named "James."

Other channelers appeared by the end of the decade, the most prominent through the 1980s being JZ Knight, who channels "Ramtha," and Jach Pursel, who channels "Lazaris." Channelling became an integral part of the **New Age** movement and numeorus New Age channels arose. Included in their number are Ken Carey, Virginia Essene, Ruth Montgomery, and Penny Torres. Their number has continued to grow.

Actress **Shirley MacLaine**'s several New Age books, especially *Out on a Limb* (1983), which was televised as a five-hour prime-time ABC mini-series in 1987, and *Dancing in the Light* (1985), further popularized the concept of spirit guides and underlined her spiritual odyssey and New Age beliefs. She also made special mention of JZ Knight. Knight began to channel "Ramtha" in the late 1980s. She now heads a school for the more serious students of "Ramtha's" gnostic teachings.

Alan Vaughan, who first became known as a writer on psychic topics, emerged as a channel in 1987. In a useful survey of the phenonenon in *New Realities,* he disclosed that he had commenced channeling in 1983. He had been teaching at a psychic seminar in Sedona, Arizona, and was asked by a couple if he could tell them something about their past lives. Although at the time he was editing *Reincarnation Report,* he was somewhat skeptical about past-life readings. He describes the incident:

"Suddenly a tremendous energy flooded over the top of my head. It was like watching a dream, as the Chinese entity Li Sung began to speak through me. He gave them [the couple] some detailed information about past lives and how they fit into their present life paths. The couple verified many specific details. For me, it was the beginning of an enlargement of consciousness."

Sixteen years earlier, Vaughan had been told by three British mediums that he would begin "channeling" the Chinese guide one day, but he was skeptical about the prospect of being invaded by some Chinese spirit. After the first channeling of "Li Sung," the Chinese guide continued to manifest and has offered treatment at healing sessions. Vaughan has now channeled "Li Sung" to thousands of people, including radio and television audiences.

Another well-known channeler is former insurance executive Jach Pursel. One day, while relaxing after a busy executive program, he went into the trance state in which he was first contacted by the entity "Lazaris." With the encouragement of his wife Penny, "Lazaris" began to manifest regularly to friends and small groups and gave both personal advice and philosophical teaching. Eventually Pursel gave up his business career and devoted himself full time to channeling "Lazaris."

It has to be admitted that the names of spirit guides are often unconvincing and seem like parodies. In the heyday of nineteenth-century Spiritualism, American Indian guides were more frequent, and even today such claimed personalities still appear to manifest, usually speaking in broken English but unable to communicate in Indian dialects. Other guides have represented themselves as famous characters in history, such as Socrates, Confucius, Abraham Lincoln, Shakespeare, St. John the Baptist, and even Jesus Christ or God. The communications channeled from such exalted guides were not always of the high intellectual or philosophical level that might be expected, and in many cases consisted merely of banal platitudes.

Many claimed entities of channeling may be regarded as fictional creations. The measure of their importance, at least to those who look to channeled entities as authorities, is whether they give information, insights, or philosophical teachings that are beyond the normal capacity of the channeler. For example, one of the spirit guides of the celebrated medium **Eileen J. Garrett** (1893–1970) was named "Uvani," a name that does not seem to belong to any known Oriental tradition of nomenclature, but the communications received through "Uvani" were of a highly evidential nature.

It may well be that in many cases a claimed spirit guide is merely a personification of an individual's unconscious or "higher self." In other cases, communications may emanate from an impersonal source of intelligence that establishes a channel by assuming a conventional personality.

Throughout history, popular religions have found it difficult to establish contact with a more austere impersonal deity, such as the concept of Brahman, the Infinite, in esoteric Hinduism, and have found it convenient to postulate a host of anthropomorphic gods and goddesses, which become a familiar focus for worshipers in societies based on interpersonal relationships. Religion requires the spiritualization of emotions, and it is very difficult to attach emotions of love or veneration to an impersonal absolute. In Christianity, the concepts of God the Father and God the Son have provided a familiar and helpful focus for worshipers, while older religions have favored the concept of a Mother Goddess. Throughout India, millions of worshipers have found the gods and goddesses of their sect or tradition a personification of divinity.

Parapsychologists have found that the personalities of communicators channeling through mediums may be manufactured consciously, and that such fictional entities can produce paranormal phenomena, as in the famous case of **"Philip."** Such experiments have validated the concept that spirit guides may often (but not invariably) be an artificial creation of subconscious mentation by the psychic or the sitters. Sometimes spirit communications are a strange mixture of genuine and false information, perhaps influenced by the conscious memory of the channeler.

The reemergence of the concept of spirit guides in North America comes at a time when popular interest in traditional Spiritualism seems less widespread than in Britain. It may be that the new name "channeling" and its disassociation from the fraud associated with Spiritualism, provides an attractive image for a new generation of spiritual seekers.

Sources:

Caddy, Eileen. *The Spirit of Findhorn.* New York: Harper & Row, 1976. Reprint, London: L. N. Fowler, 1977.

Garrett, Eileen J. *My Life As a Search for the Meaning of Mediumship.* New York, 1939. Reprint, New York: Arno Press, 1975.

Kardec, Allan. *Spiritualist Philosophy; The Spirits' Book.* London, 1893. Reprint, New York: Arno Press, 1976.

Kautz, William H., and Melanie Branon. *Channeling: The Intuitive Connection.* San Francisco: Harper & Row, 1987.

Klimo, Jon. *Channeling.* Los Angeles: Jeremy P. Tarcher, 1987.

MacLaine, Shirley. *Dancing in the Light.* New York: Bantam Books, 1986.

———. *Out on a Limb.* New York: Bantam Books, 1983. Reprint, London: Elm Tree Books; Hamish Hamilton, 1983.

Melton, J. Gordon, Jerome Clark, and Aidan Kelly, eds. *New Age Encyclopedia.* Detroit: Gale Research, 1990.

Moses, William Stainton. *Spirit Teachings, Through the Mediumship of William Stainton Moses.* London, 1883. Reprint, New York: Arno Press, 1976.

Roberts, Estelle. *Fifty Years a Medium.* London, 1959. Reprint, New York: Avon, 1972. Reprint, London: Corgi, 1975.

Roberts, Jane. *The Seth Material.* Englewood Cliffs, N.J.: Prentice Hall, 1970.

———. *Seth Speaks: The Eternal Validity of the Soul.* Englewood Cliffs, N.J.: Prentice Hall, 1972.

Silver Birch. *More Philosophy of Silver Birch.* Compiled by Tony Ortzen. London: Spiritualist Press, 1979.

Vaughn, Alan. "Channeling." *New Realities* 3, no. 3 (January/February 1987).

Westen, Robin. *Channelers: A New Age Directory.* New York: Perigee Books (Putnam), 1988.

White, Ruth, and Mary Swainson. *Gildas Communicates; The Story and the Scripts.* London: Spearman, 1971.

White, Stewart Edward. *The Betty Book.* New York: E. P. Dutton, 1930.

White Eagle. *The Path of the Soul: The Great Initiations of Every Man.* Liss, U.K.: White Eagle Publishing Trust, 1959.

Chaomancy

A branch of **aeromancy** (**divination** through aerial phenomena such as thunder and lightning) concerned with divination from apparitions or visions in the air. For instance, the shapes of clouds and the occurrence of rare aerial phenomena such as comets were interpreted in chaomancy. (See also **austromancy; meteormancy**)

Chaos: The Review of the Damned

An occasional publication devoted to detailed references connected with Forteana, the unexplained anomalous natural phenomena studied by **Charles Fort,** author of *The Book of the Damned* (1919). The "damned" were the data rejected or explained away by orthodox science, including strange falls from the sky, mysterious appearances and disappearances, unusual synchronicities, enigmatic artifacts, and astronomical ambiguities. *Chaos* explores the background detail of Fort's references and supplements them by additional in-depth material. *Chaos* is published by **Res Bureaux,** Box 1598, Kingston, Ontario K7L 5C8, Canada.

Charcot, Jean Martin (1825–1893)

French physician who studied **hypnotism** in relation to hysteria. Born November 29, 1825, in Paris, Charcot became a doctor of medicine and was later appointed physician at the Central Hospital Bureau, Paris. In 1860 he became a professor of pathological anatomy in the medical faculty, and two years later he became closely associated with the development of the Saltpêtrière, the great neurological clinic of Paris.

Charcot was responsible for notable researches in the fields of muscular disease and mental disturbance. His work, together with that of his student **Pierre Janet,** the director of the psychological laboratory of the Saltpêtrière from 1889 to 1898, marked the beginning of serious medical and scientific study of the phenomena of hypnotism (in contrast to the earlier studies of **mesmerism,** which had occult connotations). Their research forced the French Academy of Sciences to accept hypnosis as a new therapeutic instrument.

Among Charcot's most famous students was **Sigmund Freud.** Charcot died August 16, 1893.

Sources:

Charcot, Jean Martin. *Les demoniaques dans l'art.* Paris, 1887. Reprint, Amsterdam: B. M. Israel, 1972.

———. *Lectures on the Diseases of the Nervous System.* London, 1881. Reprint, New York: Hafner, 1962.

Didi-Huberman, Georges, and J. M. Charcot. *Invention de l'hysterie: Charcot et l'iconographia photographiqe de la Salpetriere.* Paris: Macula, 1982.

Chari, C(adambur) T(iruvenkatachari) K(rishnama) (1909–)

Professor and chairman of the Department of Philosophy and Psychology at Madras Christian College in India. Chari was born June 5, 1909, in Trivellore, India, and received both his M.A. (1932) and Ph.D. (1953) degrees from Madras University. He served as lecturer in philosophy at American College, Madurai (1933–40), and as assistant professor (1940–56) and associate professor (1956–58) at Madras Christian College before becoming chairman of the Department of Philosophy and Psychology in 1958. He was also a consulting editor of the *Indian Journal of Psychology.*

Chari became interested in psychical research as a teenager when he read the works of **Stainton Moses.** A Christian, he was also somewhat critical of yoga and the belief in reincarnation and emerged as a critic of the research of **Ian Stevenson.** Over the years he published numerous articles on the wide range of subjects covered by parapsychology from a philosophical perspective. In 1958 he became a corresponding member of the **Society for Psychical Research,** London. He also edited the volume *Essays in Philosophy Presented to Dr. T. M. P. Mahadevan* in 1963.

Sources:

Berger, Arthur S., and Joyce Berger. *The Encyclopedia of Parapsychology and Psychical Research.* New York: Paragon House, 1991.

Chari, C. T. K. "The Challenge of Psi; New Horizons of Scientific Research." *Journal of Parapsychology* 38 (1974).

"An Evaluation of Some Field-Theoretical Approaches to Psi." *Psychocosmos* 1 (1970).

———. "A Postscript to 'Quantum Physics and Parapsychology.'" *Journal of Parapsychology* 21 (1957).

———. "Regurgitation, Mediumship, and Yoga." *Journal* of the Society for Psychical Research 47 (1973): 156.

———. "Some Generalized Theories and Models of PSI: A Critical Evaluation." In *Handbook of Parapsychology.* Edited by B. Wolman. New York: Van Nostrand Reinhold, 1977.

Charing Cross Spirit Circle

The first Spiritualist organization in London, established in January 1857. It was later superseded by the London Spiritualist

Union, but difficulties arose centering on the activities of a medium named Jones, whose followers broke away to form a new group, the Circle of Spheral Harmony.

Chariots of the Gods

English title of a book by **Erich von Däniken,** published in 1968, that first posed the question, Was God an astronaut? and suggested that religions originated from race memories and legends of astronauts visiting the earth 40,000 years ago. Von Däniken had been given the idea of ancient astronauts from his reading of **Jacque Bergier**'s and **Louis Pauwel**'s *The Morning of the Magicians* (1960) and Robert Charroux's *One Hundred Thousand Years of Man's Unknown History* (1963) and had subsequently traveled to North Africa and the Americas to explore some of the archaeological sites. *Chariots of the Gods?* became a best-seller and popularized ancient astronaut ideas that had been surfacing in UFO litertaure for some fifteen years. Von Däniken and other writers produced a host of books on the theme over the next decade. In response, numerous books critical of these theories were published complaining of such a naive approach to both theology and archaeology. That criticism eventually led to the decline of a popular audience for ancient astronaut ideas, but not before an Ancient Astronaut Society had been formed and a cadre of followers organized. The writings of Ronald Story and Clifford Wilson make a case against von Däniken's theories.

Sources:

Clark, Jerome. *Encyclopedia of Strange and Unexplained Phenomena.* Detroit: Gale Research, 1993.

Story, Ronald. *The Space Gods Revealed: A Close Look at Erich von Däniken.* New York: Harper and Row, 1976.

Von Däniken, Erich. *Chariots of the Gods?: Unsolved Mysteries of the Past.* New York: G. P. Putnam's Sons, 1960.

Wilson, Clifford. *Crash Go the Chariots: An Alternative to "Chariots of the God."* New York: Lancer Books, 1972.

Charismatic Movement

An interdenominational Christian renewal movement that began in the 1960s and has developed an international following, especially among members of the Roman Catholic church. It takes its name from the Greek word *charisma,* meaning "gifts," and emphasizes manifestations of the gifts of the Holy Spirit as described in First Corinthians, chapter 12, as a sign of the presence of the Holy Spirit. The movement began among members of the Full Gospel Businessman's Fellowship, an independent Pentecostal brotherhood, but quickly spread to Roman Catholic and mainline Protestant churches throughout the United States. By the early 1970s it had spread to Europe and gained important support from Belgian Cardinal Suenans.

The movement has been characterized by its acceptance of the importance of speaking in tongues (also known as **glossolalia**) and divine healing, and most meetings are for prayer and spirited singing. It has become a meeting ground between followers of the older **Pentecostalism** and people who manifest the gifts but are members of older denominations. As the movement matured through the 1980s, a number of new denominations evolved from it.

Sources:

Ford, J. Massyngberde. *The Pentecostal Experience.* Paramus, N.J.: Paulist Press, 1970.

Manuel, David. *Like a Mighty River.* Orleans, Mass: Rock Harbor Press, 1977.

Poloma, Margaret M. *The Charismatic Movement: Is There a New Pentecost?* Boston, Mass: Twayne Publishers, 1982.

Quebedeaux, Richard. *The New Charismatics: The Origins, Development and Significance of Neo-Pentecostalism.* Garden City, N.Y.: Doubleday, 1976.

Ranaghan, Kevin, and Dorothy Ranaghan. *Catholic Pentecostals.* New York: Paulist Press, 1969.

Samarin, William J. *Tongues of Men and Angels.* New York: Macmillan, 1972.

Charlemagne (or Charles the Great) (742–814)

The greatest of the Frankish kings. Charlemagne was the elder son of Pepin the Short and succeeded his father in 768 C.E. He had a close connection with the supernatural according to legend. Very often in the pages of French romance, the emperor was visited by **angels** who were considered to be the direct messengers of the heavenly power.

These visitations, of course, were meant to symbolize his position as the head of Christendom in the world. He was its upholder, with the Moors on his southern borders and the pagans (Prussians and Saxons) to the north and west. Charles was regarded by the Christians of Europe as the direct representative of heaven, whose mission it was to Christianize Europe and to defend its true faith in every way. Charlemagne and his court were also connected with the realm of **fairies.** Encounters with the fairy folk by his paladins were not so numerous in the original French romances that deal with his court, but in the hands of Boiardo, Ariosto, and Pulci, the paladins dwelled in an enchanted region where at any moment they might have met with all kinds of supernatural beings.

Both in the early and late romances the powers of **magic** and enchantment are ever present, chiefly instanced in magical weapons such as the Sword Durandal of Roland, which cannot be shivered; the magic ointments of giants like Ferragus, which when applied provide invulnerablity; and armor that exercises a similar guardianship on the body of its possessor. Heroes like Ogier the Dane penetrated into fairyland itself and wedded its queens. This union with fairyland was the fate of a great many medieval heroes. The analogous cases of Tom-a-Lincolne, Tannhäuser, and **Thomas the Rhymer** are also relevant. The magic and the marvels are everywhere in use in the romances that deal with Charlemagne.

Sources:

Cabaniss, Allen. *Charlemagne.* New York: Twayne Publishers, 1972.

Easton, Steward C. *The Era of Charlemagne.* New York: Van Nostrand, 1961.

Shepard, Les. *The History of Street Literature.* Detroit: Singing Tree Press, 1973.

Charm (Carmen)

A magical formula, sung or recited to bring about a supposedly beneficial result as part of a **spell,** or to confer magical efficacy on an **amulet.** In popular usage the same word is employed to designate the incantation and the object that is charmed.

Sources:

A Gypsy Queen. *Zingara Fortune Teller.* Philadelphia: David McKay, 1901.

Lippman, Deborah, and Paul Colin. *How to Make Amulets, Charms, & Talismans.* New York: M. Evans, 1974.

Sepharial [Walter Gorn Old]. *The Book of Charms and Talismans.* New York: Arc Books, 1969.

Charnock, Thomas (1526–1581)

English alchemist born in the Isle of Thanet, Kent. As a young man Charnock traveled all over England in search of alchemistic knowledge, but eventually he fixed his residence at Oxford, and there he made the acquaintance of a noted scientist. The scientist was impressed with the youth's cleverness and appointed him his confidant and assistant. After working in this capacity for a number of years, Charnock found himself the sole legatee of his patron's paraphernalia and likewise of the various secrets written in his notebooks.

Armed with this knowledge, he proceeded to devote himself more eagerly than ever to the quest of gold production, but in 1555, just as he imagined himself on the verge of triumph, there was a sudden explosion in his laboratory.

In 1557, when he again thought that success was imminent, the press-gang arrived at his house to recruit him by force into the English army to fight the French. The alchemist was bitterly chagrined on being kidnaped in this way; he set about to destroy all his equipments so no one would lay claim to his secrets.

He subsequently proceeded to France as a soldier and took part in the disastrous campaign that culminated in the English being defeated at Calais by the Duc de Guise.

How Charnock fared during the expedition is not known, but he returned to England safely, and in 1562 he married Agnes Norton. Thereafter, he settled at Stockland, in the county of Somerset, and continued to pursue scientific researches. Neither the military nor the Church disturbed his pursuits from that point forward.

The antiquarian and historian Anthony Wood, in his *Athen Oxoniensis,* credited Charnock with a considerable amount of writing, and it is possible that several items enumerated are in reality from some other pen than the alchemist's. However, there are certain books he undoubtedly wrote, notably *Aenigma ad Alchimiam* (1572) and *Breviary of Natural Philosophy* (1557). *Breviary* was subsequently reprinted in the *Theatrum Chemicum* of Elias Ashmole.

Chartres Cathedral

A superb example of twelfth- to thirteenth-century Gothic architecture, believed by some occultists to enshrine ancient mysteries of religious inspiration. For example, in his book *The Mysteries of Chartres Cathedral* (1972), Louis Charpentier claims that the cathedral is built on the site of powerful and ancient earth currents. He examines the mystery of the amazing architecture of the cathedral, its historic connection with the Knights Templar, and its symbolic and esoteric meanings.

Sources:

Charpentier, Louis. *The Mysteries of Chartres Cathedral.* London: Research into Lost Knowledge Organization, 1972. Reprint, New York: Avon, 1972.

Chase, Warren (1813–1891)

One of the first apostles of **Spiritualism** in America. Born in Pittsfield, New Hampshire, Chase began to study **mesmerism** in Southport, Wisconsin, by 1843. He was street commissioner and road master at the time, and discussed both this subject and Charles Fourier's scheme of socialism in the local lyceum through that winter. The result was a socialist settlement in May 1844 in Fond-du-Lac County. The Wisconsin Phalanx, as the community was known, lasted for six years. It was the only one of the experiments that yielded, at the time of dissolution, substantial profit to its members. After the dissolution Chase began to take a more active part in politics, became a senator in Wisconsin in 1848, and was nominated for governor the following year.

The philosophy of **Andrew Jackson Davis** made a deep impression on him, and when the Spiritualist movement was born, he became its untiring apostle for over thirty years. His Spiritualist experiences are embodied in his *Forty Years on the Spiritual Rostrum* (1888) and his socialist activities in *The Life Line of the Lone One, an Autobiography of the World's Child* (1857).

Sources:

Chase, Warren. *Forty Years on the Spiritual Rostrum.* Boston, 1888.

———. *The Life Line of the Lone One, an Autobiography of the World's Child.* Boston: B. Marsh, 1857.

Noyes, John Humphrey. *Strange Cults & Utopias of 19th Century America.* 1870. Reprinted as *History of American Socialisms.* New York: Dover Publications, 1966.

Chauvin, Rémy (1913–)

Director of the Experimental Ethology Laboratory at Bures sur Yvette, France. Chauvin was born October 10, 1913, in Toulon, France, and earned a doctorate in 1941 from the Sorbonne. He became the research director of the French Agronomical Research Institute in 1946; two years later he was appointed director of the Experimental Ethology Laboratory. In 1954 he assumed duties as coeditor of the *Journal of Insect Physiology.* He was named a laureate of the French Academy of Science.

Chauvin wrote on a wide variety of parapsychological subjects but was especially interested in ESP in relation to animals. He wrote many articles that were published under a pseudonym.

Sources:

Berger, Arthur S., and Joyce Berger. *The Encyclopedia of Parapsychology and Psychical Research.* New York: Paragon House, 1991.

Duvall, Piere [Rémy Chauvin], and E. Montredon [Jean Mayer]. "A PK Experiment with Mice." *Journal of Papapsychology* 32 (1968): 153.

———. "Further Psi Experiments with Mice." *Journal of Parapsychology* 32 (1968): 260.

Cheiro (Count Louis Hamon) (1866–1936)

Palmist and astrologer. Cheiro was born Louis Hamon on November 1, 1866, in Dublin, Ireland, the son of Count William de Hamon, whose title he eventually inherited. He was educated privately and from his mother inherited an interest in the **occult,** especially **palmistry, astrology,** and **numerology.** At the early age of 11, much to his father's consternation, he wrote an essay on palmistry. He studied for the ministry but did not complete his academic work because of his father's bankruptcy.

As a young man he travel to India. He met a group of occultists and stayed with them for several years, during which time he did his own research on palmistry. He later moved to Egypt before he settled in England and opened an office as a palmist. To avoid any problems with his family, he worked under his pseudonym.

By the 1890s Cheiro had gained an international reputation, his own background granting him entrance into the world of royalty, many of whom were interested in the occult. In 1893 he traveled to the United States for the first of a number of visits. The following year he wrote the first of his many books, *Cheiro's Language of the Hand.* This book, and its equally popular sequel, *Cheiro's Guide to the Hand* (1900), were primary elements in the reestablishment of palmistry as a popular form of fortune-telling in the modern world.

In the late 1920s, Cheiro wrote several books on astrological predictions of world events. He spent the last part of his life in California. He died October 8, 1936.

Sources:

Cheiro [Count Louis Hamon]. *Cheiro's Guide to the Hand.* London: Nichols & Company, 1900.

———. *Cheiro's Language of the Hand.* London, 1894.

———. *Cheiro's Year Book.* Rev. ed., London: London Publishing, 1930.

———. *Mysteries and Romances of the World's Greatest Occultists.* London: Herbert Jenkins, 1935.

———. *You and Your Hand.* Garden City, N.Y.: Doubleday, Doran, 1931.

———. *You and Your Star.* Los Angeles: London Publishing; London: Herbert Jenkins, 1926.

Holden, James H., and Robert A. Hughes. *Astrological Pioneers of America.* Tempe, Ariz.: American Federation of Astrologers, 1988.

Chelidonius

A stone taken out of a swallow, said to be good against melancholy and periodical disorder. It was placed in a yellow linen cloth and tied about the neck to cure fever. Stones are sometimes found in birds and other mammals, especially in ducts and hollow organs; they are usually pathological concretions known as *calculi.*

Chemical Phenomena (in Séances)

Psychic phenomena of a chemical nature have often been reported to occur in **séance** rooms. Psychic light is one of the strangest chemical manifestations as it is cold, and its production defies human ingenuity.

Some alleged examples of chemical phenomena include: instances where blood was drawn without a break in the skin; during **materialization,** ozone and phosphorus were often smelled and fully materialized phantoms exhaled carbon dioxide; a lead whistle often melted during sittings with **Frau Silbert;** phantoms dissolved into a cloud of smoke or black vapor in the house of **Charles L. Tweedale;** Admiral Moore's ink in his bottle was changed to dirty water in a séance with the **Bangs sisters;** and in a sitting with **David Duguid** the color of a glass of water changed to the hue of wine and tasted as bitter as gall.

The book *Supramundane Facts in The Life of The Rev. J. Babcock Ferguson* (1865), edited by T. Nichols, states that the little daughter of J. B. Ferguson, under a strange spell, ordered a clean tea cup and a silver spoon. She commenced stirring the spoon in the empty cup and subjected it, after a time, to the observation of each person present. Then, returning to the center of the room in about five minutes, she presented the cup with over a teaspoonful of dark and odorous ointment with which she anointed the face of a gentleman of the house. He was suffering from neuralgia and professed to have received immediate relief.

Tosie Osanami, a Japanese medium who died in 1907, was famous for similar medical miracles. According to a statement by Wasaburo Asano, a Japanese researcher, quoted by **Harry Price** in *Psychic Research* (a journal of the American Society for Psychical Research) in 1928, she produced liquid medicine within empty glass bottles:

"Her patients would come and ask for medicine and present their own bottles. These bottles she would place in front of her family shrine. She would then kneel down before it and offer up prayers according to the Shinto rites for about ten minutes. When the prayers were ended the patients would see the bottles spontaneously fill with liquids of different colors according to the nature of the malady. Red, blue and orange were the most usual colors of these medicinal apports. . . . Accused of being a swindler, she was tried in the District Court of Kobe. In court, however, before the judge and jury she succeeded in producing a brown liquid in an empty bottle that had been sealed previously by the court. Speechless with astonishment, the court acquitted her."

In the case of **Mary Jobson,** water sprang up unaccountably through the floor and was sprinkled in the room. Previously a voice was heard calling upon the angels to perform the demonstration.

Such water sprinkling is frequently observed in poltergeist cases. Thomas P. Barkas published an account of interesting observations in the British newspaper *Newcastle Chronicle* in 1874. He witnessed water production in a private séance circle in both the dark and the daylight. During the séance a planchette and the surface of the table were covered, in less than a minute, by water drops. He placed his hat, crown downward near the center of the table and placed a sheet of clean paper in the hat. In three minutes it was found covered with waterdrops. Another time, he and his fellow experimenters tried the height at which the water fell by holding a large piece of paper at an elevation. Drops fell under the paper only until it was lowered eighteen inches. At that height they formed on the sheet. The experiment took place in broad daylight.

Seven sitters of Mme. L. Ignath fervently prayed, on the **control**'s instruction, before a picture of the Madonna of Sixtin, after which tears appeared in the eyes of the portrait and ran down the painted cheeks (*Zeitschrift für Parapsychologie,* June 1932).

Reports of chemical phenomena in séance rooms must be treated with caution. A smell like phosphorus may indeed indicate the presence of that chemical, but it may have been introduced by a fake medium. The true facts of some of the remarkable phenomena claimed in cases from past history may never be found, and skepticism should be used in measuring past claims in light of modern experiment and investigation.

Cherniack, Louis (1908–)

Physician, Department of Internal Medicine, Winnipeg Clinic, Canada, beginning in 1947. He was born November 23, 1908, and studied at the University of Manitoba (M.D., 1932; B.Sc., 1934). He was a member of the Royal College of Physicians, London (1936); a fellow of the Royal College of Physicians, Canada (1947); and a fellow of the American College of Chest Physicians (1952). He served with the rank of lieutenant colonel in the Royal Army Medical Corps from 1940 until 1947.

Cherniack took a parapsychological interest in the phenomena of mediumship.

Cherubim

An order of **angels,** often represented as figures wholly or partly human and with wings proceeding from the shoulders. The first mention of these beings was in connection with the expulsion of Adam and Eve from the Garden of Eden, and they are frequently spoken of in later biblical history. Sometimes the cherubim have two or more faces, and sometimes are of composite animal form.

Chesed

The Jewish Kabalist name for mercy. (See also **Kabala**)

Chesme

A cat-shaped well (or fountain) spirit or nymph of the Turks. She was said to lure youths to death much in the same manner as the Germanic **Lorelei.**

Chevalier, Marie George (1889– ?)

A retired engineer and director of experiments for the Association Française d'Etudes Métapsychiques. Chevalier was born September 30, 1889, in Bar-le-Duc (Meuse), France, and studied at Dijon Academy, receiving bachelor's degree in science (1908) and arts (1909). He also graduated in 1914 from the Ecole Centrale des Arts et Manufactures. Chevalier served as lieutenant in the French army in World War I, and as captain in World War II. He was awarded the Cross of the Legion of Honor.

Reports of his investigations in psychokinesis and telepathy of sensation appeared in *Sciences Métapsychiques* and *Cahiers Métapsychiques.* He was author of *La Morte, cette illusion* (1953), and co-author with Bertrand de Cressac Bachelerie of *La Métapsychique—problème crucial* (1960).

Chevaliers de l'Enfer

According to French demonologists, these are demons more powerful than those of no rank, but less powerful than titled demons—counts, marquises, and dukes. They may be evoked from dawn to sunrise and from sunset to dark. (See also **counts of hell**)

Chevreuil, Leon Marie Martial (1852–1939)

French painter, author, and Spiritualist, born March 27, 1852. Chevreuil studied at the University of Poitiers and the Ecole des Beaux-Arts, Paris. His book *On ne meurt pas* (1916) was awarded a prize by the Académie des Sciences, Paris. He also wrote *Le Spiritisme dans l'Eglise* (1923) and contributed articles to *Revue Spirite* and *Psychica.* Two of his paintings deal with Spiritualist themes. He died in December 1939.

Chevreul, Michel Eugene (1786–1889)

French chemist, expert on color theories, researcher on animal fats (culminating in discovery of margarine). Chevreul conducted experiments on behalf of the French Academy of Science on divining by means of a **pendulum.** In his book *De la baguette divinatoire* (1854) he concluded that the movements of a pendulum in response to questions are the result of involuntary muscular movements in the hand induced by mental processes.

"Chevreul's pendulum" is often cited to disprove the reality of the information obtained by such devices as pendulums or divining rods, much as **Michael Faraday**'s similar explanations for table-turning in Spiritualist séances. Although it seems likely that Chevreul was correct in his investigation of some of the mechanisms of pendulum divining, and also in his assumption that mental processes may affect the pendulum movement, there is equal evidence of paranormal information obtained by the pendulum or **divining rod** when suggestive factors are not operating.

Sources:

Bird, Christopher. *The Diving Hand.* New York: E. P. Dutton, 1979.

Ch'i

A Chinese term for life energy or spirit (Japanese *ki*), comparable with the Hindu **yoga** term *prana.* Although deriving from the breath, ch'i, like prana, is transformed by the metabolism into subtle vitality that follows certain channels in the body, and it is related to the state of health of an individual. In the recently revived ancient Chinese systems of **acupuncture** and **acupressure,** these subtle energy flows are modified by inserting needles or by specific pressures at certain body points, resulting in improved health or the alleviation of physical disorders.

In the Asian system of **martial arts,** ch'i is directed by willpower to specific points of the body, resulting in apparently paranormal feats of strength and control. (See also **breathing**)

Sources:

Palos, Stephan. *The Chinese Art of Healing.* New York: Herderand Herder, 1971.

Tohei, Koichi. *The Book of Ki: Coordinating Mind and Body in Daily Life.* San Francisco: Japan Publications, 1978.

Chiaia, Ercole (d. 1905)

Distinguished Italian psychical researcher to whom **Cesare Lombroso, P. B. Bianchi,** astronomer G. V. Schiaparelli, **Theodor Flournoy,** Prof. Porro, and **Col. Rochas** owed their introduction to the phenomena of Spiritualism. It was Chiaia who first introduced the phenomena of the famous medium **Eusapio Palladino** to the European scientific world in 1888 when he invited Lombroso to conduct investigations.

Chibbett, Harold (1900–1978)

Founder of The Probe, a pioneer British group of investigators of psychic and occult phenomena. Chibbett was born February 19, 1900, in England. He was a member of the first London science-fiction club and a friend of **Eric Frank Russell,** whom he met in 1942 and with whom he shared an interest in Fortean phenomena.

Chibbett spent some fifty years meeting occultists and collecting data on unusual phenomena. At his own expense he maintained a postal chain letter to spread information on Forteana, and during his investigations he met such famous individuals as occultist **Aleister Crowley,** psychical investigator **Harry Price,** and Kuda Bux, a fire walker. His correspondents included scientists and occultists.

Chibett suffered from ill health for some years and died February 23, 1978, after a heart attack.

Chicago and Midwest Psychic Guide

Annual Who's Who of individuals and organizations in Chicago and the Midwest. Address: 2517 W. 71st St., Chicago, IL 60629.

Chidananda, Swami (1916–)

Prominent Hindu mystic, leading disciple of the late **Swami Sivananda,** (1887–1963) and Sivananda's successor as head of the **Divine Life Society** of Rishikesh, India. Born Sridhar Rao on June 24, 1916, Chidananda was the son of Srinivasa Rao, a prosperous landowner in southern India. From an early age, Sridhar's life was influenced by Anantayya, a friend of his grandfather's, who told him inspiring stories from the Hindu religious epics Ramayana and Mahabharata and implanted the ideal of spiritual realization. He attended an elementary school at Mangalore, and in 1932 went on to the Muthiah Chetty High School at Madras, where he became a distinguished scholar. In 1936 he entered Loyola College (B.A., 1938), where he became familiar with and sympathetic to Christianity.

Rao's family had a strong tradition of charity and service to the sick and needy, and Sridhar gave special attention to the lepers in his district. He built huts for them on the vast lawns of his home and attended personally to their needs. He became engrossed by the teachings of **Sri Ramakrishna** and **Swami Vivekananda,** visiting their monastery at Madras and taking part in services. In his own neighborhood he organized spiritual instruction for young people.

In 1936 a strong desire for spiritual development led him to leave home and study in the ashram of a sage near the sacred mountain shrine of Tirupathi. His parents persuaded him to return home, but he had already set himself the goal of renunciation. In 1943 he obtained permission from Swami Sivananda to join his ashram at Rishikesh in the foothills of the Himalayas. In 1947 he founded a yoga museum at the ashram, presenting the philosophy of Vedanta and yoga development in simple pictorial form. He was put in charge of the charitable dispensary and also delivered lectures at the Yoga Vedanta Forest Academy that was established in 1948; at that time he was appointed general secretary of the Divine Life Society. He became vice-chancellor and professor of rajah-yoga instruction.

During the following year, he was initiated into the order of *sannyasa* as a renunciate by Swami Sivananda on July 10. He organized branches of the society in different parts of India and in November 1959 traveled to the United States to propagate the teachings of Yoga Vedanta. He also lectured in South American countries and made a brief tour in Europe, returning to Rishikesh in March 1962. In April 1962 he made a pilgrimage to southern India, visiting holy places and delivering spiritual lectures. Ten days after his return, in July 1963, Swami Sivananda died. In August 1963 Swami Chidananda was elected his successor as president of the Divine Life Society and chancellor of the Yoga Vedanta Forest Academy.

Swami Chidananda has made a deep impression upon thousands of devotees by his ascetic and saintly life. His wide background knowledge of Christian religious teachings has intensified his ecumenical outlook. In addition to his many official tasks at the Rishikesh ashram, he has served the lepers of the district and was elected by the government authorities to the Leper Welfare Association. In recent years he has made occasional tours in the United States and Europe, but spends most of his time in Rishikesh.

Sources:

Divine Life Society. *An Apostle of India's Spiritual Culture: Souvenir Released on the Auspices of the Sixtieth Birthday Anniversary of H.H. Sri Swami Chidaananda.* Shivanandanagar, India: Divine Life Society, 1976.

Chidananda, Swami. *Destiny of Man.* Shivanandanagar, India: Divine Life Society, 1989.

———. *Path to Blessedness.* Shivanandanagar, India: Divine Life Society, 1975.

———. *The Philosophy, Psychology, and Practice of Yoga.* Shivanandanagar, India: Divine Life Society, 1984.

———. *Truth that Liberates.* Shivanandanagar, India: Divine Life Society, 1993.

Children of God See Family, The

Children of the Night

Organization for "mature and discriminating afficionados of the **vampire** genre in art, cinema, literature, and mythology." Membership fee includes nine issues of the "coven" journal of stories, poems, artwork, and film and book reviews and a pen pal network. Address: c/o Thomas J. Strauch, 9200 S. Avers Ave., Evergreen Park, IL 60602.

Childs, Edward (ca. 1869)

Early English private medium, introduced to Spiritualism by **Mrs. Thomas Everitt.** Childs reportedly demonstrated **direct voice** and **direct writing** phenomena and played musical instruments without contact.

Chimes

Long-established Spiritualist journal that merged into the *Psychic Observer* in the 1970s. For a period it was published as the *Psychic Observer and Chimes* and served as the periodical for the **National Spiritual Science Center.** It was edited by Henry Nagorka and published by the church's ESPress imprint in Washington, D.C. The magazine ceased publication in the mid-1980s.

CHINA

Magic & Superstition

Although systems of magical practice were uncommon in ancient China, there have been many instances of the employment of magical means and the belief in a supernatural world peopled by gods, demons, and other beings. One writer comments:

"Although the Chinese mind possessed under such a constitution but few elements in which magic could strike root and throw out its ramifications and influence, yet we find many traces giving evidence of the instinctive movement of the mind, as well as of magical influence; though certainly not in the manner or abundance that we meet with it in India. The great variety of these appearances is, however, striking, as in no other country are they so seldom met with. . . .

"It is easy to understand from these circumstances wherefore we find so few of these phenomena of magic and the visionary and ecstatic state, in other parts of the East so frequent, and therefore they are scattered and uncertain. Accounts are, however, not wanting to show that the phenomena as well as theories of prophecy were known in more remote times. Under the Emperor Hoei Ti, about 304 A.D., a mystical sect arose in China calling themselves 'the teachers of the emptiness and nothingness of all things.' They also exhibited the art of binding the power of the senses, and producing a condition which they believed perfection."

Demonism and Obsession

The Chinese of former times were implicit believers in demons whom they imagined surrounded them on every hand. One writer states, "English officials, American missionaries, mandarins and many of the Chinese literati (Confucians, Taoists and Buddhist believers alike) declare that **spiritism** in some form, and under some name, is the almost universal belief of China. It is generally denominated 'ancestral worship.'" "There is no driving out of these Chinese," stated the missionary Father Gonzalo, "the cursed belief that the spirits of their ancestors are ever about them, availing themselves of every opportunity to give advice and counsel." And Justus Doolittle notes,

"The medium consulted takes in the hand a stick of lighted incense to dispel all defiling influences, then prayers of some kind are repeated, the body becomes spasmodic, the medium's eyes are shut, and the form sways about, assuming the walk and peculiar attitude of the spirit when in the body. Then the communication from the divinity begins, which may be of a faultfinding or a flattering character. . . . Sometimes these Chinese mediums profess to be possessed by some specified historical god of great healing power, and in this condition they prescribe for the sick. It is believed that the ghoul or spirit invoked actually casts himself into the medium, and dictates the medicine."

And in his work *China and The Chinese* (1869), John L. Nevins observes,

"Volumes might be written upon the gods, genii and familiar spirits supposed to be continually in communication with this people. The Chinese have a large number of books upon this subject, among the most noted of which is the 'Liau-chai-chei,' a large work of sixteen volumes. . . . Tu Sein signifies a spirit in the body, and there are a class of familiar spirits supposed to dwell in the bodies of certain Chinese who became the mediums of communication with the unseen world. Individuals said to be possessed by these spirits are visited by multitudes, particularly those who have lost recently relatives by death, and wish to converse with them. . . . Remarkable disclosures and revelations are believed to be made by the involuntary movements of a bamboo pencil, and through a similar method some claim to see in the dark. Persons considering themselves endowed with superior intelligence are firm believers in those and other modes of consulting spirits."

W. J. Plumb, a public teacher in Chen Sin Ling, states: "In the district of Tu-ching, obsessions by evil spirits or demons are very common." He further writes that "there are very many cases also in Chang-lo." Again he comments:

"When a man is thus afflicted, the spirit (*Kwei*) takes possession of his body without regard to his being strong or weak in health. It is not easy to resist the demon's power. Though without bodily ailments, possessed persons appear as if ill. When under the entrancing spell of the demon, they seem different from their ordinary selves.

"In most cases the spirit takes possession of a man's body contrary to his will, and he is helpless in the matter. The kwei has the power of driving out the man's spirit, as in sleep or dreams. When the subject awakes to consciousness, he has not the slightest knowledge of what has transpired.

"The actions of possessed persons vary exceedingly. They leap about and toss their arms, and then the demon tells them what particular spirit he is, often taking a false name, or deceitfully calling himself a god, or one of the genii come down to the abodes of mortals. Or, perhaps, it professes to be the spirit of a deceased husband or wife. There are also kwei of the quiet sort, who talk and laugh like other people, only that the voice is changed. Some have a voice like a bird. Some speak Mandarin—the language of Northern China—and some the local dialect; but though the speech proceeds from the mouth of the man, what is said does not appear to come from him. The outward appearance and manner is also changed.

"In Fu-show there is a class of persons who collect in large numbers and make use of incense, pictures, candles, and lamps to establish what are called 'incense tables.' Taoist priests are engaged to attend the ceremonies, and they also make use of 'mediums.' The Taoist writes a hand, stands like a graven image, thus signifying his willingness to have the demon come and take possession of him. Afterward, the charm is burned and the demon spirit is worshipped and invoked, the priest, in the meanwhile going on with his chanting. After a while the medium spirit has descended, and asks what is wanted of him. Then, whoever has requests to make, takes incense sticks, makes prostrations, and asks a response respecting some disease, or for protection from some calamity. In winter the same performances are carried on to a great extent by gambling companies. If some of the responses hit the mark, a large number of people are attracted. They establish a shrine and offer sacrifices, and appoint days, calling upon people from every quarter to come and consult the spirit respecting diseases. . . .

"There is also a class of men who establish what they call a 'Hall of Revelations.' At the present time there are many engaged in this practice. They are, for the most part, literary men of great ability. The people in large numbers apply to them for responses. The mediums spoken of above are also numerous. All of the above practices are not spirits seeking to possess men; but rather men seeking spirits to possess them, and allowing themselves to be voluntarily used as their instruments.

"As to the outward appearance of persons when possessed, of course, they are the same persons as to outward form as at ordinary times; but the colour of the countenance may change. The demon may cause the subject to assume a threatening air, and a fierce, violent manner. The muscles often stand out on the face, the eyes are closed, or they protrude with a frightful stare. These demons sometimes prophesy.

"The words spoken certainly proceed from the mouths of the persons possessed; but what is said does not appear to come from their minds or wills, but rather from some other personality, often accompanied by a change of voice. Of this there can be no doubt. When the subject returns to consciousness, he invariably declares himself ignorant of what he has said.

"The Chinese make use of various methods to cast out demons. They are so troubled and vexed by inflictions affecting bodily health, or it may be throwing stones, moving furniture, or the moving about and destruction of family utensils, that they are driven to call in the service of some respected scholar or Taoist priest, to offer sacrifices, or chant sacred books, and pray for protection and exemption from suffering. Some make use of sacrifices and offerings of paper clothes and money in order to induce the demon to go back to the gloomy region of Yanchow . . . As to whether these methods have any effect, I do not know. As a rule, when demons are not very troublesome, the families afflicted by them generally think it best to hide their affliction, or to keep those wicked spirits quiet by sacrifices, and burning incense to them."

An article in the London *Daily News* gave lengthy extracts from an address upon the Chinese by Mrs. Montague Beaucham, who had spent many years in China in educational work. Speaking of their spiritism, she said, "The latest London craze in using the **planchette** has been one of the recognized means in China of conversing with evil spirits from time immemorial." She had lived in one of the particular provinces known as demon land, where the natives are bound up in the belief and worship of spirits. "There is a real power," she added, "in this necromancy. They do healings and tell fortunes." She personally knew of one instance that the spirits through the planchette had foretold a great flood. The Boxer uprising was prophesied by the planchette. These spirits disturbed family relations, caused fits of frothing at the mouth, and made some of their victims insane. In closing she declared that "Chinese spiritism was from hell," the obsession baffling the power of both Christian missionaries and native priests.

Nevius sent out a circular communication for the purpose of discovering the actual beliefs of the Chinese regarding demonism through which he obtained much valuable information. Wang Wu-Fang, an educated Chinese, writes:

"Cases of demon possession abound among all classes. They are found among persons of robust health, as well as those who are weak and sickly. In many unquestionable cases of obsession, the unwilling subjects have resisted, but have been obliged to submit themselves to the control of the demon. . . .

"In the majority of cases of possession, the beginning of the malady is a fit of grief, anger, or mourning. These conditions seem to open the door to the demons. The outward manifestations are apt to be fierce and violent. It may be that the subject alternately talks and laughs; he walks awhile and then sits, or he rolls on the ground, or leaps about; or exhibits contortions of the body and twistings of the neck. . . . It was common among them to send for exorcists, who made use of written charms, or chanted verses, or punctured the body with needles. These are among the Chinese methods of cure.

"Demons are different kinds. There are those which clearly declare themselves; and then those who work in secret. There are those which are cast out with difficulty, and others with ease.

"In cases of possession by familiar demons, what is said by the subject certainly does not proceed from his own will. When the demon has gone out and the subject recovers consciousness, he has no recollection whatever of what he has said or done. This is true almost invariably.

"The methods by which the Chinese cast out demons are enticing them to leave by burning charms and paper money, or by begging and exhorting them, or by frightening them with magic spells and incantations, or driving them away by pricking with needles, or pinching with the fingers, in which case they cry out and promise to go.

"I was formerly accustomed to drive out demons by means of needles. At that time cases of possession by evil spirits were very common in our villages, and my services were in very frequent demand. . . ."

The missionary Rev. Timothy Richard writes in response to Nevius's circular:

"The Chinese orthodox definition of spirit is, 'the soul of the departed'; some of the best of whom are raised to the rank of gods. . . . There is no disease to which the Chinese are ordinarily subject that may not be caused by demons. In this case the mind is untouched. It is only the body that suffers; and the Chinese endeavour to get rid of the demon by vows and offerings to the gods. The subject in this case is an involuntary one. . . .

"Persons possessed range between 15 and 50 years of age, quite irrespective of sex. This infliction comes on very suddenly, sometimes in the day, and sometimes in the night. The demoniac talks madly, smashes everything near him, acquires unusual strength, tears his clothes into rags, and rushes into the street, or to the mountains or kills himself unless prevented. After this violent possession, the demoniac calms down and submits to his fate, but under the most heart-rending protests. These mad spells which are experienced on the demon's entrance return at intervals, and increase in frequency, and generally also in intensity, so that death at last ensues from their violence.

"Now we proceed to those, who involuntarily possessed, yield to and worship the demon. The demon says he will cease tormenting the demoniac if he will worship him, and he will reward him by increasing his riches. But if not, he will punish his victim, make heavier his torments and rob him of his property. People find that their food is cursed. They cannot prepare any, but filth and dirt comes down from the air to render it uneatable. Their wells are likewise cursed; their wardrobes are set on fire, and their money very mysteriously disappears. Hence arose the custom of cutting off the head of a string of cash that it might not run away. . . . When all efforts to rid themselves of the demon fail, they yield to it, and say 'Hold! Cease thy tormenting and we will worship thee!' A picture is pasted upon the wall, sometimes of a woman, and sometimes of a man, and incense is burned, and prostrations are made to it twice a month. Being thus reverenced, money now comes in mysteriously, instead of going out. Even mill-stones are made to move at the demon's orders, and the family becomes rich at once. But it is said that no luck attends such families, and they will eventually be reduced to poverty. Officials believe these things. Palaces are known to have been built by them for these demons, who, however, are obliged to be satisfied with humbler shrines from the poor. . . .

"Somewhat similar to the above class is another small one which has power to enter the lower regions. These are the opposite of necromancers, for instead of calling up the dead and learning of them about the future destiny of the individual in whose behalf they are engaged, they lie in a trance for two days, when their spirits are said to have gone to the Prince of Darkness, to inquire how long the sick person shall be left among the living. . . .

"Let us now note the different methods adopted to cast out the evil spirits from the demoniacs. Doctors are called to do it. They use needles to puncture the tips of the fingers, the nose, the neck. They also use a certain pill, and apply it in the following manner: the thumbs of the two hands are tied tightly together, and the two big toes are tied together in the same manner. Then one pill is put on the two big toes at the root of the nail, and the other at the root of the thumb nails. At the same instant the two pills are set on fire, and they are kept until the flesh is burned. In the application of the pills, or in the piercing of the needle, the invariable cry is; 'I am going; I am going immediately. I will never dare to come back again. Oh, have mercy on me this once. I'll never return!'

"When the doctors fail, they call on people who practice spiritism. They themselves cannot drive the demon away, but they call another demon to do it. Both the Confucianists and Taoists practice this method. . . . Sometimes the spirits are very ungovernable. Tables are turned, chairs are rattled, and a general noise of smashing is heard, until the very mediums themselves tremble with fear. If the demon is of this dreadful character, they quickly write another charm with the name of the particular spirit whose quiet disposition is known to them. Lu-tsu is a favourite one of this kind. After the burning of the charm and incense, and when prostrations are made, a little frame is procured, to which a Chinese pencil is attached. Two men on each side hold it on a table spread with sand or millet. Sometimes a prescription is written, the pencil moving of its own accord. They buy the medicine prescribed and give it to the possessed. . . . Should they find that burning incense and offering sacrifices fails to liberate the poor victim, they may call in conjurors, such as the Taoists, who sit on mats and are carried by invisible power from place to place. The ascend to a height of twenty or fifty feet, and are carried to a distance of four or five *li* (about a half mile). Of this class are those who, in Manchuria call down fire from the sky in those funerals where the corpse is burned. . . .

"These exorcists may belong to any of the three religions in China. The dragon procession, on the fifteenth of the first month, is said by some to commemorate a Buddhist priest's victory over evil spirits. . . . They paste up charms on windows and doors, and on the body of the demoniac, and conjure the demon never to return. The evil spirit answers: 'I'll never return. You need not take the trouble of pasting all these charms upon the doors and windows.'

"Exorcists are specially hated by the evil spirits. Sometimes they feel themselves beaten fearfully; but no hand is seen. Bricks and stones may fall on them from the sky or housetops. On the road they may without warning be plastered over from head to foot with mud or filth; or may be seized when approaching a river, and held under the water and drowned."

In his *Social Life among the Chinese* (2 vols., 1866), Doolittle states,

"They have invented several ways by which they find out the pleasure of gods and spirits. One of the most common of their utensils is the *Ka-pue,* a piece of bamboo root, bean- shaped, and divided in the centre, to indicate the positive and the negative. The incense lighted, the Ka-pue properly manipulated before the symbol god, the pieces are tossed from the medium's hand, indicating the will of the spirit by the way they fall."

The following manifestation is mental rather than physical:

"The professional takes in the hand a stick of lighted incense to expel all defiling influences; prayers of some sort are repeated, the fingers interlaced, and the medium's eyes are shut, giving unmistakable evidence of being possessed by some supernatural or spiritual power. The body sways back and forward; the incense falls, and the person begins to step about, assuming the walk and peculiar attitude of the spirit. This is considered as infallible proof that the divinity has entered the body of the medium. Sometimes the god, using the mouth of the medium, gives the supplicant a sound scolding for invoking his aid to obtain unlawful or unworthy ends."

And Sir John Burrowa writes, "Divination with many strange methods of summoning the dead to instruct the living and reveal the future, is of very ancient origin, as is proved by Chinese manuscripts antedating the revelations of the Jewish Scriptures."

An ancient book called *Poh-shi-ching-tsung,* consisting of six volumes on the source of true divination, contains the following preface:

"The secret of augury consists in the study of the mysteries and in communications with gods and demons. The interpretations of the transformations are deep and mysterious. The theory of the science is most intricate, the practice of it most important. The sacred classic says: 'That which is true gives indications of the future.' To know the condition of the dead, and hold with them intelligent intercourse, as did the ancients, produces a most salutary influence upon the parties. . . . But when from intoxication or feasting, or licentious pleasures, they proceed to invoke the gods, what infatuation to suppose that their prayers will move them. Often when no response is given, or the interpretation is not verified, they lay the blame at the door of the augur, forgetting that their failure is due to their want of sincerity. . . . It is the great fault of augurs, too, that, from a desire of gain, they use the art of divination as a trap to ensnare the people."

Peebles adds:

"Naturally undemonstrative and secretive, the higher classes of Chinese seek to conceal their full knowledge of spirit intercourse from foreigners, and from the inferior castes of their own countrymen, thinking them not sufficiently intelligent to rightly use it. The lower orders, superstitious and money-grasping, often prostitute their magic gifts to gain and fortune-telling. Their clairvoyant fortune-tellers, surpassing wandering gypsies in 'hitting' the past, infest the temples, streets and roadsides, promising to find lost property, discover precious metals and reveal the hidden future."

Ghosts

The Chinese were strong in the belief that they were surrounded by the spirits of the dead. Indeed ancestor-worship constituted a powerful feature in the national faith, involving the likelihood and desirability of communion with the dead. Upon the death of a person they used to make a hole in the roof to permit the soul to effect its escape from the house. When a child was at the point of death, its mother would go into the garden and call its name, hoping thereby to bring back its wandering spirit.

"With the Chinese the souls of suicides are specially obnoxious, and they consider that the very worst penalty that can befall a soul is the sight of its former surroundings. Thus, it is supposed that, in the case of the wicked man, 'they only see their homes as if they were near them; they see their last wishes disregarded, everything upside down, their substance squandered, strangers possess the old estate; in their misery the dead man's family curse him, his children become corrupt, land is gone, the wife sees her husband tortured, the husband sees his wife stricken down with mortal disease; even friends forget, but some, perhaps, for the sake of bygone times, may stroke the coffin and let fall a tear, departing with a cold smile.'

"In China, the ghosts which are animated by a sense of duty are frequently seen: at one time they seek to serve virtue in distress, and at another they aim to restore wrongfully held treasure. Indeed, as it has been observed, 'one of the most powerful as well as the most widely diffused of the people's ghost stories is that which treats of the persecuted child whose mother comes out of the grave to succour him.'

"The Chinese have a dread of the wandering spirits of persons who have come to an unfortunate end. At Canton, 1817, the wife of an officer of government had occasioned the death of two female domestic slaves, from some jealous suspicion it was supposed of her husband's conduct towards the girls; and, in order to screen herself from the consequences, she suspended the bodies by the neck, with a view to its being construed into an act of suicide. But the conscience of the woman tormented her to such a degree that she became insane, and at times personated the spirits of the murdered girls possessed her, and utilised her mouth to declare her own guilt. In her ravings she tore her clothes and beat her own person with all the fury of madness; after which she would recover her senses for a time, when it was supposed the demons quitted her, but only to return with greater frenzy, which took place a short time previous to her death. According to Mr. Dennys, the most common form of Chinese ghost story is that wherein the ghost seeks to bring to justice the murderer who shuffled off its mortal coil."

Poltergeists were not uncommon in China, and several cases of their occurrence were recorded by the Jesuit missionaries of the eighteenth century in Cochin China.

Symbolism

There are numerous mysteries of meaning in the strange symbols, characters, personages, birds, and beasts that adorn all species of Chinese art objects. For example, a rectangular Chinese vase is feminine, representing the creative or ultimate principle. A group of seemingly miscellaneous art objects, depicted perhaps upon a brush tray, are probably the *po-ku,* or "hundred antiques" emblematic of culture and implying a delicate compliment to the recipient of the tray. Birds and animals occur with frequency on Chinese porcelains, and, if one observes closely, it is a somewhat select menagerie, in which certain types are emphasized by repetition. For instance, the dragon is so familiar as to be no longer remarked, and yet his significance is perhaps not fully understood by all. There are, in fact, three kinds of dragons, the *lung* of the sky, the *li* of the sea, and the *kiau* of the marshes. The *lung* is the favorite kind, however, and may be known when met by his having "the head of a camel, the horns of a deer, the eyes of a rabbit, ears of a cow, neck of a snake, belly of a frog, scales of a carp, claws of a hawk, and palm of a tiger." His special office is to guard and support the mansions of the gods, and he is naturally the peculiar symbol of the emperor.

A less familiar beast is the *chi-lin,* which resembles in part a rhinoceros, but has a head, feet, and legs like a deer, and a tufted tail. In spite of his unprepossessing appearance, he is of a benevolent disposition, and his image on a vase or other ornament is an emblem of good government and length of days. A strange bird, having the head of a pheasant, a long flexible neck, and a plumed tail, may often be seen flying in the midst of scroll-like clouds, or walking in a grove of treepeonies. This is the *fengbuang,* the Chinese phoenix, emblem of immortality and appearing to mortals only as a presage of the auspicious reign of a virtuous emperor. The tortoise (*kuei*), which bears upon its back the seagirt abode of the Eight Immortals, is a third supernatural creature associated with strength, longevity, and (because of the markings on its back) the mystic plan of numerals that is a key to the philosophy of the unseen.

Colors have their significance, blue being the color of the heavens, yellow of the earth and the emperor, red of the sun, and white of Jupiter or the Year Star. Each dynasty had its own particular hue, that of the Chou dynasty being described as "blue of the sky after rain where it appears between the clouds."

The apparently haphazard conjunction of objects in the decorative schemes of Chinese art is far from being a matter of chance, but adds to its decorative properties the intellectual charm of symbolic significance.

China in the Modern World

In the great political and economic upheavals of modern times, culminating in the establishment of the People's Republic of China October 1, 1949, many old beliefs, superstitions, and practices have been swept away, but in the emergence of China as a modern nation many skills from the past have also been revived and developed. The references to "pricking with needles" quoted earlier can now be seen as an imperfectly understood observation of the practice of **acupuncture,** an interesting blend of mystical concepts of anatomy and medical healing. Acupuncture and its associated skills of moxibustion and **acupressure** are now gaining ground in Western countries.

Also familiar in the West is the group of Asian **martial arts,** combining mental, physical, and spiritual resources for self-defense in weaponless fighting, or the achievement of apparently paranormal feats of strength and control. These involve the concept of *ch'i* (or *ki*), a subtle vital energy that can be controlled by willpower. Also taught in Western countries is the Chinese system of physical exercises known as **t'ai chi chuan,** originally a self-defense system.

Another element of Chinese tradition to attract popular interest is the **I Ching,** a book embodying a system of philosophy and **divination,** now widely consulted in various translations in Western countries.

With the opening up of communications and cultural relations with the West, many ancient Chinese mystical teachings and practices are now becoming more widely known. Chinese **astrology** is over a thousand years old but has not been familiar in the West nearly as long. Like the Western zodiac, it comprises twelve signs. But it operates on a completely different system; it is based on a 12-year rather than 12-month cycle, and each year is symbolized by the sign of an animal—rat, bull, tiger, cat, dragon, snake, horse, goat, monkey, rooster, dog, and pig. The attributes of these animals differ radically from the pejorative associations of the West (for example, rats are intellectual, affable, generous, and fun-loving) and can be found in Chinese astrological manuals.

Buddhism was known in China from the beginning of the Christian era, and the Ch'an or **Zen** school was established in the sixth century with the arrival of the patriarch Bodhidharma. China developed its own individual forms of **yoga,** often merging with **Taoism.** Taoist yoga developed from the Hindu concepts of **kundalini** and brought together special practices of physical development, diet, and meditation. These were often characterized by the term "K'ai Men," meaning "open door," expressing the idea of Taoist yoga as the doorway to the channels of mind, spirit, and body, and reflecting the harmony and balance of the principles of yin and yang in the universe. These teachings and practices, long a secret tradition, have now gained some attention in the Western countries through such authorities as Lu K'uan Yü (Charles Luk), Mantak Chia, and Maneewan Chia. On a more popular level, the simpler mind-body exercises of t'ai chi chuan, an offshoot of the Taoist tradition, have now been revived widely in China and the rest of the world.

In the pragmatic liberalism of present-day China, religions are now widely tolerated, and in 1968, the Liaoning People's Publishing House released a series of books titled *Man and Culture,* which included the standard guide to psychical research by Ivor Grattan-Guinness, *Psychical Research; A Guide to Its History, Principles, and Practices.* This work was issued in celebration of a hundred years of the **Society for Psychical Research,** London, and its release in China signifies an interest in reputable academic study of parapsychology.

The current Chinese approach to research in claimed paranormal phenomena is in terms of materialistic philosophy, and in place of Western terms like "extrasensory perception," Chinese researchers speak of "EHF" (exceptional human function). A number of Chinese children have claimed to demonstrate such EHF faculties as identifying hidden targets of Chinese written characters, under test conditions (like Western parapsychology tests for ESP with Zener cards or other targets), psychokinesis, and teleportation. A team of five members from the **Committee for the Scientific Investigation of Claims of the Paranormal,** the skeptical debunking organization, visited China during March and April of 1988 and while there tested a number of EHF subjects and investigated claims at the Institute of Scientific and Technical Information of China, Beijing. The CSICOP findings were, as expected, largely negative. For an account of the visit, see *The Skeptical Inquirer* (12, no. 4, summer 1988).

Sources:

Academy of Traditional Chinese Medicine. *An Outline of Chinese Acupuncture.* China Books, 1975.

Carus, Paul. *Chinese Astrology.* LaSalle, Ill.: Open Court, 1907.

Cerney, J. V. *Acupressure, Acupuncture Without Needles.* Virginia Beach, Va.: Cornerstone, 1975.

Chee Soo. *Chinese Yoga: The Chinese Art of K'ai Men.* London: Gordon & Cremonesi, 1977.

Chia, Mantak. *Awaken Healing Energy Through the Tao: The Taoist Secret of Circulating Internal Power.* New York: Aurora Press, 1983.

———. *Iron Shirt Chi Kung I.* Huntington, N.Y.: Healing Tao Books, 1986.

Chia, Mantak, and Maneewan Chia. *Healing Love Through the Tao: Cultivating Female Sexual Energy.* Huntington, N.Y.: Healing Tao Books, 1986.

Da Lui. *T'ai Chu'an and I Ching.* New York: Harper & Row, 1972.

Huard, Pierre, and Ming Wong. *Oriental Methods of Mental & Physical Fitness: The Complete Book of Meditation, Kinesiotherapy & Martial Arts in China, India & Japan.* New York: Funk & Wagnall, 1971.

Latourette, K. C. *The Chinese: Their History & Culture.* 2 vols. New York: Macmillan, 1934.

Legge, James, trans. *I Ching; Book of Changes.* New York: Causeway, 1973.

Luk, Charles [Lu K'uan Yü]. *The Secrets of Chinese Meditation.* London: Rider, 1964.

———. *Taoist Yoga: Alchemy and Immortality.* London: Rider, 1970.

Morgan, Harry T. *Chinese Symbols and Superstitions.* P. D. and Ione Perkins, 1942. Reprint, Detroit: Gale Research, 1972.

Sivin, Nathan. *Chinese Alchemy.* Cambridge, Mass.: Harvard University Press, 1968.

Wilhelm, Hans. *Your Chinese Horoscope.* New York: Avon, 1980.

Yang, C. K. *Religion in Chinese Society.* Berkeley, Calif.: University of California Press, 1961.

Chinmoy, Sri (1931–)

Sri Kumar Ghose Chinmoy is a modern Hindu mystic. He was born August 27, 1931, in Chittagong, East Bengal. He is said to have had profound mystical experiences during childhood, achieving the enlightened condition of *nirvikalpa samadhi* (superconsciousness beyond subject and object) at the age of twelve. Soon afterward, he entered the Sri Aurobindo Ashram at Pondicherry, where he remained for 20 years, developing and perfecting his realization through prayer and meditation.

Sri Chinmoy immigrated to the United States in 1964 and founded a center in New York. Soon his teachings spread to Puerto Rico, then to other parts of North America, Europe, and the Far East. After establishing his mission in America, he conducted regular weekly meditations for delegates and staff at the United Nations Church Center (dedicated to creating world peace through spiritual development) in New York; later he became the first director of the U.N. Meditation Group. Sri Chinmoy has also lectured at more than 150 universities throughout the world, including Oxford and Cambridge. He had a private audience at the Vatican with Pope Paul, who presented him with a medallion.

Sri Chinmoy's basic teaching is the pathway of love, devotion, and surrender to God. He also emphasizes the value of sports, particularly running, and is himself a dedicated runner. The Sri Chinmoy Center in New York sponsors over 100 public races each year, including marathons and ultramarathons. The center also runs the Annam Brahma Restaurant in Jamaica, New York.

Sri Chinmoy has written over 300 books of spiritual aphorisms, lectures, poems, and questions and answers and has composed over 2,000 songs and musical works. He has given concerts at music centers in the United States and Europe. He has also expressed the experience of meditation in color and form in more than 130,000 mystical paintings. There are now Sri Chinmoy centers throughout the world. U.S. address: c/o Peace Runs International, 61-20 Grand Central Pky., Ste. B-408, Forest Hills, NY11375. British address: 31 Niagara Ave., Ealing, London, W5, England.

Sources:

Chinmoy, Sri. *Arise! Awake! Thoughts of a Yogi.* New York: F. Fell, 1972.

———. *Astrology: The Supernatural and the Beyond.* Hollis, N.Y.: Vishma Press,1973.

———. *Death and Reincarnation: Eternity's Voyage.* Jamaica, N.Y.: Agni Press, 1974.

———. *Mother India's Light-house.* San Francisco: Shi Chinmoy Center, n.d.

———. *The Seeker's Mind.* Jamaica, N.Y.: Agni Press, 1978.

Chintamani

A mythical wish-fulfilling stone described in ancient Hindu scriptures, clearly related to later legends of the **philosophers' stone.**

Chips of Gallows

Chips from gallows and places of execution were said to make effective **amulets** against ague.

Chirognomy

The art of estimating character by inspecting the hand. Other impressive synonyms for **palmistry** included chirology and chiromancy. The Greek word *cheir* (hand) was used by the noted palmist Count Louis Hamon (1836–1936) in his pseudonym, **Cheiro.**

Chirology

Another name for **chirognomy** or **palmistry.**

CHITON See MYANMAR

Chochurah

The Kabalist name for wisdom. (See also **Kabala**)

Choisnard, Paul (1867–1930)

Paul Choisnard, a pioneer of the modern astrological revival in France, was born February 13, 1867, at Tours. Following his graduation from L'École Polytechnique in Paris, he joined the army and rose to the rank of major in the artillery. While pursuing his military career, he also became interested in **astrology** and launched statistical research as a means of establishing the reality of planetary influence upon human affairs. In order to have his controversial sideline separate from his career, he wrote and published under the pseudonym Paul Flambert and only after his retirement went public with his astrological identity.

Choisnard's books were never translated and had little influence in the English-speaking astrological community. However, they were read by German astrologer **Karl Ernst Krafft** and underlie his research, which in turn led to the contemporary well-known work of **Michel Gauquelin** and Francoise Gauquelin. Choisnard died February 9, 1930.

Sources:

Flambert, Paul [Paul Choisnard]. *Etude nouvelle sur l'hérédité.* Paris, 1903.

———. *Influence astrale.* Paris, 1901.

———. *Langage astral.* Paris, 1903.

Holden, James H., and Robert A. Hughes. *Astrological Pioneers of America.* Tempe, Ariz.: American Federation of Astrologers, 1988.

Chov-hani

The Gypsy name for a witch. (See also **Gypsies**)

Choynowski, Mieczyslaw (1909–)

Director of the Psychometrical Laboratory, Polish Academy of Sciences. Choynowski was born November 1, 1909, in Poland and studied at Warsaw University (M.A., 1937) and Jagellonian University (Ph.D., 1946). After graduation he became the editor of the Polish journal *Life of Science* and from 1951 to 1960 was director of the Psychological Laboratory, State Hospital for Mental Illness, Krakow-Kobierzyn.

Choynowski was a visiting Ford Foundation fellow to the United States in 1957–58. He has been a member of the Polish Psychological Association, the Association Internationale de Psychologie Appliquée, the American Statistical Association, and the Association Internationale de Cybernétique; a foreign affiliate of the American Psychological Association; and a graduate member of the British Psychological Society. His acceptance of **parapsychology** is marked with skepticism, especially regarding experimental studies of **telepathy** and **clairvoyance.**

Christian, Paul (1811–1877)

Pseudonym of Jean Baptiste Pitois, who wrote *The History and Practice of Magic,* first published in France in 1870. He was born May 15, 1811, at Remiremont, France. His family wanted him to become a priest and allowed him to be raised in a monastic community. However, he eventually decided against the priesthood, and as a young man moved to Paris, where he became the associate of Charles Nodier, one of the leading literary lights of the romantic movement, which was then emerging on the Continent. Nodier's interest in the **occult** transferred to Pitois.

Pitois became a journalist and wrote largely under the pen name Paul Christian. He cowrote *Historic Paris: Walks in the Streets of Paris* (1837–1840), which was his first book, with Nodier. It was followed by his *Studies of the Paris Revolution* (1839). That same year he was appointed librarian of the Ministry of Public Education. Working with Nodier through the mass of uncataloged material opened up a new level of interest in the occult, although it was not manifested for years. Meanwhile, he took his turn in the French army (Algiers, 1843–44) and wrote several historical texts. His most important were the *History of the Terrors* (1853) and the multivolume *Heroes of Christianity* (1853–57). A hint of what was to come appeared in 1844 with his *Stories of the Marvelous from All Times and Lands.*

Pitois had read about occultism and developed a strong anticlerical stance. During his life, many Eastern texts had been translated into French, as had the works of **Emanuel Swedenborg.** In 1859 Pitois turned his attention to writing *Historie de la Magie, du monde Surnaturel et de la fatalité a travers les Temps et les Peuples* (1870). Carefully written so as not to offend his largely Catholic audience, it immediately became popular public reading. It surveyed the whole of the occult, explaining each element, and provided a history of occult practice in the West from ancient times.

Pitois wrote one additional book, *The History of the War with Prussia and of the Two Sieges of Paris, 1870–71* (1872–73). His health declined through the 1870s, and he died at Lyons on July 12, 1877. He left behind a still-unpublished work on **astrology** that reportedly contains numerous allusions to contemporary events as proof of the value of the horoscope.

Sources:

Christian, Paul [Jean Baptiste Pitois]. *Historie de la Magie, du monde Surnaturel et de la fatalité a travers les Temps et les Peuples.* 1870. Translated by Ross Nichols as *The History and Practice of Magic.* New York: Citadel Press, 1969.

Christian Fellowship Organization

Edward Lewis Hodges, a physician in San Diego, California, claimed to be the earthy representative of the Secret Order of the Christian Brotherhood and School of Christian Initiation. Similar to what has been elsewhere termed the **Great White Brotherhood,** the Secret Order of the Christian Brotherhood was seen as consisting of those evolved beings who in ages past had so spiritualized their bodies and perfected their understanding that they had been given the keys to the Kingdom Universal. Their present task is to guide the Earth. As an initiate, Hodges was given the order's teachings and told to propagate them. He founded the Christian Fellowship Organization as an instrument for the order and in 1938 published their teachings in a book, *The Teachings of the Secret Order of the Christian Brotherhood.*

The order taught a means of achieving liberation through the restoration and spiritualization of the body. Jesus headed the order during his earthly ministry and taught the means of spiritualization. The great secret of life was God, expressed through Jesus, the mortal man. We must look beyond Jesus to the Christ within. Christ within the human form is the saving potential. The first step on the path of initiation is realizing oneness with the Christ within.

The organization taught a process of liberation from death through spiritualization of the body. Students were asked to place themselves under the "cultural condition of the Christian brotherhood," by invoking its presence. They were also given a set of affirmations (positive prayers) to bring about conditions of health, prosperity, and spiritualization. Eventually, the individual should be able to take his or her body to heavenly worlds and return as he or she sees fit.

The organization functioned into the 1950s, but appears to have become defunct.

Sources:

Hodges, Edward Lewi. *Be Healed. . . A Remedy That Never Fails.* San Diego, Calif.: Christian Fellowship Organization, 1949.

———. *Teachings of the Secret Order of the Christian Brotherhood.* Santa Barbara, Calif.: J. F. Rowney Press, 1938.

———. *Wealth and Riches by Divine Right.* San Diego, Calif.: Christian Fellowship Organization, 1945.

Christian Parapsychologist, The

British journal concerned with religious aspects of **parapsychology.** Published quarterly by the **Churches' Fellowship for Psychical and Spiritual Studies,** it includes book reviews. Address: St. Mary Abchurch, Abchurch Ln., London, EC4N 7BA, England.

Christian Science See Church of Christ, Scientist

Christian Spirit Center

The Christian Spirit Center is an American branch of the Brazilian Spiritualist movement and exists primarily to translate the messages of Brazilian mediums (spoken in Portuguese) into English. Brazilian Spiritualism is derived from the French **spiritism** of **Allan Kardec** and gives central importance to **reincarnation.**

The center affirms the continuity of life after death (proved by Christ in his resurrection), the law of cause and effect, reincarnation, and the freedom and moral responsibility of people. The center may be contacted at Box 114, Elon College, NC 27244. It offers its services, including mediumship, free of charge and survives on the gifts of supporters.

Christian Spiritual Alliance, Church of

In spite of its name, the Church of the Christian Spiritual Alliance (CSA) is a Hindu organization with teachings derived from Swami Paramahansa Yogananda. However, the organization was originally founded in 1962 by H. Edwin O'Neal, formerly a Baptist; his wife, Lois O'Neal, a Religious Scientist; and William Arnold Lynn, all of whom embraced a form of metaphysical Christianity. O'Neal took over *Orion,* an older metaphysical publication founded by Ural Murphy, and made it a CSA periodical.

In the late 1960s O'Neal was joined by Roy Eugene Davis, a former minister with the Self-Realization Fellowship in Phoenix, Arizona, who had left that group to found the independent New Life World-Wide. Davis contributed his periodical, *Truth Journal,* and his national speaking tours brought many new members to CSA. In 1977 O'Neal resigned as chairman of the board and president of the CSA Press and turned the organization over to Davis. Soon after, all hint of metaphysical Christianity was dropped in favor of the kriya yoga teachings advocated by Davis.

By the early 1990s the church had centers across the United States and Canada and had expanded to Germany, Ghana, and South Africa. The headquarters complex in Lakemont, Georgia, includes facilities of the CSA Press, the Center for Spiritual Awareness, an educational arm, and the Shrine of All Faiths and Sacred Initiation Temple. Address: Lake Rabun Rd., Box 7, Lakemont, GA 30552.

Sources:

Davis, Roy Eugene. *An Easy Guide to Meditation.* Lakemont, Ga.: CSA Press, 1978.

———. *God Has Given Us Every Good Thing.* Lakemont, Ga.: CSA Press, 1986.

———. *The Teachings of the Masters of Perfection.* Lakemont, Ga.: CSA Press, 1979.

———. *The Way of the Initiate.* St. Petersburg, Fla.: New Life World-Wide, 1968.

Christian Spiritualist, The

The name of several now-defunct Spiritualist periodicals. The first was published in New York from 1854 to 1857 by the Society for the Diffusion of Spiritual Knowledge; a second was a British Spiritualist monthly, founded in 1871 by Rev. F. R. Young, that appeared for several years. The last was also a British Spiritualist journal, established in 1926 and published weekly by the Society of Communion, London; it was edited by Rev. J. W. Potter, in Wiltshire.

Christian Spiritualists

Spiritualists of the mid-nineteenth century who saw in the Bible a depiction of Spiritualist truth. They believed Jesus to be a great **medium.** In contrast, most Spiritualists were not Christians, believing that Spiritualist contact with the dead stood in contradiction to Christian doctrines of the resurrection. In the United States, Moses Hull was the first major champion of the Christian Spiritualist perspective.

Sources:

Hull, Daniel. *Moses Hull.* Wellesley, Mass.: Maugus Printing, 1907.

Christopher, Milbourne (1914–1984)

One of America's leading **conjuring** magicians and chairman of the Occult Investigation Committee of the Society of American Magicians. Christopher entered the public eye in the mid-1970s when he challenged the feats of **Uri Geller** and other psychics in his book *Mediums, Mystics and the Occult* (1975). Based upon his observations, Christopher asserted that Geller was a clever conjurer and suggested various techniques by which his apparently paranormal feats were accomplished.

Born in Baltimore, Maryland, Christopher practiced conjuring from early childhood. During the Depression years, he performed for the Roosevelts at the White House. He performed in more than 60 countries and amassed one of the world's largest private collections of magic memorabilia, including prints, paintings, letters, scrapbooks, playbills, drawings, and photographs relating to the great magicians of history. He wrote several books on the history of magic and his personal hero, **Harry Houdini.**

Although Christopher was a skeptic as far as **occult** and psychic phenomena were concerned, his writings on the subject had a precision and scholarly cast. He avoided making broad accusations against individuals; those searching for truth in paranormal research have found Christopher's skeptical writings valuable for their careful research and thoughtful presentation. Additional books on the paranormal by Christopher include *ESP, Seers & Psychics* (1970) and *Search for the Soul* (1979), a report on the continuing quest by psychics and scientists for evidence of life after death.

Christopher did much to popularize magic shows on television during the 1950s and demonstrated some amazing acts, including making an elephant vanish and the trick of catching in his mouth a bullet fired from a rifle. He also served as president of the American Society of Magicians. He died in New York, June 17, 1984, after complications following surgery.

Sources:

Christopher, Milbourne. *ESP, Seers & Psychics.* New York: Thomas Y. Crowell, 1970.

———. *Houdini: The Untold Story.* New York: Thomas Y. Crowell, 1969. Reprint, New York: Pocket Books, 1970.

———. *The Illustrated History of Magic.* New York: Thomas Y. Crowell, 1973.

———. *Mediums, Mystics and the Occult.* New York: Thomas Y. Crowell, 1975.

———. *Panorama of Magic.* New York: Dover Publications, 1962.

Christos Experience

A technique for inducing altered states of consciousness, as first described in the book *Windows of the Mind* (1974) by Australian novelist **G. M. Glaskin.** The Greek word *Christos* (anointed one) was thought by Glaskin to mean "inner self." The technique involves massaging the subject's feet and forehead before a series of visualization exercises, culminating in the experience of traveling by mind (imagination) to other places, identities, and time periods. When successful the technique produces a vivid and stimulating experience that often includes reexperiencing events believed to have happened in former lives.

The Christos experiments originated with a group in isolated Western Australia who published a magazine titled *Open Mind.* Glaskin first described the experiments in his books *Windows of the Mind; Discovering Your Past and Future Lives Through Massage and Mental Exercise* (1974) and *The Christos Experiment* (1974). He subsequently published two additional books on the subject: *Worlds Within: Probing the Christos Experience* (1976) and *A Door to Eternity; Proving the Christos Experience* (1979). (See also **Arnall Bloxham; double; dreaming true; out-of-the-body travel**)

Sources:

Glaskin, G. M. *A Door to Eternity: Proving the Christos Experience.* London: Wildwood House, 1979.

———. *Windows of the Mind; Discovering Your Past and Future Lives Through Massage and Mental Exercise.* New York: Delacorte Press, New York, 1974. Reprinted as *Windows of the Mind: The Christos Experiment.* London: Wildwood House, 1974.

———. *Worlds Within: Probing The Christos Experience.* London: Wildwood House, 1976. Reprint, Lonson: Arrow, 1978.

Chromotherapy

Chromotherapy, the practice of healing with color, emerged in the nineteenth century as the object of scientific speculation and research, out of which various practitioners created new forms of alternative healing. Modern color healing combined occult thought about color with scientific investigations of the physical properties of light and behavioral psychologists' studies of human reactions to various colors.

Early Beginnings

Augustus James Pleasanton is usually credited with beginning the contemporary enthusiasm for color healing by initiating what became known as the "blue glass craze." Pleasanton claimed that in experiments on grape vines in his laboratory, he had been able to increase the production of grapes by alternating clear sunlight with blue-filtered light. News of his findings led many to purchase blue panes of glass under which they took sunbaths, seemingly oblivious to the denunciations of many of Pleasanton's scientific colleagues. Pleasanton's work led to the first formal studies of chromotherapy in the 1870s, which led to the publication of *Blue and Red Light; or, Light and Its Rays as Medicine* (1877) by Dr. S. Pancoast.

By far the most important of the early chromotherapists, however, was Edwin Dwight Babbitt. As early as 1876 he had announced his explorations of the means of atoms interacting with "etheric" forces to produce the effects of heat, light, and electricity. He further claimed in his 1878 book, *The Principles of Light and Color,* that color directly affected humans. He suggested a method by which people could make practical use of his claims—water should be charged by putting it in a colored bottle and then placing the bottle in strong sunlight. Babbitt produced no hard data to back up his claims, and they were soon forgotten by most. Among the few who took them seriously was a young Indian scientist-inventor, Dinshah Pestanji Ghadiali (1873–1966).

Twentieth-Century Chromotherapy

As a young physician in India, Ghadiali tested the chromotherapy ideas on patients with seemingly great success. Shortly before World War I he migrated to the United States and became a citizen. He aligned himself with the emerging community of naturopathic physicians and worked on developing chromotherapy into a usable form of alternative therapy. In 1920 he announced his perfection of "Spectro-Chrome therapy," which he envisioned as an attuned color wave healing science. Meanwhile he worked on a degree in naturopathy and in 1924 he purchased land in Malaga, New Jersey, to open his institute.

Ghadiali worked quietly in Malaga through the 1920s, but in 1931, the government, which had been developing ways to combat what it considered medical quacks, moved against Ghadiali for fraud and tried to have his citizenship revoked (a real possibility under recently passed anti-Asian immigration laws). Ghadiali was at the time completing his magus opus, the three-volume *Spectro-Chrome Metry Encyclopedia,* which appeared in 1933. After almost a decade in resolving his legal problems, some of which swirled around attempts to market a color healing device, Ghadiali settled into a private practice, which he continued until his death in 1966. His son has continued his work at Malaga, but has emphasized vegetarianism rather than color therapy. Ghadiali's color healing was picked up by fellow Indian-American N. S. Hanoka of Miami, Florida.

While Ghadiali was trying to perfect a scientific perspective on color healing, Theosophist Ivah Bergh Whitten picked up on the occult speculations on color of **Annie Besant** and **Charles W. Leadbeater.** Whitten experienced a personal crisis following the death of her husband in 1907. While recovering from a nervous breakdown she was contacted by someone she later spoke of as an Elder Brother, a member of the **Great White Brotherhood.** He offered her a choice, death or a life as a lightbearer to the world. She chose the latter, soon recovered from her illness, and became an active and avid Theosophist. Eventually she became a lecturer for the **Theosophical Society** on her chosen topic, the occult meaning of color. As a result of her travels, study groups formed to examine her ideas. In the late 1920s these groups organized AMICA (the Amica Master Institute of Color Awareness).

Whitten began to publish her findings in the 1930s, beginning with a booklet, *What Color Means to You* (1932), soon followed by *The Initial Course in Colour Awareness.* She developed the theosophical perspective on color by which the highest white light is broken into the seven colors (rays) of the light spectrum. Each ray symbolizes a set of human characteristics over which a particular ascended master presides. The seven colors also correspond to various other universal structures, such as the seven subtle spiritual centers of the body, the chakras. Ultimately, this set of correspondences became the basis of an occult color healing system. Whitten was quite aware of Ghadiali, and she praised his healing devices. She also developed a form of healing meditation during which a person imagines breathing in a specific color.

During the 1930s, British Theosophist Roland T. Hunt emerged as Whitten's leading student. While he studied Whitten's writings, he was also becoming aware of the new psychological findings about the effects of color on human behavior. These were combined in his 1940 text, *The Seven Keys to Colour Healing.* Hunt moved to California following World War II and became the head of AMICA. He wrote a number of books before passing the work to Paola Hugh and the Fleur de Lys Foundation in Tacoma, Washington.

Concurrent with but independent of Hunt was the activity of Rosicrucian Corine Heline, the founder of the **New Age Bible and Philosophy Center** in Santa Monica, California. In 1943 she wrote *Healing and Regeneration through Color.* Heline, in the astrological tradition of her teacher **Max Heindel** of the **Rosicrucian Fellowship,** saw colors related to astrological signs. She also believed that illnesses affecting specific parts of the body had correspondences to astrological signs. Traditionally, for example, diseases of the head were related to Aries. Color treatment should be given in conjunction with astrological analysis. Light, she suggested, also stimulated glands. Glands serve as connecting points between the physical body and the invisible mental and causal bodies (which many occultists believe each individual possesses). Stimulating the glands with light (either visible or imagined) can lead to the glands secreting healing substances.

During the 1970s, color therapy entered the **New Age** and holistic health movements through the work of health journalist Linda Clark. Her 1975 *The Ancient Art of Color Therapy* became the first of a series of books to reintroduce the topic to a more mainstream audience after it had been pushed to the edge of the occult community in the 1960s.

Evaluating Color Therapy

Contemporary color therapy is grounded in scientific research on light and psychological findings on the beneficial effects of color. Such research has, for example, been widely utilized in the design of public institutions, possibly the most famous instance being the banishing of black boards in schools in favor of green boards. It is also widely known that sunlight, in moderate doses, stimulates the production of vitamin D by the body, that colored rooms can assist the healing of some psychological disorders, and the rights colors in offices can stimulate employees.

Physicists have explained light as part of a spectrum of electromagnetic energy. Each part of the spectrum manifests as radiation that vibrates at a specific rate. Visible light appears somewhere toward the center of the spectrum. On one side of the spectrum are cosmic rays, gamma rays, x-rays, and ultraviolet, and on the other side are infrared, electricity, radio, and television. Light is thus a form of radiant energy, and human beings can be seen as living systems that absorb and radiate energy. Many psychics and occultists claim that the body radiates energy just outside of the visible light spectrum, which surrounds the body as an aura. Some people claim the ability to see this radiation, or aura, and interpret its meaning.

While many advocate the beneficial effects of sunbaths, chromotherapists go far beyond to a sophisticated analysis of the application and use of very specific colors on specific parts of the body. Such color may be received by sitting in a spotlight shining a colored beam on the body. Alternatively, through meditation, a particular color can be imagined either to shine upon the body or be taken into the body through breaths. Color therapy has also been associated with **crystals,** which also come in a variety of colors, and some have hypothesized that crystals of varying colors radiate different healing energies. The most common explanation of the healing power of color relates to stimulating the glandular system is some way.

It should be noted that a variety of attempts to verify the healing effects of color as hypothesized by color therapists has proved unsuccessful. Thus, the sale of machines that can radiate specific beams of color for healing purposes is against the law and can lead to an arrest for fraud. To date, most of the effects with color healing can be attributed to other causes.

Sources:

Amber, Reuben. *Color Therapy.* New York: ASI Publishers, 1980.

Clark, Linda. *The Ancient Art of Color Therapy.* Old Greenwich, Conn.: Devin-Adair, 1975.

Ghadiali, Dinshah P. *Spectro-Chrome Metry Encyclopedia.* 3 vols. Malaga, N.J.: Spectro-Chrome Institute, 1933.

Heline, Corine. *Healing and Regeneration through Color.* Santa Barbara, Calif.: J. F. Rowney Press, 1943.

Hunt, Roland. *The Seven Keys to Colour Healing.* Ashington, England: C. W. Daniel, 1954.

Whitten, Ivah Bergh. *What Color Means to You.* Ashington, England: C. W. Daniel, 1932.

Chrysolite (or Chrisoletus)

A yellow-green gemstone used as an **amulet** by ancient Romans to protect the wearer from melancholy and enchantment. It was set in gold to dispel nightmares. Its virtue was also said to be enhanced if a hole was made in it and the hairs of a donkey passed through.

Chrysoprase

A semiprecious stone used in **amulets.** Its color is green and gold and it was traditionally used to combat weakness of sight and to render its possessor joyful and liberal.

Church of Christ, Scientist

Organization founded in 1879 by **Mary Morse (Baker) Eddy** (1821–1910) as the embodiment of the healing movement popularly known as Christian Science. As a young woman Eddy suffered from chronic health problems. Through the 1850s and 1860s she sought out various remedies and eventually found her way to **Phineas Parkhurst Quimby,** a mental healer in Maine. She experienced great relief for a time and was grateful for Quimby's efforts. It was not until 1866, however, that she found a new spiritual insight while recovering from an injury received in a fall. She experienced a complete recovery of health, discovering that God is all and that illness and death are unreal. She also came to believe that in the acceptance of the complete reality of God health appears.

Eddy's recovery was followed by a period of further Bible study, working with others in light of her new vision and reexamining Quimby's teachings. The result of this study was a primal booklet, *The Science of Man* (1870), and then a textbook, *Science and Health* (1875). She organized the Christian Science Association in 1876 as an organization for her students. Over the next years the healing movement grew and expanded. Several new editions of the textbook were published as *Science and Health with Key to the Scriptures.* In 1892 the movement went through a complete reorganization and the mother church structure, through which the church is currently organized, was established. The church bylaws were published in 1895 as the *Church Manual.* Leadership of the church was placed in the hands of the mother church (the First Church of Christ, Scientist), located in Boston, Massachusetts, and its pastor, Mary Baker Eddy, who had been ordained in 1881.

Included in both the textbook and the *Church Manual* are the tenets of the church. They affirm the Bible as the inspired guide to life; one God; God's Son; the Holy Ghost; and man as a being in God's image. Forgiveness of sin results from new spiritual understanding that casts out evil as having no God-ordained reality. The atonement of Jesus, "the wayshower," is evidence of God's love. Salvation comes through the truth, life, and love, as he demonstrated. Healing, following the principles laid down by Eddy in *Science and Health,* remains the most significant aspect of the doctrine of the Church of Christ, Scientist. Such healing is distinct from both psychic healing and magnetism (or **mesmerism**), both of which were condemned by Eddy.

Since Eddy's death, leadership of the church has been in the hands of a five-member board of directors that administers the affairs of the church according to the rules laid down in the *Church Manual.* Each church is autonomous but its leaders must be members in good standing with the mother church. Church headquarters are at the Christian Science Center, Boston. The Christian Science Publishing Society issues a number of books and periodicals, most notably the *Christian Science Journal* and a daily newspaper, *The Christian Science Monitor. The Herald of Christian Science* appears in a dozen languages.

The Christian Science movement has not only built a large organization but has also inspired a variety of religious healing movements in other groups. Throughout the early years of the movement a number of students withdrew from association with Eddy and the church. Some continued as independent Christian Science practitioners, and others gathered around **Emma Curtis Hopkins** and developed what would come to be known as the New Thought movement. Boston Episcopal minister **Elwood Worcester** founded the Emmanuel Movement, the organization that introduced spiritual healing into the Episcopal Church and continues today as the Order of St. Luke the Physician.

The Church of Christ, Scientist was born in controversy and has continued as a controversial organization. Members are known for their refusal to seek the services of physicians, preferring their own Christian Science practitioners. Throughout the twentieth century, church leaders have labored long and somewhat successfully to gain a legal status for their church and to have their practitioners recognized by government authorities and even insurance companies. Their success has been challenged periodically when a person who might have been helped by modern medical techniques or medicine dies. In the 1980s a score of court cases were heard, with very mixed results, concerning Christian Science parents whose children died without receiving any medical treatment.

Sources:

Christian Science: A Sourcebook of Contemporary Materials. Boston: Christian Science Publishing Society, 1990.

Eddy, Mary Baker. *Church Manual of the First Church of Christ, Scientist, in Boston, Mass.* Boston: Trustees Under the Will of Mary Baker Eddy, 1908.

———. *Science and Health with Key to the Scriptures.* Boston: Trustees Under the Will of Mary Baker Eddy, 1906.

Gottshalk, Stephen. *The Emergence of Christian Science in American Religious Life.* Berkeley: University of California Press, 1973.

Peel, Robert. *Mary Baker Eddy.* 3 vols. New York: Holt Rinehart & Winston, 1971.

Swihart, Altman K. *Since Mrs. Eddy.* New York: Henry Holt, 1931.

Church of Cosmic Science

The Church of Cosmic Science was a fellowship of Spiritualist congregations founded in 1959 at Rialto, California, by Rev. William Dickensen, Reginald Lawrence, and Josephine Dickensen. Though small (only seven congregations in the 1970s), the church made an impact among West Coast Spiritualists through its monthly publication, *Cosmic Light,* which circulated widely among independent Spiritualist congregations. The church's Cosmic Light Press also published *Awareness for Cosmic Truth,* a set of lessons in psychic development. The former headquarters in Jamul, California, have been closed, and the present status of the group, if it still exists, is unknown.

Church of Illumination

Closely associated with the **Fraternitas Rosae Crucis,** which is a very elite and exclusive fraternity, the Church of Illumination operates as an outer court that interacts with the general public. The church's program centers upon the establishment of the Manistic Age, during which the equality of male and female will be fully recognized. During this age a new world teacher will arise who will teach the five fundamentals: As ye sow so shall ye reap; talents as gifts and responsibilities; the golden rule; honesty; and the new birth as the awakening of the Christos, or divine spark, within.

Sources:

The Christic Teachings. Quakertown, Penn.: Church of Illumination, 1955.

Clymer, R. Swinburne. *Christisis.* Quakertown, Penn.: Philosophical Publishing, 1945.

———. *The Interpretation of St. John.* Quakertown, Penn.: Philosophical Publishing, 1953.

Manisis: The Interpretation of the Divine Law for the Manistic Dispensation. Quakertown, Penn.: Beverley Hall, 1955.

Church of Light

The Church of Light was one of the most important occult organizations in the United States in the mid-twentieth century. It had a special role in the modern revival of **astrology.** The church was incorporated in 1932, but it is part of the history of the Brotherhood of Light, which emerged in the nineteenth century. The Brotherhood of Light is a group of exalted beings who guide humankind (known elsewhere as the **Great White Brotherhood**). The believers in the Brotherhood of Light had representatives in Great Britain in the mid-nineteenth century. One of these, **Thomas H. Burgoyne** (1855–94), a Scotsman, came to the United States in the 1880s. He resided for a period with a Captain Norman Astley and his wife, Genevieve Stebbins, in Carmel, California. He also met Henry Wagner and his wife, Belle Wagner, who owned the Astro-Philosophical Publishing Company in San Francisco. Through the Wagners, Burgoyne published the first volume of a book he was writing on astrology and occultism, *Light of Egypt.* Burgoyne and the Wagners also agreed to found an organization, The Hermetic Brotherhood of Luxor, to give expression to the Brotherhood of Light on the visible material plane. The Hermetic Brotherhood was headed by a scribe, a seer, and an astrologer. Burgoyne was the original scribe and Minnie Higgins the original astrologer.

For a generation the organization pioneered occult and astrological thought in the United States. Then in 1909 Higgins died. A young student of the brotherhood, **Elbert Benjamine,** was called as the new astrologer. Benjamine was assigned the additional task of preparing a complete set of lessons covering the whole of occultism. These would become the textbooks of the brotherhood and introduce people to the emerging Aquarian Age. Benjamine set about the task, which would keep him busy until 1934. In the meantime, in 1913, the Hermetic Brotherhood of Luzor was formally disbanded. As the surviving leader, Benjamine inherited its mission and responsibilities, and in 1915 he began to hold informal classes, which were opened to the general public after World War I.

As Benjamine neared the completion of his lessons, he founded the Church of Light as the successor of the Hermetic Brotherhood and the visible expression of the Brotherhood of Light. The church teaches that there are two orders of truth—science and religion. Between these two there can be no true antagonism. Nature's laws provide the substance of true religions. Astrology is an especially useful tool for interpreting nature, though all occult arts contribute. The church now offers 21 courses in occult knowledge based upon the lessons prepared by Benjamine and published as a series of books by the church.

Following Benjamine's death in 1951, Edward Doane was named as president. Members are scattered across the North America and relate to the church via correspondence. The church may be contacted at Box 76862, Los Angeles, CA 90076. It publishes *The Church of Light Quarterly.*

Sources:

Astrological Research & Reference Encyclopedia. 2 vols. Los Angeles: Church of Light, 1972.

Burgoyne, Thomas H. *Light of Egypt.* 2 vols. Albuquerque, N.Mex.: Sun Publishing, 1980.

Wagner, Henry O., comp. *A Treasure Chest of Wisdom.* Denver: H. O. Wagner, 1967.

Church of Metaphysical Christianity

The Church of Metaphysical Christianity is a small Florida-based Spiritualist church founded in 1958 by Rev. Dorothy Graff Flexer and Russell J. Flexer, who were earlier associated with the Spiritualist Episcopal Church. In 1958, amid charges of fake mediumship at Camp Chesterfield, Indiana, the Flexers were among those who led the Spiritualist Episcopal Church to break with the camp. However, in that same year the Flexers also left the Spiritualist Episcopal Church to establish their independent work in Florida.

The Flexers teach what is termed Metaphysical Christianity. Metaphysical Christianity attempts to combine religion, science, and philosophy, and members live out of the spiritual truths revealed in the life and teachings of Jesus. It studies to discern the laws of nature and tries to conform to them. Obedience to natural laws constitutes the highest form of worship. Among the laws that have been discovered are the laws of life, love (the creative force of life), truth (right thinking), compensation, freedom, abundance, and perfection.

As with other Spiritualist churches, the Church of Metaphysical Christianity attempts to demonstrate the continuity of life through mediumship and encourages members to develop their own gifts of the spirit so that such communication becomes a natural part of human life. The church affirms that after death, the human spirit continues and remains conscious and can thus communicate with the visible earth plane. Also from spirit comes the power to heal. The church is headquartered at 2717 Browning St., Sarasota, FL 33577. There is a second congregation in Bradenton, Florida.

Sources:

Davis, Charles [Dorothy Flexer]. *A New Way of Life.* Sarasota, Fla.: Church of Metaphysical Christianity, 1989.

———. *Spirit Speaks.* Sarasota, Fla.: Church of Metaphysical Christianity, 1988.

Wade, Alsa Madison. *At the Shrine of the Master.* Philadelphia, Penn.: Dorrance, 1953.

Church of Satan

In the late 1960s many were dismayed to learn that one **Anton LaVey** of San Francisco, California, had founded a church dedicated to the worship of the **devil.** The media had a field day with the various events following the founding of the church on April 30, 1966, from LaVey's holding a funeral for a young sailor who died at the Treasure Island Navy Base to his use of a nude woman as an altar for a "worship" service at his home in San Francisco. The house, which served as headquarters of the church, was painted totally black. Following actress Jayne Mansfield's tragic death in a car accident, it was revealed that she had been associated with the church, and LaVey reaped the full benefit from his brief appearance as the devil in the movie version of *Rosemary's Baby.*

In 1969 LaVey issued the first of three books, *The Satanic Bible,* which presented the basic beliefs and practices of the church. It was followed by *The Compleat Witch* (1971) and *The Satanic Rituals* (1972). LaVey played on the image of a traditional Satanist and did little to counter the speculations of an exploitative press that rarely got beyond the sheer offense of the church's name or took time to look into the church's teachings or practices. Few understood the appeal of such a church in a secularized society.

Unlike traditional Satanism, which operates in a supernatural world of angels and demons, God and Satan, LaVey's assertion of Satanism was initially a statement of disbelief in supernaturalism altogether. Satan was seen not as the evil opposite of God, but as Promethean figure who represented modern secular man at his best, living in the present with little regard for the future. Satanic principle asserted that humans were simply animals who lived a time on earth and should enjoy that life. They should value indulgence, vital existence, undefiled wisdom, kindness to the deserving, vengeance, responsibility to the responsible, and the practice of those "sins" that lead to mental and physical gratification.

The church's rituals are designed to lead to members' acceptance of a perspective centered on antiestablishmentarianism, self-assertion, and gratification. The church opposes the breaking of any laws made for the common good and opposes the use of drugs, which it sees as perpetuating an escapist view of reality.

The church celebrates several main holidays. Foremost, in keeping with the self-assertive perspective, is one's own birthday. Next Walpurgisnacht and Halloween, traditional magical dates on the agricultural calendar, are also celebrated. A form of baptism includes a ceremony of glorification of the one baptized. The church uses a form of the **Black Mass,** traditionally a reversal of the Roman Catholic Mass.

The church has a policy of enrolling new members with a lifetime membership; however, active membership is renewed annually and has never been more than a few thousand. There are concentrations of members in **England, Holland,** and Denmark, and *The Satanic Bible* has been translated into Danish, Swedish, and Spanish.

The Church of Satan and its literature has given rise to a variety of Satanic groups that follow its beliefs and practices but are administratively separate. The most important group with roots in the Church of Satan is the **Temple of Set,** headed by Michael A. Aquino, which has developed a new theology based on the identification of the Christian Satan with the ancient Egyptian god Set. Address: Box 210082, San Francisco, CA 94121.

Sources:

Harrington, Walt. "The Devil in Anton LaVey." *The Washington Post Magazine,* February 23, 1986, 6–17.

Church of Satanic Brotherhood

The Church of Satanic Brotherhood grew out of the period of turmoil experienced by the **Church of Satan** in the early 1970s, during which time the majority of the church's local centers (termed grottos) revolted against the leadership of church founder **Anton LaVey.** In the Midwest, prominent grottos were functioning under the leadership of Wayne West in Detroit and John DeHaven in Dayton, Ohio. LaVey moved against the rebellious members in February 1973 by dissolving the Dayton grotto. The following month DeHaven led in the founding of the Church of Satanic Brotherhood.

The new church operated with a collective leadership of bishops. A periodical, the *True Grimoire,* was launched, and grottos soon appeared in Dayton, Indianapolis, Louisville, New York City, and St. Petersburg. The church lasted only a short time. In 1974 John DeHaven announced his conversion to Christianity and publicly renounced **Satanism.**

Church of the Final Judgment See Process Church of the Final Judgment and Foundation Faith of God

Church of the New Jerusalem

The religious organization devoted to the teachings of Swedish mystic **Emanuel Swedenborg** (1688–1772). Shortly after Swedenborg's death, Thomas Cookworthy, Rev. John Cowles, and Rev. Thomas Hartley began to translate Swedenborg's writings—all originally written and published in Latin—into English. Then in 1783 Robert Hindmarsh called together people interested in Swedenborg's ideas, and weekly meetings began. Originally called the Theosophical Society, the group was reconstituted as the New Jerusalem Church in 1787. Five years later the church was introduced into the United States.

Followers of Swedenborg believe that the Second Coming of Christ took place in 1757 in the form of the revelation of Swedenborg's esoteric interpretation of the Scriptures. They interpret the revelation as a fulfillment of St. John's vision of the New Jerusalem coming down out of heaven from God, with the declaration, "Behold, I make all things new." Salvation is regarded as deliverance from sin itself, and hell is considered a free choice on the part of those who prefer an evil life. Jesus is worshiped directly as Creator, Redeemer, the Word, and the Revelation.

The beliefs and practices for the New Jerusalem are put forth in the voluminous religious writings of Swedenborg and are summarized in the introductory chapters of *The True Christian Religion* (1950) and *The New Jerusalem and Its Heavenly Doctrine* (1938). A manuscript originally written in 1769 covering much of the same material as the first three chapters of *The True Christian Religion* was finally published in 1914 as *The Canons of the New Church.*

In England, the Church has taken the name, the New Church. It has more than forty houses of worship administered by a general conference. (Address: New Church Enquiry Centre, 20 Bloomsbury Way, London, WC1A 2TH.)

During its first quarter-century in the United States the New Jerusalem founded some 17 societies. These groups met in 1817 and founded the General Convention of the New Jerusalem. A split occurred in 1840 that led to the formation of the General Church of the New Jerusalem. This later body is now the largest of the several American churches (with more than 2,500 members). It has built a large headquarters complex and cathedral in the small community of Bryn Athyn, Pennsylvania. The General Convention with approximately 1,500 members is headquartered at 48 Sargent St., Newton, MA 02148.

In the late 1930s a movement began among members of the New Church in the Netherlands maintaining that, like the Bible, the writings of Swedenborg had an internal spiritual meaning. The immediate implication of the notion was twofold. First, not only is the Bible from the Lord, but the doctrine of the New Church is also. Second, the discovery of the internal meaning in Swedenborg's voluminous writings allows for continuous growth and change in understanding his revelation. Out of this movement emerged the Lord's New Church Which Is Nova Hierosolyma. It is the smallest of the Swedenborgian churches having less than a thousand members worldwide. (Address: c/o Rev. Philip Odhner, Box 4, Bryn Athyn, PA 19009.)

Swedenborg's teachings had strong influence on the development of the nineteenth-century Spiritualist and occult movements in both Europe and the United States. In America the church found a significant advocate in Jonathan Chapman, popularly known as "Johnny Appleseed," a Swedenborgian who wandered through nineteenth-century settlements planting apple trees and leaving Swedenborgian literature at log cabins.

Through Spiritualist medium **Andrew Jackson Davis** (1826–1910), who claimed that Swedenborg was one of three spirits who revealed the secrets of the universe to him in 1844, Swedenborgian ideas flowed into **Spiritualism.** In fact, a number of Swedenborgian leaders went on to become leaders in Spiritualism, **Theosophy,** and **New Thought.** Swedenborg's ideas concerning correspondence between the spiritual and material worlds which led him to write a number of biblical commentaries, also inspired **Mary Baker Eddy**'s *Key to the Scriptures,* which was appended to her primary Christian Science textbook, *Science and Health.*

Sources:

Block, Marguerite Beck. *The New Church in the New World.* New York: Henry Holt, 1932.

General Church of the New Jerusalem. *The General Church of the New Jerusalem: A Handbook of General Information.* Bryn Athyn, Pa.: General Church Publication Committee, 1965.

———. *Liturgy and Hymnal.* Bryn Athyn, Pa.: General Church Publication Committee, 1966.

Lord's New Church Which Is Nova Hierosalyma. *Handbook of the Lord's New Church Which Is Nova Hierosolyma.* Bryn Athyn, Pa.: The Author, 1985.

Sigstedt, C. O. *The Swedenborg Epic: The Life and Works of Emanuel Swedenborg.* New York: Bookman Associates, 1952. Reprint, London: Swedenborg Society, 1981.

Silver, Ednah C. *Sketches of the New Church in America.* Boston: Massachusetts New Church Union, 1920.

Woofenden, William Ross. *Swedenborg Researcher's Manual.* Bryn Athyn, Pa.: Swedenborg Scientific Association, 1988.

Church Universal and Triumphant

A church of the "I AM" tradition, which has emphasized its Christian Gnostic lineage. The church began in 1958 in Washington, D.C., as the Summit Lighthouse under the leadership of Mark L. Prophet. For several years Prophet had been a messenger of the Ascended Masters of the **Great White Brotherhood** and had associated with the Lighthouse of Freedom, another I AM organization. He began *Pearls of Wisdom,* a weekly periodical, as a means of disseminating the messages of the masters to the public. In 1961 Prophet was joined by Elizabeth Clare Wulf, whom he eventually married and who, after a period of training, was also named a messenger of the brotherhood.

The church developed through several stages, beginning in 1962 with the establishment of the Keepers of the Flame Fraternity at the suggestion of ascended master Saint Germain. The fraternity was created from among those who received the "pearls of wisdom," who especially dedicated themselves to the freedom and enlightenment of humanity. In 1966 the headquarters of the church was moved to Colorado Springs, Colorado. In 1971 Summit University was founded to provide more intensive and systematic training in the teachings of the masters for those associated with the Summit Lighthouse.

Mark Prophet died in 1973 and Elizabeth Clare Prophet assumed full control of the movement. She aggressively pursued the growth and development of the movement and in 1974 incorporated the Church Universal and Triumphant. Headquarters of the church were moved to California in 1976 and a decade later to Montana, on land north of and adjacent to Yellowstone National Park.

The church developed in the midst of the older I AM Religious Activity and freely admits its debt to **Guy W. Ballard,** but in its emphasis upon its Christian nature it has developed a number of differences from the I AM. It teaches that the human soul is the living potential of God. Souls are conceived in the mind of God as an initial realization of God's unity. They are then born as separate entities, a realization of the duality of God, a being of both spirit and matter. The individual is thus seen as having two parts—a higher, unchanging self and a lower, changing self. The God-identity of each individual, the I AM Presence, is extended into matter, time, and space, the church teaches.

It is the goal of each individual to evolve through many incarnations to become one with Christ—the higher self—in physical embodiment. The masters have taught a variety of disciplines that use prayers, mantras, and decrees to help purify the soul. These are used in conjunction with the violet flame of transmutation, the sacred spiritual fire of the Holy Spirit, which allows a balancing of errors of the soul in this and previous incarnations. After the process of purification is completed, the soul ascends to the Divine Source, from which it originated.

Through the 1980s the church was the subject of considerable controversy, especially from the anticult movement and from some neighbors in Montana who opposed its moving into the sparsely populated community. Also, the church has a survivalist perspective, and members built and stocked a number of underground facilities should disaster ever strike the country. It was widely (and mistakenly) reported that at one point Prophet had predicted a major disaster and ordered the membership to prepare to go underground. Slowly, as the accusations against the church proved groundless, the tension between the church and its neighbors in Montana decreased.

Address: Box A, Livingston, MT 59047.

Sources:

Lewis, James R., and J. Gordon Melton, eds. *Church Universal and Triumphant in Scholarly Perspective.* Stanford, Calif.: Center for Academic Publications, 1994.

Prophet, Elizabeth Clare. *The Great White Brotherhood in the History, Culture, and Religion of America.* Los Angeles: Summit University Press, 1976.

Prophet, Mark L., and Elizabeth Clare Prophet. *Climb the Highest Mountain.* Colorado Springs, Colo.: Summit Lighthouse, 1972.

———. *The Lost Teachings of Jesus.* 2 vols. Livingston, Mont.: Summit University Press, 1986.

Churches' Fellowship of Psychical and Spiritual Studies, The

Founded in 1953 in Britain by Lt. Col. R. M. Lester and a group of clergy and laypersons interested in psychical research and its relevance to Christianity and **mysticism.** The fellowship organizes lectures, conferences, study groups, and retreats dealing with paranormal **healing,** psychic phenomena, and mysticism and also issues a quarterly journal, *Christian Parapsychologist.* Full membership in the fellowship is limited to members of churches that belong to either the World Council of Churches or the British Council of Churches or that adhere to the orthodox theological tradition and holds Jesus Christ as Lord and Savior. Address: St. Mary Abchurch, Abchurch Ln., London, EC4N 7BA, England.

Sources:

Pearce-Higgins, John D. *Life, Death and Psychical Research: Studies on Behalf of the Churches' Fellowship for Psychical and Spiritual Studies.* London: Rider, 1973.

Churchward, James (1852–1936)

Author of several books about the lost continent of Mu or **Lemuria,** the Pacific Ocean equivalent of **Atlantis.** He stated that he became friendly with a Hindu priest during a famine in India in the nineteenth century, and the priest led him to a collection of ancient clay tablets hidden in a cave and taught him a language called Naacal, by which the tablets could be deciphered. According to Churchward, these tablets told the story of the lost continent of Mu, a primitive Garden of Eden destroyed by volcanic action.

No one ever saw the Naacal tablets, and it is likely that they never existed. More important in building Churchward's vision of Mu were the writings of Augustus Le Plongeon, an archaeologist who had spent the last decades of the nineteenth century studying the Mayan remnants in the Yucatán. He believed that he had deciphered the hieroglyphics that told the story of an ancient land, Mu. He published his results in a book *Queen Moo and the Egyptian Sphinx* (1896). Churchward inherited Le Plongeon's papers.

Churchward took Le Plongeon's speculations into the realm of pure fantasy. He picked up on the theosophical myth of Lemuria, which he identified with Le Plongeon's Mu. His first book on the subject, *The Lost Continent of Mu, the Motherland of Man,* appeared in 1926. It was followed by three additional volumes expanding upon the theme. Churchward's Mu was located in the South Pacific. It extended 500 by 300 miles in area from present-day Hawaii to Fiji and from Easter Island to the Mariana Islands. It was believed to be inhabited by a white race that worshiped the sun, believed in immortality, and built cities. The continent was home to 64 million people when it was destroyed 10,000 years ago; only a few survived.

Raymond Buckland, under the pseudonym Tony Earll, wrote a spoof on Churchward's books, *Mu Revealed* (1969).

Sources:

Churchward, James. *Children of Mu.* New York: Ives Washburn, 1931.

———. *Cosmic Forces of Mu.* New York: Ives Washburn, 1935.

———. *The Lost Continent of Mu: The Motherland of Man.* New York: Ives Washburn, 1926.

———. *The Sacred Symbols of Mu.* New York: Ives Washburn, 1933.

Earll, Tony [Raymond Buckland]. *Mu Revealed.* New York: Paperback Library, 1970.

Le Plongeon, Augustus. *Queen Moo and the Egyptian Sphinx.* New York, 1896.

Churchyard

It is not difficult to understand why the churchyard has come to be regarded as the special haunt of ghosts. The popular imagination may well be excused for supposing that the spirits of the dead continue to hover over the spot where their bodies are laid.

The ancient Greeks thought the souls of the dead were especially powerful near their graves or sepulchres, because of some natural tie binding body and soul, even after death. The more earthly a soul was, the less willing it was to leave the vicinity of its body, and in consequence, specters encountered in a churchyard were more to be feared than those met with elsewhere. The **apparitions** witnessed at the tombs of saints, however, were to be regarded as good angels rather than as the souls of the saints themselves.

CIEEPP See Comité Illusionniste D'Expertise et D'Experimentation des Phenomenes Paranormaux

Circle

Circle, one of the largest contemporary Wiccan/**neo-pagan** fellowships, began in 1974 as an informal gathering of people interested in magic and mysticism. During meditation, founder Selena Fox received the name, concept, and logo of Circle, and, with her partner Jim Alan, called the first group of people together at their home in Madison, Wisconsin. In the summer of 1975 they established Circle Farm on land near Sun Prairie, Wisconsin. There the first Circle Coven was formed, and other related groups emerged.

Fox and Alan quickly became well known in the growing neo-pagan community for their ecumenical spirit, their vibrant music, and their extensive networking activity. In 1977 they published their first tape of Wiccan music and an accompanying songbook and organized the Circle Network, an international fellowship of Wiccans. The expanding organization was incorporated as the Church of Circle Wicca in 1978; the following year it issued the first edition of the *Circle Resource Guide* (which now exists in several volumes). Circle became the largest active fellowship of neo-pagans in North America.

In 1979 Circle moved to a farm near Middleton, Wisconsin, and in 1983 a farm was purchased near Barneveld, Wisconsin. There the Circle Sanctuary was created as an all-weather nature preserve, ritual site, and gathering place for Wiccans and neo-pagans. Circle Sanctuary has the support of neo-pagans far beyond the membership of Circle. Meetings are held at the sanctuary year round. After a lengthy court battle, Circle Sanctuary won zoning status as a church.

Fox has led in the development of an ecumenical and eclectic paganism that draws on elements of indigenous land-based religions, especially the traditions and practices of Native Americans. The ever-evolving system is termed "Wiccan Shamanism" or "Nature Spirituality," a blend of Wiccan spirituality, nature mysticism, shamanistic practices from around the world, ecofeminism, and the insights of modern psychology, especially its humanistic and transpersonal branches. Fox emphasizes the divinity inherent in nature and acknowledgement of the Goddess and Mother Earth.

Through the 1980s, Circle became one of the more visible Wiccan groups, and in 1980 it launched its expansive publishing concern with *Circle Network News,* one of the more substantive of Wiccan periodicals. That same year the Pagan Spirit Alliance, a neo-pagan fellowship and friendship network, was organized and in 1981 the Circle Sanctuary hosted the first annual International Pagan Spirit Gathering. In the late 1980s, Circle also emerged as a champion of religious freedom and in 1991 established a more permanent organization, the Lady Liberty League, to focus on this continuing concern.

Currently, Circle is headed by Fox and her husband, Dr. Dennis Carpenter, both professionally trained psychotherapists. Fox heads Circle's school for priestesses, its school for women in Goddess- oriented spirituality, and its school for ministers, which trains pagan and Wiccan leadership. Circle may be contacted through Circle Sanctuary, Box 219, Mt. Horeb, WI 53572. It publishes several periodicals, including the *Circle Network Bulletin,* the *Pagan Spirit Alliance Newsletter,* and *Sanctuary Circles.* (See also **Wicca**)

Sources:

Fox, Selena. *Circle Guide to Pagan Resources.* Mt. Horeb, Wis.: Circle, n.d.

Circle of Inner Truth

The Circle of Inner Truth was a short-lived **channeling** group built around the work of trance medium Marshall Lever. Lever, a young Presbyterian seminarian, discovered his mediumistic abilities and made contact with a spirit named Chung Fu, who described himself as a student of the ancient Chinese philosopher Lao Tzu. In 1970 Lever and his wife, Quinta Lever, began the Circle of Truth as an instrument of Chung Fu's work. They gave up any home life and spent all of their time traveling and allowing Chung Fu to lecture and counsel people. In trance, Lever began to give health readings similar to those once offered by **Edgar Cayce.**

Chung Fu taught that humans have immortal spirits that live through many incarnations. The incarnating process continues until the individual identifies with a God-self during a life on Earth. Such an awareness is developed through the practices of affirmative meditation. Chung Fu also advised a regimen of nutrition and healthy practices.

The circle continued into the 1980s. The Levers issued a magazine, *Our News and Views,* from San Francisco. However, more recently, the Levers have moved on to other activities.

Sources:

Fu, Chung. *Evolution of Man.* San Francisco: Circle of Inner Truth, 1973.

Circle 77

A **séance** group in Florence, Italy, at which psychic **Roberto Campagni** has manifest physical phenomena of **materialization** of small **apports.**

Circles, Spiritualist

A group of persons who meet at intervals to hold **séances** for spirit communication. It is essential that at least one among them be a **medium,** and there may be several mediums in one circle. However, all the members of a circle must be chosen with care if the séances are to induce phenomena. The **Baron von Guldenstubbé,** in his book *Practical Experimental Pneumatology, or the Reality of Spirits and the Marvellous Phenomenon of their Direct Writing,* originally published early in the history of **Spiritualism** in French in 1857, gave directions for forming a circle after the American fashion.

"Setting aside the moral conditions, which are equally requisite, it is known that American Circles are based on the distinction of positive and electric or negative magnetic currents.

"The circles consist of twelve persons, representing in equal proportions the positive and negative or sensitive elements. This distinction does not follow the sex of the members, though generally women are negative and sensitive, while men are positive and magnetic. The mental and physical constitution of each individual must be studied before forming the circles, for some delicate women have masculine qualities, while some strong men are, morally speaking, women. A table is placed in a clear and ventilated spot; the medium is seated at one end and entirely isolated; by his calm and contemplative quietude he serves as a conductor for the electricity and it may be noted that a good somnambulist is usually an excellent medium. The six electrical or negative dispositions, which are generally recognized by their emotional qualities and their sensibility, are placed at the right of the medium, the most sensitive of all being next to him. The same rule is followed with the positive personalities, who are at the left of the medium, with the most positive among them next to him. In order to form a chain, the twelve persons each place their right hand on the table, and their left hand on that of the neighbour, thus making a circle round the table. Observe that the medium or mediums, if there be more than one, are entirely isolated from those who form the chain.

Camille Flammarion stated that the sexes are alternated to "reinforce the fluids." It has also been asserted that the séance may be as productive when the circle is composed of only a few investigators, following no rules but their own.

Although the presence of a medium is traditionally regarded as indispensable, a group of experimenters composed of members of the Toronto Society for Psychical Research in Canada obtained interesting phenomena by concentrating on "**Philip,**" an artificial personality deliberately created by the group. (See also **psychic force**)

Sources:

Post, Eric. *Communication with the Beyond: A Practical Handbook of Spiritualism.* New York: Atlantic Publishing, 1946.

Circles Effect Research Unit, The (CERES)

British organization, headed by George Terence Meaden, concerned with the phenomenon of **crop circles.** It publishes *The Journal of Meteorology.* Address: 54 Frome Rd., Bradford-on-Avon, Wiltshire, BA15 1LD, UK.

Circular, The

Periodical concerned with the phenomenon of **crop circles,** published in Great Britain by the Centre for Crop Circles Studies, 20 Paul St., Frome, Somerset, BA11 1DX, UK.

Citizens Against UFO Secrecy (CAUS)

An activist organization founded in 1977 to make public government data on **UFOs.** It has made numerous Freedom of Information requests, filed suits, and investigated UFO reports and published its findings. The organization was originally established by W. Tod Zechel, Brad Sparks, and Peter Gerstein. Zechel had edited a newsletter, *Just Cause,* which ceased when he left. CAUS briefly issued *UFORMANT* under the editorship of Larry W. Bryant. *Just Cause* was later revived by Barry Greenwood as an independent newsletter. Address: Box 218, Coventry, CT 06238

Sources:

Clark, Jerome. *The UFO Encyclopedia. I, UFOs in the 1980s.* Detroit: Apogee Books, 1990.

Fawcett, Lawrence, and Barry J. Greenwood. *Clear Intent: The Government Coverup of the UFO Experience.* Englewood Cliffs, N.J.: Prentice-Hall, 1984.

Claflin Sisters, Victoria (1838–1927) and Tennessee Celeste (1846–1923)

Early American feminists who gave Spiritualist **séances** during childhood. (See **Victoria Claflin Woodhull**)

Clairaudience

The faculty of "clear hearing," the ability to hear sounds inaudible to the normal ear, such as "spirit" voices; a faculty analogous to **clairvoyance,** but considerably less frequently met with.

One such incident occurred to the apostle Paul on the road to Damascus. He saw a light and heard a voice. As he later told of the events, "They that were with me saw the light and were afraid; but they heard not the voice of him who spoke to me" (Acts 23:9). Perhaps the best-known case is that of Joan of Arc (see **Jeanne D'Arc**). She was not the only martyr who heard the voices of saints and angels urging them to perform some special task.

In Spiritualist circles the faculty is claimed by **mediums,** but distinction must be made between the "inner voice," through which mediums are supposed to receive communications from the denizens of "the otherworld," and an externalized voice comparable to an actual physical sound. Frequently some such physical sounds form the basis of an auditory **hallucination,** just as the points of light in a crystal are said to form *points de repère* around which the hallucination of the visualizer may shape itself.

Clairaudience is considered a rare mediumistic gift, but the phenomenon has been known from ancient times: "The prophet that is in Israel telleth the king of Israel the words the king of Syria speaks in his bedchamber" (2 Kings 6). The experience of hearing inner voices was described in the age of **animal magnetism** by one of Dr. G. Billot's somnambulists:

"At first, I feel a little breath like a light zephyr, which refreshes and then chills my ear. From that instant I become deaf, and I begin to be aware of a little humming in the ear, like that of a gnat. By giving close attention I then hear a small voice which says to me that which I afterwards repeat.

"A biographer of the poet William Cowper wrote that the most important events of Cowper's later years were audibly announced to him before they occurred."

The difficulty in where to draw the line between subjective and objective experience is illustrated by the following narrative of **Vincent Turvey** in *The Beginnings of Seership* (1911):

"One afternoon a few weeks ago I went to sleep on the sofa; after a time, probably about forty minutes, I became aware that there was an indistinct conversation going on somewhere near me. Knowing that all my people were out and that my house stands detached in its own grounds, I wondered what it meant. Then I realized that I was asleep and was 'hearing' clairaudiently, and that those who were conversing were not 'spirits,' but someone inside me and someone outside me, and yet part of me, because both voices were 'Turvey' in language, etc. I caught no sentence, save here and there a word or two such as 'understand—no condition—not yet,' etc., then I heard the sentence: 'But you had better wake it up now, as there is a man coming to the house in a minute.' I woke and had just enough time to throw off my rug and smooth my hair with my hand, when the front door bell rang."

Clairaudience is either spontaneous or experimentally induced. Seashells are used for the latter purpose; most people can hear what sounds like the murmur of the sea in a shell. But the clairaudient medium soon distinguishes other voices, may hear distant friends speaking, may hear part of a conversation he or she has already heard or will soon hear, and may interpret the communications as messages from the dead or from the living. The medium **Arthur Ford** was well known as a successful platform clairaudient in the United States, whereas **Estelle Roberts** had a similar reputation in England. **Marjorie Livingston** published several books on esoteric matters that she clairaudiently received.

Clairaudience fades imperceptively into the inspiration experienced by many artists. Many poets and novelists have also claimed that they "received" their material rather than consciously constructed it. In like measure, musicians often report initially hearing in their head a new composition, which they then reproduce for their audiences.

Sources:

Hollen, Henry. *Clairaudient Transmission.* Hollywood, Calif.: Keats Publications, 1931.

Roberts, Estelle. *Forty Years a Medium.* London: Herbert Jenkins, 1959. Revised as *Fifty Years a Medium.* London: Corgi Books, 1969.

Sharp, Arthur. F. *The Spirit Saith.* London: H. H. Greaves, n.d.

Clairvoyance

The faculty of clear-sightedness, the supposed paranormal ability to see persons and events that are distant in time or place. Clairvoyance may be roughly divided into three classes—**retrocognition** and **premonition;** perceiving past and future events; and perception of contemporary events happening at a distance, or outside the range of normal vision. Clairvoyance may include **psychometry, second sight,** and **crystal gazing.**

Prophecy is a form of clairvoyance extending back into antiquity, and second sight is also an ancient form. It is notable that **Spiritualism** in Great Britain was directly heralded, about the third decade of the nineteenth century, by an outbreak of clairvoyance. Among clairvoyants of that period was **Alexis Didier,** whose phenomena suggested that **telepathy** at least entered into his feats, which included reading letters enclosed in sealed packets, playing écarté with bandaged eyes, and others of a like nature. Clairvoyance remains a prominent feature of the Spiritualistic **séance.**

Although there exists a quantity of evidence, collected by members of the **Society for Psychical Research** and other scientific investigators, that would seem to support the theory of supernormal vision, it must be acknowledged that many cases of clairvoyance lend themselves to a more mundane explanation. For instance, it has been shown that it is almost impossible to bandage the eyes of a medium so that the person cannot make some use of his or her normal vision. The possibility of hyperesthesia during **trance** should also be taken into account, as should telepathy, which may conceivably play a part in clairvoyant performances.

A private detective agency could also be a possible source of some of the knowledge displayed by the professional clairvoyant. The **crystal** is, as has been indicated, a favorite mode of exercising the clairvoyant faculty, presumably because the hypnotic state is favorable to development of supernormal vision; however, it could also be that the condition thus induced favors the rising into the upper consciousness of knowledge previously stored in the subconscious.

The term *clairvoyance* is also used to describe the power to see discarnate **spirits,** and is applied to mediumship generally.

For a discussion of the early history of clairvoyance, see **divination.**

Types of Clairvoyance

Charles Richet used the term *cryptesthesia* in a wide sense to cover a whole range of such related phenomena as clairvoyance, premonitions, monitions, psychometry, **dowsing,** and telepathy. **F. W. H. Myers** used the term "telesthesia" in a narrower context. As substitutes for "clairvoyance" **Henry Holt** suggested the word "telopsis" and Dr. Heysinger the word "telecognosis" but these terms would not include deathbed visions and other apparitions.

The clairvoyant experience may be spontaneous or induced by suggestion (as in hypnotism) or autosuggestion (as in crystal gazing and other methods of divination). There are four important subdivisions: X-ray clairvoyance, medical clairvoyance, traveling clairvoyance, and platform clairvoyance. The first is the faculty to see into closed space, such as boxes, envelopes, rooms, and books; the second is the ability to see the inner mechanism of the human body and diagnose disease; the third involves a change of the center of perception—a mental journey to a distant scene and giving a description thereof; and the fourth is seeing spirits.

The so-called X-ray clairvoyance is a frequently observed manifestation of the power. There are many cases on record in which sealed letters were read when the contents were totally unknown to the experimenter or were couched in a language of which the seer was ignorant. The clairvoyant often has to handle the envelope but not necessarily. In **pellet reading** the pellets may or may not be touched at all; they may even be burnt and the contents revealed thereafter. Conscious effort and anxiety at demonstration, however, have most often resuited mostly results in failure. Moreover, pellet reading has been notorious as a fraudulent phenomenon.

Examples of Clairvoyance

The following statement appeared in the *Report of the Experiments on Animal Magnetism,* made by the Committee of the Medical Section of the French Royal Academy of Sciences, 1831:

"We have seen two somnambulists who distinguished, with their eyes closed, the objects which were placed before them; they mentioned the color and the value of cards, without touching them; they read words traced with the hand, as also some lines of books opened at random. This phenomenon took place even when the eyelids were kept exactly closed with the fingers.

In 1837 the French Academy offered a prize of 3,000 francs for a demonstration of true clairvoyance. One of the claimants of the prize was the 12-year-old daughter of one Dr. Pigaire, a physician, whose clairvoyant faculty was admitted by the scientist Arago. At the decisive séance the jury rescued itself from the awarding the prize by stating that, according to the doctors, normal vision could not be excluded even if the girl's eyes were plastered up and covered with cotton wool and a silk mask.

In a remarkable case of clairvoyance, Thomas A. Edison, experimenting with the clairvoyant **Bert Reese,** wrote in a distant room on a piece of paper, "Is there anything better than hydroxide of nickel for an alkaline electric battery?" When he rejoined Reese, the latter at once said, "No, there is nothing better than hydroxide of nickel for an alkaline battery." In another case involving Reese, **Baron Schrenck-Notzing** wrote on five pieces of paper the questions, What is my mother's name? When will you go to Germany? Will my book be a success? What is the name of my eldest son? and an intimate question. He mixed the papers and presented them without knowing which contained which question. Reese, barely touching them, answered all the questions.

Experimenting with **Stephan Ossowiecki** in Warsaw, Charles Richet wrote this phrase: "The sea never appears so great as when it is calm. Its fury lessens it." He folded the paper and put it in an envelope. Ossowiecki kneaded it feverishly and said after 10 minutes, "I see much water, much water. You want to attach some idea to the sea. The sea is so great that beside its motion.... I can see no more." **Gustav Geley** wrote on a visiting card, under the table, "Nothing is more moving than the call to prayer by the muezzins." Ossowiecki, feeling the envelope, said, "There is a feeling of prayer, a call, from men who are being killed or wounded.... No, it is not that.... Nothing gives rise to more emotion than the call to prayer, it is like a call to prayer, to whom? A certain caste of men, Mazzi, madz.... A card. I can see no more."

Sleepwalkers furnish evidence of a clairvoyant faculty of vision. The existence of such a faculty may explain strange experiences in **dreams,** such as the oft-quoted story of Rev. Henry Bushnell (*Sunday at Home,* vol. 1875) about Capt. Youatt, a wealthy man who in a dream saw a company of emigrants perishing in the mountain snow. He distinguished the faces of the sufferers and gave special attention to the scenery; a perpendicular white rock cliff struck him particularly. He fell asleep again and the dream was repeated. He described the scenery to a comrade, who recognized its features as belonging to the Carson Valley Pass, 150 miles away. A company was collected with blankets, provisions, and mules. On arriving they found the company exactly as portrayed in the dream.

That clairvoyant vision may be independent of normal eyesight and exercised by the mind without the assistance of the senses is shown by a note by **Stainton Moses,** dated March 1, 1874:

"In the midst of the séance, when perfectly clear of influence, I saw Theophilus and the Prophet. They were as clear and palpable to the eye as human beings would be in a strong light. Placing my hand over my eyes made no difference, but turning away I could see them no longer. This experiment I repeated several times."

Darkness presents no obstruction. **Elizabeth d'Esperance** could sketch in the dark, the paper before her appearing just as well illuminated as the spirit face that she sketched.

The nature of clarivoyant perception is difficult to define. It is not seeing, it is being truly impressed. "In the clairvoyant state," wrote Alfred Vout Peters (*Light,* October 11, 1913), "all bodily sensations seem to be merged into one big sense, so that one is able to see, hear, taste, smell, and above all, know. Yet the images stand out clear and strong." In Horace Leaf's experience sometimes the images are considerably smaller than life-size, in some cases a few inches in height, although normally proportioned. He occasionally saw abnormally large forms, sometimes the face alone covering the entire field of vision. A clairvoyant may give a perfect character delineation of a man seen for the first time in his life. **Heinrich Zschokke** possessed this gift:

"It has happened to me sometimes on my first meeting with strangers, as I listened silently to their discourse, that their former life with many trifling circumstances therewith connected, or frequently some particular scene in that life, has passed quite involuntarily, and as it were dream-like, yet perfectly distinct, before me."

Medical Clairvoyance

An early allusion to medical clairvoyance, the ability to see inside the body and diagnose disease, is found in Hippocrates: "The affections suffered by the body the soul sees with shut eyes." In the age of **animal magnetism,** medical clairvoyance was widely demonstrated. The investigation committee of the French Academy of Medicine admitted the phenomena of medical clairvoyance in 1831.

With the coming of Spiritualism the magnetizer disappeared and both medical and ordinary clairvoyance found an outlet in spontaneous trance, or was exercised in the waking state. In the astounding psychic development of **Andrew Jackson Davis,** medical clairvoyance represented the initial stage.

Both in the United States and in England, the first well-attested records of medical clairvoyance involve servant girls. Mary Jane, the servant of Dr. Larkin, of Wrentham, Massachusetts, diagnosed her own state and the diseases of the doctor's patients with remarkable precision in 1844 in a trance. Emma, the maid of Dr. Joseph Haddock showed similar powers. She distinguished between arterial and venous blood in the heart, calling one the "light side" and the other the "dark side." Dr. Haddock's experiences were corroborated by Dr. William Gregory in *Letters on Animal Magnetism* (1851), in the accounts of Sir Walter Trevelyan and Dr. Elliotson, and in Dr. Herbert Mayo's *Letters on the Truths contained in Popular Superstitions* (1849, 1851).

With the unfolding of Spiritualism, it was thought less and less preposterous to employ mediums professionally for medical purposes. **Bessie Williams** was a doctor's assistant for some years, and psychic diagnosis was further developed by **Walter Kilners**'s discovery of the human **aura** and its color changes according to the state of health. The psychic healer **Edgar Cayce** diagnosed thousands of cases and is credited with many cures.

Traveling Clairvoyance

There is abundant evidence of traveling clairvoyance, the ability to mentally journey to a distant scene and observe events, in old and present-day records. Such ability was freely exercised by the **shamans** and medicine men of primitive peoples. **Sir William Barrett**'s conclusion in *Psychical Research* (1911) that the reputed evidence on behalf of traveling clairvoyance is more widespread and ancient than that for telepathy may be justified.

A well-authenticated and frequently quoted instance of traveling clairvoyance is **Emanuel Swedenborg**'s vision in 1756 at Gothenburg of a devastating fire in Stockholm. Kant wrote it down in 1758, having obtained the details from the witnesses themselves. This is a case of spontaneous traveling clairvoyance, not purposive, representing rather a psychic invasion by the medium. It resembles the experience of **Apollonius of Tyana,** who, during a lecture at Ephesus, suddenly broke off, saying that the tyrant Domitian had been killed at Rome.

The first known instance of something resembling real traveling in magnetic sleep was recorded in a letter written from Nantes to the Marquis de Puysegur in March 1785. A young girl followed the movements of her magnetizer when he went into town and described everything that was taking place around him.

In Germany some early records are to be found in Dr. Van Ghert's *Archiv für den tierischen Magnetismus.* The first carefully investigated traveling clairvoyants were the French Alexis and **Adolph Didier** and Adèle Maginot. President Seguier, without giving his name, called upon Alexis Didier for a sitting. Didier made an imaginary journey to Seguier's room and saw a tiny bell on a table. Seguier denied this. On returning home, Sequier found that in his absence a bell had been placed on the table.

The Didier brothers were widely experimented with in England. An account of 14 séances held at Brighton with Alexis Didier is to be found in Dr. Edwin Lee's *Animal Magnetism* (1866). Adolphe Didier was investigated mainly by H. G. Atkinson. Adèle Maginot's striking adventures in traveling clairvoyance were recorded by **Louis-Alphonse Cahagnet.** She not only found for his sitters distant relatives who had vanished years ago, but also claimed to have actually conversed with them.

In one instance, Maginot, "traveling" by clairvoyance to a tropical country, asked to be awakened because she was afraid of wild beasts. It is within the bounds of possibility that an encounter with a wild beast on the scene would severely affect a clairvoyant's nervous system.

In another instance, actual harm was suffered by the medium. A M. Lucas de Rembouillet was very anxious about the fate of his brother-in-law. With the mother of the vanished man he visited Adèle Maginot.

"That which astonished this good woman, not a little, as well as Mr. Lucas, and the other persons present at the séance, was to see Adèle putting her hands before the left side of her face to shelter her from the burning rays of sunshine of that climate, seeming at the same time to be overcome with heat; but what was more marvelous still was the fact that she had a violent sunstroke, which made all the side of her face, from her brow to her shoulder, a bluish red, whilst the other side remained white. This deep color only began to disappear twenty-four hours later. The heat was so violent at this time that you could not keep your hand on her.

Five thousand miles from Melbourne at sea **William Howitt** had a vision in which he clearly saw his brother's house, premises, and the landscape around. When he landed, he was so sure of his bearings that he went cross-country. All was as the vision portrayed.

Another case from an early record has some curious features. Dr. F. magnetized Jane and warned **William Eglinton** that he would send Jane to see what he was doing between eight and ten that evening. Jane said, "I see a very fat man with a wooden leg, he has no brain. He is called Eglinton. He is sitting before a table where there is brandy, but he is not drinking." The fact was Eglinton had made a fat dummy and dressed it in his own clothes.

In *Thirty Years of Psychic Research* (1923), Charles Richet describes a dramatic instance of traveling clairvoyance concerning himself. **Pierre Janet** sent Leonie B., in trance, after Richet, who had left for Paris. The clairvoyant suddenly declared that Richet's laboratory was burning. It was later determined that the laboratory was indeed burning at the time of the vision.

To exercise the faculty of traveling clairvoyance, sometimes an object belonging to a distant friend or locality is necessary, but often an index, say, the name of a friend or a place, is sufficient. The process of locating the desired person or object escapes explanation. As F. W. H. Myers writes in *Human Personality and Its Survival of Bodily Death,* 1903:

"The clairvoyant will frequently miss her way, and describe houses and scenes adjacent to those desired. Then if she almost literally gets on the scent—if she finds some place which the man whom she is sent to seek has some time traversed—she follows up his track with greater ease, apparently recognizing past events in his life as well as present circumstances. The process often reminds one of the dog who, if let loose far from home will find his way homewards vaguely at first, and using we do not quite know what instinct; then if he once gets on the scent will hold it easily across much of confusion and obstacle."

E. W. Cox in *What Am I?* (1874) observes,

"The description is rarely or never that which should be given of an object then clearly present to the sight. It is more or less wanting in definite outline, like objects seen in a fog, suggesting that the perspective faculty, whatever it may be, is exercised through more or less obstacle. The objects do not preserve their relative proportion of size or colour in the impression they make upon the mind of the patient. Whatever the perspective faculty may be it is certainly not so powerful, nor so clear as the sense of sight. Small and unimportant things are often perceived when more prominent objects are unnoticed. Moreover, the faculty seems to be subject to continuous variation during the few minutes of its exercise, as if interrupted frequently by passing clouds."

Cox also asks whether traveling clairvoyance might not be a survival of the mysterious power of orientation so well developed in animals but nearly extinguished in men.

Vincent Turvey writes in *The Beginnings of Seership?*,

"In the mental body-travelling the 'I' (the spirit) appears to leave the 'me' (the body) and to fly through space at a velocity that renders the view of the country passed over very indistinct and blurred. The 'I' appears to be about two miles above the earth, and can only barely distinguish water from land, or forest from city; and only then, if the tracts perceived be fairly large in area. Small rivers or villages would not be distinguishable."

Traveling clairvoyance may take the seer into the future. Robert James Lees' claimed visions of the crimes that Jack the Ripper was going to commit the following day, with an exact description of the locality.

Perhaps traveling clairvoyance could also be exploited for historical research in guiding the medium into the past. Many sensitives claim to be able to go back into past ages in trance, some as far back as the mythical **Atlantis** or the still older **Lemuria.** Accomplishments of this sort, however, are more psychometric than clairvoyant and defy verification.

Many trance communications are classed under traveling clairvoyance if the control is considered the subconscious self of the medium. A strange mixture of traveling clairvoyance, **clairaudience** or control by the subconscious of the living is described in the following letter from **Rosina Thompson** to **J. G. Piddington** of the **Society for Psychical Research,** May 24, 1900:

"On Monday, March 7, 1900, about 7:30 in the evening, I happened to be sitting quite alone in the dining-room and thinking of the possibility of my subliminal communicating with that of another person—no one in particular. I was not for one moment unconscious. All at once I felt someone was standing near and quietly opened my eyes, and was very surprised to see—clairvoyantly, of course—Mr. J. G. Piddington. I was very keen to try the experiment, so at once spoke to him aloud. He looked so material and lifelike I did not feel in the least alarmed. I commenced: 'Please tell me of something I may afterwards verify to prove that I am really speaking to you.'"

J. G. P. replied, "I have had a beastly row with [name witheld]."

Then Thompson asked, "What about?" but there was no answer.

J. G. P. answered, "He says he did not intend to annoy me, but I said he had been very successful in doing so whether he intended or not." And after these words he disappeared.

According to Piddington, all the details were correct. The quarrel was in correspondence. The final remark was addressed to Mrs. Piddington at breakfast. It is not possible that Thompson heard of the remark.

A curious form of clairvoyance is what Turvey (*The Beginnings of Seership*) describes as **phone-voyance,** a sort of psychic television in which the telephone wire apparently plays some part but which is nevertheless replete with elements of mystery not encountered in psychic television.

Psychical research has offered no convincing explanation for the phenomena of clairvoyance. In *Letters on the Truths contained in Popular Superstitions,* published in 1849, Herbert Mayo, professor of physiology in King's College and the Royal College of Surgeons, London, suggested an exo-neural action of the mind:

"I hold that the mind of a living person in its most normal state is always, to a certain extent, acting exo-neurally or beyond the limits of the bodily person, and in the lucid state this exoneural apprehension seems to extend to every object and person around." This hypothesis differs only in degree from another, much bolder speculation put forward by which Sir William Barrett: "It may be that the intelligence operating at a séance is a thought-projection of ourselves—that each one of us has his simulacrum in the unseen. That with the growth of our life and character here, a ghostly image of ourselves is growing up in the invisible world; nor is this inconceivable."

There are opinions in essential agreement with part of the spiritist view, according to which the sense organs of the etheric body come into play or the information is impressed on the seer's mind by the spirits. It is also suggested that in traveling clairvoyance the **double** travels to the scene. The objection to this suggestion is that the double is temporarily separated the body is usually left behind unconscious and the memory of the journey is seldom brought back, whereas in traveling clairvoyance the subject describes with living voice what transpires at a distant place. The Theosophists have speculated on an "astral tube" that the clairvoyants construct for themselves from astral matter to see through.

Vincent Turvey appeared to see through some such agency. He writes:

"In plain, long distance clairvoyance, I appear to see through a tunnel which is cut through all intervening physical objects, such as towns, forests and mountains. This tunnel seems to terminate just inside Mr. Brown's study, for instance, but I can only see what is actually there, and am not able to walk about the house, nor to use any other faculty but that of sight. In fact, it is almost like extended physical sight on a flat earth void of obstacles. (This tunnel also applies to time as well as to space.) In mental body-travelling the 'I' (the spirit) is actually on the spot and sees and hears and smells and uses all the sense of the 'me' (the body) which remains at home; although, if physical force be needed this is as a rule borrowed from a third party."

Theosophists have also suggested that the clairvoyant may see thought-pictures. Mediums themselves are at variance as to how they do it. **Bessie Williams** (Mrs. Russel-Davies) claimed that clairvoyance is vision by one's spirit. W. H. Bach, in *Mediumship and its Development,* contends that both clairvoyance and clairaudience are impressional. The gift is often noticed in children, and it may disappear later. D'Esperance, when a child, continually saw "shadow people" in the house where she lived; Bessie Williams played with spirit children in the garden; and most other gifted mediums had similar experiences. **Alfred Vout Peters** experienced a feeling of irritability or excitement before becoming clairvoyant.

Sir Arthur Conan Doyle suggested that the special atmosphere of clairvoyants might be the result of **ectoplasm** emanating from the sensitive's body and enabling the spirit to impress it. The cold chill and subsequent fainting in seeing ghosts may be due not only to terror but also to the drain on the body. In *The Coming of the Fairies* (1922) Doyle proposed a vibrational theory:

"If we could conceive a race of beings which were constructed in material which threw out shorter or longer vibrations (than ours), they would be invisible unless we could tune ourselves up or tone them down. It is exactly that power of tuning up and adapting itself to other vibrations which constitutes a clairvoyant and there is nothing scientifically impossible, so far as I can see, in some people seeing that which is invisible to others. If the objects are indeed there, and if the inventive power of the human brain is turned upon the problem, it is likely that some sort of psychic spectacles, inconceivable to us at the moment, will be invested and that we shall all be able to adapt ourselves to the new conditions. If high-tension electricity can be converted by a mechanical contrivance into a lower tension, keyed to other uses, then it is hard to see why something analogous might not occur with the vibrations of ether or other waves of light."

Dr. Daniel Frost Comstock, who was a professor at the Massachusetts Technical Institute, claimed to have known a clairvoyant woman with whom he made the discovery that her range of vision extended far past the point in the violet end of the spectrum where most of us cease to get any further retina stimuli. She therefore had an actual ultraviolet vision to a degree greatly beyond anything Comstock had ever heard of.

In the experiments of Dutch researchers **G. Heymans, Henry Brugmans,** and Weinberg with the clairvoyant D. Vandam, it was found that when certain substances, including alcohol and bromide, were ingested, clairvoyance became more intense. The reason, according to Brugmans, was that alcohol lessened the power of inhibition, of reasoning, and of attention, thereby increasing the power of the subconscious.

Charles W. Donville-Fife describes in his book *Among Wild Tribes of the Amazons* (1924) how clairvoyance could be induced by a drug named yage or peyotl (peyote). He was convinced by actual experiments of the strange workings of the drug. Since then, Louis Levin's *Phantastica* (1931) and **Aldous Huxley**'s *The Doors of Perception* (1954) have familiarized a whole generation with psychedelic **drugs.**

Dr. Norman Jeans, in experiments with himself under various anesthetics, found that under the influence of laughing gas (nitrous oxide) he became clairvoyant and was able to see events happening at various distant places.

A more complicated form of clairvoyance is shown in the case of the medium Knudsen, who, blindfolded, steered a steam-launch around the harbor of Copenhagen. For him to do it, however, somebody in the boat had to place his hand on his head. A similar feat was demonstrated by Gaston Overien in August 1928. With his face and eyes completely covered by a thick mask, he rode twice round the dirt track at White City, London, on a motorcycle and avoided numerous obstacles that had been placed in the way after he had been blindfolded.

Many clairvoyants (e.g., **Gerard Croiset**) have been consulted by the police of several countries to help trace criminals. Although startling claims of success have been made, there is some ambiguity in many instances.

Because much claimed clairvoyant faculty is of a spontaneous nature, it presents difficulties for parapsychological experimentation and testing. The personal associations and emotional stimuli of mediumship are difficult to embody in the atmosphere of laboratory testing. However, a more rigorous approach to spontaneous phenomena, involving fuller documentation (e.g., prompt recording, independent firsthand corroboration, background information on medium and sitter), can assist in tentative evaluation. Laboratory experiments have involved card guessing, target guessing, and **Ganzfeld setting,** but decades of experimentation have not yet established any consistent rationale for clairvoyant faculty, although there is some presumptive evidence for its occurrence under control conditions. Further experimentation with talented subjects is needed to determine the relationship between clairvoyance and other forms of ESP, such as telepathy and psychometry. (See also **Eyeless sight**)

Sources:

Butler, W. E. *How to Develop Clairvoyance.* New York: Samuel Weiser, 1971.

Dykshoorn, M. B., and Russell H. Felton. *My Passport Says Clairvoyant.* New York: Hawthorn, 1974.

Edmonds, Simeon. *ESP: Extrasensory Perception.* London: Aquarian Press, 1965. Reprint, North Hollywood, Calif.: Wilshire Book, 1972.

Fukurai, T. *Clairvoyance & Thoughtography.* London, 1931. Reprint, New York: Arno Press, 1975.

Geley, Gustav. *Clairvoyance & Materialisation.* London: T. F. Unwin Ltd., 1927.

Gurney, Edmund, F. W. H. Myers, and Frank Podmore. *Phantasms of the Living.* 2 vols. London: Trubner, 1886. Reprint, Gainesville, Fla.: Scholars' Facsimiles & Reprints, 1970.

Hodson, Godfrey. *The Science of Seership.* London, 1920.

Leshan, Lawrance. *Clairvoyant Reality: Toward a General Theory of the Paranormal.* Wellingborough, Northamptonshire, England: Turnstone Press, 1980.

Montague, Nell St. John. *Revelations of a Society Clairvoyante.* London, 1926.

Myers, F. W. H. *Human Personality and Its Survival of Bodily Death.* 2 vols. London: Longmans, Green, 1903. Abridged edition. New Hyde Park, N.Y.: University Books, 1961.

Osty, Eugene. *Supernormal Faculties in Man: An Experimental Study.* London: Methuen, 1923.

Pollack, J. H. *Croiset the Clairvoyant.* Garden City, N.Y.: Doubleday, 1964.

Rhine, J. B. *The Reach of the Mind.* New York: W. Sloane Associates, 1947.

Rhine, Louise E. *Hidden Channels of the Mind.* London, 1962. Reprint, New York: Apollo, 1966.

Tenhaeff, W. H. C. *Telepathy & Clairvoyance.* Springfield, Ill.: Charles C. Thomas, 1972.

Tischner, R. *Telepathy & Clairvoyance.* New York: Harcourt Brace, 1925.

Van Over, Raymond. *ESP & the Clairvoyants.* New York: Award Books, Happauge, 1970.

Clan Morna

In Irish romance one of the divisions of the Fianna, whose treasure bag containing magic weapons and precious jewels of the Danaan age was kept by Fia of that clan. (See also **Danaans**)

Clancarty, Earl of (1911–)

A writer on **UFO** and ancient astronaut themes better known under his given name **(William) Brinsley Le Poer Trench,** under which he wrote.

Claregate College

British organization offering courses and workshops on esoteric and occult subjects, directed by Dr. **Douglas M. Baker.** Subjects covered include esoteric healing, **astrology, psychology,** and **meditation.** For students unable to attend in person, Claregate offers correspondence courses with cassette tapes, textbooks, and other materials. Address: Claregate College, Great North Rd., Potters Bar, Hertfordshire, EN6 1JL, England.

Clarie, Thomas Cashin (1943–)

Author of valuable bibliographical works on the **occult** and paranormal. Clarie was born December 21, 1943, in Providence, Rhode Island. He was educated at the College of the Holy Cross (B.S., 1965), Southern Connecticut State College (M.S.L.S., 1972), and the University of Connecticut (M.A., 1973). He has produced several publications, but is best known for his bibliographical book on occultism.

Sources:

Clarie, Thomas C. *Occult Bibliography: An Annotated List of Books Published in English, 1971 through 1975.* Metuchen, N.J.: Scarecrow Press, 1978.

———. *Occult/Paranormal Bibliography: An Annotated List of Books Published in English, 1976 through 1981.* Metuchen, N.J.: Scarecrow Press, 1984.

Clark, Walter Houston (1902–1994)

Professor of psychology of religion, who took a special interest in parapsychology, psychedelic **drugs,** and religious experience. He was born July 15, 1902, in Westfield, New Jersey, and was educated at Williams College (A.B., 1925) and Harvard University (A.M., 1926; Ed.M., 1935; Ph.D., 1944). While pursuing his graduate work, he joined the staff of Lenox School in Massachusetts as an instructor in English and the Bible. He stayed at Lenox for 19 years, eventually becoming the senior master and acting headmaster. In 1945 he joined the faculty at Bowdoin College and successively taught at Middlebury College, Middlebury, Vermont (1947–51); Hartford Seminary Foundation, School of Religious Education, Hartford, Connecticut (1951–62); and Andover Newton Theological School, from 1962 until his retirement in 1967.

As a psychologist with a religious background, and the author of a standard textbook on the psychology of religion, Clark became interested in religious experience. He was among the first intellectuals affected by the psychedelic revolution and came to feel that properly administered mind-altering drugs were an instant source of intense religious experiences. His own analysis was published in 1969 as *Chemical Ecstasy; Psychedelic Drugs and Religion* and informed his later book, *Religious Experience; Its Nature and Functioning in the Human Psyche* (1973). His interest in parapsychology was manifest in his accepting the presidency of the **Academy of Religion and Psychical Research** at its founding in 1973. Clark died in December 1994.

Sources:

Clark, Walter Houston. *The Oxford Group; Its History and Significance.* New York: Bookman Associates, 1951.

———. *The Psychology of Religion; An Introduction to Religious Experience and Behavior.* New York: Macmillan, 1958.

———. *Religious Experience; Its Nature and Functioning in the Human Psyche.* Springfield, Ill.: Charles Thomas, 1973.

Clark, Walter Houstón, and M. H. Malony, J. Daane, and A. R. Tippett. *Chemical Ecstasy; Psychedelic Drugs and Religion.* New York: Sheed and Ward, 1969.

Clarke, Arthur C. (1917–)

Famous British science fiction author and technologist credited with originating the concept of communication satellites. Clarke has also presented two television series on paranormal phenomena. He was born December 16, 1917, in Minehead, Somersetshire, England, and was educated at King's College, University of London (B.Sc., 1948). He had previously been an auditor in the British Civil Service (1936–44) and a radar instructor in the Royal Air Force (1941–46), retiring as a flight lieutenant. After graduation he served as an assistant editor of *Science Abstracts* (1949–50). He began freelance writing in 1951 and has since turned out numerous nonfiction and science fiction books. He was selected to chair the Second International Astronautics Congress in London, 1951.

Clarke has received many important awards for his science fiction writing and his scientific contributions, including the Stuart Ballantine Gold Medal from the Franklin Institute in 1963 for his concept of communications satellites, the Robert Ball Award from the Aviation-Space Writers Association in 1965 for best aerospace reporting of the year, and the Westinghouse Science Writing Award from the American Association for the Advancement of Science in 1969.

Clarke became internationally famous for his screenplay (with Stanley Kubrick) for the film *2001: A Space Odyssey,* which received the Second International Film Festival special award in 1969 and an Academy Award nomination from the Academy of Motion Picture Arts and Sciences (1969).

With such a background of scientific fact and fiction, Clarke's investigation of claimed paranormal phenomena was of special interest. He was coauthor with Simon Welfare and John Fairley of two important television series: *Arthur C. Clarke's Mysterious World* (1980) and *Arthur C. Clarke's World of Strange Powers* (1984), both presented on British television and later aired on programs in the United States and other countries. The series was supported by books containing additional material not in the television programs. In both books and television programs, Clarke and his collaborators express a considerable skepticism, although granting a limited probability to certain claimed paranormal phenomena such as **apparitions,** maledictions, **poltergeists, telepathy, stigmata,** and fire walking. However, the great value of books and programs lay in the scrutiny of recent phenomena instead of simply a rehash of old material, and in the television programs rare early movie records of phenomena were shown together with recently filmed events. Both books and television programs therefore constitute a useful record of research, and even their skepticism is a healthy corrective to overcredulous writing and filming on the paranormal.

Sources:

Clarke, Arthur C. *Ascent to Orbit: A Scientific Autobiography.* New York: John Wiley, 1984.

———. *The Ghost from the Great Banks.* London: V. Gollancz, 1990.

———. *Profiles of the Future: An Inquiry into the Limits of the Possible.* New York: Holt Rinehart, and Winston, 1984.

Fairley, John. *Arthur Clarks' World of Strange Powers.* New York: G. P. Putnam's Sons, 1984.

Clavel, F. T. B. (ca. 1845)

Author of a frequently quoted history of **Freemasonry:** *Histoire pittoresque de la Franc-Maçonnerie et des sociétés anciennes et modernes* (1843). He hinted in it that when Freemasonry in Austria was suppressed by Charles VI, the Order of Mopses was established in its place. (See also **Collegia artificum**)

Claymont Society for Continuous Education

American organization stemming from the **International Academy for Continuous Education** founded by British mathematician-philosopher **John G. Bennett** propagating the **Fourth Way** methods of **G. I. Gurdjieff.** The society, founded in 1975, is based in Charleston, West Virginia.

Clear Light (Magazine)

Quarterly publication of the **Pansophic Institute** concerned with Tibetan Buddhist teachings and ideals of enlightenment and world brotherhood. Address: PO Box 42324, Portland, OR 97242.

Cledonism (or Cledonismantia)

Ancient system of **divination** based on the good or evil presage of certain words uttered without premeditation when persons come together in any way. The system also regulated the words to be used on particular occasions. Cicero stated that the Pythagoreans were very attentive to these presages, and according to Pausanius, it was a favorite method of divination at Smyrna, where the oracles of Apollo were thus interpreted.

Cleidomancy

System of **divination** using a suspended door key. It was to be performed when the sun or moon was in Virgo. The name of the individual being investigated was written upon a key tied to a Bible, and both were hung upon the nail of the ring finger of a virgin, who softly repeated certain words three times.

Depending on whether the key and Bible turned or were stationary, the person in question was considered to be innocent or guilty. Some ancient diviners added the seven psalms with litanies and sacred prayers, and then more fearful effects were produced upon the guilty, for not only were the key and the Bible supposed to turn, but the impression of the key was to be made the person or he lost an eye.

Another method was to place the key on the Fiftieth Psalm, close the Bible, and fasten it tightly with a woman's garter. It was then suspended to a nail that was said to turn when the name of a suspected thief was mentioned. In a third method, two persons suspended the Bible between them, holding the ring of the key by their two forefingers. (See also **bibliomancy**)

Sources:

Waite, Arthur Edward. *The Occult Sciences.* 1891. Reprint, Secaucus, N.J.: University Books, 1974.

Clemens, Samuel Langhorne ("Mark Twain") (1835–1910)

As a reporter-writer, Mark Twain manifested a great interest in a wide variety of contemporary events and movements. Reference to paranormal events and metaphysical movements are scattered throughout his writings. He is well known for his book on *Christian Science* (1970), upon which he poured out his scorn. He also had a great interest in **thought-transference,** or "mental telegraphy" as he called it, and wrote an essay on the subject originally intended as a chapter in *A Tramp Abroad* but later published separately in 1882. This was followed by another essay, "Mental Telegraphy Again," in 1889, in which he related personal experiences in **telepathy** and seeing an **apparition.** These essays were included in *Literary Essays* in the author's edition of *The Writings of Mark Twain.*

Sources:

Clemens, Samuel Langhorne. *The Writings of Mark Twain.* New York: Harpers, 1907.

Cleromancy

System of **divination** practiced by throwing black and white beans, little bones or dice, or stones—anything, in short, suitable for lots. A method of practicing cleromancy in the streets of Egypt is cited in the entry on **sortilege,** and similar divination was common in ancient Rome.

The Thriaejan lots meant much the same thing as cleromancy, being little more than the tossing of dice in which the objects used bore particular marks or characters and were consecrated to Mercury, who was regarded as the patron of this method of divination. For this reason an olive leaf, called "the lot of Mercury," was generally put in the urn in order to gain his favor.

Clive-Ross, Francis Fabian (1921–)

Active figure in British **occult** publishing. A justice of the peace, Clive-Ross was for many years proprietor of the Aquarian Book Service, established at Pates Manor, an ancient house in Middlesex. He relinquished his interest in Aquarian Press around 1966.

Soon after the **London Spiritualist Alliance** was reorganized as the College of Psychic Science in 1955, Clive-Ross became editor of the long-established Spiritualist journal *Light.* Under his editorship, the journal expanded its scope to include articles on **occultism,** comparative religion, and **parapsychology,** some of them highly critical and skeptical. Readers demanded that the journal revert to its former role as a Spiritualist publication. Clive-Ross pointed out that he had accepted editorship on the condition that *Light* be an independent journal. Subsequently, he resigned and Dr. V. F. Underwood took over as editor in a voluntary capacity, the journal resuming its stance of propagating the case for **Spiritualism** and **psychical research.**

Clive-Ross formed Perennial Books to specialize in **metaphysics,** philosophy, and religion. He has retained a critical faculty in dealing with occult subjects, believing that there is a good deal of **fraud** or self-deception in Spiritualism and psychical research.

Close Encounters of the Third Kind

Title of a 1977 movie about UFOs or flying saucers, produced by Columbia Pictures and directed by Steven Spielberg. The film—a story about a group of people mysteriously drawn to a site in the Western United States where government personnel hoped to communicate with a extraterrestrial craft expected to land—was fiction but drew heavily upon UFO research and theory. Astronomer and ufologist **J. Allen Hynek** served as technical consultant on the film and made a brief cameo appearance. Several of the movie's subplots were based on firsthand accounts of claimed sightings of UFOs.

The title derives from a grading of types of UFO sighting reports developed by Hynek; the first kind denotes sightings without contact, the second kind involves UFO reports that include some accompanying physical evidence, and the third kind designates claimed contacts with extraterrestrial entities.

Close Encounters of the Third Kind is particularly notable for its special effects, the creation of Douglas Trumbull, who also created the noteworthy special effects in Stanley Kubrick's film *2001: A Space Odyssey.*

Sources:

Clark, Jerome. *UFOs in the 1980s: The UFO Encyclopedia.* Vol. 1. Detroit: Apogee Books, 1990.

Closed Deck

Term used by parapsychologists in card-guessing tests, where each symbol in the deck occurs a set number of times, as in a normal pack of playing cards. The deck is randomized for each run in the test. This is in distinction to an open deck.

Cloud Busting

Popular term for controlling weather by dissipating of clouds through mental concentration or other telekinetic means. In his article "People and Weather," Les Shepard made an early comparative discussion of weather changers and techniques while reviewing the claims of **Wilhelm Reich;** Oscar Drummond of Reading, England; Judith L. Gee of London; and Dr. Rolf Alexander, author of the book *The Power of the Mind: The System of Creative Realism* (1955). Alexander, a New Zealander by birth, gave demonstrations of his claimed ability to dissipate clouds on a British television program in 1956. Alexander would stare at a chosen target of cumulus cloud and mentally concentrate on its dissipation.

Oscar Drummond was reported in the *Reading Standard* of October 1, 1948, as "attacking" the sky and stopping rain through mental action. He was quoted as saying, "Einstein's ideas of time, space, and relativity coincide somewhat with my own facts; that man is sealed down in a domeshaped sky, and he, being 90 percent water, is one with the wet sky, physically. . . . If such were not the case, I could not destroy the clouds metaphysically."

Judith L. Gee wrote, "My method is simplicity itself. It is the non-acceptance of clouds and rain. . . . So when I want sunshine, I just see the sun shining . . . the clouds parting and dispersing and blue skies triumphant."

Wilhelm Reich, an early pupil of Freud's famous for the concept of **orgone** energy, invented what he called a "cloudbuster"—an apparatus composed of hollow tubes connected with running water and pointed at the sky by the operator in a certain manner.

A more skeptical view of cloud busting was made by Denys Parsons in a 1956 article in the *Journal* of the Society for Psychical Research, London. He suggested that fair weather cumulus clouds normally dissipate within about fifteen minutes and account for the apparent effectiveness of paranormal cloud-busting activity.

Sources:

Alexander, Rolf. *The Power of the Mind: The System of Creative Realism.* London, 1955.

Parsons, Denys. "Cloud Busting: A Claim Investigated." *Journal* of the Society for Psychical Research, 38, 690 (December 1956).

Shepard, Les. "People and Weather." *Orgonomic Functionalism* 2, no. 4 (July 1955).

Cloven Foot

There is an old belief, buttressed by countless tales of apparitions, that the devil always appears with a cloven foot as a sort of distinguishing mark. It has been suggested that the Evil One, having fallen lower than any man, is not permitted to take the perfect human form but must have some sort of deformity (i.e., the cloven foot). It is also hypothesized that medieval Christian imagery of the Devil merged with that of the pagan goat-footed god Pan. The goat, of course, has a variety of **occult** associations, including its inclusion in **astrology** in the sign of Capricorn and the manifestation of incubi and succubi in the form of a **goat.**

Sources:

Cavendish, Richard. *The Black Arts.* New York: G. P. Putnam's Sons, 1967.

Russell, Jeffrey Burton. *Witchcraft in the Middle Ages.* Ithaca, N.Y.: Cornell University Press, 1972.

Clymer, R(euben) Swinburne (1878–1966)

For many years head of the *Rosicrucian Fellowship* (Fraternitas Rosae Crucis), the oldest of the contemporary Rosicrucian organizations, founded in the nineteenth century by **Pascal Beverley Randolph.** Clymer was born November 25, 1878, in Quakertown, Pennsylvania. He was educated at the College of Medicine and Surgery, Chicago, Illinois (M.D., 1902). Clymer made a special study of osteopathy and naturopathy, and in 1910 he was registered as an osteopath in New York. He soon emerged as an early champion of natural forms of medical treatment, writing several books on the subject.

Clymer had become associated with the Rosicrucian Fellowship as a young man. He enrolled as a neophyte in 1897. In 1905 he became grand master of the Rosicrucian Fellowship and later succeeded James R. Phelps as exalted grand master and Edward Brown as supreme grand master, a position he held until his death in 1966. In his work for the fellowship he created a number of associated organizations, including the Philosophical Publishing Company (1900), Royal Fraternal Association (1909), Beverly Hall Corporation (1921), Confederation of Initiates (1929), and the Beverly Hall Foundation (1941). Clymer was also a prolific author and wrote many of the books still circulated by the fellowship.

After Clymer's death in June 1966 his son Emerson M. Clymer succeeded him as head of the fellowship.

Sources:

Clymer, R. Swinburne. *The Book of Rosicrucie.* 3 Vol. Quakertown, Penn: Philosophical Publishing, 1946–49.

———. *A Compendium of Occult Law.* Quakertown, Penn.: Philosophical Publishing, 1938.

———. *Diet: A Key to Health.* Quakertown, Penn.: Humanitarian Society, 1930.

———. *The Fraternitas Rosae Crucis.* Quakertown, Penn.: Philosophical Publishing, 1929.

———. *The Rosicrucian Fraternity in America.* 2 vols. Quakertown, Penn.: Rosicrucian Foundation, 1935.

———. *The Way to Happiness.* Quakertown, Penn.: Humanitarian Society, 1920.

Coates, James (ca. 1927)

British writer on **Spiritualism** and **spirit photography.** He contributed articles to *Light* and *Two Worlds* and was the author of several books and pamphlets, including *The Practical Hypnotist* (1905), *Seeing the Invisible* (1906), and *Photographing the Invisible* (1911).

Cock

The cock has been connected with **magic** practice in various parts of the world throughout the ages. It is the herald of the dawn, and examples abound of assemblies of demons and sorcerers where its shrill cry, announcing daybreak, has put the infernal **Sabbat** to rout. It is said that to avert such a contingency, sorcerers used to smear the head and breast of the cock with olive oil or place around his neck a collar of vine-branches.

In many cases the future was divined through this bird. It was also believed that in its stomach was found a stone, called *lappilus alectorius,* from the Greek name of the bird, that gave strength and courage and is said to have inspired the gigantic might of Milo of Crotona in the sixth century B.C.E.

Originally a native of India, the cock arrived in Europe in early times via Persia, where it is alluded to in the Zoroastrian books as the *beadle* (messenger) of the sun and terror of demons. Among the Arabs, it was said that it crowed when it became aware of the presence of **jinns.** The Jews received their concept of the cock as a scarer of evil spirits from the Persians, as did the Armenians, who said that it greets the guardian angels with its clarion call, who descend to earth with the day, and that it gives the keynote to the angelic choirs of heaven to commence their daily round of song.

In **India,** too, and among the pagan **Slavs,** it was supposed to scare away demons from dwelling places and was the first living creature introduced into a newly built house. The Jews, however, believed that it was possible for the cock to become the victim of demons and that it should be killed if it upsets a dish.

The cock was used directly in magic practice. In Scotland, it was buried under the patient's bed in cases of epilepsy. The Germans believed that if a sorcerer threw a black cock into the air, thunder and lightning would follow, and among the **Chams** of Cambodia, a woman who wished to become a sorceress sacrificed a live cock on a termite's nest, cutting the bird in two from the head to the tail and placing it on an altar, in front of which she danced and sang in the nude until the two halves of the bird came together again and it came to life and crowed. The name of the cock was pronounced by the ancient Greeks as a cure for the diseases of animals, and it was said by the Romans that locked doors could be opened with its tail feathers. The bird was pictured on **amulets** in early times and also figured as the symbol of **Abraxas,** the principal deity of a Gnostic sect.

The cock was regarded as the guide of souls to the underworld, and in this respect was associated by the Greeks with Persephone and Hermes. The Slavs of pagan times sacrificed cocks to the dead and to the household serpents, in which they believed their ancestors to be reincarnated. Conversely, the cock was pictured as having an infernal connection, especially if its color was black. Indeed, it was employed in **black magic,** perhaps the earliest instance of this being in the Atharva Veda, an ancient Hindu scripture. A black cock was offered up to propitiate the Devil in Hungary, and a black hen was used for the same purpose in Germany. The Greek sirens, the Shedim of the Talmud, and the Izpuzteque, whom the dead Aztec encounters on the road to Mictlán, the Place of the Dead, all have cock's feet. Cocks are also sacrificed in the **Voudou** and Santeria ceremonies of the West Indian islands.

There is a widespread folk belief that once in seven years the cock lays a little egg. In Germany it is necessary to throw this over the roof, or tempests will wreck the homestead; but should the egg be hatched, it will produce a **cockatrice** or **basilisk.** In Lithuania the cock's egg should be put in a pot and placed in the oven. From this egg is hatched a *kauks,* a bird with a tail like that of a golden pheasant, which, if properly tended, will bring its owner great good luck. A chronicle of Basel in Switzerland mentions that in the month of August 1474 a cock in that town was accused and convicted of laying an egg and was condemned to death. He was publicly burned along with his egg, at a place called Kablenberg, in sight of a great multitude of people.

In Oldenburg, Germany, a black cock was used to divine witches. The heart, lungs, and liver were pierced with needles and placed in a sealed vessel over a fire, while everyone present kept strict silence. When the heart boiled or became ashes, the witch would be evident, since she would feel a burning pain in her body and beg to be released.

The cock was also regarded as having a connection with light and with the sun, probably because of the redness of his comb and the fiery sheen of his plumage, or perhaps because he heralds the day. It is the cock who daily wakens the heroes in the Scandinavian Asgard. (See **alectromancy**)

Cock Lane Ghost

Widely discussed disturbances of a **poltergeist** in 1762 at a house on Cock Lane, Smithfield, in London, England. They were attributed to the restless spirit of a Mrs. Kent, a former resident of the house, and **communications** were received through **raps** that she was murdered by her husband. The accused party retorted that an attempt was being made to blackmail him.

Dr. Samuel Johnson, assisted by the Reverend Douglas, later bishop of Salisbury, investigated the case. It was discovered that the phenomena of raps and furniture movements centered around 12-year-old Elizabeth Parsons, the daughter of the occupant of the house, and that the noises followed her wherever she went. But nothing occurred in the presence of the committee. By threats the child was frightened into trickery. She did it with so little art that she was immediately exposed. The story is recorded in *The Mystery Revealed* (1762), a pamphlet said to have been written by Oliver Goldsmith, and in Andrew Lang's *Cock Lane and Common Sense* (1894). Johnson's account was first published in *The Gentleman's Magazine* for 1763.

Sources:

Grant, Douglas. *The Cock Lane Ghost.* New York: Macmillan; St. Martin's Press, 1965.

Mackay, Charles. *Memoirs of Extraordinary Popular Delusions.* London: Richard Bentley, 1841. Reprinted as *Extraordinary Popular Delusions and the Madness of Crowds.* Wells, Vt.: Fraser Publishing, 1963.

Wilson, Colin. *Poltergeist: A Study in Destructive Haunting.* New York: Putnam, 1981.

Cockatrice

Another name for the fabulous and deadly reptilian monster known as the **basilisk.**

Coffin Nails

In Devonshire, England, superstition had it that a ring made from three nails or screws that have been used to fasten a coffin that was dug up in a churchyard would act as a charm against convulsions and fits of every kind.

C.O.G.

Initials for Children of God, a charismatic Christianity group founded in the late 1960s and now known as the **Family.**

Cogni, Giulio (1908–)

Author, poet, and teacher of aesthetics and the psychology of music. Cogni was born January 10, 1908, in Siena, Italy. As a member of the Italian Society for Parapsychology, he contributed articles to *Tomorrow* magazine, as well as published papers in the proceedings of the congresses and the annals of the Italian Society for Parapsychology on such topics as telepathy, clairvoyance, mediumship, and theories of survival after death. (See also **Italy**)

Coincidence

Simultaneous occurrences that connect together in a meaningful way. Such events may be the result the same prior cause or the result of sheer chance. Meaningfulness, a somewhat subjective notion, may vary from person to person. One person may see coinciding events as highly significant and another view the same events as merely of mild academic interest. Some unique coincidence may become highly important, even life-changing events, for the person who perceives them.

Unusual coincidences may be determined and assessed by calculating probabilities. When calculation shows that coincidences at a level higher than chance are occurring, and there is apparently no normal agency (error, **fraud**) to which the occurrence could be attributed, **occult** explanations (**magic, spirit intervention, clairvoyance, telepathy**) are given, and **psychical research** may shed light on the problem.

How complex calculating probabilities may be is well illustrated by a curious experience of **Sir Arthur Conan Doyle** told in his book *Through the Magic Door* (1907). He was staying in Switzerland and had visited the Gemmi Pass, where a high cliff separates a French from a German canton. On the summit of the cliff was a small inn that was isolated in winter for three months as it became inaccessible during heavy snowfalls. His imagination was stirred and he began to build up a short story of strong antagonistic characters being penned up in the inn, loathing each other, yet utterly unable to get away from each other's society, each day bringing them nearer to a tragedy. As he was returning home through France a volume of Guy Maupassant's *Tales* came into his hands. The first story he looked at was called "L'Auberge." The scene was laid in the very inn he had visited and the plot was the same as he had imagined, except that Maupassant brought in a savage hound.

Doyle experienced a most unusual coincidence. Maupassant visited the inn and wrote his story. Doyle visited the same place and evolved the same train of thought. He planned a story, then bought a book in France and saved himself from an eventual accusation of plagiarism. Was this also coincidence? He believed it to be more, an intervention by spiritual powers. But there are other explanations. For example, some might suggest that Maupassant's intense feeling about the inn amy have lingered in the psychic atmosphere and led Doyle "magnetically" to the book.

The calculation of probabilities offers little assistance in individual cases. For example, the London newspapers reported on April 1, 1930, that during the evening of the previous day two men, both named Butler, both butchers, were found shot (one in Nottinghamshire, one near London) by their cars. One was named Frederick Henry Butler, and the other David Henry Butler. They were entire strangers, unrelated, and both shot themselves with pistols by the side of their cars. In a case like this there is no chance expectation on which a calculation could be based. The probability is infinitesimal. Even if one in a billion suicides were by two strangers of the same occupation, of the same name, and under the same circumstances, there is still nothing to tell the date at which the occurrence is likely to take place. It may as well happen today as a thousand years hence. The improbability of the coincidence is therefore no barrier against its turning up in one single case.

Many similar cases of bizarre coincidences were collected by **Charles Fort** and his latter-day disciples. **Carl G. Jung** discussed the idea of personally significant coincidences under the term **synchronicity.**

Parapsychology has attempted to study repeatable coincidences and to measure their probability. A similar effort has been attempted in astrological studies. The truth of various astrological statements (e.g., people born under a prominent Mars tend to be warriors) have been tested by checking the occurrence of various planets in the birth charts of a large number of prominent people.

Sources:

Franz, Marie-Louise von. *On Divination and Synchronicity: The Psychology of Meaningful Chance.* Toronto: Inner City Books, 1980.

Jung, Carl G. *Sychronicity: An Acausal Connecting Principle.* London: Ark Paperbacks, 1985.

Koestler, Arthur. *The Roots of Coincidence.* London: Hutchinson, 1972.

Colby, Luther (1813–1894)

American Spiritualist, originally a materialist, who founded and edited the journal *Banner of Light* in Boston beginning in 1857. He also possessed mediumistic gifts.

Coleridge, Samuel Taylor (1772–1834)

English author and mystic. Coleridge was born October 21, 1772, in Ottery St. Mary, Devonshire. He was the son of John Coleridge, a clergyman and schoolmaster who enjoyed considerable reputation as a theological scholar and was author of a Latin grammar. Samuel's childhood was spent mostly at the native village. During his youth he showed a marked aversion to games and even avoided the company of other children instead giving his time chiefly to varied reading.

"At six years of age," he writes in one of his letters to his friend, Thomas Poole, "I remember to have read *Belisarius, Robinson Crusoe,* and *Philip Quarll,* and then I found the *Arabian Nights Entertainments.*" In this same letter he told how the boys around him despised him for his eccentricity, the result being that he soon became a confirmed dreamer, finding in his mind a haven of refuge from the scorn leveled at him.

By the time he was nine years old, Coleridge showed a predilection for **mysticism.** Consequently, his father decided to make him a clergyman, and in 1782 the boy left home to go to Christ's Hospital, London. There he found among his fellow pupils at least one who shared his literary tastes—Charles Lamb—and a warm friendship quickly sprang up between the two, while a little later Coleridge developed affection for a young girl called Mary Evans. The progress of the love affair was soon arrested, the poet leaving London in 1790 to go to Cambridge.

Beginning his university career as a *sizar* (undergraduate receiving an allowance from the college) at Jesus College, he soon became known as a brilliant conversationalist. He made enemies by his extreme views on politics and religion, however, and in 1793, finding himself in various difficulties, he went back to London where he enlisted in the fifteenth Dragoons. Bought out soon afterward by his relations, he returned to Cambridge, and in 1794 he published his drama *The Fall of Robespierre.* At Cambridge he met his lifelong friend Robert Southey, through whom he became acquainted with Sara Fricker, his future wife. Through her he made the necessary contacts to issue *Poems* (1796).

He began to preach occasionally in Unitarian chapels, and in 1797 he met William Wordsworth, with whom he speedily became a close friend. He joined Wordsworth in publishing *Lyrical Ballads,* which contains some of Coleridge's finest poems, notably "The Ryme of the Ancient Mariner." Scarcely before it was finished, he composed two other poems of comparable worth, "Christabel" and "Kubla Khan."

In 1798 he was appointed Unitarian minister at Shrewsbury; after holding this post for a little while, he went to travel in Germany, the requisite funds having been given him by Josiah and Thomas Wedgwood, both keen admirers of Coleridge's philosophical powers. They believed that study on the Continent would be of material service to him.

Among Coleridge's first acts on returning from Germany was to publish his translation of Schiller's "Wallenstein." At the same time he used a cottage at Keswick, intending to live there quietly for many years. But peace and quiet are benefits usually sought in vain by poets, and Coleridge was no exception. Early in life he had begun to take occasional doses of laudanum (opium), and now this practice developed into a habit that ruled his whole life.

In 1804, he sought relief by going to Malta, and afterward he visited Rome. On returning to England, he was happy to find that a small annuity had been left him by the Wedgwoods. He was quite incapable of shaking off the deadly drug habit, though it had not yet begun to weaken his gifts. After staying for awhile with Wordsworth at Grasmere, he delivered a series of lectures on poetry at Bristol and in London. His genius was quickly recognized in London, and he was made a pensioner of the Society of Literature, enabling him to take a small house at Highgate, where he spent most of his declining years. His remains were interred in Highgate Cemetery after his death in 1834.

Coleridge is representative of the romantic movement of the early nineteenth century, whose literary exponents wished to penetrate the mysteries of the inner self, and in pursuit of their goal often became mystics. That search was many times aided by the use of mind-altering drugs such as the laudanum to which Coleridge became addicted. Everything written by Coleridge is permeated with the romantic flavor. Apart from his metaphysical works, of which the most notable are *Aids to Reflection* and *Confessions of an Enquiring Spirit,* his *Biographia Literaria* and other fine contributions to critical literature are all of a mystical temper. Coleridge (more, perhaps, than any other critic, not even excepting Goethe and Walter Pater) was never content with handling the surface of things, but always reflected a striving to understand the mysterious point where artistic creation begins. For him, literature was a form of life—one of the most mysterious forms of life—and while he is supremely quick at noticing purely aesthetic merit and equally quick at marking defect, it is really the philosophical element in his criticism that gives it its transcendent value and interest.

Coleridge's metaphysical tendencies are equally marked in both his prose and his verse. In a singularly beautiful poem, "To the Evening Star," he tells that he gazes thereon, "Till I, myself, all spirit seem to grow." And in most of his poems, indeed, he is "all spirit," while often he spellbounds the reader into feeling something of his own spirituality. Waiving Coleridge's metaphysical poems altogether, it might be justly said that he introduced the **occult** into verse with a mastery rarely equaled in English literature.

The romantic had its dark side as well. Not only was the spiritual world explained, but often, in opening the unconscious, the world of nightmare and evil was also opened to the poets and novelists. Coleridge was no exception. Along with his mystical bent, Coleridge wrote the first **vampire** poem in the English language. "Christabel" tells the story of the invasion of a castle by the vampire figure Geraldine, who not only attacks the title character, but as the unfinished poem ends, has attached herself to her father.

Sources:

Coleridge, Samuel Taylor. *Selected Poems.* London: Oxford University Press, 1965.

Doughty, Oswald. *Perturbed Spirit: The Life and Personality of Samuel Taylor Coleridge.* Rutherford, N.J.: Fairleigh Dickinson University Press, 1981.

Nethercot, Arthur H. *The Road to Tryemaine: A Study of the History, Background, and Purposes of Coleridge's "Christabel."* Chicago: University of Chicago Press, 1939. Reprint, New York: Russell & Russell, 1962.

Colinon, Maurice (1922–)

Author, journalist, and lecturer in **France** who studied various aspects of **occultism** and **parapsychology.** Colinon was born February 16, 1922, at Chateau-Thierry (Aisne). He studied at the University of Paris, and his qualifications included licencié èn lettres (1943), diplòme d'études supérieures (lettres, 1943), and licencié en droit (1945). He subsequently became a journalist, lecturer, and broadcaster on French radio and television.

Colinon worked as a clairvoyant and healer. He took part in a parapsychological study group on unorthodox healing in 1954 at St. Paul de Vence. He also studied the new religious movements that were arising as a result of the occult revival of the nineteenth century and the changes wrought by the twentieth century.

Sources:

Colinon, Maurice. *Faux prophètes et sectes d'aujourd'hui.* N.p., 1953.

———. *Les Guérisseurs.* N.p., 1957.

———. *Guide de la France religieuse et mystique.* Paris: Tchou, 1969.

———. *Le Phénomène des sectes au 20ème siècle.* N.p., 1959.

Collaboration (Magazine)

Quarterly journal concerned with the teachings of **Sri Aurobindo** and his successor, The Mother (Mira Richard, 1878–1973). It carries news of **Auroville,** the **New Age** city near Pondicherry, and the various Aurobindo centers in the United States. It may be ordered through the Matagiri Sri Aurobindo Center, High Falls, NY 12470.

College of Buddhist Studies

An educational facility associated with the International Buddhist Meditation Center in Los Angeles. It was founded as the College of Oriental Studies by the Venerable Thich Thien-An (1926–1980) and offers a curriculum in advanced Buddhist studies leading to ordination to the Buddhist priesthood. It is currently headed by Thich Thien-An's successor, the Venerable Karuna Dharma. Also associated with the center is the Thien-An Institute of Buddhist Studies. Address: 928 S. New Hampshire Ave., Los Angeles, CA 90006.

College of Psychic Studies

A British organization continuing the work of the **London Spiritualist Alliance,** originally established in 1884. The organization was renamed the College of Psychic Science in 1955 and assumed its present name in 1970. It should not be confused with the **British College of Psychic Science,** which flourished from 1920 to 1947.

The College of Psychic Studies, a nonprofit body situated in London, offers facilities to both experienced investigators and the general public for research and intelligent discussion in the field of psychical phenomena, with particular emphasis on the evidence for **survival** after death and for **communication** from the dead. The college is also concerned with the relationship of psychic studies to philosophical and scientific opinion.

The college maintains an excellent library of some 10,000 volumes on all aspects of psychical science, **Spiritualism,** and related topics and organizes lectures and psychological counseling. The college currently publishes the quarterly journal *Light,* originally founded in 1881. Address: 16 Queensberry Place, South Kensington, London, SW7 2EB England.

College of Universal Wisdom

An educational facility sponsored by the ministry of Universal Wisdom, a flying saucer organization founded by **George W. Van Tassell** (1910–1978), a contactee and author of a number of books, beginning with *I Rode in a Flying Saucer* (1952). Through the school, Van Tassell published a journal, the *Proceedings of the College of Universal Wisdom.* The school was closed soon after Van Tassell's death. Address: PO Box 458, Yucca Valley, CA 92284.

Collegia artificum

Ancient Roman craftsmen's society. According to **F. T. B. Clavel,** historian of **Freemasonry,** the college of architects was from Attica, and its members established the mysteries of Bacchus at Rome.

Colley, Thomas (d. 1912)

The archdeacon of Natal and rector of Stockton, a Church of England parish, and an ardent English psychical investigator. For a period of 40 years preceding his death in 1912, Colley had many extraordinary psychical experiences. Although he participated in the exposure of the fraudulent medium **William Eglinton** in 1876, he was the firmest believer in the similar phenomena of **F. W. Monck.** He issued a challenge to the stage **magician** J. Maskelyne to produce phenomena like Monck's. When the magician claimed to have won and sued for the amount of their wager, Archdeacon Colley was awarded £75 and costs in the verdict. He lectured on Monck's **materializations** before the church congress at Weymouth in October 1903 and gave memorable defenses of physical phenomena in the annals of **Spiritualism.**

Archdeacon Colley first brought the mediumship of **William Hope,** the spirit photographer, to public attention, and later founded the famous **Crewe Circle.**

Collins, Doris (ca. 1918–)

Medium and **psychic** noted for her reported powers of **clairvoyance, prediction,** and psychic **healing.** She was born February 10, 1918 and grew up in Essex, England, the youngest of a family of nine children. Like many psychics, she said her first psychic experiences occurred during childhood. Her psychic talent seemed to have emerged at the age of five or six, when she stayed for a time with an aunt in Manor Park, East London. Collins played in the garden with a pretty little girl named

Connie, but was later told by her aunt that Connie (her daughter) had been dead for several years. Collins had also seen her own dead sister, Emmie.

At age 12, when her parents were out for the evening, Collins was in bed when she heard a voice warning her to get her sister Lily out of the downstairs room, where she was playing the piano. Collins called out to Lily, and as Lily left the room, part of the ceiling collapsed and a large slab landed on the piano stool.

Collins was reassured about the experiences by a medium who was the mother of one of her girlfriends at school. The medium explained to Collins that she had a psychic gift, and this was also confirmed when Collins attended a service at the local Spiritualist church. There a medium gave her a message for her father from Emmie. The message so impressed Collins's parents that they visited the Spiritualist church themselves. In later visits to the church, Collins went into trance.

After her first marriage and the birth of a son, she developed a talent for spiritual healing and also for clairvoyance. In 1958 she became president of Woodford National Spiritualist Church, Essex; she later became vice-president of the Union of Spiritual Mediums (now renamed the Institute of Spiritualist Mediums). Among her visitors was a government official from Trinidad and Tobago, where her fame had already spread. Collins's healing talents resulted in several visits to the West Indies to heal prominent politicians. Eventually, she became a resident psychic at the **Spiritualist Association of Great Britain,** headquarters of British Spiritualism.

As her psychic abilities became well known, she was invited to travel and made trips to the United States, the Philippines, Australia, New Zealand, Switzerland, and Finland. In London she demonstrated her psychic gifts at the prestigious Royal Albert Hall. She made many friends among stars of the entertainment world, including Peter Sellers and Michael Bentine. Together with the equally famous **Doris Stokes,** she was regarded as one of England's leading psychics through the 1980s.

Sources:

Collins, Doris. *A Woman of Spirit.* London: Panther Books, 1983.

Collins, Mabel (Mrs. Keningale Cook) (1851–ca. 1922)

An important but shadowy figure in the **Theosophical Society** during the latter part of the nineteenth century. Although her influential book *Light on the Path* (first published anonymously in 1885) is a classic work in the theosophical movement, Collins has received only scant biographical notice.

A daughter of Mortimer Collins, she became a prolific author of novels and other works, including: *Princess Clarice: A Story of 1871* (2 vols., 1872), *Blacksmith and Scholar* (3 vols., 1875), *An Innocent Sinner* (3 vols., 1877), *In the World* (2 vols., 1878), *Our Bohemia* (3 vols., 1879), *Too Red a Dawn* (3 vols., 1881), *Cobwebs* (3 vols., 1882), *The Story of Helen Modjeska* (1883), *In the Flower of Her Youth* (3 vols., 1883), *Violet Fanshawe* (2 vols., 1884), *The Prettiest Woman in Warsaw* (3 vols., 1885), and *Lord Vanecourt's Daughter* (3 vols., 1885).

Her later books, *The Idyll of the White Lotus* (1885), *Through the Gates of Gold* (1887), and *The Blossom and the Fruit: The True Story of a Black Magician* (1888), strongly manifested her growing interest in **metaphysics** and the **occult.** *The Blossom and the Fruit* was included by occultist **Aleister Crowley** as recommended reading for neophytes in working with **magic,** and it seems possible that the author had some inside knowledge of secret occult organizations.

Collins's husband, Dr. Keningale Cook, was also a writer, author of *The Fathers of Jesus: A Study of the Lineage of the Christian Doctrine and Traditions* (2 vols., 1886).

Collins became an active worker in the movement for women's suffrage in Britain and collaborated with suffragette Charlotte Despard on a novel, *Outlawed* (1908) dealing with the subject of women's rights.

She was an early member of the London Lodge of the Theosophical Society, which she joined in 1884. In the same year, she wrote *The Idyll of the White Lotus,* followed by *Light on the Path,* subtitled "A Treatise written for the personal use of those who are ignorant of the Eastern Wisdom, and who desire to enter within its influence. Written down by M.C., Fellow of The Theosophical Society." In 1887, after publication of *Through the Gates of Gold,* Collins became coeditor with **Helena Petrovna Blavatsky** of the society's journal *Lucifer,* but ceased editing it two years later as a result of a controversy in the movement connected with the authorship of her books. The ambiguous ascription on the title page of *Light on the Path* suggested to some that the work was inspired by an **adept,** and for some time it was implied that the source was Mahatma **Koot Hoomi,** one of Madame Blavatsky's mysterious "Masters." After fierce controversy over the source of the book's inspiration, Collins was expelled from the society. Later she was permitted to rejoin. Whatever the true source of the book, it seems that Collins sustained a claim to have traveled on the astral plane and encountered inspired teachers.

Another strange episode in her life revolves around allegations that in 1888 she was closely associated with the notorious murderer **Jack the Ripper.** According to Aleister Crowley in his *Confessions,* Collins had a lover who was a doctor and later evidence strongly suggested he was the infamous Ripper.

Sources:

Collins, Mabel. *The Awakening.* London: Theosophical Publishing Society, 1906.

———. *The Blossom and the Fruit: The True Story of a Black Magician.* New York: Theosophical Publishing Society, 1888.

———. *A Cry from Afar.* London: Theosophical Publishing Society, 1905.

———. *The Idyll of the White Lotus.* Adyar, Madras, India: Theosophical Publishing House, 1885.

———. *Light on the Path.* Boston: Occult Publishing, 1884.

———. *Through the Gates of Gold.* London: J. M. Watkins, 1887.

Crowley, Aleister. *The Confessions of Aleister Crowley.* Edited by John Symnonds and Kenneth Grant. New York: Hill and Wang, 1969.

Fuller, Jean Overton. *The Magical Dilemma of Victor Neuburg.* London: W. H. Allen, 1965.

Colloquy of the Ancients

A collection of Ossianic legends of ancient Ireland made into one work about the thirteenth or fourteenth century. It relates how the Fian heroes Keelta and Oisin, each with eight warriors, meet to talk over the glorious past for the last time. Then Oisin returns to the Fairy Mound of his mother, and Keelta meets with St. Patrick and his monks at Drumdreg. Keelta tells the saint many tales, interspersed with lyrics, with which he is delighted. The paint eventually baptizes Keelta and his warriors and grants them absolution.

Cölman, Arthur (ca. 1880)

Described by **Florence Marryat** as "the most wonderful **materialization medium** I ever met in England." As many as five fully materialized spirits were seen by Marryat at the same time in a **séance.** The **control** of the medium was a female spirit, "Aimee."

Cölman, a well-known figure in British **Spiritualism** in the 1880s, did not long remain before the public. Because of the drain on his strength and the adverse effect on his health, he gave up public sittings and retired. "Aimee" appears to have been inherited by the medium **F. G. F. Craddock,** who was exposed in fraudulent materialization phenomena in 1879.

Sources:

Marryat, Florence. *There Is No Death.* New York: John W. Lovell, 1891. Reprint, New York: Causeway Books, 1973.

Colombo, John Robert (1936–)

Canadian author, journalist, and consultant who has written extensively on paranormal topics, especially as they relate to Canada. Colombo was born March 24, 1936, in Kitchener, Ontario. He has edited more than 120 books for various Canadian publishing houses since 1960, and is especially known for his anthologies of poetry. He has hosted several programs on CBC-TV and had his own columns in the *Toronto Star* and *Toronto's Midtown Voice.* He has received numerous awards, including Ontario Library Association's Certificate of Merit; the Periodical Distributors of Canada's Best Paperback of the Year (1976); the Centennial Medal, Esteemed Knight of Mark Twain; and the 1985 Philips Information Systems Literary Prize. He also served as an adviser to the Canada Council and the Ontario Arts Council.

Sources:

Colombo, John Robert. *Abracadabra.* Toronto: McClelland and Stewart, 1967.

———. *Colombo's Book of Marvels.* N.p., 1979.

———. *Extraordinary Experiences: Personal Accounts of the Paranormal in Canada.* Willowdale, Ontario, Canada: Hounslow Press, 1989.

———. *Mysterious Canada.* N.p., 1988.

Columbo, John Robert, ed. *Windigo: An Anthology.* N.p., 1982.

Colville, Wilbur Juvenal (1860–1917)

British inspirational speaker and author of little education but considerable natural abilities. Little is known of Colville's early life. He was born September 5, 1860. His mother died when he was an infant and his father when he was eight. He was then raised by a guardian. As a child he saw **spirit** beings, including a beautiful lady who claimed to be his mother. The beginnings of his own mediumship date from May 24, 1874, when as a 14-year-old youth he attended an inspirational address of **Cora L. V. Richmond** at Brighton. He became conscious of spirit presence, and at home he passed into **trance** and delivered his first poetic improvisation. He described his sensations afterward:

"I suddenly felt myself lifted in the air. I seemed to have an enormous head and a very small body. My lips seemed to be moving mechanically under the pressure of some influence over which I could not exert, and could not will to exert, no power whatever. I heard someone commenting upon a poem, then I sat down and finished my supper and wondered if I had not been to sleep. That was my first experience as a medium for speaking, though from my earliest childhood I had had spiritual experiences and constantly felt, saw and heard beings around me, who were not in material form."

Colville took regular engagements from 1877. While delivering his addresses, which showed remarkable knowledge, and while answering questions on a variety of subjects, he was often unconscious. At other times he heard everything he said as if it proceeded from strange lips. He was only 18 when he traveled to the United States, and he spent most of the 1880s moving between the United States and England. Some of his more important books appeared at the end of the decade. In the early 1890s, he went to Australia for two years and then settled permanently in the United States, were he developed his early interest in alternative medicine (including chromotherapy) and mastered a broad range of subjects in the **occult** field. He continued to lecture and conduct trance sessions while writing numerous books, including *Spiritual Therapeutics; or, Divine Science* (1894), *Our Place in the Universal Zodiac* (1895), and *Light and Color* (1914).

Sources:

Coville, W. J. *Light and Color.* New York: McCoy Publishing and Masonic Supplies, 1914.

———. *Spiritual Science of Health and Healing.* Chicago: Garden City Publishing, 1888.

———. *Spiritual Therapeutics; or, Divine Science.* Chicago: Educator Publishing, 1914.

———. *Studies in Theosophy.* Boston: Colby & Rich, 1890.

———. *Universal Spiritualism.* New York: R. F. Fenno, 1906.

Comets

Throughout human history comets have been regarded as auguries of disasters such as famine, plague, or war. The most recent outbreak of widespread concern that a comet might portend disaster occurred in 1973 when the comet Kohoutek was announced. For the first time in more than a generation, there arose the possibility that a bright comet, plainly visible with the naked eye, would be seen by the majority of people. A variety of speculations on the spiritual and prophetic implications of the comet were made, but the comet did not prove to be as spectacular as hoped, and none of the predicted changes signaled by its appearance occurred. No such speculation seems to have occurred at the time of the return of Halley's Comet in 1986.

In the past century comets have also figured in speculations about the history of the earth. In *Ragnarok: the Age of Fire and Gravel* (1883), **Ignatius Donnelly** assembled legends and religious beliefs tending to show that the earth was affected by a collision with a comet that created the Pleistocene Ice Age. In the 1950s, **Immanuel Velikovsky** connected the theme of a comet disaster with biblical prophecy in his book *Worlds in Collision.*

Sources:

Donnelly, Ignatius. *Ragnarok: The Age of Fire and Gravel.* New York: Harper's, 1883. Reprinted as *The Destruction of Atlantis: Ragnarok.* Blauvelt, N.Y.: Rudolf Steiner Publications, 1971.

Melton, J. Gordon. "Comet Kouhotek: Fizzle of the Century." *Fate* 27, no. 5 (May 1974): 58–64.

Velikovsky, Immanuel. *Worlds in Collision.* Garden City, N.Y.: Doubleday, 1950.

Comité Illusionniste D'Expertise et D'Experimentation des Phenomenes Paranormaux (CIEEPP)

CIEEPP, founded in 1976, organizes conferences and demonstrations featuring experts in the field of paranormal phenomena. Publications are also issued in various languages, including English. Address: 29 rue P.V. Couturier, F-94380 Bonneuril-sur-Marne, France.

Committee for the Scientific Investigation of Claims of the Paranormal (CSICOP)

Founded April 30, 1976, at an annual meeting of the American Humanist Association devoted to "The New Irrationalism: Antiscience and Pseudoscience" and sponsored by some twenty-five scientists, authors, philosophers, and scholars. The moving spirit in this organization was Paul Kurtz, professor of philosophy at the State University of New York at Buffalo, and the formation of CSICOP was an outgrowth of a 1975 manifesto, signed by 186 prominent scientists, denouncing astrology. The following objectives were stated by the committee:

"To establish a network of people interested in examining claims of the paranormal; to prepare bibliographies of published materials that carefully examine such claims; to encourage and commission research by objective and impartial inquirers in areas where it is needed; to convene conferences and meetings; to publish articles, monographs, and books that examine claims of the paranormal; to not reject on *a priori* grounds, antecedent to inquiry, any or all such claims, but rather to examine them openly, completely, objectively, and carefully."

An initial step toward implementing these aims was the sponsorship of a journal, the *Zetetic,* originally founded by **Marcello Truzzi,** a sociologist at Eastern Michigan University, Ypsilanti. The name of the journal derived from an ancient Greek school of skeptical inquiry, although, interestingly enough, in nineteenth-century England it became synonymous with belief in a flat earth, and it is still used in that connection by the **Flat Earth Research Society International.**

Formation of CSICOP was an outcome of genuine concern of some intellectuals and scientists, most with a prior commitment to humanistic and rationalistic worldviews, about what they viewed as the uncritical public acceptance of so-called paranormal phenomena, often without any valid evidence for their genuineness. In the wake of the publicity and seeming sanctioning of paranormal phenomena by parapsychologists and other scientists, as well as the intellectual pluralism in the post–World War II West, they viewed with alarm widespread belief in highly speculative pseudoscience. They saw this belief reflected in best-selling books, television and radio programs, and even university courses that elevated such controversial subjects as ancient astronauts, **astrology,** UFOs, and so on to the status of factual science. Seeing interest in the paranormal as a reaction against science and reason, some members of the committee viewed such beliefs as threatening to civilization.

CSICOP initially included a number of outstanding individuals, such as George Abell (professor of astronomy, University of California at Los Angeles), Isaac Asimov (chemist, author of science-fiction stories), Richard Berendzen (dean, College of Arts Sciences at American University), Brand Blandshard (professor of philosophy, Yale University), Bart Bok (emeritus professor of astronomy, University of Arizona), Daniel Cohen (author, former editor of *Science Digest*), L. Sprague de Camp (engineer, author of science-fiction stories), **Eric J. Dingwall** (anthropologist, parapsychologist), Charles Fair (author), **Antony Flew** (professor of philosophy, Reading University, England), **Martin Gardner** (author, member of editorial staff of *Scientific American*), Sidney Hook (professor of philosophy, State University of New York at Buffalo), Lawrence Jerome (science writer), Philip J. Klass (engineer, science writer), Marvin Kohl (professor of philosophy, State University College at Fredonia, New York), Ernest Nagel (professor emeritus of philosophy, Columbia University), Lee Nisbet (special projects editor of *The Humanist*), James Prescott (neuro psychologist), W. V. Quine (professor of philosophy, Harvard University), **James Randi** (magician, escapologist, author), B. F. Skinner (professor of psychology, Harvard University), Martin Zelen (professor of statistical science, State University of New York at Buffalo), and Martin Zimmerman (philosopher, State University of New York at Buffalo).

The inclusion of such well-known opponents of claims for psychic phenomena as Martin Gardner and James Randi—as well as of humanists who actively discouraged belief in religion as unscientific—led to accusations that CSICOP was strongly slanted to debunking the paranormal rather than impartial investigation. Critics charged that chairman Kurtz was "exploiting the prestige lent by the names of the scientists who joined the Committee to further the aims of his American Humanist Society—which, ironically, is registered as a religion ('Atheist') for tax purposes."

However, Kurtz insisted that the CSICOP was not a "witch hunt" nor "biased or locked in by established scientific views," and claimed that it was "willing to consider and investigate areas however strange or anomalous they seem to the existing state of knowledge." He also stressed the social consequences of increasing acceptance of reports of paranormal phenomena, which might contain "inherent dangers" to society. "There is always the danger that once irrationality grows, it will spill over into other areas of society," Kurtz said.

The initial attack on astrology had garnered much news attention (and inadvertently brought a significant amount of free publicity and new business to astrologers). CSICOP proceeded to create issues that would keep its concern before the media. For example, during November 1977 the committee filed a formal complaint with the Federal Communications Commission (FCC) charging NBC Television with knowingly presenting questionable material that could result in physical harm to the public in a 50-minute program titled "Exploring the Unknown," featuring psychic surgery, communication with the dead, and other claimed paranormal events. The CSICOP's complaint alleged that the favorable presentation of such topics as psychic surgery and psychic healing could lead viewers to seek such methods of treatment to the exclusion of needed medical care. The FCC ruled that the complaint was unfounded.

Although it was true that individual members of the committee were receptive to scientific investigation of claims of the paranormal, the stance of Kurtz and others in control was amply demonstrated by their first attempt at new research. Soon after the formation of the committee, they began a project to check the claims of French researchers **Michel and Françoise Gauquelin** The Gauquelins said they had found significant correlation between the position of planets at the time of birth of a number of individuals who had been outstanding examples of success in their profession. Several members of the committee studied a sample of American athletes to see if, as the Gauquelin's had found with their sample, the planet Mars had a similarly prominent position when they were born. Kurtz's group declared that their research disproved the Gauquelins' claims, and they published their report in the committee's journal, now renamed *The Skeptical Inquirer.*

However, trouble was brewing within CSICOP. In 1979 Dennis Rawlins was excluded from the group's council, upon which he had served. Two years later, in a lengthy article published in *Fate* magazine (October 1981), Rawlins revealed that the research had in fact substantiated the Gauquelins' research, but that findings had been altered so that negative results could be reported. Rawlins accused the committee of willingness to cover up evidence of any reality of the paranormal in an effort to totally destroy public belief in it. Rawlins's revelations about the activity of some of the committee's leading members put a mark on the committee that has hampered its efforts ever since.

The "Starbaby incident," as the astrology scandal was termed, however, merely highlighted issues that had divided members of CSICOP from the beginning. Marcello Truzzi, original founder of the journal *The Zetetic* (formerly titled *Explorations*), had already resigned from the committee in 1978, relinquishing editorship of the journal, which thereafter changed its name to *The Skeptical Inquirer.* His letter of resignation told of differences between his original goals and those of the committee and the American Humanist Association, leaving him no alternative but to resign. For many years thereafter Truzzi edited the *Zetetic Scholar,* an independent scientific review of claims of anomalies and the paranormal.

Truzzi's resignation underlined a basic contradiction in the purpose of CSICOP: How could it combine an attitude of impartial inquiry with a stance of scientific authority when there was an initial assumption that *all* claims of the paranormal were erroneous or fraudulent? One searches the pages of *The Skeptical Inquirer* in vain for an instance of any paranormal phenomenon or parapsychological finding being validated or even tentatively accepted, and opposing voices or protests are quoted only in order to be relentlessly discredited without extended discussion. The tone of many articles is sarcastic and hostile, rather than impartial, and the frequent appeals to "scientific evidence" as a remedy for "false beliefs and delusions" often sound authoritarian.

Because of the skepticism of its member, however, CSICOP has made many contributions, especially through its journal. Its scope of inquiry has been a wide one. Drawing on resources far beyond the committee's membership, CSICOP has effectively refuted many dubious or fraudulent claims. Foremost among these contributions was the uncovering of several fake faith healers who were using classic Spiritualist tricks to impress their audiences.

Address: Box 703, Buffalo, NY 14226-0703.

Sources:

Clark, Jerome, and J. Gordon Melton. "The Crusade Against the Paranormal." Parts 1 and 2. *Fate* 32, 9 (September 1979): 70–76; 32, 10 (October 1979): 87–94.

Kurtz, Paul. *The Transcendental Temptation: A Critique of Religion and the Paranormal.* Buffalo, N.Y.: Prometheus Books, 1986.

Kurtz, Paul, ed. *A Skeptic's Handbook of Parapsychology.* Buffalo, N.Y.: Prometheus Books, 1985.

Melton, J. Gordon, Jerome Clark, and Aidan Kelly. *New Age Encyclopedia.* Detroit: Gale Research, 1990.

Rockwell, Theodore, Robert Rockwell, and W. Teed Rockwell. "Irrational Rationalists: A Critique of the Humanists' Crusade Against Parapsychology." *Journal* of the American Society for Psychical Research 72 (January 1971): 23–34.

Common Ground

Quarterly journal of the **Association for the Scientific Study of Anomalous Phenomena,** published during the early 1980s and concerned with a wide range of paranormal and **Fortean phenomena.** At the end of 1984, following issue number 10, *Common Ground*'s editor Kevin McClure joined the editorial panel of the quarterly journal *Magonia,* and *Common Ground* merged with it.

Commonwealth of Independent States See Russia

Communication (Between Living and Dead)

The possibility of communication between the living and the world of the dead (spirits and nonhuman intelligences) was the dominant issue raised by **Spiritualism** in the mid-nineteenth century, and the verification of Spiritualist claims dominated psychical research through the first half of the twentieth century. Spiritualist claims that certain individuals could regularly demonstrate communication with the dead and psychical research's quest for scientific proof of this alleged phenomenon emerged in response to the Enlightenment's critique of supernaturalism and demands for scientific verification of any such assertions.

Claims of communication with the dead have been an integral part of human experience since the beginning of history. Accounts of spontaneous contact date to ancient times, as do reports of specialists who claimed an extraordinary ability at regular contact with the dead. Such specialists were known by a variety of names, but in Spiritualism they have been referred to as **mediums.** Most Spiritualists have been satisfied that the human organism of a talented medium is the best mechanism for communication with spirits. The clarity and reliability of communication are usually considered dependent upon whether unseen operators can make use of the medium's sensitivity when his or her will and consciousness are passive. This function has been termed *sensory automatism* by psychical researchers.

Sometimes communication is assisted by a mechanical indicator such as a **planchette** or **Ouija board.** Throughout the twentieth century mechanical devices to effect communication without using the human organism, such as the **Ashkir-Jobson Trianion,** have been invented. Such devices, of course, involve the presence of human observers, who, it might be supposed, could exert a mediumistic element, if only subconsciously. It was long hoped that a suitable instrument could be invented that would elevate communication with the dead to the domain of pure physics, but, with some notable exceptions, few scientists have been willing to risk ridicule by devoting their energies to such a project. One exception was inventor **Thomas A. Edison,** who hoped to construct an instrument for communicating with departed spirits. A review of mechanical devices used in spirit communication follows.

Mechanical Communication

In his book *Startling Facts in Modern Spiritualism* (1874), N. B. Wolfe records a spirit prediction that a "thought indicator" instrument for spirit communication would be invented about 60 years later. In fact, during the 1930s a group of British psychical researchers formed the **Ashkir-Jobson Trianion** and devised several apparatuses, among them the **communigraph** and the **reflectograph,** to facilitate spirit communication by mechanical means.

From time to time other experimenters have also attempted to develop mechanical methods of spirit communication. In 1948 N. Zwaan, a Dutch delegate to the International Spiritualist Federation Congress in London, demonstrated an electrical device he claimed produced a field of energy capable of stimulating the psychic senses into activity. In 1949 Mark Dyne called a meeting of Spiritualists in Manchester, England, where Dennis Russell demonstrated a Zwaan ray apparatus, and the Spirit Electronic Communication Society was founded. In 1952 the Teledyne Research Unit was formed with Don Emerson as medium, and with spirit guidance the Teledyne instrument was constructed employing Zwaan ray principles.

Other devices included the **dynamistograph** and the **Vandermeulen spirit indicator.**

In the 1970s there was widespread interest expressed in the **electronic voice phenomenon** or **Raudive voices,** developed by **Friedrich Jürgenson** in Sweden and **Konstantin Raudive** in Germany. Jürgenson and Raudive claimed that voices of dead people could be recorded on a tape recorder, that these voices could answer questions and/or offer verifiable evidence of **survival.** The simplest technique involved merely making a recording in a quiet room with an open microphone, with a preliminary announcement, then to playing the tape back at maximum volume. A second method involved connecting the tape recorder to a simple diode circuit. A third method consisted of coupling an ordinary broadcast receiver to the tape recorder, which was tuned to a frequency that appeared devoid of normal signals.

Paranormal voices distinct from either radio signals, extraneous sounds, or the "white noise" backgrounds were said to have been recorded. In some cases the voices occurred at a different speed from the recording. They were sometimes noted to have broken through or interrupted radio sounds.

Because of the ambiguity of so many of the claimed paranormal voices and the susceptibility of a listener to hallucinate sounds from faint signals, there was initially a good deal of skepticism about the electronic voice phenomenon, but there was also much responsible scientific support. Interest in the phenomenon declined since it failed to produce results over a period of time.

Motor Automatism

Motor automatism refers to the action of the body, independently of the conscious will, in the production of extraordinary phenomena. Such motor automatism is seen in the movement, under the hand, of the séance table, Ouija board, planchette, coin, tumbler, or **pendulum** inside an alphabetical circle; in the striking of the pendulum against a glass; in **raps** when a nervous explosion appears to explain the phenomenon; in **automatic writing,** and in **trance** speaking. A stranger manifestation of motor automatism has been reported in some rare cases of **stigmata,** in which messages appear in raised letters on the surface of the medium's skin.

On occasion, the motor effects of the **divining rod** employed as a means of communication. According to Professor E. Garnett of the Transvaal University College is quoted in Stanley de Brath's book *The Physical Phenomena of Spiritualism* (1947), "During the past few months my son has discovered that in reply to definite question, the rod [divining rod] behaves as planchette. The method he adopts is as follows: The rod is held at forehead level, almost vertical. Questions are asked in usual tone and pitch of voice. For 'Yes' the rod moves forward and downward. For 'No' the rod moves backward and downward."

The tilting of the table in **table turning** séances or the gentle tapping by a table leg indicating a letter of the alphabet was a crude and laborious, but popular form of communication during the nineteenth century. The Ouija board and other alphabetical arrangements represent a simplification of the process. Raps are more effective, and they eliminate the medium's subconscious to a greater degree, but they are rarer. The planchette approaches automatic writing, and trance speaking is motor automatism at its most effective.

Sensory Automatism

Sensory automatism may involve some degree of mediumistic consciousness and is witnessed in the delivery of messages by **clairvoyance, clairaudience,** and **telepathy,** or in the perception of symbolic visions. The clairvoyant messages may be presented pictorially to the medium's mind, externalized in a crystal ball or other shining surface, or heard in seashells or by inner audition.

Many instances of message-bearing symbolic visions are recorded by **Ernest Bozzano** in the *Annals of Psychical Science* (volume 6, 1907). In one instance, a mother saw a little bird flying in a deserted plain whose wings suddenly fell off. Soon after the vision her son died.

Independent Physical Signals

In a third and further-developed stage of communication, Spiritualists have claimed that both motor and sensory automatism are dispensed with and messages occur in apparent independence through the operation of a mysterious psychic force. Observers have seen tables move without being touched and heard percussive sounds that could not be traced to the medium's organism.

Sir William Crookes recorded the following observations with the famous medium **D. D. Home:** "One of the most amazing things I have seen was the levitation of a glass water-bottle and tumbler. The two objects remained suspended above the table, and by tapping against each other answered 'yes' to questions. They remained suspended about six to eight inches above the table for about five minutes, moving in front of each person and answering questions."

At another time Crookes observed: "During a séance with Mr. Home a small lath moved across the table to me in the light and delivered a message to me by tapping my hand; I repeating the alphabet and the lath tapping me at the right letters. The other end of the lath was resting on the table, some distance from Mr. Home's hands.

"The taps were so sharp and clear and the lath was evidently so well under control of the invisible power which was governing its movements, that I said 'Can the intelligence governing the motion of this lath change the character of the movements, and give me a telegraphic message through the Morse alphabet by taps on my hand.' Immediately I said this the character of the taps changed and the message was continued in the way I had requested. The letters were given too rapidly for me to do more than catch a word here and there and consequently I lost the message; but I heard sufficient to convince me that there was a good Morse operator at the other end of the line, wherever it might be."

Deceiving Spirits and the Play of the Subconscious

To anyone seriously pursuing the possibility of spirit communication, the questions that present themselves are numerous. Are the communications to be accepted at their face value as emanating from spirits? Can they be explained by the subconscious powers of the medium, of the sitters, or of others?

As early as 1853 G. H. Lewes observed (and exploited for purposes of derision) that suggestion may play an important part in the shaping of the contents of mediumistic verbiage. He described a sitting for raps with **Maria B. Hayden** when, by carefully emphasized hesitation at the appropriate letters he had a conversation with one of the Eumenides. At the same sitting he induced the table to confess, in reply to his mental question, that Hayden was an impostor and that the ghost of Hamlet's father had 17 noses!

In *The Book of Mediums,* French medium **Allan Kardec** writes of an instance in which the medium evoked Tartuffe, who he showed himself in all his classical peculiarities. When the medium asked, "How is it that you are here, seeing that you never had any real existence?" Tartuffe answered "I am the spirit of an actor who used to play the part of Tartuffe."

But no such fencing was possible in the following case, also recorded by Kardec: "A gentleman had in his garden a nest of little birds. This nest having disappeared one day, he became uneasy as to the fate of his little pets. As he was a medium he went into his library and invoked the mother of the birds to get some news of them. 'Be quite easy,' she replied to him, 'my young ones are safe and sound. The house-cat knocked down the nest in jumping upon the garden wall; you will find them in the grass at the foot of the wall.' The gentleman hurried to the garden and found the little nestlings, full of life, at the spot indicated."

Highly improbable communications came sometimes even through mediums of established reputation. In a sitting with **Lenora Piper** in 1899, the biblical Moses reportedly communicated prophecies as well as a variety of meaningless utterances.

There have been numerous communications attributed to "deceiving" spirits. **Theodor Flournoy,** in his 1911 classic text *Spiritism and Psychology,* records instances in which mediumistic conversations were carried on for days with the spirits of friends who announced their sudden death. It was found afterward that they were in flourishing health and had no idea of the distress they had caused.

It was known from early times that communications allegedly coming from the spirits cannot always be trusted. **Emanuel Swedenborg** wrote in his spiritual diary: "When spirits begin to speak with man he must beware lest he believe them in any thing; for they say almost anything. Things are fabricated by them and they lie. If man then listens and believes, they press on and deceive and seduce in divers ways."

To some extent the character of an established **control** may be responsible for untrustworthy communications. **Hester Dowden** observed that the controls seem to have a private circle of acquaintances to draw from. These acquaintances always choose to come through the same control and are generally as trustworthy as the keeper of the unseen barrier. When the control was seeking a communicator Dowden often noticed that quite foolish and irrelevant little messages were spelled out as if spirits of the **poltergeist** type had been playing with the Ouija board.

Communications that seem to originate in an extraneous mind are sometimes followed by others in which the subconscious element is overwhelming. Dowden cited a case in which description of a haunted castle was given. She wanted to stop the communication as one of no interest when her guest interrupted and said that he was very much interested, since the story that came through was the plot of his new play.

Generally the communications are earnest and their tone is moral and religious. In discussing the various angles presented by the contents of mediumistic communications, **F. W. H. Myers** concluded:

"The high moral quality of these automatic communications is a phenomenon worth consideration. I must indeed confess myself unable to explain why it is that beneath frequent incoherence, frequent commonplaces, frequent pomposity of these messages, there should always be a substratum of better sense, of truer Catholicity than is usually to be heard, except from the leading minds of the generation. The almost universally high tone of genuinely automatic utterances—whether claimed as spirit communications or proceeding obviously from the automatist himself—has not, I think, been sufficiently noticed or adequately explained."

The Personal Character—Difficulties and Complications of Communications

The great question in all communications that originates in the subconscious is why they should take on the form of personal character. **William James** offered an explanation, that "all consciousness tends to personal form." He believed that genuine communications are extremely rare and that the information occasionally imparted by supernormal means is immediately seized upon by the subconscious mind and presented in a dramatized and elaborated form. His supposition is borne out by the observations of **Frederik van Eeden** with the medium **Rosina Thompson.** The sum total of his findings was that after the genuine information has ceased, the role of any spirit is easily and imperceptibly taken up by the medium.

What is the mechanism of communication? In the trance mediumship of Leonora Piper the controls took pains to give an explanation, later summarized by **Richard Hodgson:**

"We all have bodies composed of luminiferous ether enclosed in our flesh and blood bodies. The relation of Mrs. Piper's ethereal body to the ethereal world, in which communicators claim to dwell is such that a special store of energy is accumulated in connection with her organism, and this appears to them as 'light.' Mrs. Piper's ethereal body is removed by them and her ordinary body appears as a shell filled with this 'light.' Several communicators may be in contact with this light at the same time. There are two chief masses of it in her case, one connected with the head, the other in connection with the right arm and hand. Latterly, that in connection with the hand has been brighter than that in connection with the head. If the communicator gets into contact with the light and thinks his thoughts, they tend to be reproduced by movements in Mrs. Piper's organism. Very few can produce vocal effects, even when in contact with the light of the head, but practically all can produce writing movements when in contact with the light of the hand. Upon the amount and brightness of this light, *caeteris paribus,* the communications depend. When Mrs. Piper is in ill health the light is feebler and the communications tend to be less coherent. It also gets used up during a sitting and when it gets dim there is a tendency to incoherence even in otherwise clear communicators. In all cases coming into contact with this light tends to produce bewilderment, and if the contact is continued too long or the light becomes very dim the consciousness of the communicator tends to lapse completely."

Multiple Communications

To obtain communications from two different intelligences at the same time, one writing and the other speaking, was nothing unusual in Piper's mediumship. Attempts were even made at gaining the use of the left hand by a third intelligence for simultaneous communication. Hodgson reported that at a sitting where a lady was engaged in a profoundly personal conversation with Piper's control **"Phinuit"** concerning her relations, "the hand was seized very quietly and, as it were, surreptitiously, and wrote a very personal communication to myself purporting to come from a deceased friend of mine and having no relation whatsoever to the sitter; precisely as if a caller should enter a room where two strangers to him were conversing, but a friend of his is also present and whispers a special message into the ear of the friend without disturbing the conversation."

The attempt to write with the left hand was successfully made on March 18, 1895, in a sitting with a Miss Edmunds. Her deceased sister wrote with one hand and "G. P." with the other, while "Phinuit" was talking—all simultaneously on different subjects. Very little, however, was written with the left hand. The difficulty appeared to lie chiefly in the deficiencies of the left hand in writing.

Piper's case was not unique. Dr. David Underhill (later the husband of **Leah Fox**), in his story of the mediumship of **Abby Warner** (related in E. Hardinge Britten's *Modern American Spiritualism*), quotes affidavits and writes from his own experience that Warner often gave three separate communications at once—one with her right hand, another with her left, and a third through rapping.

Robert Dale Owen testified to the same versatility in **Kate Fox.** William Crookes confirmed Owen's observations: "I have been with Miss Fox when she has been writing a message automatically to one person present, whilst a message to another person on another subject was being given alphabetically by means of raps and the whole time she was conversing freely with a third person on a subject totally different from either."

Confusion and Incoherence

The incoherency of some of the messages received through mediums and the difficulties in communicating with the dead presented a very complex problem. Richard Hodgson, on the basis of his experiences with Piper, arrived at the following conclusions:

"If, indeed, each one of us is a spirit that survives the death of the fleshly organism, there are certain suppositions that I think we may not unreasonably make concerning the ability of the discarnate spirit to communicate with those yet incarnate. Even under the best conditions for communication which I am supposing for the nonce to be possible, it may well be that the aptitude for communicating clearly may be as rare as the gifts that make a great artist, or a great mathematician, or a great philosopher. Again, it may well be that, owing to the change connected with death itself, the spirit may at first be much confused, and such confusion may last for a long time; and even after the spirit has become accustomed to its new environment, it is not an unreasonable supposition that if it came into some such relation to another living human organism as it once maintained with its own former organism it would find itself confused by that relation. The state might be like that of awaking from a prolonged period of unconsciousness into strange surroundings. If my own ordinary body could be preserved in its present state, and I could absent myself from it for some days or months or years, and continue my existence under another set of conditions altogether, and if I could then return to my own body, it might well be that I should be very confused and incoherent at first in my manifestation by means of a human body. I might be troubled with various forms of aphasia and agraphia, might be particularly liable to failures of inhibition, might find the conditions oppressive and exhausting, and my state of mind would probably be of an automatic and dream-like character. Now the communications through Mrs. Piper's trance exhibit precisely the kind of confusion and incoherence which it seems to me we have some reason *a priori* to expect if they are actually what they claim to be."

Myers pointed out the resemblance of such communications to the fugitive and unstable discourse between different strata of personality of which embodied minds offer an example. He suggested that multiple personality may occur in the disembodied as well.

The explanations of Piper's control "George Pelham" presented a Spiritualist explanation of the communication process:

"In trance the ethereal body of the psychic parts from the physical body just as it does in dreams and then we take possession of it for the purpose of communication. Your conversation reaches us as if by telephone from a distant station. Our forces fail us in the heavy atmosphere of the world, especially at the end of the séance. . . . If I often blunder it is because I am making use of an organism which does not fit me well. . . . When clear communications are wanted you must not stun them with questions. In order to reveal themselves to you the spirits put themselves in an environment that discommodes them a good deal. They are like persons who have received a blow on the head and are in a state of semi-delirium. They must be calmed, encouraged, assured that their idea will immediately be of great importance. To put ourselves into communication with you we must penetrate into your sphere and we sometimes become careless and forgetful as you are. That is the reason why we make mistakes and are incoherent. I am as intelligent as I ever was, but the difficulties of communicating with you are great. In order to speak with you it is necessary for me to re-enter the body and there dream. Hence you must pardon my errors and the lacunae in my speech and memory."

A message claimed to be from the deceased **W. T. Stead,** recorded in **Julia's Bureau** on June 2, 1912, is similar: "When I see now for myself the extraordinary difficulties in getting messages through from this side, I marvel not that we got so little in all our searchings when I was with you but that we got as much as we did. For it is you, your conditions which make the barrier."

Piper's controls could not hold on long in the body of the medium and often got confused through the eagerness of the interrogator. The spirit of Robert Hyslop said to his son, "You interrupt me, I ought to go now for my power is failing me and I don't know what I am doing." Another time he said "James, I am getting weaker, wait for me, I am coming back." This experience was common with all the communicators. Free, easy chatter, safe from concentration on tests is conducive to better communications. **James H. Hyslop,** in his sixteenth sitting with Piper, when he adopted the methods of the Spiritualists, obtained more identity proofs than in all the previous 15 sittings.

The first attempts in getting through are usually fraught with greater difficulties. By a curious process of inversion, the recently dead individual reproduces the symptoms of his last bodily illness in the body of the medium without conscious effort and causes her great discomfort. At the same time the communicator lapses into the mental state he was in as he was dying. Hyslop wrote on this point:

"The mental confusion relevant to the death of my father was apparent in his first attempt to communicate through Mrs. Piper, and when I recalled this period of his dying experience, this confusion was repeated in a remarkable manner, with several evidential features in the messages. Twice an uncle lost the sense of personal identity to communicate. His communications were in fact so confused that it was two years before he became at all clear in his efforts. He had died as a result of a sudden accident. Once my father, after mentioning the illness of my living sister and her name, lost his personal identity long enough to confuse incidents relating to himself and his earthly life with those that applied to my sister and not to himself." Hyslop further observed:

"We may well suppose it possible that this coming back produces an effect similar to the amnesia which so often accompanies a shock or sudden interference with the normal stream of consciousness. The effect seems to be the same as that of certain kinds of dissociation which are now being studied by the student of abnormal psychology, and this is the disturbance of memory which makes it difficult or impossible to recall in one mental state the events which have been experienced in another."

The extent to which the medium is affected by the psychic state of the communicator at the moment of death is well illustrated by **Emma Hardinge Britten**'s description of her famous prediction of the loss of the steamer *Pacific:*

"That evening, just as my mother and myself were about to retire for the night, a sudden and unusual chill crept over me, and an irresistible impression possessed my mind that a spirit had come into our presence. A sensation as if water was streaming over me accompanied the icy chilliness I experienced and a feeling of indescribable terror possessed my whole being. I begged my mother to light up every lamp we had at hand; then to open the door that the proximity of people in the house outside our room might aid to dissipate the horror that seemed to pervade the very air. At last, at my mother's suggestion, I consented to sit at the table, with the alphabet we had provided turned from me and towards her, so that she could follow the involuntary movements of my finger, which some power seemed to guide in pointing out the letters. In this way was rapidly spelt out: 'Philip Smith: Ship *Pacific.*' To my horror I distinctly felt an icy cold hand lay hold of my arm; then distinctly and visibly to my mother's eyes, something pulled my hair, which was hanging in long curls; all the while the coldness of the air increasing so painfully that the apartment seemed pervaded by Arctic breezes. After a while my own convulsed hand was moved tremblingly but very rapidly to spell out: 'My dear Emma, I have come to tell you I am dead. The ship *Pacific* is lost and all on board have perished; she and her crew will never be heard from any more.'"

Just as the medium may prove hypersensitive to the thoughts of the sitters when in trance, so it appears that thought impressions of the spirits congregating around the "light" may have a garbling influence on the message of the control. This possibility was strongly borne out by the attitude of Piper's control "**George Pelham,**" who many times asked the waiting sitters to withdraw until he was through with his first messages. The assumption was that at the same time the spirits on the other side also left and saved him much confusion. Hyslop noted several instances in which the communication came through unintentionally.

The communication of names that have no special meaning is usually difficult for the controls when the messages are sent by telepathic or pictorial impressions. There is often confusion of the letters.

Hyslop also believed that the nature of the communicator's mind can present another difficulty in clear communication. If, for instance, the communicator was a good visualizer and the medium is a poor one, the pictorial messages impressed on the medium may come through imperfectly.

Hyslop made statistical calculations regarding the more important communications through Piper in 15 sittings. There were 205 in all; of these 152 were found to be true, 16 false, and 37 indecisive. In regard to 927 matters of detail alluded to in these communications, 717 were true, 43 false, and 167 undecided.

According to Hodgson, three kinds of confusion could be distinguished in the Piper communications: (1) confusion of the spirit as to whether it was communicating or not, primarily because of mental or bodily conditions when living; (2) confusion in the spirit produced by the conditions into which it came when in the act of communicating; and (3) confusion about the result because of lack of complete control over the writing (or other) mechanism of the medium.

Hodgson found that the best communicators were recently deceased children and adults who had died in the prime of a healthy life, like George Pelham, who only complained that the dreams of the medium got in his way.

In his first report on Piper, **Sir Oliver Lodge** stated that when "Dr. Phinuit" vacated his place for another communicator the speeches were "more commonplace, and so to say 'cheaper' than what one would suppose likely from the person himself." Phinuit said that after "entering the medium" he only remembered the messages entrusted to him for a few minutes and then became confused. Apparently he was not able to depart at once and kept on repeating incoherent statements.

Considering that in messages from the living the agents do not appear to exercise control over the contents any more than thoughts in dreams are controlled, it is a legitimate supposition that, in some cases, the dead may not be more conscious of sending a message than the living. Again, the communicator may be perfectly conscious of the message, yet uncertain of its receipt. The deceased Myers, purporting to communicate to **Alice Kipling Fleming** (Mrs. Holland), said, "Does any of this reach you, reach anyone, or am I only wailing as the wind wails—wordless and unheeded?" (*Proceedings* of the Society for Psychical Research, vol. 21, p. 233).

Other Forms of Communication

Communication from the dead may come in dreams. One of the oldest instances is given by Cicero in *De Divinatione:* Two friends go to Megare, one lodges at an inn, the other at a private house. The latter, in his dream, hears his comrade call him for assistance against an assassin. He awakens, then sleeps again. The friend appears and tells him he has been killed and thrown into a wagon by the innkeeper and that manure had been thrown over his body. In the morning the friend finds the story true in every detail.

Communicating with the spirits through raps is commonly dated from the time of the so-called **Rochester rappings** at Hydesville, New York, in 1848. Four months after the Hydesville outbreak Isaac Post, a Quaker, revived David Fox's idea of asking the spirits to rap at the corresponding letter of the alphabet. The Hydesville discovery was not without precedent, however, as early as 858 C.E. it was described in a chronicle, *Rudolf of Fulda.* Also, before 1848 a spiritualistic interpretation was accepted by many for the phenomena of magnetic trance. The **Shakers** experienced a special influx of spirit manifestation between 1837 and 1844.

The Rochester rappings and the physical phenomena followed only appeared to confirm the existence of another world. At first it seemed to be inhabited by nonhuman spirits, angels, and other exalted beings. The manifestation of "**John King**" in the log house of **Jonathan Koons** marked a transition between nonhuman and human communicators. At first King said he was semidivine, one of "the most ancient angels," and claimed kingly attributes. Later he confessed to have been Morgan, the pirate king. From his early identity as the ruler of a primeval Adamic race, King evolved into a more humble entity who, in manifesting through mediums succeeding Jonathan Koons, laid no more claim to royalty.

Sources:

Bander, Peter. *Carry on Talking: How Dead are the Voices?* U.K.: Colin Smythe, 1972.

Beard, Paul. *Survival of Death: For and Against.* London, 1966.

Broad, C. D. *Personal Identity and Survival.* London: Society for Psychical Research, 1968.

Cummins, Geraldine. *Swan on a Black Sea: A Study in Automatic Writing: The Cummins-Willett Scripts.* London: Routledge & Kegan Paul, 1965. Reprint, New York: Samuel Weiser, 1970.

Ducasse, C. J. *A Critical Examination of the Belief in a Life after Death.* Springfield, Ill.: Charles Thomas, 1961.

Ellis, D. J. *The Mediumship of the Tape Recorder.* Harlow, England: David J. Ellis, 1978.

Hart, Hornell. *The Enigma of Survival: The Case for and against an After Life.* Springfield, Ill.: Charles Thomas, 1959.

Hill, J. Arthur. *Spiritualism: Its History, Phenomena and Doctrine.* New York: George H. Doran, 1919.

Holms, A. Campbell. *The Facts of Psychic Science and Philosophy Collated and Discussed.* London, 1925. Reprint, New Hyde Park, N.Y.: University Books, 1969.

Hyslop, James H. *Contact With the Other World: The Latest Evidence as to Communication with the Dead.* New York: Century, 1919. Reprint, Finch Press, 1972.

Kautz, William H., and Melanie Branon. *Channeling: The Intuitive Connection.* San Francisco: Harper & Row, 1987.

Leonard, Gladys Osborn. *My Life in Two Worlds.* London: Cassell, 1931.

Myers, Frederic W. H. *Human Personality and Its Survival of Bodily Death.* 2 vols. London: Longmans Green, 1903, 1954.

Piper, Alta L. *The Life and Work of Mrs. Piper.* London: Kegan Paul, 1929.

Richmond, Kenneth. *Evidence of Identity.* London: G. Bell, 1939.

Salter, W. H. *Trance Mediumship: An Introductory Study of Mrs. Piper and Mrs. Leonard.* London: Society for Psychical Research, 1962.

Sargent, Epes. *Planchette: or the Despair of Science.* Boston, 1869.

Communigraph

An instrument for mechanical **communication** with spirits of the dead. Known as the Ashkir-Jobson Communigraph, it consists of a small table with a free pendulum underneath. The pendulum may make contact with a number of small metal plates representing the alphabet. The contact closes a circuit and makes the corresponding letter appear illuminated upon the face of the table. According to the inventors' claim, no medium is necessary for the instrument to work. If a circle sits around the table, the pendulum will begin swinging by what seems to be its own volition. The communigraph was developed by the **Ashkir-Jobson Trianion**—A. J. Ashdown, B. K. Kirby, and George Jobson.

After the death of Sir Vincent Caillard (1856–1930), a prominent British diplomat, industrialist, and writer, his widow, Lady Zoe Caillard, transcribed a book on the communigraph said to be dictated by the spirit of her husband and entitled *A New Conception of Love* (1934). She had previously written a book of her own, *Sir Vincent Caillard Speaks from the Spirit World* (1932).

Sources:

Ashdown, A. J. "The Communigraph and Other Early Psychic Aids for Communications." *The Psychic Researcher* supplements 2 and 3 (1975).

Gaillard, Lady Zoe. *A New Conception of Love.* London, 1934.

———. *Sir Vincent Caillard Speaks from the Spirit World.* London, 1932.

Communion

Title of a bestselling book by **Whitley Strieber,** author of such fantasy/horror stories as *The Wolfen* (1978) and *The Hunger* (1981). In *Communion* (1987) Strieber describes what are claimed to be his real personal experiences of abduction and painful examination by strange creatures. These experiences date from age 12 when Strieber claims that one evening, near his backyard, he was attacked by a huge insect resembling a praying mantis, which hit his head with a silver nail.

Strieber also recalls being abducted momentarily from a train during a journey with his family from San Antonio to Wisconsin. Soon afterward, "visiting spacemen" gave him instructions for constructing an antigravity machine. When he connected it to the electrical supply there were showers of sparks and a pulsation of lights in the house. The machine exploded, burning out house lights, and the following night the roof of the house was destroyed by fire. Other nightmare experiences concerned giant insect figures and a headless figure touching him with a silver-tipped wand.

The substance of the book, however, concerns events in 1985 in an upstate New York cabin, where he claims that a number of creatures came and transported him to an alien spacecraft. There, he says, a needle was put into his brain and a triangular object inserted into his rectum. The triangular theme recurs in a later experience; while reading in bed, he had an unexplained time-lapse of four hours, and later discovered two triangles incised on his left forearm.

In 1986 Strieber met and compared notes with Budd Hopkins, who has specialized in the subject of claimed UFO abductions. Hopkins it the author of *Missing Time* (1981) and *Intruders: The Incredible Visitations at Copley Woods* (1987). These books discuss other claimed "missing time" abductions.

Following publication of his book, Strieber received more than 500 letters in six weeks, many of them claiming similar mysterious visitations or abductions. He followed the book with a sequel, *Transformation: The Breakthrough* (1988), and eventually *Communion* was made into a movie. In 1989 he created the Communion Foundation to focus further debate on his experiences and research on abduction claims. By this time Strieber had developed a more positive view of the abduction experience, a perspective that soon led to his break with the ufological community. The foundation lasted only a few years; it was discontinued as Strieber withdrew from intense debates on the abduction phenomenon.

Sources:

Clark, Jerome. *Encyclopedia of Strange and Unexplained Phenomena.* Detroit: Gale Research, 1993.

Conroy, Ed. *Report on "Communion": An Independent Investigation of and Commentary on Whitley Strieber's "Communion."* New York: William Morrow, 1989.

Taves, Ernest H. "Communion with the Imagination." *The Skeptical Inquirer* 12, 1 (Fall 1987).

Community of Sensation

A sharing of sensations between hypnotizer and subject was discovered by early experimenters in **mesmerism.** It meant that the subject became insensible in his or her own body but reacted to physical sensations experienced by the mesmerizer. Taste and smell were most commonly transferred in this way, but the transfer of sight and hearing was often reported.

Curious occurrences of the same phenomenon were claimed by Dr. **Paul Joire** in an account of his experiments in **exteriorization of sensitivity.** Community of sensation was established between a glass of water or a ball of putty, vaguely resembling human shape. If the putty was pricked, the subject experienced the pain in a corresponding part of his body. This experiment is similar to the **black magic** practice of making a small image of an enemy and pricking it with pins.

Still stranger cases have been cited involving **materialization** phenomena in séances. **Ectoplasm,** from which the materialized shapes are reported by formed, is claimed to be exuded by the medium, and the physical sensations of the phantom figures are thus keenly felt by the medium. Stories of the bad effects of "spirit grabbing" (attempts to touch the materialized figures) are often recounted and tell of serious injury to the medium as a result. Vivid descriptions can be found in **Elizabeth d'Esperance**'s autobiography. Insistence by skeptics claimed that materializations were only the medium or an accomplice in disguise led to the necessity of such stories.

Apart from the materialization sessions, however, there are a number of accounts of a community of sensation. Possibly, the most gruesome instance was experienced in the course of a hypnotic experiment by the celebrated Belgian painter Antoine Wiertz (1806–1865) who wanted to know if thought persisted in the brain of a decapitated man. According to Larelig's biography, Wiertz, with the aid of a prison doctor friend, hid himself under the guillotine during an execution and instructed his hypnotist, who was a party to the experiment, to command him to identify himself with the criminal. Reportedly, while the condemned man was led to the scaffold, Wiertz manifested extreme distress and begged to be released.

"'It was too late, however—the knife fell.' 'What do you feel? What do you see?' asked the doctor. Wiertz writhed convulsively and replied, 'Lightning! A thunderbolt falls! It thinks! It sees!' 'Who thinks and sees?' 'The head. It suffers horribly. It thinks and feels but does not understand what has happened. It seeks its body and feels that the body must join it. It still waits for the supreme blow for death, but death does not come.'"

As Wiertz spoke, the witnesses saw the head, which had fallen into the basket and lay looking at them horribly, its arteries oozing blood. It was only after some moments of suffering that the guillotined head at last seemed aware that it was separated from its body. Wiertz became calm and seemed exhausted, while the doctor resumed his questions.

The painter answered:

"I fly through space like a top spinning through fire. But am I dead? Is all over? If only they would let me join my body again! Have pity, give it back to me and I can live again. I remember all. There are the judges in red robes. I hear the sentence. Oh! my wretched wife and children. I am abandoned. If only you would put my body to me, I should be with you once more. You refuse? All the same, I love you my poor babies. Miserable wretch that I am I have covered you with blood. When will this finish—or is not a murderer condemned to eternal punishment?"

As Wiertz spoke these words, the witnesses thought they saw the eyes of the decapitated head open wide with a look of unmistakable suffering and of beseeching.

The painter continued his lamentations: "No, such suffering cannot endure for ever; God is merciful. All that belongs to earth is fading away. I see in the distance a little light glittering like a diamond. I feel a calm stealing over me. What a good sleep I shall have. What joy!" These were the last words the painter spoke. He was still entranced but no longer replied to the questions asked by the doctor. They then approached the head and the doctor touched the forehead, the temples, and the teeth and found they were cold. The head was dead.

Wiertz painted three pictures of a guillotined head. According to an account of his gruesome experience in *Catalogue Raisonné du Musée Wiertz, précédé d'une biographie du paintre par le Dr. L. Watteau* (1865), Wiertz had been closely following a murder trial that ended in two men being sent to the scaffold. It is very likely that one of them was the subject of his experiment.

Community of sensation is witnessed when the medium through whom a recently freed spirit communicates takes on the conditions of his last illness and suffers his agonies. In experiments connected with **psychometry** this occurs frequently. It may also occur in **prevision.** British psychic **Vincent Turvey** said that when he foresaw a future event in which the subject suffered pain, he experienced the victim's sensations at the moment of premission. (See also **Wirdig's Magnetic Sympathy**)

Sources:

Wiertz, Antoine Joseph. *Antoine Wiertz, 1806–1865.* Paris: J. Damase, 1974.

Comparative Psychophysiological Study of Living Adepts Project (COMPSLA)

COMPSLA was initiated in 1989 to provide comprehensive, comparative, systematic, and focused study of the psychophysiological abilities of adepts worldwide (including Hindu yogis, Moslem fakirs, Tibetan Buddhist lamas, Taoist and Zen masters, shamans, and others) by an interdisciplinary team of anthropologists, medical researchers, and religious studies specialists. Such claimed abilities include thrusting unsterilized knives and spears through the flesh without experiencing pain, bleeding, or infection; drinking or immersing parts of the body in boiling water without pain or tissue damage; drinking poison or receiving bites from poisonous creatures such as snakes and scorpions without the expected morbid effects; chewing and swallowing glass without the expected pain and tissue damage; handling fire without being burned; radically modulating body or skin temperature; all methods of controlling pain, immune function, and metabolism; and unusual longevity.

The group undertook the first-ever study of Ethiopian Christian Orthodox ascetics, who possess the last remaining substantial tradition of Christian hermetic asceticism. The tradition is retained by many Ethiopians living in mountain caves, deserts, and forests who practice rigorous seclusion, fasting, celibacy, vigils, mortification, continual prayer and meditation, and yogalike practices involving breath control. This tradition appears to have changed very little since the movement of the desert Christian fathers from Egypt and Syria into Ethiopia in the third through the fifth centuries C.E.

The study concluded that many of the practices involve either sensory deprivation or sensory overload, attention to physical sensation, self-induced pain, and automotor manipulations such as closed eyes and eye-rolling. Appetitive drives are also altered through fasting, dietary restrictions, sexual continence, and sleep deprivation. Researchers observed the ascetics using breath and posture control, dancing (similar to that of whirling dervishes), and other kinds of ritualized movements, as well as various vocalizations—chanting, singing, and reciting poetry or mantras. The ascetics also practice visualization and various forms of meditation and prayer. Musical instruments and drugs may also be employed to bring about altered states of consciousness, influencing both mind and body.

COMPSLA may be contacted through the Department of Anthropology, Columbia University, New York, NY 10027.

Compass Brothers

Between the years 1400 and 1790, a guild of this name met twice a year at Lübeck. Their badge was a compass and sector suspended from a crowned letter "C," over which was a radiated triangular plate. In 1485 they adopted chains composed of these emblems united by eagles' tails. They appear to have been a magical or Kabalistic society.

COMPSLA See Comparative Psychophysiological Study of Living Adepts Project

Compton, Elizabeth J. (1829- ?)

A washerwoman of Havanah, New York, and mother of nine children who in 1875, at age 45, was discovered to be a powerful **medium. Henry S. Olcott,** one of the founders of the **Theosophical Society,** in his *People from the Other World* (1875) describes remarkable **séances** with Compton that produced surprising discoveries.

Olcott removed the medium's earrings, passed sewing thread through the perforation in her ears, and sealed the ends to the back of her chair. He impressed his private signet on the seals, fastened her chair to the floor with thread and wax, and left the cabinet, firmly convinced that the slightest movement of the medium would be sufficient to snap the threads.

A young girl who called herself "Katie Brink" soon stepped out of the cabinet. Her weight varied between 52 and 77 pounds (the medium weighed 121); she sat on Olcott's knee, caressed him, and gave him permission to go into the cabinet while she was outside. Her only condition was that he should not touch the chair in which the medium was sitting. Olcott went in, found the chair, but both the medium and the fastenings had disappeared.

After the appearance and departure of another phantom, an Indian warrior, Olcott went in again. He wrote in his book:

"I went inside with a lamp and found the medium just as I left her at the beginning of the séance, with every thread unbroken and every seal undisturbed. She sat there with her head leaning against the wall, her flesh as pale as marble, her eyeballs turned up beneath the lids, her forehead covered with a deathlike dampness, no breath coming from the lungs, and no pulse at her wrist. When every person had examined the threads and seals, I cut the flimsy bonds with a pair of scissors and, lifting the chair by its back and seat, carried the cataleptic woman out into the open air of the chamber. She lay thus inanimate for eighteen minutes, life gradually coming back to her body, until respiration and pulse and the temperature of her skin became normal."

Given the present perspective on such **materialization** occurrences and Olcott's own incompetence as an investigator, in spite of the presence of 11 other people at the séance, there was every reason to believe that he had simply been unable to detect the **fraud.** A skeptical view would be that Compton relied on confederates, both to impersonate spirit forms and to move her and the chair in and out of the cabinet without breaking the seals, using a duplicate empty chair to suggest that the medium had been transformed.

Observers were somewhat confounded by events during the séances. It seemed as impossible to duplicate what they saw in a mundane manner as it was for a spirit to accomplish the task. The body of the spirit seemed to be Compton's. However, a **transfiguration** involved complete change of stature and bulk. She was variously elongated, compressed, became thin and then corpulent, and her impersonation of the departed was so perfect that the presence of the spirit was accepted, especially since she had intimate knowledge of personal circumstances in every such case.

Now and again, in an attempt at exposure, she was seized. In such cases she seemed to resolve into her original form, and became Elizabeth Compton again in a second of time. Such seizures, however, were always followed by her collapse.

Later, Dr. **John Ballou Newbrough,** a Spiritualist medium himself, reported on a séance. He used shoemaker's wax-end in fastening Compton to the chair and nailed the ends to the wall and her dress to the floor. The medium, dress, and nails disappeared during the materialization of a phantom outside. When she was discovered in her chair again, careful measurements revealed that the nails were in new places, the knots had been changed or untied, and the had been seals removed and returned to their places.

Sources:

Olcott, Henry S. *People from the Other World.* Hartford, Conn.: American Publishing, 1875.

Computer UFO Newsletter

European publication that discusses computer application to **UFO** research and databases. At present the newsletter is published approximately six times per year. Address: CUFON, via Matteotti 85, 22072 Carmenate (Como), Italy.

Le Comte de Gabalis

Title of a strange work published by the **Abbé de Montfaucon de Villars** (1635–1673). It reads like an **occult** novel, with mystical commentaries, and has been interpreted by some as a satire of the writings of La Calprenede (a popular French writer of the era), but with an added blend of history, philosophy, and **mysticism.**

The book became a major source of information for later discussion on **elementary spirits.** The author remarks of his principal character,

"Paracelsus says of the practice of Philosophy, 'this Art is taught by Gabalis (the spiritual perception of Man).' These words inspired the title Comte de Gabalis which veils the identity of a great Teacher. . . . The Comte's true identity will be widely recognized."

The poet Alexander Pope, in his dedication to *The Rape of the Lock,* first drafted in 1711, states,

"The Rosicrucians are a people I must bring you acquainted with. The best account I know of them is in a French book call'd *Le Comte de Gabalis,* which both in its title and size is so like a Novel, that many of the Fair Sex have read it for one by mistake. According to these Gentlemen, the four Elements are inhabited by Spirits, which they call Sylphs, Gnomes, Nymphs, and Salamanders . . . they say, any mortals may enjoy the most intimate familiarities with these gentle Spirits, upon a condition very easy to all true Adepts, an inviolate preservation of Chastity."

The book is also cited by **Bulwer Lytton** (1803–1873) in his occult novel *Zanoni.*

Sources:

de Villars, Abbé. *Comte de Gabalis.* 1821. Reprint, London: Methuen, 1941.

Lytton, Edward Bulwar. *Zanoni.* London: Saunders & Otley, 1842. Reprinted as *Zanoni: A Rosicrucian Tale.* Blauvelt, N.Y.: Rudolf Steiner Publications, 1971.

Pope, Alexander. *The Rape of the Lock.* N.p., 1821. Reprint, London: Methuen, 1941.

Conan Mac Morna

A figure in the Ossianic cycle of Irish legend, described as scoffing and deriding all that was high and noble. One day while hunting, he and other Fians entered a magnificent palace that they found empty, and began to feast. It soon became apparent, however, that the palace was enchanted, and the walls shrank to the size of a fox's hole. Conan seemed to be unaware of the danger and continued to eat, but two of the Fians pulled him off his chair, to which some of his skin stuck. A black sheepskin was placed on his back to soothe the pain. The sheepskin adhered to his back and he wore it until he died.

Conant, Mrs. J. H. (1831–1875)

American medium who, through the generosity of **Luther Colby,** editor of *The Banner of Light,* gave, for the last 17 years of her life, free public séances in Boston. Her trance messages, characterized by the impersonation of the departed, were published weekly in the *Banner.*

Conant was known in Spiritualist circles as both an inspirational speaker and a platform healer. For her medical diagnosis the medium relied on the spirit of Dr. John Dix Fisher, an old Boston physician.

While in trance she believed herself to be outside her body and wandering about, and on occasion her **double** was believed to manifest through other mediums. She also wrote automatically in trance, and reportedly spoke in many languages unknown to her especially in various Indian dialects, an ability known as **xenoglossia.**

Sources:

Putnam, Allen, comp. *Flashes of Light from the Spirit-Land.* Boston: William White, 1872.

———. *Biography of Mrs. J. H. Conant.* Boston: W. White and Co., 1873.

Conary Mor

A legendary high king of Ireland. It is said that his great-grandfather destroyed the Fairy Mound of Bri-Leith, and thus brought ill fate upon Conary Mor. As a child, he left his three foster brothers on the Plains of Liffey and followed a flock of beautiful birds down to the shore. The birds were transformed into armed men, who told him they belonged to his father and were his kin. His *geise* (**taboo**) was made known to him, and later he was proclaimed king of Erin.

His reign was prosperous, until the **Danaans** lured him to break his *geise.* It is told how Conary, dying of thirst after battle, sent his warrior Mac Cecht to bring him water. Mac Cecht had much difficulty in obtaining the water, and on his return, he found Conary had been beheaded. The water, however, was raised to the mouth of the bodiless head, which, it is said, thanked Mac Cecht for his deed.

Condon, Edward U(hler) (1902–1974)

Professor of physics at the University of Colorado, and director of the study on **UFOs** (unidentified flying objects) commissioned by the U.S. Air Force and conducted by the University of Colorado in the late 1960s. The **Condon Report,** officially titled the *Scientific Study of Unidentified Flying Objects,* was released by the U.S. government in 1969.

An outspoken and controversial figure, Condon spent two years doing research in Germany after obtaining a Ph.D. in physics from the University of California in 1926. He was assistant professor of physics at Princeton University (1928–29), professor of theoretical physics at the University of Minnesota, and associate professor at Princeton (1930–37). During World War II he was associate director of the Westinghouse Research Laboratories and participated in the development of radar and the atom bomb. After the war he became director of the National Bureau of Standards, U.S. Department of Consumers (1945–51), and subsequently headed the research and development division of Corning Glass Works (1951–54).

In the late 1940s Condon was attacked by the House Un-American Activities Committee for allegedly "consorting with communists." At the time he was a special adviser to the Special Senate Committee on Atomic Energy of the Congress. Following the "witch-hunts" of the period, and after clashing with Richard Nixon, his security clearance was revoked in 1953 and 1954. He resigned from Corning Glass Works and returned to an academic career. From 1956 to 1963, he was Wayman Crow Professor of Physics at Washington University, and he joined the University of Colorado faculty in 1963 as a professor in the Department of Physics and Astrophysics and fellow in the Joint Institute for Laboratory Astrophysics.

Condon's main conclusion was that further studies of UFO phenomena would not be of scientific benefit. He rejected the hypothesis of extraterrestrial origins of UFOs. Not surprisingly, he was condemned by many UFO enthusiasts as a debunker of the subject. He did not personally conduct field investigations while preparing this report. Condon retired after the report appeared and was named emeritus professor in 1970. He died in 1974.

Sources:

Condon, Edward U. "UFOs I Have Loved and Lost." *Bulletin of the Atomic Scientists* (December 1969).

Condon Report

Popular name for the Scientific Study of Unidentified Flying Objects, written by Edward U. Condon, edited by Daniel S. Gillmor, and released by the U.S. government in 1969. The project grew out of a critical review of Project Blue Book, the U.S. Air Force structure for reviewing **UFO** reports, by the Air Force's Scientific Advisory Board in March 1966. The next month, a hearing on UFOs was conducted by the U.S. House of Representatives Armed Services Committee.

Subsequently commissioned by the U.S. Air Force, the Condon study occupied 15 months investigation of reports of unidentified flying objects. The report was skeptical and ascribed most UFO sightings to weather balloons, stars, birds, insects, optical illusions, or atmospheric phenomena. The tone and conclusions of the report flatly repudiated earlier rumors that the U.S. government accepted the reality of flying saucers, stating, "Our general conclusion is that nothing has come from the study of UFOs in the past 21 years that has added to scientific knowledge." As a result, the U.S. Air Force canceled Project Blue Book in December 1969, and, as a whole, ufology entered a period of decline.

During the writing of the report a controversy arose as charges were made that the study was a sham and that Condon had already reached his conclusions before the project began. Several UFO groups withdrew their support. Ufologists who read the report noted that many of the cases cited had no assigned explanation. Slowly a reaction built. In 1972 **J. Allen Hynek** wrote *The UFO Experience,* in which he critiques the report and charges the Air Force with incompetence in handling UFO reports. The following year he founded the Center for UFO Studies (now the **J. Allen Hynek Center for UFO Studies**).

Sources:

Hynek, J. Allen. *The UFO Experience: A Scientific Enquiry.* Chicago: Henry Regnery, 1972.

Condon, Edward U. *Scientific Study of Unidentified Flying Objects.* Springfield, Va.: National Technical Information Service, 1968. Reprint, New York: E. P. Dutton, 1970.

Saunders, David R., and R. Roger Hawkins. *UFOs? Yes! Where the Condon Committee Went Wrong.* New York: World, 1968. Reprint, New York: New American Library, 1968.

Conferentes

Gods of the ancients. Spoken of by Arnobius (a Christian convert from saganism) and identified by **Pierre Le Loyer** with the **incubus.**

Congress of Astrological Organizations

Founded in 1973 to promote the general welfare and interest of members and to stimulate and increase their cooperation in all matters affecting their interest in astrology; to establish, improve, and promote standards in the field of astrology; to eliminate abuses of and unfair practices in the practice of astrology; to promote and cultivate a spirit of harmony among all astrologers; and to settle disputes arising among members.

The Congress of Astrological Organizations conducts research programs, provides technical assistance, maintains a collection of scientific research materials relating to astrology, and conducts a speakers bureau. It publishes *CAO Times* and an occasional newsletter. Current membership of some 50 organizations represents some 6,000 individuals. Address: PO Box 75, Old Chelsea Station, New York, NY 10113.

Conjuretors

Magicians who claimed to have the power to evoke demons and tempests.

Conjuring

To conjure originally meant to call up spirits or practice magic arts, but in the course of time a secondary meaning of sleight of hand displaced the earlier meaning, and the term now indicates trickery or deception (usually for entertainment). In the United States, the term *magic* is usually used for conjuring, although this too originally had an occult meaning. The blurring of the occult and stage magic occurred in the late nineteenth century when so many mediums passed off stage illusions as genuine Spiritualist phenomena.

Sources:

Evans, Henry Ridgeley. *The Old and New Magic.* Chicago: Open Court Publishing, 1909.

Conklin, J. B. (ca. 1862)

Nineteenth-century American "test medium" who gave answers from departed relatives to mental questions of the sitters and also did **pellet reading.**

Conklin's chief claim to fame was the patronage of President **Abraham Lincoln.** After Lincoln's election, Conklin stated in *The Cleveland Plaindealer* that the President-elect was a Spiritualist. Lincoln did not deny the statement, and it is recorded that for four successive Sundays, prior to the issue of the antislavery proclamation, Conklin was a guest at the presidential mansion. The spirit messages delivered by Conklin were reported to have greatly strengthened the president's determination to make the historic step.

Sources:

Britten, Emma Hardinge. *Nineteenth Century Miracles.* New York: William Britten, 1884.

Cooper, Robert. *Spiritual Experiences.* London: Heywood & Co., 1867.

Shelton, Harriet M. *Abraham Lincoln Returns.* New York: Evans Publishing, 1957.

Conselheiro, Antonio (1835–1897)

Brazilian millennialist and religious leader who prophesied that the world would end in the year 1900. Born Antonio Vicente Medes Macial, son of poverty-stricken landowners in northeastern Brazil, he became a wandering preacher and acquired the name "Conselheiro" (the Counsellor) from the peasants, who respected his judgment.

His influence spread rapidly, and after the establishment of the Republic of Brazil in 1889, his preaching led to skirmishes with the authorities. After proclaiming the imminent end of the world, he formed a community of the faithful in the remote northern village of Canudos. Several military campaigns were undertaken by the government against his community, but the troops were repelled.

In 1897 Conselheiro became ill (possibly through dysentery) and died. Soon afterward his millenialists were defeated.

Sources:

Cunninghame, Graham R. B. *A Brazilian Mystic: Being the Life and Miracles of Antonio Conselheiro.* London: Heineman, 1920. Reprint, Freeport, N.Y.: Books for Libraries Press, 1971.

Levine, Robert M. *Vale of Tears: Revisiting the Canudos Massacre in Northeastern Brazil.* Berkeley, Calif.: University of California Press, 1992.

Macedo, Nertan. *Antonio Conselheiro.* N.p.: Graf Record, 1969.

Contact International

Former international **UFO** organization founded in Britain in 1967 by **Brinsley Le Poer Trench** (earl of Clancarty), the British peer who introduced the first debate on UFOs in the British House of Lords, the upper chamber of the British Parliament, on January 18, 1979. During the 1980s the organization had members in more than thirty countries. It published a quarterly journal, *Awareness,* containing UFO world reports and personal experiences, as well as a biannual *UFO Register,* which sought to present accurate information on UFO phenomena.

"Le Conte del Graal"

One of the "Quest" versions of the legend of the **Holy Grail** (Graal). It was the last of a series of works of medieval romance written by Chrétien de Troyes, a twelfth-century French writer. Chrétien favored the Arthurian legends and he wrote one volume on Lancelot and King Arthur's court that formed the background of several other books. *Le Conte del Graal* told how Perceval was reared to the life of a forester by his mother, but forsaking her became a member of the court of **King Arthur.** Perceval went forth as a knight-errant, and his numerous adventures are recited.

In the middle of the story, the adventures of Gauvain, another of the knights, are fully detailed. However, in the end Chrétien returns to Perceval, who ventures forth again and wanders about for five years in a godless state of mind. One Good Friday he meets with a band of pilgrims who remonstrate him for riding armed on a holy day, and he turns aside to confess to a hermit who turns out to be his uncle. From him he learns that only the sinless can find the Grail, and that he sinned in abandoning his mother and thus causing her death. He had also taken a lady, Balncheflor, but he never returned to her from his wanderings.

Le Conte del Graal was not completed, but copies were circulated, read, and deeply influenced later writers of the Arthurian tales, who developed the story of Perceval and filled in many details of the Graal legend. Chrétien never identifies the Graal, but its juxtaposition with Good Friday caused later authors to identify it with the cup of Christ's Last Supper.

Sources:

Chrétien de Troyes. *Le Conte del Graal (Perceval).* Edited by Félix Lecoy. Paris: Champion, 1973.

Lacy, Norris J., ed. *The Arthurian Encyclopedia.* New York: Garland Publishing, 1986.

Control

A term designating the spirit entity that works with a **medium** from "the other side" and who takes charge of the **séance** proceedings while the medium is in a trance. This operator might also be called a **guide.** Generally, the term implies enduring attendance by a distinct and continuous personality who uses the entranced medium's body. Some controls, such as **Arthur Ford**'s "Fletcher," became almost as famous as the medium. In some ways, the control resembles the regular entities that speak through channels and deliver a body of teachings. In fact, controls often deliver a brief message at the beginning of séances, but their primary function is to direct the orderly contact of various spirit entities with the people present. The apparent motive of controls is to do good, to be of service, and to work out their salvation.

Spiritualists, who view the medium as a bridge to a lively world of spirit entities, believe the control performs a variety of functions during the séance: delivering direct or relayed messages to sitters, keeping order among those who rushed to the "light" (emanating from the "other side"), keeping away undeveloped or evil spirits, and occasionally getting out of the way to allow the entity to communicate directly to others.

Spiritualists claim that the body of the medium is an instrument that requires considerable practice in efficient handling.

The control is a communication expert that watches over the fluency of the proceedings and often steps in to explain or repeat unintelligible expressions. The conversational aspect of the séances is largely due to the control's presence.

The nature of the control entity and the manner in which the control functions remains unclear. There are, of course, a variety of opinions on exactly what a control is. Today, many non-Spiritualists, especially psychological scientists, consider the control a part of the medium's personality. Others—even more skeptical in light of the significant amount of fraud found among mediums in the early twentieth century—tend to write off controls as mundane creations of mediums. Spiritualists suggest that the controls' long-term attendance of mediums is considered on the other side as a kind of missionary work, or as an occasional opportunity for experimental research.

Some of the most critical pieces of evidence to be considered in assessing the nature of spirit controls suggest that some entities at séances may be artificial personalities created from the unconscious attitudes and thoughts of the sitters. In September 1972, a group of experimenters at the Toronto Society for Psychical Research in Canada created an artificial entity named "**Philip**" by meditating on his history, characteristics, and appearance as decided on by the group. After negative results for nearly a year, the group adopted the conventional Spiritualist séance method and soon received messages from Philip through table rapping. Some spirit guides and controls are obviously synthetic and illusory, as in the deliberate creation of Philip; however, it may be that the momentary acceptance of them as real personalities can favorably influence paranormal phenomena.

The Human Qualities of Controls

There is a human element in the process of establishing a control's presence. Among the spirit entities, there may be a struggle for the post, and an established control may be replaced by another, as witnessed in the case of **Leonora Piper.** The struggle for control is often conveyed to the medium by broken communications and spasmodic movements of the hand or of the traveler on the **ouija board.**

The character and limitation of the controls also bear the human stamp. They may have a large experience in life in the beyond, yet, in answer to questions, they often confess ignorance and reply that they will inquire from another who knows. They tend to be patient, and during the days of physical phenomena were ready to produce such phenomena to the sitters' satisfaction. But they seem adverse to taking orders; they expect courteous treatment, appreciation for what they do, and have their own caprices. Often they bring a religious atmosphere but few of them seem of saintly disposition. "Walter," the control of **Mina Crandon** (Margery) cursed freely if something displeased him and sent cantankerous objectors to the devil. In his righteous indignation against **Houdini** he accused him of cheating, swore terribly, called down curses on his head, and used the most fearful language.

"Eyen," the Egyptian control of Mrs. Travers Smith (**Hester Dowden**), who claimed to have been a priest of Isis in the reign of Ramses II, also cursed and swore in verse against a member of the circle who drove him out by hypnotic suggestion given to the medium. "Peter," another control of Smith, was similar to "Walter," in that he attached himself to the circle to satisfy his own curiosity and conduct psychical experiments from the other side. He was excellent in devising tests, but otherwise his character left little to be desired.

The power of constant controls is usually greater than that of incidental communicators, and often appears to be specific. "I have only power for voices," said **Cristo d'Angelo,** when he was requested to be the control at the Rossi sittings. This is a curious parallel with similar limitations on the part of mediums and supports the theory that the control, in relation to other spirits, is just as psychic as the medium in relation to the sitters. For instance, in Cristo d'Angelo's case some spirits, if too weak to reach the sitter on their own voice vibrations, came through that of the control, which resulted in a blending of accent and occasional predomination of the timbre of the control.

During the period when mediums were under widespread scrutiny, the controls became central to physical effects (an understanding of which has to be integrated with the belief that the majority of the physical mediums were discovered in some form of fraud). Consequently, the controls often had helpers (some would term them "confederates"), other spirits who prepared difficult physical phenomena while a message was being delivered. These helpers sometimes assisted in the control as well, increasing the coherence of the messages.

Many instances of blunders by controls were recorded in the scripts of **Stainton Moses.** Once, heavy volumes of phosphoric smoke were produced, scaring the medium as he was enveloped in fire. It was explained afterward that an accident happened during the production of the psychic lights (see **luminous phenomena**). Another time, a perfume-producing experiment miscarried and the sitters were driven out of the room by an unbearable stench.

Sometimes harm reportedly occurred to the medium because of the control's negligence or careless overdraft of power. Occasionally controls failed in their capacity as doorkeepers and undesirable, malignant elements invaded the séance room. In such cases they immediately ordered the closing of the sitting. When the medium awakened from trance, the control disappeared. The control could not communicate anymore but might be watchful and desirous of sending a message. Mrs. Piper occasionally received such messages through her own entranced daughters.

The presence of the control was made known by various means. The voice in direct speaking, the character of the handwriting or the sensation experienced in **automatic writing,** the peculiar style of rapping or tilting of the table, or mannerisms disclosed the control's identity. Physiological observations may have also furnished proof. **Sir Arthur Conan Doyle** found that the pulse of medium John Tichnor beat 100 when controlled by "Colonel Lee," 118 when under the control of "Black Hawk," and 82 when normal.

A curious case of two controls conversing audibly, each using his own medium, was witnessed in the Mina Crandon séances when another medium, Miss Scott, also fell into trance. The control, "Walter," who was in charge of the séance from the other side, instructed the spirit of Mrs. Scott, mother of the medium, how to proceed, when to start and when to stop talking.

The Picturesque Element

The claims by controls of prior existence in human embodiment present another problem in assessing them. Most controls have claimed a distant and inconspicuous life that defies any verification. The control of **D. D. Home** always spoke in plural and never gave his name. Stainton Moses was attended by an organized band of controls that included biblical characters, philosophers, sages, and historic personalities. The biblical characters called themselves "Imperator" (Malachias), "Preceptor" (Elijah), "The Prophet" (Haggai), "Vates" (Daniel), "Ezekiel," "Theophilus" (St. John the Baptist), "Theosophus" (St. John the Apostle), and "Theologus" (St. John the Divine).

The philosophers and sages included a prestigious selection of the famous and a few unknowns: Solon, Plato, Aristotle, Seneca, Athenodorus (Doctor), Hippolytus (Rector), Plotinus (Prudens), Alexander Achillini (Philosophus), Algazzali or Ghazali (Mentor), Kabbila, Chom, Said, Roophal, and Magus. Moses was torn by doubts for a long time as to their identity and finally concluded that, "judging as I should wish to be judged myself they were what they pretended to be."

Imperator was one of the most ancient spirit controls, but he was preceded by nearly a thousand years by "Lady Nona" (the guide of "Rosemary"), who claimed to have lived in Egypt in the time of the pharaohs. "Black Hawk," the control of **Evan Powell,** insisted that a book had been published about him in America. In 1932 the book was found; it was printed in 1834 in Boston.

There are several instances in which the same control has manifested through different mediums. They have particular favors for one medium at a time, however, and on that medium's death the loss of power is pass on to another. "**John King**," who also claimed to have been Sir Henry Owen Morgan, the buccaneer king, first appeared in the **Davenport** séances and manifested at séances of other mediums for a long time, while "**Katie King**," his daughter, appeared to have passed on to a higher sphere after her farewell from **Florence Cook.** Katie, however, made an unexpected return to the circle of Dr. **Glen Hamilton** in 1932. Roy Stemman reported that Katie King materialized in Rome in July 1974 with the medium Fulvio Rendhell.

Native American Controls

Native Americans attained a special status within Spiritualist circles, so frequently did they act as controls. Spiritualism, in fact, presents one of the earliest attempts to build a positive image of Native Americans among the European-American public. These controls bore romantic or plain Indian names; for instance, "North Star" (**Gladys Osborne Leonard**), "Red Cloud" (**Estelle Roberts**), "White Feather" (**John Sloan**), "Greyfeather" (**J. B. Johnson**), "Grey Wolf" (**Hazel Ridley**), "Bright Eyes" (**May Pepper**), "Red Crow" (**F. F. Craddock**), "Black Hawk" (**Evan Powell**), "Black Foot" (**John Myers**), "Red Jacket" (Dr. **C. T. Buffum**) and **Emily French,** "Old John" and "Big Bear" (Dr. Charles B. Kenney), "Hawk Chief" and "Kokum" (**George Valiantine**), "Moonstone" (**Alfred Vout Peters**), "Tecumseh" (**W. H. Powell**), and "Segaske" (**T. d'Aute Hopper**). Few Native American guides surpassed the fame of "White Eagle" and "Silver Birch," the controls of two famous British mediums, **Grace Cooke** and **Maurice Barbanell,** respectively.

Other nationalities, primarily those identified as cultures that taught the ancient wisdom, were also frequently encountered, such as "Tien-Sen-Tie" (the Chinese guide of **J. J. Morse**), "Eyen" (an Egyptian guide of Hester Dowden), and "Feda" (the Asian Indian guide of Gladys Leonard. In addition, Hooper was attended by a *fakir,* **Annie Brittain** by a Senegalese child, and **Eileen Garrett** by an Arab control. Nevertheless, Native American controls were in the majority.

In spirit photographs Native American controls followed popular images and appeared in scalp locks and tribal robes. Their chief organizer was said to have been John King, but before the appearance of the romantic buccaneer the first Indian controls manifested in the **Shaker** communities in America. They came collectively as a tribe. A knock was heard at the door and when the spirits were invited they possessed everyone. Indian shouts echoed in the house; the obsessed spoke Native languages among themselves and danced Native American dances.

The Native American spirits did not deliver any teaching. On the contrary, the Shakers came to the conclusion that they had to teach and convert the spirits. The Shakers' work was the beginning of what later became known in Spiritualist groups as a **rescue circle.** The visits continued from 1837 to 1844. When the spirits left, they informed their teachers that they would return soon and invade the world, entering palaces and cottages. But generally the Native American controls restricted their activity to physical manifestations.

E. W. Wallis, coauthor with M. H. Wallis of *Guide to Mediumship,* writes:

"Many Indian spirits become true and faithful friends. They act as protectors—"doorkeepers" so to speak—to their mediums. They do the hard work of development in the circle and prevent the intrusion of undesirable spirits. Sometimes they are boisterous and exuberant in their operations and manifestations and while we do not share the prejudices which are expressed against them we think it is wise to exercise a restraining influence over their demonstrations. They generally possess strong healing power and frequently put their mediums through a course of calisthenic exercises—which, although beneficial to the health of the medium and, in the presence of a few friends, may pass without adverse comment, would probably cause criticism if performed in a public assembly."

Apart from Native Americans, and in light of contemporary discussion of the child as an element in the individual's subconscious self, children furnished the most interesting group of controls. The best known include "Feda" (Gladys Osborne Leonard), "Nelly" (**Rosina Thompson**), "Dewdrop" (**Bessie Williams**), "Sunshine" (**Anne Meurig Morris**), "Little Stasia" (**Stanislawa Tomczyk**), "Nina" and "Yolande" (**Elizabeth d'Esperance**), "Belle" (Annie Brittain), "Bell" (**Florence Perriman**), "Harmony" (**Sussannah Harris**), "Snow Drop" (Maud Lord Drake), and "Pocka" **Miss C. E. Wood**).

Before **Emanuel Swedenborg,** the human element was largely lacking in spirit contact. **Paracelsus,** for example, communed with elemental creatures; the spirits seen in the "shew stone"of **John Dee** were not identified with men; and sleepwalkers believed themselves to be possessed by the devil or by the Lord. The first controls as guiding spirits appeared in the experiments of **G. P. Billot** in France about 1820. The spirits possessing his mediums claimed to be their guardian angels. Some controls claim to be pure spirits (never incarnated), such as "Little Stasia" of Stanislawa Tomczyk and "Nona" of **Lujza Linczegh Ignath.**

Control by the Living

In several recorded cases the messages delivered by the medium were proved to have emanated from *living* individuals. This introduces the important question of whether the living can act as controls. It was found that messages from the living often came without their knowledge, in most cases when they were asleep. This would suggest that occasionally the spirit entity communicating might also be unconscious of doing so—it might be dreaming through the medium. The repeated statements of Mrs. Piper's controls that they have to enter a dream state to communicate have a curious bearing on this idea.

The Frenchman **Allan Kardec** and American **John Edmonds** were the first to state that spirit communications may emanate from the living. In his *Spiritual Tracts* (October 24, 1857), Edmonds writes:

"One day while I was at West Roxbury there came to me through Laura [his daughter] as a medium, the spirit of one with whom I had once been well acquainted, but from whom I had been separated some fifteen years. His was a very peculiar character—one unlike that of any other man whom I ever knew, and so strongly marked that it was not easy to mistake his identity. I had not seen him for several years; he was not at all in my mind at the time, and he was unknown to the medium. Yet he identified himself unmistakably, not only by his peculiar characteristics, but by referring to matters known only to him and me. I took it for granted he was dead, and was surprised afterwards to learn that he was not. He is yet living. . . . I have known since then many similar manifestations so that I can no longer doubt the fact that at times our communications are from the spirits of the living as well as the dead."

Other interesting cases may be found in E. K. Bates's *Seen and Unseen* (1907), M. Monteith's *The Fringe of Immortality* (1920), **A. N. Aksakov**'s *Animismus und Spiritismus* (1890), and **Florence Marryat**'s *There Is No Death* (1892).

In one instance the spirit of Florence Marryat was summoned while she was asleep. In the experience of the author, the spirits of the living invariably beg to be sent back or permitted to go, as if they were chained by the will of the medium. Among her own mediumistic gifts Marryat claimed the power to summon the spirits of the living.

Some early clairvoyants suggested that the only perceptible difference between the spirits of the living and those of the dead was that a delicate line of light appears to proceed from the latter, apparently uniting it with the distant physical body. Some modern clairvoyants claimed to have discovered another distinction. The spirit incarnate appears lifeless, dead, statuelike, whereas the discarnate one is intensely alive.

Catherine Berry writes in *Experiences in Spiritualism* (1876):

"The table presently began rolling in a most extraordinary manner, so that we could scarcely keep it down. We asked what was the matter and it spelled out 'We have buoyed the cable and shall be home in three days.' We did not know what this meant. Someone suggested that we should ask the name which it gave. A gentleman then present at once said 'Are you Alfred?' Answer: 'Yes.' 'Then you are on board the Great Eastern?' 'Yes.' 'Then you are all safe?' 'Yes.' At this time, I should say, the vessel had not been heard of for ten days or a fortnight; and exactly at the end of three days the vessel arrived. This spirit "Alfred" was in the flesh at the time and is now; and though he has been questioned he has no knowledge of the circumstance or of having desired to send us such a communication."

The story of a communication by raps from a living man is told in the *Revue Spirite,* January 1911 by a Mrs. Bardelia. This medium reported the occurrence took place under the observation of Gustave Le Bon. It happened in 1908 in St. Petersburg. The manager of the hotel where the medium was staying asked for the favor of a séance. He was eager to get a message from his father, who had recently died. The manager was dissatisfied when, with the aid of the alphabet, the first raps spelled out a name quite different from the one he expected. The family name shortly followed, and he exclaimed, "Why, that is the name of my best friend; but he is certainly not dead, for I just lately heard from him from a hotel in Moscow, where he is employed." Both the manager and the medium were surprised, and Bardelia sought further information. The spirit confided, "I am not dead, but in a state of coma; I shall die tonight." The manager asked, "Are you at your hotel?" "No, at the hospital," was the reply. The raps ceased.

The manager, still skeptical, announced his intention of immediately telephoning to Moscow to verifying the message. About an hour later he returned, very pale and greatly excited. A hotel spokesman said that, delirious and dying, his friend had been moved to the hospital that morning and was not expected to live through the night.

Mrs. J. H. Conant, an American medium, could manifest through other mediums while her body was in trance and under spirit control.

Wsevolod Solowiof, a well-known Russian writer, and automatist who usually produced mirror scripts, on one occasion wrote the name "Vera." On inquiry it was elicited that a relative of his was communicating. "Yes; I sleep, but I am here, and I have come to tell you that we shall meet tomorrow in the summer gardens." This came to pass. Moreover, the young girl told her family that she dreamed of visiting her cousin and of having told him of their meeting.

Hereward Carrington, in his introduction to Sylvan J. Muldoon's *The Projection of the Astral Body* (1929), narrates his personal attempt at projection—to appear to a certain young lady, an accomplished pianist, with a phenomenal musical memory:

"One day, I asked her if she had ever heard of an old song, 'Sparrows Build,' made famous years ago by Jenny Lind, and a favourite of my childhood days. She stated that she never had. I said that I would get and send her a copy 'some time' as I thought she would like it. That was all that was said about it at the time and no particular importance was attached to it. A couple of nights later I attempted to appear to her, and as usual awoke in the morning without knowing whether my experiment had 'succeeded' or not. A little later I received a telephone call and the young lady in question informed me that I had appeared to her the night before—rather more vividly than usual—and that she had thereupon been seized with the impulse to write automatically—the result being a verse of poetry. That afternoon I called, was told of the experience, was shown the poetry and confess that I received quite a momentary thrill. The poetry consisted of the opening lines of the song 'When Sparrows Build,' absolutely accurate with the exception of one word."

The Gordon Davis case recorded by **S. G. Soal** in the *Proceedings* of the Society for Psychical Research (vol. 35) is one of the more famous cases in all of psychical research. In a series of séances with **Blanche Cooper** in 1922, a voice came through which Soal recognized as that of Gordon Davis, an acquaintance who he believed had died in the war. Details about home and family were given in a very convincing manner. Three years later Soal met Davis, still quite alive. He knew nothing of the communications that were said to have come from him. Several similar cases are recorded by **W. Leslie Curnow** in a 1927 article in *Psychic Science.*

Shamar, the Hindu control of Hester Dowden, specialized in bringing communicators who were living. In one instance, the name of an intimate friend came through:

"He stated that he was not sound asleep and therefore the message would come in jerks, which it did. He said he was sitting before the fire in his drawing-room; no one else was in the room. I asked him to give my sister a message from me; he said, 'Sorry, I can't; I shall forget all this when I wake.' He then said goodbye and that he could not speak any more as he was getting more wakeful."

Sir Lawrence J. Jones, in his presidential address to the Society for Psychical Research in 1928, dwelt on the mediumship of **Kate Wingfield,** saying,

"On four different occasions my youngest girl, aged nine, purported to control during her sleep, speaking with great animation and very characteristically. In the first instance she was at Ripley, some fifteen miles from Wimbledon, where K. [Wingfield] was staying. Later at Valescure she was asleep either in the same house or in a neighbouring villa. On the first occasion the child was asked, after some conversation, "What about the sailor frock?" The answer came: "We went to a shop. Mummie just said, 'You get those things out. That is her tallness.' And they got them; nothing else to be done, no altering—they just sent them home. That's what I like."

This was a correct version of what had happened that afternoon. The child had been taken by her mother to London but none of us had been at Wimbledon that day, so K. and the other members of the circle only knew that there was a plan to buy a sailor frock. Here is Herbert's (the guide) comment,

"In many cases a spirit on our side is quite unable to tell if a person is dead, or unconscious, or merely sleeping, if the spirit is outside; for after death for some little time the cord hangs loosely before it is absorbed into the soulbody and often in sleep the slackness of the cord presents the same appearance."

This instance may be compared with the "Beard" case in *Journal* of the Society for Psychical Research (vol. 23), where Mr. Beard was described as having quite recently passed over at a sitting held some eight hours before his actual decease.

Mercy Phillimore (in *Light,* May 9, 1931) told of her experience in 1917 in a sitting with Naomi Bacon when a man was described whom she recognized as a living friend:

"The moment my mind realized his presence a certain ease seemed to invade the sitting and he took direct control of the medium. The control lasted between five and ten minutes, but before it ended the communicator requested me never to refer to the experience to him in his normal state. The facts communicated were found to be correct. In another sitting a year later the living friend again purported to be present. His communications were evidential."

In a direct voice séance given by **William Cartheuser** for the **American Society for Psychical Research** on October 26, 1926, Mrs. X, a lady acquaintance of **Malcolm Bird** received what she considered communication from her former father-in-law. He said that he died of a lung condition and had tried hard to impress Mrs. X the night before. He gave a correct description of what she was doing at that particular time. After the séance, Mrs. X found out that the communicator was alive and in great mental distress on the date of the séance (*Psychic Research,* 1927).

Alfred Vout Peters, the well-known London clairvoyant, had several similar experiences. On four separate occasions, Laura Finch ("Phygia") controlled Peters while she was in Paris in the body and he in London. She promised to do so if she could. "All who know her have been unanimous in declaring it was Phygia's own self speaking; her mannerism was there; things were said of which only she had cognisance, and when tests were agreed upon beforehand in the shape of certain phrases to be uttered they were invariably used" (*Light* September 2, 1899). On another occasion it was found that a control who manifested through Peters was alive in Africa.

Admiral J. G. Armstrong related (*Light,* April 25, 1931) that on one occasion while he was in London, his mother, who lived in Devonshire, spoke to him through a medium. She was asleep at the time and had the impression, on waking, of having made a long journey. During a naval conference in London a naval officer whom he had known many years prior similarly came through and advised him to protest against the reduction of the navy. He gave facts about his recent service. On inquiry Armstrong found out that the man was alive and served in the East. Allowing for the difference in time, it was likely he was sleeping at the hour of the communication.

There are some cases on record in which a materialized apparition was discovered to be living. Alfred Vout Peters saw, in a séance with **Cecil Husk,** the phantom of a friend who must have been at home asleep at the time. Others had similar experiences with the same medium. **Stanley de Brath** saw, on four occasions, the materialized face of a lady (then in India) of whom he had lost track. Afterward he received a letter from her. A Church of England clergyman saw the materialized face of his brother who was then living in South Africa (*Light,* 1903). In the controversy that ensued, a correspondent wrote to *Light* of the materialization in the United States of General Sherman, who not only announced his identity, but also stated that he had just died. The general, however, who was at the time on his death bed, did not die until a day or two later.

Some mediums are claimed to have materialized animal phantoms. From a Spiritualist perspective, the question might arise, Is it not possible for animal spirits to control men in trance? The confession of Charles Albert Beare, a self-styled, bogus medium of Peckham, London (*Daily Express,* September 18, 1931), contains this curious passage:

"One night at Bermondsey . . . I saw a woman supposed to be controlled by an ape. She jumped on chairs, on the table and darted all over the room just like an ape—in fact, she had all the mannerism and characteristics of the ape. It was a horrifying performance, and when the woman came out of the control she had to be revived with water and by people beating her hands."

Sources:

Berger, Arthur S., and Joyce Berger. *The Encyclopedia of Parapsychology and Psychical Research.* New York: Paragon House, 1991.

Curnow, W. Leslie. "Spirits in the Flesh." *Psychic Science* (January 1927).

Marryat, Florence. *There Is No Death.* New York: John Lovell, 1891. Reprint, New York: Causeway Books, 1973.

Moore, J. D. "A Medium Appearing in a Materialized Form." *Facts* 6 (March 1887).

Owen, Iris M., and Margaret Sparrow. *Conjuring Up Philip.* New York: Harper & Row, 1976.

Stemmen, Roy. *Spirits and Spirit Worlds.* Garden City, N.Y.: Doubleday, 1975.

Convulsionaries of St. Médard

An extraordinary outbreak of convulsions and religious ecstasy occurred during the first half of the eighteenth century in the cemetery of St. Médard, Paris. It was initiated by the Jansenists, a religious group suffering much persecution at the hands of the government and the Church.

The outbreak began with a few isolated cases of miraculous healing. One was the case of a Mlle. Morsaron, a paralytic, who had for her confessor an enthusiastic Jansenist. He recommended that she seek the tomb of St. Francis de Paris in the cemetery of St. Médard. After she had gone there a few times, she recovered her health. The news spread abroad, and other cures followed.

Violent convulsions became a feature of the crisis that preceded these cures. At length, the healing of an unusually obstinate case at the tomb of St. Francis preceded by a crisis of more than ordinary severity, was the signal for a violent outburst of epidemic frenzy. People of both sexes and all ages began to visit.

People from the provinces helped to swell the ranks, until there was not a vacant foot of ground in the neighborhood of St. Médard. On January 27, 1732, the cemetery was closed by order of the king. On its closed gate a wit inscribed the lines.

De par le roi défense à Dieu
De faire miracle en ce lieu.

However, the king's ordinance did not put an end to the epidemic, which spread from Paris to many other towns. In 1741—ten years after its commencement—convulsionary healing seemed to have died away. In 1759, however, it reappeared in Paris with vigor. It disappeared once more the following year, although isolated examples persisted as late as 1787.

Sources:

Dingwall, E. J. *Some Human Oddities.* London: Home & Van Thal, 1947.

Cook, Florence Eliza (1856–1904)

The famous British **materialization** medium whom physicist and chemist **Sir William Crookes** investigated. The popular story of her mediumship opens in 1871. She claimed to have seen spirits and heard voices in her childhood, but this was attributed to vivid imagination. When she was fifteen years of age and at a tea party with friends, table-turning was proposed. She at first refused to participate, but later, with her mother's permission, consented to the experiment. Extraordinary things were reported, including the table being unmanageable and Cook being levitated.

Next, while she and her mother sat at home, Florence's hand began to write, and a message came through in mirror (reversed) image. It said she should go to a certain bookseller and there inquire about the Dalston Association. A meeting would take place in a few days and there she would make the acquaintance of the editor of the newspaper *The Spiritualist.*

For some time afterward she gave séances for the Dalston Association. She attended a few materialization sittings of the mediums **Frank Herne** and **Charles Williams** and sat with Herne in her father's house. She soon gave up the Dalston séances because the manifestations became too strong and embarrassing for a public assembly. She was said to have been carried over the heads of the sitters, and invisible hands were said to have stripped her of her clothing. Mrs. Cook decided to allow her daughter to sit only at home.

Florence often became entranced and changed personalities, calling herself "**Katie King**," the daughter of **John King** (alias Henry Owen Morgan), the buccaneer. She promised to remain for three years and reveal many strange things. The promise was generously kept. The Hackney circle—composed of Florence, her parents, her two sisters who were also mediums, and Mary, the maid—soon became famous. The young and beautiful "Florrie" gave some private sittings to Charles Blackburn, a wealthy citizen of Manchester, and he guaranteed her an annual retaining fee so she should be free to give her services when required.

She was the first English medium who exhibited full materializations in good light. The first attempt by Katie King was made in April 1872. A face like a death mask was seen between the curtains of the **cabinet.** It is curious to note from Florence's letter to Mr. Harrison that Katie "told us that we must give her a bottle of phosphorescent oil because she could not get the phosphorus that was necessary from my body because my mediumship was not sufficiently developed." The bottle of oil was employed in the place of psychic light, and lit up Katie's face. At this stage of development the medium was still conscious. Later she passed into trance.

As time went on, increased facility and practice enabled Katie King to show herself more clearly. Her resemblance to the medium in the materialization attempts was soon noticed. To prove that she was distinct from Florence, Katie changed the color of her face to chocolate and then to jet black. Moreover, Katie King was different in stature, manner and personality. As further proof, the medium was tied by the sitters or sometimes by the spirits, in the cabinet.

Katie's Separate Existence

Sir William Crookes offered what was at the time considered decisive proof of Katie's separate existence. The report of his long series of experiments, conducted in the Cook home and in his own laboratory, was published in 1874. It aroused a storm of ridicule, sarcasm, and protests.

Prior to this, Crookes felt prompted to come before the public in defense of Florence Cook in a curious incident. On December 9, 1873, the earl and countess of Caithness and Count de Medina Pomar had been the guests of Mr. Cook. W. Volckman, one of the other guests present, became suspicious of Katie King during a séance, rushed forward, and seized her hand and then her waist. A struggle ensued in which two of the medium's friends went to Katie's aid. In the testimony of Henry Dumphy, a barrister, Katie appeared to lose her feet and legs and made a movement similar to that of a seal in water. She then glided out of Volckman's grip, leaving no trace of physical existence. According to Volckman, she was forcibly freed.

The incontestable fact, however, was that five minutes later when the excitement subsided and the cabinet was opened, Florence was found in black dress and boots with the tape tightly around her waist as at the beginning of the séance, the knot still sealed with the signet ring of the earl of Caithness. She was searched, but no trace of white drapery was found.

As a result of the ordeal the medium became ill, and Crookes came forward in three letters in the *Spiritualist* press citing his own experiences with her. In his first letter he states that when Katie stood before him in the house of a Mr. Luxmoore, he distinctly heard from behind the curtain Florence Cook's sobbing and moaning from the pangs of trance. The second and third letters contained accounts of séances held in Crookes's own house and at Hackney.

Describing how Katie took his arm when walking, he also noted:

". . . the temptation to repeat a recent celebrated experiment became almost irresistible. Feeling, however, that if I had not a spirit I had at all events a lady close to me, I asked her permission to clasp her in my arms so as to be able to verify the interesting observations which a bold experimentalist had recently somewhat verbosely recorded. Permission was graciously given and I accordingly did—well as any gentleman would do under the circumstances. Mr. Volckman will be pleased to know that I can corroborate his statement that the "ghost" (not "struggling" however) was as material as Miss Cook herself."

On March 12, 1874, Katie came to the opening of the curtain and summoned Crookes to the assistance of the medium. Katie was in white. Crookes went into the cabinet and found Cook, clad in her ordinary black velvet dress, lying across the sofa. Katie vanished.

Later, in May, Crookes actually saw the two forms together during the photographic experiments. To protect herself from the injuries of the flashlight, Cook, lying on the floor, muffled her face with a shawl. Crookes's account stated,

"I frequently drew the curtain on one side when Katie was standing near and it was a common thing for seven or eight of us in the laboratory to see Miss Cook and Katie at the same time under the full blaze of the electric light. We did not on these occasions actually see the face of the medium, because of the shawl, but we saw her hands and feet; we saw her move uneasily under the influence of the intense light and we heard her moan occasionally. I have one photograph of the two together, but Katie is seated in front of Miss Cook's head."

An account of a séance on March 29 furnishes further evidence for the simultaneous appearance of the two figures. Katie allowed Crookes to go into the cabinet. He described his experience:

"I went cautiously into the room, it being dark, and felt about for Miss Cook. I found her crouching on the floor. Kneeling down, I let air enter the phosphorus lamp, and by its light I saw the young lady dressed in black velvet as she had been in the early part of the evening, and to all appearances perfectly senseless; she did not move when I took her hand and held the light quite close to her face, but continued quietly breathing. Raising the lamp I looked around and saw Katie standing close behind Miss Cook. She was robed in flowing white drapery as we had seen her previously during the séance. Holding one of Miss Cook's hands in mine, and still kneeling, I passed the lamp up and down so as to illuminate Katie's whole figure, and satisfy myself thoroughly that I was really looking at the veritable Katie whom I had clasped in my arms a few minutes before and not at the phantasm of a disordered brain. She did not speak but moved her head and smiled in recognition. Three separate times did I carefully examine Miss Cook, crouching before me to be sure that the hand I held was that of a living woman, and three separate times did I turn the lamp to Katie and examine her with steadfast scrutiny until I had no doubt whatever of her objective realty."

He also noticed that a blister on Cook's neck was not to be found on Katie's neck, and that Katie's ears were not pierced for earrings, whereas Cook's were.

Of the many precautionary measures taken by Crookes to prevent fraud, the electrical test devised by **Cromwell Varley** was perhaps the most interesting. The medium was placed in an electric circuit connected with a resistance coil and a galvanometer. The movements of the galvanometer were shown in the outer room to the sitters on a large graduated scale. Had the medium removed the wires, the galvanometer would have shown violent fluctuations. Nothing suspicious occurred, yet Katie appeared, waved her arms, shook hands with her friends, and wrote in their presence.

As an additional test Crookes asked Katie to plunge her hands into a chemical solution. No deflection of the galvanometer was noticed. Had the wires been attached to Katie the solution would have modified the current.

On May 21, 1874, Crookes witnessed the farewell meeting between Cook and Katie behind the curtain. Katie woke Cook from her trance. The farewell was very moving. They were talking affectionately and the medium shed many tears. She never saw Katie again.

After Katie departed, another spirit form, "Marie," took her place. Marie, who danced and sang in a professional style, led to Cook's exposure. During a séance on January 9, 1880, Sir George Sitwell grabbed Marie, and she did not dissolve. She was found to be the medium, wearing only her underwear, corsets, and a flannel petticoat. The discarded pieces of garment were brought out of the cabinet by another sitter.

According to Marryat, following this exposure Cook declined to sit unless someone remained in the cabinet with her. On one occasion the duty fell to Marryat. She reported being tied to Cook with a stout rope and remaining thus fastened to her the whole evening. Marie appeared and sang and danced the same as before she was seized.

Because of the many trials she had to undergo, Cook, who from 1874 was known by her married name, Mrs. Elgie Corner, for some time gave up public mediumship. During 1899, on the invitation of the Sphinx Society, she sat under test conditions in Berlin.

Following Cook's death in 1904, her husband married her sister, **Kate Cook,** also a materialization medium.

Assessing Cook's Career: The Question of Fraud

The question of whether Florence Cook was a **fraud** has been hotly debated and is still a matter of some interest in parapsychological circles. The Sitwell exposure was the primary condemnatory evidence. However, much additional material for discussion has also been uncovered. For example, French researcher **Camille Flammarion** wrote in a satiric vein that the medium **D. D. Home** "gave it to me as his personal opinion that Miss Cook was only a skillful trickster and has shamefully deceived the eminent scientist, and as for mediums, why there was only one absolutely trustworthy and that was himself, Daniel Dunglas Home."

Crookes certainly never found the least sign of deception, and when he was notified of the death of Mrs. Corner, in a letter dated April 24, 1904, he expressed his deepest sympathy and declared again that the belief in an afterlife owed so much of its certainty to her mediumship.

Cook's phenomena, like those of Home (also investigated by Crookes), remain a baffling enigma. If one accepts Crookes's careful investigations at face value, the evidence that the materialization of Katie King was real seems conclusive: yet the possibility of a fully materialized phantom form with all the characteristics of a flesh-and-blood human being is difficult to accept, and suggests impersonation by one of Cook's sisters or another accomplice.

Over the years, increasing attention has been given to the hypothesis that Crookes was either highly incompetent or, more likely, infatuated with Florence Cook to a point that weakened his judgment or integrity. This position was supported by a new report published in 1964 by the **Society for Psychical Research** in London. In it is an account of a man who claimed to have known the medium, and said she admitted fraud to him. He further hinted that the medium had an affair with Crookes. Trevor Hall, in his book *The Spiritualists* (1962), hypothesized that Florence Cook was Crookes's mistress and that the great scientist tried to cover up the affair. Cook's supporters responded that such an accusation was highly speculative, and lacked firm evidence.

Crookes made no secret of his wonder at the beauty of the phantom Katie King, which appeared to have all the attributes of a living being. He admitted having embraced the phantom to verify his perception of the spirit form as flesh and blood. Obviously, these were things it would have been prudent to conceal if there was really an illicit affair in progress. Some have suggested that a more plausible case could be made for claiming that Crookes at first believed in the reality of Katie King but later had doubts.

By then he was embroiled in an embarrassing situation from which he could only extricate himself by insisting that his experiments Katie King was a genuine materialized spirit form. After the final séance with Katie King on May 21, 1874, Crookes avoided further psychical experimentation. He became reticent about the famous materializations and devoted himself to physics, his research culminating in his development of the radiometer and the Crookes tube.

Hall's book also raises valid doubts as to the genuineness of the Cook phenomena, notably in her association with the medium **Mary Showers,** a possible accomplice in fraud. Showers also claimed to elicit materialization of spirit forms, in particular the phantom "Florence Maple," which appeared to have the same substantiality as Cook's Katie King. Showers and Cook gave a joint demonstration at the Crookes home in March 1874, when the spirit forms Florence Maple and Katie King walked around the room linked arm in arm, laughing and talking like real human beings. The possibility of two materialization mediums demonstrating the phenomenon jointly at the same séance severely strains credulity.

Also present at this remarkable séance was Sergeant E. W. Cox, who expressed his grave reservations in a letter to *The Spiritualist* (May 15, 1874):

"I have seen the forms of Katie [King] and Florence [Maple] together in the full light, coming out from the room in which Miss Cook and Miss Showers were placed, walking about, talking, playing girlish tricks, patting us and pushing us. They were solid flesh and blood and bone. They breathed, and perspired, and ate, and wore a white head-dress and a white robe from neck to foot, made of cotton and woven by a loom. Not merely did they resemble their respective mediums, they were facsimiles of them—alike in face, hair, complexion, teeth, eyes, hands, and movements of the body. Unless he had been otherwise so informed, no person would have doubted for a moment that the two girls who had been placed behind the curtain were now standing in *propiâ personâ* before the curtain playing very prettily the character of ghost.

". . .But I have one piece of evidence that goes far to throw a doubt over the whole. At a sitting with Miss Showers a few days ago, the curtain, behind which the form of Florence [Maple] was exhibiting her face, was opened by a spectator ignorant of the conditions, and a peep behind the scenes was afforded to those present. I am bound, in the interests of truth and science, to say that I, as well as all the others, beheld revealed to us, not a form in front and a lady in the chair, but the chair was empty, and the lady herself at the curtain wearing the ghost head-dress, and dressed in her own black gown! Nor was she lying on the floor as some have surmised. When the head was thrust out between the curtain the eyes were turned up with the fixed stare which has been observed in the supposed Florence [Maple], but the eyes rapidly assumed their natural position when the exposure was made, and the hands were forthwith actively employed in trying to close the curtain, and in the struggle with the inspecting lady the spirit head-dress fell off. I was witness to it all, and the extraordinary scene that followed—the voice crying out 'You have killed my medium!'—an alarm which, by the bye, was quite needless, for she was neither killed or injured beyond the vexation of the discovery. She said in excuse that she was unconscious of what she had done, being [in] a state of trance."

Another letter by Cox to **D. D. Home,** on March 8, 1876 (cited in the entry on Mary Showers), strongly suggests that both Cook and her friend Showers were frauds. The evidence suggests but does not prove conclusively that Crookes was an accomplice.

Sources:

Berger, Arthur S., and Joyce Berger. *The Encyclopedia of Parapsychology and Psychical Research.* New York: Paragon House, 1991.

D'albe, E. E. Fournier. *The Life of Sir William Crookes.* London: T. F. Unwin Ltd., 1923.

Dingwall, E. J. *The Critics' Dilemma.* Dewsbury, England: The Author, 1966.

Hall, Trevor H. *Florence Cook & William Crookes: A Footnote to an Enquiry.* London: Tomorrow Publications, 1963.

———. *The Spiritualists: The Story of Florence Cook and William Crookes.* London, 1962. Reprint, New York: Helix Press, 1963. Reprinted as *The Medium and the Scientist.* 1984.

Marryat, Florence. *There Is No Death.* New York: John W. Lovell, 1891. Reprint, New York: Causeway Books, 1973.

Medhurst, R. G. *Crookes and the Spirit World: A Collection of Writing by or Concerning the Work of Sir William Crookes, O.M., F.R.S., in the Field of Psychical Research.* London: Taplinger, 1972.

Medhurst, R. G., and K. M. Goldney. "William Crookes and the Physical Phenomena of Mediumship." *Proceedings* of the Society for Psychical Research 54 (1964): 25.

Thouless, R. H. "Crookes and Cook." *Journal* of the Society for Psychical Research 42 (1963).

Cook, Kate Selina (1859–1923)

One of the more famous British **materialization** mediums and sister of **Florence Cook,** Kate Cook was comparatively less known, as she sat more privately and did not undergo the same scrutiny as her sister.

Dr. **Alfred Russel Wallace** writes about a series of sittings he attended in *My Life* (1902):

". . . They took place in the rooms of Signor Randi, a miniature painter, living in Montague Place, W., in a large reception room, across one corner of which a curtain was hung and a chair placed inside for the medium. There were generally six or seven persons present. Miss Cook and her mother came from North London. Miss Cook always dressed in black, with a lace collar, she wore laced boots and had earrings in her ears.

"In a few minutes after she had entered the cabinet the curtains would be drawn apart and a white-robed female figure would appear and sometimes come out and stand close in front of the curtain. One after another she would beckon to us to come up. We then talked together, the form in whispers; I could look closely into her face, examine the features and hair, touch her hands and might even touch and examine her ears closely, which were not pierced for earrings. The figure had bare feet, was somewhat taller than Miss Cook, and though there was a general resemblance, was quite distinct in features, figure and hair.

"After half an hour or more this figure would retire, close the curtains and sometimes within a few seconds would say 'Come and look.' We then opened the curtains, turned up the lamp, and Miss Cook was found in trance in the chair, her black dress, laced boots, etc., in the most perfect order as when she arrived, while the full-grown, white-robed figure had totally disappeared."

Writing of a séance with Mrs. Ross in New York, Wallace adds: "But what specially interested me was that two of the figures beckoned to me to come up to the cabinet. One was a beautifully-draped female figure, who took my hand, looked at me smilingly and on my appearing doubtful, said in a whisper that she had often met me at Miss Kate Cook's séances in London. She then let me feel her ears, as I had done before, to prove that she was not the medium. I then saw that she closely resembled the figure with whom I had often talked and joked at Signor Randi's, a fact known to no one in America."

Stainton Moses sat with Kate in 1878, and **F. W. Myers** sat with her a number of times between 1878 and 1882. Both were impressed with her performance.

In 1907, three years after her sister Florences's death, Kate married her widower. In 1923 she inherited what was left of the fortune wealthy Manchester citizen Charles Blackburn originally put at Florence's and then at Kate's disposal.

Sources:

Marryat, Florence. *There Is No Death.* New York: John W. Lovell, 1891. Reprint, New York: Causeway Books, 1973.

Medhurst, R. G., and K. M. Goldney. "William Crookes and the Physical Phenomena of Mediumship." *Proceedings* of the Society for Psychical Research 54 (1964): 25.

Wallace, Alfred Russel *My Life: A Record of Events and Opinions.* London: Chapman & Hall, 1902.

Cooke, Grace (d. 1979)

Modern British Spiritualist medium who founded the Church of the **White Eagle Lodge** in 1936 under the inspiration of her Indian spirit guide, White Eagle. Cooke, known to the members of the lodge as *minesta,* began her career as a Spiritualist medium in 1913 and became progressively convinced that the spiritual and philosophical aspects of Spiritualism were more important than mere evidence of survival.

She formed a small church in Middlesex, but later separated from its activities after church leaders became more interested in proofs of survival. During the 1930s, she leased Burstow Manor in Surrey and started a White Eagle Brotherhood, later moving to Pembroke Hall. Unfortunately, the headquarters was destroyed during bombing in World War II. In 1941 new premises were acquired in London and in Edinburgh, Scotland. In 1945 Mr. and Mrs. Cooke acquired the present premises at New Lands in Liss, Hampshire, administered by a trust since 1953.

Early in her career, Grace Cooke used her psychic gifts to offer evidence of survival, and Ramsay MacDonald, British prime minister, vouched for the accuracy of her spirit communications. But, in later years, her emphasis shifted to spiritual healing and to channeling teachings from White Eagle and a few other spirit entities, including that of **Sir Arthur Conan Doyle.** Mrs. Cooke died September 5, 1979, at age 87. A special service was held at the temple at Liss, Hampshire, headquarters of the White Eagle Lodge, which she founded.

Sources:

Cooke, Grace. *The Illumined Ones.* Liss, Hampshire, England: White Eagle Publishing Trust, 1966.

———. *The New Mediumship.* Liss, Hampshire, England: White Eagle Publishing Trust, 1965.

———. *Sun-Men of the Americas.* Liss, Hampshire, England: White Eagle Publishing Trust, 1975.

Lind, Ingrid. *The White Eagle Inheritance.* Wellingborough, Northamptonshire, England: Turnstone Press, 1984.

The Wisdom of White Eagle. Liss, Hampshire, England: White Eagle Publishing Trust, 1967.

Coombe-Tennant, Winifred Margaret Serocold ("Mrs. Willett") (1874–1956)

Winifred Coombe-Tennant was better known by the pseudonym "Mrs. Willett," under which her scripts produced by **automatic writing** were published. She was born November 1, 1874, and married Charles Coombe-Tennant in 1895. In addition to her mediumship, she was chairman of the arts and crafts section of the National Eisteddfod (a Welsh cultural conference held annually), a justice of the peace, and a delegate to the Assembly of the League of Nations (1922). She was also an associate of the **Society for Psychical Research,** London.

After the death of her daughter in 1908, Coombe-Tennant corresponded with **Margaret Verrall,** also known for her automatic writing, and later produced scripts herself. She first went into trance in 1910.

She took part in a **cross-correspondence** communications study by the Society for Psychical Research in which a group of automatists (Verrall, **Helen Salter,** Mrs. Holland [**Alice Kipling Fleming**] and "Mrs. Willett") produced interlocking scripts that indicated the possibility of a disembodied intelligence.

Coombe-Tennant's mediumship is discussed in an article by G. W. Balfour in the *Proceedings* of the Society for Psychical Research. After her death in 1956 she supposedly communicated to **Geraldine Cummins** the scripts later published in the book *Swan on a Black Sea* (1965).

Sources:

Balfour, G. W. "A Study of the Psychological Aspects of Mrs. Willett's Mediumship." *Proceedings* of the Society for Psychical Research 43 (1935): 43.

Coons, Peter (1875–1955)

American pioneer of the study of **hatha yoga** under the name **Pierre Arnold Bernard.** His nephew **Theos Bernard** was responsible for an authoritative treatise on hatha yoga.

Cooper, Blanche (ca. 1927)

British **direct voice** medium at the center of the famous Gordon Davis case. In 1921–22, **S. G. Soal,** then a teacher at the University of London carried out a series of experiments and observations surrounding Cooper's mediumship. He was concerned with the remarkable communications he obtained from a deceased brother, from presumably fictitious entities, and from a friend, Gordon Davis. Davis was believed to have died in the war but was later discovered alive in 1925 and was ignorant of the communications that came through in his "voice." (See *Proceedings* of the Society for Psychical Research, vol. 35, 1926.)

In his report, Soal says Cooper:

". . . does not go into trance and in the intervals when the voice is not speaking she is apparently normal and able to converse with the sitters and sometimes even able to repeat words which the voice has just said. There is, however, right through the sittings a certain degree of absentmindedness and the medium is sometimes slow to respond to questions addressed to her by the sitter. While the voice is not speaking she keeps up a continuous humming noise with her lips, and this humming noise ceases when the voice comes into play. Throughout the period of my own experiments the medium seemed unable to sustain the voice for more than a minute or two at a time and the information was given for the most part in rapid snatches punctuated by periods of silence lasting from a minute up to a quarter of an hour. Moreover, it appeared that the voice could only be produced while the musical box was playing, and only on one or two occasions were words spoken a second or two after the music had ceased. Objective lights were seen at every sitting but these appeared in the silent intervals and were never simultaneous with the voices. These lights varied in appearance from dim amorphous patches to bright bluish discs about the size of a half a crown."

Soal noticed the peculiar feature that "questions asked by the sitter are seldom answered immediately in the case when the sitter is holding the correct answer in his conscious mind." In such cases it was usually found that the idea had to pass back into the unconscious mind of the sitter before it could emerge from the automatism of the medium. The communicator, when asked for an answer, would usually reply, "I cannot give it now, but will try to give it later." Then at a later period of the sitting, when the sitter had forgotten the question, the correct answer would be given. In cases when the correct answer was not known to the sitter, a direct question would often result in immediate success.

In the case of Gordon Davis, his voice, accent and manner of speech were reproduced fairly accurately. He described incidents of his boyhood known to Soal, and described his last meeting with Soal and the substance of their conversation. He expressed a desire to send messages of comfort to his wife and child, and though he did not give the circumstances of his death, spoke as if he were deceased. He gave an accurate description of the environment and interior arrangements of a house which he did not occupy until a year later.

In the debate over Soal's paper before the **Society for Psychical Research,** Dr. Wolley suggested that when the house was described in Davis's spirit voice (Soal) the sitter was unconsciously forseeing an event in his own life, i.e., his visit to the house in April 1925.

This theory, however, would allow almost any piece of information given by a medium and afterward verified by the sitter to be considered the sitter's forseeing the future and subconsciously passing it along to the medium.

Cooper, Irving Steiger (1882–1935)

Irving Steiger Cooper, the first regionary bishop of the Liberal Catholic Church in the United States and a leading writer of Christian esoteric literature, was born March 16, 1882, in Santa Barbara, California. He grew up in the state and graduated from the University of California. As a young adult he was introduced to **Theosophy** and within a few years had become a popular lecturer for the **Theosophical Society.** In 1911 he traveled to India for the international meeting of the society and stayed there to become the secretary of **Charles W. Leadbeater,** an Anglican priest who had become a close associate of the society's president, **Annie Besant.**

Cooper was in India in 1915 when several priests who also were Theosophists were forced out of the Old Catholic Church in England and established the Liberal Catholic Church. The church elected James Ingall Wedgewood as their first presiding bishop. He was consecrated in February 1916. Wedgewood then went to Sydney, Australia, where Leadbeater had relocated, and consecrated him as a regionary bishop for the church in Australia. While these events were taking place, Cooper remained in India, where he was writing his first books: *Methods of Psychic Development* (1912), *Theosophy Simplified* (1915), and *Reincarnation* (1917). In 1917 Cooper moved to Australia and through Leadbeater was quickly involved in the new church. He was ordained a priest in 1918. He assisted Wedgwood and Leadbeater in the preparation of *The Liturgy of the Mass* (1917), published as *The Liturgy of the Holy Eucharist* (1918).

Meanwhile, the Liberal Catholic Church had been established in the United States, and Wedgwood chose Cooper to lead it. Cooper was consecrated as reginary bishop for the United States on July 13, 1919, at St. Alban's Liberal Catholic Church in Sydney by Wedgwood and Leadbeater, and he moved to the United States in 1920. Headquarters for the church were established in Hollywood in a cathedral built adjacent to the Theosophical Society's community called Krotona.

Cooper remained active in the Theosophical Society, which became the natural recruitment pool from which members of the church were initially found. He was a firm believer in the messianic role Besant assigned to the young **Jiddu Krishnamurti,** and in the late 1920s he traveled the United States with Besant promoting Krishnamurti as the vehicle for the coming world savior.

Cooper led the Liberal Catholic Church until his death on January 17, 1935, though his activity was severely curtailed the last five years due to ill health. He worked for many years perfecting the liturgy and in 1934 saw it published as *Ceremonies of the Liberal Catholic Church,* his major literary production. It remains the standard liturgy of the church.

Sources:

Cooper, Irving Steiger. *Ceremonies of the Liberal Catholic Church.* Los Angeles: St. Alban Press, 1924.

———. *Methods of Psychic Development.* Adyar, Madras, India: Theosophical Publishing House, 1912.

———. *The Secret of Happiness.* Chicago: Theosophical Publishing House, 1925.

———. *Theosophy Simplified.* Wheaton, Ill.: Theosophical Publishing House, 1928.

Ward, Gary L. *Independent Bishops: An International Directory.* Detroit: Apogee Books, 1990.

Cooper, Margaretta S. (ca. 1850)

Early nineteenth century American medium and daughter of **La Roy Sunderland.** In July 1850 Sunderland, a former Methodist minister turned magnetist-lecturer, launched from Boston one of the first periodicals devoted to reports on Spiritualism, the *Spiritual Philosopher.* In the first issue he expressed some doubts about the validity of spiritual rappings, but a few weeks later his daughter Margaretta became a medium. In October 1850 Sunderland wrote:

"The manifestations of the spirit world have been continued in our own family in Charlestown, and our office in Boston, with increasing and wonderful interest. . . . The mysterious sounds have been made in nearly all the rooms in our house, and have been heard at different times by different people."

Sources:

Cupron, E. W. *Modern Spiritualism: Its Facts and Fanaticisms.* Boston: B. Marsh; New York: Partridge and Brittan, 1855.

Cooperator, The (Magazine)

Former journal of the **International Cooperation Council,** a coordinating body composed of educational, scientific, cultural, and religious organizations that fostered the "emergence of a new universal person and a civilization based on unity in diversity among all peoples." Many of these organizations are concerned with religion, mysticism, and occult teachings.

When the International Cooperation Council was reorganized as the Unity-in-Diversity Council, *The Cooperator* was superseded by *Spectrum,* which continued the work of linking metaphysical and New Age groups. Address: Unity-and-Diversity Council, 1010 S. Flower St., Ste. 401, Los Angeles, CA 90015-1428.

Cooper-Oakley, Isabel (1854–1914)

Theosophical writer. She was born in Amritsas, Punjab, India, her father being an official in the colonial government. Her father, Henry Cooper, was a believer in female schooling, and young Isabel received a good education for the time. Due to an injury received in 1877, she did not walk for two years, causing her to intensify her studies. During this time she read *Isis Unveiled,* the first major writing of **Helena Petrovna Blavatsky,** cofounder of the **Theosophical Society.** Her study of psychic subjects ended, however, when she recovered. She turned to women's issues and set as her goal attending Girton College, Cambridge.

While at Cambridge in 1882 she met her future husband, A. J. Oakley, and Archibald Knightley and his wife. Together they developed a new interest in **Theosophy** and joined the Theosophical Society in the spring of 1884. In the fall they accompanied Blavatsky to India. Cooper-Oakley became a dedicated Theosophist and a close associate of Blavatsky's. She remained loyal through the scandals arising from the charges of fraud by the **Society for Psychical Research,** and after Blavatsky's death in 1891 she became an international lecturer for the society.

Cooper-Oakley's first book, *Traces of a Hidden Tradition in Masonry and Medieval Mysticism* (1900), is an exploration of the Grail and Templar traditions from a theosophical perspective. In 1907 Blavatsky's successor, Annie Besant, appointed Cooper-Oakley to the presidency of the International Committee for Research into Mystical Traditions. While serving in that capacity she published further research on themes developed earlier as *Mystical Traditions* (1909). The esoteric and mystical history of the West had captured her attention for many years, and in 1912 she gathered some of her early articles into a single volume, *The Compte St. Germain,* possibly her most-remembered book, in which she assembled all of the known material about one of the more colorful and intriguing occult characters of all time.

After a full life, Cooper-Oakley died March 3, 1914, at Budapest, Hungary.

Sources:

Cooper-Oakley, Isabel. *The Compte St. Germain.* Milan, Italy: Liberia Editrice del Dr. G. Sulli-Rao, 1912.

———. *Mystical Traditions.* Milan, Italy: Liberia Editrice del Dr. G. Sulli-Rao, 1909.

———. *Traces of a Hidden Tradition in Masonry and Medieval Mysticism.* London: Theosophical Publishing Society, 1900.

Coover, John Edgar (1872–1938)

Psychologist and director of the Psychical Research Laboratory at Stanford University whose brief flirtation with psychical research had a significant negative effect upon the whole field. Cooper was born March 16, 1872, at Remington, Indiana, and was educated at Stanford University (A.B., A.M., Ph.D.).

Shortly after Harvard University received a large grant to carry out psychical research in 1912, Thomas W. Stanford gave a significant endowment for the same purpose to the university his brother had founded. Coover had just assumed a position at Stanford and was the first to receive funding from the grant, making him the first faculty member of a large American university to conduct parapsychological experiments.

He conducted a set of methodologically sound experiments in telepathy and clairvoyance with one person "sending" from a deck of playing cards to a second person in another room. Over a five-year period he carried out 10,000 trials and in 1917 presented an impressive 600 page report, *Experiments in Psychical Research at Stanford University.* The detailed report, filled with an impressive set of statistics, claimed the attention of American scientists. Its skeptical conclusions resulted in negative reactions to further efforts to develop university-based psychical studies.

After these experiments, Coover had little to do with parapsychology. He wrote an occasional article for the periodicals of the Society for Psychical Research and the American Society for Psychical Research and contributed a chapter in a book edited by Carl A. Murchison, *The Case for and Against Psychical Belief* (1927). Coover reached a somewhat agnostic position on the question, an attitude not conducive to pursuing research in a highly controversial field. He died February 19, 1938, at Palo Alto, California.

Toward the end of Coover's life a mild controversy emerged concerning his 1917 report. In 1935 **Robert Thouless** carried out a new examination of Coover's data and suggested that it contained statistically significant results. J. B. Rhine later suggested that because of the stress Thouless felt from his colleagues, he refused to report his favorable evidence. This conclusion is bolstered by a letter Thouless wrote to the president of the university, saying his research was "offensive in the nostrils of" his fellow psychologists.

Sources:

Berger, Arthur S., and Joyce Berger. *The Encyclopedia of Parapsychology and Psychical Research.* New York: Paragon House, 1991.

Coover, J. E. *Experiments in Psychical Research at Stanford University.* Palo Alto, Calif.: Stanford University Press, 1917.

Rhine, J. B. "History of Experimental Studies." In *Handbook of Parapsychology,* edited by B. Wolman. New York: Van Nostrand Rhinhold, 1977.

Thouless, Robert H. "Dr. Rhine's Recent Experiments in Telepathy and Clairvoyance and a Reconsideration of J. E. Coover's Conclusions on Telepathy." *Proceedings* of the Society for Psychical Research 43 (1935): 24.

Copyright (of Psychic Scripts)

Under the decision of Mr. Justice Eve (London, July 1926, *Bligh Bond v. Miss Cummins*), a medium who is the amanuensis for the transmission or production of any written communication made in the presence of a sitter or sitters was adjudged to be the sole author of the script produced, and therefore the sole owner of all copyright values inherent in it (subject to the absence of any special agreement to the contrary), whether the script was addressed to a sitter as recipient or otherwise, or whether it contained matter personal to the sitter.

As a result of the above ruling, in Britain the element of telepathic transmission from sitter to medium resulting in the production of writing, or of any associative influence of a like nature involving any other person, living or dead, is excluded from the purview of the law.

Coral

An organic substance formed from the hard skeletons of marine organisms, consisting mainly of calcium carbonate and magnesium carbonate. In addition to its value as a source of lime, coral has been used for jewelry and personal ornamentation, but from ancient times it has also been used in medicine and magic.

It was believed to stop bleeding, preserve houses from thunder, and protect children from goblins, evil spirits, and sorcery. It was supposed to strengthen digestion and, if taken in powder form, to protect young children from epilepsy. Coral was worn by children from Roman times.

It has also been used for rosaries as well as for bead necklaces and bracelets.

Corbenic

A magic castle in the legends of **King Arthur,** in which it is said the **Holy Grail** was kept. It was guarded by two lions. Lancelot tried to enter it by his own strength, but instead of leaning on **God** for guidance, he was struck dumb by a fiery wind. In this state he remained for fourteen days without food or drink.

Cordonnier, Gerard Anatole F. (1907–)

An engineer with the French Naval Construction Service who had an interest in parapsychology. He was born April 19, 1907, at Bailleul (Nord), France, and studied at the Ecole Polytechnique, Paris, the University of Lyons, and the Ecole Nationale Supèvieve du Génie Maritime. Honors for his work began in 1931 when he won the Arts, Sciences and Letters Silver Medal. He was presented the Chevalier, Légion d'Honneur at the end of World War

I (1945). His distinguished scientific career included assignment to the National Center for Scientific Research in 1952. He began his service in the Documentation Center of the center in 1958. He has written on **clairvoyance** and mathematics, and on levitation in relation to gravity. His parapsychological interests included telepathy, clairvoyance, levitation, and psychokinesis.

Cordovero, Moses

A famous Kabalist of the sixteenth century who was influential in the Safed school of mystical interpretations of the Torah. His writings include *Shi'ur Lomah* and *Padres Rimmonim.*

Cornell, A(nthony) D(onald) (1923–)

British business technical representative with a long-standing interest in parapsychology. Cornell was educated at Cambridge University, where he studied economics. He was active in the Cambridge University Society for Research in Parapsychology, and became successively its research officer (1956–58), senior research officer (1958–60), and president. In 1962 he became a member of the council of the **Society for Psychical Research,** London. He conducted an early study measuring public sightings of apparitions and studied hauntings, apparitions, and poltergeists, the primary literary result being the book *Poltergeists* (1979), which he cowrote with Alan Gauld.

Sources:

Cornell, A. D. "An Experiment in Apparitional Observation and Findings." *Journal* of the Society for Pyschical Research 40 (1959): 120.

Gauld, Alan, and A. D. Cornell. *Poltergeists.* London: Routledge and Kegan Paul, 1979.

Corpse Candles

Mysterious phosphorescent lights often seen over marshes or in churchyards. They are also known as "fetchlights," "jack o'lanterns" and "dead men's candles," and are termed *ignis fatuus.* They are believed by some to presage death. The size is said to indicate the age of the victim, a small light representing an infant death, especially if it is a pale blue color.

These lights are erratic, sometimes disappearing and reappearing. They may be seen on or near the earth, in the air, or over lakes, or on the sea. They may be red, white, or blue and are thought to be caused by unusual atmospheric conditions, gaseous emanations, or by luminous insects.

Corralès, Ophelia (ca. 1908)

Materialization medium of San José, Costa Rica, of whose powers the most astounding claims were made in three publications: the *Annals of Psychic Science* (1910); *El Siglo Espirita,* (March 28, 1908), the organ of the Mexican Spiritist Federation; and *La Voz de la Verdad* of Barcelona.

The séances were presided over by Dr. Alberto Brenes, professor at the law academy and a skeptic. Roberto Brenes Mesên, under secretary to the minister of public instruction, and Ramiro Aguilar, principal of the high school of San José, were attending.

Corralès was 18 years old at the time when she retained complete consciousness while an entity, giving the name "Miguel Ruiz," materialized. He could be touched, his heart could be tested, he could become tall or reduce his size, and if a match was struck, he immediately vanished. He became the guide of the séances and often came in the company of other phantoms, among whom "Mary Brown" was the most remarkable.

It was claimed that as many as five phantoms were sometimes witnessed at the same time, each talking in its mother tongue. The medium could project her **double** into the séance room while she remained outside. The double wore a different costume but exactly reproduced the voice and appearance of Corralès. When the medium, who was heard talking outside simultaneously with the double, was asked to transmit to the double a comb that was in her hair and a handkerchief, the two articles came immediately through the wall. On request, the medium herself was similarly transported.

While the medium was possessed by a spirit, her double could be seen in the room, and on command, spoke in her voice. Once, when the medium was not possessed, the double was heard accompanying Mary in song. The voice emanated far from where the body was placed by Mary.

Many other marvels, unparalleled in Spiritualist records, were said to have been performed by these spirit visitors. Mary Brown began to write, then she placed her hand on the shoulder of a sitter, who continued the writing in the same character. Similarly, if she or Miguel touched a sitter, the sitter could speak in a language of which he or she was ignorant.

In the light of a small lamp Mary often rose and floated in the air. She could also multiply herself into four personalities or psychic forms, three of which took one of the bystanders by the arms and talked about different things at the same time, acting as though they were independent of one another, while the fourth, some distance away, sang.

Mary explained the feat as a division of the **astral body,** the parts of which could materialize separately and consciously. Several flashlight photographs were taken; Mary is remarkably lifelike in some.

However, according to a letter from the medium's father to **W. T. Stead,** published by the *Voz de la Verdad,* "the photographs taken of Mary have not all the interest which at first attached to them. It is proved that she introduced a young unknown girl into the room, and she appears on the plate (phenomenon of transport and possession)."

Mary gave this explanation: "I sought amongst living persons for one who could faithfully reproduce the expression of my countenance: I found her and brought her here. My intention was a healthy one, and I am ready to repeat the phenomenon in order that you could submit it to a more severe control."

Upon visiting San José, Prof. Willy Reichel found attempts at **fraud** during the materialization séances, yet he affirmed that Corralès was a medium for independent voices and **automatic writing.**

Corralès discontinued her séances in 1914. In the absence of any reliable evidence for her phenomena, and the questionable records of other people who have attempted similar feats, the claims made for Corralès remain doubtful. (See also **Teleportation**)

Correspondences, Doctrine of

Central idea in the work of Swedish seer **Emanuel Swedenborg** (1688–1772). Swedenborg, in contrast to the new opinion of his intellectual colleagues that reality was basically found in the visible material world, argued that everything visible is but the shadow of a corresponding spiritual reality. Ultimately, he believed the nature of the connection with the spiritual world is most easily realized through a knowledge of the correspondences found in the Bible. Swedenborg devoted a considerable part of his life to writing a 12-volume commentary on the books of Genesis and Exodus (*Arcana Coelestia*) (1905–10) and several volumes on the Book of Revelation (*Apocalypse Revealed*) (1970).

In his last book, *The True Christian Religion,* originally published in 1770–71, he detailed his method of interpreting the Bible spiritually. While on cursory examination it appears similar to allegory, it differs considerably. Swedenborg said he learned from the angels that Scripture had a literal meaning and that one could not derive the higher spiritual meaning from it by allegory. He claims that the angels told him the true meaning of the Bible.

Robert A. Vaughan, author of *Hours with the Mystics* (1905), notes in regard to Swedenborg:

"According to Swedenborg, all the mythology and the symbolisms of ancient times were so many refracted or fragmentary correspondences—relics of that better day when every outward object suggested to man's mind its appropriate divine truth. Such desultory and uncertain links between the seen and the unseen are so many imperfect attempts toward that harmony of the two worlds which he believed himself commissioned to reveal. The happy thoughts of the artist, the imaginative analogies of the poet, are exchanged with Swedenborg for an elaborate system. All the terms and objects in the natural and spiritual worlds are catalogued in pairs."

For those who do not accept Swedenborg's system, his continued attempt to draw out the correspondences make the reading of his commentaries quite difficult. However, his intense affirmation of a spiritual world drew a welcome response from those satisfied with neither traditional Christianity nor the new, truncated scientific worldview.

Sources:

Woofenden, William Ross. *Swedenborg Researcher's Manual.* Bryn Athyn, Pa.: Swedenborg Scientific Association, 1988.

Worcester, William L. *Lessons in Correspondence.* 1892. Reprinted as *The Language of Parable: A Key to the Bible.* New York: Swedenborg Foundation, 1984.

Coscinomancy

A form of **divination** practiced with a sieve and a pair of tongs or shears, which are supported on the thumbnails (or the nails of the middle fingers) of two persons facing each other.

In his book *Archaeologia Graeca; or the Antiquities of Greece* (1697–99), Bishop John Potter writes:

"It was generally used to discover thieves, or others suspected of any crime, in this manner: they tied a thread to the sieve by which it was upheld, or else placed a pair of shears, which they held up by two fingers, then prayed to the gods to direct and assist them; after that they repeated the names of the persons under suspicion, and he, at whose name the sieve whirled round or moved, was thought guilty."

In the *Athenian Oracle* it is called "the trick of the sieve and scissors, the cosciomancy of the ancients, as old as Theocritus," the writer having mentioned in his third idyll a woman who was very skillful in it. Richard Saunders, in his *Physiognomie and Chiromancy* (1653), and **Agrippa** give certain mystic words to be pronounced before the sieve will turn.

Coscinomancy was also used to discover love secrets as well as to identify unknown persons.

Cosmerism

Cosmerism was the name of a short-lived **channeling** group that originated in September 1972 when a couple (given the names Luke and Mark) channeled the messages of a group of seven **angels.** These messages were later published as the *Book of Cosmer.* Following instructions from the angels, Luke and Mark gathered a group of 13, each of whom was given a Cosmerite name: Matthias, Matthew, Judas Secarius, Josephus, Ananda, Peter, James the Elder, Thomas, Paul, Thaddeus, and John the Beloved. Luke and Mark completed the circle. In the summer of 1974 this circle went public with the first study of the *Book of Cosmer* and *The Moon Monk,* a periodical.

Cosmerism advocated the Way of Cosmer, which begins with a realization of the creative force innate in all things as the source of creation. Humanity is on a course toward a oneness of people and angels within the larger unity of the creative force.

The Cosmerites were headquartered in Winter Park, Florida. They proposed the building of Ichikama, a wilderness ashram, but it was never constructed, and the group seems to have disbanded within a few years of its formation.

Cosmic Awareness Communications

Cosmic Awareness Communications is a **channeling** group that originated in 1962 when a voice describing itself as "From Cosmic Awareness" began to speak through William Ralph Duby. Duby, a former Army officer, had emerged as a medium and a small group had gathered around him. When the group asked who or what "Cosmic Awareness" was, it replied that it was "total mind that is not any one mind, but is from the Universal Mind that does not represent any unity other than that of universality." The group collected the words spoken by "Cosmic Awareness." In 1963 the voice gave instructions for the formation of an **Organization of Awareness.** The heart of the organization was seen as the 144 entities on the inner plane known as Essence, while the outer structure facilitated the dissemination of the words of "Cosmic Awareness" to the public.

The teachings of "Cosmic Awareness" were summarized in a set of laws and precepts. The universal law is the awareness that each living thing has the power to gather all things necessary for its life. The law of love places the welfare of others above one's own. It refuses to recognize the existence of evil. The law of mercy allows one to forgive all errors. The law of gratitude recognizes the sense of satisfaction from receiving a reward for energy expended.

Following Duby's death in 1967 there was a period of turmoil, and the organization splintered. Of the resulting groups, the largest and most stable is Cosmic Awareness Communications. It recognized a new channel, Paul Shockley, through whom "Cosmic Awareness" continues to speak. Through Shockley, "Cosmic Awareness" suggested that the Organization of Awareness had already accomplished a vast shift of consciousness, a return to the Godhead, which had been willed thousands of years previously by Essence. The return to the Godhead is equated with the return of **Lucifer,** the fallen angel of light.

Cosmic Awareness Communications may be contacted at Box 115, Olympia, WA 98707. It issues a periodical, *Revelation of Awareness,* and has a number of transcripts of channeling sessions available.

Sources:

Cosmic Awareness Speaks. Vol. 1. Olympia, Wash.: Servants of Awareness, n.d. Vols. 2–3. Olympia, Wash.: Cosmic Awareness Communications, 1977, 1983.

Cosmic Consciousness

A form of mystical experience characterized by consciousness of the whole cosmos, of the life and order of the universe. It was originally defined by Dr. **Richard M. Bucke** (1837–1902) in his book of the same name. Bucke considered cosmic consciousness a higher peak in human evolution that the race will universally attain in the distant future.

According to Bucke, it seemed to appear primarily in men between the ages of thirty and forty, who were highly developed, of good intellect, high moral quality, superior physique, and earnest religious belief. He considered the 13 greatest cases to be Gautama Buddha, Jesus Christ, the apostle Paul, Plotinus, Mohammed, Dante, Las Casas, John Ypes, Francis Bacon, Jacob Behmen, William Blake, Balzac, and Bucke's friend Walt Whitman.

As described by Bucke the experience comes suddenly, with a sensation of being immersed in a flame or rose-colored cloud. It is accompanied by a feeling of ecstasy and moral and intellectual illumination in which the mind has a clear concept of the meaning of the universe.

The man or woman who goes through the experience sees and knows that the cosmos is a living presence, that life is eternal, the soul of man immortal, the founding principle of the world is love, and the happiness of every individual in the long run is absolutely certain. All fear of death, all sense of sin is lost, and the personality gains added charm and becomes transformed. In a few moments of the experience the individual will learn more than in months or years of study, and will learn much that no study can teach.

Whitman spoke of cosmic consciousness as "ineffable light, light rare, untellable, lighting the very light beyond all signs, descriptions, languages." His insights correlated with the insights of a large body of mystical and religious literature, and had additional appeal because of his scientific credentials and his mystical approach to God, a perspective somewhat compatible with Eastern thought.

As described by Bucke, cosmic consciousness is equated with the early steps of **mysticism.**

Sources:

Bucke, Richard Maurice. *Cosmic Consciousness: A Study of the Evolution of the Human Mind.* 1910. Reprint, New Hyde Park, N.Y.: University Books, 1961. Reprint, New York: Citadel Press, 1970.

———. *Richard Maurice Bucke, Medical Mystic: Letters of Dr. Bucke to Walt Whitman and His Friends.* Detroit: Wayne State University Press, 1977.

Nomad, Ali. *Cosmic Consciousness.* Chicago, 1913.

Row, M. C. Nanjunda Row. *Cosmic Consciousness, or the Vedantic Idea of Realization or Mukti in the Light of Modern Psychology.* Madras, India, 1910.

Cosmic Picture Gallery

Also known as the **akashic records**—the scenic representation of every thought, feeling, and action since the beginning of the world. Light travels at the rate of 186,000 miles a second, yet the astronomic distances are so vast that it takes hundreds of thousands of years for light to reach Earth from distant stars. Suppose a person could see, through such enormity of space, what was happening on Earth. At present they could witness only the primeval past. From a great distance the creation of the whole world could be seen as a present reality. Swami Panchadasi, an early twentieth-century writer on **astral projection,** suggested:

"By travelling to a point in time, on the fourth dimension, you may begin at that point and see a moving picture of history of any part of the earth from that time to the present, or you may reverse the sequence by travelling backwards. You may also travel in the astral, in ordinary space dimensions, and thus see what happened simultaneously all over the earth at any special time, if you wish. As a matter of strict truth, however, I must inform you that the real records of the past exist on a much higher plane than the astral, and that which you have witnessed is but a reflection (practically perfect, however) of the original records. It requires a high degree of occult development in order to perceive even this reflection in the astral light. An ordinary clairvoyant, however, is often able to catch occasional glimpses of these astral pictures, and may thus describe fairly well happenings of the past."

The concept of akashic records derives from Hinduism as transmitted through the **Theosophical Society** and the teachings of Madame **Helena Petrovna Blavatsky,** who claimed that such records were accessible to a gifted percipient.

Sources:

Panchadasi, Swami. *The Astral World: Its Scenes, Dwellers, and Phenomena.* Chicago: Advanced Thought Publishing, 1915.

Cosmic Voice (Newsletter)

Monthly newsletter of the **Aetherius Society,** promulgating the teachings of psychic **George King,** and providing up-to-date information on the society's activities. Address: 6202 Afton Pl., Hollywood, CA 90028.

Cosmology Newslink

Quarterly British publication concerned with claimed extraterrestrial contacts and **UFO** sightings. Address: 37 The Close Dunmow, Essex CM6 IEW, England.

Cosmos (Newspaper)

Australian monthly periodical concerned with **New Age** topics, ranging from occultism and higher consciousness to dietary theories. Address: P.O. Box 322, Lane Cove, New South Wales 2066, Australia.

Cotlar, Mischa (1913–)

Mathematician with a special interest in parapsychology. Cotlar was born August 1, 1913, in Kiev, Ukraine. He moved to Argentina and became a research professor in the Department of Mathematics at La Plata University (1946–47) and then became a research professor in mathematics at the University of Buenos Aires (1948–50). He moved to the United States in 1951 as a Guggenheim fellow and completed his Ph.D. in mathematics at the University of Chicago in 1953. He returned to Argentina as chairman of the Institute of Mathematics at the University of Cuyo, Mendoza, Argentina (1953–56). In 1957 he became a professor of mathematics at the University of Buenos Aires.

Cotlar was a founding member of the Institute of Parapsychology created in 1972. His research is in the fields of psychokinesis, telepathy and mediumship, yoga, and Hindu philosophy.

Cottin, Angelique (ca. 1846)

A French peasant girl from a small village near Montagne, in Normandy, who as a teen exhibited remarkable phenomena of an apparently electric nature for a period of about ten weeks. Her first manifestation took place on the evening of January 15, 1846, while she was engaged in weaving gloves with three other girls. The frame at which they were working began to jump about. The parish priest was the first to investigate, since **witchcraft** was suspected. Realizing the money-making possibilities in such a mysterious power, Angelique's parents soon took her to Paris.

A Dr. Tanchou accidentally heard of her curious phenomena, investigated, and found them to be of an electrical nature. Balls of pith or feathers hung on a silken thread were alternately attracted or repelled by a force emanating from her body. She could distinguish between the poles of a magnet by touch. A compass was violently agitated in her presence. Chairs and tables leapt away from her touch in bright daylight and against strong counterpressure. A bed rocked and shook beneath her.

Tanchou sometimes noticed a cold wind during the phenomena. He reported to the scientist François Arago, who tested the girl in his laboratory. Their report revealed sudden and violent movements of the chair on which the girl was sitting. They were not satisfied, however, that these movements were not due to muscular force. But Tanchou and many others remained convinced that the phenomena was proof of the existence of a new force. According to Lafontaine, "When she brought her left wrist near a lighted candle the flame bent over horizontally, as if continually blown upon." The power was especially strong in the evening, from seven to nine o'clock. It radiated only from the front part of Cottin's body, especially at her wrist and elbow, but only on the left side. Her left arm was of higher temperature than the other. If she was seated on a chair without her feet touching the floor, made to sit down on her hands, or stood on a wax floor, a piece of oiled silk, or a plate of glass, no phenomena took place.

At every manifestation of the mysterious force Cottin was seized with terror and sought refuge in flight. During the phenomena she was extremely hyperesthetic; her muscles convulsed and her heartrate increased to 120 beats a minute. The force was so excessive that a 60-pound table would rise into the air if her apron merely touched it.

The telekinetic phenomena of **Eusapia Palladino** seem to have been similarly produced. **Frank Podmore** in his examination of the facts found this a suspicious circumstance. He also observed that when chairs were thrown about there was a double movement on the part of the girl, first in the direction of the object thrown and then away from it, the first movement being so rapid that it generally escaped attention.

Sources:

Rochas, Eugene A. A. *L'Exteriorisation de la Motricité.* 1896. Reprint, N.p., 1899.

Cottingley Fairies

In 1917 Annie Griffiths and her daughter Frances moved from South Africa to the small village of Cottingley, a suburb of Bradford in Yorkshire, England. They would live with Annie's sister, Polly Wright; her brother-in-law, Arthur; and her niece, Elsie, while her husband was in France fighting in the war. At the time Frances was nine and Elsie was 17. Despite their age difference, Elsie and Frances soon became best friends and played together in the stream at the bottom of the garden behind the Wright home. On one occasion, Frances's mother became irritated when the girls returned with wet shoes and socks. Frances responded to her mother's scolding by telling her they had gone to the stream to see fairies. To prove that they had actually seen fairies, Elsie borrowed her father's Midg camera and in July 1917 took a picture of Frances with the fairies. When they returned from the stream, Elsie's father developed the photograph they had taken, which showed Frances sitting by the stream surrounded by four dancing fairies. In September of the same year Frances took a photograph of Elsie with a gnome kneeling near her lap.

Despite the remarkable nature of these photographs, the family chose not to publicize them immediately; instead they remained silent until 1919 when Elsie's mother attended a meeting of the Theosophical Society in Bradford. Held at a time when interest in psychic phenomena was greatly increased, in the aftermath of World War I, the meeting was attended by several hundred persons. During the meeting the lecturer, a Mrs. Powell, apparently mentioned the existence of fairies, which prompted Polly to ask if it was possible that the fairy photographs taken by her daughter and niece could be valid representations of fairy life. Eventually the two photographs taken by Frances and Elsie were given to Mrs. Powell, who forwarded them to Edward J. Gardner. Gardner discussed them with **Sir Arthur Conan Doyle** who not only believed in the existence of fairies but was also coincidentally collecting material on fairies for an article he had promised to write for the *Strand.*

Doyle obtained prints of the photographs in June 1920, while he was making preparations for a trip to Australia with his family to preach the cause of **Spiritualism.** Because of the importance of the subject matter, Doyle made arrangements to meet Gardner at the Grosvenor Hotel in London to discuss the photographs. During those discussions, Doyle asked Gardner to travel to Yorkshire to meet with the family and to investigate the photographs. After completing his investigation, Gardner was convinced that the girls' story was true and that the photographs were valid representations of fairies. Before leaving for Australia, Doyle spoke with Gardner and submitted an article to the *Strand;* it appeared in December 1920. In the article Doyle used pseudonyms for Elsie (who became Iris) and Frances (who became Alice) and discussed the background of the two photographs and Gardner's visit with the family. Doyle left for Australia before the article was published, but he admitted in the published account of that trip that he took with him "the famous fairy photos—which will appear in England in the Christmas number of the *Strand.* I feel as if it were a delay-action of mine which I had left behind me. I can imagine the cry of 'Fake!' which will arise. But they will stand investigation. It has, of course, nothing to do with Spiritualism proper, but everything which can shake the mind out of narrow material grooves and make it realize that endless worlds surround us, separated only by difference of vibration, must work in the general direction of truth."

When Doyle returned from Australia in the spring of 1921, he submitted another article to the *Strand,* which appeared in the March 1921 issue. Although two additional photographs were reproduced for the first time in this article—photographs that Elsie and Frances had been urged to take by Gardner in August 1920—the article itself had been written by Doyle before he knew anything about any of the Cottingley fairy photographs. A preface to the article states: "This article was written by Sir A. Conan Doyle before actual photographs of fairies were known to exist. His departure for Australia prevented him from revising the article in the new light which has so strikingly strengthened his case. We are glad to be able to sit before our readers two new fairy photographs, taken by the same girls, but of more recent date than those which created so much discussion when they were published in our Christmas number, and of even greater interest and importance."

Following the publication of Doyle's articles, he wrote several letters to the British press to explain his belief in the fairy photographs. On June 18, 1921, he wrote to *Light,* a spiritualist magazine, and defended the photographs against charges that they were "clumsy fakes" by assuring its readers that "the photos have been enlarged and also examined in the negatives by some of the most competent professional photographers in England, who could find no flaw."

In October of the same year he wrote to the *Yorkshire Weekly Post* and repeated that the fairy photographs had been "inspected by several of the first authorities in England, who have found no flaw in them," but also added: "When one considers that these are the first photographs which these children ever took in their lives it is impossible to conceive that they are capable of technical manipulation which would deceive experts."

Despite these explanations, others advanced more skeptical theories. On December 20, 1921, an article appeared in the British newspaper *Star,* in which a representative of Price and Sons, who were candlemakers, suggested that the Cottingley fairies were almost identical to drawings the company had used to advertise their nightlights.

Despite these criticisms, Doyle utilized both *Strand* articles as chapters in the first edition of *The Coming of the Fairies* (1922), which consisted of 1,000 copies published on September 1, 1922. A second impression was made on November 23, 1922, in which an additional 500 copies were published. The first American edition of *The Coming of the Fairies,* which consisted of 1,500 copies, was published later that same year. These publications included the four previously published fairy photographs and a fifth photograph, which was also taken in 1920. Following the publication of the first edition of *The Coming of the Fairies,* the South African newspaper *Cape Argus* published an article that disclosed that Elsie Wright wrote a letter concerning her fairy photographs before making them public. Believing that this disclosure was significant, Doyle submitted a third article to the *Strand,* for their February 1923 issue, in which he writes that there is new evidence that vindicates Elsie and Frances: "There are a good many apologies due to the children for criticism which could only mean that they were dishonest little wretches. That line of comment must now be definitely abandoned by every fair-minded critic, but what other one is open?"

Following the publication of this article, Doyle relied on others to argue the case. Geoffrey Hodson, a medium who visited Elsie and Frances in Cottingley in August 1921 and whose account was included in Doyle's book, published his own book on the subject. In *Fairies at Work and Play* (1925) Hodson cites the Cottingley fairy photos as evidence that fairies exist. His book also describes other sightings of brownies, elves, gnomes, manikins, undins, sea spirits, sylphs, devas, and nature spirits. That same year Doyle wrote a letter to *The Northern Whig and Belfast Post* in which he blasted an "allusion to the 'Fairy Photographs' as if they had been in some way explained or discredited." He declared "This is not so," and reviewed the evidence that supported their veracity, including the letter that appeared in the *Cape Argus,* and the unquestioned honesty of the girls.

Although Doyle considered writing a fourth article for the *Strand* after the discovery of additional fairy photographs from other sources, he decided, instead, to publish a second edition of *The Coming of the Fairies* in 1928. This second edition, published by Doyle's own Psychic Press, added material that was not in the first edition, including a new preface in which he recommends Hodson's book, and an article by Florizel von Reuter which discusses photographs of nature sprites.

Following the publication of the second edition of *The Coming of the Fairies,* Doyle wrote nothing further on the subject until

1929. In *Our African Winter*—the account of his missionary adventures in Africa—he recognizes that:

"... there are thousands of people who still believe the wild assertion made years ago that the fairy photographs were taken from a well-known advertisement. I took the line in my lecture that I was prepared to consider any explanation of these results, save only one which attacked the character of the children. I am sure that when I had explained the facts there were few in the Hall who were not prepared to accept the photographs.... There have been many objections made to the Cottingley photographs, most of them palpably absurd. The one which merits most attention is that they are cleverly cut-out figures which have been held up by invisible threads. Such an explanation is conceivable, but the balance of probability seems to me to be greatly against it."

In the same book Doyle also explains why he continued to reject the skeptical explanations advanced concerning the Cottingley fairy photographs:

"1. Frances, the younger girl, wrote at the time (1917) that Cottingley was a nice place on account of the butterflies and fairies. This card was sent to her friend in South Africa (who came from South Africa) and was unearthed in 1923, or thereabouts, and published in the *Cape Argus*. For what possible reason would she, a child of ten, write thus, if she knew it was a deception?

"2. If the figures were cut out, then similar figures must be in existence in other copies of the book or paper. These have not been found.

"3. There is a great difference in solidity between the 1920 figures and those of 1917, which could be accounted for by waning mediumship, but which is inconsistent with faking.

"4. Experts have reported signs of movement in the figures.

"5. Mr. Gardner formed a high opinion of the character of both of the children and of their father. The latter would certainly have known if there were deception."

Until his death in 1930, Doyle continued to believe that the photos were genuine and that Elsie and Frances were telling the truth. Edward J. Gardner, who first interviewed the girls, also wrote a book on the subject in 1945, in which he includes all five fairy photographs and describes the events that led to their publication.

Although Doyle, Gardner, and Hodson all died believing that the photographs were genuine, the controversy survived them, and more than 60 years after the initial photographs were taken, Frances and Elsie finally admitted that "for the most part, the Cottingley fairy episode was a fraud."

Following Gardner's death in 1970, at age 100, the British press revived the Cottingley fairy story. Beginning in 1971, television programs were produced in which Elsie appeared and described her first conversations with the fairies. Of course, most of these programs were tongue in cheek attempts by the British press to report the historical facts of the episode while, at the same time, leaving no doubt that it was all in good fun. In 1973 the president of the Folklore Society in Yorkshire delivered his annual address, in which he assured his audience that he did not believe the photographs actually depicted real fairies. He concluded this after watching Elsie's 1971 interview.

In 1976, another interview with both Frances and Elsie was televised in Yorkshire. During this program both women confirmed the events recorded by Doyle, Hodson, and Gardner.

Shortly thereafter, Fred Gettings discovered a picture in a book entitled *Princess Mary's Gift Book* (London: Hodder & Stoughton, 1914), which, unlike the Price & Sons advertisement, depicted dancing fairies very similar to those in the first of the photographs. Ironically, *Princess Mary's Gift Book* also contained an article by Doyle. In 1982 James Randi, the famous magician, published blowups of the photographs to demonstrate that the fairy figurines in the Cottingley photos were cutouts and that the last photograph was a double exposure.

The same year Randi's book appeared, a series of articles by Geoffrey Crawley, entitled "The Astonishing Affair of the Cottingley Fairies," began running as a series in *The British Journal of Photography*. These articles examine the history of the episode, give an analysis of each of the photographs, and detailed discussions of the Midg camera used by Frances and Elsie and of the source material the girls could have used in constructing the photographs. It also describes Elsie's artistic abilities. The articles become truly "astonishing" in Part 9, which contains a letter from Elsie in which she admits, apparently for the first time, that the fairy photograph episode was a "practical joke that fell flat on its face." She also writes that:

"My dad said really you must tell right now how you got these photos, so I took Frances aside for a serious talk, as the joke had been my own invention. But she begged me not to tell as the *Strand Magazine* had brought her so much teasing at school, and I was also feeling sad for Conan Doyle, we had read in the newspapers of his getting some jarring comments, first about his interest in Spiritualism and now laughter about his belief in our fairies, there was also a critical cartoon of him in a newspaper chained to a chair with his head in a cloud and Sherlock Holmes stood beside him, he had recently lost his son in the war and the poor man was probably trying to comfort himself with unworldly things."

In the same issue, Frances also admits that the first four photographs were staged but, unlike Elsie, she maintains that the pictures were taken "to help establish that fairies did exist" and that as a child "she did indeed see real fairies very close." In addition, she says she believed that the final photograph was "a genuine one of real fairies."

Apparently, Frances had made a similar confession to Joe Cooper, who published an article on the subject in the British magazine *The Unexplained*—before its appearance in *The British Journal of Photography*. Geoffrey Crawley later admitted that he was aware of the confession when he wrote his articles but that he believed that the subsequent confessions made by Frances and Elsie, published in *The British Journal of Photography*, established for the first time in written form, the reason for the charade. Crawley also sets forth in the articles the first detailed analysis of each of the five photographs and concludes that only one of the photographs, the first one, contained material similar to the illustration found in *Princess Mary's Gift Book*. The fairy figurines in the next three photographs were drawings made by Elsie from other sources, he says. The first four photographs were taken while the fairy figurines were planted in the earth with hat pins. Crawley, unlike James Randi, offers no solution for the last photograph.

Ironically, Geoffrey Hodson died in January 1983, at age 97 shortly after the beginning of *The British Journal of Photography*'s investigation.

The final chapter in the Cottingley fairy episode was written by Joe Cooper in 1990 when he published his recollections of Frances's first confession. According to Cooper, Frances first confessed in September 1981 during a discussion with him in Canterbury. During this conversation she claimed that the final photo was of real fairies. She also admitted, however, that she brought a copy of *Princess Mary's Gift Book* with her from South Africa in 1917, and that Elsie in fact copied the figures for the first photograph from that book. Apparently, the first confession made by Elsie was her letter to *The British Journal of Photography*, which appeared in the April 1, 1983, issue.

Although Frances and Elsie steadfastly maintained that the photographs were valid for most of their lives, they both eventually admitted they were faked. However, Frances only admitted that four of the five were fake. She maintained that the last photograph, which she took, was not faked and, to her dying day, believed in the existence of fairies. Elsie, on the other hand, stated in her last interview that she did not believe in fairies.

In Doyle's December 1920 *Strand* article he alludes to his Sherlock Holmes character when he writes, "I will now make a few comments upon the two pictures which I have studied long and earnestly with a high powered lens." Cooper, in his 1990 book, also mentions Holmes in his discussion of the fairy photos in a four-page pastiche in which Holmes solves the Cottingley fairy mystery. One telling incident occurs after Holmes solves the mystery and Doyle recalls that he wrote an article in *Princess Mary's Gift Book.* In hindsight, he laments that he should have realized that the figures in that book could have been copied by the girls for their fairy pictures.

Sources:

Cooper, Joe. *The Case of the Cottingley Fairies.* London: Robert Hale, 1990.

Crawley, Geoffrey. "The Astonishing Affair of the Cottingley Fairies." *British Journal of Photography* 24 (December 1982–April 1983; 24 May 1985; 25 July 1986).

Doyle, Arthur Conan. "The Cottingley Fairies: An Epilogue." *Strand Magazine* 65 (February 1923).

———. "The Evidence for Fairies; with More Fairy Photographs." *Strand Magazine* 61 (March 1921): 199–206.

———. "Fairies Photographed: An Epic-Making Event." *Strand Magazine* 60 (December 1920): 463–68.

Gardner, Edward L. *Fairies: The Cottingley Photographs and Their Sequel.* London: The Theosophical Publishing House, 1945.

Hodson, Geoffrey. *Fairies at Work and Play.* London: Theosophical Publishing House, 1925.

Coué, Emile (1857–1926)

Founder of a popular system of autosuggestion that reportedly had great success in healing many illnesses and diseases. The essence of autosuggestion was that Coué himself was not a healer, but taught techniques by which his patients could heal themselves. His system is quite similar to **New Thought** and directly influenced modern ideas about the power of the mind.

Coué was born February 26, 1857, in Troyes, in the Aube district of France. He attended the town school until age 15 before studying in the high school, where he showed great aptitude for science. At the age of 19, he was apprenticed in a drugstore in Troyes, later studying chemistry at the École de Pharmacie in Paris. In 1882 he returned to Troyes and became proprietor of a drugstore. He married in 1884.

Soon afterward he was persuaded to listen to a lecture by a Dr. Liebault at the Nancy School of Hypnotism. Coué developed a great interest in hypnotism, but he thought Liebault's procedures lacked systematic method. He took an American correspondence course in hypnotism and practiced on patients who came to his drugstore. He observed that many subjects were not completely hypnotized although they were beneficially affected by simple drugs in a degree far beyond the actual medical potency of the drugs. From observation of his patients, Coué developed a theory of suggestion. He abandoned traditional hypnosis, requiring his patients to make their own suggestion for healing.

In 1910 he retired from business and moved to Nancy, where he concentrated on his practice of autosuggestion, sometimes treating as many as 15,000 people a year. He became well known after the celebrated psychologist Charles Baudoin described his methods in the book *Suggestion and Autosuggestion* (1920), which he dedicated to Coué. In 1921 the British physician Dr. Monier-Williams traveled to Nancy and studied Coué's methods. Upon returning to London, he opened a clinic for the practice of conscious autosuggestion, The Coué Institute for the Practice of Conscious Autosuggestion, in London treated thousands of patients annually. In 1923 a similar institute was established in Paris.

Coué toured America, where he popularized the phrase "Every day in every way, I get better and better" as part of his therapeutic method. This was a conscious suggestion that the subject was required to repeat in early morning and before going to sleep at night. Coué died at Nancy July 2, 1926. Conscious suggestion has since become an integral element in many popular systems of healing and self-improvement.

Sources:

Brooks, C. Harry. *The Practice of Autosuggestion by the Method of Emile Coué.* New York: Dodd, Mead, 1922.

Coué, Emile. *My Method, Including American Impressions.* Garden City, N.Y.: Doubleday, Page, 1923.

———. *Self Mastery through Conscious Autosuggestion.* New York: American Library Service, 1922.

Kirk, Ella Boyce. *My Pilgrimage to Coué.* New York: American Library Service, 1922.

MacNaghten, Hugh. *Emile Coué: the Man and his Work.* New York: Dodd, Mead, 1922.

Count Dracula Fan Club

Founded in 1965 by Dr. Jeanne K. Youngson, with a membership of individuals interested in the literary and historical aspects of **Bram Stoker**'s book *Dracula,* and related topics of **vampire** and horror lore. Youngson became interested in the historical Dracula in college and, while touring Romania, she made the decision to start the club. The club disseminates information, issues newsletters and books to members, and sponsors movie showings, trips, and meetings. It maintains a large research library, opened in 1970, which includes books on vampires and of the horror genre.

The club provides a wide range of services for its members including assistance in locating hard-to-find books and helping authors working on books about Count Dracula or vampirism. The club also sells vampire memorabilia and artifacts. Among its unique endeavors is the Dracula Museum, which includes a broad collection of Dracula, vampire, and Bram Stoker memorabilia.

The club is organized into a number of divisions, including the Research Referral Centre, Dracula Press, Vampire Bookshop, Booksearch, the Moldavian Marketplace, Dracula World Enterprises, the Vampire Institute, Vampire Pen Friends Network, and the Bram Stoker Memorial Association. Young members (age 16 and under) are enrolled in Vampires Are Us, the junior division. There are also Werewolf in Fact, Fiction, and Fantasy and International Frankenstein Society divisions.

The 5,000-member club publishes four newsletters: *The Dracula News-Journal, Bites & Pieces, Leterzine,* and *Undead Undulations.* Address: 29 Washington Square W., Penthouse N., New York, NY 10011.

Sources:

The Count Dracula Fan Club Handbook. New York: Count Dracula Fan Club, 1992.

Polidori, John, et al. *The Count Dracula Fan Club Book of Vampire Stories.* Chicago: Adams Press, 1980.

Youngson, Jeanne, ed. *A Child's Garden of Vampires.* Chicago: Adams Press, 1980.

———. *The Count Dracula Book of Classic Vampire Tales.* Chicago: Adams Press, 1981.

Youngson, Jeanne, and Shelley Leigh Hunt, ed. *Do Vampires Exist? A Special Report from Dracula World Enterprises.* New York: Dracula World Enterprises, 1993.

Count Dracula Society

Founded in 1962 by Dr. Donald A. Reed for the serious study of horror films and gothic literature. It is closely associated with the Academy of Science Fiction, Fantasy and Horror Films, dedicated to honoring films and filmmakers in the several genres. The society hosts regular screenings of **vampire** and horror films and also sponsors an annual gathering at which the Ann Radcliffe Award is given.

The Count Dracula Quarterly (also known at various times as *The Castle Dracula Quarterly* and *The Gothick Gateway,*) has been discontinued. Address: 334 W. 54th St. Los Angeles, CA 90037.

Sources:

Reed, Donald. *The Vampire on the Screen.* Inglewood, Calif.: Wagon & Star Publishers, 1965.

Count Ken Fan Club, The

Founded in 1984 by Ken Gilbert as a **vampire** interest organization. It issues a newsletter and may be contacted at 18 Palmer St., Salem, MA 01970.

Counter Charms

Charms employed to counteract the effect of other charms. When magicians wished to disenchant animals, they sprinkled salt in a porringer (a small basin) with some blood from one of the bewitched creatures and repeated certain formulas for nine days.

Counts of Hell

Demons of superior order in the infernal hierarchy, who are said to command numerous legions. They may be evoked at all hours of the day, provided the evocation takes place in a wild, unfrequented spot. (See also **Chevaliers de l'Enfer**)

Courmes, Dominique Albert (1843–1914)

French naval officer and pioneer French Theosophist. Courmes was born on August 4, 1843, at Rouen. He joined the navy when he was 17 years old and after an outstanding career became its commandant. He was awarded the Legion of Honor at the time of his retirement in 1896.

In his middle years, Courmes studied **Spiritualism, Spiritism,** and **Theosophy** successively. He is credited with saving the records of Spiritist leader **Allan Kardec** when they were threatened during the days of the Paris Commune (1871). He also wrote the first article on Theosophy published in France, in 1877–78 in the *Revue Spirite.* In 1880 he joined the **Theosophical Society** and that same year translated the *Buddhist Catechism,* prepared by theosophical president **Henry Steel Olcott,** into French. He finally met **Helena Petrovna Blavatsky,** cofounder of the society, in 1884 and promised to translate her key work, *The Secret Doctrine,* into French. Sections of the translation began to appear serially in a French theosophical magazine in 1889 and were finally issued in a six-volume edition (1899–1910).

Courmes's retirement from the navy was prompted by the Theosophists' need of an editor for *Le Lotus Bleu,* their French-language journal. He made a number of notable contributions, including further translations of Blavatsky's writings and original essays of his own. He also translated the Hindu classic the *Bhagavad Gita* (1910). Courmes was the titular head of the theosophical movement in Paris until the organization of the French section of the Theosophical Society in 1900, when he proposed a colleague as the first general secretary.

Sources:

Courmes, D. A. *A Theosophical Question Book.* Translated from the French by Elin Salzer and Harry Banbery. Adyar, Madras, India: Theosophist Office, 1898.

Covenant of the Goddess

The Covenant of the Goddess (COG) is the largest Wiccan fellowship in North America. It was founded in 1975 by ten otherwise autonomous covens, all in California, to foster cooperation between covens and secure (where needed) legal recognition and tax exemption for **witchcraft** groups. During the 1980s the fellowship grew into a national organization with seven regional groups.

Membership is open to all followers of **Wicca** and includes both covens and individual Wiccans practicing as solitaires. New members must be recommended by at least two present members. While there is no creedal statement, members follow the Wiccan Rede, "An ye harm none, do as ye will," and a set of guidelines on finances. Members support the autonomy, secrecy, and diversity of local covens.

There is an annual COG gathering during which the Grand Council meets, business is conducted, and elections are held. Covens in close proximity to each other are encouraged to form local councils for cooperative efforts. COG may be contacted at Box 1226, Berkeley, CA 94704. It publishes *The Covenant of the Goddess Newsletter,* which appears eight times annually. In 1992 there were 65 affiliated covens.

Sources:

Starhawk. *The Spiral Dance.* San Francisco: Harper & Row, 1979.

Cox, Edward William (1809–1879)

Lawyer and well-known British psychical investigator in the days preceding the foundation of the **Society for Psychical Research.** Cox's career in psychical research was concentrated during the last decade of his life. He was a member of the investigating committee of the **London Dialectical Society,** which published its famous *Report on Spiritualism* in 1871. He did not accept the "spirit" hypothesis and in its stead argued for the existence of a psychic force that would explain many forms of psychic phenomena. His idea was explained in a booklet, *Spiritualism Scientifically Examined with Proofs of the Existence of a Psychic Force* (1872), and in a larger work, *The Mechanism of Man: An Answer to the Question "What Am I?"* (1876). For systematic research into the mystery of psychic phenomena, he founded, in 1875, the **Psychological Society for Great Britain.**

Cox is most remembered for his work with **William Crookes** in his first experiments with **D. D. Home.** He was a shrewd and most capable investigator and well aware of most of the tricks used by fraudulent mediums in the production of fake **materialization** phenomena. Cox was supportive of Home's mediumship and shared his opinions in a letter to Crookes:

"In the investigations in which you so kindly assisted me there was nothing of this precaution and mystery. You sat with me anywhere, at any time, in my garden, and in my house; by day and by night; but always, with one memorable exception, in full light. You objected to no tests; on the contrary you invited them. I was permitted the full use of all my senses. The experiments were made in every form ingenuity could devise, and you were as desirous to learn the truth and the meaning of it as I was. You sat alone with me, and things were done which, if four confederates had been present, their united efforts could not have accomplished. Sometimes there were phenomena, sometimes there were none. When they occurred they were often such as no human hand could have produced without the machinery of the Egyptian Hall [the scene of conjuring magician J. N. Maskelyne's shows]. But these were in my own drawing-room, and library, and gardens, where no mechanism was possible. In this manner it was that I arrived at the conviction—opposed to all my prejudices and preconceptions—that there are forces about us of some kind, having both power and intelligence, but imperceptible to our senses, except under some imperfectly known conditions. . . ."

However, he was highly critical of **Florence Cook** and **Mary Showers.** Cox's letter to the medium D. D. Home, published in Home's *Lights and Shadows of Spiritualism* (1877), is thought to refer to these two mediums. He was present on the occasion in which Cook and Showers appeared in what was supposed to be a joint materialization. He noted that both materialized forms were solid flesh and breathed and perspired.

Sources:

Berger, Arthur S., and Joyce Berger. *The Encyclopedia of Parapsychology and Psychical Research.* New York: Paragon House, 1991.

Cox, Edward W. *The Mechanism of Man: An Answer to the Question "What Am I?"* London: Longman, 1876.

———. *What Am I?: A Popular Introduction to Mental Philosophy and Psychology.* London: Longman, 1974.

Dingwall, E. J. *The Critic's Dilemma: Further Comments on Some Nineteenth Century Investigations.* Dewsbury, England: The Author, 1966.

Hall, Trevor H. *Florence Cook & William Crookes: A Footnote to an Enquiry.* London: Tomorrow Publications Ltd., 1963.

———. *The Spiritualists: The Story of Florence Cook and William Crookes.* New York: Helix Press, 1962.

Cox, William Edward (1915–1994)

Mechanical engineer and psychical researcher and lecturer. He was born September 12, 1915, at Wilmington, North Carolina, and was educated at Louisburg College, Antioch College, and the University of the South. As a young man he became interested in stage magic, which led him into the study of psychic phenomena and parapsychology. His primary research was devoted to **psychokinesis,** in which he developed some innovative experiments. In 1951 he introduced the PK-Placement method, a technique by which objects are released mechanically over an equally divided surface. The subject attempts to make the object fall to one side of the division. Cox also adapted ESP techniques for use in psychokinesis experiments. He was credited with keeping psychokinesis research alive during a period when it had largely been abandoned by parapsychology. In 1957 he won a prize presented by the **Society for Psychical Research** for the most original essay in parapsychology. Cox also became a research associate at the **Parapsychology Laboratory** at Duke University and from that time on devoted the majority of his time to parapsychology. He later worked at the **Institute for Parapsychology.**

Cox wrote more than 50 articles on parapsychology. He was a charter member of the Parapsychological Association, a board member of the **Foundation for Research on the Nature of Man,** a member of various psychical research organizations, and an associate member of the Society of American Magicians. Cox died in 1994.

Sources:

Berger, Arthur S., and Joyce Berger. *The Encyclopedia of Parapsychology and Psychical Research.* New York: Paragon House, 1991.

Cox, William E. "The Effects of PK on the Placement of Falling Objects." *Journal of Parapsychology* 15 (1951): 40–48.

———. *Mentalis and Magicians: Some Conclusive Arguments about a Modern Problem.* Singapore: Stamford College Press, 1972.

———. "Precognition and Intervention." *Journal* of the American Society for Psychical Research 50 (1956): 47–58.

Cox, William Sebron (1939–)

American parapsychologist on the research staff of the Parapsychology Laboratory at Duke University, 1958–59. He was born January 11, 1939, at Laredo, Texas, and was educated at St. Mary's University, San Antonio, Texas (B.A., 1956). He is a member of the American Association for Advancement of Science, the **Parapsychological Association,** and the Speleological Society. He founded and was the first president of the Austin (Texas) Parapsychology Society. In collaboration with **Christianne Vasse,** he developed a new test for **psychokinesis** using colored cubes.

Sources:

Cox, William S. "An Experiment in Extra-Sensory Perception." *Journal of Experimental Psychology* 19 (1936): 429–37.

Craddock, Frederick G. Foster (ca. 1920)

British **materialization medium** with a colorful career, several times exposed in imposture. As early as 1879, in Manchester, the materialized spirit "Rosetta" was grabbed and the light revealed the medium in his shirt and one stocking. Craddock recovered from this incident and went on to practice his mediumship for many years. In 1904 he came back into the public limelight when Henry Llewellyn and Gambier Bolton related their experiences in Bolton's book *Psychic Force* (1904).

In 1906 Craddock was dragged into court by the *Daily Express* newspaper for obtaining money under false pretenses. Lt. Col. Mark Mayhew, writing in *Light,* March 24, 1906, described how the spirit "Abdullah" was seized and found to be the medium. Those present at the session also saw Craddock remove a false moustache and put it in his pocket.

Admiral Usborne Moore, also present at the sitting, then had the doors locked, took the key, and commanded a search. Craddock placed himself in a fighting position and his wife attacked the admiral with a fire shovel. The search was conducted anyway. In a drawer a small electric torch was found, the instrument of spirit lights. Craddock would not allow the search of his person. For this reason Moore, in *Glimpses of the Next Slate* (1911), could not excuse him.

Moore concluded, however, that Craddock was apparently in **trance** at the moment he was seized for when he scrambled up into his chair he chattered in the voice of "Graem," his principal **control.** Moore believed that Graem was an undesirable **spirit.** Admiral Moore concluded that Craddock was a sensitive who had prostituted his gift. Even if the voices of Graem and "Red Crow," a Native American control, could be assumed, he argued that it would be impossible to reproduce constantly and faithfully the voices and special modes of speech of "Adler," "Sister Aimee," "Joey Grimaldi" and the French girl "Cerise."

Moore's opinion now seems somewhat naive, considering the varied performances of stage ventriloquists who can reproduce a number of different voices at high speed. As for the impersonated spirit Abdullah, Moore recorded that he saw him twice in Toledo, through the mediumship of **Mr. and Mrs. J. B. Jonson.**

As a consequence of the exposure by Mayhew, Craddock was fined in the Edgware Police Court 10 pounds or one month's imprisonment. A week after Mayhew's article, William McDougall, of Oxford, told the story in *Light,* March 31, 1906, of a similar experience with Craddock six years before. Abdullah, the spirit, was found to be identical to Craddock. The story was originally related in the spiritualist magazine, *The Two Worlds,* but the editor withheld the name of the medium.

As a result of the scandal surrounding his 1906 exposures, Craddock withdrew from the limelight, but he did not give up professional mediumship. H. Dennis Bradley in *The Wisdom of the Gods* (1925) describes a **direct voice** sitting with him on December 5, 1924. Seemingly oblivious to the mechanisms of **materialization** and unaware of his former exposure, Bradley asserts,

"Throughout I could not help feeling a suggestion of supernormal impersonation. On the whole I am inclined to think that Craddock has considerable powers but I should imagine that these powers vary. His guides appeared to me to be very evasive in their replies to questions verging on any evidential point. I am inclined to think his mediumship is more upon the physical than the mental plane."

A few years later, in his *The Tragedy of the Heavens* (1930), Walter Gibbons described Craddock as one of the greatest **direct voice** mediums, as:

"the possessor of a power that is unique in strength and quality, and should he choose to utilize his exceptional gifts for gain, he could, by reason of so doing, be an exceedingly wealthy man. However, this could never be, so he lives the life of a recluse in a small country cottage in very humble circumstances, mainly supported by one or two friends."

Reading all the evidence, however, one would have to be excessively charitable to believe that Craddock was other than a persistent fraud.

Sources:

Bradley, H. Dennis. *The Wisdom of the Gods.* London: T. Werner Lavrie Ltd., 1925.

"Exposures of Mr. Craddock." *Journal* of the Society for Psychical Research 12.

Gibbons, Walter. *The Tragedy of the Heavens.* N.p., 1930.

Cramp-Rings, Hallowing

A ceremony that took place in **England** on Good Friday. It consisted of the repetition of certain psalms and prayers, during which the king rubbed the rings between his hands. It was said that rings consecrated on Good Friday by the kings of England had the power of curing cramp. The rings, which were given away, were much in request even by foreign ambassadors. (See also **king's evil**)

Crandon, Mina Stinson ("Margery") (1889–1941)

Famous American medium of Boston, whose phenomena became the focus of a major controvery over **fraud** and physical mediumship. Mina Stinson was born July 29, 1889 on a farm in Princeton, Ontario. She moved to Boston in 1904 and worked as a secretary to the Union Congregational Church. In 1910 she married Earl P. Rand, a local grocer, and bore him a son. They were divorced in 1918, and soon afterward Mina married Dr. L. R. G. Crandon, professor of surgery at Harvard Medical School and author of a textbook on post surgical treatment. "Margery" had met Crandon when he performed surgery on her in 1917.

Crandon was a materialist, but one day he read **W. J. Crawford**'s book on the **Goligher Circle,** and partly as a joke, partly out of curiosity, he began to experiment in his home. His wife, in a chance visit to a clairvoyant, received a communication from the alleged spirit of her older brother Walter Stinson, who was killed in a railroad accident years before. The first sitting in the Crandon house was held during May 1923. Out of six sitters Margery alone was found to have the power of animating the table. Answers were "tilted out" and gradually she developed as a medium.

Raps came as the second stage and **trance** as the third. Joining hands replaced table contact and Margery withdrew into a **cabinet.** But the trance was only intermittent. She remained alert for the better part of the sitting and only went into a trance when "Walter," the spirit, had a lot to say. He was in full charge of the proceedings; messages of lesser spirits had to be relayed through him.

Automatic writing, psychic **music,** and finally **direct voice** completed the development of Margery's mediumship. With the advent of the latter the trance phase was abandoned. Power ran high and the cabinet, as a demonstration, was wrecked by invisible hands. Clocks were stopped at announced times and Walter's activity was noticed all over the house.

At this stage, a Harvard group conducted the first of many trying scientific investigations into Margery's mediumship. Anxiously trying to find a normal explanation for the puzzling phenomena, the group accused Margery of using a carpet thread to make a piano stool appear to move by itself.

The charge was soon withdrawn, but though Walter agreed to restrict the phenomena to a single room for the purposes of better control, no progress was made. At the end of 1923 Margery and Dr. Crandon visited Europe. In Paris Margery sat for **Gustav Geley, Charles Richet,** and others. With the strictest control, excellent phenomena were produced.

Still more successful was a **séance** before the **Society for Psychical Research** in London. **Harry Price**'s famous fraud-proof table was, in white light, twice levitated to a height of six inches. Other sittings at the **British College of Psychic Science** and **psychic photography** obtained with **William Hope** and **Ada Emma Deane** established Margery's reputation as a powerful medium.

It appeared that while in Europe, Margery learned some of the tricks of fraudulent mediumship and upon her return to America, she resolved to develop **materialization.** Psychic lights signalled the first phase; ghostly fingers lit up the darkness and produced contacts; curious forms, which Walter called his psychic pet animals, were observed; and independent writing developed on a phosphorescent background. Materialized hands performed pickpocketing stunts and—as a further evolution in vocal phenomena—tunes were produced by whistling and raps.

On April 12, 1924, the widely discussed investigation of the *Scientific American* committee began. Scientific instruments were introduced and recorded brand new phenomena.

Despite many striking demonstrations, however, the committee came to a deadlock and the only thing approaching a verdict was a series of individual statements published in the November 1924 issue of the magazine. **Hereward Carrington** pronounced the mediumship genuine; **Harry Houdini** fraudulent; **Walter Franklin Prince, William McDougall,** and another member were noncommittal.

J. Malcolm Bird, the secretary of the committee, was satisfied after 10–12 sittings that the phenomena were genuine. McDougall and Prince, however, even after further sittings, were unwilling to make a public commitment, though Prince had become convinced privately that Margery was a fraud, an opinion he would soon publish.

Another Harvard Committee also refused a final decision, and precise conclusions were absent from the report of **E. J. Dingwall** published in the *Proceedings* of the Society Psychical Research. From his sittings in January and February 1925, in Boston, Dingwall observed that "phenomena occurred hitherto unrecorded in mediumistic history . . . the mediumship remains one of the most remarkable in the history of psychical research," but troubled by the possibility of undetected hoaxing, he concluded that the mediumship "may be classed with those of Home, Moses and Palladino as showing the extreme difficulty of reaching finality in conclusions, notwithstanding the time and attention directed to the investigation of them."

Finally, **J. B. Rhine,** Prince, and others published an attack on Margery's mediumship. Dr. Crandon defended his wife in a pamphlet *Margery, Harvard, Veritas* published in 1925. The controversy over Margery had become so intense within the **American Society for Psychical Research** that the society was split. Those who had become her detractors, including Murphy and Prince, withdrew and founded the **Boston Society for Psychic Research.**

Sittings and experiments continued through the late 1920s, however, and two important experimental apparatus were introduced. One, a voice-cut-out machine offered evidence that Walter's voice was independent of the medium and sitters. The second, a glass cabinet, resembled a telephone booth and had small holes on the sides for the hands, which, together with Margery's ankles and neck, were wired to screw eyes.

Much excitement was produced in these sittings by a series of thumbprints obtained in wax that experts pronounced to be fraud-proof. They were partially identified with remains found on a razor of the thumbprints of Margary's dead brother Walter.

It was partly by such fingerprints that **R. J. Tillyard,** the famous Australian entomologist, became convinced—in a sitting alone with Margery on July 13, 1928. These experiments were repeated. On March 11, 1931, William H. Button, president of the American Society for Psychical Research, obtained a thumbprint he described as one of the best Walter prints yet obtained.

Later developments, however, considerably destroyed this part of Walter's achievements. Bulletin 18 (*Fingerprint Demonstrations*) of the Boston Society for Psychical Research, which contained a foreword by Prince and three articles by E. E. Dudley, Hereward Carrington, and Arthur Goadby, disclosed that the Walter fingerprints corresponded exactly with those of a Mr. Kerwin, an early sitter of the Margery circle. As the chances of the fingerprints of two persons being identical are said to be nil, Dudley inferred that Kerwin was "Walter." As the promised investigation by the American Society for Psychical Research continued without a definite conclusion, Prince, in Bulletin 19 (January 1933), alleged fraud, asserting, "For six years Walter has been claiming that the scores of issuing thumbprints, with a few exceptions, were his own, explaining the processes employed. In the light of the proved facts that claim is fraudulent."

The **cross-correspondence,** devised by Walter and reported by Dr. Mark Wyman Richardson in *Psychic Research* (May–September 1928) provided more evidence for evaluation, as they seemed to be methodologically sound and provided a fraud-proof technique to bar any eventual allegation of a collusion between experimenters and automatist.

The cross-correspondences occurred in March, 1928; several Chinese scripts came through. R. F. Johnson, of the Society for Psychical Research, attacked them and concluded that:

"whoever the communicator on this occasion may have been, he was certainly not the great Chinese sage (Confucius) whose name he adopted. It is also too obvious to need emphasis that the style of the writing is not ancient, that the whole contents of the script consist of ordinary modern Chinese written by a very poor scribe; that both pages of the script contain not a single word or line (barring a trifling exception) that is not a quotation."

Johnson's critique was answered by Malcolm Bird, who was research officer of the American Soceity for Psychical Research (ASPR). In an article in *Psychic Research* (August 1929), he pointed to important, unconsidered facts. First, he noted that the scripts did not identify their author as Confucius. Walter never made such a claim. He declared that Chinese spirits, the disciples of Confucius, helped him to get the test through. The important point, he said, was that the scripts were supernormally produced.

Margery delivered the first Chinese script on March 17, 1928, in red light, with closed eyes. She did not know Chinese, nor did the sitters. The very reason of the test was to demonstrate that minds other than the medium and sitters were at work. At the next séance, on March 22, two columns of Chinese were written in total darkness, on specially marked paper. Walter announced that he would try a Chinese-English cross-correspondence with Henry Hardwicke, of Niagara Falls, a distance of 450 miles from Boston. He asked Bird to pick out a sentence, which should be given through Hardwicke in Chinese. Bird chose "A rolling stone gathers no moss." The sitting was hardly over when a telegram arrived from Niagara Falls. A few days later it was followed by the original witnessed copy of Hardwicke's script. It showed a Maltese cross within the circle, a rectangle enclosing the name Kung-fu-tze, the symbols for Bird and Hill, and the Chinese sentence, the general meaning of which was, "A travelling agitator gathers no gold." Johnson's analysis revealed further important element. In the left hand column are found the words, "I am not dead, Confucius." The duplicate of this is in the right hand column of the Margery script of March 17.

In addition to that of Hardwicke, cross-correspondences were effected in Chinese through Sarah Litzelmann, who knew no Chinese either and lived in Ogunquit, Maine, a distance of 80 miles from Boston. Never before had she been in a trance.

In *The Story of Psychic Science* (1930), Hereward Carrington thus summarized his own conclusions about Margery:

"It certainly is one of the most baffling and extraordinary cases in history—and this is true, no matter how we choose to regard it. For my own part I occupy the same position as I did when rendering my formal Report in the *Scientific American,* which is that, despite the difficulties involved in arriving at any just estimate of this case, and despite the uncertainty of many of the phenomena and the complicated social, ethical, personal, physical and psychological factors involved, a number of seemingly genuine, supernormal manifestations yet remain, which are of the profoundest interest to psychical, as well as to ethico-sociological science."

As **parapsychology** has moved forward in its appraisal of Margery and other materialization mediums, however, Carrington's hesitancy appears to be a mixture of credulity and a will to believe.

Few today would attempt a defense of Margery. Possibly the final blow to her reputation came when it was revealed that in 1930 J. Malcolm Bird had submitted a report to the American Society for Psychical Research indicating that he was not only convinced that a measurable portion of the phenomena were fraudulently produced, but that he had been asked to participate in creating it. Shortly after producing that report, Bird resigned and disappeared. The American Society for Psychical Research, which had become committed to Margery, suppressed the report and published another in its place.

Sources:

Berger, Arthur S., and Joyce Berger. *The Encyclopedia of Parapsychology and Psychical Research.* New York: Paragon House, 1991.

Bird, J. Malcolm. *Margery the Medium.* Boston: Small, Maynard, 1925.

Murchison, Carl A., ed. *The Case For and Against Psychical Belief.* Worchester, Mass.: Clark University, 1927. Reprint, New York: Arno Press, 1975.

———. *Psychical Belief.* Worcester, Mass.: Clark University, 1927.

Tabori, Paul. *Companions of the Unseen.* London: H. A. Humphrey, 1968. Reprint, London: Souvenir Press, 1972.

Tietze, Thomas R. *Margery.* New York: Harper & Row, 1973.

Crawford, William Jackson (1881–1920)

Engineering professor at Queens University, Belfast, Ireland, and researcher in psychic phenomena. Crawford was born in New Zealand. He received his doctorate from the University of Glasgow. He resided in Belfast when around 1914 he began to investigate the physical phenomena of Kathleen Goligher and the group around her, known as the **Goligher Circle.** His investigation continued until his death in 1920.

From his research, he developed a set of speculations on the scientific laws behind the phenomenon of **telekinesis** (now known as **psychokinesis** or "PK"), which he presented in his books, *The Reality of Psychic Phenomena* (1916), *Experiment in Psychic Science* (1919), and *The Psychic Structures in the Goligher Circle* (1921). During his research, he converted to **Spiritualism,** though his theories played down the role of spirits in favor of a psychic force.

Crawford first tackled the problem of the alteration of weight as objects were lifted and displaced. He found that the weight of the levitated table was beared by the **medium.** Her increase in weight was usually well within five percent of that of the table. The difference was beared by the sitters. Similarly, if the table was glued down to the floor by the psychic force, the medium's weight decreased in proportion to the pressure borne by the floor. The **levitation** itself was effected, he reasoned, by an invisible substance that streamed out of the medium's body and became more or less solidified into what he called "psychic rods." These rods, which consisted of **ectoplasm,** found leverage in the medium's body and acted as cantilevers. If the weight to be lifted was too big, an elbow formation, transferring the pressure to the floor, was used. These psychic rods evolved with great rapidity and they could assume any shape and size. They were invisible but the ends were dense enough to be felt. This psychic substance according to Crawford, could rap, grip an object by suction, and perform delicate mechanical effects. If Crawford passed his hand in front of the medium's ankle, he could intercept the psychic rod and stop the **raps.** In so doing, he said, he felt something cold and clammy.

Putting the medium on a weighing machine he measured the amount of substance withdrawn for raps of varying loudness. The raps reacted on the medium's body, apparently in the region of the chest, but she was unconscious of the effect. He found that the withdrawal of ectoplasm was but a temporary loss. The medium, at the end of the séance, lost less in weight and was less exhausted than the sitters.

Crawford concluded from this that the psychic force that vitalizes the ectoplasm is drawn mostly from the sitters and used up. The sitters lost between five and ten ounces of weight. The maximum loss of weight, when ectoplasm was experimentally withdrawn in fluxes from the medium, was 54 pounds, nearly half of her normal weight. At the same time, the medium perceptibly shrank, her pulse gradually rose, and her muscles convulsed.

The flow of ectoplasm could carry particles of paint. By a colored track Crawford traced the flow from the ankles up to the hip and to the base of the spine. Powdered carmine was used for this purpose. When it was placed on the knickers, the track extended to the shoes and upward to the lower part of the trunk. This showed that the flow started from her trunk, passed down her feet, and returned. The fabric of her knickers and stockings was abraded in places. Crawford inferred that some frictional resistance was encountered. He also found that it was not the ectoplasm, but the medium which suffered from sudden exposures to light. By shielding her with black cloth he obtained many good flashlight photographs.

Crawford's conclusions were challenged by E. E. Fournier d'Albe in his book *The Goligher Circle* (1922). In 20 sittings with the same medium he obtained almost no results. He expressed the belief that the levitations recorded by Crawford were accomplished by the medium's legs.

Crawford committed suicide on July 30, 1920. Four days before his death he wrote, "I have been struck down mentally. I was perfectly all right up to a few weeks ago. It is not the psychic work. I enjoyed it too well. I am thankful to say that the work will stand. It is too thoroughly done for any material loopholes to be left."

In this belief Crawford relied in part upon the opinion of colleagues such as **Sir William Barrett,** who wrote on March 24, 1917, "I can testify to the genuineness and amazing character of these physical manifestations and also to the patient care and skill which have characterized Crawford's long and laborious investigations."

Sources:

Barham, A. "Dr. W. J. Crawford: His Work and Legacy in Psychokinesis." *Journal* of the Society for Psychical Research 55 (1988): 113.

Berger, Arthur S., and Joyce Berger. *The Encyclopedia of Parapsychology and Psychical Research.* New York: Paragon House, 1991.

Crawford, E. F. *Experiment in Psychic Science.* N.p., 1919.

———. *The Psychic Structures in the Goligher Circle.* New York: E. P. Dutton & Co., 1921.

———. *The Reality of Psychic Phenomena.* London: J. M. Watkins, 1919.

Crehore, John Davenport (1891– ?)

Publisher, writer, and organic farmer with a background in languages and general science who took a special interest in parapsychology. He was born May 14, 1891, in Pottstown, Pennsylvania. Crehore wrote several items on the subject of **telepathy,** especially as it related to his interest in **healing** and organic foods.

Sources:

Crehore, John D. *Mental Telepathy: Radiesthesia or Radesia, Our Sixth Sense.* Cleveland, Ohio: J. E. Johnson, 1956.

Creme, Benjamin (1922–)

Scottish-born professional artist who paints images of an inner reality perceived through meditation and claims to be a herald of "the reappearance of the Christ" at the end of the twentieth century. Early in his life Creme became attracted to theosophical literature, especially the writings of **Alice A. Bailey.** In the 1950s he also joined the **Aetherius Society,** an occult-oriented flying saucer contact group founded by **George King,** in which he learned a form of meditation called "transmission" meditation.

Throughout the 1950s Creme was in direct contact with the **Great White Brotherhood,** the assembly of beings believed by Theosophists to guide the destiny of humankind. Creme claimed that in 1959 he received a telepathic communication from his own master, a member of the divine hierarchy, who told him that he would have a part to play in the return of Maitreya, the Christ. (In Theosophy, the person who walked the earth as Jesus, and is called the Christ by Christians, is identified as Maitreya, the bodhisattva whom many Buddhists expect to appear in the near future.) A constant and conscious telepathic link was established with this master, by which Creme received precise and up-to-date information about the reappearance of the Christ, which Bailey had predicted to occur toward the end of the twentieth century.

In 1974 Creme began to lecture extensively on the subject throughout Europe and North America. Also in 1974 Creme formed Share International Foundation, a group to prepare for the coming of the Christ, and according to Creme, messages and contacts with the Christ took place soon afterward. In an information sheet, "The Reappearance of the Christ and the Masters of Wisdom," Creme noted:

"There now lives among us a man who embodies in Himself the hope and aspiration of the religious groups as well as the practical aspirations of the political and economic thinkers for a better life for all.

"Awaited also by Buddhists as the Lord Maitreya, by Moslems as the Imam Mahdi, as the Bodhisattva by Hindus and as the Messiah by the Jews, the World Teacher made known in June 1945 . . . His intention to return to the world at the earliest possible moment. In Palestine, 2000 years ago, He manifested through His Disciple Jesus (Who is now the Master Jesus) by a process of overshadowing. This time he comes Himself, as World Teacher for the Aquarian Age.

"On July 19, 1977, Maitreya, the Christ, entered the modern world. Since then, He has been living as a member of the Asian Community of East London: an ordinary man, not known as the Christ, and not using His name Maitreya. . . .

"A number of TV and radio programs in which the Christ has taken part have already been broadcast. The Plan was that through media coverage of His public meetings He would gradually become well-known, first nationally and then internationally. However, due to the lack of response on the part of the media, this has not taken place.

"As part of a contingency plan, therefore, Benjamin Creme was allowed to disclose the Christ's location. At a press conference in Los Angeles on May 14, Benjamin Creme announced that the Christ had been living in London since 1977. . . ."

Creme predicted the appearance of the Christ in 1982 and offered many hints to the press as to where he could be found. Some journalists searched the Indian community in London for him, but the person did not appear. Benjamin Creme subsequently claimed that "materialistic forces, seen and unseen, planetary and cosmic" had opposed the appearance, and a decision was made to postpone the actual appearance. Afterward, Creme was dismissed by many people and through the remainder of the 1980s he redirected the program of the Share International Foundation and made few public appearances. In the 1990s he has again made announcements of the presence of Maitreya and has even published photographs of his appearances to different groups around the world.

Creme published a number of books about the reappearance of the Christ. However, as of 1995 the identity of the Christ has yet to be revealed, and there is still some doubt about the ultimate direction that Creme and the group will take.

Sources:

Creme, Benjamin. *Maitreya's Mission.* Amsterdam, The Netherlands: Share International, 1986.

———. *Messages from Maitreya the Christ.* 2 Vols. London: Tara Press, 1980.

———. *The Reappearance of the Christ and the Masters of Wisdom.* London: Tara Press, 1980.

———. *Transmission: A Meditation for the New Age.* North Hollywood, Calif.: Tara Center, 1983.

Melton, J. Gordon, Jerome Clark, and Aidan Kelly. *New Age Encyclopedia.* Detroit: Gale Research, 1990.

Crewe Circle (ca. 1906)

The friends of medium **William Hope,** whose psychic abilities were discovered in 1906. Two years later, Archdeacon **Thomas Colley** called together a group of people to sit for **spirit photogra-**

phy. This group, which gathered in Crewe, England, became known as the Crewe Circle.

Sources:

Tweedale, Charles L. *Man's Survival after Death.* London: Psychic Book Club, n.d.

"Cristo d'Angelo"

Famous spirit **control,** first manifested in a **direct voice séance** of the medium **George Valiantine** in 1922 in the United States. Five years later, on March 25, 1927, the voice of "Cristo d'Angelo" was recorded on gramophone in Lord Charles Hope's apartment in London. It was heard a month later by the Italian **Marquis Carlo Centurione Scotto** in the apartment of **H. Dennis Bradley** at a Valiantine séance.

On request of the Marquis, "Cristo d'Angelo" established himself as his control from May 12, 1927, the day of the first Millesimo séance onward but also manifested several times at the **"Margery"** séances in Boston when Valiantine was present. The spirit control figured in some interesting **cross-correspondences** between Millesimo Castle and Boston records.

Cristo d'Angelo claimed he was a Sicilian shepherd on earth, a native of Sant Anselmo al Monte in the neighborhood of Palermo, and was with Garibaldi at Calatifimi. He died at age 76 of acute pneumonia. Dr. Carlo Marchese, a physician of Catania, attempted to trace his life. He found a village of the name in the province of Palermo, but obtained no further proof of the real existence of Cristo d'Angelo.

Sources:

Hack, Gwendolyn Kelley. *Modern Psychic Mysteries; Millesimo Castle, Italy.* London, 1929.

———. *Venetian Voices.* London, 1937.

Critomancy

Ancient method of **divination** by means of observing meats and cakes. The paste of cakes that were offered in sacrifice was closely examined, and from the flour spread upon them, omens were drawn, after being strewn upon sacrificial victims.

Croiset, Gerard (1909–1980)

A Dutch sensitive and healer who lived at Enschede, Netherlands. He was extensively tested by Professor **W. H. C. Tenhaeff,** director of the Parapsychology Institute of the University of Utrecht, and by **Hans Bender** of the University of Freiburg in Germany. Croiset worked unobtrusively with the chief justice of Leeuwarden and with the chief of police at Harlem in tracing criminals or missing persons. He was not a professional psychic.

Croiset was born on March 10, 1909, in the town of Laren, North Holland. He manifested clairvoyant faculty as a child, but it was not until the mid-1930s that he began to use his psychic talents. He became associated with a Spiritualist group in Enschede, where he had settled as a young man. He gradually became known as a psychic and healer and was able to make his living in that manner through World War II. At the time he was discovered by parapsychologist Tenhaeff in 1945, Croiset was running a small healing clinic. After a series of tests over several months in Utrecht, Tenhaeff concluded that Croiset was one of the most remarkable subjects he had encountered, and he devoted much time and energy to developing and testing Croiset's unusual abilities. As these abilities matured, Tenhaeff concluded that they might be applied to solving social problems, and accordingly contacted Dutch police officials, who were sufficiently broadminded to cooperate. Eventually Croiset was consulted regularly to assist in locating missing children or solving crimes, and his successes became widely known.

Tenhaeff's career rose along with that of Croiset. He quickly moved from his unsalaried position to instructor (1951) and full professor (1953) at the Utrecht State University and then to director of the university's new Parapsychology Institute. In 1956 Croiset moved from Enschede, near the German border of the Netherlands, to Utrecht, where he was more conveniently situated close to Tenhaeff and the institute. To maintain himself and his family Croiset reestablished his spiritual healing clinic, but did not charge for his parapsychological work, and even when consulted by police he paid his own traveling expenses. He did, however, sometimes charge individuals for private consultations.

One of Croiset's most remarkable achievements in the field of parapsychological testing was the famous "chair test," which involved random selection of a chair number from a seating plan for a future meeting at which seats were not reserved or allocated to specific individuals. At a period of anywhere from one hour to 26 days before the meeting, Croiset would describe the individual who would sit in that chair at the meeting. These predictions were sealed and then opened at the meeting and checked detail by detail against the characteristics of the individual actually occupying the seat. Croiset's first chair test was in Amsterdam in October 1947 before the **Studievereniging voor Psychical Research** (Dutch Society for Psychical Research). Croiset seems to have had remarkable successes in this unusual type of clairvoyance.

In cases where Croiset himself was allowed to choose a chair number, his descriptions sometimes included information on the individual's past and future. Subsequent chair tests were set up in Austria, Italy, and Switzerland, as well as Holland. Some of these tests are described in detail in Tenhaeff's 1961 book *De Voorschouw* (Precognition). Other cases have been reported in the Dutch *Tijdschrift voor Parapsychologie.*

Croiset's international reputation was spread by the publication of Jack Pollack's *Croiset the Clairvoyant* (1964) which was translated into German and French editions. The book discusses some seventy cases of various types, all verified by Tenhaeff. In the meantime, other Dutch parapsychologists were questioning Croiset's abilities. Dutch researcher Piet Hein Hoebens emerged as Croiset's and Tenhaeff's major critic. He claimed that in many of the cases, such as those reported by Pollack, Tenhaeff had misrepresented or even fabricated the facts. He also uncovered a number of cases on which Croiset had worked that had turned out to have been complete failures.

Hoebens also criticized the chair tests, noting their subjectivity (Croiset's descriptions of people were vague and could apply to a wide variety of individuals), and again alleged falsification of data by Tenhaeff. The discrediting of Tenhaeff, not only in relation to Croiset but in other work as well, has done much to tarnish the reputation of Croiset and cost doubt on the early evaluations of his abilities.

A biography of Croiset (in Dutch) titled *Croiset Paragnost* appeared in 1978. Croiset died July 20, 1980. His son has continued the work of the healing clinic.

Sources:

Berger, Arthur S., and Joyce Berger. *The Encyclopedia of Parapsychology and Psychical Research.* New York: Paragon House, 1991.

Hoebens, Piet Hein. "Croiset and Professor Tenhaeff: Discrepancies in Claims of Clairvoyance." *Zetetic Scholar* 6, no. 2 (Winter 1981–82): 32–40.

Lyons, Arthur, and Marcello Truzzi. *The Blue Sense: Psychic Detectives and Crime.* New York: Mysterious Press, 1991.

Pollack, J. H. *Croiset, the Clairvoyant.* Garden City, N.Y.: Doubleday, 1964.

Tenhaeff, W. H. C. "Psychoscopic Experiments on Behalf of the Police." *Conference Report No. 41.* Paper presented at the First International Conference of Parapsychological Studies, Utrecht, Holland, 1953.

Crollius, Oswaldus (1580–1609)

A disciple of the school of **Paracelsus** and author of *Basilica Chymica* (1612), the third part of which is the *Book of Signatures.* The preface contains a sketch of hermetic philosophy. The writer sought to demonstrate that God and Nature have "signed" all their works, that every product of a given natural force is as the sum of that force printed in indelible characters, so that he who is initiated in the **occult** writings can read as in an open book the sympathies and antipathies of things, the properties of substances, and all other secrets of creation. In his *The History of Magic* (1860), occultist **Éliphas Lévi,** summarizes the doctrine of signatures:

"The characters of different writings were borrowed primitively from these natural signatures existing in stars and flowers, in mountains and the smallest pebble. . . . King Solomon alone is credited with having accomplished the dual labor; but the books of Solomon are lost. The enterprise of Crollius was not a reconstitution of these, but an attempt to discover the fundamental principles obtaining in the universal language of the creative world.

"It was recognized in these principles that the original hieroglyphics, based on the prime elements of geometry, corresponded to the constitutive and essential laws of forms, determined by alternating or combined movements, which, in their turn, were determined by equilibrator attractions. Simples were distinguished from composites by their external figures; and by the correspondence between figures and numbers it became possible to make a mathematical classification of all substances revealed by the lines of their surfaces. At the root of these endeavors, which are reminiscences of Aldonic science, there is a whole world of discoveries awaiting the sciences. Paracelsus had defined them, Crollius indicates them, another who shall follow will realize and provide the demonstration concerning them. What seemed the folly of yesterday will be the genius of tomorrow, and progress will hail the sublime seekers who first looked into his lost and recovered world, this Atlantis of human knowledge."

The doctrine of signatures has been a persistent one in folk medicine, where the shapes of plants have been considered symbolic of their medicinal virtues.

Sources:

Lévi, Éliphas. *The History of Magic.* 1860. Reprint, New York: Samuel Weiser, 1969.

Pettigrew, T. J. *Superstitions Connected with Medicine or Surgery.* N.p., 1844.

Cromlech Temple

A British **occult** society contemporary with the Hermetic Order of the **Golden Dawn,** with rituals and initiations based on a mixture of **Kabala** and Christian **mysticism.**

Sources:

Howe, Ellic. *The Magicians of the Golden Dawn.* London: Routledge & Kegan Paul, 1972.

King, Francis. *Ritual Magic in England, 1887 to the Present Day.* London: Neville Spearman, 1970.

Cromniomancy

Form of **divination** by means of **onions.** It was usually practiced on Christmas Eve to obtain information about absent persons. One method was to inscribe the names of absent friends on individual onions and leave them undisturbed on a table until they began to sprout. The onion that sprouted most rapidly indicated that the person whose name had been inscribed on it was enjoying vigorous health.

Another method was to obtain an answer to a question by inscribing alternative answers on individual onions; the correct answer was said to be that on the onion which sprouted first. Some also believed that wishes would come true if they burned onion skins on a fire.

Crookall, Robert (1890–1981)

Geologist with the National Coal Board in London, England, who was an early British authority on **astral projection** or **out-of-the-body travel.** He examined the evidence that people can leave their physical bodies and reenter them after traveling unseen in subtle bodies. In his many books he collated hundreds of cases from various individuals and established the characteristic features and implications of this strange phenomenon.

Crookall concluded that the accumulated evidence for out-of-the-body travel validated religious concepts of the soul and an afterlife. He promoted his views in a number of books through the 1960s and 1970s. The mass of data he collected is impressive, but his objectivity has been questioned and he tended not to consider alternative explanations of the astral travel experience. Crookall died in January 1981.

Sources:

Crookall, Robert. *Casebook of Astral Projection.* Secaucus, N.J.: University Books, 1972.

———. *During Sleep: the Possibility of "Cooperation."* London: Theosophical Publishing House, 1964.

———. *Interpretation of Cosmic & Mystical Experiences.* London: James Clarke, 1969.

———. *More Astral Projections.* London: Aquarian Press, 1964.

———. *The Study and Practice of Astral Projection.* London: Aquarian Press, 1961. Reprint, New Hyde Park, N.Y.: University Books, 1966.

———. *The Supreme Adventure: Analyses of Psychic Communications.* London: James Clarke, 1961.

———. *The Techniques of Astral Projection.* London: Aquarian Press, 1964.

Crookes, Sir William (1832–1919)

One of the greatest physicists of the last century and an early exponent of scientific investigation of psychic phenomena. He was born June 17, 1832, in London, England, and educated at Chippenhurst Grammar School and the Royal College of Chemistry, London. Even without a graduate education, he became one of the most decorated scientists of his era.

In 1855 he became superintendent of the Meterological Department, Radcliffe Observatory, Oxford. In 1961 he made his first great discovery, the element thallium. Two years later, he became an Elected Fellow of the Royal Society.

Crookes seems to have been led into research on **Spiritualism** because of the untimely death of his brother Philip in 1867. He first came into contact with psychic phenomena in July 1869 in a sitting with **Mary Marshall.** He was further intrigued by **trance** speaker **J. J. Morse** in December, and in July 1870, after the arrival of **Henry Slade** in London, he announced his intention to investigate the phenomena of Spiritualism. In an early article (1870), he declares:

"Views or opinions I cannot be said to possess on a subject I do not pretend to understand. . . . I prefer to enter upon the inquiry with no preconceived notions whatever as to what can or cannot be, but with all my senses alert and ready to convey information to the brain; believing, as I do, that we have by no means exhausted all human knowledge or fathomed the depths of all the physical forces."

The investigation had been suggested to him "by eminent men exercising great influence on the thought of the country." Another sentence of the article throws light on his expectations:

"The increased employment of scientific methods promote exact observation and greater love of truth among inquirers, and will produce a race of observers who will drive the worthless residuum of spiritualism hence into the unknown limbo of magic and necromancy."

Newspaper reporters received the announcement with jubilation. It was taken for granted that Spiritualism would be shown as clear and simple humbug. They were disappointed. The investigation began in May 1871, after the return of **D. D. Home** from

Russia. It was witnessed by Crookes's chemical assistant, Williams; his brother Walter; Sir William Huggins, the eminent physicist and astronomer, and ex-president of the Royal Society; and Sergeant **E. W. Cox,** a prominent lawyer.

The secretaries of the Royal Society refused Crookes's invitation to participate. His report was submitted to the Royal Society on June 15, 1871, but his communications were refused because they did not demonstrate the fallacy of the alleged marvels of Spiritualism. Even the inscription of the title of the paper in the society's publications was denied.

It was only from the July 1871 issue of the *Quarterly Journal of Science* that the public became acquainted with the first account of Crookes's observations. This account contained the description of a **séance** held at Crookes's house in a well lit room, in which the alteration of the weight of bodies and the playing of an accordion without hands was attested by specially designed apparatus. Said Crookes, "Of all the persons endowed with a powerful development of this Psychic Force . . . Mr. Daniel Dunglas Home is the most remarkable, and it is mainly owing to the many opportunities I have had of carrying on my investigation in his presence that I am enabled to affirm so conclusively the existence of this force."

In a subsequent article, "Notes of an Enquiry into the Phenomena Called Spiritual, during the years 1870–73," (*Quarterly Journal of Science,* January 1874), Crookes observes,

"The phenomena I am prepared to attest are so extraordinary, and so directly oppose the most firmly rooted articles of scientific belief—amongst others, the ubiquity and invariable action of the force of gravitation—that, even now, on recalling the details of what I witnessed, there is an antagonism in my mind between *reason,* which pronounces it to be scientifically impossible, and the conciousness that my senses, both of touch and sight—and these corroborated, as they were, by the senses of all who were present—are not lying witnesses when they testify against my preconceptions."

The description of these experiments and the summary produced a furious anonymous attack, now known to have emanated from Dr. W. B. Carpenter, in the October 1871 issue of the *Quarterly Review.* The article described Crookes as a "specialist of the specialists," an investigator whose ability was "purely technical," and added, "We speak advisedly when we say that the Fellowship of the Royal Society was conferred on him with considerable hesitation." (In a special resolution the council of the Royal Society expressed its regret over this statement.)

Many other scientists questioned the experiments on every conceivable ground. **Balfour Stewart** in *Nature* (July 3, 1871) referred to the illusions produced by mesmerists and conjectured that the observers had been fooled. E. B. Tyler quoted **Alfred Russel Wallace,** who suggested, for a different purpose, that the **werwolf** superstition might have been due to mesmeric influence. Extending the suggestion to Spiritualistic marvels, he conjectured that Home and **Agnes Guppy** might have been werewolves, capable of influencing sensitive spectators.

But nothing could shake Crookes' belief in the accuracy of his scientific observations. He continued his experiments, and in an article in the January 1874 issue of the *Quarterly Journal of Science,* he gave a detailed account of all the phenomena he had tested.

While Crookes's report of 1874, based chiefly on experiments with D. D. Home and **Kate Fox,** was met with skepticism, accounts of his next adventure, attempting to establish the separate existence of the medium (**Florence Cook,** 1856–1904) and the materialized **spirit** (**"Katie King"**), would stretch their credulity to the breaking point.

Crookes held a series of sittings with the young and beautiful "Florrie" between December 1873 and May 21, 1874. As part of his observations of Cook and King, he measured the difference in height, noted the absence of a blister on Katie's neck, the absence of perforation in Katie's ears, and the difference in complexion, bodily proportion, manner, and expression. He had himself photographed with Katie King and Florence Cook in the same position and while his picture was the same in the two photographs, the discrepancy between the girls' photos was obvious. Later Crookes reported that he had been allowed to enter the study with Katie and saw, by the light of a phosphorus lamp, the medium in trance, while Katie was standing by her side. Another time, in the full blaze of the electric light, Katie and Cook were seen together by Crookes and eight other people.

Forty-four photographs showed differences between the medium and the apparition. In a letter published in *The Spiritualist* (June 5, 1874), Crookes describes the photographing of Katie King:

"But photography is as inadequate to depict the perfect beauty of Katie's face, as words are powerless to describe her charms of manner. Photography may, indeed, give a map of her countenance, but how can it reproduce the brilliant purity of her complexion, or the ever-varying expression of her most mobile features, now overshadowed with sadness when relating some of the bitter experiences of her past life, now smiling with all the innocence of happy girlhood when she had collected my children round her, and was amusing them by recounting anecdotes of her adventures in India?

Round her she made an atmosphere of life;
the very air seemed lighter from her eyes,
They were so soft and beautiful, and rife
With all we can imagine of the skies;
Her overpowering presence makes you feel
It would not be idolatory to kneel."

In the same letter, Crookes deals with accusations of fraud on the part of Cook:

"Every test that I have proposed she has at once agreed to submit to with the utmost willingness; she is open and straightforward in speech, and I have never seen anything approaching the slightest symptom of a wish to deceive. Indeed, I do not believe she could carry on a deception if she were to try, and if she did she would certainly be found out very quickly, for such a line of action is altogether foreign to her nature."

After the Cook experiments, Crookes conducted another set of experiments in his home with the American medium **Annie Eva Fay.** She produced a variety of psychokinetic effects and Crookes wrote a favorable report on her which was published in the March 12, 1875, issue of *The Medium.* In 1876 Fay faced the first of a series of exposures and ultimately finished her career as a stage magician.

After the Fay examination, Crookes abandoned the attempt to validate psychic phenomena by scientific method and concentrated on his more conventional scientific research, although from time to time affirming that he would not retract his earlier endorsement of psychic phenomena. He served as president of the **Society for Psychical Research** (SPR) for the years 1896–99. It was not generally known, however, that from time to time he attended séances, and at one of these, around 1916, the spirit of his late wife apparently manifested.

Crookes went on to become one of England's most celebrated and decorated scientists. He was awarded the Royal Gold Medal (1875), the Davy Medal (1888), and the Sir Joseph Copley Medal (1904). He was knighted in 1897 (while president of the SPR) and received the Order of Merit in 1910. At different times he served as president of the Royal Society, the Chemical Society, the Institution of Electrical Engineers, and the British Association. The honors were acknowledgment of his numerous scientific accomplishments, including invention of the radiometer, the spinthariscope, and the Crookes tube. He was the founder of the *Chemical News,* and editor of *Quarterly Journal of Science.*

In the mid-1870s, Crookes abandoned his attempt to convince his scientific peers of the truth of his observations, but he never withdrew or modified his opinions. He responded to the fury of the controversy and became cautious. For example, he never allowed the circulation of a photograph in which he stood arm-in-arm with Katie King. In a letter to **Angelo Brofferio** in 1894 he said, "All that I am concerned in is that invisible and intelligent beings exist who say that they are the spirits of dead persons. But proof that they really are the individuals they assume to be I have never received" (*Für den Spiritismus,* Leipzig, 1894).

Before the British Association at Bristol in his presidential address in 1898, Crookes declared:

"Upon one other interest I have not yet touched—to me the weightiest and farthest-reaching of all. No incident in my scientific career is more widely known than the part I took many years ago in certain psychic researches. Thirty years have passed since I published an account of experiments tending to show that outside our scientific knowledge there exists a Force exercised by intelligence differing from the ordinary intelligence common to mortals. I have nothing to retract. I adhere to my already published statements. Indeed, I might add much thereto."

As late as 1917, in an interview published in *The International Psychic Gazette,* he reiterated: "I have never had any occasion to change my mind on the subject. I am perfectly satisfied with what I have said in earlier days. It is quite true that a connection has been set up between this world and the next."

The Continuing Controversy

While much of the controversy surrounding Crookes died as he withdrew from further **psychical research,** it never entirely disappeared. On occasion throughout his later life Crookes was questioned about his opinions on psychic phenomena.

No matter what extensive precautions Crookes employed, his results, in the eyes of the skeptics, were always unevidential. Charles Richet in his *Thirty Years of Psychical Research* (1923), published several years after Crookes's death, defended his colleague: "Until I had seen [**Eusapia Palladino**] at Milan I was absolutely sure that Crookes must have fallen into some terrible error. And so was **[Julien] Ochorowicz;** but he repented, and said, as I do, smiting my breast *"Pater, peccavi."*

The accusations against Crookes were fed by the fact that **Mary Showers**—who occasionally had performed joint séances (including one for Crookes, with Cook)—was later caught in a fraudulent **materialization** attempt and that Cook herself was caught cheating on two occasions in 1880 and 1889.

Cook continued to operate as a medium through the rest of the century and her sister **Katie Cook** succeeded her.

The most damaging allegations were made in June 1922, long after the death of Florence Cook. Francis G. H. Anderson, called at the offices of the **Society for Psychical Research** (SPR), London, and made a statement to **E. J. Dingwall,** then the research officer of the society, that he had had an affair with Cook many years ago, and that one night she told him that her mediumship was fraudulent. Further more, he testified that she had confided in him that she had had an affair with William Crookes, and the famous séances were staged as a cover. In 1949 Anderson repeated and expanded his story to Mrs. K. M. Goldney of the Society for Psychical Research.

Assuming his recollection of what Florence Cook said was reasonably accurate, the claim that the mediumship was fraudulent carried more weight than charges that William Crookes had been an accomplice in order to carry on a love affair. Crookes's defenders argued that, if the materialization of Katie King was fraudulent, it is more likely that Crookes was deceived. He became convinced of the reality of the phenomena of Home. Also, some of the Cook séances were conducted at Crookes' own home, near his wife and children. Crookes wrote enthusiastic letters to the press about the séances, openly admitting that he embraced the phantom Katie King, which appeared as flesh and blood. He took photographs of himself and the phantom. None of these actions seem consistent with organizing the séances as a cover for a love affair.

The view that Crookes was simply duped by (rather than an accomplice with) the mediums he tested was given weight by Houdini, who in his book claimed that Fay described to him the way she had gotten around all of Crookes's gadgets and tricked him.

The controversy was continued in 1962 when Trevor H. Hall, in his book *The Spiritualists,* presented persuasive evidence that Cook was fraudulent, and also repeated Anderson's claims that Crookes connived at **fraud** to hide a love affair with her.

Crookes did not hide his attraction to Cook's beauty. Hall built his case more upon Cook's association with Showers, who, he suggests, was possibly an accomplice in fraud. Showers also claimed to materialize spirit forms, in particular the phantom "Florence Maple," which reportedly had the same substantiality as Florence Cook's "Katie King."

Showers and Cook gave a joint demonstration at the house of William Crookes in March 1874, when the spirit forms Florence Maple and Katie King walked around the room outside the cabinet, linked arm in arm, laughing and talking like real human beings. E. W. Cox, who was present at this astonishing séance, expressed his extreme skepticism in a letter published in *The Spiritualist* (May 15, 1874). In a letter to Home in November 1875, Crookes stated Showers had confessed to Fay that she was a fraud, and he had later obtained a written confession from Showers. Fraud on the part of Showers provided valid doubts on the genuineness of the phenomena of Cook. Whether Crookes can be regarded as an accomplice in such fraud in order to carry on an illicit love affair with Cook is a separate issue.

Many find it is hard to believe that Crookes, with his reputation as a scientist at stake, would make such imprudent statements as he made if he was indeed an accomplice in fraud for the sake of sexual favors. Others find it just as hard to believe that Crookes was deceived by the "innocent schoolgirl," who would have to have been a remarkable actress, capable of outwitting Crookes's tests and sustaining a phantom role with a variety of anecdotes of a past life in foreign countries.

Crookes was certainly fascinated by Katie King and/or Florence Cook. It may be that his fascination overrode his scientific and personal judgment. Cook may have mesmerized him much as Madame Blavatsky dazzled **Henry Steel Olcott** with her apparently miraculous powers. If Anderson's recollection is correct, Cook's claim of an illicit love affair may have been no more than a boastful recollection of the glamour cast over Crookes by Katie King, especially Crookes's public embracing of the phantom.

It is likely that Crookes's career in psychical research and his relation to Cook will remain a topic of discussion in parapsychological circles. In the last generation the discussion has shifted as the defenders of physical phenomena, especially materialization, have retreated from the scene.

Sources:

Berger, Arthur S., and Joyce Berger. *The Encyclopedia of Parapsychology and Psychical Research.* New York: Paragon House, 1991.

Crookes, William. "Address by the President." *Proceedings* of the Society for Psychical Research 12 (1896): 338.

———. "Notes of an Enquiry into the Phenomena called Spiritual." *Quarterly Journal of Science* (January 1874).

———. *Researches in the Phenomena of Spiritualism.* London, 1874.

———. *Researches in Spiritualism.* London: J. Burnes, 1875.

———. "Spiritualism Viewed by the Light of Modern Science." *Quarterly Journal of Science* 7 (July 1870).

Dingwall, E. J. *The Critics' Dilemma: Further Comments on Some Nineteenth Century Investigations.* Dewsbury, England: The Author, 1966.

Fournier d'Albe, E. E. *The Life of Sir William Crookes, O.M., F.R.S.* London: T. F. Unwin, 1923.

Hall, Trevor. *Florence Cook & William Crookes: A Footnote to an Enquiry.* London: Tomorrow Publications, 1963.

———. *The Spiritualists: The Story of Florence Cook and William Crookes.* New York: Helix Press, 1963. Reprinted as *The Medium and the Scientist.* Buffalo, N.Y.: Prometheus Press, 1984.

Medhurst, R. G. *Crookes and the Spirit World.* London: Taplinger, 1972.

Medhurst, R. G., and K. M. Godney. "William Crookes and the Physical Phenomena of Mediumship." *Proceedings* of the Society for Psychical Research 54, 195 (March 1964).

Thouless, R. H. "Crookes and Cook." *Journal* of the Society for Psychical Research 42 (1963).

Crop Circles

Mysterious phenomena reported from Great Britain beginning in 1980. Large, wide circles, sometimes more than 100 feet in diameter, have appeared overnight in fields of grain. The grain in the circle is not dead, but the plant stems are flattened and sometimes darker in color than the surrounding grain. The first report of the circles appeared in the *Wiltshire Times* on August 15, 1980. It told of several circles that had appeared in the oat fields of John Scull farm near the town of Bratton. A year later a set of circles was discovered in Hampshire, near Cheesefoot Head. Unlike the earlier set, which had been randomly placed, this second set of three circles was in a straight line.

Most of the circles have been reported from the southern counties of Hampshire and Wiltshire, the same area already noted for its monolithic structures such as Stonehenge and Avebury. There are some occasional reports of similar phenomena in France, Canada, Australia, and the U.S. Between 1980 and 1987 approximately 120 circles appeared in the original area west of London. Then a dramatic increase occurred in 1988 with 112 reported. Over 300 were reported in 1989 and in 1990 over 1,000.

Over the years, the original circles gave way to ever more complex patterns, called "pictograms," which included circles arranged in geometric patterns, rectangles, crescents, and dumbbell shapes. In the case of concentric rings, the grain is sometimes flattened uniformly, at other times in contrary directions.

Typically, a new circle appears completely formed over one evening. The area forming the pattern is flattened, while the surrounding grain shows no sign of disturbance. The flattened grain shows no sign of damage other than being bent.

Explanations of the phenomenon include giant hailstones, crazed hedgehogs, too much or too little fertilization, and UFOs. There was even a suggestion that the circles may have been formed by helicopters flying upside down, but the absence of widespread helicopter wrecks disproved any dangerous practice of this kind. It is well known that small rings in grass meadows and lawns are known to be caused by mushrooms, but there is no evidence that the giant crop circles result from any known fungi. One theory that is distinct from speculations of paranormal effects is that of physicist George T. Meaden. He proposes a theory of atmospheric vortices that are electrically charged.

In 1991 Doug Bower and David Chorley claimed to have personally produced more than 250 of the circles. With the assistance of the British tabloid *Today,* they created a circle and invited Pat Delgado, the author of a popular text on the phenomenon, to inspect it. Once he pronounced the new circle genuine, the hoax was revealed. Other hoaxers had also produced circles that were judged genuine. However, those who believe in the mystery of the circles have suggested that hoaxing would only account for a few of the more than 2,000 circles. No one has been caught making a crop circle and none appear to have been left half finished. Additionally, it seems difficult to create some of the more complex pictograms in the dark. To date, monitoring of the area has failed to catch the formation of a circle on film or instrumentation.

Sources:

Clark, Jerome. *Encyclopedia of Strange and Unexplained Phenomena.* Detroit: Gale Research, 1993.

Delgado, Pat, and Colin Andrews. *Circular Evidence: A Detailed Investigation of the Flattened Swirled Crop Phenomenon.* London: Bloomsbury Publications, 1989.

———. *Crop Circles: The Latest Evidence.* London: Bloomsbury Publications, 1990.

Meaden, George Terence. *The Circles Effect and its Mysteries.* Bradford-on-Avon, England: Artetech Publishing, 1989.

———. *Circles from the Sky.* London: Souvenir Press, 1991.

Randles, Jenny, and Paul Fuller. *The Controversy of the Circles.* London: British UFO Research Association, 1989.

———. *Crop Circles: A Mystery Solved.* London: Robert Hale, 1990.

Crop Watcher, The

One of several British periodicals concerned with the phenomenon of **crop circles.** Address: 3 Selbourne Ct., Tavistock Close, Romsey, Hampshire, SO51 7TY, UK.

Crosland, Camilla (1812–1895)

Well-known author who, under her maiden name, Camilla Toulmin, became one of the early champions of **Spiritualism** in England. During the 1850s a constant guest of her house, a young lady, was discovered as the possessor of remarkable mediumistic powers. Three years of investigation brought conviction of **survival** to both Camilla and her husband. In 1856 Newton Crosland published a small book entitled *Apparitions.* This was followed in 1857 by the more important work of Camilla's, *Light in the Valley: My Experiences in Spiritualism.* Because of strong public prejudice against the new Spiritualist ideas filtering into the country at the time, the Croslands suffered both financially and socially for publishing their opinions. As a result, however, several people, including **Robert Chambers,** Mr. and Mrs. S. C. Hall, and Mary and **William Howitt,** came to investigate. They all became convinced of the genuineness of the manifestations. **Michael Faraday** was invited to test his unconscious muscular action theory regarding table movement, but he sent John Tyndall instead. In *Fragments of Science for Unscientific People* (1871) Tyndall published a derisive account of the sitting.

Crosland went on to write a number of books. In her last work, *Landmarks of a Literary Life* (1893), she devoted a chapter to the bold defense and elucidation of Spiritualism.

Sources:

Crosland, Newton. *Apparitions.* N.p., 1957.

Toulmin [Crosland], Camilla. *Light in the Valley: My Experiences in Spiritualism.* London; New York: G. Routledge & Co., 1957.

Tyndall, John. *Fragments of Science for Unscientific People.* New York: Appleton, 1872.

Cross-Correspondence

Concordant automatism, a scheme allegedly originated by the spirit of **F. W. H. Myers** to eliminate the hypothesis of **telepathy** from psychic communications.

Alice Johnson, research officer of the **Society for Psychical Research** (SPR), London, first discovered that such an idea was in operation when messages were received through various mediums at about the same times in places as far apart as India, New York, and London. In the scripts of **Rosina Thompson,** Mrs. Forbes, **Margaret Verrall, Winifred Willett** (pseudonym of Winifred Coombe-Tennant), **Leonora Piper,** and others, she found fragmentary utterances that had no point or meaning but supplemented one and other when put together, forming coherent ideas.

Reflecting on her find, she noted:

"Thus, in one case, Mrs. Forbes' script, purporting to come from her son, Talbot, stated that he must now leave her, since he was looking for a sensitive who wrote automatically, in order that he might obtain corroboration of her own writing. Mrs. Verrall, on the same day, wrote of a fir-tree planted in a garden, and the script was signed with a sword and a suspended bugle. The latter was part of the badge of the regiment to which Talbot Forbes had belonged, and Mrs. Forbes had in her garden some fir-trees, grown from seed sent to her by her son. These facts were unknown to Mrs. Verrall."

She concluded:

"We have reason to believe that the idea of making a statement in one script complementary of a statement in another had not occurred to Mr. Myers in his lifetime—for there is no reference to it in any of his written utterances on the subject that I have been able to discover. Neither did those who have been investigating automatic script since his death invent this plan, if plan it be. It was not the automatists themselves that detected it, but a student of their scripts; it has every appearance of being an element imported from outside; it suggests an independent invention, an active intelligence constantly at work in the present, not a mere echo or remnant of individualities of the past."

After the death of A. W. Verrall, the eminent Greek scholar and psychical researcher, an intricate Greek mosaic and literary puzzle called the "Ear of Dionysius" was transmitted as cross-correspondence. In the opinion of **Gerald Balfour,** and other competent judges, this was one of the most striking evidences of **survival** yet obtained. In the *Proceedings* of the Society of Psychical Research, hundreds of pages are devoted to cross-correspondences. They are so ingenious and subtle that their disentanglement requires considerable literary skill.

The subject was thoroughly studied by the Verrall family, **"Mrs. Holland"** (pseudonym of Alice Fleming), **J. G. Piddington,** and **Eleanor Sidgwick. Frederik Van Eeden** obtained cross-correspondences between his own dreams and the **trance** utterances of "Nelly," Rosina Thompson's control. **James H. Hyslop** used it for research in cases of **obsession.**

Many experiments were made to establish cross-correspondence in **thought-transference**—to find out another's thoughts over distance.

Among the more baffling cases of cross-correspondences came from the mediumship of Margery (i.e., **Mina Crandon**). They were instigated by her control "Walter," and given simultaneously through Margery in Boston, **George Valiantine** in New York, Henry Hardwicke at Niagara Falls, and Sarah Litzelmann in Maine. Drawings, geometrical figures, and sentences were given in part through each medium, in some cases in Chinese characters. Their reception was immediately verified by telephone or telegraph and the message deciphered by joining the pieces into a whole.

The ingenuity of these cross-correspondences was illustrated by a single instance: A cardboard box was brought into the séance room. It contained slips of paper with certain symbols, and a calendar, the sheets of which could be torn off a sheet at a time, which show a desired number. Walter declared that he had torn off a sheet and added: "Margery will make up a problem and Valiantine and Hardwicke will each make half the answer." He then closed the box.

The sitter placed in charge of the box after the séance did not open it. Margery and the company moved into the library. There Margery passed into a light trance and wrote automatically: "11 x 2—to kick a dead." The box was now opened; they found in it at the left the calendar, the top sheet of which showed the date of the 11th, and next to it an X from the enclosed symbols and last the torn-off sheet which bore the number 2. The internal arrangements of the box, therefore, completely agreed with the part of the cross-correspondence Margery wrote.

In New York, Judge Cannon, who was in charge of the Valiantine circle, reported by telephone that they received from Walter the following message: "2—no one stops." The next morning a telegram from Hardwicke from Niagara Falls announced this fragment: "2 horse." The fragments put together show that the problem Walter worked out was this: "11 x 2 = 22. No one stops to kick a dead horse."

While many psychical researchers have been impressed by the cross-correspondence evidence, Eric J. Dingwall, for one, scoffed at the evidence presented since researchers not connected with the project were not allowed to examine the original documents.

Sources:

Dingwall, E. J. "The Need for Responsibility in Parapsychology." In *A Skeptic's Handbook of Parapsychology,* edited by Paul Kurtz. Buffalo, N.Y.: Prometheus Books, 1985.

Douglas, Alfred. *Extra Sensory Powers: A Century of Psychical Research.* Woodstock, N.Y.: Overlook Press, 1977.

Hall, Elizabeth. *Possible Impossibilities: A Look at Parapsychology.* Boston: Houghton Mifflin, 1977.

Haynes, Renée. *The Society for Psychical Research, 1882–1982: A History.* London: MacDonald, 1982.

Heywood, Rosalind. *Beyond the Reach of Sense: An Inquiry into Extra-Sensory Perception.* New York: E. P. Dutton, 1961.

Saltmarsh, H. F. *Evidence of Personal Survival from Cross Correspondences.* London: G. Bell & Sons, 1938.

Tietze, Thomas R. *Margery.* New York: Harper & Row, 1973.

Cross-Reference

Simultaneous delivery of **spirit** messages through different **mediums** with a request to forward them to the right person. The idea, originated by the communicators themselves, was to disprove the suggestion that messages were merely the working of the medium's subconscious mind.

The earliest instance of cross-reference is registered in E. W. Capron's *Modern Spiritualism* (1885) from February 12, 1850. The medium was a Mrs. Draper. A large company was divided into two groups and sent to different rooms. The spirit of **Benjamin Franklin** purported to be present and spelled out a message telling the company not to move. The same message was then spelled out in the other room with instructions to go and compare. This method of communication was called "spiritual telegraphy" and was soon practiced between New York and Philadelphia or Washington, D.C., and between Baltimore and Pittsburgh.

A deceased sister announced herself to **Robert Hare** at Cape May, nearly a hundred miles from Philadelphia. Hare asked the spirit to go to Philadelphia and ask Mrs. B. Gourlay, a medium, to get her husband to go to a certain bank and inquire about a certain bill. On his return Hare found out that Dr. Gourlay had received the message and the bank testified that he came to inquire about the the bill.

Sources:

Bradley, H. Dennis. *The Wisdom of the Gods.* London: T. Werner Larvie Ltd., 1925.

Hare, Robert. *Experimental Investigations of the Spirit Manifestations.* New York: Partridge & Brittan, 1855.

Crosse, Andrew (1784–1855)

British amateur scientist and early experimenter with electricity, who may have been the model for Mary Shelley's creation of the main character in her novel, *Frankenstein.* In addition to his remarkable experiments in collecting atmospheric electricity in his laboratory, Crosse aroused fierce controversy through reports that he had spontaneously generated insect life through electrochemical experiments.

Crosse was born on June 17, 1784, at Fyne Court, Broomfield, Somersetshire, England. Fyne Court was the ancestral home of his family, whose forbears were granted a coat of arms in the seventeenth century. In 1793 he attended Dr. Seyer's School, Bristol, where he took a great interest in natural science and the developing study of electricity. His father was a friend of both **Benjamin Franklin** (1706–1790) and the scientist Joseph Priestley (1733–1804). In 1802 Crosse continued his education at Brasenose College, Oxford, as a gentleman commoner. He was not happy there, finding many of the students foolish and intemperate and the tutors unsatisfactory.

In 1805 the death of his mother left him an orphan; he had already lost his father, sister, uncle, and two of his best friends. He retired to a solitary life at Fyne Court, where he continued to study electricity, chemistry, and mineralogy. He became friendly with George Singer, who was then compiling his book *Elements of Electricity and Electro-Chemistry,* published in 1814. Starting in 1807, Crosse experimented in the formation of crystals through the action of electrical currents. The stimulus for this research was study of the formation of stalactites and stalagmites in Holywell Cavern at Broomfield. Crosse took some water from the cavern and connected it to the poles of a voltaic battery. After ten days, he observed the formation of crystals. This was the forerunner of a development 30 years later when he claimed to have observed the formation of insect life through electrocrystallization.

Crosse married Mary Anne Hamilton in 1809, and over the next ten years they had seven children, three of whom died in childbirth. In 1817 Crosse's friend Singer also died, three years after publication of his book on electricity. Crosse became increasingly reclusive and devoted himself to his scientific research. He erected a mile and a quarter of copper wires on poles at Fyne Court, connected to his "electrical room," where he experimented on the amount and nature of electricity in the atmosphere. He was regarded with awe by the local residents, who named him "the thunder and lightning man" and "the Wizard of the Quantocks" (the nearby Quantock Hills).

Crosse was linked with the poet Percy Bysshe Shelley and his young mistress Mary Wollstonecraft Godwin (later author of the novel *Frankenstein*) after they attended a lecture by Crosse in December 1814 in London, in which he explained his experiments with atmospheric electricity.

An account of a visit to Fyne Court by **Edward W. Cox** published in the *Taunton Courier* in Autumn 1836 reads like a description of a Hollywood film set for a Frankenstein film:

"But to proceed now into the penetralia of the mansion, the philosophical room, which is about sixty feet in length and upwards of twenty in height, with an arched roof—it was built originally as a music hall—and what wonderful things you will see . . . a great many rows of gallipots and jars, with some bits of metal, and wires passing from them into saucers containing some dirty-looking crystals. . . . It was the invention of a battery by which the stream of the electric fluid could be maintained without flagging, not for hours only, but for days, weeks, years, that was the foundation of some of Mr. Crosse's most remarkable discoveries. . . . Crystals of all kinds, many of them never made before by human skill, are in progress. . . . But you are startled in the midst of your observations, by the smart crackling sound that attends the passage of the electrical spark; you hear also the rumbling of distant thunder. The rain is already splashing in great drops against the glass, and the sound of the passing sparks continues to startle your ear. Your host is in high glee, for a battery of electricity is about to come within his reach a thousandfold more powerful than all those in the room strung together. You follow his hasty steps to the organ gallery, and curiously approach the spot whence the noise proceeds that has attracted your notice. You see at the window a huge brass conductor, with a discharging rod near it passing into the floor, and from the one knob to the other, sparks are leaping with increasing rapidity and noise, rap, rap, rap—bang, bang, bang; you are afraid to approach near this terrible engine, and well you may; for every spark that passes would kill twenty men at one blow, if they were linked together hand in hand, and the spark sent through the circle. Almost trembling, you note that from this conductor wires pass off without the window, and the electric fluid is conducted harmlessly away. On the instrument itself is inscribed in large letters the warning words,

"'Noli me tangere.' (Do not touch me)

"Nevertheless, your host does not fear. He approaches as boldly as if the flowing stream of fire were a harmless spark. Armed with his insulated rod, he plays with the mighty power; he directs it where he will; he sends it into his batteries: having charged them thus, he shows you how wire is melted, dissipated in a moment, by its passage; how metals—silver, gold and tin—are inflamed, and burn like paper, only with most brilliant hues. He shows you a mimic aurora, and a falling star, and so proves to you the cause of those beautiful phenomena; and then he tells you, that the wires you had noticed, as passing from tree to tree round the grounds, were connected with the conductor before you; that they collected the electricity of the atmosphere as it floated by, and brought it into the room in the shape of the sparks that you had witnessed with such awe."

Crosse's work on electrocrystallization appears to have anticipated that of A. C. Becquerel (1788–1878). Although Crosse did not disclose his discoveries to the British Association until 1836, he had been working on the subject before 1820. His fascination with the power of electricity and magnetism dated from early life, and as early as 1816, at a party of local residents, had exclaimed, "I prophesy that, by means of the electric agency, we shall be enabled to communicate our thoughts *instantaneously* with the uttermost ends of the earth."

In 1837 Crosse was working on electrocrystallization experiments when he observed tiny insects in metallic solutions believed to be fatal to life. Crosse made no formal report at the time, but confided his observations to an acquaintance, who spread the news—later featured in an unauthorized newspaper report, that Crosse had claimed to create life. Crosse was reviled all over England and Europe as a blasphemer for daring to usurp divine creative powers.

The appearance of the insects, of the genus *acarus* (mites) under conditions which seemed to preclude contamination of the solutions, has remained one of the anomalies of science, and was a forerunner of the spontaneous generation controversies of Béchamp and Pasteur. At the height of the Crosse uproar, Faraday stated that he had noted similar appearances, although he was reluctant to ascribe them to production or revivification. An amateur experimenter named W. H. Weeks, of Sandwich, Kent, also repeated Crosse's experiments under stringent conditions and reported that the insects appeared.

Crosse reported his findings in the *Transactions* of the London Electrical Society (1838) and in the *Annals of Electricity* (October 1836–October 1837). Years later, in a letter to the writer Harriet Martineau dated August 12, 1849, he summarized these findings as follows:

"In a great number of my experiments, made by passing a long current of electricity through various fluids (and some of them were considered to be destructive to animal life), acari have made their appearance; but never excepting on an electrified surface kept constantly moistened, or beneath the surface of an electrified fluid. In some instances these little animals have been produced two inches below the surface of a poisonous liquid. . . . Their first appearance consists in a very minute whitish hemisphere, formed upon the surface of the electrified body, sometimes at the positive end, and sometimes at the negative, and occasionally between the two, or in the middle of the electrified current; and sometimes upon all. . . . Then commences the first filaments, they immediately shrink up and collapse like zoophytes upon moss, but expand again some time after the removal of the point. Some days afterwards these filaments become legs and bristles, and a perfect acarus is the result, which finally detaches itself from its birth-place, and if under a fluid, climbs up the electrical wire, and escapes from the vessel, and afterwards feeds either on the moisture or the outside of the vessel, or on paper or card, or other substance in its vicinity."

Crosse was also aware of the possibility that apparent insect formations might have been mineral crystallizations that have a strong resemblance to animal form. Such "osmostic growths" were investigated by Dr. Stéphane Leduc of Nantes, in the twentieth century. Leduc demonstrated that "artificial" structures formed in crystalloid solutions imitate the appearance and some of the properties of organic life. Leduc's experiments revived the concept of spontaneous generation in an evolutionary theory of life.

Andrew Crosse was hurt by the hostility that his experiments aroused, since he had never sought publicity or made any claims beyond the facts as he observed them. As he explained in his letter to Martineau:

"As to the appearance of the acari under long-continued electrical action, I have never in thought, word, or deed, given any one a right to suppose that I considered them as a creation, or even as a formation, from inorganic matter. To create is to form a something out of a nothing. To annihilate, is to reduce that something to a nothing. Both of these, of course, can only be the attributes of the Almighty. In fact, I can assure you most sacredly that I have never dreamed of any theory sufficient to account for their appearance. I confess that I was not a little surprised, and am so still, and quite as much as I was when the acari made their appearance. Again, I have never claimed any merit as attached to these experiments. It was a matter of chance. I was looking for silicious formations, and animal matter appeared instead. . . ."

In addition to the unwelcome notoriety caused by this controversy, Crosse's wife and brother died in January 1846. He continued his experiments at Fyne Court, although he lived more like a recluse than ever.

However, on July 22, 1850, he married for the second time. His new wife was Cornelia Burns, who took a great interest in his experiments and assisted him with great competence. Crosse also researched a mode of extracting metals from their ores and methods of purification of sea water and other fluids by electricity. He contributed a paper, "On the Perforation of Non-conducting Substances by the Mechanical Action of the Electric Fluid," and also investigated the connection between the growth of vegetation and electric influence. In 1854 he gave a paper to the British Association meeting at Liverpool, "On the Apparent Mechanical Action accompanying Electric Transfer."

He died at Fyne Court on July 6, 1855. In her *Memorials . . . of Andrew Crosse, the Electrician* (1857), his widow published details of the life and work of Crosse and included a selection of poems written by him.

Sources:

[Crosse, Cornelia A. H.] *Memorials, Scientific and Literary, of Andrew Crosse, the Electrician.* London: Longman, 1857.

Gould, Rupert T. *Oddities: A Book of Unexplained Facts.* London, 1928. Reprint, New Hyde Park, N.Y.: University Books, 1965.

Haining, Peter. *The Man Who Was Frankenstein.* London: Frederick Muller, 1979.

Leduc, Dr. Stéphane. *Théorie Physicochimique de la Vie et Générations Spontanées.* Translated as *The Mechanism of Life.* London: William Heinemann, 1911.

Crow

The cawing of a crow is said to be an omen of evil. Another superstition claims that if a crow croaks an odd number of times, the weather will be bad; if even, the weather will be fine. In general, the crow has been considered a messenger of death since ancient times.

Crowley, Aleister (1875–1947)

The most renowned magic practitioner and theoretician of the twentieth century. He was born Edward Alexander Crowley, the son of Exclusive Plymouth Brethren parents. As he grew up, Crowley found himself unsympathetic with the faith of his father—an elder in the fundamentalist group—and mother. For his refusal to fall into line both in belief and practice, his mother called him "the Beast 666" (the Antichrist, from Revelation 13:18), a title he eventually accepted with some pride. Following his father's death in 1887, Crowley was sent to public school.

In 1894 he entered King's College and went on to Trinity College, Cambridge, the next year. During his college years he emerged as a poet of some merit. He also spent his leisure time exploring the joys of sexuality, a theme that strongly influenced his poetry and led to some trouble with college authorities. He also discovered and made his first ventures into magic and the occult. He left college before completing his degree.

In 1898 he was initiated into the Hermetic Order of the **Golden Dawn,** the pioneering ceremonial magic group, into which he was introduced by George Cecil Jones. He was an avid pupil and quickly progressed until he became involved in the split that had developed between the bulk of the members, who resided in England, and the head of the order, **S. L. MacGregor Mathers,** who lived in Paris. He sided with Mathers, which cut him off from fellow believers in London.

In 1903 Crowley married Rose Kelly, and in 1904 they traveled to Egypt. There, at his wife's insistence, he sat for a period on each of three days (April 9–11) and received (channeled) material from a spirit entity, Aiwass. The finished product, *The Book of the Law,* would provide the philosophical distinctives for what would become Crowley's own system of magic. The keynote of the new system would be *thelema* or will, and its basic admonition, "Do what thou will shall be the whole of the Law." This ambiguous phrase was often misunderstood by other magicians and by critics alike as promoting an amoral libertinism, but that was not Crowley's teaching or meaning. Rather, he taught that it was the magician's duty to discover his or her destiny (or true will), and, having discovered it, he or she had no choice but to align actions with the accomplishment of that true will.

Having left the Golden Dawn, in 1907 Crowley founded the Argentum Astrum (A.·. A.·. ; Silver Star). On its behalf he began issuing a periodical, the *Equinox,* a semiannual journal in which he began to publish the teachings of the A.·.A.·.. The journal attracted attention, however, because Crowley also began to publish the secrets of the Golden Dawn, which he denounced as a juvenile organization.

Crowley was diverted from developing the A.·. A.·. in 1912, following an encounter with **Theodore Reuss,** the outer head of the **Ordo Templi Orientis** (OTO), a German **sex magic** group. Crowley had independently discovered sex magic and made his first experiments in it several years earlier. In *The Book of Lies* he had published a brief section that indicated to Reuss that he knew about the sex magic teaching of the OTO, and Reuss invited Crowley into its membership. He was immediately accepted into the highest levels of the OTO and appointed head of its British branch, which he organized under the name Mysteria Mystica Maxima. Crowley also rewrote the OTO rituals, adding an eleventh degree reflective of his own homosexuality.

In 1914 Crowley moved to America, where he waited for World War I to end. During his stay he conducted extensive sex magic experiments, established an OTO lodge in Vancouver, British Columbia, and initiated **Charles Stanfeld Jones** (later known publicly as "Frater Achad") into the order. Because of his own accomplishments and the unexpected coordination of Frater Achad's magic work, Crowley declared Achad his "magical child" and assumed the title of magus, the second-highest grade.

In 1919 Crowley moved to Sicily and established a small magic colony at Cefalu. He remained there for four years, during which time he proclaimed himself an *ipsissimis.* Banished by Mussolini in 1923, he resided for a while in Tunis and France before settling down in England, where he spent the last 15 years of his life.

All through his life Crowley continued his experimentation with magic, which soon led him into the use of consciousness-expanding drugs. Along the way he became a heroin addict, a condition he fought but was never able to overcome.

During his mature years he expended much energy in building the OTO and in getting his writings published though in both endeavors he was only partially successful. Not until the 1970s—about thirty years after his death—was the order successfully organized and lodges established across Europe and North America. Simultaneously, most of his writings, including his magic diaries, were published, and they have remained in print.

Following Crowley's death on December 1, 1947, Karl Germer became the new outer head of the order of the OTO but did little to assist its growth. Germer died in the 1960s, and in the 1970s Grady McMurtry, having learned of Germer's death, assumed leadership and built the order into a substantial international body.

Sources:

Crowley, Aleister. *Confessions.* New York: Hill & Wang, 1969.

———. *The Holy Books of Thelema.* York Beach, Maine: Samuel Weiser, 1983.

———. *Magick in Theory and Practice.* New York: Castle Books, 1965. Reprint, St. Paul, Minn.: Llewellyn Publications, 1989.

———. *Magick without Tears.* St. Paul, Minn.: Llewellyn Publications, 1973.

———. *The Secret Rituals of the O.T.O.* New York: Samuel Weiser, 1973.

King, Francis. *The Magical World of Aleister Crowley.* New York: Coward, McCann & Geoghegan, 1978.

Melton, J. Gordon, and Isotta Poggi. *Magic, Witchcraft, and Paganism in America: A Bibliography.* New York: Garland Publishing, 1992.

Parfitt, Will, and A. Drylie. *A Crowley Cross-Index.* Avon, England: ZRO, 1976.

Suster, Gerald. *The Legacy of the Beast.* York Beach, Maine: Samuel Weiser, 1989.

Symonds, John. *The King of the Shadow Realm.* London: Duckworth, 1989.

Crucifixion, Gnostic Conception of

Gnosticism was a pre-Christian religious movement that competed with Christianity for a number of centuries, beginning in the first century C.E. Gnosticism developed its own form of Christian theology, an alternative to that presented in the writings later assembled as the New Testament.

A basic tenet of Gnosticism is that the created, material world is evil. It was not created by the true God but by a lesser being. Only by escape from the material into the spirtual world can there be salvation. The Gnostics believed that this explained the presence of evil in the world, because the true God could not have created anything less than perfect.

Because the material body is inferior and evil, the spirit of an individual is dwelling in an alien environment. This belief led the Gnostics to view Jesus as a human who received his Christ component during his lifetime, probably at the moment of his baptism in the river Jordan. From that time forth, being supernaturally gifted, Jesus began to work miracles. Before that, he had been completely ignorant of his mission.

At the Crucifixion, therefore, Christ ascended to God, from whom he had come, for he did not (and could not) physically suffer on the cross and die; rather, Simon of Cyrene, who bore his cross, suffered in his place: "And they compel one Simon a Cyrenian, who passed by, coming out of the country, the father of Alexander and Rufus, to bear his cross" (Mark 15:21). The Gnostics contended that a portion of the real history of the Crucifixion was never written.

At the Resurrection, the gnostics believed, the man Jesus was given another body, made up of ether, which was why the disciples did not recognize him after the Resurrection. During his sojourn on earth after he had risen, he received from God the perfect knowledge of spiritual truth, or gnosis, which he communicated to the small number of the apostles who were capable of receiving it.

Sources:

Lacarriére, Jacques. *The Gnostics.* London, 1977.

Mead, G. R. S. *Pistis Sophia: A Gnostic Miscellany.* London, 1921. Reprint, New Hyde Park, N.Y.: University Books, 1974.

Crumbaugh, James C(harles) (1912–)

American psychologist and parapsychologist. He was born December 11, 1912, in Terrell, Texas, and educated at Baylor University (B.A., 1935), Southern Methodist University (M.A., 1938), and the University of Texas (Ph.D., 1953). Crumbaugh's education was interrupted by World War II, when he served as an assistant psychologist in the U.S. Army Air Force Aviation Cadet Classification Program (1941–45). After the war he became an instructor in psychology at Memphis State University, a post he held while finishing his doctorate (1947–56). He served in the Veterans Administration Post-Doctoral Training Program in Clinical Psychology (1956–57); as chairman of the Department of Psychology, MacMurray College, Jacksonville, Illinois (1957–59); and as research director of the Bradley Center, Columbus, Georgia (1959–64). In 1964 he became a staff psychologist at the VA Hospital at Gulfport, Mississippi.

During the 1960s Crumbaugh received two grants from the **Parapsychology Foundation** for work on the repeatability of experiments in **ESP.** In spite of many years experimentation, Crumbaugh did not discover significant psi effects, but stressed the importance of the experimenter and repeatability in **parapsychology.** His research resulted in articles contributed to various psychological and parapsychological journals.

Sources:

Crumbaugh, James C. "A Scientific Critique of Parapsychology." *Behavior Psychology* 2 (September–October 1966).

Cryptesthesia

A term coined by **Charles Richet** meaning a hidden sensibility, a perception of things by a mechanism unknown to us of which we are cognizant only of its effects. It indicated an all-inclusive psychic sense which comes into action by some mysterious external vibrations which Richet termed the "vibrations of reality," the so-called **sixth sense.** It includes **clairvoyance, premonition, monition, psychometry, dowsing,** and **telepathy,** for Richet believed that among the unknown vibrations that bring cryptesthesia into action, human thought is one that can most easily be transmitted.

He argued that telepathy as a hypothesis comes before cryptesthesia, since the reception of thought vibrations implies a new faculty. Psychometry and dowsing disclose knowledge of facts, so Richet classified them as pragmatic cryptesthesia.

The theory of cryptesthesia as a human faculty aimed at barring the spirit hypothesis. It did so at the price of investing the living with flashes of omniscience.

With the establishment of parapsychology as the dominant school within psychical research, the term **psi** has largely superseded *cryptesthesia* as an overall term for the psychic faculty.

Cryptomnesia

A term coined by **Theodore Flournoy** and used in psychical research to denote unconscious memory. It may be accessible in **trance** and explain much unusual information, or knowledge recalled under special circumstances.

Italian researcher **Cesare Lombroso** says in his book *After Death—What?* (1909):

"Under certain circumstances, i.e. when I am at great altitude, say six or seven thousand feet, I remember Italian, Latin and even Greek verses which had been forgotten for years. But I know very well that I read them in early youth. Similarly, during certain dreams in nights when I am afflicted with conditions showing intestinal poisonings disagreeable memories of years previous . . . are reproduced with precision, and with particulars so minute and exact that I could not possibly recall them when awake. Yet I observed that they are always fragmentary and incomplete recollections and depend more on the conditions of the sentiments than on the intelligence."

Cryptomnesia has been encountered in instances of plagiarism in which authors use material from other writers, without any conscious memory that they have acquired such material from their prior reading, rather than from their own creativity. Through the twentieth century, cryptomnesia has been increasingly used to explain some extraordinary information given by entranced persons.

It played an important role in explaining the case of Bridey Murphy. In a hypnotic state, Ruth Simmons (pseudonym of Virginia Tighe) described in some detail a former life as a person who lived in Ireland in the early nineteenth century. M. V. Kline was one of several psychologists who suggested that Simmons had compiled a number of forgotten memories to create the character of Bridey. It was also discovered that as a girl, Simmons had lived across the street from an Irish family which included a woman whose maiden name was Bridie Murphy. The critique of the Bridey Murphy case suggested cryptomnesia as an explanation of many past-life and similar memories produced by people under hypnotism. It has also been invoked to explain some instances of **xenoglossis,** in which people speak a language they have never learned.

Sources:

Reed, Graham. *The Psychology of Anomalous Experience.* Boston: Houghton Mifflin, 1974.

Cryptozoology

Term coined by zoologist Bernard Heuvelmans to characterize the study of "hidden animals." It includes the study of the existence of known animals in places where they were not expected to occur as well as the persistence of animals presumed to be extinct. The key trait of animals considered the object of cryptozoology is their *unexpected* nature. The idea of cryptozoology was suggested by the discovery of exotic animals through the nineteenth and early twentieth centuries. They include the gorilla, the giant squid, and the coelecanth (a fish thought to be extinct for many millenia).

The primary interest of present-day cryptozoologists are such animals as the **Loch Ness Monster** and other lake monsters, Bigfoot and other living hominoids, and the possibility of various dinosaur survivals.

Heuvelmans established a **Centre de Cryptozoologie** in France.

Sources:

Heuvelsmans, Bernard. "What Is Cryptozoology?" *Cryptozoology* 1 (Winter 1982): 1–12.

Mackal, Roy P. *Searching for Hidden Animals.* Garden City, N.Y.: Doubleday, 1980.

Michell, John, and Robert J. M. Rickard. *Living Wonders: Mysteries and Curiosities of the Animal World.* New York: Thames and Hudson, 1982.

Cryptozoology (Journal)

Official journal of the **International Society of Cryptozoology,** concerned with the study and discussion of anomalous animal phenomena (i.e., animals at present unknown to science, but occasionally reported to exist, and that could be legitimate new species). The journal includes expedition and field reports, scholarly theorizing, and in-depth studies relating to **cryptozoology.** The journal is issued by the International Society of Cryptozoology. Address: Box 43070, Tucson, AZ 85733.

Crystal Gazing (or Crystallomancy)

A mode of **divination** practiced from very early times with the aid of a crystal globe, a pool of water, a mirror, or indeed any transparent object. Divinations by means of water, ink, and such substances are also known by the name of **hydromancy.** The crystal gazer is often known as a "scryer" and the operation of gazing known as "scrying." Crystal gazing may be a very simple or a very elaborate performance, but in every case the object is to induce in the clairvoyant a form of hypnosis, so that he may see **visions** in the crystal.

The "crystal" most in favor among crystal gazers is a spherical or oval globe, about four inches in diameter, and preferably a genuine rock crystal. The crystal may be white, blue, violet, yellow, green, opalescent, or transparent. Blue or amethyst colored crystals are less tiring to the eyes. As a genuine rock crystal of this size and shape is necessarily expensive, a sphere of glass is frequently substituted, with very good results. It must, however, be a perfect sphere or oval, free from speck or flaw, highly polished, and traditionally based in a stand of polished ebony, ivory, or boxwood. Precious stones were also used by crystallomancers of the past, the favorite stone being beryl in pale sea green or reddish tints. Among the Hindus, a cup of treacle or a pool of ink was made to serve the same purpose.

Crystallomancy was practiced by the ancients to invoke spirits, and elaborate preparations and ceremonials were considered necessary. A practitioner had to first be a man of pure life and religious disposition. During the days immediately preceding inspection of the crystal, he made frequent ablutions and subjected himself to strict religious discipline, with prayer and fasting.

The crystal and its stand were inscribed with sacred characters, as was the floor of the room in which the invocation was to take place. A quiet spot where the gazer was free from all disturbances was suggested. The gazer's mental attitude was no less important than the material preparations. Perfect faith was an essential condition of success. If the magician wished to be accompanied by one or two of his friends, they had to conform to the same rules and be guided by the same principles.

The time of the invocation was chosen according to the position in the heavens of the various planets, all preparations having been made during the waxing of the moon. All instruments and accessories to be used in the performance—the sword, rod and compasses, the fire and the perfume to be burned thereon, as well as the crystal itself—were consecrated or "charged" prior to the actual ceremony.

During the process of invocation, the magician faced the east and summoned from the crystal the spirit he desired. Magic circles were inscribed on the floor, and the crystallomancer remained within these for some time after the spirit had been dismissed. It was essential that no part of the ceremonial be omitted; otherwise, the invocation would be a failure.

If the person on whose behalf the divination was to be performed was not clairvoyant, he or she sought a suitable **medium,** the best being a young boy or girl, born in wedlock, and perfectly pure and innocent. Prayers and magic words were said prior to the ceremony, and incense and perfumes were burned. Sometimes the child's forehead was anointed, and he himself provided garments suitable to the impressive nature of the ceremony.

Some early writers mention a formula of prayers, known as the "Call," that preceded the inspection of the crystal. After the crystal was "charged," it was handed over to the medium. The first indication of clairvoyant vision was the appearance of a mist or cloud in the crystal. This gradually cleared away, and the vision appeared.

Paracelsus and others declared that such elaborate ceremonies prior to crystal gazing were unnecessary, and that the *magnes microcosmi* (the magnetic principle in man) was sufficient to achieve the desired objective.

Modern crystal gazing is carried on in much the same manner as in ancient times, although the preparations are simpler. The crystal is spherical and of the size of an orange. When in use it may be held between the agent's finger and thumb, or, if the end is slightly flattened, placed on a table; alternatively, it may be held in the palm of the hand against a background of black cloth.

The operation is more readily carried out in a subdued light. A medium or clairvoyant acts as the seer and if the divination is made for anyone else it is advisable that he or she be allowed to hold the crystal in his or her hand for a few minutes before it is passed into the hands of the clairvoyant.

The object of crystal gazing is the induction of a kind of self-hypnotic state giving rise to visionary hallucinations, the reflection of light in the crystal forming *points de repère* for such hallucinations. The value of elaborate ceremonials and impressive rituals thus lies in their potency to affect the mind and imagination of the seer.

It has been widely reported that the appearance of a crystal vision is heralded by a milky clouding of the ball. This clouding is a kind of picture in itself. It depends on no optical conditions and is not the result of a strain on the eye; it persists and will be visible even after the scryer turns his head away. After the first pictures it acts as a kind of drop scene. It has been compared to the cloud in **materialization** séances; phantasmal figures reportedly emerge.

The pictures to which the cloud gives way may be small or may fill the sphere. The visions are often symbolic, and the pictures are either vague images or they have a clear sense. Lifelike visions are comparatively rare. In the majority of cases, crystal gazing is only an amusing psychical entertainment provided by the subconscious self.

According to **Charles Richet,** about one person in 20 may succeed in the experiment but perhaps one among 20 successful experimenters will receive genuine impressions that could not have been obtained by normal means. **F. W. H. Myers** considered crystal gazing a form of automatism by which the subconscious self may send messages to the conscious self. Misplaced objects may be found through the use of the crystal ball; forgotten dreams may be revived, and a systematic exploration of the subconscious mind may take place.

Margaret Verrall, a lecturer at Newnham College, England, concluded from personal experiences that the picture is created from the bright points of light reflected in the crystal. Once formed, she said, the picture has a reality and spontaneity quite unlike an imaginary scene called up voluntarily with closed eyes. The pictures are mostly colored but occasionally resemble black and white sketches. She was successful in tracing most of her visions to recent memories.

"Miss X" (Ada Goodrich-Freer), author of *Essays in Psychical Research* (1899) and an experienced crystal gazer, said the best way to begin scrying was to look about the room and observe some brightly colored object, close the eyes, and try to transfer the picture to the ball. If this is successful, the next stage should be an attempt to recall a vivid memory picture and to transfer it into the ball in the same way. After this it is very likely that spontaneous images will also appear. Miss X often traced her visions to forgotten memories, which she used the crystal to recall. Occasionally, she could see in the ball the characters of a work of fiction she was writing. If she did not know how to proceed with the plot she looked into the crystal and watched the figures enact the next steps of the story.

She also related a curious instance showing how unconscious observation may become externalized in the crystal:

"I saw, as if in a cutting from *The Times,* the announcement of the death of a lady, intimate with near friends of my own, and which I should certainly have regarded as an event of interest and consequence under whatever circumstances communicated. The announcement gave me every detail of place, name and date, with the additional statement that it was after a period of prolonged suffering. I had heard nothing of the lady—resident in America—for some months, and was quite willing to suppose the communication prophetic or clairvoyant. Of this flattering notion I was soon disabused. An examination of the paper of the day before soon showed that the advertisement was there, just as I had seen it in the crystal, and though at first I was inclined to protest that 'I had never looked at yesterday's paper' I presently remembered that I had, in fact, handled it, using it as a screen to shade my face from the fire, while talking with a friend in the afternoon. I may add the fact that we have since discovered that the lady in question is alive and well, and that the announcement related to someone else of the same name, by no means a common one."

The range of such unconscious observation may be very wide. "I have," stated Goodrich-Freer, "for example, occasionally been able to reproduce in the crystal the titles of books in a bookcase or of engravings on a wall, which after-experiment has shown to be beyond my range of vision." She also noted the play of possible thought transference in the origin of crystal images:

"We were talking of a house she had never seen, and I was describing the entrance hall. Presently she said: 'Wait, I see it; let me go on. Is there a curtained archway opposite the front door? And is there a gong in a recess by the stairs?' This was perfectly correct, and knowing my friend to have psychic faculty, I wondered how far this might be clairvoyance. On the other hand, so keen is my own power of visualizing, that I had all the time a vivid picture of the scene in my own mind. I looked into the crystal and planned my little test. 'Go into the dining room' I said. A correct description followed. 'The table is laid for lunch,' she proceeded, 'but why have they lighted the candles in broad daylight?' The fact was that, as soon as I saw that her attention was fixed on the table, I lighted the candles in my crystal picture. Hers followed suit, proving some, at least, of her impressions telepathic."

The most arresting question, of course, is whether the pictures are ever objective. There have been a very few instances in which the pictures have been reported to be reflected in a mirror, seen by several persons, and even photographed. There are, however, no verified cases of these reports.

A series of experiments and observations on the physiological changes in the eye that accompany crystal vision were recorded by **Hereward Carrington** in his book *Modern Psychical Phenomena* (1919). He found, for example, that the seer sometimes looks at a point in space nearer or further off than the crystal, and if the scene is distant the focus of the eye adjusts itself to the apparent perspective.

One of the most famous gazing crystals was that of the Elizabethan magician **John Dee** (1527–1608), kept for many years in the British Museum, London, but recently transferred to the Museum of Mankind in London. This "shew-stone" appears to be of polished coal. It was only one of several crystals possessed by Dee, one of which he claimed was brought to him by angels.

Sources:

Besterman, Theodore. *Crystal-Gazing: A Study in the History, Distribution, Theory and Practice of Scrying.* London: William Rider, 1924. Reprint, New Hyde Park, N.Y.: University Books, 1965.

Frater Achad [Charles Stansfeld Jones]. *Crystal Vision Through Crystal Gazing.* Chicago: Yogi Publication Society, 1923.

Melville, John. *Crystal-Gazing and The Wonders of Clairvoyance.* London: Nichols, 1897. Reprinted as *Crystal Gazing and Clairvoyance.* Wellingborough, England: Aquarium Press, 1979.

Pelton, Robert W. *Ancient Secrets of Fortune-Telling.* South Brunswick, N.J.: A. S. Barnes, 1976.

Sepharial [W. G. Old]. *How to Read the Crystal.* London, 1922.

Seward, A. F. *The Art of Crystal Gazing or Secrets of the Crystal Revealed.* Chicago: A. F. Seward, 1873.

Thomas, Northcote W. *Crystal Gazing: Its History and Practice, with a Discussion of the Evidence for Telepathic Scrying.* London: Alexander Moring (The De La More Press), 1905.

X, Miss [Ada Goodrich-Freer]. *Essays in Psychical Research.* London: George Redway, 1899.

Crystal Healing

In recent years there was a surge of popular interest in the use of crystals for healing purposes, harking back to ancient times when priests and shamans of many cultures used crystals for healing, as well as for summoning the dead and scrying (i.e., **crystal gazing**) to obtain knowledge of distant events or to foretell the future.

Quartz crystals are a natural product formed by movements in the earth's crust. Silica in a molten state is moved toward the earth's surface. When it rises and cools, it changes structure, forming crystals on surrounding granite or sandstone cavities. The molecular structure of quartz crystal involves a perfect alignment and symmetry and imports unusual physical properties. Crystals can receive, amplify, convert, and focus energy, or store an electrical charge. If an electric current is passed through crystal it vibrates. If rubbed, a crystal generates an electrical current. Such properties have made crystals essential components of many modern devices, such as phonograph needles, watches, and microcomputers. Lasers use quartz crystal to convert electrical current into light and focus it as a beam of great intensity. These many interesting scientific properties and technological uses underlie much of the recent metaphysical attention to crystals.

Much of the modern interest in crystals in the **New Age** movement is rooted in the psychic readings of **Edgar Cayce.** In his readings mentioning **Atlantis,** Cayce described a large crystalline structure that supplied the power to run the Atlantean culture. He also spoke of the use of various crystals for individual personal needs. The references to crystals were later compiled in a booklet, *Gems and Stones: Based on the Edgar Cayce Readings* (1960).

In 1976 psychic channel Frank Alper began to convey a series of readings said to be from spirit entities. These readings were later published in a three-volume set and described the power system of Atlantis and the use of crystals in great healing temples. Alper claimed that crystals can actually absorb and store energy, which can later be discharged as a healing power.

According to Alper, crystals come in different shapes and sizes. Those with many facets are best for storing energy. Some crystals in the form of inverted pyramids were supposedly used for surgery on Atlantis. Flat, rectangular-shaped (emerald cut) crystals were used to filter light that rejuvenated the body. Alper also described the way in which a set of small crystals can be placed on or around the body of someone who desires to use the crystals' energy to either restore the body or elevate the consciousness.

Alper provided a comprehensive text on crystals. Through the 1980s his work was the basis of numerous texts on crystal power and elaborate speculations on the properties of crystalline structures. In his wake a considerable body of theory and practice has grown up around the use of crystals for healing purposes.

Marcel Vogel, a former research scientist at IBM, established a Psychic Research Institute in San Jose, California, to study, among other subjects, the claimed healing effects of crystals. He developed special techniques for "balancing and harmonizing" the body's energy field by means of crystals and claimed that many physicians and other healers were using such techniques. He videotaped his own experiments with hundreds of individuals and alleged improvements in relieving a variety of diseases, including Parkinson's disease, bursitis, arthritis, chronic back pain, and even blindness.

In spite of the efforts of people such as Vogel, however, acceptable evidence for the use of crystals as powerful storage batteries was not forthcoming, and only claims of its spiritual and metaphysical properties survived. Supporters still claim, for example, that a crystal placed in a room will bring harmony and peace to the environment, in drinking water will improve the flavor, and set in a refrigerator will help keep food pure. Crystals are also believed to relieve mental and emotional tension if held in the hand and to bring about harmony and clarity if worn during meditation.

For such applications, the crystal must first be "cleared," that is, subjected to a process to neutralize existing vibrations and energies, usually by placing the crystal in a clear running stream, soaking it in salt water, or "charging" it with one's own breath. A new word, *crystaphile,* has been coined to indicate lovers of crystals who believe that they may have occult applications.

Without scientific backing for crystals' physical properties, however, interest in them largely died out by the beginning of the 1980s. As William Jarvis of the National Council Against Health Fraud in Loma Linda, California, has noted,

"As far as I know, there is no convincing published data to indicate that crystals have any efficacy in healing. The effects that are claimed are more in the realm of the metaphysical than the physical. They cannot really be measured, and can be readily understood as placebo effects. Until there is scientific documentation, these treatments should be presented only as medical experiments, not as valid medical therapy." Meanwhile, the Chiropractic Board of Examiners in Massachusetts has banned the use of crystals in chiropractic work in the state.

Sources:

Baer, Randall, and Vicki Baer. *The Crystal Connection: A Guidebook for Personal and Planetary Ascension.* New York: Harper & Row, 1986.

Bonewitz, Ra. *Cosmic Crystals: Crystal Consciousness and the New Age.* Van Nuys, Calif.: Newcastle Publishing, 1983.

Gems and Stones: Based on the Edgar Cayce Readings. Virginia Beach, Va.: Association for Research and Enlightenment, 1960.

Gold, Gari. *Crystal Energy.* Chicago: Contemporary Books, 1987.

Raphaell, Katrina. *Crystal Enlightenment: The Transforming Properties of Crystals and Healing Stones.* Sante Fe, N.Mex.: Aurora Press, 1985.

———. *Crystal Healing: The Therapeutic Application of Crystals and Stones.* Santa Fe, N.Mex.: Aurora Press, 1987.

Crystal Skull

Ancient Mayan skull shaped from rock crystal, discovered at Lubaantun, British Honduras, in 1927 by explorer F. A. Mitchell-Hedges. The skull may be anywhere from 3,600 to 12,000 years old, and is believed to have been laboriously shaped by a succession of Mayan priests from a large block of pure rockcrystal by rubbing with sand. Such a method might have taken many years to complete.

Like the so-called curse of the Pharaohs, the skull is supposed to bring doom upon those who mock it. Reliable observers have reported extraordinary light effects, sounds and odors, suggesting **occult** properties. Extensive laboratory tests by the Hewlett-Packard Company, Santa Clara, California, revealed that the skull had remarkable optical properties that it would be virtually impossible to duplicate with modern equipment.

The only counterpart to this strange artifact is a rock crystal skull in the British Museum discovered in Mexico in 1889. It is much cruder in execution than the Mitchell-Hedges skull, and may have been a rough model for it. After the death of Mitchell-Hedges in 1959, the skull became the property of his adopted daughter Anna Le Guillon Mitchell-Hedges.

Sources:

Bowen, Sandra, F. R. Nick Nocerino, and Joshua Shapiro. *Mysteries of the Crystal Skulls Revealed.* Pacifica, Calif.: Aquarian Networking, 1887. Revised edition, 1988.

Garvin, Richard. *The Crystal Skull.* Garden City, N.Y.: Doubleday, 1973. Reprint, New York: Pocket Books, 1974.

Mitchell-Hedges, F. A. *Danger My Ally.* Boston: Little-Brown, 1955.

Morrill, Sibley. *Ambrose Bierce, F. A. Mitchell-Hedges and the Crystal Skull.* San Francisco: Cadleon Press, 1972.

Crystal Well, The

Former neopagan journal published by the Labrys Foundation that sought to restore interest in "the ancient religion" of **magic** and mystery. It was published in the 1970s from Seal Beach, California.

Crystal Well: A Journal of the Old Religion

Neopagan periodical originally titled *Waxing Moon.* It was published through the 1970s from Philadelphia, Pennsylvania.

Crystallization of the God Flame (Magazine)

Former monthly publication presenting the teachings of Elizabeth Clare Prophet, the leader of the **Church Universal and Triumphant.**

Crystals

Solid mineral objects having naturally formed plane faces. Their orderly external appearance derives from the regularity of their internal structure.

According to folk belief, crystals prevailed against unpleasant dreams, dissolved enchantments, and served as a medium for magical visions. Crystals bruised with honey were believed to fill the breasts with milk. Before the manufacture of glass, rock crystal was widely used for bowls, figurines, and drinking vessels. Magicians in Australia and elsewhere used rock crystal in rainmaking ceremonies. Rock crystal shaped into polished balls was also the favorite material for **crystal gazing.** (See also **Crystal Skull.**)

From ancient times crystal objects have been used as amulets and talismans. In ancient Israel, 12 stones (one for each of the 12 tribes) were placed on the breastplate of the high priest (see Exodus 39). Later, 12 gemstones were identified with the 12 signs of the zodiac. These survive today as birthstones.

Sources:

Bonewitz, Ra. *Cosmic Crystals: Crystal Consciousness and the New Age.* Van Nuys, Calif.: Newcastle Publishing, 1983.

Crow, W. B. *Precious Stones.* New York: Samuel Weiser, 1968.

Crystaphile

Term used to indicate a lover of crystal who believes that it may have **occult** applications. (See also **crystal healing**)

CSAR See Center for Scientific Anomalies Research

CSICOP See Committee for the Scientific Investigation of Claims of the Paranormal

Cthulhu Mythos

Term coined by August Derleth, biographer and editor of **H. P. Lovecraft,** writer of supernatural fiction. The term denotes the mythology invented by Lovecraft for a group of horror stories. According to Derleth, Lovecraft once told him, "All my stories, unconnected as they may be, are based on the fundamental lore or legend that this world was inhabited at one time by another race who, in practicing black magic, lost their foothold and were expelled, yet live on the outside, ever ready to take possession of this earth again."

Sources:

Carter, Lin. *Lovecraft: A Look Behind the Cthulhu Mythos.* New York: Ballantine Books, 1972.

Schweitzer, Darrell. *The Dream Quest of H. P. Lovecraft.* San Bernardino, Calif.: Borgo Press, 1978.

Cuadernos de Parapsicologia Journal

Quarterly journal of parapsychology published in Argentina. Address: Ramon Lista 868, Villa Sarmiento, Haedo, Buenos Aires, Argentina.

Cuchulain

Legendary hero warrior of Irish romance, son of the solar god Lugh and Dectera. His name means "Hound of Cullan," and his mighty deeds dominate Ulster lore. In order to marry Emer, daughter of Forgall, he was obliged to pass through the ordeals of the Land of Shadow and the warrior goddess Skatha, cross the Bridge of Leaps, learn the arts of war, and slay 100 men. Cuchulain also featured in the great Cattle Raid of Quelgny, described in the *Book of Leinster* of Finn MacGorman, bishop of Kildare, recorded in 1150.

In the twelfth century *Book of the Dun Cow,* Cuchulain is summoned from hell by St. Patrick to describe the terrors of hell to the pagan king of Ireland Laery MacNeill. As a result, the King was converted to Christianity and Cuchulain allowed to enter heaven. The deeds of Cuchulain as related in the *Ulster Cycle of the Knights of the Red Branch* are thought to have influenced the development of traditions of **King Arthur** in Wales and England.

Cuddon, Eric (1905–)

British barrister, hypnotist, and writer who engaged in parapsychological investigations. He was born January 18, 1905, in London, educated at Oxford University (B.A., 1927; B.C.L., 1928; M.A., 1931), and became a barrister in 1928. During World War II he was a squadron leader in the Royal Air Force Volunteer Reserve (General Service and Defense medals). He practiced hypnotherapy and was particularly interested in **telepathy** and mediumship. He was a member of the council of the **International Institute for Psychical Research,** London, and took part in investigations of **poltergeist** phenomena with **Nandor Fodor.**

Sources:

Cuddon, Eric. *Hypnosis: its Meaning and Practice.* N.p., 1938.

CUFOS

Acronym for **J. Allen Hynek Center for UFO Studies,** founded by astrophysicist **J. Allen Hynek** (1910–1986) to study **UFO** data.

Cuisinier, Jeanne A(dele) L(ucie) (1890– ?)

French anthropologist and research worker at the French National Center for Scientific Research, who also wrote on parapsychological subjects. She was born October 30, 1890, in Neuilly-sur-Seine, and studied at the Ecole des Langues Orientales Vivantes, Paris, the Institut de Phonétique Malais, and the Sorbonne, where she received her doctorate in 1944. Cuisinier studied magic beliefs and rituals among Asian peoples and published books on social geography and sociology, sacred dance in Indochina and Indonesia, and the shadow play in Kelantan. She also reviewed books for the *International Journal of Parapsychology.*

Culpepper, Nicolas (1616–1654)

Nicolas Culpepper, one of the most influential astrologers of all time, was born in Ockley, Surrey, England, on October 18, 1616. His father died shortly before he was born and he was raised by his mother and her father, a Church of England minister who taught him Greek and Latin. His good elementary education allowed him to attend Cambridge, where a life-changing tragedy afflicted him. Engaged to a young woman, he planned to run away with her and be married. However, on the way to their rendezvous point, she was killed in a freak accident. Culpepper suffered a nervous breakdown and refused to return to school. When he was disowned by his mother's family and left financially destitute, he apprenticed himself to an apothecary.

While becoming an accomplished apothecary, Culpepper also mastered **astrology,** and he began to link the two. His prosperity ensured by his 1640 marriage to a wealthy woman, he settled in London as herbalist. In 1649 Culpepper took the step that would earn him both his long-standing fame and the hostility of his colleagues. He published an English translation of the *Pharmacopea,* the book of healing remedies, a closely guarded secret of doctors and pharmacologists. He added to the volume his own astrological reflections, and his enemies used it as a means to ridicule him.

Culpepper developed tuberculosis probably in 1642 when he participated in the Battle of Edgehill with forces opposed to King Charles I. He was only 38 when on January 10, 1654, his illness caught up with him. His single book lived on as a standard medical reference book for several centuries and is still used today by people who prefer natural forms of healing. During the darkest days of astrology, in the late eighteenth and early nineteenth centuries, it remained in print and was a major source for people who began the astrological revival in the nineteenth century. It remains in print to the present.

Sources:

Culpepper, Nicolas. *Culpepper's English Physician and Herbal Remedies.* North Hollywood, Calif.: Wilshire, 1971.

Inglis, Brian, and Ruth West. *The Alternative Health Guide.* New York: Alfred A. Knopf, 1983.

Cults

A term used for many years in social science to refer to religious groups whose basic religious beliefs and practices differ markedly from those dominant in the particular culture in which they are found. The term *cult* has, however, since the 1970s become a pejorative term used to describe unpopular religious groups. Many groups labeled as "cults" are Spiritualist, occult, and metaphysical groups. The **Theosophical Society,** the **Spiritualist** movement, **Christian Science,** and occult groups such as the **Rosicrucians** were among the first groups so negatively labeled. In social science, the term has been replaced by the less prejudicial terms "new religion," **new religious movement,** or "alternative religion."

Contemporary use of *cult* was nurtured for many decades by Evangelical Christian organizations, some organized as late as the 1930s, to oppose groups that deviated from Christian orthodoxy. In the mid-1970s, a more secular anticult movement developed in the United States to oppose several new religions that focused their attention on young adult recruits. The major organization of the contemporary anticult movement is the **Cult Awareness Network,** which grew out of the older Citizens Freedom Foundation. It has nurtured a number of similar organizations in Europe and South America.

The anticult movement has encouraged the publication of a vast literature denouncing "cults." This literature is characterized by adoption of the "brainwashing" hypothesis to explain the destructive nature of the groups under attack. Such groups are said to have an unusual power to control the minds of their members to the extent that they lose the ability to think straight and evaluate their experience. According to the literature, members have been "programmed" and act like robots following every command of their leaders; they cannot choose to leave the harmful situation in which they have been trapped. This analysis justifies an intrusion into their lives by anticult forces. In extreme cases, such intrusions take the form of "deprogramming," a forceful removal of the person from the group and the application of social and psychological pressure to convince the person to break his or her relationship with the group.

In 1987–88, the American Psychological Association examined the issue of brainwashing or mind control in relation to new religions and other groups, such as psychological training groups, that had been accused of using techniques of "coercive persuasion" against their adherents. The association concluded that such theories were based on insufficient scientific data and that the work done was severely flawed methodologically. This opinion was confirmed by the American Sociological Association and the Society for the Scientific Study of Religion. Most scholars on new religions had rejected the brainwashing hypothesis shortly after its proposal in the early 1980s, and those opinions by the several scholarly bodies have been decisive in moving discussion of the so-called cults to other issues.

The anticult movement has joined the ranks of various opposition groups (anti-Catholic, anti-Mormon, anti-Semitic) that have dotted the religious landscape in recent centuries. In the meantime, scholars have noted a radical jump in religious pluralism in Western society.

Sources:

Ellwood, Robert S., Jr. *Alternative Altars: Unconventional and Eastern Spirituality in America.* Chicago: University of Chicago Press, 1979.

———. *Religious and Spiritual Groups in Modern America.* Englewood Cliffs, N.J.: Prentice-Hall, 1973.

Melton, J. Gordon. *The Encyclopedic Handbook of the Cults.* New York: Garland Publishing, 1992.

Melton, J. Gordon, and Robert L. Moore. *The Cult Experience.* New York: Pilgrim Press, 1982.

Cummins, Geraldine Dorothy (1890–1968)

Medium, channel, and Spiritualist author. Cummins was born January 24, 1890, in Cork, Ireland, the daughter of Prof. Ashley Cummins. She had a modest education and was well traveled. The development of her mediumship began in December 1923 in sittings with E. B. Gibbs. Ordinarily her work of composition was very slow, but her **automatic writing** speed was remarkable. On March 16, 1926, for example, she channeled 1,750 words in one hour and five minutes.

Her first books, beginning with *The Spirits of Cleophas* (1928), claimed to supplement the biblical books of the *Acts of the Apostles* and the epistles of St. Paul. It was a historic narrative of the early church and the work of the apostles from immediately after the death of Jesus to St. Paul's departure from Berea for Athens.

In the production of the first two sections of the book, Cummins was associated with *F. Bligh Bond,* but she received the scripts independently afterward. In her second volume, *Paul in Athens* (1930), the narrative is taken up and continued. The third, *The Great Days of Ephesus* (1933), followed the same line of thought.

The production of these automatic scripts was witnessed by several theologians, and the scholars who edited her books endorsed their intrinsic merit. They offered new interpretations of several obscure passages in the Acts of the Apostles, apparently showing close acquaintance with the early church and that age. For example, it was claimed that only a profound student could have given the head of the Jewish community in Antioch the title "Archon," because the usual title was "ethnarch" not long before the time referred to in the chronicle of Cleophas. Cleophas was not the immediate agent in the production of the scripts. They came through "the messenger." A total of seven scribes were said to be guided by Cleophas. The chronicle stated that it had been used in the early church but the existing few copies had perished. A more skeptical approach was adopted by **Rodger I. Anderson,** who examined Cummins's work in an article for *Theta* in 1983.

Cummins's fourth book, *The Road to Immortality* (1932), a series of communications purportedly from **F. W. H. Myers,** gives a stupendous vision of the progression of the human spirit through eternity. **Sir Oliver Lodge** offered his observations of Cummins's genuineness in the book's preface: "I believe this to be a genuine attempt to convey approximately true ideas, through an amanuensis of reasonable education, characterized by ready willingness for devoted service, and of transparent honesty."

Cummins wrote a detailed study of her automatic scripts received from the deceased "Mrs. Willett" (pseudonym of **Winifred Coombe-Tennant**) in the *Swan on a Black Sea; a Study in Automatic Writing; the Cummins-Willett Scripts* (1970). This highly regarded work contains a foreword by parapsychologist Professor **C. D. Broad.** Cummins also wrote *The Fate of Colonel Fawett* (1955), dealing with psychically acquired information about the fate of the famous missing explorer, and worked with doctors on a project to heal neurotic patients through extrasensory exploration of the subconscious mind. Her book *Unseen Adventures* (1951) contains autobiographical material.

Sources:

Anderson, R. I. "The Mediumship of Geraldine Cummins." *Theta* 11, 3 (Autumn 1983).

Connell, R., and Geraldine Cummins. *Perceptive Healing.* London: Psychic Book Club, 1945.

Cummins, Geraldine. *Beyond Human Personality.* London: Psychic Press, 1935. Revised edition, 1952.

———. *The Fate of Colonel Fawett.* London, 1955.

———. *The Road to Immortality.* London: Ivor Nicholson & Watson, 1933.

———. *Swan on a Black Sea: a Study in Automatic Writing: the Cummins-Willett Scripts.* New York: Samuel Weiser, 1970.

———. *Travelers in Eternity.* Compiled by E. B. Gibbs. London: Psychic Press, 1984.

———. *Unseen Adventures.* London: Rider, 1951.

Heywood, Rosalind. "Notes on the Mediumship of Geraldine Cummins." *Journal* of the Society for Psychical Research 45, 746 (December 1970).

Cunning

In addition to normal usage implying "crafty," *cunning* has an ancient meaning of "skillful" or "wise," especially when applied to occult or magic knowledge. The Anglo-Saxon term *wortcunning* means a knowledge of the medical and occult properties of plants (*wort*) and was applied to herbalists. In the course of time, the term *cunning-man* or *cunning-woman* was applied to so-called white witches, who practiced simple spells and claimed to discover those putting "the evil eye" on cattle, and who also cured ailments by herbs and magic practices.

Sources:

Cockayne, T. O., ed. *Leechdoms, Wortcunning, & Starcraft.* 2 vols. London: Longman, Green, 1864–66. Reprint, n.p., 1968.

Curnow, W. Leslie (d. 1926)

Australian-born journalist who became prominent as a Spiritualist in Britain. He was born in New South Wales and studied at Sydney University (B.A.). He was a journalist on the staff of the Sydney *Morning Herald* and then moved to London in 1913 to write for the *Times.*

Curnow became a member of the Society for Psychical Research and was assistant editor of the Spiritualist journal *Light.* He contributed articles to a variety of psychic periodicals and was responsible for several books, including *The W. T. Stead Borderland Library Catalogue* (1923) and *The Physical Phenomena of Spiritualism: A Historical Survey* (1925).

He is chiefly remembered for his involvement with **Sir Arthur Conan Doyle**'s famous two-volume work *The History of Spiritualism,* first published at the author's own expense in 1924 and reprinted in 1975. In this work Doyle gratefully acknowledges his indebtedness to Curnow, pointing out that such a history needed more research than his own busy life permitted. Doyle also states in his preface, "I cannot admit too fully the loyal assistance which he (Curnow) has given me, and if I have not conjoined his name with my own upon the title-page it is for reasons which he understands and in which he acquiesces." Curnow died February 11, 1926.

Sources:

Doyle, Arthur Conan. *The History of Spiritualism.* 2 vols. London: The Author, 1924. Reprint, New York: Arno Press, 1975.

Curran, Pearl Lenore (Pollard) (1883–1937)

A housewife in St. Louis, Missouri, through whom the **Patience Worth** books were produced. On July 8, 1913, Curran and a friend Emily Grant Hutchings were playing with the **Ouija board** when it moved under her hands at a rapid rate. A message was spelled out that read, "Many moons ago I lived. Again I come—Patience Worth my name." Patience Worth, whoever or whatever she was, continued to communicate through Curran for the next quarter-century, at first through the Ouija board and then directly. She produced poems, prayers, and several full-length novels. Of the novels, *The Sorry Tale,* set in the time of Jesus, elicited the most response, including praise from a reviewer in the *New York Times.* During the early years, Worth communicated in an archaic English that, although it proved to be a language never spoken, nevertheless consisted almost entirely of Anglo-Saxon root words and no modernisms.

Some psychical researchers found much to praise in Curran's work. They noted that she had received material from sources far beyond her knowledge while in a waking state. Walter Franklin Prince believed that if the Spiritualist hypothesis that Patience Worth was a disembodied spirit communicating through Curran was not accepted, then a reappraisal of our understanding of the subconscious must be revised. Of course, over the last few decades that is exactly what has happened, and Curran's production, while notable, has been duplicated and does not seem as extraordinary.

Sources:

Hickman, Irene. *I Knew Patience Worth.* Sacramento, Calif.: The Author, 1971.

Litvag, Irving. *Singer in the Shadows: the Strange Story of Patience Worth.* New York: Macmillan, 1972.

Prince, Walter F. *The Case of Patience Worth.* Boston: Boston Society for Psychical Research, 1927.

Worth, Patience. *Hope Trueblood.* New York: Henry Holt, 1918.

———. *Light from Beyond: Poems of Patience Worth.* Compiled by Herman Behr. New York: Patience Worth Publishing, 1923.

———. *The Pot Upon the Wheel.* St. Louis, Mo.: Dorset Press, 1921.

———. *The Sorry Tale.* New York: Henry Holt, 1917.

Cursed Bread

Used in ancient times for **divination** or "ordeal by flour or bread." A piece of bread, about an ounce in weight, over which a spell had been cast, was administered to the suspected person. If it caused sickness or choking, the person was said to be guilty; if not, he or she was regarded as innocent. Barley bread was often used for this form of divination, since it was more likely to cause choking. This method of trial was practiced among the Anglo-Saxons.

Curtiss, Harriette Augusta (1856–1932)

Harriette Augusta Curtiss was the author of a number of influential occult books and the cofounder, with her husband, F. Homer Curtiss, of the Order of Christian Mystics. She was given a good education and was headed for a career on the stage when her mother asked her not to pursue such a course. She eventually became a clairvoyant. She was 51 years old when she married F. Homer Curtiss and they began a very successful collaboration as occult leaders and teachers. The year of their marriage they founded the Order of the 15, whose task was the correlation of theosophical and orthodox Christian teachings. Through it she issued monthly lessons for students.

The Order of the 15 evolved into the Order of Christian Mystics. Curtiss assumed the role of teacher for the order and operated under the religious name Rahmea. Meanwhile, Homer Curtiss served as the order's secretary. Hariette Curtiss's first book was assembled from correspondence to students and published as *Letters from the Teacher.* The monthly lessons were later gathered into the order's basic text, *The Voice of Isis,* and the more advanced text, *The Message of Aquaria.*

During World War I the Curtisses formed the Church of the Wisdom Religion, a more esoteric group, to work alongside the Order of Christian Mystics. The church was later incorporated as the Universal Religious Foundation. Through the fruitful years of leading these two organizations, Curtiss wrote more than 20 books and booklets covering a variety of occult topics.

Sources:

Curtiss, Harriette Augusta, and Homer Curtiss. *The Key of Destiny.* New York: E. P. Dutton, 1991.

———. *Letters from the Teacher.* 2 vols. Hollywood, Calif.: Curtiss Philosophic, 1918.

———. *The Message of Aquaria.* San Francisco: Curtiss Philosophic, 1921.

———. *The Voice of Isis.* Washington, D.C.: Curtiss Philosophic, 1935.

Cutten, John H(ector)

British author of textbooks on radar and psychical researcher. Cutten served for a number of years as secretary of the **Society for**

Psychical Research, London, and had a special interest in **telepathy, clairvoyance,** and the evidence for existence of the human **aura.**

Cutten invented what he called the "Ghost Detector," a complex apparatus consisting of a main control box containing the electronics, a camera loaded with infrared film, a wind vane and vibrator, an ordinary flash unit, a flash unit with an infrared filter, a tape recorder, a photoelectric cell, a microphone, a pilot light, and a thermostatic control.

It is often claimed that ghostly visitations are accompanied by drafts of air, vibrations, changes in the illumination of the room, noises, changes in temperature, or physical disturbances. If any such changes took place in a haunted room, the ghost detector operated automatically. The first camera took a photograph with infrared film. Simultaneously, a buzzer was automatically switched on. The investigator could then press the remote control bulb to take an ordinary photograph with the standard film unit. The arrangement also included a thin wire trained around the room that triggered the equipment if touched.

Sources:

Haynes, Renée. *The Society for Psychical Research, 1882–1982: A History.* London: Macdonald, 1982.

Cyamba

The chief of the **Egbo Society,** a secret council of tribes in Calabar, near the Niger delta, in earlier times. The Egbo practiced a form of sorcery and magic called **Obeah.**

Cycles (Journal)

Journal of the Foundation for the Study of Cycles, published in nine issues per year. Includes information on conferences, articles, and news items. Address: 900 W. Valley Rd., Ste. 502, Wayne, PA 19087.

D

D'Abadie, Jeannette (ca. 1609)

Self-confessed 16-year-old witch from the village of Sibôurre, in Gascony, France. According to **Pierre De Lancre,** she once claimed to have been transported to sea by a demon, where she saw other sorcerers raising storms to sink ships.

One day as she was sleeping a demon carried her off to the devil's sabbath, where she awoke to find herself in the midst of a large company. She saw that the principal demon had two faces, like the Roman god Janus. She did not participate in the revelry, and was transported home. On the threshold she found her **amulet,** which the demon had removed from her bosom before taking her away. She confessed all that had happened, renounced her practice of **witchcraft,** and saved herself from the common fate of witches and sorcerers of her day.

Dactylomancy

A term covering various forms of **divination** practiced with the aid of rings. One method resembles the **table-tipping** or **raps** of **Spiritualism.** A round table is inscribed with the letters of the alphabet, and a ring suspended above it. The ring, it is said, will indicate certain letters, which make up the message required. According to the historian Ammianus Marcellinus (320–390 C.E.), this method was used to find the successor to Flavius Valens (d. 378 C.E.); the name Theodosius was correctly indicated. Solemn religious services accompanied this mode of divination.

Another form of dactylomancy, of which there is no detailed account, was practiced with rings of gold, silver, copper, iron, or lead, placed on the fingernails in certain conjunctions of the planets.

Today a wedding ring is most popular for this purpose. Another way to divine an answer is to suspend the ring near a glass tumbler so that it touches the glass when swung. A code may then be arranged, the ring striking the glass once for an affirmative, twice for a negative answer, and so on. (See also **pendulums**)

Sources:

Waite, Arthur Edward. *The Occult Sciences.* 1891. Reprint, Secaucus, N.J.: University Books, 1974.

Dactyls

A class of sorcerers and scientific physicians originating in ancient Phrygia around the fifth century B.C.E. The number of members was given differently by different sources. Some said it equaled the number of fingers on the hands—five male and five female. Pausanias said five, Perecydes 52 (20 right and 32 left), while Orpheus the Argonaut mentioned a larger number.

The dactyls were magicians, exorcists, conjurers, and soothsayers. Plutarch said they made their appearance in Italy as sorcerers. Their mysterious practices threw the people of Samothrace into consternation. They were credited with the first a use of minerals and with developing the notes of the musical scale, as well as with the discovery and use of the Ephesian mines.

They supposedly introduced fire into Crete and musical instruments into Greece. They were good runners and dancers and were skilled in science and learning. They were said by some to have been the magnetic powers and spirits, whose head was Hercules.

Sources:

Eliade, Mircea. *Forgerons et Alchimistes.* Flammarion, 1965. Translated as *The Forge and the Crucible.* New York: Harper & Brothers, 1962.

"Daemonologie"

A book by James VI, king of Scotland (later James I of England). The king's books were greatly admired in his day, winning the praise of Bacon, Izaak Walton, and numerous equally eminent men of letters. Published in 1597, *Daemonologie* is written in "[the] forme of ane dialogue," the speakers being Philomathes a skeptic of magic, and Epistemon, who enlightens Philomathes on the subject. Epistemon names many famous acts of **witchcraft** for the sake of analysis, but when Philomathes asks why the black art is considered wicked Epistemon fails to give a satisfactory answer. He merely rails against the practice, making trite statements. Epistemon is converted to the other speaker's point of view, declaring loudly that all sorcerers and the like "ought to be put to death according to the law of God, the civill and imperiall Law, and municipall Law of all Christian Nations."

The book was indicative of James's credulity toward witchcraft. He attended some witchcraft trials in Scotland and was impressed with the evidence presented. Later, Puritan Bible translators seeking James I's approval of their work translated the Hebrew word *ob* as "witch" to gain his favor. That translation in the King James Version of the Bible provided the English-speaking world with phrases such as "Thou shalt not suffer a witch (*ob*) to live" and the "witch (*ob*) of Endow."

Sources:

James I. *Daemonologie.* 1597. New York: De Capo Press, 1969.

Macdougall, Norman. *James IV.* Edinburgh: John Donald Publishers, 1989.

Dahl, Ingeborg (Mrs. Koeber)

Daughter of Judge Ludwig Dahl of Fredrikstad, Norway, whose **trance** mediumship provided many in the 1930s with what they considered impressive evidence for spirit return.

Thorstein Wereide, a professor at the University of Oslo, describes his experiences in an article in *Psychic Science* (April 1931). In 1925 Wereide and his wife moved into an apartment in an old wooden house in Oslo. On February 23, 1926, in the middle of the night, Mrs. Wereide was awakened by three loud knocks on the front door. Thinking that guests of the family below had mistaken the apartment, she ignored the knocks, but soon afterward was startled by the same knocking at the door of her sitting room. She entered the room and saw no one, but when she went into the entrance hall she saw a tall man in evening dress with a sad expression. He asked her to help him, and specifically to remember a date. "It was the 23rd of February yesterday," he said, then suddenly vanished. The electric light was on and the doors were closed. The man was seen again on three occasions, and he always disappeared near a small room in the corner of the apartment.

The following year, on the same day, Wereide awoke to hear his wife holding a loud conversation with an invisible person while she was sitting up in bed. She was in a state of trance, which lasted half an hour. Wereide wrote down her side of the conversation, from which it emerged that the ghost claimed to be a man who had lived in the house. He said he was not really dead, and told Mrs. Wereide, "I cannot get into contact with other people who are dead."

The Wereides then decided to experiment with Ingeborg Dahl, a medium they knew. Without mentioning their experience, they invited her to spend an evening with them during the autumn of 1928. Dahl went into a waking trance and her control "Ludvig" immediately contacted the ghost. The control requested that on a certain day Dahl sit down in her home with paper and pencil. When she did this, a name was written on the paper.

On May 29, 1929, the Wereides again invited Dahl to their home. She went into a waking trance; the ghost said there was something in the house that must be destroyed and that he needed her help. She took the hand of the ghost and went to the small room where he always disappeared. At her suggestion, the door to another room was closed, so that light entered only from the street through a window. The medium then asked, "Was it here?" A slight tap was heard and in a moment there appeared in her hand two old letters, tied together with red ribbon. The medium went back into the bedroom and stood in front of a stove, insisting that the letters be burned. The Wereideses hesitated, noting that the paper was yellow with age and the ink very pale, then reluctantly burned them.

Through the medium the ghost then said,

"Now I have reached what I tried to do all this time. I understand very well that you were eager to have the letters, but then all my work would have been done in vain. The letters concerned a lady who has lived in the house, and her honor was threatened as long as the letters were there. It was my fault."

Afterward there were no further ghostly phenomena, and Wereide, who had formerly accepted the possibility of all psychic phenomena except **apports,** now accepted apport phenomena.

Dahl (by that time known under her married name, Ingeborg Koeber) was also the subject of a strange trial at the Oslo Criminal Court in 1935. On August 8, 1934, her father, Judge Ludwig Dahl, the mayor of Bergen, drowned while swimming in the sea. She reportedly heard him call for help and swam out to rescue him. She brought him safely to shore, but he died in her arms. At the inquest, the mayor's deputy, Christian Apenes, told the coroner that on December 4, 1933, he attended a Spiritualist séance with Judge Dahl. The medium was Koeber, and in a trance she communicated a message allegedly from her dead brother, Regnar Dahl. The message was that their father would die within a year, but that Apenes must not tell anyone this, including Koeber, who would not remember the message when she came out of the trance. The spirit also stated that the same message would be communicated to another medium, a Mrs. Stolt-Nielsen, who was to make a note of it and place it in a sealed envelope.

After Judge Dahl's death, Apenes asked Stolt-Nielsen if she had received the message, and she produced a sealed envelope. Opened in the presence of witnesses, it contained the message, "In August 1934 Mayor Ludwig Dahl shall lose his life in an accident." When these prophecies were revealed by the press, there was considerable scandal and controversy. Some people thought the mayor might have committed suicide under subconscious suggestion, others that his daughter had drowned him before bringing him back to shore. It was even suggested that Apenes had hypnotized her and suggested that she murder her father.

Koeber took the matter to court to clear her name of such rumors. The investigation lasted three years, during which it was revealed that her father's life insurance policy had expired on the day of his death. The court then found that Judge Dahl's death accidental, but the judge's wife, who had suffered great strain, committed suicide before her daughter's name was cleared.

The case was discussed in a book by Cornelius Tabori, as well as by Harry Price, who had attended a séance with the Dahl family in 1927. Price had been so impressed by the Dahls' sincerity that he helped Judge Dahl find a London publisher for his book *We Are Here* (1931), to which **Sir Oliver Lodge** contributed a foreword.

Sources:

Price, Harry. *Fifty Years of Psychical Research.* N.p., 1939.
Tabori, Cornelius. *My Occult Diary.* London, 1951.

Dahne, Micki

A modern sensitive whose predictions about famous people were covered by the *National Enquirer* in the mid-1970s and who has since hosted her own radio shows. A bright, cheerful blonde, she interpreted **ESP** as "extra-sensitive perception" and has stated that she dislikes psychic connotations. She believes this sensitivity to be present in many individuals, and has encouraged her own children to develop it.

After coverage by the tabloid press began, she delivered alleged communications from such deceased celebrities as Mary Jo Kopechne (of the Kennedy-Chappaquiddick tragedy) and Marilyn Monroe.

Daim, Wilfried (1923–)

Austrian psychologist and psychotherapist who investigated areas of **parapsychology.** He was born July 21, 1923, in Vienna, and received his Ph.D. at the University of Vienna in 1948. He began the practice of psychotherapy and in 1958 was named head of the Institute for Political Psychology, Vienna. Apart from several books on psychology, Daim has written on experimental dream telepathy and various related topics and published a book describing his interest in the psychic realm, *Experimente mit der Seele* (1949).

Sources:

Pleasants, Helene, ed. *Biographical Dictionary of Parapsychology.* New York: Helix Press, 1964.

Dalan

A druid who figures in the medieval Irish legend of **Conary Mor,** high king of Ireland.

Dale, Laura A(bbott) (1919–1983)

Prominent member of the **American Society for Psychical Research** (ASPR) who for 25 years edited the society's *Journal.* Dale was born August 22, 1919, in Cornwall, New York, and attended private schools in New York City before studying at the Sorbonne in Paris. Her research included experiments in dream telepathy and proxy sittings with medium **Eileen Garrett.** She was also closely concerned with the medical section of the society beginning in 1948.

Dale was author or coauthor of a score of papers in the *Journal* of the ASPR and collaborated with Gardner Murphy on his book *Challenge of Psychical Research: A Primer of Parapsychology* (1966). She became editor of the society's *Journal* in 1941 and was later appointed research associate and publications editor for the ASPR. She resigned as editor of the *Journal* in 1947 to devote time to her research projects and work as a clinical assistant at the Department of Psychiatry, Maimonides Hospital, Brooklyn, New York. She continued to be actively involved in production of the *Journal* and the *Proceedings.*

In 1960, Dale left the ASPR staff for three years when she moved from New York to a house on Long Island. She became an editorial associate at **University Books** in New York, concerned with its publication program devoted to psychical research. In 1963 she returned to the ASPR as editor of the *Journal* and *Proceedings.* She was a charter member of the **Parapsychological Association.** She died February 2, 1983, on Long Island, New York. (For a bibliography of her publications, compiled by Rhea A. White, see the *Journal* of the ASPR October 1983.)

Sources:

Berger, Arthur S., and Joyce Berger. *The Encyclopedia of Parapsychology and Psychical Research.* New York: Paragon House, 1991.

Dale, Laura A., and Gardner Murphy. *Challenge of Psychical Research: A Primer of Parapsychology.* New York: Harper & Row, 1966.

Dale, Laura A., and Rhea A. White. *Parapsychology: Sources of Information.* Metuchen, N.J.: Scarecrow Press, 1973.

Pleasants, Helene, ed. *Biographical Dictionary of Parapsychology.* New York: Helix Press, 1964.

Dallas, Helen Alexandria (1856–1944)

An early British investigator of psychical research and author of several books on the subject. Dallas was born July 12, 1856, in India, and was educated privately. Deeply religious, she was preoccupied with the question of evidence for **survival** and its connection with religion. Her interests led her to translate **Gabriel Delanne**'s *L'Ame est immortelle* into English, as *Evidence for a Future Life* (1904). She also sat with such famous mediums as **Florence Cook** and wrote many articles published in British periodicals such as *Light* and *Psychic Science.* She died May 10, 1944, in London.

Sources:

Dallas, Helen A. *Across the Barrier.* N.p., 1913.

———. *Comrades on the Homeward Path.* N.p., 1930.

———. *Comrades on the Homeward Way.* N.p., 1929.

———. *Human Survival and Its Implications.* N.p., 1930.

———. *Leaves from a Psychic Notebook.* N.p., 1927.

———. *Mors Janus Vitae? A Discussion of Certain Communications Purporting to be from Frederic W. H. Myers.* London: William Rider and Son, 1910.

———. *The Nurseries of Heaven.* N.p., 1920.

———. *Objections to Spiritualism Answered.* Manchester, England: Two Worlds Publishing, 1916.

———. *The Victory that Overcometh.* N.p., 1901.

Pleasants, Helene, ed. *Biographical Dictionary of Parapsychology.* New York: Helix Press, 1964.

Dalton, Joseph Grinnell (1828–1898)

Boston astronomer and astrologer who became an important figure in the development of astrology by developing and publishing an accurate ephemeris and table of houses, the two basic tabulations needed by astrologers to prepare a horoscope chart. The ephemeris charts the position of the sun, moon, and planets for each day of the year. The table of houses shows the astrologer how to rotate the chart to accurately reflect the exact minute of the client's birth, thus representing the heavens on the client's birthday. Dalton's table of houses, originally published as *The Spherical Basis of Astrology* (1893), has continued to be reprinted and used throughout the twentieth century under the title *Dalton's Table of Houses.* Dalton also published the first ephemeris of the newly discovered planets Neptune and Uranus.

Sources:

Dalton, J. G. *The Boston Ephemeris.* Boston: Occult Publishing, 1898.

———. *The Sixteen Principal Stars.* Boston: Occult Publishing, 1898.

———. *The Spherical Basis of Astrology.* Boston: Arena Publishing, 1893.

Holden, James H., and Robert A. Hughes. *Astrological Pioneers of America.* Tempe, Ariz.: American Federation of Astrologers, 1988.

Dalton, Thomas (ca. 1450)

The history of this alchemist is veiled in obscurity, but he appears to have lived about the middle of the fifteenth century. Since he is mentioned in the *Ordinall of Alchimy* by **Thomas Norton,** who died in 1477, it is likely that he studied **alchemy** with, or at least was friends with, Norton.

Dalton was a churchman, resident at an abbey in Gloucester, and it is believed that he was once brought before King Edward IV, and charged with the secret practice of **magic,** in those days a capital crime. His accuser was one Debois, to whom Dalton had at one time been chaplain; Debois affirmed on oath that he had seen the alchemist create a thousand pounds of pure gold in a day. Dalton reminded his accuser that he had sworn never to reveal this or any such facts. Debois acknowledged his breach of trust, but added that he was acting for the good of the commonwealth.

The alchemist then addressed the king, telling him that he had been given the power of projection by a certain canon of Litchfield, and that since then he had been in such a constant state of trepidation that he had ultimately destroyed the precious gift. Edward granted him his freedom, and gave him money for his journey home.

On his way there he was seized by Thomas Herbert, who had heard of the accusation brought against the churchman and was naturally inquisitive. Herbert carried his victim to the castle of Gloucester, and, incarcerating him there, tried every means to make him disclose the secret. His efforts were in vain, however, and Dalton was condemned to death by his persecutor.

When he was brought out to be beheaded in the courtyard of the castle, he placed his head on the block and cried to God to receive his soul. He asked the executioner to strike speedily, but the axe was barely raised when Herbert sprang forward to avert it, declaring that he dared not shed innocent blood. The projected execution was no more than a plot conceived by Herbert to make the alchemist confess all when his life was at stake. Since the plan failed, Dalton was allowed to go free. He returned to his abbey in Gloucestershire and lived quietly for the rest of his days.

Damaran-Nata (or Dumbarim Nardir)

One of the classes of attendants or companions of the Hindu **devas,** whose special duty was to play upon a kind of drum. (See also **Deva-Loka**)

Damcar

According to **Rosicrucian** legend, Damcar was a mystical city of secret Arabia, inhabited by a group of **adepts.**

Damian, John ("Master John") (ca. 1500)

Alchemist who first appeared at the court of James IV, king of **Scotland,** as a surgeon around 1500. He was originally from Lombardy and practiced surgery in France. He was also employed by James in the practice of **alchemy** and was later appointed abbot of Tungland in Galloway, Scotland.

Danaans, The

The people of the goddess Dana, often mentioned in Irish medieval romance. They were one of the three Nemedian families who survived the Fomorian victory and returned to Ireland at a later period. Some said they came "out of heaven," and others that they sprang from four cities, where they learned science and craftsmanship. They were said to have brought a treasure from each city: from Falias the **Lia Fail** (Stone of Destiny), from Gorias an invincible sword, from Finias a magical spear, and from Murias the cauldron of the Dagda. They were believed to have been wafted to Ireland on an enchanted cloud, carrying their treasures with them. After a victorious battle they took possession of the whole of Ireland, except Connacht, which was given to the vanquished.

The Danaans represented power, beauty, science, and poetry to the writer of the myth; to the common people they were gods of earth. In their battles they were subject to death, but they conquered their mortal foes with special powers.

D'Anania (or D'Agnany, Giovanni Lorenzo) (d. 1458)

A lawyer of the fifteenth century who wrote a four-volume work entitled *De Naturà Daemonum* and a treatise on magic and witchcraft, neither of which is well known. He died in Italy in 1458.

Daphnomancy

Ancient method of **divination** by means of the laurel. A branch was thrown into the fire, if it crackled in burning, it was a happy sign, but if it burned without crackling, the prognostication was false.

D'Aquin, Mordecai (d. 1650)

A learned rabbi of Carpentras who died in 1650. He became a Christian and changed his name from Mordecai to Philippe. He was the author of an *Interpretation of the Tree of the Hebrew Kabala.*

Dark, The

A druid of Irish medieval legend who turned Saba into a fawn because she did not return his love. When the fawn was protected by the hero **Finn Mac Cummal,** she changed back to a beautiful woman and became Mac Cummals' wife.

Dark They Were And Golden Eyed

Well-known British bookshop formerly in St. Anne's Court, London, specializing in science fiction, **occultism, Atlantis, UFOs,** and **yoga.** It was started by "Bram" Stokes and Diane Lister in 1969. The name was taken from the title of a science-fiction story by Ray Bradbury. The bookshop closed in 1981.

D'Ars, Curé (1786–1859)

Jean Marie Baptiste Vianney, a French minister of deep religious beliefs and fervent faith whose life was replete with extraordinary psychic manifestations. He built chapels, homes for destitute children and friendless women, and provided for the poor. He did not have a penny in the world, yet he regularly maintained more than 100 poor women and children, for help always seemed to come in answer to his prayer.

Persons afflicted with disease soon began to experience sudden cures while praying before the altar or making confessions to the Curé. According to the biographer Abbé Monnin, upward of 20,000 persons came annually from Germany, Italy, Belgium, all parts of France, and even from England to be cured by him. His church was open day and night, and immense crowds waited for hours and days. Omnibuses were established to convey patients from Lyons to d'Ars, and the Saone was covered with boats full of anxious pilgrims.

His powers of **clairvoyance** developed to such a degree it was reported that by walking in the crowd he could tell the names, connections, and circumstances of the patients as soon as he cast his eye upon them.

For 35 years he was persecuted by violent **poltergeist** disturbances. Loud knocks resounded at the gate, a storm of blows descended upon the furniture, and sometimes there were sounds as if a wild horse were rearing in the hall below his room, striking the ceiling with its hoofs and stamping with all four feet on the tiled floor. At other times a great flock of sheep appeared to be passing above his head, or a gendarme seemed to be ascending the stairs in heavy boots. He always expected these disturbances when someone was on his way to seek consolation from him and attributed it to the envy of the demons for the good he was going to do. He said that once the devil amused himself by pushing him about his chamber all night on a bed on castors. The next day when he entered his confessional he felt himself lifted up and tossed about as though he had been in a boat on a rough sea.

According to **William Howitt,**

"The truth probably is that M. Vianney had so reduced his body by fasting, penance and enormous exertion, that he had opened himself to all kinds of spiritual impressions, to which the devil was sure to have his share. But most likely many of these ghostly visitors were merely spirits of a low order who like to amuse themselves, as they found the curé accessible to them. Many, no doubt, like those who visited the Seeress of Prevorst, would have been glad of his prayers, had he not been so completely shut up on that head, by his catholic demonophobia."

Vianney was the subject of a papal process beginning in 1862, as a result of which he was declared venerable in 1872, blessed in 1905, and canonized in 1925.

Sources:

De Saint Pierre, Michel. *The Remarkable Cure of Ars: The Life and Achievement of St. John Marie Vianney.* Garden City, N.Y.: Doubleday, 1963.

Fourrey, René. *The Curé D'Ars.* London: Burns & Oates, 1959.

Trochu, Francis. *The Curé D'Ars.* London: Burns & Oates, 1936. Reprint, Westminster, Md.: Newman Press, 1950.

———. *The Insight of the Cure D'Ars.* London: Burns Oates & Washburn, 1934.

Trouncer, Margaret. *Miser of Souls.* London: Hutchinson, 1959.

Das Gupta, Narenda Kumar (1910–)

University lecturer in India, at Visva-Bharati University, Santiniketan, West Bengal, beginning in 1954, with a special interest in **parapsychology.** He was born January 1, 1910, in Barisal, Bengal, and was educated at the University of Calcutta. In 1937 he married Gouri Sen Gupta. His research in parapsychology centered on **telepathy, psychokinesis,** and parapsychology in relation to **yoga** and religion, about which he published a number of papers.

He served as the secretary of the Parapsychology Club, Santiniketan, and was a member of the editorial board of the *Indian Journal of Parapsychology.* He was a life member of the Indian Psychological Association and contributed a number of articles to its *Journal.* He also published a book on problems of tribal education among the Santals. Das Gupta was a member of the Indian Science Congress and the academic council of Visva-Bharati University.

Sources:

Pleasants, Helene, ed. *Biographical Dictionary of Parapsychology.* New York: Helix Press, 1964.

D'Aspilette, Marie (ca. sixteenth century)

Witch of Andaye, in the Labourd area of the Basque country, who lived during the reign of Henry IV. She was arrested at age 19 and confessed that she had been led to the **sabbat** and made to perform various **witchcraft** rites.

Davenport Brothers, Ira Erastus (1839–1877) and William Henry (1841–1911)

Famous American demonstrators of claimed spirit mediumship who performed before large audiences on the theatrical stage. Their father was a police official in Buffalo, New York.

In 1846—two years before an outbreak of paramormal activity at **Hydesville,** New York—"raps, thumps, loud noises, snaps, crackling noises" were reportedly heard at the Davenport home during the night. In 1850, in the wake of the widely reported events in Hydesville, the Davenport boys and their younger sister Elisabeth tried **table-turning.** According to their father, the table soon moved, raps were heard, messages were spelled out, and Ira's hand began to write automatically. A little later a simultaneous **levitation** of the three children was witnessed by all present. On the fifth night of the experiments, to comply with rapping directions, Ira fired a pistol into a vacant corner of the room. At the instant of firing the pistol was taken from his hand and in the flash a human figure was seen holding it and smiling at the company. The apparition was the first appearance of **"John King,"** their self-appointed **control.** It lasted for an instant only, and with the extinction of the flash the figure vanished, the pistol falling to the floor.

A short time later a public rope-tying performance, for which the brothers became famous, was instituted on direction from the spirits. The brothers released themselves from the most complicated knots remarkably quickly. In due course both **direct-writing** and **direct voice** phenomena developed, and the brothers took to the road as performers, holding public séances amid challenging circumstances. Public committees were set up to examine the Davenports' phenomena, and their rope tying developed into an art of torture.

In 1857 the *Boston Courier* offered a reward of $500 for the production of genuine physical phenomena. Dr. H. F. Gardner of Boston accepted the challenge and arranged, before a committee of Harvard professors (consisting of Benjamin Pierce, Louis Agassiz, B. A. Gould, and E. N. Horsford), a series of séances with the sisters **Kate Fox** and **Leah Fish,** J. W. Mansfield, Dr. G. A. Redman, and the Davenport brothers. The Davenports were tied in the most brutal manner, the ropes drawn through holes bored in the **cabinet** and firmly knotted outside to make a network; the knots were tied with linen. Pierce sat in the cabinet between the mediums. As soon as he entered, an invisible hand shot the bolt, and the din of musical instruments began. A phantom hand was thrust through a small, curtained opening near the top of the middle door of the wardrobelike cabinet, and the professor felt it touch his head and face.

At the end of the séance, the mediums were found released, and (according to T. L. Nichols's biography) the ropes were found twisted around Pierce's neck. (The latter statement, however, was pronounced "shamelessly false" by the *Boston Courier.*) The committee issued only a brief negative report; a complete report was never published. It was countered by the report of Dr. Loomis, a professor of chemistry and toxicology at Georgetown Medical College, who also investigated the brothers. He concluded that the manifestations were produced through some new unknown force.

A Professor Mapes also had interesting experiences with the Davenports in Buffalo. He conversed with "John King" in direct voice for half an hour. His hand was seized in a powerful grasp, and when it was taken a second time, the phantom hand increased in size and was covered with hair. A large table on the elevated platform where the mediums were sitting was carried in an instant over the heads of the sitters and deposited in the most distant part of the room.

While some found the phenomena inexplicable, charges and evidence of **fraud** soon emerged. For example, a letter from Dr. John F. Gray, a well-known New York Spiritualist, to **Epes Sargent** (June 7, 1864) states: "I have not seen the Davenports this time here; but I entertain no doubt of the genuineness of the manifestations made in their presence. When they were here some years ago they were detected in making spurious manifestations when the genuine failed."

As a means of control, investigators often filled the hands of the mediums with flour or placed pennies on their shoes after carefully drawing the outline of the shoes on a piece of paper beneath them. When the door of the cabinet was opened, the flour was found in the brothers' hands as before, no white spots were on their clothes, and the pennies were in place.

The performance while sitting in the cabinet was called the light séance. There was a second part, the dark séance, in which the lights in the room were extinguished and the mediums sat tightly bound to their chairs between the other sitters. Tying and releasing occurred as in the cabinet. The swishing of rope was heard. The knots presented no obstacle. Sometimes every intermediate knot was left undone, with the seal at the end, yet the mediums were found free. As an additional amusement the rope was often coiled around the neck of some sitter. Then through the ropes, in some mysterious way, the coats of the mediums, or their waistcoats underneath, were whisked off and on again.

Those who entered the cabinet to sit with the brothers in the light séance were usually victims of strange pranks. Their handkerchiefs were taken, their breast pins removed and stuck into their coats, and their spectacles transferred to the face of one of the mediums.

"I have, at different times," wrote Robert Cooper, who spent seven months with the Davenport brothers in England and on the Continent, "seen at least three hundred persons enter the cabinet, all of whom certified that there was no movement on the part of the Brothers."

The Davenport brothers arrived in England in 1864. They were accompanied by the Rev. J. B. Ferguson, a former pastor from Nashville, Tennessee, who was famous throughout the South; D. Palmer, their operatic manager, who acted as secretary; and **William M. Fay,** another physical medium. Their stay in England was strenuous. Public opposition was violent, but interest in their feats was tremendous, and the Spiritualists reaped rewards of favorable press.

Their first séance in London was held privately at the residence of Dion Boucicault, the famous actor and author, in the presence of scientists and members of the press. In a report on the séance, after describing the babel generated by the musical instruments playing in the light and dark séances, a correspondent for *The Times* continues:

"A new experiment was now made. Darkness having regained its supremacy, one of the brothers expressed a desire to be relieved of his coat. Returning light showed him in his shirtsleeves, though his hands were still firmly bound behind the chair. It was now stated that he was prepared to put on the coat of any one of the company willing to 'loan' that article of attire, and an assenting gentleman having been found, the coat, after a short interval of darkness, was worn in proper fashion by a person for whom it had not been designed by the tailor. Finally, the brothers desired a release, and one of the company, certainly not an accomplice, requested that the rope might fall into his lap. During the interval of darkness a rushing sound as of swiftly-drawn cords was audible, and the ropes reached the required knees, after striking the face of the person in the next chair."

The Times correspondent said he was not sure that he had witnessed simple conjuring. An account in *The Standard* says the knots were tied by a sailor who was "profound" at knot tying, and the reporter of the *Daily Telegraph* was not certain whether the feats were "the annihilation of what are called material laws" or a display of some extraordinary physical dexterity. He was unsure whether to regard the believers in Spiritualism as "the embodiment of a mutual and colossal self-deceit, or the silent heralds of a social revolution which must shake the world."

The Davenport public séances began in October 1864 at the Queen's Court Concert Rooms, Hanover Square, London. They continued almost nightly until the end of the year. No committee could pinpoint the brothers' fraud, though a group of stage magicians attempted to prove that the performance was fraudulent.

It is probable that a sailor could tie a magician so that he could not free himself. "But no person," declares T. L. Nichols in *Supramundane Facts in the Life of the Rev. J. B. Ferguson* (1865), "of all the hundreds who have tried, has ever tied the Davenports or Mr. Fay so that they were not freed in a few minutes, nor so that the manifestations, which must have been made either by them or by an intelligent, invisible force attending them, did not occur in two seconds."

Although their stay in London was somewhat successful, the Davenports and Fay met with open hostility in the countryside. In Liverpool, for example, two members selected from the audience tied the mediums with a peculiarly intricate knot. The mediums protested that it was unfairly tight and injured their circulation. A doctor from the audience made an examination and pronounced against them. The Davenports refused to sit and asked Ferguson to cut the knot. The next night a riot broke out and the party left town. At Hull, Huddersfield, and Leeds they found a hostile public, inclined to lynch them. Since they did not find the police protection sufficient, they broke off their engagements. In a letter to Ferguson, the Davenports later wrote:

"Were we mere jugglers we should meet with no violence, or we should find protection. Could we declare that these things done in our presence were deception of the senses, we should, no doubt, reap a plentiful harvest of money and applause. As tricks they would transcend, according to the testimony of experienced observers, any ever exhibited in Occident or Orient. The wonders of the cabinet, or still more, of the dark séance, surpass all pretentions of conjurers. We should safely defy the world to equal them, and be honoured for our dexterity. But we are not jugglers, and truthfully declare that we are not, and we are mobbed from town to town, our property destroyed and our lives imperilled."

The truth of these wonders was solemnly promulgated by Ferguson:

"I have in their presence had articulate and audible conversation with a voice which was not theirs, nor that of any living person. With this I have conversed as a man talks with his friend, while the power or being from which the voice proceeded made its presence and reality known to me by other physical manifestations. In railway carriages, when in company with the Brothers Davenport and Mr. Fay, in passing through dark tunnels, I have been manipulated all over my body by hands seemingly human, sometimes unexpectedly, others at my request, when no one present could have touched me without my knowledge."

Robert Cooper's *Spiritual Experiences* (1867) thus sums up seven months' of close observation:

"I can truly say that during the whole time I was with them, extending over a period of seven months, I never saw aught to indicate that they were anything but passive instruments, the manifestations being produced by a power outside themselves. Indeed, I feel quite sure they could not accomplish these things by natural means without being detected every week of their lives; and I give it as my deliberate conviction after all the opportunities I have had of forming an opinion, that their manifestations are a reality; if they are not, then all creation is a myth and our senses nothing worth."

In France, where the Davenports traveled after their misadventures in England, they could not get the necessary permit to exhibit in public for some time, since the authorities feared similar disturbances. When the time finally arrived for their first performance, an emissary of a conjurer named Robin stepped onto the platform. Under pretense of examining the cabinet, he tore off the rail that supported one of the seats and, holding it up before the excited crowd, asserted that he had discovered a secret spring. Because of the confusion that arose, the police cleared the room. A few days later the séances continued, but by order of the prefect attendance was restricted to 60 persons.

Some magicians were more friendly, however. The famous conjurer Hamilton, and one Rhys, a manufacturer of conjuring implements, state in letters to the Davenports published in the *Gazette des Etrangers* (September 27, 1865) that the phenomena were inexplicable and could not be attributed to fraud. In later years a Professor Jacobs similarly testified that the phenomena seen in Paris "were absolutely true and belonged to the spiritual order of things in every respect." Before they left Paris, the Davenports were summoned to appear before the Emperor and the Empress Napoleon at the palace of St. Cloud. A party of 40 witnessed their demonstration with astonishment. They were well received in Belgium and appeared in St. Petersburg before the czar in the Winter Palace. Their first public séance in St. Petersburg was attended by a thousand people.

In 1868 they returned to England. At Cooper's initiative the Anthropological Society appointed a committee to investigate their phenomena. A trial séance was held, which the committee considered a failure. The conditions they proposed were found unacceptable by the mediums, and the investigation was broken off.

In 1876 the Davenports visited Australia. The following year Ira Davenport died in Sydney. His brother had the cabinet, ropes, and so forth engraved on Ira's tombstone. William returned to Mayville, New York, and continued to give stage demonstrations with another partner in Boston, Washington, and Pennsylvania. In 1906 he toured Jamaica and Cuba. His last performance was on November 19, 1906, for an American regiment near Santiago de Cuba.

The general conclusion regarding the Davenport brothers' pheonomena is that their performance was simple stage conjuring. Trick cabinets and rope tying were standard items of stage magic at the time, and **Harry Houdini** and his students demonstrated feats equal to and surpassing those of the Davenports. The brothers' refusal to continue with a performance in England when their wrists were tied too tightly argues against spirit agency, since this should have operated even in such unfavorable circumstances considering other marvels that were demonstrated. They escaped any exposure of trickery though, in spite of observation by alert and intelligent investigators (which other mediums also accomplished only to be caught later), and their release from binding with strong ropes was phenomenally rapid—often taking only two or three minutes.

Futhermore, during their long and checkered career the Davenports never claimed to know how their phenomena occurred. In a letter he wrote to Houdini, Ira Davenport declares,

"We never in public affirmed our belief in spiritualism. That we regarded as no business of the public, nor did we offer our entertainment as the result of sleight-of-hand or, on the other hand, as spiritualism. We let our friends and foes settle that as best they could between themselves but, unfortunately, we were often the victims of their disagreement."

In *A Magician Among the Spirits* (1924) Houdini claims that Ira Davenport admitted that he was a fraud and described how the rope trick was performed. There is no independent confirmation of this admission, however, and Houdini privately voiced different opinions to **Sir Arthur Conan Doyle.** In *The Edge of the Unknown* (1930), Doyle asserts, "I was an intimate friend of Ira Erastus Davenport. I can make the positive assertion that the Davenport Brothers never were exposed. . . . I know more about the Davenports than anyone living."

Sources:

Berger, Arthur S., and Joyce Berger. *The Encyclopedia of Parapsychology and Psychical Research.* New York: Paragon House, 1991.

Cooper, Robert. *Spiritual Experiences, Including Seven Months with the Brothers Davenport.* London, 1867.

Doyle, Arthur Conan. *The Edge of the Unknown.* N.p., 1930.

Ferguson, J. B. *Supramundane Facts of the Life of Rev. J. B. Ferguson.* London, 1865.

Houdini, Harry. *A Magician Among the Spirits.* New York: Harper & Brothers, 1924. Reprinted as *Houdini: A Magician Among the Spirits.* New York: Arno Press, 1972.

Nichols, T. L. *A Biography of the Brothers Davenport.* London, 1864.

Randolph, P. B. *The Davenport Brothers.* Boston, 1869.

Davey, S. T. (1864–1891)

A member of the **Society for Psychical Research,** London, who in 1886 gave imitations of the **slate-writing** performances of mediums **William Eglinton** and **Henry Slade,** with a view to exposing what he believed to be their **fraud.** Such fraud was a major problem in evaluating **Spiritualism.** By simple conjuring he succeeded in emulating all their feats, his successes becoming the subject of a series of important articles. Davey's future as a valuable force in psychical research ended abruptly when he died of typhoid fever at age 27.

Sources:

Berger, Arthur S., and Joyce Berger. *The Encyclopedia of Parapsychology and Psychical Research.* New York: Paragon House, 1991.

Davey, S. T. "Spurious Mediumship." *Journal* of the Society for Psychical Research 3 (1888): 199–207.

Hodgson, Richard. "Mr. Davey's Imitations by Conjuring of Phenomena Sometimes Attributed to Spirit Agency." *Proceedings* of the Society for Psychical Research 8, 22 (1892): 253–310.

David-Neel, Alexandra (1868–1969)

French traveler, author, and Tibetan scholar. David-Neel was a practicing Buddhist and the first European woman to enter the forbidden city of Lhasa in Tibet. She spent 14 years in Tibet, living simply and studying Tibetan religion and occultism. Her two major books, translated into English as *Magic and Mystery in Tibet* and *Initiations and Initiates in Tibet,* are accounts of her first-hand observation of Tibetan occult and religious feats and have been frequently reprinted.

David-Neel received many honors for her books, including the gold medal of the Geographical Society of Paris, the French Legion of Honor, the Insigne of the Chinese Order of the Brilliant Star, and the silver medal of the Royal Belgian Geographical Society. She died September 8, 1969.

Sources:

David-Neel, Alexandra. *Buddhism: Its Doctrines and Its Methods.* New York: St. Martin's, 1939. Reprint, London: Bodley Head, 1977.

———. *Initiations and Initiates in Tibet.* London, 1932. Reprint, New Hyde Park, N.Y.: University Books, 1959.

———. *Magic and Mystery in Tibet.* Rev. ed., New Hyde Park, N.Y.: University Books, 1956. Reprint, New York: Dover Publications, 1971.

———. *My Journey to Lhasa.* New York: Harper & Brothers, 1927.

———. *The Secret Oral Tradition in Tibetan Buddhist Sects.* San Francisco: City Lights, 1964. Reprint, Calcutta: Maha Bodhi Society of India, 1971.

Davies, Lady Eleanor (1603–1652)

Eleanor Touchet, daughter of George, Lord Audley, and wife of Sir John Davies, an eminent lawyer in the time of James I and author of a poem of considerable merit, "Immortality of the Soul." Sir John Davies seems to have highly valued Eleanor's gift of prophecy, which led to her publishing a book, *Strange and Wonderfull Prophesies* (1649). She claimed to receive her prophecies from a spirit that communicated to her audibly (i.e., by **clairaudience**), although the voice could be heard by no other person. Amid her numerous other writings are *Amend; Amend; Gods Kingdome is at Hand; Amen, Amen* (1643) and *Before the Lord's Second Coming: Of the Last Days to be Visited* (1650).

Sir John Davies was nominated lord chief justice of the king's bench in 1626. Before he was inducted into office, Lady Eleanor, sitting with him at dinner, suddenly burst into tears. Sir John asked her what made her weep, and she replied, "These are your funeral tears." Sir John dismissed the prediction. Within a few days he suffered a stroke and died.

Lady Eleanor also predicted the death of the duke of Buckingham the same year. For the assumption of the gift of prophecy, she was cited before the high commission court in 1633 and was imprisoned briefly and fined.

Sources:

Davies, Lady Eleanor. *Great Britains Visitation.* London, 1645.

———. *The Revelation Interpreted.* London, 1645.

———. *Of Times and Seasons, Their Mystery.* London, 1651.

Davis, Andrew Jackson (1826–1910)

Medium, channel, and one of the founders of modern **Spiritualism.** He was born August 11, 1826, at Blooming Grove, Orange County, New York. Young Davis had gifts of **clairvoyance** and heard voices at an early age. On advice so obtained he pursuaded his father in 1838 to move to Poughkeepsie, New York (Andrew would later be known as "the Poughkeepsie Seer"). Up to age 16 he received no formal education. Apprenticed to a shoemaker named Armstrong, he worked at the trade for two years.

In 1843 Dr. J. S. Grimes, professor of jurisprudence in the Castleton Medical College, visited the city and delivered a series of lectures on **mesmerism.** Davis attended and was tried as a subject with no result. Later, a local tailor, William Livingston, made fresh attempts; he threw Davis into "magnetic sleep" and discovered that in this state the human body became transparent to Davis's eyes, enabling him to give accurate diagnosis of disease.

In 1844 Davis had a strange experience that was to have an enduring effect on his life. In a state of semitrance he wandered away from home and awoke the next morning 40 miles away in the mountains. There he claimed to have met two venerable men—whom he later identified as the ancient physician Galen and the Swedish seer **Emanuel Swedenborg**—and experienced a state of mental illumination.

He began teaching and published a small pamphlet, *Lectures on Clairmativeness,* about the mysteries of human magnetism and electricity. He did not include this pamphlet among his later works but explained in his *Autobiography* that the title was meant to be *Clairlativeness.*

During a professional tour he met a Dr. Lyon, a Bridgeport musician, and the Reverend William Fishbough. Lyon was appointed his magnetizer (i.e., mesmerist) and Fishbough his scribe. With their assistance, in November 1845 Davis began to dictate his great work, *The Principles of Nature, Her Divine Revelations, and a Voice to Mankind.* The dictation lasted for 15 months. Lyon repeated each trance utterance, and Fishbough transcribed them. They both insisted that except for grammatical corrections they performed no editing. During the dictation, the sole means of livelihood for the trio was the seer's earning power in giving medical diagnoses. When this proved insufficient the lady whom Davis later married came to their assistance.

There were many enthusiastic witnesses to the delivery of the dictation. Dr. George Bush, professor of Hebrew at the University of New York, declared that he heard Davis correctly quote Hebrew. The seer's good faith was also established by his answers to impromptu questions put to him as tests while he was in the clairvoyant state. Bush said, "Taken as a whole the work is a profound and elaborate discussion of the philosophy of the universe, and for grandeur of conception, soundness of principle, clearness of illustration, order of arrangement and encyclopaedic range of subjects, I know no work of any single mind that will bear away from it the palm."

It was partly due to Bush's enthusiasm that the book, published in 1847, was received with such interest. Within a few weeks of its appearance, however, Bush published a pamphlet, *Davis' Revelations Revealed,* warning the public against being misled by the numerous errors, absurdities, and falsities contained in Davis's work. It was clear to him, he said, that Davis, although apparently an honest and singlehearted young man, had been made the mouthpiece of uninstructive and deceiving spirits. This rapid change of opinion was later explained by **Frank Podmore** in his book *Modern Spiritualism* (1902) as stemming from the seer's attitude toward Christianity in the section of the book on divine revelations, which Bush probably did not read in advance and which contradicted Davis's views as expressed in his *Lectures on Clairmativeness.*

The book soon went through many editions, which testified to the appeal of the style and the remarkable qualities of this extraordinary work. This opening passage about the Creation is an example:

"In the beginning the Univercoelum was one boundless, undefinable, and unimaginable ocean of Liquid Fire. The most vigorous and ambitious imagination is not capable of forming an adequate conception of the height and depth and length and breadth thereof. There was one vast expanse of liquid substance. It was without bounds—inconceivable—and with qualities and essences incomprehensible. This was the original condition of Matter. It was without forms, for it was but one Form. It had not motions, but it was an eternity of Motion. It was without parts, for it was a Whole. Particles did not exist, but the Whole was as one Particle. There were not suns, but it was one Eternal Sun. It had no beginning and it was without end. It had not circles, for it was one Infinite Circle. It had not disconnected power, but it was the very essence of all Power. Its inconceivable magnitude and constitution were such as not to develop forces, but Omnipotent Power.

"Matter and Power were existing as a Whole, inseparable. The Matter contained the substance to produce all suns, all worlds, and systems of worlds, throughout the immensity of Space. It contained the qualities to produce all things that are existing upon each of those worlds. The Power contained Wisdom and Goodness, Justice, Mercy and Truth. It contained the original and essential Principle that is displayed throughout immensity of Space, controlling worlds and systems of worlds, and producing Motion, Life, Sensation and Intelligence, to be impartially disseminated upon their surfaces as Ultimates."

The first part of the book is the exposition of a mystical philosophy, the second reviews the books of the Old Testament, contests their infallibility, and describes Christ as a great moral reformer but not divine. The third advances a system of socialism.

The originality of the book as a whole was never contested. Bush, however, pointed out a strange coincidence. The revelations, for the most part, express views similar to Emanuel Swedenborg's; the language is in several cases "all but absolutely verbal [verbatim]," and there is a striking similarity to Swedenborg's book *The Economy of the Animal Kingdom,* a few English copies of which had just reached the United States.

Bush used this as an argument for Davis's supernatural powers, because it was doubtful the book could have reached him. In fact, Davis believed he was controlled by Swedenborg while he produced the book. In his publication *Mesmer and Swedenborg* (1847) Bush printed a letter from Davis accompanying a paper written in a cave near Poughkeepsie, on June 15, 1846. The paper accurately quoted long passages from Swedenborg's *Earths in the Universe.* Bush was satisfied that Davis had never heard of the book, but it is difficult to believe that Davis had not read it.

An apparently more serious charge could have been leveled against Davis's *The Great Harmonia* (1852). There are long passages in the book that correspond with the text of Sunderland's *Pathetism* (1847). But even Frank Podmore, a noted skeptic, believed that Davis could not have copied these passages and that the explanation lay in an extraordinary memory.

The statements concerning astronomy in the divine revelations section of *The Principles of Nature* are revealing. In March 1846, when the existence of an eighth planet was yet an astronomical supposition (the discovery of Neptune, verifying Leverrier's calculations, did not take place until September 1846), the book spoke of nine planets. The density of the eighth planet as given by Davis agreed with later findings. (The ninth planet, Pluto, was discovered in 1933.) On the other hand, Davis spoke of four planetoids—Ceres, Pallas, Juno, and Vesta—whereas there are now believed to be hundreds. He also said that the solar system revolves around a great center together with all the other stars. Davis further believed Saturn to be inhabited by a more advanced humanity than ours, Jupiter and Mars were also inhabited, and on Venus and Mercury the development of humanity was less advanced than on Earth. The three outer planets he declared lifeless.

His prediction of the coming of Spiritualism was often quoted: "It is a truth that spirits commune with one another while one is in the body and the other in the higher spheres—and this, too, when the person in the body is unconscious of the influx, and hence cannot be convinced of the fact; and this truth will ere long present itself in the form of a living demonstration. And the world will hail with delight the ushering-in that era when the interiors of men will be opened, and the spiritual communion will be established such as is now being enjoyed by the inhabitants of Mars, Jupiter, and Saturn."

In his notes dated March 31, 1848, the following statement occurs: "About daylight this morning a warm breathing passed over my face and I heard a voice, tender and strong, saying: 'Brother, the good work has begun—behold, a living demonstration is born.' I was left wondering what could be meant by such a message."

The publication of *The Principals of Nature* made Davis famous and he was soon surrounded by a band of enthusiasts. As their mouthpiece, on December 4, 1847, the first issue of the *Univercoelum* (apparently coined from Swedenborg's "universum coelum") appeared. Universalist minister S. B. Brittan became editor in chief. Assisting were a number of outstanding contemporaries, including Fishbough, **Thomas Lake Harris,** W. M. Fernald, J. K. Ingalls, Dr. Chivers, and Frances Green. The object of the publication was "the establishment of a universal system of truth, the reform and the reorganization of society." Davis contributed many articles that were later incorporated into *The Great Harmonia.*

After 12 months in existence, the *Univercoelum* absorbed the *Christian Rationalist,* a similar organ, however, its publication came to an end in July 1849. It was succeeded by W. M. Channing's *The Present Age,* a largely socialist organ to which Davis and his friends no longer contributed. They accepted as their new mouthpiece *The Spirit Messenger* of Springfield, Massachusetts, which was jointly edited by Rev. R. P. Ambler and Apollos Munn. As Davis's friends were scattered, other periodicals were founded and his "harmonial philosophy" was independently carried on.

About the time the *Univercoelum* was founded, Davis disposed of the services of his mesmerizer. By an effort of will he could by that time throw himself into what he called "the superior condition." He also remembered his experiences while in trance and wrote his subsequent books in his own hand. He disclaimed dictation by the spirits and said that he could write them by a process of inner perception. Except for seeing **apparitions,** he was unacquainted with abnormal physical phenomena until 1850, when he paid a visit to Dr. **Eliakim Phelps**'s house in Stratford, Connecticut, which was the scene of violent **poltergeist** disturbances. In the same year he published a pamphlet on his observations, entitled *The Philosophy of Spiritual Intercourse.*

Davis's teachings left a deep impression on his age. *The Great Harmonia* passed through 40 editions. His autobiography *The Magic Staff* extended only to the year 1857, but was later supplemented with a sequel, *Beyond the Valley* (1885). In 1860 he started the *Herald of Progress,* a weekly that absorbed the *Spiritual Telegraph.* In the late years of his life he had a small bookshop in Boston. There he sold books and, having earned a degree in natural medicine, prescribed herbal remedies for his patients.

Davis died January 13, 1910. He was an important influence in the early development of Spiritualism, particularly in his association of mediumistic revelations with religious principles. His concepts of after-death spheres for departed spirits, which he named "Summerland," are still part of the beliefs of many modern Spiritualists. He influenced most subsequent Spiritualist movements, including those of Thomas Lake Harris. It even seems possible that Edgar Allan Poe's "Eureka" owes its inception to Davis's *Principles of Nature.*

In his practice of diagnosing and treating illness in a trance condition, Davis also anticipated the rationale of the modern seer **Edgar Cayce.**

Sources:

Brown, Slater. *The Heyday of Spiritualism.* New York: Hawthorn Books, 1970.

Davis, Andrew J. *Answers to Ever-Recurring Questions from People: A Sequel to the Penetralia.* Boston: Banner of Light Publishing, 1862.

———. *Beyond the Valley; A Sequel to the Magic Staff: An Autobiography.* Boston: Colby & Rich, 1885.

———. *The Great Harmonia.* New York: J. S. Redfield, Fowler & Wells, 1853.

———. *The Magic Staff: An Autobiography of Andrew Jackson Davis.* New York, 1857.

———. *Penetralia: Being Harmonial Answers to Important Questions.* Boston: Bela Marsh, 1858.

Doyle, Arthur Conan. *The History of Spiritualism.* 2 vols. London, 1926. Reprint, New York: Arno Press, 1975.

Podmore, Frank. *Modern Spiritualism.* 2 vols. London, 1902. Reprinted as *Mediums of the 19th Century.* 2 vols. New Hyde Park, N.Y.: University Books, 1963.

Dawn (Magazine)

Quarterly magazine devoted to **yoga, meditation,** philosophy, **psychology,** and holistic living. *Dawn* is the official organ of the **Himalayan International Institute of Yoga Science and Philosophy.** Address: R.R. 1, Box 400, Honesdale, PA 18431.

Dawn Horse Communion See **Free Daist Communion**

Dawson-Scott, Catharine Amy (d. 1934)

Author of more than 20 novels and founder of several Spiritualist organizations, including the P.E.N. Club, the To-morrow Club, and the **Survival League.** She believed in **survival** and communication with the departed and wrote two psychic books: *From Four Who are Dead* and *Is This Wilson?* She also edited three small volumes of *The Guide to Psychic Knowledge,* containing questions and answers on the problems of afterlife obtained through mediums. She died November 4, 1934.

De Biragues, Flaminio (ca. 1580)

Author of a work entitled *L'Enfer de la mere Cardine* (Paris, 1585), which treats the dreadful battle in hell on the occasion of the marriage of Cerberus and Cardine. It is a satire on the demonography of the times. Didot reprinted the work in 1793. The author was a nephew of a chancellor of France, Rene de Biragues, and also published a volume of his own poems.

De Boni, Gastone (1908–1986)

Italian physician, author, and editor. He was born January 22, 1908, in Padua, Italy, and was educated at the University of Padua (M.D. 1932). He inherited the substantial library of psychical researcher **Ernesto Bozzano** (1862–1943), to which he added some six thousand volumes. After World War II he opened the library, which contains both his and Bozzano's correspondence and papers, for public research.

De Boni's own literary contribution to Italian **parapsychology** included editing translations of 40 volumes by psychical researchers and parapsychologists. In 1941 he published the first book on psychical research in Italy. He also edited *Luce e Ombra,* an Italian journal of parapsychology, from 1947 until his death 30 years later. His own books include *Metapsychics: Science of the Soul* (1947) and *Man and the Conquest of the Soul* (1960).

De Boni favored **Spiritualism** and imposed such a perspective on *Luce e Ombra.* In spite of criticism from other parapsychologists, he was able to remain a vital part of the parapsychological community. He became president of Società Italiana di Parapsicologia in 1955 and was an honorary associate of the **Society for Psychical Research,** London. He died September 23, 1986, at Verona, Italy.

Sources:

Berger, Arthur S., and Joyce Berger. *The Encyclopedia of Parapsychology and Psychical Research.* New York: Paragon House, 1991.

Pleasants, Helene, ed. *Biographical Dictionary of Parapsychology.* New York: Helix Press, 1964.

De Bonnevault, Maturin

Father of **Pierre Bonnevault.** De Bonnevault was accused of sorcery when he was visited by experts who found on his right shoulder a mark resembling a small rose, into which a long pin was thrust. He displayed such signs of distress that the experts judged that he must be a sorcerer. He confessed his betrothal to Berthomée de la Bedouche, who with her father and mother practiced sorcery, and related how he sought serpents and toads for their sorceries.

De Bonnevault testified that the witch **sabbat** was held four times yearly, at the feasts of Saint John the Baptist, Christmas, Mardi Gras, and Pâques. He confessed to having slain seven persons by sorcery and avowed that he had been a sorcerer since he was seven years of age. Like his son Pierre, he was put to death.

De Boville (or **Bovillus** or **Bovelles**), **Charles** (ca. 1470–1550)

A French mathematician and philologist who also wrote on **occult** philosophy. De Boville promulgated in his work *De sensu* the opinion held in ancient times that the world is alive, an idea also imagined by Felix Nogaret. (Twentieth-century books on this theme include *The Living Universe,* by **Sir Francis Younghusband** (1933), and *The Earth is Alive,* by François Derrey (1968).) Other works by De Boville include his *Lettres,* the *Life of Raymond Lully, Traite des douze nombres,* and *Trois Dialogues sur l'Immortalitè de l'Ame, le Rèsurrection, et la Fin du Monde.*

De Brath, Stanley (1854–1937)

British psychical researcher, author, and translator. De Brath was born in October 1854. He was trained as a civil engineer and spent 20 years in government service in India before becoming headmaster of a preparatory school in England. In 1890 he attended a séance by **Cecil Husk** (later exposed as a **fraud**) and thereafter became intensely interested in psychical research and **Spiritualism.** His own contributions centered upon his writing, editing, and translating work. His early books include *Psychic Philosophy* (under the pseudonym "C. Desertis") (1909), *The Mysteries of Life* (1915), and *The Science of Peace* (1916).

In 1918 he began spending time in Paris, collaborating with the French researcher **Gustave Geley** at the **Institut Métapsychique International.** During this period he was responsible for the English translation of Geley's *From the Unconscious to the Conscious* (1920), as well as *Supernormal Faculties in Man* (1923), by **Eugèn Osty,** and *Thirty Years of Psychical Research* (1923) by **Charles Richet.**

In 1924 he assumed editorship of the journal *Psychic Science,* published by the **British College of Psychic Science,** London. De Brath's books include *Psychical Research, Science and Religion* (1925), *Religion of the Spirit* (1927), and *The Drama of Europe* (1930). He died December 20, 1937, at Kew, London.

Sources:

Pleasants, Helene, ed. *Biographical Dictionary of Parapsychology.* New York: Helix Press, 1964.

De Crespigny, Rose Champion (1860–1935)

Daughter of the Right Honorable Sir Astley Cooper-Key (First Sea Lord of the Admiralty) and author of more than 20 novels. After the death of her husband, Philip de Crespigny, she consulted a medium, **Etta Wriedt,** through whom she believed to have obtained evidence of **survival.** As a result she became a Spiritualist, the honorary principal of the **British College of Psychic Science,** and a national lecturer on psychic subjects.

Her experiences became the substance of many of her novels. For example, *The Dark Sea* (1927) deals with **direct voice** experiences and *The Mark* with **reincarnation.** She also wrote several pamphlets on Spiritualist themes. She died February 10, 1935.

Sources:

Pleasants, Helene, ed. *Biographical Dictionary of Parapsychology.* New York: Helix Press, 1964.

De Cressac Bachelerie, Bertrande (1899– ?)

French engineer and author who lectured extensively on **parapsychology** in France, Belgium, Morocco, Algeria, and Italy. De Cressac Bachelerie was born January 2, 1899, at Limoges (Haute-Vienne). He received his B.S. degree in 1916 and an engineering degree in 1922 from l'Ecole Centrale des Arts et Manufactures, Paris. He wrote a number of books and many articles on parapsychology for French, Italian, and Belgian journals.

Sources:

De Cressac Bachelerie, Bertrande. *Démonstrations experimentales de la télépathie* (Experimental demonstrations of telepathy). N.p., 1946.

———. *Etudes sur la télépathie des sensations* (Studies on the telepathy of sensations). N.p., 1954.

———. *Etudes sur la voyance* (Studies in clairvoyance). N.p., 1942.

———. *La Métapsychique devant la science* (Parapsychology in relation to science). N.p., 1948.

———. *Le Miracle, illusion ou réalite* (The miracle, illusion or reality). N.p., 1961.

———. *Mise en évidence de l'effet psychocinétique* (Revelation of the psychokinetic effect). N.p., 1960.

De Cressac Bachelerie, Bertrande, and Marige George Chevalier. *La Métapsychique—probleme crucial* (Parapsychology: a crucial problem). N.p., 1960.

De Fontenay, Guillaume (1861–1914)

Prominent French psychical investigator, especially known for his researches into **psychic photography.** In important works such as *Action des encres sur la plaque photographique, La Chimicographie et la Prétendue Photographie du Rayonnement vital,* and *Note relative aux prétendues radiations organiques du commandant Dorget,* he offers an explanation for **emanation** photographs of the human body. He also wrote excellent books on the mediumship of **Eusapia Palladino** and **Linda Gazzera.** He died in 1914 in France.

Sources:

De Fontenay, Guillaume. *Apropos d'Eusapia Palladino.* N.p., 1898.

De Gasparin, Count Agenor (1810–1871)

French politician, minister plenipotentiary, and one of the first investigators of **table-turning** and **telekinesis.** His book *Des Tables Tournantes, du Surnaturel engénéral, et des Esprits* (1854) describes his experiments at Velleyres, Switzerland, which were constructed under stringent test conditions.

The results of his research were quite positive and seemed to support a Spiritualist explanation (i.e., he demonstrated to his own satisfaction the intelligence manifesting behind the phenomena). Because of his own orthodox Christian commitments, however, he could not accept the spirit hypothesis. Instead he settled for a more mundane conclusion suggestive of what later would be termed *telekinesis.* He suggested that the will—in a certain condition of the human organism—can act, from a distance, upon inert bodies, and by an agency different from that of the muscular. He also believed that, under the same conditions, thought can be communicated directly, though unconsciously, from one individual to another.

In a preface to an 1888 edition of his book he states that the problem had not been resolved in the 30 years that had elapsed but that "some day an edifice would be erected on the same stone which was laid in 1854."

De Gerson, Jean Charlier (1363–1429)

French theologian and chancellor of the University of Paris. De Gerson was the author of many works, including the *Examination of Spirits,* which contains rules for distinguishing true revelations from false, and the popular *Astrology Reformed.*

De Gert, Berthomine (ca. 1608)

A sorceress of the town of Préchac in Gascony who confessed about the year 1608 that when a sorceress returning from the **sabbat** is killed, the devil takes her shape and makes her reappear and die in her own dwelling so as to preserve her good reputation. But if the murderer has a wax candle and with it makes the sign of the cross on the witch's body, the devil cannot with all his strength remove her and is forced to leave her there.

De La Warr, George (1905–1969)

British expert in **radionics,** a subject related to **radiesthesia** and **dowsing,** and which uses an apparatus to identify claimed subtle radiation in humans and objects. The primary use of the tool was to diagnose illnesses. De La Warr's device was developed from the **black box** of **Albert Abrams** but used the method of stroking a rubber pad with the fingers instead of tapping the abdomen of a patient. The rubber detector pad was set in a frame with a wire circuit connection to a box containing various knobs and dials. A blood sample from the patient was placed in this circuit, and the rubber pad was stroked by the operator's finger until it indicated a "sticking" sensation at various dial readings. It was claimed that the dial markings denoted various pathological conditions of the patient whose blood sample was being tested.

In addition to diagnosis of disease, the apparatus was used for absent treatment of the patient by "correcting wave forms," sometimes in conjunction with exposure of a photographic plate inserted in the box, resulting in a kind of "psychic photograph." There was no conventional electric or magnetic circuit in black boxes, so their inventors (including De La Warr) were often charged with **fraud.**

De La Warr founded a research laboratory at Oxford, England, and developed various black boxes for medical purposes. He also experimented with photographs related to radiation from blood samples. His theories about subtle radiation are presented in detail in the book *New Worlds Beyond the Atom* (1956). He received considerable support from a variety of eminent individuals, including Air Marshal Sir Victor Goddard, Methodist minister **Leslie Weatherhead,** and **Kenneth Walker** (a student of **Georgei I. Gurdjieff**). None had medical credentials nor could their enthusiasm stop the medical community from condemning De La Warr's work (as it had earlier denounced Abrams's).

De Lancre, Pierre (1553–1631)

French judge at witchcraft trials who claimed to have discovered that virtually the entire population (30,000) of a Basque area, including priests, was affected by **witchcraft.** Born in Bordeaux, De Lancre studied law at Turin and Bohemia and became a lawyer at the Parlement of Bordeaux in 1588. In 1608 he was commissioned by Henry IV to investigate witchcraft in the Basque territories. He actually boasted that as a trial judge he had sentenced 600 to be burned.

His writings include *Tableau de l'inconstance des mauvaisanges* (1612), *L'incredulité et mescréance dusortilé* (1622), and *Du Sortilege* (1627). He died at Loubeur-sur-Garonne in 1631.

Sources:

Robbins, Rossell Hope. *The Encyclopedia of Witchcraft and Demonology.* New York: Crown Publishers, 1959.

De Launoy, Jean (1603–1678)

A celebrated doctor of the Sorbonne, canonist, and historian, De Launoy was born in Valdesie, Normandy, France. He studied at the University of Paris and after being ordained as a priest was admitted as a doctor of divinity at Navarre. He resisted the claims of the court of Rome and specialized in exposing legendary religious fables and demolishing dubious claims for saints. He thinned the ranks of sainthood by his keen scrutiny. One commentator remarked, "He suspected the whole martyrology, and examined all the saints as they do the nobility of France." In spite of his severe judgments, he was known as a kindhearted and benevolent man. He wrote several books based upon his work.

De Lisle (ca. 1710)

De Lisle was a French alchemist. Both Lenglet du Fresnoy, in his *Histoire de la Philosophie Hérmetique* (ca. 1742), and nineteenth-century alchemist G. Louis Figuier wrote about De Lisle; neither supplied his first name or his date and place of birth. Some believe he was a Provençal.

De Lisle was known to have been active during the first decade of the eighteenth century, so it may be assumed that he was born toward the close of the previous century. He seems at an early age to have entered the service of a scientist who apparently was a pupil of the alchemist **Lascaris.** This unnamed scientist got into trouble of some sort, probably because of his predilection for the **occult.** He left Provence and set out for Switzerland, taking with him his young pupil, De Lisle. On the way the youth murdered his patron and employer and took all his alchemistic property, notably some precious transmuting powder. Then, about the year 1708, he returned to his native France, where he soon attracted attention by supposedly changing masses of lead and iron into silver and gold.

Noble and influential people now began to seek his company and his scientific services, and he soon found himself safely and comfortably housed in the castle of La Palud. There he received many visitors and demonstrated his skill before them.

He eventually grew weary of this and began an affair with a Madame Alnys, a married woman. He traveled with her from place to place, and a son was eventually born to the pair. Madame Alnys's husband was still alive, but that did not prevent De Lisle from continuing to elicit patronage and favor from the rich and famous.

For example, in 1710, at the Château de St. Auban, he performed a curious experiment in the presence of a Monsieur St. Maurice, then president of the royal mint. Going into the grounds of the château one evening, De Lisle showed St. Maurice a basket sunk in the ground and had him bring it into the dining hall, where it was opened, revealing some earth of a blackish color. After distilling a yellow liquid from the earth, De Lisle projected this on hot quicksilver and quickly produced three ounces of gold, later also succeeding in concocting a quantity of silver. Some of the gold was sent to Paris to be refined. Three medals were struck from it; one, bearing the inscription *Aurum Arte Factum,* was placed in the cabinet of the king.

As a result of the incident at St. Auban, De Lisle was invited to visit the court in Paris, but he declined, saying the southern climate in which he lived was necessary to the success of his experiments, since the preparations he worked with were purely vegetable. It is probable that, having been successful in impressing his clientèle so far, he felt it wise to refrain from further endeavors that might prove futile and destroy his reputation.

Nothing is written of De Lisle later than 1760, so presumably he died about that time. His son by Madame Alnys, however, seems to have inherited some of his father's predilections and a fair amount of his skill. Wandering for many years through Italy and Germany, Alnys was reported to have affected transmutations successfully before various petty nobles. In Vienna he attracted the attention of the Duc de Richelieu, then acting as French ambassador to the Viennese court. Richelieu afterward assured the Abbé Lenglet that he not only saw the operation of gold making performed, but did it himself by carrying out instructions given him by the alchemist.

Alnys latter gradually acquired great wealth, but, falling under suspicion, he was imprisoned for a time at Marseilles. He ultimately escaped to Brussels. There he continued, not altogether unsuccessfully, to engage in **alchemy.**

It was in Brussels that he became acquainted with Percell, the brother of Lenglet du Fresnoy, to whom he is said to have confided some valuable scientific secrets. Eventually the mysterious death of one Grefier, known to have been working in Alnys's laboratory, made the Brussels authorities suspicious about Alnys's character, so he left the town stealthily, never to be heard from again.

Sources:

Waite, Arthur Edward. *The Secret Tradition in Alchemy.* London, 1926.

De Marigny, Enguerrand (d. 1315)

A minister of Louis X, king of France. De Marigny entered the stream of occult history after having been arrested and imprisoned. Soon after his arrest his wife and her sister were accused of using various enchantments to harm the king, his brother Charles, and other barons. Their ultimate intention was to free de Marigny. The ladies were arrested and along with them Jacques Dulot, a magician, who was believed to have helped in these sorceries. Dulot committed suicide in prison, after his wife was burned.

Dulot's death convinced many that de Marigny was guilty, and the ex-minister was tried and condemned. On April 30, 1315, he was hanged on a gibbet that he had erected during his term of office. The tide of popular opinion turned at the sight of his misfortune, however, and the judges refused to condemn his wife and sister-in-law. The king himself repented of having abandoned de Marigny to his enemies and in his will left a sum of money to his family.

De Martino, Ernesto (1908–1965)

Italian professor of the history of religions. De Martino was born December 1, 1908. He developed an active interest in **parapsychology** as related to ethnology and anthropology, about which he wrote several books.

Sources:

De Martino, Ernesto. *Morte e Pianto rituale nel Mondo antico* (Death and ritual dirge in the ancient world). N.p., 1958.

———. *Sud e Magia* (South Italy and magic). 2nd ed. Milan: Feltrinelli, 1971.

———. *La Terra del Rimorso* (The land of remorse). N.p., 1961.

De Morgan, Augustus (1806–1871)

A famous English mathematician, de Morgan was one of the first English scientists who investigated the phenomena of **Spiritualism** and became convinced of its paranormal nature. He was born in 1806 in Madura, Madras, India. At the age of seven months, his family moved to England. At an early age he lost the use of one eye. He attended several schools, eventually entering Trinity College, Cambridge University, in 1823. It was there that he displayed his mathematical ability. After earning his M.A., he began a career in law, but soon abandoned that and was elected as the first professor of mathematics at the University of London (later known as University College, London).

De Morgan was a brilliant mathematician and was responsible for the complete geometrical interpretation of the square root of minus one. He had a great love of algebra, puzzles, puns, and paradoxes. Beyond his long career at the university, he was secretary to the Royal Astronomical Society for 18 years and was the author of such standard works as *Formal Logic, The Differential Calculus,* and the *Theory of Probabilities.*

His first paranormal experience occurred in 1849. Ellen Dawson, a clairvoyant patient of a London surgeon named Hands, was sent, in a state of trance, on a clairvoyant journey after de Morgan. The sitting took place in the house of Mrs. de Morgan. The clairvoyant gave a description of de Morgan's acts and surroundings in a house where he was a guest. The description corresponded with the facts to the minutest details.

The first continuing series of investigations in which de Morgan participated took place with the well-known American medium **Maria B. Hayden** in de Morgan's own house. In 1854 Mrs. de Morgan discovered that her young servant Jane was a medium. She produced **raps** and **movement** of the table and saw visions. Her phenomena lasted for two years.

A report of this and the previous investigation with Hayden was published anonymously in 1863 under the title *From Matter to Spirit, the Result of Ten Years' Experience in Spirit Manifestations,* by C. D. (i.e., Mrs. de Morgan), with a preface by A. B. (i.e., de Morgan). In his preface, de Morgan writes:

"I am perfectly convinced that I have both seen and heard, in a manner which should make unbelief impossible, things called spiritual which cannot be taken by a rational being to be capable of explanation by imposture, coincidence or mistake. So far I feel the ground firm under me. But when it comes to what is the cause of these phenomena, I find I cannot adopt any explanation which has yet been suggested."

Writing anonymously, he shows some concern for the opinions of his colleagues: "My state of mind, which refers the whole either to some unseen intelligence, or something which man has never had any conception of, proves me to be out of the pale of the Royal Society." He was more definite and outspoken in his work *Mind,* published later the same year. He declared that he had come to believe that the only satisfactory hypothesis to explain the facts was that they occurred through some superhuman intelligence.

He finally gave up his anonymity by allowing the second edition of *From Matter to Spirit* to be advertised under his true name. At the Lyon-Home trial in 1868 (see **D. D. Home**) extracts from his preface were read in the court. He died March 18, 1871.

Sources:

Berger, Arthur S., and Joyce Berger. *The Encyclopedia of Parapsychology and Psychical Research.* New York: Paragon House, 1991.

De Morgan, Augustus. *A Budget of Paradoxes.* La Salle, Ill.: Open Court, 1915. Reprinted as *Encyclopedia of Eccentrics.* N.p., 1971.

De Morgan, Sophia Elizabeth. *Three Score Years and Ten; Reminiscences of the Late Sophia Elizabeth De Morgan.* London: R. Bentley, 1895.

Prince, Walter F. *Noted Witnesses for Psychic Occurrences.* Boston: Boston Society for Psychical Research, 1928. Reprint, New Hyde Park, N.Y.: University Books, 1963.

De Rupecissa, Johannes (or Jean de Roquetaillade) (d. ca. 1362)

Alchemist and ancestor of Montfauçon, the distinguished archaeologist. His name suggests that he was a man of gentle birth, while it is commonly supposed that he was a French monk of the order of St. Francis.

In 1357, presumably because of his alchemistic predilections, De Rupecissa was imprisoned by Pope Innocent VI. Much mystery surrounded his life and death. Some said he was released from prison in 1378 by Pope Urban VI, others that he died in prison. Another rumor was that he was burned at the stake in 1362.

De Rupecissa contributed four volumes to the literature of **alchemy** and hermetic philosophy: *Coelum Philosophorum* (1543), *De Quinta Essentia Rerum Omniam* (1561), *De Secretis Alchemiae* (1579), and *Livre de Lumière* (n.d.). These were admired by a number of the author's successors, but their value is literary rather than scientific.

De Tonquedec, Joseph (1868–1962)

Jesuit priest and writer on **parapsychology.** De Tonquedec was born December 27, 1868, at Morlaix (Finistère), France. He received his doctorate in philosophy in 1899 and his doctorate in theology in 1905. He was the professor of philosophy at Collège St. Grégoire, Tours, from 1899 to 1901. He died November 21, 1962.

Sources:

De Tonquedec, Joseph. *La Critique de la connaissance* (Criticism of knowledge). N.p., n.d.

———. *Introduction a l'étude du merveilleux et du miracle* (Introduction to the study of the marvelous and the miracle). N.p., n.d.

———. *Maladies neuveuses ou mentales et manifestations diaboliques* (Nervous or mental diseases and diabolical manifestations). N.p., n.d.

———. *Merveilleux métapsychique et miracle Chrétien* (The marvelous in parapsychology and the Christian miracle). N.p., n.d.

———. *La Notion de Verite dans la "Philosophie Nouvelle"* (The concept of truth in the "new philosophy"). N.p., n.d.

———. *La Philosophie de la natur* (Philosophy of nature). N.p., n.d.

De Tromelin Cylinder

A device for the detection of psychic forces was invented by the Count de Tromelin at the opening of the twentieth century. A paper cylinder with a crosspiece of straw revolves on a fine point when a human hand is in the vicinity or when the operator wills the device to move. It is also known as the **fluid motor.**

Many variant devices of this kind have been made to demonstrate the supposed action of psychic force or willpower on a lightly suspended object. One such indicator is a square of paper, folded across the diagonals so that it can revolve on a firmly fixed needle point.

One problem with all such devices is the lack of controls to exclude the possibility of the movement being caused by air currents or the heat of the operator's hand. The most impressive devices are those enclosed within a glass cover to exclude air movements (see **sthenometer**).

One very interesting instrument of this kind was developed by the British physician Charles Russ and was described by him in the July 3, 1931, issue of the respected British medical journal the *Lancet* as "An Instrument Which is Set in Motion by Vision." (See also **biometer of Baraduc; magnetometer**)

Sources:

Russ, Charles. "An Instrument Which is Set in Motion by Vision." *Lancet,* July 3, 1931.

De Vesme, Count Cesar Baudi (1862–1938)

A distinguished European author and psychical researcher, de Vesme was born November 12, 1862, in Turin, Italy. He was secretary general of the Société des Amis de l'Institut Métapsychique Internationale (Paris) from 1934 to 1938. He was drawn to the study of psychical phenomena upon reading the narrative of the following incident:

"One night in 1871 cries of despair were heard from M. de M.'s mother. She was found in a state of terror, declaring that she was carried by spirits to the foot of her bed. At seven o'clock the following morning Col. Daviso, a stranger [,] called. He was informed at a spiritistic séance that the spirits were about to play a trick upon a lady in the house of M. de M. He came to verify the information."

In 1898, after the death of **Giovanni Ermacora,** the renowned psychical researcher **Cesare Lombroso** entrusted de Vesme with the editorship of the *Rivista di Studi Psichici.* He arranged for a simultaneous French edition under the title *Revue des Etudes Psychiques* which he also edited. In 1905 this journal was merged with the *Annales des Sciences Psychiques,* of which **Charles Richet** and Dr. X. Dariex were the directors, and de Vesme became its editor in chief. He made extensive studies with **Eusapia Palladino, Stanislawa Tomczyk, Eva C.,** and other famous mediums. He acknowledged mediumistic phenomena and sympathized with the Spiritualist hypothesis. He still had serious reservations, however.

In 1930 de Vesme published an excellent book on predictions in games of chance (*Le Merveilleux dans les jeux de hasard*) that is extensively quoted by Richet in *L'Avenir et la Premonition.* His main work, however, was *A History of Experimental Spiritualism* (1931), a book lauded by the French Academy of Science. Versions appeared in English, Italian, and German. The first volume of this two-volume work, *Primitive Man,* discusses the nature and origin of religious beliefs. The second, *Peoples of Antiquity,* deals with the experimental elements in the spiritualistic doctrines of early civilizations.

De Vesme died July 18, 1938, in Paris.

Sources:

De Vesme, Cesar. *A History of Experimental Spiritualism.* 2 vols. London, 1931.

De Villanova, Arnold (or **Arnuldus**) (d. ca. 1313)

Arnold de Villanova was a physician by profession and is reported to have been a theologian and a skilled alchemist. His place of birth has never been determined, but Catalonia (Spain), Milan, and Montpellier (France) have been suggested; the approximate date was the middle of the thirteenth century.

De Villanova studied medicine for many years at the Sorbonne in Paris, which in medieval times was the principal European school training physicians. Thereafter he traveled extensively in Italy and Spain.

In Spain he heard that a friend was in the hands of the dreaded Inquisition, and, fearing that he might be arrested, de Villanova quickly returned to Italy. He lived in Naples for a long period, enjoying the friendly patronage of the Neapolitan sovereign and spending his time compiling various scientific treatises. Later he was appointed physician in ordinary to Pope Clement V, so presumably the rest of his life was spent in Rome, or possibly in Avignon.

His interest in **alchemy** became widely known. Many people declared that his skill was derived from communication with the devil, and the physician deserved nothing less than burning at the stake. He also attracted particular enmity from the clergy by sneering openly at the monastic regime and declaring boldly that works of charity are more acceptable to God than the repetition of *paternosters.*

Thanks to papal favor, de Villanova remained unscathed by his enemies. However, soon after his death, about the year 1313, the Inquisition decided that they had dealt too leniently with him and ordered certain of his writings burned publicly at Tarragona.

De Villanova was acquainted with the preparation of oil of turpentine and oil of rosemary, while the marcasite frequently mentioned by him is said to be identical to the element bismuth. His most important treatises are *Thesaurus Thesaurorum, Rosarium Philosophorum, Speculam Alchemiae* and *Perfectum Magisterum,* while two others of some importance are his *Testamentum* and *Scientia Scientiae.* A collected edition of his works was issued in 1520, and several of his writings are included in the *Bibliotheca Chemica Curiosa* of Mangetus, published in 1702.

De Villars, l'Abbe de Montfaucon (1635–1673)

This churchman, author, and mystic was a native of southern France. He was born in Alet, near Toulouse and the seaport town of Bordeaux. At an early age he took holy orders, and in 1667 left the south and moved to Paris, eager to win fame as a preacher. His eloquence in the pulpit won him numerous admirers, but he grew more interested in literature than in clerical affairs, and in 1670 he published his first and most important book, *Comte du Gabalis.*

Ostensibly a novel, this volume seems largely a veiled satire on the writings of La Calprenède, then very popular both in France and England. The satirical element in de Villars's work, however, is supplemented by a curious blend of history, philosophy, and **mysticism.** Since much of the mysticism was of a nature distinctly hostile to the dogmas of Rome, the author soon found himself out of favor with his brother clerics. Probably it was for this reason that he renounced the pulpit. De Villars's literary activities were not impaired by persecution; in 1671 he issued *De la Délicetesse,* a speculative treatise, couched in the form of dialogues, in which the author takes the part of a priest who has been writing in opposition to Port Royal (Jansenist) doctrines.

Like its predecessor this new book made a considerable stir, and de Villars began to write voluminously. At the same time he plunged deeply into the study of various kinds of mysticism, but his activities were terminated suddenly. In 1673 he was murdered on the public high road not far from Lyon, on his way from Paris.

Within the first decade succeeding his death three posthumous works appeared. *L'Amour sans Faiblesse, Anne de Bretague et Ailmanzaris,* and *Critique de la Bérénice de Racine et de Corneille,* the latter winning the praise of Mme. de Sévigné, a shrewd judge.

As late as 1715 a further work by de Villars was issued, a sequel to the *Comte de Gabalis,* bearing the significant title *Nouveaux Entretiens sur les Sciences secrètes.* This volume elicited wide interest among eighteenth-century thinkers and may be defined as a treatise opposing the philosophical theories of Descartes, or rather, opposing the popular misapprehension and abuse of those theories.

Sources:

De Villars, Abbe. *Comte de Gabalis.* London: Printed for B. M., Printer to the Cabalistical Society of the Sages, at the Sign of the Rosy-Crucian, 1680. Reprint, New York: Macoy Publishing & Masonic Supply, 1922.

De Wohl, Louis (1903–1961)

German-born astrologer who escaped to Britain from the Nazis and played a prominent part in the British psychological warfare campaign. Born January 24, 1903, in Berlin, as Ludwig von Wohl, he was a novelist, journalist, and film scriptwriter shortly before Hitler came to power. He learned astrology from Baron Harald Keun von Hoogerwoerd and became a professional astrologer. In 1937, he wrote *I Follow My Stars.* In his book *The Stars of War and Peace* (1952), de Wohl states that in 1935 he was invited to advise members of the Nazi party on astrological matters. He escaped to Britain as a refugee in the same year, where he practiced as an astrologer and wrote books on the subject.

Because of his inside knowledge of the German astrological scene and Hitler's astrologer **Karl Ernest Krafft,** he was recruited by British intelligence and served with the rank of captain, taking part in psychological warfare projects that used astrology to further the Allied cause. One of the special projects on which de Wohl worked was a fake edition of the prophecies of **Nostradamus,** used to spread subversive rumors in Germany. He died in Lucerne, Switzerland, June 2, 1961.

Sources:

Howe, Ellic. *Astrology & Psychological Warfare during World War II.* Reprinted as *Urania's Children.* N.p., n.d.

Dean, Eric Douglas (1916–)

British physical chemist and parapsychologist. He was born June 21, 1916, at Rock Ferry, Cheshire, England. He was educated at Liverpool University (B.S., 1937; B.S., 1938; M.S., 1939) and did graduate work at Cambridge University. He moved to the United States in 1951 as a fellow of the American Electrochemical Society at Princeton University.

Dean conducted research at the Educational Testing Service in Princeton, New Jersey (1954–59), and then became the assistant director of research for the **Parapsychology Foundation** (1959–62). In 1962 he became a research associate at Newark College of Engineering in Newark, New Jersey. There he and his associate John Mihalasky initiated the PSI Communications Project, out of which a number of papers were generated concerned with different ways that psychic communications can be monitored and measured. The major product of the research, however, was a volume describing how psychic activity supports successful businesspeople. *Executive ESP* appeared in 1974. While at Newark College, Dean also served a term as president of its Parapsychological Association (1967–69) and oversaw the affiliation with the American Association for the Advancement of Science.

He left Newark in 1976 and held several positions in industry. He served as head of the Parapsychology/Paraphysics department of the International College in Montreal, Canada. Dean also served as president of the **International Kirlian Research Association,** which focused on **kirlian aura** photography (a line of research that has proved a dead end). His interest in kirlian effects was part of a larger interest in psychic healing that led him to assume the presidency of the **American Healers Association** in 1976. In 1977 he was elected vice president of the World Federation of Healing. He was also active in and a board member of the **Academy of Religion and Psychical Research.**

Sources:

Berger, Arthur S., and Joyce Berger. *The Encyclopedia of Parapsychology and Psychical Research.* New York: Paragon House, 1991.

Dean, E. Douglas, John Mihalasky, Sheila Ostrander, and Lynn Schroeder. *Executive ESP.* Englewood Cliffs, N.J.: Prentice-Hall, 1974.

———. *The Mystery of Healing: Still a Mystery after 60,000 Years.* New York: Search, 1987.

Pleasants, Helene, ed. *Biographical Dictionary of Parapsychology.* New York: Helix Press, 1964.

Deane, Ada Emma (ca. 1930)

Well-known British exponent of **spirit photography.** In June 1920 an extra face was discovered on a photograph taken by her. Her subsequent psychic career was the subject of much criticism and suspicion because of her strange habit of keeping the plates for "magnetising." This objection lessened as the years passed, and after November 1924 Deane—in her sittings at the **W. T. Stead Borderland Library**—never had the plates in her possession or handled them in any way before the sitting. It was, however, discovered even before that if the plates were exchanged without her knowledge the supernormal effects still appeared.

The *Journal* of the American Society for Psychical Research (ASPR) reported in 1921 a remarkable sitting that Dr. Allerton Cushman, director of the National Laboratories of Washington, had with Deane. He obtained on his own plate a striking portrait of his daughter, who had died the previous year.

In the following year the Occult Committee of the **Magic Circle** published a report in which they claimed to have caught Deane in **fraud.** Wide publicity was given in the *Daily Press* to Deane's experiment in taking a photograph on November 11, 1922, during the two-minute Armistice silence at the Cenotaph in Whitehall, London. She was assisted by Estelle Stead. Many spirit faces appeared on the plate. The experiment was repeated during three successive years. In several cases people claimed to recognize the faces.

A remarkable communication was received by **H. Dennis Bradley,** apparently from the spirit of his brother-in-law, W. A., regarding the Armistice photograph taken in 1923. As told in Bradley's book *Towards the Stars* (1924), the communicator said in the **direct voice** that he was in the right-hand side of the photograph, near the top. On the following day Bradley obtained a copy of the photograph. To his astonishment, among the 50 spirit heads visible in the picture, he found one in the position described, which, under a magnifying glass, looked surprisingly like W. A.

The 1924 picture drew extraordinary revelations. The Topical Press Agency declared that "the spirit extras" were reproductions of the agency's well-known photographs of living sportsmen. The alleged exposure was published in the newspaper *Daily Sketch,* but the story was never fully told. In *Proceedings* of the SPR (vol. 41, 1933), Fred Barlow, in a report on **psychic photography,** also charged Deane with **fraud.**

Stead, in her booklet *Faces of the Living Dead,* printed some unpublished documents, among them **Sir Arthur Conan Doyle**'s letter to the editor of the *Daily Sketch.* In it he states that he submitted the two sets of faces published in the *Daily Sketch* to Sir Arthur Keith, the greatest authority on anthropometric matters. Keith replied, "Not one of the photographs reproduced by the *Daily Sketch* is identical with any of the representations or photos reproduced in the spirit photographs." Stead give the following testimony in her booklet:

"I have known Mrs. Deane and worked with her for the last four years and have the highest regard for her honesty and integrity of purpose. I know her cameras well, both inside and out, having examined them so often—also the dark slides used for these sittings. Both cameras and slides are continually left in my studio for days together, and I and others have plenty of opportunities to examine them at our leisure. The plates are always developed in my darkroom, and I can assure those doughty champions who explain so glibly how these are 'faked' that there are no developing dishes with transparent xylonite bases let into the dark room table, nor any concealed electric lights in my dark room. We use porcelain dishes, which are washed out after every sitting."

Hereward Carrington writes in the *Journal* of the ASPR (May 1925) of his experiences with Deane on September 5, 1921:

"Upon six of my plates curious marks appeared. On two plates these marks are mere smudges, which are not evidential, though I think curious. On the next plate, however, the result is quite striking. I had silently willed that a shaft of white light should emerge from my right shoulder, and appear on the plate. Sure enough, upon development, a column of white light, surmounted by a sort of psychic cabbage, was distinctly visible. It will be remembered that this was upon my own plate, placed in the camera, and afterwards removed and developed by myself. The odd thing to my mind is why I should have willed so curious a thing: what prompted me to wish for it? Was it a pure thought photograph? Or did some external intelligence first of all impress upon my mind this idea, and afterwards produce the image upon the plate? A very similar result was obtained by a friend of mine, Miss M., the following year at a sitting with Mrs. Deane. She was looking intently at her own hand and thinking about it, during the exposure of the plate (thinking of her new ring, as a matter of fact, which had just been given to her) and when the plate was developed, a hand appeared on the sitter's head, surrounded by an ectoplasmic cloud. The resemblance to her own hand is quite striking, and it is certainly a feminine hand."

The following year Carrington obtained further curious results, peculiar cometlike lights and a woman's face on his own plates. They were secretly marked by X-rays, but since Deane had kept them for some time, he did not accept the pictures as evidential. However, he notes:

"Nevertheless, I am inclined to regard these results with considerable interest for two reasons. In the first place, if these plates had been 'doctored' by Mrs. Deane in her own home, before the sitting, she would almost certainly have imprinted faces upon the plates instead of these bizarre lights, it seems to me. Further, knowing that Cushman was to have a sitting, and knowing of her own brilliant success in producing, at a previous séance, under excellent conditions, a psychic extra recognised by Cushman and members of his family as his daughter Agnes (the case is a celebrated one) she would, I submit, have seen to it that Agnes appeared. Again, these lights are intrinsically striking, interesting, when studied closely."

Sources:

Carrington, Hereward. *The Physical Phenomena of Spiritualism: Fraudulent and Genuine.* Boston, 1907. Reprint, New York: Dodd, Mead, 1920.

Coates, James. *Photographing the Invisible.* London, 1911.

Doyle, Arthur Conan. *The Case for Spirit Photography.* London, [1922].

———. *The History of Spiritualism.* New York: Charles H. Doran, 1926. Reprint, New York: Arno Press, 1975.

Death

Accounts of the moments before and after death abound with reports of paranormal phenomena, including **apparitions** of the dying in distant places and phantom forms seen by the dying and occasionally by others. Such near-death apparitions remain a topic of intense debate in both psychological and parapsychological circles. Those who accept a psychic explanation of near-death experiences assert that the individual's spirit, when near to being freed from its connection to the body, is immersed in two planes of existence and acts in both the material and spiritual worlds. Many reports also exist in which persons who were dead returned to life and remembered their experience of death. They verify an often-told story that in the last moments of earthly existence a panorama of the person's life flashes by.

Near-Death Experiences

A Professor Heiron of Zurich slipped in the Alps on a snow covered crag, slid head first about a mile, and then shot 60 feet through the air, landing on his head and shoulders. He was not killed. Returning to consciousness, he not only testified to having seen a panoramic view of his life but also said he had heard the most delightful music. He interviewed many people who had a similar experiences; the great rapidity of mental action and the absence of terror and pain was narrated by all of them.

Prof. A. Pastore of the Royal Lyceum at Genoa relates his experience in the *Annals of Psychic Science* of February 1906:

"I have been through a very severe illness. At the crisis, when I had entirely lost consciousness of physical pain, the power of my imagination was increased by an extraordinary degree, and I saw clearly in a most distinct confusion (two words which do not accord, but which, in this case, are the only ones which will express the idea). I saw myself as a little boy, a youth, a man, at various periods of my life; a dream, but a most powerful, intense living dream. In that immense, blue, luminous space my mother met me—my mother who had died four years previously. It was an indescribable sensation. Rereading the *Phaedo* of Plato after that experience, I was better able to understand what Socrates meant."

Still more is told by Leslie Grant Scott in *Psychic Research* (March 1931):

"Dying is really not such a terrifying experience. I speak as one who has died and come back, and who found Death one of the easiest things in life—but not the returning. That was difficult and full of fear. The will to live had left me and so I died. I had been ill for some time but not seriously so. I was in a rundown condition, aggravated by the tropical climate in which I was then living. I was in bed, a large old fashioned bed, in which I seemed lost. I lay there quietly thinking and feeling more at peace than I had felt for some time. Suddenly my whole life began to unroll before me and I saw the purpose of it. All bitterness was wiped out for I knew the meaning of every event and I saw its place in the pattern. I seemed to view it all impersonally, but yet with intense interest and, although much that was crystal clear to me then has again become somewhat veiled in shadow, I have never forgotten or lost the sense of essential justice and rightness of things."

After telling of the doctor's visit and his attempts at reviving him, Scott continues:

"My consciousness was growing more and more acute. It seemed to have expanded beyond the limits of my physical brain. I was aware of things I had never contacted. My vision was also extended so that I could see what was going on behind my back, in the next room, even in distant places. I wondered if I should close my eyes or leave them open. I thought that it would be less gruesome for those around me if they were closed, and so I tried to shut them—but found that I could not. I no longer had any control over my body. I was dead. Yet I could think, hear and see more widely than ever before. From the next room came great engulfing waves of emotion, the sadness of a childhood companion. My increased sensitiveness made me feel and understand these things with an intensity hitherto unknown to me. The effort to return to my body was accompanied by an almost unimaginable sensation of horror and terror. I had left without the slightest struggle. I returned by an almost superhuman effort of will."

Sometimes, it appears, the return is automatic and against the will of the dying. In the *Proceedings* of the Society for Psychical Research (SPR) (vol. 8, 1892), F. W. H. Myers published the narrative of a Dr. Wiltse (first printed in the *St. Louis Medical and Surgical Journal,* November 1889), who, in a state of apparent death, lost all power of thought or knowledge of existence. Half an hour later, his narrative continues,

"I came again into a state of conscious existence and discovered that I was still in the body and I had no longer any interests in common. I looked with astonishment and joy for the first time upon myself—the me, the real Ego, while the not me closed upon all sides like a sepulchre of clay. With all the interest of a physician I beheld the wonders of my bodily anatomy, intimately interwoven with which even tissue for tissue, was I, the living soul of that dead body. . . . I realised my condition and calmly reasoned thus, I have died, as man terms death, and yet I am as much a man as ever. I am about to get out of the body. I watched the interesting process of the separation of soul and body. By some power, apparently not my own, the Ego was rocked to and fro, laterally as the cradle is rocked, by which process its connection with the tissues of the body was broken up. After a little while the lateral motion ceased, and along the soles of the feet, beginning at the toes, passing rapidly to the heels, I felt and heard, as it seemed, the snapping of innumerable small cords. When this was accomplished I began slowly to retreat from the feet, towards the head, as a rubber cord shortens. I remember reaching the hips and saying to myself: 'Now there is no life below the hips.' I can recall no memory of passing through the abdomen and chest, but recollect distinctly when my whole self was collected in the head, when I reflected thus: 'I am all the head now, and I shall soon be free.' I passed around the brain as if I were hollow, compressing it and its membranes slightly on all sides towards the centre and peeped out between the sutures of the skull, emerging like the flattened edges of a bag of membranes. I recollect distinctly how I appeared to myself something like a jelly-fish as regards colour and form. As I emerged, I saw two ladies sitting at my head. I measured the distance between the head of my cot and the knees of the lady opposite the head and concluded there was room for me to stand, but felt considerable embarrassment as I reflected that I was about to emerge naked before her, but comforted myself with the thought that in all probability she could not see me with her bodily eyes, as I was a spirit. As I emerged from the head I floated up and down and laterally like a soap bubble attached to the bowl of a pipe, until I at last broke loose from the body and fell lightly to the floor, where I slowly rose and expanded to the full stature of a man. I seemed to be translucent, of a bluish cast and perfectly naked. With a painful sense of embarrassment, I fled towards the partially open door to escape the eyes of the two ladies whom I was facing, as well as others whom I knew were about me, but upon reaching the door I found myself clothed, and satisfied upon that point, I turned and faced the company. As I turned, my left elbow came in contact with the arm of one of two gentlemen who were standing in the door. To my surprise, his arm passed through mine without apparent resistance, the severed parts closing again without pain, as air reunites. I looked quickly up at his face to see if he had noticed the contact but he gave me no sign—only stood and gazed toward the couch I had just left. I directed my gaze in the direction of his, and saw my own dead body. . . .

"Suddenly I discovered that I was looking at the straight seam down the back of my coat. How is this, I thought, how do I see my back? and I looked again, to reassure myself, down the back of the coat or down the back of my legs to the very heels. I put my hand to my face and felt for my eyes. They are where they should be, I thought. Am I like an owl that I can turn my head half way round? I tried the experiment and failed.

"No! Then it must be that having been out of the body but a few moments I have yet the power to use the eyes of the body, and I turned about and looked back in at the open door where I could see the head of my body in a line with me. I discovered then a small cord, like a spider's web, running from my shoulders back to my body and attaching to it at the base of the neck, in front.

"I was satisfied with the conclusion that by means of that cord, I was using the eyes of my body and turning, walked down the street. . . . a small, densely black cloud appeared in front of me and advanced toward my face. I knew that I was to be stopped. I felt the power to move or to think leaving me. My hands fell powerless at my side, my shoulders and my head dropped forward and I knew no more.

"Without previous thought and without great effort on my part, my eyes opened. I looked at my hands and then at the little white cot upon which I was lying and, realising that I was in the body, in astonishment and disappointment I exclaimed: What in the world has happened to me? Must I die again?"

The clairvoyant description by Spiritualist medium **Andrew Jackson Davis** of the process of dying in *Death and the After Life* (1865) is often quoted. He writes:

"Suppose the person is now dying. It is to be a rapid death. The feet first grow cold. The clairvoyant sees right over the head what may be called a magnetic halo, an ethereal emanation, in appearance golden, and throbbing as though conscious. The body is now cold up to the knees and elbows, and the emanation has ascended higher in the air. The legs are cold to the hips and the arms to the shoulders; and the emanation, though it has not risen higher in the room, is more expanded. The death-coldness steals over the breast and around on either side, and the emanation has attained a higher position near the ceiling. The person has ceased to breathe, the pulse is still, and the emanation is elongated and fashioned in the outline of the human form. Beneath it is connected with the brain. The head of the person is internally throbbing—a slow, deep throb—not painful, like the beat of the sea. Hence, the thinking faculties are rational, while nearly every part of the person is dead. Owing to the brain's momentum, I have seen a dying person, even at the last feeble pulsebeat, rouse impulsively and rise up in bed to converse with a friend; but the next instant he was gone—his brain being the last to yield up the life principle. The golden emanation, which extends up midway to the ceiling, is connected with the brain by a very fine life-thread. Now the body of the emanation ascends. Then appears something white and shining, like a human head; next, in a very few moments, a faint outline of the face divine; then the fair neck and beautiful shoulders; then, in rapid succession, come all parts of the new body down to the feet—a bright shining image, a little smaller than its physical body, but a perfect prototype, or reproduction in all except its disfigurements. The fine life-thread continues attached to the old brain. The next thing is the withdrawal of the electric principle. When this thread "snaps" the spiritual body is free and prepared to accompany its guardians to the Summer Land. Yes, there is a spiritual body; it is sown in dishonor and raised in brightness."

The description is paralleled by the curious case sent by a Dr. Burgers to **Richard Hodgson** in 1902 and published in the *Journal* of the SPR (vol. 13, 1908). In it a Mr. G. gives this account of the death of his wife:

"At half-past six I urged our friends, the physician and nurses to take dinner. . . . All but two left the room in obedience to my request.

"Fifteen minutes later . . . I happened to look towards the door, when I saw floating through the doorway three separate and distinct clouds in strata. Each cloud appeared to be about four feet in length, from six to eight inches in width, the lower one about two feet from the ground, the others at intervals of about six inches.

"My first thought was that some of our friends . . . were standing outside the bedroom smoking, and that the smoke from their cigars was being wafted into the room. With this idea I started up to rebuke them, when lo! I discovered there was no one standing by the door, no one in the hall-way, no one in the adjoining rooms. Overcome with astonishment I watched the clouds; and slowly, but surely these clouds approached the bed until they completely enveloped it. Then, gazing through the mist, I beheld standing at the head of my dying wife a woman's figure about three feet in height, transparent, yet like a sheen of brightest gold; a figure so glorious in its appearance that no words can be used fitly to describe it. She was dressed in the Grecian costume, with long loose and flowing sleeves—upon her head a brilliant crown. In all its splendour and beauty the figure remained motionless with hands uplifted over my wife, seeming to express a welcome with a quiet glad countenance, with a dignity of calmness and peace. Two figures in white knelt by my wife's bedside, apparently leaning towards her; other figures hovered above the bed, more or less distinct.

"Above my wife, and connected with a cord proceeding from her forehead, over the left eye, there floated in a horizontal position a nude, white figure, apparently her astral body. At times the suspended figure would lie perfectly quiet, at other times it would shrink in size until it was no longer than perhaps eighteen inches, but always was the figure perfect and distinct; a perfect head, a perfect body, perfect arms and perfect legs. When the astral body diminished in size it struggled violently, threw out its arms and legs in an apparent effort to escape. It would struggle until it seemed to exhaust itself, then become calm, increase in size, only to repeat the same performance again and again.

"This vision, or whatever it may be called, I saw continuously during the five hours preceding the death of my wife. Interruptions, as speaking to my friends, closing my eyes, turning away my head, failed to destroy the illusion, for whenever I looked towards that deathbed the spiritual vision was there. All through these five hours I felt a strange feeling of oppression and weight upon my head and limbs; my eyes were heavy as if with sleep, and during this period the sensations were so peculiar and the visions so continuous and vivid that I believed I was insane, and from time to time would say to the physician in charge: 'Doctor, I am going insane.'

"At last the fatal moment arrived; with a gasp, the astral figure struggling, my wife ceased to breathe, she apparently was dead:

however, a few seconds later she breathed again, twice, and then all was still. With her last breath and last gasp, as the soul left the body, the cord was severed suddenly and the astral figure vanished. The clouds and the spirit forms disappeared instantly, and, strange to say, all the oppression that weighed upon me was gone; I was myself, cool, calm and deliberate, able to direct, from the moment of death, the disposition of the body, its preparation for a final resting place."

Mr. G. was known to be hostile to **Spiritualism,** and the physician in attendance appended a statement to the effect that he had known him long enough to affirm that he had no tendency to any form of mental delusion.

Phenomena at Death

Watchers by the deathbed have often claimed to hear rushing sounds and see some kind of curious luminosity. **Hyppolite Baraduc** attempted to secure a photographic record when his son and wife died. He found that in each case a luminous, cloud-like mass apparently hovered over the bodies and appeared on the photographic plate.

Telekinetic phenomena (see **movement**) have been known to occur before death. A Mme. Martillet and a Mme. Claudet, who nursed Alfred de Musset in his last illness, said that as he lay in his armchair they saw by the light of the lamp that he was looking at the bell near the mantelpiece. But he was so feeble that he could not rise. "At the moment," says Martillet, "we were surprised and frightened; the bell-pull that the sick man had not reached, moved, as if by an invisible hand, and my sister and I took each other's hands, saying: 'Did you hear? Did you see? He did not leave his chair.' The servant came, having heard the bell" (*Annales des Sciences Psychiques* [1899]).

Charles Richet, in a report on the case, inquires,

"Should the singular phenomena mentioned in all ages as accompanying a death or serious event be considered as akin to hauntings? There are legends of clocks stopping, pictures falling, some object noisily breaking, etc., but it is difficult to determine the part played by chance coincidence."

George Micklebury reported in the *Daily Graphic* (October 4, 1905) a startling instance of clairaudient premonition of impending death that occurred as he was listening to the High Mass in London. He suddenly heard his daughter's distressful voice: "Pray for me, father, I am drowning." Two friends, between whom he was kneeling, heard nothing, but asked him whether he was ill, because he looked so startled. After the mass he took a train to the farm where his daughter was working and found her in bed, alarmed, but safe. She had fallen into the river from a capsized boat and become entangled in weeds. She had lost consciousness before she was rescued. During the moments of unconsciousness, she said, she saw her father at High Mass between two friends, whom she named, and also saw Father Pycke, the celebrant. Then she saw no more.

The vision of traditional family apparitions, **death-coaches, banshees,** and phantasmal animals often proves to be a true premonition of death. In the *Proceedings* of the Society for Psychical Research (vol. 10, 1894), Mrs. E. L. Kearney narrates:

"My step-grandfather was lying ill in my father's house. I was coming downstairs when I saw a strange cat coming towards me along the hall. When it saw me it ran behind a green baize door which separated one part of the hall from the other. This door was fastened open, and I went forward quickly to hunt the strange cat (as I thought) away, but to my utter astonishment there was no cat there, or anywhere else in the hall. I at once told my mother (and she told me the other day that she remembers the occurrence). My grandfather died the next day. Taken in connection with the above the following is interesting. My mother told me that the day before he died she saw a cat walk round her father's bed: she also went to hunt it out, but it was not there."

After Death

The question, what happens immediately after death? is more difficult to answer since it is beyond observation and researchers must rely on accounts of after-death communications. They do not even know for certain whether the apparitions of the dead are the result of a voluntary effort or a simple repercussion of strong thought and emotions on the material plane.

Death-compact cases and purposive apparitions, conveying in some form a definite message, suggest conscious action of which the living remain ignorant. Such cases imply that the thoughts and emotional reactions of the dead may greatly depend on the circumstances of their dying. For example, a Private Dowding, who died by shell explosion, said through a medium.

"Something struck, hard, hard, hard against my neck. Shall I ever lose the memory of that hardness? It is the only unpleasant incident that I can remember. I fell, and as I did so, without passing through any apparent interval of unconsciousness, I found myself outside myself. You see, I am telling my story simply; you will find it easier to understand. You will know what a small incident dying is."

"Pelham" (the **control** of **Leonora Piper**), who claimed to have died in a horse-riding accident, described his death as follows: "All was dark to me. Then consciousness returned but in a dim, twilight way as when one wakens before dawn. When I comprehended that I was not dead at all I was very glad." Significance should be attached to the phrase "When I comprehended."

According to numerous communications, many of those who died did not realize that they were dead at all, and finding themselves fully conscious and in a body which, to their perception, was just as material as the earthly one, refused to believe they were in the Beyond. It is still said that these "ghosts" keep performing their former actions in an aimless, automatic way—the physician continues to visit his patients, the minister continues preaching. It is usually not until they meet the spirit of someone who died before them that they realize what has happened and begin to learn the conditions of their new existence.

Of the nature of this life, in spite of scores of descriptive accounts, man has only vague notions. **William T. Stead,** in a message quoted by Estelle Stead in a magazine article "My Father," is reported to have said, "When I think of the ideas that I had of the life I am now living, when I was in the world in which you are, I marvel at the hopeless inadequacy of my dreams. The reality is so much, so very much greater than ever I imagined. It is a new life, the nature of which you cannot understand."

A deceased friend of Richard Hodgson's gave an incoherent communication through Leonora Piper's husband. The control Pelham insisted that they should not go on because the spirit would be confused for some time, having suffered from headaches and neurasthenia while on Earth. Sometimes even the clearest minds give the impression of mental debility if they communicate too soon after death. Pelham said on this, "The words of the wisest persons who have left the material world but a short time ago are incoherent and inexact owing to the severe shock of being disincarnated and their arrival in a new environment where everything is unintelligible."

Public interest in death and claimed after-death communications is regularly stimulated by the loss of so many by unnatural causes during and immediately after wars. The intense interest in communicating with loved ones who have died frequently overrides a more rational approach to death. Many of the learned through the early twentieth century saw the secular approach as leading to an abandonment of belief in the afterlife by the public. However, numerous contemporary studies, such as those of **Robert Crookall,** who collected and collated hundreds of accounts of **out-of-the-body travel** experiences, have given a sense of scientific support to belief in **survival** of death and have contributed some knowledge of after-death consciousness. Whereas **astral projection** or out-of-body travel can be regarded as a temporary release from the physical body, death is the final release. Through the 1960s Crookall drew attention to many accounts from individuals who nearly died, or who were briefly dead but revived. Their accounts of another sphere of existence may have been colored by their religious background or expectations, but still demand careful consideration. In particular Crookall drew attention to reports of paradise and hell-like conditions in the accounts.

Since World War II a number of specialists in studies of death and dying (**thanatology**) have arisen. While most of these studies have been rather mundane, the work of pioneering thanatologist **Elisabeth Kübler-Ross** has caught the popular imagination. Kübler-Ross is a psychiatrist who has spent many years dealing with dying patients and studying related states of consciousness. Her work since the early 1970s has added a spiritual dimension to the purely physical and medical aspects of death in dealing with terminally ill patients.

Experiences of the clinically dead have been widely reported by Raymond A. Moody, Jr., in his books *Life After Life* (1975) and *Reflections on Life After Life* (1977). A similarly conducted study by Kenneth Ring in 1978–79 confirmed many of Moody's observations (see *Theta*, vol. 7, no. 2, 1979).

A more specialized area of research into death has been the study of claims of **reincarnation** by psychiatrist **Ian Stevenson** and several associates at the University of Virginia. In the face of a growing belief in reincarnation by Westerners, a wide variety of attempts to demonstrate its reality have been made including those of hypnotists, such as **Arnall Bloxham**, who have obtained accounts from hypnotized subjects claiming to remember former earthly lives.

Sources:

Baird, Alexander T. *One Hundred Cases for Survival After Death.* New York: Bernard Ackerman, 1944.

Barker, Elsa. *Letters From A Living Dead Man.* London, 1914.

Barrett, Sir William. *Death Bed Visions.* London, 1926.

Beard, Paul. *Survival of Death: For and Against.* London, 1966.

Carington, W. W. *The Foundations of Spiritualism.* New York: E. P. Dutton, 1920.

Carrington, Hereward, and J. Meader. *Death, Its Causes & Phenomena.* London, 1911.

Crookall, Robert. *Case-Book of Astral Projection.* New Hyde Park, N.Y.: University Books, 1972.

———. *The Study & Practice of Astral Projection.* London, 1960. Reprint, New Hyde Park, N.Y.: University Books, 1966.

Delacour, J. B. [Hanns Kurth]. *Glimpses of the Beyond.* New York: Delacorte Press, 1974.

Ducasse, C. J. *A Critical Examination of the Belief in a Life After Death.* Springfield, Ill.: Thomas, 1961.

Flammarion, Camille. *Death and Its Mystery.* 3 vols. London: Century, 1921–23.

Guirdham, Arthur. *The Cathars & Reincarnation.* London, 1970. Reprint, Theosophical Publishing House, 1978.

Knight, David C., ed. *The ESP Reader.* New York: Grosset & Dunlap, 1969.

Kübler-Ross, Elisabeth. *Death; The Final Stage of Growth.* Englewood Cliffs, N.J.: Prentice-Hall, 1975.

———. *On Death & Dying.* New York: Macmillan, 1970.

———. *Questions & Answers on Death & Dying.* New York: Macmillan, 1974.

Kutscher, M. L., et al., eds. *A Comprehensive Bibliography of the Thanatology Literature.* New York: Irvington Publications, 1975.

Lodge, Sir Oliver. *Raymond, or Life and Death.* London, 1917.

Lombroso, Cesare. *After Death—What?* Cambridge, Mass.: Small Maynard, 1909.

Mead, G. R. S. *The Doctrine of the Subtle Body in Western Tradition.* London, 1919.

Miller, Albert J., and M. J. Acrí. *Death: A Bibliographical Guide.* Metuchen, N.J.: Scarecrow Press, 1977.

Moody, Raymond A., Jr. *Life After Life.* Covington, Ga.: Mockingbird Books, 1975. Reprint, New York: Bantam Books, 1976.

———. *Reflections on Life After Life.* New York: Bantam Books, 1977.

Muldoon, Sylvan, and Hereward Carrington. *The Phenomena of Astral Projection.* London: Rider, 1951. Reprint, New York: Samuel Weiser, n.d.

Myers, F. W. H. *Human Personality & Its Survival of Bodily Death.* 2 vols. London: Longmans, Green, 1954.

Osis, Karlis. *Deathbed Observations by Physicians and Nurses.* New York: Parapsychology Foundation, 1961.

Ring, Kenneth. *Life at Death: A Scientific Investigation of the Near-Death Experience.* New York: William Morrow, 1980.

Simpson, M. A. *Death and Grief: A Critically Annotated Bibliography & Source Book of Thanatology and Terminal Care.* New York: Plenum, 1979.

[Stead, William T.] *Letters from Julia; or Light from the Borderland: A Series of Messages as to the Life Beyond the Grave Received by Automatic Writing.* London, 1897.

Stevenson, Ian. *Twenty Cases Suggestive of Reincarnation.* New York: American Society for Psychical Research, 1966.

Stokes, Doris. *Voices in My Ear.* London: Futura, 1980.

Tyrrell, G. N. M. *Apparitions.* London, 1943. Reprint, New York: Macmillan, 1962.

Death Coach

There is a widespread superstitious belief that Death goes around in a coach picking up souls. The form of the belief varies, of course, with the locality. In some parts of England and Wales, for example, the death coach passes silently at midnight, without sound of hoof or wheels. Both coach and horse are black, and a black hound runs in front. In some localities the horses and coachman are headless, which doubtless adds to the effectiveness of the apparition. In Ireland, when the coach with headless driver stops at the door of a house, this means someone in the house will die the following day. The Breton peasant hears the approach at midnight of a cart with a creaking axle. It is the *Ankou* (Death), and when the cart stops before a dwelling someone within must die.

Deathwatch Beetle

The ticking or tapping sound of the deathwatch beetle, a small insect found in decaying wood, is thought by the superstitious to presage death. In reality the sound is believed to be a call from one beetle to another, made by beating its head against the wood.

Decline Effect

Term used by parapsychologists to indicate a falling off in frequency of high scores when a test of **psi** is repeated. It is also called the "decline curve," referring to the appearance when the data is put into graphical form.

Dectera

A figure of Irish medieval romance. She was the daughter of Cathbad the Druid and mother of **Cuchulain.** Dectera and 50 other maidens disappeared from the court of Conor mac Nessa. Three years later, while pursuing a flock of birds that were spoiling the crops, the king and courtiers came upon a magnificent palace inhabited by a youth of noble mien, a beautiful woman, and 50 maidens. These were recognized as Dectera and her companions, and the youth as Lugh, the sun god. Conor summoned Dectera to him, but she sent him instead her newborn son, Cuchulain.

Dee, John (1527–1608)

Renowned sixteenth-century mathematician and astrologer most remembered for his numerous experiments with **crystal gazing.** He was also a scholar, a fellow of Trinity College, Cambridge, England, and the author of 49 books on scientific subjects. His delving into the occult made him a person of strange reputation and career.

Born in London July 13, 1527, Dee is said to have descended from a noble old Welsh family, the Dees of Nant y Groes in Radnorshire. He claimed that one of his direct ancestors was

Roderick the Great, Prince of Wales. Dee's father appears to have been a gentleman server at the court of Henry VIII and therefore affluent and able to give his son a good education. So at age 15, John Dee went to Cambridge University and after two years there took his bachelor of arts. Soon afterward he became intensely interested in **astronomy** and decided to leave England to study abroad. In 1547 he went to the Low Countries (modern Belgium, Luxembourg, and the Netherlands), where he consorted with numerous scholars. He returned to England with the first astronomer's staff of brass and also with two globes constructed by geographer Gerard Mercator (famed for his cartographic projection).

In 1548 he traveled to France, living for some time at Louvain. In 1550 he spent several months in Paris, lecturing on the principles of geometry. He was offered a permanent post at the Sorbonne, but declined, returning in 1551 to England, where on the recommendation of Edward VI he was granted the rectory of Upton-upon-Severn, Worcestershire.

Dee was now in a delightful and enviable position, having a comfortable home and assured income, and was able to devote himself exclusively to the studies he loved. But he had hardly begun to enjoy these benefits when, on the accession of Queen Mary in 1553, he was accused of trying to take the new sovereign's life by means of magic and was imprisoned at Hampton Court.

He gained his liberty soon afterward, but he felt that many people looked at him with distrust because of his scientific predilections. In a preface he wrote for an English translation of Euclid, he complains bitterly of being regarded as "a companion of the hellhounds, a caller and a conjuror of wicked and damned spirits."

During the reign of Queen Elizabeth I his fortune began to improve again, and after making another long tour abroad (going on as far as St. Helena), he returned and took a house at Mortlake on the Thames.

While staying there he rapidly became famous for his intimate knowledge of astronomy. In 1572—on the advent of a new star—people flocked to hear Dee speak on the subject; when a mysterious comet appeared five years later, the scholar was again granted ample opportunity to display his learning. Queen Elizabeth herself was among those who came to ask him what this addition to the stellar bodies might portend.

First Crystal Visions

The most interesting circumstances in Dee's life are those dealing with his experiments in crystallomancy. Living in comparative solitude, practicing astrology for bread, but studying **alchemy** for pleasure, brooding over Talmudic mysteries and **Rosicrucian** theories, immersed in constant contemplation of wonders he longed to penetrate, and dazzled by visions of the **elixir of life** and the **philosophers' stone,** Dee soon reached such a condition of mystic exaltation that his visions seemed real, and he persuaded himself that he was the favored of the invisible world. In his *Diary* he recorded that he first saw spirits in his crystal globe on May 25, 1581.

One day in November 1582, while on his knees and fervently praying, Dee became aware of a sudden glory that filled the west window of his laboratory and in the midst of which shone the bright angel Uriel. It was impossible for Dee to speak. Uriel smiled benignly upon him, gave him a convex piece of crystal, and told him that when he wished to communicate with the beings of another world he had but to examine it intently, and they would immediately appear and reveal the mysteries of the future. Then the angel vanished.

Dee used the crystal but discovered that it was necessary to concentrate all his faculties upon it before the spirits would obey him. Also, he could never remember what the spirits said in their frequent conversations with him. He resolved to find a fellow worker, or a neophyte, who would converse with the spirits while he recorded the interesting dialogue. He found the assistant he sought in Edward Kelley, who unfortunately possessed the boldness and cunning for making a dupe of the amiable and credulous enthusiast.

Kelley was a native of Lancashire, born, according to Dee, in 1555. Nothing is known of his early years, but after having been convicted at Lancaster of coining, he was punished by having his ears cropped. He concealed the loss of his ears by a black skullcap. He later moved to Worcester and established himself as a druggist. Carnal, ambitious, and self-indulgent, he longed for wealth; and despairing of getting it through honest work, he began to seek the philosophers' stone and to employ what secrets he picked up in taking advantage of the ignorant and extravagant.

Before his acquaintance with Dee, he obtained some repute as a necromancer and alchemist who could make the dead utter the secrets of the future. One night he took a wealthy man and some of his servants into the park of Walton le Dale, near Preston in Lancashire, and alarmed him with the most frightening incantations. He then exhumed a recently interred corpse from the neighboring churchyard and pretended to make it utter wisdom.

Dee is believed to have employed a scryer, or seer, named Barnabas Saul before he met Kelley. He recorded in his *Diary* on October 9, 1581, that Saul was strangely troubled by a "spiritual creature" about midnight. On December 2 he willed his scryer to look into the "great crystalline globe" for the apparition of the holy angel Anael. Saul looked and apparently saw, but when he confessed the following March that he neither saw nor heard spiritual creatures any longer, Dee dismissed him. Then came Kelley (who was also called Talbot), and the conferences with the spirits rapidly increased in importance as well as curiosity.

The Visions of Edward Kelley

In his work with Kelley, Dee saw nothing. The visions seemed to exist solely in Kelley's fertile imagination. The entities who reportedly communicated through Kelley bore names such as Madini, Gabriel, Uriel, Nalvage, Il, Morvorgran, and Jubanladace. Some of them were said to be **angels.**

A record of the séances held in 1582–87 was published in Meric Casaubon's *A True and Faithful Relation of What Passed between Dr. Dee and Some Spirits; Tending, Had it Succeeded, to a General Alteration of Most States and Kingdoms in the World* (1659). The spirits offered occult instructions—how to make the elixir of life, how to search for the philosophers' stone, how to involve the spirits. They also gave information on the hierarchy of spiritual beings and disclosed the secrets of the primeval tongue that the angels and Adam spoke, which was corrupted into Hebrew after the Fall. This original speech bore an organic relation to the outer world. Each name expressed the properties of the thing spoken of, and the utterance of that name had a compelling power over that creature. Dee was supposed to write a book in this tongue under spirit influence. He was later relieved of the task, however. The prophecies that were given through the crystal mostly failed. The physical phenomena were few—occasional movements of objects, **direct writing,** and **direct voice.**

In light of Kelley's low moral character the séance records must be considered dubious documents, but the extraordinary detail and scope of these claimed visions (including the complex angelic language) seems to go beyond mere fraudulent invention. Kelley's later activities, however, were undoubtedly suspect.

Dee and Kelley acquired a considerable reputation for the occult, which spread from Mortlake to continental Europe. Dee declared that he possessed the elixir of life, which he claimed to have found among the ruins of **Glastonbury** Abbey, so the curious were drawn to his house by a double attraction. Gold flowed into his coffers, but his experiments in the transmutation of metals absorbed a great portion of his money.

At that time the court of England was visited by a Polish nobleman named Albert Laski, Count Palatine of Siradz, who wanted to see the famous "Gloriana." Queen Elizabeth received him with the flattering welcome she always accorded to distinguished strangers and placed him in the charge of the earl of Leicester. Laski visited all the England of the sixteenth century worth showing, especially its two universities, but was disappointed at not finding the famous Dr. Dee at Oxford. "I would not have come hither," he said to the earl, "had I wot that Dee was not here." Leicester promised to introduce him to the learned philosopher on their return to London, and so soothed his discontent.

A few days afterward Laski and the earl of Leicester were waiting in the antechamber at Whitehall for an audience with the queen when Dee arrived. Leicester embraced the opportunity and introduced him to Laski. The interview between two genial spirits was interesting and led to frequent visits from Laski to Dee's house at Mortlake. Kelley consulted the "great crystalline globe" and began to reveal hints and predictions that excited Laski's fancy. He claimed to see in the globe magnificent projects for the reconstruction of Europe, to be accomplished with Laski's help. According to Kelley's spirit revelations, Laski was descended from the Anglo-Norman family of the Lacies and was destined to effect the regeneration of the world. After that disclosure the two men could talk about nothing but hazy politics.

A careful perusal of Dee's *Diary* suggests that he was duped by Kelley and that he accepted all his revelations as the actual utterances of the spirits. It seems that Kelley not only knew something of the optical delusions then practiced by pretended necromancers, but also may have possessed considerable ventriloquial powers, which assisted him in deceptions.

It did not serve Kelley's purposes to bring matters too suddenly to an end, and hoping to show the value of his services, he renewed his complaints about the wickedness of dealing with spirit and his fear of the perilous enterprises they might enjoin. He threatened to abandon his task, which greatly disturbed Dee. Where indeed could he hope to meet with another scryer of such infinite ability?

Once when Kelley expressed his desire to ride from Mortlake to Islington on some business, the doctor grew afraid that it was only an excuse to cover his escape. Following is Dee's only account of the events:

"Whereupon, I asked him why he so hasted to ride thither, and I said if it were to ride to Mr. Harry Lee I would go thither, and to be acquainted with him, seeing now I had so good leisure, being eased of the book writing. Then he said that one told him the other day that the duke (Laski) did but flatter him, and told him other things both against the duke and me. I answered for the duke and myself, and also said that if the forty pounds annuity which Mr. Lee did offer him was the chief cause of his mind setting that way (contrary to many of his former promises to me), that then I would assure him of fifty pounds yearly, and would do my best, by following of my suit, to bring it to pass as soon as I possibly could; and thereupon did make him promise upon the Bible.

"Then Edward Kelley again upon the same Bible did swear unto me constant friendship, and never to forsake me; and moreover said that unless this had so fallen about he would have gone beyond the seas, taking ship at Newcastle within eight days next.

"And so we plight our faith each to the other, taking each other by the hand, upon these points of brotherly and friendly fidelity during life, which covenant I beseech God to turn to his honour, glory, and service, and the comfort of our brethren (his children) here on earth."

Kelley then returned to Dee's crystal and his visions and soon persuaded Laski that he was destined by the spirits to achieve great victories over the Saracens and win enduring glory. To do he needed to return to Poland.

Adventures in Europe

Laski returned to Poland, taking with him Dee and Kelley and their wives and families. The spirits continued to respond to their inquiries even while at sea. They landed at the Brill on July 30, 1583, and traversed Holland and Friesland to the wealthy town of Lubeck. There they lived sumptuously for a few weeks, and with new strength set out for Poland. On Christmas Day they arrived at Stettin, where they stayed until the middle of January 1584. They reached Lasco, Laski's estate, early in February.

Immediately work began for the transmutation of iron into gold, since boundless wealth was obviously needed for so grand an enterprise as the regeneration of Europe. Laski liberally supplied them with means, but the alchemists always failed on the very threshold of success.

It became apparent to the swindlers that Laski's fortune was nearly exhausted. At the same time, ironically, the angels Madini, Uriel, and their comrades in the crystal began to doubt whether Laski was, after all, the great regenerator intended to revolutionize Europe.

The whole party lived at Cracow from March 1584 until the end of July and made daily appeals to the spirits in reference to the Polish prince. They grew more and more discouraging in their replies, and Laski began to suspect that he had been duped. He proposed to furnish the alchemists with sufficient funds for a journey to Prague and letters of introduction to Emperor Rudolph. At that very moment the spirits revealed that Dee should bear a divine message to the emperor, and so Laski's proposal was gladly accepted.

At Prague the two alchemists were well received by the emperor. They found him willing to believe in the existence of the famous philosophers' stone. He was courteous to Dee, a man of European celebrity, but was very suspicious of Kelley. They stayed several months at Prague, living on the funds Laski had supplied and hoping to be drafted into the imperial service.

At last the papal nuncio complained about the tolerance afforded to heretical magicians, and the emperor was obliged to order them to leave within 24 hours. They complied, and so escaped prison or the stake, to which the nuncio had received orders from Rome to consign them in May 1586.

They traveled to the German town of Erfurt, and from there to Cassel. Meeting with a cold reception, however, they made their way once more to Cracow. There they earned a scanty living by telling fortunes and casting nativities.

After a while, they found a new patron in Stephen, king of Poland, to whom Kelley's spirits predicted that Emperor Rudolph would soon be assassinated and that the Germans would elect him to the imperial throne. But Stephen, like Laski, grew weary of the ceaseless demands for pecuniary support. Then came a new disciple, Count Rosenberg, a wealthy nobleman of Trebona, in Bohemia. At his castle they remained for nearly two years, eagerly pursuing their alchemical studies but never coming any closer to the desired result.

Dee's enthusiasm and credulity had made him utterly dependent on Kelley, but the trickster was nevertheless jealous of the superior respect that Dee enjoyed as a man of remarkable scholarship and considerable ability. Frequent quarrels broke out between them, aggravated by the passion Kelley had developed for the doctor's young and beautiful wife—which he was determined to gratify. He concocted an artful plan to get what he wanted.

Knowing Dee's dependence upon him as a scryer, he suddenly announced his intention of resigning, and only consented to remain when the doctor begged him. That day, April 18, 1587, they consulted the spirits. Kelley pretended to be shocked at the revelation they made and refused to repeat it. Dee's curiosity was aroused, and he insisted on hearing it, but was extremely upset when Kelley said that the spirits had commanded the two philosophers to have their wives in common.

Dee rebuked the spirit Madini for such an improper proposal, but eventually reluctantly consented to the arrangement. Accordingly Dee, Kelley, and their wives signed an agreement on May 3, 1587, pledging obedience to the angelic demand.

Soon afterward, Dee requested permission from Queen Elizabeth to return to England and left the castle of Trebona after finally separating from Kelley. The latter, who had been knighted at Prague, proceeded to the Bohemian capital, taking with him the elixir found at Glastonbury Abbey. He was immediately arrested by order of the emperor and imprisoned.

Kelley was later released and wandered throughout Germany, telling fortunes and propagating the cause of **magic.** He was again arrested as a heretic and sorcerer. In a desperate attempt to avoid imprisonment he tried to escape, but fell from the dungeon wall and broke two ribs and both his legs. He died of his injuries in February 1593.

Dee's Final Years

Dee set out from Trebona with a splendid train, the expenses of his journey defrayed by the generous Bohemian noble Count Rosenberg. In England he was well received by the queen and settled again at Mortlake, resuming his chemical studies and his pursuit of the philosophers' stone.

But nothing went well with the unfortunate enthusiast. He employed two scryers—a rogue named Bartholomew and a charlatan named Heckman—but neither could discover anything satisfactory in the "great crystalline globe." He grew poorer and poorer; he sank into indigence and wearied the queen with his importunity. At length he obtained a small appointment as chancellor of St. Paul's Cathedral, which in 1595 he exchanged for the wardenship of Manchester College. He served in this position until age and failing intellect compelled him to resign it about 1602 or 1603.

He then retired to his old house at Mortlake, where he practiced as a fortune-teller, gaining little in return but an unenviable reputation as a wizard, "a conjuror, a caller, or invocator of devils." On June 5, 1604, he petitioned James I for protection against such calumnies, declaring that none of the "very strange and frivolous fables or histories reported and told of him (as to have been of his doing) were true."

Dee was an exceptionally interesting figure, and he must have been a man of rare intellectual activity. His calculations facilitated the adoption of the Gregorian calendar in England, and he foresaw the formation of the Historical Manuscripts Commission, addressing to the Crown a petition on the desirability of preserving the old, unpublished records of England's past, many of which were kept in the archives of monasteries. He was a voluminous writer on science, his works including *Monas Hieroglyphica* (1564), *De Trigono* (1565), *Testamentum Johannis Dee Philosophi Summi ad Johannem Guryun Transmissum* (1568) and *An Account of the Manner in which a Certayn Copper-smith in the Land of Moores, and a Certayn Moore Transmuted Copper to Gold* (1576).

It is usual to dismiss Kelley as a rogue and Dee as his dupe, but if the angelic visions were purely for money, they both could have done better for themselves. Dee seemed to be an honest man of unusual talents, devoting his life to science and the pursuit of mystical knowledge. The angelic language called Enochian, which Dee and Kelley used when invoking spirits in the crystal, is a construction of great intricacy, far beyond the capacity or the requirements of simple **fraud.** It combines magic, mathematics, astrology, and cryptography. An intriguing suggestion is that the angelic conversations were a system of codes to convey secrets, and that Dee and Kelley's visits in Europe were for purposes of espionage. In later times, Enochian rituals were revived by the magical Hermetic Order of the **Golden Dawn** and became a common element in **ceremonial magic.** Some Enochian rituals were adapted by **Anton LaVey** and the **Church of Satan,** which he founded.

Dee's reputation suffered much from the scorn of Meric Casaubon, who published some of the angelic conversations and represented them as delusive. The scholar **Theodore Besterman,** however, in his book *Crystal-Gazing* (1929), adopted Dee as a pioneer Spiritualist, and contemporary magicians have seen him as one of their ancestors.

Dee was miserably poor in his last years and was even obliged to sell his precious books in order to sustain himself. He was planning a journey to Germany when he died in December 1608; he was buried in the chancel of Mortlake Church. The seventeenth-century antiquary John Aubrey assembled an interesting character description of Dee:

"He had a very fair, clear, sanguine complexion, a long beard as white as milke. A very handsome man. . . . He was a great peacemaker; if any of the neighbours fell out, he would never lett them alone till he had made them friends. He was tall and slender. He wore a gowne like an artist's gowne, with hanging sleeves, and a slitt. A might good man he was."

One of his crystals used for scrying was supposed to have been given to Dee by an angel. It is on display in the British Museum, London, which also houses some of the mystical cakes of wax consecrated by Dee for his ceremonies and some of his manuscripts in the Cottonian collection.

Several centuries after his death, on April 18, 1873, Dee supposedly communicated via **automatic writing** through the mediumship of **Stainton Moses.** The communications gave some evidential details of his life that were verified by research at the British Museum Library, but his signature was found to be dissimilar to the one preserved there.

Sources:

Besterman, Theodore. *Crystal-Gazing.* London, 1929. Reprint, New York, 1965.

Burland, C. A. *The Arts of the Alchemists.* London, 1967.

Clulee, Nicholas H. *John Dee's Natural Philosophy: Between Science and Religion.* New York: Routledge, 1988.

Deacon, R. *John Dee: Scientist, Astrologer & Secret Agent to Elizabeth.* London: Frederick Muller, 1968.

Dee, John. *The Hieroglyphic Monad.* Translated by J. W. Hamilton Jones. London, 1847.

———. *A True and Faithful Relation of What Passed for Many Years Between Dr. John Dee . . . and Some Spirits. . . .* London, 1659. Reprint, Askin, 1974.

French, Peter J. *John Dee: The World of an Elizabethan Magus.* London: Routledge & Kegan Paul, 1972.

Halliwell, J. O., ed. *The Private Diary of Dr. John Dee, and the Catalogue of His Library of Manuscripts.* London: Camden Society, 1842.

Turner, Robert. *Elizabethan Magic.* Longmead, Dorset, U.K.: Element Books, 1989.

Yates, Frances A. *The Rosicrucian Enlightenment.* London: Routledge & Kegan Paul, 1972.

Deitton

An astrological book of Indian origin in use in Myanmar, similar to the *Dittharana.* (See also **astrology**)

Déjà Vu

A French term used by psychical researchers to characterize the feeling people sometimes have that some scene or experience in the present also occurred in the past. *Déjà vu* (already seen) is often coupled with *déjà entendu* (already heard). Through the years, many have related the feelings of déjà vu to the phenomenon of **astral projection** or **out-of-the-body travel,** when individuals apparently visit a distant place in an astral or etheric body during sleep. Déjà vu is also associated with fulfillment of a prior **premonition** of a forthcoming event.

More recently, déjà vu has been connected to experiences of **reincarnation,** when a feeling of prior knowledge is so strong that people feel sure it must have come from a former incarnation. In a celebrated case in India, a little girl named Shanti Devi, born in Delhi in 1926, claimed that she had lived elsewhere in a former birth, and even named the city. When taken there, she correctly identified the house, family, and other circumstantial details.

Feelings of déjà vu are rarely evidential or even reliable. Scenes in the present may only appear familiar because they contain some element connected with a past experience and reactivate the sensation of familiarity. Psychologists have characterized the phenomenon of false remembering as "postidentifying paramnesia."

Sources:

Berger, Arthur S., and Joyce Berger. *The Encyclopedia of Parapsychology and Psychical Research.* New York: Paragon House, 1991.

Del Rio, Martin Antoine (1551–1608)

Famous Jesuit scholar regarded as an authority on **witchcraft** during the great persecutions of the sixteenth century. Del Rio was born at Antwerp, Belgium, of a distinguished Spanish family.

He studied classical literature and works in Hebrew, Chaldean, and other languages. At age 19, he published an edition of Seneca, and was only 24 when he became vice-chancellor and attorney general for the Belgian province of Brabant.

In 1580 he entered the Jesuit order, teaching at various Jesuit centers and gathering material for his major work on witchcraft and **demonology,** *Disquisitionum Magicarum Libri Sex,* published in 1599. This encyclopedic work discusses **magic, alchemy,** witchcraft, **prophecy,** and **apparitions,** and gives instructions to judges at witchcraft trials, reviving the intolerance caused a century earlier by the sinister *Malleus Maleficarum* (1486) of Jakob Sprenger and Heinrich Kramer.

Sources:

Del Rio, Martin Antoine. *Disquisitionum Magicarum Libri Sex.* Moguntiae: Typis Joannis Albini, 1600.

Delanne, Gabriel (1857–1926)

A leading French Spiritualist and psychical researcher. He was born March 23, 1857, in Paris. He became an engineer, and his experience assisted him in becoming what **Theodore Flournoy** called "the most scientific of French spiritists."

Delanne pioneered the use of paraffin casts to obtain evidence of **materialization.** He also collected evidence of **reincarnation.** For many years he edited the *Revue Scientifique et Moderne de Spiritisme.* He wrote several books based on his investigations that marshall a case for life after death. Though he gradually went blind, he continued to participate in psychical research until shortly before his death on February 15, 1926.

Sources:

Berger, Arthur S., and Joyce Berger. *The Encyclopedia of Parapsychology and Psychical Research.* New York: Paragon House, 1991.

Delanne, Gabriel. *L' Ame est Immortelle.* N.p., 1904.

———. *Les Apparitions Materialisées des Vivants et des Morts.* N.p., 1909.

———. *L'Evolution Animique.* N.p., 1897.

———. *Le Phenom Agene Spirite.* N.p., 1894.

———. *Récherches sur la Mediumnité.* N.p., 1896.

———. *Le Spiritisme devant la Science.* N.p., 1895.

Pleasants, Helene, ed. *Biographical Dictionary of Parapsychology.* New York: Helix Press, 1964.

Deleuze, Jean Philippe François (1753–1835)

French naturalist and adept in **animal magnetism** or **mesmerism.** He was born at Sisteron, Lower Alps, in March 1753. He became an early advocate of magnetism, which he believed to be a function of the **rapport** between patient and magnetizer. He also came to believe in the ability of clairvoyants to diagnose disease.

Sources:

Deleuze, Jean P. F. *Défense du Magnétisme.* N.p., 1819.

———. *Histoire Critique du Magnétisme.* N.p., 1813–19.

———. *Instruction Pratique sur le Magnétisme Animale.* 1819. Translated as *Practical Instruction in Animal Magnetism.* New York: Samuel R. Wells, 1879.

———. *Mémoire sur la Faculté de Prevision.* N.p., 1836.

DeLouise, Joseph (1927–)

Successful Chicago psychic famous for his predictions of future events. DeLouise was born in Gibellina, Sicily, on November 10, 1927. Both his father and grandfather were healers, and his grandfather introduced him to meditation and psychic experiences. At age five, DeLouise had his initial psychic "feeling," which led to the family's securing enough money to move to the United States.

DeLouise grew up in Chicago. He dropped out of school after finishing the elementary grades and on his seventeenth birthday joined the navy. His career was marked by service in the Pacific. In an incident shortly before his discharge in 1946, he had a "feeling" of a major disaster in an ammo depository on Guam where he was working. Refusing to return to work saved his life when the place exploded.

After the war, he married, attended beauty school, and settled down to a normal life. He was divorced in 1950, which led to his separation from the Roman Catholic Church. He began to receive psychic impressions from the women whose hair he styled, and he practiced giving brief readings to them, gaining a reputation as a psychic. He also attended séances and eventually became a Spiritualist minister. He learned to work with a crystal ball to increase his concentration.

In November 1967, during an interview on a Chicago radio show, DeLouise predicted a major bridge collapse before the year was out. Twenty-one days later, the Silver Bridge across the Ohio River at Point Pleasant, West Virginia, collapsed. It matched in every detail the collapse described by DeLouise on the air. Then in 1969 he predicted a major train crash, the drowning of Mary Jo Kopechne (while a passenger in a car being driven by Sen. Edward Kennedy), and an airplane disaster in Indianapolis and gave his insights into the connection of the Manson Family to the murder of actress Sharon Tate. Whereas the 1967 prediction had made him famous in Chicago, the 1969 predictions established his reputation across America.

DeLousie has since operated as a professional psychic with offices in Chicago. He sees individual clients and also works with groups.

Sources:

Delfano, M. M. *The Living Prophets.* New York: Dell, 1972.

DeLouise, Joseph, and Tom Valentine. *Psychic Mission.* Chicago: Henry Regnery, 1971.

Delphi

The famous **oracle** of ancient **Greece,** where the priestess Pythia was consulted concerning the future and gave her answers in a state of **trance,** induced by intoxicating fumes. According to Justinian, "In a dark and narrow recess of a cliff at Delphi there was a little open glade and in this a hole, or cleft in the earth, out of which blew a strong draft or air straight up and as if impelled by a wind, which filled the minds of poets with madness." Lake Avernus, Heraclea, and Phigaleia were qualified for the evocation of the dead by similar intoxicating fumes.

According to Plutarch, the Delphian oracle had not been convicted of falsehood in a single instance. On the contrary, the verification of the oracles has filled the temple with gifts from all parts of Greece and foreign countries. In discussing the question "Why the Prophetess Pythia giveth no Answers now from the Oracle in Verse," Plutarch explained that the replies were always couched in enigmatical language when kings and states consulted the oracle on weighty matters that might have done harm if made public, but that private persons always received direct answers in the plainest terms.

Herodotus told of a successful test of the oracles by Croesus, King of Lydia. He dispatched envoys to the best six oracles: Delphi, Dodona, Branchidae, Zeus Ammon, Trophonius, and Amphiaraus. The envoys were instructed to ask on the hundredth day of their departure what Croesus was doing at home in Sardis at a particular moment. Four oracles entirely failed. Delphi was perfectly right. Herodotus quoted the reply:

I can count the sands, and I can measure the Ocean;
I have ears for the silent, and know what the dumb man meaneth;
Lo! on my sense there striketh the smell of shell-covered tortoise,
Boiling now on fire, with the flesh of a lamb, in a cauldron,
Brass in the vessel below, and brass to cover above it.

Croesus wished to think out an action that could not be guessed at. He took a tortoise and a lamb, cut them to pieces, and boiled them in a covered brazen cauldron.

The decline of the oracles began two or three centuries before Christ. That of Delphi was closed in the fourth century by a decree of Theodosius. After a long period of disuse, attempts were made to revive the oracle at the opening of the second century C.E. under Plutarch's priesthood. During the period of Christianity under Constantine the oracle became finally silent.

Delphic Circle

A regular gathering of mediums at Hertford Lodge, Battersea, England, organized by Frederick Thurstan to promote collective mediumistic development. Mrs. Thompson, **Alfred Vout Peters,** and Laura I. Finch (**Charles Richet**'s subject) were developed at these reunions. The group flourished about 1930 and no longer exists.

Dematerialization

The phenomenon of disappearance of phantom forms, human beings, or objects after being manifested or materialized. The terms **apports** and **asports** refer to the **materialization** and dematerialization of objects, involving their disappearance at one place and reappearance at another place some distance away. No satisfactory scientific theory for reported materialization or dematerialization has yet been offered, and little evidence has been produced to suggest that such phenomena in fact occur.

There are, of course, numerous anecdotal tales of materialization and dematerialization. Cases have been reported of disappearance and reappearance of persons, sometimes over hundreds of miles, often referred to as **teleportation** and **transfiguration.**

In the case of phantoms or spirits of the dead, the materialization is said to be formed from **ectoplasm,** a mysterious psychic substance exuded by a medium. Ectoplasm was often faked by mediums through the use of phosphor-covered cheesecloth and similar artifacts. Cases have also been reported of partial materialization and dematerialization by mediums such as **Elizabeth d'Esperance.**

Dement, William Charles (1928–)

Psychiatrist and researcher into phenomena relating to **dreams.** He was born in Wenatchee, Washington, July 29, 1928, and received his education at the University of Washington (B.S., 1951) and the University of Chicago (M.D., 1955). He joined the faculty of the Stanford University Medical School in 1963 as director of the Sleep Laboratory.

Dement and his colleagues found that sleep was essential for physical and psychological health and that deprivation tended to make individuals irritable or subject to memory loss. With his colleagues he investigated the phenomenon of the connection between a sleeper's rapid eye movements and the imagery of dreams. Although external sensory stimuli could influence dream imagery, Dement concluded that the themes of dreams arose primarily from the sleeper's mental or emotional processes.

Sources:

Dement, William C. *Some Must Watch While Some Must Sleep.* Stanford, Calif.: Stanford Alumni Association, 1972.

Demonius

A stone so called from the supposed demoniacal rainbow said to appear in it.

Demonocracy

The government of demons, the immediate influence of evil spirits, or the religion of certain peoples of the Americas, Africa, and Asia who claim to worship devils.

Demonography

The history and description of demons and all that concerns them. Authors who write about this subject—such as **Johan Weyer, Pierre De Lancre,** and **Pierre Le Loyer**—are sometimes called demonographers.

Demonology

The study of demons or evil spirits; also a branch of magic that deals with such beings. In religious science it has come to indicate knowledge regarding supernatural beings that are not deities. The Greek term *daimon* originally indicated "genius" or "spirit," and Socrates claimed to have had intercourse with his daimon. However, with the advent of Christianity it came to mean a malevolent spirit entity. Demonology was especially developed during the Middle Ages.

Ancient demonology is discussed in the entries **Egypt, Semites, Genius,** and **Devil Worship,** and the demonology in preindustrial societies is examined in the entries on the various countries and peoples of its origin.

According to Michael Psellus (1018–ca. 1079), author of *De Operatione Daemonum Dialogus,* demons are divided into six main bodies: the demons of fire; of the air; of the earth; those of the waters and rivers, who cause tempests and floods; the subterranean who prepare earthquakes and excite volcanic eruptions, and the shadowy ones who are somewhat like ghosts. (St. Augustine (354–430 C.E.) considered all demons under the last category.) Psellus's classification is not unlike the system of the Middle Ages, which divided all spirits into those belonging to the four elements: fire, air, earth, and water (salamanders, sylphs, gnomes, and undines, respectively).

Early Concepts of Demonology

The medieval idea of demons, of course, evolved from ancient Christian and Gnostic belief, especially from the accounts of demons in the Bible. Among the Jews, the gods of the surrounding nations were called demons, and those nations were condemned for making sacrifices to demons instead of to the one God, Yahweh (Deut. 32:17; Ps. 106:37). The Christian New Testament speaks of demons as inferior spirits who operate as subjects of the devil. Such demons can take possession of a human being, causing various illnesses and physical ailments. Demons were named as causative factors in disease in a prescientific age.

Demons have an expansive role in the biblical record. They can affect the behavior of swine (Matt. 8:30–32) and speak with a knowledge beyond that of an ordinary person (Mark 1:23–24). Biblical authors did understand demons as objectively present in the world and pictured the apostles as trying to drive them away. Considering demons as having an objective existence placed many questions about the nature of their origin, existence, operation, and habitation on the theological agenda. By the third century, the angel Lucifer, who fell from heaven (Isa. 14:12), was identified with Satan, and the fallen angels with demons.

The Gnostics (who competed for members with the early Christians), imitating Plato's classification of the orders of spirits, attempted a similar arrangement with respect to a hierarchy of **angels.** The first and highest order was named seraphim; the second, cherubim; the third was the order of thrones; the fourth, dominions; the fifth, virtues; the sixth, powers; the seventh, principalities; the eighth, archangels; and the ninth, and lowest, angels.

This classification was censured by the Christian church, yet almost outlived the pneumatologists of the Middle Ages. These scholars—studying the account in which the angel Lucifer rebelled against heaven (Isa. 14:12), and that in which Michael, the archangel, warred against him (Rev. 12:7)—long asked the momentous question, "What orders of angels fell on this occasion?"

At length it became the prevailing opinion that Lucifer was of the order of seraphim. It was also asserted, after laborious research, that Agares, Belial, and Barbatos, each of whom deposed angels of great rank, had been of the order of virtues; that Bileth, Focalor, and Phoenix had been of the order of thrones; that Goap had been of the order of powers; that Purson had been of both the order of virtues and the order of thrones; and that Murmur had belonged to both the order of thrones and the order of angels. The pedigree of many other noble devils was likewise determined.

As the centuries progressed, theologians began to inquire, "How many fallen angels were engaged in the contest?" This was a question of vital importance, and it gave rise to the most strenuous research and to a variety of discordant opinions.

Others asked, "Where was the battle fought—in the inferior heaven, in the highest region of the air, in the firmament, or in Paradise?" and "How long did it last?" These were difficult questions, but the notion that ultimately prevailed was that the engagement was concluded in exactly three seconds, and that while Lucifer, with a number of his followers, fell into hell, the rest were left in the air to tempt man.

A newer question rose out of these investigations: whether a greater number of angels fell with Lucifer or remained in heaven with Michael. Noted scribes were inclined to think that the rebel chief had been beaten by a superior force, and that consequently devils of darkness were fewer in number than angels of light.

These discussions, which for centuries interested the whole of Christendom, exercised the talents of some of the most erudite persons in Europe. The last objective of demonologists was to assess Lucifer's routed forces and reorganize them into a decided form of subordination or government. Hence, extensive districts were given to certain chiefs who fought under the general Lucifer.

There was Zimimar, "the lordly monarch of the north," as Shakespeare calls him, who had his distinct province of devils; Gorson, the king of the South; Amaymon, the king of the East; and Goap, the prince of the West. These sovereigns had many noble spirits subordinate to them whose various ranks were settled with all the preciseness of heraldic distinction. There were devil dukes, devil marquises, devil counts, devil earls, devil knights, devil presidents, and devil prelates.

As a picture of the infernal kingdom was constructed, it was determined that the armed host under Lucifer had been composed of nearly twenty-four hundred legions, of which each demon of rank commanded a certain number. Beleth for instance, who has been described as "a great king and terrible, riding on a pale horse, before whom go trumpets and all melodious music," commanded 85 legions; Agares, the first duke under the power of the East, commanded 31 legions; Leraie, a great marquis, 30 legions; Morax, a great earl and a president, 36 legions; Furcas, a knight, 20 legions. The forces of the other devil chieftains were enumerated after the same manner.

The Appearance of Demons

The strange and hideous forms connected with the popular image of demons were derived from the descriptive writings of the early demonologists, who maintained that demons possessed a decidedly corporeal form and were mortal, or that, like Milton's spirits, they could assume any sex and take any shape they chose. In the Middle Ages, when conjuration was regularly practiced in Europe, devils of rank were supposed to appear under characteristic forms by which they were as well recognized as the head of any ancient family would be by his crest and armorial bearings.

Along with their names and characters were registered the shapes they were said to adopt. A devil would appear like an angel seated in a fiery chariot or riding on an infernal dragon and carrying a viper in his right hand; or he would assume a lion's head, a goose's feet, and a hare's tail; or put on a raven's head and come mounted on a strong wolf.

Among other forms taken by demons were those of a fierce warrior, or of an old man with a hawk in his hand riding upon a crocodile. A human figure would arise having the wings of a griffin or sporting three heads, two of them like those of a toad and one like a cat's; or displaying huge teeth and horns and armed with a sword; or exhibiting a dog's teeth and a large raven's head; or mounted upon a pale horse and exhibiting a serpent's tail; or gloriously crowned and riding upon a dromedary; or presenting the face of a lion; or bestriding a bear while grasping a viper.

Other forms were those of a goodly knight, or of one who bore lance, ensigns, and even a scepter, or of a soldier, either riding on a black horse and surrounded by a flame of fire, or wearing a duke's crown and mounted on a crocodile.

Hundreds of such varied shapes were assumed by devils of rank. In his *Sketches of the Philosophy of Apparitions* (1824), Dr. S. Hibbert comments:

"It would therefore betray too much of the aristocratical spirit to omit noticing the forms which the lower orders of such beings displayed. In an ancient Latin poem, describing the lamentable vision of a devoted hermit, and supposed to have been written by St. Bernard in the year 1238, those spirits, who had no more important business upon earth than to carry away condemned souls, were described as blacker than pitch; as having teeth like lions, nails on their fingers like those of a wild-boar, on their forehead horns, through the extremities of which poison was emitted, having wide ears flowing with corruption, and discharging serpents from their nostrils. The devout writer of these verses has even accompanied them from drawings, in which the addition of the cloven feet is not omitted. But this appendage, as Sir Thomas Brown has proved, is a mistake, which has arisen from the devil frequently appearing to the Jews in the shape of a rough and hairy goat, this animal being the emblem of sin-offering."

The form of the demons described by St. Bernard (1090–1153) differs little from that which was no less carefully portrayed by English writer Reginald Scot 450 years later, and, perhaps, by the demonologists of modern times. "In our childhood," says Scot, "our mother's maids have so terrified us with an ouglie divell having horns on his head, fier in his mouth, and a tail on his breech, eies like a bason, fangs like a dog, clawes like a beare, . . . and a voice like a roaring lion."

The Powers of Demons

Although the leading tenets of the occult science of demonology may be traced to the Jews and early Christians, they matured through communication with the Moors of Spain, who were the chief philosophers of the early Middle Ages. There was much intercultural exchange between the moors and the natives of France and Italy. Toledo, Seville, and Salamanca became the great schools of **magic.** At Salamanca discourses on the black art were, in keeping with the solemnity of the subject, delivered within the walls of a vast and gloomy cavern.

The instructors taught that all knowledge and power might be obtained from the fallen angels. They were skilled in the abstract sciences, in the knowledge of precious stones, in **alchemy,** in the various languages of mankind and of the lower animals, in *belles lettres,* in moral philosophy, pneumatology, divinity, magic, history, and prophecy, it was told. The demons could control the winds, the waters, and the influence of the stars; they could raise earthquakes; induce diseases or cure them; accomplish vast mechanical tasks; and release souls from purgatory. It was said that they could influence the passions of the mind, procure the reconciliation of friends or foes, engender mutual discord, induce mania and melancholy, or direct the force and objects of sexual affection.

Hierarchy of Demons

According to **Johan Weyer,** the prominent sixteenth-century Protestant demonologist, demons were divided into a great many classes, into regular kingdoms and principalities, and into mobility and commoners. According to Weyer, Satan was by no means the great sovereign of this monarchy; this honor was held by Beelzebub. Satan was alluded to by Weyer as a dethroned monarch and chief of the opposition; Moloch was called chief of the army; Pluto, prince of fire; and Leonard, grand master of the sphere. The masters of these infernal courts were Adramelech, grand chancellor; Astaroth, grand treasurer; Nergal, chief of the secret police; Baal, chief of the satanic army.

Weyer maintained that each state in Europe also had its infernal ambassadors. Belphegor is assigned to France, Mammon to England, Belial to Turkey, Rimmon to Russia, Thamuz to Spain, Hutjin to Italy, and Martinet to Switzerland.

According to Weyer's calculations the infernal regions contained an army of 7,405,926 devils and demons, organized into 1,111 divisions of 6,666 each.

One of the strangest authorities on demonology was surely Alexis Vincent Charles Berbiguier, known as "the Scourge of the Demons," author of the three-volume encyclopedic work *Les Farfadets, ou tous les démons ne sont pas de l'autre monde* (1821). In this great study, he describes the infernal court: "This court has representatives on earth. These mandatories are innumerable. I give nomenclature and degree of power of each: Moreau, magician and sorcerer of Paris, represents Beelzebub; Pinel, a doctor of Saltpétrière, represents Satan; Bouge, represents Pluto; Nicholas, a doctor of Avigum, represents Moloch." But Berbiguier was not just a theorist, since he claimed to have caught thousands of demons, impaling them on pins like a butterfly hunter and sealing them in bottles.

Modern Demonology

Belief in demons possibly reached its lowest ebb in the nineteenth century, though occultists such as William Barrett proposed their own demonic hierarchies. By the beginning of the twentieth century, demonology was unfashionable, even in occult circles, but during the occult boom of the 1960s and 1970s, the theme of demonic possession was revived in conservative Christian circles and given widespread coverage in books and movies like *The Exorcist,* by William P. Blatty. The idea of demons became a divisive force in the church, with some churchmen reviving rituals of exorcism and others remaining adamant in their unwillingness to endorse ancient concepts of demonology. At any rate, the sensationalist aspect of possession by demons is in keeping with the apocalyptic character of modern life, and demons have once again become part of theological discourse.

Sources:

Bodin, Jean. *De la démonomania des sorciers.* Paris, 1580.

Conway, Moncure D. *Demonology and Devil-Lore.* 2 vols. London: Chatto & Windus, 1879.

Ebon, Martin, ed. *Exorcism: Fact Not Fiction.* New York: New American Library, 1974.

Irvine, Doreen. *From Witchcraft to Christ.* London: Concordia Press, 1973.

Nauman, St. Elmo, Jr. *Exorcism Through the Ages.* New York: Philosophical Library, 1974.

Neil-Smith, Christopher. *The Exorcist and the Possessed.* Cornwall, England: James Pike, 1974.

Remy, Nicolas. *Demonolatry.* 1595. Reprint, New Hyde Park, N.Y.: University Books, 1974.

Robbins, Rossell Hope. *The Encyclopedia of Witchcraft and Demonology.* New York: Crown Publishers, 1959.

Scott, Sir Walter. *Letters on Demonology and Witchcraft.* London, 1830. Reprint, New York: Citadel Press, 1970.

Shepard, Leslie. *How to Protect Yourself Against Black Magic and Witchcraft.* New York: Citadel Press, 1978.

Strachan, Francoise. *Casting Out the Devils.* London: Aquarian Press, 1972.

Wall, J. Charles. *Devils.* London, 1904. Reprint, Detroit: Singing Tree Press, 1968.

Weyer, Johan. *Witches, Devils and Doctors in the Renaissance: Johan Weyer, De Praestigiis.* Edited by George Mora. Binghamton, N.Y.: Medieval & Renaissance Texts & Studies, 1991.

Demonology and Witchcraft (by Sir Walter Scott)

This work, first published in 1830 under the full title *Letters on Demonology and Witchcraft,* occupies a curious place in Sir Walter Scott's vast literary output. Four years after his financial collapse in 1826, the author sustained a mild stroke; shortly after, John Murray, who was then issuing a series known as The Family Library, asked Scott to contribute a volume on demonology. He readily consented, but—as an entry in Scott's journal makes clear—he did not greatly care for the work and really engaged in it to help pay off his debts.

The book attempts to develop broad theories on such subjects as the prevalence of belief in **witchcraft** in the Middle Ages. Scott was far more accomplished in dealing with particular instances of occult history—such as his account of demonology in France and in Sweden and his assessment of Joan of Arc. Moreover, his intimate knowledge of early Scottish literature gives a singular importance to chapters concerned with his native land, and it is interesting to find that here and there he offers something of a sidelight on his own novels (e.g., when he discusses the specters he dealt with in *Woodstock*).

Demonology and Witchcraft is written in the form of a series of letters to the author's son-in-law. Scott died two years after publication in 1832. The book has been reprinted frequently.

Sources:

Scott, Sir Walter. *Letters on Demonology and Witchcraft.* London: J. Murray, 1830.

Demonomancy

Divination by means of demons. Such divination takes place by the oracles they make or by the answers they give to those who evoke them.

Demonomania

The mania of those who believe all that was told concerning demons and sorcerers, such as **Jean Bodin, Pierre De Lancre, Pierre Le Loyer,** and others. Bodin's 1580 book *Demonomania of the Sorcerers,* on devilry, is a vivid account of demonomania.

Denis, Leon (1846–1927)

The apostle of French **Spiritism** (the name by which **Spiritualism** is generally termed in France, distinguished by its acceptance of the ideas surrounding **reincarnation**) on whom the mantle of **Allan Kardec** fell. He claimed to have been directly inspired by the spirit of Kardec in his activity as a tireless propagandist, teacher, and author of important and popular books. Another influence was a spirit, "Jerome of Prague," that communicated through **typtology** beginning in 1892 and addressed Denis as "my son."

Sources:

Baumard, Claire. *Leon Denis intime.* N.p., n.d.

Denis, Leon. *D'Apres la Mort.* N.p., n.d.

———. *Dans l'Invisible (Spiritisme et Mediumnité).* N.p., n.d.

———. *Genie Celtique, et le Monde Invisible.* N.p., n.d.

———. *Jeanne d'Arc Medium: L'Au-delà et la Survivance de l'Etré, La Grande Énigme.* Translated as *The Mystery of Joan of Arc.* New York: E. P. Dutton, 1925.

Luce, Gaston. *Leon Denis l'apotre du spiritisme, sa vie, son oeuvre.* N.p., n.d.

Le Probleme de l'Etre et de la Destinée: Christianisme et Spiritisme. Translated as *Christianity & Spiritualism.* London, [1904].

Denis, Lorimer (1904–1957)

Ethnologist, born in Haiti October 24, 1904, who wrote several books and various articles on Haitian history, folklore, and ethnology. He was also concerned with the subject of **parapsychology,** on which he wrote two books: *Bapteme de feu dans le vodou* (*Baptism of Fire in Voodoo*) and *La religion populaire: Evolution stadiale du vodou* (*The Popular Religion: The Evolution in Stages of Voodoo*).

Dentistry, Psychic

A special area of psychic healing involving paranormal dental filling or even tooth renewal, associated with spiritual faith and the power of prayer. This extraordinary form of healing was first practiced in the United States by a traveling evangelist, A. C. McCabe, who would conduct a service and then announce to his audience, "If you have cavities in your teeth, . . . if you have gum disorders, whatever it is, you come and I'll pray for you and God will meet your dental needs." McCabe then laid hands on each person in turn and prayed. He offered a mirror and flashlight so that individuals could see dental healing taking place.

One of these healing services, at Shreveport, Louisiana, was attended by **Willard Fuller,** another evangelist who practiced spiritual healing. Fuller witnessed more than two hours of dental healing and saw one woman receive a silver filling in a tooth cavity through paranormal means. McCabe told Fuller that he could also perform such healing, but it was several weeks before Fuller found the courage to invite members of his own congregations to come forward for dental treatment. After curing a man of a stomach ulcer, the same man came back to his services and asked him to pray for the healing of a tooth cavity. Fuller laid hands on the man's head and prayed, "In the name of Jesus, be thou everywhere whole," and the man confirmed that his tooth cavity was healed.

Fuller reportedly began demonstrating significant numbers of dental healings in 1960. They involved instantaneous filling of cavities with gold, silver, or porcelain, straightening of crooked teeth, and healing of decayed teeth or gums. Eyewitnesses described the paranormal filling as beginning with a small bright spot that rapidly enlarged until it filled the whole cavity. Journalist Bryce Bond (associate editor of the *Psychic Observer* magazine) testified to witnessing such dental healing and even experienced healing in his own gums. Fuller simply touched the subject on both cheeks at the same time, saying, "In the name of Jesus, be thou whole." Not all the healing was instantaneous, however. Fuller stated that in some cases healing took several days or weeks.

Analysis of some of the gold of these paranormal fillings shows it to be purer than that normally used for dental work. Some subjects even claim that earlier silver fillings turned to gold.

During a demonstration at the **Spiritual Frontiers Fellowship** summer conference at Wagner College, Staten Island, New York, in 1979, Dr. Audrey Kargere of Stockholm, Sweden, claimed that she received several paranormal gold dental fillings, as well as healing of one leg that had become swollen after a fall.

British psychic **Matthew Manning** attended one of Fuller's demonstrations in New York with great skepticism, but afterward testified that he witnessed a paranormal filling. He said that one woman had "a very decayed tooth which was black" and he "saw it fill with something white which appeared to be a kind of ceramic substance. When finished, she had a new white tooth." (Bond has stated that several dentists and scientists have witnessed such healing but would not allow their names to be used for testimonies.)

This type of healing is bound to attract skepticism from individuals who have had no firsthand experience of the healing sessions. Such healing goes beyond that claimed by other spiritual healers and is not subject to explanations such as spontaneous remission because the alleged paranormal production of porcelain and rare metals in dental cavities would have to be either fraudulemt or real, with little room for other non-paranormal explanations. There is little written from a scientific perspective. Fuller appeared to be a sincere individual with a simple lifestyle and did not charge a fee for his healing work. His ministry was maintained only by voluntary contributions. Bond claimed that about 25,000 people in the United States experienced Fuller's allegedly miraculous dental healing.

Sources:

St. Clair, David. *Psychic Healers.* Rev. ed., New York: Bantam Books, 1979.

Denton, William (1823–1883)

Professor of geology in Boston famous for his research in **psychometry,** begun for the purpose of controlling **Joseph Rhodes Buchanan**'s experiments. His sister, Anna Denton Cridge, developed the gift of giving descriptions of character, surroundings, and personal appearance—to the color of the hair and eyes—of the writers of letters she held in her hand.

Denton applied this mysterious ability to geology and found that the history of geological specimens passed before the gaze of the seer like a grand panoramic view. Cridge's vision was sometimes rapid, like lightning; sometimes it could be easily followed. All sources of error apparently were carefully excluded. From thousands of experiments conducted from 1853 until his death in 1883, Denton concluded that the existence of psychometric ability is unquestionable.

From a fragment of lava from Kilauea, Hawaii (the sensitive had no idea of the origin and nature), the following picture was sensed:

"I see the ocean and ships are sailing on it. This must be an island, for water is all around. Now I am turned from where I saw the vessels, and am looking at something most terrific. It seems as if an ocean of fire were pouring over a precipice, and boiling as it pours. The sight permeates my whole being, and inspires me with terror. I see it flow into the ocean and the water boils intensely."

A pebble of a limestone, with glacial scratches on its surface, was given to Cridge. She said:

"I feel as if I were below an immense body of water—so deep that I cannot see down through it, and yet it seems that I could see upward through it for miles. Now I am going, going, and there is something above and around me. It must be ice; I am frozen in it. The motion of the mass I am in is not uniform; it pitches forward then halts and pitches again, then goes grinding, pressing and rushing along—a mountain mass.

Fossils and minerals also brought forth lengthy descriptions. In *Nature's Secrets* (1863), Denton states, "From the first dawn of light upon this infant globe, when round its cradle the stormy curtains hung, Nature has been photographing every moment. What a picture gallery is hers!" A further exposition of his psychometric studies is given in *The Soul of Things* (1863) and in *Our Planet, Its Past and Future* (1869).

Denton was also concerned with psychical research, and in 1875 in Boston, working with the medium **Mary M. Hardy,** he produced what was said to be the impression of a spirit face in paraffin wax. This experiment anticipated the later researches of **Gustav Geley** and **Charles Richet** with the medium **Franek Kluski.**

Sources:

Denton, William. *Our Planet, Its Past and Future; or, Lectures on Geology.* Wellesley, Mass.: Denton Publishing, 1868.

———. *The Soul of Things: Psychometric Experiments for Re-living History.* 1863. Reprint, Wellingborough, Northampton, England: Aquarian Press, 1988.

Deoca (or The Woman of the South)

A princess of Munster, mentioned in Irish medieval legend. It is said that she was betrothed to Lairgnen and asked of him as a marriage gift the children of Lir, who had been magically changed by their stepmother into four wonderful singing swans. The hermit who looked after them refused to give them to Lairgnen, who then seized them. When brought into the presence of Deoca they were transformed into their human form—withered, white-haired, miserable beings. The hermit baptized them before they died, and sorrowed for them so much that he himself was laid in their grave.

Department of Personality Studies, University of Virginia

Formerly known as "Division of Parapsychology, University of Virginia," the Department of Personality Studies was established in 1968 to develop a broad program of investigations into various aspects of **parapsychology.** The founding director was **Ian Stevenson,** noted for his scientific search for evidence of **reincarnation.** Address: Division of Personality Studies, Department of Behavioral Medicine & Psychiatry, Box 152, Medical Center, University of Virginia, Charlottesville, VA 22908. (See also **Division of Personality Studies, University of Virginia**)

Department of Psychology and Parapsychology, Andhra University, India

Established in 1967 by the University Grants Commission of Andhra University, and at the time the only university-level department of **parapsychology** in the world. Students are admitted for graduate study and a Ph.D. in parapsychology is awarded. Noted parapsychologist **K. Ramakrishna Rao** headed the department at the time of its founding until he moved to the United States as a staff member of the **Institute for Parapsychology** in Durham, North Carolina. In 1984 he returned to India for five years and resumed leadership of the department. The department publishes the *Psi Newsletter* for private circulation. Address: Andhra University, Visakhapatam 530003, Andhra Pradesh, India.

Dermatoglyphics

A term used in **palmistry** to indicate the connection between markings on the hand and illness in the subject.

Dermo-Optical Perception

One form of **eyeless sight,** the ability to perceive without the use of the eyes, or "seeing with the skin." Work on dermo-optical sensitivity was pioneered by Jules Romains in the early twentieth century and continued by A. C. Novomeyshy in the 1970s. This ability is usually distinguished from *paroptic vision* (a term coined by Romains), which means eyeless sight in which there is no direct contact with the skin.

Related terms are hyperesthesia, synesthesia, cutaneous vision, and extraretinal vision. Russian researchers on the subject use a term translated as "biointroscopy," an ability demonstrated by Russian psychic **Rosa Kuleshova.**

Sources:

DuPlessis, Yvonne. "Differences between ESP of the Blind and Dermo-Optical Perception." *International Journal of Paraphysics* 10, no. 3 (1976): 51–60.

Dermography

The psychic phenomenon of skin writing, related to **stigmata** but with one essential difference—stigmatic writings last for months, years, or throughout a lifetime, whereas skin writing disappears in a few minutes or in a few hours at the most. For that very reason the possibilities of **fraud** in skin writing are high. Given the sensitive skin of neuropsychopaths, writing may appear in a few minutes after the letters are directly traced by any blunt instrument or the fingernails.

As a preliminary to a skin writing demonstration, or **pellet reading,** some mediums burn up the pellet on which a name or question is written and rub their arm or forehead with the ashes. The rubbing process may give a good opportunity for covertly tracing the intended message.

However, in at least one case on record this tracing was reportedly done via **telekinesis.** In 1869 Manuel Eyre testified before a committee of the **London Dialectical Society** on his experience with a Mrs. Seymour at Waukegan, near Chicago, as follows:

"In trance she would hold out one arm, and with the forefinger of the other hand make a rapid motion as if writing, the movement of the finger being in the air about a foot from the arm; a few minutes after she stripped off her sleeve, and there on her arm, so distinctly written that it could be read across the room, was the peculiar signature of the spirit giving the communication."

According to the American Spiritualist newspaper *Spiritual Telegraph,* the writing on Seymour's arm appeared in raised letters and could both be seen and felt distinctly for 15 or 20 minutes. Gradually it faded away, leaving the skin natural, smooth and uncolored. Seymour appeared several times before an investigating committee in Milwaukee, but the committee could find no explanation.

In the case of a Miss Coggswell of Vermont, the writing appeared on her arms and forehead in answer to mental questions. Skin markings have also been produced by suggestion in experiments with **hypnotism.** The part that **suggestion** may play in such demonstrations was shown in 1933 at the **Institute Métapsychique International** of Paris, where Olga Kahl produced on her skin a mentally communicated word or image.

Psychologist Richard von Kraft-Ebing recorded that the writing traced on the anesthetic right side of d'Ilma S. appeared reversed on the left side.

Thomas Killigrew testified to the appearance of the names of St. Joseph and the Virgin upon the hands of the prioress of the Ursuline nuns at **Loudun** in France about the year 1635. He said, "I saw her hand, white as my hand, in an instant change color all along the vein and become red and all of a sudden a word distinctly appeared, and the word was Joseph."

During a period of religious revival in Northern Ireland, writing on the skin was a common occurrence.

In the case of mediums, the demonstration of skin writing, while interesting, is of little value for contemporary parapsychology because of the variety of mundane ways in which it can be produced. It was reported occasionally in the nineteenth-century Spiritualist press, however. British medium **Stainton Moses** reported October 12, 1873, that the following names appeared on his arm: "Imperator," "Mentor," "Solon" and "Plato." Solon's name was impressed with a capital Sigma. The names were those of Moses' spirit controls. **Charles H. Foster,** "the Salem Seer," gave abundant demonstrations of the phenomenon. Before the London Dialectical Society, Edward Laman Blanchard told the story of how the name of his father appeared in red letters on the arm of the medium and immediately afterward, in answer to a question, the number 24 appeared on the palm of his hand, indicating the number of years since his father's death. The phenomenon was very rapid, the letters and numbers disappearing in the sight of those present without the arm of the medium being withdrawn. A Dr. Ashburner examined Foster's skin letters under a magnifying glass. He observed clearly that they were in relief and that the coloring matter was under the skin. The color disappeared after two or three minutes.

Foster's biographer, George C. Bartlett, described an amusing incident. A certain Mr. Adams came to consult Foster. He saw the room was filled with spirits in Foster's presence. About two o'clock the next morning he woke up, complaining to Bartlett that he could not sleep because the room was still filled with spirits of the Adams family. They were writing their names all over the seer. To his astonishment Bartlett counted 11 distinct names, one written across Foster's forehead, others on his arms, and several on his back.

In 1926 psychical researcher **Harry Price** carried out a series of careful tests on the psychic **Eleonore Zügun** and obtained stigmatic marking phenomena under laboratory conditions.

On occasion, skin writing is pictographic. One such case was reported in the American *Spiritual Telegraph* regarding the appearance of a clearly defined human heart with a wound, as if made by a bullet, on the arm of one Coggewell in answer to the request by a sitter that his friend, who died when shot in the heart, should manifest.

A more graphic phenomenon was exhibited in New England by an African-American woman then working as a servant to Lewis Burtis. As narrated by **Emma Hardinge Britten** in *Modern American Spiritualism* (1870), red lines had formed "into a distinct and beautifully-represented picture of a kneeling man, with a woolly head and African cast of features, a chain round his waist terminating in two balls, which were ingeniously fitted into the veins at the end of the arm, whilst above the whole was written in fine character the words: 'A poor old slave.'" The woman servant was nearly illiterate. Messages frequently appeared on her arm while she was at her household work and would disappear after having been read by the Burtises.

Dermography differs from stigmata, where as, for example in the case of **Thérèse Neumann** and **Padre Pio,** actual bleeding appeared on their hands and feet, indicating identification with the suffering of Christ. Stigmata reproduces the wounds of Christ as reported in the Bible's New Testament.

Dermot of the Love-spot (Dermot O'Dyna)

A typical lover in Irish legend and the hero of the myth of Dermot and Grania. One night Dermot and three companions entered a hut for a night's shelter. In the hut lived an old man, a young girl (Youth), a wether (the World), and a cat (Death). During the night, the girl put the love-spot on Dermot's forehead, and thenceforth, it was said, no woman could see him without loving him. He came to be loved by Grania, the betrothed of **Finn Mac Cummal,** and she forced him to run away with her.

The couple was pursued all over Ireland, but after 16 years of outlawry, Dermot was allowed to return to his patrimony. He was killed by his stepbrother, who through an enchantment had taken the form of Bulben, the Boar of Ben. His body was borne away on a gilded bier by the people of Dana, and it was given a soul by Angus Og, the Irish god of love, so that he might return each day and talk with the god. Dermot may represent the sun in this legend, and the bearing away of his body may symbolize the sunset.

Dero

"Detrimental Robot"—a term coined by writer **Richard Shaver** to indicate malevolent dwarfs living in underground caverns. In his story "I Remember Lemuria," first published as a series in *Amazing Stories* beginning in March 1945 (and reprinted in *The Hidden World* in the 1960s), the deros used advanced machinery to harass human beings. This series of stories, which hypothesized a **hollow earth** and underground civilization, was presented as fact rather than fiction and stimulated paranoid fantasies on the part of many readers.

Sources:

Palmer, Ray. "Invitation to Adventure." *The Hidden World* A-1 (Spring 1961): 4–14.

Shaver, Richard. "I Remember Lemuria." *Amazing Stories* March 1945. Reprinted in *The Hidden World* A-1 (Spring 1961): 52–134.

Dervishes

A subgroup within **Sufism,** the mystical movement in Islam distinguished by a form of ecstatic whirling dance. When first observed by Westerners they were described as the "whirling dervishes." The word *dervish* indicates a poor man, religious mendicant, or ecstatic. The dervishes follow a semiesoteric doctrine. Their various "paths" or systems may date back as far as the ancient rites of Persia and Egypt.

The Bektash Sufis offer a representative example of the dervishes. In the fifteenth century Bektash of Bokhara received his mantle from Ahmed Yesevee, who claimed descent from the father-in-law of Mohammed. Bektash established a "path" to spiritual truth consisting nominally of seven degrees, only four of which, however, were essential. These aimed to establish an affinity between the aspirant and the sheik, the latter leading the aspirant, through the agency of the spirit of Bektash, and that of Mohammed, to Allah.

The initiation ceremony provided a severe test. The aspirant was tried for a year with false secrets. When his time of probation expired, a lamb was slain, from the carcass of which a cord was made for his neck and a girdle for his loins. Two armed attendants then led him into a square chamber, where he was presented to the sheik as "a slave who desires to know truth." He was then placed before a stone altar, on which were 12 scallops.

The sheik, attended by 11 others, gripped the hand of the aspirant in a particular way and administered the oath of the order, in which the neophyte promised to be poor, chaste, and obedient. The aspirant was then informed that the penalty for betraying the order was death. He then stated, "Mohammed is my guide, Ali [Mohammed's son-in-law] is my director," and was asked by the sheik, "Do you accept me as your guide?" The reply being made in the affirmative, the sheik added, "Then I accept you as my son."

Among the Bektosh sect's important symbols were the double triangles and two triangles joined at the apex. One of their maxims was, The man must die that the saint may be born. For a jewel they made use of a small marble cube with red spots, to typify the blood of the martyred Ali.

The dervish sects were held suspect by many orthodox Moslems, who said they devoted themselves entirely to the well-being of their order rather than to Islam as a whole.

The whirling dervishes originated in Konya, on the Anatolian plateau of Turkey. They were organized by Jalal al-din Rumi (born in Afghanistan in 1207), also known to his disciples as Mevlana (Our Master). Rumi was a theological scholar who came under the spiritual influence of the wandering dervish Shams Tabriz. Tabriz was murdered by disciples who were jealous of Rumi's devotion. After this, Rumi adopted the mourning costume of the period (tall felt hat, white skirt, and black cloak) and gyrated in his garden, repeating the name of God until he passed into an ecstatic trance.

Rumi's dance became the basis of the *sema,* a sacred ceremony of the dervishes that has survived into modern times. It commences with the sound of a reed flute, symbolizing a longing for reunion. The costume worn is also regarded as symbolic of the tomb, the shroud, and the tombstone. The floor is said to indicate the Last Judgment. The whirling dance itself symbolizes the movement of the planets in relation to the sun (represented by the sheik, who supervises the dance).

The whirling dervishes are also known as Mevlevis, and their organization has recently spread to other parts of the world through a revival of interest in Sufi doctrines. Today there are British and American Sufis who have learned to practice the sema.

Sources:

Brown, John P. *The Darvishes; or Oriental Spiritualism.* London, 1927. Rev. ed., London: Frank Cass, 1968.

Burke, O. M. *Among the Dervishes.* New York: E. P. Dutton, 1973.

Farzan, Massud. *The Tale of the Reed Pipe.* New York: E. P. Dutton, 1974.

Friedlander, Ira. *The Whirling Dervishes.* New York: Macmillan, 1975.

Desertis, V. C.

Pseudonym of **Stanley De Brath** for his book *Psychic Philosophy* (1909).

Desmond, Gerald (d. 1583)

Sixteenth earl of Desmond, in Ireland, who was killed in 1583. He had some reputation as a magician and was known as "the Great Earl." Many curious stories have been told about him.

He lived in a castle on a small island in Lough Gur, and there he took his young bride, to whom he was so passionately attached that he could deny her nothing. Seeking him one day in the chamber where he worked his **magic** spells, she demanded to know the secret of the black cat. In vain he told her of the terrible things she must witness. She would not be dissuaded, so he warned her solemnly that if she uttered a word the castle would sink to the bottom of Lough Gur. Then he set to work with his magic spells.

Terrible indeed were the sights she beheld, but she stood firm and uttered neither word nor cry, until her husband lay down on the floor and stretched till he reached almost from end to end of the room. Then she uttered a wild shriek, and the castle sank instantly to the bottom of Lough Gur, where it still remains.

The legend says that once in every seven years Desmond, mounted on a white horse, rises from the water and rides around the Lough. His horse is shod with silver shoes, and when they wear out the spell will be broken. Desmond will return, and his vast estates will be restored to him.

Desmond, Shaw (1877–1960)

Irish novelist and dramatist who studied psychic phenomena for 25 years. He was president of the **Survival League** and once said that he believed it impossible for anything to stop him from surviving. He was an eloquent propagandist of **Spiritualism** and lectured around the world. Three of his books, *Passion, Gods,* and *Echo,* have a psychic background, while *Tales of the Little Sisters of Saint Francis* is based on the author's experience with **fairies.** *Windjammer: The Book of the Horn* is an account of a 7,000-mile journey, undertaken partly to study **black magic.**

Desmond was born in county Waterford, Ireland, January 19, 1877, and was educated by Irish monks. At the age of 15 he left school to go into business in London, but returned to Ireland to farm. In 1909 he concentrated on literature and journalism. He wrote more than 60 books, many of which have psychic themes. He died December 23, 1960.

Sources:

Desmond, Shaw. *Healing: Psychic and Divine.* London: Rider, 1956. Reprinted as *The Power of Faith Healing.* New York: Award Books, 1969.

———. *Ragnarok.* N.p., 1926.

———. *Reincarnation for Everyman.* N.p., 1939.

———. *Spiritualism?* N.p., 1941.

———. *We Do Not Die.* N.p., 1934.

———. *You Can Speak With Your Dead.* N.p., 1941.

Pleasants, Helene, ed. *Biographical Dictionary of Parapsychology.* New York: Helix Press, 1964.

D'Espagnet, Jean (ca. 1640)

A Hermetic philosopher who left two treatises, *Enchiridion Physicae Restitutae* (1623) and *Arcanum Philosophiae Hermitacae* (ca. 1623), which were also said to be the works of one who called himself "the Chevalier Imperial." *The Secret of Hermetic Philosophy* embraces the practical side of the magnum opus, and the *Enchiridion* explores the physical possibility of transmutation of metals. D'Espagnet also wrote the preface to the *Tableau de l'inconstance des démons* by **Pierre De Lancre.**

The *Arcanum* is better known as *The Canons of Espagnet* and has been called a treatise on mystical **alchemy.** The author states, however, that "the science of producing Nature's grand Secret is a perfect knowledge of nature universally and of Art, concerning the realm of Metals; the practice whereof is conversant in finding the principles of Metals by analysis."

The authorities cited by Espagnet were those who, like **Bernard Trévisan,** are known to have devoted their lives to practical alchemy. While much of the treatise discusses physical objects, it may also be extended to the psychic side of the hermetic or alchemical art.

D'Esperance, Elizabeth (1855–1919)

Pseudonym of Elizabeth Hope Reed, a nonprofessional **medium,** the story of whose life and work was recounted by William Oxley in *Angelic Revelations* (1885) and by Reed in her autobiography *Shadow Land* (1897). The latter work is particularly important for the account of her own experiences. In his preface, Russian psychical researcher **Alexander Aksakof** describes the book as the frank but sorrowful story of the author's search for the truth at the mercy of unknown but potent powers.

Born Elizabeth Hope, her earliest recollections included seeing (in the ancient house where the family lived) "strangers" continually passing to and fro, some of whom nodded and smiled as she held up her doll for their inspection. These shadow people were her earliest friends. She did not associate them with ghosts, of which she was told frightful tales by the maid. For her there was nothing supernatural about them, although they shrank from her touch and she could not feel anything if her hand came into contact with them. They for months at a time vanished and on the whole they made her life miserable. Her mother discouraged her telling "stories" of unseen visitors, and the family doctor terrorized her by warning that those who see things that do not exist are usually mad and become dangerous.

A long cruise in 1867 on a boat that her father captained was the brightest recollection of her teens. The sleepwalking that had troubled her earlier was now cured and the shadow people stayed away, but the happiness that was hers for many weeks was finally marred by the terrifying vision of a shadow ship that passed right through their own.

Another unusual experience befell her later at the end of the school term. She had to write an essay on "nature." She could not manage a single thought. The last night came and even then she went to bed in despair, praying in tears and crying until she fell asleep, leaving sheets of paper and some pencils littered across her desk. In the morning she found the sheets covered with her own handwriting, containing an astonishing essay on the subject. The teacher was greatly surprised by the quality of the essay, and when she heard the story she spoke to the rector about it. On examination day, the rector himself read the essay and explained it as a direct answer to prayer.

At age 19, she married and settled at Newcastle-on-Tyne, England. After her marriage the shadow people came back into her life. By chance she heard of **Spiritualism** and table rapping, which she then considered tomfoolery. Challenged by a friend, she sat in a circle of six. The table soon began to vibrate, heave, and answer questions. It even disclosed the unknown whereabouts of her father, which was found afterward to be correct.

More extraordinary phenomena followed. A pair of studs disappeared from before their eyes and from information rapped out by the table they were found in the next room beneath the undisturbed, compacted soil in a flower pot. The wanderings of these studs amazed the circle. Once they were found in a locked Japanese box on a high shelf; another time they dropped from the ceiling into the cup of a guest at coffee time.

An experiment in **clairvoyance** was crowned with remarkable success. Reed's eyes were covered by a Mr. F. in the dark and she described an incident in his life that occurred 12 years earlier. She recognized him in the vision.

Her interest was now thoroughly aroused. She spoke of the shadow people to friends, and though the idea that she was a medium was at first repugnant to her, she agreed to play the part. It was suggested that she should attempt **automatic writing** to establish a more efficient means of communication. It soon came about with a tingling, pricking, and aching sensation in her arm, and thereafter the circle reported contact with spirit visitors:

"Walter Tracey," a bright, jovial American, "Humnur Stafford," the self-constituted philosopher guide, and "Ninia," a child of seven. The **control** of each could be distinguished by the sensation in Reed's arm and hand.

The next phase of her development came when she saw a luminous cloud concentrated in the darkness of the room slowly evolve into the form of a child. No one else could see the strange apparition that she sketched, but the new development was hailed with delight. People soon began to talk about it in Newcastle and overwhelmed d'Esperance (the name she began to use in her new public life) with requests for the portraits of their dead friends. To better her art she studied for a few months, but as her sketching improved her power of seeing the luminous figures diminished and violent headaches followed the attempts at drawing.

Then T. P. Barkas, an intellectual of Newcastle, joined the circle. One evening he introduced a series of popular lectures on science, illustrated with practical experiments which he intended to deliver. The medium's hand passed remarks through automatic writing that claimed the theories advocated by Barkas were wrong.

This was the beginning of a scientific period of mediumship that lasted for several months. Hammer Stafford described in detail an instrument that proved later to be the telephone, and another by which messages could be forwarded to great distances in the original handwriting. Barkas delivered his lectures and closed them with one titled "Recent Experiments in Psychology: Extraordinary Replies to Questions on Scientific Subjects by a Young Lady of Very Limited Education."

After a year, the medium's failing health put an end to the scientific séances. She went to the south of France to recuperate. On her recovery she became filled with the missionary spirit, but in trying to make converts for the new truth of Spiritualism that she had glimpsed, she discovered—to her dismay—that the psychic powers could not be consciously summoned. Her ability to write on scientific subjects appeared to fail, and her clairvoyant faculty became feeble when conscious exhibition was needed.

Yet she achieved one result—the reconciliation between a Professor Friese of Bremen and **Johann Zöllner.** The alienation had taken place when Zöllner accepted Spiritualism. It was Zöllner who wrote to Friese about her. As a result she spent weeks in the professor's house. One day he publicly declared that he had become a Spiritualist, resigned his chair, and began to write books, later published under the titles *Jenseits des Grabens* and *Stimmen aus der Geister Reich.* A visit to Bremen by d'Esperance was followed by a long stay in Sweden. A new line of experiment was tried there. She read letters, written in various languages and enclosed in seven envelopes, the words of which she had to spell out letter by letter. This power also fluctuated, and determined efforts usually resulted in failure.

It was here that she first tried to sit for **materialization.** In the darkness of the **cabinet,** she reported, she soon became conscious of a curious disturbance; the air seemed to be agitated as though a bird were fluttering about and at the second attempt she felt as if fine threads were being drawn out of the pores of her skin.

A face was seen by the sitters outside the curtains, but she did not see it from within. So she stood up, feeling her knees strangely weak, put her head out, and above her head she recognized the merry, laughing eyes of "Walter." During a six-week trial Walter learned the art of full materialization.

During his visits she felt strangely listless. Thoughts and impressions swirled like lightning through her brain. She was conscious of the thoughts and feelings of everyone in the room. While d'Esperance was in this state any movement required a great effort, which invariably compelled the materialized forms to retire into the cabinet, as though deprived of power to stand or support themselves.

"Yolande," a young Arab girl of 15, soon made an appearance and remained a constant visitor. She was inquisitive and continually mystified her audience by making things in the room invisible and producing a variety of **apports** in the form of flowers and plants. It took her about ten to fifteen minutes to build up her body from a cloudy patch on the floor, while the process of melting away usually took place in two to five minutes, the drapery being the last to disappear, in one-half to two minutes.

Yolande's flower apports were very strange. She usually asked in advance for water, sand, and a water carafe. After the water and sand were mixed in the carafe she covered it with a part of her drapery. In a séance held on August 4, 1880, an exotic plant grew up in the carafe. It was an *Ixora crocata,* 22 inches high, with a thick woody stem that filled the neck of the bottle, the roots firmly planted inside the glass. The natural home of this plant is India. It was produced for William Oxley of Manchester, and it lived for three months in his gardener's care.

Sitters frequently brought fern leaves and asked Yolande to match them. She always complied. Roses were produced from nothing and freely given away. Yolande's last and greatest work was achieved on June 28, 1890, when she apported a seven-foot high golden lily with 11 blossoms. The feat was witnessed by Professors Boutlerof, Fiedler, Aksakof, and others. The power was not sufficient for its dematerialization (Yolande insisted that the plant was borrowed and she had to return it), and she instructed the sitters to keep it in darkness. The lily remained in the house for eight days and then vanished in an instant, filling the room with an overpowering perfume.

Materialization Fraud

Bitter experiences were also in store for d'Esperance. The first befell her in Newcastle in 1880. It came after observations that one of the materialized phantoms, "the French lady," bore a bewildering resemblance to the medium.

A suspicious sitter seized the form of Yolande while the medium was believed sitting inside the cabinet. D'Esperance describes her experience when this occurred:

"All I knew was a horrible excruciating sensation of being doubled up and squeezed together, as I can imagine a hollow gutta percha doll would feel, if it had sensation, when violently embraced by its baby owner. A sense of terror and agonizing pain came over me, as though I was losing hold of life and was falling into some fearful abyss, yet knowing nothing, hearing nothing, except the echo of a scream I heard as at a distance. I felt I was sinking down, I knew not where. I tried to save myself, to grasp at something, but missed it; and then came a blank from which I awakened with a shuddering horror and sense of being bruised to death."

The result of this experience was the outbreak of the earlier hemorrhage of her lungs and a prolonged illness. In Sweden, after her recovery, successful photographic experiments were conducted to obtain portraits of the materialized entities and spirit photographs without a formal séance. These experiments proved to be a drain on her nervous energy, so they were dropped after a while.

In the later materialization séances she invariably observed the rule of sitting before the cabinet and exhibiting herself and the phantom at the same time. Her unique description of double identity dates from these days and reads:

"Now comes another figure, shorter, slenderer, and with outstretched arms. Somebody rises up at the far end of the circle and comes forward and the two are clasped in each other's arms. Then inarticulate cries of "Anna! Oh, Anna! My child! My loved one!

"Then somebody else gets up and puts her arms round the figure; then sobs, cries and blessings get mixed up. I feel my body swayed to and fro and all gets dark before my eyes. I feel somebody's arms round me although I sit on my chair alone. I feel somebody's heart beating against my breast. I feel that something is happening. No one is near me except the two children. No one is taking any notice of me. All eyes and thoughts seem concentrated on the white slender figure standing there with the arms of the two black-robed women around it.

"It must be my own heart I feel beating so distinctly. Yet those arms round me? Surely never did I feel a touch so plainly. I begin to wonder which is I. Am I the white figure or am I the one in the chair? Are they my hands round the old lady's neck, or are these mine that are lying on the knees of me, or on the knees of the figure if it be not I, on the chair?

"Certainly they are my lips that are being kissed. It is my face that is wet with the tears which these good women are shedding so plentifully. Yet how can it be? It is a horrible feeling, thus losing hold of one's identity. I long to put one of these hands that are lying so helplessly, and touch some one just to know if I am myself or only a dream—if Anna be I, and I am lost as it were, in her identity."

In 1893 at the house of a Professor E. of Christiana, an Egyptian beauty calling herself "Nepenthes," materialized in the midst of the circle and was seen at the same time with the medium. At the sitters' request she dipped her hand into a paraffin wax bucket and left behind a plaster mold of rare beauty, which the modeler said must have been produced by sorcery as it was obviously impossible to extricate the hand from the wax glove without ruining it.

Nepenthes vanished from their presence as she came. She lowered her head, on which a diadem shone, little by little became a luminous cloud, and gradually faded away. Before her disappearance she wrote a message in her own hand in ancient Greek in the pocketbook of one of the sitters. All present were ignorant of ancient Greek letters. The translation read: "I am Nepenthes thy friend; when thy soul is oppressed by too much pain, call on me, Nepenthes, and I will come at once to relieve thy trouble."

From time to time d'Esperance felt greatly troubled. The theories of subliminal consciousness and orthodox religious objections that the phenomena had to do with the devil disturbed her to a growing extent. An **out-of-the-body travel** experience, however, enlightened her; she realized the great truth behind the phenomenal side of Spiritualism and, fortified in courage, continued her missionary work.

Three times her life was endangered because of injuries received by those who tried to catch her in **fraud.** The worst experience befell her in Helsingfors in 1893, when an attempt to violate Yolande caused nearly two years of indisposition, turning her hair white and grey.

The outrage followed the most enigmatic phenomenon of her mediumship: the partial dematerialization of her body from the waist down. Aksakof made an investigation and, with the testimonies of those present, published the full story in his book *A Case of Partial Dematerialization* (1898). This alleged phenomenon occurred on the evening of December 11, 1893, at the house of a Professor Seiling, with some 15 people present at the séance.

Fourteen years later, **Hereward Carrington** published a lengthy criticism of the case in the *Proceedings* of the American Society for Psychical Research (March 1907), which was answered by **James H. Hyslop.** Carrington discussed how the incident might have been achieved by trickery. If d'Esperance was using deception, she was never caught.

Materialization mediumship has largely disappeared under the impact of numerous revelations of fraud and the inability of mediums to produce such phenomena as described in relation to d'Esperance under controlled conditions with competent observers. At best, her case must remain open, though there is every reason to believe that she simply was never caught.

In addition to many articles she wrote for the Spiritualist press, d'Esperance wrote two books, *Shadow Land* (1897) and *Northern Lights* (1900), the latter a collection of psychic stories and experiences. At the outbreak of the World War I d'Esperance found herself virtually a prisoner in Germany, where she then resided. All her papers were seized, among them the manuscript of a second volume to *Shadow Land.* It was destroyed, probably along with a quantity of séance reports in shorthand.

Sources:

Aksakof, Alexander. *A Case of Partial Dematerialization.* N.p., 1898.

Berger, Arthur S., and Joyce Berger. *The Encyclopedia of Parapsychology and Psychical Research.* New York: Paragon House, 1991.

Carrington, Hereward. "An Examination and Analysis of the Evidence for Dematerialization as Demonstrated in Mons. Aksakof's Book." *Proceedings* of the Society for Psychical Research (March 1907).

Oxley, William. *Angelic Revelations.* 5 vols. N.p., 1885.

Dessoir, Max (1867–1947)

German psychologist who had a special interest in **parapsychology**—he coined the term during or before 1889. He also had both talent and interest in art and aesthetics. A precocious child, he was an accomplished musician who played the violin for the German emperor. His experiments in **muscle reading** and **thought-transference** were undertaken in 1885 at the age of 18 and reported in the *Proceedings* of the Society for Psychical Research (1885). Three years later he founded the Gesellschaft fur Experimental Psychologie (Society for Experimental Psychology), dedicated to the study of hypnosis and paranormal phenomena.

Dessoir collaborated with Albert Moll on experiments in hypnotic rapport. He originated a theory of "Doppel-Ich" or double ego, suggesting that human consciousness is not a unit merely to our own consciousness, but actually consists of at least two distinguishable personalities, each held together by its own chain of memories. Because of this, an action that is quite intelligible can be performed unconsciously (i.e., without the agent noticing what he or she is doing, or even breaking off a conversation).

As he matured, Dessoir saw himself as an instrument for educating the German public on psychical research. He founded the periodical *Zeitschrift für kritischen Okkultismus.* He also investigated several mediums including **Eusapia Palladino.**

Sources:

Berger, Arthur S., and Joyce Berger. *The Encyclopedia of Parapsychology and Psychical Research.* New York: Paragon House, 1991.

Dessoir, Max. *Aesthetics and the Theory of Art.* Detroit: Wayne State University Press, 1970.

———. *Einleitung in die Philosophie.* N.p., 1946.

———. "Experiments in Muscle-Reading and Thought-Transference." *Proceedings* of the Society for Psychical Research 4 (1889): 111.

———. *Das Ich, der Traum, der Tod.* N.p., 1947.

———. *Psychologische Briefe.* N.p., 1948.

———. *Die Rede als Kunst.* N.p., 1948.

Hövelman, G. H. "Neglected Figures in the History of Parapsychology. I. Some General Reflections." In *Liber Amicorum in Honoue of G. A. M. Zorab,* edited by F. W. J. J. Snel. Amsterdam: Nederlander Vereniging voor Parapsychologie, 1986.

"Deuce Take You"

A saying of ancient origin. *Deuce* is practically synonymous with the devil, the word being derived from *Dusins,* the ancient name given by the Gauls to a sort of demon or devil.

Deva-Loka (or Daiver-Logum)

The world of Hindu gods, especially Indra, also known as Swarga. Said to be situated between the sun and polar star, it is a region of splendor and magnificence, inhabited by many gods, nature spirits, and angels.

Devas (or Daivers)

Hindu gods, who inhabit their world of *Deva-Loka.* The term derives from the root *div* (to shine) and may be related to the Persian **divs.** Indra was foremost among the ancient Hindu gods and Deva-Loka was his heaven. In later mythology, Indra became inferior to Agni, Vayu, and Surya, but remained in power over other gods and spirits. The Deva-Loka of the gods included many nature spirits and angels.

According to theosophical teachings (which partially derive from Hinduism) devas constitute the ranks or orders of spirits who compose the hierarchy that rules the universe under the deity. Their numbers are vast and their functions are not all known to mankind, though generally these functions may be said to be connected with the evolution of systems and of life.

Of devas there are three kinds—bodiless devas, form devas, and passion devas. Bodiless devas belong to the higher mental world; their bodies are composed of mental elemental essence, and they belong to the first elemental kingdom. Form devas belong to the lower mental world; while their bodies are composed also of mental elemental essence, they belong to the second elemental kingdom. Passion devas belong to the astral world and their bodies are composed of astral elemental essence. Devas are superlatively great and glorious creatures; they have vast knowledge and power, are calm yet irresistible, and are in appearance altogether magnificent.

Devas at Findhorn

Devas came into Western thought in a powerful way at the **New Age** community of Findhorn. In 1963, while struggling to survive in the trailer camp that would later become the community site, Peter and Eileen Caddy and Dorothy MacLean were gardening. In her meditations that spring, MacLean's attention was called to the presence of the forces of nature. She was told to cooperate with nature by thinking about the higher nature spirits, the spirits of different forms from the clouds to the varieties of different plants.

Getting over some initial skepticism, she made contact and began to receive instructions from the devas that allowed them to produce a spectacular garden in the spartan conditions of northern Scotland. Over the next few years hundreds of messages were received and published from the devas which also began to articulate a philosophy of the wholeness of creation.

Sources:

Findhorn Community. *The Findhorn Garden.* New York: Harper & Row, 1975.

Hawken, Paul. *The Magic of Findhorn.* New York: Harper & Row, 1975.

MacLean, Dorothy. *To Hear the Angels Sing.* Middleton, Wisc.: Lorian Press, 1980.

Devereux, George (1908–)

Professor of research in ethnopsychiatry, author, and editor who engaged in parapsychological research. He was born September 13, 1908, in Lugos, Hungary. He studied at the School of Oriental Languages in Paris and the Institute of Ethnology, University of Paris (Ph.D., anthropology, 1935), and later at the University of California and the Topeka Institute for Psychoanalysis, Topeka, Kansas. After World War II he accepted a position as the director of research and staff ethnologist at Winter Veterans Hospital. Subsequently he became a professor of research in ethnopsychiatry, at Temple University School of Medicine, Philadelphia.

In addition to his many publications in anthropology and psychology, Devereaux made several contributions to parapsychology. He edited the important volume *Psychoanalysis and the Occult* (1953) and contributed a variety of articles on **levitation,** Haitian **voudou,** superstitions, and **dreams**–many of which grew out of his early anthropological fieldwork—to parapsychological journals.

Sources:

Devereux, George. "Bridey Murphy, a Psychoanalytic View." *Tomorrow* (Summer 1956).

Devereux, George, ed. *Psychoanalysis and the Occult.* New York: International Universities Press, 1953.

Pleasants, Helene, ed. *Biographical Dictionary of Parapsychology.* New York: Helix Press, 1964.

Devi, Indra (1899– ?)

Pioneer teacher, writer, and lecturer on **hatha yoga.** She was born on May 12, 1899, in Riga, Russia, as Eugenie Petersen of Russian and Swedish parentage. Petersen was educated in St. Petersburg. Her first marriage was to a diplomat, her second to Sigfrid Knauer, a medical doctor, on March 14, 1953. She was fascinated by Oriental philosophy and mysticism and lived in India for 12 years and in Shanghai, China, for seven years.

While in India Petersen actively supported the movement for Indian freedom and was friends with Mahatma Gandhi, Rabindranath Tagore, and Pandit Nehru. She suffered from a supposedly incurable heart disease for some years, but was cured miraculously by yogic healing. As a result she studied hatha yoga under **Swami Kuvalanayananda,** one of two yogis who helped revive hatha yoga as a new "scientific" health discipline. Petersen took the name Indra Devi. She started a school of yoga in Shanghai, which she maintained throughout the Japanese occupation and introduced to Australia.

After the war she returned to India, where she was the first Western woman to teach yoga. In 1947 she went to the United States, where she started the Indra Devi Yoga Foundation, a yoga school in Los Angeles. She also traveled widely, lecturing on yoga. During her lecture tours she visited the U.S.S.R. and lectured on yoga to a group that included members of the presidium. She also introduced yoga to the health spa created by Edmond Bordeaux Szekely in Tecate, Baja California, Mexico. In 1958 she became a consultant to the Instituto de Filosofia Yoga in Mexico. Along the way she met Sai Baba, the contemporary Indian teacher, and became one of his early advocates in America.

Sources:

Devi, Indra. *Forever Young, Forever Healthy.* New York: Prentice-Hall, 1954.

———. *Renew Your Life through Yoga.* Englewood Cliffs, N.J.: Prentice-Hall, 1963.

———. *Yoga for Americans.* Englewood Cliffs, N.J.: Prentice-Hall, 1959.

———. *Yoga—the Technique of Health and Happiness.* Kitabistan, India, 1948.

Devil

A name derived from the Greek *diabolos,* meaning "slanderer." The name is used for the supreme spirit of evil, the enemy of God and man, also known as Satan (or "adversary") in Mat. 4:8–11 and Rev. 12:9.

The idea of Satan was most fully developed in postapostolic Christianity, but as the personification of evil, Satan has many precursors and analogous representations in other religions. Possibly the clearest precursor was Set (or Seth), the antagonist of the Egyptian god of light, Horus. Set was the deity of the desert; Horus, of the life-giving Nile. Set's color was red, and red-haired and ruddy-complected people were on occasion sacrificed because they were identified with him.

In early polygamous religious systems, the gods were pictured in quite human terms, possessing both admirable and detestable attributes at the same time. Very few of them were seen as evil like the devils in Christianity or Islam. In **Egypt** and Babylon, figures like Apepi and Tiawath, although clearly in the line of evolution toward a satanic personality, were by no means rulers of the infernal regions. Again, the **Hades** of the Greeks is merely a ruler of the ghosts of the dead, not an enemy of Olympus or of mankind.

It is strange that in Mexico, Mictlantecutli, lord of hell, is a much more directly satanic figure than any European or Asiatic ruler of the realms of the dead. But in some mythologies, there are frequent allusions to monsters that may quite easily have colored the modern concept of Satan. Such is the Hindu serpent Ahi, the Hebrew Leviathan, and the principle of Chaos. Teutonic mythology has the menacing Loki, originally a god of fire, but afterward the personification of evil.

The concept of Satan, too, appears to have some deeply rooted connection with ancient serpent worship, which seems to have penetrated most Oriental countries. Thus we find the Tempter in the Old Testament (Gen. 3) in the guise of a serpent. The serpent or dragon is generally regarded as the personification of night, who swallows the sun and envelops the world in darkness.

It is generally thought that the Hebrew concept of Satan really developed in the postexilic period, though Satan is a major character in the Book of Job, one of the earliest Hebrew writings, and exhibits traces of Babylonian or Assyrian influence. It is unlikely that before the captivity any specific doctrine respecting evil spirits was held by the Hebrews. Writing on this subject, F. T. Hall in his book *The Pedigree of the Devil* (1883) states:

"The term 'Satan' and 'Satans' which occur in the Old Testament, are certainly not applicable to the modern conception of Satan as a spirit of evil; although it is not difficult to detect in the Old Hebrew mind a fruitful soil, in which the idea, afterwards evolved, would readily take root. The original idea of a 'Satan' is that of an 'adversary,' or agent of 'opposition.' The angel which is said to have withstood Balaam is in the same breath spoken of as 'The angel of the Lord,' and a 'Satan.' When the Philistines under Achish their king were about to commence hostilities against the Israelites under Saul and David and his men were about to march with the Philistines; the latter objected, lest, in the day of battle, David should become a 'Satan' to them, by deserting to the enemy. When David, in later life, was returning to Jerusalem, after Absalom's rebellion and death; and his lately disaffected subjects were, in turn, making their submission; amongst them came the truculent Shimei; Abishai, David's nephew, one of the fierce sons of Zeruiah, advised that Shimei should be put to death: this grated upon David's feelings, at a time when he was filled with exuberant joy at his own restoration; and he rebuked Abishai as a 'Satan.' Again Satan is said to have provoked David to number Israel, and at the same time, that 'the Lord moved David to number Israel;' a course strenuously opposed by Joab, another of the sons of Zeruiah. Solomon in his message to Hiram, king of Tyre, congratulated himself on having no 'Satans' and that this peaceful immunity from discord enabled him to build the Temple, which had been forbidden to his warlike father, David. This immunity was not, however, lasting; for Hadad, the Edomite, and Regon, of Zobah, became 'Satans' to Solomon, after his profuse luxury had opened the way for corruption and disaffection. In all these cases, the idea is simply identical with the plain meaning of the word: a Satan is an opponent, an adversary. In the elaborate curse embodied in the 109th Psalm, the writer speaks of his enemies as his 'Satans' and prays that the object of his anathema may have 'Satan' standing at his right hand. The Psalmist himself, in the sequel, fairly assumes the office of his enemy's 'Satan,' by enumerating his crimes and failings, and exposing them in their worst light. In the 71st Psalm, enemies (v. 10) are identified with 'Satans' or adversaries (v. 13).

"The only other places in the Old Testament where the word occurs, are in the Book of Job, and the prophecy of Zechariah. In the Book of Job, Satan appears with a distinct personality, and is associated with the sons of God, and in attendance with them before the throne of Jehovah. He is the cynical critic of Job's actions, and in that character he accuses him of insincerity and instability; and receives permission from Jehovah to test the justice of this accusation, by afflicting Job in everything he holds dear. We have here the spy, the informer, the public prosecutor, the executioner; all embodied in Satan, the adversary: these attributes are not amiable ones, but the writer does not suggest the absolute antagonism between Jehovah and Satan, which is a fundamental dogma of modern Christianity."

In later Judaism the concept of Satan is strongly colored by Persian dualism, and it has been supposed that Asmodeus of the Book of Tobit is the same as Aeshara Daewa of the ancient Persians. Both "Satan" and "Satans" are mentioned in the *Book of Enoch;* in Ecclesiasticus, Satan is identified with the serpent of Genesis; and in the *Book of the Secrets of Enoch* his revolt against God and expulsion from heaven are described. In the Jewish Targinn, Samael, highest of the angels, merges with Satan into a single personality.

Satan in the Christian New Testament clearly builds on these later Jewish forms. In Matthew he is alluded to as the "Prince of Demons," and in Ephesians he is spoken of as ruling over a world of evil beings who dwell in the lower heavens. Thus he is prince of the powers of the air. In Revelation the war in heaven between God and Satan is described, and Satan's imprisonment is foreshadowed after the overthrow of the Beast and the kings of the earth; he will be chained in the bottomless pit for 1,000 years (Rev. 20). After another period of freedom he will be cast into the lake of brimstone forever.

The orthodox doctrine of Satan developed over a number of centuries. Satan as an independent topic of theological inquiry was not prominent. Christ was seen as gaining the victory over Satan and his kingdom, and only in the early Middle Ages did theologians turn their attention to a consideration of Satan's continuing influence in the world. Over the centuries a complete picture of Satan and his cohorts would grow, and with his emergence would come a new appreciation of the devil's continued active opposition to the Church.

A major step in the definition of Satan occurred in the late fifteenth century with the new definition of **witchcraft**—previously understood as a surviving remnant of paganism—as Satanism, (i.e., devil worship). During the three centuries of the great witch-hunts, the devil was assigned a new and significant role as the supernatural cause of evil in the mundane world. That belief was not disturbed by the Reformation of the sixteenth century, and the Protestants shared Roman Catholic ideas about the devil and his demonic assistants. These beliefs were assailed in seventeenth- and eighteenth-century critiques of the antiwitchcraft crusades and in the post-Enlightenment theologies of the nineteenth century. Supernatural explanations of evil gave way to more natural interpretations.

Modern Belief in Satan

Of course, belief in the existence and power of Satan never disappeared, and in the 1960s various forces converged to produce a revival of belief in the devil. In the 1960s conservative Protestantism, which had been pushed out of the power centers of the major denominations in the 1930s, experienced a resurgence. At the same time, Western culture was undergoing a quantum leap in religious pluralism. New religions appeared in significant numbers, among them a new nature-oriented religion that took the name witchcraft.

In 1966 Anton LaVey announced the formation of the Church of Satan. Though he preached a very sanitized and secularized form of Satanism, and he never had more than a few thousand followers, the very existence of public Satanists provided a prominent symbol used by conservative Christians to argue for the existence of supernatural evil.

The 1970s became a decade of popular attention to issues of supernatural evil and the work of the devil. Two movies, *Rosemary's Baby* (1968) and *The Exorcist* (1973) helped define an era in which public discourse on Satanism reached a new peak, and numerous books on Satan, demonic possession, exorcism, and devil worship were published. The faddish interest in Satan soon died, but belief in the existence of Satan continues high in the general public, and exorcism is still practiced in both conservative Roman Catholic circles and Pentecostal Protestant churches.

Sources:

Ashton, John. *The Devil in Britain and America.* London, 1896. Reprint, Detroit: Gale Research, 1974.

Baskin, Wade. *Dictionary of Satanism.* New York: Philosophical Library, 1972.

Carus, Paul. *History of the Devil and the Idea of Evil.* LaSalle, Ill.: Open Court Publishing, 1974. Reprint, Bell Publishing, 1974.

Kelly, Henry Ansgar. *The Devil, Demonology, and Witchcraft: The Development of Christian Beliefs in Evil Spirits.* Garden City, N.Y.: Doubleday, 1968.

Lyons, Arthur. *Satan Wants You: The Cult of Devil Worship.* New York: Dodd, Mead, 1970. London: Hart-Davis, 1971.

Michelet, Jules. *The Sorceress.* London, 1905. Reprinted as *Satanism and Witchcraft: A Study in Medieval Superstition.* New York: Dell, 1971. Reprint, New York: Citadel Press, 1973.

Nauman, St. Elmo, Jr., ed. *Exorcism Through the Ages.* New York: Philosophical Library, 1974.

Olson, Alan M., ed. *Disguises of the Demonic: Contemporary Perspectives on the Power of Evil.* New York: Association Press, 1975.

Philpott, Kent. *Manual of Demonology and the Occult.* Grand Rapids, Mich.: Zondervan, 1973.

Remy, Nicolas. *Demonolatry.* 1595. Reprint, New Hyde Park, N.Y.: University Books, 1974.

Rhodes, H. T. F. *The Satanic Mass.* New York: Citadel, 1955. Reprint, London, 1973.

Robbins, Rossell Hope. *The Encyclopedia of Witchcraft and Demonology.* New York: Crown Publishers, 1959.

Rudwin, Maximilian J. *The Devil in Legend and Literature.* LaSalle, Ill.: Open Court Publishing, 1973.

Russell, Jeffrey Burton. *The Devil: Perceptions of Evil from Antiquity to Primitive Christianity.* Ithaca, N.Y.: Cornell University Press, 1977.

———. *Lucifer: The Devil in the Middle Ages.* Ithaca, N.Y.: Cornell University Press, 1984.

———. *Satan: The Early Christian Tradition.* Ithaca, N.Y.: Cornell University Press, 1981.

Thompson, Richard Lowe. *The History of the Devil.* New York: Harcourt, Brace, 1929.

Wall, J. Charles. *Devils.* London, 1904. Reprint, Detroit: Singing Tree Press, 1968.

Woods, William H. *History of the Devil.* London, 1973. New York: G. P. Putnam's Sons, 1974.

Devil Worship

Satanism, or devil worship, refers to two distinct phenomena: (1) the worship of Satan or Lucifer, the Christian antideity, and (2) the worship by non-Christian peoples of deities that to Christian observers have a devil-like character. The worship of Satan has never been a widespread activity, and most reports of Satanism seem to originate in the imagination of Christian believers.

The idea of devil worship emerged in the fifteenth century when for various reasons the powers of the Inquisition were turned upon "witchcraft." The task of the inquisitors was to ferret out heretics, Christians who held unorthodox opinions, and apostates, former Christians who had renounced the faith. Outside the mandate of the Inquisition were those believers in other religions who had never been Christians. Before the year 1484, witchcraft had been defined as paganism, the worship of the old pre-Christian deities. Pagans had never been Christians and were thus immune to the mandate of the Inquisition.

However, in 1484 Pope Innocent VIII issued an encyclical that redefined witchcraft as devil worship, hence apostasy. The encyclical was followed two years later by publication of the *Malleus Maleficarum* (The Witch's Hammer), a volume that defined devil worship as an elaborate parody of Christian worship. *Malleus Maleficarum* became the sourcebook for the massive action against people identified as witches/Satanists. Substance was added to the perspective by the numerous confessions extracted under duress from the accused. Although *Malleus Maleficarum* was published only a generation before the Reformation, Protestants accepted its perspective and were as active as Roman Catholics in the persecution of people believed to be worshiping the devil and practicing malevolent magic.

As devil worship came to be understood, it included gatherings of people, often in groups of 13 (a parody of Christ and the 12 apostles), and the performance of a "black mass" that might include the repetition of the Lord's Prayer backward, the profanation of a eucharistic host, the sacrifice of a baby, or sexual debauchery. While many were accused of participation in devil worship, the first solid evidence of the existence of a devil-worshiping group came in the court of French king Louis XIV (1638–1715). With the assistance of a defrocked priest, Catherine Deshayes, better known as "La Voisin," constructed black masses to help members of the court—including one of the King's mistresses—retain their positions in the royal society. La Voisin was also a purveyor of poisons and assisted women in aborting unwanted babies. The situation came to light at the end of the 1670s but created little impact because of the relatively quiet manner in which the investigation and judicial proceedings were carried out. A star chamber was established that considered evidence and issued verdicts in secret in order to keep the scandal from destroying the government.

In the years since the La Voisin affair, the worship of Satan or diabolism has emerged periodically, only to quickly pass from the scene. In the twentieth century, it became the subject of some successful novels, especially those of **Dennis Wheatley,** who wrote a series of stories based on the existence of a worldwide satanic conspiratorial organization. There is no evidence that such an organization exists (or ever existed) outside of Wheatley's imagination.

A new era for devil worship began in 1966 with the organization of the **Church of Satan.** The church redefined Satanism as the epitome of American values of individualism and promoted a philosophy built around hedonism, pragmatism, and ego development. The traditional Black Mass was celebrated, but it too had been transformed into a psychodrama aimed at teaching participants to release inhibitions that kept them from reaching personal fulfillment. **Anton LaVey,** the church's founder, also operated openly and demanded that church members do nothing to violate the law.

The Church of Satan enjoyed a period of growth and publicity through the early 1970s, but soon fell victim to a series of schisms that cost it many members and led to its adopting a low profile. Among the several divisions, the most substantial and the only one to survive into the 1990s is the Temple of Set. Temple founder Michael Aquino rejected the neo-Satanism of LaVey and developed a more traditional approach built upon identifying the Christian Satan as the Egyptian deity Set (or Seth). Aquino has constructed the most sophisticated form of modern Satanism and has attracted to the temple a small but faithful following. Like the Church of Satan, the Temple of Set and Aquino (an officer in the U.S. Army) renounce all actions that break the law.

Public interest in the Church of Satan had largely died by the end of the 1970s, although a new wave of concern about Satanism emerged. Through the 1980s a number of individuals, primarily women, came forward with stories of, as children and teenagers, having participated in satanic rites at the insistence of their parents. The abuse they received had been forgotten, but several decades later was being remembered. At the same time, a number of accusations were made that various people with control over children—day care workers, divorced spouses, grandparents—were practicing satanic rituals on young children.

By the mid-1980s rumors and accusations of satanic ritual abuse emerged in every part of the United States and by the end of the decade had been transplanted to Europe. They led to several trials, the most important being the lengthy trial of the owners and workers of the McMartin Day School in Manhattan Beach, California. All defendants in the McMartin case were acquitted, and further research on the growing number of accusations found no basis for the widespread allegations of Satanism. The issue was seemingly laid to rest in 1994 when two researchers—Phillip Shaver, a psychologist at the University of California-Davis, and Pamela Freyd of the False Memory Syndrome Foundation—reported after their investigation of more than twelve thousand accusations that no evidence of any satanic cults had been uncovered.

Modern Satanism is largely the product of Christian theology, as Satan is primarily an inhabitant of the Christian religious worldview. For the most part, the documents on Satanism—descriptions of its reported beliefs and practices—were written by professing Christians who never met a Satanist or attended a satanic gathering. Their descriptions of Satanism were an admixture of material drawing from older Christian texts and their own imaginations.

A Satanic Hoax

Much of the literature of diabolism is written from the point of view of the Roman Catholic church, and in fact much satanic practice, especially the so-called Black Mass, parodies Catholic worship. Belief in the existence of Satanists and devil worship as a possibly powerful force opposing the church set the church up for an elaborate hoax in France at the end of the nineteenth century. Through the nineteenth century, the church had made an issue of its opposition to **Freemasonry,** a movement that had aligned itself against the monarchial governments of western Europe.

In the years before the hoax, the church had witnessed several Satanist-related scandals. In 1894, for example, 100 consecrated hosts (eucharistic bread) were stolen from Nôtre Dame by an old woman under circumstances that clearly proved that the vessels containing them were not the objects of the theft. An extraordinary number of such larcenies occurred in all parts of France around the end of the nineteenth century, with no less than 13 churches in the Diocese of Orleans being thus despoiled. In the Diocese of Lyons, measures were taken to transform the tabernacles into strongboxes, and in 11 of the dioceses similar acts were recorded. In Italy, Rome, Liguria, and Solerus there were similar desecrations, and even on the island of Mauritius an outrage of peculiar atrocity occurred in 1895.

Meanwhile, it had been asserted by many writers, including Archbishop Meurin and "Dr. Bataille," that Freemasonry was merely a mask for Satanism, that is, that an organization had developed of which the ordinary Mason was ignorant and that had diabolism as its special object. Members of this organization, it was asserted, were recruited from the higher branches of Masonry, although it also initiated women. Needless to say, the charge was indignantly denied by Masons.

"Bataille" and "Margiotta" claimed that the order of the Palladium, or Sovereign Council of Wisdom, had been constituted in France in 1737, and this, they inferred, was one and the same as the legendary Palladium of the **Templars,** better known by the name of **Baphomet.** In 1801 Isaac Long, a Jew, was said to have carried the "original image" of Baphomet to Charleston, South Carolina, in the United States, and it was alleged that the lodge he founded then became the chief in the Ancient and Accepted Scotch Rite. He was succeeded in due course by **Albert Pike,** who, it was alleged, extended the Scotch Rite and shared the anti-Catholic Masonic chieftainship with the Italian patriot Giuseppe Mazzini. This new directory was established, it was asserted, as the new Reformed Palladium Rite, or Reformed Palladium. Assisted by Gallatin Mackey and others, Pike built the new rite into an occult fraternity with worldwide powers and practiced the occult arts so well that the head lodge at Charleston was supposed to be in constant communication with Lucifer.

These revelations by "Dr. Bataille" in the wholly ludicrous work *Le Diable au XIX Siècle* (1896) included the claim that in March 1881 his hero, "Dr. Hacks," in whom his own personality is but thinly disguised, visited Charleston, where he met Pike, Mackey, and other Satanists. Mackey was supposed to have shown him his *Arcula Mystica,* in appearance like a liqueur stand, but in reality a diabolical telephone, operated like the **Urim and Thummim.** These revelations were supported by "Miss **Diana Vaughan,**" once a Palladist, grand mistress of the temple and grand inspectress of the Palladium, who later converted to Roman Catholicism. In *Memoirs of an ex-Palladist* (1895) she gives a colorful and exhaustive account of her dealings with the "Satanists of Charleston." She claimed to be descended from the alchemist **Thomas Vaughan,** and recounted her adventures with Lucifer.

It was later disclosed that all the revelations of "Dr. Bataille" were an elaborate invention of the French journalist **Gabriel Jogand-Pàges.** Jogand-Pàges also embroidered his inventions by writing under the pseudonym Léo Taxil and also wrote the detailed "confessions" of the fictional "Diana Vaughan."

This elaborate and mischievous hoax both deceived the Roman Catholic church and embarrassed the Freemasons. It also confused the issue so far as nineteenth- and early-twentieth-century devil worship revivals were concerned. As with other hoaxes of a literary nature, this one came back to life as people in the late twentieth century rediscovered Jogand-Pàges's books and, in their ignorance of the hoax, used them to weave new theories of contemporary diabolism.

Sources:

Bois, Jules. *Le Petites Religions de Paris.* Paris, 1894.

———. *Le Satanisme et la Magie.* Paris, 1895.

Gerber, H. *Léo Taxil's Palladismus-Roman. Oder Die "Enthüllungen" Dr. Battaille's, Margiotta's and "Miss Vaughan's" Über Freimaureri kritisch beleuchtet.* Berlin, 1897.

Huysmans, J. K. *Là-Bas.* 1891. Translated as *Down There: A Study in Satanism.* New Hyde Park, N.Y.: University Books, 1958.

LaVey, Anton Szander. *The Satanic Bible.* New York: Avon, 1964.

Lea, H. C. *Léo Taxil and Diana Vaughan.* Paris, 1901.

Margiotta, D. *Souvenirs d'un Trente-Troisieme. Adriano Lemmi, chef supreme des francsmaçons.* Paris, 1896.

Papus [G. Encausse]. *Le Diable et l'occultisme.* Paris, 1895.

Rhodes, H. T. F. *The Satanic Mass.* London, 1954.

Vaughan, Diana [Gabriel Jogand-Pages]. *Mémoire d'une Ex-Palladiste.* Paris, 1895.

Waite, Arthur E. *Devil Worship in France.* London, 1896.

Devils—Afraid of Bells

It was an old superstition that evil spirits were afraid of bells and fled from the sound of them. This seems to arise from the belief that hosts of devils lurked in the atmosphere waiting to seize souls or to create storms.

In *The Golden Legend* of Jacobus de Voragine, archbishop of Genoa (printed by Caxton about 1483), it states:

". . . the evil spirits that be in the region of the air doubt much when they hear the bells ringing; thus the bells are rung when it thunders, or when great tempest and outrages of weather happen; to the end that the fiends and wicked spirits should be abashed and flee, and cease of the moving of tempests."

The *Rationale Divinorum Officiorum* of Druandus (1459), a popular work dealing with the origin and meaning of ecclesiastical services, states that the church rings the bells on the approach of a storm, so that the devils, hearing the trumpets of the Eternal King, might flee in fear and cease from raising the storm.

Bells were baptized and blessed to consecrate them. In 1521 it was stated that "suffragans used to baptise bells under pretence of driving away devils and tempests." Many old bells in Britain were inscribed with the sign of the cross and the statement, "By my lively voice I drive away all harm."

As early as ancient Roman times, bronze bells were used to repel demons. The geographer Strabo (64 or 63 B.C.E–23 C.E.) recorded that Roman herdsmen attached bells to the necks of their flocks to keep away evil spirits and wild beasts. The Roman poet Ovid (43 B.C.E.–17 C.E.) stated that people used to beat bronze vessels during an eclipse and at the death of a friend to scare away demons.

Devil's Bridge

A bridge across the Afon Mynach, near Aberystwyth, Wales. The story goes that an old woman who had lost her cow saw it on the opposite side of the chasm but did not know how to reach it.

The Evil One appeared to her in the shape of a monk and promised to throw a bridge across if she would give him the first living thing that passed over it.

The old lady agreed. The bridge was completed and the crafty fiend begged her to try it but the old woman had observed his cloven hoof and his knee bent backward. She took a crust from her pocket and flung it across the ravine, bidding her little dog go fetch it. The devil was outwitted, as he generally is in such tales.

Devil's Cauldron

An abyss at the summit of the peak of Tenerife, Canary Islands. A stone cast into the gulf resounds as though a copper vessel were being struck by a huge hammer; thus the Spaniards gave it its name. The inhabitants of the island believed that the infernal regions were there, where the souls of the wicked dwell forever.

There is another Devil's Cauldron in Perthshire, Scotland, a waterfall on the River Lednock near Loch Earn.

Devil's Chain

There is a tradition in Switzerland that St. Bernard has the devil chained in some mountains in the neighborhood of the Abbey of Clairvaux. From this comes the farmers' custom of striking three blows with a hammer on an anvil every Monday morning before going to work. By this means the devil's chain is strengthened, so that he cannot escape.

Devil's Girdle

Witches in medieval times were often accused of wearing "the devil's girdle," probably as a mark of allegiance to the Evil One. Magic girdles were commonly worn, and it has been suggested that the magnetic belts advertised in modern times had their origin in this practice.

Devil's Jaw

Name given to an area off the coast of California near Point Arguello, supposed to be the scene of numerous mysterious disappearances in the manner of the famous **Bermuda Triangle** or Devil's Sea. In 1923 seven U.S. Navy destroyers were lost there within little more than five minutes. The name "Devil's Jaw" is a translation of the Spanish *Mandibula del Diablo,* derived from the appearance of the jagged rocks north of the Santa Barbara Channel. Although many vessels have been wrecked off this treacherous coast over the years, there is no reliable evidence that these disasters were due to anything more mysterious than weather conditions, treacherous rocks, or human error. Writer Richard Winer claimed that many wrecks associated with the area took place on a Saturday.

Sources:

Winer, Richard. *From the Devil's Triangle to the Devil's Jaw.* New York: Bantam Books, 1977.

Devil's Jelly

A mysterious substance observed falling from the sky, accounts of which were assembled by researcher of anomalous phenomena **Charles Fort.** It usually appears to be a slime composed of numerous globules and dissolves upon contact with the ground, like the equally mysterious of **angel's hair.** Devil's jelly has also been associated with **UFO** phenomena.

Devil's Pillar

There are preserved at Prague three stones of a pillar that the devil is said to have brought from Rome to crush a priest with whom he had made a compact. The devil planned to kill him while he said mass, but, says the legend, St. Peter threw the devil and his pillar into the sea three times in succession, which gave the priest time for repentance. The devil was so chagrined that he broke the pillar and saved himself.

Devil's Triangle

One of several labels applied to an area of the western Atlantic between Bermuda and Florida where ships and planes are said to vanish without trace. It is more popularly known as the **Bermuda Triangle.**

Sources:

Winer, Richard. *The Devil's Triangle.* New York: Bantam Books, 1974.

———. *The Devil's Triangle 2.* New York: Bantam Books, 1975.

Devon, Witchcraft in

Belief in **witchcraft** persisted into relatively modern times in Devonshire, England, as shown in a curious case heard in Crediton County Court during the nineteenth century when a young woman alleged that she was given a potion in a grocer's shop, and that as a result either of the draught or of the incantation delivered while she was in the shop, she was getting thinner every day.

Only those who have lived long in Devon can recall the widespread belief that still existed early in the twentieth century in remote corners of the county of the power of the **evil eye** and of the credence given to all kinds of weird superstitions. Witches were believed to be able to exercise a malign influence even after death unless they were buried with their toes pointing downward. Also in the twentieth century, a woman suspected of being a witch was buried in this way within 20 miles of Tiverton.

In no part of the country was witchcraft given more credence than in the Culm Valley. There was a local saying that there were enough witches in the valley to roll a hogshead of cider up Beacon Hill, at Culmstock, and old people living in the locality were not ashamed to say that they believed in witchcraft.

The witches were considered to be of two kinds—"black" and "white." The former professed to have the power to condemn to all kinds of misfortunes those on whom they were asked to cast a spell; the latter claimed that they could remove evil spells and bring good fortune. Visits to witches tended to be kept confidential, but every now and again particulars leaked out.

For example, a late nineteenth century report from the Culmstock district concerns a young girl who went with her mother to a witch to get a spell cast over an errant admirer who was suspected of bestowing his affections on another young lady. The witch professed to be able to bring the young man back to his first love or to condemn him to all kinds of torture, but her price was prohibitive, so the young man was left to marry whom he would.

Farmers were the witches' most reliable clients, and it is a noteworthy fact that they generally contrived to visit "the wise woman" when they were away from home, at market. Farmers used to go to Exeter from many miles around to consult a witch whenever they had misfortune, and it was commonly reported that they could get the same sort of advice in the city.

At many farmhouses, Bibles were kept in the dairies to prevent witches from retarding the butter-making operations. "I'm 'witched'" or "I must have been 'witched,'" were expressions often heard in Devon. Generally speaking, it was animals that were supposed to sustain the most harm from being "overlooked." Cattle deaths were attributed to the power of evil spirits; and according to many superstitious people, witches had a peculiar power over pigs. A man who believed his pigs had been bewitched was told to take the heart of a pig, stick it full of pins and needles, and roast it over a fire. He did so, believing it would check the mortality among his swine.

For an account of late nineteenth and early twentieth century traditions of witchcraft in Devonshire, see the chapter "White

Witches" in *Devonshire Characters and Strange Events,* by S. Baring-Gould (1908).

Sources:

Baring-Gould, S. *Devonshire Characters and Strange Events.* Rev. ed., London: John Lane, 1926.

Di Liscia, Julio C(esar) (1912–)

Industrialist and parapsychologist. He was born January 10, 1912, at Santa Rosa, Argentina. He became a member of the Argentine Institute of Parapsychology (AIP) founded in 1952, but resigned from the Institute with other members who believed that it lacked scientific interest. He led in the formation of a new organization, the Association of Friends of Parapsychology, which initiated the journal *Revista Argentina de Parapsicologia.* As a result, the AIP was reorganized and Di Liscia was appointed secretary. He frequently lectured on parapsychology at the institute and conducted research on precognition.

Diadochus

According to Marbodaeus (1035–1123), this gem resembled the **beryl** in its properties and was most valuable in **divination.** It served for the invocation of spirits, and oracular responses could be discovered in it. **Albertus Magnus** called it "diacodos," and it is possibly to this stone that Braithwaite alludes in *English Gentleman:* "For as the precious stone Diacletes, though it have many rare and excellent sovereignties in it, yet loseth them all if put in a dead man's mouth."

Leonardus's remarks about the "Diacodas" or "Diacodus" are too curious to omit: "It disturbs devils beyond all other stones, for, if it be thrown in water, with the words of its charm sung, it shows various images of devils, and gives answer to those that question it. Being held in the mouth, a man may call any devil out of hell, and receive satisfaction to such questions as he may ask."

Diakka

A term used by **Andrew Jackson Davis** to signify wicked, ignorant, or undeveloped spirits. Davis believed that at death no sudden or violent change takes place in the character and disposition of an individual. Those who were mischievous, unprincipled, or lascivious during their lives remained so, for a time at least, after they died. The American Spiritualist **Hudson Tuttle** stated, "As the spirit enters the spirit world just as it leaves this, there must be an innumerable host of low, undeveloped, uneducated, or in other words, evil spirits." Davis believed there was a special sphere or plane for these *diakka* where they were put on probation. He said they were responsible for the **fraud** and trickery often witnessed at séances; they not only deceived the sitters, but the **medium** as well. Davis believed the way to avoid their influence is to live a pure, refined, and religious life, for these evil spirits are naturally attracted to those whose minds most resemble their own.

Sources:

Davis, Andrew Jackson. *The Diakka and Their Earthly Victims.* New York, 1873.

———. *The Harmonial Philosophy: A Compendium and Digest of the Works of Andrew Jackson Davis.* London: Rider, 1917.

Diamond

This gem was believed to possess the most marvelous virtues. It gave victory to whomever carried it on his left arm, whatever the number of his enemies. Panics, pestilences, enchantments were all said to fly before it; hence, it was good for sleepwalkers and for the insane. It deprived the lodestone of its virtue, and one variety, the Arabian diamond, was said to attract iron more powerfully than a magnet.

The diamond is the hardest substance known, a property referring to its resistance to being scratched, rather than its resistance to other forces, such as the strike of a hammer. Ancient peoples believed that neither fire nor blows would overcome its hardness, unless the diamond was macerated with fresh goat's blood. Cyprian, Austin, Isidore, and other church fathers, adopting this notion, used it to illustrate the method by which the blood of the Cross softens the heart of man.

If bound to a magnet, the diamond, according to the belief of the ancients, would deprive it of its magnetic property.

Diancecht

A **Danaan** magician of Irish medieval legend. He restored to Nuada of the Silver Hand his lost limb and thus his throne.

Dianetics

A system of mental health therapeutics devised in the 1940s by writer **L. Ron Hubbard.** Announced in 1950, for several years dianetics survived as an independent practice. However, it was soon taken up into the much broader program of the Church of **Scientology,** founded in 1954, which embodies the more comprehensive spiritual philosophy developed by Hubbard.

Diaphane

The kabalistic term for the imagination. (See also **Kabala**)

Dickens, Charles (1812–1870)

The great novelist Charles Dickens had a keen interest in the supernatural, although he was skeptical of **Spiritualism,** and wrote several thrilling ghost stories, notably *To Be Taken with a Grain of Salt* and *The Signalman.*

His novel *The Mystery of Edwin Drood* was interrupted in its monthly publication by the death of Dickens on July 8, 1870. Shortly thereafter, T. P. James, an uneducated American mechanic of Brattleboro, Vermont, obtained messages in **automatic writing** that he claimed emanated from the author.

Between Christmas 1872 and July 1873, scripts came from under his hand that continued Dickens's unfinished novel. The posthumous section was longer than the first and presented a surprising continuity of the manner of thought, style, and peculiarities of Dickens's writing. The two sections were published together in 1874 as *The Mystery of Edwin Drood,* with Charles Dickens given as the author.

Spiritualists the world over hailed the book as a most convincing proof of spirit return. However, psychologist **Theodore Flournoy,** in *Spiritism and Psychology* (1911), undertook to demonstrate that Dickens himself had nothing to do with the affair and that everything was easily explained by processes of latent incubation and subconscious imagination in the medium himself. He quoted the conclusions of Mme. K. Fairbanks, a distinguished member of the Geneva University, who observed that "there are certainly very successful passages such as the scenes between the two women, Billickin and Twinkleton. But there are others which are just the contrary."

Furthermore, John Forster, author of *The Life of Charles Dickens* (1911), discovered among the papers of the deceased author a whole scene in *Edwin Drood,* written in advance and destined to figure later in the novel. Flournoy found it incredible that the "spirit" of the author, who remembered so clearly the part of the volume already published that no more than three new persons are introduced in any part of the second section, should have completely forgotten the chapter written and left in manuscript.

Forster averred that as a striking proof of identity Dickens would have made an allusion to it from the spirit world. In the book itself and in the cover blurb, T. P. James does not pretend that he has not read Dickens and his last novel. "Now it is evident," stated Flournoy, "that if he had not read Dickens he would most probably have boasted of his accomplishment, because that would have rendered his performance much more extraordinary. Let us not forget," he finally remarked, "that the medium had two and a half years to imbibe the original work of the author, and in letting this 'simmer'—without counting the six months afterwards employed in automatic writing—three years in all were completed. We must confess that this greatly reduces its marvelous character."

Even **Sir Arthur Conan Doyle,** in his book *The Edge of the Unknown* (1930), concludes that "the actual inspiration of Dickens is far from being absolutely established. . . . It reads like Dickens gone flat." In the same book he record some personally obtained automatic contributions to the solution of the mystery of Edwin Drood.

Dickens had a special interest in **mesmerism** or **animal magnetism,** through his friendship with **John Elliotson.** In 1838 Dickens witnessed a demonstration by Elliotson of the "mighty curative powers of animal magnetism." During his tour in Italy in 1844, Dickens became acquainted with the family of Emile de la Rue, a Swiss banker residing in Genoa. Dickens actually practiced mesmerism on Madame de la Rue as a treatment for her neurasthenic disorders, even experimenting with treatment at a distance. On one such occasion, while he was concentrating on sending this force over a distance, his wife, Catherine, seated nearby, fell into a "mesmeric trance," her senses numbed and her extremities cold. When Dickens awakened her, she said she had been "magnetized."

Dickens's interest of in such occult subjects was often masked by his popular writings in a jocular vein. In 1848 he practiced mesmerism on the artist John Leech, who had suffered from a severe fall. Afterward, Dickens wrote to John Forster with the jocular comment, "What do you think of my setting up in the magnetic line with a large brass plate? 'Terms twenty-five guineas per nap.'"

Sources:

Fairbanks, K. "Le Cas Spirite de Dickens." *Arch. de Psychol.* T.I. (June 1892).

Jacobson, Wendy S. *The Companion to "The Mystery of Edwin Drood."* London: Allen & Unwin, 1986.

Kaplan, Fred. *Dickens and Mesmerism: The Hidden Springs of Fiction.* Princeton, N.J.: Princeton University Press, 1975.

Dicker, The

A group adhering to the teachings of **G. I. Gurdjieff** and **P. D. Ouspensky.** Based in Britain, the organization was founded by Beryl Pogson, who had been pupil and secretary to the Jungian psychologist **Maurice Nicoll** (1884–1953), who was closely involved with Gurdjieff's work and was responsible for the authoritative *Psychological Commentaries on the Teaching of G. I. Gurdjieff and P. D. Ouspensky* (5 vols., 1952–56).

The group formed a center in the village of Upper Dicker, Sussex, England, at a large house named "The Dicker," with facilities for group activities and arts and crafts. The center is associated with other study groups elsewhere in Britain. Like all the Gurdjieff centers, it is intended only for those who take a serious interest in Gurdjieff's work and are prepared to study Nicoll's *Psychological Commentaries.* Address: The Secretary, The Dicker, Upper Dicker, Hailsham, Sussex GN27 3QH, England.

Dickhoff, Robert Ernest

Tibetan Buddhist and author of several books with Buddhist reflections on **UFOs** and the **hollow earth** theory. Dickhoff was an early champion of the idea that UFOs were hostile, a view that has gained ascendancy in UFO circles in the 1990s. He believed them to be winged *garudas,* a birdlike demon of Buddhist mythology. His book *Agharta* (1951) is a romance of subterranean races. Dickhoff founded the American Buddhist Society and fellowship in 1947 and headed the small organization for many years.

Sources:

Dickhoff, Robert Ernest. *Behold . . . the Venus Garuda.* New York: The Author, 1968.

———. *The Eternal Fountain.* Boston: Bruce Humphries, 1947.

Dickinson, Edmund (1624–1707)

Physician to King Charles II, a seeker of the hermetic knowledge, and professed **Rosicrucian,** who published a text on **alchemy** entitled *Epistola ad T. Mundanum de Quintessentia Philosophorum,* which was printed at Oxford in 1686, and a second time in 1705. A third edition was printed in Germany in 1721.

In correspondence with Theodore Mundanus, a French **adept,** Dickinson explained that the Brothers of the Rosy Cross had access to the universal medicine, the **elixir of life,** but that by the time they discovered it, they had ceased to desire it and declined to avail themselves of the promise of life for centuries.

He added that the adepts were obliged to conceal themselves for the sake of safety, because if their gifts seemed more than human they would become abhorrent to the average man. Thus, there were excellent reasons for their conduct; they proceeded with caution instead of making a display of their powers. They lived simply as mere spectators in the world and desired to make no disciples, converts, or confidants. They submitted to the obligations of life and enjoyed the fellowship of none, admired none, followed none but themselves. They obeyed all codes, were excellent citizens, and only preserved silence in regard to their own private beliefs, Dickinson said, giving the world the benefit of their knowledge up to a certain point.

It is believed by some that after laboring many years Dickinson finally succeeded in alchemical transmutations and that the king had a private laboratory where he took pleasure in watching Dickinson at work.

Didier Brothers, Alexis & Adolph (mid-nineteenth century)

The best-known clairvoyants of the age of **animal magnetism.** In hypnotic state they apparently could read closed books, recover lost objects, play billiards blindfolded or cards face downward, and achieved feats of traveling **clairvoyance.**

For Pierre Seguier, president of France, Alexis described his room and mentioned that there was a handbell on the table. The President found the description correct, but was unsure about the bell. On arriving home he found, to his surprise, that during his absence a handbell had been placed on his table.

In 1847, at the request of Marquise de Mirville, Robert Houdin, the famous conjurer, paid two visits to the Didier brothers. He drew a book from his pocket and asked Alexis to read a line eight pages back at a certain height which he marked by sticking in a pin. When Alexis did so correctly Houdin signed a declaration: "I affirm that the above facts are scrupulously accurate."

Lord Adare attended a sitting in the company of a Col. Llewellyn on July 2, 1844. According to his notes, Alexis took from the skeptical colonel a morocco case, placed it on his stomach and said, "The object is a hard substance, not white, enclosed in something more white than itself; it is a bone from a greater body; a human bone; yours. It has been separated and cut so as to leave a flat side." Alexis opened the case, took out a piece of bone wrapped in silver paper and said, "The ball struck here; it was an extraordinary ball in effect; you received three separate injuries at the same moment; the bone was broken in three pieces; you were wounded early in the day whilst engaged in charging the enemy." He also described the dress of the soldiers and was right in all respects.

Alexis Didier was always accompanied by his hypnotist Marcillet. He never claimed assistance from spirits. His views are outlined in *Le Sommeil Magnétique expliqué par le somnambule Alexis en état de lucidité* (1856). His brother Adolph wrote *Animal Magne-*

tism and Somnambulism (1856); *Mesmerism and Its Healing Power* (1875); and *Clairvoyance* (1876).

A long series of experiments conducted by Dr. Edwin Lee in 1849 at Brighton and Hastings is recorded in Lee's *Animal Magnetism* (1866). H. G. Atkinson also subjected the Didier brothers' gift to careful scrutiny. E. W. Cox noted:

"A party of experts was planned to test M. Alexis. We prepared a packet containing a single word of twelve letters and enclosed it in six envelopes of thick brown paper, each of which we carefully sealed. Handing him this packet he placed it, not before his eyes which were bound with handkerchiefs and wool, but upon his forehead, and in three minutes and a half he wrote the contents correctly, imitating the very handwriting. The word was by arrangement placed in the first envelope by a friend in a distant town, who was not informed of the object and who did not inform us what the word was; and none of us knew until the envelopes were opened and the word found to be that which the Somnambule had written."

Frank Podmore reflects on Alexis's work in *The Newer Spiritualism* (1910): "Many of these feats are so precisely recorded and so well authenticated that it is difficult to doubt their genuineness. They stand on the same evidential level as many of the similar incidents recorded in the *Proceedings* of the S.P.R." He observed that Alexis was in an abnormal state of consciousness during his performances, a conclusion he reached from reference to the fact that as a rule, he did not speak the answers but preferred to write them. From this he concluded that Alexis was an **automatic writer** and that his feats of clairvoyance were genuine and that they involved no conscious deception on his part.

Sources:

Cox, E. W. *What Am I? A Popular Introduction to Mental Physiology and Psychology.* N.p., 1874.

Didot Perceval

So named because the only manuscript of this legend discovered belonged to A. F. Didot, the famous collector. This version of the legend of the **Holy Grail** greatly emphasizes the illness of the Fisher King. It tells how **King Arthur**'s Round Table was constructed and relates the adventures of Sir Perceval, which are much the same as those told in the *Conte del Graal.* Included is the Good Friday incident in which Perceval and Brons are instructed in the mystical expressions that Christ was said to have whispered to Joseph of Arimathea on the cross.

Sources:

Lacy, Norris J., ed. *The Arthurian Encyclopedia.* New York: Garland Publishing, 1986.

Roach, William, ed. *The Didot Perceval.* Philadelphia: University of Pennsylvania Press, 1941.

Diepenbrock, Melchior von

Author of two treatises on *chirothesy* or laying on of hands by the Roman Catholic popes. (See also **Healing by Touch**)

Dimensione Psi

Quarterly journal of Associazione Italiana Studi del Paranormale. Includes scientific papers on psi phenomena and psychical research. Address: Via Puggia 47, 16131 Genova, Italy.

Dingle, Edwin John (1881–1972)

Founder of the Institute of Mentalphysics. He was born April 6, 1881, in Cornwall, England. He became a journalist, and in 1900 he moved to Singapore to cover affairs in the Orient. There he met a teacher from whom he learned meditation and yoga. In 1910 Dingle went to Tibet, where he studied for nine months and reportedly learned *pranayama* (breathing control), the remembrance of past lives, and other advanced spiritual disciplines. He returned to England to write books on his experiences and published the important *Dingle's New Atlas and Commercial Gazetteer of China* (1914), which was a standard reference for many years.

In 1921 Dingle settled in Oakland, California. He began his career as a teacher after being asked to lead an informal class on what he had learned from his teachers in Singapore and Tibet. He taught informally for more than a decade before incorporating the Institute of Mentalphysics in 1934. Dingle taught his students out of his belief that the Tibetans had preserved the ancient wisdom of the Aryans, the founders of the Indian, Mediterranean, and Anglo-Saxon cultures. He taught them the disciplines he had learned and advised a vegetarian diet.

Dingle developed a center in Los Angeles, the International Church of the Holy Trinity, where he not only taught classes but sent out a correspondence course to students across North America. He was generally known by his students as Ding Le Mei, his religious name. In 1941 he founded a retreat center in Yucca Valley, California, now the headquarters of the institute. Following his death on January 27, 1972, he was succeeded by Donald L. Waldrop.

Sources:

Dingle, Edwin John. *Borderlands of Eternity.* Los Angeles: Institute of Mentalphysics, 1939.

———. *Breathing Your Way to Youth.* Los Angeles: Institute of Mentalphysics, n.d.

———. *The Voice of the Logos.* Los Angeles: Econolith Press, 1951.

Dingwall, E(ric) J(ohn) (1890–1986)

Anthropologist, author, and one of the most experienced psychical investigators of modern times. Born in Ceylon (now Sri Lanka), he was educated at Pembroke College, Cambridge University, England (M.A., 1912), and the University of London (D.Sc., Ph.D.). He joined the staff of the Cambridge University Library. The son of a Scot living in Ceylon in 1890, he was reticent about his personal affairs, and did not publicize his exact birth date. He appears to have had some private wealth in his earlier years, since he was able to travel and follow his intellectual interests.

As a young man, Dingwall became interested in psychical phenomena and in 1921 was named the director of the department of Psychical Phenomena for the **American Society for Psychical Research.** The following year he became the research officer for the **Society for Psychical Research,** London, where he served for five years. While there he wrote his first books on psychical research, including (edited with Harry Price) *Revelations of a Spirit Medium* (1922) and *How to Go to a Medium* (1927).

Through the 1920s and 1930s Dingwall traveled widely through Europe and to the United States to investigate mediums, among whom were such famous ones as "**Eva C.,**" **Rudi and Willi Schneider, Stephan Ossowiecki,** and "Margery" (**Mina Crandon**). He also researched social and religious conditions relating to abnormal mental phenomena in Spain in 1935, and in the West Indies in 1936. These provided additional material for his articles and one additional book, *Ghosts and Spirits in the Ancient World* (1930).

Besides his work as a psychical investigator, Dingwall continued his academic interest in anthropology, making himself knowledgeable on some of the more bizarre aspects of the human personality. His publications in these areas include *Studies in the Sexual Life of Ancient and Medieval Peoples* (1925), *The Girdle of Chastity* (1931), *Artificial Cranial Deformation* (1931), and, with H. H. Ploss and other colleagues, *Woman: An Historical, Gynecological and Anthropological Compendium* (1935).

During World War II he worked at the Ministry of Information and British Foreign Office (1941–45), and resumed his writing after the war. Dingwall's numerous titles include *Racial Pride and Prejudice* (1946); *Some Human Oddities* (1947); *Very Peculiar People* (1950); with K. M. Goldney and T. H. Hall, *The Haunting of Borley Rectory* (1956); with J. Langdon-Davies, *The Unknown: Is It Nearer?;*

The American Woman (1956); and, with T. H. Hall, *Four Modern Ghosts* (1958).

During the 1960s Dingwall coedited the four-volume set *Abnormal Hypnotic Phenomena* (1967–68). He died at St. Leonards-on-Sea, East Sussex, England, on August 7, 1986. As one of Britain's oldest psychical researchers, he was widely respected for his careful reports and judgment in the field of the paranormal during some sixty years' investigation of some of the most famous and controversial mediums of the twentieth century. Although tending to skepticism, he did not hesitate to affirm the possibility of the genuineness of psychical phenomena and was scathing about the limitations of fellow researchers. As a body, he claimed, "they are hardly distinguished by the accuracy of their observations, the correctness of their records or the scrupulous care required in the conduct of their experiments."

He also cautioned against prima facie belief in **fraud,** even though claimed phenomena might seem suspect. In his article "The Hypothesis of Fraud," published in the *Proceedings* of the Society for Psychical Research (SPR), he comments on the controversial phenomena of the famous medium "Eva C." that "it may be thought that the case against the phenomena is so strong that the subject may be at once dismissed. Such a standpoint would in my opinion be entirely mistaken and would show clearly that its supporter had not the smallest appreciation of the difficulties . . . ."

At other times, he testified to observing such controversial phenomena as the production of **ectoplasm** by mediums. However, according to **Sir Arthur Conan Doyle,** he was always reluctant to make public admission of the genuineness of phenomena that he had endorsed in private.

In a tribute by parapsychologist **Guy Lyon Playfair** (*Journal* of the Society for Psychical Research, vol. 54, no. 807), Dingwall is quoted as stating (in a letter to Playfair in 1976), "We know practically nothing about the 'real' nature of the material world in which we live. We knew less 500 years ago. 500 years hence we may know a little more, but the more we peer into our surroundings the most indefinite becomes the boundary. The investigation of the relationship between matter and what you call spirit is only just beginning. Hardly any progress at all has been made since Myers laid down the guide rules in 1903. Indeed, things seem to be more mysterious now than they were then. So I think that the best position is not to hurry. The scrap heap of science is high with discarded theories derived from insufficient experimentation."

Sources:

Berger, Arthur S., and Joyce Berger. *The Encyclopedia of Parapsychology and Psychical Research.* New York: Paragon House, 1991.

Dingwall, Eric J. *Ghosts and Spirits of the Ancient World.* London: Kegan, Paul, 1930.

Direct Drawing and Painting

A development of **automatic drawing and painting** in which the hand of the automatist is not made use of, and sometimes even drawing and painting materials are dispensed with, the sketch being precipitated in the darkness in a time that is usually too short for normal execution. It is a fairly well known mediumistic phenomenon but also one that is always open to suspicion of **fraud** as the transcendental pictures are often found to be feeble copies of existing works of art and since practitioners of direct drawing and painting have often been caught in deception.

Mary Marshall's direct pencil portrait of Goethe was a close copy of an engraving in *The Life of Goethe;* many illustrations of **David Duguid**'s *Hafed* were identical with pictures in Cassell's *Family Bible;* and still-life paintings of **Mrs. E. J. French,** of New York, were similarly wanting in originality.

Taken to task, the **controls** of Duguid defended themselves by saying that they often took impressions from the medium's subconscious. His defense drew support from the hypothesis that the mind of the sitter may also contribute the subject. On occasion, for example, visitors to Duguid recognized, in the direct paintings, scenes they were acquainted with in America and Australia, which the medium could not have seen. An art dealer found a direct painting strangely familiar and later discovered its facsimile among some pictures he had bought. Frank Miller writes in the *Journal* of the American Society for Psychical Research of a well-known artist who could paint scenes he never saw but that *she* remembered having seen.

Duguid specialized in miniature paintings in oil. They were done under the alleged control of the spirits of Dutch painters Jakob Ruysdael and Jan Steen. The size of the pictures was sometimes as small as a sixpence and the execution, done in the dark, was always very fine. While the medium was tied to his chair, or held by the hands, the noise of the brushes was heard above the table and sometimes half a minute later the brushes or pencils and the picture fell down. Occasionally the drawings were obtained in a few seconds in sealed envelopes on folded sheets of paper.

Mrs. E. J. French excelled in still life paintings done under a small table that was surrounded by a shawl. For eight to fifteen minutes furious scraping and rubbing was heard, then a signal, then the brushes and pencils dropped out and, fresh with paint, a brightly colored picture was produced from under the table.

Samuel Guppy, in his anonymously published *Mary Jane, or Spiritualism Chemically Examined* (1863), describes drawings of varicolored flowers obtained, often without any drawing or painting material, in the presence of his first wife. Specially bought and marked paper was placed in a box that was itself carefully wrapped in paper and sealed to remove any chance of deception. Yet the picture appeared occasionally in as many as seven colors, covered with a varnish of unknown origin.

In one instance the effect appeared to have been produced at a distance. In a letter to the **London Dialectical Society,** Countess Panigai described a visit to **D. D. Home** during which she was promised a distinct sign from her deceased child the following day. The promise was well kept. At her home, which the medium never visited, she heard raps, apparently coming from a drawer where, unknown to all, the last pair of boots her child wore was hidden in a box. "Unlocking the drawer and the box, on the elastic of one boot was imprinted a perfect star, and in the centre of the star an eye," the countess recalled. The substance with which it is drawn is black. It has since faded slightly, but remains still thoroughly distinct. So mathematically perfect is the drawing that great skill and precision is necessary for an accurate copy to be taken." Letters at each point of the star formed the name of the child, "Stella."

The most unusual demonstrations in direct art were given by the **Bangs sisters** of Chicago. On paper-mounted canvases held against the light near the windows, they produced spirit portraits in plain sight of the sitter, who was usually advised to keep about his person a photograph of the departed friend whose spirit picture he desired to obtain. Admiral Usborne Moore often witnessed the phenomenon and describes it in *Glimpses of the Next State* (1911):

"We had to wait some time. After a few minutes the canvas assumed various hues, rosy, blue and brown; it would become dark and light independently of the sun being clouded or not.

"Dim outlines of faces occasionally appeared in different parts of the canvas. . . . We had been sitting forty minutes when the right and left edges of the canvas began to darken, and the face and bust suddenly appeared. It was finished in thirty-five minutes—i.e., one hour and fifteen minutes from the time we first sat down. On separating the two canvases it was found that the picture was on the further side of the one nearest to me, and the material was quite damp; the other canvas, which had been pressing against it all the time, was unsoiled. The stuff comes off on the finger, a smutty, oily substance. . . .

"The actual picture therefore, took thirty-five minutes to precipitate. It is richer in tone now than it was when put on a sofa after the sitting, but in other respects just the same. The likeness to the *cartes-de visiti* in my dollarpocke is not remarkable, but there are points about it which show that the invisible workers had access to these photographs."

Reported pictorial appearances of the Virgin Mary in churches and other places of worship have caused some to hypothesize that the phenomena under this heading also occur in a spontaneous manner. It was reported in the *London Press* in the summer of 1923 that, on the plaster wall in Christchurch Cathedral, Oxford—under the Burne Jones window that Dean Liddell had caused to be placed there as a memorial of a dearly loved daughter and close to three tablets erected to the memory of the dean and his family—there had gradually emerged, over a period of two years, a remarkable likeness to the late dean, whose life and work were so closely associated with Christchurch.

Relating the Liddell portrait to the phenomenon of **psychic photography. Frederick Bligh Bond** argues in the October 1923 issue of *Psychic Science* that ". . . instead of a photographic plate and the chemical changes in salts of silver, there is in the smooth white plaster wall and the mineral salts contained in the plaster, a combination susceptible to slow chemical change; and instead of the presence of a physical medium required in psychic photography, there is the physical atmosphere of a building constantly dedicated to prayer and aspiration, full of spiritual and psychical emanations of countless worshippers tending to provide the conditions necessary for the accomplishment of a process in which the alchemy of thought may succeed in affecting the grosser particles of matter."

This portrait of Dean Liddell remained unaffected by the passing of years. Barbara McKenzie, wife of **James Hewat McKenzie,** writes in *Psychic Science,* October 1931, that "the Dean's face is beautifully clear and there certainly seems an emergence of other outlines close by which bear a resemblance to two human heads." One of these was noticed to be forming in 1923; the other is more recent.

Similar appearances have been noticed in other parts of the building. Mrs. McKenzie was shown a gray marble pedestal base. About a foot from the floor a white patch appears on the marble, containing a very clear face of an elderly man with bushy hair and full whiskers and beard. An even clearer face was to be seen on a wall behind the organ and within twenty yards of the choir stall. It was popularly associated with a chorister who for many years sang in the cathedral.

The evidence for the genuineness of direct drawing and painting is far from satisfactory. Both Duguid and the Bangs sisters were exposed in mediumistic frauds, and the amateur conjurer **David P. Abbott** successfully duplicated the sisters' direct painting phenomena by trickery.

Direct Voice

Theoretically, an isolated paranormal voice in space without visible source of agency. In classical Spiritualist séances, the voice issued primarily from a **trumpet** that sailed about the séance room in the dark and appeared to serve as a condenser. At other times mediums dispensed with the trumpet, and the voice could be heard from the center of the floor or from any part of the room.

H. Dennis Bradley records an experience in which the communicator began his sentence in the middle of the room; halfway up he dropped the trumpet while his voice traveled upward to the extreme right-hand corner of the ceiling and there ended on the pronouncement of the last syllable of his last word (*Towards the Stars,* 1924, p. 20).

Physically the phenomenon requires the supposition that some material more solid than air is withdrawn from the medium's or from the sitter's body to produce the necessary vibrations in the surrounding atmosphere. Séance room communications speak of improvisation of a larynx—a strange notion, yet the improvisation of human limbs and entire bodies is even stranger.

The first vague description of a "voice box" is to be found in an **out-of-the-body** experience of **Stainton Moses,** who stated, "I did not observe how the sound was made, but I saw in a distant part of the room near the ceiling something like a box round which blue electric light played, and I associate the sound with that."

The "voice box" of "Walter," the **control** of Margery (i.e., **Mina Crandon**) has been photographed as a white mass on the medium's shoulder, connected to her left ear and nostril with tubes of the mysterious substance **ectoplasm.** This psychic microphone seems to be very closely associated with the medium's organism. "John Watt," the control of **Mrs. Thomas Everitt,** claimed that he used the medium's breath in speaking. If Everitt held her hand over her mouth the volume of the voice diminished, and it ceased entirely if Everitt placed her palm on her mouth. The spirit of **Cecil Husk** warned Dennis Bradley not to smoke excessively on the days he was sitting in séances, since smoking sometimes affected the vocal organs from which part of the ectoplasmic force was taken.

Thomas Colley described an instance in which **Frank W. Monck** was wakened from a trance to greet a materialized fellow student. He and the spirit had to speak in turn; there was an impasse if they tried to speak at once. **Harry Bastian**'s direct voice was heard when his mouth was full of water, but it immediately ceased if his nose was temporarily stopped. Everitt could never speak simultaneously with the spirits. Her lips and tongue moved but no sound was made. Other mediums felt no handicap.

Multiple Spirit Voices

Signor Damiani, in his testimony before the **London Dialectical Society** in 1870, spoke of a séance with **D. D. Home** in which two voices were heard besides that of the persistently speaking medium.

David Duguid often spoke simultaneously. **George Valiantine** and **Etta Wriedt** had no difficulty in joining with the spirit voices. According to **Noel Jaquin,** the problem consisted not so much in the use of the physical voice, but in the coordination of thought. He experienced an incoherence in thinking while the direct voice was heard and could only master through strong mental effort.

Independent conversation by two or three voices was occasionally carried on in the Wriedt séances. **J. A. Findlay** reported the same with the medium **John C. Sloan.** Admiral Usborne Moore was told that the spirits seemed to speak with his voice. During that time he often experienced a slight cough and irritation of the throat. Others observed that the sitters' voices weakened after a prolonged direct voice conversation. An interesting experiment was tried with Wriedt. She was asked to sit with seven deaf mutes from Flint, Michigan. No one in the room could utter an articulate word except for herself. No voices were heard.

Dr. Eugene Crowell writes of séances with a Mrs. Andrews in *The Identity of Primitive Christianity and Modern Spiritualism* (1875–79): "One of the common forms of manifestations at Moravia is singing by spirits. This generally occurs when the persons assembled sing with animation, the spirits seizing the moment when they are 'with one accord' raising their voices, to join in the strain, and generally the spirit voice is heard clearly above all others." He continued later: "When our spirit friends had conversed more freely than usual, the medium afterwards complained of much soreness and tenderness of the throat and lungs, evidently without any definite idea of its cause. It seemed to me that the spirits . . . were compelled to draw directly from the vocal and pulmonary organs of the medium those elements that are liberally supplied by public circles, and which are necessary for the production of spirit voices."

Findlay's *On the Edge of the Etheric* (1931) states that the communicators often make use of a psychic tube from the mouth of the medium to the trumpet. This might explain why the independent voice resembled that of the medium and also why moisture was sometimes found within the trumpet it but is consistent with the medium's speaking directly into the trumpet. Findlay's spirit communicators also offered a description of how the artificial larynx is made. It read:

"From the medium and those present a chemist in the spirit world withdraws certain ingredients which for want of a better name is called ectoplasm. To this the chemist adds ingredients of his own making. When they are mixed together a substance is formed which enables the chemist to materialize his hands. He then, with his materialized hands, constructs a mask resembling the mouth and tongue. The spirit wishing to speak places his face into this mask and finds it clings to him, it gathers round his mouth, tongue and throat. At first, difficulty is experienced in moving this heavier material, but by practice this becomes easy. The etheric organs have once again become clothed in matter resembling physical matter, and by the passage of air through them your atmosphere can be vibrated and you hear his voice."

Findlay's explanation received confirmation two years later at a séance recorded by the Rev. V. G. Duncan in his book *Proof: An Account of Spiritualistic Séances* (1933). The mediums in this instance were the Misses Moore. When asked how it was possible to speak to us on earth the communicator stated,

"I can only explain it like this. You know when you have been to the dentist for an extraction and been given an anaesthetic, he puts that queer mask over your face for you to breath the gas into your lungs. I have to use a contrivance like that in order to speak to you. This contrivance is composed of etheric matter, partly provided by the mediums and sitters, and partly supplied from our side. It is a kind of transformer, and it has a double purpose. It helps to retard my vibrations and so allows me to make my voice audible to you and provides a temporary set of vocal organs."

Findlay's views are further enlarged upon in his second book, *The Rock of Truth* (1933).

The Nature of Direct Voice

The process of direct voice speaking appears to be similar to ordinary speech. After a long sentence the controls would pause for breath, and the indrawing sound became distinctly audible. However, the phenomena differed from medium to medium, and the vocal effects varied from one to the other. The invisible communicator could laugh, whistle, or sing. "Walter," the control of Mina Crandon ("Margery"), could give expression to all sorts of moods—surprise, contentment, joy, anger, and melancholy—by whistling. Once Margery and "Walter" reportedly laughed at the same instant. The two chuckles came from a common point in space and gave the impression of being tangled together, as though conceivably from a common physical organism.

The language spoken may be unknown both to the medium and to the sitters. Yet the nationality of the medium may have a curious influence. English, for instance, is easier spoken when the medium is English than of another tongue. As an explanation it has been suggested that the material to build up the artificial larynx may be drawn from the oral cavity and therefore may be less adaptable to unusual inflections. The experience of Abraham Wallace with the spirit entity **"John King,"** who unexpectedly spoke to him in broad Scotch, suggested to some a participation on the part of the sitter. When interrogated on the subject, King replied, "Why, I got it from you."

The bewildering variety of strange languages spoken through some mediums remain mysteries, though secret knowledge by the medium or collusion with sitters has been hypothesized as a likely explanation. In the séances of **George Valiantine** (repeatedly caught in fraud), Portuguese, Basque, Welsh, Japanese, Russian, Hindustani, and "ancient pure" Chinese was supposedly spoken. Neville Whymant, a famous orientalist, studied this linguistic phenomenon, and on March 25, 1927, it was recorded on a gramophone in Lord Charles Hope's apartment in London after a special telephone cable was laid to the Columbia Gramophone Company's recording house. A megaphone was connected to the recording machine and two assistants stationed outside the séance room gave the signals at various times. In the presence of Lord Hope and H. Dennis Bradley and his wife, three voices spoke in English, one in an Indian dialect, one in Hindustani, one in Italian, and two in Chinese. Whymant said the latter, which claimed to be the voice of Confucius, was apparently the same one he heard in New York.

Was Confucius actually present? When the question was asked in the Crandon circle in Boston, **"Walter"** explained the matter this way: "When K'ung-fu-T'zu manifests in our séance room he is not necessarily personally present. However, at the time of Whymant's interview with K'ung-fu-T'zu through Valiantine in trance, the Master was actually present in person."

Further suggestions relating to the problem are found in Mrs. E. Duffey's book *Heaven Revised* (1889). In answer to her doubts as to the presence of illustrious spirits a vision was given to her, of which she writes: "I beheld, or seemed to behold—for it was not sight, it was a perception as strong as the sense of seeing—a succession of links extending from sphere to sphere and from spirit and spirit, until it had finally found utterance on earth."

Colley heard direct voices in the darkness of the night when sleeping in the same room with Monck, while holding his hand over the mouth of his sleeping companion. During an operation on **Eileen Garrett** in 1931, while she was unconscious and gagged, the doctors in attendance heard voices in her proximity. One voice spoke in a tongue that none of the doctors understood. According to Reid Clanny's account of the strange case of **Mary Jobson,** individuals connected with the Jobsons were sometimes accosted in their own homes by a voice that spoke in the presence of the girl and they were told to go and see her.

In the first attempts at communication or when the spiritual power was insufficient, the direct voice was feeble or hoarse, writers said. With an increase of power or practice it became characteristic in tone and distinctive in enunciation. It had a conspicuous selective intelligence, tending to address itself to the right person in the right language.

As soon as the power began to ebb, the trumpet was used increasingly. This waning of power is curiously described in Mrs. G. K. Hack's notes of the July 8, 1928, séance in **Millesimo Castle:** "The power suddenly failed and consequently the pronunciation of the words he used became confused and the sounds almost inarticulate, until at last they became a sort of prolonged whistle which gradually extinguished itself and formed itself into a mournful sigh."

The general strength of the voice varied individually. **Sir Arthur Conan Doyle** heard a voice in Chicago that he could only compare to the roar of a lion. Duguid's voices were usually husky. But on one occasion his speaking was so loud and harsh that the sitters became alarmed and asked the spirit to retire. Similarly, in Mrs. Robert Johnson's séances, remonstrations had to be made because of the volume of the voice.

In **Elizabeth Blake**'s case the voices were occasionally heard at a distance of one hundred feet. "Kokum" and "Hawk Chief" (Valiantine) had tremendous, resounding voices. H. Dennis Bradley recorded that their voices were heard by his wife in a bedroom on the upper floor thirty to forty yards away with all the doors closed. "Kokum's" voice carried to a distance of two hundred yards. Mediums such as Blake, Valiantine, Wriedt, Hazel Ridley, and Mrs. Murphy Lydy often produced the phenomenon in full light. The usual demonstration was to shut the light out of the trumpet with the palm of the medium and hold the small end to the sitter's ear. Mrs. Lydy gave several successful platform demonstrations in this manner in May 1931, in London.

J. B. McIndoe of Glasgow constructed a telephonic apparatus for the hearing of the voice in daylight. A sensitive telephone transmitter was placed under a tightly buttoned, high, black oilskin coat, on the larynx of the medium Andrew McCreadie. The sitters were connected with a telephone receiver through which they could hear voices in daylight. The result was the same if a trumpet was placed with the small end under the oilskin coat on the medium's larynx. Through the large end, if one closely listened, voices came through.

Many and varied experiments were conducted to attempt to prove the reality of the phenomenon. Ventriloquism on the medium's part was the first natural explanation. This was, however, rejected by researchers **James H. Hyslop** and **Hereward**

Carrington in their respective experiments and was also discounted by **J. Malcolm Bird** as part of his séances with "Margery."

According to Carrington, at a near range it is impossible for a ventriloquist to produce the illusion of distant sounds or voices; he must then depend upon near ventriloquism, and the nearer the listener's ear to the mouth of the performer the less perfect the illusion, until at quite close range the illusion vanishes altogether and the sounds are correctly located as issuing from the ventriloquist's mouth. There is no such thing as "throwing the voice" across the room, or to any distant location in space he said. The voice merely seems to issue from the spot because the performer distracts the attention of his audience to it. Deprived of light to aid the view, the illusion cannot be produced and the investigators who sit quite close to the medium can immediately locate the voice at its point of origin.

The medium was often asked to hold water in her mouth to see whether the voices were independent. With **Emily French,** of Buffalo, New York, the voices were tested by Hyslop, Dr. **Isaac Kauffmann Funk,** and others for a full week. Findlay recorded how often he had his ear at the mouth of the medium Sloan when one or more voices were speaking, yet no sound came from the mouth. In other experiments a special solution was used which, under the effect of the saliva, changed color in proportion to the time during which it was held in the mouth. If one of the sitters also took an amount into his mouth and ejected it at the same time as the medium, the color should be identical. It was by this test that Abraham Wallace claimed to have established the good faith of **Susannah Harris.**

The Voice Control Machine, designed by Mark Richardson, of Boston, for use in the "Margery" séances was a modern control apparatus. It consisted of a U-shaped tube in which small luminous floats were placed on the surface of the water. The medium blew into a flexible tube that had a specially constructed mouthpiece and caused, by the pressure of air, the second column of water to rise. This position was retained as long as the mouthpiece was tightly held by the medium's lips and tongue. The collapse of the column of water could be immediately detected in the dark by means of the luminous floats.

An even more satisfactory control was devised by psychical investigator **B. K. Thorogood.** This was a cubical box, made of layers of seven different materials, completely sound proof, closed and padlocked, containing a large, very sensitive microphone, connected by two wires emerging from the box to a distant loudspeaker. While sitters in the séance room heard nothing, the voice of "Walter" issued from the loudspeaker in the distant room, suggesting that the voice had its origin through the microphone in the box. Under such conditions the independence of the voices in the "Margery" séances seemed proved.

In direct voice communications there are two elements of the paranormal—the voice in space and the contents of the message. If it turns out that the trumpet was actually used by the medium in the dark the validity of the communication may yet be established by the other criterion. Hereward Carrington, whose book *The Physical Phenomena of Spiritualism* (1907) described many possibilities of fraud, pointed out that many investigators attended trumpet séances quite convinced that the medium did the talking. They contended that the content of the messages was the important thing.

There are many reports of voices heard in daylight with no obvious human source. In *The Blue Room* (1927), Clive Chapman describes séances with the New Zealand medium **Pearl Judd,** when direct voices were heard in a well-lighted room. Contemporary researcher **D. Scott Rogo** also reports similar cases in his book *An Experience of Phantoms* (1974). Well-researched **poltergeist** cases occasionally include voices originating in space in daylight.

Direct voice whispers in semidarkness were heard at sittings with **Gladys Osborne Leonard.** Her control "Feda" claimed to hear communicators talking in front of the medium. She conveyed their messages, which were not heard by sitters. Later confirmation came when sitters also heard the entities talking in whispered words. Robert Blatchford was convinced that his wife is spirit spoke to him in her particular manner of speech. Medium **Leslie Flint** was tested by C. Drayton Thomas in 1948 and by Robert Chapman of the *Sunday Express* newspaper and members of the Society for Psychical Research in 1971 and 1972, when use was made of throat microphones and night-sight binoculars.

Historically, the **Davenport brothers** and **Jonathan Koons** of Ohio were the first mediums through whom direct voice phenomena were reported. It was "John King" who introduced it, and it was also this control who invented the use of the trumpet in séances.

Voice mediumship is one of the most dramatic forms of supernormal manifestations. In view of the ease with which it was acquired by H. Dennis Bradley, one may understand his enthusiastic forecast in *The Wisdom of the Gods* (1925): "Communication with the spirits in their actual voices may, within this century, become as simple as the telephone or wireless. In fact, it seems to me that it is a new and phenomenal form of wireless communication." In recent times, the **electronic voice phenomenon,** popularly known as **Raudive voices** seems to have partially realized this hoped-for development. It uses a simple diode circuit and records claimed paranormal voices on a tape recorder.

Sources:

Bailey, Wilson, G. *No, Not Dead, They Live.* Camden, N.J.: I. F. Huntzinger, 1923.

Barbanell, Maurice. *The Trumpet Shall Sound.* London, Psychic Press, 1933.

Bayless, Raymond. *Voices from Beyond.* New Hyde Park, N.Y.: University Books, 1975.

Bradley, H. Dennis. *—And After.* London, 1931.

———. *Towards the Stars.* London, 1924.

Drouet, Bessie C. *Station Astral.* New York: G. P. Putnam's Sons, 1932.

Flint, Leslie. *Voices in the Dark: My Life as a Medium.* New York: Bobbs-Merrill, 1971.

Hack, Gwendolyn K. *Modern Psychic Mysteries: Millesimo Castle, Italy.* London, 1929.

Moore, W. Usborne. *The Voices.* London, 1913.

Pincock, Jenny O'Hara. *Trails of Truth.* London, 1930.

Randall, Edward E. *The Dead Have Never Died.* London, 1918.

Sewell, May W. *Neither Dead nor Sleeping.* London, 1921.

Smith, Susy. *She Spoke to the Dead.* New York: Award Books, 1972.

Thomas, C. Drayton. "A New Hypothesis Concerning Trance-Communications." *Proceedings* of the Society for Psychical Research 48 (May 1947).

Direct Writing

The claimed phenomenon in **Spiritualism** of spirit writing that is produced directly without visible physical contact with the medium and sometimes without writing material. It dispenses with mechanical contrivances such as the **planchette** and **Ouija board** and bypasses table tipping or **table turning.**

Eusapia Palladino is reported to have rubbed the end of her finger with blue chalk, asked **Charles Richet** to hold it, and, advancing to the table, drew two crosses over the tabletop in the air. The blue marks disappeared from her finger, and the crosses were found on the underside of the table. She also drew scrawls on Richet's jacket with the fingers of **F. W. H. Myers,** who was present. A blue mark was found on Richet's shirt front under the waistcoat. Then, holding Richet's clean finger as though it were a pencil, she drew a blue line on a piece of white paper in good light. A Professor Schiaparelli bought a block of new writing paper and asked Palladino to write her name. She grasped his finger and moved it over the paper as if it were a pen; the writing was found inside the block.

One of the most well known forms of direct writing was that made popular by the mediums **Henry Slade** and **William Eglinton—slate writing.** Slate writing was, of course, one of the easiest of phenomena to fake and Slade and Eglington were caught in their attempts. In any case, the proximity of the medium to the writing on the slate would throw doubt on the reality of the spirit hypothesis. The most convincing direct writing was that which was not solely dependent upon prepared materials but was produced anywhere and under any circumstances.

Thus, during a **poltergeist** disturbance in Stratford, Connecticut, in 1850 and 1851, direct writing was found on turnips that sprang apparently from nowhere. An unfinished letter left for a few moments would be found completed in a different hand, although of course during the interval it could easily have been accessible to another human.

In 1856 experiments in direct writing were carried out by the noted Spiritualist **Baron L. von Guldenstubbe.** He locked paper and pencil in a small box and carried the key around with him. At the end of 13 days he found some writing on the paper; he repeated the experiment with similar success. Later he visited galleries, churches, and other public places, leaving writing materials on the pedestals of statues, on tombs, and so on.

In this way he claimed to obtain direct writing in English, French, German, Latin, Greek, and other languages, purporting to come from Plato, Cicero, St. Paul, Juvenal, Spencer, and Mary Stuart. The baron was accompanied on these expeditions by Comte d'Ourches and other friends, and on one occasion a medium was mentioned as being present. Of course, such communications are in no way evidence of spirit agency, since under such circumstances anybody could have written messages for the baron. However, another experiment on November 24, 1856, was at the baron's own apartment. He recorded that while waiting for two other witnesses to join a séance, the furniture began to creak. Then the medium seated herself at the piano, directing the group to place an untouched packet of paper in a particular spot. The medium played for 15 minutes, then stopped. The packet of paper was opened and communications from "Cicero," "Plato," and "Spencer" were revealed. The baron's book *La Realité des Esprits et le phénomène merveilleux de leur Écriture directe* (1857) created a sensation.

The Rev. **Stainton Moses,** a medium with experience of **direct voice** phenomena, published the first study devoted entirely to direct writing, which he named "psychography." In his *Direct Spirit Writing* (1878), he discusses his own experiences and those of other individuals. It is an uncritical book, but of great interest for its discussion of the circumstances surrounding the phenomenon. Moses notes that in his own experience there were convulsive movements associated with the writing: "I was slightly convulsed, and my hands were moved under the table while the writing was going on beneath."

Moses' investigation of the direct writing of Slade is particularly valuable. Slade's hands were sometimes feverishly hot, and emitted during the writing (which was nearly always in his own hand), crackling and detonating sounds. These detonations occasionally amounted to veritable explosions and even pulverized the slate at times. The pulsations, throbs, and convulsive shudders of Slade's body were frequently communicated to those holding his hands. The claimed "exposure" of Slade by a Professor Lankester was partly based on the observation that the tendons of his wrist were in motion.

Charles E. Watkins of Cleveland, another slate-writing medium, always wrote as if in torture. He claimed he felt a sudden "drawing" from his body and was unable to articulate distinctly. As soon as the writing was finished, with a jerk he was himself again.

This invisible link between medium and direct writing may not be solely physical. Most of the direct scripts of **Mrs. Thomas Everitt** proved to be quotations from various, sometimes inaccessible books, bearing on the teachings of Swedish seer **Emanuel Swedenborg.** Because the medium belonged to the **Church of the New Jerusalem,** her subconscious mind may have had some part in the contents. There is much reason for this supposition—C. C. Massey's experience with Eglinton on April 23, 1884, suggests that even the sitter's subconscious mind may be tapped.

As quoted in John S. Farmer's *Twixt Two Worlds* (1886), the contents of a very private letter that Massey had written alone in his own room and mailed himself a week before had been rifled, and, taken out of context, passages were woven into a censorious communication. "The postscript was of a peculiarly malicious character, referring to other confidential correspondence of mine of a very delicate and personal nature," Massey complains. "I must own that this particular shot took effect and caused me no small embarrassment and annoyance." Massey at once wrote to his friend in Paris and received the assurance that nobody other than himself saw, read, or heard of the letter.

In *Experiences in Spiritualism with D. D. Home* (1869), **Lord Adare**'s father is quoted: "A sheet of paper was lying on the edge of the table next to the window, on which a pencil was placed. We presently saw the pencil moving about on the paper. Mr. Home saw the fingers holding it. Adare noticed it also more than once, but of undefined form."

Sir William Crookes recorded his first experience in direct writing with Kate Fox-Jencken: "A luminous hand came down from the upper part of the room, and after hovering near me for a few seconds, took the pencil from my hand, rapidly wrote on a sheet of paper, threw the pencil down, and then rose up over our heads, gradually fading into darkness."

Robert Dale Owen saw, in a sitting with Slade on February 9, 1874, in sufficient gas light, a white, feminine, marblelike hand, detached and shaded off at the wrist, creep up his knees, write on the notepaper placed there on a slate, then slip back with the pencil under the table. Five minutes later the performance was repeated by a smaller hand that resembled the first.

Such experiences are reminiscent of that most dramatic account in the biblical book of Daniel (5:5): "In the same hour came forth fingers of a man's hand, and wrote over against the candlestick upon the plaster of the wall of the king's palace; and the king saw the part of the hand that wrote."

There are many instances on record when apparently fully materialized phantoms have left written messages behind. The spirits of **George Spriggs** sat down to write letters, **"Katie King"** left behind farewell messages when she took her leave. "Friedrich," a materialized form different from the medium **S. F. Sambor** both in stature and gesture, wrote something on the inside of a watch belonging to "Mr. S." in Petersburg.

There is a case so unique that it can only be called an instance of direct automatic writing. "The Mahedi," a materialized phantom associated with the medium **Francis W. Monck,** wrote in Egyptian characters. The Mahedi was then controlled by Monck's guide, "Samuel," who spoke through him and wrote with his hand in English characters that **Thomas Colley,** from comparison with pieces of direct writing, found to be in "Samuel's" hand. Colley observed that, while the writing was going on, the medium, standing some seventeen feet away, involuntarily or absentmindedly moved his hand and said afterward that he felt his hand wanting to write, yet he did not know what was being written.

During a séance with **D. D. Home,** Crookes desired to see the actual production of a written message. Crookes noted:

"Presently, the pencil rose up on its point, and after advancing by hesitating jerks to the paper, fell down. It then rose and again fell. A third time it tried but with no better results. After three unsuccessful attempts, a small wooden lath, which was lying near upon the table, slid towards the pencil and rose a few inches from the table; the pencil rose again, and propping itself against the lath, the two together made an effort to mark the paper. It fell, and then a joint effort was again made. After a third trial the lath gave it up and moved back to its place, the pencil lay as it fell across the paper, and an alphabetic message told us—'We have tried to do as you asked, but our power is exhausted.'"

Led by a similar desire, Moses made the following observations in an **out-of-the-body** experience from "the other side":

"It was not done, as I had imagined, by guiding my hand or by impressing my mind, but was by directing on to the pen a ray which looked like a blue light. The force so directed caused the pen to move in obedience to the will of the directing spirit. In order to show me that the hand was a mere instrument not essential to the experiment, the pen was removed from the hand, and kept in position by the ray of light which was directed upon it. To my great astonishment it moved over the paper and wrote as before. I cried out with astonishment and was warned to keep still lest I should break the conditions.''

Horace Greeley quoted in *Putnam's Monthly Magazine* the experience of former Senator James F. Simmons of Rhode Island in obtaining direct writing by a pencil dropped through the ring of a pair of scissors. The pencil stood firmly poised and slowly and deliberately traced the words ''James D. Simmons.'' The handwriting was a facsimile of his deceased son's signature. It was obtained in daylight.

In direct-writing séances with Everitt, Crookes noticed that no matter how thin the paper was, the pencil produced no indentation. Nevertheless, it was clear that the pencil had been used, since once, the words appeared double, because the lead had a double edge. Another supernormal phenomenon was the speed with which the scripts were delivered and the success in overcoming the handicaps that had been experimentally set up. The paper had often been placed in a closed book, in a locked box and slates; the sheets were marked and writing was demanded on a given page in a book or on folded sheets in a sealed envelope. In Everitt's case, the writing often covered one side of the marked sheet and when, after examination, the light was again extinguished, it was continued on the back side of the same paper. Everitt's husband, Thomas, declared during meeting of the Marylebone Association of Inquirers into Spiritualism that he had known as many as 936 words to be written in a second.

To test the powers of the medium Sambor, a cone of sheet iron was prepared under the direction of the head of the printing works at Petersburg. A piece of paper and a pencil were placed inside. The engineers had an iron lid fixed on with special rivets. The cone was then left for several days in a room that Sambor never entered. In a later séance Sambor declared that writing would be found in the cone. After much difficulty, the cone, which was found intact, was opened. The paper was inscribed with a few words.

The direct writing produced by **Lujza L. Ignath** in Oslo (September 30, 1931) on wax tablets in a closed box appeared, under microscopic enlargement, to have been ''melted'' into the wax by fine rays, swinging together from the direction of the sitters.

The writing may be in the medium's hand or in strange characters. The language of the writing may also vary and the script may contain words or sentences desired by the company.

The Beginning of Direct Writing

The scene of the most ancient instance of direct writing was perhaps Mount Sinai, where Moses obtained the Ten Commandments. The first modern record of experiments is to be found in Baron von Guldenstubbe's book *La Réalité des Esprits.* The phenomenon was observed during the poltergeist disturbances in the house of a Rev. Phelps at Stratford in 1850. Direct scripts were delivered in the locked spirit room of the Koon log house in Vermont.

Mary Marshall, the first English professional medium, produced direct writing on sheets of glass that were smeared over with a composition of oil and whitening and kept under the table. This was the rudimentary beginning of **slate writing,** of which the first English account, with Marshall in 1861, was published by Thomas P. Barker.

The explanation often given as to why slate writing came into vogue is that it furnished a comparatively quick message from departed friends without an excessive drain on the medium, since the space between the slates served as a convenient dark chamber. However, the process was abandoned in the early twentieth century. **Laura Pruden,** of Cincinnati was one of the last mediums claiming to produce the phenomenon. **Hereward Carrington** perhaps explains its loss of popularity: ''Now there are so many different ways by which such writing [slate writing] may be obtained by trickery that it is almost impossible to obtain conclusive evidence by this means. Personally, I have never seen a genuine example, in all the years during which I have been investigating this question.'' This statement also refers to his experiences with **Pierre Keeler,** with whom he had two sittings at **Lily Dale,** the Spiritualist camp, in 1907 (he came to the conclusion that **fraud** was practiced on both occasions) and the sitting with Laura Pruden, of Cincinnati. In the latter case, Carrington admitted that the evidence was not so conclusive; indeed, his detailed account fails to show anything but a strongly imaginative possibility of fraud.

Henry Slade, Monck, Eglinton, Watkins, and **W. H. Powell** were the best-known exponents of slate writing. The commotion caused by the Slade trial resulted in some interesting public testimonies. William Barrett, in a letter quoted in the book *Psychography* by Moses, declares that he noted the same suspicious circumstances to which a Lankester alluded and also that Slade always sat with his back to the light and sideways, so that the front of his person was in comparative shade, though generally in full view. Barrett suspected fraud, but instead of forcibly interrupting Slade to discover whether the writing was already on the slate when it was not supposed to be, he took a clean slate, placed a crumb of a slate pencil below, held it firmly down with his elbow and only allowed the tips of Slade's fingers to touch the slates. He observes:

''While closely watching both of Slade's hands which did not move perceptibly, I was much astonished to hear scratching going on apparently on the under side of the table, and when the slate was lifted up I found the side facing the table covered with writing. A similar result was obtained on other days; further, an eminent scientific man obtained writing on a clean slate when it was held entirely in his own hand, both of Slade's being on the table.''

In a letter to the *Spectator* of October 6, 1877, **Alfred Russel Wallace** describes a remarkable experiment. The sitting was held in a private house with the medium Monck. Two slates were examined, cleaned, and tied together by Wallace and placed on the table, never out of his sight. Monck asked Wallace to name a word he wished to be written on the slate inside. He named the word ''God.'' Monck then asked how it should be written. He replied: ''lengthways of the slate and with a Capital G.'' In a very short time writing was heard on the slate. The medium's hands were convulsively withdrawn, Wallace himself untied the cord, and on opening the slates found on the lower one the word written in the manner he asked.

The general procedure with Slade was to place the slates under the table against the slab or lay his hands over them on top of the table. The process of writing (a scratching sound) was not only heard, but the tremors could be felt if a hand was placed over the locked slate. The finishing of the message was usually indicated by raps. The crumb of slate pencil, worn away, was usually found at the end of the written line.

With other slate-writing mediums the conditions varied. In Mrs. Harman's case, as reported by J. L. O'Sullivan (former American minister in Portugal), a steady stream of rapid little ticks was audible. In the case of Mrs. Francis, of San Francisco, the direct movement of the pencil on the slate was seen by Elliot Cowes and E. Coleman. Charles E. Watkins was offered $50,000 by Hiram Sibley, of Rochester, for the secret of his slate-writing trick. He claimed he did not know it himself. E. Crowell asked how the writing was effected and received the following answer in a séance with Slade: ''The smaller the pencil the more easily we can write, the larger the pencil the greater the difficulty. We move the point by our willpower entirely, and that enables us to write. Very few spirits can directly control the pencil. That is the reason why the medium's wife comes so often to show other spirits how to do this.''

Precipitated Writing

Fred P. Evans, of San Francisco, obtained slate writing in colored chalk. The phenomenon was witnessed by Wallace in San Francisco in 1887. Two thick lines drawn across the slate with a slate pencil seemed to prove that the colored chalk, not provided by the medium, was precipitated after the slates had been locked. Examples of precipitated writing offer some of the more curious instances of psychic phenomena on record.

There is, for example, the case of Moses' interaction with his several spirit **controls.** Moses wrote a note beneath the signature of "Imperator" under a communication received on March 3, 1876: "While I was writing the above automatically, the under-written pencil letters grew under my hand. No pencil was near me. I watched them from time to time, merely covering the page so as to get darkness." On his inquiry he was told by "Prudens" that it was not necessary for the communicators to have the materials for direct writing. As a demonstration, "Magus" wrote in blue when there was no blue pencil in the room and produced a red message in a closed book. When Moses asked for a message in multicolors, the names of various controls were signed in a closed book after a count of five in red, blue, and black pencils.

Henry Steel Olcott also obtained colored slate writing with the medium Cozine without the use of pencil or crayon "Papus" (pseudonym of **Gérard Encausse**) in a lecture before the Society d'Etudes Psychiques at Nancy in 1907, related:

"In 1889 a well-known magnetiser, named Robert, had succeeded in putting two subjects to sleep, a man and a girl, and he placed them in such a state of hypnosis that these subjects projected characters and lines of writing on blank sheets of paper, without using a pencil or pen. The characters appeared of themselves on the paper. Dr. Gibier and I went to study this phenomenon. During this séance we were able to obtain in full light on a sheet of paper, signed by twenty witnesses, the precipitation of a whole page of written verses signed 'Corneille.' I examined the substance which formed the writing under the microscope and I was led to the conclusion that it consisted of globules of human blood, some altered and as if calcined, others still quite distinct. 'Papus' believed that the blood of the medium and his nervous force exteriorized itself and reconstructed itself at a distance. The medium was preparing for the stage and had studied Corneille during the whole of the preceding day" (*Annales des Sciences Psychiques,* 1907).

Sometimes direct writing was witnessed in strange forms. *Blavatsky's Posthumous Memoirs,* published by Joseph M. Wade (1896) in Boston, is claimed to have been produced by the direct spiritual operation of a typewriter. Direct typewriting was also claimed by the **Bangs sisters** of Chicago.

Sheets of unexposed bromide paper or photographic plates may also be impressed with direct scripts. These messages are called **psychographs.** They may appear to the medium's eyes like luminous scrolls. The theory is that they are built on ectoplasmic patches. They have been found on the plates of spirit photographers.

In **poltergeist** cases the phenomenon has also occurred. In *The Great Amherst Mystery,* Dr. Carritte is standing by Esther Cox's bedside when all present hear the sound of writing on the wall and looking round they see cut deeply into the plaster on the wall the terrible words: "Esther Cox, you are mine to kill." The writing remained visible for years afterward.

Frau Gilbert's control, "Dr. Franciscus Nell," apparently produced direct writing by engraving his name on cigarette cases held under the table.

Writing in fire (i.e., by psychic lights) is another variety of direct writing. In a séance with **Ada Bessinet,** Admiral Usborne Moore saw names traced in the air in front of the sitter in letters of bright light. The effect was not permanent and the beginning of a letter disappeared before the end was completed. **James Hyslop** writes in *Contact with the Other Worlds* (1919) of his experiences with the medium Miss Burton: "The messages were written in letters of fire in the air in pitch darkness and gave cross-references with other psychics. They had to be read sometimes a letter at a time and repeated until I could be certain of them."

Dermography, or skin writing, may also be considered a form of direct writing, related to some aspects of **stigmata.**

Sources:

Cholmondely-Pennell, H. *"Bringing it to Book": Facts of Slate-Writing through Mr. W. Eglinton.* London, 1884.

Holms, A. Campbell. *The Facts of Psychic Science and Philosophy Collated and Discussed.* London, 1925. Reprint, New Hyde Park, N.Y.: University Books, 1969.

Olcott, Henry Steel. *Old Diary Leaves, First Series.* Madras, India, 1895.

Owen, J. J. *Psychography.* San Francisco, 1893.

Disappearances (Paranormal)

History has recorded many instances of mysterious disappearances, sometimes with equally mysterious reappearances. Such incidents are not, however, generally thought of as paranormal, since the evidence is usually anecdotal, reports uncorroborated, and incidents subject to more mundane explanations. In the case of well known or important individuals in the history of politics and religion, kidnapping, secret imprisonment, or assassination may have been responsible for many disappearances. In the case of ordinary folk, many young people throughout history have quarreled with their parents and left home, sometimes dying in foreign wars, or, more likely today, on the streets, victims of crime, prostitution, or drugs. Adults in one kind of difficulty or another have often had good reason for disappearing. There have also been many cases of genuine amnesia, or loss of memory, resulting in the victim's traveling far from home and reappearing without any clear recollection of what happened.

Many such explanations are equally valid for the thousands of disappearances every year in many countries of the world in modern times. However, there are a number of cases that remain intriguing mysteries.

For example, in November 1809 Benjamin Bathurst, a member of the British diplomatic service, vanished while returning from a mission to the court of Emperor Francis at Vienna. Bathurst stopped for a meal at an inn in Perleberg, a small German town, and in the evening checked the horses of his carriage. He was seen by witnesses to walk around to the far side of the horses and then disappear. He was never seen or heard of again, in spite of the most extensive investigations.

In the 1550s, in the French town of Artigues, Martin Guerre left his wife and young son one morning, walking in the direction of his father's farm. He disappeared without a trace. Eight years later, he returned and was welcomed by his wife, his four sisters, and his uncle Peter. His father had died. Martin resumed married life and fathered two more children. Three years later, another Martin Guerre turned up, a soldier with a wooden leg who had served in the Flanders war. The first Martin was arrested for impersonation, and even Uncle Peter changed his mind and said he was an impostor. At the trial, 150 witnesses were examined, and their evidence was conflicting. Martin's brothers took the side of the arrested man, who presented his case convincingly. Eventually Martin's wife changed her mind and said the man with the wooden leg was the real Martin. The other was imprisoned and executed.

In his books *Lo!* (1931) and *Wild Talents* (1932), **Charles Fort,** the chronicler of the anomalous and inexplicable, recorded a number of mysterious disappearances and reappearances, including other cases with a strange resemblance to the story of Martin Guerre. Fort cited the case of a New York woman around 1920 whose husband was in an insane asylum. The woman was visited by a man who greeted her fondly, claiming to be her husband. The woman accepted him and settled down with him. Some time later she learned that her husband was still in the asylum, and thereupon had the other man arrested. How could she have made a mistake in the first place? Fort noted another case where a man came to a woman whose husband was a sailor and claimed that he was the husband. "Go away!" said she, "you are darker than my husband." "Ah!" said he, "I have had yellow fever." So she accepted him, but later changed her mind and this case also ended in a police court.

Although a wife should surely know her own husband, even after a prolonged absence, it is reasonable to suppose that she might still be mistaken, or have preferred an impostor for reasons of her own. Some other cases of disappearance are apparently inexplicable, especially when various people have disappeared in exactly the same mysterious circumstances.

The Vanishing Children

One night in November 1878, at Quincy, Illinois, Charles Ashmore, age 16, was sent to fetch water from a well. When he did not return his father went to look for him with a lantern. The boy's footprints in the snow ended abruptly. A few days later, his mother heard his voice, as did other members of the family and neighbors, but the boy was never seen again.

On Christmas Eve 1889, 11-year-old Oliver Larch of South Bend, Indiana, also went to a well to fetch water. After a short while, his parents heard him crying out, "Help! Help! They've got me! Help!" The cries seemed to be coming from overhead. Oliver's father and others in the house went to look for the boy, carrying a lamp. Halfway to the well, about 75 feet from the house, the boy's footprints in the snow ended abruptly, and there were no other tracks. The boy had vanished forever.

By an astonishing coincidence, another 11-year-old named Oliver, son of a Mr. Thomas, a farmer at Rhayader in Wales, also vanished while going to fetch water from a well on Christmas Eve 20 years later, in 1909. The boy's footsteps also stopped in the snow, and he too was heard to cry out in terror before disappearing forever.

What happened to these children who vanished under such amazingly similar circumstances? They appeared to have been lifted up into the air. But explanations involving kidnapping balloonists or predatory eagles are too far-fetched to consider. An 11-year-old boy weighs some 75 pounds, far beyond the lifting capacity of an eagle. No balloonists were reported in the areas.

Mass Disappearances

It is not unusual for armies to be decimated in combat, particularly in view of the awesome destructive capabilities of modern armaments, but in most military campaigns there are reasonably satisfactory accounts of the fate of regiments, with a tally of corpses or survivors. However, there have been a few instances in both ancient and modern history where whole armies have disappeared without trace.

An early example dates from the Roman conquests of Britain. About the year 119 C.E., the Ninth Roman Legion, known as "Hispana," was sent to subdue one of several revolts in Brigantia, a confederacy of tribes in northern Britain. The Ninth Legion, Composed of some six thousand men, disappeared without a trace.

Some historians do not accept the evidence for this mass disappearance, but there are other cases in more recent history. During the Gallipoli campaign in World War I, the British First-Fifth Norfolk Regiment under Col. Sir Horace Beauchamp pursued the enemy through forest territory and disappeared without a trace. The regiment was composed of 250 soldiers and 16 officers. Their strange story was reported in an eyewitness account by Gen. Sir Ian Hamilton in a dispatch to Secretary-at-War Earl Kitchener. On the fiftieth anniversary of the Gallipoli landings, former sapper Frederick Reichardt (who had been in the New Zealand Engineers) signed a statement in which he recalled the appearance of a strange, huge cloud about 800 feet long and 220 feet high, into which the ill-fated regiment marched. When this cloud lifted soon afterward, the men had disappeared.

During the Spanish War of Succession (1701–14), an army of four thousand fully equipped troops was reported to have marched into the foothills of the Pyrenees Mountains and disappeared without a trace.

As recently as 1939 a Chinese army of nearly three thousand troops disappeared overnight. They were stationed 16 miles south of Nanking and had orders to fight to the finish. One hundred and thirteen men were detailed to guard a strategically important bridge over which the enemy could advance; the other troops, 2,988 men, dug in at their front line. Col. Li Fu Sien gave the troops their orders and returned to headquarters, a couple of miles behind the front line. In the morning he found no response from the army field telephones and went to investigate. The detachment guarding the bridge was in position and assured the colonel that no enemy forces had passed across the bridge, but the 2,988 men in the front line had all disappeared. If they had deserted en masse, it is strange that they were never heard of again.

Disappearance and Reappearance

There are many stories of mysterious disappearances with equally mysterious reappearances at a great distance, and some old and new examples are discussed elsewhere as incidents of **teleportation.**

In the case of Spiritualist mediums, the claimed phenomenon usually involves theories of dematerialization (rendering physical matter intangible) with rematerialization at a distance. In the case of inanimate objects or small living creatures (such as insects, birds, snakes), the appearance or disappearance over a distance is termed an **apport.** To date there is neither a satisfactory theory to account for paranormal transportation, nor any verified case illustrative of its occurrence. Reports of such cases must be considered highly questionable, especially in light of the numerous verified cases of fraudulently produced apports.

The books of **Charles Fort** meticulously list many accounts of objects or groups of objects that have appeared or disappeared suddenly, including insects, fish, blocks of ice, and unusual artifacts, some the subject of mysterious **falls** from the sky. Many of these have been explored as products of infrequent but natural phenomena.

Ancient accounts of teleportation of human beings are more impressive than modern ones, insofar as limited means of transport would preclude conventional rapid transit as an explanation. They are, of course, countered by the inability to verify what often comes across as a tall tale. According to Philostratus the Elder (ca. 170–245 C.E.), the great mystic **Apollonius of Tyana** vanished from a crowded courtroom in Rome and reappeared the same afternoon at Puteoli, 100 miles away. Similar stories are told in the Bible. In the Acts of the Apostles, the apostles were delivered from a prison, though the officers testified "the prison house we found shut in all safety, and the keepers standing before the doors; but, when we opened, we found no man within" (Acts 5:23). St. Philip, after baptizing the Ethiopian, was "caught away by the spirit" and "found at Azotus" (Acts 8:39).

In modern times, an astonishing story was reported of Armando Valdes, corporal in the Chilean army. On April 25, 1977, he was said to have disappeared in front of six of his men, reappearing minutes later. But the calendar on his watch was dated five days ahead and he had grown something like a five-day beard! He could remember nothing of what had happened. Had he been taken five days into the future before being returned? This telescoping of time recalls the folklore of supernatural time in the kingdom of **fairies** and the legend of Rip Van Winkle.

Another case of apparent time anomaly is the strange story of Rudolph Fentz. In the book *Vanishings* (1981), author Michael Harrison states that Fentz left his home in Florida in 1876 because his wife objected to his smoking in the house. Fentz went for a walk and was missing for 74 years. In June 1950 he appeared in Times Square, New York City, dressed in the formal wear of 1876—shepherd's plaid trousers, button boots, Prince Albert coat, glossy "plug" hat. He stepped off the pavement and was knocked down by a taxi, dying instantly. His pockets contained $70 in outdated bank notes and two gold certificates. His calling cards showed an address on Fifth Avenue. There was a bill from a livery stable in Lexington Avenue for "feeding and stabling one horse and washing one carriage, $3," but the stables had long ceased to exist and the premises were now occupied by a shop.

In his book *Lo!*, Fort records that in the town of Romford, Essex, in England, no less than six individuals were found wandering in the streets between 1920 and 1923. All of them "were unable to tell how they got there, or anything else about themselves.'' Even stranger was the report of a man who was walking down Euston Road in west central London one day, but nine months later found himself working on a farm in Australia.

Many stories have been told of ships that vanish at sea, or even crews that disappear, as in the case of the famous ''**Mary Celeste.**'' Claims have been made that certain ocean areas, like the so-called **Bermuda Triangle,** have mysteriously snatched ships and aircraft, though most of these claims have now been laid to rest. One of the most time-honored legends of the sea is that of the **Flying Dutchman,** condemned to sail his ship from age to age until redeemed by the love of a pure maiden.

One of the strangest disappearances of modern history is surely that of the famous writer Ambrose Bierce (1842–1914?). He had written many strange stories himself, including three about mysterious disappearances. One of these was based on the real-life story of David Lang, a farmer in Gallatin, Tennessee, who was said to have vanished in full view of five other people while crossing a field. A year later, his two children were out walking and heard a man's voice calling for help. They shouted ''Father, are you there?'' and Lang's voice answered. The children fetched Lang's wife and the calls for help persisted, but got fainter and eventually died out. Bierce visited the farm in Gallatin and based his story ''The Difficulty of Crossing a Field'' on the incident.

Bierce himself disappeared without a trace some time after 1913. One theory is that he died in Mexico during the civil warfare between Villa and Carranza, but no one really knows how, where, or when he died.

Sources:

Begg, Paul. *Into Thin Air: People Who Disappear.* North Pomfret, Vt.: David & Charles, 1979.

Berlitz, Charles, and J. M. Valentine. *Without a Trace.* Garden City, N.Y.: Doubleday, 1977.

Fort, Charles. *The Books of Charles Fort.* New York: Henry Holt, 1941. Reprinted as *The Complete Books of Charles Fort.* New York: Dover Publications, 1974.

O'Donnell, Elliott. *Strange Disappearances.* London, 1927. Reprint, New Hyde Park, N.Y.: University Books, 1972.

Phillips, G. Ragland. *Brigantia: A Mysteriography.* London: Routledge & Kegan Paul, 1976.

Steiger, Brad. *Strange Disappearances.* New York: Magnum Books, 1972.

Displacement

A term used in parapsychology for a form of **extrasensory perception (ESP)** in a test series, in which correct information about targets is displaced backward or forward from the actual target. If there is a consistent pattern of scoring one or two places from the target, this might have significance for ESP instead of just being a series of misses.

Dithorba

Brother of Red Hugh and Kimbay of Irish medieval legend. He was killed by his niece Macha, and his five sons were expelled from Ulster. They resolved to force the sovereignty of Ireland from Macha, but she discovered them in the forest, overpowered them by her magical influence, and carried them to her palace on her back. They are said to have built the famous Irish city of Emain Macha under her supervision.

Divination

The method of obtaining knowledge of the unknown or the future by means of omens. **Astrology** and the utterances of **oracles** are usually regarded as branches of divination. The derivation of the word supposes a direct message from the gods to the diviner. Divination was practiced in all grades of primitive communities and civilizations. The methods are many and various, and, strangely enough, in their variety are confined to no one portion of the world.

Crystal gazing and such allied methods as shell hearing may be classed as divination that arises from the personal consciousness of the diviner. Of the same class is divination by **dreams, automatic writing,** and so forth. What might be called divination by ''luck'' is represented by the use of cards, the casting of lots, the use of knuckle bones as in **Africa** and elsewhere, or coconuts as in **Polynesia. Haruspicy,** or the inspection of entrails, divination by footprints in ashes, by the flight of birds, or by meeting with ominous animals, represents still a third class of divination.

The art of divination is usually practiced among primitive races by the **shaman** caste; among more sophisticated peoples by the professional diviner—as in **Rome** and ancient **Mexico**—and even among modern civilized people by persons who claim the faculty of divination, such as the Spiritualist medium or the witch.

The art is undoubtedly of great antiquity. It was employed in ancient **Egypt** side by side with astrology, and divination by dreams was constantly resorted to, a class of priests being kept apart, whose office it was to interpret dreams and visions. Instances of dreams are recorded in the ancient Egyptian texts; for example those of Thothmes IV, king of Egypt in 1450 B.C.E., and Nut-Amen, king of the Eastern Soudan and Egypt about 670 B.C.E. The Egyptian magician usually set himself to procure dreams for his clients by such devices as the drawing of magic pictures and the reciting of magic words, and some of these are still extant. In Egypt, however, divination was usually effected by astrological methods.

In ancient **China** the principal method of divination was by means of the oracles, but such forms as the examination of the marks on the shell of a tortoise, are also found; they are similar to the examination of the back of a peccary by the **Maya** of Central America. Chinese monarchs consulted the fates in this manner in 1146 B.C.E. and found them unfavorable, but as in Egypt, most soothsaying was accomplished by means of astrology. Omens, however, were by no means ignored, and were given great prominence, as many tales in the ancient books testify.

In ancient Rome a distinct caste or college of priests called augurs was set apart to interpret the signs of approval or disapproval sent by the gods in reference to any coming event. This college probably consisted originally of but three members, of whom the king himself was one, and it was not until the time of Caesar that the members were increased to 16. The college remained in existence as late as the fourth century, and its members held office for life.

A tenet of the Roman augurs was that for signs of the gods one must look toward the sky and glean knowledge of the intentions of the divine beings from such omens as the flash of lightning and the flight of birds.

On a windless night, the augur took up a position on a hill that afforded an extensive view. Marking out a space for himself, he pitched a tent, seated himself and covered his head, asked the gods for a sign, and waited for an answer. He faced southward, thus having the east (lucky) quarter on his left, and the west (unfavorable) portion of the sky on his right. He carefully observed every sign that came within the scope of his vision, such as lightning, the appearance of birds, and so forth. Birdsong was carefully listened to and divided into sounds of good or evil omen. The reading of omens was also effected by feeding the birds and observing the manner in which they ate. The course of animals and the sounds they made were also closely watched, and all unusual phenomena were regarded as omens or warnings. Sortilege, or the casting of lots, was often resorted to by the caste of augurs.

The election of magistrates was nearly always referred to the diviners, as was the dispatching of an army for war and the passing of laws.

In the East divination generally appears to have been effected by crystal gazing, dreams, and similar methods of self-hallucination or self-hypnotism. Divination flourished in Chaldea and Assyria among the Babylonians and Ethiopians, and appears to have been much the same as in Egypt. In the Jewish *Talmud* witches were said to divine by means of bread crumbs. Among the Arabs, the future was often foretold by means of the shapes seen in sand. The Burmese and Siamese pierced an egg at each end, and having blown the contents onto the ground, traced within them the outline of things to be. Divination by astrology too was common in oriental countries, as were the predictions of prophets.

It is remarkable that among the native races of America the arts of divination known to the peoples of the Old World were, and still are, used. These arts, as a rule, were the preserve of the medicine man and priestly class. In ancient Mexico there was a college of augurs like the auspices of ancient Rome; the members occupied themselves with observing the flight of birds and listening to their songs, from which they drew their conclusions. In Mexico, the *Calmecac,* or college of priests, had a department where divination was taught in all its branches, but there were many *ex officio* prophets and augurs.

In Peru, still other classes of diviners predicted by means of the leaves of tobacco, or the grains or juice of coca, the shapes of grains of maize, taken at random, the forms assumed by the smoke rising from burning victims, the viscera of animals, the course taken by **spiders,** and the direction in which fruits might fall. The professors of these methods were distinguished by different ranks and titles, and their training was long and arduous.

The American tribes as a whole were keen observers of bird life. Strangely enough the bird and serpent are combined in their symbolism and in the names of several of their principal deities. The bird appeared to the American primitive as a spirit, in all probability under the spell of some potent enchanter—a spell that might be broken only by some great sorcerer or medicine man.

As among the ancient Romans, the birds of America were divided into those of good and evil omen, and certain Brazilian tribes apparently thought the souls of dead Indians entered into the bodies of birds. The shamans of certain tribes of Paraguay acted as go-betweens for the members of their tribes and such birds as they imagined enshrined the souls of their departed relatives. This usage would appear to combine the acts of divination and **necromancy.**

The priesthood of Peru practiced oracular methods by "making idols speak," and this they probably accomplished through ventriloquial arts. The *piagés* or priests of the Uapés of Brazil had a contrivance known to them as the *paxiuba,* which consisted of a tree trunk about the height of a man, on which the branches and leaves had been left. Holes were bored in the trunk beneath the foliage, and when the priests spoke through these the leaves trembled and the sound was interpreted as a message from Jurupari, one of their principal deities.

But all over the American continent, from the land of **Eskimos** to that of the Patagonians, the methods of oracular divination were practically identical. The shaman, or medicine man, raised a tent or hut that he entered, carefully closing the aperture after him. He then proceeded to make his incantations, and in a little while the entire lodge trembled and rocked; the poles bent to a breaking point, as if a dozen strong men were straining at them, and the most violent noise came from within, seeming first to emanate from the depths of the earth, next from the air above, and then from the vicinity of the hut itself.

The reason for this disturbance has never been properly explained, and medicine men who were converted to Christianity assured workers among the Native American tribes that they had not the least idea of what occurred during the time they occupied these enchanted lodges, for they were plunged into a deep sleep. After the supernatural sounds had to some extent faded away, the medicine man proceeded to question the spirit he had evoked. The answers were generally ambiguous, like those of the Pythonesses of ancient Greece.

Divination by hypnosis was well known in America. Jonathan Carver, who traveled among the Sioux about the latter part of the eighteenth century, mentioned it was used among them. The Ghost Dance religion of the Native Americans of Nevada had for one of its tenets the belief in hypnotic communion with the dead.

Divination by means of dreams and visions was extremely common in both subcontinents of the Western Hemisphere, as exemplified by the derivation of the word *priest* in the native languages. The Algonquians called them "dreamers of the gods;" the Maya, "listeners," and so forth. The ability to see visions was usually quickened by the use of drugs or the swallowing or inhalation of cerebral intoxicants, such as tobacco, *maguey,* coca, the snake plant, and others. Indeed many Native American tribes, such as the Creeks, possessed numerous plants that they cultivated for this purpose. A large number of instances are on record in which Native American medicine men were said to have divined the future in a most striking manner.

For example, in his autobiography, Black Hawk, a celebrated Sac chief, related that his grandfather had a strong belief that in four years' time "he should see a white man, who would be to him as a father." Supernaturally directed, he traveled eastward to a certain spot, and there, as he had been informed in dreams, met with a Frenchman who concluded an alliance between France and the Sac nation. Coincidence is certainly possible in this case, but not in the circumstances of Jonathan Carver. While was dwelling with the Killistenoes they were threatened with a famine, and their very existence depended on the arrival of certain traders, who brought them food in exchange for skins and other goods. The diviners of the tribe were consequently consulted by the chief, and announced that the next day, at high noon exactly, a canoe would make its appearance with news of the anxiously awaited expedition. The entire population came down to the beach in order to witness its arrival, accompanied by the incredulous Carver, and, to his intense surprise, at the very moment forecast by the shamans a canoe rounded a distant headland, and, paddling speedily shorewards, the navigators brought the patient Killistenoes news of the expedition they expected.

John Mason Brown recorded an equally singular instance of the prophetic gift of an American medicine man (see *Atlantic Monthly,* July 1866). Difficulties experienced while searching for a band of Native Americans the Mackenzie and Coppermine rivers had forced the majority of Brown's band to return home, until out of ten men who originally set out only three remained. They had almost decided to abandon their search when they stumbled upon a party of braves of the tribe they sought. These men had been sent out by their medicine man to find three white men. The shaman had given them an exhaustive account of the men's horses, equipment, and general appearance before they set out, and this the warriors related to Brown before they saw his companions. Brown asked the medicine man how he had been able to foretell their coming. The shaman, who appeared to be "a frank and simple-minded man," could only explain that "he saw them coming, and heard them talk on their journey."

Crystal gazing was in common use among many Native American tribes. The Aztecs of Mexico used to gaze into small polished pieces of sandstone, and a case is on record in which a Cherokee Indian kept a divining crystal wrapped in buckskin in a cave, occasionally "feeding" it by rubbing over it the blood of a deer. At a village in Guatemala, the traveler John L. Stephens saw a remarkable stone that had been placed on the altar of a temple, but that had previously been used as a divining stone by the Indians of the village.

Divination by arrow was also common. According to Fuentes y Guzmán, the chronicler of Guatemala, the reigning king of Kiche, Kicah Tanub, when informed by the ambassador of Montezuma II that a race of irresistible white men had conquered Mexico and were proceeding to Guatemala, sent for four diviners, whom he commanded foretell the result of the invasion. Taking their bows they discharged some arrows against a rock. They returned to inform their master that, because no impression had been made upon the rock by the arrowheads, they foresaw the worst and predicted the ultimate triumph of the white man—an incident that shows that the class to which they belonged stood in no fear of royalty. Kicah Tanub, dissatisfied, sent for the "priests," obviously a different class of diviners, and requested their opinions. From the omen of an ancient stone (brought from afar by their forefathers) having been broken, they also foretold the fall of the Kiche empire.

Many objects such as small clay birds, boats, or boat-shaped vessels, have been discovered in sepulchral mounds in North America, and it is conjectured that these may have been used for purposes of divination.

Portents, too, were implicitly believed in by the American races. Nezahualpilli, king of Tezcuco, near Mexico, was accomplished in this type of divination. Montezuma consulted him concerning the terrible prodigies that startled his people before the advance of the Spaniards upon his kingdom, and that were supposed to predict the return of Quetzalcoatl, the legendary culture-hero of Anahuac, to his people. These included earthquakes, tempests, floods, and the appearance of comets and strange lights while mysterious voices were heard in the air.

Divination has persisted in modern civilizations. Perhaps one of the most remarkable diviners was **Nostradamus** (Michael de Nostradame, 1503–66) who published hundreds of prophecies in enigmatic verses. Many believe these prophecies refer to events that have occurred through the centuries and that some will be fulfilled in the near future. The seventeenth-century astrologer **William Lilly** predicted the Great Plague of London in 1665 and the Great Fire in the following year.

In addition to such gifted individuals who seemed to be able to discern future events through signs and visions, there are also popular techniques by which ordinary people believe they can gain knowledge of the hidden present or future. As well as the popular practice of astrology, there are many fortune-telling systems such as dream interpretation, **palmistry,** and the **tarot** cards. Many such systems were successfully revived in the occult boom of the 1960s. Perhaps one of the most interesting revivals was that of the ancient Chinese system of the **I Ching,** where divination of present and future events is associated with a deeper philosophy of the function of destiny in human affairs.

Psychical researchers have recorded many cases of spontaneous prevision of future events, although there is as yet no satisfactory explanation for such phenomena involving clairvoyance, telepathy, or dreams.

Dowsing, or water-witching, is another form of divination, although it relates mainly to the discovery of hidden water, metals, or other information. The use of a twig or rod by the operator is reminiscent of the magic wand or the tripod of occult magicians in the practice of **necromancy.** It also seems related to the rationale of **table turning, planchette** and **Ouija board** in **Spiritualism.** Divination proper, however, is a system of interpreting hidden knowledge rather than eliciting information through the intervention of spirits. One development of dowsing of special interest is the art of **radiesthesia,** where pendulums are used instead of a dowsing rod, for the purpose of eliciting a wider range of information, such as ascertaining states of health or disease, prescribing remedies, tracing missing persons, or even divining distant events.

Some of the seventy or so most well defined systems of divination such as **axinomancy, belomancy,** and **capnomancy** are the subject of separate entries in this encyclopedia, as are such specialized related studies as astrology, crystal gazing, and **palmistry.**

Popular interest in divination continues to flourish in modern times and even to increase with the uncertainties and anxieties of economic and political life. **Gypsies** are still reputed to have hereditary talents for fortune-telling.

National newspapers carry daily astrological indications, and the use of tarot cards is widespread, but the art of divination still seems to require some basic or developed talent that no mechanistic system can entirely dispense with. A pertinent statement is that of the psychical researcher Count Cesar de Vesme: "Any system . . . is good for the man gifted with supernormal powers, and any system is bad for the man not so gifted."

Sources:

Aylesworth, Thomas. *Astrology and Foretelling the Future; A Concise Guide.* Danbury, Conn.: Watts, 1973.

Barrett, Sir William, and Theodore Besterman. *The Divining Rod: An Experimental and Psychological Investigation.* London, 1926. Reprint, New Hyde Park, N.Y.: University Books, 1926.

Besterman, Theodore. *Crystal Gazing.* London, 1924. Reprint, New Hyde Park, N.Y.: University Books, 1965.

Black Hawk. *Autobiography.* St. Louis, Mo., 1882.

Bouche-Leclerq, Auguste. *Histoire de la Divination dans l'Antiquite.* 4 vols. Reprint, New York: Arno Press, 1975.

Collins, Rodney. *The Theory of Celestial Influence.* London: Stuart & Watkins, 1955.

Connor, W. R. *Roman Augury and Etruscan Divination.* New York: Arno Press, 1976.

Deutch, Yvonne, ed., and F. Strachan, comp. *Fortune Tellers.* London, 1976. Reprint, New York: Black Watch, 1974.

Ebon, Martin. *Prophecy in Our Time.* New York: New American Library, 1969. Reprint, London: Alhambra, 1971.

Freedland, Nat. *The Occult Explosion.* New York: G. Putnam's Sons, 1972.

Gibson, W. B., and L. K. Gibson. *The Complete Illustrated Book of Divination and Prophecy.* Garden City, N.Y.: Doubleday, 1973. Reprint, London: Souvenir Press, 1974.

Grand Orient [A. E. Waite]. *Complete Manual of Occult Divination.* 2 vols. Reprint, New Hyde Park, N.Y.: University Books, 1972.

Halliday, W. R. *Greek Divination: A Study of Methods and Principles.* London: Macmillan, 1913.

Hill, Douglas. *Fortune Telling.* London: Hamlyn, 1972.

Jahoda, G. *The Psychology of Superstition.* London, 1969. Reprint, Baltimore, Md.: Penguin, 1971.

Kao, James. *Chinese Divination.* Smithtown, N.Y.: Exposition Press, 1980.

Legge, James, trans. *I Ching; Book of Changes.* 1899. Reprint, New York: Dover Publications, 1963.

Manas, John H. *Divination: Ancient and Modern.* New York: Pythagoran Society, 1947.

McIntosh, Christopher. *The Astrologers and Their Creed.* London: Hutchinson, 1969. Reprint, New York: Praeger, 1970.

Miall, A. M. *Complete Fortune Telling.* Greenberg, 1950. Reprint, Hackensack, N.J.: Wehman, 1962.

Rakoczi, Basil Ivan. *Foreseeing the Future.* New York: Harper & Row, 1973.

Saltmarsh, H. F. *Foreknowledge.* London: G. Bell, 1938.

Schoenholtz, Larry. *New Directions in the I Ching.* New Hyde Park, N.Y.: University Books, 1975.

Waite, Arthur Edward. *The Occult Sciences.* 1891. Reprint, Secaucus, N.J.: University Books, 1974.

Divine, Father Major Jealous (ca. 1889–1965)

The man known as Father Divine, the leader of a metaphysical communal group, the Peace Mission Movement, has an obscure origin. The most reliable of several stories that have circulated about his early life is that he was born George Baker in the 1880s on a rice plantation on Hutchinson Island in the Savannah River in Georgia, the son of sharecroppers. Around the turn of the century he appeared in Baltimore, Maryland, where he became the assistant to Samuel Morris, an itinerant preacher who called himself Father Jehovia.

He emerged on his own in 1914 in Brooklyn, New York, as the leader of a small group. Divine had absorbed teachings from Christian Science and **New Thought** and emphasized healing in his preaching. Around 1919 he moved to Sayville, New York, and in the early 1920s had fewer than 50 followers. However, by this time he had been accepted by his followers as God, a much easier affirmation from a New Thought perspective, which emphasized an impersonal imminent divine reality rather than the personal deity of traditional Christianity. Through the late 1920s and into the early 1930s, his following grew steadily, made up primarily of black people but with a measurable number of whites.

In 1931 an incident occurred that lifted him from obscurity. In response to complaints from Divine's neighbors, the police arrested him for disturbing the peace. He complained of racial discrimination, but was tried and convicted. Overriding the jury's request for leniency, the judge sentenced him to a year in jail. Two days later the judge died of a heart attack. When told of the judge's death, Divine was reported to have remarked, "I hated to do it!" The widely reported remark made him a nationally known figure, especially in the African American community. (To this day the Peace Mission publishes accounts of disasters suffered by people whose behavior does not conform to the mission's teachings.) His conviction was reversed a few days later and Divine moved with his followers to Harlem. The country was then in the midst of the Great Depression, and the movement spread and prospered. He offered people very inexpensive food and shelter, opened an employment service, and most importantly, daily demonstrated God's abundance by throwing lavish banquets at which good food was served in generous portions. When people adhered to the movement, they were expected to conform their life to its economic teachings. They had to get a job, pay off their debts, and give their employer a good day's labor for their pay. They had to cancel all insurance, return any stolen money, and for the future pay their own way. They also moved into one of Divine's communal centers, called heavens, and live a celibate communal life. To further assist members, the group formed a variety of businesses in which many members were employed.

In 1946 Divine married Canadian Edna Rose Ritchings, now known as Mother Divine, and their wedding day remains an important holiday for the movement. Around this time he relocated his headquarters to Philadelphia, Pennsylvania, and in 1954 moved to Woodmont, an estate in suburban Philadelphia, which was named the Mount of the House of the Lord. Following his death on September 10, 1965, he was enshrined at the estate. Mother Divine succeeded him as head of the movement.

The Peace Mission Movement was one of the most controversial movements of the 1930s and became one of the first groups labeled as a "cult." Its metaphysical teachings were little understood by most observers, and white writers had little sympathy for Divine and his interracial ideals. Only in recent years has he been studied in the context of his metaphysical perspective and his role as an African American leader. The Peace Mission Movement may be contacted c/o The Woodmont Estate, 1622 Spring Mill Rd., Glaswyne, PA 19035. Members can be found in Canada, Germany, Switzerland, Australia, and Nigeria.

Sources:

Burnham, Kenneth E. *God Comes to America.* Boston: Lambeth Press, 1979.

Divine, Mother. *The Peace Mission Movement.* Philadelphia: Imperial Press, 1982.

Weisbrot, Robert. *Father Divine and the Struggle for Racial Equality.* Urbana: University of Illinois Press, 1983.

Divine Life Society

Founded in March 1933 by the late **Swami Sivananda** in Rishikesh, India, as an ashram or spiritual retreat for the teaching of traditional Hindu **yoga** and **Vedanta.** Situated on the banks of the sacred river Ganges in the foothills of the Himalayas, the ashram is on the main pilgrim route to holy places high in the mountains. Originally, a small group of huts surrounded by jungle, the ashram rapidly grew into a self-contained community with temple, hospitals, pharmacy, printing press, and post office. A Yoga Vedanta Forest Academy was established in 1948, and instruction was also given in the study and practice of spiritual music.

Although not the first ashram of this kind (the settlement of **Sir Aurobindo** at Pondicherry dates from 1910), the society played a prominent part in reviving the Hindu tradition of forest academies in a modern context, long before the contemporary Western wave of interest in Eastern teachings and mass-media gurus.

In addition to resident monks, the ashram has continued to receive a stream of visitors from abroad as well as devotees from all over India. Some are members of the society, spending a short period of time in *sadhana,* or spiritual disciplines, others are pilgrims and casual visitors. As a highly concentrated microcosm, the ashram has provided intense spiritual experience for many individuals. Some of the resident swamis later established ashrams in other parts of the world. One of the most famous of these swamis is **Vishnudevananda,** an exponent of hatha yoga, who established the **Sivananda Yoga Vedanta Centers** in communities across North America, with headquarters in Quebec.

Upon the death of Swami Sivananda on July 14, 1963, Swami **Chidananda** succeeded him; the secretarial work of the ashram continued in the hands of Swami Krishnananda, author of several books.

Little known outside India are two ashram music professors. **Swami Nadabrahmananda Saraswati,** who demonstrated extraordinary applications of **kundalini** energy to spiritual music, recorded a cassette, *Science of Thaan,* issued by Ashram Records (Box 9, Kootenay Bay, B.C., Canada VOB 1XO). Another important Hindu musician staying at the ashram seasonally is Swami Parvatikar, an exponent of **nada,** the yoga of music. He has made a number of recordings, and is included on the record album, *Religious Music of India,* recorded by Alain Danielou on Folkways Records.

There are also sound recordings of life at the Sivananda Ashram, including *The Sounds of Yoga-Vedanta: A Documentary of Life in an Indian Ashram* (Folkways Records) and *Sounds of Sivananda Ashram,* issued by Ashram Records, Canada.

There are now Divine Life Society branches or related organizations on every continent. The Sivananda Ashram may be reached c/o the Divine Life Society, P.O. Sivanandanagar, Dt. Tehri-Garhwal, U.P., Himalayas, India. Related organizations within the Sivananda heritage headquartered in North America include the **Yasodhara Ashram,** established by Swami Sivananda **Radha;** Integral Yoga International, headed by Swami Satchidananda; the Holy Shankaracharya Order, founded by Swami Lalshmy Devyashram; the IndoAmerican Yoga-Vedanta Society, headed by Swami Satchidananda Bua Ji; the prana Yoga Ashram, headed by Swami Sivalingam; the Raj-Yofa Math and retreat, headed by Fr. Satchakrananda Bodhisattvaguru; and the Yoga Research Foundation, headed by Swami Jyotirmayananda.

Sources:

Chidananda, Swami. *Forest Academy Lectures on Yoga.* Rishikish, India: The Author, 1960.

Krishnananda, Swami. *Swami Sivananda and the Spiritual Renaissance.* Rishikish, India: Sivananda Literature Research Institute, 1959.

Melton, J. Gordon. *Encyclopedia of American Religion.* Detroit: Gale Research, 1992.

Sivananda, Swami. *Autobiography of Swami Sivananda.* Shivanandanagar, India: Divine Life Society, 1983.

Divine Name, The

In Jewish mysticism great emphasis is placed upon the importance of the Divine Name. It is said to consist of 42 letters; not, as Moses Maimonides pointed out, comprised in one word, but in a phrase of several words that convey an exact notion of the essence of God. With the priestly decadence in the last days of the Temple, a name of 12 letters was substituted for the Divine Name, and as time went on even this secondary name was not divulged to every priest, only to a few. The longer name was sometimes said to contain 45 or 72 letters. The ten Sefiroth are also supposed, in a mystical sense, to be the names of the Deity (see **Kabala**). The Divine Name *Yahveh* is greater than "I am that I am," since the latter signifies God as he was before the creation, the Absolute, the Unknowable, the Hidden One, while but the former denotes the Supreme Manifestation, the immanence of God in the Cosmos.

In the course of time, the Divine Name was preserved as a tradition but only whispered aloud once a year by the high priest when he entered the Holy of Holies in the temple on the Day of Atonement. In general usage, the Name was indicated by secondary terms such as *Elohim* (the god), Adonai (the Lord), or Sabaoth (Lord of Hosts) to avoid the true name's being profaned.

The **Shemhamforash** (Name That Rusheth Through the Universe) was the greatest of mysteries of kabalistic folklore, which contains many stories of its power, telling how correct utterance of this supreme sound could hasten the redemption of a sick and sinful world. The creative power of divine utterance is indicated in Genesis in the phrase "and God said," which precedes creation; this is repeated in the Christian fourth gospel: "In the beginning was the Word, and the Word was with God and the Word was God" (John 1:1).

The concept of the *Logos* as the Word of God, immanent and creative, derived from Philo Judaeus of Alexandria in the first half-century of the Christian era. Philo fused together traditional Jewish teachings from the *Talmud* and the Hellenistic philosophy of Greece (influenced by Hindu mysticism). The 72-syllable name became the Tetragrammaton of four-syllable form. A Christian Kabalist of the sixteenth century developed a Pentagrammaton said to increase the power of the Tetragrammaton by adding the letter *S* to express the name of Jesus.

According to Hindu mysticism, the universe was created through divine utterance, symbolized by a Trigrammaton of three letters: A-U-M. This sacred sound prefixes and concludes reading of Hindu scriptures, and a whole scripture (*Mandukya Upanishad*) is devoted to its symbolism. **AUM** is often rendered as OM, the middle syllable being implicit in correct pronunciation, and its repetition constitutes one of the more popular Indian **mantras.**

Sources:

Schaya, Leo. *The Universal Meaning of the Kabbalah.* Baltimore, Md.: Penguin Books, 1973.

Wood, Thomas E. *The Mandukya Upanishad and the Agama Shastra: An Investigation into the Meaning of the Vedanta.* Honolulu: University of Hawaii Press, 1990.

Divine World

Formerly known as the Adi Plane—is in theosophic belief, the first or highest world, that first formed by the divine impulse in the creative process. It is unattainable by man in his present state according to Theosophy. (See also **Solar System; Theosophy**)

Divining Rod

A forked rod, or branch of tree, that in the hands of certain people is said to indicate, by means of spasmodic movements of varying intensity, the presence of water and minerals underground. Traditionally the rod is of hazel wood and V-shaped. The ends are held by the operator. Other materials such as right-angle wire rods are claimed to be equally effective. Diviners claim that under the effect of "rhabdic force," the rod twists or revolves when the operator passes over underground water or minerals. The term *rhabdic* derives from the Greek for rod.

Mention of the rod used for purposes of divination are to be found in the records of ancient Egypt. Cicero and Tacitus both wrote of the rod "virgula divina." This ancient divining rod was a form of **rhabdomancy** or divination by means of little pieces of stick.

In Germany it was known as the *wünschelrute* or "wishing-rod" and was used just as fortune-tellers use cards, coffee, or tea grounds today. Agricola's *De Re Metallica,* published at Basle at the beginning of the sixteenth century, makes reference to another rod, that he calls the "virgula furcata," the forked rod, to distinguish it from the "virgula divina." This rod, he says, was used by miners to discover mineral lodes.

Sixteenth-century Lutheran theologian Phillip Melancthon mentioned this use of the rod and ascribed the behavior of the "instrument" in the discovery of metallic ores to the law of sympathy—the belief that metals, trees, and other natural objects had certain subtle relationships with each other. Believers in this theory pointed to the fact that trees that grew above mineral lodes drooped as though attracted downwards; the scientific explanation attributes this natural phenomenon to the poverty of the soil.

In Sebastian Münster's *Cosmography,* also written during the sixteenth century, may be found engravings of "mineral diviners" at work. The priests of that time persecuted them as demons in disguise; they were also included in the **witchcraft** persecutions, suffering tortures and being burned to death.

Among miners on the continent the use of the "virgula furcata" became universal, especially in the Harz Mountains and throughout Saxony. In Germany it was called the *Schlagruthe,* "striking-rod," because it appeared to strike when held over mineral ores.

Robert Boyle (1627–91), called the "father of chemistry," was one of the first to mention the divining rod in England, in an essay published in 1663. He writes:

"A forked hazel twig is held by its horns, one in each hand, the holder walking with it over places where mineral lodes may be suspected, and it is said that the fork by dipping down will discover the place where the ore is to be found. Many eminent authors, amongst others our distinguished countryman Gabriel Plat, ascribe much to this detecting wand, and others, far from credulous or ignorant, have as eye-witnesses spoken of its value. When visiting the lead-mines of Somersetshire I saw its use, and one gentleman who employed it declared that it moved without his will, and I saw it bend so strongly as to break in his hand. It will only succeed in some men's hands, and those who have seen it may much more readily believe than those who have not."

Some authorities on the subject state that it was first brought to England during the time of Queen Elizabeth. Commissioners were sent to Germany to study the best methods of mining and brought back with them German miners from the Harz Mountains; these foreigners probably introduced the divining rod into England. It was first used to find water in Southern France, but not until a century later was it used in England for that purpose.

It became the "dowsing rod" in England, and Somersetshire might be called the home of the "dowser." The philosopher John Locke, a Somersetshire native, referred in 1691 to the dowsing rod and De Quincey, also from Somersetshire, told of singular cases of "jousers" as he called them. Today this means of finding water is used by farmers and owners of large estates. Dowsers are not geologists who might have a scientific knowledge of the locality—they may be from all walks of life. Among amateur dowsers were Lord Farrer and **Andrew Lang.**

The rods are mostly cut from hazel, but all kinds of nut and fruit trees have been used; white and black thorn and privet are also favorites. Pieces of watch spring and copper wire are also used, and in some cases the forked rod is dispensed with, the peculiar sensation felt in the arms, hands, and body being enough to indicate the water.

Dowsers wander over the ground with the ends of the fork grasped in the palms of the hands and the rod downward, and when it moves—turning suddenly upward in the hand for water or downward for minerals—at that spot will be found the desired object.

Attempts were often made to investigate the phenomenon scientifically. The electrical or magnetic theory was exploded by Father Kircher in 1654, who balanced the rod on a frictionless support like a delicate pair of scales and found that in this position nothing would induce it to move over hidden water or metal—it must be held by a human being before the movements can occur. In 1854 the French savant Michel Chevreul proposed the theory of involuntary muscular action.

Toward a Theory of Dowsing

Since then there have been many contradictory theories about the agent behind water divining, and there is still no general consensus. Many dowsers claim that they respond to earth "rays" or magnetism. Some believe that a kind of clairvoyant faculty is involved. It is possible that various factors are involved, varying with the talent and skill of the diviner.

It is widely believed that some force acts on the muscles through the nervous system, and that it is stopped by certain materials, such as a silken or woolen glove, rubber shoes, or tight bandages on the arms or legs. The effect has some resemblance to the sensations experienced by sitters in Spiritualist séances.

The diviner is warned that the rod is about to move by a sensation of tingling in the arm and legs, muscular contractions, giddiness, or profuse perspiration. If a particular spot of ground is passed these phenomena immediately cease, leaving a feeling of exhaustion. During the nineteenth century, the Spiritualist investigator **Edward W. Cox** pointed to the curious analogy that trance subjects are sometimes very sensitive to the touch of steel; they drop it instantly and declare that it feels red hot. Copper affects them similarly, while silver feels cool and gold positively cold.

That some kind of psychic perception is primarily involved, with the movement of the rod only an indicator of that perception, is suggested by the fact that many dowsers do not need to use a rod but rely upon an analysis of their sensations. In her book *Essays in Psychical Research* (1899), **A. Goodrich-Freer** reports that the dowser Leicester Gataker relied solely on the sensations experienced in his arm: "His hands, hung down, extended a little outwards, and on observing closely, we could see, from time to time a vibration in the middle fingers which appeared to be drawn downwards, just as in the case of the apex of the twig. His movements throughout were brisk and energetic and his statements were equally definite and decided." Abbé Bouly stated in a lecture in 1928, "I no longer require a rod, I can see the stream with my eyes; I attune my mind; I am looking for lead, I fix my eyes; I feel a wavy sensation like hot air over a radiator; I see it."

There have also been dowsers who react to the presence of underground oil, sometimes reporting sensations of fainting, and their operations have not required the use of a rod.

In the case of John Timms, studied by Oxford scientists in 1924, the demonstration was further complicated by a foreknowledge of where the hidden streams would be found. The attraction of hidden metals on his rod varied in this order: nickel, gold, silver, copper, bronze. Researchers Henri Mager and Lemoine found, independently of each other, that to produce as much action on the divining rod as one gram of gold does, one had to bury 1.2 grams of silver, 6 grams of nickel, 15 of aluminum, 40 of zinc, 75 of lead, and 125 grams of copper.

Depending on what the dowser desires to find he may hold a bottle of water, a piece of metal, an empty tube (in searching for caverns), or a personal object (for a corpse in water) in his hand. Once a stream has been found it is possible, by varying the mineral substances or by holding tubes of bacterial cultures, to determine its alkaline content or infectious state. From the latter discovery the idea was developed in France (by Mlle. Chantereine, a follower of Henri Mager) of using the divining rod for medical diagnosis. Promising results have been recorded in noting human reactions to disease germs, to remedies and foods, and also in noting the difference between radiation produced by a healthy organ as compared with that of an unsound one.

The following physiological explanation was advanced by Dudley Wright:

"All living beings have in their nervous systems cells with retractile branching processes which correspond to the movable condensers in wireless sets and, in addition, the cells of the body are capable of self-induction (on the same principle as wireless) through coiled structures in the nucleus. It is through these that the bodies of men and animals are capable of tuning into the various wavelengths emitted by other people, by other living things, and even by water, minerals and oil. The muscles are supplied by two sets of nerves, viz., (1.) from the cerebro spinal system which controls the voluntary movement of the muscles; (2.) the sympathetic nervous system which controls tension of the muscles both voluntary and involuntary. The rod moves because a change in the tension of our muscles of the hand holding the rod is brought about reflexly through the nervous system by the radiations received."

Mager claimed to have demonstrated two currents traversing the rod, opposite in direction, repelling one another: a discharge current passing from the body of the dowser into the earth on one side, and a return current passing from the earth to the other side of the dowser's body, to his other arm and to the other branch of the rod. He formed the conclusion that the movements of the rod are governed by the laws of electro dynamics as formulated by Ampère in 1820.

Dowsing in France

There has been active interest in dowsing in France for several centuries. In 1635 the Baron and Baroness Beausoleil discovered 150 mineral veins in this manner. They may have been the first to apply the diving rod to finding water as Chevreul in *Les Baguettes Divinatoires* fixes 1630 as "the most remote date which may be cited for the application of the rod to the discovery of springs, at least in France." The Beausoleils published a book in 1640 (*La Restitution de Pluton*) and dedicated it to Richelieu. A few years later both the baron and his wife were put into prison on charges of **sorcery.**

One of the strangest stories of dowsing is that of the French diviner Jacques Aymar, who in 1692 apparently traced murderers through a divining rod and discovered other criminals in the same way.

On July 25, 1692 (the story goes), a wine seller and his wife were murdered. Aymar was asked to help with the investigation. His divining rod became violently agitated at the scene of the crime and led him, like the scent leads a hound, for several days on the track of the murderers. One of them was discovered in a prison and confessed; two others escaped from France.

The procurator general subjected Aymar to other severe tests. He secretly buried the blood-stained hedging bill with which the murder was committed, in different places in the garden. The divining rod indicated the place of burial every time. Despite these successes, Aymar's faculty was a complete failure when subjected to tests in Paris. However, even in modern times, psychic faculties have often failed in an atmosphere of skepticism or hostility.

In 1853 the French Academy of Sciences delegated a commission of inquiry into the divining rod. The immediate reason for the inquiry was D'Hyères Riondet's *Memoire sur la Baguette Divinatoire.* The report, prepared by Michel Chevreul and published in book form under the title *Les Baguettes Divinatoires* (1854), is a classical study. It attributes the movement of the rod to the muscular force of the dowser.

Dowsing Researched

Psychical researchers neglected dowsing for some time. **Sir William Barrett** was its first modern investigator. He experimented with a dowser who successfully found coins placed under inverted saucers on the table. He published two lengthy reports in the *Proceedings* of the Society for Psychical Research. Published posthumously was Barrett's book *The Divining Rod: An Experimental and Psychological Study* (1926). Written in cooperation with **Theodore Besterman,** it became a standard work on the subject. Like Chevreul, Barrett attributed the twisting of the rod to motor automatism and considered it a phenomenon allied to **automatic writing.** Since then considerable progress has been made in validating the phenomena of dowsing.

The Honorable M. E. G. Finch Hatton gives a remarkable account in the *Proceedings* of the Society for Psychical Research (vols. 2, 13, 15) of his experiments with J. Mullins, in which his brother, the Hon. Harold Finch Hatton, participated:

"1. I took him on the grass in front of the house, across which the water-supply pipe passed. There was no indication of its presence on the surface, nor did I previously mention its existence to Mullins. On crossing it the twig moved in the manner described and he could trace the water to right and left by its means along the path actually taken by the pipe.

"2. On our way to the kitchen garden, Mullins discovered a spring on the open lawn, whose existence was unknown to me—it had been closed in so long—but was subsequently attested by an old laborer on the place who remembered it as a well, and had seen it bricked in many years before.

"3. On reaching the kitchen garden I knew that a lead pipe, leading water to a tap outside the wall, crossed the gravel path at a certain spot. On crossing it the twig made no sign. I was astonished at first, until I remembered what Mullins had said about stagnant water and that the tap was not running. I sent to have it turned on, re-conducted Mullins over the ground, when the twig immediately indicated the spot. When Mullins had passed on I carefully marked the exact spot indicated by the twig. When he had left the garden, I said: 'Now, Mullins, may we blindfold you and let you try?' He said 'Oh yes, if you don't lead me into a pond or anything of that sort.' We promised. I then reconducted him blindfolded to the marked spot by a different route, leaving the tap running, with the result that the stick indicated with mathematic exactness the same spot. At first he slightly overran it a foot or so and then felt round, as it were, and seemed to be led back to the exact centre of influence by the twig."

Radiesthesia

In 1913, before the International Congress of Experimental Psychology in Paris, Joseph Mathieu asked to be tested for a strange ability divining water from maps alone. The claim was proved later. E. M. Penrose, official water diviner to the government of British Columbia (*Occult Review,* March 1933), was also successful in duplicating the feat. Since then many modern dowsers use a pendulum instead of a rod, and their practice is named **radiesthesia.** French dowsers were pioneers in this field.

In Gallipoli, during World War I, the British Expeditionary Force was nearing exhaustion because of the intense heat and lack of water. Sapper S. Kelley, the former head of Kelley & Bassett, civil engineers from Melbourne, attempted to find water by a piece of bent copper band. Within 100 yards of the divisional headquarters he found a spring that gave 2,000 gallons of pure, cold water per hour. In a week he discovered 32 wells giving sufficient water to supply 100,000 men with a gallon of water daily.

The Abbé Bouly restored large areas of war-devastated land in France to cultivation by localizing buried shells. He was able to discriminate between German and Allied ammunition. Another man claimed success in determining the sex of eggs by the use of the divining rod. Maria Mattaloni, a 24-year-old Italian peasant girl, located many old Etruscan tombs at Capena, near Rome.

The Abbé Gabriel Lambert, the well-known French water diviner, was the subject of some interesting experiments in London. As narrated by **Harry Price** in *Psychic Research* (October 1930) the Abbot used a bobbin (like a fisherman's cork float, cone-shaped and painted in stripes of bright colors) suspended from a thread in his right hand. Over hidden springs in Hyde Park, the bobbin which Lambert was purposely swinging laterally "would make a spasmodic movement, change its course, and commence spinning furiously, describing a larger and larger circle the longer we stood over the source of activity. When we reached the bank of the subterranean river the bobbin would stop dead—just as if it had been hit by a stone. The cessation of the spinning was even more spectacular than the commencement. . . . When we came to a nappe (a pool of still water) the bobbin would make quite a different movement. The Abbé could tell the depth of the hidden supplies, their approximate volume and directional characteristics. . . . The Abbé considers that his gift is partly physical and partly psychic. For instance, if he is looking for a nappe, he will pass over a dozen running springs without becoming aware of the fact. And the reverse is the case. He will be likewise unconscious of a flowing river (or water of any description) if he is looking for minerals of a metallic lode. . . . To provide the other 'pole' when using his bobbin, he carries in his free hand a small bottle of pure water (if looking for drinking water), a bottle of mineral water if seeking a chalybeate spring or a piece of ore similar to the metallic lode he is trying to find."

On March 22, 1931, a congress of water diviners was held in Verona by the National Society of Rhabdomancy of Italy. Nearly two hundred members assembled. It was stated by one of them that the king of Italy had water divining powers.

Since then associations of dowsers have been formed in many countries, using either name—"dowsing" or "radiesthesia." The French society L'Association des Amis de la Radiesthé was founded in 1930, followed by the **British Society of Dowsers** in 1933. Similar associations have been founded in Germany, Italy and other European countries, and in the United States the **American Society of Dowsers** was formed in 1961. A number of journals have been published, including *Journal of the British Society of Dowsers, The American Dowser, La Chronique des Souciers, Radiesthesie Magazine, Les Amis de la Radiesthesie, Zeitschrift für Radiästhesie, and Radiästhesie—Geopathie—Strahlenbiologie.*

A specialized branch of dowsing is **radionics,** in which an apparatus is used to detect or treat illnesses, involving theories of wavelengths and vibrations, and using coils, condensers, and other devices associated with electronics but without conventional electronic construction.

Although many earlier theories about "earth rays" have not been satisfactorily resolved from a scientific point of view, they persist in one form or another, and the divining faculty has been associated with the earth and stone energies claimed in the study of **leys.**

The subject is a vast one, and so far the only comprehensive survey of the scientific factors involved is the monumental study by Prof. S. W. Tromp entitled *Psychical Physics; A Scientific Analysis of Dowsing, Radiesthesia and Kindred Divining Phenomena* (1949). The book contains a bibliography of nearly fifteen hundred references. The Barrett and Besterman study, *The Divining Rod* (1926), remains a basic reference in the field of water divining itself, supplemented by Besterman's later book, *Water Divining: New Facts and Theories* (1938). A valuable work published by the U.S. Geological Survey, Department of the Interior, is *The Divining Rod: A History of Water Witching* (1917; 1938), which contains a chronological bibliography up to the year 1916. For an uncritical skeptical view of dowsing, see the chapter "Dowsing Rods and Doodlebugs" in *Fads and Fallacies in the Name of Science* (1957), by Martin Gardner. For a skeptical survey of dowsing see *Water Witching, U.S.A.* (1959), by Evon Z. Vogt and Ray Hyman.

Sources:

Benedikt, M. *Ruten- und Pendel-lehre.* Vienna; Leipzig, 1917.

Besterman, Theodore. *Water Divining; New Facts and Theories.* London: Metheun, 1938.

Bird, Christopher. *The Divining Hand.* New York: E. P. Dutton, 1979.

Cameron, Verne L. *Aquavideo: Locating Underground Water.* Santa Barbara, Calif.: El Cariso, 1970.

———. *Map Dowsing.* Santa Barbara, Calif.: El Cariso, 1971.

———. *Oil Locating.* Santa Barbara, Calif.: El Cariso, 1971.

Carrié, Abbé. *L'hydroscopographie et métalloscopogragie, ou l'art de découvrir les sources et les gisement metallifers au moyen de l'électromagnétisme.* Saintes, France, 1863.

Chambers, Howard V. *Dowsing, Water Witches and Divining Rods for the Millions.* Los Angeles: Sherbourne Press, 1969.

Chevreul, M. E. *De la Baguette divinatoire, du pendule dit explorateur, et des tables tournantes.* Paris, 1854.

De France, Henry. *The Elements of Dowsing.* London, 1948.

De Morogues, Baron. *Observations sur le fluide organo-électrique.* Paris, 1854.

De Vallemont, Abbe. *La physique occulte, ou Traité de la baguette divinatoire.* Paris, 1693.

Ellis, Arthur J. *The Divining Rod: A History of Water Witching, with a Bibliography.* Washington, 1917; 1938.

Klinckowstroem, Graf von. *Virgula divina. Ein Beitrag zur Geschichte der Wünschelrute.* Berlin, 1910.

Maby, J. Cecil, and T. B. Franklin. *The Physics of the Divining Rod.* London, 1939.

Mager, Henri. *Water Diviners and Their Methods.* London, 1931.

Maury, Marguerite. *How to Dowse: Experimental and Practical Radiasthesia.* London: G. Bell and Sons, 1953.

Mermet, Abbe. *Principles and Practice of Radiesthesie.* London, 1967.

Nicolas, Jean. *La verge de Jacob, ou l'art de trouver les trésors les sources, les limites, les métaux, les mines, les minéraux et autres cachées, par l'usage du baton fourché.* Lyons, France, 1693. Translated as *Jacob's Rod.* London: Thomas Welton, 1875.

Nielsen, Greg, and J. Polansky. *Pendulum Power.* New York: Warner, 1977.

Roberts, Kenneth. *Henry Gross and His Dowsing Rod.* Garden City, N.Y.: Doubleday, 1952.

Stark, Erwin E. *A History of Dowsing and Energy Relationships.* North Hollywood, Calif.: BAC, 1978.

Underwood, Peter. *The Complete Book of Dowsing and Divining.* London, 1980.

Wayland, Bruce, and Shirley Wayland. *Steps to Dowsing Power.* Howell, Mich.: Life Force Press, 1976.

Weaver, Herbert. *Divining, the Primary Sense: Unfamiliar Radiation in Nature, Art, and Science.* London: Routledge & Kegan Paul, 1978.

Willey, Raymond C. *Modern Dowsing.* Cottonwood, Ariz.: Esoteric Publications, 1976.

Wyman, Walker D. *Witching for Water, Oil, Pipes, and Precious Minerals.* River Falls: University of Wisconsin Press, 1977.

Division of Personality Studies, University of Virginia

In 1968 the Department of Psychiatry at the University of Virginia established a new Division of Parapsychology to develop a broad program of investigation into various aspects of the paranormal. It was given its initial impetus by the longstanding interest in **survival** of death, specifically in the form of reincarnation, by **Ian Stevenson,** a member of the faculty, who was placed in charge of the new structure. Stevenson, noted for his scientific approach to the evidence for **reincarnation,** had previously won recognition for his essay "The Evidence for Survival from Claimed Memories of Former Incarnations" (1961), and had previously pursued the research leading to his monumental book, *Twenty Cases Suggestive of Reincarnation* (1966). As head of the division he continued his investigations of reincarnation cases and also conducted studies in telepathy.

More recently, following Stevenson's retirement, the division has been absorbed into the Division of Personality Studies, and research on the paranormal deemphasized. Address: Division of Personality Studies, Department of Behavioral Medicine & Psychiatry, Box 152, Medical Center, University of Virginia, Charlottesville, VA 22908.

Sources:

Stevenson, Ian. *Cases of the Reincarnation Type.* 4 vols. Charlottesville: University of Virginia Press, 1975, 1977, 1980, 1983.

Divs

The *div* of ancient Persia, pronounced "deo, deu," or "dive," is thought to be equivalent to the European devil of the Middle Ages. In the romances of Persia *divs* are represented as male and female, but the male *divs* are considered the more dangerous. It is from their character, personified in a supposed chief, that the devil is portrayed with his well-known attributes.

The male *divs,* according to the legends of Persia, were entrusted with the government of the world for 7,000 years anterior to the creation of Adam, and they were succeeded by the female divs or *peris,* who under their chief, Gian ben Gian, ruled another 2,000 years. The dominion of the peris was terminated by Eblis (the devil of the Koran) who had been created from the elements of fire, and whose abode was previously with the angels.

Eblis or "Haris," as he was also called, became the leader of the rebellious angels when they were commanded to pay homage to the first created man. Joined by the whole race of *genii,* the male and female *divs,* that he had formerly subjugated, he was, like them, deprived of grace. Eblis and his immediate followers were condemned to suffer for a long period in the infernal regions, but the remainder were allowed to wander over the earth, a constant source of misery to themselves and to the human race.

Divs were supposed to assume various forms, especially that of the serpent, and in the drawings annexed to the Persian romances they are represented much as our own devils, ogres, and giants, in the tales of the Middle Ages. The writers of later times, both Arabian and Persian, localized the abode of these evil genii in the mountain Kaf. Their capital was Aherman-abad, the abode of Aherman their chief, who is identified with the Ahremanes of the Manicheans, that remarkable sect said to have borrowed their doctrines from Zoroaster.

The distinction of sex is a remarkable characteristic of the *divs,* and its evil results in a system of diabolic superstition may be read in the stories of the Ephialtae and Hyphialtae, or nightmare.

Possibly the same in origin as the Persian *divs,* are the **devas** or *daivres* of the Hindus, who are said to inhabit a world called, after them, **Deva-Loka.** There is a brief account of them in N. E. Kindersley's *Specimens of Hindoo Literature* (1794):

"The daivers perpetually recur in their romances, and other literary works, and are represented as possessing not only material bodies, but as being subject to human frailties. Those saints and heroes who may not as yet be considered worthy of the paradises of Shivven or of Veeshnoo, are represented as inhabiting the Daiver-Logum (or Sorgum). These daivers are in number no less than three hundred and thirty million. The principal are—I. 'Daivuntren' or 'Indiren' their king; to whom report is made of all that happens among them. His court of audience is so capacious as to contain not only the numerous daivers, but also the prophets, attendants, etc. They are represented in the mythological romances of the Hindoos, as having been engaged in bloody wars, and with various success against the giants (Assoores). The family of Daivuntren consists of his wife 'Inderaunee,' and his son 'Seedera-budderen' (born from a cow), who records the actions of men, by which they are finally to be judged. II. The attendants or companions of these daivers are—1. The 'Kinnarer,' who sing and play on musical instruments. 2. 'Dumbarim Nardir,' who also perform on a species of drum. 3. 'Kimprusher,' who wait on the daivers are represented with the wings and fair countenances of angels. 4. 'Kundagaindoorer,' similar winged beings who execute the mandates of Veeshnoo. 5. 'Paunner,' a species of jugglers, who amuse the daivers with snake dancing, etc. 6. 'Viddiaser,' their bards, who are acquainted with all arts and sciences, and entertain them with their histories and discourses. 7. 'Tsettee,' who attend them in their aerial journeys. 8. 'Kanuanader,' or 'Dovdanks,' messengers, who conduct the votaries of Veeshnoo and Shivven to their respective paradises, and the wicked to hell (*Narekah*), of which 'Eemen' is sovereign. III. The third class of daivergoel, daivers, or genii, are the eight keepers of the eight sides of the world, literally signified by their general name of 'Aushtatikcu-Pauligaur;' they are—1. 'Indiren,' who is no other than Daivuntren, named above. 2. 'Augne-Baugauven,' the god of fire. 3. 'Eemen,' king of death and the infernal regions. 4. 'Nerudee,' the element of earth represented under the figure of a giant. 5. 'Vaivoo,' god of air and winds. 6. 'Varoonen,' god of clouds and rain. 7. 'Gooberen,' god of riches. 8. 'Essaunien,' or Shivven himself, in one of his 1,008 appearances on earth."

To these principal daivers, Kindersley adds without sufficient reason the "Reeshees" of the Hindoos, and their tutelary god of virtue, "Derma-Daive."

For the true oriental doctrine of these evil genii the *Zend-Avesta* may be consulted; it associates the idea of evil more especially with the *peris* or female *divs,* contrary to the later romances of the Arab world. This anomaly reappears in our own fairy tales, the same characters that at times are invested with the most malignant attributes, being often described as having sylphlike grace and beauty.

Dixon, Jeane (1918–)

American sensitive and prophesier. Dixon's rise to prominence began when she predicted the assassination of President John F. Kennedy in 1963. She also predicted the deaths of Carole Lombard, Dag Hammarskjöld, and Mahatma Ghandhi, and the suicide of Marilyn Monroe.

Dixon was born January 5, 1918, to Frank and Emma Pickert in Medford, Wisconsin; she moved with her family to California at an early age. A gypsy told the eight-year-old Dixon that she had a sensitivity to events around her and presented her with a crystal ball, in which she saw visionary pictures. Dixon's family moved again and she attended high school in Los Angeles, later training to become a singer and actress. At age 21, she married James L. Dixon, who was then in partnership with the film producer Hal Roach in an automobile agency. During World War II, Dixon entertained servicemen with her predictions through the Home Hospitality Committee, which was organized by Washington socialites.

Being a devout Roman Catholic, Dixon believes that she has a God-given gift that must be used for the good of humankind. She is also the founder of the charity known as Children to Children Inc.

Her astrological forecasts are syndicated by the Chicago Tribune–New York News Syndicate, Inc. Her books include *Jeane Dixon, My Life and Prophecies: Her Own Story as Told to Rene Noorbergen* (1969), *Reincarnation and Prayers to Live By* (1970), *Jeane Dixon's Astrological Cookbook* (1976), *Horoscopes for Dogs* (1979), and *The Riddle of Powderworks Road* (1980). Newspaper reporter **Ruth Montgomery** published Dixon's biography, *A Gift of Prophecy,* in 1965. It sold nearly three million copies in hardback and became a number one best-seller in paperback.

Some critics belittle Dixon for her inaccuracy in predicting events. Most prophesiers, however, have a certain failure rate, often based on the faulty interpretation of symbols, visions, and psychic reactions; Dixon freely admits to these errors. It is said that **extrasensory perception** is too unpredictable for prophecy to be an exact science.

Dixon can be reached c/o James L. Dixon & Co., 1765 N St. NW, Washington, DC 20036.

Djemscheed, The Cup of

A **divination** cup that has been the subject of many of the poems and myths of ancient Persia. It was believed to have been found while digging the foundations of Persepolis and was filled with the elixir of immortality. In this magical cup was mirrored the whole world, and everything, good and evil, was revealed therein. The Persians had great faith in these revelations and attributed the prosperity of their empire to the possession of this famous cup.

Djual Khul, Master

One of the masters originally contacted by **Helena Petrovna Blavatsky,** cofounder of the **Theosophical Society.** According to theosophical teachings there exists a spiritual hierarchy composed of individuals who have finished their round of earthly reincarnations and have evolved to the spiritual planes, from which they guide the affairs of humanity. Those members of the hierarchy closest to humanity are the "lords of the seven rays" (of the light spectrum). Each ray represents a particular virtue, which the lord of that ray exemplifies.

Djual Khul, generally known simply by his initials, DK, is a master of the second ray along with the master **Koot Hoomi,** who, in the theosophical perspective, was DK's direct teacher. Theosophists believe DK currently inhabits a Tibetan body and resides in Tibet near Koot Hoomi. In his previous incarnations he was Dharmajyoyi, a follower of Gautama the Buddha; Kleinias, a follower of Pythagoras; and Aryasanga, a seventh-century Buddhist who founded a monastery in the Himalayas once visited by Blavatsky. Charles W. Leadbeater claims to have met him in Cairo when DK traveled there to meet with Blavatsky and also to have worked with DK at Adyar, India, at the international headquarters of the Theosophical Society. DK was one of the three main communicators (the others being the masters **Morya** and Koot Hoomi) of what were compiled as *The Mahatma Letters,* the ultimate source for many theosophical ideas.

DK, already one of the more important of the theosophical masters, was given new life early in the twentieth century when **Alice A. Bailey** claimed regular contact with him. Her channeled material eventually contributed to her separating from the Theosophical Society and founding the **Arcane School.** Through the 1920 and 1930s she channeled a number of books from DK, whom she generally called "The Tibetan." Bailey's books are used by a number of groups that have emerged since her death in 1949.

Among others who have claimed contact with Djual Khul is Hope Troxell, founder of the Church of Cosmic Origin and School of Thought; Muriel R. Tepper (also known as Muriel Isis), founder of the Lighted Way; Zelrun Karsleigh, founder of the Universariun Foundation; and Pauline Sharpe, the primary channel for Mark-Age, a flying saucer contactee group.

Sources:

Barker, A. Trevor, ed. *The Mahatma Letters to A. P. Sennett from the Mahatams M. & K.H.* London: T. Fisher Unwin, 1923. 3rd rev. ed. Adyar, Madras, India: Theosophical Publishing House, 1962.

DK [through Alice A. Bailey]. *Serving Humanity.* New York: Lucis Trust, 1972.

———. *The Soul, The Quality of Life: From the Writings of the Tibetan Teacher (Djwhal Khul).* New York: Lucis Trust, 1972.

Melton, J. Gordon. *Encyclopedia of American Religions.* Detroit: Gale Research, 1992.

Nada-Yolanda [Pauline Sharper]. *Mark-Age Period and Program.* Miami: Mark-Age Metacenter, 1970.

Ransom, Josephine. *A Short History of the Theosophical Society.* Adyar, Madra, India: Theosophical Publishing House, 1938.

Thirty Years Work: The Books of Alice Bailey and the Tibetan Master Djwhal Khul. New York: Lucis Publishing, n.d.

Doane, Doris Chase (1913–)

Doris Chase Doane, one of America's outstanding astrologers, was born April 4, 1913, at Mansfield, Massachusetts. After high school she left New England for California to attend the University of California, Los Angeles, from which she received her B.S. in psychology in 1944. She had previously become interested in **astrology** and associated herself with **Elbert Benjamine** and the **Church of Light.** She taught astrology while going through the complete Church of Light curriculum, which she completed the same year as her work at UCLA.

She emerged as one of the organization's leading figures. She began writing in astrology and the next year was ordained by the church and married to one of the church's ministers, Edward Doane, who succeeded Benjamine as its head in 1951. Besides her works in astrology, at a time when the selection of even basic books was extremely limited, Doane gave a considerable amount of time to changing laws that prevented astrologers from operating in some states and cites by equating astrology with fortunetelling. In that endeavor she became a strong advocate for training, professionalism, and certification of astrologers. In her mature years Chase has received many honors from astrological organizations. She was elected president of the American Federation of Astrologers in 1979.

Sources:

Doane, Doris Chase. *Astrological Rulerships.* Redondo Beach, Calif.: Foundation for Scientific Spiritual Understanding, 1970.

———. *Astrology: Thirty Years of Research.* Los Angeles: Church of Light, 1956.

———. *Astrology as a Business.* Tempe, Ariz.: American Federation of Astrologers, 1986.

———. *Horoscopes of the Presidents.* Hollywood, Calif.: Professional Astrologers, 1971.

Holden, James H., and Robert A. Hughes. *Astrological Pioneers of America.* Tempe, Ariz.: American Federation of Astrologers, 1988.

"Doctor"

One of the spirit controls of the medium **Stainton Moses** (1839–1882). "Doctor" was said to have been the stoic philosopher Athenodorus, who instructed Emperor Tiberius in his youth. He was the supervisor of the philosophic teachings delivered through Moses and claimed to have invisibly attended him for 21 years. He was the alleged author of some of the *Spirit Teachings* published by Moses.

Dodds, Eric Robertson (1893–1979)

Professor of Greek who was closely associated with psychical research. He was born July 26, 1893, in Northern Ireland, studied at Belfast, and did postgraduate work at University College, Oxford. He began his teaching career in 1924 as a professor of Greek at the University of Birmingham. He then became a regius professor of Greek at Oxford University in 1936, a post he retained until his retirement in 1960. Dodds then served as president of the **Society for Psychical Research,** London, from 1961 to 1963.

In his presidential address in 1962, Dodds stated that his first introduction to psychical research was through the book *Human Personality & Its Survival of Bodily Death,* by **F. W. H. Myers.** Although impressed by the evidence in this work, he said he saw no prospect of making "even a modest livelihood by psychical research" and so became a professional Greek scholar "with psychical research as a spare time occupation." He contributed a number of articles to the *Journal* of the Society for Psychical Research as well as to other publications. He discussed the problem of **psi** phenomena in his autobiography *Missing Persons* (1977).

Dodds is remembered as one of the more rigorous thinkers in psychical research. His most famous paper concerned **survival** and his disbelief in the acceptability of the reported evidence for it. He concluded that all of the paranormal data collected in the search for evidence of survival could be explained by super **extrasensory perception.**

He died April 8, 1979, in England.

Sources:

Berger, Arthur S., and Joyce Berger. *The Encyclopedia of Parapsychology and Psychical Research.* New York: Paragon House, 1991.

Dodds, Eric R. *The Greeks and the Irrational.* Berkeley, Calif.: University of California Press, 1951.

———. *Missing Persons: An Autobiography.* Oxford: Clearendon Press, 1977.

———. "Supernormal Phenomena in Classical Antiquity." *Proceedings* of the Society for Psychical Research 55 (1971): 189.

———. "Why I Do Not Believe in Survival." *Proceedings* of the Society for Psychical Research 42 (1934): 147.

Pleasants, Helene, ed. *Biographical Dictionary of Parapsychology.* New York: Helix Press, 1964.

Dommeyer, Frederick C(harles) (1909–)

Professor of philosophy and writer on parapsychology and philosophy. Dommeyer was born January 12, 1909, in Warrington, Florida. He studied at Union College, Schenectady, New York (B.A., 1932), and Brown University (M.A., 1935; Ph.D., 1937) and did postgraduate study at Oxford and Hamburg Universities. His professional career began as an instructor at Brown (1937–38) followed by 20 years at Syracuse University (1938–58), during which time he served as head of the philosophy department for 14 years (1944–58). He then moved to San Jose State College as head of the department of philosophy.

During his career, Dommeyer wrote several books and a number of articles for professional journals on philosophy. He also wrote articles on parapsychology, primarily for the *Journal* of the American Society for Psychical Research. He was a member of the board of review of *Psychic.*

Sources:

Dommeyer, Frederick C. *Body, Mind and Death.* N.p., 1965.

Dommeyer, Frederick C., ed. *Current Philosophical Issues: Essays in Honor of Curt John Ducasse.* N.p., 1966.

———. "Some Ostensibly Precognitive Dreams." *Journal* of the Society for Psychical Research (July 1955).

Pleasants, Helene, ed. *Biographical Dictionary of Parapsychology.* New York: Helix Press, 1964.

Don Juan

The mysterious, probably fictional Yaqui Indian sorcerer whose metaphysical doctrines were recorded by **Carlos Castaneda** in his best-selling book *The Teachings of Don Juan: A Yaqui Way of Knowledge* (1968) and in numerous subsequent writings. No evidence has been produced for the actual existence of Don Juan outside the pages of Castaneda's books.

Sources:

Castaneda, Carlos. *Journey to Ixtlan.* N.p., 1972.

———. *A Separate Reality.* N.p., 1971.

———. *The Teachings of Don Juan: A Yaqui Way of Knowledge.* N.p., 1968.

Donn

An Irish hero of medieval legend, son of Midir the Proud. *The Colloquy of the Ancients,* a thirteenth- to fourteenth-century collection of Ossianic stories, tells how Finn and Kelta and five other champions were out hunting one day and followed a beautiful fawn until it vanished under ground. Seeking shelter in a noble's mansion, they were entertained by *Donn mac Midir* and his brother, and their aid was requested against the rest of the **Danaans.**

Three times that year they had to fight their fairy foes, and all their followers were killed except the 28 warriors. The fawn they had followed had been an enchanted maiden sent to entice them. After a year of successful fighting, the Danaans were obliged to make peace.

Donnars, Jacques (1919–)

French physician who studied parapsychological phenomena. He was born September 8, 1919, in St. Mandé (Seine), France. In 1944 he married Geneviève Herdud. He was a member of the French Homeopathic Society, Acupuncture Society, and the French Society of Osteopathy. His book *Inhibition: Facteur de vie* deals with possible connections between **parapsychology** and inhibition processes.

Sources:

Pleasants, Helene, ed. *Biographical Dictionary of Parapsychology.* New York: Helix Press, 1964.

Donnelly, Ignatius (1831–1901)

Popular writer of books offering an alternative view of human history. Donnelly was born in Philadelphia, November 3, 1831. A farmer-politician, he became lieutenant governor of Minnesota and then a state senator. At one point he was nominated for the vice president of the United States.

Donnelly wrote several novels but is best remembered for reviving interest in the lost continent of **Atlantis** in his book *Atlantis, the Antediluvian World* (1882). Using nineteenth-century ethnological and archeological data, Donnelly argued that the likenesses noted in the ancient cultures on either side of the Atlantic pointed to a common origin, a sunken continent whose survivors populated lands to the east and west.

In his next book, *Ragnarök: The Age of Fire and Gravel* (1883), he claimed that the Pleistocene Ice Age resulted from a collision between the earth and a comet. This was the first statement of a theme to be developed many decades later by **Immanuel Velikovsky.** Donnelly's two books have become classics of **occultism** and have been reprinted in modern times. Atlantis has been especially favored by followers of **Edgar Cayce,** who had much to say about Atlantis.

Continuing his foray into alternative histories, Donnelly also wrote *The Great Cryptogram* (1888) designed to show that the plays of Shakespeare were written by Bacon. Donnelly died January 2, 1901.

Sources:

Donnelly, Ignatius. *Atlantis: The Antediluvian World.* 1882. Rev. ed., edited by Egerton Sykes. New York: Gramercy, 1949.

———. *The Great Cryptogram: Francis Bacon's Cipher in the So-called Shakespeare Plays.* Chicago: R. S. Peale, 1888.

———. *Ragnarök: the Age of Fire and Gravel.* Reprint, New Hyde Park, N.Y.: University Books, 1970. Reprinted as *The Destruction of Atlantis; Ragnarök.* Blauvelt, N.Y.: Rudolf Steiner Publications, 1971.

Ridge, Martin. *Ignatius Donnelly: The Portrait of a Politician.* Chicago: University of Chicago Press, 1962.

DOP See Dermo-Optical Perception

Doreal, Maurice (d. 1963)

Maurice Doreal was the name adopted by Claude Doggins as head of the **Brotherhood of the White Temple,** an occult fraternity headquartered in Sedalia, Colorado. Doreal was born in Sulfur Springs, Oklahoma. As a youth he became interested in Tarzan, which quickly broadened into a general interest in fantasy and science fiction literature, and by 1950 his library included some 5,000 titles. His interests also expanded to the **occult.** He served in World War I, after which, he claimed, he spent eight years in Tibet. He also claimed to have visited the occult center in the middle of Mt. Shasta in northern California.

Doreal founded the Brotherhood of the White Temple in 1930, and spent much of his life writing the brotherhood lessons and a series of pamphlets, called the Little Temple Library, on a wide variety of occult-related topics from **Atlantis** to **UFOs.** He claimed to have gained his knowledge from his contact with the Great White Lodge of Masters, those who have passed beyond their earthly experience and now seek to guide humanity in its evolution.

Doreal began work on new headquarters for the brotherhood in Sedalia in 1946, during the height of anxieties over possible atomic war. The location, a valley enclosed by 1,500-foot mountain walls, was believed to be a protected site. Headquarters moved in 1951. Two years later Doreal predicted that the biblical Battle of Armageddon would begin very soon, and residents stored foods against the coming hard times.

Doreal died in 1963, and the brotherhood has continued to the present using his many writings as their authoritative literature.

Sources:

Kossy, Donna. *Kooks: A Guide to the Outer Limits of Human Belief.* Portland, Oreg.: Feral House, 1994.

Doten, Elizabeth (1829–1913)

American inspirational speaker considered the greatest female improvisator of the nineteenth century. She was born in Plymouth, Massachusetts, April 1, 1829. For many years she spoke from the platform under what she claimed to be the influence of spirits. From the poems she recited on these occasions, two compilations were published: *Poems from the Inner Life* and *Poems of Progress* (1871). On one occasion she claimed to be under the direct influence of Edgar Allan Poe and rendered "Resurrexi," a poem noted for its resemblance to Poe's style and manifesting the same intensity of feeling. Some of her poems were also printed in the gift book *The Lily of the Valley for 1855* (Boston, 1855), which she edited.

During the last 28 years of her life Doten withdrew from the lecture field and mediumistic work because she had become unable to determine the point at which she ceased to act and the spirit influence began.

Sources:

Doten, Elizabeth. *Poems of Progress.* Boston: White & Company, 1871.

Double

The etheric counterpart of the physical body which, when out of coincidence, may temporarily move about in space in comparative freedom and appear in various degrees of density to others. The belief in the existence of the double, or **astral body,** is ancient, and its modern use as a "working hypothesis" solves many puzzling problems in psychical research.

The Roman Catholic Church gave tacit approval to such an idea in its consideration of the bilocation of several saints. St. Anthony of Padua, for example, preaching in the Church of St. Pierre du Queyroix at Limoges on Holy Thursday in 1226, suddenly remembered that he was due at that hour at a service in a monastery at the other end of the town. He drew his hood over his head and knelt down for some minutes while the congregation reverently waited. At that moment the saint was seen by the assembled monks across town to step forth from his stall in the monastery chapel, read the appointed passage in the office, and immediately disappear. Similar stories are recorded of St. Severus of Ravenna and St. Ambrose and St. Clement of Rome. The best-known case is dated September 17, 1774. Alphonse de Liguori, imprisoned at Arezzo, remained quiet in his cell and took no nourishment. Five days later he awoke in the morning and said that he had been at the deathbed of the pope.

Experimental Findings

Though testimonies of seeing doubles and of **out-of-the-body travel** experiences are numerous, rigid experimental proof is scarce. **Colonel Eugerne August-Albert D'Aiglun Rochas** was one of the first to attempt to furnish some. During his experiments in the **exteriorization of sensitivity** he noticed that in subjects in a state of deep hypnosis, the concentric strata around the body—which he induced by suggestion—condensed, right and left, into poles of sensitivity that finally united in a phantasmal enlargement of the body.

This phantom form, which could be lengthened under the order of the magnetizer and could pass through material objects, became the seat of sensation. It could be modeled like wax in the sculptor's hands and when Rochas suggested that a female subject give it her mother's form, the suggestion was successfully carried out. One of these experiments was made in Paris in the presence of **A. N. Aksakof** with **Elizabeth d'Esperance** as the seeing subject and a Ms. Lambert as the exteriorizing subject.

Henri Durville was the next experimenter. By means of passes he built up a double around his subjects Ninette and Martha and observed that the double was capable of motor effects at a distance of several rooms. Finally, from an effluvium from the forehead, the bregma, the throat, the epigastrium, and even the spleen, he saw a true phantom take shape at a distance of 20 to 24 inches from the medium. It had the appearance of the medium, became more or less luminous, and was united with the medium's body by a little cord at the navel, the bregma, or the epigastrium.

The phantom could see through opaque bodies in the distance and its objectivity was demonstrated by the increasing brilliance of a calcium sulphide screen when it was asked to approach it. The sensory organs of the medium were seated in the phantom. When approached it produced a sensation of cold, was humid to the touch, and made the fingers luminous in the dark.

The experiments of Dr. Duncan McDougall of Haverhill, Massachusetts, in weighing dying patients appeared to furnish some confirmation. He found that at the moment of death the beam of his scale would suddenly go up. Out of six cases the weight lost at death averaged between 2 and 2.5 ounces, but this might also be accounted for by changes in body fluids or evaporation.

On the basis of some experiments in regression of memory, Rochas believed that the double is only complete at seven years of age and that the astral shape enters the body a little while before birth and then only partially. Dr. **Joseph Maxwell** studied a very sensitive young woman who was entrusted with bringing up a child from birth. She saw at its side a luminous shadow with features larger and more formed than those of the child. This shadow was further away from the child at its birth. It seemed to penetrate gradually into the body. At 14 months of age the penetration was about two-thirds complete.

Photographic evidence for the double was presented in the works of **Gabriel Delanne,** Rochas, Durville, Commandant Darget, and Aksakof. The first such pictures were obtained by **William H. Mumler,** the American practitioner of **spirit photography.** He was promptly accused of **fraud** because it was the photograph of someone dead that was expected to appear on his plate. The double of **Stainton Moses** was photographed in 1875 in Paris by another spirit photographer, **Édouard Buguet,** while the medium lay in trance in London. This picture, however, was discredited by subsequent disclosures about Buguet.

The experiments of **Julien Ochorowicz** on the radiography of the etheric body stand in a class of their own. On September 11, 1911, he obtained the photograph of a spirit hand on a sensitive film rolled up and enclosed in a bottle. The film, as it lay rolled in the bottle, measured about three-quarters of an inch in diameter. The bottle had an orifice of about two-thirds of an inch. It was closed with the palm of Ochorowicz's right hand. With his left he laid it on his knee and held it there firmly. The medium, **Stanislawa Tomczyk,** then placed her two hands on the bottle between his. She seemed excited and exclaimed that she wished that a small hand would appear. Then she said, "It is strange! The bottle seems to enlarge under my fingers; but perhaps this is an illusion. My hands swell, I cease to feel them." An attack of cramping ensued. The medium screamed; a moment or two later Ochorowicz broke the bottle, developed the film, and found on it the imprint of a large hand with the thumb posed in line with the index finger, so that it had room to appear on the film, which was 13 cm wide. The hand looked like that of the medium.

In **automatic writing** the following explanation came through: "I crept in by a chink between your hand and the orifice of the bottle. Then I slipped my hand flat between the folds of the roll, and the light caused itself, I do not know how, I merely took care to make the film opaque." This communication came from "Little Stasia," Tomzyck's **control,** whom Ochorowicz suspected for a long time to be the medium's double.

Continuing his experiments, Ochorowicz tried to discover the thickness of the etheric hand. He found that, when materialized, the hand was less than a millimeter thick, and that it was at least very probable that it was flat, and could therefore find room in a space too narrow for a normal hand. The same experiments also assured him that the double could, by autosuggestion, diminish the size of its hand if it met with obstacles (see **thoughtforms**).

Projection of the Double

Supposed proof of the double is its experimental projection, often described as "astral" projection, but now classified as "out-of-the-body" travel. Reportedly the usual method of such experiments is to decide before going to sleep to visit someone during the night.

One case, reported in *Phantasms of the Living* by **Edmund Gurney, F. W. H. Myers,** and **Frank Podmore** (1886) is corroborated by the testimony of Stainton Moses, the "Z" of the account:

"One evening early last year, I resolved to try to appear to Z, at some miles distance. I did not inform him beforehand of the intended experiment; but retired to rest shortly before midnight with thoughts intently fixed on Z, with whose room and surroundings, however, I was quite unacquainted. I soon fell asleep, and awoke next morning unconscious of anything having taken place. On seeing Z a few days afterwards, I inquired: 'Did anything happen at your rooms on Saturday night?' 'Yes,' replied he, 'a great deal happened. I had been sitting over the fire with M. smoking and chatting. About 12:30 he rose to leave, and I let him out myself. I returned to the fire to finish my pipe, when I saw you sitting in the chair just vacated by him. I looked intently at you, and then took up a newspaper to assure myself that I was not dreaming, but on laying it down I saw you still there. While I gazed, without speaking, you faded away.'"

The Rev. P. H. Newnham, also quoted in *Phantasms of the Living,* had a singularly vivid dream. He saw the family of his fiancée, chatted with the father and mother in his dream, bade them goodnight, took a candle, and went off to bed. The he says:

"On arriving in the hall, I perceived that my fiancée had been detained downstairs, and was only then near the top of the staircase. I rushed upstairs, overtook her on the top step, and passed my two arms round her waist, under her arms, from behind. Although I was carrying my candle in my left hand, when I ran upstairs, this did not, in my dream, interfere with this gesture. On this I woke, and a clock in the house struck 10 almost immediately afterwards. So strong was the impression of the dream that I wrote a detailed account of it the next morning to my fiancée. *Crossing my letter,* not in answer to it, I received a letter from the lady in question: 'Were you thinking about me, very specially, last night just about 10 o'clock? For, as I was going upstairs to bed, I distinctly heard your footsteps on the stairs, and felt you put your arms around my waist.'"

The methods of experimental projection are discussed in **Hector Durville**'s *Le Phantôme des vivants* (1909) and in Charles Lancelin's *Méthode de dédoublement personel* (1913). Another contribution to the subject is in *The Projection of the Astral Body,* (1929) by Sylvan J. Muldoon and **Hereward Carrington.** According to this book special exercises are necessary to retain consciousness during projection. Reportedly projection nearly always occurs in the dream state. Muldoon claims that "what is thought to be an 'aura,' resting above sleepers and seen by seers, is in reality the etheric body, out of coincidence a few inches. As a rule, in normal persons, consciousness is lost before this phenomenon begins."

The astral and physical bodies are joined by a cord that may be the "silver cord" in Ecclesiastes (12:16). According to Muldoon and others who claim to have seen it, this cord or cable, which is similar to a newborn's umbilical cord, is attached at various parts of the head or, according to some claims, at the solar plexus; it is a whitish gray color, elastic, and similar to a single strand of cobweb when extended.

Supposedly when slightly out of coincidence, the cord is the diameter of a silver dollar, yet the aura surrounding it gives the impression that it is about six inches thick. It is the conductor of cosmic energy into the physical body, for which the astral body acts as condenser. It delivers "the breath of life" while the finer body is projected.

The awakening of consciousness during any unconscious projection thrusts the astral body back into the physical. Adolphe d'Assier's *Posthumous Humanity* (1887) contains material about repercussions in general and those claimed to have occurred in **witchcraft.**

Spontaneous Projection

Supposedly in the majority of cases, the projection of the double is involuntary and due to emotional stress. "Examples have come to my knowledge," wrote Jung Stilling, at an early age, "in which sick persons, overcome with an unspeakable longing to see some absent friend, have fallen into a swoon and during that swoon have appeared to the distant object of their affection."

Believers claim danger, anxiety, and mental agony are causes of projection. In *Phantasms of the Living* more than 40 cases of apparitions of the drowned or nearly drowned are cited. Sometimes they remembered seeing near relations who experienced a visual or auditive sensation or felt sudden fear coupled with the idea of their relative's danger.

Mental preoccupation may also be sufficient to result in such an apparition. According to J. G. Swift M'Neill, M.P., the double of T. P. O'Connor was seen in 1897 in the British House of Commons in his accustomed place, while he was on his way to Ireland to visit a dying parent. There are other cases recorded of members of Parliament being seen in the House of Commons when actually elsewhere.

The so-called **premonitions** of approach belong to this group. In a letter written from St. Petersburg in 1865 (published in Mrs. Home's biography, p. 240) the famous medium **D. D. Home** told the story of how his own double was seen by Count Alexis Tolstoy at the railroad station three hours before his actual arrival. In the hotel he found a note waiting from Count Tolstoy expressing joy at his return, and he was mildly reproached by the countess, who also saw him, for not seeming to know her at the station.

The following experience of the poet Goethe is narrated in *Phantasms of the Living:*

"Wolfgang Goethe was walking one rainy summer evening with his friend K., returning from the Belvedere at Weimar. Suddenly the poet paused as if he saw someone and was about to speak to him. K. noticed nothing. Suddenly Goethe exclaimed: 'My God! If I were not sure that my friend Frederick is at this next moment at Frankfort I should swear that it is he!' The next moment he burst out laughing. 'But it is he—my friend Frederick. You here at Weimar? But why are you dressed so—in your dressing gown, with your nightcap and my slippers here on the public road?' K., as I have just said, saw absolutely nothing and was alarmed, thinking that the poet had lost his wits. But Goethe, thinking only of what he say, cried out again: 'Frederick, what has become of you? My dear K., did you notice where that person went who came to meet us just now?' K., stupefied, did not answer. Then the poet, looking all round, said in a dreamy tone: 'Yes, I understand . . . it is a vision. What can it mean though? Has my friend suddenly died? Was it his spirit?' Thereupon Goethe returned to the house and found Frederick there already. His hair stood on end. 'Avaunt, you phantom!' he exclaimed, pale as death. 'But my friend,' remonstrated Frederick, 'is this the welcome that you give to your best friend?' 'Ah, this time,' exclaimed the poet, with such emotion, 'it is not the spirit, it is a being of flesh and blood.' The friends embraced warmly. Frederick explained that he had arrived at Goethe's lodging soaked by the rain, had dressed himself in the poet's dry clothing and having fallen asleep in his chair, had dreamed that he had gone out to meet him and that Goethe had greeted him with the words: 'You here! At Weimar? What! With your dressing gown, your nightcap and my slippers here on the public road?' From this time the great poet believed in a future life."

Supposedly sometimes the appearance serves a purpose. **James Coates** quoted a story from *T. P.'s Weekly,* for which the editor vouched, of a woman who was on her way to Cambridge to meet her fiancé. At every station where the train stopped she saw the apparition of her fiancé, beckoning her to get out. Finally she told her traveling companion, a gentleman, what she saw. He advised her to get out at the next station if she saw the apparition again. The woman saw the apparition again. She got out at once. So did the gentleman. Shortly afterward the train wrecked and the car in which they had been sitting was demolished. During the time her fiancé was sound asleep in the waiting room at Cambridge, and did not remember having dreamed anything unusual.

Sometimes it is a state of illness that facilitates projection. **Andrew Lang** saw his friend Q. opening his garden gate and coming up the path, which led toward the window where he was writing, but when he got up to let him in there was nobody there. The same day he learned that Q. was ill in bed at the time his double was seen.

There are instances that indicate that projection may be the result of an accident or a violent impact. **William Denton** quoted the statement of a man who fell from the scaffolding of a building: "As I struck the ground I suddenly bounded up, seeming to have a new body, and to be standing among the spectators looking at my old one. I saw them trying to bring it to. I made several fruitless efforts to re-enter my body, and finally succeeded."

Quite often there seems to be no known reason for the temporary separation. A. N. Aksakof told of the story of Emilie Sagée, a French schoolmistress in Livonia. For a period of 18 months her double was seen, sometimes at her side, making the same gestures, sometimes out in the garden while Sagée was in the room. The double did not always imitate her movements; sometimes it remained seated while she rose from her chair. As the double became clearer and more consistent, Sagée became more rigid and feeble. She was always unconscious of what happened.

Seeing One's Own Double

Dr. Paul Sollier in his *Les Phénomènes d'autoscope* (1903) gave a summary of the cases of "vision de soi" of Goethe, Alfred de Musset, Shelley, de Maupassant; of the experiences of Drs. Lassegue, Féré, Rouginovitch, and Lemaitre; and of 12 of his own cases.

Goethe's experience was described in *Aus meinem Leben, Dichtung und Wahrheit* (1811–22):

"I rode now on the footpath toward Drusenheim, and there one of the strangest presentiments surprised me. I saw myself coming to meet myself, on the same way, on horseback, but in a garment such as I had never worn. It was of light grey mingled with gold. As soon as I had aroused myself from this dream, the vision entirely disappeared. Remarkable, nevertheless, it is that eight years afterward I found myself on the same road, intending to visit Frederika once more, and in the same garment which I had dreamed about and which I now wore, not out of choice but by accident. This wonderful hallucination had a quieting effect on me."

Comparing a large number of cases, Sollier found that the apparition had many degrees—from the simple impression of being in one's own presence to a vision as if seen in a mirror. Any disturbance would make it disappear. When the phantom had different attributes—was smaller in stature, wore different clothes—it might persist for hours in varying intensity. The apparition appeared usually during the evening hours, in states of deep meditation, self-concentration, or under anesthesia. The distance at which it was seen varied from a few yards to close proximity. Sometimes it walked before the subject and vanished all at once; sometimes it turned about or moved to the side and imitated his movements. In most cases it was silent. Occasionally there was a dialogue and difference of opinion between phantom and self.

Exchange of Consciousness

Sollier explained these experiences as hallucinations resulting from a loss of sensibility. In discussing the question in the *Revue métapsychique* (May–June 1930), **Eugèn Osty** states that in some cases there is an exchange of consciousness, the double becoming the thinking self.

Tradition says that a vision of self is a sign of approaching death. Queen Elizabeth I of England was said to have been warned of her death by the apparition of her own double. It has been suggested that such cases, by a invention of time, may be phantasmal appearances after death.

In a few instances on record, the double was apparently solid; it could hold a hymn book in the church and could speak. The double of **Ophelia Corralès** of San Jose, Costa Rica, was heard to sing while the girl was somewhere far away and had no knowledge of her appearance. However, this medium was accused of fraud.

Memories of out-of-the-body travel experiences were reported by many mediums. **Emanuel Swedenborg, Andrew Jackson Davis,** D. D. Home, Stainton Moses, Elizabeth d'Esperance, **Gladys Osborne Leonard,** and many others have published descriptions. **Cora L. Richmond** was said to have remained projected for many days. Supposedly she could perceive and receive the answer to every question—even before its complete formation in thought.

Materialization and the Double

The phantom hands and limbs seen in séances are often believed to be the duplication of the medium. Paraffin molds matched a materialized leg of **William Eglinton** and impressions of a face and fingers in putty matched **Eusapia Palladino** (see **plastics**).

According to occult philosophy, the double is to be distinguished from the spirit or soul. The double is a vehicle of the spirit and, like the physical body, will later be cast off and deteriorate.

Do animals have doubles? Elliott O'Donnell in his *Animal Ghosts* (1913) asserts that they do. He states that some friends of his had a cat that was frequently seen in two places at the same time; further, he affirms that there are phantasms of both living and dead dogs in just the same proportion as there are phantasms of both living and dead human beings. He claims of a Virginia lady who had a horse that frequently appeared simultaneously in two places.

Since the mid-twentieth century, the subject of the human double and astral (or etheric) projection has been considered under the designation "out-of-body experience" (OBE). The British scientist **Robert Crookall** collated and classified hundreds of cases of OBEs and various parapsychologists have conducted experiments in the field, including **Charles T. Tart** and **Karlis Osis.** In 1956 **Hornell Hart** made a survey of reported apparitions of the dead, which he compared with apparitions of living persons when having OBEs.

In 1932 **Eileen J. Garrett,** who established the **Parapsychology Foundation** in New York, took part in a successful scientific experiment that involved projecting her double from New York to Iceland under test conditions. This case is described in Garrett's book *My Life as a Search for the Meaning of Mediumship* (1938).

In the 1970s psychic Ingo Swann worked with Karlis Osis at the **American Society for Psychical Research** on a series of experiments aimed at demonstrating the existence of the double. Swann, seated in a chair and attached by electrodes to a monitoring device, attempted to project his double to a hidden target. The vision of the double, as opposed to simple clairvoyance, was determined by the angle of vision at which the target objects were viewed. These tests proved most successful and provide some of the best data available on the existence of a human double. **Robert A. Monroe,** also known for his OBEs, has allowed himself to be tested on various occasions.

Sources:

Battersby, H. F. Prevost. *Man Outside Himself.* London, 1942. Reprint, New Hyde Park, N.Y.: University Books, 1969.

Black, David. *Ekstasy: Out-of-the-body Experiences.* New York: Bobbs-Merrill, 1976.

Crookall, Robert. *The Study & Practice of Astral Projection.* London, 1961. Reprint, New Hyde Park, N.Y.: University Books, 1966.

Fox, Oliver [Hugh G. Callaway]. *Astral Projection.* London, 1939. Reprint, New York: University Books, 1962.

Garrett, Eileen J. *My Life as a Search for the Meaning of Mediumship.* New York: Oquaga Press, 1938. Reprint, New York: Arno Press, 1975.

Green, Celia E. *Out-of-the-Body Experiences.* Oxford: Institute of Psychophysical Research, 1968. Reprint, New York: Ballantine Books, 1973.

Greenhouse, Herbert B. *Astral Journey: Evidence for Out-of-the-Body Experiences from Socrates to the ESP Laboratory.* Garden City, N.Y.: Doubleday, 1975.

Monroe, Robert A. *Journeys Out of the Body.* Garden City, N.Y.: Doubleday, 1971.

Muldoon, Sylvan J., and Hereward Carrington. *The Projection of the Astral Body.* London: Rider & Company, 1929.

Rogo, D. Scott. *Welcoming Silence; A Study of Psychical Phenomena and Survival of Death.* New Hyde Park, N.Y.: University Books, 1973.

Shirley, Ralph. *The Mystery of the Human Double.* London, 1938. Reprint, New Hyde Park, N.Y.: University Books, 1965.

Smith, Susy. *The Enigma of Out-of-Body Travel.* Garrell Publications, 1965. Reprint, New York: New English Library, 1968.

———. *Out-of-Body Experiences for the Millions.* New York: Dell, 1968.

Walker, George B. *Beyond the Body: The Human Double and the Astral Planes.* London: Boston, 1974.

Double Blind

Term used in **parapsychology** for a situation where all the participants in a test are unaware of any information or cues relating to the **target** of the test or **psi** responses to it.

Doubt (Magazine)

The journal of the **Fortean Society,** devoted to highlighting and discussing "Fortean data,"—strange and anomalistic scientific phenomena collected by **Charles Fort.** It was first published as the *Fortean Society Journal* in September 1937. The name was changed to *Doubt* with the eleventh issue (Winter 1944–45). It ceased publication with issue no. 61 after the death of editor Tiffany Thayer. The Fortean community is now served by a number of succeeding publications, including the *Fortean Times,* **Chaos: The Review of the Damned,** and **INFO.**

Doupe, Joseph (1910–)

Pioneer researcher on psychic healing. Doupe was born March 10, 1910, in Winnipeg, Manitoba. He attended the University of Manitoba (M.D., 1934) and the Royal College of Physicians, London, (M.R.C.P., 1938). During World War II he served as a major in the R.A.M.C. (1940–46). Then in 1946 he became a professor of physiology with interests in **parapsychology** and head of the Department of Physiology at the University of Mannitoba, Winnipeg, Canada. He is most remembered for his supervision in 1960 of experiments concerned with unorthodox methods of treating wound-healing in mice, which would later form a basis for similar experiments by **Bernard Grad.**

Sources:

Pleasants, Helene, ed. *Biographical Dictionary of Parapsychology.* New York: Helix Press, 1964.

D'Ourches, Comte (ca. 1856)

Nineteenth-century French occultist who experimented with **mesmerism** and **animal magnetism.** During the 1850s he and his friend the **Baron L. von Guldenstubbe** pioneered the formation of Spiritualist circles in France similar to those being formed in America. The baron describes such séances in his book *La Réalité des Espirits et le Phénomène merveilleux de leur écriture directe* (1857), stating that the Comte D'Ourches succeeded in making tables rise without contact, in addition to the phenomena of **table-turning, raps,** and vibration of piano chords. D'Ourches was also associated with the baron's experiments in obtaining **direct writing.**

Dowden, Hester (Mrs. Travers-Smith) (1868–1949)

Professional medium whose psychic development was marked by the successive appearance of five spirit personalities: "Peter," "Eyen," "Astor," "Shamar," and "Johannes." She was later known for her experiments in **automatic writing.** She was the daughter of Prof. Edward Dowden. Her first circle was formed during the winter of 1914. At the second or third sitting an entity calling himself "Peter Rooney" made his appearance. He claimed to be an Irish American who had spent most of his life in jail. Rooney committed suicide by throwning himself under a tramcar in Boston.

Reportedly **Sir William Barrett** made inquiries and found inconsistencies in the tale. Rooney was questioned at a subsequent séance and admitted that he had lied because he had no desire to communicate his real name. He claimed to have been interested in psychical research during his life and wished to assist investigations now. He introduced many features to the séance, initiated blindfold sittings on the **Ouija board,** and tried experiments in **telepathy.**

Eyen claimed to have been an Egyptian priest in the temple of Isis in the reign of Rameses II. He was attracted to the medium by a piece of cerecloth in which his mummy was wrapped. Astor, the third control, professed to be the guide of **Geraldine Cummins,** with whom Dowden often sat. She was chiefly interested in the activities of Cummins and **clairvoyance** and prophecies.

Shamar, the fourth control was a Hindu. She claimed to be the medium's spirit guide, Eyen being "the guide of her astral." She sent communications from living persons who were asleep or drowsy.

Johannes was the latest development as a spirit **guide.** He claimed to have lived 200 years before Christ and studied in the Alexandrian Library. He gave philosophical teachings that were similar to the Neoplatonic philosophy of Plotinus (205–270 C.E.). **H. Dennis Bradley** became convinced of the reality of Johannes as an independent personality as a result of a **direct voice** sitting with the medium **George Valiantine** in February 1924.

Reportedly Bradley had many sittings with Dowden and later developed automatic writing himself. He could not keep pace with the terrific speed of the communications from Johannes, although he wrote in shorthand. Leaving his hand limp, he discovered that he could write at an infinitely quicker pace and without exhaustion.

Of the existence of the first four controls, Barrett, in his introduction to Mrs. H. Travers-Smith's book *Voices from the Void* (1919), states, "I am strongly disposed to consider many of them as distant psychic entities and not in all cases mere phases of the personality of the automatist."

The author Lennox Robinson and Rev. Savell Hicks were sitting with Dowden when this message came through: "Pray for Hugh Lane." Then, on being asked who was speaking: "I am Hugh Lane; all is dark" came through. Shortly after, it continued: "It is Sir Hugh Lane, drowned. Was on board the Lusitania." At that moment boys were selling the evening newspapers in the street. Robinson ran out. When he came back he pointed to the name of Sir Hugh Lane in the story of the disaster, reported for the first time. The communications from Sir Hugh Lane described the scene on the Lusitania: "Panic. Boats lowered. Women went first. Lost in an overcrowded boat, fell over. Lost all memory until I saw a light at the sitting."

The medium knew Sir Hugh Lane personally but had heard that he had gone to America before the sinking of the Lusitania. On her way home that day Dowden saw posters: "Lusitania reported sinking" but had no personal interest in the news as she knew no one on board. Lane continued to come through in séances afterward and wanted several of his wishes communicated to his executors.

In a similar instance, the following message was spelled out rapidly: "Ship sinking; all hands lost. William East overboard. Women and children weeping and wailing—sorrow, sorrow, sorrow." The newspaper stop press was heard being called out in the street. The medium bought a paper. It contained the news that the Titanic had gone down. She believed that the name William East was incorrect and that it must have been **William Stead.** Dowden later served as the amanuensis for *The Life Eternal,* supposedly written by Stead from the spirit world in 1933.

Reportedly Dowden channeled several romantic scripts: descriptions of King Arthur's Round Table and of the missionary journeys of St. Philip the Evangelist. When she sat with **Frederick Bligh Bond,** a group of **Glastonbury** monks came through and recited details of the burial of abbey relics in 1080. Cummins's writing mediumship developed in her sittings. The communications often referred to the future. Events in her life were sometimes foretold years ahead. Her first book, *Voices from the Void* (1919), contains an account of her own experiences. Her second volume, *Psychic Messages from Oscar Wilde* (1923), was featured in the *Daily News,* on July 27, 1923. The article claimed he gave criticisms of many writers. Of George Bernard Shaw, he writes:

"I had a kindly feeling for poor Shaw. He had such a keen desire to be original that it moved my pity. He was without any sense of beauty or even a sense of the dramatic side of life. And yet there was the passionate yearning to be a personage, to force his person on the world, to press in, in spite of the better taste of those who went before him. I have a very great respect for his work. After all, he is my fellow-countryman. We share the same misfortune in that matter. I think Shaw may be called the true type of pleb. He is so anxious to prove himself honest and outspoken that he utters a great deal more than he is able to think. He is ever ready to call upon his audience to admire his work, and his audience admires it from sheer sympathy with his delight."

The Oscar Wilde script was produced in cooperation with psychical researcher **S. G. Soal** (also an automatist), who held the pencil. He later wrote a critical reflection upon his experience.

Sources:

Bentley, Edmund. *Far Horizon: A Biography of Hester Dowden, Medium and Psychic Investigator.* London: Rider & Company, 1951.

Dowden, Hester. *Psychic Messages from Oscar Wilde.* London: T. Werner Laurie, 1923.

———. *Voices from the Void.* London: Rider & Company, 1919.

Soal, S. G. "Note on the 'Oscar Wilde' Script." *Journal* of the Society for Psychical Research (July 1926).

Dowding, Hugh Caswall Tremenheere (1882–1970)

First Baron Dowding, air chief marshal in charge of Fighter Command in Britain during World War II and author of several books on psychic phenomena and **survival** of death. Lord Dowding was born April 24, 1882. He was educated at Winchester and the Royal Military Academy, Woolwich, London, and joined the Royal Artillery in 1900. In 1914, as World War I began, he joined the Royal Flying Corp (after 1918 the Royal Air Force). He commanded Fighting Area, Air Defense of Great Britain (1923–30), during which time he also was director of training at the Air Ministry, London (1926–29). He subsequently served as the air member for research and development of Air Council (1930–36), air officer commander-in-chief of Fighter Command (1936–40), and principal A.D.C. to the king (1937-43). He retired in 1943.

Soon after his retirement, Dowding wrote a series of books on psychic phenomena, including *Many Mansions* (1943), *Lychgate: The Entrance to the Path* (1945), and *The Dark Star* (1951). He was also a member of the **Fairy Investigation Society.** He died February 15, 1970.

Many people believed that Dowding's major contribution to the defense of Britain in World War II was not sufficiently honored. A statue of him was eventually erected in 1988 at St. Clements Dane, the Royal Air Church in the Strand, west central

London. It was unveiled by the Queen Mother on Sunday, October 30, 1988.

Sources:

Dowling, Lady. *Beauty—Not the Beast.* St. Helier, Spearman, 1980. Reprinted as *The Psychic Life of Muriel, the Lady Dowling: An Autobiography.* Wheaton, Ill.: Theosophical Publishing House, 1981.

Dowling, Lord. *The Dark Star.* London: Museum Press, 1951.

———. *Lychgate: The Entrance to the Path.* N.p., 1945.

———. *Many Mansions.* London: Rider, 1943.

Dowding, Lady Muriel (1908–1993)

Born in London on March 22, 1908, Muriel Albino became a Spiritualist at age 15. She had a psychic gift, and during her childhood in World War I she often saw a vision of "a tall soldier in khaki," whom she consulted about her problems and assumed she would one day meet and marry. In 1935 she married Max Whiting, who became a pilot during World War II and died when his plane was shot down.

Meanwhile Lord **Hugh C. T. Dowding,** who was convinced of the reality of human **survival** after death, received remarkable evidence of survival through the mediumship of **Estelle Roberts.** When Muriel Whiting became aware of Dowding's interest in **Spiritualism** she wrote to him, and as a result Dowding invited her to lunch. When they met she recognized him as the soldier of her childhood visions, and although he was 26 years older than she was, they were married in 1951.

Lady Dowding became a strong supporter of animal welfare and in 1959 launched a campaign called "Beauty Without Cruelty," dedicated to persuading women to renounce cosmetics produced from mistreated animals and to stop wearing animal furs. She published a magazine, *Compassion,* and opened a shop in Baywater, London, specializing in cosmetics obtained without mistreating animals. In 1964 she started an animal sanctuary at Nettlestead, Kent, and became president of the National Anti-Vivisection Society.

Lord Dowding died in 1970 at age 85. During her last two years, Lady Dowding resided at a nursing home in Hove, Sussex. She died in November 1993.

Sources:

Dowding, Lady Muriel. *Beauty—not the Beast.* St. Helier, Jersey: Neville Spearman, 1980. Reprinted as *The Psychic Life of Muriel, The Lady Dowding: An Autobiography.* Wheaton, Ill.: Theosophical Publishing House, 1981.

Dowsing

The study and detection of human response to water, minerals, and other underground materials. Dowsing, or "water witching," is usually distinguished from the related subject of **radiesthesia** by its focus on nonliving materials such as water, metals, minerals, or buried objects. Both dowsing and radiesthesia operators employ a **divining-rod, pendulum,** or similar device as an indicator of unconscious human sensitivity to hidden materials. Radiesthesia extends such detection to medical diagnosis and treatment, discovery of missing persons, telepathy, clairvoyance, and related paranormal phenomena. In Europe (particularly in France), however, the two terms are used synonymously.

The traditional form of dowsing is with a Y-shaped hazel branch. The operator holds the two ends in his hands and walks over an area thought to contain underground water. When crossing water, the branch turns over, often with considerable force, and the dowser is able to map the course of the underground water.

For some years it was hypothesized that some underground emanation or occult force moved the branch, but modern researchers tend to favor the idea that the operator responds to the hidden water in such a way that his own nervous energy moves the branch. Some theorists have compared this effect with **table-turning** or the **raps** often reported within **Spiritualism.** This does not preclude the possibility that some electromagnetic impulse stimulates the dowser's muscles through the nervous system, although there is no evidence of such an impulse.

Modern dowsers have developed considerable sensitivity and skill and will venture to estimate both the depth and possible yield of underground water. In addition to branches, dowsers employ many other forms of indicators—rods made of whalebone or wire, twisted coathangers, rods with cavities for a "sample" of the material sought for, and especially small pendulums. Since international agreements now outlaw whale hunting, plastic indicators are being substituted for whalebone.

Some dowsers even search for hidden materials over a scale map of a district, using a small suspended pendulum instead of a rod, and "map dowsing" has become synonymous with teleradiesthesia; (i.e., the tracing of materials or persons using a representation of an area instead of visiting the actual area). Some kind of psychic or other paranormal link is suggested between a district and its representation on a map.

Although dowsing and radiesthesia remain controversial, there seems to be considerable successes in water witching and the discovery of buried minerals. Water diviners have been widely employed by governments and businesses. One skilled dowser, Major C. A. Pogson, was official water diviner to the government of India between October 1925 and February 1930. During this period Pogson traveled thousands of miles locating sites for wells and bores and was a consultant on all matters relating to underground water.

The oldest organization in the field is the **British Society of Dowsers,** founded in the 1930s. There is also an American Society of Dowsers, which can be contacted at P.O. Box 24, Brained St., Danville, Vermont.

Sources:

Barrett, William, and Theodore Besterman. *The Divining Rod: An Experimental and Psychological Investigation.* London, 1926. Reprint, New Hyde Park: University Books, 1968.

Benedikt, M. *Ruten- und Pendel-lehre.* Vienna; Leipzig, 1917.

Besterman, Theodore. *Water Divining: New Facts & Theories.* London: Methuen, 1938.

Bird, Christopher. *The Diving Hand.* New York: E. P. Dutton, 1979.

Cameron, Verne L. *Aquavideo; Locating Underground Water.* Santa Barbara, Calif.: El Cariso, 1970.

———. *Map Dowsing.* Santa Barbara, Calif.: El Cariso, 1971.

———. *Oil Locating.* Santa Barbara, Calif.: El Cariso, 1971.

Carrié, Abbé. *L'hydroscopographie et métalloscopographie, ou l'art de découvrir les sources et les gisement metallifers au moyen de l'électromagnétisme.* Saintes, France, 1863.

Chambers, Howard V. *Dowsing, Water Witches & Divining Rods for the Millions.* Los Angeles: Sherbourne Press, 1969.

Chevreul, M. E. *De la Baguette divinatoire, du pendule dit explorateur, et des tables tournantes.* Paris, 1854.

De France, Henry. *The Elements of Dowsing.* London, 1948.

De Morogues, Baron. *Observations sur le fluide organo-électrique.* Paris, 1854.

De Vallemont, Abbe. *La physique occulte, ou Traité de la baguette divinatoire.* Paris, 1693.

Ellis, Arthur J. *The Divining Rod: A History of Water Witching, with a Bibliography.* Washington, 1917.

Klinckowstroem, Graf von. *Virgula divina. Ein Beitrag zur Geschichte der Wünschelrute.* Berlin, 1910.

Maby, J. Cecil, and T. B. Franklin. *The Physics of the Divining Rod.* London, 1939.

Mager, Henri. *Water Diviners and Their Methods.* London, 1931.

Maury, Marguerite. *How to Dowse: Experimental and Practical Radiasthesia.* London: G. Bell and Sons, 1953.

Mermet, Abbe. *Principles & Practice of Radiesthesie.* London, 1967.

Nicolas, Jean. *La verge de Jacob, ou l'art de trouver les trésors les sources, les limites, les métaux, les mines, les minéraux et autres cachées, par l'usage du baton fourché.* Lyons, France, 1693. Translated as *Jacob's Rod.* London: Thomas Welton, 1875.

Nielsen, Greg, and J. Polansky. *Pendulum Power.* New York: Warner, 1977.

Roberts, Kenneth. *Henry Gross and His Dowsing Rod.* Garden City, N.Y.: Doubleday, 1952.

Stark, Erwin E. *A History of Dowsing and Energy Relationships.* North Hollywood, Calif.: BAC, 1978.

Tromp, S. W. *Psychical Physics: A Scientific Analysis of Dowsing, Radiesthesia & Kindred Divining Phenomena.* New York: Elsevier, 1949.

Underwood, Peter. *The Complete Book of Dowsing & Divining.* London, 1980.

Vogt, Evon Z., and Ray Hyman. *Water Witching, U.S.A.* 2nd ed. Chicago: University of Chicago Press, 1979.

Wayland, Bruce and Shirley Wayland. *Steps to Dowsing Power.* Life Force Press, 1976.

Weaver, Herbert. *Diving, the Primary Sense: Unfamiliar Radiation in Nature, Art and Science.* London: Routledge & Kegan Paul, 1978.

Willey, Raymond C. *Modern Dowsing.* Cottonwood, Ariz.: Esoteric Publications, 1976.

Wyman, Walker D. *Witching for Water, Oil, Pipes, and Precious Minerals.* River Falls: University of Wisconsin Press, 1977.

Doyle, Arthur Conan (1859–1930)

Arthur Conan Doyle was born on May 22, 1859, in Edinburgh, Scotland, into a very strict Roman Catholic family. He was educated in Jesuit schools in the United Kingdom (Stoneyhurst) and in Austria (Stella Matutina) until he was 17. Although he was apparently attracted by the mystical, sacramental, and eucharistic aspects of Catholicism, he began to doubt his faith during his years at the Jesuit schools.

When Doyle entered the University of Edinburgh at age 17, he was, by his own account, a nonbeliever. "I found that the foundations not only of Roman Catholicism but of the whole Christian faith, as presented to me in nineteenth century theology, were so weak that my mind could not build upon them." These conditions had, according to Doyle, "driven me to agnosticism." It was during his university years that he came under the influence of materialists such as Joseph Bell, his self-proclaimed prototype for Sherlock Holmes, who taught his students the process of deductive reasoning through the observation of material phenomena.

As a result of this training, Doyle became convinced that every mystery of life could be solved through observation and deductive reasoning. Yet despite this training, his previous rejection of Catholicism, and his self-professed agnosticism, he continued to investigate religions, because without a religious foundation he felt a void in his life.

In 1881 Doyle received his medical degree and in 1882 set up a medical practice in Southsea (a suburb of Portsmouth), where he remained until 1890. Even while attending medical school, Doyle had actively investigated "new religions" in an effort to fill the void created when he left the Roman Catholic Church. He attended his first **séance** in 1880, and many of his short stories published in the 1880s reflect his interest in **Spiritualism** and his growing acceptance of it. Before the turn of the century Doyle had become interested in **Theosophy,** the **Rosicrucians,** the Hermetic Order of the **Golden Dawn,** and Mormonism.

In 1887 Doyle published *A Study in Scarlet,* which was the first of 60 Sherlock Holmes stories he eventually wrote. Holmes proved to be his most popular fictional character. That same year he wrote two letters to the weekly Spiritualist periodical *Light,* in which he recounted his conversion to Spiritualism. In these letters Doyle wrote that he became convinced that Spiritualism was true after reading books on the subject by **John W. Edmonds, Alfred Russel Wallace,** and Alfred Drayson.

To put their writings to a test, he formed a circle of six that met at a Southsea residence on nine or ten occasions. This group received messages through **table turning** and **automatic writing,** but the significance of these events was inconclusive until an experienced medium with "considerable mediumistic power" was invited to sit with the circle. This medium, writing under control, told Doyle not to read a book by Leigh Hunt that he found convincing because neither the medium nor any of his group knew he was debating whether he should read the book.

Because of this experience, Doyle became convinced that Spiritualism taught the truth:

"[T]he incident which, after many months of inquiry, showed me at last that it was absolutely certain that intelligence could exist apart from the body.... After weighing the evidence, I could no more doubt the existence of the phenomena than I could doubt the existence of lions in Africa, though I have been to that continent and have never chanced to see one.... Let me conclude by exhorting any other searcher never to despair of receiving personal testimony but to persevere through any number of failures until at last conviction comes to him, as, it will."

Several weeks later he wrote another letter to *Light,* which he wrote "[a]s a Spiritualist" and in which he opined that "Spiritualism in the abstract has no 'weak points'" but admitted that "respectable Spiritualists persist in supporting and employing men who have been proved, as far as anything mundane is capable of proof, to be swindlers of the lowest order." Although he was ready to accept that "they have real but intermittent psychical powers," he was also convinced that such charlatans were "noxious parasites" who were the "greatest bane" of Spiritualism. Doyle had received his "definite demonstration," which he believed was necessary before he could embrace any new religion. Spiritualism provided the evidence that life continues after death and that a form of religion exists that is consistent with primitive Christianity and all its attendant miracles.

From 1887 to 1916 Doyle continued to participate in the Spiritualist movement. He wrote letters concerning religious issues, joined the **Society for Psychical Research,** and contributed thousands of pounds to the Spiritualist periodical *Light.* Although he did not proselytize the cause of Spiritualism, as he later would, Doyle did attend séances and studied psychic phenomena as part of his continuing search for truth. Many of his short stories published before 1916 also portray Spiritualist ideas and concepts in a favorable light.

Doyle also wrote three books during this period that his biographers have described as autobiographical: *Beyond the City* (1893), *The Stark Munro Letters* (1895), and *A Duet With an Occasional Chorus* (1899). In the most important of these works, *The Stark Munro Letters,* Doyle's hero, Stark Munro, reveals that he has only the "vaguest idea as to whence I have come from, whither I am going, or what I am here for. It is not for want of inquiry, or from indifference. I have mastered the principles of several religions. They have all shocked me by the violence which I should have to do to my reason to accept the dogmas of any one of them.... I see so clearly that faith is not a virtue, but a vice. It is a goat which has been headed with the sheep." And yet Doyle, through Munro, also admits that his loss of faith was traumatic: "When first I came out of the faith in which I had been reared, I certainly did feel for a time as if my life-belt had burst. I won't exaggerate and say that I was miserable and plunged in utter spiritual darkness." Munro also reflects Doyle's optimism for the future of religions: "The forms of religion will be abandoned, but the essence will be maintained; so that one universal creed will embrace the whole civilized earth...."

Doyle's most productive period for writing fiction occurred after his conversion to Spiritualism. His best-known Sherlock Holmes stories were *The Sign of Four* (1890); *The Adventures of Sherlock Holmes* (1892); *The Memoirs of Sherlock Holmes* (1894); and *The Hound of the Baskervilles* (1902). Doyle also "killed off" Sherlock Holmes—to concentrate on more serious literary efforts and his studies of Spiritualism—by drowning him in Reichenbach Falls in Switzerland. Ironically, Holmes was resurrected, or at least "born again," from the waters of Reichenbach in 1905 in *The Return of Sherlock Holmes* to help supplement Doyle's income. Later books on Holmes—*The Valley of Fear*

(1915), *His Last Bow* (1917), and *The Case-Book of Sherlock Holmes* (1927)—helped enable Doyle to actively pursue his missionary efforts on behalf of Spiritualism.

Even though Doyle was a believer in Spiritualism beginning in the late 1880s, in 1916 he wrote an article in *Light* in which he enthusiastically proclaimed a new dedication to it. Subsequently he began to actively proselytize for the Spiritualist cause. World War I had finally convinced him to more fully embrace the movement: "I might have drifted on for my whole life as a psychical Researcher . . . [b]ut the War came, and . . . it brought earnestness into all our souls and made us look more closely at our own beliefs and reassess our values."

As a result of this "earnestness," he finally recognized that "this subject with which I had so long dallied was not merely a study of a force outside the rules of science, but that it was really something tremendous, a breaking down of the walls between two worlds, a direct undeniable message from beyond, a call of hope and of guidance to the human race at the time of its deepest affliction." Doyle also realized, apparently for the first time, that "the physical phenomena . . . are really of no account, and that their real value consists in the fact that they . . . make religion a very real thing, no longer a matter of faith, but a matter of actual experience and fact." As such, he turned with great zeal from the objective study of Spiritualism to proselytism.

Shortly after his second "conversion" he wrote two books, *The New Revelation* and *The Vital Message,* in which he proclaimed his personal belief in the movement. In addition, he wrote numerous letters to the press on the subject of Spiritualism in which he summarized the beliefs and practices of Spiritualists and claimed that he could not "recall any miracle in the New Testament which has not been claimed, upon good authority, as having occurred in the experience of spiritualists"; that Spiritualism is nothing more than what one would find "if he goes back nineteen hundred years and studies the Christianity of Christ"; that the date Spiritualism was organized in upstate New York in 1848 "is in truth the greatest date in human history since the great revelation of two thousand years ago"; and that no faith is necessary to realize that Spiritualism is true.

During the last decade of his life Doyle began spending great sums of money and traveled many thousands of miles to proselytize for the Spiritualist cause in Australia and New Zealand (1920–21), the United States and Canada (1922–23), France (1925), South Africa, Rhodesia, Uganda, Tanganyika and Kenya (1928–29), Scandinavia and Holland (1929), and, of course, England (1916–30). He also recorded a famous Movietone interview in 1927 that has never before been published in its entirety.

In 1924 Doyle also translated a book, *Jeanne D'Arc Medium* (Paris: Librairie des Sciences Psychiques, 1910), written by Leon Denis. Denis, like Doyle, was an adherent of Spiritualism. In his introduction to the translation Doyle extols Joan of Arc's virtues:

"[M]y personal conviction [is] that, next to the Christ, the highest spiritual being of whom we have an exact record upon the earth is the girl Joan. . . . Apart from the question of Christ's divinity, and comparing the two characters upon a purely human plane, there was much analogy between them. Each was sprung from the laboring class. Each proclaimed an inspired commission. Each was martyred while still young. Each was acclaimed by the common people and betrayed or disregarded by the great. Each excited the bitter hatred of the Church of their time, the high priests of which in each case conspired for their death."

But Doyle does not stop there. He notes that Denis was a student of psychic matters and that his work is valuable since it gives us "some intelligible reason for the obvious miracle that a girl of nineteen, who could neither read nor write, and knew nothing of military affairs, was able in a few months to turn the tide of a hundred years' war and to save France from becoming a vassal of England."

In 1926, two years after publishing *Jeanne D'Arc,* Doyle published a two-volume work on the history of Spiritualism in which he attempted to present Spiritualism in a historical and topical perspective. Perhaps the most ironic development in Doyle's quest for a new religion occurred when he began to see himself increasingly as "a prophet of the future of the whole world. . . ." The Doyles were now put in personal contact with the guide to this uncertain future, an Arabian spirit called Pheneas, who communicated through Jean Doyle's [Arthur's wife] automatic writing.

Doyle's belief in the hereafter became increasingly premised on very specific communications from Pheneas through his wife, Jean. Receiving such messages caused him to state his absolute belief in the hereafter: "I have not only received . . . prophecies [concerning the end of the world] in a very consistent and detailed form, but also so large a number of independent corroborations that it is difficult for me to doubt that there lies some solid truth at the back of these."

Although Doyle remained committed to Spiritualism, he apparently became discouraged when the prophecies and revelations concerning the end of the world that had been communicated through Pheneas were not fulfilled, and he speculated that he and his wife may have become "victims of some extraordinary prank played upon the human race from the other side."

Doyle was still a dedicated Spiritualist at the time of his death in 1930. Until his death Doyle remained convinced that life continued after death, because of ongoing communications from deceased family members who assured him that they lived in the spirit world. These communications remained the "definite demonstration" that he had sought since his days at the University of Edinburgh. He believed that these apparitions and other evidence of Spiritualism provided a factual basis from which he could deduce, in the same manner that Sherlock Holmes would have deduced, that life continues after death. Given his acceptance of these apparitions, it is hardly surprising that Doyle was also convinced that his acceptance of Spiritualism was completely consistent with the deductive reasoning of Sherlock Holmes and Holmes's observation that "there is nothing in which deduction is so necessary as in religion. . . . It can be built up as an exact science by the reasoner."

Sources:

Carr, John Dickson. *The Life of Sir Arthur Conan Doyle.* London: John Murray, 1949.

Doyle, Arthur Conan. *Letters to the Press.* Edited by John M. Gibson and Richard L. Green. Iowa City: University of Iowa Press, 1986.

Edwards, Owen Dudley. *The Quest for Sherlock Holmes, A Biographical Study of Arthur Conan Doyle.* Edinburgh: Mainstream Publishing, 1983.

Jones, Kelvin I. *Conan Doyle and the Spirits: The Spiritualist Career of Sir Arthur Conan Doyle.* Wellingborough, England: Aquarian Press, 1989.

Lellenberg, Jon L. *The Quest for Sir Arthur Conan Doyle.* Carbondale: Southern Illinois University Press, 1987.

McCearney, James. *Arthur Conan Doyle.* Paris: La Table Ronde, 1988.

Nordon, Pierre. *Conan Doyle.* London: John Murray, 1966.

Pearson, Hesketh. *Conan Doyle, His Life and Art.* London: Methuen, 1943.

Stavert, Geoffrey. *A Study in Southsea.* Portsmouth, England: Milestone Publications, 1987.

Draconites

Stones also known as dentrites, draconius, or obsianus. According to **Albertus Magnus** a draconite is a shining black stone of pyramidal shape that is obtained from the head of a **dragon,** cut off while the animal is still panting. It subdues poison and endows its possessor with invincible courage. The kings of the East were said to have esteemed it a great treasure.

Dracula

Fictional vampire in a book of that name by Irish author **Bram Stoker** (1847–1912). The Count Dracula character has become an archetype for scores of books, films, and plays on the vampire theme since first appearing in Stoker's version of May 1897.

Stoker's character was supposedly based in part on the real-life Prince Dracula (Vlad V) in fifteenth-century Wallachia, but the historical original was reportedly a sadist rather than a vampire. According to legend, during his rule one of his punishments was to impale his victims on stakes and gloat over their sufferings. Stoker wedded the image of the literary vampire developed in the stories of John Polidori and Sheridan Le Fanu with information about the medieval Romanian ruler.

Stoker possibly became aware of the real Dracula through conversations with the Hungarian scholar **Arminius Vambéry** and supplemented his stories with research in Whitby, Yorkshire, and at the British Museum Library, London. There is thus considerable authenticity in much of the background detail of Stoker's book, including vampire folklore and actual locations in Transylvania (now Romania).

Dracula was first performed as a play on May 18, 1897, at the Lyceum Theatre, London (where Stoker was manager to the actor Henry Irving), but this first production was an adapted reading for copyright purposes, lasting four hours.

In 1923 permission for a dramatization of *Dracula* was given by Stoker's widow to Irish actor Hamilton Deane, and this version was first produced in June 1924 at the Grand Theatre, Derby, opening in London at the Little Theatre, John Street, Adelphi, February 14, 1924.

It is believed that the first screen versions were a Russian and then a Hungarian silent film, but copies of neither have survived. However, the 1922 German film, *Nosferatu, oder Eine Symphonie des Grauens* (a slightly disguised Dracula made by the famous silent film director F. W. Murnau), did survive in spite of Florence Stoker's attempt to squelch it. The role of the vampire was played by Max Schreck and the film achieved a doom-laden atmosphere, chiefly through the photography of cameraman Fritz Arno Wagner. After Florence Stoker's successful prosecution for infringement of copyright, the production company went into bankruptcy, but some prints survived and have been made available for public showings.

The Movies

The first official *Dracula* movie was made in Hollywood in 1930, directed by Tod Browning and starring Bela Lugosi in the title role. Lugosi became the most famous Dracula, appearing in many plays and films in this role. In 1972 a California court upheld the copyright of the heirs of Bela Lugosi in his own characterization of the part of Dracula. Over the years, the Dracula vampire theme has proliferated in movies all over the world, Christopher Lee and John Carradine playing the part most often. *Dracula,* the novel, has been brought to the screen more than a dozen times, and several hundred movies have featured the main character. In 1992, film director Francis Ford Coppola released his version of the classic entitled *Bram Stroker's Dracula,* with Gary Oldman in the title role supported by Anthony Hopkins and Winona Ryder. The film won Academy Awards for best costume design, makeup, sound effects, and editing.

In March 1968 the magazine *Fate* published an interview with Count Alexander Cepesi, who claimed to be a descendant of Vlad Dracula. Cepesi was a Romanian, living in Istanbul since 1947. He operated a blood bank and collected plasma for Turkish hospitals.

The traditional tomb of Dracula is in a monastery at Snagov, Romania. It was opened in 1931 but was found to contain only animal bones. A second grave in the same church contained a casket with a skeleton in a purple shroud embroidered with gold. However, the Weird Museum in Hollywood, California, exhibited what is claimed to be the authentic skeleton of Vlad Dracula, believed to have been removed from Bucharest.

In Britain, the **Dracula Society** exists to promote the study and appreciation of the work of Bram Stoker and Gothic themes in literature, theater, and film. In the Republic of Ireland, a **Bram Stoker Society** was formed with similar aims and fraternal association with the British Dracula Society. In the United States both the **Count Dracula Fan Club** and the **Count Dracula Society** carry on the appreciation of Dracula and his vampire cousins. Most recently, the Transylvanian Society of Dracula, headquartered in Bucharest, has brought together a worldwide network of Dracula enthusiasts.

The modern revival of interest in the undead vampire of Bram Stoker's famous novel has continued to grow through the twentieth century but has increased since the 1972 publication of a biography of the real Dracula by historians Raymond T. McNally and Radu Florescu. In May 1977, during ceremonies held in Bucharest to celebrate the 100th anniversary of Romanian independence, President Nicolae Ceausescu solemnly honored fifteenth-century warrior-prince Vlad Dracula (prototype of Stoker's thriller) by inclusion in the nation's Hall of Fame. Prince Vlad is a tourist attraction in Romania for hundreds of foreign visitors who join the tours of sites related to both Prince Vlad and the novel's Transylvanian count. The real Dracula, Vlad Tepes or "Vlad the Impaler," killed his enemies by impaling them on sharply pointed wooden stakes. This is an inversion of the traditional method of setting a vampire to rest, as told in *Dracula.*

Vlad the Impaler was captured by Turks in 1476, and after decapitation his head was exhibited in Constantinople, on a stake. His status as a national hero stems from his opposition to the Turks and "love for the fatherland" as an authoritarian.

As the centennial of the novel *Dracula* approaches (1997), Vlad Tepes has become a well-known historical figure to contemporary audiences, while the literary Dracula has become an immediately recognizable figure in popular culture. The image of Dracula regularly appears on products from greeting cards to mass media advertisements. Dracula books, comic books, movies, jewelry, dramas, candy, and toys appeal to an ever increasing audience.

Sources:

Florescu, Radu & Raymond T. McNally. *Dracula: A Biography of Vlad the Impaler 1391–1476.* New York: Hawthorn Books, 1973.

Glut, Donald. *The Dracula Book.* Metuchen, N.J.: Scarecrow Press, 1975.

McNally, Raymond T. & Radu Florescu. *In Search of Dracula: A True History of Dracula and Vampire Legends.* New York: New York Graphic Society, 1972.

Melton, J. Gordon. *The Vampire Book: The Encyclopedia of the Undead.* Detroit: Gale Research, 1994.

Summers, Montague. *The Vampire: His Kith and Kin.* Reprint, London: Routledge, Kegan Paul, Trench, Trubner, 1928. Reprint, New Hyde Park, N.Y.: University Books, 1960.

———. *The Vampire in Europe.* London: Routledge, Kegan Paul, Trench, Trubner, 1929. Reprint, New Hyde Park, N.Y.: University Books, 1966.

Wolf, Leonard. *The Annotated Dracula.* New York: Clarkson N. Potter, 1975.

Dracula Society, The

Founded in Britain October 23, 1973, by Bernard Davies and Bruce Wightman to promote the study and appreciation of the life and works of **Bram Stoker; vampire, werwolf,** and **monster** themes in fiction; stage and movie adaptations of *Dracula, Frankenstein,* and their derivatives; the sources of Stoker and similar writers; and possible links between fictional and historical persons and places concerned with Gothic literature. Honorary life members of the society include Christopher Lee and the late Vincent Price, famous for their roles in horror movies.

The society holds meetings, lectures, and film showings and has organized tours to Transylvania by arrangement with the Romanian Tourist Ministry. These tours have traced the route of Jonathan Harker in Stoker's novel *Dracula* and visited localities associated with the book. During the latter part of 1976, the society's newsletter, *Voices from the Vaults,* was amplified by publication of the magazine *The Dracula Journals* (now discontinued). Address: The Hon. Secretary, The Dracula Society, 36 Elliston House, 100 Wellington St., London, SE18 GQF, England.

Dragon

A monster of enormous size, common to almost all countries. Descriptions of its appearance vary, but it is of reptilian nature, often red or green in color, sometimes with several heads that spew fire and vapors, and a large tail, not unlike some dinosaurs.

It is of enormous strength, but the ancients believed that it could be charmed by music, and the dragon that guarded the Golden Fleece of Greek legend was soothed by the voice of Medea. In India at the time of Alexander the Great, a dragon was worshiped as a god, while in **occult history** it is the manifestation of hell.

The dragon, however, is best known in legendary history as the monster whose duty it is to provide the hero with opportunities of valor. There is a legend of St. George and the Dragon and also the dragon that was slain by Sir Lancelot, one of the knights of **King Arthur**'s Round Table.

In the Hebrew Bible (the Christian Old Testament) the word *tannin,* commonly rendered "dragon" in older English translations, generally refers to a variety of animals such as crocodiles, jackals, and serpents, but occasionally to the dragon (Ezek. 29:3; 32:3). In Chapter 12 of the biblical book of Revelation, the dragon, a representation of the Evil One, is overcome by the archangel Michael.

The dragon became a symbol of great strength in the European Middle Ages. In the fifteenth century, the emperor of the Holy Roman Empire founded the Order of the Dragon to unite Christian rulers against the incursions of the Turkish Muslims into the Balkans. Among those invested with the order was Prince Vlad of Wallachia (Romania). He assumed the name Vlad Dracul, *dracul* being the Romanian word for dragon. His son took the diminutive form of the name as Prince Vlad Dracula.

During the time of Henry VII (1457–1509), a coin was given to those who were cured of **possession** with one side featuring an angel standing with both feet on a dragon.

The idea of the dragon is perhaps evolved from the concept of the earth as a living being, a notion that gained currency from earthquakes and related phenomena.

"Draumkvaede"

The "Dream Song" of medieval Norway, which describes the mystical visions of Olav Asteson in the 13 holy nights from Christmas to Epiphany. In a trance, Asteson travels through earth, water, air, and fire; crosses the perilous Gjaller Bridge, guarded by a serpent, a hound, and a bull; and sees heaven and hell and the judgment of souls. He returns to tell his visions to the congregation at church.

This folk ballad with pagan and Christian symbols was first known in the Telemark region about 1200 C.E. and remained in oral tradition until modern times. It has always been a source of inspiration in Norwegian poetry, painting, and music. Reportedly a traditional rendering of *Draumkvaede* has a mystical power in its tones and melody. In 1955 a limited edition recording of the singing of Gudrun Grave Norland was issued by the Norsk Folksmuseum. An English language version of *Draumkvaede* was made in 1961 by anthroposophist Eleanor C. Merry, with color illustrations from her own paintings.

Sources:

Barnes, Michael. *Draumkvaede.* Oslo, 1974.

Merry, Eleanor. *The Dream Song of Olaf Asteson.* England: New Knowledge Books, 1961.

Dream Body

A hypothetical duplicate of the physical body similar to the **double** or **astral body.** Reportedly the experience of the astral body is most commonly accessed during sleep and its reality often experienced as a dream.

Dr. F. van Eeden of Holland attempted to transfer his consciousness to his dream body so that he could remember everything that transpired during sleep and also attempted to control this body to manipulate physical objects. **Hereward Carrington** states in *Higher Psychical Development* (1920):

"He did not succeed in doing so, but came very near it—and succeeded to the extent that he induced a complete dual consciousness. He remembered clearly that he was asleep in bed, with his arms folded across his breast; and *at the same time* he remembered clearly that he was looking out of the window and saw a dog run up and look at him through the glass, and run away again—and details of that character. He then remembered gliding towards the couch on which his physical body was lying, lying down beside it—and a moment later woke up and was again, of course, in the physical body. But he had the extreme sense of duality of consciousness of the two bodies."

In the book *The Projection of the Astral Body* (1929) **Sylvan Muldoon** claims that he met with similar experiences and at first he, too, believed that his consciousness was in both bodies simultaneously. Further experiments, however, convinced him that a double functioning of vision through the cord connecting the astral body with the physical sufficiently explained the experience.

Muldoon claims that during a conscious projection, within cord activity range, the sense of sight can function in three ways: from the eyes of the phantom, from the spot occupied by the physical eyes, and from both simultaneously. As regards moving physical objects in dreams, Muldoon states: "I know it to be the truth, viz., one can move an object in his dream, but that the object does not move until about two seconds later in reality."

Supposedly Muldoon started a metronome in his dream. The metronome was in another room on the piano. After his return to consciousness a little time elapsed before the metronome began to tick. He points out the connection to the synchronization of movement, observed between the medium **Eusapia Palladino**'s limbs and the objects moved as observed by **Sir Oliver Lodge:**

"When six or seven feet away the time interval (between the push and the movement of the object) was something like two seconds. When the accordion is being played, the fingers of the medium are moving in a thoroughly appropriate manner, and the process reminds one of the twitching of a dog's legs when he is supposed to be dreaming that he is chasing a hare. It is as if Eusapia were dreaming that she was fingering the instrument, and dreaming it so vividly that the instrument was actually played. It is as if a dog dreamt of the chase with such energy that a distant hare was really captured and killed, as by a phantom dog; and, fanciful as for the moment it may seem, and valueless as I suppose such speculations are, I am, I confess, at present more than half disposed to look in some such direction for a clue to these effects. In an idealistic conception of nature it has by many philosophers been considered that thought is the reality, and that material substratum is but a consequence of thought. So in a minor degree it appears here; it is as if, let us say, the dream of the entranced person were vivid enough physically to effect surrounding objects and actually produce objective results; to cause not only real and permanent movements of ordinary objects, but also temporary fresh aggregations of material particles into extraordinary objects—these aggregations being objective enough to be felt, heard, seen and probably even photographed while they last."

A number of experiments have been carried out by parapsychologists in modern times to attempt to establish whether there is a measurable objective reality to the "astral body," but without decisive evidence. Various techniques have been used, including magnetometers, ultraviolet and infrared detectors, strain gauges, thermistors, and other electronic devices; animals have also been used as detectors.

Use of the terms *astral body, double, etheric body,* and *dream body* as more or less synonymous is somewhat confusing. For general purposes, the term *astral body* is more widespread, although astral projection is now being superseded by **out-of-the-body travel** because parapsychologists have begun taking increased interest in the phenomenon. (See also **lucid dreaming.**)

Sources:

Morris, R. L., S. B. Harry, J. Janis, J. Hartwell, and William G. Roll. "Studies of Communication during Out-of-body Experiences." *Journal* of the American Society for Psychical Research 72 (1978).

Muldoon, Sylvan J., and Hereward Carrington. *The Projection of the Astral Body.* London: Rider, 1929.

Dream Laboratory

Established by **Montague Ullman** in 1962 "to explore the problem of telepathy and dreams by means of the newly discovered Rapid Eye Movement monitoring technique." The laboratory's principal function is research, but it also brings together scholars concerned with **parapsychology** and organizes lectures to outside groups. It has conducted a number of experiments on altered states of consciousness and **psi** faculty during sleep that have been reported in various professional journals. It was directed for ten years by **Stanley Krippner.** Address: Department of Psychiatry, Maimonides Medical Center, 4802 10th Ave., Brooklyn, NY 12219.

Sources:

Ullman, Montague. *Dream Telepathy.* Rev. ed. Jefferson, N.C.: McFarland, 1989.

———. *The Varieties of Dream Experience: Expanding Our Ways of Working with Dreams.* New York: Continuum, 1987.

Ullman, Montague, and Stanley Krippner. *Dream Studies and Telepathy: An Experimental Approach.* New York: Parapsychology Foundation, 1970.

Dreaming True

The ability to have control and consciousness in the dream state, also known as **lucid dreaming.** According to **Hereward Carrington** (in his book *Higher Psychical Development,* 1924) dreamers can keep conscious control up to the moment of falling asleep. He advises:

"When you have learned to do that, then construct before yourself, mentally, a definite scene, which you must hold firmly in mind. Then, as you are falling to sleep hold this scene before you, and at the very last moment, before you fall asleep, consciously transfer yourself into the scene—in other words, step into the picture; and if you have developed yourself to the requisite point, you will be enabled to carry over an unbroken consciousness into the dream state; and in this way you have a perfect continuity of thought; there is no break in the consciousness; you step into the dream picture and go on dreaming consciously. That is the process of dreaming true, and after this dream is fully enacted, then you should remember perfectly all that has transpired during the sleep period."

In the book *The Projection of the Astral Body* by **Sylvan J. Muldoon** and Carrington (1929), Muldoon remarks that these instructions are in harmony with the method of dream control used to induce the astral body to move out into space. An article in the *Proceedings* of the Society for Psychical Research (vol. 26, July 1913) records van Eeden's experiments in dreaming true. The British psychical researcher **J. Arthur Hill** vouches for the truthfulness of the experiences in *The Dreams of Orlow* (1916), by A. M. Irvine.

Sources:

Muldoon, Sylvan J., and Hereward Carrington. *The Projection of the Astral Body.* London: Rider, 1929.

Dreams

The **occult** significance of dreams was a matter of speculation among the wise at an early period in the history of civilization. The entries on **Babylonia** and **Egypt** to some extent outline the methods by which the wise men of those countries divined the future from **visions** seen in sleep, and articles dealing with other countries include data relating to dreams and dreamlore. This entry addresses some of the more outstanding theories of antiquity regarding the nature and causes of dreams and the manner in which the ancient diviners generally interpreted them.

Historical Views of Dreaming

Dreams were regarded as of two kinds—false and true, in either case emanating from a supernatural intelligence, evil or good. Sleep was regarded as a second life by the ancients, a life in which the soul was freed from the body and was therefore much more active than during the waking state. The acts it observed and the scenes through which it passed were thought to have a bearing on the future life of the dreamer, but it is also believed that the dream life was regarded as supernatural and "inverted," and that the events that the bodiless spirit beheld were the opposites of those that would later occur on the earthly plane. The idea thus originated that "dreams go by contraries," as both popular belief and many treatises upon the subject of nightly visions assure us is the case.

A belief in the divinatory character of dreams arose, and their causes and nature occupied some of the greatest minds of antiquity. Aristotle, for example, believed them to arise solely from natural causes. Posidonius the Stoic was of the opinion that there were three kinds: the first was automatic and came from the clear sight of the soul, the second from spirits, and the third from God. Cratippus, Democritus, and Pythagoras held doctrines almost identical to this or differing only in detail.

Later, Macrobius divided dreams into five kinds: the dream, the vision, the ocular dream, the insomnium, and the phantasm. The first was a figurative and mysterious representation that required an interpretation; the second was an exact representation of a future event in sleep; the third was a dream representing some priest or divinity who declared to the sleeper things to come; the fourth was an ordinary dream not deserving of attention; and the fifth was a disturbing half-awake dream, a species of nightmare.

Other writers divided dreams into accidental dreams and those induced for the purposes of divination. Herodotus wrote that in the temple of Bel in Babylon, a priestess lay on a bed of ram skin ready to dream for divination. The ancient Hebrews obtained such dreams by sleeping among tombs. Dreams are believed to be as successful as hypnosis and other methods of reaching the supernatural world and hearing its pronouncements.

Sleep was, of course, often induced by **drugs,** whether the soma of the Hindus, the peyotl of the ancient Mexicans, the hashish of the Arabs, or the opium of the Malays or Chinese. These narcotics, which have the property of inducing speedy sleep and of heightening inward visions, were and are still prized by professional dreamers all over the world, especially as they render dreaming almost immediately possible.

Ancient Methods of Dream Interpretation

As stated, interpretation of dreams was generally undertaken by a special class of diviners, who in ancient Greece were known as *oneiocritikoi,* or "interpreters of dreams." The first treatise on the subject was that of Artemidorus (ca. 100 C.E.). He differentiated between the dreams of kings and those of commoners, since he believed that the visions of royalty referred to the commonwealth and not to the individual. Dreams that represented something happening to the dreamer revealed a personal significance, whereas a dream relating to another concerned him alone. He detailed the numerous species of dreams throughout five books, giving numerous examples. The rules of Artemidorus are far from clear, and according to them, any dream might signify any event, and any interpretation might be considered justifiable.

The method of testing dreams according to Moses Amyraldus in his *Discours sur les songes divins* (1625) was to determine whether the instructions and advice they contained made for good or ill—a test impossible to apply until after the result is known. But Amyraldus addressed this difficulty by proposing to test dreams by the evidence of divine knowledge they showed—

by asking whether the dream gave any evidence of things such as God alone could know.

It seems from an examination of dreams submitted to the ancient diviners that the exhibited symbolism could only be interpreted through divine aid, as in the cases of Moses and Daniel in the Bible. Many improbable interpretations were given to most epochal dreams of antiquity. There are some students of the occult who doubt the occult significance of dreams and do not classify dreams generally with **vision, second sight,** or **ecstasy.**

Dreams and Psychical Phenomena

Dreams of a supernormal character fall within the purview of psychical research. The dividing line between normal and supernormal dreams is not easy to draw. It is believed that subconscious elaboration often presents supernormal effects.

Reportedly Goethe solved scientific problems and composed poetry in his dreams. Jean de La Fontaine composed *The Fable of Pleasures* and **Samuel Taylor Coleridge** wrote "Kubla Khan" (1816) as a result of dreams. Bernhard Palissy made a piece on dream inspiration. Matthew Maury confessed, "I have had in dream ideas and inspiration that could never have entered my consciousness when awake." Giuseppe Tartini heard his "Sonate del Diavolo" played by Beelzebub in a dream, Holden composed *La Phantasie* in his sleep; and Charles Nodier's *Lydia* was similarly born. Robert Louis Stevenson's most ingenious plots were evolved in the dream state. Reportedly Kruger, Corda, and Maignan solved mathematical problems in dreams and Condillac finished an interrupted lecture. For many of the Romantic writers, such as Coleridge and Nodier, these creative dreams were induced by the ingestion of opium.

A dream of Louis Agassiz is frequently quoted. He tried for two weeks to decipher the obscure impression of a fish fossil on the stone slab in which it was preserved. In a dream he saw the fish with all the missing features restored. The image escaped him on awakening. He went to the Jardin des Plantes in the hope that an association with the fossil would recapture it. It did not. The next night he again dreamed of the fish, but in the morning the features of the fish were as elusive as ever. On the third night he placed paper and pencil near his bed. Toward morning the fish again appeared in a dream. Half dreaming, half awake, he traced the outlines in the darkness. On awakening he was surprised to see details in his nocturnal sketch that he thought impossible. He returned to the Jardin des Plantes and began to chisel on the surface of the stone using the sketch as a guide. Reportedly Agassiz found the hidden portions of the fish as indicated in the drawing.

The dream of a Professor Hilprecht, a Babylonian scholar who tried to decipher writing on two small pieces of agate, is more complicated and belongs to the clairvoyant order. As reported in the *Proceedings* of the Society for Psychical Research (August 1900), he went to sleep and dreamt of a tall, thin priest of the old pre-Christian Nippur who led him to the treasure chamber of the temple and went with him into a small, low-ceilinged room without windows in which there was a large wooden chest; scraps of agate and lapis lazuli lay scattered on the floor. Here the priest addressed Hilprecht as follows:

"The two fragments which you have published separately belong together, and their history is as follows: King Kruigalzu [c. 1300 B.C.] once sent to the temple of Bel, among other articles of agate and lapis-lazuli, an inscribed votive cylinder of agate. Then we priests suddenly received the command to make for the statue of the god Nidib a pair of ear rings of agate. We were in great dismay, since there was no agate as raw material at hand. In order for us to execute the command there was nothing for us to do but cut the votive cylinder into three parts, thus making three rings, each of which contained a portion of the original inscription. The first two served as ear rings for the statue of the god; the two fragments which have given you so much trouble are portions of them. If you will put the two together you will have a confirmation of my words."

The continuation of the story is given by Mrs. Hilprecht, who testified to having seen her husband jump out of bed, rush into the study and cry out, "It is so, it is so."

The scientist **Nikola Tesla** had waking visions in which a complex electrical engineering apparatus was perceived in total details of design and construction.

There are many cases of bits of information obtained in dreams. **William James** was impressed by the Enfield case, in which the discovery of the body of a drowned woman was effected through a dream of a Mrs. Titus of Lebanon, a stranger to the scene.

Charles Richet recounts the following instance of dream cognition:

"I saw Stella on the 2nd of December during the day, and on leaving I said 'I am going to give a lecture on snake poison.' She at once replied: 'I dreamt last night of snakes, or rather of eels.' Then, without of course giving any reason, I asked her to tell me her dream, and her exact words were: 'It was about eels more than snakes, two eels, for I could see their white shining bellies and their sticky skin; and I said to myself I do not like these creatures, but it pains me when they are hurt.' This dream was strangely conformable to what I had done the day before, December 1. On that day I had, for the first time in twenty years, experimented with eels. Desiring to draw from them a little blood, I had put two eels on the table and their white, shining, irridescent, viscous bellies had particularly struck me."

A case of dream **clairvoyance,** possibly under spirit influence, is that of a Miss Loganson, 19, of Chicago. She saw in a dream the murder of her brother, Oscar, who was a farmer of Marengo, about 50 miles northwest of Chicago. She accused a farmer neighbor named Bedford for days, but no one paid attention to her. At length she was permitted to send a telegram; the reply was, "Oscar has disappeared." Starting for Oscar's farm, accompanied by another brother and by the police, she went directly to Bedford's house. Traces of blood were found in the kitchen. Proceeding to the hen house, the yard of which was paved, the girl said, "My brother is buried here." Because of the girl's insistence and her agitation, consent was given to dig. Under the pavement they first found the brother's overcoat; five feet down they came upon the body. Bedford was arrested at Ellos, Nebraska, and hanged in due course. Miss Loganson, in explanation, said that the spirit of her brother haunted her for seven days in dreams.

Lost objects are frequently found in dreams. In most cases subconscious memory sufficiently explains the mystery. There are, however, more complicated cases. According to legend Hercules appeared in a dream to Sophocles and indicated where a golden crown would be found. Sophocles got the reward promised to the finder.

Supposedly the paranormal character of dreams is clearest in telepathic and prophetic dreams. They often produce an impression lasting for days. Sweating and trembling are occasionally experienced on waking from a dream of this character. The dreams tend to be repeated. One case of prophetic dreams announced the murder of a Chancellor Perceval. It is thus narrated by one Abercrombie:

"Many years ago there was mentioned in several of the newspapers a dream which gave notice of the murder of Mr. Perceval. Through the kindness of an eminent medical friend in England I have received the authentic particulars of this remarkable case, from the gentleman to whom the dream occurred. He resides in Cornwall, and eight days before the murder was committed, dreamt that he was in the lobby of the House of Commons, and saw a small man enter, dressed in a blue coat and white waistcoat. Immediately after, he saw a man dressed in a brown coat with yellow basket metal buttons draw a pistol from under his coat, and discharge it at the former, who instantly fell; the blood issued from the wound a little below the left breast. He saw the murderer seized by some gentlemen who were present, and observed his countenance; and on asking who the gentleman was that had been shot, he was told that it was the Chancellor. He then awoke, and mentioned the dream to his wife, who made light of it; but in the course of the night the dream occurred three times without the least variation in any of the circumstances. He was now so much impressed by it, that he felt much inclined to give notice to Mr. Perceval, but was dissuaded by some friends whom he consulted, who assured him that he would only get himself treated as a fanatic. On the evening of the eighth day after, he received the account of the murder. Being in London a short time after, he found in the print-shops a representation of the scene, and recognised in it the countenance and dresses of the parties, the blood on Mr. Perceval's waistcoat, and the yellow basket buttons on Bellingham's coat, precisely as he had seen them in his dreams.''

J. W. Dunne's *An Experiment with Time* (1927) is a study of how future events are foreshadowed in our dreams. By keeping a record of his dreams, putting them down immediately on awakening, he found that a considerable part of his dreams anticipated future experiences, and this was corroborated by fellow experimenters.

Many other dreams, difficult to classify, bear the stamp of paranormal. **Camille Flammarion** in his *Death and its Mystery* (1922–23) quoted the curious dream of a Mrs. Marechal, who between sleeping and waking, saw a specter taking her arm and saying, ''Either your husband or your daughter must die. Choose!'' After great mental sufferings she decided for her child. Five days later her husband, who was in good health, suddenly died.

The experience of **déjà vu** to which advocates of **reincarnation** often refer, may be explained by traveling clairvoyance in dreams. Another explanation, a theory of ancestral dreams, is offered in the *Bulletins et Mémoires de la Societé d'Anthropologie de Paris* by Letourneau, as follows:

''Certain events, external or psychic, which have made a deep impression on a person, may be so deeply engraved upon his brain as to result in a molecular orientation, so lasting that it may be transmitted to some of his descendants in the same way as character, aptitudes, mental maladies, etc. It is then no longer a question of infantile reminiscences, but of ancestral recollections, capable of being revived. From that will proceed not only the fortuitous recognition of places which a person has never seen, but, moreover a whole category of peculiar dreams, admirably co-ordinated, in which we witness as at a panorama, adventures which cannot be remembrances, because they have not the least connection with our individual life'' (Paul Joire, *Psychical and Supernormal Phenomena,* 1936).

Hereward Carrington called attention in *The Story of Psychic Science* (1930) to the neglect shown for the dreams of mediums. It is believed that if the communicators are subconscious personalities, some connection may be established between them and the dreams of the medium. In the **Lenora Piper** trances the communicators themselves alleged that they were in a dreamlike state. In one instant a statement came through that was quite wrong, but upon investigation, it turned out to be a remark that the communicator made in the delirium of death.

Modern Views on Dreaming

Modern scientists have studied the relationship of eye movements to dreaming. Professors N. Kleitman and E. Aserinsky of the Department of Physiology, University of Chicago, monitored eye movements of sleepers using electroencephalographic records. They distinguished four types of brain wave and sleep periods, ranging from lightest sleep to deep coma. In stage 1 there were rapid eye movements; in stages 2, 3, and 4, eye movements were slow. They concluded that rapid eye movements (REMs) were related to dreaming, when the eyes move like a spectator watching a theater play or reading a book.

This relationship between eye movement and mental states makes interesting comparison with Eastern religious techniques of **meditation.** In both Indian and Chinese **yoga** meditation exercises, eye rolling and focusing is linked to techniques of concentration and visionary experience.

The dream state plays a prominent part in Hindu religious philosophy, which recognizes four states of consciousness—waking, dreaming, deep sleep, and a fourth condition of higher consciousness that embraces the first three. Hindu mystics have stressed that since the essential self (the unconditioned sense of ''I'') is constant in all states of consciousness, identification with the body, mind, emotions, memories, age, sex, and so on in waking life is illusory—a false ego—since such characteristics are transitory. The pure self is always present, and this essential ''I-ness'' is the same in all individuals. Awareness of this true self in the fourth condition of higher consciousness (*turiya*) is known as self-realization, in which there is unity with all creation. The significance of dreaming, deep sleep, and waking states is discussed in the Hindu scripture Mandukya Upanishad.

Many **out-of-the-body travel** experiences (**astral projection**) appear to be stimulated by vivid dreams, particularly when waking consciousness is aroused by some irregularity in the logic of a dream. For example, a dreamer recognizes the familiar environment of his own room, but notices that the wallpaper is the wrong design and color, and immediately thinks ''This must be a dream!'' This gaining of waking consciousness while still in a sleeping condition sometimes results in a subtle or **astral body** moving independently of the physical body. (See **dreaming true; lucid dreams**)

Some experimenters have claimed that release of the subtle body may be stimulated by deliberately induced images of release (e.g., taking off in an airplane, traveling upward in an elevator), just before passing into the sleep state. Such out-of-the-body experiences were also recognized in Hindu religious philosophy and are described in ancient scriptures. The subtle body was named the *sukshma sharira.*

Freudian and Jungian psychoanalysis have moved in a different direction in their interpretation of the significance of dreams. Certain elements in dreams are said to be wish fulfilling, or to contain clues to psychic problems of the individual. In Jungian analysis, dream symbols are also understood as universal archetypes of human experience. **Carl G. Jung** drew heavily upon Eastern religious philosophies in his exposition of the concept of a collective unconscious.

Scientific research indicates other fascinating areas of dreaming. In 1927 J. W. Dunne, a British airplane designer, published his remarkable book *An Experiment with Time,* in which he analyzes a dream experiment suggestive of the occurrence of future elements in dreams, side by side with images from past experience.

In 1970 the Soviet psychiatrist Dr. Vasily Kasatkin reported on a 28 year study of 8,000 dreams and concluded that dreams could warn of the onset of a serious illness several months in advance, through a special sensitivity of the brain to preliminary physical symptoms.

At the **Dream Laboratory,** founded at Maimonides Medical Center, New York, in 1962, volunteers submitted to controlled experiments in dreaming, studying the rapid eye movements noticeable in people as they dream. One of the most interesting projects was a statistical study with pairs of subjects, which tended to show that telepathic dreams could be produced experimentally.

It would seem that dreaming and the elements in dreams have many different aspects of a physiological and psychological nature, with certain paranormal characteristics. Many of these aspects differ widely in various individuals. There have been well-authenticated prophetic dreams, as well as fragmentary elements of future events of the kind described by J. W. Dunne. Many aspects of dream imagery appear to be a visual presentation of individual psychic problems. Increasing evidence from out-of-the-body travel experiences has convinced some researchers of the reality of astral travel and of its stimulus through dream images. It may well be, as noted in several religious traditions, that there are also meta-physical dimensions to dream experience.

Newstands still carry simplistic dream manuals that offer interpretations of any and every symbol or image seen in a dream. Modern dream studies have demonstrated, if anything, that the evaluation of dreams is far more complex than these popular dream interpretation manuals even begin to suggest.

Sources:

Artemidorus. *The Interpretation of Dreams: Oneirocritica.* Translated by Robert White. Park Ridge, N.J.: Noyes Press, 1975.

Cartwright, Rosalind D. *Night Life: Explorations in Dreaming.* Englewood, N.J.: Prentice-Hall, 1977.

Christmas, Henry. *The Cradle of the Twin Giants, Science and History.* 2 vols. London, 1849.

Colquohoun, John C. *An History of Magic, Witchcraft & Animal Magnetism.* 2 vols. N.p., 1851.

De Becker, R. *The Meaning of Dreams.* London, 1968.

Diamond, E. *The Science of Dreams.* London, 1962.

Dunne, J. W. *An Experiment with Time.* London, 1927.

Ellis, Havelock. *The World of Dreams.* Boston: Houghton Mifflin Company, 1922. Reprint, Detroit: Gale Research, 1976.

Faraday, Ann. *Dream Power.* New York: Coward, McCann & Geoghegan, 1972. Reprint, New York: Berkeley, 1973.

Freud, Sigmund. *The Interpretation of Dreams.* London, 1942.

Garfield, Patricia L. *Creative Dreaming.* New York: Simon & Schuster, 1974.

Green, Celia E. *Lucid Dreams.* London: Hamish Hamilton, 1968.

Hutchinson, H. *Dreams and their Meanings.* London, 1901.

Jung, C. G. *Archetypes and the Collective Unconscious.* Collected Works, vol. 9. Princeton, N.J.: Princeton University Press, 1959.

Kelsey, Morton T. *God, Dreams, and Revelation: A Christian Interpretation of Dreams.* Minneapolis, Minn.: Augsburg Publishing House, 1974.

LaBerge, Steven. *Lucid Dreaming: The Power of Being Awake and Aware in Your Dreams.* Los Angeles: Jeremy P. Tarcher, 1987.

Lang, Andrew. *The Book of Dreams & Ghosts.* London, 1897. Reprint, New York: Causeway Books, 1974.

Lincoln, J. S. *The Dream in Primitive Cultures.* London, 1935. Reprint, Academic Press, 1970.

Luce, Gay Gaer. *Body Time.* Pantheon, 1961.

Luce, Gay Gaer, and J. Segal. *Sleep.* New York: Coward, McCann, 1966.

Muldoon, Sylvan J., and Hereward Carrington. *The Projection of the Astral Body.* London, 1929. Reprint, New York: Samuel Weiser, 1967.

Nikhilananda, Swami, trans. *Mandukya Upanishad.* Chicago: Vedanta Press, 1972.

Priestley, J. B. *Man and Time.* London, 1964. Reprint, New York: Dell, 1971.

Ratcliff, A. J. J. *A History of Dreams.* London, 1913.

Sabin, Katharine C. *ESP and Dream Analysis.* Chicago: Henry Regnery, 1974.

Seafield, Frank. *The Literature & Curiosities of Dreams.* 2nd ed. London, 1877.

Staff, V. S. *Remembered on Waking; Concerning Psychic & Spiritual Dreams & Theories of Dreaming.* Crowborough, U.K.: V. S. Staff, 1975.

Tart, Charles, ed. *Altered States of Consciousness.* Garden City, N.Y.: Doubleday, 1969.

Ullman, Montague, Stanley Krippner, and Alan Vaughan. *Dream Telepathy.* New York: Turnstone Books; London: Macmillan, 1973.

Dreams of Animals

It was believed by many people in ancient times that animals had dreams. According to **Pliny the Elder**:

"Evident it is, that horses, dogs, kine, oxen, sheepe and goats, doe dreame. Whereupon it is credibly also thought that all creatures that bring forth their young quicke and living, doe the same. As for those that lay egges, it is not so certian that they dreame; but resolved it is that they doe sleepe."

Dress, Phantom

The question of the apparel worn by **apparitions** has often aroused considerable controversy. Psychical researcher **Frank Podmore** provides some reflections upon the issue:

"The apparition commonly consists simply of a figure, clothed as the percipient was accustomed to see the agent clothed; whereas to be true to life the phantasm would as a rule have to appear in bed. In cases where the vision gives no information as to the agent's clothing and surroundings generally—and, as already said, such cases form the great majority of the well attested narratives—we may suppose that what is transmitted is not any part of the superficial content of the agent's consciousness, but an impression from the underlying massive and permanent elements which represent his personal identity. The percipient's imagination is clearly competent to clothe such an impression with appropriate imagery, must indeed so clothe it if it is to rise into consciousness at all. . . . The ghosts, it will have been observed, always appear clothed. Have clothes also ethereal counterparts? Such was and is the belief of many early races of mankind, who leave clothes, food, and weapons in the graves of the dead, or burn them on the funeral pile, that their friends may have all they require in the spirit world. But are we prepared to accept this view? And again, these ghosts commonly appear, not in the clothes which they were wearing at death—for most deaths take place in bed—but in some others, as will be seen from an examination of the stories already cited. Are we to suppose the ethereal body going to its wardrobe to clothe its nakedness withal? or that, as in the case of Ensign Cavalcante's appearance to Frau Reiken, the ghost will actually take off the ethereal clothes it wore at death and replace them with others? It is scarcely necessary to pursue the subject. The difficulties and contradictions involved in adapting it to explain the clothes must prove fatal to the ghost theory."

In *The Ghost World* (1893), Thistleton Dyer summarizes a large body of reported apparitions that mention the figures' appearance:

"It is the familiar dress worn in lifetime that is, in most cases, one of the distinguishing features of the ghost, and when Sir George Villiers wanted to give a warning to his son, the Duke of Buckingham, his spirit appeared to one of the Duke's servants 'in the very clothes he used to wear.' Mrs. Crowe, [in her *Night Side of Nature,*] some years ago, gave an account of an apparition which appeared at a house in Sarratt, Hertfordshire. It was that of a well-dressed gentleman, in a blue coat and bright gilt buttons, but without a head. It seems that this was reported to be the ghost of a poor man of that neighbourhood who had been murdered, and whose head had been cut off. He could, therefore, only be recognised by his 'blue coat and bright gilt buttons.' Indeed, many ghosts have been nicknamed from the kinds of dress in which they have been in the habit of appearing. Thus the ghost at Allanbank was known as 'Pearlin Jean,' from a species of lace made of thread which she wore; and the 'White Lady' at Ashley Hall—like other ghosts who have borne the same name—from the white drapery in which she presented herself. Some lady ghosts have been styled 'Silky,' from the rustling of their silken costume, in the wearing of which they have maintained the phantom grandeur of their earthly life. There was the 'Silky' at Black Heddon who used to appear in silken attire, oftentimes 'rattling in her silks;' and the spirit of Denton Hall—also termed 'Silky'—walks about in a white silk dress of antique fashion. This last 'Silky' was thought to be the ghost of a lady who was mistress to the profligate Duke of Argyll in the reign of William III, and died suddenly, not without suspicion of murder, at Chirton, near Shields—one of his residences. The 'Banshee of Loch Nigdal,' too, was arrayed in a silk dress, green in colour. These traditions date from a period when silk was not in common use, and therefore attracted notice in country places. Some years ago a ghost appeared at Hampton Court, habited in a black satin dress with white kid gloves. The White 'Lady of Skipsea' makes her midnight serenades clothed in long, white drapery. Lady Bothwell, who haunted the mansion of Woodhouselee, always appeared in white; and the apparition of the mansion of Houndwood, in Berwickshire—bearing the name of 'Chappie'—is clad in silk attire.

"One of the ghosts seen at the celebrated Willington Mill was that of a female in greyish garments. Sometimes she was said to be wrapped in a mantle, with her head depressed and her hands crossed on her lap. Walton Abbey had its headless lady who used to haunt a certain wainscotted chamber, dressed in blood-stained garments, with her infant in her arms; and, in short, most of the ghosts that have tenanted our country houses have been noted for their distinctive dress.

"Daniel Defoe, in his *Essay on the History and Reality of Apparitions,* has given many minute details as to the dress of a ghost. He tells a laughable and highly amusing story of some robbers who broke into a mansion in the country, and, while ransacking one of the rooms, they saw, in a chair, 'a grave, ancient man, with a long full-bottomed wig, and a rich, brocaded gown,' etc. One of the robbers threatened to tear off his 'rich brocaded gown,' another hit at him with a firelock, and was alarmed at seeing it pass through the air; and then the old man 'changed into the most horrible monster that ever was seen, with eyes like two fiery daggers red hot.' The same apparition encountered them in different rooms, and at last the servants, who were at the top of the house, throwing some 'hand grenades' down the chimneys of these rooms, the thieves were dispersed. Without adding further stories of this kind, which may be taken for what they are worth, it is a generally received belief in ghost lore that spirits are accustomed to appear in the dresses which they wore in their lifetime—a notion credited from the days of Pliny the Younger to the present day.

"But the fact of ghosts appearing in earthly raiment has excited the ridicule of many philosophers, who, even admitting the possibility of a spiritual manifestation, deny that there can be the ghost of a suit of clothes. George Cruikshank, too, who was no believer in ghosts, sums up the matter thus: 'As it is clearly impossible for spirits to wear dresses made of the materials of earth, we should like to know if there are spiritual outfitting shops for the clothing of ghosts who pay visits on earth.'

"Whatever the objections may be to the appearance of ghosts in human attire, they have not hitherto overthrown the belief in their being seen thus clothed, and Byron, describing the 'Black Friar' who haunted the cloisters and other parts of Newstead Abbey, tells us that he was always 'arrayed in cowl, and beads, and dusky garb.' Indeed, as Dr. Tylor remarks in [*Primitive Culture*] it is 'an habitual feature of the ghost stories of the civilised, as of the savage world, that the ghost comes dressed, and even dressed in well-known clothing worn in life.' And he adds that the doctrine of object-souls was held by the Algonquin tribes, the islanders of the Fijian group, and the Karens of Burmah—it being supposed that not only men and beasts have souls, but inorganic things. Thus Mariner, describing the Fijian belief, writes: 'If a stone or any other substance is broken, immortality is equally its reward; nay, artificial bodies have equal good luck with men, and hogs, and yams. If an axe or a chisel is worn out or broken up, away flies its soul for the service of the gods. The Fijians can further show you a sort of natural well, or deep hole in the ground, at one of their islands, across the bottom of which runs a stream of water, in which you may clearly see the souls of men and women, beasts and plants, stocks and stones, canoes and horses, and of all the broken utensils of this frail world, swimming, or rather tumbling along, one over the other, pell-mell, into the regions of immortality.' As it has been observed, animistic conceptions of this kind are no more irrational than the popular idea prevalent in civilized communities as to spirits appearing in all kinds of garments."

With the development of **spirit photography** around 1862 as a corroborative aspect of Spiritualist phenomena, the question of phantom apparel appeared finally to have some objective basis. However, later experiments in projecting mental pictures onto photographic materials suggested that mental impressions might still color representations of the clothing of phantoms. More important, spirit photography was so deeply involved in **fraud** that any data derived from it is at best suspect.

The question of ghost attire is a puzzling one, and it may be more useful to regard individual cases on their own merit. Above and beyond spirit photographs, there were many undoubted examples of deliberate fraud in the representation of spirit forms produced in **materialization** séances clothed in a drapery of **ectoplasm,** which turned out to be a person covered with cheesecloth. There were, of course, many examples in which scientific observers testified to seeing ectoplasm develop into spirit forms with vague clothing, and there are photographic records of such materializations in motion, showing progressive stages of formation and later dissolution. (See the discussions in *From the Unconscious to the Conscious* by **Gustave Geley,** 1920, and *Phenomena of Materialisation* by **Baron von Schrenck-Notzing,** 1923.) These have, however, been questioned in this century as more of the clever devices and techniques for producing materializations have been uncovered.

The experiments of talented exponents of **out-of-the-body travel** (**astral projection**) suggest that phantom clothing may be a mental creation or in some cases simply the human **aura.** The question is discussed by **Sylvan J. Muldoon** and Hereward Carrington in the book *The Projection of the Astral Body* (1929). According to Muldoon,

"I have noticed that, as a rule, if my physical body were clad in a certain garb, my astral counterpart would be clothed in an identical garb. I say *as a rule.* But again, there have been many exceptions to that rule—which demonstrates the eccentricities of the controlling intelligence! Sometimes the physical body will be clothed, and the astral body will be clothed in a different manner, e.g. a sort of flimsy gauzy white. This is not at all unusual, and is perhaps the reason why 'ghosts' have invariably become identified with white garments. Sometimes this astral garment is mistaken by observers for an 'aura,' and sometimes the aura is mistaken for the garment of white. There is a distinction. . . . One can be nude in the astral body and the aura would then act as clothing. In fact, it is my belief that the clothing is formed from the aura."

Sources:

Muldoon, Sylvan J., and Hereward Carrington. *The Projection of the Astral Body.* London: Rider, 1929.

Driesch, Hans (1867–1941)

Embryologist, professor of philosophy at the University of Leipzig, pioneer in many domains of science, and one of the most influential psychical investigators in Germany. Driesch was born in Bad Kreuznach, Germany, October 28, 1867, and had a distinguished academic and scientific career.

In his *Philosophie des Organischen* (1905) he expresses the opinion that behind psychic phenomena there may be a truth; and in his *Wirklichkeitslehre* (1917) he states, referring to the work of the **Society for Psychical Research,** that anyone who declares these things impossible has given up the right to be listened to by serious people.

He mainly meant mental phenomena, but he included physical phenomena as well after his sittings with **Willi Schneider** in 1922. In his report he saw no reason to deny the objectivity and the genuineness of the phenomena and in a lecture before the London University in 1924 he declared that "the actuality of psychical phenomena is doubted today only by the incorrigible dogmatist."

In the second edition of his *Ordnungslehre* (1926) a special part is devoted to **parapsychology** and parapsychophysics. In *Grundprobleme der Psychologie,* published in the same year, the problems also receive elaborate discussion. In answer to a questionnaire sent out by Oreste Parfumi, published in *Luce e Ombra* (1926), he states: 1. The mediumistic phenomena are not effects of simple hallucination; 2. It appears to me that they depend exclusively upon the organism of the medium; 3. The spirit theory does not seem to me proven; but spiritism, were it proven, would be a scientific theory. In acknowledgment of Driesch's contribution to psychical research the Society for Psychical Research elected him to the presidential chair for 1926–27, the first German so honored.

Driesch lectured widely on philosophy at universities throughout the world and associated with such pioneers of psychical research as **Gustave Geley, Eugene Osty, Baron von Schrenck-Notzing, Sir Oliver Lodge,** and **Walter Franklin Prince.** He also sat with such famous mediums as Willi and **Rudi Schneider,** "Margery" (**Mina Crandon**), and **Gladys Osborne Leonard.**

Driesch retired from his position as lecturer at the University of Leipzig in 1933 under pressure from the Nazis following his support of Jewish scientists. Thereafter he devoted time to his writings, which include a translation into German of **J. B. Rhine**'s book *New Frontiers of the Mind* (1938). He died April 16, 1941, at Leipzig.

Sources:

Berger, Arthur S., and Joyce Berger. *The Encyclopedia of Parapsychology and Psychical Research.* New York: Paragon House, 1991.

Driesch, Hans A. E. *Alltagraetsel des Seelenlebens Psychical Research* (Everyday Enigmas of the Mind). N.p., 1938.

———. *The Crisis in Psychology.* N.p., 1925.

———. *Leib und Seele.* (Body and Mind). N.p., 1916.

———. *Parapsychologie, die Wissenschaft von den "occulten" Erscheingen* (Parapsychology, Science of "Occult" Phenomena). N.p., 1932.

Pleasants, Helene, ed. *Biographical Dictionary of Parapsychology.* New York: Helix Press, 1964.

Sudre, R. "The Ideas of Hans Driesch." *Journal* of the American Society for Psychical Research 20 (1926).

Drop-in Communicator

Term coined by parapsychologist **Ian Stevenson** to indicate an uninvited entity or communicator at a séance, usually unknown to medium or sitters.

Sources:

Berger, Arthur S., and Joyce Berger. *The Encyclopedia of Parapsychology and Psychical Research.* New York: Paragon House, 1991.

Stevenson, Ian. "A Communicator Unknown to Medium and Sitter." *Journal* of the American Society for Psychical Research 64 (1970).

Drown, Ruth B. (1891–ca. 1943)

American chiropractor who developed the pioneer work of **Albert Abrams** (1863–1924) in **electronics** (later known as **radionics**), involving the correction of disease conditions by shortwave low-power electromagnetics and alternating magnetic currents. Dr. Drown was born in Greeley, Colorado, on October 21, 1891.

Drown called her treatment radio therapy and founded the Radio Therapy Institute as an outlet for her work. It involved placing a blood sample from a patient in a machine "tuned" to the patient and "broadcasting" healing radiations. This controversial system of treatment was developed further by **George De la Warr** in England. He describes her technique in several books, including *The Science & Philosophy of the Drown Radio Therapy* (1938) and *The Theory & Technique of the Drown Radio Therapy & Radio Vision Instruments* (1939).

Her apparatus was granted a British patent but declared "fraudulent" by the Food and Drug Administration in the 1940s. In 1950, at the request of several of Drown's supporters, an investigation was conducted at the University of Chicago. With blind controls, she was unable to make accurate diagnoses, and the American Medical Association reported on the negative results. These texts made Drown and anyone using her techniques open to charges of medical malpractice, and she soon disappeared from the public eye and lived the rest of her life in relative obscurity.

Through most of her life, Drown was also a metaphysical teacher and she developed her own system, which is presented in her book *The Forty-Nine Degrees* (1957). The "Gnostic" system discusses the soul's journey from heaven to earth and its eventual return, and the knowledge needed for that return.

Sources:

Drown, Ruth, ed. *The Forty-Nine Degrees: The Road to Divine Truth.* New York: Greenwich Book Publishers, 1957.

Inglis, Brian. *The Case for Unorthodox Medicine.* New York: Berkley Books, 1965.

Drugs (Psychedelic)

The use of hallucinatory drugs to enhance or alter consciousness has been known for centuries. Cannabis or hemp plant was cited in Chinese literature about 2737 B.C.E. and was used in India before 800 B.C.E. Primitive peoples used hallucinogens sacramentally in religious ceremonies. Much of the Romantic literature of the nineteenth century was written from drug experiences. Drawing primarily upon laudanum, a form of opium, novelists and poets created not only fantasy works, but the classical horror literature as well.

The publication of an English translation of Louis Levin's *Phantastica; Narcotic and Stimulating Drugs, Their Use and Abuse* (1931) drew the attention of physicians and other specialized readers to such vision-producing agents as peyote (from Mexican cactus) named *anhalonium Lewinii* because of Lewin's pioneer scientific researches. However, it was not until Aldous Huxley's *The Doors of Perception* (1954) and *Heaven and Hell* (1956) that the subject of the visionary powers of drugs like mescaline became more widely known in Britain and North America.

LSD (lysergic acid diethylamide), the active principle in peyote, had been discovered accidentally by the Swiss researcher Dr. Albert Hoffman in 1943. Huxley's *The Doors of Perception* mentioned LSD in relation to the work of psychiatrists like Humphrey Osmond, who had experimented with the drug in order to elucidate problems of schizophrenia. Psychiatrists and doctors began to experiment cautiously and observed the strange changes of consciousness and vision experienced through taking LSD. Hoffman also synthesized psilocybin, the active principle in a Mexican mushroom used in religious ceremonies by certain tribes.

It was Huxley's description of his own visionary experiences with mescaline and his sophisticated discussion of the possibilities of chemical ecstasy as a kind of religious experience that stimulated American intellectuals to initiate experiments. The mass media society of the fifties and sixties, with its instant communication geared to a bandwagon of populist trends, helped to spread the concept of instant chemical mysticism, and the growing availability of drugs like LSD and marijuana rapidly created a mass counterculture.

At the spearhead of the psychedelic revolution were two Harvard psychologists, **Timothy Leary** and **Richard Alpert,** who had instituted experiments with psilocybin at the beginning of the 1960s. Their own use of the drug and their conclusion that it should be available broadly with control given over to the public eventually led to their dismissal from their research and teaching positions. Subsequently, believing that psychedelics opened individuals to an awareness of their own inner psychic structures, they eagerly took leadership roles in the emerging psychedelic subculture with a manifesto that ran:

"The game is about to be changed, ladies and gentlemen. Man is about to make use of that fabulous electrical network he carries around in his skull. Present social establishments had better be prepared for the change. Our favorite concepts are standing in the way of a floodtide, two billion years building up. The verbal dam is collapsing. Head for the hills, or prepare your intellectual craft to flow with the current. . . ."

Many individuals elected to flow with the current and began to press for legalization of certain drugs like marijuana. With the backing of millionaire investment banker William Hitchcock, Leary and Alpert campaigned vigorously for the new world of inner space revealed by LSD. Psychedelic religious groups sprang up combining insights from their drugs experiences, **yoga,** the *Tibetan Book of the Dead,* and other mystical literature.

At first the new democracy of psychedelic drug consumption was characterized by the presence of a creative artistic culture nurtured by the glamour of an awakening mystical experience. It soon provided the opening for an underworld of hard drug pushers to invade the psychedelic scene, with its associated crime and violence. Although many discriminating LSD and marijuana users claimed that their lives were changed by a single beatific drug experience that illuminated new dimensions of existence, their testimonies were countered by horror stories of the bad trips and anti-social behavior of LSD users.

Leary became a counterculture hero, evading police and imprisonment and preaching a gospel of "Tune in, turn on, drop out." Alpert eventually went off drugs and made a trip to India, returning shortly as Baba Ram Dass, a Hindu guru with a message of conventional Hindu mysticism. He found a large following among what would soon be known as the **New Age** movement. While leaving drugs behind, he continued to believe, on the authority of his guru, that LSD had served a valuable function in introducing the spirituality to a society dominated by materialistic pursuits.

The psychedelic era came to an end. For many it had been a time of awakening that led them to a range of mature spiritual visions from orthodox Christianity to occultism and Eastern mysticism. The possibilities of the use of mind-altering drugs such as LSD were, however, distorted beyond recognition by the intrusion of legal structures that made continued controlled use and experimentation impossible, an underground culture which became solely dependent on the drugs as a source for spirituality rather than using them as a help in the spiritual quest, and the popular confusion of psychedelic drugs with hard drugs in both the psychedelic community and among the public at large.

In the aftermath of the psychedelic revolution it now seems clear that the primary benefit from the consumption of psychedelic substances came from garnering the wisdom of native cultures that to some extent limit and control their use and advise consumption only within a meaningful system of mystical development. There are significant qualitative differences between the bare chemical experiences of an ecstatic nature and the traditional mystical experience to which they were frequently compared. Sudden changes of consciousness can be life-changing, but also addictive; one experience creates a demand for its repetition. However, when mysticism is sought for its own sake at any cost, particularly with chemical shortcuts, this perpetuates the self-serving egoism of the affluent society, in which one buys metaphysics with the same attitude with which one buys a new automobile.

Within the patient gradual character transformations that come with the mystical life (in all of the traditional world religions) a maturity of physical, mental, and emotional life is attained. It may be the case, as many native peoples suggest, that some drugs assist that process. However, a chemical experience that emphasizes spirituality-upon-demand quickly ceases to expand consciousness and merely reproduces the initial heightened feelings as the by-product of its intense sensory and emotional stimuli.

A remnant of the psychedelic culture remains in such groups as the Neo-American Church and the Peyote Church of God, and in the continued popularity of the writings of **Carlos Castaneda** (even though his original writings have been demonstrated to have been fraudulently produced.)

Sources:

Baudelaire, Charles. *Artificial Paradise: On Hashish & Wine as Means of Expanding Individuality.* New York: McGraw-Hill, 1971.

Leary, Timothy. *Flashbacks: An Autobiography.* Los Angeles: J. P. Tarcher, 1983.

———. *Politics of Ecstasy.* New York: G. P. Putnam's Sons, 1968.

Masters, Robert E., and Jean Houston. *Varieties of Psychedelic Experience.* New York: Holt, Rinehart & Winston, 1966. Reprint, New York: Dell, 1967.

Osmond, Humphry, and B. Aaronson. *Psychedelics: The Uses & Implications of Hallucinogenic Drugs.* Garden City, N.Y.: Doubleday, 1970.

Slack, Charles W. *Timothy Leary, the Madness of the Sixties and Me.* New York: Peter H. Wyden, 1974.

Zaehner, R. C. *Mysticism; Sacred & Profane.* London: Clarendon Press, 1957. Reprint, London: Galaxy Book; Oxford University Press, 1961.

Drummer of Tedworth

A **poltergeist** manifestation that disturbed Magistrate John Mompesson's household at Tedworth, Wiltshire, England, from 1661 to 1663. It was believed to be caused by a vagrant drummer who was aggrieved at his drum being confiscated.

The drummer was William Drury, a vagrant who "went up and down the country to show hocus-pocus [juggling], feats of activity, dancing through hoops and such like devices." In March 1661 Drury was accused of using counterfeit documents and taken before a justice of the peace. Drury was freed, but his drum was confiscated, and during Mompesson's temporary absence of the drum was taken to the magistrate's house. When Mompesson returned, he was told that night after night thumping and drumming noises were heard in the house. An invisible drum beat the rhythms of "Roundsheads," "Cuckolds," and "Tat-too," and knocks were heard.

This was the beginning of a period of extraordinary phenomena, reminiscent of the claimed disturbances of the modern **Amityville Horror.** The drumming was heard inside and outside the house, children were lifted up in the air, a Bible was hidden in ashes, shoes flung at a man's head, and chamberpots emptied onto beds. Mysterious lights were seen, a servant was terrified by "a great body with two glaring eyes," and there were sulphurous smells and drops of blood. A horse was found with one of its rear legs forced into its mouth.

In 1663 Drury was arrested in Gloucester and charged with pig stealing. He was found guilty and sentenced to deportation instead of the customary penalty of hanging. For a time, the poltergeist phenomena ceased. However, Drury jumped overboard from the convict ship and escaped to Uffcot, a few miles from Tedworth. The poltergeist phenomena started again. Surprisingly enough, Drury also continued his earlier nuisance, acquiring a new drum and beating it recklessly. On the orders of Mompesson he was seized and jailed. This time Drury was accused of witchcraft, but was acquitted due to a lack of evidence. On the earlier charge of pig stealing he was found guilty and sentenced to deportation to Virginia. Once again, the phenomena ceased, this time for good.

The case was investigated by **Joseph Glanvill** and reported in his book *Saducismus Triumphatus* (1668). According to Glanvill:

"The noise of thumping and drumming was very frequent, usually five nights together, and then it would intermit three. It was on the outside of the house, which is most of it board. It constantly came as they were going to sleep, whether early or late. After a month's disturbance without, it came into the room where the drum lay, four or five nights in seven, within half an hour after they were in bed, continuing almost two. The sign of it, just before it came was . . . an hurling in the air above the house, and at its going off, the beating of a drum like that at the breaking up of a guard. . . .

"On the fifth of November, 1662, it kept a mighty noise, and a servant observing two boards in the children's room seeming to move, he bid it give him one of them. Upon which the board came (nothing moving it that he saw) within a yard of him. The man added, 'Nay, let me have it in my hand.' Upon which, it was shoved quite home to him. He thrust it back, and it was driven to him again, and so up and down, to and fro, at least twenty times together, till Mr. Mompesson forbade his servant such familiarities. This was in the daytime, and seen by a whole room full of people. . . .

"Mr. Mompesson perceiving that it so much persecuted the little children, he lodged them at a neighbor's house, taking his eldest daughter, who was about ten years of age, into his own chamber, where it had not been a month before. As soon as she was in bed, the disturbance began there again, continuing three weeks drumming, and making other noises, and it was observed that it would exactly answer in drumming anything that was beaten or called for. After this, the house where the children were lodged out, happening to be full of strangers, they were taken home, and no disturbance having been known in the parlor, they were lodged there, where also their persecutor found them, but then only plucked them by the hair and night clothes without any other disturbance. . . .

"After this, it was very troublesome to a servant of Mr. Mompesson's, who was a stout fellow and of sober conversation. This man lay within, during the greatest disturbance, and for several nights something would endeavor to pluck his clothes off the bed, so that he was fain to tug hard to keep them on, and sometimes they would be plucked from him by main force, and his shoes thrown at his head. And now and then he should find himself forcibly held, as it were bound hand and foot, but he found that whenever he could make use of his sword, and struck with it, the spirit quitted its hold. . . .

"The drummer was tried at the Assizes at Salisbury upon this occasion. He was committed first to Gloucester Jail for stealing, and a Wiltshire man coming to see him, he asked what news in Wiltshire. The visitant said he knew of none. 'No,' saith the drummer, 'Do not you hear of the drumming at a gentleman's house at Tedworth?' 'That I do enough,' said the other. 'I,' quoth the drummer, 'I have plagued him (or to that purpose) and he shall never be at quiet, till he hath made me satisfaction for taking away my drum.'"

Glanvill reports: "During the time of the knocking, when many were present, a gentleman of the company said, 'Satan, if the drummer set thee to work, give three knocks and no more;' which it did very distinctly, and stopped."

Glanvill himself heard some of the unusual sounds, stating:

"At this time it used to haunt the children, and that as soon as they were laid in bed. . . . I heard a strange scratching as I went up the stairs, and when we came into the room I perceived it was just behind the bolster of the children's bed, and seemed to be against the ticking. It was as loud a scratching as one with long nails could make upon a bolster. There were two little modest girls in the bed, between seven and eight years old, as I guessed. I saw their hands out of the clothes, and they could not contribute to the noise that was behind their heads; they had been used to it, and had still somebody or other in the chamber with them, and therefore seemed not to be much affrighted. I, standing at the bed's head, thrust my hand behind the bolster, directing it to the place whence the noise seemed to come, whereupon the noise ceased there, and was heard in another part of the bed; but when I had taken out my hand it returned, and was heard in the same place as before. I had been told it would imitate noises, and made trial by scratching several times upon the sheet, as five and seven and ten, which it followed, still stopping at my number." Glanvill searched the room and was unable to find any evidence of trickery.

Mr. Mompesson suffered as word of these manifestations spread. Those who did not believe in spirits and witches declared him an impostor; other people considered the visitations to be the judgment of God upon him for some wickedness or impiety. As a result, he was continually exposed to censure and harassed by the curious people who gathered around the house.

The essayist Joseph Addison (1672–1719) wrote a comedy on the affair, "The Drummer, or the Haunted House," first performed at Drury Lane Theater on April 14, 1713. (See also **Cock Lane Ghost**)

Sources:

Wilson, Colin. *Poltergeist: A Study in Destructive Haunting.* New York: Perigree Books, 1981.

Du Potet de Sennevoy, Baron (Jules Denis) (1796–1881)

A leading exponent of **animal magnetism** in nineteenth-century France, familiar with the whole range of paranormal phenomena that later figured prominently in **Spiritualism.**

Du Potet began his experiments in 1821 and recorded his experiences in *Le Propagateur du Magnétisme animal,* a journal founded in 1827, and in the *Journal de Magnétisme,* which was founded in 1845 and continued until 1861 and was subsequently revived by **Hector Durville.**

He claimed to have discovered in animal magnetism "the magic of antiquity." **Apports, fire** resistance, **levitation** of the human body, and **spirit** communications were frequently observed and studied by him. On a visit to England he introduced Dr. **John Elliotson,** the first exponent of animal magnetism in Great Britain, to the phenomena. Over the years he wrote a number of books that kept the issue of animal magnetism alive in France.

Sources:

Du Potet de Sennevoy, Baron. *Cours de magnétisme animal.* N.p., 1834. 1840.

———. *Discours sur le magnétisme animal.* N.p., 1833.

———. *Essai sur l'enseignement philosophique du magnétisme.* N.p., 1845.

———. *Exposé des expériences sur le magnétisme animal.* N.p., 1821.

———. *La Magie dévoilée ou principes des sciences occultes.* 1852. Translated as *Magnetism and Magic.* Edited by A. H. E. Lee. London, 1927.

———. *Le magnétisme animal opposé à la médecine, mémoire pour servir a l'histoire du magnétisme en France et en Angleterre.* N.p., 1840.

———. *Manuel de l'étudiant magnétiseur ou nouvelle instruction pratique du magnétisme fondée sur 30 années d'observations.* N.p., 1846.

Du Prel, Baron Carl (1839–1899)

German philosopher, author of *Die Philosophie der Mystik* (1885), translated as *The Philosophy of Mysticism* (2 vols., 1889), dealing with latent human powers, the phenomena of **dreams, trance,** and hypnotic sleep. Du Prel conducted many experiments on the phenomena of **hypnotism** (then known as **animal magnetism**) before investigating the newer fields of **Spiritualism** and psychical research.

He investigated such famous mediums as John Eglinton and **Eusapia Palladino** and concluded that the phenomena of Spiritualism furnished empirical evidence of the existence of transcendental beings. He also accepted that belief in human **survival** was justified by his research.

However, he laid himself open to criticism by his argument that comparisons between mediums and conjurers were fallacious. His treatise *Ein Problem für Taschenspieler* emphasized that skilled conjurers had declared mediums they had investigated to be free from imposture. He neglected to note that conjurers had also exposed fake mediums. Du Prel's defense of psychography (**slate writing**) did not incluce the techniques used by fraudulent mediums. According to Du Prel:

"One thing is clear, that is, that Psychography must be ascribed to a transcendental origin. We shall find (1) that the hypothesis of prepared slates is inadmissible. (2) The place on which the writing is found is quite inaccessible to the hands of the medium. In some cases the double slate is securely locked, leaving only room inside for the tiny morsel of slate pencil. (3) That the writing is actually done at the time. (4) That the medium is not writing. (5) The writing must be actually done with the morsel of slate, or lead pencil. (6) The writing is done by an intelligent being, since the answers are exactly pertinent to the questions. (7) This being can read, write, and understand the language of human beings, frequently such as is unknown to the medium. (8) It strongly resembles a human being, as well in the degree of its intelligence as in the mistakes sometimes made. These beings are, therefore, although invisible, of human nature or species. It is no use whatever to fight against this proposition. (9) If these beings speak, they do so in human language. If they are asked who they are, they answer that they are beings who have left this world. (10) Where these appearances become partly visible, perhaps only their hands, the hands seen are of human form. (11) When these things become entirely visible, they show the human form and countenance.... Spiritualism must be investigated by science. I should look upon myself as a coward if I did not openly express my convictions."

Du Prel also claimed to know three private mediums "in whose presence direct writing not only takes place inside double slates, but is done in inaccessible places."

We know that conjurers can fake spirit messages on slates under conditions that seem to preclude trickery, and the whole phenomenon of slate writing remains questionable. In spite of his credulity on the issue of slate writing, Du Prel declared his belief in the reality of Spiritualist phenomena. He was also ahead of his time in recommending psychical research by state-appointed and paid commissions.

Other publications by him include *Studien aus dem Gebiete der Geheimwissenchaften* (2 vols., 1890, 1891) and *Die vorgeburtliche Erziehung als Mittel zur Menschenzüchtung* (1899). He contributed to such journals as *Die Übersinnliche Welt.*

Dual Personality

What is popularly termed dual, split, or multiple **personality** is one form of what psychologists call disassociation. Two or more mental process in the individual can be said to be disassociated if they either coexist or alternate without apparently influencing one another or becoming connected. In the nineteenth century, disassociation described a host of phenomena from dreams to neurotic symptoms. Neurosis was explained as a constitutional weakness in the person that prevented their integrating their personality. Thus daydreaming was condemmed as a symptom of nonintegration. A more extreme example would be what had previously been called spirit **possession.**

When Freud proposed the existence of an underlying unconscious, the idea of an underlying constitutional weakness was abandoned in favor of a discussion of various mechanisms by which the ego, the central waking personality, suppressed or isolated unwanted elements and kept them out of the ongoing ego formation.

However, Freudian categories do not handle well the most extreme of disassociation phenomena characterized by the subject maintaining for an extended length of time some action not apparently initiated by the conscious self and the memory of which is not available to the conscious self. Such phenomena includes forms of amnesia, sleepwalking, and post-hypnotic suggestions. It would also include the **trance** phenomena of a Spiritualist medium or someone engaged in **channeling,** and the now well-known phenomena of multiple personality, in which the person appears to change from one person to another. This last phenomena challenges some basic assumptions about self identity, that each individual is just that, a single person with a single memory, a more or less unified being.

Sometimes, in trance state, there occurs a split so pronounced that the subject seems to have two or more distinct personalities. The secondary personality may differ from the primary in many ways, and possess entirely distinct intellectual and moral characteristics. The entranced subject may allude to his normal consciousness in the third person, may criticize its opinions and attitude, or even express direct antagonism towards it.

This secondary personality sometimes alternates with the primary in such a way as to suggest that two spirits are struggling to possess the same physical organization. (For an example, see **William Sharp.**) Another peculiarity of this state is that whereas the normal consciousness generally knows nothing of the others, the secondary personalities usually have full knowledge of each other and of the normal consciousness.

The more extreme disassociation is by no means confined to the trance state, but may arise spontaneously. Robert Louis Stevenson made effective use of the philosophical implications of dual personality in his science fiction horror story *The Strange Case of Dr. Jekyll and Mr. Hyde* (1886). In a less horrendous setting, it became familiar to many through the book and movie *The Three Faces of Eve.* Sometimes the appearance of a dual personality leads to other multiple personalities. In the famous case of Sally Beauchamp, investigated by **Morton Prince,** four well-defined personalities developed, as described in Prince's book *Dissociation of a Personality* (1905).

In many cases the emergence of secondary personalities is due to a patient's response to his or her counselor, an attempt to fulfill a real or imagined request.

While much work and discussion has been done on the dysfunctional multiple personality as a disassociation disorder, little effort has been put into understanding mediumship and **channeling** in the same way. Mediumship differs significantly from multiple personality both in the control of the medium over the appearance of the secondary personality and its nonpathological nature.

Sources:

Prince, Morton. *The Disassociation of a Personality.* 1905. Reprint, Oxford: Oxford University Press, 1978.

Ducasse, C(urt) J(ohn) (1881–1969)

Philosopher and parapsychologist. Ducasse was born July 7, 1881, in Angoulême, France. He was educated in France and England, but migrated to the United States in 1900 and was naturalized in 1910. He began teaching at the University of Washington, Seattle, in 1912 and remained there until 1926 when he moved to Brown University, Providence, Rhode Island. He rose from associate professor to chairman of the Department of Philosophy (1930–1951). He was named professor emeritus at the time of his retirement in 1951.

Ducasse served as president of the Association for Symbolic Logic (1936–38), the American Philosophical Association (1939), the American Society for Aesthetics (1945–46), and the Philosophy of Science Association (1958–61).

As a scholar, Ducasse argued for the legitimacy of psychical research, stating that such research had established a body of facts with implications for philosophy. He read about psychic phenomena, conducted fieldwork with mediums, and regularly attended parapsychological gatherings. He joined the board of the **American Society for Psychical Research** in 1951 and served a term as vice president beginning in 1966.

Ducasse was most concerned about **survival** of death. He argued that survival was not only philosophically possible but that the evidence of psychical research was impressive as proof of such survival. He also was impressed by the evidence for **reincarnation.**

Ducasse established his place in American philosophy quite apart from his concerns for psychical matters. He wrote a number of books over the years. Only during the 1950s did his concern with **parapsychology** become evident, in such books as *Nature, Mind and Death* (1951) and *A Philosophical Scrutiny of Religion* (1953). He is remembered for his text *A Critical Examination of the Belief in a Life After Death* (1961). Shortly before his death he wrote *Paranormal Phenomena, Science, and Life After Death* (1969). He died September 3, 1969.

Sources:

Berger, Arthur S., and Joyce Berger. *The Encyclopedia of Parapsychology and Psychical Research.* New York: Paragon House, 1991.

Dommeyer, Frederick C., ed. *Current Philosophical Issues: Essays in Honor of Curt John Ducasse.* N.p., 1966.

Ducasse, C. J. *A Critical Examination of the Belief in a Life After Death.* Springfield, Ill.: Charles C. Thomas, 1961.

———. *Nature, Mind and Death.* LaSalle, Ill.: Open Court Publishing, 1951.

Pleasants, Helene, ed. *Biographical Dictionary of Parapsychology.* New York: Helix Press, 1964.

Duguid, David (1832–1907)

Scottish medium, chiefly famous for his automatic and direct drawings. Duguid was born in Glasgow and became a cabinet-maker by trade.

His two brothers, Robert, of Glasgow, and Alexander, of Kirkcaldy, also claimed psychic powers, but David eclipsed them both with phenomena comprising the whole scale of séance-room manifestations. Above and beyond the more common **raps,** he supposedly moved objects without contact; heavy music boxes sailed about in the room in the dark and invisible hands wound them up when they ran down. Sitters reported hearing **direct voices,** usually in husky whispers but sometimes in thunderous tones. Reportedly on one occasion, the medium was levitated, placed on the table in his chair, to which he was bound, and a coat was put on him without disturbing the knots. Often objects were brought out from closed rooms, psychic lights were seen, phantom hands touched the sitters, redolent perfumes were produced, and, according to the testimony of Thomas S. Garriock, as quoted in E. T. Bennett's *Direct Phenomena of Spiritualism* (1908), "On one occasion Mr. Duguid put his hand into the blazing stove, took out a large piece of coal and walked round the room with it for five minutes."

The beginnings of all these marvels dated from 1865, when, out of curiosity, he took part in table-sitting experiments at the house of H. Nisbet, a publisher of Glasgow. At one of these sittings he felt his arm shake and a cold current ran down his spine. When Nisbet's daughter, who was an automatic writer, placed her right hand on his left it at once began to move and drew rough sketches of vases and flowers, and then the section of an archway. Duguid began to sit in his home for **automatic painting.** The influence that manifested claimed to feel Duguid hampered by absolute lack of artistic education. On his suggestion Duguid took lessons at a government school of arts for four months.

Later the influence suggested that after his usual work on large pictures Duguid should draw or paint on little cards in the presence of onlookers. In eight to ten minutes he turned out complete pictures. Working in total darkness, sitters reported that the "spirits" would arrive in less than a minute and, independently of the medium's hands, produce a new picture in as short a time as 35 seconds. They were tiny and sometimes so fine in execution that their merit was enhanced if viewed under a magnifying glass. Now and then, many of these little oil paintings were found on a single card. The noise of the brushes and paper, prepared in light, would be heard by those present as coming from well above the table. When the paintings were completed, everything was dropped. Invariably the paper would be found with painted side up, wet and sticky. As a rule these little paintings were then freely distributed among the sitters.

To ensure control, Duguid allowed himself to be held or tied. When the light was put on, the bindings were often found exchanged. If the medium was too tightly bound he was liberated in a few seconds in the darkness and the ligatures were quietly dropped into the lap of one of the sitters. On several occasions the little cards were found missing. As soon as the darkness was restored they were heard to drop onto the table from above.

To prevent substitution, the cards were usually signed at the back with the initials of the sitters. Later, a better method of identification was employed. A corner of the card was torn off and handed to a sitter before the painting began. For several years, Duguid took no fee for his séances.

In August 1878 **Frank Podmore** attended a sitting at which this method of control was already employed and discerned the method of its subversion. Describing how he placed the fragments of the cards securely in his pocket and how the medium was fastened with silk handkerchiefs, with adhesive paper on the ends, he writes in *Modern Spiritualism* (2 vols., 1902):

"After a quarter of an hour the lights were turned up and two small oil paintings, one circular, about the size of a penny, the other oval and slightly larger, were found on the two cards. The colours were still moist and the fragments in my pocket fitted the torn corners of the cards. The two pictures, which lie before me as I write, represent respectively a small upland stream dashing over rocks, and a mountain lake with its shores bathed in a sunset glow. The paintings, though obviously executed with some haste, were hardly such as one can imagine to have been done in such a short interval and in almost complete darkness. For many years I was quite at a loss to understand how the feat could have been accomplished by normal means. The explanation, which I have now no doubt to be correct, is an extremely simple one. Duguid, it has been seen, would not suffer profane hands to touch the cards; and, when he had torn off the corner of a card, he no doubt dropped into the sitter's hand not the piece torn from the blank card on the table, but a piece previously torn from a card on which a picture had already been painted."

Podmore's explanation also suggests other methods that could have been employed in the dark and often were employed by mediums such as Duguid.

The first extended publicity to David Duguid's mediumship was given by the *North British Daily Mail* in 1873 in a series of articles entitled *A Few Nights with the Glasgow Spiritualists.* It was later followed by the report of a subcommittee of the Psychological Society of Edinburgh. They claimed to witness 11 distinctly different forms of manifestation that they could not explain as normal. **Direct writing** that began to alternate with direct painting and drawing was among the phenomena observed. Hebrew, Greek, Latin, and German scripts were produced, sometimes on a folded sheet of paper enclosed in a sealed envelope.

(It was by this method that the frontispieces of three volumes of William Oxley's *Angelic Revelations* were allegedly illustrated.) Thomas Power was quoted by Bennett as saying:

"The plain paper was put into an envelope. The three gentlemen placed their fingers on the sealed envelope and turned off the gas. In three minutes the gas was turned on, the envelope cut open and the drawing was found in its complete state."

The **control** who worked through Duguid did not disclose his identity for a long time. He called himself "Marcus Baker." Eventually he promised a copy of one of his masterpieces. The medium worked for four days, four hours at a time, on a large painting. It was initialed "J.R.," and from Cassell's *Art Treasures Exhibition* it was recognized as "The Waterfall," by Jakob Ruysdael. The copy was not exact, however; some figures were omitted. The control, when questioned, said those figures were added later by Bergheim. When they consulted Ruysdael's biography this was found to be true.

The second of Duguid's painting controls also claimed a famous name, that of Jan van Steen. Apparently neither of them had taken the trouble to always produce original compositions. Great inconvenience arose from this for the medium after the arrival on the scene, in August 1869, of "Hafed," the third of Duguid's famous guides.

From the book that he dictated in 46 sittings between 1870 and 1871 it appears that Hafed lived nearly 2,000 years ago as a warrior-prince of Persia. At an early age he fought against an invading Arabian army, was later admitted to the order of the Magi, and was ultimately chosen arch magus. He described the creeds and social life of ancient Persia, Tyre, Greece, Egypt, Judea, Babylon, and many other long perished civilizations that he studied in travels.

The climax of his story was reached when he revealed that he conducted the expedition of the Three Wise Men to Judea to the cradle of Jesus. He was summoned by his guardian spirit to go on the journey with two brother magi and take rich gifts to the babe. He described the youthful years of Jesus that are not chronicled in the Gospels. According to his story, he traveled with Jesus in Persia, India, and many other countries and marveled at the miracles the young child performed. After the martyrdom of Jesus he became a Christian himself, met Paul in Athens, preached the gospel in Venice and Alexandria, and finally perished at age 100 in the arena at Rome.

The book, as taken down in notes by Hay Nisbet, was published in 1876 under the title *Hafed, Prince of Persia: His Experiences in Earth Life, being Spirit Communications Received Through Mr. David Duguid, the Glasgow Trance Speaking Medium, with an Appendix, containing Communications from the Spirit Artists Ruisdael and Steen, illustrated by Facsimiles of Forty-Five Drawings and Writings, the Direct Work of the Spirits.* Reportedly the book was produced in trance. Trouble arose, however, over the illustrations, and the first edition of the book had to be withdrawn as some of the sketches were discovered to be copies from Cassell's *Family Bible.* In the second edition, published in the same year, eight full-page plates had been withdrawn, although Cassell's protest only applied to three full-page and one half-page plates.

Suspicion of the rest of the expunged drawings appears to be justified. E. T. Bennett submitted an Arabic doorway inscription that supposedly came in direct writing but is also visible in an illustration in the *Family Bible* according to the expert examination of Stanley Lane-Pool. He found the text to read, "There is no conqueror but God," the characteristic motto of the Moorish kings of Granada, which occurs on all their coins and all over the Alhambra. "But the writer of the direct card," he says, "evidently had not the Alhambra nor the Syrian Gateway in his mind, but Cassell's *Family Bible.* The engraver of the cut in the Bible, which you sent me, made a muddle of the lower line of inscription under the lintel, not knowing Arabic, and the direct card exactly reproduces the engraver's blunders."

There was a sequel to *Hafed,* titled *Hermes, a Disciple of Jesus: His Life and Missionary Work; also the Evangelistic Travels of Anah and Zitha, two Persian Evangelists, sent out by Hafed; together with Incidents in the Life of Jesus given by a Disciple through Hafed* (1887). Thomas Garrioch, a member of Duguid's circle, acted as recorder. According to Hay Nisbet's preface, this book was only one-third finished by 1887. The remainder was composed of the life and missionary work of a Brahmin priest who was raised from the dead by Jesus, the autobiographies of an ancient Mexican priest and a red Indian chief, and various other spirit autobiographies, tales, addresses, and answers to questions.

Hermes—after the lesson learned from the publication of *Hafed*—was not illustrated. Supposedly, the misadventure of the *Hafed* illustrations was brought to the attention of the controls. They defended themselves by saying that the memory of these pictures was retained in Duguid's subconscious mind. If so, these impressions were apparently subject to elaboration in the reproduction as, for instance, a ruined church nave of the *Family Bible* appears in a restored condition in Duguid's book. A similar incident occurred in Duguid's demonstrations of **spirit photography.** His Cyprian priestess, a recurring spirit photograph, was found to be the exact copy of a German picture, *Night.*

Sir William Crookes conducted some experiments with this phase of Duguid's mediumship. According to Podmore, he failed to obtain conclusive results. But Podmore kept silent over the experiments of J. Traill Taylor, the editor of the *British Journal of Photography,* who first experimented with Duguid in 1892 in Glasgow, and then, on Myers' request, in London.

He writes in his report:

"The psychic figures behaved badly. Some were in focus, others not so; some were lighted from the right, while the sitter was so from the left; some were comely others not so; some monopolised the major portion of the plate quite obliterating the material sitters; others were as if an atrociously badly vignetted portrait, or one cut oval out of a photograph by a can-opener, or equally badly clipped out, were held up behind the sitter. But here is the point—not one of these figures which came out so strongly in the negative was visible in any form or shape to me during the time of exposure in the camera, and I vouch in the strongest manner for the fact that no one whatever had an opportunity of tampering with any plate anterior to its being placed in the dark slide or immediately preceding development. Pictorially they are vile, but how came they there?"

On April 1, 1905, at age 73, after nearly two thousand séances, Duguid was finally caught in **fraud** in Manchester. He had brought "spirit paintings" ready-made to the séance room and attempted to exchange them for the blank cards the sitters provided. On being forcibly searched, the original cards were discovered in his trousers. The Spiritualists were stunned by the exposure and offered the common explanation that Duguid's powers had lapsed and he was prompted by vanity to substitute spurious phenomena for the genuine. Two years after his exposure, Duguid died.

Sources:

Duguid, David. *Hafed, Prince of Persia; his Experiences in Earth Life, being Spirit Communications Received Through Mr. David Duguid, the Glasgow Trance Speaking Medium, with an Appendix, containing Communications from the Spirit Artists Ruisdael and Steen, illustrated by Facsimiles of Forty-Five Drawings and Writings, the Direct Work of the Spirits.* London: James Burn, Glasgow: Nisbet, 1876.

Duk-Duk, The

Members of a secret society of New Pomerania (originally New Britain), an island of the Bismarck Archipelago, northeast of New Guinea. These hideously masked or chalk-painted members executed justice or exacted fines. They set houses on fire or killed people as punishment.

Dukes, Sir Paul (1889–1967)

British author, secret agent, and pioneer of **yoga** in Western countries. He was educated at Caterham School, England, and Petrograd Conservative, Russia. Dukes was always seeking and affirming a higher purpose in life than everyday existence. His first marriage, in 1922, was to Margaret Rutherford; his second, in 1959, to Diana Fitzgerald.

As a young man he took a position as a language teacher in Riga, Latvia. He later moved to St. Petersburg, where he was a secret agent in prerevolutionary Russia. In 1913 he spent a season in the Russian province of Tula, acting as a tutor, and briefly claimed an ability for psychic healing.

After World War I, in 1921 he became a special correspondent of *The Times* newspaper in Eastern Europe. Under the name "Paul Dukaine" he appeared on stage in a ballet act. He also studied yoga. Dukes lectured, wrote a number of books on a variety of topics, and traveled widely. He was director of a company manufacturing components for the British Ministry of Aircraft Production. During his travels he met mystics and wonder workers, and also spent a night alone in the Great Pyramid of Gizeh in Egypt. He died August 27, 1967.

Sources:

Dukes, Paul. *Come Hammer, Come Sickle.* N.p., 1947.
———. *Red Dusk and the Morrow.* N.p., 1922.
———. *The Unending Quest.* London, 1950.
———. *Yoga for the Western World.* N.p., 1953.
———. *The Yoga of Health, Youth and Joy.* N.p., 1960.

Dumas, Andre A(lfred) (1908–)

French engineer and author of *La Science de l'âme* (1947) and many articles on parapsychological subjects. He was born November 1, 1908, in Levullois-Perret (Seine) and was educated at the Fine Arts School and the Professional and Technical School, Geneva.

Duncan, Helen Victoria (1898–1956)

Controversial British **materialization** medium exposed on several occasions as a fraud. Born in Perthshire, Scotland, she had a working-class background. She later married and became the mother of six children. Duncan became well known as a materialization medium, manifesting spirit forms.

Controversy ensued in the journal *Light* in 1931 following her sittings for the London Psychic Laboratory, the research department of the **London Spiritualist Alliance. Ectoplasm** (a psychic substance supposedly exuded from mediums) was reportedly seen in quantities, and specimens were obtained for analysis. In addition, figures of adults and children appeared under voluminous drapery, and movements of objects beyond the reach of the medium were observed. As a means of control the medium was placed nude into a sleeved sack with stiff buckram fingerless gauntlets sewn to the sleeves of her suit. The sack was sewn together at the back and fastened with tape and cords to the chair. At the end of the sitting the medium was often found outside the bag, the seals, tape, and stitching remaining intact.

The first report of the London Psychic Laboratory was published in *Light,* May 16, 1931. It advanced no definite conclusion but disclosed a favorable impression. Meanwhile, Duncan also gave sittings at the **National Laboratory of Psychical Research.** In the July 14, 1931, *Morning Post,* a long article was published on her exposure there and psychical researcher **Harry Price** branded her in a statement "as one of the cleverest frauds in the history of Spiritualism."

A portion of her **teleplasm** (another term for ectoplasm) was found to be composed of woodpulp and egg white. Photographs taken during the séance disclosed rubber gloves and rough portraits wrapped in cheesecloth. An X-ray examination revealed that Duncan possessed a remarkable faculty of regurgitation and merely swallowed the necessary paraphernalia before the séance.

Two days after this article the second report of the London Psychic Laboratory appeared in *Light.* It also branded Duncan as a clear-cut fraud and quoted a statement by her husband that was interpreted as a confession. In subsequent issues of *Light* many Spiritualists supported the medium. Dr. Montague Rust, who was responsible for introducing Duncan to London, deplored the hasty conclusions and despite the adverse report maintained that Duncan was the most remarkable physical medium in Europe. Many other impressive testimonies were given on her behalf. Will Goldston, the famous magician, confessed to having witnessed astounding results that no system of trickery could achieve (*Psychic News,* May 28, 1932).

However, another exposure followed on January 5, 1932, in Edinburgh. "Peggy," the materialized child **control,** was seized and found to be identical to the medium. "I see no escape from the conclusion," writes J. B. Mc Indoe, president of the **Spiritualists' National Union,** in *Light,* "that Mrs. Duncan was detected in a crude and clumsy fraud—a pitiable travesty of the phenomena she has so frequently displayed. I have no doubt that the fraud was deliberate, conscious and premeditated."

Yet in the Edinburgh Sheriff Court, where the exposers carried the case, he said that he had considerably modified his view because of the evidence of the Crown witnesses. **Ernest W. Oaten** and Montague Rust were the chief witnesses for the defense, the latter describing amazing experiences of the partial dematerialization of Duncan's body. The court found Duncan guilty of fraud and sentenced her to a fine of 10 pounds or a month's imprisonment. After she was convicted for "obtaining money from a sitter by false pretences," her followers declared that she was wrongly condemned. On a later occasion she was tried under the old British legislation of Section 4 of the Witchcraft Act of 1735 (see **fortune-telling**). Between December 1943 and January 1944 she gave public séances in Portsmouth. At one of these sittings she was grabbed by a policeman acting in concert with an investigator who believed the proceedings fraudulent. As a result, Duncan was tried at the Central Criminal Court in London.

A detailed account of the proceedings was published in *The Trial of Mrs. Duncan,* edited by C. E. Bechhofer Roberts, (London, 1945). Duncan was sentenced to nine months imprisonment. After her release she resumed mediumistic activities, and in October 1956 was seized by police at a séance in Nottingham. She became ill and died five weeks later. It is possible that her death (from diabetes and heart failure) may have been accelerated by the shock of the police raid.

The records of the séances at the National Laboratory for Psychical Research, with impressions of the phenomena by several professors, were published by Harry Price in book form under the title *Regurgitation and the Duncan Mediumship* (1931). Although Price concluded that her phenomena were fraudulent, Duncan continued to be endorsed by some Spiritualists, including **Maurice Barbanell,** editor of *Psychic News.*

At the time of her trials, there was considerable official opposition to **Spiritualism** in Britain, and the treatment of mediums accused of fraud verged on persecution. Convictions were often obtained by use of an outdated vagrancy act and the Witchcraft Act of 1735. Duncan's case became a focus for the Spiritualists' campaign for the abolition of prosecution of mediums under outdated and punitive legislation.

Sources:

Cassiver, Manfred. "Helen Victoria Duncan: A Reassessment." *Journal* of the Society for Psychical Research 53, 801 (October 1985).

Crossley, Alan E. *The Story of Helen Duncan.* N.p., 1975.

Roberts, C. E. Bechhofer, ed. *The Trial of Mrs. Duncan.* London, 1945.

Dunne, J(ohn) W(illiam) (1875–1949)

Parasychologist who studied the implications of **dreams** for **survival** of death. Dunne was born in Roscommon, Ireland, but lived and worked in Britain. He was a pioneer aeronautical engineer and in 1904 invented the stable, tailless airfoil, which was named after him. Between 1906 and 1907 he built and flew the first British military airplane.

In the field of parapsychology he achieved a lasting position through his theories on dreams. In his book *An Experiment with Time* (1927) he describes his own experiments with dreaming, from which he concluded that precognitive elements frequently occur in dreams. The book has been frequently reprinted.

Dunne developed a theory called "serialism," which postulates an infinite series of dimensions within time, giving any present moment extensions into the past and future. His later books developing this theory are *The Serial Universe* (1934), *The New Immortality* (1938), and *Nothing Dies* (1940). He died August 24, 1949, in Banbury, England.

Sources:

Dunne, J. W. *An Experiment with Time.* New York: Macmillan, 1927.

Prince, Walter Franklin. *Noted Witnesses for Psychic Occurrences.* Boston: Boston Society for Psychical Occurrences, 1928. Reprint, New Hyde Park, N.Y.: University Books, 1963.

Dupuis, Charles François (1742–1809)

French author and politician who studied ancient civilization and anthropology. He was born at Trie le-Chateau and was tutored by his father until he was able to enter the College d'Harcourt. At age 24 he was made professor of rhetoric at Lisieux, but his inclination led him into the field of mathematics. Several of his anthropological writings had **occult** implications. In *Origine de tous les Cultus* (3 vols., 1795) he attempts to explain not only all the mysteries of antiquity, but also the origin of all religious beliefs. In his *Memoire explicatif du Zodiaque chronologique et mythologique* (1806) he maintains a common origin for the astronomical and religious opinions of the Greeks, Egyptians, Chinese, Persians, and Arabians.

Durandal

A magical sword belonging to Roland, hero of medieval legends relating to Charlemagne and the Twelve Peers of France.

Durville, Gaston

Son of **Hector Durville,** brother of **Henri Durville,** jointly involved in publications concerned with **animal magnetism** and nature therapy. His publications included *Les Succès de la Médecine psychique, Le Sommeil provoqué et les Causes qui le déterminent: Magnétisme, Hypnotisme, Suggestion, Etude étiologique de l'hypnose.* With Hector and Henri Durville, he founded the International Psychical Society and codirected the *Journal du Magnétisme* and the *Revue du Psychisme Expérimental.*

Durville, (Marie-François) Hector (1849–1923)

Author, healer, and experimenter in the field of **animal magnetism** and other occult subjects. Durville also investigated the phenomenon of **astral projection** (**out-of-the-body travel**). He was born April 8, 1849, in Mousseau, France. With his sons Henri and Gaston, he played a significant part in popularizing occult studies in France. The publishing house of Hector & Henri Durville in Paris issued a wide range of books and journals dealing with animal magnetism, **occultism, Spiritism,** divining, and nature therapies, a number of which he wrote. With his son Henri, he directed the Institut du Magnétisme et du Psychisme expérimental, founded in 1878. In 1887 he founded the Societé Magnétique de France, and in 1893, the Ecole Pratique de Magnétisme et de Massage. With his sons Henri and Gaston he continued the *Journal du Magnétisme,* originally founded by **Baron du Potet.**

He also published the *Revue du Psychisme expérimental* and *Psychic Magazine.* He died September 1, 1923, in Montmorency, France.

Sources:

Durville, (Marie-François) Hector. *Almanach spirite et magnétique illustre pour 1893.* N.p., 1893.

———. *Bibliographie du Magnétisme et des Sciences Occultes.* N.p., 1895.

———. *Le Fantôme des Vivants, Anatomie et physiologie de l'àme; Recherches expérimentales sur le dédoublement du corps de l'homme.* N.p., 1909.

———. *Le Magnétisme considéré comme agent lumineux.* N.p., 1896.

———. *Le magnétisme des animaux; Zootherapie (Polarité des animaux morts et vivants; Zoothérapie, Biothérapie, etc.).* N.p., 1896.

———. *Le Magnétisme humain considéré comme agent physique.* N.p., 1890.

———. *Le massage et le magnétisme menacés par les médecins; le proces Moureux à Angers; necessite d'un amendement a la loi du 30 Nov. 1892, sur l'exercice de la médecine.* N.p., 1897.

———. *Le Massage et le magnétisme sous l'empire de la loi du 30 Nov. 1892, sur l'exercice de la médecine; Règlement statutaire de l'Ecole pratique de Magnétisme et de Massage: statuts du syndicate des Masseurs et Magnétiseurs de Paris.* N.p., 1894.

———. *Lois physiques du magnétisme; Polarité humaine; Traité expérimental et thérapeutique de magnetisme.* N.p., 1886.

———. *Magnétisme personnel; Education de la Pensée—Développement de la Volonté—Pour être heureux, fort, bien portant et réussir en tout.* N.p., 1905.

———. *Pour combattre la surdité, les bourdonnements, l'otite, etc. . . . par le magnétisme.* N.p., 1906.

———. *Pour combattre les maladies par suggestion et auto- suggestion, se débarrasser de ses mauvaises habitudes, prendre de l'Energie et de la Confiance en soi, dominer les autres, et éviter leurs suggestions.* N.p., 1896.

———. *Pour combattres les maladies par l'application de l'aimant.* N.p., 1906.

———. *Traité expérimental de Magnétisme avec Portrait de l'auteur et Figures dans le texte; Cours professé a l'Ecole pratique de Magnétisme et de Massage.* 2 vols. N.p., 1895–1896.

———. *Traité Expérimental de Magnétisme . . . Cours professé a l'école Pratique de Magnetisme et de Massage par Hector Durville; Théories et Procédés.* 2 vols. N.p., 1898–1904.

Durville, Henri (1888– ?)

Writer, psychotherapist, and son of occult publisher **Hector Durville.** He was born November 30, 1888, in Paris. He founded the International Psychical Society and (with his father Hector and brother Gaston) edited the *Journal du Magnétisme,* originally founded by **Baron du Potet.** He wrote a number of books and organized international study conferences on **animal magnetism.**

Sources:

Durville, Henri, ed. *1er Congres international de Psychologie expérimentale.* N.p., 1910.

———. *2e Congres international de Psychologie expérimentale, La Science secrete.* N.p., 1923.

———. *Cours de magnétisme personnel.* N.p., 1933.

———. *La Magie divine.* N.p., 1930.

———. *Mystères initatiques.* N.p., 1929.

Durville, Henri, and Andre Durville, eds. *Les Trucs de la Prestidigitation dévoilés.* A series of 17 titles reprinted from *Revue du Psychisme expérimental* and *Journal du Magnétisme* 1911–1914.

Du-Sith

The Black Elf, a little man believed to be of fairy origin who killed Sir Lachlan Mor M'Clean in 1598 at the battle of Trai-Gruinard in Islay, Scotland. According to legend this little man offered his services to Sir James Macdonald, the opponent of Sir Lachlan, and that the latter's death was caused by an arrow that struck him on the head, afterward found to be an elf bolt (see also **elf arrows**). In answer to a question of Macdonald's the little man said, "I am called *Du-sith,* and you were better to have me with you than against you."

Dwyer, Walter W(illiam) (1894– ?)

Leader during the 1950s of the **Spiritual Frontiers Fellowship.** He was born on August 11, 1894, in New York City, and educated at Columbia University (M.A., 1916). In 1918 he married Geraldine Grace McKeown. He was a charter member of Academy of Religion and Mental Health, New York, and a member of the Order of St. Luke the Physician and the Institute of Pastoral Care, Worchester, Massachusetts. He developed a particular interest in spiritual healing.

Sources:

Dwyer, Walter W. *The Churches' Handbook for Spiritual Healing.* 9th ed. New York: Ascension Press, 1965.

Dykshoorn, Marinus Bernardus (1920–)

Dutch **psychic** whose passport uniquely bears the occupation entry "clairvoyant." According to **Paul Tabori,** in his book *Crime and the Occult* (1974), Dykshoorn has:

"... solved some extremely complex crimes, has located graves that have been "lost" since 1917, foretold a great many events that defied probability, and once tracked a thief in a distant country by telephone. His fame is solidly established in his native Holland and in a number of European countries. He has actually been licensed by the Dutch government authorities as a 'practitioner of the psychic arts.'"

He was born on July 10, 1920 in Gravenzande, near The Hague, and claimed to have had clairvoyant and precognitive gifts as a child. In 1938 a German scientist diagnosed his condition as being a result of **ESP,** and Dykshoorn decided to become a professional clairvoyant. At first he practiced in Holland, moving to Australia in 1960. His reception there was somewhat unsympathetic, and in 1970 he traveled to the United States, where he became widely known.

In his autobiography, Dykshoorn claimed extraordinary success in tracking criminals, finding buried treasure, and in other clairvoyant and precognitive feats. Some of these claims, however, depend upon Dykshoorn's own statements and have proved difficult to verify independently. For a skeptical view of Dykshoorn's claims, see Piet Hein Hoebens's 1982 article in the *Zetetic Scholar.*

Sources:

Dykshoorn, Marinus Bernardus, as told to Russell H. Felton. *My Passport Says Clairvoyant.* N.p., 1974.

Hoebens, Piet Hein. "The Mystery Men From Holland, III: The Man Whose Passport Says Clairvoyant." *Zetetic Scholar* 10 (December 1982).

Tabori, Paul. *Crime and the Occult.* N.p., 1974.

Dynamistograph

An instrument said to have been constructed under spirit guidance by the Dutch physicists Dr. J. L. W. P. Matla and Dr. G. J. Zaalberg Van Zelst of The Hague to obtain direct **communication** with the spirit world without using a medium. The device consisted of a cylinder into which the spirit influence was supposed to enter, a table isolated by a sheet of glass and charged with an electric current, a pair of scales, and a writing apparatus arranged on the Morse system. Enclosed in a room, the action of the instrument was observed through a small glass window. Long communications were allegedly spelled out by spiritual intelligences using a lettered dial at the top of the machine.

The result of these investigations was detailed by the inventors in their work *Het Geheim van den Dood* (5 vols., ca. 1911). A one-volume version was issued in French under the title *La Solution du Mystère de la Mort* (1930). A report of the Dutch Physical Society objected that no sufficient allowance was made for possible earth tremors and other normal causes. Nevertheless, such objections do not give satisfactory explanation for the curious communications received from the deceased father of Zaalberg Van Zelst.

For a discussion of the work and apparatus of Matla and Van Zelst, see **Hereward Carrington,** *Laboratory Investigations into Psychic Phenomena* (1939). (See also **Ashkir-Jobson Trianion; Communigraph; Reflectograph**)

E

E. F. Benson Society, The

British society organized to arrange social and literary events relating to **E. F. Benson,** his writings, and the Benson family's. It publishes a journal, *The Dodo,* named after Benson's very successful 1893 novel, for members. Address: Allan Downend, 88 Tollington Park, London, N4, England.

E-Meter

Common term for a device known as an "electropsychometer," invented by Volney Mathison in the United States. It measures galvanic skin response through changes in the electrical conductivity of the skin when the subject is emotionally aroused. The subject holds a handle in each hand, and strongly emotive thoughts cause a meter needle to register a dramatic change from zero. In the 1950s, the E-meter became an established part of the procedures of **Dianetics** and **Scientology.** Use of the E-meter by the members of the Church of Scientology is explained in a series of books written by church founder **L. Ron Hubbard.**

Sources:

Hubbard, L. Ron. *The Book Introducing the E-meter.* Los Angeles: Church of Scientology of California, 1975.

———. *The Book of E-meter Drills.* Compiled by Mary Sue Hubbard. Los Angeles: Church of Scientology of California, 1965.

———. *E-Meter Essentials.* Los Angeles: Church of Scientology of California, 1975.

———. *Understanding the E-Meter.* Los Angeles: Bridge Publications, 1981.

EA See BABYLONIA

Eaglesfield, Francis

Pseudonym of **Arthur Guirdham,** physician, novelist, and writer on ESP and reincarnation.

Ear Magazine

Journal concerned with music and related literature that has given special attention to the esoteric aspects of music and the use of sound for healing. It is published five times per year. Address: New Wilderness Foundation, 365 West End Ave., New York, NY 10024.

Earth Laid upon a Corpse

Old Scottish superstition described by eighteenth-century writer Thomas Pennant. It was the custom in the Highlands to lay on the breast of the deceased a wooden platter containing a little earth and a little salt—the former to symbolize the corruptibility of the body, the latter the incorruptibility of the soul.

Sources:

Pennant, Thomas. *A Tour in Scotland and Voyage to the Hebrides, MDCCLXXII.* 1774. Reprint, Chester, U.K.: J. Monk, 1969.

Earth Religion News

Short-lived magazine focused on **magic** and **witchcraft** published by Herman Slater (d. 1993), founder of the Magical Childe, an occult bookstore in Brooklyn, New York. The store was later moved and is now located in Manhattan.

Earthquake Prediction

Human sensitivity to earth tremors over vast distances at the time of seismic disturbance, or hearing the ominous rumbling days before, is an unclassified psychic phenomenon. *Conversations with Goethe* (1838) by Johann P. Eckermann, relates one such account concerning Goethe: "During the night of February 5–6, 1783, my master rang for me. I went to his room and saw him dragging his bed from the end of the room to the window. Then he looked up at the sky and said, 'Listen, we are at a very serious hour, for earthquakes are happening at this very moment.'" The next day, at the court of Weimar, Goethe repeated to several persons what he had said in the night, but he was laughed at, and one lady cried, "Goethe is raving." However, two weeks later accounts of a terrible earthquake arrived. It had occurred in Calabria and Sicily at the very time Goethe called to his valet.

Lady Conan Doyle claimed possession of the same gift that Eckermann recorded of Goethe. As many as five days preceding she stated that she could hear the rumbling of the earth over thousands of miles, especially in the quiet of the night. It broke in on her usual activity at unexpected moments, stopped, then recommenced and often continued up to the hour of the earthquake. She could tell the comparative distance but not the geographical position. She felt normal during such episodes and considered her ability to be a kind of predictive **clairaudience.**

Since ancient times, it has been popularly believed that **animals** are able to sense the approach of earthquakes. One of the earliest writers to record this belief was **Pliny the Elder** (ca. 23–79 C.E.), and it has persisted even until today. It was reported that weeks before the great West Indian earthquake with the eruption of Mount Pelée in Martinique in 1902 cattle became so uneasy that they could hardly be managed, dogs were fearful and howled continually, snakes left the vicinity of the volcano, and even the birds ceased to sing and left the trees on the mountainside. Such claims were often considered superstitious folklore, but are now taken seriously by scientists and parapsychologists, who refer to the phenomenon as *anpsi,* the psi faculty in animals.

There is ample evidence that animals do in fact behave in an unusual way prior to earthquakes, and Western scientists have taken great interest in the study of animal sensitivity in the People's Republic of China. In 1976 a group of ten United States' geologists and geophysicists visited China under the auspices of the National Academy of Sciences' Committee for Scholarly Communication with the People's Republic of China to investigate new techniques of predicting earthquakes. In addition to using electronic equipment to monitor earth sounds and the study of fluctuating water levels, the Chinese also study unusual animal behavior in an attempt to scientifically verify folk beliefs. Chinese farmers have believed for centuries that the onset of earthquakes is signaled by such unusual animal behavior as dogs howling, fish leaping, and snakes and rats emerging from hiding.

Similar observations have been reported from other countries. In Japan, fish have been reported to appear in large numbers in areas where they were normally scarce. Japanese householders in earthquake areas often keep goldfish in a bowl; if the fish swim about in a frantic manner, it is believed to signal an approaching earthquake. Rabbits and deer have been observed to run in terror from epicenter zones some hours before an earthquake. The Soviet publication *U.P.I. Report on Soviet Studies* (March 24, 1969) states that a Russian woman in Tashkent survived the earthquake of 1966 when her dog dragged her to safety minutes before her house was destroyed.

Various explanations have been advanced to account for the seeming ability of animals to predict earthquakes. Since animals are aware of super- and subsonic frequencies, it has been suggested that they hear the initial sound waves of an earthquake, which are inaudible to humans. Another suggestion is that animals perceive electromagnetic field variations. Another theory proposes that earthquakes produce an intensification of positive ions in the atmosphere, acting on the nervous system of creatures rather in the same way that some people claim to be able to perceive the onset of a storm. James B. Beal, in *Extrasensory Ecology,* discusses electrostatic and electromagnetic phenomena of this kind, including the "sky glow" that may precede an earthquake by several hours, and suggests that an earthquake causes a buildup in pressure in surrounding rocks.

Sources:

Beal, James B. "The Formerly 'Supernatural': Electrical and Psi Fields in Medical Anthropology." In *Extrasensory Ecology: Parapsychology & Anthropology,* edited by E. K. Long. Metuchen, N.J.: Scarecrow Press, 1977.

Cornell, James C., Jr., and John Surowiecki. *The Pulse of the Planet: A State of the Earth Report from the Smithsonian Institution Center for Short-lived Phenomena.* Harmony Books, 1972.

Gribben, John R., and Stephen H. Plageman. *The Jupiter Effect.* New York: Vintage Books, 1975.

James, Paul. *California Superquake, 1975–77: Scientists, Cayce, Psychics Speak.* New York: Exposition Press, 1974.

Schul, Bill. *The Psychic Power of Animals.* Greenwich, Conn.: Fawcett, 1976.

East West; The Journal of Natural Health & Living See Natural Health

Eber Donn

Chief of the Milesian invaders of ancient Ireland. According to mythology, many Milesian ships were lost in a storm that the **Danaans** raised by magic.

Ebertine, Reinhold (1901–1988)

German astrologer, born on February 16, 1901, in Görlitz, Saxony, Germany. Ebertine became interested in **astrology** during World War I and in the early 1920s became a professional astrologer. He became a student of Alfred Witte's (1878–1943) and cofounder of the Uranian (Hamburg) School of Astrology. Ebertine appreciated the scientific rigor of the Uranian system but came to reject various elements of it, especially the postulation of hypothetical planets that Witte and his colleague Friedrich Sirggrün had developed. In 1928 Ebertine began the periodical *Mensch in All.*

Through the 1930s Ebertine developed "cosmobiology," an approach to astrology based on, but distinct from, the Uranian system. Its distinguishing trait was its use of a simplified form of the midpoint combinations originally utilized by Witte (midpoint theories suggest that halfway between two planets a mutual influence converges that can then form a significant relationship with another planet in the horoscope chart).

Ebertine's work was suppressed by the Nazis, but he survived the war and began anew with a new periodical, *Cosmobiologie.* He died on March 14, 1988. Over the years he wrote more than sixty books, most of which have yet to be translated into English.

Sources:

Ebertine, Reinhold. *Applied Cosmobiology.* Aalen, Germany: Ebertin Verlag, 1972.

———. *Combination of Solar Influences.* Aalen, Germany: Ebertin Verlag, 1972.

Holden, James H., and Robert A. Hughes. *Astrological Pioneers of America.* Tempe, Ariz.: American Federation of Astrologers, 1988.

Eblis (or Iblis)

The "Satan" of the Mohammedans. It was said that Eblis was an inmate of Azaze, the heaven nearest God, and when the **angels** were commanded to bow down to the first man, he was the chief of those who rebelled. They were cast out of Azaze, and Eblis and his followers were sentenced to suffer in hell for a long time. It was supposed that he was composed of the elements of fire and that he succeeded the peris (fairylike nature spirits) in the government of the world.

Ebon, Martin (1917–)

Author and editor of popular books on parapsychology and related subjects. Ebon was born May 27, 1917, in Hamburg, Germany. In 1938 he moved to the United States, where he served as a managing editor of the Foreign Language Division of the Overseas News Agency. During World War II, he was on the staff of the U.S. Office of War Information. He became an expert on the Soviet Union and wrote and lectured widely on it. However, his interest in the paranormal became the more dominant part of his life.

After the war he was associated with the **Parapsychology Foundation** and for 11 years (1954–65) served as its administrative secretary. He was managing editor of the foundation's periodical, *Tomorrow* (1953–62), and executive editor of the *International Journal of Parapsychology* (1959–65). For a brief period beginning in 1969, he also served as executive editor of the quarterly *Spiritual Frontiers.*

Throughout the sixties and seventies, he wrote and edited numerous books and articles on all fields of parapsychology, the occult, and other anomalous phenomena, and he served as book review editor for several periodicals. Ebon first became known to many through his "true experiences" series of the late 1960s, which included *True Experiences in Prophecy* (1967), *True Experiences in Telepathy* (1967), *True Experiences with Ghosts* (1968), and *True Experiences in Exotic ESP* (1968).

Ebon's major contributions to parapsychology include *Communicating with the Dead* (1968), *What's New in ESP* (1976), *The Evidence for Life After Death* (1977), and *The Signet Handbook of Parapsychology* (1978). He also wrote two books that combined his knowledge of parapsychology and the Soviet Union: *Psychic Discoveries by the Russians* (1971) and *The Soviet Propaganda Machine* (1987). Ebon's books have always been very timely, as he possessed an accurate sense of specific public interests in paranormal subjects.

Sources:

Ebon, Martin. *Communicating with the Dead.* New York: New American Library, 1968.

———. *The Evidence for Life After Death.* New York: New American Library, 1977.

———. *Psychic Discoveries by the Russians.* New York: New American Library, 1971.

———. *Psychic Warfare: Threat or Illusion?* New York: McGraw-Hill, 1983.

———. *The Signet Handbook of Parapsychology.* New York: New American Library, 1978.

———. *The Soviet Propaganda Machine.* New York: McGraw-Hill, 1987.

———. *True Experiences in Exotic ESP.* New York: New American Library, 1968.

———. *True Experiences in Prophecy.* New York: New American Library, 1967.

———. *True Experiences in Telepathy.* New York: New American Library, 1967.

———. *True Experiences with Ghosts.* New York: New American Llibrary, 1968.

———. *What's New in ESP.* New York: New American Library, 1976.

Ech-uisque

A Gaelic word meaning "water horse." The Ech-uisque was a goblin of Scottish Highland folklore, understood to be a favorite form assumed by the **kelpie** in order to lure souls to his master, the Devil. In the disguise of a fine steed, beautifully accoutered, the kelpie grazed innocently by the wayside. The weary traveler, passing by and believing this splendid animal to have strayed from his master, would be tempted to make use of him to help him on his way. The deceitful kelpie, remaining quiet as a lamb until the traveler was mounted, would then, with a fiendish yell of triumph, plunge headlong into an adjacent pool.

It was believed that the soul of the unfortunate man, who had no time to prepare for death, would thus be safely secured to the Evil One, while the kelpie received the body in payment for his trouble.

ECK

A term used by members of the religious organization **ECKANKAR,** founded by **Paul Twitchell** in October 1965. *ECK* (Hindi word for "one"; Sanskrit *eka*) is defined as "the totality of all awareness," "the audible life stream," "the living power that embraces the whole universes of God;" in brief, the essence of the Divine.

ECKANKAR

ECKANKAR, "the religion of light and sound of God," is a variation of the Radha Soami Sant Mat (tradition of the masters), a major religious tradition in the Punjab area of northern India. It was founded in 1965 by Paul Twitchell, a former student of Sant Mat Master Kirpal Singh. In 1964 Twitchell moved to San Francisco, California, and began to teach what he considered an advanced form of *surat shabd yoga,* the Sant Mat system of spiritual disciplines, which allows the student to hear the divine sounds and see the divine light and prepares the student's soul to travel on what are considered the inner planes of reality.

Twitchell claimed that he had come into contact with the Vairagi order of *mahabtas* (masters) and especially with their representatives Sudar Singh of India and ECK Master Rebazar Tarzs in the Himalayas. In 1965 Twitchell was named the 971st Living ECK Master, the lineage of the order dating back to prehistory. As the ECK master, he wrote a number of books and brought to publication two volumes of the *Shariyat-Ki-Sugmad,* the scripture of ECKANKAR. After his death in 1971 he was succeeded by Darwin Gross and then by the current ECK master, Harold Klemp.

ECKANKAR offers a picture of the inner worlds divided into an order of ascending levels through which the student may travel to the realm of God's presence. The student, or *chela,* is aided in this process by the work of the ECK master, who is believed to be able to meet and assist the student as he or she traverses the planes, especially in the nighttime while sleeping. The many ECK exercises (more than a hundred different techniques are now taught to students at different levels) assist students in their awareness of the planes, and the literature explains what they will encounter at the different levels of the inner reality. To travel the planes it is necessary to be able to see and hear the "divine light and sound."

Devotees of ECKANKAR consider it a living, growing religion headed by a master who continues to bring forth new teachings. Under Harold Klemp, the present ECK master, the organization moved into a new headquarters complex and temple in suburban Minneapolis, Minnesota. The religion is now international in scope, and in 1991 more than ten thousand attended an ECK seminar in Africa.

In the 1980s substantive charges were leveled that Twitchell had fabricated his spiritual career, had plagiarized some of his books from the writings of Julian Johnson, a prominent Sant Mat writer, and had attempted to cover up his early associations with Kirpal Singh and other spiritual teachers. Harold Klemp has largely acknowledged Twitchell's borrowing from Johnson and ECKANKAR's place in the Sant Mat tradition. Several ECKANKAR students have also left to found rival organizations, including Ancient Teachings of the Masters (Darwin Gross), The Divine Science of Light and Sound (Jerry Mulvin), and, most prominently, the Movement of Spiritual Inner Awareness (John-Roger Hinkins). ECKANKAR address: Box 27300, Minneapolis, MN 55427.

Sources:

Klemp, Harold. *Soul Travelers of the Far Country.* Minneapolis, Minn.: ECKANKAR, 1987.

Lane, David Christopher. *The Making of a Spiritual Movement.* Del Mar, Calif.: Del Mar Press, 1983.

Twitchell, Paul. *All about ECK.* Las Vegas, Nev.: Illuminated Way Press, 1969.

———. *ECKANKAR, the Key to Secret Worlds.* New York: Lancer Books, 1969.

Eckartshausen, Karl von (1752–1803)

Author of *Der Wolke vor dem Heiligthume* (1802), a classic work of Roman Catholic mysticism, translated into English as *The Cloud Upon the Sanctuary.* Eckartshausen, by nature and education an intensely religious man, began his writing career with several small books of devotion that had great vogue in France and Germany. He later turned his attention to larger works of a more profound character.

According to Eckartshausen, the requisite faculty of true communion with the "interior church" is the inward conception of things spiritual; this sense makes possible the beginning of regeneration understood as the process of gradually eliminating Original Sin. His consideration of the interior church proceeds at two levels, beginning with an elucidation of his doctrine and moving to a series of assertions derived therefrom.

Isabelle de Steiger's translated *The Cloud Upon the Sanctuary,* which was first published in 1895 in *The Unknown World* was edited by **Arthur Edward Waite.** It was later issued in book form. The English version was soon adopted not only by spiritual seekers but also by many occultists. It had some influence on the development of the modern occult revival, finding some favor among the leadership of the Hermetic Order of the **Golden Dawn.** The book also impressed magician **Aleister Crowley,** who was attracted to its idea of the mystical interior church. Crowley was eventually consecrated into an independent Gnostic tradition, and he wrote a Gnostic mass for the church he founded as an auxiliary organization to the magical order he led.

Sources:

Eckartshausen, Karl von. *The Cloud upon the Sanctuary.* Translated by Isabel de Steiger. Introduction by Arthur E. Waite. London: Philip Wellby, 1903.

Eclectic Theosophist (Journal)

Bimonthly publication of the independent Point Loma Theosophical Institute, presenting theosophical teachings, news, and book reviews. Address: Point Loma Publications, P.O. Box 6507, San Diego, CA 92106.

Eclesia Católica Cristiana

The Eclesia Católica Cristiana is a Spanish-speaking Spiritualist church operating in the Bronx, New York. It was founded in 1956 as the Spiritualist Christian Church by Delfin Roman Cardona (b. 1918). The church was reorganized and renamed in 1969 to keep down any confusion between it and other Spiritualist centers. Cardona was born and raised in Puerto Rico. Raised a Roman Catholic, he was introduced to **Spiritualism** in his teens and gained some renown on the island because of his healing abilities. After moving to the United States, he founded the church to combine Roman Catholic and Spiritualist emphases. The Roman Catholic element is most evident in the development of a hierarchy that includes cardinals, bishops, and lay members.

Spiritualism in Puerto Rico derived from Brazil, which in turn derived its Spiritualist beliefs from the French **spiritism** of **Allan Kardec,** differentiated by its early acceptance of reincarnation. It has added elements of science (**parapsychology**) and **Theosophy** to create what it considers to be universal Christianity. The resulting synthesis of thought, termed the Delfinist Thought, places great emphasis on the virtues of love, comprehension, compassion, justice, humility, and faith.

Cardona has taught that women and men are equals in the spiritual as in the material world. Following the example of ancient Atlantis and the ancient Druids, the church ordains females and welcomes them into the bishopric. The first woman cardinal, Rev. Mother Olga Roman, was elevated in 1974.

Ecsomatic Experiences

One of many terms for **out-of-the-body travel,** also known as OOB, **astral projection,** or etheric projection. The term *ecsomatic* is used by parapsychologist **Celia E. Green,** director of the **Institute of Psychophysical Research,** Oxford, England, in conjunction with related technical terms, including *parasomatic* (in which the percipient appears to have another body as distinct from the normal physical body) and *asomatic* (in which the subject is unaware of having a body).

Sources:

Green, Celia E. *Out-of-the-body Experiences.* Proceedings of the Institute of Psychophysical Research, vol. 2. London, 1968.

Ecstasy

Described by parapsychologist **F. W. H. Myers** as "a change in the centre of perception from the material into the spiritual world," ecstasy is a state of rapture in which insights and visions of the invisible world unfold. It is characterized by an exaltation of sensory faculties. It is common to all religions and is one of the most-attested psychic experiences in both civilized and primitive countries.

The **Waldenses,** Italian Protestants of the twelfth century, sustained persecution from Roman Catholic forces with the superhuman strength and energy that came to them in ecstastic states. They routed French and Savoyard troops that were fifty times more numerous. During the war in the Cevennes, three thousand religious enthusiasts stood their ground against sixty thousand men of the king commanded by the best generals of France. In like measure, the **Convulsionaires of St. Médard** in the eighteenth century endured frightful blows—which could have felled an ox—on their chests and stomachs while in the ecstatic state.

Ecstatic states were frequently reported of Christian saints and were integral to the experience of such mystics as St. Teresa of Avila. In evaluating claims of visions of the Virgin Mary, officials of the Roman Catholic Church ask, among other things, whether or not the person was in a state of ecstasy during the vision.

In Hindu mysticism, *ananda* is the name given to the blissful condition of higher consciousness, and gurus often adopt a name extolling the virtue of such activities as meditation in producing that state.

It is clear that there are degrees of ecstasy, ranging from euphoric to transcendental states. Hindu mystical teachings have charted the different stages of *samadhi,* mystical trance, with their qualitative degrees of ecstasy. Samadhi is the aim of traditional **yoga** systems, in which body, mind, and spirit are controlled and purified.

In some forms of **tantric yoga,** the vital energy known as **kundalini,** commonly the dynamic of sexual experience, is transformed into spiritual force as it follows its pathway through subtle channels along the spine and through the vital centers in the body (*chakras*) to the crown of the head, culminating in mystical experience accompanied by blissful sensations. However, this particular yoga is said to be more likely to result in sexual fixation and obsession.

Similar to tantric yoga is the **sex magic** of Western occultists developed in the late nineteenth century out of the alchemical tradition. **Aleister Crowley,** best known for his experimentation and development in this field, viewed sex as the primary tool available to the magician in raising magic energy.

In both the Eastern and Western mystical tradition, many have argued that celibacy is the more rewarding lifestyle for those on the mystical path. In such celibate systems, the mundane ecstatic pleasure of sex has supposedly been sublimated into spiritual force, and the ecstastic experience has been transcended in mystical union.

In the 1960s, as transpersonal psychology developed, consciousness studies became a primary area of research. Ecstasy was pigeonholed under such categories as the "highest state of consciousness" or "expanded state of consciousness." Note was made of the many ways of inducing such states of their desirability. Attempts have also been made to correlate such states with various measurable body states, but progress has been difficult because most such states occur spontaneously and in the context of sacred activity.

Sources:

Avalon, Arthur [Sir John Woodroffe]. *The Serpent Power.* Madras, India, 1922.

Bucke, R. M. *Cosmic Consciousness: A Study of the Evolution of the Human Mind.* N.p., 1910.

Danielou, Alain. *Yoga: The Method of Re-Integration.* London: Christopher Johnson, 1949. Reprint, New Hyde Park, N.Y.: University Books, 1955.

Gopi Krishna. *Kundalini: The Evolutionary Energy in Man.* Boulder, Colo: Shambhala, 1970.

James, William. *The Varieties of Religious Experience.* London, 1902.

Row, M. C. Nanjunda. *Cosmic Consciousness, or the Vedantic Idea of Realisation of Muktu in the Light of Modern Psychology.* Madras, India, 1910.

Underhill, Evelyn. *Mysticism: A Study in the Nature and Development of Man's Spiritual Consciousness.* London: Methuen, 1911.

White, John, ed. *The Highest State of Consciousness.* Garden City, N.Y.: Doubleday Anchor, 1972.

Ectenic Force

A supposed physical force emanating from the person of the **medium** and directed by his or her will, by means of which objects may be moved without contact in apparent defiance of natural laws. The existence of such a **psychic force** was postulated by **Count Agenor de Gasparin** in the mid-nineteenth century to explain the phenomena of **table-turning** and **rapping,** and the term *ectenic force* was bestowed upon the supposed agency by de Gasparin's colleague **Marc Thury.**

The experiments of Thury and de Gasparin were widely cited as among the most convincing evidence that **Spiritualism** could produce, and influenced many eminent students of psychic research. If tables can be moved without contact, then such a theory is plausible, but the evidence for this type of phenomena is not abundant. During the latter twentieth century, the phenomenon postulated by Thury and de Gasparin has been placed under the broad label of **psychokinesis.**

Ectoplasm

A term coined by psychical researcher **Charles Richet** and widely used in **Spiritualism,** derived from the Greek *ektos* and *plasma* (meaning "exteriorized substance"). It denotes a mysterious vaporlike substance that, Spiritualists claimed, streamed out of the body of entranced mediums. The manipulation of ectoplasm, either by the subconscious self or by discarnate intelligences, resulted in the phenomena of a superphysical order (including partial and complete **materializations.**) *Psychoplasm* and *teleplasm* are terms similarly used to convey the same meaning, the latter denoting action at a distance from the medium's body, while ideoplasm progresses a step further and means the molding of the ectoplasm into the likeness of a self.

From the eighteenth century through the early twentieth century, numerous reports of an ectoplasmic substance were reported. **Emanuel Swedenborg,** for example, in his first vision spoke of "a kind of vapour steaming from the pores of my body." It was a visible watery vapor and fell downward to the ground upon the carpet. **Eugene A. D. Rochas** compared the luminous vapor he saw arising from the breast of **Elizabeth d'Esperance** to the Milky Way. **Paul Lecour** likened the process to the condensation of a nebula. The same idea is suggested by Venzano's description of a mass of swirling vapor at the side of **Eusapia Palladino.** In the case of **Franek Kluski** and that of **Eva C.,** the substance was observed as white luminous spots from the size of a pea to that of a crown piece on the medium's clothes. In Kluski's case they were much brighter than in Eva's. **Gustav Geley** described a dimly phosphorescent column that formed beside him, out of which a luminous hand, perfectly formed and of natural size, appeared and patted him several times on the forearm in a friendly way. At the slight shock, a drop of luminous liquid fell on his sleeve and shone there for 15 to 20 minutes after the disappearance of the hand.

D'Esperance wrote of her experiences with ectoplasm:

"As soon as I have entered the mediumistic cabinet, my first impression is of being covered with spider webs. Then I feel that the air is filled with substance, and a kind of white and vaporous mass, quasi luminous, like the steam from a locomotive, is formed in front of the abdomen. After this mass has been tossed and agitated in every way for some minutes, sometimes even for half an hour, it suddenly stops, and then out of it is born a living being close to me."

Another time she added, "It seemed that I could feel fine threads being drawn out of the pores of my skin." This is significant in view of the cloudy, faintly luminous threads between the phantom and the medium that are sometimes observed in materialization séances. Such séances may help in understanding telekinetic phenomena.

The claimed discovery of ectoplasm is, of course, not recent. In the works of the alchemist Thomas Vaughan (1622–1666) is found a description under the term *first matter* or *mercury* of a substance, drawn from the body, that has some of the characteristics of ectoplasm. However, the first systematic study of ectoplasm was a joint effort by **Baron Albert von Schrenck-Notzing** and **Juliette Bisson,** who experimented with Eva C. Prior to this, **Gabriel Delanne, Enrico Morselli,** and **Charles Richet** published descriptions of the different evolutionary states of ectoplasm. Subsequently, important contributions to the discussion were made by Gustav Geley.

The questions that entertained psychical researchers, besides the basic one of establishing the very existence of ectoplasm, were its properties, the effect of its outflow upon the medium, and the means by which it could be manipulated. It was originally hypothesized that ectoplasm was a form of matter, invisible and intangible in its primary state but assuming vaporous, liquid, or solid condition in various stages of condensation. It was said to smell like ozone and to possess a number of extraordinary properties.

Experimental Findings and Inferences

A variety of photographs of what was supposed to be ectoplasm were put forward, some of which are rather repulsive. They show gelatinous, viscous material oozing from all the natural orifices of the medium's body—from the mouth, ears, nose, eyes, and lower orifices, and also from the top of the head, from the breasts, and from the fingertips. Most often it comes from the mouth. The form of the substance varies, according to Geley, between threads, cords, rigid rays, membranes, and fabriclike or woven material with indefinite and irregular outlines. The most curious picture is that of a widely expanded membrane with fringes and rucks and resembling a net in appearance. This resemblance to such materials as cheesecloth often provoked allegations of **fraud,** and, in fact, many mediums were caught in attempts to simulate ectoplasm.

The amount of ectoplasm found in the experiments varied greatly. It seemed at times to be conditioned by psychological factors of will and emotion. It could completely envelop the medium as in a mantle. It had different colors—white, black, or grey. White was the most frequent, or perhaps the most easily observed. Sometimes the three colors appeared simultaneously. Visibility varied a great deal. The impression to the touch was sometimes moist and cold, sometimes viscous and sticky, more rarely dry and hard. The substance was mobile, slow, reptilelike, or at other times quick as lightning. It was sensitive to light. The production could affect the general temperature of the room, a change being particularly noticeable near the medium or any object touched by the exuding substance.

Schrenck-Notzing in his book *The Phenomena of Materialisation* (1920) sums up hundreds of experiments conducted for a period of five years with Eva C.: "We have very often been able to establish that by an unknown process there comes from the body of the medium a material, at first semi-fluid, which possesses some of the properties of a living substance, notably that of the power of change, of movement and of the assumption of definite forms."

In Munich, with the Polish medium **Stanislawa P.,** the baron succeeded in making a cinematographic record of ectoplasm as it flowed out of the medium's mouth.

The similarity between these observations and those of a Mrs. Davidson at the haunted **Willington Mill** is of interest. She saw:

". . . what she supposed was a white towel lying on the ground. She went to pick it up, but imagine her surprise when she found that it rose up and went behind the dressing table over the top, down on the floor across the room, disappeared under the door, and was heard to descend the stairs with a heavy step" (*Journal* of the Society for Psychical Research, vol. 5).

In séances in Boston with **Mina S. Crandon,** ectoplasm was photographed as it was being reabsorbed by the medium's body through the openings of the mouth, nose, and ears. In several of these photographs the ectoplasm still had the form it had first assumed in the materialization, a form then reduced to a species of placenta attached to the medium by a cord similar to an umbilical cord.

Dr. F. Schwab, in his experiments with **Maria Vollhardt,** made a photographic record of telekinetic movements and found ectoplasm on them. The matter was usually streaming out of Vollhardt's mouth. Her teethmarks were often found in it, suggesting it was a plastic substance.

The sensation of touch produced by ectoplasm also varied in the experiments. According to the invisible operators of the séance room, it could be made to have any desired "feel."

"Walter," the control of Margery (Mina Crandon), put an ectoplasmic terminal in the hand of Dr. Crandon, telling him to feel and squeeze it gently. It was a more or less conical mass, half an inch wide at its tip, getting rapidly wider, up to about an inch and a quarter where it left Dr. Crandon's hand. The mass was ice cold, somewhat rough on the surface, and yielded slightly as a rubber eraser might do. On repetition with another sitter, named Conant, he was required to scrape his hand carefully, and he stated that through this process he recovered and put down on the table at Walter's command something that acted much like the finer inner membrane of an egg.

Sir Arthur Conan Doyle also spoke of an occasion with Eva C. when, in good light, he was allowed to squeeze a piece of ectoplasm between his fingers. It gave him the impression of a living substance, thrilling and shrinking under his touch.

When ectoplasm was suddenly exposed to light, mediums reported being thrown into agony. However, it was suggested by Dr. **W. J. Crawford** that it is not so much the ectoplasm as the medium that cannot bear the light. If the medium is shielded with black cloth, the pain is considerably reduced and flashlight photographs become easily procurable. Juliette Bisson confirmed these observations with Eva C. Sudden flashes of light were avoided. Warnings were normally given before taking a picture, in the understanding that a sudden flash would drive the substance back into the medium's body with the force of a snapped elastic band.

Franek Kluski reportedly received an open wound from a violent retreat of ectoplasm. Doyle quoted the case of a medium who exhibited a bruise from the breast to the shoulder caused by the recoil of the ectoplasm. The medium **Evan Powell,** at the **British College of Psychic Science,** suffered a bad injury on the chest owing to an unintended violent movement of a sitter touched by an ectoplasmic arm. Hemorrhage was also reported as a result of sudden exposure to light. **H. Dennis Bradley** spoke of an instance in which the medium **George Valiantine** got a black bruise, measuring about two inches by three, on the stomach by the shock of returning ectoplasm when a powerful electric light was suddenly switched on in his garage, which faced one of the windows of the séance room. The substance was seen and described by the writer Caradoc Evans as a slimy, frothy bladder "into which you could dig a finger but through which you could not pierce."

Galey gives this report in *From the Unconscious to the Conscious* (1920):

"To its sensitiveness, the substance seems to add a kind of instinct not unlike that of the self-protection of the invertebrates; it would seem to have all the distrust of a defenseless creature, or one whose sole defence is to re-enter the parent organism. It shrinks from all contacts and is always ready to avoid them and to be reabsorbed."

Many observations led to the hypothesis that ectoplasm has an immediate and irresistible tendency toward organization and, as a natural sequel, tends to assume the shape of the medium's body. This hypothesis was supported by the frequently noted duplication of the medium's face in materialization séances as a preliminary to individualized forms and also the frequent identification of a phantom hand with that of the medium.

An alternative to this theory was that the **double** of the medium serves as a pattern on which the new creations are actually built up. The double, wholly or partially detached, might magnetically attract the ectoplasm; and one observer suggested that the initial stimulation of the medium's body before the double's detachment contributes to the ejection of the ectoplasm, but only when the double is fully withdrawn does it attract the ectoplasm and clothe itself with it.

In a series of interesting experiments in the **Goligher Circle,** W. J. Crawford traced the flow of ectoplasm by using powdered carmine. He found that the ectoplasmic stream carries coloring matter. Staining various parts of the medium's body, he discovered that in this particular case the flow started at the base of the spine and passed down to the feet. On returning, it encountered frictional resistance; the fabric of the medium's clothing was found abraded in places. After staining Miss Goligher's blouse with carmine and asking for a rap on the wall, Crawford found carmine spots at the location of the raps.

Materialized hands produced wonderful paraffin molds in séances with Franek Kluski. He was amply controlled, yet once he was found smeared with wax. On another occasion, particles of wax were found in out-of-the-way corners of the séance room and even in the adjoining room, indicating a long extension of psychic structures.

It was not only particles of paint but also particles of clothing material that were believed to have been carried along by the ectoplasmic flow. At least, this conclusion was suggested to Crawford when he found that the fabric of the medium's stockings was nearly always impressed in the soft clay when he asked for an impression to be produced by the psychic rods. Because these particles were not deposited, they apparently flowed back giving rise to the possibility that ectoplasm acts as a solvent on material particles through which it passes, reducing them to an unknown fluidic state.

Crawford also noticed that if he passed his hand between the medium's ankle and the levitated table, the table dropped to the floor. If his hand was gloved, the table dropped more slowly. If he passed a glass rod between the table and the medium, the levitation was unaffected. Similarly, he found that if the medium touched the levitated table, the psychic energy became short-circuited and the table dropped. The medium's touch with a gloved hand retarded the drop, whereas a touch with wood or paper had no appreciable effect.

Schrenck-Notzing was able to get a fragment of ectoplasm into a tube. The moment he tried to trap it, it vanished with lightning speed. Occasionally, however, with the medium's consent, specimens were amputated for chemical and microscopic analysis. Of the result Schrenck-Notzing wrote:

"Very probably the formation of the substance, which appears in the sittings as liquid material, and also as amorphous material, or filmy net-like and veil-like material in the form of shreds, wisps, threads, and cords, in large or small packets, is an organised tissue which easily decomposes—a sort of transitory matter which originates in the organism in a manner unknown to us, possesses unknown biological functions, and formative possibilities, and is evidently peculiarly dependent on the psychic influence of the medium. . . . As regards the structure of the teleplasm, we only know this: that within it, or about it, we find conglomerates of bodies resembling epithelium, real plate epithelium with nuclei, veil-like filmy structures, coherent lamellar bodies without structure, as well as flat globules and mucus. If we abstain from any detailed indications concerning the composition and function of teleplasm we may yet assert two definite facts:—(1) In teleplasm, or associated with it, we find substances of organic origin, various cell-forms, which leave behind cell detritus. (2) The mobile material observed, which seems to represent the fundamental substance of the phenomena, does not consist of india rubber or any other artificial product, by which its existence could be fraudulently represented. For substances of this kind can never decompose into cell detritus, or leave a residue of such."

Schrenck-Notzing also analyzed ectoplasm obtained from Stanislawa P. This analysis was made in February 1916. It was controlled by a Dr. Dombrowski, who obtained half of the ectoplasm in Warsaw, Poland. He found leucocytes and epithelial cells, but otherwise the analysis yielded no secret. The summary of a bacteriological report published by the Polish Society for Psychical Research concluded, "The substance to be analyzed is albuminoid matter accompanied by fatty matter and cells found in the human organism. Starch and sugar discoverable by Fehling's test are absent." **Camille Flammarion** described Eusapia Palladino's sensation during the withdrawal of ectoplasm:

"She suddenly experiences an ardent desire to produce the phenomena; then she has a feeling of numbness and the gooseflesh sensation in her fingers; these sensations keep increasing; at the same time she feels in the lower portion of the vertebral column the flowing of a current which rapidly extends into her arms as far as her elbow, where it is gently arrested. It is at this point that the phenomenon takes place.''

As regards telekinetic effects produced by psychic rods, Conan Doyle suggested that the psychic rods may not be strong in themselves. They may be conveyors of strength, similar to a copper wire carrying electricity. According to all indications the ectoplasmic lines are conveyors of feeling and emotion, too, not only between the materialized figure and the medium, but between the medium and the sitters as well. **Elizabeth d'Esperance** writes in *Shadow Land* (1897) of the period when she was conscious during materialization: ''I felt conscious of the thoughts, or rather the feelings, of everyone in the room, but had no inclination to as much as lift a finger to enable me to see anything.'' She also states that her brain apparently became:

''. . . a sort of whispering gallery where the thoughts of other persons resolved themselves into an embodied form and resounded as though actual substantial objects. Was anyone suffering, I felt the pain. Was anyone worried or depressed, I felt it instantly. Joy or sorrow made themselves in some way perceptible to me. I could not tell who among the friends assembled was suffering, only that the pain existed and was in some way reproduced in myself. If anyone left his or her seat, thus breaking the chain, this fact was communicated to me in a mysterious but unmistakable manner.''

In a lecture reported in *Light* (November 21, 1903), she added:

''I lost physical strength, but no particle of my individuality. On the contrary, the loss of physical power seemed but to intensify that of the senses. Distant sounds, beyond hearing at other times, became painfully audible; a movement of any of the sitters sent a vibration through every nerve; a sudden exclamation caused a sensation of terror; the very thoughts of the persons in the room made themselves felt as though they were material objects.''

The exteriorization of ectoplasm seemed to require a state of passivity on the part of the medium. D'Esperance had no strength to exert herself during the process of materialization; but if she made a great effort, this invariably compelled the materialized forms to retire to the **cabinet,** as though deprived of the power to stand or support themselves.

It also seemed that feelings of pain could be transferred from the medium to the materialized phantom. Once, d'Esperance scorched her arm prior to a séance and felt herself fainting, during the séance, from pain. Suddenly she felt a series of something like electric shocks and the pain left her; but the phantom ''Yolande'' carried her arm as though she were in pain, and when accidentally touched she flinched as though hurt. Another time, however, when a dislocated shoulder required d'Esperance to wear a surgical bandage for a few days, Yolande appeared with both arms uninjured. Nor did she exhibit any sign of weakness, for she lifted with ease a pitcher of water in her right hand, a feat that, under the circumstances, would have been quite impossible for the medium. D'Esperance conjectured that Yolande had sufficient material on that occasion from the persons in the circle, who numbered more than 20. On the occasion of the burnt arm fewer than 10 persons formed the circle.

The physiological effect of the sitters on the medium was again curiously demonstrated in a case with d'Esperance. After sittings for **spirit photography** in Sweden, she felt prostrate. The symptoms were those of nicotine poisoning. Through experiments it was discovered that none of the uncomfortable sensations were felt when the séances were conducted with nonsmokers.

Partial Dematerialization

W. J. Crawford, in his study of the Goligher Circle, decided that the sitters also contributed to the ectoplasmic flow. He measured the variation in weight during the séance of both the medium and the sitters. Ordinarily the loss of the medium's weight did not amount to more than 10–15 pounds. In one case, however, it amounted to 54 pounds, the normal weight of the medium being 128 pounds. At 30 pounds the stress on the medium appeared to be severe. The withdrawal of her bodily substance went on with difficulty, in fluxes, as if an elastic resistance had to be overcome. There was a distinct collapse in the hips of the girl; however, they filled back out when the ectoplasm was reabsorbed.

The medium **Charles Williams,** whose normal weight was 153 pounds, was weighed while the materialized spirit ''Peter'' left the cabinet. His weight shrank to 35 pounds and remained there for half an hour. **Annie Fairlamb Mellon** and Miss **C. E. Wood** were several times observed to have lost half of their weight during the apparition of phantoms. It was noticed with **George Spriggs,** in Melbourne, Australia, that when there were tall people in the circle the forms were taller than when the sitters were of lower stature.

The apparent contraction of the medium's body was seen to reach further stages, even to the point of disintegration of the extremities and, in certain exceptional cases, the temporary disappearance of the entire body. On one occasion Eusapia Palladino was described by **Julien Ochorowicz** as ''all shrunken together'' during physical phenomena. Her hand seemed to be contracted. Arthur Levy, at a séance on November 16, 1898, similarly observed, ''Her burning hands seemed to contract or shrivel. Eusapia seems shrunken together and is very much affected. . . . when the lamps are again lighted she is seen to be very much changed, her eyes dull, her face apparently diminished to half its usual size.'' A Dr. Vezzano also once stated that he noticed the disappearance of the lower limbs of Eusapia. The **control ''John King''** claimed to have dematerialized them to gain more power.

Of the medium **Charles Eldred,** before his exposure as a fraud, Charles Letort and Ellen S. Letort report as follows in *Light:*

''He had shrunk up like a mummy; his head seemed to have sunk in between his shoulders and his legs seemed to have become shorter. When he had sat down at the beginning of the sitting we had seen his feet reach out under the curtains; now they scarcely touched the floor. He seemed all shrivelled up, but on his cheeks there was a feverish red spot.''

Willie Reichel, in the journal *Psychische Studien* (1905), writes of one of **Charles Victor Miller**'s séances in San Francisco, ''In the space of about three minutes the head of the medium became like that of a child, and after further shrinking disappeared altogether.''

Florence Marryat claimed that she was led by the materialized spirit ''Florence'' behind the curtains to see the medium **Mary Showers.** She observed:

''The first sight of her terrified me. She appeared to be shrunk to half her usual size and the dress hung loosely on her figure. Her arms had disappeared, but putting my hands up the dress sleeves I found them diminished to the size of those of a little child—the fingers reaching only to where the elbows had been. The same miracle had happened to her feet, which only occupied half her boots. She looked in fact like the mummy of a girl of four or six years old. The spirit told me to feel her face. The forehead was dry, rough and burning hot, but from the chin water was dropping freely on the bosom of her dress.''

The famous case of the partial dematerialization of d'Esperance's body in Helsinki on December 11, 1895, is described in **Alexander Aksakof**'s book *A Case of Partial Dematerialization* (1898). He was not present himself, but he collected testimonies of 15 witnesses. As he reconstructed the case, the lower part of the medium's body, from the waist downward, disappeared. Her skirt was lying flat on the chair for about 15 minutes, and her trunk was apparently suspended in the air above the seat. The light was sufficient to see by, and d'Esperance permitted five persons to verify the phenomenon by passing their hands below her trunk. This examination caused her great distress, and she was ill for three months after the occurrence.

D'Esperance's account of her feelings is especially interesting. Aksakof quotes her as follows:

"I relaxed my muscles and let my hands fall upon my lap, and I then found out that, instead of resting against my knees, they rested against the chair in which I was sitting. This discovery disturbed me greatly, and I wondered if I was dreaming. I patted my skirt carefully, all over, trying to locate my limbs and the lower half of my body, but found that although the upper part of it—arms, shoulders, chest, etc.—as in its natural state, all the lower part had entirely disappeared. I put my hand where my knees should have been, but nothing whatever was there but my dress and skirts. Nevertheless, I felt just as usual—better than usual, in fact; so that if my attention had not been attracted by accident, I should probably have known nothing of the occurrence. Leaning forward to see if my feet were in their proper place, I almost lost my balance. This frightened me very much, and I felt that it was absolutely necessary to assure myself whether I was dreaming, or the victim of an hallucination. To this end I reached over and took Prof. Seiling's hand, asking him to tell me if I was really seated in the chair. I awaited his answer in a perfect agony of suspense. I felt his hand, just as if it touched my knees; but he said: 'There is nothing there—nothing but your skirts.' This gave me a still greater fright. I pressed my free hand against my breast and felt my heart beating wildly."

Fifteen minutes later her skirts filled out and her lower limbs appeared in full view of the sitters.

Professor Haraldur Neilsson, of the University of Reykjavik, Iceland, states (*Light,* October 25, 1919) that he witnessed the entire disappearance of the left arm of **Indridi Indridason.** It occurred three times. The medium was examined in light and the absence of the arm in the sleeve was also plainly felt. It reappeared half an hour later. Other professors testified to the same phenomenon.

In the *Journal* of the American Society for Psychical Research (March 1925), there is an account by Miss Helen C. Lambert of a sitting in an experimental circle where the medium's forearm shrank in length and finally vanished. The hand appeared to grow out of the elbow. The return to normal was slow and the medium was badly scarred.

Ectoplasm in Scientific Perspective

The foregoing experimental findings appear as incredible to contemporary researchers as they were to the people who originally reported them. They attained some attention in psychical research circles because they often came from reputable observers, whose reports could not be simply dismissed as hallucination or fraud. It seemed reasonable to propose as a working hypothesis that something like the ectoplasmic process occurred during séances. The attempt to investigate that possibility was fraught with difficulties.

In the early investigations, psychical researchers speculated on the nature of such a mysterious and strange substance. French scientist Gustav Geley, for example, highlighted four striking analogies of the ectoplasmic process in the organic realm: the chrysalis, in which the body of the caterpillar is resolved into a creamy mass and reformed into the butterfly; the cold light of insects and microbes; the pseudopods of some protozoa; and certain similarities in the evolution of animal forms and dermoid cysts. In his last book, *Clairvoyance and Materialisation* (1927), he reaches the following conclusions:

"The primary condition of ectoplasmic phenomena is an anatomo-biologic decentralisation in the medium's body and an externalisation of the decentralised factors in an amorphous state, solid, liquid or vaporous. This decentralisation is accompanied by a considerable expenditure of vital energy. The vital energy thus released may take the form of mechanical energy, thus producing telekinesis or raps. It may be transformed into luminous energy, producing living lights in all respects similar to normal animal lights. Sometimes the luminous energy seems to be condensed in some organ either already materialised or in process of materialisation; sometimes it is connected with a phosphorescent secretion which can agglomerate and form actual living lamps; and sometimes it may manifest as discharges or flashes. The same vital energy which is manifested by telekinesis and bioluminescence may ultimate in the organisation of amorphous ectoplasm. It then creates objective but ephemeral beings or parts of beings. Complete materialisations are the final product of the ectoplasmic process."

On the question of whether "telekinetic" ectoplasm is a purely human contribution or if animals might also have a share in it, a séance with the medium "Margery" (Mina Crandon) shed some light. She took a cat with her into the cabinet. As told by **F. Bligh Bond** in *Psychic Research* (1929), ". . . presently we all observed a luminous appearance over the table, like a tall pale flame. This seemed to move slightly and vary in height. Then came Walter's voice, 'Here, someone take this animal out; it's croaking.' The sitter on Margery's left bent over and took up the cat from her lap. It was quite comatose and stiffened. . . ." Walter then explained that he had borrowed the cat's ectoplasm and that was what we had seen as a flame on the table. However, the strong presumption of fraud at some of the Mina Crandon's séances makes it difficult to place any reliance on this single claim of animal ectoplasm.

The evidence for the reality and the nature of telekinetic ectoplasm rests largely on the claims of the generation of psychical researchers at the end of the nineteenth and beginning of the twentieth century who examined the several Spiritualist mediums who claimed to produce the different forms of physical phenomena. This era came to an end as one after another of those mediums were discovered to be engaged in fraudulent mediumship and as more sophisticated forms of detection were developed. For example, even though most physical mediums wanted to operate in the dark, infrared cameras can take pictures as if it were daylight. Even the most capable manipulations can be quickly revealed. **Harry Houdini** was one of those who wrote against mediums faking ectoplasm.

Although many have bemoaned the inability of mediums in more recent decades to reproduce the feats reported by mediums in the decades prior to World War II, it is evident that such manifestations were largely the product of stage magic rather than any paranormal ability. Such manifestations either disappeared under controlled conditions or were uncovered by competent observers. Parapsychologists abandoned the search for telekinetic ectoplasm and have largely abandoned any belief that it exists.

Sources:

Carrington, Hereward. "An Examination and Analysis of the Evidence for 'Dematerialization' as Demonstrated in Mons. Aksakof's Book." *Proceedings* of the American Society for Psychical Research (March 1907).

Crawford, W. J. *The Psychic Structures at the Goligher Circle.* London, 1921.

D'Esperance, Elizabeth. *Shadow Land.* London, 1897.

Geley, Gustav. *Clairvoyance and Materialisation: A Record of Experiments.* London, 1927. Reprint, New York: Arno Press, 1975.

———. *From the Unconscious to the Conscious.* London, 1927.

Gray, Isa. *From Materialisation to Healing.* London: Regency Press, 1973.

Holms, A. Campbell. *The Facts of Psychic Science.* London, 1925. Reprint, New Hyde Park, N.Y.: University Books, 1969.

Houdini, Harry. *A Magician Among the Spirits.* New York: Harper, 1924. Reprinted as *Houdini: A Magician Among the Spirits.* New York: Arno Press, 1972.

Hyslop, J. H. "Replies to Mr. Carrington's Criticism of M. Aksakof." *Proceedings* of the American Society Psychical Research.

Olcott, Henry S. *People from the Other World.* Hartford, Conn.: American Publishing Company, 1875. Reprint, Rutland, Vt.: Charles E. Tuttle, 1972.

Schrenck-Notzing, Baron A. *The Phenomena of Materialisation.* London, 1920. Reprint, New York: Arno Press, 1975.

Eddy, Mary Baker (1821–1910)

Founder of the **Church of Christ, Scientist,** the organizational center of the Christian Science movement. She was born on July

16, 1821, in Bow, New Hampshire. She grew up a member of the Congregational Church. She married George W. Glover in 1843, but he died suddenly the next year, though not before one child was born. In 1853 she married Daniel Patters. For a while the health problems that had plagued her off and on for many years receded, but they eventually returned. While her husband was away during the Civil War she visited a water cure sanitorium. She then heard about mental healer **Phineas Parkhurst Quimby** and eventually went to visit him in Maine.

Learning and applying Quimby's ideas about the mind as the key to health, Eddy found some real relief from her health problems, but she also discovered that soon after leaving his presence her symptoms returned. Then in 1866 she slipped and fell on the ice and for three days was largely immobile. During this period she read the Bible, and the truth about healing, that "God is all," the only reality, came to her. As a result, she was healed immediately.

She spent a period developing her new insight and working with individuals. In 1870 she put her ideas in a booklet, *The Science of Man,* which she used while writing her textbook, *Science and Health,* which appeared in 1875. By 1876 she had trained enough students as practitioners to warrant organizing the Christian Science Association as a fellowship and professional organization. Three years later she founded the Church of Christ, Scientist, and in 1881 she organized the Massachusetts Metaphysical College in Boston. Her work blossomed, and *The Journal of Christian Science* was begun in 1883.

The 1880s were a time of expansion, but also of controversy. Eddy was especially upset with students who taught personal variations on her system or separated from her organization and continued to function as practitioners of either Christian Scientists or under other names. One of her most promising students, **Emma Curtis Hopkins,** left in 1884 and eventually became the founder of what has become known as New Thought. In 1889 Eddy dissolved most of the structures she had founded and in 1892 reorganized her followers under a new church structure headed by herself. The organization was anchored by the First Church of Christ Scientist, the mother church in Boston, of which Eddy was pastor. The mother church chartered local congregations whose leaders had to be members in good standing with the mother church.

In the 1890s a major controversy erupted involving a lawsuit charging that Eddy had simply plagiarized the work of Phineas Quimby. The suit was settled in her favor, but unfortunately Quimby's mostly unpublished papers were not available in court, and Annetta and Julius Dresser, both former Quimby students, and their son Horatio Dresser perpetuated the idea that Eddy would have lost had the material been available.

Eddy's church had spread to every section of United States and Canada by the time of her death on December 3, 1910. She left behind a church manual, published in 1908, to guide the administration of the organization, which is now headed by a self-perpetuating board of directors.

Sources:

Beasley, Norman. *The Cross and the Crown.* Boston: Little, Brown, 1952.

Eddy, Mary Baker. *Church Manual of the First Church of Christ, Scientist, in Boston, Mass.* Boston: Trustees Under the Will of Mary Baker Eddy, 1908.

———. *Poetical Works.* Boston: Trustees Under the Will of Mary Baker Eddy, 1936.

———. *Prose Works.* Boston: Trustees Under the Will of Mary Baker Eddy, 1925.

———. *Science and Health with Key to the Scriptures.* Boston: Trustees Under the Will of Mary Baker Eddy, 1906.

Peel, Robert. *Mary Baker Eddy.* 3 vols. New York: Holt Rinehart and Winston, 1971.

Eddy Brothers, Horatio (1842–1922) and William (1832–1932)

American farmer mediums of Chittenden, a small hamlet near Rutland, Vermont. In 1874 the New York *Daily Graphic* assigned **Henry Olcott** to investigate the rumors of strange happenings in the house of the Eddy family. After ten weeks in the Vermont home, Olcott, who had no previous psychic experience, came away with a dislike of his gruff hosts and a remarkable story, which he told in 15 articles. These articles were later published in book form under the title *People from the Other World* (1875). This book and another, M. D. Shindler's *A Southerner Among the Spirits* (1877), are the primary sources for our knowledge of the Eddy brothers.

According to Olcott, the family tree showed psychic powers for generations back. In 1692, in Salem, their grandmother four times removed was sentenced to the pyre as a witch. In Horatio and William, the psychic "taint" made its appearance in infancy. A fanatical father tried to suppress it with the utmost cruelty. He employed means of torture to break their trances, poured boiling water over them, or placed red-hot coal on their heads. When the children grew older, their father realized the money-making possibilities in their strange gift and hired them out as mediums.

As eloquent evidence of the savage treatment the boys had received at the hands of ignorant investigators, Olcott saw grooves of ligatures, scars of hot sealing wax, and marks of handcuffs on their limbs. The boys exhibited every phenomenon of physical mediumship, from **raps** to **materialization.**

During ten weeks of investigation, Olcott claimed that he saw about 400 apparitions of all sizes, sexes, and races issue from their **cabinet.** The chief apparition was a giant Indian named "Santum" and an Indian woman by the name of "Honto." Olcott had every facility for investigation, measured the height and weight of the apparitions, roamed freely about, and became quite satisfied that the explanation of impersonation was insufficient. He found that the production of materialized forms was William Eddy's strong feature. Horatio Eddy usually sat before a cloth screen, not a cabinet, and, unlike his brother, was always in sight. Musical instruments were played behind the screen, and phantom hands showed themselves over the edge. If the same séance was held in darkness, the phenomena became very powerful. Vigorous Indian dances shook the floor, and the room resounded with yells and whoops. "As an exhibition of pure brute force," Olcott writes in one of the articles, "this Indian dance is probably unsurpassed in the annals of such manifestation."

Frank Podmore, in his book *Modern Spiritualism* (1902), characterizes Olcott's account as an imaginative history and quotes in confirmation C. C. Massey's account of a fortnight stay with the Eddy brothers, which thus describes the nightly apparition of a deceased relative of someone present:

"A dusky young man would look out and we had to say in turn, all round the circle 'Is it for me?' When the right person was reached three taps would be given and the fortunate possessor of the ghost would gaze doubtfully, upon which the ghost would look grieved, and that generally softened the heart of the observer, and brought about a recognition in the remark 'Lor, so you be.' And that sort of thing went on night after night at the Eddy's."

Because of Olcott's later adventures in **Theosophy,** some credence is lent to the charge that he was gullible.

Sources:

Olcott, Henry S. *People from the Other World.* Hartford, Conn.: American Publishing, 1875. Reprint, Rutland, Vt.: Charles E. Tuttle, 1972.

Podmore, Frank. *Modern Spiritualism.* London: Methuen, 1902. Reprinted as *Mediums of the Nineteenth Century.* New Hyde Park, N.Y.: University Books, 1963.

Shindler, M. D. *A Southerner Among the Spirits.* Memphis, Tenn., 1877.

Eden, Jerome (1925-)

Writer on **UFO** phenomena who claims to have observed UFOs on several occasions and has interpreted them in light of the **orgone** energy theories of **Wilhelm Reich.** Eden was born August 23, 1925, in New York City. He studied at New York University (B.A.) and Columbia University (M.A.). He served in World War II and the Korean War, later becoming managing editor of the *American Water Works Association Journal,* the city and military editor of the *Idaho Falls Post Register,* and the director of the Eastern Idaho Special Services Agency. He also edited and published the *Eden Bulletin.*

In 1971 he claimed he suffered severe conjunctivitis and high fever following observation of a beam of light from a UFO. His 25-year study of UFOs led him to believe that they are responsible for drought conditions on Earth. His conclusions are in line with those of the later work of Wilhelm Reich in the field of weather changing (**cloud busting**) and **flying saucers.** Eden himself was registered with Idaho's Department of Agriculture as a weather modification operator. He has experimented with a cloud-busting apparatus similar to one described by Wilhelm Reich.

He founded the PPCC (Planetary Professional Citizens Committee), which is concerned with the problem of UFOs in relation to the development of global deserts, and publishes the quarterly *PPCC Bulletin* (which superseded the *Eden Bulletin*). Address: P.O. Box 34, Careywood, ID 83309.

Sources:

Eden, Jerome. *Animal Magnetism and the Life Energy.* Hicksville, N.Y.: Exposition Press, 1974.

———. *The Desert Makers: A Study of the Creation of Deserts in Man, His Atmosphere and Planet.* N.p.: PPCC, 1981.

———. *Do Not Disturb: The Emotional Plague in Education.* Valdez, Ala.: Eden Press, 1959.

———. *Orgone Energy—The Answer to Atomic Suicide.* N.p., 1972.

———. *Planet in Trouble—The UFO Assault on Earth.* Hicksville, N.Y.: Exposition Press, 1973.

———. *Suffer the Children.* New York, 1959.

———. *View From Eden—Talks to Students of Orgonomy.* N.p., 1976.

Mesmer, F. A. *Memoir of F. A. Mesmer, Doctor of Medicine, On His Discoveries, 1799.* Translated by Jerome Eden. Mount Vernon, N.Y.: Eden Press, 1957.

Edinburgh College of Parapsychology

Originally founded under the name Edinburgh Psychic College and Library by Ethel Miller in 1932 at 30 Heriot Row, Edinburgh, Scotland. The college was affiliated with the **British College of Psychic Science,** London, and organized along similar lines. It became the representative psychic organization in Scotland.

Following the death of her husband, Miller received evidence of **survival** through such well-known mediums as Annie Johnson, **Hester Dowden,** and **Estelle Roberts** and decided to make such psychic assistance and knowledge available to other seekers. She placed special importance on providing a good library for study and a quiet, sympathetic, and friendly atmosphere. She was especially solicitous of the welfare and procedures of mediums and insisted that they should not be overworked or be given the names of sitters or other information concerning them. The Edinburgh College outlived the British College of Psychic Science and became widely known as a leading center of psychical studies. Many well-known mediums, including **Geraldine Cummins,** Lilian Bailey, Helen Hughes, and **Helen Duncan,** visited the college.

In 1973 the Heriot Row address was sold, and the college moved to its present address under the new name Edinburgh College of Parapsychology. Its current aims are summarized as "the study of psychic or parapsychological phenomena and their implications, and the development of psychic or parapsychological powers in its members." Address: 2 Melville St., Edinburgh, EH3 7NS, Scotland.

Edinburgh Psychic College and Library See Edinburgh College of Parapsychology

Edmonds, John Worth (1799–1874)

One of the most influential early American Spiritualists. Edmonds was born March 13, 1799, at Hudson, New York, and educated at local public schools. In 1814 he entered Williams College, Williamstown, Massachusetts, moving a year later to Union College, Schenectady, New York, where he graduated in 1816. He went on to read law at Cooperstown, New York. After a great public career in the course of which he was a member of both branches of the state legislature of New York, president of the senate, and judge of the supreme court of New York, he resigned the latter position on account of the outcry raised against him because of his beliefs in **Spiritualism.**

His interest in the phenomena called the **Rochester rappings** was aroused in January 1851; the first account of his experiences was published on August 1, 1853, in the *New York Courier* in an article entitled "To the Public." To meet the continual attacks of the press against Spiritualism, he confessed his complete conversion to this belief and told the story of his investigation. This bold step produced a great sensation. His subsequent copious writings aroused a furious controversy.

In a letter published in the *New York Herald* on August 6, 1853, he writes:

"I went into the investigation originally thinking it a deception, and intending to make public my exposure of it. Having from my researches come to a different conclusion, I feel that the obligation to make known the result is just as strong. Therefore it is, mainly, that I give the result to the world. I say mainly because there is another consideration which influences me, and that is, the desire to extend to others a knowledge which I am conscious cannot but make them happier and better."

He witnessed both physical and mental phenomena, kept a careful record running to 1,600 pages, struggled against conviction, and resorted to every expedient he could devise to detect fraud and to guard against delusion. He told the story of his experiences and conversion again and again in his *Appeal to the Public* (published in answer to the abuse heaped upon him) and in his series of letters on Spiritualism, published in the *New York Tribune.*

Later his experiences became more direct. He himself developed the gift of mediumship. Between 1853 and 1854, in a small circle formed with a few chosen friends, he received many spirit communications. The chief communicators were alleged to be **Emanuel Swedenborg** and Francis Bacon. Their messages were published in the two-volume *Spiritualism* (1852–53), by Edmonds and George T. Dexter, which had an enormous sale.

Laura, the daughter of Edmonds, also became a medium. She developed great musical powers and the gift of tongues. Although she knew only English and a smattering of French, she spoke in nine or ten different languages in trance with the fluency of a native. Spanish, French, Greek, Italian, Portuguese, Latin, Hungarian, and Indian dialects were identified.

These phenomena and many others were carefully recorded by Edmonds. The account of his experiences with raps, as given in the *New York Tribune,* March 1859, is especially illustrative:

"And finally after weeks of such trials, as if to dispel all idea in my mind as to its being done by others, or by machinery, the rappings came to me alone, when I was in bed, when no mortal but myself was in the room. I first heard them on the floor, as I lay, reading. I said 'It's a mouse.' They instantly changed their location from one part of the room to another, with a rapidity that no mouse could equal. 'Still, it might be more than one mouse.' And then they came upon my person—distinct, clear, unequivocal. I explained it to myself by calling it a twitching of the nerves, which at times I had experienced, and so I tried to see if it was so. It was on my thigh that they came. I sat up in bed, threw off all clothing from the limb, leaving it entirely bare. I held my lighted lamp in one hand near my leg and sat and looked at it. I tried various experiments. I laid my left hand flat on the spot—the raps would be then on my hand and cease on my leg. I laid my hand edgewise on the limb and the force, whatever it was, would pass across my hand and reach the leg, making itself as perceptible on each finger as on the leg. I held my hand two or three inches from my thigh and found that they instantly stopped and resumed their work as soon as I withdrew my hand. But, I said to myself, this is some local affection which the magnetism of my hand can reach. Immediately they ran riot all over my limbs, touching me with a distinctness and rapidity that was marvelous, running up and down both limbs from the thighs to the end of the toes.''

Edmonds never wavered in his belief in later years. His reputation and fearless championship of the cause for a period of more than two decades was an important factor in the growth and spread of American Spiritualism. In addition to his legal work, *Report of Select Law Cases* (1868), he also published *Letters and Tracts on Spiritualism* (1874). He died April 5, 1874, in New York City.

Edmunds, Simeon (1917–)

British hypnotist and writer on psychical research. Edmunds was research secretary of the **College of Psychic Science,** London, 1956–62, and contributed articles to *Light,* the journal of the **Society for Psychical Research.** He became associate editor of *Tomorrow* magazine in 1962. He also wrote several books.

Sources:

Edmunds, Simeon. *Hypnosis: Key to Psychic Powers.* London: Aquarian Press, 1968.

———. *Hypnotism and the Supernormal.* Hollywood, Calif.: Wilshire Book Co., 1968.

———. *The Psychic Power of Hypnosis.* New York: Samuel Weiser, 1968.

———. *Spiritualism: A Critical Survey.* London: Aquarian Press, 1966.

Edwards, Frank (Allyn) (1908–1967)

Journalist, broadcaster, and author who publicized anomalous mysteries, bizarre events, and **flying saucers** (**UFOs**). Born August 4, 1908, in Mattoon, Illinois, Edwards became a golf professional and then a technical adviser in a shipyard before beginning a radio career with KDKA in Pittsburgh, Pennsylvania, in 1924. Starting in 1925 he worked for WHAS and WLAP in Louisville, Kentucky. He was a news analyst for the Mutual Broadcasting System from 1942 to 1952. Between 1949 and 1954 he was a White House correspondent. From 1955 to 1959 and from 1961 to 1962 he was a commentator for WTTV in Indianapolis; from 1964, for WXLW; and from 1965, for WLWI-TV. He subsequently lectured at Butler University on broadcast journalism.

In the *Radio Daily* poll of 1953, he was cited, along with Edward R. Murrow and Lowell Thomas, as one of the nation's top broadcasters. His ''Strange to Relate'' column was widely syndicated throughout the world, and he was a contributing editor to *Fate* magazine for a decade beginning in 1957. He was also a member of the Board of Governors of NICAP (**National Investigations Committee on Aerial Phenomena**) from 1957 until his death on June 23, 1967.

Edwards is most remembered for the many popular books in which he compiled brief accounts of extraordinary and paranormal events. Beginning with *Strange World* in 1954, he produced a series of popular books featuring short summaries of numerous anomalous occurrences, a format that served him well for the next decade. In the mid-1960s he wrote two popular books on flying saucers that rode the wave of public interest but were considered disasters by the UFO community for their numerous factual errors.

Sources:

Clark, Jerome. *The Emergence of a Phenomenon: UFOs from the Beginning through 1959.* Vol. 2 of *The UFO Encyclopedia.* Detroit: Omnigraphics, 1992.

Edwards, Frank. *Flying Saucers Here and Now.* New York: Lyle Stuart, 1967.

———. *Flying Saucers—Serious Business.* New York: Lyle Stuart, 1966.

———. *My First Ten Million Sponsors.* New York: Ballantine Books, 1956.

———. *Strange World.* New York: Lyle Stuart, 1964.

———. *Stranger Than Science.* New York: Lyle Stuart, 1959.

———. *Strangest of All.* Secaucus, N.J.: Citadel Press, 1958.

Edwards, Harry (1893–1976)

British spiritual healer (born Henry James Edwards on May 29, 1893) who also did much to publicize the subject of spiritual healing. He treated patients directly at his Healing Sanctuary in Britain or on the platform at public meetings, and also by ''absent healing'' through correspondence.

Edwards was born on May 29, 1893, in Islington, London, and grew up in various sections of the metropolitan area. At the age of 14 he was apprenticed to a printer and his seven years of service were up just in time for him to join the army in 1914. He was sent to India the following year and for a time worked in a construction project in Persia (Iran). While there he had his first experiences as a healer, as he was the one in charge of handing all of the minor work-related injuries. However, even the few medicines he had available led to his gaining a local reputation as a healer of note.

He returned to England in 1921 and established himself as a printer and was actively involved in local politics. In 1936, in the wake of the untimely death of a nephew, he visited a Spiritualist meeting. Years ago he had on one occasion attended such a gathering, but it had made little impression. This time, however, he was intrigued and began to attend a development class from which he emerged as a **medium.**

He and his wife soon formed a home circle they called the Fellowship of Spiritual Service. Told by a medium that he was to become a healer, he followed instructions to concentrate upon the recovery of the next account of a sick person described to him. It happened to be of a person with tuberculosis who experienced a recovery after Edwards' intervention. Edwards was just becoming known as a healer when World War II began. He joined the Home Guard. His home was destroyed during the bombing of London, and Edwards relocated to Surrey, eventually giving up his printing business and purchasing a large house, Burrows Lea, which became the sight of his Spiritual Healing Sanctuary.

Edwards operated as a Spiritualist healer, and believed that the late Louis Pastuer and Lord Lister worked through him from the spirit world. He was in great demand for the rest of his life and frequently gave lectures and led healing services throughout Great Britain.

He received some two thousand letters daily, many from patients in distant countries. His records indicated close to a 80 percent recovery rate dealing with such diseases as cancer, tuberculosis, arthritis and epilepsy, although, only a minority of these cases were documented to the level required to verify the healing claimed.

Edwards worked closely with physicians. He believed that spiritual healing power passed through him with the assistance of discarnate spirit helpers, and also claimed to have traveled outside his body to visit distant patients. He authored a number of books and published a monthly magazine *The Spiritual Healer* from his home.

Edwards died December 7, 1976, but his healing work has been continued at his Burrows Lea sanctuary by Joan and Ray Branch, whom he designated as his successors. The Branches have stated that they feel Edwards is still with them in their work of healing. The journal *The Spiritual Healer* continues publication from the Healer Publishing Company, Ltd., Burrows Lea, Shere, Guildford, Surrey G5 9QG.

Sources:

Branch, Ramus. *Harry Edwards: The Life Story of the Great Healer.* Burrows Lea, Guildford, Surrey, UK: Healer Publishing, 1982.

Edwards, Harry. *The Evidence for Spirit Healing.* London: Spiritualist Press, 1952.

———. *The Healing Intelligence.* New York: Taplinger, 1971.

———. *The Science of Spirit Healing.* London: Rider and Co., 1945.

———. *Spirit Healing.* London: Herbert Jenkins, 1960.

———. *Thirty Years a Spiritual Healer.* London: Herbert Jenkins, 1968.

———. *The Truth about Spiritual Healing.* London: Spiritualist Press, 1956.

Miller, Paul. *Born to Heal.* London: Spiritualist Press, 1948.

Eel

The eel, popularly known for the electrical properties of some species, has been credited with many marvelous virtues. If left to die out of the water, its body steeped in strong vinegar and the blood of a vulture, and the whole placed under a dunghill, the composition is said to be able to raise from the dead anything brought to it and give it life as before. It has also been said that anyone who eats the still-warm heart of an eel will be seized with the spirit of prophecy and will predict things to come.

Eels figure in the folklore of many countries. The Egyptians worshiped the eel, which their priests alone had the right to eat. In Polynesian, Melanesian, and Indonesian stories, men are sometimes transformed into eels. In the Philippines, eels were believed to be the souls of the dead. In New Zealand, an eel head was eaten to cure toothache. In other countries, eel skins were laid on wounds to heal them. In the United States, there was a folk tradition that eels eat human flesh, and some fishermen were reputed to have caught large quantities of eels with human bait.

In the eighteenth century, magic eels were made of flour and the juice of mutton. There is an anecdote told by William of Malmesbury about a dean of the church of Elgin, in the county of Moray in Scotland, who, having refused to cede his church to some pious monks, was changed, with all his canons, into eels, which the brother cook made into a stew.

Egg, Orphean

The cosmic doctrine of the legendary Greek hero Orpheus, who claimed that "God, the uncreated and incomprehensible Being, created all things; the ether proceeded from him; from this the unshapely chaos and the dark night arose, which at first covered all things. The unshapen mass was formed into the shape of an egg, from which all things have proceeded."

According to this belief, the whole universe has the form of an egg, and everything in it strives to attain the same form. The Orphean concept of a universal soul permeating all nature has something in common with the doctrines of **animal magnetism** and other pantheistic beliefs.

Eglamour of Artoys, Sir

An English magic legend of medieval French origin. The story tells of the winning of Christabell by Eglamour. Christabell's father agrees to their union if Eglamour will fulfill three tasks. He must conquer the giant Sir Maroke, bring from a distant land the head of an enormous boar, and kill a powerful **dragon** that has been devastating the country around Rome. In these adventures he is successful, but is kept in Rome by illness. In the meantime, Christabell has given birth to a son and is banished by her angry father. Her son is stolen from her by a griffin and taken to Israel, where he is adopted by the king and named Degrabell.

Many years afterward, Eglamour and Degrabell meet in a tournament for the hand of Christabell. Eglamour is successful, and eventually their identities are revealed. Eglamour and Christabell are married and return to their native country with their son.

Versions of this legend survived in the English ballad of Sir Lionel (Child No. 18) and in modern times in the American ballad "Old Bangham." It has been suggested that the conquest of the giant boar has an ancient origin in the Hindu myth of Lord Vishnu in the form of the gigantic boar Vahara, who created the mighty Himalayan mountain range in his battle with a demon.

Eglinton, William (1858–1933)

Famous British medium who convinced statesman W. E. Gladstone of the reality of psychic phenomena. Eglinton was born in Islington, London, July 10, 1858, and showed no sign of psychic power in his boyhood. He first heard of **Spiritualism** in February 1874 at a debate in the Hall of Science, London, between a Dr. Sexton and a Mr. Foote.

Moved by curiosity, Eglinton's father formed a home circle. For seven or eight evenings there were no manifestations, and William expressed his feelings by placing upon the door of the séance room large cards with the sarcastic inscription, "There are lunatics confined here; they will be shortly let loose; highly dangerous!" His father was highly offended and told him to either join the circle or leave the house during the investigation. He elected to join the circle and sat down at the table "determined that if anything happened I would put a stop to it. Something did happen, but I was powerless to prevent it." The table became animated and answered questions intelligently.

The evening following the séance, William himself passed into trance for the first time, and in a few months' time very strong phenomena developed under the guidance of a spirit calling himself "Joey Sandy." Eighteen months later another guide, "Ernest," appeared, and very good materializations were obtained in moonlight.

The news of Eglinton's powers soon spread. He was besieged with so many requests for séances that he gave up his job in a printing firm and became a professional medium. The earliest record of his séances was published in *The Medium* for September 1875. At the end of the year, several séances were given to the Dalston Association of Spiritualists, which later elected him an honorary member.

Many eminent men of the day attended his later sittings at the Brixton Psychological Society and at the British National Association of Spiritualists at 38 Great Russell Street, Bloomsbury, London. These were the so-called Blackburn séances, three series of 12 sittings each, Eglinton being one of the first mediums engaged. They were made possible by the generosity of Charles Blackburn of Manchester and represented the beginnings of organized psychical research.

The sittings were mostly held in light, which greatly impressed the early observers of his work. It was also noted that from the time he turned professional until 1883 he never gave a séance in his own rooms and complied with all conditions of control, his hands restricted by his sleeves being sewn to his knees or behind his back to his coat.

His first levitation is described by Archdeacon **Thomas Colley** in *The Spiritualist,* June 2, 1876:

"The medium was next entranced and carried by invisible power over the table several times, the heels of his boots being made to touch the head of our medical friend [Dr. Malcolm]. Then he was taken to the further end of the dining room, and finally, after being tilted about as a thing of no weight whatever, was deposited quietly in his chair."

The general impression created by his power is conveyed in the *Western Morning News* of July 28, 1876: "If Mr. Eglinton is a conjurer he is undoubtedly one of the cleverest who ever lived. Maskelyne and Cook are not a patch upon Mr. Eglinton. The Egyptian Hall exposure of Spiritualism is mere child's play compared with what we witnessed." The *Daily Telegraph* reported on October 10, 1876, that the Scientific Research Committee of the **British National Association of Spiritualists** had obtained direct spirit writing under absolute test conditions through the membership of Eglinton.

Marvels of Materialization

Among the many remarkable séances for **materialization** he gave at this time, the most surprising results were obtained during his stay at Malvern as the guest of a Dr. and Mrs. Nichols. In a written account of the séances Nichols observes:

"All our séances are held under test conditions. They are held in a small upper room in my own house, with its one door locked, and its one window, thirty feet from the ground, fastened. The number of persons present never exceeds six, all of whom I know intimately. I know pretty accurately what can be done by sleight-of-hand, ventriloquism, palmistry or otherwise."

He sums up his experiences thus:

"Four times I have seen a white-robed form standing by Willie Eglinton. I have seen "Joey" make yards of muslin. I have seen him standing beside his medium, and I have heard him speak in a brilliantly-lighted room, when Mr. Eglinton was with us and no more entranced than the rest of us. I have seen hands and arms and the face only, and I have seen full forms appear and disappear. I have seen a tall man appear and after many minutes with us, and in good light, I have seen him gradually sink down and become invisible, all but a few inches of form, and then that seemed to snap out. I have seen a full form dissolve and leave the drapery suspended as if held up by a hand; and I have seen the form shrink away to nothing visible and leave the garments lying about the floor. These not long after disappeared."

Nichols's descriptions of Eglinton's open-air materializations in his garden, related in the appendix to **Epes Sargent**'s *The Scientific Basis of Spiritualism* (1881), are among the most extraordinary accounts in the history of Spiritualism. In one he relates that,

"Mr. Eglinton lay on a garden bench in plain sight. We saw the bodies of four visitors form themselves from a cloud of white vapour and then walk about, robed all in purest white, upon the lawn where no deception was possible. One of them walked quite around us, as we sat in our chairs on the grass, talking as familiarly as any friend . . . [and] took my hat from my head, put it on his own, and walked off with it where the medium was lying; then he came and put it on my head again; then walked across the lawn and up a gravel walk to the foot of the balcony and talked with Mrs. Nichols. After a brief conversation he returned to the medium and gradually faded from sight."

According to this narrative, the medium was constantly in sight, no confederate could have come over the wall without being seen or heard, and the maximum distance of the materialized spirit from the medium was 66 feet in the direct line, whereas altogether about 400 feet were covered by the spirit from the time he first left the medium to his final return.

The accounts published in the Spiritualist periodicals of the time also describe Eglinton's one-armed control "Abdullah" who on occasion was reported to have materialized. He was adorned with amazingly rich jewels, which he allowed to be examined. He was bedecked with precious stones, rings, crosses, and clusters of rubies that were worth a fortune. A description by John S. Farmer, Eglinton's biographer, of a materialization séance so much agrees with observations of the flow of **ectoplasm** that it created a strong presumption for Eglinton's genuine psychic powers in many researchers' minds:

"All this time the breathing of the psychic had been increasingly laboured and deep, accompanied at times with groans. Now standing, in full view . . . I saw him, by a quick movement of the fingers, gently draw, apparently from under his morning-coat, the top button of which was fastened, a dingy, white-looking substance. . . . The movement of the fingers was such as to draw it at right angles from him, allowing it to fall and hand by its own weight down his left side. As it emerged from under his coat and fell, it gradually increased in volume until it reached the ground, covering Mr. Eglinton's left leg from the knee downwards, the connecting link between this portion and his side being preserved the whole time. The mass of white material on the ground increased in breadth, and now commenced to pulsate and move up and down, also swaying from side to side, the motor power being underneath the mass of material, and concealed from sight by it. . . . The height increased to three feet, and shortly afterwards, the 'form' quickly and quietly grew to its full stature, carrying the above-mentioned dingy white material with it. . . .

"All this time the link (of the same white appearance as already described) was maintained between the growing 'form' and Mr. Eglinton, who had remained in sight of all of us during the whole operation. The connecting link was either now completely severed, or became so attenuated as to be invisible, and the 'form' [a bearded man of middle age] . . . advanced to Mr. Everitt, shook hands with him, and passed round the circle, treating nearly every one in the same manner . . . then re-approached Mr. Eglinton, who was now partially supported from falling by Mr. Rogers, and, taking the psychic firmly by the shoulders, dragged him into the cabinet."

There is a strange contrast between the foregoing testimonies and Elington's subsequent exposure by Archdeacon Thomas Colley. During a séance in Owen Harris's house, Colley cut a piece of the robe and a piece of the beard of the materialized figure. The pieces fitted to perfection the muslin and beard that he found in the medium's portmanteau. The story of this exposure was published in the *Journal* of the Society for Psychical Research (SPR). Eglinton was in South Africa when the revelation was made public and denied the charge on his return. The Council of the British National Association of Spiritualists ordered an investigation, which, at the end, dismissed the charge on the basis that no direct evidence could be obtained from the accusers. Colley's exposure presaged events yet to come, but before Eglinton's fraudulent ways were decisively known, he presented some dramatic performances.

The most extraordinary phenomenon Eglinton produced was his own **teleportation** on March 16, 1878, at Mrs. Makdougall Gregory's house, through the ceiling into the room above, an account of which was published in *The Spiritualist* of March 22, 1878. He followed this with a year of travel. On July 5, 1878, on the invitation of a Dr. Hutchinson, Eglinton left for Cape Town, South Africa. He spent nine months with his host, giving many séances, of which copious notes were made. He studied dentistry in his leisure time and was enrolled in 1879 in England as a duly qualified practitioner.

After his return to England in May 1879, Eglinton produced some interesting results while the guest of Colonel and Mrs. Francis Lean (**Florence Marryat**) at Bruges, Belgium, in a haunted house, the ghost of which he finally laid to rest.

Shortly after this he received an invitation to visit Sweden. He gave 19 séances in Stockholm, which were attended by many scientific and literary men. Professors Tornebom and Edland, both of them skeptical previously, published a favorable report on his mediumship in the *Aftonblad* of October 30, 1879. He also gave sittings at Upsala University and then left for Denmark, Germany, and Bohemia. In Munich he was the guest of Gabriel Max, the eminent painter, and furnished the inspiration for his impressive painting *Geistesgrüss*.

After his return he gave striking séances at Cambridge University under the auspices of the Psychological Society, during which he was handcuffed to one person and held by another. It was in this month that **Florence Cook** was exposed by Sir George Sitwell and Carl von Buch. The atmosphere was decidedly hostile, and in March 1880 Eglinton again left for the Continent. He was engaged in Leipzig by Baron von Hoffman to give séances to **Johann C. F. Zöllner** and others connected with the University of Leipzig.

Zöllner was very satisfied with the result of his 25 sittings and intended to publish a book on his experiences, but death intervened. In Vienna Eglinton gave more than 30 séances to **Baron Hellenbach.**

After traveling again to Munich to carry out an engagement for 12 séances, the 11th of which was marred by some evidence of fraud, Eglinton returned to England. He gave no more professional séances that year, but the Spiritualist press was kept informed by Nichols of the many experiments in **direct writing** and drawing that were conducted in his house. In February 1881 Eglinton sailed for New York and remained in the United States until the middle of May.

Miracles in India—and a Disaster

In October 1881, following an invitation from J. G. Meugens, a wealthy Indian merchant, Eglinton left for Calcutta. He was apparently very successful in his Indian séances, some of which were held at the residence of the Maharajah Sir Jotendro Johun Tagore and reported in the daily *Indian Mirror,* but it is noteworthy that with the increase in distance from London there was a proportionate increase in the marvels.

The spirit "postmastership" that Eglinton "established" between London and Calcutta was almost unprecedented in the annals of Spiritualism. According to the narrative of a Mr. Meugens, privately marked sheets of paper were whisked by the spirits to London and returned shortly after to Calcutta with the handwriting of a close friend describing how his room had been suddenly filled with light and how the spirit "Ernest" stood by and waited for the letter to carry it back. It was claimed that this happened on several occasions. Indeed, once Meugens asked that the ring of a Mrs. Fletcher, who was then in Tothill Fields Prison (in Meugens's belief unjustly convicted), be brought to him. The spirits complied. The ring could not be identified, but a few days later the spirits brought a letter in Fletcher's own handwriting telling Meugens that she had sent the ring.

Such accounts of Eglinton's phenomena were so eagerly received that for the period of his stay in Calcutta a new fortnightly journal, similar to the *Light,* was started to meet the demand. The venture was said to have met with considerable success. Throughout Eglinton's visit to Calcutta, Harry Kellar, the famous conjurer, was also there, giving stage exposures of fraudulent Spiritualism. He issued a challenge to Eglinton in the *Indian Daily News* for January 13, 1882, and promised an unbiased opinion as to the natural explanations of the phenomena.

An invitation was duly extended. Afterward Kellar publicly stated, "I went as a skeptic, but I must own that I came away utterly unable to explain, by any natural means, the phenomena that I witnessed on Tuesday evening." He held the medium's left hand and was half levitated with Eglinton. He had no doubt that this phenomenon was genuine and reiterated this conviction in print many years later. But he wavered on endorsing independent **slate writing,** of which he also obtained a convincing demonstration.

After Meugens left India, Eglinton went to Howran, across the Hooghly River from Calcutta, as the guest of a Colonel and Mrs. Gordon and remained with them for the rest of his stay. He converted Lord William Beresford to Spiritualism and left for England in April 1882.

Eglinton sailed for England on the SS *Vega.* He claimed that during the voyage he was visited by **Koot Hoomi** (or Kut Humi). He described this meeting in a letter that was mysteriously transported from the open seas to Bombay and fell into the center of a room where **Helena Petrovna Blavatsky,** cofounder of the **Theosophical Society,** held company. The letter was addressed to Mrs. Gordon in Calcutta. Blavatsky wrote some notes on visiting cards and wrapped them up with the letter, which was then transported by the same mysterious agency to Calcutta and dropped from the ceiling in the company of Olcott and the Gordons. It was later claimed that the **Mahatma letters** were written by Blavatsky, and it appears likely that Eglinton was in concert with her and left a letter, identical to the one written on the ship, with her, and that she made careful arrangements for its mysterious appearance at the appropriate moment. There is indirect proof of this supposition in the fact that J. E. O'Conor, a Theosophist on board ship, unexpectedly asked Eglinton to enclose, as an additional test, a letter from himself to Blavatsky. Eglinton undertook the task. Blavatsky, however, at the time of the alleged delivery of Eglinton's letter, made no communication of O'Conor's note. In excuse she said that O'Conor's letter was private and she did not know whether he wished it to be made public. In further explanation she added that for some unaccountable reason, O'Conor's letter arrived an hour after the one from Eglinton was received.

Eglinton denied that he had met Blavatsky in India at all, but it appears to be a fact that he took many letters of introduction to her and to her colleague, **Henry S. Olcott,** then president of the society, and that he met Blavatsky in Calcutta. In light of this and considering that the evidence of the manufacture of the Koot Hoomi letters by Blavatsky appears to be strong, the grossness of the **fraud** seemed clear. He was also accused, in the *Proceedings* of the SPR (vol. 3, p. 254), of conspiring with Blavatsky.

This highly damaging incident was hardly touched upon in John Farmer's biography. He contented himself "with putting on record the maturer conclusions of Mr. Eglinton with regard to the 'appearance' on board the Vega. He now believes the apparition to have been a spontaneous materialization, of a somewhat unusual order, of someone who called himself 'Koot Hoomi.' "

After his return from India, Eglinton attempted to retire from professional mediumship by entering into partnership with a gentleman in a publishing firm, operating under the name Ross Publishing Company. In August 1883, however, he severed his connection and fell back again on mediumship as a means of living.

The Great Slate-Writing Problem

From 1884 on Eglinton concentrated on slate writing, which he suggested was simply a far easier means of bringing conviction than materializations (and also offered less chance of detection in fraudulent activity). According to biographer Farmer, he sat almost daily for this phenomenon for upward of three years before he obtained any results at all. His slate-writing séances were impressive, as he subjected himself to every test condition posed to him and, in contrast to **Henry Slade,** remained passive and quiet throughout the performance. As a result of some very successful sittings, W. P. Adshed of Belper, in northern England, offered a challenge of £500 to anyone who was not a medium and could produce the same results under the same conditions.

On October 29, 1884, British Prime Minister W. E. Gladstone had a séance with Eglinton. He obtained answers to his questions, which were privately written on the hostess's own slates, both when the slates were held under the table and when they were laid upon the table in full view of all present, as well as when the slates were locked. Some of the questions were put in Spanish, French, and Greek and answered in the same language. Gladstone was so impressed that soon after he joined the **Society for Psychical Research** (SPR).

On two occasions in 1884 Eglinton gave public performances from the stage at a meeting of the **London Spiritualist Alliance** and at a lecture of his own in St. James's Hall, London. Both séances were eminently successful.

In 1885 Eglinton left again for the Continent. In Paris he made the acquaintance of **J. Tissot,** the celebrated French genre painter, and in a materialization séance on May 20 completely convinced him of spirit return. Tissot's mezzotint *Apparition Medianimique,* later hung at the offices of the London Spiritualist Alliance, was an idealized conception of his experience.

During Eglinton's stay in Paris, **Charles Richet** had some sittings with him. He obtained what was for him further verification of Eglinton's powers on a subsequent visit to London in company with a Dr. Myers, brother of **F. W. H. Myers.**

Richet nevertheless did not attribute much importance to his slate-writing experiences, as revealed in his book *Thirty Years of Psychical Research* (1923):

"I drew a design on the slate so that Eglinton could not see the drawing. The slate was reversed and a small piece of chalk placed on it. I took the slate in my hand and without letting it go, held it under the table, Eglinton holding the other end of the slate. After two or three minutes a curious facsimile of my sketch was reproduced, but I think that a skillful illusionist could have done as much."

Yet Richet admitted, in the same book, that "Eglinton was a very powerful medium, and though he has been suspected of fraud, he was able, finally, to prove that the allegations of his enemies were calumnies."

Alfred Russel Wallace was convinced of the genuineness of Eglinton's materializations. He had seen his phantom "Abdullah" in a private house while Eglinton was also visible, sitting in evening dress in an armchair. A careful search was made, but no paraphernalia were discovered.

From Paris Eglinton left for Vienna, where he met **Baron du Prel,** who published some of his experiences under the title *A Problem for Conjurers,* in which he concludes: "Through Eglinton I have received the proof that [Johann] Zöllner, who was the first in Germany to have courage to speak of these slate writings, discovered a grand truth and that all his opponents who have neither read nor seen anything in this domain are in the wrong."

In 1886 a bitter fight over slate writing was waged between the SPR and Spiritualists in general. **S. T. Davey,** an associate of the SPR and also an amateur conjurer, was most impressed by Eglinton's performances, but soon became suspicious. He studied the subject from the point of view of conjuring and, placing himself in the hands of the SPR, came out, with **Richard Hodgson** as manager, under an assumed name as a medium. Owing to the ensuing sensation caused by Davey's performances, **Eleanor Sidgwick,** writing in the *Journal* of the SPR, claimed "no hesitation in attributing the performances of Eglinton to clever conjuring."

In Davey's account of his actions, which was published in the SPR's *Proceedings,* he told the story of about 20 sittings in which he rivaled the feats of professional slate writers. He produced messages on the sitters' own slates and in screwed, sealed, and locked double slates; wrote them in colors; answered questions in various languages; performed successful reading tests; produced written numbers on mental request; made a tumbler walk across the table in strong gaslight; floated music boxes; and produced materialized figures in a séance room.

Davey's explanation of his slate-writing feats was that he either substituted prepared slates with a message already written or wrote the message himself noiselessly under the table by means of a fragment of pencil fixed in a thimble that he slipped on his finger. For many of his phenomena, however, he failed to furnish a satisfactory explanation. Spiritualists took this as a confirmation of their belief that Davey himself was a renegade medium.

Alfred Russel Wallace, who responded to Davey in the 1891 issue of the *Journal* of the SPR, writes, "Unless all can be so explained, many of us will be confirmed in our belief that Mr. Davey was really a medium as well as a conjurer, and that in imputing all his performances to trick he was deceiving the society and the public."

In the same volume of the *Proceedings* in which the Davey report was published, Carvill Lewis reported that, by purposely turning his head away and pretending to divert his attention, he heard Eglinton write on a slate and occasionally saw the movements of the tendons of the wrist in the act of writing. The SPR also requested "Professor Hoffmann" (well-known conjurer Angelo J. Lewis) to report in his professional capacity on Eglinton's performances. He conducted 12 sittings and studied the reports furnished by others, concluding that, although many of the circumstances suggested occasional trickery,

". . . on the other hand, I do not believe the cleverest conjurer could, under the same conditions, use trickery in the wholesale way necessary to produce all these phenomena without exposing himself to constant risk of detection. If conjuring were the only explanation of the slate-writing phenomena, I should certainly have expected that their secret would long since have become public property."

As a result of the bitter controversy that arose over the accusations of the SPR, many Spiritualists resigned their membership. Eglinton invited testimonies from his sitters. They came forth in abundance. Eglinton had given nearly 3,500 sittings up to this period, and only three claims of fraud were made against him. Then assistant secretary to the SPR, Edward T. Bennett, in his *Physical Phenomena of Spiritualism* (1906), states: "What I may call the Eglinton problem was, at least so it seems to me, left not only in an incomplete, but in an unsatisfactory state after the death of Mr. S. T. Davey."

In 1887 Eglinton visited Russia and gave a séance for Emperor Alexander III. Spiritualist leader **Alexander Aksakof** had opportunities for repeated experiments, and he also maintained that Eglinton possessed great and genuine psychic powers. After returning from Russia, Eglinton married and started a new career. He abandoned mediumship and Spiritualism for journalism. He became editor of well-known publications such as *The New Age* and *The Tatler.* In 1890 he traveled in South Africa and indulged a passion for game shooting, acquiring a large private collection of trophies. In 1895 he was vice-chairman of the Anglo-African Writers Club, and he was chairman in 1896. He founded the *British and South African Export Gazette,* which he also edited, and was proprietor of the *British Export Gazette.* As a notable journalist his former association with mediumship was never referred to, and he achieved the distinction of entry in the prestigious publication *Who's Who,* where his recreations were listed as shooting, yachting, golf, and croquet. He died March 10, 1933.

Sources:

Farmer, John S. *Twixt Two Worlds.* London, 1886.

Marryat, Florence. *There Is No Death.* New York: John W. Lovell, 1891. Reprint, New York: Causeway Books, 1973.

Egregore

A folklore term denoting a collective ritual designed to accumulate group magical energy for successful hunting, rainmaking, or planting of crops. Occultists have used the term to denote an astral entity evoked by group energies.

EGYPT

To people throughout history, Egypt has seemed the very mother of magic. In Egypt the peoples of the ancient world found a magical system much more sophisticated than any they were aware of, and the emphasis on death and the care of the human corpse, so central to Egyptian religion, appeared to outsiders strongly suggestive of magic practice. Like all other systems, the magic of the Egyptians was of two kinds: that which was supposed to benefit either the living or the dead, and that which has been known throughout the ages as **black magic** or **necromancy.**

The contents of the Westcar Papyrus show that as early as the fourth dynasty the working of magic was a recognized art in Egypt, but evidence suggests Egyptian magic practice began in neolithic times. Egyptians used magic for numerous purposes, including exorcizing storms and protecting themselves and their loved ones against wild beasts, poison, disease, wounds, and the ghosts of the dead. Throughout the centuries, the practice varied considerably, but the principal means for its working remained the same: **amulets; spells;** magic books, pictures, and formulas; magical names and ceremonies; and the general apparatus of the occult sciences. One of the most potent methods of guarding against misfortune of any kind was the use of amulets.

It must not be assumed that all ornaments or objects discovered on the mummy are of magical potency. These are frequently the possession of the *ka* or **double,** necessary to its comfort in a future existence. The small crowns, scepters, and emblems of Osiris, usually executed in faience, were placed beside the dead person in order that he might wear them when he became one with the god Osiris, and therefore a king. The scarab, fashioned in the likeness of a scarabaeus beetle, symbolized resurrection. The *dad* symbolized the human skeleton, and, therefore, perhaps, the dead and dismembered Osiris. It was thought to have an influence on the restoration of the deceased. The *uza,* or eye, signified the health necessary to the dead man's soul.

The so-called palettes, at one time supposed to have been employed for the mixing of paint, are now known to have been amulets inscribed with words of power and placed on the breasts of the dead in neolithic times. The *menat* was worn, or held, with the sistrum (a musical instrument) by gods, kings, and priests and was supposed to bring joy and health to the wearer. It represented the vigor of the two sexes.

The simplest type of magic spell used in Egypt was that in which the exorcist threatened the evil principle, or assured it that he could injure it. Generally, however, the magician requested the assistance of the gods, or pretended that *he* was a god. Invocations, when written, were usually accompanied by a note to the effect that the formula had once been employed successfully by a god—perhaps by a deified priest.

An incomprehensible and mysterious jargon was employed that was supposed to conceal the name of a certain deity, who was thus compelled to do the will of the sorcerer. These gods were almost always those of foreign nations, and the invocations themselves appear to be attempts at various foreign idioms, employed perhaps because they sounded more mysterious than the native speech. Great stress was laid upon the proper pronunciation of these names, and failure in all cases was held to lie at the door of mispronunciation. The Book of the Dead contains many such "words of power," and these were intended to assist the dead in their journey in the underworld of Amenti.

It was believed that all supernatural beings, good and evil, possessed a hidden name; and if a person knew the name he could compel that being to do his will. The name, indeed, was as much part of the man as his body or soul. The traveler through Amenti had to not only tell the divine gods their names but also prove that he knew the names of a number of the supposedly inanimate objects in the dreary underworld.

Many books of magic in Egypt contained spells and other formulas for **exorcism** and necromantic practice. The priestly caste who compiled those necromantic works was known as Kerheb, or "scribes of the divine writings," and even the sons of pharaohs did not disdain to enter their ranks.

The Ritual of Egyptian Magic

In many instances the ritual of Egyptian magic possessed strong similarities to the ceremonial practices of other systems and countries. Wax figures were employed to represent the bodies of persons to be bewitched or harmed, and models of all kinds were used in the belief that the physical force directed against them might injure the person or animal they represented.

But the principal rite in which **ceremonial magic** was employed was the very elaborate one of mummification. As each bandage was laid in its exact position, certain words of power were uttered that were supposed to help preserve the part swathed. After evisceration, the priest uttered an invocation to the deceased and then took a vase of liquid containing ten perfumes, with which he smeared the body twice from head to foot, taking special care to anoint the head thoroughly. The internal organs were then placed on the body, and the backbone immersed in holy oil, supposed to be an emanation from the gods Shu and Seb. Certain precious stones were then laid on the mummy, each of which had its magical significance. Crystal, for instance, lightened his face, and cornelian strengthened his steps.

A priest who personified the jackal-headed god Anubis then advanced, performed certain symbolic ceremonies on the head of the mummy, and laid certain bandages upon it. After a further anointing with oil the deceased was declared to have "received his head." The mummy's left hand was filled with 36 substances used in embalming, symbolic of the 36 forms of the god Osiris. The body was then rubbed with holy oil, the toes wrapped in linen, and after an appropriate address the ceremony was completed.

Dreams

The art of procuring **dreams** and their interpretation was much practiced in Egypt. The Egyptian magician procured dreams for his clients by drawing magic pictures and reciting magic words. The following formulas for producing a dream are taken from British Museum Papyrus, no. 122, lines 64ff and 359ff:

"To obtain a vision from the god Bes: Make a drawing of Bes, as shewn below, on your left hand, and envelope your hand in a strip of black cloth that has been consecrated to Isis and lie down to sleep without speaking a word, even in answer to a question. Wind the remainder of the cloth round your neck. The ink with which you write must be composed of the blood of a cow, the blood of a white dove, fresh frankincense, myrrh, black writing ink, cinnabar, mulberry juice, rain-water, and the juice of wormwood and vetch. With this write your petition before the setting sun, saying, 'Send the truthful seer out of the holy shrine, I beseech thee Lampsuer, Sumarta, Baribas, Dardalam, Iorlex: O Lord send the sacred deity Anuth, Anuth, Salbana, Chambré, Breith, now, now, quickly, quickly. Come in this very night.'

"To procure dreams: Take a clean linen bag and write upon it the names given below. Fold it up and make it into a lamp-wick, and set it alight, pouring pure oil over it. The word to be written is this: 'Armiuth, Lailamchouch, Arsenophrephren, Phtha, Archentechtha.' Then in the evening, when you are going to bed, which you must do without touching food (or, pure from all defilement), do thus: Approach the lamp and repeat seven times the formula given below: then extinguish it and lie down to sleep. The formula is this: 'Sachmu . . . epaema Ligotereench: the Aeon, the Thunderer, Thou that hast swallowed the snake and dost exhaust the moon, and dost raise up the orb of the sun in his season, Chthetho is the name; I require, O lords of the gods, Seth, Chreps, give me the information that I desire.'"

Medical Magic

Magic played a great part in Egyptian medicine. On this point, A. Wiedemann stated:

"The Egyptians were not great physicians: their methods were purely empirical and their remedies of very doubtful value, but the riskiness of their practice arose chiefly from their utter inability to diagnose because of their ignorance of anatomy. That the popular respect for the human body was great we may gather from the fact that the Paraskhistai who opened the body for embalmment were persecuted and stoned as having committed a sinful although necessary deed. The prescribed operations in preparing a body for embalmment were never departed from, and taught but little anatomy, so that until Greek times the Egyptians had only the most imperfect and inaccurate ideas of the human organism. They understood nothing about most internal diseases, and especially nothing about diseases of the brain, never suspecting them to be the result of organic changes, but assuming them to be caused by demons who had entered into the sick. Under these circumstances medicines might be used to cause the disappearance of the symptoms, but the cure was the expulsion of the demon. Hence the Egyptian physician must also practise magic.

"According to late accounts, his functions were comparatively simple, for the human body had been divided into thirty-six parts, each presided over by a certain demon, and it sufficed to invoke the demon of the part affected in order to bring about its cure—a view of matters fundamentally Egyptian. In the *Book of the Dead* we find that different divinities were responsible for the well-being of the bodies of the blessed; thus Nu had charge of the hair, Râ of the face, Hathor of the eyes, Apuat of the ears, Anubis of the lips, while Thoth was guardian of all parts of the body together. This doctrine was subsequently applied to the living body, with the difference that for the great gods named in the *Book of the Dead* there were substituted as gods of healing the presiding deities of the thirty-six decani, the thirty-six divisions of the Egyptian zodiac, as we learn from the names given to them by Celsus and preserved by Origen. In earlier times it was not so easy to be determined which god was to be invoked, for the selection depended not only on the part affected but also on the illness and symptoms and remedies to be used, etc.

"Several Egyptian medical papyri which have come down to us contain formulas to be spoken against the demons of disease as well as prescriptions for the remedies to be used in specified cases of illness. In papyri of older date these conjurations are comparatively rare, but the further the art of medicine advanced, or rather, receded, the more numerous they became.

"It was not always enough to speak the formulas once; even their repeated recitation might not be successful, and in that case recourse must be had to other expedients: secret passes were made, various rites were performed, the formulas were written upon papyrus, which the sick person had to swallow, etc. . . . But amulets were in general found to be most efficacious, and the personal intervention of a god called up, if necessary, by prayers or sorcery."

Magic Figures

As has been said, the Egyptians believed that it was possible to transmit to the image of any person or animal the soul of the being that it represented. The Westcar Papyrus relates how a soldier who had fallen in love with a governor's wife was swallowed by a crocodile when bathing, the saurian being a magical replica of a waxen one made by the lady's husband. In the official account of a conspiracy against Rameses III (1200 B.C.E.) the conspirators obtained access to a magical papyrus in the royal library and employed its instructions against the king with disastrous effects to themselves. Others made waxen figures of gods and of the king for the purpose of slaying the latter.

Astrology

The Egyptians were fatalists and believed that a man's destiny was decided before he was born. The people therefore had recourse to astrologers. The great Egyptologist Sir E. A. Wallis Budge stated:

"In magical papyri we are often told not to perform certain magical ceremonies on such and such days, the idea being that on these days hostile powers will make them to be powerless, and that gods mightier than those to which the petitioner would appeal will be in the ascendant. There have come down to us fortunately, papyri containing copies of the Egyptian calendar, in which each third of every day for three hundred and sixty days of the year is marked lucky or unlucky, and we know from other papyri *why* certain days were lucky or unlucky, and why others were only partly so."

From the life of Alexander the Great by Pseudo-Callisthenes we learn that the Egyptians were skilled in the art of casting horoscopes. Nectanebus employed for the purpose a tablet made of gold and silver and acacia wood, to which were fitted three belts. Upon the outer belt was Zeus with the 36 *decani* surrounding him; upon the second the 12 signs of the zodiac were represented; and upon the third the sun and moon. He set the tablet upon a tripod, and then emptied out of a small box upon it models of the seven stars that were in the belts, and put into the middle belt eight precious stones; these he arranged in the places wherein he supposed the planets they represented would be at the time of the birth of Olympias, and then told her fortune from them.

But the use of the horoscope is much older than the time of Alexander the Great, for to a Greek horoscope in the British Museum is attached "an introductory letter from some master of the art of **astrology** to his pupil, named Hermon, urging him to be very exact and careful in his application of the laws which the ancient Egyptians, with their laborious devotion to the art, had discovered and handed down to posterity."

Ghosts

The motion that the *ka* or double of man wandered about after death greatly fostered the Egyptian belief in ghosts. E.A. Wallis Budge observed as follows:

"According to them a man consisted of a physical body, a shadow, a double, a soul, a heart, a spirit called the *khu*, a power, a name, and a spiritual body. When the body died the shadow departed from it, and could only be brought back to it by the performance of a mystical ceremony; the double lived in the tomb with the body, and was there visited by the soul whose habitation was in heaven. The soul was, from one aspect, a material thing, and like the *ka*, or double, was believed to partake of the funeral offerings which were brought to the tomb; one of the chief objects of sepulchral offerings of meat and drink was to keep the double in the tomb and to do away with the necessity of its wandering about outside the tomb in search of food. It is clear from many texts that, unless the double was supplied with sufficient food, it would wander from the tomb and eat any kind of offal and drink any kind of dirty water which it might find in its path. But besides the shadow, and the double, and the soul, the spirit of the deceased, which usually had its abode in heaven, was sometimes to be found in the tomb. There is, however, good reason for stating that the immortal part of man which lived in the tomb and had its special abode in the statue of the deceased was the 'double.' This is proved by the fact that a special part of the tomb was reserved for the *ka*, or double, which was called the 'house of the *ka*,' and that a priest, called the 'priest of the *ka*,' was specially appointed to minister the therein."

Esoteric Knowledge of the Priesthood

The esoteric knowledge of the Egyptian priesthood is believed to have been similar to that for which the Indian medicine man is credited, with a philosophy akin to that of ancient India added in. W. H. Davenport Adams observed as follows:

"To impose upon the common people, the priesthood professed to lead lives of peculiar sanctity. They despised the outer senses, as sources of evil and temptation. They kept themselves apart from the *profanium vulgus*, and, says Iamblicus, 'occupied themselves only with the knowledge of God, of themselves, and of wisdom; they desired no vain honours in their sacred practice, and never yielded to the influence of the imagination.' Therefore they formed a world within a world, fenced round by a singular awe and wonder, apparently abstracted from the things of earth, and devoted to the constant contemplation of divine mysteries. They admitted few strangers into their order, and wrapt up their doctrines in a hieroglyphical language, which was only intelligible to the initiated. To these various precautions was added the solemnity of a terrible oath, whose breach was invariably punished with death.

"The Egyptian priests preserved the remaining relics of the former wisdom of nature. These were not imparted as the sciences are, in our age, but to all appearances they were neither learned nor taught; but as a reflection of the old revelations of nature, the perception must arise like an inspiration in the scholar's mind. From this cause appear to have arisen those numerous preparations and purifications the severity of which deterred many from initiation into the Egyptian priesthood; in fact, not infrequently resulted in the scholar's death. Long fasting, and the greatest abstinence, appear to have been particularly necessary: besides this, the body was rendered insensible through great exertions, and even through voluntary inflicted pain, and therefore open to the influence of the mind. The imagination was excited by representations of the mysteries; and the inner sense was more impressed by the whole than—as is the case with us—instructed by an explanation of simple facts. In this manner the dead body of science was not given over to the initiated, and left to chance whether it would become animated or not, but the living soul of wisdom was breathed into them.

"From this fact, that the contents of the mysteries were rather revealed than taught—were received more from inward inspiration and mental intoxication, than outwardly through endless teaching, it was necessary to conceal them from the mass of the people."

Commenting on the same subject the egyptologist W. Schubart stated:

"The way to every innovation was closed, and outward knowledge and science could certainly not rise to a high degree of external perfection; but that rude sensuality, inclination for change and variety, was suppressed as the chief source of all bodily and spiritual vices, is clear, as well as that here, as in India, an ascetic and contemplative life was recommended.

"They imparted their secret and divine sciences to no one who did not belong to their caste, and it was long impossible for foreigners to learn anything; it was only in later times that a few strangers were permitted to enter the initiation after many severe preparations and trials. Besides this, their functions were hereditary, and the son followed the footsteps of his father.

"Concerning that which passed within the temples, and of the manner in which the sick were treated, we have but fragmentary accounts; for to the uninitiated the entrance was forbidden, and the initiated kept their vows. Even the Greeks, who were admitted to the temples, have been silent concerning the secrets, and have only here and there betrayed portions. Jablonski says, 'but few chosen priests were admitted into the sanctum, and . . . admission was scarcely ever permitted to strangers even under the severest regulations."

Modern Views of Egyptian Magic

Beginning in the nineteenth century, scholarship removed much of the mystery surrounding ancient Egyptian magic while at the same time making it an object of increasing occult and magic exploration. Modern work on Egypt really began in 1822, after J. F. Champollion (1790–1832) successfully deciphered the hieroglyphics through his work on the Rosetta Stone and thus opened the way to understanding of ancient Egyptian inscriptions on monuments and papyrus. Champollion's basic work was supplemented by other philologists, such as Richard Lepsius (1810–1884), Heinrich Brugsch (1827–1894), and Adolf Erman (1854–1916). Other great egyptologists included Sir Gaston Maspero (1846–1916), Sir E. A. Wallis Budge (1857–1934), J. H. Breasted (1865–1935), and Sir William Flinder Petrie (1853–1942). Popular interest in ancient Egypt was piqued by the discovery and excavation of the tomb of Tutankhamun (died ca. 1352 B.C.E.) by Lord Carnarvon and Howard Carter. (See also **Tutankhamun Curse**)

Modern Egyptian magical practice was largely initiated by **Aleister Crowley** who in 1904 in Cairo received a supposedly channeled book, *The Book of the Law,* and later proclaimed its reception as the beginning of a new era, the Aeon of Horus, the Crowned and Conquering Child. Since that time, ritual magicians have been poring over the Western translations of Egyptian texts to ferret out their modern implications. The Church of Eternal Source, headquartered in Burbank, California, is one prominent revivalist Egyptian magic religion, founded in the 1960s.

Much speculation has also revolved around the Great Pyramid of Giza (built in the reign of Cheops of the Fourth Dynasty). Ever since Col. Howard Vyse forced an entry into the pyramid and took measurements, an eccentric school of pyramidology focused upon speculation concerning pyramids in general and Egyptian pyramids in particular has grown up. It drew most interest in its association of various pyramid measurements with biblical prophecies (see **pyramids and pyramidology**). Other writers, most recently the devotees of the **ancient astronauts** hypothesis, have attempted to perpetuate the myth that the remarkable engineering achievements of pyramid building were the product of a long-lost occult secret (or ancient science) by which great blocks of stone could be levitated into position by the magical power of sound vibration. Such romantic speculations can be made only by ignoring archaeological and hieroglyphical evidence.

Sources:

Breasted, James. *A History of Egypt: From the Earliest Times to the Persian Conquest.* New York: Charles S. Scribner's Sons, 1919.

Brunton, Paul. *A Search in Secret Egypt.* London, 1935. Reprint, New York: Samuel Weiser, 1970.

Budge, E. A. Wallis. *The Book of the Dead.* London, 1898. Reprint, New York: Dover, 1967. Reprint, New York: Causeway, 1974.

———. *Egyptian Magic.* London, 1899.

———. *The Gods of the Egyptians.* 2 vols. London, 1898.

———. *A History of Egypt.* 8 vols. London, 1902. 4 vols. Reprint, The Netherlands: Anthropological Publications.

———. *The Mummy.* London, 1925.

de Camp, Sprague. *The Ancient Engineers.* Garden City, N.Y.: Doubleday, 1960. Reprint, New York: Ballantine, 1974.

Erman, Adolf. *Life in Ancient Egypt.* London, 1894. Reprint, New York: Dover, 1971.

Ghalioungui, Paul. *The House of Life: Magic and Medical Sciences in Ancient Egypt.* Rev. ed., New York: Wittenborn, 1975.

Hornung, Erik. *Conceptions of God in Ancient Egypt: The One and the Many.* Ithaca, N.Y.: Cornell University Press, 1982.

Knight, Alfred E. *Amentet: An Account of the Gods, Amulets and Scarabs of the Ancient Egyptians.* London: Longmans, Green, 1915.

Massey, Gerald. *Ancient Egypt, the Light of the World.* 2 vols. London, 1907. Reprint, New York: Samuel Weiser, 1974.

Seiss, Joseph. *The Great Pyramid: A Miracle in Stone.* Blauvelt, N.Y.: Multimedia (Steiner Books), 1972.

Spence, Lewis. *Mysteries of Egypt.* London, 1929. Reprint, Baluvelt, N.Y.: Multimedia (Steiner Books), 1972.

Tompkins, Peter. *Secrets of the Great Pyramid.* New York: Harper & Row, 1971.

Ehrenberg, Wolfgang (1909–)

Chemist and lecturer on atomic physics with special interest in parapsychology. Ehrenberg was born January 8, 1909, in Munich, Germany. He attended the University of Munich and joined the teaching staff following his graduation in 1936. He became an industrial consultant and researcher in the fields of chemistry and physics and published many scientific papers on these subjects and on the psychophysics of color. From 1950 to 1953 he was a staff member of the thermonuclear pilot plant at the Argentine Atomic Energy Commission in Bariloche and also lectured on atomic physics in Argentina.

He was a founder of the Psychophysical Society and became its president in 1954. Ehrenberg's interest in parapsychology is reflected in his numerous articles on its relation to physics, many of which were published in *Psychophysikalische Zeitschrift.*

Ehrenwald, Jan (1900–1988)

Psychotherapist, psychiatrist, and author. Ehrenwald was born March 13, 1900, in Bratislava, Czechoslovakia, and studied at the University of Prague. He moved to England and practiced in London. While there, an interest in parapsychology emerged and he joined the **Society for Psychical Research.** He was elected a fellow of the Royal Society of Medicine and became a member of the Royal Medico-Psychological Association. He later moved to the United States, where he became a fellow of the New York Academy of Medicine, a member of the American Academy of Psychotherapists, a charter member of the **Parapsychological Association,** and a trustee of the research committee of the **American Society for Psychical Research.**

For 25 years he served as chief of the Psychiatric Outpatient Department of Roosevelt Hospital, New York City. After retirement in 1975 he lectured to adult audiences in Florida on the psychodynamics of creative individuals and in New York gave talks on professional methods and patient needs at Weschester Institute for Training in Psychoanalysis and Psychotherapy at Mount Kisco.

Ehrenwald took a special interest in telepathy in relation to psychoanalysis. He contributed articles on parapsychology to various journals and wrote several books. He died June 15, 1988.

Sources:

Berger, Arthur S., and Joyce Berger. *The Encyclopedia of Parapsychology and Psychical Research.* New York: Paragon House, 1991.

Ehrenwald, Jan. *Anatomy of Genius: Split Brains and Global Minds.* New York: Human Sciences Press, 1984.

———. "An Autobiographical Fragment." In *Men and Women of Parapsychology,* edited by R. Pilkington. Jefferson, N.C.: McFarland, 1987.

———. *The ESP Experience: A Psychiatric Validation.* New York: Basic Books, 1978.

———. *The History of Psychotherapy: From Healing Magic to Encounter.* New York: J. Aronson, 1976.

———. *New Dimensions in Deep Analysis.* New York: Grune & Stratton, 1955.

———. *Psychotherapy, Myth and Method.* New York: Grune & Stratton, 1966.

———. *Telepathy and Medical Psychology.* New York: W. W. Norton, 1948.

Eikerenkoetter II, Frederick I. (1935–)

Popularly known as "Rev. Ike," a metaphysical healing and prosperity consciousness teacher in the African American community. Rev. Ike was born June 1, 1935, in Ridgeland, South Carolina, and as a young man became a Baptist minister. After graduation from the American Bible College in Chicago in 1956 he served two years in the U.S. Army chaplain's corps. In 1958 he founded the United Church of Christ for All People but over the next few years came to the conclusion that the over-emphasis on other worldly rewards was wrong and began to search for a way to help parishioners, many of whom where quite poor, in the present world.

The answer to Eikerenkoetter's quest came from New Thought and especially from their understanding that healing and prosperity came from changing one's mental attitude. He moved to Boston in 1964 and open a Miracle Temple. Without closing the work in Boston, he moved to New York City in 1966, and in 1969 he purchased a headquarters for his church, the United Church and Science of Living Institute and its outreach structure, the United Christian Evangelistic Association.

He developed a radio ministry and during the 1970s was on more than 80 stations nationwide. Along with Johnnie Coleman of Chicago, he became the leading voice of New Thought within the African American community nationally and developed strong support outside of the community. He became a controversial figure for advocating that members of the Black community spend their tie in changing their consciousness rather than concentrating upon social reform. The colorful preacher was a popular target for the press for his presenting metaphysical affirmations in highly quotable, catchy phrases which his audience could easily remember.

Sources:

Eikerenkoetter, Frederick. *Reverend Ike's Secrets of Health, Happiness, and Prosperity—For You.* New York: Reverend Ike Prayer Tower, n.d.

Martin, William. "This Man Says He's the Divine Sweetheart of the Universe." *Esquire* (June 1974): 76–78, 140–43.

Eisenbud, Jule (1908–)

Physician, psychiatrist, and parapsychologist. Eisenbud was born November 20, 1908, in New York, New York, and studied at Columbia College (B.A., 1929), Columbia College of Physicians and Surgeons (M.D., 1934), and Columbia University (D.Med.Sc., 1939). In 1950 he became a professor of psychiatry at the University of Colorado Medical School and an attending psychiatrist at the U.S. Veterans Administration Hospital in Denver.

Eisenbud was a charter member of the **Parapsychological Association** and wrote numerous articles on psychiatry and psychoanalysis based on his experiments on telepathy and the psi faculty. His first paper on a parapsychological subject led to a move (unsuccessful) to have him expelled from the New York Psychoanalytic Society. He attracted even more attention with his book *The World of Ted Serios: "Thoughtographic" Studies of an Extraordinary Mind* (1967), which deals with his investigation of **Ted Serios,** a former Chicago bellhop who claimed to imprint mental images on photographic film. His support of Serios provoked a controversy about his claimed abilities that in the end left a variety of unanswered questions amid charges of Serios's producing the effects by **fraud.**

Sources:

Berger, Arthur S., and Joyce Berger. *The Encyclopedia of Parapsychology and Psychical Research.* New York: Paragon House, 1991.

Eisenbud, Jule. *Paranormal Foreknowledge: Problems and Perplexities.* New York: Human Sciences Press, 1982.

———. "Paranormal Photography." In *Handbook of Parapsychology,* edited by B. B. Wolman. New York: Van Nostrand Reinhold, 1977.

———. *Psi and Psychoanalysis.* New York: Grune & Stratton, 1970.

———. "Psychic Photography and Thoughtography." In *Psychic Exploration: A Challenge for Science,* edited by Edgar D. Mitchell and John White. New York: Putnam, 1974.

———. *The World of Ted Serios: "Thoughtographic" Studies of an Extraordinary Mind.* 2d ed. Jefferson, N.C.: McFarland, 1989.

Ekisha

Term for a Japanese street fortune-teller, usually employing a system of **astrology** and **palmistry.**

Ekpe or Egbo

An African secret society that originated in the eighteenth century in Calabar, a section of Nigeria around the Niger River delta. The name means "leopard" and referred to a mysterious forest being that could be seen only by the initiates. On those occasions when the "leopard" was brought to town for ceremonies, the people could not see the animal but could hear its tremendous roar. Whenever an Ekpe day was announced, slaves, women, and children would remove themselves from the area of the ceremony, as the messenger of Ekpe, armed with a heavy whip, went through the village and lashed everyone he encountered.

The society was divided into eleven grades, of which the first three were not open to slaves. Members, as a rule, bought themselves into the higher grades in their turn, and the money thus obtained was shared among the Nyampa, who formed the inner circle. The king was president of the society under the title of Cyamba. Each grade had its special festival day, on which their *Idem* or spirit-master exercised complete control.

The Idem was usually a hermit who lived in the distant bush, and when he appeared it was in a fantastic guise of mats and branches that covered him from head to foot, and with a black mask on his face. The principals of the order were linked together by a garb of leaves so gathered up that they seemed to move in a connected mass. Ethnologist L. Froebenius observes:

"The Order of *Free Egbos,* is said to have originated at the fairs which were held at a great palm-oil market in the interior, midway between Calabar and the Kamerun. As the place became the scene of much disorder, while the European trade made it necessary for the maintenance of public credit that all engagements should be strictly carried out, this institution was formed as a sort of Hanseatic Union under the most influential traders, for the mutual safe-guarding of their interests. Later it acquired the political character of a *Vehmgericht* or secret tribunal, by bringing within its sphere of action the whole police of the Calabars and the Kamerun. The kings always sought to secure for themselves the Grand-mastership of the Order, since otherwise their authority would sink to a mere shadow. European skippers have frequently found it to their advantage to be enrolled in the lower grades, in order thereby the more easily to recover their debts. A member of the *Egbo* has the right to claim as his own property the slave of his debtor, wherever he may find him, merely by fastening a yellow strip to his dress or loincloth. Even in the interior of the continent the standing of an *Egbo* is still respected and feared, and affords one a certain immunity from molestation, such as is absolutely needed for the extensive commercial speculations in Africa.

"In the Kamerun, as a preliminary to their acceptance into the *Free Egbos,* the young men are sent for a protracted period to the Mokokos, a bush tribe in the interior; with these they live naked in the fields, and only now and then dart out, clad in green leaves, to have a bath in the river. All women, and especially slaves, are prohibited, under heavy penalties, from approaching the forest where they reside. In the Kamerun, it is customary to pay particular honour to a visitor, above all if he be a European, by introducing the *Egbo* goat, which the people are otherwise seldom allowed to set eyes upon.

"Holman reports that the whole of the Old Calabar district is subject to the rule of the so-called *Egbo* laws. These are promulgated at a secret Council, the *Egbo* Assembly, which is held in the 'Palaver-house' erected for this special purpose. In virtue of his sovereign rights, the head-chief presides, under the title of *Cyamab,* over this assembly. Amongst the members of the *Egbo* there are different ranks, which must be acquired in their due order, one after the other. Holman quotes Englishmen who state that Europeans have bought themselves into the *Egbo,* and even into the Yampai, in order to be thus better able to get in their money. He gives the following as the names and prices of the different grades of *Egbo:*

1	Abungo	"	"	"	125 bars
2	Aboko	"	"	"	75 bars
3	Makairo	"	"	"	440 copper bars
4	Bakimboko	"	"	"	100 bars
5	Yampai	"	"	"	850 copper bars

"To these must be added rum, clothes, membo, etc. The Yampai is the only grade whose members are allowed to sit in Council. The sums paid for the various titles of the *Egbo* are distributed exclusively amongst the Yampai, who, however, are not limited to a single share, since every Yampai can multiply his title as often as he can purchase shares, and these give him a claim to the receipt of the corresponding quotas from the profits of the whole institution."

The society emerged as a powerful force in nineteenth-century Calabar society and is still quite strong, though it must now compete with Christianity and a host of new religions for the hearts of the people. Much of the ceremony and belief of the society remains a secret kept from outsiders.

Sources:

Hackett, Rosalind I. J. *Religion in Calabar.* Berlin: Mouton de Gruyter, 1989.

Elbegast

A dwarf mentioned in the medieval semitraditional saga-cycle *Dietrich of Bern.* He was friendly toward Dietrich and helped him in his search for the giant Grim.

Elberfeld Horses

The mathematical wonders of the animal world in Elberfeld, Germany. The case was described by E. Clarapède, of Geneva University, as "the most sensational event that has happened in the psychological world."

The discovery of equine mathematical genius was made by William von Osten in 1891. The horse "Kluge Hans" (Clever Hans) was taught to count skittles (pins used in the bowling game of ninepins) by striking with his hoof as many times as there were skittles on the table. Von Osten first pronounced the numbers aloud and later wrote them on a blackboard. The results soon proved to be astonishing. The horse began to perform mathematical operations.

In 1904 von Osten invited cavalry officers to witness his experiments and exhibited the feats of Clever Hans without charge. As a result of the publicity that these performances attracted, scientists began to take an interest in the subject of animal intelligence. A scientific committee headed by C. Stumpf (director of the Institute of Psychology at Berlin University) investigated Clever Hans in 1904 and did not find trickery.

Their report was attacked by Albert Moll, a dogmatic specialist in hypnotism. Moll had visited Elberfeld and, as is often the case with unsympathetic or prejudiced observers, every experiment he made was a failure. He theorized that this proved that the animal could only perform the tasks by noting infinitesimal signs from the trainer or other persons present, and without any firm evidence Moll persuaded Stumpf to change his mind. A second committee reached a more positive conclusion concerning the horse's abilities. Thereafter, although Moll was not on either the first or second investigating committee, the myth of the "Clever Hans Error" of overlooking "unconscious signaling" passed into the psychology textbooks.

This view was reinforced by Stumpf's assistant Oskar Pfungst who, with the permission of von Osten, conducted his own experiments with the horse. Pfungst virtually took over the horse's training, eliciting any response he desired by movements of his head, eyes, or hands. Eventually the horse paid little attention to its groom or even to its master. Pfungst's publication of his detailed experiments duly "proved" the unconscious signaling theory of Moll and gave scientific credence to the claim that animals cannot think. Even in modern times, Pfungst's work is cited as a model of reliable scientific investigation, although some years after publication of his work Pfungst himself was aware that it was not above criticism. In his book *Clever Hans* (1911) he writes:

"Someone could say that the horse had only been 'mechanized' and rendered useless for independent thinking by our experiments, and that previously the horse had been able to count, and simply became accustomed in my lessons to the bad habit of following my signals. But Herr von Osten never achieved results without error, as I did in my experiments."

The conclusion that, consciously or unconsciously, Pfungst retrained the horse to fit his own theories seems a likely one.

Von Osten became an irritable recluse, convinced that his lifework had been destroyed. In a newspaper article of August 1904 he states: "In spite of everything one can hardly see in these experiments more than a kind of scholarly jest which has no special value for science or practical life." He died in 1909.

The horse Clever Hans passed to Karl Krall, a jeweler in Elberfeld, who decided to continue von Osten's work and disprove the unconscious signaling theory. In his stables near Wuppertal, Krall taught four more horses: "Muhamed," "Zarif," "Berto," and "Hänschen." The last horse was blind and clearly unable to perceive visual signals but learned to calculate as rapidly as the other horses. Krall also put blinders on the eyes of the others during lessons so that they could only see a blackboard and not their trainer. At times he gave lessons in complete darkness. Krall improved on von Osten's training by introducing a phonetic system for language communication.

The horses not only learned the fundamental mathematical operations of addition, subtraction, multiplication, and division, but after only four months' training they extracted square and cube roots. They answered questions by stamping with their hoofs. To give the number 34, for instance, they struck three times with the left and four times with the right hoof. Krall's book *Denkende Tiere* (1912) stirred the world of science. Commissions and investigators from all over the world journeyed to the stables. Many scientists persisted in stubborn negations; others went away in awe and wonder. One committee of 24 scientists could not tolerate the suggestion that horses could calculate like men, which would be "subversive of the evolutionary theory." They drew up a document of protest against the facts reported earlier by the investigator Clarapède, although in fact only two of the scientists on the committee had ever seen the horses.

The famous author **Maurice Maeterlinck** paid a visit. The horse Muhamed, after a formal introduction, phonetically spelled out his name with his hoofs and solved almost instantaneously problems to which even Maeterlinck did not know the answer, refused to give the square root of a chance number that was afterward found to have none, and even expressed thoughts and feelings by spelling. On one occasion Muhamed complained, "The groom struck Hänschen."

Unless one is prepared to discount the evidence of Maeterlinck and the many distinguished scientists who confirmed that the horses could correctly answer questions when the answer was not even known to the inquirer, the "unconscious signaling" theory of Pfungst must be considered unproved. His own detailed experiments with Clever Hans and other animals, however consistent in results, probably proved what he expected them to prove and so cannot be considered impartial or definitive.

There are some interesting aspects about Krall's horses. Sometimes they gave messages that they were tired and would not answer. Sometimes they could not answer quite simple questions, such as the number of individuals present. If uncertain, they made a timid blow with their hoofs, and generally their intelligence and behavior appeared to be on the level of a six- to eight-year-old child.

In the experiments, care was taken to exclude the possibility of mind reading. As a precaution to prevent "unconscious signals," the questions were sometimes asked by telephone, the receiver being hung on the ear of the horse; frequently the problem was written on the blackboard and the horse left alone to solve it. Sometimes the figures were traced with a finger on the back of the animal. It is a curious fact that after six months of schooling, the horses made no further progress. They could only do what they had been taught, and they appeared to do it without any conscious effort.

No satisfactory conclusion was ever reached, although in more recent times experiments have been conducted on communication between human beings and dogs, chimpanzees, gorillas, and dolphins. Where there is a strong and friendly relationship between teacher and animal, the results indicate animal intelligence, although not amenable to formal scientific validation. An interesting development is the attempt to bypass tapping and language codes by establishing direct communication with the animal's mind, as suggested in the work of Barbara Lysedeck in the United States.

The horses of von Osten and Krall were not the first to appear to demonstrate intelligent communication. As early as 1591, in Shropshire, England, a certain Master Banks exhibited a white horse named "Morocco" that communicated by tapping with his hoofs, apparently able to tell how much money was in a spectator's purse. Shakespeare referred to the animal in his play *Love's Labour's Lost* (act 1, scene 2). It is possible that this particular case was one of fake "mind reading" similar to modern mentalist stage shows, but according to dramatist Ben Jonson, Banks and his horse were later burned at the stake for witchcraft.

In the twentieth century the "mind-reading horse 'Lady Wonder'" was investigated by parapsychologist **J. B. Rhine** in the winter of 1927–28. The horse gave answers to questions by touching her nose to letter or number blocks and seemed to be most successful when her owner, Claudia Fonda, was near. Rhine concluded that Lady Wonder was responding telepathically. Professional magician **Milbourne Christopher** believed that the horse was receiving visual cues from Fonda.

At any rate the evidence for the genuineness of the Elberfeld horses is strong, even if opposed by various scientists like Pfungst. Many scientists testified to the reality of the phenomena. Other favorable testimony came from members of the International Society of Animal Psychology.

The psychical researcher **Count Cesar De Vesme** speculated that the Elberfeld horses may have solved their problems in a mediumistic way, since they often spelled in the reverse order, suggesting mirror-writing, which is a characteristic of automatic scripts. De Vesme did not mean to suggest the intervention of spirits, but something like a manifestation of an equine subliminal self by **motor automatism,** unhampered by the limitation of the animal brain. Curiously enough, the system of communicating by tapping of hoofs is strongly reminiscent of **table-turning** séances.

Krall also experimented with training a young elephant, but the animal refused to learn. Since then, attempts have been made to teach dogs to communicate in a manner similar to that of Krall's horses. Between 1974 and 1975 two dogs, "Elke" and "Belam," were given some 500 lessons by Dorothy Meyer in the Berchtesgaden region of Bavaria. The dogs were owned by Hilde Meilmaier, founder of a dog school. For an account of the impressive achievement of these dogs see Maurice Rowdon's 1978 book *The Talking Dogs.*

Sources:

Christopher, Milbourne. *ESP, Seers, and Psychics.* New York: Thomas Y. Crowell, 1970.

Gaddis, Vincent, and Margaret Gaddis. *The Strange World of Animals and Pets.* Cowles, 1970. Reprint, New York: Pocket Books, 1971.

Kindermann, Henny. *Lola; or, the Thought and Speech of Animals.* New York: E. P. Dutton, 1923.

Krall, Karl. *Denkende Tiere.* Leipzig, 1912.

Maeterlinck, Maurice. *The Unknown Guest.* London, 1914. Reprint, New Hyde Park, N.Y.: University Books, 1975.

Pfungst, Oskar. *Clever Hans (The Horse of Mr. Von Osten): A Contribution to Experimental Animal and Human Psychology.* New York, 1911. Reprint, New York: Holt, Rinehart & Winston, 1965.

Rhine, J. B. "An Investigation of a 'Mind-Reading' Horse." *Journal of Abnormal and Social Psychology* 23 (1929).

Rowdon, Maurice. *The Talking Dogs.* New York: Macmillan, 1978.

Woodhouse, Barbara. *Talking to Animals.* Croxley Green, England: Campions, 1970.

Elder Tree

Many superstitions and legends are associated with the elder tree and shrub (genus *Sambucus*). In some cultures, it is identified with the tree on which Judas hanged himself as well as with the wood used for the Cross. In some parts of Scotland and Wales, it was believed that the dwarf elder grew only on ground that had been soaked in blood. Elder was not used for a child's cradle because it could cause the child to pine or be harried by **fairies.** In Germany it was considered unlucky to bring an elder branch into a house, because it might also bring ghosts, or, in England, the Devil himself.

However, elder was also believed to protect against evil, and it was thought that wherever it grew witches were powerless. In England gardens were sometimes protected by having elder trees planted at the entrance, or in hedges around the garden. In some parts of the United States, an elder stick was burned on the fire at Christmas Eve to reveal witches, sorcerers, and other evil wishers in the neighborhood. In the Tyrol, it was believed that an elder stick cut on St. John's Eve (June 23) would detect witchcraft.

Many old gardens in Britain retained into the twentieth century some of the protective elder trees. The folklorist James Napier recalled:

"In my boyhood, I remember that my brothers, sisters, and myself were warned against breaking a twig or branch from the elder hedge which surrounded my grandfather's garden. We were told at the time as a reason for this prohibition, that it was poisonous; but we discovered afterwards that there was another reason, viz., that it was unlucky to break off even a small twig from a bourtree bush [old name for elder]."

In some parts of Europe, this superstition was so strong that before pruning the elder, the gardener would say, "Elder, elder may I cut thy branches?" If no response was heard, it was considered that permission had been given, and then, after spitting three times, the pruner began his cutting. Another writer claimed that elderwood formed a portion of the fuel used in burning human bodies as protection against evil influences, and drivers of funeral hearses had their whip handles made of elder for a similar reason.

In some parts of Scotland, people would not put a piece of elderwood into the fire. Napier observed one instance where "pieces of this wood were lying around unused when the neighbourhood was in great straits for firewood; but none would use it, and when asked why? the answer was: 'We don't know, but folks say it is not lucky to burn the bourtree.'"

Elderberries gathered on St. John's Eve were believed to ward off witchcraft and to bestow magic powers. If the elder was planted in the form of a cross upon a new grave and it bloomed, this was a sure sign that the soul of the dead person was happy.

Various magic powers against illness were claimed for elder. In Massachusetts, elder pulp in a bag worn around the neck was thought to cure rheumatism. Elsewhere elder was also used as an amulet, small pieces being cut up and sewn into a knot and hung around the neck or sewn in a knot in a piece of a man's shirt. Elder was also believed to be of medicinal value for deafness, faintness, strangulation, sore throat, ravings, snake and dog bites, insomnia, melancholy, and hypochondria.

Eldred, Charles (ca. 1906)

Notorious false **materialization** medium of Nottingham, England, during the early years of the twentieth century. He came into public notice when the journal *Light* (September 2, 1905) published a description of one of his early séances. The following year Eldred was unmasked at a séance in London by Abraham Wallace. A cavity was found in the back part of the chair on which he was sitting and in it was discovered, after the séance, a collapsible dummy head of stockinette with a flesh-colored mask, six pieces of white Chinese silk measuring 13 yards in all, and other "properties" of fake mediumship. Eldred had claimed that this chair was "highly magnetized," enabling spirit entities to manifest readily.

According to a friend of Eldred's, the unmasked medium asserted that the first phenomena of materialization that he produced were quite authentic but that afterward he could not satisfy the demands made upon him but by simulation. Even if this was true, the carefully premeditated **fraud** of Eldred's "magnetized" traveling chair completely negated any claim to genuine mediumship on his part.

Sources:

"Exposure of Mr. Eldred." *Journal* of the Society for Psychical Research 12: 242–52.

Letort, Ellen. "The Frauds of Mediums." *Annals of Psychic Science* 3, no. 6 (1906).

Eleazar of Garniza

A Hebrew author who left many manuscripts, several of which have been printed. His books include *Treatise on the Soul* and *Kabalistic Commentary on the Pentateuch.*

Electric Girls

Girls in whose presence certain phenomena occurred, similar in nature to the time-honored phenomena of the **poltergeist,** but ascribed to the action of some physical force akin to electricity. The best known of these electric girls was perhaps **Angelique Cottin,** a Normandy peasant girl whose phenomena were first observed about 1846. She was later taken to Paris and placed under the observation of a Dr. Tanchon and others, who testified to the actuality of the phenomena. These included the movement of objects without contact, or at a mere touch from Cottin's petticoats, the agitation in her presence of a magnetic needle, and the blowing of a cold wind. In addition, chairs and sofas held down by one or more men were violently moved away when Cottin sat on them. She was also able to distinguish between the poles of a magnet by touch.

A commission appointed by the Academy of Sciences to examine Cottin, however, could observe nothing but the violent movements of her chair, which were possibly caused by muscular force.

Other electric girls practiced about the same time; even after the beginning of the Spiritualist movement in the United States, they were occasionally heard of. They are worthy of note as a possible link between the poltergeist and the Spiritualist medium. They include the American stage performers Lulu Hurst and Angie Abbott, and also Mary Richardson. However, Lulu Hurst was clearly an illusionist rather than a medium.

For an account of Cottin's remarkable phenomena, see the *Journal des Debats* (Paris, February 1846) and also the account by **George Vale Owen** in *The Two Worlds* (1891, p. 669).

Electric Phenomena

Phenomena with properties resembling electricity have sometimes been observed in **animal magnetism** and also in psychical mediumship.

Radioactivity was suggested when the medium **Eusapia Palladino** impressed with her fingers photographic plates wrapped in dark paper. The white fluctuating clouds or luminous vapors in the séance room were believed to be additional evidence of radioactivity, because it is a property of cathode rays to excite the formation of vapor or mist when they traverse a stratum saturated with humidity.

Enrico Imoda of Turin, Italy, wondered if the emanations of radium, of cathode rays in a Crookes tube, and of mediums were not fundamentally identical, in that the latter appear to render air a conductor of electricity. He discovered that Palladino had no influence over the electroscope in her normal state. One evening, however, when she woke from a trance and held her hands above the electrodes in the air, she was able, after three or four minutes, to produce a lowering of the gold leaf.

In the experiments of **W. J. Crawford,** an electroscope was immediately discharged when it was touched by a psychic rod. The rods, however, could not conduct a low-tension electric current.

Fritz Grünewald, a Berlin engineer who designed precision instruments, disputed the conductivity of the psychic fluid as he obtained raps upon an electrometer needle carrying a charge of 500 volts without producing the slightest discharge. The objection would seem to be scientifically valid only if the raps were physically struck upon the needle.

Psychical researcher **Julien Ochorowicz** came to the conclusion that the "rigid rays" of medium **Stanislawa Tomczyk** did conduct electricity. He formed an open electrical circuit of two silver plates four millimeters apart, a voltaic pile, and a galvanometer. Tomczyk was able to close the circuit by holding her hands at either side of the silver electrodes at a distance of one or two centimeters. He also found that the medium could decrease the electrical resistance of her own body; his own resistance was two or three times as great as that of the medium. This confirmed the experiments of E. K. Müller of Zürich, which led to the discovery of the "anthropoflux" (see **emanations**). Ever since the psychogalvanic reflex was scientifically demonstrated by O. Verdguth in 1909, it had been well known that emotions produce changes in the electrical conductivity of the tissues of the hand.

W. J. Kilner, who attempted to experiment with the human **aura,** reported that it also was sensitive to electric currents; the aura completely vanished under a negative charge.

Many mediums reportedly had electrical sensations before their séances. Sensations similar to holding the poles of a strong electric battery started eight or nine hours before the sitting in the case of **Elizabeth d'Esperance.** The hair of **Florence Cook** emitted sparks before a sitting. **Mrs. J. H. Conant** observed an electrical fullness hours before a séance. One Professor Winther wrote of an electrically charged atmosphere in séances with **Anna Rasmussen.** Finally **Lord Adare** gives the following account in *Experiments with D. D. Home in Spiritualism* (1869): "My chair began to vibrate rapidly in the most violent way; it gave me a curious tingling sensation up my arm to the elbow and up my legs as though I was receiving an electric shock." He also quotes the following communication from the control of **D. D. Home:** "Remember, Dan must not sit on a silk cushion while the hot weather lasts. To-night the atmosphere is so surcharged with electricity that it appears to us quite thick, like sand. We feel like men wading through a quicksand—slipping back as fast as we advance."

Similar sensations to those recorded by Adare have been experienced by people engaged in **automatic writing** when the power bursts upon them. The emanoscope of E. K. Müller, which detected the susceptibility of persons to electricity, disclosed much more powerful reactions in the presence of the medium Oscar Schlag than Müller had previously observed.

Several **electric girls** were known in the history of **Spiritualism.** The name of **Angelique Cottin** is the most famous. An earlier instance was furnished by two electric girls of Smyrna who landed at Marseilles in November 1838. According to E. C. Rogers in his book *Philosophy of Mysterious Rappings* (1853), various men of science and professors visited the girls and ascertained the following phenomena:

"The girls stationed themselves, facing each other, at the ends of a large table, keeping at a distance from it of one or two feet, according to their electrical dispositions. When a few minutes had elapsed a crackling, like that of electric fluid, spreading over gilt paper, was heard, when the table received a strong shake, which always made it advance from the elder to the younger sister. A key, nails or any piece of iron, placed on the table instantaneously stopped the phenomena. When the iron was adapted to the under part of the table it produced no effect upon the experiment. Save this singularity, the facts observed constantly followed the known laws of electricity, whether glass insulators were used or whether one of the girls wore silk garments. In the latter case the electric properties of both were neutralised. Such was the state of matters for some days after the arrival of the young Greeks, but the temperature having become cooler and the atmosphere having loaded itself with humidity, all perceptible electric virtues seemed to have deserted them."

Catherine Berry, a developing medium of the 1870s, was said to be the possessor of similar powers. A footnote signed by "Editor, *Human Nature,*" in Berry's *Experiences in Spiritualism* (1876), states: "Mrs. Berry has the power of causing persons with a mediumistic temperament to fall down, or reel about, by the simple motion of her hand. At times, in her hands, a stick becomes a 'magic wand,' causing objects to move in a surprising manner."

Hector Durville, in his *Traité Experimental de Magnétisme* (2 vols., 1895–96) wrote of an infant, born at Saint Urbain in January 1869, who was always charged like a Leyden jar. No one could go near the baby without getting a shock, more or less violent, and luminous rays escaped now and then from the baby's fingers. The infant died in its ninth month.

The stage performances of Annie Abbot, "The Little Georgia Magnet," were unfavorably discussed by **Sir Oliver Lodge** in the *Journal* of the Society for Psychical Research (vol. 5). The demonstrations of Lulu Hurst (Mrs. Paul Atkinson) in New York in 1884 were of a similar nature. By a mere touch of her fingertips she repelled strong men and lifted Hardinge Britten with his chair a foot from the floor by touching the back side of the chair with one hand. Britten felt what was described as the strength of a condensed cyclone. No psychic powers were claimed by Lulu Hurst herself, however, in her *Autobiography* (1897), and more mundane explanations of her performances were proposed by Walter B. Gibson and J. N. Maskelyne.

Sources:

Adare, Lord. *Experiments with D. D. Home in Spiritualism.* Privately published, 1869.

Gibson, Walter B. *The Georgia Magnet.* St. Louis, 1922.

Hurst, Lulu. *Lulu Hurst Writes Her Autobiography.* Rome, Ga., 1897.

Maskelyne, J. N. *The Magnetic Lady; or, a Human Magnet Demagnetised.* Bristol, 1892.

Electrobiology

A mode of inducing **hypnotism** by having the subject look steadily at metallic disks. The process originated about the middle of the nineteenth century, and its fame was spread by numerous lecturers in England and the United States.

Electronic Video Phenomenon

Similar to the **electronic voice phenomenon.** Reports have been made of paranormal images appearing on television sets. There is no firm evidence for such claims, since faulty tuning, interference patterns, and other obvious technical reasons may explain unusual images on a television tube.

Electronic Voice Phenomenon (EVP)

Preferred term for the phenomenon discovered by **Friedrich Jürgenson** in 1959 and extensively developed by the experiments of **Konstantin Raudive** (1909–1974). The phenomenon is often referred to as **Raudive voices.** Raudive voices, apparently from dead individuals, are electronically impressed on tape recordings made on standard apparatus (sometimes enhanced by a simple diode circuit). The voices have also been discovered on the "white noise" of certain radio bands. This discovery, backed by thousands of experiments, has been seen as a way of obtaining communications from dead persons through electronic apparatus instead of Spiritualist mediums. However, some experimenters believe that the voice phenomenon is ambiguous or capable of mundane explanation, such as being the result of radio sources or even wishful thinking. George W. Meek developed an apparatus, the "spiricom," for use in testing the possibilities of more unambiguous Raudive voice data.

Sources:

Bander, Peter. *Carry On Talking: How Dead are the Voices?* Colin Smythe, 1972. Reprinted as *Voices from the Tapes: Recordings from the Other World.* New York: Drake Publishers, 1973.

Ellis, D. J. *The Mediumship of the Tape Recorder.* Polborough, West Sussex, England: The Author, 1978.

Raudive, Konstantin. *Breakthrough: An Amazing Experiment in Electronic Communication.* New York: Taplinger, 1971.

Electronics

A later development of the work of **Albert Abrams** (1863–1924) that employs therapeutic apparatus to produce shortwave low-power electromagnetic and alternating magnetic currents to correct disease conditions. Abrams believed that diseases produced peculiar radiations, and that these radiations in turn produce a reflex in living tissue that can be detected by apparatuses and normalized by the appropriate electromagnetic energy produced by other apparatuses.

In 1922 the College of Electronic Medicine was founded in San Francisco. It was superseded in 1947 by the Electronic Medical Foundation. The magazine *Physio-Clinical Medicine,* started in 1916, later became the *Electronic Medical Digest,* reviewing a wide range of developments relating to electromagnetic theories and research in cell radiation and disease therapies.

Sources:

Abrams, Albert. *Human Energy.* San Francisco: The Author, 1914.

Barr, James. *Abrams' Methods of Diagnosis and Treatment.* London, 1925.

Electrum

Amber is the subject of some curious legends under this name, but there is also a metallic electrum, sometimes called orbas by the French. Electrum is an alloy of gold and silver in the proportion of four parts gold to one of silver. The pale yellow color resembles amber.

According to Pliny, a cup of this metal has the property of discovering poison by exhibiting certain semicircles like rainbows in the liquor, which it also keeps sparkling and hissing as if on the fire. A black species of electrum or amber is the *gargates* spoken of by Pliny and the jet sometimes used in jewelry.

Elementals

A term usually used synonymously with **elementary spirits,** but sometimes given a special connotation by Spiritualists to indicate discarnate entities of a malicious nature. Theosophists use the word elemental to denote the "astral remains" or "shell" of one who has lived an evil life on Earth and who is loath to leave the scene of his pleasures. With some occultists, again, elemental really signifies a subhuman being, probably identical to an elementary spirit, but of a mental and moral status considerably lower than that of a human.

Sources:

Lévi, Éliphas. *Transcendental Magic.* London: Redway, 1896. Reprint, New York: Samuel Weiser, 1970.

Elementary Spirits

The unseen entities said to inhabit the four elements; they are composed of the finest essence of each element. The creatures of the air are called sylphs; of the earth, gnomes; of fire, salamanders; and of water, nymphs or undines. The **Abbé de Villars** (1635–ca. 1673) is often cited as an authority on the subject, since he published a treatise entitled *Comte de Gabalis* (1670), from which a good deal of what follows is drawn.

According to this work, before the Fall, the creatures of the elements were subject to Adam in all things. By means of certain performances this ancient communication may be restored, and man may once more have at his command the elementary spirits. The abbot gives a brief sketch of the nature of these spirits.

The air, he says, is filled with a great number of sylphs, beings of human form, somewhat fierce in appearance, but really of a docile nature. They are interested in the sciences and are subtle. They are officious toward the sages and hostile toward the foolish and the ignorant. Their wives and daughters are of a masculine type of beauty, such as that of the Amazons.

The seas and rivers are inhabited as well as the air, and the beings dwelling there are designated undines, or nymphs, by the sages. The female population much exceeds the male, the women being so exceedingly beautiful that among the daughters of men there is none to equal them.

The Earth is filled almost to the center with gnomes, beings of small stature that guard subterranean treasure, minerals, and precious stones. They are ingenious, friendly toward men, and easy to command. They provide the children of the sages with all the money they require, asking no other reward for their services than the glory of performing them. The gnomides, their wives, are small of stature but very good-looking, and they dress very curiously.

As for the salamanders, the inhabitants of the region of fire, they serve the philosophers, but are not overanxious for their company. Their daughters and wives are rarely seen. Their women are very beautiful, beyond all the other elementals, since they dwell in a purer element. Their habits, mode of life, manners, and laws are admirable, and their mental brillance is even greater than their physical beauty. They know and religiously adore the Supreme Being, but have no hope of eternal enjoyment of him, since their souls are mortal. Being composed of the purest parts of the elements wherein they dwell, and having no contrary qualities, they can live for several centuries, yet they are much troubled because of their mortal nature.

It was revealed to the philosophers, however, that an elementary spirit could attain immortality by marrying a human being. The children born of such unions are more noble and heroic than the children of human men and women, and some of the greatest figures of antiquity—Zoroaster, Alexander, Hercules, and Merlin, to mention a few—are declared to have been the children of elementary spirits.

The salamanders, the *Comte de Gabalis* goes on to say, are composed of the most subtle particles of the sphere of fire, conglobated and organized by the action of the Universal Fire, so called because it is the principle of all the motions of nature. The sylphs are composed of the purest atoms of the air; the nymphs, of the most delicate particles of water; the gnomes, of the finest essence of earth. Adam was in complete accord with these creatures because, being composed of that which was purest in the four elements, he contained in himself the perfections of these four species and was their natural king. But since by reason of his sin he was cast into the excrements of the elements, there no longer existed the harmony between him, so impure and gross, and these fine and ethereal substances.

The abbot goes on to give instructions on how this state of things can be remedied and the ancient order restored. To attain this end mankind must purify and exalt the element of fire that is within all humans. All that is necessary is to concentrate the fire of the world, by means of concave mirrors, in a globe of glass. There will then be formed within the globe a solar powder that, having purified itself from the mixture of other elements, will become in a very short time a sovereign means of exalting the fire within us and make us, so to speak, of an igneous nature. Thereafter, the creatures of the fire will become our inferiors, and, delighted at the restoration of mutual harmony between themselves and the human race, they will show toward man all the goodwill they have for their own kind.

Sylphs, gnomes, and nymphs are more familiar with humans than are the salamanders, on account of their shorter term of life, and it is therefore easier to get in touch with them. To restore its dominion over the sylphs, gnomes, or nymphs, the human race must close a glass full of air, earth, or water and expose it to the sun for a month, after which its various elements must be separated according to science. This process is easiest in the case of water and earth. "Thus," states the *Comte,* "without characters, without ceremonies, without barbarous words, it is possible to rule absolutely over these peoples."

Other authorities prescribe other means of obtaining dominion over the spirits of the elements. The occultist Éliphas Lévi, for instance, stated that anyone desiring to subjugate the elementals must first perform "the four trials of antique initiation," but as the original trials are no longer known, similar ones must be substituted. Thus, he who would control the sylphs must walk fearlessly on the edge of a precipice; he who would win the service of the salamanders must take his stand in a burning building, and so on, the point of the ordeals being that the man should show himself unafraid of the elements whose inhabitants he desires to rule.

In medieval times the evocation and exorcism of elementary spirits was practiced extensively, the crystal being a favorite means of evoking them. The exorcism of earth was performed by means of breathing, sprinkling water, burning incense, and repeating a certain prayer to the gnomes. Air was exorcised by breathing toward the four cardinal points and by reciting prayers to the air spirits (sylphs). Casting salt, incense, sulphur, camphor, and white resin into a fire was considered efficacious in exorcising that element. In the case of water, breathing and laying on of hands, repeating formulas, mixing salt and ashes of incense, and other ceremonies were to be observed. In every instance, a special consecration of the four elements was a primary and essential part of the proceedings.

As stated, it was thought possible for a human being to confer immortality on an elementary spirit through marriage. This does not always occur, however. Sometimes the reverse is the case, and the elementals share their mortality with their human mate. In literature, at all events, countless stories relate how men have risked and lost their immortality by marrying a sylph or an undine. According to the *Comte de Gabalis,* however, it would seem to be a matter of choice whether a man confers his immortality on his ethereal partner or whether he partakes of her mortal nature, for it suggests that those who have not been predestined to eternal happiness would do well to marry an elemental and thus spare themselves an eternity of woe.

Not every authority has painted so attractive a picture of the creatures of the elements as has the Abbé de Villars. Some have contended that there are innumerable degrees among these beings, the highest resembling the lower **angels,** while the lowest may often be mistaken for demons, which they are not. Not only do multitudinous variations of form and disposition characterize the elementals of this planet, the other planets and the stars are also the abode of countless hosts of elementary spirits, differing from those of our world perhaps more than the latter differ from one another.

All the forms of beasts, insects, and reptiles, as well as strange combinations of the shapes of different animals, may be taken by the lower elementals of Earth. The inhabitants of each element have their peculiar virtues and vices that serve to distinguish them. The sylphs are capricious and inconstant, but agile and active; the undines, jealous and cold, but observant; the salamanders, hot and hasty, but energetic and strong; and the gnomes, greedy of gold and treasures, but nevertheless hardworking, good-tempered, and patient. Anyone who would seek dominion over any of these must practice their virtues but carefully avoid their faults, thus conquering them, as it were, on their own ground.

Each species can dwell only in its own proper element. Thus a sylph may not invade the sphere of a salamander, or vice versa, while both would be decidedly out of their element in the regions of the nymphs or the gnomes. Four rulers have been set over the four species—Gob, ruler of the gnomes; Paralda, of the sylphs; Djin, of the salamanders; and Necksa, of the nymphs. The dwellers in each element are assigned a point of the compass, which is where their special kingdom lies. To the gnomes is given the north, to the salamanders, the south, to the sylphs, the east, and to the undines, the west. The gnomes influence those of a melancholic disposition, because they dwell in the gloom of subterranean caverns. The salamanders have an effect on those of sanguine temperament, because their home is in the fire. The undines influence the phlegmatic, and the sylphs those of a bilious temperament. Although the elementals are invisible to human eyes, they may on occasion become visible to those who invoke them, to the sages and philosophers, and even to the multitude.

It is said that in the reign of King Pépin, Zedekias, a ninth-century physician, suggested to the sylphs that they should appear to men, whereupon the air was seen to be full of them, sometimes ranged in battle, or in an aerial army. It was said by the people that they were sorcerers—an opinion to which Charlemagne and his son Louis the Débonnaire subscribed, the latter at least imposing heavy penalties on the supposed sorcerers. To witness the admirable institutions of the sylphs, certain men were raised up in the air, and while descending were seen by their fellowmen on Earth. The latter regarded them as stragglers of the aerial army of sorcerers and thought that they had come to poison the fruits and fountains. These unfortunate persons were thereupon put to death, along with many others suspected of ties to the sorcerers.

The nature of these spirits was collated in the *Comte de Gabalis* with the oracles of antiquity, and even with the classic pantheons of Greece and Rome. Pan, for example, was the first and oldest of the nymphs, and the news of his death, communicated by the people of the air to the inhabitants of the waters, was proclaimed by them in a voice that was heard sounding over all the rivers of Italy—"The great Pan is dead!"

The scholar of occultism and mysticism **A. E. Waite** considered the "angels" evoked in medieval magic, as well as the "devils" of the **witchcraft** sabbat, to be higher or lower elementals. Others see in the brownies and domestic spirits of folklore some resemblance to the subjugated elementary spirits. Even the familiar **poltergeist,** when not clearly identified as the spirit of a deceased person, may be regarded as an elemental. Spiritualists believe that elementals occasionally manifest as mischievous or evil spirits at séances.

Although the book *Comte de Gabalis* is probably an imaginative or allegorical work, it brings together preexisting legends of elementary spirits in an entertaining and philosophical format.

Sources:

Barrett, Francis. *The Magus.* London: Lackington, Allen, 1801. Reprint, New Hyde Park, N.Y.: University Books, 1967.

De Villars, l'Abbé de Montfaucon. *Comte de Gabalis.* 1670. Reprint, New York: Macoy Publishing and Masonic Supply, 1922.

Lévi, Éliphas. *Transcendental Magic.* London: Redway, 1896. Reprint, New York: Samuel Weiser, 1970.

Waite, Arthur Edward. *The Book of Black Magic and of Pacts Including the Mysteries of Goëtic Theurgy, Sorcery, and Infernal Necromancy.* London: George Redway, 1898. Revised as *The Book of Ceremonial Magic.* New Hyde Park, N.Y.: University Books, 1961.

Elf Arrows (or Elf Bolts)

The superstitious name given to small triangular flints, known as Belemnites, found in many countries, but notably in Scotland. It was believed that these stones were arrows shot by the elves, which usually prove fatal to cattle—the cure being to touch the cow with the arrow with which it had been hit and give it water in which the arrow had been dipped to drink.

In his book *The Secret Commonwealth of Elves, Fauns, and Fairies* (1691), Robert Kirk describes the fairy arrow as being tipped with yellow flint and states that it inflicts a mortal wound without breaking the skin. He also says that he examined such wounds. It is even on record that an Irish bishop was thus shot at by an evil spirit, and it was said that the arrows were manufactured by the devil with the help of attendant imps who rough-hewed them while the archfiend finished the work.

Cases are on record of elf arrows allegedly made and used by the witches of Scotland within historic times. In 1662 Isobel Gowdie confessed that she had seen such elf arrows made. Similar superstitions regarding these remnants of the Stone Age prevail in Italy, Africa, and Turkey.

Sources:

Kirk, Robert. *The Secret Commonwealth of Elves, Fauns, and Fairies.* 1691. Reprint, London: D. Nutt, 1893.

Elf-Fire

The *ignis fatuus,* or "foolish fire," a name also given to fire obtained by rubbing two pieces of wood together, used in superstitious ways. The elf-fire proper is the phosphorescent light seen hovering over marshy ground. When approached, it appears to recede or vanish suddenly, reinforcing the superstition that it is a mischievous spirit. When seen in graveyards the *ignis fatuus* is known as a "corpse candle." Among the Russian peasantry it was believed that these wandering lights were the souls of stillborn children, who did not desire to lure people from the path but who got no rest until they found their bodies.

Eliade, Mircea (1907–1986)

Noted scholar of the history of religions and for many years a professor at the University of Chicago. Eliade was born March 9, 1907, in Bucharest, Romania, and was educated at the University of Bucharest (M.A., 1928) and the University of Calcutta (Ph.D., 1933). He was a cultural counselor for the Romanian Legation, Lisbon (1941–44) during World War II, and after hostilities ended he became a visiting professor at the Ecole des Hautes Etudes, the Sorbonne, Paris (1946–49), before moving to University of Chicago, where he served first as the Haskell lecturer (1956) and later as a professor.

From his broad examination of the religious life of various peoples and his study of the nature of religious experience, Eliade wrote several important books dealing with topics related to parapsychology and the occult. He is most remembered for his studies of alchemy and shamanism and the monumental *Encyclopedia of Religion,* which he edited during the last years of his fruitful life.

Sources:

Eliade, Mircea. *1907 to 1937: Journey East, Journey West.* Vol. 1 of *Autobiography.* San Francisco: Harper & Row, 1981.

———. *Forgerons et alchemistes.* 1956. Translated as *The Forge and the Crucible.* New York: Harper & Brothers, 1962.

———. *Occultism, Witchcraft and Cultural Fashion: Essays in Comparative Religion.* Chicago: University of Chicago Press, 1976.

———. *Patanjali et le Yoga.* 1962. Translated as *Patanjali and Yoga.* New York: Funk and Wagnall's, 1969.

———. *Shamanism: Archaic Techniques of Ecstasy.* Princeton, N.J.: Princeton University Press, 1964.

———. *Two Tales of the Occult.* New York: Herder and Herder, 1970.

———. *Le Yoga: Immortalité et liberté.* 1954. Translated as *Yoga: Immortality and Freedom.* New York: Pantheon Books, 1958.

———. *De Zalmoxis à Genghis Khan.* 1970. Translated as *Zalmoxis, the Vanishing God.* Chicago: University of Chicago Press, 1972.

———, ed. *Encyclopedia of Religion.* 16 vols. New York: Macmillian, 1987.

Eliezar (ca. 70–79 C.E.)

Legendary Jewish exorcist. According to the historian Josephus (ca. 37–ca. 100 C.E.), who claimed to have witnessed an exorcism in the presence of Emperor Vespasian, Eliezar applied to the possessed person a ring to which was attached a magical root prescribed by King Solomon. This drew out the devils, which Eliezar caused to pass into a basin of water, which was immediately poured away.

Elixir of Life

Medieval alchemists and mystics believed they were justified in their search for the mythical elixir of life, a universal medicine supposedly containing a recipe for the renewal of youth. The search for this elixir and a quest for gold became the grand goals of **alchemy.**

There was no standard method of manufacturing the elixir of life. In the **grimoire,** *Le Petit Albert,* for example, one is instructed to use eight pounds of sugar of mercury as the foundation of such a mixture. Fifteenth-century alchemist Bernard Trévisan said that dropping **philosophers' stone** into mercurial water would create the elixir. This process would, when "elaborated to the Red," transmute copper and other metals into pure gold, he stated; if "elaborated to the White" it would produce pure silver.

The possibility that the elixir could prolong life was undoubtedly the chief reason alchemists continued their search. The aged alchemist, weary with his quest for gold, craved the boon of youth and desired renewed health and strength to assist him in carrying out his great purpose. As an illustration of the alchemical concept of the elixir of life, the following extract from a work dealing with the secret of rejuvenescence (originally supposed to have been written by **Arnuldus de Villanova** and published by Longueville-Harcourt of Paris in 1716) is instructive:

"To renew youth is to enter once more into that felicitous season which imparts to the human frame the pleasures and strength of the morning. Here it is to no purpose that we should speak of that problem so much discussed by the Wise, whether the art can be carried to such a pitch of excellence that old age should itself be made young. We know that Paracelsus has vaunted the metamorphic resources of his Mercury of Life which not merely rejuvenates men but converts metals into gold; He who promised unto others the years of the sybils, or at least the 300 winters of Nestor, himself perished at the age of thirty-seven. Let us turn rather to Nature, so admirable in her achievements, and deem her not capable alone of destroying what she has produced at the moment she has begotten them. Is it possible that she will refuse unto man, for whom all was created, what she accords to the stags, the eagles, and the serpents, who do annually cast aside the mournful concomitants of senility, and do assume the most brilliant, the most gracious amenities of the most joyous youth? Art, it is true, has not as yet arrived at the apex of perfection wherefrom it can renew our youth; but that which was unachieved in the past may be accomplished in the future, a prodigy which may be more confidently expected from the fact that in isolated cases it has actually already taken place, as the facts of history make evident. By observing and following the manner in which nature performs such wonders, we may assuredly hope to execute this desirable transformation, and the first condition is an amiable temperament, such as that which was possessed by Moses, of whom it is written that for one hundred and twenty years his sight never failed him."

Trithemius (1462–1516) on his deathbed dictated a recipe that which he said would preserve mind, health, and memory with perfect sight and hearing, for those who made use of it. It consisted of, among other things, calomel, gentian, cinnamon, aniseed, nard, coral, tartar, and mace. Five grams of it were to be taken morning and night in wine or brodium during the first month; during the second month it was to be taken in the morning only; during the third month three times a week, and so on continuing throughout life. This was a more comprehensible recipe than that of **Eugenius Philalethes** (1622–1666), who stated:

"Ten parts of coelestiall slime; separate the male from the female, and each afterwards from its own earth, physically, mark you, and with no violence. Conjoin after separation in due, harmonic vital proportion; and straightway, the Soul descending from the pyroplastic sphere, shall restore, by a mirific embrace, its dead and deserted body. Proceed according to the Volcanico magica theory, till they are exalted into the Fifth Metaphysical Rota. This is that world-renowned medicine, whereof so many have scribbled, which, notwithstanding, so few have known."

In his *History of Magic* (1913) **Éliphas Lévi** describes **Cagliostro**'s great secret of rejuvenescence in the following terms:

"Let us now turn to the secret of physical regeneration to attain which—according to the occult prescription of the Grand Copht—a retreat of forty days, after the manner of a jubilee, must be made one of every fifty years, beginning during the full moon of May in the company of one faithful person only. It must be also a fast of forty days, drinking May-dew—collected from sprouting corn with a cloth of pure white linen—and eating new and tender herbs. The repast should begin with a large glass of dew and end with a biscuit or crust of bread. There should be slight bleeding on the seventeenth day. Balm of Azoth should then be taken morning and evening, beginning with a dose of six drops and increasing by two drops daily till the end of the thirty-second day. At the dawn which follows thereafter renew the slight bleeding; then take to your bed and remain in it till the end of the fortieth day.

"On the first awakening after the bleeding, take the first grain of Universal Medicine. A swoon of three hours will be followed by convulsions, sweats and much purging, necessitating a change both of bed and linen. At this stage a broth of lean beef must be taken, seasoned with rice, sage, valerian, vervain and balm. On that day following take the second grain of Universal Medicine, which is Astral Mercury combined with Sulphur of Gold. On the next day have a warm bath. On the thirty-sixth day drink a glass of Egyptian wine, and on the thirty-seventh take the third and last grain of Universal Medicine. A profound sleep will follow, during which the hair, teeth, nails and skin will be renewed. The prescription for the thirty-eighth day is another warm bath, steeping aromatic herbs in the water, of the same kind as those specified for the broth. On the thirty-ninth day drink ten drops of Elixir of

Acharat in two spoonsful of red wine. The work will be finished on the fortieth day, and the aged man will be renewed in youth.

"By means of his jubilary regimen, Cagliostro claimed to have lived for many centuries. It will be seen that it is a variation of the famous Bath of Immortality in use among the Menandrian Gnostics."

Aristaeus is said to have left to his disciples a secret rendering all metals diaphanous and man immortal. The process apparently consisted of a mystic treatment of the atmosphere, which was to be congealed and distilled until it developed a "divine sparkle" and then became liquefied. After the air was subjected to heat and underwent several other processes, the elixir supposedly emerged.

The great sixteenth-century physician **Paracelsus** was reputed to have discovered the elixir of life. In the *De Tintura Physicorum* (1570), ascribed to him, there is a description of a tincture that enabled individuals to live for centuries.

For an account of a modern claim to have made the elixir of life, see the entry on **Rev. W. A. Ayton.**

Sources:

Lévi, Éliphas. *The History of Magic.* London: Rider, 1913. Reprint, New York: Samuel Weiser, 1971.

Ellide

The dragon-shaped ship of Frithjof, the hero of the Icelandic legend the *Frithjof Saga.* It was said to be golden-headed, with open jaws, its under part scaled with blue and gold, its tail twisted and of silver, and its sails red-bordered and black. When its wings were outspread, it could skim the calmest seas. This ship was said to have been given to one of Frithjof's forefathers as a reward for kindness by Aegir, the sea god.

Elliotson, John (1791–1868)

President of the Royal Medical and Chirurgical Society of London and the first great exponent of **animal magnetism** in England. Elliotson was born October 29, 1791, in London. He later studied medicine at Edinburgh and Cambridge Universities, continuing after his M.D. degree with studies at Guy's Hospital, London. He became a professor of principles and practice of medicine at University College Hospital, which he helped to establish and where he lectured and served as a physician for a brief period (1834–38). In 1837 he became president of the Medico-Chirurgical Society, London, and was also a fellow of the Royal Society, Royal College of Physicians.

He was introduced to the subject of animal magnetism in 1837 by **Baron Du Potet,** whom he allowed to experiment at University College Hospital. His curiosity aroused, he himself began to study the phenomena and in 1838 found two wonderful somnambules in the **O'Key sisters,** Jane and Elizabeth. The success of his experiments created a stir. When he applied for a demonstration in one of the theaters of the college, he was refused permission, and he was finally requested to discontinue mesmeric practice in the hospital. Following this, in the autumn of 1838, he resigned his professorship and severed his connections with the hospital.

Elliotson's enthusiasm sustained the first serious blow when Thomas Wakeley, the editor of the medical journal *The Lancet,* invited the O'Key sisters to his own house and demonstrated that the violent convulsions into which the patients were sent were produced when, unknown to Elliotson and the patients, the mesmerized piece of money that was supposed to call forth the phenomena was resting in the waistcoat pocket of one of the company. He also proved that if the subjects were kept in ignorance, unmesmerized water could produce sleep, whereas mesmerized water had no effect.

After this the O'Keys were considered exposed and *The Lancet* closed its columns to mesmerism. Elliotson, nevertheless, was not discouraged. The year 1843 witnessed the birth of the journal *The Zoist,* which continued under the direction of Elliotson and one Engledue until 1856. It was a journal of **mesmerism** and **phrenology,** Elliotson being also an enthusiastic phrenologist. In 1824 he founded the Phrenological Society of London and was its president until 1843.

In mesmerism he saw a powerful means for phrenological research. Nevertheless, *The Zoist* was mainly concerned with the therapeutic aspects of mesmerism. With the advent of **Spiritualism,** it opened its columns to many critical articles on the phenomena. Elliotson himself attended a few sittings with **Maria Hayden** and described his experiences in an article, "The Departed Spirits." He was somewhat skeptical and attributed everything to the agency of the medium. **Table-turning,** however, meant something different to him. It fitted into the magnetic effluence theory, and Elliotson, on the basis of observations of others alone, concluded that: "there probably is true movement of the table independent of muscular force."

In 1863 he was introduced at Dieppe, France, to the famous medium **D. D. Home,** with the result that, according to the *Morning Post* of August 3, 1868 ". . . he expressed his conviction of the truth of the phenomena, and became a sincere Christian, whose handbook henceforth was the Bible. Some time after this he said he had been living all his life in darkness and had thought there was nothing in existence but the material."

Elliotson's first step after his conversion was to seek a reconciliation with John Ashburner, from whom he had become alienated by the latter's advocacy of Spiritualism. In 1867 Ashburner had published *Notes and Studies on Animal Magnetism and Spiritualism.* Elliotson now advocated what he saw as the truth of Spiritualism with the same zeal that he had formerly opposed it. Both Elliotson and Ashburner are of importance as representing the transition from animal magnetism to Spiritualism by the British. Elliotson died the next year on July 29, 1868, in London.

Elliott, G(raeme) Maurice (1883–1959)

Clergyman in the Church of England who explored the relationship between Christianity and psychical research. Elliott was born October 1, 1883, in London, and studied at the University of London and Hackney College. He was ordained a deacon in 1915 and a priest in 1917. From 1915 until his retirement in 1952 he served as curate, vicar, or rector of various parishes.

Through his religious studies, Elliott became interested in the psychical as a tool for interpreting the Bible and understanding what is commonly understood to be the "supernatural" element in Christianity, about which he wrote several important books: *The Psychic Life of Jesus* (1938), *Spiritualism in the Old Testament* (1940), *In Search of Faith* (1948), and *The Bible as Psychic History* (1959). He participated in the founding of the **Churches' Fellowship for Spiritual and Psychical Studies** and beginning in 1954 served as its secretary for many years. He was also a cofounder of the Confraternity, an association of laity and clergy concerned with **Spiritualism,** and a member of the directorate of the Order of the Preparation of Communion of Soul (a psychical research body). From 1954 to 1959 he served on the Commission on Divine Healing set up by the archbishop of Canterbury. He died June 8, 1959, in London.

Sources:

Elliott, G. Maurice. *The Psychic Life of Jesus.* 1938. Reprint, New York: London Press, 1974.

———. *Spiritualism in the Old Testament.* London: The Psychic Book Club, 1940.

Elm Tree

The elm tree (genus *Ulmus*) is prominent in Teutonic mythology, where it was said to have been given a soul by the god Odin, senses by Hoenir, and blood and warmth by Lodur, becoming Embla, the first woman. In Finno-Ugric mythology the elms were believed to be the mothers of the fire goddess Ut. In England the tree was associated with elves and sometimes known as "elven." At Lichfield, England, choristers of the cathedral used to deck the cathedral, close, and houses with elm boughs on Ascension Day.

It was also generally believed that the falling of the leaves of an elm tree out of season predicted a murrain (disease) among cattle. The elm was also used to cure cattle disease by means of the "need fire," when two pieces of wood were rubbed together until they ignited and a bonfire was built, through the smoke of which the cattle were driven. The leaves were used medicinally as a poultice for swellings, and the inner bark of the tree was used for skin and venereal infections. The slippery elm (*U. fulva* or *rubra*), mixed with milk, is still used by herbalists as a demulcent drink.

"Éloge de l'Enfer"

A critical, historical, and moral work, an edition of which was published in two volumes at the Hague in 1759. The title means "The Praise of Hell," and an English translation was published in 1760, with authorship ascribed to "Bénard." The book is very satirical, very heavy, and somewhat lacking in wit.

Elongation of the Human Body

A comparatively rare but by no means modern psychical phenomenon. The Neoplatonists observed it in certain obsessed men. The Neoplatonist Jamblichus (ca. 363 C.E.) in a work on divination writes: "The person of the subject has been known to dilate and tower to supernormal height." J. J. von Görres, in *La Mystique Divine, Naturelle et Diabolique* (5 vols., Paris, 1854) states that one night while the blessed Ida of Louvain occupied a bed with a very devout nun, Ida assumed monstrous proportions until she was lying in all but a very narrow strip of the bed. So great was the strain that the skin of one of her legs burst and she had a scar there from then on. Suddenly, her body began to diminish until at last it was reduced to an extremely minute size. The phenomenon was repeated as she returned from church with her friend.

Among modern mediums it was the famous **D. D. Home** (1833–1886) who most often demonstrated it. The expansions and contractions of his body were witnessed by 50 people at the very least. He felt exceedingly sick after elongations. His maximum growth was found by the **Master of Lindsay** to be 11 inches. On being questioned by the members of the committee of the **London Dialectical Society,** he said:

"The top of the hip bone and the short ribs separate. In Home they are unusually close together. There was no separation of the vertebrae of the spine; nor were the elongations at all like those resulting from expanding the chest with air; the shoulders did not move. Home looked as if he was pulled up by the neck; the muscles seemed to be in a state of tension."

Lord Adare saw a Mr. Jencken, a taller man, standing beside Home when the phenomenon took place. Home's feet remained fairly level on the ground. His unbuttoned coat showed a space of about four inches between his waistcoat and the waistband of his trousers. Lord Adare estimated the entire growth to be six to eight inches. Home appeared to grow also in breadth and size all over. If an observer placed a hand flat upon Home's waist, the observer felt the lower rib pass under his hand until it was some inches above it, the whole flesh and muscle apparently moving and stretching. On the contraction taking place, the lower rib came down until it pressed against the upper edge of the observer's hand and moved into its proper position.

After two elongations—at another time—Home was shortened to less than his natural height. He could also elongate his arms. Lord Adare placed himself in front of Home when he stood against the wall and made a pencil mark at the tip of his extended arms. First his left, then his right arm was elongated. When the distance between the pencil marks was measured, it was ascertained that the total elongation amounted to nine and one half inches. During this elongation Home's chest expanded greatly.

H. T. Humphreys, a journalist, published in 1868 the following account: "Mr. Home was seen by all of us to increase in height to the extent of some eight or ten inches, and then sink to some six or eight inches below his normal stature. Having returned to his usual height, he took Lord Adare and the Master of Lindsay and placing one beside each post of the folding doors lay down on the floor, touching the feet of one with his head and the feet of the other with his feet. He was then again elongated and pushed both Lord Adare and the Master of Lindsay backward along the floor with his head and feet as he was stretched out, his arms and hands remaining motionless by his side." The distance, as measured by Mrs. S. C. Hall, was more than 7 feet.

H. D. Jencken in his account in *Human Nature* (1869) also describes the elongation of Home's legs:

"The right leg of Mr. Home was then elongated about six inches, then shortened, the foot literally shrinking into the trousers. I carefully examined the leg from the ankle joint to the hip. The limb felt shrunk and withered and, gradually elongated, it felt as if it were being expanded by air being inflated. Whilst the leg was so shortened he walked about the room, proving that, though lessened in size, the function of the limb was unimpaired. The final and most satisfactory test, however, was the lengthening and shortening of the hand. I caused Mr. Home to place his hand firmly on a sheet of paper, and then carefully traced an outline of the hand, causing the pencil point to be firmly kept at the wrist. I am, I believe, rendering the first positive measurement of the extension and contraction of the human organism."

Home could also impart the power of elongation to others. Miss Bertolacci, a medium herself, was once elongated together with him. The phenomenon was also witnessed in the mediumship of other individuals.

In an article in *Light* (May 10, 1902, p. 223), John E. Purdon writes that:

"On one occasion in my quarters at the Sandown Hospital, Isle of Wight, I held the feet of Miss Florence Cook firmly against the floor, and can certify that there was no lifting of the heels, either with or without her boots, and that there was such an elongation that my brother-in-law, the late assistant-surgeon, Mark A. Kilroy, whose hands were on her shoulders, cried out 'She is dragging me up to the ceiling.' As he was over five feet nine inches in height there could have been no posturing that would account for his experience. Further, I most distinctly remember Miss Cook coming back with a jerk to her normal stature. My wife, who was present and heard her brother make the above remark, fully endorses my statement."

Florence Marryat described a séance with **Katie Cook** in which the medium's arm, which she held, was elongated to such an extent that it reached the sitters on the other side of the table, where it would have been impossible for her own much longer arms to follow it. She believed that the limb must have been stretched to three times its natural length and in sight of everybody.

The mediums **Frank Herne, J. J. Morse, Eusapia Palladino,** and (in her early career) **Rosina Thompson** were also reported to have demonstrated the strange gift of elongation. In his book *Modern Spiritualism* (1902), **Frank Podmore** quotes Rev. C. J. M. Shaw for an account of the elongation in his house of a professional clairvoyant named Peters. The arm of the medium was said to have grown six inches.

Pepito Arriola, the Spanish infant musical prodigy, when three and a half years old, sounded full octaves on the piano. His hands did not stretch more than five notes. It seemed to the onlookers that his hand increased during the time he played.

In the case known as the Great Amherst Mystery (see **poltergeist**), Esther Cox's body repeatedly puffed out to an abnormal size. She was screaming with pain, but the physicians could do nothing to relieve her agony. In a short time, however, the trouble always subsided.

In the case of Rosina Thompson, the elongation was said to be an attempt to quiet an "angry nerve," as the medium complained of violent neuralgic pains. The attempt was successful and the medium, on coming to herself, found all her pain gone.

There are difficulties in assessing the validity of the phenomenon of elongation. It is well known that there are variations in height when the musculature of the vertebrae are relaxed or tensed. The seventeenth-century British posture master Joseph Clark could voluntarily dislocate the vertebrae of his back and other parts of his body, exhibiting apparent deformity or variation in appearance. Some acrobatic entertainers can appear to lengthen or shorten their limbs through skillful manipulation of their muscles and clothing. On the other hand, one is reluctant to impute such deceptions in the case of saints of whom the phenomenon was reported, though, of course, in all cases a question of what the reporters observed remains pertinent.

In the case of mediums, the evidence is variable. Mediums like Herne or Palladino have been accused of **fraud.** On the other hand, D. D. Home, in spite of his many unusual feats, escaped any detection in fraud, and the claims of elongation in his case rest upon various reputable witnesses.

Sources:

Dunraven, Earl of. *Experiences in Spiritualism with D. D. Home.* 1969. Reprint (enlarged), Glasgow: Society for Psychical Research and Robert Maclehose, 1924.

Marryat, Florence. *There Is No Death.* New York: John W. Lovell, 1891. Reprint, New York: Causeway Books, 1973.

Podmore, Frank. *Modern Spiritualism.* London: Methuen, 1902. Reprinted as *Mediums of the Nineteenth Century.* New Hyde Park, N.Y.: University Books, 1963.

Elvis

Following the death of Elvis Presley on August 16, 1977, numerous reports of contact with him began to surface. One set of these reports concluded that he was still alive and for whatever reason had made some random contact with different individuals. The exploration of that hypothesis even became the subject of a prime-time television special on United States television.

At the same time, a number of mediums and other people with some psychic abilities claimed to have contacted Elvis and to have received messages from him in the spirit world. (It is not unusual for mediums to claim contact with famous people who have recently died.) Among the first to claim contact was Milwaukee medium June Young, who claims to have begun receiving messages within days of Elvis's death. She published a magazine, *Elvis Still Lives,* which included texts of her ongoing contacts.

Journalist Hans Holzer received information on a variety of people with messages, but was most impressed with those received by Dorothy Sherry, who seems to have begun contact in January 1978. The account became the basic story of his recent book *Elvis Speaks from the Beyond and other Celebrity Ghost Stories* (1993).

Such stories have appeared regularly in the weekly tabloids, among the most recent being a 1995 account of a woman who claimed that she was cured by the ghost of Elvis.

Sources:

Holzer, Hans. *Elvis Speaks from the Beyond and other Celebrity Ghost Stories.* New York: Dorset Press, 1993.

"I Was Cured by Ghost of Elvis." *Sun* (January 24, 1995).

Elymas the Sorcerer (ca. 47 C.E.)

As reported in the Christian New Testament (Acts 13:7–12), a magician of Paphos, in Cyprus, who openly defied the Apostle Paul before the Roman governor. "Oh, full of all subtlety and mischief," said Paul in righteous anger, "child of the devil, enemy of all righteousness, wilt thou not cease to pervert the right ways of the Lord? And, now, behold, the hand of the Lord is upon thee, and thou shalt be blind, not seeing the sun for a season."

How Elymas exercised his talents is not related, nor are the characteristics of his sorceries, but we are told that the sentence of Paul immediately took effect, and "there fell on him a mist and a darkness; and he went about, seeking some to lead him by the hand."

"Elymus the Sorcerer Struck with Blindness" is the title of a famous cartoon by Raphael Sanzio (1483–1520), from which tapestries in the Vatican were executed.

Emanations

Supposedly perceived by psychics and identified by some parapsychologists, but largely unrecognized by mainstream science, emanations play a significant part in theories about psychic phenomena. Throughout history, subtle emanations have been postulated under a variety of names, such as the *prana* of ancient India, the *mana* of Polynesian primitives, the *telesma* of **Hermes Trismegistus,** the *pneuma* of Gallien, the *astral light* of the Kabbalists, and the *spiritus* of **Robert Fludd.** Since the late eighteenth century and **Franz Anton Mesmer**'s proposals concerning magnetic fluid, a variety of terms for emanations have been proposed, such as "odic force," "animal magnetism," "ether," "radiations," and "vibrations." At various times emanations were said to proceed from and surround everything in nature. When living things were brought into contact through this medium the result was either interpenetration or repulsion.

Early Theories

Analogies with magnetism were inevitable because the properties of the magnet were known to ancient peoples, some authorities claiming that it was used in religious rites in Egypt, Greece, and Rome. They offered as evidence the iron rings and wings used in the Samothracian mysteries, the iron wings worn by priests of Jupiter to increase their magic power, and the various symbols ascribed to the paganistic gods.

It was said too that meteoric stones, because of a force they radiate, were used in religious rites, either as objects of worship or as tools for **divination** and soothsaying. Small stones were worn by the priests, and Pliny described the temple of Arsinoe as being vaulted with magnetic stone in order to receive a hovering statue of its patron. Cedrenus gave an account of an ancient image in the Serapium at Alexandria suspended by magnetic force.

The most ancient writing extant in which a theory of emanations may be found is ascribed to Timaeus of Locris (ca. 420–380 B.C.E.). He assigns the creation of the universe to divine emanations of God, an imparting of his being to unformed matter. By this union a world-soul was created that vitalized and regulated all things he said. Claudian, in his *Idyl of the Magnet,* uses the concept of emanations as a symbol of the informative spirit of things, the laws of nature, creative and existent.

The mysticism of the seventeenth and eighteenth centuries mainly depended on ideas of radiation emanating from all things, but especially from the stars, magnets, and human beings—of a force that would act on all things and was controlled by an indwelling spirit. The writings of **Paracelsus** abound with instances of the theory. He asserted that every substance in itself contained something of the nature of the lodestone, that an "astral light"—one of the finer media of nature, finer than the luminiferous ether—existed throughout planetary space and especially around the human brain and spinal cord. He wrote that humans are simply organized magnets, each with poles that attract and repel, that our thoughts are magnetic emanations projected from our minds.

According to Paracelsus, the universe emanated from a great First Being and there was a reciprocity in all things. In man too there existed an "astral quality" emanating from the stars, which, when compared with the physical body, might be considered a spirit. He wrote that this life stood in connection with the stars from which it sprang and drew to it their power like a magnet. Paracelsus called this sidereal life the *magnes microcosmi* and made use of it to explain the manifestations of nature—it glowed in the flower, glided in the stream, moved in the ocean, and shone in the sky.

The alchemist **Jean Baptiste Van Helmont** wrote of an ethereal spirit, pure and living, that pervades all things. Robert Fludd explained sympathy and antipathy by the action of the emanatory spheres surrounding man: in sympathy the emanations proceed from the center; in antipathy the opposite movement takes place. He maintained that these sensitive emanations could also be found among animals and plants, drawing an argument from the fact that if inert substances, such as the earth and magnet seem to be, have their emanations and their poles, living forms must also have them. William Maxwell, a seventeenth-century Scottish physician, wrote: "There is a linking together of spirits, an incessant outpouring of the rays of our body into another."

The philosopher Descartes asserted that all space is filled with a fluid matter that he held to be elementary, the foundation and fountain of all life, enclosing all globes and keeping them in motion. The idea of emanation and magnetism is also found in Newton's doctrine of attraction, which he called the "Divine Sensorium." As he suggests in his *Principles of Natural Philosophy,*

"Here the question is of a very subtle spirit which penetrates through all, even the hardest bodies and which is concealed in their substance. Through the strength and activity of this spirit, bodies attract each other and adhere together when brought into contact. Through it electrical bodies operate at the remotest distances as well as near at hand, attracting and repelling; through this spirit the light also flows and is refracted and reflected and warms bodies."

Mesmer, in detailing his theoretical work for the committee of the French Academy of Science, broke down his ideas into a series of propositions. One was the following:

"Between the heavenly bodies, the earth and human beings, there exists a mutual or interchangeable influence. The medium of this influence is an universally distributed fluid which suffers no vacuum, is of a rarity with which nothing can compare and has the property of receiving and transmitting all impressions of movement. Animal bodies experience the mutual effect of this agent, because it penetrates the nerves and affects them directly. In the human body particularly are observed properties analogous to those of the magnet. It is shown by experiment that a matter flows out so fine that it penetrates all bodies without apparently losing any of its activity. This may be communicated to other bodies, animate or inanimate, such as mirrors; it is communicated, propagated, augmented by sound. Its virtues may be accumulated, concentrated and transported."

These propositions were basic to Mesmer's larger understanding of **animal magnetism** and its use in curing disease. Some experimenters in the field who followed Mesmer began to place increasing emphasis on the "mesmeric trance" and the phenomena associated with a mesmerized subject rather than the claimed physical properties of animal magnetism. In the trance condition, many sensitive individuals were said to exhibit clairvoyant and other paranormal faculties, as well as insensitivity to pain and susceptibility to suggestion. This direction of research culminated in two contradictory developments: a natural association between the psychic faculties of mesmerized subjects and the phenomena of **Spiritualism;** and the medical transition from mesmerism to **hypnotism,** in which psychic faculties were discredited and emphasis was given to abnormal physical phenomena.

Reichenbach Phenomena

During the nineteenth century, these different directions of research and theory coexisted and were often inextricably entangled. From 1840 on, German chemist **Baron Karl von Reichenbach** conducted experiments in electromagnetic phenomena in relation to a vital force which he called **od** or "odyle." Reichenbach maintained that this force was perceptible to sensitives, or psychic individuals, who could identify the poles of magnets as well as lines of force from human, animal, mineral, and vegetable sources in a totally dark room. These emanations were perceived by the sensitives as differing in color, size, intensity, and temperature according to the nature of the object examined. The poles of a magnet emitted flames which were reddish-yellow from the south pole and bluish-green from the north; similar polarity was perceived in the luminous emanation from crystal. He said that human fingers also radiated patterns of light. His claims have a unique bearing on the phenomena of psychical research and parapsychology because they deal with the question of special sensitivity of certain individuals to subtle force.

Dowsing or water witching, with its associated fields of **radionics** and **radiesthesia,** is specifically concerned with a claimed sensitivity to subjective and objective aspects of subtle force and polarity. The visual indications of subtle force allegedly perceived by Reichenbach's sensitives also have relevance to **aura** research, where lines of force and colors are described by psychics as surrounding the human body. Theories of emanations are also invoked for such phenomena as **psychometry. Sir Oliver Lodge,** lecturing before the Literary and Philosophical Society of Liverpool, speculated:

"Here is a room where a tragedy occurred, where the human spirit was strung to intense anguish. Is there any trace of that agony still present, and able to be appreciated by an attuned or receptive mind? I assert nothing, except that it is not inconceivable. If it happens, it may take many forms—that of vague disquiet perhaps, or even imaginary sounds or vague visions, or perhaps a dream or picture of the event as it occurred. Relics again. Is it credible that a relic, a lock of hair, an old garment retains any indication of the departed—retains any portion of his personality? Does an old letter? Does a painting?—an old master we call it. Aye, much of the personality of an old master may be thus preserved. Is not the emotion felt looking at it a kind of thought transference from the departed?"

Writing on the psychic gifts of the medium **Stephan Ossowiecki, Charles Richet** stated:

"There is something profoundly unknown in a line of our writing, other than the lines traced on the paper. This unknown something may be called an emanation. I have called it pragmatic emanation, which would act on our cryptesthesis and stimulate cognition. It resembles somewhat the emanation from subterranean water that provokes the movements of the dowsing rod."

The simile is suggestive. Running water, metals, crystals, and magnets produce strange sensations in some sensitives. In hypnotic and in hysteric cases the sensitivity to metals is very pronounced. The magnetism of the earth is felt by some sleepers according to whether they lie in the north-south or in the east-west position. Reichenbach discussed all these phenomena.

His famous work *Researches on Magnetism, Electricity, Heat, Light, Crystallisation and Chemical Attraction in their Relations to the Vital Force* was published and translated in 1849 and 1850. However, his *Letters on Od and Magnetism* (1852) provides a less complex introduction.

In the 1880s the **Society for Psychical Research** (SPR) investigated and replicated Reichenbach's claims. In trials with 45 subjects of both sexes, with ages ranging between 16 and 60, three professed to see something luminous. With one subject 14 consecutive successes were recorded. The SPR's committee concluded:

"In view of these apparent confirmations of previous testimony, the committee is inclined to the opinion that, among other unknown phenomena associated with magnetism, there is a *prima facie* case for the existence, under conditions not yet determined, of a peculiar and unexplained luminosity resembling phosphorescence, in the region immediately around the magnetic poles, and visible only to certain individuals" (*Proceedings,* vol. 1, 1883: 230).

However, another, more exhaustive, investigation on behalf of the **American Society for Psychical Research** by Prof. Joseph Jastrow and Dr. George Nutthal was entirely negative.

Other Turn-of-the-Century Experimenters

During the decades before World War I, the first generation of psychical researchers devoted a signifcant amount of energy in attempts to verify the existence of various forms of emanations from the human body. Among the more famous of these efforts center upon the experiments on the human aura by the physician **Walter J. Kilner.**

An interesting analogy can be found in the experiments of Dr. **Joseph Maxwell** regarding a "digital effluvium," the colored perception of which, according to his conclusions, indicated a highly psychical temperament. He advised that a dark object (e.g., an armchair covered with dark velvet) be placed between the light and the experimenter; the subject's hands were joined at the fingertips, palm toward the chest, and then slowly withdrawn, with the fingers kept stretched out. Seven or eight out of ten subjects, if their heads were on a level with the operator's head, perceived a sort of gray mist uniting the fingertips. Maxwell found that out of three hundred people of both sexes 240 to 250 perceived the effluvium; two or three out of a sample of one hundred saw it blue. Two saw it yellow and one saw it red. If the hands ceased to move, the effluvium disappeared. If the movements of withdrawal ceased when the fingertips were within 10 to 15 centimeters' proximity, the effluvium remained visible for a longer time.

Maxwell's experiments were conducted in daylight. One of his mediums saw the effluvium escape from the hands of the sitters and spread itself over the séance table. Putting out all light, Maxwell traced letters on the table with the tip of his finger. The medium was able to read five-lettered words thus traced.

This effluvium recalls the magnetic fluid of mesmerizers about which controversy ran high through much of the nineteenth century. Charles Richet believed that no satisfactory answer could be given to the question of whether the old method of mesmeric passes sets free some special human power that acts on other human beings. **Eugene A. D. Rochas, Hyppolite Baraduc,** and **Emile Boirac** claimed photographic evidence for its existence, though this evidence has proved inconclusive.

E. K. Müller, an engineer of Zürich and director of the Salus Institute for electromagnetic treatment of nervous disorders, also indicated the existence of an emanation from the human body that is capable of decreasing the resistance of an electric circuit. The experiments were further supported by the work of a Professor Farny of the Zürich Polytechnicum, who gave the name "anthropoflux" to the emanation. The maximum emission came from the inner surfaces of the fingers of the left hand. Its source appeared to be in the blood, but the breath was also charged with it. It penetrated a large number of substances, many of which gave off a secondary radiation and it could be stored in an inverted test tube in the same way as a gas.

Other mysterious emanations were claimed by Prosper Blondlot of the University of Nancy, France, in 1903. He asserted that the human brain and nerves give off rays that are capable of penetrating aluminum, black paper, and other opaque objects. He named them "N-rays" after the town of Nancy. The rays were believed to consist of at least four groups of ether vibrations. They were said to be of long wavelength and near electromagnetic waves in frequency. They could be obtained from various sources other than the Roentgen tube, and certain bodies seemed to have the property of retaining or storing the rays for a considerable amount of time. The human body was said to emit them continuously. Although nonluminous in themselves, the rays would increase the glow of any phosphorescent body they touched. A small spark or flame was similarly influenced. The existence of "N-rays" was supposedly demonstrated in photography; pictures taken without the rays were very faint, while those obtained while the "N-rays" were in action were much stronger.

Dr. Jules Regnault held it probable that the "N-rays" only constituted part of the radiation studied under the name "odic force." The reports of "N-rays" were followed by those of "N_1-rays" and by the demonstration of Gustave LeBon that all bodies emit effluvia, which he called "dark light." In 1893 a Dr. Luys published a book on the direct visibility of cerebral effluvia.

Of the several attempts to substantiate the existence of human emanations, the "N-rays" were most singularly proven nonexistent. A few months after Blondlot had been honored by the French Academy of Science, he was visited by an American physicist, Robert W. Wood. Wood slyly removed a prism from Blondlot's apparatus while the latter was describing an "N-ray" spectrum. According to Wood, this had no effect on Blondlot's observations, which he concluded could only be imaginary. The ridicule that followed this "exposure" (see *Nature,* vol. 70, 1904, p. 530) culminated in Blondlot's madness and death.

In 1896 Commandant Darget of Tours, France, claimed to have proven the existence of vital emanations in plants by placing a freshly cut small fern on a photographic plate in a dark room. After two days he obtained the exact portrait of the plant, effluvia thrown from each leaflet and zones of contracting during its loss of vitality. His experiments led him to propose that a photographic plate be placed on the head and heart of a man who was believed to be dead but might be in danger of being buried alive. Darget believed that traces of life would show themselves on the plate. But G. de Fontenay advised caution, saying there might be "perfidies of the sensitive plate" and the interchange of gaseous matter between living bodies and the atmosphere, the influence of secretions, or the action of radiant heat that might well be responsible for some of the phenomena.

Dr. Louis Favre, experimenting with Agnes Schloemer, claimed to have discovered powerful vital emanations of the human body. By the imposition of her hands, Schloemer could allegedly destroy such resistant bacteria as the *Bacillus subtilis* and the *bacillus anthracis.*

Dr. H. Durville published similar results with the typhoid bacillus in the *Bulletin General* of the Psychological Institute of Paris, but the most sensational experiments in this field were conducted by Drs. L. Clarac and B. Llaguet of Bordeaux with a Mme. X. The report of their seven-year investigations, published in 1912, appeared to prove the existence of a fluid emanation by certain individuals that prevented the decomposition of plants or animals and preserved them in a desiccated but much finer state than any mummification process could.

The experiments were conducted in the doctors' own laboratory; the various objects were provided by the physicians and placed immediately under lock and key. The treatment took place in light, under perfect control, each experiment taking about twenty minutes and consisting of placing the hands of Mme. X in contact with the object or sometimes only near it. Plants dried up with the preservation of perfect color; wine showed no signs of acid fermentation; in oysters the process of putrefaction was prevented, or stopped if the treatment began at a later stage; and fish and birds were preserved in their form, color, and brightness of the eyes. The blood of a rabbit (without being drained) was preserved in a liquefied state for 25 days and remained as a solid red mass afterward.

Similar phenomena were demonstrated by Joanny Gaillard, a shoe dealer of Lyons. He claimed that from his youth he had been able to heal burns and bruises of any sort by laying on his right hand. He observed that when he juggled with oranges they became hardened. He believed that a fluid that counteracted putrefaction and had germicidal qualities emanated from his hands. He made experiments beginning in January 1928, one being to mummify animal corpses and perishable commodities in general. He found that even fish, after treatment, were perfectly preserved. Oranges and lemons became as hard as wooden balls.

He made a little museum of such objects, which René Sudre in *Psychic Research* (March 1929) admits having seen. Lyons physicians tested Gaillard's "fluid" on seeds and microbes. It appeared that he had succeeded in arresting the germination of lentil seeds. When he tried his fluid on a bacterial culture, however, it seemed to be reflected in some curious fashion and he got the sensation of having burned his hands. A committee of physicians in Paris before whom Gaillard appeared came to the conclusion that the existence of his fluid had not been demonstrated.

A. Bue, in his *Le Magnétisme curatif* (1894), narrates interesting experiments in hastening the growth of plants by "magnetic passes." Bulbs of hyacinths were used. According to Bue, "By magnetizing every day, for about five or ten minutes, the water in the vases where the roots of these tubercles are immersed, one is able to give such vitality to the sap, that stem and flower will speedily assume extraordinary appearances."

Similar experiments were reported by Dr. Louis Favre at a meeting of the Psychological Institute at Paris in 1905. According to his findings, the human hand exercised an action over the germination and growth of plants, the right hand being the most active. It strengthened feeble vitality and the influence of six minutes' action on the first day extended to the whole period of germination. The better the health of the plant, the stronger the action.

Heinrich Nusslein, the German automatic painting medium, claimed the power to prolong the life of fresh-cut flowers for several days by making passes over them.

Gambier Bolton, in his book *Psychic Force* (1906), recommends the flower-healing test to discover mediumistic powers. In this test a dying blossom is put into fresh water in a place where it is sheltered from the full rays of the sun. The experimenter rubs the palms of his hands together sharply for half a minute and then, standing in front of the flower, places the palms of both hands behind the flower and draws the hands in a semicircle toward his body. This action is repeated slowly and steadily, with concentration, from 12 to 20 times, remembering that it is not at all necessary to touch the flower. As a further test, another dying blossom might be placed in water three feet away from the first. When the 20 passes have been made over the first blossom, both should be placed out of reach, in a moderate temperature, and left there for 24 hours. If at the end of that period the one treated shows any signs of improvement, the experimenter has some powers; if both look better, he is likely to be a good medium.

Hyppolite Baraduc spent many years studying the emission of human "fluid" and photographed the emanations of human hands. He also invented a **biometer** to register vibrations emitted from the hands. In the hands of psychics he found luminosity radiating from the base of the palm. The subjects' mental state had great influence over the lines of light he obtained.

Mental distress was disclosed by confused lines. Baraduc also photographed his son and his wife, one four minutes after death and the other 24 hours after death. In each instance there was seen stretching from the lifeless body a great stream of force that extended to the ceiling of the room and then turned down again. The son's face allegedly could be recognized in the stream, seen close to the body, by anyone who had known him. A profile of his wife was also seen in the room.

Albert Nodon, president of the Bordeaux Astronomical Society, tested the radioactivity of living substances by a specially constructed electrometer. He found that the radioactivity of vegetable matter was of the same order as that of uranium. It was found to be greater in the reproductive organs than in other parts of the plants, and was greater in newly cut plants than in dried ones. Freshly dug earth had similar radioactivity. The insects showed three to five times greater radioactivity by unit of weight than uranium. Unfortunately Nodon's instrument, because of its construction, could not be applied to humans.

As reported in *The Lancet* in 1931, British physician Charles Russ constructed an instrument to demonstrate that an energy radiates from the human eye. He suspended in a jar a delicate solenoid of mica covered with strips of aluminium. Electrically charged metal plates were fixed to the outside of the glass vessel. When a person's gaze was focused intently on one end of the cylinder it moved away from the eye. When the gaze was fixed on the other end it moved toward the eye. When the gaze was directed at the center it remained stationary.

The destructive effect of the human gaze on séance room phenomena was claimed frequently. **D. D. Home,** before his levitations, usually asked the sitters not to look at him. The fire-resistance test was sometimes similarly handicapped by the spectators' earnest stares. Experiments suggest that when sitters blindfold their eyes, psychical phenomena gain in strength, and **direct voice** may be obtained in fair visibility. Unfortunately, preventing close observation in séances also facilitates the production of fraudulent phenomena.

Recent Experiments

In spite of years of research and thousands of experiments there has been no completely satisfying scientific demonstration of emanations of psychic force nor any definitive explanation. Most of the earlier experiments have not proved repeatable under strict control conditions.

The best of recent work on emanations began with the efforts of Bernard Grad, a gerontologist at McGill University in Montreal. In the 1960s he began work with Oscar Estabany, a Hungarian immigrant who claimed healing powers. Utilizing his large laboratory and trained staff, Grad was able to put Estabany through a series of tests involving the stimulation of plant growth and the healing rate of mice, all with positive results. His work was followed by that of biochemist M. Justa Smith, who also worked with Estabany. By using nonhuman targets in their work, they were able to isolate the healing "power" as the causative agent and eliminate human suggestibility. Their research has stood for several decades without refutation and has been supported by parapsychological research on psychokinesis.

Sources:

Academy of Parapsychology and Medicine. *The Dimensions of Healing: A Symposium.* Palo Alto, Calif.: The Author, 1972.

Burr, Harold S. *The Fields of Life.* New York: Ballantine, 1973.

Crile, George. *The Phenomena of Life: A Radio-Electric Interpretation.* London: William Heinemann, 1936.

Grad, Bernard. "Healing by the Laying on of Hands: Review of Experiments and Implications." *Pastoral Psychology* 21 (September 1970): 206.

Hasted, John. *The Metal-Benders.* London: Routledge and Kegan Paul, 1981.

Kilner, Walter J. *The Human Atmosphere.* London, 1911. Reprinted as *The Human Aura.* New Hyde Park, N.Y.: University Books, 1965.

Krippner, Stanley, and D. Rubin. *The Kirlian Aura; Photographing the Galaxies of Life.* Garden City, N.Y.: Doubleday Anchor, 1974.

Maby, J. Cecil, and T. B. Franklin. *The Physics of the Divining Rod.* London: G. Bell and Sons, 1939.

Maxwell, Joseph. *Metapsychical Phenomena.* London, 1905.

Presman, A. S. *Electromagnetic Fields and Life.* New York: Plenum Press, 1970.

Price, Harry. *Fifty Years of Psychical Research.* London: Longmans, Green, 1939.

Rahn, Otto. *Invisible Radiations of Organisms.* Berlin, 1936.

Reichenbach, Karl, Baron von. *Letters on Od and Magnetism.* London, 1926. Reprinted as *The Odic Force: Letters on Od and Magnetism.* New Hyde Park, N.Y.: University Books, 1968.

———. *Researches on Magnetism, Electricity, Heat, Light, Crystallization and Chemical Attraction in Their Relations to the Vital Force.* London, 1850. Reprint, New Hyde Park, N.Y.: University Books, 1974.

Russ, Charles. "An Instrument Which is Set in Motion by Vision." *The Lancet* (July 3, 1931).

Tromp, S. W. *Physical Physics; A Scientific Analysis of Dowsing, Radiesthesia, and Kindred Divining Phenomena.* New York: Elsevier, 1949.

Emants, Marcellus (1848–1923)

Dutch author and poet who took a special interest in psychical phenomena. With the physiologist G. A. van Rijnberk, Emants took part in experiments with the famous medium **Eusapia Palladino** and became convinced of the genuineness of her phenomena. As a result, in 1903 Emants published an article in the Hague journal *Het Vaderland* proposing the foundation of a Dutch Society for Psychical Research. However, this did not take place at the time, and it was not until the efforts of **G. Heymans** of Groningen University that such a society was founded in 1920.

Emerald

One of the most highly esteemed precious stones, known to ancient Egyptians, Hindus, Greeks, and Romans. In India emeralds were used to adorn images in temples, and Moslems used emeralds as **amulets,** inscribed with verses from the Koran. Emeralds were believed to change color when surrounded by deception and treachery. They were also believed to be preservatives against decay, dysentery, and the bites of venomous creatures and to promote easy childbirth. In ancient Rome the emperor Nero was said to have had an unusually large emerald that he used for viewing gladiatorial contests. Presumably he was shortsighted and used it as a lens.

Emerald Table (of Hermes), The

A brief document believed to be the earliest statement of the principles of spiritual alchemy, ascribed to **Hermes Trismegistus,** after whom **alchemy** has been named "the hermetic art."

Hermes Trismegistus is a shadowy figure, possibly mythical. The old alchemists believed him to have been an Egyptian living about the time of Moses; others have claimed him to have been a personification of Thoth, the Egyptian god of learning. There is a legend that the Emerald Table (also known as the Smaragdine Table) was discovered by Alexander the Great in the tomb of Hermes in a cave near Hebron.

The earliest printed version in Latin dates from an alchemical work of 1541, but a commentary on it was known three centuries earlier, and the table might well be ancient. The original was believed to have been inscribed on emerald (smaragdine) in Phoenician letters, later translated into Greek and Latin. It has been translated into English as follows:

"True, without error, certain and most true; that which is above is as that which is below, and that which is below is as that which is above, for performing the miracles of the One Thing; and as all things were from one, by the mediation of one, so all things arose from this one by adaptation; the father of it is the Sun, the mother of it is the Moon; the wind carries it in its belly; the nurse thereof is the Earth. This is the father of all perfection, or consummation of the whole world. The power of it is integral, if it be turned into earth. Thou shalt separate the earth from the fire, the subtle from the gross, gently with much wisdom; it ascends from earth to heaven, and again descends to earth; and receives the strength of the superiors and of the inferiors—so thou hast the glory of the whole world; therefore let all obscurity flee before thee. This is the strong fortitude of all fortitudes, overcoming every subtle and penetrating every solid thing. So the world was created. Hence were all wonderful adaptations of which this is the manner. Therefore am I called 'Thrice Great Hermes,' having the Three Parts of the philosophy of the whole world. That which I have written is consummated concerning the operation of the Sun."

This statement's theme of "as above, so below" became a keystone of occult philosophy.

Sources:

Mead, G. R. S., ed. *Thrice-Greatest Hermes.* 3 vols. London: J. M. Watkins, 1964.

Emma

The servant girl of Joseph Haddock, a well-known English exponent of **animal magnetism** before the advent of **Spiritualism.** Emma was the first English somnambule or **trance** subject whose powers of **clairvoyance** and trance visions were carefully recorded. These were published in Haddock's book *Somnolism and Psychism* (1851) and in such journals of the time as *The Zoist* and the *Boston Chronicle.*

Haddock narrated that one day, trying to put a patient into magnetic (mesomeric) sleep, he thought of suspending a magnet from the ceiling and directing the patient to look steadfastly at it. Emma was in the kitchen under the room where he was practicing and knew nothing of his movements. In a few minutes Haddock smelled burning and called out to his daughter to look for the cause. She found Emma on fire. Haddock quickly ran down and found her mesmerized, on her knees before the kitchen fire, engaged in sweeping the hearth and with her apron burning from contact with a glowing coal. She was unconscious of the fire and her attention was wholly directed to a point in the kitchen ceiling. When asked what she was doing, she replied, "I want that magnet." When Haddock pretended not to understand, she replied, "that magnet hanging up there" and accurately described its position.

Subsequent experiments disclosed that Emma had remarkable powers both in medical and in traveling clairvoyance. Haddock freely employed her for making diagnoses. She could describe the diseased structures in the patient's body without medical terms. Looking at the heart she called the auricles the "ears" and the ventricles the "meaty part." She distinguished between arterial and venous blood in the heart by calling one the "light side" and the other the "dark side." She could see events at a distance and described the whereabouts of lost or stolen property.

One case attracted considerable attention at the time. A Mr. Arrowsmith of Bolton, England, was considerably worried over a sum of £650 that one Mr. Lomax the cashier remembered to have paid into the bank but which the bank denied receiving. Emma was consulted. On being given the envelope that had contained the money, she correctly described the contents and how they were handed in at the bank counter and finally described the missing banknotes and the bill of exchange in an envelope with other papers in an inner room of the bank. Arrowsmith went to the bank and demanded another search, and on the directions given by Emma, the money was found among some old circulars in the manager's private room.

Like her contemporary **Adèle Maginot,** Emma had visions of the future life and spiritual matters, which Haddock also recorded in his book.

Sources:

Haddock, Joseph. *Somnolism and Psychism.* 1851. Reprint, New York: Arno Press, 1975.

Emmanuel

Emmanuel, an entity who speaks through channel Pat Rodegast, emerged in the early 1980s as a being of golden light. Once he was comfortable with Emmanuel's presence, Rodegast worked with Emmanuel regularly, and some of the material from the channeling sessions were published in 1985 as *Emmanuel's Book: A Manual for Living Comfortably in the Cosmos.*

Emmanuel emphasizes a message of humans coming into a new relationship with God as co-creators. Separation from God had served a purpose and was now coming to an end. The clarity and simplicity with which Emmanuel spoke attracted popular **New Age** teacher Baba Ram Dass (**Richard Alpert**), who backed Rodegast in her channeling activity and wrote the introduction to *Emmanuel's Book.* He was convinced of Emmanuel's reality because of the perceived differences between Rodegast and her channeled entity.

Sources:

Rodegast, Pat, and Judith Stanton. *Emmanuel's Book: A Manual for Living Comfortably in the Cosmos.* New York: Some Friends of Emmanuel, 1985.

Emmerich, (Anne) Catherine (1774–1824)

German nun of the Augustine order who had ecstatic visions. Born September 8, 1774, at Flamske, Westphalia, Emmerich grew up in a peasant family. She became a servant in the household of an organist named Söntgen, and when his daughter Clara entered the convent of Agnetenberg at Dülmen, the sisters there were persuaded to take Catherine Emmerich as well. She was admitted as a postulant November 13, 1802, and professed a year later.

At the end of 1811, however, the government of Jerome Bonaparte, king of Westphalia, suppressed the convent. The church was closed and the community dispersed. Emmerich was destitute and ill, and for a few months stayed in the convent buildings, ministered to by Abbé Jean Martin Lambert (an elderly priest) and a servant girl. The three were later obliged to vacate the premises, and in 1812 the priest and Emmerich were lodged in the house of a widow.

Here she experienced frequent and prolonged ecstatic states. They were discovered accidently by Clara Söntgen, who went to visit her and found her in **ecstasy** with **stigmata,** blood falling from her outstretched hands. Clara at first thought she had met with an accident, but when she mentioned it to Emmerich afterward, Emmerich begged her to keep it secret.

On December 31, 1813, Emmerich's confessor, Father Limberg, also saw the stigmata when giving her Holy Communion. He discussed it with Father Lambert, and the two priests agreed to keep the matter secret, as they were uncertain what should be done.

Meanwhile Clara reported the matter to her father, and soon everyone in Dülmen was talking about it. The local physician visited Emmerich, determined to end her "hysteria," but came away convinced of the genuineness of the phenomena. He made an official report, and soon the administrator of the diocese of Münster took up the matter. Priests and doctors examined the girl, and as the news spread far and wide, famous visitors also came to see her, including the poet Clemens Brentano.

During her ecstasies, Emmerich experienced and described detailed scenes of Jesus' passion and crucifixion, including the story of the woman Seraphia said to have wiped the face of Jesus with a cloth, which later bore a miraculous picture of Jesus formed from the blood and sweat. Such sacred images came to be called **veronicas** (from the Greek *icon,* "image," and the Latin *vera,* "true"), the most famous being the **Turin Shroud.** The visions were approved by a number of theologians and priests, and highly regarded by Pope Pius IX, who requested that an Italian translation of them appear with the German original.

Emmerich continued to experience ecstasies and stigmata with severe wounds. She died February 9, 1824, after much agony caused by a wound in her side. She died murmuring the name of Jesus. She was buried on February 13, and six weeks later was exhumed, after a rumor that the body had been stolen. It was found that there was no corruption. The grave was opened again 32 years later, on October 6, 1856, and the body was still intact.

Sources:

Emmerich, Anne Catherine. *The Dolorous Passion of Our Lord Jesus Christ.* Springfield, Ill.: Templegate, 1951.

———. *Leben der Heil, Jungfrau Maria.* Munich: Literarisch-artistische Anstalt, 1852. Translated as *The Life of the Blessed Virgin Mary* by Michael Paliret. Springfield, Ill.: Templegate, 1954.

Schmöger, Carl E. *The Life of Anna Catherine Emmerick.* 2 vols. Los Angeles: Maria Regina Guild, 1968.

Encausse, Gérard (1865–1916)

Physician and occultist who wrote under the pseudonym "Papus." He was born July 13, 1865, at La Corogne, Spain, the son of a French chemist and Spanish woman. At the age of four, he went to France with his parents and was educated in Paris. As a young man he spent much time at the Bibliothèque Nationale, studying **magic** and **alchemy.** He became a physician and also joined the **Theosophical Society,** but resigned from it because of its emphasis on Eastern occult teachings.

In 1888 Papus published his *Traité élémentaire de science occulte,* the first of a number of books, and that same year founded the journal *L'Initiation* (1888–1914). He was an associate of such other well-known occultists as Joséphin Peladan, Stanislas de Guaita, and Oswald Wirth and founded the Independent Group for Esoteric Studies, which attracted a large number of students of the occult. He later directed the Martinist Order, based on the teaching of **Louis Claude de Saint-Martin** (1743–1803).

The many books by Papus cover the whole realm of occult thought, but his works on the **tarot** have remained by far his most popular. Three of his works were edited by his son Philippe Encausse.

Papus played a part in exposing the famous **Leo Taxil** hoax against **Freemasonry** and the Roman Catholic Church in France. Notwithstanding his occult activities, Encausse remained a popular and devoted physician. He served in the French army medical corps during World War I and died of a pulmonary infection October 25, 1916.

Sources:

Papus [Gérard Encausse]. *Le tarot des bohémiens.* 1889. Revised edition as *The Tarot of the Bohemians.* Translated by A. P. Morton. Edited by A. E. Waite. London: Rider & Son, 1910.

———. *Le tarot divinatoire* (The divinatory tarot). 1909. Reprint, Paris: Dangles, 1969.

———. *The Qabalah.* New York: Samuel Weiser, 1977.

———. *Traité élémentaire de science occulte* (Elementary treatise on occult science). 10th ed. Paris: A. Michel, 1926.

———. *Traité méthodique de magie pratique* (Systematic treatise on practical magic). 1924. Reprint, Paris: Dangles, 1969.

Waite, A. E. "Papus: A Biographical Note." *Occult Review* 25 (January 1917): 34–36.

Enchiridion of Pope Leo III, The

A collection of **charms,** cast in the form of prayers, that have nothing in common with those of the Roman Catholic Church. The *Enchiridion* is concerned chiefly with worldly, rather than spiritual, advantages. It is said to have been printed in Rome in 1523, and again in 1606. Its magical virtue rests on a supposed letter from Charlemagne to Pope Leo, in which the former states that since receiving the *Enchiridion* he has never ceased to be fortunate. However, no such letter appears to be in the Vatican library, where it was supposed to be lodged. The charms that the *Enchiridion* contains are supposed to be effectual against all the dangers to which human flesh is heir—poison, fire, wild beasts, and tempests.

When a copy of the book has been secured, it must be placed in a small bag of leather, carried on the person, and one page at least read daily. The reading must be done upon the knees with the face turned to the east, and works of piety must be performed in honor of the celestial spirits, whose influence it is desired to attract. The first chapter of the Gospel according to St. John is declared to be the most potent in the book. As for the symbols, they are mostly of Oriental origin.

The book also includes what are claimed as the mysterious prayers of Pope Leo III and certain conjurations of a semimagical character, including the seven mysterious orisons, which are merely clumsy imitations of the Roman ritual. From an extant edition of 1633, it seems unlikely that this book was the work of Pope Leo III and is more likely a compilation by a maker of **grimoires** (textbooks of black magic).

Sources:

Waite, Arthur Edward. *The Book of Black Magic and of Pacts Including the Mysteries of Goëtic Theurgy, Sorcery, and Infernal Necromancy.* London: George Redway, 1898. Revised as *The Book of Ceremonial Magic.* New Hyde Park, N.Y.: University Books, 1961.

End of the World

One of the most common concepts in prophetic literature, especially in the apocalyptical literature of Judaism and Christianity. The term can denote either the end of the physical world (*cosmos*) or the end of the social order (*aeon*). The theological term *eschatology* refers to teachings about the "last things," (from the Greek *eschaton*). Eschatology includes a consideration not only of the destiny of the world but of the individual (death, judgment, heaven, hell).

The most dramatic form of eschatology is apocalypticism. The apocalyptic vision views the world as essentially on a downward path. It will soon reach such a negative state that divine powers will intervene and bring the present order to an end. Only the faithful will be saved from destruction. There are a number of biblical passages representative of the apocalyptic viewpoint. In the Hebrew Bible (the Christian Old Testament) passages in Isaiah, Jeremiah, Ezekiel, Joel, Zechariah, and especially Daniel speak in apocalyptic terminology. In the Christian New Testament, passages in Mark and Thessalonians have strong apocalyptic overtones, while the Apocalypse or book of Revelation is an entire apocalyptic tract, demonstrably the most influential apocalyptic text in Western culture. Apocalyptic reflections also dominate some of the apocryphal literature, books written by ancient Hebrews but not included in the Bible. Such writings embody inspirational visions of the coming or second advent of a messiah, the state of faith, and interpretations of the future.

The most well-known apocalyptic book is that "channeled" by St. John of Patmos, the book of Revelation, which describes in some detail a vision of the endtime. It circulated widely among Christians at a time when they were under severe persecution for their faith. Like many older apocalyptic works, it is written in highly metaphorical language and describes a climatic cosmic war between the forces of good and evil. The forces of good are represented by the Church and God's angels and the forces of evil by the **Antichrist,** the beast whose name can be determined by **numerology,** "666," and their respective human supporters. The powerful images of this book constantly reappear in Western prophetic and apocalyptic literature over the centuries. One persistent theme in apocalyptic literature, for example, is the figure of the Antichrist, the mighty ruler opposed to God, as cited in the Epistles of John. This image harks back to the historical figure of Antiochus IV, a persecutor of the Jews.

The apocalyptical concept of the end of the world and the Antichrist figure have analogies in pre-Christian religions, such as Iranian mythology of the final conflict between Ahura Mazda and Ahriman. However, it is within the Jewish and Christian traditions that apocalyptic enthusiasm has been most notable.

In the West, in almost every generation there have arisen groups with an apocalyptic worldview and an expectation that they are witnessing the last days of human history. Not infrequently, these groups go so far as to set a specific date on which the endtime events will be initiated. Basic to such groups have been a "historicist" reading of the apocalyptic passages of the Bible, in which the prophetic texts are seen as referring to contemporary events. The failure of the proposed events to occur on time always creates a crisis in apocalyptic groups. Only rarely do they admit any significant error. Rather, they suggest that the date was incorrect and propose a new date, or, more often, they spiritualize the prophecy and suggest that it really occurred, but in an invisible spiritual realm.

In recent centuries, a number of apocalyptic date-setting groups arose from the teachings of British visionaries **Joanna Southcott** and, more notably, William Miller. Miller led an Adventist movement in the United States in the 1830s, a forerunner of both the Jehovah's Witnesses and the Seventh-Day Adventists. Miller proclaimed the Day of Judgment as March 21, 1843, but the date passed without apocalypse, and a revised calculation by one of the Adventist leaders proposed a new date of October 22, 1844. Many Adventists made special preparations for the coming of Christ, and most gathered for all-night prayer meetings on the eve of the expected event, but did not, as was widely reported by their theological enemies, don ascension robes and gather on hilltops. All were disappointed. Many, including Miller, admitted their mistake. Some posed new dates, and out of their subsequent failures have come a host of small Adventist groups (including the Advent Christian Church and the Jehovah's Witnesses).

Others found a means of reinterpreting Miller's teachings in a spiritualizing direction. Among them, Ellen G. White suggested that the date did not refer to a terrestrial event, but to a cleansing of a heavenly sanctuary. That event, which began in 1844, presages the more visible return of Christ in the indefinite but imminent future. White's teachings became the interpretation accepted by the Seventh-day Adventist Church.

In Britain in 1881 there was a panic in country districts during which people left their houses and spent the night in prayer, convinced that the world was coming to its end. This was occasioned by a fake prophecy ascribed to the legendary prophetess **Mother Shipton:** "The world to an end shall come, in eighteen hundred and eighty one." In fact, these and similar lines were invented by an eccentric bookseller named Charles Hindley, who had published them for a prank. He had already confessed to the hoax years earlier, but by then the prophecies had passed into folklore, and ordinary country people did not have access to the learned journals in which the hoax was discussed.

The end of the world concept figures in Eastern religions such as Hinduism and Buddhism, but Eastern and Western eschatology differ radically in their concepts of time. In esoteric Hinduism, time is regarded as a limitation of human consciousness and as illusory as the material world itself, designated as *maya.* On a popular level, Hindu mythology proposes vast cycles of time (*yugas*) in the ages of the world, during which there are great periods of creation, righteousness, decline, and eventual dissolution, part of an infinite cycle of creation and destruction of the cosmos. In the period of decline, there is the messianic concept of the rebirth of the divine Shree Krishna, who will redeem the world.

However, all these cycles are only a dreamlike moment of time in divine consciousness, of which the individual souls are myriad fragments; and in self-realization, or *moksha,* the individual consciousness goes beyond the duality of subject and object and is subsumed in a timeless and blissful divine consciousness, independent of time, space, and causality, which fall away as illusory.

It is of some interest that astrology has been the basis of apocalyptic speculations. For example, at the end of the seventeenth century, a group of German **Rosicrucians** settled in Pennsylvania and established an astrological observatory to search for the signs of Jesus' return. The group, known as the Woman in the Wilderness, died out, disappointed, in the early eighteenth century. More recently, with the alignment of most of the planets in the solar system in 1982, many astrologers predicted significant changes. Their predictions were bolstered by the predictions of two geophysicists, John R. Gribbin and Stephen H. Plageman, who termed their discovery of the effects of such events "the Jupiter effect," which became the title of a popular book they wrote. Gribbin and Plageman dealt honestly with the flaws in their predictions in a sequel, *The Jupiter Effect Reconsidered.* (See also **Malachy Prophecies**)

Sources:

Balleline, G. R. *Past Finding Out: The Tragic Story of Joanna Southcott and Her Successors.* New York: Macmillan, 1957.

Chamberlin, E. R. *Antichrist and the Millennium.* New York: E. P. Dutton, 1975.

Clark, Doug. *Earthquake—1982: When the Planets Align—(Syzygy).* Garden Grove, Calif.: Lyfe Production Publications, 1976.

Gribbin, John R. *Beyond the Jupiter Effect.* London: MacDonald, 1983.

———. *The Jupiter Effect.* New York: Walker, 1974. Revised as *The Jupiter Effect Reconsidered.* New York: Vintage, 1982.

Griffin, William, ed. *Endtime: The Doomsday Catalog.* New York: Macmillan, 1979.

Lowery, T. L. *The End of the World.* Cleveland, Tenn.: Lowery Publications, 1969.

Nichol, Francis D. *The Midnight Cry.* Washington, D.C.: Review & Herald Publishing Association, 1944.

Robinson, Douglas. *American Apocalypses: The Image of the End of the World in American Literature.* Baltimore, Md.: Johns Hopkins University Press, 1985.

Endless Cord, Tying Knots in

Around 1877–78 **J. C. F. Zöllner** (1834–1882) of Leipzig, Germany, investigated the phenomena of the medium **Henry Slade,** looking particularly for anything that might prove a fourth dimension of space, a hypothesis in which Zöllner was greatly interested.

Tying in an endless cord such knots as could ordinarily only be made if the ends of the cord were free was to provide such a test. In December 1877 Zöllner visited Slade with two pieces of hempen cord, the free ends of each being sealed to a piece of cardboard. To ensure that the cord was always in sight, Zöllner hung it round his neck, and kept Slade's hands continually in view. Under these circumstances four knots were produced, apparently on the original sealed cord. This experiment was in no way conclusive in the light of Slade's later reputation as a **fraud** and in view of the startling tricks performed by stage magicians with cords and rings. Zöllner reported on his experiment in his book *Transcendental Physics* (1880), which became the object of much ridicule by his colleagues.

Enfield Poltergeist, The

A contemporary British haunting that bears some resemblance to the reports of the **Amityville Horror,** although it does not appear to be the hoax that Amityville was. The house in question was a very ordinary suburban house in Enfield, North London, and the phenomena centered around the Hodgson family—divorcée Peggy Hodgson and her four children.

Poltergeist phenomena commenced August 31, 1977, at about 9 A.M. with shuffling and knocking noises. Hodgson was alarmed and took the children next door to her neighbor, a Mr. Nottingham, who was a builder. He checked the house to see if there were air locks in pipes or other natural causes, but found no explanation. Moreover, the knocks continued and even followed him up the stairs. When the police were called the knocks followed a policeman upstairs, and when he descended, an ordinary kitchen chair moved across the room without apparent contact. The police left, somewhat puzzled.

The following day Hodgson saw a chest of drawers move toward her. On September 4 two newspaper reporters made a visit at 2:30 A.M. together with a photographer. As they entered the house, children's toys, marbles, and other small objects began flying around. A child's building block struck the photographer. Although the photographer spent several months visiting the house and trying to get pictures of the phenomena, his equipment malfunctioned, the flashguns losing their charge. The phenomena were investigated by members of the **Society for Psychical Research,** including author **Guy Lyon Playfair,** but cameras and video equipment frequently malfunctioned. However, during the course of investigations, a remarkable photograph was obtained of teenager Janet Hodgson apparently flying through the air, one of many alleged incidents of **levitation.**

In addition to the knockings and movement of objects, the phenomena included gruff voices that appeared to come from Janet and her sister Margaret, clothes being whipped off beds, curtains blowing into the room and twisting themselves around Janet's neck, coins dropping from ceilings, and furniture being propelled through the air. Janet claimed that she floated about the room and even on one occasion went through the wall into the adjoining house. It was thought for a time that Janet was the center of the disturbances, but they continued even when she was away from the house for three months.

Playfair spent two years investigating the phenomena. He has stated that he caught the children faking some effects, but that this did not explain the rest of the phenomena, for which there seemed no possible physical explanation. In his book on the matter, *This House Is Haunted* (1980), he writes: "If the children decided to add a few tricks of their own this is to be expected." In such a highly charged atmosphere, this would not be remarkable, and it hardly seems reasonable to conclude on the strength of this that all the other phenomena could be traced to faking. More than 2,000 uncanny events are said to have occurred.

The case, which might fruitfully be compared with the **Ashtabula Poltergeist,** the **Cock Lane Ghost,** and the **Drummer of Tedworth,** is discussed in a set of correspondence in the *Proceedings* of the Society for Psychical Research (vols. 49–50, 1979–81).

Sources:

Fodor, Nandor. *On The Trail of the Poltergeist.* New York: Citadel Press, 1958.

Playfair, Guy Lyon. *This House Is Haunted: An Investigation of the Enfield Poltergeist.* London: Souvenir, 1980.

Rickard, Robert, and Richard Kelly. *Photographs of the Unknown.* London: Book Club Associates, 1980.

Rogo, D. Scott. *The Poltergeist Experience.* New York: Penguin, 1979.

Roll, William G. *The Poltergeist.* Garden City, N.Y.: Doubleday, 1972.

Wilson, Colin. *Poltergeist!* London: Hodder & Stoughton, 1981.

Engelbrecht, Johann (1599–1642)

German religious visionary. Engelbrecht acquired his psychic gifts after an illness, when he announced that he would live forever. In an account of his visions he states:

"I heard for 41 nights the holy angels singing and playing on the heavenly music to my bodily ears. Those would be wise witlings who are unable to believe anything but what they hear or grasp themselves. Our Lord has been beforehand with, for he opened the corporeal ears of the widow Shamann, who, sitting up with me one night and being in profound devotion, clapping her head to mine heard such a grand heavenly concert of music that she was not able to express it sufficiently. Anyone inquiring of her she will give the same account."

The ecstatic visions of Engelbrecht were followed by physical and other psychic phenomena. Troopers fired at him and broke a lance to splinters on his head, but he walked off uninjured. In ecstatic condition he preached for weeks without food, weariness, or loss of strength. To prove that his abstinence from food was genuine, and that he was fed spiritually, he went voluntarily to prison, guarded for a week or so from all possibility of material sustenance, and came out as strong as when he entered.

He predicted and foresaw in a vision in 1625 the events that the French Revolution brought about. When the vision was explained to him, he writes that he heard a voice say,

"'John, get up and write down what thou hast seen.' But as I kept lying still in my bed I received a blow upon my face, and heard a voice say: 'Thus shall it be with all who do the work of God negligently.' Upon which I got up, lit a candle and wrote down the vision and exposition. Now when the day came and the pastor saw me, observing my eye to be black and blue, he asked me which way it became so. On explaining he was greatly surprised."

Sources:

Engelbrecht, Johann. *The Divine Visions of Johann Engelbrecht.* 2 vols. Northampton, England, 1780.

ENGLAND

This entry covers Anglo-Saxon practices of magic and witchcraft through the Middle Ages in England. See also separate entries for **Scotland, Wales,** and the pre-Saxon inhabitants of England, the **Celts.** For the modern period, see separate entries on **magic** and **witchcraft.**

Early Magic and Witchcraft

The Anglo-Saxon system of magic was based on the Teutonic. Witchcraft practitioners were called *wicca* (or *wicce,* feminine), *scin-laeca, galdor-craeftig, wiglaer,* and *morthwyrtha.* A wiglaer (from *wig,* idol or temple, and *laer,* learning) was a wizard, and a wicca or wicce was a witch. Scin-laeca (a shining dead body) was a species of phantom or apparition; the term was also used to identify someone who had the power of producing such phantoms. Galdor-craeftig implies one skilled in incantations, and morthwyrtha is, literally, "a worshiper of the dead." Another general appellation for such personages was *dry* (magician).

The laws prohibiting these practices carried severe penalties. The best account given of them is found in a passage written during the reign of Edward and Guthrun (tenth century):

"If any *wicca,* or *wiglaer,* or false swearer, or *morth-wyrtha,* or any foul, contaminated, manifest *horcwenan* [whore queen or strumpet], be any where in the land, man shall drive them out. We teach that every priest shall extinguish all heathendom, and forbid *wilweorthunga* [fountain-worship], and *licwiglunga* [incantations of the dead], and *hwata* [omens], and *galdra* [magic], and man-worship, and the abominations that men exercise in various sorts of witchcraft, and in *frithspottum,* and with elms and other trees, and with stones, and with many phantoms."

From subsequent regulations, it is clear that witchcraft and magic were used for violence, for penitentiary penalties were levied against anyone who injured or killed another by *wiccecraefte* (witchcraft).

Witches apparently used philters (love potions), for it was also a crime to gain another's love through enchanted food or drink. Wicca were also forbidden to *wiglian* (divine) by the moon. King Canute renewed the prohibitions. He declared it illegal to worship the sun or the moon, fire or floods, wells or stones, or any sort of tree; to love wiccecraefte, or to frame death spells, either by lot or by torch; or to effect anything by phantoms. The *Poenitentiale* of Theodore reveals that witches also claimed the power of letting loose tempests.

Another name for magic among the Anglo-Saxons was *unlybban wyrce* (destructive of life). Penitence was prescribed for a woman who killed a man by unlybban. In one account a woman who had resolved to kill her stepson, or at least to alienate him from his father's affection, sought a witch who knew how to change minds by arts and enchantments. Offering the witch rewards, the stepmother inquired how the father's mind might be turned from the child and fixed on her. The witch immediately made a magic medicament and it was mixed with the husband's meat and drink. The episode ended with the murder of the child and the stepmother's exposure.

The Anglo-Saxons used numerous charms. They trusted in their incantations to cure disease, for successful planting and harvest, for the discovery of lost property, and for the prevention of casualties. Specimens of their charms have been preserved. The Venerable Bede recorded that "many, in times of disease (neglecting the sacraments) went to the erring medicaments of idolatry, as if to restrain God's chastisements by incantations, phylacteries, or any other secret of the demoniacal arts."

Their prognostications—from the sun, from thunder, and from dreams—were so numerous that they perpetuated superstition. Every day of every month was cataloged as a propitious or unpropitious date for certain transactions. There were Anglo-Saxon treatises that contained rules for discovering the future and disposition of a child from the day of birth. One day was useful for all things; another, though good to tame animals, was poor for sowing seeds. One day was favorable to business, another to let blood; on others these things were forbidden.

On a particular day it was said that one must buy, on a second sell, on a third hunt, on a fourth do nothing. If a child was born on a certain day it would live; if on another, it would be sickly; if on still another, it would perish early. The future could be predicted by noticing on what day of the week or month it first thundered, or when the new moon appeared. Dreams likewise had regular interpretations and applications, and thus life, instead of being governed by counsels of wisdom, was directed by those solemn rules of superstition.

Beginnings of Witchcraft in England

Prior to the Reformation, little official notice was given to the practice of witchcraft, "the craft of the wise," but authorities were always on the lookout for anyone believed to be practicing sorcery (i.e., malevolent magic). It was regarded as a political offense to employ sorcery against the ruling powers and it was punished severely, as is witnessed by the execution of the duchess of Gloucester in Henry VI's reign and the duke of Buckingham in 1521. In Henry VI's time Lord Hungerford was beheaded for consulting certain soothsayers concerning the duration of the king's life.

Witchcraft was widespread and of early origin in England, but it seems those practicing it were not systematically punished until after the sixteenth-century Reformation period. Prosecution may have taken place against witches in Plantagenet and early Tudor times, but the popularity of sorcery was probably so widespread and the protection against it by the Church was supposed to be so powerful that nothing like a crusade was directed against it.

At very early periods the Church had fulminated against those who practiced witchcraft. In 696 C.E. a canon of council held at Berkhampstead condemned to corporal punishment those who made sacrifices to evil spirits.

According to James I. F. A. Inderwick, in *Side-Lights on the Stuarts* (1888),

"For centuries in this country strange as it may now appear, a denial of the existence of such demoniacal agency was deemed equal to a confession of Atheism and to a disbelief in the Holy Scriptures themselves. But not only did Lord Chancellors, Lord Keepers, benches of Bishops and Parliament attest the truth and the existence of witchcraft, but Addison writing as late as 1711, in the pages of the *Spectator,* after describing himself as hardly pressed by the arguments on both sides of this question expresses his own belief that there is and has been, witchcraft in the land."

It was in the twelfth century that pagan witchcraft practices were first associated with the devil. The tale of the old woman of Berkeley that Southey's ballad familiarized was earlier related by William of Malmesbury (ca. 1125) on the authority of a professed eyewitness. When the devil informed the witch of the near expiry of her contract, she summoned the neighboring monks and her children, and, after confessing her criminal compact, displayed great anxiety lest Satan should take her body as well as her soul.

She asked that her body be sewn in a stag's hide and placed in a stone coffin closed with lead and iron. The coffin was then to be loaded with heavy stones and the whole fastened down with three iron chains. In order to baffle the power of the demons, she further directed that 50 psalms be sung by night, and 50 masses be sung by day, and at the end of three nights, if her body was still secure it could be buried with safety.

All these precautions, however, proved of no avail. The monks bravely resisted the efforts of the fiends on the first and second nights, but on the third night in the middle of a terrific uproar an immense demon burst into the monastery and in a voice of thunder commanded the dead witch to rise. She replied that she was bound with chains, but the demon snapped them like thread. The coffin lid fell aside, and when the witch arose the demon bore her off on a huge black horse, galloping into the darkness while her shrieks resounded through the air.

The first trial for witchcraft in England is beleived to have occurred during the tenth year of the reign of King John (Robin Hood's opponent) when, according to the *Abbreviato-Placitorum,* Agnes, the wife of Odo the merchant, accused one Gideon of the crime. He proved his innocence, however, by the ordeal of the red-hot iron.

A trial for sorcery was reported with more detail in the year 1324. Certain citizens of Coventry had suffered at the hands of the prior, whose extortions were approved of and supported by two of Edward II's favorites. By way of revenge they plotted the death of the prior, the favorites, and the king.

To carry out their plot they consulted John of Nottingham, a famous magician of the time, and his servant Robert Marshall of Leicester. Marshall, however, betrayed the plot and stated that he and his master fashioned images of wax to represent the king, his two favorites, the prior, his caterer and steward, and one Richard de Lowe—the latter being brought in merely as an experimental figure to test the effect of the charm.

At an old ruined house near Coventry on the Friday following Holy Cross Day, John gave Marshall a sharp-pointed leaden branch and commanded him to plunge it into the forehead of the figure representing Richard de Lowe. This being done, John dispatched his servant to Lowe's house to find out the result of the experiment. Lowe it seems had lost his senses and went about screaming "Harrow!" On the Sunday before Ascension, John withdrew the branch from the image's forehead and thrust it into the heart, where it remained until the following Wednesday, when the unfortunate victim died. Such was Marshall's testimony, but the judges gave it little credence, and after several adjournments the trial was abandoned.

The first enactment against witchcraft in England was by the Parliament of 1541 and was annulled six years later. In 1551 further enactments were leveled at it, but it was not until 1563 that Parliament defined witchcraft as a capital crime. The regular persecution of witches followed. Many burnings occurred during the last years of Elizabeth's reign.

Early Witchcraft Trials

At the village of Warboys, in Huntingdon county, in 1589 lived two country gentlemen, Robert Throgmorton and Sir Samuel Cromwell. Throgmorton's family consisted of his wife and five daughters, of whom the eldest, Joan, a girl of 15, was well versed in ghost and witch lore.

On one occasion Joan had to pass the cottage of a laboring family by the name of Samuel. This family consisted of a man, his wife, and their grown daughter. Mother Samuel was sitting at the door, where she was busily engaged in knitting. Joan accused her of being a witch, ran home, and fell into strange convulsive fits, swearing that Mother Samuel had bewitched her. In due course the other Throgmorton daughters were beseiged by similar fits and placed the blame on Mother Samuel.

The parents began to suspect that their children were really bewitched and reported the matter to Lady Cromwell, who, as an intimate friend of the family, took up the matter. She and Sir Samuel ordered that the alleged witch be put to ordeal. Meanwhile the children let loose their imaginations and invented all sorts of weird and grotesque tales about the old woman.

Eventually Throgmorton had the poor old woman dragged to his grounds, where she was subjected to torture, pins being thrust into her body to see if blood could be drawn. Lady Cromwell tore out a handful of the woman's hair, which she gave to Mrs. Throgmorton to burn as an antidote to witchcraft. Suffering under these injuries the old woman invoked a curse against her torturers that was afterward remembered, although she was allowed her liberty. She suffered much persecution thereafter at the hands of the two families; every misfortune occurring among their cattle and livestock was blamed on her.

Eventually Lady Cromwell was seized with an illness that caused her death, and Mother Samuel was blamed. Repeated efforts were made to persuade her to confess and amend what she had done. At last, tormented beyond endurance, she let herself be persuaded to pronounce an exorcism against the spirits and confessed that her husband and daughter were associates with her and had sold themselves to the devil. On the strength of this confession the whole family was imprisoned in the Huntingdon jail.

At the following court session the three Samuels were put on trial and indicted with various offenses, among them, "bewitching unto death" the Lady Cromwell. In the agony of torture the old woman confessed all that was required, but her husband and daughter strongly asserted their innocence. All were sentenced to be hanged and burned. The executions were carried out on April 3, 1593.

With the accession of James I, (the former James IV of Scotland) the Continental crusade against witchcraft that had begun in the late fifteenth century came to England. James, who believed deeply in the negative power of witches, became greatly concerned about the spread of witchcraft in his land. He studied the nature of witchcraft and wrote a significant polemic against the practice. His book *Daemonologie* (1547) gave great impetus to the persecution of witches in England. Some 50 witches were executed during his reign. (English Protestants, who needed the approval of James, a Roman Catholic, to get their new translation of the Bible published, not only dedicated it to him but improperly translated the Hebrew word *ob* as "witch" as an additional means of gaining his support.)

The famous case of the **Lancashire witches,** notable for its accounts of witch covens (as opposed to the actions of individual sorcerers) arose in 1612. Twenty-two years later, when a boy called Robinson claimed that he had witnessed a witches' Sabbat at the Hoare Stones, some 17 women were brought to trial at Lancaster assizes.

Witchfinders

As a result of the severe legislation against witchcraft, there arose a class of self-appointed witchfinders who used their power for personal advantage and caused the sacrifice of many innocent lives.

The most famous of these witchfinders was **Matthew Hopkins** of Manningtree, in Essex. He assumed the title "Witch-finder General," and, with an assistant and a woman whose duty it was to examine female suspects for devil's marks, he traveled about the counties of Essex, Sussex, Huntingdon, and Norfolk. In one year, from 1645 to 1646, Hopkins brought about the death of 60 people.

His general test was that of swimming. The hands and feet of the accused were tied together crosswise. She was wrapped in a sheet and thrown into a pond. If she sank—as frequently happened—she was deemed innocent, but at the cost of her life; if she floated she was pronounced guilty and immediately executed.

Another test was to repeat the Lord's Prayer without a single falter, a thing said to be impossible for a witch. Sometimes the suspect was weighed against the Bible, obtaining her freedom if she outweighed it. There is an apocryphal legend that when Hopkins's frauds were discovered an angry crowd subjected him to his own test by swimming. Hopkins retired to his home in Manningtree, Essex, in 1646, where he died about a year later.

In his book *Witch, Warlock, and Magician* (1889), W. H. D. Adams states:

"I think there can be little doubt that many evil-disposed persons availed themselves of the prevalent belief in witchcraft as a cover for their depredations on the property of their neighbours, diverting suspicion from themselves to the poor wretches, who through accidental circumstances had acquired notoriety as the devil's accomplices. It would also seem probable that not a few of the reputed witches similarly turned to account their bad reputation."

Decline of the Witchcraft Superstition

Toward the close of the seventeenth century, the tide began to turn and witchcraft convictions began to be discouraged by the courts. An old superstition dies hard, however, and in the early part of the eighteenth century, witchcraft was still considered credible, even among the educated classes of England. The last execution of witches in England took place at Northampton, where two were hung in 1705 and five others in 1712.

Francis Hutchison, commenting on this in his *Historical Essay Concerning Witchcraft* (1718), states, "This is the more shameful as I shall hereafter prove from the literature of that time, a disbelief in the existence of witches had become almost universal among educated men, though the old superstition was still defended in the Judgment Seat, and in the pulpit."

According to John Wesley (1703–1791), who had considerable influence as a bishop,

"It is true likewise that the English in general, and, indeed, most of the men of learning in Europe, have given up all accounts of witches and apparitions as mere old wives' fables. I am sorry for it. The giving up of witchcraft, is in effect giving up the Bible. But I cannot give up to all the Deists in Great Britain the existence of witchcraft, till I give up the credit of all history sacred and profane."

Judge and legal authority Sir William Blackstone (1723–1780) claimed that "to deny the possibility, nay, the actual existence of witchcraft and sorcery is at once flatly to contradict the revealed Word of God in various passages of the Old and New Testaments, and the thing itself is a truth to which every nation in the world hath in its turn borne testimony."

With every passing year, however, the old belief diminished, and in 1736, decades before Wesley stated his foregoing opinion, the laws against witchcraft were repealed. Yet the superstition was long-lived. In 1759 Susannah Hannaker of Wengrove was put to the ordeal of weighing, but she fortunately outweighed the Bible. Cases of ducking supposed witches occurred in 1760 at Leicester, in 1785 at Northampton, and in 1829 at Monmouth, while as late as 1863 a Frenchman died as the result of an illness caused by his having been ducked as a wizard. On September 17, 1875, an old woman named Ann Turner, a reputed witch, was killed at Long Compton in Warwickshire.

Magic

Magic in England in early times coexisted with witchcraft; only **Roger Bacon,** scientist-philosopher, displayed a separation between the two. Of course the occult traditions concerning Bacon are merely legendary, but they help to crystallize the popular idea of an English magician of medieval times. The Elizabethan *History of Friar Bacon* was probably the first to place these legends on record. It has no factual concern with the Bacon of science, for the Bacon of superstitious belief is a magician who cheated the devil, made a brazen head that spoke, and engaged in all manner of black magic.

In England the popular belief in magic was strengthened by the extraordinary effects of natural processes then known only to a small number of individuals who concealed their knowledge with the most profound secrecy. In England before the Reformation, the study of magic and alchemy were extremely common among the Roman clergy.

The rapid rise to power of statesmen like Cardinal Thomas Wolsey and Thomas Cromwell led people to think that they had gained their high positions through diabolical assistance. There were a great number of magicians during the reign of Henry VIII, as is witnessed by documents in the Public Record Office in London.

According to Thomas Wright in his *Narratives of Sorcery and Magic* (2 vols., 1851), at the height of Wolsey's career a magician described as "one Wood, gent." was dragged before the privy council, charged with some misdemeanor that was connected with the intrigues of the day. In a paper addressed to the lords of the council, Wood stated that William Neville had sent for him at his house at Oxford, it being the first communication he had ever had with him. After he had been at Weke a short time, Neville took him by the arm and led him privately into the garden. Wood said Neville then asked him to make a ring that would bring him favor with the king, but he declined and left.

Neville sent for him again and entered into further communication with him on the subject, telling him that he had another conjurer (occult magician) named Wade who could show him more than Wood could. Among other things, Neville said, the conjurer had shown him that "he should be a great lord." This was an effective attempt to move Wood to jealousy, and Neville then prevailed upon him to make "moldes" (probably images) of a woman on whom he seemed to have set his love. Wood again refused, declaring that, although at the desire of "some of his friends," he had "called to a stone for things stolen," he had not undertaken to find or make treasures.

The search for treasure, which the conjurer Wood so earnestly disclaimed, was, however, one of the most usual occupations of magicians of this period. The frequent discoveries of Roman, Saxon, or medieval deposits in the course of accidental digging (then probably more common than today) was enough to whet the appetites of the needy or the miserly. The belief that the sepulchral barrow, or the long-deserted ruin, or even the wild and haunted glen concealed treasures of gold and silver was carried down in a variety of local legends. Hidden treasures were said to be under the charge of spirits who obeyed the magician's call. These searches were not always successful, as is evident from the following narrative, abridged from the account of William Stapleton, the main character in the story.

In the reign of Henry VIII, a priest named William Stapleton was placed under arrest as a conjurer, having been involved in some court intrigues. At the request of Cardinal Thomas Wolsey he wrote an account of his adventures, which is preserved in the Roll's House records (it is addressed to Wolsey, and not, as has been supposed, to Thomas Cromwell). Stapleton stated that he was a monk of the mitred abbey of St. Benet in the Holm, in Norfolk, where he lived in the nineteenth year of Henry VIII's reign (i.e., in 1527 or 1528), at which time he borrowed from one Dennys of Hofton a book called *Thesaurus Spirituum,* and after that another, called *Secreta Secretorum,* a little ring, a plate, a circle, and also a sword for the art of digging, and spent six months in studying their use.

Stapleton disliked rising early, and after having been frequently punished for being absent from matins and negligent of his duty in church he obtained a leave of six months from the abbot to go into the world and try to raise money to buy a dispensation from an order that did not suit him.

The first person Stapleton consulted with was his friend Dennys, who recommended he try his skill in finding treasure. Dennys introduced Stapleton to two "knowing men" who had "placards" or licenses from the king to search for treasure troves, which were not infrequently bought from the crown at this period. These men lent him other books and instruments related to the "art of digging," and they went together to a place named Sidestrand in Norfolk to search and mark out the ground where they thought treasure should lie. It happened, however, that the lady Tyrry, to whom the estate belonged, learned of their trespassing, and after sending for them and subjecting them to a close examination, ordered them to leave her grounds.

After several more futile attempts at "conjuring" treasure at other towns, a disappointed and disgusted Stapleton gave up the pursuit. Back in Norfolk, however, he soon met with some of his old treasure-seeking acquaintances, who urged him to go to work again, which he refused to do unless he had better books. They told him of a man called Leech who had a book to which the parson of Lesingham had bound a spirit called "Andrea Malchus." Stapleton went to see the man.

Leech gave Stapleton all his instruments, and told him that the parson of Lesingham and Sir John of Leiston (another ecclesiastic) as well as others, had recently used the book to call up three spirits: Andrea Malchus, "Oberion," and "Inchubus."

After Stapleton acquired Leech's instruments he journeyed to Norwich, where he was soon found by a messenger from Lord Leonard Marquees, who lived at "Calkett Hall" and wanted a person expert in the art of digging. Stapleton met him at Walsingham; the lord promised him that if he would take pains in exercising the dig he would request a dispensation that would make Stapleton a secular priest and the lord's own chaplain.

Leonard proceeded rather shrewdly to test the searcher's talents: he directed one of his servants to hide a sum of money in the garden, and Stapleton dug for it, and one Jackson "scryed" (invoked the treasure's "spirit" through a crystal), but they were unable to find the money. Undaunted, Stapleton went directly with two other priests, Sir John Shepe and Sir Robert Porter, to a place beside Creke Abbey, where treasure was supposed to be, and "Sir John Shepe called the spirit of the treasure, and I shewed to him, but all came to no purpose."

Stapleton went to hide his disappointment in London, where he remained some weeks, until Leonard, who had arranged the dispensation he promised, sent for him to pass the winter with him in Leicestershire. Toward spring Stapleton returned to Norfolk. There he was informed that there was "much money" hidden in the neighborhood of Calkett Hall, especially in the Bell Hill (probably an ancient grave). After some delay, he obtained his instruments and went to work with the parish priest of Gorleston but reported, "of truth we could bring nothing to effect." After this Stapleton returned to London, carrying his instruments with him; on his arrival he was thrown into prison at the suit of Leonard, who accused him of leaving his service without permission, and all his instruments were seized. He never recovered them, but he was soon released from prison and obtained temporary employment in the church. The number of such treasure hunters appears to have been far greater among Stapleton's contemporaries in almost all classes of society than one might believe.

A few years before these events, in the twelfth year of Henry VIII's reign (1521) the king granted to Robert, Lord Curzon, the monopoly of treasure seeking in the counties of Norfolk and Suffolk. Curzon immediately delegated to a man named William Smith of Clopton, and to a servant or retainer of his own named Amylyon, not only the right of search given to him but also the power to arrest and press charges against any other person they found seeking treasure within the two counties.

Smith and Amylyon apparently used this delegated authority for purposes of extortion, and in the summer of 1521 Smith was brought before the court of the city of Norwich, at the suit of William Goodred of Great Melton.

It appears that the treasure diggers, who had received their "placard" (license) from Curzon in March, went to Norwich about Easter and paid a visit to the schoolmaster George Dowsing, who, they had heard, was skilled in magical arts. They showed him their license for treasure seeking, which authorized them to press into their service any persons they might find who had skill in the science; so it appears that they were not capable of raising spirits themselves without the assistance of "scholars."

The schoolmaster entered willingly into their project, and they went, about two or three o'clock in the morning, with one or two other persons who were admitted into their confidence, and dug in the ground beside "Butter Hilles," within the walls of the city, but found nothing there. (These "hilles" were probably ancient games.) They next proceeded to a place called "Seynt William in the Wood by Norwich," where they excavated two nights but with no better success.

They then held a meeting at the house of one Saunders in the market of Norwich and called to their assistance two ecclesiastics, one named Sir William, the other Sir Robert Cromer, the former being a parish priest. At this meeting, Dowsing allegedly raised "a spirit or two" in a scrying glass, but Cromer "began and raised a spirit first." Spirit or no spirit, however, they seem to have had as little success as ever in discovering the treasure.

Unable after so many attempts to find the treasure themselves, they resolved to extort a general contribution from everybody who followed the same calling. They accused a person of the name of Wikman of "digging of hilles" and by threatening to take him before Curzon they obtained ten shillings from him.

With the era of **John Dee** and Edward Kelley (middle to late sixteenth century), a much more definite system of magico-astrology evolved on English soil. Although Kelley was a rogue, there is little doubt that Dee possessed psychic gifts of no mean character. His most celebrated followers were **William Lilly** and Elias Ashmole. Lilly gathered about him quite a band of magicians—Ramsey, Scott, Hodges, and others, as well as his "skryers" (crystal gazers) Sarah Skelhorm and Ellen Evans. These may be said to be the last of the practical magicians of England. Their methods were those of divination by **crystal gazing** and evocation of spirits, combined with practical **astrology.**

The mid-seventeenth century also produced such individuals as **Robert Fludd,** who wrote concerning the secrets of mysticism and magnetism. Fludd was a Paracelsian (after sixteenth-century Swiss alchemist **Paracelsus**) and regarded man as a microcosm of the universe. He was an ardent defender of the **Rosicrucians** and wrote two spirited works about them, as well as his great *Tractatus Apologeticus* and many other alchemical and philosophical treatises. The part of the *Tractatus* that deals with natural magic is one of the most definitive ever written on the subject.

Thomas Vaughan is likewise a figure of intense interest from this period. He was a supreme expert of spiritual alchemy, and his works written under the pseudonym "Eugenius Philalethes" show he possessed an exalted mind. It is through men of this type that a mystical or spiritual dimension was added to the earlier uncritical and superstitious belief in magic.

(For the development of **Spiritualism, psychical research,** and **parapsychology** in Britain, see entries under those headings.)

Sources:

Adams, W. H. Davenport. *Witch, Warlock, and Magician: Historical Sketches of Magic and Witchcraft in England and Scotland.* London and New York, 1889. Reprint, Detroit: Gale Research, 1973.

Ashton, John. *The Devil in Britain and America.* London, 1896. Reprint, Detroit: Gale Research, 1974.

Cockayne, T. O. *Leechdoms, Wortcunning, and Starcraft.* 2 vols. London, 1864–1866. Reprint, London: Holland Press, 1968.

Gleadow, Rupert. *Magic and Divination.* London: Ryerson Press, 1941.

Hole, Christina. *Witchcraft in England.* New York: Charles Scribner's Sons, 1947.

Kittredge, George Lyman. *Witchcraft in Old and New England.* Cambridge, Mass.: Harvard University Press, 1929. Reprint, New York: Atheneum, 1972.

L'Estrange, Ewen C., *Witch Hunting and Witch Trials: The Indictments for Witchcraft from the Records of 1373 Assizes Held for the Home Circuit,* A.D. *1559–1736.* London: Kegan Paul, 1929.

Mackay, Charles. *Memoirs of Extraordinary Popular Delusions and the Madness of Crowds.* London, 1841. Reprint, New York: Farrar, Strauss & Giroux, 1932.

Maple, Eric. *The Dark World of Witches.* London: Robert Hale; New York: A. S. Barnes, 1962. Also reprinted with two other Eric Maple books in one volume as *The Complete Book of Witchcraft and Demonology.* New York: A. S. Barnes, 1964.

Notestein, Wallace. *A History of Witchcraft in England from 1558 to 1718.* Washington, 1911. Reprint, New York: Russel & Russel, 1965.

Peel, Edgar. *The Trials of the Lancashire Witches: A Study of Seventeenth-Century Witchcraft.* Nelson, England: Hendon Publishing, 1985.

Robbins, Rossell Hope. *The Encyclopedia of Witchcraft and Demonology.* New York: Crown Publishers, 1959.

Summers, Montague. *Witchcraft and Black Magic.* London: Rider, 1946. Reprint, New York: Causeway Books, 1974.

Thomas, Keith. *Religion and the Decline of Magic.* New York: Charles Scribner's Sons, 1971.

Valiente, Doreen. *An ABC of Witchcraft Past and Present.* New York: St. Martin's Press; London: Macmillan, 1973.

Wright, Thomas. *Narratives of Sorcery and Magic.* 2 vols. London, 1851. Reprint, Detroit: Gale Research, 1974.

Ennemoser, Joseph (1787–1854)

Distinguished physician at the University of Bonn, Germany, from 1820 to 1841. He subsequently practiced in Munich. Ennemoser was an early investigator of **animal magnetism** and compiled an encyclopedic work titled *The History of Magic* (1854).

Sources:

Ennemoser, Joseph. *The History of Magic.* Translated by William Howitt. 1854. Reprint (2 vols.), New Hyde Park, N.Y.: University Books, 1960.

Enoch, Book of

A Hebrew apocryphal book. It was originally written in Aramaic rather than Hebrew and hence was not included in the canon of the Hebrew Bible or in the Christian Old Testament. It was included in the collection of other materials generally called *pseudepigrapha* (various pseudonymous or anonymous Jewish religious writings of the period 200 B.C.E. to 200 C.E.). The original version was lost about the end of the fourth century, and only fragments remained, but James Bruce, the Scottish explorer, brought back a copy in Ethiopian from Abyssinia in 1773, which was probably made from the version known to the early Greek fathers. In this work the spiritual world is minutely described, as is the region of Sheol, the place of the wicked.

The book also deals with the history of the fallen angels, their relations with the human species, and the foundations of magic. The book says that:

"There were angels who consented to fall from heaven that they might have intercourse with the daughters of Earth. For in those days the sons of men having multiplied, there were born to them daughters of great beauty. And when the angels, or sons of heaven, beheld them, they were filled with desire; wherefore they said to one another: 'Come let us choose wives from among the race of man, and let us beget children.'

"Their leader Samyasa, answered thereupon and said: 'Perchance you will be wanting in the courage needed to fulfil this resolution, and then I alone shall be answerable for your fall.' But they swore that they would in no wise repent and that they would achieve their whole design.

"Now there were two hundred who descended on Mount Armon, and it was from this time that the mountain received its designation, which signifies Mount of the Oath. Hereinafter follow the names of those angelic leaders who descended with this object: Samyasa, chief among all, Urakabarameel, Azibeel, Tamiel, Ramuel, Danel, Azkeel, Sarakuyal, Asael, Armers, Batraal, Anane, Zavebe, Sameveel, Ertrael, Turel, Jomiael, Arizial. They took wives with whom they had intercourse, to whom also they taught Magic, the art of enchantment and the diverse properties of roots and trees. Amazarac gave instruction in all secrets of sorcerers; Barkaial was the master of those who study the stars; Akibeel manifested signs; and Azaradel taught the motions of the moon."

In this account, which harkens back to several biblical passages (Genesis 6:4; Isaiah 14:12), there is a description of the profanation of mysteries. The fallen angels exposed their occult and heaven-born wisdom to earthly women, whereby it was profaned, and brute force, taking advantage of the profanation of divine law, reigned supreme. Only a deluge could wipe out the stain of the enormity and pave the way for a restitution of the balance between the human and the divine, which had been disturbed by these unlawful revelations.

According to tradition, Enoch did not die, but was carried up to heaven (Genesis 5:18–24), from where he will return at the end of time. He has also been identified with Thoth of the Egyptians, Cadulus of the Phoenicians, and Palamedes of the Greeks. According to some occultists, he inspired the **Kabala** and the symbols of the **tarot.**

The Book of Enoch is one of the most important works of the pseudepigrapha and is actually a set of books. The first book of Enoch was known from a surviving Ethiopian translation, parts of which were found in the caves of Qumran among the Dead Sea Scrolls. In 1892, however, R. H. Charles found a second manuscript of the Book of Enoch, which existed in a Slavonic text. Upon seeing the book, he also discovered that it was an entirely different Book of Enoch, and he soon translated and published it. Finally, a third Book of Enoch, which has circulated among the Babylonian Jews, was discovered and published in 1928 by Hugo Odeburg.

Sources:

Andrews, H. T. *An Introduction to the Apocryphal Books of the Old and New Testament.* Grand Rapids, Mich.: Baker Book House, 1964.

Charles, R. H., ed. *The Book of Enoch [Ethiopic text].* London: Society for Promoting Christian Knowledge, 1917.

Laurence, Richard, trans. *The Book of Enoch the Prophet . . . from an Ethiopian Manuscript.* London: Kegan Paul, Tench, 1883.

Morfill, W. R., trans. *The Book of the Secrets of Enoch.* Oxford, England: Clarendon Press, 1896.

Enochian Calls

The magic incantations used by **John Dee** and **Edward Kelley** in the sixteenth century to invoke "angels" or **elementary spirits.** The Enochian language, in which the calls were spoken, has a consistent grammar and syntax and curiously impressive sound values.

There are 19 Enochian calls or keys. The first two conjure spirits; the next 16 the elements earth, fire, air, water; the nineteenth any of the "30 Aethyrys." The calls were supposed to have been dictated backward to Kelley, as direct communication from the "angels" would have invoked forces that were too powerful.

In 1912 magician **Aleister Crowley,** in the company of **Victor Neuburg,** worked a series of magic operations using the Enochian calls. During the midst of these Crowley discovered the principles of what he would later develop into a system of sex magic. He recorded his work in a lengthy article originally published in his journal *Equinox* and later published a separate book *The Vision and the Voice.* The writings of Crowley made Enochian magic widely known to twentieth-century magicians, several of whom have developed it as a variation of modern ceremonial magic. Among those who have discovered and utilized Enochian magic is **Anton La Vey,** who adapted it to his Satanic system as described in his book *The Satanic Bible* (1969).

Sources:

Crowley, Aleister. *The Vision and the Voice.* Dallas, Tex.: Sangreal Foundation, 1972.

La Vey, Anton S. *The Satanic Bible.* New York: Avon, 1969.

Regardie, Israel. *Enochian Dictionary.* Dallas, Tex.: Sangreal Foundation, 1971.

Schueler, Gerald J. *An Advanced Guide to Enochian Magic: A Complete Manual for Angelic Magic.* St. Paul, Minn.: Llewellyn Publications, 1987.

———. *Enochian Magic: A Practical Manual.* St. Paul, Minn.: Llewellyn Publications, 1985.

———. *Enochian Physics: The Structure of the Magical Universe.* St. Paul, Minn.: Llewellyn Publications, 1988.

Turner, Robert. *Elizabethan Magic.* Londmead, Dorset, England: Element Books, 1989.

Zalewski, Patrick J. *Golden Dawn Enochian Magic.* St. Paul, Minn.: Llewellyn Publications, 1990.

Epworth Phenomena

The psychic disturbances of a **poltergeist** nature at Epworth Vicarage, England, in 1716 during its occupancy by Rev. Samuel Wesley, father of Methodist Church founder John Wesley. The phenomena lasted for several months and were first attributed to trickery, then to the devil, although Samuel's wife, Susannah Wesley, disagreed with the latter hypothesis. Instead, she connected it with the fate of her brother who, in the service of the East India Company, disappeared and was never heard of again. It was not proved that the rappings were caused by his discarnate agency, but the members of the family took it for granted after a while that "Old Jeffrey" was involved in the manifestations, which appeared to be connected mostly with Hetty Wesley. She was noticed to tremble strongly in her sleep when the knockings occurred.

The main disturbances lasted with intervals for two months, December and January 1716–17, and broke out occasionally afterward. The contention that they still recurred a generation later is based on a letter by Emily Wesley, dated February 16, 1750, containing this passage: "Another thing is that wonderful thing called by us Jeffrey. You won't laugh at me for being superstitious if I tell you how certainly that something calls on me against any extraordinary new affliction; but so little is known of the invisible world that I am at least not able to judge whether it be friendly or an evil spirit."

The records of the phenomena consist mostly of family letters and an account written by Samuel Wesley. The disturbances began with knockings. Susannah Wesley wrote on January 12, 1717:

"One night it made such a noise in the room over our heads as if several people were walking; then run up and down the stairs, and was so outrageous that we thought the children would be frightened, so your father and I rose and went down in the dark to light a candle. Just as we came to the bottom of the broad stairs, having hold of each other, on my side there seemed as if somebody had emptied a bag of money at my feet and on his as if all the bottles under the stairs (which were many) had been dashed into a thousand pieces. We passed through the hall into the kitchen and got a candle and went to see the children. The next night your father would get Mr. Hoole to lie at our house and we all sat together till one or two o'clock in the morning and heard the knocking as usual. Sometimes it would make a noise like the winding up of a jack; at other times, as that night Mr. Hoole was with us, like a carpenter planning deals; but mostly commonly it knocked three and stopped and then thrice again and so many hours together."

Her daughter Hetty heard "something like a man in a loose nightgown trailing after him" coming down the stairs behind her, and sometimes a shape like a "badger" was seen under the bed. The noises answered knock for knock and came in any part of the house. At family prayers they became very agitated at the names of King George and the Prince. Samuel Wesley often tried to speak to them but the only answer he received was "two or three feeble squeaks a little louder than the chirping of a bird, but not like the noise of rats which I have often heard."

Another daughter, Nancy, was once lifted up with the bed in which she sat. She leapt down and said that surely Old Jeffrey would not run away with her. She was persuaded to sit down again when the bed was lifted several times successively to a considerable height. The noise affected the mastiff of the household. It whimpered in terror and strove to get between the people of the house. (See also **Ashtabula Poltergeist; Cock Lane Ghost; Drummer of Tedworth; Enfield Poltergeist; haunted houses;** and **Eliakim Phelps**)

Sources:

Clarke, Ada. *Memoirs of the Wesley Family.* 4th ed. London: W. Tegg, 1860.

Priestley, Joseph. *Original Letters by the Rev. John Wesley and his Friends.* Birmingham, England, 1791.

Wilder, Franklin. *Good News for Martha Wesley.* Hicksville, N.Y.: Exposition Press, 1976.

Wright, Dudley. *The Epworth Phenomena.* London: William Rider & Son, 1917.

Equilibrium (in Occultism)

According to occultist **Éliphas Lévi,** magic harmony is said to depend upon equilibrium. In **ceremonial magic** operations, if the will of the operator is always at the same tension and directed along the same line, moral impotence will ensue. On the other hand, mediums who submit themselves passively to psychic forces are equally unbalanced. Lévi extols the all-powerful action of harmony in exalting the soul and giving it rule over the senses, guided by the will.

Sources:

Lévi, Éliphas. *Transcendental Magic.* New York: Samuel Weiser, 1972.

Equinox, The

Official organ of the A.·.A.·., subtitled "The Review of Scientific Illuminism," originally published by magician **Aleister Crowley** beginning in March 1909. Each issue amounted to a book-length journal. It contained the official materials of the A.·.A.·., articles and stories by Crowley, and book reviews. Crowley, who had recently left the Hermetic Order of the **Golden Dawn,** published many of the secrets of his former colleagues. The ten issues of the first volume appeared biannually at the equinoxes, beginning in March 1909.

It appears that Crowley projected alternating five-year periods of publication and silence. The second volume was thus designated a volume of silence and was never published.

The issues of the third volume appeared sporadically, the first in March 1919. The third volume is usually designated the *The "Blue" Equinox,* as it was published with a blue cover. It followed the general format of the earlier volumes. The second issue made it to galley proofs, but was never published. The succeeding issues took the form of a series of occasional monographs. Number three did not appear until 1937. It includes a commentary on Crowley's major revelatory work, *The Book of the Law.* Number four appeared in 1938 under the title *Eight Lectures on Yoga* and number five as *The Book of Thoth,* Crowley's commentary on the **tarot.** The original edition of *The Book of Thoth* was limited to 200 signed and numbered copies.

Crowley died in 1947. His successor as outer head of the order, **Karl Germer,** saw to the publication of issue number six of the third volume, which appeared in 1962 as *Liber Aleph.* The last four issues were published by Grady McMurty ("Caliph Hymenaeus Beta"), who took charge of the order and revived it through the 1970s. The first three of these appeared as *The Shih Yi* (1971), the *Tao Teh King* (1975), and *The Holy Books of Thelema* (1983). A tenth issue, containing a variety of brief articles, appeared in 1986.

In 1975 the Society Ordo Templi Orientis, a rival organization headed by Marcelo Ramos Motta that for a while also claimed to be the official Ordo Templi Orientis (**OTO**) headed by Crowley, began to issue a new series of *The Equinox.* Four issues of what was projected as volume five were published before legal action by McMurty and the OTO stopped further publication.

Sources:

Crowley, Aleister. *The Book of Thoth: A Short Essay on the Tarot of the Egyptians.* New York: Samuel Weiser, 1974.

———. *Eight Lectures on Yoga.* 1938. Reprint, Phoenix, Ariz.: Falcon Press, 1985.

The Equinox. 1, nos. 1–10. London, 1909–1913. Reprint, New York: Samuel Weiser, 1972.

The Equinox. 3, no. 1. Detroit: Universal Publishing, 1919. Reprint, New York: Samuel Weiser, 1972.

The Equinox. 5, nos. 10–4. New York: Samuel Weiser, 1975–1981.

The Equinox of the God. London: Ordo Templi Orientis, 1936.

Hymenaeus Beta, Caliph [Grady McMurtry]. "Introduction: Culture vs. Cult." *Equinox* 3, 10 (1986): 9–12.

———. *Tao Teh King.* London: Askin Publishers; New York: Samuel Weiser, 1976.

Erfahrungswissenshaftliche Blätter (Journal)

Quarterly German-language journal published by Psychophysikalische Gesellschaft V. Reports scientific research connected with psychology and parapsychology. Address: Klarastrasse 22, D-8000 München 19, Germany.

Erhard, Werner (1935–)

Public name adopted by John Paul Rosenberg, who developed a modern system of experiential philosophy known as **est** (Erhard Seminars Training). Erhard was born September 5, 1935 in Philadelphia. He was baptized an Episcopalian, his family having converted to Christianity a short time previously.

He left home in 1960, and to keep his family from finding him, he changed his name to Werner Erhard. Over the next few years, he held a variety of jobs and also examined a variety of the new spiritual disciplines and self-help programs, including the Church of Scientology, Zen Buddhism, and Mind Dynamics. Erhard's own system, distilled from his involvement in the many movements, coalesced for him one morning in 1971 while driving on the 101 highway in Marin County, California. Basic to his insight was that each individual is the source of their own experience, they were not the labels that others had put on them.

Understanding this insight would later be labeled "getting it" in the est training. Shortly after his receiving this new insight, he founded est.

Nearly 500,000 people attended the est seminars usually given on two consecutive weekends. Most people were not dissuaded by a small chorus of detractors who noted cases of psychological problems experienced by attendees, accused est of brainwashing tactics, or were upset with the large sums of money Erhard was making.

In 1978 Erhard created The Hunger Project, a motivational program to get people to see the situation with world hunger as an opportunity to make a difference in the world and to commit themselves to ending hunger in the next twenty years.

In 1984 Erhard replaced est with a new program, The Forum. It represented an evolvement of his understanding as well as answering some of his critics, especially those who had complained of the rigid rules forced upon the attendees of the est training. He also founded Transformational Technologies to market training courses to corporations for employees.

All of Erhard's ventures came to an end in 1991. The IRS attached liens on seven million dollars worth of property; he faced a law suit from a former top employee he discharged; and he was accused of child molestation on a national news show. Est was sold by Erhard to a group of 150 employees and he disappeared from public view.

Sources:

Bartley, William Warren. *Werner Erhard: The Transformation of a Man, the Founding of est.* New York: C. N. Potter, 1978.

Bry, Adelaide. *est, Erhard Seminars Training: 60 Hours That Transform Your Life.* New York: Avon, 1976.

Fenwick, Sherida. *Getting It: The Psychology of est.* Philadelphia: J. P. Lippencott, 1976.

Self, Jane. *60 Minutes and the Assassination of Werner Erhard: How America's Top Rated Television Show Was Used in an Attempt to Destroy a Man Who Was Making a Difference.* Houston, Tex.: Breakthru Publishing, 1992.

Eric of the Windy Hat

According to Hector of Boëce, Eric (or Henry), an early king of Sweden, was surnamed "the Windy Hat" because it was believed that he could change the wind merely by turning his hat on his head to show his demon which way he wished the wind to blow. The demon obeyed the signal so promptly that the king's hat might have served the people for a weathercock. This story gave rise to the expression "a capful of wind."

Ermacora, Giovanni Battista (1869–1898)

An Italian scientist who abandoned his research in electricity (which had already caused him to be looked upon as a successor to Faraday and Maxwell) for psychical research and who became a fervent exponent and defender of paranormal phenomena when the subject was looked upon with contempt by official science. In his first work, *I fatti spiritici e le ipotesi affrettate* (1892), he severely criticized the neuropathological interpretation of mediumistic phenomena, which **Cesare Lombroso** had adopted after his first series of sittings with the medium **Eusapia Palladino** in Naples. Ermacora took part in the memorable Milan investigation with the same medium.

After the failure of his first attempt to establish an Italian Society for Psychical Research, he founded with Giorgio Finzi in January 1895 the *Rivista di Studi Psichici,* a periodical analogous to the British **Society for Psychical Research** *Proceedings,* in which most of his studies were published.

Ermacora devoted himself to all branches of psychical science, but especially to **telepathy,** to the experimental demonstration of which he made important contributions. His work on the subject was cut short by his murder. The 150-page work titled *La Telepatice,* posthumously published in 1898, is considered one of the best and most systematic treatises of the period on the subject.

Sources:

Berger, Arthur S., and Joyce Berger. *The Encyclopedia of Parapsychology and Psychical Research.* New York: Paragon House, 1991.

Ermacora, Giovanni B. *I fatti spiritici e le ipotesi affrettate* (Spiritistic facts and hasty hypotheses). Padua, Italy, 1892.

Eromancy

One of six kinds of **divination** by means of air and water practiced by the Persians. They enveloped their heads in a napkin and exposed to the air a vase filled with water, over which they muttered in a low voice the objects of their desire. If the surface of the air showed bubbles, it was regarded as a positive prognostication.

Erto, Pasquale (1895– ?)

Also known as "the human rainbow," Erto was an Italian chemist who claimed to be a medium for unique colored-light phenomena and other less striking psychical and trance effects. According to his own story, he attended a séance at age 14 at the house of an Egyptian woman. She told him that he was a medium. Shortly afterward he was able to produce **direct voice** mediumship and **automatic writing.**

In 1924 he gave a series of séances at the **Institut Métapsychique International** in Paris. Streaks of light resembling electric flashes lit up the room and luminous spheres zigzagged in the dark. The phenomena appeared to defy human production. But, as stated by **Gustav Geley** in a letter to *Le Matin* dated April 7, 1924, one of his colleagues had been able to produce a minute instrument with which Erto's lights were reproduced to perfection. In addition, more direct evidence of fraud was also discovered: 1) A small rectangular block of ferro-cerium, one centimeter long, was found in the syphon of a sink in which Erto washed immediately after a séance and before the final X-ray examination that Erto was to undergo; 2) Analysis of the workings of the medium revealed the presence of minute but unmistakable traces of ferro-cerium; 3) At the close of the last séance Erto refused to allow himself to be examined at the level of the pelvis by the doctors present; and 4) A circular hole sufficient to enable a small pencil to be pushed through was found in Erto's tights at the pelvic level. Although Erto's methods would be easily discerned today, Geley could find no explanation for the fingerprints that he could produce on photographic plates in sealed enclosures. They resembled those used as identification in criminology.

In 1924 Erto was invited once more to Paris by a committee formed by *L'Opinion* and *Le Matin.* The investigation took place at the Sorbonne and resulted in a complete exposure. Several pen nibs were found in his clothes and a piece of ferro-cerium in his shoes. By scratching the ferro-cerium with a pen nib in the dark, Erto's light effects could be easily reproduced.

For many years nothing further was heard of Erto's psychic adventures. In 1931, however, Emanuele Sorge, a prominent Italian scientist, requested the **National Laboratory of Psychical Research** of London to undertake an investigation. Erto arrived in London during December and under conditions of increasing severity gave a series of sittings under the auspices of psychical researcher **Harry Price.**

When left to himself, Erto produced brilliant flashes of light in the dark. Under conditions of strict control, however, beyond the roaring voice of "Near," a claimed trance personality, and whisperings of a female voice, no phenomena came forth. Erto was investigated by **Emilio Servadio** in 1932, but although the sittings were considered more satisfactory, the results were still ambiguous, and Erto is generally considered a fake medium on the basis of the damaging evidence from his 1924 sittings in Paris.

Sources:

Mackenzie, William. "Les Experiences de Genes avec le medium Erto." *Revue Métaphysique* (November–December 1922).

Price, Harry. *Leaves from a Psychist's Case-Book.* London: Gollancz, 1933.

Esalen Institute

A center at Big Sur, California, formed to explore trends in the behavioral sciences, religion, and philosophy that emphasize the potentialities and values of human existence. It was founded in 1962 by Michael H. Murphy to devise ways of extending human potential. The name derives from a tribe of Indians who once lived along the California coast.

Murphy spent three years in study and meditation before creating Esalen and lived for 18 months at the **Sri Aurobindo** ashram in Pondicherry, India. His associates have included Baba Ram Dass (**Richard Alpert**), William C. Schutz, Ida P. Rolf, and Frederick S. Perls. Many famous individuals have given lecture courses or acted as advisers, including veteran mythologist Joseph Campbell, Alan Watts, Ralph Metzer, and Bishop John Robinson (of Britain). Esalen made *encounter group* a universally recognized term and has conducted courses in mythology, mysticism, meditation, psychotherapy, group awareness, emotional reeducation, and expansion of consciousness. Michael Murphy has also been associated with the formation of **Quaesitor,** a European center with programs similar to Esalen's.

Inevitably, the wide range of activities and lecturers at Esalen has invited criticism that the center has sometimes sensationalized sensitive areas of human experience and potential. In addition to reputable and accredited individuals, workshops have also been conducted by self-styled mystics, shamans, and experimenters. For example, one staff member of Esalen whimsically claimed in a brochure current or previous bouts as "a drug user, village idiot, thief, madman, carny, masseur, and shaman." However, Esalen has undoubtedly pioneered and popularized new directions in human awareness and relationships and introduced methods of "turning on" without drugs. It has been considered a power center of the human potential movement.

Esalen grew out of an exciting discussion between **Aldous Huxley,** Michael Murphy, and Richard Price in Santa Monica in the summer of 1961. The story of the founding and history of Esalen, and the many famous names associated with it as the consciousness revolution swept the United States and influenced the world, is chronicled by Walter Truett Anderson in his book *The Upstart Spring: Esalen and the American Awakening* (1983). The title derives from the play *A Sleep of Prisoners,* by British playwright Christopher Fry, which describes a dark and frozen winter of centuries that begins to thaw in the "upstart spring." The quotation occurred in an introduction to the 1965 Esalen brochure. The book describes Esalen's beginnings; its exploration of new lifestyles; its development as a gathering place for such individuals as **Alan Watts,** Gregory Bateson, **Timothy Leary,** and Abraham Maslow; and the triumphs, mistakes, tragedies, and controversies of Esalen's heady history.

Anderson is a political scientist, journalist, author of books on American politics and social movements, and a former contributing editor to *Human Behavior* magazine. He has also served on the editorial board of the *Journal of Humanistic Psychology.* He visited Esalen in the mid-1960s and later became an instructor there.

Esalen maintains a wide range of programs and continues to pioneer new approaches to the development of human consciousness. Address: Esalen Institute, Big Sur, CA 93920.

Sources:

Anderson, Walter Truett. *The Upstart Spring: Esalen and the American Awakening.* Reading, Mass.: Addison-Wesley, 1983.

Miller, Stuart. *Hot Springs.* New York: Viking Press, 1971.

Esbat

A term adopted by the modern Gardnarian Wicca or **witchcraft** movement for the regular bimonthly coven meetings at the new and full moons. Esbats are distinguished from the eight major festivals, or **sabbats.** The esbats are a time for magic feats, fellowship, training of members, and feasting. According to Margaret A. Murray, the term was used as early as 1567.

Sources:

Murray, Margaret. *The Witch-cult in Western Europe: A Study in Anthropology.* Oxford: Clarendon Press, 1921.

Valiente, Doreen. *An ABC of Witchcraft Past and Present.* New York: St. Martin's Press, 1973.

Esdaile, James (1808–1859)

Scottish surgeon and mesmerist. Esdaile was born February 6, 1808, at Sydenham, England, and educated at Edinburgh University (M.D., 1830). After graduation he took a position as a physician for the East India Company (1831–35). He initially developed an interest in **mesmerism** from reading reports on the medical uses of mesmerism by **John Elliotson,** who originally introduced the subject into Britain.

Esdaile became a pioneer of surgical operations under mesmeric trance. As director of Hooghley Hospital, Calcutta, India, he performed many operations using mesmerism at the same time that another surgeon, **James Braid,** was using similar techniques in Britain. In support of his work, he wrote a series of books: *Mesmeric Facts* (1845), *Mesmerism in India and its Practical Application to Surgery and Medicine* (1846), and *Record of Cases Treated in Mesmeric Hospital, 1846–47, with Reports by Official Visitors* (1847). In 1848 Esdaile was appointed Bengal presidency surgeon. That same year chloroform and ether became available as anesthetics in India, but Esdaile recommended caution in their use, on the basis of his successful use of mesmerism.

He returned to Scotland in 1851 and wrote two books—*The Introduction to Mesmerism as an Anesthetic and Curative Agent into the Hospitals of India* (1852) and *Natural and Mesmeric Clairvoyance* (1852)—detailing his work in an attempt to introduce his successful procedures into Great Britain. He found that his mesmeric techniques were not nearly as successful with Europeans as they had been with Indians. He died January 10, 1859, in England.

Sources:

Esdaile, James. *Mesmerism in India and its Practical Application to Surgery and Medicine.* 1846. Reprint, Chicago: Psychic Research, 1902.

———. *Natural and Mesmeric Clairvoyance.* New York; London: H. Bailliere, 1852.

Eskimos

Traditional religion among the Eskimo people had a strong element of magic centered on the **shamans,** whom they called *angekok.* Eskimos consulted their shamans at important times, such as before a hunting expedition or when ill. The nature of the ceremonies employed on those occasions may be inferred from the account of Captain G. F. Lyon, who once employed an angekok named Toolemak to summon a *tomga* (familiar spirit) in the cabin of a ship. He gave an account of the ceremony that was used, as follows.

In complete darkness the sorcerer began vehemently chanting to his wife, who responded with the *Amna-aya,* the favorite song of the Eskimo. This song lasted throughout the ceremony. Toolemak began to spin around, shouting for the tomga while blowing and snorting like a walrus. His noise, agitation, and impatience increased steadily, and at length he seated himself on the deck, varying his tones, and rustling his clothes.

Suddenly the voice seemed smothered, as if the shaman was retreating beneath the deck. It became more distant, ultimately sounding as if it were many feet below the cabin. Then it ceased entirely. In answer to Lyon's queries, the sorcerer's wife declared that the shaman had dived and would send up the tomga.

In about half a minute a distant blowing was heard, approaching very slowly, and a voice different from the shaman's was mixed with the blowing. Eventually both sounds became distinct, and the old woman said that the tomga had come to answer the stranger's questions. Lyon asked several questions of the sagacious spirit, receiving what he understood to be an affirmative or favorable answer by two loud slaps on the deck.

A hollow yet powerful voice, certainly not Toolemak's, chanted for some time. A medley of hisses, groans, shouts, and gobblings like a turkey's followed in swift succession. The old woman sang with increased energy, and because Lyon conjectured that the exhibition was intended to astonish "the Kabloona," he said repeatedly that he was greatly terrified. As he expected, this admission added fuel to the flame until the spirit, exhausted by its own might, asked leave to retire. The voice gradually faded and an indistinct hissing followed. At first it sounded like the tone produced by wind on the bass cord of an Eolian harp. This was soon changed to a rapid hiss like that of a rocket, and Toolemak, with a yell, announced the spirit's return.

At the first distant sibilation Lyon held his breath, and twice exhausted himself; but the Eskimo conjurer did not breathe once. Even his returning, powerful yell was uttered without previous pause or inspiration of air.

When light was admitted Toolemak was in a state of profuse perspiration and exhausted by his exertions, which had continued for at least half an hour. Lyon then observed two bundles, each consisting of two strips of white deerskin and a long piece of sinew, attached to the back of the shaman's coat. He had not seen them before and was told that they had been sewn on by the tomga while Toolemak was below.

The performance had much in common with that of a Western medium at a spirit séance. The angekoks claim to visit the dwelling places of the spirits they invoke and give circumstantial descriptions of these habitations. They have a firm belief in their own powers.

The explorer Dr. Elisha Kane (1820–1957) considered it interesting that wonder-workers from indigenous cultures and postindustrial societies had so much in common. He observed:

"I have known several of them personally, and can speak with confidence on this point. I could not detect them in any resort to jugglery or natural magic; their deceptions are simply vocal, a change of voice, and perhaps a limited profession of ventriloquism, made more imposing by the darkness." They had, however, like the members of the learned professions everywhere else, a certain language or jargon of their own, in which they communicated with each other.

"While the *angekoks* are the dispensers of good, the *issintok,* or evil men, are the workers of injurious spells, enchantments, and metamorphoses. Like the witches of both Englands, the Old and the New, these malignant creatures are rarely submitted to trial until they have suffered punishment—the old 'Jeddart justice'—*castigate auditque.* Two of them, in 1818, suffered the penalty of their crime on the same day, one at Kannonak, the other at Upernavik. The latter was laudably killed in accordance with the 'old custom'. . . . custom being everywhere the apology for any act revolting to moral sense. He was first harpooned, then disembowelled; a flap let down from his forehead to cover his eyes and prevent his seeing again—he had, it appears, the repute of an evil eye—and then small portions of his heart were eaten, to ensure that he should not come back to earth unchanged."

Kane's observations of Eskimo shaman practice have special interest because he became the husband of **Margaretta Fox,** one of the **Fox sisters,** the first modern Spiritualist mediums.

Sources:

Kane, Elisha. *Arctic Explorations in Search of Sir John Franklin.* London: T. Nelson, 1885.

Merkur, Daniel. *Becoming Half Hidden: Shamanism and Initiation among the Inuit.* New York: Garland, 1992.

Walker, Daniel E. *Witchcraft and Sorcery of the American Native Peoples.* Moscow, Idaho: University of Idaho Press, 1989.

Esoteric Society

British organization founded in 1974 to present a wide range of esoteric studies, including **Kabala,** the **Rosicrucians,** exorcism, magic, alchemy, Stonehenge, astrology, and the Holy Grail. The society organizes meetings as well as arranges tours to such sites as Stonehenge, Avebury, and Glastonbury. It issues a quarterly newsletter, *Esoterica.* Address: 40 Buckingham Gate, London, SW1, England.

ESP See Extrasensory Perception

ESP Laboratory of Texas

Not a laboratory for research in the scientific sense of the term, but a mystical organization founded as the ESP Laboratory by Alcie Gwyn Manning in Los Angeles, California, in 1966. With the help of a spirit guide, "Professor Reinhardt," Manning wrote his initial book. He also became a minister of Spiritual Science and opened a church. He developed a program of psychic development designed to bring success, prosperity, and healing.

In 1970 Manning introduced a course on the I Ching and the following year one on white magic and witchcraft. His practical approach was emphasized in a new book, *Helping Yourself with White Witchcraft* (1972). In the early 1980s Manning moved the laboratory to Texas. He also made a most endearing and original contribution to contemporary mythology with the felicitously named Gronkydoddles, a race of invisible pixies helpful to the human race. Address: ESP Laboratory of Texas, Box 216, 219 S. Ridge Dr., Edgewood, TX 75117.

Sources:

Manning, Alcie G. *Helping Yourself with White Witchcraft.* West Nyack, N.Y.: Parker Publishing, 1972.

———. *Helping Yourself with the Power of Gnostic Magic.* West Nyack, N.Y.: Parker Publishing, 1979.

ESP Magazine

A short-lived 1970s American newsstand publication featuring articles on psychic phenomena and parapsychology.

ESP Research Associates Foundation

A psychic phenomena research and interest organization founded in 1962 with a membership of individuals who believed they had genuine ESP experiences and wished to learn more about the functioning of these powers of the mind. President and guiding force of the foundation was Harold Sherman (b. 1898), a leading figure in the psychic community in America through the mid-twentieth century.

Sherman began his adult life as a journalist and novelist. Then in 1935 he wrote a short metaphysical book, *Your Key to Happiness,* which led to his radio show by the same name. In 1937 and 1938 Sherman conducted an ESP experiment with Arctic explorer Sir Hubert Wilkins that yielded a significant account of telepathic communication of interest to parapsychologists. A log of Wilkins's thoughts and actions compared with Sherman's received impressions provide a startling record of the possibilities of psychic comunication. This served as a model for a similar experiment conducted by **Edgar Mitchell** during his voyage to the Moon on *Apollo 14* in 1971.

Through the 1940s and 1950s Sherman continued to write metaphysical and psychic books that brought him a great following. They became the basis for the formation of ESP Research Associates Foundation, which among other activities provided a contact point for people who wished to have psychic readings from Sherman. Through the 1980s, the foundation conducted conferences but was unable to continue effectively after Sherman's death and was discontinued.

Sources:

Sherman, Harold. *How to Foresee and Control Your Future.* Greenwich, Conn.: Fawcett, 1970.

———. *How to Know What to Believe.* Greenwich, Conn.: Fawcett, 1976.

———. *How to Make ESP Work for You.* Los Angeles: DeVorss, 1964.

———. *You Live After Death.* New York: C. R. Anthony, 1949.

———. *Your Key to Happiness.* New York: G. P. Putnam's Sons, 1935. Reprint, Greenwich, Conn.: Fawcett, 1964.

Sherman, Harold, and Sir Hubert Wilkins. *Thought through Space.* Greenwich, Conn.: Fawcett, 1972.

"Esplandian"

A medieval Spanish legend that tells how Amadis of Gaul and his wife Oriana of the Firm Island had the wicked enchanter Archelous in their keeping but set him free in answer to his wife's entreaties. Certain calamities occurred that were attributed to Archelous, and Amadis's son Esplandian was carried off by the enchantress Urganda. The legend goes on to relate the adventures of Esplandian, including how he was given a magic sword and killed a dragon. With this sword he also succeeded in killing Archelous himself and his nephew, and he then set free a kinsman. His next opponent was Matroed, son of Arcobone, whom he also vanquished. Finally, he utterly destroyed the stronghold of Archelous and freed the land from the pagan influence of Matroed.

Essenes, The

An esoteric Jewish sect that flourished in Palestine in the century immediately prior to the emergence of the Christian movement and from whom the early Christians may have drawn some of their basic ideas. They were very exclusive and possessed an organization peculiar to themselves. The earliest mentions of the Essenes come from the writings of Philo and Josephus, both contemporaries of Jesus. According to Philo, they lived separated lives apart from the cities, had a voluntary communal life with a subsistence level of existence, and avoided temple worship. They had a threefold rule of love of God, love of virtue, and love of humankind. Pliny, most importantly, located a holy of Essenes on the west bank of the Dead Sea at a point far enough away as to escape its noxious fumes.

Josephus was for a short period an Essene, which he described as one of three sects among the Palestinian Jews. He also notes their communalism and their voluntary poverty. He dealt with their tendency to adopt celibacy and to make room for orphans, which they treated as their own children. They had their own worship and beliefs, within a larger Jewish context. As to their peculiar beliefs, Josephus notes: ". . . they firmly believe that their bodies perish and their substance is not enduring, but that the souls are immortal. . . and that when released from the bounds of the body, they, as if released from a long servitude, rejoice and mount upwards." Josephus was criticized for trying to explain the Essene belief in such a way as to make it appear similar to Greek thought.

The Dead Sea Scrolls

We knew little of the Essenes until the late twentieth century. In 1947 a Bedouin boy discovered a cave near the northwest shore of the Dead Sea. In the cave was a jar with scrolls in it. After the initial discovery, eventually a number of other caves and an enormous number of additional scrolls were found. Slowly, texts of the scrolls have been published, and while various ideas were explored as to the identity of the community at Qumran, the site of the caves, there is now general consensus that the scrolls were gathered and reflect the beliefs and practices of at least one segment of the Essene community. Qumran existed from around the middle of the second century B.C.E. to the time of the Jewish anti-Roman revolt, 66–70 C.E.

The members of the group began their day with a prayer facing the rising sun, as Josephus described it, "as though entreating it to rise." They ate a communal meal several times during the day and spent their evenings (and all of the Sabbath) in prayer and biblical exposition. They followed the rites and festivals laid out in the Jewish Bible (the Christian Old Testament). It may be that a calendar question occasioned by the adoption of a Hellenized calendar in Jerusalem may have led to the formation of the Essenes.

Membership in the group was by initiation, which was predated by a year's probation. The initiation ceremony included baptism and the beginning of daily purification rites within the group. The purification was followed by the evening meal. The meal had an eschatological significance, a foretaste of the meal to be presided over by the Messiah.

They believed the soul to be in the midst of a war between good and evil, the Angel of Darkess viewing with the Prince of Light. They also believed in **astrology** to some degree, ascribing a place in the battle based upon the day of one's birth. They saw themselves as collectively a militia in the service of light and individually at war with the darkness that entered through the body. Their understanding of the body led them to celibacy and asceticism.

The understanding of the life and teachings of the Essenes, at least those at Qumran, will be more fully explicated as the additional texts only recently released to the larger scholarly world are translated and debate proceeds.

Sources:

Cohen, Shaye J. D. *From the Maccabees to the Mishnah.* Philadelphia: Westminster Press, 1987.

Cross, Frank Moore. *The Ancient Library of Qumran.* Minneapolis, Minn.: Fortress Press, 1995.

Ginsburg, Christian D. *The Essenes: Their History and Doctrines.* London: Routledge and Kegan Paul, 1863.

Knibb, Michael A. *The Qumran Community.* Cambridge: Cambridge University Press, 1987.

Kraft, Robert A., and George W. E. Nickelsburg. *Early Judaism and Its Modern Interpreters.* Philadelphia: Fortress Press, 1986.

Simon, Marcel. *Jewish Sects at the Time of Jesus.* Philadelphia: Fortress Press, 1967.

est

Popular name for Erhard Seminars Training, a system of experiential philosophy developed by **Werner Erhard.** Through the 1960s Erhard explored a variety of self-help courses and spiritual disciplines, including Dale Carnegie, the Church of Scientology, Subud, Zen Buddhism, and Mind Dynamics. In 1971, he had an enlightenment experience, during the time he was a mind Dynamics instructor.

Erhard concluded he must take responsibility for his life. In the seminars, through lectures and various activities, he tried to assist people to understand that they were not the labels put on them by others, but the product of their own decisions. This act of insight was termed "getting it."

The est basic program consisted of some 60 hours of training over two weekends for which attendees were charged $250.00. Some 500,000 people took the course from Erhard or his assistants between 1971 and 1984. In 1984 est was discontinued and replaced with The Forum. In 1991 Erhard sold his corporation to a group of employees and retired from public life. He was at the time under attack from several points, including the IRS and a former employee who was suing him.

Sources:

Bartley, William Warren. *Werner Erhard: The Transformation of a Man, the Founding of est.* New York: C. N. Potter, 1978.

Hargrove, Robert A. *est: Making Life Work.* New York: Delacorte Press, 1976.

Estabrooks, George Hoban (1895–1973)

Professor of psychology. Estabrooks was born December 16, 1895, at St. John, New Brunswick, Canada, and educated at Acadid University, Wolfville, Nova Scotia. He was a Rhodes scholar at Oxford University (1921–24) and completed his Ph.D. at Harvard University in 1926. He was a professor of psychology at Springfield College in Massachusetts (1926–27) and then moved on to Colgate University, where he became chairman of the Department of Psychology in 1938.

Estabrooks was introduced to psychical research during his doctoral program at Harvard when he engaged in research on telepathy with **William McDougall, Morton Prince,** and **Gardner Murphy,** who had established the **Boston Society for Psychic Research** following a dispute within the **American Society for Psychical Research.** During his years of teaching at Colgate his interest in telepathy resulted in a number of books. He died December 30, 1973.

Sources:

Berger, Arthur S., and Joyce Berger. *The Encyclopedia of Parapsychology and Psychical Research.* New York: Paragon House, 1991.

Estabrooks, George H. *Hypnosis: Current Problems.* New York: Harper, 1962.

———. *Hypnotism.* New York: Dutton, 1957.

———. *Man, Mechanical Misfit.* New York: Macmillan, 1941.

———. *Spiritism.* New York: Dutton, 1947.

Estabrooks, George H., and Nancy Gross. *The Future of the Human Mind.* New York: Dutton, 1961.

Estabrooks, George H., and Richard Lockbridge. *Death in the Mind.* New York: Dutton, 1947.

Pleasants, Helene, ed. *Biographical Dictionary of Parapsychology.* New York: Helix Press, 1964.

ET

Extraterrestrial—a being allegedly from outer space, usually traveling in a **UFO** or **flying saucer** and occasionally making contact with individuals on earth. ETs are also known as extraterrestrial biological entities (EBEs). Many modern-day theories have posited that contact with alien intelligences from flying saucers may be related to psychic phenomena, or folklore stories of such protean forms as **fairies** and **elementals,** or perhaps to parallel universes and extra dimensions of space.

The possibility of extraterrestrial life continues to dominate the ufological community, which still gives primary attention to the cases of reported abduction of humans by ETs and documented cases of UFO sightings. Also, a close examination of several abduction cases has yielded a consensus picture of the size and shape of the entities most commonly reported. To quote folklorist Thomas Bullard, "The standard being in an abduction has a bulging, hairless head often tapering to a pointed chin, large unblinking eyes, a hole or slit for a mouth, a tiny nose or holes only, and vestigial ears. With great consistency, the skin is gray or pale and sunless." He goes on to note that they generally dress in a one-piece uniform that leaves only their head and hands visible. This type of being became familiar to the public following the 1982 release of Steven Spielberg's popular movie *E.T.*

Sources:

Bullard, Thomas E. *On Stolen Time: A Summary of a Comparative Study of the UFO Abduction Mystery.* Bloomington, Ind.: The Author, 1987.

Clark, Jerome. *UFOs in the 1980s.* Vol. 1 of *The UFO Encyclopedia.* Detroit: Omnigraphics, 1990.

Fitzgerald, Randall. *The Complete Book of Extraterrestrial Encounters.* New York: Collier, 1979.

Etain

In ancient Irish romance, the second wife of Midir the Proud. The sorceress Fuamnach, Midir's first wife, became jealous of her beauty and turned her into a butterfly, and she was blown out of the palace by a magic storm. For seven years she was tossed throughout Ireland, but then was blown into the fairy palace of Angus on the Boyne. He could not release her from the spell, but during the day she fed on honey-laden flowers, and by night in her natural form gave Angus her love. Fuamnach discovered her hiding place and sent a dreadful tempest that blew Etain into the drinking cup of Etar, wife of an Ulster chief. Etar swallowed her, but she was reborn as Etar's daughter, and as such married Eochy, high king of Ireland.

Ether

Late nineteenth-century hypothesis suggested by physicists as a means of accounting for the propagation of light as a wave motion through otherwise empty space. The idea of ether meshed with the teachings of the mesmerists and Theosophists, who spoke of subtle substructures of matter sometimes referred to as *koilon*—all-pervading, filling all space, and interpenetrating all matter. Ether was supposedly of very great density, 10,000 times more dense than water and with a pressure of 750 tons per square inch.

According to Theosophical teaching, ether was said to be capable of being perceived only by clairvoyants with the most highly developed powers. It was said to be filled with an infinitude of small bubbles, much like the air bubbles in treacle or some other viscid substance. The bubbles were supposedly formed at some ancient time by the infusion of the breath of the Logos into the ether. Of these bubbles—not of the ether—matter was said to be built, its density varying with the number of bubbles combined to form each objects.

Ether became the subject of one of the more famous experiments in physics, by Albert Abraham Michelson and E. W. Morley. Their experiment involved the splitting and reintegration of a light wave in such a manner that the presence of ether would slow one of the waves. They disproved the existence of ether and brought America its first Nobel Prize for physics. The experiment also contributed to the development of Einstein's theory of relativity. The abandonment of ether by science led to its eventual abandonment by Spiritualists and Theosophists.

Etheric Double

According to theosophical teaching, derived from ancient Hindu philosophy, the etheric double is an invisible part of the ordinary, visible, physical body, which it interpenetrates and beyond which it extends a little, forming with other finer bodies the **aura.** The etheric double is not made of the supposed omnipresent ether of space, but is composed of physical matter known as etheric, superetheric, subatomic, and atomic.

The term **double** is used because the etheric double is a replica of the denser physical body. The sense organs of the etheric double are the **chakras,** and it is through the chakras that the physical body is supplied with the vitality necessary for its existence and its well-being during life. The etheric double thus plays the part of a conductor, and a bridge between the physical and astral bodies, for without it humans could have no communications with the **astral world** and hence neither thoughts nor feelings.

Anesthetics are said to drive out the greater part of the double, and the subject is then impervious to pain. During sleep the double does not leave the physical body; indeed, in **dreams** the etheric part of the brain is extremely active, especially when, as is often the case, the dreams are caused by attendant physical circumstances, such as noise. Shortly after death, the etheric double finally quits the physical body though it does not move far away from the body, but is composed of the four subdivisions of physical matter alluded to earlier. With the decay of the physical body, the double reportedly also decays.

Those who have claimed experience of **astral projection** or **out-of-the-body travel** state that the etheric or astral body is connected to the physical body by a subtle, infinitely extensible cord. Aside from their specialized use in **Theosophy,** the terms etheric double and etheric body are often used synonymously with **astral body.**

Sources:

Mead, G. R. S. *The Doctrine of the Subtle Body.* London: John M. Watkins, 1919. Reprint, Wheaton, Ill.: Theosophical Publishing House, 1967.

Powell, A. E. *The Etheric Double.* 1926. Reprint, Wheaton, Ill.: Theosophical Publishing House, 1969.

Etheric Vision

According to theosophical teaching, the power of sight peculiar to the **etheric double,** a subtle counterpart of the physical body. Etheric vision is of considerably greater power than physical vision, and by its aid many of the phenomena of the physical world may be examined, as well as many creatures of a nonhuman nature that are ordinarily just outside the range of physical vision. It responds readily to stimuli of various kinds and becomes active under their influence.

Sources:

Powell, A. E. *The Etheric Double.* 1926. Reprint, Wheaton, Ill.: Theosophical Publishing House, 1969.

Ethlinn

Daughter of Balor, king of the Fomorians of ancient Irish magic legend. She was Balor's only child, and because he had been informed by a Druid that he would be killed by his grandson, Balor had Ethlinn imprisoned in a tower and guarded by 12 women who were forbidden to tell her that such beings as men existed. Balor stole a magic cow from Kian, who in revenge obtained access, disguised as a woman, to Ethlinn. They had three children, whom Balor ordered to be drowned. But one of them fell from the napkin in which they were being taken to their doom and was carried off by the Druidess Birog to its father, Kian. This child became Lugh, the great sun god, who eventually fulfilled the prophecy and killed his grandfather Balor.

"Etteilla" (ca. 1790)

An eighteenth-century student of the **tarot.** By profession he was a hairdresser, his true name being Alliette, but on entering upon his occult studies he changed his name to read backward: "Etteilla." He had little education and was ill-acquainted with the philosophy of the initiates. Nevertheless, he possessed a profound intuition, and according to the famous occultist **Éliphas Lévi,** he came very near to unveiling the secrets of the tarot. Lévi stated that his writings, however, were "obscure, wearisome, and in style barbarous." Etteilla claimed to have revised the *Book of Thoth* (i.e., the tarot) but in reality obscured its meaning by regarding as blunders certain cards whose meaning he had failed to grasp.

It is commonly admitted that he failed in his attempt to elucidate the tarot and ended by transposing the keys, thus destroying the correspondence between the numbers and the signs. It is also said that he degraded the science of the tarot into mere fortune-telling by cards for credulous people. The publications of Etteilla include *Manière de se récréer le jeu de cartes nommés Tarots* (4 pts., 1783–85), *Philosophie des hautes sciences* (1785), and *Science, Leçons Théoriques et pratiques du livre de Thot* (1787).

Sources:

Douglas, Alfred. *The Tarot: The Origins, Meaning, and Use of the Cards.* New York: Taplinger, 1972.

Lévi, Éliphas. *Transcendental Magic.* New York: Samuel Weiser, 1972.

European Journal of Parapsychology

Semiannual professional journal of the **Parapsychology Laboratory,** University of Utrecht. Includes authoritative articles on experimental and theoretical aspects of parapsychology. Address: University of Utrecht, Parapsychology Laboratory, Sorbonnelaan 16, 3584 CA, Utrecht, Netherlands.

Eva C.

Famous French **materialization** medium, known also as "Marthe Béraud." Eva's real name was Eva Carrière (Waespé by marriage). She was the daughter of an officer and the fiancée of one General Noel's son Maurice, who died in the Congo before the marriage could take place. Her psychic powers were discovered by the general and his wife.

General and Mrs. Noel were greatly interested in psychical research and, in the presence of invited mediums, at the Villa Carmen witnessed the materialization of a helmeted phantom, "Bien Boa," a Brahman Hindu said to have died some 300 years previously and who styled himself as the spiritual guide of the Noel family. A "sister" of the phantom, "Bergoglia," who also manifested, later hinted that "Bien Boa" was an assumed name of someone who had figured in Mrs. Noel's life in an earlier incarnation. Indeed, Mrs. Noel claimed a share of credit for Bien Boa's appearances and said that either by the séance table or by direct writing Bien Boa always declared that she was the true medium at early séances.

When the powers of Marthe Béraud were first discovered, a period of two years of experimentation commenced, and Mrs. Noel published many notes on the phenomena in **Gabriel Delanne**'s *Revue Scientifique et Morale du Spiritisme.* Then the Noels and Béraud invited **Charles Richet** and Delanne to visit Algiers as their guests.

The séances were held in an isolated building over a stable behind bolted windows and doors. A curtain was thrown across one corner of the room to improvise a **cabinet.** As a rule a young black woman, Aischa, sat with Béraud behind the curtain, but Richet has said that in the more effective experiments Aischa was not present. Béraud was not tied and wore a thin dress. By making magnetic (i.e., mesmeric) passes to awaken her from her trance, Richet passed his hand all over her body and made sure that she had nothing hidden on her. The presence of Aischa, of which Mrs. Noel made a point, greatly annoyed the medium, who complained that in the tropical heat the odor of the woman was unbearable.

The materializations produced were very complete. Bien Boa appeared five or six times and offered opportunities for many important observations and experiments. Richet's report, published in the April 1906 issue of the *Annales des sciences psychiques,* created an immense sensation. He was satisfied that he had witnessed genuine phenomena and that Marthe Béraud could not have masqueraded in a helmet and sheet in the guise of Bien Boa. Besides, he asserts in the report, the medium and the phantom were also seen together when no stranger could have entered the room:

"I make a point of this, because of the assertions of Areski, an Arab coachman dismissed by General Noel for theft, who said that he 'played the ghost.' A certain starveling practitioner of Algiers, Dr. R., was ill-advised enough to entertain this man and to exhibit him in public at Algiers in a white mantle to play the ghost before spectators. That is the most that had been said against the experiments at the Villa Carmen. The general public blinded by ignoble newspaper tales, imagined that the **fraud** had been exposed. All that was really proved was that an Arab thief could lie impudently, that he could put on a sheet, could appear thus on a stage, and could get a doctor to endorse his lies. It is averred also that Marthe confessed fraud to an Algerian lawyer who took a pseudonym. But even if this anonymous allegation were true, we know the value to be placed on such revelations, which only show the mental instability of mediums."

Futhermore, according to a Dr. Z., Areski entered the séance room with the rest of the company, and when their attention was diverted by the examination of the furniture, he slipped behind the cabinet and hid behind the curtain. Richet replied to this specific charge, "Now, I declare formally and solemnly that during the séances—twenty in number—at which I was present, Areski was not once permitted to enter the séance room." The later "confession" of Marthe Béraud was alleged to contain a statement about a trapdoor. According to Richet, Béraud has never wrote or said that there was a trapdoor.

Besides the phantom of Bien Boa, a beautiful Egyptian girl also materialized and allowed Richet to cut a lock of her hair. "As I was about to cut a lock high up" stated the professor, "a firm hand behind the curtain lowered mine so that I cut only about six inches from the end. As I was rather slow about doing this, she said in a low voice 'quick, quick' and disappeared."

The second important phase of Béraud's mediumship developed under the care of sculptor **Juliette Bisson,** to whom Béraud had been introduced in 1908. It has been suggested that Bisson and Béraud shared a lesbian relationship following the death of Bisson's husband in 1910. In any case, they lived and worked together.

Between 1909 and 1913 Béraud, by then known as "Eva C.," centered her mediumship on materializations. Joint experiments by Richet and **Baron Schrenck-Notzing,** with Bisson always present, built upon previous observations and elucidated several obscure points. The period also afforded an added opportunity for Richet to check his earlier findings. During her trances the medium appeared to suffer much, writhing like a woman in childbirth, and her pulse rose from 90 to 120. The materializations, under the control of an entity named "Berthe," were always slow and seemingly difficult. Very few forms were well developed or remained for a long time. All this was in striking contrast with the ease of former years. Perhaps the rigor of the control had to do with this. Eva C. had to put on special dresses. She was subject, both before and after the séance, to meticulous medical examination and often sat nude. A battery of eight photographic cameras, two of them stereoscopic, were trained on her, and 225 valuable photographs were secured when it was discovered that the séances could be held in comparatively good light, provided the medium was shielded from a sudden flash. At certain times the ectoplasmic mediumship alternated with remarkable phenomena of the intellectual type. She read automatically on an imaginary screen (like that of a cinema) pages of philosophy that greatly exceeded her normal knowledge and power.

Regarding a séance of April 15, 1912, held in the presence of **Count Cesar de Vesme** and Bisson, Richet is quoted as follows:

"The manifestations began at once. White substance appeared on the neck of the medium: then a head was formed which moved from left to right and placed itself on the medium's head. A photograph was taken. After the flashlight, the head reappeared by the side of Eva's head, about sixteen inches from it, connected by a long bunch of white substance. It looked like the head of a man, and made movements like bows. Some 20 appearances and reappearances of this head were counted; it appeared, retreated into the cabinet, and emerged again. A woman's head then appeared on the right, showed itself near the curtains, and went back into the cabinet, returned several times and disappeared."

Richet adds, "Marthe was examined and searched before and after the experiments. I never lost sight of her for a moment and her hands were always held and visible."

To eliminate every possibility of fraud Baron Schrenck-Notzing employed detectives for several months to watch for any suspicious circumstances in Eva's life. To answer the charge that the **ectoplasm** of Eva C. was regurgitated material, a strong emetic was administered on November 26, 1913, after the ectoplasmic flow reentered her mouth. Ten minutes later the experimenters were satisfied that the medium swallowed nothing with which the phenomena could have been produced.

Another important series of experiments took place in 1917–18 in the laboratories of **Gustav Geley** with Bisson's collaboration. About 150 representative individuals, including many scientists, witnessed the phenomena. In his *From the Unconscious to the Conscious* (1920), Geley observes:

"It is needless to say that the usual precautions were rigorously observed during the séances in my laboratory. On coming into the room where the séances were held, and to which I alone had previous access, the medium was completely undressed in my presence, and dressed in a tight garment, sewn up the back and at the wrists; the hair, and the cavity of the mouth were examined by me and my collaborators before and after the séances. Eva was walked backwards to the wicker chair in the dark cabinet; her hands were always held in full sight outside the curtains and the room was always quite well lit during the whole time. I do not merely say: There was no trickery; I say there was no possibility of trickery. Further, and I cannot repeat it too often, nearly always the materializations took place under my own eyes, and I have observed their genesis and their whole development."

He adds in a footnote:

"I am, moreover, glad to testify that Eva has always shown, in my presence, absolute experimental honesty. The intelligent and self-sacrificing resignation with which she submitted to all control and the truly painful tests of her mediumship, deserve the real and sincere gratitude of all men of science worthy of that name."

The results of these experiments were the subject of a conference at the College of France, published under the title *La Physiologie dite Supranormale (Bulletin de l'Institut Physiologique,* January–June 1918.

In 1920 Eva C. and Bisson spent two months in London. Of 40 séances given to the **Society for Psychical Research,** half were entirely blank, the rest very weak. As a result, the **regurgitation** theory was again put forward as a possible explanation. Of the London work, in his *Thirty Years of Psychical Research* (1923), Richet states:

"The official reports of the séances lead to very distinct inferences; it seems that though the external conditions were unfavorable to success, some results were very clear and that it is impossible to refer the phenomena to fraud. Nevertheless, our learned colleagues of the SPR came to no conclusion. They admit that the only possible trickery is regurgitation. But what is meant by that? How can masses of mobile substance, organized as hands, faces and drawings, be made to emerge from the oesophagus or the stomach? No physiologist would admit such power to contract those organs at will in this manner. How, when the medium's hands are tied and held, could papers be unfolded, put away, and made to pass, through a veil? The members of the SPR, when they fail to understand, say 'It is difficult to understand how this is produced.' Mr. Dingwall, who is an expert in legerdemain, having seen the ectoplasm emerge as a miniature hand, making signs before disappearing, says 'I attach no importance to this.' We may be permitted to remark that very great importance attaches to Mr. Dingwall's testimony."

In 1922, 15 sittings with Eva C. took place at the Sorbonne. Thirteen sittings were totally blank and the committee returned a negative report.

After the death of Geley in 1924, there was a whispering campaign that some very suspicious photographs of Eva C. had been found among his papers, suggesting the possibility of fraud by the medium and contradicting Geley's published laudatory reports. In fact, his unpublished papers revealed that Bisson had been Eva C.'s active accomplice in fraud, and his pictures plainly showed wires attached to her hair that supported the materialized forms. However, Eva C.'s supporters countered with the published evidence of the 200 photographs and the careful reports of Schrenck-Notzing.

On the whole, the mediumship of Eva C. remains a matter of controversy. The materializations of Bien Boa in 1905 appear crude and suggest fraud, as do the Geley papers and pictures. On the other hand, the careful investigations and remarkable photographs of materialization obtained by Schrenck-Notzing cannot be so easily dismissed. In the end, Eva C. seems to be another clever fraud who was able to confound some of those who observed her séances and lacked the training or resolve to uncover her methods. The inability of Eva C. to manifest under tightly controlled conditions, along with the lack of supporting evidence for the existence of ectoplasm, make a most damning case against her.

Sources:

Berger, Arthur S., and Joyce Berger. *The Encyclopedia of Parapsychology and Psychical Research.* New York: Paragon House, 1991.

Brandon, R. *The Spiritualists.* New York: Alfred A. Knopf, 1983.

Geley, Gustav. *Clairvoyance and Materialisation: A Record of Experiments.* London, 1927. Reprint, New York: Arno Press, 1975.

Houdini, Harry. *A Magician Among the Spirits.* New York: Harper, 1924. Reprinted as *Houdini: A Magician Among the Spirits.* New York: Arno Press, 1972.

Lambert, Rudolf. "Dr. Geley's Report on the Medium Eva C." *Journal* of the Society for Psychical Research 37, no. 682 (November 1954).

Richet, Charles. *Thirty Years of Psychical Research.* London, 1923. Reprint, New York: Arno Press, 1975.

Schrenck-Notzing, Baron A. von. *Phenomena of Materialisation: A Contribution to the Investigation of Mediumistic Teleplastics.* London and New York, 1920. Reprint, New York: Arno Press, 1975.

Evans, Christopher (Riche) (1931–1979)

British psychologist and anthropologist who conducted research in parapsychology. Born May 29, 1931, in Aberdovey, Wales, Evans trained as a psychologist at University College, London, and the University of Reading, receiving a doctorate in psychology. He was a founder and secretary of the Brain Research Association and a member of the British Psychological Association, the Behavioral Psychotherapy Association, and the Ergonomics Research Society.

He took a special interest in computer technology and helped to develop the "computer doctor" Mickie, which elicited diagnostic information from patients by asking computerized questions. Evans was Principal Scientific Officer of the National Physical Laboratory, London, and a contributing editor to the U.S. magazine *Omni.* He acted as an investigative reporter and news correspondent at scientific conventions in Britain, Europe, and the United States.

As a member of the Society for Psychical Research, London, he conducted parapsychological investigations. Evans was responsible for a questionnaire that got 1,500 responses from readers about psychic phenomena. His conclusions were published in *New Scientist* January 25, 1973, and showed that 63 percent of the respondents possessed degrees, and of those 29 percent had advanced degrees. In February 1974 he conducted a survey of telepathic or ESP faculties on West German television. Over 50,000 viewers participated, and the results threw doubt on the **sheep-goat hypothesis** of parapsychologist **Gertrude Schmeidler,** which posits that believers in ESP score higher than disbelievers.

Evans published several books but is best remembered for his attack upon new religions, *Cults of Unreason* (1973), which examines a variety of newer religions and belief systems, including **Scientology, UFOs, black boxes** (devices for diagnosing disease), and some popular Eastern religions. Although mainly skeptical in tone, and while critical of some of the unfounded scientific claims, such as those supporting the black boxes, the book often veers into mere rhetoric directed against those holding religious ideas with which Evans disagrees. Evans died October 10, 1979.

Sources:

Evans, Christopher. *Cults of Unreason.* London: Harrap, 1974.

———. *Cybernetics.* Baltimore: University Park Press, 1968.

———. *The Mighty Micro.* London: Gollancz, 1979.

———. *Psychology: A Dictionary of the Mind, Brain, and Behavior.* London: Arrow Books, 1978.

———. *Understanding Yourself.* New York: A & W Visual Library, 1977.

Evans, Fred P. (1862– ?)

Slate-writing medium of San Francisco, California. Evans went to sea as a young man, and his mediumistic gifts developed while he was in marine service. He is most remembered for producing 30 different spirit messages in as many hands on a single slate at a public séance on June 21, 1885, in San Francisco. Many of the signatures were identified as correct. He demonstrated **slate writing** to British naturalist **Alfred Russel Wallace,** who testified to his abilities. On May 18, 1887, he produced five differently colored writings in the presence of Wallace and also colored portraits on paper between two slates.

Evans lived for many years in San Francisco, but in 1922 traveled to England, where he held séances. He stated that because he was impatient of the criticism that he had used his mediumship for making money, he had spent several years mining in California so that he could accumulate enough income to make him independent and give his services free.

Sources:

Owen, J. J. *Psychography: Marvelous Manifestations of Psychic Power Given Through The Mediumship of Fred P. Evans.* San Francisco, 1893.

Evans, Hilary (1929–)

British pictorial archivist and writer on paranormal and anomalous subjects. He was born in Shrewsbury, England, March 6, 1929 and attended Cambridge University (B.A.) and Birmingham University (M.A., English literature). He worked for 12 years as an advertising copywriter, first in agencies, then freelance. In 1964, with his wife, he founded the Mary Evans Picture Library, a historical illustration archive, and Evans now serves as the library curator. He has written several books about illustration and picture research.

Evans's interest in anomaly research began during his student years, but he became actively involved in the late 1960s. He has been a council member of the **Society for Psychical Research** as well as a committee member. In 1981 he helped to found ASSAP (Association for the Scientific Study of Anomalous Phenomena). He lectures frequently in Europe and the United States.

Evans has taken a special interest in **UFOs,** largely for what science can learn from observing and investigating a widespread and ongoing anomaly. He has become a major exponent of the psychosocial hypothesis that explains UFO reports primarily as culturally shaped visionary experiences. He is a council member of **BUFORA** (British UFO Research Association) and has written widely on the subject of UFOs. His research has been one aspect of a larger concern with alleged visions of, and encounters with, otherworldly beings, which he has explored in several comparative studies.

He regards himself as rather skeptical but believes that many claims of the paranormal are based on fact and that scientific anomaly research may dramatically extend our knowledge of ourselves and the universe we inhabit.

Sources:

Clark, Jerry. *UFOs in the 1980s.* Vol. 1 of *The UFO Encyclopedia.* Detroit: Apogee Books, 1990.

Evans, Hilary. *Alternate States of Consciousness: Unself, Otherself, and Superself.* Wellingborough, Northampton, England: Aquarian Press, 1989.

———. *Gods, Spirits, Cosmic Guardians.* Wellingborough, Northampton, England: Aquarian Press, 1987.

———. *Intrusions: Society and the Paranormal.* London and Boston: Routledge & Kegan Paul, 1982.

———. *UFO's 1947–1987: The 40-year Search for an Explanation.* London: Fortean Times, 1987.

———. *Visions, Apparitions, Alien Visitors.* Wellingborough, Northampton, England: Aquarian Press, 1984.

Evans, Hilary, and John Spencer, eds. *Phenomena: Forty Years of Flying Saucers.* New York: Avon Books, 1989.

Evans, John Wainwright (1883– ?)

Journalist and author who published various articles on parapsychological subjects. He was born October 13, 1883, in Alpena, Michigan. He studied at Princeton University (B.A., 1907), afterward becoming a reporter on the *New York Herald* (1908–10) and the *St. Louis Globe-Democrat* (1910). He then became an instructor in English at the University of Arkansas (1911–15), an assistant professor of journalism at the University of Kansas (1915–17), and a staff writer for *Nation's Business* (1917–19). In 1921 he became a freelance writer, the occupation he held for the rest of his life. Besides several books, including two written with Judge Ben B. Lindsey, *The Revolt of Modern Youth* (1925) and *The Companionate Marriage* (1928), he turned out numerous articles on occult subjects over the years for the *American Weekly.*

Sources:

Evans, John W. "Conan Doyle Still Lives." *American Weekly,* November 2, 1952.

———. "Haunted by the Ghost of Bernard Shaw." *American Weekly,* June 7, 1953.

———. "Patrice Munsel's Neon Ghost." *American Weekly,* November 8, 1953.

———. "The Phantom Model." *American Weekly,* April 4, 1954.

———. "When the Clocks Stood Still." *American Weekly,* June 13, 1954.

Evans, W. H. (1877– ?)

Trance and inspirational medium and exponent of the harmonial philosophy of **Andrew Jackson Davis.** A psychic from childhood, Evans began speaking at public meetings in 1898 and contributed many useful articles on the philosophy of **Spiritualism** to English and American Spiritualist periodicals. He was editor of the London monthly *Beyond* and published many books.

Sources:

Evans, W. H. *Constructive Spiritualism.* Manchester, England: Two Worlds, 1917.

———. *Modern Spiritualism.* Rochdale, England: British Spiritualists' Lyceum Union, 1923.

Evans, Warren Felt (1817–1889)

Warren Felt Evans, Swedenborgian minister and early practitioner of mind cure, was born December 23, 1817, at Rockingham, Vermont. He attended Dartmouth College but left after his junior year (1840) to become a Methodist minister. He served a number of different congregations in New England during the next 24 years. During these years he also began to read widely in the writings of seer **Emanuel Swedenborg,** and in 1863, he affiliated with the Church of the New Jerusalem. He formally left the Methodist Episcopal Church the following year.

At the time he was changing denominations, he was also experiencing some ill health described as "a nervous affection, complicated by a chronic disorder." He heard of healer **Phineas Parkhurst Quimby** and visited Quimby in Maine. Under Quimby's care he experienced a healing and adopted some of Quimby's ideas. He also became convinced that he could perform mental healing himself. He began work in Claremont, New Hampshire, later moved to Boston, Massachusetts, and in 1869 settled in Salisbury, a Boston suburb, where he would receive patients for the next twenty years.

In 1869 Evans also published his first book, *The Mental Cure,* an important work for several reasons. It introduced Quimby's ideas to the rest of world, Quimby having never published his writings. It was the first book in the field of mental healing and would become very popular as the century progressed. It would also provide a context for the publication of the writings of **Mary Baker Eddy,** whose books on healing would appear in the next decade.

Evans wrote five other books: *Mental Medicine* (1873), *Soul and Body* (1876), *The Divine Law of Cure* (1881), *The Primitive Mind Cure* (1885), and *Esoteric Christianity and Mental Therapeutics* (1886). As his thought matured, Evans took Quimby's healing practice into the Swedenborgian theology that dominated his thought. In the end he created a pantheistic system that provided a context for his healing work. His thought would later be seen as a precursor of **New Thought** metaphysics. He died in Salisbury on September 4, 1889.

Sources:

Evans, Warren Felt. *The Divine Law of Cure.* Boston: H. H. Carter, 1881.

———. *Esoteric Christianity and Mental Therapeutics.* Boston: H. H. Carter & Karick, 1886.

———. *The Mental Cure.* Boston: Colby & Rich, 1869.

———. *Mental Medicine.* Boston: H. H. Carter, 1873.

———. *The Primitive Mind Cure.* Boston: H. H. Carter & Karrick, 1885.

———. *Soul and Body.* Boston: H. H. Carter, 1876.

Leonard, William J. *The Pioneer Apostle of Mental Science: A Sketch of the Life and Work of Rev. Warren Felt Evans, M.D.* N.p.: The Author, n.d.

Teahan, John F. "Warren Felt Evans and Mental Healing: Romantic Idealism and Practical Metaphysics in Nineteenth-Century America." *Church History* 48, no. 1 (March 1979): 63–80.

Evans-Wentz, W(alter) Y(eeling) (1878–1965)

American scholar who became an authority on fairy lore and the mysticism of Tibet and India. Evans-Wentz was born February 2, 1878, in Trenton, New Jersey. Later he moved to La Mesa, California, where he lived with his family for several years. He studied at Stanford University, California (B.A. English, 1906; M.A., 1907). He traveled to Britain, where he studied social anthropology at Oxford University under Sir John Rhys, professor of Celtic.

Two other scholars had an important influence on him: **William James,** whose lectures on psychology Evans-Wentz had attended at Stanford and who had early encouraged his studies in fairy lore; and **Andrew Lang,** authority on folklore and psychical research, who was one of Evan-Wentz's examiners at Oxford University when he presented his thesis on fairy lore. From this thesis, supported by fieldwork in Wales, Ireland, Scotland, and Brittany, grew his major work, *The Fairy-Faith in Celtic Countries* (1911). After further expeditions in Brittany, Ireland, Wales, the Isle of Man, and Cornwall, he was awarded a D.S. at Oxford University in 1910.

His research into common traditions of fairy faith led to more detailed study of pagan and Christian religious beliefs and practices, and then to comparative religion. In 1917 he traveled in India, studying the mysticism and religious practices he believed were once closely connected in both East and West. In one account of those travels, he writes:

"I have spent more than five years in such research, wandering from the palm-wreathed shores of Ceylon, and thence through the wonderland of the Hindus, to the glacier-clad heights of the Himalayan Ranges, seeking out the Wise Men of the East. Sometimes I lived among city dwellers, sometimes in jungle and mountain solitudes among *yogis,* sometimes in monasteries with monks, sometimes I went on pilgrimages."

These travels took him throughout India and to Tibet, where he lived as a Buddhist monk and spent three years with Tibetan Lama Kazi Dawa-Sandup until the lama died in March 1922. As a result of these researches, Evans-Wentz published several important texts on Tibetan mysticism, including *The Tibetan Book of the Dead* (1927).

In 1931 Oxford University conferred upon him the degree of D.S. in comparative religion, a rare honor, because at that time he was one of only six persons, and the first American, to receive that degree.

A year later he attended meetings of the **Self-Realization Fellowship** in San Diego, California, under **Paramahansa Yogananda,** a famous yogi whom he had met in India. During his travels, Evans-Wentz had also met Sri Yitkeshwar Giri, a guru of Yogananda, in Puri, Orissa. In 1935 he visited the ashram of the famous Sri Ramana Maharishi at Tiruvannamalai in southern India. He also maintained close contact with Buddhist organizations and was welcome in many different religious groups; he hoped to unite East and West in mutual understanding and religious insight.

Toward the end of his life, he retired to San Diego, California, for 23 years. He was drawn to the Self-Realization Fellowship, which had a colony at Encinitas. In 1946 he wrote a warm tribute to Paramahansa Yogananda as a foreword to the yogi's *Autobiography of a Yogi.* At the Self-Realization Fellowship, Evans-Wentz worked with a secretary on his final book, *Sacred Mountains of the World,* which he completed before his death, in his 88th year, on July 17, 1965.

In his will he made generous bequests to various religious organizations. He also left 2,000 acres of land near Tecate to the state of California to be used as an experimental reforestation and recreational area; this estate included Coochama, a mountain sacred to Native Americans. He also assigned mineral rights in his property (some 5,000 acres) to Stanford University to establish a professorship in Oriental philosophy, religion, and ethics. Some of his Oriental manuscripts were left to the Bodleian Library at Oxford University, England; others he gave to Stanford.

At his cremation service on July 21, 1965, there was a reading in English from his own edition of *The Tibetan Book of the Dead,* invoking the Perfect Enlightenment of Pure Reality.

Sources:

Evans-Wentz, W. Y. *The Fairy-Faith in Celtic Countries.* 1911. Reprint, New York: Lemma, 1973.

———. *The Tibetan Book of the Dead.* 1927. Reprint, London: Oxford University Press, 1957.

———. *The Tibetan Book of the Great Liberation.* New York: Oxford University Press, 1954.

———. *Tibetan Yoga and Secret Doctrines; or, Seven Books of Wisdom of the Great Path.* 2d ed. London: Oxford University Press, 1958.

———. *Tibet's Great Yogi . . . Milarepa.* 2d ed. London: Oxford University Press, 1969.

Evergreens

The custom of decorating houses at Christmastide with evergreen plants—holly, ivy, box, laurel, mistletoe—is sometimes said to have originated when Christianity was introduced into Europe in order to typify the first British church, built of evergreen boughs. More probably it extends back into antiquity. In Druidic times, people decorated their houses with evergreen plants so that the sylvan spirits might come there to shelter from the severity of winter until their leafy bowers were renewed in the coming year. It was a widespread superstition that it was unlucky to remove evergreen Christmas decorations until after Twelfth Night.

Everitt, Mrs. Thomas (1825–1915)

One of the earliest and best British private mediums and the first to produce **direct voice** in England. She was the wife of a North London tailor. She began to give séances in 1855 but was little known to the public before 1867. She produced a variety of physical phenomena, **raps, movement** without contact, psychic lights, and **direct writing,** in addition to the direct voice of "John Watts" and of "Znippy," a South Sea Islander, who was heard through a cardboard tube. The earliest such record of "Znippy" dates from 1867 when, at a dark séance with **Agnes Guppy-Volckman,** Everitt was thrown for the first time into trance.

Many descriptions of Everitt's phenomena were published in **Morell Theobald**'s *Spirit Workers in the Home Circle* (1887). The Theobald and Everitt families were close friends. The book describes how Everitt, on returning to consciousness, frequently told what she had seen in the spirit world, that cool breezes and scents were frequent phenomena, and that she had considerable powers of **psychometry.** On one occasion, in Cornwall, she placed a piece of rock to her forehead and entertained her friends by descriptions of antediluvian monsters, boiling masses, and upheaving rocks.

Theobald compared the sounds that accompanied her direct-writing phenomena to a quickly working electric needle. In close and legible characters he had seen 500 or more words produced in five or six seconds.

E. Dawson Rogers, in a letter to E. T. Bennett, states:

"The most completely proven cases of direct writing of which I know are those of Mrs. Everitt. As to many of them I can personally testify their genuineness is beyond dispute. My first séance with Mrs. Everitt was on May 3, 1870. I thought I would ask a question which Mrs. Everitt herself could not possibly answer. 'John Watts' spoke, and promised to give us some direct writing and I thereupon said 'Please give us a definition of the distinction between the Will and the Understanding.' Paper and pencil had been placed on the table and in eight seconds, or perhaps ten, on lighting up, we found a direct and intelligent answer to the question, containing over 150 words. Its phrasing was peculiar. I afterwards found it was an extract from one of Swedenborg's writings, with a few slight alterations, and an extract such as it would be extremely difficult for anyone to carry in his memory. Certainly Mrs. Everitt could never do it. One of Mrs. Everitt's spirit attendants is said to be a gentleman who had been a distinguished Swedenborg Minister."

Several other pieces of direct writing proved to be quotations from books, sometimes from ancient ones. Once, in the presence of **Sir William Crookes** and **Edward William Cox,** the following quotation was given in direct writing: "Religentum esse oportet Religiosum nefas. You will find the meaning in Incerti Autoris Aprice Aut. Gell." After considerable search, the passage was found in *Autus Gellius,* book 4, canto 9. (Gellius was a poet who lived in the reign of Adrian in the second century.)

Writing in *Light,* July 7, 1894, Mr. Everitt describes a cold wind and strange sounds that preceded the approach of the "influence" and states:

"Then the paper and pencil are whisked up into the air, a rapid tick-tick-ticking is heard, lasting barely a few seconds, paper and pencil fall to the table, and a light is called for. The writing is done. The speed of production varies from 100 to 150 words a second. The exceeding minuteness of the writing is striking, also the closeness together of the words and the lines. Crookes was the first to draw attention to the fact that no indentation whatever is produced by this writing. Even with the thinnest paper there is not the slightest perceptible mark on the back."

Everitt being a private medium, test conditions were not applied.

Sources:

Theobald, Morell. *Spirit Workers in the Home Circle.* Boston: Colby & Rich, 1887.

Evidence

The two main sources of evidence in **psychical research** and **parapsychology,** as in other sciences, are observation and experiment. The question of observation is a peculiarly difficult one. Because claimed paranormal phenomena of a spontaneous nature, often produced by human beings, are involved, it is difficult to devise conditions that will preclude **fraud** or a misreading of what is observed. The borderlines between preconception, expectation, and actual observation are often very fuzzy, and even well-trained scientific observers have been deceived by hoaxes or by their own conscious or subconscious desire to prove or disprove the reality of claimed phenomena. Even the best of scientific observers are but amateurs in the arts of conjuring and stage magic and may easily be deceived by the skillful tricks of amateur or professional conjurers, and it is often dangerous to trust the apparent evidence of one's senses. The special effects developed by the movie industry, and available at some levels to the general public, now make the observation of various kinds of psychic phenomena even more questionable.

It is also not surprising that the observations of believers tend to endorse the paranormal, while the observations of skeptics tend in the opposite direction. Skeptics will go out of their way to protect their comfortable world. However, psychical researchers are frequently less than rigorous in applying Occam's razor (i.e., the simplest of competing theories is the preferred) and seeking the most parsimonious explanation for what is observed.

Experimenting with the psychic also presents a unique set of problems. Paranormal phenomena are not producible at the experimenter's will as in a chemical laboratory, and the human element involves numerous difficulties. "One good experiment," said Humphrey Davy, "is of more value than the ingenuity of a brain like Newton's. Facts are more useful when they contradict, than when they support received theories." Because nearly all the facts that psychical research has tried to establish contradict received theories, the importance of experimental data cannot be overemphasized.

From Psychical Research to Parapsychology

Although many areas of psychical research and parapsychology are virtually identical, their main distinction is one of emphasis, with psychical research emphasizing observation and parapsychology focusing upon experiments under laboratory conditions. It has been the hope of parapsychology that paranormal realities might be demonstrated or disproved under control conditions and evaluated by quantitative statistical methods. This approach came to the fore in the 1930s when championed by **J. B. Rhine** (1895–1980) and his associates in the United States, although the groundwork for such an approach had been laid by such British psychical researchers as **G. N. M. Tyrrell** (1897–1952), **W. W. Carington** (1884–1947), and **S. G. Soal** (1889–1975). It has to be admitted, however, that after decades of thousands of laboratory experiments over a wide range of claimed paranormal faculties and phenomena, there is still little generally accepted scientific evidence. This does not mean that the paranormal is disproved, only that it remains difficult to capture within the rigorous demands of laboratory scientific method and evidence. Such a situation has led many to move toward more open methods used successfully in the various branches of psychology.

The search for scientific understanding of paranormal experiences such as spiritual **healing, out-of-the-body travel, telepathy, clairvoyance,** seeing phantoms, and various forms of mystical states of consciousness may seem irrelevant to some. In such personal instances, objective scientific evidence is inaccessible. However, the qualitative nature of the experience itself, often accompanied by special knowledge, exaltation, wonder, or inspiration, is convincing to the person having the experience, even if unsatisfactory to observers.

Although there are obvious dangers in overemphasizing subjective experience at the expense of objective evidence, they need not be mutually exclusive approaches. Too great an emphasis on experimental data glosses over the problem that scientists are often as prejudiced as the general public, and it is now possible to discuss the "experimenter effect," where the hostile skepticism or uncritical beliefs of scientific investigators may respectively inhibit or enhance paranormal phenomena. Moreover, there is disturbing evidence that scientists can also cheat; review of the evidence for the paranormal has disclosed some probable manipulation of data.

Sources:

Barrett, W. F. *On the Threshold of a New World.* London: Kegan Paul, 1908. Revised as *On the Threshold of the Unseen: An Examination of the Phenomena of Spiritualism and of the Evidence for Survival After Death.* New York: E. P. Dutton, 1971.

Dingwall, Eric J., and John Langdon-Davies. *The Unknown—Is It Nearer?* New York: New American Library, 1956.

Ducasse, C. J. *Paranormal Phenomena, Science, and Life After Death.* New York: Parapsychology Foundation, 1969.

Garrett, Eileen J. *My Life As a Search for the Meaning of Mediumship.* London: Rider, 1939. Reprint, New York: Arno Press, 1975.

Heywood, Rosalind. *ESP: A Personal Memoir.* London: Chatto & Windus, 1964. Reprint, New York: E. P. Dutton, 1964.

Leonard, Gladys Osborne. *My Life in Two Worlds.* London: Cassell, 1931.

Marbewick, Betty. "The Soal-Goldney Experiments with Basil Shackleton: New Evidence of Data Manipulation." *Proceedings* of the Society for Psychical Research 56, no. 211 (May 1978).

Murchison, Carl A., ed. *The Case For and Against Psychical Belief.* Worcester, Mass.: Clark University, 1927. Reprint, New York: Arno Press, 1975.

Neff, H. Richard. *Psychic Phenomena and Religion: ESP, Prayer, Healing, Survival.* Philadelphia: Westminster Press, 1971.

Podmore, Frank. *Studies in Psychical Research.* New York: G. P. Putnam's and Son, 1897. Reprint, New York: Arno Press, 1975.

Prince, Walter Franklin. *The Enchanted Boundary: Being a Survey of Negative Reactions to Claims of Psychic Phenomena, 1820–1930.* Boston, Mass.: Boston Society for Psychic Research, 1930. Reprint, New York: Arno Press, 1975.

Rao, K. Ramakrishna. *Experimental Parapsychology: A Review and Interpretation.* Springfield, Ill.: Thomas, 1966.

Rhine, Louisa E. *Mind Over Matter: Psychokinesis.* New York: Macmillan, 1970. Reprint, New York: Collier, 1972.

Smythies, J. R., ed. *Science and ESP.* New York: Humanities Press, 1967.

Tuckett, Ivor L. *The Evidence for the Supernatural.* London, 1911.

Tyrrell, G. N. M. *Science and Psychical Phenomena.* New York: Harper, 1938. Reprint, New York: Arno Press, 1975.

Evil Eye

Belief in the malevolent effects of the evil eye is ancient and universal. A common form of this belief held that people with unusual eyes could cause harm by looking at other people, and such defects as squinting, a cast, or even cataracts were thought to be signs of an evil eye. Others attributed the evil eye to conscious malice on the part of witches or magicians.

The evil eye could, it was believed, bring about illness, poverty, or other afflictions and even death. An outgrowth of the evil eye notion was the belief that praise of children could have an adverse effect; hence, parents discouraged praise of their children's appearance or talents. Traditional ways of averting the evil eye were by wearing **amulets** or charms, or reciting counterspells.

Sources:

DiStasi, Lawrence. *Mal Occhio (Evil Eye): The Underside Vision.* San Francisco: North Point Press, 1981.

Elworthy, F. T. *The Evil Eye.* London, 1894. Reprint, New York: Julian Press, 1958.

MacLaglan, R. C. *The Evil Eye in the Western Highlands.* London: David Nutt, 1902.

Maloney, Clarence, ed. *The Evil Eye.* New York: Columbia University Press, 1976.

Evil Spirits

According to occultist and Spiritualist philosophy, evil spirits do exist. There are many intelligent entities in the higher and lower spheres that may not be of human origin and may not be benevolent. But the evil spirits commonly spoken of are the spirits of bad people and inhabit the lower spheres, from which, either owing to the locality to which they are earthbound or to the attraction of bad, immoral séance sitters, they may easily reach the medium. Their appearing may be accidental. They may see the "light" of the medium and attempt to oust the **control.** The controls, as a rule, are able to keep evil spirits away; but sometimes, for unknown reasons, their power fails. In such cases they urgently ask for the breaking of the circle and the suspension of the sitting.

On the other hand, if an evil spirit has already taken possession of the medium, it is considered imperative to maintain the circle unbroken until the invader can be ousted. **Possession** by evil spirits is usually manifested by fits, violent convulsions, and uncouth ravings, which may cause harm to the medium.

J. J. Morse, lecturing in trance, asserted in a speech later printed in *Light* (July 11, 1903):

"So long as evil men live on earth, pass from it at death, and live beyond, so long will it be possible for them to obtrude among you. What then is the preventive? The cultivation of your will power; the absolute determination to be master of yourself; the assertion of your unquestionable right to select your own associates among the people of either world. The exercise of your duty 'to try the spirits' as you do men before deferring to their advice or leading. And, most of all, in this connection to refuse entrance, or harbour, to unclean thoughts of any kind into your minds. The complete discontinuance of gross living, intoxicants and narcotics and a rigid obedience to personal cleanliness must also be adopted. Purity of mind must have its complement in purity of body. By aspiration, prayer and cleanliness men may not only ward off but prevent the influence of undesirable spirits and in conjunction with a steadfast will no better exorcism can be practised."

If, in spite of all, an evil spirit has gained possession, how should it be exorcised? A curious experiment was recorded by G. H. Lock in *Light* (November 28, 1903). It occurred to him that through the ages some mystic power had been associated with the Cross as a symbol, and that the very common belief in the virtue of the sign of the cross may have had its origin in the spirit world. He therefore tried the efficacy of this sign on the spirit plane with remarkable success. But, he affirmed, the mere wearing of a material cross upon the person is useless for the purpose. The medium—or, if the medium is in trance, the leader of the circle—must will the sign at or toward the spirit or draw the sign mentally upon the spirit, at the same time willing it or adjuring it to stand revealed, or to go.

Should the request be unavailing, the sign of the cross should be made firmly and deliberately upon the breast of the medium and on the back about the region of the shoulders. At a first attempt only a cringing may result, but, stated Lock, "I have never known failure at the third attempt."

An early case of control by an evil entity was recorded by **Ernesto Bozzano** from the mediumship of "L.D." The medium was controlled by his father, Luigi. Once he declared in terror that evil spirits were near the medium. Before the sitting could be closed, L.D. began to glare and, foaming at the mouth, assaulted a sitter and tried to strangle him while shouting, "I have found you at last, wretch. I was a soldier of the royal marines. Do you remember Oporto? You murdered me and I will avenge myself and strangle you." It was with difficulty that the sitter's life was saved. His story was that he had killed a drunken sailor who attacked him in Oporto and was sentenced to six years' detention for the deed.

Willie Reichel, in his *Occult Experiences* (1906), described the sudden intrusion of a female spirit that went around the circle of 14 persons striking and spitting on nearly all of them and using horrible language.

Besides injuring the medium or the sitters, the danger of an enduring possession is possible. Such possession, or **obsession,** would be called demoniacal. As a rule, however, cases of obsession do not originate in the séance room. It would be unwise, however, to deny the possibility.

Regarding the issue of evil influences on this life from the other world, **Andrew Jackson Davis,** in commenting on a book, *The Great Psychological Crime,* is very emphatic:

"I deny utterly and for all time that individuals are led into evil and crimes by persons in the other world. I know the pranks and college-boy mischievousness of the **Diakka** but even for them and all such, I know that the police regulations of the other world are adequate and universally effective."

During the 1870s Spiritualist **Carl Wickland** and his wife began to treat evil spirits believed to be possessing mental patients. The publication of his book *Thirty Years Among the Dead* in 1924 led to the spread within **Spiritualism** of **rescue circles,** to which evil spirits were invited to attend and then sent toward the Spiritualist equivalent of heaven.

Sources:

Davis, Andrew Jackson. *The Diakka, and Earthly Victims.* Boston: Colby & Rich, 1880.

Wickland, Carl. *Thirty Years Among the Dead.* Los Angeles, 1924.

Evolution of Life

According to **Theosophy,** life began when the **Logos,** in the second aspect, sent forth the second life wave. This life wave descended from above through the various worlds, causing an increasing heterogeneity, and thereafter ascended, causing a return to its original homogeneity.

Our present state of knowledge of life in these worlds extends no further than the mental world. In the higher division of that world is ensouled the relatively fine matter appropriate thereto. If that matter is atomic it is known as "monadic essence"; if nonatomic, as "elemental essence," and this is the first elemental kingdom. What we may call the inhabitants of this kingdom are the higher order of **angels.**

Having functioned sufficiently long in the higher mental world, the life wave now presses down to the lower level of that world, where it appears as the second elemental kingdom, the inhabitants of which are some of the lower orders of angels, the form **devas.**

Again pressing down, the life wave manifests itself in the **astral world,** forming the third elemental kingdom, the inhabitants of which are the lowest orders of angels, the passion devas. It then enters the physical world and, in the fourth elemental kingdom, ensouls the etheric part of minerals with the elementary type of life that these possess. The middle of this kingdom represents the farthest descent of the life wave, and thereafter its course is reversed and it begins to ascend.

The next kingdom into which it passes is the fifth elemental kingdom, the vegetable world, whence it passes to the sixth elemental kingdom, the animal world, and lastly to the seventh elemental kingdom, humanity.

During its stay in each kingdom, the life wave progresses gradually from elementary to highly specialized types, and when it has attained these, it passes to the next kingdom. This means that successive currents of this great second life wave have come forth from the Logos, since otherwise there would be only one kingdom in existence at a time.

Also, in each kingdom the souls of the bodies that inhabit it differ from those of the other kingdoms. In the seventh kingdom, that of man, each individual has a soul. In the animal kingdom, on the contrary, one soul is distributed among different bodies, the number of which varies with the state of evolution. To one soul may be allotted countless bodies of a low type of development, but as the development increases the soul comes to have fewer bodies allotted to it until in the kingdom of man there is only one.

Sources:

Clodd, Clara M. *The Ageless Wisdom of Life.* Adyar, India: Theosophical Publishing House, 1956.

Introductory Study Course in Theosophy. Wheaton, Ill.: Theosophical Society of America, 1967.

Pearson, E. Norman. *Space, Time and Self.* Adyar, India: Theosophical Publishing House, 1957.

EVP See Electronic Voice Phenomenon

Exceptional Human Experience

Term used by parapsychologist **Rhea A. White** to indicate a desirable change from studying **psi** (paranormal phenomena) experiments to studying psi experiences. In a presidential address to the **Parapsychological Association,** August 8, 1984, titled "The Spontaneous, the Imaginal, and Psi; Foundations for a Depth Parapsychology," White reviewed the long-standing impasse in progress toward validating psi in spite of improved methodology and experimental techniques. She drew attention to the difficulties of the objective scientific approach, which somehow fails to capture an elusive psi effect in repeatable, valid experiments. She suggested that depth psychology—an exploration of the inner world, the development of some feeling for psychic reality—might offer a solution to this impasse. She also proposed that the occurrence of spontaneous psi is not so much the end of a process as the beginning of one, that parapsychologists should try to examine the nature of that process as it manifests in the life of the individual.

Exceptional Human Experience (Abstracts)

A publication, formerly known as *Parapsychology Abstracts International,* commenced in 1983, edited by **Rhea A. White.** This semiannual journal contains about 250 abstracts of varying length and covers both current and historical material. Some 100 parapsychology journals are covered, as well as material in major nonparapsychological journals and books.

The first issue in 1983 was retrospective in scope, abstracting material from the *Journal of Parapsychology* from 1937 to 1960. PAI indexes its abstracts by authors and subjects. This is particularly helpful, since many of the abstracted original publications were not indexed in detail. Address: Exceptional Human Experience Network, Inc., 414 Rockledge Rd., New Bern, NC 28562.

Exceptional Human Experience Network, Inc.

Formerly known as the Parapsychology Sources of Information Center or Psi Center. It was established by noted librarian/parapsychologist **Rhea A. White** in 1983. It was organized as "a clearinghouse for information, research findings, theories, organizations, publications, and persons involved in parapsychology and its interface with psychology, psychiatry, physics, religion, medicine, mysticism, philosophy, and education."

The network publishes a semiannual journal **Exceptional Human Experience** (Abstracts), that covers abstracts of the contents of all parapsychology journals, some of which commenced publication in the nineteenth century, to date.

White also created **Psiline Database System,** a computerized database, to contain bibliographical citations, abstracts, and subsector descriptors for all important books in parapsychology and the major English-language journals from earliest times to date. Added as time and resources allow are English abstracts of many foreign language parapsychological journals; articles on parapsychology in monographs, non-parapsychological journals and magazines; proceedings, dissertations and chapters. Psiline also covers parapsychological newsletters, with selective abstracts. Address: 414 Rockledge Rd., New Bern, NC 28562.

Exorcism

To exorcize, according to the received definitions, states Edward Smedley in *The Occult Sciences* (1855), is "to bind upon oath, to charge upon oath, and thus, by the use of certain words, and performance of certain ceremonies, to subject the devil and other evil spirits to command and exact obedience. Minshew calls an exorcist a conjuror; and it is so used by Shakespeare; and exorcism conjuration. It is in the general sense of casting out evil spirits, however, that the word is now understood."

The History of Exorcism

The trade of exorcism has probably existed from very early times. In Greece, Epicurus and Aeschines were sons of women who lived by this art, and each was bitterly reproached, the one by the Stoics, the other by Demosthenes, for having assisted his parent in her "dishonorable" practices. A reference in the biblical Acts of the Apostles (19:13) concerns the failure and disgrace of "certain of the vagabond Jews, exorcists," who, like the apostles, "took upon them to call over them that had evil spirits the Name of the Lord Jesus."

The ancient Jewish historian Josephus observed:

"God enabled Solomon to learn that skill which expels demons, which is a science useful and sanative to men. He composed such incantations also, by which distempers are alleviated, and he left behind him the manner of using exorcisms, by which they drive away demons, so that they never return. And this method of cure is of great force unto this day; for I have seen a certain man of my own country, whose name was Eleazar, releasing people that were demoniacal, in the presence of Vespasian and his sons, and his captains, and the whole multitude of his soldiers. The manner of the cure was this. He put a ring that had a root of one of those sorts mentioned by Solomon to the nostrils of the demoniac, after which he drew out the demon through his nostrils; and when the man fell down immediately, he adjured him to return unto him no more, making still mention of Solomon, and reciting the incantation which he composed. And when Eleazar would persuade and demonstrate to the spectators that he had such a power, he set, a little way off, a cup or basin full of water, and commanded the demon as he went out the man to overturn it, and thereby to let the spectators know that he had left the man."

Some alleged fragments of these incantations of Solomon appear in the *Codex Pseudepigraphus* of Fabricus, and Josephus himself has described one of the antidemoniacal roots, in a measure reminiscent of the perils attendant on gathering the mandrake. Another fragment of antiquity bearing on this subject is the exorcism practiced by Tobit, the father of the Jewish hero Tobias, upon which it is by no means easy to pronounce judgment. The seventeenth-century Dutch scholar Grotius, in a note on that history, states that the Hebrews attributed all diseases arising from natural causes to the influence of demons. (These facts are derived in great measure from the Dutch theologian Balthasar Bekker's ingenious, though forgotten, four volumes *Le Monde Enchanté* (1694), which discuss the necessity of exorcism.)

Belthasar Bekker related an instance of exorcism practiced by Jews to avert the evil influence of the demon Lilis (or **Lilith**), whom some rabbis claimed was the wife of Satan. During the 130 years (states Elias, in the *Thisbi*) that elapsed before Adam was married to Eve, he was visited by certain she-devils, of whom the four principal were Lilis, Naome, Ogére, and Machalas; these encounters produced a fruitful progeny of spirits. Lilis visited the bedroom of women recently delivered and endeavored to kill their babies, boys on the eighth day after their birth, girls on the twenty-first. To chase her away, the attendants drew circles on the walls of the room with charcoal and within each they wrote, "Adam, Eve, Lilis, avaunt!" On the door of the room they also wrote the names of the three angels who preside over medicine (Senoi, Sansenoi, and Sanmangelof), a secret that was apparently taught them, somewhat unwittingly, by Lilis herself.

A particular ecclesiastical order of exorcists does not appear to have existed in the Christian church until the close of the third century, and the eighteenth-century German theologian Johann Mosheim attributed its introduction to the prevalent fancies of the Gnostics. In the tenth canon of the Council of Antioch, held in 341 C.E., exorcists were expressly mentioned in conjunction with subdeacons and readers, and their ordination described by the fourteenth Council of Carthage. It involved delivery by the bishop of a book containing forms of exorcism and directions that the exorcists should exercise the office upon *energumens,* (demoniacs), whether baptized or only catechumens. The fire of exorcism, as St. Augustine termed it, always preceded baptism. Catechumens were exorcised for 20 days previous to the administration of this sacrament. In the case of catechumens who were not also energumens, these exorcisms were not directed against any supposed demoniacal possession. They were, as Cyril described them, no more than prayers collected and composed from Holy Writ to beseech God to break the dominion and power of Satan in new converts and to deliver them from his slavery by expelling the spirit of wickedness and error.

In the Greek Church, before baptism the priest blew three times on the child to displace the devil from his seat, and this may be understood as symbolic of the power of sin over the unbaptized, not as an assertion of their real or absolute possession.

The exorcists formed one of the minor orders of the Roman Catholic Church. At their ordination the bishop addressed them as to their duties, and concluded with these words: "Take now the power of laying hands upon the energumens, and by the imposition of your hands, by the grace of the Holy Spirit, and the words of exorcism, the unclean spirits are driven from obsessed bodies."

One of the most complete manuals for Roman Catholic exorcists ever compiled was a volume of nearly 1,300 pages entitled *Thesaurus Exorcismorum et Conjurationum* . . . (1608). It contained the following tracts: "Practica Exorcistarum" (two parts), "Flagellum Daemonum," "Fustis Daemonium," "Complementum Artis Exorcistiae," and "Fuga Satanae."

From the first of these treatises, it appears that the energumens were subjected to a very severe corporal as well as spiritual discipline. They first underwent "pre-exorcisms" consisting of confessions, postulations, protestations, concitations, and interrogations. The exorcisms themselves were eight in number.

All these were accompanied with appropriate psalms, lessons, litanies, prayers, and adjurations. Then followed eight "postexorcisms." The first three were to be used according to how determined the demon was to retain possession. If the demon was very obstinate, an effigy of it, vile and horrible, was to be drawn, with its name inscribed under it, and be thrown into the flames, after having been signed with the cross, sprinkled with holy water, and fumigated. The fourth and fifth were forms of thanksgiving and benediction after liberation. The sixth referred to **incubi** and **succubi.** The seventh was for exorcising a haunted house, in which the service varied during every day of the week. The eighth was to drive away demoniacal storms or tempests and called for throwing into a huge fire large quantities of various herbs.

The "Flagellum Daemonum" treatise contained in the *Thesaurus Exorcismorum* gave numerous cautions to the exorcist himself not to be deceived by the arts of the demon, particularly when dealing with possessed women. If the devil refused to tell his name, the demoniac was to be fumigated. If it was necessary to break off the exorcism before the evil spirits were wholly expelled, they were to be adjured to quit the head, heart, and stomach of the energumen and to abscond themselves from the lower parts of the body.

In the "Fustis Daemonum" the exorcist was directed to verbally abuse the evil spirit if it persisted in staying. After this railing latinity, redoubled precaution was necessary, and if the demon still refused to tell its name, the knowledge of which facilitates an exorcism, it was to be called the worst names imaginable and the demoniac fumigated. The seventh exorcism in this treatise called for, among other things, anointing the demoniac with holy oil, and if all adjurations failed, the possessed was to be strenuously exhorted to patience. In the last form, dumbness was attacked; a very effectual remedy against this infirmity was declared to be a draught of holy water with three drops of holy wax, swallowed on an empty stomach.

Father Zacharias Vicecomes, in his *Complementum Artis Exorcistiae* (1608), explains the signs of possession or bewitchment. He also discusses how to discern the evil spirit's departure; sometimes it puts out the light, now and then it issues like a flame, or a very cold blast, through the mouth, nose, or ears. Vicecomes then enumerates various prescriptions for emetics, perfumes, and fumigations calculated to promote these results. He concludes with a catalog of the names of some of the devils of commonest occurrence: Astaroth, Baal, Cozbi, Dagon, Aseroth, Baalimm, Chamo, Beelphegor, Astarte, Bethage, Phogor, Moloch, Asmodaeus, Bele, Nergel, Melchon, Asima, Bel, Nexroth, Tartach, Acharon, Belial, Neabaz, Merodach, Adonides, Beaemot, Jerobaal, Socothbenoth, Beelzebub, Leviathan, Lucifer, Satan, and Mahomet.

Petrus Stampa's "Fuga Satanae" treatise in the *The Sauvus Exorcismorum* is very brief and does not contain any significant additional information.

According to a treatise on practical exorcism entitled *Histoire admirable de la possession et conversion d'une Penitente. . . .* (1613), Sr. Madeleine de Demandolx de la Palud was exorcised over a four-month period. She was under the power of five princes of the devils—Beelzebub, Leviathan, Baalberith, Asmodeus, and Astaroth—as well as many lesser demons. Beelzebub lived in her forehead, Leviathan in the middle of her head, Astaroth in the back of it. Her head made unnatural, perpetual movements and pulsations. After the exorcism her head barely moved.

A second sister of the same convent, Louise Capeau, was also possessed by three devils of the highest degree: Vérin, Grésil, and Soneillon. Vérin, through the proceedings of the exorcists, appears to have turned state's evidence, for, in spite of the remonstrances and rage of Beelzebub, he gave important information and instruction to his enemies and appeared to sincerely repent that he was a devil. The daily Acts and Examinations, from November 27 to the following of April 23, were specially recorded by the exorcist himself, and all the conversations of the devils were recorded verbatim. The whole business ended in tragedy, and **Louis Gaufridi,** a priest from Marseilles who was accused of **witchcraft** on the occasion, was burned alive at Aix-en-Provence.

An exorcism case of almost unparalleled atrocity occurred at **Loudun** in 1634 when **Urbain Grandier,** cure and canon of that town, was mercilessly brought to the stake partly by the jealousy of some monks, partly to gratify the personal vengeance of Cardinal Richelieu, who had been persuaded that this ecclesiastic had lampooned him, an offense he never forgave. Some Ursuline nuns were tortured and confessed themselves possessed, and Grandier was the person accused of effecting their possession. A certain Tranquille, one of the exorcists, died within four years of the execution of his victim, in a state of reputed possession, perhaps distracted by self-accusations of remorse.

The last acknowledgment of exorcism in the Anglican Church during the progress of the Reformation occurs in the first liturgy of Edward VI, which gives the following form of baptism:

"Then let the priest, looking upon the children, say, 'I command thee, unclean spirit, in the name of the Father, of the Son, and of the Holy Ghost, that thou come out and depart from these infants, whom our Lord Jesus Christ has vouchsafed to call to His holy baptism, to be made members of His Body and of His Holy congregation. Therefore, thou cursed spirit, remember thy sentence, remember thy judgment, remember the day to be at hand wherein thou shalt burn in fire everlasting prepared for thee and thy angels. And presume not hereafter to exercise any tyranny towards these infants whom Christ hath brought with His precious blood, and by this His holy baptism calleth to be of His flock.'"

On the remonstrance of Martin Bucer (1491–1551), arguing that exorcism was not originally used for any but demoniacs, and that it was uncharitable to imagine that all who came to baptism were demoniacs, it was thought prudent by reformers to omit it altogether in subsequent liturgies.

The seventy-second canon issued the following restriction on exorcism: "No minister shall, without the license of the bishop of the diocese, first obtained and had under his hand and seal . . . attempt upon any pretence whatever, either of obsession or possession, by fasting or prayer, to cast out any devil or devils: under pain of the imputation of imposture or cosenage, and deposition from the ministry."

Exorcism in the Modern World

Exorcism became news in modern times with the publication of William Peter Blatty's novel *The Exorcist* in 1971 and the subsequent Warner Brothers movie, scripted by Blatty and released in 1974. Much of the powerful background of Blatty's book and the film stem from authentic research, using as a source the classic study *Possession: Demoniacal and Other,* by **T. K. Oesterreich** (1930). Blatty's book was a best-seller, clearing 200,000 hardcover copies in the summer of 1971 and several million in paperback in the two following years.

The runaway success of the movie revived the interest in the role of the devil in Christian theology and created a industry of paperbacks on **Satanism, black magic,** and related topics. Devil possession became almost fashionable, and priests revived long-forgotten rites of exorcism. Many churchmen and psychologists were divided over whether treating devils as real entities aided the recovery of psychoneurotic individuals or actually encouraged the spread of hysterical possession.

In Britain, a 17-year-old boy claimed that he was possessed by evil after seeing the movie *The Exorcist* and afterward killed a girl, age 9. In 1975, 31-year-old Michael Taylor was exorcized at St. Thames Church, Barnsley, England, but went home "possessed with the devil" and brutally murdered his wife. He was found guilty but insane. Similar cases have been reported in other countries.

Christopher Neil-Smith, a London vicar, has performed more than three thousand exorcisms in Britain since 1949. In his book *The Exorcist and the Possessed* (1974), he claims that evil should be treated as an actual force rather than an abstract idea.

In 1963 the bishop of Exeter, England, convened a commission to consider the theology, techniques, and the place of exorcism in the life of the Christian Church. The commission's findings were published in 1972 and included suitable forms of prayer and exorcism. It was suggested that every diocesan bishop should appoint a priest as diocesan exorcist, and suitable training should be established. No exorcism should take place without the explicit permission of the diocesan bishop, nor should exorcism be performed until possible mental or physical illness had been excluded. A program of training and safeguards was drawn up by which the theological and liturgical questions could be properly evaluated without sensationalism.

Through the 1980s the subject of exorcism was kept alive within evangelical Christianity, especially Pentecostalism. Quite the contrary to the official oversight given exorcism within the Roman Catholic, Anglican, and mainline Protestant traditions, any minister (and on occasion layperson) could emerge as an exorcist, and exorcism services, such as those conducted by Bible teacher Derek Prince, became attractions at Pentecostal events. Exorcism services also became a part of missionary activity in places where either **Spiritualism** (Philippines) or polytheistic faiths (Africa) were widespread. Exorcism has become somewhat institutionalized in charismatic churches, where it is referred to as "spiritual warfare."

Sources:

Basham, Don. *A Manual for Spiritual Warfare.* Greensburg, Pa.: Manna Books, 1974.

Blatty, William Peter. *The Exorcist.* New York: Harper & Row, 1971.

Brooks, Pat. *Out! In the Name of Jesus.* Carol Stream, Ill.: Creation House, 1972.

Deutch, Richard. *Exorcism: Possession or Obsession?* London: Bachman & Turner, 1975.

Ebon, Martin, ed. *Exorcism: Fact Not Fiction.* New York: New American Library, 1974.

Huxley, Aldous. *The Devils of Loudon.* London: Chatto & Windus, 1952. Reprint, New York: Harper & Row, 1971.

Nauman, St. Elmo, Jr. *Exorcism Through the Ages.* New York: Philosophical Library, 1974.

Neil-Smith, Christopher. *The Exorcist and the Possessed.* Cornwall, England: James Pike, 1974.

Oesterreich, T. K. *Possession: Demoniacal and Other.* London: Kegan Paul; New York: R. R. Smith, 1930. Reprint, New Hyde Park, N.Y.: University Books, 1966. Reprint, New York: Causeway Books, 1974.

Petitpierre, Dom Robert. *Exorcism: The Findings of a Commission Convened by the Bishop of Exeter.* London: Society for Promoting Christian Knowledge, 1972.

Shepard, Leslie. *How to Protect Yourself Against Black Magic and Witchcraft.* New York: Citadel, 1978.

Strachan, Françoise. *Casting Out the Devils.* London: Aquarian Press, 1972.

White, Elijah. *Exorcism as a Christian Ministry.* New York: Morehouse-Barlow, 1975.

Expanding Horizons (Organization)

British organization concerned with promoting lectures, seminars, workshops, and conferences on health, healing, self-development, and spiritual awareness. Founded by Celia Macnab, Expanding Horizons has attempted to enlarge public awareness of healing, psychic development, meditation, fire walking, and psychophysical techniques. Speakers have included a wide variety of British and American authorities on the entire range of **New Age** topics. Address: 95 Constantine Rd., Hampstead, London, NW3, England.

Expanding Human Awareness Directory

Publication listing individuals and organizations in the Illinois area. Address: EHA, Inc., P.O. Box 1533, Peoria, IL 61655.

Experimenter Effect

Term used by parapsychologists to indicate an experimental result that has been influenced by the conscious or unconscious attitudes or behavior of the experimenter, rather than by the characteristics or **psi** factors relating to the subject. Such an effect could involve the expectations (positive or negative) of the experimenter or the particular methods used in dealing with subjects.

Exploring the Supernatural (Magazine)

British monthly periodical inaugurated in 1986. It treats a wide range of subjects of popular interest, such as **psychometry, healing, hypnosis, UFOs,** earth mysteries, mind over matter, **divination, astrology, tarot,** and the afterlife. Useful features include a book review section and a news roundup covering lectures, courses, fairs, and products. Address: Aceville, Ltd., 89 East Hill, Colchester, Essex, C01, 20N, England.

Exteriorization of Motricity

Term used by early psychical researchers to denote action of the medium's motor force outside the periphery of the body. It was offered as an explanation of **telekinesis** (now known as **psychokinesis**). The term appears to have originated with **Eugene Rochas** in his book *L'Exteriorisation de la motricité* (1896) and was later adopted by other researchers, including **Paul Joire.** Evidence for Rochas's theory was derived from observation of the curious synchronization between the movements of the medium **Eusapia Palladino** and her physical phenomena. The extinguishing and relighting of a lamp, for instance, corresponded with a slight movement of the index finger of Palladino in the hollow of the hand of Italian researcher **Cesare Lombroso.** Many such sympathetic movements were recorded.

To prove that the motor nerves of mediums were at work, various apparatuses were constructed. The best known were the **biometer** of **Hyppolite Baraduc** and the **sthenometer** of Paul Joire. Others included the dynamoscope of Dr. Collongues, the **magnetometer** of Abbé Fortin, the galvanometer of Puyfontain, the spiritoscope of **Robert Hare,** the magnetoscope of Ruter, and the **fluid motor** of the Count de Tromelin.

These instruments show, wrote **Charles Lancelin,** "that there is a repulsive force generated from one side of the body and an attractive force from the other side. In normal human beings these forces should be equal. When they are not, odd things are likely to happen in their immediate environment. Their relative power may be tested by means of these instruments."

With the sthenometer, Joire claimed to have proved that the exteriorized nervous force could be stored for a short time, like heat, light, and electricity, in wood, water enclosed in bottles, linen, and cardboard. Objects were said to be charged with the force by simply holding them for a time in the hand. Placed near the sthenometer, they affected the needle in proportion to the intensity of the source that produced it. A British physician, Charles Russ, constructed an instrument, described in the *Lancet* (July 3, 1931), to demonstrate that energy radiates from the human eye.

The idea of **psychic force** is a difficult one to substantiate, as there is a significant difference between a force that might cause deviation in a delicately suspended needle and the energy required to move solid objects at a distance as in pychokinesis, or to cause stress and deformation in metals as in **metal bending.** It is not clear whether one force in different modalities or different forces are involved.

Exteriorization of Sensitivity

Term used to denote sensory power of the medium operating outside the periphery of the body. The term was used by **Eugene Rochas** as the title of his book on the subject in 1896, but it was **Paul Joire** who called broad attention to the phenomenon in his treatise on hypnology, *Précis Théorique and pratique de neurohypnologie* (1892).

The phenomenon was on the confines of hypnotic and psychical phenomena. Approaching his hypnotic subject with a pointed instrument, Joire found him sensitive a short distance from the skin. The distance at which the sensation was perceived and the range of the sensitive surface varied with the nervous sensibility of the subject on an average from one to ten centimeters. The sensibility of the skin itself disappeared. In deep hypnosis a series of sensitive layers appeared to be formed around the body, and the sensibility could also be transferred into various objects, such as a glass of water, glass plates covered with velvet, wood, or a ball of putty. Joire gave the putty the vague contour of the subject, and as he pricked parts of the putty that represented the parts of the subject's body, the subject experienced a corresponding sensation.

Some of the subject's hair was cut off while he was asleep and stuck into the putty. When they were later pulled, the patient strongly protested, saying his hair was being pulled out. When a glass of water, charged with sensibility, was held by the subject, the reaction to the pricking of the water was instantaneous. If it was held by an assistant, removed from the subject in a chain, there was an increasing slowness in the sensation. The delay between the pricking and the sensation was two seconds when five persons formed a chain.

Joire claimed that he could also transfer the sensibility to a living man or to the subject's shadow on the wall. Care was taken to prevent the working of suggestion. The exteriorization of sensation to this degree, however, was a very rare phenomenon.

Joire also found that the excitation produced at a distance in a subject whose sensibility had been externalized left a persistent painful trace, like a contusion or a mosquito sting. A few moments after the first movement the subject began to stroke the sensitive spot as though he still felt the sensation; and although he remembered nothing in the waking state, in the night he often dreamed that he was being pricked or pinched.

Rochas obtained similar results to those of Joire and described during the magnetizing process the formation of a series of equidistant layers separated by an interval of six or seven centimeters around the body of his subject. They extended sometimes as far as two or three meters, and their sensibility diminished in proportion to their distance from the body. He noticed that when a glass of water was placed across a zone of sensibility the layers beyond the glass were interrupted, whereas the water in the glass became rapidly luminous throughout its mass and later a sort of luminous mist was liberated from it. Taken to some distance, the glass of water retained its sensibility.

Experimenting further on these lines, Rochas found that sensibility appeared to be stored in those substances that store odors: liquids; viscous substances, especially those derived from animals, like gelatin and wax; wadding; and stuffs of loose or plushy texture, such as velvet.

As the **emanations** seemed to spread themselves in a manner analogous to light, he tried to focus them on a plate of gelatino-bromide film. The subject of these experiments was a Mrs. Lux. She was photographed awake, then asleep but not exteriorized, and afterward asleep and exteriorized. In the latter case the plate was briefly left for sensitivity inside her belt in contact with her body.

According to Rochas, "I observed that when I pricked the first plate with a pin Mme. Lux felt nothing, when I pricked the second she felt it slightly, and when I pricked the third she felt it sharply, and this was a few minutes after the operation." Three days later, "wishing to discover to what extent this plate was sensitive, I gave two sharp blows with the pin on the hand depicted in the picture in such a manner as to tear the film of gelatino-bromide. Lux, who was two metres distant from me, and could not see what part I had pricked, fell back at once with cries of pain. I had some difficulty in restoring her to her normal state; her hand hurt her, and a few seconds afterwards I saw appear on her right hand—the one I pricked in the photograph—some little red marks whose position corresponded to the pricks. Dr. P., who was present during the experiment, observed that the epidermis was not broken and the redness was in the skin." These experiments were verified by Jules Bernard Luys (1828–1897), a famous brain specialist.

According to Rochas, exteriorization of sensibility may be gradually pushed to the formation of two luminous phantoms on the left and right of the subject, and finally to their union. This is the exteriorization of the **astral body.** While the astral body of his subject was thus exteriorized, Rochas unintentionally struck the astral hand with his hand. In a few seconds the corporeal hand became very red. It is possible that the special hypnotic conditions may have been responsible for this result.

Among those refuting Rochas and Joire, **Sylvan Muldoon,** in his remarkable book *The Projection of the Astral Body* (cowritten with **Hereward Carrington,** 1929), describes his experiences in self-projection and declares that he never experienced sensitivity as described by the French experimenters. There is some point in his question: wouldn't an astral entity have to be constantly on the watch, dodging pointed material objects? If not, these pointed objects would make contact with the entity's sensibility. Muldoon felt certain that if repercussion of sensibility took place it did so while the phantom was within cord-activity range.

Elizabeth d'Esperance wrote of her phantom "Yolande": "When she touches some object I feel my muscles contract as if it were my hands that touched it. When she put her hands into melted paraffin I felt my hands burn and when a thorn penetrated her finger I experienced great pain. When I touch the hands of Yolande I believe I am feeling my own, but perceive my error afterwards when I see four hands."

The psychical researcher **Emile Boirac** believed that there was no reason for supposing that exteriorization of sensibility is a rare, accidental, abnormal phenomenon that requires a particular hypnotic condition for its production. It might be a normal phenomenon but not in evidence because a special developer is necessary to note it.

In his book *Psychic Science* (1918) Boirac mentions some experiments with a glass of water that the experimenter held for a short time in his hand, then handed to the somnambulist subject in the first experiment and placed it on a table in the second. If the somnambulist plunged his fingers into the water and the experimenter was pinched, the somnambulist felt it in his own hand. If the experimenter held the somnambulist's hand and the glass of water was pricked by one of the spectators, the subject again declared the corresponding sensation. Everything happened as though the experimenter, and not the subject, had externalized his sensibility into a material object and remained in communication with this object by some kind of force so that every impression made on his nervous system was immediately experienced by the object and reciprocally every impression made on the object was immediately experienced in his nervous system.

Historically the beginning of the concept of exteriorized sensitivity may be traceable to the idea of sympathetic medicine in magic. In 1658 Sir Kenelm Digby published *A Late Discourse . . . Touching The Cure of Wonders by The Powder of Sympathy,* and even earlier, Sir Francis Bacon had discussed the subject in his book *Sylva Slyvarum* (1627). In Sir Walter Scott's *Last Minstrel* (1805) the Ladye of Branksome takes the broken lance from Deloraine's wound and treats the lance with a salve, instead of the wound, whereupon "William of Deloraine, in trance, whenever she turned it round and round, twisted as though she'd galled his wound."

Sources:

Joire, Paul. *Précis Théorique and pratique de neuro-hypnologie.* Paris, 1892.

Extispicy (or Extispicium)

An ancient term derived from the root word *specere,* to view, consider. It was applied chiefly to the inspection of entrails for purposes of augury. Inspection officials were extispices or aruspices, and one of the instruments they used was called by the same name as the craft, extispicium.

The ancient Etrurians were the first and also the most learned people who practiced extispicy, and the fifth-century Roman emperor Romulus is said to have chosen his first aruspices from among them. The art was also practiced throughout Greece, where it had a consecrated priesthood confined to two families.

The Roman aruspices had four distinct duties: to examine the victims before they were opened, to examine the entrails, to observe the flame as the sacrifice was burned, and to examine the meat and drink offering that accompanied it. It was a fatal sign when the heart was wanting, and this is said to have been the case with two oxen that were immolated on the day Caesar was killed.

If the priest let the entrails fall, or if there was more bloodiness than usual, or if the entrails were livid in color, it was understood to be a portent of instant disaster.

The first-century B.C.E. Roman architect Vitruvius attempted to account for the origin of extispicy by pointing to the custom of examining the viscera of animals before settling an encampment to ascertain if the neighborhood was healthy.

Extra

A paranormally imposed face or figure on a photographic film or plate. Such extras were alleged to appear on pictures produced through **psychic photography** and **spirit photography.**

Extrasensory Perception (ESP)

A term used in **parapsychology** to denote awareness apparently received through channels other than the usual senses. The term was launched by **J. B. Rhine** in his book *Extrasensory Perception* (1934), published by the **Boston Society for Psychic Research.** The book attracted the interest of the science editor of the *New York Times,* who wrote a favorable notice. After that, public interest was aroused and the term extrasensory perception, or ESP, was firmly established. Phenomena related to ESP include **clairvoyance, telepathy,** and **precognition.** Prior to Rhine's popularization of the term, a German equivalent, *außersinnliche Wahrnehmung,* had been used by Gustav Pagenstecher and **Rudolf Tishner** in the 1920s.

Extraterrestrial Earth Mission

The organization today known as the Extraterrestrial Earth Mission can be traced to March 3, 1986, when an extraterrestrial spirit named Avinash "walked into" the body of a person named John, according to the mission's literature. John was a channel and teacher of metaphysics in the Seattle, Washington, suburb of Bellevue. He had been **channeling** an entity named Elihu.

The concept of a "walk-in" was popularized by **New Age** author and channel **Ruth Montgomery,** who described situations in which the spirit of an individual would, for whatever reason, abandon a body and a disembodied spirit would walk in and take over. In that change, the memory of the person who left would be left behind, but the personality of the new entity would dominate. Thus it was that "Avinash" walked in and took over John's body. Shortly after Avinash appeared, the person that had been John moved to Hawaii. He was accompanied by a second walk in, a female named "Alezsha." In Hawaii they met a third walk-in, "Ashtridia." During the remainder of 1986, the primary teaching channeled by Avinash concerned the concept of mastery of limitation. The universe, he taught, tended to rearrange itself according to one's concept of reality. By changing one's reality, removing a sense of limitation, the world would change.

The three also have contact with a huge extradimensional space ship, which resulted in their becoming conscious of their ability to operate in other dimensions. Before the year was out, the three had decided to move to Sedona, Arizona. Soon after relocating they met a fourth walk-in, "Arthea." Avinash and Arthea soon discovered that they were divine design mates, i.e., a couple divinely created to work together. By 1987 the group of walk-ins had grown to twelve but disbanded as each found his or her mission elsewhere. By October of that year, only Avinash, Arthea, and a third person, "Alana," remained.

The three remaining people would experience what is not a totally unique occurrence but certainly an uncommon one. Over the next years, a series of new entities would walk into their bodies as others departed, thus the same body would become known by different names. In this way, John, once known as Avinash, would soon become known as Aktivar, Alarius, Savizar, and most recently ZaviRah. Arthea became known as Akria, Polaria, Silarra, and most recently Ziva'rah. Alana became known as Akrista and then as Tantra. It is believed that each of these names refers to an extraterrestrial person who inhabits the body of the Earth person. The emergence of Aktivar, Akria, and Akrista occurred at the end of the summer of 1987. During the last three months of 1987 and into 1988, these three entities toured the United States, during which time the Extraterrestrial Earth Mission began to make its initial public impact. The three made a videotape on humanity's role as a co-creator of heaven on Earth and a series of cassette tapes aimed at overcoming particular individual dysfunctions.

In March 1988 a new phase of work began when Aktivar, Akria, and Akrista left and were replaced by three new walk-ins, Alarius, Polaria, and Tantra. Shortly thereafter Tantra exited from the trio and began to work separately. Alarius and Polaria described their work as temporary, as preparing the way for Savizar and Silarra. Under the guidance of the couple known as

Savizar and Silarra, the Extraterrestrial Earth Mission matured into a New Age organization announcing the planetary shift of humans from dense physical bodies into bodies of light. According to Savizar and Silarra, there are many masters present on Earth today. It was their job to awaken these masters to the nature of their true selves and to cooperate with them in the co-creation of a new Earth. Assisting in this process, the pair taught a technique, the superconscious technique, which allows people to manifest their desires by altering their picture of reality.

In 1990, Savizar and Silarra were replaced by ZaviRah and Ziva'rah. Each change is believed to announce a new phase in the mission. In this case, the newcomers represented a change from an exclusive emphasis on opening and awakening to a stance of mobilization. Those who have been awakened to their true nature should begin the process of creation and manifestation. In 1993 Zavirah and Ziva'rah were replaced by Drakar and Zrendar, and very soon after their appearance the Extraterrestrial Earth Mission moved from Arizona to Hawaii. Included in the new phase of the mission is the ChristStar Project, the work of a group of people on Maui to build a prototype of the new civilization. Public events have been developed to present techniques (usable technologies) of consciousness that assist individuals to see the divinity in all life and to manifest their own roles as a co-creators of heaven on Earth.

In response to the lectures, workshops, and the printed, audio, and video materials published by the mission, groups have formed around the United States and Canada to share in the mission's work. Currently, ChristStar Project Mastery Events are being held at which many extraterrestrial entities speak through Drakar and Zrendar to the assembled group. Extraterrestrial Earth Mission has been chartered through the Universal Life Church in Arizona.

The Extraterrestrial Earth Mission may be contacted at P.O. Box 959, #0432, Kihei, HI 96753. It publishes a newsletter, *ChristStar.*

Sources:

Savizar and Silarra. *Conscious Channeling.* Sedona, Ariz.: Earth Mission, 1989.

———. *Extraterrestrial Earth Mission. Book I: The Awakening.* Sedona, Ariz.: Earth Mission, 1989.

———. *The Superconscious Technique.* Sedona, Ariz.: Earth Mission, 1989.

Eye-Biters

According to Reginald Scot in his *The Discoverie of Witchcraft* (1584), during the reign of Queen Elizabeth I an epidemic causing blindness afflicted the cattle of Ireland. This malevolence was attributed to witches, who were called eye-biters, and some of them were executed.

Sources:

Scot, Reginald. *The Discoverie of Witchcraft.* 1584. Reprint, New York: Dover Publications, 1972.

Eyeless Sight

The ability to see without using the eyes, also known as paroptic vision, dermo-optical perception (DOP), hyperesthesia, synesthesia, cutaneous vision (skin vision), extraretinal vision, and biointroscopy. The term eyeless sight was first popularized through the English translation of a book by the famous French author **Jules Romains** (Louis Farigoule) titled *Vision Extra-Rétinienne* (1920), which detailed Romains's research in developing the extraordinary and little-known faculty of seeing without the use of the eyes. The book was not well received, however, and was ridiculed by his colleagues. Refused access to subjects for further experiments, Romains abandoned his scientific research, turned his attention to the literary arts, and went on to become a world-famous poet, dramatist, and novelist.

Prior to Romains's book there had been scattered references to eyeless sight from the seventeenth century on. British scientist Robert Boyle referred to a doctor's report about a blind man who could distinguish colors by touch. In the eighteenth century, Jonathan Swift included a strange reference in *Gulliver's Travels* (1726) to a blind man who could distinguish paint colors by feeling and smelling. Throughout the nineteenth century there were occasional medical accounts of transposition of sight to different areas of the body.

Ten years after publication of Romains's book, Manuel Shaves of São Paulo, Brazil, tested four hundred blind patients and reported that about a dozen of them seemed to have the faculty of "skin vision," some being able to distinguish colors.

During the 1930s a Kashmiri fire-walking performer named **Kuda Bux** demonstrated what was claimed to be eyeless sight before a distinguished medical panel. Although heavily blindfolded, with lumps of dough over his eyes, and with metal foil, woollen bandages, and layers of gauze, Bux had no difficulty reading from books. He gave a similar demonstration in Montreal, Canada, in 1938, and in 1945 during a U.S. tour he rode a bicycle through Times Square, New York, while heavily blindfolded. However, much doubt has arisen concerning Kuda Bux's performances owing to claims such as those of stage magician **Milbourne Christopher,** who suggested there were defects in the blindfolding.

In 1963 Russian scientist I. M. Gol'dberg reported his experiments with **Rosa Kuleshova** in an article in *Soviet Psychology and Psychiatry.* During the previous September, Gol'dberg had demonstrated Kuleshova's ability to read ordinary printed text with the fingers of her right hand when normal vision was completely excluded. Rosa could also determine color tones on paper and objects. The term dermo-optical perception became established.

After publication of the experiments with Kuleshova, Richard P. Youtz, a psychologist at Barnard College, Columbia University, New York, experimented with a Mrs. P. Stanley, a 42-year-old housewife. Youtz concluded that color sensing through the fingertips was a real phenomenon and believed that some 10 percent of a female college population tested by him had the ability in rudimentary form.

Even before the reports on Kuleshova, an April 1965 story from the Associated Press reported that Vichit Sukhakarn of Bangkok was teaching blind people to see by **hypnosis.** Sukhakarn claimed that if volunteers concentrated deeply on the thought of "seeing through the cheeks," the nerve endings of the skin became so sensitive that impulses were transmitted to the brain and converted into visual images. Some of his blind subjects were reported able to "read" a newspaper or "watch" a movie with their cheeks. He opened an institution for blind children in Thailand and found 8- to 14-year-old subjects very susceptible to training. His findings were in line with Romains's experiments suggesting that some light hypnotic or suggestible factor assisted the development of eyeless sight.

In 1966 Yvonne Duplessis at the Centre D'Eclairagisme began reviving French research into eyeless sight with the aid of a grant from the **Parapsychology Foundation.** Duplessis trained blind volunteers to "see" objects both at a distance (paroptic perception) and by touch (dermo-optical perception). Volunteers also developed the faculty to distinguish colors by eyeless sight, which some investigators believe is capable of development mainly through use of the fingers, cheeks, or epigastric region, all sensitive skin areas. The faculty seems facilitated by light hypnotic suggestion.

The research of Duplessis was presented in a paper at the First International Conference on **Psychotronics,** held at Prague, Czechoslovakia, in 1974. At the conference, a small research group from Poland, headed by Lech Stefanski (founder of the International Section on Parapsychology), reported similar experiments. Although there have been counterreports suggesting that such results were obtained because of imperfect control or cheating, the significant number of positive results has encouraged some parapsychological researchers. (See also **Stomach, Seeing with the**)

Sources:

Duplessis, Yvonne. "Dermo-optical Sensitivity and Perception." *International Journal of Biosocial Research* 7, no. 2 (1985).

Gol'dberg, I. M. "On Whether Tactile Sensitivity Can be Improved by Exercise." *Soviet Psychology and Psychiatry* 2, no. 1 (1963).

Romains, Jules [Louis Farigoule]. *Vision Extra-Rétinienne.* 1920. Translated by C. K. Ogden as *Eyeless Sight: A Study of Extra-Retinal Vision and the Paroptic Sense.* New York: G. P. Putnam's Sons, 1924. Reprint, New York: Citadel Press, 1978.

Eysenck, H(ans) J(urgen) (1916–)

Research psychologist whose specialized work in the fields of personality, neurosis, and experimental psychology has relevance to parapsychological research. He was born March 4, 1916, in Berlin, Germany. He was educated at the University of London (B.S., 1938; Ph.D., 1940) and did postgraduate work at the University of Dijon, France, and the University of Exeter, England.

From 1942 to 1945 Eysenck was a research psychologist at Mill Hill Emergency Hospital, England, and in 1945 moved to Maudsley Hospital's Institute of Psychiatry as a psychologist. In 1950 he became a reader in psychology and director of the department of the Institute of Psychiatry, University of London. In 1955 he was named professor of psychology, a position he held until his retirement, when he was named professor emeritus. Over the years he wrote more than 40 books and 800 articles on personality and its relation to various social phenomena.

Within parapsychological circles, Eysenck is known for his development of the Eysenck Personality Scale, still in wide use among parapsychologists. In 1967 he suggested that extroverts would produce higher ESP scores, a factor still noted by parapsychologists in setting up ESP tests. Through the 1980s Eysenck became more vocal on paranormal phenomena and argued that evidence for its existence is quite good. He also worked to improve the design of ESP tests.

Sources:

Berger, Arthur S., and Joyce Berger. *The Encyclopedia of Parapsychology and Psychical Research.* New York: Paragon House, 1991.

Eysenck, Hans J. *Astrology: Science or Superstition?* London: Maurice Temple Smith, 1982.

———. *Handbook of Abnormal Psychology: An Experimental Approach.* New York: Basic Books, 1961.

———. "Personality and Extrasensory Perception." *Journal* of the Society for Psychical Research 44 (1967).

Eysenck, Hans J., and C. Sargent. *Explaining the Unexplained.* London: Weidenfield and Nicholson, 1982.

———. *Know Your Own PSI-IQ.* New York: World Almanac Publications, 1983.

Pleasants, Helene, ed. *Biographical Dictionary of Parapsychology.* New York: Helix Press, 1964.

F

F. Marion Crawford Memorial Society

Founded in 1975, dedicated to the study and appreciation of novelist F. Marion Crawford (1854–1909), author of the occult novel *Mr. Isaacs* (1882), and to other fantasy literature and postromanticism (see also occult English **fiction**). The society maintains the F. Marion Crawford Memorial Library of more than a thousand items (books, letters, autograph materials) and publishes a journal, *The Romanticist.* Address: c/o Jesse Knight, 2148 Avenida de los Flores, Santa Clara, CA 95054. (See also **Mr. Jacobs of Simla**)

Sources:

Sullivan, Jack, ed. *The Penquin Encyclopedia of Horror and the Supernatural.* New York: Viking Press, 1986.

Fabre, Pierre Jean (ca. 1590–1650)

French alchemist, a native of Castelnaudary in Languedoc. Fabre was a doctor of medicine and was renowned in his own time as a scholar of chemistry, a subject on which he compiled several treatises. Because he practiced in Montepellier, he has been confused with a painter named Fabre who was born in Montepellier and gave his name to the Musée Fabre in that town.

There is no evidence that Pierre Jean Fabre had any practical success in the field of **alchemy,** but he wrote numerous works dealing with that topic.

Of these the most important are *Alchimista Christianus* and *Hercules Piochymicus,* both published at Toulouse, the first in 1632. In the latter he maintains that the mythological "labors of Hercules" are allegories, embodying the arcana of hermetic philosophy. The **philosophers' stone,** he declares complacently, may be found in all compounded circumstances and is formed of salt, mercury, and sulphur.

Faculty of Astrological Studies

British astrological school. The Faculty of Astrological Studies was established in 1948 largely at the instigation of **Charles E. O. Carter,** for many years head of the Astrological Lodge of the Theosophical Society (now the **Astrological Lodge of London**). The lodge sponsored the founding of the school, and Carter served as its first principal (1948–54). He was succeeded in that task by Margaret Hone (1954–69). Hone had earlier been commissioned to produce *The Modern Textbook of Astrology* (1951), a basic text for students. Most of the school's coursework is by correspondence. Address: BM7470, London WC1N 3XX, England.

Faculty X

A term coined by British author **Colin Wilson** in his book *The Occult: A History* (1971) to indicate a latent power in human beings enabling awareness of a higher reality beyond immediate sense perception. The term is synonymous with the more generally used **ESP.**

Sources:

Wilson, Colin. *Mysteries: An Investigation into the Occult, the Paranormal, and the Supernatural.* New York: G. P. Putnam's Sons, 1978.

———. *The Occult: A History.* New York: Random House, 1971.

Fagail

The "parting gift" of **fairies** of Gaelic origin. This could be of a pleasant or unpleasant nature—it might be death, or the transformation of a lazy, ugly, ill-spoken man into the best workman, the best looking man, and the best speaker in the village.

Fagan, Cyril (1896–1970)

Irish astrologer, born in Dublin on May 22, 1896, into a wealthy medical family. Fagan attended Belvedere and Castlenook Colleges. He wanted to become a physician but was hampered by a condition of almost total deafness. He tried several alternatives and finally became a professional astrologer after World War I. In 1930 he founded the Irish Astrological Society and served as its president for many years. During the late 1930s he began to study the historical aspects of astrological theory, which led him to propose and champion what is known as the "sidereal" zodiac.

Fagan was concerned with adjusting the horoscope chart to reflect the "procession of the equinoxes." The "tropical" zodiac, still used by most astrologers, begins each year at the point where the sun is located at the spring equinox. However, that position, in relation to the constellations that gave the 12 signs of the zodiac their names, changes slightly each year. Over the centuries the drift has been considerable, and the divisions of the zodiac no longer reflect the actual position of the constellations in the heavens. The sidereal zodiac adjusts for the actual position of the 12 signs.

Fagan presents his argument for the sidereal zodiac in several books, beginning with *Fixed Zodiac Ephemeris for 1948.* His argument is most persuasive in *Zodiac Old and New* (1950). Initially Fagan found few supporters, but among the few were three important figures: **Donald Bradley,** a young American astrological researcher; R. C. Firebrace, a British military leader and astrologer; and Rupert Gleadow, a popular astrologer and writer. Firebrace supported Fagan in his journal *Spica* (founded in 1961). Bradley conducted his significant statistical research using Fagan's ideas.

Fagan eventually moved to Tucson, Arizona, where Bradley had become editor of *American Astrology,* a leading astrological periodical. He died there on January 5, 1970. Unfortunately Bradley, Firebrace, and Gleadow all died in 1974. The loss of the four most prominent advocates of siderealist astrology led to its decline through the 1970s and 1980s, although it has shown some new life in the 1990s.

Sources:

Fagan, Cyril. *Astrological Origins.* St. Paul, Minn.: Llewellyn Publications, 1971.

———. *Fixed Zodiac Ephemeris for 1948.* Washington, D.C.: National Astrological Library, 1948.

———. *Zodiacs Old and New.* Los Angeles: Llewellyn Publications, 1950.

Holden, James H., and Robert A. Hughes. *Astrological Pioneers of America.* Tempe, Ariz.: American Federation of Astrologers, 1988.

Fahler, Jarl Ingmar (1925–)

Finnish psychologist, hypnotherapist, parapsychological researcher. Fahler was born December 27, 1925, in Mariehamn, Finland, and studied at the University of Helsinki (B.A., 1952; M.A., 1953). He served successively as a staff member of the Foreign Department and the Finnish Police (1950–54); as a visiting research fellow at the Parapsychology Laboratory, Duke University, and the Research Laboratory, Parapsychology Foundation (1957–58); and as a staff member of the Finnish Ministry of Home Affairs (1960–62). He served as president of the Society for Psychical Research, Finland (1951–62), and was a charter member of the Parapsychological Association.

Fahler experimented with **ESP** and psychokinesis, psychological aspects of ESP in hypnosis, and precognitive factors in relation to introspective awareness. He also studied spontaneous psi phenomena in Finland. Beginning in 1959 he concentrated his research on the states of awareness induced by mescaline, LSD, and psilocybin, about which he published several articles in Finnish and Swedish journals.

Sources:

Fahler, Jarl I. "ESP Card Tests With and Without Hypnosis." *Journal of Parapsychology* 21 (1957).

Fahler, Jarl I., and R. J. Cadoret. "ESP Card Tests of College Students With and Without Hypnosis." *Journal of Parapsychology* 22 (1958).

Fahler, Jarl I., and H. H. J. Keil. "Nina S. Kulagina: A Strong Case for PK Involving Directly Observable Movements of Objects Recorded on Cine Film." *Research in Parapsychology, 1974.* Edited by J. D. Morris, William G. Roll, and R. L. Morris. Metuchen, N.J.: Scarecrow Press, 1975.

Fahler, Jarl I., and Karlis Osis. "Checking for Awareness of Hits in a Precognition Experiment with Hypnotized Subjects." *Journal* of the American Society for Psychical Research 60 (1966).

Pleasants, Helene, ed. *Biographical Dictionary of Parapsychology.* New York: Helix Press, 1964.

Fairchild, Helen

Nineteenth-century American **materialization** medium. Fairchild's mediumship was somewhat unconventional inasmuch as she stood outside her **cabinet,** from which a variety of phantom forms emerged, allegedly under the influence of her **control.** According to E. A. Brackett in his book *Materialized Apparitions* (1886), this forced "the skeptic or investigator to the conclusion that the forms are either genuine materializations or confederates." Brackett, who attended some of Fairchild's séances, reported that **dematerialization** of the phantom forms was sometimes witnessed before the cabinet in full view of the sitters.

Fairfax, Edward (d. 1635)

An English scholar of the sixteenth century, translator of Tasso's *Gerusalemme Liberata* and author of *Daemonologia: A Discourse on Witchcraft,* in which he claims that in 1621 two of his daughters were bewitched through the malice of six witches.

Sources:

Fairfax, Edward. *Daemonologia: A Discourse on Witchcraft.* Harrogate, England: R. Ackrill, 1882. Reprint, New York: Barnes & Noble, 1971.

Fairies

A species of supernatural beings or nature spirits, one of the most beautiful and important of mythological concepts. Belief in fairies is ancient and widespread, and similar ideas concerning them are found in primitive as well as civilized societies. Fairies have been celebrated in folklore, stories, songs, and poems. The term fairy comes from the Latin *fata* and *fatum* (fate), and in Middle English implied enchantment, or an enchanted land and its inhabitants. Fairies were known as "fays" or "fées" in the British Isles and Europe.

Fairies were often said to be invisible, usually of smaller stature than humans. It was believed they could be helpful to humans, but might be dangerous and evil if offended. They were often considered just mischievous and whimsical in a childlike manner, but were believed to have magical powers.

The strongest traditions of fairies are those of the British Isles and Europe, but belief in fairies has also been found in Asia, America, and Africa. There are scores of characteristic fairies in the European tradition, but the main types include the trooping fairies, who are the aristocrats of the fairy world, living in palaces or dancing and feasting underground; the hobgoblin fairies of a rougher, workman type; nature spirits of rivers, gardens, and woods; and deformed monsters, like hags and giants. For a comprehensive listing of pixies, nixies, elves, fauns, brownies, dwarfs, leprechauns, bogies, banshees, and other fairies, see the excellent work *A Dictionary of Fairies* (1976), by **Katharine Briggs,** a modern authority on the subject.

Typical activities of fairies in relation to human beings include abducting babies and putting changelings in their place; helping plants and flowers to grow; sweeping floors; bestowing miraculous gifts for friendship (such as removing deformities or breaking the spells of witches); performing mischievous pranks like milking cows in the fields, soiling clothes put out to dry, curdling milk, and spoiling crops.

Fairyland was usually underground or in some magical other dimension. Here time became mystically changed—one night in fairyland might equal a lifetime in the human world. Some of the most romantic and poignant folktales concern mortals who fall in love with a fairy queen and are transported to the magical world of fairyland where all wishes come true, but through breaking some taboo or indulging in homesickness for earthly existence, the mortal is suddenly returned to his world, in which scores of years have passed.

In the seventeenth century, Rev. Robert Kirk investigated the fairies of Aberfoyle in Scotland, much as a visiting anthropologist might study a native tribe. In his book *The Secret Commonwealth of Elves, Fauns, and Fairies* (1691), Kirk confidently describes the life, occupations, and activities of the fairies in their subterranean world. Kirk's tomb is in Aberfoyle, but legend has it that he swooned away while crossing a fairy hill and after apparent death and burial appeared in a dream to a relative, stating that he was a prisoner in fairyland. He gave instructions for his release, but his cousin was too frightened to complete them, and Kirk was lost forever.

There are many folklore stories of fairies assisting humans, mainly in a bucolic setting. Household fairies were said to assist in everyday tasks like washing dishes, laying the fire, sweeping the floor, making bread bake properly, and so on but asked to be treated respectfully and given a cup of milk for their trouble.

Other fairies played mischievous pranks of a **poltergeist** nature, pelting mortals with stones, preventing bread from rising, blowing out candles, knocking pans off shelves, sending gusts of smoke, or annoying horses and cattle. Often this was deemed a punishment for lack of respectful treatment. In rural areas, fairies were often referred to in flattering terms as "the good people" to avoid offending them.

According to superstition, the fairies would sometimes steal a human baby and put a changeling fairy child in its place, often ugly and bad-tempered. The changeling might be tricked into a sudden admission of its fairy origin, but there was also a folk superstition that it should be set on fire for this purpose. Undoubtedly some temperamental babies were fatally burned because of this belief, which persisted until some two centuries ago in isolated peasant districts.

Fairy traditions have been strongest in Celtic countries. In Scotland and Ireland, fairies were called *daoine sithe* (men of peace) and it was believed that every year the devil carried off a tenth part of them. In Scotland and Ireland, Neolithic flint arrowheads were believed to be fairy weapons, and water in which they were dipped was said to be a cure for many ills. The Celts believed fairy music could be heard in certain spots, and it was usually described as sublime. Some folk music airs are said to have originated in fairy music.

"Fairy rings" are small dark green circles in the grass of meadows, fields, or lawns caused by a certain fungus. These rings were once said to be the dancing places of the fairies. In Ireland, mound burials were believed to be the haunts of fairies.

Theories of Fairies

There were many different beliefs concerning fairies. Peasant traditions said they were fallen angels who were neither good enough to be saved nor bad enough to be lost. Folklorists hypothesize that fairies are a folk recollection of an ancient pygmy race, are mythological personifications of natural phenomena, or are remnant figures from ancient religious beliefs. Household tales of folk heroes like Jack the Giant-Killer are probably transplanted from ancient Indo-European folklore, and folk traditions have been made sophisticated in the tales of the Countess d'Aulnoy and Hans Christian Andersen.

Different beliefs and folk memories have no doubt merged, but when all this is sifted and evaluated there remains a body of tradition and testimony, even today, of an elusive ghostly order of life on the borderland of mind and matter, usually depicted in the natural setting of wild and lonely places rather than in the skeptical materialistic bustle of towns and cities.

W. Y. Evans-Wentz, in his *The Fairy-Faith in Celtic Countries* (1911) presents a living testimony of fairies, the recorded traditions of Celtic literature and mythology, an examination of various theories for fairies, and a case for the reality of fairy life. In the final section, Evans-Wentz correlates fairy life with the ghosts and spirits of psychical phenomena, quoting the French researcher **Camille Flammarion,** who suggests in his book *Mysterious Psychic Forces* (1907):

"Either it is we who produce these phenomena, or it is spirits. But mark this well: these spirits are not necessarily the souls of the dead; for other kinds of spiritual beings may exist, and space may be full of them without our ever knowing anything about it, except under unusual circumstances. Do we not find in the different ancient literature, demons, angels, gnomes, goblins, sprites, spectres, elementals, etc.? Perhaps these legends are not without some foundation in fact."

Evans-Wentz concludes that "we can postulate scientifically, on the showing of the data of psychical research, the existence of such invisible intelligences as gods, genii, daemons, all kinds of true fairies, and disembodied men." In his assertions, Evans-Wentz goes far beyond the territory usually covered by his colleagues, who usually limit themselves to the study of folklore traditions.

In his foreword to the 1966 reissue of Evans-Wentz's book, Leslie Shepard cites the protean aspect of fairies (i.e., their ability to change form in accordance with the convention of the viewer) and says, "I have a strong suspicion that in the newer mythology of flying saucers some of those 'shining visitors' in spacecraft from other worlds might turn out to be just another form of fairies." Since then, similar views have been advanced by **UFO** commentators like **Jacques Vallee** and **Brad Steiger.** Other ufologists have suggested that fairies and **flying saucer** phenomena can be correlated with such miraculous religious apparitions as those of **Fatima** or **Lourdes.**

Real Fairies

Claims of contact with fairies are numerous. In 1907 Lady Archibald Campbell interviewed an old blind man and his wife living in an Irish glen who claimed to have caught a fairy and kept it captive for two weeks before it escaped (see *Occult Review,* 6, no. 5, November 1907). A friend of the couple claimed he had seen fairies on the Hill of Howth at early morning, "little men about three feet high, riding on donkeys to scale." Around the same time a reporter on Irish radio interviewed a woman in the west of Ireland who had been "infested with fairies" for several weeks after cutting down a fairy thornbush. The thornbushes believed to be jealously cherished by fairies are still sometimes left undisturbed in Irish fields.

The most famous case of alleged fairy contact came in 1917, when Elsie Wright, age 16, and Frances Griffiths, 10, who lived in the small Yorkshire village of Cottingley, England, claimed they saw and played with fairies near a brook in the local countryside. No one believed them, so they borrowed a camera and produced photographs of their fairies. These pictures later came to the attention of the author **Sir Arthur Conan Doyle** and became the basis of his book *The Coming of the Fairies* (1922). Doyle accepted the girls' story. The evidence for the genuineness of these photographs was quite strong, and a number of attempts were made to disprove them. Skeptics suggested a number of explanations (all of which proved wrong) and it was not until a thorough study of the photographs was made in the 1980s that the source and means of the hoax became known. Shortly before their deaths, the women admitted the hoax.

Doyle's book continues to be reprinted and circulated, primarily in theosophical circles. Many Theosophists became convinced of the truth of the girls' story after independent claims regarding the reality of the **Cottingley fairies** came from Theosophist Geoffrey Hodson, who visited the Cottingley glen with the two girls in 1921 and affirmed that he saw wood elves, gnomes, goblins, and other nature spirits.

In her book *The Real World of Fairies* (1977), theosophical leader Dora van Gelder, who grew up in Java, states that she played with fairies and later even saw them in New York's Central Park.

Other British psychics, including **Vincent Turvey** and **Horace Leaf,** also claimed to see fairies, and in 1927 the **Fairy Investigation Society** was formed in Britain to collate information on fairy sightings of that time. The society eventually became inactive, largely as a result of unwelcome newspaper reports ridiculing the subject. Other organizations that take an interest in fairies include the **Gnome Club of Great Britain** and **Gnome International.**

Sources:

Arrowsmith, Nancy, and G. Moorse. *A Field Guide to the Little People.* New York: Macmillan, 1977.

Baring-Gould, S. *A Book of Folk-Lore.* London, [1913].

Briggs, Katharine M. *The Anatomy of Puck: An Examination of Fairy Beliefs Among Shakespeare's Contemporaries and Successors.* London: Routledge & Kegan Paul, 1959.

———. *A Dictionary of Fairies.* London: Allen Lane, 1976. Reprint, London: Penguin, 1977.

———. *The Personnel of Fairyland.* Oxford, England: Alden Press, 1953. Reprint, Singing Tree Press, 1971.

———. *The Vanishing People: A Study of Traditional Fairy Beliefs.* London: B. T. Batsford, 1978.

Cooper, Joe. *The Case of the Cottingley Fairies.* London: Robert Hale, 1990.

Doyle, Arthur Conan. *The Coming of the Fairies.* London: Hodder & Stoughton, 1922. 2nd ed., rev. and enl. London: Psychic Press, 1928. Reprint, New York: Samuel Weiser, 1972.

Edwards, Gillian. *Hobgoblin and Sweet Puck: Fairy Names and Natures.* London: Geoffrey Bles, 1974.

Evans-Wentz, W. Y. *The Fairy-Faith in Celtic Countries.* Oxford: Oxford University Press, 1911. Reprint, New Hyde Park, N.Y.: University Books, 1966.

Froud, Brian, and Alan Lee. *Faeries.* London: Souvenir Press, 1978. Reprint, New York: Bantam Books, 1979. Reprint, London: Pan Books, 1979.

Gardner, Edward L. *Fairies: The Cottingley Photographs and Their Sequel.* London: Theosophical Publishing House, 1945.

Haining, Peter. *The Leprechaun's Kingdom.* London: Souvenir Press, 1979.

Halliwell-Phillipps, J. O. *Nursery Rhymes and Nursery Tales of England.* London, 1853.

Hartland, Edwin, W. *The Science of Fairy Tales: An Enquiry Into Fairy Mythology.* London, 1891. Reprint, Detroit: Singing Tree Press, 1968.

Kirk, Robert. *The Secret Commonwealth of Elves, Fauns, and Fairies.* 1691. Reprint, London: D. Nutt, 1893.

Latham, M. W. *The Elizabethan Fairies.* New York: Columbia University Press, 1931.

Mac Manus, D. A. *The Middle Kingdom: The Faerie World of Ireland.* London: Max Parrish, 1959.

O'Donnell, Elliot. *The Banshee.* London: Sands, 1919.

Ritson, Joseph. *Fairy Tales, Now First Collected: To Which Are Prefixed Two Dissertations: 1. On Pygmies; 2. On Fairies.* London, 1831.

Sikes, Wirt. *British Goblins.* London, 1880. Reprint, Wakefield, England: EP Publishing, 1973.

Spence, Lewis. *British Fairy Origins.* London: Watts, 1946.

———. *The Fairy Tradition in Britain.* London: Rider, 1948.

Van Gelder, Dora. *The Real World of Fairies.* London: Theosophical Publishing House, 1977.

White, Carolyn. *A History of Irish Fairies.* Ireland: Mercier Press, 1976.

Yearsley, Macleod. *The Folklore of Fairy-Tale.* London: Watts, 1924. Reprint, Detroit: Singing Tree Press, 1968.

Yeats, W. B., ed. *Fairy and Folk Tales of the Irish Peasantry.* London & New York, 1888.

Fairlamb, Annie See Annie Fairlamb Mellon

Fairy Investigation Society

Founded in Britain in 1927 by Sir Quentin Craufurd, M.B.E., to collate information on fairy sightings. Craufurd, himself, claimed to have observed nature spirits.

During its heyday, the society organized meetings, lectures, and discussions, collecting evidence of fairy life. With the outbreak of World War II, however, members were dispersed and the society's records were largely lost or destroyed by enemy action, and so the society became inactive. In 1955, with an energetic secretary, the society was revived and began to issue a regular newsletter, listing reports from members or other individuals. During the 1950s, there were some 50 members, including such famous persons as author Alasdair Alpin MacGregor, **Hugh Dowding** (of the Battle of Britain in World War II), Walter Starkie (of gypsy lore fame), and Walt Disney.

As the society grew and became known, newspaper articles ridiculing the study of **fairies** appeared, saying they were only a superstition of past centuries. As a result, the society once again became inactive.

Fairy Stroke

A strange enchantment, administered through touch or through *blasting* (raising a fairy eddy or wind), said to be practiced by **fairies.** A fairy stroke had a paralyzing effect, the victim being deprived of speech or movement. This spell might be broken by the use of certain flowers or herbs, such as foxglove, water lily, cow parsnip, or dock, but the latter might also predispose an individual to be fairy-struck.

One strangely impressive painting by the talented but troubled artist Richard Dadd (1817–1886) is titled *The Fairy-Feller's Master Stroke.* It hangs in the Tate Gallery, London.

Faith Healing

A general term for all nonmedical cures, ranging from suggestion to psychic and spiritual therapy. (See also **Christian Science; Dentistry, Psychic; Harry Edwards; Healing by Faith; Healing by Touch; Healing, Psychic; Kathryn Kuhlman; Seventh Son**)

Faithist Journal

Quarterly publication for followers of the teachings of the New Age bible *Oahspe.* Address: Kosmon Publications, P.O. Box 4670, Hualapai, AZ 86412-4670.

Fakirs

Moslem religious mendicants. The term literally means "poor man" in Arabic. As with Hindu wandering holy men, many legends have grown up around alleged psychic miracles of fakirs. Most of these claimed miracles prove to be rumors or conjuring tricks, but there is an important element that suggests talents similar to those of Western psychics. Fakirs are distinguished by their disciplined attempt to obtain mastery over the physical body and control over psychic forces, as opposed to becoming passive instruments for the transmission of psychic power.

In 1870 a troup of fakirs from Algeria gave performances in London, but the public reacted negatively to their act, which included inflicting wounds upon their own bodies. Similar demonstrations were given at a Paris exhibition in 1900 by a troup of Aissauas—Algerian Moslems. A detailed description of their self-mutilations was published in the German newspaper *Übersinnliche Welt* in the following year by a Dr. Nagel, who, with two other doctors, witnessed and photographed the performance.

Later, the visit of Tarah Bey, Rahman Bey, and Hamid Bey attracted great attention in Europe and in the United States. Their chief demonstrations were of insensibility to pain, control over the physiological functions of the body, and survival of burial while alive but in a cataleptic state. They could inflict on their bodies deep wounds with long pins or daggers, stop the flow of blood at will, and cause the wounds to heal in a short time. They could desynchronize their pulse, making it different in each wrist and different again in the heart. They could voluntarily throw their bodies into a cataleptic state in which they could withstand being buried alive—remaining without a coffin, under the soil, without being the worse for the ordeal.

There was little doubt that these feats were genuine. They were witnessed by committees of journalists and physicians, who chose the ground for burial. The cataleptic states were real—the pulse ceased to beat, respiration appeared to be suspended, the ears and nose were stopped with cotton—yet the individuals emerged in the same condition. The body was completely dry and in five minutes the normal physiological functions were fully restored.

Hereward Carrington compared the cataleptic state of the fakirs to artificial hibernation. This similarity was first noticed by the hypnotist **James Braid.** The fakir concentrates upon the heart, slows its circulation by an effort of will, presses upon certain nerve centers on the head and neck, throws back his head, retracts his tongue, and, having cut the air supply off, falls into a cataleptic sleep. The time of return to consciousness is either impressed on his subconscious mind (which, as known from hypnotic experiments, has a remarkable appreciation of time) or the fakir relies upon his assistants to wake him.

Harry Houdini, who attempted to rival the live burial feat of Rahman Bey by normal means, succeeded in remaining in a large metal coffin under water for an hour and a half. He was in constant telephonic communication with his assistant and explained that his achievement was because of slow breathing.

Records of several well-attested earlier cases of living burials were published in a brief book, *Observations on Trance: Or, Human Hibernation,* by James Braid, in 1850. Braid traces the idea of these demonstrations to the following passage in the *Dabistan,* a learned Persian work on the religious sects in India:

"It is an established custom amongst the Yogis that, when malady overpowers them, they bury themselves. They are wont, also, with open eyes, to force their looks towards the middle of their eyebrows, until so looking they perceive the figure of a man; if this should appear without hands, feet or any member, for each they have determined that the boundaries of their existence would be within so many years, months or days. When they see the figure without a head, they know that there certainly remains very little of their life; on that account, having see the prognostic they bury themselves."

Braid comments,

"Now it appears to me no very improbable supposition to allege, that accident had revealed to them the fact, that some of those who were thus buried might be restored to life after exhumation—the action of the air restoring respiration and circulation, on an accidental disinterment of the body of someone thus interred, and the fact once observed would encourage others to try how much they could accomplish in this way, as the newest and most striking achievement which they would perform in token of the divine origin and efficacy of their religion over that of all others."

As interesting as these feats are, many Indian religious leaders have observed that there is nothing inherently spiritual about them and indeed they may become an obstacle to the realization of spiritual progress. In the treatise *The Yoga Sutras of Patanjali* (ca. 300 B.C.E.), various occult powers, such as **levitation, invisibility,** and mastery over the senses, are said to result from the practice of **yoga.** However, the author also warns that such powers should be ignored lest they prove an obstacle to spiritual progress.

Among the phenomenal feats attributed to fakirs, who operate in India as entertainers, is levitation, the so-called Indian rope trick. Reports of this phenomena emerged in England in the 1880s, and in 1919 the British Magic Circle, a professional association of stage magicians, offered a £500 reward to anyone who could perform the trick. No one accepted the offer. The Indian rope trick does exist but is rarely performed, as it is a difficult illusion to accomplish. The secret lies in doing it late in the day under poor lighting, using wires obscured by the poor illumination. The major skills required (e.g., climbing the rope with a boy hidden under a robe) account for the infrequent attempts.

There are some reports of levitation by fakirs, however, that are not so easily explained. For example, Harry Kellar, himself a magician, witnessed a performance in which an entranced fakir of Calcutta was placed upon the upturned blades of several swords. The swords were then removed, leaving the body floating in the air. The feat was performed outdoors, with people viewing it from all sides and angles.

Sources:

Braid, James. *Observations on Trance: Or, Human Hibernation.* N.p., 1850.

Jacolliot, Louis. *Occult Science in India and Among the Ancients.* London: William Rider, 1919.

Ormand, Ron, and Gill Ormond. *Into the Strange Unknown.* Hollywood, Calif.: Esoteric Foundation, 1959. Reprinted as *Religious Mysteries of the Orient.* New York: A. S. Barnes, 1976.

Rawcliffe, D. N. *Illusions and Delusions of the Supernatural and Occult.* Rev. ed. New York: Dover Publications, 1959.

Stein, Gordon. *Encyclopedia of Hoaxes.* Detroit: Gale Research, 1993.

Falcomer, Marco Tullio (d. 1924)

Noted Italian researcher, Spiritualist, and professor of law in the Regio Instituto Tecnico e Nautico at Venice. In *An Introduction to Modern Spiritualism,* a 56-page pamphlet, Falcomer summarizes the development of the movement up to 1895. He dedicated the second edition of this pamphlet to the Third International Congress of Psychology, held at Munich in 1896. He intended to speak there on the subject of **Spiritualism** but his paper was not admitted. In a later brochure, *Phenomenography* (Paris, 1903), he describes a series of remarkable phenomena produced through the mediumship of Signorina Nilda Bonardi between 1900 and 1904.

Sources:

Falcomer, Marco T. *An Introduction to Modern Spiritualism.* [Venice], 1895.

———. *Phenomenography.* Paris, 1903.

Falconet, Noel (1644–1734)

French physician and medical writer. He was born at Lyons and became consulting physician to the king. Falconet's works included *Letters and Remarks on the So-Called Potable Gold.* Gold has been used medicinally since ancient times, and potable gold, often prepared by alchemists, was gold prepared in a drinkable form, usually through the addition of some volatile oil.

Falls

The study of materials or objects falling onto the earth was first initiated by **Charles Fort** in his remarkable work *The Book of the Damned* (1919). Fort collected and correlated accounts of the most astonishing variety of falls, including black rain, red snow, butter, manna, large blocks of ice, frogs, periwinkles, and hailstones with portraits on them. He also distinguished selective falls in which different objects were apparently sorted before descent. Fort was not only concerned with the bizarre nature of authenticated falls, but also by the principle of selectivity that appeared to govern descent.

Since Fort's death, further data on falls and other **Fortean phenomena** have been collected by groups such as the **Fortean Society** and the **International Fortean Organization** and by such individuals as William R. Corliss and Robert J. M. Rickard, editor of the **Fortean Times.**

Sources:

Clark, Jerome. *Encyclopedia of Strange and Unexplained Phenomena.* Detroit: Gale Research, 1993.

Corliss, William R., ed. *Handbook of Unusual Natural Phenomena.* Glen Arm, Md.: The Sourcebook Project, 1977.

———. *Tornados, Dark Days, Anomalous Precipitation, and Related Weather Phenomena: A Catalog of Geophysical Anomalies.* Glen Arm, Md.: The Sourcebook Project, 1983.

Fort, Charles. *The Books of Charles Fort.* New York: Henry Holt, 1941.

False Memory Syndrome Foundation

Organization formed in March 1992 by a group of psychologists and psychiatrists to combat "a fast-growing epidemic of dubious therapy that is ripping thousands of families apart, scarring patients for life, and breaking the hearts of innocent parents and other relatives." The False Memory Syndrome Foundation is concerned primarily with false memories of childhood sexual abuse generated by inept or distrustful therapists and welfare workers. Address: 3401 Market St., Philadelphia, PA 19104. Phone: (215) 387-1865.

Sources:

Gardner, Martin. "Notes of a Fringe-Watcher: The False Memory Syndrome." *Skeptical Inquirer* 17 (summer 1993).

———. "The Tragedies of False Memories: The Accused Are Striking Back, But Grave Injustices Have Been Done." *Skeptical Inquirer* 18 (fall 1994).

Familiars

Spirits that live with, travel with, and assist magicians, sorcerers, and witches. The idea seems to have emerged in the thirteenth or fourteenth century from the idea of **fairies** and **kobolds,** the mischievous spirits who could be paid or cajoled into assisting people in various ways. Familiars, it was believed, could take the form of animals or birds. The black dog of **Cornelius Agrippa** was one of the best-known familiars. His story rested on the authority of the sixteenth-century Italian biographer Paulus Jovius, and it was copied by Thevet, among others, in his *Hist. des Hommes plus Illustres et Scavans.*

Jovius relates that Agrippa was always accompanied by the devil in the shape of a black dog, and that, perceiving the approach of death, he took a collar that was ornamented with nails arranged in magical inscriptions from the neck of the animal and dismissed him with these memorable words, "Abi perdita Bestia quae me totum perdidisti" (Away, accursed beast, through whose agency I must now sink into perdition). The dog, it is said, ran hastily to the banks of the Saone, into which he plunged headlong and was never seen again.

According to **Pierre Le Loyer,**

"With regard to the demons whom they imprisoned in rings and charms, the magicians of the school of Salamanca and Toledo, and their master Picatrix, together with those in Italy who made traffic of this kind of ware, knew better than to say whether or not they had appeared to those who had been in possession or bought them. And truly I cannot speak without horror of those who pretend to such vulgar familiarity with them, even to speaking of the nature of each particular demon shut up in a ring; whether he be a Mercurial, Jovial, Saturnine, Martial, or Aphrodisiac spirit; in what form he is wont to appear when required; how many times in the night he awakes his possessor; whether benign or cruel in disposition; whether he can be transferred to another; and if, once possessed, he can alter the natural temperament, so as to render men of Saturnine complexion Jovial, or the Jovials [Saturnine], and so on. There is no end of the stories which might be collected under his head, to which if I gave faith, as some of the learned of our time have done, it would be filling my paper to little purpose. I will not speak therefore of the crystal ring mentioned by Joalium of Cambray, in which a young child could see all that they demanded of him, and which eventually was broken by the possessor, as the occasion by which the devil too much tormented him. Still less will I stay my pen to tell of the sorcerer of Courtray, whose ring had a demon enclosed in it, to whom it behoved him to speak every five days. In fine, the briefest allusion must suffice to what they relate of a gentleman of Poitou, who had playfully taken from the bosom of a young lady a certain charm in which a devil was shut up. Having thrown it into the fire, he was incessantly tormented with visions of the devil till the latter granted him another charm, similar to the one he had destroyed, for the purpose of returning to the lady and renewing her interest in him."

Sometimes the familiar attached itself voluntarily to a master, without any exercise of magic skill or invocation on the master's part, nor could such a spirit be disposed of without **exorcism,** as illustrated by the following story cited by **Martin Antoine Del Rio:**

"A certain man [*paterfamilias,* head of a family] lived at Trapani, in Sicily, in whose house it is said, in the year 1585, mysterious voices had been heard for a period of some months. This familiar was a daemon, who, in various ways, endeavoured to annoy man. He had cast huge stones, though as yet he had broken no mortal head; and he had even thrown the domestic vessels about, but without fracturing any of them. When a young man in the house played and sung, the demon, hearing all, accompanied the sound of the lute with lascivious songs, and this distinctly. He vaunted himself to be a daemon; and when the master of the house, together with his wife, went away on business to a certain town, the daemon volunteered his company. When they returned, however, soaked through with rain, the spirit went forward in advance, crying aloud as he came, and warning the servants to make up a good fire."

In spite of these "services,"the father called in the aid of a priest and expelled the familiar, though not without some difficulty.

The Swiss alchemist **Paracelsus** was believed to carry a familiar about with him in the hilt of his sword. According to the seventeenth-century physician and historian Gabriel Naudé, Paracelsus never laid this weapon aside even when he went to bed, and he often got up in the night and struck it violently against the floor. Frequently when the night before he was without a penny, he would show a purseful of gold in the morning (*Apologie pour les Grands Hommes soupconnez de Magie,* xiv, p. 281). Although other alchemists attributed these events and other of Paracelsus's feats to the **philosophers' stone,** Naudé thought it more rational to believe that it was two or three doses of laudanum (opium) that Paracelsus never went without, and with which he effected many strange cures.

Familiars in Witchcraft

In the late thirteenth century, the idea of the fairy was demonized, and through the next century it became a popular belief that sorcerers and witches had spirit familiars. Among the earliest appearances of the familiar was in 1303 when Philip IV of France had Pope Boniface VIII deposed. Among other charges listed against Boniface, Philip accused him of sorcery and possession of a familiar.

In return for a pact with the devil, a witch was said to be given a personal demon in the form of a domestic animal that would assist the witch in carrying out malevolent magic. The Scottish witch Isobel Gowdie stated, "Each one of us has a spirit to wait upon us, when we please to call upon him." The most common form for a witch's familiar was a cat, and since so many old women kept cats as companions in their loneliness, it was not difficult for witch hunters to make accusations of sorcery. The familiars had pet names, again a characteristic of domestic cats and dogs.

During the **witchcraft** trials at Chelmsford, England, in March 1582, Ursula Kemp confessed that she "had four spirits, whereof two of them were hes, and the other two shes were to punish with lameness and other diseases of bodily harm. . . . One he, like a gray cat, is called Tittey; the second, like a black cat, is called Jack; one she, like a black toad, is called Pigin; and the other, like a black lamb, is called Tyffin." Elizabeth Bennet said she had a familiar called "Suckin, being black like a dog." Alice Manfield had four imps, Robin, Jack, William, and Puppet, "two hes and two shes, all like unto black cats." Agnes Heard had six familiars that were blackbirds, white-speckled and all black.

Sources:

Gleadow, Rupert. *Magic and Divination.* Wakefield, England: EP Publishing, 1976.

Maple, Eric. *The Complete Book of Witchcraft and Demonology: Witches, Devils, and Ghosts in Western Civilization.* South Brunswick, N.J.: A. S. Barnes, 1966.

———. *Dark World of Witches.* New York: A. S. Barnes, 1964.

Russell, Jeffrey Burton. *Witchcrft in the Middle Ages.* Ithaca, N.Y.: Cornell University Press, 1972.

Valiente, Doreen. *The ABC of Witchcraft Past and Present.* New York: St. Martin's, 1973.

Family, The

Founded in 1968 as Teens for Christ, the group now known as The Family adopted the name Children of God (COG), the name by which it became well-known, the following year. COG grew up around David Berg, a former minister in the Christian and Missionary Alliance. With several of his teenage children he began evangelistic work in Huntington Beach, California. In 1969 several of the group received revelations concerning possible earthquakes, and the entire group left to wander across the United States. During this exodus, Berg became known as Moses David and the group as the Children of God.

The group adopted fundamental Christian belief with an emphasis on the endtime, and Berg was accepted as the prophet of the endtime. They attained some initial fame after conducting a series of demonstrations warning people of the evils of American society. They dressed in sackcloths and covered their faces with ashes. Opposition to the youth participation in the group began to grow from parents who called COG a cult, and from their actions against the group the term "cult" began to take on the negative connotations it has today.

The COG soon parted from the other Jesus People groups that had arisen contemporaneously along the West Coast of the United States. The Jesus People objected to the role assigned Berg, and to the fact that he claimed contact with several spirits. As early as 1970, for example, he let it be known that he had come into contact with someone he termed a "spirit helper," named Abrahim, who described himself as a Bulgarian Christian gypsy who had been killed by the Turks. Subsequently, usually in dreams, he spoke with spirit beings, usually understood to be angel messengers. Also, Berg offered prophecies of the future that were used to guide the group.

By the mid 1970s, COG had largely left the United States, the few who remained having taken a very low profile. In 1976 they instituted their most controversial practice, flirty fishing, the use of sexual allure to attract potential converts. Some of the people the group was trying to convert would be offered sexual favors as a symbol of the love of the person trying to win them to God. Several years later, sharing, the free sexual contact of adult members of the group, became widely practiced.

The sexual freedoms and practices of COG were sharply curtailed in 1983 (by which time the group had assumed its present name) and several years later, it became known that during this period of sexual freedom some adult-minor sex had occurred in the group. In 1987, very strict guidelines concerning sexual behavior were introduced with severe penalties for infractions. The Family continues to practice the law of love, which, as they interpret it, permits some freedom of sexual contact between adult members, but have adopted strong regulations against any involvement of minors in sexual activities. After learning of the several unfortunate incidents of sexual child abuse that occurred, different governments moved against The Family in separate actions during the early 1990s. While giving The Family much bad publicity, in the end, the investigations produced no evidence of any ongoing abuse in The Family homes and no subsequent actions were taken against the group or any of its members.

The Family lives communally. David Berg died in 1994, and the group is now headed by his widow, Maria. Homes are found in a number of countries with significant numbers in South America and continental Europe. In 1994 there were approximately 3,000 adult members and 6,000 youth and children.

Sources:

Lewis, James R., and J. Gordon Melton. *Sex, Slander, and Salvation.* Goleta, Calif.: Center for Academic Publication, 1994.

Pritchett, W. Douglas. *The Children of God, Family of Love: An Annotated Bibliography.* New York: Garland Publications, 1985.

Fancher, Mollie (1848–1910)

A Brooklyn girl who, because of two serious accidents, became blind and bedridden at age 17, yet lived another 44 years exhibiting remarkable phenomena of clairvoyance and multiple personality. Fancher became known as "the Brooklyn Enigma." She took no food for nine years and lay on her right side in a paralyzed state with twisted limbs; all the natural functions of her body ceased, at times no pulse was felt, and, except for the region of the heart, her body became entirely cold. In this state she was possessed by a different personality that executed delicate fancywork with her crippled hands, wrote beautifully, read books under her pillow clairvoyantly, saw colors in the dark, discovered lost articles, and exhibited astounding traveling **clairvoyance.** Henry M. Parkhurst, the eminent American astronomer, testified to her reading a torn-up letter that was fished out of a wastepaper basket and enclosed in a sealed envelope.

Fancher's original personality returned after nine years; the bodily rigidity relaxed and she became prey to frightful fits of convulsions. Between such fits, Fancher was possessed by various new invading personalities, called "Sunbeam," "Idol," "Rosebud," "Ruby," and "Pearl." Her personality changed five times in one night, the invaders keeping up a constant quarrel among themselves.

The story of her strange life was narrated by Judge Abram H. Dailey in *Mollie Fancher,* published in Brooklyn in 1894. The case was also reviewed by **Walter Franklin Prince** in Bulletin XI of the Boston Society for Psychic Research.

Fantasmagoriana

The title of a collection of popular stories in two volumes dealing mainly with apparitions and specters that was published in Paris in 1812. The contents were translated from the original German by Jean Baptiste Eyriès. Lord Byron read these stories aloud to Percy Shelley, Mary Wollstonecraft (later Mrs. Shelley), Claire Clairmont, and John William Polidori in the summer of 1816 at the Villa Diodati by Lake Geneva in Switzerland. Subsequently, Byron proposed that each member of the company, amid their ingestions of laudanum, attempt to write a ghost story. As a result Mary Wollstonecraft began her novel **Frankenstein.** Several years later Polidori expanded the story begun by Byron and turned it into the first modern **vampire** story, published as *The Vampyr* in 1819. These stories generated a whole genre of gothic literature with special reference to vampire themes.

Fantl, Kurt (1914– ?)

Psychiatrist and lecturer on parapsychology. Fantl was born January 25, 1914, in Vienna, Austria, educated at the University of Vienna, and did postgraduate work at St. Mary's Hospital, Racine, Wisconsin (1939). During World War II he worked at the American Hospital in Chicago (1939–41), St. Anthony's Hospital, Effingham, Illinois (1941–44), and the Los Angeles Tuberculosis Sanatorium, Duarte, California (1944–45). After the war he interned and did his residency in psychiatry at Bellevue Hospital, New York (1945–48).

He served successively as an assistant in psychiatry, New York University, New York (1947–48); an instructor, University of Southern California (1948–50); a consultant in psychiatry at Los Angeles City Health Department (1948–51); Long Beach City Health Department (1951–53); U.S. Public Health Service, San Pedro, California (1952–53); and was a staff member at San Pedro Community Hospital and at Clearview Sanatorium, Gardena, California.

Fantl developed a special interest in psychokinesis, **telepathy, clairvoyance,** table-rapping, **yoga,** and evidence of **survival** after death. He lectured on parapsychology at Tokyo University and at Poona and Lucknow Universities in India. In 1960 he became president of the Consciousness Research Foundation, a position he held for a number of years.

Sources:

Pleasants, Helene, ed. *Biographical Dictionary of Parapsychology.* New York: Helix Press, 1964.

Faraday, Michael (1791–1867)

Famous British physicist, born in London on September 22, 1791. He became an assistant to Sir Humphry Davy and later became celebrated for his brilliant discoveries relating to electricity and chemistry. Faraday's well-known saying, "Nothing is too amazing to be true," apparently was not meant to cover **table turning.** It was, for him, too amazing to be true. His noted theory that table movements were caused by unconscious muscular pressure was first advanced in a letter to the *Times* of June 30, 1853. To prove it, he prepared two small flat boards a few inches square, placed several glass rollers between them and fastened the whole together with a couple of rubber bands so that the upper board would slide under lateral pressure to a limited extent over the lower one. A light index fastened to the upper board would betray the least amount of sliding.

During experiments this is just what happened. The upper board always moved first, which demonstrated that the fingers moved the table and not the table the fingers. Faraday also found that when the sitters learned the meaning of the index and kept their attention fixed on it, no movement took place. When it was hidden from their sight it kept on wavering, although the sitters believed that they always pressed directly downward. However, the pressure of the hands was trifling and was practically neutralized by the absence of unanimity in the direction. The sitters never made the same movement at the same moment.

For this reason, and for the weightier one that tables moved without contact as well, his theory was soon found inadequate. According to **Charles Richet,** it was **Michel Chevreul,** the famous French chemist, who originally evolved the theory of unconscious muscular pressure. Chevreul's book, however, did not appear until 1854, a year after Faraday's explanation was published.

In later years many attempts were made to prove to Faraday the reality of psychic phenomena, but he was too obstinate. "They who say these things are not competent witnesses of facts," he wrote in 1865. To an invitation to attend the first séance of the **Davenport brothers** he returned the answer, "If spirit communications, not utterly worthless, should happen to start into activity, I will trust the spirits to find out for themselves how they can move my attention. I am tired of them."

Faraday was a member of the Sandemanians, an obscure religious sect holding rigid biblical views. When **Sir William Crookes** inquired of Faraday how he reconciled science with religion, he received the reply that he kept his science and religion strictly apart.

At the time of the Home-Lyon trial (see **D. D. Home**), a Professor Tyndall, in a letter in *Pall Mall Gazette* (May 5, 1868), wrote that, years before, Faraday had accepted an invitation to examine Home's phenomena, but his conditions were not met and the investigation fell through. When the original correspondence on the subject between Faraday and Sir Emerson Tennant was published, it appeared that one of Faraday's conditions was, "If the effects are miracles, or the work of spirits, does he (Home) admit the utterly contemptible character, both of them and their results, up to the present time, in respect either of yielding information or instruction or supplying any force or action of the least value to mankind?" Robert Bell, the intermediary for the proposed séance, found Faraday's letter so preposterous that, without consulting Home, he declined his intervention. Home, when he learned about it, was duly indignant.

Professor Tyndall—as an arch skeptic—commended Faraday's attitude, but those interested in psychical research assumed the contrary position. "The letter," writes **Frank Podmore** in *Modern Spiritualism* (1902), "was, of course, altogether unworthy of Faraday's high character and scientific eminence, and was no doubt the outcome of a moment of transient irritation. The position taken was quite indefensible. To enter upon a judicial inquiry by treating the subject-matter as a *chose jugée* was surely a parody of scientific methods."

Faraday died August 25, 1867. In a series of séances between 1888 and 1910 in Spring Hall, Kansas, the presiding spirit claimed to be Faraday, and his communications were published in four books by A. Aber: *Rending of the Veil, Beyond the Veil, The Guiding Star,* and *The Dawn of Another Life.* A second set of communications reportedly from Faraday were received by an anonymous medium who called herself (or himself) the "Mystic Helper." The messages were received sporadically beginning in 1874 and were finally published in 1924.

Sources:

Berger, Arthur S., and Joyce Berger. *The Encyclopedia of Parapsychology and Psychical Research.* New York: Paragon House, 1991.

Mystic Helper, The. *The Evolution of the Universe, or, Creation According to Science.* Los Angeles: Cosmos Publishing, 1924.

Podmore, Frank. *Modern Spiritualism.* London: Methuen, 1902. Reprinted as *Mediums of the Nineteenth Century.* New Hyde Park, N.Y.: University Books, 1963.

Farajou Data Base

Iranian research center and scientific data bank for conducting research on **psychology, parapsychology, hypnotism, yoga, zen, meditation,** and natural treatments. It sponsors translations into Farsi (a Persian language of Iran) of works in these areas from around the world and provides other countries with articles on science practices and tribal customs of the Middle East. Address: P. O. Box 13185-1354, Tehran, Iran.

Fascination

The term generally signifies the charming or enchanting of another by the eyes or the looks; to hold or keep in subjection by charms, by powers of pleasing. It is derived from the Latin *fascinare* (enchant). A belief in the power of fascination appears to have been prevalent in most ages and countries. In ancient Greece and Rome there is the example of Theocritus's wish that an old woman might be with him to avert this danger by spitting, and the complaint of Menalcas (in Virgil) that some **evil eye** had fascinated his lambs.

The Romans, with their usual passion for increasing the host of heaven, deified this power of evil, and enrolled a god, "Fascinus" among their objects of worship. Although he was a *numen* (presiding spirit), the celebration of his rites was entrusted to the vestal virgins, and his phallic attribute was suspended around the necks of children and from the triumphal chariots.

Lucretius, in *Of Natural Witchcraft for Love,* states:

"But as there is fascination and witchcraft by malicious and angry eyes unto displeasure, so are there witching aspects tending contrariwise to love, or, at the least, to the procuring of good will and liking. For if the fascination or witchcraft be brought to pass or provoked by the desire, by the wishing or coveting any beautiful shape or favour, the venom is strained through the eyes, though it be from afar, and the imagination of a beautiful form resteth in the heart of the lover, and kindleth the fire where it is afflicted. And because the most delicate, sweet and tender blood of the beloved doth there wander, his countenance is there represented, shining in his own blood, and cannot there be quiet, and is so haled from thence, that the blood of him that is wounded, reboundeth, and slippeth into the wounder."

Vairus, prior of the Benedictine Convent of Ste. Sophia in Benevento, published a treatise, *De Fascino,* in 1589. In it he first points to whole nations that have been reported to possess the power of fascination. The idolatrous "Biarbi" and "Hamaxobii," on the authority of Olaus Magnus, are represented as "most deeply versed in the art of fascinating men, so that by **witchcraft** of the eyes, or words, or of aught else [a very useful latitude of expression] they so compel men that they are no longer free, nor of sane understanding, and often are reduced to extreme emaciation, and perish by a wasting disease."

He then proceeds to similar marvels concerning animals:

"Wolves, if they see a man first, deprive him of all power of speech; a fact yet earlier from Theocritus. The shadow of the hyaena produces the same effect upon a dog; and this sagacious wild beast is so well acquainted with its own virtue, that whenever it finds dog or man sleeping, its first care is to stretch its length by the side of the slumberer, and thus ascertain his comparative magnitude with its own. If itself be larger of the two, then it is able to afflict its prey with madness, and it fearlessly begins to nibble his hands or paws (whichever they may be) to prevent resistance; if it be smaller, it quietly runs away."

In the tenth chapter of the *First Book of Vairus* the author inquires, "An aliqui se fascinare possint?" a question that is decided in the affirmative by the example of the Basilisk of Narcissus, and of one less known, though equally unfortunate, Eutelis. In the twelfth chapter Vairus states that the more wicked a person is, the better he is adapted to exercise evil fascination. This book offers two cautions: "Let no servant ever hire himself to a squinting master, and let jewellers be cautious to whose hands, or rather eyes, they intrust their choicest wares."

Additionally, Vairus stresses that all those individuals who are immoderately praised, especially behind their backs, persons of fair complexion and of handsome face or figure, particularly children, are most exposed to fascination. This notion probably arose from such children attracting more attention from strangers than others less indebted to nature. It was an impression of his own personal beauty that induced Polyphemus to put into practice the spitting charm that Cotattaris had taught him.

In *The Second Book of Varius,* after disputing against "natural" fascination, which he treats as visionary, Vairus concludes that all fascination is an evil power, attained by tacit or open compact with the devil.

A second writer on this matter is John Lazarus Gutierrez, a Spanish physician who may be believed to be equally well qualified for the consideration of mystery. His *Opusculum de Fascino* appeared in 1653. Of his own experience he does not say much, but in his *Dubium* he cites an account of a servant who could bring down a falcon from her highest flight by steadily looking at her. He also cites two other wonders: the first of a man in Guadalazara who was in the habit of breaking mirrors into minute fragments solely by looking at them; the second, of another in Ocana, who killed horses and even children by the contagion of his eyes.

From **Jerome Cardan,** Gutierrez extracted the following symptoms by which a physician determined that his patient was fascinated: loss of color; heavy and melancholy eyes, either overflowing with tears or unnaturally dry; frequent sighs and lowness of spirits; watchfulness; bad dreams; and falling away of flesh. The patient was also diagnosed as fascinated if a coral or jacinth worn by him lost its color, or if a ring made from the hoof of an ass, when put on his finger, grew too big for him after a few days. According to the same writer, the Persians used to determine the sort of fascination under which the patient labored by binding a clean linen cloth around his head, letting it dry there, and analyzing any spots that arose on it.

But the most curious fact stated by Gutierrez is that the Spanish children in his time wore **amulets** against fascination, somewhat resembling those in use among the Romans. The son of Gutierrez himself wore one of these; it was a cross of jet, (agavache) and it was believed that it would split if regarded by evil eyes, thus transferring venom from the child to itself. The amulet worn by the Gutierrez boy did split one day while a person was steadfastly looking at him; in justice to Gutierrez it must be added that he attributed the occurrence to some accidental cause. He expressed his conviction that the same thing would have happened under any other circumstances. Throughout his volume, indeed, Gutierrez uses all his reasoning to explode the superstition.

A third similar work is that of John Christian Frommann, a physician of Saxe-Coburg, who published his *Tractatus de Fascinatione* in 1675. Frommann quotes Theocritus, who claimed that children in unwashed baby linen were easily subject to fascination, as was any beauty who employed two lady's maids to dress her hair; moreover, all those who lay in bed very late in the morning, especially if they wore nightcaps; all who broke their fast on cheese or peas; and all children who, having been once weaned, were brought back to the breast would, even against their will, be gifted with the power of fascinating both men and beasts.

In order to ascertain whether a child was fascinated, three oak apples could be dropped into a basin of water under its cradle, the person who dropped them observing the strictest silence. If the apples floated the child was free, if they sank it was affected. In another test a slice of bread was cut with a knife marked with three crosses, and both the bread and the knife were left on the child's pillow for a night; if marks of rust appeared in the morning, the child was fascinated. Some also believed that if on licking a child's forehead with the tongue a salt taste was perceived, it was proof of fascination.

Protection Against Fascination

The following remedies against fascination rest upon the authority either of Vairus or Frommann, or both, and several may be traced to Pliny: an invocation of Nemesis; the root of the *Satyrios orchis;* the skin of a hyena's forehead; the kernel of the fruit of a palm tree; Alyssum (madwort) hung up anywhere in the house; the stone *Catochites;* spitting on the right shoe before it was put on; hyssop; lilies; fumigations; sprinklings; necklaces of jacinth, sapphire, or carbuncle; washings in river water, provided silence be kept; licking a child's forehead, first upward, next across, and lastly up again, and then spitting behind its back; sweeping the child's face with the bough of a pine tree; laying the child on the ground, covered with a linen cloth, and then sprinkling it with earth in the form of a cross; laying turf from a boy's grave under a boy's pillow, from a girl's under a girl's; silently placing near a child the clothes in which it was baptized; if, as is sometimes the case, a child appears to derive no benefit from washing, taking three scrapings from the plaster of each of the four walls of its bedroom, and sprinkling them on its linen; three "lavements" of three spoonfuls of milk; giving in a drink the ashes of a rope with which a man has been hanged; drawing water silently, and throwing a lighted candle into it in the name of the Holy Trinity, then washing the patient's legs in this water, and throwing the remainder behind his or her back in the form of a cross; hanging up the key of the house over the child's cradle; laying on the child crumbs of bread, a lock with the bolt shut, a looking-glass, or some coral washed in the font in which it was baptized; and hanging round the child's neck fennel seeds, or bread and cheese.

Vairus states that huntsmen, as a protection against fascination, used to split an oak plant and pass themselves and their dogs between it. As amulets against love fascination, he recommends a sprinkling with the dust in which a mule had rolled itself; a bone which may be found in the right side of a toad; or the liver of a chameleon.

Some instances of more recent belief in fascination than those referred to above may be found collected in John Brand's *Popular Antiquities* (1849). Such belief was prevalent among the inhabitants of the western islands of Scotland, who used nuts called Molluca beans as amulets against fascination. James Dallaway, in his *Constantinople Ancient and Modern* (1797), remarks that "Nothing can exceed the superstition of the Turks respecting the evil eye of an enemy or infidel. Passages from the Koran are painted on the outside of the houses, globes of glass are suspended from the ceiling, and a part of the superfluous comparison of their horses is designed to attract attention and divert a sinister influence."

Martin Antoine Del Rio wrote a short notice of fascination, which he divided into "Poetica seu Vulgaris," that resulting from obscure physical causes, which he treated as fabulous; "Philosophica," which he considered to be contagion; and "Magica," to which he heartily assented.

The Evil Eye

A belief in the destructive power of human vision was once widespread, and the power was called "casting the evil eye" or "overlooking." Individuals with eyes of a different color from others in their community, or with such defects as a squint or cataracts were suspected of causing harm by overlooking. People believed this could affect animals, individuals, or objects and result in illness, poverty, injury, death, or other evils. During the great witch-hunting manias, hundreds of individuals were burned after being accused of causing injury through casting the **evil eye.**

The evil was believed to be averted by countercharms, amulets, or ritual actions. Making an image of the person believed to be overlooking and sticking pins into it was one way of removing the evil eye. Another method was to go out at night and collect nine toads, which had to be tied together with string and buried in a hole. As the toads languished, so the person casting the evil eye would pine away and die. An ancient remedy was to make gestures having a sexual connotation. It is possible that the veil worn by the bride in European marriage was originally a protection against the malice of the evil eye.

Mesmerism

The term fascination has also been used in reference to the more hypnotic aspect of the practice of **mesmerism** or **animal magnetism** in order to induce a **trance.** The operator gazes steadily into the subject's eyes for five or ten minutes. It is possible, however, that trance is induced more by the subject's concentration upon the eyes of the operator than by any mysterious power from the operator's eyes, since trance can be induced by having the subject stare fixedly at a bright object. Fascination is also evident among animals and reptiles, as in the often quoted instance of a snake fascinating a bird.

Psychic Force and Vision

Psychical researchers have often claimed that there is a **psychic force** exerted by human vision, and some psychics are believed to have influenced objects at a distance by gazing at them. Various instruments have been devised to demonstrate this claimed psychic force, exerted by willpower, by proximity of the hands, or by vision (see **biometer of Baraduc; De Tromelin cylinder; sthenometer**). One of the most interesting instruments of this kind was developed by British physician Charles Russ, described by him in an article in the British medical journal the *Lancet* (July 3, 1931) as "an instrument which is set in motion by vision."

Sources:

Brand, John. *Popular Antiquities.* 1849. Reprint, London: J. R. Smith, 1870.

Dallway, James. *Constantinople Ancient and Modern.* N.p., 1797.

Fascinum

An artificial male phallus reportedly used in **witchcraft** ceremonies. Evidence of the artificiality of claimed copulation with the devil is the frequent reference to the coldness of the phallus. Centuries before the great witchcraft manias of Europe, the fascinum was used in ancient religious rituals, such as those connected with worship of the god Priapus; such phalli were also known in ancient Egypt. Probably the earliest known is that of the fertility god Min at Koptos, around 5500 B.C.E.

Sources:

Knight, Richard Payne. *A Discourse on the Worship of Priapus.* 1786. Reprint, Secaucus, N.J.: University Books, 1974.

Fat of the Sorcerers

It was believed at one time that the devil made use of human fat for his sorceries. Witches rubbed themselves with an **ointment** made from this fat in order to go to the **Sabbat,** a gathering of members of their **witchcraft** group. Other ingredients of the witch unguent were said to be blood of the lapwing and bat, soot, aconite, and deadly nightshade. Francesco-Maria Guazzo, author of *Compendium Maleficarum* (1608) states that the witch unguent was made from a thick stew of boiled children, preferably unbaptized. This was a fantastic allegation made earlier by Sylvester Prierias, in 1521. It was claimed that this ointment gave witches the power of **transvection,** flying through the air.

Fata Morgana

A mirage often seen in the Strait of Messina, Sicily, once attributed to the **fairies.** It took its name from the Italian form of **Morgan le Fay,** sister of **King Arthur** in Arthurian legend.

FATE (Magazine)

Preeminent American journal devoted to articles and true stories of the strange and unknown. It was originally launched by **Raymond A. Palmer** and **Curtis Fuller** in the spring of 1948. Previously both had worked for Ziff-Davis, a Chicago-based publishing company that was in the process of moving to New York. Palmer and Fuller decided to stay in the Midwest. Palmer had concluded from his prior publishing experience that there was a market for a magazine offering true stories of mysterious occurrences. The first issue featured the story of Kenneth Arnold's **UFO** sightings and *FATE* regularly thereafter carried UFO stories.

In 1955, after Palmer had moved to Amherst, Wisconsin, and started a second magazine, *Mystic,* Fuller bought his share of the publication and became sole owner. He published and edited the magazine until 1966, when Mary Margaret Fuller became the editor. She was succeeded by Jerome Clark in 1988. *FATE* emerged as a unique publication. On the one hand it promoted, through its very existence, all areas of inquiry on matters psychic, occult, and Fortean. It also became known for its large advertisement section covering a wide range of occult and other curious publications and services representative of the contemporary scene. At the same time *FATE* took the lead in exposing hoaxes and printing articles presenting evidence of mundane explanations of supposed mysterious phenomena.

In 1989 Fuller relinquished *FATE* to its present owner, **Carl L. Weschcke.** Address: P.O. Box 64383, St. Paul, MN 55164-0383. Back issues from the first volume on are available on microfilm from *FATE* #5876, Periodicals, Order Entry, University Microfilms, 300 North Zeeb Rd., Ann Arbor, MI 48106.

Sources:

Clark, Jerome. *The Emergence of a Phenomenon: UFOs from the Beginning through 1959.* Vol. 2. of *The UFO Encyclopedia.* Detroit: Omnigraphics, 1992.

———. *Encyclopedia of Strange and Unexplained Phenomena.* Detroit: Gale Research, 1993.

Father Divine See **Divine, Father Major Jealous**

Father's House

The Father's House was a small organization that served for many years as a dissemination point for the teachings of the Universal Link, the original international organization spreading the **New Age** movement. It was founded by Ralph F. Raymond (d.1984) in the mid-1960s as the Universal Link Heart Center in Los Angeles. In 1968 Raymond made a tour of Universal Link centers in Europe and upon his return settled in San Jose, California. Under his religious name, Brother Francis, he published a booklet of his travels, now an important chronicle of the beginning of the New Age. He also began to issue the *Father's House Journal,* in which he reprinted selections, primarily channeled material, from many of the early New Age groups such as the **Findhorn Foundation** in Scotland. Raymond believed in the coming **Aquarian Age** and saw himself as one facilitator assisting people into its reality. The Father's House ceased to exist soon after his death.

Sources:

Brother Francis [Ralph F. Raymond]. *The Universal Link Concept.* Los Angeles: Universal Link Heart Center, 1968.

Faust

A legendary occult magician of the sixteenth century, famous in literature. There is some evidence that such a person existed. **Trithemius** mentioned him in a letter written in 1507, in which he referred to him as a fool and a mountebank who pretended he could restore the writings of the ancients if they were wiped out of human memory, and blasphemed concerning the miracles of

Christ. In 1513 Konrad Mudt, a canon of the German Church, also alluded to Faust in a letter as a charlatan.

In 1543 Johann Gast, a Protestant pastor of Basel, apparently knew Faust, and considered a horse and dog belonging to the magician to have been **familiar** spirits.

Johan Weyer, who opposed the excesses of witch-hunters, mentioned Faust in a work of his as a drunkard who had studied magic at Cracow. He also mentioned that in the end Satan strangled Faust after his house had been shaken by a terrific din.

From other evidence it seems likely that Faust was a wandering magician or necromancer whose picturesque character won him notoriety. No doubt the historic Faust was confused in legend with Johan Fust, the pioneer of early printing, whose multiplication of books must have been ascribed to magic. By the end of the century in which Faust flourished, he had become the model of the medieval magician, and his name was forever linked with those of Virgil, **Roger Bacon, Pope Silvester II,** and others.

The origins of the Faust legend are ancient. The essentials underlying the story are the pact with Satan, and the supposed vicious character of purely human learning. The idea of the pact with Satan belongs to both Jewish and Christian magico-religious belief, but is probably more truly Kabalistic. The belief can scarcely be traced further back, unless it resides in the idea that a sacrificed person takes the place of the deity to which he gives up his life.

The Faust tale soon spread over Europe and the story of Faust and his pact with the devil was celebrated in broadside ballads. The first dramatic representation of the story was Christopher Marlowe's *Tragicall History of Dr. Faustus.* The dramatist G. E. Lessing wrote a Faust play during the German literary revival of the eighteenth century, but it remained for **Goethe** to grant Faust some degree of immortality through the creation of one of the great psychological dramas of all time. Goethe differed from his predecessors in his treatment of the story in that he gave a different character to the pact between Faust and Mephistopheles, whose nature is totally at variance with the devils of the old Faust books. Goethe took the idea of Faust's final salvation from Lessing. It may be said that although in some respects Goethe adopted the letter of the old legend he did not adopt its spirit. Probably the story of Faust has given to thousands their only idea of medieval magic, and this idea has lost nothing in the hands of Goethe, who cast about the subject a much greater halo of mystery than it contained.

Sources:

Bates, Paul A., ed. *Faust: Sources, Works, Criticism.* New York: Harcourt, Brace, and World, 1968.

Grim, William E. *The Faust Legend in Music and Literature.* Lewiston, N.Y.: Edwin Mellen Press, 1988.

Palmer, Philip M., and Robert P. More. *Sources of the Faust Tradition from Simon Magus to Lessing.* Oxford: Oxford University Press, 1936. Reprint, New York: Haskell House, 1965.

Fay, Annie Eva (ca. 1855–1927)

Famous American medium who demonstrated on the theatrical stage, where she produced phenomena quite similar to that of the **Davenport brothers.** Born as Anna Eva Heathman in Southington, Ohio, she was driven from home by her stepmother. She gave her first exhibition in an old schoolhouse in Ohio. Her first husband, Henry Cummings Melville Fay, had been denounced as a fraud by Spiritualists, and his appearance on the stage with Annie Fay immediately threw doubt on the authenticity of Annie's performance, billed as "The Indescribable Phenomenon."

Her public performances in London in 1874 at the Crystal Palace aroused the interest of researcher **Sir William Crookes,** who was then finishing a series of tests on the mediumship of **Florence Cook.** The phenomena involved the movement of objects and playing of musical instruments in the dark. Annie Fay was tested by Crookes at his house in London in February 1875. Crookes had Fay hold two electrodes in an electrical circuit connected with a galvanometer in an adjoining room, which indicated any variation in the medium's grip. Under these circumstances, a heavy musical box was moved across the room, opened, wound up, started, and stopped again. A handbell was rung, and a hand holding it was thrust through a curtained doorway into the laboratory, where the bell dropped in full view. Crookes's locked bureau was opened, odd things were placed on it, and all the drawers were opened. Crookes was convinced that his electrical control was not broken. An account of the experiment was published in the *Medium* (March 12, 1875).

An exposure of the Fay stage séances was published in the *New York Daily Graphic* (April 12, 1876), based on material supplied by Washington Irving Bishop, who had been a member of the Fay troupe and was later dismissed. Bishop demonstrated the methods by which Fay worked her marvelous feats, which required some difficult but very natural physical exertions. Later both Fay and Bishop were satirized under the names "Evalina Gray" and "W. S. Bischoff" in the 1877 novel *Spiritualists and Detectives* by private detective Alan Pinkerton. The exposures did little to slow Fay, who continued to travel as a performer working on the border between stage magic and **Spiritualism.**

Annie Fay's son John Truesdale Fay (born in Ohio in 1877) traveled with his mother's show and was suspected of assisting with "manifestations" while hidden under Annie's dress. In 1881 Annie married David H. Pingree, who promoted her performances, which included a stage clairvoyant act called "Somnolency," now known to have been an ingenious trick.

Some confusion has been caused by the fact that Annie's son John married Anna Norman in 1898 and taught his wife the same stage clairvoyance act, which they performed together as "The Fays." Earlier, another American stage performer using the name "Annie Fay" had copied the "Indescribable Phenomenon" act.

In her later years, Annie Fay made money answering letters by mail, in addition to continuing her stage appearances. In 1913 she was honored by the famous conjurer's association *The Magic Circle* in London, which elected her first honorary lady associate. She continued to draw large crowds for her stage shows until an accident in 1924 in Milwaukee, after which she retired.

The great **Houdini** claimed that she told him how she had tricked Crookes during his experiments in London by holding a handle with one hand and gripping the other with the bare flesh under her knee, thus enabling her to produce raps and play musical instruments. Fay died May 20, 1927.

Sources:

Christoper, Milbourne. *Mediums, Mystics and the Occult.* New York: Thomas Y. Crowell, 1975.

Fay, Mrs. H. B. (ca. 1885)

American materialization medium of the nineteenth century, described by **Florence Marryat** in her book *There is No Death* (1891). According to Marryat, some 30 or 40 different forms materialized at a séance, ranging from babies and children to adults, male and female. These materializations included Marryat's late brother Frederick, drowned at sea. The figures came from the séance **cabinet** into the room.

E. A. Brackett of Boston records interesting séances with Fay in his book *Materialized Apparitions* (1886). He claims that as many as 40 to 60 forms of all ages appeared during a single séance, often changing into other forms in full view of the sitters. For two years, Brackett himself regularly witnessed the materialization of his wife's niece, who had died young. At one sitting, the Spiritualist **Alfred Russel Wallace** also recognized the niece.

Sources:

Marryat, Florence. *There is No Death.* New York: John W. Lovell Company, 1891. Reprint, New York: Causeway Books, 1973.

Fay, William M. (1839- ?)

Nineteenth-century medium who took part in stage demonstrations by the **Davenport brothers,** which were claimed to be caused by spirit agency. He was born in Darmstadt, Germany, and emigrated to the United States at age 11. Fay claimed that he initially experienced physical mediumship while residing with his widowed mother in Buffalo, New York, and that the phenomena led to his association with the Davenports. He took part in their performances, which involved rapid release from rope tying.

An exposure of Fay as fraudulent, published in the Toronto *Globe* during 1864, was later proved unfounded, since he was not in America at the time and had been confused with H. Melville Fay, husband of the claimed medium **Annie Eva Fay.**

Sources:

Houdini, Harry. *A Magician Among the Spirits.* New York: Harper & Brothers, 1924. Reprinted as *Houdini: A Magician Among the Spirits.* New York: Arno Press, 1972.

"Feda"

Gladys Osborne Leonard's **control.** "Feda" was said to have been married to an ancestor of the medium in India and to have died about 1800 at age 13.

Feedback

Term used in parapsychology to indicate information relating to a subject's performance that may be relayed by the experimenter or indicated by apparatus and can be immediate or (in a test series) delayed.

Feilding, (Francis) (Henry) Everard (1867–1936)

A barrister and pioneer psychical researcher, Feilding attended Oxford and received a degree in law. His interest in psychic phenomena was sparked by a visit to **Lourdes** in 1892 and deepened by the death of his sister three years later. The evidence for **survival** of death presented by his Catholic faith proved insufficient in the face of his personal loss.

Feilding became an early member of the **Society for Psychical Research** (SPR) in London and served as its secretary from 1903 to 1920. He investigated the phenomena of **Florence Cook,** the famous materialization medium also investigated by **Sir William Crookes.** Feilding also reported on the phenomena of the Italian medium **Eusapia Palladino** with whom he sat in Naples in 1908. His reports on the sittings with Palladino were among the most important of the various articles he contributed to both the *Proceedings* and the Journal of the SPR.

In 1919 Feilding married the Polish medium **Stanislawa Tomczyk.** He gradually withdrew as an active member of the SPR but followed with interest the investigations of **Rudi and Willi Schneider** and **Mina Crandon** (Margery). He died February 8, 1936.

Sources:

Berger, Arthur S., and Joyce Berger. *The Encyclopedia of Parapsychology and Psychical Research.* New York: Paragon House, 1991.

Feilding, F. E. *Sittings with Eusapia Palladino and Other Studies.* New York: University Books, 1963.

Feilding, F. E., W. W. Baggally, and Hereward Carrington. "Report on a Series of Sittings with Eusapia Palladino." *Proceedings* of the Society for Psychical Research 23, no. 59 (1909); 25, no. 62 (1911).

Pleasants, Helene, ed. *Biographical Dictionary of Parapsychology.* New York: Helix Press, 1964.

Fellowship of Isis

Irish-based neopagan religious organization founded in 1976 by author and painter Olivia Robertson to revive worship and communion with the feminine principle of the deity in the form of the goddess Isis and to promote knowledge of the world's matriarchal religions.

The fellowship is organized on a democratic basis and there are no vows of secrecy (though member groups may have their own secrets). It professes religious toleration and members are free to maintain other religious allegiances. Communication between members is maintained through literature and correspondence and through local sister centers and groups, in addition to the main center in Ireland.

The quarterly magazine *Isian News* includes news, lists of members, temples, shrines, and centers, as well as articles on rites, festivals, and formation and hallowing of temples. Other publications include a festival calendar and books on rites and mysteries of the Goddess. In the early 1990s the loosely organized fellowship had 83 affiliated centers in 22 countries with a total combined membership of approximately 3000 individuals. The Fellowship of Isis may be contacted at Huntingdon Castle, Clonegal, Enniscorthy, Eire.

Sources:

Durdin-Robertson. *The Goddesses of Chaldea, Syria and Egypt.* Enniscorthy, Eire: Cesara Publications, 1975.

Robertson, Olivia. *The Call of Isis.* Enniscorthy, Eire: Cesara Publications, 1975.

———. *The College of Isis Manual.* Enniscorthy, Eire: Cesara Publications, n.d.

———. *Handbook of the Fellowship of Isis.* Enniscorthy, Eire: Cesara Publications, n.d.

Robertson, Olivia, and Lord Strathloch. *The Fellowship of Isis Directory for 1980.* Enniscorthy, Eire: Cesara Publications, 1979.

Fellowship of Ma-Ion

Secret magic order founded by "Frater Achad" (**Charles Stansfeld Jones**), a close associate and magical child of magician **Aleister Crowley.** The order was based on interpretations of the Kabalistic Tree of Life and *The Book of the Law,* the thelemic magic text channeled by Crowley. *The Book of the Law* announces the new aeon of Horus, the Egyptian deity referred to by Crowley as "the Crowned and Conquering Child." Jones announced the coming of the Ma-Ion or Aeon of Maat, the Egyptian goddess of truth and justice. The Ma-Ion was to succeed the Aeon of Horus, an idea that proved unacceptable to most thelemic magicians. The fellowship as such no longer exists, but its impetus has been carried on by contemporary Maatian magic groups such as the Ordo Adeptorum Invisiblum.

Sources:

Achad, Frater. *Anatomy of the Body of God.* Chicago: Collegium ad Spiritum Sanctum, 1925.

———. *Liber 31.* San Francisco: Level Press, 1974.

———. *XXXI Hymns to the Star Goddess.* Chicago: Will Ransom, 1923. Reprint, Kenilworth, Ill.: Ordo Adeptorum Invisiblum, 1983.

Skia, Persona. *O.A.I. Manifesto: Origin, History, Organization.* Kenilworth, Ill.: Ordo Adeptorum Invisiblum, 1982.

Fellowship of the Inner Light

The Fellowship of the Inner Light is a **channeling** group founded in 1972 in Atlanta, Georgia, by the followers of Paul Solomon, a trance channel believed by his followers to be like **Edgar Cayce.** Solomon first began to channel from what was termed the "Source" in February 1972. Further sessions produced a variety of information for the treatment of diseases, accurate prophecies, and a complete system for the development of "Inner Light Consciousness." The fellowship was organized to disseminate the teachings concerning the Inner Light Consciousness and to provide a vehicle for Solomon's continued work.

In 1974 headquarters were shifted to Virginia Beach, Virginia, where Cayce had lived the last years of his life and where the **Association for Research and Enlightenment** continued the study of the Cayce transcripts. Here the fellowship became associated with the Heritage Store and Heritage Publications. Heritage Store was formed in 1969 to make the remedies suggested by the Cayce readings available to the general public. The store began to make Solomon's material available to its customers both in the immediate area and around the country. Through the 1980s, the fellowship also operated Carmel-in-the-Valley, a 13-acre retreat center near New market, Virginia, though in recent years all of the fellowship activities have been centered in Virginia Beach.

Solomon's channeled material parallels that of Cayce at many points. The source of his information is believed to be the Universal Mind and the **Akashic records.** All of human thought is believed to be recorded on the Akashic records, or the universal ethers, and hence remains available for someone like Solomon to draw on. The fellowship discourages contact with the spirits of the dead.

According to Solomon's teachings, humans are children of God trapped in a material bodies, first manifest on ancient **Atlantis.** By spiritual growth and bodily cleansing, the trapped soul can stop the cycle of reincarnations and become one with God. Reincarnations allow time for the growth of the soul.

The fellowship can be reached at The Fellowship Center, 620 14th St., Virginia Beach, VA 23451, where a file of the Solomon readings are available for perusal. It is active through affiliated study groups across North America and Europe and publishes a periodical, *Reflections on the Inner Light.*

Sources:

A Healing Consciousness. Virginia Beach, Va.: Master's Press, 1978.

Spiritual Unfoldment and Psychic Development through Inner Light Consciousness. Atlanta: Fellowship of the Inner Light, n.d.

Fellowship of Universal Guidance

The Fellowship of Universal Guidance, a metaphysical group that operated in the greater Los Angeles area, was among the early groups to align itself with the **New Age** movement. The fellowship was founded by Wayne A. Guthrie and Bella Karish in 1960. Both channelled entities who were viewed as great sources of light. After operating in Los Angeles for several decades, the fellowship moved to suburban Glendale. Among the people associated with the fellowship in the 1960s was **David Spangler.** As a young student, Spangler learned to channel under the guidance of the fellowship and was still associated with them when the entity "John" began to speak through him. Spangler carried an understanding of the New Age developed in relationship to Guthrie and Karish with him to **Findhorn** in 1970. He stayed at Findhorn for several years and eventually became one of the major spokespeople for the New Age movement in the United States.

No contact has been made with the fellowship in recent years and it is assumed that it has disbanded.

Sources:

Wisdom Workshop Lessons. 12 vols. Los Angeles: Fellowship of Universal Guidance, n.d.

Fendeurs

A supposed French Rosicrucian society that flourished in the mid-seventeenth century. It appears to have been formed in the twelfth century as a league to combat severe forest laws in France. The fendeurs were hewers, and their organization was similar to that of the Italian Carbonari or charcoal burners.

Feng-shui

A form of **geomancy** practiced in China, frequently employed to determine the location and orientation of buildings, and particularly of tombs. It is concerned with the "dragon lines" or subtle energies of the earth. Feng-shui was consulted not only so that each dwelling could be most auspiciously placed, but so the total configuration of a village would be harmonious. For example, if a man built so that the corner of his house faced the side of a house belonging to someone else, the latter believed that the worst misfortune would befall him. Longstanding feuds might result from the unfortunate action. A remedy consisted in placing in a chamber a dragon or other monster in terra-cotta, facing the corner of the contrary building. The terrible gaze of the monster would repulse the evil influence. Incense was burned before the dragon, and it was treated with much respect.

Sources:

Eitel, E. J. *Feng-shui: The Rudiments of Natural Science in China.* Bristol, England: Pentacle Books, 1979.

Rossbach, Sarah. *Feng Shui: The Chinese Art of Placement.* New York: E. P. Dutton, 1983.

Skinner, Stephen. *The Living Earth Manual of Feng-shui: Chinese Geomancy.* London: Routledge & Kegan Paul, 1982.

Fennel

A common herb (*Foeniculum vulgare*) credited in folklore with mysterious and vivifying properties. According to Pliny, serpents eat fennel to shed the skin and thus renew youth and vision. In humans it has been said to improve the eyesight, increase the milk of nursing mothers, and reduce corpulence. In ancient times fennel leaves were used to crown victors in games, and fennel was also used in the rites of Adonis.

Feola, Jose M(aria) (1926–)

Argentine radiobiologist and parapsychologist. Feola was born May 30, 1926, in Buenos Aires and served in Argentine army research in the 1940s, earning the rank of lieutenant. Feola was a radiobiological researcher at the Argentine Atomic Energy Commission in Buenos Aires (1956–64) before moving to the United States in 1965 as a researcher at Donner Laboratory, University of California, Berkeley (1965–69). He was awarded a fellowship from the National Academy of Sciences and International Atomic Agency for 1959–61.

He subsequently became an instructor in radiobiology at the University of Minnesota, Minneapolis (1970–73), and an instructor in parapsychology at the University of Minnesota extension division (1972–75), before accepting a position as an assistant professor of clinical medicine at the University of Kentucky in 1975. Feola became a naturalized citizen in 1974.

His interest in parapsychology developed early in his professional career. Before his move to the United States he served as director of the Argentine Institute for Parapsychology (1957–64). He subsequently joined the **American Society for Psychical Research,** the **Parapsychological Association,** the **California Society for Psychical Studies** (president, 1968–70), and the Minnesota Society for Parapsychological Research (president, 1971–73).

His writings include *PK, Mind Over Matter* (1975), the column "Parapsychology Today" in *Gnostica,* beginning in 1974, and various articles in scientific journals and in *Psychic* magazine.

Sources:

Berger, Arthur S., and Joyce Berger. *The Encyclopedia of Parapsychology and Psychical Research.* New York: Paragon House, 1991.

Pleasants, Helene, ed. *Biographical Dictionary of Parapsychology.* New York: Helix Press, 1964.

Feraferia

An early neopagan group that pioneered the development of goddess worship in southern California. It was founded by Frederick M. Adams in 1967. Adams, who had studied Greek and Celtic folklore, as well as the works of **C. G. Jung,** had a mystical experience in 1956 when he was suddenly seized by a realization of "the sacred feminine principle." In 1957 he devoted himself to establishing a "nature celebration" group known as the Fellowship of Hesperides. He also met and was deeply influenced by the poet Robert Graves and Graves's book *The White Goddess.* In 1959 Adams started a multifamily commune in the Sierra Madre, with seasonal festivals at a goddess temple. The temple and commune became the predecessors of Feraferia, an organization which continued into the 1980s.

Ferguson, Rev. Jesse Babcock (d. 1870)

Noted American minister in the antebellum South whose early studies of **animal magnetism** beginning in 1842 led him to **Spiritualism.** He initially experimented by hypnotizing his wife. In 1853 he had his first experience with a rapping **medium** in Ohio, and soon afterward both his wife and daughter developed psychic powers, wrote and spoke automatically, and saw visions. Ferguson recounted these events in his book *Spirit Communion: A Record of Communications from the Spirit Spheres* (1854). They later became the subject of a second volume, *Supramundane Facts in the Life of the Rev. J. B. Ferguson,* by T. L. Nichols (1865).

In 1864 he traveled to England as part of the entourage of the **Davenport brothers.** The tone of the press toward him was courteous and respectful. He even accompanied the Davenports to France, but because he could not speak French he soon returned to London. Robert Cooper describes him in his *Spiritual Experiences* (1867) as "a giant in intellect, a child in simplicity and an angel in goodness and one of Nature's noblemen."

Sources:

Ferguson, Jesse Babcock. *Spirit Communion: A Record of Communications from the Spirit Spheres.* Nashville, 1854.

Nichols, T. L. *Supramundane Facts in the Life of the Rev. J. B. Ferguson.* London, 1865.

Ferguson, Marilyn (1938–)

New Age publisher, editor, and author. Ferguson was born April 5, 1938, in Grand Junction, Colorado, and is known for her best-selling book *The Aquarian Conspiracy: Personal and Social Transformation in the 1980s* (1980). In 1973 she wrote *The Brain Revolution,* and her study for the book led her to found a newsletter, the *Brain/Mind Bulletin* in 1975. Her interest in human potential expanded through the rest of the decade and into the New Age movement. She came to believe that society was undergoing a profound paradigm shift, a change in the basic metaphor used to explain life. She documented the rationale for her new belief in *The Aquarian Conspiracy* (1980), in which she uses a conspiracy metaphor to postulate a consciousness revolution as distinct from a political, economic, or religious revolution. Through this quiet revolution an informal network of enlightened individuals is creating radical change in modern culture, based on a greatly enlarged concept of human potential.

Sources:

Ferguson, Marilyn. *The Aquarian Conspiracy: Personal and Social Transformation in the 1980s.* Los Angeles: J. P. Tarcher, 1980.

———. *The Frontiers of Mind Research.* New York: Taplinger, 1973.

Ferguson, Marilyn, and Michael Ferguson. *Champagne Living on a Beer Budget.* New York: G. P. Putnam's Sons, 1968.

Taylor, Peggy. "Life at the Leading Edge: A New Age Interview with Marilyn Ferguson." *New Age* 8, no. 1 (August 1982): 30–35, 52–53.

Fern

Many occult beliefs have adhered to the common fern. In ancient times the fern was thought not to have seed. Later on, people thought that the seed was invisible, and if a man could find this invisible seed, it would confer the power of **invisibility** upon him. The fern was also believed to flower at midnight on St. John's Eve, one of the more magical days of the year in medieval Europe. Legend said that anyone who gained possession of the flower would be protected from all evil influences and would obtain a revelation of hidden treasure.

Fernández, José S(alvador) (1893–1967)

A civil engineer and for many years the president of Colegio Argentino de Estudios Psiquicos (Argentine College of Psychic Studies). Fernández was born February 16, 1893, in Buenos Aires and studied at Buenos Aires University. His wife was a **clairvoyant,** and through the 1930s Fernández championed the cause of both **Spiritualism** and **parapsychology** in Argentina. He was the first Argentinian to adopt the quantitative methodology as advocated by **J. B. Rhine,** and made early statistical studies of clairvoyance and precognition. He also founded the ATMAN Spiritualist Circle in 1933 and attended meetings of the Psyke Circle to sit with mediums and clairvoyants. He helped revive psychical studies after World War II and served successively as the president of the Sociedad Argentina de Parapsicologia (1948–53), the Instituto Argentino de Parapsicologia (1953–55), and the Argentino de Estudios Psiquicos (1957–67).

Fernández was a member of the Sociedad Constancia and was assistant editor of the psychic journal *Constancia.* He contributed many articles on parapsychology to journals in Argentina, Brazil, Portugal, Mexico, and Great Britain. He died March 14, 1967.

Sources:

Berger, Arthur S., and Joyce Berger. *The Encyclopedia of Parapsychology and Psychical Research.* New York: Paragon House, 1991.

Fernández, José S. *Application of the Statistical Method to the Study of Cryptesthetic Phenomena.* N.p., 1942.

———. *Clairvoyance and Probability.* N.p., 1941.

———. *Experimental Parapsychology.* N.p., 1953.

———. *A Mathematical Preface to the Study of ESP.* N.p., 1949.

———. *Parapsychology and the Existence of the Soul.* N.p., 1959.

———. *Philosophical and Scientific Bases for Survival and Reincarnation.* N.p., 1957.

———. *The Photoelectric Cell and Perception of the Spiritual World.* N.p., 1932.

Ferrarius (or Efferariaus or Eufarius) (ca. 1200)

Italian alchemist, believed to have been an abbot or monk of Ferrara. His works on **alchemy** include *De Lapide Philosophorum* (The Philosophers' Stone) and *Thesaurus Philosophiae,* which is included in the collection *Theatrum Chemicum* (1659).

Fetch

According to Irish and British belief, the spirit **double** or apparition of a living person, also known as the **wraith.** It resembles in every particular the individual whose death it is supposed to foretell, but is generally of a shadowy or ghostly appearance. The fetch may be seen by more than one person at the same time and, like the wraith of England and Scotland, may even appear to the person it represents. There is a belief, too, that if the fetch is seen in the morning, it indicates long life for the person, but if seen at night, a speedy death may be expected.

The fetch enters largely into the folktales of Ireland, and it is hardly surprising that so many tales have been woven around it, for there is something gruesome in the idea of being haunted by one's own double (an idea that has frequently been explored by more sophisticated writers than the inventors of folk tales).

Patrick Kennedy, in his *Legendary Fictions of the Irish Celt* (1866), referring to the Irish fetch, quotes the tale of *The Doctor's Fetch,* based on authentic sources:

"In one of our Irish cities, and in a room where the mild moonbeams were resting on the carpet and on a table near the window, Mrs. B., wife of a doctor in good practice and general esteem, looking towards the window from her pillow, was startled by the appearance of her husband standing near the table just mentioned, and seeming to look with attention on the book which was lying open on it. Now, the living and breathing man was by her side apparently asleep, and, greatly as she was surprised and affected, she had sufficient command of herself to remain without moving, lest she should expose him to the terror which she herself at the moment experienced. After gazing on the apparition for a few seconds, she bent her eyes upon her husband to ascertain if his looks were turned in the direction of the window, but his eyes were closed. She turned round again, although now dreading the sight of what she believed to be her husband's fetch, but it was no longer there. She remained sleepless throughout the remainder of the night, but still bravely refrained from disturbing her partner.

"Next morning, Mr. B., seeing signs of disquiet on his wife's countenance while at breakfast, made some affectionate inquiries, but she concealed her trouble, and at his ordinary hour he sallied forth to make his calls. Meeting Dr. C., in the street, and falling into conversation with him, he asked his opinion on the subject of fetches. 'I think,' was the answer, 'and so I am sure do you, that they are mere illusions produced by a disturbed stomach acting upon the excited brain of a highly imaginative or superstitious person.' 'Then,' said Mr. B., 'I am highly imaginative or superstitious, for I distinctly saw my own outward man last night standing at the table in the bedroom, and clearly distinguishable in the moonlight. I am afraid my wife saw it too, but I have been afraid to speak to her on the subject.'

"About the same hour on the ensuing night the poor lady was again roused, but by a more painful circumstance. She felt her husband moving convulsively, and immediately afterwards he cried to her in low, interrupted accents, 'Ellen, my dear, I am suffocating; send for Dr. C.' She sprang up, huddled on some clothes, and ran to his house. He came with all speed, but his efforts for his friend were useless. He had burst a large blood-vessel in the lungs, and was soon beyond human aid. In her lamentations the bereaved wife frequently cried out, 'Oh! the fetch, the fetch!' and at a later period told the doctor of the appearance the night before her husband's death."

Sources:

Kennedy, Patrick. *Legendary Fictions of the Irish Celt.* 1866. Reprint, Detroit: Singing Tree Press, 1968.

Fetishism

A term formerly used to discuss various aspects of African religions, especially the use of objects believed to be inhabited by spirit beings. It was a term that grew out of an inadequate understanding of traditional African religious faith and was abandoned in the late twentieth century.

Sources:

Durkheim, Emile. *The Elementary Forms of the Religious Life.* New York: Collier, 1961.

Fey

A term with various meanings: cowardly, doomed, or gifted with **second sight.** The most common definition is possessing second sight, in which sense the term is more widely used in Scotland. The word seems to mean "fated" (i.e., possessing some special occult destiny), which indicates either the doom of early death or the faculty of second sight.

Fiction, English Occult

The literary form of English-language occult fiction emerged from the folklore of supernatural beings and heroic events and was made possible by the secular understanding of the ancient mythology of gods, devils, and heroes. During the Elizabethan Age, penny balladsheets and prose chapbooks told of sorcerers, ghosts, monsters, and warning signs in the heavens against the sins of the day. A favorite story was that of the sorcerer Dr. Faustus and his pact with the devil. The great **witchcraft** persecutions from the Middle Ages on provided archetypal themes of terror, wonder, and the eternal play of good and evil.

Themes of magic and enchantment from earlier Arthurian legends were developed in Malory's *Morte d'Arthur.* There were also magic elements in some of Chaucer's stories: "The Franklin's Tale," "The Squire's Tale," and "The Wife of Bath's Tale." Dragons and enchantment occur in Spenser's *Faerie Queene.* Supernatural elements were common in drama from Elizabethan times on, as amply illustrated by the ghost in *Hamlet,* the witches in *Macbeth,* and Marlowe's *Tragicall History of Dr. Faustus.*

Early collections of ghost stories include Ludwig Lavater's *De Spectris* (1570), translated in 1572 as *Of Ghostes and Spirites Walking by Nyght and of Strange Noyses, Crackes, and Sundry Forewarnynges* and Thomas Nashe's *The Terrors of the Night, or, a Discourse of Apparitions* (1594). An influential work was Joseph Glanvil's *Saducismus Triumphatus, or, Full and Plain Evidence Concerning Witches and Apparitions* (1681), which includes the famous **poltergeist** story of the **Drummer of Tedworth.**

It was in the eighteenth century that occult fiction came into its own in the creation of the Gothic novel genre. Horace Walpole's *The Castle of Otranto,* first published in 1764, was subtitled "A Gothic Story." Walpole was obsessed with the Gothic. In 1747 he leased the Strawberry Hill estate near Twickenham, where he spent a decade building what he called "a little Gothic castle." He lived in a dream world of revival Gothic architecture and mock medievalism. Other country gentlemen followed Walpole in remodeling their estates with mock castles, follies, and grottoes. Some even employed old men to live as hermits in artificially constructed caverns—a kind of Gothic Disneyland.

Walpole's novel launched a thousand imitations and variations. After *Otranto* came Clara Reeve's *The Old English Baron: A Gothic Story* in 1778, Ann Radcliffe's *The Mysteries of Udolpho* (1794), and Matthew Gregory Lewis's successful sensation *The Monk* (1794). Such "horrid mysteries" became the mainstay of the rapidly developing circulating libraries that were replacing the old-time ballad and chapbook peddlers in every large town and city in England.

Stock ingredients of the Gothic novel were such plot elements as pure young virgins and chivalrous heroes embroiled with scoundrels of Continental origin (usually Italians), base monks, cruel Inquisitors, and ruthless bandits. They struggled in a fantasy medieval world of gloomy castles, ruined abbeys, dismal dungeons, bloodstained daggers, skulls, sliding panels, secret rooms, magic books, and animated portraits, all in a twilight setting of dark forests, pale moonlight, and nameless terrors lurking behind rocks. Walpole wrote *Otranto* as a reaction against realism in literature. He initiated a literary form of fantasy fiction, combining mystery, romance, supernaturalism, and sentimentality in a setting of mock medievalism.

The success of the Gothic novel among the upper and middle classes in England soon led to their merchandising at a more popular level, in abridged and pirated versions in cheap paper-covered pamphlets. These forerunners of today's paperback books sold at sixpence or a shilling each and were known as "bluebooks" (from the blue paper covers) or "shilling shockers."

Shilling shockers went out of fashion around the opening of the nineteenth century, largely through sheer exhaustion of their stereotyped characters and plots. Meanwhile the Gothic impulse had also passed into serious literature in the romantic movement, which in Britain included poets like Shelley, Byron,

Wordsworth, and **Coleridge** and novelists like Sir Walter Scott. For example, in Scott's *The Monastery*, a mysterious sylph rises from a fountain; astrology is introduced into *Guy Mannering, The Fortunes of Nigel* and *Quentin Durward;* a ghost story is told in *Redgauntlet;* and ghosts figure in *Woodstock.* In *The Bride of Lammermoor,* Scott deals with the Scottish belief in prophecy, and in *Waverley* a Highland chief is awestruck by a peculiar omen.

Perhaps the most influential expression of the Gothic impulse in English literature was formed at that strange opium-soaked literary house party of Shelley, Byron, Mary Wollstonecraft (later Shelley's wife), Claire Clairmont (Mary's stepsister), and J. W. Polidori, at the Villa Diodati, Geneva, in the summer of 1816. Byron had been reading a book of ghost stories by Jean Baptiste Eyriès titled **Fantasmagoriana** (1812) and proposed, "We will each write a ghost story." Byron himself drafted a fragment that Polidori later expanded into *The Vampyre*; Polidori produced a trifle about a skull-headed lady who was punished for peeping through a keyhole, but Wollstonecraft began her masterpiece published in 1818 as *Frankenstein or the Modern Prometheus.* **Frankenstein** relied less upon Gothic ruins than emotions of wonder and terror generated by the mysterious powers of nature and science, and so led the Gothic novel into a science-fiction genre. Meanwhile folklore themes of monsters and vampires became new stereotypes of the Gothic impulse. In the twentieth century these gave birth to hundreds of horror stories and sensationalist movies.

Another offshoot of the Gothic imagination during the nineteenth century was the mystery novel of such writers as Wilkie Collins. In *The Woman in White* (1860) and *The Moonstone* (1868), a Gothic architectural setting was metamorphosed into a Gothic *atmosphere* of strange hidden mysteries, motives, crime, and sensational suspense. Out of this was born the romance of large country mansions, culminating at the end of the nineteenth century in such Gothic novels as Daphne du Maurier's *Rebecca.* The country house detective thriller of writers like Agatha Christie also has roots in the Gothic story as developed by writers like Wilkie Collins and Edgar Allan Poe.

In "The Fall of the House of Usher," "The Pit and the Pendulum," and "Premature Burial," all published in the 1840s, Poe reverted to a classic Gothic format expressed in the short story rather than the full-length novel.

Three Irish writers made a notable contribution to the Gothic novel with supernatural elements: Charles Robert Maturin (1782–1824), Joseph Sheridan Le Fanu (1814–1873), and **Bram Stoker** (1847–1912). In Maturin's novel *Melmoth the Wanderer* (1820) there is strong emphasis on episodes of terror, but the complex plot structure hinges upon the classic theme of a pact with the devil. Le Fanu wrote several short stories on supernatural themes, "Green Tea" being one of the most outstanding, but his Gothic masterpiece was undoubtedly the longer story "Carmilla," in which he developed the vampire theme. It is a brilliantly atmospheric story of a female vampire, with a strong suggestion of lesbian love, set in a dreamlike landscape in an old castle in Styria, a region in Austria. "Carmilla," first published in 1871, was read by another Irishman, Bram Stoker, when he was a young part-time drama critic in Dublin. It was to stay in his mind for 25 years before he wove the vampire theme into his own masterpiece, *Dracula,* first published 1897. Stoker's novel has since had a lasting influence on stories, plays, and movies all over the world.

Other nineteenth-century British writers of notable occult fiction include James Hogg (1770–1835), Frederick Marryat (1792–1848), **Bulwer Lytton** (1803–1873), **Charles Dickens** (1812–1870), William Morris (1836–1896), and Robert Louis Stevenson (1850–1894). Hogg, known as "the Ettrick Shepherd," was a peasant poet and protégé of Sir Walter Scott. Hogg's *The Private Memoirs and Confessions of a Justified Sinner* (1824) is a strange and powerful story of diabolical split personality. Frederick Marryat's *Snarleyyow, or the Dog Fiend* (1836) contains an episode dealing with a werewolf, often reprinted as a self-contained story; *The Phantom Ship* (1839) is based on the **Flying Dutchman** legend.

Lytton published some classic supernatural stories, including the thrilling "The Haunted and the Haunters" (1859), originally titled "The House and the Brain." His book *Zanoni* (1842) is concerned with a secret occult society; *The Coming Race* (1871) portrays an underground race.

Dickens wrote a number of short stories on supernatural themes, such as "A Child's Dream of a Star" (1850), "The Haunted House" (1849), "No. 1 Branch Line: The Signalman" (1866), *Nurse's Stories* (1860), and of course the immortal "A Christmas Carol" (1843).

Morris, a founder of the pre-Raphaelite art movement, translated Scandinavian sagas and also published such fantasy stories as "The Wood Beyond the World" (1894), "The Well at the World's End" (1896), and "The Water of the Wondrous Isles" (1897).

Stevenson, a brilliant stylist, published some excellent stories of the supernatural, including the renowned "The Strange Case of Dr. Jekyll and Mr. Hyde" (1888). Less well known but equally brilliant are his short stories "Thrawn Janet," "Will o' the Mill," and "Markheim." In the latter story, Stevenson touches a deeper metaphysical note.

The popular novelist H. Rider Haggard (1856–1925) was celebrated for his great adventure stories like *King Solomon's Mines,* but there are themes of fantasy and reincarnation in his stories *She* (1886) and *Ayesha* (1905).

Another great nineteenth-century writer was the playwright Oscar Wilde (1854–1900), who also wrote a whimsical ghost story, *The Canterville Ghost* (1887), and the terrifying Gothic story *The Picture of Dorian Gray* (1890).

The ghost short story flourished during the nineteenth century, encouraged by numerous magazines and Christmas supplements. The journal *All the Year Round,* founded by Dickens, published a number of stories of the supernatural.

At a more popular level, writers like G. W. M. Reynolds (with *Wagner, the Wehr-Wolf* and *The Necromancer*) and Thomas Preskett Prest (with *Varney the Vampire, or The Feast of Blood*) had replaced the old sentimental Gothic romances with extravagantly written full-length shockers.

Other writers of the period included Mrs. J. H. Riddell (with *Weird Stories,* 1884, and *The Banshee's Warning,* 1894), and Margaret Oliphant (*A Beleagered City,* 1880, and *Stories of the Seen and Unseen,* 1889). On a lighter note, F. Anstey (1856–1934) created his own characteristic genre of humorous fantasy with *Vice-Versa* (1882), *The Tinted Venus* (1885), and *The Brass Bottle* (1900). Another innovative writer was E. Nesbit (1858–1924) with her fairy-tale fantasies for children: *The Phoenix and the Carpet* (1904) and *The Enchanted Castle* (1908). She also published three adult fantasy collections: *Something Wrong* (1893), *Grim Tales* (1893), and *Fear* (1910).

American Gothic

American writers who made important contributions to the English language supernatural story include Washington Irving (1783–1859), F. Marion Crawford (1854–1909), Ambrose Bierce (1842–ca. 1914), Henry James (1843–1916), and Lafcadio Hearn (1850–1904).

Irving was persuaded by his friend Sir Walter Scott to publish *The Sketch Book of Geoffrey Crayon, Gent.* (1819–20), which included "Rip Van Winkle" and "The Legend of Sleepy Hollow." Other favorite Irving tales include "The Spectre Bridegroom" (1819) and "The Devil and Tom Walker" (1824).

Crawford was justly celebrated for his uncanny and horrific short stories such as "The Upper Berth," "For the Blood Is the Life," and "The Screaming Skull" from the late nineteenth century, collected posthumously in *Wandering Ghosts* (1911). His first novel, *Mr. Isaacs* (1882), was based upon a real-life wonder worker in India; *The Witch of Prague* (1891) was concerned with the misuse of hypnotism.

Bierce was famous for his psychological explorations in short story format: "The Death of Halpin Frayser," "The Realm of the Unreal," and "The Middle Toe of the Right Foot." His collections include *Can Such Things Be?* (1893) and *In the Midst of Life* (1898).

The great novelist Henry James wrote a classic ghost story in *The Turn of the Screw* (1898). A posthumously published collection is *The Ghostly Tales of Henry James* (1948).

Hearn published several strange and macabre stories, many of which were collected in *Fantastics* (1914).

Into the Twentieth Century

Writers who bridged the nineteenth and early twentieth centuries included **Sir Arthur Conan Doyle** (1859–1930), Rudyard Kipling (1865–1936), H. G. Wells (1866–1946), and May Sinclair (1865?–1946).

Many of Conan Doyle's earliest short stories had supernatural themes before he turned his attention to the deductive logic of the great Sherlock Holmes. But after World War I, Conan Doyle became a champion of Spiritualism and his novel *The Land of Mist* (1925) fictionalizes an investigation into the subject. An early novel *The Parasite* (1894), deals with a psychic vampire. Some of Doyle's short stories on occult themes were collected in *Tales of Twilight and the Unseen* and included in *The Conan Doyle Stories* (1929).

Kipling wrote several impressive short stories of the eerie and supernatural, including "The Mark of the Beast" (1890), "The House Surgeon" (1909), "The Brushwood Boy" (1898), and "They" (1904). These are contained in his various collections.

Wells was a prolific writer of short stories, many of which were on occult and fantasy themes, including "The Red Room," "A Moth," "The Apple," "Under the Knife," "Skelmersdale in Fairyland," "The Door in the Wall," and "A Dream of Armageddon." These are contained in such collections as *The Stolen Bacillus* (1895), *The Red Room* (1896), *The Plattner Story and Others* (1897), and *Thirty Strange Stories* (1897). Six early collections were reissued in one volume as *Famous Short Stories of H. G. Wells* in 1938.

Sinclair began writing novels in 1895 and later became interested in Spiritualism. A collection of her short stories on occult themes, *Uncanny Stories* (1923), contains "Where Their Fire is Not Quenched," a brilliant evocation of the afterlife.

Among minor writers of occult fiction from the nineteenth to twentieth centuries, Richard Middleton (1882–1911) was responsible for the humorous story "The Ghost Ship" (1912) and the more serious "On the Brighton Road" in the same volume. W. W. Jacobs (1863–1943), famous for his humorous "Night Watchman" stories, also wrote the classic story "The Monkey's Paw," which was dramatized. M. P. Shiel (1865–1947) wrote horror and fantasy tales, including *Prince Zaleski* (1895), *Shapes in the Fire* (1896), and the posthumously published collections *Best Short Stories of M. P. Shiel* (1948) and *Xelucha and Others* (1975).

Twentieth-Century Fiction

Important writers of occult stories during the twentieth century include M. R. James (1862–1936), Arthur Machen (1863–1947), **E. F. Benson** (1867–1940), **Algernon Blackwood** (1869–1951), Walter de la Mare (1873–1956), Lord Dunsany (1878–1957), and Charles Williams (1886–1945).

The scholarly M. R. James, provost of Eton, wrote ghost stories for the amusement of his friends. The stories were later published in the collections *Ghost Stories of an Antiquary* (1904), *More Ghost Stories of an Antiquary* (1911), *A Thin Ghost* (1919), and *A Warning to the Curious* (1925). These classics of the genre are some of the most powerful and disturbing ghost stories in the English language. A later volume, *The Collected Ghost Stories* (1931), includes most of them.

The stories of Arthur Machen are haunted by fear of natural forces and the horror of evil from an ancient world. One of his best stories is "The Terror" (1917), in which the world of nature rebels against man's destructiveness in war, but his many shorter stories of horror and the supernatural are also masterpieces. These include "The Great God Pan," "The White People," and "The Shining Pyramid." These were reprinted in the collection *Tales of Horror and the Supernatural* (1949).

Benson is justly regarded as a master of the supernatural short story. "The Room in the Tower" and "Mrs. Amworth" are classic vampire stories; other well-written horror tales include "Caterpillars," "Negotium Perambulans," and "And No Bird Sings." These were published in the collections *The Room in the Tower* (1912), *Visible and Invisible* (1923), *Spook Stories* (1928), and *More Spook Stories* (1934). A representative selection was published as *The Horror Horn* (1974).

Blackwood specialized in occult fiction that drew upon his own psychic sensitivity. *John Silence* (1908) is based on the casebook of an occult detective. Some of Blackwood's best stories are "The Wendigo" (about a demon of lonely places), "Ancient Sorceries" (about cats and their witches), "The Man Whom the Trees Loved" (about the absorption of a man into nature), and "The Transfer" (on psychic vampirism), but he also wrote many other stories with psychic and ghostly themes. These are included in such collections as *Tongues of Fire* (1924), *The Lost Valley* (1910), *Pan's Garden* (1912), *Incredible Adventures* (1914), and *Day and Night Stories* (1917). His own selection, *Strange Stories* was published 1929, but a later comprehensive collection is *Tales of Terror and Darkness* (1977).

De la Mare was a famous poet of great sensitivity who also published several beautifully written short stories of the supernatural, including "All Hallows," "The Recluse," and "The Looking-Glass." Collections of his short stories include: *The Riddle* (1923) and *On the Edge* (1930). A later collection is *Ghost Stories* (1956).

Williams was a sensitive writer of fantasy stories. "War in Heaven" (1930) and "The Place of the Lion" (1931) deal with demonic themes. Other stories include "Descent Into Hell" (1937), "Witchcraft" (1941), and "All Hallow's Eve" (1945).

The Irish writer Lord Dunsany was an acclaimed master of fantasy fiction. His books include *Time and the Gods* (1906), *The Sword of Welleran* (1908), *A Dreamer's Tales* (1910), *The Book of Wonder* (1912), *The Last Book of Wonder* (1916), *The King of Elfland's Daughter* (1924), and *The Blessing of Pan* (1927).

Another creator of fantasy worlds was J. R. R. Tolkien (1892–1973) with his famous *The Lord of the Rings* trilogy: *The Fellowship of the Ring* (1954), *The Two Towers* (1955), and *The Return of the King* (1955). These books involve a fictitious mythology reminiscent of Arthurian romance and generated a worldwide cult following.

There is a strong element of fantasy mythology in some of the short stories of the American writer **H. P. Lovecraft** (1890–1937), who appears to have been strongly influenced by Machen and Lord Dunsany. Lovecraft's style is uneven and mannered, but his stories of ancient evil, monsters, and horror have secured a cult following. Many of his stories were originally published in magazines like *Weird Tales;* others were collected and published posthumously through the initiative of fantasy writer August Derleth. Representative collections are *The Dunwich Horror and Others* (1963) and *Dagon and Other Macabre Tales* (1965).

One important British writer of fantasy and horror fiction much neglected in his lifetime was William Hope Hodgson (1877–1918). His terrifying short stories of the sea include "From the Tideless Sea" (1906), "The Thing in the Weeds" (1912) and "The Voice in the Night" (1907). These are included in the collection *Men of the Deep Waters* (1914). His full-length stories *The House on the Borderland* (1908) and *The Night Land* (1912) are full of terrifying fantasy.

L. P. Hartley (1895–1972) was an established novelist who also wrote some macabre supernatural short stories, notably "A Visitor From Down Under" (1927). His first collection was *Night Fears* (1924); his *Collected Short Stories* was published in 1968.

Another great writer of ghostly short stories was Oliver Onions (1873–1961); his best-known story is "The Beckoning Fair One." Collections of his stories include *Widdershins* (1911) and *Ghosts in Daylight* (1924); there is also a *Collected Ghost Stories* (1935).

Practicing occultists who have also written fiction include **Violet M. Firth** (best known under her public name, Dion Fortune; 1890–1946) and the famous **Aleister Crowley** (1875–1947). Fortune was a member of the Hermetic Order of the **Golden**

Dawn occult society and also founded her own **Fraternity of the Inner Light.** She fictionalized some of her own psychic experiences in *The Secrets of Dr. Tavener* (1926). Her other occult fiction includes *The Demon Lover* (1927), *The Winged Bull* (1935), *The Goat-Foot God* (1936), *The Sea Priestess* (1938), and *Moon Magic* (1956).

Crowley, the most outstanding magician of the twentieth century, was also a member of the Golden Dawn before he founded his own society, the **A∴A∴**, and became the Outer Head of the **Ordo Templi Orientis** (OTO). In addition to his treatises on the practice of occultism, Crowley published two volumes of occult fiction: *Moonchild* (1929) and *The Stratagem* (1929). These were inferior to some of his other prose and his brilliant poetry.

One of the most prolific writers on the subject of black magic and occultism was **Dennis Wheatley** (1897–1977). His most popular books were *The Devil Rides Out* (1935), *Strange Conflict* (1941), *To the Devil a Daughter* (1953), *The Satanist* (1960), and *They Used Dark Forces* (1964). As well as these and other novels on occult themes, he edited the *Dennis Wheatley Library of the Occult,* a series of reprints of significant occult books by other writers.

Although the demise of many short story magazines during the period following World War II restricted the market for short stories on occult subjects, the popularity of the horror movie generated a new outlet.

Richard Matheson published many macabre short stories before becoming a prominent scriptwriter of horror films. Some of his most well-known stories include *I Am Legend* (1954), about vampires, and *A Stir of Echoes* (1958), dealing with psychic invasion of the mind. As a movie scriptwriter, Matheson adapted some of the works of Edgar Allen Poe, such as the story "The Pit and the Pendulum" and the poem "The Raven," as well as also his own novel *Hell House* (1971).

Robert Bloch, who wrote *Psycho* (1959), filmed by Alfred Hitchcock, also published many novels on occult themes, as well as scripting his own radio and movie stories. His film credits include *The House That Dripped Blood* (1970) and *Asylum* (1972).

The explosion of mass interest in occultism during the 1960s and 1970s slackened during the 1980s, perhaps through literary overkill of a basically elusive phenomenon, but has generated a romantic popular interest in fictional occultism, reflected in blockbuster novels of the occult adapted into movies. Typical of this trend are Ira Levin's sensational witchcraft stories **Rosemary's Baby** (1967) and *The Stepford Wives* (1972), which became successful movies.

Stephen King became the leading novelist of horror and the occult in America by the end of the 1970s. Beginning with *Carrie* (1974) about a teenager with paranormal powers, *Salem's Lot* (1975), a vampire story, and *The Shining* (1977), about an evil entity in a deserted hotel, King has produced a shelf of worldwide best-sellers, many of which have been made into movies.

Meanwhile, the **Dracula** theme has continued to proliferate all over the world in scores of books and movies. All this is a long way from the leisured sentimental Gothic tales of the eighteenth century and the cultured *frisson* of the Victorian and Edwardian ghost story. If the fantasy has become more imaginative, merging with the newer genre of science fiction, the thrills of the movie horror film have become more sensational. The vampire theme is the most successful single subgenre of contemporary Gothic fiction, with more than 650 vampire movies having been made during the twentieth century. As of 1994 more than 50 new vampire novels were being published annually.

Sources:

Ashley, Mike. *Who's Who in Horror and Fantasy Fiction.* London: Elm Tree Books, 1977.

Barclay, Glen St. John. *Anatomy of Horror: The Masters of Occult Fiction.* London: Weidenfeld & Nicolson, 1978.

Birkhead, Edith. *The Tale of Terror: A Study of the Gothic Romance.* London: Constable, 1921.

McNutt, Dan J. *The Eighteenth-Century Gothic Novel: An Annotated Bibliography of Criticism and Selected Texts.* New York: Garland Publishing, 1975.

Messent, Peter B., ed. *Literature of the Occult.* Englewood Cliffs, N.J.: Prentice-Hall, 1971.

Scarborough, Dorothy. *The Supernatural in Modern English Fiction.* New York: G. P. Putnam's Sons, 1917.

Sieger, James R. *Ghost Stories Index.* Denver: Opar Press, 1973.

Siemon, Fred. *Ghost Story Index: An Author-Title Index to More than 2,200 Stories of Ghosts, Horrors, and the Macabre Appearing in 190 Books and Anthologies.* San Jose, Calif.: Library Research Associates, 1967.

Sullivan, Jack, ed. *The Penguin Encyclopedia of Horror and the Supernatural.* New York: Viking Press, 1986.

Summers, Montague. *A Gothic Bibliography.* London: Fortune Press, 1940.

———. *The Gothic Quest: A History of the Gothic Novel.* London: Fortune Press, 1938.

Watt, William W. *Shilling Shockers of the Gothic School: A Study of Chapbook Gothic Romances.* Cambridge: Harvard University Press, 1932.

Fields Within Fields (Journal)

Former quarterly journal for "ongoing creative thinking about solutions to mankind's problems from the viewpoint of the human being as a complex of intellectual, material and spiritual resources in interplay of multiple systems."

Fifth Epochal Fellowship

The Fifth Epochal Fellowship continues the work of the **URANTIA Brotherhood.** It was originally founded in 1955 by students of *The URANTIA Book,* a large volume of channeled material published that same year. The brotherhood operated for many years as an association to nurture people who had been attracted to the Urantia teachings, and several of its members had published helpful study tools. However, in 1989, the brotherhood had a disagreement with the URANTIA Foundation, which owned the trademarks of the name URANTIA and the publishing rights to *The URANTIA Book.* The foundation withdrew the right of the brotherhood to use the name or the symbols associated with the book. The brotherhood reorganized, changing its name to the Fifth Epochal Fellowship, and continued much as before. The fellowship publishes a newsletter, the *Fifth Epochal Fellowship Bulletin,* and may be contacted at 529 Wrightwood Ave., Chicago, IL 60614.

Sources:

Bedell, Clyde. *Concordex to the URANTIA Book.* Leguna Hills, Calif.: The Author, 1980.

Faw, Duane L., comp. *The Paramony.* Malibu, Calif.: The Author, 1986.

The URANTIA Book. Chicago: URANTIA Foundation, 1955.

Figuier, Louis (Guillaume) (1819–1894)

French chemist and writer on occult subjects. He was born at Montpellier, France, where his uncle Pierre Figuier was professor of chemistry at the School of Pharmacy. Louis, having taken his doctorate in medicine and having completed his postgraduate study in chemistry at the laboratory of Balard in Paris, was made professor of chemistry at the same school in his hometown. In 1853 he exchanged this post for a similar one in the School of Pharmacy of Paris. Many honorary degrees in science and medicine were conferred upon him by various faculties during his career.

In 1857 he left teaching and devoted himself to writing, specializing in the popularizing of science, mainly physiology and medical chemistry. He published many notable works and was equally distinguished for his prodigious output and literary quality. Those works having a bearing on occult matters include *Le Lendemain de la mort, ou La Vie future selon la science* (1872, dealing with the transmigration of souls), *L' Alchimie et les Alchimistes* (1854), *Histoire du merveilleux dans les temps modernes* (1859–60), and *Les Bonheurs d' outre tombe* (1892). In 1889 he published a volume of dramas and comedies, *La Science au Théatre.*

Figuier's four-volume *Histoire du merveilleux* was a well-documented study of the Jansenist *convulsionaires,* the religious revival of the Cevennes, the divining rod, **animal magnetism,** table turning, mediums, and spirits. He died in Paris in 1894.

Sources:

Figuier, Louis. *The Day After Death, or, Our Future Life, According to Science.* London: R. Bentley, 1874.

Fillmore, Charles Sherlock (1854–1948)

Charles S. Fillmore, cofounder of the Unity School of Christianity, the largest of the **New Thought** metaphysical groups in North America, was born August 22, 1854, in St. Cloud, Minnesota. He had little formal schooling in his childhood years and was largely self-educated. Reading widely during his youth, he was fascinated by the few books he could find on **Spiritualism,** Eastern religions, and the **occult.** He moved about the West during his young adult years and eventually settled in Colorado in 1881, where he went into business with the brother-in-law of Nona Brooks, an early Divine Science leader in the state. While there, he married Mary Caroline Page, who, as **Myrtle Fillmore,** would work as Charles's partner in the development of the Unity School.

In 1884 the Fillmores moved to Kansas City. Two years later, E. B. Weeks, the student and representative of an independent Christian Science college in Chicago, came to Kansas City to lecture. Myrtle Fillmore attended the lectures and, taking their teachings to heart, was over the next year healed of the tuberculosis that had hobbled her young life. She gradually convinced Charles of the truth of the teachings, and thereafter Charles became an enthusiastic supporter of Christian Science. He began a magazine, *Modern Thought,* which went through several name changes over the next few years. It survives today as *Unity.*

In the meantime, the Fillmores became aware of the work of **Emma Curtis Hopkins** and gradually became convinced that she was the best of the many Christian Science and mind cure lecturers they had heard. They traveled to Chicago to study with her and in 1891 were ordained by her. Their magazine, which had been open to all of the varied interests of Charles, finally focused on the healing principles as taught by Hopkins. As suggested by Myrtle, Charles began the Society of Silent Help to tie together the readers of the magazine who could not travel to Kansas City. In 1891, while in Chicago, the two also decided upon a name for their work, Unity, and soon all of their activities were combined under that heading. The growth of the work allowed the launching in 1909 of a second magazine, *Weekly Unity,* as well as Charles's first book, *Christian Healing,* written from the notes of his healing classes in Kansas City.

By the end of World War I, Unity had become a large movement with a national following. A vegetarian restaurant opened, and Fillmore became one of the early radio preachers, beginning broadcasts in WOQ in 1922. In 1924 Unity purchased its own radio station. That same year Fillmore began one of the most important Unity projects, *Unity Daily Word,* now *Daily Word,* a day-by-day devotional booklet and the organization's most popular publication over the years.

During the 1930s Fillmore wrote a number of the books for which he is widely remembered today. They include *The Twelve Powers of Man* (1930), which explores some of humanity's psychic potentials; *Metaphysical Bible Dictionary* (1931), a guide to metaphysical Bible interpretation; *Prosperity* (1934), the Fillmores' answer to the Depression; and *Jesus Christ Heals* (1931). In 1933 Myrtle died, and Charles married Cora G. Dedrick. He retired from the pulpit of Unity Church and began a period of lecturing and traveling until his death on July 5, 1948, at the age of 93.

Sources:

D'Andrade, Hugh. *Charles Fillmore: Herald of the New Age.* New York: Harper & Row, 1974.

Fillmore, Charles S. *Christian Healing: Science of Being.* Kansas City, Mo.: Unity School of Christianity, 1909.

———. *Jesus Christ Heals.* Kansas City, Mo.: Unity School of Christianity, 1931.

———. *Metaphysical Bible Dictionary.* Kansas City, Mo.: Unity School of Christianity, 1931.

———. *Prosperity.* Kansas City, Mo.: Unity School of Christianity, 1936.

———. *The Twelve Powers of Man.* Lee's Summit, Mo.: Unity School of Christianity, 1930, 1955.

Fillmore, Mary Caroline "Myrtle" Page (1845–1931)

Myrtle Fillmore, cofounder of the Unity School of Christianity, was born Mary Caroline Page on August 6, 1845, in Pagetown, Ohio. She was raised in a devout Methodist family and given the best education available for females in her day. She attended Oberlin College and upon graduation moved to Clinton, Missouri, to become a schoolteacher.

In the 1870s she moved to Dennison, Texas, where she met her future husband, **Charles Fillmore.** They were married in 1881 and settled in Colorado, where Charles had previously moved. They moved to Kansas City in 1884, but Myrtle's life entered a downward spiral. She had tuberculosis, at the time an incurable wasting disease. However, in 1886 she attended some lectures given by an independent Christian Science teacher, E. B. Weeks of Chicago. Charles attended reluctantly, but Myrtle's life was changed by what she heard. She began to apply the teachings and over the next year was cured of her illness. Her recovery captured Charles's imagination and enthusiasm. While Myrtle was sharing with others the teachings to which she attributed her healing, Charles was studying. In 1889 he began a magazine that presented Christian Science in the context of his various interests in the **occult** and Eastern religions.

Soon after founding the magazine, Myrtle and Charles met **Emma Curtis Hopkins,** the independent Christian Science teacher, and became her students. Under her tutelage, they focused their work in healing. In 1891 they were ordained by Hopkins and decided to organize their work under the general name Unity. By this time the Fillmores had three children, Lowell (1882), Rickert (1884), and Royal (1889). Myrtle founded the Unity Sunday School and in 1893 launched and for over thirty years edited *Wee Wisdom,* a children's magazine published for almost a century by the movement. She took the lead in the formation of the Society of Silent Help, today known as Silent Unity, the movement's prayer ministry. In 1903 she cofounded with Charles the Unity School of Christianity, the central organization of the movement. She lived to celebrate her fiftieth wedding anniversary and passed away on October 3, 1931.

Sources:

Fillmore, Myrtle. *How to Let God Help You.* Lee's Summit, Mo.: Unity School of Christianity, 1956.

———. *The Letters of Myrtle Fillmore.* Kansas City, Mo.: Unity School of Christianity, 1936.

Witherspoon, Thomas E. *Myrtle Fillmore, Mother of Unity.* Unity Village, Mo.: Unity Books, 1977.

FIND See **Friends in New Directions**

Findhorn Community

Early New Age center in northern Scotland. The New Age movement began with the linking (networking) of a number of theosophical/metaphysical centers across the United Kingdom in the 1960s. All of these communities were in sympathy with the theosophical ancient wisdom tradition but were also involved in channeling, either channeling spiritual energy to the world or channeling messages from various spiritual entities, or both. Eileen and Peter Caddy and a friend, Dorothy McLean, had settled at a small trailer court near the village of Findhorn outside Inverness, Scotland, during a period of financial lack. Through 1963 and 1964 they survived in part by gardening. During this period Eileen Caddy regularly channeled messages from what were believed to be nature spirits, or **devas,** and when their advice was followed the garden blossomed abundantly.

In 1965 Peter Caddy attended a meeting of other spiritual group leaders organized by **George Trevelyan,** later the founder of the **Wrekin Trust.** The visit with Trevelyan became a catalyst for the formal organization of the Findhorn Community, which was to become an object of pilgrimage. Its fame was generated by the extraordinary results of the garden, which was producing growth out of season and spectacularly large vegetables, in spite of the harsh climate. The garden became the visible focus of the paranormal and miraculous claims that grew up around the small but growing community. Caddy's channeled messages were published in a small volume, *God Spoke to Me,* and McLean, who had begun to channel, also published her messages.

The Findhorn Trust was created in 1971 and the Findhorn Foundation incorporated in 1972. In the 1970s an American student of the Alice Bailey literature, David Spangler, joined the community and developed its education program. Spangler's 1976 book, *Revelation: the Birth of a New Age,* became the early manifesto of both Findhorn and the New Age movement. Drawing on channeled messages received by himself and others at Findhorn, he declared that a New Age was beginning. It was already evident in the vast scientific advances and technological improvements that so separated twentieth-century humanity from previous generations. According to Spangler, in the last half of the twentieth century, in part owing to astrological realignments, new cosmic spiritual energies were available that could bring humanity into contact with the masters of the **Great White Brotherhood** and initiate a new era of light and love, the New Age.

Spangler returned to the United States, as did McLean, and initiated the movement in North America. As the movement became known through the 1970s, Findhorn was seen as a major source of inspiration and a popular site to visit. The community grew to include around 250 resident members. In 1975 the nearby Clung Hotel was purchased to accommodate conferences and other activities. Peter Caddy moved to the United States in 1982, and although Eileen Caddy remained at Findhorn, leadership was increasingly passed to the community as a whole. Members have developed a diversified program of educational activities for the burgeoning New Age community and the general public. Peter Caddy died February 18, 1994.

Address: The Park, Forres, Moray IV36 0TZ Scotland.

Sources:

Caddy, Eileen. *The Dawn of Change.* Forres, Scotland: Findhorn Publications, 1979.

Findhorn Community. *Faces of Findhorn.* Forres, Scotland: Findhorn Publications, 1980.

Hawken, Pauul. *The Magic of Findhorn.* New York: Harper & Row, 1975.

Findlay, J. Arthur (1883–1964)

Prominent British Spiritualist who wrote extensively on finance, economics, and psychic subjects. He was a justice of the peace for the counties of Essex and Ayrshire and in 1913 received the Order of the British Empire for his organizational work for the Red Cross during the war. In 1920 he was a founder and vice president of the Glasgow Society for Psychical Research and took a leading part in the Church of Scotland's inquiry into psychic phenomena in 1923. He was chairman of *Psychic News,* a leading British Spiritualist periodical, and was well known as a speaker, lecturer, and researcher. For five years he made a special study of the **direct voice** phenomena of the medium John C. Sloan. His book *An Investigation of Psychic Phenomena* (1924), which was followed by *On the Edge of the Etheric* (1931) and *The Rock of Truth* (1933), explains how the direct voice is produced and discusses the subject and teachings obtained by this mediumship.

On the Edge of the Etheric ran into 30 printings within the first year of publication. Findlay argues for the claims of **Spiritualism** on the basis of the growing extension of physics. He proposes that the universe is a gigantic scale of vibrations of which the physical is in but a small range. As mind constitutes the highest range of vibrations, so individual consciousness consists of the interaction of mind vibrations with physical vibrations. When we discard our physical bodies, says Findlay, our minds interact with etheric vibrations through the **etheric double.** The book presents teachings based on data recorded at direct voice séances describing the etheric world, upon the philosophy of which Findlay's *The Rock of Truth* further enlarges. This book also contains a lucid review of the various world religions, including Christianity, and Findlay claims a common origin for all religious beliefs. He also argues for the development of Christianity out of the beliefs prevailing in countries adjoining Palestine during the first 300 years of the Christian era. Findlay's conclusion is that religious instinct originates in man's psychic structure.

Sources:

Findley, Arthur J. *The Curse of Ignorance.* 2 vols. London, 1947.

———. *An Investigation of Psychic Phenomena.* London, 1924.

———. *Looking Back: the Autobiography of a Spiritualist.* London: Psychic Press, 1955.

———. *On the Edge of the Etheric.* London: Psychic Press, 1931.

———. *The Psychic Stream.* London, 1939.

———. *The Rock of Truth, or Spiritualism, the Coming World Religion.* London: Rider, 1933.

———. *The Unfolding Universe.* London, 1935.

———. *The Way of Life* London, 1953.

Fingitas

The tradition concerning this legendary stone is remarkable. It is described as quite transparent and hard like marble. A certain king supposedly built a temple of it that needed no windows, the light being admitted into it as if it were open to the day.

Finias

One of the four great cities from which the Irish mythical **Danaans** were said to have sprung. The other cities were Falias, Gorias, and Murias. From Finias, the Danaans brought a magic spear.

Finn Mac Cummal

In ancient Irish romance, captain of the Fianna warrior band and the center of the Ossianic tales. His father, Cumhal, chief of the clan Basena, was slain at Castle Knock by the rival clan Morna, but his mother succeeded in saving him from the enemy. He was brought up in hiding and given the name of Finn from the clearness of his skin.

He learned science and poetry from the druid Finegas, who lived on the river Boyne. The druid had been unable to catch the salmon of knowledge until Finn became his pupil, and when he did succeed in catching it, he told Finn to watch it while it was cooking but not to partake of it. Finn, however, burned his fingers as he turned the spit and put one of them in his mouth. Seeing this, Finegas bade him eat the salmon and he became filled with the wisdom of all ages.

Afterward Finn took service with King Cormac, to whom he revealed his name and lineage. Cormac promised him the leadership of the Fianna if he succeeded in killing the fire-blowing demon that came yearly to set Tara in flames. Finn slew the demon and carried its head back to Tara. The Fianna were therefore ordered to swear allegiance to Finn as their captain.

Under Finn the Fianna rose to great eminence that at length became tyrannical, and they were defeated at the battle of Bowra.

Finn's death is shrouded in mystery. According to popular tradition he and his great companions lie sleeping in an enchanted cave and will arise in the hour of their country's need, like Arthur, Barbarossa, and Charlemagne.

Fioravanti, Leonardi (d. 1588)

Italian alchemist, doctor, and surgeon of the sixteenth century. Fioravanti was born in Bologna, studied medicine, and practiced in Palermo from 1548 to 1550. He traveled to Africa with the Spanish fleet, returning in 1555 and going on to Rome, Venice, and Bologna, where he was appointed a doctor and count. He published a number of books, the most well known being *Il compendio dei secreti di scienza rationali intorno alla medicina, cirugia et alchimia* (Summary of the Arcana of Medicine, Surgery, and Alchemy). Published in Venice in 1564, it was reprinted in many editions. This venture into **alchemy** included an application of the principles and methods of **hermetica** to medicine. Fioraranti's account of the *petra philosophorum* or **philosophers' stone** claimed its designation to be purely arbitrary. It was a mixture of mercury, potassium nitrate, and other ingredients intended as a stomachic and had no connection with the transmuting *lapis* of the alchemists, he said.

Fire Immunity

A most dramatic claimed paranormal manifestation, frequently witnessed in the course of history. An early instance recorded in the Bible is that of Meschach, Shadrach, and Abednego, who were thrown into Nebuchadnezzar's furnace:

"Lo, I see four men loose walking in the midst of the fire and they have no hurt. And the princes, governors and captains and the king's counsellors, being gathered together saw these men upon whose bodies the fire had no power, nor was a hair of their heads singed, neither were their coats changed, nor the smell of fire had passed them." (Dan. 3:25–27)

Fire Immunity and Religion

Immunity to fire has often been recorded as a religious miracle, especially as an element in the life of saints. St. Francis of Paula (1508), in whose arms Louis XI of France died, held red-hot cinders in his hands and said to the amazed spectators, "All creatures obey those who serve God with a perfect heart." According to the theologian St. Bonaventura, St. Francis was told that nothing could relieve the inflammation in his eyes but cauterization from the jawbone to the eyebrow. He addressed the flame in the brazier, "My brother Fire, the Most High hath created thee beyond all other creatures, mighty in thine enviable glory, fair and useful. Be thou clement unto me in this hour and courteous. I beseech the great Lord who created thee that he temper thy heat unto me, so that I may be able to bear thy gentle burning." He made the sign of the cross over the cauterizing iron and felt no pain whatever on its application.

St. Catherine of Siena fell into a trance with her face in the midst of burning coals on a hearth. When she was discovered and dragged away she was found unhurt. On another occasion, in church, a lit candle fell on her head while she was in a state of contemplation and was not extinguished until it was entirely consumed. She was not burned in the least.

The Camisard leader Claris, during the rise of the Huguenots against Louis XIV, in a state of possession and in the presence of 600 men, put himself on top of a pyre. The flames rose above his head. He continued to speak all the while and did not stop until the wood was consumed and there was no more flame. He was unhurt; there was no mark of fire on either his clothes or hair. One Colonel Cavalier, when in London in 1706, affirmed this as a fact; he was the leader of the troop that had surrounded the fire. Durand Page corroborated his statement. He had helped to fetch wood for the fire and did his best to comfort Claris's shrieking wife.

The **Convulsionnaires of St. Medard** exhibited similar phenomena. P. F. Mathieu states in his *Histoire des Miracles:*

"Marie Sonet, called the Salamander, on several occasions, in the presence of Carré de Montgeron and others, stretched herself on two chairs over a blazing fire, and remained there for half an hour or more at a time, neither herself nor her clothing being burnt. On another occasion, however, she thrust her booted feet into a burning brazier until the soles of both boots and stockings were reduced to a cinder, her feet remaining uninjured."

Bernadette Soubirous, the girl who had a vision of the Virgin Mary at **Lourdes,** was seen by a Dr. Dozous in prayer in the grotto. P. J. Boisserie, quoting Dozous in his book *Lourdes* (1891), notes:

"During her ecstasy, she put her hands together, and her fingers were loosely crossed above the flame of a taper which they enveloped in the cavity between the two hands. The taper burnt; the flame showed its point between the fingers and was blown about at the time by a rather strong current of air. But the flame did not seem to produce any alteration in the skin it touched. Astonished at this strange fact I did not allow anyone to put a stop to it, and taking out my watch I could observe it perfectly for a quarter of an hour. Her prayer ended, Bernadette rose, and prepared to leave the grotto. I kept her back for a moment and asked her to show me her hand, which I examined with the greatest care. I could not find the slightest trace of a burn anywhere. I then tried to place the flame of the taper beneath her hand without her observing it; but she drew her hand quickly back, exclaiming 'You burn me!'"

The **fire ordeal** of the Middle Ages to establish the innocence of a suspected person was performed, according to the famous jurist Sir William Blackstone, either by taking up in the hand unhurt a piece of red-hot iron of one, two, or three pounds weight, or else by walking barefoot and blindfolded over red-hot ploughshares laid lengthwise at unequal distances. If the party escaped being hurt he was judged innocent; if not he was condemned as guilty.

Fire ordeals as a kind of religious ceremony still took place as late as the 1920s. According to an article by Victor Forbin in the *Revue Aristote,* there was a demonstration of fire walking at Maritzburg, South Africa, in September 1929. Twelve tons of wood were burned in a ditch 14–15 meters long. Eight Hindus and four Englishmen walked through this bed of flames with bare feet. One of the Englishmen, two or three feet from the edge of the brazier, was seized with feebleness, fell on his knees, then recovered and finished the course. He fainted when he was beyond the ditch and was taken to the hospital where the doctors found the soles of his feet badly burned. When he regained consciousness he declared to reporters that his misfortune was because of the shouts of the public, which prevented him from concentrating on the Supreme Being (see also the contribution on the fire walk by Victor Forbin in the *Journal* of the Society for Psychical Research [SPR], vol. 26, p. 83.).

In 1935 the psychical researcher **Harry Price** arranged a scientific investigation of fire walking in Surrey, England, with the cooperation of **Kuda Bux,** a Moslem **fakir** from Kashmir. The tests were successful, but two other individuals who attempted the walk suffered blisters on their feet (see *Bulletin II* of the University of London Council for Psychical Investigation, 1936).

Psychic Immunity to Fire

Among mediums none was more famous for handling fire with impunity than **D. D. Home.** In the report of a subcommittee for the **London Dialectical Society** (1871), five witnesses stated that they had seen red-hot coals applied to the hands or heads of several persons by Home without producing pain or scorching.

A Mrs. Honeywood and the **Master of Lindsay,** the earl of Crawford, described how in a séance on March 17, 1869, Home placed a red-hot coal on his hostess's white muslin dress without harming it and how he held a spray of white flowers, taken from a vase on the table, in the fire of the grate. Smoke rose from the coals, but the flowers remained uninjured and their pure white color undimmed. In the same séance, intensely hot lampglass was easily handled by Honeywood and Lindsay while Home thrust the heated glass (which instantly ignited a match held to it) into his mouth. Lindsay later reported:

"Eight times I myself have held a red-hot coal in my hands without injury, when it scorched my face on raising my hand. Once, I wished to see if they really would burn, and I said so, and touched a coal with the middle finger of my right hand, and I got a blister as large as a sixpence; I instantly asked him [Home] to give me the coal, and I held the part that had burnt me, in the middle of my hand, for three or four minutes, without the least inconvenience."

On one occasion Home knelt down and held his face in the flames of a bright coal fire. **Lord Adare,** in *Experiences in Spiritualism with D. D. Home* (1869), thus describes the incident:

"Having apparently spoken to some spirit, he went back to the fire, and with his hand stirred the embers into a flame; then kneeling down, he placed his face right among the burning coals, moving it about as though bathing it in water. Then, getting up, he held his finger for some time in the flame of the candle."

Sir William Crookes witnessed Home handling fire on two or three occasions. In the *Proceedings* of the SPR (vol. 6) he reports his experience, also shared by Sir W. Huggins, former president of the Royal Society, as follows:

"Mr. Home then waved the handkerchief about in the air two or three times, held it above his head and then folded it up and laid it on his hand like a cushion; putting his other hand into the fire, took out a large lump of cinder, red-hot at the lower part, and placed the red-hot part on the handkerchief. Under ordinary circumstances it would have been in a blaze. In about half a minute, he took it off the handkerchief with his hand saying, "As the power is not strong, if we leave the coal longer it will burn." He then put it on his hand and brought it to the table in the front room where all but myself had remained seated."

On this occasion, with another piece of red-hot coal nearly as big as an orange, Home improvised a furnace in his hand by covering the coal with his left hand and blowing at it until it was nearly white-hot. "Then," continues Crookes, "he drew my attention to the lambent flame which was flickering over the coal and licking round his fingers; he fell on his knees, looked up in a reverent manner, held up the coal in front, and said, 'Is not God good? Are not his laws wonderful?'"

William Stainton Moses also saw Home's strange abilities with fire:

"He then went to the fireplace, removed the guard, and sat down on the hearth rug. Then he seemed to hold a conversation by signs with a spirit. He repeatedly bowed, and finally set to work to mesmerize his head again. He ruffled his bushy hair until it stood out like a mop, and then deliberately lay down and put his head in the bright wood fire. The hair was *in* the blaze, and must, under ordinary circumstances, have been singed off. His head was in the grate, and his neck on a level with the top-bar. This was repeated several times. He also put his hand into the fire, smoothed away the wood and coal and picked out a live coal which he held in his hand for a few seconds; but replaced soon, saying the power was not sufficient. He tried to give a hot coal to Mr. Crookes, but was unable to do it. He then came to all of us to satisfy us that there was no smell of fire on his hair. There was absolutely none."

F. W. H. Myers showed this account to Crookes, who declared that he was unable to explain how it was that Home was not severely burned. Crookes then told Myers:

"I do not believe in the possibility of the ordinary skin of the hand being so prepared as to enable hot coals to be handled with impunity. Schoolboys' books and medieval tales describe how this can be done with alum or certain other ingredients. It is possible that the skin may be so hardened and thickened by such preparations that superficial charring might take place without the pain becoming great, but the surface of the skin would certainly suffer severely. After Home had recovered from the trance I examined his hand with care to see if there were any signs of burning or of previous preparation. I could detect no trace of injury to the skin, which was soft and delicate like a woman's. Neither were there signs of any preparation having been previously applied. I have often seen conjurers and others handle red-hot coals and iron, but there were always palpable signs of burning."

Mrs. S. C. Hall's testimony of an occurrence on July 5, 1869, is often quoted. In this case the burning coal was placed on the head of Mr. Hall. He felt it warm but not hot. Home

"then proceeded to draw up Mr. Hall's white hair over the red coal. Mr. Home drew the hair into a sort of pyramid, the coal, still red, showing beneath the hair; then, after, I think, four or five minutes, Mr. Home pushed the hair back, and taking the coal off Mr. Hall's head, he said . . . addressing Mrs. Y.: 'Will you have it?' She drew back; and I heard him murmur, 'Little faith, little faith!' Two or three attempted to touch it, but it burnt their fingers. I said, 'Daniel, bring it to me; I do not fear to take it.' It was not red all over. . . . but it was still red in parts. I put out my right hand but he murmured, 'No, not that; the other hand.' He then placed it in my left hand. . . . I felt it. . . . 'warm'; yet when I stooped down to examine the coal my face felt the heat so much that I was obliged to withdraw it."

The source usually cited for this incident is S. C. Hall's *Retrospect of a Long Life.* It does not appear in that work, however, and may simply be an apocryphal tale.

Another fire test was reported by **Frank Podmore** from a letter written to him by Mrs. William Tebb in June 1882:

"Only on Friday I was in a circle with five others when one fell apparently in deep trance and put his hands over a flame and held them for some time without apparent injury. He also held the flame close to his eyes, to our horror, and we had to beg for the fire test to be dropped. It seemed too much to risk the eyesight in such a way. The burning of the hands we had been able to bear. The man afterwards was apparently no worse."

An American woman named Suydam handled hot iron and live coals and lamp chimneys at their most intense heat in public séances. "While she is under the control of the 'Fire Queen'," reported the *Religio Philosophical Journal* of Chicago, "her hands are cold and clammy; as cold as ice."

James Robertson, in his book *Spiritualism, an Open Door to the Unseen Universe* (1908) describes a séance with John Hopcroft, a London shoemaker, in his own house in Glasgow in which "he placed his hands amidst the ruddy coals in the fireplace, and lifting a piece which was perfectly red, he walked through the room so that its glow was reflected by the pictures on the wall."

The *New York Herald* of September 7, 1871, published the remarkable case of Nathan Coker, a 58-year-old African blacksmith of Easton, Maryland, who in the presence of a committee placed an iron shovel heated to a white heat upon the soles of his feet and kept it there until the shovel became black. When it was again red hot he laid it on his tongue and licked it until it became cooled. He poured a large handful of melted squirrel shot into the palm of his hand and then put it into his mouth, allowing it to run all around his teeth and gums. He repeated the operation several times, each time keeping the molten lead in his mouth until it solidified. After each operation he was carefully examined by physicians and was found unhurt.

The British newspaper *Daily Express* published a story in 1917 about an interesting experience **Rose de Crespigny** had with the medium Annie Hunter, in the presence of the paper's correspondent. The control of the medium was said to be a Persian fire worshiper. A log that the reporter brought up from the cellar when red hot was lifted out of the fire by the entranced medium. Talking in an excited way in a foreign language, she carried it about the room. The reporter shrank away. His hair was singed. De Crespigny also held the log across her arms for some seconds without the least harm. Another man, encouraged by what he had seen, allowed her to put the log near his head without any bad results.

There are a variety of different explanations of fire immunity and a variety of conjuring tricks that include apparent fire immunity. A substance called Mallot's metal melts at very low temperatures and can be handled safely for relatively brief periods. It has been noted that under hypnosis, a person can be made to produce a blister on his body after being touched by a pencil and told that it is a lit cigarette. In various altered states of consciousness the body reacts differently to its environment and can, for example, develop an immunity to pain. Few today attempt such feats, except for the well-documented fire-eating by circus performers, and from the sketchy descriptions of reporters it is often difficult to discern exactly what occurred in past generations.

Sources:

Boisserie, P. J. *Lourdes.* Paris, 1891.

Carrington, Hereward. "Psychical Phenomena Among Primitive Peoples." *Psychic Research* (October 1930).

Lang, Andrew. "The Fire Walk." *Proceedings* of the Society for Psychical Research 15, p. 36.

Leroy, Oliver. *Les hommes salamandres: Recherches et réflexions sur l'incombustibilité du corps humain.* Paris, 1932.

Michell, John, and Robert J. M. Rickard. *Phenomena: A Book of Wonders.* London: Thames and Hudson, 1977. Reprint, New York: Pantheon Books, 1977.

Price, Harry, and E. J. Dingwall, eds. *Revelations of a Spirit Medium.* London: Kegan Paul, Trench, Trubner, 1922.

Rickard, Robert, and Richard Kelly. *Photographs of the Unknown.* London: Book Club Associates, 1980.

Stein, Gordon. *Encyclopedia of Hoaxes.* Detroit: Gale Research, 1993.

Fire Ordeal

The fire ordeal is of great antiquity and probably arose from the concept of the purifying influence of fire. Among the Hindus, from the earliest times until comparatively recently, those who were suspected of wrongdoing were required to prove their guilt or innocence by walking over red-hot iron. If they escaped unharmed their innocence was proved beyond a doubt. In the great Hindu religious epic the *Ramayana,* after Sita, wife of Rama, has been rescued from the demon Ravana, Sita proves her purity by the fire ordeal. The priestesses of Cappodocian goddess Diana Parasya walked barefoot on red-hot coals, attributing their invulnerability to the powers of the divinity.

In Europe, trial by fire was of two kinds—traversing the flames, or undergoing the ordeal of hot iron. The latter comprised carrying red-hot irons in the hand, walking over iron bars or glowing ploughshares, and thrusting the hand into a red-hot gauntlet. An early instance of the former trial method in European history was the case of Pierre Barthelémy, who in 1097 declared to the Crusaders that heaven had revealed to him the place where the spear that had pierced the Savior's body was concealed. To prove his assertion he offered to undergo the ordeal by fire and was duly required to walk a path about a foot in width and some fourteen feet in length, on either side of which were piled blazing olive branches. The judgment of the fire was unfavorable, and 12 days later the rash adventurer died in agony.

Books were also sometimes submitted to trial by fire. This method was adopted to decide the claims of the Roman and Mozaratian liturgies, the former emerging victorious from the flames. The fire ordeal was also widely known in New Zealand, India, Fiji, and Japan.

In may be suspected that the outcome of such ordeals was not always left to the gods. There is no doubt that the ancient Egyptians were acquainted with substances that rendered the body temporarily impervious to fire. **Albertus Magnus** gives a recipe for this purpose. The concoction was made up of powdered lime made into a paste with the white of an egg, radish juice, marshmallow juice, and fleabane seeds. A first coat of this mixture was applied to the body and allowed to dry, then a second coat was applied. If the feet were constantly oiled or moistened with sulphuric acid they could be rendered impervious. Possibly the ancients were not unaware of the fire-resistant properties of asbestos.

The fire ordeal persisted into relatively modern times as one of the phenomena of **Spiritualism.** The famous medium **D. D. Home** frequently handled live coals and laid them on a handkerchief without damaging the material in the least. On one occasion he enclosed a glowing coal in his hands and blew upon it until it became white-hot.

In an account given by a Mrs. Honeywood and the **Master of Lindsay** of a séance with the same medium, Home took a chimney from a lighted lamp and put it into the fire—making it so hot that a match applied to it ignited instantly—and then thrust it into his mouth, touching it with his tongue, without any apparent ill effects. Another account stated that Home placed his face right into the fire among the burning coals, "moving it about as though bathing it in water." Other mediums in England and America emulated this feat with some measure of success.

It has been suggested that the state of trance generally accompanying such exploits, and corresponding to the ecstasy of the shaman performing a similar feat, may produce an anesthesia like insensibility to the pain of burning. How skin remains unscorched and a handkerchief unmarked by burning coals, however, is not easy to say.

Contemporary Fire Walking

Fire walking is still practiced in many parts of the world, including India, Pakistan, Japan, Malaya, Fiji, Tonga, Samoa, and Tahiti. Fire walkers believe that their faith protects them from injury and undergo the ordeal for purification, to fulfill vows, or to prove innocence. In 1935 **Harry Price** arranged a scientific investigation of fire walking in Surrey, England, with the cooperation of **Kuda Bux,** a Moslem from Kashmir. The tests were successful, but two volunteers who attempted the walk suffered blisters on the feet. Price concluded that the secret of fire walking involved three factors: the short contact time of each foot on the glowing embers (with a limit of two steps per foot); the low thermal conductivity of burning or burned wood embers; and confidence and steadiness in walking.

Interest in fire walking has been revived in the second half of the twentieth century. The 50-year-old film made by Harry Price of his investigation of Kuda Bux's fire walking was reproduced on the British television series *Arthur C. Clarke's World of Strange Powers.* A discussion of timely experiments and theories concerning scientific aspects of the subject followed the airing of the film. Various experiments were also detailed in the accompanying book to the series by John Fairley and Simon Welfare, *Arthur C. Clarke's World of Strange Powers* (1984). One notable citation was the work of Jearl Walker, professor of physics at Cleveland State University, Ohio. Walker had studied fire walking and was particularly intrigued by the research of Johann Gottlieb Leidenfrost, a German doctor who published a paper on the properties of water in 1756. Leidenfrost observed that if water was dropped onto a very hot surface, the drops danced about for a longer period than if the surface was cooler. Walker's own experiments showed that at 2100° centigrade the drops would last a minute or more on a hot surface, whereas they would evaporate in a few seconds at a lower temperature. Walker also discovered that the water drops were kept from contact with the hot surface by a thin vapor layer. He concluded that this "Leidenfrost effect" must be the secret of fire walking—that at a high temperature perspiration on the fire walker's feet forms a protective layer long enough to prevent injury.

Walker was courageous enough to put his theories to a personal test. He constructed a five-foot bed of hot coals in his back garden. He stated, "I suddenly found it remarkably easy to believe in physics when it is on paper, but remarkably hard to believe in it when the safety of one's own feet is at stake." Nevertheless, he later reported, "Clutching my faded copy of Halliday & Resnick's *Physics* in one hand, I strode over the five feet of hot coals. Apparently I am a true believer in physics. I have to report, however, that my feet did get a bit hot."

A German scientific team from Adubingen subsequently investigated the annual fire-walk ceremony at Langadhas, in northern Greece. The ceremony is held on May 21 each year at the festival of St. Constantine and St. Catherine to celebrate the traditional belief that Emperor Constantine successfully removed sacred relics from a burning church without injury to himself. In May 1980 the scientific team ensured that the fire was four yards long, with some two inches of hot coals with a surface temperature of 5000° Celsius. Three of the fire walkers agreed to have electrodes taped to their heads to secure an electroencephalogram (EEG), with thermocouples on their feet to give temperature readings. Both records were relayed from a backpack transmitter to the scientists with EEG recorder and tape recorder for temperature readings.

Two significant results were noted. First, although the surface of the fire was 5000°, the soles of the walkers' feet recorded only 1800°; second, increased theta activity was registered in the brain during the fire walk. Unfortunately a definitive physical explanation of the phenomenon of fire immunity proved elusive; when two of the scientific team ventured the fire walk, they suffered third-degree burns.

Evidence that immunity in fire walking is due solely to religious faith is also inconclusive. In 1982 a team of doctors and students from the medical faculty at Colombo University, Sri Lanka, took part in an extraordinary event designed to highlight the superiority of medical science to magic and superstition. As well as sponsoring vasectomies for family planning and medical treatment for snake-bite and venereal disease, the doctors staged demonstrations of fire walking. These deliberately flouted religious taboos as the doctors ate pork and imbibed alcohol (both forbidden by religion) while walking on red-hot coals without harm. The intention was to show that such fire immunity is a scientific phenomenon and not related to spiritual faith.

Another interesting case, quoted by **Arthur C. Clarke** and his co-authors, was that of Methodist minister Jon Munday from Katonan, New York, who took part in a fire walk in 1970 at the summer ashram retreat of **Swami Vishnudevananda** near Montreal, Canada. Munday described how he prepared himself by "chaotic meditation"—a combination of dancing, singing, and meditation—before joining others in a fire walk. Munday stated, "I didn't feel like I'd gone into a trance. Then, seconds before we stepped onto the coals I felt like something had happened and just walked right across, probably no more than six steps. I wasn't burned at all. I remember I fell on the ground face forward and held there kicking my feet. It was the exhilaration of having done something so incredible."

New Age Fire Walking

Fire walking has been revived in the United States and Britain as a kind of **New Thought** technique for raising human potential. It is claimed that by proving that the mind can control pain and physical reaction, individuals can liberate hidden potential for other achievements. In the United States, Eric Best, an industrial systems analyst, has been conducting seminars in which students are taught to overcome their fears through fire walking. Psychological techniques are used to prepare students by helping them face their longstanding fears before fire walking. Eventually the group surrounds a large bonfire that is later dismantled and used to feed a bed of glowing coals three feet wide and ten feet long.

The fire walkers are taught to internalize energy, to concentrate on it, then to assure themselves that the walk is on "cool moss." They shout, "Energy in!" then, "Strong focus!" "Eyes up!" and then, "Cool moss!" as they walk confidently over the glowing coals (a variant final chant used by some fire walkers is "Cool green moss!"). Walkers are instructed not to proceed with the ordeal unless they "feel right."

The technique was introduced to Britain by Hugh Bromiley, a karate black belt and member of the British Society of Hypnotherapists, after observing a fire-walking workshop in California. Participants are prepared by a "Power and Personal Research Training" course at which they are taught to confront their fears and successes before walking across burning embers. Local council authorities in London have banned fire walking, however, and medical authorities on burns have strongly discouraged the project.

In a valuable report on his own fire-walking experience, parapsychologist **Charles T. Tart** tells how he successfully maneuvered through the fire without injury. In his discussion of the various theories of immunity he concludes that a key factor is the *belief* of the fire walker that he or she can walk over the coals without being burned. This belief may be rationalized in many different ways, depending upon the disposition of the participant and whether he holds a religious or scientific philosophy. Tart questions the simplistic explanation of the Leidenfrost effect and points out discrepancies in the theory based on his own experience.

For a valuable collection of papers on fire walking, see *Psi Research* (vol. 4, no. 2, 1985). For a bibliography of articles on fire walking, see *Bulletin II* of the University of London, Council for Psychical Investigation (London, 1936).

Sources:

Burkan, Tolly. *Guiding Yourself into a Spiritual Reality.* Twin Harte, Calif.: Reunion Press, 1983.

Danforth, Loring M. *Firewalking and Religious Healing: The Anastenaria of Greece and the American Firewalking Movement.* Princeton, N.J.: Princeton University Press, 1989.

Michell, John, and Robert J. M. Rickard. *Phenomena: A Book of Wonders.* London: Thames and Hudson, 1977. Reprint, New York: Pantheon Books, 1977.

Rickard, Robert, and Richard Kelly. *Photographs of the Unknown.* London: Book Club Associates, 1980.

Sandwith, George, and Helen Sandwith. *Research in Fiji, Tonga & Samoa.* Surrey, England: Omega Press, 1954.

Stein, Gordon. *Encyclopedia of Hoaxes.* Detroit: Gale Research, 1993.

Tart, Charles T. "Firewalk." *Parapsychology Review* 18, no. 3 (May–June 1987).

Truzzi, Marcelo. "A Bibliography on Fire-Walking." *Zetetic Scholar* 11 (1983): 105–07.

Firebrace, Roy Charles (1889–1974)

British researcher in psychical science, **radionics, hypnostism,** and **astrology.** Born August 16, 1889, at Halifax, Nova Scotia, Firebrace served in the British army for almost four decades (1909–46) and retired with the rank of brigadier. Firebrace took special interest in the study of mediumship and the evidence for **survival** of personality after death and also edited booklets on astrology. He was president of the Astrological Association, Britain, in 1958 and played a valuable part in the development of the College of Psychic Science (now **College of Psychic Studies**).

During his period as a British military attache at Riga, Latvia, he took part in séances with a **direct voice** circle, at which he became convinced of the reality of survival of personality after death. He also attended séances with **Helen Duncan** (at which a materialized figure conversed with him in Russian), with Alec Harris (at which 18 materializations are said to have formed), and with voice medium **Leslie Flint.**

Firebrace practiced healing by radionics, the system originally developed by **Albert Abrams** involving diagnosis of blood spots by the use of a **black box** device. He was president of the College of Psychic Studies for 13 years, after supervising its change of name. He died November 10, 1974.

Sources:

Pleasants, Helene, ed. *Biographical Dictionary of Parapsychology.* New York: Helix Press, 1964.

Fires, Paranormal

Spontaneous combustion or "auto-oxidation" of human beings is one of the most baffling types of unexplained phenomena. For centuries, cases have been reported of individuals who burst into flames for no apparent reason; although their bodies were destroyed by fire, their clothes and surrounding objects were often unaffected. For example, on December 16, 1904, Mrs.

Thomas Cochrane, a widow of Falkirk, Scotland, was burned to death in her bedroom. There was no fire in the grate but she was burned almost beyond recognition, although the chair in which her body was found and the pillows and cushions with which she was surrounded were not even scorched. In January of the same year Elizabeth Clark of Hull, England, was found with her body covered with burns. There was no fire and her bed was not scorched. Although still alive when found, she could not explain what had happened, and she soon died. On December 13, 1959, Billy Thomas Peterson was found burning in his garaged automobile in Pontiac, Michigan. His left arm was so badly burned that the skin rolled off; his nose, mouth, and ears were burned; and his genitals were charred to a crisp. The hairs on his body were unsinged, however, and all his clothing remained unscorched, although the heat involved was so intense that a plastic religious statue on the auto dashboard had melted.

Such cases are usually explained away by rationalizations that do not meet the facts. For example, when a victim of spontaneous combustion has been seated near a fireplace, the usual explanation is that a cinder from the fire ignited the clothing—ignoring the fact that the calcined body indicates tremendous heat but often clothing is unaffected. In some cases of victims who were seated in autos, the instrument panel and fuel tanks were unaffected in spite of the great heat required to burn up a human body. Of course there are cases that are less ambiguous, where clothing and surroundings have been burned and some natural explanation is indicated.

The phenomenon of spontaneous combustion has been recognized by the medical profession over many years, although it is frankly admitted that a coroner's verdict of "death by spontaneous combustion" or even "accidental death" explains nothing in such cases.

Early Cases

The first professional recognition of spontaneous combustion recorded in print appears to be in the book *Acta Medica & Philosophica Hafniensia Ann. 1671 & 1672,* by Thomas Bartholin, published in Copenhagen in 1673. The earliest detailed account of spontaneous combustion of a human body is in *De Incendiis Corporis Spontaneis,* by Jonas Dupont, published in Leyden in 1763. During the nineteenth century, the phenomenon was often discussed in medical works and journals, but there was a tendency to dogmatize on insufficient evidence. An 1833 paper by M. J. Fintelle for the French Academy of Sciences suggested that the victims were usually corpulent women who were addicted to alcohol, thus generating "inflammable gases" in the stomach, and were usually seated near a source of heat or flame. Examination of numerous cases of spontaneous human combustion has shown these assumptions to be little more than inaccurate generalizations. There have been many male victims, most not heavy drinkers and often not seated near a source of flame.

The case of John Greley, helmsman of the S.S. *Ulrich* is instructive. On April 7, 1938, he was steering the ship toward Liverpool, England, when the second mate noticed it was beginning to yaw. The second mate ran to the wheelhouse, where he found the helmsman burned to a crisp at the wheel. The compass, varnished wooden wheel, and even the holystoned deck were not scorched. Interestingly enough, on the *same day* two other individuals died of spontaneous combustion. George Turner, a British truck driver, was heading for Liverpool from southeast England when the vehicle stopped and rolled into a ditch. Turner was later found calcined in his cab, but nothing else was burned—not even a grease stain on the passenger side of the truck. Willen ten Bruik, an 18-year-old Dutchman, also similarly died at the wheel of his vehicle while driving into Ubbergen, Holland.

The extraordinary coincidence of these three similar deaths on the same day is heightened by the fact (pointed out by Michael Harrison in his book *Fire From Heaven*) that the deaths were geographically linked, taking place in a triangular area with two sides roughly 340 miles long. Is this another "fatal triangle" mystery? No other similar coincidences have been recorded in the same area, although the mystery remains. As journalist Michael McDougall wrote in the *Newark Sunday Star-Ledger:* "It was as if a galactic being of unimaginable size had probed Earth with a three-tined fork: three fingers of fire, which burned only flesh."

Little is known of the reason for spontaneous combustion, but the *Transactions of the Medical Society of Tennessee* for 1835 reports a remarkable case of *partial* combustion that offers clues to the onset of the phenomenon. On January 5, 1835, on a very cold day, James Hamilton, professor of mathematics of the University of Nashville, walked home, a distance of about three-quarters of a mile. Forty minutes later he was inspecting a hygrometer that he had hung outside his house when he felt a sudden pain in his left leg "like a hornet sting, accompanied by a sensation of heat." He looked down and saw a bright flame, several inches long, "about the size of a dime in diameter," issuing like a gas flame from his trousered leg. After slapping the flame several times, he eventually extinguished it by cupping his hands around it to cut off oxygen. After putting out the flame he found that his leg had an injury that resembled an abrasion; the wound was very dry and the scar tissue had gathered in a roll at the lower edge of the abraded surface. Other writers have stated that spontaneous combustion begins with a bluish flame that extends rapidly all over the body until all parts are blackened and burned to a cinder. Throwing water on this flame only aggravates it, they say.

During the nineteenth century the phenomenon of spontaneous combustion was so familiar that it was referred to in various works of fiction, such as Frederick Marryat's *Jacob Faithful* (1833), Honore de Balzac's *Le Cousin Pons* (1847), Herman Melville's *Redburn* (1849), Charles Dickens's *Bleak House* (1853), and Mark Twain's *Life on the Mississippi* (1833).

Cases of human spontaneous combustion are still reported. Various theories have been advanced to account for this weird phenomenon, such as unusual effects of ball lightning, static electricity, or even psychical effects related to levitation and telekinesis. If this latter theory should seem far-fetched, it is worth quoting a comment of Soviet parapsychologist Genady Sergeyev about the telekinetic subject **Nina Kulagina,** reported in the British newspaper *Sunday People* (March 14, 1976): "She can draw energy somehow from all around her. . . . On several occasions the force rushing into her body left burn-marks up to 4 inches long on her arms and hands. . . . I was with her once when her clothing caught fire from this energy-flow—it literally flamed. . . ."

Of the many recorded cases of spontaneous human combustion it is probable that there is no single appropriate explanation but rather various types of phenomena. In some cases there may be a simple explanation, in others a mysterious and as yet inexplicable reason. Joe Nickel and John F. Fischer, skeptics of the paranormal, tried their hand at explanations, but fared little better than previous observers. Jerome Clark suggested that spontaneous human combustion may be a manufactured mystery bringing together a series of unrelated cases, each of which has its own explanation.

Sources:

Bartholin, Thomas. *Acta Medica & Philosophical Hafniensia Ann. 1671 & 1672.* Copenhagen, 1673.

Clark, Jerome. *Encyclopedia of Strange and Unexplained Phenomena.* Detroit: Gale Research, 1993.

Gaddis, Vincent H. *Mysterious Fires and Lights.* New York: McKay, 1967.

Harrison, Michael. *Fire From Heaven.* London, 1976. Reprint, New York: Methuen, 1977. Rev. ed. London: Pan, 1977.

Lair, Pierre. *Essai sur les combustions humaine, produites par l' abus des liqueurs spiritueses.* Paris, 1808.

Michell, John, and Robert J. M. Rickard. *Phenomena: A Book of Wonders.* London: Thames and Hudson, 1977. Reprint, New York: Pantheon Books, 1977.

Nickell, Joe, and John F. Fischer. *Secrets of the Supernatural: Investigating the World's Occult Mysteries.* Buffalo, N.Y.: Prometheus Press, 1988.

Rickard, Robert, and Richard Kelly. *Photographs of the Unknown.* London: Book Club Associates, 1980.

Russell, Eric Frank. *Great World Mysteries.* London, 1957.

United States Army. *Index-Catalogue of the Library of the Surgeon-General's Office.* Washington, D.C., 1882.

Firman, Mr. and Mrs. A. H. (ca. 1876)

British mediums who claimed to be controlled by **"John King"** and produced **direct voice** phenomena. Mrs. Firman produced wax molds (see **plastics**) and **materialization** of spirit forms.

William Oxley, author of *Modern Messiahs and Wonder Workers* (1889), claimed to have observed a total dematerialization of the medium while the phantom was outside the **cabinet.** The phantoms either shrank through the floor or rose to the ceiling and slowly disappeared. Similarly, **Emma Hardinge Britten** wrote of the production of the mold of a spirit foot in her *Nineteenth Century Miracles* (1883). The Honorable J. L. O'Sullivan recorded in *The Spiritualist* an instance of May 4, 1877, when four spirits were present at once with the sleeping form of the medium plainly visible.

Unfortunately, when mediums claimed to do materializations, discovery of **fraud** usually followed, and the Firmans were no exception. There was a very serious disclosure in the *Procès des Spirites* by Mme. P. G. Leymarie (Paris, 1875), according to which Mr. Firman was detected in Paris masquerading as an Indian spirit and left his mantle in the hands of the woman who seized him.

Firth, Violet Mary (1890–1946)

Leading British occultist, author, and founder of the **Fraternity of the Inner Light.** Firth was born December 6, 1890, at Bryn-y-Bia, Llandudno, Wales. She manifested some mediumistic abilities in her teens. She later became interested in psychoanalysis and studied the work of Freud, but came to prefer **C. G. Jung**'s perspective. She worked for a time at the Medico-Psychological Clinic in London. She also became interested in the writings of **Helena Petrovna Blavatsky** but was put off by the Eastern style of occultism dominant in the **Theosophical Society.**

About 1919 she joined the Alpha and Omega Lodge of the **Stella Matutina,** an outer order of the Hermetic Order of the **Golden Dawn,** a ritual magic group under the guidance of **J. W. Brodie-Innes.** He instructed her in various magic practices. Firth's pseudonym, "Dion Fortune," was derived from her period as a member of the Stella Matutina. She took the motto *Deo Non Fortuna* (By God, not luck), and this was condensed to "Dion Fortune" when she began to write. Under her own name she wrote one early book, *Machinery of the Mind* (1922).

In 1924 she founded the Community (later Fraternity) of the Inner Light to attract recruits for the Golden Dawn but eventually split off from the main body as warden of the new order. She taught her own variation of magic, based on claimed contacts from the "inner planes" of wisdom.

Firth wrote several books on magic and the occult and several occult novels, notably *The Secrets of Dr. Traverner* (1926), *The Demon Lover* (1927), *Through the Gates of Death* (1932), *The Winged Bull* (1935), *The Goat-Foot God* (1936), *The Sea Priestess* (1938), and *Moon Magic* (ca. 1939). Her books of occult instruction include *Sane Occultism* (1929), *Psychic Self-Defence* (1930), *The Training and Work of an Initiate* (1930), and *The Mystical Qabalah* (1935).

Sources:

Chapman, Janine. *Quest for Dion Fortune.* York Beach, Maine: Samuel Weiser, 1993.

Fielding, Charles, and Clark Collins. *The Story of Dion Fortune.* York Beach, Maine: Samuel Weiser, 1985.

Fortune, Dion. *Applied Magic.* New York: Samuel Weiser, 1962.

———. *The Esoteric Orders and Their Work.* London: Rider, 1929. Reprint, St. Paul, Minn.: Llewellyn Publications, 1971.

———. *The Mystical Qabalah.* London: Ernest Benn, 1935.

———. *Psychic Self-Defence.* London: Rider, 1930.

———. *Sane Occultism.* London: Rider, 1929.

———. *The Secrets of Dr. Traverner.* London: Noel Douglas, 1926.

———. *The Training and Work of an Initiate.* London: Rider, 1930.

———. *The Winged Bull.* London: Williams & Norgate, 1935.

Richardson, Alan. *Priestess: The Life and Magic of Dion Fortune.* Wellingborough, England: Aquarian Press, 1987.

Fischer, H(enri) Thèodore (1901–)

Dutch professor of anthropology who was also active in the field of **parapsychology.** Born April 6, 1901, at Poerwakarta, Dutch East Indies, Fischer was awarded a Ph.D. in cultural anthropology in 1929 and became professor of cultural anthropology at the University of Utrecht in 1936.

He was also director of the Volkenkundig Institut, Utrecht; president of the Dutch Society for Psychical Research (1945–56); and a charter member of the **Parapsychological Association.** He took a special interest in **clairvoyance** and the evidence for **survival** after death. In addition to his papers for various periodicals dealing with anthropology, Fischer published several books on anthropology and ethnology.

Sources:

Pleasants, Helene, ed. *Biographical Dictionary of Parapsychology.* New York: Helix Press, 1964.

Fish, (Ann) Leah (ca. 1814–1890)

The eldest of the famous **Fox sisters,** whose claimed spirit raps at Hydesville, New York, in 1848 launched the Spiritualist movement in the United States. Her birth date is not known, but is believed to be around 1814. Leah Fox was only 14 when she married Bowman Fish. He deserted her and she was living in Rochester teaching music when the rappings began in the family home in Hydesville. Leah later married Calvin Brown, and after his death in 1853 she married Daniel Underhill in 1858.

In 1885, as Leah Underhill, she published *The Missing Link in Modern Spiritualism* (1885), detailing her recollections of the **Rochester rappings** and the development of **Spiritualism** as a link between the living and the dead. The book was severely criticized by her younger sister Kate Fox (Jencken) in 1888 as "a string of lies." That was also the year in which Kate allied herself with her sister Margaret in a confession of **fraud.** They blamed Leah for continuing the fraud past the first weeks, but they retracted everything in the following year.

Fisk, G(eorge) W(illiam) (1882–1972)

British parapsychologist and lecturer in physics. Fisk was born January 9, 1882, at Liverpool, England. He studied at London University (B.D., 1906) and Victoria University (B.A., 1907). After graduation, Fisk moved to China where he lectured in physics at Chi-lu University, Shantung, China (1908–1915), and served as British vice-consul at the Chinese Emigration Bureau Center, North China (1915–19), and as labor superintendent of Kailan Mining Administration (1919–30). While in China, Fisk joined the **Society for Psychical Research** (SPR). He became fascinated with the examples of paranormal activity he saw in the Orient. Later, upon his return to England, he became a charter member of the Parapsychological Association, joined the SPR Council (1950), and served as editor of the *Journal* and *Proceedings* of the SPR (1957–66). In 1958 he and **Donald J. West** received the McDougall Award for their paper "Psychokinetic Experiments with a Single Subject."

Fisk spent more than 30 years in quantitative research on ESP. His articles were published in the *Journal* of the SPR and the *Journal of Parapsychology.* He also wrote a Chinese-English-French phrase book for mining engineers.

Sources:

Berger, Arthur S., and Joyce Berger. *The Encyclopedia of Parapsychology and Psychical Research.* New York: Paragon House, 1991.

Fisk, George W. "How Primitive is ESP?" *Tomorrow* (spring 1957).

———. "We Card-Guessers." *Tomorrow* (winter 1957).

Fisk, George W., and Donald J. West. "Psychokinetic Experiments with a Single Subject." *Parapsychology Newsletter* (November–December 1957).

Heywood, Rosalind. "G. W. Fisk and ESP." *Journal* of the Society for Psychical Research 47 (1973).

Pleasants, Helene, ed. *Biographical Dictionary of Parapsychology.* New York: Helix Press, 1964.

Fitzlar, Martin von (ca. 1750)

German alchemist who lived in the first half of the eighteenth century. He was probably a Hessian, residing chiefly at the village of Fitzlar. While a young man he studied pharmacy, intending to make it his profession, but he soon grew interested in the quest of gold-making, and when the celebrated alchemist **Lascaris** came to Germany, Fitzlar hastened to see him hoping to glean his secrets.

Along with several other young men, Fitzlar was allowed to witness numerous experiments, and it seemed that the great secret lay open before him, but afterward, when he made attempts on his own, he found that Lascaris had duped him shamefully and had even taken advantage of his ignorance. Then—unlike the majority of thwarted alchemists—he renounced the futile search altogether and resumed his original calling as a pharmacist.

Fitzsimons, Frederick William (1875– ?)

South African scientist and Spiritualist. Fitzsimons was an expert on snakes and was curator of the Natal Society Museum, Pietermaritzburg, Natal. His interest in **Spiritualism** led him to investigate psychic photographer **William Hope** and to sit with **Etta Wriedt** while in London in 1920. He later published one book, *Opening the Psychic Door* (1933).

Flagellation

Flagellation (usually with whips) has been associated with religious fervor from pagan times. In ancient Egypt devotees of the goddess Isis scourged themselves at an annual festival. According to Pausanias, women were flogged in the temple of Dionysus. Plutarch states that the priests of Cybele were flogged in the temple of the goddess.

In the Christian religion, flagellation found many rationalizations. It was used as an official punishment for priests and monks, a self-inflicted penance, and a dramatization of the sufferings of Christ. There was an epidemic of flagellant sects in Europe during the tenth and fourteenth centuries, associated with penance and love of Christ, and the Catholic authorities took extreme measures to suppress what they considered a morbid enthusiasm for the act. In Latin American countries, flagellation still occurs at religious processions of *penitentes.*

Symbolic whippings have also been associated with certain Tibetan and Mongolian sects, and some American Indian tribes used whipping to test the endurance of young males in ritual ordeals. In the witchcraft movement of the mid-twentieth century, flagellation was introduced by **Gerald Gardner;** it is used both as a means of exciting psychic awareness and as a disciplinary measure.

The persistent and widespread practice of flagellation both as a religious ritual and in sadomasochistic deviations appears to be based on the intense emotional and sexual sensations it arouses, sometimes culminating in paranormal consciousness. Although there is widespread sadomasochistic literature for those addicted to flogging and related practices, there has been little attempt to analyze the psychosomatic basis of flagellation.

In his book *The Function of the Orgasm* (1942) **Wilhelm Reich** explains masochism as a compulsion neurosis arising from sexual anxiety; he does not accept that real pain is desired—rather that the suggestion of pain evokes inhibited pleasure sensations in individuals with long-established sexual inhibitions. This inhibited pleasure, Reich says, is a longing for release from tensions and is expressed biologically in the organism as in well as the psyche. The historical facts of the association of actual pain and injury with flagellation, however, would indicate that Reich's explanation does not go far enough.

On a more everyday level, devotees of the sauna bath will testify to the overall tonic effect of scourging with twigs. It would seem that flagellation certainly elicits biological and psychic excitation, sometimes involving intense sexual and emotional release, and when associated with religious fervor it may induce almost mystical states of transport, although of a psychopathological kind.

Sources:

Cooper, William M. [James Glass Bertram]. *Flagellation and the Flagellants: A History of the Rod in All Continents from the Earliest Period to the Present Time.* London, 1868. Rev. ed. Paris: C. Carrington, 1900.

Gibson, Ian. *The English Vice: Beating, Sex, and Shame in Victorian England and After.* London: Duckworth, 1978.

History of Flagellation Among All Nations. New York: Medical Publishing, 1903.

Reich, Wilhelm. *The Function of the Orgasm: Sex-Economic Problems of Biological Energy.* New York: Orgone Institute Press, 1942. Reprint, New York: Farra, Straus and Giroux, 1973.

Valiente, Doreen. *An ABC of Witchcraft Past and Present.* New York: St. Martin's, 1973.

Weigle, Marta. *Brothers of Light, Brothers of Blood: The Penitentes of the Southwest.* Albuquerque: University of New Mexico Press, 1976.

Flamel, Nicholas (ca. 1330–1418)

One of the most famous alchemists. Flamel was said to have been born at Pontoise of a poor but respectable family, about the beginning of the fourteenth century. Very little is certain about his life, but it is believed that he received a good education, of which his natural abilities enabled him to make the best use. Moving to Paris, he obtained employment as a public scrivener. The occupation provided a modest income, and Flamel also had some skill in poetry and painting. Eventually he prudently married a well-to-do widow named Pernelle.

One day he came across a remarkable book of **alchemy** written on leaves made from the bark of trees and with a cover made of brass. The book cost two florins. The calligraphy was as admirable as the language was cryptical. Each seventh leaf was free from writing but emblazoned with a picture; the first representing a serpent swallowing rods, the second, a serpent crucified on a cross, and the third, the arid expanse of a desert in whose depths a fountain bubbled, with serpents trailing their slimy folds from side to side.

The author of this mysterious book purported to be "Abraham, the patriarch, Jew, prince, philosopher, Levite, priest, and astrologer." He had included a complete exposition of the art of transmuting metals—describing every process, explaining the different vessels, and pointing out the proper seasons for making experiments. The book was addressed not so much to the novice as to the expert, however, and took it for granted that the reader was already in possession of the **philosophers' stone.**

Flamel showed the book to scholars and learned men, but they were unable to interpret the text, until one day it was suggested that a rabbi might be able to translate it. Since the chiefs of the Jews were principally located in Spain, Flamel went there and from one of the Hebrew sages obtained some hints that afforded a key to the mysteries. Returning to Paris, he resumed his studies with a new vigor and was rewarded with success.

On February 13, 1382, according to the story, Flamel made a projection on mercury and produced some virgin silver. During the following April he converted some mercury into gold and found himself the fortunate possessor of an inexhaustible treasure. His wife assisted in his experiments. As they had no children, they spent their wealth on churches and hospitals, and several of the religious and charitable institutions of France still attest to their well-directed benevolence.

One of Flamel's works on the fascinating science of alchemy—a poem entitled *The Philosophic Summary*—was printed as late as 1735. William Salmon's valuable and unusual *Medicina Practica* (1691) preserves some specimens of the drawings in Abraham's treatise on metallurgy and some of his handwriting.

More skeptical writers have suggested that Flamel used his alchemical studies to disguise his financial activities, primarily his usurious practices. The writers also say he used alchemy to account for immense wealth acquired by money-lending to young French nobles and by transacting business between the Jews of France and those of Spain, and they accuse him of inventing the story of his discovery of the philosophers' stone. For an argument against this theory, see *Alchemists Through The Ages* (1970), a reprint of A. E. Waite's *Lives of the Alchemystical Philosophers* (1888).

Sources:

Federmann, Reinhard. *The Royal Art of Alchemy.* New York: Chilton, 1964.

Magre, Maurice. *The Return of the Magi.* London: P. Allen, 1931.

Waite, A. E. *Lives of the Alchemystical Philosophers.* London: George Redway, 1888. Reprinted as *Alchemists Through The Ages.* Blauvelt, N.Y.: Rudolf Steiner Publications, 1970.

Flammarion, Camille (1842–1925)

Famous French astronomer who also became a notable psychical researcher. Flammarion was born February 26, 1842. He was a student astronomer from 1858 to 1862 and from 1876 to 1882 he was an astronomer at the Paris Observatory. In 1882 he founded Juvisy Observatory, which he directed for the rest of his life. That same year he also founded the French Astronomical Society. As a scientist he made balloon ascents to study the upper atmosphere and was celebrated for his research on double and multiple stars and the topography of Mars. He was named a commander of the Legion of Honor, one of France's highest nonmilitary honors.

His first contact with psychical phenomena was during November 1861. When writing his first book, *The Plurality of Inhabited Worlds,* he came across Spiritualist **Allan Kardec**'s *Le Livre des Esprits,* paid him a visit, and joined the Society for Psychologic Studies, of which Kardec was president. The weekly séances of the society were devoted to inspirational writing. Flammarion himself tried to practice it and succeeded, after several attempts, in obtaining words and phrases.

The scripts were mostly on astronomical subjects and were signed by Galileo. Flammarion, however, believed them to be wholly the product of his own intellect and had no doubt that the illustrious Florentine astronomer had nothing to do with them. These communications remained in the possession of the society and were published in 1867 in Kardec's *Genesis* under the head of "General Uranography."

Flammarion soon obtained entrance to the chief Parisian spiritistic circles and even acted as honorary secretary to one of them for several years. Nevertheless, he did not become a Spiritist. After two years of experience in automatic writing, in the use of the **planchette,** and in rapping communications, he came to the conclusion that the method practiced by Kardec's society permitted a margin for doubt and that the automatic scripts did not prove the intervention of another mind from the spirit world at all.

In 1865, under the title *Des Forces naturelles inconnues* (Unknown Natural Forces), he published his first book on the subject of psychical research, a monograph of 150 pages that was meant as a critical study "apropos of the phenomena produced by the **Davenport brothers** and mediums in general." It was not so much about the Davenport brothers that he wrote, but about psychic (he used this word in his early writings) matters, stating that, "these forces are as real as the attraction of gravitation and as invisible as that." His book *Les Forces Naturelles Inconnues,* published in 1906 (translated as *Mysterious Psychic Forces,* 1907), is in a sense an enlarged edition of this early work.

Allan Kardec died March 30, 1869, and Flammarion was asked to deliver the funeral oration. In the eulogy he impressed upon all students of the mysterious phenomena that "spiritualism is not a religion but a science, of which we as yet scarcely know the a.b.c."

In 1899, through the *Annales Politiques et Litteraires,* the *Petit Marseilles,* and the *Revue des Revues,* Flammarion started to make his own census of hallucinations. Of 4,280 people questioned 1,824 answered that they had had phantasmal visions. Of these, 786 cases were selected as having evidential value. They were dealt with in the *Annales Politiques et Litteraires,* for which Flammarion was writing articles on psychic subjects. Revised and amplified, these articles formed the substance of *L'Inconnu,* published in 1900 in an attempt to prove the reality of **telepathy, apparitions** of the dying, premonitory **dreams,** and **clairvoyance.** Flammarion concludes that the soul exists as a real entity independent of the body; it is endowed with faculties still unknown to science; and it is able to act at a distance without the intervention of the senses.

He reaffirmed his belief in the reality of psychical phenomena in *Mysterious Psychic Forces* on the basis of very wide experience. "During a period of more than forty years," he writes "I believe that I have received at my home nearly all of them [mediums], men and women of divers nationalities and from every quarter of the globe." He met Italian medium **Eusapia Palladino** for the first time on July 27, 1897, at Montfort l'Amaury. The report of the séances conducted there form the subject of Guillaume de Fontenay's *Apropos d'Eusapia Palladino* (1898).

In cooperation with the editor of the *Annales Politiques et Litteraires,* Flammarion extended an invitation to Palladino to come to Paris. She accepted and gave eight séances in Flammarion's home during November 1898. Many scientists were present and surprising manifestations were witnessed. Additional opportunities for observation with the same medium were afforded by a later series of séances in 1905, and especially in 1906 under Flammarion's own conditions in his home, often in the full light of a gas chandelier. He felt no hesitation in declaring that "mediumistic phenomena have for me the stamp of absolute certainty and incontestability, and amply suffice to prove that unknown physical forces exist outside the ordinary and established domain of natural philosophy."

Nevertheless, he was not yet convinced of **survival,** and in *Mysterious Psychic Forces* he makes the following conclusions: "The universe is a dynamism. . . . Matter is only a mode of motion. Life itself . . . is a special kind of movement, a movement determined and organized by a directing force. . . . The vital force of the medium might externalize itself and produce in a point of space a vibratory system which should be the counterpart of itself in a more or less advanced degree of visibility and solidity. . . .

"It is not the body which produces life; it is rather life which organizes the body. . . .

"As to beings different from ourselves—what may their nature be? Of this we cannot form any idea. Souls of the dead? This is very far from being demonstrated. The innumerable observations which I have collected during more than forty years all prove to me the contrary. No satisfactory identification has been made.

"The communications obtained have always seemed to proceed from the mentality of the group, or, when they are heterogeneous, from spirits of an incomprehensible nature. The being evoked soon vanishes when one insists on pushing him to the wall and having the heart out of his mystery. . . .

"That souls survive the destruction of the body I have not the shadow of a doubt. But that they manifest themselves by the processes employed in séances the experimental method has not yet given us absolute proof. I add that this hypothesis is not at all likely. If the souls of the dead are about us, upon our planet, the invisible population would increase at the rate of 100,000 a day, about 36 millions a year, 3 billions 620 millions in a century, 36 billions in ten centuries, etc.—unless we admit re-incarnations upon the earth itself.

"How many times do apparitions or manifestations occur? When illusions, auto-suggestions, hallucinations are eliminated what remains? Scarcely anything. Such an exceptional rarity as this pleads against the reality of apparitions."

As the years passed Flammarion was forced to surrender his old stand. His trilogy *La Mort et son mystère* (*Death and Its Mystery*), its three volumes subtitled *Before Death, At the Moment of Death,* and *After Death* (1921–23), aims mainly at demonstrating the continuity of existence. His *Les maisons hantées* (*Haunted Houses*) (1924) discusses the activities of the dead under exceptional circumstances. In his presidential address before the **Society for Psychical Research** in October 1923, he summed up his conclusions after 60 years of psychical research: "There are unknown faculties in man belonging to the spirit, there is such a thing as the double, thought can leave an image behind, psychical currents traverse the atmosphere, we live in the midst of an invisible world, the faculties of the soul survive the disaggregation of the corporeal organism, there are haunted houses, exceptionally and rarely the dead do manifest, there can be no doubt that such manifestations occur, telepathy exists just as much between the dead and the living as between the living."

Flammarion died at Juvisy Observatory, Paris, on June 3, 1925. His return was soon claimed by Spiritualists, the most notable account being published in *Egoland* (1932), by Emily Loweman, through the mediumship of her father, A. H. Loweman, a shopkeeper and the postmaster of Little Glemham. "Egoland" was Flammarion's name for the spirit world.

Sources:

Berger, Arthur S., and Joyce Berger. *The Encyclopedia of Parapsychology and Psychical Research.* New York: Paragon House, 1991.

De Fontenay, Guillaume. *Apropos d'Eusapia Palladino.* Paris, 1898.

Flammarion, Camille. *Death and Its Mystery: After Death.* New York: Century, 1923.

———. *Death and Its Mystery: At the Moment of Death.* New York: Century, 1922.

———. *Death and Its Mystery: Before Death.* New York: Century, 1921.

———. *Haunted Houses.* Detroit: Tower Books, 1971.

———. "The Unknown of Yesterday and the Truth of Tomorrow." *Journal* of the Society for Psychical Research 29 (1935).

Loweman, Emily. *Egoland.* London, 1932.

Flat Earth Research Society International

Organization founded in 1800. Members are individuals whose outlook is *zetetic,* or characterized by a seeking for truth and the denial of "imaginary" theories. They rely only on provable knowledge and consequently believe that the "spinning ball" theory regarding Earth is absurd and that, in reality, the Earth is flat and infinite in size. Members maintain that Australia is not under the world; Australians do not hang by their feet, nor do ships sail over the edge of the world to get there. They also assert that continental drift is really the result of the earth and water being "shaken asunder by God."

The society gathers information, disseminates the results of its findings, and generally seeks to "push forth the frontiers of knowledge in geophysical matters."

The society conducts research programs, confers a Seeker for Truth Award, and publishes the *Flat Earth News.* Address: Box 2533, Lancaster, CA 93539.

Sources:

Larsen, David. "Society Flatly Denies Global Theory." *Los Angeles Times,* May 15, 1978.

Fleming, Alice Kipling (1868–1948)

Sister of British author Rudyard Kipling who became a well-known psychic, producing **automatic writing** under the name "Mrs. Holland." Born June 11, 1868, Alice Kipling was privately educated. She went to India at age 16 and married British army officer John Fleming.

While in India she wrote a number of poems, and in 1893 initially experimented with automatic writing. After a long illness she returned to England in 1902 and in the following year read the classic study *Human Personality and Its Survival of Bodily Death,* by **F. W. H. Myers.** As a result she contacted the secretary of the **Society for Psychical Research** (SPR), London, regarding her own automatic writing.

She took part in the SPR's **cross-correspondence** tests, in which several automatic writers produced scripts that only became meaningful when combined. Her contribution was described in several papers by **Alice Johnson** in the *Proceedings* of the SPR (1908–09).

Sources:

Berger, Arthur S., and Joyce Berger. *The Encyclopedia of Parapsychology and Psychical Research.* New York: Paragon House, 1991.

Johnson, Alice. "On the Automatic Writing of Mrs. Holland." *Proceedings* of the Society for Psychical Research 21 (1908).

———. "Second Report on Mrs. Holland's Script." *Proceedings* of the Society for Psychical Research 24 (1910).

———. "Supplementary Notes on Mrs. Holland's Scripts." *Proceedings* of the Society for Psychical Research 22 (1909).

———. "Third Report on Mrs. Holland's Scripts." *Proceedings* of the Society for Psychical Research 25 (1911).

Saltmarsh, H. F. *Evidence of Personal Survival from Cross Correspondences.* London: G. Bell & Son, 1938.

Fletcher, John William (1852–1913)

American clairvoyant and trance medium. His mother possessed the gift of **second sight.** As a boy he was a puzzle to his teachers; instead of the lesson he would recite a paper presented to him in a vision. When barely 17 he was known and sought out as a trance speaker.

As a young man he married Susie Willis, who was a clairvoyant and had been a public lecturer since age 15. In 1873 both embarked on professional mediumship at the Lake Pleasant camp meeting. Fletcher's control was an Indian girl, "Winona," and some of her sitters claimed to have seen her materialized.

In 1877 Fletcher visited London. Because of the **Henry Slade** trial, American mediums were not popular there at the time. At **James Burns**'s Spiritual Institution he was coldly received. Although *The Spiritualist* newspaper never ceased to attack him, Fletcher continued his tour and gave test sittings at the house of **Agnes Guppy-Volckman,** at the **British National Association of Spiritualists,** and at the Dalston Association. In Cavendish Rooms and in Steinway Hall he delivered many platform addresses on the religion and philosophy of **Spiritualism** and instituted Sunday class meetings on the plan of the Children's Lyceums of America.

In 1881 the Fletchers were overtaken by disaster. Mrs. Fletcher was sentenced to 12 months' hard labor for obtaining, by undue influence, the property of Mrs. Hart Davies. Her defense was that she was sheltering the woman, who appealed to her for refuge and protection, and only reluctantly consented to take charge of her property as long as Davies desired it, since she and her husband were paying Davies's expenses while she stayed in their home. At the time of his wife's trial Fletcher was addressing an audience of three thousand in Boston. He never went back to England, fearing the same fate that befell his wife.

In his later years Fletcher practiced as a palmist in New York. In June 1913 the police made a sudden raid with a warrant for his arrest. He collapsed and died from heart failure.

Sources:

Gay, Susan E. *John William Fletcher, Clairvoyant.* London, 1883.

Marryat, Florence. *There is No Death.* New York: John W. Lovell, 1891. Reprint, New York: Causeway Books, 1973.

Flew, Antony G(arrard) N(ewton) (1923–)

British author, humanist, and professor of philosophy who has written widely on parapsychological subjects. Flew was born February 11, 1923, in London. He became a lecturer at Christ Church College, Oxford, and at King's College, Aberdeen, Scotland. In 1954 he became a professor of philosophy at the University of Keele, Staffordshire, England. He was a distinguished research fellow at the Social Philosophy and Policy Center, Bowling Green State University, and a professor emeritus of the University of Reading, in England.

Flew is a humanist-rationalist and is known internationally as a skeptic regarding paranormal claims. Over the years he has contributed many articles on philosophy and parapsychology, especially on issues of personal **survival,** to various journals, including the *Cambridge Journal,* the *British Journal of Sociology,* the *Philosophical Quarterly, New Biology,* and the *Rationalist Annual,* and contributed articles for several anthologies.

His many books include *A New Approach to Psychical Research* (1953), his main text touching on the paranormal; *Hume's Philosophy of Belief* (1961); *God and Philosophy* (1966); *Evolutionary Ethics* (1967); *An Introduction to Western Philosophy* (1971); *Crime or Disease?* (1973); *Thinking About Thinking* (1975; reissued as *Thinking Straight,* 1977); *The Presumption of Atheism* (1976); *Sociology, Equality and Education* (1976); *The Warren-Flew Debate* (1977); *A Rational Animal* (1978); *Philosophy: An Introduction* (1979); *The Politics of Procrustes* (1981); and *The Logic of Mortality* (1987). He also edited the 1964 book *Body, Mind and Death.*

Sources:

Berger, Arthur S., and Joyce Berger. *The Encyclopedia of Parapsychology and Psychical Research.* New York: Paragon House, 1991.

Flew, Antony G. N., ed. *Body, Mind and Death.* New York: Macmillan, 1964.

———. "Is There a Case for Disembodied Spirit?" *Journal* of the American Society for Psychical Research 66 (1972).

———. *The Logic of Mortality.* Oxford: Blackwell, 1987.

———. *A New Approach to Psychical Research.* London: C. A. Watts, 1953.

Ludwig, J. K., ed. *Philosophy and Parapsychology.* Buffalo, N.Y.: Promethus Books, 1978.

Flint, Leslie (ca. 1911–1994)

Noted British **medium** who specialized in independent **direct voice** communications (i.e., voice phenomena purported to be from dead individuals that originate a little above the medium's head and to one side, without the use of his or her vocal cords). In some 35 years of mediumship, Leslie Flint was tested by a number of psychical researchers using electrical devices, but nothing of a fraudulent nature was discovered. William R. Bennett, professor of electrical engineering at Columbia University, New York, tested Flint in 1970 and stated, "My experience with Mr. Flint is first hand; I have heard the independent voices. Furthermore, modern investigation techniques not available in earlier tests corroborate. . . . that the voices are not his."

Bennett also discounted the possibility of accomplices. In a few instances Flint conveyed messages from living individuals who were either in a coma or deep sleep at the time. Flint, a dedicated Spiritualist, places emphasis on providing evidence of **survival** after death.

During the 1940s Flint had several private sittings with film star Mae West when she visited London. He also visited her in Hollywood during his short American tour in 1949. He retired from public séance work in 1976. The next year he was named "Spiritualist of the Year" by readers of the British newspaper *Psychic News.*

Sources:

Flint, Leslie. *Voices in the Dark.* New York: Bobbs-Merrill, 1971.

Flournoy, Theodore (1854–1920)

Professor of psychology at the University of Geneva, Switzerland, and a noted psychical researcher. Flournoy was born August 15, 1854, and studied at the University of Strasbourg Medical School. From 1891 to 1919 he taught physiological psychology, experimental psychology, and the philosophy of science at the University of Geneva. He published many important works on medicine and psychology, including *Des Phénomènes de Synapsie* (Phenomena of Synapsis) (1893), *Les Principes de la psychologie religieuse* (1903), and *Le Genie religieux* (1904).

He became interested in mediumship, which led to his writing one of the more famous books in psychical research, *Des Indes à la Planète Mars* (1900), translated as *From India to the Planet Mars* in 1901. This was the sensation of the year, and the passage of time has in no way affected its unusual scientific worth or mitigated its absorbing interest. The book deals with the mediumship of **Hélène Smith,** to whose circle Flournoy was first admitted in the winter of 1894–95. It was published at a time when the work of the **Society for Psychical Research** (SPR), London, and information on the mediumship of **Lenora Piper** had prepared a large part of the public for scientific revelation regarding another life.

Flournoy's book, written with erudition and a vivid sense of humor and irony, questioned many Spiritualistic beliefs and threw great doubt on the ascertainability of the extramundane existence of the entities that appear to communicate through mediums. He admitted many puzzling phenomena in the history of Smith's mediumship, however. He found the Hindu reincarnation remarkably real, and he could not offer an explanation for the medium's knowledge of remote historical incidents and traces of the Sanskrit language.

The arguments he advanced to prove that the communicators were subconscious impersonations were most impressive. He saw no reason to surrender this attitude in his subsequent *Nouvelles Observations sur un cas de Somnambulisme* (Geneva, 1902).

The reality of other psychic phenomena, such as **telekinesis, telepathy,** and **clairvoyance,** he did not doubt. He became convinced of telekinesis through his experiences with **Eusapia Palladino** and he found sufficient proof of telepathy in the research of the SPR.

Flournoy investigated the question of apparitions of the dying and the dead as early as 1898 by addressing a questionnaire to the members of the Societé des Études Psychiques and others concerning their personal experiences. He received 72 replies and published his conclusions in February 1899 in the *Revue philosophique.* Because he did not accept the narratives at their face value he was accused of suppressing evidence.

Feeling honor-bound to publish the correspondence in full, he included it in a later work, *Esprits et Médiums, Mélanges de Métapsychique et de Psychologie* (Paris, 1911), translated into English in an abridgment under the title *Spiritism and Psychology* in the same year. It is a book of reference and contains a detailed exposition of his conclusions regarding psychical research and **survival.** Flournoy believed in the survival of the soul but not in experimental communications with the dead. He referred briefly to Lenora Piper's mediumship and the evidence of **cross-correspondence** but was hesitant in offering telepathy as an explanation.

Flournoy died November 5, 1920.

Sources:

Berger, Arthur S., and Joyce Berger. *The Encyclopedia of Parapsychology and Psychical Research.* New York: Paragon House, 1991.

Flournoy, Theodore. *Esprits et Médiums, Mélanges de Métapsychique et de Psychologie.* Geneva: Libraire Kundig, 1911. Translated by Hereward Carrington and abridged as *Spiritism and Psychology.* New York: Harper & Brothers, 1911.

———. *Des Indes à la Planète Mars.* 1900. Translated as *From India to the Planet Mars.* New York: Harper, 1901.

———. *The Philosophy of William James.* Freeport, N.Y.: Books for Libraries Press, 1969.

LeClair, R. C. *The Letters of William James and Theodore Flournoy.* Madison, Wis.: University of Wisconsin Press, 1966.

Flower, Amanda Cameron (1863–1940)

Amanda Cameron Flower was a **medium** and the founder of the **Independent Spiritualist Association of the United States of America.** She was born October 15, 1863, at Owen Sound, Ontario, and at the age of 27 moved to the United States. She was attracted to **Spiritualism** as a young woman and became a medium with the **National Spiritualist Association of Churches** (NSAC), the oldest of several Spiritualist churches in the United States. Her first pastorate was located in Owosso, Michigan. Around the turn of the century, with money given her by her husband, she built the Church of Truth in Grand Rapids, Michigan. It was incorporated in 1908 as the Spiritualist Temple Society (Church of Truth) in Grand Rapids.

Flower proved a popular medium and contributed greatly to the growth of the movement in Michigan and throughout the Midwest. However, in the 1920s she began to bristle under some of the NSAC rules, especially those that prevented her from speaking or doing mediumship work in congregations not associated with the NSAC. She had also absorbed some elements of **Theosophy** into her thinking, including a belief in reincarnation, an idea actively opposed by the NSAC. In 1924 she had a vision of a new association of churches bound together in a loose fellowship. She withdrew from the NSAC and founded the Independent Spiritualist Association of the United States of America. The association grew rapidly through several states of the Midwest. She founded and edited the association's newsletter. In 1931 she was elected president for life. She died November 20, 1940.

Sources:

Corey, Kathleen. *Rev. Amanda C. Flower.* Holly, Mich.: The Author, n.d.

Judah, J. Stillson. *The History and Philosophy of the Metaphysical Movement in America.* Philadelphia: Westminster Press, 1967.

Fludd (or Flud), Robert (1574–1637)

English Rosicrucian and alchemist who was born at Milgate House, in the parish of Bearsted, Kent, England. His father was Sir Thomas Fludd, a knight who enjoyed the patronage of Queen Elizabeth and served her for several years as "treasurer of war in the low countries."

At age 17 Robert entered St. John's College, Oxford. Five years later he took his bachelor of arts degree. Soon afterward he decided to take up medical science and left England to study on the Continent. Going first to Spain, he traveled to Italy and subsequently stayed for some time in Germany, where he is said to have supported himself by acting as a teacher. Upon returning home his alma mater, Oxford, conferred on him the degrees of bachelor of medicine and doctor of medicine; five years later, in 1609, he became a fellow of the College of Physicians.

Having prepared himself thoroughly for the medical profession, Fludd went to London and took a house in Fenchurch Street. He soon gained an extensive practice, his success attributable not merely to his genuine skill but also to his having an attractive and even magnetic personality. Although he kept busy with his medical practice, Fludd found time to write at length on medicine. He also became an important and influential member of the Fraternity of the Rosy Cross and began experiments in **alchemy.** He preached the great efficacy of the magnet, of sympathetic cures, of the weapon salve, and declared his belief in the **philosophers' stone,** the universal alkahest or solvent, and the *elixir vitae.*

Fludd maintained that all things were animated by two principles: condensation, the boreal, or northern virtue; and rarefaction, the austral, or southern virtue. He asserted that the human body was controlled by a number of demons, that each disease had its peculiar demon, and each demon his particular place in the frame of humanity, and that to conquer a disease—say, in the right leg—one must call in the aid of the demon who ruled the left, always proceeding by this rule of contraries.

As soon as the doctrines of the **Rosicrucians** were promulgated in the early seventeenth century Fludd embraced them with eagerness, and when several German writers attacked them he published a defense in 1616, under the title *Apologia Compendiaria Fraternitatem de Rosea-Cruce Suspicionis et Infamiæ Maculis Aspersam Abluens,* which procured him a widespread reputation as one of the apostles of the new fraternity.

Fludd met with the usual fate of prophets and was lustily denounced by a host of critics, including Pierre Gassendi and Johann Kepler. Fludd retorted in an elaborate treatise, *Summum Bonum, quod est Magiæ, Cabalæ, Alchimiæ, Fratrum Roseæ-Crucis Verorum, et adversus Mersenium Calumniatorem.* At a later period he made an adventurous attempt to identify the doctrines of the Rosicrucians with what he called the "philosophy of Moses" in his new volume, *Philosophia Mosaica, in quâ sapientia et scientia Creationis explicantur* (1638), and wrote numerous treatises on alchemy and medical science. His *Philosophia Mosaica* is notable for a discussion of the relationship between a rod and the mineral and vegetable world (i.e., the **divining rod** or **dowsing** rod). He also founded an English school for Rosicrucians.

Fludd was one of the high priests of the magnetic philosophy and learnedly expounded the laws of austral medicine, the doctrines of sympathies, and the fine powers and marvelous effects of the magnet. According to his theory, when two men approach each other their magnetism is either active or passive, that is, positive or negative. If the emanations that they send out are broken or thrown back, there arises antipathy, or *magnetismus negativus;* when the emanations pass through each other, positive magnetism is produced, for the magnetic rays proceed from the center to the circumference. Humans, like the earth, have their poles, or two main streams of magnetic influence, according to Fludd's theory. Like a miniature world, humans are endowed with a magnetic virtue that is subjected to the same laws as those of the universe. How these principles could be developed in the cure or prevention of disease is described at length in Fludd's books.

Fludd died September 8, 1637, at a house in Coleman Street, London, to which he had moved a few years before. Before his death he had won a fairly wide reputation founded on his chemical ability and had also written a number of books that contributed to the establishment of Rosicrucianism in Europe.

Sources:

Fludd, Robert. *Medicina Catholica.* Frankfurt: William Fitzer, 1629.

———. *Monochordum Mundi Symphoniacum.* Frankfurt, 1622.

———. *Philosophia Mosaica, in quâ sapientia et scientia Creationis explicantur.* Gouda: Peter Rammazen, 1638. Translated as *Mosaicall Philosophy.* London: Humphrey Moseley, 1659.

———. *Tractatus Apologeticus integritatem Societatis de Rosae Cruce defendans.* Leiden: Gottfried Basson, 1617.

———. *Veritatis Proscenium.* Frankfurt: Johann Theodore de Bry, 1621.

Godwin, Joscelyn. *Robert Fludd: Hermetic Philosopher and Surveyor of Two Worlds.* Boulder, Colo.: Shambhala, 1979.

Fluid Motor

A simple device invented by the Count de Tromelin, described in his book *Les Mysteres de l'Univers* (ca. 1908). It was supposed to demonstrate the existence of human energy **emanations** analagous to the subtle "fluid" of **animal magnetism.** It was composed of a paper cylinder about two inches in diameter, open at each end and crossed diametrically at its upper part by a piece of straw. A needle was stuck through the middle with the point resting on the bottom of a small, inverted porcelain or glass jar. The paper cylinder was suspended outside and concentric with the inverted jar, the point of the needle acting as a pivot and enabling it to turn easily under the slightest impulse.

Count de Tromelin claimed that if the right hand was placed behind this apparatus it would turn counterclockwise. If the left hand was placed behind, it would turn in the other direction. W. Warcollier, writing in the *Annals of Psychical Science* (August–September 1908), observes that this motion has nothing to do with the polarity of the two hands. The left hand produces the same effect as the right in the same position, writes Warcollier; moreover the heat of the hand is sufficient to create an air current that is capable of producing the rotation.

A more satisfactory instrument of this kind was invented by **Paul Joire** and was known as a **sthenometer.** (See also **biometer of Baraduc; magnetometer**)

Flute, Charm of the

The flute is often mentioned in history as being used for the purpose of charming animals, and serpents were said to have been peculiarly delighted with its music. It was claimed that adders would swell at the sound of the flute, raising themselves up, twisting about, and keeping proper time. An early Spanish writer stated that in India he had often seen people leading enchanted serpents, making them dance to the sound of a flute, putting them around their necks, and touching them without harm, and to this day a musical instrument of this nature is used by the snake charmers of that country.

However, it is now known that serpents cannot hear music, but instead are captivated by the swaying movements of the snake charmer, although some have suggested it is possible that snakes somehow perceive musical vibrations.

Flying Dutchman, The

Sailors in Holland long believed that a Dutch skipper named van Straaten was condemned as a penalty for his sins to sail for year after year through the seas around the Cape of Storms (an early name for the Cape of Good Hope). Crews returning to the Zudyer Zee (the northern coast of the Netherlands) after voyaging in this region used to declare that they had seen van Straaten's mysterious craft and fled from it in terror. The legend is a very old one, although its exact date is not known. The story is found in Dutch, German, and other folklore.

Several German versions call the ill-fated seaman von Falkenberg and maintain that it was not near South Africa but in the North Sea that his spectral ship commonly hovered. Others contend further that the devil paid periodic visits to the captain on board his ship and frequently the two were seen playing dice on deck, the stakes being von Falkenberg's soul.

The tale soon found its way from folklore into actual literature; among the greatest of writers utilizing it was Heinrich Heine. In his rendering the sailor has a chance of salvation; that is, the fates allow him to walk on land again once every seven years. If during his brief period of respite he contrives to win the affection of a pure maiden, liberation from perennial sea-wandering will be granted him as reward.

Heine's form of the story appealed greatly to the composer Richard Wagner, who always regarded women devoutly as a regenerating force, and the great composer based his opera *Der Fliegende Holländer* on Heine's version. It is set in the North Sea, and the sailor is called van Derdecken; the maiden to whom he makes advances is Senta. This opera was first staged at Dresden in 1843, and although it did not win speedy appreciation, it became popular in the course of time. The novelist Frederick Marryat also wrote his story *The Phantom Ship* (1839) on the subject of the *Flying Dutchman.*

During the nineteenth century, there were reliable reports of sightings of the *Flying Dutchman.* An English ship's log of 1835 stated that the captain and ship's crew saw the vessel bearing down on them "with all sails set" during a heavy gale. Another entry in the log of the *Bacchante* in 1881 reported that the *Flying Dutchman* crossed their bows, glowing with a strange red light before suddenly disappearing into a clear, calm night. Thirteen persons saw the phantom vessel, and two other ships in the vicinity reported seeing a strange red light. (See also **sea phantoms and superstitions**)

Sources:

Basset, W. *Wanderships.* Chicago, 1917.

Jal, A. *Scènes de la vie maritime.* Paris, 1830.

Rappoport, Angelo S. *Superstitions of Sailors.* London, 1928. Reprint, Ann Arbor, Mich.: Gryphon Books, 1971.

Flying Saucer Chronicle

Publication formerly issued ten times per year, connected with the investigations of the United Aerial Phenomena Agency, reporting **UFO** sightings in the United States and elsewhere.

Flying Saucer News

Journal concerned with flying saucers and **UFOs,** published for many years by Flying Saucer News Company in New York City.

Flying Saucer Review

Prominent British publication on **UFOs.** The *Flying Saucer Review* was founded in 1955 in London by Derek Dempster, a former Royal Air Force pilot. Under the editorship of **Brinsley le Poer Trench** (1956–59) it developed a reputation as an uncritical periodical, but during the tenure of Charles Bowen it became one of the most influential journals serving the UFO community. Bowen retired because of illness in 1982 and was succeeded by Gordon Creighton. Creighton, influenced by various conspiracy theories, has aliented many in the UFO establishment who no longer consider the *Flying Saucer Review* a serious UFO organ. Address: FSR Publications, Box 162, High Wycombe, Bucks. HP13 5D2, England.

Sources:

Clark, Jerome. *The Emergence of a Phenomenon: UFOs from the Beginning through 1959.* Vol. 2 of *The UFO Encyclopedia.* Detroit: Omnigraphics, 1992.

Flying Saucers

Popular term for Unidentified Flying Objects or **UFOs.** The terms flying saucer and UFO were used somewhat synonymously in the 1950s, but the former term was eventually adopted by those who claimed to have positive evidence that what others called UFOs were in fact extraterrestrial crafts. The term originated from a report by Kenneth Arnold, whose 1947 sightings of UFOs near Mt. Rainier in Washington began the modern UFO era.

Sources:

Clark, Jerome. *The Emergence of a Phenomenon: UFOs from the Beginning through 1959.* Vol. 2 of *The UFO Encyclopedia.* Detroit: Omnigraphics, 1992.

Flying Saucers International

Former quarterly publication of the **Amalgamated Flying Saucer Clubs of America.** It was published from 1962 to 1969.

Sources:

Clark, Jerome. *The Emergence of a Phenomenon: UFOs from the Beginning through 1959.* Vol. 2 of *The UFO Encyclopedia.* Detroit: Omnigraphics, 1992.

Fodor, Nandor (1895–1964)

Prominent psychoanalyst and psychical researcher. Fodor was born May 13, 1895, at Beregszasz, Hungary. He studied law and took his LL.D. degree at the Royal Hungarian University of Science in 1917 and served as a law assistant during World War I (1917–21). From 1921 to 1928, he worked as a journalist and in 1921 visited the United States as a staff reporter on the New York Hungarian language daily *Amerikai Magyar Nepszava.* His chance discovery of a book on psychic phenomena by researcher **Hereward Carrington** led to an interview with Carrington and a meeting with veteran Spiritualist **Sir Arthur Conan Doyle.** Fodor's interest was aroused and he began to correspond with Carrington.

In 1926 Fodor interviewed Sandor Ferenczi, prominent psychoanalyst and associate of Freud, and became interested in psychoanalysis. Later Fodor was to integrate three professions as journalist, psychoanalyst, and psychical researcher.

He was employed as a secretary by British press magnate Lord Rothermere in 1929. During this period in England, Fodor was able to compile his monumental *Encyclopaedia of Psychic Science.* Fodor also became assistant editor of the *Light,* the oldest British Spiritualist journal. He was also appointed research officer of the **International Institute for Psychical Research** and undertook careful investigations into mediumistic transfiguration, **apports, direct voice, levitation, hauntings, materializations,** and **poltergeist** phenomena.

Fodor lectured extensively on such subjects and wrote a number of books and articles. In 1938 he was responsible for a number of highly skeptical newspaper articles on mediumship and **Spiritualism,** which aroused a good deal of opposition from Spiritualists. Soon afterward Fodor returned to the United States, where he renewed his friendship with Hereward Carrington and practiced as a psychoanalyst. He took a profound interest in the psychological aspects of mediumship and published a number of important studies on the subject. He also advocated a more open methodology in studying mediumship as opposed to the attempts to control the environment of the séance room with ropes and other devices then used by investigators.

During his lifetime Fodor was an honorary member of the Danish Society for Psychical Research and the Hungarian Metaphysical Society, a member of the New York Academy of Science, the American Psychological Association, and the New York State Psychological Association. He wrote a number of books and contributed more than 70 articles to various psychoanalytic, neurological, and psychiatric journals. He died May 17, 1964.

Sources:

Berger, Arthur S., and Joyce Berger. *The Encyclopedia of Parapsychology and Psychical Research.* New York: Paragon House, 1991.

Fodor, Nandor. *Between Two Worlds.* New York: Paperback Library, 1964.

———. *Encyclopedia of Psychic Science.* London: Arthurs Press, 1934.

———. *The Haunted Mind: A Psychoanalyst Looks at the Supernatural.* New York: Garrett Publications, 1959.

———. *New Approaches to Dream Interpretation.* New York, 1951. Reprint, New Hyde Park, N.Y.: University Books, 1951.

———. *On the Trail of the Poltergeist.* New York: Citadel Press, 1958.

———. *These Mysterious People.* London: Rider, 1936.

———. *The Unaccountable.* New York: Award Books, 1968.

Fodor, Nandor, and Hereward Carrington. *Haunted People.* New York: Dutton, 1951.

———. *The Story of the Poltergeist down the Centuries.* London: Rider, 1953.

Pleasants, Helene, ed. *Biographical Dictionary of Parapsychology.* New York: Helix Press, 1964.

FOG Newsletter

Former bimonthly newsletter of the **International Society for the Investigation of Ghosts.** FOG is an acronym for "Friends of Ghosts." The society may be contacted at P.O. Box 5011, Salinas, CA 93901.

Fohat

In **Theosophy,** a term for the primal life force or power of the **Logos.** It was adapted from the Tibetan in the writings of **Helena Petrovna Blavatsky.**

Folklore Frontiers

British quarterly publication concerned with new frontiers of urban belief stories, tall tales, and folklore, including **Fortean phenomena,** Earth mysteries, and modern shamanism. Edited by Paul Screeton. Address: 6 Egton Dr., Seaton Carew, Hartlepool, Cleveland, TS25 2AT, England.

Folk-Lore Society

Pioneer British scholarly society for the study of oral traditions and cultures, founded in 1878. The term *folk-lore* was coined by the antiquary W. J. Thomas (1803–1885) to denote old-world manners, customs, and popular superstitions. The Folk-Lore Society had as its objectives the preservation and publication of popular traditions, legendary ballads, local proverbial sayings, superstitions, and old customs, both British and foreign, as well as other related subjects. Over the years many distinguished scholars have been associated with the society, including Max Müller, E. B. Tylor, and **Andrew Lang.** In 1912 **Sir William Crookes,** famous for his research in **Spiritualism,** was president of the society.

The society has published many specialized studies of various aspects of folklore, as well as its periodicals *Folk-lore Record* (from 1878) and *Folk-lore Journal* (from 1883). Address: University College, Gower Street, London, WC1E 6BT, England.

Fongities

According to ancient belief this was a gem said to assuage anger.

Fontaine, Jean de la (or John Fontaine) (ca. 1413)

Flemish alchemist and poet who lived at Valenciennes toward the close of the thirteenth century. Two books are ascribed to him, *La Fontaine des Amoureux de Science* and *La Fontaine Perilleuse,* both of which were written in French and published in Paris, the first in 1561 and the second in 1572.

Fontaine's claims to the authorship of the latter work have frequently been disputed, but the former is almost certainly his, and is a curious production. At the outset the author professes himself an expert in hermetic philosophy, and thereafter he proceeds, in poetry of an allegorical style that recalls *The Roman of the Rose,* to describe the different processes involved in achieving a transmutation. There is little in this metrical treatise that indicates that the writer was an alchemist of any great ability, but he certainly possessed a distinct gift for writing pleasant verse.

Sources:

Fontaine, Jean de la. *La Fontaine des Amoureux de Science.* Paris, 1561.

———. *La Fontaine Perilleuse.* Paris, 1572.

Fontenettes, Charles

Author of a *Dissertation sur une fille de Grenoble, qui depuis quatre ans ne boit ni ne mange* (1737). This prodigy was commonly attributed to the devil, but Fontenettes explains that it was due to a less sinister cause.

Ford, Arthur A(ugustus) (1896–1971)

American Spiritualist **medium** and founder of the **International General Assembly of Spiritualists.** Ford was born January 8, 1896, at Titusville, Florida. As a youth he followed a pilgrimage that took him from Episcopalianism to the Baptists to Unitarianism and finally to the Disciples of Christ. He attended Transylvania College, a Disciples of Christ school in Lexington, Kentucky. Ordained as a Disciples minister, he served a church in Barbourbville, Kentucky.

Ford realized his psychic abilities during World War I. While in the army he would "hear" the names of people he served with, and those names would appear on the casualty lists several days later. In the years after the war he investigated psychic phenomena and eventually joined the Spiritualists. Around 1921 Ford emerged as a trance medium, and "Fletcher," his control for the rest of his life, made his first appearance in trance sessions. He developed a popular following and in 1927 traveled to Great Britain. One of his lectures was attended by veteran Spiritualist **Sir Arthur Conan Doyle,** who enthusiastically told people the next day, "One of the most amazing things I have ever seen in 41 years of psychic experience was the demonstration of Arthur Ford."

Ford founded a congregation in New York City, but soon experienced conflict with the National Spiritualist Association, the main Spiritualist organization of the time. Ford had come to believe in **reincarnation,** a belief the association rejected. After many years of tension, in 1936 Ford led in the founding of the General Assembly, which had a more open perspective on reincarnation.

Ford achieved fame far beyond the Spiritualist community in 1928 by allegedly breaking the secret code between the late **Houdini** and his wife Beatrice. Houdini had arranged with his wife that if he died before she did he would attempt to communicate through a secret code known only to them. Arthur Ford is credited with revealing that code through his control, "Fletcher."

As a result of a tragic auto accident in 1931, in which his sister died, Ford was severely injured and became addicted first to morphine and then to alcohol. In his autobiography *Nothing So Strange* (1958) he states that it took him 20 years and much suffering to overcome his addiction. (In fact, he never overcame his addiction and suffered from alcoholism until the end of his life.)

In spite of his affliction he impressed numerous people with his abilities, including prominent researchers **William McDougall** and **William G. Roll, Jr.** of the **Psychical Research Foundation.** He also traveled widely to demonstrate his mediumship and in Britain visited the **Churches' Fellowship for Psychical and Spiritual Studies.** In 1955 Ford was active in the formation of a similar organization in the United States, the Spiritual Frontiers Fellowship, now the **Spiritual Frontiers Fellowship.**

In 1967 Ford again came into public prominence during a television discussion on life after death, when he went into a trance and delivered several messages to Episcopal bishop **James Pike.** One claimed to be from Pike's son and another from the prominent theologian Paul Tillich. Duly impressed, Pike later publicly affirmed his belief in the reality of psychic phenomena in his book *The Other Side* (1968). The television program also revived public interest in **Spiritualism** and psychic phenomena, and within a month Ford received more than 12,000 letters. It was only after Ford's death that Allen Spraggett and William Rauscher, while compiling materials for his biography, discovered his notes for the session among his papers, revealing the fact that he faked the famous séance.

Ford died in Miami, Florida, January 4, 1971. Shortly after his death, **Ruth Montgomery** claimed to have received messages from Ford, which were later published in her book *A World Beyond* (1971).

The most decisive incident in evaluating Ford's mediumship seems to be his relationship to the Houdini code. The evidence for the authenticity of the code message from the deceased Houdini received through Ford's mediumship is contradictory. The message itself involved a secret code that was supposed to have been known only to Houdini and his wife. The stage magician Dunninger, however, claimed that the code had been published earlier.

The testimony of Houdini's widow is contradictory. She was said to have told a reporter that she did not know what the message would be, although she later wrote an impassioned private letter to columnist Walter Winchell stating emphatically that the message received from Ford was definitely the one agreed upon with Houdini and that she had not previously revealed it to Ford. She insisted it was not a **fraud,** as some had claimed.

However, *New York Graphic* reporter Rea Jaure, in a story headlined "Houdini Message A Big Hoax!" (January 10, 1929) stated that Ford had come to her apartment for an interview and admitted that Mrs. Houdini had supplied the code to him. Jaure produced two witnesses who confirmed her story with sworn statements. Ford's attorney produced three witnesses who affirmed that Ford had been elsewhere at the time of the claimed interview. An anonymous man stated that he had been paid to impersonate the medium.

Sources:

Christopher, Milbourne. *Mediums, Mystics & The Occult.* New York: Thomas Y. Crowell, 1975.

Ford, Arthur. *The Life Beyond Death.* New York: G. P. Putnam's Sons, 1971.

———. *Nothing So Strange.* New York: Harper, 1958.

———. *Spiritual Vibrations.* New York: H.P.B. Publishers, 1926.

———. *Unknown But Known.* New York: Harper, 1968.

———. *Why We Survive.* Cooksburg, N.Y.: 1952.

Montgomery, Ruth. *A World Beyond.* New York: Coward, McCann & Geoghegan, 1971.

Spraggett, Allen, with William V. Rauscher. *Arthur Ford, The Man Who Talked with the Dead.* New York: New American Library, 1973.

Formative Causation

A bold theory concerned with the origin and growth of form and characteristics in nature. This theory was proposed by biochemist and plant researcher **Rupert Sheldrake** in his book *A New Science of Life: The Hypothesis of Formative Causation.*

For many years, embryologists have used the general term *morphogenetic fields* to indicate the mysterious factors that influence the development of growth and characteristics in plants and animals. The term is derived from the Greek *morphe* (form) and *genesis* (coming into being) and is usually assumed to embrace a complex of inherited characteristics programmed in DNA molecules. Sheldrake's theory, however, proposes a literal interpretation of morphogenetic fields as structures independent of time and space. All the past fields of a given type are available instantly to, or coexist with, subsequent similar systems.

The genes only define parameters within which development takes place and do not determine the future form of the organism. The fertilization of a seed or egg, says Sheldrake, is a "morphogenetic germ" for development that is influenced by "previous systems of which structures similar to these morphogenetic germs were a part. [It] thus becomes surrounded by, or embedded within, the morphogenetic field of the higher-level system [i.e., the cell is influenced by the tittuse-field, the tissue by the organ-field], which then shapes or moulds the process of development towards the characteristic form."

Sheldrake calls the influence of one morphogenetic field upon another "morphic resonance," involving a new kind of action at a distance, independent of space and time. This influence does not appear to be electromagnetic and may involve some as yet undiscovered method of action, a theory that clearly has relevance to such parapsychological phenomena as **telepathy** and **clairvoyance.**

Sheldrake's theory applies to crystals as well as to animals and plants. If a new organic compound is crystallized the shape may be merely a matter of chance. Once crystallization has taken place, however, it establishes a morphogenetic field affecting all subsequent crystallizations of that substance, influencing them to take the same form. Successive crystallizations reinforce the field, facilitating future formation of a particular crystal shape. In the same way, future developments of animal or plant species are affected by the establishment of morphogenetic fields in the past. In simplest outline the theory suggests that it is easier to learn something because others have learned it before.

Although Sheldrake does not discuss the implications for parapsychology in detail in his book, his references make it clear that since morphogenetic fields are claimed as independent of space and time they could also act as channels for transmission of information, and are thus related to telepathy and clairvoyance.

The theory had an astonishingly hostile reception by the editors of the journal *Nature* (September 1981):

"What is to be made of Dr. Rupert Sheldrake's book. . . . This infuriating tract has been widely hailed by the newspapers and popular science magazines as the 'answer' to materialistic science, and is now well on its way to being a point of reference for the motley crew of creationists, anti-reductionists, neo-Lamarckians and the rest. The author, by training a biochemist and by demonstration a knowledgeable man, is, however, misguided. His book is the best candidate for burning there has been for many years. In reality, Sheldrake's argument is in no sense a scientific argument but is an exercise in pseudoscience. Preposterously, he claims that his hypothesis can be tested . . . and the text includes half a dozen proposals for experiments that might be carried out to verify that the forms of aggregations of matter are indeed moulded by the hypothetical morphogenetic fields that are supposed to pervade everything. These experiments have in common the attributes of being time-consuming, inconclusive in the sense that it will always be possible to postulate yet another morphogenetic field to account for some awkwardly inconclusive result, and impractical in the sense that no self-respecting grant-making agency will take the proposals seriously. . . . His book should not be burned (nor even confined to closed shelves in libraries) but, rather, put firmly in its place among the literature of intellectual aberrations."

In correspondence in subsequent issues of *Nature,* however, readers deplored this "emotional outburst." Clearly the suggestion that experiments should not be undertaken to test a theory because they would be "time-consuming" or "inconclusive" seemed thoroughly unscientific, they wrote, since many scientific theories that appeared at first sight to be "preposterous" were validated by later experiments.

A thoughtful discussion of Sheldrake's theory is a comprehensive article by R. J. M. Rickard in *Fortean Times* (Spring 1982), which printed a detailed interview and discussion with Sheldrake himself at the home of John Mitchell.

Sources:

Sheldrake, Rupert. *A New Science of Life: The Hypothesis of Formative Causation.* London: Blond & Briggs, 1981.

———. *The Presence of the Past: Morphic Resonance and the Habits of Nature.* New York: Vintage Books, 1989.

Fort, Charles (Hoy) (1874–1932)

American journalist, writer, and explorer of scientific anomalies. He was the archenemy of dogmatic science. Fort was born on August 9, 1874, in Albany, New York. As a boy he wanted to be a naturalist. Instead he became a journalist at age 17. Two years later he decided to see the world and spent two years traveling, from New York to New Orleans, Nova Scotia, England, Scotland, Wales, and South Africa. His vast store of travel impressions over 30,000 miles laid the foundation for his later preoccupation with accumulating and analyzing data.

Back in New York he married Anna Filing, an English girl, on October 26, 1896. They lived in poverty while Fort took various nondescript jobs and worked on his writing. He sold feature stories to the New York press, then began to write humorous short stories. He also started a number of large-scale novels, only one of which was ever published, *The Outcast Manufacturers* (1909).

He read widely, took thousands of notes and destroyed them, trying to hammer out a personal philosophy. He decided that science consisted of believers and cranks, and out of his skepticism he said whimsically that he would be a crank. He wrote a strange book titled X, which was never published, and the manuscript was probably destroyed. He corresponded with novelist Theodore Dreiser, who appreciated Fort's restless originality.

In 1916 Fort inherited a share of his grandfather's estate, and the following year, after his brother's death, he inherited that share. Freed from the financial problems that had dominated his adult life, he was able to devote his time to what had become a growing obsession: to explain the unexplained. He had collected many notes on odd phenomena that had been reported but remained outside the explanation of science as it existed in his day. The result of his early research was his first book, *The Book of the Damned* (1919). The "damned" were the data rejected or explained away by mainstream science. He relentlessly chronicled strange falls from the sky, mysterious disappearances and reappearances, strange synchronicities, enigmatic artifacts, and astronomical ambiguities.

Dreiser took the manuscript to Boni & Liveright of New York and insisted that they publish it. When the book was first published in 1919 it attracted favorable comments from Booth Tarkington, John Cooper Powys, Ben Hecht, and other notable persons. It was followed by *New Lands* (1923), *Lo!* (1931), and *Wild Talents* (1932). By the time the last book was published Fort's health was failing. He died on May 3, 1932. His wife died five years later.

Shortly before Fort's death Tiffany Thayer organized the **Fortean Society** to promote the study of his books and continue the work of gathering "Fortean data." Thayer urged the one-volume reprinting of Fort's books a decade later and wrote the introduction to *The Books of Charles Fort* (1941). After Thayer's death in 1959 the society essentially ceased to exist, but a new group, the **International Fortean Organization,** was founded in 1965.

Charles Fort was the first individual to gather and make a systematic study of many unusual physical phenomena. He studied **UFOs** long before the modern UFO era, which began in 1947. He called attention to many unusual phenomena and the extent of their occurrence. Among many topics now studied as "Fortean phenomena" are falls of frogs, stones, blood, or ice from the sky, mysterious fires, **stigmata,** invisible assassins, UFOs, **poltergeists,** ancient technologies, **levitation,** teleportation, monsters, fireballs, meteors, and ancient artifacts. Until Fort began to write, no one realized how many strange events were occurring and how weak "scientific" explanations of them were. In the years since, many of the mysteries he addressed have been examined and brought into the body of scientific knowledge. Many remain unexplained, however, and new ones are continually being added to the list.

Sources:

Fort, Charles. *The Complete Books of Charles Fort.* New York: Henry Holt, 1941. Reprint, New York: Dover, 1974.

———. *The Outcast Manufacturers.* B. W. Dodge, 1909.

Gross, Loren E. *Charles Fort, the Fortean Society, and Unidentified Flying Objects.* Fremont, Calif.: The Author, 1976.

Knight, Damon. *Charles Fort, Prophet of the Unexplained.* Garden City, N.Y.: Doubleday, 1970.

Fortean News, The (Journal)

A British journal devoted to "Fortean data," i.e., strange phenomena, curiosities, prodigies, portents, coincidences, and mysteries in the spirit of the late **Charles Fort,** who first correlated and studied such things. Originally issued as *The News* beginning in November 1973, the name was changed to *The Fortean News* with issue 16 in June 1976. It is published and edited by Robert J. M. Rickard and may be contacted at its editorial offices at 96 Mansfield Rd., London NW3 2HX, United Kingdom. (See also **INFO**)

Fortean Society

Founded by author Tiffany Thayer to honor **Charles Fort,** chronicler of the unexplained, promote the study of his books, preserve his notes and papers, and continue the work of collecting "Fortean data." Founded January 26, 1931, the society was the forerunner of organizations studing unidentified flying objects and other bizarre phenomena. The first issue of the *Fortean Society Magazine* appeared in September 1937. With the eleventh issue (Winter 1944–45) the title was changed to *Doubt,* emphasizing Fort's characteristic preoccupation with healthy skepticism toward dogma. Thayer died in 1959 and the society languished. *Doubt* owed much to Thayer's indefatigable enthusiasm, and issue no. 61 was the last.

Although the society was never officially dissolved, its work was superseded by INFO, the **International Fortean Organization,** headed by Paul and Ron Willis, which publishes *INFO Journal* (P.O. Box 367, Arlington, VA 22210-0367). A related journal of Fortean curiosities is the **Fortean Times** (originally *The News*), published by Robert J. M. Rickard and Paul Sievking. A one-act play, *The Great Caper,* dealing with Fortean mysteries, was written by Ken Campbell and produced at the Royal Court Theatre, London, in October 1974.

Sources:

Fort, Charles. *The Complete Books of Charles Fort.* New York: Henry Holt, 1941. Reprint, New York: Dover, 1974.

Fortean Times

British journal devoted to "Fortean data," (i.e., strange phenomena, curiosities, prodigies, portents, mysteries) in the spirit of the late **Charles Fort.** It was founded in November 1973 and originally titled *The News.* The name change dates from issue no. 16 (June 1976). The journal is published by Robert J. M. Rickard and Paul Sievking. Rickard has compiled several books from data assembled for the magazine. Address: The Boathouse, Crabtree Ln., London SW6 6LU, England.

Sources:

Michell, John, and Robert J. M. Rickard. *Phenomena: A Book of Miracles.* London: Thames and Hudson, 1977. Reprint, New York: Pantheon Books, 1977.

Rickard, Robert J. M., and Richard Kelly. *Photographs of the Unknown.* London: Book Club Associates, 1980.

Forteana

Quarterly publication (in Danish language) of the Scandinavian Fortean Organization (SCANFO), concerned with reports of unusual phenomena (e.g., **UFO** sightings, apparitions). Address: Classensgade 17-A-4TH, DK-2100, Copenhagen, Denmark.

Forthuny, Pascal (1872–1962)

Pseudonym of Georges Cochet, French author, musician, poet, painter, art critic, and possessor of remarkable powers of **psychometry.** The loss of a son in an aviation accident at the end of World War I induced Forthuny to take an interest in table sittings. The result was not strictly evidential, yet it had a soothing effect on the grieving father. Then in July 1921, while engaged in ordinary writing, his hand was seized by what appeared to be an extraneous power. Strokes and loops were followed by mirror writing and scripts, delivered at an extreme speed, full of high thoughts and affection, which he believed emanated from the spirit of his son.

Soon, however, claimed Forthuny, the influence gave way to an obsessive entity that demanded entire command over his life, representing itself as having a mandate from Christ and driving Forthuny to strange acts. By an effort of will Forthuny regained his self-control; but when banished, the obsessive entity predicted that Forthuny would lose his mediumship.

Forthuny's phenomenon of **automatic writing** did disappear in about six months, but more important gifts took its place. During a visit to the **Institut Métapsychique** in 1922 Forthuny picked up an envelope containing an autograph of Landru, the Bluebeard murderer, which **Gustav Geley** had prepared for another psychic, and gave an accurate description of the cottage at Gambais where Landru committed his crimes.

Mrs. Geley then picked up a fan and asked jokingly, "Where does this fan come from?" Forthuny answered, "I feel as though I were choking and I hear Elisa by my side." The fan had belonged to an old lady named Elisa who died of congestion of the lungs.

Eugèn Osty's *Supernormal Faculties in Man* (1923) and **Charles Richet**'s *Our Sixth Sense* (1929) deal extensively with Forthuny's powers, which were tested in many experiments at the institute. For instance, walking among 50 unknown persons Forthuny addressed each as he felt inspired and disclosed amazingly accurate facts about their lives.

He was actually stimulated by a large audience. He did not go into trance nor call himself a medium, was ignorant of the machinery through which he got his supernormal knowledge, and preserved a remarkable spirit of criticism in his moments of intuition. He was sensitive to hostile attitudes, but they only made him more convinced of the exactness of his vision and induced him to publicly denounce the hostility. He did not "fish" for information nor ask leading questions but wanted to be stopped if he ran off the subject, since, he said, he often experienced the blending of two influences. Generally he "heard" the names, at other times he saw colored pictures or written names.

In April 1924 he was appointed general secretary of the *Union Spirite Française* and gave regular clairvoyant sittings at the Maison des Spirites, Paris. On one occasion he visited Geley and, very much moved, told him that he had just had a vision of an airplane crash in Poland in which a physician was killed. Forthuny insisted that his vision be recorded at the institute. He said he did not know who the physician was—possibly a "Voronoff" but he was not sure. On July 14 of the same year Geley was killed in an airplane crash near Warsaw.

In 1919 Forthuny paid a visit to the **Society for Psychical Research** (SPR). V. J. Woolley concludes in his report (*Proceedings* of the SPR, vol. 39) that "we are driven to assume that his knowledge comes from some supernormal faculty, and it seems reasonable to suppose that this faculty consists mainly in a supernormal knowledge of what is in the minds of people present with him, whether we call such knowledge telepathic or clairvoyant."

The archskeptic **Harry Price** met Forthuny in Paris in 1927 and was impressed by his "remarkable psychic powers." Price became friendly with Forthuny, whom he described as a "fine clairvoyant."

Fortune, Dion

Pseudonym of **Violet M. Firth** (1890–1946), the prominent British occultist and author who founded the **Fraternity of the Inner Light.**

Fortune-Telling

Fortune-telling in Britain was formerly included under the crime of **witchcraft** and was made punishable by death under the Statute of 1563. This act was repealed by George II (1683–1760), who ordained that no prosecution should thereafter be made on a charge of witchcraft and that all persons professing to occult skill or undertaking to tell fortunes might be sentenced to imprisonment for one year, made to stand pillory, and pledge future good behavior.

Punishment by pillory was later abolished. Under George IV (1762–1830) fortune-tellers were included along with other vagrants under the general category of "rogues and vagabonds" and were liable to imprisonment for three months. This provision was made applicable to Scotland also and provided that "every person pretending or professing to tell fortunes or using any subtle craft, means, or device, by palmistry or otherwise to deceive, and impose on any of His Majesty's Subjects" would be deemed a vagabond and rogue and be punished accordingly.

The first case to be prosecuted under this law was the Smith case. A woman named Jone Lee Smith was charged in the police court at Glasgow with a violation of the enactment. She was convicted of the violation and drew a suspension. The court overturned the conviction, on the grounds that the complaint was irrelevant in that it did not set forth that the accused had pretended to tell fortunes with intent to deceive anyone. Lord Young, one of the judges, said,

"It has never been imagined, so far as I have ever heard, or thought, that writing, publishing, or selling books on the lines of the hand, or even on astrology—the position of the stars at birth and the rules upon which astrologers proceed in telling fortunes therefrom. I say that I have never heard of publishing, or selling such books is an offence, or that reading such books, and telling fortunes therefrom is an offence. Roguery and knavery might be committed that way, but it would be a special case. I am not in any way suggesting that a spae wife or anyone else may not through that means commit knavery and deception, and so be liable to punishment."

It thus appears that fortune-telling was of itself no offense unless accompanied by **fraud.** While it might be an offense for the palmist or fortune-teller to knowingly accept payment from a foolish or ignorant person, it could hardly be said that the ordinary person who consulted and then paid a professional fortune-teller or crystal gazer should feel imposed upon if the character delineations were faulty or the forecast inaccurate.

British Spiritualists continued to be harassed under the Vagrancy Act of 1824 throughout the first half of the twentieth century. Psychical research might be quite respectable, but until as recently as 1951 a **medium** could be prosecuted under sections of the Witchcraft Act of 1735 and the Vagrancy Act of 1824. In a 1921 case a judge stated, "I cannot reverse the decision on the claim that the intention to deceive was not necessarily to be proved. *The act of fortune-telling is an offence in itself.*"

Perhaps the most deplorable type of prosecution was that in which undercover agents were employed by the police to obtain evidence. Disguised policewomen posing as bereaved parents would approach a medium, begging for some consolatory message. A small sum of money would be proffered as a "love offering," and if this was accepted the medium could be prosecuted—often for as little as the equivalent of a 25-cent "donation" to the Spiritualist church. Unsympathetic magistrates, convinced that all Spiritualists were frauds, often imposed a fine, or a sentence of up to three months' imprisonment.

As late as 1944 the medium **Helen Duncan** was prosecuted for "pretending to communicate with spirits." Duncan was found guilty and served a sentence of nine months' imprisonment. After her release she resumed mediumistic activities and in October 1956 was seized by police at a séance in Nottingham. She became ill and died five weeks later. This case stimulated efforts by Spiritualists to get the old punitive legislation repealed, since it could theoretically make any séance illegal.

In 1951 the old witchcraft and vagrancy legislation was finally repealed by the new Fraudulent Mediums Act, which, although not wholly satisfactory, at least implicitly acknowledged that there might be genuine mediumship. In New York comparable outdated legislation had been amended in 1929 to exempt ministers and mediums of Spiritualist associations acting in good faith without personal fees.

The dropping of the old witchcraft law had a second, and unplanned, effect: the revival of a new form of witchcraft. Following the repeal of the anti-witchcraft legislation, **Gerald Gardner** published several books announcing the continued existence of witchcraft followers in England.

Sources:

Gardner, Gerald. *Witchcraft Today.* London: Rider, 1954.

Forum for Death Education and Counseling, Inc. Newsletter

Publication concerned with the relatively new field of **thanatology,** emphasizing information on various alternative approaches to death and dying. Address: 638 Prospect Ave., Hartford, CT 06105-4298.

Forwald, Haakon Gabriel (1897–1978)

Scandinavian electrical engineer, inventor, and parapsychologist. Born August 21, 1897, at Mandal, Norway, Forwald was educated at the Technical College of Oslo. From 1918 to 1923 he was a pilot with the Norwegian Naval Air Force. In 1925 he received his B.A. from the Technische Hochschule, Danzig, and later studied at the Swiss Federal Institute of Technology, Zurich, and the Royal Institute of Technology, Stockholm. He worked as a consulting engineer and held many patents for his engineering and electrical work.

In 1950 he began experimenting in the field of parapsychology, particularly **psychokinesis.** In 1957 he was a research fellow at Duke University and in 1959 a research fellow at the University of Pittsburgh. He was given the William McDougall Award for Distinguished Work in Parapsychology for his paper (with **J. G. Pratt**) on "Confirmation of the PK Placement Effect" (1958).

Forwald became a charter member of the Parapsychological Association and wrote a number of articles on parapsychology. In 1969 he contributed *Mind, Matter and Gravitation: A Theoretical & Experimental Study* to the Parapsychology Foundation monograph series. In this paper he discusses his experiments in psychokinesis and states that they "led to the recognition of mathematical structures which are the same in PK-forces as those observed in physics. The findings suggest that PK-forces are of a gravitational kind, and that they originate from a mental influence on atomic nuclei in the material which is used in the moveable bodies in the experiments." He died September 16, 1978, at Ludvika, Sweden.

Sources:

Berger, Arthur S., and Joyce Berger. *The Encyclopedia of Parapsychology and Psychical Research.* New York: Paragon House, 1991.

Forwald, Haakon G. "An Approach to Instrumental Investigation of Psychokinesis." *Journal of Parapsychology* (1954).

———. "Experiments with Alternating PK Placement and Control Tests." *Journal of Parapsychology* (1955).

———. "A Further Study of the PK Placement Effect." *Journal of Parapsychology* 16 (1952).

———. *Mind, Matter and Gravitation.* New York: Parapsychology Foundation, 1970.

———. "A Study of Psychokinesis in its Relation to Physical Conditions." *Journal of Parapsychology* 19 (1955).

Forwald, Haakon G., and Joseph G. Pratt. "Confirmation of the PK Placement Effect." *Journal of Parapsychology* 22 (March 1958).

Pleasants, Helene, ed. *Biographical Dictionary of Parapsychology.* New York: Helix Press, 1964.

Foster, Charles H. (1838–1888)

American medium who had a controversial career. The claim put forward in *The Salem Seer* (1891) by his enthusiastic biographer, George C. Bartlett, that he was the greatest spiritual medium since **Emanuel Swedenborg** seems somewhat exaggerated, and whatever powers he possessed he probably magnified through **fraud.**

Foster was born in Salem, Massachusetts, and educated at a public school there. According to Bartlett, the first indications of his mediumship were noticed at age 14. During school hours **raps** were heard on his desk. At night he was awakened by violent noises and the furniture was tossed about in his room. Some time later the phenomena began to occur in daylight, and furniture was heard moving about in rooms where no one was present. Skin writing (see **dermography**) and **pellet reading** were the special features of his mediumship. Both were subjects of lively discussion and controversy.

According to an amusing story told in his biography, Foster was once rudely seized by the arm when skin writing was produced. Two men asked for a test in plain sight. While they were holding him, in large round characters the words "Two Fools" appeared on the medium's arm. In such skin writing the letters were blood-red and, as a rule, displayed the name of the communicating spirit. They appeared mostly on Foster's forearm.

In pellet reading the usual procedure was to ask the sitters to write the names of their deceased relatives on slips of paper while the medium was out of the room, roll them up, and put as many blank pellets as they liked together with them in a heap on the table. On his return the names on the slips were spelled out by raps, and Foster picked out the writing, delivered trance addresses, and gave clairvoyant and clairaudient descriptions of spirits. He claimed that Virgil, Camoens, Cervantes, and many other illustrious entities were among his communicators.

In 1861 Foster visited England and while there **materialization** phenomena were added to his performances. His first séance was given in the house of William Wilkinson, the editor of *Spiritual* magazine. He became friendly with the **Master of Lytton,** with whom he stayed at Knebworth. The literary elite—Charles Dickens, Thackeray, Tennyson, Robert Chambers, and William Howitt—came to him for sittings. John Ashburner, an authority on **animal magnetism** and **Spiritualism,** recorded unusual phenomena. He saw nine materialized hands floating over the dining table and witnessed a **levitation** of the medium and of the piano on which he was playing.

In January 1862, at the invitation of Thomas P. Barkas, Foster gave four séances in Newcastle-upon-Tyne. At each of these, ten persons participated. Their names were kept in a private book and withheld from the medium. With these 40 people the errors in the communications, according to Barkas, did not exceed three percent, and these usually happened during some trifling confusion or controversy.

Nevertheless, Barkas had the impression that, although Foster was a genuine medium, he occasionally, perhaps frequently, heightened the effects by trickery and deception. In support of this surmise, Barkas points out, in his *Outlines of Ten Years Investigations into the Phenomena of Modern Spiritualism* (1862), that the names of the departed spirits were written by the medium according to the spelling on the pellets, which was sometimes wrong; the communications were extraordinarily similar; his rapid entrancement and sudden relief were more likely to be apparent than real; and the writing, whether obtained directly or automatically, always resembled the normal writing of the medium.

Sentiment eventually turned against Foster. In 1863 *Spiritual* magazine stated that the editor had received from a Judge Edmonds such "sickening details of his criminality in another direction that we should no longer soil our pages with his mediumship." Foster simply left England for the Continent. He went to Paris, appeared before Napoleon III, toured Australia, and finally returned to New York.

Epes Sargent records convincing personal experiences in pellet reading with Foster in *Planchette, or the Despair of Science* (1869). On the other hand, John W. Truesdell, in *The Bottom Facts Concerning the Science of Spiritualism* (1883), tells of an exposure in 1872 in New York. Foster palmed the pellets and read them by continually relighting his cigar, the match being held in the hollow of his hand.

The case of Charles Foster well illustrates the difficulty of assessing the phenomena of psychic people. It seems likely that Foster was often guilty of fraud, particularly in such phenomena as pellet reading, which is peculiarly amenable to simple magic tricks. On the other hand there is strong testimony of some genuine mediumistic insights.

Foster was a convivial character who enjoyed drinking alcohol and smoking long cigars in barrooms with his companions as much as he did transmitting messages from the dead. His biographer, Bartlett, summarizes his observations of Foster thus: "He was extravagantly dual. He was not only Dr. Jekyll and Mr. Hyde, but he represented half-a-dozen different Jekylls and Hydes. . . . He was an unbalanced genius, and at times, I should say, insane. . . . He wore out many of his friends. He seemed impervious to the opinions of others, and apparently yielded to every desire."

Some of Foster's strangest phenomena, like skin writing, appear to have been involuntary. During Foster's tour of England in 1861 Dr. John Ashburner was called to Foster's bedside by one of his companions, who stated that Foster was near death. Ashburner found him in a drunken stupor, following a night of unrestrained drinking with friends. After Ashburner examined the medium, then in a drunken torpor, an extraordinary phenomenon occurred, as Ashburner narrates in his book *Philosophy of Animal Magnetism and Spiritualism* (1867):

"Suddenly the bedclothes were tightly rolled downwards as far as his groin. The shirt was then rolled tightly, like a cord, exposing to our view the skin of the chest and abdomen. Soon there appeared in large red letters raised on the surface the word 'DEVELOPMENT,' which extended from the right groin to the left shoulder, dividing the surface into two triangular compartments. These were filled up with sprigs of flowers, resembling fleur-de-lys. The phenomenon lasted nearly ten minutes, when the shirt and bedclothes were unrolled gently and replaced as they were at first."

In his later years Foster became addicted to alcohol. In 1881, at age 48, he was taken to Danvers Insane Asylum, suffering, according to reports, from advanced alcoholism and softening of the brain. For the last four years of his life he apparently lived a vegetable existence under the care of an aunt, simply staring into space most of the time.

A few days after his death the equally controversial psychic **Kate Fox** was practicing automatic writing with her friend Mrs. Taylor and found her hand galvanized into frantic, incoherent messages that were signed "Charles Foster, medium."

Sources:

Ashburner, John. *Philosophy of Animal Magnetism and Spiritualism.* London, 1867.

Bartlett, George C. *The Salem Seer.* New York, 1891.

Brown, Slater. *The Heyday of Spiritualism.* New York: Hawthorn Books, 1970.

Truesdell, John W. *The Bottom Facts Concerning the Science of Spiritualism.* New York: G. W. Carleton, 1883.

Foster, Esther Bond (1913–1963)

American school psychologist who worked at the Duke University Parapsychology Laboratory and wrote several papers published in the *Journal of Parapsychology.* Foster was born March 16, 1913, at Apalachicola, Florida. She studied at Florida State College for Women, Tallahassee (B.S., 1932; M.S., 1933). After her graduation she worked as a secondary school teacher at Sarasota, Florida (1933–38), and as an assistant psychologist at the Department of Veterans Affairs, Ottawa, Canada, (1945–46). In 1948 she became a research assistant at the Parapsychology Laboratory at Duke, where she remained for the next eight years. She died March 1, 1963.

Sources:

Foster, Esther B. "General Extrasensory Perception with a Group of Fourth and Fifth Grade Retarded Children." *Journal of Parapsychology* 2 (1937).

———. "A Re-examination of Dr. Soal's Clairvoyance Data." *Journal of Parapsychology* 20 (1956).

Foster, Esther B., and Karlis Osis. "Multiple Aspect Targets in Tests of ESP." *Journal of Parapsychology* 16 (1952).

———. "A Test of ESP in Cats." *Journal of Parapsychology* 17 (1953).

Foster, Esther B., and J. G. Pratt. "Displacement in ESP Card Tests in Relation to Hits and Misses." *Journal of Parapsychology* 14 (1950).

Pleasants, Helene, ed. *Biographical Dictionary of Parapsychology.* New York: Helix Press, 1964.

Foundation Church of the Divine Truth

The Foundation Church of the Divine Truth is one of two organizations that emerged out of the organizational chaos that beset the **Foundation Church of the New Birth** beginning in 1982. In that year, the sole surviving trustee of the church, Rev. John Paul Gibson, died. Leadership passed to Victor Summers. Since its founding, the headquarters and most of the leadership of the church had been in Washington, D.C. However, in 1983 Summers moved first to San Diego, California, and then to Lake Helen, Florida. He then resigned from all church offices and disbanded the church.

Members in the Washington, D.C., area who did not accept Summers's actions reorganized as the New Birth Christian Healing Sanctuary and were granted permission to receive the mail directed to the former church's postal mail box. Then in 1985 nine former members founded the Foundation Church of Divine Truth as the successor to the former Foundation Church of the New Birth.

The Foundation Church is based upon channeled messages believed to be from Jesus Christ, a selection of high celestial spirits, and other spirits received through James Edward Padgett (1852–1923). Padgett was a Methodist Sunday School teacher who had become interested in **Spiritualism** following the death of his wife in 1914. Advised to begin practicing **automatic writing,** he soon became adept at it. Shortly thereafter, he received a message, purportedly from Jesus Christ, telling him to pray for an inflowing of the Father's divine love. Padgett was told that he had been selected to disseminate the Father's truths to humankind.

Padgett channeled some 1,500 messages between 1914 and 1923. The manuscripts were left in the care of an associate, Leslie R. Stone. Stone saw to the publication in 1940 of a selection of the channeled material under the title *True Gospel Revealed Anew by Jesus.* Subsequently three other volumes, the last published in 1972, appeared. These four volumes are believed by church members to constitute Christ's second coming.

The message of the Padgett channelings flows from Spiritualism and affirms the continuity of the soul after death, and its life and continued growth in the spirit realm. The soul progresses through various realms to paradise (the sixth realm). Should it seek to be filled with the divine love of the Creator, it may then progress to the celestial heavens. In heaven it is conscious of its immortality and continues to receive inflowings of the divine essence of the Father. Jesus' mission on Earth was to make known the possibilities of divine love to all persons.

The Foundation Church may be contacted at Box 66003, Washington, D.C. 20035-6003. It has several hundred members in the United States, Canada, England, Nigeria, and Togo. It has published a new edition of Padgett's writings under the title *Angelic Revelations of Divine Truth.* A second group of followers of the Padgett teachings was organized in 1991 under the church's original name.

Sources:

Padgett, James E. *True Gospel Revealed Anew by Jesus.* 4 vols. Washington, D.C.: Foundation Church of the New Birth, 1958–72.

Foundation Church of the New Birth

The Foundation Church of the New Birth is one of two organizations that grew out of the turmoil among the followers of the revelations of channel James Edward Padgett (1852–1923). Beginning in 1914, Padgett received some 1,500 messages, believed to be from Jesus Christ and other spirit entities. These messages affirmed the immortality of the human spirit. Following Padgett's death, a close associate, Leslie R. Stone, took charge of the manuscripts. He saw to the publication of an initial volume drawn from the material in 1940. In 1958 the Foundation Church of the New Birth was incorporated in Washington, D.C. The small church was headed by a board of trustees. The last of those trustees, Rev. John Paul Gibson, died in 1982. Leadership passed to Victor Summers, but in 1983 Summers resigned all connection with the church and formally dissolved it.

Summers's actions were opposed by the majority of members. One group in Washington, D.C., moved to reorganize. They founded the New Birth Christian Healing Sanctuary and were eventually incorporated as the **Foundation Church of the Divine Truth,** under which name they continue to exist. A second group reorganized in 1991 using the original name, the Foundation Church of the New Birth. The church upholds the beliefs of the original body and disseminates the teachings of the Padgett revelations, contained in the four-volume set *True Gospel Revealed Anew by Jesus.*

The Foundation Church of the New Birth may be contacted at Box 996, Benjamin Franklin Station, Washington, DC 20044.

Sources:

Padgett, James E. *True Gospel Revealed Anew by Jesus.* 4 vols. Washington, D.C.: Foundation Church of the New Birth, 1958–72.

Foundation Faith of God

The Foundation Faith of God was founded in 1974 by former members of the **Process Church of the Final Judgment,** including the great majority of the leadership. Many in the Process Church had become increasingly discouraged by the direction being taken by church founder Robert de Grimston. He had come to focus more and more on a dualist doctrine of the unity of Christ and Satan, and the church had been identified as a Satanist religion in the popular press. The leaders collectively withdrew, leaving the church an empty shell, and reorganized as the Foundation Church of the Millennium. They later changed names to the Foundation Faith of the Millennium (1977) and adopted the present name in 1980.

The Foundation Faith of God has a doctrine approaching orthodox Christianity and affirms a belief in the Christian Trinity, the deity of Christ, salvation from sin, and the necessity of a new birth. The church is strongly focused on endtime issues of the Second Coming of Christ and the coming kingdom of God. It has a healing ministry and many of the ministers offer spiritual (psychic) consultations. The church also maintains a strong social ministry.

Address: Faith Center, 6209 Shadywood Dr., Las Vegas, NV 89102.

Foundation for Mind Research

Organization formed by the husband and wife team **Robert E. L. Masters** and **Jean Houston** in New York to conduct experiments on the border between mental and physical experience. Houston is a professor of psychology, and Masters is a poet and sexologist and the author of many books. Both have experimented with clinically controlled hallucinogenic drugs.

Masters and Houston also developed the ASCID (Altered States of Consciousness Induction Device), better known as "the witches' cradle." It was suggested by historical accounts of witches being suspended from tree branches in swinging bags. Masters and Houston developed a metal swing in which the subject is secured blindfolded with ear baffles and swings in various directions. In this situation of sensory deprivation and confusing movement, the subject experiences enhanced fantasies and alteration in consciousness. A more primitive and dangerous form of this activity has long been called "dervish dangling" and has been reported to result in paranormal perception.

Sources:

Houston, Jean. *Lifeforce: The Psycho-historical Recovery of the Self.* New York: Delacorte Press, 1989.

Masters, Robert E. L., and Jean Houston. *Mind Games.* New York: Viking Press, 1972.

———. *The Varieties of Psychedelic Experience.* New York: Holt, Rinehart & Winston, 1966.

Foundation for Mind-Being Research

A research facility established in 1980 to further consciousness studies and to bring this field into wider recognition as a bona fide science. Its interdisciplinary nature is reflected in the wide range of interests of the membership, including engineering, science, medicine, the humanities, and the arts. The foundation holds regular meetings and issues a newsletter. Address: 442 Knoll Dr., Los Altos, CA 94024.

Foundation for Reincarnation and Spiritual Research

The Foundation for Reincarnation and Spiritual Research was founded in India in 1985 to focus empirical research on **reincarnation.** It especially aims to follow up on the technique developed by American parapsychologist **Ian Stevenson** for in-depth investigation of cases suggestive of reincarnation, several volumes of which were published through the 1970s. The leading researcher connected with the foundation is Jamuna Prasad, its research adviser who through the 1960s and 1970s established an impressive record in studying life after death, especially in his cooperation with **Karlis Osis** of the **American Society for Psychical Research** in his study of deathbed experiences. Also integral to the program of the foundation is the attempt to discover correlates between the results of scientific research and the teachings of the ancient Hindu (Vedic and yogic) literature of India.

The foundation is a membership organization that draws most of its members from India but coordinates its research with that of other like organizations around the world. It may be contacted at 109 Rami Mundi, Allahabad 211003, Uttar Pradeshm, India.

Foundation for Research on the Nature of Man (FRNM)

Institution established in 1962 by parapsychologist **J. B. Rhine** and his wife, **Louisa Rhine,** after the discontinuance of support by Duke University of the former Parapsychology Laboratory. The foundation had a broad purpose, being "devoted to advancing the understanding of the human individual, particularly to the discovery of what it is that distinguishes him as a person." The board of directors derived primarily from the Parapsychology Laboratory, which has now been directly replaced by the **Institute for Parapsychology,** a division of FRNM. FRNM is currently directed by **K. Ramakrishna Rao.**

The foundation is intended as an international center for the advancement of parapsychology and its integration with other scientific studies on the nature of humanity and to serve as a clearinghouse for research information and a training base for individuals studying psi.

FRNM publishes the quarterly **Journal of Parapsychology** through its own Parapsychology Press, which also publishes books and collections of papers on parapsychological topics. Address: 402 N. Buchanan Blvd., Durham, NC 27701-1728.

Founding Church of Scientology See Scientology, Church of

Fountain Spirits

According to German mystic **Jakob Boehme** (1575–1624) there were in nature seven active principles, the "Fountain Spirits" or "Mothers of Existence": the astringent quality, the sweet quality, the bitter quality, the quality of fire, the quality of love, the quality of sound, and the quality of essential substance. The reciprocal action of these antipathetic qualities resulted in supreme unity. Each was at once the parent and the child of all the rest, being generated and generating one another. They were typified by the seven golden candlesticks of Rev. 1:20.

Boehme's mystical visions are detailed in his books, notably *Aurora,* first published in 1612, translations of which have been reissued.

Sources:

Boehme, Jacob. *The Life and Doctrines of Jacob Boehme.* New York: McCoy Publishing, 1929.

Fountain of the World Fellowship See WFLK Fountain of the World

Fourth Dimension

A "higher" form of space that mathematicians conceive as another direction from which a fourth line may be drawn at right angles to each of the three lines (mutually at right angles) that three-dimensional space permits to be drawn through any point in it. A highly speculative form of the theory that such a higher form of space exists has been employed in the attempt to solve certain questions concerning psychic phenomena.

For beings living on a flat surface, having no thickness, and possessing all their nerve endings on the periphery of their bodies, only two directions could exist. A circle drawn on their plane with chalk would be a closed space into which they could not penetrate except through a cut in it. Having no concept of a third dimension, they could not picture objects passing out of and into the circle if the objects did not pass through the cut.

From a third dimension, however, both the inside and outside of the circle are visible and accessible. Similarly, for beings living in a four-dimensional world, enclosed spaces would appear open. Persons could make objects mysteriously vanish in the direction of the fourth dimension and make them reappear again in an apparent transgression of the law of impenetrability.

A similar explanation is presented for **apport** phenomena, the reported materialization of an object in the midst of a séance. **Johann Zöllner** made the first attempt at the experimental demonstration of the fourth dimension in his sittings with the medium **Henry Slade. Cesare Lombroso** considered it an ingenious solution to many perplexing psychic problems. **W. W. Carington,** in *A Theory of the Mechanism of Survival* (1920), hypothesizes that after physical death the individual consciousness is embodied in a vehicle made not from physical matter, but from four-dimensional matter (i.e., that which in four-dimensional space corresponds to what we call matter in three-dimensional space). The connecting link between the physical body and the four-dimensional vehicle is the **etheric double.**

Clairvoyants who see the front, sides, back, and every internal point of three-dimensional objects simultaneously are thus believed to employ a four-dimensional organ of sight. Traveling and medical **clairvoyance** are better understood by using this hypothesis.

If the four-dimensional vehicle is so pliable that it is capable of being molded by the mere power of will, **apparitions** will find a ready explanation, provided the percipient is receptive to supernormal impressions. Another application is the phenomenon of **prevision,** bound up with the riddle of time. Its adoption as a working hypothesis has also been offered as a way to bridge the gap between religious and scientific thought.

Sources:

"A. Square" [E. A. Abbott]. *Flatland: A Romance of Many Dimensions.* 1884. 6th ed. New York: Dover Publications, 1953.

Hinton, C. H. *The Fourth Dimension.* London: G. Allen & Unwin, 1934.

———. *Scientific Romances.* London, 1886.

Rucker, Rudy von Bitter. *The Fourth Dimension: Toward a Geometry of Higher Reality.* Boston: Houghton-Mifflin, 1984.

Fourth Way

The system of mystic and occultist **Georgei I. Gurdjieff** (1872–1949), which he contrasted to the three traditional ways of mysticism—those of the fakir, the monk, and the yogi. Gurdjieff maintained that human beings are "asleep" (i.e., not living at full potential of awareness and performance). To develop greater awareness requires hard work in removing illusory or limited experience and awakening to higher reality, he said. This evolution can be assisted by special work involving a system of psychophysical exercises including movement, music, and dance. Gurdjieff's system was especially concerned with achieving evolution in everyday life, rather than retreating from society.

An early enthusiast for the work of Gurdjieff was the journalist **Peter D. Ouspensky.** Later disciples included **Maurice Nicoll, J. G. Bennett,** and **Thane Walker,** each of whom founded schools concerned with teachings stemming from the philosophy and methods of Gurdjieff. A leading group concerned with Gurdjieff work in the United States is the Gurdjieff Foundation of New York.

Traditional Gurdjieff schools carry on unobtrusively and avoid publicity. There is little centralized organization, and proselytizing attempts are low key. Prospective followers of the Fourth Way are usually expected to have studied books dealing with the life and thought of Gurdjieff.

Sources:

Bennett, J. G. *Gurdjieff, A Very Great Enigma: Three Lectures.* New York: Samuel Weiser, 1973.

———. *Gurdjieff: Making a New World.* New York: Harper & Row, 1974.

De Hartmann, Thomas. *Our Life with Gurdjieff.* New York: Penguin, 1972. Rev. ed. San Francisco: Harper & Row, 1983.

Driscoll, J. Walter. *Gurdjieff: An Annotated Bibliography.* New York: Garland Publishing, 1985.

Gurdjieff, G. I. *All and Everything.* New York: Harcourt, Brace, 1950. Reprint, New York: E. P. Dutton, 1963.

———. *Meetings With Remarkable Men.* New York: E. P. Dutton, 1964.

———. *Views From the Real World: Early Talks in Moscow, Essentuku, Tiflis, Berlin, London, Paris, New York, Chicago as Recollected by His Pupils.* New York: Triangle Editions; London: Routledge & Kegan Paul, 1973.

Webb, James. *The Harmonious Circle.* New York: G. P. Putnam's Sons, 1980.

Fowler, Edward P. (ca. 1852– ?)

Principal **medium** of the **New York Circle,** established as the first Spiritualist organization in the summer of 1851. Fowler was a medical student, brother of a well-known phrenologist, and the first medium who produced **direct writing** in the United States. Suspicion of fraud was aroused, however, because a Hebrew text that he claimed to have received while asleep and alone in his room did not withstand the criticism of experts.

Much publicity was given to another script, "Peace, but not without freedom," similarly obtained in December 1951. It was signed by 56 spirits, including many of the original signatories of the Declaration of Independence, in their characteristic handwriting. The autographs are reproduced by **Emma Hardinge Britten** in her *Modern American Spiritualism* (1869). According to Britten, one Professor Bush desired to test the possibility of communicating in Hebrew through **raps,** called out the alphabet in that language, and received highly satisfactory answers.

Fowler's mediumship was the subject of a debate between S. B. Brittan, editor of the *Shekinah,* and B. W. Richmond. The case chiefly rested on the medium's own testimony and the internal evidence of his scripts.

Sources:

Britten, Emma Hardinge. *Modern American Spiritualism.* 1869. Reprint, New Hyde Park, N.Y.: University Books, 1979.

Fowler, Lottie (1836–1899)

Professional name of Charlotte Connolly, American clairvoyant and medical diagnoser. While biographical details are scarce, Fowler attained brief fame during a trip to England in 1872. During this tour, in April 1872, she initially introduced **Stainton Moses** to **Spiritualism.** Florence Marryat often acted as transcriptionist for Fowler in taking down trance answers to letters as dictated by "Annie," her German guide. According to Marryat, Fowler was consulted by physicians of the court at the time of the Prince of Wales's dangerous illness, and from the beginning predicted his recovery.

It was through her mediumship that the body of the late **Master of Lindsay** of Balcarres, which had been stolen from the family vault, was eventually recovered. She predicted a London riot and the Tay Bridge disaster. Among her more unusual stories, in *Medium and Daybreak* (1872), is her claim that on February 17, 1872, she was paranormally transported from a bus near Oxford Circus, London, to an apartment in Bloomsbury, about three miles away.

Sources:

"Fritz." *Where Are the Dead?* London, 1873.

Hellenbach, Baron. *Eine Philosophie des Gesunden Menschenverstandes.* N.p., 1876.

Marryat, Florence. *The Spirit World.* London, 1894.

———. *There is No Death.* London, 1892. Reprint, New York: Causeway Books, 1973.

Fox, George (1624–1691)

Mystic and founder of The Society of Friends (Quakers). In his *Journal,* one of the great religious autobiographies, he testifies to many extraordinary psychic experiences. In the 1920s Walter Prince cited him as one of the "noted witnesses for psychic occurrences." Once he lay in trance for 14 days, had great spiritual struggles and ecstasies, heard voices that he believed to be of the Lord, and proclaimed by direct revelation the doctrine of the Inner Light: "I saw that Christ enlightened all men and women with his divine and saving light, and I saw that the manifestation of the spirit of God was given to every man to profit withal."

It was said that there was a wonderful magnetism and power about the eyes of George Fox. He had gifts of healing and himself made many wonderful recoveries. He foretold the fall of the Rump Parliament; he had a striking presentiment of the approaching death of Cromwell; he had a vision of the fire of London years before it happened; and he had a foreshadowing of the coming revolution of 1689. He reportedly had so much psychic power that during some of the meetings at which he was present the house was shaken, and on one occasion a clergyman ran out of the church fearing it would fall on his head.

Fox's journal contains accounts of the miraculous events of his life.

Sources:

Cadbury, H. J. *George Fox's "Book of Miracles."* Cambridge: Cambridge University Press, 1948.

Fox, George. *Journal.* Edited by John L. Nickalls. Cambridge: Cambridge University Press, 1952.

Prince, Walter F. *Noted Witnesses for Psychic Occurrences.* Boston: Boston Society for Psychic Research, 1928. Reprint, New Hyde Park, N.Y.: University Books, 1963.

Fox, Marietta Newton (1928–)

American psychologist active in the field of parapsychology. Fox was born January 18, 1928, at Bradford, Pennsylvania. She studied psychology at the College of Wooster, Wooster, Ohio (B.A., 1950), after which she became a researcher at the **Parapsychology Laboratory** at Duke University. She joined the staff of the Institute of Living, Hartford, Connecticut, in 1952. From 1953 to 1954, she was a schoolteacher in Wheaton, Illinois. She was a charter associate of the Parapsychological Association.

Sources:

Fox, Marietta N., and Kenneth Bates. "An Experimental Study of ESP Capacity in Mental Patients." *Journal of Parapsychology* (December 1951).

Pleasants, Helene, ed. *Biographical Dictionary of Parapsychology.* New York: Helix Press, 1964.

Fox, Oliver

Pseudonym of **Hugh G. Callaway** (1885–1949), pioneer British exponent of **astral projection,** or **out-of-the-body travel.** His book *Astral Projection: A Record of Out-of-the-body Experiences* (1939) was the first major British publication on the subject.

Fox Sisters, Kate [Catharine] (1836–1892) and Margaret(ta) (1833–1893)

The pioneers of modern **Spiritualism,** along with a third sister, (Ann) Leah (1814–1890), variously known by marriage as Mrs. Fish, Mrs. Brown, and Mrs. Underhill. According to Leah Fox's book *The Missing Link in Modern Spiritualism* (1885), psychic power ran in the family.

Their great-grandmother was a somnambulist (sleepwalker). She attended phantom funerals of people yet living and described every detail about the officiating minister and the persons present. Her descriptions corresponded with the facts as they were later observed. An aunt, Elisabeth Higgins, as told in **Robert Dale Owen**'s *Footfalls on the Boundary of Another World* (1860), saw in a dream her own tombstone; she died on the day inscribed in her vision.

The events that made the Fox family name historic date from December 11, 1847, the day on which John D. Fox took the tenancy of a house in Hydesville, New York. The house had a mysterious reputation. Michael Weakman, the former tenant who had moved in two years before, left it because of strange noises, but the family of John D. Fox did not experience serious discomfort until March 1848. At that time **raps,** knocks, and noises as of moving furniture were heard at night. They increased in intensity. On March 31 there was a very loud and continued outbreak of inexplicable sounds. Fox's wife suggested that the sashes might have rattled since the night was windy. John Fox got up and tried the sashes, shaking them to see if they were loose. Kate, the youngest girl, happened to remark that when her father shook the window sash the noises seemed to reply. The idea came to her to ask for an answer by imitating the sounds.

John's wife, Margaret, in a testimony signed four days later, described the occurrences as follows:

"On the night of the first disturbance we all got up, lighted a candle and searched the entire house, the noises continuing during the time and being heard near the same place. Although not very loud, it produced a jar of the bedsteads and chairs that could be felt when we were in bed. It was a tremulous motion, more than a sudden jar. We could feel the jar when standing on the floor. It continued on this night until we slept. I did not sleep until about twelve o'clock. On March 30 we were disturbed all night. The noises were heard in all parts of the house. My husband stationed himself outside the door while I stood inside, and the knocks came on the door between us. We heard footsteps in the pantry, and walking downstairs; we could not rest, and I then concluded that the house must be haunted by some unhappy restless spirit. I had often heard of such things, but had never witnessed anything of the kind that I could not account for before.

"On Friday night, March 31, 1848, we concluded to go to bed early and not permit ourselves to be disturbed by the noises, but try and get a night's rest. My husband was here on all these occasions, heard the noises and helped in the search. It was very early when we went to bed on this night—hardly dark. I had been so broken of my rest I was almost sick. My husband had not gone to bed when we first heard the noise on this evening. I had just lain down. It commenced as usual. I knew it from all the other noises I had ever heard before. The children, who slept in the other bed in the room, heard the rapping and tried to make similar sounds by snapping their fingers.

"My youngest child, Cathie, said: 'Mr. Splitfoot, do as I do,' clapping her hands. The sound instantly followed her with the same number of raps. When she stopped the sound ceased for a short time. Then Margaretta said, in sport, 'No, do just as I do. Count one, two, three, four,' striking one hand against the other at the same time; and the raps came as before. She was afraid to repeat them. Then Cathie said in her childish simplicity, 'Oh, mother, I know what it is. To-morrow is April-fool day and it is somebody trying to fool us.'

"I then thought I could put a test that no one in the place could answer. I asked the noise to rap my different children's ages, successively. Instantly each one of my children's ages was given correctly, pausing between them sufficiently long to individualize them until the seventh, at which a longer pause was made, and then three more emphatic raps were given, corresponding to the age of the little one that died, which was my youngest child.

"I then asked: 'Is this a human being that answers my questions so correctly?' There was no rap. I asked 'Is it a spirit? If it is make two raps.' Two sounds were given as soon as the request was made. I then said: 'If it was an injured spirit, make two raps,' which were instantly made, causing the house to tremble. I asked: 'Were you injured in this house?' The answer was given as before. 'Is the person living that injured you?' Answered by raps in the same manner. I ascertained by the same simple method that it was a man, aged 31 years, that he had been murdered in this house and his remains were buried in the cellar; that his family consisted of a wife and five children, two sons and three daughters, all living at the time of his death, but that the wife had since died. I asked: 'Will you continue to rap if I call my neighbors that they may hear it too?' The raps were loud in the affirmative.

"My husband went and called in Mrs. Redfield, our nearest neighbor. She is a very candid woman. The girls were sitting up in bed clinging to each other and trembling with terror. I think I was as calm as I am now. Mrs. Redfield came immediately (this was about half past seven), thinking she would have a laugh at the children. But when she saw them pale with fright and nearly speechless, she was amazed and believed there was something more serious than she had supposed. I asked a few questions for her and she was answered as before. He told her age exactly. She then called her husband, and the same questions were asked and answered.

"Then Mr. Redfield called in Mr. Duesler and wife, and several others. Mr. Duesler then called in Mr. and Mrs. Hyde, also Mr. and Mrs. Jewell. Mr. Duesler asked many questions and received answers. I then named all the neighbors I could think of and asked if any of them had injured him and received no answer. Mr. Duesler then asked questions and received answers. He asked 'Were you murdered?' Raps affirmative. 'Can your murderer be brought to justice?' No sound. 'Can he be punished by law?' No answer. He then said: 'If your murderer cannot be punished by the law manifest it by raps,' and the raps were made clearly and distinctly. In the same way Mr. Duesler ascertained that he was murdered in the east bedroom about five years ago and that the murder was committed by a Mr.— on a Tuesday night at twelve o'clock; that he was murdered by having his throat cut with a butcher's knife; that the body was taken through the buttery, down the stairway and that it was buried ten feet below the surface of the ground. It was also ascertained that he was murdered for his money by raps affirmative.

"'How much was it—one hundred?' No rap. 'Was it two hundred?' etc., and when he mentioned five hundred the raps replied in the affirmative.

"Many called in who were fishing in the creek, and all heard the same questions and answers. Many remained in the house all night. I and my children left the house. My husband remained in the house with Mr. Redfield all night. On the next Saturday the house was filled to overflowing. There were no sounds heard during the day, but they commenced again in the evening. It was said that there were over three hundred persons present at the time. On Sunday morning the noises were heard throughout the day by all who came to the house.

"On Saturday night, April 1, they commenced digging in the cellar; they dug until they came to water and then gave it up. The noise was not heard on Sunday evening nor during the night. Stephen B. Smith and wife (my daughter Marie) and my son David S. Fox and wife, slept in the room this night.

"I have heard nothing since that time until yesterday. In the forenoon of yesterday there were several questions answered in way by rapping. I have heard the noise several times to-day.

"I am not a believer in haunted houses or supernatural appearances. I am very sorry there has been so much excitement about it. It has been a great deal of trouble to us. It was our misfortune to live here at this time; but I am willing and anxious that the truth should be known and that a true statement should be made. I cannot account for these noises; all that I know is that they have been heard repeatedly as I have stated. I have heard this rapping again this (Tuesday) morning, April 4. My children have also heard it."

John D. Fox then signed the following statement:

"I have also heard the above statement of my wife, Margaret Fox, read, and hereby certify that the same is true in all its particulars. I heard the same rappings which she has spoken of, in answer to the questions, as stated by her. There have been a great many questions besides those asked, and answered in the same way. Some have been asked a great many times and they have always received the same answer. There has never been any contradiction whatever.

"I do not know of any way to account for those noises, as being caused by any natural means. We have searched every nook and corner in and about the house at different times to ascertain if possible whether anything or anybody was secreted there that could make the noise and have not been able to find anything which would or could explain the mystery. It has caused a great deal of trouble and anxiety.

"Hundreds have visited the house, so that it is impossible for us to attend to our daily occupations; and I hope that, whether caused by natural or supernatural means, it will be ascertained soon. The digging in the cellar will be resumed as soon as the water settles, and then it can be ascertained whether there are any indications of a body ever having been buried there; and if there are I shall have no doubt but that it is of supernatural origin."

The digging could not be resumed until summer. Then, at a depth of five feet, they found a plank, along with charcoal and quicklime, and finally hair and some bones, which were pronounced by medical men to belong to a human skeleton.

The rest of the skeleton was believed to be found 56 years later. According to a report of the *Boston Journal,* November 23, 1904, some parts of a rough wall built one yard from the true wall of the cellar fell down. Excavations were made by the owner of "the spook house" and an almost complete human skeleton was found. It was thought that the murderer first buried the body in the middle of the cellar, then became alarmed, dug it up, and buried it in the space between the two walls.

As the murder victim's spirit continued to communicate with the Foxes in 1848, Mrs. Fox's hair turned white as a result of the disturbances in the house. The phenomena soon assumed the character of formal haunting. The sound of a death struggle, the gurgling of a throat, and the heavy dragging of a body across the room was heard night after night. Finally the family could not stand it any longer and moved out. But the raps continued in the house even after they left, and one night more than 300 people conversed with the invisible entity.

From Raps to the Message of Spiritualism

Kate took refuge at her brother's house in Auburn, and her sister Margaret went to Leah's house in Rochester. The raps broke out again in both places. In Rochester they were especially violent. Calvin Brown, who afterward became Leah's second husband and who lived in the same house, was opposed to the manifestations and became the object of **poltergeist** attacks. Things were thrown at him, but without causing him injury. Blocks of wood were found scattered in the rooms, sometimes with sentences written on them. The manifestation was intelligent and spiteful.

"We had become satisfied," writes Leah in *The Missing Link,* "that no earthly power could relieve us. While on our knees pins would be stuck into different parts of our persons. Mother's cap would be removed from her head, her comb jerked out of her hair and every conceivable thing done to annoy us." The spirits "carried on the manifestations on the very peak of the roof. It sounded like the frequent discharge of heavy artillery. It was stated to us the next day that the sounds were heard a mile away. We feared that the roof would fall in upon us."

These violent disturbances went on until Isaac Post, a visiting friend, suddenly remembered that Leah's brother David "conversed with the Hydesville spirits by using the alphabet." Tremendous raps came in answer to the first question and this message was spelled out: "Dear Friends, you must proclaim this truth to the world. This is the dawning of a new era; you must not try to conceal it any longer. When you do your duty God will protect you and good spirits will watch over you." From that time on, communications began to pour through and the manifestations became orderly. The table rocked, objects moved, guitars were played, and psychic touches were experienced.

On November 14, 1849, the first meeting of a small band of Spiritualists took place in the Corinthian Hall in Rochester. The excitement grew. Public investigation was demanded. The report of a committee of five that could not explain the phenomena as **fraud** was rejected and another committee was delegated. They were also forced to report that when the girls "were standing on pillows with a handkerchief tied round the bottom of their dresses, tight to the ankles, we all heard rapping on the wall and floor distinctly."

Passions rose to fury; once the girls were nearly lynched, but in spite of a hostile atmosphere and denunciation in the press, the movement kept growing. Other mediums sprang up. Mrs. Tamlin and **Mrs. Benedict** of Auburn, the first two well-known mediums who were developed in the circle of Kate Fox (see **Apostolic Circle**), were followed by a host of others, and on November 28, 1849, because of the increasing demand for sittings, Leah became a professional medium.

The first public sittings were soon followed by a propaganda tour to Albany in May 1850, then to Troy, where their lives were threatened and they were fired on. On June 4, 1850, they took the message of Spiritualism to New York City.

Horace Greeley, the editor of the *New York Tribune,* was their first caller. Fearing for their safety, he advised them to charge a

$5 admission fee. Later, under the aegis of the **Society for the Diffusion of Spiritual Knowledge,** free public sittings were initiated, for which Mr. H. H. Day paid $1,200 per annum to Kate. Interest ran high from the very first.

Greeley's report in the *Tribune* was enthusiastic:

"We devoted what time we could spare from our duties out of three days to this subject, and it would be the basest cowardice not to say that we are convinced beyond a doubt of their perfect integrity and good faith in the premises. Whatever may be the origin or cause of the 'rappings,' the ladies in whose presence they occur do not make them. We tested this thoroughly and to our entire satisfaction."

The phenomena in these first séances were not spectacular in light of later occurrences associated with the Fox sisters. Raps were heard, the table and chairs moved, and the sitters were touched by invisible hands. Perhaps their most powerful early manifestation was recorded in 1853 by Governor Talmadge. It was the complete levitation of the table with the governor himself on top. He also claimed to have received a communication in direct writing from the spirit of John C. Calhoun. According to Robert Dale Owen, Leah was the best medium for raps. With her he obtained them on the seashore on a rock, in a sailing boat (sounding from underneath), on tree trunks in the woods, and on the ground beneath their feet in open air. Spirit lights and **materializations** were a comparatively late development, and they were produced by both Kate and Leah Fox.

"Exposures," Tests, and Confessions

Claimed exposures from time to time were common. In February 1851 the "snapping of the knee joints" explanation of the raps was advanced for the first time. Dr. Austin Flint, Dr. Charles A. Lee, and Dr. C. B. Coventry of the University of Buffalo published in the *Commercial Advertiser* of February 18, 1851, the disclosure that the raps were produced within the sisters' anatomies. A second investigation upheld this theory, and an alleged confession of Margaret Fox, published in April 1851 by a relation named Mrs. Norman Culver, threatened to bury both the Fox sisters and the fledgling Spiritualistic movement.

There was, however, a flagrant contradiction in the allegation, which claimed that when the committee held the ankles of the Fox sisters in Rochester a Dutch servant girl rapped with her knuckles under the floor of the cellar. She was instructed to rap whenever she heard their voices calling on the spirits. Yet the investigation to which the revelation referred was held in the houses of the members of the committee or in a public hall, the girls did not keep a servant, and Kate Fox was not present at these meetings at all. Nevertheless, the effect of the revelation was that "the Rochester impostors" were at the mercy of the press, having but one significant defender—Horace Greeley. His interest was so deep, however, that he furnished funds for Kate Fox to polish up her imperfect education.

Investigations into the reality of the phenomena were numerous. Test after test was applied. The skeptics faced two problems: explaining what they believed were the "fraudulent" production of the rappings and determining the nature of the intelligence that answered the questions, which were in many cases asked mentally. The second problem was seldom tackled; the first was addressed often and with very great ardor. One popular explanation was that the raps were produced by flexing the knee joints. In 1857, as a result of the challenge to mediums in the *Boston Courier,* several mediums appeared before a committee of Harvard professors in Boston. Kate and Leah Fox were among them. The committee was difficult to satisfy and their promised report was never published.

There is much in the personal history of the Fox sisters in these early years that remains obscure. Years of public mediumship in a hostile atmosphere, the drain of too-frequent sittings on their energy, the commercial exploitation of their talents, and the absence of understanding regarding the religious implications of Spiritualism combined to produce a deteriorating influence.

Margaret Fox married Dr. Elisha Kane, the famous Arctic explorer. With marriage, she retired from public mediumship. Before his marriage to Margaret, Kane was skeptical. He never arrived at any satisfactory solution to the phenomena, and apparently was convinced that Margaret was exploited in a mercenary spirit by her elder sister, Leah. When he was away in the Arctic he had Margaret stay with his aunt for the purpose of polishing up her education and married her on his return. Some time after Kane's death in 1857, under the title *The Love Letters of Dr. Elisha Kane* (1865), was published a book that exacerbated suspicion of the Fox sisters. Kane, in his letters, continually reproached Margaret for living in deceit and hypocrisy. He also strongly objected to the sisters' indulgence in alcohol.

In 1861 Kate Fox was engaged as a medium exclusively for Charles F. Livermore, a rich banker from New York whose wife, Estelle, had died a year before. Over a period of five years Kate gave him nearly 400 sittings of which detailed records were kept. The doors and windows were carefully locked and the séances, witnessed by prominent men, were often held in Livermore's own house.

The medium retained consciousness while "Estelle" gradually materialized. She was not recognized until the 43rd sitting when she was illuminated by a psychic light. Later the materialization became more complete, but the figure could not speak except for a few words. The communication took place through raps and writing. Estelle and another phantom, calling himself "Benjamin Franklin," wrote on cards brought by Livermore. Kate Fox's hands were held while she wrote. The script was said to be a perfect reproduction of the characters "Estelle" used when on earth. At the 388th séance, "Estelle" declared that she was appearing for the last time. Livermore never saw her again. In gratitude for the consolation he derived from these sittings, he enabled Kate Fox to visit England in 1871. In a letter to Benjamin Coleman he praised Kate's irreproachable character and detailed her idiosyncrasies.

The career of Kate Fox in England was undisturbed. She sat for many important people, gave excellent opportunities to **Sir William Crookes** for investigation, and often held joint sittings with **D. D. Home** and **Agnes Guppy-Volckman.** On December 14, 1872, Kate married H. D. Jencken, a barrister-at-law. They had two sons, both strongly psychic at an early age. Jencken died in 1881. In 1883 the widowed medium visited Russia on the invitation of **Alexander Aksakof** and was consulted about the auspices of the coronation of the czar.

Financial circumstances forced Margaret Fox back into professional mediumship. According to **Isaac Funk,** she lived in poverty.

Leah died in 1890, Kate in 1892, and Margaret in 1893. Kate (known as Mrs. Sparr from her last marriage) and Margaret were buried in the Brooklyn Cypress Hill Cemetery.

In 1916 the old Hydesville house where the Fox family had lived in 1848 was moved to Lily Dale, a campground in Western New York that has served at times as an informal headquarters for American Spiritualists. Unfortunately it burned to the ground in 1955. The house was reconstructed in 1968 as a tourist attraction on the Hydesville site, which bears a marker erected in 1927 reading: "Birthplace of Modern Spiritualism 1848." The reconstructed building includes a niche in the cellar wall where the skeleton was found.

Sources:

Brown, Slater. *The Heyday of Spiritualism.* New York: Hawthorn Books, 1970.

Davenport, Reuben Briggs. *The Death Blow to Spiritualism.* New York: G. W. Dillingham, 1888.

Doyle, Arthur Conan. *The History of Spiritualism.* 2 vols. London, New York, 1926. Reprint, Arno Press, 1975.

Fornell, Earl Wesley. *The Unhappy Medium: Spiritualism and the Life of Margaret Fox.* Austin, Tex.: University of Texas Press, 1964.

Jackson, Herbert G., Jr. *The Spirit Rappers.* Garden City, N.Y.: Doubleday, 1972.

Lewis, E. E. *A Report of the Mysterious Noises Heard in the House of Mr. John D. Fox.* Canandaigua, N.Y.: The Author, 1848.

Pond, Mariam Buckner. *Time Is Kind: The Story of the Unfortunate Fox Family.* New York: Centennial Press, 1947. Reprinted as *The Unwilling Martyrs.* London: Psychic Book Club, 1947.

Taylor, W. G. Langworthy. *Katie Fox, Epochmaking Medium and the Making of the Fox-Taylor Record.* Boston: Bruce, 1933.

Underhill, A. Leah. *The Missing Link in Modern Spiritualism.* New York: T. R. Knox, 1885. Reprint, New York: Arno Press, 1976.

Fragarach (The Answerer)

In ancient Irish legend, a sword that could pierce any armor. It was one of the magical gifts brought by Lugh from the Land of the Living. Another gift was the horse of Mananan, named Aonbarr, able to travel on land and sea. (See also **Danaans**)

FRANCE

Early Belief in Sorcery

According to occultist **Éliphas Lévi,** the practice of magic in pre-Roman France originated with the Druids and was nearly identical to that of the Draids in Britain, from which it drew its inspiration. It is unlikely that Roman magic gained any footing in Gaul, but there is little evidence of whether this was or was not the case.

In his book *The History of Magic* (1913), Lévi states that in the early Frankish period of the Merovingian dynasty, Fredegond, wife of Hilperic, king of Soissons, destroyed many people apparently through **sorcery,** or malevolent magic. She also experimented with **black magic,** the calling up of spirit entities, and protected many practitioners of the art, Lévi says. On one occasion, she saved a sorceress who had been arrested by Ageric, bishop of Verdun, by hiding her in the palace.

The practice of **magic** was not punished under the rule of the early French kings, except on those occasions when (usually through poisonings) it intruded into the royal caste and thus became a political offense, as in the case of the military leader Mummol, who was tortured by command of Hilperic for sorcery. One of the Salic laws attributed to Pharamond by Sigebert stated: "If any one shall testify that another had acted as *hèrèburge* or *strioporte* [titles applied to those who carry the copper vessel to the spot where the vampires perform their enchantments] and if he fail to convict him, he shall be condemned hereby to a forfeit of 7,500 deniers, being 180 1/2 sous. . . . If a **vampire** shall devour a man and be found guilty, she shall forfeit 8,000 deniers, being 200 sous."

The Christian church also legislated against sorcerers and vampires, and the Council of Agde in Languedoc, held in 506 C.E., pronounced excommunication against them. The first Council of Orleans, convened in 541, condemned divination and augury. The Council of Narbonne, in 589, excommunicated all sorcerers and ordained that they be sold as slaves for the benefit of the poor. Those who allegedly had dealings with the devil were condemned to be whipped.

Some extraordinary phenomena are said to have occurred in France during the reign of Pepin le Bref (714?–768): the air seemed to be alive with human shapes, mirages filled the heavens, and sorcerers were seen among the clouds, scattering powders and poisons with open hands. Crops failed, cattle died, and many people perished. Such visions may have been stimulated by the teachings of the famous Kabbalist Zedekias. He presided over a school of occult science, where he withheld the secrets of his art and contented himself with postulating his ideas about elemental spirits. The spirits he stated, had been subservient to him before the fall of man. The aforementioned visions might have been caused by mass belief that sylphs and salamanders were descending in search of their former masters. Lévi wrote as follows:

"Voyages to the land of sylphs were talked of on all sides as we talk at the present day of animated tables and fluidic manifestations. The folly took possession even of strong minds, and it was time for an intervention on the part of the Church, which does not relish the supernatural being hawked in the public streets, seeing that such disclosures, by imperilling the respect due to authority and to the hierarchic chain of instruction, cannot be attributed to the spirit of order and light. The cloud phantoms were therefore arraigned and accused of being hell-born illusions, while the people—anxious to get something into their hands—began a crusade against sorcerers. The public folly turned into a paroxysm of mania; strangers in country places were accused of descending from heaven and were killed without mercy; imbeciles confessed that they had been abducted by sylphs or demons; others who had boasted like this previously either would not or could not unsay it; they were burned or drowned, and, according to Garinet, the number who perished throughout the kingdom almost exceeds belief. It is the common catastrophe of dramas in which the first parts are played by ignorance or fear.

"Such visionary epidemics recurred in the reigns following, and all the power of Charlemagne was put in action to calm the public agitation. An edict, afterwards renewed by Louis the Pious, forbade sylphs to manifest under the heaviest penalties. It will be understood that in the absence of the aerial beings the judgments fell upon those who had made a boast of having seen them, and hence they ceased to be seen. The ships in air sailed back to the port of oblivion, and no one claimed any longer to have journeyed through the blue distance. Other popular frenzies replaced the previous mania, while the romantic splendors of the great reign of Charlemagne furnished the makers of legends with new prodigies to believe and new marvels to relate."

Mysterious legends grew around the figure of **Charlemagne.** It was said that the **Enchiridion of Pope Leo III,** a collection of written magic charms, was presented to Charlemagne. Lévi illustrates the condition of affairs in Charlemagne's France:

"We know that superstitions die hard and that degenerated Druidism had struck its roots deeply in the savage lands of the North. The recurring insurrections of Saxons testified to a fanaticism which was (a) always turbulent, and (b) incapable of repression by moral force alone. All defeated forms of worship—Roman paganism, Germanic idolatry, Jewish rancour—conspired against victorious Christianity. Nocturnal assemblies took place; thereat the conspirators cemented their alliance with the blood of human victims; and a pantheistic idol of monstrous form, with the horns of a goat, presided over festivals which might be called *agap* of hatred. In a word, the Sabbat was still celebrated in every forest and wild if yet unreclaimed provinces. The adepts who attended them were masked and otherwise unrecognisable; the assemblies extinguished their lights and broke up before daybreak, the guilty were to be found everywhere, and they could be brought to book nowhere. It came about therefore that Charlemagne determined to fight them with their own weapons.

"In those days, moreover, feudal tyrants were in league with sectarians against lawful authority; female sorcerers were attached to castles as courtesans; bandits who frequented the Sabbats divided with nobles the bloodstained loot of rapine; feudal courts were at the command of the highest bidder; and the public burdens weighed with all their force only on the weak and poor. The evil was at its height in Westphalia, and faithful agents were despatched thither by Charlemagne entrusted with a secret mission. Whatsoever energy remained among the oppressed, whosoever still loved justice, whether among the people or among the nobility, were drawn by these emissaries together, bound by pledges and vigilance in common. To the initiates thus incorporated they made known the full powers which they carried from the emperor himself, and they proceeded to institute the Tribunal of Free Judges."

Lévi's observations must be taken with a grain of salt, however. It is unlikely that the **Sabbat** was celebrated to such an extreme. Also, the Vehmgericht was founded 450 years after Charlemagne's reign.

From the reign of Robert the Pious to that of St. Louis (1215–70), there is not much to stimulate the student of occult history. In St. Louis's time flourished the famous Rabbi Jachiel, a celebrated master of the **Kabbalah.** There is some reason to believe that he had glimmerings of electricity, because a radiant star was said to appear in his home at night, the light so brilliant that no one could look at it without being dazzled, and it darted rainbow colors. It appeared to be inexhaustible and was never replenished with oil or any other combustible substance. When the rabbi was annoyed by intruders at his door he struck a nail fixed in his cabinet, producing a blue spark on the head of the nail and on the door-knocker, to which, if the intruder clung, he received a severe shock.

German scholar and scientist **Albertus Magnus** lived during the same period.

The twelfth century had seen the founding of the Knights Templars of the Temple of Solomon, a French-based religious order of military men dedicated to protecting pilgrims on their way to the Holy Land. The order prospered until its prosecution by Philip the Fair (1268–1314), who accused the order of various occult crimes, including the worship of the devil in the form of an idol, **Baphomet.** Another prosecution for sorcery was that of the sadistic **Gilles de Laval** (1404–40), lord of Rais, the prototype of Bluebeard. Laval was a renowned sorcerer who, with two assistants, practiced diabolical rites at his castle of Machecoul, celebrating the black mass in a revolting manner. He slaughtered children as part of a ritual he hoped would assist him in his search for the **philosophers' stone. Jeanne d'Arc,** under whom Gilles had fought at the siege of Orleáns, was suspected of sorcery but was actually condemned as a heretic.

The Fourteenth and Fifteenth Centuries

As early as the thirteenth century, a charge of sorcery was made as a means of branding the **Waldenses,** who were accused of selling themselves to the devil and of holding sabbatical orgies. About the middle of the fifteenth century France became the scene of wholesale oppression of suspected sorcerers.

In 1315 **Enguerraud de Marigny,** a minister of Philip the Fair who had conducted the execution of the Templars, was hanged along with an adventurer named Paviot for attempting to bring about the deaths of the counts of Valois and St. Paul. In 1334 the countess of Artois and her son were thrown into prison on suspicion of sorcery.

In 1393, during the reign of Charles VI, his sister-in-law, the duchess of Orleans, who was the daughter of the Duke of Milan, was accused of driving the king mad by sorcery. The ministers of the court resolved to pit a magician against her, and a certain Arnaud Guillaume was brought from Guienne as a suitable adversary to the noble lady. He possessed a book *Smagorad,* and said the original was given to Adam by God to console him for the loss of his son Abel. Guillaume claimed that the possessor of this volume could hold the stars in subjection and command the four elements. He assured the king's advisers that Charles was suffering because of a sorcerer's malice but in the meantime the young monarch recovered, and Gillaume fell back into his original obscurity.

Five years later the king had another attack, and two Augustine friars were sent from Guienne to cure him. But their conduct was so outrageous that they were executed.

A third attack in 1403 was combated by two sorcerers of Dijon. They established themselves in a thick wood near the gates of Dijon, where they made a magic circle of iron that was supported by iron columns the height of an average man, to which 12 chains of iron were attached. The King's subjects were so anxious for his recovery that the two sorcerers were able to persuade 12 of the town's principal persons to enter the circle and allow themselves to be chained. The sorcerers then proceeded with their incantations, but without result. They were arrested and burned for their pretenses.

After the duke of Burgundy ordered the duke of Orleans murdered, he attempted to justify his crime by alleging that the dead duke had attempted to kill him by means of sorcery.

Witchcraft Persecutions

By the year 1400 belief in the nightly meetings of the witches' **Sabbat** was widespread. In Paris alone, in the time of Charles IX, there were said to be no less than thirty thousand sorcerers, and it was estimated that France contained more than three times that number during the reign of Henry III. Not a town or village was exempt from accusations and trials. The accused belonged to all classes, and generally met the same fate, regardless of rank, age, or sex. Children of the tenderest years and nonagenarians alike were committed to the flames. The terror of being publicly accused as a sorcerer hung like a black cloud over the life of every successful man because it was a charge readily available to an envious enemy who wished him destroyed.

England no edict regarding **witchcraft** had at this period, but in France and other Continental countries (especially Germany) a law had been taking shape. By the end of the fifteenth century there was an international belief in the efficacy of sorcery and a conviction that witchcraft was a religion of devil worshipers. In the 1480s the pope gave his official approval for the Inquisition to move against the supposed witches, and two Dominican fathers wrote a textbook describing them, their crimes, and the method of proceeding against them.

During the early sixteenth century witchcraft trials were rare in France, and there are few cases recorded before the year 1560. The first instance would almost be humorous if it were not a taste of things to come. In 1561 a number of persons were brought to trial at Vernon, accused of having held their Sabbat gathering in a ruined castle. The "witches" were accused of having arrived at the castle in the shape of cats. Witnesses were deposed who claimed to have seen the assembly and to have been attacked by the pseudofeline conspirators. After a good laugh and the proper expression of righteous indignation, the court dismissed the charges as worthy only of ridicule.

In 1564 three men and a woman were executed at Poitiers, having been forced to confess to various acts of sorcery. They said they had regularly attended the witches' Sabbat held three times a year, and that the demon who presided at it ended by burning himself to make powder for his agents to use in mischief. These first executions were followed by a series of others in the 1570s.

In 1571 a mere conjurer who played tricks with cards was thrown into prison in Paris, forced to confess that he was an attendant on the Sabbat. He was executed. In 1573 a man was burned at Dôle on the charge of changing himself into a wolf and devouring children. Several persons who confessed to having been at the Sabbats were condemned to be burned that same year in different parts of France. In 1578 another man was tried and condemned in Paris for changing himself into a wolf, and a man was condemned at Orleans for the same supposed crime in 1583.

Wolves were prolifie in France and people often connected their ravages with witchcraft. The belief in what were in England called **werewolves** (men-wolves) and in France *loups-garous* was ancient and widespread.

In 1578 a woman was burned at Compiègne after she confessed that she had given herself to the devil, who appeared to her as a great black man on horseback, booted and spurred. Another avowed witch was burned the same year; she also stated that the Evil One came to her in the shape of a black man. In 1582 and 1583 several witches were burnted all frequenters of the Sabbats.

Local councils of the time passed severe laws against witchcraft, and a significant number of victims were put to death in France under such accusations. In the course of only 15 years, from 1580 to 1595, in the province of Lorraine alone, the president Remigius burned nine hundred witches, and as many more fled the country to save their lives. About the close of the century, a French judge stated that the crime of witchcraft had become so common that there were not enough jails to hold the prisoners or judges to hear their cases. A trial he witnessed in 1568 induced physician **Jean Bodin** to write *De la Demonomanie des Sorciers*

(1580), which became a standard French textbook on the subject of witchcraft.

Among English witches, the devil was generally said to come in person to seduce his victims, but in France and other countries this seems to have been unnecessary. Once initiated each person became seized with an uncontrollable desire to make converts, whom he or she carried to the Sabbat to be duly enrolled as witches. According to Bodin's imaginings, one witch was enough to corrupt five hundred honest persons. The infection quickly ran through a family and was generally carried down from generation to generation, which explained satisfactorily, according to his commentary on **demonology,** the extent to which witchcraft had supposedly spread in his day. The novice received a burlesque rite of baptism and was marked with the sign of the demon on some unexposed part of the body. The first act of compliance with the devil was then performed, and it was frequently repeated, the evil one presenting himself to the converts as a member of the opposite sex, as Bodin tells it.

Toward the end of the sixteenth century, infatuation with witchcraft had risen to its greatest height in France. Not only the lower classes but also persons of the highest rank in society were liable to suspicion of dealing in sorcery. Such charges were publicly made against King Henry III and Queen Catherine de Medici and early in the following century became grounds for state trials that had fatal conclusions.

In 1610, during the reign of Louis XIII, the *cause c lèbre* of the marechale d'Ancre occurred. Among Marie de Medici's servants was a certain Eleanora Dori, who married Concini, a prodigal spendthrift. As guardian to her son, Marie de Medici was ruler of France and considerable power was exercised by these favorite servants. Because of this favor the peers of France joined together against the upstarts, but with little result at first. Concini was named marechal of France, with the title of marquis d'Ancre.

His wife, who was very superstitious, fell sick and attributed her ill health to the effects of sorcery. The result was that d'Ancre was assassinated by the nobles during a hunting expedition. The mob dragged d'Ancre's corpse from its grave and hanged it on the Pont Neuf. His wretched widow was accused of sorcery and of having bewitched the Queen Mother.

The exorcists who had helped her free herself from illness advised the sacrifice of a cock, and it was represented as a sacrifice to the infernal powers. Added to this, the astrological nativities of the royal family were found in her possession, as, it was said, were several occult books, and a great number of magic characters. After being tortured without result, she was beheaded and burned. Strangely enough the anger of the Parisian mob then turned to general commiseration.

Many other interesting cases occurred in France in the seventeenth century, including several cases of reputed demoniac possession among the Ursulines at Aix (see **Louis Gaufridi**), the **nuns of Louviers,** and the nuns of Auxonne. The case of the **nuns of Loudon** resulted in the burning alive of **Urbain Grandier.**

The Rise of Modern Occultism

The eighteenth century in France is rich in occult history. At a time when the Enlightenment was destroying the older supernatural magic, a new magic was beginning to evolve that made use of scientific categories and information. While the eighteenth century was the low point in practice of the occult in Europe, the founders of modern occultism were emerging. Perhaps the most striking personality of this age was the **Comte de Saint Germain,** who was credited with possessing the secrets of **alchemy** and magic. His family connections were unknown, and his conversation suggested that he had lived for many centuries. Another mysterious adept was an alchemist calling himself **Lascaris,** who literally sowed his path through Europe with gold.

Then followed **Cagliostro,** who attained a fame unrivaled in the history of French occultism. He founded many Masonic lodges throughout the country, Freemasonry being credited with spreading the democratic beliefs underlying the French Revolution and the democratic upheavals across the continent during the next century.

A school of initiates was founded by **Martinez de Pasqually,** which appeared in some measure to have incorporated the teachings of the later European adepts. Another important figure at this time was **Louis Claude de Saint-Martin,** known as "le Philosophe Inconnu" (the unknown philosopher), who came under the influence of Pasqually, and later that of the writings of the mystical **Jakob Boehme,** whose works Saint-Martin translated. **Jacques Cazotte** was one of the first men associated with both magic and the Revolution. Much of the Revolutions inception is owed to those mysterious brotherhoods of France and Germany, which during the eighteenth century sowed the seeds of equality and Illuminism throughout Europe.

Loiséaut, a parishioner of Sainte-Mandé, formed a mystical society in 1772 that met in great secrecy, awaiting a vision of John the Baptist, who supposedly came to them to foretell the Revolution. The spiritual director of this circle was a monk named Dom Gerle, one of the first mesmerists in Paris, who was said to have foretold the dreadful fame of Robespierre through the seeress Catherine Théot. He was expelled by the members of the circle, who acted on the advice of member Sister Françoise André, who cherished a notion to preserve the crown for the future reign of Louis XVII.

The appearance of **Marie Lenormand** as a prophetess at the end of the eighteenth century may be said to have ended a chapter of the occult history of that age. With the beginning of the nineteenth century the influence of Austrian physician **Franz A. Mesmer** (1733–1825) had led to a widespread interest in **animal magnetism,** which in turn culminated in the growth of **Spiritualism.** The **Baron du Potet de Sennevoy** did much to advance Mesmer's views which by this time were being seriously pursued by **Cahagnet** and others.

By the middle of the nineteenth century the new occultism was well established in Paris. A story by Alphonse Esquiros titled *The Magician* (1838) led to the founding of a school of magic fantasy, which was assiduously developed by Henri Delaage, who was said to have the gift of ubiquity and who collected recipes for acquiring physical beauty from the old magicians. In his works *The Reform of Philosophy* and *Yes or No,* **J. M. Hoene-Wronski** claimed to have discovered the first theorems of the Kabbalah and later beguiled rich persons of weak intellect into paying him large sums in return for knowledge of the Absolute.

Spiritual Healing

The celebrated **Curé D'Ars,** founder of the D'Ars "Providence," and many other noble works of charity, was born Jean Baptiste Vianney in the vicinity of Lyons in 1786. At school he was remembered as a somewhat dull student. Circumstances opened the way for his becoming a priest, although he had only enough Latin to say mass and no learning beyond the routine of his profession. His amiable nature and unaffected piety won him friends wherever he went. After some changes of fortune and the rejection of two good offers of rich positions, he accepted the pastoral charge of the little agricultural village of D'Ars, now in the arrondisement of Trevoux.

Very soon his reputation for beneficence drew to him a much larger circle of poor dependents than he could provide for, and it was then that he began his extraordinary life of faith, supplicating in fervent prayer for whatever means were necessary to carry out his divine mission of blessing his unfortunate fellow creatures. In this way the sphere of his benevolence and the wonderful results of the prayer he employed to maintain it reached remarkable proportions.

But a more wonderful thing was to happen in the blessed region of D'Ars. The sick began to experience sudden cures while praying before the altar or making confessions to the curé. The fame of this new miracle soon spread abroad, until the Abbé Monnin declared that more than twenty thousand persons annually came from Germany, Italy, Belgium, all parts of France, and even from England to see the cure, and that in less than six years, this number increased to an average of eighty thousand. Diseases of every kind that had been pronounced incurable were dissipated at once. The indefatigable curé gave himself up to the work, heart and soul. His church stood open day and night, and the immense crowds that surrounded it were obliged to wait for hours and sometimes days to reach the healer.

No one was allowed to take precedence over others except in cases of extreme poverty or extreme suffering. Princes, nobles, and great ladies often drove up as near as they could to the church in grand carriages and were astonished when informed that they could not be admitted except in turn.

The curé only permitted himself to take four hours sleep, namely from 11:00 to 3:00, and when he came to the confessional again the church and all the approaches to it were crowded with those who had waited all night to secure their places. Omnibuses were established to convey patients from Lyons to D'Ars, and the Saône was crowded with boats full of anxious pilgrims.

Spiritualism and Animal Magnetism

The Comte d'Ourches was the first to introduce **automatic writing** and **table turning** to France. **Baron Ludwig von Guldenstubbe,** in his *Practical Experimental Pneumatology; or, the Reality of Spirits and the Marvellous Phenomena of their Direct Writing* (first published in French in 1857) gives an account of his discovery:

"It was in the course of the year 1850, or about three years prior to the epidemic of table-rapping, that the author sought to introduce into France the circles of American spiritualism, the mysterious Rochester knockings and the purely automatic writings of mediums. Unfortunately he met with many obstacles raised by other mesmerists. Those who were committed to the hypothesis of a magnetic fluid, and even those who styled themselves Spiritual Mesmerists, but who were really inferior inducers of somnambulism, treated the mysterious knockings of American spiritualism as visionary follies. It was therefore only after more than six months that the author was able to form his first circle on the American plan, and then thanks to the zealous concurrence of M. Rousaan, a former member of the Socièté des Magnètiseurs Spiritualistes, a simple man who was full of enthusiasm for the holy cause of spiritualism. We were joined by a number of other persons, amongst whom was the Abbé Châtel, founder of the Eglise Française, who, despite his rationalistic tendencies, ended by admitting the reality of objective and supernatural revelation, as an indispensable condition of spiritualism and all practical religions. Setting aside the moral conditions which are equally requisite, it is known that American circles are based on the distinction of positive and electric or negative magnetic currents.

"The circles consist of twelve persons, representing in equal proportions the positive and negative or sensitive elements. This distinction does not follow the sex of the members, though generally women are negative and sensitive, while men are positive and magnetic. The mental and physical constitution of each individual must be studied before forming the circles, for some delicate women have masculine qualities, while some strong men are, morally speaking, women. A table is placed in a clear and ventilated spot; the medium is seated at one end and entirely isolated; by his calm and contemplative quietude he serves as a conductor for the electricity, and it may be noted that a good somnambulist is usually an excellent medium. The six electrical or negative dispositions, which are generally recognised by their emotional qualities and their sensibility, are placed at the right of the medium, the most sensitive of all being next him. The same rule is followed with the positive personalities, who are at the left of the medium, with the most positive next to him. In order to form a chain, the twelve persons each place their right hand on the table. Observe that the medium or mediums, if there be more than one, are entirely isolated from those who form the chain.

"After a number of séances, certain remarkable phenomena have been obtained, such as simultaneous shocks, felt by all present at the moment of mental evocation on the part of the most intelligent persons. It is the same with mysterious knockings and other strange sounds; many people, including those least sensitive, have had simultaneous visions, though remaining in the ordinary waking state. Sensitive persons have acquired that most wonderful gift of mediumship, namely, automatic writing, as the result of an invisible attraction which uses the nonintelligent instrument of a human arm to express its ideas. For the rest, non-sensitive persons experience the mysterious influence of an external wind, but the effect is not strong enough to put their limbs in motion. All these phenomena, obtained according to the mode of American spiritualism, have the defect of being more or less indirect, because it is impossible in these experiments to dispense with the mediation of a human being or medium. It is the same with the table-turning which invaded Europe in the middle of the year 1853.

"The author has had many table experiences with his honourable friend, the Comte d'Ourches, one of the most instructed persons in Magic and the Occult Sciences. We attained by degrees the point when tables moved, apart from any contact whatever, while the Comte d'Ourches has caused them to rise, also without contact. The author has made tables rush across a room with great rapidity, and not only without contact but without the magnetic aid of a circle of sitters. The vibrations of pianochords under similar circumstances took place on January 20, 1856, in the presence of the Comte de Szapary and Comte d'Ourches. Now all such phenomena are proof positive of certain occult forces, but they do not demonstrate adequately the real and substantial existence of unseen intelligences, independent of our will and imagination, though the limits of these have been vastly extended in respect of their possibilities. Hence the reproach made against American spiritualists, because their communications with the world of spirits are so insignificant in character, being confined to mysterious knockings and other sound vibrations. As a fact, there is no direct phenomenon at once intelligent and material, independent of our will and imagination, to compare with the direct writing of spirits, who have neither been invoked or evoked, and it is this only which offers irrefutable proof as to the reality of the supernatural world."

Spiritualism enjoyed great popularity in France for the rest of the century.

Mesmerism

After public attention was drawn to animal magnetism by Mesmer and D'Eslon, several distinguished scientists followed their experiments with great success. Among them was the Baron Du Potet, whose deep interest in the subject of magnetism led him to publish the periodical *Journal de Magnètisme,* which forms a treasury of insight on the age.

Du Potet's investigations began about 1836, and for the next decade he chronicled the production of remarkable phenomena and their attestation by scientific and eminent witnesses. The baron's magnetized subjects reportedly experienced **clairvoyance, trance** speaking, healing, **stigmata** (raised letters and figures on the subject's body), **levitation,** and insensibility to fire, injury, or touch. In the presence of the magnetized subjects, heavy bodies were moved without human contact and distant objects materialized through walls and closed doors (generally termed **apports**). Sometimes the "lucides" (magnetized clairvoyants) described scenes in the spirit world, found lost property, prophesied, and spoke in foreign languages.

In 1840 Du Potet wrote that he had "rediscovered in magnetism the magic of antiquity.

"Let the savants," he stated, "reject the doctrine of spiritual appearances; the enquirer of to-day is compelled to believe it; from an examination of undeniable facts. . . . If the knowledge of ancient magic is lost, all the facts remain on which to reconstruct it."

But of all those to whom French Spiritualism was indebted for evidence of supermundane intercourse, none was more prominent than **Alphonse Cahagnet,** author of *Magnètisme: Arcanes de la vie future dévoilés* (2 vols., 1948–49), which was translated into English in 1850.

Cahagnet was a mechanic, though he was a sensible and interesting writer. He said he was a "materialist" when he was first attracted to the subject of animal magnetism, but he determined to devote all his leisure time to a thorough examination of its possibilities. When he found that he could induce the magnetic sleep in others, he proceeded with a task generally adopted by mesmerists—to substitute his own senses, mind, and will for those of the sleeper.

Cahagnet discovered that he could cure disease and determined to put all his energy into healing. However, a new obstacle arose to confound his philosophy and scatter his theories to the winds: some of his subjects, instead of representing what he willed, began to wander off to regions they persisted in calling the "land of spirits" and to describe people whom they emphatically affirmed to be the souls of the dead.

For a long time Cahagnet fought what he termed these "wild hallucinations," but when he found them recurring and saw that many of those who came to witness the experiments in magnetism recognized dead individuals in descriptions given by the somnambulists, he was compelled to admit there was another dimension to clairvoyance. After a long series of experiments Cahagnet wrote *The Celestial Telegraph; or, Secrets of the Life to Come.*

In her book *Nineteenth Century Miracles* (1884), **Emma Hardinge Britten** quotes from the anonymous author of *Art Magic* (1876):

"The narrow conservatism of the age, and the pitiful jealousy of the Medical Faculty, rendered it difficult and harassing to conduct magnetic experiments openly in Europe within several years of Mesmer's decease. Still such experiments were not wanting, and to show their results, we give a few excerpts from the correspondence between the famous French Magnetists, MM. Deleuze and Billot, from the years 1829 to 1840. By these letters, published in 1836 [*sic*], it appears that M. Billot commenced his experiments in magnetizing as early as 1789, and that during forty years, he had an opportunity of witnessing facts in clairvoyance, ecstasy, and somnambulism, which at the time of their publication transcended the belief of the general mass of readers. On many occasions in the presence of entranced subjects, spirits recognised as having once lived on earth in mortal form would come *in bodily presence* before the eyes of an assembled multitude and at request bring flowers, fruits, and objects, removed by distance from the scene of the experiments.

"M. Deleuze frankly admits that his experience was more limited to those phases of somnambulism in which his subjects submitted to amputations and severe surgical operations without experiencing the slightest pain. . . . In a letter dated 1831 M. Billot, writing to Deleuze, says, 'I repeat, I have seen and known all that is permitted to man. I have seen the stigmata arise on magnetized subjects; I have dispelled obsessions of evil spirits with a single word. I have seen spirits bring those material objects I told you of, and when requested, make them so light that they would float, and, again, a small *boiteau de bonbons* was rendered so heavy that I failed to move it an inch until the power was removed.'

"To those who enjoyed the unspeakable privilege of listening to the somnambules of Billot, Deleuze, and Cahagnet, another and yet more striking feature of unanimous revelation was poured forth. Spirits of those who had passed away from earth strong in the faith of Roman Catholicism—often priests and dignitaries of that conservative Church, addressing prejudiced believers in their former doctrine—asserted that there was no creed in Heaven, no sectarian worship, or ecclesiastical dogmatism there prevailing.

"They taught that God was a grand Spiritual Sun—life on earth a probation—the spheres, different degrees of comprehensive happiness or states of retributive suffering, each appropriate to the good or evil deeds done on earth. They described the ascending changes open to every soul in proportion to his own efforts to improve.

"They all insisted that man was his own judge, incurred a penalty or reward for which there was no substitution. They taught nothing of Christ, absolutely denied the idea of vicarious atonement, and represented man as his own Saviour or destroyer.

"They spoke of arts, sciences, and continued activities, as if the life beyond was but an extension of the present on a greatly improved scale. Descriptions of the radiant beauty, supernal happiness, and ecstatic sublimity manifested by the blest spirits who had risen to the spheres of Paradise, Heaven, and the glory of angelic companionships melts the heart, and fills the soul with irresistible yearning, to lay down life's weary burdens and be at rest with them." (The reference to the correspondence between Deleuze and Billot is probably to G. P. Billot's *Recherches psychologiques sur la cause de phénomenes extraordinaires,* published in two volumes in 1839, and the correspondence would have ceased before that date.)

Spiritualism and Spiritism

Spiritualism emerged in France, as in Germany, out of the awakening interest in psychic powers resulting from experiments in animal magnetism. It appears that although Spiritualism gained an immense foothold and exerted an influence upon the popular mind, one of the chief obstacles to its general acceptance was its lack of internal unity and the antagonism among its leaders.

Two leaders who figured most prominently in the drama of French Spiritualism, and in all probability exerted more influence upon public opinion than any other members of its *dramatis personae,* were **Allan Kardec** and **A. T. Pierart,** the respective editors of the movement's two leading journals: *La Revue Spirite* and *La Revue Spiritualiste.* Pierart and Kardec may also be regarded as the representatives of the two opposing factions generally known as Spiritualists and Spiritists, the former teaching that the soul undergoes only one mortal birth and continues its progress through eternity in spiritual states, the latter affirming the doctrine of **reincarnation** and claiming that the human spirit can and does undergo many incarnations in different mortal forms. Kardec and his followers represented **Spiritism,** and Pierart led the opposing faction commonly called Spiritualists.

Kardec derived his communications chiefly from writings and trance mediums who proved the most susceptible to his influence, and is said to have persistently banished from his circles not only **D. D. Home,** M. Brédif, and other physical mediums but all those who did not endorse his favorite dogma through their communications.

In *Nineteenth Century Miracles* Britten noted how the schism in French Spiritualism reached out across Europe. In France, Kardec's personal influence fitted him for a propagandist and his opinions were generally accepted by his readers. Little or no Spiritualist literature had been disseminated in the French language when Kardec's works were first published. He pursued his beliefs with an indomitable energy that his harassed rival Pierart lacked.

The doctrines of the reincarnationists, although defended ability by their propagandists—who included many of the most capable minds of France—were not allowed to pass without severe castigation by their English neighbors. In the *London Spiritual Magazine* of 1865 the editor, commenting on the ominous silence of the *Spirite* journals concerning Maldigny's opera, *Swedenborg,* states:

"It is worthy of note that the journals of the Kardec school, so far as we have seen them, do not take the least notice of this opera. The *Avenir* of Paris, which appears weekly, but greatly wants facts, has not a word to say about it. . . . It is greatly to be regretted that the main object of the Kardecian journals seems to be, not the demonstration of the constantly recurring facts of Spiritualism, but the deification of Kardec's doctrine of reincarnation.

"To this doctrine—which has nothing to do with Spiritualism, even if it had a leg of reason or fact to stand on—all the strength, and almost all the space of these journals is devoted.

These are the things which give the enemies of Spiritualism a real handle against it, and bring it into contempt with sober minds. Reincarnation is a doctrine which cuts up by the roots all individual identity in the future existence. It desolates utterly that dearest yearning of the human heart for reunion with its loved ones in a permanent world. If some are to go back into fresh physical bodies, and bear new names, and new natures, if they are to become respectively Tom Styles, Ned Snooks, and a score of other people, who shall ever hope to meet again with his friends, wife, children, brothers and sisters? When he enters the spirit-world and enquires for them, he will have to learn that they are already gone back to earth, and are somebody else, the sons and daughters of other people, and will have to become over and over the kindred of a dozen other families in succession! Surely, no such most cheerless crochet could bewitch the intellects of any people, except under the most especial bedevilment of the most sarcastic and mischievous of devils."

In the January 1866 issue a stronger article on this subject was written by **William Howitt,** who protests Spiritualists toying with the doctrine of reincarnation:

"In the *Avenir* of November 2nd, M. Pezzani thinks he has silenced M. Pierart, by asserting that without Reincarnation all is chaos and injustice in God's creation: 'In this world there are rich and poor, oppressed and oppressors, and without Re-incarnation, God's justice could not be vindicated.' That is to say, in M. Pezzani's conception, God has not room in the infinite future to punish and redress every wrong, without sending back souls again and again into the flesh. M. Pezzani's idea, and that of his brother Re-incarnationists is, that the best way to get from Paris to London is to travel any number of times from Paris to Calais and back again. We English believe that the only way is to go on to London at once. . . . As to M. Pezzani's notions of God's injustice without Re-incarnation, if souls were re-incarnated a score of times, injustice between man and man, riches and poverty, oppression and wrong, all the enigmas of social inequality would remain just then as now.

"In noticing these movements in the Spiritist camp in France, we should be doing a great injustice if we did not refer to the zealous, eloquent, and unremitting exertions of M. Pierart in the *La Revue Spiritualiste,* to expose and resist the errors of the *Spirite* to which we have alluded. The doctrine of Re-incarnation, M. Pierart has persistently resisted and denounced as at once false, unfounded on any evidence, and most pernicious to the character of Spiritualism."

Allen Kardec died in 1869. Even though receiving communications through physical mediumship was not favored by his followers, physical phenomena of all kinds were recorded in Pierart's journal and others. Characteristic aspects of non-Kardecean Spiritualism in France may be found in such sources.

French Spiritualism

The first well marked impulse that Spiritualism received in France was owed to the visits of D. D. Home, the celebrated medium, and subsequently to the large influx of professional mediums who found in France an excellent field for the demonstration of their gifts.

Home's séances remain the most remarkable of their kind. His manifestations were given almost exclusively in the presence of persons of rank or those distinguished by literary fame. During his residence in Paris, under the Imperial régime, he was a frequent visitor at the court of Emperor Louis Napoleon. A record of the manifestations produced through his mediumship was kept by command of the empress and frequently read to her favored friends. Among these memoranda is one published in the papers when it occurred. It concerns a séance held at the Tuileries when only the emperor, the empress, the duchess of Montebello, and Home were present:

Pen, ink, and paper were placed on the table and a spirit hand was seen. It dipped the pen into the ink and wrote the name of the first Napoleon, in a perfect facsimile of that monarch's handwriting. The emperor asked if he might be permitted to kiss this wonderful hand. It instantly rose to his lips, subsequently passing to those of the empress, and Home. The emperor preserved this precious autograph, and inscribed with it a memorandum that the hand was warm, soft, and resembled that of his great predecessor and uncle.

As evidence of the wide popularity Spiritualism had attained by 1869, Pierart quotes an article by Eugène Bonnemère from the *Siécle,* a leading paper that editorialized against the movement:

"Although somnambulism has been a hundred times annihilated by the Academy of Medicine, it is more alive than ever in Paris; in the midst of all the lights of the age, it continues, right or wrong, to excite the multitude. Protean in its forms, infinite in its manifestations, if you put it out of the door, it knocks at the window; if that be not opened, it knocks on the ceiling, on the walls; it raps on the table at which you innocently seat yourselves to dine or for a game of whist. If you close your ears to its sounds, it grows excited, strikes the table, whirls it about in a giddy maze, lifts up its feet, and proceeds to talk through mediumship, as the dumb talk with their fingers.

"You have all known the rage for table-turning. At one time we ceased to ask after each other's health, but asked how your table was. 'Thank you, mine turns beautifully; and how goes yours on?' Everything turned; hats and the heads in them. One was led almost to believe that a circle of passengers being formed round the mainmast of a ship of great tonnage, and a magnetic chain thus established, they might make the vessel spin round till it disappeared in the depth of the ocean, as a gimlet disappears in a deal board. The Church interfered; it caused its thunders to roar, declaring that it was Satan himself who thus raised the devil in the tables, and having formally forbade the world to turn, it now forbade the faithful to turn tables, hats, brains, or ships of huge size. But Satan held his own. The sovereign of the nether world passed into a new one, and that is the reason that America sends us mediums, beginning so gloriously with the famous Home, and ending with the Brothers Davenport. One remembers with what a frenzy everyone precipitated himself in pursuit of mediums. Everyone wished to have one of his own; and when you introduced a young man into society, you did not say, 'He is a good waltzer,' but, 'He is a medium.' Official science has killed and buried this Somnambulism a score of times; but it must have done it very badly, for there it is as alive as ever, only christened afresh with a new name."

Among the many distinguished adherents of Spiritualism in France, most prominent were astronomer **Camille Flammarion,** authors **Victor Hugo** and Alexandre Dumas, and **Victorien Sardou,** the renowned writer of French comedy. Sardou was himself a talented medium. He executed a number of drawings purporting to represent scenes in the spirit world. Among them was an exquisite and complex work of art entitled *The House of Mozart.*

In addition to Home and the **Davenport brothers,** many other famous mediums visited France, including **Henry Slade, William Eglinton, Elizabeth d'Esperance, Florence Cook** and **Lottie Fowler.** They stimulated interest in the scientific investigation of claimed phenomena.

Psychical Research and Parapsychology

The formation of the **Society for Psychical Research** (SPR) in Britain in 1882 led to scientific interest in Spiritualism all over the world. One of the pioneers of French psychical research was the physiologist **Charles Richet,** who was elected president of the SPR in 1905. Another notable Frenchman with an interest in the findings of psychical research was the philospher **Henri Bergson,** elected president of the SPR in 1913. (Bergson's sister was a devoted practitioner of magic.)

The engineer **Gabriel Delanne** had founded the Societé d'Etude des Phénomènes Psychiques and studied various mediums. In 1890 the *Annales des Sciences Psychiques* was first published under the direction of a Dr. Dariex and Richet (an English edition was published beginning in 1905).

In 1918, through the generosity of **Jean Meyer,** the **Institut Métapsychique International** was founded and Richet became its first honorary president. Meyer, a follower of Kardec, had founded Le **Maison des Spirites** to propagate knowledge of Spiritism, and he founded the Institut Métapsychique for psychical research. In 1920 the *Revue Métapsychique* became the official publication of the Institut and continued the excellent work of the earlier *Annales des Sciences Psychique.* The *Revue Métapsychique* is still the leading publication of its kind.

Richet's interest in **psychical research** stemmed from the work of **Col. Eugen Rochas,** who had experimented with hypnosis and human radiation. Other workers in the field of human radiations included Dr. **Paul Joire, Hippolyte Baraduc, Emile Boirac,** Dr. **Joseph Maxwell,** Prof. Blondlot, Jules Regnault, Louis Favre, and G. de Fontenay.

French workers in the field of psychical research included **Paul Gibier,** Alfred Binet, **Pierre Janet, Gustav Geley, Theodore Flournoy, Eugèn O ty,** René Sudre, and **Rene Warcollier.** Another notable researcher was **Cesar de Vesme,** whose *Histoire du Spiritualisme experimentale* (History of Experimental Spiritualism, 1928) was awarded a prize by the Paris Académie des Sciences. Geley experimented with the famous medium **Eva C.,** who specialized in **materialization** phenomena; Flournoy investigated the strange talents of the medium **Hélène Smith.**

In the transition from psychical research to **parapsychology,** a later development was the formation of the Groupe d'Etudes et de Recherches en Parapsychologie (GERP) in 1971. GERP experimenters studied animal parapsychology and possible **psychokinesis.** Other experiments include those of **Paul and Christiane Vasse,** who have studied plant germination and growth in relation to mental effects.

The Laboratory of Parapsychology was founded in Bordeaux by Dr. Jean Barry, who experimented with PK effects on fungi virus. Other PK experiments have been conducted by engineers G. Chevalier and De Cressac. Another modern researcher is Dr. R. Dufour, who experimented with clairvoyance and psychometry.

Among the more noteworthy modern developments was the establishment of the Centre d'Eclairagisme headed by Yvonne Duplessis, aided by a grant from the **Parapsychology Foundation** in New York. The center specialized in the subject of **eyeless sight,** first propagated by the great novelist Jules Romains, and volunteers have discovered the ability of blind persons to distinguish colors.

Radiesthesia and Out-of-the-Body Travel

An offshoot of interest in "human radiation" through the research of Baraduc and others has been French interest in such subjects as **radiesthesia** and **astral projection.** It has always been difficult to draw a line between such subjects as psychical research, Spiritualism, and radiesthesia, and in the past many prominent French psychical researchers endorsed Spiritualist beliefs and astral projection out of their belief in the reality of the human soul or subtle body. Some researchers who claim to have detected human radiation have also propagated concepts of the subtle body; Baraduc claimed to have photographed it.

Radiesthesia, a French term for **dowsing** and divining for water and metals, is specifically concerned with subtle radiation, not only human but also animal and mineral. French experimenters have specialized in the use of the **pendulum** in place of the divining rod, and a number of exponents of radiesthesia were priests. Radiesthesiests developed the use of the pendulum in prospecting over a map of an area in order to trace minerals, water, or even detect the movement of individuals. Another interesting application of radiesthesia is in diagnosis of health and disease in individuals. In 1930 a society was formed under the name L'Association des Amis de la Radiesthesie, including among its members were engineers and doctors. The monthly journal *La Chronique des Sourciers* was issued under the editorship of its president le Vicomte Henry de France. It was superseded by two currently published journals: *Radiésthesie* and *Les Amis de la Radiésthesie.*

Closely associated with radiesthesia is the comprehensive study of **psychotronics,** described as the study of the relationship of man to the universe, interaction with other physical bodies and matter, and fields of energy, known or unknown. The Organisation pour la Recherche en Psychotronique publishes the *Revue Française de Psychotronique* at Siége Social Bureau 644, U.E.R. de Mathématiques, Universite Toulouse le Mirail.

A pioneer experimenter in **out-of-the-body travel** was a Frenchman, Marcel Louis Forhan, whose book *Le Médecin de l'Âme* was first published in English as *Practical Astral Projection* in 1935, under the pseudonym Yram. Yram's record of his personal experiences antedated the 1938 book *Astral Projection,* by Oliver Fox (**Hugh G. Callaway**), so important to the launching of research on the topic in English-speaking countries.

Sources:

Baraduc, Hippolyte. *L'Âme humaine.* Paris, 1896.

Cauzons, Theodore de. *La Magie et la Sorcellerie en France.* 4 vols. Paris, 1900.

De France, Henri Vicomte. *The Elements of Dowsing.* London: G. Bell & Son, 1948.

Delanne, Gabriel. *Evidence for a Future Life.* London: Philip Wellby/New York: G. P. Putnam's Sons, 1904.

Deleuze, J. P. F. *Practical Instruction in Animal Magnetism.* Rev. ed. New York: Samuel R. Wells, 1846.

De Vesme, Cesar. *A History of Experimental Spiritualism.* 2 vols. London: Rider, 1931.

Du Potet, Baron. *Magnetism and Magic.* London: Allen & Unwin, 1927.

Geley, Gustav. *From the Unconscious to the Conscious.* London: William Collins Sons, 1920.

Flournoy, Theodore. *From India to the Planet Mars.* New York & London, 1900.

Huxley, Aldous. *The Devils of Loudon.* London, 1952. Reprint, New York: Harper, 1971.

Joire, Paul. *Psychical and Supernormal Phenomena.* London: William Rider & Son, 1916.

Kardec, Allan. *The Mediums' Book (Experimental Spiritism).* London, 1876.

Michelet, Jules. *The Sorceress.* London, 1905. Reprinted as *Satanism and Witchcraft.* Wehman, 1939.

Richet, Charles. *Thirty Years of Psychical Research.* London: W. Collins Sons, 1923. Reprint, New York: Arno Press, 1975.

Summers, Montague. *The Geography of Witchcraft.* London, 1927. Reprint, New Hyde Park, N.Y.: University Books, 1958.

———. *The Werewolf.* London, 1933. Reprint, New Hyde Park, N.Y.: University Books, 1966.

Yram [Marcel Louis Forhan]. *Practical Astral Projection.* London: Rider, 1935. Reprint, New York: Samuel Weiser, n.d.

Franck (or **Frank**), **Sebastian** (ca. 1499–ca. 1543)

Sixteenth-century visionary and freethinker. In 1531 he published the treatise *L'Arbu de la science du bien et du mal, dont Adam a mangé la mort, et dont encore aujourd'hui tous les hommes la mangent.* According to this work, the sin of Adam is an allegory and the Tree of Knowledge represents the person, will, knowledge, and life of Adam.

Franck's major publication was his *Chronica, Zeitbuch und Geschichtsbibel* (1536), based on the Nuremberg Chronicle. His *Guldin Arch* (1538) discusses pagan parallels to Christian sentiments and caused Franck trouble with religious authorities, who accused him of heresy. He was contemptuously criticized by Luther as "a devil's mouth."

Sources:

Franck, Sebastian. *Paradoxa.* Jena, Germany: E. Diederichs, 1909.

Williams, George H. *The Radical Reformation.* Philadelphia: Westminster Press, 1962.

Wollgast, Siegfried. *Der deutsche Pantheismus im 16. Jahrhundert.* Berlin: Deutscher Verlag der Wissenschaften, 1972.

Francke, Christian (1549–ca. 1595)

A sixteenth-century visionary who frequently changed his religion, which gained him the nickname "Weathercock." He believed the religion of Japan to be the best because he had read that its ministers were ecstatic. He published *Colloquium Jesuiticum* in 1579.

Frankenstein

The name of the creator of the archetypal zombielike artificial man, as well as the moniker given his creation. *Frankenstein; or, the Modern Prometheus,* by Mary Wollstonecraft Shelley (1797–1851), a classic of English occult **fiction,** was first published in London in 1818 in three volumes. It tells the story of how Dr. Victor Frankenstein creates an artificial man out of fragments of bodies from churchyards and dissecting rooms—a human form without a soul. The monster longs for love and sympathy but inspires only horror and loathing and becomes a powerful force for evil. It seeks revenge against its creator, murdering his friend, brother, and bride and ultimately bringing death to Frankenstein himself.

The book owes much to discussions of the time regarding the scientific work of Darwin and to theories of spontaneous generation and the power of electricity, and is thus also an early science-fiction story. In her introduction Mary Shelley writes of the possibility that a corpse might be reanimated.

The book also contains powerful writing with an overall theme of the moral limits of science and technology. The subtitle refers to the question of whether science has the right to usurp the divine function of creation. (Prometheus was a mythological Greek who stole fire from heaven and thereafter suffered a horrible punishment from the god Zeus.) The book was also popular as a modern myth of the dangers of the industrial era and the many unplanned horrors created by human inventions manufactured to be a boon to the race.

Mary Wollstonecraft wrote a first draft of the story of Frankenstein in the company of Percy Shelley, Lord Byron, John Polidori, and Claire Clairmont when the group spent a week taking opium while vacationing at the Villa Diodati, Geneva, in the summer of 1816. Polidori's *The Vampyre,* came from a suggestion by Byron that weekend and generated interest in another monster theme, culminating in such later thrillers as **Bram Stoker**'s *Dracula* (1897).

Sources:

Baldrick, Chris. *In Frankenstein's Shadow: Myth, Monstrosity, and Nineteenth-Century Writing.* Oxford: Oxford University Press, 1987.

Florescu, Radu. *In Search of Frankenstein.* New York: New York Graphic Society, 1975.

Forry, Steven Earl. *Hideous Progenies: Dramatizations of Frankenstein from Mary Shelley to the Present.* Philadelphia: University of Pennsylvania Press, 1990.

Glut, Donald F. *The Frankenstein Catalog.* Jefferson, N.C.: McFarland, 1984.

Troop, Martin. *Mary Shelley's Monster.* Houghton Mifflin, 1977.

Franklin, Benjamin (1706–1790)

A versatile statesman, printer, inventor, scientist, and diplomat, Franklin was also associated with the occult doctrine of his time, although his attitude was largely skeptical. He was familiar with **astrology,** and while at college he calculated the horoscope of another student named Titus Leads, allegedly predicting the exact time of his death.

In 1784 Franklin was a member of the committee of the Academie des Sciences in Paris, which reported on the phenomena of **Franz Anton Mesmer** during the furor created by **animal magnetism.** Although certain aspects of animal magnetism were acknowledged by the committee, the report attributed these to other causes. Franklin associated with **Rosicrucians** and became a Freemason in February 1730, a member of the Lodge of the Nine Muses, which was said to have influenced the French Revolution.

Franklyn, Julian (1899–1970)

British author, lecturer, and editor, active in the field of parapsychology. Born December 30, 1899, in London, Franklyn became an expert on London Cockneys and their slang, as well as heraldry. He was a member of the Heraldry Society and the Society of Genealogists.

He was editor of an important compilation titled *A Survey of the Occult* (1935), reprinted as *A Dictionary of the Occult* (1973). He also published articles on parapsychological topics in *Tomorrow* magazine and wrote a variety of nonoccult books, including *The Cockney* (1953), *A Dictionary of Rhyming Slang* (1960), *Shield and Crest* (1960), and *A Dictionary of Nicknames* (1962). His final book, on **witchcraft,** was *Death by Enchantment,* published posthumously in 1971.

Sources:

Franklyn, Julian. *Death by Enchantment.* New York: G. P. Putnam's Sons, 1971.

———. *A Survey of the Occult.* London, 1935. Reprinted as *A Dictionary of the Occult.* New York: Causeway Books, 1973.

Pleasants, Helene, ed. *Biographical Dictionary of Parapsychology.* New York: Helix Press, 1964.

Fraser-Harris, David (Fraser) (1867–1937)

Professor of physiology and histology who also took an active interest in psychical research. Born in Edinburgh, Scotland, in February 1867, Fraser-Harris had a distinguished career in Scotland, Birmingham, and later in Nova Scotia.

His first experiences in psychical research were at the **National Laboratory of Psychical Research,** founded by **Harry Price,** in May 1931 while investigating the claimed **materialization** phenomena of **Helen Duncan.** Following this he attended séances with the medium **Rudi Schneider** from February to May 1932 and testified (*Hibbert Journal,* October 1932) to Schneider's genuine telekinetic powers. He suggested the term *teledynamist* for physical mediums.

In addition to his books on medical and technical subjects, Fraser-Harris published *Sixth Sense* (1928) and *The Rhythms of Life* (1929). He contributed articles to the *Journal* of the **Society for Psychical Research** and occasionally lectured at the **British College of Psychic Science.** He died January 3, 1937.

Sources:

Fraser-Harris, David. *The Great Design: Order and Progress in Nature.* New York: Macmillan, 1934.

Fraternitas Rosae Crucis

The Fraternitas Rosae Crucis is the oldest of the several presently existing Rosicrucian bodies. Founded by **Paschal Beverly Randolph** (1825–75) in 1868, its first lodge was opened in San Francisco in 1861. The fraternity had an unstable history through the nineteenthth century, as Randolph moved around the country; on three occasions it was closed for a period and reopened first in Boston (1871), then again in San Francisco (1874), and following Randolph's death in Philadelphia (1895).

According to Randolph's claim, he became the Supreme Hierarch of the Rosicrucian Fraternity in 1846, the same year he retired from the sea due to an accident and settled in Philadelphia. However, it was not until 1861 that he organized the First Grand Lodge. As American **Rosicrucianism** developed, Randolph formulated his ideas in dialogue with Spiritualism. He championed the act of volition as a central element in occult development and decried the need of mediums to go into **trance** and lose control in order to obtain results. The mature mystical system now forms the teachings given out to members of the fraternity. Randolph developed a process of occult transmutation, by which the base self is transformed into the finest spiritual gold. The teachings include a belief in **reincarnation** and the development of a healthy body through natural means. The inner circle of the fraternity, to whom its hightest teachings are given, is called the Aeth Priesthood. Closely associated with the fraternity is the **Church of Illumination.**

Randolph died at a relatively young age in 1875. He was succeeded by Freeman B. Dowd, and he in turn by Edward H. Brown (1907), **R. Swinburne Clymer** (1922), and Emerson M. Clymer. The order was largely moribund during the last decades of the nineteenth century, but was revived primarily through the efforts of Swinburne Clymer, a natural physician and writer, who wrote numerous books and led the fight to legitimize the fraternity, whose place was challenged by newer groups such as the Ancient and Mystical Order of the Rosae Crucis (**AMORC**) and the **Rosicrucian Fellowship,** both founded in the early twentieth century.

The fraternity is headquartered at a rural complex near Quakertown, Pennsylvania. It is headed by a Council of Three and the Hierarch of Eulis. Included in that complex are the Humanitarian Society and the Clymer Health Clinic, both of which continue Randolph's and Clymer's concern for naturalistic health services. The fraternity may be contacted c/o Beverly Hall, Quakertown, PA 18951.

Sources:

Clymer, R. Swinburne. *The Age of Treason.* Quakertown, Penn.: Humanitarian Society, 1959.

———. *The Rose Cross Order.* Allentown, Penn.: Philosophical Publishing, 1916.

———. *The Rosicrucian Fraternity in America.* 2 vols. Quakertown, Penn.: Rosicrucian Foundation, 1935.

———. *The Rosy Cross: Its Teachings.* Quakertown, Penn.: Beverly Hall, 1965.

Fraternitas Saturni

An influential occult group in Germany before World War II, headed by Albin Grau as grand master, accepting much of the teachings of **Aleister Crowley.** The group was disbanded by the Nazis in 1933 but reorganized in 1945.

A German ritual magic group the Fraternitas Saturni grew out of the spread of Crowley's ideas in Germany in the 1920s among members of the Grand Pansophical Lodge, a Masonic occult order. Among the leaders of the lodge was Eugen Grosche, better known as Gregir A. Gregorius. Gregorius was favorably impressed by Crowley's ideas of a new aeon of magic activity characterized by the law of thelema (will) and his teachings on sexual magic, but did not wish to associate directly with Crowley or any of the organizations he headed. In 1926 he led in the dissolving of the Pansophical Lodge and the formation of the Fraternitas Saturni, drawing additional inspiration from reports of Saturnian lodges that had existed in Germany in earlier centuries.

Gregorius began to write a series of books and documents for the new fraternity, borrowing heavily from Crowley's works. The lodge was suppressed shortly after Hitler came to power in 1933 and Gregorius moved to Switzerland. He was extradited to Germany in 1943 but survived the war and refounded the group in 1945. Its growth was delayed by its location in Soviet territory through the late 1940s. The lodge was not truly revived until 1950, when Gregorius was able to move to west Germany. In 1957 a grand lodge was established in Berlin and Gregorius was declared its grand master, a position he held until his death in 1964.

After Gregorius's death the lodge went through a period of dissension and split into three factions. Copies of materials that had been kept secret were handed over to Dr. Aldolf Hemberger, who published them along with his study of the group. Finally, in 1971, the three factions of the fraternity reunited and returned to their secret ritual life. The order continues to exist in Germany, according to reports.

In the 1970s the Fraternitas Saturni emerged in Toronto, Ontario, under the leadership of Frater Set-Orion, the North American grand master. Its present status is uncertain. Copies of the pre-1969 rituals were published in English in 1990 by Edred Flowers, who manifested no knowledge of any North American lodge.

Sources:

Flowers, S. Edred. *Fire and Ice: Magical Teachings of Germany's Greatest Secret Occult Order.* St. Paul, Minn.: Llewellyn Publications, 1990.

Fraternity of the Inner Light

Founded by British occultist "Dion Fortune" (**Violet Mary Firth**) in 1922, but originally called the Community of the Inner Light. Firth was a member of the **Stella Matutina,** an outer order of the famous Hermetic Order of the **Golden Dawn** occult society, and the Community of the Inner Light was originally intended by Golden Dawn members as a recruitment body for suitable prospects. Firth came into conflict with Golden Dawn leaders, however, and she split away from the parent body. Firth remained warden of the fraternity until her death in 1946.

The fraternity was headquartered at Community House, 3 Queensborough Terrace, Bayswater, London, and maintained a library of occultism and mysticism, including the various works on occultism by Fortune herself. Public lectures were organized, and the fraternity published a monthly journal, the *Inner Light Magazine,* devoted to esoteric Christianity, occult science, and the psychology of superconsciousness.

The fraternity also purchased a site at **Glastonbury,** long considered a holy place in Britain, a power center associated with legends of Joseph of Arimathea. A guest house was established on this site on the side of the Tor, the famous Hill of Vision supposed to overlook the Isle of Avalon. Here, Fortune could retreat from the continued tensions she experienced from her interactions with the older, male-dominated magic community. The guest house became a meeting place and social center for those interested in mysticism.

After the death of Dion Fortune, the fraternity continued her teachings virtually unchanged for a time, but eventually its scope broadened, embracing a wider range of occult practices and dispensing with the initiation oath.

Sources:

Chapman, Janine. *Quest for Dion Fortune.* York Beach, Me.: Samuel Weiser, 1993.

Fielding, Charles, and Clark Collins. *The Story of Dion Fortune.* York Beach, Me.: Samuel Weiser, 1985.

Richardson, Alan. *Priestess: The Life and Magic of Dion Fortune.* Wellingborough, England: Aquarian Press, 1987.

Fraud

Spiritualism is unique as a religious community. In no other religious group have substantive charges of fraud played such a large part, and within no other group has the need to confront fraud had such an effect upon its development. Soon after the founding of the movement charges of deliberate fraud were leveled against a growing number of mediums, and the movement itself was charged with complicity in the fraud and a refusal to rid itself of obviously fraudulent leaders.

The frequency with which mediums were exposed in acts of trickery and even convicted of fraud induced many people—concluding the bulk of the phenomena to be fraudulently produced—to abandon both the movement and **psychical research.** The era of systematic research on Spiritualist phenomena came to a close in the 1930s when psychical researchers concluded that there was little, if anything, real in physical phenomena. Psychical research was gradually superseded by laboratory-oriented **parapsychology.** In most countries Spiritualism was pushed to the fringes of the community of people interested in paranormal phenomena and has never regained its credibility. It is conspicuously absent from the **New Age** movement.

The question of fraud is an interesting and complicated one, however, worthy of the student's attention. Simple deception practiced for money was founded, but there were also many instances of apparently deliberate trickery in which there was no reward to be obtained, and even some cases in which the medium seemed entirely innocent and ignorant of the fraud.

The great majority of fraud was related to the production of physical phenomena, especially **materialization, apports,** and the **levitation** of **trumpets** and other objects. A significant portion of the mental phenomena remains that provides an interesting arena for research and explains the continuing fascination with the paranormal.

Conscious and Unconscious Fraud

It is helpful to distinguish between conscious and unconscious fraud, although at times one seemed to shade imperceptibly into the other. During the century (1850–1950) when researchers turned their attention to Spiritualism, conscious fraud most often appeared in connection with physical phenomena. Almost at the outset of the spiritualistic movement (i.e., in 1851) three doctors demonstrated that the rappings that attended the **Fox sisters** were produced by manipulation of the knee and toe joints, a fact that was soon afterward corroborated by a relative of the Fox family. In the wake of the sisters' contradictory claims, confessions, and recantations the evidence was declared inconclusive, but the possibility of fraud had been shown.

After that many mediums have at one time or another been detected in fraud, and every phase of physical mediumship was eventually discredited. **Slate writing, spirit photography,** and **materialization** were all in turn exposed, and now exist only in the fringes of Spiritualism, primarily at Camps Chesterfield in Indiana and Silver Belle in Pennsylvania and in the several churches associated with them. A major exposure of materialization fraud was published as late as 1960 in the *Psychic Observer* by **Andrija Puharich.** The result of the exposure was the bankruptcy of the periodical. In the 1970s Lamar Keene, a Spiritualist medium heavily involved in the production of fraudulent phenomena, left the profession and published his memoirs. In the 1980s magician **James Randi** discovered several faith healers operating on the fringe of the Pentecostal community using some old conjuring tricks to convince their audiences that miracles were occurring.

Time and again, sitters beheld the form and features of the medium in the materialized spirit; shadowy figures in filmy draperies were shown to be dummies wrapped in muslin. False beards and white draperies were found on the medium's person. **Apports**—jewels, flowers, perfumes, *objects d'art*—were smuggled into the séance room in order to be showered upon the sitters by generous "spirits." Threads and human hairs were used to move furniture and other objects. More elaborate and complicated machinery was sometimes provided, but more often the fake medium depended upon sleight of hand and skillful suggestion to accomplish his ends. Some of the mediums were so skilled that professional magicians admitted to séances failed to discover the *modus operandi* of the phenomena, which would only be revealed at a later date.

Fraud can also be illustrated by many instances of self-styled clairvoyance where the medium acquired information by **muscle-reading,** or by judicious inquiry before the séance. Fraud of this kind may have been either conscious or unconscious.

A large group of automatic phenomena occuring when the medium was in a **trance** state must be classed under the heading of unconscious fraud. In many of the more pronounced cases of **automatism,** the agent was not consciously responsible for his or her acts. There was a slighter degree of automatism where the agent may have been partly conscious of, and responsible for, the phenomena. The latter state, if frequently induced and if the automatist's willpower was somewhat relaxed, may have passed into the more profound stage, so that fraud that was at first conscious and voluntary may have become unconscious and spontaneous. Thus it is extremely difficult to know when an accusation of fraud was fairly brought against a medium.

There is evidence that many trance mediums reproduced in their discourses information subconsciously acquired at some more or less remote period. The trance utterances of **Leonora Piper, Rosina Thompson,** and others revealed this peculiarity. It is true that extensive and apparently fraudulent arrangements were sometimes made before a séance. It is possible, though unlikely, that such preparations were made automatically in a state similar to the mediumistic trance.

Spiritualists themselves were often called to face exposures of undoubted fraud, and on such occasions various apologies of a more or less ingenious nature were sometimes offered for the fraudulent medium. Sometimes it was said that the medium was controlled by a mischievous, lying, or lower spirit who made use of the medium's physical organism to perform tricks and deceptions, an apology that opened Spiritualists to charges of demonic possession from Christian detractors. It was sometimes stated that the medium felt an irresistible impulse to perform the action that he or she knew was in the mind of the **control.**

Italian medium **Eusapia Palladino** sometimes extended her hand involuntarily in the direction in which movement of furniture was to take place, although without actual contact. Perceiving that the spirits desired to move the object, she was impelled to attempt a physical (and fraudulent) forestalling of the action, it was said. Other investigators who examined this medium's phenomena declared that their production caused Palladino a great deal of pain and fatigue, and that she therefore seized an opportunity to produce them easily and without trouble. Such an opportunity, they held, only presented itself when their rigorous precautions were relaxed.

The same explanation was given in connection with other mediums. Following cases of materialization séances when the spirit form was grasped and found to be the medium, apologists attempted an elaborate if ultimately unsatisfying explanation. A certain amount of the medium's physical energy, it was suggested, was imparted to the spirit. If the latter was roughly handled, spirit and medium would unite for their joint benefit, either within or outside of the cabinet. If the medium possessed the greater amount of energy she drew the spirit to herself. If most of the energy belonged to the materialized spirit the medium would instantly be attracted to the spirit. The fact that the latter invariably happened had no significance for committed Spiritualists.

Alternatively, Spiritualists suggested, as did **Sergeant Cox,** on one occasion, that the medium was controlled in order to impersonate a spirit entity.

Whatever the reason for fraud, it became clear to psychical researchers that even the most honorable medium could not be trusted without reserve, even if his character in normal life was blameless and there was no apparent objective for committing fraud. Investigators had to rely on the strictest vigilance and the most up-to-date scientific methods and apparatus.

The Mechanics of Fraud

While some Spiritualists were apologists for the most questionable phenomena and proved themselves the exponents of an intense "will to believe," a few manifested an eagerness to challenge and expose fraudulent mediumship and proved themselves far from gullible. On a few occasions Spiritualists joined in the exposure of fraudulent colleagues, such as the celebrated rogue **William Roy,** although these instances were rare.

From the time of the Hydesville phenomena many mediums, including most all the physical mediums, were accused of cheating and fell victim to compromising exposures. In the attempt to test the genuineness of the extraordinary claims of Spiritualism, mediums were pursued both by people who hoped the phenomena proved true and skeptics eager to uncover fraud. The means of fraudulent production of phenomena has a literature of its own. **Hereward Carrington** aptly stated:

"The ingenuity of some of these methods is simply amazing, and in some respects the race between fraudulent mediums and psychical investigators has resembled that between burglars and police—to see which could outwit the other. It may be said, however, that these trick methods are now well known. To take one simple example, it may be pointed out that Mr. David O. Abbot's book *Behind the Scenes with the Mediums* and my own *Psychical Phenomena of Spiritualism* have between them explained more than a hundred different methods of fraudulent slatewriting."

More efficient controls evolved with the development of the science of deception. Wooden sleeves and pants were tied on the **Davenport brothers** in Bangor, Maine. **Augustus Politi** was brought before the psychical research society of Milan in a woolen sack. **Elizabeth d'Esperance, Mrs. C. E. Wood,** and **Annie**

Fairlamb were meshed in nets like fish to prevent masquerading during their séances of materialization. **Florence Cook** was closed into an electrical circuit. **Charles Bailey** was shut in a cage with mosquito netting. Eusapia Palladino was tied by **Enrico Morselli** to the couch with a thick, broad band of surgical tape like that used in asylums to fasten down violent lunatics. **Rudi Schneider** was under a formidable triple control while being tested at the **National Laboratory of Psychical Research.**

From the simple method of holding the medium (one of the most efficient methods of control) to the electrical indicators and infrared cameras of modern psychical research laboratories (as in the **Institut Métapsychique**), a long line of evolution might be traced to the point where fraud was reduced to a negligible factor. To operate fraudulently under the conditions thus imposed might be a far greater marvel than a genuine physical phenomenon.

With mental phenomena the control was more laborious and fraught with many psychological difficulties. There is no doubt, however, that persevering examination of an imposture inevitably leads to the discovery of the source of deception. Through the early twentieth century many physical mediums avoided detection primarily because of the ineptness of the observers.

As early as 1894 pioneering researcher **F. W. H. Myers** divided séance-room phenomena into three classes. The first and by far the largest class consisted of tricks whose mechanism was perfectly well known—as well known as the way in which the ordinary conjurer produced the rabbit from the hat. These tricks, indeed, were generally on a lower level than those of the conjurer at a fair, but in spite of repeated exposures they deceived the great mass of seekers hoping and expecting to contact the supernatural.

The second class consisted of phenomena somewhat similar to those of the first class, but that confounded the average magician, who was unable to reproduce the phenomena. If these phenomena were genuine, the first class may be called imitations of them. If they were fraudulent, they indicate that here and there a so-called medium had professional secrets of his own.

The third class consisted of a few rarely attested phenomena, of which Home fire-tests are examples, which were not imitated with any kind of plausibility, even by the most accomplished conjurers. This leads to the hypothesis that genuine mysterious phenomena have occurred, or, equally interesting, that some kind of hallucination was induced in the observers in some readily imitable manner.

In the past, charges of fraud often resulted from a lack of knowledge of unsuspected possibilities. **William H. Mumler,** the first spirit photographer, was promptly accused of trickery when, instead of the spirit of the dead, the double of the living appeared on his plate. The famous third limbs or "pseudopods" of Eusapia Palladino were first ascribed to movement of her hands.

The suggestion that a mysterious substance, **ectoplasm,** existed as an agent for physical phenomena provided some critical examples of the problem of fraud in psychical research. For example, in his experiments with the Goligher Circle, **William J. Crawford** posited the existence of ectoplasm to account for some otherwise odd phenomena carring minute particles of fresh paint discovered on objects and on the medium's body. It was later discovered that the phenomena in the circle was fraudulently produced. The idea of ectoplasm was later abandoned altogether, but before that searching out the substance and attempting to define its properties proved a formidable task for psychical researchers.

Charles Richet, for example, suggested that "there is a quasi-identity between the medium and ectoplasm, so that when an attempt is made to seize the latter a limb of the medium may be grasped; though I make a definite and formal protest against this frequent defence of doubtful phenomena by the spiritualists. More frequently the ectoplasm is independent of the medium, indeed, perhaps it is always so."

Apologies for Fraud

The resemblance of the materialized phantom to the medium was a frequent source of the accusations throughout the history of materializations. The more dedicated argued that the **double** of the medium served as a model for the first materialization and appeared before the manifestation of true phantoms.

Sir Arthur Conan Doyle suggested that the medium's double served as a pattern on which the temporary new body was built. He carried the suggestion too far, however. In pointing out that in certain cases so much ectoplasm was taken from the medium that hardly anything was left behind than an invisible simulacrum, he conjectured that when a materialized figure was seized it might not dematerialize into the simulacrum but absorb the residue of the medium. The acceptance of such a naive explanation would have opened the gates of fraud and made it nearly impossible to present evidence in case of brazen fraud.

The problem, however, was not so complicated as Doyle suggested. The simple truth was that nearly all materializing mediums were from time to time exposed by spirit grabbing. The "ectoplasm" was often seen to disappear, but quite often the medium was found in undergarments and without shoes, so that conscious or unconscious masquerade appeared to be incontestable.

It was suggested that many genuine mediums, when they felt their powers ebbing, could not resist the temptation of supplementing then by artifice. Some, in an extreme state of suggestibility, might have obeyed the secret urging of a deceitful person. Such was the defense of Eusapia Palladino in an instance in Genoa before **Cesare Lombroso. Julien Ochorowitz** said, "When it is understood that the medium is but a mirror for reflecting and directing the nervous energies of the sitters to an ideoplastic purpose, it will not be found surprising that suggestion should play an important part. With controllers imbued with the notion of fraud the medium will be dominated by the suggestion of fraud."

Gustav Geley was forced to declare that "when a medium tricks the experimenters are responsible." Hereward Carrington's advice in the case of genuine mediums who resorted to trickery was "to say nothing but to let the medium see by one's manner that one is displeased and the phenomena evidently not convincing. If she perceives that such attempts are useless, she will settle down, pass into a trance, and genuine phenomena will be obtained." In his *Mysterious Psychic Forces* (1907), Camille Flammarion notes:

"One may lay it down as a principle that all professional mediums cheat. But they do not always cheat; and they possess real, undeniable psychic powers. Their case is nearly that of the hysterical folk under observation at the Salpêtrière or elsewhere. I have seen some of them outwit with their profound craft not only Dr. Charcot, but especially Dr. Luys and all the physicians who were making a study of their cases. But because hysterics deceive and simulate it would be gross error to conclude that hysteria does not exist."

Unconscious fraud was facilitated by the anesthetic condition observed by **William James** in **automatic writing,** which involved the medium's hands and arms to a considerable degree. **James H. Hyslop** found this as an explanation when, with the medium's consent, he made several flashlight photographs of the production of physical phenomena. The medium was dumbfounded when the pictures were shown to her. They showed plainly that she produced every manifestation.

The unconscious impulse to cheat is sometimes quite beyond control. Laura I. Finch, editor of the *Annals of Psychic Science,* confessed that once, during a materialization séance, she felt a nearly overpowering impulse to roll up her sleeve in the cabinet and pass her arm out between the curtains.

Andrew Jackson Davis adduced the impulse as a partial explanation of the Stratford Poltergeist phenomena that occurred in the home of **Eliakim Phelps**. The testimonial given to **Henry Gordon** by the Springfield Harmonial Circle in January 1851 attempted an explanation:

"It may be stated, however, as a circumstance which seems to have been the cause of some misapprehension, that the individual referred to is highly susceptible to the magnetic power of the spirits, and that under the influence of an impression which he is unable to resist, he occasionally endeavors to perform the very action which he perceives to be in the mind of the spirit."

Professor Haraldur Neilsson of Iceland quoted a case in *Psychic Science* (July 1925) in which a perfectly senseless fraud was committed by one of the circle and a spirit afterward confessed to instigating the fraud.

A few have suggested, though it stretches credulity, that a state of dissociated consciousness prompting automatic preparations for fraud before a séance be considered as a possibility for understanding a medium's tricks. Such activity might be attributed to a form of "posthypnotic promise." **Frank Podmore** suggested that in trance the medium may promise to apport flowers in the next séance and then, in the waking state, might buy them and hide them in the séance room without conscious knowledge. Some hint of this possibility is given in Philippe Tissé's book *Les Rèves* (Paris, 1890), which narrates the case of a man who repeatedly commits thefts in the daytime under the effect of a dream in the night before.

Fraud by Psychical Researchers and Parapsychologists

Accredited scientists who performed psychical research were expected to have training in various disciplines that made them reliable observers and experimenters. It was assumed that only mediums were likely to practice fraud and that it was the task of the scientist to expose any fraud. Many scientists approached the paranormal already convinced that claimed phenomena *must* be fraudulent (or the result of some other mundane explanation), since they not only violated accepted physical laws but contradicted their own personal experience. Thus, to the average scientist examining mediums, it was only a matter of finding out *how* a medium cheated.

In the nineteenth century many scientists had a devout religious heritage, a heritage they felt had been stolen from them by science. When the opportunity of using science to reconstruct the lost foundations upon which their traditional religious beliefs had been constructed, they eagerly pursued it. The biographies of the founders of psychical research suggest that just such a motivation energized their investigations.

The possibility of rebuilding a lost faith coupled with the genuine scientific breakthrough that would result if their work proved fruitful was enough to test the integrity of any individual. The contemporary awareness of fraud in every area of scientific endeavor testifies to the temptation to cheat, even when the likely reward was far less than that afforded by any positive data in psychical research. It is to the credit of psychical research that no serious charges of fraud were leveled at the primary people involved in leading the Society for Psychical Research and the American Society for Psychical Research during its foundational years.

Within the last decade or so, however, a formidable attack on the credibility of **Sir William Crookes** was sustained. He allegedly was a party to deception by the medium **Florence Cook** because he was sexually involved with her, and the séances were a coverup for the affair.

There is every reason to doubt much of Cook's phenomena; the claim that Crookes was her lover is not conclusive, but does explain why he reported so favorably on them, given his scientific training and later unquestioned accomplishments. Crookes's defenders have argued that he was scrupulous in his other investigations of psychical phenomena, and that it would be absurd to attempt to invalidate his work with Daniel Dunglas Home, for example, on the grounds that he was sexually involved with him. Yet the question remains: if Cook was a fraud, why was Crookes so completely taken in?

After the death of veteran psychical researcher **Harry Price,** other researchers declared that Price had been guilty of deception in the famous case of the haunting of **Borley Rectory,** and that doubt must therefore be cast upon his other investigations. In his biography *The Search for Harry Price* (1978), author Trevor H. Hall (who also made the substantive charges against Crookes), even questions Price's personal integrity. Hall seems to go beyond the evidence of Price's shortcomings as a researcher in extending his critique to Price's basic honesty.

The modern era of parapsychology has also been affected by evidence of error and deception. In the summer of 1974 **J. B. Rhine** announced that **Walter J. Levy, Jr.,** the director of the **Institute for Parapsychology,** had been discovered deliberately falsifying experimental results. This announcement was clearly a challenge to parapsychology, then in the midst of a controversy surrounding charges of fraud directed at **S. G. Soal,** a leading British parapsychologist. Soal died in 1975, and three years later hard evidence of fraud (conscious manipulation of computer data) was uncovered and publicized. Fortunately for the field, such cases have been rare, and parapsychologists have not been hesitant in reporting them when found.

Conjuring Campaigns Against Parapsychology

By World War I awareness of the depth of fraud that beset Spiritualism had become common knowledge within psychical research, though hope remained that some elements of real phenomena existed and could be isolated. It was during this time that **Harry Houdini** introduced his magic show, and it became evident that his conjuring skills would be helpful in uncovering Spiritualist tricks the average untrained researcher would miss.

Many intelligent Spiritualists and psychical observers were led to believe that what they perceived was the result of psychic faculty. Doyle thought Houdini's tricks so inexplicable that he declared him a psychic.

Trained stage magicians were especially helpful in the observation and denouncement of fraudulent psychics and healers whom laboratory-oriented parapsychologists considered outside their concern. Such phenomena is often found in worship services and thus difficult to fully examine as one might in an experimental situation, but the religious setting has not proved insurmountable.

Assuming the mantle of Houdini during the late twentieth century as the archenemy of fake psychics and miracle workers is the magician James Randi (known as "the Amazing Randi"). He has never acknowledged observing any genuine psychical phenomena, and operates out of a stated desire to destroy belief in the paranormal. He has become a leading public spokesperson for the **Committee for the Scientific Investigation of Claims of the Paranormal.** While his work has rarely spoken to the claims and efforts of mainstream parapsychology, he has demonstrated that he can ostensibly perform ESP, psychic surgery, metal bending and other parapsychological phenomena by trickery. He also demonstrated that at least some who call themselves parapsychologists were incompetent in detecting fraud.

To prove his point Randi planted magicians in tests by parapsychologists. At a press reception in New York in 1982, he revealed that two young "metal benders," Steve Shaw and Mike Edwards, had deceived parapsychologists at the **McDonnell Laboratory for Psychical Research,** Washington University, St. Louis, for four years. On various occasions Randi himself was present at some sessions in disguise. The researchers at McDonnell believed that Shaw and Edwards had demonstrated genuine paranormal talent in metal bending and psychokinesis.

Randi's point was driven home in 1984 when **Masuaki Kiyota,** hailed as the Japanese **Uri Geller,** revealed in a television interview that he had faked the phenomena that had been verified by both American and Japanese researchers. Randi had long denounced Geller as a fake, but had been unable to provoke a decisive confrontation. Kiyota claimed that he had reproduced the primary Geller phenomenon, **metal bending,** as well as another frequently hailed phenomenon associated with psychic **Ted Serios**—the paranormal creation of pictures on film.

The incidents in which researchers did not discover fraud are important, but must also be placed in the larger context of parapsychology. Even before Randi revealed his scheme at the McDonnell Laboratory, for example, parapsychologists had called attention to methodological problems in their research that would have to be solved before they could accept any optimistic initial findings. The application of those proper controls tied the hands of the two magician/subjects and they were unable to perform.

During his research of fake ministers operating as Pentecostal healers, Randi investigated several in whom he could find no evidence of deceit, even though he found their faith naive and personally unacceptable.

Sources:

Berger, Arthur S., and Joyce Berger. *The Encyclopedia of Parapsychology and Psychical Research.* New York: Paragon House, 1991.

Christopher, Milbourne. *ESP, Seers, and Psychics.* New York: Thomas Y. Crowell, 1970.

Houdini, Harry. *A Magician among the Spirits.* New York: Harper & Brothers, 1924. Reprinted as *Houdini, A Magician among the Spirits.* New York: Arno Press, 1972.

Keene, M. Lamar. *The Psychic Mafia.* New York: St. Martin's Press, 1976.

Price, Harry, and Eric J. Dingwall. *Revelations of a Spirit Medium.* London: Kegan Paul, Trench, Trubner, 1922.

Randi, James. *The Faith Healers.* Buffalo, N.Y.: Prometheus Books, 1987.

———. *Flim-Flam: Psychics, ESP, Unicorns, and Other Delusions.* Buffalo, N.Y.: Prometheus Books, 1982.

———. *The Magic of Uri Geller.* New York: Random House, 1975.

Stein, Gordon. *Encyclopedia of Hoaxes.* Detroit: Gale Research, 1993.

Free Daist Communion

An Advaita Vedanta (Hindu) religious community founded and headed by Avadhoota Da Love-Ananda (born Franklin Jones). It was previously known as the **Dawn Horse** fellowship and the **Johannine Daist Communion.** A religious seeker, in 1960 Jones began to study with Swami Rudrananda (1928–73), an American-born disciple of Indian spiritual teacher **Swami Muktananda** (1908–82). Rudrananda guided him to a Lutheran seminary. Then in 1968 he went to India to visit Muktananda's ashram. While there he had a deep experience that led two years later to his entering what he called a permanent state of "Sahaj Samadhi" (trance). It is believed by his followers that he had surrendered that condition at the time of his entering this present incarnation at birth, and that his lifetime of seeking was an attempt to recover it while still in the embodied condition.

Jones began to teach small groups of students shortly after the 1970 experience. Then in 1973 he made a pilgrimage to India, during which journey he changed his name to Bubba Free John, understanding "Bubba" to be a familial way of denoting "brother." Later in the 1970s he became one of the most well known of the new spiritual teachers (gurus) to emerge in America. He was distinctive for his confrontational style of teaching, especially for placing his students in stressful conditions to enhance their learning. All his lessons were meant to show the futility of the search for meaning in sexuality, material possessions, and various psychic and spiritual experiences.

The teachings were leading toward a form of Advaita Vedanta that he called "the way of radial understanding." At the heart of Vedanta is denial of the illusion of the separateness of our individual selves from the "all-comprehensive divine reality." We are aware of this illusion but live in a somewhat forgetful state. Our realization of our true state tends to occur in stages.

In his attempt to bring his students through the various stages of enlightenment Bubba Free John has on several occasions changed his name, indicating a new phase of his work. In 1979 he withdrew from public work and became known as Da Free John, "Da" being understood as "giver." In the mid-1980s he took his present name, more informally known as Heart Master Da Love-Ananda.

In 1991 there were approximately twelve hundred members of the Free Daist Community, the majority in North America. Heart Master Da Love-Ananda resides at the group's retreat center in the Fiji Islands. American headquarters are located at 750 Adrian Way, San Rafael, CA 94903.

Sources:

Bubba Free John [Franklin Jones]. *No Remedy.* Lower Lake, Calif.: Dawn Horse Press, 1976.

Da Free John [Franklin Jones]. *The Dawn Horse Testament.* San Rafael, Calif.: Dawn Horse Press, 1985.

Da Love-Ananda. *The Holy Jumping Off Place.* San Rafael, Calif.: Dawn Horse Press, 1986.

Jones, Franklin. *The Method of the Siddhas.* Los Angeles: Dawn Horse Press, 1973.

Free Spirit; Resources for Personal and Social Transformation (Directory)

Quarterly **networking** publication of **New Age** topics and information, primarily for the New York metropolitan area. Similar networking periodicals now serve most major urban areas in North America. *Free Spirit* covers the arts, business services, children and childbirth, events and gatherings, healing and bodywork, intuitive arts and sciences, movement, **martial arts** and **yoga,** natural foods and nutrition, schools, certification and degrees, spiritual practices, social change, therapy and counseling, tools of life, and women's concerns. It includes "Yellow Pages of Consciousness," addresses of organizations, and a comprehensive calendar of events. Free Spirit is distributed free in locations in the area it serves, but subscriptions may be secured from Living Network Production, 34 Prospect Pl., Brooklyn, NY 11217.

Freeman, John Albert (1920–)

Psychologist and parapsychologist. He was born January 15, 1920, and studied at Ouachita College, Arkadelphia, Arkansas; Southern Baptist Theological Seminary, Louisville, Kentucky; and Oklahoma State University, Stillwater.

Freeman was a staff member of the Department of Psychology at Oklahoma Baptist University in Shawnee (1953–56) and head of the Department of Psychology at Wayland Baptist College in Plainview, Texas (1956–60). A charter member of the Parapsychological Association, Freeman set up the parapsychology laboratory at Wayland Baptist College. In 1960 he became a research associate at the **Parapsychology Laboratory** at Duke University, and became the author of many papers on the paranormal.

Freemasonry

An occult movement of the seventeenth century. Freemasonry emerged as the British form of revived **gnosticism** analogous to the **Rosicrucian** movement in Germany. While having its roots in the architectural and construction guilds of the Middle Ages, modern masonry is rooted in the post-Reformation revival of Gnostic thought and occult practice. The mythical history of masonry served to protect it in the religiously intolerant atmosphere operative in Great Britain at the time of its founding.

History and Mythic Origin

Although it would not be exactly correct to say that the history of Freemasonry was lost in the mists of antiquity, it is possible to say that although to a certain degree traceable, its records are of a scanty nature, and so crossed by the trails of other mystical brotherhoods that disentanglement is an extremely difficult process.

The ancient legend of its foundation at the time of the building of the Temple at Jerusalem is manifestly mythical. If one might hazard an opinion, it would seem that at a very early epoch in the history of civilization, a caste arose of builders in stone, who jealously guarded the secret of their craft. Where such a caste of operative masons might have arisen is altogether a separate question, but it must obviously have been in a country where working in stone was one of the principal arts. It is also almost certain that this early brotherhood must have been hierophantic with a leadership adept in the ancient mysteries. Its principal work to begin with would undoubtedly consist in the raising of temples and similar structures, and as such it would come into very close contact with the priesthood, if indeed it was not wholly directed by it.

In early civilization only two classes of dwelling received the attention of the architect—the temple and the palace. For example, among the ruins of **Egypt** and Babylon, remains of private houses are rare, but the temple and the royal residence are conspicuous everywhere, and we know that among the ruins of Central America temples and palaces alone remain, the huts of the surrounding dwellers having long ago disappeared. The temple was the nucleus of the early city. Commerce, agriculture, and all the affairs of life revolved around the worship of the gods.

A medieval cathedral took more than one generation to erect, and in that time many masons came and went. The lodge was invariably founded near the rising cathedral or abbey, and apprentices and others started work as opportunity offered. Indeed, a man might serve his apprenticeship and labor all through his life on one building, without ever seeing any work elsewhere.

The evidence as to whether the master-masons were also architects is very conflicting, and it has been held that the priests were the architects of the British cathedrals, the master-masons and operatives merely carrying out their designs. There is good evidence, however, that this is not wholly true. Of all arts, architecture is by far the most intricate. It is undoubtedly one that requires a long and specific training. Questions arise of stress and strain of the most difficult description, and it is obvious that ecclesiastics, who had not undergone any special training, would not be qualified to compose plans of the cathedrals.

Professional architects existed at a very early period, though instances are on record where the priests of a certain locality have taken upon themselves the credit of planning the cathedral of the diocese. Be this as it may, the "mystery" of building was sufficiently deep to require extensive knowledge and experience and to a great extent this justifies the jealousy with which the early masons regarded its secrets. Again, the jealousy with which it was kept from the vulgar gaze may have been racial in its origin, and may have arisen from such considerations as the following: "Let no stranger understand this craft of ours. Why should we make it free to the heathen and the foreigner?"

Masonry in Great Britain

In Great Britain, prior to the founding of the Grand Lodge, York and the north of England in general were regarded as the most ancient seat of the fraternity. Indeed, without stretching probabilities too far, the line of evolution so far as York is concerned is quite remarkable. In the early days of that city a temple of Serapis existed there, which was afterward a monastery of the Begging Friars, and the mysteries of this god existed beside the Roman Collegia or Craftsmen's Society.

Some have argued that the crypt of York Minster affords evidence of the progress of masonry from Roman to Saxon times. It is stated that it has a mosaic pavement of blue and white tiles laid in the form employed in the first degree of masonry. Undoubted is the fact that the craft occasionally met in this crypt during the eighteenth century.

Masonic tradition goes to show that even in the beginning of the fourteenth century, masonry in Britain was regarded as a thing of great antiquity. Lodge records for the most part only date back to the sixteenth century in the oldest instances, but ancient manuscripts are extant which undoubtedly relate to masonry.

Thus the old charges embodied in the Regius manuscript, which was unearthed in 1839 by Halliwell Phillips, are dated at 1390 and contain a curious legend of the craft that tells how the necessity of finding work of some description drove men to consult Euclid, who recommended masonry as a craft to them. It goes on to tell how masonry was founded in Egypt, and how it entered England in the time of King Athelstan (d. 940). The necessity for keeping close counsel as regards the secrets of the craft is insisted upon in rude verse.

The Cooke manuscript from the early fifteenth century likewise contains versions of the old charges. Egypt was regarded here as the motherland of masonry, and King Athelstan the medium for the introduction of the craft into the island of Britain. But that this manuscript was used among masons at a later date was proved by the 1890 discovery of a more modern version dated about 1687 and known as the William Watson manuscript. In all, about 70 of these old charges and pseudohistories have been discovered since 1860. They all have much in common and are of English origin.

The Birth of Speculative Masonry

Whatever the ancient and medieval roots of masonry, in the seventeenth century it was given a new direction by the widespread acceptance into the lodges of non-masons who used the lodges as a home for their pursuit of spiritual wisdom apart from the theology of the established church, often while keeping a nominal membership in the Church of England. (By 1723, for example, all specific references to Christianity were removed from the movement's constitution; members had only to acknowledge God, the Great Architect of the Universe.) The first prominent speculative Freemason was astrologer Elias Ashmole (1617–1692), an officer in the court of Charles II. Ashmole, and his contemporaries such as **Robert Flud** (1574–1637), helped spread the revived gnosticism represented on the continent by Rosicrucianism. Through the century, speculative lodges consisting primarily if not exclusively of accepted masons spread throughout England and Scotland where they existed as a condoned (and somewhat unrecognized) form of religious dissent.

The coming of age of speculative masonry was signaled by the formation of the Grand Lodge of England, inaugurated on St. John the Baptist's Day 1717 by four of the old London lodges. Rev. John Theophilus Desguliers, who became Grand Master in 1719, was the chaplain to the Prince of Wales, and used his considerable influence to spread the movement both in England and France. The Grand Lodge provided the fraternity with its first central governing body, as prior to this time each lodge was self-governing. Many lodges speedily came under its aegis, and Ireland formed a Grand Lodge of her own in 1725, but Scotland did not follow until 1736, and even then many lodges held aloof from the central body, only 33 out of 100 falling into line.

From one or other of these three governing bodies all the regular lodges and variant rites throughout the world have arisen, so that modern masonry may truthfully be said to be of British origin. To say that Continental masonry is the offspring of the British lodges is not to say that no masonic lodges existed in France and Germany before the formation of the English Grand Lodge, but underscores the break between the masonry of the builders of the medieval architectual wonders and the speculative masonry of the seventeenth century. All of the modern speculative lodges in Europe date from the inception of the English central body. However, the Continental masonry possesses many rites that differ entirely from those found in the British craft.

In Germany, which existed at this time as a number of independent states, it was said that the Steinmetzin approximated very strongly in medieval times to the British masons, if they were not originally one and the same, but again, the modern lodges in Germany all dated from the speculative lodge founded in 1733.

We find the beginnings of modern French masonry in the labors of **Martine de Pasqually, Louis Claude de Saint-Martin,** and perhaps to a some extent **Cagliostro** who toiled greatly to found his Egyptian rite in France. It is noticeable, however, that Cagliostro had become a member of a London lodge before attempting work on the Continent. In France, masonry had a more political complexion, being a source of the democratic thought underlying the French (and later the Italian) Revolution. Because of the political alignment of continental Freemasonry, an extreme enmity developed between Freemasonry and the Roman Catholic Church, which had aligned itself to the royal families of Europe. Masonry in England, a country that broke with Rome during the Reformation of the sixteenth century, had a much more apolitical stance.

Official opposition to Freemasonry by the Roman Catholic Church dates back to Papal bulls of 1738 and 1751 and is a tangled story of suspicion and intrigue relating to masonic secrecy and to complex political developments of the time. Much antagonism has been deliberately fostered by mischief makers. For example, during the nineteenth century, the French journalist **Gabriel Jogand-Pagés,** writing under the name **Leo Taxil,** perpetrated an extraordinary and prolonged hoax in which he claimed to have exposed a Satanist activity within Freemasonry. The motive appears to have been to embarrass the Roman Catholic Church, but it also added to traditional Church prejudices against Freemasonry and caused much trouble for masons.

The plot involved the claim that a certain Diana Vaughan, claimed to have been a High Priestess of Satanic Freemasonry and dedicated to overthrowing Christianity and winning the world for Satanism, had been converted to the Roman Catholic faith. The memoirs of "Diana Vaughan," written by Jogand, were read by Pope Leo XIII, and Jogand himself was received in private audience by the pope, and an anti-masonic congress was summoned in 1887 at Trent.

On Easter Monday 1897, at a press conference to present Diana Vaughan, Jogand confessed to his conspiracy and the details of his complex hoax are now generally known. But, great damage had already been done to relations between Roman Catholics and Freemasons. In 1917 the Church declared that anyone who joined a masonic lodge was automatically excommunicated.

The Masonic Worldview

The Freemasons instituted an initiatory degree system by which members were step-by-step brought into the inner working of the lodge. Initially there were three degrees, but these could never satisfy the true gnostics. Various elaborate systems of degrees were developed to picture the levels leading from this world to God and to symbolize the journey of the knowing soul back home. The most famous, due to its success and longevity, was the 300 system placed upon the original three degrees that emerged as the 33O system of the Ancient and Accepted Rite, the system operative in the United Grand Lodge. This system became integral to the dominant American masonic body, the Ancient and Accepted Scottish Rite, and its teachings as illustrated in the writings of **Albert Pike,** its dominant intellectual leader.

As speculative masonry emerged, it espoused the idea that masonry was a restatement of the ancient religion of humankind. At one time, the masons suggested, there were two religions, one for the educated and enlightened and one for the masses. The one religion of the enlightened became the base upon which the various historic faiths emerged. Through the centuries, however, adepts (masters) kept the original teachings intact, and they were eventually passed in their purity to the masonic leadership. In the modern age, due to the evolution of the race, more people are now capable of receiving and safely handling that secret wisdom that is now being disseminated by the masonic lodges. That secret wisdom came from the ancient East and Middle East, and both Eastern religions (especially Hinduism) and Western mystical systems such as Kabalism assist the process of describing it.

The ancient wisdom myth of Freemasonry found an origin in the Bible, a significantly more acceptable source to a Christian establishment than Arabia and the Muslim countries of Rosicrucianism. In 1 Kings 7:13–45, the masons found the story of Hiram. Hiram was employed by King Solomon to work on the temple in Jerusalem. After his work, he disappeared from both the pages of the Bible and from history. Freemasons, however, developed his biography that included a murder by his artisan colleagues. Hiram, in working on the temple, became aware of the "Word of God" inscribed in the secret parts of the temple. He would not reveal what he had learned and his noncollegial reticence cost him his life. His death then became integral to the ritual initiation of members who symbolically die and are reborn into the craft.

The masonic worldview begins with three fundamental realities. First, there is a omnipresent, eternal, boundless, and immutable principle that is ineffable, beyond any limiting descriptors of human language, the end-point of all metaphysical speculation, the rootless root and the uncaused cause. Natural law is a representation of the permanency of the absolute. Second, there exists what we term space in the abstract. Space is a symbol of divinity as it is basic to all experience; it is fathomless but at the same time integral to all human concepts. Third, there exists motion, another abstract notion, representing unconditioned consciousness that manifests as spirit and matter. Spirit and matter are two facets of the absolute.

The universe is seen as a boundless plane, a playground upon which numerous universes come and go. There is an eternal flex in which new universes begin to develop and are absorbed back into the boundless space out of which they were formed. Creation of a universe begins as space becomes turgid and produces a first or potential matter called the akasa. Operating on this matter is absolute abstract motion, latent potential energy, consciousness, and cosmic ideation.

Thus at the beginning is the universal energy (fofat) and the universal substance (akasa) behind which stands consciousness and ultimately the absolute. As creation proceeds, it will occur in steps of seven. Seven plans of creation will be formed from the purely spiritual to physical substance. These seven planes of existence are reflected throughout the universe. Each human also possesses these seven levels. The seven levels are: atma, buddhi, manas, kama, astral, life principle, and physical. The operation of these seven planes in the universe and in the individual provide much room for speculative elaboration and would later provide material upon which Theosophy would build.

Masonry in America

Through the eighteenth century, Freemasonry had aligned itself with the Enlightenment and with the anti-monarchial ideals of the late-century revolutionaries. Masonic and Rosicrucian ideals flowed through the salons of France and supplied vital ideological components of the new revolutionary ethos that allowed the complete overthrow of an obsolete government system and the institution of a new democratic system. The Marquis de Lafayette, who joined in the American Revolution, was a mason. In the United States James Madison; James Monroe; Benjamin Franklin, who financed much of the revolution; and George Washington, who led its armies, were Freemasons. The input of Freemasonry in the founding of the republic can now be found on the dollar bill, which hails the coming of the "ordo nuevo seculorum," the "new order of the ages" and the pyramid topped with the all-seeing eye.

But masonry had established itself in America long before the revolution. The Grand Lodge of Massachusetts dates from 1733 and that of South Carolina was founded just four years later. The General Grand Chapter of the Royal Arch Masons of the U.S.A. was founded in Boston in 1797 by representatives from Massachusetts and New York. The Supreme Council 33 of Ancient and Accepted Scottish Rite of Freemasonry for the Southern Jurisdiction of the United States of America was formed in Charleston, South Carolina, in 1801. Albert Pike, the most noteworthy of nineteenth century masons, was the leader of this latter organization for many years (1859–1891). The Order of the Eastern Star, an auxiliary for female relatives of masons, was founded in 1876. The masonic movement now encompasses millions of members primarily in lodges affiliated to its larger organizations, but also in a variety of smaller masonic groups that follow various patterns of different speculative rites.

Understanding the origins of speculative masonry as an occult movement, and the essentially gnostic nature of its thought, does much to explain why many prominent occultists such as Manly Palmer Hall trumpeted their masonic connections. It also shows how masonic thought served as a basis for Theosophy, and the manner in which masonic organizations provided the substructure upon which modern Rosicrucianism emerged at the end of the nineteenth century. Masonry supplied the organizational model not only for Rosicrucianism, but for ceremonial magic groups such as the Hermetic Order of the **Golden Dawn** and the **Ordo Templi Orientis.**

Sources:

Coil, Henry. *Coil's Masonic Encyclopedia.* Richmond, Va.: Macoy Publishing, 1961.

———. *Freemasonry Through Six Centuries.* 2 vols. Richmond, Va.: Macoy Publishing, 1961.

Hall, Manly P. *Lost Keys of Freemasonry.* Richmond, Va.: Macoy Publishing, 1923.

Haywood, H. I. *The Newly Made Mason.* Richmond, Va.: Macoy Publishing, 1948.

Knight, G. Norman, and F. Smyth. *The Pocket History of Freemasonry.* London: Fred K. Muller, 1977.

Knight, Stephen. *The Brotherhood: The Secret World of the Freemasons.* New York: Stein & Day, 1984.

Mackey, Albert G. *Mackey's Revised Encyclopedia of Freemasonry.* Richmond, Va.: Macoy Publishing, 1909.

Mellor, Alec. *Our Separated Brethren: The Freemasons.* London: George G. Harp, 1964.

Voorhis, Harold V. B. *Masonic Organizations and Allied Orders and Degrees.* N.p.: Press of Henry Emmerson, 1952.

Waite, A. E. *A New Encyclopedia of Freemasonry.* 2 vols. London: William Rider; New York: David McKay, 1921. Reprint, New Hyde Park, N.Y.: University Books, 1970. Reprint, New York: Weatherwane, 1971.

Freer, Ada Goodrich See Ada Goodrich-Freer

Frei, Gebhard (1905–1967)

Roman Catholic priest and professor of philosophy and comparative religion. He was born March 24, 1905, at Lichtensteig, St. Gallen, Switzerland. He took his Ph.D. in 1935 at the University of Innsbruck and then became a professor of philosophy and comparative religion at the Theological Seminary of Schöneck/Beckenried, Switzerland, in 1933. He founded and served as a professor at the C. G. Jung Institute in Zürich. He also acted as president of the Swiss Society of Philosophy and the Swiss Society of Catholic Psychotherapeutists.

Frei served a term as president of Imago Mundi, the international society of Catholic parapsychologists. He wrote many articles on parapsychological subjects and edited a series of books titled *Grenzfragen der Psychologie* (Borderline Questions of Psychology). He served as the Vatican's consultant on parapsychology and contributed to **Konstantin Raudive**'s study of **electronic voice phenomenon.** Frei died October 27, 1967.

Sources:

Berger, Arthur S., and Joyce Berger. *The Encyclopedia of Parapsychology and Psychical Research.* New York: Paragon House, 1991.

Frei, Gebhard. "Psychologie, Parapsychologie and Weltanschaung." *Schweizer Rundschau.* N.p., 1946.

———. "Die Heutige Situation in der Parapsychologie" (The Present Situation of Parapsychology). *Neue Wissenchaft.* N.p., n.d.

Pleasants, Helene, ed. *Biographical Dictionary of Parapsychology.* New York: Helix Press, 1964.

Raudive, Konstantin. *Breakthrough.* New York: Taplinger, 1971.

French, Mrs. E. J. (ca. 1860)

Nineteenth-century medium of New York who specialized in psychic painting. The pictures—brightly colored flowers, birds, or insects—were produced in a curtained-off dark **cabinet** under a small table with prepared pencils, brushes, and paints. The speed of execution was remarkable, pictures of considerable artistic merit being produced within 8 to 15 seconds. Scraping and rubbing sounds, suggesting extremely rapid movement, were distinctly heard by the sitters. It was discovered, however, that many of the pictures produced in this way were copies of existing pictures and suspicions of **fraud** were entertained by some sitters. In light of other exposures of similar phenomena, such as those produced by **David Duguid,** it seems likely that French operated fraudulently.

Benjamin Coleman describes his experiences with French in his book *Spiritualism in America* (1861). (See also **direct drawing and painting**)

French, Emily S. (1830–1912)

Direct voice medium of Buffalo, New York, and a relative of President Grover Cleveland. French was investigated for 20 years by **Edward C. Randall** of Buffalo. **Isaac Funk** and **James H. Hyslop** also conducted remarkable experiments to prove that the voices did not originate in the vocal organs of the medium.

Her Indian **control** "Red Jacket" had an exceedingly loud, masculine voice that would have easily filled a hall with a seating capacity of 2000 people. The medium at that time was a frail old woman with a weak heart and was deaf, yet the sitters could hear every remark of the communicators.

For 22 years French assisted Randall's **"rescue circle,"** where "earthbound spirits" were helped. She gave her mediumistic services without charge. Randall's book *The Dead Have Never Died* (1917) describes their work and contains biographical information. French died July 24, 1912.

Sources:

Funk, Isaac. *The Psychic Riddle.* London/New York: Funk & Wagnalls, 1907.

Freud, Sigmund (1856–1939)

Founder of psychoanalysis. Freud conducted some experiments in parapsychology but was unsympathetic to public discussion of the occult, which he believed to be enveloped in dangerous superstition. Freud was born at Freiburg, Moravia, on May 6, 1856. He graduated from Vienna University, Austria, and became a demonstrator at the physiological institute and an assistant physician at Vienna General Hospital. In 1885 he worked under the neurologist J. M. Charcot in Paris and, after returning to Vienna, started to treat patients by hypnosis. In 1902, while a professor of neurology at Vienna University, he also treated patients in his private clinic.

In 1904 he abandoned hypnosis and developed his own theories of psychoanalysis using techniques of free association in the treatment of neurosis. He later attached great significance to the role of dreams and the importance of the sexual drive, both in individuals and in the development of civilization. His sexual theories were supported and developed in new directions by his pupil **Wilhelm Reich.**

It was Freud's emphasis on sex and mistrust of mystical and occult areas that caused the defection of another pupil, **C. G. Jung,** who later established his own system of psychotherapy with elaborate theories of the significance of mythology and symbolism in human affairs. Jung himself had personal occult experiences.

By 1921 Freud had reached a reluctant private conclusion that there might be something to **telepathy;** he experimented with the Hungarian psychoanalyst Sandor Ferenczi but did not wish his interest to be made public. His papers on the paranormal were later gathered and published by **George Devereaux.** He died in London, September 23, 1939.

Freud once wrote to **Hereward Carrington,** "If I had my life to live over again, I should devote myself to psychical research rather than to psychoanalysis."

Sources:

Berger, Arthur S., and Joyce Berger. *The Encyclopedia of Parapsychology and Psychical Research.* New York: Paragon House, 1991.

Devereaux, George, ed. *Psychoanalysis and the Occult.* New York: International Universities Press, 1953.

Fodor, Nandor. *Freud, Jung, and Occultism.* New Hyde Park, N.Y.: University Books, 1971.
Freud, Sigmund. *Studies in Parapsychology.* Edited by Philip Rieff. New York: Collier Books, 1963.
Pleasants, Helene, ed. *Biographical Dictionary of Parapsychology.* New York: Helix Press, 1964.

Friar Rush

A character in medieval German folklore, Friar Rush (Brüder Rausch) was the devil disguised as a friar. He was a mischief-maker who entered monasteries to cause trouble for the monks by confusing and tempting them. His pranks were described in English chapbooks of the sixteenth century, and he is also mentioned in an anonymous farce, *Gammer Gurton's Needle* (ca. 1575), ascribed to John Still or William Stevenson. In English folklore Friar Rush is associated with drunkenness, playing such pranks as turning on the wine taps in the cellars.

Frick, Harvey Lee (1906–)

School psychologist who was a student of **J. B. Rhine** and **William McDougall** at Duke University and an early worker in the field of **parapsychology.** Frick was born November 15, 1906, at Gold Hill, North Carolina, and took his M.A. in 1931 at Duke.

After graduation he was successively a laboratory instructor at Wayne University College of Medicine, Detroit, Michigan (1933–35); school psychologist for the Detroit public schools (1935–42); and, during World War II, a personnel consultant (military psychologist) for the U.S. Army (1942–46).

Frick's primary work in parapsychology occurred during his college days. At Duke he took part in some of the experiments that later culminated in the establishment of the **Parapsychology Laboratory.** He also participated in telepathy tests conducted by **John F. Thomas.** Frick's master's thesis, *Extrasensory Cognition,* was one of the first on such a subject and was taken from his own experiments. It also includes an historical survey of the field.

Sources:

Frick, Harvey Lee. *Apostate Physician.* New York: House of Field, 1937.
Pleasants, Helene, ed. *Biographical Dictionary of Parapsychology.* New York: Helix Press, 1964.

Fricker, Edward G. (1910–)

British psychic healer. When his mother died from cancer, Fricker prayed that he might be able to heal others. A Spiritualist medium brought him a message from his mother that Fricker indeed had such a healing gift. His first healing was the removal of warts from his daughter.

His autobiography, *God Is My Witness* (1977), tells of his humdrum life as shop assistant, butcher, and costermonger (hawker of fruit or vegetables) before he developed his healing gift. He writes that he was inspired by a "voice" that put him in touch with a team of doctors in the spirit world. He claims to have healed over a million people during the last 25 years, although he has no medical knowledge.

After Fricker was featured on a television program, the station that broadcast the program was swamped with thousands of calls from sufferers. His clients have included such well-known personalities as British TV presenter Katie Boyle, actor Christopher Lee (famous for his **Dracula** roles), and actress Ann Todd. He operates from a clinic in the Westminster area of London. Address: Fricker's Healing Centre, 15 Wyndham Pl., London, W1, England.

Friendly Contacts Associates

Organization founded in 1965, comprised of state and local groups, that brought together professionals interested in studying **parapsychology,** healing, hypnosis, and **reincarnation.** Through the 1970s it conducted research and held seminars on nonsectarian psychical, metaphysical, and religious issues; sponsored a speakers bureau; and maintained a library at its Florida headquarters. It published the *Friendly Contacts* newsletter.

Friends in New Directions (FIND)

A Canadian organization of individuals concerned with fostering public awareness of **kundalini,** the powerful life force believed by many Hindus to be possessed by all human beings, as understood in the teachings of **Pandit Gopi Krishna.** It was originally described in ancient Hindu treatises on **yoga** and spiritual development. FIND (Friends in New Directions) believes this energy to be the divine guiding force behind the continuing evolution of human beings toward higher dimensions of consciousness and, as such, the mechanism responsible for all extraordinary talents, intuition, genius, inspiration, and spiritual illumination. The group encourages the scientific investigation of kundalini and is confident that such research will inevitably lead to a new understanding of evolution, religion, psychic gifts, insanity, and all other normal and abnormal phenomena of the mind.

FIND members are active in literary research concerned with kundalini and also support other groups concerned with related studies and the promotion of a cleaner environment and world peace. FIND publishes the books and audiotapes of Gopi Krishna, who wrote a number of books based on his more than 45 years of personal experience of higher consciousness states, after arousing kundalini energy through yoga meditation. Address: R.R. 5, Flesherton, Ontario, Canada, NOC 1EO.

Friends of Astrology

The oldest astrological organization currently operating in the Chicago area. It was founded in 1938 with Mary Adams as its first president, and it was incorporated two years later. It functions to raise the standards of **astrology** and to educate students of astrology. It provides a gathering place where serious students of the subject can continue their learning and improve their competence. It currently operates through several branches in Chicago and its suburbs and publishes a monthly newsletter. Address: c/o Gladys Hall, 525 Woodside Ave., Hinsdale, IL 60521.

Friends of God

A mystical school founded in Germany in the fourteenth century for the purpose of ministering to the poor by preaching, sacrament, and meditation. Those associated with it included men and women of every rank and station, not only monks and nuns but knights, farmers, artisans, and merchants.

The name Friends of God derived from the Christian New Testament (John 15:15): "Henceforth I call you not servants; for one servant knoweth not what his lord doeth; but I have called you friends." The Friends of God were not organized as a formal society but rather as a school of thought with a strongly mystical trend. Their law was, "That universal love, commanded by Christ, and not to be gainsaid by his vicar."

Many Dominicans were Friends of God, and notable mystics associated with the school included Meister Eckhart (1304–1328), Nicolas of Basle (1330–1383), and John Tauler (1290–1361). Their teachings roused antagonism among the establishment clergy of their time, who strongly condemned them. They influenced the first generation of Protestant thinkers.

Sources:

Inge, William Ralph. *Christian Mysticism.* London: Methuen, 1899.

Friends of the Garden Central Seed Centre

Loosely organized group of individuals seeking **New Age** mystical experience, deriving their name from **Gandalf's Garden.** Founded by Muz Murray, the group became a focal point for New Age seekers in Chelsea, London, before its dispersal in 1971 into various "seed centers" in different parts of the world. Friends of the Garden Central Seed Centre was established at 24 St. Margaret's Close, Norstead, Norwich, England.

Sources:

Murray, Muz. *Seeking the Master: A Guide to the Ashrams of India.* London: Neville Spearman, 1980.

Friends of the Wisdom Religion

Community of students of the teachings on higher consciousness of **Franklin Merrell-Wolff.** It was originally known as the Assembly of Man. Merrell-Wolff is the author of *Pathways Through to Space: A Personal Record of Transformation in Consciousness* (1976).

Sources:

Merrell-Wolff, Franklin. *Pathways Through to Space: A Personal Record of Transformation in Consciousness.* New York: Warner, 1976.

———. *The Philosophy of Consciousness without an Object.* New York: Julian Press, 1973.

Friendship Centre, The

Founded by Stephen Foster in 1929 at 85 Lancaster Gate, London, W2, England. It became the new home of the Conan Doyle Memorial Psychic Library and Museum and held regular meetings for **psychometry,** psychic demonstrations, healing, and classes for development of psychic ability. Unfortunately the Conan Doyle Museum collection was later dispersed and some of the items were lost or destroyed. The center closed during World War II.

FRNM See Foundation for Research on the Nature of Man

FRNM Bulletin

Former publication of the Parapsychology Press, giving information and news related to the **Foundation for Research on the Nature of Man** (FRNM), directed by **J. B. Rhine.** With issue no. 14 (autumn 1969) it became the *Parapsychology Bulletin.* Back issues are available from the Foundation for Research on the Nature of Man (402 N. Buchanan Blvd., Durham, NC 27701-1728) or from University Microfilms, Zeeb Rd., Ann Arbor, MI 48106.

Fronczek, Janusz (ca. 1926)

Polish mining engineer of Warsaw who was a medium for telekinetic, teleplastic, and luminous phenomena. **Eric J. Dingwall,** then research officer of the **Society for Psychical Research** (SPR), had three sittings with Fronczek in August and September 1923 and was impressed. Lights appeared to "come from the medium's mouth and to remain apparently unsupported in space two or three inches from the lips. The brilliancy of each appearance varied, not only as compared with others but apparently in itself when still in view," Dingwall said.

Fronczek was invited to London to sit at the SPR. He arrived April 17, 1925. According to the report of V. J. Woolley and Dingwall in the society's *Proceedings* (vol. 36), before he entered the séance room he disrobed entirely and offered himself unreservedly for examination. He sat in a pajama suit, and his hands and legs were controlled. He preferred silence or low conversation during the sitting.

The phenomena seemed to be preceded by vigorous grinding of the teeth. Greenish, bright spherical sparks were seen, lights appeared on Fronczek's arm and jerked up toward his mouth. The floating lights were about one to two inches from his lips; a bell was telekinetically moved while both hands and both feet were under control.

Throughout the sittings the medium constantly rubbed his chest with his hands (still controlled) and soon afterward a light appeared. Since the investigators could not discover the modus operandi for the supposed fraudulent production of the phenomena, they summed up their conclusions as follows:

"(1) At three sittings out of a total of nine given by Mr. Fronczek at the Society's rooms, phenomena occurred which purported to be produced supernormally.

(2) At one of these three the phenomena consisted of the movements of small luminous objects provided by us for the purpose and we suppose these movements to have been brought about by the employment of a cushion held in the medium's mouth.

(3) At the other two sittings the phenomena consisted of the appearance of small luminous objects which appeared to come from the medium's mouth and to be attached to it, but we were unable to discover their nature or the method of their introduction into the séance room."

Frontiers of Science Newsletter

Bimonthly newsletter of the **Mankind Research Foundation.** The publication is concerned with parapsychology and parascience. It includes articles by researchers and reports on activities of the foundation. Address: 1315 Apple Ave., Silver Spring, MD 20910.

Fry, Daniel (1908–)

One of the early 1950s flying saucer **contactees.** Fry was born July 19, 1908, in Vernon, Minnesota. A former technician of White Sands Proving Grounds, Fry claimed that in 1950 while he was walking in the New Mexico desert he found a **flying saucer** that had landed. He said he held a conversation by telepathy with an invisible spaceman called "Alan" and took a ride in the saucer over New York. Following the publication of his books *White Sands Incident* and *Alan's Message: To Men of Earth* in 1954, Fry became a celebrity in the contactee movement. He went on to found Understanding, Inc. (now World Understanding) in 1955, through which he teaches the metaphysical perspective he has derived from his space contacts.

Sources:

Fry, Daniel. *Alan's Message: To Men of Earth.* Los Angeles: New Age Publishing, 1954.

———. *Atoms, Galaxies, and Understanding.* El Monte, Calif.: Understanding Publishing, 1960.

———. *Can God Fill Teeth? The Real Facts Behind the Miracle Ministry of Evangelist Willard Fuller.* Lakemont, Ga.: CSA, 1970.

———. *The Curve of Development.* Lakemont, Ga.: CSA, 1965.

———. *White Sands Incident.* Los Angeles: New Age Publishing, 1954.

Fukurai, Tomobichi

President of the Psychical Institute of Japan, professor of Kohyassan University, and former professor at the Imperial University of Tokyo. He was obliged to resign because of a book he published in 1913 on his experiments with Chizuko Mifune and Ikuko Nagao, declaring **clairvoyance** to be a fact.

With Nagao's assistance, Fukurai also conducted experiments in thought photography. Other mediums with whom he experimented included three women, Tetsuko Moritake, Sadako Takahashi, and Tenshin Takeuchi, and one man, Kohichi Mita. His results were presented in the 1913 book, translated into English in 1921 under the title *Clairvoyance and Thoughtography.* The book was reissued with additional matter in 1931 and again in 1975. The implications of Fukurai's pioneer work were not pursued in the West for many years. **Jule Eisenbud**'s work with the "thought photography" of **Ted Serios** in 1964 had parallels to Fukurai's investigations.

Sources:

Fukurai, Tomobichi. *Clairvoyance and Thoughtography.* 1921. Rev. ed. London: Rider, 1930. Reprint, 1975.

Otani, Soji. "Past and Present Situation of Parapsychology in Japan." In *Parapsychology Today: A Geographic View.* Edited by Allan Angoff and Betty Shapin. New York: Parapsychology Foundation, 1973.

Fuller, Curtis (1912–1991)

Cofounder and publisher of **FATE** magazine. Fuller was born March 2, 1912, in Necedah, Wisconsin, and was educated at the University of Wisconsin (B.A., 1933) and Northwestern University (M.S., 1937). He married Mary Margaret Stiehm on September 24, 1938. After a period as a newspaper writer, he was an editor on several magazines in the late 1930s and 1940s. By the mid-1940s he was working for Ziff-Davis, a large Chicago-based publisher.

In the wake of Ziff-Davis's contemplated move to New York and the sighting of flying saucers by Kenneth Arnold in 1947, Fuller and **Ray Palmer** (also a Ziff-Davis employee) decided to start a new company, Clark Publishing, and issue *FATE* magazine to explore **UFOs** and other mysteries. In 1955 he bought out Ray Palmer, who had already withdrawn from active editorial work. In 1966 Mary Margaret Fuller was named editor and Curtis Fuller assumed duties as publisher. He also created a second company, Woodall, Inc., which operated in the travel field and issued directories for trailers and campers.

Fuller had a sympathetic but skeptical view of paranormal phenomena and always insisted on high editorial standards and supporting data on any extraordinary claims made in the magazine's pages. He was a member of the Illinois Society for Psychical Research (president 1961–64) and was active in the **Spiritual Frontiers Fellowship** (treasurer 1962–69). The Fullers directed *FATE* together through the 1970s and 1980s, but following Mary Margaret's retirement in 1988 the magazine was sold to Llewellyn Publications. The March 1989 issue of *FATE* contained a farewell editorial from Curtis Fuller. He died April 29, 1991.

Sources:

Clark, Jerome. *Encyclopedia of Strange and Unexplained Phenomena.* Detroit: Gale Research, 1993.

Fuller, Jean (Violet) Overton (1915–)

Actress, writer, and member of a group that included poet Dylan Thomas and novelist Pamela Hansford Johnson. Fuller was born March 7, 1915, at Iver Heath, Buckinghamshire, England. She studied at the Royal Academy of Dramatic Art (1930–31), was a student of painting at Academie Julien, Paris, and finished college at the University of London (B.A. honors English, 1945). She later studied astronomy (because of an interest in astrology) at Goldsmith's College (1962–64).

Her varied career included a period as an actress, government service with the British Ministry of Information, and lecturing at the Speech Fellowship, London. She was a member of the British Astronomical Association, the Society of Authors, PEN, Poetry Society, Manifold Group of Poets, and the Dulwich Group of Poets. She also served as vice-president of the Astrological Lodge of the Theosophical Society.

Besides her involvement with **Theosophy,** in the circle of Dylan Thomas during the 1930s she became a close friend of occultist and poet **Victor Neuburg** and wrote a sympathetic biography of him, *The Magical Dilemma of Victor Neuburg* (1965). This volume contains one of the most complete accounts of the magic work of Neuberg and **Aleister Crowley,** including the story of Crowley's rediscovery of "sex magick" in 1912 in the Cairo workings. (Fuller was not related to **J. F. C. Fuller,** who also knew Neuburg and Aleister Crowley.)

Fuller also wrote biographies of **Helena Petrovna Blavatsky** and Noor Inayat Khan.

Sources:

Fuller, Jean Overton. *Blavatsky and Her Teachers: An Investigative Biography.* London: East-West Publications, 1988.

———. *Madeleine: The Story of Noor Inayat Kahn.* London: Gollancz, 1952. Reprinted as *Noor-un-nisa Inayat Kahn (Madeleine).* Rotterdam: East-West Publications, 1971.

———. *The Magical Dilemma of Victor Neuburg.* London: W. H. Allen, 1965.

Fuller, J(ohn) F(rederick) C(harles) (1878–1966)

Distinguished British soldier and friend of magician **Aleister Crowley.** As a young man he became impressed by Crowley's poems and occult philosophy and wrote a eulogistic book, *The Star in the West* (1907), in which he hailed Crowley as "more than a new-born Dionysis, he is more than a Blake, a Rabelais or a Heine; for he stands before us as some priest of Apollo . . ."

"Crowleyanity" was to be the new religion of mankind. It was Fuller who introduced Crowley to poet **Victor Neuburg,** who was to become Crowley's foremost disciple. (Fuller was not related to **Jean Overton Fuller,** who wrote an excellent biography of Victor Neuburg.)

Fuller parted company with Crowley in 1911 after a disagreement over a court action and later repudiated *The Star in the West* as "a jumble of undigested reading with a boyish striving after effect." Before he died, however, in the year of his death, Fuller stated that Crowley "remains one of the greatest of English lyric poets."

Fuller's long career included service in the Boer War (1899–1902) and World War I. He wrote several books on military strategy, including *Tanks in the Great War, 1914–18* (1920). Stationed in India for a period, he developed an interest in Eastern philosophy and yoga mysticism. He rose to the rank of major-general in 1930. He also continued to write on occult topics, his later books including *Yoga: A Study of the Mystical Philosophy of the Brahmins and Buddhists* (1925) and *The Secret Wisdom of the Qabalah* (1937). He died February 10, 1966.

Sources:

Fuller, John F. *The Secret Wisdom of the Qabalah.* London, 1937.

———. *The Star in the West.* London: Walter Scott Publishing, 1907. Reprint, Mokelumne Hill, Calif.: Health Research, 1969.

———. *Yoga: A Study of the Mystical Philosophy of the Brahmins and Buddhists.* London, 1925.

Fuller, Willard (1915–)

Spiritual healer specializing in the astounding phenomenon of psychic **dentistry.** Born in Grant Parish, Louisiana, Fuller was brought up as a Baptist and hoped to become a minister, but suffered from a pronounced stammer. After graduating from college with a B.A. in business administration and a B.E. in electrical engineering, he joined the army, where he reached the rank of master sergeant. By the time he returned to civilian life in his own town his stammer had ceased. When a traveling evangelist preached on two consecutive nights on the theme "Go Preach," Fuller decided that this had a special meaning for him. He determined to enter the ministry.

In 1946 he studied at the Southern Baptist Theological Seminary in New Orleans, where he graduated in theology. During one of his own revivalist meetings a stranger told him that he would be used "as a funnel through which God would pour blessings on His people." Later Fuller felt impelled to leave the Baptist ministry and become a Pentecostal. One day he felt a sudden surge of spiritual force and heard a voice declare that he was given the gift of healing and would heal people in the name of Jesus. At his next service he invited those who needed healing to come forward, and a number of remarkable cures took place.

He attended a service by evangelist A. C. McCabe, who practiced dental healing. McCabe told Fuller that he would also perform dental healing. Fuller was at first reluctant to attempt this, but a man he had cured of a stomach ulcer returned to his meetings and asked him to pray for a tooth cavity. Fuller laid hands on the man's head and prayed, "In the name of Jesus, be thou everywhere whole," and the man confirmed that his tooth cavity was healed. From March 1960 on, Fuller demonstrated this strange healing ability at his meetings. Those who attended his services stated that they saw or personally experienced dental healing, involving instantaneous filling of cavities with gold, silver, or porcelain, straightening of crooked teeth, and healing of decayed teeth and gums. On various occasions such phenomena were witnessed by professional dentists in the congregation.

Although such dental healing phenomenon seems incredible to skeptics, the suggestion of fraud seems even more incredible in the face of numerous eyewitness reports and considering the large sums of money that would be involved in skillful conjuring with substantial quantities of gold, silver, and other cavity fillings.

Fuller organized the **Lively Stones World Healing Fellowship** to give focus to his ministry. He was assisted by his wife, Margaret, a trained psychologist. She worked for several years in the area of counseling within the realm of the ministry and was herself a healer. She used the same method as her husband—that of laying on of hands and praying in the name of Jesus.

The Fullers were devoted to a healing ministry based on spiritual faith and the power of prayer. Although a number of those who attended their services claimed to receive miraculous dental healing, the Fullers did not become rich through their healing. They had a simple lifestyle and lived for some time on a houseboat. They did not charge for their healing, and their ministry was sustained only by voluntary contributions. They traveled wherever they were invited if their schedule permitted. They moved freely among groups of all persuasions and beliefs. They believed and taught that we are living in the New Age in which God's kingdom will be established on this Earth and perfect order in all things will once again be a reality.

Sources:

Fry, Daniel W. *Can God Fill Teeth? The Real Facts Behind the Miracle Ministry of Evangelist Willard Fuller.* Lakemont, Ga.: CSA Press, 1970.

St. Clair, David. *Psychic Healers.* Garden City, N.Y.: Doubleday, 1974. Rev. ed. New York: Bantam, 1979.

Fumigation (in Exorcism)

One of the most important rites during the **exorcism** of an evil spirit appears to have been the fumigation of the victim, and for this various prescriptions were given throughout occult history. If it was found difficult to dislodge the demon, a picture of him would sometimes be drawn, which was to be thrown into a fire after having been "signed with the cross, sprinkled with holy water, and fumigated."

At other times if the evil spirit refused to give his name the exorcist would fumigate the possessed person. The recipe for fumigation included such substances as asafoetida, sulphur, and salt. Fumigation was sometimes enhanced by **flagellation.**

Fund for UFO Research

Founded in the District of Columbia in 1979 to provide grants for **UFO** research and public education. The chairman since its beginning has been physicist Bruce Maccabee. It reviews research proposals and approves those that promise to advance scientific knowledge and public awareness of UFO phenomena. It grants interviews to news media, bestows awards, and conducts research programs. It is not a membership organization nor does it publish a magazine, although it issues occasional reports. It does not investigate UFO reports, but it works with and funds groups that do. Address: P.O. Box 277, Mt. Rainier, MD 20712.

Sources:

A Brief History of the Fund for UFO Research. Washington, D.C.: Fund for UFO Research, n.d.

Clark, Jerome. *UFOs in the 1980s.* Vol. 1 of *The UFO Encyclopedia.* Detroit: Apogee Books, 1990.

The Government UFO Collection: A Collection of UFO Documents from the Government of the USA and Canada. Mount Rainier, Md.: Fund for UFO Research, 1981–85.

Fung Hwang

Fabulous bird to which the ancient Chinese attributed almost the same qualities as other cultures did to the phoenix. It was said to have a cock's head, a snake's neck, a swallow's beak, a tortoise's back, and to be of five different colors and more than six feet high. According to the *Lun Yü Tseh Shwai,* "its head resembles heaven, its eye the sun, its back the moon, its wings the wind, its foot the ground, and its tail the woof." Like the dragon, tortoise, and unicorn, the fung hwang was considered to be a spiritual creature.

The appearance of the fung was always regarded as an auspicious augury. Women adorned themselves with the image of this bird in gold, silver, or brass, according to their means.

Sources:

Gould, Charles. *Mythical Monsters.* London, 1886. Reprint, Detroit: Singing Tree Press, 1969.

Funk, Isaac Kauffmann (1839–1912)

Director and principal proprietor of the publishing house Funk and Wagnalls, well-known psychical investigator, and author of several books on the paranormal. Funk was converted to a belief in **Spiritualism** by the medium **May Pepper** of Brooklyn, New York, through whom he received a manifestation from **Richard Hodgson** a few weeks after Hodgson's death, and by numerous other important incidents. **James H. Hyslop,** in his book *Contact with the Other World* (1919), devotes a chapter to claimed spirit communication from Funk through the mediumship of **Minnie Meserve Soule** (Mrs. Chenoweth).

Sources:

Funk, Isaac K. *The Next Step in Evolution; The Present Step.* London/New York: Funk & Wagnalls, 1902.

———. *The Psychic Riddle.* London/New York: Funk & Wagnalls, 1907.

———. *The Widow's Mite and other Psychic Phenomena.* London/New York: Funk & Wagnalls, 1904.

G

Gagates

Ancient term for **jet** (a velvet-black coal often used for jewelry), believed to be a black species of **electrum** or amber. The name derives from the area of Gagas, in Lycia, where the substance was found in classical times. Various occult properties are ascribed to it.

Gaia

Pre-Olympian Greek earth goddess, worshiped as mother of all. She mated with her son Uranus and bore Titans, the Cyclops, and Hectoncheires. Worship of Gaia continued after the rise of the Olympians, and she was regarded as a powerful influence in marriage, healing the sick, and divination. She was represented as a gigantic female form. Earlier cultures also had religious concepts of a great earth goddess.

The concept of Gaia as earth goddess has been revived in **New Age** ecological and mystical beliefs. On September 6, 1970, Otter G'Zell, founder of the Church of All Worlds, one of the early modern Neo-Pagan organizations, had a vision of the unity of the Earth's planetary biosphere—a single organism. He shared the vision with other church members and wrote about it in 1971 in the periodical he edited, *The Green Egg.*

Atmospheric biochemist James E. Lovelock had a very similar idea at somewhat the same time and through his books *Gaia* (1979) and *The Ages of Gaia* (1988) emerged as the leading proponent of this modern Gaia hypothesis of the earth as a living organism. His books propose a dynamic interaction between life and environment, with earth regulating life, and life regulating earth, virtually a single self-regulating entity.

The controversial aspect of Lovelock's concept is the extent the earth may be regarded as a living organism in which life and environment form one dynamic interacting whole. Although not unsympathetic to modern environmentalism, Lovelock proposes a broader frame of reference, and in *The Ages of Gaia* states: "At the risk of having my membership card of the Friends of the Earth withdrawn, I say that only by pollution do we survive. We animals pollute the air with carbon dioxide, and the vegetation pollutes it with oxygen. The pollution of one is the meat of the other." The Gaia hypothesis has stimulated New Age and Neo-Pagan veneration of Gaia as a living earth goddess and become an integral part of the revival of goddess worship in the last two decades.

The modern Gaia hypothesis was earlier prefigured by such writers as Gustav Fechner (1801–1887) and Francis Younghusband.

Sources:

Derrey, Francois. *The Earth is Alive.* London Arlington Books, 1968.

G'Zell, Otter. *Gaia: A New Look at Life on Earth.* London: Oxford University Press, 1979.

———. "Theogenesis: The Birth of the Goddess." *Green Egg* 21, 81 (May 1, 1988): 4–7, 27.

Olson, Carl. *The Book of the Goddess, Past and Present.* Philadelphia: J. P. Lippincott, 1983.

Pedlar, Kit. *Quest for Gaia.* UK: Sovereign Press, 1979.

Stein, Diane. *The Women's Spirituality Book.* St. Paul, Minn.: Llewellyn Publications, 1987.

Younghusband, Sir Francis. *The Living Universe.* London: John Murray, 1933.

Galactites (or Galaricides)

A precious stone of white color. According to ancient belief it was greatly valued by magicians, its property being to make magical writings known and ghosts to appear and also to return answers to questions. It was said to promote love and friendship.

Galbreath, Robert (Carroll) (1938–)

Writer and editor on folklore, popular culture, and the occult. He was born October 24, 1938, in Cincinnati, Ohio. He attended the University of Michigan (A.B. with high honors; Ph.D., 1970) and Harvard University (A.M., 1961). He was awarded a Woodrow Wilson fellowship for 1960–61. He taught at Bowling Green State University, Ohio (1965–70) and then became a postdoctoral fellow at the Center for Twentieth Century Studies at the University of Wisconsin, Milwaukee (1972–74). He taught at the University of Wisconsin for several years before moving to a position at the Northwestern University library in Evanston, Illinois.

Galbreath has had a longstanding interest in the occult and has published a number of articles in various scholarly journals. He is a member of the **American Society for Psychical Research** and the Popular Culture Association. Through the latter he published his main book, *The Occult: Studies and Evaluations* (1972). He also served as the associate editor for *Explorations: A Newsletter of Research into the Occult.*

Sources:

Galbreath, Robert C. "Arthur Edward Waite, Occult Scholar and Christian Mystic: A Chronological Bibliography." *Bulletin of Bibliography* 30, no. 2 (April–June 1973).

———. "History of Modern Occultism: A Bibliographical Survey." *Journal of Popular Culture* 5, no. 3 (winter 1971).

———, ed. *The Occult: Studies and Evaluations.* Bowling Green, Ohio: Bowling Green University Popular Press, 1972.

Galeotti, Marzio (or Martius) (ca. 1440–ca. 1494)

Italian astrologer and theologian who appears to have been a native of Narni, in Umbria. It seems that while a young man he settled for a while at Bologna, where he gave grave offense to the Church of Rome by promulgating the doctrine that good works are not the road to salvation, which is only to be obtained by faith in Christ. Finding the priests around him growing daily more and more hostile, Galeotti left for Hungary, where be became secretary to the king, Matthias Corvinus, and also tutor to the king's son, Prince John.

His secretarial and tutorial duties did not occupy all his time, so he was able to study **astrology** and also wrote a book, *De jocose Dictis et Factis Regis Matthiae Corvini.* Some of the tenets in this work caused further offense to the clergy, and eventually their rancor was such that the writer was seized and taken to Venice, where he was imprisoned for a while.

He was eventually released, chiefly through the influence of Pope Sixtus IV, whose tutor he is said to have been at an earlier, indeterminate date. Thereupon, Galeotti left for France, where he came under the notice of the king, Louis XI, who appointed him his state astrologer. He acted in this capacity for many years, sometimes living within the precincts of the royal castle of Plessis-les-Tours, sometimes at the town of Lyons. In 1478, while staying at Lyons, he was informed that Louis was approaching and he rode out to meet him, but fell from his horse and died shortly afterward as a result of injuries sustained in the fall.

A special interest attaches to Galeotti in that he appears in Sir Walter Scott's inimitable story of medieval France, *Quentin Durward.* Early in the tale, soon after Quentin has entered the Scots Guard of Louis XI, the latter and his new guardsman are depicted as visiting the astrologer, the king being anxious for a prophecy regarding Quentin's immediate future. The scene is a very memorable and graphic one, among the best in the whole book, and it is historically valuable because it contains what is probably a fairly accurate description of the kind of study used generally by an astrologer in the Middle Ages.

Galeotti is represented "curiously examining a specimen, just issued from the Frankfurt Press, of the newly invented art of printing," and the king questions him about this novel process, whereupon the seer speaks of the vast changes it is destined to bring about throughout the whole world.

This scene has a special point, since although the novelist himself did not refer to the matter in his notes, nor did Andrew Lang refer to it in his annotations to the Border Waverley edition, it is known that Louis was keenly interested in printing. Soon after the craft first made its appearance, the king commissioned the director of his mint (one Nicholas Janson or Jenson) to give up his post in favor of studying typography, with a view to its being carried on in France.

Galigai, Leonora (d. 1617)

Wife of the Maréchal d'Ancre Concinoc, who was killed by King Louis XIII's men April 24, 1617. The queen's niece and foster sister, she was believed to be a sorceress and was said to have bewitched the queen, becoming one of her favorites. She was found with three volumes full of magic characters, in addition to charms and amulets. At her trial, it was established that the marshal and his wife had consulted magicians, astrologers, and sorcerers, had made use of waxen images, and had brought sorcerers from the town of Nancy to sacrifice cocks.

It is said that she was condemned on her own confession and beheaded and burned. When President Courtin had asked her by what charm she had bewitched the queen, she had replied, proudly, "My spell was the power of a strong mind over a weak one."

Gallagher, Danny

Irish healer, the **seventh son** of a seventh son, and thus, according to folk tradition, destined to heal by touch. Although aware of this tradition, Gallagher did not attempt to practice healing until 1974, when he was working as an ice cream vendor in Coalisland, Northern Ireland. He had often saved an ice cream for a young girl who was paralyzed from the waist down. One day the girl was late in meeting the ice cream van, and Gallagher had a sudden premonition that he should help the child. He entered the house of her parents and told them he believed he could cure the girl. He succeeded, and when the news spread rapidly, Gallagher was overwhelmed by requests from scores of sick people for his healing touch. He sold his ice cream van and began a new life as a healer.

At the beginning of his ministry thousands of invalids traveled miles and waited in line for hours to spend just a few moments with the healer. Many remarkable cures have been claimed. Invalids have stood up from their wheelchairs and walked, terminal cancer patients have recovered, the deaf have regained hearing, and the blind have recovered their sight. For example, Jean Pritchett had been blind for 22 years, and a specialist had even recommended removal of one of her eyes. Jean's brother Peter went to a faith healing meeting in Birmingham, England, and just happened to take Jean along with him. After treatment by Gallagher, Jean recovered her sight.

Gallagher's healing technique normally involves three sessions with a patient. In the first session he lays his hands on the afflicted part of the body and requests that the patient bring soil from consecrated ground for the second visit. On that visit he "blesses" the soil and asks the patient to mix it with water and bathe the troubled area with it. On the third visit the treatment is normally completed.

Danny does not consider what he does **healing by faith.** Rather, he observes, "A person can come with faith in me, or God, or themselves, or none at all. It doesn't matter." He says he believes he acts only as a channel for divine healing power.

After traveling through Ireland, England, Australia, and the United States giving healing sessions, Gallagher set up a clinic at the house of his friends Mr. & Mrs. Jim Shannon at 49 Crouch Hill, Finsbury Park, London, N4. His address in Ireland is 122 Glen Rd., Maghera, Co. Derry, Northern Ireland.

Gandalf's Garden

A British experimental community of the sixties situated in Chelsea, London, embracing popular **mysticism, yoga, meditation, gurus,** and **occultism.** It was a meeting place for young people interested in such topics, with a craft shop and free food. The center was founded by Muz Murray, an art student who spent seven years hitchhiking in Europe, the Middle East, and Africa. He claims that while in Cyprus during 1964 he experienced mystical awareness, which he later compared with the LSD experience, finding the latter inferior. He developed Gandalf's Garden (named after author Tolkien's white wizard in *Lord of the Rings*) to create a spiritual and mystical lifestyle for young people. Their journal, *Gandalf's Garden,* included articles on new and old systems of developing changes in consciousness presented in the somewhat sensationalist pop style of the sixties.

Gandalf's Garden was dispersed in 1971 into various "seed centers" in different parts of the world, and the journal ceased publication. The "Friends of the Garden" described their centers as "gatherings of people who are not restricted by or to any one spiritual viewpoint, religion, sect or path, and who are open to the totality of things to be discovered in this incredible state of existence, whether it be from the intuitive mystical experience or the aware scientific investigation of the Cosmos." There is a **Friends of the Garden Central Seed Centre** at 24 St. Margaret's Close, Norstead, Norwich, England.

Gandillon Family (Pierre, Georges, Antoinette, Perrenette) (d. 1598)

French **werewolves** of St. Claude, in the Jura region, France, one of the major historical cases of **lycanthropy.** Perrenette believed that she was a wolf and one day in 1598 attacked two children who were picking wild strawberries. One of the children, a four-year-old boy, defended his sister with a knife, but Perrenette wrenched the knife from him and gashed his throat. He died of the wound after communicating the news that the wolf had human hands. Perrenette was found in the vicinity and torn to pieces by the enraged villagers.

Antoinette confessed to being a werewolf, and also to sleeping with the devil (who had taken the form of a goat), attending a

Sabbat, and producing magical hailstorms. Her brother Pierre was also accused of making hailstones, luring children to a Sabbat, turning himself into a wolf, and killing and eating people. He stated that Satan clothed them as wolves and that they hunted on all fours. Pierre's son Georges also confessed to changing into a wolf by smearing himself with a salve and killing two goats.

Antoinette, Pierre, and Georges were all convicted as werewolves and burned in 1598. The presiding judge was Henri Boguet whose *Discours des sorciers* became a standard guide to witchcraft.

Ganguly, Sachindra Nath (1932–)

Indian university lecturer in philosophy who has explored the connections between **yoga** and **parapsychology.** Ganguly was born on September 1, 1932, at Calcutta, India. He attended Presidency College, Calcutta University, graduating with an M.A. in philosophy in 1953.

He was appointed lecturer in philosophy at Jadavpur University, Calcutta, and between 1960 and 1962 researched at the Department of Philosophy of the University of Bristol, England. He is a founding member of the Narsingdas Academy of Yoga and Parapsychology, Calcutta, and a member of the **Society for Psychical Research,** London. He has taken a special interest in the development of **psi** faculty in relation to repeatable tests.

Sources:

Pleasants, Helene, ed. *Biographical Dictionary of Parapsychology.* New York: Helix Press, 1964.

Ganzfeld Setting

A development in modern parapsychological techniques popularized by **Charles Honorton,** director of research at the Division of Parapsychology and Psychophysics at Maimonides Medical Center, New York. The term *Ganzfeld* roughly translates as "total field," and the Ganzfeld Setting is basically a sensory isolation situation used for testing ESP. The subject, wearing earphones and blinders, sits in a comfortable chair in a soundproof booth and is instructed to stare at a bold red light, creating a diffused glow. Over the headphones comes a soft hiss of white noise.

The subject normally stays in the isolation booth for about 35 minutes and is instructed to think aloud, describing mental images, thoughts, and feelings. This monologue is monitored by an experimenter on an intercom system. Meanwhile another assistant (often a friend or associate of the subject) starts looking at pictures (often on slides held to the light). Experimenters have found frequent similarity between the images viewed by the assistant and the reveries of the subject in the Ganzfeld Setting.

In the first 30 tests initiated by parapsychologists Honorton and Harper in 1973, 43.3 percent of the subjects demonstrated a match with selected targets, as against a 25 percent chance expectation. In other cases, there was a suggestion of possible clairvoyant or precognitive faculty. Remarkable results were also achieved by parapsychologist **D. Scott Rogo** in California with the gifted subject Claudia Adams, a Los Angeles actress. During tests, Adams displayed such uncanny prescience that problems arose in *limiting* her ESP faculty to the disciplines of a given test. For example, in one test Rogo had prepared four pictures in sealed envelopes, only one of which was to be used, leaving the other three for later tests. However, Adams accurately described all four pictures during one test.

Sources:

Berger, Arthur S., and Joyce Berger. *The Encyclopedia of Parapsychology and Psychical Research.* New York: Paragon House, 1991.

Blackmore, Susan. "A Report of a Visit to Carl Sargent's Laboratory." *Journal* of the Society for Psychical Research 54, no. 808 (July 1987).

Harley, Trevor, and Gerald Matthews. "Cheating, Psi, and the Appliance of Science: A Reply to Blackmore." *Journal* of the Society for Psychical Research 54, no. 808 (July 1987).

Rogo, Scott. "ESP in the Ganzfeld: An Exploration of Parameters." In *Research in Parapsychology 1975,* edited by J. D. Morris, W. G. Roll, and R. L. Morris. Metuchen, N.J.: Scarecrow Press, 1976.

———. "Free Response Ganzfeld Experiments With a Selected Subject." In *Research in Parapsychology 1975,* edited by J. D. Morris, W. G. Roll, and R. L. Morris. Metuchen, N.J.: Scarecrow Press, 1976.

Garabandal

San Sebastian de Garabandal is a village in Spain, located 90 kilometers from Santander, where beginning in 1961 four young girls claimed to see **apparitions** of the Virgin Mary. In July 1961 Maria Cruz Gonzalez, Jacinta Gonzalez, Mari Loli Mazon, and Maria Conception (known as Conchita) Gonzales, ages 11 and 12, astonished villagers by declaring that an angel had appeared to them, followed by an apparition of the virgin. These visions came several times in a week, when the girls went into trance, oblivious to the crowds surrounding them. Afterward they said they were talking to the Blessed Mother, the Virgin Mary. In the course of time, their trances were witnessed and recorded by priests and psychologists, even filmed. When the girls were pricked with pins and bright lights flashed in their faces they did not respond.

In October 1961 the message from the Virgin Mary was that they had been chosen to receive a message for the world: "We must make many sacrifices, perform much penance and visit the Blessed Sacrament frequently, but first we must lead good lives. The cup is already filling up and if we do not change, a very great chastisement will come up on us."

During such visions the girls were shown part of the chastisement threatened to the world, and they screamed in terror. The visions continued until 1965, when Conchita was 15 years old. Conchita asked the Virgin Mary to send proof that these visions were truly from God and was told that a great miracle would take place. Conchita reported,

"The only thing I can tell is that it's going to be something that will happen in my village. . . . [T]he people who are sick are going to be cured. The day after there is going to be a sign in the pine trees . . . something we can see is gonna be there for ever."

This miracle was to be announced eight days in advance.

By this time Conchita was the only one of the four girls to continue to see visions, and early in 1965 she stated that she was to receive a second worldwide message. It came late at night on June 18 before a large, expectant crowd. The following morning Conchita stated that the message was similar to the earlier one but much stronger:

"Before the cup was filling up, now it is flowing over. Many cardinals, many bishops, and many priests are on the road to perdition and taking many souls with them. I, your Mother, ask you to amend your lives. You are now receiving the last warnings. I love you very much and do not want your condemnation. You should make more sacrifices, think about the passion of Jesus."

By November 1965 the visions ceased entirely, but Conchita was constantly pressed to reveal the date of the promised miracle, known only to her. Then quite suddenly Conchita lost faith in her visions, feeling it was all a dream. The village priest sent her to the bishop, who simply advised her not to talk further about the apparitions. She decided to leave the village, feeling she could not stay there with people wanting to talk to her and not knowing what to say to them. She emigrated to the United States and lived anonymously.

An advocacy center for the Garabandal visions was founded in New York, and a branch was formed in London. The center declares that before the "chastisement" there will be great miraculous signs that the world will accept as supernatural. There will be a worldwide warning that everyone will be aware of, regardless of race, color, or creed. Conchita will announce the great miracle eight days in advance. It will take place at Garabandal, where the sick will be cured and sinners converted, and in this spectacular miracle God will manifest at the pine trees a visible sign that will remain until the end of time for the conversion of the world.

Meanwhile Conchita lives quietly and avoids publicity, trying to escape the attention of the public. She did, however, take part in a British Broadcasting Corporation (BBC) television feature on Garabandal (telecast in the "Everyman" series in 1980), although she declined the standard fee for her appearance. This program highlighted the extraordinary challenge of such apparitions of the Virgin Mary and the dilemma they pose for those who see them.

Whereas the story of **Lourdes** now depends upon hearsay accounts and traditions of a century ago, the case of Garabandal is so topical that film records were actually taken of the girls during their trances, and direct interviews were recorded with Conchita herself. In the BBC feature it was clear from interviews with Conchita that she faces a strange problem, intensified as the date of the miracle, known only to her, presumably approaches. If there is no miracle, she will be branded a fake or hysteric. If there *is* a miracle, her privacy and family life will be invaded and disrupted by publicity.

Even the simple life of the villagers of Garabandal has changed as the village has become a great pilgrim center. Speculators have bought up land and new houses are being built to accommodate pilgrims. Every year thousands visit the pine trees where the miracle is scheduled. In the United States, Conchita Gonzales waits with her family and dedicates herself to "love God and do his work."

Fr. Robert Pelletier, the strongest advocate for the Garabandal visions in North America, has attempted to liken Garabandal to **Fatima,** even recounting a similar miracle of the sun's dancing in the sky. Unlike Fatima in neighboring Portugal, however, Garabandal has not received the endorsement of the Catholic Church. An initial inquiry under the bishop of Santander in 1967 reported to Rome negatively about the events at Garabandal. Rome did not act on these findings, and thus the church has made no official pronouncement on the validity of the apparitions.

Sources:

Gonzalez, Conchita, and Harry Daley. *Miracle at Garabandal: The Story of Mysterious Apparitions in Spain and a Message for the Whole World.* Garden City, N.Y.: Doubleday, 1983.

McClure, Kevin. *The Evidence for Visions of the Virgin Mary.* Wellingborough, England: Aquarian Press, 1983.

Pelletier, Robert A. *God Speaks at Garabandal.* Worcester, Mass.: Assumption, 1970.

———. *The Sun Dances at Garabandal.* Worcester, Mass.: Assumption, 1973.

Perry, Nicholas, and Loreto Echeverria. *Under the Heel of Mary.* London: Routledge, 1988.

Garatronicus

A red-colored stone that Achilles is believed to have carried with him in battle. It was said to render its possessor invincible.

"Garden of Pomegranates"

A sixteenth-century tract, *Pardis Rimonim,* by Rabbi Moses Cordovero reflecting the later spirit of the **Kabala.** The title derives from the biblical *Song of Songs:* "Thy plants are an orchard of pomegranates." The pomegranate has been a favorite Eastern symbol of mystics in the context of the garden of the soul. The title *A Garden of Pomegranates* was also given to a modern outline of kabbalistic teachings by magician **Israel Regardie.**

Sources:

Cordovero, Moses ben Jacob. *Moses Cordovero's Introduction to Kabbalah: An Annotated Translation of His Or na'errav.* New York: Michael Sharaf Publishing Trust of the Yeshiva University Press, 1994. (Originally published sixteenth century.)

Regardie, Israel. *A Garden of Pomegranates.* London: Rider, 1936. Reprint, St. Paul, Minn.: Llewellyn Publications, 1970.

Gardner, F(rederick) L(eigh) (1857–ca. 1930)

British occultist, member of the Hermetic Order of the **Golden Dawn** occult society. Gardner's private papers and correspondence have helped to throw light on some aspects of the Golden Dawn and its members, such as **W. W. Westcott, S. L. M. Mathers,** and **W. A. Ayton.**

Gardner was born in Highbury, North London, March 31, 1857, the son of an accountant. His parents were Spiritualists and held séances at their home, at one of which young Gardner was controlled by an Indian guide.

Gardner began employment as a stockbroker's clerk, becoming a member of the Stock Exchange in 1886. He joined the **Theosophical Society** around 1884 and was informed that his mahatma (a master or adept of the Society) was "Koot Hoomi." He married soon after this, and his wife shared his theosophical interests. Gardner knew **Helena Petrovna Blavatsky** personally and became a member of the Blavatsky Lodge in 1890. He lost interest in the Theosophical Society after joining the Golden Dawn in 1894.

He corresponded frequently with Rev. W. A. Ayton, another member of the Golden Dawn, who was a student of **alchemy,** and their letters (a collection of which, edited by Ellie Howe, was published in 1985) are valuable for their sidelights on the order. Gardner was also a Freemason, later joining the **Societas Rosicruciana in Anglia** and becoming its librarian. He became financially involved in sponsoring publication of the English translation by Mathers of the important occult treatise *The Book of the Sacred Magic of Abra-Melin* in 1898.

Gardner retired from membership of the Stock Exchange in 1903 and thereafter was an antiquarian bookseller, with special interest in occult works. He edited and privately published the limited edition, three-volume *Catalogue Raisonné of Works on the Occult Sciences,* consisting of *Rosicrucian Books* (1903), *Astrological Books* (1911), and *Freemasonry: A Catalogue of Lodge Histories* (1912). These remain very useful bibliographical contributions.

Sources:

Howe, Ellic, ed. *The Alchemist of the Golden Dawn: The Letters of the Revd W. A. Ayton to F. L. Gardner and Others 1886–1905.* Wellingborough, England: Aquarian Press, 1985.

———. *The Magicians of the Golden Dawn.* London: Routledge & Kegan Paul, 1972.

Gardner, G(erald) B(rosseau) (1884–1964)

Pioneer of the modern **witchcraft** revival. Gardner was born at Blundell Sands near Liverpool, England, June 13, 1884. Beginning at age 16, he spent much of his life in the East, as a tea planter in Ceylon (1900–19), a rubber planter in Borneo and Malaya (1923), and a customs official in Malaya (1936). In the East he took the opportunity to study magic practices and even became an expert on the kris, a Malay ceremonial dagger, about which he wrote a definitive text. In Ceylon he also became a Mason.

On his retirement from Malaya, Gardner and his wife settled in New Forest in Hampshire, England, where he associated with members of a theosophical group, the Crotona Fellowship of **Rosicrucians.** One of the members supposedly had belonged to a secret witch coven and introduced Gardner to witchcraft. In fact, it appears that Gardner set out to construct a new popular occult religion, drawing upon all the things he had learned in the East. Elements of this new religion were first published in 1949 in a novel, *High Magic's Aid,* issued under a pseudonym, Scire. Then in 1951 the last of the archaic antiwitchcraft laws (which had in this century been used primarily to attack Spiritualists) were removed from British law. Three years later Gardner completed his most important book, *Witchcraft Today.* By this time he had created a working coven, but he presented his new religion as the faith of an old witchcraft group that was dying out. The book was a means of contacting people who wanted to be members of the witchcraft faith. It was followed by *Meaning of Witchcraft* (1959).

Throughout the 1950s the practice of witchcraft spread in England. Gardner opened a witchcraft museum on the Isle of Man and made himself available to the press and to prospective new witches. In 1962, shortly before Gardner's death, the Americans Rosemary and Raymond Bucklad traveled to his home and were initiated as priestess and priest and returned to found the Gardnerian movement in the United States. Gardner died at sea on February 12, 1964. After his death the contents of the museum were sold to Ripley's Believe It or Not and were subsequently disbursed to various Ripley's museums and sold to private collectors.

Gardner's form of witchcraft was based on a polytheism centered on the Great Mother Goddess and her consort, the Horned God. In the coven, the basic organizational and worshiping group of the movement, the two deities are symbolized by the priestess and priest. The priestess has clear dominance, and the lineage of authority is passed through her. The ritual is in three degrees, Gardner having assembled ritual elements from a variety of sources. Much of the third degree is taken from the writings of **Aleister Crowley.**

As Gardner's movement spread, a number of variations developed, first by former members **Alexander Sanders** and **Sybil Leek,** and in the United States by various self-described "traditionalists." In North America upward of fifty thousand people have been attracted to the Gardnerian or Neopagan Wiccan movement.

Sources:

Bracelin, L. L. *Gerald Gardner: Witch.* London: Octagon Press, 1960.

Gardner, Gerald. *A Goddess Arrives.* London: A. W. Stockwell, 1948.

———. *Meaning of Witchcraft.* London: Aquarian Press, 1959.

———. *Witchcraft Today.* London: Jerrolds, 1954.

Kelly, Aidan A. *Crafting the Art of Magic: A History of Modern Witchcraft, 1939–1964.* St. Paul, Minn.: Llewellyn Publications, 1991.

Valiente, Doreen. *The Rebirth of Witchcraft.* London: Robert Hale, 1989.

Gardner, Martin (1924–)

Journalist and writer, born in Tulsa, Oklahoma, on October 21, 1914. Gardner graduated from the University of Chicago (B.A., 1936). His first job was as a reporter for the *Tulsa Tribune.* In the 1950s he moved to New York and in 1957 became associated with *Scientific American,* for which he has written a column on mathematical games for many years.

In 1952 Gardner wrote what has become the most famous and enduring of his many books, *In the Name of Science* (reprinted in 1957 as *Fads and Fallacies in the Name of Science*), a skeptical book dealing with numerous scientific deadends, hoaxes, and religious groups that made scientific claims to support their beliefs. The volume has become a classic of debunking literature relative to the occult.

Gardner continued to turn out books, primarily on mathematics, over the years. Periodically he gathered his columns into what has turned into a series of books on mathematical games. In the 1980s he returned to the debunking role and turned out three new volumes: *Science, God, Bad, and Bogus* (1981), *New Age Notes of a Fringe Watcher* (1988), and *How Not to Test a Psychic: Ten Years of Remarkable Experiments with Renowned Psychic Pavel Stepanek* (1989). In this debunking role he has identified with the **Committee for the Scientific Investigation of Claims of the Paranormal,** of which he was an original member.

Sources:

Gardner, Martin. *How Not to Test a Psychic: Ten Years of Remarkable Experiments with Renowned Psychic Pavel Stepanek.* Buffalo, N.Y.: Prometheus Books, 1989.

———. *In the Name of Science.* New York: George Putnam's Sons, 1952. Reprinted as *Fads and Fallacies in the Name of Science.* New York: Dover Publications, 1957.

———. *New Age Notes of a Fringe Watcher.* Buffalo, N.Y.: Prometheus Books, 1988.

———. *Science, God, Bad, and Bogus.* Buffalo, N.Y.: Prometheus Books, 1981.

Garinet, Jules (1797–ca. 1877)

French bibliophile and author of *Histoire de la Magie en France* (1818), in which he includes a description of the **Sabbat,** a dissertation on demons, and a discourse on the superstitions connected with magic among the ancients and his contemporaries.

Sources:

Garinet, Jules. *Histoire de la Magie en France.* Paris, 1818.

Garland, Hamlin (1860–1940)

Author, lecturer, and psychical researcher. Born at LaCrosse, Wisconsin, September 14, 1860, he was educated at Cedar Valley Seminary, Iowa, the University of Wisconsin (Hon. LL.D., 1926), and the University of California (1927).

As a young man Garland spent his early life in farming. At age 24 he moved to Boston for further formal education and became established as a critic and lecturer. He was a staunch defender of farmers and also of women's rights. His book *Daughter of the Middle Border* (1921) won a Pulitzer Prize. While in Boston, Garland joined the **American Society for Psychical Research** and conducted his own investigations into psychic matters. He also wrote many articles on the subject. His books include *Forty Years of Psychic Research* (1936) and *The Mystery of the Buried Crosses* (1939). He died March 4, 1940.

Sources:

Garland, Hamlin. *Forty Years of Psychic Research.* New York: Macmillan, 1936.

Holloway, Jean. *Hamlin Garland, a Biography.* Austin, Tex.: University of Texas Press, 1960.

Pleasants, Helene, ed. *Biographical Dictionary of Parapsychology.* New York: Helix Press, 1964.

Garlic

A member of the lily family that has been used worldwide as a Garlic herb and medicine. It was cultivated throughout Europe, where it was believed that using it or even mentioning its name was a sure charm against **witchcraft,** the **evil eye,** and **vampires.** Newly built houses and the sterns of boats belonging to Greece and Turkey once had long bunches of garlic hanging from them as a preventive against the fatal envy of any ill-disposed person. In ancient Rome soldiers believed that eating garlic gave them courage in battle. In addition to its use as an amulet, garlic was also credited with medical virtue as an antiseptic, salve, and water purifier.

Garlic also appeared in the folklore of Mexico, South America, and China, where it emerged as an antivampire agent. It was also long believed to have aphrodisiac properties and was forbidden in the diet of yogis in higher spiritual development in ancient India.

Sources:

Lehrer, Ernst, and Johanna Ernst. *Folklore and Odysseys of Food and Medicinal Plants.* New York: Tutor Publishing, 1962.

Melton, J. Gordon. *The Vampire Book: An Encyclopedia of the Undead.* Detroit: Visible Ink Press, 1994.

Garnet

Gemstone that was popularly believed to preserve health and promote joy, but in the case of lovers might cause discord.

Garnett, Richard (1789–1850)

British philologist who maintained a secret interest in **astrology.** He was born July 26, 1789, in Otley, Yorkshire, and educated at Otley Grammar School. In time he mastered several languages—French, Italian, German, Latin, and Greek—and became a curate at Blackburn and assistant master of the grammar school. He also contributed articles to the *Protestant Guardian.* After the death of his first wife and their infant daughter, he moved to Lichfield, where he became priest-vicar of Lichfield Cathedral in 1829 and absorbed himself in the study of comparative philosophy. He contributed important papers to the *Quarterly Review* dealing with English lexicography, dialects, and the Celtic languages. In 1834 he married his second wife, Rayne Weaks.

In 1838 he became assistant keeper of printed books at the British Museum Library. He became a member of the Philological Society and contributed important papers to its *Transactions.* He died September 27, 1850.

Few suspected that this eminent scholar of philology and important official at the august British Museum Library was secretly fascinated by astrology. However, he not only studied early accounts of this subject but also experimented himself with research on the association of planetary positions with mental illness. He published his findings under the pseudonym A. G. Trent (an anagram of his own name).

Garnier, Gilles (d. 1574)

Notorious French **werewolf** of the Dôle area of France-Comté during the sixteenth century and a classic instance of **lycanthropy.** Following an epidemic of attacks on young children in 1573, Garnier and his wife were arrested and tried as werewolves. Garnier confessed that he had killed a 12-year-old boy and was about to eat his flesh but was interrupted by villagers. Garnier and the villagers testified that Garnier appeared in human form, although in other instances it was claimed that he appeared as a wolf.

Garnier confessed that on another occasion he killed a ten-year-old girl while in the shape of a wolf, tearing her flesh with his teeth and claws, and then devoured her, and that on another occasion he attacked a girl while in the shape of a wolf but was interrupted and had to flee. He then claimed that a few days later he strangled a ten-year-old boy while in the shape of a wolf, tearing off a leg with his fangs and eating the flesh. In reaction to his confession, the authorities burned him alive at Dôle on January 18, 1574, and scattered his ashes to the winds.

Garrett, Eileen J(eanette Vancho Lyttle) (1892–1970)

Psychic medium, foundation executive, writer, editor, publisher, and one of the most important figures of the early parapsychological scene. She is believed to have been born March 14, 1892, in Meath, Ireland, and given the name Emily Jane Savage. In later years, Emily became known variously as "Jane Savage" or "Jean Lyttle" (or "Little"). The latter name was the pseudonym for her four published novels.

Garrett was a natural sensitive from an early age. Her psychic ability was further developed by Spiritualist **James Hewat McKenzie** at the **British College of Psychic Science,** London, between 1924 and 1928. Garrett, however, was unique among mediums in developing an objective approach to her own phenomena. She also enlisted the assistance of qualified researchers and scientists in investigating paranormal phenomena. She was invited to the United States by the **American Society for Psychical Research** in 1931, and from time to time visited Duke University, working under the guidance of **William McDougall** and **J. B. Rhine.** She worked with many famous investigators of the paranormal, including **Alexis Carrel, Nandor Fodor,** and **Hereward Carrington.** She experimented with **telepathy, trance,** psychic controls, **poltergeist, ESP,** and many other phenomena.

Her own powers of telepathy and **clairvoyance** were remarkable. As a medium she attracted world interest when she received a communication apparently from the dead captain of the airship R101 after the airship had crashed but before the news was reported.

In 1941 Garrett started the publishing house Creative Age Press in New York with her own book *Telepathy,* written in five weeks. She also launched *Tomorrow* magazine, one of the most intelligent journals on paranormal topics of the time, and established Helix Press, another publishing house.

In 1951 she set up the **Parapsychology Foundation** in New York to encourage organized scientific research through grants and international conferences. The foundation published the *International Journal of Parapsychology,* the first issue of which appeared in the summer of 1959. The foundation organized its first international conference on **parapsychology** at the University of Utrecht, Holland, on July 29, 1953, under the chairmanship of **Gardner Murphy.**

Garrett had been married twice before her marriage to J. W. Garrett in 1918. During her lifetime she encountered many famous literary figures and worked with the greatest parapsychologists of her time. She died September 15, 1970, and was buried at Marseilles, France.

Sources:

Angoff, Allen. *Eileen Garrett and the World Beyond the Senses.* New York: William Morrow, 1974.

Garrett, Eileen J. *Adventures in the Supernormal.* New York: Garrett Publications, 1949.

———. *Awareness.* New York: Creative Age Press, 1941.

———. *Life is the Healer.* Philadelphia: Dorrance, 1957.

———. *Many Voices: The Autobiography of a Medium.* 1968. Reprint, New York: Dell, 1969.

———. *My Life as a Search for the Meaning of Mediumship.* London: Rider, 1939.

———. *The Sense and Nonsense of Prophecy.* New York: Farrar, Straus & Giroux, 1950. Reprint, New York: Berkley, 1968.

———. *Telepathy: In Search of a Lost Faculty.* New York: Creative Age Press, 1945.

———, ed. *Beyond the Five Senses.* Philadelphia: J. B. Lippincott, 1957.

———. *Does Man Survive Death?* New York: Helix Press, 1957.

Progoff, Ira. *The Image of an Oracle: A Report on Research into the Mediumship of Eileen Garrett.* New York: Helix Press, 1964.

Gastromancy

Divination from the belly, an ancient method now generally believed to have been ventriloquism, the voice sounding low and hollow, as if issuing from the ground. Eusèbe Salverte, author of *Des sciences occultes* (1834), put forward this opinion, adding, "The name of *Engastrimythes,* given by the Greeks to the Pythie (priestesses of Apollo)[,] indicates that they made use of this artifice."

Another method of practicing gastromancy connects it with **crystal gazing.** At one time vessels of glass, round and full of clear water, were placed before several lighted candles. In this case, a young boy or girl was generally the seer, and the demon was summoned in a low voice by the magician. Replies were then obtained from the magical appearances seen in the illuminated glass vessels.

Sources:

Salverte, Eusèbe. *Des sciences occultes.* Paris, 1834.

Waite, Arthur Edward. *The Occult Sciences.* 1891. Reprint, Secaucus, N.J.: University Books, 1974.

Gaufridi, Louis (Jean Baptiste) (d. 1611)

French priest burned as a sorcerer at Aix-en-Provence in 1611. He was a cure at Marseilles, where his personality and manners gained him a footing in high society. He became friendly with a 14-year-old girl, Madeleine de Demandolx, who had attended the Ursuline convent school at Aix for two years. Madeleine fell in love with the personable 34-year-old Gaufridi, who was already much in demand as a confessor by the women of the district.

After some gossip, Madeleine entered a convent in 1607, where she confessed to intimacies with Gaufridi. About two years later, Madeleine exhibited convulsive fits and claimed visions of devils. After an unsuccessful exorcism, her symptoms spread to other nuns at the convent. The girls were removed and examined by other exorcists. Madeleine accused Gaufridi of obscene bewitchment. Gaufridi attempted to clear his name, appealing to the bishop of Marseilles and the pope.

In 1611 the Parliament at Aix held a trial at which Madeleine was a star witness, exhibiting demoniacal possession and affirming her lascivious desire for Gaufridi. Meanwhile the unfortunate priest had spent a year chained in an underground dungeon with rats. Three devil's marks were said to have been found on his body. After torture he confessed to magic, sorcery, and fornication but later retracted his confession. He was sentenced to be burned alive on a slow fire. Before this was carried out, he was tortured so horribly that he was willing to confess to any atrocity—even eating roasted babies! Before being burned, he was dragged through the streets. (See also **Urbain Grandier; Loudun, Nuns of; Louviers, Nuns of**)

Gauher-abad

The "Abode of Jewels," the name given to one of the capitals of the *peris* of Persian romance. The peris were beings of an angelic or pleasant disposition who were believed to inhabit the earth, along with the **divs** or evil-doers, before the creation of man. After this event, they became inhabitants of the aerial regions and had three capitals: Shad-u-kam (Pleasure and Desire), Gauher-abad, and Amber-abad (City of Ambergris).

Gauld, Alan

Contemporary British parapsychologist and historian of psychical research. Gauld became a member of the **Society for Psychical Research,** London, in 1954, was co-opted to its Council in 1962, and elected to the Council in 1966. From 1965 to 1970 he edited the SPR's *Journal* and *Proceedings.* He is also senior lecturer in psychology at the University of Nottingham, England. He is the author of several books, including *Mediumship and Survival* (1982).

Sources:

Gauld, Alan. *The Founders of Psychical Research.* New York: Schocken Books, 1968.

———. *Human Action and its Psychological Investigation.* London: Routledge & Kegan Paul, 1977.

———. *Mediumship and Survival.* London: Heineman, 1982.

Gauld, Alan, and A. D. Cornell. *Poltergeists.* London: Routledge & Kegan Paul, 1979.

Gauld, Alan, and J. D. Shotter. *Human Action and its Psychological Investigation.* Boston and London: Routledge & Kegan Paul, 1977.

Gauquelin, Françoise Schneider (1929–)

Swiss astrologer and statistician, born in French-speaking Switzerland. She attended the University of Paris, where she received a degree in statistics. In Paris she met and married **Michel Gauquelin.** While still in school, the two began to collect birth dates of large groups of people to determine if there was any relationship between the positions of the planets in the solar system and such factors as a person's choice of profession.

In their search for correlations they concentrated on outstanding professionals—sports champions, army officers, scientists, and so on. One of the first patterns they found was the presence of the planet Mars at either the horizon or the midheaven (two significant positions in the birth chart) at the time of birth. The frequency of these occurrences far exceeded any normal distribution due to chance alone and gave rise to the name "Mars effect" denoting a significant correlation between the position of the planets and professional achievement. Writers, for example, had a significantly positioned Moon, and scientists a significantly placed Saturn.

The Gauquelins' findings began to appear in publications in the 1960s. Michel published an initial book in 1967, *The Cosmic Clocks,* and then through the 1970s more than 25 volumes of statistical data were published by the couple from the Laboratoire d'Etude des Relations entre Rythmes Cosmiques et Psychophysiologiques, which they had founded in Paris. Their collaboration, however, as well as their marriage, came to an end in the 1980's.

Since that time Françoise has continued to write and publish (Michel died in 1991). For a number of years she edited *Astro-Psychological Problems* (1982–88). Her 1982 *Psychology of the Planets* emphasizes the agreement of her and Michel's statistical results and traditional astrology, the differences having been emphasized in several of Michel's writings.

Sources:

Lewis, James L. *The Astrology Encyclopedia.* Detroit: Gale Research, 1994.

Series A: Professional Notabilities. 6 vols. Paris: Laboratoire d'Etude des Relations entre Rythmes Cosmiques et Psychophysiologiques, 1970–71.

Series B: Heredity Experiments. 6 vols. Paris: Laboratoire d'Etude des Relations entre Rythmes Cosmiques et Psychophysiologiques, 1970–71.

Series C: Psychological Monographs. 5 vols. Paris: Laboratoire d'Etude des Relations entre Rythmes Cosmiques et Psychophysiologiques, 1972–77.

Series D: Scientific Documents. 10 vols. Paris: Laboratoire d'Etude des Relations entre Rythmes Cosmiques et Psychophysiologiques, 1976–82.

Gauquelin, Michel (Roland) (1928–1991)

French psychologist and writer who attempted to put **astrology** on a scientific basis through his special studies of correlation between personality and cosmic influences. Gauquelin was born November 13, 1928, in Paris and was educated at the Sorbonne, University of Paris (Ph.D., 1954). In 1954 he married Françoise Schneider, a science writer and psychologist, who collaborated with him on research and writing. Gauquelin served in the French Military Reserve (active duty, 1953–54) and attained the rank of lieutenant. He began practicing psychology and writing in 1956.

With his wife he established the Laboratory for Study of the Relations between Cosmic Rhythms and Psychophysiologics in Paris. In 1949, having found that previous quantitative studies in astrology lacked sufficient controls, the Guaquelins began collecting large pools of birth data and analyzed planetary positions in relation to various factors, especially career choice and performance. Among the statistically significant factors they discovered was a correlation between the position of Mars in the natal chart and success in sports. This correlation became known as the Mars effect.

The research was published in a series of books beginning with *The Cosmic Clocks* in 1967. The research was hailed by the astrological community as good news, even though the findings contradicted many standard astrological affirmations. It served as part of the catalyst for the formation of the Committee for the Scientific Investigation of the Claims of the Paranormal, which began a project to refute the data presented by the Gauquelins. The project, in fact, replicated the Gauquelins' results, but rather than publish its findings, the committee falsified the results. The ensuing "Starbaby" scandal severely damaged the credibility of the committee. The controversy was aired quite thoroughly in several issues of the **Zetetic Scholar.**

Regarding his studies in "cosmopsychology," Gauquelin wrote:

"Until the beginning of this century, science believed that man was in isolation on earth, separated from the rest of the universe. Now we know that the biological clocks of our brain and our body are attuned to the movement of the cosmic forces. . . . This new conception should have not only scientific but also philosophical and even poetical implications for modern thought."

The Gauquelins divorced in the 1980s, and each continued to pursue an independent line of research. Michel Gauquelin went on to work with astrologers on a revised neoastrology that would embody the results of his research. Besides writing numerous books, he contributed articles to periodicals and wrote television programs on psychology and cosmic influences. He died in Paris on May 20, 1991.

Sources:

Curry, Patrick. "Research on the Mars Effect." *Zetetic Scholar* 9 (1982): 34–52.

Dean, G. *Recent Advances in Natal Astrology.* Cowes, England: The Author, 1977.

Gauquelin, Michel. *The Cosmic Clocks: From Astrology to a Modern Science.* Chicago: Henry Regnery, 1967. Reprint, New York: Avon, 1969.

———. *Cosmic Influences on Human Behavior.* 2nd ed. New York: ASI Publishers, 1978.

———. *Dreams and Illusions of Astrology.* Buffalo, N.Y.: Prometheus Books, 1979.

———. *How Atmospheric Conditions Affect Your Health.* New York: Stein and Day, 1971.

———. *The Scientific Basis of Astrology: Myth or Reality?* New York: Stein and Day, 1969.

Gauquelin, Michel, and Françoise Guaquelin. *The Mars Effect and Sports Champions: A New Replication.* Paris: Laboratorie d'études des relations entre rhythmes cosmiques et psychophysiologiques, 1979.

Lewis, James. *Encyclopedia of Astrology.* Detroit: Visible Ink Press, 1994.

Seymour, Percy. *The Scientific Basis of Astrology.* New York: St. Martin's, 1992.

Gauthier, Jean

Self-described alchemist of the sixteenth century. Charles IX (1550–1574) of France, deceived by his promises, provided him with 120,000 pounds with which to make gold. After he had worked for a week, he ran away with the king's money. He was pursued, captured, and hanged.

Gauthier of Bruges

According to medieval legend, Gauthier, a Franciscan monk made a bishop by Pope Nicholas III and deposed by Clement V, appealed to God against his deposition and asked to be buried with his act of appeal in his hand. Some time after his death, Pope Clement V visited Poitiers and, finding himself one day in a Franciscan monastery, asked to see Gauthier's remains. He caused the tomb to be opened and was horrified to see Gauthier of Bruges presenting his act of appeal with a withered hand.

Gaveshana Journal

Hindi quarterly journal of philosophy, **psychology,** sociology, religion, **mysticism,** and **parapsychology,** published by J. P. Atreya, Moradabad 19, India.

Gay, Kathleen Agnes Robson (1890–1969)

British parapsychologist. She was born June 22, 1890. During World War I, she was a voluntary worker for the Invalid Children's Aid Association (1914) and a member of the British Red Cross Society (1914–16). Later she worked at the British Treasury Department (1916–18) and the School of Oriental Studies, London (1920–22). Once World War II began she served with the British Red Cross Society and the Soldiers' and Sailors' Families Association (1939–45).

During the last years of her life, she became interested in psychical research. She joined the Council of the **Society for Psychical Research,** London, in 1950 and served as chairperson of the Sir Oliver Lodge Posthumous Test Committee. She took special interest in work with mediums. From her research she wrote articles for the *Journal* of the SPR.

Sources:

Pleasants, Helene, ed. *Biographical Dictionary of Parapsychology.* New York: Helix Press, 1964.

Gayatri Mantra

The most famous and powerful **mantra** ("power sound prayer") of Hinduism. It is said to have been revealed to the great sage Vishwamitra, preceptor of Prince Rama of the *Ramayana* religious epic. Its origin, however, is believed to have been the supreme creative force Brahma, before the Vedic scriptures were revealed. Thus the Gayatri mantra has been named "Vedamata" (Mother of the Vedas).

Every devout Brahmin is required to perform the Gayatri mantra each morning and evening. The mantra is addressed to the sun as "Savitri," personified as a goddess, wife of Brahma. The mantra translates roughly as "Earth, sky, heaven, we meditate on these and the ineffable light and power of the resplendent sun, may it guide our understanding."

The three regions of earth, sky, and heaven are also associated with physical, emotional, and mental states. Mantras, when properly intoned, vibrate the body. Some practitioners have combined the repetition of the Gayatri mantra with *pranayama* (breathing techniques) in order to activate the psychic body, especially as it is pictured in the *chakras* or mystical centers, and thus arouse *kundalini* energy (which is seen as resting latent at the base of the spine) to transform consciousness.

Gazzera, Linda (ca. 1900–)

Nonprofessional Italian medium discovered by psychical researcher **Enrico Imoda,** who published an important book, *Fotographie di fantasma* (1912), on his experiments with her at Turin in the house of the Marquise de Ruspoli. Gazzera produced impressive **telekinesis** and **materialization** phenomena. Her primary **control** was a deceased cavalry officer, "Vincenzo," and at times "Carlotta," a child of four.

Charles Richet describes her powers in *Thirty Years of Psychical Research* (1923):

"I hold Linda's two hands, her head and knees. A hand, seemingly from behind me, strikes me heavily. I think I can distinguish its fingers and this is repeated a second time. I hold the left hand firmly, Imoda holding the right, which I frequently verify by touch. The objects were taken from the cupboard behind, a thimble was put on the first finger of my left hand, a sheath [étui] was put on my nose, and I felt fingers touching my nose and face."

Richet compared her phenomena to that of **Eusapia Palladino:**

"Telekinetic experiments succeed well with Linda as she is more easily controlled than Eusapia, for she scarcely moves at all, while Eusapia is in continual jerky movement. In the first experiment the ectoplasmic hand that I felt was cold and stiff; in the fourth experiment it was warm, articulated and supple."

A notable feature of Gazzera's mediumship was the rapidity with which phenomena were manifest, often within a few moments of the light being extinguished during dark séances. Richet's colleague **Guillaume de Fontenay** took some excellent photographs of phenomena, and Richet enthusiastically endorsed her mediumship as genuine.

Sources:

Imoda, Enrico. *Fotographie di fantasma.* Turin, 1912.

Gbalo

A former order of priests among the Ga people of the Gold Coast, west of Togoland in West Africa.

Geber (d. ca. 776 C.E.)

Arabian alchemist whose real name has been variously stated as Dschabir Ben Hayyan or Abou Moussah Djafar al Sofi. According to the tenth-century *Kitab-al-Fihrist,* Geber was born at Tarsus and lived at Damascus and Kufa. Very little is known of his early life. He undertook wide experiments in metallurgy and chemistry with the object of discovering the constituent elements of metals, in the course of which he stumbled upon nitric acid and red oxide of mercury. It is upon such actual discoveries that his reputation is based, not upon the many spurious treatises that have been attributed to him and embrace the entire gamut of eighth-century science.

His alleged extant works, which are in Latin, are regarded with suspicion, especially since several other medieval writers adopted his name. It is believed, however, that the library at Leyden and the Imperial Library at Paris contain Arabic manuscripts that might have been written by him. His books *Sum of Perfection* and *Investigation into the Perfection of Metals* are his most important works. Complete editions were published at Dantzic in 1682 and are included in the *Bibliotheca Chemica Curiosa* of Mangetus, published at Cologne in 1702.

Sum of Perfection professes to draw its inspiration from alchemical authors who lived before Geber, but because **alchemy** was not advanced at that time the derivation is an unlikely one. The book states that success in the great art is only to be achieved by rigid adherence to natural law. A spirit of great strength and a dry water are spoken of as the elements of the natural principle. The philosophical furnace and its arrangement are dealt with in detail, as is the "philosopher's vessel," a glass vase with several intricate details.

Sources:

Federman, Reinhold. *The Royal Road of Alchemy.* New York: Chilton, 1969.

Gehenna

One of the words in the Christian New Testament for hell, the place of destruction. The word is derived from the Hebrew *ge* and *hinnom,* the Valley of Hinnom—originally a valley in Palestine where the Hebrews passed their children through the fire to Moloch, the god of the Ammonites (1 Kings 11; 2 Kings 23:10).

Gehenna was popularly regarded as a place of destruction to which the wicked were consigned when they died (Matt. 18:7–8). Gehenna is usually translated as "hell fire" in the New Testament (Mark 9:43; Luke 12:5). Over the centuries it was merged with other terms for the abode of the dead, and through the writings of novelists such as Dante and John Milton the Christian world was given a description of hell as a place of unutterable anguish, horror, and despair.

The locality of hell and the duration of its torments have for centuries been the subject of much speculation. Some imagined there was a purgatorial region—a kind of upper Gehenna "in which the souls of just men are cleansed by a temporary punishment" before being admitted to heaven. It was believed that during this period the soul could revisit the places and persons it had loved. The Persians understood Gehenna as the place inhabited by the **divs** (rebellious angels), to which the rebels were confined when they refused to bow down before the first man.

Geley, Gustav (1868–1924)

Distinguished French psychical researcher. Geley was born in 1868 at Montceau-les-Mines, France, and became a physician. In his first book, *l'Etre Subconscient* (1899), he expounded a theory of "dynamo-psychism," a sort of soul energy by which he sought to escape from the difficulties of materialistic philosophy. In his second book, *De l'Inconscient au Conscient* (1919), published in English as *From the Unconscious to the Conscious,* he developed his idea into a more comprehensive treatise and admitted an external direction and intention in the phenomena of trance that could not be referred to the medium or the experimenters.

Shortly before the publication of his second book, which is considered by many the most important contribution to psychical research since **F. W. H. Myers**'s *Human Personality and its Survival of Bodily Death* (1903), Geley abandoned his medical practice at Annecy and accepted the post of director of the **Institut Métapsychique International** founded by Jean Meyer.

Geley was a keen and indefatigable investigator. When, under fraud-proof circumstances, paranormal results were apparently produced in his laboratory, he had to defend himself against the accusation of medical colleagues that he was an accomplice of the medium. He consented to having his premises examined for secret doors and to being chained up with other investigators.

The most palpable evidence he produced for the reality of metapsychical phenomena were plaster casts from the mediumship of **Franek Kluski,** which were put on view in the institute. Geley's last book, *L'Ectoplasmie et la Clairvoyance* (1924), based chiefly on his experiences with **Eva C.,** marked another milestone in psychical research. It was to have been followed by a second volume, "The Genesis and Meaning of Metapsychic Phenomena," which, unfortunately, was never written because of Geley's death in an airplane accident on July 15, 1924.

Geley was essentially a spiritist, because he accepted the reality of **survival, reincarnation,** and communication with the dead. He was careful not to declare his opinion on subjects that would have alienated the scientific community. However, his belief system seems to have made him a target for tricks by the mediums he studied and, in the end, capable of suppressing negative evidence. After his death it was reported that some very suspicious photographs of the mediumship of Eva C. were found among his papers, and it was suggested that these indicated the possibility of **fraud.** For a discussion of the facts and speculations involved, see Rudolf Lambert's article in the November 1954 issue of the *Journal* of the Society for Psychical Research.

Sources:

Geley, Gustave. *L'Etre Subconscient.* Paris: Editions Pygmalion, 1899.

———. *De l'Inconscient au Conscient.* Paris: F. Alcan, 1919. Translated as *From the Unconscious to the Conscious.* New York and London: Harper & Brothers, 1921.

Lambert, Rudolf. "Dr. Geley's Reports on the Medium 'Eva C.'" *Journal* of the Society for Psychical Research 37, 682 (November 1954).

Geller, Uri (1946–)

One of the most famous exponents of claimed ESP and paranormal phenomena in the 1970s. Geller was born in Tel Aviv, Israel, December 20, 1946. As a boy he performed feats of stopping the hands of watches through paranormal means. In 1969 he demonstrated **telepathy** and became a full-time professional performer. In August 1971 his feats were witnessed in Tel Aviv by parapsychologist **Andrija Puharich,** who then became closely associated with Geller, assisted him in traveling to America, and conducted scientific investigations of his phenomena.

At the Stanford Research Institute, California, during November 1972 Geller demonstrated **metal bending,** guessing contents of metal cans and numbers on dice (shaken in a closed box), and telepathy. Some of the tests were supervised by former astronaut **Edgar D. Mitchell,** who had become actively involved in the study of paranormal phenomena. The most publicized talent demonstrated by Geller was the ability to cause metal objects to bend or break without direct physical pressure—the so-called **Geller effect,** a form of **telekinesis.** This deformation of metals (particularly the bending of forks, spoons, nails, or keys) was demonstrated on television programs in the United States and Britain. During such television shows in Britain many viewers reported that they shared the same ability. Geller also involved viewers in the starting of clocks and watches that had not functioned for some time.

In his book *Uri,* a biography published in 1974, Puharich claims that Geller's powers came from outer space intelligences on a planet millions of light-years distant, and also claims that Geller dematerialized objects. Geller's autobiography, published soon afterward, claims additional phenomena such as **teleportation.** While some American and British scientists reported favorably on Geller phenomena, some commentators (notably stage magicians **Milbourne Christopher** of the Occult Investigation Committee of the Society of American Magicians and **James Randi** of the **Committee for the Scientific Investigation of Claims of the Paranormal**) alleged sleight of hand and other conjuring tricks as the probable explanation. In 1983 it was revealed that James Randi had organized fake metal-bending accomplices in an undercover operation to discredit parapsychologists investigating the phenomenon. In 1991, in response to a remark by Randi accusing Geller of fakery, Geller filed a multimillion-dollar lawsuit claiming defamation. As of 1994, that suit was still under adjudication.

The strongest scientific support for the reality of Geller's phenomena came from British mathematician **John Taylor,** who tested Geller during 1974 and also investigated children and adults who manifested similar paranormal ability after seeing Geller's appearances on British television programs. However, Taylor, a distinguished scientist, largely retracted his support of Geller's phenomena in his book *Science and the Supernatural* (1980). Another British scientist, **John Hasted,** was more sympathetic to the genuineness of the "Geller effect."

After Geller's visit to Tokyo in 1973, thousands of Japanese children apparently manifested similar paranormal powers. Eight of these children were investigated in 1974 by Shigemi Sasaki, professor of psychology at Denki Tsushin University, Tokyo, with a team of 15 researchers. Laboratory tests were devised to test PK (psychokinetic ability) and metal bending. One 12-year-old, Jun Sekiguchi, demonstrated an amazing ability to bend spoons paranormally and also recharged dead electric batteries by merely holding them. **J. B. Rhine** of Durham, North Carolina, commented: "The tests in Tokyo have shown that PK power exists among many of their children. The research is of great significance."

In the mid–1970s, at the height of his fame, Geller was earning approximately $5,000 a session for his media performances involving spoon bending, telepathy, and clock or watch restarting, generating intense public enthusiasm and also hostile criticism from stage **magicians** and other critics who claimed that his apparently paranormal feats were ingenious trickery. At the height of worldwide interest in his claimed powers, Geller suddenly disappeared from the public scene for ten years. There were various rumors—that he had lost his powers, that he had been finally exposed in **fraud** and silenced, or even that he had been recruited for secret psychic warfare.

In 1986 the newspaper *Financial Times* (a British equivalent of the *Wall Street Journal*) published a report by Margaret van Hatten revealing that in 1974 Geller had been persuaded to put his psychic talents at the disposal of industrialists by **dowsing** for oil and minerals. The report stated that Geller had met the late Sir Val Duncan, then head of the prestigious Rio Tinto-Zinc Corporation and himself an amateur dowser, who suggested that Geller try psychic prospecting. At Duncan's homes in Britain and Majorca, Geller experimented successfully with dowsing for bottles of olive oil and mineral objects that had been buried in gardens. From this Geller progressed to experimenting with dowsing over scale maps (*teleradiesthesia*) and distinguishing the various types of valuable mineral deposits in different parts of the world.

When Geller developed accuracy in dowsing Duncan eventually told him, "You're on your own—go out and make some money." Geller's first attempts at dowsing for a South African mining group were given free of charge although they apparently resulted in a large-scale discovery of coal deposits near Zimbabwe. In time Geller had sufficient confidence to ask for a standard fee of one million pounds sterling as an advance against royalties. Geller says he has always found something, even if not a mineral deposit of commercial viability. Of 11 projects over ten years, he maintains that four were highly successful, resulting in royalties way beyond the original one million pound advance. He also advised companies where drilling would be ineffective, so they could save money.

In general, oil and mining companies have been reluctant to substantiate these remarkable claims. Understandably, directors and shareholders might feel that this expensive and unconventional method of prospecting sounds bizarre. Peter Sterling, chairman of Zanex, an Australian mineral exploration company, did confirm, however, that Geller was flown to the Solomon Islands to help pinpoint gold deposits, at Geller's standard fee, and that the company was successful in finding alluvial gold in the Solomons. In addition the company sent Geller some topographical maps and received the response that the company should look for diamonds on Malaita. Although the company had never considered that area to be geologically appropriate for diamonds, Geller insisted, and samples taken there were "very encouraging," according to Sterling. Diamond-like kimberlite rock was located, as were all the minerals usually associated with diamond deposits.

The *Financial Times* report quoted Peter Sterling as stating that it was not easy to explain the employment of Geller to his board of directors and shareholders. He said:

"Most mining people are pretty down to earth and materialistic, and the sort of work Uri does doesn't fit current scientific knowledge. I'm an engineer—I have no idea how it works, though I think that in 20 to 30 years time science will know, and will be building machines to do the same thing. But now—well the reaction is a bit like witch hunters in the dark ages, or flat earthers. There are a lot of flat earthers around."

In October 1986 Geller launched a new book, cowritten with parapsychologist Guy Lyon Playfair, titled *The Geller Effect.* The book tells Geller's story from 1976 to 1986, recounting jet-set friendships, approaches by the CIA, FBI, customs, and narcotics agents, and Geller's activities in prospecting for mining companies. To publicize the book Geller appeared on television talk shows where he presented exactly the same phenomena he had ten years earlier—spoon bending, telepathy, and starting clocks and watches that had been inactive for a long time. Many of these performances were quite impressive, although staged informally without rigid controls. Coming in the same breath as the revelations about million-pound fees, these familiar activities were something of an anticlimax. Stage magicians can and do duplicate such effects under similar circumstances by conjuring.

From time to time, sensational reports are circulated that Geller significantly changed the course of world events, such as mentally influencing Gorbachev's top aide so that the Soviet leader made an offer of dramatic cuts in nuclear weapons. It seems more credible that the Soviets would be influenced by traditional diplomacy or the enlightened efforts of such private negotiators as the late Armand Hammer.

Geller's book itself offers little new material to resolve the fierce controversies over the genuineness of his talents beyond his anecdotal claims and the reputed faith of wealthy and highly placed friends or officials of mining companies. In it he tries to distance himself from (without denying) some of the more sensational claims Puharich makes in his 1974 biography, for instance, that Geller was an instrument of extraterrestrial intelligences. Geller writes:

"Although much of his [Puharich's] book was accurate factual reporting, many people were put off by the space-fantasy passages, and I admit that they caused me some embarrassment. . . . You must remember that all of this fantasy material was obtained while I was under hypnosis. One reason I wrote *My Story* was to give my own version of events, though I must emphasize that there is a slight possibility that some of my energies do have extraterrestrial connection. Andrija and I are still the closest of friends and I have never forgotten how much of my success is due to him."

Sources:

Christopher, Milbourne. *Mediums, Mystics & the Occult.* New York: Thomas Y. Crowell, 1975.

Geller, Uri. *My Story.* New York: Praeger, 1975.

Geller, Uri, and Guy Lyon Playfair. *The Geller Effect.* London: Jonathan Cape, 1986.

Hasted, John. *The Metal-Benders.* London: Routledge & Kegan Paul, 1981.

Panati, Charles, ed. *The Geller Papers.* Boston: Houghton Mifflin, 1976.

Randi, James. *The Truth about Uri Geller.* Buffalo, N.Y.: Prometheus Books, 1982.

Taylor, John. *Science & the Supernatural.* London: Temple Smith, 1980.

———. *Superminds: An Investigation into the Paranormal.* New York: Warner Books, 1975.

Geller Effect

Term used to indicate the apparent ability to bend metal paranormally, as in the demonstrations by **Uri Geller.** Alternative terms used are **metal bending** or "PK-MB" (psychokinesis-metal bending).

Gematria

A form of **numerology.** In Jewish mysticism gematria was the study of Hebrew letters in association with numbers. The method was used to discover hidden meanings in Hebrew words. Prominent words could be systematically converted into numbers and linked to other words with the same numerical value, which were then regarded as comments upon the original words. This kind of numerology was also used with the Greek alphabet.

A related system of gematria is *Notarikon,* in which letters taken from phrases form mystical acronyms, or words are developed into mystical phrases. A more complicated procedure is *temurah,* in which letters of words are transposed or replaced according to complex rules. Some modern occultists have applied gematria to the **tarot** cards, associating the 22 trump cards with the Hebrew letters, a practice suggested by **Éliphas Lévi,** author of *The History of Magic* (1913).

Gematria became an integral part of modern ceremonial magic as practiced in the Hermetic Order of the **Golden Dawn** and by **Aleister Crowley.** Crowley and **William Westcott** of the Golden Dawn wrote several books on the subject, and Crowley published a key word guide to numerological meanings of words titled *777.*

Sources:

Bond, Bligh, and Thomas Simcox Lea. *Gematria: A Preliminary Investigation of the Cabala.* London: Research into Lost Knowledge Organization, 1977.

Crowley, Aleister. 777. London: Walter Scott Publishing, 1909. Revised as *777 Revised.* London: Neptune Press, 1952.

Ginsburg, Christian D. *The Kabbalah* (with *The Essenes*). London: Routledge, 1863. Reprint, New York: Samuel Weiser, 1970.

Kozminsky, Isidore. *Numbers—Their Meaning and Magic.* New York: Samuel Weiser, n.d.

Westcott, William W. *An Introduction to the Study of the Kabalah.* New York: Allied Publications, n.d.

———. *Numbers: Their Occult Power and Mystic Virtues.* New York: Allied Publications, n.d.

General Assembly of Spiritualists

The General Assembly of Spiritualists originated in 1930 when its members withdrew from the National Spiritualist Association of Churches (NSAC) and reorganized independently. The NSAC was in the midst of a reoccurring debate over **reincarnation.** The traditional Spiritualist position in North America and England opposed reincarnation, which seemed to deny the possibility of spirit contact (if the spirit was reincarnated). However, a belief in reincarnation had become entrenched in the New York area. The Declaration of Principle of the General Assembly of Spiritualists is identical to that of the parent body except that it lacks the statement on prophecy, which was only added to the NSAC statement after the schism. The General Assembly of Spiritualists is headquartered at the Ansonia Hotel, 2107 Broadway, New York, NY 10023.

Sources:

General Assembly of Spiritualists, State of New York. New York: Flying Saucer News, n.d.

Lomaxe, Paul R. *What Do Spiritualists Believe?* New York: General Assembly of Spiritualists, 1943.

General Church of the New Jerusalem

The General Church of the New Jerusalem is the largest of the several churches in North America that have grown out of the teachings of **Emanuel Swedenborg** (1688–1772). Its origins can be traced ultimately to the 1838 decree adopted by the **General Convention of the New Jerusalem** requiring all member societies to organize under the same rule of order. Rev. George De Charms, then pastor of the society in Philadelphia and editor of an influential magazine, the *Precursor,* rejected the new rule, which he saw as a move by the Boston headquarters church to set itself up as the mother church of the convention and require all societies to acknowledge its primacy. De Charms and his congregation left the convention, and in 1840 he founded the Central Convention, which emphasized the writings of Swedenborg.

In reaction, the General Convention changed its rules. It loosened its control over the societies, adopted a structure granting more equitable representation from the societies, and renounced any spiritual authority inherent in the Boston headquarters. With his basic objection now resolved, De Charms dissolved the Central Convention in 1852 and his Philadelphia church and rejoined the General Convention.

The independent impulse of the Central Convention was preserved, however, by William Benade, a young pastor who—like De Charms—stressed the authority of Swedenborg's writings. In 1859 he proposed the formation of an academy of scholars to study Swedenborg's writings and to train young men for the priesthood. The idea of a priesthood was plainly stated in Swedenborg's writings, but the General Convention never implemented it as many did not like the idea of priests.

Benade formed the academy in 1874 and started a periodical, *Words for the New Church.* Over the years it developed a unique stance within the convention, with controversy centering on its liberal view of sexuality and its stance against temperance. A break between the academy and the convention occurred in stages beginning with the formation of a school in Philadelphia. In 1882 Benade became a bishop of the church in Philadelphia, which included seven societies. Other societies favorable to Benade's views associated themselves with the Philadelphia church. The final break came in 1890, and those affiliated with the academy reorganized as the General Church of the New Jerusalem.

The church is headed by its bishops and a general assembly who elect the national church officers. Affiliated congregations are found in Europe, Australia and New Zealand, South Africa, and Brazil. In the 1980s there were 2,618 members and 31 congregations in North America and an additional 1,157 members worldwide. Headquarters are located in suburban Philadelphia in the small community of Bryn Athyn, PA 19009.

Sources:

De Charms, George. *The Distinctiveness of the New Church.* Bryn Athyn, Pa.: Academy Book Room, 1962.

The General Church of the New Jerusalem: A Handbook of General Information. Bryn Athyn, Pa.: General Church Publication Committee, 1965.

General Convention of the New Jerusalem in the United States of America

The ecclesiastical organization that grew out of the response to the writings of seer **Emanuel Swedenborg** (1688–1772). It began in the United States in 1792 when members of the New Church migrated from England to Baltimore, Maryland, and formed the first society. Over the next 25 years, 17 societies formed in cities along the East Coast and as far west as Madison Town, Indiana. These were brought together for a convention in 1817 following a call from the society in Philadelphia. At that time delegates regularized the ordination of ministers and strategized on spreading their message west of the Allegheny Mountains. The church spread across the eastern half of the United States through the 1800s, but it was severely weakened by a schism in 1890 which led to the founding of the **General Church of the New Jerusalem.**

The organization is a Christian one, but it interprets the Bible and Christian doctrine according to Swedenborg's basic perspective. Swedenborg believed the Bible to have two levels of meaning, the material and the spiritual. He learned the true spiritual meaning of the Bible from his conversations with the angels, the results of which fill numerous volumes. Swedenborg compiled a condensed statement of his belief in a small booklet, *The New Jerusalem and Its Heavenly Doctrine,* which serves as a doctrinal statement for the convention.

The convention believes in a divine Trinity, not of persons, but of principle. Salvation is open to all who cooperate with God by faith and obedience. When people die, they immediately pass to judgment and enter either heaven or hell, their fate depending on the spiritual character they acquired on earth. Worship is liturgical, and both the Lord's Supper and baptism are administered.

The church is organized with a modified episcopacy. Local societies manage their own affairs. The convention meets annually and elects a president and other national officers. A board of missions oversees work in Europe, Japan, and Guyana. In 1990 there were 1,546 members and 35 societies in the United States and 460 members and 10 societies in Canada. The convention is headquartered at 48 Sargent St., Newton, MA 02158.

Sources:

Zacharias, Paul. *Insights into the Beyond.* New York: Swedenborg Publishing Association, n.d.

Genesa Update

Newsletter of the Genesa Foundation, concerned with energies generated by pyramidical and other geometrical shapes. Address: P.O. Box 327, Bonsall, CA 92003.

Genius

Generally used to denote a human being of extraordinary intelligence, but historically indicating a superior class of entities holding an intermediate rank between mortals and immortals. The latter meaning appears to be the signification of *daemon,* the corresponding term in Greek. It is probable that the whole system of **demonology** was invented by the Platonic philosophers and grafted by degrees onto popular mythology.

The Platonists, however, professed to derive their doctrines from the "theology of the ancients," so this system may have come originally from the East, where it formed a part of the tenets of Zoroaster. This sage ascribed all the operations of nature to the agency of celestial beings, the ministers of one supreme first cause, to whose brilliant image—fire—homage was paid.

Some Roman writers referred to the *genius* as "the God of Nature," or "Nature" itself, but their notions seem to have been modified by, if not formed from, etymological considerations more likely to mislead than to afford a clue to the real meaning of the term. At a later period they supposed almost every created thing, animate or inanimate, to be protected by its guardian genius—a sort of demigod who presided over its birth and was its constant companion until death. Censorinus, who lived about the middle of the third century, noted:

"The *genius* is a god supposed to be attendant on everyone from the time of his birth.... Many think the *genius* to be the same as the *lars* of the ancients.... We may well believe that its power over us is great, yea, absolute.... Some ascribe two *genii* at least to those who live in the houses of married persons."

Euclid, the Socratic philosopher, gave two genii to everyone, a point on which Lucilius, in his *Satires,* insists we cannot be informed.

To the genius, therefore, so powerful through the whole course of one's life, yearly sacrifices were offered. As the birth of every mortal was a peculiar object of his guardian genius's solicitude, the marriage bed was called the genial bed (*lectus genialis*). The same invisible patron was also supposed to be the author of joy and hilarity, hence a joyous life was called a genial life (*genialis vita*).

There is a curious passage relating to the functions of the Greek demons in the *Symposium* of Plato, in which he has Socrates state:

"... from it [i.e., the agency of genii] proceed all the arts of divination, and all the science of priests, with respect to sacrifices, initiations, incantations, and everything, in short, which relates to oracles and enchantments. The deity holds no direct intercourse with man; but, by this means, all the converse and communications between gods and men, whether asleep or awake, take place; and he who is wise in these things is a man peculiarly guided by his *genius.*"

Plato highlights the connection between demonology and **magic,** an association characteristic of the romances of the East if the **jinns** of the Moslems are compared to the genii of the Platonists.

A modern understanding of the term *genius* is well illustrated by **F. W. H. Myers** in his book *Human Personality and its Survival of Bodily Death* (1903):

"Genius should be regarded as a power of utilising a wider range than other men can utilise of faculties in some degree innate in all; a power of appropriating the results of subliminal mentation to subserve the supraliminal stream of thought; so that an 'inspiration of genius' will be in truth a subliminal uprush, an emergence into the current of ideas which the man is consciously manipulating of other ideas which he has not consciously originated but which have shaped themselves beyond his will, in profounder regions of his being."

Theodore Flournoy said he considered Myers's chapter on genius one of the most remarkable and strongest of the work because it made one feel the insufficiency of all the naturalistic explanations advanced up to that time.

In *The Road to Immortality* (1932), claimed to be composed of posthumous communications from Myers through the mediumship of **Geraldine Cummins,** the discarnate "Myers" expands on genius with reference to the idea of a **group-soul:**

"If a certain type of psyche is continually being evolved in the one group, you will find that eventually that type, if it be musical, will have a musical genius as its representative on earth. It will harvest all the tendencies in those vanished lives, and it will then have the amazing unconscious knowledge that is the property of genius."

The often-quoted dictums of Jane Ellice Hopkins, "Genius only means an infinite capacity for taking pains," and Thomas Edison, "genius is one percent inspiration and ninety-nine percent perspiration," draw attention to the phenomenon that prolonged absorption and study often result in an inspirational leap of awareness and insight. Many new concepts and discoveries have taken place in this way. This is comparable to the mystic's experience in which meditation leads to enhancement of consciousness, sometimes to ecstatic conditions of so-called cosmic consciousness.

Sources:

Cummins, Geraldine. *The Road to Immortality.* London: Ivor Nicholson & Watson, 1933.

Galton, Francis. *Hereditary Genius.* London, 1869. Reprint, London: Watts, 1950.

Kenmore, Dallas. *The Nature of Genius.* Westport, Conn.: Greenwood Press, 1972.

Lombroso, Cesare. *The Man of Genius.* London: Scott, 1889.

Storr, Anthony. *The School of Genius.* London: A. Deutsch, 1988.

Geomancy

A system of divination by means of scattering pebbles, dust, sand grains, or seeds on the earth and interpreting their shape and position. A later development by occultist **Cornelius Agrippa** involved making marks on the ground with a stick (currently practiced with a pencil on paper). Interpretations are partly intuitive and partly by means of a system of positions reminiscent of the **I Ching** hexagrams.

The term *Geomancy* is also applied to the Chinese practice of *feng-shui* (wind and water), and was used by nineteenth-century writers to translate feng-shui. This Chinese art is concerned with the relationship between human beings and the subtle energies of nature. In classical Chinese sources the term *ti li* (land patterns) was also used; another related term is *kan-yü* (cover or support), with special reference to relationships between heaven and earth.

Feng-shui and ti li are concerned with the "dragon lines" or subtle energies of the earth in relation to the placement of buildings and the interaction between human life and earth currents. Feng-shui experts would determine the most suitable places for roads, bridges, canals, wells, and mines in relation to earth currents; the sites of graves were especially important. Bodies might be kept unburied for some time until a suitable burial place with harmonious currents was determined, and in some cases bodies were reburied.

It seems likely that the Western form of geomancy for divinatory purposes grew out of feng-shui concepts, since the position of pebbles, dust, or seeds has something in common with **acupuncture** pressure points on the "body" of nature and its energies. Chinese concepts of the subtle energies of the earth also parallel the Western concepts of **leys** and **dowsing.**

Sources:

Asher, Maxine. *Ancient Energy: Key to the Universe.* New York: Harper & Row, 1979.

Cole, J. A. Abayomi. *Astrological Geomancy in Africa.* London, 1898.

Hartmann, Franz. *Geomancy: The Art of Divining by Punctuation According to Cornelius Agrippa and Others.* London: William Rider & Son, 1913.

Pennick, Nigel. *Geomancy.* Cambridge: Cokayne Publishing, 1973.

Skinner, Stephen. *The Oracle of Geomancy.* London: Routledge & Kegan Paul, 1977.

———. *Terrestrial Astrology: Divination by Geomancy.* London: Routledge & Kegan Paul, 1980.

Watkins, Alfred. *The Old Straight Track.* 1925. Reprint, London: Garnstone Press, 1970.

George, Llewellyn (1876–1954)

Prominent astrologer and founder of the Llewellyn Publishing Company. He was born in Swansea, Wales, on August 17, 1876. After his father's death his mother remarried and the family moved to the United States. He grew up in Chicago, but moved to Portland, Oregon, around the turn of the century. He studied **astrology** with L. H. Weston and in 1901 founded the Llewellyn Publishing Company and the Portland School of Astrology. In 1908 he began issuing the *Astrological Bulletina.* He later moved his business to Los Angeles.

George emerged as the champion of a more scientific astrology. He attempted to move away from an astrology based on hermetic philosophy and build instead upon newer understandings of gravitational and other forces operating in the solar system. Eventually, however, as science had little to offer, he had to fall back on occult speculations.

George wrote a score of works on astrology, beginning with, *The Planetary Hour Book* in 1907. He followed with a set of books to assist the new astrological student, *The A to Z Horoscope Delineator* (1910), *Practical Astrology for Everyone* (1911), and *The Student's Chart Reader* (1912). Among his more important books are *How Planets Affect People* (1921) and *Astrology: What It Is and What It Is Not* (1931).

His most well known publications are the *Moon Sign Book* (published annually since 1905) and the *Astrological Bulletin,* a quarterly magazine, which he edited for nearly twenty years. He also founded the Llewellyn College of Astrology, which greatly expanded the audience for astrology by offering home study courses.

Llewellyn Publications emerged as a major center of astrological publishing. Prominent astrologers published by George over the years include Donald Bradley (*Solar and Lunar Returns*) and Grant Lewi (*Astrology for the Millions* and *Heaven Knows What*).

After George's death in 1954, the *Moon Sign Book* was edited by **Sydney Omarr.** In 1960 the company was purchased by Minnesota businessman **Carl Llewellyn Weschcke,** well known as an astrologer and occultist, who moved the company to St. Paul, Minnesota, as **Llewellyn Publications,** now one of the largest publishing and wholesaling organizations of occult books in the United States.

Sources:

George, Llewellyn. *The A to Z Horoscope Delineator.* Portland, Oreg.: Portland School of Astrology, 1910.

———. *Astrology: What It Is and What It Is Not.* Los Angeles: Llewellyn Publishing, 1931.

———. *How Planets Affect People.* Los Angeles: Llewellyn Publishing, 1921.

———. *Practical Astrology for Everyone.* Portland, Oreg.: Portland School of Astrology Bulletina Publishing, 1911.

———. *The Student's Chart Reader.* Portland, Oreg.: Portland School of Astrology Bulletina Press, 1912.

Lewis, James R. *The Astrology Encyclopedia.* Detroit: Gale Research, 1994.

George Adamski Foundation

Foundation formed after the death of flying saucer contactee **George Adamski** (1891–1965) in 1965 to keep his work alive, especially his philosophical teachings. It was founded by Alice Wells (d. 1980), a close associate. She was succeeded in leadership by Fred Steckling. The foundation is headquartered in Vista, California.

Sources:

Adamski, George. *Cosmic Philosophy.* Freeman, S.D.: Pine Hill Press, 1971.

———. *Wisdom of the Masters of the Far East.* N.p.: Royal Order of Tibet, 1936.

Steckling, Fred. *We Discovered Alien Bases on the Moon.* Vista, Calif.: GAF International Publishers, 1981.

———. *Why Are We Here?* New York: Vantage Press, 1969.

Gerhardie, William (Alexander) (1895–1977)

Famous British novelist who was also intensely preoccupied with the paranormal. He was born William Gerhardi, on November 21, 1895, in St. Petersburg, Russia, of British subjects. He was educated in St. Petersburg (1900–13), Kensington College, London (1913–16), and Worcester College, Oxford (M.A., B. Litt.). He added an *e* to his name in 1971.

His novels include *Futility* (1922), *The Polyglots* (1925), *Pending Heaven* (1930), *Resurrection* (1934), *Of Mortal Love* (1937), *My Wife's the Least of It* (1938), and *This Present Breath* (4 vols., 1975). He also wrote several plays as well as volumes of short stories and miscellaneous literature. A gifted author, he was awarded an Order of the British Empire and an Order of St. Stanislas of Russia.

An acute observer of the tragedy and comedy of human intercourse, Gerhardie gave little hint in his books of his profound interest in psychic manifestations, **extrasensory perception, bilocation, synchronicity,** time anomalies, and other aspects of the paranormal. Only a few friends were aware of such preoccupations, and since Gerhardie lived a hermitlike existence, seldom leaving his London apartment, he held long telephone conversations with his friends on a wide range of anomalous topics.

His novel *Resurrection* relates his own **out-of-the-body travel** experience, which must have had a profound effect on his philosophy of life and death. He died July 15, 1977.

Sources:

Gerhardie, William A. *Memoirs of a Polyglot.* London: Macdonald, 1973.

———. *The Memoirs of Satan.* Garden City, N.Y.: Doubleday, Doran, 1933.

———. *Resurrection.* London: Macdonald, 1973.

Gerloff, Hans (1887– ?)

Teacher, author, and parapsychologist. Born May 31, 1887, in Berlin, Germany, he obtained his Ph.D. from the University of Jena in 1911. Gerloff lectured on German language and literature at the University of Lund, Sweden (1912–13 and 1915–16), before becoming a cultural exchange officer in Germany and Scandinavia (1916–37).

In 1932 Gerloff began a special study of physical mediumship and worked with **Einer Nielsen** and Anna Rasmussen in Copenhagen, Maria Sukfull in Austria, and Hela Zimmermann in Germany. He lectured on parapsychology throughout Europe and wrote a number of books, his work being ended by the rise of Nazi power in his homeland. Gerloff also contributed articles on parapsychology to *Natur und Kulter* and *Neue Wissenschaft.*

Sources:

Gerloff, Hans. *The Crisis in Parapsychology: Stagnation or Progress?* Tittmoning, Obb., Germany: W. Pustet, 1965.

———. *Die Heilungen von Lourdes im Lichte der Parapsychologie* (The Healings at Lourdes in the Light of Parapsychology). Budingen-Geltenbach: Verlag Welt und Wissen, 1959.

———. *Materialisation: Die Phantome von Kopenhagen* (Materialization: The Phantoms of Copenhagen). N.p., 1956.

———. *Das Medium Carlos Mirabelli: Eine kirtische Untersuchung* (The Medium Carlos Mirabelli: An Investigation.) N.p., 1960.

Pleasants, Helene, ed. *Biographical Dictionary of Parapsychology.* New York: Helix Press, 1964.

Germain, Walter (1889–1962)

American author who wrote and lectured on **parapsychology.** Born February 23, 1889, at Saginaw, Michigan, Germain worked as a businessman, and from 1930 to 1950 was an officer with the Saginaw Police Department. In 1950 he began writing on **ESP** and other aspects of parapsychology. He describes his own experiences in his book *The Magic Power of Your Mind* (1956). He also contributed articles to *Fate* magazine and *Science of Mind.* He died June 22, 1962, at Saginaw.

Sources:

Germain, Walter. *The Magic Power of Your Mind.* New York: Hawthorn Books, 1956.

GERMANY

Magic & Witchcraft

For an account of the magical beliefs of the early Teutonic peoples, see the entry on **Teutons.** Magic as formulated and believed in by the Germans in the Middle Ages bears, along with traces of its unmistakable derivation from the ancient Teutonic religion, the impress of the influence brought by the natural characteristics of the country upon the mind of its inhabitants.

Deep forests, mountains, limitless morasses, caverned rocks, and springs all helped to shape the imagination which may be traced in Teutonic mythology, and later in aspects of **magic** and in Christian fears of **witchcraft,** which first arose in Germany and obtained ready credence there.

As the clash and strife of Teuton and Roman, of Christian and others left records in folklore and history, so they have also characterized the magical belief of the Middle Ages. Earlier monkish legends are replete with accounts of magic and sorcery, indicating how ancient deities became evil following the introduction of the newer religion. Miracles were recounted, where these evil ones were robbed of all power in the name of Christ, or before some blessed relic, then chained and prisoned beneath mountain, river, and sea in eternal darkness. At the same time, tales were told of how misfortune and death were the consequence to those who still might follow the outcast gods.

Again, the sites and periods of the great religious festivals of the Teutons were perpetuated in those localities said to be the place and time of the witches' sabbat and other mysterious meetings and conclaves. Mountains especially retained this character. The Venusberg, the Horselberg, and Blocksberg now became the Devil's realm and an abode of the damned. Chapels and cathedrals were full of relics to exorcise the spirits of evil, while the bells must be blessed, as ordained by the Council of Cologne, in order that "demons might be affrighted by their sound, calling Christians to prayers; and when they fled, the persons of the faithful would be secure; that the destruction of lightnings and whirlwinds would be averted, and the spirits of the storm defeated."

Storms were held to be the work of the devil, or the conjuration of his followers. In their fury might be heard the trampling of his infernal train above the tossing forests or holy spires, and thus were Odin and his associated deities transformed.

In like measure the Valkyries, the Choosers of the Slain, riding to places of battle, became the medieval witches riding astride broomsticks on their missions of evil. Castles of flames, where the devil held wild revels; conclaves of corpses revivified by evil knowledge; unearthly growths, vitalized by hanged men's souls, springing to life beneath gallows and gibbets; little men of the hills, malicious spirits, with their caps of mist and cloaks of invisibility; from these stories it is possible to trace the origins of the belief in dire consequences for those who believed in magic to the combination "heathen" and christian.

Witchcraft was at first derided as a delusion by church leaders, and belief in it was forbidden by some of the earlier councils. It was in the fourteenth century in the form of sorcery (malevolent magic), and then in the fifteenth and sixteenth centuries as witchcraft that it attained prominence, especially after the practice of witchcraft was declared a crime in the eyes of the Church (heresy and apostasy) in 1484—a crime punishable by confiscation and death. In their rumination on witchcraft the inquisitors first systematized and formulated an understanding of **black magic.** Under such authority, belief in black magic flourished, filling people with either an abject fear or unholy curiosity.

Once placed on the books, the motives for charging a person with sorcery and/or witchcraft were many besides that of care for their soul. Individuals otherwise involved in personal feuds, political enmities, and religious conflict, not to mention rulers facing empty treasuries, found the charges of black magic an unfailing and sure means of achieving their ends. For several centuries, the charges were hurled at high and low, and death the consequence.

The Council of Constance (1414) began with its proscription of the doctrines of Wyclif and the burning of John Huss and Jerome of Prague. Less known, at this time, too, a multivolume work was published by one of the inquisitors, called the *Formicarium,* a comprehensive list of the sins against religion. The fifth volume contained an account of **sorcery.** The list of crimes accomplished by witches was also detailed: second sight, the ability to read secrets and foretell events; the power to cause diseases and death by lightning and destructive storms; the ability to transform themselves into beasts and birds; and powers to bring about illicit love or barrenness of living beings and crops. Finally, it detailed their enmity against children and practice of devouring them (a crime often brought against socially proscribed groups).

Witchcraft Persecutions

Papal bulls appeared for the appointment of inquisitors, who must not be interfered with by the civil authorities, and the emperor and reigning princes took such under their protection. The persecutions rose to a ferocity unparalleled in other countries until the following century, and hundreds of alleged witches were burned in a few years. Immediately after the redefinition of witchcraft in 1484, two inquisitors, **Jakob Sprenger** and **Heinrich Kramer,** compiled the **Malleus Maleficarum** (first published in 1486), a complete system of witchcraft along with a detailed method of how to prove any accused capable and guilty of any and every crime.

Persecutions in Germany were intermittent throughout the fifteenth and sixteenth centuries, Germany being more concerned with the split occasioned by the activity of reformers Martin Luther and John Calvin. However, persecution broke out with renewed vigor in the seventeenth century stimulated by the increasing strife between Catholics and Protestants and the condition of the country, devastated by wars, plague, and famine. Two cities in particular, Bamberg and Würzburg, attained notoriety for trials and the number of victims.

In Bamberg, Prince-Bishop George II, and his suffragan Frederic Forner, prosecuted the holy inquisition with such energy that between the years 1625 and 1630 over 900 trials took place and some 600 people were burned. Confessions were extracted from the victims under extreme torture. Rich and poor were gathered into the jails, the number often being so great that names were never taken and written down, the prisoners being cited as No. 1, 2, 3, and so on.

In other parts of Germany, Lutheranism was gaining ground, and here the charge of sorcery was brought against its followers. Protestants had no disagreement with Roman Catholics on the issue of witchcraft. At Würzburg, the bishop, Philip Adolph, in 1623, did not prosecute them openly, but nevertheless acted against the accused. In Eberhard David Hauber's *Bibliotheca, Actaet Scripta Magica* (1738–45) is a list of 29 burnings from the 1620s. Each burning consisted of several victims, the numbers ranging from two up to ten or more, which included: old men and women; little girls and boys and infants; noble ladies; washerwomen; vicars; canons; singers and minstrels; Bannach, a senator; a wealthy man; a keeper of the pot-house; the bishop's own nephew and page; a huckster; and a blind girl.

At Würzburg, in 1749, the last trial for witchcraft took place, that of Maria Renata of the Convent of Unterzell. She was condemned and burned in June that year for consorting with the devil and being the focus of bewitchments and other infernal practices.

Toward the end of the seventeenth century, disbelief in the truth of witchcraft and criticism of the wholesale burnings began to be heard, although earlier than this some had dared to speak against the injustice and ignorance. Before 1593, Cornelius Saos, a priest in Mainz, had stated his doubt of the whole proceedings, but suffered for his temerity. **Johann Weyer,** physician to the Duke of Cleves, Thomas Erast, another physician, Adam Tanner, a Bavarian Jesuit, and Frederick Spree, also a Jesuit, all attempted to put forward rational views about witchcraft persecution.

Alchemy and Occultism

Alchemy, one medieval form of Gnosticism, was seen as operating from the realm of magic, and many believed it satanic in its derivation. Though few were charged unless caught in fraud for trying to make gold, alchemists were liable to the charge of sorcery and the death penalty if found guilty. Yet alchemy attracted emperors and princes who took up the study themselves, or, more frequently who hired well-known practitioners of the art. For example, Joachim I had **Johannes Trithemius** as teacher of **astrology** and "defender of magic," and the Emperor Rudolph employed **Michael Maier** as his physician.

Germany supplies numerous names famous for their discoveries in magic, men who by their philosophical pursuits were open to suspicion. Here we find **Paracelsus**—who in his search for the **elixir of life** discovered laudanum, a form of opium distilled from poppies; **Cornelius Agrippa; Basil Valentine,** prior and chemist; **Henry Khunrath,** physician and philosopher; and a host of students, all searching for the mysteries of life, the innermost secrets of nature.

Some people believed the activities of these men to be nothing more than infernal dealings and pacts with the devil. Such knowledge as the alchemists gained could only be acquired by infernal means, and religious people reasoned that the soul of the magician was the price promised and demanded by the Evil One. These myths and imaginings centered around one magician especially, and in the **Faust** legend we may find the general attitude and belief of the Middle Ages regarding the interaction of learning and supernatural beliefs.

Mystical Societies

While the alchemist conducted rudimentary scientific research, they were Gnostic mystics, as their writings testify. Their work fits into the larger Gnostic world whose exponents were **Rosicrucians** and theosophists. Among the more notable mystics was the shoemaker, **Jakob Boehme,** the son of peasants.

During the Thirty Years' War (1618–1648), many preachers, seers, and fanatics appeared, exhorting and prophesying. It is believed the condition of the country contributed towards producing the hallucination and hysteria. Reportedly there are accounts of ecstatics absorbed in supernatural visions, such as Anna Fleischer of Freiburg, and Christiana Poniatowitzsch, who traveled throughout Bohemia and Germany relating her visions and prophesing.

At the end of the seventeenth century the old tenets of magic were undergoing a gradual change, except alchemy. The Gnostic magical beliefs found new expression in secret societies, many of which were founded on those of the Middle Ages. **Freemasonry**—whose beginnings are attributed by some to a certain guild of masons banded together for the building of Strasburg Cathedral, but by other authorities to Rosicrucianism—formed the basis and pattern for many other secret societies.

In the eighteenth century, occultism flourished. There were stories of Frederick William who worked with Steinert in a house specially built for evocations; Schroepfer, proprietor of a café with his magic punch and circles for raising the spirits of the dead; the physiognomist J. K. Lavater, said to have two spirits at his command; the **Mopses,** a society whose rites of initiation were said to resemble those of the Templars and witches' sabbat in a mild and civilized form; and Carl Sand, the mystical fanatic who killed the dramatist August Kotzebue.

The **Illuminati,** whose teachings spread to France and underlay the French Revolution, was banded together as a society by Adam Weishaupt and fostered by Baron von Knigge, a student of occultism. This society was said to have originated as an attempt to circumvent the authority of the Jesuits, but in its development its absorbed mysticism and supernaturalism, finally becoming political and revolutionary as it applied its philosophies to civil and religious life. Though the Illuminati was disbanded and dispersed in 1784, its ideas continued through other occult groups and reappeared in the democratic wave that swept Europe in the next century.

Mysticism and Animal Magnetism

In the transition from occultism to a more scientific view of the paranormal largely accomplished in the nineteenth century, many occult elements reemerged in the development of **animal magnetism** and **Spiritualism.** Some of the significant names of the period included: **Johann Heinrich Jung** (1740–1817), better known as Jüng Stilling, a seer, prophet, and healer; **Franz Anton Mesmer** (c. 1733–1815), the discoverer and apostle of animal magnetism; the Marquis de Puységur, magnetist and spiritualist; Madame von Krudener, preacher of peace and clemency to monarchs and princes; **Heinrich Zschokke,** the Gothic novelist; and Dr. **Justinus Kerner** (1786–1862), believer in magnetism and historian of two cases of **possession** and mediumship, the "Maid of Orlach" and **Frederica Hauffe,** the "Seeress of Prevorst."

Early in the nineteenth century occurred the cures said to be affected by **Prince Hohenlohe,** a dignitary of the church. He was led to believe in the power of healing through the influence of a peasant named Martin Michel. Most of these cures took place at Würzburg, the scenes of former witch-burnings, and it is said that upwards of 400 people, deaf, mute, blind, and paralytic, were cured by the power of prayer.

About this time also occurred the case of **stigmata** with **Catherine Emerich,** the nun of Dülmen. Supposedly there was an appearance of a bloody cross encircling the head; marks of wounds on her hands, feet, and side; and crosses on her breast that frequently bled.

In nineteenth-century occultism we find, as in the earlier periods, stories of hauntings and spirits existing side by side with learned disquisitions, such as that on the "fourth dimension in space" by **Johann C. F. Zöllner** in his *Transcendental Physics* (1880) and another on the luminous emanations from material objects in **Baron Karl von Reichenbach**'s treatise on *od* or *odylic force,* similar to some aspects of the magic of the Middle Ages.

Spiritualism

It was some years after the original **Rochester Rappings** in America before the Spiritualism movement surfaced in German-speaking lands. Several intellectual leaders made note of the movement, including the philosopher J. G. Fichte, a proponet of Spiritualism; **Edward von Hartmann,** author of *Philosophy of the Unconscious* (1869), who gave the phenomena a place in his philosophy; and **Carl du Prel,** who, in his *Philosophy of Mysticism* (1889), held up Spiritualistic manifestations as evidence of a subconscious region in the human mind. Du Prel also founded a monthly magazine, *The Sphinx,* devoted to the interest of Spiritualism, and **Alexander Aksakof,** the Russian Spiritualist, published the results of his research in Germany and in the German language because he was not permitted to publish them in Russian. **Baron Lazar De Baczolay Hellenbach,** integrated Spiritualist teachings in his hypothesis that no change of world or "sphere" occurs at birth or death, but merely a change in the mode of perception.

Psychical Research and Parapsychology

German psychical research owes much to the work of **Baron Albert Schrenck-Notzing,** who conducted investigations of such mediums as **Eva C., Stanislawa Tomczyk, Franek Kluski, Linda Gazzera, Willi and Rudi Schneider,** and **Eusapia Palladino.** His book *Phenomena of Materialisation* (London, 1920) reports on the claimed phenomenon of **materialization.**

The engineer **Fritz Grünewald** (d. 1925) was a pioneer of scientific testing of **mediums,** and maintained a laboratory in Charlottenburg, Berlin with various recording instruments. With the British investigator **Harry Price,** he tested such psychics as **Jan Guzyk** and **Eleonore Zügun.**

Other German researchers include **Karl Grüber** (1881–1927), who investigated the Schneider brothers, **Traugott Konstantin Oesterreich** (1880–1949), who published a comprehensive study of **possession; Rudolph Tischner** (1879–1961); General Josef Peter (1852–1939); Dr. Albert Moll (1862–1939), a psychiatrist who contributed a study on **hypnotism;** Max Dessoir, who first used the term "parapsychologie" in 1889; and **Hans Driesch** (1867–1941). **Graf Carl von Klinckowstroem,** even though skeptical regarding some psychical phenomena, wrote on water-divining and published a history of the **divining rod.**

In 1874, **Alexander Aksakof** founded the journal *Psychische Studien* in Leipzig, published until 1934. It was superseded by the *Zeitschrift für Parapsychologie.*

Parapsychology was largely destroyed during the nazi era, but quickly rose again. **Hans Bender,** a post-war German researcher, was instrumental in founding the **Institut für Grenzgebiete der Psychologie und Psychohygiene** (the Institute for Border Areas of Psychology and Mental Health) in Freiburg in 1950, and held the chair for Border Areas of Psychology established at Freiburg University. In 1966, a Department for the Border Areas was established at the university's Psychological Institute and in 1968, the 11th Convention of the Parapsychological Association was held. The Institute has conducted investigations into **psychokinesis, poltergeist, electronic voice phenomenon,** and qualitative and quantitative **extra sensory perception** research.

Sources:

Driesch, Hans. *Psychical Research: The Science of the Supernormal.* London, 1933. Reprint, Arno Press, N.Y., 1975.

Du Prel, Carl. *Die Magie als Naturwissenschaft.* Leipzig: M. Altmann, 1912.

Grüber, Karl. *Parapsychologische Erkenntnisse.* Munich: Drei Masken Verlag, 1925.

Gulat-Wellenburg, W. von et al. *Der Physikalische Mediumismus.* Berlin: Ullstein, 1925.

Hansen, Joseph. *Zauberwahn, Inquisition und Hexenprozess in Mittalalter und die Entstehung der grossen Hexenverfolgung.* Munich/Leipzig: R. Oldenbourg, 1900. Reprint, Aalen: Scientiia, 1983.

Lea, Henry Charles. *Materials Toward a History of Witchcraft.* 3 vols. Philadelphia, 1939. Reprint, New York: Thomas Yoseloff, 1957.

Moll, Albert. *Hypnotism.* London: W. Scott, 1901.

Oesterreich, T. K. *Possession, Demoniacal & Other, Among Primitive Races, In Antiquity, the Middle Ages, and Modern Times.* London, 1930. Reprint, New Hyde Park, N.Y.: University Books, 1966.

Reichenbach, Karl von. *Researches on Magnetism, Electricity, Heat Light, Crystallization, and Chemical Attraction, in Their Relations to the Vital Force.* London, 1851. Reprint, New Hyde Park, N.Y.: University Books, 1966.

Tischner, Rudolf. *Geschichte der Parapsychologie.* Titmoning (Pustet), 1960.

Germer, Karl Johannes (1885–1962)

Karl Johannes Germer, successor to **Aleister Crowley** as outer head of the order of the **Ordo Templi Orientis** (OTO), was born January 22, 1885, in Germany. His college career at the Sorbonne, University of Paris, was interrupted by World War I, when he was drafted into the German army. He served as a reserve officer and was awarded the Iron Cross, both first and second class, possibly for intelligence activity in regards to Russia.

After the war Germer joined the publishing firm Barth Verlag in Munich as a manager. In the early 1920 he worked with Tränker, a member of the OTO in the publication of several short works by Crowley, including *Der Meister Therion: Eine biographische Nachricht* (1925). By this means Germer became acquainted with Crowley and moved to England, where he worked publishing Crowley's writings. Also with the help of Martha Küntzel, a former Theosophist, he founded Thelema-Verlag in Leipzig to publish German translations of Crowley's books. In 1935, on a visit to Leipzig, he was arrested by the Nazi government, which was in the process of suppressing occult work. Germer was confined at Alexanderplatz prison and Esterwegen concentration camp for ten months and kept his sanity by reciting the Thelemic Holy Books, the essential writings of thelemic magic as taught by Crowley. Shortly before his release, he was given a vision of his Holy Guardian Angel, a major early magical step for all thelemites. (The word *thelema,* the central concept of Crowley's magic, is derived from the Greek word for will.)

Germer then moved to Brussels and tried to keep in touch with the scattered OTO groups, but all of these were finally closed in 1937. In 1941 he was arrested again and spent ten months in an internment camp before he was allowed to get out of the country. He migrated to the United States, and Crowley named him the Grand Treasurer of the order. Germer concentrated on raising money to continue the fragile publication program of the OTO. He wrote an account of his experiences in prison but was never able to find a publisher. Among his duties as the highest ranking officer in the United States was mediating a dispute in the Pasadena lodge concerning the magical work of Jack Parsons. Germer worked through Grady McMurtry as his representative.

Crowley named Germer his successor as head of the order, then died in 1947. Germer lived quietly in rural California and seemed unwilling and uninterested in carrying out his duties as chief administrator of the OTO. In 1955 he chartered a lodge in England under Kenneth Grant, who formed the New Isis Lodge with instructions to limit his work to the first three of the eleven OTO degrees. When Grant began to work higher degrees, Germer withdrew his charter. He also chartered a Swiss lodge, but otherwise remained aloof from the members, many of whom were unaware for several years of his death on October 25, 1962.

Germer died without naming a clear successor or establishing a process for appointing a successor. His work was carried by several claimants, including Metzger in Switzerland, Kenneth Grant in England, Marcelo Ramos Motta in Brazil, and eventually Grady McMurtry in California, each of whom would head a separate branch of the OTO.

Sources:

King, Francis. *Sexuality, Magic, and Perversion.* Secacus, N.J.: Citadel Press, 1972.

Gervais, Bishop (d. 1067)

Archbishop of Rheims. His death was said to have been revealed to a Norman knight, returning from a pilgrimage to Rome, by a hermit he met on the way. According to popular belief, the hermit told the knight that on the previous night he had been disturbed by a vision of demons making a great noise. He said the demons told him they had been carrying the body of Gervais from Rheims, but because of his good deeds in life the body had been taken from them. On his return to Rheims the knight learned that Gervais was dead, and that the time of his death corresponded exactly with the time of the hermit's vision.

GESP

Abbreviation for *general extrasensory perception,* a term used by parapsychologists to cover both **telepathy** (in which there is an apparent transfer of information paranormally from one mind to another) and **clairvoyance** (in which apparent paranormal cognition relates to an object or event).

Gestefeld, Ursula Newell (1845–1921)

Ursula Newell Gestefeld, an independent Christian Science teacher and one of the founders of **New Thought,** was born April 22, 1845, in Augusta, Maine. As a child she was quite sickly and her family had doubts that she would live to adulthood. She did survive, however, and eventually married newspaperman Thomas Gestefeld. They had four children and settled in Chicago.

Early in 1884 Gestefield obtained a copy of *Science and Health with Key to the Scriptures,* the Christian Science textbook written by **Mary Baker Eddy.** Attracted to what she read, she joined the class Eddy taught in Chicago in the spring of that year. Soon after the class she became a practitioner and a popular teacher in her own right. She wrote for the *Christian Science Journal* and in the late 1880s wrote three books, *Mental Medicine?* (1887), *Ursula Gestefeld's Statement of Christian Science* (1888), and *Science of the Christ* (1889). These books brought her into conflict with Eddy, who accused Gestefeld of distorting her teachings. Gestefeld was dismissed from Eddy's church and responded with an attack on Eddy in *Jesuitism in Christian Science* (1888).

Gestefeld developed her own variation on Christian Science, which she termed the Science of Being. For several years she functioned as an independent teacher and writer. Besides a number of books, in 1896 she began the magazine *Exodus* (1896–1904). She also founded informal Science of Being groups, one of which was in England. In 1897 she founded the Exodus Club, which grew in 1904 into the Church of New Thought, one of the first metaphysical churches to use that name. As the pastor of the church, she was recognized as one of the leading figures of the emerging New Thought Movement, which had developed out of the independent Christian Scientists of the previous decade. In 1901 she wrote the most important statement of her mature position, *The Builder and the Plan.* She addressed the first meeting of the International New Thought League in 1899 in Boston. That organization was a precursor to the International New Thought Alliance, founded in 1914.

She continued to lead her church until her death on October 22, 1921, in Chicago, but it dissolved soon after her passing. She was cremated, and her ashes were buried in Chicago.

Sources:

Gestefeld, Ursula N. *The Builder and the Plan.* Chicago: Exodus Publishing, 1901.

———. *Jesuitism in Christian Science.* Chicago: The Author, 1888.

———. *The Science of the Christ.* Chicago: The Author, 1889.

———. *A Statement of Christian Science.* Chicago: The Author, 1888.

Ghadiali, Dinshah Pestanj (1873–1966)

Dinshah Pestanji Ghadiali, an Indian American, pioneered vegetarianism and chromotherapy (healing with color) in twentieth-century America. Born November 28, 1873, into a Zoroastrian family in Bombay, India, he developed an early interest in chemistry and trained himself through his reading. He was only 11 when he became an assistant in math and science at Wilson College.

During his teen years Ghadiali became a rational materialist, then in 1891 he encountered the **Theosophical Society.** At the time of his initiation he had a visionary experience of one of the mahatmas, the superhuman entities who are believed to guide the work of the society. Ghadiali studied with a Hindu neighbor and gave up meat and alcohol. Through the society, he was introduced to the world of religion, and for a time became a student of Hindu guru Swami Murdhan Shastri.

After finishing college, Ghadiali practiced medicine. He moved to the United States in 1911 and was naturalized in 1917. His medical degree was not recognized in the United States, and he was also alienated from medicine as it then existed. He had adopted the Hindu virtue *ahimsa,* harmlessness, as a basic principle of living and was led to naturopathy, which had developed out of older natural schools of healing. In 1919 he became vice president of the National Association of Drugless Practitioners and actively participated in efforts to have the government recognize alternative medical practices.

In 1920 Ghadiali announced that he had perfected the techniques of spectro-chrome therapy, a method of healing using attuned color waves. The machine he developed could project beams of light upon the body of an ill person. In addition, Ghadiali received his medical degree in chiropractic, naturopathy, and several other healing practices, and two years later he purchased land in Malaga, New Jersey, and opened the Spectro-Chrome Institute. He wrote several books over the next few years, but his primary text, the three volume *Spectro-Chrome Metry Encyclopedia,* was finished in 1933. Meanwhile, Ghadiali faced a series of court actions as the government moved against his healing practices. He was arrested for fraud in 1931 but was acquitted. In 1934 an attempt was made to strip him of his citizenship, as had happened to so many Indian Americans under provisions of the 1924 anti-Asian immigration law. He argued that though he was an Indian, he was of Persian ancestry, and thus was able to retain his citizen's status.

During the next decade, Ghadiali was able to train more than 100 students in the techniques of spectro-chrome therapy, but in 1945 the government acted again. Ghadiali faced charges that he had made false claims about his spectro-chrome healing device. In 1947 he was convicted but not sent to prison on the condition that he cease practicing chromotherapy. His books and unsold devices were destroyed, and those that had been sold were confiscated from their owners. In the 1950s he resumed his healing practice and operated quietly until his death on April 30, 1966. His son, H. Jay Dinshah, continues Ghadiali's work, but concentrates on veganism, a strict form of vegetarianism. Dinshah founded and heads the American Vegan Society.

Sources:

Ghadiali, Dinshah P. *Spectro-Chrome Metry Encyclopedia.* 3 vols. Malaga, N.J.: Spectro-Chrome Institute, 1933.

The Life of a Karmi-Yogi. Malaga, N.J.: American Vegan Society, 1973.

Ghirardelli, Cornelio (ca. 1610)

Originally listed in the *Encyclopedia of Occultism* by **Lewis Spence** (1920) as "Quiradelli, Corneille." Ghirardelli was a Franciscan monk born in Boulogne, France, toward the end of the sixteenth century. He studied **astrology** and was the author of several works on astrology, physiognomy, and other subjects.

Sources:

Ghirardelli, Cornelio. *Cefalogia fisonomica divisa in dieci Doche, dove conforme a'documenti d'Aristotile, e d'altri filosofi naturali. . . .* Bologna, Italy, 1630.

———. *Compendio della cefalogia fisonomica; nella quale si contiene cento sonetti di diversi eccellenti posti sopra cento teste humane.* Bologna, Italy, 1673.

Ghor-Boud-Des, The

The people of Ghor-bund-land. Edward Pococke in his book *India in Greece* (1852) maintains that these people were the same as the Corybantes, or ministers of the gods, otherwise known as the **Cabiri.** Pococke claims, on somewhat slender evidence of place-names, that Palestine and Greece were colonized from India in ancient times.

Sources:

Pococke, Edward. *India in Greece.* London: J. J. Griffin & Co., 1852.

Ghost

The disembodied spirit or image of a deceased person, appearing to be alive. The term does not include apparitions of the living. Reports of appearances of ghosts go back to ancient times, and ghost stories have always been popular as a special genre of literature. Ghosts are believed to be ethereal, able to penetrate doors and walls, and are often said to appear at the moment of death to a distant relative or friend. Ghosts are also believed to haunt specific localities, either dwellings associated with their earthly life or locales with a tragic history. Children are often reported to have encountered ghostly playmates.

Although the evidence for ghosts is largely anecdotal, it is widespread and persistent. For a detailed discussion of various types of ghosts and related appearances, see **apparitions.** (See also **double; haunting;** and **dress, phantom**)

Ghost Club, The

One of the original psychical research organizations. It was founded in 1862 by individuals interested in ghost phenomena. Its membership (by invitation only) has included prominent psychical researchers, as well as actors, actresses, authors, and poets. Today the club, which has been superseded as a research organization, holds an annual dinner at which members relate personal experiences concerned with ghosts. Membership is not limited to believers in ghostly phenomena. Address: Peter Underwood, The Savage Club, Fitzmaurice Place, Berkeley Square, London, W1X 6JD, England.

Ghost Research Society

Founded in 1981 for individuals interested in supernatural or preternatural phenomena. The society seeks to substantiate proof that humans exist after death and that ghosts inhabit the earth. It investigates reports of **ghosts, hauntings,** and **poltergeists,** conducts expeditions to "haunted" sites, and attempts to compile data. It sponsors lectures, speaking engagements, psychic discussions, and ghost tours in the greater Chicago area and publishes the quarterly *Ghost Trackers Newsletter.* Address: P.O. Box 205, Oak Lawn, IL 60454.

Ghost Seers

European folklore belief maintains that persons born at a particular time of the day have the power to see ghosts. For example, British folklorist T. F. Thiselton Dyer in *The Ghost World* (1893), observes:

"Thus it is said in Lancashire that children born during twilight are supposed to have this peculiarity, and to know who of their acquaintance will next die. Some say that this property belongs also to those who happen to be born exactly at twelve o'clock at night, or, as the peasantry say in Somersetshire, 'a child born in chime-hours will have the power to see spirits.' The same belief prevails in Yorkshire, where it is commonly supposed that children born during the hour after midnight have the privilege through life of seeing the spirits of the departed. Mr. Henderson [T. F. Henderson, *Notes on the Folk-lore of the Northern Counties,* 1866] says that a Yorkshire lady informed him she was very near being thus distinguished, but the clock had not struck twelve when she was born. When a child she mentioned this circumstance to an old servant, adding that 'Mamma was sure her birthday was the 23rd, not the 24th, for she had inquired at the time.' 'Ay, Ay,' said the old woman, turning to the child's nurse, 'mistress would be very anxious about that, for bairns born after midnight see more things than other folk.'"

This idea, part of a much larger belief in the significance of various days in explaining little-understood phenomena such as luck, prevailed on the Continent. In Denmark, children born on Sunday had prerogatives far from enviable. The antiquarian Benjamin Thorpe tells how:

". . . in Fryer there was a woman who was born on a Sunday, and, like other Sunday children had the faculty of seeing much that was hidden from others. But, because of this property, she could not pass by a church at night without seeing a hearse or a spectre. The gift became a perfect burden to her; she therefore sought the advice of a man skilled in such matters, who directed her, whenever she saw a spectre to say, 'Go to Heaven!' but when she met a hearse, 'Hang on!' Happening sometime after to meet a hearse, she, through lapse of memory cried out, 'Go to Heaven!' and straightway the hearse rose in the air and vanished. Afterwards, meeting a spectre she said to it, 'Hang on!' when the spectre clung round her neck, hung on her back, and drove her down into the earth before it. For three days her shrieks were heard before the spectre would put an end to her wretched life."

It used to be a popular belief in Scotland that those who were born on Christmas Day or Good Friday had the power to see spirits and even command them, a superstition to which Sir Walter Scott alludes in his poem "Marmion" (stanza 22). The Spaniards attributed the haggard and downcast looks of their Philip II to the disagreeable visions to which this privilege subjected him.

Among primitive tribes it was supposed that spirits are visible to some persons and not to others. The people of the Antilles used to believe that the dead appeared on the road when one went alone but not when people went together; among the Finns the ghosts of the dead were to be seen by the shamans and not by men generally, unless in dreams. It was also a popular theory with primitive races that the soul appeared in dreams to visit the sleeper, and hence it was customary for tribes to drink various intoxicating substances under the impression that when thrown into the state of ecstasy they would have pleasing visions.

On this account certain tribes of the Amazon used narcotic plants, producing an intoxication lasting 24 hours. During this period they were said to be subject to extraordinary visions, in the course of which they acquired information on any subject they wished.

For a similar reason the inhabitants of northern Brazil, when anxious to discover some guilty person, administered narcotic drinks to seers, in whose dreams the criminal made his appearance. Californian Indians gave children certain intoxicants to gain from the ensuing vision information about their enemies. The Darien Indians used the seeds of the *Datura sanguines* to produce in children prophetic delirium, during which they were said to reveal the whereabouts of hidden treasures.

One of the most famous seers in the British Isles was Kenneth Ore, the **Brahan Seer** of the Highlands of Scotland. The faculty of such prophetic vision was generally known in Scotland as **second sight.** Other seers favor inducing visions by such means as **crystal gazing.**

Sources:

Campbell, John L., and Trevor H. Hall. *Strange Things: The Story of Fr. Allan McDonald, Ada Goodrich Freer, and the Society for Psychical Research's Enquiry into Highland Second Sight.* London: Routledge & Kegan Paul, 1968.

Dyer, T. F. Thiselton. *The Ghost World.* London: Ward & Downey, 1893.

Henderson, William. *Notes on the Folk-lore of the Northern Counties, and the Borders.* London, 1866. Reprint, London: Folk-Lore Society, 1879.

Mackenzie, Alexander. *The Prophecies of the Brahan Seer Doinneach Odhar Fiosaiche.* Stirling, Scotland: Eneas Mackay, 1935. Rev. ed., Golspie, Scotland: Sutherland Press, 1970. Reprint, London: Constable, 1977.

Ghost Tours

Regular weekend "supernatural tours" of Chicago, Illinois, are organized by lecturer/researcher Richard T. Crowe, who broadcasts on occult topics and has appeared on television shows. The tours include visits to a reputedly haunted church, a cemetery, the grave of a miracle child, the locale of a hitchhiking ghost, and sites of other historic mysteries. International ghost tours are also arranged. Similar tours of haunted sites in Britain have been arranged by A. Hippesley Coxe. Crowe may be reached at P.O. Box 29054, Chicago, IL 60629.

Ghost Trial of the Century

Term given by the *New York Times* to the legal contest in Arizona from March to October 1967 in which 134 individuals and organizations competed for the funds of the late **James Kidd** (1879–ca. 1949), a prospector and miner who left nearly a quarter of a million dollars for "research on scientific proof of a soul of the human body." The judge's decision of October 20, 1967, awarded the funds to the Barrow Neurological Institute, Phoenix, Arizona.

Sources:

Fuller, John G. *The Great Soul Trial.* New York: Macmillan, 1969.

Ghoul

An evil spirit or revived corpse supposed to rob graves and feed on human corpses. It is similar to the **vampire,** but differs in that it not only drinks blood but also consumes flesh. The term is from the Arabic *ghul* (feminine form, *ghulah*) meaning "to seize," and the story of the ghoul has been widely disseminated in Moslem countries, ranging from India to Africa. Some people believe that the superstition stems from wild animals that disturb graves at night, others that its origin is the terror of death in the lonely desert. The idea of the ghoul entered into the West in the nineteenth century through translations of the *Arabian Nights.*

Among Hindus there are similar beliefs in ghoul-like figures, such as the *vetala,* a demon that haunts cemeteries and animates dead bodies, and the *rakshasas,* a whole order of evil demons that disturb sacrifices, harass devout people, and devour human beings. Even lower than the rakshasas are the *pishachas,* the vilest and most malignant of fiends. In India the line between ghoulish and vampire figures is often unclear. In Hinduism the eating of human flesh is a forbidden and degrading act, but certain **tantric yoga** groups (who find enlightenment by indulging in what other groups avoid) in India and Tibet practice a necrophilistic rite of lying upon a corpse, or eating a portion of the flesh.

In modern times the concept of the ghoul has become commonplace in Hollywood horror movies. Ghouls made probably their best-known appearance in George Romero's 1968 horror classic *Night of the Living Dead* and its sequels.

Sources:

Barber, Richard, and Anne Riches. *A Dictionary of Fabulous Beasts.* New York: Walker, 1971.

Giant Rock Space Convention

Organized annually by **George Van Tassell** from 1954 until just before his death in 1977 at Giant Rock airport near Valley, California. The 1954 and 1958 events attracted more than ten thousand attendees. Van Tassell, author of the book *I Rode in a Flying Saucer* (1952), claimed that the Giant Rock area was a "natural cone of receptivity" for flying saucers and that he received telepathic messages from **UFO** "crew members," who were also said to visit him.

The space conventions resembled old-time Spiritualist camp meetings, with lectures by "contactees" or speakers on the metaphysical and religious aspects of UFOs. The conventions declined in attendance through the 1960s and were discontinued after Van Tassell's death.

Sources:

Clark, Jerome. *The Emergence of a Phenomenon: UFOs from the Beginning through 1959.* Vol. 2 of *The UFO Encyclopedia.* Detroit: Omnigraphics, 1992.

Van Tassell, George. *I Rode in a Flying Saucer.* Los Angeles: New Age Publishing, 1952.

Gibier, Paul (1851–1900)

French scientist, director of the American branch of the Pasteur Institute of New York, who became interested in psychical research in 1885 and found a remarkable medium in Mrs. Salmon (pseudonym of **Carrie M. Sawyer**), with whom he conducted experiments for ten years both in his New York laboratory and at his country home.

Gibier established the reality of some surprising phenomena and planned to take his medium to England, France, and Egypt, but his plans were cut short when he was killed by a runaway horse. The night before the accident he reportedly dreamed that he rode out alone, was thrown from his buggy, and died; he told his dream to his wife and laughed at her fears.

Sources:

Gibier, Paul. *Physiologie transcendentale: Analyse des choses.* 1890. Translated as *Psychism: Analysis of Things Existing.* N.p., 1890.

———. *Le Spiritisme (Fakirisme occidental).* Paris: C. Doin, 1887.

Gibran, Kahlil (1883–1931)

Metaphysical poet and philosopher. He was born in the town of Bshar e, Lebanon, traditionally the area of the forest of the Holy Cedars, which furnished timber for King Solomon's temple in ancient Jerusalem. Gibran was baptized in the Maronite (Eastern Rite) branch of the Roman Catholic Church and named after his paternal grandfather as Gibran Kahlil Gibran, a name he retained in Arabic, although he used the simpler "Kahlil Gibran" in his English writings.

He was educated in Lebanon and emigrated to the United States with his family, settling in Boston in 1895. There he attended a public school for two and a half years, then studied at night school.

He returned to Lebanon to study at the Madrasat Al-Hikmat (The School of Wisdom), founded by the Maronite bishop Joseph Debs in Beirut. After graduation he traveled in Syria and Lebanon, visiting historic places.

In 1902 he returned to the United States to dedicate himself to painting, and in 1908 went to Paris to study under famous sculptor Auguste Rodin at the Academy of Fine Arts. He then returned to the United States once again, where he continued to paint. Gibran wrote many books of mystical inspiration, of which *The Prophet* (1923) is by far the most popular.

Sources:

Gibran, Kahlil. *Beloved Prophet: The Love Letters of Kahhil Gibran and Mary Haskell and her Private Journal.* New York: Alfred A. Knopf, 1972.

———. *Earth Gods.* New York: Alfred A. Knopf, 1931.

———. *Gibran: A Self-Portrait.* New York: Citadel, 1959.

———. *Jesus the Son of Man.* New York: Alfred A. Knopf, 1956.

———. *The Prophet.* New York: Alfred A. Knopf, 1923.

———. *Sand and Foam.* New York: Alfred A. Knopf, 1926.

———. *Wisdom of Kahlil Gibran.* New York: Philosophical Library, 1966.

Hawi, Khalil. *Kahlil Gibran: His Background, Character, and Works.* Beirut, 1963.

Nu'aymah, Mikha'il. *Kahlil Gibran: A Biography.* New York: Quartet, 1988.

Sherfan, Andrew Dib. *Kahlil Gibran: The Nature of Love.* New York: Philosophical Library, 1971.

Young, Barbara. *This Man from Lebanon: A Study of Kahlil Gibran.* New York: Alfred A. Knopf, n.d.

Gibson, Edmund P(aul) (1898–1961)

American writer, engineer, and researcher in **parapsychology.** Born May 20, 1898, in Grand Rapids, Michigan, he took part in **ESP** card research in Grand Rapids (1932–37) and conducted experiments in **precognition** and **psychokinesis** at Duke University (1938–40). In 1946 he investigated the mediumship of William H. Thatcher.

Gibson was a member of the **Society for Psychical Research** and the **American Society for Psychical Research** and an associate member of the **Parapsychological Association.** In addition to numerous articles on archaeology, he contributed writings on psychical subjects to *Tomorrow, Light, FATE, Blue Book,* and the *Journal of Parapsychology.* He died March 19, 1961.

Sources:

Pleasants, Helene, ed. *Biographical Dictionary of Parapsychology.* New York: Helix Press, 1964.

Gichtel, John Georg (1683–1710)

German theosophical mystic in the tradition of **Jakob Boehme.** He was born at Ratisbon, Germany, on March 14, 1638. He attributed his leaving a legal career to a meeting with Baron Justinianus von Weltz, who presented a vision for the union of Christianity. As a result Gichtel became the head of a small society, the Christerbauliche Jesusgesellschaft. It was not long before the church authorities expressed their disapproval, and Gichtel moved to Holland, the most religiously tolerant country on the Continent at the time. There he discovered Boehme's mystical writings and became an ardent disciple. He saw to the publication of the writings in 1682 and organized a Boehmist society called the Brethren of the Angels. Gichtel's own major literary contribution lay primarily in a number of letters he wrote that were gathered and published by one of his followers as *Theosophia practica* (1701).

Giffard, Ellen Hovde (1925–)

Film editor with special interest in parapsychology. Giffard was born March 9, 1925, at Meadville, Pennsylvania, and attended the Carnegie Institute of Technology at Pittsburgh. She worked as an assistant in marine ecology at the Marine Biological Laboratory, Woods Hole, Massachusetts; as secretary to the New York Aquarium; and as a freelance film editor (1950–63). She was a member of the Conference on Parapsychology and Psychedelics held in New York during 1958.

Sources:

Pleasants, Helene, ed. *Biographical Dictionary of Parapsychology.* New York: Helix Press, 1964.

Gilbert, Mostyn (d. 1992)

Noted psychical researcher and active member of the **Society for Psychical Research** (SPR). Although born in the United States, he lived and worked in Britain. Gilbert had special interests in table turning, mediumship, materialization, electronic voice phenomena, and the history of nineteenth-century **Spiritualism.** He became secretary of the Survival Joint Research Committee (SJRC) of the SPR in 1963 and prepared its quarterly agenda and minutes of meetings. The SJRC, now a trust, was concerned with investigating evidence for **survival** after death, and Gilbert was actively involved in its formation, together with such Spiritualists friends as **Maurice Barbanell** (former editor of the newspaper *Psychic News*). The committee brought together Spiritualists and scientists.

Gilbert was a friend of **Eric J. Dingwall** and helped him prepare his book *The Critic's Dilemma* (1966), dealing with the research of **Sir William Crookes,** a subject on which Gilbert also made contributions to the *Journal* of the SPR (in volumes 41–44). He did valuable work in editing the society's *Combined Index,* part IV (1973), and also cataloged the collection of the Britten Memorial Library in Manchester prior to its transfer to the **Spiritualists' National Union** headquarters at Stansted.

Gilbert did not hesitate to criticize what he considered shortcomings in council proceedings, but many members believed that his comments were a valuable stimulus. He was extremely helpful for several years in the organization of the **Association for the Scientific Study of Anomalous Phenomena** (ASSAP).

Gilbert, R(obert) A(ndrew) (1942–)

Book dealer and authority on the history of magic and esoteric organizations. He was born October 6, 1942, in Bristol, England, and attended the University of Bristol (B.A. honors, 1964). Since 1966 Gilbert and his wife have been antiquarian book dealers. Gilbert is also a trustee of the Yarker Library Trust and the Hermetic Research Trust and is a member of the **Churches' Fellowship for Psychical and Spiritual Studies.** He has written a number of books and articles, but is possibly most known for his work on the Hermetic Order of the **Golden Dawn** and in particular one of its members, occult author **Arthur E. Waite.**

Gilbert has stated that his aim is:

"to promote those elements within the esoteric traditions of Western Europe and of the Judeo-Christian tradition which have been unjustly neglected on account of their presumed unorthodoxy. I wish to demonstrate their compatibility with orthodox Christianity. In addition, I continue to work on the questions of the nature and communication of mystical experience, the distribution of life within the universe, and the religious implications of cosmology."

He has been an incisive critic of the pretentious and the charlatanic in occultism.

Sources:

Gilbert, Robert A. *A. E. Waite: A Bibliography.* Wellingborough, England: Aquarian Press, 1983.

———. *A. E. Waite: Magician of Many Parts.* Wellingborough, England: Aquarian Press, 1987.

———. *The Golden Dawn Companion.* Wellingborough, England: Aquarian Press, 1986.

———. *The Golden Dawn: Twilight of the Magicians.* Wellingborough, England: Aquarian Press, 1983.

———, ed. *The Sorcerer and His Apprentice: Hermetic Writings of S. L. McGregor Mathers & J. W. Brodie Innes.* Wellingborough, England: Aquarian Press, 1983.

——— [Edward Dunning]. *Selected Masonic Writings of A. E. Waite.* Wellingborough, England: Aquarian Press, 1988.

Gilbert, Robert A., and Michael A. Cox, eds. *The Oxford Book of English Ghost Stories.* Oxford: Oxford University Press; New York: Oxford University Press, 1989.

Gilbert, Robert A., and W. N. Birks. *The Treasure of Montsegur.* Crucible, 1987.

Waite, Arthur Edward. *Hermetic Papers of A. E. Waite.* Edited by R. A. Gilbert. Wellingborough, England: Aquarian Press, 1987.

Gill, Madge (d. 1961)

British psychic and London housewife who practiced **automatic drawing and painting** and produced work claimed to be inspired by spirit guidance. Gill's mediumship began after the death of her eight-year-old son. She said she felt "impelled to execute drawings on a large scale on calico." These drawings were complex, with a mysterious atmosphere. In 1942 one of the drawings, measuring 36 feet by 5 feet, was priced at 1,000 pounds. The London borough of Newham sponsored an exhibition of her works. In 1977 another exhibition was arranged at the Central School of Art and Design, London.

Gilles de Rais (1404–1440)

Lord of Rais (or Retz) and marshal of France, the "Bluebeard" of nursery legends, and a famous sorcerer. He was born Gilles de Laval in September or October 1404 at Machecoul to one of the most outstanding families of Brittany. His father, Guy de Montmorency-Laval, died when Gilles was 20 years old, and the impetuous young man found himself possessed of unlimited power and wealth.

After his father's death he became Gilles de Rais, the lord of 15 princely domains, yielding a revenue of 300,000 livres. He was handsome and distinguished by a beard of bluish-black. His appearance was fascinating, his erudition extensive, and his courage unimpeachable. All this seemed to ensure him a splendid career, yet the name of Bluebeard came to be associated with horror and atrocious crimes.

At the outset of his career de Rais did nothing to suggest an evil predisposition. He served with zeal and gallantry in the wars of Charles VI against the English and fought under Joan of Arc in the Siege of Orléans. His exploits won him the dignified title marshal of France.

From that point de Rais's career drifted downward. He retired to his castle of Champtocé and indulged in the display of his luxury. Two hundred horsemen accompanied him on his travels, and the magnificence of his hunting entourage exceeded that of the king himself. His retainers wore the most sumptuous clothing; his horses were caparisoned with the richest trappings; his castle gates were open day and night to all comers. A whole ox was roasted daily for his guests. Sheep, pigs, poultry, mead, and hippocras (wine) were provided for five hundred persons.

De Rais carried the same love of pomp into his devotion. His principal chaplain, a dean, a chanter, two archdeacons, four vicars, a schoolmaster, twelve assistant chaplains, and eight choristers comprised his ecclesiastical establishment. Each of these had his own horse and servant; all were dressed in robes of scarlet and furs and had costly appointments. Sacred vessels and crucifixes, all of gold and silver, were transported with them wherever their lord went, as were many organs, each carried by six men. De Rais was intent on having all the priests of his chapel wear the mitre; he sent many embassies to Rome to obtain this privilege, but without success.

He maintained a choir of 25 young children of both sexes, who were instructed in singing by the best masters of the day. He also had comedians, morris dancers, and jugglers, and every hour was crowned with some sensual gratification or voluptuous pleasure.

In 1420 Lord de Rais wedded Catherine, the heiress of the noble House of Thouars. The wedding afforded him a fresh occasion to display his passion for luxurious pomp. He gave splendid banquets and participated in chivalric tournaments.

History or Legend?

From this point on it is difficult to separate fact from popular tradition. The folklore version of the horrific events that transpired is related by **Éliphas Lévi** in *The History of Magic* (1913). Lévi writes: "He had espoused a young woman of high birth and kept her practically shut up in his castle at Machecoul, which had a tower with the entrance walled up."

Since de Rais had spread a report that the tower was in a ruinous state, no one sought to enter it. Madame de Rais—who was frequently alone during the dark hours—saw red lights moving to and fro in the tower but did not venture to question her husband, whose bizarre and somber character filled her with terror.

De Rais's expenses were so extensive that they eventually exhausted even his apparently inexhaustible revenues, and to procure the funds for his pleasures and extravagance he was compelled to sell several of his baronies.

For de Rais, unable to live in diminished splendor, money became the principal object of desire, and to obtain it he decided to turn to **alchemy.**

He sent accordingly into Italy, Spain, and Germany and invited the alchemical experts to the splendors of Champtocé. Among those who obtained the summonses, and continued attached to de Rais during the remainder of his career, was Prélati, an alchemist of Padua. At their instigation de Rais built a stately laboratory and, joined by other alchemists, they eagerly began the search for the **philosophers' stone.** For 12 months the furnaces blazed brightly and a thousand chemical combinations disposed of the marshal's gold and silver.

Impetuous, de Rais could not abide such lingering processes. He wanted wealth and he wanted it immediately. If the grand secret could not be discovered by any quicker method, he would have none of it, nor, as his resources were fast melting away, would it avail him much if the search occupied several years. At this junction the Poitousan physician and the Paduan alchemist whispered to de Rais that there were quicker methods of obtaining the desired alkahest if he had the courage to adopt them.

De Rais immediately dismissed the inferior alchemists and put himself in the hands of the two abler and subtler masters, one a physician. They persuaded him that the devil could at once reveal to them the secret and offered to summon him so that the marshal could conclude with him whatever arrangement he thought best. Short of sacrificing his soul, the lord of Rais professed himself willing to do anything the devil might command.

In this frame of mind he went to the physician at midnight to a solitary spot in the neighboring woods where the physician drew a magic circle and made the customary conjurations. De Rais listened to the invocation with wonder, expecting that at any moment the Spirit of Darkness would burst upon the startled silence. After a lapse of 30 minutes, the physician manifested signs of the greatest alarm—his hair seemed to stand on end, his eyes glared with unutterable horror, he talked wildly, his knees shook, a deadly pallor overspread his countenance, and he sank to the ground.

The lord of Rais was a dauntless man and gazed upon the strange scene unmoved. After awhile the physician seemed to recover. He arose and, turning to his master, inquired if he had not seen the wrathful countenance of the devil. De Rais replied that he had seen no devil, whereupon the physician declared that the Evil One had appeared in the form of a wild leopard and had growled at him horribly.

Lévi quotes the physician: "You would have been the same, and heard the same, but for your want of faith. You could not determine to give yourself up wholly to his service, and therefore he thrust a mist before your eyes." De Rais acknowledged that his resolution had indeed somewhat faltered, but said that he would believe if the Evil One could really be coerced into revealing the secret of the universal alkahest.

The physician said certain herbs grew in Spain and Africa that possessed the power necessary to coerce the devil, and offered to go in search of them himself if the lord of Rais would supply the funds. Since no one else would be able to identify the herbs, de Rais thanked the physician for volunteering and loaded him with all the gold he could spare. The man then took leave of his credulous patron, who never saw him again.

As soon as the physician left Champtocé, de Rais was once more seized with the fever of unrest. His days and nights were consumed in ceaseless visions of gold.

He now turned for help to the alchemist Prélati, who agreed to undertake the enterprise if de Rais furnished him with the necessary charms and talismans. The marshal was to sign with his blood a contract that he would obey the devil in all things and offer up a sacrifice of the hands, eyes, blood, heart, and lungs of a young child. The madman having willingly consented to these terms, Prélati went out alone on the following night. After an absence of three hours, he returned to his impatient lord. His tale was a monstrously extravagant one, but de Rais believed it.

The devil, Prélati improvised, had appeared in the shape of a comely young man of 20 who desired to be called "Barron" and had pointed out to him a store of ingots of pure gold buried under an oak in the adjacent woods. It was to become the property of the lord of Rais if he fulfilled the conditions of his contract. But this bright prospect was clouded by the devil's injunction that the gold was not to be searched for until a period of seven times seven weeks had elapsed, or it would turn to slates and dust.

Gilles was by no means willing to wait so many months for the realization of his wishes and asked Prélati to inform the devil that he would decline any further dealings with him if matters could not be expedited. Prélati persuaded de Rais to wait for seven times seven days, and then the two went with pickax and shovel to dig up the treasure.

They eventually dug up a load of slates inscribed with hieroglyphical characters. Prélati broke into a fit of rage and branded the Evil One a liar, a knave, and a rogue—de Rais heartily joining in his fierce denunciations. Prélati persuaded his master to give the devil a further trial, however, and led him on from day to day with dark oracular hints and pretended demoniac intimations until he had obtained nearly all de Rais's remaining valuables. He was preparing to escape with his plunder when a catastrophe occurred that involved him in his lord's ruin.

On Easter Day in the year 1440, Gilles de Rais received Communion solemnly in his chapel and bade farewell to his wife, telling her that he was departing to the Holy Land. The poor woman was even then afraid to question her husband. She was also several months along in her pregnancy. The marshal permitted her sister to come on a visit as a companion during his absence. Madame de Rais took advantage of this indulgence, after which de Rais mounted his horse and departed.

Madame de Rais communicated her fears and anxieties to her sister. The two women wondered what went on in the castle. Why was her lord so gloomy? What signified his repeated absences? What became of the children who disappeared day by day? What were those nocturnal lights in the walled-up tower? These and other questions caused both women to burn with curiosity. But what could they do?

The marshal had expressly forbidden them even to approach the tower, and before leaving he had repeated this injunction. It must surely have a secret entrance, Madame de Rais and her sister Anne agreed, and they proceeded to search through the lower rooms of the castle, corner by corner, stone after stone. At last, in the chapel, behind the altar, they came upon a copper button hidden in a mass of sculpture. It yielded under pressure, a stone slid back, and the trembling curiosity seekers distinguished the lowermost steps of a staircase, which led them to the condemned tower.

At the top of the first flight there was a kind of chapel, with an inverted cross and black candles; on the altar stood a hideous figure, no doubt representing the devil. On the second floor they came upon furnaces, retorts, alembics, charcoal—all the apparatuses of alchemy. The third flight led to a dark chamber where the heavy and fetid atmosphere compelled the young women to retreat. Madame de Rais bumped into a vase, which fell over. She then became aware that her robe and feet were soaked by some thick liquid. On returning to the light at the head of the stairs, she found that she was bathed in blood.

Anne would have fled from the place, but Madame de Rais's curiosity was stronger than her disgust and fear. She descended the stairs, took a lamp from the infernal chapel, and returned to the third floor, where a frightful spectacle awaited her. Copper vessels filled with blood lined the whole length of the walls, bearing labels with a date on each. In the middle of the room was a black marble table on which lay the body of a child, obviously murdered recently. It was one of the gory basins that had fallen, and black blood spread over the grimy and worm-eaten wooden floor.

The two women were horrified. Madame de Rais endeavored at all costs to destroy the evidence of her indiscretion. She used a sponge and water to wash the boards, but she only extended the stain, and that which at first seemed black became all scarlet. Suddenly a loud commotion echoed through the castle, mixed with the cries of people calling to Madame de Rais: "Here is Monseigneur come back!" The two women made for the staircase, but at the same moment they were aware of footsteps and the sound of other voices in the devil's chapel. Sister Anne fled upward to the battlement of the tower; Madame de Rais rushed down the stairs trembling and found herself face to face with her husband, accompanied by an apostate priest and Prélati.

De Rais seized his wife by the arm and without speaking, dragged her into the infernal chapel. According to Lévi, Prélati told the marshal: "It is needs must, as you see, and the victim has come of her own accord. . . ." "Be it so," answered his master. "Begin the Black Mass. . . ." The apostate priest went to the altar while de Rais opened a little cupboard inside and drew out a large knife. He sat down close to his swooning spouse, who was crumpled in a heap on a bench against the wall. The sacrilegious ceremonies began.

Lévi explains that the marshal, instead of taking the road to Jerusalem, had proceeded only to Nantes, where Prélati lived, and had attacked the miserable traitor with the utmost fury, threatening to slay him if he did not reveal the means of extracting from the devil the long-sought gold. Stalling, Prélati declared that terrible conditions were required by the infernal master; first would be the sacrifice of the marshal's unborn child, after tearing it from the mother's womb. De Rais made no reply but returned at once to Machecoul, the Florentine sorcerer and his accomplice the priest on his heels.

Meanwhile, Anne, left to her own devices on the roof of the tower and not daring to come down, had used her veil to send distress signals. These were answered by two cavaliers accompanied by a posse of armed men, who were riding toward the castle. They proved to be her two brothers, who, on learning of the spurious departure of the marshal for Palestine, had come to visit and console Madame de Rais. Soon after, they arrived with a clatter in the court of the castle, Lévi narrates, whereupon Lord de Rais suspended the hideous ceremony and said to his wife:

"Madame, I forgive you, and [put] the matter at an end between us if you do now as I tell you. Return to your apartment, change your garments, and join me in the guest-room, whither I am going to receive your brothers. But if you say one word, or cause them the slightest suspicion, I will bring you hither on their departure; we shall proceed with the Black Mass at the point where it is now broken off, and at the consecration you will die. Mark where I place this knife."

De Rais rose and led his wife to the door of her chamber, then received her brothers, saying their sister was preparing herself to come and greet them. Madame de Rais appeared almost immediately, pale as a specter. Her husband never took his eyes off her, seeking to control her by his glance. When her brother suggested that she was ill, says Lévi, she answered that it was the fatigue of pregnancy, but added in an undertone, "Save me, he seeks to kill me."

At the same moment Sister Anne rushed into the hall, crying, "Take us away; save us, my brothers, this man is an assassin," and she pointed to de Rais. The marshal summoned his men, but the visitors' escort surrounded the women with drawn swords. The marshal's people disarmed instead of obeying him. Madame de Rais, with her sister and brothers, crossed the drawbridge and left the castle.

Terrible rumors spread through all the countryside. Many young girls and boys had disappeared; some had been traced to the castle of Champtocé and not beyond. The public accused de Rais of murder and of crimes even worse than murder. It was true that no one dared openly accuse a baron so powerful as the lord of Rais. Whenever the disappearance of so many children was mentioned in his presence, he reacted with the greatest astonishment. Suspicions aroused are not easily allayed, however, and the castle of Champtocé and its lord had acquired a fearful reputation and were shrouded in mystery.

The continued disappearance of young boys and girls had caused so bitter a feeling in the neighborhood that the Church felt compelled to intervene. At the urging of the bishop of Nantes, the duke of Brittany ordered de Rais and his accomplices arrested.

De Rais's Trial

Their trial took place before a commission composed of the bishop of Nantes, the chancellor of Brittany, the vicar of the Inquisition, and Pierre l'Hôpital, the president of the provincial parliament. De Rais was accused of sorcery, sodomy, and murder. At first he stood his ground, denouncing his judges as worthless and impure and declaring that rather than plead before such shameless knaves he would be hung like a dog, without trial. But overwhelming evidence brought against him day after day—terrible revelations by Prélati and de Rais's servants about his unquenchable sexual lust, his sacrifices of young children for the supposed gratification of the devil, and the ferocious pleasure with which he gloated over the throbbing limbs and glazing eyes of those who were the victims of both his sensuality and his cruelty—shook even de Rais's imperturbability and he confessed everything.

The final count showed that 140 children had fallen victim to de Rais and his insane lust for the philosophers' stone. Both de Rais and Prélati were doomed to be burned alive, but in consideration of rank, the punishment of the marshal was somewhat mitigated—he was strangled before he was given over to the flames.

The sentence was executed at Nantes, on October 26, 1440. The chronicler Monstrelet states:

"Notwithstanding his many and atrocious cruelties, he made a very devout end, full of penitence, most humbly imploring his Creator to have mercy on his manifold sins and wickedness. When his body was partly burned, some ladies and damsels of his family requested his remains of the Duke of Brittany, that they might be interred in holy ground, which was granted. The greater part of the nobles of Brittany, more especially those of his kindred, were in the utmost grief and confusion at his shameful death."

The records of the trial and judgment are preserved in the Bibliothèque Nationale in Paris, and at Nantes.

The castle of Champtocé stands in a beautiful valley, and many a romantic legend flowers about its gray old walls. Novelist Anthony Trollope described it thus:

"The hideous, half-burnt body of the monster himself circled in flames, pale, indeed, and faint in colour, but more lasting than those the hangman kindled around his mortal form in the meadow under the walls of Nantes—is seen on bright moonlight nights, standing now on one topmost point of craggy wall, now on another, and is heard mingling his moan with the sough of the night-wind. Pale, bloodless forms, too, of youthful growth and mien, the restless, unsepulchred ghosts of the unfortunates who perished in these dungeons unassoiled, may at similar times be seen flitting backwards and forwards in numerous groups across the space enclosed by the ruined walls, with more than mortal speed, or glancing hurriedly from window to window of the fabric, as still seeking to escape from its hateful confinement."

Sources:

Bataille, Georges. *Procès de Gilles de Rais.* Paris, 1959.

Gabory, Emile. *Alias Bluebeard.* New York: Brewer & Warren, 1930.

Lévi, Éliphas. *The History of Magic.* London: Rider, 1913.

Wilson, Thomas. *Blue-Beard: A Contribution to History & Folk-Lore.* London, 1899. Reprint, New York: B. Blom, 1971. Reprint, New York: Arno Press, 1981.

Wolf, Leonard. *Bluebeard: The Life & Crimes of Gilles de Rais.* New York: Crown, 1980.

Gillespie, William Hewitt (1905–)

British psychiatrist and psychoanalyst who also wrote on parapsychological subjects. Gillespie was born August 6, 1905, at Pei-Tai-Ho, China. He later attended the University of Edinburgh (Scotland). He held important positions in the LCC Mental Hospitals Service, London; the Institute of Psychiatry; and the London Clinic of Psychoanalysis before being appointed to the Maudsley Hospital, London, where after a long tenure he was named emeritus physician. During his career he wrote a number of articles on parapsychological subjects.

Sources:

Gillespie, William H. "Extrasensory Elements in Dream Interpretation." *Psychoanalysis and the Occult.* Edited by George Devereaux. New York: International Universities Press, 1953.

Ginnungagap

In Norse mythology, the unfathomable gap between Niflheim (the region of eternal cold, mist, and darkness) and Muspellsheim (the realm of fire)—the void before the creation. Cold winds from the abyss changed the streams into blocks of ice, which fell into the void with the sound of thunder, the legends say. Sparks from Muspellsheim turned the ice into streams, forming layers of frost that filled the gap. The inchoate mass became animate, taking the form of the primeval giant Ymir. Ymir was slain by Odin, Villi, and Ve, who threw his body into the chasm, where his blood became the sea, his flesh the earth, his bones the mountains and rocks, his skull the sky, and his brains the clouds.

During the eleventh century, the sea between Greenland and America was named Ginnungagap.

The name was also used by author James Webb as the title of the first chapter of his book *The Occult Establishment* (1976) to denote the political and economic chaos in Western Europe after World War I, from which arose occult and political cults and their leaders, profoundly influencing modern society.

Ginseng

Pronounced "jin-seng," a plant of the genus Panax, family Aralia, indigenous to China, Korea, and North America. The Chinese and Korean species, *Panax ginseng,* is said to have curative properties, including the ability to prolong life.

The roots sometimes resemble the human form, rather like the **mandragoras** or **mandrake,** and a legend similar to that of the mandrake says that ginseng also screams when uprooted. Chinese tradition claims that ginseng absorbs a special earth vitality that is communicated to those who consume the plant (usually in the form of an infusion); hence in former times its use was restricted to emperors.

Although the plant's medicinal value is still disputed in Europe and the United States, it is now cultivated widely for sale in health food stores.

The American general William Westmoreland reportedly took ginseng tea at breakfast during the Vietnam War, and Russians gave it to cosmonauts to combat infectious disease.

Sources:

Harriman, Sarah. *The Book of Ginseng.* New York: Pyramid Books, 1975.

Melton, J. Gordon, Jerome Clark, and Aidan Kelly. *New Age Encyclopedia.* Detroit: Gale Research, 1990.

Girard, Jean-Baptiste (1680–1733)

A Jesuit born at Dôle in France. Girard was persecuted by the Jansenists, who accused him of seducing a girl named Catherine Cadière, who showed symptoms of possession and had to be sent to a convent of Ursulines at Brest. His enemies found it impossible to implicate him in the affair, and the Parliament of Aix-en-Provence, before which he was tried in 1731, was forced to acquit him. He returned to his native Dôle, where he died two years later. The case resembles similar accusations against priests by nuns that occurred at **Loudon** and **Louviers.**

Gladen, The Root of

Regarded as a remedy for a disease called the "elf cake," which caused a hardness in the side. Thomas Lupton's *A Thousand Notable Things* (1595) gives the following prescription for making up the medicine: "Take a root of gladen, and make powder thereof, and give the diseased party half a spoonful thereof, to drink in white wine, and let him eat thereof so much in his pottage at one time, and it will help him within awhile." *Gladen* or *Gladdon* is an old name for both varieties of iris—the garden flower (*Iris pseudo-acorus*) and the wild iris (*Iris foetidissima*). The root of the former was reputed to be effective for dropsy and the root of the latter for hysterical disorders.

Gladstone, William Ewart (1809–1898)

The great Victorian statesman, four times prime minister of Great Britain, who was interested in psychical research, which he considered "the most important work which is being done in the world—by far the most important." Gladstone came to that belief rather late in his life. On October 29, 1884, he had a successful **slate-writing** sitting with the medium **William Eglinton.** After the séance he was quoted as saying:

"I have always thought that scientific men run too much in a groove. They do noble work in their own special line of research, but they are too often indisposed to give any attention to matters which seem to conflict with their established modes of thought. Indeed, they not infrequently attempt to deny that into which they have never inquired, not sufficiently realising the fact that there may possibly be forces in nature of which they know nothing."

Shortly after the Eglinton sitting, Gladstone joined the **Society for Psychical Research.**

Sources:

Feuchtwanger, E. J. *Gladstone.* Blasingtoke, U.K.: Macmillan, 1989.

Tweedale, Violet. *Ghosts I Have Seen and Other Psychic Experiences.* New York: Frederick A. Stokes, 1919.

Glamourie

The state of mind in which witches were said to see **apparitions** and **visions** of many kinds. (See also **witchcraft**)

Glanvill, Joseph (1636–1680)

Chaplain to Charles II, prebendary of Worcester, philosopher, and one of the earliest fellows of the Royal Society. He was the author of several books, including *Scepsis Scientifica* (1665) and *Sorcerers and Sorcery* (1666). He is best remembered as a precursor of modern psychical researchers and the author of *Sadicismus Triumphatus* (1681), which contains accounts of remarkable cases of **witchcraft** and details of the author's personal investigation into the **poltergeist** known as the **Drummer of Tedworth.**

Sources:

Glanvill, Joseph. *Sadicismus Triumphatus.* London: Printed for J. Collins and S. Lownds, 1681.

Redgrove, H. Stanley, and I. M. L. Redgrove. *Joseph Glanvill and Psychical Research in the Seventeenth Century.* London: William Rider & Son, 1921.

Taylor, Sascha. *Glanvill: The Uses and Abuses of Skepticism.* New York: Pergamon Press, 1981.

Glas Ghairm

A rhyme or spell of Scottish origin to keep a dog from barking or to open a lock. The glas ghairm was also supposed to be of special value to young men in their courtship days. About 1900 a well-known character in Skye (Hebrides, Scotland) named Archibald the Lightheaded was believed to know this incantation but repeated it so quickly that no one could understand what he said. The man was insane, but the fear that dogs had of him was ascribed to his knowledge of the glas ghairm. It was believed that this rhyme had some reference to the safety of the children of Israel on the night before the biblical Exodus: "against any of the children of Israel shall not a dog move his tongue, against man or beast" (Exod. 11:7). (See also **hand of glory**)

Glaskin, G(erald) M(arcus) (1923–)

Australian novelist who has experimented with the **"Christos experience,"** a method of inducing altered states of consciousness. Born December 16, 1923, in Perth, Western Australia, Glaskin traveled widely. During World War II, he served in the

Australian navy and air force. He began to write short stories and articles at age 18 in a military hospital.

After the war he worked as a stockbroker in Singapore for ten years, then returned to Perth in 1959 as a full-time writer. Beginning with *A World of Our Own* (1955), Glaskin wrote a number of novels and other books, as well as several dramas. His writing has brought him numerous honors in his homeland. He first encountered the Christos experience through a group at Mahogany Creek, Western Australia, who published several volumes of a magazine titled *Open Mind.* In his first Christos experience, Glaskin appeared to be transported to a life in ancient Egypt. In his 1974 book *Worlds Within,* he describes the techniques for inducing the Christos experience.

Glaskin wrote three books dealing with the Christos experience: *Windows of the Mind: Discovering Your Past and Future Lives through Massage and Mental Exercise* (1974), *Worlds Within: Probing the Christos Experiment* (1974), and *A Door to Eternity: Proving the Christos Experiment* (1979).

Sources:

Glaskin, G. M. *A Door to Eternity: Proving the Christos Experience.* London: Wildwood, 1979.

———. *Windows of the Mind: Discovering Your Past and Future Lives through Massage and Mental Exercise.* New York: Delacorte, 1974.

———. *Worlds Within: Probing the Christos Experiment.* 1976. Reprint, London: Arrow, 1978.

Glastonbury

A town in Somerset, England, that has become the focus of romantic legends of both Paganism and Christianity. It is situated among orchards and water meadows in the fen country surrounding Glastonbury Tor, a hill on what was once an island. Although there is an old Christian chapel on the Tor, Celtic legends state that this was the entrance to a pagan underworld, home of the fairy folk. The ruined abbey at Glastonbury is associated with the legend of Joseph of Arimathea, who is said to have brought the Holy **Grail** to the Vale of Avalon and planted a staff in the ground, which grew as a thorn, flowering on Christmas Eve.

The Glastonbury thorn actually existed until Reformation times, when it was destroyed, but varieties exist in other parts of Britain. Glastonbury is also believed to be the resting place of **King Arthur.**

During the early decades of this century, **Frederick Bligh Bond** received a number of messages—published as the **Glastonbury Scripts**—that directed his excavations of the abbey. In the 1920s, Katherine Maltwood began to examine reports that the land around Glastonbury was laid out as a giant horoscope, which became known as the **Glastonbury zodiac.** More recently Glastonbury became the home of magician Dion Fortune.

This "power complex" of traditions and legends has attracted many young people to Glastonbury as a pilgrimage center in the contemporary occult and mystical revival. New mythologies crossed with the old as thousands of young pilgrims spend magical weekends at Glastonbury, combining flying saucer cults, Hare Krishna incantations, and rock music with legends of King Arthur and Joseph of Arimathea.

Glastonbury is now regarded as a power center of the New Age of Aquarius, and a community magazine, *Torc,* has been founded to further knowledge of Glastonbury and its associations. (Address for subscription information: 3 Jacobs Close, Windmill Hill, Glastonbury, Somerset, U.K.) In 1989 the "alternative" community of Glastonbury, through an organization called Unique Publications, launched a journal, *The Glastonbury Gazette.*

For a skeptical account of the Glastonbury legends, see *Christianity in Somerset* (1976), by Robert Dunning. Dunning claims that all the stories of King Arthur and St. Joseph were twelfth-century fabrications used to attract funds for the rebuilding of the abbey.

Sources:

Ashe, Geoffrey. *The Quest for Arthur's Britain.* London, 1968.

Greed, John A. *Glastonbury Tales.* Bristol, England: St. Trillo Publications, 1975.

Howard-Gordon, Francis. *Glastonbury: Maker of Myths.* Glastonbury, England: Gothic Image, 1982.

Lewis, Lionel. *St. Joseph of Arimathea at Glastonbury.* London: James Clarke, 1955.

Michell, John. *New Light on the Ancient Mystery of Glastonbury.* Glastonbury, England: Gothic Images Publications, 1990.

Reiser, Oliver L. *This Holyest Erthe: The Glastonbury Zodiac and King Arthur's Camelot.* Bedford, England: Perennial Books, 1976.

Treharne, R. F. *The Glastonbury Legends.* London, 1967.

Williams, Mary. *Glastonbury: A Study in Patterns.* Hammersmith, England: Research into Lost Knowledge Organization, 1969.

Glastonbury Scripts

Title given to a series of nine booklets edited by **Frederick Bligh Bond** containing various **automatic writing** communications concerning Glastonbury Abbey and its history: (1) *The Return of Johannes,* (2) *Pages from the Book of Immortal Remembrance,* (3 and 7) *Life of Hugh of Avalon,* (4) *Life of Abbot Ailnoth,* (5) *The Vision of Mathias,* (6) *The Rose Miraculous,* (8) *The Founding of the First Christian Church,* and (9) *King Arthur and the Quest of the Holy Grail.*

Number 1 contains writing obtained by Bond with the medium **John Alleyne** (psudonym of J. Allen Bartlett). The communicator claimed to be "Johannes Bryant," a monk of Glastonbury of the period 1497–1534. Numbers 3, 4, and 7 are the work of two American sitters to whom the history of the abbey was unknown.

Number 2 records the writings of a Winchester medium whose hand was allegedly used automatically without her volition. The communicators claimed to be monks of the eleventh and twelfth centuries. According to psychical researcher **Nandor Fodor,** "they were veridical in scores of cases, the most famous of which is the discovery of the Norman wall of Herlewin's Chapel, recorded by Bond in his book *The Company of Avalon*" (1924). It was the public's linking this discovery with psychical research (in Bond's publications) that led to the abrupt closing of the excavations in 1922. Bond was suspended from his directorship of the excavations and forfeited his privileges. In the atmosphere of the times, when Spiritualism was considered a crackpot belief by many, the abbey trustees were alienated. Several of Bond's findings were allegedly obliterated by the removal of stones and the filling of trenches.

Numbers 5, 6, 8, and 9 of the Glastonbury Scripts were obtained by Bond in his sessions with **Hester Dowden,** who claimed that his presence and the contact of his fingers on her hand or wrist was a *sine qua non* in the process of obtaining them. The mental contact came through Bond, Dowden said. Her contribution was the motor power of transmission and the more mechanical side of the word formation. For this reason the automatist disclaimed sole **copyright,** alleging "dual mediumship."

This view was energetically contested by **Sir Arthur Conan Doyle** who in conjunction with the Authors' Society gave his support to the chancery court action of July 1926 (*Cummins* v. *Bond*), which established the ruling that all automatic scripts are the sole copyright of the amanuensis, who is thus regarded by law as the only author.

The story of the Glastonbury Scripts carried on the record of prediction and discovery as told by Bond in a series of earlier books: *The Gate of Remembrance* (1918), *The Hill of Vision* (1919), and *The Company of Avalon* (1924). These examples of **cross-correspondence** were obtained through four far-separated mediums. To these a fifth may be added, since the monk "Johannes" again wrote, in his old style, through the hand of **Mina Crandon** of Boston in 1926–27. Part of the record is printed in the *Clark University Symposium* of 1926.

Sources:

Bond, F. Bligh. *The Glastonbury Scripts.* 9 vols. Glastonbury, England: Abbot's Leigh, n.d.

Kenawell, William W. *The Quest at Glastonbury: A Biographical Study of Frederick Bligh Bond.* New York: Garrett Publications, 1965.

Lambert, G. W. "The Quest at Glastonbury." *Journal* of the Society for Psychical Research 43, 728 (June 1960).

Glastonbury Zodiac

One of the strangest features of legend-haunted **Glastonbury** in Britain is the so-called zodiac formation of earthworks, field tracks, river banks, and other ground markings over an area of some 30 miles, resembling a gigantic star map. An early mention of the Glastonbury zodiac was made by **John Dee,** famous Elizabethan scholar and occultist, but it was not until comparatively recent times that the subject was examined in detail.

In her book *A Guide to Glastonbury's Temple of the Stars* (1929), Katherine E. Maltwood maps a giant zodiac from the features of the Glastonbury landscape with additional features suggestive of symbols of the Holy **Grail** tradition.

Although this theory has been received with some skepticism, aerial surveys have tended to support the ground markings as suggestive of a zodiac. (See also **leys**)

Sources:

Caine, Mary. *The Glastonbury Zodiac: Key to the Mysteries of Britain.* Torquay, England: Grael Communications, 1978.

Maltwood, Katherine E. *A Guide to Glastonbury's Temple of the Stars.* London, 1929.

Glauber, Johann Rudolph (ca. 1604–1670)

German apothecary and alchemist. Glauber was born at Karlstadt and grew up in Franconia. He traveled widely in Germany seeking alchemical knowledge and eventually settled in Amsterdam, Holland, in 1648. He was a prolific writer and left many treatises on medicine and **alchemy.** He discovered and prepared medicines of great value to pharmacy, some of which are still in common use, for example the familiar preparation known as Glauber's salt.

He was a firm believer in the **philosophers' stone** and the **elixir of life.** Concerning the former, he stated:

"Let the benevolent reader take with him my final judgment concerning the great Stone of the Wise; let every man believe what he will and is able to comprehend. Such a work is purely the gift of God, and cannot be learned by the most acute power of human mind, if it be not assisted by the benign help of a Divine Inspiration. And of this I assure myself that in the last times, God will raise up some to whom He will open the Cabinet of Nature's Secrets, that they shall be able to do wonderful things in the world to His Glory, the which, I indeed, heartily wish to posterity that they may enjoy and use to the praise and honour of God."

According to fellow alchemist Goossen van Vreeswych, Glauber died in Amsterdam, March 14, 1670. Some of Glauber's principal works include *Philosophical Furnaces; Commentary on Paracelsus; Heaven of the Philosophers, or Book of Vexation; Miraculum Mundi; The Prosperity of Germany;* and *Book of Fires.*

Glosopetra (or Gulosus)

A miraculous stone said to fall from heaven in the wane of the moon. It was supposed to be shaped like a human tongue and was used by magicians "to excite the lunar motions."

Glossolalia

A form of religious speech generally called "speaking in tongues" or "pseudo-tongues." It is also occasionally confused with **xenoglossis,** which refers to speaking in tongues unknown to the medium or psychic.

Glottologues

Mediums or ecstatics who speak in unknown tongues. (See **Xenoglossis**)

Gloucester, Duchess of (Eleanor Cobham) (d. ca. 1443)

Wife of Humphrey of Gloucester, who was uncle of Henry VI and lord protector of England during the king's minority. Although Humphrey was very popular in England, he was not without enemies, and one of the most bitter of these was Henry Beaufort, cardinal of Winchester, great-uncle to the king. Beaufort brought a charge of **witchcraft** against the duchess of Gloucester, hoping thus to destroy her husband's power as the actual head of the realm and heir to the throne in the event of the king's death.

It was supposed that the duchess had first resorted to witchcraft in order to gain the affections of Humphrey. When she became his second wife and the death of the duke of Bedford had removed all but one barrier between her and a crown, she set about to secretly remove that barrier—the unfortunate king.

To assist in her plot, she was said to have sought the advice of Margery Jourdain (the Witch of Eye), Roger Bolingbroke, Thomas Southwell, and Fr. John Hun, a priest. All five were accused of summoning evil spirits and plotting to destroy the king. They were also suspected of making a waxen image, which was slowly melted before a fire in the expectation that as the image was consumed the king would also waste away.

The five were tried. Father Hun turned informer and was pardoned. Bolingbroke was publicly humiliated, then hanged and drawn and quartered. Southwell died in prison, Margery Jourdain was burned as a witch, and in 1441 the duchess of Gloucester was disgraced and sentenced to walk through the streets of London on three separate occasions bearing a lighted taper in her hand and attended by the lord mayor, sheriffs, and others.

She was imprisoned for life, first in Chester Castle, then from October 1443 in Kenilworth. She died around 1443.

Early in 1443 Humphrey had set out for parliament in the hope of securing a pardon for the duchess, but he was arrested on suspicion of treason and died in custody. Known as "Good Duke Humphrey," he is remembered chiefly for his love of books; he made generous gifts to the library of Oxford University.

Gnome Club of Great Britain, The

A British-based organization with an international section (Gnome International), founded in 1978 by Ann Atkin of Devon, who claimed that her contact with gnomes revealed their wish to communicate with humans on a global scale to benefit the ecology of the planet and widen human consciousness in the forthcoming new age.

The organization was featured in national newspapers and on BBC Television. It was also concerned with various forms of fairy life, like the **Fairy Investigation Society.** The Gnome Club issued a regular newsletter from the Old Rectory, West Putford, Devon, England.

After 1983 the Gnome Club was reorganized as **Gnomes Anonymous,** now based at the Gnome Reserve, 224 Kingston Rd., New Malden, Surrey, KT3 3UH, England. (See also **Cottingley fairies; fairies**)

Gnome International

The international section of the **Gnome Club of Great Britain,** founded in 1978 by Ann Atkin at the Old Rectory, West Putford, Devon, England. In 1983 Gnome International was reorganized as **Gnomes Anonymous,** now based at the Gnome Reserve, 224 Kingston Rd., New Malden, Surrey, KT3 3UH, England.

Gnomes Anonymous

British organization that developed from a reorganization of the **Gnome Club of Great Britain** and **Gnomes International,** both founded in 1978 by Ann Atkin at the Old Rectory, West Putford, Devon.

In 1983 the Gnome Reserve was moved to Surrey under the administration of Alex Adams, "gnome-in-chief." The purpose of Gnomes International is to "unite gnomes and their human keepers," and membership is open to people of all ages interested in gnomes. The organization offers children's services, conducts research, and maintains a speakers' bureau. It publishes *Gnome News* three times a year. Address: Alex Adams, Gnome Reserve, 224 Kingston Rd., New Malden, Surrey, KT3 3UH, England.

Gnostic Association of Cultural and Anthropological Studies

The Gnostic Association of Cultural and Anthropological Studies is one of the largest occult groups to operate among Spanish-speaking people. It was founded in 1952 by Samuel Aun Weor (d. 1977), a native of Colombia. Weor had studied with German esotericist Arnold Krumm Heller, a leader in the **Ordo Templi Orientis.** Over the years Weor became an accomplished esotericist and teacher and began to write books in Spanish. His central teachings appeared in his 1961 volume, *The Perfect Matrimony.*

Weor sought to synthesize the many occult, magical, and yogic materials he had absorbed, resulting in a system of occult sexuality. He believed that humanity could be redeemed by the transmutation of sexual energies and that God manifests as both Father (knowledge) and Mother (love). The "perfect marriage" occurs when two people who know how to love unite. Individuals can transform themselves into gods with the fire of love. Weor taught that during the sexual act, individuals are charged with universal magnetism. The true white magician practices what is known as karazza and ends the union before any semen is spilled. Transmuting the creative energies, so that orgasm does not occur and therefore semen is not released, is equated with the committing of an act of sexual magic. The success of the magic is experienced by the awakening of the kundalini energy, which is pictured as stored at the base of the spine, which then travels up the spine. When it reaches the brain, individual consciousness awakens.

The association spread first through South and Central America, then traveled to Spain and Portugal before it penetrated Europe. It came to New York and Los Angeles in the 1970s and spread across the United States in the Spanish-speaking communities. Through the 1970s and 1980s, many of Weor's books were translated into English and other languages. An English language periodical, *The Gnostic Arhat,* was begun in 1987. The first international congress of the association occurred in 1986 in Montreal. In 1988 the association reported work in 25 countries. It may be contacted at Box 291488, Los Angeles, CA 90029.

Sources:

Almarez, Anita Ford. *Simple Introduction to the Ancient Science of Gnosis.* Chicago: Gnostic Association, n.d.

Weor, Samuel Aun Weor. *Manual of Practical Magic.* Los Angeles: Gnostic Association, 1988.

———. *Manual of Revolutionary Psychology.* Los Angeles: Gnostic Association, 1987.

———. *The Perfect Matrimony.* New York: Adonai Editorial, 1980.

Gnostica

Bimonthly journal that appeared through the 1970s and covered all aspects of the contemporary occult scene. It was edited by **Carl L. Weschcke** and was published by Llewellyn Publications, 213 4th St., St. Paul, MN 55101.

During the 1980s *Gnostica* was superseded by *Llewellyn's New Times,* published from the same address.

Gnosticism

Gnosticism, from the Greek "Gnosis," meaning "to know," refers to a number of different groups in the second century C.E. Roots of the movement are evident in the Christian New Testament writings of the first century; they drew on various Pagan, Jewish, and occult ideas current in the Mediterranean Basin. Some have seen the roots of Gnosticism in the writings of **Apollonius of Tyana** and the biblical magician **Simon Magus,** mentioned in Acts 8:9–24. However, the emergence of gnostic thinking is seen most clearly in passages such as the opening verses of the Gospel of John, Paul's epistle to the Collossians 2:18, and I John 4:1, where gnostic themes are denounced.

Among some of the Gnostics, a priesthood of the mysteries existed and these initiated priests practiced **magic, astrology,** incantations, exorcisms, the fashioning of charms, talismans, and **amulets,** of which many are in museums and special collections. These priests were viewed as heretics by the church, which in the second and third century struggled to separate itself from them. Upon gaining control of the Roman Empire, Christian leaders periodically suppressed Gnostic groups and occasionally these movements provided the ideology for revolutionary groups.

Manicheism, a later movement of Gnosticism that emphasized its dualistic tendencies, was founded by a prophet named Mani (216–276 C.E.), who was noted for his skill in astrology, medicines, and magic.

The most notable gnostic teacher was Valentinus, a second-century Alexandrian who moved to Rome around 140 C.E. He became a teacher in the church of Rome before being expelled as a heretic. He continued to teach as a rival of the church for the next two decades. His major literary production was the *Gospel of Truth,* known only from quote in Christian polemical writings until a copy was discovered in the Egyptian desert in the twentieth century.

Magical and Occult Element in Gnosticism

The **Carpocratians,** one of the Gnostic sects, seem to have derived some of their mysteries and rites from Isis worship, and used theurgic incantations, symbols, and signs. The Ophites also adapted Egyptian rites, and, as their name indicates, these included serpent symbolism, an actual serpent being the central object of their mysteries. Marcos, a disciple of Valentinus, and founder of the Marcian sect, reportedly celebrated Mass with two chalices, pouring wine from the larger into a smaller, and on pronouncing a magical formula, the vessel was filled with a liquor like blood. Other sects practiced divination and prophecy by using female somnambules. Some of the sects engaged in rituals of a sexual nature.

The Gnostic talismans were mostly engraved on gems, the color and traditional qualities of the jewel being part of its magical efficacy. They used spells and charms and mystic formulas, said to "loose fetters, to cause blindness in one's enemies, to procure dreams, to gain favor, to encompass any desire whatsoever."

In a Greek Gnostic papyrus the following spell of Agathocles for producing dreams was found:

"Take a cat, black all over, and which has been killed; prepare a writing tablet, and write the following with a solution of myrrh, and the dream which thou desirest to be sent, and put in the mouth of the cat. The text to be transcribed runs: 'Keimi, Keimi, I am the Great One, in whose mouth rests Mommom, Thoth, Nauumbre, Karikha, Kenyro, Paarmiathon, the sacred Ian icê ieu aêoi, who is above the heaven, Amekheumen, Neunana, Seunana, Ablanathanalba,' [here follow further names, then] 'Put thyself in connection with N.N. in this matter [as to the substance of the dream named] but if it is necessary then bring for me N.N. hither by thy power; lord of the whole world, fiery god, put thyself in connexion with N.N. . . . Hear me, for I shall speak the great name, Thoth! whom each god honours, and each demon fears, by whose command every messenger performs his mission. Thy name answers to the seven (vowels) a, e, ê, i, o, u, ô, *iauoeêaô oueê ôia.* I named thy glorious name, the name for all needs. Put thyself in connection with N.N., Hidden One, God, with respect to this name, which Apollobex also used.' ''

The repetition/chanting of various syllables, otherwise apparently meaningless, was always held to be of great efficacy in magical rites, either as holding the secret name of the powers invoked, or of actual power in themselves. A similar practice, japa **yoga,** may be found in Hinduism with the repetition of mantras.

In Atanasi's *Magic Papyrus,* Spell VII directs one to place the link of a chain upon a leaden plate, and having traced its outline, to write around the circumference the common Gnostic legend in Greek characters (reading both ways) continuously. Within the circle should be written the nature of what was to be prevented. The operation was called "The Ring of Hermes." The link was then to be folded up on the leaden plate, and thrown into the grave of one dead before his time, or else into a disused well. After the formula was to follow in Greek: "Prevent thou such and such a person from doing such and such a thing"—a proof that the string of epithets all referred to the same power.

These instances might be multiplied, although much of the Gnostic teachings were lost as the gnostic lost out in the religious struggles of the era. Gnosticism was passed on through the centuries in various groups usually described a heretical groups such as the Cathars and Bogomils. It reemerged in the late Middle Ages in **alchemy** and the **kabala.** With the rise of Rosicrucianism and nineteenth-century Theosophy, it became well established in the emerging pluralistic culture and has enjoyed a new life in the **New Age** movement.

Many of the lost gnostic texts were recovered in 1945 in the accidental discovery of a fourth-century gnostic library in the Egyptian desert at Nag Hammadi. Many complete copies of books, such as the *Gospel of Truth,* previously known only from a few surviving quotes in other books, were discovered intact. This discovery has stimulated modern gnostic studies, and one book, *The Gospel of Thomas,* a collection of lost sayings attributed to Jesus, has been adopted as holy writ by several contemporary gnostic churches.

Sources:

Doresse, Jean. *The Secret Books of the Egyptian Gnostics.* London: Hollis and Carter, 1960. Reprint, New York: AMS Press, 1972.

Lacarriere, Jacques. *The Gnostics.* London: Peter Owen, 1977.

Mead, G. R. S. *Fragments of a Faith Forgotten.* London, 1931. Reprint, New York: University Books, 1964.

Mead, G. R. S. *Pistis Sophia; A Gnostic Miscellany.* London, 1921. Reprint, New Hyde Park, N.Y.: University Books, 1974.

Goat

The devil was frequently represented as a goat, and as such presided over the witches' **Sabbat.** The goat was also the "emblem of sinful men at the day of judgment." (See also **Baphomet; she-goat; witchcraft**)

Goblin

A spirit formerly supposed to lurk in houses. Goblins were generally of a mischievous and grotesque nature. Hobgoblins, according to Junius, were so called because they used to hop on one leg. (See also **fairies**)

God (in Occult Perspective)

According to the ancient magical conception of God in the scheme of the universe, evil is the inevitable contrast and complement of good. God permits the existence of the shadow in order that it may intensify the purity of the light. He has created both and they are thus inseparable, the one being necessary to and incomprehensible without the other.

The very idea of goodness loses its meaning if considered apart from that of evil—Gabriel is a foil to Satan and Satan to Gabriel. The dual nature of the spiritual world penetrates into every department of life, material and spiritual. It is typified in light and darkness, cold and heat, truth and error, in brief, the names of any two opposing forces will serve to illustrate the primary law of nature—namely, the continual conflict between the positive or good and the negative or evil.

For a scriptural illustration of this point, the story of Cain and Abel can be used. The moral superiority of his brother is at first irksome to Cain, finally intolerable. He murders Abel, thus bringing on his own head the wrath of God and the self-punishment of the murderer. For in killing Abel, Cain has done himself harm. Cain has not done away with Abel's superiority, but has added to himself a burden of guilt that can end only by much suffering.

Suffering is shown in the Judaeo-Christian scriptures to be one means evil is overcome by good. Cain reappears in the story of the prodigal son, who after deprivation and suffering is restored to his father who forgives him fully and freely.

It is believed that the possibility of sin and error is consistent with and inseparable from life. The great sinner is a more vital being than the colorless character, because having greater capacity for evil he has also greater capacity for good, and in proportion to his faults so will his virtues be when he turns to God. "There is more joy in heaven over one sinner that repenteth than over ninety and nine just persons," because more force of character, more power for good or evil is displayed by the sinner than by the feebly correct. And that power is the most precious thing in life. The apostle Paul specifically rejected this approach to understanding sin and redemption in Romans 6: 1-2.

This dual law of right and wrong, two antagonistic forces, is designated by the term "duad." It is the secret of life and the revelation of that secret means death. This secret is embodied in the myth of the Tree of Knowledge in Genesis. At death the discord will be resolved, but not until then.

From the duad is derived the triad based on the doctrine of the Trinity. Two forces producing equilibrium, the secret of nature, are designated by the duad, and these three—life, good, and evil—constitute one law. By adding the conception of unity to the triad the tetrad is produced, the perfect number of four, the source of all numerical combinations.

According to orthodox theology there are three persons in God, Father, Son and Holy Ghost, and these three form one Deity. In occult speculations, three and one make four, the fourth reality being the unity required to explain the Three. Hence, it is suggested, in many languages (most notably Hebrew), the name of God is symbolized by four letters. Again, two affirmations make two negations either possible or necessary. According to the Kabalists the name of the Evil one consisted of the same four letters spelled backward, signifying that evil is merely the reflection or shadow of good—"The last reflection or imperfect mirage of light in shadow." Everything exists in light or darkness, good or evil, and exists through the tetrad. The triad or trinity, then, is explained by the duad and resolved by the tetrad.

Such occult interpretations of God echo the ancient mysticism such as the Eastern religion of Hinduism, where the pairs of opposites like good and evil are regarded as twin poles of a larger reality, where anthropomorphic concepts of God the creator are considered legal fictions for a divine infinity, beyond time, space, and causality.

Sources:

Achad, Frater. *The Anatomy of the Body of God.* Chicago: Collegium ad Spiritum Sanctum, 1925.

Akiba ben Joseph Rabbi. *The Book of Formation.* (Sepher Yetzirah). London: William Rider, 1923.

Angeles, Peter A. *The Problem of God; A Short Introduction.* Buffalo, N.Y.: Prometheus Books, 1981.

Arya, Ushbarbudh. *God.* Honesdale, Pa.: Himalayan International Institute, 1979.

Brightman, Edgar S. *The Problem of God.* New York: Abingdon Press, 1930.

Goblet D'Alviella, E. F. *Lectures on the Origin and Growth of the Conception of God.* London, 1892. Reprint, New York: AMS Press, 1982.

Pereira, Jose, ed. *Hindu Theology: A Reader.* Garden City, N.Y.: Image Books, 1976.

Godfrey (or **Gaufridi**) (d. 1611)

A priest of Provence, France, who was accused of seducing several women, one of them a nun. To save herself the nun asserted that Godfrey had bewitched her. Arrested and imprisoned, Godfrey was tortured until he confessed that he was a magician and that he had, through his breathing and other enchantments, corrupted the woman and several more. He was even induced, in his extreme agony, to speak of his presence at the witches' **Sabbat** and to give a long description of it.

After these confessions had been extorted from the priest, the Parliament of Aix-en-Provence condemned him. On April 30, 1611, Godfrey was burned alive as guilty of **magic, sorcery,** impiety, and abominable lust. This horrible affair gave rise to an adventure related by the abbé of Papon:

"The process contained many depositions upon the power of the demons. Several witnesses protested that after being anointed with a magic oil, Godfrey transported himself to the Sabbat, and afterwards returned to his chamber down the shaft of the chimney. One day, when these depositions had been read to the Parliament, and the imagination of the judges excited by a long recital of supernatural events, there was heard in the chimney an extraordinary noise, which suddenly terminated with the apparition of a tall black man. The judges thought it was the devil come to the rescue of his disciple, and fled away swiftly, with the exception of a councillor Thorton, their reporter, who finding himself entangled in his desk, could not follow them. Terrified by what he saw, with trembling body and staring eyes, and repeatedly making the sign of the cross, he in his turn affrighted the pretended demon, who was at a loss to understand the magistrate's perturbation. Recovering from the embarrassment he made himself known, and proved to be a chimney sweeper who, after having swept the chimney of the Messieurs des Comptes, whose chimneys joined those of the Tournelle, had by mistake descended into the chamber of the Parliament."

(For further details, see entry on **Louis Gaufridi,** the name by which the notorious priest is better known.)

Goethe, Johann Wolfgang von (1749–1832)

Probably the most celebrated of all German writers. Goethe had strong interest in **mysticism** and **occult** subjects. He was born at Frankfurt-on-Main, August 28, 1749. His father was a lawyer of some eminence. At an early age the boy showed a persistent fondness for drawing and learned with surprising ease. In 1759 a French nobleman of aesthetic tastes came to stay with the Goethes, and a warm friendship developed between him and the future author. The friendship accelerated young Goethe's intellectual development.

Shortly after this, a French theater was founded at Frankfurt, and there Goethe became conversant with the plays of Racine; he also made some early attempts at original writing and began to learn Italian, Latin, Greek, English, and Hebrew.

He soon moved from his native town to Leipzig, where he entered the university, intending to become a lawyer. At Leipzig, Goethe showed little affection for the actual curriculum; instead he continued in essay writing and drawing and even took lessons in etching. He also found time for a love affair, but this was cut short in 1768 when he developed a serious illness. On his recovery he decided to leave Leipzig and go to Strasbourg.

There he became friendly with Jung-Stilling (see **Johann Heinrich Jung**), and his taste for letters was strengthened, Homer and Ossian being his favorites among the masters. Although he continued to appear indifferent to the study of law, he succeeded in becoming an advocate in 1771 and returned to Frankfurt.

Goethe had already written a quantity of verse and prose, and he began to write critiques for some of the newspapers in Frankfurt. At the same time he started writing *Goetz von Berlichingen* and *Werther.* These works were soon followed by *Prometheus,* and in 1774 the author began working on *Faust.*

The following year saw the production of some of Goethe's best love poems, written for Lilli Schönemann, daughter of a Frankfurt banker. Nothing more than poetry, however, resulted from this new devotion. Scarcely had it come and gone before Goethe's whole life was changed, for his writings had become famous. As a result the young duke Carl August of Weimar, anxious for a trusty page, invited the rising author to his court. The invitation was accepted. Goethe became a member of the privy council; subsequently he was raised to the rank of Geheimrat (privy counselor) and then ennobled.

Goethe's life at Weimar was a very busy one. Trusted implicitly by the duke, he directed the construction of public roads and buildings, attended to military and academic affairs, and founded a court theater. As occupied as he was, he continued to write voluminously. Among the most important works he produced during his first years at the duke's court were *Iphigenie* and *Wilhelm Meister.*

In 1787 he had a lengthy stay in Italy, visiting Naples, Pompeii, Rome, and Milan. Returning to Weimar, he began writing *Egmont.* In 1795 he made the acquaintance of poet and dramatist Friedrich von Schiller, with whom he quickly became friendly and with whom he worked on the *Horen,* a journal designed to elevate the literary tastes of the masses.

About this period, too, Goethe wrote his play *Hermann und Dorothea* and also began translating Voltaire, Diderot, and Benvenuto Cellini.

(For an account of a strange psychic experience at Weimar, when Goethe saw the projected double of a friend, see **double.**)

The year 1806 was a significant one in Goethe's life, marked by his marriage and also by the entry of Napoleon into Weimar. The conquering general and the German poet found much in each other to admire, and Napoleon decorated Goethe with the cross of the Legion of Honour.

In 1811 Goethe wrote *Dichtung und Wahrheit, Wilhelm Meister's Wanderjahre;* in 1821 he began working at a second part of *Faust.* During this time he had two famous visitors—Beethoven from Vienna and Thackeray from London. Although the composer thought himself coldly received, the novelist spoke with enthusiasm of the welcome accorded him. Goethe was then well advanced in years, however, and his health was beginning to fail. He died March 22, 1832.

Few great writers—not even Disraeli or Sir Walter Scott—had fuller lives than Goethe. His love affairs, besides those mentioned here, were many, and his early taste for the graphic arts continued to the end of his days, resulting in a vast collection of treasures.

His interest in mysticism manifested itself in various forms besides the writing of *Faust.* With a temperament aspiring to the unattainable, Goethe's mind was essentially a speculative one. During his childhood at Frankfurt he did symbolic drawings of the soul's aspirations to the deity, and he later became immersed in the study of the Christian religion. Eventually he grew skeptical on this subject, his ideas being altered not only by his own ruminations but by reading various iconoclastic philosophers, especially Rousseau. Later his intellect was seemingly less engaged by Christianity than by ancient Eastern faiths, as demonstrated by some of his works, notably *Westöstliche Divan.*

One of his notebooks shows that, while a young man at Strasbourg, Goethe made a close study of Giordano Bruno and other early scientists. As a boy he was a keen student of **alchemy,** reading deeply in Welling, **Jean Baptiste van Helmont, Basil Valentine,** and **Paracelsus,** and even fitting up a laboratory where he spent long hours in arduous experiments. No doubt it was while thus engaged that Goethe first conceived the idea of writing a drama on the subject of *Faust,* and his alchemistic and other scientific research certainly proved advantageous when he was composing that work.

The story's main outlines are visible in Calderon's and Marlowe's versions, as well as in the operas of Gounod, Schumann, and Berlioz. It is mainly because of *Faust* that Goethe is considered a great mystic, for his rendering of the immortal theme is acknowledged as among the finest in the whole of mystical literature.

Sources:

Cottrell, Alan P., ed. *Goethe's Faust: Seven Essays.* Chapel Hill, N.C.: University of North Carolina Press, 1976.

Davidson, Thomas. *Philosophy of Goethe's Faust.* Boston, 1906. Reprint, Haskell, 1969.

Goethe, Johann Wolfgang von. *The Autobiography of Johann Wolfgang von Goethe.* 2 vols. Chicago: University of Chicago Press, 1975.

Gray, Ronald D. *Goethe, the Alchemist: A Study of Alchemical Symbolism in Goethe's Literary & Scientific Works.* Cambridge: Cambridge University Press, 1952. Reprint, New York: AMS Press, 1979.

Lewes, George H. *The Life of Goethe.* London, 1864. Reprint, Norwood Editions, 1979.

Reed, T. J. *Goethe.* Oxford: Oxford University Press, 1984.

Steiner, Rudolph. *Goethe's Conception of the World.* Reprint, Brooklyn: Haskell, 1972.

———. *The Theory of Knowledge Implicit in Goethe's World Conception.* Hudson, N.Y.: Anthroposophic Press, 1978.

Golden Dawn, Hermetic Order of the

Fountainhead of the modern revival of ceremonial magic. As a secret order it attracted some of the most interesting and talented personalities of its time, including poet **William Butler Yeats,** Annie Horniman (who sponsored the Abbey Theatre, Dublin), Florence Farr (mistress of G. B. Shaw), **S. L. MacGregor Mathers, Aleister Crowley, Israel Regardie, A. E. Waite, Algernon Blackwood, Arthur Machen, Violet Firth,** and many others.

The order dated from the discovery in 1887 of a cipher manuscript, bought from a bookstall in Farringdon Road, London, by **William Wynn Westcott.** He was a coroner and a member of the **Societas Rosicruciana in Anglia** (Rosicrucian Society of Freemasons). Westcott deciphered the manuscript, which contained a series of mystical rituals. With the aid of his occultist friend MacGregor Mathers, these rituals were expanded and systematized. Also among the pages of the manuscript was a slip of paper with the address of **Fräulein Anna Sprengel,** a Rosicrucian adept living in Germany.

Reportedly, Westcott corresponded with Sprengel, who authorized him to found an English branch of the occult society Die Goldene Dämmerung (The Golden Dawn). It has been suggested, however, that Sprengel did not exist and that Westcott fabricated the correspondence to establish the new secret order.

The Isis-Urania Temple of the Hermetic Order of the Golden Dawn was established in London in 1888, with Westcott, Mathers, and W. R. Woodman (another occultist Freemason) as chiefs. Between 1888 and 1896 the Osiris Temple was formed at Weston-super-Mare, Somerset; the Horus Temple at Bradford, Yorkshire; the Amen-Ra Temple at Edinburgh, Scotland; and the Ahathoor Temple in Paris. A total of 315 initiations took place during this period.

The Golden Dawn consisted of ten main grades, associated with the symbolism of the **Kabala:** zelator $10^\circ = 100^\circ$, theoricus $20^\circ = 90^\circ$, practicus $30^\circ = 80^\circ$, philosophus $40^\circ = 70^\circ$, adeptus minor $50^\circ = 60^\circ$, adeptus major $60^\circ = 50^\circ$, adeptus exemptus $70^\circ = 40^\circ$, magister templi $80^\circ = 30^\circ$, magus $90^\circ = 20^\circ$, and ipsissimus $100^\circ = 10^\circ$.

Selected candidates who passed the adeptus minor grade might qualify for admission to a secret second order—the **Ordo Rosae Rubeae et Aureae Crucis** (Order of the Red Rose and Cross of Gold). Behind the second order loomed the so-called secret chiefs, equivalent to the fabled mahatmas of the **Theosophical Society.** These chiefs might be contacted on the astral plane.

The complex rituals of the order were partially revealed in the journal ***The Equinox*** by Aleister Crowley, who joined the Golden Dawn in November 1898 and left early in 1900. A more detailed record of the teaching, rites, and ceremonies was later published by Israel Regardie in four volumes (1937–40).

Although the rituals of the Golden Dawn were little more than a rather complicated Freemasonry embroidered with occult symbolism, the special studies related to them developed the individual's insight into **occultism** and **mysticism.** The poet W. B. Yeats placed a high value on his magic studies with the order and once wrote, "If I had not made magic my constant study I could not have written a single word of my Blake book, nor would *The Countess Kathleen* have ever come to exist."

Yeats played a prominent part in a conflict with Aleister Crowley, who tried to take over the London lodge in 1900. Crowley was expelled from the Golden Dawn, and Yeats took charge of the Rosae Rubeae et Aureae Crucis and also became imperator of the Isis-Urania Temple Outer Order. Crowley eventually founded his own order (the A∴A∴) in 1905, using material he had first encountered in the Golden Dawn.

The Golden Dawn continued to fragment as leadership of the various branches changed hands and new orders were formed. Several Golden Dawn offshoots are still in existence; possibly the most substantive is the Los Angeles–based Builders of the Adytum. In addition several new groups have organized, in part to offer an alternative to the magic practiced in those groups that derive from Aleister Crowley.

Sources:

Colquhoun, Ithell. *The Sword of Wisdom: MacGregor Mathers and the Golden Dawn.* New York: G. P. Putnam's Sons, 1975.

Gilbert, Robert A. *The Golden Dawn: Twilight of the Magicians.* Wellingborough, England: Aquarian Press, 1983.

Harper, George Mills. *Yeats's Golden Dawn.* New York: Macmillan, 1974.

Howe, Ellic. *The Magicians of the Golden Dawn.* London, 1972.

King, Francis. *Astral Projection, Ritual Magic & Alchemy: Being Hitherto Unpublished Gold Dawn Material.* London: Neville Spearman, 1971.

———. *Ritual Magic in England (1887 to the Present Day).* London, 1970.

Regardie, Israel. *The Golden Dawn.* 4 vols. Chicago: Aries Press, 1937–40. Reprint, St. Paul, Minn.: Llewellyn Publications, 1989.

———. *What You Should Know About the Golden Dawn.* Phoenix, Ariz: Falcon Press, 1983.

Roberts, Marie. *British Poets and Secret Societies.* Totowa, N.J.: Barnes & Noble, 1986.

S.M.R.D., Frater, et al. *The Secret Workings of the Golden Dawn: Book "T" the Tarot.* Cheltenham, England: Helios Book Service, 1967.

Torrens, Robert George. *The Inner Teachings of the Golden Dawn.* London: Neville Spearman, 1969.

———. *Secret Rituals of the Golden Dawn.* Wellingborough, England: Aquarian Press, 1973.

Wang, Robert. *An Introduction of the Golden Dawn Tarot.* New York: Samuel Weiser, 1978.

Wang, Robert, and Chris Zalewski. *Z-Five: Secret Teachings of the Golden Dawn.* St. Paul, Minn.: Llewellyn Publications, 1991.

Zalewski, Patrick J. *Golden Dawn Enochian Magic.* St. Paul, Minn.: Llewellyn Publications, 1990.

———. *Secret Inner Order Rituals of the Golden Dawn.* Phoenix, Ariz.: Falcon Press, 1988.

"Golden Key"

Many volumes have been published under this title purporting to reveal an infallible method of attaining success in a lottery. *La Clef d'or,* or *La Véritable trésor de la fortune* (1810), reprinted from time to time at Lille, Belgium, is based on the doctrine of sympathetic numbers, which the anonymous author claims to have discovered from study of the works of **Cagliostro, Cornelius Agrippa,** and others. Each number drawn, he declares, has five sympathetic numbers that directly follow it. For example, the number 4 has for its sympathetic numbers 30, 40, 50, 20, and 76. With this knowledge it is claimed to be an easy matter to win a lottery.

Golden Path, The

Nonprofit organization founded in 1963 by psychic **Irene Hughes** to teach students to develop their psychic talents. It operated out of Chicago, Illinois, through the 1970s.

Goldney, Kathleen M(ary) H(ervey)

Noted British worker in the fields of **psychical research** and **parapsychology.** Goldney joined the **Society for Psychical Research** in 1927 and became a council member in 1943. She served as organizing secretary from 1949 to 1957.

Through the 1950s and 1960s Goldney worked on a number of notable research projects. She assisted **S. G. Soal** in his pioneer investigations into **ESP** with Basil Shackleton, and also investigated the celebrated haunting of Borley Rectory with **Harry Price.** She then collaborated with **Eric J. Dingwall** and **Trevor Hall** on their book *The Haunting of Borley Rectory* (1956), which raised doubts about the part played by Price. Goldney also discussed the evidence for charges that **Sir William Crookes** was misled or falsified his investigations into the mediumship of **Florence Cook.**

Sources:

Medhurst, R. G., and K. M. Goldney. "William Crookes and the Physical Phenomena of Mediumship." *Proceedings* of the Society for Psychical Research 54, 195 (March 1964).

Golem

An artificial man-**monster** of Jewish legend created from clay by a magic religious ceremony. The word *golem* was first used in talmudic references to the creation of Adam to indicate formless matter before the inception of a soul. Talmudic stories of the third and fourth centuries suggest that certain rabbis might have been able to create a manlike creature by magic that followed the divine process of creation. In medieval kabbalistic legends, such stories revolved around the symbolism of the *Sepher Yetsirah* (Book of Creation), in which numbers and letters are associated with parts of the body and astrological correspondences. Much of Western occult practice is related to such texts.

Jakob Grimm refers to such legends in his 1808 book *Zeitung für Einsiedler* (Journal for Hermits): "The Polish Jews, after having spoken certain prayers and observed certain Feast days, make the figure of a man out of clay or lime which, after they have pronounced the wonderworking *Shem-ham-phorasch* over it, comes to life. It is true this figure cannot speak, but it can understand what one says and commands it to do to a certain extent. They call it Golem and use it as a servant to do all sorts of housework; he may never go out alone. On his forehead the word *Aemaeth* (Truth; God) is written, but he increases from day to day and can easily become larger and stronger than his house-comrades, however small he might have been in the beginning. Being then afraid of him, they rub out the first letters so that nothing remains but *Maeth* (he is dead), whereupon he sinks together and becomes clay again."

In the sixteenth century, such legends crystallized around Rabbi Judah Loew of Prague (ca. 1520–1609), who was said to have created a golem who not only worked as a servant but also saved the Jews from persecution arising from false accusations of ritual murders. The tomb of Rabbi Loew may still be visited in the old Jewish Cemetery of Prague in Czechoslovakia.

In the seventeenth century, such stories were recorded in a manuscript titled "Nifloet Mhrl" (Miracles of Rabbi Loew), which formed the basis of the enchanting *Der Prager Golem* of Chayim Bloch, translated into English by Harry Schneiderman as *The Golem: Legends of the Ghetto of Prague,* published in Vienna in 1925. The book contains photographs of the Altneuschul and the monument to Rabbi Loew in Prague. One of the legends related by Bloch is "The Golem as Water Carrier," and there is a tradition that this story inspired Goethe's ballad *The Sorcerer's Apprentice* during his visit to Prague.

The Prague legends also stimulated production of the German silent film *Der Golem,* directed by Henrik Galeen and Paul Wegener, released in 1915 and remade in 1920, as well as later Czech and French films on the same theme. It also seems likely that golem legends may have influenced British novelist Mary Shelley in the creation of her famous novel *Frankenstein,* first published in 1818. A later literary work influenced by the legend was the powerful occult novel *The Golem,* by Gustav Meyrink (1928).

Sources:

Bloch, Chayim. *Der Prager Golem.* Translated by Harry Schneiderman as *The Golem: Legends of the Ghetto of Prague.* Vienna, 1925.

Meyrink, Gustav [G. Meyer]. *The Golem.* London, 1928. Reprint, New York, 1964.

Scholem, Gershom G. *On the Kabbalah and Its Symbolism.* New York: Schocken Books, 1965.

Sherwin, Byron L. *The Golem Legend: Origins and Implications.* Lanham, Md.: University Press of America, 1985.

Wiesel, Elie. *The Golem: The Story of a Legend.* New York: Summit Books, 1983.

Winkler, Gershon. The Golem of Prague. New York: Judaica Press, 1980.

Goligher Circle

A small Spiritualist group in Ireland that became the subject of a series of experiments by Dr. **W. J. Crawford.** The circle was created from a poor Belfast family consisting of a father, four daughters, a son, and a son-in-law. The girls were all mediumistic, Kathleen Goligher (b. 1898) being the most noteworthy among them. The experiments lasted from 1914 until Crawford's death in 1920. For four years the family accepted no payment since Spiritualism was their religion. The séances were held in dim red light either in the Goligher home or in Crawford's house.

Six members of the family formed the circle, while Crawford retained liberty of movement for better observation and experiments. Communication with the invisible operators was maintained through raps. Kathleen only went into trance when prolonged discussion on the phenomena became necessary. The explanation then came through trance speaking.

Crawford wrote enthusiastically of the phenomena he witnessed and speculated broadly about its implication for understanding the nature of the world. Psychic researchers William Barrett and Whateley Carington witnessed the phenomena and also believed it real. Two years after Crawford's death, however, E. E. Fournier d'Albe sat with the circle and suggested **fraud** as the better explanation for the unusual manifestations. After his book appeared, Kathleen Goligher (by then Lady G. Donaldson) discontinued sittings for outside inquirers.

Sources:

Crawford, W. J. *Experiments in Psychical Science: Levitation, "Contact," and the "Direct Voice."* London: John M. Watkins, 1919.

———. *The Psychic Structures at the Goligher Circle.* London: John M. Watkins, 1921.

———. *The Reality of Psychic Phenomena: Raps, Levitations, etc.* 2nd ed. London: John M. Watkins, 1919.

D'Albe, E. E. Fournier. *(Psychical Research). The Goligher Circle: May to August, 1921.* London: John M. Watkins, 1922.

Gomes, Alair de Oliveira (1921–)

Brazilian engineer who wrote on parapsychological topics. He was born December 20, 1921, in Rio de Janeiro and was educated at the University of Brazil. Gomes was a contributor to the *Brazilian Journal of Philosophy* and published an article, "A Parapsicologia e um Problema Classico de Ciencia e Filosofia" (Parapsychology and a Classical Problem of Science and Philosophy), in the *Bulletin of the Institute of Psychology* of the University of Brazil in 1956.

Sources:

Pleasants, Helene, ed. *Biographical Dictionary of Parapsychology.* New York: Helix Press, 1964.

Gonzalez-Quevado, Oscar

Director of the Centro Latino-Americano de Parapsicologia, São Paulo, Brazil. Gonzalez-Quevado is a Spanish-born Jesuit priest, residing in São Paulo, who condemns Spiritualist miracles, which he ridicules by performing his own (which he claims to be phoney). His public demonstrations of such feats as apparently levitating a young girl in the open air, however, have tended to encourage belief in miraculous powers by many in his audiences. He has also parodied **psychic surgery** and reportedly has summarized his experience with the paranormal by saying, "Everything is in the mind. Clairvoyance is just a trick, and if people have visions or hear voices, it is just a hallucination."

Sources:

Gonzalez-Quevado, Oscar. *A face Oculta da Mente.* São Paulo, Brazil: Edicos Loyola, 1967.

———. *As Forcas Fisicas da Mente.* São Paulo, Brazil: Edicos Loyola, 1968.

Good, Sarah (d. 1692)

One of the first women to be declared a witch in the famous proceedings at Salem Village, Massachusetts. Discovered using an egg white as a scrying (divining) instrument, the two young daughters of parish minister Samuel Parris began to complain of being victims of **witchcraft.** They accused Tituba, a slave who had showed them the scrying technique, Sarah Osburn, and Sarah Good of bewitching them. Good already had a reputation for possessing a sharp tongue and a short temper. Neighbors sometimes accused her of cursing them and causing various malevolent incidents, including the death of a cow.

Good was arrested on a warrrant issued on February 29, 1692. Her age is not known, but at the time of her arrest and trial she was the mother of a four-year-old daughter, Dorcas, and a recently born infant, whom she was still nursing. Before her trial, Sarah Osburn died in prison, but four others, including **Rebecca Nurse,** were arrested. The five were tried on June 30 and condemned together. Good and the others were executed by hanging on July 19, 1692.

Good is remembered not only for being the first of those killed at Salem Village (now Danvers, Massachusetts) but also for her last words to the crowd, "If you take away my life, God will give you blood to drink."

Sources:

Ericson, Eric. *The World, The Flesh, and The Devil: A Biographical Dictionary of Witches.* New York: Mayflower Books, 1981.

Hansen, Chadwick. *Witchcraft at Salem.* New York: George Braziller, 1969.

Goodavage, Joseph F. (1925–)

Journalist and astrologer, born in Philadelphia on October 29, 1925. Goodavage served in the South Pacific during World War II and was awarded both the Bronze Star and the Silver Star. After the war he attended the Philadelphia Museum College of Art, Temple University, and the University of Pittsburgh (B.A., 1953). He began his journalistic career in 1954 with the *Pittsburgh Sun-Telegraph* and later worked for such papers as the *Cleveland Plain-Dealer,* the *Chicago Tribune,* and the *New York Times.*

Along the way Goodavage became interested in **astrology** and joined the **American Federation of Astrologers.** His first major writing in the field, *Astrology: The Space Age Science,* appeared in 1965. The next year that book was picked up as the first title in the New American Library paperback "Mystic Arts Series." It was followed by *Write Your Own Horoscope* (1969), the *Astrology Guide Almanac for 1970* and *The Comet Kohoutek* (1974).

Goodavage has also written two astrological columns for *Saga* magazine and the Bell McClure syndicate. His significant production of books through the 1970s slowed in the 1980s, but he has continued to write popular articles on astrology and related topics.

Sources:

Goodavage, Joseph F. *Astrology: The Space Age Science.* Englewood Cliffs, N.J.: Prentice-Hall, 1965. Reprint, New York: New American Library, 1966.

———. *The Comet Kohoutek.* New York: Pinnacle Books, 1974.

———. *Our Threatened Planet.* New York: Simon and Schuster, 1978.

———. *Seven by Seven.* New York: New American Library, 1978.

———. *Storm on the Sun.* New York: New American Library, 1979.

———. *Write Your Own Horoscope.* New York: New American Library, 1969.

Goodman, Linda (1925–1995)

American astrologer, born Linda Kemery on April 9, 1925, in Parkersburg, West Virginia. She emerged into public notice in 1958 as the writer-broadcaster for a Pittsburgh radio show, "Letter from Linda." She moved to New York City in 1964 and later became a speechwriter for the National Urban League.

In 1968 Goodman published her first book, *Sun Signs,* a massive work on **astrology** and human relationships offering advice for changing one's responses to the actions of others in accordance with one's own astrological characteristics as well as those of whomever one is dealing with. It became one of the best-selling astrology texts of the period. It went into 17 hardback printings prior to paperback publication in the fall of 1971. By the end of the decade it had sold more than four million copies. From having no prior connection to the astrological community, Goodman became one of the most influential astrologers in America, and her clients included a number of celebrity personalities.

Additional astrological texts by Goodman include *Venus Trines at Midnight* (1970) and her equally popular *Linda Goodman's Love Signs: A New Approach to the Human Heart* (1978).

Less known, Goodman founded a new religion she termed Mannitou, a synthesis of teachings from St. Francis of Asissi and some Native American tribes. She put a large percentage of the income from her books into establishing her new faith.

Sources:

Goodman, Linda. *Linda Goodman's Love Signs: A New Approach to the Human Heart.* New York: Harper, 1978.

———. *Sun Signs.* New York: Taplinger, 1968. Reprinted as *Linda Goodman's Sun Signs.* New York: Bantam Books, 1971.

———. *Venus Trines at Midnight.* New York: Taplinger, 1970.

Goodrich-Freer, Ada (1857–1931)

Pioneer psychical researcher who wrote under the pseudonym "Miss X." Goodrich-Freer was born May 15, 1857, in Rutland, England. Mystery surrounds much of her life and parentage, and she appears to have been responsible for the deliberate clouding of many details, probably to impress influential patrons and associates. However, she was also noted for useful research and for her valuable editorial association with **W. T.**

Stead, with whom she coedited the magazine *Borderland.* In 1905 she married the Reverend Hans H. Spoer, although continuing to be known professionally as "Miss Freer" or "Miss Goodrich-Freer."

She was an early member of the **Society for Psychical Research** in Britain and an associate of **F. W. H. Myers,** one of its founders. She was also a member of the Folklore Society. Between 1918 and 1920 she was assistant to her husband, who was then district commander under the Allied high commissioner in Armenia.

In addition to her collaboration with Stead on *Borderland,* Goodrich-Freer wrote a variety of articles for different journals in folklore and in psychical research, most of which appeared under the pseudonym "Miss X."

In 1897 Goodrich-Freer became involved in an investigation of a **haunting** at Bellechin. The affair turned into a fiasco, and she and Myers had a heated quarrel that led to a permanent break in relations. The period proved critical for her, since her employment with Stead at *Borderland* ended and three years later her patron, Lord Bute, died. In 1901 she left England for Palestine and eventually settled in the United States. She dropped out of psychical research during this period, though she wrote a number of books on her travels in the Middle East. She died in New York on February 24, 1931.

History has not treated Goodrich-Freer kindly. John L. Campbell and **Trevor H. Hall,** who looked over the body of material she left, accused her of a lifetime of falsification and deception, the pseudonym being only a small part of the ruse. She regularly plagiarized from others in her publications, said Campbell and Hall, and was accused of using fraud in her sittings.

Sources:

Campbell, John L., and Trevor H. Hall. *Strange Things.* London: Routledge & Kegan Paul, 1968.

Goodrich-Freer, Ada. *Arabs in Tent and Town.* London: Seeley, Service, & Co. Int., 1924.

———. *Essays in Psychical Research.* 2nd ed., London: G. Redway, 1899.

———. *Inner Jerusalem.* New York: E. P. Dutton, 1904.

———. *Outer Isles.* London: A. Constable, 1902.

———, and John, Marquess of Bute. *The Alleged Haunting of B. House.* London: G. Redway, 1899.

Gopi Krishna, Pandit (1903–1984)

A modern Hindu teacher who focused attention on the **kundalini,** the latent force in the human organism said to be responsible for sexual activity and (in a sublimated form) higher consciousness or mystical experience.

In Hindu mythology kundalini is personified as a goddess with creative and destructive aspects and serpentlike movement. Kundalini is often described as a serpent that sleeps at the base of the spine, darting upward when aroused, bringing sexual excitement or enlightenment or pain. This concept has been loosely correlated with the biblical story of Adam and Eve and the serpent and has analogues in other religions as well.

Gopi Krishna was born in Kashmir in 1903. After failing his college examinations he devoted himself to a personal discipline of **yoga** and meditation while working as a minor civil servant.

In 1937 he experienced the sudden arousal of kundalini energy. The experience was a shattering one, because the energy was aroused prematurely in a negative form. Although the pandit had strange visions and insights, the shock resulted in his suffering ill health for a number of years. He sustained the ordeal, however, and after years of practice he discovered that the energy had transformed him gradually and manifested a positive aspect, with states of higher consciousness, mystical insight, and some paranormal side effects.

Gopi Krishna's first book, *The Shape of Events to Come* (1968; reissued 1979), describes a New Age–like vision of human affairs characterized by materialism and decadence. He writes of an impending nuclear war, after which human beings will rediscover the importance of the moral and ethical principles that are the basis of most great religions and thereby prepare the way for a great evolutionary surge.

Several of the pandit's books are in verse format, "dictated by a Higher Intelligence" at great speed. At the apex of the pandit's condition of higher consciousness in 1950 he spontaneously dictated poems in German, French, and Italian, languages that he had never learned. His prose works concerned with the concept of kundalini transcended his own simple education and average intelligence. Like his poetry they were written during full consciousness, not in the trance condition of a psychic or channeler. Yet his writings were a product of his higher consciousness.

Although accounts of the arousal of kundalini through yoga practice—culminating in mystical consciousness—have appeared in Hindu Scriptures for centuries, firsthand accounts are so rare in modern times that some consider kundalini a mere fable. Gopi Krishna was one of several mid-twentieth-century gurus who succeeded in arousing kundalini and as a result wrote a number of books on the subject. He was known for his detailed description of the aroused kundalini state. His writings draw upon his outgoing personal experience of higher consciousness.

He claimed that kundalini is a biological force with an important role in human evolution and believed that the goal of higher consciousness may eventually lead humankind away from materialistic ambition and world conflicts toward new goals for religion and science.

Gopi Krishna's books attracted the serious attention of such eminent thinkers as Carl von Weizsäcker of the Max Planck Institute for the Life Sciences, Germany. The Indian government also expressed interest in the subject of kundalini. In 1974 Dr. Karan Singh, minister of health, announced an ambitious kundalini research project, to be sponsored by the All-India Institute of Medical Science, to research "kundalini concept and its relevance to the development of higher nervous functions." Unfortunately the project was discontinued with a change in the Indian government.

Meanwhile sympathizers with the work of Pandit Gopi Krishna founded the Central Institute for Kundalini Research at Srinagar, Kashmir, India, and the **Kundalini Research Foundation** was established in New York (later relocated to P.O. Box 2248, Darien, CT 06820) and in Switzerland at Gemsenstrasse 7, CH-8006 Zürich.

Gopi Krishna died in Srinagar, Kashmir, on July 31, 1984, at age 81. During the last week of his life, he met with Hindu leaders in order to convince them of the importance of strengthening and unifying the Hindu community so that adequate social services could be developed in case of difficult times in Kashmir.

During his lifetime he made great efforts to interest scientists in investigating and verifying the phenomenon of kundalini as a biological force in human affairs, with implications for the study of the paranormal as well as the intellectual and ethical evolution of humanity.

Sources:

Gopi Krishna. *The Awakening of Kundalini.* New York: E. P. Dutton, 1975.

———. *Biblical Prophecy for the 20th Century.* Toronto: Kundalini Research Institute of Canada, 1979.

———. *The Biological Basis of Religion and Genius.* New York: Harper & Row, 1972.

———. *Kundalini: The Evolutionary Energy in Man.* New Delhi, 1967. Reprint, Boulder, Colo.: Shambhala, 1970.

———. *Living with Kundalini: The Autobiography of Gopi Krishna.* Boston: Shambhala, 1993.

———. *The Secret of Yoga.* New York: Harper & Row, 1972.

———. *The Shape of Events to Come.* New Delhi: Kundalini Research and Publication Trust, 1979.

Gordon, Henry C. (ca. 1850)

One of the earliest American physical mediums to claim to demonstrate **levitation.** At a New York conference on June 18,

1852, he seemed to levitate in the crowded assembly room; at another time he was apparently carried through the air over a distance of 60 feet. Gordon was scientifically tested by **Robert Hare** in 1853 and demonstrated to Hare's satisfaction the existence of a **psychic force.**

Gordon was several times accused of **fraud,** however. He was exposed at a New York séance when he was discovered in the **cabinet** with faces painted on cardboard, luminous cloth, and other fraudulent properties.

Sources:

Hare, Robert. *Experimental Investigation of the Spirit Manifestations.* 1854. Reprint, Elm Grove, Wis.: Sycamore Press, 1963.

Gormogons

A Jacobite society, perhaps related to the lodges of **Harodim.** They employed pseudonyms like the Harodim and had an ambassador at Rome. The duke of Wharton and the chevalier Ramsay, who were well-known Jacobites, were members of the order. Gormogons had a cipher and secret reception of their own and used a jargon in which the names of places and individuals were transposed. An extant engraving by William Hogarth lampoons the order under the title "The Mystery of Masonry brought to light by ye Gormogons." The intention of the Gormogons, apparently, was to establish a countertradtion to **Freemasonry.**

Gow, David (d. ca. 1939)

Scottish journalist, poet, and Spiritualist. As a poet Gow contributed to such journals as *Cassell's Saturday Journal, London Magazine,* and *London Scotsman* and his poems were included in such anthologies as *Modern Scottish Poets* and *Book of Highland Verse.* He was author of *Four Miles From Any Town* (1929) and edited *Ask the Spirits* (1934).

Gow was an outstanding figure in British Spiritualism. In January 1914 he took over editorship of the famous Spiritualist journal the *Light* following the death of editor **E. W. Wallis.** Gow continued in that position until 1930. He was a lucid and prolific writer on psychic literature and philosophy and knew many of the leading figures in the field, including **Agnes Guppy-Volckman** and **Emma H. Britten.**

Graal, The Lost Book of the

The alleged origin of the Christian form of the Graal (**Holy Grail**) legend. Seven ancient books are cited as being the possible source of the story, but not one has been so proven. The Huth Merlin refers to a "Book of the Sanctuary," but this volume is a book of records, not containing any special spiritual allusion. If the lost book of the Graal ever existed it may have been a mass book used about 1100. Its contents would have related to a mass following the Last Supper.

The mystery of the Graal is threefold: (1) its origin, which is part of the mystery of the Incarnation; (2) its manifestation, which would have taken place had the world been worthy; and (3) its removal—this world being unworthy, the Graal was said to be removed, yet not hidden, for it is always discernible by anyone worthy of seeing it.

It seems unlikely that such a mass book ever existed.

Sources:

Waite, Arthur E. *The Holy Grail: The Galahad Quest in the Arthurian Literature.* London: J. M. Watkins, 1921. Reprint, New Hyde Park, N.Y.: University Books, 1961.

Grad, Bernard (1920–)

Canadian biologist who experimented in the field of paranormal healing. Grad was born February 4, 1920, Montreal, Canada. He attended McGill University (B.S., 1944; Ph.D., 1949), where he remained through his professional career. He was a research assistant, lecturer, and assistant professor at McGill. In 1985 he became an associate professor at the University of Quebec, Montreal. He became well known for his research on cancer.

As early as the 1940s Grad became interested in the **orgone** energy theories as postulated by **Wilhelm Reich.** The death of his daughter further stimulated his interest in spiritual healing, and in 1957 he came to know Oscar Estabany, a Hungarian refugee who professed to have healing powers. Working with Estabany in the 1960s, he carried out a series of experiments on plant seeds and mice that resulted in some of the strongest evidence of a healing power to arise in parapsychology. In a series of more complicated tests, all carried out with double blinds, Grad was able to isolate a healing power that seemed to radiate from Estabany. It could be transferred to plant seeds to stimulate their growth, to mice to speed healing, and even to water used for plants.

Sources:

Grad, Bernard. "Paranormal Healing and Life Energy." *American Society for Psychical Research Newsletter* 7 (1981).

———. "Some Biological Effects of the 'Laying on of Hands': A Review of Experiments with Animals and Plants." *Journal* of the American Society for Psychical Research 59 (1965).

———. "A Telekinetic Effect on Plant Growth." *International Journal of Parapsychology* 3 (1961); 5 (1963).

Grad, Bernard, Remi J. Cadoret, and G. I. Paul. "The Influence of an Unorthodox Method of Treatment on Wound Healing in Mice." *International Journal of Parapsychology* 3, no. 2 (1961).

Grail, Holy

A portion of the Arthurian cycle of romance, of late origin, embodying a number of tales dealing with the search for a certain vessel of great sanctity called the "Grail" or "Graal." Versions of the story are numerous, the most celebrated of them being the *Conte del Graal,* the *Grand St. Graal, Sir Percyvalle, Quete del St. Graal,* and *Guyot,* but there are also many others. These overlap in many respects, but the standard form of the story may perhaps be found in the *Grand St. Graal,* one of the latest versions, which dates from the thirteenth century.

It tells how Joseph of Arimathea employed a dish used at the Last Supper to catch the blood of the Redeemer, which flowed from his body before his burial. The wanderings of Joseph are then described. He leads a band to Britain, where he is cast into prison, but is delivered by Evelach or Mordrains, who is instructed by Christ to assist him. Mordrains builds a monastery where the Grail is housed. Brons, Joseph's brother-in-law, has a son Alain, who is appointed guardian of the Grail. Alain, having caught a great fish with which he feeds the entire household, is called "the Rich Fisher," which becomes the perpetual title of the Grail keepers. Alain places the Grail in the castle of Corbenic and in time, various knights of King Arthur's court come in quest of the holy vessel. Only the purest of the pure could approach it, and in due time the knight Percival manages to see the marvel.

It is probable that the idea of the Grail originated with early medieval legends of the quest for talismans that conferred great boons upon the finder, for example, the shoes of swiftness, the cloak of invisibility, and the ring of Gyges, and that these stories were interpreted in the light and spirit of medieval Christianity and mysticism.

The legends may be divided into two classes: those that are connected with the quest for certain talismans, of which the Grail is only one, and that deal with the personality of the hero who achieves the quest; and second, those that deal with the nature and history of the talismans.

A great deal of controversy has raged around the possible Eastern origin of the Grail legend. Much erudition has been employed to show that Guyot, a Provençal poet who flourished in the middle of the twelfth century, found at Toledo, Spain, an Arabian book by an astrologer, Flegitanis, which contained the Grail story. But the name "Flegitanis" can by no means be an

Arabian proper name. It could be the Persian *felekedânêh,* a combined word which signifies "astrology," and in that case it would be the title of an astrological work. Some believed the legend originated in the mind of Guyot himself, but this conclusion was strongly opposed by the folklorist Alfred Nutt. There is, however, some reason to believe that the story might have been brought from the East by the Knights Templar.

The Grail legend has often been held by various ecclesiastical apologists to support theories that either the Church of England or the Roman Catholic Church has existed since the foundation of the world. From early Christian times the genealogy of these churches has been traced back through the patriarchs to numerous apocryphal persons, although it is not stated whether the religions possessed hierophants in neolithic and paleolithic times, or just how they originated. Such theories, which would logically identify Christianity with the grossest forms of paganism, are confined only to a small group.

The Grail legend was readily embraced by those who saw in it a link between Palestine and England and an argument for the special separate foundation of the Anglican Church by direct emissaries from the Holy Land. **Glastonbury** was fixed as the headquarters of the Grail immigrants, and the finding of a glass dish in the vicinity of the cathedral there some years ago was held to be confirmation of the story by many of the faithful. The exact date of this vessel was not definitely estimated, but there seemed little reason to suppose that it was more than a few hundred years old.

A new conspiratorial interpretation of the Grail legend is offered in the book *The Holy Blood and the Holy Grail* (1982), by Michael Baigent, Richard Leigh, and Henry Lincoln. Their speculation involves suggestions that Jesus did not die on the Cross, but married and had children. His wife, they postulate, fled to the south of France with her family, taking with her the "Royal and Real Blood," the "Sang-real" or Grail of medieval romance. This line will supposedly culminate in a second Messiah, all this being the secret of an order named the Prieure de Sion. Apparently the investigation of this amazing story began with the mystery of Berenger Sauniere, a parish priest at Rennes-le-Château in the Pyrenees, who seemed to have discovered a secret that gave him access to a vast sum of money before his death, under mysterious circumstances, in 1917. That secret involved the history of Rennes-le-Château and its association with the Templars, the Cathars, and the royal bloodline of the Merovingian dynasty. The story has too many jumps in history and logic to ever be researched, and only time will show whether its major claims can be independently substantiated.

Patricia and Lionel Fanthorpe refute the theory of Baigent, Leigh, and Lincoln in their 1982 book *The Holy Grail Revealed: The Real Secret of Rennes-le-Château.*

Sources:

Bruce, James Douglas. *The Evolution of Arthurian Romance, From the Beginnings Down to the Year 1300.* Baltimore, Md.: Johns Hopkins University Press, 1923.

Cooper-Oakley, Isabel. *Traces of a Hidden Tradition in Masonry and Medieval Mysticism.* London, 1900.

Fanthorpe, Patricia, and Lionel Fanthorpe. *The Holy Grail Revealed: The Real Secret of Rennes-le-Château.* North Hollywood, Calif.: Newcastle Pub. Co., 1982.

Lacy, Norris J., ed. *The Arthurian Encyclopedia.* New York: Garland Publishing, 1986.

Loomis, Roger Sherman. *The Grail: From Celtic Myth to Christian Symbol.* Cardiff: University of Wales Press, 1963.

Nutt, Alfred. *Studies on the Legend of the Holy Grail.* London: Folklore Society, 1888. Reprint, New York: Cooper Square Publishers, 1965.

Rhys, Sir John. *Studies in the Arthurian Legend.* Oxford: Clarendon Press, 1891.

Waite, Arthur Edward. *The Holy Grail: The Galahad Quest in the Arthurian Literature.* London, 1933. Reprint, New Hyde Park, N.Y.: University Books, 1961.

Weston, Jessie L. *From Ritual to Romance.* Cambridge: Cambridge University Press, 1920. Reprint, Garden City, N.Y.: Doubleday Anchor, 1957.

———. *The Quest of the Holy Grail.* London: G. Bell & Sons, 1913; London: Frank Cass, London, 1964.

Grail Foundation

The Grail Foundation emerged in the 1920s to disseminate the material written by Oskar Ernest Bernhardt (1875–1941). In 1924 Bernhardt moved to Bavaria, where he wrote and lectured under the pen name Abd-ru-shin. He moved to Austria in 1928 and began publishing *In the Light of Truth,* but his work was suppressed by the Nazis in 1938. Bernhardt died during the war. Followers attracted to the writings reorganized after the war, and the foundation has continued unabated ever since, spreading throughout Europe and North America. The first U.S. center was founded in 1939 in Mt. Morris, Illinois.

According to Bernhardt, God created human beings and sent them in search of self-consciousness and maturity. They wandered into gross matter and acquired physical bodies in which to function on Earth. All are to learn to live by the original laws of creation and eventually return to God as mature, self-conscious entities.

The Grail Foundation may be contacted through the Grail Movement of America, 2081 Partridge Ln., Binghamton, NY 13903. It publishes the English edition of *In the Light of Truth* and other writings by Bernhardt. In recent decades the foundation has become an international movement with followers on every continent.

Sources:

Abd-ru-shin [Oskar E. Bernhardt]. *Awake! Selected Lectures.* Vomperberg, Austria: Maria Bernhardt Publishing, n.d.

———. *In the Light of Truth.* 3 vols. Vomperberg, Austria: Maria Bernhardt Publishing, 1954.

Grail Sword

Associated with the Holy **Grail** in Arthurian legend. Its supposed history begins with King David, who bequeathed the sword to Solomon, who was bidden to recast the pommel. In Solomon's time it was placed in a ship built and luxuriously furnished by Solomon's wife. Subsequently discovered by the Knights of the Quest, it was assumed and worn by Sir Galahad.

Gram

In medieval legend, a magic sword thrust into a tree by Odin and pulled out by Sigmund. It bestowed upon its possessor exceptional powers and performed many miracles. The story is told in *The Lay of the Volsungs.*

Grand Grimoire, The

A **grimoire,** or text of instruction for use in **ceremonial magic.** It was supposedly edited by one Antonia del Rabina from a copy transcribed from the genuine writings of King Solomon. *The Grand Grimoire* is divided into two parts, the first containing the evocation of "Lucifuge Rocofale" and the second concerned with the rite of making pacts with demons.

The first portion of *The Grand Grimoire* describes a process for evoking evil spirits to assist the operator in discovering hidden treasure. The second part suggests the surrender of the magician's body and soul to the demon, but the pact is grossly unfair to the devil, for it is such that the magician can readily slip through his fingers.

The work has been regarded as one of the more atrocious grimoires.

Sources:

Le Grand Grimoire, ou l'art de commander les esprits célestes. Paris, 1845.

McIntosh, Christopher. *The Devil's Bookshelf.* Wellingborough, England: Aquarian Press, 1985.

Grand Lodge of England

For the foundation of The Grand Lodge of Masons in England in 1717, see **Freemasonry.**

Grandier, Urbain (d. 1634)

Urbain Grandier, a canon of the French church and a popular preacher of the town of **Loudun** in the district of Poitiers, was brought to trial in the year 1634, accused of practicing **magic** and causing demonic possession of the Ursuline nuns of Loudun. The prime cause of the accusations, however, seems to have been the envy of his rival preachers, whose fame was eclipsed by Grandier's superior talents. The second cause was a libel upon Cardinal Richelieu falsely attributed to Grandier.

In addition to his eloquence, Grandier was distinguished for his courage and resolution, for his physical appearance, and for the extraordinary attention he paid to his dress, which gave him the reputation of being a ladies' man.

In 1633 certain nuns of the convent of Ursulines at Loudun were attacked with a disease that manifested extraordinary symptoms, suggesting to many that they were possessed by devils. A rumor was spread that Grandier, prompted by some offense he had conceived against the nuns, had caused the possessions through his skill in sorcery.

Unfortunately the same Capuchin friar who assured Richelieu that Grandier was the author of the libel against him also told the cardinal the story of the possessed nuns. The cardinal seized this opportunity for private vengeance and wrote to the counselor of state at Loudun, asking him to begin a strict investigation of the charges, plainly implying that what he sought was the destruction of Grandier.

According to an authorized transcript of the trial, Grandier was convicted on the evidence of Astaroth, a devil of the order of seraphims and chief of the possessing devils, and sentenced to be burned alive. In fact, he was convicted upon the evidence of 12 nuns who, being asked who they were, gave 12 demonic names and professed to be possessing devils compelled by the order of the court to testify. Sentence was passed on August 18, 1634, and Grandier was condemned to torture so severe that his legs were smashed, followed by burning at the stake.

Grandier met his fate with constancy. At his death an enormous drone fly was said to be seen buzzing about his head and a monk who was present at the execution attested that the fly was Beelzebub (in Hebrew the god of flies), come to carry away to hell the soul of the victim. Such stories may have been circulated to justify a cruel and unjust persecution. The nuns involved in the accusations continued to exhibit the signs of demonic possession after Grandier's execution.

Sources:

Carmona, Nichel. *Les diables de Loudun: sorcellerie et politique sous Richelieu.* Paris: Fayard, 1988.

Huxley, Aldous. *The Devils of Loudun.* London: Chatto & Windus, 1952.

Granny-Wells

A folk term for sacred wells dedicated to St. Anne, mother of the Virgin Mary and grandmother of Christ. According to a Breton legend, St. Anne lived in Brittany in her old age and was visited by Christ, of whom she requested help for the sick in her district. Christ pierced the ground with a staff and opened a healing spring, later named St. Anne-de-la-Palue.

Grant, Ernest A. (1893–1968)

Astrologer and cofounder of the **American Federation of Astrologers** (AFA). Grant was born in Detroit, Michigan, on June 4, 1893. As a teenager he moved to Washington, D.C., and held a variety of jobs as stenographer, court reporter, and eventually secretary to a U.S. senator. He married and through the 1920s both he and his wife, Catherine, studied **astrology.** She became a prominent astrologer and had a number of prominent Washingtonians among her clients. Through the 1930s they increasingly saw the need for a professional organization for astrologers, whose work was still held in disdain by many. Numerous laws against fortune-telling hampered the development of the profession in many parts of the country.

Together with Anna May Cowan and Swen Erickson, Grant led in the founding of the AFA, now the largest and most prestigous of the several professional associations for astrologers. He was its first president (1938–41) and then became its first executive secretary (1941–59). The association was headquartered in the Grant home. In 1949 he quit his other jobs and devoted full time to the AFA. Two years later he led in the purchase of a small parcel of land adjacent to the Library of Congress where a new headquarters was erected.

With his wife, Grant began work on a set of basic textbooks in astrology, and he published a set of ephemeris volumes for the important years associated with the founding of the nation (1776, 1777, and 1781). Together they also founded the National Astrological Library, a publishing house and retail book outlet. While Catherine Grant continued to see clients, Ernest Grant specialized in teaching astrology and research. He also developed a special interest in political astrology.

Grant died on March 6, 1968. His wife continued as an astrologer and eventually sold the library to the AFA. In the early 1970s, along with the AFA, she moved to Tempe, Arizona, and worked there into her early 90s. She died in 1988.

Sources:

Grant, Ernest. *Astrological America.* Washington, D.C.: National Astrological Library, 1949.

———. *Ephemeris for the Year 1776.* Washington, D.C.: National Astrological Library, 1944.

———. *Tables of Diurnal Planetary Motion.* Washington, D.C.: National Astrological Library, 1948.

Grant, Ernest, and Catherine T. Grant. *Grant Textbook Series.* 4 vols. Washington, D.C.: National Astrological Library, n.d.

Holden, James H., and Robert A. Hughes. *Astrological Pioneers of America.* Tempe, Ariz.: American Federation of Astrologers, 1988.

Grant, Joan (Joan Marshall Kelsey) (1907–1989)

Author of various fictional works dealing with **reincarnation** that she claimed were partly biographical. In her book *Many Lifetimes* (1969), written in collaboration with her third husband, Dr. Denys Kelsey, Grant describes claimed memories of former existences revealed when she was hypnotized by her husband.

Sources:

Grant, Joan. *Eyes of Horus.* London: Methuen, 1942. New York: Arno Press, 1980.

———. *Far Memory.* Reprinted as *Time Out of Mind, A Lot to Remember.* New York: Arno Press, 1980.

———. *Life as Carola.* London: Methuen & Co. Ltd., 1939; New York & London: Harper & Brothers, 1940; New York: Arno Press, 1980.

———. *Lord of the Horizon.* London: Methuen & Co. Ltd., 1943.

———. *Return to Elysium.* New York: Arno Press, 1980.

———. *So Moses Was Born.* London: Methuen, 1952; New York: Arno Press, 1980.

———. *Winged Pharaoh.* New York: Harper & Brothers, 1938.

Kelsey, Denys, and Joan Grant. *Many Lifetimes.* Garden City, N.Y.: Doubleday, 1967.

Grant, Kenneth

Founder of a branch of the **Ordo Templi Orientis** (OTO), a ceremonial "magick" group in the tradition of **Aleister Crowley,** in Great Britain. Grant was initiated into Crowley's own order, the A∴A∴, and the OTO.

After Crowley's death in 1947 he was succeeded by Karl Germer as outer head of the order. Germer was at that time living in the United States. He presented Grant a charter to open the **New Isis Lodge** of the OTO in 1955. Grant was limited to teaching the first three OTO grades. After Germer died in 1962 Grant claimed leadership of the OTO. While members in America did not acknowledge him, there was no one in England to oppose his authority. Grant began to accept initiates for all ten working degrees of the order (the eleventh being purely administrative).

Grant worked with **John Symonds,** Crowley's literary executor, to produce *The Confessions of Aleister Crowley* (1969). Grant also published *The Magical Revival* (1972), an informative survey of occult theory and practice in modern times. A particularly valuable chapter is concerned with the work of occult artist **Austin Osman Spare.** Grant also published *Images and Oracles of Austin Osman Spare* (1975), a study of the work of this strange and talented artist.

Grant's wife, Steffi, contributed beautiful illustrations to five *Carfax Monographs* issued by the Grants in London in a limited edition, dealing with *The Tree of Life, The Golden Dawn, Aleister Crowley, Austin Osman Spare,* and *Vinum Sabbati.*

Sources:

Grant, Kenneth. *Aleister Crowley and the Hidden God.* London: Muller, 1973.

———. *Cults of the Shadow.* New York: Samuel Weiser, 1976.

———. *Images and Oracles of Austin Osman Spare.* London: Muller, 1975.

———. *The Magical Revival.* New York: Samuel Weiser, 1972.

———. *Nightside of Eden.* London: Muller, 1977.

———. *Outside the Circles of Time.* London: Frederick Mueller, 1980.

Symonds, John, and Kenneth Grant. *The Confessions of Aleister Crowley.* New York: Hill & Wang, 1969.

Grapevine (Newsletter)

(1) Former monthly newsletter of the Psychic Information Exchange. Included articles on the paranormal, self-development lessons, notices of meetings, and book reviews. Apparently no longer active.

(2) Monthly newsletter of the Movement for a New Society, devoted to alternative and nonviolent living. Address: 6722 Baltimore Ave., Philadelphia, PA 19143.

Graphology

The study of handwriting, involving the interpretation of character and personality traits. Empirical interpretation of handwriting dates back to ancient times. Aristotle claimed that he could define a person's soul by his way of writing. Suetonius noted that Emperor Augustus did not separate his words when writing and concluded that this demonstrated a neglect of detail when forming a picture of a whole situation.

In the seventeenth century Camillo Baldi published a small Latin treatise called *De Signis ex Epistolis* (1622). Graphology was systematized in nineteenth-century France when the Abbé Flandrin (1809–64) made a detailed study of autographs. In 1872 Adolphe Desbarolles published *Les mystères de l'écriture; art de juger les hommes sur leurs autographes.* Since then there have been many books on graphology, often falling somewhere between scientific principle and popular occultism.

Although modern graphologists have evolved a scientific rationale that assigns particular significance to the slope of handwriting, the formation of individual letters, size of characters, joinings and disjoinings of letters, and so on, interpretation remains largely subjective and allows considerable room for the practitioner's psychic ability to operate and add material. Some graphologists allow the handwriting itself to convey impressions in much the same way as objects function in **psychometry.** Perhaps one's signature is the most characteristic piece of handwriting, for consciously or unconsciously it becomes a kind of symbolic self-portrait, indicating the personality as a whole. In this it resembles the magic **sigil** of celestial intelligences. Part of the perennial attraction of autograph collecting and book signing is the emotional association with great or famous individuals as represented by their signatures.

Graphology is to be sharply delineated from handwriting analysis. The latter is concerned with establishing the authenticity of writing and signatures, and such analysts are frequently called upon to make judgments in legal situations. Graphology has made some progress toward respectability, however. Some corporations now employ graphologists to elucidate staff applications, and police authorities have been known to hire graphologists to analyze the writing of criminals.

Sources:

Byrd, Anita. *Handwriting Analysis: A Guide to Personality.* New York: Arco, 1982.

Casewit, Curtis. *Graphology Handbook.* Rockport, Mass.: Para Research, 1980.

Friedenhain, Paula. *Write and Reveal: Interpretation of Handwriting.* London, 1959.

Golson, K. K. *Presidents Are People.* New York: Carlton Press, 1964.

Jacoby, H. J. *Analysis of Handwriting.* London: Allen & Unwin, 1929.

Kurdsen, Stephen. *Graphology: The New Science.* Washington, D.C.: Acropolis Books, 1971.

Lowengard, Manfred. *How to Analyze Your Handwriting.* London: Marshall Cavendish, 1975.

Marcuse, Irene. *The Key to Handwriting Analysis.* New York: R. M. McBride, 1959.

Moretti, Girolamo M. *The Saints Through Their Handwriting.* New York: Macmillan, 1964.

Schang, F. C. *Visiting Cards of Celebrities.* Paris: Gale Research, 1973.

Solomon, Shirl. *How to Really Know Yourself Through Your Handwriting.* New York: Taplinger, 1974. Reprint, London: Coronet, 1975.

Grattan-Guinness, Ivor (1941–)

Reader in mathematics at Middlesex Polytechnic, England, and a council member of the Society for Psychical Research, England. His main areas of research have concerned the history and philosophy of mathematics, the history of psychical research, and the relationship of parapsychology to established science and ufology. His paper "What Are Coincidences?" was published in the *Journal* of the Society for Psychical Research (vol. 49).

Sources:

Berger, Arthur S., and Joyce Berger. *The Encyclopedia of Parapsychology and Psychical Research.* New York: Paragon House, 1991.

Grattan-Guinness, Ivor. *Psychical Research: A Guide to its History, Principles and Practices, in Celebration of 100 Years of the Society for Psychical Research.* Wellingborough, England: Aquarian Press, 1982.

Gray Barker's Newsletter

Fanzine edited during the 1970s by the late Gray Barker, author of *They Knew Too Much About Flying Saucers* (1975). The newsletter covered UFO sightings, news of personalities in the

UFO field, activities of organizations, and book and magazine reviews.

Great White Brotherhood

The group of superhuman **adepts** or **masters** who many Theosophists and other occultists believe guide the development of the human race. The brotherhood is occasionally associated with a "great white lodge" situated in astral realms. Modern **Rosicrucians** define the Great White Brotherhood as "the school or Fraternity of the Great White Lodge and into this invisible Brotherhood of visible members every true student of the Path prepares for admission."

Sources:

Garver, Will. *Brother of the Third Degree.* Halcyon, Calif.: Halcyon Temple Press, 1929.

Great White Brotherhood. *The Books of Azrael: Teachings.* Santa Barbara, Calif.: J. F. Rowney Press, n.d.

Johnson, K. Paul. *The Masters Revealed: Madam Blavatsky and the Myth of the Great White Lodge.* Albany, N.Y.: State University of New York Press, 1994.

Leadbeater, Charles W. *The Masters and the Path.* Chicago: Theosophical Press, 1925.

Perkins, Lynn F. *The Masters as New Age Mentors.* Lakemont, Ga.: CSA Press, 296.

Prophet, Elizabeth Clare. *The Great White Brotherhood in the Culture, History and Religion of America.* Los Angeles: Summit University Press, 1983.

Greater World, The (Newspaper)

London Spiritualist weekly established in 1928 by **Winifred Moyes** and C. A. Aeschimann to spread the teachings of the Zodiac Circle. It led to the foundation in 1931 of the **Greater World Christian Spiritualist Association.** It had as its aim "the spreading in all directions of the truth of survival after death under the banner of Jesus Christ." *The Greater World* ceased publication in March 1989 and was superseded by a newsletter.

Greater World Christian Spiritualist Association

British Spiritualist organization founded in 1931 as the Greater World Christian Spiritualist League. It grew out of the Zodiac Circle, which was organized in the early 1920s around the mediumship of **Winifred Moyes.** Moyes was a channel who transmitted teachings from the entity "Zodiac," who claimed he was a temple scribe at the time of Christ. These teachings were at first transmitted to a small home circle held on Sunday evenings, but the movement grew rapidly to claim a membership of twenty thousand in Britain. Moyes was president of the league until her death in 1957, after which F. M. Tolkin became president until 1963, when he was succeeded by Margaret Hoare.

In addition to the weekly newspaper *The Greater World,* discontinued in 1989, the association also published *The Children's Greater World* and in 1933 launched French (*Le Monde Superior*) and German (*Die Größere Welt*) editions. The newspaper was replaced by a newsletter.

Members of the association must subscribe to eight basic beliefs, arising from the teachings of "Zodiac": (1) I believe in one God, who is Love; (2) I accept the leadership of Jesus Christ; (3) I believe that God manifests through the illimitable power of the Holy Spirit; (4) I believe in the **survival** of the human soul and its individuality after physical death; (5) I believe in the communion with God, with his angelic ministers, and with the soul's functioning in conditions other than the Earth life; (6) I believe that all forms of life created by God intermingle, are interdependent, and evolve until perfection is attained; (7) I believe in the perfect justice of the divine laws governing all life; and (8) I believe that sins committed can only be rectified by the sinner himself or herself, through the redemptive power of Jesus Christ, by repentance and service to others. There is also the following pledge: "I will at all times endeavour to be guided in my thoughts, words, and deeds by the teaching and example of Jesus Christ."

The league is now administered through the Greater World Spiritualist Association Trust and has a board of literature responsible for official publications. In 1961 the league affiliated with the **National Federation of Spiritual Healers.**

Very early in its life the league was involved in social work. In 1937 the league organized a convalescent home for elderly women at Leigh-on-Sea, and more recently added another at Bridlington, Yorkshire. The league's night shelter for homeless women in Lambeth, London, was destroyed by German bombs during World War II, but a new shelter and rest home was opened at Deptford in South London in 1948. That shelter continued its work until 1955, when a new law made it an offense for women to be on the streets at night without a lodging. A night shelter opened in Leeds in 1935 and continues as a home for women and children.

The London headquarters at 3–5 Conway Street, London, W1P 5HA, includes a sanctuary and a church with accommodation for nearly 150 people. Services, lectures, healing meetings, and circles are held regularly. There is also a Greater World Healing Fellowship, concerned with spiritual healing through accredited healers. Each of the affiliated churches throughout Britain has at least one medium. Affiliated congregations are also found in Canada, the United States, and New Zealand. The association offers a diploma to mediums who meet the league's standards and for long-standing service to the league.

Sources:

Edmunds, Simeon. *Spiritualism: A Critical Survey.* London: Aquarian Press, 1966.

Greatrakes, Valentine (1629–1683)

Irish mesmerist, born in the county of Waterford. In 1662 Greatrakes dreamed that he had received the gift of healing by laying on of hands. He ignored the dream, but when it recurred on several occasions he experimented on his wife, which proved quite successful. He subsequently practiced the laying on of hands for practically all diseases and in 1666 went to London, where he was summoned to court. While there he healed many persons, but the insults of the courtiers proved too much for him and he was forced to withdraw to a house near London, where he continued his cures. In his *Critical History of Animal Magnetism* (2 vols., 1813, 1819), J. P. F. Deleuze states: "Amongst the most astonishing cures which history records, are those of an Irish gentleman in London, Oxford, and other cities of England and Ireland. He himself published in London in 1666 a full account of them: *Val. Greatrakes Esq., of Waterford, in the kingdom of Ireland, famous for curing several diseases and distempers by the stroak of his hand only: London, 1660.*

Joseph Glanvill, a chaplain to Charles II, stated in a letter that Greatrakes was a simple, amiable, and pious man, a stranger to all deceit. A similar testimony was offered by George Rust, bishop of Dromore in Ireland, who stated that Greatrakes was at his house for three weeks, giving him an opportunity to observe his sound morals and many of his cures. Through the simple laying on of hands, said the bishop, he drove pain to the extremities. Many times the effect was very rapid and as if by magic. If the pain did not immediately subside he repeated his rubbings and always drove the pain finally into the limbs to expel it.

The Bishop further stated that "I can as eyewitness assert that Greatrakes cured dizziness, very bad diseases of the eyes and ears, old ulcers, goitre, epilepsy, glandular swellings, scirrhous indurations, and cancerous swellings. I have seen swellings disperse in five days which were many years old, but I do not believe by supernatural means; nor did his practice exhibit anything sacred. The cure was sometimes very protracted, and the diseases only gave way through repeated exertions; some altogether resisted his endeavours."

It appeared to the bishop that "something healing, something balsamic" flowed from the healer. Greatrakes himself believed that his power was a special gift of God. He healed even epidemic complaints by his touch and believed it his duty to devote himself to the cure of diseases.

To the bishop's testimony may be added that of two physicians, Faireklow and Astel, who assiduously inquired into the reality of his cures. Faireklow noted, "I was struck with his gentleness and kindness to the unhappy, and by the effects which he produced by his hand." Astel stated, "I saw Greatrakes in a moment remove most violent pains merely by his hand. I saw him drive a pain from the shoulder to the feet. If the pains in the head or the intestines remained fixed, the endeavor to remove them was frequently followed by the most dreadful crises, which even seemed to bring the patient's life into danger; but by degrees they disappeared into the limbs, and then altogether. I saw a scrofulous child of twelve years with such swellings that it could not move, and he dissipated merely with his hand the greatest part of them. One of the largest, however, he opened, and so healed it with his spittle."

Astel stated that he saw a number of other cures, and repeated the testimonies of Rust and Faireklow on the character of Greatrakes.

The celebrated Robert Boyle, president of the Royal Society of London, stated, "Many physicians, noblemen, clergymen, etc., testify to the truth of Greatrakes' cures, which he published in London. The chief diseases which he cured were blindness, deafness, paralysis, dropsy, ulcers, swellings, and all kinds of fevers."

Greatrakes was one of the most celebrated of the early mesmerists, and there is no question that mesmerism owed some of its popularity to his cures. According to accounts, he cured the **king's evil,** palsy, dropsy, epilepsy, ulcers, gallstones, wounds and bruises, lameness, deafness, and partial blindness by laying on of hands, stroking the pain out of its seat, and finally driving it out at the extremities. The Royal Society published accounts of his cures in their *Transactions.*

After several years of spectacular cures, Greatrakes seemed to lose his power.

Sources:

A Brief account of Mr. Valentine Greatrakes, and divers of the strange cures by him lately Performed; written by himself in a letter addressed to the Honourable Robert Boyle Esq. London, 1666. Reprint, Dublin: Samuel Dancer, 1688.

Greatrakes, V. *Val. Greatrakes, Esq., of Waterford, in the kingdom of Ireland, famous for curing several diseases and distempers by the stroak of his hand only.* London: The Author, 1660.

Henry Stubbe: The Miraculous Conformist; or an account of Several Marvailous Cures performed by Mr. Valentine Greatarick. Oxford, England, 1666.

Pechlin, J. N. *Observationes Physico-Medicae.* Hamburg, Germany, 1691.

GREECE

Magic in Ancient Greece

Magic in its widest sense was native to the imagination and genius of the Greeks, as was the case with most ancient peoples. This is apparent in their theogony, mythology (essentially magical in conception and meaning), literature, sculpture, and history. The natural features of the country appealed powerfully to the quality of their imagination. Mountains and valleys, mysterious caves and fissures, vapors and springs of volcanic origin, and sacred groves were all, according to their character, dedicated to the gods. Parnassus was the abode of the sun-god Apollo; the lovely vale of Aphaca that of Adonis; the oak-groves of Dodona favored of Zeus; and the gloomy caves with their roar of subterranean waters the Oracle of Trophonius.

Innumerable instances of magical wonder-working are found in the stories of Greek deities and heroes. The power of transformation is shown in a multitude of cases, among them that of Bacchus who, by waving a spear, could change the oars of a ship into serpents and the masts into heavy-clustered vines. He could also cause tigers, lynxes, and panthers to appear amidst the waves and the terrified sailors leaping overboard to take the shape of dolphins. In the story of Circe, the enchantress took her magic wand and with her enchanted philter turned her lovers into swine.

The serpent-staff of Hermes gave, by its touch, life or death, sleep or waking; Medusa's head turned its beholders into stone; Hermes gave Perseus wings that he might fly and Pluto a helmet which conferred **invisibility.** Prometheus molded a man of clay and to give it life stole celestial fire from heaven; Odysseus, to peer into the future, descended to Hades in search of Tiresias the Soothsayer; Archilles was made invulnerable by the waters of the Styx.

Dedicated by immemorial belief, there were places where the visible spirits of the dead might be evoked and where men in curiosity, longing, or remorse strove to call back those who had passed beyond mortal ken. In March, when the spring blossoms appeared and covered the trees, the Festival of the Flowers was held at Athens. The Commemoration of the Dead also occurred in the spring. It was thought that the spirits of the deceased rose from their graves and wandered about the familiar streets, striving to enter the dwellings of men and the temples of the gods but were shut out by the magic of branches of whitethorn, or by knotted ropes and pitch.

Oracles

Of great antiquity and eminently of Greek character and meaning were the Oracles. For centuries they ministered to that longing ingrained in human nature to know the future and to invoke divine foresight and aid in the direction of human affairs, from those of a private citizen to the multitudinous needs of the state. **Divination** and **prophecy** became the great features of the oracles. They were inspired by various means, including intoxicating fumes, natural or artificial mind-altering drugs, the drinking of mineral springs, signs and tokens, and dreams.

The most famous Oracles were those at **Delphi,** Dodona, Epidaurus, and that of Trophonius, but others of renown were scattered over the country. Perhaps one of the earliest was that of Aesculapius, son of Apollo and called the Healer, the Dreamsender, because his healing was given through the medium of dreams that came upon the applicant while sleeping in the temple-courts, the famous temple-sleep. This temple, situated at Epidaurus, was surrounded by sacred groves and whole companies of sick persons lingered there in search of lost health and enlightenment through divine dreams.

Famous above all was that of Apollo, the Delphian oracle, on the Southern Slopes of Parnassus, where kings, princes, heroes, and slaves of all countries journeyed to ask the questions as to the future and what it might hold for them. The temple was built above a volcanic chasm, amid a wildness of nature that suggested the presence of the unseen powers. Here the priestess, the Pythia, so named after the serpent Pytho whom Apollo slew, was seated on a tripod placed above the gaseous vapors rising from the chasm. Intoxicated to a state of frenzy, her mouth foaming, wild torrents of words fell from her lips. These words were shaped into coherence and meaning by the attendant priests and given to the waiting questioner crowned with laurel, the symbol of sleep and dreams, who stood before the altar.

Priests and priestesses were also crowned with these leaves, which were sacred to Appollo and burned as incense. Before the Pythias chamber hung a falling screen of laurel branches, while at the festival of the Septerion every ninth year a bower of laurel was erected in the forecourt of the temple. One writer has left strange details, such as the rule that the sacred fire within the temple must only be fed with firwood, and although a woman was chosen as the medium of the prophetic utterance, no woman might question the oracle.

The Oracle of the Pelasgic Zeus at Dodona was the oldest of all. It answered by signs rather than inspired speech, by means of lots and the falling of water, or by the wind-moved clanging of brazen-bowls, two hollow columns standing side by side.

The three priestesses or Peliades (meaning doves) were given titles signifying the Diviner of the Future; the friend of man, Virtue; and the virgin-ruler of man, Chastity. For 2,000 years this oracle existed. It was consulted by those heroes of the ancient myths struggling in the toils of Fate—Hercules, Achilles, Ulysses and Aeneas—down to the later vestiges of Greek nationality.

The Oracle of Trophonius was also of great renown. Here there were numerous caverns filled with misty vapors and troubled by the noise of hidden waters far beneath. In this mysterious gloom the supplicants slept sometimes for nights and days, coming forth in a somnambulic state from which they were aroused and questioned by the attendant priests. Frightful visions were generally recounted, accompanied by a terrible melancholy, so that it passed into a proverb regarding a sorrowful man "He has been in the cave of Trophonius."

Thus it may be seen that magic, in the sense of secret revelations, miraculous cures, prophetic gifts, and unusual powers, had always existed for the Greeks; the oracles were a purely natural human way of communicating with their gods upon earth.

But magic in the sense of **sorcery** was introduced into Greece from Asia and Egypt. It had to fit into a conception of Fate as inexorable and inescapable for gods, rulers, and slaves alike, a belief which warred a form of magic that had for its primary aim a certain command of the destinies of man.

Good and evil and the perpetual strife between these two principles and the belief in **demonology** gradually evolved within Greek thought. It was said that the first mention of good and evil demons could be traced to the Pythagorean school, and not until after the Persian War was there a word in the Greek language for "magic." As these beliefs emerged, however, they were ascribed to the native deities, gradually becoming incorporated with the ancient histories and rites.

Sorcery and Enchantment

After the invasion by the Persians, Thessaly, where their stay was of lengthy duration, became famous for its sorceresses and their practices, which embraced a wide thaumaturgical field, from calling down the moon to brewing magical herbs for love or death. Thus Apuleius in his romance *The Golden Ass* stated that when in Thessaly he was in the place,

". . . where, by common report of the world, sorcery and enchantments were most frequent. I viewed the situation of the place in which I was, nor was there anything I saw that I believed to be the same thing which it appeared to be. Insomuch that the very stones in the street I thought were men bewitched and turned into that figure, and the birds I heard chirping, the trees without the walls, and the running waters, were changed from human creatures into the appearances they were. I persuaded myself that the statues and buildings could move; that the oxen and other brute beasts could speak and tell strange tidings; that I should hear and see oracles from heaven conveyed in the beams of the Sun."

Homer told the tale of Circe the enchantress, with her magic philters and magic songs, but made no mention of Medea, the arch-sorceress of later times. Around her name the later beliefs clustered. To her were attributed all the evil arts and she became the witch par excellence, her infamy increasing from age to age.

The same may be said of Hecate, the moon-goddess, at first sharer with Zeus of the heavenly powers, but later an ominous shape of gloom, ruler and lover of the night and darkness, of the world of phantoms and ghouls. Like the Furies she wielded the whip and cord; she was followed by hell hounds, by writhing serpents, by lamiae, strygae and empusae, figures of terror and loathing. She presided over the dark mysteries of birth and death; she was worshipped at night in the flare of torches. She was the three-headed Hecate of the crossroads where little round cakes or a lizard mask set about with candles were offered to her in propitiation, that none of the phantom mob might cross the threshold of man.

Love-magic and death-magic, the usual forms of sorcery, became common in Greece as elsewhere. Love philters and charms were eagerly sought, the most innocent being bitten apples and enchanted garlands. Means of protection against the evil eye became a necessity, tales of bewitchment were spread abroad, and misfortune and death were being brought upon the innocent and unwary by means of a waxen figure molded in their image and tortured by the sorceress.

In tombs and secret places, leaden tablets were buried with inscriptions of the names of foes and victims and pierced through with a nail in order to bring disaster and death upon them. At this time it became law that no one who practiced sorcery might participate in the Eleusinian Mysteries, and at Athens a Samian Sorceress, Theoris, was cast to the flames.

Orphic Magic

The introduction of Egyptian influences were due generally to the agency of Orpheus and Pythagoras, who, while in Egypt, had been initiated into the mysteries. The story of Orpheus shows him as preeminently the wonder-worker, but one of beneficence and beauty. To men of his time, everything was enchantment and prodigy. By the irresistible power of his music he constrained the rocks, trees, and animals to follow him; at his behest storms arose or abated. He was the necromancer, who by his golden music overcame the powers of darkness, and, descending to the world of shades, found his beloved Eurydice. They gained the upper air that brought her back to the living world.

Jealous women tore him limb from limb, and his head floated down the waters of the Hebrus and was cast on the rocky shores of Lesbos where, still retaining the power of speech, it uttered oracles that gave guidance to people. Orpheus was said to have instructed the Greeks in medicine and magic, and for long afterward remedies, magical formulas, incantations, and charms were engraved upon Orphean tablets and the power of healing was ascribed to the Orphean hymns.

Pythagoras, a philosopher, geometrician, and magician who was indefatigable in the pursuit of knowledge, wielded an immense influence on the thought of his time. After his return from Egypt he founded a school where to those who had previously undergone severe and drastic discipline he communicated his wide and varied knowledge. He was also credited with miraculous powers such as being visible at the same hour in places as far apart as Italy and Sicily, taming a bear by whispering in its ear, and calling an eagle from its flight to alight on his wrist.

Mysteries

Among the greatest features of religious life were the **mysteries** held at periodic intervals in connection with the different deities, such as the Samothracian, the Bacchic, and, most famous of all, the Eleusinian. Their origin is to be traced mostly to a prehistoric nature-worship and vegetation-magic.

All these mysteries had three trials or baptisms by water, fire, and air, and three specially sacred emblems, the phallus, egg, and serpent, generative emblems sacred in many secret rites.

The Samothracian centered around four mysterious deities: Axieros, the mother; her children: Axiocersos, male; Axiocersa, female; and Casindos the originator of the universe. The festival probably symbolized the creation of the world and also the harvest and its growth. Connected with this mystery was the worship of Cybele, goddess of the earth, cities, and fields. Her priests, the Corybantes, dwelt in a cave where they held their ceremonies, including a wild and orgiastic weapon-dance, accompanied by the incessant shaking of heads and clanging of swords on shields.

The cult of Bacchus was said by some to have been carried into Greece from Egypt by Melampus. He was the god of the vine and vegetation, and his mysteries typified the growth of the vine and the vintage—the winter sleep of all plant life and its renewal in spring. Women were his chief attendants—the Bacchantes, who, clashing cymbals and uttering wild cries in invocation of their god, became possessed by ungovernable fury and homicidal mania.

Greatest of all in their relation to Hellenic life were the Eleusinian Mysteries. These were the paramount interest and function of the state religion exerting the widest, strongest influence on people of all classes. The rites were secret and their details are practically unknown, but they undoubtedly symbolized the myth of Demeter, corn-goddess, and were held in spring and September.

Prior to initiation, a long period of purification and preparation was enforced, during which the higher meaning of the myth was inculcated, the original meaning having become exalted by the genius of the Greeks into an intimate allegory of the soul of man, its birth, life, death, descent into Hades, and subsequent release therefrom. After this came the central point of the mysteries, the viewing of certain holy and secret symbols; next, a crowning of garlands, signifying the happiness that arises from friendship with the divine. The festival also embodied a scenic representation of the story of Demeter, the rape of Persephone, the sorrow of the mother, her complaints before Zeus, and the final reconciliation.

Women played a great part in this, the reason being that as they themselves "produce," so by sympathetic magic their influence was conveyed to the corn, as when crying aloud for rain they looked upward to the skies, then down to the earth with cries of "Conceive!" These priestesses were crowned with poppies and corn, symbolical attributes of the deity they implored.

Divination

Besides the priests and priestesses attached to the different temples, there was an order of men called "interpreters," whose business it was to divine the future by various means such as the flight of birds and entrails of victims. These men often accompanied the armies in order to predict the success or failure of operations during warfare and thus avert the possibility of mistakes in the campaign. They fomented or repressed revolutions in state and government by their predictions.

The most celebrated interpreters were those of Elis, where in two or three families, notably the Iamidae and the Clytidae, this peculiar gift or knowledge was handed down from father to son for generations. But there were others who were authorized by the state, both men and women, who professed to read the future in natural and unnatural phenomena, eclipses, thunder, dreams, unexpected sight of certain animals, convulsive movement of eyelids, tingling of the ears, sneezing, and a few words casually dropped by a passerby.

In the literature and philosophies of Greece, magic in all its forms is found as a theme for imagination, discussion, and belief. In the hands of the tragic poets, sorceresses such as Circe and Medea became figures of terror and death, embodiments of evil.

Pythagoras left no writings but on his theories were founded those of Empedocles and Plato. In the verses of Empedocles he teaches the theory of **reincarnation,** he himself remembering previous existences wherein he was a boy, a girl, a plant, a fish and a bird. He also claimed to teach the secrets of miraculous medicine, of the reanimation of old age, of bringing rain, storm, or sunshine, and of recalling the dead.

Aristides, the Greek orator, gave exhaustive accounts of the many dreams he experienced during sleep in the temples and the cures prescribed therein. Socrates told of his attendant spirit or genius who warned him, and others through his agency, of impending danger, also foretelling futurity. Xenophon, treating of divination by dreams, maintained that in sleep the human soul reveals her divine nature, and, being freed from trammels of the body, gazes into futurity.

Plato, while inveighing against sorcery, took the popular superstitions relating to magic, demons, and spirits and used them as a basis for a spiritual and magical theory of things. On his teaching would be founded the Neo-Platonists school, which was among the most fervid defender of magic.

Aristotle stated that prediction is a purely natural quality of the imagination, while Plutarch in his writings (wherein much may be found on magic and dreams) gave an exhaustive account on the somnambulic states of the oracular priestess, Pythia, attributing them to possession by the divinity.

Vampirism

Some of the later superstitions of the Hellenic archipelago partake more of the nature of Slavonic tradition than that of the ancient inhabitants of Greece. One of the most notable circumstances in later Greek superstition relates to vampirism.

The **vampire** was called *vroucolaca* or *broucolack* by the Greeks, and appears to have come into Greek thought from the Slavic world in early medieval times. French researcher Augustine Calmet, author of *Dissertations Upon the Apparitions of Angels, Daemons and Ghosts, and concerning . . . Vampires* (1759) stated,

"It is asserted by the modern Greeks, in defence of their schism, and as a proof that the gift of miracles, and the episcopal power of the keys, subsists in their church more visibly and evidently than in the church of Rome, that, with them, the bodies of excommunicated persons never rot, but swell up to an uncommon size, and are stretched like drums, nor ever corrupt or fall to dust, till they have received absolution from some bishop or priest. And they produce many instances of carcasses which have been in their graves uncorrupted, and which have afterwards putrefied as soon as the excommunication was taken off.

"They do not, however, deny that a body's not corrupting is sometimes a proof of sanctity, but in this case they expect it to send forth an agreeable smell, to be white or ruddy, and not black, stinking, and swelled like a drum, as the bodies of excommunicated persons generally are. We are told, that in the time of Manuel, or Maximus, patriarch of Constantinople, the Turkish emperor having the mind to know the truth of the Greek notion concerning the incorruption of excommunicated bodies, the patriarch ordered the grave of a woman, who had lived in a criminal commerce with an archbishop of Constantinople, to be opened. Her body being found entire, black and much swelled, the Turks put it into a chest, under the emperor's seal, and the patriarch having repeated a prayer, and given absolution to the deceased, the chest was opened three days after and the body was found reduced to ashes. It is also a notion which prevails among the Greeks, that the bodies of these excommunicated persons frequently appear to the living, both day and night, and speak to them, call upon them, and disturb them several other ways.

"Leo Allatius is very particular upon this head, and says, that in the isle of Chio, the inhabitants never answer the first time they are called, for fear of its being a spectre; but if they are called twice, they are sure it is not a Broucolack (this is the name they give these spirits). If any one appears at the first call, the spectre disappears, but the person certainly dies.

"They have no way to get rid of these evil genii, but to dig up the body of the person that has appeared, and burn it after having repeated over it certain prayers. By this means the body being reduced to ashes, appears no more. And they look upon it as a clear case, that either these mischievous and spiteful carcasses come out of their graves of their own accord, and occasion the death of the persons that see or speak to them; or that the devil himself makes use of these bodies to frighten and destroy mankind. They have hitherto discovered no remedy which more infallibly rids them of these plagues, than to burn or mangle the bodies which were made use of for these cursed purposes. Sometimes the end is answered by tearing out the heart and letting the bodies rot above ground before they burn them again, or by cutting off the head, or driving a large nail through the temples."

Sir Paul Rycaut in his *The Present State of the Greek & Armenian Churches* (1679) observed that the opinion that excommunicated bodies are preserved from putrefaction prevails not only among the Greeks, but also among the Turks, and he gives us a fact that he had from a caloyer (monk) of Candia, who confirmed it to him upon oath. The caloyer's name was Sophronius, a man well known and respected in Smyrna.

A man, who was excommunicated for a fault that he had committed in the Morea, died on the island of Milo and was buried in a private place, without any ceremonies, and in unconsecrated ground. His relations and friends expressed great dissatisfaction at his being treated in this manner, and very soon after the inhabitants of the island were tormented every night by frightful apparitions, which they attributed to this unhappy man. Upon opening the grave his body was found entire; his veins swelled with blood and a consultation was held upon the subject with the caloyers dismembering his body, cutting it in pieces, and boiling it in wine, which, it seems, is the usual manner of proceeding there in those cases.

However, the friends of the deceased prevailed upon them, by dint of entreaty, to delay the execution, and in the meantime sent to Constantinople to get absolution for him from the patriarch. Until the messenger could return, the body was laid in the church, and prayers and masses were said daily for the repose of his soul. One day while Sophronius, the caloyer above mentioned, was performing the service, there was suddenly heard a great noise in the coffin and upon examination the body was found reduced to ashes, as if it had been dead seven years. Particular notice was taken of the time when the noise was heard, and it was found to be the very morning when the absolution was signed by the patriarch. Sir Paul Rycaut, who has recorded this event, was neither a Greek nor Roman Catholic, but a staunch Protestant of the Church of England.

He observes upon this occasion that the notion among the Greeks is that an evil spirit enters into the excommunicated carcass and preserves it from corruption by performing the usual functions of the human soul in a living body. They fancy, moreover, that these corpses eat by night and actually digest and are nourished by their food; that several have been found of a fresh, ruddy color, with their veins ready to burst with blood, full forty days after their death; and that upon being opened there has issued from them as large a quantity of warm, fresh blood as would come from a young person of the most sanguine constitution. And this opinion prevails so universally, that everyone is furnished with a story to this purpose.

Father Theophilus Raynard, a Roman Catholic author of a particular treatise upon this subject, asserted that this coming again of deceased persons is an undoubted truth and is supported by unquestionable facts. But he also argued that to pretend that these specters are always excommunicated persons, and that the Church of Greece has a privilege of preserving from putrefaction the bodies of those that die under her sentence, is what cannot be maintained, since it is certain that excommunicated bodies rot as well as others, and that several who have died in the communion of the church, Greek as well as Roman, have continued uncorrupted. (In the Western Roman tradition, to die and remain uncorrupted was a sign of great sanctity.) There have even been instances of this nature among the heathens, and frequently among other animals, whose carcasses have been found unputrefied in the ground, and among the ruins of old buildings.

In his book *A Voyage Into the Levant* (1741), J. Pittonde Tournefort gave an account of the digging up of a believed *broucolack* in the island of Mycone, where he was January 1, 1701.

"We were present at a very different scene in the same island, upon occasion of one of those dead corpses, which they suppose to come to life again after their burial. The man, whose story I am going to relate, was a peasant in Mycone, naturally ill-natured and quarrelsome (a circumstance of consequence in such cases); he was murdered in the fields, nobody knew how, or by whom.

"Two days after his being buried in a chapel in the town it was noised about that he was seen in the night walking about in a great hurry; that he came into houses and tumbled about their goods, gripped people behind, and played a thousand little monkey tricks. At first it was only laughed at, but it soon grew to be a very serious affair when the better sort of people joined in the complaint. The Papas themselves gave credit to it, and no doubt had their reasons for so doing. Masses, to be sure, were said, but the peasant was incorrigible, and continued his old trade. After several meetings of the chief people of the town, and of the priests and monks, it was concluded to be necessary, in obedience to some old ceremonial, to wait till nine days after the burial.

"On the tenth day, a mass was said in the chapel where the body lay, in order to drive out the devil, which was imagined to have taken possession of it. When the mass was over the body was taken up, and preparations were made for pulling out its heart. The butcher of the town, an old clumsy fellow, began with opening the belly instead of the breast. He groped a long while among the entrails without finding what he looked for, till at last somebody said he should cut up the diaphragm, and then the heart was pulled out, to the admiration of the spectators. In the meantime the carcass stunk so abominably that they were obliged to burn frankincense but the smoke mixing with the fumes of the corpse, increased the stink and began to heat the poor people's brains. Their imagination, already affected with the spectacle before them, grew full of whimsies, and they took it into their heads that a thick smoke came from the body; nor durst we say that it was only the smoke of the incense.

"In the chapel and the square before it they were incessantly bawling out Broucolack, which is the name they give to these pretended redivivi. From hence the bellowing was communicated to the streets and seemed to be invented on purpose to split the roof of the chapel. Several there present averred that the blood of the offender was red, and the butcher swore that the body was still warm, whence they concluded that the deceased was guilty of a heavy crime for not being thoroughly dead, or rather for suffering himself to be reanimated by the devil, which is the notion they have of a Broucolack. They then roared out that word in a stupendous manner. Just at this time there came in a flock of people, who loudly protested that they plainly saw the body was not grown stiff when it was carried from the fields to the church to be buried, and that consequently it was a true Broucolack, which word continued to be the burden of the song.

"I question not but they would have sworn it did not stink if we had not been there so thoroughly were their heads turned upon this occasion, and so strongly were they infatuated with the notion of these specters. As for us, we got as close to the body as we could, that we might observe what passed more exactly, and were almost poisoned with the stink. When they asked us what we thought of the corpse we told them we believed it to be completely dead, and having a mind to cure, or, at least, not to exasperate their prejudices, we presented to them that it was no wonder the butcher should feel some warmth, by groping in the entrails, which were then putrefying, that it was no extraordinary thing for it to emit fumes since the same will happen upon turning up a dunghill, and that as for the pretended redness of the blood, it was still visible by the butcher's hands, that it was a mere stinking nasty smear.

"After all our reasoning they resolved upon going to the seashore, and there burning the dead man's heart. But, notwithstanding this execution, he did not grow more peaceable, but made more noise than ever. He was accused of beating people in the night, breaking down doors, and even roofs of houses, shattering windows, tearing clothes, and emptying casks and bottles. It was a ghost of a very thrifty constitution; nor do I believe that he spared any house but the consul's, where we lodged. In the meantime nothing could be more deplorable than the condition of this island. Not a head in it but was turned; the wisest among them were seized like the rest. In short, it was a real disorder of the brain, as dangerous as lunacy or madness. Whole families quitted their houses, and brought their beds from the remotest parts of the town into the great square, there to spend the night. Every one complained of some fresh insult, and nothing could be heard but groans at the approach of night. The most sensible people among them thought proper to retire into the country.

"When the prepossession was so general, we thought it our best way to hold our tongues. Had we opposed it we should have been treated not only as fools, but as infidels. Indeed, how was it possible to bring a whole nation to its senses? Those who believed in their hearts that we doubted the truth of the fact, came and reproached us with our incredulity, and endeavoured to prove that there were such things as Broucolacks, by quotations out of the *Buckler of Faith,* written by Father Richard, a Jesuit missionary. Their argument was this: He was a Latin, and therefore you ought to believe him, nor should we have got anything by denying the consequence. We were entertained every morning with a recital of the new pranks of this night-bird, who was even charged with being guilty of the most abominable sins.

"Some of the citizens, who were most zealous for the public good, took it into their heads that there had been a defect in the most essential part of the ceremony. They were of opinion that mass ought not to have been said, till after the heart had been pulled out. With this precaution they insisted that the devil must needs have been worsted, and would not have ventured to come again; whereas, by mass being said first, he had time enough given him to make off, and return to his post when the danger was over.

"After all these wise reflections, they were as much perplexed as at first setting out. They meet night and morning, debate, and make processions for three days and three nights. The Papas are obliged to fast, and run from house to house with sprinklers on their hands. Holy water is plentifully scattered about, even to the washing of the doors, and filling the mouth of the poor Broucolack.

"We repeated it so often to the magistrates, that we should not fail in Christendom to appoint a watch by night upon such an occasion, in order to observe what passed in the town, that at last they apprehended some vagabonds who had certainly a hand in these disorders; but either they were not the principal agents, or they were dismissed too soon. For two days after, to make themselves amends for the fast they had kept in prison, they begun to empty the wine casks of such as had been silly enough to leave their houses in the night, so that nothing was left but to have recourse again to prayers.

"One day, as they were repeating a certain form, after having stuck a number of naked swords in the grave where the carcass lay (which they dug up three or four times a day to gratify the whim of whoever came by), an Albanian, who happened to be at Mycone, took upon him to pronounce with an air of great wisdom, that it was ridiculous to make use of the swords of Christians in such a case as this. 'Are you so blind,' says he, 'as not to see that the hilt of these swords, being made in the form of a cross, hinders the devil from coming out of the carcass? I am surprised that you do not take the Turkish sabres.' But the expedient of this wise personage had no effect: the Broucolack was still unruly; the whole island continued in a strange consternation, and they were utterly at a loss what saint to invoke, when all of a sudden, as if they had given one another the word, they begun to bawl all over the city that they had waited too long, that the Broucolack should be burned to ashes, and then they defied the devil to harbour there any longer, and that it was better to have recourse to this extremity, than to have the island totally deserted. For, in fact, several whole families had begun to pack up in order to retire to Syra or Tinos.

"The magistrates, therefore, gave orders to carry the Broucolack to the point of St. George's Island, where they got ready a great pile, with pitch and tar, for fear the wood should not burn fast enough of itself. The remnant of this miserable carcass was thrown into it and soon consumed. It was the 1st of January, 1701, and we saw the flame as we returned from Delos. It might properly be called a rejoicing bonfire, as no more complaints were heard of the Broucolack. They only said that the devil had at last met with his match, and some ballads were made to turn him into ridicule.

"It is a notion which prevails all over the Archipelago that the devil reanimates no carcasses but those of the Greek communion. The inhabitants of Santorini are terribly afraid of these bugbears: those of Mycone, after their whims were dissipated, were equally afraid of a prosecution from the Turks, and from the bishop of Tinos. Not a single Papas would venture to be at St. George's when the body was burnt, for fear the bishop should insist upon a fee for their taking up and burning a body without his leave. As for the Turks, they did not fail, at their next visit, to make the Myconians pay heavily for their treatment of this poor devil, who became in every respect an object of abomination and horror to all the country."

Psychical Research & Spiritualism

Because of the religious control asserted by the Greek Orthodox Church in the decades since modern Greece attained independence from Turkey, Greece has been one of the most hostile countries to the emergence of religious pluralism. Spiritualism, Theosophy, and other new religious impulses, occult and otherwise, have found little fertile ground in the country. However, in common with other European countries, Greek scientists took an active interest in psychical studies during the 1920s and 1930s. Prominent societies included the Hellenic Society of Psychical Research and the **Society for Psychical Research** and the Society for Psychic Studies. The most prominent researcher was **Angelos Tanagras,** a high ranking naval officer who edited the *Revue Psychikae Creonae* of Athens from 1925 onward. He proposed a theory of precognition which involved the psychokinetic action of the percipient, thus sidestepping the issue of determinism.

At the present time, there are two active societies: The Society for the Scientific Study of Metaphysics, Rue Agathoupoleus 104, Athens; and the Psychic Society of Athens, 32 Tsiller-str., Athens 905. Both publish periodicals.

Sources:

Abbott, G. F. *Macedonian Folklore.* Chicago: Argonaut, Inc., 1909.

Apuleius. *The Golden Ass.* Trans. Adlington. London: William Heineman, 1935.

Berger, Arthur S., and Joyce Berger. *The Encyclopedia of Parapsychology and Psychical Research.* New York: Paragon House, 1991.

Fontenrose, Joseph. *Python: A Study of Delphic Myth and Its Origins.* Berkeley, Calif.: University of California Press, 1959.

Lawson, John C. *Modern Greek Folklore and Ancient Greek Religion.* 1910. Reprint, New Hyde Park, N.Y.: University Books, 1964.

Melton, J. Gordon. *The Vampire Book: An Encyclopedia of the Undead.* Detroit: Gale Research, 1994.

Schwab, Gustav. *Gods and Heroes: Myths and Epics of Ancient Greece.* New York: Pantheon Books, 1946.

Tanagras, A. *Psychophysical Elements in Parapsychological Transactions.* New York: Parapsychology Institute, 1967.

Greeley, Horace (1811–1872)

Famous American political writer, editor of the *New York Tribune,* and an important figure in early American Spiritualism. He was the first to call upon the **Fox Sisters** on their arrival in New York in June 1850, and he admitted publicly that he was puzzled by the phenomena he observed and that he thought the good faith of the mediums could not be questioned.

The Fox sisters were guests at Greeley's home in New York for three days. During that period he became convinced of the genuineness of their mysterious rappings, although he did not accept the spirit hypothesis. "Whatever may be the origin of the cause of the rappings," he wrote, "the ladies in whose presence they occur do not make them. We tested this thoroughly and to our entire satisfaction."

The columns written in Greeley's paper were fair and impartial during periods of the wildest controversy. In his *Recollections of a Busy Life* (1868), he admits that "the jugglery hypothesis utterly fails to account for occurrences which I have personally witnessed," and that "certain developments strongly indicate that they do proceed from departed spirits." He submitted, however, that nothing of value was obtained from the investigation, that the spirits "did not help to fish up the Atlantic cable or find Sir John Franklin."

Sources:

Berger, Arthur S., and Joyce Berger. *The Encyclopedia of Parapsychology and Psychical Research.* New York: Paragon House, 1991.

Moore, Lawrence R. *In Search of White Crows.* New York: Oxford University Press, 1977.

Van Deusen, Glyndon G. *Horace Greeley: Nineteenth-Century Crusader.* Philadelphia: University of Pennsylvania Press, 1953.

Green, Celia Elizabeth (1935–)

Director of the Institute of Psychophysical Research, Oxford, England, founded in 1961 to undertake research in the field of **parapsychology.** Green was born November 26, 1935, in London. She studied at Oxford University, from which she received her B.A. (1957), M.A. (1961), and B. Litt. (1961). From 1958 to 1960 she studied at Trinity College, Cambridge, on a Perrott studentship in psychical research, and from 1957 to 1962 she was research secretary of the **Society for Psychical Research** (SPR), London. She is a fellow of the Royal Society of Medicine.

During the 1950s Green participated in the SPR study of spontaneous paranormal phenomena in Britain, covering some fifteen hundred cases. She wrote several books and a number of articles and contributed to the encyclopedia *Man, Myth, and Magic.* Green also translated the English edition of **René Sudre**'s book *Traité de Parapsychologie,* published as *Treatise on Parapsychology* (1960) in Britain and as *Parapsychology* (1960) in the United States.

Sources:

Berger, Arthur S., and Joyce Berger. *The Encyclopedia of Parapsychology and Psychical Research.* New York: Paragon House, 1991.

Green, Celia. *The Decline and Fall of Science.* London: Hamilton, 1976.

———. *The Human Evasion.* London: Hamilton, 1969.

———. *Lucid Dreams.* Oxford: Institute of Psychophysical Research, 1968.

———. *Out-of-the-Body Experiences: Proceedings of the Institute of Psychophysical Research.* London: Hamilton, 1968.

———. "Report on the Spontaneous Cases Enquiry." *Proceedings* of the Society for Psychical Research 53, no. 191 (November 1960).

Green, Celia, and Charles McCreely. *Apparitions.* London: Hamilton, 1975.

Pleasants, Helene, ed. *Biographical Dictionary of Parapsychology.* New York: Helix Press, 1964.

Green Man, The

A mysterious legendary character in British folklore dating back to medieval times, deriving from a pagan god of vegetation and the woodlands. Although his origins are shrouded in antiquity, he may also be related to myths of the Arcadian goat-god, Pan. The Green Man is usually represented by a human face embedded in foliage, but some ancient representations depict him as horned, suggesting a connection with a **witchcraft** deity. He has even been depicted in carved decorations on old churches and cathedrals, suggesting that at some period, pagan deities were supplanted by Christianity.

During the Christian eras, the Green Man survived in folk plays and folklore customs, such as the May Day revels, when he was called "Jack in the Green" or some similar name. Traditions of the Green Man may also have merged with the legends of Robin Hood.

Greenbank, Richard Kelly (1924–)

Psychiatrist and psychoanalyst who wrote on parapsychology. He was born April 23, 1924, in Washington, D.C., and studied at George Washington University, Washington, D.C.; the Medical College of Virginia, Richmond; and the Philadelphia Psychoanalytic Institute. Before entering private practice as a psychiatrist and psychoanalyst in 1955, he was a resident psychiatrist at Norways Foundation Hospital, Indianapolis, Indiana, and a resident in psychiatry and research fellow at Jefferson Medical School and Hospital, Philadelphia. In 1968 he became chief of section of the Department of Psychiatry, Philadelphia General Hospital. In addition to many articles on psychiatric subjects, including hypnosis and the psychotherapy of schizophrenia, Greenbank wrote various articles on parapsychological subjects.

Sources:

Greenbank, Richard K. "Allegedly Prophetic Dreams in Psychotherapeutic Treatment." *International Journal of Parapsychology* (Summer 1960).

———. "Communication of Suicidal Thoughts." *Canadian Psychiatric Association Journal* (July 1957).

———. "My Wolf." *Journal of Abnormal and Social Psychology* (May 1957).

———. "Unexplained Mental Phenomena Regarding Suicide." *Journal of Nervous and Mental Diseases* (January 1957).

Pleasants, Helene, ed. *Biographical Dictionary of Parapsychology.* New York: Helix Press, 1964.

Greenwood, Joseph Albert (1906–1988)

Mathematician who worked in the field of **parapsychology.** He was born September 18, 1906, at Breckenridge, Missouri, and studied at the University of Missouri (B.A., 1927; M.A., 1929; Ph.D., 1931).

He was an instructor and later an assistant professor of mathematics at Duke University (1930–42). While there he worked with **J. B. Rhine,** who recruited him to provide the statistical work for his research on parapsychology. Greenwood emerged as a major spokesperson answering criticisms of the statistical work being carried on at Duke, about which he wrote a number of articles. After the war began in 1942, he left Duke to serve in the United States Navy (1942–46). He spent his postwar career in government employ. He became a charter associate of the **Parapsychological Association.**

Sources:

Berger, Arthur S., and Joyce Berger. *The Encyclopedia of Parapsychology and Psychical Research.* New York: Paragon House, 1991.

Foundation for Research on the Nature of Man. "Joseph A. Greenwood, 1906–1988." *Foundation for Research on the Nature of Man Bulletin* 37 (Spring 1988).

Greenwood, Joseph A. "Analysis of a Large Chance Control Series of ESP Data." *Journal of Parapsychology* 2 (1938).

———. "A Co-Variation Statistic." *Journal of Parapsychology* 3 (1939).

———. "An Empirical Investigation of Some Sampling Problems." *Journal of Parapsychology* 2 (1938).

———. "Mathematical Techniques Used in ESP Research." *Journal of Parapsychology* 1 (1937).

———. "A Reply to Dr. Feller's Critique." *Journal of Parapsychology* 4 (1940).

———. "Some Mathematical Problems for Future Consideration Suggested by ESP Research." *Journal of Parapsychology* 3 (1939).

———. "Variance of the ESP Call Series." *Journal of Parapsychology* 2 (1938).

Greenwood, Joseph A., and C. E. Stuart. "Review of Criticisms of the Mathematical Evaluation of ESP Data." *Journal of Parapsychology* 1 (1937).

Pleasants, Helene, ed. *Biographical Dictionary of Parapsychology.* New York: Helix Press, 1964.

Gregory, Anita (Kohsen) (1925–1984)

British parapsychologist with a background in psychology; her late husband, C. C. L. Gregory, was also a parapsychologist. Anita Gregory was principal lecturer in education at the Polytechnic of North London, where she taught psychology and philosophy. Gregory was born Anita Kohsen on June 9, 1925, in Berlin, Germany. Because her parents were Jewish, it was soon necessary for her to leave Germany. For a time she was entrusted to a Belgian convent before eventually moving to England, where she studied at Birkbeck College, University of London, taking an honors degree in languages before studying politics, economics, philosophy, psychology, and physiology at St. Hugh's College, Oxford University. In 1949 she became interested in psychical research through Dr. **William Brown,** a reader in mental philosophy at Oxford, who discussed with her the phenomena of the Austrian medium **Rudi Schneider.**

In 1954 Kohsen married Clive Gregory, emeritus director of the University of London Observatory, and the two formed the Institute for the Study of Mental Images at their home in Hampshire and published various joint papers on psychology and cosmology. Between 1961 and 1964 they issued their own journal, *Cosmos,* which included contributions on Clive Gregory's concept of the "O-Structure," a theory of psychophysical cosmology.

In 1962 Anita Gregory translated a study of **ESP** by the Russian parapsychologist **L. L. Vasiliev,** which was published the following year by the Institute for the Study of Mental Images under the title *Experiments in Distant Influence.* An expanded edition was published in 1976. Gregory also edited a collection of the writings of Sir **Cyril Burt** on psychical research, published as *ESP and Psychology.* Her own study of the Rudi Schneider case occupied a full issue of the journal *Annals of Science* in 1977 and was later published as a separate book. She also contributed various articles to *Psychic News,* using the pseudonyms "Zebedee" and "John Barnes."

She was an active member of the **Society for Psychical Research,** serving on the council and becoming honorary secretary for a period. While with the society, Gregory conducted a series of experiments with British psychic **Matthew Manning,** resulting in an 85-page report in 1982. This included some valuable observations on the role of the experimenter by Manning himself. In 1981 Gregory participated in the **Parapsychology Foundation**'s Thirtieth Annual International Conference in New York, presenting a paper on "Investigating Macro-Physical Phenomena."

In August 1983 she was awarded a doctorate by the Council for National Academic Awards. She taught a course on psychical research at the School of Education in the North London Polytechnic. She suffered from illness for a long period after the death of her husband in 1964 and died November 7, 1984.

Sources:

Berger, Arthur S., and Joyce Berger. *The Encyclopedia of Parapsychology and Psychical Research.* New York: Paragon House, 1991.

Gregory, Anita. "London Experiments with Matthew Manning." *Proceedings* of the Society for Psychical Research 56 (1982).

———. "Psychical Research as a Social Activity." *Journal* of the Society for Psychical Research 51 (1981).

———. *The Strange Case of Rudi Schneider.* Metuchen, N.J.: Scarecrow Press, 1985.

Pleasants, Helene, ed. *Biographical Dictionary of Parapsychology.* New York: Helix Press, 1964.

Gregory VII, Pope (ca. 1023–1085)

A pope of the eleventh century against whom a charge of **necromancy** was brought. Gregory was chiefly noted for his bitter and prolonged struggle with Henry IV, emperor of Germany. A quarrel arose between them regarding a gift by Henry of ecclesiastical dignities. Henry was summoned before Gregory to account for the gifts. He refused to appear, was excommunicated, and, in return, had the pope kidnapped by brigands.

Gregory, however, was rescued by the people of Rome and on his release commanded the Germans to elect a new emperor, Rudolph, duke of Swabia. Henry, attended by a very small retinue, went to Canossa, where Gregory resided, to arrange for terms of peace. He was treated with such severity and neglect that he lost his desire to come to terms with the pope, and on his return he elected an antipope, Clement III. In the struggle that ensued, Henry defeated Rudolph in battle and Gregory was sentenced as a sorcerer. He died in exile at Salerno.

Gregory's fame rests not in magic but chiefly on a prophecy he made publicly that Rudolph would be victorious "before St. Peter's day," a statement on which he staked his papal crown. The unfortunate Rudolph, entirely trusting Gregory's prediction, renewed the battle six times and finally died without having obtained the promised victory.

Other stories credit Gregory with the power of making lightning with a motion of his hand and causing thunder to dart from his sleeve. It was related by Benno that on one occasion he left his magic book behind him at his villa. Entrusting two of his servants with the task of returning for it, he warned them not to look into it on pain of the most awful punishment. Curiosity overcame the fears of one of them, and, opening the book, he pronounced some words. Immediately a band of imps appeared and asked what they commanded. The terrified servants begged the demons to cast down as much of the city wall as lay in their way; thus they escaped punishment for their disobedience. Notwithstanding such folklore, there is no real evidence that Gregory practiced sorcery.

Grenzgebiete der Wissenschaft (Journal)

German-language quarterly journal of **parapsychology,** the organ of the Austrian organization Grenzgebiete der Wissenschaft und von Imago Mundi, edited by Professor Andreas Resch. Address: Resch Verlag, Maximilianstr. 8, Postfach 8, A-6010 Innsbruck, **Austria.**

Greville, T(homas) N(all) E(den) (1910– ?)

Mathematician who took part in statistical evaluation of experiments on **ESP.** He was born December 27, 1910, in New York City and studied at the University of the South in Sewanee, Tennessee (B.A., 1930), and the University of Michigan (M.A., 1932; Ph.D., 1933). After graduation Greville became an instructor in mathematics at the University of Michigan (1937–40) and then worked for the United States Bureau of the Census during World War II (1940–46). After the war he spent his career as a mathematician and statistician for various government agencies.

Greville compiled the United States Life Tables and Actuarial Tables 1939–41 (1946), one of several books on statistics. His parapsychological interest was largely in statistical evaluation of ESP experiments, on which he wrote a number of papers. He was a member of the **Parapsychological Association** and served as statistical editor of the *Journal of Parapsychology.*

Sources:

Berger, Arthur S., and Joyce Berger. *The Encyclopedia of Parapsychology and Psychical Research.* New York: Paragon House, 1991.

Greville, T. N. E. "Exact Probabilities for the Matching Hypothesis." *Journal of Parapsychology* 2 (1938).

———. "A Method of Evaluating the Reinforcement Effect." *Journal of Parapsychology* 15 (1951).

———. "On Multiple Matching with One Variable Deck." *Annals of Mathematical Statistics* 15 (1944): 432–34.

———. "A Reappraisal of the Mathematical Evaluation of the Reinforcement Effect." *Journal of Parapsychology* 18 (1954).

———. "A Summary of Mathematical Advances Bearing on ESP." *Journal of Parapsychology* 3 (1939).

———. "A Survey and Appraisal of the Statistical Methods Used in Parapsychological Research." *Journal of Parapsychology* 13 (1949).

Pleasants, Helene, ed. *Biographical Dictionary of Parapsychology.* New York: Helix Press, 1964.

Grimoire of Honorius, The

A **grimoire,** or text of magic instructions, published in Rome in 1629, and not, as is generally thought, connected in any way with kabbalistic magic. The work is actually permeated with Christian ideas. It is extremely unlikely that it is the work of the Roman bishop known as Honorius. The work has been called "a malicious and somewhat clever imposture," since it pretends to convey the sanction of the papal chair to the operators of **necromancy.** It deals with the evocation of the rebellious **angels.**

Sources:

Lévi, Éliphas. *The History of Magic.* New York: Samuel Weiser, 1971.

McIntosh, Christopher. *The Devil's Bookshelf.* Wellingborough, England: Aquarian Press, 1985.

Grimoires

Detailed books of magic rituals and spells, often invoking spirit entities. The term derives from *grammarye* or grammar, as magic was in times past intimately connected to the correct usage of language. Several of the more important grimoires were attributed the wise biblical king Solomon, while others were said to be the work of other ancient notables.

Grimoires began to appear during medieval times, when Western society was controlled by the Roman Catholic church, and the early grimoires reflect the conflict with Catholicism's supernaturalism. The grimoires called upon spirits generally thought to be evil by the church and were thus often branded as instruments of **black magic.** Some grimoires directly challenged church authority. One book of black magic was attributed to a pope. In the last century, a new form of **ceremonial magic** that operates outside the Christian sphere has arisen. Grimoires have thus taken on the trappings of an alternative religious worldview that assumes a neutral position with regard to Christianity.

Throughout the nineteenth and twentieth centuries, students of magic have tracked down many grimoires, some rare copies of which survived in the British Museum and the Bibliotheque de l'Arsenal in Paris, and made them available to the public. *The Magus,* published by **Francis Barrett** in London in 1801, stands as the fountainhead of these efforts. Barrett had access to a number of magic documents from which he took bits and pieces to construct a section of his book, which he titled *The Cabala* or *The Secret Mysteries of Ceremonial Magic Illustrated.* It includes not only instructions for working magic but also imaginative drawings of the various evil spirits he discusses. *The Magus* is important in being the first modern publication with sufficient instruction to actually attempt magic rituals.

The next major step in preserving grimoires came in the mid-nineteenth century with the writings of **Éliphas Lévi.** His 1856 book, *The Ritual of Transcendent Magic,* enlarges upon Barrett's presentation and discusses several grimoires. In *The History of Magic* (1971) he includes a lengthy discussion of **The Grimoire of Honorius** (1629). Lévi's books did much to create a revival of magic which then took embodiment in the Hermetic Order of the **Golden Dawn,** the first modern group to create a whole system of ritual magic. As a result of the order's activities, several of its members took important steps in publishing grimoires.

The Work of MacGregor Mathers

Among the most important works attributed to Solomon was **The Key of Solomon.** A manuscript of the work in Greek found in the British Museum may date from as early as the thirteen century, and other copies in various languages can be found around Europe. In 1559 the Inquisition pronounced the *Key* a dangerous book and prohibited its being published or read. Many of the later grimoires, however, show its influence. In 1889 Golden Dawn leader **S. L. MacGregor Mathers** published an abridged edition of the work collating some seven different versions of it from the British Museum collection. His translation then became a major source for Golden Dawn rituals. It was reprinted in 1909, and a slightly revised, pirated American edition was published by L. W. deLaurence. The book, even in its abridged version, offers detailed instructions for preparing and executing various magic rituals involving the summoning and control of spirit entities.

Mathers also began work on a new edition of the *Lemegeton,* or *Lesser Key of Solomon,* (1916) a shorter book that lists a large number of spirit entities and gives instructions for summoning them. It seems to date from the sixteenth century. For whatever reason, the *Lemegeton* was not published and existed only in a manuscript version, which Mathers lent to **Aleister Crowley.** In 1903 Crowley and Mathers had a falling out, and Crowley published Mathers's work in 1904. As with *The Key of Solomon,* deLaurence published a pirated American edition.

Mathers then turned to his most impressive translating work, *The Book of the Sacred Magic of Abra-Melin the Mage,* (1974) a grimoire attributed to **Abraham the Jew,** a fourteenth-century German magician. In the introduction, Abraham claims that he met Abra-Melin in Egypt, where the older sage entrusted him with the secrets embodied in the text of *The Book of Sacred Magic.* The volume lays out in some detail the prerequisites for doing magic and then offers instructions on the rather rigorous process by which it is accomplished. The chief operation it describes leads one toward knowledge and communication with one's guardian angel (what some would call the higher self), an essential occurrence in the development of any ritual magician. Mathers's translation appeared in 1898 and, as with his other works, was also reprinted in a pirated American edition.

Mathers's work inspired others to action, not the least being **Arthur E. Waite,** who in 1898 published *The Book of Black Magic and of Pacts Including the Mysteries of Goëtic Theurgy, Sorcery and Infernal Necromancy.* Waite included a lengthy survey of the history and origin, as far as it could be known, of the various grimoires and then provided a working summary, with copious quotes and illustrations, of some of the more important grimoires. In addition to *The Key of Solomon* and the *Lemegeton,* the following grimoires are discussed in the book:

Arbatel, a sixteenth-century work published in Basle in 1575. It was supposed to include nine sections, but only one was ever published. That initial section, the "Isagoge," deals with fundamental magic instructions. Basic instructions for summoning the seven Olympic spirits believed to rule the planets are given.

The Grand Grimoire, also known as the *Red Dragon.* This grimoire had also been discussed at length by Éliphas Lévi. It had been published in the seventeenth century in France and was notable as a true work of black magic, for it included instructions on how to make a pact with the devil.

The Grimorium Verum, an eighteenth-century work claiming sixteenth-century origins. It is based in part on *The Key of Solomon* and claims Solomon as its ultimate source. It describes the characters and seals of the demons, their powers, and the method of invoking them.

The *Grimoire of Honorius,* attributed to an eighth-century bishop of Rome. It seems, however, to be a seventeenth-century product first published in 1629. It purportedly gave the sanction of the papal office to the practice of ritual magic.

The Black Pullet (1972), a product of the late eighteenth century and a type of popular romantic piece of the period. It is allegedly the product of a French soldier in Egypt during the Napoleonic excursion. Left for dead near the pyramids, he was rescued by a man who came out of one of them. The soldier was allowed to go into the pyramid, where he discovered a vast magic center. He was given information on the use of 22 talismans and the secret of manufacturing the black pullet, or the hen with the golden eggs.

Waite's discussions were continued by Idries Shah in *The Secret Lore of Magic* (1957) and to a lesser extent by Migene González-Wippler in *The Complete Book of Spells, Ceremonies & Magic* (1978).

Since World War II there has been a large market in magical texts, including grimoires, which has led to a number of reprintings of older editions. There have also been effort to create new grimoires, such as *The Master Grimoire of Magickal Rites & Ceremonies* (1982), by Nathan Elkana, which integrates material from the older works into a modern perspective with little mention of spirits and demons. A few completely new grimoires have appeared, and there have been several attempts to create **The Necronomicon** (1977), the book first mentioned in the fictional works of horror writer **H. P. Lovecraft.**

Sources:

Barett, Francis. *The Magus.* London: Lackington, Allen, 1801. Reprint, New Hyde Park, N.Y.: University Books, 1967.

The Grimoire of Raphael. Edited by Fra. Zarathustra [Nelson White]. Pasadena, Calif.: The Technology Group, 1987.

Lemegeton; Clavicula Salomonis: or, The Complete Lesser Key of Solomon the King. Edited by Nelson White and Anne White. Pasadena, Calif.: The Technology Group, 1979.

Simon, ed. *The Necronomicon.* New York: Schlangekraft/Barnes Graphics, 1877. Reprint, New York: Avon Books, 1977.

The Sword Book of Honourius the Magician. Translated and edited by Daniel J. Driscoll. Gilette, N.J.: Heptangle Books, 1977.

Grimorium Verum, The

A **grimoire,** or textbook of magic instructions, first published in 1517 and purported to be translated from the Hebrew. It is based to some extent upon the **"Key of Solomon the King"** and is quite honest in its statement that it proposes to invoke devils. It refers to the four elements, so these would appear to be **elementary spirits.** A part of the account it gives regarding the hierarchy of spirits is taken from the *Lemegeton,* or Lesser Key of Solomon.

The work is divided into three portions. The first describes the characters and seals of the demons, with the forms of their evocation and dismissal; the second gives a description of the supernatural secrets that can be learned by the power of the demons; and the third is the key of the work and its proper application. But these divisions only outline what the *Grimorium Verum* purports to place before the reader, since the whole work is a mass of confusion. The plates that supply the characters do not apply to the text. The book really consists of two parts—the *Grimorium Verum* itself, and a second portion consisting of magic secrets. The first supplies directions for the preparation of the magician based on those of the Clavicle of Solomon. Instructions are given for the manufacture of magic instruments and for the composition of a parchment on which the characters and seals are to be inscribed, as well as the processes of evocation and dismissal.

The second part contains the "admirable secrets" of the pretended **Albertus Magnus,** the "Petit Albert," and so forth. The work is only partially diabolical in character, and some of its processes might be classified as white magic.

Gronkydoddles

A race of invisible pixies, first described by the **ESP Laboratory,** a group founded by Alcie Gwyn Manning of Los Angeles, California, and now known as ESP Laboratory of Texas. Address: 219 Southridge Dr., Edgewood, TX 75117.

Gross, Don Hargrave (1923–)

American clergyman with special interests in paranormal healing, on which he wrote extensively. Gross was born on February 16, 1923, at Pittsburgh, Pennsylvania, and studied at Carnegie Institute of Technology, Pittsburgh (B.S. in physics, 1944).

He finished college just as World War II began and he joined the United States Naval Reserve as a technical radar officer (1944–46). He completed his seminary training at the Episcopal Theological School, Cambridge, Massachusetts, in 1949. He served several parishes before returning to school to earn a master's degree in psychology from the University of Pittsburgh (1959). From 1959 to 1960 he was assistant rector at Emmanuel Church, Boston, Massachusetts, the famous church from which the healing movement in the Episcopal Church originated. In 1960 he became the associate rector at Christ Church, Hamilton, Massachusetts.

Through the 1950s Gross wrote one book, *The Case for Spiritual Healing* (1958), and a variety of articles on healing. He contributed to the symposium "Spiritual Healing" in the spring 1956 issue of *Religion in Life* and wrote the section "Questions and Answers on the Healing Ministry" for *The Churches' Handbook for Spiritual Healing* (1957). He had a special interest in Kathryn Kuhlman, a healer from his hometown. He was a member of the Society for the Scientific Study of Religion and a charter associate of the **Parapsychological Association.**

Sources:

Gross, Don H. *The Case for Spiritual Healing.* New York: T. Nelson, 1958.

———. "Kathryn Kuhlman: Another Point of View." *The Pittsburgher* (October–December 1954).

———. "Prayer That Heals." *Religion in Life* (Spring 1955).

———. "Spiritual Healing and the Archbishop's Commission." *International Journal of Parapsychology* (Autumn 1959).

Grosseteste, Robert (ca. 1175–1253)

Bishop of Lincoln, England, from 1235, generally known as Robert of Lincoln. A notable statesman and philosopher, he was also rumored to be proficient in the art of magic. Born of poor parents, he was compelled early to earn his own living and even at times to beg for bread. He was at length "discovered" by the mayor of Lincoln, who was attracted by his appearance and the shrewdness of his remarks and had him sent to school, where his capacity for study was so great that he was able to complete his education at Oxford, Cambridge, and Paris.

The illustrious **Roger Bacon** described Grosseteste and his friend Friar Adam de Marisco as the most learned men of their time. Grosseteste was well skilled in the sciences of mathematics and astronomy and was a master of Greek and Hebrew. As a member of the clergy he distinguished himself chiefly by his vigorous denunciation of the abuses in the court of Rome, particularly those of the pope, Innocent IV, whose rule added little to the Church. Grosseteste did not hesitate to point out the misdeeds of the ecclesiastical dignitaries, many of whom had never even visited their various sees. He openly declared Innocent to be the Antichrist.

In addition to reputedly publishing a treatise entitled *Magick* (probably a false ascription), legend also has it that he constructed a brazen head that would answer questions and foretell the future. (This story was also told of both Pope Silvester II and Roger Bacon.)

Ground Saucer Watch

Founded in 1957 with a membership of scientists, engineers, professionals, and educated laymen interested in taking scientific action to resolve the controversial elements in **UFO** reports. Its objectives are as follows: to provide an accessible outlet for all interested persons who wish to report any aerial phenomena experiences without fear of ridicule or undue publicity; to "edify a confused media" with factual press releases, lectures, conferences, and interviews; to research and evaluate all UFO cases to which scientific criteria can be applied and analyzed with the use of specialized talents and instrumentation; to continue to pursue legal action against the federal government with lawsuits and Freedom of Information Act requests for release of UFO materials; and to bring forth workable hypotheses and theories of UFO origin and reasons for their continuing surveillance.

In addition to technical papers, GSW publishes *News Bulletin* three times a year. Address: 13238 N. Seventh Dr., Phoenix, AZ 85029.

Group Soul

A philosophical concept expounded in *The Road to Immortality* (1932), a script purporting to be from the deceased and discarnate **F. W. H. Myers** as channeled through British medium **Geraldine Cummins.** The concept posits a number of souls bound together by one spirit, acting and reacting upon one another in the ascending scale of psychic evolution. There may be contained within that spirit any number of souls, according to Cummins:

"It is different for each man. But what the Buddhists would call the karma I had brought with me from a previous life is, very frequently, not that of my life, but of the life of a soul that preceded me by many years on earth and left for me the pattern which made my life. I, too, wove a pattern for another of my group during my earthly career. . . . I shall not live again on earth, but a new soul, one who will join our group, will shortly enter into the pattern or karma I have woven for him on earth. . . . Here, in the After-death, we become more and more aware of this group-soul as we make progress. Eventually brethren . . . its spirit feeds, with life and mental light, certain plants, trees, flowers, birds, insects, fish, beasts, men and women; representatives of living creatures in varying stages of evolution. It inspires souls who are on various planes, various levels of consciousness in the After-death. It feeds also creatures on other planets. For the spirit must gather a harvest of experience in every form."

Sources:

Cummins, Geraldine. *The Road to Immortality.* London: Ivor Nicholson & Watson, 1932.

Gruagach

"The long-haired one," from the Gaelic *gruag,* a wig. The *gruagach* was a fairy being with protective duties in Scottish legends, apparently of either sex, but generally female. The *gruagach* was particularly associated with cattle, and milk was laid aside for him or her every evening—otherwise no milk would be given at the next milking. Usually this being was of a beneficent nature, although it occasionally made mischief by loosing the cattle so that the herders had to get up, sometimes several times during a night, to tie them up. This apparently caused the *gruagach* much impish delight.

Among the many stories of **fairies,** there are tales in different parts of **Scotland** about the *gruagach.* It seems that this fairy commonly had long hair and was well dressed, whichever sex it happened to be.

Sources:

Thompson, Francis. *The Supernatural Highland.* London: Robert Hale, 1976.

Gruber, Karl (1881–1927)

Professor of biology and zoology at Munich Polytechnic, Germany, and a noted psychical researcher. Gruber was born in Freiburg on October 30, 1881. His background in biology led to an interest in the claims of paranormal abilities in **animals.** In 1923 he studied the **Elberfeld horses,** and later investigated Rolf, the "talking" dog of Mannheim. He also studied supernormal phenomena in conjunction with **Rudolf Tischner** and **Baron Schrenck-Notzing.** He did valuable work in the elucidation of the problem of clairvoyance and psychometry. His conclusions were detailed in his *Parapsychologische Erkenntnisse* (1925) and in a posthumously published volume, *Okkultismus und Biologie.*

Sources:

Gruber, Karl. *Okkultismus und Biologie.* Munich, 1930.

———. *Parapsychologische Erkenntnisse.* Munich, 1925.

Grünewald, Fritz (d. 1925)

German engineer who pioneered instrumental control for testing psychical phenomena. His ingenious laboratory instruments were exhibited at the 1921 International Congress for Psychical Research in Copenhagen, and they served as a model for research laboratories in Paris, London, Berlin, Munich, and Vienna. Grünewald mostly experimented with psychics Johannsen, **Einer Nielsen,** Jan Guzyk, and **Anna Rasmussen.** He also investigated the case of **Eleonore Zügun.**

Sources:

Grünewald, Fritz. *Physikalisch-Mediumis-tische Untersuchungen.* N.p., 1920.

Guadalupe Apparitions (of the Virgin Mary)

Guadalupe, Mexico, is the site of a claimed miraculous appearance of the Virgin Mary in 1531 that has become part of the folklore of Central and South America. According to the popular account of the **apparition,** a young Aztec Indian named Juan Diego was making his way to a Christian church at Tlateloco to study his catechism on December 9, 1531. He was a recent convert to Catholicism, and the church was a few miles from his uncle's home, where the boy lived following the death of his parents.

While taking a shortcut over the hill of Tepeyac, he heard his name called. He also heard music and the songs of birds. He followed the sounds and was confronted by a beautiful Indian girl about 19 years old, dressed in the robes the boy had seen adorning saints in the church. She declared herself to be "the eternal Virgin, holy Mother of the true God" and "merciful Mother" of men. She told the boy to go to the bishop of Mexico, the Spaniard Fray Juan de Zumarraga, and tell him that she wished to have a church built on the hill of Tepeyac.

The boy made his way to the bishop's palace about four miles away and, after some difficulty with the guards, was eventually admitted to the bishop's study and told his story. Zumarraga was sympathetic but not convinced. As the first Catholic bishop of Mexico, he had heard many wild stories from converted Indians. He said he would need time to think about it.

Juan returned to the hill somewhat crestfallen, where he saw the Virgin and suggested that it would be better for some more important person to convince the bishop. The Virgin told him that he was the chosen one and directed him to visit the bishop again the following day.

The next day the bishop listened carefully but said he would need some proof before building a church. He directed the boy to bring back an unmistakable sign of the genuineness of the apparition. After the boy had gone he instructed two of his staff to follow him and report back. After the boy had climbed the hill at Tepeyac the observers lost sight of him. Annoyed at being outwitted by a mere Indian boy, they returned to the bishop and said that the boy was unreliable and should not be believed. Meanwhile Juan had again seen the Virgin, who told him to come back the following day and she would give him a sign for the bishop.

When he returned home Juan found his uncle seriously ill and at the point of death. He nursed him through the night, and in the morning, finding no improvement, decided to fetch a priest from the church at Tlateloco to administer the last rites. Juan was worried that he had failed to keep the appointment with the Virgin and took the longer lower road to Tlateloco instead of the shortcut over the hill of Tepeyac. But the Virgin appeared on the lower path and told him that there was no need to worry about his uncle, who was now cured. Juan was to go back to the top of the hill, where he would find many flowers growing. He was to pick a bunch, wrap them in his cape, and take them to the bishop. The Virgin stressed that the flowers must be concealed and not shown to anyone else.

At the top of the hill the boy found some beautiful and fragrant roses growing, out of season in the frosty weather. He picked a bunch, wrapped them in his cloak, and made his way to the bishop's palace again, where the guards demanded to know what he was carrying in his cape. They could smell the flowers, but when they took hold of the cape and opened it, the roses had become painted flowers on the inside of the cape. They took the boy to the bishop and when Juan opened his cape the fresh roses spilled out onto the floor. The bishop saw that on the inside of the cape, where the painted flowers had been, was now a portrait of the Virgin.

The bishop took the cape to his chapel, where he prayed and thanked God and the Virgin for the miracle. The church was built on the hill at Tepeyac. The miraculous cape survived and more than four centuries later is still venerated in the cathedral at Guadalupe. The Virgin became the patron saint of Mexico.

The cape is made of woven grass, which normally has a lifespan of about 30 years. In November 1921 it survived a gelignite attack from a distance of eight feet. The nearby altar, large crucifix, and candlesticks were damaged and every window in the building blown out, but the image, behind a glass shield, was untouched.

Aside from this relic there is no factual evidence to support the legend. In 1532 Bishop de Zumarraga returned to Spain, where he gave a detailed account of his life in Mexico, but there is no record of any reference by him to Juan Diego and the miraculous cape. The celebrated historian Fray Bernardino de Sahagún was in Mexico at the time and described the Indians and their religious beliefs, but did not report the case of Juan Diego. The story first appeared in print in 1648—127 years after the claimed miracle—in a booklet titled *The Image of the Virgin Mary,* by Manuel Sánchez.

The Spanish soldier Bernal Diaz del Castillo, who traveled with Cortez, wrote a book, *Historia verdadera de la Conquista de la Nueva-España* (True History of the Conquest of New Spain, ca. 1632), in which he reports that Mexican Indian painters had been trained by a Franciscan father to copy sacred images and paintings, and that their work compared with the best in Italy and Spain. During the 1930s the Mexican artist Jorge González Camarena was engaged to restore murals at the Hujotingo Convent in Puebla. Hidden under layers of later paint he uncovered a picture of the Virgin Mary that appeared identical to that of the Virgin of Guadalupe.

Skeptics may claim that the story of Juan Diego is a pious legend and that the image on the cape is typical of others of the period by skilled Indian religious artists. However, the cloth has been examined by historians, art experts, and scientists from the Massachusetts Institute of Technology and has not been discredited. It is also of great interest that this early account of apparitions of the Virgin Mary has features common to other claimed apparitions even in modern times, such as those at **Fatima** and **Medjugorje:** a simple child is chosen to receive the apparitions and messages rather than a sophisticated adult; the messages are often at variance with the opinions of the established ecclesiastical authorities; and a miraculous sign is given to authenticate the visitation.

Although such apparitions are normally within the conventions of the Catholic religion, it is interesting to note that when the Spaniards first arrived at Tepeyac, there was an Aztec temple on the hill honoring Tenotzin, virgin mother of the gods. Each year, on a date equivalent to December 22, Indians came from far and wide to honor this Aztec goddess just as modern Mexicans assemble on December 12 to honor the Virgin of Guadalupe. Every year, some ten million visitors go to see the cape with the portrait of the Virgin of Guadalupe. Among famous visitors were United States President John F. Kennedy and President Charles de Gaulle of France.

Sources:

Demarest, Donald, and Coley Taylor. *The Dark Virgin: The Book of Our Lady of Guadalupe.* Freeport, Maine: Coley Taylor, 1956.

Johnston, Francis M. *The Wonder of Guadalupe.* Rockford, Ill.: TAN, 1981.

Smith, Jody Brant. *The Image of Guadalupe: Myth or Miracle?* Garden City, N.Y.: Doubleday, 1983. Reprinted as *The Guadalupe Enigma: Myth or Miracle?* London: Souvenir Press, 1983.

Watson, Simone. *The Cult of Our Lady of Guadalupe: A Historical Study.* Collegeville, Minn.: Liturgical Press, 1964.

Gualdi, Signor

A Rosicrucian who, according to the book *Hermippus Redivivus; or The Sage's Triumph over Old Age and the Grave* (1744), by J. H. Cohausen, lived for several hundred years.

Gualdi lived in Venice for several months and was called "the Sober Signor" among the common people because of the regularity of his life, the composed simplicity of his manners, and his simple dress. He always wore dark clothes of a plain, unpretentious style.

Gualdi had a small collection of fine pictures, which he readily showed to anyone who was interested. He was versed in all arts and sciences and spoke with astonishing detail. It was observed that he never sent or received mail. He never desired any credit, paid for everything in ready money, and made no use of bankers, currency, or letters of credit. He always seemed to have enough, and he lived respectably, although with no attempt at splendor or show.

Shortly after his arrival in Venice, Gualdi met—at a coffeehouse he frequented—a Venetian nobleman who was fond of art. This pair had many conversations concerning various objects and pursuits of mutual interest. They became friends and the nobleman, who was a widower, invited Gualdi to his home, where he first met the nobleman's daughter, a beautiful maiden of 18, intelligent and accomplished. Constantly in his company and fascinated by his narratives, the young lady gradually fell in love with the mysterious stranger.

Gualdi was a well-educated gentleman, a thinker rather than a man of action. At times his countenance seemed to glow during conversation, and a strange aura surrounded him when he became more than usually pleased and animated. Altogether he seemed a puzzling person of rare gifts.

The Venetian nobleman was now sufficiently intimate with Gualdi to say to him one evening that he understood that he had a fine collection of pictures, and that if agreeable, he would pay him a visit one day to see them. The nobleman's daughter, looking down at the table and thinking deeply of something Gualdi had just said, raised her eyes eagerly at her father's proposal and showed her desire to go with him to see the pictures.

Gualdi was very polite and readily invited the nobleman to his house. He also extended the invitation to his daughter.

On the day agreed upon, the father and daughter went to Gualdi's home. They were received warmly and Gualdi showed them his rooms graciously. The nobleman viewed Gualdi's pictures with great attention and remarked that he had never seen a finer collection, considering the number of pictures.

They were about to leave Gualdi's own chamber, the last of his set of rooms, when the nobleman by chance noticed over the door a picture evidently of Gualdi himself. The Venetian looked at it suspiciously, but after a while his face cleared, as if with relief. The daughter's gaze was also riveted upon the picture, which was very like Gualdi, but she regarded it with a blush. The Venetian looked from the picture to Gualdi, and back again from Gualdi to the picture. It was some time before he spoke.

"That picture was intended for you, sir," he said at last, hesitatingly, to Gualdi. A slight cold change passed over the latter's eyes, but he only replied by a low bow. "You look a moderately young man—to be candid with you, sir, I should say about forty-five, or thereabouts—and yet I know, by certain means of which I will not now further speak, that this picture is by the hand of Titian who has been dead nearly a couple of hundred years. How is this possible?" he added, with a polite, grave smile.

"It is not easy," replied Gualdi quietly, "to know all things that are possible, for very frequent mistakes are made concerning such, but there is certainly nothing strange in my being like a picture painted by Titian."

The nobleman easily perceived by his manner and his countenance that Gualdi felt offense. The temporary misunderstanding was soon put to an end by Gualdi himself, however, who in a moment or two resumed his ordinary manner and saw the father and daughter downstairs to the entrance of his house with his usual composed politeness. The nobleman, however, could not help feeling uneasy; his daughter experienced a considerable amount of discomfort and could not look at Gualdi for a while. When she did look, she looked too much.

This little occurrence remained in the mind of the nobleman. His daughter felt lonely and dissatisfied afterward, eager for the restoration of friendly feelings with Gualdi. The Venetian went in the evening to the usual coffeehouse and spoke of the incident among the group of people collected there. Their curiosity was roused, and one or two resolved to satisfy themselves by looking at the picture attentively. In order to do so it was necessary to see Gualdi somewhere and be invited to his home. The only likely place to meet him was at the coffeehouse, and the gentlemen went there the next day at the usual time, hoping that Gauldi would stop in as was his habit.

But he did not come—nor had he been heard from since the nobleman's visit to his house the day before. Since they did not meet with him at the coffeehouse, one of their number went to his lodgings to inquire after him. The owner of the house came to the street door and stated that Gauldi had gone, having left Venice early that morning, and that he had locked up his pictures with certain orders and taken the key to his rooms with him.

This affair caused much gossip at the time in Venice, and an account of it found its way into most of the newspapers of the year in which it occurred. Gualdi's story is also found in *Les Mémoires historiques* for the year 1687.

Hermippus Redivivus, which includes other strange anecdotes of triumph over old age, is not a reliable source and may in fact be a satirical work.

Guardian Angels

More common term for what Spiritualists call **guiding spirits,** claimed to watch over or inspire individuals and intervene in moments of crisis or danger. (See also **Angels**)

Guecubu

Among the Araucanians, an Indian tribe of Chile, the *guecubu* were evil spirits who did all in their power to thwart and annoy the Great Spirit Togin and his ministers.

Guide

A continually benevolent, protective, ethereal influence acting through mediums in Spiritualist séances. The term is more comprehensive than *control,* as the latter may apply to any chance communicator who gets through. The guide usually delivers lofty philosophical or religious instruction beyond the normal intellectual capacity of the medium. It may operate while the medium is either awake or in **trance.**

A number of claimed guides have been Native Americans; others have Greek or similarly impressive names, often untraceable. Since the 1950s, some guides have claimed to be from outer space or from planets known to be uninhabited. Some are clearly fictional entities, but acceptance of their claims may result in remarkable and sometimes verifiable communications.

Since the **New Age** occult revival of the 1980s, there has been a widespread renewal of interest in the teachings of **trance personalities** under the general term **channeling.**

Guide to Psi Periodicals

A directory of magazines, newsletters, and journals concerned with **parapsychology, occultism, astrology, witchcraft, UFOs**, and **New Age** spiritual studies, edited by Elizabeth M. Werner during the 1970s. Listings included a brief description of each source, U.S. and overseas subscription rates, and addresses. The guide was eventually incorporated into the *Whole Again Research Guide,* a comprehensive annual resource guide concerned with various New Age topics and issued by Sourcenet in Santa Barbara, California. Only a few issues were published.

Sources:

Werner, Elizabeth, ed. *Directory of Psychic Sciences Periodicals.* Burbank, Calif.: Inner-Space Interpreters Services, 1973.

Guide to Psi Tape Recordings

A directory of tape recordings dealing with **psychic science, meditation,** spiritual development, **healing, UFOs**, **yoga,** esoteric studies, and related topics edited by Elizabeth M. Werner of Burbank, California.

Guiding Spirits

The claimed existence of guiding spirits or guardian angels escapes experimental verification. According to séance-room communications, everyone has guiding spirits and they are often relatives who have risen to a high spiritual level in the beyond. The *daimon* of Socrates who forewarned him of dangers is the best historical example of the claimed existence of guiding spirits. In *Theages* Plato has Socrates say, "By the favor of the Gods I have, since my childhood, been attended by a semi-divine being whose voice, from time to time, dissuades me from some undertaking, but never directs me what I am to do."

In the *Apology* Socrates further notes, "This prophetic voice has been heard by me throughout my life; it is certainly more trustworthy than omens from the flight or the entrails of birds; I call it a God or a daimon. I have told my friends the warnings I have received, and up to now the voice has never been wrong."

As an instance of the daimon's clairvoyance, **F. W. H. Myers** declares as follows in *Human Personality and its Survival of Bodily Death* (1903): "As the philosopher was in conversation with Eutyphron, he suddenly stopped and warned his friends to turn into another street. They would not listen; but misfortune overtook them—they met a drove of swine that jostled them and threw them down."

"Few facts in history possess such documentary evidence as the Daimon," concludes Dr. Lelut of the Institut de France in *Du Démon de Socrate* (1836).

Edward Everett Hale, in his book *James Russell Lowell and His Friends* (1899), writes of Josiah Quincy II (1772–1884), an American statesman:

"It is interesting to know, what I did not know till after his death, that this gallant leader of men believed that he was directed in important crises, by his own 'Daimon,' quite as Socrates believed. In the choice of his wife, which proved indeed to have been made in heaven, he knew he was so led. And in after life, he ascribed some measures of importance and success to his prompt obedience to the wise Daimon's directions."

The novelist Julian Hawthorne writes of his mother, the wife of Nathaniel Hawthorne, in *Nathaniel Hawthorne and His Wife* (1884): "My mother always affirmed that she was conscious of her mother's presence with her on momentous occasions during the remainder of her life, that is, following her mother's death."

According to Hoole's *Life of Tasso,* Torquato Tasso ended his career believing that he had a familiar spirit with whom he conversed and from whom he learned things that he had never read or heard of, and that were unknown to other persons. (See also: **angels; control; genius; guide**)

Guillaume de Carpentras (ca. 15th century)

An astrologer who made for King René of Sicily and for the duke of Milan astrological spheres from which horoscopes were drawn. He made one for Charles VIII of France at a price of twelve hundred crowns. The sphere contained many parts and was designed so that all the movements of the planets, at any hour of the day or night, could be observed within it.

Guillaume de Paris (ca. 1180–1249)

French prelate and philosopher who was rumored by some demonologists to have made talking statues, like those made by **Roger Bacon,** a thing which, it was believed, could only be done by diabolical agency. Similar legends have been told of other individuals, often as a kind of tribute to their reputation as wise men.

Guinefort, St.

A strange story was recorded by Father Etienne Bourbon, a Dominican who died in 1262. He related that while he was preaching in the diocese of Lyons, many women came to him confessing that they had taken their children to a St. Guinefort. Curious to know what sort of saint it might be whose cult called for confession, Bourbon inquired into the matter and found that Guinefort was a dog!

It was the dog in the well-known fable of the dog and the serpent, wherein a dog is killed under the suspicion that it has slain a child, when in reality it has saved the child from the attack of a serpent. It was this dog-martyr to whose "shrine" the women brought their children.

A similar story was told of a dog named Ganelon whose tomb was in Auvergne, near a fountain. The dog was buried during the reign of Louis le Debonnaire. Two or three centuries later it was found that the waters of the fountain possessed medicinal virtues. Cures were attributed to the unknown occupant of the tomb—until a certain bishop found among the archives of the château the anecdote of the dog Ganelon.

Guirdham, Arthur (1905– ?)

British physician, psychiatrist, novelist, and writer on **ESP** and **reincarnation.** He also wrote under the pseudonym "Francis Eaglesfield." Born March 9, 1905, in Workington, Cumberland, England, he was educated at Keble College, Oxford University, and at Charing Cross Hospital, London (B.S., M.A., M.D.). He was senior consulting psychiatrist in the Bath Child Guidance Clinic, retiring from the National Health Service in 1968.

During his adult life Guirdham became increasingly interested in the history and teachings of the Cathar sect of thirteenth-century France. Cathar doctrine regarded the world as a kind of hell for rebellious angels, condemned to human existence until redeemed by unification with Christ. This doctrine was related to **Gnosticism** and Manichean teachings. The Cathars were persecuted and murdered by the established Church, culminating in their final destruction in 1243 at Montségur, France, when 200 Cathars were burned alive on one day.

Guirdham became convinced that he had been a Cathar priest named Roger de Grisolles in a former incarnation. In his book *The Cathars and Reincarnation* (1970) he describes the strange circumstances leading to this belief. He had a woman patient who was referred to him for treatment as a possible epileptic. She had vivid nightmares of life in the thirteenth century as a peasant girl in Toulouse, France, in a family that befriended a priest named Roger de Grisolles. Grisolles was arrested and died in prison; the girl was burned at the stake.

Extraordinarily enough Guirdham had also had similar nightmares since childhood, and when he met the patient, a Mrs. Smith, she revealed that he was the priest de Grisolles she had seen in her own dreams. Guirdham was sufficiently impressed with the factual aspects of her narrative to undertake research, in which he was able to confirm events and names in Smith's nightmares. There *was* a Roger de Grisolles who was murdered in 1242, and the details of the family who befriended him before betrayal were correct. In addition, Smith's own notes, written earlier, contained much background material on the Cathars not then known to scholars and only subsequently verified.

Guirdham also published *The Lake and the Castle* (1976), which surveys evidence of "far memory" from himself and a group of friends, suggesting various incarnations at different periods of history. His book *The Great Heresy: The History and Beliefs of the Cathars* (1977) compares his own scholarship on Cathar history with claimed evidence from discarnate entities. In addition to his fascinating works on Cathar reincarnation, Guirdham also published *A Theory of Disease* (1957), in which diseases are related to a realistic assessment of personality.

Sources:

Guirdham, Arthur. *The Cathars and Reincarnation.* Wellingborough, England: Turnstone Press, 1982.

———. *Christ and Freud.* London: Allen & Unwin, 1959.

———. *Cosmic Factors in Disease.* London: Duckworth, 1963.

———. *A Foot in Both Worlds: A Doctor's Autobiography of Psychic Experience.* [St. Helier] Jersey, Spearman, 1973.

———. *The Great Heresy.* St. Helier: Neville Spearman, 1977.

Wilson, Colin. *Strange Powers.* New York: Random House, 1973.

Guldenstubbe, Baron L(udwig) von (1820–1873)

Prominent nineteenth-century Spiritualist who wrote several influential books on Spiritualistic phenomena. He was a Scandinavian nobleman who appears to have had mediumistic talents himself. Because he spent time in Paris, he is often mentioned as "de Guldenstubbe." He was interested in **animal magnetism** for many years and was anxious to find evidence of the immortality of the soul. When he heard of the American Spiritualist movement in 1850 he promptly formed a circle at his own house in Paris, and soon obtained phenomena of **raps,** mysterious noises, and movements of furniture.

In August 1856 he began to experiment in the phenomenon of **direct writing** without the intervention of a medium. He placed paper and pencil in a small locked box, carrying the key with him. After 13 days he opened the box and found some written characters on the paper; the experiment was repeated successfully ten times on the same day.

Later, with his friend the comte d'Ourches and other acquaintances, Guldenstubbe visited churches, cemeteries, and public galleries and obtained writing on pieces of paper left on tombs or on the pedestals of statues. These writings were in various languages including Latin, Greek, Russian, French, German, and English and claimed to be from illustrious figures such as Mary Stuart, St. Paul, Cicero, Melchisedec, Plato, and Juvenal. Some of these communications were reproduced in the baron's book *La Réalité des Esprits* (1857). The French and German letters were small, regular, and perfectly legible, but the Latin and Greek characters were large, irregular, and badly formed. Such spirit messages foreshadowed the famous **mahatma letters** of **Helena Petrovna Blavatsky.**

Among the distinguished witnesses who repeatedly assisted Guldenstubbe in his experiments were Delamarre, editor of the *Patrie;* Choisselat, editor of the *Univers;* **Robert Dale Owen;** Lacordaire, brother of the great orator; the historian Bonnechose; the Swedish painter Kiorboe; Baron von Rosenberg, German ambassador at the court of Wurttemberg; and Prince Leonide Galitzin.

During 1867 Guldenstubbe had a house in London at which Spiritualist séances were held. The medium was Agnes Nichol (later **Agnes Guppy-Volckman**). At one of these séances, a sister of the Baron was discovered to have a wreath of flowers and ferns on her head, presumably placed there by spirit hands.

Sources:

Guldenstubbe, Baron Ludwig von. *Pensées d'Outre-Tombe.* 1858.

Goldenstubbe, Baron Ludwig von, and J. von Guldenstubbe. *La Morale Universelle.* 1863.

Guppy, Mary Jane (ca. 1860)

The first wife of Spiritualist Samuel Guppy and a medium for physical phenomena, **apports, automatic drawings,** and psychic lights. Accounts of her phenomena are given in *Mary Jane; or Spiritualism chemically explained, with Spirit Drawings,* a book published anonymously in 1863. Samuel Guppy was known to be its author.

Sources:

Guppy, Samuel. *Mary Jane; or Spiritualism chemically explained, with Spirit Drawings.* London, 1863.

Guppy-Volckman, Agnes (1838–1917)

Formerly Miss Agnes Nichol and the second wife of Spiritualist Samuel Guppy. She was originally discovered to be a powerful medium by naturalist **Alfred Russel Wallace** in the house of his sister, a Mrs. Sim, about a year after he started his investigation into Spiritualism in 1865. The young girl, a professional mesmerist, produced movements without contact. The power was strongest if she and Sim were alone. Remarkable phenomena were observed after a séance in an empty room. The famous naturalist learned that Nichol saw phantoms as a child and, in carefully watching her mediumistic development, had strange experiences. **Raps** and table movement were followed by **levitations.**

Nichol was a heavily built woman. In the darkness, while holding the sitters' hands, she was several times lifted on top of the table in her chair. Independent music and **apport** phenomena came next. On many occasions flowers and fruits, sometimes in large quantities, fell onto the séance table from an unknown source.

The requests of the sitters were often honored. When a friend of Wallace asked for a sunflower, one six feet high with a mass of earth around the roots fell upon the table. In the house of **E. W. Cox** a mass of snow and hothouse flowers was precipitated. It was sufficient to make a mental request. Princess Marguerite of Naples desired specimens of a prickly cactus. More than 20 dropped on the table and had to be removed with tongs. Stinging nettles and ill-smelling white flowers that had to be burned arrived on other occasions. The duchess d'Arpino wished for sea sand. It soon splashed down with seawater and live starfishes. The sea was about a hundred yards from the house. Not infrequently live eels and lobsters appeared.

Nichol married Samuel Guppy in 1867. For some time afterward they resided on the Continent. More marvels were witnessed on their return. The first spirit photograph of **Frederick A. Hudson** was obtained in March 1872, through Agnes's mediumship (see also **spirit photography**). In the same year she produced **materializations.**

Catherine Berry, in *Experiences in Spiritualism* (1876), writes of many strange happenings. A white cat and a Maltese dog belonging to Guppy appeared in a séance in Berry's house where Guppy sat. Three ducks prepared for cooking were brought into the circle in Guppy's home. Showers of butterflies descended from the ceiling. On another occasion a shower of feathers fell to the depth of several inches. In a mischievous spirit Guppy asked for tar, whereupon Berry, looking like a magpie in her black dress, rushed out. She became estranged for years from Guppy.

The most incredible incident in Guppy-Volckman's career was her claimed **transportation** from her house at Highbury, London, to 61 Lamb's Conduit Street, a distance of three miles. The most humorous occurred when **Frank Herne** and **Charles Williams,** with eight sitters, were holding a séance. On the half-humorous request of a Mr. Harrison to transport Guppy to the room, she was precipitated to the room. Unfortunately, she was half dressed, with her shoes off, and in a state of deep trance.

Samuel Guppy was a very rich man. The complete absence of financial motives in Agnes Guppy's case greatly puzzled **Frank Podmore,** the skeptical author of *Modern Spiritualism* (2 vols., 1902), who considered most mediums frauds out for financial gain. Not understanding the equal appeal of power and fame, he ponders, "But Mrs. Guppy, even during the few months in which, as Miss Nichol, she practised as a professional Mesmerist, can scarcely have found her main incentive in the hope of gain. On the assumption of fraud, the mere cost of the flowers lavished on her sitters must have swallowed up any probable profit from her increased mesmeric clientele. And even such a motive would have ceased with her marriage."

After Samuel Guppy's death, his widow married again and was afterward known as Mrs. Guppy-Volckman. She died in December 1917.

Gurdjieff, Georgei Ivanovitch (1872–1949)

Mystic and spiritual teacher of Greek ancestry, born at Alexandropol, near the borders of Russia and Persia. When still a young man, Gurdjieff left home to spend 20 years searching for the esoteric truths of life in Tibet, India, and the Arabian countries. His quest is described obliquely in his own book *Meetings with Remarkable Men* (1963), but much of this book must be regarded as parable rather than strict fact or autobiography.

In 1912 Gurdjieff launched his own system of psychophysical culture in Russia. Early disciples included Dr. de Stjoernval, a Finnish physician, composer Thomas de Hartmann and his wife, sculptor Vladimir Pohl, and journalist **Peter Demianovitch Ouspensky.** It was Ouspensky who later developed his own interpretation of the work of Gurdjieff and became the leading publicist for his system.

In spite of the Russian Revolution, the Gurdjieff group continued to grow, and Gurdjieff established his Institute for the Harmonious Development of Man in Tiflis, later moving to Constantinople, then to France, where the group became firmly established at a chateau in Fontainebleau. Many well-known intellectuals spent time with the group, including Katherine Mansfield, Clifford Sharp (editor of the *New Statesman*), and A. R. Orage (editor of the *New Age*).

Gurdjieff's system was a flexible one, employing both systematic and variable techniques to break habits of thought and emotion and awaken a higher consciousness. He would often shock his pupils out of routine reactions by a kind of westernized Zen technique. Fastidious intellectuals might be obliged to clean out stables, teetotalers to drink alcohol. In addition Gurdjieff devised psychophysical group exercises, involving breathing techniques, music, and dance. He called his system the **Fourth Way,** as distinct from that of the fakir, monk, and yogi, and was especially concerned with involvement in everyday life.

In 1924 he visited the United States with his disciples, who gave astonishing demonstrations of physical and mental control. Various writers and editors of the day supported his work, including Hart Crane, Jane Heap, and Margaret Anderson.

His influence has been widespread and survives in modern times through such individuals as **Maurice Nicoll** and **J. G. Bennett** and a continuing tradition of Gurdjieff groups that carry on unobtrusively. The books of P. D. Ouspensky have attracted many seekers to the work of Gurdjieff, although Ouspensky himself tended to intellectualize a system that depended upon firsthand experience.

Gurdjieff himself was an enigmatic figure, whose lifestyle often appeared at variance with that of a mystic master. He enjoyed good food and wine and was capable of apparently inconsistent behavior, usually explained away by his disciples as being designed deliberately to shock individuals out of habitual reactions.

His book *All and Everything: Beelzebub's Tales to His Grandson* (1950) can be variously interpreted as turgid writing or a tongue-in-cheek attack on the reader's level of consciousness. *Time* magazine once aptly described Gurdjieff as a "remarkable blend of P. T. Barnum, Rasputin, Freud, Groucho Marx, and everybody's grandfather."

Sources:

Bennett, John Godolphin. *Gurdjieff: Making a New World.* New York: Harper & Row, 1974.

———. *Is There Life on Earth?—An Introduction to Gurdjieff.* New York: Stonehill, 1973. 1st Bennett Books ed., Santa Fe, N. Mex.: Bennett Books, 1989.

De Hartmann, Thomas. *Our Life with Gurdjieff.* New York: Penguin, 1972.

Driscoll, J. Walter. *Gurdjieff: An Annotated Bibliography.* New York: Garland Publishing, 1985.

Lefort, Rafael. *The Teachers of Gurdjieff.* New York: Samuel Weiser, 1973.
Ouspensky, P. D. *Tertium Organum (the third organ of thought): A key to the enigmas of the world.* Rochester, N.Y.: Manas Press, 1920.
Pauwels, Louis. *Gurdjieff.* New York: Samuel Weiser, 1972.
Speeth, Katherine Riodan. *The Gurdjieff Work.* Berkeley, Calif: And/Or Press, 1976. Rev. ed., Los Angeles: Jeremy P. Tarcher, 1989.
Webb, James. *The Harmonious Circle: The Lives and Work of G. I. Gurdjieff, P. D. Ouspensky, and Their Followers.* New York: G. P. Putnam's Sons, 1980.

Gurdjieff Foundation of California

Organization devoted to study and practice of the teachings of mystic **G. I. Gurdjieff** (1877?–1949) in transforming inner and outer life. Address: P.O. Box 549, San Francisco, CA 94101.

Gurney, Edmund (1847–1888)

Distinguished English psychical researcher whose work was one of the mainstays of the early period of the **Society for Psychical Research.** Gurney was born March 23, 1847, at Hersham, Surrey. He was a classical scholar, a musician, and a student of medicine, but he did not definitely adopt any profession. Between 1874 and 1878 he attended a great number of Spiritualist séances. He never discussed what he had seen and learned, but when the Society for Psychical Research (SPR) was founded in 1882 he readily assumed the post of honorary secretary.

It was the discovery of **thought-transference** that aroused his enduring interest in psychical research, and hypnotism the primary tool. According to **F. W. H. Myers,** "he was the first Englishman who studied with any kind of adequate skill the psychological side of hypnotism in England."

Between 1885 and 1888 Gurney devised a large number of experiments by which he sought to prove that there is sometimes, in the induction of hypnotic phenomena, an agency at work that is neither ordinary nervous stimulation nor suggestion conveyed by any ordinary channel to the subject's mind.

He next attacked the problem of the relation of the memory in one hypnotic state to the memory in another hypnotic state and of both to the normal or waking memory. His research along this line preceded Pierre Janet's similar explorations in France.

Gurney then proceeded to consider **hallucinations.** His treatise on the telepathic induction of hallucination in *Phantasms of the Living* (1886) was the first serious discussion of the problem. His investigations were done in consultation with Myers and **Frank Podmore.** The actual writing of *Phantasms of the Living* was done by Gurney, and during the three years of sifting evidence and hearing witnesses he performed an immense amount of work. He was also editor of the SPR's *Proceedings,* to which he contributed many important papers. He died June 23, 1888.

His work did not, it seems, end with his death. Shortly afterward, communications were received by a lady through **automatic writing** that purported to come from him. The following year **William James** obtained similar messages in a sitting with **Lenora Piper.**

Other messages again pointed to the trance intelligence of the medium. **Margaret Verrall** also received occasional messages from Gurney, while "Mrs. Forbes" was entirely under a Gurney influence. The Gurney **control** of "Mrs. Holland" (pseudonym of **Alice Kipling Fleming**) appeared to be a different type. Edmund Gurney, while alive, knew both Verrall and Forbes, but not Fleming.

Sources:

Gurney, Edmund. "Account of Some Experiments in Mesmerism." *Proceedings* of the Society for Psychical Research 2, no. 6 (1884).
———. "Hallucinations." *Proceedings* of the Society for Psychical Research 3, no. 8 (1885).
———. "Hypnotism and Telepathy." *Proceedings* of the Society for Psychical Research 5, no. 12 (1888–89).
———. "Peculiarities of Certain Post-Hypnotic States." *Proceedings* of the Society for Psychical Research 4, no. 11 (1886–87).
———. *The Power of Sound.* 1880. Reprint, New York: Basic Books, 1966.
———. "The Problems of Hypnotism." *Proceedings* of the Society for Psychical Research 2, no. 7 (1884).
———. "Recent Experiments in Hypnotism." *Proceedings* of the Society for Psychical Research 5, no. 12 (1888–89).
———. "Some Higher Aspects of Mesmerism." *Proceedings* of the Society for Psychical Research 3, no. 10 (1885).
———. "Stages of Hypnotic Memory." *Proceedings* of the Society for Psychical Research 4, no. 11 (1886–87).
———. "The Stages of Hypnotism." *Proceedings* of the Society for Psychical Research 2 (1884).
———. *Tertium Quid: Chapters on Various Disputed Questions.* London, K. Paul, Trench & Co., 1887.
Gurney, Edmund, F. W. H. Myers, and Frank Podmore. *Phantasms of the Living.* London: Trubner, 1886.
Hall, Trevor H. *The Strange Case of Edmund Gurney.* London: Duckworth, 1964.

Guru

Though many spiritual teachers from India settled in the West through the twentieth century, during the 1970s, the term "guru" (or "teacher," the Indian equivalent of "rabbi") first became well known in America and Europe through the rapid growth of Indian movements built around such figures as **Maharishi Mahesh Yogi,** and **Guru Mahara Ji** who attracted many thousands of young adult followers. In the process of moving to America and Europe, the guru concept underwent a change.

In traditional Indian religious life, the guru-chela (teacher-pupil) relationship is a very personal one, restricted to a few followers and usually involving strict austerities, religious observances, study of scriptures, and/or **yoga** exercises. And although many gurus (for example, Satya Sai Baba) have been reputed miracle workers and the subject of numerous anecdotal accounts of supernormal feats, the goal of mysticism, union with the divine, was generally regarded as paramount and miracles merely incidental. That relationship remained the case with most Indian teachers in the West. However, many in the West were unfamiliar with the nature of spiritual guidance offered by gurus and were put off by the absolutist language of obedience used in traditional literature to describe that relationship.

In the wake of the unexpected favorable reception of **Swami Vivekananda** at the World's Parliament of Religions in Chicago in 1893, many eastern spiritual teachers settled in America and developed relatively small followings. Gurus were often associated in the public mind with miracles, even though their teachings emphasized spiritual development. Following World War II and the declaration of Indian independence from England in 1948, and especially the opening of the United States to Asian immigration in 1965, a number of gurus developed missions in the West. The pop cultures and mass advertising techniques of postwar America and Europe facilitated the spread of large international movements. Some of the more popular leaders presented a Westernized Hinduism with roots in the nineteenth-century Hindu Renaissance developed in reaction to the critique of colonial powers to abhorrent (to westerners) practices in popular Hinduism. Some of these teachers promised world peace, success in life, achievement, personal relaxation and/or spiritual advancement through simple meditation techniques or prayers, while other Hindu gurus like **Swami Muktananda** and **Satya Sai Baba** attracted thousands of followers through "demonstrating" paranormal phenomena.

The transition from the Hindu concept of the family type guru, rather like a local priest and psychoanalyst, teaching a few followers, to the charismatic leader of millions adopting Western movements, represented a significant transition of the guru-chela relationship. In such a setting traditional admonitions to sacrifice everything to the guru in return for spiritual instruction took on a different meaning.

Sources:

Greenfield, Robert. *The Spiritual Supermarket.* New York: Saturday Review Press/E. P. Dutton, 1975.

Murray, Muz. *Seeking the Master; A Guide to the Ashrams of India.* Jersey, U.K.: Neville Spearman, 1980.

Uban, Sujan Singh. *The Gurus of India.* London: Fine Books (Oriental)/New Delhi, India: Sterling Publishers, 1977.

Guru Bawa Muhaiyaddeen Fellowship

Founded by Guru Bawa, a Sufi teacher from Sri Lanka (Ceylon), said to be over a hundred years old. Around 1940 he established an ashram on a farm in Sri Lanka, teaching a traditional Sufi doctrine. He traveled to the United States about 1971 to help found a Serendib Sufi study circle in Philadelphia. Other small fellowship groups sprang up around his teachings. He spoke Tamil and seems to have spent some time in South India. A Singalese doctor translated his Tamil discourses into English. His followers established the Guru Bawa Muhaiyaddeen Fellowship, now headquartered at 5820 Overbrook Ave., Philadelphia, PA.

Sources:

Muhaiyadden, Guru Bawa, Shaikh. *God, His Prophets, and His Children.* Philadelphia: Fellowship Press, 1978.

———. *Guidebook.* 2 vols. Philadelphia: Fellowship Press, 1976.

———. *Mata Veeram, or the Forces of Illusion.* York Beach, Maine: Samuel Weiser, 1982.

———. *Truth and Light.* Philadelphia: Guru Bawa Fellowship of Philadelphia, 1974.

Gustenhover (17th century)

A goldsmith who resided at Strasbourg, Germany, in 1603. In a period of much danger he gave shelter to one M. Hirschborgen, who was described as "good and religious." In return for the hospitality of his host, Hirschborgen gave Gustenhover some **powder of projection** and departed on his journey. Gustenhover indiscreetly used the powder to perform alchemical transmutation before many people, and news of this reached Rudolph II, himself an amateur alchemist. He ordered the Strasbourg magistrates to send the goldsmith to him. Gustenhover was accordingly arrested.

On learning that he was to be sent to the emperor at Prague, Gustenhover requested that the magistrates meet after procuring a crucible and charcoal. Without coming near them, he had them melt some lead. When the lead was molten, he then gave them a small quantity of a reddish powder that, when thrown into the crucible, produced a considerable amount of pure gold from the lead. On being brought into the presence of the emperor, Gustenhover confessed that he had not himself prepared the magic powder and that, being but a beginning student of **alchemy,** was wholly ignorant of the nature of its composition. This the emperor refused to believe in spite of the repeated protests of the goldsmith.

After the powder was exhausted, Gustenhover was set to the now impossible task of making more gold. Still convinced that the alchemist was concealing his secret, the emperor had him imprisoned for the rest of his life.

It is believed that Hirschborgen, who presented Gustenhover with the powder, was none other than the alchemist **Alexander Seton,** who at that period was traveling through Germany in various disguises.

Guyon, Madame (1648–1717)

Jeanne Marie Bouvières de la Mothe, a celebrated mystic and quietist who suffered persecution at the hands of the Roman Catholic Church. She was born at Montargis on April 13, 1648, and showed an early and passionate interest in martyrdom and religious exercises. At age 16 she was forced into a marriage with the wealthy M. Guyon, more than 20 years her senior, in whose household she was exposed to insult and cruelty. Broken in spirit, she turned to religion and consulted a Franciscan, who advised her to seek God in her heart rather than in outward observances.

From that time on, she became a mystic, aiming at the suppression of all human hopes, fears, and desires and the attainment of a completely disinterested love of God. She embraced every form of suffering, physical and mental, and even eschewed spiritual joys.

In 1680 Guyon's husband died and she was released from bondage. She embraced the doctrine of quietism. "In losing the gifts," she writes in her autobiography, "she had found the Giver, and had reached an ideal state of resignation and self-suppression." She went to Paris, expounded her theories with earnestness and charm, and gathered an illustrious circle about her. There also she made friends with fellow mystic Francois Fénélon.

But the persecutions of the Church increased. She requested that a commission be appointed to examine her doctrine and writings. Three commissioners were chosen, among them Bossuet, the champion of the Church, her erstwhile friend and now her bitter enemy. Her writings were condemned, and she was incarcerated at Vincennes. For four years she lay in the dungeons of the Bastille, while Bossuet used every means to malign her name and doctrine.

In 1702, her health broken, she was released and sent to Blois, where she died June 9, 1717. Her last years were blessed with peace and resignation and a continued acceptance of her trials.

Sources:

Guyon, Jeanne Marie. *Autobiography of Madame Guyon.* St. Louis, Mo.: B. Herder, 1897.

Guzyk, Jan (1875–1928)

Polish **materialization** medium, the son of a weaver, whose fraudulent production of phenomena fooled several prominent psychical researchers into the conclusion that he possessed strange powers. He first began to show his mediumistic tendencies during his years of apprenticeship in the tanning trade at Warsaw. There were **raps,** blows on the walls, and a stirring of objects as soon as evening approached. At age 15, under the tutelage of a Mr. Chlopicki, a Spiritualist, he became a professional medium. Russian Spiritualist and psychical researcher **Alexander N. Aksakof** took him to St. Petersburg, where he achieved great success although he did not impress **Julien Ochorowicz.**

A systematic study of Guzyk's mediumship, however, did not take place until **Gustav Geley** had a series of 50 sittings with him in Warsaw in September 1921. Geley became convinced of the reality of the phenomena. He witnessed the perfect materialization of a human face, alive and speaking, and the displacement of heavy objects. He took Guzyk to Paris for further experiments at the **Institut Métapsychique International.** Since Guzyk's phenomena only took place in complete darkness, the measures to avoid fraud were very strict. He was disrobed and medically examined before the séance, put into a pajama suit without pockets, and his wrists were joined to those of the controllers by sealed ribbons.

After a series of séances during 1922 and 1923 a very cautious report was issued. Among its 34 signatories were Geley, **Eugèn Osty,** Roux, Moutier, **Charles Richet, Rocco Santoliquido, Camille Flammarion, René Sudre,** and **Sir Oliver Lodge.** Only those facts are mentioned that were positively observed by all present and the report concluded, "We simply affirm our conviction that the phenomena obtained with Jan Guzyk are not explicable by individual or collective illusion or hallucination, nor by trickery." Altogether more than 80 highly placed persons attended the séances and, with the exception of three or four, declared themselves convinced of the genuine nature of the occurrences.

Footsteps were heard passing around the circle when everyone's position was accounted for and no confederate could have entered the room. Psychic lights were seen near the sitters; they formed couples and became two eyes, with expressive and mobile pupils that regarded the sitter fixedly. A mass of cloudy matter formed around the eyes and finally took a human shape.

The most noteworthy and convincing, at least to the sitters, were manifestations that occurred toward the end of the séances, at the moment when Guzyk awoke from the trance. René Sudre writes in *Psychic Research* (1928, p. 605) "At such a moment as he mumbled some unintelligible words, Guzyk brought my hand into contact with a hairy creature, just as somebody turned on the red light. Between the medium and myself I saw a sort of dark nebulous mass, which disappeared rapidly like a melting fog." The **apparition** was what Geley termed the "Pithecanthropus," an ape-man with a hairy, tough skin who often licked the hands of the sitters. At other times sounds were heard as if of a materialized dog. Sudre further observes, "These phenomena of animal materialisation may appear incredible to those who have not experienced the proof of them, but in all honesty of conscience and in all scientific equanimity it is impossible for me to make any reservation whatever against their actuality."

Sudre was once embraced by a human figure of which he hardly saw anything more than the eyes and lips. The lips were quite cold. His wife, similarly embraced, perceived an odor of alcohol. Guzyk always drank brandy before the séances, but it appeared impossible for him to produce the phenomenon under the conditions of control.

It appears that Guzyk had fooled Geley, Sudre, and their colleagues at the Institut. In November 1923 a series of ten séances was held with Guzyk at the Sorbonne in Paris. The report, signed by four investigators, stated that their conviction of **fraud** was "complete and without reserve." The phenomena—**touches** and displacement of objects—were produced by Guzyk's elbows and liberated leg. Yet it does not appear from the report that he was actually caught in fraud, and some observations cannot be explained by the liberation of a leg.

It is well known that Guzyk was often caught in fraud. His powers were highly commercialized, and he gave as many as five séances a day. **Harry Price** sat with him in August 1923 in Warsaw and found the phenomena childishly fraudulent. Max Dessoir wrote in *Von Jenseits der Seele* (1920) that he and a colleague repeatedly caught Guzyk using his foot for psychic touches and sounds. At Cracow in December 1924 the Metapsychical Society took a flashlight photograph at an unexpected moment. The picture showed Guzyk with his left hand raised to the height of the curtain, which he seemed to be grasping.

Following these séances M. Szczepansky wrote an article in *Psychische Studien* (June 1925), "The Career and Exposure of Guzyk." He drew a sharp reply from **Baron Schrenck-Notzing** who defended him by pointing out that Guzyk's frauds had been well known for years and did not detract from his genuine faculties. In 1927 **Walter Franklin Prince** sat with Guzyk in Warsaw. In Bulletin VII of the Boston Society for Psychical Research he gave an entirely negative report.

Gwion Bach

In ancient Welsh romance and myth, son of Gwreang. Assigned to stir the magic brew in the cauldron of science and inspiration intended for Ceridwin's son, Gwion tasted the liquid and became gifted with supernatural sight.

He fled, pursued by Ceridwin, and the pair were changed successively into a hare and a greyhound, a fish and an otter, a bird and a hawk, and a grain of wheat and a black hen, which ultimately swallowed the wheat. (Compare the metamorphoses of Ceridwen and Gwion Bach with that of the Queen of Beauty and the Djinn in the *Arabian Nights* Tale of the Second Calendar).

This pursuit and magical metamorphosis is a recurrent theme in folklore in the Indo-European tradition and survives also in the Scottish ballad "The Two Magicians" (Child No. 44).

Later, Gwion was placed in a bag and flung into the sea by Ceridwin. He was drawn out by Elphin, son of Cwyddus, and was then called Taliesin (Radiant Brow). (See also **Wales**)

Gypsies

The name Gypsy, an abbreviation of "Egyptian," has been used for centuries by English-speaking people to denote a member of a group of wanderers who traveled Europe during the Middle Ages, and whose descendants are still found in most European countries.

Many other names, such as "Saracen" and "Zigeuner," or "Cigan," have been applied to these people, but "Egyptian" is the most widespread. It does not, however, relate to Egypt, but to the country of "Little Egypt" or "Lesser Egypt," whose identity has never been clearly established. Two Transylvanian references from the years 1417 and 1418 suggested that Palestine is the country in question, but there is some reason to believe that "Little Egypt" included other regions in the East. It is now almost unanimously agreed that the Gypsies came into Europe from India.

There are strong resemblances between Indian and gypsy language. Gypsies speak of themselves as "Romany" and of their language as Romani-tchib (*tchib*=tongue). Physically they are black-haired and brown-skinned, their appearance, like their language, suggesting affinities with Hindustan.

In recent centuries, if not in earlier times, many of their overlords were not of Gypsy blood, but belonged to the nobility and *petite noblesse* of Europe, and were formally appointed by the kings and governments of their respective countries to rule over all the Gypsies resident within those countries. The title of baron, count, or regent of the Gypsies was no proof that the official so designated was of Gypsy race.

The appointed rulers, were empowered by Christian princes, and under Papal approval, were necessarily Christian. Moreover, their vassals were at least Christian by profession. Although their behavior was often inconsistent with such a profession, it was in the character of Christian pilgrims that they asked and obtained hospitality from the cities and towns of Medieval Europe.

This twofold character is illustrated in connection with the services held in the crypt of the church of Les Saintes Maries de la Mer, in the Ile de la Camargue, Bouches-du-Rhône. In this church many Gypsies annually celebrate the Festival of the Holy Marys on May 25. The crypt is specially reserved for them, because it contains the shrine of Saint Sara of Egypt, whom they regard as their patron saint. Throughout the night of the 24th-25th May they keep watch over her shrine, and on the 25th they leave. Among the Gypsy votive offerings presented in the crypt, some are believed to date back to about the year 1450.

All this would appear to indicate that the Gypsies were Christians. Another statement, however, tends to qualify such a conclusion. The assertion that the shrine of Saint Sara rests upon an ancient altar dedicated to Mithra, that the Gypsies of that neighborhood who are known as "Calagues," are descended from the Iberians formerly inhabiting the Camargue, and that their cult is really the Mithraic worship of fire and water, upon which the veneration of Saint Sara is superimposed.

Many believe that confirmation of this view is the worship of fire still existing among the Gypsies of Southern Hungary although this is also characteristic of India. There are special ceremonies observed at childbirth, in order to avert evil during the period between birth and baptism. Prior to the birth of the child, the Gypsies light a fire before the mother's tent, and this fire remains until the rite of baptism has been performed. The women who light and feed the fire recite the following chant:

"Burn ye, burn ye fast, O Fire!
And guard the babe from wrathful ire
Of earthy Gnome and Water-Sprite,

Whom with thy dark smoke banish quite!
Kindly Fairies, hither fare,
And let the babe good fortune share,
Let luck attend him ever here,
Throughout his life be luck aye near!
Twigs and branches now in store,
And still of branches many more,
Give we to thy flame, O Fire!
Burn ye, burn ye, fast and high,
Hear the little baby cry!"

It is noted that the spirits of the Earth and Water here are regarded as malevolent, and only to be overcome by the superior aid of fire. These women who are believed to have learned their occult lore from the unseen powers of Earth and Water are held to be the greatest magicians of the tribe.

Moreover, the water-being is not invariably regarded as inimical, but is sometimes directly propitiated. As when a mother, to charm away convulsive crying in her child, goes through the prescribed ceremonial details, including casting a red thread into the stream and repeating the following: "Take this thread, O Water-Spirit, and take with it the crying of my child! If it gets well, I will bring thee apples and eggs!"

The water-spirit appears again in a friendly character when a man, in order to recover a stolen horse, takes his infant to a stream, and, bending over the water, asks the invisible genius to indicate, by means of the baby's hand, the direction in which the horse has been taken. These two instances demonstrate the worship of water and the watery powers. Although these rites may be ascribed to Mithraism in its later stages, they may have an earlier origin.

Joseph Glanvill's observation of a young Gypsy inspired Matthew Arnold's poem, "The Scholar-Gypsy." In his *Vanity of Dogmatising* (1661), Glanville states, "There was lately a lad in the University of Oxford who was, by his poverty, forced to leave his studies there, and at last to join himself to a company of vagabond Gypsies.... After he had been a pretty while exercised in the trade," this scholar-gypsy chanced to meet two of his former fellow-students, to whom he stated, "that the people he went with were not such imposters as they were taken for, but that they had a traditional kind of learning among them, and could do wonders by the powers of imagination, their fancy binding that of others; that himself had learned much of their art, and when he had compassed the whole secret, he intended," he said, "to leave their company, and give the world an account of what he had learned."

It is believed that ancient Gypsies had knowledge and exercised **hypnotism.** Even among modern Gypsies this power is said to be exercised. **Col. Eugene De Rochas** stated that the Catalan Gypsies were mesmerists and clairvoyants, and the writer **Lewis Spence** supposedly experienced an attempt on the part of a South Hungarian Gypsy to exert this influence.

The same power, under the name of "glamour," was formerly an attribute of the Scottish Gypsies. Glamour was defined by Sir Walter Scott as "the power of imposing on the eyesight of the spectators, so that the appearance of an object shall be totally different from the reality."

Scott in explanation of a reference to "the Gypsies' glamour'd gang," in one of his ballads, he remarks: "Besides the prophetic powers ascribed to the Gypsies in most European countries, the Scottish peasants believe them possessed of the power of throwing upon bystanders a spell to fascinate their eyes and cause them to see the thing that is not. Thus in the old ballad of 'Johnnie Faa,' the elopement of the Countess of Cassillis with a Gypsy leader is imputed to fascination—

"Sae soon as they saw her weel-faur'd face,
They cast the glamour o'er her."

Scott also relates an incident of a Gypsy who "exercised his glamour over a number of people at Haddington, to whom he exhibited a common dunghill cock, trailing, what appeared to the spectators, a massy oaken trunk. An old man passed with a cart of clover, he stopped and picked out a four-leaved blade; the eyes of the spectators were opened, and the oaken trunk appeared to be a bulrush." Supposedly the quatrefoil, owing to its cruciform shape, acted as an antidote to witchcraft. Moreover, in the face of this sign of the cross, the Gypsy had to stop exercising the unlawful art. As to the possibility of hypnotizing a crowd, or making them "to see the thing that is not," that feat has often been ascribed to African witch doctors. What is required is a dominant will on the one hand and a sufficiently plastic imagination on the other.

Scott introduces these statements among his notes on the ballad of "Christie's Will," in relation to the verse:

"He thought the warlocks o' the rosy cross,
—Had fang'd him in their nets sae fast;
Or that the Gypsies' glamour'd gang
—Had lair'd his learning at the last."

This association of the **Rosicrucians** with Gypsies is not inapt, for hypnotism appears to have been considered a Rosicrucian art. Scott has other suggestive references including:

"Saxo Grammaticus mentions a particular sect of Mathematicians, as he is pleased to call them, who, 'per summam ludificandorum oculorum peritiam, proprios alienosque vultus, varus rerum imaginibus, adumbraie callebant; illicibusque formis veros obscurare conspectus.' Merlin, the son of Ambrose, was particularly skilled in this art, and displays it often in the old metrical romance of Arthour and Merlin. The jongleurs were also great professors of this mystery, which has in some degree descended, with their name, on the modern jugglers."

Various societies are credited with possession, of the art of hypnotism, during the Middle Ages. Presumably, it was inherited from one common source. How much the Gypsies were associated with this power may be inferred from a Scottish Act of Parliament of the year 1579, which was directed against "the idle people calling themselves Egyptians, or any other that fancy themselves to have knowledge of prophecy, *charming*, or other abused sciences." For the term "charming," like "glamour" and other kindred words (e.g., "enchantment," "bewitched," "spellbound") bore reference to the mesomeric influence.

The statement made by Glanvill's scholar-gypsy would lead one to believe that the Gypsies inhabiting England in the seventeenth century possessed other branches of learning. They have always been famed for their alleged prophetic power, exercised through the medium of **astrology** and chiromancy or **palmistry,** and also by the interpretation of **dreams,** this last named phase being distinctly specified in Scotland in 1611. It does not appear that any modern Gypsies profess a traditional knowledge of astrology. Nevertheless, it is interesting to note that the scholar Francis H. Groome was shown by a Welsh Gypsyman the form of the written charm employed by his mother in her fortune-telling, and that form was unquestionably a survival of the horoscope. Both mother and son were obviously unaware of that fact, and made no profession of astrology, but they had inherited the scheme of the horoscope from ancestors who were astrologers.

The practice of palmistry is still identified with the Gypsies, as it has been for ages. A curious belief was current in medieval times to the effect that the Three Kings or Magi who came to Bethlehem were Gypsies, and in more than one religious play they were represented as telling the fortunes of the Holy Family by means of palmistry. This circumstance evoked the following suggestive remarks from **Charles Godfrey Leland.**

"As for the connection of the Three Kings with Gypsies, it is plain enough. Gypsies were from the East; Rome and the world abounded in wandering Chaldean magi-priests, and the researches which I am making have led me to a firm conclusion that the Gypsy lore of Hungary and South Slavonia has a very original character as being, firstly, though derived from India, not Aryan, but Shamanic, that is, of an Altaic, or Tartar, or 'Turanian' stock.... Secondly, this was the old Chaldean-Accadian 'wisdom' or sorcery. Thirdly—and this deserves serious examination—it was also the old Etruscan religion whose magic formulas were transmitted to the Romans. . . .

"The Venetian witchcraft, as set forth by Bernoni, is evidently of Slavic-Greek origin. That of the Romagna is Etruscan, agreeing very strangely and closely with the Chaldean magic of Lenormant, and marvelously like the Gypsies'. It does not, when carefully sifted, seem to be like that of the Aryans. . . . nor is it Semitic. To what degree some idea of all this, and of Gypsy connection with it, penetrated among the people and filtered down, even into the Middle Ages, no one can say. But it is very probable that through the centuries there came together some report of the common origin of Gypsy and 'Eastern' or Chaldean lore, for since it *was* the same, there is no reason why a knowledge of the truth should not have been disseminated in a time of a traditions and earnest study in occultism."

These surmises on the part of a keen and accomplished student of every phase of magic, written and unwritten, are deserving of the fullest consideration. By following the line indicated by Leland it may be possible to reach an identification of the "traditional kind of learning" possessed by the Gypsies in the seventeenth century.

Leland also identified the gypsy language **Shelta** (as distinct from Romany) surviving in Ireland.

Gypsies have also been noted for their folk music, especially for the Flamenco style surviving in Andalucia (Spain).

Sources:

Bercovici, Konrad. *The Story of the Gypsies.* Cosmopolitan Book Corp., 1928. Reprint, Detroit: Gale Research, 1974.

Black, George F. *A Gypsy Bibliography.* London: Gypsy Lore Society, 1914. Reprint, Ann Arbor, Mich.: Gryphon Books, 1971.

Borrow, George. *Lavengro; the Scholar, the Gypsy, the Priest.* 3 vols. London, 1851.

———. *The Romany Rye.* London, 1957.

Clébert, Jean-Paul. *The Gypsies.* London: Vista Books, 1963. Reprint, Harmondsworth, Middlesex, U.K.: Penguin Books, 1967.

Leland, Charles G. *The English Gipsies and Their Language.* London, 1893.

———. *Gypsy Sorcery.* New York: Tower, n.d.

Starkie, Walter. *Raggle Taggle; Adventures With a Fiddle in Hungary and Roumania.* London, 1933.

Trigg, E. B. *Gypsy Demons and Divinities: The Magical and Supernatural Practices of the Gypsies.* Secaucus, N.J.: Citadel Press, 1973. Reprint, London: Sheldon Press, 1975.

Gyromancy

A form of **divination** performed by going round continually in a circle, the circumference of which was marked by letters. The presage was drawn from the words formed by the letters on which the inquirers stumbled when they became too giddy to stand. This practice has a curious connection with the familiar technique of psychic circles, in which the sitters place a finger on a glass surrounded by letters of the alphabet, when the glass touches letters in turn to give words or messages.

The object of this routine was simply to exclude the interference of the will and reduce the selection of letters to mere chance. In some species of enchantment, however, the art of turning round was to produce a prophetic delirium. The religious dances, and the rotation of certain devotees on one foot, with their arms stretched out (for example, the (see **Dervishes**), are of this nature. These cases really indicate a kind of mystical secret.

In the phenomenon known as St. Vitus' Dance, and the movements of the convulsionaries, manifestations of spirit intelligence were quite common. The tendency of the spiritual force is to act spirally, rhythmically, whether in the use of language or of the bodily members. (See **planchette**)

Sources:

Waite, Arthur Edward. *The Occult Sciences.* 1891. Reprint, Secaucus, N.J.: University Books, 1974.

H

Haas, George C(hristian) O(tto) (1883– ?)

Archbishop (primate of Universal Spiritual Church) who took an active interest in psychical science and lectured on the subject. Born March 28, 1883, in New York, New York, he attended Columbia University (M.A., 1903; Ph.D., 1909). He worked as a tutor at the College of the City of New York (1904–16) and then went to work for the U.S. Department of Justice as a translator (1917–51). As a member of the American Oriental Society, he served as coeditor of the *Journal of the American Society* (1916–18).

Throughout his adult life Haas was an active Spiritualist. In 1927 he founded the Universal Spiritual Church. Haas was responsible for the theory of "hyperphysics," intended to reorient science, and was founder and director of the Institute of Hyperphysical Research (IHR). He also directed the Institute of Life, a division of IHR.

During his retirement years he became active in the Fellowship of Faiths, an interfaith organization, and in 1956 was consecrated as archbishop of the Universal Spiritual Church. The church affiliated with the Catholic Apostolic Church, headquartered in England, and in 1959 the synod of the Catholic Apostolic Church named him primate of all the Americas.

Sources:

Haas, George C. O. *The Key to Enrichment of Life.* N.p., 1949.

———. "The New Orientation of Science." *IS* 23 (1960).

Ward, Gary. *Independent Bishops: An International Directory.* Detroit: Apogee Books, 1990.

Habondia (or Habundia)

The queen of the witches, presiding over the **Sabbat.** She was also identified with Diana or Herodias. She was referred to as "Habonde" in the thirteenth-century poem *Le Roman de la Rose.* In his work *Tableau de l'inconstance des mauvais anges* (Description of the inconstancy of evil angels, 1612), the demonologist **Pierre de Lancre** refers to Habondia rather sweepingly as "Queen of the fairies, witches, harpies, furies; and ghosts of the wicked."

Hades

Greek god of the underworld and of wealth, also identified with Pluto. Hades abducted Persephone (daughter of the corn goddess Demeter) and made her his wife. In his intimidating character as lord of death, Hades was mysterious and terrifying, but in his benign aspect he was the generous god of wealth. His attention could be secured by striking the ground, and he could be propitiated by an offering of a black-fleeced sheep.

Entrance to the domain of Hades was through the groves of Persephone, where the gates were guarded by the great dog Cerberus, who admitted visitors without difficulty but would not let them leave. After passing through the gate, one had several rivers to cross, including Lethe, the river of forgetfulness. For a small fee, the ferryman Charon would take the traveler across.

In later history, the domain of Hades became synonymous with **hell,** although Hades' domain was not referred to as a place of torment.

Hag of the Dribble

Welsh **banshee** named Gwrach y Rbibyn, who was said to carry stones across the mountains in her apron, then untie the string, letting the stones shower down, thus making a "dribble." It was believed that at twilight this hag flapped her raven wing against the windows of those doomed to die, and howled "A-a-a-ui-ui-Anni!"

Haggadah

The general name for the narrative or fabular portion of rabbinical literature. The most familiar use of the term is in the household service of *seder* at Passover, dramatizing the Jewish exodus from Egypt led by Moses.

Haines, Frederick H(enry) (1869–1944)

Prominent British Spiritualist, insurance broker, and author of *Chapters on Insurance History* and *The Insurance Business,* which were considered classics in their field. He was converted to **Spiritualism** during World War I, and after careful investigations, begun in a spirit of skepticism, he developed powers of **clairvoyance.**

In the mid-1920s he began to receive by **automatic writing** a large number of scripts that were later published, including *He Became Man,* an inspirational script on the life of Christ. He also published his autobiography, *Nothing But the Truth: The Confessions of a Medium* (1931). Haines contributed many articles to British psychic journals and was in demand as a lecturer. He founded the Watford Christian Spiritualist Fellowship and edited a monthly periodical, *Spiritual Vision.* He died February 6, 1944.

Sources:

Haines, Frederick H. *The Book of Spiritual Wisdom.* N.p., 1928.

———. *A Lamp to the Feet.* N.p., 1928.

———. *Locusts and Wild Honey.* N.p., 1928.

———. *Thus Saith Celphra.* N.p., 1928.

———. *A Voice from Heaven.* Watford, England: Pure Thought Press, [1932].

Haining, Peter (1940–)

British novelist, writer on occult subjects, and anthologist of horror stories. Born April 2, 1940, in Enfield, England, Haining was educated in Buckhurst Hill. He worked as a journalist and magazine writer (1957–63) and successively as editor, senior editor, and editorial director of New English Library (1963–72) in London. Since 1972 he has been an editorial consultant, writer, and anthologist. He is a member of the International Association of Poets, Playwrights, Editors, Essayists and Novelists (PEN).

Haining's family lived for many generations in Scotland, but he now resides in the "witch county" of Essex, England. His research into witchcraft and black magic resulted in a ritual curse from a group of devil worshipers in London, but that did not interfere with Haining's literary success. He claims that one of his ancestors was burned at the stake for possessing a "book of spells," and his publication *The Warlock's Book* is said to include materials based on records of this ancestor.

Haining's investigation of a desecrated graveyard in Essex led to his first book, *Devil Worship in England* (1964), coauthored with A. V. Sellwood. Since that time he has written or edited several titles annually. His early **vampire** anthology, *The Midnight People* (1966), also known as *Vampires at Midnight,* has been frequently reprinted. His work has covered the fields of occultism, science fiction, fantasy, and horror. Most memorable among Haining's almost 100 titles are *Anatomy of Witchcraft* (1972), *Ghosts: An Illustrated History* (1974), *The Craft of Terror: Extracts from the Rare and Infamous Gothic "Horror" Novels* (1966), *A Circle of Witches: An Anthology of Victorian Witchcraft Stories* (1971), *The Necromancers: The Best of Black Magic and Witchcraft* (1971), *The Hashish Club* (1974), *The Sherlock Holmes Scrapbook* (1974), *The Edgar Allen Poe Bedside Companion* (1980), *The Vampire Terror* (1981), and *Shades of Dracula* (1982). Haining edited *The Complete Ghost Stories of Charles Dickens* (1982), *Vampire!* (1984), *The "Doctor Who" File* (1986), *Elvis in Private* (1987), and *Supernatural Tales of Sir Arthur Conan Doyle* (1987).

Sources:

Ashley, Mike. *Who's Who in Horror and Fantasy Fiction.* London: Elm Tree Books, 1977.

Melton, J. Gordon. *The Vampire Book: The Encyclopedia of the Undead.* Detroit: Visible Ink Press, 1994.

Reginald, Robert. *Science Fiction and Fantasy Literature, 1975–1991.* Detroit: Gale Research, 1992.

Hair

Hair has had an occult significance since ancient times. It seems to have a life of its own, since it may continue to grow after the death of the body. It has been regarded as a source of strength and sexuality and has played a part in religion and magical rituals. The Hebrews developed a number of customs relative to hair that served to separate them from their pagan neighbors, a fact which is played out in the story of Samsom and Delilah (Judg. 16:4–22)

In various cultures, individuals dedicated to service of the priesthood have undergone ritual cutting of hair, and the tonsure of priests is said to have originated in Egypt (see the writings of Herodotus). In Hinduism, there are hair rituals for youths, and those who become celibates have their heads formally shaven. The association of hair with sexuality has given hair as a symbol remarkable force, and distinctions between male and female hair have emphasized sexual attraction.

Since the hair is believed to be intimately related to the life of an individual, it has magical significance in witchcraft rituals, and people in many civilizations have been at pains to prevent their hair from falling into the hands of an enemy, who might use it for **black magic.**

There is even a school of character reading from the hair, known as trichsomancy.

Extreme fright or ecstatic states have caused hair to literally "stand on end" in the goose-flesh condition of horripilation.

Sources:

Berg, Charles. *The Unconscious Significance of Hair.* London: Allen & Unwin, 1951.

Cooper, Wendy. *Hair: Sex Society Symbolism.* London: Aldus Book, 1971.

Hajoth Hakados

According to the mystical teachings of the **Kabala,** one of the spheres of angels by whose agency Jehovah's providence is spread. It was believed that these angels inhabited one of the hierarchies named Jehovah, and that the simple essence of the divinity flowed through the Hajoth Hakados to the angel Metatron and to the ministering spirit Reschith Hajalalim.

Ha-Levi, Judah ben Samuel (ca. 1085–ca. 1140)

Celebrated Jewish theologian and mystic. Ha-Levi seems to have had some conception of **elementary spirits,** for he said that some angels are "created for the time being, out of the subtle elements of matter." He was chiefly noted for his liturgical hymns, used extensively in sephardic rites.

Hal

A Moslem term meaning "now," given to a condition of mystical ecstasy often involving violent physical activity, such as wild dancing, shouting, or even foaming at the mouth. Hal sometimes ensues when extremely devout and emotional Moslems visit the grave of a famous saint.

Hall, James A(lbert) (1934–)

Medical student who experimented with **ESP.** Born February 13, 1934, Hall studied at the University of Texas (B.A., 1955) and Southwestern Medical School, University of Texas. He is a member of the **American Society for Psychical Research,** an associate member of the Parapsychological Association, and an associate of the **Society for Psychical Research,** London.

In 1958 he experimented with elementary school children in Gladewater, Texas, to ascertain the effect of teacher and pupil attitudes on ESP scores. The results were reported in the *Journal of Parapsychology* (vol. 22, no. 4, December 1958). He contributed papers to the annual convention of the Parapsychological Association in 1981 ("Unconscious Cultural Influences and Psi: A Jungian Footnote") and 1986 ("Ethical Structure in Clinical Applications of Parapsychology").

Sources:

Hall, James A. "The Works of J. B. Rhine: Implications for Religion." *Journal of Parapsychology* (1981).

Hall, James A., and H. B. Crasilneck. "Physiological Changes Associated with Hypnosis." *International Journal of Clinical and Experimental Hypnosis* 7, no. 1 (January 1959).

Pleasants, Helene, ed. *Biographical Dictionary of Parapsychology.* New York: Helix Press, 1964.

Hall, Manly Palmer (1901–1990)

Writer and lecturer on **astrology** and the occult. He was born on March 18, 1901, in Peterborough, Ontario, Canada, and moved to the United States in 1904. He had an early interest in matters occult and as a young man joined the **Theosophical Society,** the Freemasons, the **Rosicrucians,** and the **American Federation of Astrologers.**

Hall moved to California in 1923 and was ordained to the ministry in a metaphysical church. He became the pastor of the Church of the People, an independent occult and metaphysical congregation in Los Angeles, California; established the Hall Publishing Company; and began a magazine, *The All-Seeing Eye.* Hall, though lacking formal higher education, wrote a series of occult titles that became known for their erudition. Possibly the most important book from his early writings is *An Encyclopedic Outline of Masonic, Hermetic, Qabalistic, and Rosicrucian Symbolical Philosophy* (1928) in which he attempted to correlate the teachings of various alternative occult traditions.

In 1934, Hall, who had harbored a dream of creating a school modeled on the ancient one headed by Pythagoras, founded the Philosophical Research Society, which he hoped would become a major center for the dissemination of ancient wisdom throughout North America. It became the home to a large library, including many rare texts, collected by Hall.

Through the last 60 years of his life Hall lectured and wrote widely, his texts ranging over the broad field of the occult and topics relative to it, including history and comparative religion. He died on August 29, 1990, in Los Angeles, and his work is being continued by the society. Hall avoided writing autobiographical material during his life, and his volume on his grandmother is the only autobiographical information he left.

Sources:

Hall, Manly Palmer. *Growing Up with Grandmother.* Los Angeles: Philosophical Research Society, 1985.

———. *The Little World of PRS.* Los Angeles: Philosophical Research Society, 1982.

———. *Reincarnation: The Cycle of Necessity.* Los Angeles: Philosophical Research Society, 1942.

———. *Self-Unfoldment by Disciplines of Realization.* Los Angeles: Philosophical Research Society, 1945.

Melton, J. Gordon. *Religious Leaders of America.* Detroit: Gale Research, 1991.

Hall, Prescott F(arnsworth) (1868–1921)

American lawyer, author, and psychical researcher. Born September 27, 1868, in Boston, Massachusetts, Hall took his LL.B. in 1892 at Harvard. He was in law practice in Boston from 1892 to 1921 and was a founder of the Immigration Restriction League and a member of the **American Society for Psychical Research.** In addition to his various writings on law, immigration, and economics, he took a special interest in mediumship.

Sources:

Hall, Prescott F. "Experiments with Mrs. Caton." *Proceedings* of the American Society for Psychical Research 8 (1914).

———, ed. "The Harrison Case." *Proceedings* of the American Society for Psychical Research 13 (1919).

Pleasants, Helene, ed. *Biographical Dictionary of Parapsychology.* New York: Helix Press, 1964.

Hall, Trevor H(enry) (1910–)

Surveyor and noted British author of books on parapsychological subjects. Hall was born May 28, 1910, at Wakefield, England. He was chief surveyor of the Huddersfield Building Society (1935–39), was a major in the British army during World War II (1939–45), and became director of the Huddersfield Building Society in 1958.

Hall was a Perrott student in psychical research at Trinity College, Cambridge (1954–56). He had special interest in conjuring and compiled *A Bibilography of Conjuring Books in English from 1580 to 1850* (1957). His expert knowledge of conjuring was, in part, responsible for the skeptical attitude that became evident as he began to write about physical mediums, many of whom had been caught in **fraud.** In his early book *The Spiritualists,* Hall confirmed the belief of many that the phenomena of famous medium **Florence Cook** were fraudulent and suggested that she was having an affair with **Sir William Crookes.**

His other books on psychical researchers were equally critical. His book on **Edmund Gurney,** for example, investigated the claimed trickery of G. A. Smith and Douglas Blackburn, whose second-sight act Gurney investigated. Hall's book, though, on the whole was sympathetic to Gurney. His book *Strange Things* ruined the reputation of **Ada Goodrich-Freer** (known in psychical research literature as "Miss X"), and *The Search for Harry Price* effectively denigrates the character and work of the famed psychical researcher.

Hall also contributed articles on the history of psychical research to the *International Journal of Parapsychology.* He went on to write several texts on ghosts. During the late 1960s an interest in Sherlock Holmes (whose creator, **Arthur Conan Doyle,** was a confirmed Spiritualist) emerged, and Hall wrote several popular volumes, including *Sherlock Holmes: Ten Literary Studies* (1969), *The Late Mr. Sherlock Holmes* (1971), and *Sherlock Holmes and His Creator* (1974).

Sources:

Berger, Arthur S., and Joyce Berger. *The Encyclopedia of Parapsychology and Psychical Research.* New York: Paragon House, 1991.

Hall, Trevor H. *The Enigma of Daniel Home.* Buffalo, N.Y.: Prometheus Books, 1984.

———. *The Search for Harry Price.* Dallas: Southwest Book Services, 1978.

———. *The Spiritualists.* 1962. Reprinted as *The Medium and the Scientist.* Buffalo, N.Y.: Prometheus Books, 1984.

———. *The Strange Case of Edmund Gurney.* London: Duckworth, 1964.

Hall, Trevor H., and J. L. Campbell. *Strange Things.* London: Routledge & Kegan Paul, 1968.

Hall, Trevor H., and E. J. Dingwall. *Four Modern Ghosts.* London: Duckworth, 1958.

Hall, Trevor H., E. J. Dingwall, and K. M. Goldney. *The Haunting of Borley Rectory.* London: Duckworth, 1956.

Medhurst, R. G., and K. M. Goldney. "William Crookes and the Physical Phenomena of Mediumship." *Proceedings* of the Society for Psychical Research 54, no. 195 (March 1964).

Pleasants, Helene, ed. *Biographical Dictionary of Parapsychology.* New York: Helix Press, 1964.

Hallowed Grounds Fellowship of Spiritual Healing and Prayer

The Hallowed Grounds Fellowship of Spiritual Healing and Prayer is a Spiritualist Center in Santa Barbara, California, founded in 1961 by British **medium** Heroge Daisley. An outstanding medium, Daisley traveled widely lecturing and holding séances in the 1950s, during which time he accumulated a large mailing list. After settling in Santa Barbara, his new home became the base from which he traveled the continent and to which he welcomed people who wished to utilize his talents at contacting the spirit world. For many years he also issued a quarterly journal, *The Witness* (1961–73).

Daisley teaches a form of Christian Spiritualism, emphasizing biblical teachings about the nature of the afterlife. He believes that at death, the physical body is discarded and replaced with a spiritual body. The soul continues to exist on several planes, each invisible to the physical eye. Mediums and certain gifted individuals can contact and communicate with the souls of the dead. The fellowship is headquartered at its single center at 629 San Ysidro Rd., Santa Barbara, CA 93108.

Halloween See **All Hallow's Eve**

Hallucination

A false perception of sensory vividness arising without the stimulus of a corresponding sense impression. In this it differs from illusion, which is merely the misinterpretation of an actual sense perception. Visual and auditory hallucinations are the most common, but hallucinations of the other senses may also be experienced. Human figures and voices most frequently form the subject of a hallucination, but in certain types other classes of objects may be seen, as, for instance, the rats and insects of delirium tremens.

Although hallucination is often associated with various mental and physical diseases, it may nevertheless occur spontaneously while the agent shows no departure from full vigor of body and mind. It may also be induced (i.e., in **hypnotism**) in a high percentage of subjects. The essential difference between sane and insane hallucinations is that in the former case the agent can, by reflection, recognize the subjective nature of the impression, even when it has every appearance of objectivity, whereas in the latter case the patient cannot be made to understand that the vision is not real.

Until the early twentieth century, hallucinatory percepts were regarded merely as intensified memory images; however, the most intense of ordinary representations do not possess the sensory vividness of the smallest sensation received from the external world. It follows that other conditions must be present besides the excitement of the brain, which is the correlate of representation. The seat of excitement is the same in actual sense perceptions and in memory images, but in the former the stimulus is peripherally originated in the sensory nerve, whereas in the latter it originates in the brain itself.

When a neural system becomes highly excited—a state which may be brought about by emotion, ill health, drugs, or a number of other causes—it may serve to divert from their proper paths any set of impulses arising from the sense organs. Because any impulse ascending through the sensory nerves produces an effect of sensory vividness—normally, a true perception—the impulses thus diverted gives to the memory image an appearance of actuality not distinguishable from that produced by a corresponding sense impression—a hallucination.

In hypnosis a state of cerebral dissociation is induced, whereby a neural system may be abnormally excited and hallucination thus readily engendered. **Drugs,** especially **hallucinogens,** which excite the brain, also induce hallucinations.

In 1901 the British physician Sir Henry Head demonstrated that certain visceral disorders produce hallucinations, such as the appearance of a shrouded human figure. The question of whether there is any relationship between the hallucination and the person it represents is, and has long been, a vexing one. Countless well-authenticated stories of **apparitions** coinciding with a death or some other crisis are on record and would seem to establish some causal connection between them. In former times apparitions were considered to be the **doubles** or "ethereal bodies" of real persons, and Spiritualists believe that they are the spirits of the dead (or, in some instances, of the living) temporarily forsaking the physical body.

The dress and appearance of the apparition does not necessarily correspond with the actual dress and appearance of the person it represents. Thus a man at the point of death, in bed and wasted by disease, may appear to a friend miles away as if in ordinary health and wearing familiar clothing. Nevertheless, there are notable instances where some remarkable detail of dress is reproduced in the apparition. It seems clear, however, that it is the agent's general personality that is, as a rule, conveyed to the percipient, and not, except in special cases, his or her actual appearance.

It has been suggested that those images that do not arise in the subliminal consciousness of the agent may be telepathically received by him or her from other minds. A similar explanation has been offered for the hallucinatory images that many people can induce by **crystal gazing** or staring into a pool of water, a drop of ink, or a magic mirror in search of information about scenes or people they know nothing about.

Collective hallucination is a term applied to hallucinations shared by a number of people. There is no firm evidence, however, of the operation of any agency other than **suggestion** or telepathy.

Hallucination and Psychical Research

One of the most succinct definitions of hallucination occurs in *Phantasms of the Living* (2 vols., 1886), by **Edmund Gurney, F. W. H. Myers,** and **Frank Podmore:** "percepts which lack, but which can only by a distinct reflection be recognised as lacking, the objective basis which they suggest." If the sensory perception coincides with an objective occurrence or counterpart, the hallucination is called veridical, (truth-telling), as in the phantasm of the dying. If the apparition is seen by several people at the same time, the case is called collective veridical hallucination.

In the years following the foundation of the **Society for Psychical Research** (SPR), London, the hallucination theory of psychic phenomena was in great vogue. If no other explanation was available the person who had had a supernormal experience was told it was a hallucination, and if several people testified to the same occurrence it was said that the hallucination of one was communicated to the others. **Sir William Crookes** counters that idea in his *Researches in the Phenomena of Spiritualism* (1870): "The supposition that there is a sort of mania or delusion which suddenly attacks a whole roomful of intelligent persons who are quite sane elsewhere, and that they all concur, to the minutest particulars, in the details of the occurrences of which they suppose themselves to be witnesses, seems to my mind more incredible than even the facts which they attest."

Charles Richet, in *Thirty years of Psychical Research* (1923), omits hallucination completely in his discussion of metapsychical phenomena (a term for paranormal). He believed that hallucination should be reserved to describe a morbid state when a mental image is exteriorized without any exterior reality. According to Richet,

"It is extremely rare that a person who is neither ill, nor drunk, nor hypnotised should, in the walking state, have an auditory, visual, or tactile illusion of things that in no way exist. The opinion of alienists that hallucination is the chief sign of mental derangement, and the infallible characteristic of insanity seems to me well grounded. With certain exceptions (for every rule there are exceptions) a normal healthy individual when fully awake does not have hallucinations. If he see[s] apparitions these correspond to some external reality or other. In the absence of any external reality there are no hallucinations but those of the insane and of alcoholics."

An instance recounted by Sir John Herschel did not conform to Richet's idea. He had been watching with some anxiety the demolition of a familiar building. On the following evening, in good light, he passed the spot where the building had stood. "Great was my amazement to see it," he wrote, "as if still standing, projected against the dull sky. I walked on, and the perspective of the form and disposition of the parts appeared to change as they would have done if real."

In the case of hauntings where a ghost is seen, Gurney suggests that a person thinking of a given place that is at the time actually experienced in sense perception by others may be imparting into the consciousness of the others a thought existing in his own.

Of course, data provided by a registering apparatus or photography may rule out the hallucination theory as applied to hauntings, provided that there is some proper scientific control. Similarly, if objects are displaced, as in **poltergeist** cases, the theory of hallucination is no longer tenable. As Andrew Lang writes in *Cock Lane and Common Sense* (1896), "Hallucinations cannot draw curtains, or open doors, or pick up books, or tuck in bedclothes or cause thumps."

The things seen during a psychic experience of an otherwise normal person should also be distinguished from the hallucinations of the mentally deranged, of the sick, drunk, or drugged. The latter are not veridical, nor telepathic, nor collective. In the "Census of Hallucinations," published in the *Proceedings* of the SPR (1894), the committee excluded, as far as possible, all pathological subjects. J. G. Piddington (see *Proceedings,* vol. 19), in testing this census for cases that would show the same nature as hallucinations arising from visceral diseases, concluded that there was not a single case in the census report that fell into line with the visceral type.

In hypnotic hallucinations the hypnotized subject may see apparitions if so suggested and may not see ordinary people who are in the same room. But the subject may hear the noises they make, see the movement of objects they touch, and be frightened by what appears to be poltergeist phenomena. If the suggestion is posthypnotic the subject may also see a phantom shape when given a signal or at a prescribed time.

The visions seen by some people on the verge of sleep were called "**hypnagogic** hallucinations" by F. W. H. Myers. The after-images on waking from sleep he named "hypnopompic hallucinations." A comprehensive study of both classes of phenomena was published by G. E. Leaning in the *Proceedings* of the SPR, (vol. 35, 1926).

The difference between hallucination and illusion is that there is an objective basis for the illusion, which is falsely interpreted. In hallucination, although more than one sense may be affected, there is no external basis for the perception.

Sources:

Besterman, Theodore. *Crystal-Gazing.* London, 1924. Reprint, New Hyde Park, N.Y.: University Books, 1965.

Bramwell, J. M. *Hypnotism: Its History, Practice, and Theory.* London, 1903.

Gurney, Edmund, F. W. H. Myers, and Frank Podmore. *Phantasms of the Living.* 2 vols. London: Trubner, 1886. Reprint, Gainesville, Fla.: Scholars Facsimiles Reprints, 1970.

Huxley, Aldous. *The Doors of Perception.* London, 1954.

Johnson, Fred H. *The Anatomy of Hallucinations.* Chicago: Nelson Hall, 1978.

MacKenzie, Andrew. *Apparitions and Ghosts.* London: Barker, 1971. Reprint, New York: Popular Library, 1972.

———. *Hauntings and Apparitions.* London: Heinemann, 1982.

Myers, F. W. H. *Human Personality and Its Survival of Bodily Death.* 2 vols. London: Longmans Green, 1903. Reprint, New York: Arno Press, 1975.

Podmore, Frank. *Apparitions and Thought Transference.* London, 1894.

Reed, Graham. *The Psychology of Anomalous Experience.* Boston: Houghton Mifflin, 1974.

Richet, Charles. *Thirty Years of Psychical Research.* London: W. Collins, 1923. Reprint, New York: Arno Press, 1975.

Rogo, D. Scott. *Mind Beyond the Body: The Mystery of ESP Projection.* New York: Penguin, 1978.

Samuels, Mike. *Seeing With the Mind's Eye: The History, Techniques, and Uses of Visualization.* New York: Bookworks; Random House, 1975.

Tyrrell, G. N. M. *Apparitions.* London: Duckworth, 1953. Reprint, London: Society for Psychical Research, 1973.

Hallucinogens

Drugs that induce profound changes in consciousness through interference with normal sensory perception. Typical **drugs** of this kind are mescaline, LSD, and psilocybin. The dissemination of knowledge of hallucinogens and their widespread availability in the 1960s created a significant subculture in the West. The use of LSD and related substances opened many to the spiritual life, even though most soon dropped their use.

The public was first alerted to the possibilities of psychedelics through **Aldous Huxley**'s books *The Doors of Perception* (1954) and *Heaven & Hell* (1956), which suggest that drug experience is related to states of mysticism. His insights were developed at great length by numerous writers in the following two decades.

Opponents of the use of psychedelics have noted that their use tends to make individuals dependent upon them for the production of ecstatic experiences, and that they are no substitute for the development of a mature mystical lifestyle.

Sources:

Lewin, L. *Phantastica, Narcotic and Stimulating Drugs.* New York: E. P. Dutton, 1964.

Masters, R. E. L., and Jean Houston. *The Varieties of Psychedelic Experience.* New York: Holt, Rinehart & Winston, 1966. Reprint, London: Anthony Blond, 1967.

Wasson, R. G. *Soma: The Divine Mushroom.* New York: Harcourt Brace, 1971.

Zaehner, R. C. *Mysticism Sacred and Profane.* London, 1957.

Halomancy

A branch of **pyromancy** (**divination** by fire) involving throwing salt into flames. Indications were obtained from the nature of the flames, their color, speed, and direction.

Ham

According to Norwegian legend, Ham was a storm fiend in the shape of an eagle with black wings, sent by Helgi to engulf Frithjof as he sailed for the island of Yarl Angantyr. The story is told in the Saga of Grettir.

Hambaruan

Among the Dayaks of Borneo the hambaruan, or soul of a living man, was believed to be able to leave the body at will and go where it chose; however, it was vulnerable to capture by evil spirits. If this should happen, the man would fall ill, and if his soul was not speedily liberated, he would die. The belief represents an awareness of the experience today termed **out-of-the-body travel.**

Hamilton, T(homas) Glen(dinning) (1873–1935)

Medical practitioner of Winnipeg and former president of the Winnipeg Society for Psychical Research. Over a period of 15 years, Hamilton carried on systematic research in his own laboratory under scientific conditions and often in the presence of distinguished guests from across Canada and the United States.

He was born in Agincourt, Ontario, Canada, on November 26, 1873, into a farming family. He studied at Manitoba Medical College, after which he spent a year as house surgeon at Winnipeg General Hospital. In 1904 he established a private medical practice in Elmwood, Winnipeg. He took a great interest in community life, serving as chairman of the Winnipeg Playground Commission and in 1915 serving on the Manitoba Legislative Assembly.

His interest in psychical phenomena dated from his days as a medical student, and through the 1920s he studied **Pearl L. Curran,** the medium of the entity known as **"Patience Worth."** In Winnipeg he formed a **circle** consisting of four medical doctors, a lawyer, a civil engineer, and an electrical engineer. His wife, an experienced nurse, also assisted. He secured the services of several nonprofessional mediums known only as Elizabeth M., Mary M., and Mercedes. Through regularly attending the séances, some of the sitters also developed mediumship and fell occasionally into trance. The supposed spirits of author Robert Louis Stevenson, missionary David Livingstone, Spiritualist medium **W. T. Stead,** Baptist minister Charles H. Spurgeon, and psychical researcher **Camille Flammarion** acted as regular **controls.**

Many of the phenomena were simultaneously photographed by a large group of cameras, several stereoscopic, and Hamilton obtained a unique collection of photographs of table levitations, telekinetic movements, teleplasmic structures, and materialized hands, faces, and full figures. The success of the circle was credited to the harmonious conditions that prevailed. It allowed Hamilton to make an important contribution to the study of **direct voice** and psychic lights. Apart from the photographs, the most valuable contribution was a critical analysis of trance that, in the hands of a competent observer, would be invaluable to researchers in eliminating imposition and fraud, whether deliberate or unintentional.

Hamilton died April 7, 1935.

Sources:

Hamilton, Margaret L. *Is Survival a Fact? Studies of Deep-Trance Automatic Scripts.* London, 1969.

Hamilton, T. Glen. *Intention and Survival: Psychical Research Studies and Bearing of Intentional Acts by Trance Personalities on the Problem of Human Survival.* Toronto: Macmillan, 1942. Rev. ed. London: Regency Press, 1977.

———. "A Lecture to the British Medical Association." *Psychic Science* 9, no. 4 (January 1931).

———. "The Mary M. Teleplasm of Oct. 27, 1929." *Psychic Science* 10, no. 4 (January 1932).

———. "Teleplasmic Phenomena in Winnipeg." *Psychic Science* 8, no. 3 (1929); 8, no. 4 (January 1930); 9, no. 2 (July 1930).

Hammurabi, Law of

Hammurabi's famous system of law included an injunction against **black magic.** It was propounded during the reign of Hammurabi, sixth king of the Amoritic or West Semitic dynasty of Babylonia, 2067–2025 B.C.E. (See **Semites**)

Hamon

A legendary sacred stone like gold, shaped like a ram's horn. If its possessor was in the posture of contemplation, it was believed to give the mind a representation of all divine things.

Hamon, "Count" Louis See Cheiro

Hand, Robert S. (1942–)

Contemporary American astrologer, born on December 5, 1942, in Plainfield, New Jersey. Hand grew up in Massachusetts and attended Brandeis University (B.A., magna cum laude, 1965). He later attended the University of California and Princeton University. During his teen years Hand had become fascinated with **astrology,** which his father had used successfully in analyzing the stock market. He began studying astrology seriously in 1960.

Hand became a professional astrologer in 1972. He was an active member of the **National Council for Geocosmic Research** (NCGR) serving successively as its publications chairman, research director, and, beginning in 1973, board member. Through the mid-1970s he wrote a set of detailed astrological texts hailed by his colleagues. *Planets in Composite* (1975) was followed by *Planets in Transit* (1976) and *Planets in Youth* (1977). These volumes have been translated into several foreign languages.

Hand has become well known for his scientific research on astrology, especially the application of astrology to economic conditions. He also became one of the first to program computers to do astrological charts, and in 1979 he cofounded Astro-Graphics Services (now Astrolabe Software). He has continued to write books and numerous articles. In 1980 he became the chairperson of the NCGR. In 1989 he was given the Regulus Award by the United Astrological Congress for his research and in 1992 received the Neil F. Michaelssen Award from the Global Research Forum for his work on astrology and financial cycles.

Sources:

Hand, Robert. *Essays on Astrology.* Rockport, Mass.: Para Research, 1982.

———. *Horoscope Symbols.* Rockport, Mass: Para Research, 1981.

———. *Planets in Composite.* Rockport, Mass.: Para Research, 1975.

———. *Planets in Transit.* Rockport, Mass.: Para Research, 1976.

———. *Planets in Youth.* Rockport, Mass.: Para Research, 1977.

Hand of Glory

The hand of a dead man (preferably hanged) in which a lighted candle was placed. In Ireland and Mexico it was formerly believed to be an instrument of magic. If the candle with its gruesome candlestick was taken into a house, the sleeping inhabitants were believed to be prevented from waking, and the candle itself remained invisible. To be truly effective, however, both hand and candle had to be prepared in a special manner. The term hand of glory is believed to derive from the French *main de gloire* or **mandragoras** and be related to legends of the mandrake. The mandrake plant was believed to grow under the gallows of a hanged man. Belief in the efficacy of the hand of glory to facilitate robbery persisted as late as 1831 in Ireland. (See also **Glas Ghairm**)

Sources:

Ingoldsby, Thomas. *The Ingoldsby Legends or Mirth and Marvels.* London: R. Bentley, 1840.

Robbins, Rossell Hope. *The Encyclopedia of Witchcraft and Demonology.* New York: Crown Publishers, 1959.

Thompson, C. J. S. *The Hand of Destiny.* London, 1932. Reprint, Detroit: Singing Tree Press, 1970.

Hands of Spirits

There are various instances in occult history where the hand of a spirit has been said to become visible to the human eye. During the reign of James I of England a vision of this kind came to a certain clerk who was writing a will that was to disinherit a son. A fine white hand appeared between the candle and the parchment, casting a shadow on the latter. It came three times, until the clerk, becoming alarmed, threw down his pen and refused to finish the work.

In the biblical book of Daniel (5:5) appears the famous instance of the handwriting on the wall: "In the same hour came forth fingers of a man's hand, and wrote over against the candlestick upon the plaster of the wall of the king's palace: and the king [Belshazzar] saw the part of the hand that wrote." Also in Daniel (10:10), it is recorded that Daniel, after a certain vision, was touched by a hand, which set him upon his knees and the palms of his hands.

There are also other instances of writing being done without human hands, and in his book *Startling Facts in Modern Spiritualism* (1874), N. B. Wolfs stated that he shook hands with spirits, as "substantially" as one man shakes hands with another.

Sir William Crookes described the appearance of a phantom hand, which appeared during a séance with **Kate Fox:** "A luminous hand came down from the upper part of the room, and after hovering near me for a few seconds, took the pencil from my hand, rapidly wrote on a sheet of paper, threw the pencil down, and then rose up over our heads, gradually fading into darkness."

A similar séance took place with Fox at the home of S. C. Hall, editor of the *Art Journal,* on September 6, 1876, in the presence of nine individuals. A report in *The Spiritualist* (October 13, 1876) states: "A luminous, small, beautifully shaped hand then descended from the side at which was sitting, that is to say, at the opposite side to Mrs. Jencken [Fox]. The hand seized a pencil which was lying on the table and wrote the letters 'E.W.E.'"

Phantom hands were also reported to have materialized during séances with the medium **D. D. Home,** in sittings with Napoleon III in 1857, as well as on many other occasions with other sitters, including Crookes.

Sources:

Crookes, William. "Notes of an Enquiry into the Phenomena Called Spiritual." *Quarterly Journal of Science* (January 1874).

Medhurst, R. G., comp. *Crookes and the Spirit World: A Collection of Writings by or Concerning the Works of Sir William Crookes D.M., F.R.S., in the Field of Psychical Research.* New York: Taplinger; London: Souvenir Press, 1972.

Moses, W. Stainton. *Direct Spirit Writing (Psychography).* London, 1878. Reprint, London: Psychic Book Club, 1952.

Hankey, Muriel W(inifred) Arnold (1895–1978)

Prominent British researcher and organizer in the field of psychical science. She was born May 17, 1895, in London. She became secretary to **J. Hewat McKenzie,** founder of the **British College of Psychic Science,** and for a period served as principal and secretary of the college (1952–60). Over her long life she investigated psychic phenomena and assisted in the training of mediums in Britain. She cooperated with **John F. Thomas** of Detroit, Michigan, by acting as a "proxy sitter" in experiments over a period of 16 years. (A proxy sitter substitutes for the individual seeking information from a medium in order to eliminate the possibility of telepathy between the medium and sitter.) Hankey died in April 1978.

Sources:

Hankey, Muriel A. *James Hewat McKenzie, Pioneer of Psychical Research.* London: Aquarian Press, 1963.

Pleasants, Helene, ed. *Biographical Dictionary of Parapsychology.* New York: Helix Press, 1964.

Hanon-Tramp

German name for a classical type of **nightmare.** This particular nightmare took the form of a demon that suffocated people during sleep. It was called "Dianus" by the French peasantry and was believed to be what is referred to in Psalm 91 as "the destruction that wasteth at noon-day," since it was supposed that people were most exposed to its attacks at that time. It suffocated by pressing on the breast and thus restricting the lungs. This kind of nightmare is related to belief in the **incubus,** a demon having intercourse with human beings during sleep, the Scandinavian *mara,* and the **vampire.**

Hansel, C(harles) E(dward) M(ark) (1917–)

British lecturer in psychology who wrote many articles on parapsychology. Hansel was born on October 12, 1917, at Bedford, England. He attended Cambridge University (M.A., 1950) and joined the faculty at the University of Manchester, England, as a lecturer in psychology in 1949.

Hansel emerged as a leading critical voice in parapsychology. Quite outspoken concerning psychical research in general, he concluded from his study of its history that "the first forty years of psychical research produced nothing that could be regarded as scientific evidence for supernatural processes. It was in the main, a history of fraud, imposture, and crass stupidity." In 1966 he published his most important book in the field, *ESP: A Scientific Evaluation.* He also wrote a number of articles and participated in the **Committee for the Scientific Investigation of Claims of the Paranormal.**

Sources:

Hansel, C. E. M. "A Critical Analysis of the Pearce-Pratt Experiment." *Journal of Parapsychology* (June 1961).

———. "A Critical Analysis of the Pratt-Woodruff Experiment." *Journal of Parapsychology* (June 1961).

———. "A Critical Review of the Experiments on Mr. Basil Shackleton and Mrs. Gloria Stewart." *Proceedings* of the Society for Psychical Research (May 1960).

———. *ESP: A Scientific Evaluation.* New York: Charles Scribner's Sons, 1966. Rev. ed. as *ESP and Parapsychology: A Critical Reevaluation.* Buffalo, N.Y.: Prometheus, 1980.

———. "Experimental Evidence for Extrasensory Perception." *Nature* (1959–60).

———. "Experiments on Telepathy." *New Scientist* (February 1959).

———. "Experiments on Telepathy in Children: A Reply to Sir Cyril Burt." *British Journal of Statistical Psychology* (November 1960).

Pleasants, Helene, ed. *Biographical Dictionary of Parapsychology.* New York: Helix Press, 1964.

Hansen, F. C. C.

Danish scholar known as the proponent of a theory of "involuntary whispering" to account for apparent thought transference (i.e., **telepathy**). The theory, originally published as a pamphlet in German, was discussed at some length in the *Journal* of the Society for Psychical Research (SPR) (vol. 9) and the *Proceedings* of the SPR (vols. 12 and 14).

Sources:

Hansen, F. C. C., and Alfred Lehmann. "Über unwilkürliches Flüstern: Eine kritische und experimentelle Untersuchung der sogenannten Gedankenübertragung." *Philosophische Studien* 11, no. 4 (1895).

Hantu Penyardin

Term for a **vampire** in Malayan superstition.

Hantu Pusaka

Term for a demon in Malayan superstition.

Hanussen, Erik Jan (1889–1933)

Extraordinary stage clairvoyant who made a great reputation in Germany during the 1920s and 1930s, combining blatant trickery with the most astounding mental phenomena. Because of the accuracy of his predictions he became known as "the Devil's Prophet." Born Heinrich Steinschneider on July 2, 1889, he was the son of a synagogue caretaker. At an early age he left school to join a circus, where he became a knife thrower, fire eater, and professional strong man. He served in World War I, and when his company was cut off from water supplies Hanussen demonstrated a weird talent for water witching without apparatus. He was eventually transferred to headquarters to entertain troops.

After the war he built up a reputation as strong man at the Ronacher Circus in Vienna and demonstrated stage **clairvoyance** at music halls. During one routine performance he suddenly foretold details of the discovery of a local murderer before they were printed in newspapers. At the same demonstration he privately informed an elegant woman that she was the baroness Prawitz, unhappily married, and that within a month she would leave her husband and become his mistress in Berlin, although the affair would eventually break up.

Meanwhile Hanussen found himself on trial in the Czech town of Leitmeritz, charged with extracting money under false pretenses by claiming to forecast the future. With arrogant poise Hanussen correctly told the state prosecutor the contents of his pockets, the judge the contents of his attache case, and gave other information about court officials. When the judge protested that this was just music hall telepathy, Hanussen retorted that he would give further proof of his powers. He stated that at that moment there was a man standing on platform 2 at the Leitmeritz railway station who had just burgled the Commercial Bank and had the money in his briefcase, and that the train was due in four minutes' time. Police rushed to the station and found that Hanussen was right! The bank robber was arrested and Hanussen acquitted.

This case made Hanussen famous, and he became a star at the Scala Theatre in Berlin during the 1920s. The baroness Prawitz also felt an irresistible compulsion to join him as his mistress and was further humiliated by being obliged to dress in a revealing costume and act as his stage assistant "Jane."

In 1929, at a Scala performance, Hanussen told a banker that there was a short circuit in his strong room, which had 360,000 marks in the safes, and there were just over three minutes left to telephone for the fire engines. It happened just as Hanussen predicted. There was no evidence of fraud or collusion, and an electrical fault in a secure strong room of a securely locked bank would have been difficult to fake.

In spite of such sensationally accurate predictions, Hanussen also cold-bloodedly engaged an assistant to ferret out information and gossip for his regular stage performances to avoid having to rely solely on clairvoyance.

With the Nazi rise to power, Hanussen obtained a favorable status as an honorary Aryan, but overreached himself at a séance for party members at which his medium predicted the burning of a large building as a signal for revolt. With the burning of the

Reichstag, Hanussen became an embarrassment to the Nazis, and in March 1933 he was taken for a car ride and murdered by three Nazi party members. As it happens, he had earlier told one of his mistresses that he felt his end was near.

Although little known outside Europe, Hanussen was a celebrity in prewar Germany and Austria, and in 1955 a German film company made a film about his life in which this strange charlatan and clairvoyant was represented as an anti-Nazi martyr. In 1989, he was the subject of another movie in the United States.

Sources:

Hanussen, Erik Jan. *Meine Lebenslinie.* Berlin, 1930.

Tabori, Paul. *Companions of the Unseen.* London, 1968.

Haraldsson, Erlendur (1931–)

Icelandic psychologist and parapsychologist, born in 1931 near Reykjavik, Iceland. Haraldsson graduated from Reykjavik Gymnasium in 1954, studied languages and philosophy at the University of Edinburgh, Scotland (1955–56), and completed his studies at the University of Freiburg, Germany (1957–58). He was a journalist for a few years in Reykjavik, then worked as a freelance writer in Berlin, the Middle East, and India.

After being away from school for a number of years, he returned to college to study psychology at the University of Freiburg (1964–66) and then at the University of Munich (1966–69), where he graduated with an advanced degree in psychology. While completing a doctorate, he spent two years in the United States as first a research fellow at the **Institute for Parapsychology** in Durham, North Carolina (1969–70), and then as an intern in clinical psychology in the Department of Psychiatry at the University of Virginia Medical School (1970–71). He obtained his Ph.D. from the University of Freiburg (under parapsychologist **Hans Bender**) in February 1972. His dissertation dealt with vasomotor reactions as indicators of extrasensory perception.

Haraldsson returned to the United States for two years (1972–74) as a research associate at the **American Society for Psychical Research** (ASPR) before assuming a position in psychology at the University of Iceland. Over the years he contributed many papers to *Journal* of the ASPR, the *Journal* of the Society for Psychical Research (SPR), London, and other publications. His interests ranged from the phenomena of Sri Sathya Sai Baba to ESP scores to psychic healing in Iceland and the investigation of mediums. He is best known for his work with Karlis Osis of the ASPR on deathbed observations.

Sources:

Berger, Arthur S., and Joyce Berger. *The Encyclopedia of Parapsychology and Psychical Research.* New York: Paragon House, 1991.

Haraldsson, Erlendur. *Miracles Are My Visiting Cards: An Investigative Report on Psychic Phenomena Associated with Sri Sathya Sai Baba.* 1978. Reprinted as *Modern Miracles.* New York: Fawcett Columbine, 1988.

———. "Representative National Surveys of Psychic Phenomena: Iceland, Great Britain, Sweden, USA and Gallup's Multinational Survey." *Journal* of the Society for Psychical Research 53, no. 801.

———. "The Sai Baba Enigma." In *Miracles,* edited by Martin Ebon. New York: New American Library, 1981.

Haraldsson, Erlendur, and L. R. Gissurarson. "The Icelandic Medium Indridi Indridason." *Proceedings* of the Society for Psychical Research 57 (1989).

Osis, Karlis, and Erlendur Haraldsson. *At the Hour of Death.* New York: Avon, 1977. Rev. ed. New York: Hastings House, 1980.

———. "Deathbed Observations by Physicians and Nurses: A Cross-cultural Survey." In *Signet Handbook of Parapsychology,* edited by Martin Ebon. New York: New American Library, 1978.

Harary, Keith (1953–)

Parapsychologist, born February 9, 1953, best known as a subject in parapsychological experiments in out-of-body experiences. During the early 1970s, under the name Stuart Blue Harary, he worked with the Psychical Research Foundation on experiments during which he seemed to interact with a kitten while out of his body. During these same years, he was research consultant with the **American Society for Psychical Research** (1970–71) and was a research consultant with the **Foundation for Research on the Nature of Man** (1972). He graduated magna cum laude from Duke University (B.A., 1975) and completed his doctorate at the graduate school of the Union Institute (1986).

Since 1982, when he changed his name to Keith Harary, he has had a dual role as a trained psychologist and a subject of parapsychological research. Following graduation he became a writer and lecturer on parapsychological topics. It has been his hope to promote the practical applications of **psi.** In the early 1980s he worked with **Russell Targ** and became known for his predictions concerning silver futures for one of Targ's clients. In 1985 he cowrote *The Mind Race* with Targ. Through the 1980s he worked to popularize parapsychology and to educate people about their individual abilities to experience psychic events of an uplifting and expansive nature. In this endeavor he wrote a series of popular texts with Patricia Weintraub. He has written widely for parapsychological journals as well as for more popular mass-circulation periodicals. In 1984 he was chairman and organizer of the first national "Psychology of Extended Abilities" conference at the **Esalen Institute.**

Sources:

Harary, Stuart Blue [Keith Harary]. "A Personal Perspective on Out-of-Body Experiences." In *Mind Beyond the Body: The Mystery of ESP Projection,* edited by D. Scott Rogo. New York: Penguin Books, 1978.

Harary, Keith, and Patricia Weintraub. *The Creative Sleep Program.* New York: St. Martin's Press, 1989.

———. *The Erotic Fulfillment Program.* New York: St. Martin's Press, 1990.

———. *The Free Flight Program.* New York: St. Martin's Press, 1989.

———. *Have an Out-of-Body Experience in 30 Days.* New York: St. Martin's Press, 1990.

Targ, Russell, and Keith Harary. *The Mind Race: Understanding and Using Psychic Abilities.* New York: Villard Books, 1984.

Harbinger of Light, The

The first Australian Spiritualist magazine, founded by William Terry in 1870 in Melbourne, published monthly.

Harding, Douglas E. (1909–)

British mystic whose teaching resembles a very practical application of Hindu jnana yoga and Zen Buddhist teachings. Harding was born at Lowestoft, Sussex, England, into a fundamentalist Christian family, his parents being members of the Plymouth Brethren. He studied architecture at University College, London. After breaking with the Plymouth Brethren, he was disowned by his parents and suffered a loss of religious faith until he spontaneously rediscovered the secret of mystical identity taught in various religions.

His own awakening was a matter of patient trial and error, which he went through while still pursuing his profession as an architect in India and Britain, as is described in his books *On Having No Head* (1971) and *Me, The Science of the 1st Person* (1975). Harding pursued the method of direct first-person experience of "headlessness," involving exercises in achieving identity and awareness. In this endeavor, Harding recalled the classic Hindu mystical question "Who am I?" expounded by **Sri Ramana Maharshi** and other sages, but beginning at a pragmatic level of physical awareness and culminating in a kind of Western-style Zen insight.

Harding lived in Suffolk, England, but spent time traveling through Europe and the United States lecturing and conducting experiential workshops.

Sources:

Harding, Douglas E. *The Hierarchy of Heaven and Earth.* Gainesville, Fla.: University of Florida Press, 1979.

———. *On Having No Head.* 1971. Reprint, Boston: Arkana, 1986.

Hardy, Mary M. (ca. 1875)

Boston, Massachusetts, medium through whom, in 1875, the first paraffin casts of **hands of spirits** were obtained. Hardy gave séances in public halls before hundreds of spectators. On the platform there was a table, the cloth of which reached to the ground. Two vessels, containing liquid paraffin and cold water, were placed under the table. The lights were turned down, but spectators were able to see the medium sitting motionless. After about a quarter of an hour **raps** were heard and a paraffin mold was found floating on the water.

Hardy was investigated by **William Denton,** who conducted many careful experiments.

In 1875 Hardy visited Europe and gave séances in England and on the Continent. For an account of a séance in 1876 under rigid test conditions, during which molds of spirit hands were produced, see the British periodical *The Spiritualist* (1878, p. 168).

Hardy, Sir Alister Clavering (1896–1985)

Zoologist who was very active in the field of parapsychology. Hardy was born February 10, 1896, at Nottingham, England. He attended Oundle School and Exeter College, Oxford (M.A., D.Sc.). In 1920 he was a Christopher Welch Biological Research Scholar and Oxford Biological Scholar at Stazione Zoologica, Naples, Italy, after which he became an assistant naturalist with the Fisheries Department, Ministry of Agriculture and Fisheries, in England (1921–24) and chief zoologist on the *Discovery* expedition (1924–28).

In 1928 Hardy began his lengthy tenure (1928–42) as professor of zoology and oceanography at University College, Hull. In 1939 he was awarded the Scientific Medal of the Zoological Society of England. He spent three years (1942–45) as regius professor of natural history at the University of Aberdeen, Scotland, and in 1946 settled at Oxford University as Linacre Professor of Zoology and Comparative Anatomy, where he spent the rest of his life. He was knighted in 1957.

In addition to his work on zoology, oceanography, and marine ecology, Hardy took a keen interest in the significance of psychical research for biology, and as a member of the council of the **Society for Psychical Research** (SPR), London, he sought to bring psychical and biological studies closer together. He made his views clear in his 1953 article "Biology and Psychical Research." He went on to write several important books, including *The Living Stream: A Restatement of Evolution Theory and its Relation to the Spirit of Man* (1965); *The Divine Flame* (1966); *The Challenge of Chance* (with R. Harvie and A. Koestler, 1973); *The Biology of God* (1975); and *The Spiritual Nature of Man* (1979). He served as president of the SPR from 1965 to 1969.

In 1969 Hardy founded the **Religious Experience Research Unit** at Manchester College, Oxford, and as its director he collected and analyzed firsthand accounts of religious experiences. These he specifically distinguished from psychical experiences involving **ESP.** He held a firm religious belief in "a Power which is greater than, and in part lies beyond the individual self."

Hardy died in Oxford May 23, 1985, at age 89. The Alister Hardy Research Center is located at 29-31 George St., Oxford OX1 2BR, England.

Sources:

Berger, Arthur S., and Joyce Berger. *The Encyclopedia of Parapsychology and Psychical Research.* New York: Paragon House, 1991.

Hardy, Sir Alister. "Biology and Psychical Research." *Proceedings* of the Society for Psychical Research 50, no. 183 (1953).

———. *The Biology of God.* London: Jonathan Cape, 1975.

———. *The Divine Flame.* London: Collins, 1966.

———. *The Living Stream: A Restatement of Evolution Theory and its Relation to the Spirit of Man.* London: Collins, 1965.

———. *The Spiritual Nature of Man.* Oxford: Clarendon, 1979.

———. "Telepathy and Evolutionary Theory." *Journal* of the Society for Psychical Research 35 (1950).

Hardy, Sir Alister, R. Harvie, and Arthur Koestler. *The Challenge of Chance: Experiment and Speculations.* London: Hutchinson, 1973.

Pleasants, Helene, ed. *Biographical Dictionary of Parapsychology.* New York: Helix Press, 1964.

Hare, Robert (1781–1858)

Nineteenth-century professor of chemistry at the University of Pennsylvania and early advocate of **Spiritualism.** Among his scientific discoveries was the oxy-hydrogen blowpipe. He wrote more than 150 scientific papers as well as additional papers on various political and moral questions.

Hare was born in Philadelphia January 17, 1781, and studied at the University of Philadelphia, where he filled the chair of chemistry from 1818 to 1847. As a high-ranking scientist of the day, he was one of the first scientific authorities to denounce early American Spiritualism in the press. In 1853 he wrote that he considered it "an act of duty to his fellow creatures to bring whatever influence he possessed to the attempt to stem the tide of popular madness which, in defiance of reason and science, was fast setting in favour of the gross delusion called spiritualism." So at age 72 he began his investigations and devised a number of instruments that, contrary to his expectations, conclusively proved, he believed, that a power and intelligence other than that of those present was at work.

His first apparatus was a wooden board about four feet long, supported on a fulcrum about a foot from one end, and at the other end attached by a hook to a spring balance. A glass vessel filled with water was placed on the board near the fulcrum; a wire gauze cage attached to an independent support, not touching the glass at any point, was placed in the water. The medium would affect the balance by simply placing his hand into the wire cage. The medium Hare tested was **Henry Gordon.** The balance showed variations of weight amounting to 18 pounds. This apparatus had similarities to that used later by **Sir William Crookes** to test the medium **D. D. Home.**

A second apparatus consisted of a revolving disk attached to a table in such a manner that the movements of the table actuated the pointer, which ran around the letters of the alphabet printed on the circumference of the disk and spelled out messages. The disk was arranged so that the medium could not see the letters. Hare's book *Experimental Investigation of the Spirit Manifestation,* published in 1855, sums up the results:

"The evidence may be contemplated under various phases; first, those in which rappings or other noises have been made which could not be traced to any mortal agency; secondly, those in which sounds were so made as to indicate letters forming grammatical, well-spelt sentences, affording proof that they were under the guidance of some rational being; thirdly, those in which the nature of the communication has been such as to prove that the being causing them must, agreeably to accompanying allegations, be some known acquaintance, friend, or relative of the inquiry.

"Again, cases in which movements have been made of ponderable bodies of a nature to produce intellectual communications resembling those obtained, as above-mentioned, by sounds.

"Although the apparatus by which these various proofs were attained with the greatest possible precaution and precision, modified them as to the manner, essentially all the evidence which I have obtained tending to the conclusions above mentioned, has likewise been substantially obtained by a great number of observers. Many who never sought any spiritual communications and have not been induced to enrol themselves as

Spiritualists, will nevertheless not only affirm the existence of the sounds and movements, but also admit their inscrutability."

The book, the second part of which describes the afterlife as depicted by the communicators, passed through five editions. Reaction was quick to set in against its influence. The professors of Harvard University passed a resolution denouncing Hare and his "insane adherence to a gigantic humbug." He was howled down by the American Association for the Advancement of Science when, in Washington in 1854, he tried to address members on the subject of Spiritualism. He finally paid for his convictions by resigning from his chair.

A. D. Ruggles, a professional medium who often wrote in languages unknown to him, was one of the subjects with whom Hare experimented. Later Hare himself evidently became a medium, as deduced from a letter he wrote to **John Worth Edmonds,** which contains this paragraph: "Having latterly acquired the powers of a medium in sufficient degree to interchange ideas with my spirit friends, I am no longer under the necessity of defending media from the charge of falsehood and deception. It is now my own character only that can be in question." The revelations Hare believed he received from the otherworld he took at face value. There was no careful sifting or criticism, and the belief that they apparently came from spirits appears to have attested their credibility for Hare. This simplistic acceptance of Spiritualism diminished Hare's reputation, especially among his former colleagues, in his later years. He died in Philadelphia May 15, 1858.

Sources:

Hare, Robert. *Experimental Investigation of the Spirit Manifestations.* New York: Partridge & Britten, 1855. Reprint, Elk Grove, Wis.: Sycamorte Press, 1963.

Harmonial Society

A Spiritualist organization founded in Benton County, Arkansas, in 1855 by former American Methodist minister T. E. Spencer and his wife. It was called Harmony Springs, and admission to membership was subject to the approval of the **controls** of the founder. Spencer taught that many spirits perished with the body, and that some languished after death but soon expired. However, those who followed his system, he expounded, would arrive at immortality here on Earth. Part of the price of that immortality was the surrender of the members' property to the founders. In the course of events some initiates began to doubt and made known their intentions to take legal measures to recover their property. The Spencers thereupon disappeared but were soon apprehended and sentenced to imprisonment.

Harodim

A degree of **Freemasonry** very popular in the north of England, especially in the county of Durham, and probably founded in Gateshead in 1681. It was brought under the Grand Lodge in 1735. Members were the custodians of the Ritual of All Masonry, or the Old York Ritual. There were nine lodges in all. A London version of this society was the Harodim-Rosy-Cross, of Jacobite origin, probably carried to London by the earl of Derwentwater. In 1787 a Grand Chapter of the Ancient and Venerable Order of Harodim was founded by William Preston, author of *Illustrations of Masonry* (1775).

Sources:

Preston, William. *Illustrations of Masonry.* London, 1775.

Harris, Melvin (1940–)

Contemporary British author, researcher, and radio commentator who has investigated claimed paranormal phenomena. His position is skeptical and has been bolstered by his own personal detailed research. After years of teaching and lecturing, Harris became a full-time broadcaster with BBC Radio, presenting dozens of programs on such topics as the history of the phonograph, unusual inventions, the telephone centenary, magnetic recording, and the story of the bassoon. He actually makes baroque oboes as a hobby, and the Melvin Harris Collection of early recordings of performances on wind instruments, at the University of Washington, Seattle, is the largest in the world.

He was a researcher for the television series *Arthur C. Clarke's Mysterious World* and *Strange Powers,* and was described by the producer Simon Welfare as "a great detective of the supernatural." His radio series *Strange to Relate* dealt with many classic mysteries and bizarre events of history, and his book *Sorry, You've Been Duped!* (1986) debunks many misconceptions about such well-known mysteries as the **Amityville Horror,** the **Bloxham Tapes,** the **Angels of Mons,** and mediums.

Based on scores of earlier books and articles about the celebrated **Jack the Ripper** case by other writers, his own book *Jack the Ripper: The Bloody Truth* (1987) exposes fake documents, doctored quotations, and falsified references on the subject. Harris concludes, in a well-argued presentation, that the probable identity of the Ripper was an occultist with a medical background who committed his grisly crimes as part of a black magic ritual. Harris claims that the Ripper was known to Theosophist **Mabel Collins** and also to journalist **W. T. Stead.**

Sources:

Harris, Melvin. *Jack the Ripper: The Bloody Truth.* London: Columbus Books, 1987.

———. *Sorry, You've Been Duped!* London: Weidenfeld and Nicolson, 1986.

Harris, Susannah (ca. 1920)

American direct voice medium (later known as Mrs. Harris Kay), pastor of a Spiritualist church in Columbus, Ohio, whose control was a child, "Harmony." The last years of her life were spent in England. After accusations of **fraud** against Harris, Abraham Wallace applied the water test, filling her mouth with water, which changed color according to the length of time it was affected by saliva. Wallace claimed to have established the independence of the medium's voices.

In 1913 and 1914 the Spiritualist journal *Light* contained many testimonies in favor of Harris's mediumship. In 1919 at Steinway Hall, London, while blindfolded, she executed a painting in oils upside down and nearly completed another in about two hours. However, in 1920 the Norwegian Society for Psychical Research published a very unfavorable report on 25 sittings held in Christiania. Proof was adduced that the German voice of "Rittmeister Hermann" was a fraud to which "Harmony" was an accomplice (*Light,* May 1, 1920). Harris was also accused of fraud at séances in Holland in 1914. She was defended by James Coates in *Is Spiritualism Based on Facts or Fancy?* (1920).

Sources:

Jong, K. H. "The Trumpet Medium Mrs. Harris." *Journal* of the Society for Psychical Research 16 (1914).

Harris, Thomas Lake (1823–1906)

Spiritualist mystic, poet, medium, and religious reformer. He was born at Fenny Stratford, England, May 15, 1823, and moved to the United States as a child. He became a Universalist minister at age 20 and was one of the small band of enthusiasts who gathered around **Andrew Jackson Davis** after the publication of *The Principles of Nature, Her Divine Relations, and a Voice to Mankind* in 1847.

In the same year Harris formally withdrew from the Universalist church and went on a lecture tour to spread the knowledge of the new revelation. On his return he broke off relations with Davis over his sexual views and behavior. Davis had associated with a married woman whose husband was still living and taught that if married partners discovered that they were no longer adapted to each other they ought to separate and seek truer affinities. Although Harris and Davis became reconciled after Davis married the woman in question, they never again worked together.

Harris became pastor of the First Independent Christian Society of New York. In 1851 he joined the **Apostolic Circle** at Auburn, New York, under the leadership of J. L. Scott, a Baptist preacher. Scott, a trance speaker, had come to believe that he was the chosen vessel of St. John. Harris's imagination was fueled by messages coming through a Mrs. Benedict, the official medium of the movement, stating that St. Paul was expected to communicate and that Harris might be the fortunate mouthpiece. He went to Auburn and in joint editorship with Scott published a new periodical, *Disclosures from the Interior and Superior Care of Mortals.*

The **Mountain Cove Community** was founded soon afterward. The faithful band of settlers yielded themselves and all their possessions to Scott, the "perfect medium." Harris did not join the community. When dissent arose and a break was threatening, however, Scott went to New York and induced Harris to come to the rescue. Because Harris prevailed upon several men of property to follow them, the crisis was averted. There were now two "perfect mediums," and Harris, as the representative of St. Paul, assumed directing influence. His autocratic rule did not last long, however, and after a revolt developed, he left for New York to preach **Spiritualism** at Dodworth Hall, then the headquarters of the movement.

During November and December 1853, in a state of trance or inspiration, he dictated his first great poetic composition: *An Epic of the Starry Heavens.* According to Arthur A. Cuthbert's biography, the poem germinated in Harris's subconscious three years and nine months before its dictation, and its 6,000 lines were delivered in 21 sittings from November 24 to December 8, 1853, in 26 hours and 16 minutes. Cuthbert also recorded that Harris was, from his earliest childhood, a remarkable poetical improvisatore. In proof of this he quotes a letter from Richard M'Cully's *The Brotherhood of the New Life* (1893), which states: "When in Utica he would come to my sitting room of an evening, and sitting down in a rather high chair, he would compose poetry by the mile; and it was really poetry—exquisite thoughts exquisitely worded."

An Epic of the Starry Heavens was followed by *The Lyric of the Morning Land* and *A Lyric of the Golden Age,* both similarly dictated in a state of trance. Of the former, a poem of 5,000 words of great beauty, Harris claimed entire ignorance in his conscious state. He spoke and sang it during parts of 14 days in about 30 hours. It was finished by August 4, 1854. *A Lyric of the Golden Age* reflects the higher ideals of the British romantics—Lord Byron, Percy Shelley, Samuel Taylor Coleridge, and others—whom Harris actually claimed, along with Dante, as his inspirers.

In view of such impressive performances, Harris aspired to be the leader of the Spiritualist movement. Rebuffed, his attitude underwent a singular change. He professed to be the champion of Christianity versus Spiritualistic Pantheism and published his *Song of Satan,* in which the communicating spirits, with the exception of those who visited Harris's "Sacred Family," are declared to be demons in the worst sense of the word. Yet apparently he himself was not immune to the influence of these demons. In his life work, *Arcana of Christianity* (1857), he complains of obsession in writing: "It was resolved upon by Evil Spirits that my physical existence should be destroyed, the demon, by name Joseph Balsamo, planned a subtle scheme to bring to bear upon the enfeebled physical system the magic of the Infernal World."

Fairies occupied a large place in Harris's esoteric system. There is a long discussion of them in the *Arcana* under the title "The Divine Origin of the Fay." He claimed constant intercourse with fairyland and poured forth a number of communications in which the "Little Brothers" playfully called him "Little Yabbit." The publication of Harris's own following, *The Herald of Light* (1857–61), was called "a journal of the Lord's New Church" and was almost entirely written by Harris.

In 1859 he announced to his congregation in New York that the spirits had entrusted him with the mission of going to England and preaching there. He arrived in May 1859, and, in inspirational addresses of striking eloquence, preached his mystic Christianity in both London and various provincial centers. In his first sermon he presented "in bold relief the danger of Spiritualists giving themselves up to production of physical phenomena, and allowing their minds to be held captive by the teachings of the low forms of Spiritualism." The *Morning Advertiser* interpreted the sermon as "an extraordinary and triumphant exposure of Spiritualism."

In his *History of the Supernatural* (1863), **William Howitt** waxes eloquent in paying great tribute to Harris's oratorical mastery:

"His extempore sermons were the only realisation of my conceptions of eloquence; at once full, unforced, outgushing, unstinted and absorbing. They were triumphant embodiments of sublime poetry, and a stern unsparing, yet loving and burning theology. Never since the days of Fox were the disguises of modern society so unflinchingly rent away, and the awful distance betwixt real Christianity and its present counterfeit made so startlingly apparent. That the preacher was also the prophet was most clearly proclaimed, by his sudden hastening home, declaring that it was revealed to him that the nethermost hells were let loose in America. This was before the public breach betwixt North and South had taken place. But it soon followed, only too deeply to demonstrate the truths of the spiritual intimation."

Laurence Oliphant, a brilliant writer and politician, and Lady Oliphant, his mother, the widow of former chief justice of Ceylon, came under Harris's influence during his stay in England. Oliphant was a man of varied career. He had been on various diplomatic missions, was private secretary to Lord Elgin during his vice-royalty of India, was secretary of legation in Japan, was special correspondent of *The Times* in Crimea, and was a member of Parliament for the Stirling Burghs in 1865. During his two years of parliamentary life he observed unbroken silence in obedience to Harris's influence.

In 1867 Harris decided to impose a more severe probation. Oliphant disappeared from London and was not seen until 1870. He was summoned to the United States to work as a manual laborer at "The Use," the theo-socialistic community and the headquarters of Harris's own movement, the Brotherhood of the New Life. Harris had founded the community in 1861 on a small farm near Wassaic, New York. The Holy Ghost (i.e., the "Divine Breath") was expected to descend in seven stages upon the members of this community. It appears, however, that Harris and subsequently his wife were the only ones who attained the seventh stage. The practice of "open breathing," a form of respiration to bring the divine breath into the body, resembles *pranayama* or yoga breathing.

In 1863 The Use moved to Amenia, about four miles from Wassaic, where a mill was purchased and the First National Bank of Amenia was founded under Harris's presidency. This site was soon given up for a settlement in Brockton, on the shore of Lake Erie, which was bought largely with Lady Oliphant's money. Laurence Oliphant was ordered to report to Brockton, and the first task he was assigned was to clean a stable. According to **Frank Podmore,** the stable must have been of Augean dimensions, because Oliphant was engaged in it for many days in absolute loneliness, sleeping in a loft that was furnished with only a mattress and empty orange boxes. His meals were brought to him by a silent messenger. He was rarely allowed to see his mother, to whom he was very much attached.

After a period of probation, Harris allowed Oliphant to go out into the world. During the Franco-Prussian war Oliphant acted as correspondent for *The Times* but always held himself in readiness to return if Harris summoned him. He met his future wife in 1872. Harris withheld his consent to the marriage and only agreed when the woman placed all her property in his hands. After the marriage had taken place, the couple were summoned to Brockton. Harris's wife was assigned to housework, and Oliphant was quickly dispatched to New York to labor for the community as director of a cable company. For years husband and wife were kept apart. For a period of three years Oliphant was not even allowed to see his wife. During that time Mrs. Oliphant was sent out of the community penniless and alone to earn her living.

In 1880 Harris permitted their reunion in Europe, after his community had migrated to Santa Rosa, California. The grape and wine culture that they had begun in Amenia was developed to a profitable industry in the new settlement.

In the meantime Oliphant's mother was reported to be dying. Laurence went to bid her farewell. When she died, the spell in which he was held by Harris was broken. He charged Harris with fraud and, with the help of friends, recovered a considerable part of his fortune.

Nevertheless, until the end of his days in December 1888, Oliphant persisted in the belief that Harris had genuine psychic powers. Harris's hold on his followers was very strong. They implicitly believed him when in 1891 he announced that he had discovered the **elixir of life** and had thereby renewed his youth. Consequently, when he died March 23, 1906, his disciples refused to believe in his death and only acknowledged the fact three months later.

Sources:

Cuthbert, Arthur A. *The Life and World Work of Thomas Lake Harris, Written from Direct Personal Knowledge.* Glasgow, Scotland, 1908.

Harris, Thomas Lake. *Brotherhood of the New Life: Its Fact, Law, Method, and Purpose.* Fountain Grove, Calif.: Fountain Grove Press, 1891.

———. *An Epic of the Starry Heaven.* New York: Partridge & Britten, 1854.

———. *A Lyric of the Golden Age.* New York: Partridge & Britten, 1856.

———. *The New Republic.* Santa Rosa, Calif.: Fountain Grove Press, 1891.

Hine, Robert V. *California's Utopian Colonies.* New Haven, Conn.: Yale University Press, 1966.

Kagan, Paul. *New World Utopias.* Baltimore, Md.: Penguin, 1975.

Noyes, John Humphrey. *History of American Socialisms.* Lippincott, 1870. Reprinted as *Strange Cults and Utopias of 19th-Century America.* New York: Dover, 1966.

Schneider, Herbert Wallace. *A Prophet and a Pilgrim, Being the Incredible History of Thomas Lake Harris and Laurence Oliphant: Their Sexual Mysticisms and Utopian Communities.* New York: Columbia University Press, 1942.

Swainson, William P. *Thomas Lake Harris and His Occult Teaching.* London: William Rider & Son, 1922.

Hart, Hornell (Norris) (1888–1967)

American professor of sociology and parapsychologist. Hart was born August 2, 1888, in St. Paul, Minnesota. He studied at Oberlin College, Ohio (B.A., 1910), the University of Wisconsin (M.A. sociology, 1914), and the State University of Iowa (Ph.D. child welfare and sociology, 1921). He was a faculty member successively at Bryn Mawr College (1924–33), Hartford Theological Seminary (1933–38), Duke University (1938–57), Centre College of Kentucky (1957–60), and Florida Southern College (1960–67). He developed an early interest in parapsychology and was a charter member of the **Parapsychological Association** and a member of the **American Society for Psychical Research** and the **Society for Psychical Research.**

Hart was a widely published and respected scholar in sociology. Also, as early as the 1930s he began to publish in parapsychology. His special concerns were apparitions and the evidence for **survival,** the latter topic being the subject of his major book, *The Enigma of Survival: The Case For and Against an After-Life* (1959). He discusses the question of **out-of-the-body travel** or "astral projection" in his article "Man Outside His Body?" (*Tomorrow,* winter 1954). His culminating statements about his explorations are presented in his final book, *Toward a New Philosophical Basis for Parapsychological Phenomena* (1965). He died in 1967.

Sources:

Berger, Arthur S., and Joyce Berger. *The Encyclopedia of Parapsychology and Psychical Research.* New York: Paragon House, 1991.

Hart, Hornell N. *The Enigma of Survival: The Case For and Against an After-Life.* Springfield, Ill.: Charles C. Thomas, 1959.

———. "ESP Projection: Spontaneous Cases and the Experimental Method." *Journal* of the American Society for Psychical Research (1954).

———. *Living Religion.* New York: Abingdon Press, 1937.

———. "The Psychic Fifth Dimension." *Journal* of the American Society for Psychical Research (1953).

———. "Psychical Research and the Methods of Science." *Journal* of the American Society for Psychical Research (1957).

———. "Six Theories About Apparitions." *Proceedings* of the Society for Psychical Research (May 1956).

———. *Skeptic's Quest.* New York: Macmillan, 1938.

———. *Toward a New Philosophical Basis for Parapsychological Phenomena.* New York: Parapsychological Foundation, 1965.

———. "Visions and Apparitions Collectively and Reciprocally Received." *Proceedings* of the Society for Psychical Research (May 1933).

———. *Your Share of God: Spiritual Power for Life Fulfillment.* Englewood Cliffs, N.J.: Prentice Hall, 1958.

Pleasants, Helene, ed. *Biographical Dictionary of Parapsychology.* New York: Helix Press, 1964.

Hartlaub, Gustav Friedrich (1884–1963)

German museum director and professor of art who studied the relationship of occultism and magic to art. He was born March 12, 1884, at Bremen, Germany, and later obtained his Ph.D. at Heidelberg University. In 1921 he became the director of the Municipal Art Museum in Mannheim, Germany, where he remained until fired by the Nazis in 1933. After World War II, he became a professor of art history at Heidelberg University in 1946. He worked there until his death on April 30, 1963.

Sources:

Hartlaub, Gustav Friedrich. *The Inexplicable: Study of the Magic World View.* N.p., 1951.

———. *Magic of the Mirror.* N.p., 1950.

———. *The Philosopher's Stone: Character and Image of Alchemy.* N.p., 1959.

Pleasants, Helene, ed. *Biographical Dictionary of Parapsychology.* New York: Helix Press, 1964.

Hartmann, (Carl Robert) Eduard von (1842–1906)

German philosopher and author of *The Philosophy of the Unconscious,* which laid the groundwork of both modern psychoanalysis and of phenomenology. Born February 23, 1842, in Berlin, Hartmann was originally educated for an army career but later turned to philosophy and was awarded his doctorate by the University of Rostock in 1867.

He was among the first to investigate **Spiritualism** in Germany. He tried to give a definite place to both physical and mental phenomena in his philosophy. In his book *Der Spiritismus* (1885), he offers the following analysis of Spirtualistic phenomena:

"A nervous force producing outside the limits of the human body mechanical and plastic effects. Duplicate hallucinations of this same nervous force and producing also physical and plastic effects. A latent, somnambulistic consciousness, capable (the subject being in his normal state) of reading in the intellectual background of another man, his present and his past, and being able to divine the future."

Hartmann died at Grosslichterfelde on June 5, 1906.

Sources:

Hartmann, Eduard von. *Der Spiritismus.* Translated by C. C. Massey as *Spiritism.* London: Psychological Press, 1885.

Hartmann, Franz (1838–1912)

Noted Theosophist and writer on occultism. Hartmann was born November 22, 1838, in Bavaria, Germany, though he claimed descent on his mother's side from the old Irish kings of Ulster. He became a physician and immigrated to the United States in 1865, traveling as a doctor to various cities and also visiting Indian tribes and studying their religious beliefs. He became interested in **Spiritualism** and later corresponded with leading Theosophists after the founding of the **Theosophical Society** in 1875.

Hartmann was invited to the society's headquarters at Adyar, India, where he lived during the furor over **Helena Petrovna Blavatsky**'s alleged miracle working. He published his own *Report of Observations During a Nine Months' Stay at the Headquarters of the Theosophical Society at Adyar (Madras), India* (1884).

When **Richard Hodgson** of the **Society for Psychical Research,** London, published his devastating exposure of claimed trickery and fraudulent phenomena by Blavatsky in 1885, Hartmann accompanied her to Europe and then returned to his hometown in Bavaria. There he claimed to have encountered a sect of secret **Rosicrucians** from whom he acquired many mystical insights. He was president of the Theosophical Society in Germany for a brief period, but eventually resigned to found independent societies. During his later years he spent much time in the Untersberg Mountains near Salzburg, Austria, where he believed he encountered gnomes, water nymphs, and other nature spirits and also wrote his more memorable books. He died at Kempten, Bavaria, August 7, 1912.

Sources:

Hartmann, Franz. *An Adventure Among the Rosicrucians.* Boston: Occult Publishing, 1887.

———. *In the Pronaos of the Temple of Wisdom.* London: Theosophical Society, 1890. Reprint, Chicago: Aries Press, 1941.

———. *Life and Doctrines of Paracelsus.* N.p., 1891.

———. *Magic, Black and White.* 1885. Reprint, New Hyde Park, N.Y.: University Books, 1970.

———. *Occult Science in Medicine.* N.p., 1893.

———. *The Principles of Astrological Geomancy.* Boston: Occult Publishing, 1889. Reprint, Mokulumne Hill, Calif.: Health Research, 1965.

———. *Report of Observations During a Nine Months' Stay at the Headquarters of the Theosophical Society at Adyar (Madras), India.* Madras, India: Scottish Press, 1884.

Haruspicy

Ancient system of **divination** using the entrails of animals. One method was to sacrifice animals to the gods, then inspect the intestines, spleen, kidneys, lungs, gall bladder, and liver. The shapes, colors, and markings of entrails were interpreted. Skilled haruspices or diviners also claimed to be able to interpret the condition of entrails from the outward appearances of animals, such as colors and shapes of eyes, ears, and other organs.

Haruspicy was practiced by ancient Assyrians, Babylonians, and Etruscans, as well as by African and South American tribes. Alternative terms for haruspicy include aruspicy and extispicy. Divination involving the liver of animals is a special branch of haruspicy called hepatoscopy.

Hasted, John B(arrett) (1921–)

British physicist who conducted important research in parapsychology and paraphysics. Hasted began his professional training as a chemist, then worked in the field of physics at the Clarendon Laboratory, Oxford, England, during World War II. He was responsible for important developments in the microwave region of the electromagnetic spectrum in communications and was a reader in physics at the University College of London. His published works include *Physics of Atomic Collisions* (1964) and *Aqueous Diaelectrics* (1973). He was also a professor of experimental physics at Birkbeck College, University of London.

Hasted conducted experiments on **psychokinesis** with the psychic **Uri Geller.** These experiments, together with those of colleagues David Bohm, Edward W. Bastin, and Brendan O'Regan, took place between February and September 1974 at Birkbeck College and were designed to investigate Geller's abilities in **metal bending,** deforming crystals, and activating a Geiger counter without touching it. Witnesses at some of the sessions included authors **Arthur Koestler** and **Arthur C. Clarke.** The results, which were largely successful, were reported in the paper "Experiments on Psychokinetic Phenomena," by Bohm, Bastin, Hasted, and O'Regan (1976). Hasted subsequently conducted experiments with many children who claimed to be able to reproduce the Geller effect.

Because there have been frequent criticisms that metal-bending experiments are not properly controlled and that children, in particular, are given to blatant **fraud,** Hasted took care to experiment under conditions in which touching the targets was ruled out and observers closely watched the experiments, some of which were videotaped.

Hasted also devoted special attention to what happens to metal during paranormal bending. The targets are connected with a strain gauge to register the strength of the deformation. Hasted suggests that children may have special aptitude in paranormal bending in the same way that they are often centers of disturbance in **poltergeist** phenomena. In contrast to **John Taylor,** author of *Superminds* (1975), who discounted the possibility of an electromagnetic phenomenon being involved, Hasted believes there is evidence of an electromagnetic field in paranormal metal bending.

Sources:

Hasted, John B. *The Metal-benders.* London: Routledge & Kegan Paul, 1981.

Hasted, John B., David Bohm, Edward W. Bastin, and Brendan O'Regan. "Experiments on Psychokinetic Phenomena." In *The Geller Papers: Scientific Observations on the Paranormal Powers of Uri Geller,* edited by Charles Panati. Boston, Mass.: Houghton Mifflin, 1976.

Taylor, John. *Science and the Supernatural.* New York: E. P. Dutton, 1980.

———. *Superminds.* London: Macmillan, 1975.

Hastings, Arthur Claude (1935–)

Assistant professor of speech and drama who has investigated paranormal phenomena. Born May 23, 1935, at Neosho, Missouri, Hastings studied at Tulane University (B.A., 1957) and Northwestern University (M.A., 1958). In 1960 he became a professor at the Department of Speech and Drama, University of Nevada. He is a member of the **Parapsychological Association.** In 1960 he investigated poltergeist phenomena in Gutenberg, Iowa, for the **Parapsychology Laboratory** at Duke University. In the 1970s he became associated with the Institute of Noetic Sciences and was a professor at the Institute of Transpersonal Psychology.

Sources:

Hastings, A. C. "Expectancy Set and 'Poltergeist' Phenomena." *ETC* 18, no. 3 (October 1961).

Hastings, A. C., James Fadiman, and James B. Gordon. *Health for the Whole Person.* Boulder, Colo.: Westview Press, 1980.

Hastings, A. C., and Stanley Krippner. "Poltergeist Phenomena and Expectancy Set." *Northwestern Tri-Quarterly* 3, no. 3 (Spring 1961).

Pleasants, Helene, ed. *Biographical Dictionary of Parapsychology.* New York: Helix Press, 1964.

Hastraun

A small mystical sect of Judaism located in some parts of Palestine and Babylon. Members practiced a form of communism and were also known as "fearers of sin."

Hatha Yoga

The ancient Hindu practice of physical exercise. Hatha yoga differs essentially from Western gymnastics in featuring static postures (**asanas**) instead of active movements and in being related to spiritual development. Though described in ancient Indian literature, the practice of hatha yoga had largely died out before being revived in the late nineteenth century.

The rebirth of hatha yoga, in large part a reaction to the emergence of modern science in India under British rule, can be traced to the careers of two men, Yogi Madhavdas and Shyam Sundar Goswami. After establishing an ashram near Guzrat in Western India, they trained two important students: Sri Yogendra, who introduced hatha yoga to the West, and Swami Kuvalayanand. Most of their students established schools in Bombay, and almost all modern practice of hatha yoga can be traced to people trained by the two men. In the 1920s, Shyam Sundar Goswami established work in Calcutta.

The Sanskrit syllable *ha* indicates the sun and *tha* the moon. The "yoga" or union of the sun and moon is through *pranayama,* believed to be the subtle vitality of breath and essence of food. Pranayama is induced by actual practice of the asanas and also by special breathing exercises and cleansing techniques.

Good physical health is regarded as an important step toward spiritual development rather than an end in itself. Thus, the traditional hatha yoga treatises insist upon *yama* and *niyama* (moral observances and ethical restraints) as an essential preliminary to yoga practice. These include: non-violence, not stealing, truthfulness, abstinence from sexual impropriety and greed, observance of purity, austerity, religious study, and faith in God. Without such observance, hatha yoga becomes merely a gymnastic achievement.

Of the theoretical 8,4000,000 asanas, 84 are said to be the best, and 32 the most useful for good health. Most of these are named after living creatures, e.g., cow, peacock, locust, cobra, lion, etc. An asana is considered to be mastered when the yogi can maintain the position without strain for three hours. Asanas develop flexibility in associated muscle groups throughout the body, and also affect the tone of veins and arteries, particularly through inverted positions such as the yoga headstand. Many asanas help develop maximum flexibility of the spine through a series of backward and forward bending positions at different points of gravity. Asanas are also claimed to improve the function of the ductless glands through persistent gentle pressure.

The mastery of basic asanas and associated cleansing techniques prepares the yogi for meditative positions, and the practice of mental concentration prepares him for detachment and meditation itself. When associated with special breathing techniques, the subtle current of the body (termed **prana**) flows through nerve channels, culminating in the arousal of a latent energy called **kundalini,** often pictured as a coiled snake resting at the base of the spine. The task of the yogi is to induce the kundalini energy to flow up the spine to a subtle center in the head, resulting in mystical or transcendental experience.

Sources:

Bernard, Theos. *Hatha Yoga.* New York: Columbia University Press, 1944. Reprint, London, 1950. Reprint, New York: Samuel Weiser, 1970.

Dvivedi, M. N., trans. *The Yoga-Sutras of Patanjali.* Madras, India: Theosophical Publishing House, 1890.

Iyangar, Yogi S., trans. *Hatha-Yoga-Pradipika of Svatmarama Svamin.* Madras, India: Theosophical Publishing House, 1893.

Iyengar, B. K. S. *Light on Yoga.* New York: Schrocken Books, 1977.

Majumdar, S. M. *Introduction to Yoga Principles & Practices.* New Hyde Park, N.Y.: University Books, 1964.

Vishnudevananda, Swami. *The Complete Illustrated Book of Yoga.* New York: Bell, 1960. Reprint, New York: Pocket Books, 1971.

Hauffe, Frederica (1801–1829)

"The Seeress of Prevorst," as described in *Die Seherin von Prevorst* (1829) by **Justinus Kerner.** Hauffe was born in the village of Prevorst near Löwenstein, Wüttemburg, Germany, in 1801. She married in 1819, and from that time until her death ten years later she was bedridden, subject to various ailments. She had convulsive fits and became rigid like a corpse; in this state she was possessed by spirits. She saw clairvoyantly, made predictions, and exhibited a wide range of psychic phenomena. At one time she spoke only in verse for three days. Occasionally she reportedly saw her own **double,** clad in white and seated on a chair, while she was lying in bed.

She drew with tremendous speed perfect geometrical designs in the dark, used the **divining rod** with great skill, exhibited disturbances of a **poltergeist** character, and communicated extraordinary revelations from the spirit world. The spirits of the dead were said to be in constant attendance on her and allegedly were occasionally seen by others. Kerner himself once observed in her bedroom a grey pillar of cloud that seemed to have a head. Kerner also recorded an instance of Hauffe's seeing with the **stomach,** which is related to **eyeless sight.**

Troubled spirits of the dead came to Hauffe for help and disclosed secrets of the doings on Earth that had made them restless. They made various noises, rapped, threw things about, pulled off Hauffe's boots with violence (in Kerner's presence), extinguished the nightlight, and made the candle glow.

Hauffe's Teachings

Hauffe taught while in a trance state, primarily emphasizing the triune doctrine of body, soul, and spirit. She taught that the soul is clothed by an ethereal body ("Nervengeist") that carries on the vital processes when the body is in trance and the soul wanders about. After death it withdraws with the soul but later decays and leaves the soul free.

The unique part of the spiritual revelations of the Seeress of Prevorst consisted of her description of systems of circles—sun circles and life circles—corresponding to spiritual conditions and the passage of time. They were illustrated by amazing diagrams. The interpretation was furnished partly by ciphers, partly by words of a primeval language written in primitive ideographs. On the basis of these revelations, a mystic circle was founded and members claimed that the teachings disclose analogies with the philosophical ideas of Pythagoras, Plato, and others. They issued a journal, *Blätter aus Prevorst,* 12 volumes of which were published from 1832 to 1839.

Universal Language

The "universal language" described by the Seeress of Prevorst compares, as in the case of **John Dee,** with Hebrew. A philologist also discovered in it a resemblance to Coptic and Arabic. Hauffe claimed that it was the language of the inner life. The written characters, preserved by Kerner, were always connected with numbers. Some of them are as complicated as an Egyptian hieroglyph. Hauffe said that the words with numbers had a much deeper significance than those without numbers. In this respect the language had affinity with Hebrew **gematria,** a forerunner of modern **numerology.** The names of things in this language expressed the properties and qualities of the things. Hauffe spoke it quite fluently and in time her listeners vaguely understood her. Kerner quoted a few words of the language in his book.

In 1823 Hauffe gave birth to a child who was also seized with spasms and convulsions and died within a few months. In January 1829 Hauffe, in trance state, announced that she had only four months to live, but in spite of severe illness she was still living in May. She stated, "It is hard to know the moment of one's death" and continued to see visions of specters and a coffin. Three days before her death she stated that she could not endure another three days. She died August 5, 1829.

Sources:

Kerner, Justinus. *Die Seherin von Prevorst.* 1829. Abridged and translated as *The Seeress of Prevorst.* London, 1845. Reprint, Stuttgart: J. F. Steinkopf, 1963.

Smith, Eleanor Touhey. *Psychic People.* New York: William Morrow, 1968.

Haunt Hunters

Founded in 1965 as a division of the Psychic Science Institute to serve as a clearinghouse for experiences and information on **ghosts, hauntings, extrasensory perception,** and other psychic phenomena. It seeks to improve the image of psychical research through public relations techniques and strives to bring together the qualified psychical researcher and the individual who has had a psychic experience. It maintains a speakers bureau and a file of more than 300 case histories of psychic phenomena. It has published *The Haunt Hunters Handbook for the Psychic Investigator.* Address: c/o Goodwilling, 2188 Sycamore Hill Ct., Chesterfield, MO 63017.

Haunted Houses

About 1919, a number of British newspapers contained an advertisement offering for sale "an ancient Gothic Mansion, known as Beckington Castle, ten miles from Bath and two from Frome." After describing the noble scenery around Beckington and the rare architectural beauty of the house itself, the writer of this advertisement proceeded to say that the place was all the more desirable because it was reported to be haunted.

No doubt there are people who long for a house containing a genuine ghost, and it was sometimes said that the rich tradesman, anxious to turn himself into a squire, used to look for a haunted manor, while humorists declared that ghosts were on sale at department stores and that the demand for them among American millionaires was stupendous.

But if the purchaser of Beckington Castle had to pay an additionally high price because the place had a veritable ghost, in reality anything of the sort used to make a house almost unsalable. At Lossiemouth, on the east coast of Scotland, a fine old mansion stood untenanted for years and was eventually sold for a merely nominal sum. The reason was, simply, that according to popular tradition, the building was visited nightly by a female figure draped in white, her throat bearing an ugly scar, and her hands tied behind her back with chains. Nor was it merely concerning old country mansions that stories of this nature were current. Even in many densely-populated towns there were houses, reputed to be haunted, that could not be sold. Following World War II, the acute housing shortage in Britain made homebuyers less finicky and agents less forthcoming about ghosts.

Royal palaces, closely watched and guarded as they invariably have been, are popular residences of such inhabitants. Legend contends, for example, that Windsor Castle is frequently visited by the ghost of Sir George Villiers, and it is said that in the reign of Charles I, this ghost appeared to one of the king's gentlemen-in-waiting and informed him that the Duke Buckingham would shortly fall by the hand of an assassin—a prophecy that was duly fulfilled soon after, as all readers of *The Three Musketeers* will doubtless remember.

At Hackwood House, near Basingstoke Hampshire, there is a room in which no one dares to sleep, all dreading "the grey woman" supposed to appear there nightly, while Wyecoller Hall, near Colne, boasts a specter horseman who visits the place once a year, and rides at full speed through the garden.

Very different is the legend attached to Dilston, in Tyneside, where a bygone Lady Windermere is said to appear from time to time and indulge in loud lamentations for her unfortunate husband, who was executed for his share in the Jacobite rising of 1715. Dilston Hall is now an educational establishment, but permission can be obtained to visit the castle ruins.

At Salmesbury Hall, Blackburn, there is a ghost of yet another kind, neighborhood tradition affirming that a weird ghostly lady and her knight promenade the grounds of the hall, indulging all the while in silken dalliance. At the present time, the hall houses an exhibition center and may be visited by tourists.

There are also more gruesome apparitions and among these is the ghost of Amy Robsart, which haunts the manor of Cumnor, in Oxfordshire. Amy was a real woman, not a mere creation of novelist Sir Walter Scott. She was married in 1550 to the Earl of Leicester and her tragic death is commonly attributed to him, but a tradition exists to the effect that Queen Elizabeth was really the responsible person, and recalling an authentic portrait of Amy, which depicts her as a woman of charm and of no ordinary beauty, it is easy to believe that the ill-favored queen hated her and took strong measures to get her out of the way.

Numerous rectories rejoice in the ghost of a clergyman murdered by his parishioners, while at Holy Trinity Church at York a phantom nun was said to appear occasionally on winter evenings and walk about muttering paternosters. The story concerning her is that, on one occasion during the Civil War, a band of soldiers intended to loot the church. On approaching it with this intention they were confronted by an abbess, who warned them of the divine wrath they would surely incur if they committed such an act of sacrilege. They laughed at her piety, never thinking that she would offer any resistance as they tried to march *en masse* into the building, but hardly had they commenced the assault when their opponent snatched a sword from one of them and stood bravely on the defensive. A fierce battle ensued, the abbess proving herself a fierce warrior by killing a number of the soldiers. Ultimately she lost her life, and her ghost was supposed to frequent the church she sought to defend.

There are few parts of England so rich in romance as Sherwood Forest in Nottinghamshire, once the scene of Robin Hood's exploits. One place in this region that claims a number of ghosts is Newstead Abbey, the seat of Lord Byron's ancestors. A part of the garden there is popularly known as "the devil's wood," a name which points to the place having been infested once by minions of the foul fiend, while one of the rooms in the house was haunted by a certain "Sir John Byron, the little, of the grey beard," who presumably ended his days in some uncanny fashion. His portrait hung over the hall in the dining room, and a young lady staying at Newstead about the middle of the nineteenth century insisted that once she had entered this room to find the portrait gone, and its subject seated by the fireside reading a black-letter folio volume.

The poet Byron himself cherished very fondly all the ghostly traditions that clung to his home and it is recorded that, on his learning that there were stone coffins underneath the house, he immediately had one of them dug up and then opened. He used some of its gruesome contents to"decorate" his own library, while he had the coffin itself placed in the great hall through which thereafter the servants were afraid to pass by night. He also utilized the supernatural lore of Newstead in one of his poems, and from this we learn that a specter friar used to parade about the mansion whenever some important event was about to occur to one of its owners:

When an heir is born he is heard to mourn,
And when aught is to befall
That ancient line, in the pale moonshine
He walks from hall to hall.
His form you may trace, but not his face,
'Tis shadowed by his cowl;
But his eyes may be seen from the folds between,
And they seem of a parted soul.
Say nought to him as he walks the hall,
And he'll say nought to you:
He sweeps along in his dusky pall,
As o'er the grass the dew.
Then, gramercy! for the black friar;

Heaven sain him, fair or foul,
And whatsoe'er may be his prayer,
Let ours be for his soul.

There are many stories of hauntings at that grim ancient fortress, the Tower of London, but visitors must remember that those were usually reported at night, when the gates were closed to tourists.

Passing from England to **Ireland,** we find many traditions of haunted houses. For instance, at Dunseverick in Antrim dwells the soul of a bygone chief so wicked in his lifetime that even hell's gates were closed to him. Other haunted houses in Ireland, now open to visitors, include castle Matrix in Limerick, castle Malahide in county Dublin and Springhill Manor in county Londonderry.

Scotland

In Scotland there are also numerous haunted buildings, notably Holyrood Palace and the castles of Hermitage and Glamis. The ghost of Hermitage is considerably addicted to exercise and in truth his story marks him as having been a man of rare activity and ambition. Lord Soulis was his name, and, possibly hearing of the exploits of **Faust,** he vowed that he too would invoke the devil, who generously made his appearance. "Vast power will be yours on earth," said the devil to Soulis, "if you will but barter your soul therefor," so his lordship signed the requisite compact with his life's blood and from then on his days were given over to the enjoyment of every conceivable pleasure.

Soon, however, he felt that his end was near, and calling some of his vassals around him he told them of the awful fate awaiting him after death. They were thunderstruck, but soon after Soulis was gone it occurred to them that, if they could destroy his mortal remains completely, they might save his soul from the clutches of Beelzebub. So having sheathed the corpse in lead they flung it into a furnace, and (so the story goes) manifestly this cremation saved his lordship from the nether regions, for had he gone there his soul could not have been active still at Hermitage.

The ghost story associated with Glamis Castle, the family seat of the Earl of Strathmore, is quite different from the rank and file of supernatural tales and bears a more naked semblance of veracity than pertains to any of these. It is a matter of tradition that there is a secret chamber at Glamis, a chamber that enshrines a mystery known only to a few members of the Strathmore family, and three or four generations ago a lady, staying as a visitor at Glamis, vowed she would solve the riddle.

Her first difficulty was to locate the actual room, but one afternoon, when all the rest of the household were going out, she feigned a headache and thus contrived to be left completely alone. Her next move was to go from room to room, putting a handkerchief in the window of each, and having done this she went outside and walked around the castle to see whether any room had evaded her search.

Very soon she observed a window that had no handkerchief in it, so she hastened indoors again, thinking that her quest was about to be rewarded. But try as she might she could not find the missing room, and while she was searching the other guests returned to the house, along with them the then Lord Strathmore.

He was fiercely incensed on learning what was going on and that night shrieks were heard in a long corridor in the castle. The guests ran out of their rooms to find out what was wrong, and in the dim light they perceived a curious creature with an inhuman head, wrestling with an aged manservant who eventually managed to carry the monster away. There the story ends, but as remarked before, it bears a semblance of truth, the probability being that some scion of the Glamis castle family was mad or hideously deformed, and was accordingly incarcerated in a room to which access was difficult and secret.

Another explanation was offered by the nineteenth-century writer F. G. Lee, who claimed that strange, weird, and unearthly sounds were regularly heard in the castle. The then head of the family unlocked the haunted room, then swooned away in the arms of his companions. What had he seen? The story goes that there had been a feud between the Ogilvie and Lindsay clans, and that one day a party of fleeing Ogilvies demanded sanctuary in the castle. The lord of the day could not refuse, but feared to offend the Lindsays. He thereupon led the Ogilvies to a remote room and locked them in—forever. What the later head of the family saw was the skeletons of the starved Ogilvies, who still had the bones of their arms clenched in their teeth, having been driven in desperation to eat their own flesh.

Be that as it may, there are traditions of other ghosts at Glamis, including a White Lady, a tall thin man known as "Jack the Runner," and a small black servant. Glamis is Scotland's oldest inhabited castle and has many dark and gloomy legends. As a stately home, it is accessible to visitors at the present time.

Borley Rectory

The reputation of "The Most Haunted House in England" was bestowed upon Borley Rectory in Suffolk by psychical researcher **Harry Price** in his book *"The Most Haunted House in England": Ten Years' Investigation of Borley Rectory* (1940). Price rented the rectory for a year and advertised for observers. Over a period of 14 months, 2,000 paranormal phenomena were reported: voices, footsteps, ringing of bells, locking and unlocking of doors, messages on walls, transportation of objects, crashes, breaking of windows, starting of fires, lights in a window, the apparitions of a nun, and a ghost coach with a headless coachman.

Price died in 1948, two years after publication of another book *The End of Borley Rectory,* following the demolition of the rectory. Seven years later, psychical investigators **Eric J. Dingwall,** Kathleen M. Goldney, and **Trevor H. Hall** published another book, *The Haunting of Borley* (1956), alleging that Price deliberately faked phenomena and distorted the Borley story. Hall later followed this work by *The Search for Harry Price* (1978) in which he attempted methodically to demolish Price's reputation not only as a psychical researcher but also as an individual, but in the end simply overstated his case against Price. So far as Borley Rectory is concerned, the claimed hauntings stretch back in time to the period of its construction, long before the appearance of Price on the scene.

The study of the phenomenon of **haunting** was a popular exercise of psychical research, but has dropped out of popularity with the rise of laboratory-based parapsychology.

Visiting Haunted Houses

British ghosts have been well documented in a series of books. *Haunted Britain* by Antony Hippisley-Coxe (1973) lists the haunts of varied ghosts of the British countryside, including grey ladies, headless horsemen, phantom hounds, healing wells, and witches. The pretty village of Pluckley in Kent has no fewer than 12 phantoms, including a White Lady, a Red Lady, a poltergeist, a monk, the Mistress of Rose Court, a schoolmaster who hanged himself, a miller, a watercress woman who burned to death, a highwayman impaled to a tree by a sword, a screaming man who died in a clay pit, and a coach and horses in the main street. Hippisley-Coxe also conducted a weekend ghost safari in conjunction with Grand Metropolitian Hotels and Boswell and Johnson Travel of New York. A coach trip took tourists to supernatural sites in the West Country frequented by ghosts, witches, and poltergeists. (In the United States, similar **ghost tours** were organized by Richard T. Crowe in Chicago, Illinois.)

Jack Hallam, former picture editor of the British *Sunday Times* newspaper, published *The Ghost Tour: A Guidebook to Haunted Houses Within Easy Reach of London* (1967), and *The Ghost Who's Who* (1977) which lists some 500 frequently reported apparitions in England and Wales, ranging from a Bronze Age ghost through kings and queens to a man in a bowler hat haunting a runway at London Airport. Hallam claims that Britain is the most haunted country in the world, with 25,000 phantoms in England and Wales as well as thousands more in Scotland and Ireland. He states that the most haunted English village is Bramshott in Hampshire, with 300 living residents and 17 ghosts.

Other useful guides to ghost-ridden Britain include *Ghost Over Britain* by Peter Moss (1977) and **Peter Underwood**'s *Hauntings* (1977), *Gazetteer of British Ghosts* (1975), and *Gazetteer of Scottish & Irish Ghosts* (1973). Irish ghosts are documented in *Haunted Ireland: Her Romantic & Mysterious Ghosts* by John J. Dunne (1977), which lists 52 traditional Irish phantoms.

Of course, hauntings are not confined to the stately homes of the British Isles. In the United States there have also been celebrated haunted houses, including the Audubon House of Key West, Florida, San Antonio's Brooks House, Fort Sam Houston's Service Club, the Dakota Apartments in New York City (which inspired the setting of **Rosemary's Baby**), and the Governor's Mansion in Delaware, right up to modern times with the claimed phenomena of the **Amityville Horror.** Some of the most famous earlier hauntings, such as the Great Amherst Mystery, are more accurately classified as cases of **poltergeist,** though most people have trouble distinguishing poltergeists from ghosts.

Sources:

Alexander, Marc. *Haunted Houses You May Visit.* London: Sphere Books, 1982.

Anson, Jay. *The Amityville Horror.* New York: Bantam; London: Pan Books, 1978.

Bennett, E. T. *Apparitions and Haunted Houses: A Survey of Evidence.* London: Faber & Faber, 1939. Ann Arbor, Mich.: Gryphon Books, 1971.

Dunne, John J. *Haunted Ireland: Her Romantic & Mysterious Ghosts.* Belfast: Appletree Press, 1977.

Dyer, T. F. Thiselton. *The Ghost World.* London: Ward & Downey, 1893.

Flammarion, Camille. *Haunted Houses.* London: T. Fisher Unwin, 1924. Reprint, Detroit: Tower Books, 1971.

Hallam, Jack. *The Ghost Tour: A Guidebook to Haunted Houses Within Easy Reach of London.* London: Wolfe Publishing, 1967.

Harper, Charles G. *Haunted Houses: Tales of the Supernatural, With Some Account of Hereditary Curses and Family Legends.* London: Palmer, 1924. Reprint, Detroit: Tower Books, 1974.

Hippisley-Coxe, A. D. *Haunted Britain: A Guide to Supernatural Sites Frequented by Ghosts, Witches, Poltergeists & Other Mysterious Beings.* London: Hutchinson; New York: McGraw Hill, 1973. Reprint, London: Pan, 1975.

Holzer, Hans. *Hans Holzer's Haunted Houses: A Pictorial Register of the World's Most Interesting Ghost Houses.* New York: Crown, 1971.

Lang, Andrew. *The Book of Dreams and Ghosts.* London: Longmans Green, 1897. Reprint, New York: Causeway, 1974.

Moss, Peter. *Ghost Over Britain.* U.K.: Elm Tree Books, 1977.

Price, Harry. *The End of Borley Rectory.* London: George G. Harrap, 1946.

———. *"The Most Haunted House in England": Ten Years' Investigation of Borley Rectory.* London: Longmans, 1940.

Smith, Susy. *Ghosts Around the House.* New York: World Publishing, 1970. Reprint, Pocket Books, 1971.

Tabori, Paul, and Peter Underwood. *The Ghosts of Borley: Annals of the Haunted Rectory.* Newton Abbot, U.K.: David and Charles, 1973.

Underwood, Peter. *Gazetteer of British Ghosts.* London: Souvenir Press; New York: Walker, 1975.

———. *Gazetteer of Scottish and Irish Ghosts.* London: Souvenir Press, 1973. Reprint, New York: Walker, 1975.

Haunting

Disturbances of a paranormal character, attributed to the spirits of the dead. Tradition established two main factors in haunting: an old house or other locale and restlessness of a spirit. The first represents an unbroken link with the past, the second is believed to be caused by remorse over an evil life or by the shock of violent death.

The manifestations vary greatly. In most cases, strange noises are heard alone (auditory effects); in some others objects are displaced, and lights are seen (visual effects); also, a chilliness is sometimes felt in the atmosphere, not infrequently unbearable stench pervades the room, and an evil influence imparts feelings of unspeakable horror (sensory effects); and phantoms, both human and animal, appear in various degrees of solidity. The more noise they make the less solid they are.

The phenomena of haunting are often classed as objective and subjective. This classification is rather arbitrary as it does not take count of auditive hyperesthesia. Sounds below the ordinary limit of audition may be heard objectively although nobody else is aware of a beginning disturbance. The phantoms themselves are often harmless and aimless, sometimes malevolent. "Since the days of ancient Egypt, ghosts have learned, and have forgotten nothing," stated **Andrew Lang,** noted folklorist and writer on psychical manifestations. The usual type display no intelligence, appear irregularly, and act like sleepwalkers or mechanical recordings.

A. W. Monckton, in his *Some Experiences of a New Guinea Resident Magistrate* (1927) told the story of ghostly footsteps at Samarai, in the house where he was staying. In brilliant illumination he could see depressions at the spots from which the sound of the footsteps came.

Perhaps the most ancient case of haunting is attributed to the spirit of the traitorous general Pausanias (second century C.E.) who was immured in the Temple of Athene of Sparta to die of starvation. Terrifying noises were heard in the temple until a necromancer finally laid the ghost to rest.

John H. Ingram, in *The Haunted Homes and Family Traditions of Great Britain* (1890), published many accounts of haunting. According to him there are at least 150 haunted houses in Britain. From one account published in *Notes and Queries* (1860) Ingram noted that Edmund Lenthal Swifte, who was appointed keeper of the crown jewels in the Tower of London in 1814, experienced various unaccountable disturbances. One night one of the sentries saw a huge phantom bear issue from underneath the jewel room door. The bear dissolved into the air after the sentry thrust at it with his bayonet. The sentry died of fright the next day.

Haunted "B. House"

Sir Oliver Lodge, F. W. H. Myers, L. M. Taylor, the marquis of Bute, and Miss X. (**Ada Goodrich-Freer**) did the research for the book *The Alleged Haunting of B. House* (1899). Goodrich-Freer, who was in charge of the investigation, spent about three months at Ballechin House, Perthshire, Scotland. In her diary she states,

"I was startled by a loud clanging sound which seemed to resound through the house. The mental image it brought to my mind was of a long metal bar, such as I have seen near iron foundries, being struck at intervals with a wooden mallet. The noise was as of metal struck with wood; it seemed to come diagonally across the house. It sounded so loud, though distant, that the idea that any inmate of the house should not hear it seemed ludicrous."

Several phantoms were seen, most often a nun whom the investigators named "Ishbel" and a lay woman dressed in grey who was called "Margaret." The nun was sketched by a member of the party. She often appeared to be talking with the lay woman, who seemed to upbraid or reprove her. The attempt to catch their words was unsuccessful. The phantoms were seen by the dogs, who were terrified.

The clanging sounds sometimes continued for a long time and were succeeded by other sounds.

"It might have been made by a very lively kitten, jumping and pouncing, or even by a very large bird; there was a fluttering noise too. It was close, exactly opposite the bed. . . . We heard noises of pattering in Room No. 8 and Scamp [the dog] got up and sat apparently watching something invisible to us, turning his head slowly as if following the movements of some person or thing across the room from West to East. During the night, Miss Moore had heard footsteps crossing the room, as of an old man or invalid man shuffling in slippers."

Attempts to produce the same noises naturally were unsuccessful.

The phantoms apparently desired to be noticed. Goodrich-Freer, absorbed in writing, was gently, then firmly and more decidedly pushed to make her look up. Nothing was visible, but the dog was gazing intently from the hearth-rug at the place where the phantoms might have been expected.

Once the phantom of a living man, Rev. Father H., was seen. He was supposedly sleeping at the time. Twice the vision of a wooden crucifix presented itself, preceded by an acute chill on the part of someone present. Phantom dogs were heard pattering and bounding in play, and one was seen. Goodrich-Freer and a Miss Moore felt more than once that they were being pushed as if by a dog, and on one occasion two forepaws of a large black dog were seen resting on the edge of a table. Gradually the manifestations died down and finally ceased altogether.

Animal Ghosts

The family history of the owners of this haunted house appears to bear out the theory that the animals seen in haunted houses have also lived there. Major S., who was commonly believed to be one of the haunting spirits, was convinced in his lifetime that the spirits of the dead can enter the bodies of animals, and intended to possess, after his death, the body of a favorite black spaniel from among his many dogs. The family was so distressed by the idea that they had all his dogs shot after his burial. Curiously enough, among the dog apparitions at B. House several witnesses saw a black spaniel.

Elliott O'Donnell suggested that there are as many animal phantasms as human, the most frequent being the cat, as cats meet more often with a sudden and violent end in the house in which they live than any other animal. When investigating a haunted house, he generally used to take a dog with him as a dog seldom fails to give early "notice—either by whining, or growling, or crouching shivering on one's feet, or springing on one's lap and trying to bury its head in one's coat—of the proximity of a ghost." O'Donnell stated that belief in spectral dogs was common all over the British Isles.

Haunted Hampton Court

Goodrich-Freer claimed to have seen ghost manifestations in Hampton Court, the famous London palace built for Cardinal Wolsey but taken over by Henry VIII. "In the darkness before me there began to glow a soft light. I watched it increase in brightness and in extent. It seemed to radiate from a central point, which gradually took form, and became a tall, slight woman, moving slowly across the floor." She asked the phantom whether she could help her. "She then raised her hands, which were long and white, and held them before her as she sank upon her knees and slowly buried the face in her palms, in the attitude of prayer—when, quite suddenly, the light went out, and I was alone in the darkness."

Goodrich-Freer nevertheless did not believe that the visitor in this case was a departed spirit. She conjectured that it was a telepathic impression of the dreams of the dead, "just as the figure which, it may be, sits at my dining-table, is not the friend whose visit a few hours later it announces but only a representation of him, having no objective existence apart from the truth of the information it conveys—a thought which is personal to the brain which thinks it."

A Haunted Chateau

At the Chateau T. in Normandy, near Caen, a resident recorded in a diary various knocking phenomena (later published in *Annales des Sciences Psychique,* 1892–93).

"One o'clock. Twelve blows followed by a long drumming, then 30 rapid single knocks. One would have thought that the house was shaken; we were rocked in our beds on every storey . . . then a long rush of feet; the whole lasting only five minutes. A minute later the whole house was shaken again from top to bottom; ten tremendous blows on the door of the green room. Twelve cries outside, three bellowings, followed by furious outcries. Very loud drumming in the vestibule, rhythmical up to 50 knocks. 1.30 A.M. The house shaken 20 times; strokes so quick that they could not be counted. Walls and furniture alike quivered; nine heavy blows on the door of the green room, a drumming accompanied by heavy blows. At this moment bellowings like those of a bull were heard, followed by wild non-human cries in the corridor. We rang up all the servants and when all were up we again heard two bellowings and one cry."

The Laying to Rest of Uneasy Spirits

There are many cases of hauntings by uneasy spirits that required certain acts to take place before the manifestation ceased. A highly curious mixture of haunting, poltergeist, and obsession phenomena is found in the old case of The Maid of Orlach, told in Justinus Kerner's *Geschichten Besessener neurer Zeit* (1834). The disturbances began in the cowhouse. The cows were found tied up in unusual ways and places. Sometimes their tails were finely plaited together, as if by a lace weaver. Strange cats and birds came and went and invisible hands boxed the cowmaid Magdalene's ears while she was milking and struck her cap off with violence. Mysterious fires broke out from time to time in the cottage and a contest between a black and a white spirit ensued.

There was a white spirit, a benign influence, a nun born at Orlach in 1412, who was guilty of many crimes. She tried to give protection against the increasing violence of the black spirit and asked for the house to be pulled down. The black spirit threw Magdalene into a cataleptic state and obsessed her. The persecution suddenly stopped when the house was demolished. Under an ancient piece of masonry a mass of human bones, among them the remains of several infants, was discovered. The girl never saw ghosts thereafter.

According to **Emma Hardinge Britten**'s *Modern American Spiritualism* (1869) the **Hydesville** phenomena developed into a formal haunting some time after the discovery of the rapping intelligence.

"The furniture was frequently moved about; the girls were often clasped by hard, cold hands; doors were opened and shut with much violence; their beds were so shaken that they were compelled to "camp out" as they termed it, on the ground; their bed-clothes were dragged off from them, and the very floor and house made to rock as in an earthquake. Night after night they would be appalled by hearing a sound like a death struggle, the gurgling of the throat, a sudden rush as of falling blood, the dragging as if of a helpless body across the room, and down the cellar stairs; the digging of a grave, nailing of boards, and the filling in of a new-made grave. These sounds have been subsequently produced by request."

The *Proceedings* of the Society for Psychical Research (vol. 11, p. 547–549) contains one of the most curious and well-authenticated cases in which a haunting spirit established communication with a living person and was laid to rest after its wishes were carried out. The incident occurred in 1893 to a Mrs. Claughton, a resident of 6 Blake Street, a house reputed to have been haunted by the spirit of its former owner, a Mrs. Blackburn.

Claughton was awakened in the night by a female apparition, which was also perceived by her elder child. The apparition bid her "follow me," led her to the drawing room, said "tomorrow" and disappeared. The next night the apparition returned, made a statement to Claughton and asked her to do certain things. To prove to her the reality of her experience, the apparition gave the date of Blackburn's marriage, which, on subsequent inquiry, was found to be correct.

During this period, a second phantom appeared who stated himself to be George Howard, buried in Meresby churchyard, and gave the date of his marriage and death. He asked Claughton to go to Meresby (she had never heard of the place before), verify the dates and wait at Richard Hart's grave in the aisle of the church after midnight. He also said that her railway ticket would not be taken, that Joseph Wright, a dark man to whom she should describe him, would help her, and that she would lodge with a woman who had a drowned child buried in the same churchyard. The rest of the story would be told to her at the churchyard.

A third phantom also appeared. He was in great trouble and stood with his hands on his face, behind Blackburn. Thereafter the three phantoms disappeared. Claughton found that such a place as Meresby existed, went there, and found lodgings with Joseph Wright, who turned out to be the parish clerk. The woman who lost a child was Wright's wife. She spoke to Joseph Wright about George Howard, and he took her to Howard's and Richard Hart's graves. Richard Hart appeared and made a communication that Claughton did not feel at liberty to disclose. She carried out the desires of the dead in full and received no communications from them thereafter.

Justinus Kerner's book *The Seeress of Prevorst* (1845) includes an account of a poor German family in Weinsberg that was disturbed by a ghost. Kerner brought the women of the house to see **Frederica Hauffe.** The ghost attached itself to Hauffe and told her that he had lived in about 1700 under the name Belon in the house he haunted, had died at the age of 79, and could not rest because he had defrauded two orphans. After a search in the records it was found that the information tallied with a burgomaster of the town who died in 1740 at the age of 79 and had been guardian of orphans.

Premonitory Haunting

Premonitory haunting, foretelling death or another catastrophe, is in a class by itself. The White Lady of the Royal Palace in Berlin and of the Castle of Schönbrunn, the White Lady of Avenel (in Sir Walter Scott's book *The Monastery*), the Dark Lady of Norfolk, and the Grey Lady of Windsor are all said to be heralds of death. The White Lady of the Royal Palace of Berlin is supposed to be the ghost of the Countess Agnes of Orlemunde, who murdered her two children. She appeared in 1589, eight days before the death of the Prince Elector John George, in 1619, 23 days before the death of Sigismund, and also in 1688. In 1850 her appearance preceded the attempt on the life of Count Frederick Williams. The White Lady of Schönbrunn was seen in 1867 before the tragic death of Emperor Maximilian of Mexico in 1889, prior to the Mayerling drama and before the news arrived that John Orth, the ex-Archduke, was lost at sea.

The forms of premonitory haunting show great variety, from death lights and phantom funeral processions to symbolic sounds, the stopping of clocks, the apparition of banshees, and ominous **animals.** Deathbed visions are in a different class as there is no periodicity in their occurrence.

Augustus Hare, in his book *The Story of My Life* (1896), tells of the visit of Sir David Brewster to the Stirling family at Kippenross, in Scotland. Brewster was so terrified by strange noises heard in the night that he fled to his daughter's room. His daughter then saw at the head of the stairs a tall woman leaning against the banisters. She asked her to send her maid. She nodded three times and, pointing to a door in the hall, descended the stairs. When the daughter spoke of the matter to Miss Stirling she became deeply agitated. A Major Wedderburn and his wife were sleeping in the room the spirit had pointed to. The tradition said that whoever was pointed out by the ghost died within the year. Strangely enough, before the year was out both the major and his wife were killed in the Sepoy rebellion in India.

The Vanishing Bread and Other Weird Phenomena

The British Spiritualist publication *Light* (October 24, 1903), reprinted an account from the *Daily Express* newspaper of the mystery of the vanishing bread of Raikes Farm, Beverley, Yorkshire. The Websters, a family with seven children, apparently lived in a haunted farmstead. Strange noises, footsteps, and mysterious choir singing were heard in the night but what really disturbed the family was that the bread, from the first week of March 1903, crumbled away during the night. It looked as if it had been gnawed by rats or mice.

All sorts of precautions were taken but nothing could arrest the dwindling of the loaves. They were set in a closed pan, with a rat-trap set inside and another on top of the lid, the floor was sprinkled with flour, two lengths of cotton were stretched across the room, and the doors were locked. In the morning, everything was found intact, but one of the loaves had entirely disappeared, and the other had dwindled to half of its original size. For nearly three months the Websters kept the mystery to themselves. The situation became desperate. Mrs. Webster had seen the end of a loaf waste to nothingness on the kitchen table within an hour.

The family requested the services of a former police constable named Berridge, and he was put in sole charge of the dairy for several days. But Berridge frankly confessed that he was baffled. He came with two loaves of bread to the farm, and locked them in the dairy with his own special lock. The next day they appeared to be all right, but a day after, cutting them open, he found the loaves quite hollow. He suspected faulty baking but the cavity gradually grew wider and wider, and the second loaf began to dwindle before his eyes.

He secreted pieces of bread in other places about the house, but in every instance they wasted away to nothing. Ten leading chemists of Beverley and Hull visited the farm and analyzed the bread. Microscopic examination did not reveal the presence of any microbe or fungus, and the bread was pronounced absolutely pure.

When Mrs. Webster resorted to baking cakes for the household, she was relieved to find that although they lay side by side with the blighted bread they showed no sign of harmful contact. But when the last crumb of bread disappeared, the mysterious destroyer of the loaves attacked the cakes as well. The decay of a loaf was immediately arrested if it was removed from the precincts of the farmhouse. This proved that the blight was local and possibly a bizarre form of haunting.

The gruesome traits of the traditional ghost are well reflected in the story the Earl of Bective told British psychical researcher **Harry Price.** As reported in *Psychic Research* (June 1930), the earl was staying with some friends at a Scottish castle and wished to explore a certain wing, which had been closed for generations. In the state ballroom, he saw to his amazement,

"The trunk of a man near the door by which he had just entered and which he had closed after him. No head, arms or legs were visible, and the trunk was dressed in red velvet, with slashings of white across the breast and a good deal of lace. The period was perhaps Elizabethan and the trunk was undoubtedly that of a man. . . .

"The apparition gradually became less distinct and finally vanished, apparently through the closed door. Lord Bective then hurried to the other end of the room with the intention of ascertaining whether the phantom had passed into the next apartment. . . .

"And now comes the most extraordinary part of the story. Although he had a few minutes previously passed through the doorway (the door swinging very easily and with a simple latch), he now found that something was on the other side of the door which prevented his opening it. He could still raise the latch and the door would give a fraction of an inch, with a pronounced resilience, exactly as if someone were on the far side attempting to bar his entry into the room. After two or three good pushes he gave an extra powerful one and the door flew open and he was alone."

The story of the haunted vaults at Barbados sounds like fiction, yet Commander R. T. Gould, R.N., assures us in his book *Oddities: A Book of Unexplained Facts* (1928) that it is a true tale. Time after time, heavy leaden coffins were found standing on end and tossed about as if by the hand of a giant. Lord Combermere, governor of Barbados, decided to test the matter. The six coffins of the haunted vault were placed in order, a stone weighing five tons was cemented into the doorway and Combermere and others placed their seals on the vault. On April 18, 1820, eight months later, the vault was opened. The sand on the floor bore no mark, yet the six coffins were found thrown all over the vault.

A recurring spectral light, subsequently named the Fire of St. Bernardo, was seen in Italy in Quargnento by Signor Sirembo during the early months of 1895, and afterward by one Professor Garzino, the civil engineer Capello and others. At about half past eight in the evening, a luminous mass, sometimes of a diameter of 24–28 inches, appeared and moved by leaps from the little church of St. Bernardo to the cemetery and about midnight returned to the church. The event took place at all seasons, but it was not seen by everybody. The case was described in **Cesare Lombroso**'s book *After Death—What?* (1909).

The medium **Elizabeth d'Esperance,** as a young girl, was greatly frightened on the Mediterranean in 1867 seeing a "strange ship . . . her white sails gleaming rosy red in the light of the setting sun," looming full over the bows of the S.S. *Sardinian,* on which she was sailing. "One man on her deck was leaning with folded arms against the bulwarks watching the on-coming of our vessel." The strange ship passed through their own. D'Esperance saw the vessel in the wake of her boat, with sails fully set; she saw each rope of the rigging, men moving about on the deck, and the pennant flying at the mast-head. Lieutenant N., standing next to the girl, saw nothing.

To **Charles Richet,** the idea that nonhuman intelligences might be behind the phenomena of haunting was greatly appealing. However, almost nothing that would amount to evidence is available of such haunting. The German "Berg Geister," (the spirits of mountains and mines) or the "little people" (fairies) would be of this class.

In *Nineteenth Century Miracles* (1884), Emma Hardinge Britten related that a Mr. Kalozdy, a Hungarian author on mineralogy and teacher in the Hungarian School of Mines, collected many narratives of knockings in Hungarian and Bohemian mines. He and his pupils often heard these knockings. The miners took them for signals from the Kobolds (underground goblins) not to work in the direction against which they were warned. The materialized appearance of these Kobolds was seen by Mrs. Kalozdy, herself an author, in the hut of a peasant, Michael Engelbrecht. Lights the size of a cheese plate suddenly emerged; surrounding each one was the dim outline of a small human figure, black and grotesque. They flitted about in a wavering dance and then vanished one by one. This visit was announced to Engelbrecht by knockings in the mine. The more prosaic explanation of underground knockings is that they are caused by seismic disturbances.

Speculations of the Early Psychical Researchers

Such instances, complemented with **poltergeist** disturbances and other famous cases (such as the **Bealings bells,** the **Drummer of Tedworth,** the **Epworth phenomena,** the house of **Eliakim Phelps,** and **Willington Mill**), give a comprehensive idea of the complexity of haunting. What did psychical researchers make out of it? Early investigation pointed to a disapproval of the general belief that some great crime or catastrophe is always to be sought as the cause of haunting.

The chapter on "Local Apparitions" in the *Report on the Census of Hallucinations* published by the **Society for Psychical Research,** London, in 1894, concludes:

"The cases we have given, in addition to others of the same kind to be found in previous numbers of the Proceedings, constitute, we think, a strong body of evidence, showing that apparitions are seen in certain places independently by several percipients, under circumstances which make it difficult to suppose that the phenomena are merely subjective, or that they can be explained by telepathy without considerable straining of our general conception of it. It appears, however, that there is in most cases very little ground for attributing the phenomena to the agency of dead persons, but as we have said, in the great majority of cases they are unrecognised; and in these cases, if they really represent any actual person, there is often no more reason to suppose the person dead than living."

Folklorist Andrew Lang objected to the SPR's investigation mainly on the grounds that the committee "neglected to add a seer to their number." This he considered a wanton mistake. He added that ghosts do not have benefit nights, that they are not always on view, and even where they have appeared there are breaks of years without any manifestations. **Eleanor Sidgwick,** who drew up the report, was the first to make a serious attempt to face the difficulties of the problem of hauntings. In an 1885 paper she offers four hypotheses for consideration:

1. The apparition is something belonging to the external world that, like ordinary matter, it occupies and moves through space, and would be in the room whether the percipient were there to see it or not.
2. The apparition has no relation to the external world but is an hallucination caused in some way by some communication, without the intervention of the senses, between the disembodied spirit and the percipient, its form depending on the mind of either the spirit or of the percipient, or of both. This hypothesis does not account for the apparent dependence of the haunting on the locality.
3. The first appearance in haunted houses is a purely subjective hallucination, and subsequent similar appearances, both to the original percipient and to others, are the result of the first appearance, unconscious expectancy causing them in the case of the original percipient and in the case of others. This hypothesis assumes that a tendency to a particular hallucination is very infectious.
4. There is something in the actual building itself which produces in the brain that effect which, in its turn, becomes the cause of hallucination.

Personally, she did not find any of these hypotheses satisfactory and concludes,

"I can only say that having made every effort—as my paper will, I hope, have shown—to exercise a reasonable scepticism, I yet do not feel equal to the degree of unbelief in human testimony necessary to avoid accepting, at least provisionally, the conclusion that there are in a certain sense, haunted houses, i.e., that there are houses in which similar quasi-human apparitions have occurred at different times to different inhabitants, under circumstances which exclude the hypothesis of suggestion or expectation."

Frank Podmore believed that the story of a haunting was begun by some subjective **hallucination** on the part of a living person, which lingered on in the atmosphere and was telepathically transmitted to the next occupant of the room or house in question. Ada Goodrich-Freer, in her *Essays in Psychical Research,* aptly remarks that on this theory the story of her vision in Hampton Court Palace ought to be transmitted to future occupants of her room whether she really saw or only imagined what she saw, or mistook what she saw, or even if she told lies as to what she saw.

F. W. H. Myers defined the ghost as a manifestation of persistent personal energy. He made many interesting suggestions. One was that haunting may be the result of past mental actions that may persist in some perceptible manner, without fresh reinforcement, just as the result of our bodily actions persist. The perception may be retro-cognition owing to some curious relation of supernormal phenomena in haunted houses to time. In another suggestion he attributed the phenomena to the dreams of the dead, which are somehow being made objective and visible to the living. In his *Human Personality and its Survival of Bodily Death* (1903) he went much further and offered for consideration his theory of "psychorrhagic diathesis" as applied to a spirit. He defined it as "a special idiosyncrasy which tends to make the phantasm of a person easily perceptible; the breaking loose of a psychical element, definable mainly by its power of producing a phantasm, perceptible by one or more persons in some portion of space."

The theory is a bolder exposition of what **Edmund Gurney** suggested: that spectral pictures, like the recurring figure of an old woman on the bed where she was murdered, may be veridical after-images impressed we know not how on what we cannot guess by that person's physical organism and perceptible at times to those endowed with some cognate form of sensitiveness. The image is veridical because it contains information regarding the former inhabitant of the haunted place.

Earthbound Spirits?

The same suggestion was contained in **Ernesto Bozzano**'s "psychical infestation" theory. Bozzano made a special study of haunting and compiled statistics that indicated that out of 532 cases of haunting, 374 were caused by ordinary ghosts and 158 by the poltergeist type. Psychometric impressions are frequently referred to as another possibility of explanation. As Longfellow writes, "All houses wherein men have lived and died are haunted houses, through the open doors the harmless phantoms on their errands glide, with feet that make no sound upon the floors."

To explain how psychometric impressions may become intensified, the theory may be combined with the emotional energy of the dreams or the remorse of the dead. Remorse is said to make a spirit earthbound, but additional theories have also been brought forth.

Plato quotes Socrates in *Phaedo,*

"And in this case [impure life] the soul which survives the body must be wrapped up in a helpless and earthy covering, which makes it heavy and visible, and drags it down to the visible region, away from the invisible region of spirit world, Hades—which it fears. And thus these wandering souls haunt, as we call it, the tombs and monuments of the dead, where such phantoms are sometimes seen. These are apparitions of souls which departed from the body in a state of impurity, and still partake of corruption and the visible world, and therefore are liable to be still seen. And these are not the souls of good men, but of bad, who are thus obliged to wander about suffering punishment for their former manner of life which was evil."

In *Per Amica Silentia Lunae* (1918), poet **W. B. Yeats** was less censorious in suggesting that "We carry to Anima Mundi our memory, and that memory is for a time our external world; and all passionate moments recur again and again, for passion desires is own recurrence more than any event."

In the book *The Projection of the Astral Body,* written in collaboration with **Hereward Carrington** (1929), **Sylvan J. Muldoon** states, ". . . the most upright earthly being is just as apt to become the victim of an earthbound condition as the most wicked." It is not the moral but the psychic conditions that make a spirit earthbound. "How often do we hear of the murderer haunting a place? No, it is always the victim—the innocent party, who figures in haunted house phenomena." This is not always true, however, as there have been many accounts of hauntings by murderers.

Spirits may be earthbound for four reasons: desire, habit, dreams, and insanity. Revenge may be just as potent a factor in making a spirit earthbound as love. Often the haunter appears to be dreaming, yet occasionally he can be drawn into conversation. According to Muldoon, it is the "crypto-conscious" mind which does the talking, while the conscious mind is engaged in the dream.

The crypto-conscious mind of Muldoon is a department of the unconscious which has a will of its own. Violent death is, however, the most frequent cause of haunting. It results in a stress on the mind that influences the crypto-conscious mind to re-enact the last scene on earth. As an analogy Muldoon pointed to the "very common occurrence during the World War to see soldiers, while dreaming, jump from their beds and re-enact terrors which they had met with and which had left a deep stress in their subconscious minds."

Lombroso investigated many cases of haunting and always found a certain purpose: inflicting punishment for the reoccupation of the house, revenging the honor of the family, or moral or religious warning. The disturbances are especially powerful if the victims of the tragedy, enacted perhaps centuries before, died a violent death in the flower of their life. Lombroso called the haunted houses "necrophanic houses."

Vexed by the problem of how haunting spirits obtain matter for their materializations in uninhabited houses where no human organism is available, he asked for an explanation from the **control** during a séance and twice received the answer that the haunters derive the material for their incarnations from the animals and plants of the deserted house. Nevertheless, human organisms, if available, may be drawn upon by the haunters.

R. C. Morton, in her record of a haunted house (*Proceedings* of the SPR, vol. 8, p. 311) states:

"I was conscious of a feeling of loss, as if I had lost power to the figure. Most of the other percipients speak of a feeling of cold wind, but I myself had not experienced this." The ghosts Morton saw sometimes appeared to be so solid that they were mistaken for the living. A dog mistook the phantom for a living man and fled in abject terror after discovering his mistake. However solid the phantoms are, material objects do not apparently impede their progress.

Successful experiments were conducted in haunted houses by crystal gazers to locate the source of the trouble. The picture of the haunter was often disclosed when no materialization took place. J. Grasset recorded a case in the *Proceedings* of the SPR (vol. 18, p. 464) in which a girl saw the haunting spirit in a glass of water.

Experience shows that a decent burial of the remains of the victims of foul deeds, division of an ill-gotten treasure, **exorcism,** prayer, or mass often lays the ghost to rest. This suggests that the haunters are conscious of causing the disturbance, that the physical effects are not simple repercussions of the spirit's tormented mental state. But, as Andrew Lang remarked, "the ghost can make signs, but not the right signs." They suffer from what he calls "spectral aphasia," imperfect expression on the physical plane. He believed that lights in haunted houses are partial failures of ghosts to appear in form. The possibility of causing physical effects often disappears if the haunted house is rebuilt, or if the furniture is taken out. The psychical researcher Col. Taylor once cured a haunted house by ordering the inhabitants to burn an old, moth-eaten bed he had discovered in the attic. Whether the bed was a focal point of evil or not, the manifestations soon ceased.

Ancient laws made special dispositions in the case of haunting. In *Cock Lane and Common Sense* (1894) Andrew Lang gave a summary of old cases carried to court. Lawsuits over haunting were started in 1915 at Altavilla (Italy), in 1907 at Naples, and in 1907 at Egham, England, in the latter case by the author Stephen Philips. In November 1930, the question came up before the Berlin courts in Germany whether one had the right to keep his family ghosts on the premises. An eleven-year-old girl, Lucie Regulski, was pursued by poltergeist disturbances that purported to emanate from her dead uncle. As the house acquired the reputation of being haunted, the owner applied for an order of eviction. The court decided in favor of the tenant, stating that Lucie's father could harbor as many ghosts as he pleased and that they did not lessen the value of the house.

Present Position

Cases of haunting are still reported in modern times and old-fashioned apparitions are said to appear occasionally in their traditional locales. However, in spite of the development of scientific apparatus superior to that of the past, such as tape recorders, temperature measurement devices, infra-red photography, etc., investigation of haunting is still difficult. Ghosts do not appear to order, and many individuals do not report their experiences for fear of ridicule. On the other hand, the tendency of the mass media to sensationalize claims of haunting raises doubts about cases that are reported or that become publicized in bestselling paperbacks (such as the fraudulent **Amityville Horror**).

Apparitions possess a strong subjective aspect, and most informants speak of reactions that suggest energy being drawn from themselves to assist the manifestations in haunting. In this sense those who perceive apparitions appear to function like mediums in séances and such subjective factors do not register on cameras and tape recorders. Moreover spontaneous cases and anecdotal reports are difficult for modern parapsychologists to evaluate.

Much more frequent than traditional hauntings are reports of poltergeist phenomena, which appear to be impersonal, as distinct from the personalities of apparitions. Poltergeist phenomena is more accessible to psychical investigation with cameras and tape recorders.

Although there are many well-authenticated cases of haunting over a long period of time, there is still no evidence to show how apparitions are produced and why they persist. An intriguing aspect of apparitions is the question of those of living individuals, of which there are many reliable reports (see *Phantasms of the Living* by Gurney, Myers, and Podmore, 1886). It should be mentioned that hypnotists have shown that apparently real apparitions may be evoked in subjects by suggestion and one subject was able to produce such images at will (see *The Story of Ruth* by Morton Schatzman, 1980). The term "hallucination" (without popular misconceptions of lunacy) still seems a useful scientific description of apparitions until there is decisive evidence of how haunting takes place.

In 1970, a team of sociologists at Birmingham University, England, investigated religious beliefs and behavior in one Shropshire town and found that 15 percent of the 8,000 inhabitants accepted the existence of ghosts, while ten percent claimed to have seen or felt a ghost. Another survey by the **Institute of Psychophysical Research** in Oxford, England, collated 1,500 first-hand accounts of encounters with ghosts reported by individuals in all walks of life. This report, edited by **Celia Green** and Charles McGreery under the title *Apparitions* (1977), emphasized that the majority of ghost sightings are in the familiar surroundings of people's homes rather than at eerie old sites.

Sources:

Anson, Jay. *The Amityville Horror.* New York: Bantam Books; London: Pan Books, 1978.

Automobile Association of Great Britain. *Haunts and Hauntings.* Basingstoke, England: Publications Division of the Association, 1974.

Bell, Charles Bailey. *The Bell Witch, A Mysterious Spirit.* Nashville, Tenn.: Lark Bindery, 1934.

Bord, Janet. *Ghosts.* Newton Abbot, England: David & Charles, 1974.

Bozzano, Ernesto. *Dei Fenomeni d'Infestazione.* Rome, 1919.

Cox, Katharine. *Haunted Royalties.* London: W. Rider, 1916.

Crowe, Catherine. *The Night Side of Nature; or Ghosts & Ghost Seers.* 2 vols. London, 1848. Reprint, Folcroft, Pa., 1976.

Dingwall, Eric J. *Ghosts and Spirits in the Ancient World.* London: Kegan Paul, 1930.

Flammarion, Camille. *Haunted Houses.* London: T. Fisher Unwin, 1924. Detroit: Tower Books, 1971.

Gauld, Alan, and A. D. Cornell. *Poltergeists.* London: Routledge & Kegan Paul, 1979.

Green, Andrew M. *Ghost Hunting: A Practical Guide.* London: Garnstone Press, 1973.

Green, Celia, and Charles McGreery. *Apparitions.* London: Hamish Hamilton; New York: State Mutual Book, 1977.

Gurney, Edmund, F. W. H. Myers, and Frank Podmore. *Phantasms of the Living.* 2 vols. London, 1886. Rev. ed. New Hyde Park, N.Y.: University Books, 1962. Reprint, Delmar, N.Y.: Scholars Facsimiles and Reprints, 1970.

Haining, Peter. *Ghosts: The Illustrated History.* London: Sidgwick & Jackson, 1974. Reprint, New York: Macmillan, 1975.

Harper, Charles G. *Haunted Houses.* London: Cecil Palmer, 1927.

Harris, John W. *Inferences from Haunted Houses and Haunted Men.* London, 1901.

Hubbell, Walter. *The Great Amherst Mystery.* New York, 1888.

Ingram, John H. *Haunted Houses and Family Traditions of Great Britain.* London, 1884.

Ingram, M. V. *An Authenticated History of the Famous Bell Witch.* Clarksville, Tenn.: W. P. Titus, 1894.

Lombroso, Cesare. *After Death—What?* London: T. Fisher Unwin, 1909.

Mackenzie, Andrew. *Apparitions and Ghosts.* London: Barker; New York: Popular Library, 1971.

———. *Hauntings and Apparitions.* London: Heinemann, 1982.

Middleton, Jessie A. *The White Ghost Book.* London: Cassell, 1918.

Moore, Edward. *Bealings Bells.* Woodbridge, England, 1841.

O'Donnell, Elliot. *The Banshee.* London: Sands, 1920.

———. *Family Ghosts & Ghostly Phenomena.* London: Philip Allan, 1933.

———. *Haunted Places in England.* London: Sands, 1919.

Podmore, Frank. *Apparitions and Thought-Transference.* London: Walter Scott Publishing, 1894.

Prince, Walter F. *The Psychic in the House.* Boston: Boston Society for Psychical Research, 1926.

Roll, W. G. *The Poltergeist.* Metuchen, N.J.: Scarecrow Press, 1976.

Schatzman, Morton. *The Story of Ruth.* London: Duckworth, 1980.

Smith, Susy. *Haunted Houses for the Million.* New York: Bell Publishing, 1967.

———. *Prominent American Ghosts.* New York: World Publishing, 1967.

Stead, William T. *Real Ghost Stories.* London, 1891. Reprinted as *Borderland: A Casebook of True Supernatural Stories.* New Hyde Park, N.Y.: University Books, 1970.

Thompson, C. J. S. *The Mystery and Lore of Apparitions.* London: Shaylor, 1930. Reprint, Detroit: Gale Research, 1975.

Tweeddale, Violet C. *Ghosts I Have Seen.* London: Herbert Jenkins, 1919.

Tyrrell, G. N. M. *Apparitions.* Rev. ed. London: Duckworth, 1953. Reprint, London: Society for Psychical Research, 1973.

Walter, W. Grey. *The Neurophysiological Aspects of Hallucinations and Illusory Experience.* London: Society for Psychical Research, 1963.

Wright, Dudley. *The Epworth Phenomena.* London, 1917.

X, Miss [Ada Goodrich-Freer], and John, Marquess of Bute. *The Alleged Haunting of B. House.* London, 1899. Rev. ed. 1900.

Zingaropoli, F. *Case Infestate degli Spiriti.* Naples, 1907.

Hauser, Kaspar (ca. 1812–1833)

Mysterious teenage boy who appeared in the streets of Nuremberg, Germany, on May 26, 1828. He could give no clear account of how he came there or where he was from, and some months later claimed that he had been imprisoned in a small, dark room all his life and fed on bread and water. At the time of his appearance in Nuremberg he appeared to be unstable on his legs and largely incoherent. The boy had a letter in his possession, ostensibly from a poor laborer, which stated that the writer first took charge of the boy as an infant in 1812 and had never let him "take a single step out of my house . . . I have already taught him to read and write, and he writes my handwriting exactly as I do." There was also a note purporting to come from Hauser's mother, stating that the boy was born on April 30, 1812, that his name was Kaspar, and his father, now dead, had been a cavalry officer. Both letters appeared to be fakes.

A citizen took Hauser to the house of a local cavalry captain, where the boy is supposed to have said, "I want to be a horseman, like my father," but speaking in a parrot fashion. His vocabulary was otherwise limited to phrases like "I don't know." He was at first believed to be an imbecile.

Hauser was adopted by the town of Nuremberg and educated by a schoolmaster named Daumer, at whose house he lived. The boy's education progressed rapidly, and he soon wrote his own account of his strange life. He claimed that until age 16 he was kept in a prison, perhaps six or seven feet long, four feet broad, and five feet high. There were two small windows, with closed black wooden shutters. He lay on straw, lived on bread and water, and played with toy horses, confined in darkness. He never saw his captor, but "the man" taught him letters and about nine words, after many years taught him to stand and walk, and finally released him.

Hauser's case was studied by Paul John Anselm von Feuerbach, a legal reformer, who published a passionate and not wholly accurate work about Hauser. Both Feuerbach and Daumer claimed that Hauser was an excellent example of a mediumistic subject, sensitive to animal magnetism and able to see in the dark.

Romantic rumors circulated about Hauser, including one claiming that he was really the crown prince of Baden, a legitimate son of the grand duke Charles, and that he had been kidnaped in 1812 by servants of the countess of Hochberg (morganatic wife of the grand duke) to secure succession by her own offspring.

In 1831, the British Earl Stanhope visited Nuremberg and became interested in Hauser, believing him to be the victim of criminals. He undertook to sponsor the lad's higher education, and in the following year Hauser was sent to Anspach in the charge of a Dr. Meyer, who became his tutor. Hauser eventually became a clerk in the office of Feuerbach, who was then president of the court of appeal. Feuerbach died in May 1833, and rumors circulated that he had been poisoned by mysterious enemies. (Back in 1829, when in the care of Daumer, Hauser had claimed to be the victim of a mysterious assassin who had wounded him on the forehead.)

Hauser became increasingly dissatisfied with his clerical post, believing himself destined for higher things. Like Meyer, he had hopes that Lord Stanhope would take him to England and adopt him into high society. Meanwhile Meyer became increasingly disillusioned with Hauser, finding him incurably untruthful. He had strong misgivings about Stanhope's imminent visit to Anspach.

On December 14, 1833, Hauser suddenly rushed into Meyer's room, clutching his side, and led Meyer to a point about five hundred yards from the house. Hauser was unable to answer questions, but on returning to the house gasped out, "Went court garden . . . man . . . had a knife . . . gave a bag . . . struck . . . I ran as I could . . . bag must lie there." It was found that he had a narrow wound under the center of his left breast, caused by a sharp, double-edged weapon. He claimed that on the morning of the fourteenth, a man brought him a message from the court gardener, asking him to look at some clay from a newly bored well. When he went there, another man came forward, gave him a bag, stabbed him and fled. There was snow in the vicinity of the stabbing, but no footprints beyond a single track, perhaps Hauser's own. The bag contained a note in mirror writing containing vague phrases about coming from the Bavarian frontier. Hauser died within three or four days, his heart having been injured.

Rumors multiplied—that Hauser was once more the victim of a sinister plot connected with the prince of Baden, that Lord Stanhope himself was the ringleader and Meyer was an accomplice. The Countess Albersdorft saw visions and published an accusation. Stanhope himself believed that Hauser might have injured himself deliberately to attract attention and perpetuate romantic legends, and that the weapon may have penetrated farther than intended. Hauser undoubtedly had a neurotic and hysterical temperament, and mysterious attacks seemed to occur after quarrels with his guardians.

Sources:

Lang, Andrew. *Historical Mysteries.* London: Smith Elder, 1904.

Sampath, Ursula. *Kaspar Hauser: A Modern Metaphor.* Columbia, S.C.: Camden House, 1991.

Singh, Joseph Amrito Lal. *Wolf-children and Feral Man.* Hamden, Conn.: Archon Books, 1965.

Stanhope, Earl. *Tracts Relative to Caspar Hauser.* London: James S. Hodson, 1836.

Hawaiian Society for Psychical Research

Nonprofit organization established to promote, encourage, and participate in the scientific study of **psi** phenomena. Address: Gharith Pendragon, Hawaiian Society for Psychical Research, P.O. Box 4620, Honolulu, HI 96813.

Haxby, W. (ca. 1878)

Nineteenth-century English physical medium who was a postal employee. **Alfred Russel Wallace** writes of Haxby's psychic side in *My Life* (1902):

"He was a small man, and sat in a small drawing-room on the first floor separated by curtains from a larger one, where the visitors sat in a subdued light. After a few minutes, from between the curtains would appear a tall and stately East Indian figure in white robes, a rich waistband, sandals, and large turban, snowy white, and disposed with elegance. Sometimes this figure would walk round the room outside the circle, would lift up a large and very heavy musical box which he would wind up and then swing around his head with one hand.

"He would often come to each of us in succession, bow and allow us to feel his hands and examine his robes. We asked him to stand against the door-post and marked his height, and on one occasion Mr. Hensleigh Wedgwood brought with him a shoemaker's measuring rule and at our request, Abdullah, as he gave his name, took off a sandal, placed his foot on a chair and allowed it to be accurately measured with the sliding rule. After the séance Mr. Haxby removed his boot and had his foot measured by the same rule, when that of the figure was found to be full one inch and a quarter the longer, while in height it was about half a foot taller. A minute or two after Abdullah had retired into the small room, Haxby was found in a trance in his chair, while no trace of the white-robed stranger was to be seen. The door and window of the back room were securely fastened and often secured with gummed paper which was found intact."

It was recorded in the contemporary Spiritualist press that Haxby materialized dogs that ran about the room. However, **Charles Richet** in *Thirty Years of Psychical Research* (1923) states: "Haxby cheated impudently."

Sources:

"Alleged Mediumship of W. Haxby." *Proceedings* of the Society for Psychical Research 4.

Wallace, Alfred Russel. *My Life.* London: Chapman & Hall, 1905.

Hayden, Maria B. (ca. 1852)

Influential American medium of Boston and wife of W. R. Hayden, editor of the *Star Spangled Banner.* Maria Hayden was the first American medium to visit England after the beginnings of modern **Spiritualism** in the United States, and subsequently had a great influence on the development of the Spiritualist movement. She arrived in England in October 1852 in the company of a man named Stone, who professed to be a lecturer on "electro-biology," the art of inducing hypnotism by gazing at metallic disks.

Hayden was an educated woman and possessed a limited type of mediumship consisting mainly of **raps;** however, they furnished information beyond the knowledge of the sitters. In the British press she was treated as an American adventuress. The magazine *Household Words* was the first to ridicule her. *Blackwood's Magazine, The National Miscellany,* and other papers followed. Many disclosures were published claiming that the medium could not give correct answers unless she saw the alphabet.

The first man who confessed he was puzzled and unable to account for the phenomena was **Robert Chambers.** He describes his visit to Hayden in an unsigned article in *Chamber's Journal* on May 21, 1853, and admitted to having witnessed correct information when the alphabet was behind the medium's back. *The Critic* was the next to call attention to the inadequacy of the theory put forward by the skeptics. A Dr. Ashburner, one of the royal physicians, came forward for the defense and so did Sir Charles Isham. Other people of importance admitted that the phenomena were worthy of serious investigation, although they were unwilling to commit themselves.

Hayden's most important conquest was the conversion to Spiritualism of **Augustus de Morgan,** the famous mathematician and philosopher. The book by Mrs. de Morgan *From Matter to Spirit* (1863, first edition anonymous), the preface of which was written by her husband, gives a detailed account of Hayden's séances. Additional notes were published in Mrs. de Morgan's *Memoir of Augustus de Morgan* (1882).

The veteran socialist Robert Owen, age 83 at the time, also had several sittings. As a result he boldly embraced Spiritualism and proclaimed in the *Rational Quarterly Review* a formal profession of his new faith. The publication of the first English periodical on Spiritualism dates from Hayden's visit. The publisher was W. R. Hayden, who joined his wife in England, and the periodical was titled *The Spirit World.* The first and last issue appeared in May 1853.

After a year's stay in England Maria Hayden returned to the United States, graduated as a doctor of medicine, and practiced for 15 years with such remarkable healing powers that **James Rhodes Buchanan,** the famous pioneer in **psychometry,** declared her to be "one of the most skillful and successful physicians I have ever known." She was later offered a medical professorship in an American college.

The great medium **D. D. Home** gave one of his first public séances at the Haydens' home in March 1851. It is possible that Hayden's mediumship dated from that visit.

Sources:

De Morgan, Augustus. *A Budget of Paradoxes.* Chicago: Open Court Publishing, 1915. Reprinted as *The Encyclopedia of Eccentrics.* La Salle, Ill.: Open Court Publishing, 1974.

Haynes, Renée (Oriana) (1906–1994)

British novelist, historian, and writer on psychical research. Haynes was born on July 23, 1906, in London and was educated at private schools and an open-air establishment run by Theosophists. She then attended St. Hugh's College, Oxford (B.A. honors, 1927), where she majored in law and history. From 1928 to 1930 she worked for the publishers Geoffrey Bles, Ltd., London. Her literary career began in 1928 with her book *Neopolitan Ice.* Through the 1930s she wrote *Immortal John* (1932), *The Holy Hunger* (1935), and *Pan, Caesar and God: Who Spake by the Prophets* (1938). She worked for over a quarter-century for the British Council, London, becoming director of book reviews (1941–67).

She joined the **Society for Psychical Research** (SPR), London, in 1946, edited the society's *Journal* and *Proceedings* for more than a decade (1970–81), and served a tenure as a vice president. She was most interested in spontaneous phenomena and shied away from statistical studies. She argued that the psychic aspect of existence was an integral part of human life, an observation made in part from incidents in her own life, including some vivid precognitive dreams. She wrote a number of books on psychical research, but is most remembered for her centennial history of the society. Haynes died in 1994.

Sources:

Berger, Arthur S., and Joyce Berger. *The Encyclopedia of Parapsychology and Psychical Research.* New York: Paragon House, 1991.

Haynes, Renée. *The Hidden Springs: An Enquiry into Extra-Sensory Perception.* London: Hollis and Carter, 1961. Rev. ed. Boston: Little, Brown, 1973.

———. *Philosopher King: The Humanist Pope Benedict XIV.* London: Weidenfeld & Nicolson, 1970.

———. *The Seeing Eye, The Seeing I: Perception, Sensory and Extra-Sensory.* New York: St. Martin's Press, 1976.

———. *The Society for Psychical Research: A History 1882–1982.* London: McDonald, 1982.

Omez, Reginald. *Psychical Phenomena.* Translated by Renée Haynes. New York: Hawthorn, 1958.

Hazel Tree

The hazel was dedicated to the god Thor and was esteemed a plant of great virtue for the cure of fevers. Hazel branches were a favorite for use as a **divining rod.** Cutting a rod on St. John's Day or Good Friday was believed to ensure its success as an instrument of divination. A hazel rod was also a badge of authority, and it was probably this notion that that caused it to be used by schoolmasters. A hazel rod was also a symbol of authority among ancient Romans.

Hazelrigg, John (1860–1941)

American astrologer, born on June 20, 1860. He was the younger of twins, his brother being one hour older. Hazelrigg moved to New York as an actor but later abandoned the stage to become an astrologer. His first book, *Metaphysical Astrology,* was published in 1900, and in 1901 he launched a magazine, *Astro-Herald.* In 1916 he led in the formation of the American Academy of Astrologians, an elite group of astrologers who met periodically to discuss the more esoteric aspects of astrology. Hazelrigg edited the proceedings.

Hazelrigg wrote several additional books over the years. He also worked with Geroge J. McCormack in astrometeorological research for 15 years (1917–32).

Sources:

Hazelrigg, John. *Astrosophia: Being Metaphysical Astrology.* New York: The Author, 1915.

———. *Astrosophical Principles.* New York: Hermetic Publishing, 1917.

———. *Fundamentals of Hermetic Science: Being the Bona Fides of Astrology.* New York: Hermetic Publishing, 1925.

———. *Metaphysical Astrology.* New York: Metaphysical Publishing, 1900.

———. *The Sun Book; or, the Philosopher's Vade Mecum.* New York: Hermetic Publishing, 1916.

Yearbook of the American Academy of Astrologians. 2 vols. New York: Hermetic Publishing, 1917, 1918.

HDI See Human Dimensions Institute

Head of Baphomet

An interesting discovery was made public in 1818 dealing with the history of secret societies. According to Baron Joseph von Hammer-Purgstall (in his essay "Mysterium Baphometis Revelatum" in volume 6 of *Fundgruben des Orients*), there was found among the antiquities of the Imperial Museum of Vienna some idols named Heads of **Baphomet,** which the **Templars** were said to have venerated. These heads represented the divinity of the Gnostics, named *Mêté* (Wisdom). For a long time one of these gilded heads was preserved at Marseilles. It had been seized during a Templar retreat, at a time when they were pursued by the law.

Healing, Psychic

A popular early theory of psychic healing was that it was effected by a sudden and profound nervous change. The conception of the therapeutic power of such a change we owe to **Franz Anton Mesmer** (1733–1815). He brought it about by a combination of passes, unconscious suggestion, and supposed metallotherapy in an aparatus called the **baquet.** The baquet involved an oak tub filled with water, iron filings, and flasks of "magnetized water." Patients were connected to this baquet by holding rods or cords, which supposedly conveyed the "magnetism." The atmosphere was enhanced by music. Mesmer contended that a nervous effluence was passing into the patients.

There are many sensitives even now who claim curative power by such a fluid. But the discovery of magnetic action was put forward long before Mesmer as the basis of the sympathetic system of medicine.

The magnet itself was an illustration of the interaction of living bodies. Every substance was supposed to radiate a force. This force was guided by the in-dwelling spirit of the body from which it proceeded. A dissevered portion of a body retained something of the virtue of the body. This led to the deduction that instead of the wound, the weapon that caused it should be anointed, as the wound cannot heal while a portion of the vital spirit remains in disastrous union with the weapon and exerts an antipathetic influence upon its fellow spirit in the body (see **powder of sympathy**).

The sway of mesmerism was long and powerful. It yielded place to **hypnotism** after **James Braid** proved that **somnambulism** can be induced without passes by mere suggestion, or moreover that the patients can bring it about by themselves by staring at bright objects.

This discovery threw the nervous effluence theory overboard, although its possibility as a coordinating factor was by no means ruled out. Indeed **animal magnetism** has often, in one form or another, been rediscovered. A. A. Liébeault (1823–1901), for example, from his work treating children under four and curing some under three, claimed that magnetic healing was not due to suggestion. Similar successes were registered later by psychologist **Julien Ochorowicz** (1850–1917) on children under two. Liébeault even came to the conclusion that a living being can, merely by his presence, exercise a salutary influence on another living being quite independently of suggestion.

However that may be, the mysterious power that after Braid was ascribed to suggestion did not bring us any closer to understanding the curative process. It is more than likely that the ordinary hypnotizer has no curative power at all, and that his command simply starts a train of self-suggestion from the conscious mind, which otherwise would not have penetrated sufficiently deeply to bring about a nervous change.

It is even legitimate to suppose that the same power may be at work in charms, **amulets,** and incantations. **E. W. Cox** may have hit upon the truth when he wrote: "The use of the passes is to direct the attention of the patient to the part of the body then being operated upon. The effect of directing the attention of the mind to any part of the frame is to increase the flow of nerve force [or vital force] to that part."

The healer himself may have no knowledge of the process. The supposition that when he lays his hand on the diseased part of the body a magnetic current passes through may not be correct at all, even if the patients often experience a feeling of warmth, as of an electric shock. The healer's influence appears to be rather a directive one for the patient's own powers, which the healer turns into a more efficient channel. If the hypnotizer is more successful than the average psychic healer, an explanation may be found in the trance state into which the patient is thrown, giving him direct access to the subconscious self to which, to use the words of **F. W. H. Myers,** "a successful appeal is being made through suggestion." In the *Proceedings* of the Society for Psychical Research, he suggests,

"Beneath the threshold of waking consciousness there lies, not merely an unconscious complex of organic processes but an intelligent vital control. To incorporate that profound control with our waking will is the great evolutionary end which hypnotism, by its group of empirical artifices, is beginning to help us to attain."

This vital control he believed to be the result of some influx from the unseen world; the efficacy of suggestion was dependent on the quantity of new energy that could be imbibed from the spiritual world by directing subliminal attention to a corporeal function.

The problem of psychic healing, however, is much more complex than it appears. It bristles with interesting and stubborn facts that refuse to be fitted into convenient pigeonholes. Suggestion appears to be ruled out when healers cure animals. The process of healing seems interwoven with psychical manifestations, the success of healing often serving as evidence of the paranormal. Medical **clairvoyance, psychometry,** and direct and indirect action by spirits are concepts that demand consideration.

The somnambules of the early magnetizers diagnosed their own diseases. This was known later as **autoscopy.** It is now a rare phenomenon. As an intermediate instance between autoscopy and clairvoyant diagnosis, the curious case in Baron Carl du Prel's *Experimental-Psychologie* (1890) is worth mention. To a hypnotic subject it was suggested that, in his dream, he would find a certain cure for his ailments. The dream was very vivid, a voice giving medical advice was heard, and when these instructions were followed the patient's health considerably improved.

To the eyes of medical clairvoyants, the human body appears to be transparent. They see and describe in lay terms the seat and appearance of the disease. Some have a more restricted power and diagnose from the changes in the **aura** of the patient, the color being allegedly affected by illness.

Psychometrists do not require the presence of the patient at all. A lock of hair may be sufficient to put the medium on the right track. Sometimes an index, i.e., the mere mention of the name, will suffice. The medium, however, sometimes suffers sympathetically. Temporarily he or she often assumes the bodily conditions of the afflicted man and vividly experiences his ailments.

The therapeutic services of psychical research are now often acknowledged by psychoanalysts and physicians. **Crystal gazing** and **automatic writing** help to explore the subconscious mind. Long forgotten memories may be recalled and events of importance may be traced to their source and enable the psychoanalyst to form conclusions without hypnotic experiments. The **divining rod** (the diviner holding bacterial cultures in his hand) has also been discovered as a means of successful diagnosis, and the use of the pendulum in place of the rod has developed into the art of **radiesthesia.**

Spirit Healing

Often diagnosis and cure take place through alleged spirit influence, advice, or direct action. A physician, Josiah A. Gridley of Southampton, Massachusetts, confessed in his *Astounding Facts from the Spirit World* (1854) to have often known a patient's disease and the treatment to be followed before he ever went to see that patient. He attributed the remarkable success of his practice to his communion with the spirit world.

In England, the first spiritual healer, a lecturer on mesmerism named Hardinge, became convinced through spirit communications that epilepsy was due to demonic **possession** and undertook to cure such cases by spirit instruction. J. D. Dixon, a homeopathic doctor, was the next English healer who, after being converted to Spiritualism in 1857, treated his patients with prescriptions obtained by raps. Daniel Offord, a nine-year-old English boy, wrote prescriptions in Latin, a language which he did not know. He predicted the 1853 cholera epidemic two months in advance and prescribed a daily dose of half a teaspoonful of carbon as an antidote.

The spirits who assist mediums mostly claim to have been physicians on earth who have attained to a higher knowledge in the beyond. **A. H. Jacob** ("Jacob the Zouave") actually saw the spirits ministering to his patients. **Mrs. J. H. Conant** attributed Jacob's curative powers to the knowledge of "Dr. John Dix Fisher" in spirit; similarly "Dr. Lascelles" who worked through C. A. Simpson in the **Seekers** group in London; and **"Dr. Beale,"** a spirit entity who claimed to have followed the medical profession on Earth and who worked through one Miss Rose, a medium. The strange cure of Mme X. (as recorded in the *Proceedings* of the SPR, vol. 9) was effected by a spirit doctor; the healing controls were Native Americans who were said to have been medicine men in their tribes.

The methods of Native American controls were quite interesting. As the medium **Gladys Osborne Leonard** describes in *My Life in Two Worlds* (1931),

"Mrs. Massey's chair was a wooden rocking one. Suddenly her chair began to rock backwards and forwards gently at first, then gathering speed, till it rocked at a tremendous rate. Then, to our horror, the chair turned a complete somersault. So did Mrs. Massey. She fell right on her head, and lay where she fell. I rushed to her, and before I realised what was happening North Star had taken control of me. A lump, the size of an egg, had come up on Mrs. Massey's head. North Star placed my hands upon it; in a few moments it had gone. North Star then left her head alone and proceeded to make passes over her body, particularly over the heart. He gave loud grunts of satisfaction, and seemed extremely well pleased with something. After about half an hour's hard work he stopped controlling me, and Mrs. Massey then disclosed the fact that she had felt very ill for some days past, and she felt better now than she had for months."

Further on, Leonard states,

"When North Star controlled me for healing, he always appeared to appeal to someone far higher than himself before commencing his treatment. He never spoke, but he used to hold his hands upward and outward as if he expected something to be put, or poured into them. His attitude was so obviously one of prayer, or supplication, though he was usually in a standing position."

The most well-known psychic healer was **Edgar Cayce** (1877–1945) who diagnosed and prescribed for thousands of ailments in a state of self-induced trance.

Healing at a Distance

Cases of healing at a distance are also on record. When the healer's magnetism is said to be transferred into water, paper, or cloth one may argue for suggestion as an explanation; there are, however, more difficult instances. According to a letter from E. W. Capron, quoted in Leah Underhill's *The Missing Link in Modern Spiritualism* (1885) on the occasion of Capron's first visit to the **Fox sisters** in Rochester, he mentioned casually that his wife was affected with a severe and troublesome cough. Leah Fox in trance suddenly declared: "I am going to cure Rebecca of the cough." She then gave an accurate description of Rebecca and pronounced her cured. Returning home, Capron found her extremely well and the trouble never returned. Absent healing, through prayer groups, is now a regular activity of healing centers.

Cases are recorded in which an apparition at the bedside of a sick person effects a cure by the laying on of hands or by giving instructions. Materialized spirit hands made passes over the head, throat, chest, and back of **Stainton Moses** to relieve his bronchitis. While it may have been Stainton Moses's faith in the powers of his guides that effected the cure, this does not, however, explain how the healing took place.

Neurologist J. M. Charcot (1825–1893) notes,

"The faith which was healing power seems to me to be the greatest of medicines, for it may succeed where all other remedies have failed. But why should faith, which works on the soul, be considered more miraculous than a drug, which acts on the body? Has anyone yet understood how a drug can cure?"

St. Bernard, the Abbot of Clairvaux (1090–1153), **Valentine Greatrakes** (1662), Jacob The Zouave (1828–1913), **J. R. Newton** (1810–1883), the **Earl of Sandwich** (1839–1916), author of *My Experiences in Spiritual Healing* (London, 1915), and such modern healers as the late **Harry Edwards** (1893–1976) to mention a few names only, put many astonishing cures on record that seem to be authentic.

The Nature of Healing

The mind-cures of Christian Science must also be considered. These are wrought by the perception of God as the sole reality and the belief that neither matter nor evil exist. Reports of spectacular healings come from the records of the **Church of Christ Scientist,** just as they come from Roman Catholicism, evangelical Christianity, and various Spiritualist, occult, and metaphysical groups. There appears to be little objective difference between spiritual healing, divine healing, mind-cure, and faith-cure (the removal of pain by faith in God's power and by prayer). In this respect, one may go back to the ancient days when sleeping in the temple, after having invoked the help of God, often brought about healing at the shrines of Aesculapius, Isis, and Seraphis.

Astonishing instances of healing are recorded in Carré de Montgeron's book *La Verité des Miracles opérés par l'intercession de M. de Paris* (Cologne, 1745–47), dedicated to the king of France. Miracles took place at the tomb of the Abbé Paris, the Jansenist, in 1731 and the three or four years following. The cure of Mlle. Coirin was without precedent. Cancer had completely destroyed her left breast, and the case seemed utterly hopeless. A visit to the tomb not only cured her, but restored the breast and nipple without any trace of a scar. She was examined in Paris by the royal physician, M. Gaulard, who declared the restoration of the nipple an actual creation. Other physicians deposed before notaries that the cure was perfect. Other amazing cures followed.

The cemetery of St. Médard became so famous for this occurrence that the ire of the Jesuits was aroused and soon afterward, according to Voltaire, it was inscribed on the churchyard wall:

De par le Roi—défense à Dieu
De faire miracle en ce lieu.

Voltaire said that God obeyed and the miracles stopped. This, however, is contradicted by the cures, which kept on occurring for a space of 25 years. And miraculous cures were effected at Treves in Germany by touching a relic known as the **Holy Coat of Treves** in 1891. Holywell in Wales was called the Welsh Lourdes for similar occurrences. **Lourdes** itself has become an established site for miracles in healing.

Recent Developments

The most sensational modern development of psychic healing is **psychic surgery,** which takes two forms. The first, in which the medium mimes operations, is allegedly guided by the spirit of a dead doctor; in the second, in which psychic healers appear to perform real operations, either with their bare hands or with primitive instruments, wounds heal instantaneously. The latter type of psychic surgery, practiced widely in the Philippines and Brazil, remains highly controversial, with conflicting evidence of authenticity and fraud.

Since the rise of paraposychology, psychic healing has been considered under the general heading of psychokinesis. During the 1960s, some interesting healing research was carried out, as various people who claimed healing powers were put to the test in laboratories in attempts to effect living objects. The most spectacular of these experiments used Oscar Estabany, a Hungarian immigrant, who worked with cancer researcher Bernard Grad of McGill University, Montreal. Through the 1960s, Grad involved Estabany in a set of ever more complicated experiments that had as their object the stimulation of the growth of plants and the increase of the rate of healing in wounds on mice. Biochemist Justa Smith also found that Estabany could stimulate the growth of enzymes. The choice of targets in these carefully controlled experiments was made in each case to take the factor of suggestion away.

In one of the most interesting of experiments, Estabany was not allowed near the plants, but merely held the water used to water the plants in his hands. As with other experiments, the plants watered with Estabany's water grew taller.

The Estabany experiments stand as among the most impressive in psychokinesis and are a demonstration of the healing power inherent in at least some human beings. The understanding of a healing power in some persons underlies the popular practice of therapuetic touch developed by Dolores Krieger, a nursing instructor, during the mid-1970s.

Sources:

Carter, Mary Ellen, and William McGarey. *Edgar Cayce on Healing.* New York: Warner, 1972.

Dooley, Anne. *Every Wall a Door.* London: Abelard-Schuman, 1973. Reprint, Bergenfield, N.J.: E. P. Dutton, 1974.

Edwards, Harry. *A Guide to the Understanding and Practice of Spiritual Healing.* Surrey, England: Spiritual Healing Sanctuary, 1974.

———. *Thirty Years a Spiritual Healer.* Surrey, England: Spiritual Healing Sanctuary, 1968.

Flammonde, Paris. *The Mystic Healers.* New York: Stein & Day, 1974.

Guirdham, Arthur. *Obsession: Psychic Forces and Evil in the Causation of Disease.* London: Neville Spearman, 1972.

Hammond, Sally. *We Are All Healers.* New York: Harper & Row, 1973. Reprint, New York: Ballantine, 1974.

Hutton, Bernard. *Healing Hands.* London: W. H. Allen, 1966.

James, R. L. L. *The Church and Bodily Healing.* Essex, England: C. W. Daniel, 1929.

Kiev, Ari. *Magic, Faith and Healing.* New York: Macmillan, 1964.

Macmillan, W. J. *The Reluctant Healer.* London: Victor Gollancz, 1952.

Melton, J. Gordon. *A Reader's Guide to the Church's Ministry of Healing.* Independence, Mo.: Academy of Religion and Psychical Research, 1977.

Melton, J. Gordon, Jerome Clark, and Aidan Kelly. *New Age Encyclopedia.* Detroit: Gale Research, 1990.

Montgomery, Ruth. *Born to Heal.* New York: Coward, McCaan & Geoghan, 1973.

Nolen, William. *Healing: A Doctor in Search of a Miracle.* New York: Random House, 1975.

Rose, Louis. *Faith Healing.* London: Victor Gollancz, 1952.

Sherman, Harold. *Wonder Healers of the Philippines.* Los Angeles: DeVorss, 1966. Reprint, London: Psychic Press, 1967.

Tenhaeff, W. H. C. *Paranormal Healing Powers.* Olten, 1957.

Valentine, Tom. *Psychic Surgery.* Chicago: Henry Regnery, 1974.

Healing by Faith

Faith healing, the idea that faith in God is the operative agent in miraculous healings of the body, is large part a misnomer. Most Christian ministers and evangelists who practice healing understand clearly that God, through the power of the Holy Spirit, is the operative force in healing. In Christian theology, faith is the name given to the trusting relationship the Christian hopefully has with God. Given the omnipotence of God, faith is often seen as the element that allows the believer to receive God's healing power.

The practice of healing in evangelical churches has often received bad press. It has been attacked by those who believe it is an exercise in ignorance. The image of healing ministers has not been helped by those few who have advocated a complete break with doctors, an attitude carried over from the days prior to the scientific medicine of this century. Given the successes of medicine, the miracles reported have not dealt with the question of those who failed to receive any healing. A few have cited lack of faith as a reason why some people are not healed.

Divine healing, the more proper designation of what is popularly called faith healing, emerged in force in the 1870s, contemporaneously with Christian Science and **New Thought.** Physicians were scarce and their cures still haphazard at best. The leader of the new healing movement was an Episcopal physician, Charles Cullis, who held healing meetings each summer beginning in the 1880s. Among those who were healed at his hand was Rev. Albert Benjamin Simpson, a Presbyterian minister who had responded to the new Holiness movement that had emerged among the Methodists. Members of the Holiness movement saw themselves living in the last days, when God would pour his spirit out anew on his people (Acts 2). They thought they lived in a time of miracles.

Simpson joined hands with G. O. Barnes, also a former Presbyterian minister, who had worked with evangelist Dwight L. Moody and also had been affected by Holiness preachers. In 1876, Barnes traveled through Kentucky, saving souls and healing the sick by laying on hands in the name of the Lord. By 1882, Barnes and A. B. Simpson were working together. Simpson began a magazine, the first step toward founding the Christian and Missionary Alliance, the first modern denomination to advocate healing as a central tenet. Simpson developed an understanding of Christ's fourfold ministry as Saviour, Sanctifier, Healer, and Coming King.

Another influential evangelist healer was John Alexander Dowie, an Australian Congregationist minister who came to the United States from Australia in 1888 as head of the international Divine Healing Asssociation. He eventually settled in Zion, Illinois, north of Chicago, and founded the independent Christian Catholic Church. Dowie was a controversial figure, constantly in conflict with authorities, and lost control of his own movement following an illness in 1906. His community was a frequent stop on the tours of initerant healing evangelists and several of the residents emerged to became evangelists of note.

Healing in the Holiness movement was passed along to the Pentecostal movement. That movement began with Holiness evangelist Charles Fox Parham. Parham opened the Bethel Healing Home and Bible School in Topeka, Kansas, and it was here in 1901 that people began "speaking in tongues," the definitive experience of Pentecostalism. In his revival campaigns, Parham practiced healing through the laying on of hands, and hundreds of cures were claimed. Among Parham's Bible school students was African American Holiness preacher William J. Seymour, who became pastor of a small holiness congregation located on Azusa Street in Los Angeles.

The healing emphasis in Pentecostalism set the stage for the emergence of Aimee Semple McPhearson, one of the most colorful healing evangelists of the 1920s. Unable to find a home in the older denominations, she founded the independent Church of the Foursquare Gospel, drawing her doctrinal perspective from A. B. Simpson. Although MacPherson's following was initially small, a revival campaign in San Diego became immensely successful through claims of miraculous healing under her ministry, and her followers eventually provided funds for a huge Angelus Temple in Los Angeles. A charismatic figure, McPherson had a flair for publicity, and was one of the early evangelists to take advantage of the new communication possibilities provided by radio. She purchased a radio station in Los Angeles, and her services were broadcast to thousands of followers across the United States. In 1926, she was supposed to have been kidnaped for a month, but critics have stated that this story covered a "love-nest" scandal.

During the Great Depression, healing evangelism suffered something of a decline, although there were still many missions and itinerant preachers. There was a great upsurge in evangelism after World War II with the ministry of William Marrion Branham, an independent Baptist preacher who attracted huge crowds with his healing during the 1940s. There were rumors that he had even raised a man from the dead. Amongst those influenced by Branham's gospel campaigns were Oral Roberts, O. L. Jaggers, Gayle Jackson, T. L. Osborn, and Gordon Lindsay, all of whom developed their own ministries. In spite of a great expansion of such evangelism during the 1950s, there was again some decline through the 1960s, largely attributed to the development of air conditioning, which virtually killed independent itinerant evangelism of all kinds until the emergence of large air conditioned facilities in the 1980s.

Marjoe Gortner, a healing evangelist as a teenage preacher, left the field and appeared in a documentary film (*Marjoe,* 1972) in which he exposed the tricks used by some evangelists to support their highly competitive work. His exposure of the underbelly of healing ministries, and the disgusting practices of some ministers, disillusioned thousands of would-be followers and threw doubt on other evangelists.

By 1970, the end of the traveling tents was in sight, as increasingly sophisticated audiences expected comfortable seats and air conditioning. However, a recovery was seen as revival services were shifted to hotel auditoriums and the new civic centers built to house seasonal sports events. Experienced evangelists such as Oral Roberts, W. V. Grant, and Rex Humbard found a new life.

New life for the healing evangelists also came from the emergence of the charismatic movement, a new spread of Pentecostalism within the older mainline denominations. As Baptists, Methodists, and Presbyterians found the baptism of the Holy Spirit and spoke in tongues, they became open to the Pentecostal message of healing. A new generation of healers emerged, including Don Stewart, **Kathryn Kuhlman,** Roxanne Brandt, and many others. Included among them was the sister of the former president, **Ruth Carter Stapleton.** One notable evangelist healer is **Willard Fuller,** who specializes in dental healing. An eyewitness reported: "He prays for people and God fills their teeth. I have actually seen fillings appear in teeth that had cavities; some gold, some silver, some white enamel-like substances, and some are completely restored to their original condition."

Is Faith Healing Genuine?

Healing as practiced by the Pentecostal and Charismatic evangelists raises all of the questions that any form of nonconventional or psychic healing does. Do healings occur? If paranormal healings occur, do they happen because of some psychokinetic force? By definition, consideration of God and the Holy Spirit stands outside of any scientific discourse, but might it be that the results of any divine intervention in the life of an individual have measurable consequences that could be documented? Could it be that subtle psychokinetic forces are active but misunderstood as miraculous or divine?

Given current knowledge of the mundane healing forces, quite apart from drugs, available to the average individual, from placebos to the body's own healing capacity, those skeptical of divine healing have made a strong case that all religious healing can be ascribed to natural forces—the placebo effect (operative in most cases of fraud), delayed action by medications, temporary or spontaneous remission, or, as often as not, misdiagnosis of the person's condition. On such grounds, for example, physician William Nolan attacked the ministry of Kathryn Kuhlman.

The most recent attack upon the legitimacy of healing ministries followed the discovery and exposure in the mid-1980s of several healers, most notably Peter Popoff and W. V. Grant, Jr., who were using fraudulent techniques derived from **Spiritualism** to bolster their appearance as people possessed of unusual powers. Magician **James Randi** surveyed the activities of numerous evangelists. He found most of them to be naive people of integrity, but discovered several engaged in fraud.

Defenders have countered with reports, complete with medical records, of people who have been healed in their meetings. These are, however, relatively few in number given the amount of effort required to properly document a case. Also, in most cases today, the proper records do not exist, the condition is largely stress related (psychosomatic), or the causes operative in the healings are not clear.

Many who defend healing in the religious context no longer argue that such healing is miraculous. Rather they cite the value of a life in which community, intimacy, fellowship, forgiveness, order, and compassion operate to destroy the guilt, alienation, and chaos that contributes to diseased conditions.

Sources:

Allen, A. A. *Bound to Lose, Bound to Win.* Garden City, N.Y.: Doubleday, 1970.

Berger, Arthur S., and Joyce Berger. *The Encyclopedia of Parapsychology and Psychical Research.* New York: Paragon House, 1991.

Harrell, David Edwin, Jr. *All Things Are Possible With God.* Bloomington, Ind.: Indiana University Press, 1975.

Hart, Ralph. *Doctors Pronounced Me Dead in Dallas.* Detroit: The Author, n.d.

Lindsay, Gordon. *William Branham, A Man Sent From God.* Dallas, Tex.: Voice of Healing Publishing, 1950.

Melton, J. Gordon. *A Reader's Guide to the Church's Ministry of Healing.* Independence, Mo.: Academy of Religion and Psychical Research, 1977.

Randi, James. *The Faith Healers.* Buffalo, N.Y.: Prometheus Books, 1987.

Roberts, Oral. *My Story.* Tulsa, Okla.: Oral Roberts Evangelistic Association, 1961.

Rose, Louis. *Faith Healing.* London: Victor Gollancz, 1968.

Simpson, Eve. *The Faith Healer: Deliverance Evangelism in North America.* St. Louis, Mo.: Concordia, 1977. Reprint, New York: Pyramid, 1977.

Spraggett, Allen. *Kathryn Kuhlman: The Woman Who Believes in Miracles.* New York: Thomas Y. Crowell, 1970. Reprint, New York: New American Library, 1971.

Stegall, C., and C. C. Harwood. *The Modern Tongues and Healing Movement.* Western Bible Institute, n.d.

Tenhaeff, W. H. C. *Paranormal Healing Powers.* Olten, 1957.

Healing by Touch

In England, Scotland, and also in France, the idea that a touch of the royal hand was a sure remedy for scrofula was long prevalent, and consequently this complaint acquired the now familiar name "**king's evil.**" In France, so far as can be ascertained, this interesting practice dates from the reign of Louis IX, and in England from that of Edward III, who is recorded to have performed a considerable number of cures. He initially would wash the affected part of the sufferer, but gradually the actual bathing was discontinued, and most subsequent kings merely touched while offering prayers on behalf of the patient.

Eventually the religious ceremony used on such occasions grew more elaborate, and during the reign of Henry VII a special "king's evil" petition was drawn up. It is found in some editions of the Service Book printed as late as the beginning of the eighteenth century.

The belief that kings ruled by divine right was strong in Scotland, and so it is natural to assume that the early inhabitants of that land regarded their sovereigns as capable of miracles. There is little or no evidence, nevertheless, that the Stuarts, prior to the union of the Crowns, practiced touching for king's evil. Scarcely was Charles I on the British throne, however, before he began to demonstrate his powers, and scrofulous persons flocked from far and near accordingly. They came in such numbers that early in the fifth year of his reign Charles found it essential to specify certain times for their reception at court; the proclamation that he issued on the subject is found in the *Historical Collections* of John Rushworth, sometime secretary to Oliver Cromwell.

In the proclamation the king spoke at length of the many cures wrought by his "royal predecessors." This may allude purely to the Plantagenets or Tudors, but it is equally possible that these references indicate touching for scrofula on the part of the early Stuarts.

John Evelyn, in his *Diary,* writes repeatedly of Charles II's activities in this relation, while Samuel Pepys refers to the same thing, and in one passage states that the sight failed to interest him in the least, for he had seen it often before. The practice of healing by the royal touch did not end with the ousting of the Stuarts in 1689. The lexicographer Dr. Samuel Johnson was taken by his father when a boy to London from Litchfield to be touched "for the evil" by Queen Anne, in 1712. The Chevalier de St. George attempted healing by touch on several occasions, and his son Prince Charles, when in Scotland in 1745, made at least one attempt.

At a late period, coins that had been touched by the king were believed to ward off evil or scrofula. These were known as "royal touch-pieces" and specimens of several are preserved in the British Museum, London.

Healing by Touch in Ancient Times

The natural process of healing was thought by early peoples to be effected by a mysterious power possessed only by God and his servants—emperors, kings, priests, and saints. The common man believed he must have faith in order to be healed, and great ceremony often accompanied healing "miracles." Healers used the laying on of hands and special words and prayers, as well as objects like **talismans, amulets,** rings, and images of saints.

The healing of the sick by touch and the laying on of hands was found among the people of India and Egypt, and especially among the Jews. Egyptian sculptures depict healers placing one hand on the patient's stomach and the other on his back. The Chinese, according to the accounts of early missionaries such as Athanasius Kircher, in *China . . . Illustrata* (1667), healed sickness by the laying on of hands. In the Hebrew Bible (the Christian Old Testament) are numerous examples of healing by touch.

One instance is the healing of a seemingly dead child by Elisha, who stretched himself three times upon the child and prayed. The manner in which Elisha raised the dead son of a Shunamite woman was even more remarkable. He told Gehazi to go before him and lay his staff upon the face of the child. When that failed, Elisha laid himself upon the child, placing his hands upon the child's hands so that the child's body became warm again and he opened his eyes.

Elisha's healing powers survived his death:

"And Elisha died, and they buried him, and the bands of the Moabites invaded the land in the coming of the year. And it came to pass, as they were burying a man that, behold, they spied a band of men; and they cast the man into the sepulchre of Elisha, and when the man was let down, and touched the bones of Elisha, he revived and stood upon his feet" (2 Kings 13:20, 21).

Naaman the leper, when he stood before Elisha's house with his horses and chariots, having been told to wash seven times in the Jordan said, "Behold I thought, he will surely come out to me, and stand, and call upon the name of the Lord his God, and strike his hand over the place, and recover the leper" (2 Kings 5:11).

The Christian New Testament is particularly rich in examples of the efficacy of the laying on of hands, healing by this method being a major theme in the early Christian church. "Neglect not the gift that is in thee, which was given thee by prophecy, with the laying on of the hands of the presbytery" (1 Tim. 4:14) was the principal maxim of the apostles, for the practical use of their powers for the good of their brethren in Christ.

St. Paul was remarkable for his powers: "And it came to pass that the father of Publius lay sick of a fever and of a bloody flux; to whom Paul entered in, and prayed and laid his hands on him and healed him" (Acts 28:8). And again:

"And Ananias went his way, and entered into the house, and putting his hands on him, said, Brother Saul, the Lord, even Jesus that appeared unto thee in the way as thou camest, hath sent me that thou mayest receive thy sight and be filled with the Holy Ghost. And immediately there fell from his eyes as it had been scales, and he received sight" (Acts 9:17–8).

Among the many stories of Jesus' healings are several from the Gospel of Mark:

"And they brought young children to him, that he might touch them, and his disciples rebuked those who brought them. But Jesus said, 'Suffer the little children to come unto me, for of such is the kingdom of heaven.' And he took them up in his arms, put his hands upon them, and blessed them" (Mark 10:13–14,16).

Also:

". . . they brought unto him one that was deaf and had an impediment in his speech, and they besought him to put his hand upon him. And he took him aside from the multitude, and put his fingers into his ears, and he spit and touched his tongue and, looking up to heaven, he sighed, and said unto him, 'Ephphatha'—that is, Be opened. And straightway his ears were opened, and the string of his tongue was loosed, and he spake plain" (Mark 7:32–35).

Other passages on healing are scattered throughout the four gospels. In the histories of the saints, innumerable examples are recorded. They took their lead from Jesus' words: "In my name shall they cast out devils; they shall speak with new tongues; they shall take up serpents, and if they drink any deadly thing it shall not hurt them; they shall lay their hands on the sick and they shall recover" (Mark 16:17–18).

The saints are said to have accomplished everything through absolute faith in Christ, and were therefore able to perform miracles. St. Patrick, the Irish apostle, healed the blind by laying on his hands. St. Bernard is said to have restored 11 blind persons to sight and 18 lame persons to the use of their limbs in one day at Constance. At Cologne he healed 12 lame individuals, caused 3 dumb persons to speak, and made 10 who were deaf to hear; when he himself was ill, St. Lawrence and St. Benedict appeared to him and cured him by touching the affected part. Even his plates and dishes were said to have cured sickness after his death.

The miracles of Saints Margaret, Katherine, Elizabeth, and Hildegarde, and especially the miraculous cures of the two holy martyrs Cosmas and Damianus, belong to this class. They were said to have freed the emperor Justinian from an incurable sickness. St. Odilia embraced a leper who was shunned by all, warmed him, and restored him to health.

Remarkable above all others are those cases where persons who were at the point of death have recovered by holy baptism or extreme religious fervor. The emperor Constantine is one of the best examples. Pyrrhus, king of Epirus, was reputed to have the power of assuaging colic and afflictions of the spleen by laying the patients on their backs and passing his big toe over them (Plutarch, *Vita Pyrrhi*). The emperor Vespasian cured nervous conditions, lameness, and blindness solely by the laying on of his hands (Suelin, *Vita Vespas*). According to Coelius Spartianus, Hadrian cured those afflicted with dropsy by touching them with the points of his fingers, and recovered himself from a violent fever by similar treatment. King Olaf healed Egill on the spot by merely laying his hands upon him and singing proverbs, according to the *Edda*.

The kings of England and France cured diseases of the throat by touch. It is said that the pious Edward the Confessor of England and Philip I of France were the first who possessed this power. The French formula used on such occasions was "the King touches you, go and be healed," and the phrase was spoken with the act of touching. In France this power was retained until the time of the Revolution, and it is said that at the coronation the exact manner of touching and the formula "the King touches you, God heals you" were imparted to the new monarch.

Among German princes this curative power was ascribed to the counts of Hapsburg, and it was also believed that they were able to cure stammering by a kiss. According to Pliny, "There are men whose whole bodies possess medicinal properties, as the Marsi, the Psyli, and others, who cure the bite of serpents merely by the touch." He claimed this was especially true of the island of Cyprus, and later travelers confirmed these cures. In later times the Salmadores and Ensalmadores of Spain became famous for healing almost all diseases by prayer, laying on of hands, and by breathing upon the sick.

In Ireland, **Valentine Greatrakes** cured king's evil and other diseases by touch. One Richter, a nineteenth-century innkeeper at Royen, in Silicia, cured many thousands of sick persons in the open fields by touching them with his hands. Under the popes, laying on of hands was called *chirothesy*. **Franz Anton Mesmer** and his assistants also employed touch for healing purposes.

Sources:

Greatrakes, Valentine. *A Brief Account of Mr. Valentine Greatrake's, and Divers of the Strange Cures by Him Lately Performed.* London, 1666.

Hocart, A. M. *Kingship.* London: Humphrey Milford, 1927.

Rose, Louis. *Faith Healing.* London: Victor Gollancz, 1968.

Thompson, C. J. S. *Magic and Healing.* London: Rider, 1947. Reprint, Detroit: Gale Research, 1973.

Healing Center for the Whole Person

The project during the 1970s of a religious corporation that met at the **International Cooperation Council** (now the **Unity-in-Diversity Council**) world headquarters, Northridge, California. The Healing Center for the Whole Person was directed by various types of professional people who specialized in healing and sought to transcend traditional disciplines, incorporating all valid methods of healing the whole person "in the spirit of the emerging new age." The center grew out of the conference

"Healing the Whole Person," held in Los Angeles in May 1974. The center functioned for several years and then dissolved.

Healing Our World (Organization)

Organization devoted to linking groups and individuals all over the world in contemplation and cultural celebration in order to liberate love and healing energies. Healing Our World (HOW) creates "high games," celebrations, and other joyful experiences that allow individuals to remember "the source," love unconditionally, and connect with others.

Activities include "global healing events" (celebrating the connectedness of all life); "resonating cores" (effective technologies for bonding in small groups); a "love corps" (providing opportunities for meaningful service to others); local celebrations and events (celebrating the joy of being with family and supporting one another); and communication vehicles (a newsletter, computer network, and speakers bureau).

Leaders of the organization have affirmed, "We know that each of us has a deep mission to experience wholeness and to heal our world. We can best do this by accessing the Source within, opening ourselves to unconditional love, and linking up with other members of our Global Family, wherever they may be."

Address: 540 University Ave., Ste. 225, Palo Alto, CA 94301.

Heard, Gerald (Henry Fitz Gerald Heard) (1889–1971)

British author and lecturer with special interest in parapsychology. Heard was born October 6, 1889, in London. He studied at Cambridge University (B.A. honors in history, graduate work in philosophy and philosophy of religion, 1908–13) and lectured for the Oxford University Board of Extramural Studies from 1926 to 1929. Apart from his writing and lecturing, he was also a science commentator for the British Broadcasting Corporation (BBC) and lecturer for the British Ethical Society (1930–34). He lectured on historical anthropology at Duke University, Durham, North Carolina, in 1937. He was a council member of the **Society for Psychical Research,** London (1932–42), and studied on a Bollingen Trust grant (1945–47). Heard lived in California during his later years.

He wrote one of the early flying saucer books, *Is Another World Watching?* (1951), in which he suggests that the saucers themselves might be living entities. His other books include *The Social Substance of Religion* (1930), *Pain, Sex, and Time* (1939), *Is God in History?* (1950), *The Human Venture* (1955), and *Training for a Life of Growth* (1959). He died August 14, 1971.

Sources:

Heard, Gerald. *Is Another World Watching?* New York: Harpers, 1951.

Pleasants, Helene, ed. *Biographical Dictionary of Parapsychology.* New York: Helix Press, 1964.

Heart

Belief in the heart as a psychic structure dates to ancient times and stems from the characteristic responses of that organ to emotional crises. Some mystical writers have posited the idea of a subtle or spiritual heart center located slightly to the right of the physical heart.

In the Bible (Eccles. 10:2) it is said that the heart of the wise is at the right side and the heart of the foolish at the left. This proverb parallels the ancient Hindu yoga concept of the *anahata chakra,* or subtle heart center, which yogis have experienced as slightly to the right side in the body.

Heat and Light (Journal)

American Spiritualist journal published in Boston in the 1850s.

Heavenly Man, The

A concept of the Jewish mysticism of the **Kabala.** According to the Zohar, the "heavenly man" was the first of the sephiroth or divine emanations. Before the creation, God was without form, above and beyond all attributes. But after he created the heavenly man, he used him as a chariot in which to descend. And desiring to make himself known by his attributes, "He let Himself be styled as the God of pardon, the God of Justice, the God Omnipotent, the God of Hosts and He Who Is (Jahveh)."

The heavenly man is to be distinguished from the "earthly man." The creation of the earthly man was, indeed, the work of the heavenly man—that is, of the first emanation from God.

Sources:

Halevi, Z'ev ben Shimon. *AAM and the Kabbalistic Tree.* London: Rider, 1974.

Hecate

A Greek goddess, daughter of Zeus and Demeter, but of uncertain origin. She appears to have been one of the original Titans, who ruled the heaven, earth, and sea and could bestow gifts on mortals as they pleased. Later she was confused with other goddesses until she became known as a mystic goddess having all the magic powers of nature at her command. Magicians and witches sought her aid, and sacrifices of dogs, honey, and female black lambs were offered to her where three ways met, at crossroads, or in graveyards. Festivals were held in her honor annually at Egina.

In appearance she was frightful, and serpents hung hissing around her shoulders. As a dark goddess of ghosts and moonlight, her propitiation was an early form of **black magic** and **witchcraft.** In Shakespeare's play *Macbeth,* Hecate is the leader of three witches who plot Macbeth's downfall.

Sources:

Valiente, Doreen. *An ABC of Witchcraft Past and Present.* New York: St. Martin's Press, 1973.

Hefferlin, Gladys

Along with her husband, promoter of a story of a mysterious underground world culminating in an Antarctic kingdom called Rainbow City, supposed to have been constructed two and a half million years ago of plastic. It is warmed by hot springs and has eluded discovery by polar explorers because it is surrounded by ice walls 10,000 feet high, according to the story.

As distinct from the evil **deros** of the **Shaver mystery,** Rainbow City and its subterranean world are said to be ruled by "the Ancient Three," originally from the planet Mars, who take a benevolent interest in world politics and use their occult influence on behalf of humanity.

Sources:

Barton, Michael X. *Rainbow City and The Inner Earth Story.* Los Angeles: Futura Press, 1960. Reprint, Clarksburg, W. Va.: Saucerian Press, 1969.

Hefley Report, The

Former psychic newspaper edited by Carl D. Hefley. It reported on and discussed a wide range of paranormal topics for popular readership. It was published in the 1970s by U.S. Research, Inc., in Burbank, California. (See also **Hefley's Secret Journal**)

Hefley's Secret Journal

Publication edited by Carl D. Hefley. It supplemented his now-defunct newspaper **The Hefley Report** with in-depth stories and research on paranormal topics.

Heim, Roger (1900–)

French botanist who specialized in cryptogamy and contributed to knowledge of the hallucinogenic properties of **mushrooms.** He was born on February 12, 1900, in Paris. He studied at the University of Paris (D.Sc., 1931) and Uppsala University, Sweden (Hon. Ph.D.). Heim was appointed director of the French National Museum of Natural History, and also served as director of the laboratory for the study of mycology and tropical phytopathology at the Ecole Pratique des Hautes Etudes. His interest in parapsychology was stimulated by his studies of psychedelic **drugs,** especially those to be found in mushrooms. He wrote scholarly articles on the sacred mushroom rites of Mexican Indians.

Sources:

Heim, Roger, and R. B. Wasson. *Les champignons hallucinogens du Mexique.* Paris: Editions du Museum National d'Histoire Naturelle, 1958.

———. *Les champignons toxiques et hallucinogens.* Paris: Boubee, 1978.

Pleasants, Helene, ed. *Biographical Dictionary of Parapsychology.* New York: Helix Press, 1964.

Heindel, Max (1865–1919)

Public name of Carl Louis van Grasshoff. He was born in Germany to an aristocratic family. He became a maritime engineer and emigrated to the United States in 1895. Settling in Los Angeles in 1903, he joined the **Theosophical Society** and became vice president of the Los Angeles lodge in 1904. Through Theosophy he learned of **astrology,** a continuing interest throughout the rest of his life.

While visiting Europe in 1907, Heindel claimed that he encountered a mysterious **Rosicrucian** who took him to a Rose Cross temple on the border of Germany and Bohemia. There he was initiated into the order. He soon publicized the secret wisdom in his book *The Rosicrucian Cosmo-Conception* (1909).

However, his basic concepts were drawn from Theosophy in general and from **Rudolf Steiner** in particular. Steiner might have been his real "Rosicrucian" mentor. After publication of his book, Heindel founded various centers and created a headquarters and temple of what became known as the Rosicrucian Fellowship at Mount Ecclesia, Oceanside, California. Integral to his Rosicrucian work was astrology, and through his books Heindel became one of the early popularizers of the wisdom of the stars in the United States. He died in 1919. His two main books, *The Message of the Stars* (1919) and *Simplified Scientific Astrology* (1928), were published posthumously and remain in print. His wife, Augusta Foss Heindel, was also an editor and writer on Rosicrucian subjects and succeeded her husband as head of the organization. She died in 1938.

The Mount Ecclesia temple was the subject of a 50-year lawsuit by various factions, resolved only by the deaths of the principals.

Sources:

Heindel, Augusta Foss. *The Birth of the Rosicrucian Fellowship.* Oceanside, Calif.: Rosicrucian Fellowship, n.d.

Heindel, Max. *The Rosicrucian Cosmo-Conception.* Oceanside, Calif.: Rosicrucian Fellowship, 1909.

———. *The Rosicrucian Mysteries.* Oceanside, Calif.: Rosicrucian Fellowship, 1911.

———. *The Rosicrucian Philosophy, Questions and Answers.* Oceanside, Calif.: Rosicrucian Fellowship, 1922.

———. *Simplified Scientific Astrology.* Oceanside, Calif.: Rosicrucian Fellowship, 1928.

Hekalot

According to the Jewish mysticism of the **Kabala,** the Zohar, the seven halls of the world of Yetsirah, the divine halls into which the seekers for the chariot ("merkabah") strive to enter. Here dwell the angels, presided over by the angel Metatron, as well as the souls of men not especially noted for their piety. (The souls of the pious dwell in the world of Beriah.)

Hel (or Hela)

In Teutonic mythology, the goddess of death, one of the offspring of Loki and the giantess Angurbodi. The gods became alarmed at her and the other monsters that were coming to life in Jotunheim, so All-father advised that they be brought before him. Hel was cast into Niflheim, the realm beneath the roots of the world tree Yggdrasil, reserved for all those who die of sickness or old age. According to the myth, Hel governs this world, which is composed of nine regions into which she distributes those who come to her and in which she inhabits a strongly protected abode.

Niflheim is said to be "a dark abode far from the sun," its gates open to the "cutting north;" its walls "are formed of wreathed snakes and their venom is ever falling like rain," and it is surrounded by dark and poisonous streams. "Nidhog, the great dragon, who dwells beneath the central root of Yggdrasil, torments and gnaws the dead."

It is said that one-half of Hel's body is livid and the other half flesh-colored. Hunger is her table, starvation her knife, delay her man, slowness her maid, precipice her threshold, care her bed, and burning anguish forms the hangings of her apartments.

Heliocentric Astrologers of North America

Practitioners of **astrology** in the twentieth century face a common problem. Astrology is predicated on Earth as the center of the solar system, when in fact the planets, including Earth, revolve around the sun. Most astrologers have made some adjustment for this fact, but a small number have been working on a new astrological system based on the sun's central position in the solar system. Some of these astrologers, largely from Detroit and Windsor, Ontario, came together in 1982 and founded the Heliocentric Astrologers of North America.

The organization has as its purpose promoting heliocentric astrology and reestablishing lines of communication between astrologers and members of the scientific community, especially astrophysicists and astronomers. It also publishes a newsletter. Address: 4115 Echo Dr., West Bloomfield, MI 48033.

Heliotrope

A plant that follows the sun with its flowers and leaves and is popularly known as "turnsole." Heliotrope was believed to render its possessor invisible if the body was rubbed all over with the juice of this herb, which was also reputed to stop bleeding and avert danger from poison.

Hell

This word is believed to be from the Teutonic root *helan* (to cover), designating a subterranean or hidden place. It is sometimes used in the form of **Hel** to mean simply a place of the dead, with no mention of punishment. "Hel" or "Hela" is also the name of the mythical Teutonic goddess who was guardian of the dead.

This concept has a somewhat clear train of evolution. The Christian idea of a place of punishment was directly colored by the Jewish concept of "Sheol," which in turn took shape from Babylonian sources. When exactly hell began to be perceived as a place of punishment is not clear, as among the ancient Semites, Egyptians, and Greeks the underworld was regarded only as a place of the dead.

In Egypt "Amenti" is distinctly a place of the dead, one in which the tasks of life are for the most part duplicated. This was also the case among primitive people, who merely regarded the land of the dead as an extension of human existence in which people led a more or less shadowy life. The primitives did not generally believe in punishment after death and conceived that any breach of moral rule was summarily dealt with in this life. It was usually when a higher moral code emerged from totemic or similar beliefs that the idea of a place of punishment was invented by a priesthood.

However, this was not always the case. In Greece, Rome, and Scandinavia, Hades was merely looked upon as a place of the dead, where shadowy ghosts flitted to and fro, gibbering and squeaking as phantoms were believed to do. According to the Greeks, Hades was only some twelve feet under the surface of the ground, so Orpheus would not have had a long journey from the subterranean sphere to reach Earth once more. Hell was generally regarded as a sovereignty, a place ruled in an ordinary manner by a monarch set there for that purpose by the celestial powers.

Thus the Greek Hades ruled the Sad Sphere of the Dead, Osiris was lord and governor of the Egyptian Amenti, while in Central America there were twin rulers in the Kiche Hades, Xibalba, whose names were given as Hun-came and Vukub-came. The latter were malignant, unlike the Mictlán of Mexico, whose empire was for the generality of the people. These could only exist for four years, after which they became extinct.

The Mexicans represented Mictlán as a huge monster with open mouth ready to devour his victims; this was paralleled in the Babylonian Tiawith. It seems that at a certain stage in all mythologies the concept of a place of the dead was confounded with the idea of a place of punishment.

The Greeks generally bewailed the tragedy of humanity, being condemned to dwell forever in semidarkness after death. The possibility of the existence of a place of reward seems never to have appealed to them. To the Greek mind, life was everything; it was left to the Semitic conscience to evolve in the near East the concept of a place of punishment. Thus Sheol, a place of the dead, became a fiery abyss into which the wicked and unjust were thrust for their sins.

This was foreshadowed by Babylonian and Egyptian ideas, for Egyptians believed that those unable to pass a test of justification were simply refused admittance to Amenti. From the idea of rejection sprang the idea of active punishment. The Semitic concept of hell was probably reinforced with the introduction of Christianity into Europe, and colored by concepts of the underworld belonging to European mythologies.

"Hela" (Death) in Teutonic mythology was cast into the underground realm of Niflheim and given power over nine regions into which she distributed all who died through sickness or old age.

The ideas concerning the Celtic otherworld probably played only a small part in forming the British concept of hell. The Brythonic "Annwyl" was certainly subterranean, but it was by no means a place of punishment; rather, it was merely a microcosm of the world above, where folk hunted, ate, and drank, as in early Britain. The Irish otherworld was much the same.

In southern Europe the idea of hell appears to have been strongly influenced by both classical and Jewish concepts. The best picture of the medieval idea of the place of punishment is undoubtedly found in Dante's *Inferno.* Basing his description on the teachings of contemporary schoolmen, Dante also acknowledged Virgil as his master and followed him in many descriptions of Tartarus. The Semitic idea crops up here and there, however, such as in the beginning of one of the cantos, where what looks suspiciously like a Hebrew incantation is recorded.

In later medieval times the ingenuity of the monkish mind introduced many apparently original concepts. For instance, hell obtained an annex: purgatory. Its inhabitants took on a form that may be alluded to as European, in contrast to the more satyrlike shape of the earlier hierarchy of Hades. It featured grizzly forms of birdlike shape, with exaggerated beaks and claws, and the animal forms and faces of later medieval gargoyles could well be what the denizens of Hades seemed like in the eyes of the superstitious of the sixteenth and seventeenth centuries.

A modified version of these ideas was passed to later generations, and one may suspect that such superstitions were not altogether disbelieved by our forefathers.

Most Eastern mythological systems possess a hell that does not differ in any fundamental respect from that of most barbarian races, except that it is perhaps more specialized and involved. Many later writers, such as **Emanuel Swedenborg, Jakob Boehme, William Blake,** and others (including John Milton), have given us vivid pictures of the hierarchy and general condition of hell. For the most part these are based on patristic writings. In the Middle Ages endless controversy took place as to the nature and offices of the various inhabitants of the place of punishment (see **Demonology**), and the descriptions of later visionaries are practically mere repetitions of the conclusions arrived at then.

The locality of hell has also been a question of endless speculation. Some believed it to be in the sun, because the Greek name for the luminary is "Helios," but such etymologies have been in disfavor with most writers on the subject, and the popular idea that hell is subterranean has had no real rival.

Sources:

Bernstein, Alan E. *The Formation of Hell: Death and Retribution in the Ancient and Early Christian Worlds.* Ithaca, N.Y.: Cornell University Press, 1993.

Fox, Samuel J. *Hell in Jewish Literature.* Wheeling, Ill.: Whitehall, 1969.

Kohler, Kaufmann. *Heaven and Hell in Comparative Literature.* Folcroft, Pa., 1923.

Kvanvig, Jonathan L. *The Problem of Hell.* New York: Oxford University Press, 1993.

Lehner, Ernest, and J. Lehner. *Picture Book of Devils, Demons, and Witchcraft.* New York: Dover Publications, 1972.

MacCullough, John A. *The Harrowing of Hell: A Comparative Study of an Early Christian Doctrine.* London: T. & T. Clark, 1930. Reprint, New York: AMS Press, 1981.

Mew, James. *Traditional Aspects of Hell.* London: Swan, Sonnenschein, 1903. Reprint, Detroit: Gale Research, 1971.

Swedenborg, Emanuel. *Heaven and Hell.* 1758. Reprint, New York: E. P. Dutton, 1931.

Walker, Daniel P. *Decline of Hell: Seventeenth Century Discussions of Eternal Torment.* London: Routledge, 1964.

Hellawes

A medieval sorceress, lady of the castle Nigramous. She attempted to win the love of Lancelot, but being unable to do so, she perished. Her story is told in Sir Thomas Mallory's *Morte d'Arthur,* first published in 1485.

Hellenbach, Baron Lazar De Baczolay (1827–1887)

Hungarian philosopher whose numerous important works, including *Birth and Death* and *The Philosophy of Sound Common Sense* closely concern psychical research. In *Birth and Death,* which was translated into English in 1886, Hellenbach proposes the original idea that no change of world occurs at the moment of birth and death, except in the method of perception. In *The Philosophy of Sound Common Sense,* published in 1876, he tells the story of his psychical investigations.

Hellenbach's first convincing mediumistic experience was in 1857 at a Countess D.'s castle in Croatia. For six years thereafter, he engaged the services of two women as mediums. Through one of them he supposedly communicated with the philosopher Schopenhauer.

In 1870 he made the acquaintance of **Baroness Adelma Vay,** whose powers as a seeress opened up new fields of research for him.

In 1875 Hellenbach witnessed impressive physical manifestations with **Lottie Fowler.** Following these he invited many well-known mediums to Vienna. **Henry Slade** visited in 1878, and the results of the sittings were published in a pamphlet, *Mr. Slade's Residence in Vienna: An Open Letter to My Friend.* In February 1880 Karl Hansen, the famous hypnotist, went to Vienna. In response to the controversy that arose in the press, Baron Hellenbach contributed another pamphlet, *Is Hansen a Swindler? A Study of Animal Magnetism.* In the same year he stood up with similar vigor for the medium **William Eglinton,** who had been charged with **fraud.**

The medium **Harry Bastian** paid Hellenbach two visits, of which he gives an account in a leaflet entitled *The Latest Communications from the "Intelligible" World.* In 1884 Bastian went to Vienna for the third time. The sitters were Crown Prince Rudolph and Archduke John. The archduke seized the "materialized spirit," and it was found to be the medium. The archduke himself published a pamphlet about this exposure, *A Glimpse into Spiritism.* Hellenbach countered with another, *The Logic of Facts,* in which he attempted a defense of the medium.

In 1885, after a second visit from Eglinton, Hellenbach gave up his residence in Vienna and returned to his second home in Croatia, where he began another book. However, he only completed a series of essays, published in the periodical *The Sphynx* under the title "Ether as a Solution of the Mystic Problem."

Hell-Fire Club

An eighteenth-century British Satanist society of rich men, politicians, and eccentrics based at Medmenham Abbey in Buckinghamshire and later in caves at High Wycombe. The founder was the notorious profligate Sir Francis Dashwood (1708–1781), a member of parliament who was appointed chancellor of the exchequer in 1762. His ignorance and incapacity for the latter post resulted in his resignation a few months later.

As a young man Dashwood plunged into a life of pleasure and dissipation. When only 17, he became a member of one of the earlier Hell-Fire clubs, which conducted secret orgies in a cellar. There were rumors that during Dashwood's subsequent European travels he was initiated into a diabolic cult in Venice and brought back to England various magical grimoires and manuals.

About 1745, Dashwood founded the brotherhood known as the Knights of St. Francis of Wycombe or the Franciscans of Medmenham, more popularly known as the Hell-Fire Club. In 1750 Dashwood rented the old Cistercian abbey of Medmenham on the river Thames, near Marlow, originally founded in 1201. He made costly renovations to the premises, which he furnished with an altar in the chapel, candlesticks, and pornographic pictures. The entrance to the abbey bore the inscription *Fay ce que voudras* (Do what thou wilt), derived from the Abbey of Thelema in Rabelais's *Gargantua.* The same motto was adopted by **Aleister Crowley** for his own Abbey of Thelema nearly two centuries later.

Although it has been claimed that Dashwood's "Franciscans" (derived from his own forename) were largely rakes of the period seeking drunken sex orgies, there was an inner circle or "superior order" of 12 members who held obscene parodies of Catholic ritual in the chapel as an elementary form of Satanism. As grand master, Dashwood used a communion cup to pour libations to pagan gods, and even administered the sacrament to a baboon in a contemptuous mockery of sacred ritual. Members of this superior order included Lord Sandwich, the libertine Paul Whitehead, the debauchee George Selwyn, and Thomas Potter (son of the archbishop of Canterbury). A fictionalized account of the Franciscans was published in Charles Johnston's novel *Chrysal* (1760).

The brotherhood flourished at Medmenham for 12 years, until it was exposed by John Wilkes, who had joined in 1762 but was later expelled, probably through political quarrels. At one of the Satanic rituals, Wilkes secretly brought an ape with horns tied on its head, dressed in a long black cloak. The creature was released at the height of the ceremony and sprang upon the Satanists, who screamed with fear at the devil they thought they had raised by their mockery. Wilkes and the politician Charles Churchill exposed the brotherhood in an issue of the *North Briton* newspaper, and a satirical print appeared entitled "The Saint of the Convent."

In the face of public exposure, the Medmenham chapel was hastily stripped and its contents taken away to West Wycombe, where Dashwood attempted to revive his ceremonies. He built a church on Wycombe Hill, where he and his companions drank heavily and blasphemed the Psalms. In the caves underneath the hill, they attempted to revive the orgies and rituals of Medmenham, but some of Dashwood's friends had died and others tired of their activities.

After resigning from the post of chancellor of the exchequer, Dashwood retired from the ministry, and in 1763 became the fifteenth Baron Le Despencer, premier baron of England. In 1763 he became lord-lieutenant of Buckinghamshire. He died at West Wycombe after a prolonged illness on December 11, 1781, and was buried in the mausoleum he had built there.

Other Hell-Fire clubs existed in eighteenth-century England at Oxford and Cambridge, as well as in Scotland (Edinburgh) and Ireland (Dublin). The contemporary influences that brought about such societies were an increasing religious skepticism, the growth of free thought, romantic Gothic literature with mad monks and devils, and male chauvinism in an atmosphere of class privilege and debauchery.

Sources:

McCormick, Donald. *The Hell-Fire Club.* London: Jarrolds Publishers, 1958. Reprint, London: Sphere Books, 1975.

Mannix, Daniel P. *The Hell Fire Club.* New York: Ballantine Books, 1959.

Towers, Eric. *Dashwood: The Man and the Myth.* U.K.: Crucible, 1986.

Hellström, Eva Backström (1898– ?)

Founder of Sällskapet för Parapsykologisk Forskning, the Swedish psychical research organization, in 1947. Hellström also served as secretary of the society. She was born on September 26, 1898, at Stockholm. She was educated at Djursholm College, Sweden.

Hellström became a member of the **Society for Psychical Research,** London, and a charter member of the **Parapsychological Association.** Her interests included mediumship, **psychokinesis,** and **psychometry,** and she studied the work of various Swedish, Dutch, and Danish mediums. She was herself a clairvoyant and manifested faculties of precognition.

Sources:

Hellström, Eva Backström. "Collection of Spontaneous Cases." *Journal* of the Society for Psychical Research 43.

———. "Precognition of Girls Dancing." *Journal* of the Society for Psychical Research 41; 44.

Pleasants, Helene, ed. *Biographical Dictionary of Parapsychology.* New York: Helix Press, 1964.

Helvetius, John Friedrich (1625–1709)

A physician of the Hague, Holland, who in 1667 published a work concerning a strange adventure in which he claims to have taken part in a veritable act of metallic transmutation by **alchemy.** The book was translated into English and published in London in 1670 under the title *The Golden Cult Which the World Adores and Desires: In Which is Handled the Most Rare and Incomparable Wonder of Nature, in Transmuting Metals.* It is one of the few exact descriptions of such an experiment.

"On the 27th December, 1666, in the afternoon, a stranger, in a plain, rustic dress, came to my house at the Hague. His manner of address was honest, grave authoritative; his stature was low, with a long face and hair black, his chin smooth. He seemed like a native of the north of Scotland, and I guessed he was about 44 years old. After saluting me he requested me most respectfully to pardon his rude intrusion, but that his love of the pyrotechnic art made him visit me. Having read some of my small treatises, particularly that against the sympathetic powder of Sir Kenelm Digby (see **Powder of Sympathy**) and observed therein my doubt of the Hermetic mystery, it caused him to request this interview. He asked me if I still thought there was no medicine in Nature which could cure all diseases, unless the principal parts, as the lungs, liver, etc. were perished, or the time of death were come. To which I replied I never met with an adept, or saw such a medicine, though I read of much of it and often wished for it. Then I asked if he was a physician. He said he was a founder of brass, yet from his youth learned many rare things in chemistry, particularly of a friend—the manner to extract out of metals many medicinal arcana by the use of fire.

"After discoursing of experiments in metals, he asked me, would I know the **philosophers' stone** if I saw it? I answered, I would not, though I read much of it in Paracelsus, Helmont, Basil, and others, yet I dare not say I could know the philosophers' matter. In the interim he drew from his breast pocket a neat ivory box, and out of it took three ponderous lumps of the stone, each about the size of a small walnut. They were transparent and of a pale brimstone color, whereto some scales of the crucible adhered when this most noble substance was melted. . . . When I had greedily examined and handled the stone almost a quarter of an hour, and heard from the owner many rare secrets of its admirable effects in human and metallic bodies, also its other wonderful properties, I returned him this treasure of treasures, truly with a most sorrowful mind, like those who conquer themselves, yet, as was just, very thankfully and humbly.

"He asked me for a little piece of gold, and, pulling off his cloak, opened his vest, under which he had five pieces of gold. They were hanging to a green silk ribbon, and were of the size of breakfast plates. . . . I was in great admiration, and desired to know where and how he obtained them. He answered, 'A foreigner, who dwelt some days in my house, said he was a lover of this science, and came to reveal it to me. He taught me various arts—first, of ordinary stones and chrystals, to make rubies, chrysolites, sapphires, etc., much more valuable than those of the mine; and how in a quarter of an hour to make oxide of iron, one dose of which would infallibly cure the pestilential dysentery, or bloody flux; also how to make a metallic liquor to cure all kinds of dropsies, most certainly and in four days; as also a limpid, clear water, sweeter than honey, to which in two hours of itself, in hot sand, it would extract the tincture of garnets, corals, glasses, and such like.' He said more, which I Helvetius did not observe, my mind being occupied to understand how a noble juice could be drawn out of minerals to transmute metals. He told me his said master caused him to bring a glass of rain-water, and to put some silver leaf into it, which was dissolved therein within a quarter of an hour, like ice when heated. 'Presently he drank to me the half, and I pledged him the other half, which had not so much taste as sweet milk, but whereby, methought, I became very light-headed. I thereupon asked if this were a philosophical drink, and wherefore we drank this potion; but he replied, I ought not to be so curious.' By the said masters directions, a piece of a leaden pipe being melted, he took a little sulphureous powder out of his pocket, put a little of it on the point of a knife into the melted lead, and after a great blast of the bellows, in a short time he poured it on the red stones of the kitchen chimney. It proved most excellent pure gold, which the stranger said brought him into such trembling amazement that he could hardly speak; but his master encouraged him saying, 'Cut for thyself the sixteenth part of this as a memorial and give the rest away among the poor,' which the stranger did, distributing this alms, as he affirmed if my memory fail not, at the Church of Sparenda. 'At last,' said he, 'the generous foreigner taught me thoroughly this divine art.'

"As soon as his relation was finished, I asked my visitor to show me the effect of transmutation and so confirm my faith; but he declined it for that time in such a discreet manner that I was satisfied, he promising to come again in three weeks, to show me some curious arts in the fire, provided it were then lawful without prohibition. At the three weeks end he came, and invited me abroad for an hour or too. In our walk we discoursed of Nature's secrets, but he was very silent on the subject of the great elixir, gravely asserted that it was only to magnify the sweet fame and mercy of the most glorious God; that few men endeavoured to serve Him, and this he expressed as a pastor or minister of a church; but I recalled his attention, entreating him to show me the metallic mystery, desiring also that he would eat, drink, and lodge at my house, which I pressed, but he was of so fixed a determination that all my endeavours were frustrated. I could not forbear to tell him that I had a laboratory ready for an experiment, and that a promised favour was a kind of debt. 'Yes, true,' said he, 'but I promised to teach thee at my return, with this proviso, if it were not forbidden.'

"When I perceived that all this was in vain, I earnestly requested a small crumb of his powder, sufficient to transmute a few grains of lead to gold, and at last, out of his philosophical commiseration, he gave me as much as a turnip seed in size, saying, "Receive this small parcel of the greatest treasure of the world, which truly few kings or princes have ever seen or known.' 'But,' I said, 'this perhaps will not transmute four grains of lead,' whereupon he bid me deliver it back to him, which, in hopes of a greater parcel, I did, but he, cutting half off with his nail, flung it into the fire, and gave me the rest wrapped neatly up in blue paper, saying, 'It is yet sufficient for thee.' I answered him, indeed with a most dejected countenance, 'Sir, what means this? The other being too little, you give me now less.'

"He told me to put into the crucible half an ounce of lead, for there ought to be no more lead put in than the medicine can transmute. I gave him great thanks for my diminished treasure, concentrated truly in the superlative degree, and put it charily up into my little box, saying I meant to try it the next day, nor would I reveal it to any. 'Not so, not so,' said he, 'for we ought to divulge all things to the children of art which may tend alone to the honour of God, that so they may live in the theosophical truth.' I now made a confession to him, that while the mass of his medicine was in my hands, I endeavoured to scrape away a little of it with my nail, and could not forbear; but scratched off so very little, that, it being picked from my nail, wrapped in paper, and projected on melted lead, I found no transmutation, but almost the whole mass sublimed, while the remainder was a glassy earth.

"At this unexpected account he immediately said, 'You are more dexterous to commit theft than to apply the medicine, for if you had only wrapped up the stolen prey in yellow wax, to preserve it from the fumes of the lead, it would have sunk to the bottom, and transmuted it to gold; but having cast it into the fumes, the violence of the vapour, partly by its sympathetic alliance, carried the medicine quite away.' I brought him the crucible, and he perceived a most beautiful saffron-like tincture sticking to the sides. He promised to come next morning at nine o'clock, to show me that this tincture would transmute the lead into gold. Having taken his leave, I impatiently awaited his return, but the next day he came not, nor ever since. He sent an excuse at half-past nine that morning, and promised to come at three in the afternoon, but I never heard of him since.

"I soon began to doubt the whole matter. Late that night my wife, who was a most curious student and inquirer after the art, came soliciting me to make an experiment of the little grain of the stone, to be assured of the truth. 'Unless this be done,' said she, 'I shall have no rest or sleep this night.' She being so earnest, I commanded a fire to be made, saying to myself, 'I fear, I fear indeed, this man hath deluded me.' My wife wrapped the said matter in wax, and I cut half an ounce of lead, and put it into a crucible in the fire. Being melted, my wife put in the medicine, made into a small pill with the wax, which presently made a hissing noise, and in a quarter of an hour the mass of lead was totally transmuted into the best and finest gold, which amazed us exceedingly. . . . I ran with this aurified lead, being yet hot, to the goldsmith, who wondered at the fineness, and after a short trial by the test, said it was the most excellent gold in the world.

"The next day a rumour of this prodigy went about the Hague and spread abroad, so that many illustrious and learned persons gave me their friendly visits for its sake. . . . We went to Mr. Brectel, a silversmith, who first mixed four parts of silver with one part of the gold, then he filled it, put *aquafortis* to it, dissolved the silver, and let the gold precipitate to the bottom; the solution being poured off and the calx of gold washed with water, then reduced and melted, it appeared excellent gold, and instead of a loss in weight, we found the gold was increased, and had transmuted a scruple of the silver into gold by its abounding tincture.

"Doubting whether the silver was now sufficiently separated from the gold, we mingled it with seven parts of antimony, which we melted and poured out into a cone, and blew off the regulus on a test, where we missed eight grains of our gold; but after we blew away the red of the antimony, or superfluous *scoria,* we found nine grains of gold for our eight grains missing, yet it was pale and silverlike but recovered its full colour afterwards, so that in the best proof of fire we lost nothing at all of this gold, but gained, as aforesaid. These tests I repeated four times and found it still alike, and the silver remaining out of the *aquafortis* was of the very best flexible silver that could be, so that in the total the said medicine or elixir had transmuted six drams and two scruples of the lead and silver into most pure gold."

Helvetius died at the Hague August 29, 1709.

Henslow, George (1834–1925)

A clergyman of the Church of England and noted scholar. Henslow was a medalist of Christ College, Cambridge, vice president of the British Association for the Advancement of Science (1919), and a celebrated authority on botany, on which he wrote 16 learned works. He was also a dedicated Spiritualist. In his research he was closely associated with Archdeacon **Thomas Colley** and took much interest in **psychic photography.** He died December 20, 1925, at age 92.

Sources:

Henslow, George. *The Proofs of the Truth of Spiritualism.* New York: E. P. Dutton, 1919.

———. *The Religion of the Spirit World.* Chicago: Marlow Press, 1920.

Henslow, George, and D. J. D'Aute Hooper. *Spirit Psychometry.* London: W. Rider, 1914.

Hepatoscopy

A branch of **haruspicy** or extispicy (**divination** from the entrails of animals). In ancient times the liver was regarded as the focal point of life and thus of special occult significance. It was studied in detail, being divided into a number of zones, each associated with particular deities. The markings in these zones were considered to have special significance.

Herbert, Benson (1912–1991)

British psychical researcher and director of the **Paraphysical Laboratory,** London. He joined the **Society for Psychical Research** before World War II and with friends took part in séances for mental and physical phenomena at his house in Chelsea, London. It transpired that he had mediumistic talent himself, and for a time he manifested a Chinese spirit entity with healing powers.

Herbert founded the Paraphysical Laboratory in Wiltshire, with his friend Manfred Cassirer as the honorary research officer. The laboratory investigates paranormal phenomena of all kinds but has specialized in physical phenomena. In addition to conducting many original experiments, Herbert and Cassirer traveled in eastern Europe for further investigations, becoming founder members of the **International Association for Psychotronic Research** in Prague. Herbert also visited Russia and conducted important tests with the famous psychic Nina Kulagina.

He died April 21, 1991.

Hereburge

Frankish title for a witch. (See **France**)

Hermes Trismegistus

"The thrice greatest Hermes," the name given by the Greeks to the Egyptian god Thoth or Tehuti, the god of wisdom, learning, and literature. Thoth was alluded to in later Egyptian writings as "twice very great" and even as "five times very great" in some demotic or popular scripts (ca. third century B.C.E.).

As "scribe of the gods," Hermes was credited with the authorship of all Greek sacred books, which were thus called "hermetic." There were 42 of these, according to Clemens Alexandrinus, and they were subdivided into six portions, the first dealing with priestly education, the second with temple rituals and the third with geographical matters. The fourth division treated **astrology,** the fifth recorded hymns in honor of the gods and was a textbook for the guidance of kings, and the sixth was a medical text.

It is unlikely that these books were all the work of one individual; more likely they represent the accumulated wisdom of Egypt, attributed in the course of ages to the great god of wisdom.

As "scribe of the gods," Hermes was also the author of all strictly sacred writings. For convenience the name of Hermes was placed at the head of an extensive cycle of mystic literature produced in post-Christian times. Most of this hermetic or trismegistic literature has perished, but all that remains of it has been gathered and translated into English. It includes the *Poimandres,* (Shepherd of Men), the *Perfect Sermon,* or the *Asclepius,* excerpts by Stobacus, as well as fragments from the church fathers and from the philosophers Zosimus and Fulgentius.

These writings were neglected by theologians, who dismissed them as the offspring of third-century Neoplatonism. According to the generally accepted view, they are eclectic compilations, combining Neoplatonic philosophy, Philonic Judaism, and Kabalistic Theosophy in an attempt to supply a philosophic substitute for Christianity. The many Christian elements to be found in these mystic scriptures were ascribed to plagiarism.

Examination of early mystery writings and traditions has shown that the main source of the Trismegistic tractates is probably the wisdom of Egypt and that they "go back in an unbroken tradition of type and form and context to the earliest Ptolemaic times."

Sources:

Bell, H. Idris. *Cults and Creeds in Graeco-Roman Egypt.* Liverpool, England: Liverpool University Press, 1957.

Hermes Trismegistus. *Hermetica.* Edited by Brian Copenhaver. Cambridge: Cambridge University Press, 1992.

———. *Hermetica.* Edited by Walter Scott. Vol. I. Oxford: Oxford University Press, 1924. Reprint, Boston: Shambhala, 1985.

———. *Theological & Philosophical Works.* Edited by J. D. Chambers. 2 vols. London, 1882.

Mead, G. R. S. *Thrice-Greatest Hermes.* London, 1906. Reprint, New Hyde Park, N.Y.: University Books, 1964.

Hermetic Society (Dublin)

Founded in 1898 by mystical poet "AE" (**George W. Russell**) in Dublin, Ireland, after he left the **Theosophical Society.** The Hermetic Society placed great emphasis on meditation. It was not connected with the **Hermetic Society (London).**

Hermetic Society (London)

Founded by **Anna Kingsford** and **Edward Maitland** in London, England, in 1884, connected with the **Theosophical Society** of **Helena Petrovna Blavatsky.** Occultists **S. L. MacGregor Mathers** and **W. Wynn Westcott** lectured to the society before launching the famous Hermetic Order of the **Golden Dawn.**

Sources:

Mitland, Edward. *The Story of Anna Kingsford and Edward Maitland and of the New Gospel of Interpretation.* Birmingham, England: Ruskin Press, 1905.

Hermetica

The body of secret mystical wisdom that honored **Hermes Trismegistus** ("Thrice-Greatest Hermes") between the third century B.C.E. and first century C.E., identifying the Greek god Hermes with the Egyptian god Thoth. This wisdom literature involved two levels of writing: a popular Hermetic teaching of **astrology,** magic, and **alchemy,** and a later higher religious philosophy. The Hermes-Thoth literature had a profound effect on the development of Western magic. Hermetic works include *Poimandres* (Shepherd of Men), *Asclepius,* and *The Secret Discourse on the Mountain.*

Sources:

Atwood, M. A. *A Suggestive Inquiry into the Hermetic Mystery.* Belfast, Ireland, 1918. Reprint, New York: Arno Press, 1976.

Hermes Trismegistus. *The Divine Pymander.* Translated by Dr. Everard. London: Theosophical Publishing Society, 1894.

———. *Hermetica.* Edited by Brian Copenhaver. Cambridge: Cambridge University Press, 1992.

———. *Hermetica.* Edited by Walter Scott. Vol. 1. Oxford: Oxford University Press, 1924. Reprint, Boston: Shambhala, 1985.

———. *Theological and Philosophical Works.* Edited by J. D. Chambers. 2 vols. Edinburgh: T. and T. Clark, 1882.

Hernandez Montis, Vicente (1925–)

Associate professor of physics, University of Seville, who published papers on parapsychology. Montis was born April 23, 1925, at Seville, Spain. He studied at the University of Seville and the University of Madrid. He was a member of Colegio Official de Doctores y Licenciados en Letras y Ciencias, Seville, and the **Parapsychological Association.** He studied **ESP** in relation to the hypnotic state, as well as **dowsing** or water witching.

Sources:

Pleasants, Helene, ed. *Biographical Dictionary of Parapsychology.* New York: Helix Press, 1964.

Herne, Frank (ca. 1870)

Famous nineteenth-century English medium. His first séances were given in January 1869. He began with clairvoyant descriptions of spirits and of the sitter's aura, but physical manifestations soon developed. In 1870 at the house of a Dr. Dixon he was said to have manifested **elongation of the human body. Florence Cook** held her first sittings with Herne, from whom she may have learned some of the techniques of physical mediumship.

In 1871 Herne joined partnership with **Charles Williams.** Their séances at 61 Lamb's Conduit Street, London, were very impressive. Voices, psychic lights, independent music, **apports,** and **levitations** were often allegedly witnessed. **Agnes Guppy-Volckman**'s famous **transportation** occurred in one of these joint sittings. In 1875 St. George Stock made an attempt to expose Herne as a **fraud** but did not succeed, and two years later in *The Spiritualist* apologized for the attempt.

Much suspicion surrounded the mediumship of Herne and Williams. Williams, who worked closely with Herne, was caught cheating in séances in Paris in 1874 and in Amsterdam in 1879.

Sources:

"Alleged Mediumship of F. Herne." *Proceedings* of the Society for Psyhical Research 7; *Journal* of the Society for Psychical Research 10.

Hesse, Hermann (1877–1962)

Famous German novelist (he later acquired Swiss nationality) whose books on mystical themes were quite influential in the spiritual and occult revival among young adults in the 1960s and 1970s. His novel *Siddhartha* deals with the relationship between father and son and the quest for self-discovery through a journey to India. His novel *Das Glasperlenspiel* (1943, translated as *Magister Ludi,* 1950) resolves world disorder through a religious game played by rulers.

Sources:

Hesse, Herman. *Siddhartha.* New York: New Directions, 1951.

Hettinger, J(ohn)

Pioneer British psychical researcher with special interest in **telepathy.** Hettinger was active in the physical sciences and electrical engineering. He was one of the first individuals in Britain to receive a Ph.D. degree for a dissertation concerned with paranormal phenomena. He studied psychology at Kings College, London University (1933–38), exploring what he named the "ultra-perceptive faculty" of telepathy, employing a pictorial method.

He devoted much time to "object reading," in which a subject is given some object, concentrates on it, and describes impressions received that relate to it or to the owner. Object reading is more popularly known as **psychometry.** Hettinger conducted psychometric tests to discover the sealed message left by **Sir Oliver Lodge** before his death, and pieced together the purported message in 17 test sittings (described in his book *Telepathy and Spiritualism*). His work received mixed reviews from his colleagues.

Sources:

Berger, Arthur S., and Joyce Berger. *The Encyclopedia of Parapsychology and Psychical Research.* New York: Paragon House, 1991.

Hettinger, John. *Exploring the Ultra-Perceptive Faculty.* London: Rider, 1941.

———. *Telepathy and Spiritualism.* London: Rider, 1952.

———. *The Ultra-Perceptive Faculty.* London: Rider, 1938.

Scott, Christopher. "Experimental Object-Reading: A Critical Review of the Work of Dr. J. Hettinger." *Proceedings* of the Society for Psychical Research 49 (1949).

Hex (or Hexerai)

General term for **witchcraft** spells among the Pennsylvania Dutch settlers of America, especially those of southeastern Pennsylvania. Beliefs in magic were brought to the area in the later seventeenth century and given focus in the Rosicrucian group that settled on Wissahikon Creek in Germantown. The group, generally referred to as the Woman in the Wilderness, dissolved in the early eighteenth century, but its members became practitioners of magic, astrology, and healing in the area and were the forerunners of the later hex meisters.

The standard textbook of hex spells and folk remedies used by hex meisters, *The Long Lost Friend or Pow-Wows,* was published by John George Hohman of Berks County, Pennsylvania, in 1820. The book includes instruction for a variety of magic formulas to accomplish practical tasks, as indicated by some of the topics covered: "Against Mishaps and Dangers in the House," "Treating a Sick Cow," "To Stop Bleeding at Any Time," and "To Charm Enemies, Robbers, and Murderers." Many Pennsylvania barns are still decorated with "hex signs," known as hexafoos, originally placed to keep away evil spirits, but today largely a decorative addition.

Sources:

Hark, Ann. *Hex Marks the Spot in Pennsylvania Dutch Country.* Philadelphia: J. B. Lippincott, 1938.

Hohman, John George. *The Long Lost Friend or Pow-Wows.* N.p., 1820.

Lewis, Arthur H. *Hex.* New York: Pocket Books, 1972.

Sachse, Julius F. *The German Pietists of Provencial Pennsylvania.* Philadelphia, 1895. Reprint, New York: AMS Press, 1970.

Hexenhaus

A prison for witches built in Bambert, Germany, in 1627 during the rule of the "witch-bishop" Prince Gottfried Johann George II Fuchs von Dornheim. It contained two chapels, a torture chamber, and cells to accommodate 26 witches.

Heyd

A Norwegian sea witch or storm fiend in the shape of a white bear, alluded to in the *Frithjof Saga.* With the other storm fiend Ham, she was sent by Helgi to engulf Frithjof as he sailed for the island of Yarl Angantyr.

Heydon, John (1629–ca. 1668)

English astrologer, Rosicrucian, and attorney. He was born in London on September 10, 1629, and was educated at Tardebigg in Worcestershire. Because of the outbreak of the Civil War, he did not go on to the university, but joined the king's army. He is said to have been successful as a soldier, but after the triumph of the Roundhead party he left England and for some years lived in various countries on the Continent, notably Spain and Turkey. He is said to have visited Zante, the island in the Levant praised by Edgar Allan Poe, but by 1652 Heydon was back in England. In 1655 he studied law and later established a practice.

Law was not his only study, however, for he became deeply involved in **astrology.** According to Thomas Carte in his biography of the marquis of Ormonde, Heydon was imprisoned for two years for his prophecy that one Cornwell would die by hanging.

In 1656 Heydon married the widow of **Nicolas Culpepper,** who, after fighting for Parliament in the Civil War, had devoted a wealth of energy to compiling elaborate treatises on astrology and pharmacopia, arts which went hand in hand in the seventeenth century.

Heydon became intimate with many of the great scientists of the Restoration but quarreled with a number of them, and although he always maintained that he was not actually affiliated with the **Rosicrucians,** he explained their theories publicly. In 1667 he was imprisoned for "treasonable practices in sowing sedition in the navy, and engaging persons in a conspiracy to seize The Tower [of London]." He died the following year.

In spite of the ups and downs of Heydon's life, while out of jail he wrote a number of books and pamphlets, those on Rosicrucian themes dominating any contributions to astrology. Among his Rosicrucian texts are *A New Method of Rosie-Crucian Physick* (1658), *The Rosie-Crucian Infallible Axiomata* (1660), *The Wise Man's Crown, The Glory of the Rosie-Cross* (1664), and *The Rosie-Cross Uncovered* (1662). In addition he was author of *Theomagia or The Temple of Wisdom* (1664) and *The Prophetic Trumpeter, Sounding an Allarum to England* (1655), the latter being dedicated to Henry Cromwell. According to Wood's *Athen Oxonicsis,* Heydon was also the compiler of *A Rosiecrucian Theological Dictionary.*

Sources:

Heydon, John. *Eugenius Theodidactus.* London, 1655.

Heym, Gerard (d. ca. 1974)

Scholar, bibliophile, and student of the occult during the 1930s in Britain. Although Heym was a close associate of **S. L. MacGregor Mathers** and other members of the Hermetic Order of the **Golden Dawn,** he does not appear to have been a member himself.

Heym had a special interest in **alchemy** and in 1937 became a founding member of the Society for the Study of Alchemy and Early Chemistry, established for "the scientific and historical study of the branches of learning named in its title." Heym contributed to the society's journal, *Ambix.*

Heymans, Gerardus (1857–1930)

Psychologist, philosopher, and pioneer of parapsychology in the Netherlands. Heymans established a laboratory for research in 1892 and led in the spread of experimental parapsychology in Holland in the years immediately after World War I. He was one of the founders of the **Studievereniging voor Psychical Research** (SPR), inaugurated on April 1, 1920, and served as its first president. The Dutch SPR served as a meeting ground for scientists, scholars, Spiritualists, and Theosophists.

Having discovered a psychically gifted student, Heymans conducted telepathy experiments at the University of Groningen, tests widely cited for both design and positive results.

Sources:

Berger, Arthur S., and Joyce Berger. *The Encyclopedia of Parapsychology and Psychical Research.* New York: Paragon House, 1991.

Heymans, Gerardus. "Psychische Monismus und 'Psychical Research.'" In *Zeitschrift für Psychologie.* Leipzig: J. A. Barth, 1912.

Heymans, Gerardus, Henry J. F. W. Brugmans, and A. Weinberg. "Une communication sur des expériences télépathiques au laboratorie de psychologie a Groningue." In *Compte Rendu Officiel du Primier Congres International des Recherches Psychiques.* Copenhagen, 1922.

Pleasants, Helene, ed. *Biographical Dictionary of Parapsychology.* New York: Helix Press, 1964.

Heyn, F(rans) A(driaan)(1910–)

Dutch professor of nuclear physics who studied telepathy. Heyn was born November 2, 1910, at Delft, Netherlands, and studied science at the University of Delft. In 1947 he joined the faculty of the University of Delft, where he taught in the area of nuclear physics and electrical engineering. He had a strong interest in psychical research and became a charter member of the **Parapsychological Association.** He was coauthor with **S. Mulchuyse** of *Vorderingen en Problemen van de Parapsychologie* (Progress and Problems in Parapsychology, 1950).

Sources:

Pleasants, Helene, ed. *Biographical Dictionary of Parapsychology.* New York: Helix Press, 1964.

Heywood, Rosalind (Hedley) (1895–1980)

Prominent British researcher in the field of psychical science. She was born February 2, 1895, at Gibraltar, and she attended London University. During World War I, as a nurse's aide, she had some initial and intense psychic experiences. She would be given an "order" for unusual treatments for dying patients that would lead to their recovery. She had several deathbed visions and began to experience telepathic contact with a man, Frank Heywood, whom she married during the war.

It was not until 1938 that Heywood joined the **Society for Psychical Research** (SPR), but she was an active member for the rest of her life, including a tenure on the council. She experimented with **Whateley Carington** on **ESP,** and was also a subject for physicians studying the effects of mescaline. She contributed a number of articles to the *Journal* of the SPR, including many memoirs of deceased members, but is most remembered for her two books, *The Sixth Sense* (1959) and her autobiography, *The Infinite Hive* (1964). She died June 27, 1980, in England.

Sources:

Berger, Arthur S., and Joyce Berger. *The Encyclopedia of Parapsychology and Psychical Research.* New York: Paragon House, 1991.

Heywood, Rosalind. *The Infinite Hive.* London: Chatto & Windus, 1964. Reprinted as *ESP: A Personal Memoir.* New York: E. P. Dutton, 1972.

———. *The Sixth Sense: An Enquiry into Extrasensory Perception.* London: Chatto & Windus, 1959. Reprint, London: Pan Books, 1971. Reprinted as *Beyond the Reach of Sense.* New York: E. P. Dutton, 1974.

Pleasants, Helene, ed. *Biographical Dictionary of Parapsychology.* New York: Helix Press, 1964.

Hickling, Alan Micklem (1936–)

British aeronautical engineer who has experimented in the field of **ESP**. He was born on February 22, 1936, in London. He studied at Cambridge University (B.A. honors, mechanical sciences, 1958) and joined the Royal Navy as a pilot in 1959. He became a charter member of the **Parapsychological Association.**

Sources:

Pleasants, Helene, ed. *Biographical Dictionary of Parapsychology.* New York: Helix Press, 1964.

Hieroglyphs

This term, normally applied to ancient Egyptian picture writing, is also used for the symbolic illustrations in astrological almanacs and for symbols produced by **automatic** and **direct writing** through mediumship. Direct writing (i.e., messages produced without contact between mediums and writing materials), although sometimes produced at séances, has also occurred during outbreaks of **poltergeist** phenomena, when the poltergeist distributes messages throughout a house. For example, in a disturbance in the house of **Eliakim Phelps,** in Stratford, Connecticut (1850–51), hieroglyphs were found on the walls and ceilings. The matter was investigated by Spiritualist medium **Andrew Jackson Davis,** who claimed to recognize the hieroglyphs as spiritual symbols. He interpreted them as friendly messages from spiritual powers.

Sources:

Capron, E. W. *Modern Spiritualism: Its Facts and Fanaticisms.* Boston: B. Marsh; New York: Patridge and Brittan, 1855.

Higgins, Godfrey (1772–1833)

British archaeologist, humanist, social reformer, and author. Early in his life Higgins became convinced that there was an ancient universal religion from which later creeds developed, and he devoted 20 years to a search for a secret tradition. The result of his research was his monumental volume *Anacalypsis, An Attempt to Draw Aside the Veil of the Saitic Isis; or An Inquiry into the Origin of Languages, Nations and Religions,* first published posthumously in two volumes in 1933 and 1936. A work of more than 1,250 pages, it supplied material and inspiration for the early theosophical writings of **Helena Petrovna Blavatsky,** who even echoed the title in her own book *Isis Unveiled* (1877).

Sources:

De Morgan, Augustus. *The Encyclopedia of Excentrics.* La Salle, Ill.: Open Court Press, 1974.

Higgins, Godfrey. *Anacalypsis, An Attempt to Draw Aside the Veil of the Saitic Isis; or An Inquiry into the Origin of Languages, Nations and Religions.* 2 vols. London, 1933, 1936. Reprint, New Hyde Park, N.Y.: University Books, 1965.

Higginson, Gordon (1918–1993)

President of the **Spiritualists' National Union** (SNU) in Britain for 23 years and one of the country's leading mediums. In Spiritualist circles he was popularly known as "Mr. Mediumship."

Higginson first sat in a Spiritualist circle with his mother at age 3. He manifested mediumship at age 12. His mother, Fanny Higginson, demonstrated clairvoyant mediumship for some seventy years. At age 14, she had been told by the trance medium **Annie Brittain** that she would become a medium, that she would bear a son, and that mother and son would span two lifetimes in the service of the Spiritualist Church. Gordon Higginson took his first Spiritualist service at age 14 in Nantwich, Cheshire.

During World War II he served as a lance corporal and took part in the Dunkirk landings. Although at that time the British army did not recognize Spiritualism as a religion, Higginson fought for such recognition.

He became president of the SNU in 1970 and came to be its longest-serving president, holding that office for more than 23 years. He was a tireless worker in the cause to "put the spirit back into Spiritualism."

Higginson died in January 1993 at age 74. His place as president of the SNU was filled by Eric Hatton.

Hilarion, Master

One of the masters originally contacted by **Helena Petrovna Blavatsky,** cofounder of the **Theosophical Society.** According to theosophical teachings, there exists a spiritual hierarchy composed of individuals who have finished their round of earthly reincarnations and have evolved to the spiritual planes, from which they guide the affairs of humanity. Those members of the hierarchy closest to humanity are the "lords of the seven rays" (of the light spectrum). Each ray represents a particular virtue, which the lord of that ray exemplifies.

Master Hilarion is the lord of the fifth ray and an exemplar of science, or detailed knowledge. He influences scientists, and those who identify with him are known for their ability at research and scientific investigation. During the first decades of the Theosophical Society he channeled *The Voice of Silence* through Blavatsky and *Light on the Path* through **Mabel Collins.** In a former life he is believed to have been Iamblichus, the Neoplatonic philosopher. Today he supposedly inhabits a Greek body but resides in Egypt. Blavatsky claimed to have first met him in 1860 and said he helped her with some of her short stories.

Francis A. LaDue and William H. Dower, cofounders of the Temple (which grew out of the Syracuse, New York, Lodge of the Theosophical Society), claimed Master Hilarion as the primary member of the hierarchy with whom they were in contact. In 1968 Rev. Wayne Taylor claimed that Master Hilarion had guided him in the founding of the City of the Sun Foundation in Columbus, New Mexico. Most recently, Maurice B. Cooke has channeled a set of books allegedly from Master Hilarion.

Sources:

Hilarion, Master [through Maurice B. Cooke]. *The Nature of Reality.* Toronto: Marcus Books, 1978.

Pallas Athena and the Master Hilarion Speak. Part I: The Master Hilarion. Kings Park, N.Y.: Bridge to Freedom, 1975.

Ransom, Josephine. *A Short History of the Theosophical Society.* Adyar, Madras, India: Theosophical Publishing House, 1938.

Taylor, Wayne. *Pillars of Light.* Columbus, N. Mex.: The Author, 1965.

Temple Messages. Halcyon, Calif.: Temple of the People, 1983.

Theogenesis. Halcyon, Calif.: Temple of the People, 1981.

Hill, J(ohn) Arthur (1872–1951)

British psychical researcher and author. Hill was born on December 4, 1872, at Halifax, England. He attended Thornton Grammar School, Bradford, and worked as a business manager until 1898, when he suffered a heart ailment and was unable to work full time. He then spent his time studying the literature of psychical research and also sat with various mediums.

Hill joined the **Society for Psychical Research,** London, and served on the council between 1927 and 1935. He assisted **Sir Oliver Lodge** in his work but is most remembered for his many writings. Hill wrote both books and articles on psychical research and **Spiritualism.** He died March 22, 1951.

Sources:

Hill, J. Arthur. *Emerson and His Philosophy.* 1919. Reprint, Folcroft, Pa.: Folcroft Library Editions, 1971.

———. *From Agnosticism to Belief.* London: Methuen, 1924.

———. *Man Is a Spirit.* New York: George H. Doran, 1918.

———. *New Evidences in Psychical Research.* London: W. Rider and Son, 1911.

———. *Psychical Investigations.* New York: George H. Doran, 1917.

———. *Psychical Miscellanea.* New York: Harcourt, Brace and Howe, 1919.

———. *Psychical Science and Religious Belief.* London: Rider, 1929.

———. *Religion and Modern Psychology.* N.p., 1911.

———. *Spiritualism: Its History, Phenomena and Doctrine.* New York: George H. Doran, 1919.

———. *Spiritualism and Psychical Research.* London: T. C. and E. C. Jack; New York: Dodge Publishing, 1913.

Pleasants, Helene, ed. *Biographical Dictionary of Parapsychology.* New York: Helix Press, 1964.

Hillman, James (1926–   )

Analytical psychologist who studied the relationship of parapsychology to depth psychology. Hillman was born on April 12, 1926, at Atlantic City, New Jersey. He studied at Trinity College, Dublin, Ireland (B.A., 1950; M.A., 1953), and at the University of Zurich (Ph.D. summa cum laude, 1958). After graduation he became an analytical psychologist and director of studies at the C. G. Jung Institute, Zurich. He returned to the United States in 1970 as an editor for Spring Publications in New York (1970–78). He became a professor at the University of Dallas in 1979.

Hillman was the founding associate editor of *Envoy: An Irish Review of Literature and Art* (1949–51), and wrote a number of books on psychology. His most famous work, however, was initiated during a visit to India when he met the Hindu teacher **Gopi Krishna.** Gopi Krishna was a retired civil servant from Srinagar who attained a condition of higher consciousness through arousing the legendary **kundalini** energy of Hindu mysticism. Hillman was favorably impressed and contributed a psychological commentary for Gopi Krishna's book *Kundalini: The Evolutionary Energy in Man.* The commentary interprets the experiences of Gopi Krishna in relation to Jungian psychology.

Sources:

Gopi Krishna. *Kundalini: The Evolutionary Energy in Man.* New Dehli: Ramadhar and Hopman, 1967. Reprint, Boulder, Colo.: Shambala, 1970.

Hillman, James. *A Blue Fire: Selected Writings.* New York: Harper & Row, 1989.

———. *The Dream and the Underworld.* New York: Harper & Row, 1979.

———. *Emotion: A Comprehensive Phenomenology of Theories and their Meanings for Therapy.* 1960. Reprint, Evanston, Ill.: Northwestern University Press, 1961.

———. *The Feeling of Function.* N.p., 1971.

———. *Insearch: Psychology and Religion.* New York: Charles Scribner's Sons, 1967.

———. *Loose Ends.* Dallas: Springhill Publications, 1975.

———. *The Myth of Analysis.* Evanston, Ill.: Northwestern University Press, 1972.

———. *Pan and The Nightmare.* New York: Spring Publications, 1972.

———. *Re-visioning Psychology.* New York: Harper & Row, 1975.

———. *Suicide and The Soul.* New York: Harper and Row, 1964.

Pleasants, Helene, ed. *Biographical Dictionary of Parapsychology.* New York: Helix Press, 1964.

Hills, Christopher

New Age teacher and director of the **University of the Trees.** Born in England, he left home at an early age and attended a naval school, serving in World War II. By age 30, Hills had become a businessman in the West Indies with an international organization of ten companies, but in 1957 he became concerned with psychic and spiritual life after his son was miraculously healed through prayer. Hills retired from his business practice and spent two years in India, studying **yoga** and Hindu philosophy.

In 1960 he became honorary director of research at the Indian Institute of Philosophy, Psychology and Psychical Research and was elected president of the World Conference on Scientific Yoga, attended by 800 yogis and 50 Western scientists. In 1962 he formed the Commission for Research into the Creative Faculties of Man, bringing together the work of scientists, psychical researchers, philosophers, holy men, educationalists, and politicians.

One aspect of this project was the formation in 1965, with Professor Hiroshi Nakamura, of the International Union of Leading Microbiologists, advising on production of edible algae as a means of solving world food problems.

During 1966 Hills founded the **Centre House** community in England, a free fellowship for those interested in spiritual development, serving a social and educational program aimed at "a conscious evolution towards a society based on love and peace." Training was given in yoga, meditation, awareness, sensitivity development, and related subjects. Hills left Centre House after a few years and spent some time as a lecturer. Then in 1973 he established the University of the Trees in Boulder Creek, California, an institution offering a comprehensive program of New Age teachings and granting degrees in consciousness research. The university has also formed the **Research Institute for Supersensonic Healing Energies** for practical research into subtle energy therapeutics.

Sources:

Hills, Christopher. *The Christ Book.* Boulder Creek, Calif.: University of the Trees, 1980.

———. *Christ Yoga of Peace: Proposal for a World Peace Center.* 1970. Rev. ed. as *Universal Government by Nature's Laws.* N.p., 1978.

———. *Creative Conflict.* Boulder Creek, Calif: University of the Trees, 1980.

———. *Exploring Inner Space.* Boulder Creek, Calif.: University of the Trees, 1978.

———. *The Golden Egg.* Boulder Creek, Calif.: University of the Trees, 1979.

———. *Nuclear Evolution: A Guide to Cosmic Enlightenment.* London: Centre Community Publications, 1968.

———. *Rays from the Capstone.* Boulder Creek, Calif.: University of the Trees, 1976.

———. *Rejuvenating the Body Through Fasting With Spirulina Plankton.* Boulder Creek, Calif.: University of the Trees, 1980.

———. *The Secrets of Spirulina.* Boulder Creek, Calif.: University of the Trees, 1980.

HIM See Human Individual Metamorphosis

Himalayan International Institute of Yoga Science and Philosophy

Organization teaching the yoga-centered Hinduism espoused by Swami Rama, a Indian spiritual leader who first came to the United States in 1970. Swami Rama was at one time a monk, but left that life behind in order to pursue his teaching work. He founded the institute in India and brought the organization with him to the United States.

The reason Swami Rama came to the United States was the work of Elmer E. and Alyce M. Green in the Voluntary Controls Research Project at the Menninger Foundation. The project conducted experiments with autogenic training, involving the use of **biofeedback** instrumentation. Swami Rama cooperated with them on psychophysiological programs. Swami Rama's spiritual work received a significant boost from his spectacular success in the Greens' experiments.

At the institute, yoga, **meditation,** and holistic health are taught with a special emphasis on **hatha yoga** as a means of balancing the body-spirit dichotomy. The practice of yoga, it is felt, will lead to a spiritual worldview. The institute sponsors seminars on a wide range of personal growth topics, maintains a speakers bureau, operates a children's school, and runs a program in Eastern studies and comparative psychology in affiliation with the University of Scranton Graduate School. The program culminates in a Master of Science degree. The institute has established the Eleanor N. Dana Research Laboratory and the Himalayan Institute Teachers Association, which certifies yoga teachers. The Honesdale Institute maintains a library of 20,000 volumes. Publications include: *Dawn* magazine, quarterly; *Himalayan Institute Quarterly,* bimonthly; and *Research Bulletin of the Himalayan International Institute/Eleanor N. Dana Laboratory,* annual. The institute also publishes a large number of books and audiotapes on all aspects of yoga, meditation, and holistic health.

The address of the 422-acre campus of the Himalayan International Institute is RR 1, Box 400, Honesdale, PA 18431. In 1992 there were 21 branch centers in North America.

Sources:

Green, Elmer M. "How to Make Use of the Field of Mind Theory." In *The Dimensions of Healing: A Symposium.* Los Altos, Calif.: Academy of Parapsychology and Medicine, 1972.

Rama, Swami. *Lectures on Yoga.* Arlington Heights, Ill.: Himalayan International Institute of Yoga Science and Philosophy, 1972.

———. *Path of Fire and Light.* Honesdale, Pa.: Himalayan International Institute of Yoga Science and Philosophy, 1986.

Himalayan News

Former bimonthly publication of the **Himalayan International Institute of Yoga Science and Philosophy,** which has been superseded by the *Himalayan Institute Quarterly.*

Hindu Spiritual Magazine

A Spiritualist journal founded in Calcutta, India, March 1906. The *Hindu Spiritual Magazine* was edited by Babu Shishir Kumar Ghose (1840–1911), a Bengali scholar, until his death. It continued to appear through July 1916.

Hippomancy

A method of **divination** practiced by the ancient Celts, who kept certain white horses in consecrated groves. The horses were made to walk immediately behind sacred carts and auguries were drawn from their movements. The ancient Germans kept similar steeds in their temples. If the horses crossed the threshold with the left forefoot first on leaving the temples at the outbreak of hostilities, it was regarded as an evil omen and the war was abandoned.

Sources:

Waite, Arthur Edward. *The Occult Sciences.* 1891. Reprint, Secaucus, N.J.: University Books, 1974.

Hmana Zena

Slavonic name for a witch in Dalmatia (present-day Croatia). The term means "common woman."

Hmin Nat

A Burmese evil spirit.

Hobgoblins

British domestic **fairies** or brownies of nocturnal habits. In past centuries they were said to be the most populous species of elves in England and were said to stay in houses close to warm fires. Each section of the land had its own name for them—Hob-Gob, Robin Round Cap, and Hob-Thrush, for example. Today they are best known from their appearance in literary works, the most famous hobgoblin being Puck, of Shakespeare's *A Midsummer Night's Dream.* Puck has a merry disposition, and he says he is a jester at the court of Oberon, king of the fairies.

In *Discovery of Witchcraft* (1584) Reginald Scot states, "Your grandames maids were wont to set a bowl of milk for him for his pains in grinding of malt and mustard, and sweeping the house at midnight. This white bread, and bread and milk, was his standard fee."

In some folklore traditions hobgoblins were malicious rather than mischievous, and in medieval times they were associated with the devil. The hobgoblin was believed by some to be a demon who led men astray during the night. Sometimes he was represented as clothed in a suit of leather, and sometimes he wore green. He was usually considered to be full of tricks and mischief.

Sources:

Arrowsmith, Nancy, with George Moorse. *A Field Guide to the Little People.* New York: Wallaby, 1977.

Hockley, Frederick (1809–1885)

British occultist who was a member of the **Societas Rosicruciana in Anglia.** Hockley collected some important occult texts, including a Rosicrucian manuscript belonging to **Sigismond Bacstrom,** who was initiated into an occult society in Mauritius in 1794. This text had a great influence on British occultism. Hockley had some gift of **crystal gazing** and was a close friend of **Kenneth R. H. Mackenzie** and other British **Rosicrucians** and occultists of his period. He was a pupil of Francis Barrett, author of *The Magus* (1801). Hockley died November 10, 1885.

Sources:

Hockley, Frederick. *The Rosicrucian Seer: Magical Writings of Frederick Hockley.* Wellingborough, England: Aquarian Press, 1986.

King, Francis. *The Rites of Modern Occult Magic.* New York: Macmillan, 1970.

Hocus Pocus

Words of pseudomagical import. According to Sharon Turner in *The History of the Anglo-Saxons* (4 vols., 1799–1805), they were believed to be derived from "Ochus Bochus," a magician and demon of the north. It is more probable, however, that they are a corruption of the Latin *hoc est corpus* (this is my body), words spoken during the act of transubstantiation in the Roman Catholic Mass. The term has been used since the seventeenth century as a preface to the tricks of **conjuring** magicians. Conjurers used to introduce tricks with the sham Latin formula, "Hocus pocus, tontus talontus, rade celeriter jubeó."

Hod

The name assigned in the Jewish mysticism of the **Kabala** to the number eight. It means "eternity"—that is, the eternity of the conquest achieved by mind over matter, active over passive, or life over death.

Hodgson, Richard (1855–1905)

One of the leading members of the **Society for Psychical Research** (SPR), London. Hodgson was born September 24, 1855, in Melbourne, Australia. He studied at the University of Melbourne (B.A., 1874; L.L.B., 1875; M.A., 1876; L.L.D., 1878). His interest in psychical research began in Australia during his college years. He moved to England in 1878 to continue his legal studies at Cambridge University, where he took an active part in the undergraduate Ghost Society, which investigated psychical phenomena. His name appears in the first published list of the members of the SPR (1882–83), and in 1885 he was a council member. His legal training and personal attainments made him especially qualified for the detection of **fraud.**

In November 1884, as a member of the SPR committee, he was sent to India to investigate the paranormal phenomena being reported from the heart of the theosophical movement, especially that initiated by **Helena Petrovna Blavatsky.** His "Report on Phenomena Connected with Theosophy," published in the *Proceedings* of the SPR in December 1885 charged Blavatsky with widespread fraud. The report created a pubic scandal for **Theosophy** and ensured Hodgson's place in the history of psychical research. (The report continues to embarrass Theosophists, and there were unsuccessful attempts to discredit it as recently as the mid-1980s.)

A short time later, in conjunction with **S. T. Davey,** Hodgson undertook important experiments into the possibilities of malobservation and lapse of memory in connection with séance phenomena. While not well known, this paper is actually his most original work in the field. He developed an extremely skeptical attitude toward all physical phenomena. He remarked that "nearly all professional mediums form a gang of vulgar tricksters, who are more or less in league with one another." All his early investigations ended with a negative opinion.

Hodgson was among the first to become convinced that **Eusapia Palladino,** whose sittings he attended at Cambridge in 1895, was an impostor, although investigations by other psychical researchers indicated that she produced genuine phenomena when properly controlled, but cheated on other occasions.

He was sent to the United States in 1887 to act as secretary to the **American Society for Psychical Research** in Boston. (He would continue in this capacity until his sudden death of heart failure while playing a game of handball at the Boat Club in Boston on December 20, 1905.) A change in Hodgson's general attitude toward the phenomenal side of **Spiritualism** was brought about—very slowly and after much resistance—by his unparalleled opportunities to investigate the mediumship of **Leonora Piper** for a period of 15 years. His systematic study of the Piper mediumship cannot be overestimated in importance.

Piper was introduced to the SPR by **William James,** a lifelong friend of Hodgson's. Hodgson, being extremely skeptical, had Piper watched by detectives to learn whether she attempted to collect information by normal means. He took every precaution to prevent such acquisition of knowledge and finally became convinced not only of the genuineness of her mediumship, but also of spirit return.

His first report on the Piper phenomena was published in 1892 in the *Proceedings* of the SPR (vol. 8). In it no definite conclusions were announced. Yet at this time Hodgson had already obtained convincing evidence of Piper's genuineness. It was of a private character, however, and since he did not include the incident in his report he did not consider it fair to point out its import. As he later told **Hereward Carrington** (who later printed the account in his *The Story of Psychic Science*), Hodgson, when still a young man in Australia, had fallen in love with a girl and wished to marry her. Her parents objected on religious grounds. Hodgson left for England and never married. One day, in a sitting with Piper, the girl suddenly communicated, informing Hodgson that she had died shortly before. This incident, the truth of which was verified, made a deep impression on Hodgson.

In his second report, published in the *Proceedings* of the SPR (vol. 13, 1897), his tone is definite in stating:

"At the present time I cannot profess to have any doubt that the chief communicators to whom I have referred in the foregoing pages are veritably the personages that they claim to be, that they have survived the change we call death, and that they have directly communicated with us whom we call living, through Mrs. Piper's entranced organism."

After ten years spent in these investigations Hodgson returned to England for one year and became editor of the SPR *Journal* and *Proceedings.* Then he went back to the United States and resumed his Piper studies. He intended to publish a third report but he did not live to do so.

His personal experiences changed his whole outlook on life. He lived in one room in Boston, dependent on an inadequate salary. Nevertheless, in order to devote all his time to psychical research, he refused remunerative offers from colleges and universities. In his latter years he lived an austere life and eagerly anticipated his own death.

It appears from the revelations of Carrington that, like so many other famous psychic investigators, Hodgson developed mediumship at the end. In the last years of his life he allowed no one to enter his room at 15 Charles Street. In the evenings when alone there, he received direct communications from "Imperator," "Rector," and Piper's other controls. These communications were convincing, but he told few people about them. The room was closed to everyone so as not to disturb the "magnetic atmosphere."

The Hodgson Memorial Fund was created at Harvard University in 1912 and was used to fund research by such investigators as **Gardner Murphy.**

Hodgson in the Afterlife

After Hodgson's death, alleged communications from him were received in England by **Alice Kipling Fleming** (then known under her pseudonym, "Mrs. Holland"). They contained a cipher similar to entries found in Hodgson's notebook, but it could not be solved. Not even by the dramatic and very lifelike "Hodgson" control of Mrs. Piper was the key ever given. Through Piper he first communicated eight days after his death and delivered many messages claimed to be from his surviving self.

However, many test questions were left unanswered. "If we could suppose," writes **Frank Podmore,** "that sometimes the real Hodgson communicated through the medium's hand, and that sometimes, more often, when he was inaccessible, the medium's secondary personality played the part as best it could, these difficulties would, no doubt, be lessened."

Many evidential messages bearing on the continued identity of Hodgson were received by **James Hyslop.** One of the first came through a friend who asked Hodgson, the communicator, if he would get in touch with him through another "light." The reply was, "No, I will not, except through the young light. She is all right." Later in the sitting, one of the other controls remarked that Hyslop would know what the statement meant. It referred to a young, nonprofessional medium whose powers were a subject of discussion between the living Hodgson and Hyslop. It appears that the surviving Hodgson investigated her case from "the other side," since the young lady's control about the time of the incident remarked that he had seen Hodgson. The news of his death was carefully kept from the medium at the time.

The detailed records of these séances, held from the time of Hodgson's death until January 1, 1908, were handed over to William James for examination. In his paper "Report on Mrs. Piper's Hodgson Control," he says,

"I myself feel as if an external will to communicate were probably there, that is, I find myself doubting . . . that Mrs. Piper's dreamlife, even equipped with 'telepathic' powers, accounts for all the results found. But if asked whether the will to communicate be Hodgson's or be some mere spirit-counterfeit of Hodgson, I remain uncertain and await more facts, facts which may not point clearly to a conclusion for fifty or a hundred years."

In England the Hodgson messages were studied by **Eleanor Sidgwick, J. G. Piddington,** and **Sir Oliver Lodge** during Piper's visit to England. They did not find them authentic.

Sources:

Baird, A. T. *Richard Hodgson: The Story of a Psychical Researcher and His Times.* London: Psychic Press, 1949.

Berger, Arthur S., and Joyce Berger. *The Encyclopedia of Parapsychology and Psychical Research.* New York: Paragon House, 1991.

Harrison, Vernon. "J'Accuse. An Examination of the Hodgson Report." *Journal* of the Society for Psychical Research 53 (1986).

Hodgson, Richard. "An Account of Personal Investigations in India, and Discussion of the Authorship of the 'Koot Hoomi' Letters." *Proceedings* of the Society for Psychical Research 3 (1885).

Hodgson, Richard, and S. J. Davey. "The Possibilities of Malobservation and Lapse of Memory from a Practical Point of View." *Proceedings* of the Society for Psychical Research 4 (1887).

James, William. "Report on Mrs. Piper's Hodgson Control." *Proceedings* of the Society for Psychical Research 23 (1909).

Pleasants, Helene, ed. *Biographical Dictionary of Parapsychology.* New York: Helix Press, 1964.

Hoebens, Piet Hein (1948–1984)

Dutch journalist who wrote a number of skeptical reports on parapsychological phenomena. He was a staff member of the Amsterdam newspaper *De Telegraaf* for 13 years and served as the Dutch representative on the **Committee for the Scientific Investigation of Claims of the Paranormal.**

In spite of his skepticism about parapsychology, Hoebens took a keen interest in the subject and was regarded as a fair-minded critic. In the early 1980s, he contributed to *Zetetic Scholar* a valuable series of articles, "The Mystery Men From Holland," concerning the phenomena claimed for **Peter Hurkos, Gerard Croiset,** and **Marinus Dykshoorn.** Hoebens died in the Netherlands, October 22, 1984.

Sources:

Hoebens, Piet Hein. "The Mystery Men From Holland." *Zetetic Scholar* 8 (July 1981); 9 (March 1982); 10 (December 1982).

Hoene-Wronski, Jozef Maria (1776–1853)

Polish mathematician and inventor who developed a philosophy of messianism, derived from the **Kabala** and **Gnosticism.** He claimed to have discovered "the secret of the Absolute," which he revealed for 150,000 francs to Pierre Arson, a businessman who agreed to publish Hoene-Wronski's messianic works. When Arson backed out of the deal, Hoene-Wronski declared him to be the beast of the Apocalypse and published a pamphlet with the immortal title *Yes or No—that is to say, have you or have you not, yes or no, purchased from me for 150,000 francs my discovery of the Absolute?* Not surprisingly, Hoene-Wronski lost his court battle to obtain the remainder of the money, but the unfortunate Arson had already expended some 40,000 francs on the works of Hoene-Wronski.

About 1850 Hoene-Wronski became the occult teacher of Alphonse Louis Constant, who later wrote many books on the occult under the pseudonym **Éliphas Lévi.**

Sources:

Hoene-Wronski, Jozef Maria. *Hoene-Wronski: Une philosopie de la creation.* Paris: Seghers, 1970.

Hoffer, Abram (1917–)

Psychiatrist who studied the effect of psychedelic drugs on human consciousness. Hoffer was born on November 11, 1917, in Saskatchewan, Canada. He studied successively at the University of Saskatchewan (B.S., 1938; M.S., 1940), the University of Minnesota (Ph.D., 1944), and the University of Toronto (M.D., 1945). After graduation he took a position as director of psychiatric research in the Psychiatric Services Branch, Department of Public Health, Saskatchewan.

Hoffer began work on the effects of **hallucinogens** in the 1950s. In 1959 he addressed the Conference on Parapsychology and Psychedelics in New York, and in the following year published, with **Humphrey Osmond,** the *Chemical Concepts of Psychiatry* (1960). He and Osmond also worked together on *Hallucinogens* (1967) and both contributed to *Clinical and Other Uses of the Hoffer-Osmond Diagnostic Test* (1975).

In the 1970s he concentrated his research on problems of nutrition. His books include *How to Live with Schizophrenia* (1978), *Orthomolecular Nutrition* (with Morton Walker, 1978), *Nutrients to Age Without Senility* (1980), and *Ortho-Molecular Nutrition* (with Morton Walker, 1981).

Sources:

Hoffer, Abram, and Humphrey Osmond. *Megavitamin Therapy: In Reply to the American Psychiatric Association Task Force Report on Megavitamins and Orthomolecular Psychiatry.* Regina, Sask., Can.: Canadian Schizophrenia Foundation, 1976.

Pleasants, Helene, ed. *Biographical Dictionary of Parapsychology.* New York: Helix Press, 1964.

Hohenlohe, Prince (1794–1849)

A priest and claimed miracle healer whose full title was Alexander Leopold Franz Emmerick, Prince of Hohenlohe-Waldenburg-Schillings-Furst. He was born at Kupferzell, near Waldenburg, now in Bavaria, on August 17, 1794. He was ordained as a Catholic priest in 1815 and went to Rome, where he entered the Society of the Fathers of the Sacred Heart.

Prince Hohenlohe gained a great reputation as a miraculous healer at Bamberg and Munich and attracted large crowds. Eventually the authorities intervened to prevent his healing work. He traveled to Vienna and Hungary, becoming titular bishop of Sardica in 1844. He died at Vöslau, near Vienna, November 17, 1849.

Sources:

Baur, F. N. *A Short and Faithful Description of the Remarkable Occurrences and . . . Conduct of . . . Prince Alexander of Hohenlohe.* N.p., 1822.

Brunner, S. *Aus dem Nachlasse des Furstein Aloysius von Hehenlohe.* Regensburg: G. J. Manz, 1851.

Doyle, J. *Miracles Said to Have Been Wrought by the Prince Hohenlohe.* N.p., 1823.

Hohenwarter, Peter (1894– ?)

Theologian who conducted important research into mediumistic phenomena. He was born May 18, 1894, at Obervellach, Austria, and studied at Graz University, Austria (Theol.D., 1924). He worked as a professor of mathematics, physics, and philosophy at Klagenfurt until removed by the Nazis in 1938.

After the war Hohenwarter became vice president of Imago Mundi, the International Society of Catholic Parapsychologists, and joined the Austrian Society for Psychical Research. He organized a great many sittings with the Viennese medium **Maria Silbert** and with the Danish medium **Einer Nielsen,** whose phenomena he endorsed in lectures.

Sources:

Hohenwarter, Peter. "The Experiments of Astro-Physicist Dr. Alois Gatterer, S. J., with Maria Silbert." *Vergorgene Welt* 2, no. 3 (1957).

———. "Germany's Leading Parapsychologist: The 100th Anniversary of Schrenck-Notzing's Birth." *Vergorgene Welt.* 3–5 (1959).

———. "Hauntings at Schwarzach in the Voralberg Region." *Neue Wissenschaft* (July 1954).

———. "Our Experiments with Maria Silbert." *Schweizer Rundschau* (February 1954).

———. "Should We Study Parapsychology?" *Der Seelsorger* (March 1958).

Pleasants, Helene, ed. *Biographical Dictionary of Parapsychology.* New York: Helix Press, 1964.

Holistic

A **New Age** term implying an integrated approach to life. For many it embodies a pretechnological life that supports, for example, alternative healing practices in place of contemporary established medicine, or unprocessed (whole) foods instead of canned or frozen products. It has also been identified with environmentalism, nonpolluting alternative energy sources, communal living arrangements, and intense spirituality.

The term *holism* derives from the Greek *holos* (whole), and was first used by Jan Christian Smuts in his book *Holism and Evolution* (1926), in which he states, "Both matter and life consist of unit structures whose ordered grouping produced natural wholes. . . . The rise and self-perfection of wholes in the Whole is the slow but unerring process and goal of this Holistic universe."

This notion prefigures the theory of theologian Theilhard de Chardin that the human race is "evolving mentally and socially, towards a final spiritual unity."

Holism has been mostly associated with healing processes. At its best, it reaches for a patient-centered medicine in which the physician treats the person as a whole being, rather than focusing only on a set of symptoms. Generally, however, holistic medicine is simply a catch phrase referring to a range of healing practices, some beneficial and some questionable.

Sources:

Hastings, Arthur C., James Fadiman, and James S. Gordon. *Health for the Whole Person.* Boulder, Colo.: Westview Press, 1980.

Miller, Don Ethan. *Bodymind: The Whole Person Health Book.* Englewood Cliffs, N.J.: Prentice-Hall, 1974.

Pathways to Wholeness: A Healing Guide. Berkeley, Calif.: Clear Light Publications, 1975.

Pelletier, Kenneth R. *Mind as Healer/Mind as Slayer: A Holistic Approach to Preventing Stress Disorder.* New York: Delta, 1977.

St. Aubyn, Lorna, ed. *Healing.* London: Heineman, 1983.

HOLLAND

For general early occultism among German peoples, see the entry **Teutons.**

Spiritualism

Spiritualism was introduced into Holland in about 1857. The first Dutch Spiritualist on record is J. N. T. Marthese, who, after studying psychic phenomena in foreign countries, finally returned to his native Holland, taking with him the American medium **D. D. Home.** The latter held séances at The Hague before several learned societies, and by command of Queen Sophia a séance was given in her presence. The medium himself, in an account of the performance, stated that the royal lady was obliged to sit seven séances on consecutive evenings before any results were obtained. These results, however, were apparently satisfactory, for the queen was thereafter a staunch supporter of the movement.

During Home's visit Spiritualism gained a considerable following in Holland and the practice of giving small private séances became fairly widespread. Allegedly, spirit voices were heard at these gatherings, the touch of spirit hands was felt, and musical instruments were played by invisible performers.

Séances held at the house of J. D. van Herwerden in The Hague were particularly notable and were attended by many enthusiastic students of the phenomena. Van Herwerden recruited a 14-year-old Javanese boy of his household as the medium. The manifestations ranged from spirit rapping and **table turning** in the earlier séances to **direct voice, direct writing, levitation,** and **materializations** in later ones. The séances were described in van Herwerden's book *Ervaringen en Mededeeling op een nog Geheimzinnig Gebied* and took place between 1858 and 1862. One of the principal spirits purported to be a monk, Paurellus, who was assassinated some 300 years previously in that city. Afterward van Herwerden was induced by his friends to publish his diary, under the title *Experiences and Communications on a Still Mysterious Territory.*

For a time Spiritualist séances were conducted only in family circles and were of a private nature. But as the attention of intellectuals became more and more directed to the new phenomenon, societies were formed to promote research. Oromase, or Ormuzd, the first of these societies, was founded in 1859 by Major J. Revius, a friend of Marthese's, and included among its members many people of high repute. They met at The Hague, and the records of their transactions were carefully preserved. Revius was president until his death in 1871. He was assisted by the society's secretary, **A. Rita.** They assembled a fine collection of works on Spiritualism, mesmerism, and kindred subjects.

Another society, the Veritas, was founded in Amsterdam in 1869. The studies of this association were conducted in a somewhat less searching and scientific spirit than those of the Oromase. Its mediums specialized in trance utterances and written communications from the spirits, and its members inclined to a belief in **reincarnation,** an opinion at variance with that of the older society. Rotterdam had for a time a society known as the Research after Truth, which had similar manifestations and tenets, but it soon came to an end, although its members continued to devote themselves privately to the investigation of spirit phenomena.

Other equally short-lived societies were formed in Haarlem and other towns. In all of these, however, there was a shortage of mediums able to produce form materializations. To supply this demand a number of foreign mediums hastened to Holland, including Margaret Fox Kane (of the **Fox sisters**), the **Davenport brothers, Florence Cook,** and **Henry Slade.**

Before this the comparatively private nature of the séances and the high standing of those who took part in them had prevented the periodicals from making any but the most cautious comments on the séances. The appearance of professional mediums on the scene, however, swept away the barrier and let loose a flood of journalistic ridicule and criticism. This in turn provoked the supporters of Spiritualism to retort, and soon a lively battle was in progress between the Spiritualists and the skeptics. The consequence was that "the cause" was promoted as much by the articles that derided it as by those that were in favor of it.

Among the defenders of Spiritualism was Madame Elise van Calcar, who not only wrote a novel expounding Spiritualist principles but also published a monthly journal, *On the Boundaries of Two Worlds,* and held a sort of Spiritualist salon where enthusiasts could meet and discuss their favorite subjects. Dutch intellectuals, such as Drs. H. de Grood, J. Van Velzen, Van der Loef, and Herr Schimmel, were among authors who wrote in defense of the same opinions, and the writings of **C. F. Varley, Sir William Crookes,** and **Alfred Russel Wallace** were translated into Dutch.

A mesmerist, Signor Donata, carried on the practice of **animal magnetism** in Holland and endeavored to identify the magnetic force emanating from the operator with the substance of which disembodied spirits were believed to be composed. Progress of the movement was hampered by the many exposures of unscrupulous mediums, but on the whole the mediums, professional or otherwise, were well received. Haunted houses and **poltergeists** were also noted.

Psychical Research and Parapsychology

Some of the pioneers of psychical research in Holland were **Frederik van Eeden** (1860–1932), K. H. E. de Jong (1872–1960), P. A. Dietz (1878–1953), and Florentin J. L. Jansen (b. 1881). Van Eeden was an author and physician who sat with the English medium **Rosina Thompson** and was also acquainted with **F. W. H.**

Myers. Van Eeden contributed "A Study of Dreams" to the *Proceedings* of the Society for Psychical Research (vol. 26, p. 431), in which he used the term *lucid dream* to indicate those conditions in which the dreamer is aware that he is dreaming. This condition of consciousness in the dream state was emphasized by the British writer **Oliver Fox** as a frequent preliminary to **astral projection.**

Jong was a classical student whose doctoral thesis dealt with the mysteries of Isis. As World War II began, he was a lecturer in parapsychology at the University of Leiden and was responsible for a number of books and articles dealing with **psi** faculty.

Dietz attempted to organize a student social group for psychical research when studying biology at the University of Groningen. Although this was short-lived, Dietz went on to investigate parapsychological card tests, using himself as the subject. After qualifying as a medical doctor in 1924, he became a neurologist in The Hague. A few years later he and **W. H. C. Tenhaeff** founded the periodical *Tijdschrift voor Parapsychologie.* In his book *Wereldzicht der Parapsychologie* (Parapsychological View of the Universe) Dietz coined the terms *paragnosy* for psychical phenomena and *parergy* for physical phenomena. He became a lecturer in parapsychology at the University of Leiden in 1931 and had a reputation as an excellent speaker.

Jansen seems to have established a parapsychological laboratory as early as 1907, while still a medical student. He founded the quarterly periodical *Driemaandelijkse verslagen van het Psychophysisch Laboratorium te Amsterdam.* He took a special interest in experiments with **Paul Joire**'s **sthenometer** and conducted a number of experiments to verify the **od** force proposed by **Baron von Reichenbach.** In 1912 he emigrated to Buenos Aires, where he worked as a physician.

Other pioneers included Marcellus Emants (1848–1932), a novelist who experimented with the famous medium **Eusapia Palladino;** engineer Felix Ortt (1866–1959), who published articles on parapsychology and a book on the philosophy of occultism and Spiritualism; and Captain H. N. de Fremery, who published a manual of Spiritualism and also contributed to *Tijdschrift voor Parapsychologie.*

In 1920 the **Studievereniging voor Psychical Research,** the Dutch Society for Psychical Research, was founded in Amsterdam through the enterprise of **Gerardus Heymans** (1857–1930) of Groningen University. Although the society began well, it was soon criticized for an unsympathetic atmosphere for mediums, but in 1927 it received a new impetus from the psychologist W. H. C. Tenhaeff and the journal *Tijdschrift voor Parapsychologie.* Some notable investigations over the years included studies of **dowsing** (water witching), physics and parapsychology, and precognitive elements in dreams.

The society was suppressed during World War II, and the Germans took the library to Germany and destroyed it. After the war the society was reconstructed and soon numbered a thousand members, including Javanese parapsychologist **George Zorab.** Some of the work in this period included observations on the noted psychic **Gerard Croiset,** an attempt to replicate the **Whately Carington** tests with **Zener cards,** and the investigation of "objective clairvoyance." Meanwhile, in 1933 Tenhaeff founded the Parapsychology Institute of the State University of Utrecht, later known as the **Parapsychological Division of the Psychological Laboratory, Utrecht.**

In 1953 the First International Conference of Parapsychological Studies, sponsored by the **Parapsychology Foundation,** New York, was held in Utrecht. In 1959 the Amsterdam Foundation for Parapsychological Research was established and began an investigation of the influence of psychedelics on **ESP.** Another investigation was a widely conducted inquiry into the occurrence of spontaneous phenomena.

In 1960 a controversy erupted in the Studievereniging voor Psychical Research over Tenhaeff's authoritarian control of the organization. Some members withdrew and founded the **Nederlandse Vereniging voor Parapsychologie,** which now provides the primary focus for parapsychological research in the country. By 1967 there was growing interest in parapsychology among students of five major universities, and various societies were set up. These were later grouped into the Study Center for Experimental Parapsychology.

The Federation of Parapsychological Circles of the Netherlands emerged as an umbrella for several small local parapsychological groups, including the Amsterdamse Parapsychologische Studiekring, the Haarlemse Parapsychologische Studiekring, the Haagse Parapsychologische Studiekring, and the Rottendamse Parapsychologische Studiekring.

Sources:

Berger, Arthur S., and Joyce Berger. *The Encyclopedia of Parapsychology and Psychical Research.* New York: Paragon House, 1991.

Dykshoorn, M. B., with Russell H. Felton. *My Passport Says Clairvoyant.* New York: Hawthorn Books, 1974.

Hurkos, Peter. *Psychic.* London: Arthur Baker, 1962.

Pleasants, Helene, ed. *Biographical Dictionary of Parapsychology.* New York: Helix Press, 1964.

Pollack, Jack Harrison. *Croiset the Clairvoyant.* Garden City, N.Y.: Doubleday, 1964. Reprint, New York: Bantam Books, 1965.

"Holland, Mrs." (1868–1948)

Pseudonym of **Alice Kipling Fleming,** who took part in famous "cross correspondence" tests of the **Society for Psychical Research,** London, and produced significant **automatic writing** scripts.

Holleran, Eugene M(artin) (1922–)

Professor of chemistry who investigated psychokinesis. Holleran was born June 25, 1922, in Kingston, Pennsylvania. He attended Scranton University (B.S., 1943) and Catholic University, Washington D.C. (Ph.D. chemistry, 1949). In 1950 he became a professor of chemistry at St. John's University, Jamaica, New York. He joined the Parapsychological Association, and during the 1960–61 school year Holleran worked on a Parapsychology Foundation grant on tests to establish psychokinetic ability.

Sources:

Pleasants, Helene, ed. *Biographical Dictionary of Parapsychology.* New York: Helix Press, 1964.

Hollis, Mary J. (Mrs. Hollis-Billing) (1837– ?)

American **direct voice** and **materialization** medium of the nineteenth century, controlled by spirit guides "James Nolan" and "Skiwaukee" (a Native American). In 1874 and 1880 she visited England, where she demonstrated **slate writing,** the script frequently said to be produced by a materialized hand in full view. Hollis was born April 24, 1837, in Jeffersonville, Indiana, into a wealthy family. She was an exemplary member of the Episcopal Church until she began to see and talk with spirits.

During the years 1871 to 1873 N. B. Wolfe of Chicago made exhaustive investigations into her phenomena. The account is included in his *Startling Facts in Modern Spiritualism* (1873). According to Wolfe, Hollis's direct voice mediumship was well developed. As many as 30 or 40 spirits were said to have come in a single sitting. They spoke only in the dark, but they could sing along with the sitters. Sometimes the sitters were given the **Freemasonry** challenge. Objects frequently moved. Sometimes the medium was levitated to the ceiling and left a pencil mark there. One of her manifesting spirits was fond of making dolls and rosettes from the material provided for this purpose, and the sewing was done accurately in the dark.

Hollis produced materialized forms from a **cabinet** without going into trance. Phantom hands quickly appeared. As a test the medium's right hand was blackened with cork. The spirit hand was clean. The faces were often flat, and the sitters looked at them through opera glasses. On one occasion six heads materialized simultaneously. Famous people were claimed to have manifested at the Hollis séances, including Napoleon and Empress Josephine, who wore a jeweled crown and strings of pearls.

Hollow Earth

Many occult speculations revolve around variant cosmologies in which the Earth is not simply a solid sphere in a universe of other celestial bodies. One of them is the idea that the Earth is to some degree hollow. This theory takes two basic forms. The first, "the cellular cosmogony," proposes that we live on the inside of a sphere or oval, with sun, moon, and planets in the center. The second suggests that we live on the outside of a hollow sphere with a mysterious inner kingdom known only to a few initiates or intrepid travelers.

An early hollow Earth theory was proposed by the English astronomer Edmund Halley (of comet fame) in 1692. He suggested that the Earth is a shell 500 miles thick with two inner shells and a solid inner sphere, all capable of sustaining life. In 1721 Congregationalist minister **Cotton Mather** put forward a similar theory.

In 1818 Captain John Cleves Symmes, a retired army officer, spent the last years of his life trying to prove that the Earth consisted of five concentric spheres with holes several thousand miles in diameter at the poles. His theories are explained in detail in the books *Symmes' Theory of Concentric Spheres* (1826), by James McBridge, and *The Symmes' Theory of Concentric Spheres* (1878), by Americus Symmes, son of the captain.

In 1820 a writer with the probably pseudonymous name "Captain Seaborn" published a fictional narrative about a hollow Earth under the title *Symzonia.* In the book Seaborn finds his steamship drawn by strong currents to a southern polar opening, where he finds an inner world of happy utopiates. Edgar Allan Poe's "Narrative of Arthur Gordon Pym" develops a similar theme.

A later development of the Symmes theories was propounded with messianic zeal by Cyrus Reed Teed (1839–1908), who spent 38 years lecturing and writing on the hollow Earth theme. He had a laboratory for the study of **alchemy,** and claimed that in 1869 he had a vision of a beautiful woman who revealed to him the secret of the hollow Earth. This discovery was given to the world in a pamphlet titled *The Illumination of Koresh: Marvelous Experience of the Great Alchemist at Utica, N.Y.* In 1870 he published *The Cellular Cosmogony* under his religious name "Koresh" (Cyrus) and after many years of enthusiastic lecturing established a College of Life in Chicago in 1886. This was the beginning of a communal society called the Koreshan Unity. By the 1890s this had blossomed into the town of Estero, near Fort Myers, Florida, under the name The New Jerusalem.

In the 1930s, long after Teed's death and the decline of his Koreshan communities in the United States, his ideas were merged with theosophical and occult notions and also became part of some eccentric Nazi cosmologies. Remnants of the *Hohlweltlehre* (hollow Earth teaching) still have some following in Germany. Teed's ideas were later exploited by two famous occult swindlers, Mr. and Mrs. Frank Jackson, operating under the names **Theodore and Laura Theodore Horos.** The name "Horos" was taken from the writings of Cyrus Reed Teed. Mrs. Jackson (also known as "Mrs. Diss Debar," "Angel Anna," and "Editha Gilbert Montez") appears to have been born as Editha Salomon. In addition to representing herself as a founder of "Koreshan Unity," she stole the rituals of the Hermetic Order of the **Golden Dawn.**

Another hollow Earth theorist was Marshall B. Gardner, an Illinois maintenance engineer who worked for a corset manufacturer. His book *Journey to the Earth's Interior* (1906) might have been influenced by Jules Verne's story *Journey to the Center of the Earth* (1864). It rejects the theory of several concentric spheres and claims fact that there is only one hollow Earth and that we live on the outside of it. Gardner's "Earth" is 800 miles thick, and the interior has its own sun. There are openings at the poles, each 1,400 miles wide, through which the mammoths of Siberia and the Eskimoan people came. An enlarged edition of Gardner's book was published in 1920, with many impressive illustrations showing the everlasting summer of the interior.

Six years after the publication of the second edition of Gardner's book, Admiral Richard E. Byrd flew over the North Pole. Three years later Byrd flew over the South Pole, but he found no holes in either of the poles. Incredibly enough, however, his statements about his explorations have since been quoted out of context to make it seem as if he actually endorsed the hollow Earth myth. Claims that **flying saucers** really come from inside the Earth through the polar openings are made by, among others, Raymond Bernard in his book *The Hollow Earth* (1969).

A persistent variant of the hollow Earth cosmology is the idea that the Earth is honeycombed with a network of secret **subterranean cities** and caverns, the home of underground kingdoms. Such notions have been articulated by **Richard Shaver.** These are modern versions of older folklore about fairies and gnomes.

Sources:

Gardner, Marshall B. *A Journey to the Earth's Interior; or, Have the Poles Really Been Discovered?* Aurora, Ill.: The Author, 1913.

Lang, Johannes. *Die Hohlwelttheorie.* Franfurt am Main, Germany: Goethe Verlag, 1938.

Teed, Cyrus Reed. *The Cellular Cosmogony; or, the Earth, a Concave Sphere.* Chicago: Guiding Star, 1899.

Walton, Bruce A. *A Guide to the Inner Earth.* Jane Lew, W. Va.: New Age Books, 1983.

Holly

This name is probably a corruption of the word *holy* since this plant has been used from time immemorial as a protection against evil influence. It was hung around or planted near houses as a protection against lightning. Its common use at Christmas apparently originated in an ancient Roman festival in which holly was dedicated to the god Saturn. While the Romans were holding this feast—which occurred about the time of the winter solstice—they decked the outsides of their houses with holly. At the same time the Christians were quietly celebrating the birth of Christ, and to avoid detection they outwardly followed the custom of their heathen neighbors and decked their houses with holly as well. In this way holly came to be connected with Christmas customs. The plant was also regarded as a symbol of the Resurrection.

The use of mistletoe along with holly probably came from the notion that in winter the **fairies** took shelter under its leaves and that they protected all who sheltered the plant. The origin of kissing under the mistletoe is considered to have come from Saxon ancestors of the British, who regarded this plant as dedicated to Freya, the goddess of love.

Holmes, Ernest Shurtlett (1887–1960)

Ernest S. Holmes, the founder of Religious Science, was born January 21, 1887, in Lincoln, Maine. His poor family provided little incentive for education, and at the age of 15 he left home for Boston to make his way in the world. He pursued a course in public speaking and discovered that one of his instructors was a Christian Scientist. He was given a copy of **Mary Baker Eddy**'s *Science and Health with Key to the Scriptures.* This basic Christian Science textbook fit easily into Holmes's reading of philosopher Ralph Waldo Emerson.

In 1912 Holmes moved to Southern California where his brother Fenwicke had become the pastor of a Congregational church. Shortly after his arrival he discovered the Metaphysical Library in Los Angeles, which had become the center for the distribution of **New Thought** metaphysical literature. He avidly devoured the works of writers such as Thomas Troward, William Walker Atkinson, and Christian Larsen. In 1916 he gave his first public lecture at the Metaphysical Library, and the following year he and his brother opened the Metaphysical Institute and began issuing a magazine, *Uplift.* Within a short time he was lecturing regularly in Los Angeles and Long Beach, California, and began to travel nationally. His first book, *Creative Mind,* appeared in 1919. A final step in his mature development occurred in 1924 when he briefly settled in New York City and became the last student to be accepted by **Emma Curtis Hopkins,** the founder of New Thought.

In 1925 Holmes returned to Los Angeles and finished writing his major work, *The Science of Mind* (1925), a summary of his thought and the textbook embodying his own perspective on New Thought. The "Science of Mind" was the study of spirit, the reality underlying the visible cosmos. Mastery of the Science of Mind led to happiness, health, and prosperity. He also developed a simple technique of healing prayer. In 1927 he founded the Institute of Religious Science and School of Philosophy and began to train people in his methods. They in turn established themselves as Science of Mind practitioners in a manner similar to Christian Science practitioners.

The movement Holmes began prospered over the next several decades. He continually had to move his Sunday lectures into larger facilities. In 1949 he began a radio show, "This Thing Called Life." New books appeared regularly.

Holmes resisted attempts to see Religious Science as a church movement. However, in 1949, giving in to requests from some of his closest associates, he oversaw the formation of the International Association of Religious Science Churches. In 1954 Holmes moved to reorganize the very loosely organized association directly under the institute, whose name was changed to the Church of Religious Science. While most congregations went along with the plan, some, including those led by several of Holmes's closest colleagues, saw the move as a power grab and continued the association as a separate movement.

Holmes died April 7, 1960, in Los Angeles. The Church of Religious Science continues as the United Church of Religious Science and the association continues as Religious Science International.

Sources:

Armor, Reginald C. *Ernest Holmes: The Man.* Los Angeles: Science of Mind Publications, 1977.

Holmes, Ernest S. *How to Use the Science of Mind.* New York: Dodd, Mead, 1948.

———. *The Science of Mind.* 1925. Rev. ed. New York: R. M. McBride, 1938.

———. *This Thing Called Life.* Los Angeles: Institute of Religious Science and Philosophy, 1943.

———. *What Religious Science Teaches.* Los Angeles: Church of Religious Science, 1944.

Holmes, Fenwicke L. *Ernest Holmes: His Life and Times.* New York: Dodd, Mead, 1970.

Holmes, Mr. and Mrs. Nelson (ca. 1874)

Materialization mediums of Philadelphia who claimed **"Katie King"** and **"John King"** as their **controls.** The claim was supported by Henry T. Child, another medium, who published particulars of the two controls' corporeal lives as privately communicated to him in his study.

In 1873 the Holmeses—of longstanding good reputation—traveled to England, where they were charged with dishonorable attempts to raise money. The accounts of their powers of mediumship varied between séances. One family recognized a spirit face as that of a departed relative; in an account of that experience in *The Spiritualist,* the Reverend **Stainton Moses,** stated that the light was good and the face was only a few feet away from the sitters. After their return to the United States, a General Lippitt publicly endorsed the Holmeses' mediumship in *The Galaxy* in December 1874.

The Holmeses' fall from grace is amply demonstrated in the change undergone by their once-powerful advocate, **Robert Dale Owen,** who initially wrote:

"I have seen Katie on seven or eight different occasions, suspended, in full form, about two feet from the ground for ten or fifteen seconds. It was within the cabinet, but in full view; and she moved her arms and feet gently, as a swimmer upright in the water might. I have seen her, on five different evenings, disappear and reappear before my eyes, and not more than eight or nine feet distant. On one occasion, when I had given her a calla lily, she gradually vanished, holding it in her hand; and the lily remained visible after the hand which held it was gone; the flower, however, finally disappearing also. When she reappeared the lily came back also, at first a bright spot only, which gradually expanded into a flower."

On November 2, 1874, Owen additionally affirmed: "I stake whatever reputation I may have acquired, after eighteen years' study of spiritualism, as a dispassionate observer upon the genuine character of these phenomena."

Nevertheless, a month later, on December 6, 1874, he declared in *The Banner of Light*: "Circumstantial evidence, which I have just obtained, induces me to withdraw the assurances which I have heretofore given of my confidence in the genuine character of certain manifestations presented last summer, in my presence, through Mrs. and Mr. Nelson Holmes."

A similar notice was published by Henry T. Child.

The reason for the sudden change was the revelation that Eliza White, the Holmeses' landlady, claimed that she had impersonated Katie King by slipping in through a false panel of the **cabinet**. A demonstration of the impersonation was given to Owen and Child. The newspapers made a great sensation of the exposure. The Holmeses appeared to have been ruined.

Then **Henry Olcott** came to the rescue. He investigated and soon discovered very serious discrepancies in White's story. Affidavits were given to him alleging White's bad moral reputation and dishonest nature. A New Jersey justice of the peace testified to having heard White singing in another room while "Katie King" appeared before Owen and Child.

General Lippitt told of a thorough investigation of the cabinet with a professional magician who was satisfied that there was no chance of any trick. Letters were produced by the Holmeses that spoke against the probability of any conspiracy between them and Eliza White. On the contrary, they proved that White tried to blackmail them much earlier by threatening to claim that she impersonated "Katie King."

Additional evidence also seemed to vindicate the Holmeses: At the time of the mock séance before Child and Owen, the Holmeses had a real séance with 20 people at which the spirits appeared.

On the basis of these facts, and allowing for the dubious part that Child appeared to have played in the affair, Olcott concluded that the Holmeses should be tested again without reference to the past. This he did. He netted a cabinet to proof it against surreptitious entry and put Mrs. Holmes into a bag tied around her neck. The experiments were repeated in his own room. Olcott became satisfied that Mrs. Holmes was a genuine and powerful medium for materializations, an opinion he affirms in his book *People from the Other World* (1875). General Lippitt shared his conclusions.

Sources:

Olcott, Henry Steele. *People from the Other World.* Hartford, Conn.: American Publishing, 1875.

Holms, A(rchibald) Campbell (1861–1954)

Scottish expert on shipbuilding who also studied **Spiritualism** and psychic science. In addition to his classic work *Practical Shipbuilding* (1904), he also compiled one of the most valuable and comprehensive encyclopedias of psychical phenomena ever published: *The Facts of Psychic Science* (1925). Although not a critical study, it analyzed and classified every major phenomenon of psychic science, with detailed indexes.

Sources:

Holms, A. Campbell. *The Facts of Psychic Science.* 1925. Reprint, New Hyde Park, N.Y.: University Books, 1969.

Holonomics

Term coined by the **Holonomics Group,** founded in England in 1977, to denote "the unified and impartial study of the pattern of law and purpose of the universe as a whole," deriving from the ancient Greek words *holon* (whole) and *nomos* (law). Holonomics, a **holistic** theory, is considered "a new approach to fundamental knowledge, adopting a holistic mode of thinking and action, and aiming to coordinate and integrate the approaches of science, philosophy, religion, personal experience, ethics, and the arts, and to have direct applications to the human situation."

Holonomics Group, The

Founded in November 1977 by **Alan J. Mayne** and others to help promote a unified approach to science, parascience, philosophy, religion, the arts, human development, and human affairs and to provide a forum for the discussion of ideas relevant to this theme. The group issues a newsletter, *Holon,* presenting concepts and principles of Holonomics, as well as notices of relevant societies, meetings, reports, and projects. The group maintains a register of interests and personal statements of members to assist them in contacting each other on related interests and experiences and to stimulate the exchange of ideas. A communication network allows members and other interested individuals to arrange informal discussions and meetings.

The group also aims to provide an environment that encourages relevant interdisciplinary research. Address: The Holonomics Group, c/o Alan Mayne, 63A Muswell Ave., London, N10 2EH, England.

Holt, Henry (1840–1926)

American publisher who encouraged the publication of books on psychic phenomena. Holt was born on January 3, 1840, in Baltimore, Maryland. He attended Yale University (B.S., 1862) and the Columbia University Law School (LL.B., 1864). In 1866 Holt became a partner in the publishing company of George P. Putnam, and later founded Henry Holt and Company. He also became a council member of the **American Society for Psychical Research.**

Holt's interest in psychic phenomena led him to promote research and to publish books on the subject, including his own work *On the Cosmic Relations* (2 vols., 1914). A revised edition was issued after World War I with additional matter on immortality, under the title *The Cosmic Relations and Immortality* (1918). He died February 13, 1926.

The company continued in existence, and in 1941 published the important one-volume edition of *The Books of Charles Fort,* dealing with bizarre, inexplicable, and mysterious phenomena. (See also **Charles Fort**)

Sources:

Holt, Henry. *Calmire.* New York: Macmillan, 1892.

———. *Garrulities of an Octogenarian Editor.* Boston: Houghton Mifflin, 1923.

———. *Man and Man.* N.p., 1905.

———. *Man and Nature.* N.p., 1892.

———. *On the Cosmic Relations.* 1914. Rev. ed. as *The Cosmic Relations and Immortality.* Boston: Houghton Mifflin, 1919.

Holy Coat of Treves

Sacred relic believed to be the seamless robe worn by Jesus Christ at the time of crucifixion. It is displayed in the cathedral at Treves, on the river Moselle in the Rhineland of Germany. The coat has been venerated by many thousands of pilgrims. For details of a similar but more famous reputed relic, see **Turin Shroud.**

Sources:

Clark, Richard J., S.J. *The Holy Coat of Treves.* London, 1892.

Holy Rosicrucian Church

The Holy Rosicrucian Church was a small, short-lived Rosicrucian group that functioned briefly early in the twentieth century in the western United States. It was founded and headed by a man known as Sergius Rosenkruz. The church taught a method of liberation, the awakening of knowledge of unity with the One. As a means to liberation, Rosenkruz advocated a series of practices that included study, two daily baths, charitable works, the avoidance of frivolous activities, and meditation.

The order was headquartered in Los Angeles. It was associated with the Order of the Knights of the Golden Circle, which offered a series of ceremonies aimed at preparing members for either a favorable reincarnation or safety in the life beyond death. The church is known primarily through one pamphlet, *Rosikrucinism,* issued in 1915.

Sources:

Rosenkruz, Sergius. *Rosikrucinism.* Los Angeles: The Author, 1915.

Holzer, Hans W. (1920–)

Popular writer on paranormal topics. Holzer was born on January 26, 1920, in Vienna, Austria, and later attended Vienna University and Columbia University. In 1945 he became a free-lance writer. He was also a playwright and composer, a drama critic for the *London Weekly Sporting Review* (1949–60), and a television consultant.

He was a member of the **American Society for Psychical Research,** the **Society for Psychical Research,** London, the British College for Psychic Science, the Authors Guild, and the Dramatists Guild, and was research director of the New York Committee for the Investigation of Paranormal Occurrences.

Holzer wrote hundreds of newspaper and magazine articles on psychic phenomena, the occult, and related subjects. Through the 1970s he turned out numerous books on ghosts, the occult, and psychical topics that reached a popular audience despite continual complaints by reviewers and some people he wrote about of numerous errors. At his peak he wrote three to four books a year. Several books in the 1970s helped promote the spread of **witchcraft** and neopaganism. In the early 1980s Holzer wrote two books that perpetuated the **Amityville** hoax.

Sources:

Holzer, Hans. *The Directory of the Occult.* Chicago: Henry Regnery, 1974.

———. *The Great British Ghost Hunt.* Boston: G. K. Hall, 1975.

———. *The New Pagans.* Garden City, N.Y.: Doubleday, 1972.

———. *Pagans and Witches.* New York: Manor Books, 1979.

———. *The Prophets Speak.* Indianapolis, Ind.: Bobbs-Merrill, 1971.

———. *The Truth about Witchcraft.* Garden City, N.Y.: Doubleday, 1969.

———. *Wicca: The Way of the Witches.* New York: Manor Books, 1979.

Pleasants, Helene, ed. *Biographical Dictionary of Parapsychology.* New York: Helix Press, 1964.

Home, Daniel Dunglas (1833–1886)

The most notable physical medium in the history of **Spiritualism.** There was a certain mystery about Home's parentage. According to a footnote in his *Incidents in My Life* (1863), his father was a natural son of Alexander, the tenth earl of Home. Through his mother he was descended from a Highland family in which the traditional gift of **second sight** had been preserved. He was born on March 20, 1833, in Scotland.

Home was a sensitive, delicate child of a highly nervous temperament and of such weak health that he was not expected to live. Adopted by Mrs. McNeill Cook, a childless aunt, he passed his infancy at Portobello, Scotland, and was taken to the United States at the age of nine, growing up in Greeneville, Connecticut, and Troy, New York. It was noticed that he had keen powers of observation and a prodigious memory. He saw his first vision at age 13. A schoolfellow, Edwin, died in Greeneville and appeared to him in a bright cloud at night in Troy, thus keeping a childish promise with which they had bound themselves that he who died first would appear to the other. Home's second vision came four years later. It announced the death of his mother to the hour.

From that time on his thoughts turned more and more to the life beyond. One night he heard loud, unaccountable blows, the next morning a volley of **raps.** His aunt, remembering the **Hydesville** rappings that had occurred two years before, believed him to be possessed by the devil and called for a Congregationalist, a Baptist, and a Methodist minister for exorcism. This being unsuccessful, she turned him out of doors. Thenceforth, although he never asked for or received direct payment, Home appears to have lived on the hospitality of friends attracted by his curious gift.

The first scientist to investigate Home's phenomena was George Bush, a distinguished theologian and Oriental scholar from New York. The celebrated American poet William Cullen Bryant and a Professor Wells of Harvard University testified in a written statement to the reality of the phenomena. Professors **Robert Hare** and **James Mapes,** both famous chemists, and **John Worth Edmonds** of the United States Supreme Court owed much of their conversion to Spiritualism to this young man of frail health.

Home's first **levitation** occurred in the South Manchester house of Ward Cheney, an eminent American manufacturer. Strains of music were heard when no instrument was near.

Nobody understood at that time the part the physical organism plays in the production of the phenomena. The demands made on Home were very heavy and the drain of nervous energy excessive. His intended medical studies had to be broken off because of illness; a trip to Europe being advised, Home went to England in April 1855. He first stayed at Cox's Hotel in Jermyn Street, London, and was later the guest of J. S. Rymer, an Ealing solicitor.

The conversion of many of the later leaders of the Spiritualist movement in England was attributed to Home's phenomena. When these phenomena attracted public attention Home found himself in the midst of a press war. Among the first who asked Home to attend a séance was Lord Brougham, who came to the sitting with **Sir David Brewster.** Home was proud of the impression he made upon these two distinguished men and wrote about it to a friend in the United States. The letter was published in the United States and found its way to the London press, whereupon Brewster at once disclaimed all belief in Spiritualism and set down the phenomena to imposture. At the same time his statements in private supported Home, and they too found their way into the newspapers.

More lasting harm was done to Home's reputation by **Robert Browning**'s poem, "Mr. Sludge, the Medium," which was generally taken to refer to Home. Browning and his wife, who accepted Spiritualism, had attended séances with Home. The poem was a malignant attack, since Browning had never claimed in public to have caught Home at trickery and in private admitted that imposture was out of the question. The reason for this vicious attack may have been jealousy over his wife's enthusiasm for Home's phenomena.

Other famous men of the day, such as **Bulwer Lytton** and **William Thackeray,** never spoke of their experiences in public. Thackeray made Home's acquaintance in the United States when he lectured there. Both there and in London Thackeray availed himself of every opportunity of sitting with Home. He admitted to have found a genuine mystery and warmly endorsed Robert Bell's anonymous article "Stranger than Fiction," published in the *Cornhill Magazine,* which Thackeray then edited.

Bell's account of a séance with Home starts with a quotation of a Dr. Treviranus to Coleridge: "I have seen what I would not have believed on your testimony, and what I cannot therefore, expect you to believe upon mine." Thackeray was bitterly attacked for the publication of the article and it was said that the *Cornhill Magazine* dropped considerably in circulation as a consequence.

In the early autumn of 1855 Home went to Florence to visit **Thomas A. Trollope.** His name and fame soon spread there, too. False rumors arose among the peasants that he was a necromancer and administered the sacraments of the Church to toads in order to raise the dead by spells and incantations. This rumor may explain an attempt against his life on December 5, 1855, when a man ambushed him late at night and stabbed him three times with a dagger. Home had a narrow escape. The attacker was never arrested, but Home was warned the following month by Signor Lan Ducci, minister of the interior to the grand duke of Tuscany, of his sinister reputation among the populace.

About this time he was told by the spirits that his power would leave him for a year. In Home's state of seclusion from supernormal contact, Catholic influences found an easy inroad into his religious ideas. He converted to Catholicism and decided to enter a monastery. He was received by Pius IX and treated with favor. Home changed his mind, however, and left Italy for Paris, where, to the day from the announced suspension, his powers returned. The news reached the French court and Napoleon III summoned him to the Tuilleries.

The story of Home's séance with Napoleon was not made public. The curiosity of the press was aroused, however, when the first séance was followed by many others.

An account of the first séance in Home's autobiography, *Incidents in My Life,* tells how Napoleon followed every manifestation with keen and skeptical attention and satisfied himself by the closest scrutiny that neither deception nor delusion was possible. His and the empress's unspoken thoughts were replied to, and the empress was touched by a materialized hand that, from a defect in one of the fingers, she recognized to be the hand of her late father.

The second séance was more forceful. The room was shaken; heavy tables were lifted and then held down to the floor by an alteration of their weight. At the third séance a phantom hand appeared above the table, lifted a pencil, and wrote the single word *Napoleon* in the handwriting of Napoleon I.

Prince Murat later related to Home that the Duke de Morny told Napoleon III that he felt it a duty to contradict the report that the emperor believed in Spiritualism. The emperor replied, "Quite right, but you may add when you speak on the subject again that there is a difference between believing a thing and having proof of it, and that I am certain of what I have seen."

When, soon after these séances, Home left Paris for the United States, rumors were rife that his departure was compulsory. On his return, however, he was speedily summoned to Fontainebleau, where the king of Bavaria was interested in a séance. Home was in great power at the time and so much sought after that the Union Club, where fashionable sophisticates congregated, offered him 50,000 francs for a single séance. Home refused. A book, privately printed in France, recorded the strange experiences of the high society with Home's mediumship.

Earlier, in Italy, Home had been introduced to the king of Naples. The German emperor and the queen of Holland soon joined the ranks of the curious who were besieging Home with requests for séances.

While enjoying the benevolence of crowned heads and the highest members of the aristocracy, Home had to wage a desperate struggle against the scandalmongers. Fantastic stories began to circulate as soon as he left Paris, and while he was regaining his shattered health in Italy it was even rumored that he was in the prison of Mazas.

In Rome during the spring of 1858 Home was introduced to Count Koucheleff-Besborodka and his wife. Soon after he became engaged to Alexandrina de Kroll, the count's sister-in-law. The wedding took place in St. Petersburg. It was a great society affair. Count Alexis Tolstoy, the poet, and Count Bobrinsky, a chamberlain to the emperor, acted as groomsmen. Alexandre Dumas, a guest of Count Koucheleff-Besborodka, was one of the witnesses.

Many of Dumas's fantastic stories about spirits entering into inanimate objects were derived from Home's mediumship. In Russia, as well as in many other countries, rumors circulated regarding Home's mysterious powers. For instance, it was said that a great number of cats slept with him and by this means his body became so charged with electricity that he could produce raps at pleasure! In Paris the favorite story was that he carried a trained monkey in his pocket to twitch dresses and shake hands during the séances. From chloroforming and magnetizing the sitters, to possessing a magic lantern, to hiring secret police to obtain information for the sittings—every sort of wild explanation was attempted. Yet none of them could match the inspired inanity of one woman who was reported to have said, "Lor, sirs, it's easy enough, he only rubs himself all over with a gold pencil first."

From Home's marriage to Alexandrina de Kroll a son was born. Shortly after Home returned to England, friends tried to bring about a meeting between him and **Michael Faraday,** the famous scientist and proponent of the involuntary muscular action theory to explain table movement. As the *Morning Star* reported, Faraday was not satisfied with demanding an open and complete examination, but wished Home to acknowledge that the phenomena, however produced, were ridiculous and contemptible. Thereafter, the idea of giving him a sitting was abandoned.

Home derived more satisfaction from his experiences with Dr. Ashburner, a royal physician, and **John Elliotson,** sometime president of the Royal Medical and Chirurgical Society of London, a character study of whom, as "Dr. Goodenough," was drawn by Thackeray in *Pendennis,* and to whom the work was dedicated. When Ashburner became a believer in Spiritualism, Elliotson, who was one of the hardest materialists, became estranged from him and publicly attacked him for his folly. A few years later, however, Home and Elliotson met in Dieppe. The result was a séance, a strict investigation, and the conversion of Elliotson. On his return to London he hastened to seek reconciliation with Ashburner and publicly declared that he was satisfied of the reality of the phenomena and that they were tending to revolutionize his thoughts and feelings.

Home's phenomena also radically changed **Robert Chambers,** coauthor, with Leitch Ritchie, of the anonymous *Vestiges of the Natural History of Creation* (1844), which startled the public by its outspoken skepticism. Chambers attended the séance Robert Bell wrote about in *Cornhill Magazine.* He was too afraid of losing his reputation to make a public statement, although he allegedly received startling evidence of continued personal identity from his deceased father and daughter. Nevertheless, Chambers anonymously wrote the preface to Home's autobiography in 1862. Eight years later, during the Lyon-Home trial, he abandoned his attitude of reserve and gave an affidavit in Home's favor.

For a time during 1859 to 1860, Home gave frequent joint séances with the American medium **J. R. M. Squire,** an editor of the Boston *Banner of Light.* Squire was introduced to London society under Home's auspices and later in the year he was presented at court.

Home's wife died in July 1862. Six months later his book *Incidents in My Life* was published. It attracted widespread notice in the press. The *Morning Herald* remarked, "We must note also the strangeness of the fact that Mr. Home has never been detected, if indeed he is an imposter." The book sold very well and a second edition was published in a few months. This, however, did not relieve the money problems Home began to experience. Relatives disputed his right of inheritance to the fortune of his wife, and, looking about for a means of livelihood, he decided to develop his keen artistic perception. He hoped to become a sculptor and went to Rome to study.

The papal government, however, had not forgiven the breaking of his promise to enter a monastery. In January 1864 he was summoned before the chief of the Roman police and ordered, on the grounds of "sorcery," to leave Rome within three days. Home claimed the protection of the English consul, and the order of expulsion was suspended on his promise that, during his stay in Rome, he would have no séance and would avoid—as much as possible—all conversations about Spiritualism. Because the manifestations were beyond his control, however, he was soon ordered to quit the papal territory. He left for Naples, where he was received by Prince Humbert, and returned in April to London to demand diplomatic representations on the subject of his expulsion. There was a debate in the House of Commons, but no representation was agreed upon.

Soon after, Home made another trip to the United States, hoping to achieve success as a reader because he had talent as a stage reciter. His public rendering of Henry Howard Brownell's poems was very well received; on returning to Europe he continued this new career with a lecture on Spiritualism in London.

His health, however, could not stand the strain. Friends came to the rescue with the post of residential secretary at the foundation of the **Spiritual Athenaeum,** a kind of headquarters for London Spiritualists.

Then came the disastrous proposition of Jane Lyon, a wealthy widow, that she adopt Home, with the intention of securing his financial stability. Lyon took a fancy to Home and proposed to adopt him if he added her name to his own, in which case she was prepared to give him substantial wealth. Home assented and changed his name to Home-Lyon. Lyon transferred £60,000 to Home's account and drew up a will in his favor. Later she repented her action and sued him for the recovery of her money on the basis that she was influenced by spirit communications coming through Home from her late husband.

While the suit was in progress, an attempt was made against Home's life. He parried the blow of the assassin's stiletto with his hand, which was pierced. The fantastic stories that were circulated around this incident are best illustrated by a reminiscence in the *New York World* on the report of his death, in which the paper stated that Lyon had a false left hand and Home actually made her believe that by mediumistic power he could create life in the artificial limb.

Lord Adare, in his privately published *Experiences in Spiritualism with D.D. Home* (1869), covers most of Home's work for the period 1867 to 1869, including some 80 séances. In 1869 the **London Dialectical Society** appointed a committee for the investigation of Spiritualistic phenomena. The committee, before which Home appeared, had some of the most skeptical members of the society on its list, including atheist spokesman **Charles Bradlaugh.** Four séances were held, but because of Home's illness the manifestations did not extend beyond slight raps and movements of the table. The committee reported that nothing material had occurred, but added that "during the inquiry Mr. Home afforded every facility for examination."

In May 1871 **Sir William Crookes** began an investigation of Home and reached a very favorable opinion of what he saw. Before this investigation other important events took place in Home's life. He won the lawsuit for his deceased wife's fortune, became engaged to an aristocratic lady of wealth, and gave several séances in the Winter Palace in St. Petersburg. During a lecture on Spiritualism he referred to some particulars of a séance held in the presence of a distinguished professor at the University of St. Petersburg. At the end of the lecture a Professor Boutlerof rose from his place and announced that he was the investigator to whom Home had referred. This dramatic scene was followed by an investigation by a committee from the university. The results were negative, since Home's powers were alledgly at an ebb because of recurring illness.

In 1872 Home published the second series of his *Incidents in My Life,* including the principal affidavits in the Lyon lawsuit, and in 1873 he published his *Lights and Shadows of Spiritualism.* His opinions on fraudulent mediumship and his protest against holding séances in the dark were bitterly resented by other mediums. They said that he had little experience of the powers of others.

Kate Fox Jencken, of the **Fox sisters,** was the only medium with whom he was friendly. On a few occasions he sat jointly with **William Stainton Moses.** After the first such sitting, on December 22, 1872, Moses wrote in his notebook:

"Mr. D. D. Home is a striking-looking man. His head is a good one. He shaves his face with the exception of a moustache, and his hair is bushy and curly. He gives me the impression of an honest, good person whose intellect is not of high order. I had some talk with him, and the impression that I have formed of his intellectual ability is not high. He resolutely refuses to believe in anything that he has not seen for himself. For instance, he refuses to believe in the passage of matter through matter, and when pressed concludes the argument by saying 'I have never seen it.' He has seen the ring test, but oddly enough, does not see how it bears on the question. He accepts the theory of the return in rare instances of the departed, but believes with me that most of the manifestations proceed from a low order of spirits who hover near the earth sphere. He does not believe in Mrs. Guppy's passage through matter, nor in her honesty. He thinks that regular manifestations are not possible. Consequently he disbelieves in public mediums generally. He said he was thankful to know that his mantle had fallen on me, and urged me to prosecute the inquiry and defend the faith. He is a thoroughly good, honest, weak and very vain man, with little intellect, and no ability to argue, or defend his faith."

Home slowly broke with nearly all of his friends and spent most of his time on the Continent. In 1876 his death was falsely reported in the French press. He lived in declining health for ten more years and died on June 21, 1886. His grave is at St. Germain, Paris, and his tombstone is inscribed "To another discerning of Spirits." In the Canongate of Edinburgh there is a fountain erected to his memory. It is not known who erected it nor why it was placed opposite the Canongate Parish Church.

Evaluating Home's Work

Home demonstrated every known physical phenomenon of Spiritualism except **apports** and **direct voice.** He even possessed a latent faculty of direct voice. Faint whisperings were sometimes heard in his séances, but only of single words. He was mostly in a normal state during the phenomena but went into trance during the fire test, **elongations,** and occasionally during levitations.

The spirit teachings delivered through Home's mouth by his control were sometimes absurd. The control, criticizing the knowledge of scientists, said that the sun was covered with beautiful vegetation and was full of organic life. When Lord Adare asked, "Is not the sun hot?" the control answered "No, the sun is cold; the heat is produced and transmitted to the earth by the rays of light passing through various atmospheres."

Lord Adare, then earl of Dunraven, describes Home's character in the 1924 edition of *Experiences in Spiritualism with D. D. Home:*

"He had the defects of an emotional character, with vanity highly developed (perhaps wisely to enable him to hold his own against the ridicule and obloquy that was then poured out upon spiritualism and everyone connected with it). He was liable to fits of great depression and to nervous crisis difficult at first to understand; but he was withal of a simple, kindly, humorous, lovable disposition that appealed to me. . . . He never took money for séances, and séances failed as often as not. He was proud of his gift but not happy in it. He could not control it and it placed him sometimes in very unpleasant positions. I think he would have been pleased to have been relieved of it, but I believe he was subject to these manifestations as long as he lived."

Sir William Crookes summed up his opinion as follows:

"During the whole of my knowledge of D. D. Home, extending for several years, I never once saw the slightest occurrence that would make me suspicious that he was attempting to play tricks. He was scrupulously sensitive on this point, and never felt hurt at anyone taking precautions against deception. . . . To those who knew him Home was one of the most lovable of men and his perfect genuineness and uprightness were beyond suspicion. . . ."

Frank Podmore, a most skeptical psychical researcher, said of Home:

"A remarkable testimony to Home's ability whether as medium or simply as conjurer, is the position which he succeeded in maintaining in society at this time [1861] and indeed throughout his later life, and the respectful treatment accorded to him by many leading organs of the Press. No money was ever taken by him as the price of a sitting; and he seemed to have had the entree to some of the most aristocratic circles in Europe. He was welcomed in the houses of our own and of foreign nobility, was a frequent guest at the Tuilleries, and had been received by the King of Prussia and the Czar. So strong, indeed, was his position that he was able to compel an ample apology from a gentleman who had publicly expressed doubts of his mediumistic performance (Capt. Noble in the *Sussex Advertiser* of March 23, 1864) and to publish a violent and spiteful attack upon Browning on the occasion of the publication of Sludge (*Spiritual Magazine,* 1864, p. 315). His expulsion from Rome in 1864 on the charge of sorcery gave to Home for the time an international importance."

Podmore added: "Home was never publicly exposed as an imposter; there is no evidence of any weight that he was even privately detected in trickery."

Between the publication of his *Modern Spiritualism* in 1902 and *The Newer Spiritualism* in 1910, Podmore nevertheless succeeded in unearthing a single piece of so-called evidence of imposture in a letter from a Mr. Merrifield, dated August 1855 and printed in the *Journal* of the Society for Psychical Research (1903), in which the writer claims to have noticed that the medium's body or shoulder sank or rose in concordance with the movements of a spirit hand and to have seen afterward "the whole connection between the medium's shoulder and arm and the spirit hand dressed out on the end of his own." This highly speculative statement was sufficient for Podmore to proceed to talk of Home as a practiced conjurer who dictated his own conditions in the experiments and produced his feats by trickery. The only admission Podmore made was that "we don't quite see how some of the things were done and we leave the subject with an almost painful sense of bewilderment."

Long after Home's death various writers speculated on how Home's feats might have been achieved by trickery, imputing that there must have been trickery. It is generally conceded that Home was never detected in trickery.

Attempts were also made to discredit Home's unfortunate association with Jane Lyon and to suggest that Home tried to take advantage of a wealthy widow. But the evidence suggests that Home was pressured by a foolish and unstable woman. Her claim that Home used undue influence "from the spirit world" is refuted by her transferring allegiance to a Miss Nicholls, another medium, at the time she reneged on her commitment to Home. It was also claimed that Lyon wanted Home to be "something nearer than an adopted son," and her change of heart stemmed from his repulsing her advances.

As far as Browning's spiteful attack in "Mr. Sludge, the Medium" is concerned, the veteran psychical researcher E. J. Dingwall suggests in his book *Some Human Oddities* (1947) that Home might have given the impression of latent homosexual tendencies, which might have incensed Browning.

Home remains an enigma. He was never caught in fraud but accomplished things far beyond that which even contemporary scientific opinion admits are possible. He operated at a time when numerous others where doing similar things and were caught in fraud, often after successfully deceiving many learned and seemingly competent observers. There are two possibilities: he was either a very unusual person, capable of doing the phenomenal things reported of him, or he was one of the most clever frauds in the history of humanity. We may never know which one he was.

Sources:

Adare, Viscount. *Experiences in Spiritualism with D. D. Home.* U.K.: Privately printed, 1869. Reprint, London: Society for Psychical Research, 1924.

Alexander, Patrick P. *Spiritualism: A Narrative with a Discussion.* Edinburgh, Scotland, 1871.

Browning, Elizabeth Barrett. *Letters to her Sister, 1846–1859.* Edited by Laura Huxley. London: John Murray, 1929. Reprint, New York: E. P. Dutton, 1930.

Burton, Jean. *Heyday of a Wizard: Daniel Home the Medium.* London: George G. Harrap, 1948.

Chevalier, J. C. *Experiments in Spiritualism; or, The Adjuration of Spirits, by a late member of Mr. Home's Spiritual Athenaeum.* London, 1867.

Cox, Edward W. *Spiritualism Answered by Science.* London, 1871.

Crookes, William. *Research in the Phenomena of Spiritualism.* London: J. Burns, 1874. Reprint, London and Manchester, 1926.

Dingwall, E. J. *Some Human Oddities.* London: Home and Van Thal, 1947. Reprint, New Hyde Park, N.Y.: University Books, 1962.

Gordon, Mrs. M. M. *The Home Life of Sir David Brewster.* Edinburgh, Scotland, 1869, 1870.

Home, D. D. *Incidents in My Life.* London: Longman, Green, 1863. 2nd series. New York: A. K. Butts, 1874. Reprint, New Hyde Park, N.Y.: University Books, 1972.

Jenkins, Elizabeth. *The Shadow and the Light: A Defence of Daniel Dunglas Home, the Medium.* London: Hamish Hamilton, 1982.

Medhurst, R. G., ed. *Crookes and the Spirit World.* London: Souvenir Press; New York; Taplinger, 1972.

Molloy, J. Fitzgerald. *The Romance of Royalty.* London, 1904.

Pleasants, Helene, ed. *Biographical Dictionary of Parapsychology.* New York: Helix Press, 1964.

Porter, Katherine H. *Through a Glass Darkly: Spiritualism in the Browning Circle.* Lawrence, Kans.: University of Kansas Press, 1958.

Rymer, J. Snaith. "Spirit Manifestations." A lecture presented in London, 1857.

Stein, Gordon. *Encyclopedia of Hoaxes.* Detroit: Gale Research, 1993.

Verax [J. J. Garth Wilkinson]. *Evenings with Mr. Hume and the Spirits.* Keighley, England, 1855.

Wyndham, Horace. *Mr. Sludge: The Medium.* London: G. Bles, 1937.

Homunculus

An artificial man supposedly made by the alchemists, and especially by **Paracelsus.** To manufacture one, Paracelsus stated that the needed spagyric (a term probably coined by Paracelsus implying an alchemical process using semen) substances should be sealed in a glass vial and placed in horse dung to digest for 40 days. At the end of this time something will begin to live and move in the bottle. This is sometimes a man, said Paracelsus, but a man who has no body and is transparent.

Nevertheless, he exists, and nothing remains but to bring him up—which is not more difficult than making him. This may be accomplished by feeding him daily (over a period of 40 weeks, and without extricating him from his dung hill) with the arcanum of human blood. At the end of this time there should be a living child, having every member as well proportioned as any infant born of a woman. He will be much smaller than an ordinary child, though, and his physical education will require more care and attention.

Early in the twentieth century, magician **Aleister Crowley** wrote a novel that deals with the production of a kind of homunculus he terms a *Moonchild,* the name under which the novel was eventually published. Crowley wrote of a magic rite to induce a particular type of spirit to incarnate in an embryo, which a woman would then carry until birth.

During the 1940s, Jack Parsons, head of the **OTO** (Ordo Templi Orientis) lodge in Pasadena, California, carried out this sexual ritual with Marjorie Cameron and a third person who acted as a seer for the process. Crowley, angered by reports of what Parsons had done, ordered an investigation of the lodge, by which time the operation had been completed.

Sources:

King, Francis. *The Rites of Modern Occult Magic.* New York: Macmillan, 1970.

Hone, Margaret (1892–1969)

British astrologer, born October 2, 1892. Hone was associated with the Astrological Lodge of the Theosophical Society (now the **Astrological Lodge of London**) in the 1930s and was associated with **Charles E. O. Carter** for many years. She assisted him in founding the **Faculty of Astrological Studies** (FAS) in 1948 and in 1954 succeeded him as dean, a post she held for the rest of her life. She also wrote *The Modern Textbook of Astrology* (1951), adopted as the basic text by the FAS. It has now become a widely used textbook in astrology throughout the English-speaking world. She followed it with a companion volume, *Applied Astrology,* in 1953.

Sources:

Hone, Margaret. *Applied Astrology.* London: L. N. Fowler, 1953.

———. *The Modern Textbook of Astrology.* Rev. ed., London: L. N. Fowler, 1967.

Honorton, Charles (1946–)

Parapsychologist. Born at Deer River, Minnesota, Honorton studied at the University of Minnesota from 1965 to 1966, during which time he was research coordinator for the Minnesota Society for Psychic Research. In 1966 he became a research fellow at the Institute for Parapsychology, Foundation for Research on the Nature of Man, and the following year was named a senior research associate at the Maimonides Medical Center Dream Laboratory. A short time later he became the director of research and joined with Stanley Krippner and Montague Ullman in receiving the first federal grant for research in parapsychology, from the Public Health Service, National Institute of Mental Health. In 1979 Honorton became director of the Psychophysical Research Laboratories in Princeton, New Jersey.

Honorton has written widely on parapsychological subjects but is best known for his experiments with the **Ganzfeld setting,** a procedure that establishes an environment of reduced sensory alertness. (Strong sensory input is believed to impede **ESP**.) Honorton has argued that the Ganzfeld procedure is the most effective way to produce the kind of repeated ESP results parapsychology seeks. The **Parapsychology Association** awarded Honorton its Exceptional Contribution Award in 1988.

Honorton has been a longtime member of the Parapsychological Association. He served on its council and has held the offices of secretary, vice president, and president (1975). He is also a member of the Board of Trustees of the **American Society for Psychical Research.**

Sources:

Honorton, Charles. "Has Science Developed the Competence to Confront Claims of the Paranormal?" In *Research in Parapsychology 1975,* edited by J. D. Morris, W. G. Roll, and R. L. Morris. New York: Parapsychological Association, 1976.

———. "Meta-Analysis of Psi Ganzfield Research: A Response to Hyman. *Journal of Parapsychology* 49 (1981).

———. "Psi-Mediated Imagery and Ideation in an Experimental Procedure for Regulating Perceptual Input." *Journal* of the American Society for Psychical Research 68 (1974).

———. "Separation of High- and Low-Scoring ESP Subjects Through Hypnotic Preparation." *Journal of Parapsychology* 28 (1964).

———. "Significant Factors in Hypnotically-Induced Clairvoyant Dreams." *Journal* of the American Society for Psychical Research 66 (1972).

———. "State of Awareness Factors in Psi Activation." *Journal* of the American Society for Psychical Research 68 (1974).

Hoodoo Sea

One of many terms for an area of the western Atlantic between Bermuda and Florida where ships and planes are said to have vanished without a trace. (See **Bermuda Triangle**)

Hooper, T. d'Aute (ca. 1910)

Extraordinary British medium of the early twentieth century. Although a busy physician in Birmingham, England, Hooper was also credited with a wide range of psychic phenomena, physical and mental.

Hooper's Indian **control,** "Segaske" (Rising Sun), produced scents and **apports.** An Indian **fakir** demonstrated the fire test, made articles appear and vanish in daylight, and spoke in Hindustani. A deceased Chicago preacher, calling himself "Ajax," and many other frequent spirit visitors produced **direct voice** manifestations and **psychic photography.**

In the anonymously published *Spirit Psychometry and Trance Communications by Unseen Agencies through a Welsh Woman and Dr. T. d'Aute Hooper* (1914) the medium recorded important investigations in **psychometry.**

Sources:

Henslow, George. *The Proofs of the Truths of Spiritualism.* London: K. Paul, Trench, Trubner; New York: E. P. Dutton, 1919.

Hope, William (1863–1933)

A carpenter of Crewe, England, and famous spirit photographer, whose abilities were discovered accidentally about 1905. Hope and a friend photographed each other on a Saturday afternoon. The plate that Hope exposed showed an extra figure, a transparent woman, behind whom a brick wall was visible. It was the sister of Hope's comrade, dead for many years. With the help of a Mr. Buxton, the organist at the Spiritualist Hall at Crewe, a circle of six friends was formed to sit for **spirit photography.**

Fearful of being accused by devout Catholics of being in league with the devil, the circle destroyed all the original negatives until Archdeacon **Thomas Colley** came on the scene. He tested Hope's powers, endorsed them, and gave him his first stand camera, which Hope refused to give up long after it had become old-fashioned, its box battered and its leg broken.

The first controversy about Hope and his psychic photographs arose in 1908 in connection with Colley's first sitting. He recognized his mother in the psychic "extra." Hope thought it was more like a picture he had copied two years earlier. A Mrs. Spencer, of Nantwich, recognized her grandmother in the image. Hope informed Colley of his mistake. Colley said it was madness to think that a man did not know his own mother and advertised in the Leamington paper asking all who remembered his mother to meet him at the rectory. Eighteen persons selected the photograph from a group of several others and testified in writing that the picture was a portrait of the late Mrs. Colley, who had never been photographed.

The second case of public controversy arose in 1922 and was, on the surface, damning for Hope. In a report published in the *Journal* of the Society for Psychical Research (vol. 20, pp. 271–283), Hope was accused of imposture by **Harry Price.** The accusations were later published in a sixpenny pamphlet. The basis of the revelation was that Price, in a sitting at the **British College of Psychic Science,** caught Hope in the act of replacing the dark slide holding the exposed plates with another. Price also said that Hope handed him two negatives (one of which contained a psychic extra) that did not bear the secret mark of the Imperial Dry Plate Company (impressed on the packet of film by X-rays) and that were different in color and thickness from the original plates.

Subsequent investigation proved that the counteraccusation by Spiritualists claiming an organized conspiracy against Hope deserved examination. The wrapper of the packet was found, and it bore marks of tampering. Moreover, one of the original marked plates was returned anonymously and undeveloped to the **Society for Psychical Research** (SPR) a week after the experiment and three weeks before the revelation. On being developed, it showed an image. Since the packet of marked plates had been lying about for four weeks in the office of SPR it was open to tampering and substitution. It was also likely, in the view of the Hope apologists, that the missing plate was sent back out of pure mischief.

Immediately after the accusation of **fraud** Hope offered new sittings and declared his willingness to submit to stringent tests. The offer was refused. Harry Price, however, signed a statement to the effect that the test of February 24, 1922, "does not rule out the possibility that Hope has other than normal means."

Many prominent people supported Hope. For example, **Sir William Crookes** gave an authorized interview published in the *Christian Commonwealth* on December 4, 1918. On his own marked plates, under his own conditions, Crookes obtained a likeness of his wife different from any he possessed. **Sir William Barrett** claims to have received with Hope "indubitable evidence of supernormal photography" in the *Proceedings* of the Society for Psychical Research (vol. 34, 1924). After the exposure by Harry Price, Allerton F. Cushman of Washington also claimed to have obtained psychic extras on his own plates, similarly marked by the Imperial Dry Plate Company, and also on plates purchased before the sitting by **Hereward Carrington.**

Sir Oliver Lodge, however, was emphatic concerning a test of his own with a sealed packet sent to Hope: "I have not the slightest doubt that the envelope including the plates had been opened." The most signifcant charges of fraud were advanced by Fred Barlow and Major W. Rampling Rose in an article in the *Proceedings* of the Society for Psychical Research (vol. 41, 1933). Previously, on January 21, 1921, in *Budget No. 58* of the **Society for the Study of Supernormal Pictures,** Barlow had asserted that he "got results with Mr. Hope here in my own home under conditions where fraud was absolutely impossible. I have loaded my dark slides in Birmingham and taken them to Crewe with my own camera and apparatus, have carried out the whole of the operation myself (even to the taking of the photograph) and have secured supernormal results."

Then, in 1923, Barlow had associated with **Sir Arthur Conan Doyle** in the publication of *The Case for Spirit Photography* (1923), a book written in answer to the Hope exposure. At that time, he says, he could not "get away from the fact that many of these photographic effects are produced by discarnate intelligences."

But in 1933 Barlow asserted that "a further ten years of careful continuous experimenting has enabled me to say quite definitely that I was mistaken. During the whole of this period no single instance has occurred, in my experience, that would in any way suggest that Hope has genuine gifts" (*Light,* April 14, 1933).

Hope never commercialized his gift. He charged about 50 cents for a dozen prints. This was calculated on the basis of his hourly earnings as a carpenter. He was very devout—almost fanatical—and relied blindly on the advice of his spirit guides. "During all his career as a medium," writes **David Gow** in *Light,* March 17, 1933, "he had become so accustomed to accusation and abuse that he had grown case-hardened. His attitude seemed to be that, knowing himself to be honest, it did not matter how many people thought otherwise. I found, too, that in his almost cynical indifference, he was given to playing tricks on skeptical inquirers by pretending to cheat and then boasting that he had scored over his enemies in that way. . . . Mr. Hope, in my view, was a genuine medium, but of a type of mentality which might easily lead to the opposite conclusion on the part of an unsympathetic observer."

During his lifetime Hope obtained more than 2,500 claimed spirit photographs. He died March 7, 1933.

Hope Diamond

Famous precious stone with a reputation of bringing disaster to its owners. The Hope diamond is one of the largest colored diamonds known, a vivid blue and weighing 44.4 carats. It is believed to have been cut from an even larger stone of more than 67 carats. The name is derived from Henry Thomas Hope, a former owner who bought it for £18,000.

Fact and legend are inextricably tangled in the story of this unlucky diamond. The known history begins in the seventeenth century with the explorer Jean Baptiste Tavernier (1605–1689), who is reputed to have acquired the stone from the Indian mines of Killur, Golconda, around 1642. He sold the stone to Louis XIV in 1668 and subsequently lost all his money through his son's speculations.

The diamond was worn by Madame de Montespan at a court ball, and she fell from favor soon afterward. From this time on, the diamond had a sinister reputation. It was worn by Marie Antoinette, who had misfortune in connection with diamonds when the celebrated Affair of the Diamond Necklace preceded the French Revolution.

Princess de Lamballe, who was lent the diamond, was executed on the guillotine and her head was paraded on a pike under the windows of the prison in which Louis XVI and his family were imprisoned.

The diamond disappeared for 30 years, reappearing in the possession of a Dutch lapidary named Fals. As in the case of Tavernier, a son brought Fals misfortune. He stole the diamond and left his father to die in poverty. The son entrusted the diamond to a Frenchman named Beaulieu, who committed suicide after selling it to London dealer Daniel Eliason, who died under mysterious circumstances. It was then that the diamond was acquired by Henry Thomas Hope, and it remained in the Hope family for 70 years.

Lord Francis Hope, last of the line, married an actress but divorced her and lost all his money. The diamond disappeared for a time, but was later acquired by an American who went bankrupt, a Russian who was stabbed, and a French dealer who committed suicide. A Greek merchant sold it to Abdul Hamid II, sultan of Turkey, who lost his throne. In 1908 the diamond was bought by Habib Bey for £80,000 but was auctioned the following year at a fifth of the price.

The diamond got to the United States through a New York jeweler who was said to have arranged a sale to a man who was a passenger on the ill-fated **Titanic.**

The next owner was a millionaire named McLean. His wife, Evalyn, published a book, *Father Struck It Rich* (1938), in which she describes the misfortunes that befell the family in spite of having the diamond blessed by a priest.

The diamond was finally bought by Harry Winston, a jeweler in New York. He displayed it for several years and donated it in November 1958 to the Smithsonian Institution, Washington, D.C. Interestingly enough, Winston sent it through the U.S. mail system and it arrived without incident at the Smithsonian.

Sources:

Cohen, Daniel. *Encyclopedia of the Strange.* New York: Dodd, Mead, 1985.

Hopedale Community

A Spiritualist community founded by Rev. **Adin Ballou** (1828–1886) in 1841 near Milford, Massachusetts. From 1850 on, this religious and socialistic community was the scene of various spirit manifestations and helped spread **Spiritualism** in the United States. Ballou proclaimed his new faith in *Modern Spirit Manifestations,* published in 1852, the year in which he first received communications from his deceased son.

Hopedale was a remarkable experiment in social engineering, a community with admirable ideals of religious, moral, and social cooperation: total abstinence, opposition to slavery, war, and violence; it was dedicated to liberty, equality, and fraternity. It flourished until 1857 but eventually failed through its structure as a joint stock company.

Ballou's presidency was superseded by that of E. D. Draper, an enterprising businessman who, with his brother, made successful investments outside the community. As the community capital dwindled, Draper bought up three quarters of the joint stock, obtaining legal control. He expressed dissatisfaction with the management of the community, and some time around 1858 informed Ballou that the community must come to an end. With the stipulation that Draper would pay off its debts, the Hopedale experiment was terminated.

Sources:

Holloway, Mark. *Heavens on Earth: Utopian Communities in America, 1680–1880.* London: Turnstile Press, 1951.

Noyes, John Humphrey. *History of American Socialisms.* Philadelphia: J. B. Lippincott, 1870. Reprinted as *Strange Cults and Utopias of 19th-century America.* New York: Dover Publications, 1966.

Perry, Lewis. "Adin Ballou's Hopedale Community and the Theology of Anti-slavery." *Church History* 39 (September 1970): 372–389.

Hopkins, Budd (1931–)

Budd Hopkins, the major exponent of the importance of the abduction phenomenon within ufology, was born June 15, 1931, in Wheeling, West Virginia. He graduated from Oberlin College in 1953 and moved to New York City, where he began a successful career as an artist. His paintings now hang in many outstanding museums, and he has been a frequent contributor to art magazines and a lecturer at colleges on art.

Hopkins became interested in **UFOs** in 1964 when he and two other people observed for several minutes a disc flying in broad daylight. He joined the National Investigations Committee on Aerial Phenomenona and began reading in ufology. He published an initial article in 1975 in the *Village Voice* on the case of a UFO landing in New Jersey. This led to his receiving additional reports, and he began studying incidents of claimed UFO contact with other UFO investigators and several psychologists. His first book, *Missing Time: A Documented Study of UFO Abductions,* published in 1981, placed the issue of abductions before the ufological community. He had become convinced by the sheer number of people who reported such abductions; he found it entirely credible that their stories of being abducted by visitants from outer space were accounts of actual events.

As described by Hopkins, many people, now in their middle years, have experienced one or more abductions earlier in their lives, the first occurrence often happening in childhood. These early abductions have been forgotten and are recovered only through hypnosis or dream recall techniques over a period of time. These abductions occurred for the purpose of medical experimentation and study. The victim of an abduction frequently reports a "cell sampling," in which tissue is removed and he or she is left with an identifying scar. The aim of the abductions might be to produce a hybrid alien-human race, considering that human female abductees supposedly have become pregnant as a result of their encounters.

Hopkins's first book not only sparked popular interest in the field but led to further research by ufologists that tended to confirm Hopkins's data, the most important being that of T. Eddie Bullard, a folklorist who conducted a comparative study of abduction stories and confirmed their high level of similarity in spite of the abductees' lack of contact with each other. By the time Hopkins published his second book, *Intruders: The Incredible Visitations at Copley Woods* (1987), abductions had become the central focus of ufology. He has found strong support from such leading UFO figures as David M. Jacobs, and his work has prompted studies by psychiatrists such as such as Rima E. Laibow (who founded an organization, Treatment and Research on Experienced Anomalous Trauma, to study abductions). Popular attention to Hopkins's work was provided by author **Whitley Streiber,** whose 1987 account of his own abduction, *Communion,* became a best seller and was made into a movie.

Hopkins has not, of course, been without his critics. Included are milder critics such as ufologist Michael D. Swords, who argued that UFO abduction accounts are shield fantasies, which hide traumatic experiences from the abductee's earlier life that are too painful to discuss directly. Arguments over the abduction phenomena continue to dominate ufology as of the mid-1990s. Meanwhile Hopkins has produced a third book.

Sources:

Hopkins, Budd. *Intruders: The Incredible Visitations at Copley Woods.* New York: Random House, 1987.

———. *Missing Time: A Documented Study of UFO Abductions.* New York: Richard Marek, 1981.

Hopkins, Emma Curtis (1849–1925)

Emma Curtis Hopkins, founder of the popular metaphysical movement known as **New Thought,** was born September 2, 1849, in Killingly, Connecticut, of an old New England family. She received a good education and became a schoolteacher. Attracted by reading *Science and Health with Key to the Scriptures,* the Christian Science textbook, she traveled to Boston in 1883 to attend a class under **Mary Baker Eddy.** She established herself as a practitioner and the following year was made editor of the *Christian Science Journal.* However, by fall 1885, Hopkins and Eddy were in conflict over several of Hopkins's ideas, including her opinion that Christian Science was not so much a new revelation as it was a new expression of a perennial philosophy that had been stated many times previously.

Late in 1885 Hopkins moved to Chicago and established an independent Christian Science practitioner's office. The next year, in spite of her never having taken the advanced course under Eddy, Hopkins began to teach classes, and her students began establishing offices as practitioners. Hopkins also began to hold Sunday services at what became known as the Hopkins Metaphysical Institute. Her students were organized into an association similar to that joined by Eddy's students. Students were attracted to her from around the country, and Hopkins traveled to San Francisco and New York in 1887 to teach. By the end of 1887, branches of her institute could be found across the United States from Maine to California. As the work matured, the institute in Chicago was reorganized as the Christian Science Theological Seminary.

Hopkins began her work as an independent Christian Science practitioner and teacher. Her several original deviations from Eddy's thought led to the development of her own system, which centered upon mysticism and dropped many particularly Christian elements. She was intensely antiorganization, a stance held by many who had come out of the very hierarchically organized **Church of Christ, Scientist.** Over the years she attracted a number of outstanding students, whom she encouraged to establish independent movements. As independent Christian Science matured into New Thought, these movements founded by her students became the leading organizations of New Thought. Among her students were Malinda Cramer (founder of Divine Science); **Charles and Myrtle Fillmore** (founders of the Unity School of Christianity); Annie Rix Militz (founder of the Homes of Truth); and **Ernest Holmes** (founder of Religious Science).

After a decade in Chicago as an elder of a school and church, Hopkins turned the work over to her students and in 1894 retired to New York City and lived quietly as a private tutor to those who wished to study with her one-on-one. During this period of her life she wrote her mature work, *High Mysticism,* which she circulated informally to her students then published as a series of booklets and as a book.

Because of her withdrawal from the public spotlight and the desire of several of the founders of the International New Thought Alliance to project the image that New Thought was not the offshoot of Christian Science, Hopkins's role was largely pushed aside. **Phineas Parkhurst Quimby,** who had taught Mary Baker Eddy for a period, was assigned the role of founder of New Thought, in spite of his lack of association with the movement. Only in the 1980s was Hopkins's role rediscovered and her place in New Thought history recovered.

Hopkins died April 8, 1925, at her home in Connecticut. Her work was continued by her sister Estelle Carpenter under the name High Watch Fellowship. Hopkins's writings are now again in print.

Sources:

Harley, Gail. "Emma Curtis Hopkins: 'Forgotten Founder' of New Thought." Ph.D. diss., Florida State University, 1991.

Hopkins, Emma Curtis. *Class Lessons, 1888.* Marina del Rey, Calif.: DeVorss, 1977.

———. *High Mysticism.* Cornwall Bridge, Conn.: High Watch Fellowship, n.d.

———. *Scientific Christian Mental Practice.* Cornwall Bridge, Conn.: High Watch Fellowship, 1958.

Hopkins, Matthew (d. 1647)

The infamous English "witchfinder" who, with his equally evil accomplices, persecuted, imprisoned, tortured, or killed hundreds of unfortunate individuals he believed to be involved in the horrors of **witchcraft.** Given the amount of damage he accomplished, it is difficult to realize he operated for only 14 months. The English philosopher and writer William Godwin commented:

"Nothing can place the credulity of the English nation on the subject of witchcraft in a more striking point of view, than the history of Matthew Hopkins, who, in a pamphlet published in 1647 in his own vindication, assumes to himself the surname of the Witchfinder. He fell by accident, in his native county of Suffolk, into contact with one or two reputed witches, and, being a man of an observing turn and an ingenious invention, struck out for himself a trade, which brought him such moderate returns as sufficed to maintain him, and at the same time gratified his ambition by making him a terror to many, and the object of admiration and gratitude to more, who felt themselves indebted to him for ridding them of secret and intestine enemies, against whom, as long as they proceeded in ways that left no footsteps behind, they felt they had no possibility of guarding themselves."

Hopkins began to operate as a witchfinder in March 1645. He had as a text King James I's book *Demonology.* After two or three successful experiments, Hopkins engaged in a regular tour of the counties of Norfolk, Suffolk, Essex, and Huntingdonshire. One of his confederates was a man named John Stern. They visited every town in their route that invited them and were paid 20 shillings and their expenses, as well as whatever they received from the spontaneous gratitude of those who deemed themselves indebted to Hopkins and his gang.

By this expedient they won a favorable reception and a set of credulous persons who would listen to their dictates as if they were oracles. They were able to play the game into one another's hands and were sufficiently strong to overcome all timid and irresolute opposition. In every town they visited they inquired for reputed witches. Having taken them into custody the witchfinders could be sure of a certain number of zealous abettors and obtained a clear stage for their experiments.

They subdued their victims with a certain air of authority, as if they had received a commission from heaven for the discovery of misdeeds. They assailed them with a multitude of artfully constructed questions. They stripped them naked in search of the "devil's marks" on different parts of their bodies, which they ascertained by running pins into those parts, saying that if they were genuine marks the "witches" would feel no pain.

They threw their victims into rivers and ponds, declaring that, if the persons accused were true witches, the water (which was the symbol of admission into the Christian Church) would not receive them.

If the persons examined remained obstinate, Hopkins and his men seated them in constrained and uncomfortable positions, occasionally binding them with cords, and compelled them to remain so without food or sleep for 24 hours. They walked the person up and down a room, one taking him or her under each arm, till the accused dropped down with fatigue. They carefully swept the room in which the experiment was made so that they might keep away spiders and flies, which were supposed to be devils or their imps in disguise.

The inquisition of Hopkins and his confederates culminated in 1646. So many persons had been committed to prison on suspicion of witchcraft that the government was compelled to take the affair in hand. The rural magistrates before whom Hopkins and his confederates brought their victims were obliged, willingly or unwillingly, to commit those accused for trial.

A commission was granted to the earl of Warwick and others to hold a session of jail delivery against them. Lord Warwick was, at the time, the most popular nobleman in England. Dr. Calamy, the most eminent divine of the period of the Commonwealth, was sent with him to see (according to Richard Baxter) that no fraud was committed or wrong done to the parties accused.

Warwick sat on the bench with the judges and participated in their deliberations. As a result of this inquisition, 16 persons were hanged at Yarmouth in Norfolk, 15 at Chelmsford, and 60 at various places in the county of Suffolk. Bulstrode Whitelocke in his *Memorials of English Affairs* (1649) writes of many witches being apprehended around Newcastle on information from a person he calls "the Witch-finder"—very likely Hopkins. In 1652 and 1653 the same author spoke of women in Scotland who were put to incredible torture to extort from them confessions of witchcraft.

The fate of Hopkins was such as might be expected. The multitude were at first horrified at the monstrous charges that were advanced against him. But, after a time, they began to reflect and saw that they had acted with too much haste. The man who they at first hailed as a public benefactor they came to regard as a cunning impostor, dealing in cold blood for personal gain and the lure of short-lived fame. The multitude rose up against Hopkins and resolved to subject him to one of his own tests. They dragged him to a pond and threw him into the water as a witch. It seems he floated on the surface, as a witch ought to do. They then pursued him and drove him into obscurity and disgrace. Whether this story is true or not, Hopkins retired to Manningtree, Essex, in 1646 and died of tuberculosis within a year.

Sources:

Kittredge, George Lyman. *Witchcraft in Old and New England.* New York: Atheneum, 1972.

Robbins, Russell Hope. *The Encyclopedia of Witchcraft and Demonology.* New York: Crown Publishers, 1959.

Horbehutet

The ancient Egyptian winged disk, symbol of a solar deity who accompanied the sun god Ra on his daily journey across Egypt to protect him from evil. His symbol was placed over the gates and doors of temples to protect them from malign influences.

Hörbiger, Hans (1860–1931)

German engineer who developed an eccentric cosmology of "cosmic ice." According to Hörbiger, space is filled with cosmic ice, a basic material from which stellar systems are generated when a large block of cosmic ice collides with a hot star. Stellar systems are governed by a law of spiral motion and propelled toward a central sun and smaller planets, eventually being captured by larger ones and becoming moons, Hörbiger said. Earth is supposed to have had several previous moons that were drawn to it, according to his theory. These earlier moons caused geological upheavals when they spiraled to Earth, and myths and legends are said to preserve race memories of such cataclysms. When a former moon circled the earth with ever-increasing rapidity during such a capture, its appearance generated legends of the Judeo-Christian devil, as well as of dragons and other monsters.

Hörbiger's complex theories included occult concepts of a "platonic world soul." With Phillipp Fauth, he published *Glazialcosmogonie* in 1912. In the 1920s, a Hörbiger cult called WEL (Welt Eis Lehre) sprang up, attracting millions of supporters. Hörbiger was intolerant of all opposition to his theories and once wrote to rocket expert Willy Ley: ". . . either you believe in me and learn, or you must be treated as an enemy." After the death of Hörbiger, Hans Schindler Bellamy, a British mythologist, continued the propaganda for WEL in his book *Moons, Myths and Man* (1936) and in further books on the subject.

Hörbiger's ideas provoked enraged opposition from German astronomers, but during the 1930s Nazi sympathizers associated it with ideas of the lost **Atlantis** and a master Aryan race. Adopted by Nazi occultists, Hörbiger's ideas eventually attained the sponsorship of none other than Heinrich Himmler. During the height of the Nazi rule in Europe, the teachings of Hörbiger and Bellamy were combined with paranoid propaganda and anti-Semitism.

Sources:

Gardner, Martin. *Fads and Fallacies in the Name of Science.* New York: Dover Publications, 1957.

Horos, Theodore (ca. 1866– ?) and Laura (1849–ca. 1906)

A notorious man-and-wife team of occult swindlers who were sentenced for fraud in Britain on December 20, 1901. Mrs. Horos—also known as "Ellora," "Madame Helana," "Swami Viva Ananda," "Mrs. Diss Debar," "Angel Anna," "Claudia D'Arvie," "Editha Gilbert Montez," and "Blanche Solomons"—appeared to have been born in Harrodsburg, Kentucky, on February 9, 1849, daughter of "Professor John C. F. R. Salomon."

In 1870, under the name Editha Gilbert Montez, she collected money by representing herself as the daughter of famous adventuress Lola Montez. In the 1880s she became a fraudulent Spiritualist medium in partnership with "General" Joseph H. Diss Debar. In 1888 she was sentenced to six months' imprisonment for fraud.

In 1898 she married Frank Dutton Jackson in New Orleans. The couple engaged in a fake mediumship partnership in Bucktown, Jefferson Parish, and, after complaints, were arrested and served a short prison sentence. At that time there were rumors of unsavory sexual practices in their "Orders of the Crystal Star."

The Jacksons reappeared in Europe in 1899 as "Mr. and Mrs. Horos," and in Paris became acquainted with **S. L. MacGregor Mathers,** from whom they stole some of the rituals of the Hermetic Order of the **Golden Dawn.** At that time they variously represented themselves as being principals of the Koreshan Unity, a communal group located in Estero, Florida, or of the Theocratic Unity.

They moved to South Africa in 1890 and opened the College of Occult Science in Cape Town. Mrs. Horos lectured and gave clairvoyant readings under the names Madame Helena and Swami Viva Ananda, assisted by her husband, who called himself Theodore Horos. The swami issued to students certificates of occult proficiency, modeled on the stolen teachings of the Golden Dawn.

In October 1900 the pair set up headquarters in Britain. Their College of Life and Occult Sciences was established in London, teaching mental and magnetic therapeutics, psychology, clairvoyance, mediumship, materialization, thaumaturgic power, and divine healing. Under this cover they operated an esoteric order using the Golden Dawn rituals, with secret mysteries of their own in which gullible young women were raped as well as swindled. Their odd career seems to have come to an end in September 1901 when the couple was arrested for fraud. Jackson was sentenced to fifteen years' imprisonment and his wife to seven.

Sources:

Dingwall, Eric J. *Some Human Oddities.* London, 1947. Reprint, New Hyde Park, N.Y.: University Books, 1962.

King, Francis. *The Rites of Modern Occult Magic.* New York: Macmillan, 1970.

Horoscope (Magazine)

Monthly magazine for popular readership, published since 1935. It includes articles, self-guidance charts, and a daily guide for horoscope signs. Address: Dell Publishing Co. Inc., 1540 Broadway, New York, NY 10036-4094.

Horoscope Guide

Monthly popular magazine featuring a year's forecast for each sign of the month. Address: J. B. H. Publishing Co., 201 E. 57th St., New York, NY 10022.

Horoscope Yearbook

Popular publication presenting world predictions, astrotrends, forecasts, solar-lunar calendar, and planetary configurations. Address: Dell Publishing Co., 245 East 47th St., New York, NY 10017.

Horseshoes

In the Middle Ages horseshoes were nailed on the thresholds of homes to keep out witches. The significance of the horseshoe, however, is probably of more ancient origin, possibly being related to the two-horn shape that was believed to repel the **evil eye** in more ancient civilizations. This shape may have derived from a belief in animal horns as a symbol of good fortune. Iron as a metal is also traditionally believed to repel witches, fairies, and evil spirits, and the horseshoe combined both the shape and the metal that would ensure good fortune and avert evil.

For protection the horseshoe charm was placed outside buildings with the prongs pointing upward, so that the luck would not "run out," but in many buildings the horseshoe was used indoors with the prongs pointing down, so that good luck would be diffused inside the house.

Gypsies, who have a special relationship to horses, saw the horseshoe as a charm against the demons of unhappiness, bad luck, bad health, and death.

Sources:

Trigg, E. B. *Gypsy Demons and Divinities: The Magical and Supernatural Practices of the Gypsies.* London: Sheldon Press, 1973.

Horseman's Word

A persistent theme in British folklore is the magic word or phrase that can tame an unruly horse. Gypsies were reputed to have this secret, and it was also known to members of a mysterious group of individuals known as the Brotherhood of the Horseman's Word. In other parts of Britain, horse handlers with the secret were said to practice **horse-whispering.** It has been suggested that the secret was in substances with an attractive smell for the horse, and that the whispering was simply a blowing in the ear of the animal.

Horse-Whispering

A secret method by which certain persons are supposed to be able to acquire power over hard-to-manage horses. As is well known to students of Gypsy lore, Gypsies are reputed to be in possession of some secret by which they can render vicious horses entirely tame.

Opinions are divided as to whether this secret consists of the application of a certain odor or balm to the horse's muzzle, or whispering into its ear a spell or incantation. It has been claimed that the Gypsy horse-charmer applies anise seed to the nose of the animal.

Horse-whispering has also been in vogue among many other peoples. The antiquary William Camden, in his recital of Irish superstitions, states, "It is by no means allowable to praise a horse or any other animal unless you say 'God save him.' If any mischance befalls a horse in three days after, they find out the person who commended him, that he may whisper the Lord's Prayer in his right ear."

It was said by Con Sullivan, a famous Irish horse-whisperer of the eighteenth century, that practitioners of the art could not explain their power. This was affirmed by those who practiced it in South America, where a couple of men could tame half a dozen wild horses in three days. The same art was widely practiced in Hungary and Bohemia, and it was from a Bohemian Gypsy that a family in the county of Cork claimed to hold a secret by which the wildest or most vicious horse could be tamed. For generations this secret was regularly transmitted as a parting legacy at the time of death from the father to the eldest son.

Throughout the north of Scotland there are members of a secret society for breaking in difficult horses, which is believed to be called the Horseman's Society and which purports to trace its origin to the Dark Ages. Only those who gain their livelihood by the care and management of horses are admitted, and the more affluent and better educated are jealously excluded. Many farmers entertain a prejudice against the members of the society, but they are forced to admit that they are always very capable in managing their teams and can perform services that would otherwise require calling in a veterinary surgeon. They are usually skilled in the knowledge of herbs and medicinal plants, and a great deal of folklore surrounds them. It is stated that they hold their meetings at night in the clear moonlight, going through various equestrian performances with horses borrowed for the occasion from their masters' stables.

There is also said to be an inner circle in the society in which the black art and all the spells and charms of **witchcraft** are studied. Members of the inner circle are said to be able to smite horses and cattle with mysterious sickness, and even cast spells over human beings. One local writer stated that the inner circle of the horsemen employ hypnotic influence both on men and animals, as it is said certain North American Indians and some of the jungle tribes of Hindustan do.

On one occasion the services of the famous Con Sullivan were requisitioned by Colonel Westenra (afterward earl of Rosmore), who possessed a racehorse called Rainbow. The horse was savage and would attack any jockey courageous enough to mount him by seizing him by the leg with his teeth and dragging him from the saddle. A friend of the colonel's told him that he knew a person who could cure Rainbow, and a wager of £1,000 was laid on the matter. Sullivan, who was known throughout the countryside as "the Whisperer," was sent for. After being shut up alone with the animal for a quarter of an hour, he gave the signal to admit those who had been waiting on the result. When they entered, they found the horse extended on his back, playing like a kitten with Sullivan, who was quietly sitting by him, but both horse and operator appeared exhausted, and the latter had to be revived with brandy. The horse was perfectly tame and gentle from that day on.

Another savage steed, named King Pippin, took an entire night to cure, but in the morning he was seen following Sullivan like a dog, lying down at the word of command, and permitting any person to put his hand into his mouth. Shortly afterward he won a race at the Curragh.

Sullivan's statement that the successful whisperer is not acquainted with the secret of his own power may well be true. As Elihu Rich (in E. Smedley's *The Occult Sciences,* 1855) states:

"The reason is obvious. A force proceeding immediately from the will or the instinctive life would be impaired by reflection in the understanding and broken up or at least diminished by one half. The violent trembling of the animal under this operation is like the creaking and shivering of the tables before they begin to 'tip,' and indicates a moral or nervous force acting physically, by projection perhaps from the spirit of the operator. None of these cases are, after all, more wonderful than the movement of our own limbs and bodies by mental force, for how does it move them with such ease? And may not the same power that places its strong but invisible little fingers on every point of our muscular frames, stretch its myriad arms a little further into the sphere around us, and operate by the same laws, and with as much ease, on the stalwart frame of a horse?"

Sources:

Trigg, E. B. *Gypsy Demons and Divinities: The Magical and Supernatural Practices of the Gypsies.* London: Sheldon Press, 1973.

Hot Cross Buns

A surviving British Easter custom is the eating of "hot cross buns"—spiced currant cakes with a cross marked on the top. In former times, the bun vendors were a familiar feature of street life on Good Friday, with their cry of "Hot cross buns, one a penny, two a penny, hot cross buns!" In modern times, the buns are sold from bakeries well before the Easter holiday.

Although the cross symbolized the Crucifixion, it had a more ancient origin. The cross was also a pagan symbol, and it was used by the Anglo-Saxons to indicate the four seasons on loaves baked for the vernal equinox and to discourage evil spirits that might prevent bread from rising.

As a Christian symbol, the buns derive from the ecclesiastical consecrated loaves given in churches as alms and to those who could not take communion. They were given by the priest to the people after the Mass, before the congregation was dismissed. They were to be kissed before being eaten.

In the 1660s, the spiced loaves were prohibited as "popish," but allowed on Good Friday for the Easter celebrations. Spiced buns replaced the loaves after the Restoration.

Houdini, Harry (1874–1926)

Escape artist and investigator of claims of Spiritualist mediums. Houdini was born Ehrich Weiss on March 24, 1874, in Budapest, Hungary, and taken to Appleton, Wisconsin, as a child, although he later claimed to have been born on April 6, 1874 (eastern Europe still being on the Julian calendar at that time). Weiss began his professional life as a trapeze performer. He went on to become the foremost conjuring magician and escape artist of his day.

Weiss derived the name Houdini from Jean Eugene Robert Houdin (1805–1871), a famous French illusionist who took pride in exposing fake performers of religious marvels. Houdini was similarly very proud of his amazing feats and spent many years exposing so-called Spiritualist frauds. The story of his many adventures are recounted in his 1924 book *A Magician Among the Spirits.* That same year he served as a member of the committee appointed by *Scientific American* to investigate the mediumship phenomena of "Margery" (i.e., **Mina Crandon**). He was later accused of allowing his eagerness to prove **fraud** to lead him to tampering with the experiments.

Sir Arthur Conan Doyle, an enthusiastic Spiritualist, claimed that some of Houdini's own incredible feats were accomplished through psychic or supernatural powers. This infuriated Houdini, and at one time caused a break in his long-standing friendship with Doyle.

Houdini's death was precipitated by a reckless blow to the stomach from a student who visited him in his dressing room at the Princess Theater in Montreal on October 22, 1926. The student, J. Gordon Whitehead, had asked if it was true that Houdini could sustain punches to his midsection without injury. When Whitehead punched him, Houdini had been sorting his mail and was somewhat distracted.

Given permission to take a few trial punches, the student struck Houdini several times with powerful blows, and Houdini was clearly unprepared. That evening he suffered severe abdominal pains but completed his stage shows and took the train to Detroit, where he was booked for two weeks.

The train stopped at London, Ontario, where a telegram was sent to Detroit to request a medical examination. The doctor diagnosed acute appendicitis and ordered an ambulance, but Houdini refused and completed his show at the theater. After the show, his wife Bess pleaded with him to go to the hospital, and eventually, on the morning of October 25, he went to Grace Hospital, where he was found to be suffering from advanced peritonitis. He died on October 31, 1926.

The Houdini Code

Houdini's uneasy feud with Spiritualism persisted after his death, when various mediums claimed to convey messages from him lamenting his arrogant denunciation of Spiritualism. But one message was quite different. Among the challenges Houdini continuously issued to mediums was one that could be met only after his death. He stated that if spirit **survival** was possible, he would communicate with his wife, Bess, in a secret two-word code message known to no one else. A reward of $10,000 was offered for successfully communicating this code message.

Three years after Houdini's death, the medium **Arthur Ford** gave Bess Houdini a two-word message, "Rosabelle believe," in the special code used by the Houdinis in an early mind-reading act. Rosabelle had been a pet name used by Houdini for his wife. Bess Houdini signed a statement that Ford was correct. This was witnessed by a United Press reporter and an associate editor of the *Scientific American,* but 48 hours later the *New York Graphic* stated that the story was untrue, that a reporter had perpetrated a hoax, possibly with the connivance of Ford and Bess Houdini.

The original scoop story evaporated in a confusion of charges, countercharges, and denials, and Bess Houdini did not refer to the matter again in public. Many believe the evidence favors the original claim that Ford really did break the Houdini code by a mediumistic message from the beyond. Bess Houdini died February 11, 1943.

Sources:

Cannell, J. C. *The Secrets of Houdini.* London, 1931. Reprint, Detroit: Gale Research, 1976.

Christopher, Milbourne. *Houdini: The Untold Story.* New York: Thomas Y. Crowell, 1969. Reprint, New York: Pocket Books, 1970.

———. *Mediums, Mystics, and the Occult.* New York: Thomas Y. Crowell, 1975.

Ernst, Bernard M. L., and Hereward Carrington. *Houdini and Conan Doyle: The Story of a Strange Friendship.* Albert and Charles Boni, 1932. London: Hutchinson, 1933.

Fitzsimons, Raymund. *Death and the Magician: The Mystery of Houdini.* London: Hamish Hamilton, 1980.

Ford, Arthur, and Margueritte Harmon Bro. *Nothing So Strange.* New York: Harper & Row, 1958.

Houdini, Harry. *A Magician Among the Spirits.* New York: Harper & Brothers, 1924. Reprint, New York: Arno Press, 1972.

———. *The Right Way to Do Wrong.* Boston: H. Houdini, 1906.

———. *The Unmasking of Robert Houdin.* New York: Publishers Printing, 1908.

Kellock, Harold. *Houdini: His Life-Story.* New York: Harcourt, Brace, 1928.

Pressing, R. G., comp. *Houdini Unmasked.* Lily Dale, N.Y.: Dale News, 1947.

Spraggett, Allen, with William V. Rauscher. *Arthur Ford: The Man Who Talked with the Dead.* New York: New American Library, 1973.

Houghton, Georgina (d. 1887)

Nineteenth-century English private medium, author of *Evenings at Home in Spiritual Séance* (1882) and *Chronicles of the Photographs of Spiritual Beings and Phenomena Invisible to the Material Eye* (1882). Houghton never sat for research and knew nothing of test conditions. Her mediumship, which developed after a visit to **Mary Marshall,** appears to have consisted of **automatic drawing,** other acts of automatism, minor telekinetic phenomena, unconfirmed cases of **levitation** or floating above the ground while apparently walking like anyone else, **apports,** and the ability to see colored **auras** about the heads of others.

She claimed a band of 70 archangels as her guardian spirits and implicitly believed and obeyed every subconscious impulse, even to the extent of leaving it to the spirits to choose the wallpapers and carpets in her house.

The spirit photographs in her book *Chronicles of the Photographs of Spiritual Beings* were taken at the studio of **Frederick Hudson,** the first in England to practice **spirit photography,** but who was later exposed as a **fraud.** The pictures themselves—which include spirit forms of Joan of Arc, the wife of Manoah (mother of Samson), and St. John the Evangelist—are for the most part obvious fakes but have a certain nineteenth-century charm.

Houghton, Michael (d. ca. 1956)

British poet and occultist, associate of **Aleister Crowley.** Houghton was proprietor of the famous **Atlantis Book Shop** in London, specializing in occultism, and also edited the journal *Occult Observer* (1945–50), with contributions from leading occultists of the period. Under the pseudonym Michael Juste, Houghton published several volumes of poetry and a volume he described as an occult biography, *The White Brother* (1927).

Sources:

Juste, Michael [Michael Houghton]. *Escape, and Other Verse.* Leeds, 1924.

———. *Many Brightnesses, and Other Verse.* London, 1954.

———. *Shoot—and Be Damned.* London, 1935.

———. *The White Brother.* London, 1927.

House of Wisdom

The *tarik* (path) of the House of Wisdom, founded by Moslem mystics at Cairo in the ninth century, had seven initiatory degrees. The original founder appears to have been Abdallah, a Persian, who, believing in the Gnostic doctrine of the aeons or sephiroths, applied the system to the successors of Mohammed, stating that Ismael was the founder of his tarik and naming one of his descendants as the seventh imam (ruler).

Abdallah established an active system of propaganda and sent missionaries far and wide. He was succeeded in his office as chief of the society by his son. After the institution had been in existence for some time it was transferred to Cairo, and assemblies were held twice a week, when all the members appeared clothed in white. They were gradually advanced through the seven degrees of the tarik over which a *dia-al-doat* (missionary of missionaries) presided. A later chief, Hakem-bi-emir-Illah, increased the degrees to nine, and in 1004 erected a stately home for the society, which he elaborately furnished with mathematical instruments.

Because the institution did not meet the approval of the authorities, it was destroyed in 1123 by the then grand vizier, but meetings continued elsewhere. The officers of the society were *sheik, dai-el-keber* (deputy), *dai* (master), *refik* (fellow), *fedavie* (agent), *lassik* (aspirant), and *muemini* (believer). The tarik taught that there had been seven holy imams, that God had sent seven lawgivers, who each had seven helpers, who in turn had 12 apostles. (See also **Assassins**)

Houston, Jean (1939–)

Professor of psychology, formerly an actress and New York City Drama Critics award-winning playwright. She was born May 10, 1939. Houston taught at Columbia University and the New York School of Social Research. She collaborated with her husband, **Robert E. L. Masters,** on the book *The Varieties of Psychedelic Experience* (1966). Together the couple organized the **Foundation for Mind Research** in New York in 1964 to conduct experiments on the borderland between mental and psychical experiences.

Sources:

Houston, Jean. *Lifeforce.* New York: Delacorte Press, 1980.

———. *The Search for the Beloved: Journeys in Sacred Psychology.* Los Angeles: Jeremy P. Tarcher, 1987.

Masters, Robert E. L., and Jean Houston. *Listening to the Body.* New York, Delacorte Press, 1978.

———. *Mind Games: The Guide to Inner Space.* New York: Viking, 1972.

———. *The Varieties of Psychedelic Experience.* New York: Holt, Rinehart & Winston, 1966.

Howe, Ellic (1910–)

British authority on printing history who also wrote on occult subjects. Howe was born on September 20, 1910, in London. He attended Hertford College, Oxford (1929–31). During World War II he served with the British army (1939–41) and was promoted to the Foreign Office (1941–45). After the war he became a director of printing companies (1947–62).

In addition to his comprehensive studies of the history of British printing, he wrote and edited several important books on the occult and the history of magic, including *Urania's Children: The Strange World of the Astrologers* (1967; U.S. title, *Astrology: A Recent History Including the Untold Story of its Role in World War II,* 1968) and *The Magicians of the Golden Dawn* (1972). The latter work is a comprehensive study of the history and membership of the Hermetic Order of the **Golden Dawn,** the fountainhead of most contemporary ceremonial magic.

Sources:

Howe, Ellic, ed. *The Alchemist of the Golden Dawn: The Letters of the Revd W. A. Ayton to F. L. Gardner and Others, 1886–1905.* Wellingborough, England: Aquarian Press, 1985.

———. *The Magicians of the Golden Dawn.* New York: Samuel Weiser, 1972.

———. *Urania's Children: The Strange World of the Astrologers.* London, 1967. Reprinted as *Astrology: A Recent History Including the Untold Story of its Role in World War II.* New York: Walker, 1968.

Howitt, William (1792–1879)

Author and pioneer British Spiritualist. Howitt was born on December 18, 1792, at Heanor, Derbyshire, England, the son of a Quaker. He published his first poem at age 13. He studied chemistry and natural philosophy at Tamworth and expanded his education by reading widely. He married Mary Botham in 1821, and they cowrote a number of works. Howitt traveled through England and Germany, extending his knowledge of foreign languages. He wrote several books during his early adulthood, including *Popular History of Priestcraft in All Ages and Nations* (1833) and *Homes and Haunts of the Most Eminent British Poets* (1847). He edited *Howitt's Journal of Literature and Popular Progress* (3 vols., 1847–49) and published a translation of J. Ennemoser, *The History of the Supernatural* (2 vols., 1854; reissued in 1970).

In 1852 Howitt went to Australia, and while there first learned of the outbreak of **Spiritualism** when digging for gold in the Australian bush. In his novel *Tallangetta or the Squatters' Home,* which he conceived there, he included many incidents of a

Spiritualist or supernatural nature. Before the novel was published (two and a half years after his return to England) he had some interesting experiences.

His wife attended a séance in April 1856 in the home of a Mrs. de Morgan (see **Augustus de Morgan**), and within a month mediumship developed in the Howitt family. It started with **automatic writing** and **automatic drawing** and continued with **clairvoyance** and spirit vision. There may have been some inherited tendency, because William Howitt's mother was a seeress and he himself was a sleepwalker in early youth. The phenomena started with his son and daughter. In January 1858 Howitt himself gained the power to write and draw automatically. It suddenly began after a visit to a Mrs. Wilkinson, who was a good drawing medium.

William Howitt's debut as a champion of Spiritualism occurred with a lively exchange of letters in *The Critic* regarding a haunted house and ghosts in general. **Charles Dickens** desired to visit some well-known haunted houses and asked for information. Howitt told him of **Willington Mill,** which he had visited, and of a house at Cheshunt, near London, of which he had read in Catharine Crowe's *Night Side of Nature* (2 vols., 1848). But the house at Cheshnut was partly pulled down, and Dickens could not find it.

When William Wilkinson's *Spiritual Magazine* was started in 1860, Howitt became a regular contributor and in the 13 years of its existence he wrote more than a hundred articles on the supernatural in the lives of men and nations, on the religious and philosophical aspects of the manifestations, and on personal experiences. In his leisure time he arranged séances with the famous medium **D. D. Home.**

His most important work was a book of two volumes, *The History of the Supernatural in All Ages and Nations and in All Churches, Christian and Pagan, Demonstrating a Universal Faith,* published in 1863. Howitt died in Rome on March 3, 1879.

Sources:

Ennemoser, Joseph. *The History of the Supernatural.* Translated by William Howitt. 2 vols. 1854. Reprint, New Hyde Park, N.Y.: University Books, 1970.

Howitt, William. *The History of the Supernatural in All Ages and Nations and in All Churches, Christian and Pagan, Demonstrating a Universal Faith.* Philadelphia: J. B. Lippincott, 1863. Reprinted as *The History of Magic.* New Hyde Park, N.Y.: University Books, 1970.

———. *Homes and Haunts of the Most Eminent British Poets.* New York: Harper & Brothers, 1847.

Howitt-Watts, Mrs. *Pioneers of the Spiritual Reform.* London: Psychological Press Association, 1883.

Howling of Dogs

It was a common superstition in Europe and Asia that the howling of dogs at night presaged death to someone in the vicinity.

HPR See Human Potential Resources, Inc.

Huaca

Peruvian oracle.

Hubbard, L(afayette) Ron(ald) (1911–1986)

Founder of the Church of **Scientology.** Hubbard was born in Tilden, Nebraska, on March 13, 1911. He spent much of his childhood in Montana on his grandfather's ranch. His father was a naval officer, and as Hubbard matured, he traveled through the Pacific and to Asia. In 1930 he enrolled in the Engineering School of George Washington University, Washington, D.C., where he studied for the next two years. During the remainder of the decade he roamed the world as a participant in various explorations and wrote over 150 articles and short stories. His first book, *Buckskin Brigades,* appeared in 1937. In 1940 he was elected a member of the Explorers Club in New York. During World War II he served in the U.S. Navy with the rank of lieutenant. He also worked briefly in naval intelligence.

After the war, he returned to writing as a career. As a writer, Hubbard had a prodigious output and was remembered for the amazing speed at which he could produce copy. Often several stories would be published in the same issue of a magazine and thus many appeared under pseudonyms. No one systematically recorded his output, and reassembling a bibliography was a tedious process, carried out through the 1980s. In the 1930s he turned out Westerns for pulp magazines under the pseudonym "Winchester Remington Colt." His early science-fiction pulp stories were under the pseudonyms "Kurt von Rachen" and "René Lafayette." He wrote for Columbia Pictures in Hollywood in 1935.

Through the 1940s, partly based upon his experiences in the war, Hubbard began to develop a new philosophy of human nature and a new approach to dealing with basic human ills. The first public notice of his thinking appeared in an article in *Astounding Science Fiction* (May 1950), later to prove an unfortunate debut. As Dianetics, the name he gave his new approach, developed into the Church of Scientology and proved both controversial and successful, it would be demeaned as a "science fiction" religion and Hubbard dismissed as just a hack science fiction writer.

Dianetics: The Modern Science of Mental Health appeared a few weeks after the *Astounding Science Fiction* article. The book created a sensation and launched a vast new industry of do-it-yourself psychotherapy. Hubbard created the Hubbard Dianetics Research Foundation and local Dianetics centers began to emerge based upon Hubbard's technique for ridding individuals of the causes of aberrant behavior patterns and leading them to a state of "clear."

As Hubbard continued to expand his thought and work out the implications of his theories, Dianetics grew into a comprehensive philosophical-religious system, Scientology. In 1954 the first Church of Scientology was opened in Los Angeles. The rest of Hubbard's life would be spent in developing and perfecting Scientology. In 1966 he resigned from any official position in the church, but he continued his research and writing for a number of years. He developed guidelines for the church and left behind writing that focused on the implications of his thought for education and business.

During the last years of his life he dropped out of public sight and remained in contact with only a few church leaders. In the years prior to his death on January 24, 1986, he returned to his love for storytelling and wrote one major novel, *Battlefield Earth,* and a ten-volume science fiction series, *Mission Earth.*

As his church became a prosperous international movement, it and Hubbard became the center of controversies involving people who left the movement to found competing organizations, former members who turned upon the church for real or imagined grievances, and the anti-cult movement, which branded the church a cult. In retrospect, early controversy with the American Medical Association, which disapproved of Dianetics, seems to have spilled over into federal government departments and covert actions against the church were instigated. Rumors of illicit actions by the church, many of which led to problems with different governments, began to emerge around the world. Legal actions, most of which were eventually resolved, became the justification for action against the church in additional countries. Some high church officials authorized the infiltration of several government agencies, and this became a major source of embarrassment for the church when the people responsible were arrested and convicted for theft of government documents.

For the Church of Scientology, the years since 1985 have been marked by intense polemics and court action between members of the church and the Cult Awareness Network, which emerged in the mid-1980s as the chief organizational expression of the anti-cult movement. These legal battles continue. However, a several-decades-old controversy with the Internal Revenue Service came to an end.

Hubbard and the OTO

During the 1940s, Hubbard became involved in one of the more bizarre happenings in the world of the occult. In the 1930s, a lodge of the **Ordo Templi Orientis,** the magical group headed by magician **Aleister Crowley,** had opened in Pasadena, California. Among its members was John W. "Jack" Parsons, a research scientist at the California Institute of Technology. At some point in 1945, Parsons decided to try a magical experiment to produce a magical child. At this point Hubbard showed up at Parson's house and was eventually invited by Parsons to become the necessary third person in the magical experiment.

The experiment consisted of Parsons and his female partner engaging in sexual intercourse while a third person, a clairvoyant, would tell them what was occurring in the invisible astral realm. The ritual would climax at what the clairvoyant seer suggested was the proper moment. Hopefully the act would result in the pregnancy of the woman and the induction of a spirit in the resulting child.

While Parsons and Hubbard seemed to have developed a strong friendship, early in 1946 they parted ways and Hubbard moved to Miami. Parsons claimed that Hubbard had skipped town with OTO funds and went to Miami to confront him. The present Church of Scientology claims that Hubbard had no attachment to either Parsons or the OTO, and that in spite of Hubbard's work with Parsons, Hubbard was never initiated into the organization. Rather, they suggest that he was acting as an undercover agent to investigate Parsons and other people associated with Cal Tech who were living in Parsons's house and working on sensitive government projects. Several of these physicists were later dismissed from government service as security risks. Hubbard did work for a period after the war as an undercover agent for the Los Angeles Police Department.

Hubbard died January 24, 1986, after years of living as a recluse.

Sources:

Hubbard, L. Ron. *Dianetics: The Modern Science of Mental Health.* New York: Hermitage House, 1950.

———. *Scientology: A New Slant on Life.* Los Angeles: Publications Organization, United States, 1965.

———. *Scientology: The Fundamentals of Thought.* Los Angeles: Publications Organization, United States, 1956.

Miller, Russell. *Bare-Faced Messiah: The True Story of L. Ron Hubbard.* New York: Henry Holt, 1987.

Huby, Pamela M(argaret) Clark (1922–)

British university lecturer in philosophy who experimented in parapsychology. She was born on April 21, 1922, in London and attended Oxford University (B.A., 1944; M.A., 1947). After graduation Huby was a lecturer in philosophy at St. Anne's College, Oxford (1947–49). She then joined the faculty at Liverpool University, where she was named a senior lecturer in 1971. Her philosophical works include *Greek Ethics* (1967) and *Plato and Modern Morality* (1972).

A member of both the **Parapsychological Association,** and the **Society for Psychical Research,** London, Huby conducted experiments in group telepathy and clairvoyance (some in collaboration with **C. W. M. Wilson**), about which she wrote several papers. She also contributed a paper to *Philosophical Foundations of Psychical Research,* edited by S. C. Thakur.

Sources:

Huby, Pamela M. C. "Case of Xenoglossy." *Journal* of the Society for Psychical Research 44.

———. "Effects of Centrally Acting Drugs on ESP Ability." *Journal* of the Society for Psychical Research 41.

———. "New Evidence About 'Rose Morton.'" *Journal* of the Society for Psychical Research 45.

Pleasants, Helene, ed. *Biographical Dictionary of Parapsychology.* New York: Helix Press, 1964.

Hudson, Frederick A. (ca. 1877)

The first British exponent of **spirit photography.** In March 1872 Samuel Guppy and his wife, **Agnes Guppy-Volckman,** who made several unsuccessful experiments to obtain psychic photographs in their own home, went on an impulse to Hudson's studio, which was nearby. A white patch resembling the outline of a draped figure was obtained behind Mr. Guppy's portrait. The experiment was repeated with increasing success.

After report of these pictures spread, the accusation of imposture soon arose, but, according to **Alfred Russel Wallace,** even those who were most emphatic about **fraud** believed that a large number of genuine pictures were taken. Wallace obtained two different portraits of his mother, representing two different periods and unlike any photograph taken during her life.

William Howitt obtained the likeness of two deceased sons, one of whom even the friend who accompanied him was ignorant. A Dr. Thompson obtained the extra of a lady whom his uncle in Scotland identified as the likeness of Thompson's mother. She had died in childbirth and no picture of her remained.

The editor of the *British Journal of Photography* investigated, using his own collodion and new plates. He found abnormal appearances on the pictures. Nevertheless, from time to time Hudson was caught cheating. Once he was exposed by **Stainton Moses,** for whom he produced many spirit photographs that agreed with his clairvoyant visions. To play the part of the ghost, Hudson occasionally dressed up or made double exposures. The duplication of the pattern of the carpet and other parts of the background showing through the legs of the sitter and of the ghost was ingeniously explained by refraction—the spirits being quoted as saying that the spirit aura differs in density and refracting power from the ordinary terrestrial atmosphere. Such resourceful explanations, coupled with the belief that Hudson produced many genuine spirit photographs, helped to reestablish his shaken credibility.

However, according to psychical researcher **Harry Price,** in his book *Confessions of a Ghost-Hunter* (1936; reprinted in 1974), Hudson used an ingenious camera manufactured by Howell, a famous London maker of conjuring apparatus. This camera was of the old square wooden type and contained a light metal frame that in its normal position rested on the bottom of the smaller of the camera's two telescopic portions. This frame held a waxed paper positive of the desired ghostly "extra." When the dark slide was pushed into the camera, it actuated a lever, raising the frame to a vertical position in contact with the photographic plate. When the picture was taken, the extra image was also printed on the plate. When the plate was drawn out of the camera the frame automatically fell back to its hidden position.

Fifty-four "spirit photographs" taken in this way are reproduced in the book *Chronicles of the Photographs of Spiritual Beings,* by **Georgina Houghton** (1882).

Sources:

Price, Harry. *Confessions of a Ghost-Hunter.* London: Putnam, 1936. Reprint, New York: Causeway Books, 1974.

Hudson, Thomson Jay (1834–1903)

American author and lecturer who attained prominence by an ingenious anti-Spiritualist theory expounded in his books. He was born on February 22, 1834, in Windham, Ohio. He attended public schools in Windham and later studied law. He was admitted to the bar at Cleveland, Ohio, in 1857 and practiced for a time in Michigan before entering a journalistic career, culminating in the editorship of the *Detroit Evening News.* In 1880 he left journalism to enter the U.S. Patent Office, becoming principal examiner. In 1893 he resigned and devoted his time to the study of experimental psychology. Hudson was awarded an honorary LL.D. by St. John's College, Annapolis, in 1896.

The essence of his special theory of psychic phenomena, developed from studies in **hypnotism,** was that man has within him two distinct minds: the objective, with which he carries on his practical daily life; and the subjective, which is dormant but is infallible as a record, registering every single impression of life. The objective mind is capable of both inductive and deductive reasoning, the subjective mind of deductive only, according to Hudson's theory.

The change of death is survival in another state of consciousness, with which, however, communication is impossible. Any attempt is simply playing the fool with the subjective mind, which presents reflections of the experimenter's complete life record and lures him on to believe that he is communicating with his departed friends, Hudson said.

The Law of Psychic Phenomena (1893), in which this theory is expounded, became very popular and made a deep impression. It was followed by *Scientific Demonstration of the Future Life* (1896), *Divine Pedigree of Man* (1900), *Law of Mental Medicine* (1903), and *Evolution of the Soul and Other Essays* (1904).

Hudson's theories attained an even greater popularity after they were picked up by Thomas Troward and became the basis of his famous Edinburgh Lectures on Mental Science (1909). Troward fed the notion of two minds into **New Thought,** where it was eventually picked up by Ernest Holmes and became the basic insight upon which Religious Science was based.

Hudson died in Detroit on May 26, 1903. Admiral Usborne Moore writes in *Glimpses of the Next State* (1911) that through Mrs. Georgie, a young dramatist of Rochester who wrote automatically in mirror writing, he received manifestations of Hudson's spirit. Details of his life, unknown to both of them, were given, and he communicated through different mediums in Detroit and Chicago, carrying as a test messages of the admiral from one medium to another and describing his activities to them.

Sources:

Hudson, Thomson Jay. *Divine Pedigree of Man.* Chicago: A. C. McClure, 1900.

———. *Evolution of the Soul and Other Essays.* Chicago: A. C. McClure, 1904.

———. *The Law of Psychic Phenomena.* London: G. P. Putnam; Chicago: A. C. McClurg, 1893. Reprint, New York: Samuel Weiser, 1969.

———. *Scientific Demonstration of the Future Life.* Chicago: A. C. McClure, 1896.

Melton, J. Gordon. *New Thought: A Reader.* Santa Barbara, Calif.: Institute for the Study of American Religion, 1990.

Huebner, Louise

Psychic and astrologer who enjoyed brief fame as the Official Witch of Los Angeles County, a title she was given in 1968. Her career as a psychic began when she was only ten years old, when she began to give palm readings at a children's carnival. She later moved to Los Angeles and opened an office as an astrologer. Through the 1960s she gained local fame as a psychic and was a frequent guest on radio and television shows. She appeared regularly on a talk show on radio station KLAC for four years (1965–69). Occasionally she was invited to assist in crime detection.

On July 21, 1968, she was presented with a scroll naming her the Official Witch of Los Angeles County. At the time of the presentation, she performed a spell to ensure the continued sexual vitality of Los Angeles. The act had some immediate consequences. Some in the county were embarrassed when Huebner began to use the title to promote her writings on **witchcraft** and attempted to stop her. The effort ended after Huebner threatened to undo the spell. Second, members of the emerging neopagan Wiccan movement were somewhat upset by Huebner, who was not a part of their movement and tended to perpetuate what they felt were negative stereotypes of witches.

Huebner continued to operate as a public psychic and witch for several years. In 1970 she traveled to Salem, Massachusetts, where the mayor presented her with a broom. She produced one record album, two books, and a series of mini-books for Hallmark Cards. By the mid-1970s, however, she had largely retired from public life, and for a period she operated an antique shop in Pasadena, California.

Sources:

Guiley, Rosemary. *The Encyclopedia of Witches and Witchcraft.* New York: Facts on File, 1989.

Huebner, Louise. *Magic Sleep.* Kansas City, Mo.: Springbok Editions, 1972.

———. *Magical Creatures.* Kansas City, Mo.: Springbok Editions, 1972.

———. *Never Strike a Happy Medium.* Los Angeles: Nash Publishing, 1971.

———. *Power through Witchcraft.* Los Angeles: Nash Publishing, 1969. Reprint, New York: Bantam Books, 1972.

———. *Your Lucky Numbers.* Kansas City, Mo.: Springbok Editions, 1972.

Huet, Pierre-Daniel (1630–1721)

A celebrated French bishop of Avranches who collected some early reports of **vampires.** Huet was born on February 8, 1630, at Caen. He was educated at a Jesuit school and by a Protestant pastor and became a great classical scholar. In addition to editing Origen's *Commentary on St. Matthew,* he studied mathematics, astronomy, anatomy, ocular research, and chemistry and learned Syriac and Arabic. With Ann Lefèvre, he edited 60 volumes of Latin classics.

Huet took holy orders in 1676 and became bishop of Soissons in 1685 and later bishop of Avranches. He died on February 26, 1721. In his *Memoirs* (translated, 2 vols., 1810) there are many interesting passages relating to the vampires of the Greek archipelago. "Many strange things," he states, "are told of the broucolagnes, or vampires of the Archipelago. It is said in that country that if one leads a wicked life, and dies in sin, he will appear again after death as he was wont in his lifetime, and that such a person will cause great affright among the living." Huet believed that the bodies of such people were abandoned to the power of the devil, who retained the soul within them for the vexation of mankind.

Father François Richard, a Jesuit employed on a mission in the islands, provided Huet with details of many cases of vampirism. On the island of St. Erini (the Thera of the ancients) occurred one of the greatest chapters in the history of vampirism. Huet states that the people of St. Erini were tormented by vampires, and were always disinterring corpses to burn them. Huet states that this evidence is worthy of credence, having come from a witness of unimpeachable honesty who saw what he wrote about. He further says that the inhabitants of these islands cut off a person's feet, hands, nose, and ears after death, and they called this act *acroteriazein.* They hung the severed parts around the elbow of the dead.

The bishop appears to have thought that the modern Greeks might have inherited the practice of burning bodies from their forebears in classical times, and that they imagined that unless the corpse was burned the soul of the deceased could not rest.

Huet died February 26, 1721.

Hughes, Irene (Finger)

Chicago psychic who attained fame in the 1960s with her predictions. Born Irene Finger in a log cabin at Saulsbury, Mississippi, Hughes claimed Cherokee Indian and Scotch-Irish ancestry. She worked in a hospital in New Orleans and married William Hughes in 1945. After the war she moved to Chicago and became a reporter. Hughes used her psychic abilities to pay for the move to Chicago by correctly forecasting horserace winners.

Following a major operation in 1961 Hughes became aware of a Japanese spirit guide. She went on to develop psychically and become a professional psychic reader. She wrote and lectured on psychic subjects and began offering private consultations. In 1963 she founded the **Golden Path** in Chicago, an organization devoted to teaching students to develop their psychic talents. In 1967 she visited the **Psychical Research Foundation** in Durham, North Carolina, where her psychic abilities were tested by parapsychologist **William Roll.**

Among her many psychic predictions was one concerning the assassination of Robert Kennedy. In 1962 she predicted the exact date of death of former Illinois governor Adlai Stevenson in 1965. Her growing reputation was enhanced in 1967 when some six months in advance she predicted the massive snowstorm to hit Chicago in January of that year. She filed other predictions with the **Central Premonitions Registry.**

During the 1970s Hughes emerged as one of the top psychics in the Chicago area. Several books by and about her appeared. She was a frequent guest on radio and television talk shows, and for several years she hosted a local television show on Chicago's WSNS. After a fruitful career, she retired from the public scene.

Sources:

Defano, M. M. *The Living Prophets.* New York: Dell, 1972.

Hughes, Irene. *ESPecially Irene: A Guide to Psychic Awareness.* Blauvelt, N.Y.: Rudolph Steiner Publications, 1972.

———. *Know Your Future Today.* New York: Paperback Library, 1970.

Psychic magazine, editors of. *Psychics.* New York: Harper & Row, 1972.

Steiger, Brad. *Irene Hughes on Psychic Safari.* New York: Warner Paperback Library, 1972.

Hugo, Victor (1802–1885)

The great French romantic novelist. He was keenly interested in **Spiritism.** He wrote, "To avoid phenomena, to make them bankrupt of the attention to which they have a right, is to make bankrupt truth itself." Hugo left an unpublished manuscript on Spiritism in the possession of Paul Meurice, who died in 1905. It appears that he had his first experiences in **table turning** in September 1853 at the home of a Mme. de Girardin during his period on the island of Jersey after he was exiled from France by Napoleon III in 1852. Hugo at first refused to attend the séance but was greatly moved when the table spelled out the name of his lost daughter Leopoldine. Soon regular communications were established.

The sitters included General Le Flo, Count Paul Teleki, Charles Hugo, one Vacquerie, and Mme. Hugo. Victor Hugo himself was never at the table, sometimes not even in the room. Many symbolical personages came through, including "the Lion of Androcles," "the Ass of Balaam," and "the Dove of Noah." "The Shadow of the Tomb" expressed itself in verse in the style and language of Victor Hugo, with all the grandiloquence of romantic poetry. Sometimes verse in the same style was signed by "Aeschylus." "Shakespeare" challenged Hugo to a poetic competition. "André Chenier," the guillotined poet, finished the fragmentary poem that was interrupted by his execution. Charles Hugo was the principal medium in all these experiments.

In 1892, seven years after Victor Hugo's death, the spirit of Victor Hugo, or a secondary **personality** assuming the name, appeared as the **control** of **Hélène Smith,** the medium, famous for her pseudo-Martian communication. "Victor" was in exclusive control for five months. After a struggle lasting for a year he was ousted by another control, "Leopold," the so-called spirit of **Cagliostro.**

Sources:

Berger, Arthur S., and Joyce Berger. *The Encyclopedia of Parapsychology and Psychical Research.* New York: Paragon House, 1991.

Ebon, Martin. *They Knew the Unknown.* New York: New American Library, 1971.

Flournoy, Theodor. *From India to the Planet Mars.* Reprint, New Hyde Park, N.Y.: University Books, 1963.

Grillet, Claudius *Victor Hugo Spirite.* Paris, 1929.

Malo, Henry. *Life of Delphine Gray.* N.p., 1925.

Sudre, René. "The Case of Victor Hugo and the Collective Psychism." *Psychic Research* 23 (1971).

Human Dimensions Institute (HDI)

New Age educational organization in Buffalo, New York, that in the 1970s pioneered research on the "whole" person—physical, emotional, mental, and spiritual. The institute operated through scientific research, publications, lectures, seminars, experience groups, and continuing courses at Rosary Hill, Buffalo, and surrounding colleges and institutions. Seminars were held at Swen-i-o, the new HDI Retreat Center at Canandaigua, New York. International authorities discussed such areas as parapsychology, consciousness expansion, nutrition, unorthodox healing, **holistic** philosophy, and spiritual experience. The institute published the *Human Dimensions Magazine,* a quarterly publication of articles and professional papers on new frontiers of human experience.

Human Dimensions Institute, West

Research center and forum concerned with scientific and metaphysical disciplines. Advisors included **Stanley Krippner,** Charles Muses, Elizabeth Rauscher, **David Spangler,** and Fred Wolfe. The center is related to the **Human Dimensions Institute** at Buffalo, New York, and provides classes, lectures, and workshops. Address: P.O. Box 5037 or 10773 Hwy. 150, Ojai, CA 93023.

Human Individual Metamorphosis (HIM)

A flying saucer cult founded in the American West by two individuals calling themselves Bo and Peep, who claimed they would lead their followers to literal ascension to heaven in a spacecraft.

Human Information Processing Group

Organized at Princeton University, New Jersey, as an interdisciplinary study of all aspects of the interaction between humans and machines. Programs include such topics as consciousness-related anomalous phenomena.

Human Nature (Journal)

Early Spiritualist monthly journal founded by **James Burns** in 1867. It was published in London for a decade as a major forum for non-Christian or "progressive" Spiritualism.

Human Potential Resources (Journal)

British quarterly journal with a wide range of subjects—spiritual pathways, environmental issues, health and therapies, education, and humanistic psychology. It includes a comprehensive resource directory and calendar of events in Britain. Address: LSG Plc., HRP Subscription Dept., P.O. Box 10, Lincoln, LN5 7JA, England.

Human Potential Resources, Inc. (HPR)

Organization founded by Michael Lach in July 1986 to publish a networking catalog of the **New Age** movement titled *Choices and Connections,* the first issue of which appeared in 1987. This large publication presents some 2,400 alternative lifestyle items in 60 categories, covering everything from solar-powered equipment to Eastern philosophy. Lach claimed that there was a real demand for information on New Age philosophies and products, stressing the need for personal development and commitment to global peace. Based in Boulder, Colorado, HPR has sold some 10,000 copies of its catalog through bookstores.

Sources:

Cott-MacPhail, Carolyn. *Choices and Connections: The First Catalog of the Global Family.* Boulder, Colo.: Human Potential Resources, 1987.

Humpfner, Winfried G(oswin) (1889–1962)

German priest who was actively interested in parapsychological studies. Humpfner was born on August 4, 1889, at Aidhausen, Bavaria, Germany, and he studied at the University of Würsburg (D. Theol., 1930). He entered the Augustinian Order in 1909 and was ordained as a priest in 1914. He studied in Rome and became the order's general archivist and subsecretary general in 1931 and was later assistant general (1936–47).

Humpfner pursued his interest in psychical research throughout his adult life. He was a life member of the **Society for Psychical Research,** London, and an associate member of the **American Society for Psychical Research.** He also joined the Societá Italiana di Parapscicologia, **Association Italiana Scientifica de Metapsichica,** and Imago Mundi, the international organization of Roman Catholic parapsychologists. He died on November 3, 1962.

Sources:

Humpfner, Winfried G. *L'Interpretazione di Fenomeni Metapsichici; ovvero, L'Anima in Metapsichica, in Psicologia, ecc.* (The Interpretation of Metapsychical Phenomena; or, The Soul in Metapsychics, Psychology, etc.). N.p., 1951.

Pleasants, Helene, ed. *Biographical Dictionary of Parapsychology.* New York: Helix Press, 1964.

Humphrey, Betty N. See Betty Humphrey Nicol

Humphreys, Eliza M. Y. (Mrs. W. Desmond) (d. 1938)

Popular British novelist and Spiritualist who wrote under the pseudonym Rita. She was a daughter of John Gilbert Gollan of Inverness-shire, Scotland. She was educated in Sydney, Australia, later returning to England. She was married twice; her second husband was W. Desmond Humphreys of Ballin, county Cork, Ireland.

She began writing at an early age and during her lifetime published more than 60 popular novels as well as several nonfiction works, including her own autobiographical *Recollections of a Literary Life* (1936). She was a convinced Spiritualist and in her book *The Truth of Spiritualism* (1918) she states that her interest began in her girlhood, "when, owing to my father's interest in the subject, we used to try for communications sitting at a table with joined hands in dim light, and received messages by means of the alphabet and raps . . . and my father used to keep a written record of communications." She died January 1, 1938.

Huna

The secret knowledge of Hawaiian-priest sorcerers known as *kahunas,* or keepers of the secret. This knowledge includes healing, weather control, and mastery of fire walking on red-hot lava.

An important aspect of Huna miracles is the concept of *mana,* a vitalistic force with close parallels to the Odic force of **Baron von Reichenbach,** the **animal magnetism** of nineteenth-century Europe, and the **orgone** energy of **Wilhelm Reich,** as well as the **kundalini** of Hindu tradition.

According to **Max Freedom Long,** who studied Huna magic in Hawaii, the kahunas recognize three entities of *aka* (bodies of the human being): a low, middle, and higher self. The low self generates mana through food and other vital processes and is concerned with the physical body and the emotions. The middle self is a reasoning entity, while the higher self transcends memory and reason.

Long later established **Huna Research.** Serge King has since founded a second Huna-based organization, **Huna International,** an organization for research and teaching in the field of Huna magic.

Sources:

King, Serge. *Kahuna Healing.* Wheaton, Ill.: Theosophical Publishing House, 1983.

———. *Mastering Your Hidden Self.* Wheaton, Ill.: Theosophical Publishing House, 1983.

———. *Urban Shaman.* New York: Simon & Schuster, 1990.

Long, Max Freedom. *Introduction to Huna.* Sedona, Ariz.: Esoteric Publications, 1975.

———. *The Secret Science Behind Miracles.* Vista, Calif.: Huna Research Publications, 1954.

Steiger, Brad. *Kahuna Magic.* Rockport, Mass.: Para Research, 1971.

Wingo, E. Ortha. *The Story of the Huna Work.* Cape Girardeau, Mo.: Huna Research, 1981.

Hundredth Monkey

Crucial to the **New Age** movement was the positing of a means or agent to bring it into existence. Some saw the New Age as due to astrological forces released by the changing movement of the stars or due to energy coming from the spiritual hierarchy. The concept of the Hundredth Monkey was an alternative to both astrological and spiritualist concepts. It suggested that when a certain number of people gave their consent and commitment to a new idea, it would spread through the population somewhat mysteriously. Thus as the number of people attuned to the New Age grew, at some point New Age consciousness would spontaneously sweep through the general population, and the New Age would arrive.

The basis for this idea was derived from a story in the 1979 book *Lifetide: A Biology of the Unconscious* by Lyall Watson. He reported on research conducted by several anthropologists on the macaques (a species of monkey) in the islands off Japan. According to the story, in 1953 one of the anthropologists observed an aged macaque female wash a potato to get the sand and grit off of it before eating. She, in turn, taught another to do the same thing. The pair taught others, and soon a number of the adult macaques were washing their potatoes. In the fall of 1958, almost every macaque was doing it. Then macaques who had had no contact with the potato-washing monkeys began to wash their food. It appeared, concluded Watson, that as the practice spread through the monkey communities, a critical mass was approached when 98 and then 99 monkeys washed their food. Then, when the hundredth monkey adopted the practice, critical mass was reached, and the practice exploded through the monkey population.

Watson's story was seized upon by New Age spokesperson Ken Keyes, founder of the Living Love Seminars. In 1982 he published the book *The Hundredth Monkey* and within a year had distributed 300,000 copies. His subject was peace, and he argued that peace consciousness could spread throughout the human race only if a sufficient number of people adopted a commitment to peace. Once a critical mass was reached, love of peace would suddenly move quickly through the race. As the idea became a well-known concept within the New Age community, other writers, such as Rupert Sheldrake, Peter Russell, and Stanislav Grof, picked up the discussion.

However, the idea of the hundredth monkey did not go unchallenged within the New Age community. As early as 1983, psychologist Maureen O'Hara confronted it in the *Journal of Humanistic Psychology.* Her article was followed two years later by another writer protesting Watson's claims, arguing that all the monkeys who washed their food had learned it from another. There was no evidence of a magical mysterious spread of the practice. Watson accepted Amundson's analysis of the situation and admitted that he had developed the hundredth monkey concept as a metaphor based on slim evidence and a great deal of hearsay. While the concept retained some supporters through the 1980s, it slowly disappeared from New Age thinking.

Sources:

Keyes, Ken, Jr., *The Hundredth Monkey.* Coos Bay, Ore.: Vision Books, 1982.

Watson, Lyall. *Lifetide: A Biology of the Unconscious.* New York: Simon & Schuster, 1979.

Huns

The people who invaded the eastern Roman Empire around 372–453 C.E. and were particularly ruthless and effective in their war campaigns under the leadership of Attila. Modern day Hungarians claim ancestry dating back to the Huns.

Ancient historians recorded legends that grew out of the severe stress the Huns created in all those whom they fought against. They credited the Huns with a supernatural origin. The Huns were referred to as "children of the devil," because it was said that they were born of a union between demons and hideous witches, the latter cast out of their own country by Philimer, king of the Goths, and his army. The old writers state that the Huns were of horrible deformity and could not be mistaken for anything but the children of demons. The German historian C. Besoldus (1577–1638) claimed that their name came from a Celtic or barbaric word signifying "great magicians." Many stories are told of their magic prowess and of their raising specters to assist them in battle.

Sources:

Manchen-Helfen, Otto. *The World of the Huns: Studies in Their History and Culture.* Berkeley, Calif.: University of California Press, 1973.

Hunt, Ernest (1878–1967)

Ernest Hunt, founder of the Western Buddhist Order and a leading figure in the introduction of Buddhism to non-Asian Americans, was born August 16, 1878, in Hoddesdon, Hertfordshire, England. He went to sea as a young man, but returned home and studied for the Anglican priesthood. As he was making preparation for his ordination, he converted to Buddhism. In 1915 he moved with his wife, Dorothy, to Hawaii (where Buddhism had its strongest presence in the West) and worked on a plantation. In the early 1920s he moved to the big island and began teaching classes in English for the children of Japanese plantation workers. His work was recognized in 1924 when he was ordained by the Honpa Hongwanji, the largest of the Buddhist groups operating in Hawaii.

In 1926, Hunt, in cooperation with the Bishop Yemyo Imamura, became head of the Honpa Hongwanji's English-language department. The school was originally established to serve Japanese youth, many of whom had begun to drop the Japanese language, but Hunt also used it to reach out to the Caucasian population and teach Buddhism. He wrote a book of Buddhist ceremonies in English, and Dorothy Hunt composed a number of poems that were adapted as hymns. By 1928 some 60 converts formed the Western Buddhist Order, a nonsectarian branch of Buddhism attached to the Honpa Hongwanji.

Hunt's ideal of a nonsectarian Buddhism found an ally in 1929 in the International Buddhist Institute founded by Chinese Buddhist abbot Tai Hsu. Tai Hsu came to Hawaii and convinced Hunt to found a branch of the institute. Hunt saw it as a perfect means of spreading his notion that the surest way to Nirvana was through *metta,* active goodwill. He was able to bring Buddhists of all persuasions together in the institute and set them to doing good deeds, from visiting the sick and imprisoned to building schools.

The late 1920s proved the period of Hunt's prime literary production, beginning with his often-reprinted pamphlet, *An Outline of Buddhism: The Religion of Wisdom and Compassion.* He edited four volumes of the *Hawaiian Buddhist Annual* as well as the institute's magazine, *Navayana.* All came to an end, however, in 1932 with the death of Bishop Imamura. His successor was both a strong sectarian Buddhist and a Japanese nationalist. He rejected Hunt's approach and in 1935 removed Hunt from the Honpa Hongwanji and disbanded the English department. Hunt moved his membership to the Soto Temple, a branch of the Japanese Zen Buddhist movement, and continued much as before. He was eventually ordained as a Soto priest (1953). He was also honored as the first Westerner to be given the title Osho, a rank acknowledging his accomplishments.

During the 1950s, Hunt produced his last two publications, *Gleanings from Soto-Zen* and *Essentials and Symbols of the Buddhist Faith.* He spent much time in his last years in the Soto Temple, where he greeted the increasing number of tourists who were coming to the islands. He died in Honolulu on February 7, 1967.

Sources:

Hunt, Ernest. *Essentials and Symbols of the Buddhist Faith.* Honolulu: The Author, 1955.

———. *Gleanings from Soto-Zen.* Honolulu: The Author, 1953.

———. *An Outline of Buddhism.* Honolulu: Hongwanji Buddhist Temple, 1929.

Hunter, Louise. *Buddhism in Hawaii.* Honolulu: University of Hawaii Press, 1971.

Peiris, William. *The Western Contribution to Buddhism.* Delhi, India: Motilal Banarsidass, 1953.

Hunt, H(arry) Ernest (d. 1946)

British Spiritualist, lecturer, and author. A tutor at St. Paul's School, London, Hunt resigned to devote his attention to the study of practical psychology. He wrote a number of books. He died January 6, 1946.

Sources:

Hunt, H. Ernest. *A Book of Auto-Suggestion.* N.p., 1923.

———. *Hidden Self and Its Mental Processes.* London: W. Rider and Son, 1921.

———. *Manual of Hypnotism.* London: W. Rider, 1917.

———. *Nerve Control.* N.p., 1923.

———. *Self Training.* Philadelphia: D. McKay, 1918.

———. *Spirit and Music.* N.p., 1922.

———. *Spiritualism For the Enquirer.* N.p., 1931.

———. *Why We Survive.* N.p., 1928.

Hurkos, Peter (1911–1988)

Prominent psychic born on May 21, 1911, as Peter Van der Hurk in Dordrecht, Holland. He worked as a merchant seaman before becoming a member of the Dutch underground movement in occupied Holland during World War II. He claimed that as a result of a fall from a ladder in 1941 he discovered a psychic faculty.

Hurkos was not able to make use of the new ability immediately, because he was arrested and imprisoned in Buchenwald, Germany, for the duration of World War II. Upon his return to Holland he found his psychic abilities too distracting for him to follow a normal occupation, and he began to appear on stage and television shows, demonstrating feats of **ESP**. In 1947 he began work as a psychic detective, his fame being derived from his abilities in tracing missing persons and objects and identifying criminals. While having some success, he also had his notable failures. For example, when he was brought in to assist the police in tracing the Boston Strangler, his psychic description had no relevance to Albert DeSalvo, who confessed to the crimes. Hurkos cooperated with police departments throughout Europe and the United States.

Hurkos was a controversial psychic. He promoted himself and his successes. He was brought to the United States in 1965 by **Andrija Puharich,** who tested his abilities over a two-and-a-half-year period. He was praised by police in New Jersey for his assistance in solving a murder case. However, various parapsychologists had different experiences with him. Tests by **Charles T. Tart** were negative, and Hurkos refused the invitations of **J. B. Rhine** to be tested at Duke University.

Hurkos died in Los Angeles, California, on May 25, 1988.

Sources:

Berger, Arthur S., and Joyce Berger. *The Encyclopedia of Parapsychology and Psychical Research.* New York: Paragon House, 1991.

Browning, Norma Lee. *The Psychic World of Peter Hurkos.* Garden City, N.Y.: Doubleday, 1970.

Hoebens, Piet Hein. "The Mystery Men From Holland, I: Peter Hurkos' Dutch Cases." *Zetetic Scholar* 8 (July 1981).

Hurkos, Peter. *Psychic: The Story of Peter Hurkos.* London: Arthur Barker, 1961.

Lyons, Arthur, and Marcello Truzzi. *The Blue Sense: Psychic Detective and Crime.* New York: Mysterious Press, 1991.

Puharich, Andrija. *Beyond Telepathy.* Garden City, N.Y.: Doubleday, 1962.

Hurley, George Willie (1884–1943)

George Willie Hurley, the founder of Universal Hagar's Spiritual Church, a prominent Spiritual denomination functioning in the African American community, was born in rural Georgia near the town of Reynolds on February 17, 1884. He was raised as a Baptist and as a young man became a preacher, though he soon switched his affiliation to Methodist. In 1919 he moved to Detroit and soon affiliated with the Triumph the Church and Kingdom of God in Christ, a holiness church functioning primarily within the African American community. Hurley became the Prince of the State of Michigan.

His life was changed by a visit to a Spiritualist church. He was converted and he soon resigned his position and became a minister for an independent Spiritual congregation. Shortly thereafter, in 1923, he had a vision of a brown-skinned damsel who was transformed into an eagle. He interpreted the vision as a prophecy concerning a church he was to found. Thus on September 23, 1923, he founded Universal Hagar's Spiritual Church. He opened the church's School of Mediumship and Psychology the next year.

Along with his traditional Spiritualist ideals, Hurley taught a form of black Judaism. He believed that blacks were God's original Hebrew people and that the mark of Cain (God's curse) was the pale skin of white people. Hurley also suggested that he was the bearer of God's spirit on earth for the emerging **Aquarian Age,** just as Jesus was the spirit bearer for the Piscean Age, and Moses and Adam had been for prior astrological ages. He believed that the Aquarian Age had begun with the signing of the armistice following World War I, that it would last 7,000 years, and that it would see the end of Protestantism, segregation, and injustice.

Hurley died on June 23, 1943. He was succeeded by his wife, who led the church until her death in 1960.

Sources:

Baer, Hans A. *The Black Spiritual Movement: A Religious Response to Racism.* Knoxville, Tenn.: University of Tennessee Press, 1984.

Husk, Cecil (1847–1920)

British professional singer and member of the Carl Rosa Opera Company. Because of failing eyesight, Husk abandoned his vocation and—having been strongly psychic from early childhood—replaced it with professional mediumship.

Husk's **materialization** séances began about 1875 and were well known for the number and varied nature of the phenomena. **"John King"** was claimed as his chief control and had five subordinates: "Uncle," "Christopher," "Ebenezer," "Tom Hall," and "Joey" (the latter apparently the same control as manifesting through medium **William Eglinton**). Their voices, according to **Florence Marryat,** were heard as soon as the medium entered the **cabinet.** The subordinates prepared the manifestations for "John King."

One of "King's" favorite phenomena was the demonstration of **matter passing through matter.** The threading of chairs or iron rings on the medium's arms while the sitters held his hands was a frequently observed manifestation.

One experiment was carried out by George Wyld of Edinburgh and is described in his book *Theosophy, or Spiritual Dynamics and the Divine and Miraculous Man* (1884). For four years, Wyld had carried with him a specially made oval-shaped iron ring of five to six inches in diameter. Wyld hoped that it would be placed on his arm or on a medium's while he held the medium's hand. The size of the ring did not allow its passage over the hand. Wyld's wish was finally satisfied by Cecil Husk in 1884. While Wyld held the left hand of the medium, the ring was taken from his right; the medium cried out in pain, and when the light was turned on it was found on Husk's left wrist. An hour later it fell onto the floor.

Encouraged by this success, Wyld had a smaller ring made. This was also put on Husk's wrist while his hand was held by a friend. The ring was identified by microscopic markings. The **Society for Psychical Research** examined the ring and undertook to force it off if the medium permitted himself to be chloroformed. When he refused they brought the verdict: "We cannot infer that it is impossible that the ring should have come into the position in which we found it by known natural means." This verdict was based on experiments conducted on three other men by etherizing them and compressing their hands with metallic tape. The ring could not be passed over. Still the investigators concluded that they might have been successful in the case of Husk.

In 1890, through Cecil Husk's mediumship, **Stanley de Brath** made his first acquaintance with psychic phenomena. During the following year, at a public séance with about 20 sitters, Husk was exposed. In the light of an electric tie-pin he was seen leaning over the table and illuminating his face with a phosphorized slate. The "spirit drapery" that enveloped his head did not disappear. The attempt at an apology by Spiritualists who suggested that a case of **transfiguration** was taking place and that the drapery was apported instead of being materialized proved unacceptable.

In an article in the July 1906 issue of the *Annals of Psychic Science,* Henry A. Fotherby describes an interesting materialization séance with Husk in which the phantasms appeared to develop from a sort of phosphorescent vapor in the air, dotted all over with countless minute points of bright light, like little glow lamps. They were rendered visible by luminous slates that rose by themselves from the table and cast a weird bluish light on the phantom faces.

Gambier Bolton recounted an instance when, in his own house in the presence of 14 investigators, the medium, while tightly held, was levitated in his chair onto the top of the table. When Admiral Usborne Moore sat in an initial séance with Husk in 1904 a zither rose from the table and soared above the circle. Its movements could be seen by the phosphorescent spots on its underside. After two or three swirls it dashed onto the floor and apparently went through, for faint music could be heard from underneath.

In the light of illuminated cards Moore witnessed the materialization of about 15 spirits. He later recounted that the faces were about two-thirds life size. "John King" always spoke in an extremely loud voice. This was not exceptional. When a sitter asked the control "Uncle," "Are you using the medium's throat?" the answer came in a bellowing voice close to him: "Do you think that this is the medium's throat? If so, he must have a long neck." The voices spoke in many languages. The singing—

tenor, bass, and all the shades between—went on in astonishing volume even when Husk had a cold.

Moore sat more than 40 times with Husk and only once suspected **fraud.** On that occasion conditions were poor and he was by no means sure that his doubts were reasonable.

Sources:

Bolton, Gambier. *Psychic Force.* N.p., 1904.

Moore, Usborne. *Glimpses of the Next State.* London: Watts, 1911.

Hutin, Serge Roger Jean (1929–)

French author who wrote extensively on occult subjects. He was born on April 2, 1929, in Paris, and he studied at the Sorbonne. Hutin joined a variety of psychic and occult organizations, including the **Institut Métapsychique International,** Paris; the Association Francaise d'Etudes Métapsychiques, Paris; the Jacob Boehme Society, New York; the Swedenborg Institute, Basel; and the Rosicrucian Order.

He is most remembered for his work on the history of the occult, especially **alchemy, Freemasonry,** and the **Rosicrucians.** He also wrote a number of articles on parapsychological topics, especially retrocognition and **reincarnation.** Many were published in *Revue Métapsychique.*

Sources:

Caron, M., and Serge Hutin. *Les Alchimistes.* 1959. Translated as *The Alchemists.* New York: Grove Press, 1961.

Hutin, Serge. *Les Civilisations inconnues* (Unknown Civilizations). N.p., 1961.

———. *Les Disciples anglais de Jacob Boehme.* Paris; n.p., 1960.

———. *Les Francs-Macons* (The Freemasons). Paris: Editions du Seuil, 1960.

———. *Histoire des Rose-Croix* (History of the Rosicrucians). Paris: G. Nizet, 1955.

———. *Histoire mondiale des sociétés secrétes* (World History of Secret Societies). N.p., 1959.

———. *A History of Alchemy.* New York: Walker, 1963.

———. *Voyages vers Ailleurs* (Travels to Elsewhere). Paris: Fayard, 1962.

Huxley, Aldous (Leonard) (1894–1963)

Eminent British novelist whose brief volumes *The Doors of Perception* (1954) and *Heaven and Hell* (1956) pioneered discussions on the relationship between drug experience and mysticism. Huxley was born in Godalming, England, on July 27, 1894, grandson of a famous biologist. He was educated at Eton and at Balliol College, Oxford University (B.A., 1916). He suffered from defective vision and about 1935 began special eye-training exercises according to the system of W. H. Bates. These involved special visualization techniques. Huxley found a remarkable improvement in vision and describes his experiences in his book *The Art of Seeing* (1942).

He went on to write a number of critically hailed novels, short stories, and essays, including *Crome Yellow* (1921), *Antic Hay* (1923), *Point Counter Point* (1928), *Eyeless in Gaza* (1936), and *Ape and Essence* (1949). His prophetic novel *Brave New World* (1932) rose above all his writings as a particularly effective statement against modern forms of totalitarianism and of the threat posed to individual liberty by technology.

Through Huxley's early friendship with novelist D. H. Lawrence he began to be interested in mystical perception, and toward the end of his life this interest deepened and mellowed his later writings. After a period of living in southern France the Huxleys eventually settled in Los Angeles. After Huxley's wife Maria died in 1955, he married Laura Archera. Huxley himself died on November 22, 1963 (the same day President Kennedy was assassinated).

Huxley's developing interest in occult themes is indicated by his books *The Devils of Loudon* (1952), *The Doors of Perception* (1954), and *Heaven and Hell* (1956). Huxley had met occultist **Aleister Crowley** in Berlin in 1930 and through him was familiar with the effects of mescaline, but it was not until summer 1953 that Huxley took the four-tenths of a gram of mescaline that resulted in his own enthusiasm for the possibilities of **hallucinogens.** Huxley's discussions of consciousness-expanding drugs were drawn upon by such apostles of the psychedelic revolution as **Timothy Leary** and **Richard Alpert,** but Huxley himself opposed indiscriminate drug-taking. According to his brother, the famous biologist Sir Julian Huxley, he realized "that LSD would not bring liberation and understanding to everyone, and in his last book, *Island,* he points out its potential danger . . . though his warnings were not heeded."

Sources:

Huxley, Aldous. *Aldous Huxley's Hearst Essays.* New York: Garland Publishing, 1994.

———. *The Devils of Loudon.* London: Chatto & Windus, 1952.

———. *The Doors of Perception.* New York: Harper, 1954.

———. *Heaven and Hell.* New York: Harper, 1956.

———. *Island.* London: Chatto & Windus, 1962.

———. *Moksha: Writings on Psychedelics and the Visionary Experience.* New York: Stonehill, 1977.

Hwyl

A special characteristic of traditional Welsh revivalist preaching, indicating a surge of intense emotional and spiritual fervor released by chanting. *Hwyl* is also Welsh for "the sails of a ship," and a possible derivation is that as a breeze (*awel*) fills the sails and transports the vessel, so a strong current of emotion lifts the spiritual awareness of the preacher and his congregation.

Traditional Welsh revivalism is comparable with the fervor of Kentucky backwoods preaching. The congregation catches the spirit of the preacher and shouts deeply felt responses of *Bendigedig!* (Praise the Lord!) or *Diolch byth!* (Amen!). The hwyl is sometimes induced by chanting the attributes of God in a rhythmic sequence.

Hydesville

A little hamlet in New York State, in the township of Arcadia 30 miles east of Rochester, New York. Hydesville is considered the birthplace of nineteenth-century **Spiritualism.** There—in the house of John D. Fox, his wife Margaret, and their daughters—mysterious rappings first took place on March 31, 1848. The two **Fox sisters,** eventually joined by a third older sister living in Rochester, asked questions to which the raps responded intelligently. Various neighbors were called in and one displayed great ingenuity in reciting letters of the alphabet and eliciting responses by raps associated with letters. The raps were a forerunner of the technique of "spirit communication" in the development of Spiritualism.

In 1915 the old Fox house was purchased by B. F. Bartlett of Cambridge, Pennsylvania, who had it dismantled and removed to the **Lily Dale** Spiritualist camp in western New York. In 1955 the building was totally destroyed by fire.

During the week of December 4–7, 1927, an International Hydesville Memorial and Spiritualist Congress was held at Rochester, and it was resolved to erect a 25-foot monument to commemorate the advent of Spiritualism at Hydesville.

In 1948 a centennial celebration of the Hydesville events was held at Lily Dale.

Sources:

Cadwallader, M. E. *Hydesville in History.* Chicago: Progressive Thinker Publishing House, 1922.

The Centennial Memorial of Modern Spiritualism Records, 1848–1948. Lily Dale, N.Y.: National Spiritualist Association of the U.S.A., 1988.

Hydromancy

Divination by water, said by Natalis Comes (d. 1582) to have been the invention of Nereus, ancient god of the sea. However, the term covers various methods of divination, ranging from forms of **crystal gazing** (using a large or small pool of water) to what is now known as **radiesthesia**—using as a **pendulum** a wedding ring suspended on a thread and held over a glass of water.

Hydromancy is, in principal, the same thing as divination by the crystal or mirror, and in ancient times a natural basin of rock kept constantly full by a running stream was a favorite medium.

The Jesuit scholar M. A. Del Rio (1551–1608) described one example of hydromancy in which the sucessor of Emperor Andronicus Comnenus was revealed.

The letters *S.I.* showed upon the water and the prediction was verified, for, within the time named, Isaac Angelus had thrown Andronicus to be torn to pieces by the infuriated populace of Constantinople. Since the devil spells backward, S.I., when inverted, would fairly enough represent Isaac, according to all laws of magic.

Del Rio cited several kinds of hydromancy. In one, a ring was suspended by a thread in a vessel of water. When the vessel was shaken, a judgment was formed according to the strokes of the ring against its sides.

In a second method, three pebbles were thrown into standing water and observations were drawn from the circles they formed. A third method depended upon the agitations of the sea.

A fourth divination was taken from the color of water and certain figures appearing in it. There arose a method of divination by fountains, since these were the waters most frequently consulted. Among the most celebrated fountains for this purpose were those of Palicorus in Sicily, which invariably destroyed the criminal who ventured to adjure them falsely in testimony of his innocence. A full account of their use and virtue is given by the Roman philosopher Macrobius (ca. 345–423 C.E.).

Pausanias (second century C.E.) described a fountain near Epidaurus, dedicated to Ino. On her festival certain loaves were thrown into the fountain. It was a favorable omen to the applicant if these offerings were retained; unlucky if they were washed up again. So, also, Tiberius cast golden dice into the fountain of Apomus, near Padua, where they long remained as a proof of the imperial monster's good fortune in making the highest throw.

Several other instances of divining springs were collected by the antiquary J. J. Boissard (1528–1602), and Del Rio ascribed to them the origin of a custom of the ancient Germans, who threw their newborn children into the Rhine, with a conviction that if they were spurious they would sink, if legitimate they would swim. This custom also sounds like a precursor of the seventeenth-century custom of "swimming witches," perhaps related to the Anglo-Saxon law, created by King Athelstan, of trial by water.

In a fifth method of hydromancy, certain mysterious words were pronounced over a cupful of water and observations were made upon its spontaneously bubbling. In a sixth method, a drop of oil on water in a glass vessel furnished a kind of mirror upon which many wonderful objects were said to become visible.

Clemens Alexandrinus mentioned a seventh kind of hydromancy in which the women of Germany watched the sources, whirls, and courses of rivers with a view to prophetic interpretation.

In modern Italy, acording to Del Rio, diviners were still to be found who wrote the names of any three persons suspected of theft upon a like number of little balls, which they threw into the water to determine the guilty party.

E. W. Lane, in his work *An Account of the Manners and Customs of the Modern Egyptians* (1836), testifies to the success of divination by a pool of water as practiced in Egypt and Hindustan. Lane witnessed the performance of this type of sorcery. The magician began by writing forms of invocation to his familiar spirits on six slips of paper. A chafing dish with some live charcoal in it was then procured and a boy summoned who had not yet reached puberty.

When all was prepared, the sorcerer threw some incense and one of the strips of paper into the chafing dish; he then took the boy's right hand and drew a square with some mystical marks on the palm. In the center of the square he poured a little ink, which formed the magic mirror, and told the boy to look steadily into it without raising his head. In this mirror the boy declared that he saw, successively, a man sweeping, seven men with flags, an army pitching its tents, and the various officers of state attending on the sultan. The rest is told by Lane himself:

"The sorcerer now addressed himself to me, and asked me if I wished the boy to see any person who was absent or dead. I named Lord Nelson, of whom the boy had evidently never heard, for it was with much difficulty that he pronounced the name after several trials. The magician desired the boy to say to the Sultan: 'My master salutes thee and desires thee to bring Lord Nelson; bring him before my eyes that I may see him speedily.' The boy then said so, and almost immediately added, 'A messenger has gone and brought back a man dressed in a black (or rather, dark blue) suit of European clothes; the man has lost his left arm.' He then paused for a moment or two, and looking more intently and more closely into the ink, said 'No, he has not lost his left arm, but it is placed on his breast.'

"This correction made his description more striking than it had been without it; since Lord Nelson generally had his empty sleeve attached to the breast of his coat; but it was the right arm that he had lost. Without saying that I suspected the boy had made a mistake, I asked the magician whether the objects appeared in the ink as if actually before the eyes, or as if in a glass, which makes the right appear left. He answered that they appeared as in a mirror. This rendered the boy's description faultless.

"On another occasion Shakespeare was described with the most minute exactness, both as to person and dress, and I might add several other cases in which the same magician has excited astonishment in the sober minds of several Englishmen of my acquaintance."

Lane's account may be compared with a similar one given by A. W. Kinglake, the author of *Eöthen* (1844).

Sources:

Waite, Arthur Edward. *The Occult Sciences.* 1891. Reprint, Secaucus, N.J.: University Books, 1974.

Hyena

A fabled many-colored stone taken from the eye of the animal so called. Put under the tongue, the hyena stone was said to enable its possessor to foretell future events. It was also supposed to cure gout and intermittent fever.

Hyle

The primordial matter of the universe; also the name used in **Gnosticism** to denote one of the three degrees in the progress of spirits.

Hynek, J(oseph) Allen (1910–1986)

Prominent astrophysicist and authority on **UFOs.** Hynek was born on May 1, 1910, in Chicago, Illinois. He attended the University of Chicago, from which he received both his B.S. (1931) and Ph.D. degrees (1935). In 1942 he married Miriam Curtis.

Following graduation he took a position on the faculty at Ohio State University, where he remained until 1956. He worked for four years with the Smithsonian Astrophysics Observatory (1956–60) and then became the director of the Dearborn Observatory at Northwestern University, Evanston, Illinois, where he served until his retirement in 1980. In 1964 he also assumed duties as director of Northwestern University's Lindheimer Astronomical Research Center.

Hynek approached the UFO question as a skeptic but eventually became convinced that some of the reports could not be explained away by conventional means. During his early days at Northwestern, several graduate students, including Jacques Vallee, encouraged his interest in the question. In 1965 he was quoted as suggesting that UFOs might be extraterrestrial craft and calling for more scientific attention. When in 1966 Hynek was asked to speak on the subject of a flurry of UFO sightings in Michigan, he dismissed them as "swamp gas." The humor provoked by that incident led to his speaking out on the need for UFO studies at a congressional hearing several weeks later.

Several years later a civilian review committee was formed. The **Condon Report,** however, was trapped in controversy and internal bickering and Hynek was among a number of scholars who rejected its final negative report. In 1972, in *The UFO Experience,* Hynek charged the air force with laxity and incompetence in its research on UFOs, and the following year he led in the founding of the Center for UFO Studies. From that time forward he took the lead in championing the cause of UFO research and nurturing scientists and other researchers around the country. The center's work peaked during the late 1970s. In 1977 Hynek served as a technical consultant on the Steven Spielberg movie *Close Encounters of the Third Kind,* which drew its name from a term coined by Hynek.

Hynek went on to write several additional books prior to his move to Arizona in 1985. Believing he had found a major source of money for UFO research, in 1984 he resigned from the center in Evanston and early in 1985 established the International Center for UFO Research in Phoenix. The financial support he had hoped for, however, proved to be dedicated more to metaphysical than scientific study, and Hynek dropped his association. Before he could recover from his mistake, he was diagnosed as having a brain tumor. The tumor took his life on April 27, 1986.

He was survived by his wife Mimi, who had been a diligent and often unheralded editor and worker behind the scenes. The Center for UFO Studies was renamed the J. Allen Hynek Center for UFO Studies.

Hynek's own career awaits final evaluation when the UFO question is finally laid to rest. In 1973 he was interviewed by Ian Ridpath for the May 17 issue of the journal *New Scientist.* Hynek modestly reflected, "I've never launched any new theories, I've never made any outstanding discoveries." When Ridpath stated that Hynek would be remembered "not as an astronomer but as the man who made UFOs respectable," Hynek replied, ". . . I wouldn't mind it. It's always nice to add one stone to the total structure of science. If I can succeed in making the study of UFOs scientifically respectable and do something constructive in it, then I would think that would be a real contribution."

Sources:

Clark, Jerome. *UFOs in the 1980s.* Vol. 1 of *The UFO Encyclopedia.* Detroit: Apogee Books, 1990.

Hynek, J. Allen. *The Hynek UFO Report.* New York: Dell, 1977.

———. *The UFO Experience: A Scientific Inquiry.* Chicago: Henry Regnery, 1972.

Hynek, J. Allen, and Jacques Vallee. *The Edge of Reality: A Progress Report on Unidentified Flying Objects.* Chicago: Henry Regnery, 1975.

Jacobs, David M. "J. Allen Hynek and the UFO Phenomenon." *International UFO Reporter* 11, no. 3 (May/June 1986): 4–8, 23.

Hyperesthesia

An actual or apparent exaltation of the perceptive faculties, or superacuity of the normal senses, characteristic of the hypnotic state. It has been observed frequently in hysterics. They may feel a piece of wire on their hands as heavy as a bar of iron. The smallest suggestion—whether given by word, look, gesture, or even breathing or unconscious movement—is instantly seized upon and interpreted by the entranced subject, who for this reason is often called "sensitive."

The phenomenon of hyperesthesia, observed but wrongly interpreted by the early magnetists and mesmerists, was largely responsible for the so-called **clairvoyance, thought reading, community of sensation,** and other kindred phenomena. In its manifestation, hyperesthesia is often difficult to distinguish from **telepathy** or clairvoyance. Theoretically the dividing line is that hyperesthesia is a peripheral perception. Telepathy or clairvoyance is a central perception that does not reach us through the sensory organs. In practice it is difficult to decide whether the perception takes place through the sensory organs or not.

The realization of a relationship between suggestion and hyperesthesia by Alexandre Bertrand and **James Braid** brought **hypnotism** into the domain of scientific fact. The significance of hyperesthesia in connection with every form of psychic phenomena can hardly be overestimated. Nor is it found only in the trance state. It enters into the normal existence to an extent that is but imperfectly understood. Dreams, for instance, frequently reproduce impressions that have been recorded in some obscure stratum of consciousness, while much that we call intuition is made up of inferences subconsciously drawn from indications too subtle to reach the normal consciousness.

Hyperesthesia has been defined as "an actual or *apparent* exaltation of the preceptive faculties," modern scientists being unsure whether the senses are actually sharpened or not. Most probably the hyperesthetic perception is merely a normal perception that, through cerebral dissociation, operates in a free field. Very slight sense impressions may be recorded in the brain during normal consciousness but other impressions may inhibit them from reaching the conscious mind.

Gilbert Murray conducted telepathic experiments by placing himself in a different room from the sensitive and having a sentence spoken to him in a very low voice. The sensitive in the other room reproduced the sentence. The British Society for Psychical Research considered this a case of telepathy. **Charles Richet** considered it exceptional auditory hyperesthesia. Similarly, the sudden movements that save people from falling objects in the street may be attributed to subconscious hearing of an almost inaudible sound that generates and sends an urgent impulse to the motor centers.

Emile Boirac recorded interesting cases of tactile and visual hyperesthesia. His subject read with his fingertips in complete darkness. Being bandaged, his back turned to Boirac, but holding his elbow, he could also read if Boirac passed his own fingertips along the lines of a newspaper. It did not make the least difference if Boirac closed his eyes. (See also **Eyeless Sight.**) Another subject could tell the time from a watch wrapped up in a handkerchief. A Mme. M., before the Medical Society of Tamboff, told the colors of 30 flasks wrapped in paper and placed under a thick cloth. Further complicating the issue, Mme. M. could also taste by the sense of touch.

James Braid found the olfactory sense so acute in some hypnotic patients that by the smell of a glove they could unhesitatingly and unerringly detect its owner in a large company. It is questionable whether auditory hyperesthesia could explain the astounding phonic imitations he observed, such as patients repeating accurately what was spoken in any language, or singing correctly in a language they had never heard before. Braid noted,

"A patient of mine who, when awake, knew not the grammar even of her own language, and who had very little knowledge of music, was enabled to follow Mlle. Jenny Lind correctly in songs in different languages, giving both words and music so correctly and simultaneously with Jenny Lind, that two parties in the room could not for some time imagine that there were two voices, so perfectly did they accord, both in musical tone and vocal pronunciation of Swiss, German, and Italian songs."

Hypnagogic State

A condition between waking and sleeping characterized by illusions of vision or sound. These appear to have been first noted by J. G. F. Baillarger (1809–1890) in France and W. Griesinger (1817–1868) in Germany about 1845. They were studied by the scholar and antiquary Alfred L. F. Maury, who gave them the name "illusions hypnagogiques." They are distinguished from "hypnopompic visions," which appear at the moment when sleep recedes and momentarily persist into waking life. Both illusions are related to the faculty of dreaming. Some hypnagogic visions have been noted as the precursor to **out-of-the-body travel** or **astral projection.**

Sources:

Monroe, Robert A. *Journeys Out of the Body.* Garden City, N.Y.: Doubleday, 1971.

Muldoon, Sylvan, and Hereward Carrington. *The Projection of the Astral Body.* London: Rider, 1929.

Tart, Charles T. *Altered States of Consciousness.* Garden City, N.Y.: Anchor/Doubleday, 1972.

White, John, ed. *The Highest State of Consciousness.* Garden City, N.Y.: Anchor/Doubleday, 1972.

Hypno-Art

Term used by professional artist Curtis Watkins to denote his artwork done under **hypnosis.** He first began drawing under hypnosis in 1971 while working at a commercial art studio in Ann Arbor, Michigan. He had earlier learned self-hypnosis as an aid to relaxation. After using self-hypnosis to make the most of a short coffee break, Watkins was astonished to find that he had made a drawing without conscious effort.

Since then Watkins has experimented widely in producing art while under hypnosis. He found that this kind of art is quite unlike his normal conscious production. He established a Hypno-Art Research Center and Studio at 519 S. Michigan Ave., Howell, Michigan 48843. Watkins's experiments in hypno-art make interesting comparison with the **automatic drawing and painting** reportedly produced by Spiritualist mediums.

Hypnotism

A peculiar altered state of consciousness distinguished by certain marked symptoms, the most prominent and invariable of which are the absence of continuous alpha waves on the electroencephograph, hypersuggestibility in the subject, a concentration of attention on a single stimulus, and a feeling of "at oneness" with the stimulus. Hypnotic states may be induced by various techniques applied to oneself or by another.

The hypnotic state may be induced in a very large percentage of normal individuals, or may occur spontaneously. It is recognized as having an affinity with normal sleep, and likewise with a variety of trance-like conditions, among which may be mentioned **somnambulism, ecstasy,** and the trances of Hindu yogis and **fakirs,** and various tribal shamans. In fact, in one form or another, hypnosis has been known in practically all countries and periods of history.

Hypnotism, once classed as an occult science, has gained, though only within comparatively recent years, a definite scientific status, and no mean place in legitimate medicine. Nevertheless its history is inextricably interwoven with occult practice, and even today much hypnotic phenomena is associated with the psychic and occult, so that a consideration of hypnotism remains a necessary component in any mature understanding of the occult world science of both our own time and the past.

The Early Magnetists

As far back as the sixteenth century, hypnotic phenomena were observed and studied by scientists, who attributed them to "magnetism," an effluence supposedly radiating from every object in the universe, in a greater or lesser degree, and through which objects might exercise a mutual influence on one another. From this doctrine was constructed the "sympathetic" system of medicine, by means of which the "magnetic effluence" of the planets, of the actual magnet, or of the physician was brought to bear upon the patient. **Paracelsus** is generally supposed to be the originator of the sympathetic system, as he was its most powerful exponent. Of the magnet he states,

"The magnet has long lain before all eyes, and no one has ever thought whether it was of any further use, or whether it possessed any other property, than that of attracting iron. The sordid doctors throw it in my face that I will not follow the ancients; but in what should I follow them? All that they have said of the magnet amounts to nothing. Lay that which I have said of it in the balance, and judge. Had I blindly followed others, and had I not myself made experiments, I should in like manner know nothing more than what every peasant sees—that it attracts iron. But a wise man must inquire for himself, and it is thus that I have discovered that the magnet, besides this obvious and to every man visible power, that of attracting iron, possesses another and concealed power."

That power, he believed, was of healing the sick. And there is no doubt that cures were actually effected by Paracelsus with the aid of the magnet, especially in cases of epilepsy and nervous affections. Yet the word "magnet" is most frequently used by Paracelsus and his followers in a figurative sense, to denote the *magnes microcosmi,* man himself, who was supposed to be a reproduction in miniature of the Earth, having, like it, his poles and magnetic properties. From the stars and planets, he taught, came a very subtle effluence that affected human intellect, while earthly substances radiated a grosser emanation that affected the body. The human Mumia (body of vitalism) especially was a "magnet" well suited for medical purposes, since it draws to itself the diseases and poisonous properties of other substances. The most effective Mumia, according to Paracelsus, was that of a criminal who had been hanged, and he suggests the manner of its application:

"If a person suffer from disease, either local or general, experiment with the following remedy. Take a magnet impregnated with Mumia, and combined with rich earth. In this earth sow some seeds that have a likeness to, or homogeneity with, the disease; then let this earth, well sifted and mixed with Mumia, be laid in an earthen vessel, and let the seeds committed to it be watered daily with a lotion in which the diseased limb or body has been washed. Thus will the disease be transplanted from the human body to the seeds which are in the earth. Having done this, transplant the seeds from the earthen vessel to the ground, and wait till they begin to flourish into herbs. As they increase, the disease will diminish, and when they have reached their mature growth, will altogether disappear."

The quaint but not altogether illogical idea of "weaponsalve"—anointing the weapon instead of the wound—was also used by Paracelsus, his theory being that part of the vital spirits clung to the weapon and exercised an ill effect on the vital spirits in the wound, which would not heal until the ointment was first been applied to the weapon. This also was an outcome of the magnetic theory.

Towards the end of the sixteenth century, Paracelsus' ideas were developed by **J. B. van Helmont,** a scientist of distinction and an energetic protagonist of magnetism. "Material nature," he writes, "draws her forms through constant magnetism from above, and implores for them the favour of heaven; and as heaven, in like manner, draws something invisible from below, there is established a free and mutual intercourse, and the whole is contained in an individual."

Van Helmont believed also in the power of the will to direct the subtle fluid. There was, he held, in all created things a magic or celestial power through which they were allied to heaven. This power or strength is greatest in the human soul, resides in a lesser degree in the body, and to some extent is present in the lower animals, plants, and inorganic matter. It is by reason of his superior endowment in this respect that humans are enabled to rule the other creatures, and to make use of inanimate objects for their own purposes. The power is strongest when one is asleep, for then the body is quiescent, and the soul most active and dominant, and for this reason dreams and prophetic visions are more common in sleep. He notes,

"The spirit is everywhere diffused, and the spirit is the medium of magnetism; not the spirits of heaven and of hell, but the spirit of man, which is concealed in him as the fire is concealed in the flint. The human will makes itself master of a portion of its spirit of life, which becomes a connecting property between the corporeal and the incorporeal, and diffuses itself like the light."

To this ethereal spirit he ascribed the visions seen by "the inner man" in ecstasy, and also those of the "outer man" and the lower animals. In proof of the mutual influence of living creatures he asserted that a human being could kill an animal merely by staring hard at it for a quarter of an hour.

That Van Helmont was not ignorant of the power of imagination is evident from many of his writings. A common needle, he declared, may by means of certain manipulations and the willpower and imagination of the operator, be made to possess magnetic properties. Herbs may become very powerful through the imagination of the person who gathers them. And he adds,

"I have hitherto avoided revealing the great secrets, that the strength lies concealed in man, merely through the suggestion and power of the imagination to work outwardly, and to impress this strength on others, which then continues of itself, and operates on the remotest subjects. Through this secret alone will all receive its true illumination—all that has hitherto been brought together laboriously of the ideal being out of the spirit—all that has been said of the magnetism of all things—of the strength of the human soul—of the magic of man, and of his dominion over the physical world."

Van Helmont also gave special importance to the stomach as the chief seat of the soul, and recounted an experience of his own in which, on touching some aconite with his tongue, he found all his senses transferred to his stomach. Several centuries later, seeing with the stomach was to become a favorite accomplishment of somnambules and cataleptic subjects.

A distinguished English magnetist was **Robert Fludd,** who wrote in the first part of the seventeenth century. Fludd was an exponent of the microcosmic theory and a believer in the magnetic influence. According to Fludd, not only were these emanations able to cure bodily diseases, but they also affected the moral sentiments, for if radiations from two individuals were flung back or distorted, negative magnetism, or antipathy resulted, whereas if the radiations from each person passed freely into those from the other, the result was positive magnetism, or sympathy. Examples of positive and negative magnetism were also to be found among the lower animals and among plants. Another magnetist of distinction was the Scottish physician William Maxwell, author of *De Medicina Magnetica* (1679), who is said to have anticipated much of Mesmer's doctrine. He declared that those who are familiar with the operation of the universal spirit can, through its agency, cure all diseases, at no matter what distance. He also suggested that the practice of magnetism, though very valuable in the hand of a well-disposed physician, is not without its dangers and is liable to many abuses.

The Healers Valentine Greatrakes and J. J. Gassner

While the theoretical branch of magnetism was thus receiving attention at the hands of the alchemical philosophers, the practical side was by no means neglected. There were, in the seventeenth and eighteenth centuries, a number of "divine healers," whose magic cures were without doubt the result of hypnotic suggestion.

Of these perhaps the best known and most successful were **Valentine Greatrakes,** an Irishman, and a Swabian priest named John Joseph Gassner. Greatrakes was born in 1628, and on reaching manhood served for some time in the Irish army, thereafter settling down on his estate in Waterford. In 1662 he had a dream in which it was revealed to him that he possessed **healing by touch,** a gift which could cure the **king's evil** (scrofula). The dream was repeated several times before he paid heed to it, but at length he experimented, his own wife being the first to be healed by him.

Many people who came to him from the surrounding country were cured when he laid his hands upon them. Later the impression came upon him strongly that he could cure other diseases besides the king's evil. News of his wonderful powers spread far and wide and patients came by the hundreds to seek his aid. Despite the fact that the bishop of the diocese forbade the exercise of these apparently magical powers, Greatrakes continued to heal the afflicted people who sought him. In 1666 he proceeded to London, and, though not invariably successful, he seems to have performed there a surprising number of cures, which were testified to by Robert Boyle, Sir William Smith, Andrew Marvell, and many other eminent people.

His method of healing was to stroke the affected part with his hand, thus (it was claimed) driving the disease into the limbs and so finally out of the body. Sometimes the treatment acted as though by magic, but if immediate relief was not obtained, the rubbing was continued. Only a very few cases were dismissed as incurable. Even epidemic diseases were healed by a touch. It was noted that during the treatment the patient's fingers and toes remained insensible to external stimuli, and frequently he or she showed every symptom of such a "magnetic crisis" as was afterward to become a special feature of mesmeric treatment.

Personally Greatrakes was a simple and pious gentleman, persuaded that his marvelous powers were a divinely-bestowed gift, and most anxious to make the best use of them.

The other healer mentioned earlier, J. J. Gassner (1727–1779), belongs to a somewhat later period—about the middle of the eighteenth century. He was a priest of Bludenz in Vorarlberg, Austria, where his many cures gained for him a wide celebrity. All diseases, according to him, were caused by evil spirits possessing the patient, and his mode of healing thus consisted of exorcising the demons.

Gassner, too, was a man of kindly disposition and piety, and made reference to the Scriptures in his healing operations. The ceremony of **exorcism** was a rather impressive one. Gassner sat at a table, the patient and spectators in front of him. A blue red-flowered cloak hung from his shoulders. The rest of his clothing was "clean, simple, and modest." On his left was a window, on his right, the crucifix. His fine personality, deep learning, and noble character inspired the faith of the patient and his friends and doubtless played no small part in his curative feats. Sometimes he made use of "magnetic" manipulations, stroking or rubbing the affected part, and driving the disease, after the manner of Greatrakes, into the limbs of the patient. He generally pronounced the formula of exorcism in Latin, with which language the demons seemed to show a perfect familiarity.

Not only could Gassner control sickness by these means, but the passions also were amenable to his treatment,

"Now anger is apparent, now patience, now joy, now sorrow, now hate, now love, now confusion, now reason—each carried to the highest pitch. Now this one is blind, now he sees, and again is deprived of sight, etc."

These curious results suggest what in the nineteenth century was termed "phreno-magnetism," where equally sudden changes of mood were produced by touching with the fingertips those parts of the subject's head which **phrenology** associated with the various emotions to be called forth.

Emanuel Swedenborg

Hitherto it will be seen that the rational and supernatural explanations of magnetism had run parallel with one another, the former most in favor with the philosophers, the latter with the general public. It was reserved for **Emanuel Swedenborg** (1688–1772), the Swedish philosopher and seer to unite the doctrine of magnetism with that of spirit agency—i.e., the belief in the action in the external world of the discarnate spirits of deceased human beings. That Swedenborg accepted some of the theories of the older magnetists is evident from some of his mystical writings, where, for example, he states,

"In order to comprehend the origin and progress of this influence [i.e., God's influence over man], we must first know that which proceeds from the Lord is the divine sphere which surrounds us, and fills the spiritual and natural world. All that proceeds from an object, and surrounds and clothes it, is called its sphere.

"As all that is spiritual knows neither time nor space, it therefore follows that the general sphere or the divine one has extended itself from the first moment of creation to the last. This divine emanation, which passed over from the spiritual to the natural, penetrates actively and rapidly through the whole created world, to the last grade of it, where it is yet to be found, and produces and maintains all that is animal, vegetable, and mineral. Man is continually surrounded by a sphere of his favorite propensities; these unite themselves to the natural sphere of his body, so that together they form one. The natural sphere surrounds every body of nature, and all the objects of the three kingdoms. Thus it allies itself to the spiritual world. This is the foundation of sympathy and antipathy, of union and separation, according to which there are amongst spirits presence and absence.

"The angel said to me that the sphere surrounded man more lightly on the back than on the breast, where it was thicker and stronger. This sphere of influence peculiar to man operates also in general and in particular around him by means of the will, the understanding, and the practice.

"The sphere proceeding from God, which surrounds man and constitutes his strength, while it thereby operates on his neighbour and on the whole creation, is a sphere of peace, and innocence; for the Lord is peace and innocence. Then only is man consequently able to make his influence effectual on his fellow man, when peace and innocence rule in his heart, and he himself is in union with heaven. This spiritual union is connected with the natural by a benevolent man through the touch and the laying on of hands; by which the influence of the inner man is quickened, prepared, and imparted. The body communicates with others which are about it through the body, and the spiritual influence diffuses itself chiefly through the hands, because these are the most outward or *ultimum* of man; and through him, as in the whole of nature, the first is contained in the last, as the cause in the effect. The whole soul and the whole body are contained in the hands as a medium of influence."

Mesmerism or Animal Magnetism

In the latter half of the eighteenth century, a new era was inaugurated in connection with the doctrine of a magnetic fluid, due in large measure to the works of **Franz Anton Mesmer,** the physician from whose name **mesmerism** was taken. Mesmer was born at Wiel, near Lake Constance, in 1733, and studied medicine at the University of Vienna, taking his doctor's degree in 1766. In the same year he published his first work, *De Planetarum Influxu* (The Influence of Planets on the Human Body). Although he claimed to have thereby discovered the existence of a "universal fluid," to which he gave the name of *magnétisme animal,* there is no doubt that his doctrine was in many respects identical to that of the older magnetists mentioned above.

The idea of the universal fluid was suggested to him in the first place by his observation of the stars, which led him to believe the celestial bodies exercised a mutual influence on each other and on the Earth. This he identified with magnetism, and it was but a step (and a step which had already been taken by the early magnetists) to extend this influence to the human body and all other objects, and to apply it to the science of medicine.

In 1776, Mesmer met with J. J. Gassner, the Swabian priest. Mesmer set aside the supernatural explanation offered by the healer himself, and declared that the cures and severe crises that followed his manipulations were attributable to nothing but magnetism. Nevertheless this encounter gave a new trend to his ideas. Hitherto he himself had employed an actual magnet in order to cure the sick, but seeing that Gassner dispensed with that aid, he was led to consider whether the power might not reside in a still greater degree in the human body. Mesmer's first cure was performed on an epileptic patient by means of magnets, but the honor of it was disputed by a Jesuit, Fr. Hell (a professor of astronomy at the University of Vienna), who had supplied the magnetic plates, and who claimed to have discovered the principles on which the physician worked.

Thereafter for a few years Mesmer practiced in various European cities and strove to obtain recognition for his theories, but without success. In 1778, however, he went to Paris, and there attained an immediate and triumphant success in the fashionable world, although the learned bodies still refused to have anything to say to him.

Aristocratic patients flocked in hundreds to Mesmer's consulting rooms, which were hung with mirrors, it being one of the physician's theories that mirrors augmented the magnetic fluid. He himself wore, it was said, a shirt of leather lined with silk, to prevent the escape of fluid, while magnets were hung about his person to increase his natural supply of magnetism. The patients were seated round a *baquet,* or magnetic tub, a description of which was left by Seifert, one of Mesmer's biographers:

"The receptacle was a large pan, tub, or pool of water, filled with various magnetic substances, such as water, sand, stone, glass bottles (filled with magnetic water), etc. It was a focus within which the magnetism was concentrated, and out of which proceeded a number of conductors. These being bent pointed iron wands, one end was retained in the *baquet,* whilst the other was connected with the patient and applied to the seat of the disease. This arrangement might be made use of by any number of persons seated round the *baquet,* and thus a fountain, or any receptacle in a garden, as in a room, would answer for the purpose desired."

For the establishment of a school of *animal magnetism* Mesmer was offered 20,000 livres by the French government, with an annual sum of 10,000 livres for its upkeep; he refused. Later, however, the sum of 340,000 livres was subscribed by prospective pupils and handed over to him.

One of Mesmer's earliest and most distinguished disciples was Charles D'Eslon, a prominent physician, who laid the doctrines of animal magnetism before the Faculty of Medicine in 1780. Consideration of Mesmer's theories was, however, indignantly refused, and D'Eslon was warned to rid himself of such a dangerous doctrine.

Another disciple of Mesmer who attained distinction in magnetic practice was the Marquis de Puységur, who was the first to observe and describe the state of induced somnambulism, now well known as the hypnotic trance.

Puységur's ideas on the subject began to supersede those of Mesmer, and he gathered about him a distinguished body of adherents, among them the celebrated Lavater. Indeed, his recognition that the symptoms attending the magnetic sleep were resultant from it was a step of no small importance in the history of mesmerism.

In 1784, a commission was appointed by the French government to enquire into the magnetic phenomena. For some reason or another its members chose to investigate the experiments of D'Eslon, rather than those of Mesmer himself. The commissioners, including Benjamin Franklin, Antoine Lavoisier, and Jean Bailly, observed the peculiar crises attending the treatment, and the *rapport* between patient and physician, but decided that imagination could produce all the effects, and that there was no evidence whatever for a magnetic fluid. The report, edited by Bailly, offers a description of the crisis,

"The sick persons, arranged in great numbers, and in several rows around the *baquet* (bath), received the magnetism by means of the iron rods, which conveyed it to them from the *baquet* by the cords wound round their bodies, by the thumb which connected them with their neighbours, and by the sounds of a pianoforte, or an agreeable voice, diffusing magnetism in the air.

"The patients were also directly magnetised by means of the finger and wand of the magnetiser, moved slowly before their faces, above or behind their heads, or on the diseased parts.

"The magnetiser acts also by fixing his eyes on the subjects; by the application of his hands on the region of the solar plexus; an application which sometimes continues for hours."

Meanwhile the patients present a very varied picture.

"Some are calm, tranquil, and experience no effect. Others cough and spit, feel pains, heat, or perspiration. Others, again, are convulsed.

"As soon as one begins to be convulsed, it is remarkable that others are immediately affected.

"The commissioners have observed some of these convulsions last more than three hours. They are often accompanied with expectorations of a violent character, often streaked with blood. The convulsions are marked with involuntary motions of the throat, limbs, and sometimes the whole body; by dimness of the eyes, shrieks, sobs, laughter, and the wildest hysteria. These states are often followed by languor and depression. The smallest noise appears to aggravate the symptoms, and often to occasion shudderings and terrible cries. It was noticeable that a sudden change in the air or time of the music had a great influence on the patients, and soothed or accelerated the convulsions, stimulating them to ecstasy, or moving them to floods of tears.

"Nothing is more astonishing than the spectacle of these convulsions.

"One who has not seen them can form no idea of them. The spectator is as much astonished at the profound repose of one portion of the patients as at the agitation of the rest.

"Some of the patients may be seen rushing towards each other with open arms, and manifesting every symptom of attachment and affection.

"All are under the power of the magnetizer; it matters not what state of drowsiness they may be in, the sound of his voice, a look, a motion of his hands, spasmodically affects them."

Although Mesmer, Puységur, and their followers continued to practice magnetic treatment, the report of the royal commission had the effect of quenching public interest in the subject, although from time to time a spasmodic interest in it was shown by scientists. M. de Jussieu, at about the time the commission presented its report, suggested that it would have done well to inquire into the reality of the alleged cures, and to endeavor to find a satisfactory explanation for the phenomena they had witnessed, while to remedy the deficiency he himself formulated a theory of "animal heat," an organic emanation that might be directed by the human will. Like Mesmer and the others, he believed in action at a distance, i.e., what is today termed **absent healing.**

Mesomeric practitioners formed themselves into Societies of Harmony until the political situation in France rendered their existence impossible. Early in the nineteenth century Pététin and **Jean Deleuze** published works on animal magnetism. But a new era was inaugurated with the publication in 1823 of Alexandre Bertrand's *Traité du Somnambulisme,* followed three years later by a treatise *Du Magnétisme Animal en France.*

From Animal Magnetism to Phreno-Magnetism and Hypnotism

Alexandre Bertrand was a young physician of Paris, and to him belongs the honor of having discovered the important part played by suggestion in the phenomena of the induced trance. He had observed the connection between the magnetic sleep, epidemic ecstasy, and spontaneous sleepwalking, and declared that all the cures and strange symptoms that had formerly been attributed to animal magnetism, animal electricity, and the like, resulted from the suggestions of the operator acting on the imagination of a patient whose suggestibility was greatly increased.

It is probable that had he lived longer (he died in 1831, at the age of 36), Bertrand would have gained a definite scientific standing for the facts of the induced trance, but as it was, the practitioners of animal magnetism still held to the theory of a "fluid" or force radiating from magnetizer to subject, while those who were unable to accept such a doctrine ignored the matter altogether, or treated it as vulgar **fraud.**

Nevertheless Bertrand's works and experiments revived the flagging interest of the public to such an extent that in 1831 a second French commission was appointed by the Royal Academy of Medicine. The report of this commission was not forthcoming until more than five years had elapsed, but when it was finally published, it contained a definite testimony to the genuineness of the magnetic phenomena, and especially of the somnambulic state, and declared that the commission was satisfied of the therapeutic value of "animal magnetism."

The report was certainly not of great scientific worth. The name of Bertrand was not even mentioned therein, nor his theory considered. On the other hand, a good deal of space was given to the more paranormal or "supernatural" phenomena, **clairvoyance,** action at a distance, and the prediction by somnambulic patients of crises in their maladies. This is the more excusable, however, since these ideas were almost universally associated with somnambulism. A **community of sensation** was held to be a feature of the trance state, as was also the transference of the senses to the stomach. Thought-transference was suggested by some of these earlier investigators, notably by J. P. F. Deleuze, who suggested that thoughts were conveyed from the brain of the operator to that of the subject through the medium of the subtle "magnetic fluid."

Meanwhile the Spiritualist theory, i.e., the activity of spirit entities, was becoming more and more frequently advanced to explain the "magnetic" phenomena, including both the legitimate trance phenomena and the multitude of supernormal phenomena that was supposed to follow the somnambulic state. This will doubtless account in part for the extraordinary animosity the medical profession showed toward animal magnetism as a therapeutic agency. Its anesthetic properties they ridiculed as fraud or imagination, notwithstanding that serious operations, even of the amputation of limbs, could be performed while the patient was in the magnetic sleep.

Thus **John Elliotson** was forced to resign his professorship at the University College Hospital, and **James Esdaile,** a surgeon who practiced at a government hospital at Calcutta, had to contend with the derision of his professional colleagues. Similar contemptuous treatment was dealt out to other medical men who were really pioneers of hypnotism, against whom nothing could be urged but their defense of mesmerism.

In 1841, **James Braid,** a British surgeon, arrived independently at the conclusions Bertrand had reached some 18 years earlier. Once more the theory of abnormal suggestibility was offered to explain the various phenomena of the so-called magnetic sleep, and once more it was largely ignored, alike by the world of science and by the public.

Braid's explanation was essentially that which is offered now. He placed the new science, which he called "hypnotism," on a level with other natural sciences, above the mass of medieval magic and superstition in which he had found it. Yet even Braid did not seem to have entirely separated the chaff from the grain, for he countenanced the practice of phreno-mesmerism, a combination of mesmerism and phrenology wherein the entranced patient whose head was touched by the operator's fingers exhibited every sign of the emotion or quality associated with the phrenological organ touched.

Braid asserted that a subject, entirely ignorant of the position of the phrenological organs, passed rapidly and accurately from one emotion to another, according to the portion of the scalp in contact with the hypnotist's fingers. His physiological explanation is a somewhat inadequate one, and we can only suppose that he was not fully appreciative of his own theory of suggestion.

In 1843, two periodicals dealing with magnetism appeared: the *Zoist,* edited by John Elliotson and a colleague, and the *Phreno-Magnet,* edited by Spencer T. Hall. The first, adopting a scientific tone, treated the subject mainly from a therapeutic point of view, while the latter was of a more popular character. Many of the adherents of both papers, and notably Elliotson himself, afterward became Spiritualists.

In 1845, an additional impetus was given to animal magnetism by the publication in that year of **Baron von Reichenbach**'s research. Reichenbach claimed to have discovered a new force, which he called **od,** odyle, or odylic force, and which could be seen in the form of flames by sensitives, i.e., psychics.

Reichenbach meticulously classified the indications of such sensitivity as a more acute form of normal human faculty.

In the human being these emanations might be seen to radiate from the fingertips, while they were also visible in animals and inanimate things. Different colors issued from the different poles of the magnet. Reichenbach experimented by putting his sensitives in a dark room with various objects—crystals, precious stones, magnets, minerals, plants, animals—when they could unerringly distinguish each object by the color and size of the flame visible to their clairvoyant eye. These emanations appeared so invariable and so permanent that an artist might paint them and, indeed, this was frequently done. Feelings of temperature, heat or cold, were also experienced in connection with the force.

Baron von Reichenbach's experiments were spread over a number of years, and were made with every appearance of scientific care and precision, so that their effect on the mesmerists of the time was very considerable. But notwithstanding the mass of dubious and occult phenomena which was associated with hypnotism at that time, there is no doubt that the induced trance, with its therapeutic and anesthetic value, would soon have come into its own had not two other circumstances occurred to thrust it into the background.

The first was the application of chloroform and ether to the purposes for which hypnotism had hitherto been used, a substitution which pleased the medical faculty greatly. Both work to induce sleep even in persons only lightly or totally unaffected by hypnotism. At about the same time, the introduction of the movement known as modern **Spiritualism** emphasized the occult associations of trance phenomena and drove many people from any study of anything closely tied to it.

Later Views of Hypnotism

But if the great body of medical and public opinion ignored the facts of hypnotism during the period following Braid's discovery, the subject did not fail to receive some attention from scientists in Europe, and from time to time investigators took upon themselves the task of inquiring into the phenomena. This was especially the case in France, where the study of mesmerism or hypnotism was most firmly entrenched and where it met with least opposition. In 1858, one Dr. Azam of Bordeaux investigated hypnotism from Briad's point of view, aided by a number of members of the Faculty of Paris. An account of his research was published in 1860, but cast no new light on the matter. Later the same set of facts was examined by E. Mesnet, M. Duval, and others. In 1875, the noted psychical researcher **Charles Richet** also studied artificial somnambulism.

It was, however, from the Bernheim and the Nancy school that the generally accepted modern view of hypnotism is taken. H. Bernheim was himself a disciple of A. A. Liébeault, who, working on independent lines, had reached the same conclusion as Bertrand and Braid and once more formulated the doctrine of suggestion. Bernheim's work *De la Suggestion,* published in 1884, embodied the theories of Liébeault as well as the result of Bernheim's own research.

According to this view, hypnotism is a purely psychological process, and is induced by mental influences. The "passes" of Mesmer and the magnetic philosophers, the elaborate preparations of the *baquet,* the strokings of Valentine Greatrakes, and all the multitudinous ceremonies with which the animal magnetists used to produce the artificial sleep were only of service in inducing a state of expectation in the patient, or in providing a soothing and monotonous, or violent, sensory stimulus. And so also the modern methods of inducing hypnosis—the fixation of the eyes, the contact of the operator's hand, the sound of his voice—are only effective through the medium of the subject's mentality.

Other investigators who played a large part in popularizing hypnotism were **J. M. Charcot,** of the Salpêtrière, Paris, a distinguished pathologist, and R. Heidenhain, professor of physiology at Breslau. The former taught that the hypnotic condition was essentially a morbid one, and allied to hysteria, a theory which, becoming widely circulated, exercised a somewhat detrimental effect on the practice of hypnotism for therapeutic purposes, until it was at length proved erroneous. As a result, prejudice lingered against the use of the induced hypnotic trance in medicine until relatively modern times.

Heidenhain laid stress on the physical operations to induce somnambulism, believing that thereby a peculiar state of the nervous system was brought about wherein the control of the higher nerve centers was temporarily removed, so that the suggestion of the operator was free to express itself automatically through the physical organism of the patient. The physiological theory also is somewhat misleading, nevertheless its exponents did good work in bringing the undoubted facts of hypnosis into prominence.

Besides these theories there was another to be met with chiefly in its native France—the old doctrine of a magnetic fluid. But it rapidly died out.

Among the symptoms which may safely, and without reference to the supernatural, be regarded as attendant on hypnotism are: the *rapport* between subject and operator, implicit obedience on the part of the former to the smallest suggestion (whether given verbally or by look, gesture, or any unconscious action), anesthesia, positive and negative hallucinations, the fulfillment of post-hypnotic promises, and control of organic processes and of muscles not ordinarily under voluntary control.

Other phenomena which have been allied from time to time with magnetism, mesmerism, or hypnotism and for which there is not the same scientific basis, are clairvoyance, telekinesis, transference of the senses from the ordinary sense organs to some other part of the body (usually the fingertips or the pit of the stomach), community of sensation, and the ability to commune with the dead.

The majority of these, like the remarkable phenomena of phreno-magnetism, can be directly traced to the effect of suggestion on the imagination of the patient. Ignorant as were the protagonists of mesmerism with regard to the great suggestibility of the magnetized subject, it is hardly surprising that they saw new and supernormal faculties and agencies at work during the trance state. To the same ignorance of the possibilities of suggestion and **hyperesthesia** may be referred the common belief that the hypnotizer can influence his subject by the power of his will alone, and secure obedience to commands which are only mentally expressed. At the same time it must be borne in mind that if belief in **telepathy** be accepted, there is a possibility that the operation of thought transference might be more freely carried out during hypnosis, and it is notable, in this respect, that the most fruitful of the telepathic experiments conducted by psychical researchers and others have been made with hypnotized percipients.

An Extraordinary Experiment

One of the most bizarre and dangerous experiments in hypnotic telepathy is related in M. Larelig's biography of the celebrated Belgium painter Antoine Joseph Wiertz (1806–1865) and also in the introductory and biographical note affixed to the *Catalogue Raisonné du Musée Wiertz,* by Dr. S. Watteau (1865). Wiertz was the hypnotic subject and a friend, a doctor, was the hypnotizer.

Wiertz had long been haunted by a desire to know whether thought persisted in a head severed from the trunk. His wish was the reason for the following experiment being undertaken, this being facilitated through his friendship with the prison doctor in Brussels and another outside practitioner. The latter had been for many years a hypnotic operator and had more than once put Wiertz into the hypnotic state, regarding him as an excellent subject.

About this time, the trial for a murder in the Place Saint-Géry had been causing a great sensation in Belgium and the painter had been following the proceedings closely. The trial ended in the condemnation of the accused. A plan was arranged and Wiertz, with the consent of the prison doctor, obtained permission to hide with his friend, Dr. D., under the guillotine, close to where the head of the condemned would roll into the basket.

In order to carry out more efficiently the scheme he had determined upon, the painter desired his hypnotizer to put him through a regular course of hypnotic suggestion, and when he was in the sleep state to command him to identify himself with various people and tell him to read their thoughts and penetrate into their psychical and mental states. An account appeared in *Le Progrés Spirite:*

"On the day of execution, ten minutes before the arrival of the condemned man, Wiertz, accompanied by his friend the physician with two witnesses, ensconced themselves underneath the guillotine, where they were entirely hidden from sight. The painter was then put to sleep, and told to identify himself with the criminal. He was to follow his thoughts and feel any sensations, which he was to express aloud. He was also 'suggested' to take special note of mental conditions during decapitation, so that when the head fell in the basket he could penetrate the brain and give an account of its last thoughts.

"Wiertz became entranced almost immediately, and the four friends soon understood by the sounds overhead that the executioner was conducting the condemned to the scaffold, and in another minute the guillotine would have done its work. The hypnotized Wiertz manifested extreme distress and begged to be demagnetized, as his sense of oppression was insupportable. It was too late, however—the knife fell.

"'What do you feel? What do you see?' asks the doctor. Wiertz writhes convulsively and replies, 'Lightning! A thunderbolt falls! It thinks; it sees!' 'Who thinks and sees?' 'The head. It suffers horribly. It thinks and feels but does not understand what has happened. It seeks its body and feels that the body must join it. It still waits for the supreme blow for death, but death does not come.'

"As Wiertz spoke, the witnesses saw the head which had fallen into the basket and lay looking at them horribly; its arteries still palpitating. It was only after some moments of suffering that apparently the guillotined head at last became aware that is was separated from its body.

"Weirtz became calmer and seemed exhausted, while the doctor resumed his questions. The painter answered: 'I fly through space like a top spinning through fire. But am I dead? Is all over? If only they would let me join my body again! Have pity! give it back to me and I can live again. I remember all. There are the judges in red robes. I hear the sentence. Oh! my wretched wife and children. I am abandoned. If only you would put my body to me, I should be with you once more. You refuse? All the same I love you, my poor babies. Miserable wretch that I am I have covered you with blood. When will this finish!—or is not a murderer condemned to eternal punishment?'

"As Wiertz spoke these words, the witnesses thought they detected the eyes of the decapitated head open wide with a look of unmistakable suffering and of beseeching.

"The painter continued his lamentations: 'No, such suffering cannot endure for ever; God is merciful. All that belongs to earth is fading away. I see in the distance a little light glittering like a diamond. I feel a calm stealing over me. What a good sleep I shall have! What joy!' These were the last words the painter spoke. He was still entranced, but no longer replied to the questions put by the doctor. They then approached the head and Dr. D. touched the forehead, the temples, and teeth and found they were cold. The head was dead."

In the Wiertz Gallery in Brussels are to be found three pictures of a guillotined head, presumably the outcome of this gruesome experiment.

Theory of Hypnotic Action

Among numerous explanations of the physiological conditions accompanying the hypnotic state there is one, the theory of cerebral dissociation, which was generally accepted by science, and which may be briefly outlined as follows. The brain is composed of innumerable groups of nerve cells, all more or less closely connected with each other by means of nervous links or paths of variable resistance. Excitement of any of these groups, whether by means of impressions received through the sense organs or by the communicated activity of other groups, will, if sufficiently intense, occasion the rise into consciousness of an idea.

In the normal waking state, the resistance of the nervous association-paths is fairly low, so that the activity is easily communicated from one neural group to another. Thus the main idea which reaches the upper stratum of consciousness is attended by a stream of other, subconscious ideas, which has the effect of checking the primary idea and preventing its complete dominance.

Now the abnormal dominance of one particular system of ideas—that suggested by the operator—together with the complete suppression of all rival systems, is the principal fact to be explained in hypnosis. To some extent the physiological process conditioning hypnosis suggests an analogy with normal sleep. When one composes oneself to sleep there is a lowering of cerebral excitement and a proportionate increase in the resistance of the neural links, and this is apparently what happens during hypnosis, the essential passivity of the subject raising the resistance of the association-paths.

But if normal sleep, unless some exciting cause be present, all the neural dispositions are at rest, whereas in the hypnotic state such a complete suspension of cerebral activities is not permitted, since the operator, by means of voice, gestures, and manipulations of the patient's limbs, keeps alive that set of impressions relating to himself. One neural disposition is thus isolated, so that any idea suggested by the operator is free to work itself out in action, without being submitted to the checks of the sub-activity of other ideas.

The alienation is less or more complete according to the degree of hypnotism, but a comparatively slight raising of resistance in the neural links suffices to secure the dominance of ideas suggested by the hypnotizer.

Hyperesthesia, mentioned so frequently in connection with the hypnotic state, really belongs to the doubtful class, since it has not yet been decided whether or not an actual sharpening or refining of the senses takes place. Alternatively it may be suggested that the accurate perception of very faint sense-impressions, which seems to furnish evidence for hyperesthesia, merely reclass the fact that the excitement conveyed through the sensory nerve operates with extraordinary force, being freed from the restriction of sub-excitement in adjacent neural groups and systems.

In putting forward this viewpoint it must be conceded that in normal life, very feeble sensory stimuli must act on nerve and brain just as they do in hypnosis, save that in the former case they are so stifled amid a multitude of similar impressions that they fail to reach consciousness. In any case the occasional abnormal sensitiveness of the subject to very slight sensory stimuli is a fact of hypnotism as well authenticated as anesthesia itself, and the term "hyperesthesia," if not entirely justified, may for want of a better term, be practically applied to the observed phenomenon.

The hypnotic state is not necessarily induced by a second person. "Spontaneous" hypnotism and "autohypnotization" are well known. Certain yogis, fakirs, and shamans can produce in themselves a state closely approximating hypnosis by a prolonged fixation of the eyes, and by other means. The mediumistic trance is also, as will be shown hereafter, a case in point.

Hypnotism and Spiritualism

The association of spirits and what is today called hypnotism was advocated by the magnetic philosophers of medieval times, and even earlier by astrologers and magi. It has been shown that at a very early date, phenomena of a distinctly hypnotic character were ascribed to the workings of spirit agencies, whether angelic or demonic, by a certain percentage of the observers. Thus Greatrakes and Gassner believed themselves to have been gifted with a divine power to heal diseases. Witchcraft, in which the force of hypnotic suggestion seems to have operated to a very large degree, was thought to result from the witches' traffic with the devil and his legions. Cases of ecstasy, catalepsy, and other trance states were given a spiritist significance, i.e., demons, angels, elementals, and so on, were supposed to speak through the lips of the possessed. Even in some cases the souls of deceased men and women were identified with these intelligences, although not generally until the time of Swedenborg.

Although the movement known as modern Spiritualism is properly dated from 1848, the year of the **Rochester rappings,** its roots lead directly to the animal magnetists. Additionally, Swedenborg, whose affinities with the magnetists have already been referred to, exercised a remarkable influence on the Spiritualist thought of America and Europe, and was also a precursor of that faith. Automatic phenomena were even then a feature of the magnetic trance, and clairvoyance, community of sensation, and telepathy were believed in generally, and regarded by many as evidences of spiritual communication.

In Germany, Professor Jung-Stilling, C. Römer, Dr. Werner, and the poet and physician **Justinus Kerner,** were among those who held opinions on these lines, the latter pursuing his investigations with a somnambule who became famous as the Seeress of Prevorst—**Frederica Hauffe.** Hauffe could apparently see and converse with the spirits of the deceased, and she gave evidence of prophetic vision and clairvoyance. Physical phenomena were witnessed in her presence, knockings, rattling of chains, movement of objects without contact, and, in short, such manifestations as were characteristic of a **poltergeist.** She was, moreover, the originator of a "primeval" language, which she declared was that spoken by the patriarchs. Hauffe, although only a somnambule or magnetic patient, possessed all the qualities later associated with successful Spiritualist mediums.

In England also there were many circumstances of a supernatural character associated with mesmerism. Dr. Elliotson, one of the best-known of English magnetists, became in time converted to a Spiritualist theory as offering an explanation of the clairvoyance and similar phenomena he thought he observed in his patients.

France, the headquarters of the rationalist school of magnetism, had indeed a good deal less to show of Spiritualist opinion. Nonetheless even in that country the latter doctrine made its appearance at intervals prior to 1848. J. P. F. Deleuze, a good scientist and an earnest protagonist of magnetism, who published his *Histoire Critique du Magnétisme Animal* in 1813, was said to have embraced the doctrines of Spiritualism before he died.

It was however, **Louis-Alphonse Cahagnet,** a man of humble origin who began to study induced somnambulism about the year 1845 and experimented with somnambules, who became one of the first French Spiritualists of distinction. So good was the evidence for spirit communication furnished by Cahagnet and his subjects that it remains among the most impressive the movement produced.

In the United States, the **La Roy Sunderland, Andrew Jackson Davis,** and others who became pillars of Spiritualism were first attracted to it through the study of magnetism. Elsewhere we find hypnotism and the consideration of the work of spirits identified with each other until 1848, when a definite split occurs, and the two go their separate ways. Even so, however, the separation is not quite complete. In the first place, the mediumistic trance is obviously a variant of spontaneous or self-induced hypnotism, while in the second, many of the most striking phenomena of the séance room have been matched time and again in the records of animal magnetism.

For instance, the diagnosis of disease and prescription of remedies dictated by the control to the "healing medium" have their prototype in the cures of Valentine Greatrakes, or of Mesmer and his disciples. Automatic phenomena—speaking in **tongues** and so forth—early formed a characteristic feature of the induced trance and kindred states.

Even some of the physical phenomena later associated with Spiritualism, **movement** without contact, **apports,** and **rappings,** were witnessed in connection with magnetism long before the movement known as modern Spiritualism was so much as thought of. In some instances, though not in all, it is possible to trace the operation of hypnotic suggestion in the automatic phenomena, just as we can perceive the result of fraud in many of the physical manifestations.

Hypnotism and Psychical Phenomena

In the 1890s, psychical researcher **Paul Joire** described the three classical states of hypnotism:

"*Lethargy,* the state of complete relaxation with variable amount of anesthesia, with neuro-muscular excitation as its fundamental characteristic. In this state the subject has the eyes closed and is generally only slightly open to suggestion.

"*Catalepsy,* the eyes are open, the subject is as though petrified in the position which he occupies. Anesthesia is complete, and there is no sign of intelligence. Immobility is characteristic of this state.

"*Somnambulism,* the condition of the eyes varies, the subject appears to sleep. Simple contact, or stroking along any limb is sufficient to render that limb rigid. Suggestibility is the main characteristic of this state. The somnambulistic state presents three degrees:

"1. Waking somnambulism, slight passivity with diminution of the will and augmentation of suggestibility.

"2. The second personality begins to take the place of the normal one. Torpor of consciousness and memory. Sensibility decreases.

"3. Complete anesthesia. Disappearance of consciousness and memory. Inclination to peculiar muscular rigidity."

It is very likely that the depth of hypnotic sleep may vary infinitely. Distinct trains of memory may correspond to each stage, presenting alternating personalities of a shallow type.

The means to induce the hypnotic state differ. In many cases simple suggestion will do, even from a distance; in others, passes and the close proximity of the hypnotizer will be necessary. Some subjects feel the old "mesmerizer" influence, some do not.

The implicit obedience to suggestion has great therapeutical and psychological significance. Bad habits may be improved, phobias, manias, criminal propensities, and diseases cured, inhibitions removed, pain banished, the ordinary working of defective senses restored, the ordinary senses vivified, intelligence and ability in professional pursuits increased, and new senses of perception developed.

Subconscious calculation discloses flashes of mathematical genius, and once the rapport is established, the possibility is open for the development of supernormal faculties. The subject may see clairvoyantly, give psychometric descriptions, see into the future, read the past, make spiritual excursions to distant places and hear and see events occurring there, and give correct medical diagnoses.

Eugèn Osty believed that the number of hypnotizable subjects was getting smaller and smaller, and in support of his contention, he refers in the *Revue Metapsychique* (November–December 1930) to the similar experiences of Berillon, Richet, and Emile Magnin. However, modern hypnotists have shown that there is no shortage of subjects and that a high percentage of ordinary individuals are susceptible to hypnosis.

The exact nature of the hypnotic trance is still somewhat unknown, although it has received additional attention as new instrumentation for measuring brain waves has been developed. Its relation to the mediumistic trance is of absorbing interest to spiritualists (though of miniscule concern to modern scientists). The medium's trance differs in that it tends to be voluntary and self-induced, although hypnotism, for the purpose of relieving the medium from the attendant physiological suffering, is sometimes employed to bring it about.

Julien Ochorowicz saved the medium **Stanislawa Tomczyk** much exhaustion by hypnotizing her. The **Didier brothers** were always accompanied by a magnetizer and the mediumship of Andrew Jackson Davis was initiated by hypnotic clairvoyance. **Juliette Bisson** facilitated the materialization phenomena of **Eva C.,** and Kathleen Goligher was hypnotized by **W. J. Crawford,** though we are now aware of the fraud inherent in Eva C.'s and Goligher's work.

The hypnotized subject has great powers of personation. But he or she does not claim, unless so suggested, communication with the dead. In the mediumistic trance such suggestion is already assumed, but works in a confined territory. Often, those whose appearance is yearned for do not communicate at all; many strangers come and go, and all the controls seem to exhibit a distinct personality far surpassing in variety the imitative efforts of any hypnotized subject. If they were subjective creations of the medium's mind, Spiritualists argue, they would not exhibit those special peculiarities by which the sitters establish their identity with their departed friends.

The hypnotic self does not normally exhibit such cunning as the personation of hundreds of individuals and the acquisition of facts deeply buried in the subconscious or totally unknown to the sitters, although there is evidence that the subconscious mind may sometimes invent plausible personalities, just like the waking consciousness of a novelist.

The hypnotic personality usually has an uncanny sense of time. Spirit controls, on the other hand, are generally very vague and uncertain on this point. Their messages are not exactly located in time, and are sometimes borne out by past or near future happenings.

William James made many attempts to see whether **Leonora Piper's** medium-trance had any community of nature with ordinary hypnotic trance. The first two attempts to hypnotize her failed but after the fifth attempt, he noted, she had become a pretty good hypnotic subject:

". . . as far as muscular phenomena and automatic imitations of speech and gesture go; but I could not affect her consciousness, or otherwise get her beyond this point. Her condition in this semi-hypnosis is very different from her medium-trance. The latter is characterized by great muscular unrest, even her ears moving vigorously in a way impossible to her in her waking state, but in hypnosis her muscular relaxation and weakness are extreme. She often makes several efforts to speak before her voice becomes audible; and to get a strong contraction of the hand, for example, express manipulation and suggestion must be practised. Her pupils contract in the medium-trance. Suggestions to the control that he should make her recollect after the medium-trance what she had been saying were accepted, but had no result. In the hypnotic trance such a suggestion will often make the patient remember all that has happened."

Hypnotic Regression

From time to time hypnotism has been used in an attempt to validate theories of **reincarnation.** A hypnotized subject is made to recall experiences that progressively regress to birth and then (allegedly) to memories of former births. An early experimenter in this technique was **Albert Rochas** in France.

In modern times, the hypnotist **Morey Bernstein** created a sensation with his book *The Search for Bridey Murphy* (1956) based on his experiences with the subject "Ruth Simmons" (Mrs. Virginia Tighe), who was alleged to have recovered memories of a previous life as an Irish girl named Bridey Murphy. Another modern experimenter is Denys Kelsey, who hypnotized his wife, novelist **Joan Grant.** Their book, *Many Lifetimes* (1969), presents Joan Grant's claimed memories of former lives. Many of these memories were given in full in the form of a series of novels by Grant.

Though permeated with methodological problems, which has led most people studying survival of death to abandon the technique, a few individual cases of hypnotic regression have been impressive. The attempt to regress people to hypothesized former lives remains a popular activity, and the literature on such attempts grows steadily.

Sources:

Ambrose, G., and G. Newbold. *A Handbook of Medical Hypnosis.* 4th ed. New York: Macmillan, 1980.

Barber, Theodore Zenophon. *Hypnosis: A Scientific Approach.* New York: Psychological Dimensions, 1976.

Bernheim, H. *Hypnosis and Suggestion in Psychotherapy: A Treatise on the Nature and Uses of Hypnotism.* London, 1888. Reprint, New Hyde Park, N.Y.: University Books, 1964.

Braid, James. *Neurypnology.* 1843. Reprinted as *Braid on Hypnotism: The Beginnings of Modern Hypnosis.* New York: Julian Press, 1960.

Brown, Slater. *The Heyday of Spiritualism.* New York: Hawthorn Books, 1970.

Cahagnet, L. Alphone. *The Celestial Telegraph.* London, 1850. Reprint, New York: Arno Press, 1976.

Crasilneck, Harold B. *Clinical Hypnosis: Principles and Applications.* Orlando: Grune & Stratton, 1985.

Deleuze, J. P. F. *Practical Instruction on Animal Magnetism.* New York, 1879.

Edmunds, Simeon. *Hypnotism and Psychic Phenomena.* Hollywood, Calif.: Wilshire, n.d.

Erskine, Alex. *A Hypnotist's Casebook.* London: Rider, 1932.

Esdaile, James. *Mesmerism in India.* 1850. Reprinted as *Hypnosis in Medicine and Surgery.* New York: Institute for Research in Hypnosis Publication Press, 1957.

Fahnestock, William B. *Statuvolism, or Artifical Somnambulism.* Chicago, 1871.

Frankau, Gilbert, ed. *Mesmerism by Doctor Mesmer (1779): Being the First Translation of Mesmer's Historic "Mémoire sur la découverte du Magnétisme Animal" to appear in English.* London: Macdonald, 1948.

Goldsmith, Margaret. *Franz Anton Mesmer: The History of an Idea.* London: Arthur Barker, 1934.

Greatrakes, Valentine. *A brief account of Mr. V. Greatrakes and divers of the strange cures by him performed, written by himself.* London, 1666.

Gregory, William. *Animal Magnetism or Mesmerism and its Phenomena.* London, 1884. Reprint, New York: Arno Press, 1975.

Grossi, Ralph. *Reliving Reincarnation Through Hypnosis.* Smithtown, N.Y.: Exposition Press, 1975.

Haddock, Joseph W. *Somnolism and Psycheisan: Of The Science of the Soul and The Phenomence of Nervation.* London, 1851. Reprint, New York: Arno Press, 1975.

Hall, James A. *Hypnosis: A Jungian Perspective.* New York: Guilford Press, 1989.

Hull, C. L. *Hypnosis and Suggestibility: An Experimental Approach.* New York: Century Psychology Service, 1933.

Milne, J. Bramwell. *Hypnotism: Its History, Practice, and Theory.* London, 1903.

Moll, Albert. *Hypnotism: Including a Study of the Chief Points of Psycho-Therapeutics and Occultism.* London: Walter Scott Publishing, 1909.

Ochorowicz, Julien. *De la Suggestion Mentale.* Paris, 1887.

Podmore, Frank. *Mesmerism and Christian Science.* London: Methuen, 1909.

Reichenbach, Karl von. *Letters on Od and Magnetism.* Translated by William Gregory. London: Hutchinson, 1928. Reprinted as *The Odic Force: Letters on Od and Magnetism.* New Hyde Park, N.Y.: University Books, 1968.

———. *Researches on Magnetism, Electricity, Heat, Light, Crystallizaton, and Chemical Attraction in their Relations to the Vital Force.* Translated by William Gregory. London, 1850. Reprint, New Hyde Park, N.Y.: University Books, 1974.

Rutter, J. O. N. *Human Electricity: The Means of Its Development.* London: Parker, 1854.

Smith, Susy. *ESP and Hypnosis.* New York: Macmillan, 1973.

Theories of Hypnosis: Current Models and Perspectives. New York: Guilford Press, 1991.

Tinterow, Maurice M. *Foundations of Hypnosis: From Mesmer to Freud.* Springfield, Ill.: Chas. C. Thomas, 1970.

Toksvig, Signe. *Emmanuel Swedenborg, Scientist and Mystic.* New Haven, Conn.: Yale University Press, 1948.

Wambach, Helen. *Reliving Past Lives: The Evidence Under Hypnosis.* New York: Harper & Row, 1978.

Hypocephalus

A disk of bronze or painted linen found under the heads of Greco-Roman mummies in Egypt. It is inscribed with magic formulas and divine figures, and its purpose was probably to secure warmth for the corpse.

Hyslop, George Hall (1892–1965)

American physician, neuropsychiatrist, and psychical researcher. He was born on December 20, 1892, in New York City. He studied at Indiana University (B.A., 1913; M.A. psychology, 1914) and Cornell University Medical College (M.D., 1919). He had a distinguished medical and psychiatric career and served as president of the New York Neurological Society (1955–56) and as chair of the section on neurology and psychiatry of the New York Academy of Medicine (1941–42).

Hyslop was the son of pioneer psychic researcher **James Hervey Hyslop.** He joined the board of the **American Society for Psychical Research** (ASPR) in 1921, the year after his father's death, and suffered through the society's disruption in the 1920s. He emerged at the end of the decade as one of the prime voices demanding the reestablishment of the high standards of research that had existed during his father's lifetime. In 1941, at the time of the merger of the **Boston Society for Psychical Research** back into the ASPR, he assumed the mantle of leadership of the organization and served as president for the next 21 years. He was also a member of the **Society for Psychical Research,** London, and the **Parapsychological Association.**

Sources:

Berger, Arthur S., and Joyce Berger. *The Encyclopedia of Parapsychology and Psychical Research.* New York: Paragon House, 1991.

Hyslop, George H. "The Biological Approach to Psychic Phenomena." *Journal* of the American Society for Psychical Research (April 1942).

———. "Certain Problems of Psychic Research." *Journal* of the American Society for Psychical Research (August 1930).

———. "An Instance of Apparent Spontaneous Telepathy." *Journal* of the American Society for Psychical Research (April 1948).

———. "James H. Hyslop: His Contribution to Psychical Research." *Journal* of the American Society for Psychical Research (October 1950).

———. "Report of the Questionnaire Committee." *Journal* of the American Society for Psychical Research (November 1930).

Pleasants, Helene, ed. *Biographical Dictionary of Parapsychology.* New York: Helix Press, 1964.

Hyslop, James Hervey (1854–1920)

Professor of logic and ethics and prominent psychical researcher. He was born on August 18, 1854, in Xenia, Ohio. He was educated at Wooster College, Ohio (B.A., 1877), the University of Leipzig (1882–84), and Johns Hopkins University (Ph.D., 1877). He was one of the first American psychologists to connect psychology with psychic phenomena. He joined the philosophy department at Columbia University as a professor in ethics and logic, during which time he became deeply involved with psychical research.

As early as 1888, in a skeptical frame of mind, he was brought for the first time into contact with the supernormal through the mediumship of **Leonora Piper.** Messages from his father and relatives poured through. Out of 205 incidents mentioned as of his sixteenth sitting, he was able to verify 152.

The personalities of the communicators were so impressive that after 12 sittings he publicly declared,

"I have been talking with my father, my brother, my uncles. Whatever supernormal powers we may be pleased to attibute to Mrs. Piper's secondary personalities, it would be difficult to make me believe that these secondary personalities could have thus completely reconstituted the mental personality of my dead relatives. To admit this would involve me in too many improbabilities. I prefer to believe that I have been talking to my dead relatives in person; it is simpler."

Early in the new century ill health forced him to retire from his teaching post. He used the occasion to found the **American Institute for Scientific Research** to stir interest and raise funds for psychical research. However, in 1905 **Richard Hodgson,** the research officer and real force in the **American Society for Psychical Research** (ASPR), died. The following year the ASPR was dissolved. Hyslop quickly revived it as a section of his institute. It soon absorbed and replaced the institute altogether.

Hyslop dominated, somewhat autocratically, the ASPR for the rest of his life. He assumed Hodgson's role as chief investigator of Piper's continuing mediumship. He issued the first *Journal* in January 1907. He recruited both **Hereward Carrington** and **Walter F. Prince** to assist in the work.

Hyslop became a significant propagandist of human **survival** of death. In his *Life After Death* (1918), for example, he forcefully states,

"I regard the existence of discarnate spirits as scientifically proved and I no longer refer to the skeptic as having any right to speak on the subject. Any man who does not accept the existence of discarnate spirits and the proof of it is either ignorant or a moral coward. I give him short shrift, and do not propose any longer to argue with him on the supposition that he knows anything about the subject."

Hyslop also contributed many ingenious theories to psychical literature. He made a deep study of multiple **personality** and of **obsession,** and came to the conclusion that in many cases it could be attributed to spirit **possession.** In his will he left money to found an institute for the treatment of obsession through the instrumentality of mediums. He died June 17, 1920, in Upper Montclair, New Jersey. The evidence of his own spirit return is discussed by his longtime secretary, Gertrude O. Tubby, in her book *James Hyslop X.—His Book* (1929).

Sources:

Berger, Arthur S., and Joyce Berger. *The Encyclopedia of Parapsychology and Psychical Research.* New York: Paragon House, 1991.

Hyslop, George H. "James H. Hyslop: His Contribution to Psychical Research." *Journal* of the American Society for Psychical Research (October 1950).

Hyslop, James H. *Borderland of Psychical Research.* London: G. P. Putnam's Sons, 1906.

———. *Contact with the Other World.* New York: Century, 1919.

———. *Enigmas of Psychical Research.* Boston: H. B. Turner, 1906.

———. *Life After Death: Problems of the Future Life and Its Nature.* New York: E. P. Dutton, 1918.

———. *Psychical Research and the Resurrection.* Boston: Small, Maynard, 1908.

———. *Psychical Research and Survival.* London: G. Bell and Sons, 1913.

———. *Science and a Future Life.* London: G. P. Putnam's Sons, 1906.

Knopf, A. Adolphus. *A Reminiscence of and a Promise to Professor James Hervey Hyslop.* New York: The Author, 1921.

Pleasants, Helene, ed. *Biographical Dictionary of Parapsychology.* New York: Helix Press, 1964.

Tubby, Gertrude. *James Hysop X—His Book.* York, Pa.: York Printing, 1929.

I

"I AM" Religious Activity

Theosophical religious movement that originated in the 1930s. It was founded by **Guy W. Ballard** (1878–1939) and **Edna W. Ballard** (1886–1971), who claimed to be the "accredited messengers" of the ascended masters of the **Great White Brotherhood.** In 1929 Guy Ballard visited Mt. Shasta, a volcano in northern California that had for several generations been the object of legends and mysterious stories, among them that it was hollow and the home to occult **adepts.** In the slope of the mountain, Ballard, as he later recounted the story, encountered the ascended master **Saint Germain.** Saint Germain supposedly assigned Ballard the task of initiating the Seventh Golden age, the permanent "I AM" age of eternal perfection on earth. The saint designated Ballard, his wife, and their son Donald as the only accredited messengers of the masters.

Staying near Mt. Shasta, Ballard wrote about his experiences in a series of letters to his wife. He returned to Chicago and they initiated the "I AM" Religious Activity and organized the Saint Germain Foundation and the Saint Germain Press. In 1934 and 1935 the press issued two initial volumes, *Unveiled Mysteries* and *The Magic Presence,* which describe Ballard's experiences with the masters. In 1934 Ballard held his first ten-day public class, in which he delivered messages for the masters by a process known today as **channeling,** though leaders of the movement reject that term. These messages were published in *The Voice of the "I AM"* beginning in 1936, and the most important were compiled into a set of books.

The "I AM" teachings build upon previous claimed contact with ascended masters by **Helena Petrovna Blavatsky.** Ballard claimed to have contacted not only the several masters who spoke to Blavatsky but also a host of additional exalted beings. By far the largest number of messages were from Saint Germain and the master Jesus.

Through Ballard the masters taught of the "I AM," the basic divine reality of the universe, God in action. Individualized, the "I AM" is the essence of each person, they said, and should be constantly invoked and activated. It is pictured as an entity residing above each person's head and surrounded by golden light and a rainbow of color. It is connected to the person by a shaft of white light. The "I AM" presence is invoked by use of decrees, affirmative commands that the "I AM" presence initiate action in the self and the world. Basic in the daily activity of an "I AM" student is the violet flame decree, in which a violet flame is pictured surrounding the person and purifying him spiritually.

The "I AM" movement has published a wide variety of decrees to be used for all life situations. Included are a set of decrees used for removing negative conditions from the individual's life or environment. These negative decrees have been occasionally misunderstood, and the movement has occasionally been accused of using them to curse someone, which the movement denies. The decrees picture the blasting away of negative energies in the world, and strict instructions are given to students not to decree against any person.

The "I AM" movement grew spectacularly during the 1930s but ran into significant problems shortly after Guy Ballard's death in 1939. Several former students began to organize against the movement, charging that its leaders were religious frauds. In 1942 Edna Ballard, Donald Ballard, and a number of leading students were charged with mail fraud. In the trial the prosecutor argued that Ballard had made up the religion and that he and other members did not believe it and operated the foundation purely as a fraudulent moneymaking scheme. Although the defendants were initially convicted, the convictions were eventually overturned in an important Supreme Court decision holding that one's religious faith could not be put on trial. Not until the early 1950s was the damage done by the initial indictments reversed.

Meanwhile Edna Ballard had assumed control of the movement, taking it out of the public spotlight. She refused to give interviews to outsiders, and through the next decades many supposed the movement had died out. It had actually expanded. As of the early 1980s there were more than three hundred "I AM" sanctuaries and centers in North America. The movement is now led by a board and several teachers appointed by the Ballards. Since Edna Ballard's death, no messages have been received from the masters.

The Saint Germain Foundation and Press are located at 1120 Stonehedge Dr., Schaumburg, IL 60194. A summer retreat center is located not far from Mt. Shasta, California. Every summer, members gather for various events, closing with the public presentation of a pageant on the life of Christ. The pageant tells the story of Jesus' life without mentioning the Crucifixion and emphasizes Christ's ascension.

Ending one's life on earth by ascending to the realm of the masters is a goal of "I AM" activity.

Sources:

Germain, Saint, through Guy W. Ballard. *The "I AM" Discourses.* Chicago: Saint Germain Press, 1935.

King, Godfre Ray [Guy W. Ballard]. *The Magic Presence.* Chicago: Saint Germain Press, 1934.

———. *Unveiled Mysteries.* Chicago: Saint Germain Press, 1935.

Melton, J. Gordon. *Encyclopedia of American Religions.* Detroit: Gale Research, 1992.

I Ching (Yi King or Y-Kim)

The ancient Chinese *Book of Changes,* attributed to the emperor Fo-Hi in 3468 B.C.E. It expounds a classical Chinese philosophy based on the dual cosmic principles of yin and yang and claims to elucidate the outcome of any given situation by a technique involving interpretation of 64 hexagrams, each composed of two groups of three lines. These lines are each either broken or solid.

Predicitions are traditionally ascertained by a detailed process of selecting sticks or yarrow stalks to indicate the appropriate hexagram and the interpretation associated with it. A bundle of 50 sticks is used. These should be kept wrapped in clean silk or cloth. When the I Ching is consulted, it is traditional to face south and incorporate the divination procedure into a ritual. Prostrations are made, then incense lighted and the sticks passed through the fumes. The question to be answered should be straightfoward, usually related to the favorable or unfavorable auguries of a given project. One of the 50 sticks is taken out and put on one side. The remaining 49 are bunched together then quickly divided into two heaps by the right hand. The inquirer then takes one stick from the right-hand pile and places it between the last two fingers of the left hand. He then pushes away four sticks at a time from the left-hand pile until only one, two, three, or four remain. This remainder is placed between the next two fingers of the left hand. Next, four sticks at a time are pushed away from the right-hand pile until only one, two, three, or four remain. The left hand should now contain either five or nine sticks, thus: 1 + 1 + 3; 1 + 2 + 2; 1 + 3 + 1; or 1 + 4 + 4. These sticks are laid in the *second* heap. The process is then repeated with the remaining sticks from the first heap, which are pushed together with the right hand and then divided as previously. This will yield a total of either four or eight sticks, thus: 1 + 1 + 2; 1 + 2 + 1; 1 + 3 + 4; or 1 + 4 + 3. These four or eight sticks are then placed on the first pile, but kept slightly apart from those already there.

The process is repeated with sticks remaining on the first heap, resulting in either four or eight, as in the second phase. After these three counts, the second heap will contain (5 or 9) + (4 or 8) + (4 or 8). These three figures indicate the bottom line of the appropriate hexagram (i.e., unbroken or broken), and whether "moving" or not. The 49 sticks are then bunched together again and the whole process repeated to discover the second line from the bottom of the hexagram, and so on until the six lines have been found. A table of interpretations of the upper and lower trigrams can then be consulted.

A quicker system of divining the appropriate hexagrams involves tossing six coins; a set of I Ching playing cards has been marketed in the United States, permitting an even more rapid divination.

There are several translations currently available, and it is advisable to study more than one, because the interpretations of the ancient Chinese concepts and symbols sometimes vary. For parallels between the I Ching and Western occultism, see **Y-Kim, Book of.**

Sources:

Baynes, C. F., and R. Wilhelm, trans. *The I Ching or Book of Changes.* Princeton, N.J.: Princeton University Press, 1967.

Blofeld, John, trans. *I Ching: The Book of Changes.* New York: E. P. Dutton, 1968.

Legge, James, trans. *I Ching: Book of Changes.* Edited by Ch'u Chai and Winberg Chai. New Hyde Park, N.Y.: University Books, 1964. Reprint, New York: Causeway Books, 1973.

Liu, Da. *I Ching Coin Prediction.* New York: Harper & Row, 1975.

Reifler, Sam. *I Ching: A New Interpretation for Modern Times.* New York: Bantam, 1974.

Schoenholtz, Larry. *New Directions in the I Ching: The Yellow River Legacy.* New Hyde Park, N.Y.: University Books, 1975.

Wincup, Gregory. *Rediscovering the I Ching.* Garden City, N.Y.: Doubleday, 1986.

IAC See **Institute for Anomalistic Criminology**

IAM See **International Association of Metaphysicians**

IANDS See **International Association for Near-Death Studies**

Iao (or **I-ha-ho**)

A mystic emblem said by Clement of Alexandria (ca. 150–ca. 213 C.E.) to have been worn by the initiates of the mysteries of Serapis. It was said to embody the symbols of the two generative principles, and is thus similar to **aum** in India. Serapis was an Egyptian divinity who, with Isis, supplanted Osiris and Apis and acquired their attributes. As a healing divinity, Serapis was a rival of Aesculapius in Rome and in vogue in the Greek cult of Asklepios at Pergamon and Alexandria.

IAPR See **International Association for Psychotropic Research**

IARP See **International Association for Religion and Parapsychology**

ICELAND

Icelandic interest in psychical research goes back many years to the founding of Salarrannsoknafelag Island, the Society for Psychical Research of Iceland in Reykjavik in 1918. The founder was Prof. Einar Hjöleifsson Kvaran (1859–1938), a well-known writer who edited *Morgunn,* a Spiritualist magazine. A prominent member was Prof. **Harald Nielsson** (d. 1928) of the University of Reykjavik, who spent five years investigating the phenomena of the medium **Indridi Indridason.**

Ichthyomancy

Divination by the inspection of the entrails of fish.

Icke, David (1952–)

British television presenter who was a familiar figure on television snooker (a form of pool) contests. Icke became a sensation when he suddenly turned visionary, promoting often bizarre channeled revelations that were featured in his books.

Born in Leicester, England, Icke's interest in sports began at an early age. He became a professional goalkeeper for the Coventry City soccer team and later for Hereford United. After his career was thwarted by arthritis, he eventually became a sports journalist and television presenter.

When his media career ended he was married, with two children. He worked for a time for a travel agency, becoming familiar with railway timetables. He was fascinated by steam trains and planned to write a history of the steam line on the Isle of Wight. He moved there in 1984 and championed the cause of the Isle of Wight Steam Railway. He was also active in other causes, notably the welfare of the handicapped. He organized a Special Olympics for children in 1987, which he persuaded BBC Television to film. Icke became the first president of the Isle of Wight Special Olympics Committee, and his associates recall his tremendous enthusiasm for that cause, which did not last. In his later visionary period he put forward the astonishing view that the mentally handicapped have brought their condition upon themselves by acts in former lives.

After his enthusiasm for steam train history and the mentally handicapped waned, Icke next entered Isle of Wight politics through the Liberal Party (since renamed Liberal Democrats), but suddenly dropped out, now converted to the cause of Green party politics. This conversion, which he claims changed his life, occurred after reading the Green party's manifesto. This new cause is documented in his book *It Doesn't Have To Be Like This* (1990). He also championed the Green cause on television programs.

In 1990, while Icke was seeking relief for his arthritis from a medium and spiritual healer, the medium channeled a message from an entity claiming to be Chinese and to have died 800 years earlier, which stated that Icke "is a healer who is here to heal the earth, and he will be world-famous." Through another channeler, Deborah Shaw (since known as Mari Schawaun), he received messages from "master souls and extraterrestrials" named Attarre and Rakorczy claiming that the Isle of Wight was a center point for life forces and ley lines (ancient straight tracks on the ground) from all over the world, that Earth was in danger of imminent destruction through geological upheavals, and that the Christian church had perverted Christ's teachings by hiding the realities of karmic **reincarnation.**

In his book *The Truth Vibrations* (1991), Icke proclaimed himself the Son of God, destined to help remedy the imbalance of Earth's energies and ensure the survival of the planet. The book was disastrous to his television career, which rapidly came to an end, and Icke was widely ridiculed for his bizarre and outlandish beliefs. In a later book, *The Robots Rebellion* (1994), Icke claimed that the controversy and criticism had served a valuable purpose in giving him a platform from which to put forward his views to a wider public.

Identity

Establishing the identity of spirit communicators has been a difficult problem for psychical researchers. Nineteenth-century Russian Spiritualist **A. N. Aksakof** conceded, "Absolute proof of spirit identity is impossible to obtain; we must be content with relative proof." Psychical researcher **Charles Richet** agreed, saying, "Subjective metapsychics will always be radically incapable of proving survival."

Sir Oliver Lodge suggested that the question of identity in spirit communication could be established (1) by gradually accumulated internal evidence based on thorough and meticulous records; (2) by **cross correspondences,** that is, the reception of unintelligible parts of one consistent and coherent message through different mediums; or (3) by information or criteria especially characteristic of the supposed communicating intelligence and, if possible, in some sense new to the world.

The role of the communicating spirit in a Spiritualist séance is somewhat complicated. The spirit acts like a prompter in the theater. The automatic script or trance speech delivered through the medium is seldom in his or her own hand or voice. The medium's organism acts like a freshly painted sieve; it tints whatever it lets through. Besides, **communication** is an art itself and has its own inherent difficulties. **Direct voice** séances, **materialization** in good light, lifelike personation of the departed, or the **transfiguration** of the medium, which afford more dramatic evidence with less opportunity for self-deception, are comparatively rare.

Many spirit entities claim to be ancient or historic personalities, and the problem of establishing the identity of such entities is almost impossible. Impersonation frequently occurs. According to the entity "Imperator," in a script of **Rev. William Stainton Moses,** "There is much insanity among lower spirits. The assumption of great names, when it is not the work of conscious deceivers, is the product of insanity. The spirit imagines itself to be some great one, fancies how he would act, and so projects his imaginings on the sphere of the medium's consciousness."

If the information claimed as proof of identity of famous personages is verifiable, it cannot be proved that such facts were not fraudulently gathered by the medium before the séance, that the information was inaccessible to the medium's subconscious mind, or that it was not obtained through **clairvoyance.** Furthermore, "Rector," another **control** of Stainton Moses, purportedly had the power to read books. Such power would open up a storehouse of pertinent information for so-called deceiving spirits.

Therefore, the difficulties of proof of spirit identity are almost insurmountable, a major reason why psychical research has largely abandoned the task. On a practical level, however, the human element—personal information embedded in the complexity of life—often provides convincing material to an individual who receives a communication through a medium.

One of the earliest cases of such convincing identity proof was registered by the Rev. J. B. Ferguson in his book *Spirit Communion* (1854). According to Ferguson's account, his cousin O. F. Parker died on August 5, 1854, in St. Louis. On the following day, in Maryville, Kentucky, Mrs. Ferguson was controlled by his spirit. Part of the communication was "My books I ordered to be sold to defray my funeral expenses, but it was not done. I am afraid, too, that there will be some flaw picked in my life policy, and if so I wish you to order my books to be sold to pay my debts, and if they fail, do not fail then from any delicacy of feeling to write to my mother, and she will have all properly settled. The policy is now in the hands of Mr. Hitchcock."

The Reverend Ferguson affirmed that until the communication the only account they had of his cousin's death was a short telegram. Because every detail was found correct, he considered the evidence of identity overwhelming.

C. H. Foster was visited in 1874 in San Francisco by the Honorable Charles E. de Long, a perfect stranger to him. Foster said he had a message for Ida and asked the visitor if this name meant anything to him. It was the name of de Long's wife. Foster asked him to bring her, and when she came he delivered the following message by means of **automatic writing**: "To my daughter, Ida. Ten years ago I entrusted a large sum to Thomas Madden to invest for me in certain lands. After my death he failed to account for the investment to my executors. The money was invested and 1,250 acres of land were bought, and one half of this land now belongs to you. I paid Madden on account of my share of the purchase 650 dollars. He must be made to make a settlement. Your father, Vineyard." This story proved to be true. Madden admitted it and made restitution.

An often-quoted case in Spiritualist literature is that of the steamroller suicide. The notes of Rev. Stainton Moses are as follows: "February 20, 1874. Dr. and Mrs. Speer and I dined with Mrs. Gregory, to meet the Baron du Potet, the celebrated magnetist and spiritualist. Mr. Percival was of the party. During dinner I was conscious of a strange influence in the room and mentioned the fact. The Baron had previously magnetised me very strongly, and had rendered me more than usually clairvoyant. He also recognised a spirit in the room, but thought it was the spirit of a living person. After dinner, when we got upstairs, I felt an uncontrollable inclination to write, and I asked the Baron to lay his hand upon my arm. It began to move very soon and I fell into a deep trance. As far as I can gather from the witnesses, the hand then wrote out 'I killed myself to-day.' This was preceded by a very rude drawing, and then 'Under steam-roller, Baker Street, medium passed,' (i.e., W. S. M.) was written. At the same time I spoke in the trance and rose and apparently motioned something away, saying 'Blood' several times. This was repeated and the spirit asked for prayer. Mrs. G. said a few words of prayer, and I came out of the trance at last, feeling very unwell.

"On the following day Dr. Speer and I walked down Baker Street and asked the policeman on duty if any accident had occurred there. He told us that a man had been killed by the steamroller at 9 A.M. and that he himself had helped to carry the body to Marylebone Workhouse."

The only flaw in this case is that the *Pall Mall Gazette* published a short account of the suicide the same evening and this might have been subconsciously seen by the medium. The name was not known, nor was it disclosed by Moses.

Dr. **Isaac Funk,** the New York editor, handed a letter to Lenora Piper containing the word *mother.* Piper gave the Christian name of Funk's mother, told him that she was walking on only one leg and asked, "Don't you remember that needle?" She had hurt herself by thrusting a needle into her foot. Piper also described a grandson, Chester, of whom Funk knew nothing. Upon inquiry, however, he found out that a grandson of that name had died 20 years earlier.

Dr. Joseph Vezzano established the identity of a materialized form in a séance given by **Eusapia Palladino** and describes it in *Annals of Psychic Science* (vol. 6, September 1907, p. 164) as follows: "In spite of the dimness of the light I could distinctly see Mme. Palladino and my fellow sitters. Suddenly I perceived that behind me was a form, fairly tall, which was leaning its head on my left shoulder and sobbing violently, so that those present could hear the sobs; it kissed me repeatedly. I clearly perceived the outlines of this face, which touched my own, and I felt the very fine and abundant hair in contact with my left cheek, so that I could be quite sure that it was a woman.

"The table then began to move, and typtology gave the name of a close family connection who was known to no-one present except myself. She had died some time before and on account of incompatability [sic] of temperament there had been serious disagreements with her. I was so far from expecting this typtological response that I at first thought this was a case of coincidence of name, but whilst I was mentally forming this reflection I felt a mouth, with warm breath, touch my left ear and whisper *in a low voice in Genoese dialect,* a succession of sentences, the murmur of which was audible to the sitters. These sentences were broken by bursts of weeping, and their gist was to repeatedly implore pardon for injuries done to me, with a fullness of detail connected with family affairs which could only be known to the person in question.

"The phenomenon seemed so real that I felt compelled to reply to the excuses offered me with expressions of affection, and to ask pardon in my turn if my resentment of the wrongs referred to had been excessive. But I had scarcely uttered the first syllables when two hands, with exquisite delicacy, applied themselves to my lips and prevented my continuing. The form then said to me: 'Thank you,' embraced me, kissed me, and disappeared."

According to **Theodore Flournoy,** this case was nothing more than the objectification of the emotional complex existing within the subconscious mind of Vezzano. There is food for thought, even for those who incline to differ, in his following remark: "The invasion or subjugation of the organism of the medium by a psychic complex belonging to a strange individual is not more easy to explain if that individuality be a spirit of the dead than if it is or belongs to one of the sitters in flesh and blood. And in this equally difficult question there is no reason to attribute to the discarnate or to the spirit world phenomena which can as readily be explained by the phenomena of our empirical world."

The pearl tie-pin case of **Sir William Barrett** has been frequently cited. Through the medium **Hester Dowden,** a Mrs. C. obtained a message spelled out on the **Ouija board:** "Tell mother to give my pearl tie-pin to the girl I was going to marry." The message allegedly came from a cousin of Mrs. C's, an officer who had been killed a month earlier. The name and address was returned and the whole message was thought ficitious. Six months later, however, it was discovered that the officer *had* been engaged to the lady. The war office returned his effects—a pearl tie-pin among them—and it was found that he put the lady's name in his will as his beneficiary.

Ernesto Bozzano recorded that in a sitting held on July 23, 1928, with the **Marquise Centurione Scotto** in **Millesimo Castle,** a voice addressed him as follows: "O Ernesto Bozzano, O my dear, my dear, I sought you in London, I sought you in Genoa, at last I find you." He immediately recognized the voice; the words carried a strong southern accent like that of Eusapia Palladino. He later noted: "This, her first manifestation, was a great revelation to me from the point of view of personal identification of the communicating spirit; because, without the faintest shadow of doubt, I recognised the person who was speaking to me the moment she pronounced my name. In life she had her own particular way of enunciating my surname, for she pronounced the two z's in an inimitable manner. Not only so, for when she spoke to me in life, she never called me simply by my surname, but invariably added my Christian name, though she never used the word 'Mr.' These small but most important idiosyncrasies of language are really what constitute the best demonstration of the real presence of the agency which affirms that it is actually present. I must add that she spoke with the identical timbre of voice which she had in life and with the very marked accent of her Italianized Neapolitan dialect."

Many visions of deceased soldiers were recorded by clairvoyants during the world wars. Mrs. E. A. Cannock of London described at a Spiritualist meeting a novel and convincing method employed by the fallen soldiers to make their identity known. In her vision they advanced in single file up the aisle, led by a young lieutenant. Each man bore on his chest a large placard with his name and the place where he lived inscribed. Cannock read the names and the place. The audience identified them one after the other. After recognition the spirit form faded and made way for the next one.

There has been no shortage of evidence of communication from servicemen who died in World War II. One of the most distinguished champions of such communication was Air Chief Marshal **Lord Dowding,** who was head of fighter command in the Battle of Britain. He obtained convincing evidence of spirit communication from servicemen at sittings with such famous mediums as **Estelle Roberts,** which he later compiled in his books *Many Mansions* (1943) and *Lychgate* (1945).

Of course, such convincing personal evidence of identity in spirit communications does not reach the level demanded by scientific criteria. However, thousands of people from all walks of life have been assured of and based their affirmation of **survival** upon such impressive clairaudient and clairvoyant messages through a medium or psychic.

Sources:

Baird, Alexander T. *One Hundred Cases for Survival After Death.* New York: Bernard Ackerman, 1944.

Christopher, Milbourne. *Search for the Soul: An Insider's Report on the Continuing Quest by Psychics and Scientists for Evidence of Life After Death.* New York: Thomas Y. Crowell, 1979.

Currie, Ian. *You Cannot Die: The Incredible Findings of a Century of Research on Death.* New York: Methuen; London: Hamlyn, 1978.

Ducasse, C. J. *Paranormal Phenomena, Science, and Life After Death.* New York: Parapsychology Foundation, 1969.

Garrett, Eileen J., ed. *Does Man Survive Death? A Symposium.* New York: Helix Press, 1957.

Hart, Hornell. *The Enigma of Survival: The Case For and Against An After Life.* Springfield, Ill.: Charles Thomas, 1959.

Hyslop, James H. *Contact With the Other World: The Latest Evidence as to Communication with the Dead.* New York: Century, 1919.

Kastenbaum, Robert, ed. *Between Life and Death.* New York: Springer, 1979.

Murphy, Gardner. *Three Papers on the Survival Problem.* New York: American Society for Psychical Research, 1945.

Richmond, Kenneth. *Evidence of Identity.* London: G. Bell, 1939.

Salter, W. H. *Zoar; or, The Evidence of Psychical Research Concerning Survival.* London: Sidwick & Jackson, 1961.

Ideoplasm

Another term for **ectoplasm,** a substance claimed to issue from the body of a **materialization** medium in a vaporous or solid form, taking on the appearance of phantom forms or limbs. The concept of ideoplasm stems from the investigations of such psychical researchers as the Frenchman **Gustav Geley** and conveys the additional idea that the substance may be molded by the operators into any shape to express ideas of the medium or of the sitters.

Idolatry

The subject of idolatry was raised as a religious polemic, a monotheistic appraisal of the polytheism. Idolatry is concerned with the rather ubiquitous belief among indigenous cultures that images of gods can become a repository of divine power, one development of animism, in which all of nature was imbued with supernatural forces. The sympathetic magic of images depended upon the image being a proper representation of the god, and also being installed through a special invocatory ceremony. Although the early Judaic commandment not to worship graven images implied a new separate form of worship, the statement that the Jewish god was "a jealous god" implied that Pagan images possessed some power but that it would be of rival demonic gods as distinct from the monotheism of Moses.

The belief in the power of images is also related to the designation of special sacred places—particularly striking natural locations or buildings such as tabernacles, synagogues, and churches where the presence of God might be enhanced. The very structure of churches and cathedrals utilized architecture to reinforce this belief, while rituals created a mental and emotional structure to invoke divine presence. Allied to the use of rituals are the geometrical shapes of *mandalas,* used as an aid in meditation.

In the history of Christianity, the Judaic commandment prohibiting images, in the face of their almost universal appeal, caused great controversies in relation to the use of icons (flat stylized picture of the saints), as opposed to statues of Christ and/or the Virgin Mary in churches, one major element in the division of Roman Catholics and Eastern Orthodox Christians. The sixteenth-century Protestant reformers banned images in their churches, and only in recent decades have they returned, but only as decorative art.

The Catholic view is that such representations are not actually worshiped, but are simply an aid for intercession with divine power, that it is a more intangible god that is worshiped. However, the concept of God as a father figure, and the tangible representations of Jesus Christ merely remove imagery to a mental and spiritual level, for which an image is a support.

Moreover, in some countries, the "veneration" of images closely approaches actual "worship," as for example, the famous "Child of Prague" image of the Carmelites Church of Our Lady of Victories in the former Czechoslovakia (a statue actually brought from Spain in the sixteenth century). This statue has become known in many countries and venerated by thousands of people, in the belief that it can render favors on those who pray to it. Interestingly enough, the robes of this image are changed regularly in accordance with the ecclesiastical calendar. This custom of dressing images is also widely practiced at the present day temples through India, indicating that customs and beliefs relating to images are common to many traditions.

Worship associated with ancient pagan Mother Goddesses has much in common with Christian adoration of the Virgin Mary. Some comparative religionists would go so far as to claim that these are but different forms of one primal maternal force in nature. Similarly the concept of a divine savior, born of a virgin and crucified for the atonement of human sin, is also found in some Pagan religions.

The belief that images might become actual centers of divine power is still common in different religions. In Hindu temples, images are installed with special ceremonies to invoke divinity, and subsequently treated as living entities. The installation ceremonies mark an important point in the opening of a temple for public worship. In **Swaminarayan** temples, for example, the installation of an image requires a ritual in which, at the high point, a mirror is held in front of the deity's eyes, so that the power may not blind observers; the mirror is said to be cracked by this force.

In Roman Catholicism, miracles continue to be associated with statues of Christ and the Virgin Mary. Such miracles involve statues that move, weep, or shed blood. In the phenomenon of **stigmata,** an intensely devout individual or a saint may become, in effect, a living statue upon which the wounds of Christ are physically reproduced—the marks of scourging, wounds on the shoulder and side, the bruising of wrist, and bleeding hands. **Apparitions** of the Virgin Mary are a related phenomenon in which a holy figure does not require the material support of an image for manifestation but appears with independent life.

Even in modern times, there are claims of moving **statues** of the Virgin Mary, notably at the village of **Ballinspittle,** in Ireland.

Sources:

Abbott, John. *The Keys of Power: A Study of Indian Ritual and Belief.* London: Methuen, 1932. Reprint, New Hyde Park, N.Y.: University Books, 1974.

Bevan, Edwyn Robert. *Holy Images; An Inquiry Into Idolatry and Image—Worship in Ancient Paganism and in Christianity.* London: George Allen, 1940.

Breasted, J. H. *Religion and Thought in Ancient Egypt.* London: Hodder & Stoughton, 1912.

Graves, Kersey. *The World's Sixteen Crucified Saviors.* Boston, Mass., 1875. Reprint, New Hyde Park, N.Y.: University Books, 1971.

Hastings, James, ed. *Encyclopaedia of Religion and Ethics.* 12 vols. Edinburgh: James Clark, 1908.

Tylor, E. B. *Primitive Culture.* 2 vols. London: John Murray, 1871.

Ifrits

Hideous specters, probably of Arabian origin, now genies of Persian and Indian mythology. They assume diverse forms and inhabit ruins, woods, and wild, desolate places for the purpose of preying upon human beings and animals. They are sometimes associated with the **jinns** or **divs** of Persia.

IFS See International Frankenstein Society

Ignath, Lujza Linczegh (b. 1891)

Hungarian clairvoyant, and healing and **apport** medium, controlled by "Nona," a pure spirit who claimed to have never been incarnated and came without **trance,** in the manner of an alternating personality. Ignath's unusual psychic powers were first described in a Hungarian pamphlet by William Tordai of Budapest. In *Tidskrift for Psykisk Forskning* (vol. 5), the journal of the Norwegian Society for Psychical Research, Lujza Lamaes-Haughseth, a high school teacher and experimental psychologist, published a long report of her observations with Ignath in Budapest. As a consequence the Norwegian Society for Psychical Research, headed by Professors Jaeger and Theostein Wereide, both of the University of Oslo, sent an invitation to Ignath, which she accepted.

According to a report in the *Tidens Tegn* (November 20, 1931), the medium produced **direct writing** in the presence of 100 people on places selected by the audience. In an experimental sitting for the Norwegian SPR conducted by Dr. Jorgen Bull, a chemist in Oslo, direct writing was produced on wax tablets in a specially prepared and closed box.

In religious ecstatic condition, stigmatic wounds were observed on Ignath's head. On such occasions "Nona" delivered moving lectures on the subject of religion.

Ignath's oddest phenomena consisted of miniature heads that she materialized in drinking glasses filled with water. "Nona" asserted that the heads, the size of walnuts, were "plastic thoughts." Having been shown a photograph of Haughseth's husband, Nona materialized his likeness. Flashlight photographs of these forms were published in the *Psykisk Forskning* (vol. 6).

In the *Proceedings* of the Society for Psychical Research (vol. 38, p. 466–71) **Theodore Besterman** describes some psychometric experiments with Ignath in Budapest. On November 18, 1928, he left a sealed vial with Lujza Haughseth for testing. His conclusion of the reading was that "the experiment is very instructive from a negative point of view."

Ignis Fatuus

A wavering luminous appearance frequently observed in meadows and marshy places, around which many popular superstitions cluster. Its folknames, Will o' the Wisp and Jack o' Lantern, suggest a country fellow bearing a lantern or straw torch (wisp). Formerly these lights were supposed to haunt desolate bogs and moorlands for the purpose of misleading travelers and drawing them to their death. Another superstition says that they are the spirits of those who have been drowned in the bogs, and yet another says that they are the souls of unbaptized infants. Science now attributes these *ignes fatui* to gaseous exhalations from the moist ground or, more rarely, to night-flying insects.

Ike, Rev. See **Eikerenkoetter II, Frederick I**

Illuminati

A term first used in the fifteenth century by enthusiasts in the occult arts, signifying those who claimed to possess light directly communicated from a higher source or because of abundant human wisdom. The term was used in Spain about the end of the fifteenth century, but probably originated from an Italian Gnostic source. All kinds of people, many of them charlatans, claimed to belong to the Illuminati. In Spain those who assumed the label had to face the rigor of the Inquisition, and many of them moved to France as refugees in the early seventeenth century.

Here and there small bodies of those called Illuminati—sometimes known as **Rosicrucians**—rose into publicity for a short period. It was through Adam Weishaupt (1748–1830), professor of law at Ingolstadt, that the movement first became identified with republicanism. Weishaupt founded the order of the Illuminati in Bavaria in 1776. It soon secured a stronghold throughout Germany. Its critics suggested that its founder's objective was merely to convert his followers into blind instruments of his will.

Weishaupt built a strong organization modeled on the Jesuits'. The Illuminati was an occult organization and had a series of classes and grades, similar to that within **Freemasonry.** It offered promise of the communication of deep occult secrets in the higher ranks. Only a few of the members knew Weishaupt personally as the society spread throughout Germany. He was able to enlist a number of young men of wealth and position, and within four or five years the members even began to have a hand in the affairs of the state. Not a few of the German princes found it to their interest to have dealings with the fraternity.

Weishaupt blended philanthropy and mysticism. He was only 28 when he founded the sect in 1776, and it began to prosper when a certain Baron Adolph von Knigge (1752–1796) joined him in 1780. A gifted person of strong imagination, von Knigge had been a master of most of the secret societies of his day, including the Freemasons. He was also an expert occultist, and the supernatural held a strong attraction for him. He and Weishaupt rapidly spread the gospel of the revolution throughout Germany. They grew fearful, however, that if the authorities discovered the existence of such a society as theirs they would take steps to suppress it. With this in mind they conceived the idea of grafting Illuminism onto Freemasonry, which they thought would protect it and help it spread more widely and rapidly.

The Freemasons were not long in discovering the true nature of those who had just joined their organization. A chief council was held to thoroughly examine the beliefs held by the Illuminati, and a conference of Masons was held in 1782. Knigge and Weishaupt attended and endeavored to capture the whole organization of Freemasonry, but a misunderstanding grew up between the leaders of Illuminism. Knigge withdrew from the society, and two years later some who discovered Weishaupt's democratic aims denounced it to the Bavarian government, which quickly moved to suppress it. The Illuminati were all but destroyed in 1785 and Weishaupt fled. However, illuminist ideas spread to occultists in France and helped in building support for the French Revolution.

The title Illuminati was later given to the French Martinists, followers of the French mystic **Louis Claude de St. Martin** (1743–1803), known as "le philosophe inconno."

A famous member of the Order of Illuminati was **Count Alessandrodi Cagliostro.** He was initiated in 1781 at Frankfurt, where the Illuminati used the name Grand Masters of the Templars, and was said to have received money and instructions from Weishaupt to influence French Masonry. Cagliostro later became associated with the Martinist order, which had been founded in 1754. Some believe that the Illuminati maintained a complex network of secret orders in the later seventeenth century, others that a variety of different independent groups used the name. A revived Order of Illuminati was founded in 1880 by Leopold Engel at Dresden, Germany. Notable names connected with this revival include **Rudolph Steiner** and **Franz Hartmann.**

Through the twentieth century, the idea of an Illuminati conspiracy became one of the more popular conspiracy myths feeding off waves of paranoia in the Western public. In the late twentieth century, popular writer Robert Anton Wilson played with the Illuminati theme in a series of books designed to shake the reader out of conventional modes of thought.

Sources:

Barruel, Augustin. *Memoirs Illustrating the History of Jacobinism.* 4 vols., London, 1797.

Daraul, Arbon. *Secret Societies, Yesterday and Today.* London: Fernhill Housen, 1961. Reprinted as *A History of Secret Societies.* New York: Citadel, 1961.

Fagan, Myron. *A Brief History of the Illuminati.* Lansing, Ill.: H.B.C., 1978.

Gould, R. F. *History of Freemasonry.* 5 vols. Rev. ed. London: Caxton, 1931.

Hackethorn, Charles William. *The Secret Societies of All Ages and Countries.* 2 vols. Reprint, New Hyde Park, N.Y.: University Books, 1965.

Holmes, Donald. *The Illuminati Conspiracy.* Los Angeles: Falcon Press, 1987.

Waite, Arthur E. *A New Encyclopaedia of Freemasonry.* 2 vols. London: Rider, 1921. Reprint, New Hyde Park, N.Y.: University Books, 1970.

Wilgus, Neal. *The Illuminoids.* New York: New American Library, 1989.

Wilson, Robert Anton. *Cosmic Trigger: Final Secret of the Illuminati.* Berkeley, Calif.: And/Or Press, 1977.

———. *The Illuminati Papers.* Berkeley, Calif.: And/Or Press, 1980.

———. *Illuminatus!* 3 vols. New York: Dell, 1975.

———. *Masks of the Illuminati.* New York: Timescape, 1981.

Illusion

Sensory perception originated by an actual sensory stimulus to which wrong interpretation is attached. (See also **Hallucination**)

Imhotep

(Also spelled "Imhetep.") An ancient Egyptian deity, son of Ptah and Nut, to whom great powers of **exorcism** were attributed. Imhotep was often appealed to in cases of demonic **possession.**

Sources:

Doumato, Lamia. *Imhotep.* Monticello, Ill.: Vance Bibliographies, 1981.

Shorter, Alan W. *The Egyptian Gods.* London: Routledge & Kegan Paul, 1937. Reprint. 1981.

Immortality

Psychical research is concerned primarily with **survival** as a matter of inference from intelligently observed and interpreted psychic phenomena. It does not attempt to answer the question whether survival means continued existence for a only a limited period or for a longer time, or even forever. With few exceptions, psychical researchers have been concerned with the authenticity of claimed phenomena and with the question of whether there is really evidence for survival of personality after death.

The issues of the continued existence of a soul or spirit and the possible perfection of that soul through evolution or **reincarnation** move from science into the realm of religion. Many religions proclaim the immortality of the soul. Christianity speaks of a continued existence in heaven with an eternity for progress and perfection (though different denominations have quite different ideas about the exact details of the afterlife). Eastern religions also offer elaborate descriptions of the existence beyond this earthly life, although, again, details vary considerably on the relationship between the human soul and God.

In advaita **Vedanta,** for example, the individual soul is perfected by infinite reincarnations to reassert its true reality as a group soul, then as the infinite Divine itself; in vishadvaita Vedanta, however, there remains some distinction between Divinity and the perfected human souls. In general Vedanta does not view immortality in terms of an achievement of individual souls in a period of time, but rather as the reassertion of an infinite divine reality when the illusions of individual ego, body, mind, time, space, and causality have disappeared. This postulates the infinite Divine as the eternal reality that is veiled by illusions of individual consciousness and the world of matter.

At its beginning **Spiritualism** offered itself as a new religion, necessarily rooted in Christianity. The question of immortality and perfectibility of the soul has been more than just another doctrine; it has been a keystone of the Spiritualist position. As the movement developed, it developed a split over the doctrine of reincarnation. Most Spiritualists now accept reincarnation.

Most of the pioneers of psychical research in the nineteenth century were religious people who had experienced a crisis of faith, largely because of the attacks of nineteenth-century science on traditional Christian doctrine. Spiritualism claimed the ability to demonstrate "scientifically" the reality of life after death. It thus offered a means, many hoped, to recover not only an affirmation of mere survival (the primary issue open to psychical research) but a firm base from which a faith in a meaningful afterlife could be reaffirmed as a religious hope.

The religious quest so evident in the life of most of the pioneer psychical researchers suggests that a will to believe was operative in their research and was a causative element in their frequently falling victim to **fraud.**

Sources:

Augustine, Saint. *Immortality of the Soul.* Reprinted in the Fathers of the Church series, vol. 4. Washington, D.C.: Catholic University of America Press, 1973.

Bernard, Theos. *Philosophical Foundations of India.* London: Rider, [1945].

Carrington, Hereward. *Death: The Causes and Phenomena with Special Reference to Immortality.* London, 1911. Reprint, New York: Arno Press, 1977.

Charles, R. H. *A Critical History of the Doctrine of a Future Life in Israel, in Judaism and in Christianity.* London, 1899. Reprinted as *Eschatology, The Doctrine of a Future Life in Israel, in Judaism, and in Christianity: A Critical History.* New York: Schocken Books, 1963.

Ducasse, C. J. *Critical Examination of the Belief in a Life After Death.* Springfield, Ill.: Charles C. Thomas, 1974.

Fournier, D'Albe. *New Light on Immortality.* London, 1908.

Hyslop, James H. *Psychical Research and the Nature of Life After Death.* Albuquerque, N. Mex.: American Institute for Psychological Research, 1980.

James, William. *The Will to Believe and Human Immortality.* New York: Dover Publications, n.d.

Lombroso, Cesare. *After Death—What?* London: T. Fisher Unwin, 1909.

Myers, Frederick W. *Human Personality and Its Survival of Bodily Death.* 2 vols. London, 1903. Reprint. New York: Arno Press, 1975.

Steiner, Rudolf. *Reincarnation and Immortality.* New York: Harper & Row, 1980.

Tugwell, Simon. *Human Immortality and Redemption.* London: Darton, Longman, & Todd, 1990.

Immortality (Magazine)

Spiritualist monthly "for progressive thinking people," founded in 1919 as the official organ of the **General Assembly of Spiritualists,** New York. It continued publication into the 1930s.

Immortality and Survival (Magazine)

British monthly, incorporated after a short existence into *Survival* magazine. No longer published.

Imoda, Enrico (ca. 1912)

Pioneer Italian psychical researcher. Dr. Imoda conducted a series of methodical experiments in Turin with the medium **Linda Gazzera** in the house of Marquise de Ruspoli. His book *Fotografie di fantasmi* (1912), with a preface by **Charles Richet,** contains photographs of what is purported to be **ectoplasm** produced by Gazzera. In 1908 Dr. Imoda experimented with the famous medium **Eusapia Palladino** and claimed that radiations resembling those of radium and the cathode rays of **Sir William Crookes** emanated from the medium.

Sources:

Imoda, Enrico. "The Action of Eusapia Palladino on the Electroscope." *Annals of Psychical Science* 7, 44/45, (August–September 1908).

"Imperator"

The famous spirit **control** of the **Rev. W. Stainton Moses,** commanding a band of spirits engaged in a missionary effort to uplift the human race by teachings through automatic writing. He first identified himself as "Imperator" on September 19, 1872, but later, yielding to entreaties by Moses, he revealed, on July 6, 1873, in *Book IV* of his writings that he was the biblical prophet Malachi. The spirit control charged the medium not to speak of his biblical identity (except to those intimately associated with Moses) without his express permission.

Imperator was seen clairvoyantly by Stainton Moses, and his appearance is described in *Book VI* of the writings. His communications were not written by Imperator himself, but by "Rector." The signature was "Imperator S. D. (Servus Dei)" or "I.S.D.," preceded by a Latin cross at first, then later by a crown.

In 1881 a story was circulated from theosophical sources maintaining that Imperator was a living man, a theosophical brother whose dealings with Moses had been known all along to **Helena Petrovna Blavatsky.** Imperator, following Moses' query, branded the whole story as false. Of Blavatsky he added, "She does not know or speak with us, though she has the power of ascertaining facts concerning us." Imperator claimed that he directed the whole course of Moses' life and had carefully prepared him for his role as a messenger.

Complaining of Moses' unquestioning acceptance of all the spirit said, Imperator summed up the case on January 18, 1874, as follows: "We are real in power over you; real in the production of objective manifestations; real in the tests and proofs of knowledge which we adduce. We are truthful and accurate in all things. We are the preachers of a Divine Gospel. It is for you to accept the individual responsibility from which none may relieve you, or deciding whether, being such as we are, we are deceivers in matters of vital and eternal import. Such a conclusion, in the face of all evidence and fair inference, is one which none could accept save a perverted and unhinged mind; least of all one who knows us as you do now."

"Imperator" and Lenora Piper

In 1897 Imperator and his band supposedly took over as the controls of **Lenora Piper.** Immediately both **Sir Oliver Lodge** and **William James** raised doubts that they were the Imperator group of Stainton Moses, since these entities could not give the names that they had given to Moses. Though Piper's other controls, the spirits of **F. W. H. Myers** and **Richard Hodgson,** endorsed them, Lodge countered, "I conjecture, however, that whatever relationship may exist between these personages and the corresponding ones of Stainton Moses, there is little or no identity" (*Proceedings* of the Society for Psychical Research, vol. 23., p. 235).

Eleanor Sidgwick (*Proceedings* of the Society for Psychical Research vol. 28, p. 71) also rejected their claims for identity. **James H. Hyslop** was slightly inclined to accept it. He argued (*Journal* of the American Society for Psychical Research, vol. 16, p. 69) that *Malachi* means "messengers" and that this is the very function that Imperator assumed through Piper and **Minnie Soule** (public name, Mrs. Chenoweth), as well as through Stainton Moses.

A. W. Trethewy, author of *The "Controls" of Stainton Moses* (London, 1923), stated that ". . . the internal evidence points to the two groups not having been identical. There are, it is true, slight resemblances, but they are either so vague as to be well within the sphere of coincidence where two good bands of controls are concerned, or they are of a nature to suggest an origin from the mind of Mrs. Piper or her sitter. On the other hand, the ignorance and the errors of her controls concerning the earth-lives of the guides of Stainton Moses whose names they bore, and concerning important features of his mediumship, are altogether inconsistent with their claim to identity."

Richard Hodgson (d. 1905), in the last years of his life, also received direct communications from the Imperator group. **Hereward Carrington** gave the following character sketch of Hodgson in *The Story of Psychic Science* (1930): "He possessed a keen sense of humour, and was always buoyant and cheerful, but would become serious when the name of Imperator was mentioned. It is now realised, perhaps, that this Personality—together with Rector and the other members of the group—played a large part in many people's lives, and that numerous old "Piper Sitters" (as they were called) *prayed* to Imperator for comfort and guidance—as one might pray to any favourite Saint."

Communications by Imperator were received at a later date through Minnie M. Soule, and in the 1920s Gwendolyn Kelley Hack also claimed the control of Imperator in her automatic scripts. (See the account in the 1929 *Modern Psychic Mysteries at Millesimo Castle.*)

Sources:

Carrington, Hereward. *The Story of Psychic Science.* 1930.

M. A. (Oxon) [W. Stainton Moses]. *More Spirit Teachings.* Manchester, England: Two Worlds Publishing, 1942.

Spirit Teachings. 1898. Reprint, London: Spiritualist Press, 1949.

Trethewy, A. W. *The "Controls" of Stainton Moses.* London, 1923.

Incommunicable Axiom, The

Occultist **Éliphas Lévi** suggested that all magic was embodied in knowledge of this secret. The axiom was to be found enclosed in the four letters of the Tetragram arranged in a certain way; in the words *Azoth* and *Inri* written kabbalistically; and in the monogram of Christ embroidered in the labarum. Whoever succeeded in elucidating it became omnipotent in the practice of magic.

Thus did Lévi deal with a Western occult interpretation of Jewish **Kabbalah** and Eastern teachings about the creative power of the Ineffable Name of God, **Aum.** (See also **Divine Name; Mantra; Shemhamphorash**)

Sources:

Lévi, Éliphas. *Transcendental Magic.* London: Rider, 1896. Reprint, New York: Samuel Weiser, 1972.

Incorporeal Personal Agency (IPA)

Rather cumbersome term used by parapsychologist **J. B. Rhine** to indicate **survival** of bodily death (i.e., aspects of personality surviving without a body).

Incubus/Succubus

A demon spirit that has sexual intercourse with mortals. The concept may have arisen from the idea of the commerce of gods with people, which was rife in pagan times. The male demon said to have intercourse with women is called the incubus and the female demon who seduces men the succubus. The demons were generally believed to appear most frequently during sleep or in nightmares. During the **witchcraft** scare of the late medieval period these demons, when associated with an individual witch or sorcerer, were known as **familiars.**

Belief in incubi and succubi goes back to ancient times but was incorporated into Christian belief in the medieval period. Such churchmen as Thomas Aquinas (1225–74) discussed the demons.

The Incubus

The *Description of Scotlande* of Hector Boethius as translated in the first volume of Holinshed's *Chronicles* (1577), has three or four notable examples of these demons, which are corroborated by Jerome Cardan. One of these, concerning an incubus, is quoted in the quaint language Holinshed used:

"In the year 1480 it chanced as a Scottish ship departed out of the Forth towards Flanders, there arose a wonderful great tempest of wind and weather, so outrageous, that the master of the ship, with other the mariners, wondered not a little what the matter meant, to see such weather at that time of the year, for it was about the middle of summer. At length, when the furious pirrie and rage of winds still increased, in such wise that all those within the ship looked for present death, there was a woman underneath the hatches called unto them above, and willed them to throw her into the sea, that all the residue, by God's grace, might yet be saved; and thereupon told them how she had been haunted a long time with a spirit dailie coming into hir in man's likenesse. In the ship there chanced also to be priest, who by the master's appointment going down to this woman, and finding her like a most wretched and desperate person, lamenting hir great misfortune and miserable estate, used such wholesome admonition and comfortable advertisements, willing her to repent and hope for mercy at the hands of God, that, at length, she seeming right penitent for her grievous offences committed, and fetching sundrie sighs even from the bottome of her heart, being witnesse, as should appeare, of the same, there issued forth of the pumpe of the ship, a foule and evil-favoured blacke cloud with a mighty terrible noise, flame, smoke, and stinke, which presently fell into the sea. And suddenlie thereupon the tempest ceased, and the ship passing in great quiet the residue of her journey, arrived in saftie at the place whither she was bound." (*Chronicles,* vol. 5, p. 146, 1808 ed)."

In another case related by the same author, the incubus did not depart so quietly. In the chamber of a young gentlewoman who was the daughter of a nobleman in the country of Mar there was found "a foule monstrous thing, verie horrible to behold." For the love of this "Deformed," nevertheless, the lady had refused sundry wealthy marriages. A priest who was in the company began to repeat St. John's Gospel, and "suddenlie the wicked spirit, making a verie sore and terrible roaring noise, flue his waies, taking the roofe of the chamber awaie with him, the hangings and coverings of the bed being also burnt therewith."

Jean Bodin, author of *Démonomaie* (1580) cites the case of Joan Hervilleria, who at age 12 was solemnly betrothed to Beelzebub by her mother, who was afterward burned alive for contriving this clandestine marriage. According to the story, the bridegroom was respectably attired and the marriage oath simple. The mother pronounced the following words to the bridegroom: "Ecce filiam meam quam spospondi tibi." Then, turning to the bride, she stated "Ecce amicum tuum qui beabit te." Joan was not satisfied with her spiritual husband alone, however. She became a bigamist by intermarrying with real flesh and blood.

In another story Margaret Bremont, in company with her mother and others, was in the habit of attending diabolic trysts. She and the others were burned alive by Adrian Ferreus, general vicar of the Inquisition.

Magdalena Crucia of Cordova, an abbess, was more fortunate. Suspected by her nuns of magic—an accusation convenient when a superior was at all troublesome—she anticipated their charge. Going before Pope Paul III, she confessed a 30-year intimacy with the devil and obtained pardon.

The Succubus

Old rabbinical writings relate the legend of how Adam was visited during a 130-year period by female demons and had intercourse with demons, spirits, specters, lemurs, and phantoms. Another legend relates how, under the reign of Roger, king of Sicily, a young man was bathing by moonlight. He thought he saw someone drowning and hastened to the rescue. Having drawn from the water a beautiful woman, he became enamored of her, married her, and had by her a child. Afterward she disappeared with her child, which made everyone believe that she was a succubus.

The historian Hector Boece (1465–1536), in his history of Scotland, relates that a handsome young man was pursued by a female demon who would pass through his closed door and offer to marry him. He complained to his bishop, who enjoined him to fast, pray, and confess his sins, and as a result the infernal visitor ceased to trouble him.

The witchcraft judge **Pierre de Lancre** (1553–1631) stated that in Egypt an honest blacksmith was occupied in forging during the night when a demon appeared to him in the shape of a beautiful woman. He threw a hot iron in the face of the demon, which at once took flight.

More Accounts of Incubi and Succubi

Among the many writers who reflected upon the incubus/succubus were Erastus, in his tract *de Lamiis;* **Jakob Sprenger** and **Heinrich Kramer** in *Malleus Maleficarum* (1486), which contains a report of a nun who slept with an incubus in the form of a bishop; H. Zanchius in *de Operibus Del,* (1597, 16, 4); G. Dandini in *Aristotelis Tres de Anima* (1610); J. G. Godellman in *Tractatus de Magis* (1591); M. A. Del Rio in *Disquisitionum Magicarum* (1599); and F. M. Guazzo in *Compendium Maleficarum* (1608).

An interesting treatise on the subject is the nineteenth-century hoax *Demoniality or Incubi and Succubi,* supposedly by one Fr. L. M. Sinistari of Ameno, first translated and published by the bibliophile Isidore Liseux in Paris in 1879. It was later translated into English by Montague Summers (Fortune Press, London, 1927; reprinted B. Blom, New York, 1972).

In the early nineteenth century the issue of the incubus/succubus, which had been dismissed by many as outdated superstition was raised again by the emerging science of psychoanalysis. Possibly the most important discussion is that of Ernest Jones, a Freudian psychoanalyst in his famous treatise *On the Nightmare* (1951).

Sources:

Barrett, Francis. *The Magus.* 1801. Reprint, New Hyde Park, N.Y.: University Books, 1967.

Jones, Ernest, *On the Nightmare.* New York: Liveright Publishing, 1951.

Robbins, Rossell Hope. *The Encyclopedia of Witchcraft and Demonology.* New York: Crown Publishers, 1959.

Independent Drawing and Painting See Direct Drawing and Painting

Independent Spiritualist Association of the United States of America

The Independent Spiritualist Association of the United States of America was founded in 1924 by **Amanda Cameron Flower** (1863–1940), a medium with the **National Spiritualist Association of Churches** (NSAC). Flower had absorbed some theosophical emphases, including a belief in **reincarnation,** an idea not consistent with NSAC belief. She also protested the NSAC rule against its mediums teaching or doing mediumistic work in non-NSAC churches. The association is currently headquartered at 5130 West 25th St., Cicero, IL 60650. It is headed by Harry M. Hilborn.

Sources:

Judah, J. Stillson. *The History and Philosophy of the Metaphysical Movement in America.* Philadelphia, Penn.: Westminster Press, 1967.

Independent Voice See Direct Voice

Independent Writing See Direct Writing

INDIA

Many occult beliefs and practices stem from the complex religious and mystical concepts of Indian people. It might be said that the mysticism of the Hindus was a reaction against the austere religion and practical ceremonial of the sacred scriptures, the *Vedas.* If its trend were summarized it might justly be said that the *Vedas* point champion detachment; the pantheistic identification of the subject and object, worshiper and worship, aimed at ultimate absorption in the Infinite; inculcating transcendence from the material world through the most minute self-examination, the cessation of physical powers; and belief in the spiritual guidance of the **guru** or mystical adept.

For the Indian theosophist there is only one Absolute Being, the One Reality. However, in popular Hinduism, the pantheistic doctrine of *Ekam advitiyam* "the One without Second" posits a countless pantheon of gods, great and small, and a rich demonology, but these should be understood ultimately as merely illusions of the soul and not realities. Upon the soul's coming to fuller knowledge, its illusions are totally dispelled. According to such a theory, to the ordinary man and woman the impersonality of the Absolute being is too remote, and they require a symbolic deity to bridge the gulf between the impersonal Absolute and the very material self, hence the numerous gods of Hinduism regarded by the initiated merely as manifestations of the Supreme Spirit.

In this way, even the everyday forms of temple idols can be seen as possessing higher meaning. As Sir Alfred Lyall stated,

"It [Brahminism] treats all the worships as outward visible signs of the same spiritual truth, and is ready to show how each particular image or rite is the symbol of some aspect of universal divinity. The Hindus, like the pagans of antiquity, adore natural objects and forces,—a mountain, a river, or an animal. The Brahmin holds all nature to be the vesture or cloak of indwelling divine energy which inspires everything that produces all or passes man's understanding."

A life time of asceticism has from the remotest times been regarded in India as a true preparation for communion with the deity. Asceticism has been extremely prevalent especially in connection with the cult of the god Siva, who is in great measure regarded as the prototype of this class.

The yogis (disciples of the **yoga** philosophy) practice mental abstraction, and are popularly supposed to attain to superhuman powers. In some cases their extreme ascetic practices have resulted in madness or mental vacancy and many claimed paranormal powers, as in Spiritualism, have turned out to be jugglery and conjuring. However, there are charlatans in all religions, and the authentic prerequisites of the training of a yogi preclude such imposture and indeed warn against the vanity of displaying supernatural powers.

The paramahamsas, that is "supreme swans," are believed to have achieved communion with the world-soul through spiritual disciplines and **meditation.** They are said to be equally indifferent to pleasure or pain, insensible to heat or cold, and incapable of satiety or want. The sannyasis are those who renounce the world and live as wandering monks or residents in an ashram or spiritual retreat. The *dandis,* or staff-bearers, are worshipers of Siva in his form of Bhairava the Terrible.

J. C. Oman in *Mystics, Ascetics and Saints of India* (1903) said of these sadhus or holy men,

"*Sadhuism,* whether perpetuating the peculiar idea of the efficacy of asceticism for the acquisition of far-reaching powers over natural phenomena, or bearing its testimony to the belief in the indispensableness of detachment from the world as a preparation for the ineffable joy of ecstatic communion with the Divine Being, has undoubtedly tended to keep before men's eyes, as the highest ideal, a life of purity, self-restraint, and contempt of the world and human affairs. It has also necessarily maintained amongst the laity a sense of the righteous claims of the poor upon the charity of the more affluent members of the community. Further, *Sadhuism,* by the multiplicity of the independent sects which have arisen in India has engendered and favoured a spirit of tolerance which cannot escape the notice of the most superficial observer."

Of the three main branches of Hinduism, the most esoteric is the Shaktas. The Shaktas are worshipers of the shakti or the female principle as a creative and reproductive agency. Each of the principal gods possesses his own Shakti, through which his creative acts are performed. The Shaktas or Tantrics developed an elaborate picture of the subtle anatomy of the individual, proposing that each person had a secondary body composed of spiritual/psychic energies. In *Tantra,* sexual energy in the yogi is manifested in a pure form as **kundalini,** a psycho-physiological force resting like a coiled snake at the base of the spine. When awakened, the kundalini travels up the spine to the several psychic centers called **chakras** and eventually to the top of the head. The rise of the kundalini to the highest chakra brings higher consciousness and spiritual enlightenment.

Tantrics can usually be divided into two distinct groups. The original self-existent gods were supposed to divide themselves into male and female energies, the male half occupying the right-hand and the female the left-hand side. From this conception we have the two groups of "right-hand" observers and "left-hand" observers. In distinction to the ascetic world-denying approach to the religious life, Tantra does not offer enlightenment as a result of denying the material world, but from using it. Tantric practice takes things specifically denied to the ascetic and accepts them as the means of overcoming the world and gaining enlightenment. The righthand path does this symbolically, the left hand path actually eats denied food and participates in denied activities. Most controversial of all is sexual activity, for which tantrics have been most frequently criticized. The left-hand path of Tantra involves participation in sexual intercourse as a means of union with the goddess.

The right hand tantrism was expounded by **Sri Aurobindo** and **Pandit Gopi Krishna.** Lefthand tantrism has found a major exponent in Swami Satyananda Saraswati whose students have moved to the west.

Brahmanism

Brahmanism is a system originated by the Brahmans, the sacerdotal caste of the Hindus, at a comparatively early date. It is the mystical religion of India *par excellence,* and represents the older beliefs of its peoples. It states that the numerous individual existences of animate nature are but so many manifestations of the one eternal spirit towards which they tend as their final goal of supreme bliss. The object of life is to prevent oneself sinking lower in the scale, and by degrees to raise oneself in it, or if possible to attain the ultimate goal immediately from such state of existence as one happens to be in.

The socio-religious Code of *Manu* concludes "He who in his own soul perceives the supreme soul in all beings and acquires equanimity towards them all attains the highest state of bliss." Mortification of animal instincts, absolute purity and perfection of spirit, were the moral ideals of the Brahman class. But it was necessary to pass through a succession of four orders or states of existence before any hope of union with the deity could be held out. These were: that of *brahmacharin,* or student of religious matters; *grihastha,* or householder; *varnaprastha* or hermit; and *sannyasin* or *bhikshu,* religious mendicant.

Practically every man of the higher castes practiced at least the first two of these stages, while the priestly class took the entire course. Later, however, this was by no means the rule, as the scope of study was intensely exacting, often lasting as long as forty-eight years, and the neophyte had to support himself by begging from door to door.

He was usually guided by a spiritual preceptor and after several years of his tuition was usually married, as it was considered absolutely essential that he should leave a son behind him to offer food to his spirit and to those of his ancestors. He was then said to have become a "house-holder" and was required to keep up perpetually the fire brought into his house upon his marriage day.

Upon his growing older, the time arrived for him to enter the third stage of life, since having fulfilled his *dharma* (social and religious obligations) he now became aware of the transitory nature of the material life and found it necessary to become preoccupied with more eternal spiritual truth. He therefore cut himself off from family ties except (if she wished) his wife, who might accompany him, and went into retirement in a lonely place, carrying with him his sacred fire, and the instruments necessary for his daily sacrifices. Scantily clothed, the anchorite lived entirely on food growing wild in the forest—roots, herbs, wild grain, and so forth. The acceptance of gifts was not permitted him unless absolutely necessary, and his time was spent in studying the metaphysical portions of the *Vedas* under the guidance of a *guru,* in making offerings, and in practicing austerities with the object of producing entire indifference to worldly desires.

In this way he fitted himself for the final and most exalted order, that of religious mendicant or *bhikshu.* This consisted solely of meditation. He took up his abode at the foot of a tree in entire solitude and only once a day at the end of his labors might he go near the dwellings of men to beg a little food. In this way he waited for death, neither desiring extinction nor existence, until at length it reached him, and he was absorbed in the eternal Brahma.

The doctrines of Brahmanism are to be found in the vedanta philosophic system, which recognizes the *Vedas,* a collection of ancient Sanskrit hymns, as the revealed source of religious belief through the visions of the ancient *rishis* or seers. The *Upanishads* are later scriptures (after 1000 B.C.E.). The *Vedas* and *Upanishads* are the most widely accepted holy writings in India. A large number of later writings are also accepted by various groups as sacred scripture. Among the most popular of these later scriptures is the *Bhagavad-Gita.*

It has been already mentioned that the Hindu regarded the entire gamut of animated nature as being traversed by the one soul, which journeyed up and down the scale as its actions in its previous existence were good or evil. To the Hindu the vital element in all animate beings appears essentially similar, and this observation gave credence to the Brahmanical theory of **reincarnation** that took such a powerful hold upon the Hindu mind.

Demonology

A large and intricate **demonology** appears as part of Hindu mythology. The gods were at constant war with demons. Vishnu slew more than one demon, but Durga appeared to have been a great enemy of the demon race. The *asuras,* probably a very ancient and aboriginal pantheon of deities, later became demons in the popular imagination, and the *rakshasas* may have been cloud-demons. They were described as cannibals, could take many forms, and were constantly menacing the gods. They haunted cemeteries, disturbed sacrifices, animated the dead, and harried and afflicted mankind in all sorts of ways. In fact they were somewhat similar to the **vampires** of Slavonic countries; and this greatly assisted the conjecture that the Slavonic vampires were originally cloud-spirits.

We find the gods constantly harassed by demons, and on the whole may be justified in concluding that just as the Tuatha-de-danaan harassed the later deities of Ireland, so did these aboriginal gods lead an existence of constant warfare with the divine beings of the pantheon of the immigrant Aryans.

Popular Witchcraft & Sorcery

The popular **witchcraft** and **sorcery** of India resembles that of Europe. The Dravidian or aboriginal peoples of India have always been strong believers in sorcery, and it is possible that this is an example of the mythic influence of a conquered people. They are, however, extremely reticent regarding any knowledge they possess of it.

It seems possible that the demands made upon the popular religious sense by Brahmanism crushed the superstitions of the popular occult practices of the very early period, and confined the practice of minor sorcery, (malevolent magic), to the castes of Dravidian or aboriginal stock. Witchcraft seems most prevalent among the more isolated peoples like the Kols, Bhils, and Santals.

The nomadic peoples were also strong believers in sorcery, one of the most dreaded forms of which was the *Jigar Khor,* or liver-eater, of whom Abul Fazl (1551–1602) stated:

"One of this class can steal away the liver of another by looks and incantations. Other accounts say that by looking at a person he deprives him of his senses, and then steals from him something resembling the seed of a pomegranate, which he hides in the calf of his leg; after being swelled by the fire, he distributes it among his fellows to be eaten, which ceremony concludes the life of the fascinated person. A *Jigar Khor* is able to communicate his art to another by teaching him incantations, and by making him eat a bit of the liver cake. These *Jigar Khors* are mostly women. It is said they can bring intelligence from a long distance in a short space of time, and if they are thrown into a river with a stone tied to them, they nevertheless will not sink. In order to deprive any one of this wicked power, they brand his temples and every joint of his body, cram his eyes with salt, suspend him for forty days in a subterranean chamber, and repeat over him certain incantations."

The witch does not, however, devour the man's liver for two and a half days, and even if she has eaten it, and is put under the hands of an exorcizer, she can be forced to substitute a liver of some animal in the body of the man whom she victimized. There are also folk tales of witches taking out the entrails of people, sucking them, and then replacing them.

All this undoubtedly illustrates, as in ancient France and Germany, and probably also in the Slavonic countries, the manner in which the witch and vampire were believed to be essentially one and the same. In India the archwitch *Ralaratri,* or "black night" has the joined eyebrows, large cheeks, widely-parted lips, and projecting teeth, of the Slavonic **werewolf** and is a veritable vampire. But she also possesses the powers of ordinary witchcraft—**second-sight,** the making of philters, the control of tempests, the **evil eye,** and so forth.

Witches also took animal forms, especially those of tigers, and stories of trials are related at which people gave evidence that they had tracked certain tigers to their lairs, which upon entering they had found tenanted by a notorious witch or wizard. For such witch-tigers the usual remedy was to knock out their teeth to prevent their doing any more mischief.

Strangely enough, the Indian witch, like her European prototype, was very often accompanied by a cat. The cat, said the jungle people, is aunt to the tiger, and taught him everything but how to climb a tree. Zalim Sinh, the famous regent of Kota, believed that cats were associated with witches, and imagining himself enchanted ordered that every cat should be expelled from his province.

As in Europe, witches were known by certain marks. They were believed to learn the secrets of their craft by eating offal of all kinds. The popular belief concerning them was that they were often very handsome and neat, and invariably applied a clear line of red lead to the parting of their hair. They were popularly accused of exhuming dead children and bringing them to life to serve occult purposes of their own. They could not die so long as they were witches and until (as in Italy) they could pass on their knowledge of witchcraft to someone else.

They recited charms backwards, repeating two letters and a half from a verse in the *Quran.* If a certain charm was repeated "forwards," the person employing it would become invisible to his neighbor, but if he repeated it backwards, he would assume whatever shape he chose.

A witch could acquire power over her victim by getting possession of a lock of hair, the paring of nails, or some other part of his body, such as a tooth. For this reason Indian people were extremely careful about the disposal of such, burying them in the earth in a place covered with grass, or in the neighborhood of water, which witches universally disliked. Some people even flung the cuttings of their hair into running water.

Like the witches of Europe, they too made images of persons out of wax, dough, or similar substances, and tortured them with the idea that the pain would be felt by the person whom they desired to injure.

In India the witches' **familiar** was known as a *bir* or the "hero," who aided her to inflict injury upon human beings. The power of the witch was greatest on the 14th, 15th, and 29th of each month, and in particular on the Feast of Lamps *(Diwali)* and the Festival of Durga.

Witches were often severely punished amongst the isolated hill-folk and diabolical ingenuity was shown in torturing them. To nullify their evil influence, they were beaten with rods of the castor-oil plant and usually died in the process. They were often forced to drink filthy water used by couriers in the process of their work, or their noses were cut off, or they were put to death. It has also been said that their teeth were often knocked out, their heads shaved and offal thrown at them. In the case of women, their heads were shaved and their hair was attached to a tree in some public place. They were also branded, had a ploughshare tied to their legs or were made to drink the water of a tannery.

During the Mutiny, when British authority was relaxed, the most atrocious horrors were inflicted upon witches and sorcerers by the Dravidian people. Pounded chili peppers were placed in their eyes to see if they would bring tears, and the wretched beings were suspended from a tree head downwards, being swung violently from side to side. They were then forced to drink the blood of a goat, and to exorcize the evil spirits that they had caused to enter the bodies of certain sick persons. The mutilations and cruelties practiced on them were sickening, but one of the favorite ways of counteracting the spells of a witch was to draw blood from her, and the local priest would often prick the tongue of the witch with a needle and place the resulting blood on some rice and compel her to eat it.

In Bombay state, the Tharus people were supposed to possess special powers of witchcraft, so that the "Land of Tharus" is a synonym for witch-land. In Gorakhpur, witches were also very numerous and the half-gypsy *banjaras,* or grain-carriers, were notorious believers in witchcraft. In his *Popular Religion and Folklore of Northern India* (1896) William Crooke, who did much to elucidate India's popular mythology, stated regarding the various types of Indian witches:

"At the present day [ca. 1895] the half-deified witch most dreaded in the Eastern Districts of the North-western Provinces is Lona, or Nona, a *Chamarin* or woman of the currier caste. Her legend is in this wise. The great physician Dhanwantara, who corresponds to Luqman Hakim of the Muhammadans, was once on his way to cure King Parikshit, and was deceived and bitten by the snake king Takshaka. He therefore desired his sons to roast him and eat his flesh, and thus succeed to his magical powers. The snake king dissuaded them from eating the unholy meal, and they let the cauldron containing it float down the Ganges. A currier woman, named Lona, found it and ate the contents, and thus succeeded to the mystic powers of Dhanwantara. She became skilful in cures, particularly of snake-bite. Finally she was discovered to be a witch by the extraordinary rapidity with which she could plant out rice seedlings. One day the people watched her, and saw that when she believed herself unobserved she stripped herself naked, and taking the bundle of the plants in her hands threw them into the air, reciting certain spells. When the seedlings forthwith arranged themselves in their proper places, the spectators called out in astonishment, and finding herself discovered, Nona rushed along over the country, and the channel which she made in her course is the Loni river to this day. So a saint in Broach formed a new course for a river by dragging his clothes behind him. . . .

"Another terrible witch, whose legend is told at Mathura, is Putana, the daughter of Bali, king of the lower world. She found the infant Krishna asleep, and began to suckle him with her devil's milk. The first drop would have poisoned a mortal child, but Krishna drew her breast with such strength that he drained her life-blood, and the fiend, terrifying the whole land of Braj with her cries of agony, fell lifeless on the ground. European witches suck the blood of children; here the divine Krishna turns the tables on the witch.

"The Palwar Rajputs of Oudh have a witch ancestress. Soon after the birth of her son she was engaged in baking cakes. Her infant began to cry, and she was obliged to perform a double duty. At this juncture her husband arrived just in time to see his demon wife assume gigantic and supernatural proportions, so as to allow both the baking and nursing to go on at the same time. But finding her secret discovered, the witch disappeared, leaving her son as a legacy to her astonished husband. Here, though the story is incomplete, we have almost certainly, as in the case of Nona Chamarin, one of the Melusina type of legend, where the supernatural wife leaves her husband and children, because he violated some taboo, by which he is forbidden to see her in a state of nudity, or the like."

The aborigines of India lived in great fear of ghosts and invisible spirits, and a considerable portion of their time was given up to averting the evil influences of these. Protectives of every description littered their houses, and the approaches to them, and they wore numerous amulets for the purpose of averting evil influences. Regarding these, W. Crooke stated:

"Some of the Indian ghosts, like the *ifrit* of the Arabian Nights, can grow to the length of ten *yojanas* or eighty miles. In one of the Bengal tales a ghost is identified because she can stretch out her hands several yards for a vessel. Some ghosts possess the very dangerous power of entering human corpses, like the Vetala, and swelling to an enormous size. The Kharwars of Mirzapur have a wild legend which tells how long ago an unmarried girl of the tribe died, and was being cremated. While the relations were collecting wood for the pyre, a ghost entered the corpse, but the friends managed to expel him. Since then great care is taken not to leave the bodies of women unwatched. So, in the Punjab, when a great person is cremated the bones and ashes are carefully watched till the fourth day, to prevent a magician interfering with them. If he has a chance, he can restore the deceased to life, and ever after retain him under his influence. This is the origin of the custom in Great Britain of waking the dead, a practice which 'most probably originated from a silly superstition as to the danger of a corpse being carried off by some of the agents of the invisible world, or exposed to the ominous liberties of brute animals.' But in India it is considered the best course, if the corpse cannot be immediately disposed of, to measure it carefully, and then no malignant *Bhut* can occupy it.

"Most of the ghosts whom we have been as yet considering are malignant. There are, however, others which are friendly. Such are the German Elves, the Robin Goodfellow, Puck, Brownie and the Cauld Lad of Hilton of England, the Glashan of the Isle of Man, the Phouka or Leprechaun of Ireland. Such, in one of his many forms, is the *Brahmadaitya,* or ghost of a Brahman who has died unmarried. In Bengal he is believed to be more neat and less mischievous than other ghosts; the Bhuts carry him in a palanquin, he wears wooden sandals, and lives in a Banyan tree."

Psychical Research and Parapsychology

The scientific study of psychical phenomena in India really belongs to the period following independence (1948). A small beginning took place in 1951 at the Department of Philosophy and Psychology of Benares Hindu University under Bhikhan L. Atreya, when parapsychology was included as a postgraduate subject, but it did not make much progress. But various other Indian scholars such as C. T. K. Chari and S. Parthasarthy of Madras, and Prof. & Mrs. Akolkar of Poona became keenly interested in psychical phenomena. Prof. Chari took a special interest in scientific and statistical approaches and published papers in the *Journal* of the American Society of Psychical Research.

Another pioneer was K. Ramakrishna Rao, professor and head of the Department of Psychology and Parapsychology at Andhra University who worked for several years at Duke University, North Carolina, and then established the department at Andhra University and collaborated with B. K. Kanthamani. Rao subsequently became president of the Parapsychological Association for 1965 and 1978, and was later director of the **Institute for Parapsychology,** Durham, North Carolina.

In North India, Dr. Sampurananand first became interested in parapsychology when Education Minister, and later initiated study of the paranormal at the University of Lucknow in conjunction with Kali Prasad, head of the Department of Philosophy and Psychology. When Sampurananand was appointed Governor of Rajasthan, he helped to establish a department of parapsychology at the Rajasthan University at Jaipur, although this was subsequently closed. Since then, however, there has been interest in the subject for postgraduate degrees in Lucknow and Agra Universities.

In 1962–63, the Bureau of Psychology in Allahabad took up a research project in parapsychology, studying (ESP) **Extra sensory perception** in schoolchildren. The results were published in the *International Journal of Parapsychology* in the Autumn 1968 issue.

In 1964, Jamuna Prasad, president of the Indian Institute of Parapsychology, Allahabad, assisted **Ian Stevenson** who visited India to investigate reported cases of reincarnation first hand. A group of researchers took part in this project, which involved a Specific Trait Questionnaire designed to assess the possible impressions of past experiences carried over to another incarnation. With the formal establishment of the Indian Institute of Parapsychology, another valuable project on "Paranormal Powers Manifested During Yogic Training" was undertaken with a grant from the **Parapsychology Foundation.**

Of a slightly different nature was "Project Consciousness" inaugurated in December 1966 by Karan Singh, Minister of Health and Family Planning. This project, conducted by the National Institute of Mental Health and Neuro Sciences, Bangalore, was largely concerned with exploration of the ancient Hindu concept of *kundalini* as a psycho-physiological force in humans related to sexual energy, and in a sublimated form, to levels of higher consciousness. Interest stemmed from the work of Pandit Gopi Krishna, one of several modern spiritual teachers who revived interest in the subject through his writing and teaching activity. The project languished after a change of government.

Indian publications concerned with parapsychology have included: *Darshana International* (quarterly journal of philosophy, psychology, psychical research, religion and mysticism), *Psychics International* (quarterly journal of psychic and yoga research), *Parapsychology* (an Indian journal of parapsychological research from the department of parapsychology, Rajasthan University, Jaipur), discontinued with the closure of the Department of Parapsychology at Rajasthan University, and the *Journal of Indian Psychology* (Andhra University).

On a more general mystical basis, the journal *Kundalini* (formerly *Kundalini & Spiritual India*) was devoted to the study of consciousness evolution arising from the work of Gopi Krishna. In this connection, a Central Institute for Kundalini Research was established at Srinagar, Kashmir, although it became inactive following the Gopi Krishna's death in 1984.

Sources:

Abbott, John. *The Keys of Power: A Study of Indian Ritual and Belief.* London, 1932. Reprint, New Hyde Park: University Books, 1974.

Atreya, B. L. *An Introduction to Parapsychology.* Banaras, India: International Standard Publications, 1957.

Bernard, Theos. *Philosophical Foundations of India.* London: Rider, 1945.

Crooke, William. *The Popular Religion and Folk-Lore of Northern India.* Allahabad, India: Government Press, 1894. Reprint, 2 vols. London: A. Constable, 1896.

Garrison, Omar. *Tantra—The Yoga of Sex.* New York: Causeway Books, 1973.

Gervis, Pearce. *Naked They Pray.* London: Cassell, 1956.

Gopi Krishna, Pandit. *The Biological Basis of Religion & Genius.* New York: Harper & Row, 1971.

———. *Kundalini: The Evolutionary Energy in Man.* London: Stuart & Watkins, n.d. Reprint, Boulder, Colo.: Shambhala, 1967.

Oman, J. Campbell. *Cults, Customs & Superstitions of India.* London: T. Fisher Unwin, 1908.

———. *The Mystics, Ascetics and Saints of India.* London: T. Fisher Unwin, 1903.

Sanyal, J. M., trans. *The Srimad Bhagavatam.* 2 Vols., New Delhi, India: Munshiram Manocharlal, 1973.

Indian Journal of Parapsychology

Published by University of Rajasthan, Department of Parapsychology, Jaipur, India.

Indian Rope Trick

A legendary illusion said to have been witnessed by travelers in India and other Oriental countries. As classically described, the demonstration starts with the magician throwing a rope high into the air. The rope stays vertical and a boy assistant of the magician climbs up the rope and disappears from sight. The magician calls to the boy in apparent anger, demanding his return, then puts a sharp knife in his teeth and also climbs the rope and disappears high into the air. There is then the sound of a fierce quarrel; the dismembered limbs of the boy, followed by his bleeding trunk and head, are thrown down to the ground. The magician comes down the rope, kicks the limbs, throws a cloth over them or puts them in a basket, and in a moment the boy reappears whole, none the worse for the experience.

Travelers' tales often included the detail that a photographer took a picture, which proved blank on developing the negative, or alternatively showed only the magician sitting on the ground without a rope, suggesting that the whole exhibition was a collective hallucination induced by the magician.

An early account of the illusion is that of the great Moslem traveler Ibn Batuta (1304–1378), who claimed to witness it in Hang-chow, China. Two centuries later a wandering juggler demonstrated a version of the trick in Germany. Pu Sing Ling, a seventeenth-century Chinese author, wrote that he saw the trick at Delhi, India, in 1630, but it was performed using a 75-foot chain instead of a rope. Edward Melton, a British sailor, saw the trick performed at Batavia by Chinese conjurers about 1670. Since then there have been several reports and numerous rumors of the trick by British travelers and residents in India, continuing until modern times. The British newspaper the *Daily Mail* carried several firsthand accounts of different versions of the trick (beginning on January 8, 1919) and even ran a photograph.

The various reports by people who have actually witnessed the trick suggest that it is an illusion accomplished by a combination of concealed wires, special lighting assisted by a sun low in the sky at the end of the day, and a dissected monkey whose parts can be thrown from the air. Given modern devices there are other methods that could be used to assist in the illusion. One version of the trick was demonstrated in India by the American illusionist **John Keel,** who used carefully suspended wires invisible to the spectators, over which a rope was thrown and secured by a hook. Keel claimed that he learned the trick from an Indian holy man who was no longer interested in illusions.

However, there are still some feats of Indian fakirs that have not been explained by simple illusion. These include various acts of levitation done in the round, with prying eyes at every angle. Some have suggested that such events argue for the existence of a rare but genuinely occult power.

According to traditional Hindu yoga teachings, **levitation** and other supernormal powers are possible at a certain stage of yogic development. The material world itself is regarded as *maya* (illusion), an inferior reality that may be transcended by advanced yogis. The great Hindu religious teacher Shankaracharya (b. eighth century C.E.) cites the classic form of the Indian rope trick in his commentary on the scripture Mandukya Upanishad, using this as an example of the illusory nature of empirical reality. He points out that although the spectators appear to witness the marvels of the trick, in reality the magician is simply seated on the ground veiled by his own magic. This discussion suggests that Shankaracharya had seen the trick performed and that he thought it to be achieved by the magician's transcending empirical reality and communicating an illusory demonstration to the spectators. In modern terms Shankaracharya is suggesting that what today would be thought of as a collective hallucination was achieved by the supernormal powers of an occultist.

Sources:

Gould, Rupert T. *The Stargazer Talks.* Reprinted as *More Oddities and Enigmas.* New Hyde Park, N.Y.: University Books, 1973.

Keel, John A. *Jadoo.* London, 1958.

Stein, Gordon. *Encyclopedia of Hoaxes.* Detroit: Gale Research, 1993.

Indridason, Indridi (1883–1912)

Powerful Icelandic medium (discovered by the novelist Einar H. Kuaran) who was the subject of systematic experiments between the years 1904 and 1909 by the Psychic Experimental Society of Reykjavik, which was established for the purpose of studying this mediumship, the first that **Iceland** had known. Indridason, who was under exclusive contract to the society, began with **automatic writing** and **trance** speaking. After that **telekinesis, levitation, materialization,** and **direct voice** developed. He also had healing powers. The phenomena was so strong that direct voice was heard and levitations took place in the presence of 60 to 70 sitters.

Indridason's chief **control** claimed to be a brother of his grandfather, a university professor at Copenhagen. The power of the medium was at its height in 1909. During the summer he contracted typhoid fever and later consumption, dying in a sanatorium in August 1912.

The experimental society disbanded after his death. **Harald Nielsson,** professor of theology at the University of Reykjavik, was the chief exponent of the genuineness of Indridason's power (*Light,* October–November 1919). The *Journal* of the American Society for Psychical Research (1924, p. 239) published a critical analysis of the phenomena by Prof. Gudmundur Hanneson of the University of Reykjavik. He concludes: "The phenomena are unquestionable realities."

Sources:

Gissurarson, Loftur R., and Erlendur Haraldsson. "The Icelandic Physical Medium Indridi Indridason." *Proceedings* of the Society for Psychical Research 57, 214 (January 1989).

Inedia

Technical term for the claimed ability to survive without taking nourishment. This ability has been reported of various saints throughout history, and in modern times of the Bavarian peasant woman **Therese Neumann,** who is said to have existed for many years without food, taking only a little water.

Infernal Court

Johan Weyer (1515–1588) and other demonologists knowledgeable in the lore of the infernal regions claimed to have discovered there princes and high dignitaries, ministers, ambassadors, and officers of state, whose names and occupations are listed as precisely as in any earthly census. Satan is no longer the sovereign of Hades but is leader of the opposition, the true leader being Beelzebub.

According to Weyer, the demons number 7,405,926, commanded by 72 princes. The anonymous author of *Le Cabinet du Roy de France* (1581) amends these figures to 7,409,127 demons and 79 princes.

Although demons are specifically named in many inspired catalogs and invoked by sorcerers from their **grimoires,** there is no real agreement on names and numbers, and in all these fantastic works it is not difficult to see that they represent a distorted reflection of social organization of the world of their time.

Sources:

Weyer, Johannes. *Witches, Devils and Doctors in the Renaissance: Johann Weyer, De Praestigiis.* Edited by George Mora. Binghamton, N.Y.: Medieval & Rensaissance Texts & Studies, 1991.

Influence

In mediumistic terminology *influence* is equivalent to "spirit." The American medium **Lenora Piper** applied it to objects that, by virtue of association of ideas or magnetism of the late owner, helped her to establish communication with the deceased. The presence of such objects, she declared, helped her to clear the ideas of the communicators. The term *influence* was used earlier by practitioners of **animal magnetism** to denote the mesmeric force between operator and subject.

INFO See International Fortean Organization

INFO (Journal)

Journal of the **International Fortean Organization,** continuing the research of the late **Charles Fort** into inexplicable events, prodigies, mysteries, and so forth. Address: INFO, P.O. Box 367, Arlington, VA 22210-0367. (See also **Doubt; Fortean Times**)

Information Services for Psi Education

A clearinghouse for information on sources and resources in parapsychology in New York City. It was formed to provide facts on individuals, organizations, and research findings for the benefit of librarians and educators. Apparently now inactive.

Informazioni de Parapsicologia

Semiannual Italian publication reporting research in parapsychology; includes news and book reviews. Published by **Centro Italiano di Parapsicologia,** Via Belvedere 87, 81027 Naples, Italy.

Inglis, Brian (1916–1993)

Irish author and journalist, an authority on alternative medicine and paranormal topics. Inglis was born on July 31, 1916, in Dublin. He attended Shrewsbury and Magdalene Colleges, Oxford (B.A., honors) and Dublin University (Ph.D.). He served in the Royal Air Force during World War II and afterward became a journalist and author. He was editor of *The Spectator* (1959–62).

His original outlook on and mistrust of scientific dogma led him to join the **Society for Psychical Research** in the early 1960s and make his own investigation into paranormal subjects. He was a founding member of the **K.I.B. Foundation,** with **Arthur Koestler,** formed to encourage and promote research in fields at present outside scientific orthodoxies, such as parapsychology and alternative medicine. (After the death of Arthur Koestler, the organization was renamed The Koestler Foundation.)

Inglis wrote numerous books on Irish history, unorthodox medicine, and the paranormal. He was also a consultant to the serial publication *The Unexplained.*

Parapsychologist Scott Roge complained that Inglis had a bad habit in his writing of suppressing negative information about psychics and researchers he favored by failing to note cases of fraud that were uncovered. Inglis died in 1993.

Sources:

Berger, Arthur S., and Joyce Berger. *The Encyclopedia of Parapsychology and Psychical Research.* New York: Paragon House, 1991.

Inglis, Brian. *Fringe Medicine.* 1964. Reprinted as *The Case for Unorthodox Medicine.* New York: Berkeley, 1969.

———. *The Hidden Power.* London: Jonathan Cape, 1986.

———. *Natural and Supernatural: A History of the Paranormal from Earliest Times to 1914.* London: Hodder & Stoughton, 1977.

———. *Natural Medicine.* London: Collins, 1979.

———. *The Paranormal: An Encyclopedia of Psychic Phenomena.* London: Granada, 1985.

———. *Science and Parascience: A History of the Paranormal, 1914–1939.* London: Hodder & Stoughton, 1984.

Inglis, Brian, and Ruth West. *The Alternative Health Guide.* New York: Alfred A. Knopf, 1983.

Initiation

The process of entry into a secret society, an occult group, or a mystical stage of religion. The idea of initiation was inherited by the Egyptians and Assyrians from Neolithic peoples who possessed secret organizations or "mysteries" analogous to those of the Medwiwin of the North American Indians or those of the Australian Blackfellows. Initiation was a stage in the various grades of the Egyptian priesthood and the mysteries of Eleusis and Bacchus. These processes probably consisted of tests of courage and fidelity (as with the ordeals of primitive peoples) and included such acts as sustaining a severe beating, drinking blood, real and imaginary; and so forth.

In the *Popol Vuh,* the saga of the Kiche Indians of Guatemala, there is a description of the initiation tests of two hero-gods on entrance to the native equivalent of Hades. Indeed, many of the religious mysteries typified the descent of man into hell and his return to earth, based on the corn mother legend of the resurrection of the wheat plant.

Initiation into the higher branches of mysticism, magic, and **Theosophy** is largely symbolic and is to be taken as implying a preparation for the higher life and the regeneration of the soul. Typical of such rites are the ceremonies for initiation and advancement of Freemasons.

The great religions instituted initiation rituals, such as the baptism and laying on of hands in Christianity, and the circumcision and bar mitzvah in Judaism.

The ordeal rituals of initiation into **Freemasonry** echo older ceremonies symbolizing the mysteries of birth, pain, death, and the life of the soul. Many trades also have traditional ordeal ceremonies for the initiation of young apprentices, similar to those instituted by college fraternities.

In esoteric traditions, both Eastern and Western, initiation refers to the entrance into various levels of purification of the individual through development at all levels of experience—body, mind, emotions, and soul—as discussed in various forms of magical and mystical traditions. Initiation can be used in a somewhat watered-down sense, and is adaptable to any new insight brought about by the ups and downs of living. However, it more properly is used to refer to those insights created by a planned system of inner development while the individual is involved in mastering a particular system of esoteric teachings.

Sources:

Allen, M. R. *Male Cults and Secret Initiation in Melanesia.* Melbourne, Australia: Melbourne University Press, 1967.

Alli, Antero, et al. *All Rites Reversed: Ritual Technology for Self-Initiation.* Boulder, Colo.: Vigilantero Press, 1987.
Danielou, Alain. *Yoga: The Method of Re-Integration.* London: Christopher, 1969. Reprint, New Hyde Park, N.Y.: University Books, 1956.
Duncan, Malcolm C. *Duncan's Masonic Ritual and Monitor.* New York: McKay, 1976.
Eliade, Mircea. *Rites and Symbols of Initiation: The Mysteries of Birth & Rebirth.* New York: Harper Torchbooks, 1968.
Fortune, Dion. *The Training and Work of an Initiate.* 1930. Reprint, New York: Samuel Weiser, 1972.
Hall, Manly P. *Secret Teachings of All Ages.* Hollywood, Calif.: Philosophical Research Society, 1962. Rev. ed. 1977.
Heard, Gerald. *Training for the Life of the Spirit.* Hankins, N.Y.: Strength Books, 1975. Distributed by Steiner Books.
Huxley, Francis. *The Way of the Sacred.* Garden City, N.Y.: Doubleday, 1974. Reprint, New York: Dell, 1976.
MacKenzie, Norman, ed. *Secret Societies.* London: Aldus Books, 1967.
Oliver, Rev. George. *The History of Initiation, in Twelve Lectures; comprising a Detailed Account of the Rites & Ceremonies, Doctrines and Discipline, of all the Secret and Mysterious Institutions of the Ancient World.* London: Richard Spencer, 1829. Rev. ed. 1841.
Sédir, Paul. *Initiations.* London: Regency Press, 1967.
Stewart, R. J. *UnderWorld Initiation: A Journey Towards Psychic Transformation.* Wellingborough, England: Aquarian Press, 1985.
Underhill, Evelyn. *Mysticism.* London: Methuen, 1911.
Young, Frank W. *Initiation Ceremonies: A Cross-Cultural Study of Status Dramatization.* Bobbs-Merrill, 1965.

Inner Circle Kethra E'Da Foundation

A foundation established in 1945 by trance medium Mark Probert. Probert was recognized as a medium by Meade Layne of the **Borderland Sciences Research Society,** who helped assist him in his development. Gradually a set of teachers emerged who expressed the desire to use him as their means of communicating with the world. The sessions at which these spirit entities spoke were recorded, transcribed, and published by the foundation.

Probert died in 1969, and since then the foundation has preserved tape recordings of his trance lectures and circulated copies of those that were published. As of 1992 there were three centers associated with the foundation where people gathered to listen to the Probert tapes. The foundation may be contacted at 152 Thompson Ave., Mountain View CA 94043.

Sources:

Probert, Mark. *Excerpts from the Mark Probert Séances: 1950 Series.* 3 vols. San Diego, Calif.: Inner Circle Press, 1950.
———. *The Magic Bag.* San Diego, Calif.: Inner Circle Kethra E'Da Foundation, 1963.
Wassen, Ralph, ed. *Yada Speaks.* San Diego, Calif.: Kethra E'Da Foundation, 1985.

Inner Forum Newsletter

Monthly publication featuring developments in parapsychology; includes sections on yoga, astrology, pyramids, and related subjects. Address: Inner Forum, Inc., P.O. Box 1611, Boise, ID 83701.

Inner-Space Interpreters

Publishers in the 1970s of three valuable guides to periodicals, recordings, and services in the fields of **psi** phenomena and New Age spiritual awareness: the *Guide to Psi Periodicals* (newspapers, magazines, newsletters); the *California Directory of Psi Services* (organizations, individuals, shops, services); and the *Guide to Psi Tape Recordings.* All three guides were edited by Elizabeth M. Werner. They were superseded by *Whole Again Resource Guide,* published by SourceNet, in Santa Barbara, California, in the 1980s.

Inner Voice

An auditory sensation covered, whether subjective or objective, by the term **clairaudience.** Clairaudience is usually conceived of as a purely mental phenomenon. One interesting description of the inner voice was offered by medium T. Herbert Noyes, before the **London Dialectical Society** in the last century: "I know that I should excite the derision of the sceptics if I were to say that I have conversed with spirits after a fashion which was asserted to be that in which spirits communicate with each other—by an "inner voice," which I could only compare to the sensation which would be caused by a telegraphic apparatus being hooked on to one of the nerve-ganglia—a distinctly audible click accompanying every syllable of the communication, which one could not say one heard, but of which one was made conscious by a new sense, and which was clearly distinguishable from thoughts originated in one's own mind."

InPSIder, The (Newsletter)

Monthly newsletter issued by the Parapsychological Services Institute (PSI), a nonprofit organization founded in 1986. PSI offers education and counseling for those wishing to explore the meaning of psychic and spiritual experiences. The first issue of *The InPSIder* was published in July 1992. Address: 5575 B Chamblee Dunwoody Rd., Ste. 323, Atlanta, GA 30338.

INPSITE (Psychical Research Database)

This computer catalog of the holdings of the **American Society for Psychical Research** is maintained in *Inmagic,* a software package designed for libraries and information centers. The software assists with serials control and circulation, and also connects with other computer systems. INPSITE contains records of the book and journal collections, the pamphlet file, and the society's archives. Initially INPSITE emphasized items that did not appear in the existing card catalog—which closed in early 1987 with some 600 books and many pamphlets not yet cataloged—but as INPSITE expands, it hopes to provide access to the complete card catalog. For information on INPSITE, contact the American Society for Psychical Research, 5 W. 73rd St., New York, NY 10023.

Insight (Journal)

Occasional publication of **Central Psi Research Institute**, 4800 N. Milwaukee Ave., Ste. 210, Chicago, IL 60630.

Insight (Magazine)

Quarterly magazine of occultism with a wide range of coverage, published by Deric Robert James, 25 Calmore Close, Stourvale Meadows, Bournemouth, Dorset, England.

Insight Northwest (Newsletter)

Bimonthly newsletter published by PsiCircle Center, concerned with New Age, holistic, and spiritual topics. Address: PsiCircle Center, P.O. Box 95341, Seattle, WA 98145.

Insights (Journal)

Monthly publication of the Jersey Society of Parapsychology, reporting on the society's activities and experiments in *psi* phenomena. Address: P.O. Box 2071, Morristown, NJ 07960.

Inspiration

A psychic state in which one becomes susceptible to creative spiritual influence or unwittingly lends oneself as an instrument for through-flowing ideas. It is the creative state of the artist, poet, and author, traditionally believed to be amenable to the wisdom of the muses or inspiring gods. In a state of inspiration, the prophets of various religions dictated scriptures or predicted future events. The term inspiration denotes a breathing in of the divine creative spirit, bringing perception of truth.

Numerous thinkers and artists have noted their own experience of inspiration. They describe states of outward passivity in which the mind becomes receptive to information that they cannot ascribe to their own intelligence. The inspiration of the muse in poets, painters, and musicians, when considered universally, resembles the experiences of mediums, channels, and psychics.

The philosopher Ferdinand Schiller wondered where his thoughts came from; they frequently flowed through him "independent of the action of his own mind." Mozart stated, "When all goes well with me, when I am in a carriage, or walking, or when I cannot sleep at night, the thoughts come streaming in upon me most fluently; whence or how is more than I can tell." Beethoven said, "Inspiration is for me that mysterious state in which the entire world seems to form a vast harmony, when every sentiment, every thought re-echoes within me, when all the forces of nature become instruments for me, when my whole body shivers and my hair stands on end."

Lord Beaconsfield, British statesman and novelist, admitted, "I often feel that there is only a step from intense mental concentration to madness. I should hardly be able to describe what I feel at the moment when my sensations are so strangely acute and intense. Every object seems to be animated. I feel that my senses are wild and extravagant. I am no longer sure of my own existence and often look back to see my name written there and thus be assured of my existence."

The two satellites of Mars were discovered in 1877 by Professor A. Hall. One hundred seventy-five years earlier, Jonathan Swift wrote in *Gulliver's Travels* of the astronomers of Laputa: "They have discovered two small stars, or satellites, which revolve round Mars. The inner one is three diameters distant from the centre of the planet, the outer one five diameters; the first makes its revolution in ten hours, the second in twenty hours and a half." These figures, cited at the time as a proof of Swift's ignorance of astronomy, show a striking agreement with the later findings of Hall.

W. M. Thackeray in one of his "Roundabout Papers" (*Cornhill Magazine,* August 1862): "I have been surprised at the observations made by some of my characters. It seems as if an occult power was moving the pen. The personage does or says something and I ask: 'How did he come to think of that?'"

Lafcadio Hearn (1850–1904) said his writing was done in "periods of hysterical trance." He said he saw and heard things that were not real.

Of the inception of the chapter "The Death of Uncle Tom" in *Uncle Tom's Cabin,* one biographer of Harriet Beecher Stowe stated, "It seemed to her as though what she wrote was blown through her mind as with the rushing of a mighty wind."

Bogdan Hasdeu, the great Romanian writer, became a convinced Spiritualist after he automatically obtained messages from his deceased daughter. His father had been a distinguished linguist and was planning a standard dictionary of the Romanian language at the time of his death. Bogdan himself was a historian. When half through his *History of the Romanian People,* he suddenly plunged into the compilation of a vast dictionary, saying he felt that he was forced to do so. It is difficult to explain this case by ordinary psychological processes, since in a séance Bogdan later atteneded the medium (who could not speak Russian) passed into trance and wrote messages from his father in Russian urging him to complete the work.

The popular novelist and playwright Edgar Wallace wrote in the London *Daily Express* (June 4, 1928): "Are we wildly absurd in supposing that human thought has an indestructible substance, and that men leave behind them, when their bodies are dead, a wealth of mind that finds employment in a new host? I personally do not think we are. I am perfectly satisfied in my mind that I have received an immense amount of help from the so-called dead. I have succeeded far beyond the point my natural talents justified. And so have you—and you. I believe that my mind is furnished with oddments of intellectual equipment that have been acquired I know not how."

Sitting with **W. T. Stead** and **Ada Goodrich-Freer,** the medium David Anderson went into trance and gave the name of the hero and some incidents from a story that Goodrich-Freer had written but never published. A similar occurrence is recorded in H. Travers Smith's *Voices from the Void* (1919).

Hannen Swaffer interviewed a number of distinguished artists and writers on the method by which their work was produced. The majority of their statements, recorded in Swaffer's book *Adventures with Inspiration* (1929) attribute the imparting of creativity to a supernormal source.

According to ancient Hindu mysticism, there is a psychophysiological mechanism in human beings by which a condition of higher consciousness may be brought about by meditation or yoga practice, and in modern times there is some evidence that this condition—the raising of the **kundalini**—has occurred spontaneously in inventors and men of genius.

Sources:

Bucke, Richard Maurice. *Cosmic Consciousness: A Study in the Evolution of the Human Mind.* Innes & Sons, 1901. Reprint, New Hyde Park, N.Y.: University Books, 1961.

Clissold, Augustus. *The Prophetic Spirit in its Relation to Wisdom and Madness.* London, 1870.

Duchesneau, Louise. *The Voice of the Muse.* Frankfurt, Germany: P. Lang, 1986.

Gopi Krishna. *The Biological Basis of Religion and Genius.* New York: Harper & Row, 1972.

Graves, Robert. *The White Goddess.* London: Faber & Faber, 1948.

James, William. *The Varieties of Religious Experience.* London: Longmans Green, 1902.

Kast, Verena. *Joy, Inspiration, and Hope.* College Station, Tex.: Texas A & M University Press, 1991.

Kennard, Nina H. *Lafcadio Hearn, His Life and Work.* New York: D. Appleton and Co., 1912.

Inspirational Speakers

Trance **mediums** who deliver impromptu platform addresses on various subjects, often chosen by the audience, the contents of which seem to greatly surpass their normal intellectual power and knowledge. The degree of difference in knowledge and erudition between the medium awake and in a trance continues to be (in the case of New Age **channeling**) one of the primary arguments in favor of the spirit hypothesis. The history of **Spiritualism** is rich in accounts of inspirational mediums. Among the most famous mediums in the United States were **Cora Richmond** (first known as "Miss Cora Scott" and later as "Mrs. Hatch" and "Mrs. Tappan"), **Emma Hardinge Britten, Thomas Lake Harris,** Thomas Gale Forster, and Nettie Colburn (also known as **"Maynard"**). They were joined in England by **William J. Colville, J. J. Morse, Anne Meurig Morris, Estelle Roberts,** and **Winifred Moyes.**

The first American inspirational speaker who visited England shortly after the arrival of **Maria B. Hayden** was Emma Frances Jay (later Mrs. Emma Jay Bullene). Emma Hardinge Britten mentions a number of additional inspirational speakers in her survey *Modern American Spiritualism* (1870), among them a Miss Sprague, Charlotte Tuttle, Hattie Huntley, Frances Hyzer, and Mrs. M. S. Townsend. Trance speaker Henrietta Maynard had a special claim to fame since her oratory reportedly influenced **Abraham Lincoln** on the issue of emancipation.

In recent times the concept of trance speaking has experienced a remarkable revival as a **New Age** phenomenon, with the deviation that the New Age channels rarely allow the audience to suggest the topic for their regular discourses. Familiar names from the modern era include **Edgar Cayce** and **Jane Roberts,** who inspired a host of contemporary channelers, such as Elwood

Babbitt, **JZ Knight** (who channels "Ramtha"), Jack Pursell ("Lazaris"), and **Ruth Montgomery.**

It is not always clear whether the trance message is coming from a real or fictitious communicating entity or whether it springs from a hidden level of consciousness of the channeler. It is therefore always wise, as with mediumship in general, to evaluate the phenomenon of channeling on the basis of the quality of inspiration and on the accuracy of information and insight.

Sources:

Garrett, Eileen J. *My Life as a Search for the Meaning of Mediumship.* New York, 1939. Reprint, New York: Arno Press, 1975.

Klimo, Jon. *Channeling: Investigations on Receiving Information from Paranormal Sources.* Los Angeles: Jeremy P. Tarcher, 1967.

Leaf, Horace. *What Mediumship Is.* London: Spiritualist Press, 1976.

Maynard, Nettie. *Was Abraham Lincoln a Spiritualist?* Philadelphia: R. C. Hartranft, 1891. Reprint, London: Psychic Book Club, 1917.

Moses, William Stainton. *Spirit Teachings Through the Mediumship of William Stainton Moses.* London, 1883. Reprint, New York: Arno Press, 1976.

Roberts, Jane. *Seth Speaks.* Englewood Cliffs, N.J.: Prentice-Hall, 1972.

Stern, Jess. *Edgar Cayce: The Sleeping Prophet.* Virginia Beach, Va.: A.R.E. Press, 1967.

Institut für Grenzgebiete der Psychologie und Psychohygiene (Institute for Border Areas of Psychology and Mental Hygiene)

German institute for parapsychology and related areas, founded in 1950 by **Hans Bender.** In conjunction with Freiburg University, West Germany, a chair in psychology and border areas of psychology was established at Freiburg University in 1953 and was held by Bender until his retirement in 1975. His successor, Johannes Mischo, installed a laboratory in the university department that works in close cooperation with the independent institute.

The institute has a library of 16,000 volumes. Since 1957 the institute has published the *Zeitschrift für Parapsychologie und Grenzgebiete der Psychologie* (Journal of Parapsychology and Border Areas of Psychology), in which many articles contain summaries in English. Address: Eichhalde 12, 7800 Freiburg i Br., Germany.

Sources:

Berger, Arthur S., and Joyce Berger. *The Encyclopedia of Parapsychology and Psychical Research.* New York: Paragon House, 1991.

Institut Général Psychologique

Founded in Paris in 1904 to pursue psychical research. The presidents of the institute were, successively, Professor Duclaux (Pasteur's successor in L'Institut Pasteur); M. d'Arsonval (member of the Academy): and a Professor Borda. Following the intervention of Czar Nicholas, the French government authorized a lottery on behalf of the institute that produced 800,000 francs. The depreciation of the franc, however, wiped out most of this capital. The institute's most memorable investigation was conducted between 1905 and 1908 with **Eusapia Palladino.** After the capital was gone the institute ceased activities.

The moving spirit of the institute was Serge Yourievitch, secretary to the Russian Embassy in Paris, and the secretarial duties were attended to by M. J. Courtier.

Institut Métapsychique International

Founded by Jean Meyer at 89 Avenue Niel, Paris, in 1918, and recognized as an institute of public utility. The first director was **Gustav Geley,** who was assisted by a committee consisting of **Charles Richet,** a Professor Santoliquido, Count de Gramont of the Institut of France, Medical Inspector General Dr. Calmette, **Camille Flammarion,** former Minister of State Jules Roche, and a Dr. Treissier of the Hospital of Lyons. Later members were **Sir Oliver Lodge, Ernesto Bozzano,** and a Professor Leclainche, a member of the institute and inspector general of sanitary services. Later, **Eugén Osty** became director and Richet was elected president. The institute published a journal, *La Revue Métapsychique.*

An important phase of the work of the institute was to invite public men of eminence in science and literature to witness the investigations. Invitations to a hundred men of science were extended by Geley to the séances with **"Eva C."** The institute installed infrared photography equipment with which it was possible to take 1,000 fully exposed pictures per second. The apparatus cost about $2,500, but was so noisy and technically impractical it could not be put to much use.

The most important experiments after Osty took office were conducted with **Rudi Schneider.** The medium produced an invisible substance that—though it could not be seen—intercepted the passage of an infrared ray emitted from an apparatus outside his reach. The interception was automatically registered on a revolving cylinder.

Institute for Anomalistic Criminology (IAC)

Specialized section of the **Center for Scientific Anomalies Research** (founded 1981). The IAC was formed by **Marcello Truzzi** to bring together behavioral science researchers and criminal investigation experts concerned with the interface between claims of scientific anomalies and criminal behavior. Concerns include such diverse topics as "occult crime" (e.g., claims of Satanic abuse), use of psychics by law enforcement agencies, spontaneous human combustion, involvement of "apparitions" in crimes, and correlation between lunar phase and crime.

Address: Center for Scientific Anomalies Research, c/o Dr. Marcello Truzzi, Director, P. O. Box 1052, Ann Arbor, MI 48106-1052.

Sources:

Lyons, Arthur, and Marcello Truzzi. *Blue Sense: Psychic Detectives and Crime.* New York: Mysterious Press; New York: Warner Books, 1991.

Institute for Parapsychology

A division of the **Foundation for Research on the Nature of Man,** housing the Duke University collection on parapsychology, comprised of more than 10,000 accounts of spontaneous **psi** experiences. The institute was founded in 1962 after Duke University discontinued its sponsorship of the controversial Parapsychology Laboratory which was headed by pioneer parapsychologist **J. B. Rhine.**

The institute conducts research and serves as an international forum. It holds meetings attended by researchers from other parapsychology centers, and many of their papers and reports are published by the institute in its **Journal of Parapsychology.** It also houses a large parapsychology library and sponsors summer study programs for graduate students and postgraduate research. The current director is Dr. **K. Ramakrishna Rao**. Address: Box 6847, College Station, Durham, NC 27708.

Institute for the Development of the Harmonious Human Being

An organization teaching a Sufi form of **Fourth Way** teachings (derived from the work of **Georgei Ivanovitch Gurdjieff**). The institute encourages a search for God that transcends human conceptuality and, by assimilation with God, the discovery of truth and happiness. The institute holds workshops on conscious birth, sex, and death, and teaches meditation techniques. Address: Box 370, Nevada City, CA 95959.

Institute for the Study of American Religion (ISAR)

Educational research organization formed to further research and the study of the numerous small religious bodies and psychic/occult organizations formed in America during the nineteenth and twentieth centuries. It existed in Evanston, Illinois, for many years before moving to Santa Barbara, California, in 1985. At the time of the move the institute donated its library of more than 30,000 volumes to the Davidson Library at the University of California, Santa Barbara (UCSB), where it now exists as the American Religions Collection. The institute continues to support and build the collection. The American Religions Collection houses more than volumes in addition to research files, magazines, and ephemeral literature. Among its unique materials is the Elmer T. Clark Memorial set of volumes used by him in writing his classic work *The Small Sects in America* (Abingdon, 1949). The collection is open to the public for research through the special collections department of the university.

Above and beyond building a research library, ISAR has worked at creating reference books and other scholarly tools for the study of new religious movements, especially occult, magic, and Eastern groups. With the relocation of the library to the university, the research and publication program took center stage. In cooperation with Gale Research and Garland Publishing Company, the institute has been responsible for producing almost 200 separate publications during the 25 years of its existence.

ISAR's director is **J. Gordon Melton,** who also serves as a research specialist with the Department of Religious Studies at UCSB. He has written and edited a number of the institute's publications. The institute also sponsors periodic conferences. Address: P.O. Box 90709, Santa Barbara, CA 93190-0709.

Sources:

Melton, J. Gordon. *Encyclopedia of American Religions.* Wilmington, N.C.: Consortium Books, 1978. 4th ed. Detroit: Gale Research, 1992.

———. *Religious Leaders of America.* Detroit: Gale Research, 1991.

Melton, J. Gordon, Jerome Clark, and Aidan Kelly. *New Age Encyclopedia.* Detroit: Gale Research, 1990.

Murphy, Larry J., Gordon Melton, and Gary L. Ward, eds. *Encyclopedia of African American Religion.* New York: Garland Publishing, 1993.

Institute for Yoga and Consciousness

The Institute for Yoga and Consciousness was established in 1985 at Andhra University, Andhra Pradesh, India, by K. Ramakrishna Rao. Earlier, in 1967, Rao had been responsible for setting up the Department of Psychology and Parapsychology at the school, which became the center for the dissemination of information about parapsychology in India. In 1977 Rao moved to North Carolina to become head of the **Institute for Parapsychology.** While there he became aware of the new interest in consciousness studies. In 1984 he returned to India to become vice chancellor at his former school. In that position he set up the first Indian center to dedicate itself to consciousness research with a special reference to yoga and the popular consciousness-altering techniques developed by the various yoga disciplines.

Rao became the first director of the new institute, but in 1987 he came back to the United States and again resumed his leadership of the Institute for Parapsychology. The Institute for Yoga and Consciousness continues its program of research in consciousness and paranormal powers in the context of Indian spiritual belief and practice. The institute also conducts a practical program assisting individuals in using its findings in a personal program of self-discovery through yoga, meditation, counseling, and psychotherapy.

Sources:

Rao, K. R. *The Basic Experiments in Parapsychology.* Jefferson, N.C.: McFarland, 1984.

Institute Magazine

A journal of **Fourth Way** teachings, stemming from the philosophy of **Georgei Ivanovitch Gurdjieff** as taught by **J. G. Bennett.** Address: Coombe Springs Press, Daglingworth Manor, Daglingworth, Gloucestershire, GL7 7AH, England.

Institute of Noetic Sciences (IONS)

Founded in 1973 by former astronaut **Edgar D. Mitchell** to encourage and conduct basic research and education programs on mind–body relationships for the purpose of gaining new understanding of human consciousness. The term **noetic** is defined as "pertaining to, or originating in intellectual or rational activity." Institute programs include research in parapsychology, healing, personal awareness, and control of interior states. Address: 475 Gate Five Rd., Ste. 300, Sausalito, CA 94965.

Sources:

Mitchell, Edgar D. *Psychic Exploration.* Edited by John White. New York: G. P. Putnam's Sons, 1974.

Institute of Parascience See International Parascience Institute

Institute of Psychophysical Research

Founded in 1962 at Oxford, England, by members of the **Society for Psychical Research,** London, at Oxford University to advance understanding of the working of the human mind by scientific research on neglected areas of psychology, including **dreams, out-of-the-body travel,** and **hallucinations.**

The Institute of Psychophysical Research is an independent group under the directorship of **Celia E. Green,** best known as the author of the book *Out-of-the-body Experiences,* published in 1968 as volume 2 of *Proceedings of the Institute of Psychophysical Research.* Address: 118 Banbury Rd. Oxford, OX2 6JU England.

Institutio "Gnosis" per la Ricérca Sulla Ipótesi della Sopravvivenza

The Institutio "Gnosis" per la Ricérca Sulla Ipótesi della Sopravvivenza (Gnosis Institute for Research on the Survival Hypothesis) was founded in 1981 in Naples, Italy, by Giorgio Di Simone, a French parapsychologist who teaches at the University of Naples. Di Simone came of age during World War II and during his whole adult life has been intrigued by the study of possible **survival** of death. He has concentrated on the study of out-of-the-body experiences, deathbed visions, and mediumship as phenomena with the greatest potential of yielding data that will increase our understanding of individual human destiny.

The institute as a research organization cooperates with the Centro Italiano de Parapsicologia, an educational organization with which it shares office space. The institute publishes a periodical, *Quaderni Gnosis,* and may be contacted at Via Belvedere, 87/80127, Naples, Italy.

Instituto Argentino de Parapsychología

The Instituto Argentino de Parapsychología (Argentine Parapsychological Society) was founded in 1949. Its foundation came in direct response to the government's establishment the year before of the Institute of Applied Psychopathology with the aim of studying the practices of Spiritualists and determining if they were injurious to public welfare. The Parapsychological Society had the support of the Spiritualist groups in the country and included several outstanding Spiritualists, such as **José S. Fernández** and **J. Ricardo Musso,** in its leadership.

In response to a growing membership, the society reorganized in 1952 to provide both lectures and classes in parapsychology. It also began the first Spanish-language parapsychological journal, the *Review of Parapsychology.* During the next 20 years the institute, which had initially garnered the support of several academics, helped spread interest in parapsychology through the nation's university system. Musso was given an appointment to teach at the Littoral National University. Then in the late 1960s the government began to reverse its support of parapsychological research and by 1970 only one course remained. Since then, the institute has continued a program of public lectures and non-university-based courses for the general public. It may be contacted at Calle Ramon Lists 868, 1706 Domingo F. Sarmiento (Haedo) Prov. Buenos Aires, Argentina.

Instituto de Estudios Parapsicologicos

The Instituto de Estudios Parapsicologicos (Institute of Parapsychological Studies) was founded in Panama in 1982, the first and only parapsychological research center in Central America. Closely tied to the University of Panama, the institute launched an expansive program of research and education that included a series of public lectures over the first three years of its existence. The research program includes both controlled laboratory experiments and observations of spontaneous psychic occurrences. As part of their study, research programs of indigenous native groups have been undertaken.

The institute had defined its task as the study of the nature of the human being as revealed by psi phenomena such as **telepathy, clairvoyance, precognition,** and psychokinesis. While it began as a membership organization, that aspect was dropped in 1985, and the institute now concentrates on research alone. It publishes a periodical, *Boletín Informativo.* It may be contacted at Apartado 8000, Panama 7, Panama.

Instituto de Parapsychología

Through the 1950s and 1960s parapsychology enjoyed the support of the Argentine government and spread through the nation's university system. However, by 1970 that support had been withdrawn and all of the courses in the subject had been discontinued except those taught at the University of Salvador. In response to the downturn of events, in 1972 several people at the university founded the Instituto de Parapsychología, modeled on the **Institute for Parapsychology** created by **J. B. Rhine** in North Carolina. The institute also began a journal, *Cuaderanos de Parapsychología,* modeled on the *Journal of Parapsychology.* The work of the institute has been largely devoted to attempts to replicate the work initiated at the Institute for Parapsychology. It may be contacted c/o Dr. Enrique Novillo Paulí, Universidad del Salvador, Hipolito Yrigoyen 2025—Sarandi 65, 1081 Buenos Aires, Argentina.

Instituto Mexicano de Investigaciones Siquicas

The Instituto Mexicano de Investigaciones Siquicas (Mexican Institute of Psychical Investigations) was founded in 1939 as the Circulo de Investigationes Metasíquicas de Mexico at the National University of Mexico. Its founding was occasioned by the fame of physical medium **Louis Martinez,** whose work it studied. It conducted a series of séances with Martinez, attended by a number of Mexico City's social and political leaders. The organization flourished for a few years and then was discontinued.

Insufflation

Occultist **Éliphas Lévi,** in his book *Transcendental Magic* (1896), defines insufflation as follows:

"[It]" is one of the most important practices of occult medicine, because it is a perfect sign of the transmission of life. To inspire, as a fact, means to breath upon some person or thing, and we know already, by the one doctrine of Hermes, that the virtue of things has created words, that there is an exact proportion between ideas and speech, which is the first form and verbal realisation of ideas. The breath attracts or repels, according, as it is warm or cold. The warm breathing corresponds to positive and the cold breathing to negative electricity.

"Electrical and nervous animals fear cold breathing, and the experiment may be made upon a cat, whose familiarities are importunate. By fixedly regarding a lion or tiger and blowing in their face, they would be so stupefied as to be forced to retreat before us.

"Warm and prolonged insufflation recruits the circulation of the blood, cures rheumatic and gouty pains, restores the balance of the humours, and dispels lassitude. When the operator is sympathetic and good, it acts as a universal sedative.

"Cold insufflation soothes pains occasioned by congestions and fluidic accumulations. The two breathings must therefore be used alternately, observing the polarity of the human organism and acting in a contrary manner upon the poles, which must be treated successively to an opposite magnetism. Thus, to cure an inflamed eye, the one which is not affected must be subjected to a warm and gentle insufflation, cold insufflation being practised upon the suffering member at the same distance and in the same proportion.

"Magnetic passes [moving the hands over something, e.g., an afflicted part of the body] have a similar effect to insufflations, and are a real breathing by transpiration and radiation of the interior air, which is phosphorescent with vital light. Slow passes constitute a warm breathing which fortifies and raises the spirits; swift passes are a cold breathing of dispersive nature, neutralising tendencies to congestion. The warm insufflation should be performed transversely, or from below upward, the cold insufflation is more effective when directed downward from above."

(See also **mesmerism**)

Sources:

Lévi, Éliphas. *Transcendental Magic.* N.p., 1896. Reprint, New York: Samuel Weiser, 1972.

Integral Yoga International (IYI)

Founded in 1966 as the Integral Yoga Institute by **Swami Satchidananda,** disciple of the late **Swami Sivananda** of Rishikesh, India. Integral Yoga combines various yoga methods such as **hatha yoga** (physical development), karma yoga (selfless service), bhakti yoga (devotion), japa yoga (mantra repetition), jnana yoga (knowledge) and raja yoga (meditation and mind control), thus harmonizing the personality and enhancing spiritual awareness. Satchidananda wrote one of the standard modern texts on hatha yoga.

There are now a number of IYI branches across the United States. These institutes offer instruction for beginners and advanced students, community service and drug rehabilitation programs, and yoga instruction in schools and prisons. Record albums, cassette tapes, and spiritual publications are available. Address: Satchidananda Ashram—Yogaville, Rte. 1, P.O. Box 1720, Buckingham, VA 23921.

Sources:

Barlow, Sita, et al. *Sri Swami Satchidananda: Apostle of Peace.* Yogaville, Va.: Integral Yoga Publications, 1986.

Satchidananda, Sri Swami. *A Decade of Service.* Pomfret Center, Conn.: Satchidananda Ashram-Yogaville, 1976.

———. *Integral Hatha Yoga.* New York: Holt, Rinehart & Winston, 1970.

Weiner, Sita. *Swami Satchidananda.* New York: Bantam Books, 1972.

Intercosmic Association of Spiritual Awareness

Founded by Dr. Rammurti S. Mishra, endocrinologist, neurosurgeon, and psychiatrist, who has also published authoritative works on **hatha yoga** and yoga philosophy. ICSA is responsible for Mishra's lectures and study groups throughout the world, operating through the **Ananda Ashram,** Rte. 3, P.O. Box 141, Monroe, NY 10950.

Sources:

Mishra, Rammurti S. *Fundamentals of Yoga.* New York: Lancer Books, 1969.

———. *Self Analysis and Self Knowledge.* Lakemont, Ga.: CSA Press, 1978.

International Academy for Continuous Education

Founded in 1971 by mathematician-philosopher **J. G. Bennett** to propagate the **Fourth Way** work of **Georgei Ivanovitch Gurdjieff.** It aimed "to achieve, in a short space of time, the effective transmission of a whole corpus of practical techniques for self-development and self-liberation, so that people could learn effectively to direct their own inner work and to adapt to the rapid changes in the inner and outer life of man." The organization was based in Sherborne House, a Victorian mansion in the Cotswold countryside of Britain. Students studied psychology, art, history, cosmology, and linguistics and practiced spiritual and psychological exercises that were demanding at all levels—mental, physical, and emotional.

After Bennett's death in 1974 the academy expected considerable changes, largely necessitated by the evolution brought about by the inner and outer work of the students. In fact the organization soon ceased to exist, though work in the Bennett tradition continues in the United States through the **Claymont Society for Continuous Education.**

International Association for Near-Death Studies (IANDS)

Founded in 1981 with a membership of medical, academic, and health care professionals, as well as laypersons and those who had undergone **near-death experiences** (phenomena occurring in individuals who are very close to death or who pass into a temporary state of clinical **death**). The first president of the association was **Kenneth Ring,** a modern pioneer in the study of the subject.

The goals of the association are to encourage, promote, and support the scientific study of near-death experiences; to inspire the exchange and communication of ideas among persons who have conducted or are conducting research on such experiences; to collect information for educational material to be dispersed in the public and popular media; and to relate knowledge emerging from research to appropriate settings, including hospitals and nursing homes.

The association serves as a fraternal organization for those who have had near-death experiences. It maintains a collection of tapes describing these experiences and holds seminars, workshops, and symposia. It also publishes a quarterly newsletter, *Revitalized Signs,* and the *Journal of Near-Death Studies.* Address: P.O. Box 502, East Windsor, CT 06028-0502. (See also **Death; Shanti Nilaya; Thanatology**)

Sources:

Ring, Kenneth. *Heading Toward Omega: In Search of the Meaning of the Near-Death Experience.* New York: William Morrow, 1984.

International Association for Psychotronic Research

Publishers of reports, bulletins, newsletters, and a journal concerned with **psychotronics**—defined as the mutual interactions of consciousness, energy, and matter. The association brings together individuals conducting experimental research and applied studies in interactions between living organisms and their internal and external environments and the energetic processes underlying their manifestations.

Originally based in Ontario, Canada, the association moved to Czechoslovakia in the 1980s. Address: c/o Association Internationale de Recherche Psychotronique, V Chaloupkach 59, HLoubetin, CS–194 01 Prague 9, Czech Republic.

International Association for Psychotropic Research (IAPR)

Eastern European organization that conducts experimental and applied research in the interdisciplinary study of distant interactions between living organisms (i.e., **telepathy**). IAPR also offers conventions and conferences and publishes two quarterly (non-English language) journals. Address: V Chaloupkach 59, Hloubetin, CS-194 01 Prague 9, Czech Republic.

International Association for Religion and Parapsychology (IARP)

A psychical research organization founded in Toyko in 1972 by parapsychologist and engineer Hiroshi Motoyama. As early as 1966 Motoyama has traveled to the Philippines to study psychic surgery, and he began to develop a model of the unification of spirit and science and to prove the non-physical basis of mind. The association was founded to verify the reality of paranormal phenomena and to provide a program for individuals to clarify truths of mind, matter, and religious experience.

Above and beyond its research, the association holds yoga classes, retreats and other programs, and maintains an acupuncuture clinic. Demonstrating the truth and basis of acupuncutre had taken a significant portion of Motoyama's research time. The association publishes a journal and a newsletter in English. It may be contacted at 4 11-7 Inokashira, Mitaka-shi, Tokyo 181, Japan.

Sources:

Motoyama, Hiroshi, and Rande Brown. *Science and the Evolution of Consciousness: Chakras, Ki, and Psi.* Brookline, Mass.: Autumn Press, 1978.

International Association of Metaphysicians (IAM)

Organization formed in 1985 to serve as a central registry of metaphysicians and establish a code of ethics. The term *metaphysician* refers to healers and other workers in various psychic areas. The association proposed a summer camp program for children with psychic abilities. Benjamin Smith, president of IAM, has a special interest in healing and past-life regression and believes that some of the world's most valuable resources are lying untapped in children. Address: 5555 Zuni Rd. SE, Ste. 297, P.O. Box 26800, Albuquerque, NM 87125.

International Association of Parapsychologists

New Age association founded in 1965 to bring together individuals in all phases of parapsychology, organic gardening, sciences, and arts and "to build a new age town incorporating new age thought with no masters, gurus, or teachers as such as leaders, and no particular teachings."

The association believes that each individual is an "instrument of light" or "temple" and not part of a commune or family.

It bestows awards, conducts charitable and specialized educational programs, and offers children's services. It maintains a library of 1,000 volumes on parapsychology, science, herbs, UFOs, and related subjects and publishes *Luminator News.* Address: P.O. Box 1450, Apache Junction, AZ 85220.

International Congress of Psychical Research

Occasional gathering of psychical researchers from all over the world. The first congress was held in Copenhagen in 1921, the second in 1923 in Warsaw, the third in 1927 in Paris, and the fourth in 1930 in Athens. World War II interrupted such international congresses, but in 1953 the first of a new series of international conferences on parapsychological studies was held at Utrecht University, Holland, sponsored by the **Parapsychology Foundation.**

International Cooperation Council

A **New Age** organization formed as an international coordinating body for educational, scientific, cultural, and religious organizations that "foster the emergence of a new universal person and a civilization based on unity in diversity among all peoples." Originally formed to propagate the ideals and activities of several such organizations during the International Cooperation Year, it was voted into being in 1965 by the General Assembly of the United Nations. It has since been reformed under the title **Unity-in-Diversity Council,** with the aim of linking metaphysical and New Age groups worldwide.

International Flat Earth Society

Successor to the Universal Zetetic Society of America and Great Britain, dedicated to the view that "so called modern astronomy is false; that no proof has been brought forth to show the earth as a spinning ball." The term *zetetic* refers to an ancient Greek school of skeptical inquiry and has also been used in the title of several periodicals that examine claims for paranormal phenomena. Address: Box 2533, Lancaster, CA 93539.

International Fortean Organization (INFO)

An organization founded in 1965 by Ronald J. Willis, with a membership of scientists, scholars, and laymen concerned with new and unusual scientific discoveries, philosophical problems pertaining to the criteria of scientific validity, and theories of knowledge. The organization is named after **Charles Hoy Fort** (1874–1932), who researched and cataloged unusual and unexplained phenomena. INFO maintains a library of 5,000 volumes in the physical, biological, and psychological sciences, and publishes a quarterly journal **INFO.** Address: P.O. Box 367, Arlington, VA 22210-0367. (See also **Fortean Society; Fortean Times**)

International Frankenstein Society (IFS)

Founded in 1980 by Dr. Jeanne K. Youngson as a division of the **Count Dracula Fan Club** to bring together enthusiasts of Frankenstein, the main character in and title of the novel by Mary Shelley (1797–1851).

The society existed separately during the 1980s but has since become a section of the Count Dracula Fan Club. IFS promotes exchange of information; sponsors "ethical, social, moral and educational activities mixed with good fun"; and offers a book search service for members. An IFS section appears in the *Count Dracula Fan Club Newsletter.* The society publishes the Frankenstein Gold Book of membership registration. Address: c/o Dr. Jeanne K. Youngson, 29 Washington Square W., Penthouse N, New York, NY 10011.

International General Assembly of Spiritualists See Light of Divine Truth Foundation

International Ghost Registry

Formed in California to preserve and investigate records of hauntings and ghostly phenomena throughout the world. The major objectives included preserving firsthand records of ghost sightings that might otherwise have been lost, cataloging and recording ghost lore from individual geographic regions, encouraging careful evaluation and documentation of ghostly phenomena, and providing a central file for use by researchers and writers in parapsychology. The registry was administered by the International Society for the Investigation of Ghosts. It was active in the 1980s but has since become inactive.

International Group of Theosophists

The International Group of Theosophists was a small group of Theosophists active during the mid-twentieth century. They tried to remain aloof from the very intense quarrels that divided the movement in the 1890s. Heading the group was Boris Mihailovich de Zirkoff (1902–1981), the grandnephew of **Helena Petrovna Blavatsky,** one of the founders of the original **Theosophical Society.** De Zirkoff spent much of his life editing and publishing Blavatsky's collected works. The group dissolved soon after de Zirkoff's death.

Sources:

The Theosophical Movement, 1875–1950. Los Angeles: Cunningham Press, 1951.

International Institute for Psychic Investigation

British organization formed in January 1939 by the merger of the **British College of Psychic Science** and the International Institute for Psychical Research (IIPR). The institute was founded in 1934 by Mrs. Dawson Scott, pupil and associate of pioneer psychical researcher **J. Hewat McKenzie; J. Arthur Findlay;** and **Shaw Desmond.** The institute had as its aim investigation of psychic phenomena by the objective methods of laboratory research. Fraser Harris was appointed as the original research officer. He was succeeded by **Nandor Fodor,** who held the post until the summer of 1938. The IIPR premises at Harrington Rd., London, SW, were later moved to Walton House, Walton St., London, SW3.

The institute emphasized the need for experimental work and secured photographic and recording apparatuses to investigate and record voice and physical phenomena. The council consisted of both Spiritualists and non-Spiritualists, ensuring a balanced approach to the investigation of paranormal phenomena.

The institute published papers on their experiments, including the following: *Bulletin I: Historic Poltergeists,* by **Hereward Carrington;** *The Saragossa Ghost,* by Nandor Fodor; *Bulletin II: The Lajos Pap Experiments,* by Nandor Fodor; and *Bulletin III: Enquiry into the Cloud-Chamber Method of Studying the "Intra-Atomic Quantity,"* by G. J. Hopper.

During January 1939 the institute was amalgamated with the British College of Psychic Science (BCPS) under the name International Institute for Psychic Investigation (IIPI). The BCPS transferred many of its workers and its excellent reference library to the IIPR at the Walton House. Publication of the college's valuable journal, *Psychic Science,* continued under the auspices of the institute. With the outbreak of war the organization had a difficult time, however, and collapsed in 1947. The library and records were dispersed or destroyed by bombing.

Its place was to a large extent filled by the **College of Psychic Science,** in London, formed in 1955 from the long-established **London Spiritualist Alliance,** originally founded in 1884. The College of Psychic Science had similar objectives to the BCPS and IIPR and at one time or another leading Spiritualists or psychical researchers connected with the earlier organizations also took part in its activities. The college also maintains an excellent loan and reference library at its premises in 16 Queensberry Pl., South Kensington, London, SW7., and arranges for experimental investigations and consultations with mediums, currently carried out under the new name **College of Psychic Studies.**

Sources:

Edmunds, Simeon. *Spiritualism: A Critical Survey.* London: Aquarian Press, 1966.

International Institute for Psychical Research See International Institute for Psychic Investigation

International Institute for the Study of Death

Organization providing an international forum for exploration of the central questions raised by the death experience. The institute maintains a research division and multilingual periodicals and also organizes conferences and seminars. Address: Box 8565, Pembroke Pines, FL 33084. (See also **Death; Near-Death Experiences**)

International Journal of Parapsychology

Former scholarly journal that appeared quarterly from the summer of 1959 through the winter of 1968, published by the **Parapsychology Foundation** "as a forum for scholarly inquiry, linking parapsychology with psychology, physics, biochemistry, pharmacology, anthropology, ethnology and other scientific disciplines." Summaries of main articles were given in French, German, Italian, and Spanish.

The purpose of the *International Journal of Parapsychology* has now been assumed by the bimonthly *Parapsychology Review,* published by the Parapsychology Foundation. Back issues of the *Journal* are available from University Microfilms, Ann Arbor, MI 48106.

International Kirlian Research Association

Founded in 1975 with a membership of physicists, electrical engineers, psychologists, parapsychologists, physicians, graduate science students, interested individuals with advanced degrees, and those engaged in scientific research. The association hoped to advance research on Kirlian photography (electrography) through multidisciplinary research or electromagnetic interactions in biological and medical functions.

Kirlian photography is named for its inventor, Semyon Kirlian, a Russian electrical engineer who developed a technique of photographing objects without the use of cameras through a high-voltage, high-frequency, low-amperage electrical discharge, thus showing an **aura** around objects. The **Kirlian aura** was frequently identified as the aura reportedly seen around individuals by psychics and that was seen by **Walter J. Kilner** through various optical effects.

The work of the association was blunted in the early 1980s by a negative laboratory opinion on the more interesting Kirlian effects that suggested they were caused by flawed experimental controls. The association maintains a speakers bureau and publishes *Communications and Acta Electragrafica* quarterly. Address: 2202 Quentin Rd., Brooklyn, NY 11229.

International Organization of Awareness

The International Organization of Awareness was one of several groups that emerged in the late 1960s following the death of William Ralph Duby, the leader of the **Organization of Awareness** (now known as **Cosmic Awareness Communications**). The International Organization of Awareness, which was headquartered in Honolulu under the leadership of Edward Young, lasted only a few years.

International Parascience Institute

Founded in 1971 in Devon, England, at the Institute of Parascience to investigate scientific aspects of parapsychology. The first president was **Alan J. Mayne.** Beginning with a mimeographed publication *Parascience,* the institute held symposia on experimental **psi** research and published *Parascience Proceedings* and *Parascience Newsletter* (1975). Subjects covered include psychical research and the theory of resonance, the macromechanics of **psychokinesis,** approaches to psi and methods of psi research, **precognition,** and mediumship. The institute is located at Spryton, Lifton, Devon, England,

International Plant Consciousness Research Newsletter

Monthly publication that reported on meetings and seminars concerned with matters relating to plant consciousness. The directors included pioneer researcher **Cleve Baxter** and Mrs. Charles Musés. It was headquartered in Long Beach, California, but is no longer active. (See also **Plants, Psychic Aspects of**)

International Psychic Gazette

Monthly magazine founded in 1912 as the official organ of the International Club for Psychical Research. It ceased publication after only a few months.

International Psychic Register

A directory of practitioners of the psychic arts in North America and Great Britain that appeared during the 1970s from Ornion Press in Erie, Pennsylvania. It included classified lists of healers, psychics, teachers, and parapsychologists, with addresses and telephone numbers.

International Society for Krishna Consciousness (ISKCON)

Hindu bhakti yoga religious group. The International Society for Krishna Consciousness (ISKCON) was founded in 1965 by A. C. Bhaktivedanta Swami Prabhupada (1896–1977), who migrated to the United States soon after the passing of new immigration laws allowing the migration of Asians into America. During his adult life as a businessman, Prabhupada was initiated into Krishna Consciousness as a member of the Guadiya Mission in Calcutta. Krishna Consciousness is a popular term given the revival movement founded by Chaitanya Mahaprabhu (1486–1534?), who taught intense devotion to the deity Krishna. Devotional activity was centered upon public dancing and chanting and temple worship before the statues of Krishna. Most characteristic of the movement was the repetition of the Hare Krishna mantra:

Hare Krishna, Hare Krishna
Hare Hare, Krishna Krishna
Hare Rama, Hare Rama
Hare Hare, Rama Rama.

In traditional Hindu teachings, Krishna and Rama are incarnations of the god Vishnu, and those who worship Vishnu as their primary deity are called Vaishnavas (one of the three large religious groups in India). Bhakti yoga is the name given to the practice of following a path to God primarily through devotional activity.

Prabhupada was told by his guru to prepare himself to take Krishna devotion to the West. Krishna Consciousness had actually been introduced into the United States soon after the beginning of the twentieth century by another teacher from Bengal, Baba Bharati, but his organization died out soon after he returned to India. Soon after his arrival, Prabhupada began anew the task of introducing Krishna Consciousness to Westerners. He settled in New York City and found his first devotees from among the street people. He had already published a translation of the Bhagavad Gita, and soon after he developed a following he began work on translation of other important books of the tradition, the *Srimad Bhagavatam* and the *Caitanya-caritamrita.*

The groups became well known in the early 1970s. Members adopted Indian garb and attracted attention on the street, dancing, chanting, and distributing literature. As the anticult movement developed in the mid-1970s, they became a major target of deprogrammings.

In the early 1970s Prabhupada appointed a governing body commission (GBC) that came to power after his death in 1977. The GBC was made up of the initiating gurus who had been installed in the various areas to which the movement had spread, as well as other prominent leaders. Through the 1980s it had to deal with attacks on the movement from outside and with the internal split between the reformists and conservatives. Conservatives found their major voice in Kirtananda Swami Bhatipada, who headed ISKCON of West Virginia, but he was excommunicated in 1987. For about three years he was occupied with court proceedings against him and the community and with accusations of child abuse.

In the early 1990s the community was finally able to have a multimillion dollar judgment (awarded at the height of the anticult struggles) overturned. The judgment in the Robin George case had threatened the movement on the West Coast. In the meantime, the movement spread internationally and now has centers in more than eighty countries. In the United States it has three thousand core members, full-time Krishna devotees, but is also supported by many thousands of constituency members, especially within the Indian American community.

Nominal headquarters from what has become a very decentralized movement is at the ISKCON International Ministry of Public Affairs, 1030 Grand Ave., San Diego, CA 92109. Its primary magazine, *Back to Godhead,* is published from the Philadelphia temple. Address: Box 18928, Philadelphia, PA 19119-0428.

Sources:

Gelberg, Steven, ed. *Hare Krishna, Hare Krishna.* New York: Grove Press, 1983.

Knott, Kim. *My Sweet Lord.* Wellingsborough, England: Aquarian Press, 1986.

Prabhupada, A. C. Bhaktivedanta Swami. *Bhagavad-Gita As It Is.* New York: Bhaktivedanta Book Trust, 1972.

International Society for the Investigation of Ghosts

An organization that through the 1970s and 1980s maintained an **International Ghost Registry** to preserve and investigate records of hauntings and related phenomena throughout the world. The society published a bimonthly newsletter **FOG,** which included ghost accounts sent by members, articles, and book reviews.

International Society for the Study of Subtle Energies and Energy Medicine (ISSSEEM)

ISSSEEM was organized informally in 1989 by a clinical psychologist, a biomedical engineer, an anthropologist, and a psychophysiologic researcher. It is concerned with the study of information systems and energies that interact with the human psyche and physiology, either enhancing or perturbing homeostasis. The society publishes a quarterly newsletter and the journal *Subtle Energies and Energy Medicine; An Interdisciplinary Journal of Informational and Energetic Interactions.* Address: 356 Golden Circle, Golden, CO 80401.

International Society of Cryptozoology (ISC)

Organization concerned with the study and discussion of anomalous animal phenomena (i.e., creatures bordering between fact and myth). The ISC published a newsletter and an official journal, *Cryptozoology.* Address: Box 43070, Tucson, AZ 85733.

Sources:

Clark, Jerome. *Encyclopedia of Strange and Unexplained Phenomena.* Detroit: Gale Research, 1993.

International Spiritual Frontiers Fellowship

An organization founded in 1956 by a group of Christian clergy and laypersons to explore an interest in paranormal phenomena—especially the evidence for life after death—and to explore the life of prayer, meditation, mysticism, and spiritual healing. Spiritual Frontiers Fellowship (SFF) had its origin in a network of Christian leaders who had been influenced by the work of Spiritualist medium **Arthur A. Ford,** with whom many had private sittings. They had come to share Ford's opinion that much of the spiritual dryness so evident in many mainstream Christian churches could be attributed to a lack of direct experience of the spiritual world. In 1953 British church leaders had founded the Churches Fellowship for Spiritual and Psychical Studies, and SFF modeled itself on the British organization.

SFF issued a statement of "principles, purposes, and programs" that called for emphases on mystical prayer, spiritual healing, and the search for evidence of personal **survival** of death. While trying to revive the spiritual life of the churches, the group has been open to parapsychological perspectives and has supported a research committee. In 1972 it sponsored the development of an affiliated academic organization, the Academy of Religion and Psychical Research, which grew out of a recommendation of the organization's field director, **J. Gordon Melton.**

Through the years the organization has undergone several changes. In the early 1970s the original interest in mediumship and survival gave way to a primary interest in meditation and spiritual healing. During this time SFF experienced a period of rapid growth. The organization experienced a major overturn in leadership in 1974–75 and a period of organizational chaos. When it stabilized in the early 1980s, it was considerably weakened. It has also taken a new direction, identifying largely with the emerging New Age movement. The organization has largely cut its ties with conventional Christian churches.

In 1987 the headquarters of SFF were moved to 33210 Baring St., Philadelphia, PA 19104. It has recently added "International" to its name. It publishes a monthly newsletter and the *Spiritual Frontiers* journal.

Sources:

Higgins, Paul Lambourne, ed. *Frontiers of the Spirit.* Minneapolis: T. S. Denison, 1976.

Rauscher, William V. *The Spiritual Frontier.* Garden City, N.Y.: Doubleday, 1975.

Spiritual Frontiers Fellowship. *Christianity and the Paranormal.* Independence, Mo. The Author, 1986.

Wagner, Melinda Boiler. *Metaphysics in Midwestern America.* Columbus: Ohio State University Press, 1983.

International Spiritualist Alliance

The International Spiritualist Alliance is a Canadian-based international Spiritualist church founded for the purpose of bringing brotherhood and unity to Spiritualists worldwide. It has succeeded in bringing congregations in Canada, the United States, and Great Britain together. The alliance operates out of a loose fellowship association. Members accept seven affirmations concerning the fatherhood of God, the brotherhood of man, the immortality of the soul, communion with the departed, personal responsibility, compensation for good and evil, and the eternal progress of the soul. These affirmations are set within a general Christian theology that accepts God as the loving creator and Jesus as the Lord incarnated for the salvation of humanity. Perfected in suffering, Jesus became Lord and Christ. The church is headed by the Rev. Beatrice Gaulton Bishop of Vancouver, British Columbia.

International Spiritualist Congress

The name of five international gatherings of Spiritualist leaders held in the years between the two world wars. The first was held at Liège (1923), the second at Paris (1925), the third in London (1928), the fourth at The Hague (1931), and the fifth in Barcelona (1934).

The Paris congress prepared and promulgated a statement of the philosophy and fundamental principles of Spiritualism. Delegates agreed that Spiritualism stood for (1) the existence of God as the intelligent and supreme cause of all things; (2) the affirmation that man is a spirit related to a perishable body by an intermediate body (the etheral or "perispirit") that is indestructible in nature; (3) the immortality of the spirit and its continuous evolution toward perfection through progressive stages of life; and (4) universal and personal responsibility, both individual and collective, between all beings. Later congresses reaffirmed these principles. The congresses were a programmatic expression of the **International Spiritualists Federation.**

International Spiritualists Federation (Fédération Spirites Internationale)

A Spiritualist organization founded in 1923 with headquarters at Maison des Spirites, 8 Rue Copernic, Paris. Its original presidents were **Sir Arthur Conan Doyle** and **Ernest W. Oaten** (editor of the journal *Two Worlds*). Affiliated associations were formed in Europe (England, France, Germany, Spain, Holland, Belgium, and Switzerland), the Americas (United States, Cuba, Costa Rica, and Mexico), and South Africa. The first International Spiritualist Congress was held at Liège, Belgium, in 1923, followed by four others in 1925, 1928, 1931, and 1934. The organization was destroyed during World War II.

International UFO Reporter (Magazine)

Bimonthly publication reporting UFO sightings, personal accounts, and book reviews concerning UFOs. It was originally edited by **J. Allen Hynek,** who was in charge of UFO investigations on "Project Bluebook," the U.S. Air Force official investigation of UFO sightings. Hynek also served as a technical consultant on the Steven Spielberg movie **Close Encounters of the Third Kind.** Address: J. Allen Hynek Center for UFO Studies, 2457 W. Peterson Ave., Chicago, IL 60659.

International Yoga Guide

Monthly magazine of the International Yoga Society. It includes extracts from Hindu scripture, yoga exercises, and news of society activities. Address: 6111 SW 74th Ave. Miami, FL 33143.

Interplanetary Space Travel Research Association (ISTRA)

Nonprofit society founded in 1957 to promote public interest in space activities (including UFOs and extraterrestrials) and science fiction. Membership is free. The first issue of *Space Digest* (1977) is available from ISTRA. Contact: Robert Morison, Editor, 30 Grosvenor Rd., London, E. 11, England.

Interspace Link Confidential Newsletter

Monthly newsletter of National Investigations Committee on UFOs. Address: 14617 Victory Blvd., #4, Van Nuys, CA 91411.

Intuition

Human faculty by which individuals are aware of facts not accessible to normal sensory or mental processes. Some apparent intuition may be attributed to unconscious sensory or mental perception or deduction. Other intuitive awareness suggests paranormal faculty. (See also **Extrasensory Perception**)

Intuitional World

Theosophical term for the Buddhic plane or the fourth world, from which come intuitions. (See also **Intuition; Solar System; Theosophy**)

Invisibility

The belief in invisibility is an ancient one in religion, folklore, and superstition. The soul or vital principle in human beings could not be established visibly, and after death was presumed to inhabit an invisible realm, also peopled by angelic and demonic entities not visible to normal human sight. Even in modern times, the concept of the **astral plane** and of heaven and hell in some invisible dimension of space rather than a distant position in the cosmos still persists, and has relevance to the belief in **apparitions** or ghosts of the dead that may become visible and then vanish under certain circumstances. In **Spiritualism,** such appearances and disappearances of phantom forms are claimed in the phenomena of **materialization** and **dematerialization.**

Although the concept of an invisible world that may sometimes be made visible is at variance with the known scientific machinery of vision and the function of the eyes, there remains the philosophical problem that the actual nature of empirical reality cannot be established scientifically through human senses, although there is consistency in the common experience of vision, touch, and other sensory impressions that are validated by sensations in the brain. The idealist school of philosophy stemming from Bishop Berkeley, Immanuel Kant, and others holds that there are no physical objects existing apart from thought and experience, and the theist claims that the consistency of mental experience derives from divine law.

Much of the great body of superstition, folklore, and sorcery relating to visibility and invisibility derives from the earliest experiences of humankind and the prescientific observation of natural phenomena incorporated in religious and magical beliefs. Many of these beliefs appear untenable to scientifically trained minds.

Invisibility in Folklore

A constant motif in folktales throughout the world is the power of becoming invisible, giving the possessor of this power special advantages in overhearing an enemy's plans, winning battles with powerful adversaries, or merely stealing valuable objects unperceived. Usually invisibility was conferred by an object or garment, such as a magic ring, stone, cap, shoes, or cloak. Such magic possessions were sometimes associated with other powers—the shoes that carry the wearer great distances in a brief moment, the ring that could be rubbed to summon up a genie, the cap that conferred wisdom, or vision of distant or future events.

In Greek legend, the hero Perseus, who slew the Gorgon, had magic shoes that carried him through the air, in addition to a cap of invisibility. In the ancient Sanskrit story book *Kathasaritsagara* (Ocean of Story) of Somadeva, the Brahmin Gunarsarman becomes invisible by putting a magic ointment on his eyes, and is thus able to penetrate the camp of King Vikramaskti.

The cloak of invisibility is known in folktales throughout Europe, and even in the Apache Indian legends of America, where Child-of-the-Water gets a cloak from Lizard, enabling him to get near to the monster Buffalo without being seen. In Arthurian legend, the king himself had a cloak of invisibility.

The *Motif-Index of Folk-Literature* (1932–36) compiled by Stith Thompson lists 28 magic objects that confer invisibility, including a stone, flower, serpent's crown, heart of an unborn child, belt, cloak, saint's cowl, ring, helmet, sword, and wand. For example, it was long believed that fern seed conferred invisibility, but the seed itself was supposed to be invisible, so anyone who could find this seed and carry it would also become invisible. The fern was said to bloom at midnight on Midsummer Eve, and to seed soon after. The seeker of the seed had to avoid touching it, or letting it fall on the ground. A white cloth had to be placed under the plant for the invisible seed to fall on. It could then be wrapped up and carried around, rendering the owner invisible. Shakespeare, Ben Johnson, Beaumont, and Fletcher all have references in their plays to fern seed conferring invisibility, and this belief continued in folklore centuries later.

Another persistent folk belief was the power of the "Hand of Glory." This was the dried or pickled hand of a dead criminal hanged on the gallows. Robbers were supposed to be invisible if they carried this gruesome hand with a candle made from the fat of a hanged man. Sometimes the fingers of the hand were used as candles, and a finger lit for each occupant of the house to be robbed, ensuring that they would remain motionless.

The Rev. Richard Barham, in his *Ingoldsby Legends* (1840 etc.) versified this belief in "The Nurse's Story, The Hand of Glory."

On January 3, 1831, a gang of thieves attempted to rob the house of a Mr. Napier in Loughcrew, County Meath, Ireland. They broke into the house carrying a Hand of Glory and a candle, believing that it would prevent the occupants from waking. However, the Hand of Glory failed to keep the inmates asleep, and the robbers fled, leaving their talisman behind.

Invisibility in Sorcery and Witchcraft

A Manuscript (No. 2350) titled "Le Secret des Secrets" in the Bibliotheque de l'Arsenal in France, contains a chapter devoted to the secret of invisibility. It consists of a spell in Latin, which opens with over thirty mystical names, preferably to be written in bat's blood, and continues in a mixture of Christian and pagan tradition with an invocation translated as:

"O thou, Pontation! master of invisibility, with thy masters [here follow names of the masters], I conjure thee, Pontation, and these same masters of invisibility, by Him Who makes the universe tremble, by Heaven and Earth, Cherubim and Seraphim, and by Him Who made the Virgin conceive and Who is God and Man, that I may accomplish this experiment in perfectibility, in such sort that at any hour I desire I may be invisible; again I conjure thee and thy ministers also, by Stabuches and Mechaerom, Esey, Enitgiga, Bellis, and Semonei, that thou come straightway with thy said ministers and that thou perform this work as you all know how, and that this experiment may make me invisible in such wise that no one may see me. Amen."

According to other **grimoires,** invisibility may be achieved by simply carrying the heart of a bat, a black hen, or a frog under the right arm.

Another method is to construct and wear the Ring of Gygès, King of Lydie. It should be made of fixed mercury, set with a little stone found in a lapwing's nest, and around the stone the words "Jésus passant par le milieu d'eux s'en allat" are inscribed. A variant instruction for the Ring of Gygès is contained in the grimoire *Le Véritable Dragon Rouge . . . plus La Poule Noire* (1521), where the inscription is in magical symbols.

The Second Book of the *Secrets of Albertus Magnus* contains the following formula:

"*If thou wilt be made Invisible.*

"LVII. Take the Stone which is called Ophethalminus, and wrap it in the leafe of the Laurell or Bay tree. And it is called Lapis Obtelmicus, whose colour is not named, for it is of many colours, and it is of such virtue that it blindeth the sights of them that stand about. Constantinus carrying this in his hand, was made invisible therewith."

The seventeenth-century grimoire *The Lemegeton of Solomon or Book of the Spirits* contains the names of spirits who may be invoked in a crystal at a set hour and used for magical purposes by means of their mystical seals. These include:

"BAAL. This is the name of one of the most powerful of all kinds of demons. He may present himself as a man with a human head—or that of a cat or toad. Occasionally he is seen with all at once. Speaking in a hoarse voice, he gives knowledge of all kinds, and tells the means to obtain invisibility.

"GLASYALABOLAS is a powerful President, whose importance is belied by his appearance as a winged dog. In addition to teaching all sciences, he causes murder, makes men invisible and knows all about the past, present and future."

The **Grimorium Verum** (True Grimoire) of the sixteenth century or earlier, contains the following **black magic** instuctions:

"*To Make Oneself Invisible.* Collect seven black beans. Begin the ritual on a Wednesday before sunrise. Then take the head of a dead man and put one of the black beans in his mouth, two in his eyes and two in his ears. Then make upon his head the character of MORAIL. Afterwards bury the head with the face upwards, and for nine days before sunrise water it each morning with good brandy. On the eighth day you will find the spirit mentioned, who will say to you: 'What wilt thou?' You will reply: 'I am watering my plant.' Then the Spirit will say: 'Give me the Bottle, I desire to water it myself.' In response, refuse him, even although he will ask you again. Then he will reach out with his hand and will show you the same figure which you had drawn upon the head. Now you can be certain that this is the right spirit, the spirit of the head. There is a danger that some other Spirit might try to trick you, which would have evil consequences—and in that case your operation would not succeed. Then you may give him the bottle and he will water the head and depart. On the next day, which is the ninth, when you return you will find that the beans are germinating. Take them and put them in your mouth, or in that of a child. Those which do not confer invisibility are to be reburied with the head."

Invisibility in Spiritual Development

Invisibility is one of the *siddhis* or occult powers traditionally marking the progress of the Indian yogi on the pathway to higher spiritual development. Other *siddhis* include knowledge of past incarnations, access to the minds of others, knowledge of the time of one's death, and of hidden things, of movements and positions of stars and planets, freedom from hunger and thirst, the ability to walk through space and time, or to enter other bodies, and to become light or heavy at will, and to levitate.

In the *Yoga-Sutras of Patanjali,* a standard yoga treatise (ca. 3rd century B.C.E., Chapter III, 21), it is stated:

"By *Samyana* [combined concentration-absorption-trance] on the form of the body, suspending the power of another to see it, there follows disappearance of the body."

However, such powers are regarded only as signs of progress, and their use for personal gain or to impress others is considered to be a serious obstacle to spiritual development.

In *The Kingdom of the Lost* (1947), J. A. Howard Ogdon offers an account of the use of such **yoga** techniques to create invisibility, The author suffered from schizophrenia, and after a period of voluntary treatment at a British mental hospital was improperly certified as a lunatic and confined to a mental institution. During his incarceration, he practiced **hatha yoga** intensively without the knowledge of the authorities, and perfected techniques of mental concentration and suggestion.

In 1941, he escaped from the institution in broad daylight in full view of some forty other patients and the hospital attendants. His pockets were bulging with food for his journey and he wore a raincoat and carried a full shopping bag, as well as a gas mask container (gas masks were issued to all civilians during World War II in Britain). He claims that through mental concentration he walked openly past fifty or sixty individuals and out through the front door of the institution without being perceived or challenged by anyone.

Naturally such a claim from a former mental patient must be treated with caution, but it is clear that Ogdon was an intelligent and well-read individual with a very rational view of his illness. The possibility of establishing an atmosphere of mass suggestion is not implausible. Some modern hypnotists have claimed to make individuals invisible to a hypnotized subject, so that he or she apparently sees right through them, even if they may be sitting in chairs.

Scientific Aspects of Invisibility

Aside from the fantasies and wish-fulfillment stories of folklore, or the interference with normal visual perception by means of **hypnosis,** the possibility of scientific techniques of invisibility has long been a matter for speculation. There are many accounts of seeing **apparitions,** but no adequate scientific explanation of how invisible forms can become visible, then again vanish. Where do they come from and where do they go? Ingenious theories have been advanced of intra-atomic space or interlocking universes, but outside the realm of science fiction literature there is no evidence for extra-dimensional worlds.

Spiritualists claim that phantom forms of the dead may manifest at séances using a subtle substance exuded by the medium in a vapor or cloud-like flow, becoming more solid and eventually taking on the form of a deceased person and having the appearance of a living individual as in the case of **"Katie King."** This substance is known as **ectoplasm,** is said to be sensitive to light, and to recoil suddenly upon the medium if handled roughly. The process of becoming visible then vanishing again is known as **materialization** and **dematerialization.** Few today would argue for the existence of ectoplasm, or materializations. Since such claimed phenomena usually occur in subdued light or darkness, there is opportunity for **fraud,** and many cases have been detected. There remain a few reported cases of apparitions appearing in daylight.

Any scientific method of producing invisibility in human beings would involve apparently insuperable difficulties of interference with the light refracting characteristics of various types of human tissue and organs, and to be fully effective, the individual would need to be transparent as well as invisible. Unless the invisibility process also applied to inanimate material such as clothing, the invisible being would be obliged to travel naked, a problem vividly portrayed in H. G. Wells' science fiction novella *The Invisible Man* (1897).

A high level of skepticism is therefore inevitable in considering the claim that a top secret U.S. Navy experiment in 1943 succeeded in rendering the destroyer *Eldridge* and its crew temporarily invisible and teleporting it from its berth in Philadelphia to Norfolk, Virginia. Some of the crew members were said to have disappeared without trace, others to have gone mad, or to have met alien beings. Authors **Charles Berlitz** and William Moore suggest that the experiment involved using an intensified force field around the ship, deriving from the principles of Einstein's Unified Field Theory.

Another book, *Invisible Horizons* (1964) by Vincent Gaddis, attempts to link the Philadelphia Experiment story with the **Bermuda Triangle** mystery. All this is fascinating but highly speculative and lacking firm evidence. The Office of Naval Research firmly denies the whole story, and the Department of the Navy, Office of Information, states: "ONR has never conducted any investigations on invisibility, either in 1943 or at any other time." A 1984 movie *The Philadelphia Experiment* further fictionalized the story.

Sources:

Berlitz, Charles, and William Moore. *The Philadelphia Experiment: Project Invisibility.* N.p., 1979.

Moore, William L., and Charles Berlitz. *The Philadelphia Experiment.* New York: Grosset & Dunlap, 1979.

IONS See **Institute of Noetic Sciences**

IPA See **Incorporeal Personal Agency**

IRELAND

Pagan and Christian Beliefs

[For information regarding ancient Ireland, see **Celts.**]

Although nominally Christianized, there is little doubt that the early medieval Irish retained many remnants of their former paganism, especially those possessing a magical tendency. This is made clear by the writings of the Welsh historian Giraldus Cambrensis (ca. 1147–1220), the first account we have of Irish manners and customs after the invasion of the country by the Anglo-Normans. His description, for example, of the Purgatory of St. Patrick in Lough Derg, County Donegal, suggests that the demonology of the Catholic Church had already fused with the animism of earlier Irish tradition. He states:

"There is a lake in Ulster containing an island divided into two parts. In one of these stands a church of especial sanctity, and it is most agreeable and delightful, as well as beyond measure glorious for the visitations of angels and the multitude of the saints who visibly frequent it. The other part, being covered with rugged crags, is reported to be the resort of devils only, and to be almost always the theatre on which crowds of evil spirits visibly perform their rites. This part of the island contains nine pits, and should any one perchance venture to spend the night in one of them (which has been done, we know, at times, by some rash men), he is immediately seized by the malignant spirits, who so severely torture him during the whole night, inflicting on him such unutterable sufferings by fire and water, and other torments of various kinds, that when morning comes scarcely any spark of life is found left in his wretched body. It is said that any one who has once submitted to these torments as a penance imposed upon him, will not afterwards undergo the pains of hell, unless he commit some sin of a deeper dye.

"This place is called by the natives the Purgatory of St. Patrick. For he, having to argue with a heathen race concerning the torments of hell, reserved for the reprobate, and the real nature and eternal duration of the future life, in order to impress on the rude minds of the unbelievers a mysterious faith in doctrines so new, so strange, so opposed to their prejudices, procured by the efficacy of his prayers an exemplification of both states even on earth, as a salutary lesson to the stubborn minds of the people."

Human Animals

The ancient Irish believed in the possibility of the transformation of human beings into animals, and Giraldus, in another narrative of facts purporting to have come under his personal notice, shows that this belief had lost none of its significance with the Irish of the latter half of the twelfth century. The case is also interesting as being one of the first recorded examples of **lycanthropy** in the British Isles:

"About three years before the arrival of Earl John in Ireland, it chanced that a priest, who was journeying from Ulster towards Meath, was benighted in a certain wood on the borders of Meath. While, in company with only a young lad, he was watching by a fire which he had kindled under the branches of a spreading tree, lo! a wolf came up to them, and immediately addressed them to this effect: 'Rest secure, and be not afraid, for there is no reason you should fear, where no fear is!' The travellers being struck with astonishment and alarm, the wolf added some orthodox words referring to God. The priest then implored him, and adjured him by Almighty God and faith in the Trinity, not to hurt them, but to inform them what creature it was in the shape of a beast uttered human words. The wolf, after giving catholic replies to all questions, added at last: 'There are two of us, a man and a woman, natives of Ossory, who, through the curse of Natalis, saint and abbot, are compelled every seven years to put off the human form, and depart from the dwellings of men. Quitting entirely the human form, we assume that of wolves. At the end of the seven years, if they chance to survive, two others being substituted in their places, they return to their country and their former shape. And now, she who is my partner in this visitation lies dangerously sick not far from hence, and, as she is at the point of death, I beseech you, inspired by divine charity, to give her the consolations of your priestly office.'

"At this wood the priest followed the wolf trembling, as he led the way to a tree at no great distance, in the hollow of which he beheld a she-wolf, who under that shape was pouring forth human sighs and groans. On seeing the priest, having saluted him with human courtesy, she gave thanks to God, who in this extremity had vouchsafed to visit her with such consolation. She then received from the priest all the rites of the church duly performed, as far as the last communion. This also she importunately demanded, earnestly supplicating him to complete his good offices by giving her the viaticum. The priest stoutly asserting that he was not provided with it, the he-wolf, who had withdrawn to a short distance, came back and pointed out a small missal-book, containing some consecrated wafers, which the priest carried on his journey, suspended from his neck, under his garment, after the fashion of the country. He then intreated him not to deny them the gift of God, and the aid destined for them by Divine Providence; and, to remove all doubt, using his claw for a hand, he tore off the skin of the she-wolf, from the head down to the navel, folding it back. Thus she immediately presented the form of an old woman. The priest, seeing this, and compelled by his fear more than his reason, gave the communion; the recipient having earnestly implored it, and devoutly partaking of it. Immediately afterwards the he-wolf rolled back the skin and fitted it to its original form.

"These rites having been duly, rather than rightly performed, the he-wolf gave them his company during the whole night at their little fire, behaving more like a man than a beast. When morning came, he led them out of the wood, and, leaving the priest to pursue his journey pointed out to him the direct road for a long distance. At his departure, he also gave him many thanks for the benefit he had conferred, promising him still greater returns of gratitude, if the Lord should call him back from his present exile, two parts of which he had already completed.

"In our own time we have seen persons who, by magical arts, turned any substance about them into fat pigs, as they appeared (but they were always red), and sold them in the markets. However, they disappeared as soon as they crossed any water, returning to their real nature; and with whatever care they were kept, their assumed form did not last beyond three days. It was also a frequent complaint, from old times as well as in the present, that certain hags in Wales, as well as in Ireland and Scotland, changed themselves into the shape of hares, that, sucking teats under this counterfeit form, they might stealthily rob other people's milk."

Witchcraft in Ireland

In Anglo-Norman times, **sorcery,** malevolent magic, seems to have been widely practiced, but records are scarce. It is only by fugitive passages in the works of English writers who constantly comment on the superstitious nature and practices of the Irish that we glean any information concerning the occult history of the country. However, the great scandal of the accused witch **Dame Alice Kyteler** shook the entire Anglo-Norman colony during several successive years in the first half of the fourteenth century. The party of the Bishop of Ossory, the relentless opponent of the Dame Alice, boasted that by her prosecution they had rid Ireland of a nest of sorcerers, but there is reason to believe that Ireland could have furnished other similar instances of **black magic** had the actors in them been of royal status—that is, of sufficient importance in the eyes of chroniclers.

In this connection St. John D. Seymour's *Irish Witchcraft and Demonology* (1913) is of striking interest. The author appears to take it for granted that **witchcraft** in Ireland is purely an alien system, imported into the island by the Anglo-Normans and Scottish immigrants to the north. This may be the case so far as the districts of the Pale and of Ulster are concerned, but surely it cannot be applied to the Celtic districts of Ireland.

Early Irish works contain numerous references to sorcery, and practices are chronicled in them that bear a close resemblance to those of the shamans and medicine men of tribes around the world. The ancient Irish cycles frequently allude to animal transformation, one of the most common feats of the witch, and in Hibernian legend most heroes have a considerable working magic available to them. Wonder-working druids also abound.

Seymour claims, "In Celtic Ireland dealings with the unseen were not regarded with such abhorrence, and indeed had the sanction of custom and antiquity." He adds that ". . . the Celtic element had its own superstitious beliefs, but these never developed in this direction" (i.e., witchcraft). He lacks support for this observation. An absence of records of such a system is no proof that one never existed, and it is possible that a thorough examination of the subject would prove that a veritable system of witchcraft obtained in Celtic Ireland as elsewhere, although it may not have been of "Celtic" origin.

Be that as it may, Seymour's book is most informative on those Anglo-Norman and Scottish portions of Ireland where the belief in sorcery followed the lines of those in vogue in the mother-countries of the immigrant populations. He sketches the famous Kyteler case, touches on the circumstances connected with the Earl of Desmond and notes the case of the Irish prophetess who insisted upon warning the ill-fated James I of Scotland on the night of his assassination at Perth. It is not stated by the ancient chronicler, Seymour quotes, where in Ireland the witch in question came from—for a witch she undoubtedly was as she possessed a **familiar** spirit, "Huthart," whom she alleged warned her of the coming catastrophe. This spirit is the Teutonic *Hudekin* or *Hildekin,* the wearer of the hood, sometimes also alluded to as *Heckdekin,* well known throughout Germany and Flanders as a species of house-spirit or brownie. Trithemius alludes to this spirit as a "spirit known to the Saxons who attached himself to the Bishop of Hildesheim" and it is cited here and there in occult history. From this circumstance it might be inferred that the witch in question came from some part of Ireland that had been settled by Teutonic immigrants, probably Ulster.

Seymour continues his survey with a review of the witchcraft trials of the sixteenth century, the burning of Adam Dubh, the Leinster trial of O'Toole and College Green in 1327 for heresy, and the important passing of the statute against witchcraft in Ireland in 1586. He notes the enchantments of the Earl of Desmond, who demonstrated to his young and beautiful wife the possibilities of animal transformation by changing himself into a bird, a hag, a vulture, and a gigantic serpent. Florence Newton, the witch of Youghal, claims an entire chapter to herself, and worthily, for her case was one of the most absorbing in the history of witchcraft.

Ghostly doings and **apparitions,** fairy possession, and dealings with **fairies** are also included in the volume, and Seymour did not confine himself to Ireland, but followed one of his countrywomen to the United States, where he demonstrated her influence on the "supernatural" speculations of Congregationalist minister **Cotton Mather.**

Seymour completes his survey with seventeenth-century witchcraft notices from Antrim and Island Magee and the affairs of sorcery in Ireland from the year 1807 to the early twentieth century. The last notice is that of a trial for murder in 1911, when a woman was tried for killing another (an old-age pensioner) in a fit of insanity. A witness deposed that he met the accused on the road on the morning of the crime holding a statue or figure in her hand and repeating three times, "I have the old witch killed. I got power from the Blessed Virgin to kill her." It appears that the witch in question had threatened to plague the woman with rats and mice. A single rodent had evidently entered her home and was followed by the bright vision of a lady who told the accused that she was in danger, and further informed her that if she received the senior citizen's pension book without taking off her clothes and cleaning them and putting out her bed and cleaning up the house, she would "receive dirt for ever and rats and mice."

Modern Occultism

During the late nineteenth and early twentieth centuries, Celtic mysticism and legends of ghosts and fairies received a new infusion from Hindu mysticism through the Dublin lodge of the **Theosophical Society** and the writings of poets **William Butler Yeats** and "AE" (pseudonym of **George W. Russell**). Through the society, Russell was profoundly influenced by Hindu scriptures such as the *Bhagavad-Gita* and came to understand that mysticism should be interfused with one's everyday social responsibilities. Russell wrote mystical poems and painted pictures of nature spirits.

Yeats became a noted member of the Hermetic order of the **Golden Dawn,** a ritual magic society, and its teachings had a primary influence on the symbolism of his poems and on his own mystical vision. He too was greatly impressed by Hindu mystical teachings, and collaborated with **Shri Purohit Swami** in the translation of Hindu religious works.

After the death of Yeats and Russell, occultism did not make much headway in Irish life and literature. The occult and witchcraft boom of the 1950s and 1960s was largely ignored in Ireland, but Janet and Stewart Farrar, both neo-pagan witches trained by **Alexander Sanders,** did take up residence in the Republic of Ireland. Stewart Farrar has written a number of books on witchcraft, including the early neo-pagan classic *What Witches Do: The Modern Coven Revealed* (1971).

The **Fellowship of Isis,** headquartered at Huntingdon Castle, Clonegal, Enniscorthy, has become an international association of neo-pagans and witches. It is devoted to the deity in the form of the goddess, and publishes material concerning matriarchal religion and mysticism.

Irish writer **Desmond Leslie** was coauthor with **George Adamski** of the influential book *Flying Saucers Have Landed* (1953) an important early book introducing the topic to the English-speaking public. The book was eventually translated into 16 languages.

Psychical Research & Parapsychology

Although Ireland is traditionally a land of **ghosts, fairies, banshees,** and haunted castles, there have been few systematic attempts to conduct psychical research there, although there has been some interest in dowsing (water-divining). However, there is a **Society for Psychical and Spiritual Studies** in Dublin that holds lecture meetings and issues an occasional newsletter. There is a Belfast Psychical Society at Gateway House, 57 Dublin Road, Belfast, Northern Ireland. Spiritualism in Ireland is based in the Belfast Spiritualist Alliance and Church of Psychic Science in Belfast.

Sources:

AE [George W. Russell]. *The Candle of Vision.* London: Macmillan, 1918. Reprint, New Hyde Park, N.Y.: University Books, 1965.

Curtin, Jeremiah. *Tales of the Fairies and of the Ghost World, Collected from Oral Tradition in Southwest Munster.* London: D. Nutt, 1895. Reprint, Dublin: Talbot Press, 1974.

Dunne, John J. *Haunted Ireland: Her Romantic and Mysterious Ghosts.* Belfast: Appletree Press, 1977.

Farrar, Stewart. *What Witches Do: The Modern Coven Revealed.* New York: Coward, McCann & Geoghegan; London: Peter Davies, 1971.

Giraldus Cambrensis. *The Historical Works of Giraldus Cambrensis, Containing the Topography of Ireland, and The History of the Conquest of Ireland.* Translated by R. C. Hoare. London: Bohn's Antiquarian Library, 1847.

Gregory, Lady. *Visions and Beliefs in the West of Ireland.* 2 vols. New York: George Putnam's Sons, 1920. Reprint, U.K.: Colin Smythe, 1970.

Harper, George Mills. *Yeats's Golden Dawn.* London: Macmillan, 1974.

McAnally, D. R., Jr. *Irish Wonders: The Ghosts, Giants, Pookas, Demons, Leprechawns, Banshees, Fairies, Witches, Widows, Old Maids and Other Marvels of the Emerald Isle.* Boston: Houghton Mifflin, 1888. Reprint, Detroit: Grand River Books, 1971.

O'Donnell, Elliot. *The Banshee.* London: Sands, 1920.

Seymour, St. John D. and Harry L. Neligan. *True Irish Ghost Stories.* London: Oxford University Press, 1915. Reprint, New York: Causeway Books, 1974.

White, Carolyn. *A History of Irish Fairies.* Cork, Ireland: Mercier Press, 1976.

Yeats, W. B., ed. *Fairy and Folk Tales of the Irish Peasantry.* London: Walter Scott Publishing, 1888. Reprint, New York: Grosset & Dunlap, 1957.

Iremonger, Lucille (d'Oyen)

British novelist, journalist, and broadcaster who wrote on parapsychological topics. Iremonger received her M.A. at Oxford University (1939) with honors. She was awarded the Society of Women Journalists' Lady Britain trophy for the best book of the year in 1948 for *It's A Bigger Life* and that same year received the Lady Violet Astor trophy for the best article of the year. She was also awarded the Silver Musgrave Medal (Jamaica) for her contributions to literature relating to the West Indies (1962). In addition to her novels, her books on occult themes include *West Indian Folk Tales: Anansi Stories* (retold for English children; 1956) and *The Ghosts of Versailles: Miss Moberly and Miss Jourdain and Their Adventure—A Critical Study* (1957).

Sources:

Pleasants, Helene, ed. *Biographical Dictionary of Parapsychology.* New York: Helix Press, 1964.

Iridis (Newsletter)

Monthly newsletter of the California Society for Psychical Study, Address: P.O. Box 844, Berkeley, CA 94709.

Irish Society of Diviners

Society composed of individuals interested in all aspects of **dowsing,** water divining, **radiesthesia,** healing, earth energies, and tracing missing persons through divining techniques. It was founded in 1958 and holds meetings with lectures. For a time it issued a journal titled *Irish Diviner,* now superseded by the society's newsletter. Address: Mrs. T. G. Grace, 23 Grange Park Walk, Raheny, Dublin 5, Republic of Ireland.

Irish UFO Organization

Society concerned with the scientific study of the UFO phenomenon. It investigates and classifies UFO reports and publishes an occasional newsletter. It is associated with **Spectrum—Society for Psychical and Spiritual Studies,** with which it shares a common address: 70 Glasmeen Rd., Glasnevin, Dublin 11, Republic of Ireland.

Iron

The occult virtues of iron are thus described in **Pliny the Elder**'s *Naturalis Historia* (in the 1601 translation by Philemon Holland):

"As touching the use of Yron and steele in Physicke, it serveth otherwise than for to launce, cut and dismember withal; for take the knife or dagger, an make an ymaginerie circle two or three times round with the point thereof upon a young child or an elder bodie, and then goe round withall about the partie as often, it is a singular preservative against all poysons, sorceries, or enchantments. Also to take any yron naile out of the coffin or sepulchre wherein man or woman lieth buried, and to sticke the same fast to the lintle or side post of a dore, leading either to the house or bed-chamber where any dooth lie who is haunted with Spirits in the night, he or she shall be delivered and secured from such phanasticall illusions. Moreover, it is said, that if one be lightly pricked with the point of sword or dagger, which hath been the death of a man, it is an excellent remedy against the pains of sides or breast, which come with sudden prickes or stitches."

In certain parts of Scotland and Ireland, there was a belief in the potency of iron for warding off the attacks of fairies. An iron poker, laid across a cradle, would, it was believed, keep fairies away until the child was baptized. The Reverend John G. Campbell in his *Superstitions of the Highlands and Islands of Scotland* (1900) relates how, when children, he and another boy were believed to be protected from a fairy that had been seen at a certain spot because one boy possessed a knife and the other a nail.

Many other countries had folklore about iron as a religious taboo or a charm against witchcraft and the supernatural. Iron tools were prohibited in Greek and Hebrew temples in ancient times. In Korea the body of the king was never to be touched by iron. Roman priests were forbidden to shave with iron blades. In India and China evil spirits were warded off by iron.

Irving, Rev. Edward (1792–1834)

Famous Scottish preacher whose Catholic Apostolic Church in London was the scene of extraordinary psychic manifestations in 1831. The "Irvingites" were seized with the gift of speaking in **tongues;** they prophesied and effected cures. The manifestations continued for about two years.

Sources:

Baxter, Robert. *A Narrative of Facts Characterising the Supernatural Manifestations in the Members of Mr. Irving's Congregation, and Other Individuals in England and Scotland, and formerly in the Writer Himself.* London, 1833.

Dallimore, Arnold A. *Forerunner of the Charismatic Movement: The Life of Edward Irving.* Chicago: Moody Press, 1983.

Drummond, Andrew L. *Edward Irving and His Circle.* London: J. Clarke, 1937.

Marricks, William S. *Edward Irving: The Forgotten Giant.* East Peoria, Ill.: Scribe's Chamber Publications, 1983.

Wilks, Washington. *Edward Irving: An Ecclesiastical and Literary Biography.* London, 1854.

Irwin, H(arvey) J(on) (1943–)

Australian parapsychologist, senior lecturer in psychology at the University of New England, Australia. Irwin was born on September 8, 1943. He studied at Sydney University (B.Sc., 1964; Dip.Ed., 1965), the University of New South Wales (B.A., 1969), and the University of New England (Litt.B., 1972; Ph.D., psychology, 1978). His dissertation was entitled *Visual Selective Attention and the Human Information Processing System: Structures, Processes, and Processing Interference in Visual Input Selection.* After graduation he was a senior tutor at the University of New England. In 1985 joined the faculty in psychology as a lecturer, a position that allowed him some freedom to teach in the overlapping area between psychology and parapsychology.

His doctoral research concerned the nature of selective attention in vision and its interpretation within an information-processing framework. He has since explored the possibility of accounting for the experiential properties of paranormal phenomena in terms of information-processing theory. In recent years he has also investigated the nature of **out-of-the-body** experiences. He has published articles and several books on parapsychology and psychology.

Sources:

Irwin, H. J. *Flight of Mind: A Psychological Study of the Out-of-Body Experience.* Metuchen, N.J.: Scarecrow Press, 1985.

———. *An Introduction to Parapsychology.* Pittsburgh: R. A. McConnell, 1983.

———. *Psi and the Mind: An Information Processing Approach.* Metuchen, N.J.: Scarecrow Press, 1979.

Isaac of Holland (fl. fifteenth century)

Little is known about the life of this alchemist, but he is commonly supposed to have lived and worked early in the fifteenth century. The main reason for assigning his career to that period is that in his writings he refers to Geber, Dastin, Morien, and **Arnaldus de Villanova,** but not to more modern authorities. Furthermore, he appears to have been acquainted with various chemical processes discovered toward the close of the fourteenth century. Therefore, it may be deduced that he did not live before that time.

According to tradition Isaac worked with his son, whose name is not recorded, and the pair are usually regarded as having been the first men to exploit chemistry in the Netherlands. They are said to have been particularly skillful in the manufacture of enamels and artificial gems, and it is noteworthy that no less distinguished an alchemist than **Paracelsus** attached value to the Dutchmen's research. Isaac and his son were also mentioned with honor by the seventeenth-century English scientist Robert Boyle.

Isaac compiled two scientific treatises on **alchemy,** one entitled *Opera Mineralia Joannis Isaaci Hollandi, sive de Lapide Philosophico* (1600), and the other *De Triplici Ordine Elixiris et Lapidis Theoria* (1608). Both were published at the beginning of the seventeenth century. The latter treatise is the more important of the two because the author sets forth his ideas on exalting base metals into *Sol* and *Luna* (gold and silver) and illustrates exactly what kind of vessel should be used for each.

ISAR See Institute for the Study of American Religion

ISC See International Society of Cryptozoology

Isian News

Quarterly publication of the **Fellowship of Isis,** an Irish-based religious organization founded in 1976 to revive worship and communion with the feminine principle in deity, in the form of the Goddess, and to promote knowledge of the world's matriarchal religions. Address: Huntingdon Castle, Clonegal, Enniscorthy, Eire.

ISKCON See International Society for Krishna Consciousness

ISKCON Review (Journal)

Short-lived biannual interdisciplinary journal of the **Bhaktivedanta Institute of Religion and Culture.** Founded in the spring of 1985, its purpose was "to stimulate and communicate—as well as to review—research and reflection on the Hare Krishna movement in all its aspects. It is intended both for those who have a direct interest in ISKCON, as well as for those whose general interest in Hindu tradition, new religious movements, or contemporary spirituality might be served by a deeper awareness of the movement. It is directed towards a wide, primarily academic and professional audience, including Hindu studies, scholars, sociologists, and psychologists of religion, students of American religious history, theologians, mental health professionals, and clergy—as well as interested members of ISKCON."

Although subsidized by the **International Society for Krishna Consciousness** through the Bhaktivedanta Book Trust, ISKCON's publishing house, the *Review* had complete editorial autonomy and was not an official publication of the Hare Krishna movement. It served as a forum both for those committed to ISKCON and for independent scholars and theologians.

ISRAEL

Beginning with the Balfour Declaration of November 2, 1917, there was a great influx of Jewish immigrants into Palestine, and this migration was intensified with the establishment of the State of Israel on May 14, 1948. Refugees from persecutions and the aftermath of two world wars brought the rich folklore of Europe into the new homeland. Stories of the Hasidim—the miracle-working mystical rabbis and their followers—existed side by side with legends of the Angel of Death, or the **golem** created by Rabbi Loew of Prague. As in the United States, mystical groups in Israel have kept alive the study of **Kabbalah.**

Beyond the legends of miracles and occult phenomena that have a basically mystical purpose, speculation on the afterlife is alien to the general trend of Judaism and there has been little basis for studies of **Spiritualism** and psychical research. Since the 1960s, however, there has been a growing interest in parapsychology in Israel, given added topical interest by the furious controversies over the phenomena of **Uri Geller,** who encountered great opposition from scientists and psychologists who were convinced that he was a fraud.

Enlightened scientific interest in parapsychology in Israel owes much to Professor H. S. Bergman, who was a great friend of the famous psychic **Eileen Garrett,** founder of the **Parapsychology Foundation** in the United States. With the cooperation of Bergman, F. S. Rothschild, Heinz C. Berendt and others, the Israel Parapsychology Society was formed. In 1965, Garrett visited the group in Jerusalem for the opening of the Parapsychology Foundation Library. Berendt published the first Hebrew-language book on parapsychology, *Parapsychology—The World Beyond* (Jerusalem, 1966).

In 1968 the Israel Society for Parapsychology was founded in Tel Aviv under the chairmanship of Margot Klausner. The society has organized lectures and courses on a wide range of subjects, such as clairvoyance, telepathy, reincarnation, dowsing, spiritual healing, meditation, and astrology. It also publishes a journal, *Mysterious Worlds,* and maintains a library of more than 1,200 volumes. The Israel Parapsychology Society can be contacted c/o Mr. Gilad Livneh, 28 Hapalmach St., 92542 Jerusalem, Israel.

Sources:

Berger, Arthur S., and Joyce Berger. *The Encyclopedia of Parapsychology and Psychical Research.* New York: Paragon House, 1991.

ISSSEEM See International Society for the Study of Subtle Energies and Energy Medicine

ISTRA See Interplanetary Space Travel Research Association

ITALY

[For information regarding ancient Italy, see **Rome, Ancient Religion and Magic.**]

Strangely enough, magic and sorcery in medieval Italy seem to have centered around the many great personalities of the church, and even several popes have been included by the historians of occult science in the ranks of notable Italian sorcerers and alchemists. There appears to have been some sort of folk tradition that the popes had been given over to the practice of **magic** ever since the tenth century, and it was alleged that Silvester II confessed to this charge on his death bed. **Éliphas Lévi** stated that Honorius III, who preached the Crusades, was an abominable necromancer, and the author of the **Grimoire of Honorius,** a book by which spirits were evoked.

Bartholomew Platina (1421–1481), quoting from Martinus Polonus, stated that Silvester, who was a proficient mathematician and versed in the **Kabbalah,** on one occasion evoked Satan himself and obtained his assistance to gain the pontifical crown. Furthermore he stipulated as the price of selling his soul to the devil that he should not die except at Jerusalem, where he inwardly determined he would never go.

He duly became pope, but on one occasion while celebrating mass in a certain church at Rome, he felt extremely ill, and suddenly remembered that he was officiating in a chapel dedicated to the Holy Cross of Jerusalem. He had a bed set up in the chapel, to which he summoned the cardinals and confessed that he had held communication with the powers of evil. He further arranged that when dead, his body should be placed upon a car of green wood drawn by two horses, one black and other white. He stipulated that the horses should be started on their course, but neither led nor driven, and that where they halted his remains should be entombed. The conveyance stopped in front of the Lateran, and at this juncture terrible noises proceeded from it, which led the bystanders to suppose that the soul of Silvester had been seized upon by Satan according to the agreement.

There is no doubt whatsoever that such legends concerning papal necromancers are simply inventions; they can be traced through Platina and Polonus to Galfridus and the chronicler Gervase of Tilbury, whom Gabriel Naudé termed "the greatest forger of fables, and the most notorious liar that ever took pen in hand!"

On par with such myths is that of Pope Joan, who for several years was supposed to have sat on the papal throne although a woman, and who was supposed to be one of the rankest sorceresses of all time. Many magic books were attributed to Pope Joan. Lévi has an interesting passage in his *History of Magic* (1913) in which he states that certain engravings in a life of this female pope, purporting to represent her, are nothing but ancient tarots representing Isis crowned with a tiara. "It is well-known that the hieroglyphic figure on the second **tarot** card is still called 'The Female Pope,' being a woman wearing a tiara, on which are the points of the crescent moon, or the horns of Isis."

But all Italian necromancers and magicians were by no means churchmen—indeed, medieval Italy was hardly a place for the magically inclined, so stringent were the laws of the church against the occult. One exception, **astrology,** however, flourished, and its practitioners were accepted into the highest levels of society. A Florentine astrologer named Basil, who flourished at the beginning of the fifteenth century, obtained some repute for successful predictions and was said to have foretold to Cosmo de Medici that he would attain exalted dignity, as the same planets had been in ascendency at the hour of his birth as at the birth of the Emperor Charles V.

Many remarkable predictions were made by Antiochus Tibertus of Romagna, who was for some time counselor to Pandolpho de Maletesta, Prince of Rimini. He foretold to his friend Guido de Bogni, the celebrated soldier, that he was unjustly suspected by his best friend, and would forfeit his life through suspicion. Of himself he predicted that he would die on the scaffold, and of the Prince of Rimini, his patron, that he would die a beggar in the hospital for the poor at Bologna. It is stated that the prophecies came true in every detail.

Although the recorded notices of **sorcery** in medieval times are few in Italian history, there is reason to suspect that although magic was not outwardly practiced, it lurked hidden in out-of-the-way places. We have an excellent portrait of the medieval Italian magician in the popular myths of Virgil the Enchanter.

The Legend of Virgil

The fame of Virgil the Poet was so great in ancient Italy that in due time his name became synonymous with fame itself. From that it was a short step to the attribution of supernatural power, and Virgil the Roman poet became in the popular mind a medieval enchanter. His myth is symptomatic of magic in medieval Italy as a whole and is therefore described here at some length.

When the popular myth of Virgil the Enchanter first grew into repute is uncertain, but probably the earliest conception arose about the beginning of the tenth century and each succeeding generation embroidered upon it some new fantastic element. Soon, in the south of Italy (for the necromancer's fame was of southern origin), mysterious legends of the enchantments he had wrought emerged.

Thus Virgil was said to have fashioned a brazen fly and planted it on the gate of fair Parthenope to free the city from the inroads of the insects of Beelzebub. On a Neapolitan hill he built a brass statue and placed a trumpet in its mouth. When the north wind blew a roar so terrible came from that trumpet that it drove the noxious blasts of Vulcan's forges back into the sea. At one of the gates of Naples, Virgil supposedly raised two statues of stone and gifted them respectively with the power of blighting or blessing the strangers who passed by one or the other of them on entering the city. He constructed three public baths for the removal of every disease afflicting the human body, but the physicians, in a dread of losing their patients and their fees, caused them to be destroyed.

Other wonders he was supposed to have wrought were woven into a biography of the enchanter, first printed in French about 1490–1520. A still fuller history appeared in English as "The Life of Virgilius," about 1508, printed by Hans Doesborcke at Antwerp. It set forth with tolerable clearness the popular type of the medieval magician, and is drawn upon in the following biographical sketch:

"Virgil was the son of a wealthy senator of Rome, wealthy and powerful enough to carry on war with the Roman Emperor. As his birth was heralded by extraordinary portents, it is no marvel that even in childhood he showed himself endowed with extraordinary mental powers, and his father having the sagacity to discern in him an embryo necromancer sent him, while still very young, to study at the University of Toledo, where the 'art of magick' was taught with extraordinary success.

"There he studied diligently, for he was of great understanding, and speedily acquired a profound insight into the great Shemaia of the Chaldean lore. But this insight was due not so much to nocturnal vigils over abstruse books, as to the help he received from a very valuable **familiar.**"

The story goes on to say that Virgil's father died and his estates were seized by his former colleagues, so his widow was sunk into extreme poverty. Virgil accordingly gathered together the wealth he had amassed by the exercise of his magical skill and set out for Rome to put his mother in a position proper to her rank. At Toledo he had been regarded as a famous student; but at Rome he was a despised scholar, and when he asked the emperor to execute justice and restore his estate to him, that potentate, ignorant of the magician's power, simply replied, "Methinketh that the land is well divided to them that have it, for they may help you in their need; what needeth you for to care for the disheriting of one school-master. Bid him take heed, and look to his schools, for he hath no right to any land here about the city of Rome."

Four years passed, and only such replies as this were given to Virgil's frequent appeals for justice. Growing at length weary of the delay, he resolved to exercise his wondrous powers in his own behalf. When the harvest came, he accordingly shrouded the whole of his rightful inheritance with a vapor so dense that the new proprietors were unable to approach it, and under its cover his men gathered in the entire crop with perfect security. This done, the mist disappeared.

Then his angry enemies assembled their swordsmen and marched against him to take off his head. Such was their power that the emperor fled out of Rome in fear, ". . . for they were twelve senators that had all the world under them, and if Virgilius had right, he had been one of the twelve, but they had disinherited him and his mother." When they drew near, Virgil once more baffled their designs by encircling his patrimony with cloud and shadow.

The emperor, with surprising inconsistency, now joined forces with the senators against Virgil, whose magical powers he should have feared far more than the rude force of the senatorial magnates, and made war against him. But who can prevail against the arts of necromancy? Emperor and senators were duly beaten, and from that moment Virgil, with marvelous generosity, became the faithful friend and powerful supporter of his sovereign.

It may not be generally known that Virgil, besides being the savior of Rome, was supposed to be the founder of Naples. This feat had its origin, like so many other great actions, in the power of love.

Virgil's imagination had been fired by the reports that reached him of the surpassing loveliness of the sultan's daughter. Now the sultan lived at Babylon (that is, at Cairo, the "Babylon" of medieval romancers) and the distance might have daunted a less ardent lover and less potent magician. But Virgil's necromantic skill was equal to magically raising a bridge in the air, and, passing over it, he found his way into the sultan's palace and into the princess's chamber. Speedily overcoming her natural modesty, Virgil bore her back with him to his Italian bower. There, he enjoyed his fill of love and pleasure, then restored the princess to her bed in her father's palace. Meanwhile, her absence had been noted, but she was soon discovered on her return, and the sultan, hastening to her chamber, interrogated her respecting her disappearance. He found that she did not know who had carried her off, nor where she had been carried.

When Virgil abducted and restored the princess on the following night, she took back with her, by her father's instructions, some fruit plucked from the enchanter's garden, and from its quality the sultan guessed that she had been carried to a southern land "on the side of France." These nocturnal journeys being several times repeated and the sultan's curiosity growing ungovernable, he persuaded his daughter to give her lover a sleeping draught. The deceived magician was then captured in the Babylonian palace and flung into prison, and it was decreed that both he and his mistress should be punished for their love by death at the stake.

Necromancers, however, are not so easily outwitted. As soon as Virgil was apprised of the fate intended for him, he made, by force of his spells, the sultan and all his lords believe that the mighty Nilus, great river of Babylon, was overflowing in the midst of them, and that they swam and lay and sprang like geese, and so they took up Virgil and the princess, tore them from their prison, and placed them upon the aerial bridge. And when they were thus out of danger, Virgil delivered the sultan and all the lords from the river, and when they recovered their wits they saw the enchanter bearing the beautiful princess across the Mediterranean, and they marveled and felt that they could not hope to prevail against such supernatural power.

And in this manner Virgil conveyed the sultan's daughter over the sea to Rome. He was infatuated with her beauty, and,

"Then he thought in his mind how he might marry her [apparently forgetting that he was already married] and thought in his mind to found in the midst of the sea a fair town with great lands belonging to it; and so he did by his cunning, and called it Naples. . ."

After accomplishing so much for his Babylonian beauty, Virgil did not marry her, but endowing her with the town of Naples and its lands, gave her in marriage to a certain grandee of Spain. Having thus disposed of her, the enchanter returned to Rome, collected all his treasures, and removed them to the city he had founded, where he resided for some years and established a school that speedily became of illustrious renown. Here he lost his wife, by whom he had no issue, built baths and bridges, and wrought the most extraordinary miracles. So passed an uncounted number of years, and Virgil at length abandoned Naples forever and retired to Rome.

Italian Witchcraft

In his *Aradia, or the Gospel of the Witches of Italy* (1899) folklorist **Charles Godfrey Leland** gives a valuable account of the life and practice of the Italian *strega*, or witch, as described by a Florentine hereditary witch named Maddalena. He states:

"In most cases she comes of a family in which her calling or art has been practiced for many generations. I have no doubt that there are instances in which the ancestry remounts to medieval, Roman, or it may be Etruscan times. The result has naturally been the accumulation in such families of much tradition. But in Northern Italy, as its literature indicates, though there has been some slight gathering of fairy tales and popular superstitions by scholars, there has never existed the least interest as regarded the strange lore of the witches, nor any suspicion that it embraced an incredible quantity of old Roman minor myths and legends, such as Ovid has recorded, but of which much escaped him and all other Latin Writers. . . . Even yet there are old people in the Romagna of the North who know the Etruscan names of the Twelve Gods, and invocations to Bacchus, Jupiter, and Venus, Mercury, and the Lares or ancestral spirits, and in the cities are women who prepare strange amulets, over which they mutter spells, all known in the old Roman time and who can astonish even the learned by their legends of Latin gods, mingled with lore which may be found in Cato or Theocritus. With one of these I became intimately acquainted in 1886, and have ever since employed her specially to collect among her sisters of the hidden spell in many places all the traditions of the olden times known to them. It is true that I have drawn from other sources but this woman by long practice has perfectly learned what few understand, or just what I want, and how to extract it from those of her kind.

"Among other strange relics, she succeeded, after many years, in obtaining the following 'Gospel,' which I have in her handwriting. A full account of its nature with many details will be found in an Appendix. I do not know definitely whether my informant derived a part of these traditions from written sources or oral narration, but believe it was chiefly the latter. . . .

"For brief explanation I may say that witchcraft is known to its votaries as *la vecchia religione,* or the old religion, of which Diana is the Goddess, her daughter *Aradia* (or Herodias) the female Messiah, and that this little work sets forth how the latter was born, came down to earth, established witches and witchcraft, and then returned to heaven. With it are given the ceremonies and invocations or incantations to be addressed to Diana and Aradia, the exorcism of Cain, and the spells of the holy-stone, rue, and verbena, constituting, as the text declares, the regular church service, so to speak, which is to be chanted or pronounced at the witch meetings. There are also included the very curious incantations or benedictions of the honey, meal, and salt, or cakes of the witch-supper, which is curiously classical, and evidently a relic of the Roman Mysteries."

Briefly, in discussing the ritual of the Italian witches, Leland reports that at the Sabbath they take meal and salt, honey and water, and say a conjuration over these, one to the meal, one to the salt, one to Cain, and one to Diana, the moon goddess. They then sit down naked to supper, men and women, and after the feast is over they dance, sing, and make love in the darkness, quite in the manner of the medieval Sabbath of the sorcerers. Many charms are given connected with stones, especially if these have holes in them and are found by accident. A lemon stuck full of pins we are told is a good omen. Love spells fill a large space in the little work, which for the rest recounts several myths of Diana and Endymion in corrupted form.

Leland's interesting book was one of the major sources used by **Gerald B. Gardner** in his reconstruction of witchcraft in the 1940s and served as a model for the *Book of Shadows,* which modern witches claim as a traditional descent in their covens.

Spiritualism

An early indication of the rise and spread of **Spiritualism** in Italy was surveyed in an article published in *Civitta Catholica,* the well-known Roman organ entitled "Modern Necromancy." It concluded,

"1st. Some of the phenomena may be attributed to imposture, hallucinations, and exaggerations in the reports of those who describe it, but there is a foundation of reality in the general sum of the reports which cannot have originated in pure invention or be wholly discredited without ignoring the value of universal testimony.

"2nd. The bulk of the theories offered in explanation of the proven facts, only cover a certain percentage of those facts, but utterly fail to account for the balance.

"3rd. Allowing for all that can be filtered away on mere human hypotheses, there are still a large class of phenomena appealing to every sense which cannot be accounted for by any known natural laws, and which seem to manifest the action of intelligent beings."

The famous medium **D. D. Home** visited the principal cities of Italy in 1852 and was so active in his propaganda that numerous circles were formed after his departure. Violent journalistic controversies arose out of the foundation of these societies, with the result that public interest was so aroused that it could only be satisfied with the publication of a paper on the subject. It was titled *Il amore del Vero,* issued from Geneva and edited by Pietro Suth and B. E. Manieri. In this journal accounts of the spiritual movements in the various countries of Europe, and the United States were published although the Church and press leveled anathemas against the journal.

In the spring of 1863, a society was founded at Palermo named Il Societa Spiritual di Palermo, which had for its president J. V. Paleolozo, and such members as Paolo Morelle, professor of Latin and philosophy.

It was about the autumn of 1864 that lectures were first given on Spiritualist subjects in Italy. They were started in Leghorn and Messina, and although of a very mixed character and often partaking largely of the lecturer's peculiar idiosyncrasies on religious subjects, they served to draw attention to the upheaval of thought going on in all directions, in connection with the revelations from the spirit world.

In the year 1870, over a hundred different societies were formed, with varying success, in different parts of Italy. Two of the most prominent flourishing at that date were conducted in Naples, and according to the French journal *Revue Spirite,* represented the two opposing schools that have prevailed in Spiritualism, namely, those who accepted the idea of **reincarnation**—associated with the **Spiritism** of **Allan Kardec** from **France**—and those who looked for the continued upward progress of the soul, known in America and England merely as "Spiritualists."

About 1868, the cause of Spiritualism was energized (at least in the higher strata of Italian society) by the visit of Samuel Guppy and his wife **Agnes Guppy-Volckman** to Naples, where they took up residence for two or three years. Guppy-Volckman was known throughout Europe for her physical mediumship. Drawing upon Guppy's wealth and social standing, she was able to place her performance at the command of the distinguished visitors who crowded his salons. It soon became a matter of notoriety that the most exalted individuals in the land, including King Victor Emmanuel and many of his nearest friends and counselors, had become convinced of the truth of the phenomena exhibited through her mediumship.

About the year 1863 Spiritualism began to enjoy the advantage of positive representation in the columns of a new paper named the *Annali dello Spiritismo* (Annals of Spiritualism). This journal was published in Turin by Niceforo Filalete. The columns of the *Annali* recorded that a Venetian Society of Spiritualists named "Atea" elected General Giuseppe Garibaldi their honorary president, and received the following reply by telegraph from the distinguished hero, the liberator of Italy,

"I gratefully accept the presidency of the Society Atea. Caprera, 23rd September."

The same issue of the *Annali* contained a verbatim report of a "grand discourse, given at Florence, by a distinguished literary gentleman, Signor Sebastiano Fenzi, in which the listeners were considerably astonished by a rehearsal of the many illustrious names of those who openly avowed their faith in Spiritualism."

The years 1863–64 appear to have been rich in Spiritualist efforts. Besides a large number of minor associations, (their existence was recorded from time to time in the early numbers of the *Annali* and *Revue Spirite*), about this time the Magnetic Society of Florence was formed. It would continue for many years to exert a marked influence in promoting the study of occult forces and phenomena. Seymour Kirkup, well known to the early initiators of Spiritualism, resided in Florence and contributed many records of spiritual phenomena to the *London Spiritual Magazine.* Nearly ten years after the establishment of the Magnetic Society of Florence, Baron Guitern de Bozzi, an eminent occultist, founded the Pneumatological Psychological Academy of Florence, but it was discontinued after his death.

Psychical Research and Parapsychology

In Italy, the divisions between Spiritualism and psychical research have tended to be blurred. Many eminent psychical researchers were sympathetic to Spiritualism if not actually endorsing its beliefs. One of the most famous investigators was the psychiatrist and criminologist **Cesare Lombroso** (1836–1909) who was convinced by the evidence for survival after death. **Marco Tullio Falcomer,** who conducted experiments with the famous physical medium **Florence Cook,** was a Spiritualist, as was also **Enrico Morselli** (1852–1929) who had investigated the phenomena of the medium **Eusapia Palladino.**

Among other Italian psychical researchers were Giovanni Batista Ermacora (1869–98), Enrico Imoda (who investigated the phenomena of **Linda Gazzera**), P. B. Bianchi, **Angelo Brofferio** (who became a Spiritualist), Ercole Chiaia, **Philippe Bottazzi,** Augusto Tamburini, and Rocco Santoliquido (1854–1930), who played a part in the founding of the **Institut Métapsychique** in Paris. Later researchers were Ernesto Bozzano (1862–1943), Giovanni Pioli of Milan, Lidio Cipriani of the University of Naples, William McKenzie of Genoa, **Count Cesar Baudi De Vesme** (1862–1938), Ferdinando Cazzamalli of Como, Fabio Vitali, G. C. Trabacchi, and Sante de Sanctis.

In 1901, the Società di Studi Psichici (Society of Psychic Studies) was founded in Milan. It was responsible for investigations of the mediums **Augustus Politi,** Eusapia Palladino and **Lucia Sordi.**

In 1937, the Società Italiana di Metapsichica (Italian Society of Metapsychics) was founded in Rome, in memory of **Charles Richet,** the noted French psychical researcher. In 1946, one group from the society headed by Ferdinando Cazzamalli formed the Association di Metapsichica, in Milan; at a later date the name was changed to Società Italiana di Parapsicologia, replacing the older term "metapsychics" with "parapsychology." It is currently headed by **Emilio Servadio,** at Via de Montecatini 7, 00186 Rome. The quarterly journal *Metapsichica Rivista Italiana di Parapsicologia* is the official organ of the Associazione Italiana Scientifica di Metapsichica headquartered at Via 5 Vittore, 19-20123 Milano.

Another active organization is the Centro Studi Parapsicologici (Center for Parapsychological Studies) established in Bologna in 1948, directed by **Piero Cassoli.** Other organizations include the Facoltà di Scienze Psichiche e Psicologiche (Faculty of Psychic and Psychological Sciences) of Academia Tiberina, established in 1960 (which may be reached at Via del Vantaggio 22, Rome), the Centro Italiano di Studi Metapsichici (Italian Center of Metapsychic Studies) founded in Pavia in 1968, which has conducted studies in psychic healing (and may be reached at Via Calascione 5/A, Naples), and the Centro Studi Parapsicologici de Bologna, Via Tamagno 2, Bologna.

Among periodicals the oldest is *Luce e Ombre* (Light and Shadow) founded in 1900 in Rome, edited from January 1932 from Milan under the title *Ricerca Psichica.* The journal *Uomini e Idee* (Men and Ideas) was launched in Naples in 1959 and in 1965 it was replaced by *Informazioni di Parapsicologia* (Parapsychology News) as a publication of the Centro Italiano di Parapsicologia. Since then, *Luce e Ombra* has been published quarterly by dell'Associazione Archivio di Documentazione Storica della Ricerca Psichica. Address: Bozzano-De Boni, Via Orfeo, 15, 40214 Bologna.

Sources:

Berger, Arthur S., and Joyce Berger. *The Encyclopedia of Parapsychology and Psychical Research.* New York: Paragon House, 1991.

The Wonderful History of Virgilius The Sorcerer of Rome. London: Daure Nutt, 1893.

Iubdan

In Ultonian romance (the Ossianic stories of Ireland), the king of the Wee Folk. One day he boasted of the might of his strong man Glower, who could hew down a thistle at one blow. His bard Eisirt retorted that beyond the sea there existed a race of giants, any one of whom could annihilate a whole battalion of the Wee Folk. Challenged to prove his words, Eisirt returned with Creda, King Fergus's dwarf and bard. He then dared Iubdan to go to Fergus's palace and taste the king's porridge.

Iubdan and Bebo, his queen, arrived at the palace at midnight, but while trying to get at the porridge so he could taste it and be gone before daybreak, Iubdan fell in. He was found in the pot the next morning by the scullions, and he and Bebo were taken before Fergus, who after a while released them in exchange for a pair of water shoes, which by wearing a man could go over or under water as freely as on land.

Ivan III (1440–1505)

Ivan, son of Vasily Vasilievich, grand duke of Moscow, became grand duke of Muscovy in the fifteenth century. According to legend, when he was at the point of death, he fell into terrible swoons, during which his soul made laborious journeys. In the first he was tormented for having kept innocent prisoners in his dungeons; in the second he was tortured further for having ground the people under heavy tasks; during the third voyage he died, but his body disappeared mysteriously before he could be buried, and it was thought that the devil had taken him.

Ivanova, Barbara (1917–)

Soviet psychic healer and parapsychologist. A former foreign-language college instructor, she was also an educator, lecturer, and author. She became known throughout the USSR for her healing skills and attended many prominent officials. Her techniques included conventional healing through holding her hands close to the patient, but she also experimented with absent healing, using telephone conversations as a contact with the subject. During the conversation Ivanova attempted to visualize the patient and the illness and form a mental healing process. During such conversations she believed she visualized former incarnations of the subject.

Ivanova became the first teacher of psychic healing in the USSR. She both conducted experiments in telepathy and allowed herself to be studied as a subject. She was an honorary member of many parapsychological societies and journals (including the editorial advisory board of *Psi Research*). She wrote on a broad range of subjects, and her articles on parapsychology, healing, human potential, and the interconnectedness in living nature have appeared in many languages, including English, German, French, Italian, Spanish, Polish, and Yiddish.

Sources:

Berger, Arthur S., and Joyce Berger. *The Encyclopedia of Parapsychology and Psychical Research.* New York: Paragon House, 1991.

Ivanova, Barbara. *The Golden Chalice.* Edited by M. Mir and L. Vilenskaya. San Francisco: H. S. Dakin, 1986.

———. "Reincarnation and Healing." *Psi Research* 5, 1,2 (March/June 1986).

———. "Some Experiments on Healing Processes." *International Journal of Paraphysics* 19, 5,6 (1985).

Ivunches

Chilean familiars. (See United States of **America**)

IYI See Integral Yoga International

Iynx

A Chaldean symbol of universal being, the name of which means "power of transmission." It was reproduced as a living sphere or winged globe and was said to be projected forth by divine mind on the plane of reality, to be followed by two other beings, called "paternal" and "ineffable," and finally by hosts of iynxs of a subordinate character, called "free intelligences."

The iynx was described by occultist **Éliphas Lévi** as "corresponding... to the Hebrew *Yod* or to that unique letter from which all other letters were formed," and thus related to the Jewish mysticism of the **Sepher Yetsirah** or Book of Creation, a primary text of the **Kabbalah**. For reference to Chaldean concepts, see the complex Gnostic emanations discussed by **G. R. S. Mead.**

J

J. Allen Hynek Center for UFO Studies

Foremost organization investigating unidentified flying objects. CUFOS was founded as the **Center for UFO Studies** in 1973 by J. Allen Hynek, a professor of astronomy at Northwestern University, and Sherman J. Larsen, an insurance salesman who had been active in the **National Investigations Committee on Aerial Phenomena** (NICAP). Through the 1960s Hynek was the chief consultant for the air force UFO project known as Blue Book, but later turned his attention to nurturing scholarly enthusiasm for the study of strange flying objects.

CUFOS grew through the 1970s and had its peak years toward the end of the decade. Allan Hendry joined the staff in 1976 as a full-time investigator. A newsletter grew into a periodical, the **International UFO Reporter.** The work of the center was hindered, however, by methodological problems, and as Hendry concluded in 1979 in a massive report on his ongoing research, its investigators lacked the tools to carry out their task. However, CUFOS carried on in an attempt to generate scholarly interest, maintain public support, and garner financial resources.

The center underwent substantial change in the mid-1980s. Hynek moved to Phoenix, Arizona, and then died a year later. The center moved to Glendale, Arizona, and then to Chicago, Illinois. Mark Rodeghier succeeded to leadership of the organization, which took a new name in honor of its founder. The organization still publishes the *International UFO Reporter,* a substantial magazine dealing with both recent sightings of interest and the more theoretical issues surrounding UFOs; occasional monographs; and the scholarly **Journal of UFO Studies.** It is an open-membership organization. Address: 2457 W. Peterson Ave., Chicago, IL 60659.

Sources:

Clark, Jerome. *UFOs in the 1980s.* Vol. 1 of *The UFO Encyclopedia.* Detroit: Apogee Books, 1990.

Hendry, Allan. *The UFO Handbook: A Guide to Investigating, Evaluating, and Reporting UFO Sightings.* Garden City, N.Y.: Doubleday, 1979.

Jachin and Boaz

The names of two symbolical pillars of King Solomon's Kabalistic temple. They were believed to explain the mystery of the meaning of life. One was black and the other white, representing the powers of good and evil. It was said that they symbolized the need of "two" in the world. Human progression requires two feet, the worlds gravitate by means of two forces, generation needs two sexes.

The symbolism of the two pillars has been discussed in the book *The Garden of Pomegranates,* by Rabbi Moses Cordovero, a book on the **Kabala** first published in Cracow, Poland, in 1591. The two pillars have also become part of the symbolism of **Freemasonry** and **ceremonial magic.**

Jachowski, Jan (1891– ?)

Polish publisher who experimented with the **divining rod** and **pendulum** and also studied in the field of **astrology.** He was born on December 13, 1891, at Jaktorowo, Chodziez Poznanskie, Poland. He served as an editor for the publications services of the University of Poznan and was the winner in 1936 of the Silver Wreath of the Polish Academy of Literature.

Sources:

Pleasants, Helene, ed. *Biographical Dictionary of Parapsychology.* New York: Helix Press, 1964.

Jacinth

A gemstone, a variety of zircon that was believed to protect the wearer from plague and from lightning, to strengthen the heart, and to bring wealth, honor, prudence, and wisdom. It was recommended by **Albertus Magnus** as a soporific on account of its coldness and was ordered by Psellus in cases of coughs, ruptures, and melancholy; it was to be drunk in vinegar. Marbodeus described the wonderful properties of three species of jacinth. Pliny and Leonardus also spoke highly of it.

Jack the Ripper

Epithet of a brutal murderer in Whitechapel, London's east side. Over a period of some ten weeks during 1888 five prostitutes were murdered and mutilated, apparently by the same psychopath. The victims were Mary Anne Nicholls, Annie Chapman, Elizabeth Stridge, Catharine Eddowes, and Mary Jeannette Kelly. Some commentators have extended the list to seven victims, others to ten. In spite of police vigilance, the murderer was never discovered.

The sensational nature of the crimes (the victims were raped and mutilated) and the fact that they remained unsolved has generated hundreds of books, articles, and stories propounding various theories about the identity of the Ripper. Some of the more bizarre involve the Russian secret police, Masonic conspiracies, or members of the royal family. In their enthusiasm to validate a cherished theory, many otherwise reputable writers falsified evidence. One of the most persistent myths is that the Spiritualist and clairvoyant **Robert James Lees** had given the police advance knowledge of the crimes and identified the murderer through clairvoyant powers. This continuing story stemmed from a hoax article in the *Chicago Sunday Times-Herald* (April 28, 1895) and was repeated in London newspapers. One constant theme throughout the speculative volumes, however, is that the murderer was someone with medical knowledge, because of the skillful mutilations.

Among the many books, that by British author **Melvin Harris,** *Jack the Ripper: The Bloody Truth* (1987), has particular interest because of the occult connections it draws. Harris advances a convincing case that the Ripper was Dr. Roslyn D'Onston (born Robert Donston Stephenson), a journalist and medical man obsessed with the occult. D'Onston himself wrote articles claiming to know the true identity of Jack the Ripper. He also claimed to know exactly how the crimes were committed and stated that they were part of a black magic ritual. In his writings, D'Onston used the pseudonym Tautriadelta.

One of these articles was published in the April 1896 issue of the journal *Borderland,* edited by Spiritualist **W. T. Stead.** In a foreword to the article, Stead writes that the author "prefers to be known by his Hermetic name of Tautriadelta" and also states:

"The writer . . . has been known to me for many years. He is one of the most remarkable persons I ever met. For more than a year I was under the impression that he was the veritable Jack the Ripper, an impression which I believe was shared by the police, who, at least once, had him under arrest; although as he completely satisfied them, they liberated him without bringing him into court."

In the article itself Tautriadelta claims to have studied occultism under the novelist **Bulwer Lytton,** celebrated for his occult stories, and to have witnessed or taken part in extraordinary occult phenomena in France, Italy, India, and Africa.

D'Onston lived in London's Whitechapel, where the Ripper murders took place, in the same lodginghouse were Theosophist **Mabel Collins** and her occultist friend Vittoria Cremers lived. Collins became infatuated with D'Onston, but subsequently experienced fear and revulsion around him. She once told Cremers about something D'Onston said to her and showed her, and said "I believe D'Onston is Jack the Ripper." Cremers had noticed a large black box in D'Onston's room, and one day, while the doctor was out, she looked inside the box. She found some books and also some black ties that had dried, dull stains at the back. She thought the stains might be blood.

Later, commenting on a newspaper report that the Ripper would kill again, D'Onston laughed and said, "There will be no more murders. Did I ever tell you that I knew Jack the Ripper?" He went on to describe in detail how the Ripper had carried out the murders, said they were "for a very special reason," and related how he had concealed the organs cut from the victims in the space between his shirt and tie.

The story of the discovery by Cremers is retold in *The Confessions of Aleister Crowley* (1969) without naming D'Onston. **Aleister Crowley** also writes:

"At this time London was agog with the exploits of Jack the Ripper. One theory of the motive of the murderer was that he was performing an Operation to obtain the Supreme Black Magical Power. The seven women had to be killed so that their seven bodies formed a 'Calvary cross of seven points' with its head to the west."

All these references are detailed by Melvin Harris in his book, and he also cites an unsigned article by D'Onston that reinforces Crowley's claim that the murders were a black magic operation. The article is titled "Who Is the Whitechapel Demon? (By One Who Thinks He Knows)" and propounds in detail a black magic theory about the murders, stemming from occultist **Éliphas Lévi**'s work *Le Dogme et Rituel de la Haute Magic.* D'Onston's precise knowledge of the methods and intentions of the murders, impudently combined with false clues while posing as an investigator of the crimes, makes a strong case that he was Jack the Ripper, as W. T. Stead, Vittoria Cremers, and Mabel Collins suspected.

Sources:

Crowley, Aleister. *The Confessions of Aleister Crowley.* Edited by John Symonds and Kenneth Grant. New York: Hill & Wang, 1969.

Tautriadelta [Roslyn D'Onston]. "A Modern Magician: An Autobiography. By a Pupil of Lord Lytton." *Borderland* 3, no. 2 (April 1896).

Jacks, L(awrence) P(earsall) (1860–1955)

British author and professor of philosophy who investigated psychical phenomena. He was born on October 9, 1860, at Nottingham, England. He was educated at University School, Nottingham; London University (M.A., 1886); Manchester College; and Harvard. He became a professor of philosophy at Manchester College, Oxford, in 1903, and for many years served as principal (1915–31).

Jacks served as president of the **Society for Psychical Research,** London (1917–18), and as vice president (1909–55). He was particularly concerned with the relationship of psychical research to philosophy. He also sat with a number of mediums, including **Gladys Osborne Leonard,** one of the outstanding British trance mediums. After an active life that included writing several books and a number of articles, Jacks died February 17, 1955.

Sources:

Berger, Arthur S., and Joyce Berger. *The Encyclopedia of Parapsychology and Psychical Research.* New York: Paragon House, 1991.

Jacks, L. P. *All Men Are Ghosts.* London: Williams & Norgate, 1913.

———. *The Confessions of an Octogenarian.* N.p., 1942.

———. "Dramatic Dreams, an Unexplored Field for Psychical Research." *Journal* of the Society for Psychical Research 17 (1915).

———. *Elemental Religion.* New York: Harper, 1934.

———. *The Inner Sentinel.* New York; London: Harper & Brothers, 1930.

———. *My American Friends.* London: Constable & Co. Ltd, 1933; New York: Macmillian, 1933.

———. *My Neighbour the Universe.* N.p., 1928.

———. *Near the Brink.* London: Allen & Unwin, 1955.

———. "Presidential Address: The Theory of Survival in the Light of Its Context." *Proceedings* of the Society for Psychical Research 29 (1918).

Pleasants, Helene, ed. *Biographical Dictionary of Parapsychology.* New York: Helix Press, 1964.

Jacob, Auguste Henri ("Jacob the Zouave") (1828–1913)

Famous French spiritual healer whose curative and clairvoyant powers became known in 1867 while he was still attached to his French regiment. He was born on March 6, 1828. As a young man Jacob volunteered to serve in the Seventh Hussars (the Zouaves). He became interested in **Spiritualism** as it began to spread throughout Europe in the mid-nineteenth century. His healing powers probably began while he was serving in the Crimea and Algeria, but his fame spread when he was stationed in central France. He was soon discharged from the army, since the crowds that assembled daily around his tent made army discipline impossible. After moving to Versailles, Jacob visited Paris to effect his cures, and at a house in the Rue de la Roquette he was besieged by crowds of the crippled and diseased.

He began a career of healing mediumship, claiming that he saw spirits ministering to the patients who called upon him and that they prescribed healing. He not only refused to charge for his healing, but also declined freewill offerings, even when it was requested that they be devoted to healing the poor. His father, however, became a self-appointed manager, standing at the door selling Jacob's photograph for one franc to all who would buy.

Jacob's method of healing often resembled that of modern evangelists—a forceful command to be well. In other cases he simply stared at the patient. Many spectacular cures were reported. He was not always successful, and in some cases he simply dismissed the sufferer with the remark, "I can do nothing for your disease." In his later years he recommended natural health treatment and condemned the use of alcohol. He ascribed his own healing powers to "the spirits of white magnetism." (See also **Animal Magnetism**)

Sources:

Britten, Emma Hardinge. *Nineteenth Century Miracles.* New York: W. Britten, 1884.

Jacob, August Henri. *L'Hygiène naturelle, ou l'art de consevèr sa santé et de se guérir soi-même.* Paris, 1868.

———. *Les Pensées du Zouave Jacob.* Paris, 1868.

———. *Poisons et contre-Poisons dévoilés.* Paris, 1874.

Jacob, Mr. ("Jacob of Simla") (ca. 1850–1921)

A reputed wonder-worker of India during the late nineteenth and early twentieth centuries. A rich diamond merchant, Jacob had a reputation for generosity and for working miracles. He was immortalized in literature, serving as the archetype for the main character in the novel *Mr. Isaacs* (1882), by F. Marion Crawford. In the novel, Isaacs is a disciple of Brahmin initiate Ram Lal, whose mystical powers include appearing and disappearing at will.

Jacob was also the model for "Lurgan Sahib," the mysterious secret agent with hypnotic powers in Rudyard Kipling's great novel *Kim* (1901). Lurgan, too, is a dealer in precious stones and describes himself as a "Healer of Pearls." He boasts, "There is no one but me can doctor a sick pearl and re-blue turquoises. I grant you opals—any fool can cure an opal—but for a sick pearl there is only me. Suppose I were to die! Then there would be no one."

Crawford first met Jacob in a hotel in Simla, India. Jacob invited the novelist to his room, where Crawford was astounded by an Aladdin's cave of wealth and beauty:

"It appeared as if the walls and the ceiling were lined with gold and precious stones. . . . Every available space, nook and cranny was filled with gold and jeweled ornaments, shining weapons or uncouth but resplendent idols. . . . The floor was covered with a rich, soft pile, and low divans were heaped with cushions of deep-tinted silk and gold . . . superbly illuminated Arabic manuscripts. . . . At last I turned, and from contemplating the magnificence and inanimate wealth, I was riveted by the majestic face and expression of the beautiful living creature, who by a turn of his want, or, to speak prosaically, by an invitation to smoke had lifted me out of the humdrum into a land peopled with all the effulgent fantasy and the priceless realities of the magic East."

After publication of Crawford's novel, wild rumors spread about the reputed magical powers of Jacob, whose operation was assisted by his spirit guide, "Ram Lal," who was said to have died 150 years earlier. An article by a European occultist calling himself "Tautriadelta (pseudonym of Dr. Roslyn D'Onston) a pupil of Lord Lytton," in *Borderland* (April 1896) recounts miracles performed by Jacob, such as growing bunches of ripe black grapes on a walking stick, thrusting a sword into a man's body without injury, and walking on water. Some time later, interviewed by a member of the **Society for Psychical Research,** Jacob was quoted as saying that the growing of buds and blossoms on a walking stick was a trick with a prepared stick, and that pushing a sword into the body was only a matter of skill and knowledge, but that his walking on water was achieved by being supported in the air by his spirit guide, who also acted as a kind of "astral postman," delivering messages over vast distances when needed.

This last phenomenon is of particular interest considering that Jacob met Theosophist **Helena Petrovna Blavatsky,** who later acquired fame for the magical precipitation of **"Mahatma letters"** over a distance. Jacob himself regarded Blavatsky as no more than "a clever conjurer."

Jacob's early life was as romantic as his later life was reputed to be. He was born a Turkish or Armenian Jew near Constantinople and sold into slavery at age ten. He was bought by a rich and intelligent pasha who saw that the boy had great abilities and instead of giving him menial tasks educated him in Eastern life, literature, philosophy, and occultism. On the death of his patron Jacob made a pilgrimage to Mecca, then took passage to Bombay, landing without money or friends. Through his knowledge of Arabic he soon obtained a position as scribe to a nobleman at the Nizam's court in Hyderabad. There he started dealing in precious stones, later moving to Delhi, then to Simla, where he became one of the most famous jewelers of the time. Maharajahs from all over India engaged his services and he became a rich man, furnishing his house in Oriental splendor with priceless and lavish possessions. At home he received Indian princes, viceroys, governors, and distinguished members of the civil and military services. Lord Lytton, then viceroy, visited him and remained for several days. In spite of his lavish surroundings, Jacob lived a simple vegetarian life, occasionally entertaining guests with occult marvels that became the gossip of Simla.

The story of his eventual downfall is equally remarkable. He had incurred the displeasure of a prime minister at Hyderabad through giving information about the brutal execution of a Hindu by the minister's brother. Knowing that the Imperial Diamond was being sold in England, Jacob offered to buy it for the nizam of Hyderabad, who agreed to pay him 46 lakhs of rupees (more than $600,000). Jacob knew that he could buy it for half that sum and saw the chance of a good bargain. The nizam paid him 20 lakhs of rupees on account. After the diamond arrived in India and was paid for by Jacob, the prime minister urged the government of India to prevent the sale, knowing that there was an official embargo on princes spending such large sums. The sale was vetoed and Jacob was left with the diamond and less than half the sum promised by the nizam. Next, the prime minister urged the nizam to sue Jacob for return of the money already paid. The trial lasted 57 days; after returning the nizam's deposit and paying legal costs, Jacob was ruined. In desperation he offered the diamond to the nizam at any price from one rupee upward and the nizam agreed to pay 17 lakhs of rupees. Jacob never received any money after handing over the diamond, however, and was penniless. He retired to Bombay, living in penury and later becoming blind.

Sources:

Fodor, Nandor. *The Haunted Mind.* New York: Garrett Publications, 1959.

Heath, Frederick W. "The Story of Mr. Isaacs' Life." *Occult Review* (October 1912).

Russell, Edmund. "'Mr. Isaacs' of Simla." *Occult Review* (March 1917).

Jacobi, Jolande Szekacs (Mrs. Andrew Jacobi) (1890– ?)

Psychologist and psychotherapist who wrote on parapsychology in the context of Jungian psychology. Jacobi was born on March 25, 1890, at Budapest, Hungary, and later studied at the University of Vienna (Ph.D. psychology, 1938). She trained as a psychotherapist with **C. G. Jung** from 1938 to 1943. In 1947 she joined the staff as a lecturer for the Institute for Applied Psychology, University of Zürich, and the C. G. Jung Institute. She published a number of articles on depth psychology, Jungian psychology, and parapsychology, and she lectured on such topics throughout Europe. She also contributed a chapter, "Dream of the Oracle," to the volume honoring Jung's eightieth birthday.

Sources:

Jacobi, Jolande S. *Case Studies in Counselling and Psychotherapy.* N.p., 1959.

———. *Komplex, Archetypus, Symbol in der Psychologie von C. G. Jung.* Zürich: Rascher, 1957; London: Routledge & Paul, 1959.

———. *Paracelsus.* Wien: P. Neff, 1951.

———. *Die Psychologie von C. G. Jung.* New Haven: Yale University Press, 1943.

———. *Vom Bilderreich der Seele.* Zürich: Rascher, 1940.

———. *The Way of Individuation.* London: Hodder & Stoughton, 1967.

———, ed. *Man and His Symbols.* Garden City, N.Y.: Doubleday, 1964.

Pleasants, Helene, ed. *Biographical Dictionary of Parapsychology.* New York: Helix Press, 1964.

Jacob's Ladder

According to the **Kabala,** Jacob's Ladder, which was disclosed to Jacob in a vision, was a metaphorical representation of the powers of **alchemy** operating through visible nature. The ladder was a "rainbow," or prismatic staircase, between heaven and earth. Jacob's dream symbolizes a theory of the hermetic creation. There were said to be only two original colors, red and blue, representing spirit and matter. Orange is red mixing with the yellow light of the sun; yellow is the radiance of the sun itself; green is blue and yellow; indigo is blue tinctured with red; and violet is produced by the mingling of red and blue. The sun is alchemic gold, and the moon is alchemic silver. It was believed that all earthly creations were produced through the interaction of these two potent ruling spirits.

Jacob's Ladder is also part of the symbolism of the high grades of **Freemasonry.**

Jade

A term covering minerals of varied color and chemical composition, credited with occult properties. Jade may be jadeite, nephrite, or chloromelanite, with a range of colors—black, brown, red, lavender, blue, green, yellow, or white. The mineral is found mainly in New Zealand, Mexico, Central America, and China. In prehistoric times jade was used for utensils and weapons, but in Mexico, Egypt, and China it was employed in burial rites. In China, Burma, and India, jade is used for **amulets.**

Jade is chiefly associated with China, where it has been carved into ornaments for thousands of years. The blue variety of jade was traditionally associated with the heavens, and Chinese emperors were said to have made contact with heaven through a disk of white jade. There was a Chinese superstition that rubbing a piece of jade in the hand would bring good fortune to any decision or business venture. The Chinese word for jade is *yü*, indicating beauty, nobility, and purity. Because of its *yang* (masculine, hot, active) qualities, jade is believed to prolong life. It is taken medicinally in water or wine, and is believed to protect against heat and cold, hunger and thirst. Powdered jade is taken to strengthen the heart, lungs, and voice. It is also considered an indicator of health and fortune, becoming dull and lusterless when its owner experiences ill health or misfortune.

In Burma, Tibet, and India, jade is considered a cure for heart trouble and a means of deflecting lightning. It has the property of bringing rain, mist, or snow when thrown into water. In Scotland it has been used as a touchstone to cure illness. The carving of jade into beautiful ornaments reached its peak in China, where even a small carving involved skilled and patient work over several months. There is still a large jade market in Hong Kong.

Jadian

A wer-tiger or human animal in Malayan superstition. (See **Malaysia**)

Jadoo

A Hindu term for magic or wonder-working, usually applied to traveling conjurers, or jadoo-wallahs. The term was popularized in the United States by writer-magician **John A. Keel** in his book *Jadoo* (1958). Keel traveled through India, where his skill as an amateur magician earned him the confidence of Indian conjurers, who disclosed their own tricks, including a version of the famous **Indian rope trick.** Most of the present-day jadoo is skillful conjuring, but this does not preclude the possibility of genuine paranormal versions of the same wonders.

Sources:

Keel, John A. *Jadoo.* London, 1958.

Jaffé, Aniela (1903–)

Jungian psychologist who wrote on parapsychology. Jaffé was born on February 20, 1903, in Berlin, Germany. After World War II she became the secretary at the C. G. Jung Institute, Zürich (1947–55), and then personal secretary to **C. G. Jung** (1955–61). She later recorded and edited the reminiscences of Jung, published as *Memories, Dreams, Reflections* (1963). In addition to her various important papers on psychology, she wrote widely on parapsychology, particularly on connections between **psi** phenomena and the unconscious, and on the psychological interpretation of paranormal phenomena.

Sources:

Berger, Arthur S., and Joyce Berger. *The Encyclopedia of Parapsychology and Psychical Research.* New York: Paragon House, 1991.

Jaffé, Aniela. *Apparitions and Precognition: A Study from the Point of View of C. G. Jung's Analytical Psychology.* New York: Harper & Row, 1971.

———. *From the Life and Work of C. G. Jung.* New York: Harper & Row, 1971.

———. *The Myth of Meaning.* New York: Putnam, 1971.

———. "The Psychic World of C. G. Jung." *Tomorrow* (spring 1961).

Pleasants, Helene, ed. *Biographical Dictionary of Parapsychology.* New York: Helix Press, 1964.

Jahagirdar, Keshav Tatacharya (1914–)

Indian professor of philosophy and psychology who studied parapsychological phenomena. He was born on April 16, 1914, at Agarkhed, Mysore, India. He studied at Allahabad University, Uttar Pradesh (M.A., 1941) and then was awarded a research scholarship in the philosophy department at Allahabad University (1941–44). He became a professor of philosophy at Nagpur University (1944–46) and a professor and head of the Departments of Psychology and Philosophy at M.T.B. College, Surat, Bombay (1946–54). In 1954 he began a long tenure as professor and head of the Departments of Psychology and Philosophy at D. & H. National College, Bombay.

Jahagirdar studied mediumship, psychokinesis, and clairvoyance, and from his studies he wrote many papers. He became a charter member and general secretary of the Society for Psychical Research, Bombay, in 1956.

Sources:

Jahagirdar, Keshav Tatacharya, and Edwin C. May. "From Where Does the Kum-Kum Come? A Materialization Attempt." In *Research in Parapsychology 1975,* edited by J. D. Morris, W. G. Roll, and R. L. Morris. New York: Parapsychological Association, 1976.

Pleasants, Helene, ed. *Biographical Dictionary of Parapsychology.* New York: Helix Press, 1964.

Jahn, Robert

Engineering professor and rocket propulsion specialist at Princeton University, who branched out into investigation, under strict laboratory conditions, of **micro-PK** effects in **parapsychology.** Following publication of his parapsychological studies, he was demoted from the post of dean of the engineering faculty at Princeton to an associate professorship. However, his studies are widely respected by parapsychologists for their scope and rigor. He continued experimenting at the Princeton Engineering Anomalies Research Laboratory, funded by the McDonnell Foundation and the Petzer Institute.

Jahn's experiments, conducted over 14 years, during which period he devised increasingly sophisticated safeguards against charges of possible error or fraud, are based on a random event generator featuring the white noise emitted by an electrical diode. The noise produced is sampled a thousand times a second to ascertain whether it is in a positive or negative value phase, the probability being roughly equal, even making allowance for occasional significant deviations, which can also be calculated. The setup amounts to a kind of electrical "heads or tails" choice. The subject sits in front of the generator and attempts to mentally effect a positive or negative registration, and the result is charted on a computer screen.

In later **macro-PK** experiments, Jahn created a random mechanical cascade, resembling a pinball machine, in which 9,000 polystyrene balls drop through a grid of nylon pegs, bouncing about to collect in time at the bottom. The balls should normally end up with a classic Gaussian (normal), bell-shaped distribution. Jahn's experiments show that **PK** subjects tend to produce slight deviations to one side.

One remarkable recent development is Jahn's experiments with subjects attempting to influence his devices from as far away as Kenya, New Zealand, England, and Russia, sitting for an hour at an agreed time and attempting to alter output according to a prearranged pattern. Distance does not appear to affect the results.

Jahn has also attempted to assist other experimenters by creating inexpensive solid-state versions of his random event generators that can be used to replicate his findings.

Jahoda, Gustav (1920–)

Lecturer in social psychology who wrote on parapsychological topics. He was born on October 11, 1920, in Vienna, Austria. He took all of his degrees at London University, England (B.S., 1945; M.S., 1948; Ph.D., 1952). After graduation Jahoda taught for four years at the University College of Ghana (Gold Coast), then became a senior lecturer in social psychology at Glasgow University, Scotland. In addition to his various papers on psychological, anthropological, and sociological subjects, Jahoda wrote on the supernatural beliefs of West Africans. His article "Emotional Stress, Mental Illness and Social Change" (*International Journal of Social Psychiatry*) describes West African healers; his "Aspects of Westernization" (*British Journal of Sociology*) analyzes West African belief in the paranormal.

Sources:

Jahoda, Gustav. *The Psychology of Superstition.* New York: J. Aronson, 1974.

———. *White Man: A Study of the Attitudes of Africans to Europeans Before Independence.* London; New York: Oxford University Press, 1961.

Pleasants, Helene, ed. *Biographical Dictionary of Parapsychology.* New York: Helix Press, 1964.

James, T. P. (ca. 1874)

Automatic writing medium of Brattleboro, Vermont, who claimed the spirit of Charles Dickens led him to complete and publish Dickens's unfinished novel *The Mystery of Edwin Drood.*

James, William (1842–1910)

Professor of psychology at Harvard University and one of the founders of the **American Society for Psychical Research** (ASPR). James was born in New York City on January 11, 1842, and obtained his M.D. in 1870 from Harvard Medical School. In 1872 he was appointed instructor in anatomy and physiology at Harvard College. He went on to study psychology and hygiene and in 1890 published his famous work *The Principles of Psychology.* In 1897 James became professor of philosophy at Harvard and lectured at universities in the United States and Britain. He developed the doctrine of pragmatism, and one of his most important philosophical books is *The Varieties of Religious Experience* (1902), which has been an influential work in the attempt to reconcile science and religion.

The first case that piqued James's interest in psychic phenomena is reported in the *Proceedings* of the American Society for Psychical Research (vol. 1, part 2, pp. 221–31). It is the case of a drowned girl whose body was seen by a Mrs. Titus of Lebanon, New Hampshire, in a dream. The girl's head was under the timber trussing of a bridge at Enfield. Divers had searched for the girl's body in vain, but following Titus's vision they found it.

The discovery of **Leonora Piper**'s mediumship for the **Society for Psychical Research** (SPR) was attributed to James. His mother-in-law, led by curiosity, paid a visit to Piper in 1885. She returned with a perplexing story. Seeking a simple explanation for the supernatural nature of the facts related to him, James took a rationalist view. Then a few days later, with his wife, he went to get a direct personal impression. The Jameses arrived unannounced, and they were careful not to make any reference to a relative who had preceded them. James later noted:

"My impression after this first visit was that Mrs. P. was either possessed of supernormal powers or knew the members of my wife's family by sight and had by some lucky coincidence become acquainted with such a multitude of their domestic circumstances as to produce the startling impression which she did. My later knowledge of her sittings and personal acquaintance with her has led me to absolutely reject the latter explanation, and to believe that she has supernormal powers."

For 18 months after his first experiments, James was virtually in charge of all arrangements for Piper's séances. When, because of other duties, he dropped his inquiries for a period of two years, he wrote to the SPR (London) and induced them to engage Piper for experiments. "The result," he wrote of his personal investigations, "is to make me feel as absolutely certain as I am of any personal fact in the world that she knows things in her trances which she cannot possibly have heard in her waking state." He admitted there was a strong case in favor of **survival** when the following message, obtained while a Ms. Robbins had a sitting with Piper, was submitted to him: "There is a person named Child, who has suddenly come and sends his love to William and to his own wife who is living. He says L . . ." Neither Robbins nor Piper knew Child, who was an intimate friend of James and whose Christian name began with L.

In the autumn of 1899 Piper visited James at his country house in New Hampshire. There he came to know her personally better than ever before. "It was in great measure," wrote Alta L. Piper in her biography of the medium, "due to his sympathetic encouragement and understanding of the many difficulties, with which she found herself confronted in the early days of her career, that my mother was able to adhere unfalteringly to the onerous course which she had set herself to follow."

In an often quoted lecture in 1890 James declared:

"To upset the conclusion that all crows are black, there is no need to seek demonstration that no crow is black; it is sufficient to produce one white crow; a single one is sufficient." Since his proclamation of Piper as his "one white crow," the concept of the single "white crow" has become a cliché in psychical research.

James published several papers in the *Proceedings* of the SPR and an important essay on psychical research in his book *The Will to Believe* (1902). In a lecture at Oxford in 1909 he announced his firm conviction that "most of the phenomena of psychical research are rooted in reality." Shortly before his death he stated in the *American Magazine* that, after 25 years of psychical research, he held the spiritistic hypothesis unproven and was inclined "to picture the situation as an interaction between slumbering faculties in the automatist's mind and a cosmic environment of other consciousness of some sort which is able to work upon them."

James served as president of the SPR, London, from 1894 to 1895 and as vice president from 1896 to 1910. His name and prestige and his open espousal of the cause of psychical research were a great benefit to the nascent science. He died at Chocorua, New Hampshire, August 26, 1910. His alleged return after death is discussed in a long chapter in **James Hyslop**'s *Contact with the Other World* (1919).

Sources:

Berger, Arthur S., and Joyce Berger. *The Encyclopedia of Parapsychology and Psychical Research.* New York: Paragon House, 1991.

James, William. *Essays in Psychical Research.* Cambridge, Mass.: Harvard University Press, 1986.

———. *Letters of William James and Theodore Flournoy.* Edited by R. C. Le Clair. Madison, Wis.: University of Wisconsin Press, 1966.

———. *William James on Psychical Research.* Edited by Gardner Murphy and Robert O. Ballou. New York: Viking Press, 1960.

Pleasants, Helene, ed. *Biographical Dictionary of Parapsychology.* New York: Helix Press, 1964.

James IV of Scotland (1473–1513)

The romantic nature of King James IV of **Scotland** led him to encourage the study of **alchemy** and the occult sciences during his reign. William Dunbar, in his *Remonstrance,* refers to the patronage that James bestowed upon alchemists and charlatans, and in the treasurer's accounts there are numerous payments for the "quinta essencia" (the "fifth essence," the spiritual goal of alchemy), including wages to the persons employed and utensils of various kinds. Following is a letter from King James to one Master James Inglis:

"We graciously accept your kindness, by which in a letter brought to us you signify that you have beside you certain books learned in the philosophy of the true Alchemy, and that although most worthy men have sought them from you, you have nevertheless with difficulty kept them for our use, because you had heard of our enthusiasm for the art. We bring you thanks . . . and we have sent our familiar, Master James Merchenistoun, to you, that he may see to the transfer hither of those books which you wish us to have; whom receive in good faith in our name. Farewell. From our Palace at Edinburgh."

In addition to promoting alchemy, James was also caught up in the **witchcraft** hysteria of his day and wrote a book that promoted witch-hunts.

Janet, Pierre (Marie Félix) (1859–1947)

French psychologist and neurologist noted for his research on hysteria and neuroses. Janet was born on May 30, 1859, in Paris. He studied at the École Normale and the École de Medecine, Paris. He became a lecturer on philosophy at the lycées of Chateauroux and The Hague, at the College Rollin, and at the lycées Louis-le-Grand and Condorcet. From 1889 to 1898 he was director of the psychological laboratory of the Saltpêtrière in Paris. He also lectured on psychology at the Sorbonne and became professor of psychology at the Collège de France in 1902. He published many important works on psychology and hysteria. His work with French neurologist **J. M. Charcot** includes a serious medical and scientific study of the phenomena of **hypnotism.**

Sources:

Berger, Arthur S., and Joyce Berger. *The Encyclopedia of Parapsychology and Psychical Research.* New York: Paragon House, 1991.

JAPAN

Magical concepts are to be found among the Japanese in their traditional religious beliefs and rites and in their conception of nature. According to such beliefs, all forms and objects, both animate and inanimate, possess, equally with man, a soul with good or evil tendencies; these forms and objects, either of their own volition or by evocation, come into close touch with man either to his advantage or detriment. Much of Japanese folklore and tradition is permeated with a belief in the supernatural.

Shinto Religion and Ancestor-Worship

A prominent feature of the Japanese religion Shintoism is the worship of ancestors, allied to the worship of nature. Each of the main sects of Shintoism includes the veneration of one's ancestors as a cardinal principle. According to that belief, the disembodied spirits acquire the powers of deities and possess supernatural attributes. They become potential for good or evil and exercise their potentialities in the same mundane sphere upon which their interests and affections centered during life. They thus become guardian divinities and the object of ceremonies to honor them, to show gratitude for their services while upon earth, and to solicit a continuance of these services beyond the grave.

On this point, Lafcadio Hearn writes,

"An intimate sense of relation between the visible and invisible worlds is the special religious characteristic of Japan among all civilized countries. To Japanese thought the dead are not less real than the living. They take part in the daily life of the people—sharing the humblest sorrows and the humblest joys. They attend the family repasts, watch over the well-being of the household, assist and rejoice in the prosperity of their descendants. They are present at the public pageants, at all the sacred festivals of Shinto, at the military games, and at all the entertainments especially provided for them. And they are universally thought of as finding pleasure in the offerings made to them or the honors conferred upon them."

Every morning, while ancient prayers are repeated, one member of the family places flowers and food-emblems as offerings of pious affection before the shrine to be found in most Japanese homes. On the shrine, beside the symbols of the sun-goddess and the tutelary god of the family, one finds the memorial tablets containing names, ages, and dates of death of members of the household. Stories circulate through the villages of the souls of ancestors taking material form and remaining visible through centuries.

In the month of July three days are set apart for the celebration of the Festival of the Dead. At this time it is thought that the disembodied souls return from the dismal region of the Shades to gaze for a while upon the beauty of their country and to visit their people. On the first morning, new mats are placed upon all altars and on the household shrine, while in the homes, tiny meals are prepared in readiness for the ghostly guests. The streets at night are brilliant with many torches. In front of the houses gaily-colored lanterns are lit in welcome. Those who have recently lost a relative go to the cemeteries to pray, burn incense, and leave offerings of water and flowers set in bamboo vases.

On the third day, the souls of those who are undergoing penance are fed, as are the souls of those who have no friends among the living to care for them. The evening of this day is the time of the ghosts' departure, and for this thousands of little boats are fashioned and laden with food-offerings and tender messages of farewell. When the night falls, tiny lanterns are lit and hung at the miniature prows and the ghosts are supposed to step aboard. Then the craft are set free upon rivers, lakes, and seas, the water gleaming with the glow of thousands of lights. On this day no sailor dreams of putting out to sea—for this one night belongs to the dead. It was believed that if a ship failed to come to port before the sailing of the ghost-fleet the dead arose from the deep and the sailors could hear their mournful whispering, while the white breakers were dead hands clutching the shores, vainly trying to return.

For the Japanese, land and life is sacred, and in the Shinto pantheon, deities represent almost everything in heaven and earth, from the mountain of Fujiyama to the household kitchen. When infants were a week old they were taken to the temple and placed under the protection of some god chosen by the parents, but in later years the child might choose a patron god for him or herself beside the tutelary one.

In remote parts of Japan traces may be found of an older form of Shinto in which phallic symbols represented life-giving power and therefore were used as a magical exorcism of evil influences, especially that of disease. In this connection a dwarf-god appears who is said to have first taught humankind the art of magic and medicine.

In Shinto there are no idols, their place being taken by *shintia,* god-bodies, concrete objects in which the divine spirit is supposed to dwell, such as the mirror, jewel, and sword of the sun-goddess, worshipped at the famous Ise shrine. Pilgrims from all parts of Japan made their way to this shrine, acquiring merit and purification thereby. These pilgrims received from the priests objects of talismanic properties called *harai* that also served as evidence of having been at the holy place. In former days they were recognized as passports.

The term harai signifies to "drive out" or "sweep away," and had reference to the purification of the individual from his sins. These objects were in the form of small envelopes or paper boxes, each containing shavings of the wands used by the Ise priests at the festivals held twice a year to purify the nation in general from the consequences of the sins of the preceding six months. The list included **witchcraft,** wounding, and homicide, these latter being regarded more as uncleanness than as a moral stigma. On the pilgrim's return home, the harai were placed upon the "god's-shelf."

On certain festival days the ancient ordeals were practiced. These were three in number: the *Kugadachi,* in which priests, wrought to ecstatic frenzy by participation in a rhythmic dance, poured boiling water upon their bodies without receiving harm from the process; the *Hiwatari,* a **fire ordeal** consisting of walking barefoot over a bed of live coals in which both priests and people alike participated; and *Tsurugiwatari,* the climbing of a ladder of sword-blades. These were regarded as tests of purity of character, purity being thought to confer an immunity from hurt in these ordeals. The attendant rites consisted of exorcism of evil spirits by the waving of wands and magical finger-knots, and invocation of the gods who were then believed to be actually present.

Possession by Divinities

In connection with some of the Shinto sects, occult rites were practiced to bring about possession of a selected person by the actual spirits of the gods. Priests and laymen alike developed and practiced this art, undergoing a period of purification by means of various austerities. **Prophecy, divination,** and the cure of disease were the objects of these rites. The ceremony took place in a temple or ordinary house where the "gods' shelf" made the shrine. In the rites, the *gohei,* Shinto symbols of consecration, were used; the pendant form was utilized for purification and exorcism of evil influences; an upright *gohei* affixed to a wand signifying the shintai, or god-body, was the central object.

The medium, called *nakaza,* took his seat in the midst. Next to him in importance was the functionary, the *maeza,* who presided over the ceremony. It was he who built the magical pyre in a brass bowl and burned in the flames strips of paper inscribed with characters, effigies of disease and trouble. There was a clapping of hands to call attention to the gods, and chants were intoned, accompanied by the shaking of metal-ringed crosiers and the tinkle of pilgrim bells.

After the fire burned out, the bowl was removed and sheets of paper placed in symbolic form, upon which was then put the upright gohei wand. There was further chanting. The medium closed his eyes and clasped his hands, into which the maeza thrust the wand. All then awaited the advent of the god, which was indicated by the violent shaking of the wand and convulsive throes on the part of the medium, who was now considered to have become the god. The maeza reverently prostrated himself before the entranced nakaza, and asked the name of the god who had deigned to come. This done and answered, he next offered his petitions, to which the god replied. The ceremony concluded with a prayer and the medium was awakened by beating his back and massaging his limbs out of their cataleptic contraction. These **possession** rites were also conducted by the pilgrims who ascended the mountain of Ontaké.

Buddhist Sects

Buddhism shared with Shinto the devotions of Japan, enjoining **meditation** as a means of attaining supernatural knowledge and **occult** power. It was said that to those who in truth and constancy put into force the doctrines of Buddha the following ten powers would be granted. (1) They know the thoughts of others. (2) Their sight, piercing as that of the celestials, beholds without mist all that happens in the Earth. (3) They know the past and present. (4) They perceive the uninterrupted succession of the ages of the world. (5) Their hearing is so fine that they perceive and can interpret all the harmonies of the three worlds and the ten divisions of the universe. (6) They are not subject to bodily conditions and can assume any appearance at will. (7) They distinguish the shadowing of lucky or unlucky words, whether they are near or far away. (8) They possess the knowledge of all forms, and knowing that form is void, they can assume every sort or form; and knowing that vacancy is form, they can annihilate and render nought all forms. (9) They possess a knowledge of all laws. (10) They possess the perfect science of contemplation.

It was said that methods were thus known by which it was possible to so radically change the psychological condition of the individual that he or she would be enabled to recognize the character of the opposition between subjective and objective. These two extremes were reconciled in a higher condition of consciousness, a higher form of life, and a more profound and complete activity that concerns the inmost depths of the self. Such beliefs parallel Hindu **yoga** philosophy, and may have been imported into Japan from India by Buddhist influence during the twelfth and fourteenth centuries C.E. Early Buddhist influence in Japan from the sixth century on was from China.

Zen Buddhism in Japan belongs to the later period of the twelfth century. Zen monasteries were instituted, to which anyone so inclined could retire for temporary meditation and for the development of special faculties, which are mainly produced by entering a calm mental state, not exactly passive, but in which the attention is not devoted to any one thing, but evenly distributed in all directions, producing a sort of void and detachment. The spirit thus obtains entire repose and a satisfaction of the thirst for the ideal. This mystical retirement was sought by politicians and generals, by business, scientific, and professional people, and it is said that the force that accumulated within them by practicing the Zen was effective even in practical life.

Customs and Occult Lore

Many of the customs of the Japanese have a magical significance. At the Festival of the New Year, extending over three days, it is considered of the first importance to ensure good luck and happiness for the coming year by means of many traditional observances. Houses are thoroughly cleansed materially and spiritually, and evil spirits are expelled by throwing beans and peas out the open slides of the houses. The gateways are decorated with straw ropes made to represent the lucky Chinese numbers of three, five, and seven. Mirror cakes, associated with the sun-goddess, are eaten, as are lobsters, longevity being symbolized by their bent and ancient appearance. The pine-tree branches used for decoration at this time also signify long life.

Divination was performed by various methods: by **divining-rods,** by the reading of lines and cracks in the shoulder-blade of a deer, and by the classical form taken from the Confucian **I Ching** or *Book of Changes,* this involving the use of eight trigrams and sixty-four diagrams.

One method of "raising spirits" used by the Japanese, especially by girls who had lost their lovers by death, was to put into a paper lantern a hundred rushlights and repeat an incantation of a hundred lines. One of these rushlights was taken out at the end of each line and the would-be ghost-seer then went out in the dark with one light still burning and blew it out when the ghost ought to appear.

Charms used to be popular, fashioned of all substances and in all forms, such as strips of paper bearing magical inscriptions to avert evil, fragments of temples, carved rice grains representing the gods of luck, *sutras* (sacred texts) to frighten the demons, and copies of Buddha's footprint. Paper tickets bearing the name of a god were often affixed outside the doors of houses to combat the god of poverty.

Nature and her manifestations are the result of indwelling soul-life, and the Japanese mind, imbued with this belief, peopled nature with multiform shapes. There were dragons with lairs in ocean and river that could fly abroad in the air, while from their panting breath came clouds of rain and tempests of lightning. In the mountains and forests were bird-like gnomes who often beset wayfaring men and women and stole away their wits.

There were also mountain men, huge hairy monkeys, who helped the woodcutters in return for food, and mountain-women, ogres with bodies grown over with long white hair, who flitted like evil moths in search of human flesh.

Legend also told of the *Senrim,* hermits of the mountains, who knew all the secrets of magic. They were attended by wise toads and flying tortoises, could conjure magical animals out of gourds, and could project their souls into space.

Supernatural powers were also ascribed to animals. The fox was believed to possess such gifts to an almost limitless extent, for he had miraculous vision and hearing, could read the inmost thoughts of man, and could transform himself and assume any shape at will. He loved to delude mankind and work destruction, often taking the form of a beautiful and seductive woman whose embrace meant madness and death. To the agency of this animal was attributed demoniacal possession.

The cat was not regarded with any kindly feeling by the Japanese, because this animal and the serpent were the only creatures who did not weep at Buddha's death. Cats also had the power of bewitchment and possessed **vampire** proclivities. Among sailors, however, the cat was held in high estimation, for it was thought to possess the power of warding off the evil spirits that haunt the sea.

The images of animals were also thought to be endowed with life. There are tales of bronze horses and deer, huge carved dragons, and stone tortoises wandering abroad at night, terrorizing the people and only laid to rest by decapitation. Butterflies were thought to be the wandering souls of the living who might be dreaming or sunk in reverie; white butterflies were the souls of the dead. Fireflies kept evil spirits afar, and an ointment compounded of their delicate bodies defied any poison.

Trees occupied a foremost place in the tradition and legends of Japan. The people regarded them with great affection, and there are stories of men who, seeing a tree they loved withering and dying, committed suicide before it, praying to the gods that their life so given might pass into the tree and give it renewed vigor. The willow is one of the most eerie of trees; the willow-spirit often became a beautiful maiden and wedded a human lover. The pine tree brought good fortune, especially in the matter of happy marriage. It was also a token of longevity. Tree spirits could sometimes be inimical to man and it is recorded that to stay the disturbing wanderings of one it was necessary to cut it down, at which time a stream of blood flowed from the stump.

The element of fire figured large in the Japanese world of marvels. It was worshiped in connection with the rites of the sun-goddess and even the kitchen furnace became the object of a sort of cult. There is the lamp of Buddha. Messages from Hades came to this world in the shape of fire wheels, phantom fires flickered about, flames burnt in the cemeteries, and there were demon-lights, fox-flames, and dragon-torches. From the eyes and mouths of certain birds such as the blue heron, fire darted forth in white flames. Globes of fire, enshrining human faces and forms, sometimes hung like fruit in the branches of the trees.

The dolls of Japanese children were believed to be endowed with life, deriving a soul from the love expended upon them by their human possessors. Some of these dolls were credited with supernatural powers. They could confer maternity upon a childless woman, and they could bring misfortune upon any who ill-treated them. When old and faded these dolls were dedicated to Kojin the many-armed who dwelt in the *enokie* tree, and they were reverently laid upon his shrine, bodies which once held a tiny soul.

New Religions in Japan

The ancient beliefs and superstitions confronted the tremendous pressures changing Japan in the decades following World War II, and although Shinto and Buddhist religions still predominate, an astonishing number of new religions, most variations of the older religions, have arisen. Many combine original Shinto and/or Buddhist beliefs with elements of Christianity. The defeat of Japan in the war was a crushing blow to national morale and weakened belief in traditional religion, especially Shintoism. Again, the post-war arrival of high technology and the intensification of industrialization created further receptivity to new directions in religious life. Many saw a need for updating and streamlining religious belief and practice. In modern times, hundreds of new religions have been registered officially, two-thirds of them developments of Shinto or Buddhism, with a combined following in the millions.

Among these sects is a group known as Omoto (Teaching of the Great Origin), which originally began in 1892 as a Messianic sect, founded by a farmer woman named Deguchi Nao. The sect was developed by Deguchi Onisaburo and featured the healing of diseases by mystical power. By 1934, it had some 2.5 million followers. Then in 1935, the Japanese government turned on the group and imprisoned the founders and leading followers; their headquarters were dynamited and for all practical purposes the group was destroyed. Not until after World War II was Omoto revived, now under the name of Aizen-en (Garden of Divine Love). Onisaburo died in 1948, but the movement continued to flourish and also gave rise to various splinter sects.

Among unrelated new religions is Tensho Kotai Jingu Kyo, more generally known as Odoru Shukyo (The Dancing Religion), founded by Kitamura Sayo, a farmer's wife regarded by followers as divinely inspired. She is addressed as "Goddess" and her son as "Young God." She is believed to have prophetic insight and power to heal diseases.

Psychical Research & Parapsychology

Although little has been published in Western countries about Japan in relation to paranormal phenomena, Japanese interest in the subject goes back to the last century. As already mentioned, shamanistic techniques and mediumistic faculty were characteristic of some Japanese religions, and from the middle of the nineteenth century on, such phenomena began to be studied objectively. One early investigator was Atsutane Hirat (1776–1843) who was a pioneer in drawing attention to reported cases of **reincarnation** and **poltergeists.**

Chikaatsu Honda (1823–1889) studied the techniques of *Chinkon,* a method of meditation involving revelation through divine possession, becoming mediumistic himself. His techniques were later developed by Deguchi Onisaburo (1871–1948), the leading figure of Omoto. The *Chinkon Kishin* technique involved spirit communication, and Wasaburo Asano, then a member of Omoto, perceived that this had much in common with European **Spiritualism.** He subsequently became independent of Omoto and promoted the study of Spiritualism.

A pioneer of psychical research was Enryo Inoue (1858–1919) who founded Fushigi Kenkyukai (the Society for Anomalous Phenomena) at the University of Tokyo in 1888. Another early investigator was Toranosuke Oguma of Meiji University, who studied abnormal **psychology,** hypnosis, and **dreams,** and who began to make Western psychical research known in Japan. Oguma published several books on psychical science.

Another pioneer was **Tomobichi Fukurai** (1869–1952) of the University of Tokyo, whose experiments on **clairvoyance** and **psychic photography** (which he called "thoughtography") commenced in 1910. An English translation of his book *Clairvoyance and Thoughtography* (1913) was published in 1921. His experiments in thoughtography were a remarkable anticipation of the phenomena of Ted Serios in modern times, investigated by **Jule Eisenbud.** Unfortunately Fukurai's experiments caused dissension at Tokyo University, and he was obliged to resign. He went to the Buddhist University of Kohyassan where he became president of The Psychical Institute of Japan. He also published a second book, *Spirit and Mysterious World* (1932), in which he attempted to reconcile psychical phenomena with Buddhism.

In 1923, the Japanese Society for Psychic Science was founded at Tokyo, under the presidency of W. Asano. Progress in psychical research was slow, however. After the war, **J. B. Rhine**'s book *The Reach of the Mind* (1947) was translated into Japanese and stimulated investigation of **ESP.** Meanwhile Fukurai, who had removed to Sendai in Honshu, organized a research group of psychologists and engineers for the study of **parapsychology.** The Fukurai

Institute of Psychology was founded after his death in 1952. Another organization formed during this period was the Institute for Religious Psychology, founded by Hiroshi Motoyama.

After a visit to Japan by **J. G. Pratt** of Duke University Parapsychology Laboratory in 1963, a Japanese Society for Parapsychology was founded through the initiative of Soji Otani, who visited Duke University and studied the techniques of the researchers there. In 1967, the society held a conference of parapsychologists in Tokyo, when Oguma lectured on the history of parapsychology in Japan. Parapsychology has since become a recognized area for research at various Japanese universities.

The showing of a program featuring psychic **Uri Geller** on Japanese television stimulated interest in the phenomena of **psychokinesis.** In 1977, experiments were reported with a 17-year-old boy, **Masuaki Kiyota,** who claimed unusual faculties in **metal bending** and in thoughtography (now investigated as "nengraphy"). Some of these experiments were filmed and shown on American television in 1977. Kiyota has since confessed that he produced the results by fraud.

Addresses for Japanese organizations concerned with parapsychological investigations are as follows:

International Association for Religion & Parapsychology, 4–11-7 Inokashira, Mitaka, Tokyo 181

Japan Nengraphy Association, Awiji-cho 2-25, Kannda, Chioda, Tokyo

Japan Association for Psychotronic Research, c/o 284-6 Anagawa-cho. Chiba-shi

Japan Society for Parapsychology, 26–14 Chuo 4-chrome, Nakano, Tokyo 164

Psi Science Institute of Japan, Shibuya Business Hotel 6F, 12-5 Shibuya 1-chrome, Shinjuki-ku, Tokyo 150

Sources:

Anesaki, Masaharu. *History of Japanese Religion.* London: Kegan Paul, 1930.

Davis, F. Hadland. *Myths and Legends of Japan.* London: Harrap, 1912.

Deguchi, Onisaburo. *Memoirs.* Japan: Kameoka, 1957.

Fukurai, Tomokichi. *Clairvoyance and Thoughtography.* London: Rider, 1931. Reprint, New York: Arno Press, 1975.

Hearn, Lafcadio. *Kokoro: Hints & Echoes of Japanese Inner Life.* Boston, Mass.: Houghton Mifflin, 1906.

Lowell, Percival. *Occult Japan.* Boston: Houghton Mifflin, 1895.

Offner, C. B., and H. van Straelen. *Modern Japanese Religions.* Leyden, Netherlands: E. J. Brill, 1963.

Thomsen, Harry. *The New Religions of Japan.* Rutland, Vt.: Charles E. Tuttle, 1963.

Uphoff, Walter, and Mary Jo Uphoff. *Mind Over Matter: Implications of Masuaki Kiyota's PK Feats with Metal and Film.* Oregon: New Frontiers Center; London: Colin Smythe, 1980.

Jaquin, Noel (1894–1974)

One of the best-known British experts in **palmistry,** who attempted to establish a scientific rationale for the study of what has so often been regarded as superstition. He was able to diagnose disease from markings on the hand and also worked with police authorities in studying palmistry indications of criminals.

Sources:

Jaquin, Noel. *The Hand and Disease.* N.p., 1926.

———. *The Hand of Man.* London: Faber & Faber Ltd., 1933.

———. *Hand-reading Made Easy.* N.p., 1928.

———. *The Human Hand.* London: Rockliff, 1956.

———. *It's in Your Hands: The Secrets of the Human Hand.* New York: R. M. McBride & Co., 1941.

———. *Man's Revealing Hand.* N.p., 1934.

———. *Scientific Palmistry.* London: C. Palmer, 1925.

———. *The Signature of Time.* London: Faber & Faber Ltd., 1940.

———. *The Theory of Metaphysical Influence: A Study of Human Attunements, Perception, Intelligence and Motivation.* N.p., 1958.

Jarman, Archibald Seymour (1909–)

Writer on parapsychological subjects. Jarman was born on June 23, 1909, at Richmond, Surrey, England. He worked as an estate administrator and was associate editor of *Tomorrow* magazine for many years, beginning in 1962. He also wrote articles for British journals dealing with parapsychology, including the *Journal* of the **Society for Psychical Research.** His article "High Jinks on a Low Level" (originally from *Tomorrow*), published in *Spiritualism: A Critical Survey,* by Simeon Edmunds (1966), is an amusing description of three séances attended by the writer and illustrates the crude methods of **fraud** carried out by bogus mediums.

Sources:

Jarman, Archie. "High Jinks on a Low Level." *Tomorrow* 2, no. 2. Reprinted in *Spiritualism: A Critical Survey,* by Simeon Edmunds. London: Aquarian Press, 1966.

———. "Physical Phenomena: Fraud or Frontier?" *Tomorrow* (autumn 1960).

———. "Unsolved Animal Mysteries." *Tomorrow* (spring 1960).

Pleasants, Helene, ed. *Biographical Dictionary of Parapsychology.* New York: Helix Press, 1964.

Jarricot, Jean (1877–1962)

French homeopathic physician and experimenter in the field of **radiesthesia.** Born July 14, 1877, at Saint Genis Laval, Rhône, France, he studied at Lyon University. Jarricot was laboratory director at the medical school of Lyon University and was on the staff for medical research in pharmodynamics at St. Rambert I'lle Barbe, Rhône.

He was honorary president of the Rhône Homeopathy Society; an honorary member of Barcelona Medico-Homeopathic Society; an associate member of the Hahnemanian Institute of Brazil; and a laureate of the Académie Française (1960). His article "A quel cadre de reférences rattacher les faits de parapsychologie?" (In what terms of reference should we consider parapsychology?) was published in *La Tour Saint Jacques* (May 1958). He died November 13, 1962.

Sources:

Jarricot, Jean. *Pendule et Médecine* (Pendulum and Medicine). Paris: G. Doin, 1949.

———. *Radiesthesie* (Radiesthesia). N.p., 1958.

Pleasants, Helene, ed. *Biographical Dictionary of Parapsychology.* New York: Helix Press, 1964.

Jasper

A variety of quartz to which many medicinal values were attributed in ancient times. It was believed to prevent fever and dropsy, strengthen the brain, and promote eloquence. It was said to prevent defluxions (discharge of catarrhal mucous), nightmares, and epilepsy and was often used in the East as a countercharm. Bishop Marbodeus mentioned 17 species of this stone but noted that, like the emerald, it was mainly sought for its magic properties. As late as 1609 it was still believed that jasper worn about the neck would strengthen the stomach.

Jastrow, Joseph (1863–1944)

Psychologist, educator, and author who was critical of psychoanalysis and psychical research. In 1910 he revealed trickery by the famous medium **Eusapia Palladino** during investigations of her phenomena by a committee of American stage magicians. Jastrow was born on January 30, 1863, in Warsaw, Poland, the son of Marcus Jastrow (1829–1903), a noted rabbi and Hebrew scholar. The family immigrated to the United States when Joseph was still a child. He was educated at Rugby Academy, the University of Pennsylvania, and John Hopkins University.

From 1888 to 1927 he taught psychology at the University of Wisconsin and then moved to the New School for Social Research, where he taught until his retirement (1927–33). He wrote a number of books on psychology and played a large part in popularizing the subject with the general public, editing the syndicated newspaper column "Keeping Mentally Fit" (1928–32) and giving regular radio broadcasts (1935–38).

Although Jastrow closely followed the work of psychical researchers, he was intensely skeptical of the possibility of establishing significant evidence for the existence of psychic phenomena, especially any that implied there was life after death. In 1926 he took part in a public symposium on the subject at Clark University, Worcester, Massachusetts, at which **Sir Oliver Lodge, Sir Arthur Conan Doyle, F. Bligh Bond,** and L. R. G. Crandon spoke as individuals "convinced of the multiplicity of psychical phenomena." **William McDougall, Hans Driesch, Walter F. Prince,** and **F. C. S. Schiller** said they were "convinced of the rarity of genuine psychical phenomena." **John E. Coover** and **Gardner Murphy** claimed to be "unconvinced as yet." Jastrow and magician **Harry Houdini** spoke as individuals "antagonistic to the claims that such phenomena occur." The papers were published in *The Case For and Against Psychical Belief* (1927), edited by Carl Murchison.

Jastrow died at Stockbridge, Massachusetts, on January 8, 1944.

Sources:

Berger, Arthur S., and Joyce Berger. *The Encyclopedia of Parapsychology and Psychical Research.* New York: Paragon House, 1991.

Jastrow, Joseph. *Error and Eccentricity in Human Belief.* New York: Dover Publications, 1962.

———. *Fact and Fable in Psychology.* Boston; New York: Houghton, Mifflin & Co., 1900.

———. *Freud, His Dream and Sex Theories.* Cleveland, Ohio; New York: The World Publishing Co., 1943.

———. *The House That Freud Built.* New York: Greenberg, 1932.

———. *The Psychology of Conviction.* Boston; New York: Houghton, Mifflin & Co., 1918.

———. *Time Relations of Mental Phenomena.* N.p., 1890.

———. *Wish and Wisdom.* New York; London: D. Appleton-Century Co. Inc., 1935.

———, ed. *The Story of Error.* N.p., 1936.

Murchison, Carl, ed. *The Case For and Against Psychical Belief.* Worcester, Mass., 1927.

Jayne, Charles (1911–1985)

Leading American astrologer, born in Jenkintown, Pennsylvania, on October 9, 1911. Jayne became interested in **astrology** as a young man and studied the subject throughout the 1930s. He published his first article in 1940 but did not become a professional astrologer until after World War II, in 1949.

Jayne is remembered as an innovative theoretician of astrology, much of his focus on a technical nature concerning the fine points of astrological interpretation. One of his more impressive studies concerned the long-term zodiacal cycles of the outermost planets, which take many years to pass around the zodiac. He found interesting correlations to cycles of history noted by historians such as Arnold Toynbee and Oswald Spengler (their theoretical work was never accepted by most historians). In recognition of his work he was given the Johndro Award in 1979 for contributions to the technical aspects of astrology.

Jayne also made contributions to astrological organizations. He was president of the **Astrologers' Guild of America** (1958–60), a professional organization. In 1958 he founded Astrological Research Associates and with his wife, Vivia Jayne, edited *In Search* (1958–62), an international astrological journal. In 1970 he founded the Association for Research in Cosmicology, an organization specializing in the reintegration of astrology into mainline science. He was also one of the founders of the **National Council for Geocosmic Research.**

Jayne died December 31, 1985, at Goshen, New York.

Sources:

Brau, Jean-Louis, Helen Weaver, and Allan Edwards, eds. *Larousse Encyclopedia of Astrology.* New York: New American Library, 1982.

Holden, James H., and Robert A. Hughes. *Astrological Pioneers of America.* Tempe, Ariz.: American Federation of Astrologers, 1988.

Jayne, Charles. *A New Dimension in Astrology.* New York: Astrological Bureau, 1975.

———. *The Technique of Rectification.* New York: Astrological Bureau, 1972.

———. *The Unknown Planets.* New York: Astrological Bureau, 1974.

Jean

According to Lewis Spence (in the *Encyclopedia of Occultism*, 1920), Jean was a French magician, votary of **Apollonius of Tyana.** He traveled from town to town, wearing an iron collar and making his living by performing deeds of charlatanry. At Lyons he attained some measure of fame by his miraculous cures and met with the sovereign, to whom he presented a magnificent enchanted sword. In battle this weapon became surrounded by ninescore drawn knives. Jean also gave this prince a shield containing a magic mirror that divulged the greatest secrets. The arms vanished or were stolen.

(Unfortunately, Spence did not state the period or the ruler involved, but this is probably a medieval legend.)

Jean d'Arras (ca. 1387)

A French writer of the fourteenth century who compiled for his patron John, duke of Berry, the *Chronique de la princesse* in 1387 from popular stories about the fairy Mélusine. Mélusine was doomed to change into the form of a serpent every Saturday unless she found a husband who would never see her on Saturdays. She married Raymond of Poitiers of the house of Lusignan. He was rich and powerful, and Mélusine was instrumental in the building of the castle of Lusignan and other family fortresses. One Saturday her husband was overcome by curiosity and spied on her, whereupon she cried out and flew away in serpent form. Thenceforth, the cry of Mélusine was said to herald death in the family of Lusignan. (See also **Banshee**)

Jean de Meung (or Mehun) (ca. 1250–ca. 1305)

French poet who owes his celebrity to his continuation of the *Roman de la Rose* of Guillaume de Saint-Amour. De Meung also wrote a rhyming treatise on **alchemy.** He was born Jean Clopinel (or Chopinel) at Meun-sur-Loire and flourished through the reigns of Louis X, Philip the Long, Charles IV, and Philip de Valois. He appears to have possessed a light and railing wit and a keen appreciation of a jest, and it may well be doubted whether he was altogether sincere in his praises of alchemy.

The poet composed a strongly stigmatic quatrain on womankind and the ladies of Charles IV's court resolved to revenge their affronted honor. Surrounding him in the royal antechamber, they ordered the courtiers present to strip de Meung before they gave him a sound flogging. Jean begged to be heard before he was condemned and punished. Having obtained an interval of grace, the poet admitted—with fluent eloquence—that he was certainly the author of the calumnious verses, but that they were not intended to disparage all women. He referred only to the vicious and debased, he insisted, and not to such models of purity as he saw around him. Nevertheless, if any lady present felt that the verses really applied to her, he would submit to a well-deserved chastisement! None, of course, accepted.

Like most of the medieval poets, Jean de Meung was a bitter enemy of the priesthood, and he contrived with great ingenuity a posthumous satire upon their inordinate greed. He bequeathed in his will, as a gift to the Cordeliers (friars), a chest of immense weight. Since his fame as an alchemist was widespread, the brotherhood accepted the legacy in the belief that the chest contained the golden results of his quest for the **philosophers' stone.** But when they opened it, their dismayed eyes rested only on a pile of slates covered with the most unintelligible hieroglyphics and kabalistic characters. The perpetrator of this practical joke was hardly, it seems, a sincere believer in the wonders of alchemy.

Jean de Meung's book on alchemy was published as *Le Miroir d'alchymie* (1557) and in German as *Der Spiegel der Alchymie* (1771), but some critics believe it is spurious. Also doubtfully attributed to de Meung are the poetical treatises *Les Remonstrances de Nature à l'Alchimiste errant* and *La Reponse de l'Alchimiste à Nature.*

Jeanne D'Arc, St. (St. Joan of Arc) (1412–1431)

Joan was born Jeanette, with the surname Arc or Romée, in the village of Domrémy, on the border of Champagne and Lorraine, on January 15, 1412. In documents of her time she is known as Jeanne.

She was taught to spin and sew but not to read or write, these accomplishments being unnecessary to people in her station of life. Her parents were devout, and she was brought up piously. Her nature was gentle, modest, and religious, but with no physical weakness or morbidity. On the contrary, she was exceptionally strong, as her later history shows.

At or about age 13 she began to experience what modern psychology calls "auditory hallucinations." In other words, she heard voices (usually accompanied by a bright light) when no visible person was present. This is a symptom that occasionally presages a mental disorder, but no insanity developed in Jeanne d'Arc. She was startled at first, but continuation of the experience led to familiarity and trust. The voices gave good counsel of a commonplace nature, for example, that she "must be a good girl and go often to church."

Soon, however, she began to have visions. She saw St. Michael, St. Catharine, and St. Margaret and was given instructions as to her mission. She eventually made her way to the dauphin, put herself at the head of 6,000 men, and advanced to the relief of Orleans, which was surrounded by the victorious English. After a fortnight of hard fighting the siege was raised and the enemy driven off. The tide of war turned, and in three months the dauphin was crowned king at Rheims as Charles VII.

At this point Jeanne felt that her mission was accomplished, but her wish to return to her family was overruled by the king and the archbishop. She took part in further fighting against the allied English and Burgundian forces, showing great bravery and tactical skill. In November 1430, however, in a desperate sally from Compiégne (which was besieged by the duke of Burgundy), she fell into the enemy's hands and was sold to the English and thrown into a dungeon at their headquarters in Rouen.

After a year's imprisonment she was brought to trial before the bishop of Beauvais in an ecclesiastical court. The charges were heresy and sorcery. Learned doctors of the Church and subtle lawyers did their best to entangle the simple girl in their dialectical webs, but she showed remarkable power in keeping to her affirmations and avoiding heretical statements. "God has always been my Lord in all that I have done," she repeated.

But the trial was only a sham, for her fate was already decided. She was condemned to the stake. To the end she solemnly affirmed the reality of her "voices" and the truth of her depositions. Her last word, as the smoke and flame rolled round her, was "Jesus." Said an English soldier, awestruck by the manner of her passing, "We are lost; we have burned a saint." The idea was corroborated in popular opinion by events that followed, for speedy death (as if by Heaven's anger) overtook her judges and accusers. Inspired by her example and claims, and helped by dissension and weakening on the side of the enemy, the French took heart once more and the English were all but swept out of the country.

Jeanne's family was rewarded by ennoblement, under the name De Lys. Twenty-five years after her death, the pope acceded to a petition that the trial by which Jeanne was condemned should be reexamined. The judgment was reversed and her innocence was established and proclaimed.

The life of the Maid of Orleans presents a problem that orthodox science cannot solve. She was a simple peasant girl with no ambitions. She rebelled pathetically against her mission, saying, "I had far rather rest and spin by my mother's side, for this is no work of my choosing, but I must go and do it, for my Lord wills it." She cannot be dismissed on the "simple idiot" theory of Voltaire, for her genius in war and her aptitude in repartee undoubtedly prove exceptional mental powers, unschooled though she was. She cannot be dismissed as a mere hysteric, for her health and strength were superb.

It is on record that a man of science said to an abbot, "Come to the Salpêtrière Hospital [the refuge for elderly, poor, and insane patients in Paris] and I will show you twenty Jeannes d'Arc." To which the abbot responded, "Has one of them given us back Alsace and Lorraine?"

Although Jeanne delivered France and her importance in history is great, it is arguable that her mission and her actions were the outcome of merely subjective hallucinations induced by the brooding of her religious and patriotic mind on the woes of her country. The army, being ignorant and superstitious, would have readily believed in the supernatural nature of her mission, resulting in great energy and valor—soldiers fight well when they feel that Providence is on their side. So goes the most common theory in explaining the facts surrounding the life of St. Joan. But it is not fully satisfactory.

How was it possible that this simple, untutored peasant girl could persuade not only the soldiers, but also the dauphin of France and the court of her divine appointment? How did she come to be given the command of an army? It seems improbable that a post of such responsibility and power would be given to an ignorant girl of 18 on the mere strength of her own claim to inspiration.

Although the materialistic school of historians conveniently ignores or belittles it, there is strong evidence to support the idea that Jeanne gave the dauphin some proof of her possession of supernormal faculties. In fact, the evidence is so strong that Andrew Lang, not known for unsupported statements, called it "unimpeachable." Among other curious things, Jeanne seems to have repeated to Charles the words of a prayer that he had said *mentally,* and she also made some kind of clairvoyant discovery of a sword hidden behind the altar of the Fierbois church. Johann Schiller's magnificent dramatic poem "Die Jungfrau von Orleans" (1801), although not historically correct in some details, is positive on these points concerning clairvoyance and mind-reading.

There is also evidence that Jeanne was connected with **fairies,** which were also part of **witchcraft** beliefs. Not far from Domrémy was a tree called "the Fairies' Tree" beside a spring said to cure fevers. The wife of the local mayor stated that it had been said that "Jeanne received her mission at the tree of the fairy-ladies" and that St. Katharine and St. Margaret came and spoke to her at the spring beside the fairies' tree. During Jeanne's trial the fourth article of accusation was that Jeanne was not instructed in her youth in the primitive faith, but was imbued by certain old women in the use of witchcraft, divination, and other superstitious works or magic arts. Jeanne herself, according the accusation, had said she heard from her godmother and other people about visions and apparitions of fairies.

Moreover, Pierronne, a follower of Jeanne d'Arc, was burned at the stake as a witch. She stated on oath that God appeared to her in human form and spoke to her as a friend, and that he was clothed in a scarlet cap and a long white robe.

It has been suggested that the voices heard by Jeanne may have been those of human beings rather than Christian saints, and Jeanne herself stated, "Those of my party know well that the Voice had been sent to me from God, they have seen and known this Voice. My king and many others have also heard and seen the Voices which came to me. . . . I saw him [St. Michael] with my bodily eyes as well as I see you." Jeanne's references to "the King of Heaven" in the original Latin and French were translated with a Christian bias as "Our Lord," and "my Lord" was translated as "Our Saviour." The scholar Margaret A. Murray in her book *The Witch-Cult in Western Europe* (1921) also suggests that if Jeanne was a member of a Dianic [witch] cult, the wearing of male clothing may have been for Jeanne an outward sign of that faith, hence the importance attached to it.

In another book, *The God of the Witches* (1931), Murray examines the tradition that Jeanne was not actually burned at the stake but survived for a number of years afterward. The *Chronique de Metz* states, "Then she was sent to the city of Rouen in Normandy, and there was placed on a scaffold and burned in a fire, so it was said, but since then was found to be the contrary." Some of the evidence for this view had been cited earlier by Andrew Lang in his essay "The False Jeanne d'Arc" in his book *The Valet's Tragedy and Other Studies* (1903).

The period between the trial at Rouen and the Trial of Rehabilitation (1452–56) is crucial. In 1436, five years after the Rouen trial, the herald-at-arms and Jeanne's brother Jean du Lys announced officially in Orleans that Jeanne was still alive. The city accounts record that on Sunday, August 6, Jean du Lys, brother of "Jehane la Pucelle" [Jeanne the Maid] was in Orleans with letters from his sister to the king. In July 1439 Jeanne's brothers were in Orleans with their sister, now married to the sieur des Armoises (or Harmoises), and the city council presented Jeanne des Armoises with 210 pounds "for the good that she did to the said town during the siege of 1429." Accounts are also recorded of the wine merchant and draper who supplied Jeanne with wine and clothing. Her own mother was in Orleans at the time. Moreover, the masses that had been celebrated in Orleans for the repose of Jeanne's soul were discontinued after her mother's visit.

It is not conclusive that this Jeanne was an impostor (as Andrew Lang believed), and it seems unlikely that many people in Orleans, including Jeanne's own brothers, could have been deceived. The riddle of conflicting evidence of burning at the stake or substantiated appearances years later has never been satisfactorily resolved. Many such questions remain unresolved, in spite of various books, mainly by French writers, dealing with the issue.

Early French books on the subject include *La Survivance et le Mariage de Jeanne D'Arc*, by Grillot de Givry and *La Legende Detruite: Indications pour essayer de suivre l'histoire de Jeanne d'Arc*, by Paraf-Javal (1929). More recently another French writer, Pierre de Sermoise, published *Jeanne d'Arc et la Mandragore* (1983), which has revived the claim that the veiled woman burned at the stake in the marketplace was a prisoner condemned to death as a witch, substituting for France's national heroine.

More speculative is the conclusion of American biologist Robert Greenblatt (reported in 1983) that Jeanne was really a man. It was also claimed that two midwives who had examined Jeanne to establish her virginity were astonished to find that she had not reached puberty.

Sources:

Barstow, Anne Llewellyn. *Joan of Arc: Heretic, Mystic, Shaman.* Lewiston, N.Y.: Edwin Mellen Press, 1986.

Marglis, Nadia. *Joan of Arc in History, Literature, and Film: A Select Bibliography.* New York: Garland Publishing, 1990.

Jehovah's Witnesses

A popular millenarian Christian religious group that grew out of the ministry of Pastor Charles Taze Russell in the late nineteenth century. It is also known by reference to its corporate entity, the Watchtower Bible and Tract Society. Its members have become a common sight in many countries as they go from door to door preaching their message and distributing their literature, especially the *Watchtower* magazine. Originally known as Bible Students, the group adopted the name Jehovah's Witnesses in 1931.

The Witnesses have, like many Christian churches, shown a marked aversion to **Spiritualism** and other occult phenomena. Very early in the group's history Russell attacked Spiritualism (which he called Spiritism), and periodically over the years the organization has published booklets and numerous articles warning members to eschew any association with the occult. The Witnesses' primary biblical doctrinal handbook, *Make Sure of All Things, Hold Fast to What Is Fine* (1965), includes an assemblage of texts believed to refute Spiritualism as well as a separate set dealing with **reincarnation.**

Sources:

Bergman, Jerry. *Can the Living Talk with the Dead? A Clear Explanation of Spiritism.* Brooklyn, N.Y.: International Bible Students, 1920.

———. *Jehovah's Witnesses and Kindred Groups: A Historical Compendium and Bibliography.* New York: Garland Publishing, 1984.

Russell, Charles Taze. *Unseen Spirits—Do They Help Us? or, Do They Harm Us?* Brooklyn, N.Y.: Watchtower Bible and Tract Society, 1978.

———. *What Do the Scriptures Say about "Survival of Death?"* Brooklyn, N.Y.: Watchtower Bible and Tract Society, 1955.

———. *What Say the Scriptures about Spiritism?* Brooklyn, N.Y.: Watchtower Bible and Tract Society, 1897.

Jensen, Wiers (1866–1925)

Norwegian dramatist who was active in the field of psychical research. Jensen was born on November 25, 1866, at Bergen, Norway, and was educated at the University of Oslo. In addition to his work as a playwright and an instructor at theaters in Bergen and Oslo, he edited the journal *Norsk Tidsskrift for Psykisk Forksning,* dealing with psychical research, from 1922 to 1925. His play *Anne Pedersdotter* is about a mediumistic woman believed to be a witch.

Jensen made a special study of the phenomenon of the psychic **double** as known in Norway and Scotland. His experiences and those of other individuals were chronicled by **Thorstein Wereide** in an article in *Tomorrow* in 1955. He died August 25, 1925. After Jensen's death, communications believed to be from him were received through the automatic writing of the medium **Ingeborg Dahl.**

Sources:

Pleasants, Helene, ed. *Biographical Dictionary of Parapsychology.* New York: Helix Press, 1964.

Wereide, Thorstein. "Norway's Human Doubles." *Tomorrow* 3, no. 2 (winter 1955).

Jephson, Ina (d. 1961)

British artist and expert in child guidance. She joined the **Society for Psychical Research** (SPR), London, in 1920 and served on the council from 1928 on. Jephson was born in London and studied art at the Slade School. She also studied psychology under Leonard Seif in Munich, Germany, and later worked with children at the Individual Psychology Clinic of Doris Rayner. During World War II she worked with disturbed children at Oxford. Jephson devoted special attention to research designed to set up repeatable experiments dealing with clairvoyance, which became the main subject of a set of articles she wrote for the *Proceedings* of the SPR.

Sources:

Jephson, Ina. "A Behaviourist Experiment in Clairvoyance." *Proceedings* of the Society for Psychical Research 128, no. 41 (January 1933).

———. "Evidence for Clairvoyance in Card-Guessing." *Proceedings* of the Society for Psychical Research 109, no. 38 (December 1928).

Jephson, Ina, S. G. Soal, and Theodore Besterman. "Report on a Series of Experiments in Clairvoyance." *Proceedings* of the Society for Psychical Research 118, no. 39 (April 1931).

Jersey Devil

Strange creature on the borderline between fact and legend, reported in southern New Jersey for more than two centuries. The Jersey devil is said to have a kangaroo body, bat's wings, pig's feet, dog's head, the face of a horse, and a forked tail. Depending on the storyteller the creature is said to be anywhere from 18 inches to 20 feet in height and is considered impervious to gunshot. It appears to have been born, at least as a legend, after the off-the-cuff remark of a woman unhappy over her pregnancy. Her curse on her child resulted in her child being devil-like. The Jersey devil appeared over the years, possibly as a running joke by bored newspaper reporters.

However, it might have remained unknown were it not for the accounts of its having terrorized inhabitants of the Delaware Valley in 1909, when people stayed home even in daylight and factories and theaters closed. When all the reports were assembled, though, descriptions of the creature varied widely. At least one person later confessed to participating in the 1909 events by creating footprints of the supposed devil. In another famous scare in 1951 the Jersey devil was said to have attacked and mutilated poultry, cats, and dogs. Some have written the Jersey devil off as a mere hoax. Others have seen it as a folk legend lost in endless variations.

Sources:

Bord, Janet, and Collin Bord. *Alien Animals.* Harrisburg, Pa.: Stackpole Books, 1981.

Clark, Jerome. *Encyclopedia of Strange and Unexplained Phenomena.* Detroit: Gale Research, 1993.

McCloy, J. F., and Ray Miller, Jr. *The Jersey Devil.* Newark, Del.: Middle Atlantic Press, 1976.

Stein, Gordon. *Encyclopedia of Hoaxes.* Detroit: Gale Research, 1993.

Jesodoth

According to Jewish mysticism, the angel through which Elohim, the source of knowledge, understanding, and wisdom, was imparted to the Earth. (See also **Kabala**)

Jesus, Master

One of the masters originally contacted by **Helena Petrovna Blavatsky,** cofounder of the **Theosophical Society.** According to theosophical teachings there exists a spiritual hierarchy composed of individuals who have finished their round of earthly reincarnations and have evolved to the spiritual planes, from which they guide the affairs of humanity. Those members of the hierarchy closest to humanity are the "lords of the seven rays" (of the light spectrum). Each ray represents a particular virtue, which the lord of that ray exemplifies.

The identity of Master Jesus is somewhat complicated in Theosophical history. According to the Theosophical Society, Master Jesus was not the same person as Jesus Christ. Rather, he took embodiment as Apollonius of Tyana.

Master Jesus is the lord of the sixth ray of purity and fiery devotion. As such he is the master of devotees, saints, and mystics of every religious tradition. He is the guardian of the Christian Church, founded by Maitreya (commonly known as Jesus Christ). He was also incarnated as the Indian teacher Ramanujacharya, who lived in the twelfth century. He currently inhabits the body of a Syrian and lives in Lebanon among the Druse people. Over the centuries his mission has been to found "magnetic centers."

Through the twentieth century, most theosophical movements have continued the original teachings tying Master Jesus to Appolonius rather than Jesus Christ, but others have quietly adopted an identification of the master with the ascended Jesus Christ. Most prominently, that identification has been made in the **I Am Movement** and in groups that have roots in the I Am Movement, such as the **Church Universal and Triumphant.**

Sources:

Ransom, Josephine. *A Short History of the Theosophical Society.* Adyar, Madras, India: Theosophical Publishing House, 1938.

Jet

A velvet-black coal that is a variety of lignite. Its occult virtues are thus described by Pliny (*Historia naturalis,* translated by Philemon Holland, 1601):

"In burning, the perfume thereof chaseth away serpents, and bringeth women again that lie in a trance by the suffocation or rising of the mother; the said smoke discovereth the falling sickness and bewraieth whether a young damsel be a maiden or no; the same being boiled in wine helpeth the toothache, and tempered with wax cureth the swelling glandules named the king's evil. They say that the magicians use this jeat stone much in their sorceries, which they practice by the means of red hot axes, which they call axinomancia, for they affirm that being cast thereupon it will burne and consume, if that ewe desire and wish shall happen accordingly."

Jet was known in Prussia as black amber. (See also **Electrum; Gagates**)

Jettatura

The Italian name for the power of the **evil eye.** To guard against it magicians said that horns must be worn on the body or the phallic gesture of horns must be made with the fingers.

Jinn

Arabian spirits, perhaps animistic, but more probably strictly mythological like the Persian **divs.** The jinn were said to have been created out of fire and to have occupied the Earth for several thousand years before Adam. They were perverse and would not reform, although prophets were sent to reclaim them; they were eventually driven from the Earth and took refuge in the outlying islands of the sea.

One of the number named Azazeel (afterward called Iblees) was carried off as a prisoner by **angels.** He grew up among them and became their chief, but when he refused to prostrate himself before Adam he was degraded to the condition of a *sheytân* (devil), and became the father of the sheytâns.

The jinn are not immortal and, according to legend, are destined ultimately to die. They eat and drink and propagate their species, live in communities, and are ruled over by princes. They can make themselves visible or invisible, and they assume the forms of various animals, such as serpents, cats, and dogs. There are good jinn and bad jinn. They are said to frequent baths, wells, latrines, ovens, ruined houses, rivers, crossroads, and marketplaces. Like the demons of Jewish traditions, they ascend to heaven and learn the future by eavesdropping. With all their power and knowledge, however, they are liable to be reduced to obedience by means of talismans or occult arts and become obsequious servants until the spell is broken.

It is far from certain that the jinn of the East were derived from the mythology or philosophy of the West, and the practice of translating the Arabic word *jinn* by the Latin term **genius** arose more from an apparent resemblance in the names than from any identity in the nature and functions of those imaginary beings.

This similarity of name, however, must have been purely accidental, for the Arabs knew little or nothing of the Latin language. Demon—not genius—is the word they probably would have used if they had borrowed this part of their creed from the West. *Jinn* appears, moreover, to be a genuine Arabic word derived from a root signifying "to veil" or "to conceal"; it therefore means properly "that which is veiled and cannot be seen."

"In one sense," states Frús-àbàdí (*Câmús,* vol. 3, p. 611), "the word Jinn signifies any spiritual being concealed from all our senses, and, for that reason, the converse of a material being. Taken in this extensive sense, the word Jinn comprehends devils as well as angels, but there are some properties common to both angels and Jinn; some peculiar to each. Every angel is a Jinn, but every Jinn is not an angel. In another sense, this term is applied peculiarly to a particular kind of spiritual being; for such beings are of three kinds; the good, which are angels; the bad, devils; and the intermediate, comprehending both good and bad, who form the class of Jinn."

Thus Arabs acknowledged good and bad jinn, in that respect agreeing with the Greeks, but differing from the Persians. The "genii" so long familiar to European readers through the *Arabian Nights* are not the same beings, but rather are the divs and dévatàs of Indian romance dressed up in a foreign attire to please the tastes of readers in Persia and Arabia.

The principal differences, therefore, between the genii of the West and the jinn of the East seem to have been as follows: the genii were deities of an inferior rank, the constant companions and guardians of men, capable of giving useful or prophetic impulses, acting as mediators and messengers between the gods and men. Some were supposed to be friendly, others hostile, and many believed one of each kind was attached from birth to every mortal. The former was called **Agathodemon,** the latter **Cacodemon.**

The good genius prompted men to good, the evil to bad actions. That of each individual was as a shadow of himself. Often the genius was represented as a serpent. His age also varied. He was generally crowned with a chaplet of plane-tree leaves. His sacrifices were wholly bloodless, consisting of wine and flowers, and the person who performed the oblation was the first to taste the cup. The birthday was placed under his special care.

Roman men swore by their genius, the women by their juno. The genius of the reigning prince was an oath of extraordinary solemnity. There were local as well as individual genii, concerning whom many particulars may be found in *De Idolatria liber* of Dionysius Vossius (editions 1633, 1641).

The jinn, on the contrary, who seem to be the lineal descendants of the dévatés and **rakshasas** of Hindu mythology, were never worshiped by the Arabs nor considered as anything but agents of the Deity. Since the establishment of Islam, indeed, they have been described as invisible spirits, and the feats and deformities that figure into romance are as little believed by Easterners as the tales of King Arthur's Round Table are by Westerners.

Jinnistan

An imaginary country that, according to a popular belief among the ancient Persians, was the residence of the **jinn** who submitted to King Solomon.

Jobson, Mary (ca. 1840)

Nineteenth-century psychic of Bishop Wearmouth, England. Her strange case is recorded in a brief book by Reid Clanny, *A Faithful Record of the Miraculous Case of Mary Jobson* (1841). At age 13, in November 1839, Mary was taken ill and had convulsions for 11 weeks. The first time she was seized her mother heard three loud knocks in the sickroom. The knocks were repeated, violent scratching was heard, and the door opened and shut violently four or five times.

While in a helpless and apparently hopeless condition, the girl heard voices and occasionally made accurate predictions. In May 1840 she foretold an attempt on the life of Queen Victoria. The voices claimed to come from the Virgin Mary, from apostles, and from martyrs. R. B. Embleton said he once heard the voice begin, "I am the Lord thy God which brought thee out of the land of Egypt."

Many other witnesses testified to a series of occult phenomena. Water appeared from nowhere and was sprinkled in the room, an astronomical design in green, yellow, and orange appeared on the ceiling, and music was frequently heard.

The latter phenomenon was confirmed by Jobson's governess, Elizabeth Gauntlett, and by a Dr. Drury. Drury stated, "On listening I distinctly heard most exquisite music which continued during the time I might count a hundred. This she told me she often heard." The girl alternately became blind, deaf, and dumb. After eight months of unaccountable illness she was mysteriously cured.

Jogand-Pagès, Gabriel (1854–ca. 1906)

Nineteenth-century French journalist who, under the name "Léo Taxil," perpetrated an extraordinary and prolonged hoax in which he claimed to have exposed **devil worship** within **Freemasonry.** Jogand's motives are not entirely clear even today, but it seems that his hoax was also designed to embarrass the Roman Catholic church.

In 1892 a book entitled *Le Diable du XIXe Siècle* was published in Paris, attributed to **"Dr. Bataille."** For a time the book was thought to be the work of Dr. Charles Hacks, who contributed a preface entitled "Revelations of an Occultist." Hacks was a real, although shadowy, figure. It was not until five years later that the hoax was revealed by Jogand himself.

The groundwork for the hoax began as early as 1885 when Jogand, as Léo Taxil, edited an anticlerical newspaper. He began to publish exposés of Freemasonry, claiming that there were lodges that practiced rites deriving from the Manichaean heresy. With the publication of "Dr. Bataille's" book, Jogand introduced a sinister high priestess of satanic Freemasons. She was **Diana Vaughan,** said to be a descendant of the seventeenth-century alchemist Thomas Vaughan. She had been chosen as a high priestess of Lucifer to overthrow Christianity and win the world over to Satanism, Jogand wrote. Diana was supposed to head a feminine cult of Freemasonry named Palladism. Periodicals claiming to emanate from the Palladium were published by Jogand.

His next audacious stroke was to announce that Diana Vaughan had been converted from Satanism to the true Roman Catholic faith. Her *Memories d'une Ex-Palladist* (1895–97) attracted enormous interest and enthusiasm. They were read by Pope Leo XIII, together with a short devotional work supposedly composed by Vaughan, and His Holiness responded with a papal benediction. It seemed that Jogand himself had repented of his former freethinking and created a saintly impression. He was received in private audience by the pope, who had expressed approval of his anti-masonic writings, and an anti-masonic congress was summoned in 1887 at Trent, famous for its sixteenth-century council.

By then there was great pressure for Diana Vaughan herself to be produced from the unnamed convent where Jogand claimed she was residing. It was announced that she would appear on Easter Monday 1897 and give a press conference in Paris. Instead, Jogand himself appeared and calmly announced that he had invented the whole conspiracy. He claimed that he himself had written Diana Vaughan's confessions, but asserted that Diana actually existed. She was his secretary, he said, and it had appealed to her sense of humor to be involved. After this astounding denouement, Jogand calmly left the hall by a side door and enjoyed a coffee and cognac in a nearby cafe, while a riot erupted in the lecture hall and the police were called in.

The whole affair was so extraordinary and deceived so many people, including exalted ecclesiastics, that much confusion still remains about Jogand's motives. Clearly he was a great liar, and even some details of his brazen confession are suspect. In general he seems to have developed the hoax to discredit both the Freemasons and the Catholic Church, but there also seem to be elements of personal neurosis. Jogand came from a deeply religious family but rebelled against his father's authority. As a young man, he early came into contact with Freemasonry and revolutionary circles, for which he was punished by being sent to a special school. He developed an aversion to authority and became a freethinker, later earning his living as a journalist concerned with freethinking publications.

Many questions remain unanswered about his great hoax as "Léo Taxil." The book by "Dr. Bataille" is a substantial work, and some of its revelations appear to be an imaginative embroidering of known facts. They provided the believable base from which the hoax could be worked. It is undoubtedly true that there were some Rosicrucian elements in certain masonic temples, and some of Taxil's inventions are not unlike the claims made against the **Templars.** Other individuals were evidently parties to the hoax, including Hacks and someone willing to pose as Diana Vaughan for photographs and for correspondence that was unlikely to have been written by Jogand.

The hoax was forgotten by all but a few students of occult history, but Taxil's books reemerged in the 1980s as source material from which contemporary anti-Mormon and anti-Satanist conspiracy books have been written.

Sources:

Bataille, Dr. [Gabriel Jogand-Pagès]. *Le Diable du XIXe Siècle.* Paris, 1892.

———. *Memoire à l' Adresse des Members du Congrès de Trent.* N.p., 1897.

Jastrow, Joseph. *Error and Eccentricity in Human Belief.* New York: Dover Publications, 1962.

Lea, H. C. *Léo Taxil, Diana Vaughan et l'Eglise romaine.* Paris, 1901.

Vaughan, Diana [Gabriel Jogand-Paqés]. *Mémoires d'une Ex-Palladiste, parfaite Initié, Indépendante.* Paris, 1895–97.

Waite, A. E. *Devil Worship in France.* London, 1896.

Johannine Daist Communion See Free Daist Communion

Johannites

A mystical sect of prerevolutionary Russia, founded on tenets from Father John of Kronstadt. The sect published a periodical and spread their propaganda by means of itinerant pamphlet sellers. They were said to abduct Jewish children, and because of this rumor they sometimes came under police supervision. On various occasions they unsuccessfully forecast the date of the Last Judgment. They declared that all the powers of heaven had descended into Kronstadt and were personified in the entourage of Father John.

They exhorted all believers to make confession to Father John, who alone could rescue sinners from the depths of hell. The orthodox clergy would not know the Lord, but Father John would gather together in Kronstadt 144,000 of the blessed and then "leave the earth." Another tenet of the Johannities was that all newborn babies were "little devils" who must be "stamped out" immediately after birth.

The Johannites urged people to sell all their possessions and send the proceeds to Father John, or entrust them to the keeping of the pamphlet sellers. It seems, however, that Father John was unaware of the abuse of his name, and on one occasion, in reply to a telegram from Bishop Nikander of Perm, he strongly repudiated any connection with certain Johannite propagandists in the Perm government.

Another well-known sect of Johannites existed in seventeenth-century Holland. They were a less rigid branch called the Mennonites. They were first known as Anabaptists, but this name became distasteful because of the excesses of the Anabaptists under such fanatics as John of Leyden, and in 1537 the priest Menno Simonis gave his name to the movement. The members of the Johannite branch were also known as "Waterlanders," from the name of the Waterland district in North Holland where they lived. Other Mennonite sects immigrated to the United States.

John, Bubba Free See Jones, Franklin Albert

John (Damian), Master, the French Leich

Among the several alchemists in the court of King **James VI of Scotland,** the most noted was the person variously styled in the Treasurer's Accounts as "the French Leich," "Maister John the French Leich," "Maister John the French Medicinar," and "French Maister John." The real name of this empiric was John Damian. He was a native of Lombardy and had practiced surgery and other arts in France before his arrival in Scotland. His first appearance at the court of James was in the capacity of a French leech, and, as he is mentioned among the persons who received "leveray" (livery) in 1501–02, there can be no doubt that he held an appointment as a physician in the royal household.

John soon succeeded in ingratiating himself with the king, and it is probable that it was from him that James absorbed a strong passion for **alchemy,** as James about this time erected at Stirling a furnace for conducting such experiments, and continued during the rest of his reign to expend considerable sums of money in attempts to discover the **philosophers' stone.** Bishop Lesley observed, "Maister John caused the king believe, that he by multiplying and utheris his inventions sold [should] make fine gold of uther metal, quhilk science he callit the Quintassence, whereupon the king made great cost, but all in vain."

There are numerous entries in the Treasurer's Accounts of sums paid for saltpeter, bellows, two great stillatours, brass mortars, coals, and numerous vessels of various shapes, sizes, and denominations, for the use of this foreign **adept** in his mystical studies. These studies, however, were not his sole occupation, for after the mysterious labors of the day were concluded, John used to play cards with the sovereign—a mode by which he probably transferred the contents of the royal exchequer into his own purse, as efficaciously as by his distillations.

Early in the year 1504, the Abbot of Tungland, in Galloway, died, and the king, with a reckless disregard of the dictates of duty, appointed the unprincipled adventurer John to the vacant office. On March 11, the treasurer paid "to Gareoch Parsuivant fourteen shillings to pass to Tungland for the Abbacy to the French Maister John." On the 12th of the same month, "by the king's command," he paid "to Bardus Altovite Lumbard twenty-five pounds for Maister John, the French Mediciner, new maid Abbot of Tungland, whilk he aucht (owed) to the said Bardus," and a few days later on the 17th, there was given "to Maister John the new maid Abbot of Tungland, seven pounds." Three years after, on July 27, 1507, occurs the following entry: "Item, lent, by the king's command to the Abbot of Tungland, and can nocht be gettin fra him £33 : 6 : 8."

An adventure that befell this dexterous impostor afforded great amusement to the Scottish court. On the occasion of an embassy setting out from Stirling to the court of France, he had the audacity to declare that by means of a pair of artificial wings he had constructed, he would undertake to fly to Paris and arrive long before the ambassadors. This incident gave rise to a satirical ballad entitled "Of the Fenyeit Friar of Tungland," in which a poet exposed in the most sarcastic strain the pretensions of the luckless adventurer, and related with great humor the result of his attempt to soar into the skies, when he was dragged to the earth by the low-minded propensities of the "hen feathers," he had inadvertently admitted into the construction of his wings.

Although John's unsuccessful attempt, according to Lesley, subjected him to the ridicule of the whole kingdom, it did not result in the loss of the king's favor. The treasurer's books, from October 1507 to August 1508, repeatedly mention him as having played at dice and cards with his majesty, and on September 8, 1508, "Damiane, Abbot of Tungland," obtained royal permission to pursue his studies abroad during the space of five years.

John must have returned to Scotland, however, before the death of James, since the last notice given to this impostor is quite in character. On the March 27, 1513, the sum of twenty pounds was paid to him for his journey to the mine in Crawford Moor, where the king had at that time artisans at work searching for gold.

"John King"

Claimed spirit entity manifesting at many Spiritualist séances. (See **"King, John"**)

John of Nottingham

Famous occult magician of fourteenth-century **England.**

John XXII, Pope (ca. 1244–1334)

Jacques Duèse, subsequently Pope John XXII, was born at Cahors, France. His parents were affluent, and it has even been suggested that they belonged to the nobility. Jacques was educated first at a Dominican priory in his native village and afterward at Montpellier. He then proceeded to Paris, where he studied both law and medicine.

Leaving the Sorbonne, Duèse was still at a loss as to what profession to follow, but, chancing to become intimate with Bishop Louis (a son of Charles II, king of Naples) the young man decided to enter the Church, doubtless prompted to this step by the conviction that his new friend's influence would help him advance in his clerical career.

The future pontiff was not disappointed, for in the year 1300, at the request of the Neapolitan sovereign, he was elevated to the episcopal see of Fréjus, then in 1308 he was appointed chancellor of Naples. He soon showed himself a man of no mean ability in ecclesiastical affairs. In 1310 Pope Clement V summoned him to Avignon, anxious to consult him on the question of the legality of suppressing the **Templars** and also on whether to condemn the memory of Boniface VIII. Duèse was in favor of suppressing the Templars but rejected condemnation of Boniface. In 1312 Duèse was made bishop of Porto, and four years later was elected to the pontifical crown and scepter as Pope John XXII.

From that time on he lived at Avignon, but his life was by no means a quiet or untroubled one. Early in his papacy the throne of Germany became vacant. Louis of Bavaria and Frederick of Austria both contended for it, and Pope John offended many by supporting Frederick. Later he raised a storm by preaching a somewhat unorthodox sermon purporting that the souls of those who die in a state of grace go straight into Abraham's bosom and do not enjoy the beatific vision of the Lord until after the Resurrection and the Last Judgment. This doctrine was hotly opposed by many clerics, notably Thomas of England, who had the courage to preach against it openly at Avignon. So great was the disfavor Pope John incurred that for several years after his death he was widely regarded as the **Antichrist.**

Pope John was frequently accused of avarice, and it is true that he made stupendous efforts to raise money, imposing numerous taxes unheard of before his papacy. He manifested considerable ingenuity in that regard, and so the tradition that he dabbled in hermetic philosophy (**alchemy**) may be founded on fact. He did issue a stringent bull against alchemists, but it was directed against the charlatans of the craft, not against those who were seeking the **philosophers' stone** with real earnestness and with the aid of scientific knowledge.

The pope may have introduced this mandate to silence those who had charged him with the practice of alchemy himself. Whatever his reason, it is probable that he believed in magic and was interested in science. His belief in magic is indicated by his bringing a charge of sorcery against Géraud, bishop of Cahors. Pope John's scientific predilections are evident from his keeping a laboratory in the palace at Avignon and spending much time there.

Doubtless some of this time was given to physiological and pathological studies, for various works of a medical nature are ascribed to Pope John XXII, in particular a collection of prescriptions, a treatise on diseases of the eye, and another on the formation of the fetus. But it may well be that the ativities in his laboratory also centered in some measure on alchemistic research. This theory is strengthened by the fact that Pope John was friends with **Arnold de Villanova,** famous physician, astrologer, and alchemist.

Among the writings attributed to Pope John XXII is the alchemical work *L'Elixir des philosophers, autrement L'art transmutatoire,* published at Lyons in 1557.

When he died the pontiff left behind him a vast sum of money and a mass of priceless jewels. It was commonly asserted among the alchemists of the day that the money, jewels, and 200 huge ingots were all manufactured by the late pope. The story of the unbounded wealth amassed in this way gradually blossomed and bore fruit, and one of the pope's medieval biographers credited him with having concocted an enormous quantity of gold.

Johnson, Alice (1860–1940)

Prominent figure in British psychical research. Johnson was organizing secretary of the **Society for Psychical Research** (SPR), London, from 1903 to 1916, research officer from 1908 to 1916, and editor of the society's *Proceedings* from 1899 to 1916. Born in Cambridge, England, she was educated at Newham College, Cambridge University (Bathurst student 1882). From 1884 to 1890 she was a demonstrator in animal morphology at the Balfour Laboratory.

Johnson became interested in psychical research through her association with **Eleanor Sidgwick** and became her personal secretary. Johnson participated in the first sittings in England with the American medium **Leonora Piper** in 1889 and assisted in the SPR **Census of Hallucinations** between 1889 and 1894. In 1901 she collaborated with **Richard Hodgson** on the preparation of the **F. W. H. Myers** book *Human Personality and Its Survival of Bodily Death,* which was published after Myers's death. Johnson also reported on the SPR group of mediums investigated in connection with automatic phenomena (writing and trance messages). She died January 13, 1940.

Sources:

Johnson, Alice. "The Education of the Sitter." *Proceedings* of the Society for Psychical Research (1908–09).

———. "Mrs. Henry Sidgwick's Work in Psychical Research." *Proceedings* of the Society for Psychical Research (1936–37).

———. "On the Automatic Writing of Mrs. Holland." *Proceedings* of the Society for Psychical Research (1908–09).

———. "Report of Some Recent Sittings for Physical Phenomena in America." *Proceedings* of the Society for Psychical Research (1908–09).

———. "Second Report on Mrs. Holland's Scripts." *Proceedings* of the Society for Psychical Research (1910).

———. "Supplementary Notes on Mrs. Holland's Scripts." *Proceedings* of the Society for Psychical Research (1910).

———. "Third Report on Mrs. Holland's Scripts." *Proceedings* of the Society for Psychical Research (1910).

Pleasants, Helene, ed. *Biographical Dictionary of Parapsychology.* New York: Helix Press, 1964.

Johnson, Douglas (ca. 1909–1988)

Modern British medium who investigated **haunted houses** in the United States and who appeared on television programs to demonstrate **clairvoyance** and **psychometry.** He was born in London, and his powers were evident as early as age six. His parents were not psychic but did not disapprove of his predictive talents; they permitted him to attend a Spiritualist public meeting at age 12. Three years later he went into **trance** for the first time, **channeling** information and advice to a circle of people.

In World War II he served with the Royal Air Force, but he was removed from active duty after an injury at the end of the war. He had corresponded with the College of Psychic Science (now the **College of Psychic Studies**) in London and afterward gave many clairvoyant sittings there. He also spent time in the United States, where he worked with **W. G. Roll, Eileen Garrett, Thelma Moss, Stanley Krippner,** and other parapsychologists. He died in October 1988.

Sources:

Editors of *Psychic Magazine. Psychics.* New York: Harper & Row, 1972.

Johnson, Mrs. Roberts (ca. 1927)

Direct voice medium of Stockton-on-Tees, England. Her powers developed after a sitting with **Mrs. Thomas Everitt.** Her principal **control** claimed to be **David Duguid,** the former trance painting medium of Glasgow.

A sitter at a séance held March 5, 1918, reported in *Light* as follows:

"I have never had two sittings alike with Mrs. Johnson. They are marked each time by some different characteristic. On this occasion, before each new speaker used the trumpet, I saw a faintly-luminous figure moving about. Then, again, all the voices were louder than is usual in ordinary conversation, so much so, that Mrs. Johnson on more than one occasion asked the male speakers to moderate their tone; otherwise neighbours and pedestrians outside might be attracted by the unusual noise. Most of our spirit visitors remained throughout the sitting, and verbally called our attention to the fact. This was the best direct-voice sitting which, so far, it has been my good fortune to attend."

Sir Arthur Conan Doyle remarked on Johnson's remarkable power with direct voice phenomena, commenting on the non-religious atmosphere of her sittings with humorous spirit communicators.

Johnson, Raynor C(arey) (1901–1987)

Master of Queen's College, University of Melbourne, Australia, author, and writer on parapsychology. Born April 5, 1901, at Leeds, England, he studied at Bradford Grammar School, Balliol College, Oxford, and the University of London (B.A., M.A., D.S.). He was also awarded an honorary doctorate by the University of Melbourne.

Johnson was successively a lecturer in physics, Queen's University of Belfast; lecturer in physics, King's College, University of London; and master of Queen's College, University of Melbourne (from 1934 on). He was a member of the **Society for Psychical Research,** London, and wrote various books on physics and on paranormal topics.

Sources:

Berger, Arthur S., and Joyce Berger. *The Encyclopedia of Parapsychology and Psychical Research.* New York: Paragon House, 1991.

Johnson, Raynor C. *The Imprisoned Splendour.* New York: Harper & Brothers, 1953.

———. *Nurslings of Immortality.* London: Hodder & Stoughton, 1957.

———. *Psychical Research.* New York: Philosophical Library, 1955.

———. *The Spiritual Path.* New York: Harper & Row, 1971.

———. *Watcher on the Hills.* New York: Harper & Row, 1959.

Pleasants, Helene, ed. *Biographical Dictionary of Parapsychology.* New York: Helix Press, 1964.

Joire, Paul (1856– ?)

Professor at the Psycho-physiological Institute of Paris, president of the Societé Universelle d'Etudes Psychiques, and distinguished psychical researcher. His studies in hypnotism and in the obscure area of the **exteriorization of sensitivity** are especially noteworthy. He invented a device named the **sthenometer** to demonstrate the existence of a force that seemed to emanate from the nervous system and was capable of acting at a distance and causing movement of objects without contact.

His book *Psychical and Supernormal Phenomena* (1916) is an important contribution to psychical literature.

Sources:

Joire, Paul. *Précis historique et pratique de Neuro-Hypnologie.* N.p., 1892.

———. *Traité de Graphologie scientifique.* N.p., 1906.

———. *Traité de l'Hypnotisme expérimental et thérapeutique.* N.p., 1908.

Jones, Charles Stansfeld (1886–1950)

British occultist and author who lived in Canada and assumed the name "Frater Achad." Jones was an accountant in Vancouver when he became a disciple of magician **Aleister Crowley.** Crowley would later come to consider Jones his "magical son" as prophesied in Crowley's early channeled text, *The Book of the Law.*

Crowley believed that Jones had discovered a kabalistic key to *The Book of the Law.* As a disciple Jones progressed to the grade of master of the temple in Crowley's secret order A.·.A.·., while Crowley moved on to become a magus. There is a record of his achievement in *Liber 165,* partially published in Crowley's journal **The Equinox** (vol. 3, p. 127).

In attempting his mystical rebirth as a "Babe of the Abyss," Jones had a nervous breakdown. He returned briefly to England and joined the Roman Catholic Church, hoping to convert other Catholics to Crowley's Law of Thelema. Upon returning to Vancouver he wandered around the city wearing only a raincoat, which he threw off in public, crying that he had renounced all the veils of illusion. After his recovery Jones became somewhat hostile to Crowley, who had expelled him from his order.

Over the years Jones wrote a number of books, including *The Anatomy of the Body of God* (1925), which attempts a three-dimensional projection of the kabalistic Tree of Life. (See also **Kabala**)

Sources:

Achad, Frater [Charles Stansfeld Jones]. *The Anatomy of the Body of God.* Chicago: Collegium ad Spiritum Sanctum, 1925.

———. *Chalice of Ecstacy.* Chicago: Yogi Publication Society, 1923.

———. *Liber 31.* San Francisco: Level Press, 1974.

———. *Q.B.L. or the Bride's Reception.* The Author, 1922.

Jones, Franklin Albert (1939–)

Currently known by his religious name Avatara Adi Da, Franklin Jones is the founder of the **Free Daist Communion,** an advaita vedanta community that has undergone a number of changes since its founding in 1972. According to his own account, Jones was a fully enlightened being who gave up that enlightenment during the early years of this incarnation. As a young man he attended Columbia University (B.A., 1961), Stanford University (1961–62), and Lutheran Theological Seminary in Philadelphia (1966–67). In 1962 he participated in some research on drugs at the Veterans Administration Hospital, Mountain View, California, an event that stimulated his recovery of his enlightened state.

In 1964 Jones sought out Swami Rudrananda (Albert Rudolph) and in 1968 traveled to India to meet Swami Muktananda, one of Rudrananda's teachers. In the summer of 1970, while meditating in the temple of the Vedanta Society in Hollywood, California, he felt a "permanent reawakening." He founded the Dawn Horse Fellowship and began a public ministry on April 25, 1972. His first book, *The Knee of Listening,* had just appeared. The following year he severed his connection with Muktananda and changed his name to Bubba Free John.

He gathered around him a small group of devoted students with whom he worked in a somewhat intense fashion reminiscent of **Georgei I. Gurdjieff.** Many of his teachings given orally were transcribed and edited into books. In 1979 he withdrew from this form of active teachings and changed his name to Da (giver) Free John. He now saw his work as that of transmitting the transcendental condition to his students. As a teacher of advaita vedanta, he emphasized the unity and identity of the human self with the Brahman, the soul of all things. He continued to speak and write, and a steady flow of his books continued to be published. He also largely withdrew from public presence to an island in Fuji.

In the late 1980s he changed his name to Heart Master Da Love Ananda (bliss) and to Da Avabhasa (the Bright). This period has been accompanied by the release of those books that are considered the most important of his earthly career, *The Dawn Horse Testament* (1985) and *Free Daism* (1992), a presentation of his mature religious perspective. Jones is also known by the name Da Kalki.

Sources:

Bonner, Saniel. *The Divine Emergence of the World-Teacher: The Realization, the Revelation and the Revealing Ordeal of Heart Master Da Love-Ananda.* Clearlake, Calif.: Dawn Horse Press, 1990.

Jones, Franklin [Heart Master Da Love Ananda]. *Dawn Horse Testament.* San Rafael, Calif.: Dawn Horse Press, 1985.

——— [Da Avabhasa]. *Free Daism: The Eternal, Ancient, and New Religion of God-Realization.* Clearlake, Calif.: Dawn Horse Press, 1992.

———. *The Heart's Shout.* Clearlake, Calif.: Dawn Horse Press, 1993.

———. *The Knee of Listening.* Los Angeles: Dawn Horse Press, 1972.

Jones, Jim (1931–1978)

Founder of the Peoples Temple 900, whose members died in a massive murder-suicide in 1978. Jones was for many years an honored pastor of the Christian Church (Disciples of Christ) before his career ended in controversy and death.

Jones was born May 31, 1931, in Lynn, Indiana. As a young man he became the pastor of a Methodist church but could not meet the Methodist standards for a minister. He left in 1954 to found an independent congregation in Indianapolis to further his vision of a church that could overcome racial barriers. He was impressed with the accomplishments of **Father Divine,** and he modeled his own church, which he called the Peoples Temple, on Father Divine's Peace Mission Movement. In the mid-1960s he had a vision of a nuclear holocaust and moved the congregation to Ukiah, California, which he believed would be a relatively safe location. In the meantime, he and the congregation had become affiliated with the Disciples of Christ.

In California, Jones became a social activist and was well known for his support of liberal social and political causes. He extended his work to Los Angeles and San Francisco, where he built predominantly African American congregations. Leadership, however, tended to fall into the hands of the minority white members. Worship followed a style common to the black community, with a gospel choir, spirited preaching, and reports of miracle healings. According to reports, Jones became increasingly autocratic in his leadership, and as he became frustrated at the lack of visible effects of his efforts to end racism, he began to lean increasingly toward Marxism.

In 1973 he founded a rural agricultural colony in the largely Marxist country of Guyana. Through the mid-1970s, as the colony seemed to prosper, there were an increasing number of rumors and accusations concerning irregularities at the temple, including charges of violence against former members and temple critics. In 1977, just before the appearance of an exposé article in *New West* magazine, Jones and many of his followers migrated to the colony, which had been named Jonestown.

Jones responded to the accusations with heightened paranoia. During this time he was also seeking a solution to the problem of financing his following and placing his followers in a harmonious environment. He explored a number of possibilities, including "revolutionary suicide,"—suicide committed in furtherance of a moral cause. During the Vietnam War, for example, several Buddhist monks killed themselves in protest of the war. Jones's situation was different, however, in that he was attempting to gain the entire community's acceptance of the idea.

In November 1978 California Congressman Leo Ryan made a visit to Guyana to observe life at Jonestown. For reasons still not well understood, immediately after he left and was preparing to return to the United States, a group of temple members attacked and killed him and his party. A short time later, most of the residents at Jonestown—approximately 900 men, women, and children—either committed suicide or were murdered.

Understanding the tragedy of Jonestown has been hindered by the confiscation and storage under lock and key of the many records concerning the investigation of the temple and Ryan's death. The lack of information has allowed a wide range of speculation about what occurred. Jonestown has since become a popular example of the pitfalls of unapproved religious groups, or cults.

Sources:

Hall, John R. *Gone from the Promised Land: Jonestown in American Cultural History.* New Brunswick, N.J.: Transaction, 1987.

Melton, J. Gordon, ed. *The Peoples Temple and Jim Jones: Broadening Our Perspectives.* New York: Garland, 1990.

Moore, Rebecca, ed. *New Religious Movements, Mass Suicide, and Peoples Temple: Scholarly Perspectives on a Tragedy.* New York: Edwin Mellen, 1989.

Reiterman, Tom. *Raven.* New York: E. P. Dutton, 1982.

Jones, Marc Edmund (1888–1980)

Well-known writer on occult and astrological subjects. Born in St. Louis, Missouri, October 1, 1888, Jones was educated privately. From 1911 to 1918 he was a pioneer motion picture writer and the author of nearly 200 original screenplays. He was ordained a minister of the United Presbyterian Church and also founded the **Sabian Assembly** (concerned with solar mysteries).

Jones was founder of the Photoplay Authors' League (later renamed Screenwriters' Guild of the Authors' League of America). He was a member of the Writers Club (New York), the Writers (Hollywood), and Playwrights Club (New York). From 1922 on, he was a freelance writer and lecturer on metaphysical subjects. He was founder-editor of the *Message,* to which he contributed regularly beginning in 1926. He was an active proponent of **New Thought** and was responsible for two weekly students' lessons of 1,200 words each before 1927, later conducting 36 correspondence courses averaging 40,000 words each. Jones died in 1980.

Sources:

Jones, Marc Edmund. *Essentials of Astrological Analysis.* Stanwood, Wash.: Sabian Publishing Society, 1970.

———. *How to Live With the Stars.* Wheaton, Ill.: Theosophical Publishing House, 1976.

———. *Key Truths of Occult Philosophy.* Los Angeles: J. F. Rowney Press, 1925.

———. *Occult Philosophy: An Introduction.* Stanwood, Wash.: Sabian Publishing Society, 1971.

———. *The Ritual of Living.* Los Angeles: J. F. Rowney Press, 1930. Rev. ed. *The Sabian Manual: A Ritual for Living.* New York: Sabian Publishing Society, 1957.

———. *The Sabian Book.* Stanwood, Wash.: Sabian Publishing Society, 1973.

———. *Scope of Astrological Prediction.* Stanwood, Wash.: Sabian Publishing Society, 1969.

Jonson, Mr. (1854– ?) and Mrs. J. B. Jonson

Celebrated American mediums of Toledo, Ohio, who later moved to Altadena, California. Jonson was a painter and paperhanger who, with his wife, sat for **materialization** and **direct voice** phenomena. He was born October 16, 1854, in Akron, Ohio. His father was said to be a lineal descendant of the British poet Ben Jonson and his great-grandmother a descendant of Thomas Paine. Both his parents were Spiritualists and held a séance on the evening before his birth. His own psychic talents developed at age seven, when, while playing with his sister, he ran right through a burly black-whiskered man on the steps of the house. His sister also saw the phantom. She died soon after the incident, but manifested at a séance with Jonson when he was only 18.

Beginning in 1876 Jonson sat regularly in a home circle with friends, and physical manifestations occurred, including materializations. He also became a trumpet medium. He married in 1901, and his wife was usually present at séances. Both usually sat outside the **cabinet,** and Jonson went into trance. His wife was reputed to be a good direct voice medium.

Homer Taylor Yaryan, chief of the secret police under the Grant government, watched the mediums carefully for years and assured Admiral Usborne Moore that they were genuine. The admiral himself, in his book *Glimpses of the Next State* (1911), reached the same conclusion. He saw 15 to 16 phantoms—in circumstances that apparently excluded confederacy—emerge from the cabinet in a single sitting. Some of them dematerialized into the floor and it was possible to follow their heads with the eye until the shoulders were level with the carpet; some came too far out into the light, doubled up and collapsed; some dissipated after falling over on one side.

Each phantom had a distinctive movement of the limbs and carriage by which, in successive séances, they were identified. They were mostly etherealizations; the faces and heads alone were tangible. The admiral put his arms around the waist of a phantom relative and found nothing.

A white-robed figure with a bright silver band on her forehead and bracelets and jewels on her arm gave her name as "Cleopatra, Queen of Egypt"; another form claimed to be "Josephine."

In 1923 the Jonsons were visited in California by **Sir Arthur Conan Doyle,** who was greatly impressed by their materialization phenomena, which he believed genuine. He describes the séance in his book *Our Second American Adventure* (1923).

The Jonsons, however, did not live up to the favorable reputation that the experiments of Yaryan and Moore established for them. Considering the experiences of **J. Hewat McKenzie** in Toledo in 1917, those who accused them of **fraud** apparently had grounds for doing so. Writing in *Psychic Science* (April 1927), McKenzie notes:

"I proved on this visit, that the daughter of the Jonsons' masqueraded as a spirit, and would appear from the back room to dance as a materialised form in highly illuminated garments, the illumination for these being produced in an adjoining room with the help of magnesium wire used on clothing impregnated with phosphorescent paint. The smoke from the magnesium wire was seen by me in clouds in the room where she danced, and my sense of smell also recognized the well-known odour. Here we have a striking instance of what the abuse of spirit intercourse may lead to."

Sources:

Yaryan, Homer T. "An Investigator's Experience of Materialization Phenomena." *Psychic Science* (October 1926).

Jonsson, Olof (1918–)

Famous Swedish-born psychic who took part in telepathic experiments with Apollo astronaut **Edgar Mitchell** during Mitchell's flight to the moon. Jonsson trained as an engineer in Sweden, qualifying in 1941. He worked with various companies and in 1946 was appointed be a design engineer at the Monarch motorcycle factory in Varberg. At this time his psychic gifts (which had been evident in childhood) became more widely manifested and he became known as "the psychic engineer" through his demonstrations of **clairvoyance, telepathy,** and **psychokinesis.**

He was tested by parapsychologists in Sweden and Denmark. He visited South America, Canada, China, Japan, and Australia, studying paranormal phenomena among primitive peoples. In 1953 **J. B. Rhine** of Duke University invited Jonsson to the United States, where he was tested by parapsychologists in such areas as telepathy, clairvoyance, precognition, psychometry, and psychokinesis.

His successful card guessing led to his being chosen to participate in the Apollo 14 tests of **ESP** with Edgar Mitchell during the three days before and after the moon landing. The tests are described in detail by Mitchell in the *Journal of Parapsychology* (June 1971). The results indicated scoring significantly above chance expectation. However, for a more skeptical view of claimed success, see the chapter "ESP in Outer Space" in *Mediums, Mystics, and the Occult,* by Milbourne Christopher (1975).

Among other psychic achievements, Jonsson is said to have elucidated 13 murder cases after visiting the scenes of the crimes and to have located three missing women. He was also supposed to have predicted accurately the time and place of death of Nasser and De Gaulle.

Sources:

Steiger, Brad. *The Psychic Feats of Olof Jonsson.* New York: Popular Library, 1971.

Jordan, Pacual (1902–)

Physicist who was concerned with the relationship of physics, psychology, and parapsychology. Jordan was born on October 18, 1902, at Hanover, Germany, and studied at Göttingen University (Ph.D., 1924). He was professor of theoretical physics at the University of Rostock (1929–44) and later a professor of theoretical physics at the University of Hamburg. Jordan conducted joint research with Niels Bohr and Werner Heisenberg in quantum mechanics and in 1942 won the Max Planck Medal for his work in physics.

Through the 1950s Jordan manifested an interest in parapsychology. He contributed articles to the *Journal* of the Society for Psychical Research, including one on "Quantum Field Theory." He was a member of the International Conference on Philosophy and Parapsychology, St. Paul de Vence, France, 1954, where he lectured on "New Trends in Physics and Their Relation to Parapsychology."

Sources:

Jordan, Pacual. "New Trends in Physics and Their Relation to Parapsychology." *Parapsychology Foundation Newsletter* (July–August 1955).

———. *Verdrängung and Komplementarität* (Repression and Complementarity). N.p., 1951.

Journal du Magnetisme et du Psychisme Experimental

Monthly publication founded by **Baron Du Potet,** covering 20 volumes (1845–61). It was later continued and edited by **Henri Durville** as the official organ of the Société Psychiques Internationale.

Journal of Automatic Writing

Published by Spiritual Press, Box 464, Don Mills, Ontario M3C 2T3 Canada.

Journal of Borderland Research

Bimonthly publication of **Borderland Sciences Research Foundation,** concerned with such subjects as psychical research, psychic surgery, radionics, radiesthesia, and related occult topics. Address: P.O. Box 429, Garberville, CA 95540.

Journal of Geocosmic Research

Journal of the National Council for Geocosmic Research, concerned with correlations between astrological observations and human behavior. Address: P.O. Box 1220, Dunkirk, MD 20754.

Journal of Holistic Health

A defunct publication that dealt with **New Age** teachings of a comprehensive and integrated approach to life, combining diet, environmental concern, personal responsibility, and spiritual growth. Contributors included Pir Vilayat Inayat Khan, **Olga Worrall, Ruth Carter Stapleton,** and Jonas Salk. Address: Mandala Holistic Health, P.O. Box 1233, Del Mar, CA 92014.

Journal of Humanistic Psychology

Quarterly professional journal of the Association for Humanistic Psychology, concerned largely with aspects of consciousness expansion from a psychological viewpoint, presenting research, theory, and discussion on various aspects of consciousness, health, and growth. Address: 325 9th St., San Francisco, CA 94103.

Journal of Instrumented UFO Research

Former journal published at irregular intervals, specializing in the detection of **UFOs** by sophisticated electronic equipment. Psychic Ray Stanford of Austin, Texas, established the site upon which a UFO detection device was placed.

Journal of Man

J. R. Buchanan's journal of research in **psychometry.** Founded in 1853 in Cincinnati, it superseded S. B. Brittan's Spiritualist monthly *The Shekinah.* No longer published.

Journal of Meteorology, The

One of several British periodicals concerned with the phenomenon of **crop circles.** It is edited by Dr. George Terence Meaden and published by the Circles Effect Research Unit, 54 Frome Rd., Bradford-on-Avon, Wiltshire, BA15 1LD, UK.

Sources:

Meaden, George Terence. *The Circles Effect and Its Mysteries.* Bradford-on-Avon, U.K.: Artetech Publishing, 1989.

Journal of Occult Studies

Short-lived quarterly publication of the Occult Studies Foundation, in cooperation with the University of Rhode Island, as "an interdisciplinary approach to Paranormal Phenomena." Beginning in May 1977 it published several issues until 1980, when its name was changed to *MetaScience Quarterly* and the foundation name to MetaScience Foundation. The change of name reflected reservations about the contemporary connotations of the word occult, since the MetaScience Foundation intends to maintain a high standard of scientific information in the field of parapsychology and related subjects. Address: MetaScience Quarterly, Box 32, Kingston, RI 02881.

Journal of Orgonomy

Biannual journal representing an authoritative view of the life, work, and writings of the late psychologist **Wilhelm Reich.** The journal is published by a group of accredited Reichian physicians and includes previously unpublished writings of Reich as well as contemporary views and research on **orgone** energy and associated topics. Address: P.O. Box 565, Ansonia Sta., New York, NY 10023.

Journal of Our Time

Canadian journal concerned with **Fourth Way** teachings deriving from the philosophy of **Georgei Gurdjieff.** Address: Box 484, Adelaide St. P.O., Toronto, Canada M5C 2K4.

Journal of Parapsychology

Quarterly journal published since 1937 and edited for many years by **Louisa E. Rhine** (1891–1983) and **Dorothy H. Pope.** It is a scholarly publication "devoted primarily to the original publication of experimental results and other research findings in extrasensory perception and psychokinesis." In addition, articles presenting reviews of "literature relevant to parapsychology, criticisms of published work, theoretical and philosophical discussions, and new methods of mathematical analysis" are included in its scope. The journal has been the major organ of academic parapsychology since its founding. It is published by the Parapsychology Press, Box 6847, College Sta., Durham, NC 27708.

Journal of Research in Psi Phenomena

Organ of the Kingston Association for Research in Parasciences, P.O. Box 141, Kingston, Ontario, K7L 4V6, Canada.

Journal of Scientific Exploration

Semiannual journal of the Society for Scientific Exploration, devoted to advancing the study of anomalous phenomena originally catalogued by **Charles Fort.** Study includes anomalies in various areas of established science as well as in areas outside of established science that are currently being investigated under controlled laboratory conditions. The society also studies anomalies in areas outside established science that have not been subjected to investigation under control conditions, such as **cryptozoology** (the study of life forms such as **Sasquatch** and **"Nessie"**), **precognition, extrasensory perception, psychokinesis,** and **UFO** phenomena.

Address: Society for Scientific Exploration, c/o Dr. Peter Sturrock, ERL 306, Stanford University, Stanford, CA 94305-4055.

Journal of the American Society for Psychical Research

The major quarterly publication of the **American Society for Psychical Research** (ASPR). It originally was published from 1906 until 1928, when volume 22 was continued under the title *Psychic Research.* In January 1932, however, the original title was resumed. The *Journal* and also the *Proceedings* of the ASPR are now published from the society's headquarters at 5 W. 73rd St., New York, NY 10023.

Journal of the American Society for Psychosomatic Dentistry and Medicine

Quarterly professional journal relating parapsychological phenomena, hypnosis, acupuncture, and similar subjects to medicine and the welfare of patients. Address: 2802 Mermaid Ave., Brooklyn, NY 11224.

Journal of the Society for Psychical Research

Published since 1884. Volumes 1 through 34 (1884–1948) were restricted to members of the society, but issues since September 1949 have been available for purchase by the public. The journal is now published quarterly by the society at 49 Marloes Rd., Kensington, London W8 6LA, England. The society also publishes a *Combined Index* to the *Journal*, and the society's *Proceedings* are also published.

Journal of Transpersonal Psychology

Semiannual journal with contributions concerned with a psychological approach to dreams, meditation, psychic experiences, biofeedback, and consciousness-expanding techniques. Address: 345 S. California, Palo Alto, CA 94306.

Journal of UFO Studies

Irregular publication of the **J. Allen Hynek Center for UFO Studies** (formerly the Center for UFO Studies). The journal is concerned with UFO research at a scholarly level, and articles include abstracts and bibliographies. Address: J. Allen Hynek Center for UFO Studies, 2457 W. Peterson Ave., Chicago, IL 60659.

Journal of Vampirism

Short-lived journal of the **Vampire Studies Society.** It was published for several years in the mid-1970s by Chicago vampirologist Martin V. Riccardo.

Journal of Vampirology

Scholarly journal founded in 1984 and edited by John L. Vellutini. This quarterly journal covered many aspects of vampires, especially vampire folklore from around the world. It was discontinued in the early 1990s.

Journal UFO

Canadian publication reporting on UFO activities and related mysteries, now incorporating *Canadian UFO Report* (formerly published from British Columbia). Address: UP Investigations Research Inc., Box 455, Streetsville, Mississauga, Ontario, Canada L5M 2B9.

Joy, Sir George Andrew (1896–1974)

Official of the British Colonial and Foreign Office, also active in the field of psychical research. He was born on February 20, 1896, in London. He served in the British army and was, successively, assistant commissioner for the New Hebrides Condominium; resident commissioner and deputy commissioner for the Western Pacific; consultant for the Hoorn and Wallace Island; resident adviser to the Quaiti and Kathiri sultans, Hadhramaut States of Arabia; civil secretary to the government of Adam, and commissioner for civil defense, governor and commander-in-chief of St. Helena. He received numerous awards.

Joy served a tenure as secretary of the **Society for Psychical Research** (SPR), London, beginning in 1958, and was a member of the SPR Council. He was later vice president of the organization.

Sources:

Pleasants, Helene, ed. *Biographical Dictionary of Parapsychology.* New York: Helix Press, 1964.

Judd, Pearl (1908–1967)

Direct voice medium of Dunedin, New Zealand, who held séances in a well-lighted room or in daylight with remarkable manifestations, as described in Clive Chapman's book *The Blue Room* (1927).

In *Psychic Research* (November 1930) psychical researcher **Harry Price** quoted the testimony of W. P. Gowland, professor of anatomy and neurologist at the Medical School, Dunedin. Gowland witnessed the **levitation** of heavy tables and the playing of a specified tune on an ordinary piano when three people were sitting on the closed and locked lid. He also heard invisible instruments and many voices.

An entity named "Sahnaei," who first manifested in 1923, stated he was an Arab who had lived hundreds of years before. Sahnaei appeared to be in charge of a band of communicators including "Captain Trevor," "Ronald," "George Thurston," "Charlie," "Grace," "Oliver," "Jack," and "Vilma." Judd's uncle, Clive Chapman, was also a medium and was present at the most impressive séances. These were held in a blue room, hence the title of Chapman's book. Pearl Judd retired some years after publication of the book. Chapman died August 10, 1967, at age 84.

Judge, William Q(uan) (1851–1896)

Prominent American Theosophist and one of the founders of the **Theosophical Society** along with **Helena Petrovna Blavatsky** and **Henry Steel Olcott.** Born April 13, 1851, in Ireland, Judge studied occult literature and immigrated to the United States, where he became a lawyer. After Blavatsky and Olcott moved to India, Judge became the leader of the American branch of the society. Following the death of Blavatsky, he was involved in the case of the **Mahatma letters,** in which communications allegedly from the **Koot Hoomi,** a mysterious adept, appeared to favor Judge's taking charge of the esoteric section of the society, as opposed to Blavatsky's choice to succeed her, **Annie Besant.**

At the 1895 convention of the American section of the Theosophical Society, members decided to secede from the parent society. Judge was elected president for life of the Theosophical Society in America. He died March 21, 1896, and passed leadership to **Katherine Tingley.**

Among his various writings Judge produced his own edition of the *Yoga Sutras of Patanjali,* study notes on the Bhagavad Gita, and a book, *The Ocean of Theosophy* (1893).

Sources:

Eek, Sven, and Boris de Zirkoff. *William Quan Judge: Theosophical Pioneer.* Wheaton, Ill.: Theosophical Publishing House, 1969.

Judge, William Q. *Echoes of the Orient.* 2 vols. San Diego, Calif.: Point Loma Publications, 1975, 1980.

———. *The Ocean of Theosophy.* Reprint, Point Loma, Calif.: Theosophical University Press, 1974.

Ju-Ju

A term applied in a variety of ways by non-African writers to describe various features and sometimes even the whole of the system of African traditional tribal religion and/or magic practice. It is a French word meaning "little doll." Like *fetishism,* it is a term that has been abandoned in the contemporary discussion of African religion.

Sources:

King, Noel Q. *African Cosmos: An Introduction to Religion in Africa.* Belmont, Calif.: Wadsworth, 1986.

Parrinder, Geoffrey. *African Traditional Religion.* Westport, Conn.: Greenwood Press, 1962.

Peek, Philip M., ed. *African Divination Systems.* Bloomington: Indiana University Press, 1991.

Julia's Bureau

A public institution founded by **William T. Stead** in 1909 in London for free communication with "the beyond." Visitors were allowed to have three sittings with three different mediums to experience communication. Shorthand records were kept. For distant inquirers, psychometric readings were given. **Robert King, Alfred Vout Peters,** Mrs. Wesley Adams, J. J. Vango, and **Etta Wriedt** were employed as mediums. In its three years' existence about 1,300 sittings were given; running the bureau cost Stead about £1,500 a year.

The idea for the bureau was suggested to Stead in his own automatic scripts by the spirit of "Julia A. Ames," an American journalist, who was his constant communicator. In 1914 the work of Julia's Bureau was taken up by a new organization, the W. T. Stead **Borderland Library,** founded by Estelle W. Stead along the lines of other Spiritualist societies.

Jung, Carl Gustav (1875–1961)

Swiss psychologist who made the study of various occult ideas valid within the framework of psychology. Jung was born on July 26, 1875, at Kesswil, Thurgau, Switzerland. He studied medicine at the University of Basel, Switzerland, (1895–1900) and completed his M.D. at the University of Zürich (1902). While still a student he became fascinated with the occult, on which he read a number of books. He also attended several Spiritualist séances. Jung's first publication was an essay on the psychology and pathology of occult phenomena.

Jung became a physician and assisted Eugene Bleuler at the Burghölzi Mental Hospital in Zürich. In 1905 he joined the faculty at the University of Zürich; about the same time he became interested in the new psychoanalysis of **Sigmund Freud.** He became a leading student of Freud and in 1911 served as president of the International Psychoanalytic Society. In 1913, however, he went his own way as a result of what he regarded as Freud's overemphasis on sexual theories and opposition to occult ideas.

Jung's break with Freudian theory was marked by his paper "Symbols of the Libido," written in 1913. He resigned from the university that year, and for the next twenty years engaged in private practice, which allowed him to develop the approach he termed "analytic psychology." In his 1921 text *Psychological Types* he introduced his understanding of personality based on a set of polarities—introvert/extrovert, feeling/thinking, and sensation/intuition. Jung saw individual personality as determined by the balance or imbalance of these polarities.

Jung developed a view of the individual as consisting of a set of personality aspects he termed the *ego* (self-awareness), the *persona* (the expected social role played by each person), the *shadow* (a dark side), the *animus* (in a female) or *anima* (in a male) (the unconscious attitude toward the opposite sex), the *self* (soul or spirit), and the *unconscious.* He believed the development of a healthy personality, a process called "individuation," occurs as the various opposites in the personality are differentiated and then balanced.

Out of this basic understanding of the self several concepts of particular relevance to the modern occult community emerged. For example, Jung saw the unconscious as consisting of two layers—the personal unconscious and the collective unconscious. The collective unconscious, he said, is a deposit of archetypes or fundamental modes of apprehension that are common to all humanity because of the universality of certain underlying experiences. Archetypes manifest themselves in ancient (and not so ancient) myths, dreams, symbols, and artistic productions. One important appearance of archetypes is in the god forms of the ancient polytheistic religions. Thus one can speak of the archetype of the sky god or the mother goddess. Also from his concept of archetype, Jung speculated on the nature of flying saucers, about which he wrote a short book.

He also introduced the concept of **synchronicity,** connecting principle between events, as distinct from conventional cause and effect, an important idea in modern **astrology,** which has attempted to break out of its deterministic mode of conceptualizing the relationship between humans and the zodiac.

Jung returned to teaching in 1933 as a professor of psychology at the Federal Polytechnical University, Zürich (1933–41) and professor of medical psychology at the University of Basel (1943–44). He spent his last years as a consultant and lecturer at the C. G. Jung Institute (1948–61). His many writings wore compiled in *Collected Works* (1953).

Jung's perception covered every major area of human experience. His occult experiences are indicated in his book *VII Sermones ad Mortuoso,* published anonymously, which dramatizes Jung's journey into the unconscious. Some of his reminiscences are recorded in *Memories, Dreams, Reflections* (1963). He died June 6, 1961, at Kuessnacht, Zürich.

Sources:

Charet, F. X. *Spiritualism and the Foundations of C. G. Jung's Psychology.* Albany: State University of New York Press, 1993.

Franz, Marie-Louise von. *On Divination and Synchronicity: The Psychology of Meaningful Chance.* Toronto: Inner City Books, 1980.

Merkur, Daniel. *Gnosis: An Esoteric Tradition of Mystical Visions and Unions.* Albany: State University of New York Press, 1993.

Pleasants, Helene, ed. *Biographical Dictionary of Parapsychology.* New York: Helix Press, 1964.

Jung, Johann Heinrich (1740–1817)

German author and physician best known under his assumed name, Heinrich Stilling. He was professor of political economy at the University of Marburg, a contemporary of **Franz A. Mesmer,** and founder of a German spiritual school of cosmology. His book *Theorie der Geister-Kunde* (1808; English translation by S. Jackson as *Theory of Pneumatology,* 1834) contains a great number of authentic narratives of **apparitions** and similar phenomena. Jung also expounded the doctrine of a psychic body, based on the luminiferous ether.

According to Jung, **animal magnetism** undeniably proves that we have an inward man, a soul, constituted of the divine spark, the immortal spirit, possessing reason and will, and of a luminous body that is inseparable from it. Light, electricity, magnetic forces, galvanic matter, and ether appear to be all one and the same body under different modifications, according to Jung. This light substance, or ether, is the element that connects body and soul and the spiritual and material worlds. When the inward man—the human soul—forsakes the outward sphere, where the senses operate and merely continue the vital functions, the body falls into an entranced state, or a profound sleep, during which the soul acts more freely and powerfully. All its faculties are elevated.

The more the soul is divested of the body, the more extensive, free, and powerful is its inward sphere of operation, Jung said. It has, therefore, no need whatever of the body in order to live and exist. The body is rather a hindrance to it. The soul does not require the organs of sense—it can see, hear, smell, taste, and feel in a much more perfect state.

The boundless ether that fills the space of our solar system is the element in which spirits live and move, according to Jung. The atmosphere that surrounds our earth, down to its center, and particularly the night, is the abode of fallen angels and of human souls that die in an unconverted state.

Jung discouraged communications with the spirit world as sinful and dangerous. He considered **trance** a diseased condition. He believed implicitly in the efficacy of prayer and claimed psychic powers himself. More than ten weeks before the event, he predicted the tragic fate of Swiss writer Johann Kaspar Lavater, who was shot by a soldier in Zürich in 1801. The first part of Jung's autobiography (*Heinrich Stillings Jugend,* 1777) was published at the instigation of Goethe.

Sources:

Jung, Johann Heinrich. *Heinrich Stilling.* Translated by S. Jackson. 1835–36. 2nd ed. 1843. Abridged ed., edited by R. O. Moon. N.p., 1886.

Jürgenson, Friedrich (1903–1987)

Russian-born Swedish painter and film producer who first discovered the paranormal voice phenomenon that has since come to be known as **Raudive voices** or the **electronic voice phenomenon.** In July 1959 Jürgenson recorded the song of a Swedish finch on his tape recorder and on playback heard what appeared to be a human voice. He thought there must be some fault in the apparatus, but subsequent recordings contained an apparent message that seemed to be from his dead mother. Jürgenson mentioned his experiences in a book that made a deep impression on the Latvian psychologist **Konstantin Raudive.**

The two men conducted further research into paranormal voices on tape recordings, collaborating with other scientists between 1964 and 1969. The collaborators included **Hans Bender** of the University of Freiburg and Friedebert Karger of the Max Planck Institute in Munich.

After 1969 Jürgenson and Raudive had some differences of opinion and conducted their further research independently.

Raudive's research was extensive and included the collection and study of more than 100,000 recordings. Following publication of his book on the subject, translated into English as *Breakthrough: An Amazing Experiment in Electronic Communication with the Dead* (1971), the phenomenon became generally known and discussed as "Raudive voices," although more recently the term electronic voice phenomenon has become preferred by parapsychologists.

Essentially this phenomenon consists of paranormal voice communications (apparently from the dead) that are heard on recordings made on standard tape recorders, sometimes enhanced by a simple diode circuit. The voices are also apparent on the "white noise" of certain radio bands.

In view of traditional opposition to Spiritualist phenomena from the Catholic Church in the past, it is significant that the work of Jürgenson on paranormal voice recordings has been known to the Holy See since 1960, and according to Jürgenson the suggestion that these recordings are voices from the dead has been sympathetically considered. In 1969 Archbishop Dr. Bruno B. Heim presented Jürgenson to Pope Paul VI for investiture as commander of the Order of St. Gregory. This honor, however, was in respect of Jürgenson's work as a filmmaker.

After the initial discovery of the paranormal voice phenomenon through tape recordings of a bird song, some confusion was caused by the announcement that Raudive later investigated mediumistic messages conveyed by a budgerigar (parrot). Such bird voices may be related to the electronic voice phenomenon discovered by Jürgenson, but are basically of a different nature. Jürgenson died October 15, 1987, at his home in Hoor, Sweden, at age 84.

Sources:

Bander, Peter. *Voices from the Tapes.* New York: Drake Publishers, 1973.

Berger, Arthur S., and Joyce Berger. *The Encyclopedia of Parapsychology and Psychical Research.* New York: Paragon House, 1991.

Raudive, Konstantin. *Sprechfunk mit Vesterbenen.* Freiburg I Br., Germany: Herman Bauer, 1967. Translated as *Breakthrough: An Amazing Experiment in Electronic Communication with the Dead.* Gerrards Cross, U.K.: Colin Smythe; New York: Japlinger, 1971.

Juste, Michael

Pseudonym of poet and occultist **Michael Houghton,** an associate of **Aleister Crowley.**

Jyotir Maya Nanda, Swami (1931–)

Disciple of the late **Swami Sivananda** of Rishikesh, India, now president of **Yoga Research Foundation** of Miami, Florida. Jyotir Maya Nanda was born February 3, 1931, in Dumari Buzurg, District Saran, Bihar, India. He became a renunciate at age 22 and served as a religious professor at the Sivananda Ashram in Rishikesh for nine years. He lectured on yoga and Vedanta and also edited the journal *Yoga Vedanta.*

In 1962, at the invitation of Swami Lalitananda (formerly Leonora Rego), also a disciple of Swami Sivananda, Jyotir Maya Nanda moved to Puerto Rico to head the Hindu religious center, Sanatan Dharma Mandir. In 1969 he moved with Swami Lalitananda to Miami as head of the International Yoga Society, now re-formed as the Yoga Research Foundation. The foundation has issued a number of publications on yoga and Hindu philosophy, as well as tape recordings and study courses. Address: 6111 S.W. 74th Ave., Miami, FL 33143.

Sources:

Jyotir Maya Nanda, Swami. *The Way to Liberation.* Miami, Fla.: Swami Lalitananda, 1976.

———. *Yoga Can Change Your Life.* Miami, Fla.: International Yoga Society, 1975.

———. *Yoga in Life.* Miami, Fla.: The Author, 1973.

———. *Yoga Vasistha.* Miami, Fla.: Yoga Research Society, 1977.

K

Ka

The human **double** or **astral body** in ancient Egyptian belief. The ka was usually depicted as a birdlike duplicate of the deceased. Egyptologist Gaston Maspero defined it as "a kind of second copy of the body in matter less dense than the corporeal, a coloured though real projection of the individual, an exact reproduction of him in every part." The ka was believed to live in the tomb. Egyptians mummified the deceased's body and filled the tomb with provisions to prolong the life of the ka. If neglected the ka was thought to come out of the tomb and haunt the guilty relatives.

The ka was not to be confused with the soul, called *ba* or *bai,* which was believed to abandon the material body and the double at the moment of death.

Sources:

Berger, Arthur S., and Joyce Berger. *The Encyclopedia of Parapsychology and Psychical Research.* New York: Paragon House, 1991.

Hornung, Erik. *Conceptions of God in Ancient Egypt.* Ithaca, N.Y.: Cornell University Press, 1982.

Kabala (or Kabbalah or Cabbalah or Cabbala or Cabala)

A Hebrew and Jewish system of **Gnosticism** or Theosophy. The word means "doctrines received from tradition." In ancient Hebrew literature the name was used to denote the entire body of religious writings, the Pentateuch excepted. It was only in the early Middle Ages that the mystical system known as Kabalism was designated by that name.

The Kabala deals with the nature of God and with the *sephiroth,* or divine emanations of angels and man. God, the *En Soph,* fills and contains the universe. As in Gnosticism, God is boundless, inconceivable, and distantly transcendent. In a certain mystical sense, God can be thought of as nonexistent or preexistent. To justify existence the deity had to become active and creative, and this was achieved through the medium of the ten sephiroth, intelligences that emanated from God like rays proceeding from a luminary.

The first sephiroth was the wish to become manifest, and this contained nine other intelligences or sephiroth, which again emanated one from the other—the second from the first, the third from the second, and so forth. These ten sephiroth were known as the "Crown," "Wisdom," "Intelligence," "Love," "Justice," "Beauty," "Firmness," "Splendor," "Foundation," and "Kingdom." From the junction of pairs of sephiroth other emanations were formed; thus from Wisdom and Intelligence proceeded Love or Justice and from Love and Justice, Beauty.

The sephiroth were also symbolic of primordial man and heavenly man, of which earthly man was the shadow. They formed three triads, representing intellectual, moral, and physical qualities: the first was Wisdom, Intelligence, and Crown; the second, Love, Justice, and Beauty; the third, Firmness, Splendor, and Foundation.

The whole was encircled or bound by Kingdom, the ninth sephiroth. Each of these triads symbolized a portion of the human frame: the first, the head; the second, the arms; the third, the legs. Although those sephiroth were emanations from God, they remained a portion of God, simply representing different aspects of the One Being.

Kabalistic cosmology posits the existence of four different worlds, each forming a sephirotic system of a decade of emanations generated thusly: from the world of emanations, or the heavenly man, came a direct emanation from the En Soph. From the emanation was produced the world of creation, or the *Briatic* world of pure nature, less spiritual than the world of the heavenly man. The angel Metatron inhabited the Briatic world and constituted a world of pure spirit. He governed the visible world and guided the revolutions of the planets. From the world of pure nature was created the world of formation or the *Yetziratic* world, the abode of angels.

Finally, from these three worlds emanate the world of action or matter, the dwelling of evil spirits. It is said to contain ten hells, each becoming lower until the depths of diabolical degradation are reached. The prince of this region is the evil spirit Samuel, the serpent spoken of in the book of Genesis, otherwise known as "the Beast."

The universe was incomplete, however, without the creation of man. The heavenly Adam (the tenth sephiroth) created the earthly Adam, each member of whose body corresponds to a part of the visible universe. The human form is said to be shaped according to the four letters that constitute the Jewish tetragrammaton: YHWH.

Souls preexist in the world of emanations, and are all destined to inhabit human bodies, according to the Kabala. Like the sephiroth from which it emanates, every soul has ten potencies, consisting of a trinity of triads—spirit, soul, and elemental soul, or *neptesh.* Each soul, before its entrance into the world, consists of male and female united into one being, but when it descends to earth, the two parts are separated and animate different bodies.

The destiny of the soul upon earth is to develop from the perfect germ implanted in it, which must ultimately return to En Soph. If the soul does not succeed in acquiring the experience for which it has been sent to earth, it must reinhabit the body three times so that it becomes duly purified. When all the souls in the world of the sephiroth have passed through this period of probation and returned to the bosom of En Soph, the Jubilee will begin. Even Satan will be restored to his angelic nature, and existence will be a Sabbath without end. The Kabala states that these esoteric doctrines are contained in the Hebrew Scriptures but cannot be perceived by the uninitiated; they are, however, plainly revealed to persons of spiritual mind.

The Kabala is sometimes regarded as occult literature, and it has been stated that the philosophical doctrines developed in its pages have been perpetuated by a secret of oral tradition from the first ages of humanity. As British Hebrew and biblical scholar Christian D. Ginsburg notes (1863):

"The Kabala was first taught by God Himself to a select company of angels, who formed a theosophic school in Paradise. After the Fall the angels most graciously communicated this heavenly doctrine to the disobedient child of earth, to furnish the protoplasts with the means of returning to their pristine nobility and felicity. From Adam it passed over to Noah, and then to Abraham, the friend of God, who emigrated with it to Egypt, where the patriarch allowed a portion of this mysterious doctrine to ooze out. It was in this way that the Egyptians obtained some knowledge of it, and the other Eastern nations could introduce it into their philosophical systems. Moses, who was learned in all the wisdom of Egypt, w[as] first initiated into the Kabala in the land of his birth, but became most proficient in it during his wanderings in the wilderness, when he not only devoted to it the leisure hours of the whole forty years, but received lessons in it from one of the angels. By the aid of this mysterious science the lawgiver was enabled to solve the difficulties which arose during his management of the Israelites, in spite of the pilgrimages, wars, and frequent miseries of the nation. He covertly laid down the principles of this secret doctrine in the first four books of the Pentateuch, but withheld them from Deuteronomy. . . . Moses also initiated the seventy Elders into the secrets of this doctrine, and they again transmitted them from hand to hand. Of all who formed the unbroken line of tradition, David and Solomon were most deeply initiated into the Kabala. No one, however, dared to write it down till Simon Ben Jochai, who lived at the time of the destruction of the second Temple. . . . After his death, his son, Rabbi Eliezer, and his secretary, Rabbi Abba, as well as his disciples, collated Rabbi Simon Ben Jochai's treatises, and out of these composed the celebrated work called *Sohar,* i.e., Splendor which is the grand storehouse of Kabalism."

This legendary account of kabalistic origins, however, has found little support from historians. The mysticism of the Mishna and the Talmud, the older Hebrew literature, must be carefully distinguished from that of the kabalistic writings.

At the time of the Protestant Reformation in the sixteenth century, the Kabala found an audience among Protestant biblical scholars who turned to the Hebrew text for their biblical translations. From writers such as Johannes Reuchlin, Old Testament professor at Wittenburg, a Christian Kabala (usually spelled Cabala or Qabala) developed and was passed into non-Jewish occult circles.

Non-Jewish occultism and magic became deeply indebted to kabalistic combinations of the divine names for the terms of its rituals, deriving from the Kabala the belief in a resident virtue in sacred names and numbers. Certain rules were employed to discover the sublime source of power resident in the Jewish scriptures. Thus the words of several verses in the Scriptures that were regarded as containing an occult meaning were placed over each other and the letters were formed into new words by reading them vertically. Often the words of the text were arranged in squares so they could be read vertically or otherwise.

Words were joined together and redivided, and the initial and final letters of certain words were formed into separate words. Every letter of the word was reduced to its numerical value, and the word was explained by another of the same value. Every letter of a word was also taken to be an initial of an abbreviation of that word. The 22 letters of the alphabet were divided into two halves, one half placed above the other, and the two letters that thus became associated were interchanged. Thus *a* became *l, b* became *m,* and so on. This cipher alphabet was called *albm,* from the first interchanged pairs. The commutation of the 22 letters was effected by the last letter of the alphabet taking the place of the first, the next-to-last the place of the second, and so forth. This cipher was called *atbah.* These permutations and combinations are much older than the Kabala and were recognized by Jewish mystics from time immemorial.

During the nineteenth century a revival of magic—based in large part upon the Kabala and the identification of the 22 letters of the Hebrew alphabet with the tarot—occurred in France, primarily around **Eliphas Lévi.** From Lévi a new appreciation of the Kabala passed to the magicians of the Hermetic Order of the **Golden Dawn** and through it to **Aleister Crowley,** a dominant practitioner of magic in the twentieth century. It would be difficult to think of modern magic without the Kabala and its related practices of **gematria** and path workings.

Within the Jewish community study of the Kabala revived in the eighteenth century with the development of the Hassidic movement under the leadership of the **Baal Shem Tov** (1700–1760). This form of Judaism was seen as a competitor by the orthodox Jews, who organized efforts to suppress it during the eighteenth and nineteenth centuries. **Hasidim** (Jewish mysticism) in Europe was largely wiped out during the Holocaust, but has survived in the United States and Israel. Some Jewish Kabalists have resented the Kabala being appropriated by non-Jewish occultists. Most, however, have participated in what has become an active dialogue with contemporary occultists. Jews and non-Jews alike, for example, appreciate the scholarship of Gershom Scholem, the greatest Kabala scholar of this century.

Sources:

Abelson, Joshua. *Jewish Mysticism: An Introduction to Kabbalah.* New York: Sepher-Hermon Press, 1981.

Achad, Frater [Charles S. Jones]. *The Anatomy of the Body of God: Being the Supreme Revelation of Cosmic Consciousness.* Chicago: Collegium ad Spiritum Sanctum, 1925. New York: Samuel Weiser, 1969.

Bension, Ariel. *The Zohar in Moslem and Christian Spain.* New York: Sepher-Hermon Press, 1932.

Berg, Phillip S. *Kabbalah for the Laymen.* New York: Research Center of Kabbalah, n.d.

Franck, Adolphe. *The Kabbalah.* New Hyde Park, N.Y.: University Books, 1967. Reprint, New York: Citadel, 1979.

Gaster, Moses. *The Origin of the Kabbalah.* New York: Gordon Press, 1976.

Halevi, Z'ev Ben Shimon. *An Introduction to the Cabala—Tree of Life.* New York: Samuel Weiser, 1972.

Kalisch, Isidor, trans. *Sepher Yezirah.* New York, 1877. Reprint, San Jose, Calif.: Rosicrucian Press, 1950. Reprint, N. Hollywood, Calif.: Symbols and Signs, n.d.

Lévi, Éliphas. *The Book of Splendors.* New York: Samuel Weiser, 1973.

Luzzatto, Moses. *General Principles of the Kabbalah.* New York: Research Center of Kabbalah, 1970.

Meltzer, David, ed. *The Secret Garden: An Anthology of the Kabbalah.* New York: Seabury Press, 1976.

Pick, Bernhard. *The Cabala.* LaSalle, Ill.: Open Court Publishing, 1903.

Rauchlen, Johannes. *On the Art of the Kabbalah.* Translated by Martin Goodman and Sarah Goodman. New York: Abaris Books, 1983.

Scholem, Gershom. *Kabbalah.* New York: Quadrangle, 1974.

———. *On the Kabbalah and Its Symbolism.* New York: Schocken, 1960.

———, ed. *Zohar—The Book of Splendor: Basic Readings from the Kabbalah.* New York: Schocken, 1963.

Sperling, Harry, and Maurice Simon, trans. *The Zohar.* 5 vols. New York: Rebecca Bennet Publishing, n.d.

Waite, Arthur E. *The Holy Kabbalah.* New Hyde Park, N.Y.: University Books, 1960. New York: Citadel, 1976.

Kabbalist, The (Journal)

Quarterly journal of the International Order of Kabbalists, devoted to study of Hebrew mysticism and related subjects. Address: 25 Circle Gardens, Merton Pk., London, SW 19 3JX, England.

Kabir (ca. 1440–1518)

One of the most celebrated mystics of fifteenth- to sixteenth-century India, who practiced **yoga** and attempted to reconcile Hindus and Moslems. After his death he was claimed by both religions. Kabir's inspirational hymns are very moving and are still popular in present-day India. Kabir was a contemporary of Guru Nanak, who founded the Sikh religion.

Sources:

Hedayetullah, Muhammed. *Kabir: The Apostle of Hindu-Muslim Unity*. Delhi, India: Motilal Banarsidass, 1977.

Kabir. *One Hundred Poems of Kabir*. Translated by Rabinadrath Tagore. London, 1915.

Kay, Frank E. *Kabir and His Followers*. London, 1931.

Lorenzen, David N. *Kabir Legendas and Ananta-das's Kabir Parachai*. Albany, N.Y.: State University of New York Press, 1991.

Westcott, G. H. *Kabir and the Kabir Panth*. Calcutta: Varanasi Bhartiya Publishing House, 1974.

Kaboutermannekens

According to the folklore of Flemish peasants, these are little spirits that play tricks on country women, particularly on those who work in the dairy. In this respect they are similar to the **fairies** of other folklore.

Kaempffert, Waldemar B(ernhard) (1877–1956)

Editor and writer associated with pioneer psychical researchers. He was born in New York City on September 23, 1877. He attended the City College of New York (B.S., 1897) and New York University (LL.B., 1903). Kaempffert was a friend of **James H. Hyslop** and **Walter Franklin Prince** and believed that psychical research could help people learn more about themselves from physical, psychological, and philosophical viewpoints.

As science editor of the *New York Times* from 1927 to 1928 and from 1931 to 1956, Kaempffert's favorable reports on the work of **J. B. Rhine** and other parapsychologists helped to spread public awareness of research in parapsychology and its implications. He died November 27, 1956, in New York.

Sources:

Allison, L. W. "In Memory of Waldemar B. Kaempffert." *Journal* of the American Society for Psychical Research 51 (1957).

Berger, Arthur S., and Joyce Berger. *The Encyclopedia of Parapsychology and Psychical Research*. New York: Paragon House, 1991.

Kaempffert, Waldemar B. *Explorations in Science*. N.p., 1953.

———. *Invention and Society*. Chicago: American Library Association, 1930.

———. *Science Today and Tomorrow*. New York: Viking Press, 1945.

Pleasants, Helene, ed. *Biographical Dictionary of Parapsychology*. New York: Helix Press, 1964.

Kaf

According to Arabian tradition, a great mountain that stretches to the horizon on every side. The earth is in the middle of this mountain, like a finger in the middle of a ring. Its foundation is the stone Sakhrat, the least fragment of which is capable of working untold marvels. Sakhrat, made of a single emerald, is said to cause earthquakes. Kaf, which is frequently referred to in Eastern tales, is said to be the habitation of genii. To reach it one must pass through dark wildernesses, and it is essential that the traveler be guided by a supernatural being.

Kagyu Dharma

Group of centers founded in the United States by the late Venerable Kalu Rinpoche, concerned with the teaching and practice of Mahayana and Vajrayana Buddhism. Rinpoche is a teacher of the Kargyupa—one of several primary sects of Tibetan Buddhism—which is revered as the most esoteric of all of the branches of Buddhism. It absorbed Hindu tantric emhases. He studied at the Palpung Monastery in eastern Tibet.

In 1957 Rinpoche established a monastery in Bhutan and later founded his own center, Samdup Tarjeyling Monastery, at Sonada, Darjeeling, India. He trained monks to establish centers in the West and during the 1970s founded centers in Europe and the United States (New York, California, Oregon, Washington, Hawaii, and Alaska). There is also a center in British Columbia, Canada. North American headquarters is 127 Sheafe Rd., Wappinger Falls, NY 12590.

Kahn, Ludwig (ca. 1925)

German clairvoyant whose faculty of "lucidity" in reading sealed messages created a sensation in Paris in 1925. In 1925 and 1926 he appeared in Paris before the **Institut Métapsychique.** In the presence of a distinguished gathering of scientists, he held a **pellet reading** session during which he read the contents of 11 mixed pellets.

When his residence permit in France was expiring he went with a letter of introduction from **Charles Richet** to the commissioner of police. Richet, in the letter, argued that Kahn's stay in France was desirable from a scientific point of view, to which the commissioner replied that he would extend the permit if Kahn proved his lucidity to him. When Kahn convinced the commissioner of his powers he received the permit.

The literature concerning Kahn is summarized by E. J. Dingwall in an article in the 1926 *Journal* of the Society for Psychical Research.

Sources:

Osty, E. "Un Homme doué de connaissance paranormale: M. Ludwig Kahn." *Revue Métapsychique* (March–April, May–June, 1925).

Kahn, S. David (1929–)

Psychiatrist who wrote on experimental parapsychology. His interest in the psychic dated from his youth, his family having been friends of seer **Edgar Cayce.** Kahn was born on February 15, 1929, in New York City. He studied at Harvard University (B.A., 1950; M.D., 1954), during which time he made his first experiments in parapsychology, overcoming resistence from behaviorist B. F. Skinner. In the years immediately after his graduation he worked with **Eileen Garrett** and finally persuaded her to fund an experimental laboratory at her Parapsychology Foundation.

In 1960 Kahn was appointed senior psychiatrist at Montefiore Hospital, New York. He continued writing about parapsychology into the 1980s. He became a member of the **Parapsychology Association** and served on the board of the **American Society for Psychical Research** for many years until he retired in 1988.

Sources:

Kahn, S. David. "Ave Atque Vale: Gardner Murphy." *Journal* of the American Society for Psychical Research 74 (1980).

———. "The Enigma of Psi: A Challenge for Scientific Method." *Journal* of the American Society for Psychical Research (July 1962).

———. "Extrasensory Perception and Friendly Interpersonal Relations." In *Explorations in Altruistic Love and Behavior*, edited by Pitirim A. Sorokin. N.p., 1950.

———. "A Mechanical Scoring Technique for Testing GESP [General Extrasensory Perception]." *Journal of Parapsychology* 13, no. 3 (1949).

———. "Studies in Extrasensory Perception: Experiments Utilizing an Electronic Scoring Device." *Proceedings* of the American Society for Psychical Research 25 (October 1952).

Pleasants, Helene, ed. *Biographical Dictionary of Parapsychology*. New York: Helix Press, 1964.

Pratt, J. G. "A Review of Kahn's 'Studies in Extrasensory Perception.'" *Journal of Parapsychology* 17 (1953).

Kai

King Arthur's seneschal, known of in the French romances as Messire Queux, or Maitre Queux or Kuex. He is prominent in Malory's *Le Morte d' Arthur*. In the tale of Kilhwch and Olwen in the *Mabinogion,* he is identified as a person whose "breath lasted nine nights and days under water" and who "could exist nine nights and nine days without sleep." A wound from his sword could not be cured; he could make himself as tall as the highest tree; and so great was his body temperature that during rain whatever he carried remained dry. Originally a rain and thunder god, he apparently degenerated through a series of mythological processes into a mere folk hero.

Kaiser, A. W. (1876– ?)

American **direct voice** medium of Detroit, Michigan, through whom "Blackfoot" and "Leota," both Native Americans, and "Dr. Jenkins," spoke as his chief controls. Some messages received through Kaiser were purportedly from the spirits of Sir Isaac Newton and from psychical researcher **Richard Hodgson,** who had died in 1905. Kaiser did not go into trance. Vice-Admiral W. Usborne Moore sat with Kaiser in Detroit in 1909 and in 1911. Moore described Kaiser as "an honest, manly young fellow . . . good to the poor, and admits many without payment." He commented, "There is not a doubt in my mind that Mr. Kaiser is a true psychic."

Sources:

Moore, W. Usborne. *Glimpses of the Next State.* N.p., 1911.

Kaivalyadhama S.M.Y.M. Samhiti

Indian center for the medical and scientific study of **hatha yoga,** established in 1924 by **Swami Kuvalayananda** for scientific and philosophico-literary research, training, and treatment in yoga.

The center has been officially recognized as a research institute by the government of Bombay. It publishes the journal **Yoga-Mimamsa** and maintains an extensive library of some twenty-one thousand volumes. Address: Yoga Mimamsa Office, Lonavla (C.R.), India 410 403.

Sources:

Kuvalayananda, Swami. *Popular Yoga Asanas.* Rutland, Vt.: C. E. Tuttle, 1972.

Kalari

An ancient Indian system of **martial arts** that appears to predate the systems of China and Japan. It includes all kinds of barehanded and weapons techniques. It is said to have been taught by the sage Agasthiya some two thousand years ago and has been kept alive by the traditional method of personal instruction from teacher to pupil. It is thought that kalari may be even older in origin, brought from the Middle East by Buddhist monks to India, China, and Japan through trade routes, where it was an essential safeguard against the dangers of such travel.

In kalari the pupil learns warm-up exercises rather like **yoga** postures, but active rather than static. Some of the postures and movements of kalari are also paralleled in Bharata Natyam, the ancient system of Indian dance. Kalari is also associated with the healing techniques called *marma,* involving specialized techniques of massage with the feet and the use of aromatic vegetable oils (see also **aromatherapy**). (Marma is concerned with pressure points in the body and is also part of the deadly barehanded martial art in which a blow to various vital points can cause serious injury or death.)

The kalari system is regarded as a religious exercise and is taught with rituals associated with gods and goddesses.

Kalé, Shrikrishna Vasudeo (1924–)

Psychologist actively concerned with parapsychology. Kalé was born on April 10, 1924, in Poona, India. He studied at the University of Bombay (B.A., 1944; M.A., 1947) and Columbia University, New York (M.A., 1950; Ph.D., 1953). In 1959 Kalé became a reader in psychology at the University of Bombay. He has written widely on psychology and has a continuing interest in parapsychology.

Sources:

Kalé, Shrikrishna Vasudeo. "Parapsychology and Science." *Indian Journal of Parapsychology* 1, no. 2 (1959).

———. "Parapsychology and Science." *Indian Journal of Parapsychology* 2, no. 1 (1961).

Pleasants, Helene, ed. *Biographical Dictionary of Parapsychology.* New York: Helix Press, 1964.

Kale Thaungto

A town of wizards in Lower Burma.

Kali Yuga

The "Iron Age" of Hindu mythology. Hindu mythology posits four ages of the world: the Krita Yuga (Golden Age of Truth), lasting 4,800 years of the gods; the Treta Yuga (Silver Age), 3,600 years of the gods; the Dwapara Yuga, 2,400 years of the gods; and the Kali Yuga (Iron or Evil Age), 1,200 years of the gods.

Since a year of the gods equals 360 years of men, the extent of Kali Yuga is said to be 432,000 years; it would have begun in 540 B.C.E. During the Kali Yuga righteousness has diminished by three-quarters, and the age is one of devolution, culminating in the destruction of the world prior to a new creation and another Krita Yuga in an endless cycle of time.

Kammerdiener, Franklin Leslie, Jr. (1932–)

Director of the Parapsychology Laboratory at Wayland Baptist College, Plainview, Texas. Kammerdiener was born on September 1, 1932, in Oklahoma City, Oklahoma. He studied at Oklahoma Baptist University (B.S., 1954); Southwestern Baptist Theological Seminary, Fort Worth, Texas (B.D., 1957; M.Th., 1959); and Stephen F. Austin State College, Nacogdoches, Texas (M.A., 1960). In 1960 Kammerdiener became an instructor in psychology at Wayland as well as director of the Parapsychology Laboratory. He was responsible for evaluation of experiments in telepathy involving objects of various shapes.

Sources:

Pleasants, Helene, ed. *Biographical Dictionary of Parapsychology.* New York: Helix Press, 1964.

KAMPUCHEA

Known for many years as Cambodia and briefly (1970–1975) as the Kymer Republic, Kampuchea is a Southeast Asian country that has been particularly and negatively affected by the rush to modernize and secularize since World War II. It is a land rich in occult history and lore, a heritage at essential conflict with the recent course of political history. In the tremendous upheavals following the Vietnamese war, many customs, traditions, and beliefs have been disrupted. Although the 1976 constitution of Kampuchea granted freedom of worship to a people traditionally following the Theravada Buddhist faith, refugees report that religious practices are not permitted in the general political change to Marxist-Leninist ideology. The horrific excesses of the Khmer Rouge under the Pol Pot regime graphically dramatized in the film *The Killing Fields* (1984), represent one of the more horrific chapters in all of human history.

In the past, **magic** was mixed up to a surprising degree with the daily life of the people. They consulted sorcerers on the most trivial matters and were constantly at great pains to discover whether any small venture was likely to prove lucky or unlucky. There were two kinds of magical practitioners, the *à thmop,* or soothsayers, and the *kru* or medicine-sorcerers. Of these the latter enjoyed the highest reputation as healers and exorcists, while the former were less respected, dealing in charms and philters for the sake of gain, or in evil incantations and spells.

The outcast kru, however, could be ministers of destruction as well as of healing. One of the means used to take the life of an enemy was the old device favored by sorcerers. They would make a wax figure of the victim, prick it at the spot where they wished to harm him or her, and thus bring disease and death upon the individual. Another plan was to take two skulls from which the tops had been removed, place them against each other, and secretly place them under the bed of a healthy man, where they were believed to have very evil results. Sometimes by means of spells the kru would transform wood shavings or grains of rice into a large beetle or worms, which were said to enter the body of the victim and cause illness, or even death. If the person thus attacked happened to possess the friendship of a more powerful sorcerer, however, a stronger magic could be obtained, and the original sorcery blocked. The more harmless occupations of the wizards consisted in making philters and **amulets** to insure the admiration of women, the favor of the king, and success at play.

The evil spirits, to whom were ascribed the most malicious intent, were called *pray,* the most fearsome variety being the *khmoc pray,* or wicked dead, which included the spirits of women who died in childbirth. From their hiding places in the trees these spirits were said to torment inoffensive passers-by with their hideous laughter, and shower stones down upon them. These practices were, of course, calculated either to kill or to drive the unfortunate recipients of their attentions insane. Among the trees there were also supposed to be concealed mischievous demons who inflicted terrible and incurable diseases upon mankind.

Those who suffered a violent death were also greatly to be feared. From the nethermost regions they would return, pale and terrible, to demand food from human beings, who dared not deny it to them. Their name, *beisac,* signifies "goblin," and they were believed to have the power to inflict all manner of evil on those who refused their request. So the average Kampuchean, to avert such happenings, used to put his offering of rice or other food in the brushwood to appease the goblins. The pray generally required to have their offerings laid on the winnowing fan that enters so largely into Kampuchean superstition.

The **werewolf,** both male and female, struck terror into the hearts of the people. By the use of certain magical rites and formulae, people could be endowed with supernatural powers, such as the ability to swallow dishes, and thereupon change into werewolves. Women who had been rubbed with oil a wizard had consecrated were said to lose their reason and to flee away to the woods. They retained their human shape for seven days. If during that time a man underwent the same process of being rubbed with consecrated oil, followed the woman to the woods, and struck her on the head with a heavy bar, then the Kampucheans claimed she would recover her reason and return home. If, on the other hand, no such drastic remedy was to be found, at the end of seven days the woman would turn into a tigress. In order to cure a man of being a werewolf, one should strike him on the shoulder with a hook.

The Kampucheans believed that **ghosts** issued from dead bodies during the process of decomposition. When this ceased the ghosts were no longer seen, and the remains changed into owls and other nocturnal birds.

Most hideous of all the evil spirits were the *srei ap,* or ghouls, who, represented only by head and alimentary canal, prowled nightly in search of gruesome orgies. They were known by their terrible and bloodshot eyes, and much feared, since even their wish to harm could inflict injury. When anyone was denounced as a ghoul she was treated with great severity, either by the authorities, who may have sentenced her to banishment or death, or by the villagers, who sometimes took the law into their own hands and punished the supposed offender.

Astrology was also widely practiced in Kampuchea. Astrologers, or, as they were called, *horas,* were attached to the court, and their direct employment by the king gave them some standing in the country. At the beginning of each year they made a calendar, which contained, besides the usual astronomical information, weather and other predictions. They were consulted by the people on all sorts of subjects, and were believed to be able to avert the calamities they predicted.

It is not surprising that in such a country, where good and evil powers were ascribed so lavishly, much attention should be paid to omens, and much time spent in rites to avert misfortune. The wind, the fog, and the trees were objects of fear and awe, to be approached with circumspection lest they send disease and misfortune, or withhold some good. For instance, trees whose roots grow under a house bring bad luck to it. Bamboo and cotton plant were also dangerous when planted near a house, for should they grow higher than the house, they would wish, out of a perverted sense of gratitude, to provide a funeral cushion and matting for the occupants.

Animals received their share of superstitious veneration. Tigers were regarded as malevolent creatures whose whiskers were very poisonous. Elephants were seen as sacred, and particularly so white elephants. Monkeys they would on no account destroy. Should a butterfly enter the house, it was considered extremely unlucky, while a grasshopper, on the contrary, indicated coming good fortune.

Kane, Elisha Kent (1820–1857)

Arctic explorer and husband of Margaret Fox, one of the **Fox sisters,** who pioneered American **Spiritualism.** Kane attended the University of Virginia and the University of Pennsylvania Medical School. In 1843 he was commissioned assistant surgeon in the U.S. Navy. He served two years in India and served with the marines in Mexico (1847–48). In 1850 he was assigned to accompany an Arctic expedition to search for the lost John Franklin expedition. In 1853 Kane set out on the trip that gave him some degree of fame. He sailed into the Arctic on a ship that became icebound. He and the crew made friends with the Eskimos and learned much of their culture. Abandoning the ship, they marched across land to a Danish settlement in the south of Greenland, arriving in 1855.

Kane met Fox soon after his return from Greenland. They were married in a simple ceremony in 1856. Kane's health had been broken by his Arctic experience and he died the next year. His relatives refused to accept the marriage or Margaret's claim to Kane's estate. In 1865 Margaret published a volume, *The Love-Life of Dr. Kane,* which contained his correspondence to her.

Kane did not believe in spirits, but there was nothing in his letters to suggest that he discovered **fraud** on Margaret's part. On the contrary, in a letter to her sister Kate he writes: "Take my advice and never talk of the spirits either to friends or strangers. You know that with my intimacy with Maggie after a whole month's trial I could make nothing of them. Therefore they are a great mystery." A lively controversy arose, however, about the meaning of his accusations against Margaret for "living in deceit and hypocrisy."

In another letter he writes: "I can't bear the thought of your sitting in the dark, squeezing other peoples hands. I touch no hand but yours; press no lips but yours; think of no thoughts that I would not share with you; and do no deeds that I would conceal from you."

Sources:

Baird, George W. *Great American Masons.* Kila, Mont.: Kessinger Publishing, 1992.

Fornell, Earl L. *The Unhappy Medium: Spiritualism and the Life of Margaret Fox.* Austin, Tex., 1964.

Kane, Margaret Fox. *The Love-Life of Dr. Kane.* New York, 1865.

Kant, Immanuel (1724–1804)

German philosopher who anticipated the modern pictographic conception of apparitions in his analysis of the experiences of **Emanuel Swedenborg** in *Dreams of a Spirit-Seer*

(1766). He was impressed with Swedenborg's attempts, with some seeming success, to communicate with the deceased brother of the wife of the king of Sweden. In his book, written several years later, Kant explores the possibility of the existence of disembodied spirits and their ability to communicate with humans: "Departed souls and pure spirits . . . can still act upon the soul of man. . . . For the ideas they excite in the soul clothe themselves according to the law of fantasy in allied imagery and create outside the seer the apparition of the objects to which they are appropriate."

Kant did not distinguish between veridical and objective apparitions and after some perfunctory speculation laid the subject aside.

In *Dreams of a Spirit-Seer* Kant expresses admiration for some of Swedenborg's insights, although he questions the seer's sanity and pokes fun at some of his more extravagant claims. He later acknowledges, albeit grudgingly, an affinity between his philosophy and Swedenborg's: "The system of Swedenborg is unfortunately very similar to my own philosophy. It is not impossible that my rational views may be considered absurd because of that affinity. As to the offensive comparison I declare we must either suppose greater intelligence and truth at the basis of Swedenborg's writings than the first impression excites, or that it is a mere accident when he coincides with my system."

Sources:

Berger, Arthur S., and Joyce Berger. *The Encyclopedia of Parapsychology and Psychical Research.* New York: Paragon House, 1991.

Broad, C. D. "Immanuel Kant and Psychical Research." *Proceedings* of the Society for Psychical Research 49 (1950).

Kant, Immanuel. *Träume eines Geistersehers erläutert durch die Träume der Metaphysik.* 1766. Translated as *Dreams of a Spirit-Seer.* N.p., 1900.

Kapila (ca. sixth century B.C.E.)

Celebrated Hindu sage and founder of the Sankya school of philosophy. He is believed by some Hindus to be the god Vishnu in the fifth of his 24 incarnations.

The Sankya system seeks to explain the creation of the phenomenal universe and the part played by spirit and matter (*purusha* and *prakriti*) and to harmonize rational analysis and the religious authority of the Vedas. It is the oldest of the Hindu philosophical systems and is regarded as the cornerstone of Hindu philosophy. The **yoga** system popularized in the *Yoga Sutras* of the sage Patanjali (ca. 200 B.C.E.) is based on the Sankya system.

Sources:

Bahadur, Krishna Prakash. *The Wisdom of Saankhya.* New Delhi, India: Sterling, 1978.

Prabhupada, Swami A. C. Bhaktivedanta. *Teachings of Lord Kapila: The Son of Devahuti.* New York: Bhaktivedanta Book Trust, 1977.

Kappers, Jan (1914–)

Dutch physician who was active in the field of parapsychology. He was born on July 30, 1914, at Rotterdam, the Netherlands. He took his medical degree at the University of Leiden (M.D., 1938). After several years as a medical officer with the Netherlands army (1938–40) he entered private practice in Amsterdam. Kappers also devoted much of his spare time to psychical research. In 1955 he became a board member of the Foundation for the Investigation of Paranormal Healing, and in 1959 he became the research officer of the Amsterdam Foundation for Parapsychological Research. He also served as president of the Parapsychological Circle, Amsterdam. In 1959 Kappers set up the Amsterdam Foundation for Parapsychological Research in order to facilitate funding.

Kappers joined the board of the **Studievereniging voor Psychical Research** (the Dutch Society for Psychical Research) in 1958. He participated in a heated controversy regarding the organization's autocratic president. He and others left the society in 1960 and Kappers became the first president of the **Nederlandse Vereniging voor Parapsychologie.**

Kappers was associated with **Arie Mak,** F. van der Berg and A. H. de Jong in investigating clairvoyance with an apparatus devised by Mak. A report on this project was published in *Tijdschrift voor Parapsychologie* (1957). Kappers also undertook a statistical evaluation of astrological findings, an inquiry into spontaneous paranormal phenomena in Amsterdam, and a study of paranormal events among subjects using **hallucinogens.** He edited the bimonthly journal *Spiegel der Parpsychologie,* to which he also contributed articles.

Sources:

Kappers, Jan. "ESP Status in 1966." *International Journal of Neuropsychiatry* (September–October 1966).

———. "The Investigation of Spontaneous Cases." *Tijdschrift voor Parapsychologie* (1954).

———. "Is It Possible to Induce ESP with Psilocybine? An Exploratory Investigation." *International Journal of Neuropsychiatry* 2, no. 5 (1966).

Pleasants, Helene, ed. *Biographical Dictionary of Parapsychology.* New York: Helix Press, 1964.

Karadja, Princess Mary (Despina) (d. ca. 1935)

Swedish poet and writer on mystical themes. Although a member of the Swedish royal family, she spent many years in Britain. Karadja was the daughter of an eminent envoy to the Ottoman Empire based in London. She lived in London and later in Sussex and wrote several books, chiefly in English. She founded the White Cross Union and was president of the Universal Gnostic Alliance, founded in January 1912 to propagate *gnosis* (knowledge) of "the Great Spiritual Laws which rule the Universe, and thus promote the spiritual evolution of the human race."

Sources:

Karadja, Mary. *Esoteric Meaning of the Seven Sacraments.* N.p., 1910.

———. *Etincelles* (French epigrams). N.p., 1890.

———. *King Solomon: A Mystic Drama.* N.p., 1912.

———. *Towards the Light.* New York: Dodd, Mead, 1909.

Karagulla, Shafica (1914–ca. 1986)

Medical doctor and psychiatrist who took a special interest in psychic perception. Karagulla was born in Turkey into a Christian family. She was educated at the American School for Girls in Beirut, Lebanon; the American Junior College for Women, Beirut; and the American University of Beirut (M.D. and surgery degree, 1940). She went on to specialize in psychiatry in Scotland, where she took her residency at the Royal Edinburgh Hospital for Mental and Nervous Disorders. She was awarded the Walter Smith Kay Research Fellowship in Psychiatry and the Lawrence McLaren Bequest by the University of Edinburgh. During this period she reported unfavorably on the effect of the then-fashionable electric shock therapy. In 1948 she was awarded the D.P.M. by the Royal College of Physicians of Edinburgh, one of the highest medical qualifications in Britain.

In 1952 she visited the neurosurgeon Wilder Penfield at McGill University, Montreal, to discuss the investigation of hallucinations by electrode probes. Later she was associated as consultant psychiatrist with the work of Penfield on temporal lobe epilepsy and the study of hallucinations by electrical stimulation of the brain. In 1956 she moved to the United States as a practicing physician and joined the faculty of the State University of New York as an assistant professor in psychiatry. She also became an American citizen.

After reading the book *Edgar Cayce: Mystery Man of Miracles* (1961), by Joseph Millard, she became interested in psychic research and sought subjects with abilities similar to **Edgar Cayce**'s for study. She spent several years researching what she called "higher sense perception" and published her findings in the book *Breakthrough to Creativity* (1967). Her book was warmly received in university circles. She moved to Beverly Hills, California, and founded the Higher Sense Perception Research Foundation. With her associate Viola P. Neal she taught courses in higher sense perception at the University College of Los Angeles. Karagulla developed an affinity for theosophical teachings and a special interest in the psychic ability of theosophical leader **Dora Van Gelder.** Karagulla died March 12, 1986.

Sources:

Bolen, J. G. "Interview: Shafica Karagulla." *Psychic* 4, no. 6 (1973).

Karagulla, Shafica. *Breakthrough to Creativity: Your Higher Sense Perception.* Santa Monica, Calif.: DeVorss, 1967.

Kardec, Allan (1804–1869)

The father of **Spiritism,** the French variation of **Spiritualism** distinguished primarily by its acceptance of **reincarnation.** Kardec's birth name was Hypolyte Léon Denizard Rivail. The pseudonym originated in mediumistic communications. Both Allan and Kardec were said to have been his names in previous incarnations. He was born on October 3, 1804, at Lyon and studied at Yverdun, Switzerland, eventually becoming a doctor of medicine.

The story of his first investigations into spirit manifestations is somewhat obscure. *Le Livre des Esprits* (The Spirits' Book), which expounds a new theory of human life and destiny, was published in 1856. According to an article by **Alexander Aksakof** in *The Spiritualist* in 1875, the book was based on trance communications received through Celina Bequet, a professional somnambulist. For family reasons she took the name Celina Japhet and, controlled by the spirits of her grandfather, M. Hahnemann, and **Franz Mesmer,** gave out medical advice under this name. In her automatic scripts the spirits communicated the doctrine of reincarnation.

In 1857 *Le Livre des Esprits* was issued in a revised form and later was published in more than 20 editions. It became the recognized textbook of Spiritistic philosophy in France. It has been translated into many different languages and has had an enormous influence in Brazil, where Kardec has been commemorated on postage stamps.

Spiritism differs from Spiritualism in that it is built on the main tenet that spiritual progress is effected by a series of compulsory reincarnations. Kardec became so dogmatic on this point that he always disparaged physical mediumship in which the objective phenomena did not bear out his doctrine. He encouraged **automatic writing,** where there was less danger of contradiction stemming from the psychological influence of preconceived ideas. As a consequence, experimental psychical research was retarded for many years in France.

Several French physical mediums were never mentioned in *La Revue Spirite,* the monthly magazine Kardec founded in 1858. Nor did the Society of Psychologic Studies, of which he was president, devote attention to them. **C. Brédif,** a heralded physical medium, acquired celebrity only in St. Petersburg. Kardec even ignored the important mediumship of **D. D. Home** after the medium declared himself to be against reincarnation. Kardec died March 31, 1869, in Paris.

In England, **Anna Blackwell** was the most prominent exponent of Kardec's philosophy. She translated his books into English and helped get them published. In 1881 a three-volume work, *The Four Gospels,* about the esoteric aspect of the Gospels, was published in London.

Sources:

Kardec, Allan. *Le Ciel et L'Enfer ou la justice divine selon le Spiritisme.* 1865. Translated as *Heaven and Hell, or the Divine Justice Vindicated in the Plurality of Existences.* N.p., 1878.

———. *Collection of Selected Prayers.* New York: Stadium, 1975.

———. *L'Evangile selon le Spiritisme.* 1864. Translated as *The Gospel According to Spiritism.* London: Headquarters Publishing, 1987.

———. *Le Livre des Mediums.* Translated by Emma E. Wood as *The Book of Mediums.* Reprint, New York: Samuel Weiser, 1970.

———. *The Spirits' Book.* Translated by Anna Blackwell. Reprint, São Paulo, Brazil: Livraria Allan Kardec Editora, 1972.

Karma

A doctrine common to Hinduism, Buddhism, and Theosophy, although not wholly adopted by Theosophists as taught in the other two religions. The word *karma* itself means "action," but implies both action and reaction. All actions have consequences, some immediate, some delayed, others in future incarnations, according to Eastern beliefs. Thus individuals bear responsibility for all their actions and cannot escape the consequences, although bad actions can be expiated by good ones.

Action is not homogeneous, but on the contrary contains three elements: the thought, which conceives the action; the will, which finds the means of accomplishment; and the union of thought and will, which brings the action to pass. It is plain, therefore, that thought has potential for good or evil, for as the thought is, so will the action be. The miser, thinking of avarice, is avaricious; the libertine, thinking of vice, is vicious; and, conversely, one thinking of virtuous thoughts shows virtue in his or her actions.

Arising naturally from such teaching is the attention devoted to thought power. Using the analogy of the physical body, which can be developed by regimen and training based on natural scientific laws, Theosophists teach that character, in a similar way, can be scientifically built up by exercising the mind.

Every vice is considered evidence of lack of a corresponding virtue—avarice, for instance, shows the absence of generosity. Instead of accepting that an individual is naturally avaricious, Theosophists teach that constant thought focused on generosity will in time change the individual's nature in that respect. The length of time necessary for change depends on at least two factors: the strength of thought and the strength of the vice; the vice may be the sum of the indulgence of many ages and therefore difficult to eradicate.

The doctrine of karma, therefore, must be considered not in relation to one life only, but with an understanding of reincarnation. In traditional Hinduism individuals were seen as immersed in a world of illusion, called *maya.* In this world, distracted from the real world of spirit, one performs acts, and those actions create karma—consequences. In traditional teaching the goal of life was to escape karma. There was little difference between good and bad karma. Karma kept one trapped in the world of illusion.

During the nineteenth century, Western notions of **evolution of life** and the moral order were influenced by Indian teachings. Some began to place significance upon good karma as a means of overcoming bad karma. The goal gradually became the gaining of good karma, rather than escape. Such an approach to reincarnation and karma became popular in Theosophy and **Spiritism,** a form of **Spiritualism.**

According to this view, reincarnation is carried on under the laws of karma and evolution. The newborn baby bears within it the seeds of former lives. His or her character is the same as it was in past existences, and so it will continue unless the individual changes it, which he or she has the power to do. Each succeeding existence finds that character stronger in one direction or another. If it is evil the effort to change it becomes increasingly difficult; indeed a complete change may not be possible until many lifetimes of effort have passed.

In cases such as these, temptation may be too strong to resist, yet the individual who has knowledge of the workings of karma will yield to evil only after a desperate struggle; thus, instead of increasing the power of the evil, he helps to destroy its potency.

Only in the most rare cases can an individual free himself with a single effort.

Sources:

Abhedananda, Swami. *Doctrine of Karma: A Study in the Philosophy and Practice of Work.* Calcutta: Ramakrishna Vedanta Math, 1965.

Carus, Paul. *Karma: A Study of Buddhist Ethics.* La Salle, Ill.: Open Court, 1894.

Glasenapp, Helmuth von. *The Doctrine of Kerman in Jain Philosophy.* Bombay: Bai Vojibai Jivanial Panalal Charity Fund, 1942.

Hanson, Virginia, ed. *Karma: The Universal Law of Harmony.* Wheaton, Ill.: Theosophical Publishing House, 1975.

Jast, L. Stanley. *Reincarnation and Karma.* Secaucus, N.J.: Castle Books, 1955.

Reichenbach, Bruce R. *The Law of Karma: A Philosophical Study.* London: Macmillan, 1990.

Sharma, I. C. *Cayce, Karma and Reincarnation.* Wheaton, Ill.: Theosophical Publishing House, 1975.

Silananda, U. *An Introduction to the Law of Karma.* Berkeley, Calif.: Dharmachakka Meditation Center, 1990.

Woodward, Mary Ann. *Edgar Cayce's Story of Karma.* New York: Coward-McCann, 1971.

Kat, Willem (1902–)

Dutch psychiatrist and neurologist who was active in the field of parapsychology. He was born on June 13, 1902, at Medemblick, the Netherlands. Kat studied at the University of Amsterdam and then spent many years on the teaching staff of the biochemical laboratory at Amsterdam University, eventually becoming head of the laboratory.

He investigated unorthodox healing. A member of the **Studievereniging voor Psychical Research** (the Dutch Society for Psychical Research) and the Netherlands Committee for the Study of Unorthodox Healing and Its Social Consequences, he contributed articles on parapsychology to *Tijdschrift voor Parapsychologie.*

Sources:

Pleasants, Helene, ed. *Biographical Dictionary of Parapsychology.* New York: Helix Press, 1964.

Katean Secret Society

A secret society of the Moluccas, or Spice Islands, of the Malay archipelago. Anyone who wished to become a member was introduced into the Katean house through an aperture in the form of a crocodile's jaws or a cassowary's beak. After remaining there for a few days, he was secretly removed to a remote spot. At the end of two months he was permitted to return to his relatives—theretofore unaware of his whereabouts—as a member of the Katean Society.

Kathari See Cathari

"Katie King" See "King, Katie"

Katika Lima

Malay system of **astrology.**

Katika Tujo

Malay system of **astrology.**

Kauks

Fabulous bird said to be hatched from a **cock**'s egg.

Keel, John A(lva) (1930–)

Conjuring magician and writer on the subjects of magic, mysteries, and **UFOs.** Keel was born in Hornell, New York, on March 25, 1930, the son of Harry Eli Kiehle, a musician. From an early age he was interested in magic tricks and idolized the great **Houdini.** After the divorce of his parents he lived with his grandparents until age ten, then returned to his mother and stepfather, working on their farm near Perry, New York. At Perry High School he edited a mimeographed one-sheet journal called *The Jester.* At age 14 he edited a column in the local weekly paper, the *Perry Herald,* using the name John A. Keel. Meanwhile he studied at Perry Public Library and planned to be a professional writer.

In 1947 he left home, hitchhiking to New York, where he earned a meager living as a writer in Greenwich Village for four years before being drafted during the Korean War. Later, while quartered in West Germany, Keel contributed to the Armed Forces Network and was responsible for a Halloween broadcast from Frankenstein Castle, which started a monster scare similar to the scare caused by Orson Welles's famous radio broadcast about a Martian invasion in 1938.

Several years later he produced another Halloween broadcast from the Great Pyramid of Giza in Egypt. Attracted by the mystery of the East, he resigned from the Armed Forces Network and, at age 24, started a series of adventurous world travels, hoping to write his way around the world, earning a living as a journalist.

Keel's travels in search of mysteries took him from Egypt to India and Tibet, searching out mystics, **fakirs,** lamas, and magicians. In India he discovered the secrets of snake charming, being buried alive, walking on water, the basket trick, and the **Indian rope trick,** as well as other feats of **Jadoo,** or conjuring illusion.

However, he also admitted there were mysteries that were not tricks. In Darjeeling he met Sherpa Tensing Norgay, hero of the Everest expeditions, who talked about the *Yeti,* or Abominable Snowman. Keel went on to Sikkim, where he saw what he believed to be the Yeti's footprints and heard the creature's strange cry. All these adventures are recounted in his entertaining book *Jadoo* (1957).

Keel came out of obscurity at the beginning of the 1970s when his series of books on UFOs and Forteana (see **Fort, Charles**) began to appear. He wrote articles both for UFO periodicals and the popular men's magazines of the period, such as *Saga* and *True.* He considered as source material many stories that were generally dismissed because they were so strange.

After a flurry of writing, Keel faded from the scene in the late 1970s but reappeared with a new book in 1988 and also became a columnist for *Fate* magazine.

Sources:

Keel, John A. *Disneyland of the Gods.* New York: Amok Press, 1988.

———. *The Eighth Tower.* New York: New American Library, 1975.

———. *The Mothman Prophecies.* New York: Saturday Review Press, 1975.

———. *Our Haunted Planet.* Greenwich, Conn.: Fawcett Gold Medal, 1977.

———. *UFOs: Operation Trojan Horse.* New York: G. P. Putnam's Sons, 1970.

———. *Why UFOs?* New York: Manor Books, 1978.

Keeler, Pierre L. O. A.

American **slate-writing** medium who sat for physical phenomena before the **Seybert Commission** in 1885. The committee did not find the phenomena unexplainable by normal means and came to no definite conclusion except that it could "dismiss the theory of a spiritual origin of the hand behind Mr. Keeler's screen."

Alfred Russel Wallace describes in his book *My Life* (2 vols., 1905) some remarkable sittings with the medium in 1886 in the company of Elliott Coues, one General Lippitt, and a Mr. D. Lyman. In good light Wallace examined the enclosed space, the curtain, the floor, and the walls. After various telekinetic demonstrations, a hand appeared above the curtain, the fingers moving excitedly. Wallace narrates:

"This was the signal for a pencil and a pad of notepaper, then rapid writing was heard, a slip of paper was torn off and thrown over the curtain, sometimes two or three in rapid succession, in the direction of certain sitters. The director of the séance picked them up, read the name signed, and asked if anyone knew it, and when claimed it was handed to him. In this way a dozen or more of the chance visitors received messages which were always intelligible to me and often strikingly appropriate. . . . On my second visit a very sceptical friend went with us and seeing the writing pad on the piano marked several of the sheets with his initials. The medium was very angry and said that it would spoil the séance. However, he was calmed by his friends. When it came to the writing the pad was given to me, over the top of the curtain, to hold. I held it just above the medium's shoulder, when a hand and pencil came through the curtain and wrote on the pad as I held it."

At another séance, according to Wallace,

". . . most wonderful physical manifestations occurred. A stick was pushed through the curtain. Two watches were handed to me through the curtain, and were claimed by the two persons who sat by the medium. The small tambourine, about ten inches in diameter, was pushed through the curtain and fell on the floor. These objects came through different parts of the curtain, but left no holes as could be seen at the time, and was proved by a close examination afterwards. More marvelous still (if that be possible) a waistcoat was handed to me over the curtain, which proved to be the medium's, though his coat was left on and his hands had been held by his companion all the time; also about a score of people looking on all the time in a well-lighted room. These things seem impossible, but they are nevertheless facts."

Later in his career Keeler concentrated solely on slate writing, which he combined with **pellet reading.** A. B. Richmond, in his book *What I Saw at Cassadaga Lake* (1888), describes a sitting in which Keeler received an answer to a pellet inside a pair of locked slates, the key to which was in his pocket.

Admiral Osborne Moore, in his book *Glimpses of the Next State* (1911), writes of a successful séance in which, on five slates, 474 words were written and two pictures drawn in a period not exceeding ten minutes. The letters signed by names on the pellets were very commonplace. They contained no proof of identity. Still, Moore believed that the sitting was a striking exhibition of spirit power because there was full light and the slates were held above the table with no cloth or covering of any sort over them. He knew the reports of past slate writing through **William Eglinton, S. T. Davey,** and others, and said he thought that no explanation he had read was applicable to Keeler's case.

Hereward Carrington, during his investigations in the **Lily Dale** camp in August 1907, came to a different conclusion. He admitted that Keeler's slate writings were the most puzzling phenomena of their kind he had ever witnessed, but, as pointed out in his report (*Proceedings* of the American Society for Psychical Research, vol. 2), there was sufficient evidence of **fraud.** In the *Journal* of the American Society for Psychical Research (July 1908) an instance is mentioned in which Keeler was seen writing on a slate held on his lap under the table.

Carrington also stated that **Richard Hodgson,** Henry Ridgely Evans, **David P. Abbott,** and others thought that Keeler was a clever trickster, yet he said he did not wish to be dogmatic on the point since he was unable to explain many stories told to him by apparently good observers. Carrington reported only on his own sittings, saying that both the slate writing and **direct voice** were certainly fraudulent.

Keeler was also exposed by **Walter F. Prince** in 1921. In retrospect it seems doubtless that Keeler's phenomena—like those of so many other exponents of slate writing—were fraudulent.

Sources:

Prince, Walter F. "A Survey of American Slate Writing Mediumship." *Proceedings* of the American Society for Psychical Research 15 (1921).

Keeler, William M.

American spirit photographer, brother of **Pierre L. O. A. Keeler,** also mentioned in the report of the **Seybert Commission.** No formal investigation took place because his terms ($300 for three sittings) and his conditions were considered unacceptable. Keeler was later exposed by **Walter F. Prince.** (See also **Spirit Photography**)

Sources:

Prince, Walter F. "Supplementary Report on the Keeler-Lee Photographs." *Proceedings* of the American Society for Psychical Research 12 (1919).

Keely, John (Ernst) Worrell (1837–1898)

Founder of the Keely Motor Company, formed to promote his inventions powered by energy claimed to be derived from "vibratory etheric force" or cosmic energy. Keely was born in Philadelphia on September 3, 1837, the son of a musician. He worked as a carpenter before developing his famous inventions. The Keely Motor Company was incorporated April 29, 1874. The company spent $60,000 on experimental work on Keely's first engine, called "the Multiplicator." The company attracted investment, which Keely spent on research, but he had no practical motor to show for the money.

In 1881 the managers threatened Keely with imprisonment if he did not disclose his secret. He did in fact spend a brief period in jail, but was befriended by Clara Sophia Bloomfield Moore, a Theosophist, who provided further funds for Keely's experiments and defended him from criticism. She wrote a stirring defense of his work: *Keely and His Discoveries* (1893).

In addition to the famous motor, Keely also demonstrated other devices, including a "compound disintegrator," a "musical ball," a "globe engine," a "pneumatic rocket gun," and a model airship, all powered by the same mysterious etheric force. He wrote articles purporting to explain this force, but they were shrouded in such resounding pseudotechnical jargon that they only deepened the mystery. For example, he spoke of "Vibro-Molecular, Vibro-Atomic, and Sympathetic Vibro-Etheric Forces as applied to induce Mechanical Rotation by Negative Sympathetic Attraction."

There was no doubt about the startling demonstrations of force given in his laboratory in Philadelphia, however, and many scientists, professors, and businessmen were greatly impressed.

After Keely's death on November 18, 1898, startling evidence of **fraud** was uncovered, and it has since been assumed that all his inventions were fraudulent. The real motive force seems to have been compressed air, concealed in cylinders in a secret basement and conveyed to each apparatus by thin hollow wires. In spite of these findings, many individuals even today believe that any fraud Keely committed may have been merely because of the intense pressure to show practical results and that there may have been some genuine basis to Keely's lifework. However, there is no evidence that Keely ever discovered a more powerful force than the inspired jargon of his theoretical expositions.

A similar mysterious motor was built by **John Murray Spear.**

Sources:

Moore, Clara Sophia Bloomfield. *Keely and His Discoveries.* London, 1893. Reprint, New Hyde Park, N.Y.: University Books, 1972.

Keely Motor

An invention of **John E. Worrell Keely** (1837–1898), who claimed that it was powered by "vibratory etheric force" or cosmic energy. The motor was developed from what was called a "Hydro-Pneumatic-Pulsating-Vacuo-Engine."

The Keely Motor Association was formed in 1873 with headquarters in New York, while Keely experimented in Philadelphia. It developed into the Keely Motor Company, incorporated the following year.

Keely gave startling test demonstrations of motor force and other inventions said to use a similar mysterious energy, and convinced many reputable individuals and investors that his discoveries were genuine. There was evidence of **fraud** after his death, however, and as a result of these disclosures the Keely Motor Company dissolved.

Sources:

Moore, Clara Sophia Bloomfield. *Keely and His Discoveries.* London, 1893. Reprint, New Hyde Park, N.Y.: University Books, 1972.

Keevan of the Curling Locks

In Irish mythology, Keevan, the lover of the **Danaan** maiden Cleena, went off to hunt in the woods, leaving Cleena to be abducted by the fairies.

Keil, H(erbert) H(ans) J(ürgen) (1930–)

Lecturer in psychology and active parapsychologist. Keil was born May 30, 1930, at Freiberg, Germany. He emigrated to Australia as a young man and studied at the University of Tasmania, Hobart, from which he earned his B.A. (1957), Dip. Ed. (1959), and B.A. hons. (1960).

After a year as a teaching fellow in psychology at the University of Tasmania (1960–61) Keil became a research fellow at the **Parapsychology Laboratory** of North Carolina's Duke University (1961–62). He later returned to the University of Tasmania as a lecturer in psychology and became an associate member of the **Parapsychological Association.**

His parapsychological investigations included studies of **psychokinesis** with improved controls and automated experimental paraphernalia. With **Montague Ullman** and **J. G. Pratt** he presented a critical evaluation of psychokinetic findings regarding the psychic **Nina Kulagina.** Keil later wrote a book about Pratt, with whom he worked on various occasions. He also published articles in the *Proceedings* of the Society for Psychical Research and the *Journal* of the American Society for Psychical Research.

Sources:

Berger, Arthur S., and Joyce Berger. *The Encyclopedia of Parapsychology and Psychical Research.* New York: Paragon House, 1991.

Keil, Jürgen. *Gaither Pratt: A Life for Parapsychology.* Jefferson, N.C.: McFarland, 1987.

Keil, Jürgen, and J. Gaither Pratt. "First Hand Observations of Nina S. Kulagina Suggestive of PK on Static Objects." *Journal* of the American Society for Psychical Research 67 (1973).

Keil, Jürgen, Montague Ullman, and J. Gaither Pratt. "Directly Observable Voluntary PK Effects." *Proceedings* of the Society for Psychical Research 56 (1976).

Pleasants, Helene, ed. *Biographical Dictionary of Parapsychology.* New York: Helix Press, 1964.

Keingala

The weatherwise mare of Asmund in the Icelandic saga of Grettir the Strong (ca. eleventh century). Asmund believed in her weather prophecies, and when he charged his second son, Grettir, with looking after the horses, he told Grettir to be guided by Keingala, who would always return to the stable before a storm. Because Keingala persisted in remaining on the cold hillside, grazing on the scanty grass until the lad was nearly frozen with cold, Grettir determined to make her return home regardless of the weather.

One morning, before turning out the horses, Grettir tore off a long strip of her skin from withers to flank. This made the mare soon seek her stable. When Keingala did the same thing the next day, no storm impending, Asmund himself let out the horses and discovered his son's cruel trick.

Kelpie, The

A water spirit of Scotland believed to haunt streams and torrents. Kelpies appear to have been mischievous and were often accused of stopping the waterwheels of mills and of swelling streams. The Kelpie's name was occasionally used to frighten unruly children, and it was believed that he devoured women. The Kelpie, taking the form of a horse, was also said to tempt travelers to mount him, then plunge them into deep water and drown them. An Irish version of the Kelpie is the Eac Visge. (See also **Phouka**)

Kelpius, Johannes (1673–1708)

Johannes Kelpius, the founder of the first occult group in North America, the Chapter of Perfection (also known as the Society of the Woman in the Wilderness), was born in a German community in Halwegen, Transylvania. He received a good education and at the age of 16 wrote a treatise on natural theology. He subsequently wrote several learned texts that eventually brought him to the attention of Johann Jacob Zimmerman, a scholar and Lutheran pietist leader. Pietism was a movement that grew within Lutheranism at a time when the state church emphasized the more formal aspects of worship and church life and tended to be aloof from the religious needs of individuals. Across Germany numerous informal groups developed, centering on prayer, singing, and encouragement in the spiritual life. While many of these groups were quite orthodox, others veered off into mysticism and occultism. Such was the group that gathered around Zimmerman, who wished to find a means of combining science (including **astrology**), Christian theology, and mystical occultism.

In the late 1680s, encouraged by increasing government disapproval of pietisim and by his own expectation of the imminent return of Christ, Zimmerman planned for his followers to migrate to the British American colonies. Pennsylvania was already the home of a number of German religious refugees. However, before the group could leave, Zimmerman died, and his successor, Kelpius, oversaw the migration of the small body to Germantown. They arrived in June 1694.

Kelpius secured land on Wissahikon Creek (now a park in Philadelphia), where they built a forty-foot cube, which became the all-male group's headquarters and home. Discovering the local children were without a school, he founded a school and became their teacher. He also set up an astrological laboratory where members of the chapter watched the heavens for astrological and other signs of Christ's coming. He developed tuberculosis in the harsh weather, but hoped for Christ to return before he died. Meanwhile, he and the brothers gained some income from providing various healing and occult services for the surrounding community.

When Christ did not appear, Kelpius grew increasingly disappointed, a condition not helped by his failing health. In bed during most of the winter of 1706–07, he composed his most substantive writing and the hymn "A Loving Moan of the Disconsolate Soul in the Morning Dawn." Kelpius finally succumbed to tuberculosis in 1708 at the age of 35. He was succeeded by Conrad Matthai. Because the hope for Christ's return was the only force that held the group together, as that hope died, the group disintegrated. Some of the men who stayed in the area continued as healers, astrologers, and occult practitioners and their presence gave rise to what became known as powwow, or hexing, the peculiar form of folk magic practiced in southeastern Pennesylvania.

Sources:

Sasche, Julius F. *The German Pietists of Provincial Pennsylvania.* Philadelphia, 1895.

Kenawell, William Wooding (1920–)

Assistant professor of history at Stroudsburg State College, East Stroudsburg, Pennsylvania, and writer on parapsychology. He was born on November 19, 1920, in Reedsville, Pennsylvania. He studied at Franklin and Marshall College, Lancaster (B.A., 1953), and Lehigh University, Bethlehem (M.A., 1955). After graduation he worked as a librarian at the Lehigh University library (1956–61) before taking his position at Stroudsburg.

Kenawell's major contribution to psychical studies came from a grant he received from the **Parapsychology Foundation,** for which he engaged in a study of the life of **Frederick Bligh Bond,** a British archaeologist who used automatic writing in connection with excavations at Glastonbury Abbey, England.

Sources:

Kenawell, William W. *The Quest at Glastonbury: A Biographical Study of Frederick Bligh Bond.* New York: Helix Press, 1965.

Pleasants, Helene, ed. *Biographical Dictionary of Parapsychology.* New York: Helix Press, 1964.

Kephalomancy (or Cephalomancy)

A method of **divination** that was practiced by interpreting various signs on the baked head of an ass. It was familiar to the Germans, and the Lombards substituted the head of a goat. The ancient diviners placed lighted carbon on an ass's head and pronounced the names of those who were suspected of any crime. If a crackling coincided with the utterance of a name, that person was believed to be guilty.

Kephu

A **vampire** of the Karen tribes of Burma.

Kepler, Johann (1571–1630)

Famous German mathematician, astronomer, and astrologer. He was born on December 27, 1571, at Weil in Württemberg and educated at a monastic school at Maulbrunn. He attended the University of Tübingen, where he studied philosophy, mathematics, theology, and astronomy. In 1593 he became professor of mathematics and morals at Gratz in Styria, where he also continued his astrological studies. He had an unhappy home life and was somewhat persecuted for his doctrines.

The famous Rudolphine tables, which he prepared with the astronomer Tycho de Brahe, were printed in 1626.

Some of Kepler's writings were influenced by occult and mystical concepts. In his work *De Harmonice Mundi* (1619) he expounded a system of celestial harmonies. His book *Somnium* (1634) was an early speculation about life on the moon. A discussion of Kepler's concept of archetypes appears in "The Influence of Archetypal Ideas on the Scientific Theories of Kepler" in the book *The Interpretation of Nature and the Psyche,* by C. G. Jung and W. Pauli (1955).

The laws of the courses of the planets, deduced by Kepler from observations made by Tycho, and known as "the three laws of Kepler," became the foundation of Newton's discoveries, as well as of the whole modern theory of the planets. His services in the cause of astronomy place him high among the distinguished people of science, and in 1808 a monument was erected to his memory at Ratisbon. Kepler's most important work is his *Astronomia nova, seu Physica Coelestis tradita Commentariis de Motibus Stellae Martis* (1609), which is still regarded as a classic by astronomers.

Kepler died November 15, 1630, at Ratisbon.

Kerheb

The priestly caste of ancient Egyptian scribes.

Kerner, Justinus (Andreas) (Christian) (1786–1862)

Noted German poet and physician, born on September 18, 1786, at Ludwigsburg, Würtemberg. Kerner studied medicine at Tübingen and practiced as a physician at Wildbad. In addition to books of poetry, he was the author of a remarkable record of supernormal phenomena and experiments in **animal magnetism** therapeutics: *Die Seherin von Prevorst, Eröffnungen über das innere Leben des Menschen und über das Hereinragen einer Geisterwelt in die Unsere* (1845). It is the story of **Frederica Hauffe,** "the Seeress of Prevorst," who arrived in Weinsberg in November 1826 and became Kerner's patient.

Hauffe was the picture of death, exhibited many frightful symptoms, and fell into trance every evening at seven o'clock. For a while Kerner ignored her somnambulant condition and declared that he was not going to take any notice of what she said in her sleep. He began treating her by homeopathic remedies.

The medicine was ineffective, and Hauffe was fast approaching death. In trance she prescribed for herself a gentle course of animal magnetism. Kerner at first wanted nothing to do with the treatment, but he finally became convinced of the extraordinary character of the case and began to study it in earnest.

His book, published in 1829, passed through three enlarged editions (1832, 1838, and 1846). Translated by Catherine Crowe, it was published in English in 1845 under the title *The Seeress of Prevorst; or, Openings-up into the Inner Life of Man, and Mergings of a Spirit World into the World of Matter.* In Germany the book caused a great sensation. Among those who inquired into the case of the Seeress of Prevorst were Kant, Schubert, Eschenmayer, Görres, Werner, and David Strauss.

A school of philosophy was built on the revelations of the seeress, and in 1831 Kerner established a periodical, *Blätter aus Prevorst; Originalien und Lesefrüchte für Freunde des innern Lebens* (Leaves from Prevorst; or, Original Literary Fruits for Lovers of the Inner Life). Its chief contributors were Eschenmayer, Frederik von Mayer of Frankfort, Gotthelf, Heinrich von Schubert, Guido Görres, and Franz von Baader. Twelve volumes were published; then in 1839 the periodical was superseded by *Magikon; Archive für Beobachtungen aus dem Gebiete der Geisterkunde und des magnetischen und magischen Lebens* (Magikon; or, Archives for Observations Concerning the Realms of the Spirit World and of Magnetic Life). It was published until 1853.

King Ludwig of Bavaria and the king of Württemberg bestowed pensions upon Kerner, while King Frederick William IV of Prussia expressed his admiration in 1848 by sending him the gold medal of art and science. King Ludwig made him the first knight of the newly instituted Maximilian Order of Science and Art.

Besides the *Seeress of Prevorst,* Kerner wrote a variety of additional volumes, including *Geschichte Zweier Somnambulen, nebst einiger andern Denkwürdigkieten aus dem Gebiete der Magischen Heilkunde und Psychologie* (The History of Two Somnambules, Together with Certain Notable Things from the Realms of Magical Cure and Psychology; 1824); *Geschichten Besessener neurer Zeit* (History of Modern Possession; 1834); *Nachricht von dem Vorkommen des Besesseins eines dämonisch-magnetischen Leidens und seiner schon im Alterthum bekannten Heilung durch magisch-magnetisches Einwirken* (News of the Appearance of Possession, Demoniacal-Magnetic Suffering and its Cure through Magnetic Treatment; 1836); *Eine Erscheinung aus dem Nachtgebiete der Natur, durch eine Reihe von Zeugen gerichtlich bestätigt* (An Appearance from the Night Realms of Nature, Proved Legally by a Series of Witnesses; 1836); *Die somnambülen Tische; Zur Geschichte und Erklärung dieser Erscheinung* (Somnambulic Tables; or, the History and Explanation of That Phenomenon; 1853); and *F. A. Mesmer aus Schwaben, Entdecker des thierischen Magnetimus* (F. A. Mesmer, the Discoverer of Animal Magnetism; 1856).

Kerner died February 21, 1862.

Sources:

Howitt-Watts, A. M. *The Pioneers of Spiritual Reformation.* London, 1883.

Reinhard, Aime. *Justinus Kerner und das Kernerhaus zu Weinsberg.* Tübingen, Germany, 1862.

Kether

The term in the **Kabala** for the number one. It means reason, the equilibrating power. Also a Hebrew occult name for one of the three essentials of God—reason.

Kettner, Frederick (d. 1957)

Founder of the Biosophical Institute and **Biosophy,** a system of spiritual self-education and self-improvement intended to create a world fellowship of peace-loving men and women who have overcome religious, national, racial, and social prejudice to work creatively for the growth of democracy and world peace.

Kettner was inspired by the writings of the philosopher Baruch Spinoza and became a leading authority on his teachings. He created the Institute for the Advancement of Cultural and Spiritual Values in cooperation with leading educators and thinkers in the United States and in 1935 inaugurated a movement to place a secretary of peace in every government. He toured the United States to lecture on his ideas. In 1936 the secretary of peace concept was partially endorsed by the Inter-American Peace Conference in Buenos Aires, where Kettner founded the Instituto Biosofico Argentino. He also founded the Biosophical Institute, which continues his teachings and which was warmly endorsed by Albert Einstein, who wrote, "Your group is the embodiment of that spirit which Spinoza served so passionately."

Key of Solomon the King (Clavicula Salomonis)

A **grimoire**—textbook on magic—of medieval origin. It is supposed to be the work of **Solomon,** but is manifestly of later origin and was probably written in either the fourteenth or fifteenth century. A number of manuscripts have survived. There are stories of a book of magic spells ascribed to Solomon as early as the first century C.E.; the historian Flavius Josephus stated that Eleazar the Jew exorcised devils with Solomon's book. Stories of a ring of Solomon's are also found in the *Arabian Nights.*

The *Key* is not an authentic Jewish work, since it contains ancient concepts that may date from earlier semitic or Babylonian times. It may have come to Europe through Gnostic channels and mixed with later kabalistic notions.

In its popular form, its chief use appears to be in finding treasure and performing magic rites with the purpose of interfering with the free will of others. The power of the **Divine Name** is much in evidence, but the work appears to combine elements of both white and **black magic.**

The *Lemegeton* (Lesser Key of Solomon) is much more noteworthy. Its earliest examples date from the seventeenth century, and it invokes the hierarchies of the abyss by legions and millions. It is divided into four parts that enable the operator to control the offices of all spirits.

The first part, *Göetia,* contains forms of conjuration for 72 demons with an account of their powers and offices; the second, *Theurgia Göetia,* deals with the spirits of the cardinal points, which are of mixed nature; the third, the *Pauline Art* (the significance of the name is unaccountable), deals with the angels of the hours of the day and night and with the signs of the zodiac; and the fourth, *Almadel,* enumerates four other choirs of spirits. The operator is required to live a pure life, and none of the conjurations may be applied to the injury of another.

Sources:

The Greater Key of Solomon. Translated by S. L. MacGregor Mathers. 1909. Reprint, Chicago: De Laurence, 1914. Reprint, London: Routledge & Kegan Paul, 1972.

The Lesser Key of Solomon/Göetia/The Book of Evil Spirits. Chicago: De Laurence, 1916.

Shah, Indres. *The Secret Love of Magic.* London: Frederick Muller, 1957. Reprint, London: Abacus, 1972.

Waite, Arthur E. *The Book of Ceremonial Magic.* New Hyde Park, N.Y.: University Books, 1961.

Keyhoe, Donald Edwards (1897–1988)

Prominent figure in early **UFO** controversies. Keyhoe was born on June 20, 1897, in Ottumwa, Iowa. He was a graduate of the U.S. Naval Academy (1919) and was commissioned a lieutenant in the marines. After an accident in 1922, he resigned from the marines. He held several jobs through the decade and emerged in 1928 as a successful freelance writer. Keyhoe returned to the marines during World War II and served with a naval aviation training division. He rose to the rank of major by the end of the war. He began writing about unidentified flying objects in 1949 when he was commissioned to write an article for *True,* a popular men's magazine. His article, "Flying Saucers are Real" (*True,* January 1950), caused a sensation with its claim that the U.S. Air Force was covering up evidence that proved flying saucers were real. He continued that theme in the three books that soon followed: *The Flying Saucers Are Real* (1950), *Flying Saucers From Outer Space* (1953), and *The Flying Saucer Conspiracy* (1955).

It was some years later that a memorandum discovered through the Freedom of Information Act revealed that Keyhoe was right about the air force's covering up its real investigation of UFOs with a public relations activity called Project Blue Book.

In 1956 Keyhoe founded **National Investigations Committee on Aerial Phenomena** (NICAP). Prominent military men and politicians on the board of governors included Senator Barry Goldwater. During his period of leadership in NICAP, Keyhoe wrote one more book, *Flying Saucers: Top Secret* (1960). He could not solve NICAP's persistent financial situation over the years, and after a stormy meeting in 1969 Keyhoe retired as director, although he remained on the board.

After he left NICAP Keyhoe wrote one last book, *Aliens From Space* (1973), in which he continued his cover-up theme but shifted primary responsibility to the CIA (Central Intelligence Agency). He served on the Mutual UFO Network board through the 1980s but was never really active in ufology again.

Keyhoe died November 29, 1988.

Sources:

Clark, Jerome. *The Emergence of a Phenomenon: UFOs from the Beginning through 1959.* Vol. 2 of *The UFO Encyclopedia.* Detroit: Omnigraphics, 1992.

Hall, Richard. "Major Donald E. Keyhoe: An Appreciation." *MUFON UFO Journal* (February 1989): 12–13.

Keyhoe, Donald E. *Aliens From Space: The Real Story of Unidentified Flying Objects.* Garden City, N.Y.: Doubleday, 1973.

———. *The Flying Saucer Conspiracy.* New York: Henry Holt, 1955.

———. *The Flying Saucers Are Real.* New York: Fawcett Publications, 1950.

———. *Flying Saucers From Outer Space.* New York: Henry Holt, 1953.

———. *Flying Saucers: Top Secret.* New York: G. P. Putnam's Sons, 1960.

Khaib

The ancient Egyptian name for the shadow, which at death was supposed to quit the body to continue a separate existence of its own.

Khérumian, Raphaël (1903–)

Painter and writer on parapsychological topics, born at Baku, Azerbaijan. He was a member of the board of directors of the **Institut Métapsychique International,** Paris, with special interest in the physiological mechanisms of telepathy and the moral implications of parapsychology. During the decade after World War II, Khérumian wrote a variety of articles for the *Revue Métapsychique* and one book, *Léonard de Vinci et les mystères* (Paris, 1952).

Sources:

Khérumian, Raphaël. "A propos de l'hypothèse cryptesthétique" (Regarding the Cryptesthetic Hypothesis). *Revue Métapsychique* 1, no. 2 (1955).

———. "Essai d'interprétation des expériences de Soal et Goldney" (Interpretative Essay on the Experiments of Soal and Goldney). *Revue Métapsychique* 8 (1949).

———. "Introduction à l'étude de la connaissance parapsychologique" (Introduction to the Study of Parapsychology Knowledge). *Revue Métapsychique* 1–3 (1948).

———. "Procédés mécaniques pour faciliter les transmissions télépathiques" (Mechanical Procedures to Facilitate Telepathic Messages). *Revue Métapsychique* 26 (1953).

———. "Les propriétés groupales des organismes et la parapsychologie" (The Group Properties of Organisms and Parapsychology). *Revue Métapsychique* 10 (1950).

———. "Réflexions sur l'état actuel et les perspectives de la parapsychologie" (Remarks on the Present Status and the Future of Parapsychology). *Revue Métapsychique* 2, nos. 8, 9 (1958–59).

Pleasants, Helene, ed. *Biographical Dictionary of Parapsychology.* New York: Helix Press, 1964.

Khu

The ancient Egyptian name for one of the immortal parts of man, probably the spirit. The word means "clear" or "luminous" and was symbolized by a flame.

Khunrath, Heinrich (1560–1605)

German alchemist and hierophant of the physical side of the *Magnum Opus.* Khunrath was certainly aware of the greater issues of Hermetic theorems and may be regarded as a follower of **Paracelsus.** Born in Saxony in 1560, Khunrath graduated in medicine from the University of Basle at age 28. He practiced in Hamburg and thereafter in Dresden. He died in poverty and obscurity in Leipzig in 1605 at age 45.

The most remarkable of his works, some of which are still in manuscript, is the *Anphitheatrum Sapientie! Eterne! solius vere, Christiano Kabbalisticum divino magicum.* This unfinished work appeared in 1602, although it is believed an earlier edition was printed in 1598. A 1609 edition contains a preface and conclusion by Khunrath's friend Erasmus Wohlfahrt. It is a mystical treatise based on the wisdom of **Solomon** describing the seven steps leading to universal knowledge. Khunrath's book has been interpreted as the voice of ancient chaos, and its folding plates are particularly odd.

Khunrath believed in the transmutation of stones and metals through **alchemy** and sought the **elixir of life.** The physician and chemist Conrad Khunrath (ca. 1594) may have been Heinrich Khunrath's brother.

Kian

In Irish mythology the father of Lugh (who was the father of the Ulster warrior-hero Cuchulain). Kian had a magic cow with a wonderful supply of milk. After the cow was stolen by Balor (king of the Fomorians), Kian took revenge by making Balor's daughter, Ethlinn, the mother of three sons. Two were drowned by Balor, and the third, Lugh, escaped by falling into a bay and being wafted back to his father, Kian.

Some years later while fighting in Ulster, Kian encountered the three sons of Turenn, whose house was at enmity with his. To escape their notice, he turned himself into a pig, but they recognized him and one of them wounded him. He begged to be allowed to restore himself to his human form before dying. This request was granted, and Kian rejoiced in having outwitted his enemies; they would have to pay the blood fine for a man instead of a pig. The brothers, determined that there should be no bloodstained weapon as evidence of the deed, stoned Kian and buried his body.

KIB Foundation See Koestler Foundation

Kidd, James (1879–ca. 1949)

American copper miner and prospector whose disappearance in 1949 led to the discovery of his will bequeathing nearly a quarter of a million dollars to "research or some scientific proof of a soul of the human body which leaves at death." As a result, there ensued what newspapers called "the Ghost Trial of the Century," in which at least 134 scientific researchers, organizations, and institutions filed a claim on the Kidd estate.

Kidd was something of a mystery man, a quiet, well-mannered, unobtrusive loner who lived in Phoenix, Arizona, and worked in the copper mines or prospected in the mountains. He vanished after undertaking a prospecting trip in the area of Superstition Mountain, claimed as the locale of the legendary Lost Dutchman gold mine. Kidd set out November 9, 1949, and his disappearance was not noticed until some weeks later. Routine inquiries ascertained that he was born July 18, 1879, in Ogdensburg, New York, and had lived in Reno, Nevada, and Los Angeles, California. He worked for the Miami Copper Company of Arizona, lived simply, and had few acquaintances.

By 1954 Kidd was officially registered as a missing person but no proof of death was established. It was not until 1957 that the contents of Kidd's unclaimed safe deposit box, including stock certificates, were delivered to the estate tax commissioner's office in Arizona. In January 1964 official examination of Kidd's papers disclosed assets totaling $174,065.69 and a will written in Phoenix, Arizona. It reads,

"This is my first and only will and is dated the second of January, 1946. I have no heirs and have not been married in my life and after all my funeral expenses have been paid and one hundred dollars to some preacher of the gospel to say fare well at my grave sell all my property which is all in cash and stocks with E. F. Hutton Co., Phoenix, some in safety deposit box, and have this balance money to go in a research or some scientific proof of a soul of the human body which leaves at death I think in time their can be a Photograph of soul leaving the human at death, James Kidd."

Even before the will was validated, the first claim to the estate came from the University of Life Church, Inc., Arizona, as an organization conducting research on scientific proof of the existence of a human soul. Meanwhile two Canadians, claiming to be blood brothers of Kidd, contested the will. By now, widespread press coverage had resulted in claims to the estate from a number of individuals and organizations, including the **Parapsychology Foundation,** the **Psychical Research Foundation,** and the Neurological Sciences Foundation of the University of Arizona College of Medicine.

On May 6, 1965, the Court of Maricopa County, Arizona, declared the will fully acceptable for probate. More petitions flooded into the court, some of them merely facetious and invalid, others from reputable organizations like the **American Society for Psychical Research.** The hearings were presided over by Judge Robert L. Myers of the Supreme Court of Maricopa County and occupied 90 days and some 800,000 words of testimony. Eventually a decision of October 20, 1967, awarded the Kidd funds to the Barrow Neurological Institute, Phoenix, Arizona.

After an appeal, the court's decision was overridden and the money was split between the American Society for Psychical Research (two-thirds share) and the Psychical Research Foundation (one-third share).

Sources:

Berger, Arthur S., and Joyce Berger. *The Encyclopedia of Parapsychology and Psychical Research.* New York: Paragon House, 1991.

Fuller, John G. *The Great Soul Trial.* New York: Macmillan, 1969.

Kilner, Walter J(ohn) (1847–1920)

British physician who first studied the phenomenon of the human **aura** and its changes in appearance during sickness and health. Kilner was born on May 23, 1847, at Bury St. Edmunds, Suffolk, England. He was educated at Bury St. Edmunds Grammar School and St. John's College, Cambridge University, and was a medical student at St. Thomas's Hospital, London. In June 1879 he took charge of electrotherapy at St. Thomas's Hospital. In 1883 he became a member of the Royal College of Physicians, then opened a private practice as a physician in Ladbroke Grove, London.

Kilner took a scientific interest in the aura, believed to be a kind of radiating luminous cloud surrounding individuals, usually perceived only by clairvoyants. Kilner's interest was inspired in part by the work of **Baron von Reichenbach,** who claimed to perceive auras around the poles of magnets and around human hands.

In 1908 Kilner said he believed that the human aura might be made visible if viewed through a suitable light filter. He experimented with dicyanin, a coal tar derivative, and after careful study reported his findings in his book *The Human Atmosphere* (1911). This book was the first to approach the study of the human aura as scientific fact instead of questionable psychic phenomenon. The revised edition of Kilner's book was published in 1920, and some medical men endorsed his findings, although the theories were very unconventional for his time. Kilner died later that year, on June 12.

After Kilner's death, his findings were endorsed by the experimenter Oscar Bagnall in his book *The Origin and Properties of the Human Aura* (1937). A special photographic technique has since been devised by which it is claimed that the aura can be reproduced.

Sources:

Berger, Arthur S., and Joyce Berger. *The Encyclopedia of Parapsychology and Psychical Research.* New York: Paragon House, 1991.

Kilner, Walter J. *The Human Atmosphere.* London, 1911. Reprinted as *The Human Aura.* New Hyde Park, N.Y.: University Books, 1965.

Kimmell, Susan C(randall) (1894– ?)

Public relations director who collaborated with **Stewart Edward White** on his channeled books. These include *Anchors to Windward* (1945), *The Stars Are Still There* (1946), *With Folded Wings* (1947), and *The Job of Living* (1948).

Born January 1, 1894, in Chicago, Crandall studied at the University of Minnesota (B.A., 1917). In 1924 she married Leslie Frederic Kimmell. From 1953 to 1962 she was director of public relations for the American Institute of Family Relations, Los Angeles.

King, Bruce (1897–1976)

A modern tycoon of **astrology** who used the pseudonym Zolar. Born in Chicago, King became an actor, stockbroker, and eventually part owner of a radio station in Los Angeles. The station had an astrologer named Kobar as general manager, and King was impressed with his financial success. In the same week that Kobar left the station to go to Hollywood, another astrologer demonstrated a dime-in-the-slot horoscope machine to King. The two men went into partnership in the Astrolograph Company, putting the machines in movie theaters.

King later conceived the idea of making horoscopes for chain stores and established a highly successful business. It was then that he took the pseudonym Zolar, derived from the word *zodiac* with echoes of "Kobar." He later sold approximately 100 million horoscopes and published a variety of popular books on astrology and occultism.

King died January 16, 1976.

Sources:

Zolar [Bruce King]. *Black Magic.* New York: Arco Publishing, 1972.

———. *Dreams and Your Horoscope.* New York: Zolar Publishing, 1970.

———. *The Encyclopedia of Ancient and Forbidden Knowledge.* Los Angeles: Nash, 1970.

———. *Fortune Telling with Cards, Palmistry.* New York: Arco Publishing, 1973.

———. *History of Astrology.* New York: Arco Publishing, 1972.

———. *It's All in the Stars.* New York: Zolar Publishing, 1962.

———. *Nature's Mysteries.* New York: Arco Publishing, 1972.

———. *Sex and the Zodiac.* New York: Zolar Publishing, 1971.

King, Cecil (Harmsworth) (1901–1987)

British newspaper tycoon who was sympathetic to **Spiritualism** and sponsored **psychical research.** King was born on February 20, 1901, in London and was educated at Christ Church, Oxford University. In 1951 he became chair of Daily Mirror Newspapers, Ltd. (1951–63), and then chairman of International Publishing Corporation, which included the *Daily Mirror* and some two hundred other papers and magazines, (1963–68). Through the 1960s he was also chair of Reed Paper Group (1963–68), a director of the Bank of England (1965–68), and chair of the Newspaper Proprietors Association (1961–68).

In addition to his newspaper and journalistic activities, King also wrote several books on history and current events. His second wife was Dame Ruth Railton, whom he married in 1962. She was a **medium,** and King publicly acknowledged her psychic gift at a meeting of the Royal Institution on the subject of **ESP** in 1969.

In 1964 readers of King's newspaper the *Daily Mirror* were invited to take part in a **telepathy** experiment. King donated a substantial sum of money to finance telepathy and **clairvoyance** experiments by three Oxford graduates who formed the Psycho-Physical Research Unit. He also provided funds for the **Society for Psychical Research,** London, which he and Dame Ruth joined in 1968. In 1970 he endorsed the phenomena of the musical medium **Rosemary Brown.**

In a speech at a *Psychic News* function in 1973, King stated: "It has seemed to me for many years that the only way out of the materialism of our society and our contempt for spiritual values will come from knowledge and wisdom in the general area covered by *Psychic News.* If we are to have a revival of religion—and this must come some day—it would seem that the work of Spiritualists may lead the way into realms of discovery ignored by ecclesiastical officialdom of today."

King was a guest of honor at a *Psychic News* dinner and dance in 1973, when he paid tribute to his wife's psychic gifts: "Her presence by my side is a constant reminder that there is more in heaven and Earth than atheists, skeptics, and some scientists suppose." King was not a Spiritualist and had never attended a **séance** but accepted the psychic gifts of his wife.

King had great affection for Ireland and the Irish people, and in 1974 he and his wife retired to Dublin. He died at his home in Dublin on April 17, 1987, at age 86. An obituary in the *Psychic News* (May 2, 1987) revealed that King had known the former editor, **Maurice Barbanell,** for some 40 years. King was quoted as saying, "We collaborated in our newspapers in reporting the psychic experiences of well-known mediums of the period, in particular **Estelle Roberts.**"

King, Francis (Xavier) (1904–)

Contemporary British author who also wrote or edited a number of important historical studies on **magic** and occultism, especially as related to **Aleister Crowley** and the **OTO** (Ordo Templi Orientis). King edited and published some of the secret ritual materials of the OTO and also made important contributions to such reference books as the *Encyclopedia of Mythology* and the *Encyclopedia of the Unexplained.*

Sources:

King, Francis. *Astral Projection, Ritual Magic, and Alchemy.* London, 1971.

———. *Magic: The Western Tradition.* London: Thames & Hudson, 1975.

———. *The Magical World of Aleister Crowley.* New York: Coward, McCann & Geoghegan, 1978.

———. *Ritual Magic in England: 1887 to the Present Day.* London, 1970. Reprinted as *The Rites of Modern Occult Magic.* New York: Macmillan, 1971.

———. *Satan and Swastika: The Occult and the Nazi Party.* London: Mayflower, 1976.

———. *Sexuality, Magic, and Perversion.* London, 1971. Reprint, New York: Citadel Press, 1972.

———. *Wisdom From Afar.* London: Aldus Books, 1975.

King, Francis, and Stephen Skinner. *Techniques of High Magic.* New York: Destiny Books, 1980.

King, Francis, and Isabel Sutherland. *The Rebirth of Magic.* London: Corgi, 1982.

King, Godfré Ray

Pseudonym of **Guy W. Ballard** (1878–1939), founder and leader of the **I Am Movement.** Under the name Godfré Ray King, Ballard wrote *Unveiled Mysteries* (1934), in which he reported meeting an ascended master, **Saint Germain,** who imparted the teachings of the I Am Movement. Ballard claimed that, "Each copy of this book carries with it the mighty Presence of the ascended Host, their radiation and sustaining power. The Masters have become a blazing outpouring of Light into which no discordant thought or feeling can enter."

"King, John"

One of the most romantic and frequently claimed spirit entities, manifesting at many Spiritualist séances of different mediums over many decades. He claimed that he had been Henry Owen Morgan, the famous buccaneer who was knighted by Charles II and appointed governor of Jamaica. **"Katie King," Florence Cook**'s control, claimed to be John King's daughter. John King first manifested with the **Davenport brothers** in 1850, his first **materialization** following the flash of a pistol fired by Ira Davenport in the dark. He remained as spirit manager with the Davenports throughout their career, and in **typtology** and **direct voice** he gave them sound advice during difficult times.

While faithfully serving the Davenport brothers, King took charge of the séances in the loghouse of **Jonathan Koons** in the wilds of Ohio. As the head of a band of 160 spirits, King claimed descent from a race of men known as "Adam," who had as leaders "the most ancient angels." They signed their communications "King No. 1," "No. 2," and so forth, and sometimes "Servant and Scholar of God." In his last incarnation King had strayed from the path of virtue and become a redoubtable pirate. He communicated in direct voice through a trumpet, his own invention, and through direct scripts. The tone of these writings was sanctimonious and upbraiding (e.g., "We know that our work will be rejected by many, and condemned as the production of their King Devil, whom they profess to repudiate, but do so constantly serve by crucifying truth and rejecting all that is contrary to their own narrow pride and vain imaginings.").

The *Telegraph Papers* of 1856 published a psychometric reading of the writing of John King by a Mrs. Kellog and a Miss Jay of New York, to whom the paper was handed in a sealed envelope. Kellog became entranced and said:

"A person of great might and power appears before me—a power unknown. I cannot compare him to anyone on earth. He wields a mighty weapon. I can neither describe nor explain the influence that emanates from him. I can only compare it to one of whom we read in the Bible. It seems like unto one who 'rules the world.' It does not seem to have been done by any human being. It does not seem to me that a mortal could have been employed even as the instrument for this writing. This is beyond human effort."

Jay gave a similar reading: "It must be a power so far exalted in the scale of development as to grasp the great laws that govern all material combinations. He does not seem to be of the Earth, but to belong to another race of beings, whose spiritual growth has continued for ages."

In the early years of British **Spiritualism** it was the aspiration of many mediums to secure the influence of John King. **Mary Marshall** was the first, **Agnes Guppy-Volckman, Georgina Houghton, Mrs. A. H. Firman, Charles Williams, William Eglinton,** and **Cecil Husk** followed. In the United States he was claimed by **Mr. and Mrs. Nelson Holmes** and **Helena Petrovna Blavatsky** during her early career as a Spiritualist. V. S. Solovyoff, in his book *A Modern Priestess of Isis* (1895), suggested that Blavatsky's Mahatma Koot Hoomi was John King transformed by Eastern garb.

On March 20, 1873, in a daylight séance conducted by Charles Williams, John King manifested so successfully that a sketch was made of him by an artist. A week later he appeared again in solid and material form. He was usually seen in the light of a peculiar lamp that he carried and that illuminated his face and sometimes the room. In Paris on May 14, 1874, a young man tried to seize him. John King eluded his grasp and left a piece of drapery behind. The medium was found entranced. He was searched, but no paraphernalia for deception was discovered.

In time John King took charge of the physical phenomena of **Etta Wriedt** in London. He greeted the sitters of Williams's and Cecil Husk's circle by their names. **W. T. Stead** once found a mislaid manuscript through communication in **automatic writing** from John King. "Feda," the control of **Gladys Osborne Leonard,** informed **H. Dennis Bradley** during a séance of his own that John King often helped with the voices and that the volume of King's voice was enormous.

Of all the public activities of John King, his association with **Eusapia Palladino** was the most remarkable. He said in many messages that Palladino was his reincarnated daughter. A curious story of his appearance in strong light is told by Chevalier Francesco Graus, an Italian engineer, in a letter to Vincent Cavalli. The letter was published in *Luce e Ombra* in April 1907. At the time of the narrative, Palladino worried herself ill over the theft of her jewels. She was so affected by the reproaches of the police inspector that she fainted. The table began to move and rapped out, "Save my daughter, she is mad." Graus later wrote of the incident:

"A minute later in full light, a phenomenon occurred which I shall never forget. On my left, in the space separating me from Mme. Palladino, appeared the form of an old man, tall, rather thin, with an abundant beard who, without speaking, laid the full palm of his right hand on my head, which he squeezed between his fingers as if to draw from it some vital fluid, and when he saw fit he raised his hand and spread over Eusapia's head the fluid he had withdrawn from my brain. He repeated this operation three times in succession, then the figure dissolved. Mme. Palladino immediately returned to her normal state. I remained for three consecutive days in such a condition of cerebral prostration, on account of the fluid that had been drawn from me, that I could not carry on the smallest intellectual work."

King and Morgan

The identification of John King with Henry Owen Morgan, the pirate, was investigated by **Sir Arthur Conan Doyle,** who had in his possession a contemporary picture of the buccaneer king. It bore no resemblance to the tall, swarthy man with a noble head and full black beard who presented himself in materialized form. But Doyle stated that a daughter of a recent governor of Jamaica was confronted in a séance in London by John King, who said to her, "You have brought back from Jamaica something which was mine." She asked, "What was it?" He answered, "My will." It was a fact. Her father had returned with the document.

Through Etta Wriedt at **Julia's Bureau** in London, John King gave many particulars in regard to his corporeal life in Jamaica and made beautiful bugle calls through the trumpet, saying that was how he used to call his men together in the old buccaneering days, one terrific blast being his signal to fight.

In February 1930 John King manifested in **Glen Hamilton**'s circle in Winnipeg, Canada, and carried on a dialogue with "Walter," who controlled another medium, feigning that they were aboard a pirate ship among a crew of ruffians. This playacting had a psychological purpose—the recovery of past memories and the imagining of a sailing ship that was afterward built out of **ectoplasm.**

The continued manifestation of John King with different mediums over a period of some 80 years raises a number of interesting questions. If the manifestations were genuine, why should a relatively unimportant individual dominate séance phenomena? Why should such a personality exist virtually unchanged for nearly a century? Was there so little progress in the spirit world? Or did the interest of mediums in a well-defined personality bring about conscious or unconscious **fraud?** Or was John King perhaps a fictitious personality like **"Philip,"** the experimental "ghost" created by members of the Toronto Society for Psychical Research?

Sources:

Berger, Arthur S., and Joyce Berger. *The Encyclopedia of Parapsychology and Psychical Research.* New York: Paragon House, 1991.

Medhurst, R. G., and K. M. Golney. "William Crookes and the Physical Phenomena of Mediumship." *Proceedings* of the Society for Psychical Research 54 (1964).

"King, Katie"

The famous spirit **control** of **Florence Cook.** Katie claimed to be the daughter of the equally famous spirit entity **"John King,"** but there is even less proof of her identity than of her father's.

Katie began to manifest in the Cook house when Florence was a girl of 15. She was seen almost daily, the first time in April 1872, showing a deathlike face between the séance curtains. Later her **materializations** became more perfect, but it was only after a year of experimental work that she could walk out of the **cabinet** and show herself in full view to the sitters.

She became a nearly permanent inhabitant of the Cook household, walked about the house, appeared at unexpected moments, and allegedly went to bed with the medium, much to Cook's annoyance. When Florence Cook married, complications arose. According to **Florence Marryat,** Captain Corner felt at first as if he had married two women and was not quite sure which one was his wife.

According to all accounts Katie was a beautiful girl. In his famous investigations of psychic phenomena, **Sir William Crookes** had 40 flashlight photographs of Katie. In most of them she noticeably resembled Cook, but Crookes had no doubt of her independent identity. He wrote:

"Photography was inadequate to depict the perfect beauty of Katie's face, as words are powerless to describe her charm of manner. Photography may, indeed, give a map of her countenance; but how can it reproduce the brilliant purity of her complexion, or the ever varying expression of her most mobile features, now overshadowed with sadness when relating some of the bitter experiences of her past life, now smiling with all the innocence of happy girlhood when she had collected my children round her, and was amusing them by recounting anecdotes of her adventures in India?"

Katie claimed that her name during her earthly existence was Annie Owen Morgan. She said she was about 12 years old when Charles I was beheaded. She married, had two children, and committed many crimes, murdering men with her own hands. She died quite young, at age 22 or 23. Katie said her attachment to Florence Cook served the purpose of convincing the world of the truth of **Spiritualism.** This work was given her on the other side as a service to expiate her earthly sins, she claimed. On her farewell appearance, after three years of constant manifestations, she declared that her years of suffering were now over; she would ascend to a higher sphere from which she could only correspond with her medium through **automatic writing** at long intervals, although Cook would be able to see her clairvoyantly.

In her early manifestations in the séances of the **Davenport brothers,** Katie King was apparently far less spiritual than at the time of the Crookes records. Robert Cooper, describing a **direct voice** consultation of the spirits by the Davenports, wrote:

"The next minute a shrill female voice was heard immediately in front of us. It was like that of a person of the lower walks of life and talked away, like many persons do, for the mere sake of talking. It was intimated that it was 'Kate' who was speaking. There was a great attempt on her part at being witty, but according to my ideas on such matters, most of what was said would come under the category of small—very small—wit."

In another passage he wrote:

"Unlike John, Kate will talk any length of time, as long in fact as she can find anything to talk about, even if it be the most frivolous nonsense; but I must do her the justice to say that she talks sensibly enough at times, and I have heard great wisdom in her utterances, and satisfactory answers given to profound philosophical questions."

The "Katie" who assisted "John King" in the séances of **Frank Herne** and **Charles Williams** was apparently not identifiable with Katie King, since the former—after the materialization of a black hand—was described as a descendant of an African. Her voice was like a whisper, but perfectly distinct. The transportation of **Agnes Guppy-Volckman** to Williams's room was put down to her achievement.

A rather dubious Katie King manifested through the mediumship of **Mr. and Mrs. Nelson Holmes,** of Philadelphia. Henry T. Child and **Robert Dale Owen** stated that they saw her materialize on May 12, 1874. Owen said he believed that she was identical to Cook's control, though her features differed from those in the photograph of the London Katie. The nose was straight, not aquiline, and the expression was more intellectual. Crookes, when he saw a photograph of the Philadelphia Katie, did not hesitate to declare her a **fraud.**

To justify her appearance in the United States, the Philadelphia Katie King declared, "Some of my English friends misinterpreted my parting words. I took final leave not of your Earth, but of dear Florrie Cook, because my continuance with her would have injured her health." This was a rather limp explanation that did not fit the fact that Cook, under the control of another spirit, "Marie," continued her materialization séances without injury to her health. On November 2, 1874, Owen reaffirmed his belief in the genuineness of the Katie King phenomena, but only a month later withdrew his assurances in the face of convincing evidence that he had been the victim of fraud. Child made a similar statement.

In October 1930 Katie King unexpectedly manifested in the circle of **Glen Hamilton** in Winnipeg, Canada. Photographs were taken. According to Hamilton,

"Obviously it was wholly impossible to say whether or not this Mary M.-Mercedes-Katie King is the same being as the entity appearing in the experiments of Crookes and others. We have the word of the controls in this case that it is so and we have seen how, so far, these controls have repeatedly established the fact that they know whereof they speak. . . . While there are, I may say, some points of similarity to be traced between Katie as photographed by Crookes and Katie as photographed in the Winnipeg experiments, both faces for instance being rather long in formation, the eyes in both being large and luminous, the angle of the jaw in both being rather pronounced, the later Katie is so much younger in appearance, her beauty so much more apparent that it is evident that we cannot use the earlier record of her presence in any way as conclusive proof that there is any connection between the two."

Meanwhile, serious doubts have been cast upon the Katie King phenomena of Florence Cook. In his book *The Spiritualists* (1962), **Trevor H. Hall** presents persuasive evidence that Crookes may have used the Katie King séances as a cover for an illicit love affair with Cook. More recently, Ray Stemman reported that Katie King materialized in Rome in July 1974 with the medium Fulvio Rendhell.

Sources:

Hall, Trevor. *The Spiritualists.* New York: Helix Press, 1963. Revised as *The Medium and the Scientist.* Buffalo, N.Y.: Prometheus Books, 1984.

Medhurst, R. G., and K. M. Golney. "William Crookes and the Physical Phenomena of Mediumship." *Proceedings* of the Society for Psychical Research 54 (1964).

Stemman, Roy. *Spirits and Spirit Worlds.* Garden City, N.Y.: Doubleday, 1975.

King, Robert (1869– ?)

British professional clairvoyant and lecturer in occult science. He sat for **Sir William Crookes,** with whom he was acquainted, worked with Theosophist **A. P. Sinnett,** with whom he served on the *Daily Mail* committee for the investigation of **psychic photography** in 1908, and served as chief psychic of **Julia's Bureau** from 1909 to 1913. King toured Europe as a lecturer. His particular psychic faculty was diagnosing cases in which emotions were related to physical disease. He prepared himself for the profession by studying biology, physiology, and chemistry. King was not a trance medium and reflected spirit messages in a perfectly still but fully conscious state.

King Robert of Sicily

English romance of unknown authorship, written during the fourteenth century. It tells the story of King Robert of Sicily, who was beguiled by pride into sneering at a priest saying mass. An angel is sent by God to punish him, and transforms the king into the likeness of his own fool, sent out to lie with the dogs. King Robert is allowed to resume his proper shape after a long and ignominious penance. The theme is an ancient one, with parallels in early Buddhist and Hindu tales. It was revived by the poet Longfellow in one of his *Tales of a Wayside Inn.*

Sources:

Baring-Gould, S. *Curiosities of Olden Times.* London: J. T. Hayes, 1869.

King's Evil

For centuries, the kings of England and France were credited with the ability to cure scrofula by touching the sufferer with their fingers, a **healing by touch** ritual known as "touching for the king's evil." Many thousands of subjects regularly assembled for this royal touch, and some English kings were credited with hundreds of cures. The custom seems to have arisen during the reign of Edward the Confessor as a result of a young woman's dream. It was discontinued in England during the Hanoverian period, when it was considered a papal gift.

Kingsford, Anna Bonus (1846–1888)

Founder of Esoteric Christianity, which combined insights from **Gnosticism,** the Sufis, and proponents of spiritual **alchemy.** She was born Anna Bonus at Stratford, Essex, England, September 16, 1846. Even as a child, she displayed unusual psychic gifts and claimed kinship with **fairies,** who were said to visit her during sleep. She told fortunes at school and seems to have been something of a seeress.

After her marriage in 1867 to the Reverend Algernon G. Kingsford, an Anglican clergyman, she edited a ladies' journal and conducted a feminist campaign with special emphasis on womanly attributes. She considered masculinity in women degrading. In 1870 she became a Roman Catholic, and ten years later took her medical degree in Paris.

About this time she discovered in **Edward Maitland** a "twin soul" for her mystical mission. Although platonic, their association resulted in some mischievous gossip. In fact the Maitland and Kingsford families were related by marriage. In 1884 Kingsford and Maitland founded the **Hermetic Society** in Britain for the study of mystical Christianity. While they were innovators in the field of mystical Christianity, their society was largely ineffectual. However, many of their inspired teachings were eventually included in the broad conspectus of Theosophy. Kingsford and Maitland placed a strong emphasis on vegetarianism and opposed experimentation on animals.

It was Kingsford who introduced the magician **S. L. MacGregor Mathers** to **Helena Petrovna Blavatsky.** Mathers sympathized with the campaign against vivisection, although his occult interests were wider than those of the **Theosophical Society.** He eventually became a leading figure in the Hermetic Order of the **Golden Dawn.**

Sources:

Kingsford, Anna Bonus. *Clothed with the Sun.* London: John M. Watkins, 1889.

Kingsford, Anna, and Edward Maitland. *The Perfect Way: or, The Finding of Christ.* London, 1882. Rev. ed. London, 1887. Reprint, Boston: Esoteric Book Company, 1988. Reprint, Mokelumne Hill, Calif.: Health Research, 1972.

———. *The Virgin of the World.* 1885. Reprint, Minneapolis, Minn.: Wizard's Bookshelf, 1977.

Maitland, Edward. *Anna Kingsford: Her Life, Letters, Diary.* London, 1896.

———. *The Story of Anna Kingsford and Edward Maitland and of the New Gospel of Interpretation.* Birmingham, England: Ruskin Press, 1905.

Kinocetus

A fabled precious stone said to be effective for casting out devils.

Kirby, Bernard C(romwell) (1907–)

Professor of sociology who conducted investigations in parapsychology. Kirby was born on October 9, 1907, in Indianapolis, Indiana. He attended Denison University, Granville, Ohio (B.A., 1929), and held various government positions through the 1930s and 1940s. In 1946 he became an instructor at Farragut (Idaho) College and Technical Institute (1946–48). He moved to Seattle to work on his master's degree at the University of Washington (M.A., 1950). While completing his Ph.D. (1953) he worked as an instructor at the University of Washington. In 1954 he joined the sociology and anthropology faculty at San Diego State College,

California. Kirby investigated the linkage effect in clairvoyance and conducted experiments in telepathy.

Sources:

Pleasants, Helene, ed. *Biographical Dictionary of Parapsychology.* New York: Helix Press, 1964.

Kirlian Aura

Although the human **aura** has long been considered a psychic phenomenon visible only to gifted sensitives, some scientists have maintained that the aura is an objective reality and that such a radiation around human beings varies in different states of the individual's health. During the nineteenth century **Karl von Reichenbach** spent many years attempting to verify the existence of the aura, although he was ridiculed by many of his colleagues. In Britain the physician **Walter J. Kilner** (1847–1920), who knew of Reichenbach's experiments, devised a method of making the aura visible through spectacle screens or goggles impregnated with the chemical dicyanin. His work was developed further by other experimenters, notably **Oscar Bagnall.**

Then in 1958 Semyon Davidovich and his wife, Valentina Khrisanova Kirlian, two Soviet scientists, described electrophotography, a photographic technique of converting the nonelectrical properties of an object into electrical properties recorded on photographic film. They spent some 13 years in painstaking research. Eventually their work was endorsed by Soviet authorities and a new laboratory was provided for them in Krasnodar in the Kuban region of Southern Russia. Their technique of photographing what has become generally known as the "Kirlian aura" became well known in the West during the 1970s.

The method was a modern development of a technique known as early as the 1890s but not formerly applied to the human aura. In 1898 a Russian engineer and electrical researcher named Yakov Narkevich-Todko had demonstrated "electrographic photos" by using high-voltage spark discharges. The modern development by the Kirlians was influenced by study of **acupuncture** after Viktor Adamenko, a Soviet physicist, demonstrated the "tobiscope," a device to detect the acupuncture points of the human body. Various Kirlian photography devices were marketed in the United States and Europe to record biological fields around human beings, animals, and even plants. One such device available in Europe was known as a "Verograph."

Intense examination of the paranormal claims for Kirlian photography has shown that most of the early effects reported can be attributed to lack of proper controls in the laboratory. During the 1980s, reports of Kirlian effects all but disappeared.

Sources:

Bagnall, Oscar. *The Origin and Properties of the Human Aura.* London, 1937. Rev. ed. New Hyde Park, N.Y.: University Books, 1970.

Berger, Arthur S., and Joyce Berger. *The Encyclopedia of Parapsychology and Psychical Research.* New York: Paragon House, 1991.

Davis, Mikol, and Earle Lune. *Rainbows of Life: The Promise of Kirlian Photography.* New York: Harper & Row, 1978.

Johnson, Kendall. *The Living Aura: Radiation Field Photography and the Kirlian Effect.* New York: Hawthorn Books, 1976.

Kilner, Walter J. *The Human Atmosphere.* London, 1911. Revised as *The Human Aura.* New Hyde Park, N.Y.: University Books, 1965.

Krippner, Stanley, and Daniel Rubin. *Galaxies of Life: The Human Aura in Acupuncture and Kirlian Photography.* Gordon & Breach, 1973. Reprinted as *The Kirlian Aura: Photographing the Galaxies of Life.* Garden City, N.Y.: Doubleday Anchor, 1974. Reprinted as *Energies of Consciousness.* New York: Interface, 1976.

Moss, Thelma. *The Body Electric: A Personal Journey into the Mysteries of Parapsychological Research, Bioenergy, and Kirlian Photography.* London: Granada, 1981.

Kischuph

In the **Kabala,** the higher magical influence. It was divide into two branches, an elementary and a spiritual, and include exorcism. Sometimes Kischuph exhibited a striking resemblanc to the **witchcraft** of medieval times. Sorcerers were said to chang themselves into animals and travel long distances in a very sho time. They might also induce pain, disease, and death in me and animals.

Further allied to witches were the "women who make a co tract with the Schedim, and meet them at certain times, danc with them, and visit these spirits who appear to them in the shap of goats." In many countries such women were killed. This for of Kischuph is true sorcery. The other form, material Kischup consists of disturbing influences on the natural elements pr duced by exciting false "rapports" in various substances.

Kiss, Bewitchment by a

Florence Newton, a notorious Irish witch of the seventeent century, was on several occasions accused of bewitching peopl by means of a kiss. The first was a maid who refused alms to he About a week later the witch kissed her violently, from which tim the servant suffered from fits and was transported from place t place, first being carried mysteriously to the top of the hous then being placed between two feather beds, and so on. Th witch was also said to have caused the death of David Jones, wh stood sentinel over her in prison, by kissing his hand, and by th same means brought about the death of the children of thre aldermen of Youghall, county Cork. Newton was tried at Cor Assizes in 1661.

Sources:

Seymour, St. John. *Irish Witchcraft and Demonology.* 1913. Re print, New York: Causeway Books, 1973.

Kitson, Alfred (1855–1934)

British pioneer of teaching **Spiritualism** to children throug the lyceum system first founded in the United States by **Andre Jackson Davis** around 1863. Kitson, son of a Yorkshire coa miner, was a veteran of the Spiritualist movement at a time whe it was violently opposed in Britain. In 1876 he organized evenin classes for children on the lyceum system as a wing of the newl formed Spiritualist Society in Yorkshire. Kitson campaigned vig orously for the lyceum movement and became known as "th Father of British Lyceums." He collaborated with Harry A. Kerse on the *English Lyceum Manual,* first published in 1887.

Kersey and Kitson were also largely instrumental in bringin into existence the Spiritualists' Lyceum Union in 1890. Th Union started a monthly *Spiritualists' Lyceum Magazine,* first pub lished in Oldham in January 1890. When this magazine ceasec publication in November 1890 it was replaced by the **Lyceum Banner,** edited by **J. J. Morse** from Liverpool until 1902, whe Kitson became editor. In 1894 the union changed its name to th **British Spiritualists' Lyceum Union.** The lyceum movement pros pered for many years, but Kitson resigned from secretaryship o the union in 1919 because of ill health.

Kiyota, Masuaki (1962–)

Remarkable young Japanese psychic born April 30, 1962 wh appears to have extraordinary talents in **metal bending** an nengraphy (**psychic photography**). Kiyota rivals famed psychic **Uri Geller** and **Matthew Manning** in his unusual demonstrations Kiyota was elaborately tested and filmed in the 1970s while pro ducing his phenomena. In addition to an appearance on a Nip pon Television program, Kiyota was also featured on the Ameri can program "Exploring the Unknown" (narrated by Bur Lancaster), presented on NBC October 30, 1977. Later in th decade, he was investigated by **Walter Uphoff** and his wife Mar Jo, who visited him in Japan.

Kiyota's reputation as a paranormal metal bender suffered considerably with his own admission that he had cheated on two occasions. In the course of a television demonstration in Tokyo on February 3, 1984, Kiyota was challenged by observers who accused him of cheating during the metal bending. Kiyota admitted that he had assisted his claimed psychic efforts by physical exertion with his hands. A month later, in the course of an interview on April 27, 1984, with a Mr. Kasahara and Soji Otani, Kiyota further admitted to cheating on one earlier occasion during a "metal-bending party" in 1983. Kiyota stated that he had used normal muscular effort to produce metal distortions. These admissions have cast doubt over other performances by Kiyota. It is possible that the great publicity given to his claimed metal bending abilities put him under pressure to supplement paranormal ability with **fraud,** as has been often claimed in the case of earlier psychics and Spiritualist mediums.

For a thoughtful discussion on the subject of Kiyota's cheating and its implications, see the correspondence from Ian Stevenson, Emily Williams Cook, Carolee A. Werner, Michael Dennis, H. H. J. Keil, and Peter Phillips, with an additional communication from Jules Eisenbud, in the *Journal* of the American Society for Psychical Research (vol. 79, no. 2, April 1985). (See also **Japan**)

Sources:

Berger, Arthur S., and Joyce Berger. *The Encyclopedia of Parapsychology and Psychical Research.* New York: Paragon House, 1991.

Eisenbud, Jules. "Some Investigations of Claims of PK Effects on Metal: The Denver Experiments." *Journal* of the American Society for Psychical Research 76 (1982).

Uphoff, Walter, and Mary Jo Uphoff. *Mind Over Matter: Implications of Masuaki Kiyota's PK Feats with Metal and Film.* Oregon, Wis.: New Frontiers Center, 1980. Reprint, U.K.: Colin Smythe, 1980.

Klinckowstroem, Graf Carl von (1884–1969)

German research scientist who wrote about water divining and other parapsychological subjects. He was born on August 26, 1884, at Potsdam, Germany. Klinckowstroem attended the University of Munich, where he studied physics, philosophy, psychology, and history. He was a corresponding member of the **Society for Psychical Research,** London, from 1928 on and an honorary member of Deutscher Erfinder-Verband, Nuremberg. As an amateur conjuring magician he was critical of many claims of psychical phenomena. He was particularly skeptical of **astrology** and **witchcraft,** but was also critical of parapsychology. He gathered data on fraudulent mediums and attacked flaws in the research of **Baron Schrenk-Notzing.**

Klinckowstroem published several books on science, such as the 1959 volume *Geschichte der Technik* (History of Technology) and a variety of books on paranormal subjects.

He died August 29, 1969.

Sources:

Berger, Arthur S., and Joyce Berger. *The Encyclopedia of Parapsychology and Psychical Research.* New York: Paragon House, 1991.

Klinckowstroem, Graf Carl von. *Bibliographie der Wünschelrute* (Bibliography of the Divining Rod). N.p., 1911.

———. *Yogi-Künste* (Yogic Arts). N.p., 1922.

———. *Die Zauberkunst* (The Art of Magic). N.p., 1954.

Klinckowstroem, Graf Carl von, and Rudolph von Maltzahn. *Handbuch der Wünschelrute* (Handbook of the Divining Rod). Müchen; Berlin: R. Oldenbourg, 1931.

Klinckowstroem, Graf Carl von, W. von Gulat-Wellenburg, and Hans Rosenbusch. *Der Physikalische Mediumismus* (Physical Mediumship). N.p., 1925.

Pleasants, Helene, ed. *Biographical Dictionary of Parapsychology.* New York: Helix Press, 1964.

Klinschor (or Klingsor)

According to tales of **King Arthur,** he was lord of the magic castle wherein Arthur's mother was kept. Klinschor was a nephew of Virgilius of Naples and was overcome by Sir Gawain. He is alluded to in the *Parsival* of Wolfram von Eschenbach.

Kloppenburg, Boaventura (1919–)

Professor of theology and Franciscan priest who studied **Spiritism** in Brazil. He was born on November 2, 1919, at Molbergen (Oldenburg), Germany, and studied at the Antonianum University, Rome (D.Th.). Besides his books on **Spiritualism,** Kloppenburg wrote pamphlets on **Theosophy** and the **Rosicrucians** in Brazil.

Sources:

Kloppenburg, Boaventura. *O Espiritismo no Brasil* (Spiritism in Brazil). Petropolis: Editoria Vozes, 1964.

———. *A Maçonario no Brasil* (Masonry in Brazil). 4th ed. N.p., 1961.

———. *Nossas Supersticoes* (Our Superstitions). N.p., 1959.

———. *O Reencarnacionismo no Brasil* (Reincarnationism in Brazil). Petropolis: Editoria Vozes, 1961.

———. *Pastoral Practice and the Paranormal.* Translated by Paul Burns. Chicago: Franciscan Herald Press, 1979.

Pleasants, Helene, ed. *Biographical Dictionary of Parapsychology.* New York: Helix Press, 1964.

Kluski, Franek (1874– ?)

Pseudonym of a distinguished Polish poet and writer whose remarkable physical powers coexisted with psychic gifts. As a child of five or six he had presentiments, visions of distant events, and saw phantoms. He thought the phantoms natural and talked with them familiarly. In 1919 Kluski's psychic gifts were discovered when he attended a séance with Jan Guzyk. His talent annoyed him at first, but curiosity prevailed and he consented to experiments. Various phases of physical phenomena developed, culminating in **materialization,** during which, like **Elizabeth d'Esperance,** Kluski retained consciousness.

For scientific research he placed himself readily at the disposition of the Polish Society for Psychic Research and the **Institut Métapsychique** of Paris, where his first sittings took place in 1920 in the presence of **Charles Richet,** Count de Grammont, and **Gustav Geley.** The paraffin casts of materialized limbs made in these séances were considered among the best objective evidence of supernormal power ever produced.

Another curious feature of Kluski's materialization séances was the appearance of animal forms, which included squirrels, dogs, cats, a lion, and a buzzard. One of the most disturbing manifestations was a large primitive creature like a huge ape or a hairy man. The face was hairy, and the creature had long, strong arms and behaved roughly to the sitters, trying to lick their hands and faces. This materialization, which Geley named "Pithecanthropus," exuded a strong odor like "a wet dog." Geley considered Kluski a universal medium, a king among his contemporaries. He found the clairvoyance that was manifest in Kluski's **automatic writing** scripts almost terrifying.

The best account of Kluski's mediumship is the 1926 book (in Polish) by Col. Norbert Ocholowicz, *Wspomnienia Z, Seansow Z (Medium Frankiem Kluskim).*

Sources:

Berger, Arthur S., and Joyce Berger. *The Encyclopedia of Parapsychology and Psychical Research.* New York: Paragon House, 1991.

Geley, Gustav. *Clairvoyance and Materialisation.* London, 1927.

Kneale, Martha Hurst (1909–)

University fellow and tutor who wrote on psychical research. Born at Skipton, Yorkshire, England, Kneale studied at Somerville College, Oxford University (B.A., 1933). Following graduation she became a Graham Kenan fellow at the University of North Carolina (1933–34) and a graduate fellow at Bryn Mawr College, Pennsylvania (1934–36). She received her master's degree at Oxford University (1936). Kneale became a tutor in philosophy at Lady Margaret Hall, Oxford University. She had a keen interest in parapsychology and wrote papers on philosophical issues related to the discipline. She was a member of the **Society for Psychical Research,** London.

Sources:

Kneale, Martha Hurst. "Is Psychical Research Relevant to Philosophy?" *Proceedings, Aristotelian Society.* Supplementary volume 24 (1950).

———. "Time and Psychical Research." *Proceedings* of Four Conferences of Parapsychological Studies (1957).

Pleasants, Helene, ed. *Biographical Dictionary of Parapsychology.* New York: Helix Press, 1964.

Knight, JZ (1946–)

Channel of **"Ramtha"** and head of Ramtha's School of Enlightenment. JZ Knight was born Judith Darlene Hampton on March 16, 1946, in Dexter, New Mexico. She grew up in poverty and was unable to go to college; after high school she married and became the mother of two children. The marriage ended when she became unwilling to continue to countenance her husband's alcoholism and infidelity. She became a businesswoman and her career led her eventually to Tacoma, Washington, and a second marriage. Along the way, a cryptic psychic reading told her that one day she would meet "the One." She did not understand, for several years, but the words proved true when in 1977 she encountered Ramtha.

Ramtha appeared to her one Sunday afternoon in 1977. Shortly thereafter he began to speak through her and there was an immediate response from people who attended her initial sessions as a channel. After she became relatively comfortable as a channel, she began **channeling** Ramtha regularly in weekend "dialogues" held at various locations around the United States. Knight eventually took the dialogues to Canada, England, Germany, Australia, and New Zealand. In the 1980s she became the most successful of the channels that grew up around the **New Age** movement.

In 1987 she discontinued the dialogues and opened Ramtha's School of Enlightenment in Yelm, Washington, on land previously used as a ranch. Many of the students moved to northeast Washington and have gathered periodically in the years since for more systematic teaching by Ramtha, who continues to speak through Knight. Approximately three thousand students are connected with the school.

During the early years of the school, Knight went through a period of intense criticism from the media, largely caused by the obvious success and built around the criticisms of former followers of Ramtha's teachings. About that same time, Knight released her own autobiography. The negative publicity continued into the 1990s, in large part occasioned by the breakup of her marriage to Jeff Knight, who contested the terms of their divorce. However, these issues have been largely decided in Knight's favor and the school has continued to grow and prosper.

Over the years of the dialogues, transcripts of Ramtha's talks were compiled and published, and several videotapes of dialogue sessions were released. While these cover some major themes in Ramtha's teachings, a more systematic presentation of Ramtha's basic philosophy and instruction on the spiritual disciplines is currently available only to students of the school.

Sources:

Knight, JZ. *A State of Mind: My Story.* New York: Warner Books, 1987.

Ramtha (as channeled by JZ Knight). *The Ancient Schools of Wisdom.* Transcribed by Diane Munoz. Yelm, Wash.: Diane Munoz, 1992.

———. *I Am Ramtha.* Edited by Cindy Black, Richard Cohn, Greg Simmons, and Wes Walt. Portland, Oreg.: Beyond Words Publishing, 1986.

Ramtha (The White Book). Edited by Steven Lee Weinberg, with Randall Weischedel, Sue Ann Fazio, and Carol Wright. Eastsound, Wash.: Sovereignty, 1986.

Ramtha's School of Enlightenment: The American Gnostic School. Yelm, Wash.: JZK, 1994.

Knock

Irish village in county Mayo that was the scene of apparitions of the Virgin Mary similar to those that occurred at **Lourdes** in the nineteenth century. On the evening of August 21, 1879, shortly before dusk, three strange figures were observed by one or two parishioners of the village. The figures were standing motionless by the gable of the Roman Catholic church. At first this occasioned no surprise, since the parishioners assumed that the figures were statues ordered by the parish priest. As the evening advanced, however, the figures appeared to be surrounded by a strange light, and soon a small crowd of villagers assembled to observe the apparitions. The main figure was a woman clothed in white, wearing a golden crown. On each side of her was a man, one wearing a bishop's mitre, the other elderly and bearded.

Because it was raining at the time the crowd eventually dispersed. Some villagers went home to dry their clothes, others to assist an elderly woman who had collapsed on her way to church. The priest's housekeeper went to tell the priest about the apparitions, but he was not impressed and did not go to the church to see for himself. Later that night the apparitions disappeared.

The apparitions had been witnessed by nearly 30 people, and a few weeks later the archbishop of Tuam set up a commission to investigate the phenomenon and interview the witnesses. Fifteen villagers were interviewed, ranging from a boy of six to an old woman of 75. Their evidence was given in a frank, down-to-earth manner that carried absolute conviction, and their accounts never changed throughout their lives. Minor variations between accounts were no more significant than might be expected from a number of individual witnesses to a remarkable event.

A Marian shrine for pilgrimages was constructed at Knock with the permission of the Roman Catholic Church. In addition to the original Knock Shrine at the apparition church, there is now a large new Church of Our Lady, and, as at Lourdes, there are mass services for healing the sick. The shrine achieved worldwide recognition when Pope John Paul II visited Knock in September 1979. In the 1980s an ambitious project was begun—the construction of an airport at Knock.

The Knock airport was the brainchild of Monsignor James Horan, parish priest of Knock, and although the plan was at first ridiculed, he managed to secure initial financial support, which was later curtailed. Critics pointed out that there was no need for an airport at Knock, that it was on the edge of a bog in the middle of nowhere. In spite of such opposition Horan's tireless enthusiasm somehow culminated in completion of the airport, now regarded as the major miracle of Knock.

On Friday, October 25, 1985, the Knock airport was operational and three Aer Lingus planes landed there. They took off with nearly 500 people on an eight-day pilgrimage to Rome, where Horan was received at St. Peter's. The 72-year-old priest made a speech calling upon the Irish transport minister to grant full recognition to Knock and create a duty-free zone there in order to develop the airport to its full potential.

On Friday, August 1, 1986, Horan died at age 74, only two days after the first transatlantic flight touched down at the new Connaught Airport at Knock. It was also the golden jubilee year of Horan's ordination to the priesthood.

On July 9, before setting out on his final pilgrimage to Lourdes, Horan had signed the remaining contract for Connaught International Airport to install lighting on the runway.

In Lourdes he celebrated public Mass and remarked, "This is the happiest day of my life." With a convivial Irish group in the hotel lounge he sang "Auld Lang Syne;" he died only a few hours later.

From time to time, skeptics have revived the theory—considered in great detail in 1879—that the apparitions at Knock were the work of a prankster projecting magic lantern slides. However, this theory is based solely on the fact that the images appeared static—as distinct from the reported living and moving images of the Virgin Mary seen at other locations—and there is no direct evidence to substantiate the slide projection theory.

Notable points from witnesses seem to negate the magic lantern theory. The apparitions were first seen in daylight, just before sunset, and continued after dark. It was raining, but this did not affect the apparitions. Various witnesses saw the apparitions from different angles of approach, and some would surely have observed a characteristic beam of light proceeding from a magic lantern, even assuming that it could project images in daylight as well as dusk and be unaffected by rain.

In 1880 a reporter for the London *Daily Telegraph* interviewed a policeman who said he saw only "a rosy sort of brightness, through which what seemed to be stars appeared. I saw no figures . . . but some women who were praying there, declared that they beheld the Blessed Virgin" he said. Asked whether he looked around to see where the brightness came from, the policeman replied, "I did, but everything was dark. There was no light anywhere, except on the gable."

The *Daily Telegraph* reporter also made a detailed investigation of all possible sources for a magic lantern projection, as other investigators had done earlier. His finding was as follows:

"The chapel stands in a rather extensive yard, which is bounded, opposite the table, and distant from it some 25 paces, by a dilapidated wall about four feet high. Beyond this is a large field and the open country. Within the yard, a little to the north of a line drawn from the north angle of the gable to the low wall, stands a schoolhouse, its gable directly facing towards the east. Obviously, therefore, if the appearances alleged to have been seen on the chapel wall were due to a magic lantern, the operator, supposing he could have focussed his picture at such a distance, must have taken post behind the low wall; or, if stationed in the school, must have thrown the image on the 'screen' at a very considered angle. The wall theory may be dismissed, because over its tumbled stones the first witness passed to get a nearer view, and the glare of the lantern would at once have been detected by the observant policeman. There remains the notion of a manipulator stationed in the schoolhouse. I gave my best attention to the windowless gable of that building, and could find no signs of hole or crack from chimney to foundation. Going inside among the children, to look at the wall from that point of view, the plaster appeared untouched, and the roof too much open to admit a man working between its apex and what there was of ceiling."

One of the witnesses, a Mrs. O'Connell, later recalled how two church commissioners took her statement in the schoolhouse and a fortnight later 20 more priests arrived, and carried out elaborate tests with magic lantern slides. "They wanted to make out," she said, "that the pictures were like the ones we saw, but they were no more like them and no one could make them like the apparitions."

The Catholic Church is normally skeptical of reported miracles and is prepared to endorse them only after most careful and extensive investigation. Moreover, in the case of Knock, the commission of inquiry had barely completed taking depositions from witnesses when further visions were reported. Amid scenes of great religious fervor, similar appearances on the same church gable were reported on February 9 and on March 25 and 26, 1880. The probability of a prankster being able to maintain a hoax over a period of several months, in the presence of investigators and newspaper reporters, seems low.

The magic lantern theory was again revived in a British television program, "Is There Anybody There?" produced by Karl Sabbagh and telecast on October 31, 1987. In this production Nicholas Humphrey demonstrated how a passable magic lantern image could be projected from within the gable of a Cambridge church, using a right-angled shaving mirror. Humphrey suggested **fraud** by Archdeacon Cavanagh, one of the three commissioners. In support of the theory, a document from the State Papers in Dublin Castle was cited in which Cavanagh, parish priest of Knock, was reported by a spy as criticizing rebels and consequently endangering his prestige in the area by championing landlords and attacking local Fenians or Land League leaders. The idea that Cavanagh, widely respected in his parish, might resort to fraud was not well received.

Over the years, many remarkable miraculous cures have been reported in connection with Knock Shrine, including cures of three archbishops, and Knock has become known as "the Lourdes of Ireland."

Sources:

Berman, David. "Knock: Some New Evidence." *The British and Irish Skeptic* 1, no. 6 (November/December 1987).

———. "Papal Visit Resurrects Ireland's Knock Legend." *The Freethinker* (October 1979). Reprinted in *The British and Irish Skeptic* 1, no. 1 (January/February 1987).

Coyne, William D. *Our Lady of Knock.* New York: Catholic Book Publishing, 1948.

MacPhilpin, John. *The Apparitions and Miracles at Knock, also Official Depositons of the Eye-Witnesses.* Tuam, Ireland, 1880. 2d ed. Dublin: M. H. Gill & Son, 1894.

Rynne, Catherine. *Knock 1879–1979.* Dublin: Veritas Publications, 1979.

Walsh, Michael. *The Apparition at Knock.* Tuam: St Jarlath's College, 1959.

Knockers

Underground sprites of Cornish folklore in England who are said to inhabit tin mines. They resemble the friendly German **kobolds,** since they knock to indicate places underground where there is a rich vein of ore. (See also **Elementary Spirits**)

Knodt, William Charles (1936–)

Administrative employee, Illinois Bell Telephone Company. He conducted experiments in psychokinesis (influencing casting of dice) and correlation between physical pain and **ESP** in hospital patients.

Sources:

Pleasants, Helene, ed. *Biographical Dictionary of Parapsychology.* New York: Helix Press, 1964.

Knorr von Rosenroth, Christian (1636–1689)

German alchemist and mystic who edited kabalistic works under the title *Kabbala Denudata* (1677, 1684). This book includes three fragments from the book *Zohar* with extensive commentary, as well as treatises by Isaac Luria, founder of a kabalistic sect in the sixteenth century, and the *Treatise on the Soul,* by Moses Cordovero. Rosenroth translated these Hebrew works into Latin and thus made them available to non-Jewish readers. An English translation of *Kabbala Denudata* was published by **S. L. MacGregor Mathers** in 1887. (See also **Kabala**)

Knowles, Elsie A(nna) G(race) (1908–)

German statistician who wrote and experimented in the field of parapsychology. She was born on July 14, 1908, in Berlin, and studied at the University of Jena (Ph.D., 1932). In 1935 she moved to England and taught mathematics at various universities through the mid-1950s. Then in 1954 she became the manager of the statistics department at Ferodo Ltd. Associates, Institute of Physics, London.

Knowles had a longtime interest in psychical research and was a charter member of the **Parapsychological Association.** She conducted experiments in **psi** dexterity.

Sources:

Knowles, Elsie A. G. "Report on an Experiment Concerning the Influence of Mind Over Matter." *Journal of Parapsychology* 13, no. 3 (September 1949).

———. "Report on the Susceptibility of Manually Operated Random Selector to Psi Dexterity." *Journal of Parapsychology* 16, no. 1 (March 1952).

Pleasants, Helene, ed. *Biographical Dictionary of Parapsychology.* New York: Helix Press, 1964.

Knowles, Frederick W(ilfred) (1911–   )

German physician and surgeon who wrote on psychic healing. Knowles was born on June 7, 1911, in Berlin. He studied at the Royal College of Surgeons, England (member 1950), and the Royal College of Physicians (licentiate 1950). His medical practice took him to Canada, India, New Guinea, Australia, and New Zealand as well as to England. He was a life member of the **Society for Psychical Research,** London, and a charter member of the **Parapsychological Association.**

Knowles's studies on psychic healing included Indian **yoga** techniques, **hypnosis,** and phenomena formerly known as **mesmerism.** In addition to his medical and anatomical papers, he published articles on paranormal healing.

Sources:

Knowles, Frederick W. "ESP Today." *Corrective Psychiatry and Journal of Special Therapy* 12, no. 2 (March 1966).

———. "Psychic Healing in Organic Disease." *Journal* of the American Society for Psychical Research 50, no. 3 (July 1956).

———. "Rat Experiments and Mesmerism." *Journal* of the American Society for Psychical Research 53, no. 2 (April 1959).

———. "Some Investigations into Psychic Healing." *Journal* of the American Society for Psychical Research 48, no. 1 (January 1954).

Pleasants, Helene, ed. *Biographical Dictionary of Parapsychology.* New York: Helix Press, 1964.

Kobolds

The sprites or **fairies** of German folklore. They are of two kinds. The first is a household sprite like the English brownie, helping with the housework if properly fed and treated, but mischievous, playing pranks on people. Kobolds are often given names, like "Chimmeken," "Heinze," or "Walther." The second type are underground sprites who haunt caves and mines and are often evil and malicious. The metallurgist George Landmann describes these spirits in his book *De Animatibus subterraneis* (1657). (See also **Elementary Spirits; Knockers**)

Koch, Walter A(lbert) (1895–   ?)

Teacher and astrologer who wrote books and articles on parapsychology. He was born on September 18, 1895, in Esslingen/Neckar, Württemberg, Germany, and studied at the University of Tübingen (Ph.D., 1920). He was scientific adviser to the Association of German Astrologers and leader of the investigation circle of the Cosmobiosophical Association, Hamburg. He served in the German army during World War I but was arrested for resistance to the Nazis in 1941 and spent three years in prisons (including the concentration camp at Dachau). Koch wrote a number of books on astrological subjects. He also contributed articles on psychokinesis, card divination, and prophecy to various journals, including *Neue Wissenschaft* and *Mensch und Schicksal.*

Sources:

Koch, Walter A. *Astrologische Farbenlehre* (Astrological Science of Colors). N.p., 1930.

———. *Deine Farbe—Dein Charakter* (Your Color—Your Character). N.p., 1953.

———. *Dr. Korsch und Die Astrologie* (Dr. Korsch and Astrology). N.p., 1956.

———. *Innenmensch und Außenmensch* (Man: Introversion and Extraversion). N.p., 1956.

———. *Prophetie und Astrologische Prognose* (Prophecy and Astrological Prediction). N.p., 1954.

———. *Psychologische Farbenlehre* (Psychological Science of Colors). C. Marhold, 1931.

———. *Regiomontanus und das Häusersystem des Geburtosorte* (Regiomontanus and the System of Houses of Birthplaces). N.p. 1960.

———. *Die Seele der Edelsteine* (The Psyche of Precious Stones) N.p., 1934.

Koestler, Arthur (1905–1983)

World-famous novelist and writer on political, scientific, and philosophical themes who was also interested in parapsychology. He was born in Budapest September 5, 1905, the only son of a Hungarian father and an Austrian mother. He described his early life as "lonely, precocious and neurotic," saying he was "admired for my brains and detested for my character by teachers and schoolfellows alike." Koestler attended the Polytechnic High School in Vienna and studied engineering, then studied science and psychology at the University of Vienna.

As a young man he became a Zionist, and when working as a journalist he joined the Communist party. He was a reporter in Spain during the Civil War, where he was imprisoned as a Communist and was only released after the intervention of the British government. In Paris during World War II, he was arrested and sent to a concentration camp. His prison experiences became the basis of his brilliant but depressing book *Darkness at Noon* (1940). In this book, as in his contribution to the later symposium *The God That Failed: Six Studies in Communism* (1949), he expresses his rejection of communism and other totalitarian regimes, which he sees as corrupted by inhuman and cynical power politics. In 1941 Koestler joined the British army and after the war became a British citizen. By 1955 he had ceased to be actively involved in political campaigning.

In addition to his novels Koestler published a series of brilliant questing works concerned with human faculty and destiny in relation to scientific findings. Although it was not widely recognized that he had a long-standing interest in parapsychology, his book *The Roots of Coincidence* (1972) touches on the question of scientific validation of psychic gifts and states that extrasensory perception might be "the highest manifestation of the integrative potential of living matter," while in *The Challenge of Chance,* published a year later, Koestler reviews possible connections between parapsychology and quantum physics. However, he maintained a characteristic skepticism, as expressed in a television interview: "I am still skeptical. I've got a split mind about it. I know from personal experience, from intuition, whatever you call it, that these phenomena exist. At the same time, my rational or scientific mind rejects them. And I'm quite happy with that split of the mind."

He participated in three annual international conferences of the **Parapsychology Foundation.** At the 1972 Amsterdam conference, "Parapsychology and the Sciences," he contributed a paper, "The Perversity of Physics," in which he states:

"I do believe that there is a positive, not only a negative rapprochement between those two black sheep: parapsychology and quantum physics. But let us not try to rush things. The great new synthesis in the history of science occurred when each component, which ultimately went into synthesis, was already there and they only needed to be together. I do not think that the time is ripe, but I think there is this affinity between parapsychology and modern physics which is more intuitive than logical, more potential than actual . . . a kind of 'gestalt' affinity."

In the 1974 conference at Geneva, he again discussed parapsychology in relation to quantum physics, stating,

"So there is now a radical wing in parapsychology, a sort of Trotskyite wing, of which I am a member, with Alister Hardy and others, who are trying really radically to break away from causality, not only paying lip service to the rejection of causality, or confining this rejection of causality and determinism to the micro-level, but who really wonder whether a completely new approach, indicated in holism, Jung's synchronicity, and so on, might not be theoretically more promising."

Koestler was also a founding member of the KIB Foundation (later renamed the **Koestler Foundation**), a British organization fostering research into unorthodox and paranormal phenomena. He wrote some 35 books.

Koestler died at his London home March 3, 1983, at age 77, in a joint suicide with his third wife, Cynthia Koestler. He had been suffering from leukemia and advanced Parkinson's disease. In his will he included a bequest to a British university for the study of paranormal faculties such as metal bending, telepathy, and healing. The Koestler bequest, equivalent to $600,000, was awarded to the University of Edinburgh, Scotland, to establish the Koestler Chair of Parapsychology. The first occupant was **Robert L. Morris** of Syracuse University, former president of the Parapsychological Association.

Koestler is generally recognized as one of the most stimulating intellects of the twentieth century. In 1968, at the University of Copenhagen, he was awarded the Sooning Prize for his political and philosophical writings, a prize earlier awarded to Bertrand Russell and Winston Churchill. Koestler was also honored with such awards as Commander of the British Empire and Companion of the Royal Society of Literature.

Sources:

Atkins, John. *Arthur Koestler.* N.p., 1956.

Berger, Arthur S., and Joyce Berger. *The Encyclopedia of Parapsychology and Psychical Research.* New York: Paragon House, 1991.

Hardy, Aleister C., Arthur Koestler, and Robert Harvie. *The Challenge of Chance: A Mass Experiment in Telepathy and Its Unexpected Outcome.* New York: Random House, 1973.

Huber, Peter Alfred. *Arthur Koestler, Das Literarische Werk.* Zürich: Fretz & Wasmuth, 1962.

Koestler, Arthur. *The Ghost in the Machine.* New York: Macmillan, 1968.

———. *The Lotus and the Robot.* London: Hutchinson, 1960.

———. *The Roots of Coincidence.* London: Hutchinson, 1972.

———. *The Yogi and the Commissar.* New York: Macmillan, 1946.

Webberly, Rob, ed. *Astride the Two Cultures: Arthur Koestler at 70.* London: Hutchingson, 1975.

Koestler Foundation

British organization founded in 1980 as the KIB Foundation to encourage and promote research in fields outside established science, especially **parapsychology** and alternative medicine. The trustees were **Arthur Koestler, Brian Inglis,** Tony Bloomfield, Michael Fullerlove, and Sir William Wood. The foundation's original name derives from initials of the first three trustees. After the death of Arthur Koestler in 1983 the foundation was given its present name.

The foundation acts as a clearinghouse for information about research in various parts of the world and as a bridge between sponsors and research projects. Selection of projects is by an advisory group that includes individuals of distinction in relevant fields of science and medicine. Among its major accomplishments has been the publication of *A Glossary of Terms Used in Parapsychology* (1982), compiled by Michael A. Thalbourne, on behalf of the Society for Psychical Research. Address: 23 Harley House, Marylebone Rd., London, NW1 5HE, England.

Koilon

The name given to **ether** by Theosophists **Annie Besant** and **Charles W. Leadbeater** in their book *Occult Chemistry* (1919).

Kommasso

Burmese evil spirits inhabiting trees.

Koons, Jonathan (ca. 1855)

A well-to-do American farmer in Millfield Township, Athens County (a remote district of Ohio), and an early American Spiritualist medium. Koons became interested in **Spiritualism** in 1852 and was told at a séance that he was "the most powerful medium on Earth" and that all of his eight children—even the seven-month-old baby—had psychic gifts. Acting on spirit instructions, he built a "spirit room," a single-room log house, 16 feet by 12, for use by the spirits and equipped it with all kinds of musical instruments. This log house soon became famous and people flocked from great distances to see a variety of curious phenomena. The eldest boy, Nahum, a youth of 18, sat at the "spirit table," the audience in benches beyond.

When the lights were put out a fearful din ensued that was sometimes heard a mile away. Surprising feats of strength were also manifested, yet no one present was struck or injured by the flying objects or target-shooting pistol bullets. The sitters were touched by materialized hands that, in the light of phosphorized paper, were seen carrying objects. Spirit faces were also seen. Through a trumpet that sailed about in the air, voices called out the names of the guests even if they concealed their identities; deceased relatives and friends spoke to them and gave proof of **survival.**

The circle was attended by a host of ministering spirits said to number 165. They claimed to belong to a race of men known under the generic title "Adam" (red clay), antedating the theological Adam by thousands of years. They represented their leaders as the most ancient angels. One of these ancient angels, who instructed the circle, was called "Oress." Generally they signed themselves in the written communications as "King" No. 1, No. 2, and No. 3, and sometimes "Servant and Scholar of God." Foremost among them was the **"John King"** who claimed to have been Henry Morgan, the pirate.

Two or three miles from the Koons' farm was another lonely farmhouse, belonging to John Tippie, where another "spirit room" was laid out on the same plan. The manifestations in the Tippie family were identical to those in the Koon log house. Each had a "spirit machine" that consisted of a complex arrangement of zinc and copper for the alleged purpose of collecting and focusing the magnetic aura used in the demonstrations. The Tippies had ten children, all mediums.

J. Everett of Athens County, Ohio, who investigated the Koons' phenomena, published the messages of the spirits under the title *Communications from Angels* (1853) and also printed a number of affidavits testifying to the occurrences in the spirit house, with a chart of the spheres drawn by Nahum Koons in trance.

Charles Partridge writes of his visit in the American *Spiritual Telegraph* of 1855:

"The spirit rooms will hold . . . 20 to 30 persons each. After the circle is formed and the lights extinguished, a tremendous blow is struck by the drum-stick, when immediately the bass and tenor drums are beaten with preternatural power, like calling the roll on a muster field, making a thousand echoes. The rapid and tremendous blows on these drums are really frightful to many persons; it is continued for five minutes or more and when ended, 'King' usually takes up the trumpet, salutes us with 'Good evening, friends' and asks what particular manifestations are desired. After the introductory piece on the instruments, the spirits sang to us. They first requested us to remain perfectly silent; then we heard human voices singing, apparently in the distance, so as to be scarcely distinguishable; the sounds gradually increased, each part relatively, until it appeared as if a full choir of voices were singing in our room most exquisitely. I think I never heard such perfect harmony. Spirit hands and arms were formed in our presence several times, and by aid of a solution of phosphorous, prepared at their request by Mr. Koons, they were seen as distinctly as in a light room."

The Koons family did not fare well at the hands of their neighbors. Their house was attacked by mobs, fire was set to their crops and barns, and their children were beaten. Finally they left the countryside and began missionary wanderings, which lasted for many years. Their mediumship was given free to the public, and they did a great service to the cause of early American Spiritualism.

The phenomenally noisy "spirit room" of the Koons bears a striking resemblance to some **shaman** performances, where the medicine man enters an enclosed area and manifests noisy spirit communications.

Koot Hoomi, Master (Kuthumi)

One of the masters originally contacted by **Helena Petrovna Blavatsky,** cofounder of the **Theosophical Society.** According to theosophical teachings a spiritual hierarchy exists, composed of individuals who have finished their round of earthly reincarnations and have evolved to a position from which they guide the affairs of humanity from the spiritual planes. Members of the hierarchy closest to humanity are the lords of the Seven Rays (of the light spectrum). Each ray is representative of a particular virtue that the lord of that ray exemplifies.

Master Koot Hoomi, generally referred to simply as "Master K. H.," is the lord of the Second Ray, and exemplar of wisdom. He is especially concerned with culture—art, religion, and education—and is the guardian of a vast museum located in the remote Tibetan valley where he and Master Morya reside. In one of his past incarnations Koot Hoomi was the philosopher Pythagoras but today he inhabits the body of a Kasmirian Indian. Like Morya, he travels frequently and many members of the Theosophical Society have reported seeing him. Blavatsky reportedly first met him in 1868. He also had a special relationship with **A. P. Sinnett,** one of the early theosophical leaders. Master Koot Hoomi was one of the three main communicators (the others being **Master Morya** and Djual Khul) of what were compiled as *The Mahatma Letters,* the ultimate source for many theosophical ideas.

K. H. has been one of the masters with whom leaders of theosophical movements independent of the Theosophical Society have claimed frequent contact.

Sources:

Barker, A. Trevor, ed. *The Mahatma Letters to A. P. Sinnett from the Mahatams M. and K.H.* London: T. Fisher Unwin, 1923. 3rd ed. Adyar, Madras, India: Theosophical Publishing House, 1962.

Jesus and Kuthumi [through Mark L. Prophet and Elizabeth Clare Prophet]. *Prayer and Meditation.* Los Angeles: Summit University, 1978.

Kuthumi [through Ann Herbstreith]. *The Nameless One.* Grass Valley, Calif.: Golden Sierra Printing, 1973.

Kuthumi, Ascended Master. *The Wisdom of the Ages.* 2 vols. St. James, N.Y.: Bridge to Freedom, n.d.

Ransom, Josephine. *A Short History of the Theosophical Society.* Adyar, Madras, India: Theosophical Publishing House, 1938.

Kooy, J(ohannes) M(arie) J(oseph) (1902–)

Lecturer in mathematics and physics who made special studies of the problems of space travel and precognition in dreams. Kooy was born on July 13, 1902, at Rotterdam, the Netherlands. He studied at the Technical University of Delft and the University of Leyden (Ph.D. physics and mathematics). He became an engineer with De Nederlandsche Staalindustrie, Rotterdam (1927–32); chief scientific adviser in the aeronautical department of the Technical University, Delft (1936–39); a lecturer in theoretical physics, mechanics, and mathematics at the Royal Military Academy, Breda (1939–59); and a lecturer in space-flight mechanics at the Technical University of Delft (1960–). Besides his publications on ballistics, space travel, and related fields, Kooy published many papers on parapsychology, especially ruminations on the relationship of time, space, and psychical events. He was a charter associate member of the **Parapsychological Association.**

Sources:

Kooy, J. M. J. "Introspectief Onderzoek naar Het Dunne-Effect" (Introspective Investigation of the Dunne-Effect). *Tijdschrift voor Parapsychologie* 6, no. 3 (March 1934).

———. "Paragnosie en Kansrekening" (Extrasensory Perception and the Calculus of Probability). *Tijdschrift voor Parapsychologie* 7, no. 3 (March 1935).

———. "Reply to Dr. Chari." *Journal of Parapsychology* 22, no. 1 (March 1958).

———. "Space, Time and Consciousness." *Journal of Parapsychology* 21, no. 4 (December 1957).

———. "Tijd, Ruimte en Paragnosie" (Time, Space and Extrasensory Perception). *Tijdschrift voor Parapsychologie* 15, nos. 3–4, (May–July 1947).

Pleasants, Helene, ed. *Biographical Dictionary of Parapsychology.* New York: Helix Press, 1964.

Koresh

Hebrew for "Cyrus" and the name assumed by Cyrus Reed Teed (1839–1908), proponent of a form of the **hollow earth** theory. Teed founded the Koreshan Unity, a communal group that constructed a settlement in Estero, Florida, in the hope that it would become the capital of the world.

Koreshan Unity

Communal group founded by Cyrus Reed Teed (1839–1908) under the name "**Koresh.**" Teed was a major exponent of the cellular cosmogony theory, which postulates that humans actually live on the inside of a **hollow earth** and the sun is in the center of the globe.

Koschei the Deathless

A demon of Russian folklore. This horrid monster is described as having a death's-head and a fleshless skeleton "through which is seen the black blood flowing and the yellow heart beating." Koschei is armed with an iron club, with which he knocks down all who come into his path. In spite of his ugliness he is said to be a great admirer of young girls and women. He is avaricious, hates old and young alike, particularly those who are fortunate. His dwelling is among the mountains of the Koskels and the Caucasus, where his treasure is concealed.

Sources:

Ralston, W. R. S. *Russian Folk-Tales.* 1873. Reprint, New York: Arno Press, 1977.

Kosh

A wicked forest fiend of the Bangala of the southern Congo.

Kosmon Unity

Semiannual publication of the Confraternity of Faithists, concerned with the teachings of the "New Age Bible," *Oahspe. Oahspe* is an automatic script received on a typewriter by **J. B. Newbrough** and published in 1882. *Kosmon Unity* may be ordered from the Kosmon Press, BM/KCKP, London, WCIV 6XX, England, or, in the United States, from the Kosmon Service Center, P.O. Box 664, Salt Lake City, UT 84110.

Kosmos

Quarterly publication of the International Society for Astrological Research, Inc. It includes a cumulative digest of astrological activities and research. The society also publishes a newsletter. Address: 70 Melrose Pl., Montclair, NJ 07042.

Kostka, Jean (d. 1903)

Pseudonym of Jules Stanislas Doinel, a former Gnostic and initiate of the 33rd degree. After being converted to Christianity, Kostka claimed to reveal his diabolic adventures in the pages of *La Verité* under the title "Lucifer démasqué" (Lucifer Unmasked). He tells of diabolic happenings in the private chapel of a lady, "Madame X," who figures frequently in his pages (she was thought to be the late countess of Caithness).

It seems probable from the evidence that "Jean Kostka" never came into personal contact with a satanic cult and that his diabolic experiences were merely the imaginings of an intellectual Satanist. Kostka's revelations came in the same period as the fake Satanist writings of "Léo Taxil" (**Gabriel Jogand-Pagès**) and seem to partake of the same contemporary anti-Masonic and anti-Semitic conspiracies.

Around 1890 Kostka founded the Universal Gnostic Church in France and assumed the role of patriarch. He claimed consecration directly from Jesus and later from two Bogomile bishops who emerged during a Spiritualist séance. He in turn consecrated other bishops and they perpetuated the Kostka succession in a variety of small Gnostic churches.

Sources:

Anson, Peter F. *Bishops at Large.* London: Faber & Faber, 1965.

Krafft, Karl Ernst (1900–1945)

Swiss astrologer of German descent born May 10, 1900 who was employed by the Nazis for propaganda work during World War II. He participated in tests by the German parapsychologist **Hans Bender** in 1937 upon moving to Germany. Krafft had formerly conducted an ambitious statistical investigation of cosmic influences on individuals and developed his own system of "typocosmy." His book *Traité d'Astro-Biologie* was printed in Brussels in 1939.

Krafft was introduced to the German Propaganda Ministry by C. Loog, another astrologer, who had worked on interpretations of the famous **Nostradamus** prophecies. Krafft's pro-German edition of *Nostradamus* was used for psychological warfare, and Krafft himself became highly regarded after he made a successful prediction of the attempt on Hitler's life November 9, 1939, in Munich. In fact, this prophecy was so remarkable that Krafft was at first interrogated by the Gestapo, who thought he might have had a hand in the plot.

After the 1941 flight of Rudolf Hess to Britain, many astrologers and occultists in Germany were arrested, including Krafft, who was imprisoned for a year. After his release he again worked for the German Propaganda Ministry, interpreting horoscopes of leaders of the Allies in a manner favorable to Germany. However, he was arrested again in 1943 and sent to Oranienburg concentration camp. He died January 8, 1945, on the way to Buchenwald.

Sources:

Howe, Ellie. *Astrology and Psychological Warfare during World War II.* London: Rider, 1972.

Kral, Josef (1887– ?)

Publisher, editor, and writer on parapsychology. He was born August 15, 1887, in Munich, Germany. During World War II he worked with the opposition to Hitler and was eventually awarded the Distinguished Service Cross of the German Federal Republic. Kral published an autobiography in 1958, *Auftrag des Gewissens: Documente Katholischen Widerstandes gegen das N. S. Regime* (Command of Conscience: Documents of Catholic Resistance to the National Socialist Regime).

After the war Kral became general secretary of Imago Mundi, the International Society of Catholic Parapsychologists, and in 1951, with **Alois Wiesinger,** he began publication of the journal *Vergorgene Welt* (Hidden World), dealing with occult and parapsychological subjects. He also wrote a number of books on the paranormal.

Sources:

Kral, Josef. *Das Heisse Eisen: Das Außersinnliche als Wissenschaft und Glaube* (The Hot Iron: The Paranormal as Science and Faith). Berlin: Verlag Harmonie, 1962.

———. *Die Irrelehre vom Zufall und Schicksal im Lichte der Wissenschaften und des Glaubens* (The Heresy of Coincidence and Fate in the Light of Science and Faith). N.p., 1953.

———. *Der Neue Gottesbeweis: Parapsychologie, Mystik, Unsterblichkeit* (New Proof of God: Parapsychology, Mysticism, Immortality). N.p., 1956.

Pleasants, Helene, ed. *Biographical Dictionary of Parapsychology.* New York: Helix Press, 1964.

Kramer, Heinrich (ca. 1430–1505)

Dominican inquisitor who played a leading part in the great **witchcraft** persecutions as coauthor with **Jakob Sprenger** of the infamous **Malleus Maleficarum,** (literally, the Witches' Hammer), the authoritative sourcebook for inquisitors, judges, and magistrates.

Born at Schlettstadt, in Lower Alsace, near Strasbourg, Kramer entered the Dominican order, where he progressed so rapidly that he was appointed prior to the Dominican House in Schlettstadt while still a young man. He became preacher-general and master of sacred theology (two Dominican Order distinctions) and around 1474 was appointed inquisitor for the districts of Tyrol, Salzburg, Bohemia, and Moravia. He received praise from Rome and from the archbishop of Salzburg, becoming spiritual director of the Dominican church in Salzburg.

In 1484 Pope Innocent VIII was responsible for the famous bull *Summis desiderantes affectibus* of December 9, which deplored the power of the witch organization and redefined witchcraft in such a way as to bring it into the scope of the Inquisition. The pope also delegated Kramer and Sprenger as inquisitors throughout northern Germany, especially in Mainz, Cologne, Treves, Salzburg, and Breman.

By 1485 Kramer had written a treatise on witchcraft circulated in manuscript; this was later incorporated into the *Malleus Maleficarum,* first published around 1486. This became the working manual for inquisitors, judges, and magistrates in the great witchcraft persecutions and went into many editions in French, Italian, and English, as well as in German.

Kramer resided for a period at the priory of Santi Giovanni e Paolo (X. Zanipolo), returning to Germany in 1497, where he lived at the convent of Rohr, near Regensburg. On January 31, 1500, he was appointed nuncio and inquisitor of Bohemia and Moravia by Alexander VI and empowered to proceed against the Waldenses and Picards as well as witches. He died in Bohemia in 1505.

Sources:

Robbins, Rossell Hope. *The Encyclopedia of Witchcraft and Demonology.* New York: Crown Publishers, 1959.

Krata Repoa

Title of a book published in Berlin in 1782 claiming to be an "initiation into the ancient mysteries of the priests of Egypt." The authors were C. F. Köppen (1734–ca. 1797) and J. W. B. von Hymmen (1725–1786). Köppen was a German official and one of the founders of the Order of **African Architects.**

The *Krata Repoa* is of a Masonic ritual nature and is divided into seven grades. The grade of Postophoris (a name used by Apuleius to signify a priest of Isis) corresponds to the apprentice or keeper of the sacred threshold. Second comes the degree of Neokaros, in which are found many ordeals and temptations. The third grade is the state of death—of judgment and passage of the soul. The candidate is restored to light in the following degree, that of the battle of the shadows. In the fifth grade, a drama of vengeance is enacted. The sixth is that of the astronomer before the gate of the gods. In the final grade, the whole scheme of initiation is expounded.

It was believed that these degrees corresponded to the actual procedure of a secret society, and it may be that in some measure they did, since one of their authors was a prominent member of the African Architects. However, although there seem to be elements of real tradition in the work, most of it is probably invention.

Sources:

Waite, Arthur E. *A New Encyclopaedia of Freemasonry*. London: William Rider & Son, 1921. Rev. ed. 1923. Reprint, New Hyde Park, N.Y.: University Books, 1970.

Kraus, Joseph (1892– ?)

Famous European performer of stage telepathy and clairvoyance during the 1930s, known under the stage name **Frederick Marion.**

Kreskin (1935–)

The mentalist magician Kreskin was born George Joseph Kresge, Jr., on January 12, 1935, in Montclair, New Jersey. He was educated at Seton Hall University (B.A., 1963). He worked for eight years as consultant to a psychologist. He disclaims supernatural powers but appears to use some form of **ESP** in such stage tricks as "influencing" a member of his audience to select a name (previously placed by Kreskin in an envelope) from a pile of telephone directories. He has described telepathy as "just a heightening of the senses," and he has suggested that "ESP" should read "PSE"—phenomena scientifically explainable.

In addition to his book *The Amazing World of Kreskin* (1973), he has also published *Use Your Head to Get Ahead! With Kreskin's Mind Power Book* (1977). Although he says he uses **telepathy** in conjunction with conventional stage magic, he also claims that his methods are purely scientific. According to Kreskin, "Everything I do is inherent in everyone. But what I have done is to learn to sensitize myself to the reactions and attitudes of people around me. Under certain conditions I can sense their thoughts as well as influence their thoughts."

Sources:

Berger, Arthur S., and Joyce Berger. *The Encyclopedia of Parapsychology and Psychical Research.* New York: Paragon House, 1991.

Kreskin [George J. Kresge, Jr.]. *The Amazing World of Kreskin.* New York: Random House, 1973.

KRF See Kundalini Research Foundation

Krieger, Delores

Delores Krieger, a professor of nursing in the Division of Nursing Education at New York University, burst into public consciousness in the late 1970s as the advocate of a somewhat traditional laying-on-of-hands technique as an additional tool for nurses in their treatment of patients. Krieger had become intrigued by the work conducted by Canadian cancer researcher Bernard Grad in the 1960s with healer Oscar Estabany. Grad published some of the most impressive data in parapsychological literature on the effects of psychic healing. Krieger decided to test Grad's findings, which had been conducted in a laboratory on plants and laboratory mice, on human beings in a hospital setting.

In 1971 Krieger set up a program with Estabany and discovered that his healing touch appeared to increase the presence of a protein pigment in the blood of the initial patients with whom he worked. The change, confirmed in a second series of experiments, led her to begin teaching the technique to the nurses in her classes. She referred to the laying-on-of-hands, a term that has significant religious connotations, as "therapeutic touch," a more nonreligious designation. Krieger's work, while presenting little new data to parapsychologists, was of significance because it spread parapsychological knowledge into an established field.

Sources:

Krieger, Delores. "Healing by the Laying-On of Hands as a Facilitator of Bioenergetic Change: The Response of In-Vivo Human Hemoglobin." *Psychoenergetic Systems* 1 (1976): 121.

———. "Therapeutic Touch: The Imprimatur of Nursing." *American Journal of Nursing* 75, no. 5 (May 1875): 784–87.

Kripalu Center for Yoga and Health

Residential community offering programs in yoga, holistic health, stress management, dance exercise, and bodywork training, founded in 1971 by Yogi Amrit Desai. Address: Box 793, Lenox, MA 02140.

Krippner, Stanley Curtis (1932–)

Psychologist and writer on parapsychology. Krippner was born on October 4, 1932, at Edgerton, Wisconsin. He studied at the University of Wisconsin (B.S., 1954) and Northwestern University (M.A., 1957; Ph.D., 1961). After completing his education he became the director of the Child Study Center at Kent State University in Ohio. Such interests were reinforced by contacts with parapsychologists **J. B. Rhine** and **Gardner Murphy** during his undergraduate and graduate years. While at Kent Krippner visited Rhine at Duke University and began to conduct parapsychological experiments with the children with whom he was working.

An internationally known humanistic psychologist, Krippner has explored dreams, altered states of consciousness, and paranormal phenomena for many years. His interest in such things began as a teenager on a Wisconsin farm: "When I was about 14 years of age, I had a very dramatic sense of my uncle's death at the very time that my parents received a phone call announcing his death. The effect of that was quite electrifying. Also I was an avid science fiction reader and an amateur magician, and all of these interests coalesced."

In 1964 Krippner left his position at Kent State University to become director of the **Dream Laboratory** at Maimonides Medical Center in Brooklyn, New York. With **Montague Ullman** and, later, **Charles Honorton,** Krippner spent ten years in a systematic exploration of dreams, including **ESP** in dreams and other altered states of consciousness. Interest in consciousness studies in the early 1970s led him to explore psychedelic drugs, yoga, meditation, and other means of altering consciousness.

He also established contact and nurtured relationships with European colleagues, and in 1973 he became the first parapsychologist to become vice president for the Western Hemisphere of the International Psychotronic Research Association. He chaired sessions of the Psychotronic Congress in Czechoslovakia in 1973 and in Monte Carlo in 1975 and became editor of the international journal *Psychoenergetic Systems.*

In 1973 Krippner became a faculty member of the Institute for Humanistic Psychology and more recently the director of the Center for Consciousness Studies at Saybrook Institute in San Francisco. Krippner has been recognized as one of the most outstanding leaders in the parapsychological field. In 1973 he became president of the **Parapsychological Association** and the following year began a tenure as president of the Association for Humanistic Psychology. He also serves as editor-in-chief of *Ad-*

vances in Parapsychological Research: A Biennial Review. He has written extensively on parapsychology and related consciousness and psychological subjects.

Sources:

Berger, Arthur S., and Joyce Berger. *The Encyclopedia of Parapsychology and Psychical Research.* New York: Paragon House, 1991.

Krippner, Stanley. *Dreamworking: How to Use Your Dreams for Creative Problem Solving.* Buffalo, N.Y.: Bearly Ltd., 1988.

———. *Human Possibilities: Mind Exploration in the USSR and Eastern Europe.* Garden City, N.Y.: Anchor Press/Doubleday, 1980.

———. *Psychoenergetic Systems: The Interaction of Consciousness, Energy, and Matter.* New York: Gordon and Breach Science Publishers, 1979.

———. *Song of the Siren: A Parapsychological Odyssey.* New York: Harper & Row, 1975.

Krippner, Stanley, and Daniel Rubin. *Galaxies of Life: The Human Aura in Acupuncture and Kirlian Photography.* Gordon & Breach, 1973. Reprinted as *The Kirlian Aura: Photographing the Galaxies of Life.* Garden City, N.Y.: Doubleday Anchor, 1974. Reprinted as *Energies of Consciousness: Exploration in Acupuncture, Auras, and Kirlian Photography.* New York: Interface, 1976.

Krippner, Stanley, and Sidney Cohen. *LSD Into the Eighties.* N.p., 1981.

Krippner, Stanley, and A. Villoldo. *The Realms of Healing.* Millbrae, Calif.: Celestial Arts, 1976.

Pleasants, Helene, ed. *Biographical Dictionary of Parapsychology.* New York: Helix Press, 1964.

Ullman, Montague, and Stanley Krippner, with Alan Vaughn. *Dream Telepathy.* New York: Macmillan, 1973.

Krishna Venta (1911–1958)

Religious name adopted by Francis Heindswater Pencovic, founder of the WFLK Fountain of the World, a Hindu-based religious community. Pencovic grew up in Utah as a Mormon but claimed that as a young man he went to the Himalayas and from there was sent to the American Indians as a new savior. He gathered a following that settled in the Box Canyon area of the San Fernando Valley in the 1940s.

During the 1950s Krishna Venta was accused of unfaithfulness to his wife with various women of the group. On December 10, 1958, several former members whose wives were still in the group encountered Krishna Venta in the administrative building of the group's communal settlement and set off a dynamite bomb that killed ten people, including Venta. His wife succeeded him as leader of the group, which continued into the early 1980s.

Krishnamurti, Jiddu (1895–1986)

Indian philosopher and spiritual teacher. Born May 12, 1895 in Madanapelle, South India, Krishnamurti was educated privately. While still a child, in 1909, he was "discovered" by Theosophist **Charles W. Leadbeater,** who had been promoting the idea that the next world teacher would appear among Theosophists. Leadbeater presented the young boy to **Annie Besant,** president of the **Theosophical Society,** who took up his cause.

Besant saw to his education and in the 1920s began to travel the world with him. She organized the Order of the Star of the East to promote his mission. Krishnamurti emerged as a talented teacher but also began to question the role that had been thrust upon him. In 1929 he publicly announced that he did not accept the messianic role and withdrew from any association with **Theosophy.** He continued from that time forward as an independent teacher to those who were attracted to him. A network of foundations formed in various countries to facilitate his teaching activity and publish transcripts of his lectures.

Krishnamurti's philosophical position stemmed from his background in Hinduism and Theosophy, but he developed his own unique iconoclastic understanding. He traveled widely and addressed audiences all over the world. He attacked many other Indian teachers then working in the West, some of whom he believed were watering down Indian thought and exploiting their followers.

Krishnamurti died in Ojai, California, on February 17, 1986, at age 90. A number of books were produced from the transcripts of his talks and dialogues with various intellectuals.

Sources:

Field, Sidney. *Krishnamurti: The Reluctant Messiah.* New York: Paragon House, 1989.

Jayakar, Pupul. *Krishnamurti.* San Francisco: Harper & Row, 1986.

Krishnamurti, Jiddu. *The Awakening of Intelligence.* New York: Harper & Row, 1973.

———. *The First and Last Freedom.* London: V. Gollancz, 1954.

———. *Life Ahead.* London: V. Gollancz, 1963.

———. *The Only Revolution.* London: V. Gollancz, 1970.

Lutyens, Emily. *Candles in the Sun.* Philadelphia: Lippincott, 1957.

———. *Krishnamurti, The Years of Awakening* . New York: Farrar, Straus, & Giroux, 1975.

———. *Krishnamurti, The Years of Fulfillment.* London: J. Murray, 1983.

Kristensen, H(arald) Kromann (1903–)

Danish engineer and chairman of the Danish Society for Psychical Research (1963). Kristensen was born on March 5, 1903, at Charlottenlund, Denmark. He studied at the Polytechnic University of Denmark (M.S., electrical engineering, 1927). From 1928 on he was a staff member of the City of Copenhagen Lighting Department. He published many technical papers on engineering.

Sources:

Pleasants, Helene, ed. *Biographical Dictionary of Parapsychology.* New York: Helix Press, 1964.

Krohn, Sven I(lmari) (1903–)

Professor of philosophy and writer on parapsychology. Krohn was born on May 9, 1903, at Helsinki, Finland, and later studied at the University of Helsinki (M.A., 1929) and the University of Turku, Finland (Ph.D., 1949). He became successively a schoolteacher, a lecturer in theoretical philosophy, and professor of philosophy and in 1960 was appointed head of the Philosophical Institution at the University of Turku.

Krohn had a lifelong interest in parapsychology. He served as president of the Society for Psychical Research, Finland (1934–40); as the Finnish representative to the International Congress for Psychical Research, Oslo (1935); and as founder and president of the Society for Parapsychological Studies in Finland.

Sources:

Krohn, Sven I., and Ake Tollet. *Jälleenlöydetty sielu: Kekusteluja parapsykologiasta* (Soul Rediscovered: Dialogues Concerning Parapsychology). N.p., 1936.

Pleasants, Helene, ed. *Biographical Dictionary of Parapsychology.* New York: Helix Press, 1964.

Krstaca

Dalmatian (Serbo-Croatian) name for a witch. (See **Slavs**)

Kübler-Ross, Elisabeth (1926–)

Contemporary physician who has become a world authority on the subject of death and after-death states. Born in Switzerland on July 8, 1926, she worked as a country doctor before moving to the United States. During World War II she spent weekends at the Kantonspital (Cantonai Hospital) in Zürich, where she volunteered to assist escaped refugees. After the war she visited Majdanek concentration camp, where the horrors of the death chambers stimulated in her a desire to help people facing death and to understand the human impulses of love and destruction. She extended her medical background by becoming a practicing psychiatrist. Her formal work with dying patients began in 1965 when she was a faculty member at the University of Chicago. She also conducted research on basic questions concerning life after death at the Manhattan State Hospital, New York.

Her studies of death and dying have involved accounts by patients who reported **out-of-the-body travel.** Her research tends to show that while dying can be painful, death itself is a peaceful condition. Her 1969 text, *On Death and Dying*, was hailed by her colleagues and also became a popular best-seller.

In 1978 Kübler-Ross helped to found Shanti Nilaya (Final Home of Peace), a healing and growth center in Escondido, California. This was an extension of her well-known "Life-Death and Transition" workshops conducted in various parts of the United States and Canada, involving physicians, nurses, social workers, laypeople, and terminally ill patients. In the mid 1980s Shanti Nilaya moved from San Diego County, California, to Head Waters, Virginia, where it continues to offer courses and short- and long-term therapeutic sessions.

Sources:

Berger, Arthur S., and Joyce Berger. *The Encyclopedia of Parapsychology and Psychical Research.* New York: Paragon House, 1991.

Gill, Derek L. T. *Quest: The Life of Elisabeth Kübler-Ross.* New York: Harper & Row, 1980.

Kübler-Ross, Elisabeth. *AIDS: The Ultimate Challenge.* New York: Macmillan, 1987.

———. *Coping With Death and Dying.* Edited by John T. Chirban. Lanham, Md.: University Press of America, 1985.

———. *Living with Death and Dying.* New York: Macmillan, 1981.

———. *On Death and Dying.* New York: Macmillan, 1969.

———. *Questions and Answers on Death and Dying.* New York: Macmillan, 1974.

———. *To Live Until We Say Good-Bye.* Englewood Cliffs, N.J.: Prentice-Hall, 1978.

———, ed. *Death: The Final Stage of Growth.* Englewood Cliffs, N.J.: Prentice-Hall, 1975.

Kuda Bux (1905–1981)

Kashmiri stage magician who demonstrated claimed feats of **eyeless sight** and **fire walking.** Born at Akhnur, Kashmir, on October 15, 1905, he moved to London in 1935. He first practiced fire walking at age 14 and subsequently devoted himself to public performances of stage magic. He normally performed fire walking only at an annual religious festival and claimed that his immunity from burns was attributable to this faith, conferred by a higher power in India. He also claimed to be able to convey his immunity to others and take them over the fire walk without burns.

During 1935 Kuda Bux cooperated with psychical researcher **Harry Price** in two fire walk tests under control conditions, on September 9 and September 17. Scientific observers carefully monitored all aspects of the fire walk. Kuda Bux's feet were examined, and no chemical or other preparation was discovered. The temperature of his feet was taken before and after the walk and was found to be slightly lower after it. His feet were not blistered or injured in any way. The skin was soft and not calloused; moreover the feet were washed and dried before the walk.

The surface temperature of the fire trench on the second day was 430c. The trench was 25 feet long by 6 feet wide and 9 inches deep. Kuda Bux walked the trench deliberately and steadily in 4.5 seconds; the estimated time of contact of each foot with the burning embers was half a second. The tests were photographed and a cinematographic record taken. A volunteer European, Digby Moynagh, attempted the walk on both days but suffered some blistering of the feet. A full report of the tests appeared in *Bulletin II* of the University of London Council for Psychical Investigation in 1936. These tests made Kuda Bux well known, and he performed in British variety theaters with his impressive act of "eyeless sight." (Fire departments would not permit fire trenches to be built on stage for demonstrations of fire walking.)

In 1938 Kuda Bux traveled to the United States to demonstrate his fire walk for a Robert Ripley "Believe It or Not" radio program and later became a member of the Society of American Magicians. He demonstrated his eyeless vision act widely and in 1945 rode a bicycle through the heavy traffic of Times Square in New York while blindfolded.

Magicians claim that such performances are tricks, in spite of the performer's being heavily blindfolded, with balls of dough placed over the eyes and secured with yards of bandages. The skeptical view is that the dough and bandages are shifted sufficiently by the performer to enable him to squint underneath them.

Kuda Bux claimed that his performance consisted of feats of mental concentration, establishing a link between his mind and outside objects, although he admitted to practicing **conjuring** tricks in his acts. (See also **Fire Ordeal; Rosa Kuleshova; Jules Romains;** Seeing with the **Stomach; Transposition of the Senses**)

Kuhlman, Kathryn (1907–1976)

Well-known Christian healer of the United States. Kuhlman was born on May 7, 1907, in Concordia, Missouri. At age 13, she had a religious experience and felt a strong call to the ministry. Though she could not find a church that would accept her, Kuhlman dropped out of school and at age 15 started preaching. She eventually became an itinerant evangelist traveling throughout the midwestern states.

Her first healing took place while she preached in Franklin, Pennsylvania, in 1946. A woman stood up and gave testimony that she had been cured of a tumor. From 1947 on, Kuhlman held regular services in the Carnegie Auditorium at Pittsburgh, where a number of cases of miraculous healing were reported during her ministry. She held services at the Carnegie Auditorium for 20 years before transferring to the First Presbyterian Church in downtown Pittsburgh.

During her services she would speak with simplicity and emotional sincerity and become transformed by what she called the Holy Spirit. Members of the congregation reported a feeling of power building up, with a healing effect. At this point Kuhlman would become clairvoyantly aware of various diseases and symptoms of ill health, which she would locate and "rebuke" from her place on the stage. "To my right in the first balcony, somebody is being healed of diabetes. . . . a growth has disappeared. It's a man up there in the top balcony." Kuhlman spoke rapidly in a kind of transported trancelike condition. She later revealed that she experienced **out-of-the-body travel** during the healing segments of her services.

She often introduced medical doctors into her programs, some of whom confirmed the reality of her miraculous cures, although one physician, William Nolen, attacked the validity of the healings.

Kuhlman died in Tulsa, Oklahoma, February 20, 1976, following open-heart surgery.

Sources:

Kuhlman, Kathryn. *I Believe in Miracles.* New York: Prentice-Hall, 1962.

———. *Nothing Is Impossible With God.* Englewood Cliffs, N.J.: Prentice-Hall, 1974.

Nolen, William. *Healing: A Doctor in Search of a Miracle.* New York: Random House, 1975.

Spraggett, Allen. *Kathryn Kuhlman: The Woman Who Believes in Miracles.* New York: Thomas Y. Crowell, 1970. Reprint, New York: New American Library, 1971.

Kulagina, Nina S. (1926–1990)

Russian psychic who demonstrated the ability to move objects at a distance, one form of **psychokinesis** (PK). Kulagina, a St. Petersburg housewife, has been tested under laboratory conditions by noted researchers, including physiologist **L. L. Vasiliev** and neurophysiologist Genady A. Sergeiev of the Uktomskii Physiological Institute, Leningrad; Czech psychical researcher Zdenek Rejdak; psychologist B. Blazek; and Dr. J. S. Zvierev.

Tested by Vasiliev in the 1960s, Kulagina caused a compass needle to spin by holding her hand a few inches above it and also moved matchboxes at a distance. She was filmed demonstrating her ability to move small objects such as a pen or cigarettes without contact. In 1968 this film was presented by Sergeiev before an international meeting of parapsychologists in Moscow. American parapsychologists who tested her, including **Montague Ullman** and **J. G. Pratt,** considered her a most successful subject with respect to producing PK regularly on demand.

Kulagina died in 1990.

Sources:

Berger, Arthur S., and Joyce Berger. *The Encyclopedia of Parapsychology and Psychical Research.* New York: Paragon House, 1991.

Kulagina, V. V. "Nina S. Kulagina." *Journal of Paraphysics* 5 (1971).

Rejdak, Z. "Nina Kulagina's Mind Over Matter." *Psychic* 2, no. 4 (June 1971).

Kuleshova, Rosa (1955–1978)

Russian psychic who demonstrated the ability to "read" printed words with the fingers of her right hand when her normal vision was completely obstructed, an ability usually termed **dermo-optical perception** or **eyeless sight.** She could also determine color tones on paper and objects by touch. Experiments with Kuleshova were reported in 1963 by Soviet scientist I. M. Gol'dberg.

Kuleshova was a relatively unimportant individual in her hometown of Nizhniy Tagil in the Urals, but after news of her remarkable abilities spread through the scientific world in the USSR she was invited to Moscow to undergo experiments at the Biophysics Institute of the Soviet Academy of Sciences. There Kuleshova demonstrated her abilities to scientists, and it seems likely that the attention and excitement went to her head.

She found it difficult to adjust to ordinary life back in Tagil and insisted on returning to Moscow for further experiments. She made wild claims that she often failed to fulfill and was even caught cheating. After this led to skepticism about "skin vision," further scientific tests were undertaken with precautions against fraud, and these validated Kuleshova's basic abilities.

In 1964 *Life* reporter Bob Brigham saw Kuleshova in Moscow and stated that she was able to read the small print on his business card accurately with her elbow when her normal vision was entirely obstructed. Soon other Soviet subjects were discovered to have the ability of eyeless sight, and new programs of scientific investigation were undertaken. The faculty of "skin vision" was renamed "bio-introscopy" in the Soviet Union.

Rosa Kuleshova died in 1978 from a brain tumor. Reports of her successful demonstrations of eyeless sight in the editorial offices of the Moscow journal *Technika Mologeji* shortly before her death were reported in *The International Journal of Paraphysics* (vol. 13, nos. 3, 4). (See also **Jules Romains;** Seeing with the **Stomach; Transposition of the Senses; USSR**)

Sources:

Berger, Arthur S., and Joyce Berger. *The Encyclopedia of Parapsychology and Psychical Research.* New York: Paragon House, 1991.

Gol'dberg, I. M. "On Whether Tactile Sensitivity Can Be Improved by Exercise." *Soviet Psychology and Psychiatry* 2, no. 1 (1963).

Ostrander, Sheila, and Lynn Schroeder. *Psychic Discoveries Behind the Iron Curtain.* Englewood Cliffs, N.J.: Prentice-Hall, 1970. Reprint, New York: Bantam Books, 1971.

Kumbha Mela

Important Hindu religious festival held every 12 years at the appropriate planetary conjunction; an *Ardh-Kumbha* (half-Kumbha) is held midway between the major Kumbha festivals. Kumbha is equivalent to the sign Aquarius, and the festival is calculated at the conjunction of Jupiter, Aquarius, Aries, and the sun. The festival takes place at either Hardwar, Allahabad, Ujjain, or Nasik. In 1977 the festival was at Allahabad, an especially holy place where the sacred river Ganges merges with the Jamuna and the Saraswati.

Ritual bathing by pilgrims is a special feature of the festival, which originated in ancient times as an occasion for spiritual instruction from great sages and yogis. Some two million pilgrims attend the festival to visit wandering holy men and yogis from all over India. The festival is divided into different camps relating to individual Hindu sects and subsects.

The Indian government has provided sanitary facilities and a system of barricades to prevent accidents caused by vast crowd movements. Kumbha Mela is one of the most colorful mass festivals of India, a kind of nongenerational super-Woodstock of the spiritual life.

Kundalini

According to ancient Hindu religious teachings and yoga science, a latent force in the human organism responsible for sexual activity and (in a sublimated form) higher consciousness. In Hindu mythology kundalini is personified as a goddess, sometimes with the aspect of Durga (a creator) and sometimes Kali (the destroyer) or Bhujangi (the serpent). Kundalini is often described as a serpent that sleeps at the base of the spine and, when aroused, darts upward, bringing enlightenment or pain.

The traditional Hindu yoga texts state that kundalini can be aroused by a combination of **hatha yoga** positions, pranayama (breathing exercises), meditation, and spiritual practices. Some claim that when kundalini is incorrectly aroused, physical disability or even death can result.

The *Panchastavi* is an esoteric Hindu scripture in which kundalini is addressed as the mother of all beings and the arousal of kundalini for mystical enlightenment is described in ecstatic terms:

"Flawless, exceedingly sweet and beautiful, soul-enchanting, fluent speech manifests in all ways in those [devotees] blessed with genius who keep Thee, O Shakti [power] of Shiva, the destroyer of Kamadeva [god of love] constantly in mind, as shining with the stainless luster of the moon in the head..." (3-12).

"O Goddess, rising from the cavity of Muladhara [chakra or center at the base of the spine], piercing the six lotuses [chakras] like a flash of lightning, and then flowing from the moon into the immovable sky-like center [in the head] as a stream of Supreme nectar, Thou then returnest [to Thy abode]" (4-6).

These descriptions, in context, indicate that kundalini is considered to be the creative force expressed in procreation, which is also responsible for mystical enlightenment when sublimated by rising up the spine through the **chakras,** or psychic centers, to the highest center in the head.

There are foreshadowings of the biblical story of the Garden of Eden in the poetic myth of the serpent and the tree with the fruit of knowledge or of sexual force, and there are similar myths in many ancient religions, suggesting a lost secret of the relationship between sex and mysticism. Esoteric groups in many countries have guarded this secret, and there is evidence of meditation systems in ancient Egypt, China, and Tibet that, under one name or another, taught the arousal of the serpentlike force for higher consciousness instead of procreation. Many other religions have emphasized a relationship between sex and mysticism by enjoining celibacy for priests and monks.

Kundalini is also believed to be connected with certain psychic powers, known to yogis as *siddhis.*

In the twentieth century the ancient concept of kundalini has been revived and spread in the West by several Indian teachers, such as Pandit **Gopi Krishna** of Srinagar, India, who aroused this legendary force and claimed to experience a continuing state of higher consciousness. He describes his experience in *Kundalini: The Evolutionary Energy in Man* (1970) and a number of other books. Among other modern Hindus who claimed to have aroused kundalini is **Swami Muktanada,** who was said to have the power to communicate this arousal by touch, a technique traditionally known in India as *shaktipat.*

The controversial psychoanalyst **Wilhelm Reich,** originally a pupil of Freud's, developed a theory of **orgone** energy expressed in different segments of the human body, closely paralleling the course of kundalini through the chakras. Reich also associated this energy with sexual activity. However, he was strongly opposed to yoga, which he mistakenly considered merely a system of fixed physical positions with rigid musculature.

In the nineteenth century B. D. Basu of the Indian Medical Service, in a prize essay entitled "The Hindu System of Medicine" (*Guy's Hospital Gazette,* London, 1889), identified kundalini and the chakras with nervous energy and the main plexi of the human body. This theory was elaborated by Dr. Vasant G. Rele in his book *The Mysterious Kundalini* (1927).

Pandit Gopi Krishna believed that kundalini is an evolutionary force that will play an increasingly important part in the development of the human race and its goals, indicating new directions for both science and religion. Unfortunately, his followers have not been able to see his goal realized. Following up on the writings of Gopi Krishna, Karan Singh, union minister of health in India, announced in 1974 an ambitious kundalini research project, to be sponsored by the All-India Institute of Medical Science, to research the "Kundalini concept and its relevance to the development of higher nervous functions." The project failed, however, to secure official funding following a general election and change of government. Meanwhile, sympathizers with the work of Gopi Krishna founded the Central Institute for Kundalini Research at Srinagar, Kashmir, India, but it too became inactive following the death of Gopi Krishna in 1984.

There are now several organizations concerned with kundalini. The **Kundalini Research Association International** is located at Gemsenstrasse 7, 8006 Zürich, Switzerland. In the United States the **Kundalini Research Foundation**'s address is P.O. Box 2248, Darien, CT 06820. In Canada the **FIND** (Friends in New Directions) research trust publishes books and audio tapes on the work and thought of Gopi Krishna. It may be reached at R.R. 5, Flesherton, Ontario, Canada, NOC IEO.

Sources:

Avalon, Arthur [Sir John Woodroffe]. *The Serpent Power.* Madras, India, 1922.

Condron, Barbara. *Kundalini Rising: Mastering Creative Energies.* Windyville, Mo.: SOM, 1992.

Gopi Krishna. *The Awakening of Kundalini.* New York: E. P. Dutton, 1975.

———. *The Biological Basis of Religion and Genius.* New York: Harper & Row, 1972.

———. *Kundalini: The Evolutionary Energy in Man.* Boulder, Colo.: Shambhala, 1970.

Kieffer, Gene, ed. *Kundalini for the New Age: Selected Writings of Gopi Krishna.* New York: Bantam Books, 1988.

Narayananda, Swami. *The Primal Power in Man of the Kundalini Shakti.* Risikesh, India: N. K. Prasad, 1950.

Rele, Vasant G. *The Mysterious Kundalini.* Bombay: Taraporevala, 1927.

Vyasdev, Brahmachari Swami. *Science of Soul (Atma Vijnana).* Gangotri, India: Yoga Niketan Trust, 1964.

Kundalini Quarterly

Quarterly publication of the Kundalini Research Institute, California, concerned with the relationship of **kundalini** energy and **yoga** techniques to the emotional, physical, and spiritual life of human beings. Address: P.O. Box 1020, Claremont, CA 91711.

Kundalini Research Association International

A Swiss-based organization for the scientific study of all aspects of **kundalini,** first described in traditional Hindu scriptures and yoga texts as a divine power latent in the human organism, and now believed to be a subtle biological force generated by the reproductive system, responsible for human evolution and states of higher consciousness and mystical experience.

The association aims to initiate, encourage, and support research into the nature and functions of kundalini; to cooperate with individuals and organizations concerned with spiritual, cultural, medical, or other aspects of kundalini; to study, translate, and publish texts from Tibet, China, Germany, Japan, or elsewhere concerned with kundalini; and to gather statistics and study case histories of people in all parts of the world who have had experience or claim talents related to the arousal of kundalini.

The association adheres to the teachings of the late Pandit **Gopi Krishna** (1903–1984), who claimed that kundalini is the basic psychosomatic mechanism responsible for genius, psychic faculties, mystical ecstasy (or *samadhi*) and (in an abnormal form) certain kinds of insanity. The association hopes to create global awareness about the scientific implications of kundalini in order to establish the unity of religions and to bridge the gulf existing between revealed knowledge and science. Address: Gemsenstrasse 7, 8006 Zürich, Switzerland.

Kundalini Research Foundation (KRF)

American organization concerned with the study of **kundalini,** believed to be the powerful life force related to procreation and higher consciousness, originally described in ancient Hindu treatises on **yoga** and spiritual development, but also known in various cultures and religions throughout history. The KRF is particularly concerned with the writings of Pandit **Gopi Krishna** (1903–1984), who wrote from personal experience of the arousal of kundalini and consequent states of higher consciousness.

The KRF acts as a clearinghouse for information on all aspects of kundalini, including correlation of traditions in various cultures, personal experiences, and scientific study of the phenomenon. Address: P.O. Box 2248, Darien, CT 06820.

Kuppuswami, B(angalore) (1907–)

Professor of psychology, active in the field of parapsychology. Kuppuswami was born on February 29, 1907, at Bangalore, Mysore, India, and studied at the University of Mysore (B.A., 1927; M.A., 1929). Beginning in 1929, he was a lecturer in psychology for two decades at Presidency College, Madras. In 1952 he became a professor of psychology at the University of Mysore.

He had an outstanding career as a psychologist. He served as, among many other positions, president of the psychology section of the Indian Science Congress (1945); editor of the journal *Psychological Studies* (Mysore); chairman of the section on social change, International Conference on Human Relations, the Netherlands (1956); president of the psychology section, All India Philosophical Conference (1956); and president of the Parapsychology Conference, Indian Science Congress (1960). In addition to his work in the fields of psychology, sociology, and education, Kuppuswami studied the effects of education and variation in distance on **psi** ability.

Sources:

Pleasants, Helene, ed. *Biographical Dictionary of Parapsychology.* New York: Helix Press, 1964.

Kusche, Lawrence David (1940–)

Author of an important critical work on the **Bermuda Triangle** mystery. His carefully researched book, *The Bermuda Triangle Mystery—Solved* (1975), examines popular theories of time warps, black holes, UFOs, and so on and opts for a rational view that there is no single overall mysterious explanation, but rather a mystery built up from inaccurate research, exaggeration, omission of important facts, and the spread of rumors.

Kusche has had considerable experience as a flight instructor and also as a research librarian. In commenting on his approach to such matters as the Bermuda Triangle question, he has stated:

"I might be called a skeptic. It's not that I disbelieve anything and everything, but I *especially* question much of the present day written and televised information that passes for 'fact.' Much of it is nothing more than a half-fact attempt to earn as much money as possible with as little regard for truth as possible."

Kusche followed his initial book with *The Disappearance of Flight 19* (1980), which discusses the disappearance on December 5, 1945, of five navy TBM Avenger torpedo bombers, carrying 14 men, after leaving Fort Lauderdale Naval Air Station on a routine flight. This event has often been cited as a basic example of the Bermuda Triangle mystery. Kusche spent seven years in careful research of all aspects of the event, including many interviews, and retraced the Flight 19 route. He provides a basically rational explanation of the tragedy.

Sources:

Kusche, Lawrence David. *The Bermuda Triangle Mystery—Solved.* New York: Harper & Row, 1975.

———. *The Disappearance of Flight 19.* New York: Harper & Row, 1980.

Kuvalayananda, Swami (1883–1966)

Famous Indian pioneer of the scientific study of **hatha yoga.** He was born Jagannath Ganesh Gune on August 30, 1883, at Dabhoi, Baroda. His first language was Marathi, but his publications on yoga all appeared in English. He was a noted scholar, educationist, and national freedom fighter. He organized the Khandesh Education Society in 1916 and was principal of the society's college (1921–23). He chaired the Physical Education Committee, appointed by the Bombay Board of Physical Education, and was a member of the Central Advisory Board of Physical Education.

Gune was one of Paramahamsa Shree Madhavadasji Maharaj's two major students at Malsar, on the banks of the river Narmada in Gujarat State. Paramahamsa Madhavadasji trained Gune and Shri Yogendra in yoga, which had died out in most of India; Paramahansa Madhavadasji was the major advocate of its revival. Yogendra founded a yoga center in Bombay, and Gune worked at it until 1932. He then left to found the Yogic Health Center at Santa Cruz, Bombay; new premises were secured in 1935 and the center was renamed Ishwardas Chunilal Yoga Health Centre, Kaivalyadhama. Later a spiritual center was added at Kanakesvara Hill in the Kolaba district of Bombay. An additional center, the Kaivalyadhama Saurashtra Mandal, was established in Rajkot in 1943.

By the end of 1943 it was decided to divide the main organization into two wings: Kaivalyadhama Ashrama with emphasis on spiritual development, and Kaivalyadhama Sreeman Madhava Yoga Mandira (SMYM) Samhiti at Lonavla, Poona, specializing in the medical and scientific investigation of yoga. The latter wing was officially recognized as a research institute by the government of Bombay and by Bombay State.

Since 1935 the Kaivalyadhama SMYM Samhiti has published the *Yoga-Mimamsa* journal, edited by Swami Kuvalayananda, with both popular and scientific sections devoted to the serious study of yoga.

Sources:

Kuvalayananda, Swami. *Asanas.* Lonavla (C.R.), India: Yoga-Mimamsa Office. Reprinted as *Popular Yoga Asanas.* Rutland, Vt.: C. E. Tuttle, 1972.

———. *Pranayama.* Lonavla (C.R.), India: Yoga-Mimamsa Office. Reprint, Bombay: Popular Prakashan, 1966.

Melton, J. Gordon, Jerome Clark, and Aidan Kelly. *New Age Encyclopedia.* Detroit: Gale Research, 1990.

Kwan Um Zen (KUZ) School

International organization concerned with the application of traditional Buddhist teachings to everyday life. The school was founded by Zen master Seung Sahn, one of the first Korean Zen masters to teach in the West. KUZ schools include some 50 associated resident centers and groups in the United States, western Europe, Poland, and Korea. Address: Kwan Um Zen School, R.F.D. 5, 528 Pound Rd., Cumberland, RI 02864.

Kyphi

An aromatic substance of the ancient Egyptians with soothing and healing properties, prepared from 16 materials according to the prescription of the sacred books. (See also **Egypt**)

Kyteler, Dame Alice (fl. fourteenth century)

Fourteenth-century accused sorcerer of Kilkenny, Ireland, of a good Anglo-Norman family. Members of her husband's family, attempting to break the will that left her in control of most of the family fortune, accused her of malevolent magic. She was indicted by Bishop de Ledrede, but with her connections and wealth she was able to defy the church. The bishop, however, moved to excommunicate her. Kyteler responded by imprisoning the bishop, who responded by indicting the whole community.

However, the lord justice, who supported Kyteler, obliged the bishop to lift his ban. The bishop eventually succeeded in instituting a case against Kyteler and others accused with her of sorcery, but she fled to England. Her maid Petronilla de Meath was arrested and flogged, only after which she confessed to various orgies involving Kyteler. Petronilla was excommunicated and burned for her part in Kyteler's supposed crimes at Kilkenny on November 3, 1324. Kyteler eventually lost her estate but spent the rest of her life peacefully in England.

The case is significant as the first **witchcraft** (i.e., sorcery) trial in Ireland. A full account is printed as volume 24 in the series of the Camden Society, England, under the title *A Contemporary Narrative of the Proceedings against Dame Alice Kyteler, prosecuted for Sorcery in 1324,* edited by Thomas Wright, 1843.

Sources:

Robbins, Rossell Hope. *The Encyclopedia of Witchcraft and Demonology.* New York: Crown Publishers, 1959.

Russell, Jeffrey Burton. *Witchcraft in the Middle Ages.* Ithaca, N.Y.: Cornell University Press, 1972.

Wright, Thomas, ed. *A Contemporary Narrative of the Proceedings Against Dame Alice Kyteler.* 1843. Reprint, New York: AMS Press, 1968.

L

Labadie, Jean (1610–1674)

A French religious leader of the seventeenth century who was born in 1610 at Bourg, on the Dordogne. He declared himself a second John the Baptist, sent to announce the second coming of the Messiah, and also claimed some measure of divinity for himself.

Labadie had pronounced taste for worldly pleasures, however, which he indulged under the mask of religion. He left the Jesuit College in Bordeaux in 1639 and became canon of Amiens. He became the favorite confessor of upper-class women but was obliged to leave Amiens after a number of scandals. He was also in trouble in Toulouse and was eventually discredited by the church.

In 1650 Labadie joined the Reformed Church and became a pastor at Montauban but was banished after charges of sedition. He was similarly ousted from Geneva and moved to Middleburg in Zealand with a band of followers. He was opposed by the Lutherans and eventually expelled with his band. He died February 16, 1674, at Erfurt.

A sect of Labadists persisted for a few years at Wiewart, North Holland, professing austerity of manners similar to early Quakers. The Labadists emphasized community of property within the church and continuance of prophecy. Among the works of Labadie (which were condemned) was *Le Veritable Exorcisme, au l'unique moyen de chasser le diable du monde chrétien.*

Labarum

A Kabalistic sign embodied in the Great Magical Monogram. The Labarum is the seventh and most important pentacle of the **Enchiridion,** a collection of sixteenth-century prayers and charms, ascribed to Pope Leo III.

Laboratoire d'études des relations entre rythmes cosmiques et psychophysiologiques

Established by psychologist **Michel Gauquelin** and his wife, Françoise, for the study of cosmic influences in relation to the psychology of personality. Over 20 publications were released during Gauquelin's life.

Laboratoire Universitaire de Parapsychologie et d'Hygiene Mental

The Laboratoire Universitaire de Parapsychologie et d'Hygiene Mental was founded in 1974 in Toulouse, France, by a group of University of Toulouse researchers interested in **parapsychology.** Psychical research had flourished in France for a century prior to World War II, but it had slowed in the 1930s and completely died out during the years of the German occupation. During the last half of the twentieth century, it has been slow to revive, but the center at Toulouse has emerged as the most vital in the nation.

The laboratory conducts a full program of laboratory experiments including card guessing experiments, psychokinetic tests, and field research in such diverse subjects as ghost hauntings and dowsing. The experimental work is complemented with an educational program that includes public lectures, workshops, and an annual conference. It is the organization's hope that sharing parapsychological data can lead the public to replace irrational opinions on the occult with scientific knowledge of the paranormal.

In 1987 the laboratory created the **Organisation pour la Recherche en Psychotronique** as an independent agency to promote parapsychological research in France and other French-speaking countries. The laboratory is currently directed by Yves Lignon. It may be contacted c/o IUER Mathématics, Université Toulouse-Le-Mirail 31058, Toulouse CEDEX, France.

Lacteus

A fabled precious stone said by ancient writers to be efficacious when applied to rheumatic eyes.

Lady of Lawers (ca. 1650)

Name given to a woman of the Breadalbane family of Scotland (possibly a Stewart of Appin), who was married to Campbell of Lawers (north shore of Loch Tay, ca. 1650). This woman was believed to be gifted with prophetic powers; her prophecies, said to be written in a book shaped like a barrel and kept in the charter room of Taymouth Castle, were known as "The Red Book of Balloch."

The prophecies all had reference to the house and lands of Breadalbane. One of these related to an ash tree planted by the lady on the north side of the church, beneath which she was said to have been eventually buried. The prophecy was: "The tree will grow, and when it reaches the gable the church will be split asunder, and this will also happen when the red cairn on Ben Lawers falls."

The tree reached the gable in the year 1833, when a great thunderstorm demolished the west loft of the church, collapsing into the middle and rendering the church derelict. At the same time, a cairn (heap of stones) built by sappers and miners on Ben Lawers fell, and the Disruption of the Church of Scotland itself took place.

Ladybug (or Ladybird)

Popular name of the colorful red-spotted beetle of the family Coccinellidae of the order Coleoptera. It is the subject of many folklore superstitions. It brings children, warns of danger, forecasts length of life by the number of its spots, or warns of death. In British and European folklore, the ladybird was captured by a young woman and bidden to fly "north, south, or east, or west" in the direction in which her lover lived. Whichever way the insect flew, there dwelled her future husband. A well-known children's rhyme is: "Ladybird, ladybird, fly away home, your house is on fire, and your children all roam."

Lafleche, Pierre (1892– ?)

French poet and government official who studied telepathy and ESP in cooperation with **René Warcollier.** Lafleche was born on February 6, 1892, in Paris, France. He studied at the Collège de Juilly (Seine-et-Marne) (Bachelier ès lettres, 1909) and at the University of Paris (licencié en droit, 1918). He served in the French army in World War I and received the Croix de Guerre and chevalier, Legion of Honor.

Lafleche worked for the French Ministry of Public Works from 1920 to 1952. He published three volumes of poetry and a number of articles on parapsychology in various journals such as *Psychica, Revue Métapsychique, Lotus Bleu,* and *Tomorrow.*

Sources:

Pleasants, Helene, ed. *Biographical Dictionary of Parapsychology.* New York: Helix Press, 1964.

Laidlaw, Robert W(ordsworth) (1901–)

Physician and psychiatrist with an interest in parapsychology. He was born on February 26, 1901, at Englewood, New Jersey. He studied at Princeton University (B.A., 1924) and Columbia University (M.D., 1931). In 1949 he served as chief of psychiatric services at Roosevelt Hospital in New York City and as consultant in psychiatry at Union Theological Seminary.

Laidlaw's interest in parapsychology led him to study hypnosis, mediumship, and the effect of chemical substances on the human mind. He presented the paper "Psychedelics: A New Road to the Understanding of Mediumistic Phenomena?" at the Conference on Parapsychology and Psychedelics held in New York in 1958. That same year his article on hypnosis and hypnoanalysis appeared in *Tomorrow* magazine (autumn 1958). Laidlaw investigated such topics as the effect on the mind of LSD 25 and the clinical aspects of spiritual healing. He also took an interest in the healing techniques of **Ambrose and Olga Worrall.**

Sources:

Pleasants, Helene, ed. *Biographical Dictionary of Parapsychology.* New York: Helix Press, 1964.

Lakshmi (Center)

Organization founded by former English professor Dr. Frederick Lenz, who was a disciple under guru **Sri Chinmoy** for 11 years. Given the name Atmananda by his guru, Lenz began teaching yoga in Los Angeles and throughout Southern California. His students reported a number of extraordinary experiences during his classes, including that Lenz was seen to levitate and disappear completely during group meditations and to radiate intense beams of light.

Lenz formed the Lakshmi center in the 1970s as an independent organization. Lakshmi is the Hindu goddess of fortune and the consort of Vishnu. In the early 1980s Lenz announced to a gathering of his students that Eternity had given him the new name "Rama." Accordingly, in 1985 Lakshmi was superseded by a new organization, Rama Seminars.

As Rama, Lenz teaches that humanity is approaching the end of a cycle. The present period is the Kali Yuga, the dark age of devolution. At the end of each cycle or age, the god Vishnu is due to become incarnated. While Rama (Lenz) does not claim to be the same conscious entity as the historic Rama (the hero of the religious epic Ramayana and a previous incarnation of Vishnu), Lenz does claim to be the embodiment of the "particular octave of celestial light which was once before incarnated as the historic Rama."

Rama Seminars was headquartered in southern California through the 1980s. However, a scandal, occasioned by accusation of abuse by several of Lenz's students, disrupted the organization, which has moved its headquarters to the East Coast.

Sources:

The Last Incarnation. Malibu, Calif.: Lakshmi Publications, 1983.

Lenz, Frederick. *Life Times.* New York: Fawcett Crest, 1979.

Rama [Frederic Lenz]. *The Wheel of Dharma.* Malibu, Calilf.: Lakshmi Publications, 1982.

Lam

A mystical word in Hindu **yoga** practice that is associated with the **Muladhara chakra,** or subtle energy center situated at the base of the human spine. Each chakra has its characteristic shape, colors, symbolic figure, and mantra (mystical sounds formed by combinations of letters). "Lam" is a *bija,* or seed, **mantra,—**a special form of natural power that can be liberated by meditation. (See also **kundalini**)

Lama Foundation

New Age communal center founded in 1968 by a small group wishing to work for the awakening of higher consciousness. Members agreed to live and work full time wherever needed, to participate in group meetings and decisions, and to cooperate in fundraising ventures. The foundation conducts programs of regular meditation, group meetings, communal meals, work projects, farming and gardening, and book publishing. The intensive study center houses 12 students and a teacher in intensive practices and studies. Lama Foundation plans seminars for music study, Vipassana (insight), meditation, and the study of various religious traditions. Address: Box 44, San Cristobal, NM 87564.

Sources:

Dass, Baba Ram. *Be Here Now.* San Cristobal, N.Mex.: Lama Foundation, 1971.

Gardner, Hugh. *The Children of Prosperity.* New York: St. Martin's Press, 1978.

Hedgepath, William, and Dennis Stock. *The Alternative.* New York: Macmillan, 1970.

Lamb, John (d. 1628)

Lamb was a noted astrologer and reputed sorcerer in the time of Charles I. In *Certainty of the World of Spirits* (1691), Richard Baxter recorded an apocryphal account in which Lamb met two acquaintances who wished to witness some examples of his skill. He invited them home with him, conducted them into an inner room, then, to their great surprise, they saw a tree spring up in the middle of Lamb's apartment. A moment later three diminutive men appeared with axes in their hands to cut down this tree. After the tree was felled, the doctor dismissed his guests.

That night a tremendous hurricane arose, causing the house of one of the guests to rock from side to side, with every appearance that the building would come down and bury him and his wife in the ruins. The wife in great terror asked, "Were you not at Dr. Lamb's to-day?" The husband confessed the truth. "And did you not bring something away from his house?" The husband admitted that, when the little men felled the tree, he had picked up some of the chips and put them in his pocket. As soon as he obtained the chips, and got rid of them, the whirlwind immediately ceased, and the remainder of the night passed quietly.

Originally a physician, Lamb became known for practicing "other mysteries, as telling fortunes, helping of divers to lost goods, showing to young people the faces of their husbands or wives that should be in a crystal glass." It is possible that popular resentment against Lamb was due less to the success of his magical practices than his position as a favorite of the duke of Buckingham. It was generally believed that Lamb used magic charms to corrupt women to serve the pleasure of the duke.

Lamb eventually was so hated for his infernal practices that a mob tore him to pieces in the street. Then, 13 years later, a woman who had worked as a maid in Lamb's house was charged with witchcraft, tried, and executed at Tyburn.

A broadside ballad by Martin Parker titled "The Tragedy of Doctor Lambe, the great supposed conjurer, who was wounded to death by saylers and other lads, on Friday the 14 of June, 1628. And dyed in the Poultry Counter, neere cheap-side, on the Saturday morning following" was sold and sung in the streets. The ballad contains two mistakes, as Lamb was mobbed on June 13 and died the following day.

Lambert, G(uy) W(illiam) (1889–1983)

A British government official who took an active interest in psychic research. He was born in London, England, on December 1, 1889, studied at St. John's College, Oxford University (B.A. with honors, 1912), and was a member of the British Civil Service (1913–51). From 1938 to 1951 Lambert was assistant undersecretary of state for war; he received the Chevalier, Legion of Honor (1920), the Silver Jubilee Medal (1935), the Coronation Medal (1937), and the Companion of the Bath (1942).

Beginning in 1925 Lambert was a council member of the **Society for Psychical Research** (SPR), London. He served as president (1955–58) and as honorary secretary beginning in 1958. He studied spontaneous phenomena involving **ESP, haunting** and **poltergeists,** and the **Glastonbury Scripts** of **Frederick Bligh Bond.** He contributed various articles to publications of the SPR.

Lambert, who died December 15, 1983, was one of the longest serving members of the Society for Psychical Research, having been a member for 70 years.

Sources:

Berger, Arthur S., and Joyce Berger. *The Encyclopedia of Parapsychology and Psychical Research.* New York: Paragon House, 1991.

Lambert, G. W. "Antoine Richard's Garden." *Journal* of the Society for Psychical Research 37 (July–October 1953, March–April 1954); 41 (June 1962).

———. "The Dieppe Raid Case." *Journal* of the Society for Psychical Research 35 (May–June 1952).

———. "Poltergeists: A Psychical Theory." *Journal* of the Society for Psychical Research 38 (June 1955).

———. "The Quest at Glastonbury." *Journal* of the Society for Psychical Research 43 (1966).

Pleasants, Helene, ed. *Biographical Dictionary of Parapsychology.* New York: Helix Press, 1964.

Lambert, R(ichard) S(tanton) (1894– ?)

Broadcasting official and author who explored the field of parapsychology and published books and articles on the subject. He was born on August 25, 1894, at Kingston-on-Thames, England, and studied at Oxford University (M.A., 1921). He tutored at the University of Sheffield (1919–23), then at the University of London (1923–28). He was editor of the *Listener,* published by the British Broadcasting Corporation (BBC) (1928–39), then moved to Canada where in 1943 he became supervisor of school broadcasts for the Canadian Broadcasting Corporation (CBC). He won the Governor General of Canada Medal for Juvenile Literature in 1949. Lambert wrote over 30 books dealing with biography, children's adventure, travel, art, crime, radio, films, propaganda, and various school textbooks.

In the field of parapsychology he investigated **poltergeist** phenomena with **Harry Price,** with whom he was joint author of *The Haunting of Cashen's Gap* (1936). The publicity around this celebrated case nearly cost Lambert his career as editor of the *Listener,* when one of the governors of the BBC concluded that an interest in the supernatural was a reflection on Lambert's competence. Lambert challenged him by suing him for defamation. Lambert tells the story of this case in his biographical works *Ariel and All His Quality* (1940). Lambert's *Exploring the Supernatural* (1955) also deals with parapsychology. (See also **Cashen's Gap**)

Sources:

Lambert, Ricahrd Stanton. *Areil and all His Quality.* London: V. Gollancz Ltd., 1940.

———. *Exploring the Supernatural.* London: A. Barker, 1955.

Price, Harry, and R. S. Lambert. *The Haunting of Cashen's Gap.* N.p., 1936.

Pleasants, Helene, ed. *Biographical Dictionary of Parapsychology.* New York: Helix Press, 1964.

Lamia

In ancient Greek folklore, Lamia was a shape-shifting monster that sucked blood and ate flesh, similar to stories of the succubus and **vampire.** Lamia, the daughter of Belus and Libya, was loved by Zeus and punished by Hera. Because Hera took Lamia's children away, Lamia took her revenge on the children of men and women, since she had no power over gods. Lamia became transformed into a class of demonic being in Greek lore, the *lamiai.* According to folk beliefs, the *lamiai* might be in the form of a beautiful woman, a snake with a woman's head, or a monster with deformed lower limbs and the power to take out her eyes. (See also **Striges**)

Sources:

Lawson, John Cuthbert. *Modern Greek Folklore and Ancient Greek Religion.* 1910. Reprint, New Hyde Park, N.Y.: University Books, 1964.

Lampadomancy

Form of **divination** based on reading the form, color, and movements of the flame of an oil lamp or a torch. A flame with a single point was believed to indicate good fortune, but two points signaled bad luck. A flame that bent might indicate illness. Sparks were said to indicate forthcoming news, and the sudden extinction of the flame portended disaster.

Sources:

Waite, Arthur Edward. *The Occult Sciences.* 1891. Reprint, Secaucus, N.J.: University Books, 1974.

Lamps, Magic

Stories of magic lamps are of great antiquity. According to G. Panciroli (1523–1599), the sepulcher of Tullia, daughter of the Roman statesman Cicero (106–43 B.C.E.), had a lamp that burned for over 1,550 years. St. Augustine described a lamp placed by the seashore that was not extinguished by wind or rain. Monsignor Guerin, the chamberlain of Pope Leo XIII, told of a lamp before the shrine of St. Genevieve in the Church of St. Denis whose oil was always consumed but never diminished in quantity.

Another lamp legend concerned Rabbi Jachiel of Paris, who was regarded by the Jews as one of their saints and by the Parisians as a sorcerer. During the night when everyone was asleep, he was believed to work by the light of a magic lamp that illuminated his chamber like the sun itself. The rabbi never replenished this lamp with oil, nor otherwise attended to it, and folks began to hint that he had acquired it through diabolic agencies. If anyone knocked at his door during the night, they reported seeing the lamp throw out sparks of light of various colors, but if they continued to rap, the lamp failed, and the rabbi would touch a large nail in the middle of his table that connected magically with the knocker on his door, giving the person who rapped on it something of the nature of an electric shock (see **France**).

One of the best-known stories is the one about Aladdin and his lamp from the *Arabian Nights Entertainment,* or *Book of a Thousand and One Nights,* in which the lamp is a magic wish-fulfilling **talisman.** Although versions of the stories in the *Arabian Nights* are of some antiquity, some of the tales, like that of Aladdin, are from late Egyptian sources.

Another well-known legend is that of the tomb of Christian Rosenkreutz, founder of the Order of the Rosy Cross, or **Rosicrucians.** According to the Rosicrucian manifesto *Fama Fra-*

ternitatis (first printed in 1614), translated together with the manifesto *Confessio Fraternitatis* (1615) by "Eugenius Philalethes" (the pseudonym used by alchemist **Thomas Vaughan**) in London, 1652, the tomb of Christian Rosenkreutz was opened many years after his death, and a secret vault was discovered with an ever-burning lamp, together with magical mirrors, sacred books, bells, more ever-burning lamps, and "artificial songs," which sounded like precursors of the phonograph record. For an attempt to separate history from legend and symbolism in this story, see Arthur E. Waite's *The Brotherhood of the Rosy Cross* (1924). Many stories of ever-burning lamps stem from phosphorescent phenomena or from spontaneous combustion caused by the sudden influx of air into a gaseous vault.

Sources:

Waite, Arthur E. *The Brotherhood of the Rosy Cross.* 1924. Reprint, New Hyde Park, N.Y.: University Books, 1961.

Lancashire Witches

A famous episode of ignorance, superstition, and persecution in Lancashire, England, which involved a mass trial of 20 alleged witches. Not far from Manchester lies Pendelbury Forest, where, at the beginning of the seventeenth century, witches were said to live. Terrified townspeople avoided the place, imaginging it to be the scene of frightful orgies and diabolical rites. Roger Nowel, a country magistrate, hit upon the plan of routing the witches out of their den and ridding the district of their malevolent influence, and he believed he would be performing a public-spirited and laudable service.

He promptly seized Elizabeth Demdike and Ann Chattox, two women of 80 years of age, one blind and the other threatened with blindness, both living in squalor and abject poverty. Demdike's daughter, Elizabeth Device, and her grandchildren, James and Alison Device, were included in the accusation, and Ann Redferne, daughter of Chattox, was apprehended with her mother.

Also seized in quick succession were Jane Bulcock and her son John, Alice Nutter, Catherine Hewitt, and Isabel Roby. All of them were induced to make a more or less detailed confession of the communication with the Devil. It is not known how these confessions were obtained, but considering the age and condition of the women, their confessions were probably extorted. Afterward they were sent to prison in Lancaster Castle, some 50 miles away, to await trial.

Soon after the authorities were informed that about 20 witches assembled on Good Friday at Malkin's Tower, the home of Elizabeth Device, in order to arrange the death of one Covel, to blow up the castle in which their companions were confined and rescue the prisoners, and also to kill a man called Lister by means of a diabolical agency.

In summer 1612, the prisoners were tried for **witchcraft** and were all found guilty. The woman Demdike had died in prison and thus escaped a more ignominious death at the gallows. The principal witnesses against Elizabeth Device were her grandchildren, James and Jannet Device. When Jannet entered the witness-box, her grandmother set up a terrible yelling punctuated by bitter execrations.

The child, who was only nine years of age, begged that the prisoner be removed so that she could proceed with her evidence. Her request was granted, and she and her brother swore that the devil had visited their grandmother in the shape of a black dog and asked what were her wishes. She said she desired the death of one John Robinson, whereupon the fiend told her to make a clay image of Robinson and gradually crumble it to pieces, saying that as she did so the man's life would decay and finally perish. On such evidence, 10 persons were hanged, including the aged Ann Chattox.

The story of the Lancashire witches became the subject of Thomas Shadwell's play of that name in 1681, and a novel by W. H. Ainsworth in 1848. Twenty-two years after the events of 1612, a similar outrage in the same area of Lancashire was narrowly avoided, by the shrewdness of the judge who tried the case. A man by the name of Edmund Robinson thought to profit by the general belief in witchcraft. He told his young son, a boy of 11, to say that he had encountered two dogs in the field, and he tried to get them to catch a hare. When the animals would not obey his bidding, he tied them to a post and whipped them, when they immediately turned into a witch and her imp.

The fiction gained such credence that Robinson declared that his son possessed a sort of **second-sight,** which enabled him to distinguish a witch at a glance. He took the boy to the neighboring churches, set him on a bench, and bade him point out the witches. The boy identified 17 persons, and the jury convicted them. They might have been hanged were it not for the judge's suspicions about the story.

The judge postponed their sentences and sent some of them to London for examination by the king's physician and by King Charles I himself. The boy's story was investigated and found to be false, and the child himself admitted the lie.

Sources:

Ainsworth, William Harrison. *The Lancashire Witches: A Romance of Pendle Forest.* London: George Routledge, 1878.

Robbins, Rossell Hope. *The Encyclopedia of Witchcraft and Demonology.* New York: Crown Publishers, 1959.

Whitaker, Thomas D. *A History of The Original Parish of Whalley.* London, 1818.

Lancaster, John B(usfield) (1891– ?)

Engineering technician who experimented in the field of parapsychology. He was born on January 19, 1891, in Philadelphia, Pennsylvania. He studied structural design and building at the Drexel Institute, Philadelphia (1914–18). He was a draftsman, power plant engineer, and chief draftsman at the Philadelphia Gas Works, 1911–55.

Lancaster developed games for testing telepathy and psychokinesis, which he presented to the **Parapsychology Laboratory** of Duke University in Durham, North Carolina. During 1959 he conducted long-distance experiments in **telepathy** with students of Cambridge and Oxford universities in England and Wayland College in Plainview, Texas.

Sources:

Lancaster, John B. "A GESP Experiment with a Dual (Color-Symbol) Target." *Journal of Parapsychology* (December 1959).

Lancelin, Charles (ca. 1927–)

French physician and occultist who was an early experimenter in the field of **astral projection,** also known as **out-of-the-body travel.** He published a number of important books in the active period of French interest in occultism that preceded World War II.

Sources:

Lancelin, Charles. *L'ame humaine: etudes expérimentales de psycho-physiologie.* Paris: H. Durville, 1921.

———. *Comment on meurt, comment on nait.* Paris: H. Durville, 1912.

———. *La fraude dans la production des phénomès mediumiques.* N.p., 1912.

———. *Histoire mythique de Shatan: de la légende au dogme.* N.p., 1903.

———. *L'humanité posthume et le monde angélique.* N.p., n.d.

———. *Méthode de dédoublement personnel.* N.p., 1913.

———. *L'occultisme et la science.* Paris: J. Meyer, 1926.

———. *L'occultisme et la vie.* Paris: Editions Adyar, 1928.

———. *Qu'est-ce l'âme?* N.p., n.d.

———. *La réincarnation.* N.p., n.d.

———. *La sorcellerie des campagnes.* N.p., 1923.

———. *La vie posthume.* Paris: H. Durville, 1922.

Landau, Lucian (1912–)

Industrial consultant who experimented and lectured in the field of parapsychology. He was born on April 13, 1912, in Warsaw, Poland. He first came to England as a business executive and consultant in the rubber, plastics, and electronics industries. He invented various devices and processes used in Britain, France, and Italy and wrote a study on latex published by the British Rubber Development Board in 1954.

Landau experimented with **dowsing, clairvoyance, psychic photography,** and **radiasthesia** and lectured on such subjects to the Medical Society for the Study of Radiesthesia, the Cambridge University Society for the Study of Parapsychology, and the **College of Psychic Science,** London. He published articles in *Light* journal, including a report on the Delawarr Camera (vol. 77, no. 3430 [March 1957]). (See also **black box**)

Sources:

Landau, Lucian. "Radionics: General Considerations." *Journal of the British Society of Dowsers* (September 1958).

Pleasants, Helene, ed. *Biographical Dictionary of Parapsychology.* New York: Helix Press, 1964.

Lane, David (Christopher) (1956–)

Philosophy professor and writer on new religious movements. He was born on April 29, 1956, and received his education at Los Angeles Valley College (Associate of Arts) and California State University, Northridge (B.A.). He did his graduate work at the Graduate Theological Union (M.A.) and the University of California at Berkeley from which he received both a M.A. and Ph.D. in sociology. While there he was a research assistant to Mark Juergensmeyer on a grant to study the trans-national Radhasoami faith. He traveled throughout North India and compiled an exhaustive genealogical tree of Radhasoami gurus and gaddis (seats of Sikh gurus). He helped to produce a documentary film on the history of Sant Mat (a transcendental Sikh movement), and was instrumental in arranging a rare interview with Baba Faqir Chand, then a 94-year-old sage in the foothills of the Himalayas. The research became the basis of his M.A. thesis (1981) and ultimately a book, *The Radhasoami Tradition* (1992). His research also helped satisfy his own spiritual quest and in 1978 he was initiated by Radhasoami master Maharaj Charan Singh.

Prior to assuming his present position, Lane taught at the University of California, San Diego, where he received a Regents Fellowship in Sociology.

Lane's research on the Radhasoami movement led to work on two modern western offshoots of the movement, **ECKANKAR** and the Movement for Inner Spiritual Awareness (MSIA), both of which had denied their contact with the larger movement. The first result was the publication in 1983 of *The Making of a Spiritual Movement* (originally presented as a term paper at California State University, Northridge, 1978), a detailed study of the intellectual roots of ECKANKAR and of its founder, **Paul Twitchell.** The book charged that Twitchell had been trained by Radhasoami master Kirpal Singh and had plagiarized extensively from Radhasoami literature in books circulated as ECKANKAR texts. Lane went on to found a journal, *Understanding Cults and Spiritual Movements,* with his colleague Brian Walsh and continued his research on various Radhasoami and Indian-based groups, some of which he felt had perverted the Radhasoami tradition. John Roger Hinkins and Da Free John especially became objects of severe criticism.

Lane's own publishing venture was interrupted in the mid-1980s by a series of events including some death threats, a break-in at his home, and the theft of his mailing lists and other documents. However, he has continued to write in the field and has recently published two volumes, including an updated text of his early study of the Radhasoami tradition and an anthology of his critical works on Indian spiritual movements.

Sources:

Lane, David Christopher. *Exposing Cults: When the Skeptical Mind Confronts the Mystical.* New York: Garland Publishing, 1994.

———. *The Making of a Spiritual Movement.* Del Mar, Calif.: Del Mar Press, 1983.

———. *The Radhasoami Tradition: A Critical History of Guru Successorship.* New York: Garland Publishing, 1992.

Lang, Andrew (1844–1912)

Philosopher, poet, scholar, and author of scholarly books on a wide range of topics, including anthropology, folklore, mythology, psychology, ghost lore, history, biography, and fairy tales. He was born at Selkirk, Scotland, on March 31, 1844, and was educated at St. Andrews University. He also studied at Glasgow University and Oxford University (Balliol and Merton colleges). Lang abandoned his fellowship at Merton College to become a journalist and author in London.

He joined the **Society for Psychical Research** (SPR) in 1906, but his interest in psychical phenomena was of longer standing. Lang studied them rather from the historic and anthropologic, than from the experimental, viewpoint.

His earliest paper was read before the SPR on the **Cock Lane Ghost** in 1894. Subsequently he was a frequent contributor to the society's *Proceedings* and *Journal.* In the *Journal* (vol. 7) he wrote on Queen Mary's diamonds; in *Proceedings* (vol. 11) on the voices of Joan of Arc. The telepathy *à trois* (involving three individuals) was his conception in a paper on the mediumship of **Leonora Piper.** His book *Custom and Myth,* published in 1884, contained a chapter on the **divining rod,** which he regarded as a mischievous instrument of superstition. However, the investigations of **William Barrett** convinced him that it was "a fact, and a very serviceable fact." Lang also contributed some valuable personal evidence on **crystal gazing.**

He wrote several articles on psychic research for the *Encyclopaedia Britannica* in 1902. His books *The Making of Religion* (1898), *Magic and Religion* (1901), *Cock Lane and Common Sense* (1894), and *The Book of Dreams and Ghosts* (1897) are regarded as valuable tools for students of psychic research. *The Mind of France* (1908) was the first attempt to consider Joan of Arc in the light of psychic phenomena. In 1911 Lang became president of the Society for Psychical Research. According to the Rev. M. A. Bayfield in *Proceedings* (vol. 26), it is fair to infer from Lang's later writings that he found the exclusion of an external agency from some phenomena increasingly difficult.

The range and content of Lang's books and writings demonstrate remarkable originality and scholarship. He was the first scholar to properly correlate the mythology of ancient society with the folklore and psychic phenomena of modern civilization. His rainbow-colored series of fairy tale books for children, beginning with *The Blue Fairy Book* in 1889, remains popular.

Lang was honored by St. Andrews and Oxford universities and was elected an honorary fellow of Merton College in 1890. The freedom of his native town of Selkirk was conferred on him in 1889. He died July 20, 1912.

Sources:

Berger, Arthur S., and Joyce Berger. *The Encyclopedia of Parapsychology and Psychical Research.* New York: Paragon House, 1991.

Lang, Andrew. *The Book of Dreams and Ghosts.* 1897. Reprint, New York: Causeway Books, 1974.

———. *Cock Lane and Common Sense.* London: Longmans, Green, 1894. Reprint, New York: AMS Press, 1970.

———. *Magic and Religion.* 1901. Reprint, New York: Greenwood Press, 1969.

———. *The Maid of France, Being the Story of the Life and Death of Jeanne d'Arc.* London: Longmans, Green, 1908.

———. *The Making of Religion.* 1898. Reprint, New York: AMS Press, 1968.

Pleasants, Helene, ed. *Biographical Dictionary of Parapsychology.* New York: Helix Press, 1964.

Lanz von Liebenfels, Jörg (1874–1954)

Austrian astrologer and member of the occult underground preceding the Nazi movement. His **Order of New Templars** only admitted members who had satisfied his racist concepts of Nordic purity. He also founded the Ariosophical Movement, another occult and anti-Semitic organization.

Born in Vienna July 19, 1874, as Adolf Lanz, he claimed to be the son of Baron Johannes Lancz de Liebenfels. He circulated an incorrect birthdate to mislead other astrologers. He became a novice at a Cistercian monastery but was expelled for improper behavior. Soon afterward he founded his Order of New Templars, which claimed divine support for Hilter's race theories and the supremacy of a master race. Lanz advocated special breeding colonies, or stud farms, for the master race, as well as the elimination of lesser breeds.

The order used the swastika symbol before it was officially adopted by the Nazi party, and Hitler met Lanz as early as 1909, when he collected some issues of Lanz's journal *Ostara.* Lanz prophesied the success of Hilter as a world figure but failed to find favor with the Nazis after their 1938 invasion of Austria. His ideas were certainly used by the Nazis, but Hitler may have been reluctant to admit their origin. Lanz died April 22, 1954.

Sources:

Daim, W. *Der Mann, der Hitler die Ideen gab* (The man who gave Hitler the ideas). München: Isar Verlag, 1958.

Sklar, Dusty. *Gods and Beasts: The Nazis and the Occult.* New York: Thomas Y. Crowell, 1977.

Webb, Janes, *The Occult Establishment.* La Salle, Ill.: Open Court, 1976.

Lapis Exilis

A fabulous precious stone believed to cause the phoenix to renew her youth. According to Wolfram von Eschenbach, the Lapis exilis was synonymous with the Holy **Grail.** (See also **Lapis Judaicus**)

Lapis Judaicus

A fabulous precious stone also identified with the Holy **Grail** and the talismanic stone of inexhaustible feeding power. It was sometimes called "Theolithos" and may have been another name for the **Lapis Exilis.** It has also been known as the Phoenix stone. Another legend claimed that it fell from the crown of Lucifer as he was banished from heaven and remained in the keeping of the angels of the air.

LAPLAND

The Laplanders acquired a reputation for magical practice that was almost proverbial throughout Europe, and certainly so among the peoples of the Scandinavian peninsula. Indeed the Finns used to credit them with extraordinary power in sorcery and divination. Many Scandinavian scions of nobility were in ancient times sent to Lapland to obtain a magical reputation, and Eric, the son of Harold Haarfager, found Gunhild, daughter of Asur Tote, living among the Lapps in 922 C.E. for that purpose. English literature abounds with references to Lapland witches. But sorcery in Lapland was a preserve of the male shamans or magicians. Like the Celtic witches, the Lapps were addicted to the selling of wind or tempests in knotted ropes.

In his *The History of Lapland* (1674), Joannes W. Scheffer describes Lapp magic,

"The melancholic constitution of the Laplanders, renders them subject to frightful apparitions and dreams, which they look upon as infallible presages made to them by the Genius of what is to befall them. Thus they are frequently seen lying upon the ground asleep, some singing with a full voice, others howling and making a hideous noise not unlike wolves.

"Their superstitions may be imputed partly to their living in solitudes, forests, and among the wild beasts, partly to their solitary way of dwelling separately from the society of others, except who belong to their own families sometimes several leagues distance. Hereafter it may be added, that their daily exercise is hunting, it being observed that this kind of life is apt to draw people into various superstitions, and at last to a correspondence with spirits. For those who lead a solitary life being frequently destitute of human aid, have ofttimes recourse to forbidden means, in hopes to find that aid and help among the spirits, which they cannot find among men; and what encourages them in it is impunity, these things being committed by them, without as much as the fear of any witnesses; which moved Mr. Rheen to allege, among sundry reasons which he gives for the continuance of the impious superstitions of the Laplanders, this for one: because they live among inaccessible mountains, and at a great distance from the conversation of other men. Another reason is the good opinion they constantly entertain of their ancestors, whom they cannot imagine to have been so stupid as not to understand what God they ought to worship, wherefore they judge they should be wanting in their reverence due to them if, by receding from their institutions, they should reprove them of impiety and ignorance.

"The parents are the masters, who instruct their own sons in the magical art. 'Those,' says Tornaeus, 'who have attained to this magical art by instructions receive it either from their parents, or from somebody else, and that by degrees which they put in practice as often as an opportunity offers. Thus they accomplish themselves in this art, especially if the genius leads them to it. For they don't look upon every one as a fit scholar; nay, some are accounted quite incapable of it, notwithstanding they have been sufficiently instructed, as I have been informed by very credible people.' And Joh. Tornaeus confirms it by these words: 'As the Laplanders are naturally of different inclinations, so are they not equally capable of attaining to this art.' And in another passage, they bequeath the demons as part of their inheritance, which is the reason that one family excels the other in this magical art. From whence it is evident, that certain whole families have their own demons, not only differing from the familiar spirits of others, but also quite contrary and opposite to them. Besides this, not only whole families, but also particular persons, have sometimes one, sometimes more spirits belonging to them, to secure them against the designs of other demons, or else to hurt others.

"Olaus Petri Niurenius speaks to this effect, when he says—'They are attended by a certain number of spirits, some by three, others by two, or at least by one. The last is intended for their security, the other to hurt others. The first commands all the rest. Some of those they acquire with a great deal of pains and prayers, some without much trouble, being their attendants from their infancy.' Joh. Tornaeus gives us a very large account of it. 'There are some,' says he, 'who naturally are magicians; an abominable thing indeed. For those who the devil knows will prove very serviceable to him in this art, he seizes on in their very infancy with certain distemper, when they are haunted with apparitions and visions, by which they are, in proportion of their age, instructed in the rudiments of this art. Those who are a second time taken with this distemper, have more apparitions coming before them than in the first, by which they receive much more insight into it than before. But if they are seized a third time with this disease, which then proves very dangerous, and often not without the hazard of their lives, then it is they see all the apparitions the devil is able to contrive, to accomplish them in the magical art. Those are arrived to such a degree of perfection, that without the help of the drum (see infra), they can foretell things to come a great while before; and are so strongly possessed by the devil, that they foresee things even against their will. Thus, not long ago, a certain Laplander, who is still alive, did voluntarily deliver his drum to me, which I had often desired of him before; notwithstanding all this, he told me in a very melancholy posture, that though he had put away his drum, nor intended to have any other hereafter, yet he could foresee everything without it, as he had done before. As an instance of it, he told me truly all the particular accidents that had happened to me in my journey into Lapland, making at the same time heavy complaints, that he did not know what use to make of his eyes, those things being presented to his sight much against his will.'

"Lundius observes, that some of the Laplanders are seized upon by a demon, when they are arrived to a middle age, in the following manner: 'Whilst they are busie in the woods, the spirit appears to them, where they discourse concerning the conditions, upon which the demon offers them his assistance, which done, he teaches them a certain song, which they are obliged to keep in constant remembrance. They must return the next day to the same place, where the same spirit appears to them again, and repeats the former song, in case he takes a fancy to the person; if not, he does not appear at all. These spirits make their appearances under different shapes, some like fishes, some like birds, others like a serpent or dragon, others in the shape of a pigmee, about a yard high; being attended by three, four, or five other pigmees of the same bigness, sometimes by more, but never exceeding nine.'

"No sooner are they seized by the Genius, but they appear in the most surprising posture, like madmen, before bereaved of the use of reason. This continues for six months; during which time they don't suffer any of their kindred to come near them, not so much as their own wives and children. They spend most of this time in the woods and other solitary places, being very melancholy and thoughtful scarce taking any food, which makes them extremely weak. If you ask their children, where and how their parents sustain themselves, they will tell you, that they receive their sustenance from their Genii.

"The same author gives us a remarkable instance of this kind in a young Laplander called Olaus, being then a scholar in the school of Liksala, of about eighteen years of age. This young fellow fell mad on a sudden, making most dreadful postures and outcries, that he was in hell, and his spirit tormented beyond what could be expressed. If he took a book in hand, so soon as he met with the name of Jesus, he threw the book upon the ground in great fury, which after some time being passed over, they used to ask him whether he had seen any vision during this ecstasy? He answered that abundance of things had appeared to him, and that a mad dog being tied to his foot, followed him wherever he stirred. In his lucid intervals he would tell them, that the first beginning of it happened to him one day, as he was going out of the door of his dwelling, when a great flame passed before his eyes and touching his ears, a certain person appeared to him all naked. The next day he was seized with a most terrible headache, so that he made most lamentable outcries, and broke everything that came under his hands. This unfortunate person's face was as black as coal, and he used to say, that the devil most commonly appeared to him in the habit of a minister, in a long cloak; during his fits he would say that he was surrounded by nine or ten fellows of a low stature, who did use him very barbarously, though at the same time the standers-by did not perceive the least thing like it. He would often climb to the top of the highest fir trees, with as much swiftness as a squirrel, and leap down again to the ground, without receiving the least hurt. He always loved solitude, flying the conversation of other men. He would run as swift as a horse, it being impossible for anybody to overtake him. He used to talk amongst the woods to himself no otherwise than if several persons had been in his company.

"I am apt to believe, that those spirits were not altogether unknown to the ancients, and that they are the same which were called by Tertullian *Paredri,* and are mentioned by Monsieur [Herride] Valois, in his *Ecclesiastical History of Eusebius.*

"Whenever a Laplander has occasion for his familiar spirit, he calls to him, and makes him come by only singing the song he taught him at their first interview; by which means he has him at his service as often as he pleases. And because they know them obsequious and serviceable, they call them Sveie, which signifies as much in their tongue, as the companions of their labour, or their helpmates. Lundius has made another observation, very well worth taking notice of, viz.:—That those spirits of demons never appear to the women, or enter into their service, of which I don't pretend to allege the true cause, unless one might say, that perhaps they do it out of pride, or a natural aversion they have to the female sex, subject to so many infirmities."

The Magic Drum

For the purposes of augury or **divination,** the Lapps employed a magic drum, which, indeed, was in use among several Arctic peoples. Writing in 1827, De Capell Brooke states that the ceremonies connected with this instrument had almost quite disappeared at that date. The encroachments of Lutheranism had been long threatening the existence of the native shamanism. In 1671 the Lapp drum was formally banned by Swedish law, and several magicians were apprehended and their instruments burned. But before that date the religion the drum represented was in full vigor.

The Lapps called their drum *Kannus* (Regnard, 1681), also *Kaunus, Kabdas, Kabdes Gabdas,* and *Keure* (Von Duben, 1873), its Scandinavian designations being *troll-trumma,* or *Rune-bomme,* "magic or runic drum," otherwise *Spa-trumma,* "fortune-telling drum." J. A. Friis has shown that the *sampo* of the Finnish national epic poem *Kalevala* is the same instrument. According to G. W. von Düben, the best pictures and explanations of the drum are to be found in *Lappisk Mythologi* (Christiania, 1871) by J. A. Friis (pp. 30–47) but there are good descriptions in G. W. von Düben's own work *Om Lappland och Lapparne* (Stockholm 1873), as also in the books of Scheffer, Leem, Jessen, and others.

The appearance of the Lapp drum was thus described by Jean François Regnard in 1681,

"This instrument is made of a single piece of wood, hollowed in its thickest part in an oval form, the under part of which is convex, in which they make two apertures long enough to suffer the fingers to pass through, for that purpose of holding it more firmly. The upper part is covered with the skin of the reindeer, on which they paint in red a number of figures, and from whence several brass rings are seen hanging, and some pieces of the bone of the reindeer."

A wooden hammer, or, as among the Samoyeds (1614), a hare's foot was used as a drumstick in the course of the incantation. An *arpa* or divining-rod was placed on a definite spot showing from its position after sounding the drum what magic inference might be drawn. By means of the drum, the priest could be placed in sympathy with the spirit world, and was thus enabled to divine the future, to ascertain synchronous events occurring at remote distances, to forecast the measure of success attending the day's hunting, to heal the sick, or to inflict people with disease and cause death. Although long obsolete in Lapland, these rites survived for a long time among the Samoyeds and other races of Arctic Asia and America. It is interesting to note how exactly the procedure described among the Vaigatz Samoyeds in 1556 (*Pinkerton's Voyages,* London, 1808, I, 63) tallied with the account of the Sakhalin Ainos in 1883 (J. M. Dixon in the *Transactions of the Asiatic Society of Japan,* Yokohama, 1883, 47). The same practices can be traced eastward through Arctic America, and the drum was used in the same fashion by the Eskimo shaman priests in Greenland (Hinrich Johannes Rink's *Tales and Traditions of the Eskimos,* 1875, pp. 60–61). The shape of the drum varied a little according to locality. The form of the Eskimo drum was that of a tambourine.

According to J. J. Tornaeus

"Their most valuable instrument of enchantment is this sorcerer's kettle-drum, which they call Kannas or Quobdas. They cut it in one entire piece out of a thick tree stem, the fibres of which run upwards in the same direction as the course of the sun. The drum is covered with the skin of an animal; and in the bottom holes are cut by which it may be held. Upon the skins are many figures painted, often Christ and the Apostles, with the heathen gods, Thor, Noorjunkar, and others jumbled together; the pictures of the sun, shapes of animals, lands and waters, cities and roads, in short, all kinds of drawings according to their various uses. Upon the drum there is placed an indicator, which they call *Arpa,* which consists of a bundle of metallic rings. The drumstick is, generally, a reindeer's horn.

"This drum they preserve with the most vigilant care, and guard it especially from the touch of a woman. When they will make known what is taking place at a distance,—as to how the chase shall succeed, how business will answer, what result a sickness will have, what is necessary for the cure of it, and the like, they kneel down, and the sorcerer beats the drum; at first with light strokes, but as he proceeds, with ever louder stronger ones, round the index, either till this has moved in a direction or to a figure which he regards as the answer which he has sought, or till he himself falls into ecstasy, when he generally lays the kettle-drum on his head.

"Then he sings with a loud voice a song which they call *Jogke,* and the men and women who stand round sing songs, which they call *Daura,* in which the name of the place whence they desire information frequently occurs. The sorcerer lies in the ecstatic state for some time—frequently for many hours, apparently dead, with rigid features; sometimes with perspiration bursting out upon him. In the meantime the bystanders continue their incantations, which have for their object that the sleeper shall not lose any part of his vision from memory; at the same time they guard him carefully that nothing living may touch him—not even a fly. When he again awakes to consciousness, he relates his vision, answers the questions put to him, and gives unmistakable evidence of having seen distant and unknown things."

The inquiry of the oracle does not always take place solemnly and completely. In everyday matters as regards the chase, etc., the Lapp consults his drum without falling into the somnambulic crisis. On the other hand, a more highly developed state of prophetic vision may take place without this instrument, as has already been stated. Claudi relates and incident from Bergen, Norway, concerning the clerk of a German merchant who demanded a Norwegian Finn-Laplander tell him what his master was doing in Germany. The Finn promised to give him the intelligence. He first began to cry out like a drunken man, and to run round in a circle, until he fell, as one dead, to the earth. After a while he woke again, and gave the answer, which time showed to be correct.

Finally, that many Lapp shamans, while wholly awake and free from convulsions, were able to become clairvoyant, is asserted by Tornaeus: "The use which they make of their power of clairvoyance, and their magic arts, is, for the most part, good and innocent; that of curing sick men and animals; inquiring into far-off and future things, which in the confined sphere of their existence is important to them. There are instances however, in which the magic art is turned to the injury of others."

Sources:

Abercromby, John. *The Pre- and Proto-historic Finns.* 2 vols. N.p., 1898.

Jessen-Schardebøl, E. J. *Afhandling om de Norske Finners og Lappers Hedenske Religion.* N.p., 1765.

Petitot, Émile. *Les Grands Esquimaux.* N.p., 1887.

Sioborg, N. H. *Tympanum Schamanico-lapponicum.* N.p., 1808.

Larcher, Hubert (1921–)

French physician and authority on industrial medicine who was also active in the field of parapsychology. Larcher was born June 26, 1921, in Paris, France. He studied at the University of Grenoble (Licencié en philosophie, 1943) and the University of Paris (M.D., 1951; diploma in industrial hygiene and industrial medicine, 1955). From 1961 onward he was professor of hygiene and safety at Ecole Normale Sociale, Paris. He became a council member of the Institut Métapsychique International.

Larcher took a special interest in paranormal psychophysiology, pathogenesis, and paranormal cures. He studied the relationship between parapsychology, psychic research, and mysticism, and investigated physiological aspects of metamorphosis and survival, as well as such parapsychological phenomena as **levitation** and **psychokinesis.** He is the author of *Le sang peut-il vaincre la mort?* and the editor of *Aux frontierès de la science* (1957).

Sources:

Larcher, Hubert. "Perspectives parapsychochimiques: La Drogue" (Parapsychochemical Outlook: Narcotics). *La Tour St. Jacques* 1 (1960).

———. "Prodiges sanguins après la mort" (Wonders of the Blood after Death). *Revue Métapsychique* (Sept.–Oct. 1953; Nov.–Dec. 1953).

———. "Towards a Science of Healing." *Proceedings* of Four Conferences on Parapsychological Studies (1957).

———. "Trois cas extraordinaires d'oncorruption de la chair" (Three Remarkable Cases of Lack of Decay of Flesh). *Revue Métapsychique* (March–April 1954).

Pleasants, Helene, ed. *Biographical Dictionary of Parapsychology.* New York: Helix Press, 1964.

Lascaris (fl. eighteenth century)

Legendary alchemist about whom limited facts are known. He was commonly supposed to have been active in Germany at the beginning of the eighteenth century, but everything recorded concerning him reads like a romance and suggests the Middle Ages.

According to popular belief, he claimed to be of Oriental origin, a native of the Ionian Isles, and a scion of the Greek royal house of Lascaris, while on other occasions he declared himself to be an archimandrite of a convent in the Island of Mytilene. His reason for coming to Europe was to solicit alms for the ransom of Christian prisoners in the East, but the alchemical achievements credited to him make this purpose unlikely. He began his wanderings in Germany around 1700. While staying in Berlin, Lascaris fell ill and sent for medical aid. It happened that Johann Friedrich Böttischer, the young apothecary who provided medical care, was deeply interested in **alchemy.** A friendship sprang up between physician and patient, and when Lascaris left the Prussian capital, he gave Böttischer a packet of transmuting powder and instructed him how to use it successfully, although he refrained from telling him how to manufacture the powder itself.

Böttischer set to work speedily, concocted considerable quantities of gold and silver, grew rich, was raised to the peerage, and began to mingle and be courted by kings and nobles, especially for his services as a scientist. The title of baron was conferred on him. When his supply of the precious powder ran short, and being unable to make more, he found his reputation waning rapidly. Because he had spent all his newly acquired wealth, Böttischer found himself reduced to penury. He was placed under house arrest, and when he attempted to escape he was removed to prison. During his detention he was allowed to experiment with chemistry. Böttischer discovered a process for the manufacture of red porcelain, and by the sale of this he eventually restored his fallen fortunes.

Why the alchemist gave the powder to Böttischer is unknown, as is the reason he made an analogous present to someone else at a later date. The second recipient was Schmolz de Dierbach, a lieutenant colonel in the Polish Army. Like the German apothecary, Schmolz succeeded in making a quantity of gold, although no more is known about him after this transmutation. A certain Baron de Creux was likewise favored by Lascaris, the baron's experiments proving just as successful as those of the others.

The alchemist bestowed his transmutatory powder on others as well, such as on Domenico Manuel, the son of a Neopolitan mason.

Manuel then wandered through Spain, Belgium, and Austria, performing alchemical operations before princes and noblemen, and reaping wealth accordingly.

Soon Manuel began styling himself Comte Gautano, then Comte di Ruggiero, and in one town he maintained that he was a Prussian major general. Elsewhere he declared that he was field marshal of the Bavarian forces. In Berlin he offered to make gold in the presence of the king, but when he failed, the king had him hanged as a charlatan.

That was in 1709, and in the same year, according to tradition, Lascaris himself performed some successful transmutations before a German politician named Liebknech, a citizen of Wurtembourg. Nothing further was ever heard of the mysterious alchemist, and his generosity had no parallel in the whole history of hermetic philosophy.

Laszlo, Laszlo (1898–1936)

One of the most famous fake mediums of Hungary during the 1920s. He was born in Budapest September 23, 1898, the son of a locksmith. At the age of 13 he was apprenticed to an electrician, by whom he was harshly treated. Laszlo ran away on several occasions but was returned by the police. After three and a half years apprenticeship, he beat up his master before finally leaving him.

Laszlo earned a living as an electrician until 1915, when he joined a Polish Legion of the Austro-German campaign against Russia. He fought at the front for nearly a year but deserted after being wounded. He was court-martialed, then escaped, later serving in a Hungarian unit on the Italian front in 1916. He deserted again when his girlfriend became a prostitute, and, since ordinary employment was barred to him, Laszlo joined a gang of burglars. He supported his girlfriend to keep her off the streets, but when he found that she was still living as a prostitute and even keeping pimps, he began to drink heavily and attempted suicide. He was arrested and imprisoned until October 1918, when the revolution in Hungary decreed a general amnesty.

After that, he continued his criminal activities, taking refuge from the police in southeast Hungary, where he became involved with an anti-Communist plot. Arrested and sentenced to be shot, Laszlo was freed by anti-Communists. He fought against Romanians until captured and taken to the death camp of Jassy, where he was beaten and starved for three months before he escaped.

Laszlo returned to Budapest, hoping that his criminal record had been lost in archives' burnings. According to his own account, he took a succession of jobs as actor, film extra, variety artist, playwright, painter, and electrical technician. The performance of a music hall hypnotist led him to become interested in **Spiritualism** and occultism.

With his background and emotional instability, it was a fatal mixture. Influenced by Laszlo's séances, several young men committed suicide in order to journey to the "Great Beyond." In 1920 Laszlo fell off a tram, and during two weeks in a hospital met a girl with whom he fell deeply in love. After recovery, he telephoned her, demanding that they become engaged, and when she refused him, he shot himself in the telephone booth. Back in the hospital, he fell in love with another girl, with whom he later formed a suicide pact. In a somewhat confused scene with a gun, the girl died, while Laszlo was only wounded. He was arrested for homicide.

The police astonishingly agreed to hold a Spiritualist séance at their headquarters with Laszlo as medium, during the course of which Laszlo claimed that he was the victim of an evil entity from the thirteenth century who desired to use psychic force to destroy victims. Laszlo was released, but he later claimed the séance to be a fake.

He then became a journalist on a Budapest newspaper, publishing articles about occultism and Spiritualism. Through them Laszlo was introduced to William Torday, president of the Hungarian Metapsychical Society. Torday and his colleagues believed that Laszlo had brilliant occult talents and persuaded him to sign an exclusive contract with them for séances. Laszlo duly produced fake spirit heads and hands and built up a reputation as a great medium.

After reading a classic work on **materialization** by famed psychic researcher **Baron Schrenck-Notzing,** Laszlo deliberately contrived to fake such effects in order to deceive the baron. The materials used by Laszlo for fake **ectoplasm** were gauze and cottonwool soaked in goose fat. These props were hidden in the furniture in the séance room, and when this became impossible through strict controls, Laszlo was impudently adroit in slipping his props into the pockets of his investigators when he was searched, then picking their pockets during the séance! It is not known whether Schrenck-Notzing was actually deceived, but many prominent psychic researchers were.

Laszlo was exposed in his **fraud** by Eugene Schenck, a music-hall hypnotist and stage clairvoyant. Anticipating publicity for his tricks, Laszlo himself admitted fraud at a public lecture and even reveled in them. In the aftermath of the scandal, Torday was discredited as a psychic researcher, and 67 of the 70 members of the Hungarian Metapsychical Society resigned. According to Laszlo, he was then visited by two young men who were members of a Spiritualist circle. They said they had received a spirit message that Laszlo should retract his confession of fraud or be killed. Laszlo accordingly drew up a public statement that his materialization phenomena were genuine, and he undertook not to combat Spiritualism in any way. This melodramatic episode may also be of Laszlo's invention. The story of Laszlo can be compared with that of the famous British fake medium **William Roy,** who was equally shameless.

Laszlo resumed his everyday work as an electrician, and in due course became a criminal again. Ten years later he was arrested for burglary and housebreaking. Before the hearing could be completed, he died of a lung hemorrhage in 1936.

Sources:

Tabori, Cornelius. *My Occult Diary.* London, 1951.

Tabori, Paul. *Companions of the Unseen.* London, 1968.

Latihan

A spiritual exercise that is a basic feature of the **Subud** movement (the term is Indonesian). The object of the latihan is worship of God. In a state of submission, contact is said to be made with the divine life force, resulting in a process of regeneration.

In principle the latihan can be practiced individually, but usually a number of individuals gather together for this purpose. The preliminary stages of the latihan are characterized by marked physical reactions. Urges to cry, weep, dance, or speak in tongues occur, but these may be stopped if need be. No particular stress is laid on such manifestations, but they are said to cause a release of tension that culminates in a state of inner quietude, in which communion with God takes place. All this is believed to have a strong resemblance to what is supposed to have occurred at the original Pentecostal scene.

In contrast to other spiritual movements and sects involving Pentecostal phenomena, there are no anticipatory stimulating speeches, music, ceremonies, or rituals; the ecstatic state emerges spontaneously. The cathartic quality of the latihan is said to manifest in a gradual integration of the entire being. In conjunction with the latihan, the problems of members are "tested," and answers are received in a state of inner receptivity.

The characteristic physical features of the latihan compare with the spiritual exercises of earlier religious movements such as the Shakers. The backwoods revivalists of Kentucky and Tennessee in the early nineteenth century often acted out "the jerks," similar to the physical convulsions of the early Methodists in Britain, who sometimes jumped and danced until they became insensible. In Hindu **yoga** practice, the onset of **kundalini,** or divine force, is also accompanied by jerking and twitching in the body.

Sources:

Van Hien, Gordon. *What is Subud?* London: Rider, 1963. Revised, 1968.

Laurel

A tree that Lucius Apuleius (ca. 126–173 B.C.E.) classed as among the plants which preserve men from the influence of evil spirits. It was also believed to give protection from lightning. The laurel was regarded as sacred to Apollo, and it was associated with purifying, since Apollo was the great purifier. An evergreen, it was a symbol of immortality; its intoxicating properties associated it with prophetic and poetic inspiration. The Pythian priestess at Delphi in **Greece** used to chew laurel leaves to enhance oracular powers. The laurel also symbolized victory and peace. The victors in the Pythian games were crowned with laurel. Roman generals sent news of their victories in messages wrapped in laurel leaves, delivered to the Senate.

"Laurin" (or "Der Kleine Rosengarten")

A Tyrolese romance of the late thirteenth century, attached to the saga-cycle of Dietrich of Bern. Laurin, a dwarf, possessed a magic rose-garden into which no one could enter without losing a hand or a foot. Dietrich and his follower Witege entered the garden, and Witege rode through the rose bushes. Laurin appeared on horseback and dismounted Witege. He was challenged by Dietrich and, because he wore his cloak of invisibility, Laurin wounded him.

Dietrich then persuaded him to try a wrestling match, during which he wrenched off Laurin's belt, the source of his superhuman strength. Thus Dietrich overthrew Laurin. Laurin invited Dietrich and his followers to his mountain home, prepared a banquet for them, made them tipsy, and threw them all into a dungeon. They were eventually released by Künhild, a mortal woman, who also returned their weapons. They took Laurin prisoner and carried him to Bern, where he converted to Christianity and received Künhild in marriage.

Sources:

MacDowall, M. W. *Epics and Romances of the Middle Ages.* London: S. Sonnenschein, 1896.

LaVey, Anton (1930–)

Founder and high priest of the **Church of Satan.** Howard Anton Szandor LaVey was born in Chicago on April 11, 1930. As a youth he became interested in magic and the occult. Shortly after World War II, he dropped out of high school and joined the circus, where he trained the big cats and learned stage magic.

In the early 1960s he married Diane Hegarty and they organized late-evening occult meetings, from which the idea for the Church of Satan, and its original members, emerged. The church was formally founded on April 30, 1966. LaVey, with years of performing behind him, brought a flare for the dramatic to his leadership. He shaved his head and donned black ritual garb to announce the first year of "Satan's era." During the first year he conducted the first satanic wedding and funeral, each with a cadre of media representatives present, and played the part of the Devil in the movie version of **Rosemary's Baby.** In 1969 he completed *The Satanic Bible,* in which the beliefs and basic rituals of the church are presented. The book has remained in print and its ideas are expanded on in two subsequent volumes, *The Compleat Witch* (1970) and *The Satanic Rituals* (1972).

LaVey had a most secularized image of Satan and Satanism. On the one hand he saw the power of the image of Satan to invoke fear in Christians and the hold the image retained even over those who had left their Christian beliefs behind. He saw the value that a focus on Satan could have in freeing people from their Christian pasts and turning them into autonomous, modern people. Thus rituals were designed not so much as a means of worshiping or invoking Satan, but as a way of affirming the self and unleashing what LaVey saw as natural human drives (such as for sex and pleasure) that had been suppressed by a culture that branded them as evil. At the same time, the church was particularly vocal about members being involved in anything that suggested they were breaking the law under the guise of following their religion.

LaVey's support was weakened by the defection of many members in the early 1970s who believed in a more literal existence of Satan and were attempting to find a more traditional Satanism. Since that time, LaVey has assumed a much lower profile and the church has tended to avoid publicity. Its high level of fame, including regular attacks from Christian ministers, has supplied it with a steady stream of prospective members.

Sources:

Barton, Blanche. *The Secret Life of a Satanist: The Authorized Biography of Anton LaVey.* Los Angeles: Feral House, 1990.

Harrington, Will. "The Devil in Anton LaVey." *The Washington Post Magazine* (February 23, 1986): 6–9, 12–17.

LaVey, Anton. *The Compleat Witch.* New York: Lancer Books, 1971.

———. *The Satanic Bible.* New York: Avon Books, 1969.

———. *The Satanic Rituals.* Secaucus, N.J.: University Books, 1972.

Wolfe, Burton H. *The Devil's Avenger.* New York: Avon Books, 1974.

Lavritch, Sophie Bentkowski (1905–)

Editor and writer on parapsychological subjects. She was born on May 8, 1905, in St. Petersburg, Russia, and studied at the University of Paris Law School (Licencié en droit, 1926). She was editorial director of the journal *Initiation et Science,* and from 1945 to 1946 was welfare officer at the United Nations Relief and Rehabilitation Administration.

Lavritch described her experimental studies in clairvoyance in the article "La Voyance: Ses limites et ses erreurs" (Clairvoyance: Its limits and errors) in *Initiation et Science* (no. 49). She wrote under the names of Sophie Bentkowski, Sonia Bentkowski-Lavritch, and Sophie de Trabeck.

Sources:

Pleasants, Helene, ed. *Biographical Dictionary of Parapsychology.* New York: Helix Press, 1964.

Law, William (1686–1761)

English mystic and theologian. William Law was born at King's Cliffe, Northamptonshire, England. His father, a grocer, managed to send William to Cambridge University in 1705. Entering Emmanuel College, he became a fellow in 1711, but on the accession of George I, felt himself unable to subscribe to the oath of allegiance. As a result, Law forfeited his fellowship.

In 1727 he went to Putney to tutor the father of Edward Gibbon, the historian of the Roman Empire. He held this post for 10 years, winning universal esteem for his piety and theological erudition.

When his employer died in 1737, Law retired to his native village of King's Cliffe and was chiefly supported by some of his devotees, notably Hester Gibbon, sister of his guardian pupil, and the widow Mrs. Hutcheson. The two women had a united income of fully 3,000 pounds a year, so Law must have been comfortable, and wealth and luxury did not corrupt him. It is recorded that he rose every morning at five and spent several hours before breakfast in prayer and meditations.

Early in his career, Law began publishing theses on mysticism and on religion in general. After he retired, he acquired fresh inspiration from reading the works of **Jakob Boehme,** of which he was an enthusiastic admirer, and produced year after year a considerable mass of writing until his death April 9, 1761.

Law's works comprise some 20 volumes. In 1717 he published an examination of the recent tenets of the bishop of Bangor, which were followed soon after by a number of analogous writings. In 1726 his attack on the theater was published as *The Absolute Unlawfulness of the Stage Entertainment Fully Demonstrated.* In the same year he issued *A Practical Treatise upon Christian*

Perfection, followed shortly thereafter by *A Serious Call to a Devout and Holy Life, Adapted to the State and Condition of All Orders of Christians,* considered his best-known work.

Other well-regarded works include: *The Grounds and Reason of Christian Regeneration* (1739), *The Spirit of Prayer* (1749), *The Way to Divine Knowledge* (1752), *The Spirit of Love* (1752), and *Of Justification by Faith and Works* (1760).

Most of Law's books, especially *A Serious Call,* have been reprinted again and again, and a collected edition of Law's works appeared in 1762. In 1893 an anthology was brought out by Dr. Alexander Whyte. In his preface Whyte spoke of Law's "golden books," declaring that "in sheer intellectual strength Law is fully abreast of the very foremost of his illustrious contemporaries, while in that fertilising touch which is the true test of genius, Law stands simply alone."

Sources:

Law, William. *The Absolute Unlawfulness of the Stage Entertainment Fully Demonstrated.* Reprint, New York: Garland Publishing, 1973.

———. *The Grounds and Reason of Christian Regeneration.* Philadelphia: Andrew Bradford, 1741.

———. *A Practical Treatise upon Christian Perfection.* Newcastle upon Tyne: J. Gooding, 1743.

———. *A Serious Call to a Devout and Holy Life, Adapted to the State and Condition of All Orders of Christians.* London: W. Innys, 1732.

———. *The Spirit of Love.* London: W. Innys and J. Richardson, 1752.

———. *The Spirit of Prayer.* London: W. Innys, 1750.

———. *The Works.* Brockenhurst: G. Moreton, 1892–93.

Rudolph, Erwin Paul. *William Law.* Boston: Twayne, 1980.

Lawrence Museum of Magic and Witchcraft

Situated in Galveston, about 50 miles north of Indianapolis, Indiana. It contains **Aleister Crowley**'s salt and water set, authentic implements from **Gerald Gardner,** and magical and psychic artifacts from the ancient Aztec and modern civilizations. For visits, contact: Merlin and Moonstone, Box 219, Galveston, IN 46932.

Lawton, George (1900–1957)

Psychologist, gerontologist, lecturer, and writer on **Spiritualism.** He was born on June 22, 1900, in New York City, took all his degrees from Columbia University (B.A., 1922; M.A., 1926; Ph.D., 1936), and entered private practice as a psychologist beginning in 1936. He authored several books, the most important being *The Drama of Life after Death* (1932), concerned with the psychological motivations behind Spiritualism. Lawton died October 9, 1957.

Sources:

Lawton, George. *The Drama of Life after Death.* New York: H. Holt, 1932.

Pleasants, Helene, ed. *Biographical Dictionary of Parapsychology.* New York: Helix Press, 1964.

Laya Yoga

That form of **yoga** in which the yogi listens to sounds that can be heard within his own body when the ears are closed. These sounds, termed **Nada,** are of various kinds, ranging from the roar of the ocean to the humming of bees. Variations on laya yoga have become central to the Radhaksoami groups in the Pubjab and to its North American derivatives such as the Diving Life Mission (now Elan Vital) and **ECKANKAR.**

Lazare, Denys (ca. 622 C.E.)

A prince of Serbia said to have lived in the year of the Hegira (flight of Mohammed from Mecca), i.e. in 622 C.E. He was author of a work entitled *Dreams,* published over a millennia later in 1686. He himself claimed to have had nocturnal visions.

"Lazaris"

The name of the nonphysical entity channeled by Jach Pursel. Pursel first became aware of this entity in the 1970s when on a business trip as part of the accelerated executive program with State Farm Insurance. He reportedly had a visionary experience while meditating, and the "Lazaris" entity manifested. Later Pursel began **channeling** "Lazaris" to his wife Peny and eventually to groups of friends and to individuals seeking guidance in life.

Since forming the home-based organization Concept Synergy, Pursel has channeled "Lazaris" to as many as 850 people in afternoon and weekend programs with visitors from Australia, Argentina, Switzerland, and Hong Kong. Pursel has traveled throughout North America, and "Lazaris" has been consulted by celebrities such as **Shirley MacLaine,** Michael York, and others.

"Lazaris" manifests without exotic settings of New Age incense, robes, and candles. Pursel simply sits on a chair, goes into trance, and the "Lazaris" speeches begin. Concept Synergy, which publishes and distributes audio and videotapes of "Lazaris," may be contacted at PO Box 3285, Palm Beach, FL 33480-3285.

Sources:

Martin, Katherine. "The Voice of Lazaris." *New Realities* 7, no. 6 (July/August 1987).

Pursel, Jach. *Lazaris Interviews.* 2 vols. Beverly Hills, Calif.: Concept Synergy, 1988.

———. *Lazaris: The Sacred Journey; You and Your Higher Self.* Beverly Hills, Calif.: Concept Synergy, 1987.

Leadbeater, C(harles) W(ebster) (1854–1934)

British clergyman, occultist, and author who played a prominent part in the **Theosophical Society.** Leadbeater was born February 16, 1854. While a curate in the Church of England in Hampshire, he became interested in **Theosophy** and eventually left the Church. In 1884 he moved to Adyar, the headquarters of the Theosophical Society near Madras, India. He devoted himself to the cause of Theosophy and the related **Liberal Catholic Church** for the rest of his life.

He traveled in Ceylon with **Henry S. Olcott,** one of the founders of Theosophy, and publicly professed himself to be a Buddhist. He returned to England in 1890 and became a tutor. After the death of **Helena Petrovna Blavatsky** in 1891, Leadbeater wielded considerable influence over **Annie Besant,** Blavatsky's successor, in part due to his reputed clairvoyant abilities.

Leadbeater's homosexuality became a matter of ongoing embarrassment to Besant and the society. In 1906 several mothers in the United States brought charges against Leadbeater for immoral practices with their sons. Besant found it impossible to accept these charges, so the mothers appealed to Olcott, then in London, and a judicial committee of the society summoned Leadbeater to appear before them. In the face of clear evidence, Leadbeater was obliged to resign from the society. However, after Olcott's death, the Leadbeater scandal took a bizarre turn. In an Open Letter, Weller van Hook, General Secretary of the American Section, vigorously defended Leadbeater's sex theories on the upbringing of young boys and even claimed that this defense was dictated to him by a Theosophical Master, or Mahatma. Leadbeater had initially designated van Hooks's son as the new World Savior and believed that he was due to appear in the immediate future.

In July 1908 the British Convention of the society carried a resolution to the president and general council requesting that Leadbeater and his practices be repudiated. The council did not agree and "saw no reason why Mr. Leadbeater should not be restored to membership." This action prompted some 700 members (including the scholar **G. R. S. Mead**) to resign. Leadbeater then rejoined the society, settled in Madras, and for several years exerted powerful influence over the Indian section, emphasizing clairvoyant teachings and an exalted lineage of reincarnation. During World War I he entered the newly formed Liberal Catholic Church and wrote many of the church's basic texts.

In 1908 Leadbeater switched allegiance and designated a young Brahmin boy, **Jiddu Krishnamurti,** as the future World Teacher, or Messiah. Besant saw to Krishnamurti's education and later founded the Order of the Star in the East to propagate his mission. After a decade of work, during which the society saw its greatest expansion and membership growth, Krishnamurti publicly renounced his messianic role in 1929, dissolved the order, and dropped his connections with Theosophy. He became an independent Indian spiritual teacher and taught all over the world.

The reemergence of the charges of active homosexuality with minor boys forced Leadbeater out of India. He moved to Australia, where he was living when Bishop James I. Wedgewood made his initial world tour establishing the Liberal Catholic Church. Wedgewood consecrated Leadbeater as bishop of Australia of the Liberal Catholic Church. Leadbeater remained in Australia, though at a distance from the local Theosophists, for the rest of his life. He died February 29, 1934. Long after his death, Leadbeater remains a controversial figure. A comprehensive biography, *The Elder Brother: A Biography of Charles Webster Leadbeater,* was published in 1982 by Gregory Tillett.

Leadbeater wrote numerous books, many of which became popular theosophical texts that are frequently reprinted.

Sources:

Leadbeater, C. W. *The Hidden Side of Christian Festivals.* Los Angeles: St. Alban Press, 1920.

———. *The Hidden Side of Things.* 1913. Reprint, London: 1968. Abridged reprint, Adyar, India: Theosophical Publishing House, 1974.

———. *Man Visible and Invisible.* Reprint, London: Theosophical Publishing House, 1920.

———. *The Masters and the Path.* Chicago: Theosophical Press, 1925.

———. *Outline of Theosophy.* Chicago: Theosophical Book Concern, 1903.

———. *The Science of the Sacraments.* Los Angeles: St. Alban Press, 1920.

———, and Besant, Annie. *Light on the Path.* N.p., 1926.

———. *The Lives of Alcyone: A Clairvoyant Investigation.* 2 vols. N.p., 1924.

———. *Man, Whence, How, and Whither.* 1913. Reprint, Wheaton, Ill.: Theosophical Press, n.d.

———. *Occult Chemistry, Clairvoyant Observations.* N.p., 1919.

———. *Talks on the Path of Occultism.* Vol. 1: *At the Feet of the Master.* 1926. Vol. 2: *The Voice of the Silence.* Adyar, India: Theosophical Publishing House, 1947.

———. *Thought-Forms: A Record of Clairvoyant Investigation.* London: Theosophical Publishing House, 1948.

Melton, J. Gordon. *Religious Leaders of America.* Detroit: Gale Research, 1991.

Tillett, Gregory. *The Elder Brother: A Biography of Charles Webster Leadbeater.* London: Routledge & Kegan Paul, 1982.

Leading Edge: A Bulletin of Social Transformation

Newsletter edited and published every three weeks by **Marilyn Ferguson,** author of the **New Age** book **The Aquarian Conspiracy** (1980). The format of the newsletter is similar to **Brain/Mind Bulletin** (also edited and published by Ferguson), but *The Leading Edge* focuses on social aspects of the New Age (politics, relationships, business, schools, law, arts, religion) and other topics related to *The Aquarian Conspiracy.* At the end of each year related articles on a particular topic are published as Theme Packs. *Leading Edge* complements the materials in *Brain/Mind Bulletin,* which covers such topics as learning, medicine, psychology, psychiatry, and right and left brain research. Address: P.O Box 42247, Los Angeles, CA 90042.

Sources:

Ferguson, Marilyn. *The Aquarian Conspiracy.* Los Angeles: J. B. Tarcher, 1980.

Leading Edge Journal

British newsstand periodical dealing with the broad range of New Age and esoteric topics. It has been published since 1990 from Runnings Park, Croft Bank, West Malvern, Worcestershire, WR14 4BP, England.

Leaf, Horace (ca. 1886–1971)

Well-known British lecturer and author in the cause of **Spiritualism** and psychic research. His own psychic abilities included **clairvoyance, psychometry,** and **healing.** Leaf traveled extensively, meeting most of the important mediums in North America and regularly contributing articles to such Spiritualist journals as *Light.*

He was well known to the pioneer Spiritualist **James Hewat McKenzie,** whom he met at the beginning of the twentieth century while a member of a debating society in North London, which discussed philosophical, political, social, and religious topics. Soon after McKenzie established the **British College of Psychic Science** in London, Leaf became a staff lecturer on psychology and the development of mediumship.

Sources:

Leaf, Horace. *Ahmed's Daughter.* N.p., 1933.

———. *Death Cannot Kill.* N.p., 1967.

———. *Psychology and Development of Mediumship.* London: Rider, 1923.

———. *Under the Southern Cross.* N.p., 1923.

———. *What is this Spiritualism?* New York: G. H. Doran, 1919.

———. *What Mediumship Is.* London: Psychic Press, 1938.

Leaf, Walter (1852–1927)

Classical scholar, banker, and pioneer of psychical research in Britain. He was born November 28, 1852, in London, England, and was educated at Trinity College, Cambridge (B.A., 1874; M.A., 1877). Leaf became successful banker and retained an amateur interest in classical studies. His banking leadership was acknowledged by his being elected president of the Institute of Bankers (1919–21) and later president of the International Chambers of Commerce (1924–26). He was also president of the Hellenic Society (1914–19), president of the Classical Association (1921), and an honorary fellow of Trinity College, Cambridge.

Leaf was also an active member of the **Society for Psychical Research** (SPR), London, and served a tenure on the council (1889–1902). He took part in the SPR sittings with the medium **Leonora Piper** in 1889–90 and frequently contributed to the *Journal* and the *Proceedings* of the SPR. He died March 8, 1927.

Sources:

Berger, Arthur S., and Joyce Berger. *The Encyclopedia of Parapsychology and Psychical Research.* New York: Paragon House, 1991.

Pleasants, Helene, ed. *Biographical Dictionary of Parapsychology.* New York: Helix Press, 1964.

Leanan Sidhe

Also "lhaiannan sidhe," Gaelic words for "fairy sweetheart" either male or female. According to one tradition, mortals are advised to have nothing to do with such beings, as no good ever comes of the connection. So long as the fairy lover is pleased with his or her mortal, all goes well, but when offended, life may be the forfeit.

In Ireland the fairy mistress has sometimes been considered the spirit of life, inspiring poets and singers but making their lives short through their all-consuming burning vision. Another tradition regards the leanan sidhe of a man as more like a **vampire** or **succubus.** (See also **genius**)

Sources:

Arrowsmith, Nancy, and George Moore. *A Field Guide to the Little People.* New York: Wallaby, 1978.

Briggs, Katherine M. *An Encyclopedia of Fairies, Hobgoblins, Brownies, Bogies, and Other Supernatural Creatures.* New York: Pantheon Books, 1976.

Leary, Timothy (1920–)

With Dr. **Richard Alpert,** Leary became a controversial figure in the psychedelic revolution of the 1960s. He was born October 22, 1920, in Springfield, Massachusetts. He attended Holy Cross College (1938–39), the U.S. Military Academy (1940–41), the University of Alabama (A.B., 1943), Washington State University (1946), and the University of California at Berkeley (Ph.D. in psychology, 1950).

He was an assistant professor at the University of California at Berkeley (1950–55), director of psychological research at the Kaiser Foundation, Oakland, California (1955–58), and a lecturer in psychology at Harvard University, Cambridge, Massachusetts (1959–63). After leaving Harvard Leary became the head and first guide of the League of Spiritual Discovery, which was based at a mansion in Millwood, New York.

Leary and Alpert were both dismissed from Harvard for their experiments with psilocybin (later revealed to have been funded by the U.S. government). They engaged in widespread psychedelic experiments and emerged as advocates for the use of LSD and other such drugs to produce altered states of consciousness. Together they launched the psychedelic revolution that in less than a decade impacted an entire generation.

The belief that mystical experience could be obtained from mind-altering drugs came from Leary's and Alpert's experiences as well as from the suggestion made a decade earlier in **Aldous Huxley**'s book *The Doors of Perception* (1954), which described the sacramental use of peyote by certain North American Indians.

Having exhausted the drug experience by 1967, Alpert went to India in search of more substantial spirituality and experienced a major transformation. He discovered a guru in the Himalayas and returned to the United States as Baba Ram Dass. His transformation became a parable of the emerging **New Age** movement, and he is a popular teacher of Hinduism and New Age values. Leary, however, continued to advocate the psychedelic revolution, and in 1969 he was an appellant in the U.S. Supreme Court decision that invalidated the federal marijuana law test case.

Various brushes with the law on drug charges resulted in Leary receiving sentences of 10 years imprisonment by a federal judge in Houston on January 21, 1970, and another ten years in Santa Ana, California, on March 22, 1970, both charges involving marijuana offenses. He began serving his sentence at the California Men's Colony West in San Luis Obispo, but escaped in September 1970 and later surfaced in Lebanon. He settled in Switzerland for a time but later returned to the United States and served his sentence at Folsom Prison in California. The 10-year jail sentence in 1970 resulted from possession of less than half an ounce of marijuana, which had a street value of ten dollars. His 42-month imprisonment (29 months in solitary confinement) seemed to reflect mainstream opinion about the psychedelic revolution initiated by Leary and his associates.

Leary's case was reviewed in the mid-1970s, and in March 1975 he was paroled but immediately began serving another sentence. Leary was finally released April 21, 1976. Separated from his wife, Rosemary, in 1971, he married his fourth wife, Barbara, after being released from jail.

Over the next 10 years Leary continued to be in the public eye as a trendsetter in ideas. He lectured widely, though he no longer advocated the psychedelic revolution or drug taking. In September 1976 he spoke to 3,000 students at Princeton University on a scientific approach to self-development. In his book *Exo-Psychology* (1977), he suggested that human beings could evolve into pure, intelligent, disembodied energy. Other lecture topics include Skylab/space shuttle activities and efforts to increase human intelligence and life-span, summed up in the acronym SMILE (Space Migration, Increased Intelligence, Life Extension). He founded an organization named Starseed, a cooperative to colonize space.

In 1982 Leary toured on a debate circuit with convicted Watergate conspirator G. Gordon Liddy, who participated in a 1966 raid on Leary's Millbrook drug community. In the 1990s Leary has taken on a role as a futurist guru, advocating ways to stimulate human development and intelligence. He has popularized the concept of SKPI (Super Knowledge, Processing Interaction), using computers as mind-expanding tools. Although Leary refrains from advocating mind-expanding drugs, he expresses no regrets for his part in the psychedelic revolution.

A comprehensive assessment of Leary, his kaleidoscopic career and philosophies, and the views of other commentators can be found in *Contemporary Authors* (Vol. 107, 1983). In addition to Leary's own biographical works, see also **Psychedelic Drugs, Hallucinogens,** and **Mushrooms.**

Sources:

Kleps, Art. *Millbrook: The True Story of the Early Years of the Psychedelic Revolution.* Oakland, Calif.: Bench Press, 1977.

Leary, Timothy. *Changing My Mind among Others: Lifetime Writings.* Englewood Cliffs, N.J.: Prentice-Hall, 1982.

———. *Flashbacks.* Los Angeles: Jeremy P. Tarcher, 1983.

———. *High Priest.* New York: World Publishing, 1968.

———. *The Politics of Ecstasy.* New York: G. P. Putnam's, 1968.

———. *The Psychedelic Experience.* New Hyde Park, N.Y.: University Books, 1964.

———. *Psychedelic Prayers after the Tao te ching.* New Hyde Park, N.Y.: University Books, 1966.

Leary, Timothy, Robert Wilson, and George A. Koopman. *Neuropolitics: The Sociobiology of Human Metamorphosis.* Los Angeles: Starseed/Peace Press, 1977.

Slack, Charles W. *Timothy Leary, the Madness of the Sixties, and Me.* New York: Peter H. Wyden, 1974.

Le Brun, Charles (1619–1690)

A celebrated French painter born in Paris February 24, 1619. When only 15 years old, he received commissions from Cardinal Richelieu, and his paintings were also praised by Poussin. Le Brun was a founder of the Academy of Painting and Sculpture (1648) and the Academy of France at Rome (1666). He also was director of the Gobelins, a famous school for the manufacture of tapestries and royal furniture.

Le Brun's treatise on physiognomy, *Traité sur la physionomie humaine comparée avec celle des aminaux,* was written at a time when the subject was considered to be an occult science. In this book Le Brun executed remarkable drawings comparing human and animal faces, a theme later developed with reference to the emotions by Charles Darwin in his book *The Expression of the Emotions in Man and Animals* (1872 etc.). Le Brun died February 22, 1690.

Lebrun, Pierre (1661–1729)

French theologian born at Brignolles. He published a book on the **divining-rod,** *Lettres qui découvrent l'illusion des philosophes sur la Baguette et qui détruisent leurs systèmes* (1693), and a work on occult curiosities and popular beliefs, *Histoire critique des pratiques superstitieuses qui ont séduit les peuples et embarrassé les savants* (1702).

Lecanomancy

A branch of crystalomancy (**divination** by water). One method was to toss an object into a full container of water and interpret either the image formed by it or else the sound it made striking the water. Another more complex method involved placing water in a silver vase on a clear, moonlit night. The light from a candle would be reflected onto the water by the blade of a knife and the inquirer would concentrate on the image formed in the water. (See also **pegomancy**)

Lecour, Paul (1871–1954)

French government official and writer on psychic research. Born on April 5, 1871, at Blois, France, he was a tax collector and head of the department of the French Ministry of Public Works from 1896 to 1934. In 1926 he organized the Society for Atlantean Studies at the Sorbonne, which issued the journal *Atlantis* beginning in 1927. He was present at sittings with the famous physical medium **Eva C.** (Marthe Beraud), and his own photographs of her reputed **ectoplasm** phenomena were reproduced in *Annales des Sciences Psychique* (No. 1, 1919). He died February 5, 1954.

Sources:

Lecour, Paul. *Hellénisme et Christianisme* (Hellenism and Christianity). Bordeaux: Editions Bierre, 1943.

———. *Ma Vie mystique* (My mystical life). N.p., n.d.

———. *Saint Paul et les mystères Chrétiens* (St. Paul and the Christian mysteries). N.p., n.d.

———. *Le Septième sens* (The Seventh sense). N.p., n.d.

Pleasants, Helene, ed. *Biographical Dictionary of Parapsychology.* New York: Helix Press, 1964.

LeCron, Leslie M. (1892– ?)

Psychologist, expert on **hypnotism,** and author on parapsychological topics. He was born on October 27, 1892, at Minneapolis, Minnesota, and studied at University of Colorado (B.A., 1916). He entered into private practice as a psychologist and became a member of the Society for Clinical and Experimental Hypnosis and the Academy of Psychosomatic Medicine. Lecron was an honorary member and a consultant of the Los Angeles Society for Psychic Research.

Sources:

Cheek, David B., and Leslie M. LeCron. *Clinical Hypnotherapy.* New York: Grine & Stratton, 1968.

LeCron, Leslie M. *Experimental Hypnosis.* New York: Macmillan, 1952.

———. "The Paranormal in Hypnosis." *Tomorrow* magazine (spring 1955).

———. *Self-Hypnosis: The Technique and Its Daily Use in Daily Living.* Englewood Cliffs, N.J.: Prentice-Hall, 1964.

———. *Techniques of Hypnotherapy.* New York: Julian Press, 1962.

LeCron, Leslie M., and Jean Bordeaux. *Hypnotism Today.* New York: Grune & Stratton, 1964.

Pleasants, Helene, ed. *Biographical Dictionary of Parapsychology.* New York: Helix Press, 1964.

Lectorium Rosicrucianum

The Lectorium Rosicrucianum, the largest of the European-based Rosicrucian groups, was founded in the Netherlands in 1924 by former members of the **Rosicrucian Fellowship,** under the leadership of Jan Van Rijckenborgh and Catharose de Petri (both pen names). The organization grew very slowly and was forced to disband during the German occupation of Holland. It revived after the war, however, and has since spread throughout Europe and into North America.

The order views itself as gnostic (from the Greek word *gnosis,* or knowledge) and is organized as a gnostic school. Following ancient gnostic learning, the order teaches that wisdom comes from the Word, the divine source of all that exists. Members follow a path of transfiguration, or return to the gnosis, for humankind is presently in a fallen state, from which it needs reawakening. Within each person is a rose of the heart, a spirit-speak atom, which can ascend to the divine. This process is aided by those who have already found knowledge, the Universal Brotherhood. The school transmits the light of the Universal Brotherhood to the members, thus allowing them to break the chain of **reincarnation** (death and rebirth) and begin the process of return to the divine.

The Lectorium Rosicrucianum is unique in its espousal of the concept of two nature orders. Humans are born into this nature order, the seventh cosmic region, that is, the world of nature. Humans also carry a remnant of their origin in the sixth cosmic region, where they exist as an immortal seed. Their purpose on Earth is to cooperate with the blossoming of the rose of the heart, the Christ principle within, in the process of transfiguration and return.

From their headquarters in Holland, the order has initiated an extensive translation and publishing program in English, German, French, Portuguese, Swedish, and other European languages. A periodical, *Pentagram,* is published in five languages. The Lectorium Rosicrucianum can be contacted at Bakenessergract 11-15, 2011JS, The Netherlands, or in the United States at the Western North American headquarters, Box 9246, Bakersfield, CA 93389. There are some 10,000 members internationally.

Sources:

Van Rijckenborgh, Jan. *The Coming New Man.* Haarlem, The Netherlands: Rozekruis-Pers, 1957.

———. *Elementary Philosophy of the Modern Rosecross.* Haarlem, The Netherlands: Rozekruis-Pers, 1961.

The Way of the Rosecross in Our Times. Haarlem, The Netherlands: Rozekruis-Pers, 1978.

Lee, Dal (1895–1973)

Prominent writer and astrologer, born Adalbert Nebel in New York City on December 7, 1895. As a young man he became attracted to **astrology** and for a decade (1917–27) studied it privately. In 1927 he became a part-time astrologer and then in 1937 became an associate editor of *Astrology Guide* magazine. The following year he also became editor of *Your Personal Astrology,* another newsstand periodical. He discontinued his private practice in 1941 and thereafter spent his life as an editor and writer of astrological literature.

Lee died in Fort Lee, New Jersey, on July 7, 1973.

Sources:

Holden, James H., and Robert A. Hughes. *Astrological Pioneers of America.* Tempe, Ariz.: American Federation of Astrologers, 1988.

Lee, Dal. *Dictionary of Astrology.* New York: Paperback Library, 1968.

———. *How to Use and Understand Astrological Predictive Systems.* New York: Astro Books, 1939.

———. *Understanding the Occult.* New York: Paperback Library, 1969.

Lee, Gloria (1926–1962)

Gloria Lee, one of the prominent flying saucer contactees of the 1950s, was born March 22, 1926, in Los Angeles. She developed an interest in flying as a teenager and became one of the early airline stewardesses, a position she held until her marriage to William H. Byrd in 1952. About this same time she developed an interest in flying saucers, then being raised as an issue by **George Adamski,** who claimed contact with extraterrestrials.

In 1953 Lee began to receive messages from the saucer brothers through the process of **automatic writing.** The first messages were received while she was at work. The contacts led her into association with several occult interest groups. The regularity of the messages increased, and eventually the automatic writing gave way to **telepathy.** The extraterrestrial identified himself as J.W., a Venusian who came from a race of people who no longer used vocal communications and in their evolution had lost their vocal cords. They communicated by telepathy alone. As the communications continued, she attempted in various ways to prove J.W.'s existence, both to herself and others. In 1959 she founded the Cosmon Research Foundation and published her first book, *Why We Are Here!* The book shows some background in Theosophy. Theosophy pictures a hierarchy of spiritual beings that stand between humanity and the divine. In Lee's thinking, that hierarchy had been transformed into a space command hierarchy. A second book, *The Changing Conditions of Your World!* appeared in 1962.

By the early 1960s Lee was a well-known figure in the contactee subculture. In the fall of 1962, accompanied by her friend and colleague Hedy Hood, Lee went to Washington to attempt to interest political leaders in her ideas about the space brothers. She wanted financing and assistance to build a spaceship, the plans of which had been given her by J.W. She found no positive response, and on September 13, the pair took a hotel room and Lee began a fast to call attention to her ideas. No one listened. On November 2, she fell into a coma and died.

Immediately after her death, several contactees claimed to have talked to Gloria Lee in her new spiritual existence. Verity of the Heralds of the New Age (New Zealand) and Yolanda of Mark-Age both produced booklets of what they claimed were communications from Lee. Lee was considered a martyr by the contactees of the 1960s but was soon forgotten as new people who did not know her moved into leadership positions.

Sources:

Lee, Gloria. *The Changing Conditions of Your World!* Palos Verdes Estates, Calif.: Cosmon Research Foundation, 1962.

———. *Why We Are Here!* Palos Verdes Estates, Calif.: Cosmon Research Foundation, 1959.

Steiger, Brad. *The Aquarian Revelations.* New York: Dell, 1971.

Verity. *The Going and the Glory.* Auckland, N.Z.: Heralds of the New Age, 1966.

Lee Penny

Famous Scottish **amulet** that belonged to Sir Simon Locard on Lockhart of Lee, ca. 1330. The story of this relic suggested the title of **Sir Walter Scott**'s novel *The Talisman,* and in his introduction to the book, Scott related the incident that led to the acquisition of the Lee penny.

After the death of Robert the Bruce, king of Scotland in 1329, his friend Lord James of Douglas set out to take the dead king's heart to the Holy Land, making the pilgrimage that the king was not able to undertake in his lifetime. While making their way through Spain, Douglas and his band of knights battled with the Saracens. Douglas died on the battlefield, but the king's heart in its silver casket was rescued by Sir Simon Locard of Lee, who brought it back to Scotland for burial (Sir Walter Scott, however, believed it was taken on to the Holy Land).

Sir Simon Locard imprisoned a wealthy emir from a battle. His aged mother ransomed him, and in the course of counting out the money, a pebble inserted in a coin fell out of the lady's purse. She was in such a hurry to retrieve it that the Scottish knight realized it must be valuable to her and insisted on this amulet being added to the ransom. The lady reluctantly agreed and also explained to Sir Simon Locard what its virtues were.

Apparently it was a medical talisman believed to drive away fever and stop bleeding. The stone was a dull, heart-shaped pebble of a semitransparent dark red color, set in a piece of silver said to be an Edward IV groat (coin). The Lockhart family tradition credits the Lee penny with the ability to cure all diseases in cattle and the bite of a mad dog. The stone should be dipped in water three times and swirled around, then the water should be given to the man or beast to be cured.

The amulet was used frequently in the past, according to tradition. In 1629 the Lee penny was used to cure sick oxen, but as a result a young woman was burned at the stake for witchcraft. There are records of an accusation of **witchcraft** against Sir Thomas Lockhart during the Reformation, but the Church Synod at Glasgow merely reproved Sir Thomas and advised him to cease using the penny as a charm.

During the reign of Charles I, the citizens of Newcastle requested the use of the penny to cure a cattle plague. Sir James Lockhart required from the corporation a bond of 6,000 pounds. The penny was used, the plague abated, and the corporation offered to purchase the amulet with the money. The offer was refused, and the Lee penny was returned to Scotland. During the eighteenth century it was housed in a gold casket presented to the head of the family by the Empress Maria Theresa of Austria. Many cures are recorded through the middle of the nineteenth century. More recently the penny has passed into the possession of Simon Macdonald Lockhart of Lee, at Dolphinton, Scotland.

Leek, Sybil (1922–1982)

Astrologer, witch, author, and one of the more popular figures in the modern occult revival. She was born on February 22, 1922 in the Midlands, England, and claimed an ancestry in **witchcraft** through both sides of her family. Through her mother the lineage could be traced to southern Ireland in the twelfth century and through her father to Russia. She was tutored at home and attended school for only four years (ages 12–16).

She claimed that she had been initiated into the craft while near Nice, in southern France, and that her initiation was to fill an opening left by the death of her aunt, who had been high priestess of a coven. She then returned to England and settled near New Forest, where she reportedly joined the Horsa Coven, which she claimed predated the Norman Conquest. She soon became high priestess of the group. There is no substantiation of that story and some evidence that it is fabricated.

In the early 1950s she claimed to have had a mystical experience in which she realized that her calling in life would be as a spokesperson for witchcraft, the old religion. Her early efforts resulted in tourists flocking to her antique shop, not to buy but to get her autograph. She had a conflict with her landlord, who demanded she renounce her religion, and she eventually had to close her shop. In the meanwhile, she had written several books, but none of them dealt with witchcraft.

In the early 1960s Leek moved to the United States. With the assistance of her publisher and a set of public relations people, she soon became famous as a public witch. She lectured widely, appeared on television, and built a large clientele as an astrologer. Quietly, she founded and for a period led several covens, two in Massachusetts, one in Cincinnati, and one in St. Louis.

Leek wrote over 60 books among which were an autobiography, *Diary of a Witch* (1968), and several on witchcraft, including *The Complete Art of Witchcraft* (1971). The material in these books conflicts. While claiming traditional witchcraft roots, prior to the neo-pagan revival of witchcraft by **Gerald Gardner,** her own presentation of witchcraft is completely Gardnerian. She talks of ritual items such as the athame (the ritual dagger) as if she had known about them before Gardner. However, we now know that they were invented by Gardner. She seems to have reproduced a variation on Gardner's ritual. It appears as if she, like many in the early decades of the Wiccan revival, created a magical lineage for herself, but in fact obtained her training and knowledge of the craft from Gardnerians.

She died in Melbourne, Florida, in 1982.

Sources:

Buckland, Raymond. *Witchcraft: Ancient and Modern.* New York: H. C. Publishers, 1970.

Leek, Sybil. *Astrology and Love.* New York: Berkley, 1977.

———. *The Best of Sybil Leek.* New York: Popular Library, 1974.

———. *Cast Your Own Spell.* New York: Pinnacle Books, 1970.

———. *The Complete Art of Witchcraft.* New York: World Publishing, 1971.

———. *Diary of a Witch.* Englewood Cliffs, N.J.: Prentice-Hall, 1968.

———. *A Shop in the High Street.* New York: David McKay, 1962.

———. *Sybil Leek's Book of Curses.* Englewood Cliffs, N.J.: Prentice-Hall, 1975.

———. *Sybil Leek's Book of Fortune Telling.* New York: Collier, 1969.

Lees, Robert James (d. ca. 1931)

British clairvoyant and pensioner of the Privy Purse who was often received at Buckingham Palace by Queen Victoria. He was also the subject of a hoax concerning the infamous **Jack the Ripper** case. An article was published in the London *Daily Express* March 9, 1931, shortly after Lees's death, claiming that Lees rendered great service to the English police. Lees, it was claimed, had unaccountable premonitions of the crimes the Ripper was going to commit. In a vision Lees saw the victim and the place. He communicated his descriptions to the police, and later findings corroborated the details in the vision. When the visions continued to reoccur, the police asked Lees to track down the murderer. Much in the same way as a bloodhound pursues a criminal, Lees set out in a state of trance, followed by an inspector and detectives. While on the trail, at four o'clock in the morning Lees halted at the gates of a West End mansion where a prominent physician was living and, pointing to an upper chamber where a faint light gleamed, declared: "There is the murderer." It was reported that the physician later confessed that he was subject to fits of obsession in which he committed acts of fiendish cruelty. Evidence consistent with victims of the Ripper was found in his rooms, and on the recommendations of a medical committee, he was confined to an insane asylum.

Later it was learned that this story stemmed from a journalistic hoax reported in the Chicago *Sunday-Times Herald* April 28, 1895, which reported that Lees had a vision of one of the killings prior to its occurrence.

During his life, Lees was best known for his healing work, his controls often diagnosing disease and effecting remarkable, instantaneous cures. Lees also published several books that he claimed were inspired psychically. He wrote a posthumous manuscript that is supposedly the autobiography of a soul in paradise.

Sources:

Berger, Arthur S., and Joyce Berger. *The Encyclopedia of Parapsychology and Psychical Research.* New York: Paragon House, 1991.

Lees, Robert J. *The Car of Phoebus: An Astral Bridegroom.* N.p., 1909.

———. *The Gate of Heaven.* N.p., n.d.

———. *The Heretic.* N.p., 1901.

———. *The Life Elysian.* N.p., 1905.

———. "My Books: How They Were Written." *Occult Review* (December 1931).

———. *Through the Mists.* London: W. Rider & Sons Ltd., 1910.

Stein, Gordon. *Encyclopedia of Hoaxes.* Detroit, Mich.: Gale Research, 1993.

Lefebure, Francis (1916–)

Physician, experimenter, and writer on parapsychological sub jects. Born September 17, 1916, in Paris, France, he studied at th Paris Medical School at the University of Paris (M.D.). Durin World War II, he was a physician in the French Army (1939–44 and after the war worked as the school physician (1944–59). H subsequently was director of "cervoscopy" (his own technique o brain exploration) at Dynam Institut, Paris.

Lefebure joined the Association Francais d'Etudes Métapsych iques in Paris. He experimented successfully with projecting hi "psychic double" at a distance to individuals who had no prio knowledge of the attempt. This conscious projection of a "dou ble" is what is elsewhere termed **out-of-the-body travel.** He au thored several books and contributed articles on clairvoyanc and occultism to the magazine *Initiation et Science.*

Sources:

Lefebure, Francis. *Expériences initiatiques.* 3 vols. N.p., 1954 1956, 1959.

———. *Les Homologies; architecture cosmique ou, La Lumièr secrète de l'Asie devant la science modern* (Homologies; or, The Secre Light of Asia in Relation to Modern Science). Paris: Edition Aryana, 1950.

Pleasants, Helene, ed. *Biographical Dictionary of Parapsychology* New York: Helix Press, 1964.

Lehman, Alfred

Danish coauthor, with **F. C. C. Hansen,** of a pamphlet prop osing a theory of "involuntary" whispering to account for appar ent thought-transference, or **telepathy.**

Lehrstuhl für Psychologie und Grenzgebiete der Psychologie, Psychologisches Institut der Universität, Freiburg

Parapsychology laboratory at the University of Freiburg in Germany under the direction of Johannes Mischo. The laboratory has a library and an experimental program and works in close cooperation with the **Institut für Grenzgebiete der Psychologie und Psychohygiene** (Institute for Border Areas of Psychology and Mental Hygiene).

Leippya

Burmese term for human soul.

Leland, Charles Godfrey (1824–1903)

Versatile American writer and folklorist who researched traditional **witchcraft** lore. He was born in Philadelphia, Pennsylvania, on August 15, 1824. He graduated from Princeton University and also studied at Heidelberg and Munich, after which he lived in Europe for a number of years. Leland became well known for his humorous dialect verse *The Breitmann Ballads* (1871) and for his research in gypsy lore and language. He first discovered and elucidated **Shelta Thari,** the secret language of the tinkers.

From 1886 onward, Leland was friendly with Maddalena, a Florentine fortune-teller and hereditary witch from Tuscany. She communicated to him the traditional witchcraft lore, which he published in *Aradia; or, The Gospel of the Witches* (1899; Weiser, 1974). The book played a prominent part as a source book in the modern revival of Wicca, or witchcraft, since the 1960s. Leland, a genial giant of a man, seemed fascinated by anything occult or mysterious. He died in Florence, Italy, March 20, 1903.

Sources:

Leland, Charles Godfrey. *The Alternate Sex; or, The Female Intellect in Man, and the Masculine in Woman.* London: P. Wellby, 1904.

———. *Aradia; or, The Gospel of the Witches.* 1899. Reprint, New York: Samuel Weiser, 1974.

———. *A Dictionary of Slang, Jargon, and Cant.* London: Ballantyne Press, 1889. Reprint, Detroit, Mich.: Gale Research, 1967.

———. *The English Gipsies and their Language.* New York: Hurd and Houghton, 1872. Reprint, Detroit, Mich.: Gale Research, 1968.

———. *The Gypsies.* Boston: Houghton, Mifflin, 1882.

Leland, Charles Godfrey, and Albert Barrére. *Gypsy Sorcery and Fortune-Telling.* London: T. Fisher Unwin, 1891. Reprint, New Hyde Park, N.Y.: University Books, 1963. Reprint, New York: Dover Publications, 1971.

———. *Memoirs.* 1893. Reprint, Detroit: Gale Research, 1968.

———. *The Mystic Will.* New York: Hero Publishers, 1972.

Pennell, Elizabeth. *Charles Godfrey Leland.* Boston: Houghton, Mifflin, 1906.

Le Loyer, Pierre (1550–1634)

Sieur de la Brosse, royal councilor, and demonographer. He was born at Huillé in Anjou, France, and later became a magistrate at Angers. Le Loyer authored *Discours et histoires des spectres, visions, et apparitions des esprits, anges, demons, et âmes se montrant aux hommes* (Discourse and Histories about Specters, Visions, and Apparitions of Spirits, Angels, Demons, and Souls that Appeared Visibly to Men), published at Paris in 1605 in one quarto volume. The work is divided into eight books dealing with the marvelous visions and prodigies of several centuries and the most celebrated authors, sacred as well as profane, who have dealt with occult subjects. It discusses the cause of **apparitions;** the nature of good and evil spirits; demons; **ecstasy**; the essence, nature, and origin of souls; **magicians** and sorcerers and the manner of their communication; **evil spirits;** and imposters.

The first book deals with specters, apparitions, and **spirits;** the second with the physics of Le Loyer's time, the illusions to which the senses are prone, wonders, and the elixirs and metamorphosis of sorceries and of philters; the third book establishes the degrees, grades, and honors of spirits, gives a resumé of the history of Philinnion and of Polycrites, and recounts diverse adventures with specters and demons; the fourth book gives many examples of spectral appearances, of the speech of persons possessed of demons, of the countries and dwelling-places of these specters and demons, and of marvelous portents; the fifth treats of the science of the soul, of its origin, nature, its state after death, and of haunting ghosts; the sixth division is entirely taken up with the apparition of souls, and shows how the happy do not return to earth, but only those whose souls are burning in purgatory; in the seventh book the case of the Witch of Endor and the evocation of the soul of Samuel are dealt with, as is evocation in general and the methods practiced by wizards and sorcerers in this science; and the last book gives some account of **exorcism, fumigations, prayers,** and other methods of casting out devils, and the usual means employed by exorcists to destroy these.

The work, though disputatious, throws considerable light upon the occult science of the times. Although often credulous, Le Loyer was most skeptical about **alchemy,** of which he wrote: "As to transmutation, I wonder how it can be reasonably defended. Metals can be adulterated but not changed. . . . Blowing [the bellows], they may exhaust their purses, they multiply all into nothing. Yes, I do not believe, and may the philosophers excuse me if they wish, that the alchemists can change any metal into gold."

Lemuria

Lemuria, the lost continent of the Pacific, has been discussed in nineteenth- and twentieth-century occult literature as the Pacific equivalent of **Atlantis.** It is distinct, however, in that it is a completely modern invention, having originated in the middle of the nineteenth century as a means to solve some problems of biology. Biologists had noted the existence of very similar flora and fauna in southern India and Ceylon (now Sri Lanka) and southern Africa. The problem was that these species did not exist on the lands between. Before scientists had arrived at an understanding of continental drift, Philip L. Schattler proposed the idea of a land bridge between southern India and southern Africa. The lemur was a prominent animal whose habitat was being researched, and Schattler gave the name Lemuria to his hypothesized land bridge. The idea was quickly adopted by a number of biologists, including Ernst Haekel (1834–1891), who further hypothesized that Lemuria was the home of the missing original hominoids. (Many yet-to-be-discovered skeletons would point in different directions.) By the 1880s, the lost continent of Lemuria would be an honest (if soon-to-be-discarded) scientific theory.

In the 1880s, however, **Helena Petrovna Blavatsky,** cofounder and major theorist of the **Theosophical Society,** integrated the idea of Lemuria into her understanding of human evolution. Humans evolved through a series of root races, she said. She claimed that the contemporary Anglo-Saxons were the fifth root race. The two previous root races had emerged on Atlantis and Lemuria, respectively. Blavatsky's account of Lemuria led to further discussion in the theosophical writings of **Charles W. Leadbeater** and to the major book, *The Story of Atlantis and the Lost Lemuria,* by W. Scott-Elliot. What had started as a hypothetical land bridge between Africa and India had become a sizable continent stretching from India to New Zealand. Australia was a remnant and the Aborigines were descendants of the continent's dwellers.

Lemuria was soon identified with the lost continent of Pan described in *Oahspe: A New Age Bible,* a channeled text from the hand of Spiritualist **John B. Newbrough.** Pan was said to be a large continent located in what is today the north Pacific. Pan's remnants theoretically included the western coast of California, whose unique flora and fauna were another problem for nineteenth-century biologists.

A third source of speculation on Lemuria derives from the work of Augustus Le Plongeon, an archaeologist working in the late nineteenth century in Central America. At the time, the Mayan hieroglyphs in the Yucatán had not been deciphered, but Le Plongeon claimed significant progress in that regard. He suggested that the writing at Chichen Itza told the story of a princess Moo and an ancient continent to the east (Atlantis) that he called Mu. He presented his findings in 1896 in a book, *Queen Moo and the Egyptian Sphinx,* but after he was given a brief hearing before his archaeological colleagues, his ideas were dismissed.

Le Plongeon would be long forgotten if his papers had not passed to one **James Churchward** (1832–1936). Churchward claimed to have seen what he called the Naacal tablets, a set of materials written in the lost Naacal language. The tablets told the story of a lost continent in the Pacific as described by a few of the survivors of the continent's fiery destruction. Churchward claimed to have seen the tablets in India, but no one else to the present day has ever seen them. Combining the Le Plongeon material with stories of the Naacal tablets in his 1926 book *The Lost Continent of Mu,* Churchward proposed the idea of a huge continent in the Pacific south of Hawaii.

The notions about Lemuria, Pan, and Mu were melded in the 1931 Rosicrucian classic, *Lemuria: The Lost Continent of the Pacific.* According to **H. Spencer Lewis** (writing under the pen name Wishar S. Cerve), Lemuria was a mid-Pacific continent. When it was destroyed, a sliver of it was jammed against North America and became California. It is especially associated with Mt. Shasta, a prominent volcano in northern California that has become the focus of occult speculation in its own right. Five years after Lewis's book was published, the **Lemurian Fellowship,** a theosophical occult group, was founded in Chicago. Its leader, Robert Stelle, expanded on the now-entrenched occult myth in two books, *An Earth Dweller Returns* (1940) and *The Sun Rises* (1952).

In the last generation Lemuria has become a standard part of **New Age** mythology and is frequently mentioned in channeled literature. Among the interesting twists on the idea of Lemuria is that attributed to **"Ramtha,"** the entity who speaks through **J. Z.**

Knight. "Ramtha" says he was a Lemurian. Lemuria, according to "Ramtha," was not a separate continent but a section of the ancient continent of Atlatia (as he calls Atlantis). An initial cataclysm, some thirty-five thousand years ago, destroyed the northern half of the continent, including Lemuria. Survivors found shelter in Onai, the great port city of Atlatia. "Ramtha" says he was born of a Lemurian mother who had escaped to Onai.

Sources:

Blavatsky, Helena P. *The Secret Doctrine.* 2 vols. London: Theosophical Publishing, 1889.

Cerve, Wishar S. [H. Spencer Lewis]. *Lemuria: The Lost Continent of the Pacific.* San Jose, Calif.: Supreme Grand Lodge, AMORC, 1931.

Churchward, James. *The Lost Continent of Mu.* New York: Ives Washburn, 1926.

Le Plongeon, Augustus. *Queen Moo and the Egyptian Sphinx.* New York: The Author, 1896.

Melton, J. Gordon. *New Age Encyclopedia.* Detroit: Gale Research, 1990.

Walton, Bruce, ed. *Mount Shasta: Home of the Ancients.* Mokelume Hill, Calif.: Health Research, 1985.

Lemurian Fellowship

The Lemurian Fellowship was founded in Chicago in 1936 by Robert D. Stelle and Howard John Zitko and named for **Lemuria,** a continent first hypothesized in the nineteenth century as a Pacific counterpart of **Atlantis.** Shortly after the fellowship formed, it moved to Milwaukee and then in 1938 to Chula Vista, California, near San Diego. In 1941, the group purchased land in rural San Diego County near Ramona.

The teachings of the Lemurian philosophy were initially presented in two books, *An Earth Dweller Returns* and *The Sun Rises.* The former was written as a sequel to *A Dweller on Two Planets* (1899). Claiming to be channeled through Frederick William Oliver by an entity known as "Phylos the Tibetan," *The Earth Dweller Returns* was one of the early books to discuss Lemuria. *The Sun Rises,* written by Stelle, goes into great detail concerning the ancient Lemurian civilization. Its philosophy is summarized in several basic laws, notably the laws of precipitation, cause and effect, compensation, correspondence, and transmutation. Zitko's early presentation of the philosophy in *The Lemurian Theochristic Conception* became the basis of the fellowship's correspondence lessons.

According to the fellowship, Christ visited Lemuria and there enunciated the Lemurian philosophy. The fellowing also teaches that Christ reigned for 1,000 years as Melchizedek, the emperor of Atlantis. When Atlantis was destroyed, all that Christ had taught was stored away in archives of the secret brotherhoods such as the **Essenes** and **Rosicrucians.** The oldest of these brotherhoods was the Lemurians. The Lemurian Fellowship is a mundane organization designed to release the information contained in the Lemurian Brotherhood archives.

The Lemurian Fellowship, which sees the **New Age** as the kingdom of God, believes that the kingdom will have a communal social structure in which the individual's and society's prosperity mutually support each other. New members in the fellowship are expected eventually to become complete participants in it.

The fellowship is located on 260 acres on two tracts of land eight miles apart. Groups of members live communally, and facilities for their welfare and for fellowship administration worldwide have been constructed. Besides Gateway, the headquarters building, there is a chapel, school, dining hall, laundry, member residences, and Lemurian Crafts, a business that helps support the community. Most students to the group begin with a set of correspondence lessons. Leadership comes from the higher plane through the Council of Elder Brothers and the Advanced Ego (Stelle). Stelle led the group until his death in 1952 and was succeeded by a board of governors. Zitko left the group to found the World University. The fellowship may be contacted at Box 397, Ramona, CA 92065. Former members the fellowship founded the Stelle Group in Illinois.

Sources:

The Lemurian Scribe. *Let It Be Resolved.* Milwaukee, Wis Lemurian Press, 1940.

Phylos the Tibetan. *An Earth Dweller Returns.* Milwaukee, Wis Lemurian Press, 1940.

Stelle, Robert D. *The Sun Rises.* Ramona, Calif.: Lemuria Fellowship, 1952.

Zitko, Howard John. *The Lemurian Theochristic Conception.* N.p n.d.

Le Normand, Marie-Anne Adélaide (1772–1843)

Famous French clairvoyant and fortune teller known as "Th Sybil of the Faubourg Saint Germain." She was born at Alenço and became one of the most celebrated occultists and diviners c her day, though it might be said that her art was much more th product of sound judgment than of any supernatural gift.

She predicted their futures to Danton, Marat, Robespierre and St. Just, but we hear no more of her under the years of th Directory (1795–99). When Josephine Beauharnais came int prominence as the intended wife of Napoleon, Le Normand wa received at all those houses and salons where the future empres had any influence.

Josephine was extremely credulous and used to read her ow fortunes to herself on the cards, but when she discovered that L Normand was an adept at this art, she often had her in attend ance to assist her in it. Even Napoleon himself, who was no without his own superstitions, had his horoscope read by her.

Le Normand soon set up her own salon in Paris, where sh read people's fortunes by means of the cards. It is not certai whether these cards were of the nature of **tarot** cards, but it i more than likely that she used various methods. She occasionall divined the fortunes of others through playing games of piquet sept, and other well-known card games of the day. There i anecdotal evidence that she told fortunes with ordinary playin cards, but there is also a tradition that she used a speciall designed pack. She did not hide her methods from others, bu the Parisian society of her day appears to have thought that he power of **divination** lay not only in the cards she manipulated bu in her personality or occult insight.

After the fall of the emperor, Le Normand was in great de mand among the Russian, German, and English officers in Paris and even Emperor Alexander and other potentates consulte her. Shortly after this she went to Brussels, where she read th fortune of the Prince of Orange, but when she was discovere trying to cheat the customs officials, she was arrested and throw into a Belgian prison.

By 1830 she had become quite forgotten, and when the news papers announced her death on June 25, 1843, a great man people failed to remember her name. Le Normand had a grea reputation for the accuracy of her predictions among all classes from revolutionary heroes to emperors and royalty. What is said to be an authentic reproduction of the "Mademoiselle Le Normand Fortune Telling Cards" has long been reprinted in Europe and elsewhere and is currently marketed by U.S. Games Systems Inc., New York, New York.

Leo, Alan (1860–1917)

Pseudonym of British astrologer William Frederick Allen, born in London August 7, 1860. His mother was a member of the conservative Plymouth Brethren, and when Allen was a child, his father abandoned him and his mother. Young Allen was apprenticed as a draper, chemist, and grocer in turn, but in each instance failed to serve out his time. At the age of 16 he was destitute in Liverpool. A few years later he was a prosperous employer, then just as suddenly was ruined by a dishonest manager. He then became a salesman for a manufacturer of sewing machines.

Eventually Allen learned about **astrology** from an old herbalist, who treated him for an illness. He also became friendly with the astrologer "Sepharial" (**Walter Gorn Old**), a Theosophist. Allen joined the **Theosophical Society** in 1890 and became a successful mail-order astrologer. In 1895 he married Bessie Phillips, a professional palmist and phrenologist.

Allen became the proprietor of the periodical *Modern Astrology,* and under his professional name, Alan Leo, compiled a number of popular books on astrology. His Modern Astrology Publishing Co. was the first large-scale venture of its kind, and he established branches in Paris and New York.

In 1914 and 1917 Allen was prosecuted for fortune-telling. He was acquitted in the first case, but convicted and fined in the second. At that date, prosecution of Spiritualist mediums and other seers was not infrequent (see **Fortune Telling Act**). He died August 30, 1917, at Cornwall, England. His wife, who published several books under the name "Bessie Leo," edited his biography, *The Life and Works of Alan Leo* (1919).

Sources:

Leo, Alan. *Astrology for All.* 2 vols. London: Modern Astrology Office, 1921.

———. *Casting the Horoscope.* London: Modern Astrology Office, 1912.

———. *The Horoscope and How to Read It.* N.p., 1902.

———. *How to Judge a Nativity.* 2 vols. 1904. Reprint, London: Modern Astrology Office, 1928.

———. *Practical Astrology.* Philadelphia: David McCay, n.d.

Leo, Bessie. *The Life and Works of Alan Leo.* N.p., 1919.

Leonard, Gladys Osborne (1882–1968)

Celebrated trance medium born May 28, 1882. **Hereward Carrington** designated her as "the British Mrs. Piper," and she had a reputation during her lifetime as one the greatest trance mediums.

In her autobiographical *My Life in Two Worlds* (1931) she recalled her life as a child:

"In whatever direction I happened to be looking, the physical view of the wall, door, ceiling, or whatever it was, would disappear, and in its place would gradually come valleys, gentle slopes, lovely trees and banks covered with flowers, of every shape and hue. The scene seemed to extend for many miles, and I was conscious that I could see much farther than was possible with the ordinary physical scenery around me."

Leonard became a professional singer early in her adult life and during this period acquired experimental acquaintance with the phenomena of **Spiritualism** through **table-turning** experiences. She sat with two girlfriends in her dressing room. After 26 futile attempts, a communicator appeared who called herself "Feda" and said that in life she had been the wife of one of Leonard's ancestors. According to her account, she was quite young at the time and lived only a brief time after the marriage; she died at the age of thirteen about 1800. Leonard abandoned her singing career and henceforth devoted much of her time to her mediumship.

From her first appearance, "Feda" remained a faithful attendant of Leonard and was always the first to come through when Leonard passed into trance. During her first manifestations, according to reports, through the table communications, her form and that of other spirit friends were quite distinctly seen in the subdued light on the white walls "like clearly-cut shadows, which showed up perfectly against the light background." However, significant physical phenomena such as **ectoplasm** or **materialization** did not develop. Leonard sometimes heard voices objectively, slight **touches,** and little manifestations when alone, being always aware of "suspended" or blank feeling whenever this happened. Her acquaintance with physical phenomena came about only after her sittings with other mediums who performed materializations and other phenomena. The first time she herself heard the voice of "Feda" was in a **direct voice** sitting in the house of **H. Dennis Bradley.** It appears that even part of her own power, necessary for the trance control, was contributed by her husband, as "Feda" was very clamorous whenever a separation came about through her husband's professional engagements. "Feda" said that she could not use the power well enough during his absence.

Occasionally, for medical purposes, "Feda" gave way to "North Star," another Indian, who did not speak through Leonard but used her "hands and arms in an extraordinary way, making passes over the patient, and certainly he cured several people of different maladies."

In March 1914, "Feda" gave instructions that Leonard must begin work as a professional medium as soon as possible. At the same time the medium was deluged with messages ending with the words: "Something big and terrible is going to happen to the world. Feda must help many people through you."

During the winter of 1914, **Hewat McKenzie,** the founder of the **British College of Psychic Science,** had some satisfactory sittings with Leonard. On his recommendation, Lady and **Sir Oliver Lodge** came, after their son Raymond was killed in World War I in autumn 1915. Their first evidence of Raymond's survival was obtained through Leonard, and the resulting publicity made Leonard a celebrity.

In 1916 two sitters, Radcliffe Hall and (Una) Lady Troubridge, approached Leonard after the death of their friend "A.V.B." Although the sitters and subject were unknown to her, "Feda" gave remarkably detailed information on the subject and the house where the ladies had lived. The sitters not only approached Leonard anonymously, but also employed a private detective to make sure Leonard had not obtained the information in a mundane way. No deception was discovered.

In 1918, for a period of three months, Leonard was exclusively engaged by the **Society for Psychical Research.** Out of 73 sittings, all but three were anonymous. The report of Mrs. W. H. Salter stated that the sitters generally agreed that good evidence of surviving personality had been obtained and the complete trustworthiness of the medium could not be questioned.

Rev. **C. Drayton Thomas** carried on experiments with Leonard for years. Important book and newspaper tests were evolved. Thomas's deceased father acquired the ability to come through without "Feda," who usually acted as interpreter for others, and he spoke directly from Leonard's mouth. Thomas reported several occasions in which he received evidential messages. For example, on one occasion he was told, "In to-morrow's *Times,* on page 8, column 5, about six inches from the bottom, you will find a name which will recall intimate associations of your youth between the ages of 16–18." The *Times* appears to have been "invaded" systematically for information by this communicator who also disclosed personal traits in referring to his favorite books, indicating passages on certain pages in answer to questions put by his son.

In her autobiography, Leonard narrated many interesting **out-of-the-body travel** experiences. She stated that she often met people in the spirit world and brought back memories of such meetings into the waking state. These spiritual excursions often received striking confirmation through other means. Leonard also cooperated with parapsychologist **W. W. Carington** in tests to establish whether "Feda" was a secondary personality or a genuine communicator. After nearly 50 years of mediumship, Leonard died March 10, 1968.

Sources:

Berger, Arthur S., and Joyce Berger. *The Encyclopedia of Parapsychology and Psychical Research.* New York: Paragon House, 1991.

"Books and Reports on Leonard Mediumship." *Psychic Science* 16, no. 4 (January 1938).

Broad, C. D. *Lectures on Psychical Research.* New York: Humanities Press, 1962.

Carington, W. W. *Telepathy.* London, 1945.

Hall, Radcliffe, and (Una) Lady Troubridge. "On a series of Sittings with Mrs. Osborne Leonard." *Proceedings* of the Society for Psychic Research 30.

Heywood, Rosallind. "Mrs. Gladys Osborne Leonard: A Biographical Tribute." *Journal* of the Society for Psychic Research 45 (1969).

Leonard, Gladys Osborne. *My Life In Two Worlds.* London: Cassell, 1931.

Lodge, Sir Oliver J. *Raymond or Life and Death.* London: Metheun; New York: George H. Doran, 1916.

Pleasants, Helene, ed. *Biographical Dictionary of Parapsychology.* New York: Helix Press, 1964.

Salter, W. H. *Trance Mediumship: An Introductory Study of Mrs. Piper and Mrs. Leonard.* London: Society for Psychical Research, 1962.

Smith, Susy. *The Mediumship of Mrs. Leonard.* Reprint, New Hyde Park, N.Y.: University Books, 1964.

Thomas, C. Drayton. *Life beyond Death with Evidence.* N.p., 1928.

———. *Some New Evidence for Human Survival.* London: Collins, 1922.

Thomas, John F. *Beyond Normal Cognition: An Evaluative and Methodological Study of the Mental Content of Certain Trance Phenomena.* Boston, Mass.: Boston Society for Psychical Research, 1937. Reprint, Ann Arbor, Mich.: University Microfilms, n.d.

Leroy, Olivier-Gilbert (1884– ?)

Author of books on the lives of the saints and on parapsychology. He was born October 9, 1884, at Tours, France, and studied at the Law School, University of Paris (LL.D., 1925) and the Sorbonne, University of Paris (docteur ès lettres, 1931). From 1941 to 1950 he was a director of education in Madagascar. As a student of hagiography, he wrote books on saints and mysticism and also contributed various articles to *Revue d'Ascétique et de Mystique.*

Sources:

Leroy, Olivier-Gilbert. "Apparitions de Sainte Thérèse de Jésus" (Apparitions of Saint Theresa of Jesus). *Revue d'Ascétique et de Mystique* 134 (1958).

———. *Le Chevalier Thomas Browne.* Paris: J. Gamber, 1931.

———. "Examen des témoignages sur la lévitation extatique chez Sainte Thérèse de Jésus" (Study of the Testimony on Ecstatic Levitation of Saint Theresa). *Revue d'Ascétique et de Mystique* 131 (1937).

———. *Les Hommes-Salamandres* (The Salamander Men). N.p., 1931.

———. *La Lévitation.* N.p., 1928.

———. "La Pénètration des consciences chez Sainte Thérèse de Jésus" (The Penetration of Consciousness in Saint Theresa of Jesus). *Revue d'Ascétique et de Mystique* 136 (1958).

———. *La Raison primitive* (Primitive Reason). N.p., 1926.

———. *Sainte Jeanne d'Arc, Les Voix* (The Voices of St. Joan of Arc). N.p., 1956.

Pleasants, Helene, ed. *Biographical Dictionary of Parapsychology.* New York: Helix Press, 1964.

Lescoriere, Marie (fl. sixteenth century)

A witch of the sixteenth century arrested at the age of 90. On being examined she declared that she was no longer a witch, that she prayed daily, and that she had not visited the **sabbat** for 40 years. Questioned on the subject of the sabbat, she confessed that she had seen the devil and that he had visited her in the shape of a dog or a cat. On one occasion, she said, she had killed a neighbor by praying to the devil.

LeShan, Lawrence (L.) (1920–)

Psychologist and parapsychologist. He was born September 8, 1920, in New York City and was educated at the College of William and Mary (B.A., 1942), the University of Nebraska (M.S., 1943), and the University of Chicago (Ph.D., 1954). His education was interrupted on two occasions by periods of service in the U.S. Army (1943–46, 1950–52). Following his graduation he became the chief of the department of psychology at the Institute of Applied Biography in New York (1954–64) and simultaneously a research associate at the Ayer Foundation, Inc., New York (1954–70).

Originally a skeptic in his attitude to paranormal phenomena, he devoted some 500 hours to testing the famous psychic **Eileen Garrett** and was particularly impressed by her powers in the field of **psychometry.** He also made a special study of psychic **healing** and since 1970 has held training seminars in New York for psychologists and students. He is a member of the **American Psychical Research Society** and the author of a number of books and articles.

In his book *The Medium, the Mystic, and the Physicist* (1974), he proposed a theory of different types of reality: sensory reality (that of everyday experience), clairvoyant reality (in which the time structure is modified and the identities of "you" and "I" become a part of a total "One" in the cosmos), and a transpsychic reality (in which there is total identification with the "All").

Sources:

Berger, Arthur S., and Joyce Berger. *The Encyclopedia of Parapsychology and Psychical Research.* New York: Paragon House, 1991.

LeShan, Lawrence. *Alternative Realities.* New York: M. Evans, 1976.

———. *Einstein's Space and Van Gogh's Sky: Physical Reality and Beyond.* New York: Macmillan, 1982.

———. *From Newton to EAP: Parapsychology and the Challenge of Modern Science.* Wellingborough, England: Turnstone Press, 1984.

———. *How to Meditate: A Guide to Self-Discovery.* New York: Bantam Books, 1975.

———. *The Medium, the Mystic, and the Physicist.* 1974. Reprinted as *Clairvoyant Reality: Toward a General Theory of the Paranormal.* Wellingborough, England: Turnstone Press, 1980.

———. *The Psychology of War: Comprehending Its Mystique and Its Madness.* Chicago: Noble Press, 1992.

Leslie, Desmond (Peter Arthur) (1921–)

Irish novelist, film scriptwriter, musician, and coauthor of a key book on **flying saucers.** Born in London, the youngest son of novelist Sir Shane Leslie, he was educated at Ampleforth, England, and Trinity College, Dublin. During World War II he served in the Royal Air Force (1940–44). Over the years he wrote a number of books, but his most famous was written with **George Adamski.** *Flying Saucers Have Landed* (1953) created a sensation and launched a trend. It passed through many editions and was translated into 16 different languages. Leslie remained friendly with Adamski and eventually wrote a sympathetic obituary for him. In addition to his novels and scripts, Leslie has composed electronic music for films and television.

Sources:

Leslie, Desmond. *The Amazing Mr. Lutterworth: A Novel.* London: Allan Wingate, 1958.

———. "Leslie Strikes Back." *Nexus* 1, nos. 2–5 (May 1955): 7–8; *Saucer News* 2, nos. 2–6 (June/July 1955): 7–8.

———. "Obituary: George Adamski." *Flying Saucer Review* 11, no. 4 (July/August 1965): 18–19.

Leslie, Desmond, and George Adamski. *Flying Saucers Have Landed.* New York: British Book, 1953.

Leventhal, Herbert (1941–)

Author of scholarly studies on occultism. He was born October 9, 1941, in Brooklyn, New York, and was educated at Brooklyn College of the City University of New York (B.A., 1962; Ph.D., 1973). His doctoral dissertation, *In the Shadow of the Enlightenment: Occultism and Renaissance Science in Eighteenth-Century America,* was published by the State University of New York Press in 1976. It grew out of his research on political thought in eighteenth-century American culture, in which he identified relics of occultism and Renaissance science that played an important part in the outlook of their time.

Sources:

Leventhal, Herbert. *In the Shadow of the Enlightenment: Occultism and Renaissance Science in Eighteenth Century America.* New York: State University of New York Press, 1976.

Lévi, Éliphas (1810–1875)

Pseudonym of Alphonse Louis Constant, a French occultist of the nineteenth century, whose work stands as the fountainhead of the contemporary magical revival. He was born in Paris, the son of a shoemaker, and through the good offices of the parish priest was educated for the church at St. Sulpice. In due course he became a deacon and took the required vow of celibacy, but shortly thereafter he was expelled from St. Sulpice for teaching doctrines contrary to those of the Church.

Obscure for a time, he emerged about 1839 under the influence of a political and socialistic prophet named Ganneau. Lévi's pamphlet entitled *The Gospel of Liberty* earned him six-months' imprisonment. In Paris he married a 16-year-old woman who later had the marriage annulled. It was probably not until after she left him that he launched his study of the occult sciences; his writings previous to this time show little trace of occult influence.

In 1850 he contributed a Dictionary of Christian Literature to a series of theological encyclopedias published by Abbé Migne. Within a year, however, Lévi was known to be giving lessons on occultism to pupils. According to a paragraph by M. Chauliac: "The Abbé Constant, for a second time repudiating his name, assumed the title of the Magus Éliphas Lévi, giving consultations in great number to credulous clients, who paid as much as twenty-five francs a time for a prediction from Lucifer." There is no evidence that Lévi was actually ordained as a priest, but the title "Abbé" was normally given to those wearing a clerical style of costume, and Lévi wore a quasi-clerical garb in his capacity of a Magus or master of magic.

In 1853 he traveled to London and met Lord **Bulwer Lytton,** whom he assisted in various magical evocations and theories. These were later fictionalized in Lytton's occult stories *Zanoni: A Strange Story* and *The Haunted and the Haunters.* Lévi's own works on occultism, which had their shortcomings, nevertheless played a prominent part in the occult revival. Waite's critical notes added considerable value. However, Lévi's knowledge of the occult sciences was often more imaginative than circumstantial, so that the reader must be on guard.

Lévi died in April 1875. There is an interesting firsthand account of Lévi during his lifetime by **Kenneth R. H. Mackenzie,** who visited the magus in Paris in 1861. (See *Occult Review,* December 1921.)

Sources:

Lévi, Éliphas. *La Clef des grands mystères.* Translated as *The Key of the Mysteries.* 1861. Translated by Aleister Crowley. London: Rider, 1959. Reprint, New York: Samuel Weiser, 1970.

———. *Dogme de la haute magie.* N.p., 1854.

———. *Histoire de la magie.* Translated as *The History of Magic.* 1860. Trans. Arthur Edward Waite. London: W. Rider, 1913. Reprint, New York: Samuel Weiser, 1971.

———. *The Magical Ritual of the Regnum Sanctum.* New York: Samuel Weiser, 1970.

———. *The Mysteries of Magic: A Digest of the Writings of Éliphas Lévi.* Trans. Arthur Edward Waite. 1886. Reprint, New Hyde Park, N.Y.: University Books, 1974.

———. *The Paradox of the Highest Science.* Adyar, India: Theosophical Publishing House. Reprint, Mokelumne Hill, Calif.: Health Research, 1969.

———. *Rituel de la haute magie.* N.p., 1856.

———. *Transcendental Magic.* Translation of *Dogme de la haute magie* and *Rituel de la haute magie.* Translated by Arthur Edward Waite. London: George Redway, 1896. Reprint, New York: Samuel Weiser, 1970.

Williams, Thomas A. *Eliphas Levi: Master of Occultism.* University, Ala.: University of Alabama Press, 1975.

Levitation

The rising of physical objects, tables, pianos, etc., or of human beings into the air, contrary to the known laws of gravitation and without any visible agency. More often the term is used in a restricted sense and refers to the levitation of the human body. As such, the phenomenon was reported from ancient times. Instances of transportation, or **teleportation,** which is levitation in its highest form, are recorded both in the Jewish Bible and the Christian New Testament, illustrated, for example, by Jesus' walking on the water, a feat reportedly accomplished by many of the saints.

The power was claimed by wizards of many primitive tribes, by mystics in the East, and it has been repeatedly claimed, in less sensational degrees, by several modern Spiritualist mediums. The mediums offered themselves as evidence to science that the miracles of rising in the air recorded in the life of saints, ecstatics, witches, and victims of demoniac possession might rest on a solid basis of fact.

Levitating Saints

In *Die Christliche Mystik* (5 vols., 1836–42), J. J. von Görres spoke of 72 levitated saints, while **Olivier Leroy** (in *Levitation,* 1928) noted that out of 14,000, at least 200 had experienced the phenomenon. Among them were St. Dunstan (918–988), St. Dominic (1170–1221), St. Francis of Assisi (1186–1226), Thomas Aquinas (1226–1274), St. Edmund, archbishop of Canterbury (d. 1242), Blessed James of Illyria (d. 1485), Savonarola (1452–1498), St. Ignatius Loyola (1491–1556), St. Philip Neri (1515–1595), St. Peter of Alcantara (1499–1562), St. Joseph of Copertino (1603–1663) and St. Alphonsius Liguori (1696–1787). They were variously reported as having been raised a short distance in the air. Leroy found the average elevation 20 inches, but in some cases, exceptional height was recorded.

St. Joseph of Copertino who, in the *Acta Sanctorum,* is credited with 70 separate flights, once flew up into a tree and perched on a branch which quivered no more than if he had been a bird. According to von Görres, St. Peter of Alcantara was, on one occasion, carried up in the air to a great height, far above the trees, when with his arms crossed on his chest he continued to soar while hundreds of little birds gathered around him, making a most agreeable concert with their songs.

St. Dunstan, archbishop of Canterbury, was observed to rise from the ground shortly before his death in 988. St. Bernard Ptolomei, St. Philip Benitas, St. Albert of Sicily, and St. Dominic, founder of the Dominican order, were all seen to be levitated while engaged in their devotions. An ecstatic nun "rose from the ground with so much impetuosity, that five or six of the sisters could hardly hold her down." It is related by his biographers that Savonarola, shortly before he perished at the stake, remained suspended at a considerable height above the floor of his dungeon, absorbed in prayer.

Levitation before the Altar

The scene of the elevation of saints and ecstatics was most often the altar in the church, and the state which seemed to condition it was the deep trance-like state known as "rapture." St. Joseph of Copertino experienced 15 levitations in front of images of the Holy Virgin; his raptures in saying mass were of frequent occurrence, and "his ecstasies and ascensions were witnessed not only by the people and the members of his order, but Pope Urban VIII saw him one day in this state and was intensely astonished. Joseph, bethinking himself that he was in the presence of the Vicar of Christ, fell into an ecstasy and was raised above the ground."

According to an official report, the original of which is in the Bibliotheque National of Paris, Françoise Fontaine, a young servant of Louviers, exorcized in 1591, was three times raised before the altar and the third time was carried through the air head downwards.

Fr. K. A. Schmöger recounted the statement of stigmatist **Anne Catherine Emmerich** (1774–1824):

"When I was doing my work as vestry-nun, I was often lifted up suddenly into the air, and I climbed up and stood on the higher parts of the church, such as windows, sculptured ornaments, jutting stones; I would clean and arrange everything in places where it was humanly impossible. I felt myself lifted and supported in the air, and I was not afraid in the least, for I had been accustomed from a child to being assisted by my guardian angel."

Of Abbé Claude Dhière (1757–1820), director of the Grand Séminaire of Grenoble, his biographer de Franclieu noted that: "when he experienced ecstasies during his Mass, it was usually at the Memento of the living and the dead, and the students who used to serve his Mass declare that, when enraptured, his feet did not touch the floor."

Lesser-known people also were reported to levitate on occasion, as was noted in the *Frankfurter Zeitung* of September 8, 1861:

"We read in the *Gegenwart* of Vienna that a Catholic Priest was preaching before his congregation last Sunday in the Church of St. Mary, at Vienna, on the subject of the constant protection of angels over the faithful committed to their charge, and this in words of great exaltation, and with an unction and eloquence which touched profoundly the hearts of numbers of the congregation. Soon after the commencement of the sermon, a girl of about 20 years of age, showed all signs of ecstasy, and soon, her arms crossed upon her bosom, and with her eyes fixed on the preacher, she was seen by the whole congregation to be raised gradually from the floor into the air, and there to rest at an elevation of more than a foot until the end of the sermon. We are assured that the same phenomenon had happened several days previously at the moment of her receiving the communion."

The French psychic investigator **Col. Rochas** received a personal testimony from Abbé Petit that once, to his great terror, he was levitated in the church.

In religious chronicles, one also meets with the antithesis of the phenomenon of levitation—excessive gravitation. G. Neubrigensis recorded the case of Raynerus, the wicked minister, who so overweighed a ship with his iniquity that in the midst of the stream it was unable to stir. As soon as he was put out of the ship they could easily sail away.

There is a seeming analogy to these questionable accounts from the past in the cases of hysterics who often claim such an increase of weight that they are unable to stir. That the feeling may not be purely imaginary is suggested by the case of the medium Alberto Fontana who, after a levitation, remained as if nailed to the floor, and nobody was able to move him.

Levitation in Witchcraft

In the tenth century, it was popularly charged that women who followed the pagan goddess Diana flew in the air to their rituals, but the church considered this a heretical delusion. However, during the **witchcraft** mania of the sixteenth and seventeenth centuries, confessions or accusations of **transvection** (flying through the air) were accepted as describing a reality. It was believed that witches smeared themselves with a special ointment which gave them the power of flight, usually mounted on a broomstick, a shovel, a distaff, or even an animal.

The inquisitors suggested that the transvection of witches was a fact and existed as a diabolical parody of the transports of saints. It now seems possible that behind some of the claimed transvection of witches may have been either vivid dreams or occasional **out-of-the-body travel** experiences, while some may have been hallucinations. Such experiences may have been induced by the special ointment, though other accounts claim that no such ointment was necessary to produce the experience. Some have argued that in light of well-attested accounts of the transvection of saints, it should be logical to consider that there may have been some genuine cases of levitation of witches.

From Witchcraft to Spiritualism

In ancient rituals, levitation was mentioned as a sign of **possession.** Charges of witchcraft or bewitchment usually followed the manifestation. Henry Jones, a 12-year-old English boy of Shepton-Mallet, England, was believed to be bewitched in 1657 as he was carried by invisible means from one room to another and sometimes was wholly lifted up, so that his body hung in the air, with only the flat of his hands placed against the ceiling. One afternoon in the garden of Richard Isles, he was raised up and transported over the garden wall for about 30 yards.

Patrick Sandilands, a younger son of Lord Torpichen, was similarly believed to be the victim of witchcraft in 1720 at Caldo in Scotland. His tendency to rise entranced into the air was so great that his sisters had to watch him and sometimes could only keep him down by hanging to his skirts.

Mary London, a hysterical servant girl who was tried for witchcraft in 1661 at Cork, Ireland, was frequently transported by an invisible power to the top of the house.

The phenomenon was frequently witnessed in **poltergeist** cases. The **Drummer of Tedworth** would lift all the children up in their beds. During the disturbances at the Epworth Vicarage in 1716, Nancy Wesley was several times successfully lifted up with the bed on which she was sitting to a considerable height. Four of her sisters were present, among them Hetty, whom the disturbances chiefly followed (see **Epworth phenomena**). Harry Phelps the 12-year-old son of the Rev. **Eliakim Phelps** around whom the Stratford, Connecticut, disturbances centered in 1850, was often lifted from the floor, was once put into a water cistern, and at another time was suspended from a tree.

During the age of **animal magnetism,** Dr. **G. Billot** reported that his somnambules sometimes rose into the air. If put into a bath during her trance, **Frederica Hauffe,** the Seeress of Prevorst, Germany, floated on the top of the water like a cork. If Dr. **Justinus Kerner** placed his fingers against her own, he could act like a magnet and lift her from the ground. In his book *Physiologie, médecine, et métaphysique du magnétisme* (1848), Louis J. J. Charpignon stated that Bourguignon, a mesmerist of Rouen, could lift several of his subjects from the ground by placing his hand over the epigastrium. Other experimenters have recorded with the same experience.

The levitation of Spiritualist mediums represents a simple continuity of an age-old phenomenon. When modern Spiritualism was introduced with the **Rochester rappings,** levitation soon appeared. It was recorded for the first time with **Henry C. Gordon** in February 1851. A year later, in Dr. Gray's house in New York, he was carried through the air to a distance of 60 feet.

If we accept Dr. R. T. Hallock's account before the New York Conference of June 18, 1852, there was an instance of Gordon's levitation in daylight in a crowded assembly room. According to Hallock, while he was delivering a lecture, Gordon, who sat at some distance from but in front of him, rose into the air, swayed from side to side, his feet grazing the top seats, and sank to the ground when the attention of the entire congregation became riveted on him. It was afterwards declared by the spirits that they intended to carry him over the heads of the sitters to the rostrum but that the audience had broken the necessary conditions of passivity.

The Levitations of D. D. Home

The next medium to exhibit the phenomenon was **D. D. Home.** His first levitation occurred August 8, 1852, in Ward Cheney's house at Manchester, Connecticut. The *Hartford Times* recorded the event:

"Suddenly and without any expectation on the part of the company, Mr. Home was taken up in the air. I had hold of his hand at the time, and I felt his feet—they were lifted a foot from the floor. He palpitated from head to foot with the contending emotions of joy and fear which choked his utterance. Again and again he was taken from the floor, and the third time he was carried to the ceiling of the apartment with which his hands and feet came in gentle contact. I felt the distance from the soles of his boots to the floor, and it was nearly three feet. Others touched his feet to satisfy themselves."

With no other medium was levitation so often and so reliably attested as with Home. In Britain, **Sir William Crookes** narrated his own experiences:

"On one occasion I witnessed a chair, with a lady sitting on it, rise several inches from the ground. On another occasion, to avoid the suspicion of this being in some way performed by herself, the lady knelt on the chair in such a manner that its four feet were visible to us. It then rose about three inches, remained suspended for about ten seconds and then slowly descended.

"At another time two children, on separate occasions rose from the floor with their chairs, in full daylight under (to me) most satisfactory conditions; for I was kneeling and keeping close watch upon the feet of the chair, observing distinctly that no one might touch them.

"The most striking instances of levitation which I have witnessed have been with Mr. Home. On three separate occasions have I seen him raised completely from the floor of the room. Once sitting in an easy chair and once standing up. On each occasion I had full opportunity of watching the occurrence as it was taking place.

"There are at least a hundred instances of Mr. Home's rising from the ground, in the presence of as many separate persons, and I have heard from the lips of the three witnesses to the most striking occurrence of this kind—the Earl of Dunraven, Lord Lindsay and Captain C. Wynne—their own most minute accounts of what took place. To reject the recorded evidence on this subject is to reject all human testimony whatever; for no fact in sacred or profane history is supported by a stronger array of proofs."

In the *Journal* of the **Society for Psychical Research** (Vol. 6, no. 15, [1889]), Crookes further stated:

"On several occasions Home and the chair on which he was sitting at the table rose off the ground. This was generally done very deliberately, and Home sometimes tucked up his feet on the seat of the chair and held up his hands in full view of all of us. On such an occasion I have got down and seen and felt that all four legs were off the ground at the same time, Home's feet being on the chair. Less frequently the levitating power was extended to those sitting next to him. Once my wife was thus raised off the ground in her chair."

The striking occurrence to which Crookes referred in the first quotation was the most famous case in history of levitation. It was witnessed on December 13 (not December 16, as first printed in **Lord Adare**'s book), 1868, at Ashley House, Victoria Street, London, in the presence of Adare, the Master of Lindsay and Charles Wynne, Adare's cousin. Home floated out of a third story window and came in through the window of another room.

Lord Adare noted: "He [Home] then said to us, 'Do not be afraid, and on no account leave your places' and he went out into the passage. Lindsay suddenly said 'Oh, good heavens! I know what he is going to do; it is too fearful.'"

Adare: "What is it?"

Lindsay: "I cannot tell you, it is too horrible! Adah [the spirit of a deceased American actress] says that I must tell you; he is going out of the window in the other room, and coming in at this window.' We heard Home go into the next room, heard the window thrown up, and presently Home appeared standing upright outside our window; he opened the window and walked in quite coolly. 'Ah,' he said, 'you were good this time'—referring to our having sat still and not wished to prevent him. He sat down and laughed."

Charlie: "What are you laughing at?"

Home: "We [the spirits; Home always was spoken of in third person when in trance] are thinking that if a policeman had been passing and had looked up and had seen a man turning round and round along the wall in the air he would have been much astonished. Adare, shut the window in the next room.' I got up, shut the window, and in coming back remarked that the window was not raised a foot, and that I could not think how he managed to squeeze through. He arose and said, 'Come and see.' I went with him; he told me to open the window as it was before. I did so; he told me to stand a little distance off; he then went through the open space, head first, quite rapidly, his body being nearly horizontal and apparently rigid. He came in again, feet foremost, and we returned to the other room. It was so dark I could not see clearly how he was supported outside. He did not appear to grasp, or rest upon, the balustrade, but rather to be swung out and in. Outside each window is a small balcony or ledge, 19 inches deep, bounded by stone balustrades, 18 inches high; the balustrades of the two windows are 7 feet 4 inches apart, measuring from the nearest points. A string-course, 4 inches wide, runs between the windows at the level of the bottom of the balus trade; and another 3 inches wide at the level of the top. Between the window at which Home went out, and that at which he came in, the wall recedes 6 inches. The rooms are on the third floor. . . . I asked Lindsay how Adah had spoken to him on the three occasions. He could scarcely explain; but said it did not sound like an audible human voice; but rather as if the tones were whispered or impressed inside his ear. When Home awoke he was much agitated; he said he felt as if he had gone through some fearful peril, and that he had a horrible desire to throw himself out of the window; he remained in a very nervous condition for a short time, then gradually became quiet." (Viscount Adare. *Experiences in Spiritualism with D. D. Home.* London: privately printed, 1870).

The Master of Lindsay gave an account of the incident before the Committee of the **Dialectical Society** in London in 1869 and wrote out an account in 1871. Before the society he stated:

"I saw the levitations in Victoria Street, when Home floated out of the window; he first went into a trance and walked about uneasily; then he went into the hall; while he was away, I heard a voice whisper in my ear 'He will go out of one window and in at another.' I was alarmed and shocked at the idea of so dangerous an experiment. I told the company what I had heard, and we then waited for Home's return. Shortly after he entered the room, I heard the window go up, but I could not see it, for I sat with my back to it. I, however, saw his shadow on the opposite wall; he went out of the window in a horizontal position, and I saw him outside the other window [that in the next room] floating in the air. It was eighty-five feet from the ground. There was no balcony along the windows, merely a string course an inch and a half wide; each window had a small plant stand, but there was no connection between them."

In his letter dated July 14, 1871, published in the *Spiritualist* newspaper, there was a further addition to the story: "The moon was shining full into the room; my back was to the light, and I saw the shadow on the wall of the window sill, and Home's feet about six inches above it. He remained in this position for a few seconds, then raised the window and glided into the room feet foremost, and sat down."

Frank Podmore, the author of *Modern Spiritualism* (2 vols., 1906) who discredited the phenomenon of levitation, stated that he looked up a Nautical Almanack of 1868 and found that the moon was new and could not have lit the room, not even faintly. But in Lord Adare's almost contemporary account there is no mention of the moon. He only stated that "the light from the window was sufficient to enable us to distinguish each other." As the moon is not mentioned in the Master of Lindsay's account before the Dialectical Committee either, Podmore's criticism is probably based on a misstatement of facts.

Another line of attack was chosen by Dr. W. B. Carpenter, vice president of the Royal Society. In the *Contemporary Review* of January 1876, he wrote:

"A whole party of believers will affirm that they saw Mr. Home float out of the window and in at another, whilst a single honest sceptic declares that Mr. Home was sitting in his chair all the time. The 'single honest sceptic' could be no other than Captain Wynne, the third witness of the occurrence. However, when he narrated to Sir William Crookes, S. C. Hall and others what he saw, he was actually in accord with Lord Adare and the Master of Lindsay. When Carpenter's assertion found echo in an American book, W. A. Hammond's *Spiritualism and Allied Causes and Conditions of Nervous Derangement* (1876), Capt. Wynne being explicitly mentioned as the honest skeptic, D. D. Home challenged his testimony. Wynne, answering him explicitly declared: 'The fact of your having gone out of the window and in at the other I can swear to.'"

A different basis of suspicion was raised by Podmore in a letter that H. D. Jencken sent to *Human Nature.* According to this letter, a few days before the much-discussed miracle of levitation, Home had opened the same window in the presence of two of his later witnesses, stepped on the ledge outside, and to the great alarm of the Master of Lindsay, remained standing there, looking down at the street some 80 feet below. Podmore believed that this was a rehearsal and "What, no doubt, happened was that Home, having noisily opened the window in the next room, slipped back under cover of darkness into the séance room, got behind the curtains, opened the curtains, opened the window, and stepped on the window ledge."

In his *Spiritualism: A Popular History from 1847* (1920), Joseph McCabe also attacked the case on the grounds of visibility and held it likely that it was only the shadow of Home which was seen. Andrew Lang took the stand that people in a room can see even in a fog a man coming in by the window, and going out again, head first, with body rigid.

The famous escapologist **Harry Houdini** (May 6, 1920) recorded in his diary: "I offered to do the D. D. Home levitation stunt at the same place that Home did it in 1868, and G. shirked and messed it up." According to the authors of *Houdini and Conan Doyle,* "he had evidently made a careful examination of the premises, with his customary thoroughness, and had decided that it would be possible to duplicate the performance, with suitable assistance. The assistant was apparently to have been G.; but the latter for some reason or other became frightened at the prospect, and backed out of the bargain." It is hardly necessary to stress that the possibility of Home having an accomplice is a most unreasonable one in the light of the circumstances of this celebrated levitation.

Subjective Sensations of Levitation

As Home was not always in trance when levitation occurred, he could give an account of his sensations. He wrote in his autobiography *Incidents in My Life* (1863):

"During these elevations, or levitations I usually experience in my body no particular sensation, than what I could only describe as an electrical fullness about the feet. I feel no hands supporting me, and since the first time, above described, have never felt fear, though if I had fallen from the ceiling of some rooms in which I have been raised, I could not have escaped serious injury. . . . At times, when I reach the ceiling, my feet are brought on a level with my face, and I am, as it were, in a reclining position. I have frequently been kept so suspended four or five minutes."

Home's account compares with that of the Rev. **Stainton Moses** of August 1872:

"I was carried up. I made a mark on the wall opposite my chest. I was lowered very gently until I found myself in my chair again. My sensation was that of being lighter than air. No pressure on any part of my body, no unconsciousness or entrancement. From the position of the mark on the wall it is clear that my head must have been close to the ceiling. The ascent of which I was perfectly conscious, was very gradual and steady, not unlike that of being in a lift, but without any perceptible sensation of motion other than that of feeling lighter than the atmosphere."

His only discomfort was a slight difficulty in breathing accompanied by a sensation of fullness in the chest. A longer account of subjective sensations appeared in the writings of St. Teresa of Avila, the famous reformer of the Carmelite Order. Explaining the difference between union and rapture, the saint wrote:

"Rapture, for the most part, is irresistible. It comes, in general, as a shock, quick and sharp, before you can collect your thoughts or help yourself in any way, and you see and feel it as a cloud or a strong eagle rising upwards and carrying you away on its wings. . . . Occasionally I was able, by great efforts, to make a slight resistance; but afterwards I was worn out, like a person who had been contending with a strong giant; at other times it was impossible to resist at all: my soul was carried away, and almost always my head with it—and now and then the whole body as well, so that it was lifted up from the ground. . . . It seemed to me when I tried to make some resistance, as if a great force beneath my feet lifted me up, I know of nothing with which to compare it . . . for it is a great struggle, and of little use, whenever our Lord so wills it. There is no power against this power. . . . When the rapture was over, my body seemed frequently to be buoyant, as if all the weight had departed from it; so much so that now and then I scarcely knew that my feet touched the ground."

Home stated: "I am generally lifted up perpendicularly, my arms frequently become rigid, and are drawn above my head, as if I were grasping the unseen power which slowly raises me from the floor."

Crookes saw him, in one instance, levitate in a sitting posture. On April 21, 1872, he recorded: "He was sitting almost horizontally, his shoulders resting on his chair. He asked Mrs. Walter Crookes to remove the chair from under him, as it was not supporting him. He was then seen to be sitting in the air, supported by nothing visible."

This account compares in an interesting manner with the deposition of the surgeon Francesco Pierpaoli about the last illness of St. Joseph of Copertino. The saint was sitting on a chair with his leg laid on the surgeon's knee. The surgeon began to cauterize it when he realized that Father Joseph was "rapt out of his senses." He said he:

"noticed that he was raised about a palm over the said chair, in the same position as before the rapture. I tried to lower his leg down, but I could not; it remained stretched out. . . . He had been a quarter of an hour in this situation when Father Silvestro Evangelista of the monastery of Osimo came up. He observed the phenomenon for some time, and commanded Joseph under obedience to come to himself, and called him by name. Joseph then smiled and recovered his senses."

A similar levitation in sitting posture was put on record by **Eugerne Rochas** in *Recueil de documents relatifs à la lévitation du corps humain* (1897), of the stigmatist from Ardeche, Victoire Claire of Coux, who died in 1883. Mrs. D., an eyewitness, testified:

"I saw her with great amazement remain with her eyes fixed but lively, and gradually raised above the chair whereon she was sitting. She stretched forth her arms, leaned her body forward, and remained thus suspended, her right leg bent up, the other touching the earth but by a toe. I saw Victoire in this position, impossible for anyone to keep up normally, every time she was in an ecstatic trance . . . more than a thousand times."

D. D. Home was often levitated in good light. Lord Lindsay categorically stated before the Dialectical Society that: "I once saw Home in full light standing in the air seventeen inches from the ground."

Strength of Levitating Power

Such contemporary testimony makes Home's levitations vie in importance with the stories of levitating saints. Olivier Leroy, manifesting his ecclesiastic bias, attributed mediumistic levitations to diabolic agency, but apart from his theological evaluation, there is no objective difference between levitating saints, demoniacs, and/or mediums. And all are equally interesting to the parapsychologist.

Also noteworthy, according to von Görres, is the impossibility of causing the levitants to descend. Thus the Blessed Gilles, while one day reading a passage relative to ecstasy, was lifted up above the table. When found in this state by some of his brethren, he was seized and pulled at with all their strength, but they could not get him down. When Curé Peller wanted to give the Sacrament to Francoise Fontaine, the girl:

"kneeling down had been almost alarmingly carried away, without being able to take the Sacrament, opening her mouth, rolling her eyes in her head in such a horrible way that it had been necessary, with the help of five or six persons, to pull her down by her dress as she was raised into the air, and they had thrown her down on the floor."

According to Dom La Taste, Miss Thevenet, the Jansenist convulsionaire, "was sometimes raised seven or eight feet high up to the ceiling, and then could carry two persons pulling down with all their might, three feet above the ground."

Joseph Glanvill quoted the testimony of **Valentine Greatrakes,** the famous healer, as given at Lady Conway's castle in 1665 in the case of a butler who rose from the ground. Notwithstanding that Greatrakes and another man caught hold of him and held him with all their strength, he was forcibly taken up, and for a considerable time floated about in the air just over their heads.

Domic de Jesus-Marie was raised up to the ceiling of his cell and remained there without earthly support for a day and night. A skeptic who seized the floating body by the feet was on another occasion borne on high. Frightened, he let go and fell to the earth.

In the days of the Salem witchcraft persecutions (see **America**), the tormentors of Margaret Rule once "pulled her up to the ceiling of the chamber, and held her there before a numerous company of spectators who found it as much as they could do to pull her down again."

In séance and table-tipping experiences, the power that effects levitation is often short-circuited as soon as the chain of hands is broken, the gaze of the sitters is too intense, the light is switched on, or the levitated body is touched.

While in the house of **Agnes Guppy-Volckman** and in the presence of **Mary Hardy,** the American medium Florence Marryat observed:

"Mrs. Guppy did not wish to take part in the séance, so she retired to the back drawing-room with the **Baroness Adelma Vay** and other visitors, and left Mrs. Hardy with the circle in the front [drawing room]. Suddenly, however, she was levitated and carried in sight of us all into the midst of our circle. As she felt herself rising in the air she called out: 'Don't let go hands, for Heaven's sake.' We were just standing in a ring, and I had hold of the hand of Prince Albert of Solms. As Mrs. Guppy came sailing over our heads, her feet caught his neck and mine, and in our anxiety to do as she told us, we gripped tight hold of each other and were thrown forward on our knees by the force with which she was carried past us into the centre. . . . The influence that levitated her, moreover, placed her on a chair with such a bump that it broke the two front legs off" (*There is No Death,* 1891).

The levitations of the medium **A. Zuccarini** were photographed. The flash of magnesium light caused the medium to fall back into the cabinet, but he was not hurt. One of the photographs showed the medium with his feet about 20–24 inches above the table. According to Prof. Murani, the duration of the levitation was about 12–14 seconds.

M. Macnab, an engineer, wrote in 1888 in Gaborieau's *Lotus Rouge* of the levitation of M. C., a sculptor: "Another time, having accidentally lighted up, while he was levitated on the music-stool, he fell heavily from a height of from fifty to sixty centimetres, so heavily that the foot of the stool was broken."

Macnab devised an ingenious means of control. He spread on the ground a square of very thin material, placed a chair in the middle and had M. C. sit on it. The sitters then held a corner of the material and, when the medium was levitated, could lift it up and test the height of the chair on which the medium was sitting in the air.

Home often asked the sitters not to look at him at the moment he was being carried up. Robert Bell touched his foot when he passed over him in the air. It "was withdrawn quickly and with a palpable shudder," he wrote; "it was floating and sprang from the touch as a bird would." In another instance, however, James Wason, a Liverpool solicitor, testified: "Laying hold and keeping hold of his hand, I moved along with him five or six paces as he floated above me in the air, and I only let go his hand when I stumbled against a stool." Apparently the conditions greatly depend upon the available power. Crookes observed instances in which it was ample to impart levitation to others.

Psychic investigator **Gambier Bolton** reported a similar experience in a séance with the medium **Cecil Husk** in his book *Psychic Force* (1904):

"At one of our experimental meetings, one of the observers (a man weighing quite 12 stones) was suddenly raised from the floor, with the chair in which he was sitting; and releasing the hands of those who were holding his hands, he was levitated in his chair, greatly to his surprise, until his feet were just above the heads of the other experimenters present. He remained stationary in the air for a few seconds and then slowly descended to the floor again. Fourteen observers were present."

Lord Lindsay witnessed Home floating with an armchair in his hand: "I then felt something like velvet touch my cheek, and on looking up, was surprised to find that he had carried with him an armchair, which he held out in his hand and then floated round the room, pushing the pictures out of their places as he passed along the walls. They were far beyond the reach of a person on the ground" (Report on Spiritualism . . . of the London Dialectical Society, 1871).

The medium **William Eglinton,** noted for his fradulent phenomena, was levitated in the presence of the emperor and empress of Russia, the grand duke of Oldenburg, and the grand duke Vladimir. "My neighbours," he wrote, "had to stand on their chairs to follow me. I continued to rise till my feet touched two shoulders on which I leaned. They were those of the Czar."

Simultaneous Levitations

At one of Eglinton's levitations in Calcutta, India, in 1882, the stage magician Harry Kellar, while holding firmly the left hand of the medium, was pulled after him: "his own body appeared for the time being to have been rendered non-susceptible to gravity."

In his book *What Am I?* (2 vols., 1873), **E. W. Cox** described a violent outburst of power:

"Mr. Williams, although held firmly by myself on one side and an F.R.S. on the other, was instantaneously lifted from his chair and placed in a sitting posture on the table. Mr. Herne was in like manner thrown flat upon his back upon the table, while his hands were held by two others of the party. While thus lying he was suddenly raised from the table, as if he had been flung by a giant, and thrown over the heads of the sitters to the corner of the room. The height to which he was actually thrown may be judged by this, that he knocked down a picture that was hung upon the wall, at a height of eight feet."

Dr. Nicholas Santangelo of Venosa wrote in a letter to psychic researcher **Dr. Paul Joire:**

"When the medium Ruggieri commenced to rise I held him firmly by the hand, but seeing myself drawn with such force as almost to lose my footing I held on to his arms, and thus I was raised in the air with my companion, who was on the other side of the medium. We were all three raised in the air to a height of at least three yards above the floor, since I distinctly touched with my feet the hanging lamp which was suspended from the centre of the ceiling. . . . The three mediums, Cecrehini, Ruggieri and Boella were also raised into space until they almost touched the ceiling."

On another occasion, Santangelo and M. Gorli, holding the hands of the medium Alberto Fontana, were suddenly lifted on the table, Gorli standing, Santangelo kneeling. Later the medium, who was seated in his chair, was suddenly thrown full length under the table with such force that Gorli was dragged with him and Santangelo was thrown down.

Accounts of such cases of simultaneous levitation are quite rare. One very early account was cited in Col. Henry Yule's *The Book of Ser Marco Polo* (1871). The story was told by Ibn Batuta, the Moor who lived in the fourteenth century, and concerned seven Indian jugglers who rose in the air in a sitting posture. However, Ibn Batuta confessed to a loss of consciousness, so it is possible that the experience was the result of hypnotic suggestion. Another yet earlier account from the second century B.C.E. is found in Philostratus' *Life of Apollonius of Tyana* and has even less evidential value. Damis, a disciple of Apollonius, stated that he had seen Brahmins suspended in the air at the height of two cubits, and that they could walk there without visible support.

The evidential value of records improves as time progresses. St. Joseph of Copertino was seen to rise in the air with a lamb on his shoulder. Once he grasped the confessor of the convent by the hand, snatched him off the floor, and began whirling round with him in midair. Another time he seized by the hair an insane nobleman who was brought to him to be healed, uttered his usual shout, and soared up with the patient who finally came down cured. St. Teresa of Avila and St. John of the Cross, while engaged in a conversation about the Trinity, were seen lifted up simultaneously.

In the mediumistic age, the first record is of the **Davenport Brothers.** The three children, Ira, William, and Elizabeth, were seen at an early age floating high up in the air at the same time. A joint levitation of **Frank Herne** and Guppy-Volckman was described in an attested record in **Catherine Berry**'s *Experiences in Spiritualism* (1876):

"After this, Mr. Herne was floated in the air, his voice being heard near the ceiling, while his feet were felt by several persons in the room, Mrs. Guppy who sat next to him being struck on the head by his boots as he sank into the chair. In a few minutes he recommenced ascending, and as Mrs. Guppy on this occasion determined, if possible, to prevent it, she held his arm, but the only result was that she ascended with him, and both floated together with the chairs on which they sat. Rather unfortunately, at this moment the door was unexpectedly opened, and Mr. Herne fell to the ground, injuring his shoulder, Mrs. Guppy alighting with considerable noise on the table where, on the production of light, she was found comfortably seated though considerably alarmed."

On occasions, the American medium **Charles Foster** also registered great anxiety. According to Dr. John Ashburner, author of *Notes and Studies on the Philosophy of Animal Magnetism and Spiritualism* (1867): "He grasped my right hand, and beseeched me not to quit my hold of him; for he said there was no knowing where the spirits might convey him. I held his hand, and he was floated in the air towards the ceiling. At one time Mrs. W. C. felt a substance at her head, and putting up her hands, discovered a pair of boots above her head."

The following case is an interesting contrast. About 1858, strong physical phenomena were recorded in the Poston Circle in America. The seven-year-old son of Charles Cathcart, an ex-congressman of Indiana, was often levitated and tossed about in the air. The spirit **control, "John King"** was credited with the manifestation. The little boy shouted with delight and cried: "Go it, old King. I am not a bit afraid; take me again." For details of the Poston Circle, see *Modern American Spiritualism* by Emma Hardinge (1869; 1970).

Another "baby story" was told by Florence Marryat about "Dewdrop," the child control of **Bessie Williams,** who grew very impatient when the medium's 15-month-old baby interrupted her chats with crying. She usually went up to quiet him, relinquishing the control of the medium for a few minutes, and reassuming it after. One day her attempt at pacifying the baby failed, for she returned saying: "It is no good, I have had to bring him down. He is on the mat outside the door." The baby, who was on the top story and could not yet walk, was found there, wailing, in his night shirt.

Cases in which the mediums have been levitated to the top of the table while sitting in a chair and holding the hands of the sitters are very numerous. **Charles Richet** classified them as semi-levitations, including as such the loss of weight of the medium also. Many physical mediums have at one time or other performed this feat. A curious testimony of the medium **Henry Slade** was given by Dr. Kettredge, a schoolmate, in *Light* (1909), according to which Slade was once levitated when sound asleep and was carried from one bed to another in a recumbent position.

The Levitations of Eusapia Palladino and Other Mediums

The levitations of **Eusapia Palladino** were among the best observed cases. **Cesare Lombroso,** Dr. **Ercole Chiaia,** Dr. **Julien Ochorowitz,** Col. Rochas, Prof. Porro, Prof. **Enrico Morselli,** and Dr. de Albertis testified to the facts. Chiaia reported a case in which he:

"found the medium stretched out, her head and a small portion of her back supported on the top of the table, and the remainder of the body extended horizontally, straight as a bar, and without any support to the lower part, whilst her dress was adhering to her legs as if her clothing was fastened or stitched around her. One evening I saw the medium stretched out rigid in the most complete cataleptic state, holding herself in a horizontal position, with only her head resting on the edge of the table for five minutes with the gas lighted in the presence of Prof. de Cinties, Dr. Capuano, the well-known writer, and Mr. Frederic Verdinois and other persons."

In Lombroso's *After Death—What?* (1909) there is an account of Palladino's levitation by a semi-materialized phantom:

"On the evening of the 28th September, while her hands were being held back by MM. Richet and Lombroso, she complained of hands which were grasping her under the arms; then, while in trance, with the changed voice characteristic of this state, she said: 'Now I lift my medium up on the table.' After two or three seconds the chair, with Eusapia in it, was not violently dashed, but lifted without hitting anything, on the top of the table and M. Richet and I are sure that we did not even assist the levitation by our force. After some talk in the trance state the medium announced her descent and (M. Finzi having been substituted for me) was deposited on the floor with the same security and precision, while MM. Richet and Finzi followed the movements of her hands and body without at all assisting them, and kept asking each other questions about the position of the hands. Moreover during the descent, both gentlemen repeatedly felt a hand touch them on the head."

At a later date, there are records by Dr. Schwab on the levitation of **Maria Vollhardt** and by **Baron Schrenck-Notzing** on **Willy Schneider.** Willy, to quote from René Sudre's *Introduction à la metapsychique humaine* (1926), "horizontally . . . seemed to rest on an invisible cloud. He ascended to the ceiling and remained five minutes suspended there, moving his legs about rhythmically. The descent was as sudden as the up-lighting. The supervision had been perfect. Geley in his last journey to Vienna also witnessed a levitation of Willy at Dr. Holub's and he told me he felt absolutely sure of the genuineness of the phenomenon."

Carlo Mirabelli, the South American medium, was fastened to an armchair in the presence of several members of the **Academia de Estudo Psychicos "Cesare Lombroso."** After that he rose from the ground and remained two minutes suspended twelve feet over the floor. The witnesses passed under the levitated body. At Santos, in the street, he was lifted up from a motor car for about three minutes.

Length of Time, Height, Luminosity

The period of mediumistic levitation seldom exceeds a few minutes. The fakir Covindassamy, of whom Louis Jacolliot wrote in *Occult Science in India* (1884), established a fairly good duration.

"As the Fakir was about to leave me, to go to his breakfast. . . . He stopped in the embrasure of the door leading from the terrace to the outside stairs, and, crossing his arms upon his chest, lifted himself up gradually, without any apparent support or assistance, to the height of about ten to twelve inches. I was able to determine the distance exactly by means of a point of comparison which I had fixed upon during the continuance of the phenomenon. Behind the Fakir's back there was a silken hanging, which was used as a portière, striped in gold and white bands of equal width. I noticed that the Fakir's feet were on a level with the sixth band. At the commencement of his ascension I had seized my chronometer; the entire time from the moment when the Fakir commenced to rise until he touched the ground again, was more than eight minutes. He remained perfectly still, at the highest point of elevation for nearly five minutes."

In this case, however, we have only Jacolliot's unsupported statements. Ten minutes is far behind the achievements of the saints. St. Joseph of Copertino was testified to have once remained suspended in the air at the height of the trees in the garden for more than two hours. And accounts of his levitations were confirmed by reliable witnesses.

The record of height attained belongs to a fakir who, according to Count Perovsky-Petrovo Solovovo in *Proceedings* of the Society for Psychic Research (Vol. 38, p. 276) was levitated in the presence of a crowd, about twice the height of a five-story building.

The levitation of saints is often accompanied by luminous phenomena, like the **aura.** The light that surrounds their body is said to be dazzling, sometimes lighting up the room. In mediumistic cases, the **luminous phenomena** are of a separate order. But they may also accompany levitation. Home wrote in *Incidents in My Life* (2nd series, 1872), "Just before this took place [levitation] we saw his whole face and chest covered with the same silvery light which we had observed on our host's [Mr. S. C. Hall's] face."

With some of the saints, intense corporeal heat was also noticed during their elevation. The difference between the ecstatic and ordinary trance state may eventually shed light on such epiphenomena.

More Recent Accounts of Levitation

During the 1930s, various mediums apparently demonstrated levitations. In 1938 the British newspaper *Daily Mirror* (June 13) published an impressive photograph of the medium Colin Evans apparently levitating. However, such photographic evidence is far from conclusive.

In his book *The Haunted Mind* (1959), Dr. **Nandor Fodor** devoted a chapter to "Phenomena of Levitation" and described his own investigation of the claimed levitation of the medium Harry Brown. A photograph of the medium apparently levitated in trance showing his coat-line dead straight and the buttons without blurring. Had the medium jumped from his chair, one would have expected the coat to have flapped and the buttons to blur.

Recent accounts of mediumistic levitation are rare. In the **Enfield Poltergeist** case in 1977, one of the children involved claimed to have floated about a room, and there is a photograph of her apparently levitated during an investigation.

A case of levitation associated with demonic possession was reported in Rome. The British newspaper *Sunday People* (May 15, 1977) described how the nun "Sister Rosa" in a Rome convent was the center of poltergeist type disturbances in which objects around her in a room would rise up and fly around, and the nun herself was levitated on several occasions. The Sisters of the convent stated to a reporter that Sister Rosa had once floated through the ceiling and was found standing on the floor above. The Mother Superior of the convent consulted Padre Candido, a leading exorcist in Rome, but the phenomena persisted. Sister Rosa was sent to no less than five different exorcists in other parts of Italy, but after returning was again surrounded by diabolic disturbances. These included persecution of the nun by inanimate objects, such as cactus thorns that became embedded in her head and could not be removed until washed with holy water. An iron bar is said to have broken loose from a door and moved through the walls to materialize in the nun's cell and commenced beating her while she slept. Kitchen knives were reported as flying from a table and trying to stab the nun in the chest. On other occasions, the nun is said to have spoken obscenities, using a gutteral "animal-like" voice, and had to be restrained by five nuns from attacking the cross and the altar.

A recent documentary film "Journey into the Beyond" (Burbank International Pictures) featured a spectacular scene of the apparent levitation of an African witch doctor. It was filmed in a small village somewhere between Dahomey and Togo. Witch doctor Togo Owaku is shown meditating on the shores of a lake, then at dusk walking in front of a large palm tree and drawing a circle in the sand with his staff. A fire is built, and as darkness falls, drummers build up an impressive rhythm. Inside the circle, Owaku spreads out his arms and begins to float upwards to height of about three feet. The scene is shown by two cameras, one in front and the other in the rear, and the ascent occupies about ten seconds. The film was directed by Frank Martin Lang, later known as "Rolf Olsen." When he was interviewed by Alan Vaughan, one of the editors of *New Realities* magazine, it seemed that the film team believed this to be a genuine case of levitation. However, some doubts remain, since the witch doctor himself picked the site, and the incident took place in darkness illuminated by the light of the fires.

In the 1970s a teaching course in levitation was offered by an academy organized by **Maharishi Mahesh Yogi** in Lucerne, Switzerland. This novel development of Transcendental Meditation was reported by various newspapers between May and July 1977. The London *Evening News* (May 16) stated that 12 individuals had just graduated from the first six-month course in levitation. One of them, Mrs. Albertine Haupt, stated:"I suddenly found myself six feet above the floor and thought, 'Heavens, I've done it.'" Although the floor was covered with foam rubber, she landed precipitately, and other students, equally successful in levitating, sustained bruises. Haupt stated: "It is just a matter of learning to control the power."

The *Daily Mirror* (July 14, 1977) stated that reporter Michael Hellicar interviewed the maharishi but was refused a demonstration of levitation. His followers refused to permit photographs being taken and stated, "We will not turn this into a circus." However, they produced their own picture taken two days earlier showing disciples apparently levitating, and this was reproduced in the *Daily Mirror* report.

In the London *Evening News* (May 18, 1977), professional magician David Berglas offered to pay £2,000 to any levitator who could hover six inches or more above the ground in a public demonstration, and up to £10,000 if as many as five of the Maharishi disciples demonstrated the ability together. The challenge was not accepted. In India, if certain yoga practices result in the ability to levitate, as well as other *siddhis,* or psychic powers, yogis are enjoined to avoid pride in such feats, which might hinder spiritual emancipation. As of the mid-1990s, no general satisfactory evidence exists that levitation is occurring among the maharishi's students, and several former *siddha* students have successfully sued the Maharishi's organization, claiming that it had failed to teach them to levitate.

Theories of Levitation

How can levitation be possible? What power or agent accomplishes it? The most obvious explanation—the possession of a word of mystical power—is little more than legendary. This appears in an ancient Jewish anti-gospel *Toledoth Jeshu: Life of Jesus,* composed about the sixth century B.C.E. which **G. R. S. Mead** quoted in his book *Did Jesus Live 100 Years B.C.?:*

"And there was in the sanctuary a foundation stone—and this is its interpretation: God founded it and this is the stone on which Jacob poured oil—and on it were written the letters of the Shem [Shem Hamephoresch, the ineffable name, of which only the consonants Y.H.V.H. are given to indicate the pronunciation as known to the initiated] and whosoever learned it, could do whatsoever he would. But as the wise feared that the disciples of Israel might learn them and therewith destroy the world, they took measures that no one should do so.

"Brazen dogs were bound to two iron pillars at the entrance of the place of burnt offerings, and whosoever entered in and learned these letters—as soon as he went forth again, the dogs bayed at him; if he then looked at them the letters vanished from his memory.

"This Jeschu came, learned them, wrote them on parchment, cut into his hip and laid the parchment with the letters therein—so that the cutting of his flesh did not hurt him—then he restored the skin to its place. When he went forth the brazen dogs bayed at him, and the letters vanished from his memory. He went home, cut open his flesh with his knife, took out the writing, learned the letters."

Queen Helene, being greatly troubled by the miracles of Jesus, sent for the wise men of Israel. They decided to use against Jesus his own medicine and taught Juda Ischariota the secret of learning the letters of the Shem. In the presence of Queen Helene and the wise men, Jesus (says the chronicle) "raised his hands like unto the wings of an eagle and flew, and the people were amazed because of him: How is he able to fly twixt heaven and earth?"

"Then spake the wise men of Israel to Juda Ischariota: 'Do thou also utter the letters and ascend after him. Forthwith he did so, flew in the air, and the people marvelled: How can they fly like eagles?' Ischariota acted cleverly, flew in the air, but neither could overpower the other, so as to make him fall by means of the Shem, because the Shem was equally with both of them."

The belief expressed in Robert Kirk's *Secret Commonwealth of Elves, Fauns and Fairies* (written 1691, published 1815 etc.), that levitation is accomplished by fairies, explains as little as crediting spirits with the feat or ascribing it to Taoist charms which, when swallowed, have the effect of carrying people to any place they think of. Nevertheless, the legend of the world of power persists alongside with the fairy agency. Writing of the teleportation of Lord Duffus, John Aubrey stated in his *Miscellanies* (1696 etc.) that the fairies cry "Horse and Hattock," and whenever a man is moved to repeat the cry he will be caught up.

At the dawn of the scientific age, early observers of psychic phenomena speculated on "electric," "magnetic," "mesmeric," and "odic" forces. They are all now antiquated notions.

From a theological viewpoint, J. J. von Görres explained nothing when he stated that the source of levitation is in the human organism and is produced by a pathological process or a mystic disposition of the soul. He described the pathological process of somnambules as a "kind of interior tempest aroused by the mechanical forces of the organism being suddenly upset." He described the mystical disposition as a condition for the reception of the Holy Ghost, with levitation due to this special gift setting the natural mechanism of the body in motion. Von Görres's idea may be a halfway house between naturalistic and supernatural theories, but it is more satisfactory than the Catholic view, which ascribed the levitation of the saints to a divine marvel and that of "demoniacs" and mediums to diabolic trickery. While the first claim is unacceptable to science, the second is too much in agreement with the extreme Spiritualistic idea that spirits have the power to act on matter directly.

Anti-Gravity Phenomena

Scientific interest in anti-gravity phenomena goes back many years. Documentation about variations of the gravitational field of the Earth were noted as early as 1672 by Jean Richer, and the first practical gravity meter was invented in 1833 by Sir John Herschel.

The repulsion effect of aluminum to electromagnetism is well known, and in 1914 the French inventor M. Bachelet demonstrated a working model of his Levitated Railway system. A Bachelet Levitated Railway Syndicate was formed to promote a full-scale layout, but the development was abandoned at the outbreak of World War I.

Scientists in various countries have conducted secret researches in "electro-gravities," the science of anti-gravity effects, and some devices have been constructed in which levitation of disk-like forms has been achieved in laboratory tests. Little has so far been published on such work, and conjecture exists that some **UFO** reports may concern such levitated devices. The Gravity Research Foundation of New Boston, New Hampshire, which was founded by Roger W. Babson, investigated various aspects of scientific inquiry into gravity and its anomalies. Recently the principle of magnetic levitation has been revived in novelty advertising displays. In Germany and Japan, researchers have investigated the feasibility of creating high-speed magnetic levitation railroads, while in Britain, a section of magnetic levitation railroad is operating at Birmingham International Airport.

The Cantilever Theory of Levitation

Some investigators have attempted to explain human levitation on the same basis as movement of objects by **psychic force** (**telekinesis** or **psychokinesis**). Between 1917 and 1920, Dr. W. J. Crawford of Belfast, Ireland, investigated the phenomena of the **Goligher Circle.** He studied alteration in weight of the medium Kathleen Goligher during levitation of a table, and claimed that the levitation was effected by "psychic rods" of ectoplasm emanating from the medium, which found leverage in the medium's body, acting as cantilevers. He obtained flashlight photographs of these psychic structures.

The parapsychologist **René Sudre** believed that Crawford's cantilever theory accounted for the movement of distant objects by the extrusion of elastic and resisting pseudopods from the body of the medium and thus sufficiently explained levitation:

"From a theoretical point of view, the levitation of a person is as easy to understand as that of an object. The teleplastic levers have naturally their fulcrum on the floor. Their shape is not definite; it may be that of a simple stay, of a cloudy cushion, or even a complete human materialization. The force of gravity is not eluded, but simply opposed by a contrary upward power. The spent amount of energy is not above that required for the production of the phenomenon of telekinesis."

According to Crawford, however, the sphere of action of pseudopods was limited to about 7 feet, the extreme mobility of the levitated body had to be accounted for, and the cantilever structure was very sensitive to light. Therefore such ectoplasm hardly lent itself as a mechanism for daylight levitation as in the case of Home or saints and stigmatics. (Later Crawford's observations were called into question due to fraud in the Giligher Circle.)

The Effect of Willpower

The possibility of the effect of willpower on levitation was suggested by Capt. J. Alleyne Bartlett in a lecture before the **London Spiritualist Alliance** on May 3, 1931. He often had the feeling that he could lighten his weight at will. He stepped on a scale and willed that his weight should be reduced, and the scale indicated, in fact, a loss of several pounds. To make such observations unobjectionable, the possible pressure of cantilever structures on the floor around the weighing machine ought to be made a matter of control.

The loss of weight in the levitated body may be an appearance due to the effect of a force which lifts or, if internally applied, makes the body buoyant. The best evidence as to the alleged extraordinary lightness of the bodies of saints and ecstatics is furnished in a case quoted by Col. Rochas of an ecstatic who lived in a convent near Grenoble. Three eyewitnesses, a parish priest, a university professor, and a student of the polytechnic school, stated that "her body would sometimes become stiff and so light that it was possible to lift her up like a feather by holding her by the elbow." According to some hypnotists, the phenomenon could be accomplished by simple hypnotic suggestion. During the early 1980s the question of possible paranormal changes of weight was the subject of experiments by parapsychologists **John B. Hasted,** David Robertson, and Ernesto Spinelli.

Special Breathing Techniques

Breathing exercises that form an important part in Eastern psychic development are believed by some practitioners to have a curious effect on the weight of the human body. According to Hindu **yoga** teachings, they generate a force that partially counteracts gravitation. They say that he who awakens the **Anahata Chakra** (a psychic and spiritual center situated in the region of the heart) "can walk in the air."

The psychic researcher **Camille Flammarion** believed that by breathing, even the ordinary sitters of a circle release a motor energy comparable to that which they release when repeatedly moving their arms. **Hereward Carrington**'s experiments with the "lifting game" seemed to show that, for some mysterious reason, rhythmical breathing may considerably reduce the weight of the human body. At the third International Psychical Congress in Paris in 1927, **Baron Schrenck-Notzing** described the case of a young man who claimed that by breathing exercises he had levitated his own body 27 times.

In **Alexandra David-Neel**'s *With Mystics and Magicians in Tibet* (1931 etc.), there is a description of a practice that especially enabled its adepts to take extraordinary long hikes with amazing rapidity. It is called *lung-gom* and it combines mental concentration with various breathing gymnastics. Meeting a *lung-gom-pa* in Northern Tibet, she noticed: "The man did not run. He seemed to lift himself from the ground, proceeding by leaps. It looked as if he had been endowed with the elasticity of a ball and rebounded each time his feet touched the ground. His steps had the regularity of a pendulum."

The breathing exercises of the *lung-gom-pa* had to be practiced for three years and three months during strict seclusion in complete darkness. It was claimed that the body of those who trained themselves for years became exceedingly light, nearly without weight: "These men, they say, are able to sit on an ear of barley without bending its stalk or to stand on the top of a heap of grain without displacing any of it. In fact the aim is levitation." One of these exercises was described as follows: "The student sits cross-legged on a large and thick cushion. He inhales slowly and for a long time, just as if he wanted to fill his body with air. Then, holding his breath he jumps up with legs crossed, without using his hands and falls back on his cushion, still remaining in the same position. He repeats that exercise a number of times during each period of practice. Some lamas succeed in jumping very high in that way."

Some initiates asserted that "as a result of long years of practice, after he has traveled over a certain distance the feet of the *lung-gom-pa* no longer touch the ground and that he glides on the air with an extreme celerity." Some *lung-gom-pas* wore iron chains around their body for "they are always in danger of floating in the air."

David-Neel discovered that during their walk the *lung-gom-pas* were in a state of trance. They concentrated on the cadenced mental recitation of a mystic formula with which, during the walk, the in and out breathing must be in rhythm, the steps keeping time with the breath and the syllables of the formula. The walker must neither speak, nor look from side to side. He must keep his eyes fixed on a single distant object and never allow his attention to be attracted by anything else. The use of a mystical formula, or *mantra*, as an adjunct to levitation recalls the legends of sacred words in the Judeo-Christian tradition.

The Elevation of Famous Dancers

The observation that the *lung-gom-pas* are able to sit on an ear of barley without bending its stalk finds a suggestive parallel in the history of famous dancers. It was said of Maria Taglioni that "she seemed to be able to walk on a cornfield without bending the ears." While such unusual lightness may be purely metaphorical hyperbole, there is evidence that the *élévation* of some famous dancers demonstrated the rudiments of levitation.

Vestris père, the "Dioux de la Dance," said of his famous son, Augustus Vestris: "Il resterait toujours en l'air, s'il ne craignait d'humilier ces camarades" (He would always remain in the air but feared to humiliate his comrades). Cyril W. Beaumont wrote of Vaslav Nijinski that "in execution of leaps he displayed a rare quality which contemporaries observed in the dancing of both Vestris and Taglioni—the ability to remain in the air at the highest point of *élévation* before descending."

There is a specific technique for dancers who try remaining in the air. Before taking a leap, the dancer breathes deeply and keeps on drawing in during the leap. He holds his breath while up and tightens his thigh muscles so that his trunk should rest on his thighs.

However, the capacity of the lungs appears to have less to do with the feat than the development of thigh muscles. Diaghilev noticed of Nijinski: "His *élévation* is nearly three feet. . . . Nature has endowed him with tendons of steel and tensile muscles so strong that they resemble those of the great cats. A real lion of the dance, he could cross the diagonal of the stage in two bounds."

Nikolai Legat, who was the leader of the class of perfection at the Imperial Theatre School of Warsaw, disclosed in *Der Tanz* (Berlin, February 1933) the following observations:

"As an example of phenomenally high, beautiful and elastic *élévation* I hold the memory of N. P. Damaschoff, the dancer of the great Imperial Theatre of Moscow. . . . I have never seen such an *élévation* in my life. The impression was that Damaschoff, after the high jump, remained for a longer time in the air. Rather smaller than of middle stature he possessed extraordinary leg muscles with respectable thighs and impressive calves. Tightening his leg muscles, especially those of the thighs in the air, he made all his moderate jumps fairly high. During the leap he held his breath, i.e., he breathed in shortly before the spring and breathed out as soon as he was down again."

It is for future research to elucidate the relationship between muscular tension in the thighs, deep breathing, and suspension in the air.

The question of levitation remains a fascinating one. The evidence for levitation of Christian saints is strong, even if anecdotal. Particular interest is attached to the subjective aspect, as expressed in the writings of St. Teresa of Avila and other saints.

There seems good ground for believing that levitation has sometimes been characteristic of possession and poltergeist cases, but the evidence is less reliable. Abnormal morbid mental states may involve uncontrolled muscular feats such as leaps in the air that could be mistaken for levitation. Moreover the spectator moods of horror or loathing could impede clear observation. It is not clear whether movement of objects without contact (psychokinesis) is related to the same mechanisms as levitation of human beings. On the face of things, it seems unlikely since the subjective human aspects of levitation are distinct from the objective application of some kind of psychic force to inanimate objects.

The Hindu yoga teachings on pranayama breathing techniques offer one line of inquiry. The concept of **prana** as the dynamic force in the human body, connected with the latent power of **kundalini,** offer a repeatable, observable situation. In this connection, the expensive special TM-Siddhi courses of the **Transcendental Meditation** movement (*siddhi* is a yoga term for special accomplishment) are clearly a packaging of the standard Hindu yoga teachings of Patanjali and others. The cross-legged position sounds like a copy of the *lung-gom-pa* exercise described by David-Neel. There is no supporting evidence, but some of the TM meditators may have achieved degrees of levitation because they were accelerated by the suggestible aura of success.

Indeed, suggestion may be a secondary factor in achieving levitation, in much the same way that **Jules Romains** claimed that it assisted the development of the special faculty of "**eyeless sight.**"

In some cases, out-of-the-body phenomena may have been confused with levitation, particularly from the point of view of the subjective sensations of floating in the air. The evidence for the reality of the claimed levitations of some psychic mediums, in particular D. D. Home, is impressive. It is possible that special aspects of breathing may play some part, as with the elevation of some dancers, but combined with states of exaltation.

Sources:

Berger, Arthur S., and Joyce Berger. *The Encyclopedia of Parapsychology and Psychical Research.* New York: Paragon House, 1991.

Crawford, W. J. *Experiments in Psychic Science.* London: John M. Watkins, 1919. New York: E. P. Dutton, 1919.

———. *The Psychic Structures in the Goligher Circle.* London: John M. Watkins, 1921. New York: E. P. Dutton, 1921.

———. *The Reality of Psychic Phenomena.* London: John M. Watkins, 1916. New York: E. P. Dutton, 1916.

Dingwall, E. J. *Some Human Oddities.* London: Home & Van Thal, 1947. Reprint, New Hyde Park, N.Y.: University Books,

1962. Includes a chapter on the levitations of Joseph of Copertino.

Dunraven, Earl of. *Experiences in Spiritualism With D. D. Home.* 1869. Reprint, New York: Arno Press, 1976.

Feilding, Everard. *Sittings with Eusapia Palladino and Other Studies.* New Hyde Park, N.Y.: University Books, 1963.

Fodor, Handor. *The Haunted Mind: A Psychoanalyst Looks at the Supernatural.* Helix Press, New York, 1959.

Forwald, Haakon. *Mind, Matter, and Gravitation: a Theoretical and Experimental Study.* New York: Parapsychological Foundation, 1969.

Goldney, Mrs. A. P., Mrs. H. Richard, and others. "Photographs of Jumping Model Imitating Levitation." *Proceedings* of the Society for Psychic Research 45, no. 158.

Hasted, John B., David Robertson, and Ernesto Spinelli. "Recording of Sudden Paranormal Changes of Body Weight." In *Research in Parapsychology 1982.* Eds. W. G. Roll, John Beloff, and Rhea A. White. Metuchen, N.J.: Scarecrow Press, 1983.

Kuvalayananda, Swami. *Pranayama.* Bombay, India, 1931. Frequently reprinted.

Leroy, Olivier. *Levitation.* London: Burns, Oates, 1928.

Patanjali. *The Yoga-Sutras of Patanjali.* Translated by M. N. Dvivedi. Adyar, India: Theosophical Publishing House, 1890.

Plinth, August. *Principles of Levitation.* New York: White Sun Prees, 1970.

Prasad, Rama. *The Science of Breath and the Philosophy of the Tattvas . . . Nature's Finer Forces.* London: Theosophical Publishing Society, 1897.

Richards, Steve. *Levitation: What It Is, How It Works, How to Do It.* Wellingborough, England: Aquarian Press, 1980.

Rogo, D. Scott. *Miracles: A Parascientific Inquiry into Wondrous Phenomena.* New York: Dial Press, 1982.

Underhill, Evelyn. *Mysticism: A Study in the Nature and Development of Man's Spiritual Consciousness.* New York: E. P. Dutton, 1911.

Von Görres, J. J. *Die Christliche Mystik.* 5 vols. Regensburg & Landshut, 1836–42.

"Leviticon"

A gospel adopted by revivalist French Templars of the nineteenth century and alleged by them to have been discovered in the Temple at Paris, along with other objects. It was supposed to have been composed in the fifteenth century by the Greek monk Nicephorus, who sought to combine Moslem tenets with Christianity. It was translated into French, with modifications, by Fabré Palaprat (a Freemason) in 1822.

Sources:

Heckethorn, Charles. *The Secret Societies of all Ages and Countries.* 2 vols. 1897. Revised ed., N.p., 1965.

Levy, Walter J., Jr.

Former director of the **Institute for Parapsychology** in Durham, North Carolina, who was accused of fraudulently manipulating data in one of his experiments. In summer 1974 **J. B. Rhine** disclosed that Levy had been discovered deliberately falsifying experimental results. This exposure threw doubt on Levy's other studies, and research was undertaken by other parapsychologists attempting independent replication of the Levy researches. The results, on the whole, were ambiguous, but as far back as 1972, parapsychologist **Helmut Schmidt** had done an independent replication of the Levy research with a lack of positive results.

While the prompt exposure of the alleged manipulation reflects credit on Levy's fellow parapsychologists who were anxious to maintain the integrity of their scientific researches, the scandal has had long-term consequences harmful to the field as a whole.

Sources:

Davis, James. "Comments on the Levy Affair." In *Research in Parapsychology 1974.* Metuchen, N.J.: Scarecrow Press, 1975.

Levy, Walter J., Jr. "Possible PK by Rats to Receive Pleasurable Brain Stimulation." In *Research in Parapsychology 1973.* Metuchen, N.J.: Scarecrow Press, 1974.

Levy, Walter J., Jr., Brian Artley, Al Mayor, and Carol Williams. "The Use of an Activity Wheel Based Testing Cage in Small Rodent Precognition Work." In *Research in Parapsychology 1973.* Metuchen, N.J.: Scarecrow Press, 1974.

Levy, Walter J., Jr., and James Davis. "A Potential Animal Model for Parapsychological Interaction between Organisms." *Research in Parapsychology 1973.* Metuchen, N.J.: Scarecrow Press, 1974.

Lewi, William Grant II (1902–1951)

Writer and astrologer who authored two of the most popular books in twentieth-century **astrology.** Grant Lewi was born in Albany, New York, on March 24, 1902. He graduated from Hamilton College, Clinton, New York, and did graduate work at Columbia University. He then became an instructor of English at the University of North Dakota, the University of Delaware, and Dartmouth College (successively).

In 1926 he married Carolyn Wallace. Wallace's mother was an astrologer and gave Lewi his first lessons in the field. Although he had written several fairly successful novels, Lewi turned to astrology in the early 1930s to supplement his income. He wrote the eminently successful *Heaven Knows What* in 1935. In the late 1930s he became editor of *Horoscope Magazine,* for which he also wrote articles through the 1940s. In 1940 he issued his first astrological text, *Astrology for the Millions* (1940), an early attempt to make astrology available to the average person who had never studied the details of horoscope construction. Like *Heaven Knows What,* it has gone into many editions and remains in print today.

Lewi eventually developed his own system of chart interpretation based on an integration of sign and house influences with some psychological insights.

In 1950 he moved to Arizona, where he began his own magazine, *The Astrologer.* He died the following year, on July 14, 1951, in Tucson.

Sources:

Holden, James H., and Robert A. Hughes. *Astrological Pioneers of America.* Tempe, Ariz.: American Federation of Astrologers, 1988.

Lewi, Grant. *Astrology for the Millions.* Garden City, N.Y.: N.p., 1940.

———. *Heaven Knows What.* New York: Doubleday, 1935.

———. *Your Greatest Strength.* New York, N.p., 1946.

Lewis, H(arvey) Spencer (1883–1939)

Founder of the Ancient and Mystic Order Rosae Crucis (AMORC), a modern revival Rosicrucian order headquartered at San Jose, California. Lewis was born in Frenchtown, New Jersey, November 25, 1883, of Welsh ancestry. He was educated in New York state and raised as a Methodist. He became a journalist and sat on a committee investigating Spiritualism in New York. He was closely associated with Elbert Hubbard and Ella Wheeler Wilcox. In 1903 he was president of the Publishers' Syndicate in New York and edited several scientific and research magazines.

In 1904 Lewis founded and served a president of the New York Institute for Psychical Research. The institute specialized in occult studies with emphasis on Rosicrucian teachings. A meeting with a British Rosicrucian resulted in Lewis traveling to Europe, and in 1909 he was initiated into the Rosicrucian order in France and given authority to organize in the United States. The AMORC was organized in several stages over the next years, and by 1917 held its first national convention in Pittsburgh, at which Lewis established his plan to develop correspondence courses.

In 1918 Lewis moved his headquarters to San Francisco, and in 1921 the order received an additional charter from the Ordo

Templi Orientis (**OTO**) in Germany. In 1925 the AMORC relocated to Florida, but soon afterward the organization moved to its present location in San Jose, California. Lewis applied his special talents in advertising to form a worldwide fraternal organization. AMORC taught philosophical and mystical practices in order to develop the latent faculties of man, and it sold literature by mail order. Lewis himself authored the basic set of correspondence lessons and a number of the books published by AMORC.

The large headquarters includes an Egyptological museum, a temple, an auditorium and modern computerized offices. Lewis, whose immediate family controlled the board of the organization, held the title imperator, or chief executive. After Lewis died August 2, 1939, his son **Ralph Maxwell Lewis** succeeded him as imperator.

Sources:

Lewis, H. Spencer. *Mansions of the Soul.* San Jose, Calif.: Rosicrucian Press, 1930.

———. *Rosicrucian Principles for the Home and Business.* San Jose, Calif.: Supreme Grand Lodge of AMORC, 1929.

———. *Rosicrucian Questions and Answers with Complete History.* San Jose, Calif.: Supreme Grand Lodge of AMORC, 1929.

———. *Self Mastery and Fate with the Cycles of Life.* San Jose, Calif.: Supreme Grand Lodge of AMORC, 1929.

The Rosicrucian Manual. San Jose, Calif.: Rosicrucian Press, 1952.

Lewis, Matthew Gregory (1775–1818)

English author commonly known as "Monk" Lewis. He was born in London July 9, 1775. His father, Matthew Lewis, was deputy secretary of war and proprietor of several valuable estates in Jamaica; his mother, Anna Maria Sewell, was devoted to music and various other arts. The future author showed precocity during childhood, and he attended Westminster School. During this period his parents separated, although Lewis remained friendly with both his parents. In 1791 he visited Paris and attempted a novel and a farce.

In 1792 he went to Weimar in Germany where he met **Johann Goethe** and also learned German thoroughly. Two years later he was appointed attaché to the British Embassy at the Hague, where he wrote his famous sensational story, *Ambrosio; or, The Monk.* Completed in ten weeks and published in 1795, it earned him his nickname of "Monk" Lewis.

In 1796 Lewis became a member of Parliament for Hindon in Wiltshire. Residing chiefly in or near London, he met most of the notable people of the day. Meantime his interest in the occult had been developing, and in 1798 his play *Castle Spectre* was staged at Drury Lane. Ghosts and the like played a prominent part in this popular production, for the public greatly enjoyed Gothic romances. In 1788 Lewis published *Tales of Terror* and in 1801 the volume *Tales of Wonder,* which anthologized popular occult verses, including some by novelist **Sir Walter Scott.**

When Lewis's father died in 1812, the author found himself a very rich man. His conscience was troubled, nevertheless, because the wealth derived from slave labor. Lewis sailed to Jamaica in 1815 to arrange for generous treatment of the workers on his estates. Returning to England in 1816, he went soon afterward to Geneva, where he met Lord Byron and Percy Shelley. Lewis made another visit to the West Indies in 1818 and died at sea May 14, 1818, while returning home.

The books of Lewis are memorable chiefly for the sensational way in which he exploited the rapidly developing public taste for gothic romance inaugurated by Horace Walpole's *The Castle of Otranto* (1764). Ann Radcliffe's *The Mysteries of Udolpho* appeared in April 1794, and Lewis was greatly impressed by it before publishing his own *Ambrosio; or, The Monk* only a few months later.

Sources:

Sullivan, Jack. *The Penguin Encyclopedia of Horror and the Supernatural.* New York: Viking, 1986.

Summers, Montague. *The Gothic Quest.* 1938. Reprint, London: Fortune Press, 1950.

Lewis, Ralph M. (1904–1987)

Ralph M. Lewis, for 48 years the imperator of the Ancient and Mystical Order of the Rosae Crucis (**AMORC**), was born in February 14, 1904, in New York City, the son of **H. Spencer Lewis,** the founder of the order. He formally joined the order in 1921 during his teen years and quickly progressed through the degrees. In 1924 he was appointed supreme secretary and in the 1930s emerged as a public lecturer for the order. He was credited with spreading the membership through North America and Europe.

In 1939 H. Spencer Lewis died and Ralph became the new imperator and took administrative control of the order. He also became a teacher in his own right and beginning in 1944 wrote a number of books, including *Behold the Sign* (1944), *The Sanctuary of the Self* (1948), *The Conscious Interlude* (1957), and *Yesterday Has Much to Tell* (1973). Lewis led the order until his death January 12, 1987, in San Jose, California.

Sources:

Lewis, Ralph M. *Behold the Sign.* San Jose, Calif.: Supreme Grand Lodge of the AMORC, 1944.

———. *The Conscious Interlude.* San Jose, Calif.: Supreme Grand Lodge of the AMORC, 1957.

———. *The Sanctuary of the Self.* San Jose, Calif.: Supreme Grand Lodge of the AMORC, 1948.

———. *Yesterday Has Much to Tell.* San Jose, Calif.: Supreme Grand Lodge of the AMORC, 1973.

Ley Hunter, The (Journal)

Publication concerned with the study of **leys,** ancient wisdom, sacred sites, cosmic energy, UFOs, and related subjects. Issued bimonthly from Box 5, Brecon, Powys LD3 7LU, Wales.

Leys

(Pronounced "lays.") A term now used to indicate ancient straight tracks formed by the alignment of burial mounds, beacon hills, earthworks, moats, and church sites in Britain. The term had long been thought by philologists to indicate a pasture or enclosed field, but this meaning was challenged by Alfred Watkins (born 1855) in his book *The Old Straight Track,* first published in London in 1925. Watkins pointed out that the word "ley" in its various place-name forms "lay," "lee," "lea," or "leigh" must have predated the enclosure of fields or pastures.

Watkins was an original thinker, an early photographer, and inventor of a pinhole camera and the Watkins exposure meter. In 1922 he published his book *Early British Trackways,* based on a lecture to the Woolhope Club of Hereford, England. Three years later he published *The Old Straight Track,* in which he detailed his investigations, which tended to show a vast network of straight tracks in Britain, aligned with either the sun or a star path. He also claimed evidence that such sighted straight tracks existed in other parts of the world.

The purpose of such tracks remains a mystery, but more recently they have been connected with occult beliefs and ancient lines of earth power. Such lines of force have been reported in primitive magical systems such as the *mana* of the Polynesian Islands. It has also been suggested that certain line marks of ground sites indicate gigantic zodiacs (see **Glastonbury Zodiac**).

Sources:

Michell, John. *The View over Atlantis.* Rev. ed. London: Abacus, 1976.

Underwood, Guy. *Patterns of the Past.* London: Museum Press, 1969.

Watkins, Allen. *Alfred Watkins of Hereford: His Life and Pioneer Work in the Three Worlds of Archaeology, Photography, and Flour Milling, 1855–1935.* England: Privately printed, 1961.

———. *The Ley Hunter's Manual: A Guide to Early Tracks.* 1927. Reprint, Wellingborough, England: Aquarian Press, 1983.

———. *The Old Straight Track.* London: Methuen, 1925. Reprint, London: Sphere Books, 1974.

Wilcock, John. *A Guide to Occult Britain: The Quest for Magic in Pagan Britain.* London: Sidgwick & Jackson, 1976.

Williamson, Tom, and Liz Bellamy. *Ley Lines in Question.* Kingwood, England: World's Work, 1983.

Lhermitte, Jacques Jean (1877–1959)

French physician and writer who also published works on parapsychology. He was born on January 20, 1877, at Mont Saint Pere, Aisne, France. He served as a staff physician at L'Hospice Paul Brouse (1919–45) and professor of medicine at the Paris Medical School (1923–47). Following his retirement he was named an honorary professor. In addition to his many books on medical subjects, he also produced a number of texts in psychic research. He died January 24, 1959.

Sources:

Lhermitte, Jacques Jean. *Le Cerveau et la pensée* (The Brain and Thought). 1951.

———. *Les Hallucinations.* N.p., 1951.

———. *Mystiques et faux mystiques* (Mystics and False Mystics). N.p., 1952.

———. *Le Problème des miracles.* N.p., 1956.

———. *Psychopathologie de la vision.* N.p., 1942.

———. *Les Reves* (Dreams). N.p., 1942.

———. *Vrais et faux possédés.* (True and False Possession). New York: Hawthorn Books, 1956.

Pleasants, Helene, ed. *Biographical Dictionary of Parapsychology.* New York: Helix Press, 1964.

Lia Fail

The Stone of Destiny in medieval Irish romance. It was said that when the feet of rightful kings rested upon it, the stone would roar for joy. According to tradition, this became the famous Stone of Scone, on which Scottish kings were formerly crowned at Scone, near Perth, removed from Scotland by Edward I in 1296 and brought to Westminster Abbey, London, where it was housed under the Chair of St. Edward. It was stolen by Scottish Nationalists on Christmas Eve 1950 as a protest, then recovered and restored to Westminster Abbey in February 1952. It is also known as the Tanist Stone, or Jacob's Stone. (See also **Danaans**)

Libanomancy

A system of **divination** by means of incense and prayers. The incense was thrown on a fire and the smoke said to carry the prayers to heaven. If the incense was consumed, the prayers would be answered.

"Libellus Merlini" (Little Book of Merlin)

A Latin tract on the subject of the prophecies of **Merlin** written by Geoffrey of Monmouth about 1135. Geoffrey prefaced his account of the prophecies with one concerning the deeds of a supernatural youth named Ambrosius whom he deliberately confounded with Merlin.

Vortigern, king of the Britons, asked Ambrose Merlin the meaning of a vision in which two dragons, one red and one white, engaged in combat. Merlin replied that the Red Dragon signified the British race, which would be conquered by the Saxon, represented by the White Dragon.

A long prophetic rhapsody follows, relating chiefly to the Saxon wars, which concludes in the Seventh Book of Geoffrey's *Historia Regum Britanniae.* The story was known in Iceland before 1218 in a form independent of the *Historia.* This tract must not be confused with the *Vita Merlini* (1145 or 1148) generally attributed to Geoffrey.

Liberal Catholic Church

Liturgical church that has attempted to blend Roman Catholic and Anglical ritual forms with a theosophical theology. The church was founded by former members of the Old Roman Catholic Church in England. The Old Roman Catholic Church was founded in 1908 following the consecration of Arnold Harris Mathew as a bishop by the bishops of the Old Catholic Church in the Netherlands. The Old Catholics were orthodox Catholics who rejected the promulgations of the Vatican Council of 1870–71, especially the declaration of the infallibility of the pope.

In England, however, there was little support for the Old Catholic movement and the church tended to be filled by a number of priests who for one reason or another did not fit in either the Church of England or the Roman Catholic Church. Among them were some who had developed a belief in **Theosophy** and were preaching a theosophical interpretation of Christianity.

Mathew was somewhat tolerant of Theosophy at first, and in 1914 consecrated a person known to be a Theosophist, Frederick Samuel Willoughby, as a bishop to assist him. He became more aware of theosophical teachings and the influence they were beginning to have in his church, however, and in 1915 he condemned it as a heresy and ordered all of his priests to sever their ties with it. The result was that the majority of the priests withdrew and largely gutted the Old Catholic Church.

The clergy who had withdrawn reorganized, and on February 13, 1916, Willoughby consecrated James Ingall Wedgwood (1883–1951) as the regionary bishop for England. At this time the group was operating as the Old Roman Catholic Church, and Wedgwood set out on a world tour to build support among ritually-oriented Theosophists around the world. In Australia he consecrated **Charles W. Leadbeater** as regionary bishop and in the United States named four new bishops, including **Irving S. Cooper,** as regionary. At a synod in London in 1918, the name Liberal Catholic was adopted as the official name of the church and Wedgwood was named as presiding bishop. The church subsequently spread to many countries.

The Liberal Catholic Church affirms a number of Christian beliefs but injects a Gnostic or theosophical meaning into them. The church believes that humans are sparks of divinity (rather than creatures of God) and believes in **reincarnation** (rather than resurrection). The church also accepts the idea of the spiritual hierarchy of masters, or highly evolved beings who guide the spiritual development of the race. In this regard, it accepts the idea that Jesus is one of the masters, but separates the human Jesus (known in the hierarchy as "the Lord Matreya") from the master Jesus (a position in the hierarchy held by the person known in his early life as Appolonius of Tyanna).

The church is headquartered in London. It is organized into a number of regionary provinces usually made up of one or two countries. In the United States the church is headquartered at Ojai, California, where the cathedral of Our Lady of the Angels has been built. *Ubique,* the church's periodical, is published by Presiding Bishop Joseph Tisch, who also serves as pastor of the congregation in Melbourne, Florida.

Sources:

The Liturgy of the Liberal Catholic Church. London: St. Alban Press, 1983.

Norton, Robert. *The Willow in the Tempest: A Brief History of the Liberal Catholic Church in the United States, 1817–1942.* Ojai, Calif.: St. Alban Press, 1990.

Ward, Gary L. *Independent Bishops: An Independent Directory.* Detroit: Apogee Books, 1990.

Wedgwood, James Ingall. *The Beginning of the Liberal Catholic Church.* Lakewood, N.J.: Ubique, 1967.

Licking a Charm

To lick the child's forehead first upward, then across, and lastly up again, and then to spit behind its back was believed to be a remedy for enchantment. It was said that if on licking a child's forehead with the tongue a salt taste was perceived, this was infallible proof of **fascination.**

Lien Hypnotique, Le (Journal)

French-language publication about **hypnotism** and related subjects. Address: L'Union Magnetique de Tersac, C.P. 482, Quebec 8 P.Q., Canada G1K 6W8.

Life Waves

According to **Theosophy,** the three creative life waves flow from the Deity (the **Logos**). The theosophical deity is pictured in three aspects, somewhat analogous to the Christian Trinity: Will, Wisdom, and Activity. Each has its definite role in the creation of a universe.

When the Logos sets about the great work of creation it sends the first life wave through the aspect of Activity into the multitude of bubbles in the **ether,** and thereby forms the various kinds of matter. The universe having been thus far prepared, the second life wave is sent through the aspect of Wisdom, which, bringing with it life as we usually understand that term and penetrating matter from above, gradually descends to the grosser forms and again ascends to the finer forms. In its descent, this life wave makes for an ever-increasing heterogeneity, but in its ascent the process is reversed and it makes for an ever-increasing homogeneity.

The work of creation is now far enough advanced to permit the creation of humanity, for matter has now been infused with the capacity of form and provided with life, and the Logos, therefore, through the aspect of Will, bears forth the Divine Spark, the **Monad,** and, along with the form and the life, ensouls man.

Light

Spiritualists believed that light had a destructive effect upon the physical phenomena of Spiritualism, which psychic research attempted to document. Quite apart from the fact that darkness hid much **fraud,** Spiritualists developed arguments to suggest that light had an inherent inhibiting effect on psychic phenomena. For example, it is known that light waves have very rapid vibrations (the visible light waves are from 3900 angstroms to 7700 angstroms; that is, the wave lengths range from 0.00000077 to 0.00000039 meters). Broadcasting practice demonstrates that the fast vibrations tend to nullify the slower vibrations on which radio is based. When the days are long and the sunlight intense, radio reception drops down. With the oncoming of night it improves again. With short waves which vibrate faster, reception is better.

It is claimed that psychic vibrations are in the same position. The slowest light vibration is red, and its destructive effect is correspondingly less. Filtering of daylight by glasses of various colors makes little difference. Cold light, devoid of actinic rays, is the least injurious. "I have had many opportunities," wrote **Sir William Crookes,** "of testing the action of light of different sources and colours, such as sunlight, diffused daylight, moonlight, gas, lamp and candle light, electric light from a vacuum tube, homogeneous yellow light, etc. The interfering rays appear to be those at the extreme end of the spectrum." He found moonlight ideal.

Sulphide of zinc or calcium screens have also been tried. They have the disadvantage that their illumination is poor unless they are extremely large, and the intensity of their phosphorescence rapidly diminishes. **Gustav Geley** experimented with biological light. It did not appear to affect the phenomena. However, the cultures of photogenic microbes are very unstable. In Brazil, luminous insects were tried with some apparent success.

Meanwhile, some of the more notable mediums worked primarily in lighted rooms and were able to produce extraordinary phenomena. **D. D. Home** seldom sat in darkness. **Eusapia Palladino** once levitated a table in blazing sunshine. French psychic researcher Dr. **Joseph Maxwell** was probably right in stating that the action of light is not such as to constitute an insurmountable obstacle to the production of telekinetic movements.

The supposed problem of light was highlighted in an incident reported in the issue of *Psychic Research* (January 1930). According to a communication by Irving Gaertner of St. Louis, Missouri, in a sitting with Eveling Burnside and Myrtle Larsen in Camp Chesterfield, Indiana, a ray of light, owing to the turning of a switch outside, penetrated through a crack between the lower edge of the door and the floor into the séance room.

"Agonized groans were heard (presumably from the entranced medium, Mrs. Larsen) and one of the two trumpets which had been levitated for the voice immediately fell at the feet of Mr. Nelson. At the same moment, Mrs. Nelson received an electric shock which formed a blister on one of her fingers, resembling one which would be produced by a burning of the skin. All the sitters testified to having felt the electric shock both in the region of the solar plexus, the back and the forehead."

Larsen was reportedly discovered prostrate on the floor, minus any heartbeat and her body rigid. It took considerable effort to restore her to consciousness. Burnside, the other medium, suffered from the shock for several days after the sitting. **Frederick Bligh Bond,** editor of *Psychic Research,* speculated about the nature of the electric shock: "Is it the light, *qua* light, which in this case causes the violent disturbance of conditions, or is it light as an avenue of conductivity, linking the psychic circuit to the current on the wires of the lamp in the hall?"

The dangers of the shock from unexpected light were considered an interesting matter in **J. Hewat McKenzie**'s report on the mediumship of **Ada Besinnet** in the April 1922 issue of *Psychic Science.* The smallest red spark burning was sufficient to prevent the medium from going into trance.

"Upon another occasion, when drawing the electric plug from the wall socket, behind a piece of furniture, and about 8 feet from the medium, the small spark, about 1/16 inch long, which usually accompanies the withdrawal of a plug of this kind when the power is on, was sufficient to create such a psychic shock that the medium immediately fell forward on the table in a cataleptic state."

That psychic structures may objectively exist beyond the range of our optical capacity was demonstrated by quartz lens photography. The quartz lens transmits ultra-violet rays to make visible on the photographic plate things not visible to the eyes. Mrs. J. H. McKenzie and Major Mowbray experimented in this field with the mediums J. Lynn and Lewis. The quartz lens not only disclosed fluorescing lights; vibrating, spinning substances; and psychic rods, but also the dematerialization of the medium's hand when added force had to be borrowed.

Similar results were achieved by Daniel Frost Comstock in séances with **"Margery the Medium"** (**Mina Stinson Crandon**) in Boston. Several of his exposed plates showed curious, indefinable white patches, one of which was fairly recognizable as a human face, although it could not be identified. The most important advance in this field of research was registered at the **Institut**

Métapsychique International in Paris with the mediumship of **Rudi Schneider** in 1931.

Over the first half of the twentieth century, critics claimed that the alleged destructive effect of light on psychic phenomena and the health of the medium were a subterfuge to cover fraud in the darkness of the séance room. In no case was any true physical harm done to mediums by the shining of light, and over the long run, physical mediumship of the type popular in the early twentieth century disappeared under the scrutiny of psychic researchers and the continued improvement of observational techniques.

Light (Journal)

The oldest British Spiritualist weekly, official organ of the **London Spiritualist Alliance,** founded in 1881 by Dawson Rogers and the Rev. **Stainton Moses.** Successive editors were **E. W. Wallis** and **David Gow.** It is now published quarterly as the journal of the **College of Psychic Studies,** London, 16 Queensberry Place, South Kensington, London SW7 2EB, England.

Sources:

Berger, Arthur S., and Joyce Berger. *The Encyclopedia of Parapsychology and Psychical Research.* New York: Paragon House, 1991.

Light of Divine Truth Foundation

A Spiritualist association of churches and mediums founded in 1936 as the International General Assembly of Spiritualists. It took its present name in 1979. The foundation issues charters to Spiritualist churches and certifies various clerical leaders—ministers, associate ministers, healers, and mediums. It also nurtures the practice of spiritual healing and conducts classes and training sessions in the art of spiritual healing and psychic unfoldment.

The foundation operates a speakers bureau and publishes an occasional newsletter. It may be contacted c/o Rev. Betty Latham, 304 Boulevard, Florence, NJ 08518.

Light of the Universe

The Light of the Universe (LOTU) is a **New Age channeling** group founded in the early 1960s by Helen Spitler, better known by her public name Maryona. In 1965 she published *The Light of the Universe,* a compilation of channeled materials from the "higher source" who spoke through her. In 1966 she launched the *Lotus,* a quarterly periodical. As membership increased and groups developed, Maryona developed a set of correspondence lessons.

LOTU places great emphasis upon the nature and the development of the human soul. It teaches that souls progress upward through a series of incarnations. The rate of progress can be increased by turning oneself away from the imperfection and impurities of this world, and this is accomplished through meditation and various cleansing exercises. LOTU teachings discourage outmoded and false traditions.

LOTU may be reached at 161 N. Sandusky Rd., Tiffin, OH 44883.

Sources:

Maryona [Helen Spitler]. *Light of the Universe.* 2 vols. Tiffin, Ohio: The Light of the Universe, 1965, 1976.

———. *Mini-Manual for Light Bearers.* Tiffin, Ohio: Light of the Universe, 1987.

Lignites

A beautiful glass-like stone. According to ancient belief, if the stone were hung about a child, it preserved him or her from witchcraft, and if it were bound on the forehead, it stopped bleeding of the nose, restored the loss of senses, and helped to foretell future events. It is not clear what stone is indicated, and it seems unlikely to have been the lignite, which is a brown or black variety of coal.

Lilith

Demonic figure in Jewish folklore. She seems to have originally been a storm demon and was later associated with the night. At a very early period, she was seen as one of several **vampire** demons in ancient Sumer. In the *Gilgamesh Epic* (approximately 2000 B.C.E.), she is pictured as a vampire harlot; though a beautiful young woman, she is unable to bear children, her breasts are dry, and she has the feet of the nocturnal owl.

In the Talmud, Lilith is given a new mythological life as the supposed first wife of Adam. Following an argument over who should have the dominant position during sexual intercourse, Lilith left and became a promiscuous wanderer. She mothered many children, called the *lilim.* She also encountered three angels sent by God, with whom she negotiated an agreement. She became a vampiric demon attacking children but would stay away from any child wearing an amulet with the name of three angels—Senoy, Sensenoy, and Semangelof.

Over the centuries Lilith was gradually transformed into a whole legion of beings who functioned as incubi and succubi, attacking men and women who were engaged in normal sexual activity. They gathered the men's sperm to father more demonic offspring. They inflicted women with barrenness and miscarriages and sucked the blood of children. A special anti-Lilith ritual was developed to banish them from homes and force them to go naked into the night.

The myth was active in the Jewish community through the centuries and flourished during the Middle Ages. It survived into the nineteenth century among conservative Jewish communities. A remnant of the story remains in the amulets with the name of the three angels, sometimes used by people who know little of the Lilith story.

In the early 1990s the Lilith myth was adopted as part of the *Midnight Sons,* the supernatural stories of the Marvel Comics universe.

Sources:

Graves, Robert, and Raphael Patai. *Hebrew Myths: The Book of Genesis.* Garden City, N.Y.: Doubleday, 1964.

Patai, Raphael. *The Hebrew Goddess.* New York: Ktav Publishing House, n.d.

Lilly, William (1602–1681)

One of the most famous early English astrologers. Born April 30, 1602, at Diseworth, Leicestershire, he was the son of a yeoman farmer, although a rival astrologer John Heydon later insisted that his father was "a laborer or ditcher." In 1613 Lilly began his education at the grammar school of Ashby-de-la-Zouch, studying Latin, Greek, and Hebrew.

In 1620 he traveled to London and worked as a servant, helping with his master's accounts. He also nursed his master's first wife, who died of cancer in 1624. The following year, his master remarried but died in 1627. Lilly accepted an offer of marriage from the widow, who was able to provide for him comfortably for the rest of his life. He was made a freeman of the Salter's Company and spent his time in angling or listening to Puritan sermons.

Lilly became interested in **astrology** in 1632 and pursued his study by reading many books on the subject and contacting the leading astrologers of the day. Soon after the death of his wife in 1633, Lilly studied the famous **Ars Notoria** grimoire, and he took part in an occult ceremony with hazel rods to locate treasure said to be buried in the cloisters of Westminster Abbey (see **divining-rod**). In this case, however, only a coffin was found.

practice. From 1670 onward he became celebrated as a physician as well as an astrologer. He published 15 major works on astrology as well as 36 almanacs and was consulted by famous individuals of the time. He died June 9, 1681. His posthumous autobiography was published in 1715.

Sources:

Lilly, William. *The History of Lilly's Life and Times.* N.p., 1715.

Lily Dale (Spiritualist Assembly)

One of the oldest camp organizations of American Spiritualism. It was established in 1880 as the Cassadaga Free Lake Association situated in beautiful countryside in the Chautauqua hills, scarcely two hours drive from the city of Buffalo. In 1906 the site was renamed Lily Dale. It comprised 80 acres with hundreds of cottages, gathering places, and a hotel for the many summer guests, as well as a post office and a library. For many years it became a focal point for world famous lecturers and mediums, including its share of fradulent mediums, demonstrating every variety of phenomena.

The old Hydesville house, which was the center of the Fox family knockings that resulted in the founding of American Spiritualism, was removed to Lily Dale in 1916 but burned to the ground in 1955. It was recreated in 1968 as a tourist attraction on the Hydesville site. Lily Dale still conducts a program through the summer. It may be contacted at 5 Melrose Park, Lily Dale, NY 14752.

Sources:

Whiting, Lilian. "The Spiritualistic Camp-Meetings in the United States." *Annals of Psychical Science* (January 1907).

Limachie

According to ancient belief, this resembled a chip of a man's nail and was squeezed out of the head of a slug, which had to be done the instant it was seen. It was said to be a good **amulet** to preserve from fever.

Lincoln, Abraham (1809–1865)

Sixteenth president of the United States, who, it has been claimed, was influenced in his decision to free the slaves by Spiritualist experiences. Immediately after his election to the presidency, an article was published in the *Cleveland Plaindealer* based on statements of medium **J. B. Conklin,** who identified Lincoln as a sympathizer with Spiritualism. Conklin said Lincoln was the unknown individual who frequently attended his séances in New York, asked mental questions, and departed as unnoticed as he had arrived. When the article was shown to Lincoln, he reportedly did not contradict it but said: "The only falsehood in the statement is that the half of it has been told. This article does not begin to tell the wonderful things I have witnessed."

In a letter to **Horace Greeley** in August 1862, Lincoln stated: "My paramount object is to save the union, and not either to save or destroy slavery." The antislavery proclamation was dated a month later, September 1862, and was issued in January 1863. The change in Lincoln's attitude was at least in part brought about by the influences of Senator Thomas Richmond, by his experiences through the mediums J. B. Conklin, Mrs. Cranston Laurie, Mrs. Miller, Nettie Colburn (later known under her married name **Henrietta Maynard**), and by Dr. Farnsworth's predictions. Senator Richmond, one of the leading businessmen of Chicago, had a controlling interest in the grain and shipping industries. While chairman of the committee on banks and corporations, he became a personal friend of Lincoln. In his book, *God Dealing with Slavery* (1870), Richmond reproduced the letters which, under psychic influence, he sent to the president.

Col. S. P. Kase claimed in the *Spiritual Scientist* that "for four succeeding Sundays Mr. Conklin, the test medium, was a guest at the presidential mansion. The result of these interviews was the President's proposition to his cabinet to issue the proclamation." Col. Kase also narrated President Lincoln's visit, in the company of his wife, in Mrs. Laurie's house. Laurie was a well-known medium. The colonel's daughter, Mrs. Miller, produced strong physical phenomena.

Colburn was another guest. She later became famous as an inspirational speaker, but then she was scarcely out of her teens. She passed into trance, approached the president with closed eyes, and addressed him for a full hour and a half. The sum total of her address was: "This civil war will never cease. The shout of victory will never ring through the North, till you issue a proclamation that shall set free the enslaved millions of your unhappy country."

In the same séance President Lincoln witnessed powerful physical manifestations. The piano on which the medium was playing rose four inches from the floor in spite of the efforts of Col. Kase, Judge Wattles, and the two soldiers who accompanied the president to weigh it down.

In 1891 Colburn (then Mrs. Maynard) published the book *Was Abraham Lincoln a Spiritualist?* in which she described her very first meeting with President Lincoln. In 1862 in Washington, Mrs. Lincoln had a sitting with her and was so much impressed that she asked her to come and see the president. According to Maynard's account in her book, she delivered a trance address in which the President:

"was charged with the utmost solemnity and force of manner not to abate the terms of its [Emancipation Proclamation] issue and not to delay its enforcement as a law beyond the opening of the year; and he was assured that it was to be the crowning event of his administration and his life; and that while he was being counselled by strong parties to defer the enforcement of it, hoping to supplant it by other measures and to delay action, he must in no wise heed such counsel, but stand firm to his convictions and fearlessly perform the work and fulfill the mission for which he had been raised by an overruling Providence. Those present declared that they lost sight of the timid girl in the majesty of the utterance, the strength and force of the language, and the importance of that which was conveyed, and seemed to realise that some strong masculine spirit force was giving speech to almost divine commands. I shall never forget the scene around me when I regained consciousness. I was standing in front of Mr. Lincoln, and he was sitting back in his chair, with his arms folded upon his breast, looking intently at me. I stepped back, naturally confused at the situation—not remembering at once where I was; and glancing around the group where perfect silence reigned. It took me a moment to remember my whereabouts. A gentleman present then said in a low tone: 'Mr. President, did you notice anything peculiar in the method of address?' Mr. Lincoln raised himself, as if shaking off his spell. He glanced quickly at the full-length portrait of Daniel Webster that hung above the piano, and replied: 'Yes, and it is very singular, very!' with a marked emphasis."

On Mr. Some's inquiry whether there had been any pressure brought to bear upon the president to defer the enforcement of the proclamation, Lincoln admitted, "It is taking all my nerve and strength to withstand such a pressure."

Sources:

Berger, Arthur S., and Joyce Berger. *The Encyclopedia of Parapsychology and Psychical Research.* New York: Paragon House, 1991.

Britten, Emma Hardinge. *Nineteenth-Century Miracles.* London & Manchester, 1883.

Fleckles, Elliott V. *Willie Speaks Out: The Psychic World of Abraham Lincoln.* St. Paul, Minn.: Llewellyn Publications, 1974.

Maynard, Nettie Colburn. *Was Abraham Lincoln A Spiritualist?* Philadelphia: R. C. Hartrampft, 1891. Reprint, London: Psychic Book Club, 1956.

Shirley, Ralph. *Short Life of Abraham Lincoln.* London, 1919.

length portrait of Daniel Webster that hung above the piano, and replied: 'Yes, and it is very singular, very!' with a marked emphasis."

On Mr. Some's inquiry whether there had been any pressure brought to bear upon the president to defer the enforcement of the proclamation, Lincoln admitted, "It is taking all my nerve and strength to withstand such a pressure."

Sources:

Berger, Arthur S., and Joyce Berger. *The Encyclopedia of Parapsychology and Psychical Research.* New York: Paragon House, 1991.

Britten, Emma Hardinge. *Nineteenth-Century Miracles.* London & Manchester, 1883.

Fleckles, Elliott V. *Willie Speaks Out: The Psychic World of Abraham Lincoln.* St. Paul, Minn.: Llewellyn Publications, 1974.

Maynard, Nettie Colburn. *Was Abraham Lincoln A Spiritualist?* Philadelphia: R. C. Hartrampft, 1891. Reprint, London: Psychic Book Club, 1956.

Shirley, Ralph. *Short Life of Abraham Lincoln.* London, 1919.

Lindisfarne

New age educational community in Southampton, New York, founded in 1973 by **William Irwin Thompson,** author of *Passages about Earth: An Exploration of the New Planetary Culture* (1974). Lindisfarne takes its name from the English monastery founded by St. Aidan on Holy Island in Northumberland in 635 C.E.

The island is now owned by Robin Henderson who keeps racing pigeons, and the monastery is a ruin, but Thompson was impressed by the symbolic associations of the place, which he described in *Passages about Earth.* He regarded Lindisfarne as typifying a historic clash between esoteric Christianity and ecclesiastical Christianity, between religious experience and religious authority.

A visit to the **Findhorn Foundation** in Scotland helped to develop Thompson's concept of a new "planetary culture" involving a synthesis of science, art, and spiritual awareness. He founded the Lindisfarne Association as an educational community "in which people of all ages could work and study together in new forms of growth and transformation." Spiritual self-discipline is regarded as a basis for artistic and cultural learning, and Lindisfarne offers seminars in science and the humanities for students rooted in daily meditational practice. All this has much in common with contemporary outlooks loosely labeled new age.

Sources:

Thompson, William Irwin. *The American Replacement of Nature: The Everyday Acts and Outrageous Evolution of Economic Life.* Garden City, N.Y.: Doubleday, 1991.

———. *Passages about Earth: An Exploration of the New Planetary Culture.* New York: Harper & Row, 1974.

———. *Reimagination of the World: A Critique of the New Age, Science, and Popular Culture.* Santa Fe, N.Mex.: Bear, 1991.

Lindsay, The Master of (1847–1913)

Also later known as the Earl of Crawford and Balcarres. A famous figure in the early history of English Spiritualism owing to his association with **Lord Adare** in testimony to the phenomena of the medium **D. D. Home.** He appeared before the committee of the **London Dialectical Society** in 1869 and testified to Home's powers. His account of Home's most famous **levitation** and floating out of the third-story window of Lord Adare's house led to sharp controversy in later literature.

Link, The

An international association of Spiritualist home circles, founded by N. Zerdin in 1931 for the interchange of psychic information obtained in the home circles. I. S. Beverley, president of the Link Association and treasurer of the Great Metropolitan Spiritualist Association for many years, died January 9, 1947. He had also edited the association's monthly journal, the *Link*.

Linton, Charles (ca. 1855– ?)

An early American writing medium of first generation **Spiritualism.** Originally a blacksmith with limited education, he became a clerk in a store in Philadelphia at the age of 22 and a bookkeeper afterward. Soon after he developed **automatic writing,** under the alleged **control** of Daniel Webster. Governor Nathaniel P. Talmadge and the actor Fenno claimed to have received, through his hand, communications from Shakespeare.

In 1853 Linton began his great work. In the space of only four months, he produced a book of religious rhapsody, published in 1855 under the title *The Healing of the Nations,* with a preface by Talmadge, who often witnessed the writing. The book consists of more than 100,000 words; it came very fluently and in a different handwriting from the medium's, who was quite conscious during its production. It was one of the most unique inspirational books of the period, although its aphorisms would now seem rather trite.

Lippares (or Liparia)

According to ancient belief, he who has this stone "needs no other invention to catch wild beasts." On the other hand, no animal can be attacked by dogs or huntsman if it looks upon it. It is not clear whether this was a known or a fabled precious stone.

Liquefaction of Blood

A famous miracle claimed for the blood of St. Januarius, executed September 19, 309 C.E. In *Lives of the Saints* (1623), E. Kinesman stated: "The most stupendous miracle is that seen to this day in the church of St. Gennaro, in Naples, viz. the blood of St. Januarius, kept in two glass vials. When either vial, held in the right hand, is presented to the head of the saint, the congealed blood first melts, and then goes on apparently to boil." Scientists have pointed out that such a miracle may be accomplished scientifically by the use of ether or other chemicals.

However, the miracle has continued into modern times. On May 6, 1989, the blood liquified on schedule in Naples, and Cardinal Michele Giordano revealed that he had allowed scientists to study the relic secretly. The liquefaction traditionally occurs twice a year, on September 19, the day of the saint's death, and on the Saturday before the first Sunday in May. Cardinal Giordano, archbishop of Naples, stated that the "May Miracle" of 1989 occurred during the religious procession that precedes the usual ceremony for the liquefaction.

Sources:

Rogo, D. Scott. *Miracles: A Parascientific Inquiry into Wondrous Phenomena.* New York: Dial Press, 1982.

Thurston, Herbert. *The Physical Phenomena of Mysticism.* London: Burns Oates, 1952.

List, Guido von (1848–1919)

Austrian occultist, author, journalist, and playwright whose racist theories preceded National Socialism in Germany. He grew up obsessed by pagan folklore of gods and demons, and after publication of his first books, a small group of admirers founded a Guido von List Society, which issued further books of a pseudo-mystical nature.

List developed a theory of a mysterious ancient race called the "Armanen," whose symbol was the swastika, and founded a secret occult lodge of the Armanen. After a press scandal, in which it was revealed that he practiced medieval black magic with blood rituals and sexual perversion, he fled from Vienna. Many of his associates, like **Jorg Lanz von Liebenfels,** were rabid anti-Semites, part of the occult underground that nourished perverted Nazi beliefs. List died in Berlin in May 1919.

Sources:

Sklar, Dusty. *Gods and Beasts: The Nazis and the Occult.* New York: Thomas Y. Crowell, 1977.

Litanies of the Sabbat

According to one account, on Wednesdays and Saturdays it was the custom to sing at the witches' **sabbat** the following litanies:

"**Lucifer,** Beelzebub, Leviathan, have pity on us. Baal, prince of the seraphim; Baalberith, prince of the cherubim; Astaroth, prince of the thrones; Rosier, prince of denominations; Carreau, prince of the powers; Belial, prince of the vertues; Perrier, prince of the principalities; Oliver, prince of the arch angels; Junier, prince of the angels; Sarcueil, Fume-bouche, Pierre-le-Feu, Carniveau, Terrier, Contellier, Candelier, Behemoth, Oilette, Belphegor, Sabathan, Garandier, Dolers, Pierre-Fort, Axaphat, Prisier, Kakos, Lucesme, pray for us."

Satan was evoked in these litanies only in company with a crowd of other demons. Accounts of different sabbats vary and many litanies appear to have been merely anti-Christian parodies. This particular litany sounds more like an evocation of demons for a magical ritual than a celebration of a **witchcraft** sabbat.

Lithomancy

A species of **divination** performed by stones, but in what manner it is difficult to ascertain. Thomas Gale, in a "Note upon Iamblichus," confessed that he did not clearly understand the nature of it; whether it referred to certain motions observable in idols, or to an insight into futurity obtained by demons [familiars] enclosed in particular stones. That these supernatural beings might be so commanded is clear from a passage of Nicephorus.

The old rabbis attributed Leviticus 25:1 to lithomancy, but the prohibition of stones given there is most probably directed against idolatry in general. J. C. Boulenger showed from Tzetzes that Helenus ascertained the fall of Troy by the employment of a magnet, and claimed that if a magnet be washed in spring water and interrogated, a voice like that of a sucking child will reply.

The pseudo-Orpheus related at length this legend of Helenus: "To him, Apollo gave the true and vocal sideritis, which others call the animated ophites, a stone possessing fatal qualities, rough, hard, black, and heavy, graven everywhere with veins like wrinkles. For one and twenty days Helenus abstained from the nuptial couch, from the bath, and from animal food. Then, washing this intelligent stone in a living fountain, he cherished it as a babe in soft clothing; and having propitiated it as a god, he at length gave it breath by his hymn of mighty virtue. Having lighted lamps in his own purified house, he fondled the divine stone in his hands, bearing it about as a mother bears her infant; and you, if ye wish to hear the voice of the gods, in like manner provoke a similar miracle, for when ye have sedulously wiped and dandled the stone in your arms, on a sudden it will utter the cry of a new-born child seeking milk from the breast of its nurse. Beware, however, of fear, for if you drop the stone upon the ground, you will rouse the anger of the immortals. Ask boldly of things future, and it will reply. Place it near your eyes when it has been washed, look steadily at it, and you will perceive it divinely breathing. Thus it was that Helenus, confiding in this fearful stone, learned that his country would be overthrown by the Atridae."

Photius, in his abstract of the life of Isodorus by Damascius, a credulous physician in the age of Justinian, wrote of an oracular stone, the *boetulum,* to which lithomancy was attributed. A physician named Eusebius used to carry one of these wonder-working stones about with him.

The story is told that one night he had an unexplained impulse to wander out from the city Emesa to the summit of a mountain dignified by a temple of Minerva. There, as he sat down fatigued by his walk, he saw a globe of fire falling from the sky and a lion standing by it. The lion disappeared, the fire was extinguished, and Eusebius ran and picked up a *boetulum.* He asked it to what god it appertained, and it readily answered, to Gennaeus, a deity worshiped by the Heliopolitae, under the form of a lion in the temple of Jupiter. During this night, Eusebius said he traveled not less than 210 stadia (more than 26 miles).

He never became the perfect master of the *boetulum* but was obliged very humbly to solicit its responses. It was of a handsome, globular shape, white, a palm in diameter, though sometimes it appeared more, sometimes less; occasionally, also, it was of purple color. Characters were to be read on it, impressed in the color called "tingaribinus." Its answer seemed as if proceeding from a shrill pipe, and Eusebius himself interpreted the sounds.

Damascius believed its animating spirit to be divine; Isodorus, on the other hand, thought it demoniacal, that is, not belonging to evil or material demons, nor yet to those which are quite pure and immaterial.

It was with one of these stones, according to Hesychius, that Rhea fed Saturnus, when he fancied that he was devouring Jupiter, its name being derived from the skin in which it was wrapped, and such the commentator supposed to have been the *Lapides divi,* or *vivi,* which the insane monster Heliogabalus wished to carry off from the temple of Diana, built by Orestes at Laodicea (AEL. Lampid, *Heliogab,* 7'). In *Geographia Sacroe* (ii, z, 1646), Samuel Bochart traced the name and the reverence paid to the *boetylia,* to the stone which Jacob anointed at Bethel. Many of these *boetylia,* Photius assured us from Damascius, were to be found on Mount Libanus.

Sources:

Waite, Arthur Edward. *The Occult Sciences.* 1891. Reprint, Secaucus, N.J.: University Books, 1974.

Little World (Society)

The name given to a secret society which was said to have conspired in England, during the eighteenth century to reestablish the Stuart dynasty. Various strange stories are told of this society, for instance, that the devil presided over their assemblies in person. The members were believed to be Freemasons.

Lively Stones World Healing Fellowship, Inc.

Organization to support the healing mission of **Willard Fuller,** famous for his psychic **dentistry.** Apparently now inactive.

Livingston, Marjorie (ca. 1935)

British inspirational writer, psychic lecturer, and author of several books received by **clairaudience.** Her first work, *The New Nuctrmeron,* (1930) was claimed to have been inspired by **Apollonius of Tyana** and to have expounded some remnants of his teachings, the originals having been lost during the famous burning of the Alexandrian Library. It was followed by *The Harmony of the Spheres* (1931), *The Elements of Heaven* (1932), and *The Outline of Existence* (1933), all containing new speculations, after-death conditions, and the scheme of life in the universe.

Llewellyn Publications

Founded as Llewellyn Publishing Co. in Portland, Oregon, by astrologer **Llewellyn George** (1876–1954). The company existed for many years in Los Angeles, becoming the leading publishing house of astrological literature in America. In the years after George's death, it was acquired by Minnesota businessman **Carl Llewellyn Weschcke** (a relative of George) and is now located in St. Paul, Minnesota, under the name Llewellyn Publications. It has emerged as one of the largest publishing and wholesaling organizations of occult, witchcraft, and magical literature in the United States.

During the early days of the Wicca revival, Llewellyn was one of the first to publish a version of the witchcraft manual, the **Book of Shadows,** and Weschske emerged as a champion of disclosing all the secrets of coven life. Llewellyn also published the periodicals *Gnostica, Astrology Now,* and *Aquarian Age Preview,* as well as the annual *Moon Sign Book,* a standard astrological text first edited by George in 1905.

The large retail bookstore Gnostica was opened in Minneapolis on January 15, 1970, but was closed after a few years. The company, however, maintains a large mail-order operation. For a few years in the 1970s it sponsored an annual Aquarian Age Festival, which included lectures, readings, and consultations.

Llewellyn's New Times (Magazine)

The periodical of **Llewellyn Publications** succeeding *Gnostica,* which was published in the 1970s. It is released at eight-week intervals and covers New Age, occult, and magic activities and publications. Each issue includes special articles on such topics as **magic, witchcraft, astrology,** and paganism, in the context of a detailed catalog and reviews of Llewellyn Publications products. Llewellyn, which began by publishing books on astrology, has emerged as one of the most prominent publishers of occult materials. It is currently headed by astrologer-occultist **Carl Llewellyn Weschcke.** Address: Box 64383-864, St. Paul, MN 55164-0383.

Loathly Damsel, The

Kundrie (or Kundry), the "Grail Messenger," a character who first appears in the eleventh-century romance by Chrétien de Troyes that developed the legend of the Holy **Grail,** *Le Conte del Graal,* also known as *Perceval.* One would imagine that the holder of the Grail would be saint-like, but Chrétien de Troyes describes her as "a damsel more hideous than could be pictured outside hell." Wolfram von Eschenbach, who elaborated on de Troyes's work, refers to her in his work as "Kundrie la Sorcière." Kundry, in Richard Wagner's music-drama "Parsifal," represents sin.

Lobb, John (1840–1921)

Prominent British businessman and public figure who became active in the cause of **Spiritualism.** Lobb was born on August 7, 1840, in Middlesex, England, and became a lay preacher in the Methodist ministry as well as editor of successful journals. He emerged into public life in 1876 after he raised a fund for the Rev. Josiah Henson, an African-American minister who inspired Hariette Beecher Stowe's *Uncle Tom's Cabin.*) Lobb lectured and preached on Henson and edited Henson's life story, which sold over 30,000 copies in the first six weeks and was later translated into 12 languages. Lobb and Henson were honored with a command to meet the queen at Windsor Castle on March 5, 1877.

Through the rest of the century Lobb maintained an active public life. He belonged to the London School Board, was guardian of the City of London Union, and served on the Metropolitan Asylums Board, the Central Markets committee, and the London city council. He succeeded in exposing many scandals and abuses in the educational system, the police force, and other areas of social and public life.

After 1903 Lobb campaigned vigorously on behalf of Spiritualism by lecturing and publishing. He traveled all over Britain and claimed to have addressed some 40,000 individuals on such subjects as survival of personality after death, **spirit photography,** and **materialization.**

Sources:

Lobb, John. *Talks with the Dead.* N.p., 1906.

———. *Uncle Tom's Story of His Life.* N.p., 1877.

Loch Ness & Morar Project

Project that grew out of the Loch Morar Expedition to investigate reports of a monster named **"Mhorag,"** similar to the **Loch Ness Monster.** Originating in 1970–72, the Loch Morar Survey investigated with manned observation equipment, then used underwater television in 1975. Later, sonar monitoring was the favored procedure. In spite of largely negative findings, the project continued to survey both Loch Morar and Loch Ness. In 1974 the project used divers and dredging in search of organic matter, on the supposition that if there had been large animals in the loch over a longer period, there should be organic remains. This search was inconclusive.

In the 1980s the project intensified its use of sonar equipment and underwater photography. An ambitious project, "Operation Deepscan," engaged more than 20 small boats to sweep the whole area of Loch Ness using sonar and video scanning. Although the results were largely ambiguous, there were three unexplained sonar contacts, indicating something that might be large fishes.

The project invites field membership. Address: Box 1, Loch Ness Centre, Drumnadrochit, Inverness-shire, Scotland.

Sources:

Campbell, Steuart Campbell. *The Loch Ness Monster: The Evidence.* Wellingborough, England: Aquarian Press, 1986.

Loch Ness Investigation Bureau

Founded in 1962 to obtain scientific evidence of the existence of the **Loch Ness Monster,** a marine animal or animals believed by some to inhabit Loch Ness and other lakes in Scotland, Ireland, Canada, Siberia, and the Scandinavian countries. Formerly titled Loch Ness Phenomena Investigation Bureau. After a decade of operation, the project concluded in 1972.

Sources:

Binns, Ronald. *The Loch Ness Mystery Solved.* Buffalo, N.Y.: Prometheus Books, 1984.

Loch Ness Monster

A persistently reported monster or colony of **monsters** in the vast area of Loch Ness in northern Scotland. The loch is some 24 miles long and about a mile wide, with a depth from 433 to 754 feet. A monster was reported here in ancient Gaelic legends as well as in a biography of St. Columba circa 565 C.E. The modern history dates from 1933, when the monster began to receive a significant amount of media attention. Research efforts to produce conclusive proof of the monster's existence were initiated by different researchers in the 1970s.

In 1972 Robert Rines, an MIT physics graduate who went to Loch Ness to search for "Nessie," obtained some now famous computer-enhanced "flipper" photographs. The photographs were taken by an underwater camera after a sonar device detected what appeared to be two large moving objects. The pictures clearly showed a rhomboid shape that appeared to resemble the flippers on seals and similar aquatic mammals.

Other films and photographs of an unidentified object in the loch have been obtained in the last few decades. An impressive picture of a large unknown creature in Loch Ness made the front page of the *New York Times* (April 8, 1976); the photograph was captured in 1975 with an underwater camera using a sonar echo technique. A scientific report by Martin Klein and Harold E. Edgerton appeared in *Technology Review* (March–April 1976).

Two widely known photographs of the head and neck of the monster were taken by monster-hunter and conjurer Tony "Doc" Shiels on May 21, 1977, near Castle Urquhart at Loch Ness, Scotland. One of these photographs was reproduced in both *Cornish Life* and the London *Daily Mirror* for June 9, 1977, and both photographs were reproduced and discussed in *Fortean Times* (No. 22, summer 1977). Interest in the Loch Ness and similar monsters was stimulated by reports and photographs of the decomposing body of a sea creature caught by Japanese fishermen April 25, 1977, off the coast of New Zealand.

In 1983, Rikkie Razdan and Alan Kielar, two young electrical engineers, visited Loch Ness and spent six weeks trying to spot the monster with 144 sonar devices, covering an area of 6,400 square feet. After failing to find any significant traces of the monster that could not be explained as gas bubbles, floating debris, etc., they decided to study the sonar tracings obtained by Robert Rines.

They contacted Alan Gillespie of the Jet Propulsion Laboratory, who had handled the computer enhancement of the Rines pictures, and asked for copies of the shots. To their surprise, the images were vague and indistinct, quite unlike the distinctive "flipper" shape that had been given such prominence in press accounts. It seems that the pictures were retouched after being returned to Rines. An unretouched picture was reproduced in the journal *Discover* (September 1984) alongside the retouched "flipper" images of Rines. However, the basic shape remains, although somewhat hazy.

After centuries of sightings, it seems reasonable to suppose that there might be a continuing colony of creatures rather than a single monster. Biologist Roy Mackal made the case for the "possibility" of the existence of the monster, though definitive evidence remains elusive. Known in Great Britain affectionately as "Nessie," the creature was recently named *Nessiteras rhombopteryx* by Sir Peter Scott and Robert Rines (see "Naming the Loch Ness Monster," *Nature,* December 11, 1976) in an attempt to secure official protection as a rare species qualifying for conservation. In the late 1970s the existence of a "nessie" religious cult was revealed by European New Religions scholars, who made contact with the priestess who led the group.

The Loch Ness Phenomena Investigation Bureau was founded at 23 Ashley Place, London S.W.1, England, in 1961, though it became inactive after 1972. It was succeeded by the **Loch Ness & Morar Project,** concerned with claims of the Loch Ness Monster as well as **"Mhorag."** On October 9–11, 1987, the project instituted "Operation Deepscan." Twenty small boats equipped with sonar apparatus were deployed abreast, sweeping up and down Loch Ness in line, forming a "sonar curtain." At a press conference on September 17, organizer Adrian J. Shine stated that the project had scientific objectives—a study of fish distribution, water temperatures, and the contents of the loch. The results of this scan were inconclusive, although there were three unexplained sonar contacts, indicating something that might be large fishes or perhaps debris. No colony of monsters was located.

The Loch Ness and Loch Morar monsters are not unique, since similar creatures have been reported in lakes in a number of different countries. Their study is one of the main objects of **cryptozoology.**

Sources:

Binns, Ronald. *The Loch Ness Mystery Solved.* London: Star (W. H. Allen), 1984.

Campbell, Steuart Campbell. *The Loch Ness Monster: The Evidence.* Wellingborough, England: Aquarian Press, 1986.

Clark, Jerome. *Encyclopedia of Strange and Unexplained Phenomena.* Detroit: Gale Research, 1993.

Costello, Peter. *In Search of Lake Monsters.* London, 1974.

Dinsdale, Tim. *The Story of the Loch Ness Monster.* London, 1973.

Gould, Rupert T. *The Loch Ness Monster.* London, 1934. Reprint, New Hyde Park, N.Y.: University Books, 1969.

Heuvelmans, Bernard. *In the Wake of the Sea Serpents.* London, 1968.

Holiday, F. W. *The Dragon and the Disc.* London, 1973.

Oudemans, A. C. *The Loch Ness Animal.* Leyden, 1934.

Witchell, Nicholas. *The Loch Ness Story.* London, 1974.

Loch Ness Monster Centre & Exhibition

Tourist attraction concerned with the traditions and investigations relating to reports of a **Loch Ness Monster** in Scotland. The facility includes a monster exhibit, animated "lair," video games, refreshment facilities, souvenirs, and books. It is situated some two miles from Urquhart Castle on Main Road A82. Address: Drumnacrochit, Inverness-shire, Scotland.

Lodestone (or Loadstone)

A magnetic stone of magnetite (oxide of iron) showing polarity when suspended. It was once believed to possess magical properties of various kinds. If one was ill, the stone should be held in the hands and shaken well. It was said to cure wounds, snakebites, weak eyes, headaches, and defective hearing. The possessor of the lodestone was supposed to be able to walk through reptiles in safety even when they were accompanied by "black death." Orpheus stated that "with this stone you can hear the voices of the gods and learn many wonderful things," that it had the property of unfolding the future, and if held close to the eyes, it would inspire with a divine spirit.

Lodge, Sir Oliver (Joseph) (1851–1940)

World famous British physicist and a fearless champion of after-death **survival.** He missed no opportunity to declare his belief that death is not the end, that there are higher beings in the scale of existence, and that intercommunication between this world and the next is possible. Lodge was born June 12, 1851, at Penkhull, Staffordshire, England, and studied at University of London (B.S., 1875; D.Sc. 1877). He was professor of physics at University of London (1877) and at University of Liverpool (1881–90) and served as principal of Birmingham University (1900–19). Lodge was elected fellow of the Royal Society in 1887, awarded the Albert Medal of the Royal Society of Arts for his pioneer work in wireless telegraphy, and was knighted in 1902. He was president of the British Association in 1913. His great reputation as a physicist was established by his research in electricity, thermoelectricity, and in wireless (radio) and theories of matter and ether. Lodge developed the spark plug that bears his name.

His first experiences in psychic research occurred in 1883–84, when he joined Malcolm Guthrie on his investigations of **thought-transference** in Liverpool. Lodge undertook similar experiments himself in 1892 in Carinthia at Portschach am See and reported them in *Proceedings* of the SPR (Vol. 7, part 20, 1892).

His most notable observations in physical research were made with the medium **Eusapia Palladino.** In **Charles Richet**'s house on the Ile Roubaud, he attended four séances and reported on them in the *Journal* of the SPR (November 1894), affirming the reality of Palladino's phenomena:

"However the facts are to be explained, the possibility of the facts I am constrained to admit; there is no further room in my mind for doubt. Any person without invincible prejudice who had the same experience would come to the same broad conclusion, viz., that things hitherto held impossible do actually occur. If one such fact is clearly established, the conceivability of others may be more readily granted, and I concentrated my attention mainly on what seemed to me the most simple and definite thing, viz., the movement of an untouched object in sufficient light for no doubt of its motion to exist. This I have now witnessed several times; the fact of movement being vouched for by both sight and hearing, sometimes also by touch, and the objectivity of the movement being demonstrated by the sounds heard by an outside observer, and by permanent alteration in the position of the objects. The result of my experience is to convince me that certain phenomena usually considered abnormal do belong to the order of nature, and as a corollary from this, that these phenomena ought to be investigated and recorded by persons and societies interested in natural knowledge."

When Palladino was exposed in **fraud** in the following year at Cambridge, Lodge, who attended two of the sittings there, defended his earlier observations. He declared that there was no resemblance between the Cambridge phenomena and those observed on the Ile Roubaud. In the field of mental phenomena, **Lenora Piper** was his chief source of enlightenment. His first investigations with Piper took place in 1889, when the medium was tested in England by the **Society for Psychical Research.** Lodge received many evidential messages, which soon convinced him that the dead were still live.

His first report was published in 1890. Nineteen years later, in discussing the evidence for the return through the mediumship of Piper of **F. W. H. Myers, Edmund Gurney,** and many others, he referred to his experiences:

"The old series of sittings with Mrs. Piper convinced me of survival for reasons which I should find it hard to formulate in any strict fashion, but that was their distinct effect. They also made me suspect—or more than suspect—that surviving intelligences were in some cases consciously communicating—yes, in some few cases consciously; though more usually the messages came, in all probability, from an unconscious stratum, being received by the medium in an inspirational manner analogous to psychometry. The hypothesis of surviving intelligence and personality—not only surviving but anxious and able with difficulty to communicate—is the simplest and most straightforward and the only one that fits all the facts" (from *The Survival of Man,* 1909).

Lodge openly stated for the first time, in 1908, that he believed he had genuinely conversed with late friends and that the boundary between the two worlds was wearing thin in places. Five years later, speaking from the presidential chair to the British Association in September 1913, he boldly declared that his own investigations convinced him that "memory and affection are not limited to that association with matter by which alone they can manifest themselves here and now, and that personality persists beyond bodily death."

The widest publicity to Lodge's belief in survival appeared in his famous book, *Raymond: or, Life and Death* (1916). The story of the return of his son, who died in action in World War I, is one of the best-attested cases of spirit identity. It begins with the celebrated "Faunus" message, delivered through Piper on August 8, 1915. It purported to come from the spirit of psychic researcher **Richard Hodgson** and began abruptly: "Now, Lodge, while we are not here as of old, i.e., not quite, we are here enough to give and take messages. Myers says you take the part of the poet, and he will act as Faunus. FAUNUS. Myers. Protect: he will U.D. (understand). What have you to say Lodge? Good work ask Verrall, she will also U.D. Arthur says so."

The message reached Sir Oliver Lodge in early September 1915. On September 17, the War Office notified him that Raymond was killed in action on September 14. Before this blow fell, Lodge wrote to **Margaret Verrall,** a well-known classical scholar and asked her, "Does the poet and Faunus mean anything to you? Did one protect the other?" She replied at once that "the reference is to Horace's account of his narrow escape from death, from a falling tree, which he ascribes to the intervention of Faunus."

The Rev. M. A. Bayfield attached to the incident the following interpretation: "Horace does not, in any reference to his escape, say clearly whether the tree struck him, but I have always thought it did. He says Faunus lightened the blow; he does not say 'turned it aside.' As bearing on your terrible loss, the meaning seems to be that the blow would fall, but would not crush; it would be 'lightened' by the assurance, conveyed afresh to you by a special message from the still living Myers, that your boy still lives."

On September 25, Lady Lodge had a sitting with **Gladys Osborne Leonard.** Raymond sent this message: "Tell Father I have met some friends of his." On asking for names, Myers was mentioned. Two days later, medium **Alfred Vout Peters** spoke about a photograph of a group of officers with Raymond among them. Various other messages came from different mediums, as did the **cross-correspondence** on the Faunus message.

On November 25, Mrs. Cheves, a complete stranger, wrote a letter saying that she had a photograph of the officers of the South Lancashire Regiment of which Raymond Lodge was a second lieutenant and offered to send it. In a séance on December 3, Gladys Leonard described the photograph, featuring Raymond sitting on the ground and an officer placing his hand on Raymond's shoulder. The photograph arrived on December 7 and corresponded with the description in every detail.

Many other messages, bearing the authentic stamp of Raymond's identity, came through. The most curious was one about "Mr. Jackson." "Feda," Leonard's **control,** said that Raymond mixed it up with a bird and a pedestal. The truth of the matter was that Jackson was a peacock which, after its death, was stuffed and put on a pedestal.

Lodge displayed the whole mass of evidential communications in his book *Raymond,* including the reference to cigars and whiskey and soda in the afterlife. Owing to this, many ridiculed the book, although many others accept the idea that dead spirits can furnish the afterlife with familiar associations of everyday physical life. Some critics suggested that Lodge's bereavement led him into **Spiritualism,** but his book repudiates this notion. "My conclusion," Lodge wrote, "has been gradually forming itself for years, though, undoubtedly, it is based on experience of the same sort of thing. But this event has strengthened and liberated my testimony. It can now be associated with a private experience of my own, instead of with the private experience of others."

The book *Raymond* was followed by other important publications on psychic research in which Lodge elaborated his previous conclusions. Before the Modern Churchmen's Conference in September 1931 in Oxford, Lodge declared:

"If I find myself an opportunity of communicating I shall try to establish my identity by detailing a perfectly preposterous and absurdly childish peculiarity which I have already taken the trouble to record with some care in a sealed document deposited in the custody of the English S.P.R. I hope to remember the details of this document and relate them in no unmistakable fashion. The value of the communication will not consist in the substance of what is communicated, but in the fact that I have never mentioned it to a living soul, and no one has any idea what it contains. People of sense will not take its absurd triviality as anything but helpful in contributing to the proof of the survival of personal identity."

He reiterated this viewpoint two years later in his book *My Philosophy:* "Basing my conclusions on experience I am absolutely convinced not only of survival but of demonstrated survival, demonstrated by occasional interaction with matter in such a way as to produce physical results."

Lodge died August 22, 1940, at Amersham, Wiltshire, England. His correspondence is preserved in the Lodge Collection of the Society for Psychical Research in London.

The post-mortal identity test of Lodge's survival involved the depositing of a set of envelopes with the Society for Psychical Research and the London Spiritualist Alliance, with instructions for consecutive opening of the envelopes. The packet in the possession of the Society for Psychical Research contained seven envelopes, one inside another, containing clues when opened consecutively. The instructions were somewhat complex and, owing to the war years following his death, could not be applied. The final envelope with the test message was opened February 10, 1947. No psychic had identified it. The test did not lead to the evidence of survival hoped for (see *Journal* of the SPR Vol. 38, pp. 121–134).

Sources:

Berger, Arthur S., and Joyce Berger. *The Encyclopedia of Parapsychology and Psychical Research.* New York: Paragon House, 1991.

Hill, J. Arthur, ed. *Letters from Sir Oliver Lodge.* London: Cassell, 1932.

Jolly, W. P. *Sir Oliver Lodge.* New Jersey: Fairleigh Dickinson University Press, 1975.

Lodge, Sir Oliver. *Christopher: A Study in Human Personality.* New York: George H. Doran, 1919.

———. *Conviction of Survival.* N.p., 1930.

———. *Past Years.* London: Hodder and Stoughton, 1931.

———. *Raymond; or, Life and Death.* London: Methuen, 1916.

———. *Raymond Revised.* N.p., 1922.

———. *The Reality of a Spiritual World.* N.p., 1930.

———. *The Substance of Faith Allied with Sciences.* London: Methuen, 1915.

———. *Survival of Man.* London: Methuen, 1909.

———. *Why I Believe in Personal Immortality.* Garden City, N.Y.: Doubleday, Doran, 1929.

Loehr, Franklin (Davison) (1912–1988)

Clergyman and parapsychologist. He was born November 19, 1912, at Oskaloosa, Iowa. He studied at Monmouth College, Illinois (B.A., 1933) and McCormick Theological Seminary, Chicago, Illinois (B.D., 1936). He was ordained as a Congregational minister, pastored various churches, and served a period as a chaplain in the U.S. Army Air Force. While serving a church in Los Angeles, in 1952 he founded and became director of research of the Religious Research Foundation.

While pastoring in Los Angeles, Loehr conducted some informal research on the power of prayer to stimulate plant growth originally as a demonstration of the power of prayer for his church members. His book *The Power of Prayer on Plants* (1959) described the development of his initial interest into what became a three-year laboratory study. His work was later duplicated under rigorous laboratory conditions by Bernard Grad at McGill University in Montreal.

In 1958 he married Grace Wittenberger, a **medium.** He began research on her mediumship, in particular her past-life readings. These readings are concerned with claimed former incarnations of individuals, throwing light on their present-day personality. In this regard, Loehr coined the term "psychography" to describe the mapping of the past life influences upon the personality in the present. Grace Loehr's work was documented in Roy C. Smith's book, *Incarnation and Reincarnation* (1975).

Loehr's work at the Religious Research Foundation focused primarily on **survival** of death, about which he wrote widely. He himself became a medium and communicated with his colleague Henry Clements for four months after Clements's death in which the spirit entity minutely described the transition of death and the new awareness he received once established on the other side.

The work of the Religious Research foundation, Box 208, Grand Island, FL 32735, has led to the production of a number of books. Loehr died on July 10, 1988 shortly after his address to the first International Conference on Paranormal Research meeting in Colorado.

Sources:

Loehr, Franklin. *Death with Understanding.* Grand Island, Fla.: Religious Research Press, 1987.

———. *Power of Prayer on Plants.* Garden City, N.Y.: Doubleday, 1959.

———. *Psychography: A Method of Self Discovery.* Grand Island, Fla.: Religious Research Press, 1990.

———. *Science, Religion, and the Development of Religion as a Science.* Grand Island, Fla.: Gnosticours, 1983.

Smith, Roy O. *Incarnation and Reincarnation.* Los Angeles: Religious Research Press, 1975.

Logan, Daniel (1936–)

Modern American psychic. Born Daniel Olaschinez on April 24, 1936, in Flushing, New York, he later changed his name after deciding upon an acting career. Then he discovered his psychic ability and gave up acting for a career as a professional psychic; he also wrote and lectured on psychic subjects. Logan successfully forecast the prolonging of the Vietnam war into the 1970s, the race riots of 1967, and, weeks in advance, named the Academy Award winners for 1966, 1967, and 1968. His first public appearance as a psychic was on David Susskind's television show, and he later appeared in an hour-long television special. He is unusual in that his insights have often been verbal rather than visual; he sometimes makes predictions before he is aware of what he is saying.

Sources:

Logan, Daniel. *America Bewitched: The Rise of Black Magic and Spiritism.* New York: William Morrow, 1973.

———. *Do You Have ESP?* N.p., 1970.

———. *The Reluctant Prophet.* Garden City, N.Y.: Doubleday, 1968.

———. *Vibrations.* N.p., 1976.

———. *Your Eastern Star.* N.p., 1972.

Logos

A Greek term generally translated in the Christian New Testament as "Word" but meaning essential thought or concept. In its theological sense, it refers to the creative power (word) of God; in logic, grammar, and rhetoric it indicates meaningful and significant statement. The concept of the ontological creative sound is common to both Hellenic and Jewish theology, which may have influenced each other. Logos is also analogous to the word **"AUM"** in Hindu mysticism.

The term has been utilized in **Theosophy.** "Fohat" is the term very commonly used in Theosophy to designate the Deity. Along with the great religions, Theosophy has, as the beginning of its scheme, a Deity who is altogether beyond human knowledge or conception, whether in the ordinary or the clairvoyant states. But when the Deity manifests to man through his works of creation, He is known as the Logos.

Essentially God is infinite, but when He encloses a "ring-pass-not" within which to build a cosmos, He has set limits to Himself, and what we can know of Him is contained in these limits.

He appears in a triple aspect, but this is, of course, merely an appearance, for in reality He is a unity. This triple aspect shows Him as Will, Wisdom, and Activity, and from each of these came forth one of the creative **life waves** that formed the universe. The third wave created matter, the second wave aggregated diffuse matter into form, and the first wave brought with it the **Monad,** that scintillation of Himself which took possession of formed matter and thereby started the process of **evolution.**

Loka

In Hindu religion, a term for a world or division of the universe. For general purposes, there are three *lokas:* heaven, earth, and hell, but different philosophical schools have enumerated seven or even eight *lokas.* The seven lokas are: *Bhur-loka* (earth), *Bhwar-loka* (space between earth and the sun, inhabited by semi-divine beings), *Swar-loka* (region between the sun and polar star, the heaven of the god Indra), *Mahar-loka* (the abode of great sages and saints), *Jana-loka* (abode of the sons of the god Brahma), *Tapar-loka* (abode of other deities), and *Satya-loka* or *Brahma-loka* (abode of Brahma, where souls are released from the necessity of rebirth).

In Buddhism, there are three worlds—or world systems—named *lokas:* the *kamaloka* (world of desire), the *rupaloka* (world of matter or form), and the *arupaloka* (world without form). These terms have been adopted by the **Theosophical Society.** (See also **Lokaloka**)

Loka (Journal)

Annual publication of the Naropa Institute, concerned with Buddhism and its meditation techniques. Address: Vajradhatu Books, 78 Fifth Avenue, New York, NY 10011.

Lokaloka

A fabulous region of Hindu mythology—"world and no world." It was said to be a chain of mountains at the edge of the seven seas, dividing the visible world from the regions of darkness. (See also **Loka**)

Lombroso, Cesare (1836–1909)

Italian psychiatrist, criminal anthropologist, and psychic investigator. He was born on November 18, 1836, at Verona, and studied at Padua, Vienna, and Paris. In 1862 he began his professional career as a professor of psychiatry at Pavia, then served successively as director of the lunatic asylum at Pesaro, professor of forensic medicine and psychiatry at Turin, and finally professor of criminal anthropology.

In 1872 he investigated the disease known as *pellagra* and concluded that in Italy it was caused by a poison in diseased maize eaten by the peasants. He also researched madness and genius, about which he authored several books, then turned his attention to psychic research. His later studies in criminal behavior were conducted concurrently with his psychic investigations.

His involvement in the paranormal resulted from an article he wrote for the July 1888 *Fanfulla della Domenica* on the "Influence of Civilization and Opportunity of Genius." In it he concluded:

"Who knows whether I and my friends who laugh at spiritism are not in error, since, just like hypnotised persons, thanks to the dislike of novelties which lurks in all of us, we are unable to perceive that we are in error, and just like many lunatics, being in the dark as regards the truth, we laugh at those who are not in the same condition."

After reading this article, **Cavaliere Ercole Chiaia** of Naples addressed an open letter to Lombroso and invited him to sittings with the medium **Eusapia Palladino** in Naples. In March 1891 Lombroso accepted the invitation. With Professors Tamburini, Bianchi, and Violi and Drs. Ascenzi, Prenta, Limoncelli, Gigli, and Ciolfi, Lombroso witnessed the extraordinary medium. In a subsequent letter to Ciolfi, the reporter of the sittings, Lombroso openly declared: "I am ashamed and grieved at having opposed with so much tenacity the possibility of the so-called spiritistic facts; I say the facts because I am still opposed to the theory. But the facts exist, and I boast of being a slave to facts."

Lombroso's admission caused a great sensation in Italy. As a direct consequence, a memorable series of sittings was held with the same medium in October 1892 at Dr. Finzi's house in Milan. The facts were completely confirmed for Lombroso, who pursued his research assiduoulsy. He conducted experiments in thought-transmission and contributed many articles on the phenomena of mediumship to the 1896 *Archivio di Psichiatria.* His investigation of a haunted house in Turin is of special interest (see **poltergeist**).

In 1900 Lombroso wrote to **M. T. Falcomer:** "I am like a little pebble on the beach. As yet I am uncovered; but I feel that each tide draws me a little closer to the sea."

In 1901 and 1902 Lombroso participated at further sittings with Palladino in Genoa and in 1907 in Turin. He came progressively to accept the spirit hypothesis, and, against the protests of friends who believed he would ruin an honorable reputation, he published his findings *After Death—What?* (1909).

The book is richly illustrated and presents a very lucid and sincere account of the phenomena of mediumship. Lombroso's chief credit was his fearless confession to the truth of his strange observations at a period when, despite the courage of **William Crookes, Alfred Russel Wallace** and **J. C. F. Zöllner,** the physical phenomena of Spiritualism were held in utter disdain. Following Lombroso's open declaration, a group of scientists resolved to put aside prejudice and investigate in a serious frame of mind.

Lombroso died suddenly at Turin on October 19, 1909.

Sources:

Berger, Arthur S., and Joyce Berger. *The Encyclopedia of Parapsychology and Psychical Research.* New York: Paragon House, 1991.

Lombroso, Cesare. *After Death—What?* Boston: Small, Maynard, 1909.

———. *The Man of Genius.* London: Scott, 1891.

London Dialectical Society

A British professional association that in the late 1800s investigated the phenomena of **Spiritualism.** Established in 1867, the London Dialectical Society was a highly regarded association of professional individuals. With the appearance and popularity of Spiritualism in England, the society resolved on January 26, 1869, "to investigate the phenomena alleged to be Spiritual Manifestations, and to report thereon." A committee was appointed on which 33 members were appointed: H. G. Atkinson, G. Wheatley Bennett, J. S. Bergheim, Charles Bradlaugh (later a famous atheist leader), G. Fenton Cameron, George Cary, E. W. Cox, Rev. C. Maurice Davies, D. H. Dyte, Mrs. D. H. Dyte, James Edmunds, Mrs. James Edmunds, James Gannon, Grattan Geary, William B. Gower, Robert Hannah, Jenner Gale Hillier, Mrs. J. G. Hillier, Henry Jeffery, H. D. Jencken, Albert Kisch, J. H. Levy, Joseph Maurice, Isaac L. Meyers, B. M. Moss, Robert Quelch, Thomas Reed, G. Russel Roberts, W. H. Sweepstone, William Volckman, **Alfred Russel Wallace** (later a famous psychic researcher), Josiah Webber, and Horace S. Yeomans. Thomas H. Huxley and George Henry Lewes were both invited but refused, Huxley stating that even "supposing the phenomena to be genuine, they do not interest me."

The report with evidence was presented to the council of the London Dialectical Society on July 20, 1870. It was accepted, but since it appeared to favor Spiritualist phenomena, the society did not publish it. However, the committee felt that it was in the public interest to be published, so it privately printed the report in 1871.

The principal work was done in six subcommittees. The general committee conducted 15 meetings to receive oral evidence of personal spiritual (i.e., psychic) experience from 33 written statements from 31 persons. The general committee stated that the report of the subcommittees:

"substantially corroborate each other, and would appear to establish the following propositions:

"1. That sounds of a very varied character, apparently proceeding from articles of furniture, the floor and wall of the room—the vibrations accompanying which sound are often distinctly perceptible to the touch—occur without being produced by muscular action or mechanical contrivance.

"2. That movements of heavy bodies take place without mechanical contrivance of any kind or adequate exertion of muscular force by the persons present, and frequently without contact or connection with any person.

"3. That these sounds and movements often occur at the times and in the manner asked for by persons present, and by means of a simple code of signals, answer questions and spell out coherent communications.

"4. That the answers and communications thus obtained are, for the most part, of a commonplace character; but the facts are sometimes correctly given which are only known to one of the persons present.

"5. That the circumstances under which the phenomena occur are variable, the most prominent fact being that the presence of certain persons seems necessary to their occurrence and that of others generally adverse; but this difference does not appear to depend upon any belief or disbelief concerning the phenomena.

"6. That, nevertheless, the occurrence of the phenomena is not insured by the presence or absence of such persons respectively."

The evidence was summarized in the report as follows:

"1. Thirteen witnesses state that they have seen heavy bodies–in some instances men—rise slowly in the air and remain there for some time without visible or tangible support.

"2. Fourteen witnesses testify to having seen hands or figures, not appertaining to any human being, but life-like in appearance and mobility, which they have sometimes touched or even grasped, and which they are therefore convinced were not the result of imposture or illusion.

"3. Five witnesses state that they have been touched, by some invisible agency, on various parts of the body, and often where requested, when the hands of all present were visible.

"4. Thirteen witnesses declare that they have heard musical pieces well played upon instruments not manipulated by an ascertainable agency.

"5. Five witnesses state that they have seen red-hot coals applied to the hands or heads of several persons without producing pain or scorching; and three witnesses state that they have had the same experiment made upon themselves with the like immunity.

"6. Eight witnesses state that they have received precise information through rappings, writings, and in other ways, the accuracy of which was unknown at the time to themselves or to any persons present, and which, on subsequent inquiry was found to be correct.

"7. One witness declares that he has received a precise and detailed statement which, nevertheless, proved to be entirely erroneous.

"8. Three witnesses state that they have been present when drawings, both in pencil and colours, were produced in so short a time, and under such conditions as to render human agency impossible.

"9. Six witnesses declare that they have received information of future events and that in some cases the hour and minute of their occurrence have been accurately foretold, days and even weeks before."

"In addition to the above[,] evidence has been given of trance speaking, of healing, of automatic writing, of the introduction of flowers and fruits into closed rooms, of voices in the air, of visions in crystals and glasses, and of the elongation of the human body.

"In presenting their report your Committee, taking into consideration the high character and great intelligence of many of the witnesses to the more extraordinary facts, the extent to which their testimony is supported by the reports of the sub-committees, and the absence of any proof of imposture or delusion as regards a large portion of the phenomena; and further, having regard to the exceptional character of the phenomena, the large number of persons in every grade of society and over the whole civilised world who are more or less influenced by a belief in their super-natural origin, and to the fact that no philosophical explanation of them has yet been arrived at, deem it incumbent upon them to state their conviction that the subject is worthy of more serious attention and careful investigation than it has hitherto received."

Two of the subcommittees reported failure to obtain phenomena, one investigated the medium **D. D. Home** with very feeble results, and three witnessed strong physical manifestations without contact and intelligence behind the operations. Dissenting opinion to the report was registered by general committee chair Dr. James Edmunds and by three other members: Henry Jeffrey, Grattan Geary, and H. G. Atkinson.

Alfred Russel Wallace stated in *On Miracles and Modern Spiritualism* (1875) that, of the 33 acting members of the committee, only 8 believed in the phenomena from the outset, while not more than 4 accepted the spiritual theory. During the inquiry, at least 12 of the complete skeptics became convinced of the reality of many of the physical phenomena through attending the experimental subcommittees, almost entirely by means of the mediumship of members of the committee. At least 3 of the previous skeptics later became thorough Spiritualists. The degree of conviction was approximately proportionate to the amount of time and care given the investigation.

Among those who gave evidence or read papers before the committee were: Wallace, **Emma Hardinge Britte,** H. D. Jencken, Benjamin Coleman (later a member of the **British National Association of Spiritualists**), **Cromwell F. Varley,** D. D. Home, and the **Master of Lindsay.** Correspondence was received from **Bulwar Lytton,** Dr. **Robert Chambers,** Dr. Garth Wilkinson, **William Howitt,** and **Camille Flammarion.**

Very little opposing evidence was brought in. Lord Lytton believed in material influences of whose nature we are ignorant, Dr. Carpenter in unconscious cerebration, and Dr. Kidd in the devil. Coverage of the report in the press, however, was largely hostile. The London *Times* pronounced it as "nothing more than a farrago of impotent conclusions, garnished by a mass of the most monstrous rubbish it has ever been our misfortune to sit in judgment upon." The *Morning Post* considered it entirely worthless. The *Saturday Review* was disappointed that it did not discredit a little further "one of the most unequivocally degrading superstitions that has ever found currency among reasonable beings." The *Standard* took a more open-minded view. The *Daily News* stated that "it may be regarded as an important contribution to a subject which someday or other, by the very number of its followers will demand more extended investigation." The *Spectator* agreed with the report's conclusion that the phenomena justified further cautious investigation.

Although the report considered only the phenomenal aspect of Spiritualism and not the question of survival, it highly influenced qualified investigators to look into the subject. Even arch skeptic **Frank Podmore** admitted so much in his book *Modern Spiritualism* (2 vols., 1902):

"The work done by the Dialectical Society was, no doubt, of value, since it has brought together and preserved for us a large number of records of personal experiences by representative Spiritualists. For those who wish to ascertain what Spiritualists believed at this time, and what phenomena were alleged to occur, the book may be of service. But, except in the Minority Report by Dr. Edmunds, there is no trace of any critical handling of the materials, and the conclusions of the committee can carry little weight."

Sources:

Berger, Arthur S., and Joyce Berger. *The Encyclopedia of Parapsychology and Psychical Research.* New York: Paragon House, 1991.

London Dialectical Society. *Report.* London: Longmans, Green, Reader & Dyer, 1871. Reprint, London: J. Burns, 1873. Reprint, London: Arno Press, 1976.

London Spiritualist Alliance

A Spiritualist association organized out of the **British National Association of Spiritualists** in 1884, incorporated under the Companies Act in 1896. The first president was the Rev. **Stainton Moses.** Many other famous names were associated with the alliance over the years, including **Sir Arthur Conan Doyle,** who served a tenure as president in the 1930s. Accepting and investigating psychic phenomena, not as a new religion, but as the basis of all religions, the group aimed "to seek, collect, and obtain information respecting, and generally to investigate the phenomena commonly known as psychical or as spiritualistic, including hypnotism, somnambulism, thought-transference, second-sight, and all matters of a kindred nature. To aid students and enquirers in their researches."

Visitors from abroad were welcomed, and consultations with psychic mediums were arranged. The Alliance's library was one of the finest of its kind in England at the time, and it published the important newspaper *Light.*

In 1955 the London Spiritualist Alliance was renamed the College of Psychic Science (CPS) (not to be confused with the **British College of Psychic Science** of 1920–47). In 1970 the CPS changed its name to the **College of Psychic Studies.**

Well over a century in age, the college continues the study of psychic and spiritual exploration, arranging lectures, study groups, conferences, and consultations with reputable psychics. It maintains its large, comprehensive library and continues to publish *Light* as a quarterly journal. It may be contacted at 16 Queensberry Place, London SW7 2EB, England.

Sources:

Edmunds, Simeon. *Spiritualism: A Critical Survey.* London, England: Aquarian Press, 1966.

Long, Max Freedom (1890–1971)

Pioneer researcher into the mystery of **Huna** magic, the secret techniques of Kahunas, or Polynesian priest-sorcerers. Long first went to Hawaii in 1917 as a schoolteacher following his graduation from Los Angeles Normal School (now the University of California at Los Angeles). Over a three-year period he was introduced to the stories of the native Hawaiians, though they refused to talk to him about the interesting occult aspects of the narratives.

In 1921, as he was planning to return to California, he stopped at the Bishop Museum in Honolulu and met William Tufts Brigham, then curator of the museum. Brigham had studied the seemingly miraculous feats of the Kahunas, including paranormal healing, weather control, and **fire ordeals** that involved walking over red-hot lava. Long stayed in Honolulu and studied with Brigham until the curator died in 1926. They were unable to discover the Kahunas' secret. Long returned to the mainland and opened a photography business. He had all but given up finding an answer to the Kahuna mystery when in 1935 it suddenly occurred to him that the secret might be indicated by the terms used for various aspects of Huna in the Polynesian language.

He published the first report on his discoveries, *Recovering the Ancient Magic,* in 1936, though most of the copies were destroyed in the German bombing of London during World War II. In 1945 he founded the Huna Fellowship, began issuing printed letters to what had become a long list of correspondents, and published a small pamphlet on the basic Huna concepts. Three years later the letters became a regular bulletin, and his most important book, *The Secret Science Behind the Miracles,* was published. A second book, *The Secret Science at Work* (1953), integrated what he had come to know of the Huna work and what he had learned in its practical modern application.

He developed the Huna concepts in various books over the rest of his life. In 1968 he met E. Otha Wingo, an instructor at Southeast Missouri State College, and for the last three years of his life groomed Wingo to succeed him. Also during the 1960s, a memorial library was established in his honor in Fort Worth, Texas, and now houses many of his mementos. Wingo continues as head of Huna Research.

Sources:

Hoffman, Enid. *Huna, A Beginner's Guide.* Rockport, Mass.: ParaResearch, 1976.

Long, Max Freedom. *Growing Into Light.* Vista, Calif.: Huna Research Publications, 1955.

———. *Recovering the Ancient Magic.* London, 1936. Reprint, Cape Girardeau, Mo.: Huna Press, 1978.

———. *The Secret Science behind Miracles.* Kosmon Press, 1948. Reprint, Vista, Calif.: Huna Research Publications, 1954.

———. *The Secret Science at Work.* Vista, Calif.: Huna Research Publications, 1953.

Wingo, E. Otha. *The Story of the Huna Work.* Cape Girardeau, Mo.: Huna Research, 1981.

Lopato, David (1911–)

South African accountant, medium, and spiritual healer. He was born October 13, 1911, and studied at the University of Witwatersrand, Johannesburg, South Africa. He began his practice as a chartered accountant and auditor in 1934. He chaired (1945–60) and was president (beginning in 1961) of the Society for Psychic Advancement, Johannesburg. Lopato lectured on parapsychology and worked as a healing medium in conjunction with physicians, treating patients who had failed to respond to orthodox treatment.

Sources:

Pleasants, Helene, ed. *Biographical Dictionary of Parapsychology.* New York: Helix Press, 1964.

Lopukhin, I. V. (1756–1816)

Russian lawyer and politician with special interests in mysticism and Freemasonry who anonymously published the work *Characteristics of the Interior Church.* This tract was first published in Russian in 1798. It was translated into English in 1912 from a French edition by D. H. S. Nicholson and occultist **Arthur E. Waite.** Lopukhin's teaching was similar to that of **Karl von Eckhartshausen.** It is a kind of Christian transcendentalism and resembles the higher literature of the **Grail.**

Loquifer, Battle of

A tale incorporated in the Charlemagne saga, supposed to have been written around the twelfth century. Its hero is Renouart, the reputed giant brother-in-law of William of Orange (died 812 C.E.) and the events take place on the sea. Renouart and his barons are on the shore at Porpaillart when a Saracen fleet is seen. He is persuaded to enter one of the ships, which immediately sets sail, and he is told by Isembert, a hideous monster, that the Saracens mean to flay him alive.

Armed only with a huge bar of wood, Renouart kills this creature and makes the Saracens let him go, while they return to their own country. It is arranged that Renouart will fight Loquifer, a fairy giant and leader of the Saracens, and on the outcome of this combat will determine the war.

They meet on an island near Porpaillart. Loquifer possesses a magical balm, which heals all his wounds immediately and is concealed in his club. But Renouart is assisted by angels, and he eventually deprives Loquifer of his club, so that his strength departs. Then Renouart slays him, and the devil carries off his soul.

The romance goes on to tell of a duel between William of Orange and Desrame, Renouart's father, in which the latter is slain. Renouart is comforted by **fairies,** who bear him to **Avalon** where he has many adventures. He is shipwrecked but is rescued by mermaids and awakes to find himself on the sands at Porpaillart, from which spot he had been taken to Avalon.

Lörber Society

The Lörber Society (in German, the Lörber Gesellschaft) is the organization of the students of Austrian seer and channel Jakob Lörber (1800–1864). Lörber was 40 years old when he claimed a voice commanded him to take up a pencil and write. He obeyed, and the voice eventually claimed to be Jesus Christ. Jesus dictated some 25 substantive books and a variety of shorter works. Supposedly, after Lörber's death, these revelations were given to Gottfried Meyerhofer (1807–1877), a retired army officer living in Trieste, Italy. After Meyerhofer died, the voice continued to speak through other individuals, including Leopold Engel, Johanne Ladner, Bertha Dudde, Johannes Widmann, Max Seltmann, Johanna Henzsel, George Riehle, and Johannes Friede. The revelations now fill over 40 volumes.

The works of Lörber were published by the Neutheosophischer Verlag, (after 1907 the Newsalems Verlag or New Jerusalem Publishing House) of Bietigheim, Germany, whose owner, Christoph Friedrich Landbeck, was a student of the materials. In 1924 Lörber's students founded the New Jerusalem Society. After the rise of Adolph Hitler and the annexation of Austria, the society was suppressed, but after the war it resurfaced as the Lörber Gesellschaft (or Lörber Society).

In 1921, Hans Nordewin von Koerber (1896–1979), for many years a professor of Asiatic studies at the University of Southern California, discovered the Lörber material and began to translate it into English. In 1962 he founded the Divine Word Society to publish and disseminate English editions of Lörber's writings. This society was very active through the 1970s but seems to have disbanded in more recent years.

Lörber's revelations amount to a revised gnostic interpretation of Christianity. According to Lörber, the universe was created by God as the environment for a society of living love. Many individuals, thought of as divine sparks, were to grow into the divine likeness. That plan was thwarted by Lucifer, who revolted and was entrapped in matter. God is now using matter as a filter through which the impure spirits can be purified. On Earth, spirits are given the opportunity to return to God. Jesus came to earth to speed the redemptive process.

Through the imitation of Christ, the individual can learn to love God and his neighbor. Reborn, the soul drops the body and ascends to the New Jerusalem. Meanwhile, on Earth, Christ will return in the near future to recreate the Earth and establish the millennium. The current social turmoil is a sign of his near return. When he appears, Lucifer and the earthbound souls will have to make an ultimate choice. Those who refuse God and continue in rebellion will be in destroyed.

Support for Lörber's revelations is strongest in German-speaking Europe, but followers can now be found around the world.

Sources:

Bunger, Fred S., and Hans N. Von Koerber. *A New Light Shines Out of the Present Darkness.* Philadelphia: Dorrance, 1971.

Lörber, Jakob. *The Three-Days-Scene at the Temple of Jerusalem.* Bietigheim, Germany: Neu-Salems-Society, 1932.

Lord, Jenny (ca. 1854)

Nineteenth-century American physical medium of Maine. Later married to J. L. Webb, she is said to have produced remarkable musical phenomena, either by herself or with her sister Annie, who was also mediumistic.

In her book *Modern American Spiritualism* (1870), Emma Hardinge (Britten) stated:

"These young ladies, both very slight, fragile persons, suffering under the most pitiable conditions of ill-health, and in their normal state unable to play upon any instrument, became mediums for various phases of "the power" requiring the most astounding physical force in execution, in addition to which, spirits, in their presence and in darkened rooms, would play upon a double bass violin cello, guitar, drums, accordion, tambourine, bells, and various small instruments, with the most astonishing skill and power. Sometimes the instruments would be played on singly, at others all together, and not infrequently the strange concert would conclude by placing the young medium, seated in her invalid chair, silently and in a single instant in the center of the table, piling up all the instruments around her, and then calling for a light to exhibit their ponderous feats of strength and noiseless agility to the eyes of the astonished circle. The sisters rarely sat together, and though it would be impossible to conceive of any persons more incapable of giving off *physical power* than these two fragile and afflicted girls, yet their manifestations with one alone acting as medium, have surpassed, in feats of vast strength and musical achievements, any that are recorded in the annals of Spiritualism."

In his book *The Scientific Basis of Spiritualism* (1882), Epes Sargent described similar amazing séances with Lord, and introduced the Scottish writer **Robert Chambers** to her phenomena on a visit to America. Sargent expressed absolute conviction of the genuineness of the phenomena of Jenny Lord.

Lord, Maud E. (1852–1924)

American **direct voice** medium who worked under her married name, Mrs. Maud Lord-Drake. She was born March 15, 1852, in Marion County, West Virginia, with a double veil, or **caul,** over her face. Her father was a Baptist deacon, her mother a Methodist.

She appeared before the **Seybert Commission** in 1885. Nothing more than hoarse whispers were heard and these were never simultaneous with the speech of the medium. Touches were also felt here and there, but the committee did not find the phenomena convincing. However, **Sir Arthur Conan Doyle** concluded that the members of the commission were prejudiced against Spiritualist phenomena.

Usually Lord sat in the middle of her circle and clapped her hands in the darkness to prove that she did not change position while the voices spoke from different parts of the room. Her favorite **control** was the Indian child "Snowdrop." She continued to work for 65 years, and she was reported to produce full-form **materializations** in daylight, independent music from a levitated guitar, independent voices and singing, **clairvoyance, clairaudience** and **psychometry.** At one point she was invited to Buckingham Palace, England, where she gave two readings to Queen Victoria.

Sources:

Lord-Drake, Maud. *Psychic Light: The Continuity of Law and Life.* Kansas City, Mo.: Frank T. Riley, 1904.

l'Ordre de la Rose Croix Catholicque, du Temple et du Graal

French **Rosicrucian** order founded in 1890 by Joséphin Péledan (1858–1918). Péladan had been one of the founders of l'Ordre Kabbalistique de la Rosecroix, but left because he found himself in unresolvable conflict with the other leaders over his religious faith. Péladan was a strict Roman Catholic and possessed a hope of bringing **occultism** back under the guidance of the church. Through his new order he hoped to carry out works of mercy that would lead members to prepare for the reign of the Holy Spirit.

Like previous groups, Péladan's order had three grades that he termed equerries, knights, and commanders. Commanders were assigned one of the sephiroth of the Kabbalistic Tree.

The order enjoyed some success during Péladan's life and he led it in assuming a role in cultural nurturance. Beginning in 1892 it sponsored a series of art exhibitions in Paris aimed at restoring the cult of the ideal, with an emphasis on beauty and tradition. The art displayed had a mystical or **occult** theme. Péladan also did much to promote Richard Wagner's music in France. Unfortunately, for the art world, the order died with Péladan's death immediately after the end of World War I.

Sources:

Aubrun, R. G. *Péladan.* Paris: Sansot, 1904.

McIntosh, Christopher. *Éliphas Lévi and the French Occult Revival.* New York: Samuel Weiser, 1972.

———. *The Rose Cross Unveiled: The History, Mythology and Rituals of an Occult Order.* Wellingborough, Northamptionshire, UK: Aquarian Press, 1980.

Péladan, Joséphin. *Comment on devient mage.* Paris, 1892.

———. *La decadence esrhétique.* Paris: Dalou, 1888.

———. *Le Vice supreme.* Paris: Labrairie de la Presse, Laurens, 1886.

l'Ordre Kabbalistique de la Rosecroix

An important French **Rosicrucian** order created in 1888, the same year of the founding of the Hermetic Order of the **Golden**

Dawn in England. It was founded by the Marquis Stanislas de Guaita and Joséphin Péladan (1858–1918). De Guaita, a poet living in Paris in the 1880s, had been introduced to the magical writings of **Éliphas Lévi.** Pélatan, a staunch Catholic, had developed an interest in **mysticism** and the **kabala.** He authored a series of novels under the collected title of *La Décadence latine,* one of which, *Le Vice supréme,* fell into de Guaita'a hands. The two struck up a correspondence which led to a friendship and the establishment of the order.

The Ordre was headed by a council of twelve, six secret chiefs and six known persons. The original six besides the two founders included Papus (**Gérard Encausse**), Marc Haven, the Abbé Alta, Paul Adam, and astrologer Francois-Charles Barlet. It was structured on three levels, and new members received in succession a baccalaureate, licentiate, and doctorate in the Qabalah (one of the alternate spellings of kabala).

The order suffered its first problem when Péladan withdrew over the other leaders' disagreement with his adherence to Roman Catholicism. He founded a rival order, l'Ordre de la Rose Croix Catholicque, du Temple et du Graal. He and de Guaita were never reconciled.

De Guaita died in 1887. He was succeeded Johnny Bricaud, author of a number of books on the history of the **occult,** and then in 1932 by Constant Martin Chevillon. Chevillon was killed in 1944 by the Gestapo.

Sources:

Guaita, Stanislas de. *Essais des sciences maudites.* Paris: Carré, 1885.

———. *La Serpent de la genese.* 2 Vols. Paris: Chamuel, 1891, 1897.

McIntosh, Christopher. *Eliphas Levi and the French Occult Revival.* New York: Samuel Weiser, 1972.

———. *The Rose Cross Unveiled: The History, Mythology and Rituals of an Occult Order.* Wellingborough, Northamptionshire, UK: Aquarian Press, 1980.

Wirth, Oswald. *Stanislas de Guaita, souvenirs de son secrétare.* Paris: Editions du Symbolisme, 1935.

Lord's New Church Which Is Nova Hierosolyma

The Lord's New Church Which Is Nova Hierosolyma was founded in 1937 by former members of the **General Church of the New Jerusalem** under the leadership of Rev. Theodore Pitcairn. The ideas leading to its formation can be traced to writings of a Dutch layman, H. D. G. Groeneveld, who began the periodical *De Hemelsche Leer* (The Celestial Doctrine) in 1929. **Emanuel Swedenborg,** whose writings form the distinctive body of material used by the General Church of the New Jerusalem, proposed the idea that the Bible had, in addition to its planned material meaning, a spiritual meaning that had been revealed through the communications between Swedenborg and the angelic realm. The General Church placed great authority on the writings of Swedenborg, but Groeneveld went further and proposed that Swedenborg's writings, like the Bible, also had an inner spiritual meaning. The Lord's New Church was founded after the General Church rejected Groeneveld's perspective.

In the United States, former General Church minister Theodore Pitcairn emerged as an early champion of the new perspective, about which he wrote *The Book Sealed with Seven Seals* in 1927 to present the idea to the American church. In 1937 he led in the formation of two congregations, one in Bryn Athyn, adjacent to the General Church headquarters, and one in Yonkers, New York. Eventually, support was found among Swedenborgians in Holland, Sweden, South Africa, Japan, and the United Kingdom. The Lord's New Church can be reached at Box 4, Bryn Athyn, PA 19009. There are fewer than 1,000 members worldwide.

Sources:

Handbook of the Lord's New Church Which Is Nova Hierosolyma. Bryn Athyn, Pa.: Lord's New Church Which Is Nova Hierosolyma, 1985.

Pitcairn, Theodore. *The Book Sealed with Seven Seals.* Bryn Athyn, Pa.: Cathedral Book Room, 1927.

———. *My Lord and My God.* New York: Exposition Press, 1967.

Lords of the Flame (or Children of the Fire Mist)

Adepts, or *manasaputras* (sons of mind), sent from the planet Venus to aid terrestrial **evolution.** According to **Theosophy,** Venus was considered in advance of the Earth in the evolution of the **Solar System.** The efforts of these adepts directed towards intellectual development enable the inhabitants of the Earth to become further advanced than could be expected in the ordinary course of events. These adepts are not permanent inhabitants of the Earth, and, while a few remain, most of them have already returned to Venus, the time of crisis during which they assisted having now passed.

Lorelei

Name of the tall rock on the right bank of the river Rhine, near St. Goar, Germany, that is noted for its remarkable echo. It has given rise to the legend of the lorelei water nymph, whose siren song lures sailors to their doom. In turn, this story has affinity with the legend of Holda, queen of the elves, who fascinates men, who become doomed to wander with her forever. The lorelei legend is of comparatively recent origin, a creation of the writer Klemens Brentano in his ballad story *Lore Lay* (1800) and retold in Heine's famous poem "Die Lorelei."

Lorian Association

New Age organization. The Lorian Association was founded in 1973 by David Spangler soon after his return to the United States after a three-year stay at the **Findhorn** community, a pioneering **New Age** community in northern Scotland. Among the 15 individuals who founded the Lorian Association was Dorothy McLean, one of the co-founders of Findhorn, who also moved to the United States that year. The purpose of Lorian was to explore and celebrate the emergence of new spiritual energies that could bring about human transformation, both personal and social. In 1982 Spangler and the founders issued a statement of interdependence affirming a commitment to such New Age values as cooperative decision making, harmlessness in interacting with the environment, the wise use of energy, a diversity of cultural expressions, and communion with superhuman intelligences.

Channeling was a vital part of the association in the early years. Just as Eileen Caddy had received messages that guided the developing Findhorn community, Spangler and McLean channeled and the messages were published by the association. The association was located in Wisconsin through the 1970s but moved to Issaquah, Washington, around 1980. There it survived into the 1990s, but the community has recently disbanded. Spangler radically revised his opinions concerning the New Age in the late 1980s and abandoned the basic New Age hope of social transformation.

Sources:

McLean, Dorothy. *To Hear the Angels Sing.* Middleton, Wisc.: Lorian Press, 1980.

Spangler, David. *Channeling and the New Age.* Issaquah, Wash.: Morningtown Press, 1988.

———. *Conversations with John.* Elgin, Ill.: Lorian Press, 1980.

Lost Word of Kabalism (in Freemasonry)

Also known as the Lost Word in Masonry. A word relating to some mystic plan, which, although it is held to have disappeared, will at some time be restored, and will then make the whole system plain. It is not really lost, only withheld for a season. In the same way the **Grail** was not lost, but withdrawn to its own place, the search for it occupying the noblest figures in chivalry. It represented the Key to the enigma of Creation, or, in terms of Christianity, the Kingdom of Heaven.

Occultist and mystic **Arthur E. Waite** associated the Lost Word with the virtues of faith, hope, and charity, stating: "The quest of the Lost Word is followed in one of the High Degrees within a spiritual area which is delineated by these Pillars [Wisdom, Strength, and Beauty], and that which is hidden within them, leading to the term of quest, is symbolical of these virtues, connoting their inward and sacramental sense."

Sources:

Waite, Arthur E. *New Encyclopedia of Freemasonry.* N.p., 1921.

Lotus Ashram

The Lotus Ashram is a Spiritualist fellowship tied together by the mediumship of Noel Street and his wife, Coleen Street. It was established in Miami, Florida, in 1917. Street was born and raised in New Zealand but moved to the United States and was ordained originally by the Universal Church of the Master. For a number of years he toured the United States annually. He and his wife lectured, and he did psychic readings and healings. He was known for drawing upon the teaching of the Maori people of his native New Zealand. Coleen, not a medium, taught yoga, physical fitness through vegetarianism, and proper food preparation.

Street wrote a number of booklets on various topics related to mediumship and reincarnation. In 1975 he opened a center in Chillicothe, Ohio. That center relocated to Texas in 1977 and more recently to its present location at 264 Mainsail, Port Lucie, FL 33452.

Sources:

The Story of the Lotus Ashram. Miami, Fla.: Lotus Ashram, n.d.

Street, Noel. *Karma: Your Whispering Wisdom.* Fabens, Tex.: Lotus Ashram, 1978.

———. *Reincarnation: One Life—Many Births.* Fabens, Tex.: Lotus Ashram, 1978.

Lou (1898–1968)

Name assumed by the Dutch fisherman Louwrens van Voorthuizen (or Voorthuyzen), who claimed to have experienced the annihilation of his human self and the taking over by a divine self, as a kind of Christian avatar. Lou was born in 1898 at Anna Paulowna, in the Netherlands. He began preaching in 1950 with the words: "I preach Jesus Christ bodily, his resuscitated body, with his new name, which is Lou. Those who accept this shall experience it and those who have experienced, shall be as Jesus Christ was on earth. Brothers and sisters of Jesus, sons and daughters of God."

A small group gathered around Lou and in 1963 produced a mimeographed magazine in English from Amsterdam, Holland. In his later years, Lou declared himself to be the immortal God and Creator of the universe. However, he died in 1968. His death created a crisis among his followers, and the group soon dispersed.

Loudun, Nuns of

The second of three cases of demonic possession reported in seventeenth-century France. The first involved **Father Louis Gaufridi** and Sister Madeleine de la Palud de Demandolx at Aix-en-Provence in 1611. The third was the case of the Nuns of the Franciscan Tertiaries at **Louviers** concerned with Sister Madeleine Bavent and Father Thomas Boullé.

In 1633 the convent of Ursulines in Loudun, France, became the scene of an outbreak of what was described as diabolical possession. The numerous nuns who inhabited the convent showed all of the signs of possession, including speaking in **tongues** and acting in a most extraordinary and hysterical manner. The affair grew in volume until practically all the nuns belonging to the institution were in the same condition.

The Mother Superior of the convent, Jeanne des Anges (Madame de Béclier), appears to have been of an unstable temperament, and she was not long in infecting the other sisters. She, a sister named Claire, and five other nuns were the first to be obsessed by the so-called evil spirits. The outbreak spread to the neighboring town and caused such scandal that Cardinal Richelieu appointed a commission to examine the affair. The "devils" resisted the process of **exorcism,** but seemed to succumb to a more imposing ceremony, then returned with greater violence than ever. Suspicion then fell upon Fr. **Urbain Grandier,** the confessor of the convent, as the instigator. He was arrested and accused of giving the nuns over into the possession of the devil by means of the practice of sorcery.

However, it came to light that the neighboring clergy were jealous of Grandier because he had obtained two benefices in their diocese, of which he was not a native, and they made up their minds to destroy him at the first possible moment. Despite his protests of innocence, the priest was hauled before a council of judges of the neighboring presidencies. They found on his body various marks said to be the undoubted signs of a sorcerer, and the inquest also brought out weaknesses in Grandier's reputation.

However, religious prejudice undoubtedly tainted this case. Papers seized from him were said to contain much material subversive to Roman Catholic religious practice. The prosecution produced a pact with Satan, promising Grandier the love of women, wealth, and worldly honor, endorsed with diabolical signatures. Some doubt as to the authenticity of this document is inevitable in view of the prosecution's claim that it was stolen by the demon Asmodeus from Lucifer's private files. This document, and a further claimed pact with the devil, apparently signed by Grandier in his own blood, survives in The Bibliothèque Nationale in Paris. Versions of it were published by credulous persons and sold as broadsheets.

Grandier was condemned to be burnt at the stake. The sentence was carried out in 1634, though only after he had been so severely tortured that the marrow of his bones oozed through his broken limbs. Through it all he persistently maintained his innocence.

However, his death did not end the symptoms among the sisters. In fact, the demons became more obstreperous than ever and flippantly answered to their names of such leading demons as Asmodeus, Leviathan, and Behemoth. A very holy brother called Surin was delegated to put an end to the affair. Frail and unhealthy, he possessed, however, an indomitable spirit, and after much wrestling in prayer succeeded in finally exorcising the demons.

A somewhat sensational movie based loosely on this incident was produced in 1971 under the title *The Devils.*

Sources:

Berger, Arthur S., and Joyce Berger. *The Encyclopedia of Parapsychology and Psychical Research.* New York: Paragon House, 1991.

Carmona, Michel. *Les Diables de Loudun: Sorcellerie et politique sous Richelieu.* Paris: Fayard, 1988.

Historie des diables de Loudun. N.p., 1839.

Huxley, Aldous. *The Devils of Loudun.* London: Chatto & Windus, 1952.

Lourdes

French watering resort famous for miracle cures. In 1858 the Virgin Mary reportedly appeared in a grotto to the peasant girl

Bernadette Soubirous (1844–1879), later canonized as St. Bernadette in 1933. A marble tablet at Lourdes records the apparition:

Dates of the Eighteen apparitions
and words of the Blessed Virgin
in the year of grace 1858.
In the hollow of the rock where her statue is now seen the
Blessed Virgin appeared to Bernadette Soubirous Eighteen times.
the 11th and the 14th of February;
Each day, with two exceptions, from February 18th till
March 25th, April 7th, July 16th.
The Blessed Virgin said to the child on February 18th,
"Will you do me the favour of coming here daily for a fortnight?
I do not promise to make you happy
In this world, but in the next;
I want many people to come.
The Virgin said to her during the fortnight:
"You will pray for sinners; you will kiss the earth for sinners.
Penitence! penitence! penitence!
Go, and tell the priests to cause a chapel to be built;
I want people to come thither in procession.
Go and drink of the fountain and wash yourself in it
Go and eat of the grass which is there."
On March 25th The Virgin said:
"I Am the Immaculate Conception."

Bernadette alone saw the apparition, and there was no coinciding objective event that would make it veridical. There was, however, a later incident of a supernormal character in the life of Bernadette, for which evidence is available in the testimony of Dr. Dozous. His advocacy is largely responsible for the credence bestowed on Bernadette and the fame of Lourdes. His testimony was quoted in Dr. Boissarie's book *Lourdes*, which gives a summary of the miraculous cures, published in the *Annales des Lourdes* from 1868 until 1891. While praying in ecstasy, the girl held her interlaced fingers over the flame of a lighted taper. The point of the flame came out between the fingers without causing her any harm.

In the story of the apparition, there was no promise of miraculous cures. Bernadette was an invalid child subject to fits, and nobody would have paid attention to her visions but for the grotto in the rocks to which she was conducted by the white angel, and the water of which made her feel lighter and stronger. The quarryman Bourriette was the first to conceive the idea that the water of the spring in the grotto uncovered by Bernadette's bare hands might benefit his eyes, which had been injured by an explosion. He was healed, and the rumor soon spread that the Virgin Mary was effecting miraculous cures.

A. T. Myers and **F. W. H. Myers** wrote an analysis of Lourdes from a psychic research perspective, which appeared in the *Proceedings* of the SPR in 1893. They concluded:

"Many forms of psycho-therapeutics produce, by obscure but natural agencies, for which at present we have no better terms than suggestion and self-suggestion, effects to which no definite limit can yet be assigned. Thus far Lourdes offers the best list of cures; but this superiority is not more than can be explained by the greater number of patients treated there than elsewhere, and their greater confidence in the treatment. There is no real evidence, either that the apparition of the Virgin was itself more than a subjective hallucination, or that it has any more than a merely subjective connection with the cures."

The Roman Catholic Church was also cautious in assessing claimed cures at Lourdes, and a Medical Bureau was established and reorganized after World War II in 1947. Claimed cures must meet strict criteria.

In the first place, the sick are expected to bring with them a diagnosis from their own doctors and are given an examination upon arrival in Lourdes. If a cure is claimed, the patient must return to Lourdes a year later for examination, and if the cure appears permanent and inexplicable by normal explanations, the case is then put to a higher medical tribunal in Paris. Even then, it is submitted to members of an ecclesiastical tribunal before being pronounced miraculous, or, in some cases, a genuine cure but still non-miraculous.

Approximately 3 million pilgrims visit Lourdes each year, and some 6,000 cures have been considered genuine but not miraculous. About 60 cures are considered in the miraculous category, and of these, some appear quite remarkable.

Lourdes is now one of the most famous pilgrim sites, and the whole area is well organized for great annual pilgrimages. In 1876 a huge basilica was constructed above the rock, and in the cave where Bernadette had her vision a marble state of the Virgin was placed. The grotto is festooned with crutches from disabled pilgrims who did not need assistance after their visits.

Of course not all pilgrims who visit the shrine come in expectation of a cure. Thousands come as an act of piety, and the grotto has a remarkable atmosphere of faith and grace. (See also **Fatima; Garabandal; Guadalupe Apparitions; healing, psychic; healing by faith;** and **Medjugorje**)

Sources:

Estrade, J. B. *The Appearances of the Blessed Virgin Mary at the Grotto of Lourdes: Personal Souvenirs of an Eyewitness.* London: Art & Book Co., 1912.

Kselman, Thomas A. *Miracles and Prophecies in Nineteenth-Century France.* New Brunswick, N.J.: Rutgers University Press, 1983.

Marchand, A. *The Facts of Lourdes and the Medical Bureau.* London: Burns Oates & Wasbourne, 1924.

Myer, A. T., and F. W. H. Myers. "Mind-Cure, Faith-Cure, and the Miracles of Lourdes." *Proceedings* of the Society for Psychic Research 9, no. 24 (1893).

Neame, Alan. *The Happening at Lourdes.* London: Hodder & Stoughton, 1968.

Trochu, Francis. *Saint Bernadette Soubirous, 1844–1879.* London: Longmans, 1957.

West, Donald J. *Eleven Lourdes Miracles.* New York: Helix Press, 1957.

Louviers, Nuns of

The third case of demonic possession reported in seventeenth-century France. The first involved **Father Louis Gaufridi** and Sister Madeleine de la Palud de Demandolx at Aix-en-Provence in 1611; the second was the great scandal of **Father Urbain Grandier** and the nuns of **Loudun** in 1633.

The case of the Nuns of the Franciscan Tertiaries at Louviers concerned Sister Madeleine Bavent and Father Thomas Boullé and was documented by Madeleine Bavent's own written confession, which included her earlier life story. Born in Rouen in 1607, she was apprenticed to a dressmaker. At the age of 18 she was seduced by a Franciscan priest who had also been intimate with other girls.

Madeleine then decided to enter the convent at Louviers. Here she found that the first chaplain, Father Pierre David, had strange, heretical ideas, believing that an illuminated individual (such as he himself) could not sin and that he should worship God naked like Adam. During three years as a novice under Father David, Madeleine was obliged to be received by him naked, although he did not have intercourse with her.

Father David was succeeded as chaplain by Father Mathurin Picard in 1628 and his assistant Father Thomas Boullé. According to Madeleine, she became pregnant by Father Picard, who also made revolting love charms from altar wafers to secure favors from other nuns. Both priests were said to have conducted a black mass at midnight sabbats with Madeleine and other nuns, involving disgusting practices, and as a result, Madeleine was visited by the devil in the shape of a huge black cat. Between 1628 and 1642, such orgies involved other nuns, who exhibited frenzied symptoms of hysterical possession by specific devils. When the scandal became public, the nuns confessed but blamed Madeleine Bavent.

Attempts at **exorcism** were made, and the Bishop of Evreux investigated the convent for **witchcraft.** Madeleine was charged with sorcery, witchcraft, and making a pact with the devil. She confessed and was expelled from the order, being punished with perpetual imprisonment in an underground dungeon with only bread and water three days of the week.

She died soon afterward in 1647. Father Picard had died in 1642, but his corpse was exhumed and excommunicated. Father Thomas Boullé was imprisoned for three years, tortured, then burned alive in 1647. The remaining nuns of Louviers were sent away to other convents.

Lovecraft, H(oward) P(hillips) (1890–1937)

Celebrated American writer of macabre supernatural fiction. He was born August 20, 1890, in Providence, Rhode Island. Both his parents suffered from insanity, and Lovecraft himself grew up as a lonely neurasthenic with a love of eighteenth-century English literature. He was also strongly influenced by the fantasy fiction of Edgar Allan Poe. He began writing stories at the age of five, and as a young man became something of an eccentric recluse. At the age of sixteen, he contributed a series of articles on astronomy to the *Providence Tribune.*

A shy, imaginative, and delicate individual, he was much influenced in his own stories by such fantasy authors as Algernon Blackwood, Lord Dunsany, Arthur Machen, and Walter de la Mare. His own somewhat Augustan prose style and highly individual preoccupation with fantasy and horror themes remained too specialized for conventional literary outlets, and much of his work was for small press magazines like *Vagrant* and *Home Brew* or the new generation of pulps like *Weird Tales, Amazing Stories* and *Astounding Stories.*

In 1924 he married Sonia Greene of New York City, also a writer, but the marriage only lasted a couple of years and he was later divorced, returning to Providence where he wrote late into the night at his stories.

His most impressive creation was the **Cthulhu Mythos,** involving a group of stories about entities from another time and space. Part of the myth was a fictitious **grimoire,** or magical instruction and ritual book, called the **Necronomicon,** also referred to as the Book of Dead Names compiled by the "mad Arab Abdul Alhazred."

In spite of his considerable literary output, Lovecraft made very little money out of his fiction, which he supplemented by editing and ghost-writing. He died from cancer March 15, 1937. After his death, his friend and biographer August Derleth revived and reissued his stories through Arkham House Press, "Arkham" being a fictional city in Lovecraft's stories.

It has been suggested that some of the fantasy inventions of Lovecraft may have had some real existence in some other plane of reality, contacted through his subconscious mind. A small group of magicians have explored the possibility of the cthulu mythos for the working of magic. No less than three Necronomicrons have been written and published.

Sources:

Burleson, Donald R. *Lovecraft: Disturbing the Universe.* Lexington: University Press of Kentucky, 1990.

de Camp, L. Sprague. *Lovecraft: A Biography.* Garden City, N.Y.: Doubleday, 1975.

Derleth, August. *H.P.L.: A Memoir.* Ben Abramson, 1945.

Long, Frank Belknap. *Howard Phillips Lovecraft: Dreamer on the Nightside.* Sauk City, Wis.: Arkham House, 1975.

Lovecraft, Howard Phillips. *At the Mountains and Other Novels.* Sauk City, Wis.: Arkham House, 1964.

———. *Collected Poems.* Sauk City, Wis.: Arkham House, 1963.

———. *The Dunwich Horror and Others.* Sauk City, Wis.: Arkham House, 1963.

———. *Haunter of the Dark, and Other Tales of Horror.* London: Gollancz, 1950.

———. *Supernatural Horror in Literature.* New York: B. Abramson, 1945.

Simon, ed. *The Necronomicron.* New York: Schjangekraft, 1977.

Lubin

The fish whose gall was used by Tobias to restore his father's sight. It was said to be very powerful against ophthalmia, and the fish's heart potent in driving away demons. The account of Tobias can be found in the extra-biblical book of **Tobit** in the *Apocrypha.*

Luce e Ombra (Light and Shade) (Journal)

The principal Italian Spiritualist monthly, founded in 1900. It was edited by Angelo Marzorati until his death in autumn 1931. The title was changed in January 1932 to *La Ricerca Psichica* (Psychic Review), with a transfer of editorial offices from Rome to Milan. Since then, *Luce e Ombra* has been published quarterly by dell'Associazione Archivio di Documentazione Storica della Ricerca Psichica. Address: Bozzano-De Boni, Via Orfeo 15, 40214 Bologna, Italy.

Sources:

Berger, Arthur S., and Joyce Berger. *The Encyclopedia of Parapsychology and Psychical Research.* New York: Paragon House, 1991.

Lucid Dreaming

Preferred modern term for **"dreaming true,"** indicating the experience of dreaming with consciousness that one *is* dreaming, i.e., experiencing a dream with waking consciousness. The condition is often associated with **out-of-the-body travel,** as it often happens that some incongruity in a dream stimulates the dreamer to conclude "Why, I must be dreaming!" and this awareness sometimes precedes an out-of-the-body event.

The term "lucid dreaming" was introduced by Frederick van Eeden in 1913 and was subsequently used by **Celia E. Green** in her study *Lucid Dreams* (1968). Early classic studies on out-of-the-body experience, such as **S. J. Muldoon**'s and **Hereward Carrington**'s *The Projection of the Astral Body,* (1929) relied upon anecdotal evidence by dreamers of the lucid state, after awakening. In modern times, parapsychologists have endeavored to clarify the lucid state and its relationship to extrasensory perception by controlled experiments.

In his work on lucid dreams, Keith M. T. Hearne of the Department of Psychology of the University of Liverpool described a technique of identifying the lucid dream in a polygraphic record by instructing the subject to signal information by predetermined ocular movements. This avoided the massive bodily paralysis of Stage REM sleep, which affects the rest of the musculature. The ocular signalling technique provided a channel of communication from the sleeping and dreaming subject to the outer world, by means of which physiological and psychological information on the dreams was obtained. The general investigation included simple testing of the subject, in a lucid dream state, for any ESP ability.

Another promising method of investigating lucid dreams that has been tried by other experimenters is the artificial inducing of lucidity and control of the dream through guided instruction on the part of the experimenter. This involved verbal communication with the dreamer to ascertain the nature of the dream imagery and the making of suggestions to guide the course of the dream.

Sleep researcher Stephen LaBerge had lucid dreams from an early age, and in 1977 started a dream journal, continued over a number of years, covering over 900 lucid dreams. In his own research at Stanford University, he concluded that the ability to dream lucidly could be important to humanity and a tool in solving problems of waking life.

The **Lucidity Association,** concerned with education and research into lucid dreaming and related phenomena, may be contacted c/o Department of Psychology, University of Northern Iowa, Cedar Falls, IA 50614.

Sources:

Green, Celia E. *Lucid Dreams.* London: Hamish Hamilton, 1968.

Hearne, Keith M. T. "'Lucid' Dreams and ESP: An Initial Experiment Using One Subject." *Journal* of the Society for Psychic Research 51, no. 787 (1981).

Kelzer, Kenneth. *The Sun and the Shadow: My Experiment with Lucid Dreaming.* Virginia Beach, Va.: A.R.E. Press, 1987.

LaBerge, Steven. *Lucid Dreaming: The Power of Being Awake and Aware in Your Dreams.* Los Angeles: Jeremy P. Tarcher, 1987.

Muldoon, Sylvan J., and Hereward Carrington. *The Projection of the Astral Body.* London: Rider, 1929. Reprint, New York: Samuel Weiser, 1967.

Ullman, Montague, Stanley Krippner, and Alan Vaughan. *Dream Telepathy.* London: Turnstone Books, 1973. New York: Macmillan, 1973.

van Eeden, Frederick. "A Study of Dreams." *Proceedings* of the Society for Psychic Research 26 (1913).

Lucidity

A faculty by which paranormal knowledge may be obtained. It is a collective term for the phenomena of **clairvoyance, clairaudience, psychometry,** and **premonitions.** It was first used by experimenters describing the condition of sensitives in relation to the phenomena of **animal magnetism** and **mesmerism** but was later used by French psychical researchers. It has generally been replaced in recent decades by ESP, or extrasensory perception.

Lucidity Association

Organization devoted to education and research into **lucid dreaming** and related phenomena. It publishes a biannual *Lucidity Letter,* dealing with research findings on lucid dreaming from researchers all over the world. The association may be contacted c/o Department of Psychology, University of Northern Iowa, Cedar Falls, IA 50614.

Lucifer

Latin term meaning "light-bringer," from the Hebrew word *helel.* The name appears in Isa. 14:12, where the king of Babylon is compared to Lucifer (or the planet Venus, the morning star) as one fallen from heaven. In the third century C.E., Lucifer was identified with Satan, and Luke 10:18, which speaks of Satan falling from heaven, was seen as a reference to the verse in Isaiah. In the West, Lucifer also survived as an independent spirit being.

According to the old magicians, Lucifer was said to preside over the East (possibly an identification with the morning star). He was invoked on Mondays in a circle in the center of which was written his name. As the price for appearing to the magician, he asked only a mouse.

Other traditions state that Lucifer rules Europeans and Asiatics. He sometimes appears in the shape of a beautiful child. When he is angry his face is flushed, but there is nothing monstrous about him.

He is, according to some students of **demonology,** the grand justice of Hades, and as such is the first to be invoked by witches in the **Litanies of the Sabbat.**

In his poetry John Milton pictured a most human Lucifer, who existed as a potent force for good or evil, one who might have done great good, intensely proud and exceedingly powerful.

The attempt to revive Lucifer in his pre-Christian positive nature occurred in **Theosophy.** Early in the twentieth century, the **Theosophical Society** named one of their prominent periodicals *Lucifer,* and the **Arcane School** called its publishing concern Lucis Publishing.

Lugh

In medieval Irish romance, son of Kian and father of **Cuchulain.** He was brought up by his uncle Goban, the Smith, and by Duach, King of Fairyland. It was prophesied that Lugh should eventually overcome his father's old enemy **Balor,** his own grandfather. So instead of killing the three murderers of his father, Kian, he put them on oath to obtain certain wonders, including the magical spear of the king of Persia and the pig-skin of the king of Greece, which, if laid on a patient, would heal him of his wound or cure him of his sickness. Thus equipped, Lugh entered the Battle of Moytura against the Fomorians, and by hurling a stone that pierced through the eye to the brain of Balor, Lugh fulfilled the Druidic prophecy.

Lugh was the Irish sun god; his final conquest of the Fomorians and their leader symbolizes the victory of light and intellect over darkness. Balor was god of darkness and brute force as embodied in the Fomorians. By his title of Ildanach, or "All Craftsman," Lugh is comparable to the Greek Apollo. He was widely worshiped by Continental Celts.

Luk, Charles (Lu K'uan Yü) (1898– ?)

Chinese-born teacher and writer on Chinese **Zen** Buddhism and the **yoga** of **Taoism.** He was born in Canton, China, and his first master was the Hutuktu of Sikang, who was the guru of two Tibetan Buddhists sects—the Kargyupas (White Sect) and the Nyingmapas (Red Caps)—and also an enlightened Great Lama. His second master was the Venerable Ch'an Master Hsu Yun, Dharma-successor of all the Five Ch'an (Zen) Sects of China and 119 years old when he died in October 1959 in a monastery in Kiangsi province.

Charles Luk was one of the leading authorities on Chinese yoga and Buddhism. He lived in Hong Kong and spent many years studying and interpreting traditional texts of Chinese Buddhism and meditational practices, so that this teaching would be preserved and made available in the West. His works on Taoist yoga and **meditation** indicated that the basic principles of **kundalini,** a teaching of Hindu tantric groups, were also known and practiced in Chinese tradition.

Sources:

Luk, Charles. *Ch'an and Zen Teachings.* Series 1, 2 & 3. London: Rider, 1960–62.

———. *Practical Buddhism.* London: Rider, 1971.

———. *The Secrets of Chinese Meditation.* London: Rider, 1964.

———. *Taoist Yoga, Alchemy, and Immortality.* New York: Samuel Weiser, 1973.

———. *The Vimalakirti Nirdesa Sutra.* Berkeley, Calif.: Shambhala, 1972.

Lully, Raymond (or Ramon Lull) (ca. 1232–1315)

An alchemist believed to possess titanic physical and mental energy, who threw himself heart and soul into everything he did. Lully's father was a Spanish knight, who won the approval of John I, king of Arragon and was granted an estate on the island of Majorca, where Lully was born about the year 1232.

His father's royal privilege earned the very young Lully the appointment of Seneschal of the Isles, but he embarrassed his parents soon thereafter by living a life of debauchery. He consorted with women of all sorts, especially the married woman Eleonora de Castello, whom he followed wherever she went, making no attempt to conceal his illicit passion. On one occasion he actually sought the lady while she was attending mass. And so loud was the outcry against this bold, if not sacrilegious act, that Eleonora found it essential to write in peremptory style to her *cavaliere servente,* and bid him desist from his present course.

The letter failed to cool the youth's ardor, but when he learned that the lady was smitten with a deadly cancer, Lully's frame of mind began to alter speedily. Sobered by the frustration of his hopes, he vowed henceforth to live differently, consecrating his days to the service of God.

Lully took holy orders, but his active and impetuous temperament left him little inclined for monastic life. Aiming to carry the Gospel far afield to convert the followers of Mahomet, he began to study Arabic. After mastering that tongue, he proceeded to Rome to enlist the pope's sympathy in his project. Lully failed to get the pope's support, yet, undaunted, he embarked on his own from Genoa in about 1291, and when he reached Tunis, he commenced his crusade. His ardor resulted in fierce persecution and ultimate banishment, so he returned for a while to Europe, visiting Paris, Naples, and Pisa, and exhorting all good Christians to aid his beloved enterprise.

In 1308 he went to Africa, and at Algiers he made a host of converts, yet was once more forced to flee for his life before the angry Moslems. He traveled to Tunis, thinking to escape from there to Italy, but his former activities in the town were remembered, and consequently he was seized and thrown into prison. Here he languished for a long time, preaching the gospel at every opportunity that presented itself. At last some Genoese merchants procured his release, and so Lully sailed back to Italy. In Rome he worked strenuously to get the pope's support for a well-equipped foreign mission, but after he failed, he rested briefly in his native Majorca, then returned to Tunis.

Proclaiming his presence publicly, he had scarcely begun preaching when he was savagely attacked, left lying on the seashore, his assailants imagining him dead. He was still breathing, however, when some Genoese found him, and they carried him to a ship and set sail for Majorca. But the zealot did not rally, and he died in sight of his home June 30, 1315.

Lully's proselytizing ardor made his name familiar throughout Europe, and while many people regarded him as a heretic for undertaking a mission without the pope's sanction, others admired him so much that they sought to make him a saint. He was eventually canonized as a martyr, and a mausoleum was erected to him.

Meanwhile he also attained some notoriety as an alchemist and was reported to have made a large sum of gold for the English king. There is really no proof that he ever visited Britain, but the remaining part of the story holds a certain significance. It is said that Lully made the money on the strict understanding that it should be utilized for equipping a large and powerful band of missionaries. There is some reason to believe that he thought to employ his alchemical skill on behalf of his missionary object. Possibly he approached some European sovereign with this goal in view, thus giving rise to the tradition about his dealings with the English monarch.

Lully's writings include a number of works on **alchemy,** most notably *Alchimia Magic Naturalis, De Aquis Super Accurtationes, De Secretis Medicina Magna* and *De Conservatione Vitoe.* It is interesting to find that several of these won considerable popularity and were repeatedly reprinted, while as late as 1673, two volumes of *Opera Alchima* purporting to be written by him were issued at London. Five years before this, a biography by De Vernon had been published at Paris, while at a later date a German historian of chemistry named Gruelin referred to Lully as a scientist of exceptional skill and mentioned him as the first man to distill rosemary oil.

Sources:

Waite, Arthur E. *Raymond Lully, Illuminated Doctor, Alchemist, and Christian Mystic.* London, 1922. Reprint, London, 1939. Reprint, New York: David McKay, 1940.

Lumieres dan la Nuit

French-language publication concerned with unidentified flying objects, published annually. Address: R. Veillith, ed., "Les Pins," 43400 Le Chambon-sur-Lignon, France.

Luminous Bodies

Dead bodies were frequently supposed to glow in the dark with a sort of phosphorescent light. Possibly the belief arose from the idea that the soul was like a fire dwelling in the body.

Luminous Phenomena

A frequent occurrence in physical mediumship. On rare occasions such phenomena have been witnessed in apparent independence of mediumistic conditions.

The chronicles of religious revivals are full of instances of transcendental lights. For example, during both the great Irish revival in 1859 and the Welsh revival in 1904 there were multiple accounts. A Mr. Jones of Peckham, editor of the *Spiritual Magazine* (1877, vol. 18), quotes a leading official belonging to the Corporation of London:

"Having heard that fire had descended on several of the great Irish assemblies during the Revivals, I, when in Ireland, made inquiry and conversed with those who had witnessed it. During the open-air meetings, when some 600–1,000 people were present, a kind of cloud of fire approached in the air, hovered and dipped over the people, rose and floated on some distance, again hovered on that which was found afterwards to be another revival meeting, and so it continued. The light was very bright and was seen by all, producing awe."

Of the Welsh Revival an interesting account was published by Beriah G. Evans in the *Daily News* (February 9, 1905). The lights he saw appeared for the first time on the night when Mary Jones began her public mission at Egryn. The first light, Evans writes, "resembled a brilliant star emitting sparklets. All saw this. The next two were as clearly subjective, being seen only by Mrs. Jones and me, though the five of us walked abreast. Three bars of clear white light crossed the road in front, from right to left, climbing up the stone wall to the left. A blood-red light, about a foot from the ground in the middle of the roadway at the head of the village street was the next manifestation."

A *Daily Mirror* correspondent confirmed Evans's account. He said he saw both sets of lights. A third confirmation was published in the July 1905 *Review of Reviews* by the Reverend Llewellyn Morgan.

These lights seem to have been the result of an outpouring of the combined psychic forces that religious ecstasy supposedly generates. Religious enthusiasm and ecstasy in general have often been reported to be accompanied by luminous phenomena. The Bible says that Jesus was transfigured before his disciples and that his face shown as the sun and his garments were white as light (Matt. 17:2). As Paul walked to Damascus, he encountered a light from heaven that shone around him (Acts 9:3). The saints and martyrs spoke of an interior illumination. St. Ignatius Loyola was seen surrounded by a brilliant light while he prayed and his body shone with light when he was levitated; St. Columba was said to have been continually enveloped in a dazzling, golden light, reminiscent of what is today termed an **aura.**

William James quotes many interesting instances in *Varieties of Religious Experience* (1902). In *Cosmic Consciousness* (1901), **R. Maurice Bucke** speaks of his heightened state being heralded by an influx of dazzling light. The body of the medium **Leonora Piper** was described by the communicators as an empty shell filled with light.

"A medium," said "Phinuit," the spirit control of **W. Stainton Moses,** "is for us a lighthouse, while you, non-mediums are as though you did not exist. But every little while we see you as if you were in dark apartments lighted by a kind of little windows which are the mediums."

This light or flame, according to communications obtained by **Hester Dowden,** appears to be pale, "a clear white fire" that seems to grow more vivid as the medium gets into better touch with the spirit world.

It has been suggested that spectral lights may have a psychic origin. The fire of St. Bernardo was studied in 1895 in Quargnento by a Professor Garzino. It was a mass of light that wandered every night from the church to the cemetery and returned after midnight. A similar light was observed at Berbenno di Valtellina. The light passed through trees without burning them.

The phenomenon has not been explained by reference to known chemical laws. The main difficulty that such lights present is the absence of a human organism to which their origin could be traced. But such an absence is also noted in uninhabited haunted houses where the human link is strongly emphasized.

As luminous phenomena emerged in a Spiritualist context, many of the accounts were tied to the rather questionable phenomena of **materialization.** Not a major concern of psychical research, the strange—even extraordinary—luminous phenomena reported by sitters could simply have been additional phenomena produced as part of a total fraudulent event.

The Psychic Lights of D. D. Home and Stainton Moses

Sir William Crookes, in *Researches in the Phenomena of Spiritualism* (1874), relates the following:

"Under the strictest test conditions I have seen a solid luminous body, the size and nearly the shape of a turkey's egg, float noiselessly about the room, at one time higher than anyone present could reach standing on tiptoe, and then gently descend to the floor. It was visible for more than ten minutes, and before it faded away it struck the table three times with a sound like that of a hard solid body. During this time the medium was lying back, apparently insensible, in an easy chair.

"I have seen luminous points of light darting about and settling on the heads of different persons; I have had questions answered by the flashing of a bright light a desired number of times in front of my face. . . . I have had an alphabetic communication given me by luminous flashes occurring before me in the air, whilst my hand was moving about amongst them. . . . *In the light,* I have seen a luminous cloud hover over a heliotrope on a side table, break a sprig off and carry the sprig to a lady."

Viscount Adare writes in his *Experiments in Spiritualism with D. D. Home* (1870): "We all then observed a light, resembling a little star, near the chimney piece, moving to and fro; it then disappeared. Mr. Home said: Ask them in the name of the Father, the Son and the Holy Ghost, if this is the work of God. I repeated the words very earnestly; the light shone out, making three little flashes, each one about a foot higher above the floor than the preceding."

The color of the lights was sometimes blue, yellow, or rose. They did not light up their surroundings. Special effort was necessary to produce an effect of illumination. When Ada Menken's spirit tried to make her form visible, writes Adare, "the surface of the wall to Home's right became illuminated three or four times; the light apparently radiating from a bright spot in the centre. Across the portion of the wall thus illuminated we repeatedly saw a dark shadow pass."

Adare saw the extended hand of Home become quite luminous. On another occasion his clothes began to shine. Once the top of his head glowed with light as if a halo surrounded it. The tongues or jets of flame described by the **Master of Lindsay** and Capt. Charles Wynne as issuing from Home's head probably refer to this experience. Lindsay and many other witnesses often saw luminous crosses in Home's presence. They were variously globular, columnar, or star-shaped.

Reading a paper before the **London Dialectical Society,** Lindsay said:

"I saw on my knee a flame of fire about nine inches high; I passed my hand through it, but it burnt on, above and below it. Home turned in his bed and I looked at him, and saw that his eyes were glowing with light. It had a most disagreeable appearance. . . . The flame which had been flitting about me now left me, and crossed the room about four feet from the ground, and reached the curtains of Home's bed; these proved no obstruction; for the light went right through them, settled on his head and then went out."

In a letter to the London Dialectical Society, Lindsay narrated a further experience:

"At Mr. Jencken's house I saw a crystal ball, placed on Mr. Home's head, emit flashes of coloured light, following the order of the spectrum. The crystal was spherical, so that it could not have given prismatic colours. After this it changed and we all saw a view of the sea, as if we were looking down at it from the top of a high cliff. It seemed to be the evening as the sun was setting like a globe of fire, lighting up a broad path over the little waves. The moon was faintly visible in the south, and as the sun set, her power increased. We saw also a few stars; and suddenly the whole thing vanished, like shutting the slide of a magic lantern; and the crystal was dead. This whole appearance lasted about ten minutes."

Many similar observations were recorded in the mediumship of Stainton Moses. Stanhope Templeman Speer observed that the light could be renewed when it grew dim by making passes over it with the hand. The light had a nucleus and an envelope of drapery. It seemed to be more easily developed if Moses rubbed his hands together or on his coat. The drapery passed over the back of his hand several times. It was perfectly tangible. These large globes of light could knock distinct blows on the table. A hand was distinctly generated in their nucleus.

These globular lights ceased after a time because the drain on Moses' strength was too great. They were supplanted by a round disk of light that had a dark side, generally turned toward the medium; the light side gave answers to questions by flashes. On rarer occasions the light was a tall column, about half an inch in width and six or seven feet high. The light was of bright golden hue and did not illuminate objects in the neighborhood. For a minute a cross developed at its top and rays seemed to dart from it.

Around Moses' head was a halo, and another cluster of light, oblong in shape, was at the foot of the tall column. It moved up and the big, luminous cross gradually traveled toward the wall until it had passed over an arc of 90 degrees. Solid objects afforded no obstacles to one's view of the lights. If they appeared under a mahogany table they could be seen from above just as well as if the tabletop were glass. Sometimes as many as 30 lights were seen flashing about like comets in the room. The big lights were usually more stationary than the smaller ones, which darted swiftly about the room.

Accidents in Light Production

The chemistry for the production of these lights misfired on April 14, 1874. Speer writes:

"Suddenly there arose from below me, apparently under the table, or near the floor, right under my nose, a cloud of luminous smoke, just like phosphorus. It fumed up in great clouds, until I seemed to be on fire, and rushed from the room in a panic. I was very frightened and could not tell what was happening. I rushed to the door and opened it, and so to the front door. My hands seemed to be ablaze and I left their impress on the door and handles. It blazed for a while after I had touched it, but soon went out, and no smell or trace remained. I have seen my own hands covered with a lambent flame; but nothing like this I ever saw. There seemed to be no end of the smoke. It smelt phosphoric, but the smell evaporated as soon as I got out of the room into the air. I was fairly frightened, and was reminded of what I had read about a manifestation given to Mr. Peebles similar to the burning bush. I have omitted to say that the lights were preceded by very sharp detonations on my chair, so that we could watch for their coming by hearing the noises. They shot up very rapidly from the floor."

The next day, "Imperator" (Moses' spirit control) explained that the phosphoric smoke was caused by an aborted attempt on the part of "Chom" (another spirit) to make a light. There were, he said, ducts leading from the sitters' bodies to the dark space beneath the table, and into this space these ducts conveyed the substance extracted for the purpose of making the light. The phosphoric substance was enclosed in an envelope that was materialized. It was the collapse of this envelope that caused the escape of the phosphoric smoke and the smell. This substance was the vital principle, he said, and was drawn mainly from the spine and nerve centers of all the sitters—except those who were of no use or would be deterrents to the process.

Another miscarriage of psychic light was described by W. H. Harrison. It occurred at a séance with the mediums **Frank Herne** and **Charles Williams.** Harrison said, "The name of the spirit was then written rapidly in large phosphorescent letters in the air near Mr. Williams. In the same rapid manner the spirits next began writing 'God Bless—' when there was a snap, like an electrical discharge, and a flash of light which lit up the whole room." At the end of the sitting a slight smell of phosphorus was perceptible. However, a more likely explanation of this phenomenon is that it was caused by the sudden striking of a match, since suspicion of **fraud** is attached to the séances of Herne and Williams.

The following description is from the Livermore records of séances with Kate Fox (of the **Fox sisters**): "A spherical ovoid of light rises from the floor as high as our foreheads and places itself on the table in front of us. At my request the light immediately became so bright as to light up that part of the room. We saw perfectly the form of a woman holding the light in her outstretched hand."

A Dr. Nichols, in whose house **William Eglinton** gave a series of sittings, wrote of "masses of light of a globular form, flattened globes, shining all through the mass, which was enveloped in folds of gauzy drapery."

"'Joey'"[a spirit control], wrote Nichols, "brushed the folds aside with his finger to show us the shining substance. It was as if a gem—a turquoise or a pearl—three inches across, had become incandescent, full of light, so as to illuminate about a yard round. This light also we saw come and go. 'Joey' allowed his larger light to go almost dark, and then revived it to its former brilliancy. I need hardly say that all the chemists of Europe could not, under these conditions, produce such phenomena, if indeed they could under any." [Nichols's account indicates that he was duped by Eglinton's trick.]

The spirit entity "John King" often brought a spirit lamp when he materialized. Once, in a séance with Williams, the lamp was placed in the hands of Alfred Smedley, who states in his book *Some Reminiscences* (1900), "To my great surprise it was like a lump of solid, warm flesh, exactly similar to my own." Others observed that the lamp was often covered with lacelike drapery. This is not surprising, since the appearance of psychic lights often heralded materializations. A disk of light could transform itself into a face, a star into a human eye. To the touch, the light was sometimes hard, sometimes sticky, sitters reported.

Later Observations

In a séance with **Franek Kluski** on May 15, 1921, **Gustav Geley** recorded: "A moment later, magnificent luminous phenomena; a hand moved slowly about before the sitters. It held in the palm, by a partial bending of the fingers, a body resembling a piece of luminous ice. The whole hand appeared luminous and transparent. One could see the flesh colour. It was admirable."

After another séance on April 12, 1922, Geley wrote:

"A large luminous trail like a nebulous comet, and about half a metre long, formed behind Kluski about a metre above his head and seemingly about the same distance behind him. This nebula was constituted of tiny bright grains broadcast, among which there were some specially bright points. This nebula oscillated quickly from right to left and left to right, and rose and fell. It lasted about a minute, disappeared and reappeared several times. After the sitting I found that the medium, who had been naked for an hour, was very warm. He was perspiring on the back and armpits; he was much exhausted."

With the same medium, a Professor Pawlowski recorded the appearance of a completely luminous figure of an old man that looked like a column of light. It illuminated all of the sitters and even the more distant objects in the room. The hands and the region of the heart were much brighter than the rest of the body.

Admiral Usborne Moore stated that he had seen tongues of spirit light issue from the body of the medium **Ada Besinnet.** They were about one-third of an inch broad at one end and tapered away, for a length of about one and a half inches, to nothing.

In a séance with the medium **Indridi Indridason, Harald Nielsson** counted one evening more than 60 tongues of light of different colors. "I could not help thinking of the manifestations described in the second chapter of the Acts of the Apostles," he writes in *Light* (October 25, 1919), "especially as a very strong wind arose before the lights appeared. Later on the whole wall behind the medium became a glow of light."

An unusual type of "psychic" light was shown by the medium **Pasquale Erto** ("the human rainbow") in séances at the Metapsychical Institute of Paris, the genuineness of which was later doubted. Flashes like electric sparks proceeded from the lower part of Erto's body, lighting up the floor and sometimes the walls of the room. He also produced luminous white rays up to eight meters in length; luminous spheres from the size of a walnut to an orange in white, reddish, or bluish color; zig-zag flashes; and rocketlike lights. They were cold lights, devoid of actinic rays.

Before each séance Erto was completely stripped and medically examined in all cavities—mouth, ears, rectum, and even urethra. Erto demanded absolute darkness and did not permit hand control. Geley found out that the phenomena could be produced by the use of ferro-cerium, and believed the medium used this trick.

Erto's phenomena were not unique. **Maria Silbert** occasionally produced somewhat similar psychic flashes, but her mediumistic reputation was far above that of Erto.

In the Boston séances of the medium "Margery" (**Mina S. Crandon**) a glowing light was seen on Margery's left shoulder. On touch, no luminous material was rubbed off, and the light continued to be seen through a black sock, though with decreased frequency and brilliance. On examination the medium's left shoulder strap was found to be luminous. There was a less distinct brightness on her chest and luminous patches on her right shoulder that soon faded and went out. When the luminous shoulder strap was brought into the séance room, a sudden increase in its intensity was noticed. During a close examination a whisper in the voice of "Walter" (the spirit control) said "goodnight." At approximately the same time, the light of the shoulder strap faded except for one tiny luminous point that seemed more persistent than the rest. At another time **Hereward Carrington,** holding Margery's left hand, noticed at the end of the sitting that *his* hand was faintly luminous.

Charles Richet attempted to imitate psychic lights with a neon tube six feet long and one inch in diameter. By rubbing the tube he induced a frictional electric charge that made a brilliant glow in the neon at the point of the tube where the hand had made contact. It looked like a realistic psychic phenomenon in the dark.

A Professor Dubois collected a number of examples to prove that under exceptional, but not paranormal, conditions, the human organism is capable of creating light. A woman suffering from breast cancer, under treatment at an English hospital, showed luminosity of the cancerous area strong enough to be recognized from several paces away and bright enough to read watch hands by at night from a few inches away. The discharge from the tumor was also very luminous. Bilious, nervous, redhaired, and, more often, alcoholic subjects have sometimes shown phosphorescent wounds.

Geley, working with the now-obsolete idea of **ectoplasm,** concluded that organic light and ectoplasmic light were rigorously analogous. They had the same properties. They were cold light, giving off neither calorific nor chemical radiations. Both were nearly inactinic and had considerable powers of penetration into opaque bodies. They impressed photographic plates through cardboard, wood, and even metal. Geley believed it likely that analysis of ectoplasmic secretion would reveal the two constituents—luciferin and luciferase—in the luminous secretions of Dubois's cancer patient.

Julien Ochorowicz, in his research into the radiography of etheric hands, found it significant that when an etheric hand radiated light it did not, and apparently could not, materialize at the same time. Upon materializing, it lost its luminosity.

Recorded experiences caution against generalization about luminous phenomena. Many lights were found to be created through fraud, and the ease with which the phenomena can be produced chemically encourages caution in assessing the genuineness of any claimed phenomena.

Sources:

Berger, Arthur S., and Joyce Berger. *The Encyclopedia of Parapsychology and Psychical Research.* New York: Paragon House, 1991.

Lusus Naturae

A general term for freaks or sports of nature, sometimes applied to the area of collecting stones and minerals that appear to contain pictures on their surfaces when cut and polished. Such pictures may appear as landscapes or even portraits, arising from the principle of duplication of shapes in nature, rather as if nature draws doodles and tests out forms. The resemblance of certain roots, notably mandrake (see **mandragoras**), to human shape is a well-known example of this strange principle.

Lutin, The

The Lutin of Normandy in many respects resembled Robin Goodfellow, the mischievous sprite also identified with Puck. Like Robin, he had many names and also the power of assuming many forms, but the Lutin's pranks were usually of a more serious nature than those of the tricky spirit of Merrie England. Many a man ascribed his ruin to the malice of the Lutin, although some neighbors were uncharitable enough to say that the Lutin had less to do with it than habits of want-of-thrift and self-indulgence.

Thus, on market days, when a farmer lingered late over his ale, whether in driving a close bargain or in enjoying the society of a boon companion, he declared the Lutin was sure to play him some spiteful trick on his way home: his horse would stumble and he would be thrown, or he would lose his purse or else his way. If the farmer persisted in these habits, the tricks of the Lutin would become more serious: the sheep pens would be unfastened, the cowhouse and stable doors left open, and the flocks and cattle found moving among the standing corn and unmown hay, while every servant on the farm would swear to his own innocence, and unhesitatingly lay the blame on the Lutin.

Similar tricks were played on the fishermen by the Nain Rouge—another name of the Lutin. He opened the meshes of the nets and set the fish free. He removed the floats and let the nets sink to the bottom, or let the nets float away on the retiring tide. True, if closely questioned, the fishermen would confess that on these occasions, the night was dark and stormy, the cottage warm, and the grog plentiful, and that instead of drawing their nets at the proper time, they had delayed until morning.

Again, the Lutin might appear like a black nag, ready bridled and saddled, quietly feeding by the wayside. Unless the nag was mounted for some charitable or holy purpose, he was borne with the speed of the wind to his destination. In this form the Lutin played his wildest pranks and was called Le Cheval Bayard. (See also **fairies; Kaboutermannekens**)

Lutoslawski, Wincenty (1863–1954)

Polish occultist and mystic. He was born in Warsaw and studied chemistry and philosophy before developing his own synthesis of psychic phenomena, sex, and mysticism. He corresponded with psychologist **William James** and with psychical researcher **Charles Richet.**

In 1902 he proposed the term "metapsychic" for studies in psychic science, independently adopted by Richet for his own investigations. Lutoslawski also founded a short-lived political party named the Philaretes.

Sources:

Lutoslawski, Wincenty. *The Knowledge of Reality.* N.p., 1930.
———. *Pre-Existence and Reincarnation.* N.p., 1928.
———. *The World of Souls.* N.p., 1924.

Lycanthropy

The transformation of a human being into an animal. The belief is an ancient one. The term derives from the Greek words *lukos,* a wolf, and *anthropos,* a man, but it is employed regarding a transformation into any animal shape. It is chiefly in those countries where wolves are numerous that we find such tales concerning them. But in India and some parts of Asia, the tiger takes the place of the wolf. In Russia and elsewhere it is the bear, and in Africa the leopard.

Such beliefs generally adhere to savage animals, but even harmless ones sometimes figure in them. There is considerable confusion as to whether such transformations were voluntary or involuntary, temporary or permanent. The human being transformed into the animal may be the physical individual or, on the other hand, may be only a double, that is, the human spirit may enter the animal but the human body remain unchanged.

Magicians and witches were credited with the power of transforming themselves into wolves and other animal shapes, and it was asserted that if the animal were wounded, then the marks of the wound would be discovered upon the wizard's body. The belief was current in many tribal cultures that every individual possessed an animal form, which could be entered at death or at will. This transformation was effected either by magic or natural agency.

As mentioned, the wolf was a common form of animal transformation in Europe. In ancient Greece, the belief was associated with the dog, which took the place of the wolf. Other similar beliefs have been found in India and Java. In the former country we find the **werwolf** in a kind of **vampire** form.

Magical Transformation

The seventeenth-century writer Louis Guyon related the history of an enchanter who used to change himself into different beasts:

"Certain people persuaded Ferdinand, first Emperor of that name, to command the presence of a Polish enchanter and magician in the town of Nuremberg to learn the result of a difference he had with the Turks, concerning the kingdom of Hungary; and not only did the magician make use of divination, but performed various other marvels, so that the king did not wish to see him, but the courtiers introduced him into his chamber. There he did many wonderful things, among others, he transformed himself into a horse, anointing himself with some grease, then he took the shape of an ox, and thirdly that of a lion, all in less than an hour. The emperor was so terrified by these transformations that he commanded that the magician should be immediately dismissed, and declined to hear the future from the lips of such a rascal.

"It need no longer be doubted [that Lucius Apuleius Plato was a sorcerer, and that he] was transformed into an ass, forasmuch as he was charged with it before the proconsul of Africa, in the time of the Emperor Antonine I, in the year 150 A.D., as Apollonius of Tyana, long before, in the year 60, was charged before Domitian with the same crime. And more than three years after, the rumour persisted to the time of St. Augustine, who was an African, who has written and confirmed it; as also in his time the father of one Prestantius was transformed into a horse, as the said Prestantius declared. Augustine's father having died, in a short time the son had wasted the greater part of his inheritance in the pursuit of the magic arts, and in order to flee poverty he sought to marry a rich widow named Pudentille, for such a long time that at length she consented. Soon after her only son and heir, the child of her former marriage, died. These things came about in a manner which led people to think that he had by means of magic entrapped Pudentille, who had been wooed in vain by several illustrious people, in order to obtain the wealth of her son. It was also said that the profound knowledge he possessed—for he was able to solve difficult questions which left other men bewildered—was obtained from a demon or familiar spirit he possessed. Further, certain people said they had seen him do many marvellous things, such as making himself invisible, transforming himself into a horse or into a bird, piercing his body with a sword without wounding himself, and similar performances. He was at last accused by one Sicilius milianus, the censor, before Claudius Maximus, proconsul of Africa, who was said to be a Christian; but nothing was found against him.

"Now, that he had been transformed into an ass, St. Augustine regards as indubitable, he having read it in certain true and trustworthy authors, and being besides of the same country; and this transformation happened to him in Thessaly before he was versed in magic, through the spell of a sorceress, who sold him, and who recovered him to his former shape after he had served in the capacity of an ass for some years, having the same powers and habits of eating and braying as other asses, but with a mind still sane and reasonable as he himself attested. And at last to show forth his case, and to lend probability to the rumour, he wrote a book entitled *The Golden Ass,* a mélange of fables and dialogues, to expose the vices of the men of his time, which he had heard of, or seen, during his transformation, with many of the labours and troubles he had suffered while in the shape of an ass.

"However that may be, St. Augustine in the book of the *City of God,* book XVIII, chapters XVII and XVIII, relates that in his time there were in the Alps certain sorceresses who gave a particular kind of cheese to the passers by, who, on partaking of it, were immediately changed into asses or other beasts of burden, and were made to carry heavy weights to certain places. When their task was over, they were permitted to regain their human shape.

"The bishop of Tyre, historian, writes that in his time, probably about 1220, some Englishmen were sent by their king to the aid of the Christians who were fighting in the Holy Land, and that on their arrival in a haven of the island of Cyprus a sorceress transformed a young English soldier into an ass. He, wishing to return to his companions in the ship, was chased away with blows from a stick, whereupon he returned to the sorceress who made use of him, until someone noticed that the ass kneeled in a church and did various other things which only a reasoning being could do. The sorceress who followed him was taken on suspicion before the authorities, was obliged to give him his human form three years after his transformation, and was forthwith executed.

"We read that Ammonius, a peripatetic philosopher, about the time of Lucius Septimius Severus, in the year 196 A.D., had present at his lessons an ass whom he taught. I should think that this ass had been at one time a man, and that he quite understood what Ammonius taught, for these transformed persons retain their reason unimpaired, as St. Augustine and other writers have assured us.

"Fulgose writes, book VIII, chapter II, that in the time of Pope Leon, who lived about the year 930, there were in Germany two sorceresses who used thus to change their guests into beasts, and on one occasion she changed a young mountebank into an ass, who, preserving his human understanding, gave a great deal of amusement to the passers-by. A neighbour of the sorceresses bought the ass at a good price, but was warned by them that he must not take the beast to a river, or he would lose it. Now the ass escaped one day and running to a near-by lake plunged into the water, when he returned to his own shape. Apuleius says that he regained his human form by eating roses.

"There are still to be seen in Egypt asses which are led into the market-place to perform various feats of agility and tricks, understanding all the commands they receive, and executing them: such as to point out the most beautiful woman of the company, and many other things that one would hardly believe; and Belon, a physician, relates in his observations that he has seen them, and others also, who have been there, and who have affirmed the same to me."

Augustin Calmet, author of *The Phantom World* (2 vols., 1850), stated:

"One day there was brought to St. Macarius, the Egyptian, an honest woman who had been transformed into a mare by the wicked art of a magician. Her husband and all who beheld her believed that she had really been changed into a mare. This woman remained for three days without taking any food, whether suitable for a horse or for a human being. She was brought to the priests of the place, who could suggest no remedy. So they led her to the cell of St. Macarius, to whom God had revealed that she was about to come. His disciples wished to send her away, thinking her a mare, and they warned the saint of her approach, and the reason for her journey. He said to them: 'It is you who are the animals, who think you see that which is not; this woman is not changed, but your eyes are bewitched.' As he spoke he scattered holy water on the head of the woman, and all those present saw her in her true shape. He had something given her to eat and sent her away safe and sound with her husband."

Modern Beliefs in Transformation

Belief in transformation of human beings into predatory animals persisted into relatively modern times in Africa, India, Java, Malaya, and other countries. In Africa there were tiger men and even a leopard society of wizards. It seems very likely, however, that many apparent cases of transformation were effected by wearing the skin of an animal when hunting victims. In some cases there may have been a perverse desire for blood-drinking or cannibalism, as in the celebrated sixteenth-century case of the French lycanthrope **Gilles Garnier.**

In July 1919 the *Journal* of the SPR published a summary of Richard Bagot's article, "The Hyaenas of Pirra" (*Cornhill Magazine,* October 1918), in which some experiences were reported by a Lieutenant F. personally and an experience of the late Capt. Shott, D.S.O. dealt with the killing of Nigerians when in the form of supposed hyenas. The main facts, which deeply impressed the officers were as follows:

"Raiding hyenas were wounded by gun-traps, and tracked in each case to a point where the hyena traces ceased and were succeeded by human footprints, which made for the native town. At each shooting a man mysteriously dies in the town, all access being refused to the body. In Lieut. F.'s experiences the death wail was raised in the town almost immediately after the shot; but Capt. Shott does not mention this. In Capt. Shott's experience the beast was an enormous brute, readily trackable, which after being hard hit made off through the guinea-corn. It was promptly tracked, and a spot was come upon where 'they found the jaw of the beast lying near a large pool of blood.' Soon after the tracks reached a path leading to the native town. The natives next day came to Capt. Shott—and this is the curious part of the affair—and told him, without any regrets, that he had shot the Nefada—a lesser head-man—who was then lying dead with his jaw shot away. The natives gave their reasons as having seen and spoken to the Nefada, as he was, by his own admission, going into the bush. They heard the gun and saw him return with his head all muffled up and walking like a very sick man. On going next morning to see what was the matter . . . they found him as stated."

Mr. Bagot, a member of the SPR, added in response to further questions:

"In the article in question I merely reproduced verbatim the reports and letters sent to the said official . . . by British officers well known to him, and said that the authenticity and good faith of the writers can be vouched for entirely. I have evidence of precisely similar occurrences that have come under the notice of Italian officers in Eritrea and Somaliland; and in all cases it would seem that a gravel patch thrown up by the small black ants is necessary to the process of metamorphosis. I drew the attention of Sir James G. Frazer (author of *The Golden Bough*) to this coincidence and asked him if he had come across in his researches anything which might explain the connection between gravel thrown up by the ants and the power of projection into animal forms; but he informed me that, so far as he could recollect, he had not done so. Italian officials and big game hunters assure me that it is considered most dangerous (by natives in Somaliland, Abyssinia, etc.) to sleep on ground thrown up by ants; the belief being that anyone who does so is liable to be possessed or obsessed by some wild animal, and that this obsession once having taken place, the victim is never afterwards able entirely to free himself from it and is compelled periodically to assume the form and habits of some beast or reptile."

Psychic Aspects

Psychic research does not normally admit such phenomena as lycanthropy within its scope, but there are two possible points of contact. The first is the projection of the **double** (or **astral body**), provided it could be proved that the double may assume any desired shape. **Eugen Rochas** asserted that the double of his hypnotic subject, on being so suggested, assumed the shape of her mother. If it were proved that the shape of animals could be assumed, we would have to consider lycanthropy as a psychic possibility. But the animal, in that case, would not be more than a phantom, and we would have to prove that this phantom can be hurt and transfer, by repercussion, the wound to the projector.

The second possibility brings us nearer to this aspect of the problem. **Paul Joire** succeeded in transferring the exteriorized sensitivity of his subject to a figure made of putty. If the hand of the putty figure was scratched by a needle, a corresponding red mark appeared on the somnambule's hand.

The question arises: would it not be possible to transfer sensitivity to a living being, to an animal? In that case it would be natural to expect a repercussion from the animal to the human body.

Sources:

Baring-Gould, Sabine. *The Book of Were-Wolves.* London, 1865. Reprint, New York: Causeway Books, 1973.

Hamel, Frank. *Human Animals.* London, 1915. University Books, 1969.

Kaigh, Frederick. *Witchcraft and Magic of Africa.* London: Richard Lesley, 1947.

Maclean, Charles. *The Wolf Children.* Hill & Wang, 1977.

Summers, Montague. *The Werewolf.* London, 1933. University Books, 1966.

Woodward, Ian. *The Werewolf Delusion.* London & New York: Paddington Press, 1979.

Lyceum Banner, The

Spiritualist publication founded in 1890 as the official monthly organ of the **British Spiritualists' Lyceum Union.** It was published by **J. J. Morse** in Liverpool until 1902, when the paper was passed to the Lyceum Union under the editorship of **Frank Kitson.** Publication continued through the 1930s.

Sources:

Kuhlig, Kathryn. *Spiritualist Lyceum Manual.* Milwaukee, Wis.: National Spiritualist Association of Churches, 1962.

Lychnomancy

A branch of **pyromancy** (**divination** by fire), concerned with interpreting the flames of three candles arranged in a triangle. Success was indicated by one flame burning brighter than the other two; a wavering flame indicated travel; a spiral flame signified plots by enemies; and uneven flame, danger; sparks signified caution; and a sudden extinction of flame indicated bad luck. Obviously such a system of divination was largely affected by currents of air in the room or by the breathing of the diviner. (See also **lampadomancy**)

Lynn, Thomas (ca. 1928)

A coal miner medium in northern England and the subject of remarkable experiments by **James Hewat McKenzie** and Major C. Mowbray in photographing the arrival and ectoplasmic mechanism of **apports.** Lynn's mediumship developed around 1913 in his home circle, but he did not exercise physical mediumship before 1926. Extrusions of **ectoplasm,** small coils or rods of varying shapes, were seen to issue from the pit of his stomach, to perform minor physical feats, and leave—after their disappearance—red marks like punctures behind on the medium's skin.

Apports of small, insignificant objects were the most impressive phenomena. In earlier séances, held in the dark, it was said that small bottles arrived containing wax in various shapes and molded images. In the experimental séances held in light by the investigators of the **British College of Psychic Science,** no such bottles were apported.

The first series of these experimental sittings took place in July 1928. Two cameras were used, one whole-plate with ordinary lens, and a half-plate with quartz lens. The medium was put in a bag and his hands were tied to his knees with tapes.

The flashlight photographs showed luminous connections between the medium's body and the apports. The sittings were continued in September 1928 and were repeated at the college in March 1929. By then, Lynn abandoned his former occupation and became a professional medium. At the time, the curious photographs secured in these séances were believed by many to throw new light on the problem of apports, though at present most believe that such apports were simply the sign of the medium's engagement in **fraud.** For a detailed report on the Lynn phenomena, including photographs, see *Psychic Science* (Vol. 8, no. 2, July 1929: 129–37).

Lyttelton, Edith (ca. 1865–1948)

Author, playwright, psychic, and past president of the **Society for Psychical Research** (SPR), London. A daughter of Arthur Balfour, she was educated privately and married in 1892. In a well-to-do position, she served in a number of social and charitable roles. She was a member of the Joint Council of the Vic-Wells and National Theatre and a governor of Stratford Memorial Theatre. During World War I she served on the War Refugees Committee and was deputy director of the Women's Branch of the Ministry of Agriculture (1917–19). She was British Substitute Delegate to the League of Nations Assembly at Geneva (1923–31) and appointed Dame Commander of the Order of the British Empire (1917). She received the Dame Grand Cross (1929).

In 1902 she joined the Society for Psychical Research, and from 1928 onward was a member of the council. In 1913, soon after her husband's death, she experimented with automatic writing and received predictions of the outbreak of World War I. Her scripts predicted the sinking of the liner *Lusitania* in 1915, and offered additional predictions that seemed to refer to World War II. Her presidential address to the SPR was published in the society's *Proceedings* (Vol. 41, part 132, 1933). She died September 2, 1948.

Sources:

Berger, Arthur S., and Joyce Berger. *The Encyclopedia of Parapsychology and Psychical Research.* New York: Paragon House, 1991.

Lyttelton, Edith. *The Faculty of Communion.* N.p., 1925.

———. *Our Superconscious Mind.* London, 1931.

———. *Some Cases of Prediction.* London: Bell, 1938.

Pleasants, Helene, ed. *Biographical Dictionary of Parapsychology.* New York: Helix Press, 1964.

Lytton, Bulwer (1803–1873)

According to his baptismal certificate, the full name of this once famous author was Edward George Earle Lytton Bulwer-Lytton. He was born in London May 23, 1803. His father was a Norfolk squire, Bulwer of Heydon Hall, and colonel of the 106th regiment (Norfolk Rangers); his mother was Elizabeth Barbara Lytton, a lady who claimed kinship with Cadwaladr Vendigaid, the semi-mythical hero who led the Strathclyde Welsh against the Angles in the seventh century.

As a child the future novelist was delicate, but he learned to read at a surprisingly early age and began to write verses before he was ten years old. Going first to a small private school at Fulham, he soon passed on to another one at Rottingdean, and here he continued to manifest literary tastes, Lord Byron and Sir Walter Scott being his chief idols at this time.

He was so talented that his relations decided it would be a mistake to send him to a public school. Accordingly he was placed with a tutor at Ealing, under whose care he progressed rapidly with his studies. Thereafter he proceeded to Cambridge, where he took his degree easily and won many academic laurels. Afterward he traveled for a while in Scotland and France, then bought a commission in the army. He sold it soon afterward, however, and began to devote himself seriously to writing.

Although busy and winning great fame, Lytton's life was not really a happy one. Long before meeting his wife, he fell in love with a young girl who died prematurely, and this loss seems to have left an indelible sorrow. His marriage was anything but a successful one, the pair being divorced comparatively soon after their union.

His first publications of note were the novels *Falkland, Pelham* and *Eugene Aram.* These won an instant success and placed considerable wealth in the author's hands, the result being that in 1831 he entered Parliament as the liberal member for St. Ives, Huntingdonshire. During the next ten years he was an active politician yet still found time to produce a host of stories, such as *The Last Days of Pompei, Ernest Maltravers, Zanoni,* and *The Last of the Barons.* These were followed shortly by *The Caxtons,* and simultaneously Lytton achieved some fame as a dramatist, perhaps his best play being *The Lady of Lyons.*

Besides further novels, he issued several volumes of verses, notably *Ismael* and *The New Union,* while he did translations from German, Spanish, and Italian. He produced a history of Athens, contributed to endless periodicals, and was at one time editor of the *New Monthly Magazine.*

In 1851 he was instrumental in founding a scheme for pensioning authors and also began to pursue an active political career. In 1852 he was elected conservative Member of Parliament for Hertfordshire and held the post until his elevation to the peerage in 1866. He became Secretary for the Colonies in Lord Derby's ministry (1858–59) and played a large part in the organization of the new colony of British Columbia. He became Baron Lytton of Knebworth in July 1866 and thereafter took his place in the House of Peers.

In 1862 he increased his reputation greatly by his occult novel entitled *A Strange Story.* Toward the end of the decade he began to work at yet another story, *Kenelm Chillingly,* but his health was beginning to fail, and he died May 23, 1873, at Torquay.

Even as a child, Lytton had evinced a predilection for mysticism, while he had surprised his mother once by asking her whether she was "not sometimes overcome by the sense of her own identity" (almost exactly the same question was put to his nurse in boyhood by another mystic, William Bell Scott). Lytton sedulously developed his leaning towards the occult, and it is frequently manifest in his literary output, including his poem *The Tale of a Dreamer,* and in *Kenelm Chillingly.* In *A Strange Story* he tried to give a scientific coloring to old-fashioned magic.

He was a keen student of psychic phenomena. The great medium **D. D. Home** was his guest at Knebworth in 1855. Home's phenomena greatly aroused Lytton's curiosity. He never spoke about his experiences in public, but his identity was at once detected in an account in Home's autobiography (*Incidents in My Life,* 1863) which reads:

"Whilst I was at Ealing, a distinguished novelist, accompanied by his son, attended a séance, at which some very remarkable manifestations occurred that were chiefly directed to him. The rappings on the table suddenly became unusually firm and loud. He asked: 'What spirit is present?' The alphabet was called over, and the response was: 'I am the spirit who influenced you to write Z (Zanoni).' 'Indeed,' said he, 'I wish you would give me some tangible proof of your presence.' 'What proof? Will you take my hand.' 'Yes.' And putting his hand beneath the surface of the table it was immediately seized by a powerful grasp, which made him start to his feet in evident trepidation, exhibiting a momentary suspicion that a trick had been played upon him. Seeing, however, that all the persons around him were sitting with their hands quietly reposing on the table, he recovered his composure, and offering an apology for the uncontrollable excitement caused by such an unexpected demonstration, he resumed his seat.

"Immediately after this another message was spelt out: 'We wish you to believe in the . . .' On inquiring after the finishing word a small cardboard cross which was lying on a table at the end of the room was given into his hand."

When the press asked Lord Lytton for a statement, he refused to give any. His wariness to commit himself before the public was well demonstrated by his letter to the secretary of the **London Dialectical Society,** February 1869:

"So far as my experience goes, the phenomena, when freed from inpostures with which their exhibition abounds, and examined rationally, are traceable to material influences of the nature of which we are ignorant.

"They require certain physical organisations or temperaments to produce them, and vary according to these organisations and temperaments."

Lord Lytton sought out many mediums after his experiences with Home and often detected imposture. His friendship with Home extended over a period of ten years, and when he commenced the wildest of his romances, *A Strange Story,* he intended first to portray Home in its pages, but abandoned this intention for the fantastic conception of Margrave. The joyousness of Home's character, however, is still reflected in the mental make-up of Margrave.

Lytton also became acquainted with the French occultist **Éliphas Lévi,** whom he assisted in magical evocations, and Lévi was clearly a model for the character of the magus in *The Haunted and The Haunters.*

Sources:

Howe, Ellic. *The Magicians of the Golden Dawn.* London: Routledge & Kegan Paul, 1972.

Lytton, Bulwar. *The Coming Race.* London: George Routledge & Sons, 1877.

———. *Complete Works.* New York: Thomas Y. Crowell, n.d.

———. *A Strange Story.* Mobile, Ala.: S. H. Goetzel, 1863. Frequently reprinted.

———. *Zanoni.* London: Saunders & Otley, 1842.